LE ROBERT & COLLINS

« les pratiques »

ANGLAIS

LE ROBERT & COLLINS

« les pratiques »

DICTIONNAIRE
FRANÇAIS-ANGLAIS
ANGLAIS-FRANÇAIS

DICTIONNAIRES LE ROBERT

Collins

An Imprint of HarperCollins*Publishers*

third edition/troisième édition en France 1999

© William Collins Sons & Co. Ltd. 1988
© HarperCollins Publishers 1995, 1997, 1999

Dictionnaires Le Robert
ISBN 2-85036-587-4

Pierre-Henri Cousin • Lorna Sinclair Knight
Jean-François Allain • Catherine E. Love

Other contributors/Autres collaborateurs
Megan Thomson
Cécile Aubinière-Robb • Harry Campbell
Keith Foley • Janet Gough • Jean-Benoît Ormal-Grenon

Editorial staff/Secrétariat de rédaction
Elspeth Anderson • Susan Dunsmore

Series editor/Collection dirigée par
Lorna Sinclair Knight

Editorial management/Chef de projet
Vivian Marr

Dépôt légal avril 1999
Achevé d'imprimer en avril 1999

Typeset by/Photocomposition Morton Word Processing Ltd, Scarborough
Printed and bound in Great Britain by/Imprimé en Grande-Bretagne par
Caledonian International Book Manufacturing Ltd, Glasgow, G64

TABLE DES MATIÈRES

CONTENTS

Les marques déposées

Les termes qui constituent à notre connaissance une marque déposée ont été désignés comme tels. La présence ou l'absence de cette désignation ne peut toutefois être considérée comme ayant valeur juridique.

Note on trademarks

Words which we have reason to believe constitute trademarks have been designated as such. However, neither the presence nor the absence of such designation should be regarded as affecting the legal status of any trademark.

INTRODUCTION

Vous désirez apprendre l'anglais ou approfondir des connaissances déjà solides. Vous voulez vous exprimer en anglais, lire ou rédiger des textes anglais ou converser avec des interlocuteurs anglophones. Que vous soyez lycéen, étudiant, touriste, homme ou femme d'affaires, vous venez de choisir le compagnon de travail idéal pour vous exprimer et pour communiquer en anglais, oralement ou par écrit. Résolument pratique et moderne, votre dictionnaire fait une large place au vocabulaire de tous les jours, aux domaines de l'actualité, des affaires, de la bureautique et du tourisme. Comme dans tous nos dictionnaires, nous avons mis l'accent sur la langue contemporaine et sur les expressions idiomatiques.

MODE D'EMPLOI

Vous trouverez ci-dessous quelques explications sur la manière dont les informations sont présentées dans votre dictionnaire. Notre objectif: vous donner un maximum d'informations sans pour autant sacrifier la clarté.

Les articles

Voici les différents éléments dont est composé un article type dans votre dictionnaire:

Transcription phonétique

La prononciation des mots figure, entre crochets, immédiatement après l'entrée. Comme la plupart des dictionnaires modernes, nous avons opté pour le système dit "alphabet phonétique international". Vous trouverez ci-dessous, aux pages viii et ix, une liste complète des caractères utilisés dans ce système.

Données grammaticales

Les mots appartiennent tous à une catégorie grammaticale donnée: substantif, verbe, adjectif, adverbe, pronom, article, conjonction, préposition, abréviation. Les substantifs peuvent être singuliers ou pluriels et, en français, masculins ou féminins. Les verbes peuvent être transitifs, intransitifs, pronominaux (ou réfléchis) ou encore impersonnels. La catégorie grammaticale des mots est indiquée en *italique*, immédiatement après le mot.

Souvent un mot se subdivise en plusieurs catégories grammaticales. Ainsi le français **creux** peut-il être un adjectif ou un nom masculin et l'anglais **early** peut-il être soit un adverbe, soit un adjectif. De même le verbe **fumer** est parfois transitif ("fumer un cigare"), parfois intransitif ("défense de fumer"). Pour vous permettre de trouver plus rapidement le sens que vous cherchez, et pour aérer la présentation, nous avons séparé les différentes catégories grammaticales par un losange noir ♦.

Subdivisions sémantiques

La plupart des mots ont plus d'un sens; ainsi **bouchon** peut être un objet servant à boucher une bouteille, ou, dans un sens figuré, un embouteillage. D'autres mots se traduisent différemment selon le contexte dans lequel ils sont employés: **couler** se traduira en anglais "to leak" ou "to sink" selon qu'il s'agit d'un stylo ou d'un bateau. Pour vous permettre de choisir la bonne traduction dans tous les contextes, nous avons subdivisé les articles en catégories de sens; ces catégories sont introduites par une "indication d'emploi" entre parenthèses et en *italique*. Pour les exemples ci-dessus, les articles se présenteront donc comme suit:

bouchon *nm* (*en liège*) cork; (*autre matière*) stopper; (*fig: embouteillage*) hold-up

couler *vi* to flow, run; (*fuir: stylo, récipient*) to leak; (*sombrer: bateau*) to sink

De même certains mots changent de sens lorsqu'ils sont employés dans un domaine spécifique, comme par exemple **puce** que nous employons généralement dans son acception de "petit insecte sauteur", mais qui est aussi un terme d'informatique. Pour montrer à l'utilisateur quelle traduction choisir, nous avons donc ajouté, en majuscules italiques entre parenthèses, une indication de domaine, à savoir dans ce cas particulier (*INFORMATIQUE*), que nous avons abrégé pour gagner de la place en (*INFORM*):

puce *nf* flea; (*INFORM*) chip.

Une liste complète des abréviations dont nous nous sommes servis dans ce dictionnaire figure ci-dessous, aux pages vi et vii.

Traductions

La plupart des mots français se traduisent par un seul mot anglais, et vice-versa, comme dans les exemples ci-dessus. Parfois cependant il n'y a pas d'équivalent exact dans la langue d'arrivée et nous avons donné un équivalent approximatif, indiqué par le signe ≈; c'est le cas par exemple pour le mot **baccalauréat** dont l'équivalent anglais est "GCE A-levels": il ne s'agit pas d'une traduction à proprement parler puisque nos deux systèmes scolaires sont différents:

baccalauréat *nm* ≈ GCE A-levels

Parfois il est impossible même de trouver un équivalent approximatif. C'est le cas par exemple pour les noms de plats régionaux, comme le plat languedocien suivant:

cassoulet *nm sausage and bean hotpot*

L'explication remplace ici une traduction (qui n'existe pas); pour plus de clarté, cette explication, ou glose, est donnée en *italique*.

Souvent aussi, on ne peut traduire isolément un mot, ou une acception particulière d'un mot. La traduction anglaise de **copain**, par exemple, est "mate, pal", cependant **être copain avec** se traduit "to be pally with". Même une expression toute simple comme **doigt de pied** nécessite une traduction séparée, en l'occurrence "toe" (et non "footfinger"). C'est là que votre dictionnaire se révélera particulièrement utile et complet, car il contient un maximum de composés, de phrases et d'expressions idiomatiques.

Registre

En français, vous saurez instinctivement quand dire **j'en ai assez** et quand dire **j'en ai marre** ou **j'en ai ras le bol**. Mais lorsque vous essayez de comprendre quelqu'un qui s'exprime en anglais, ou de vous exprimer vous-même en anglais, il est particulièrement important de savoir ce qui est poli et ce qui l'est moins. Nous avons donc ajouté l'indication (*col*) (= *colloquial*) aux expressions de langue familière dans la partie anglais-français; les expressions particulièrement grossières se voient dotées d'un point d'exclamation supplémentaire (*col!*), vous incitant à une prudence accrue. Notez également que dans la partie français-anglais, les traductions qui appartiennent au registre vulgaire sont suivies d'un point d'exclamation entre parenthèses.

Mots-clés

Une importance particulière a été accordée aux mots qui figurent dans le texte sous la mention *MOT-CLÉ*, tels que **être** et **faire** ou leurs équivalents anglais **be** et **do**. Ils constituent en effet les éléments de base de la langue. Ce petit coup de pouce supplémentaire vous permettra d'utiliser ces termes complexes en toute confiance.

Notes culturelles

Les articles séparés du texte principal par deux lignes horizontales décrivent certaines caractéristiques culturelles des pays francophones et anglophones. Les médias, l'éducation, la politique et les fêtes figurent parmi les sujets traités. Exemple: **quality papers, honours degree, Assemblée nationale** et **Toussaint**.

abréviation	**ab(b)r**	abbreviation
adjectif, locution adjective	**adj**	adjective, adjectival phrase
administration	**ADMIN**	administration
adverbe, locution adverbiale	**adv**	adverb, adverbial phrase
agriculture	**AGR**	agriculture
anatomie	**ANAT**	anatomy
architecture	**ARCHIT**	architecture
article défini	**art déf**	definite article
article indéfini	**art indéf**	indefinite article
automobile	**AUT(O)**	the motor car and motoring
aviation, voyages aériens	**AVIAT**	flying, air travel
biologie	**BIO(L)**	biology
botanique	**BOT**	botany
anglais de Grande-Bretagne	**BRIT**	British English
chimie	**CHIMIE, CHEM**	chemistry
cinéma	**CINÉ, CINE**	cinema
langue familière (! emploi vulgaire)	**col(!)**	colloquial usage (! particularly offensive)
commerce, finance, banque	**COMM**	commerce, finance, banking
informatique	**COMPUT**	computing
conjonction	**conj**	conjunction
construction	**CONSTR**	building
nom utilisé comme adjectif, ne peut s'employer ni comme attribut, ni après le nom qualifié	**cpd**	compound element: noun used as an adjective and which cannot follow the noun it qualifies
cuisine, art culinaire	**CULIN**	cookery
article défini	**def art**	definite article
déterminant: adjectif démonstratif, indéfini etc	**dét**	determiner: demonstrative etc.
économie	**ECON**	economics
électricité, électronique	**ELEC**	electricity, electronics
exclamation, interjection	**excl**	exclamation, interjection
féminin	**f**	feminine
langue familière (! emploi vulgaire)	**fam (!)**	colloquial usage (! particularly offensive)
emploi figuré	**fig**	figurative use
(verbe anglais) dont la particule est inséparable du verbe	**fus**	(phrasal verb) where the particle cannot be separated from the main verb
dans la plupart des sens; généralement	**gén, gen**	in most or all senses; generally
géographie, géologie	**GEO**	geography, geology
géométrie	**GEOM**	geometry
histoire	**HIST**	history
article indéfini	**indef art**	indefinite article
informatique	**INFORM**	computing
invariable	**inv**	invariable
irrégulier	**irrég, irreg**	irregular
domaine juridique	**JUR**	law
grammaire, linguistique	**LING**	grammar, linguistics
masculin	**m**	masculine
mathématiques, algèbre	**MATH**	mathematics, calculus
médecine	**MÉD, MED**	medical term, medicine

masculin ou féminin, suivant le sexe	**m/f**	either masculine or feminine depending on sex
domaine militaire, armée	**MIL**	military matters
musique	**MUS**	music
nom	**n**	noun
navigation, nautisme	**NAVIG, NAUT**	sailing, navigation
nom non comptable: ne peut s'utiliser au pluriel	**no pl**	collective (uncountable) noun: is not used in the plural
nom ou adjectif numéral	**num**	numeral adjective or noun
	o.s.	oneself
péjoratif	**péj, pej**	derogatory, pejorative
photographie	**PHOT(O)**	photography
physiologie	**PHYSIOL**	physiology
pluriel	**pl**	plural
politique	**POL**	politics
participe passé	**pp**	past participle
préposition	**prép, prep**	preposition
psychologie, psychiatrie	**PSYCH**	psychology, psychiatry
temps du passé	**pt**	past tense
quelque chose	**qch**	
quelqu'un	**qn**	
religions, domaine ecclésiastique	**REL**	religions, church service
	sb	somebody
enseignement, système scolaire et universitaire	**SCOL**	schooling, schools and universities
singulier	**sg**	singular
	sth	something
subjonctif	**sub**	subjunctive
sujet (grammatical)	**su(b)j**	(grammatical) subject
techniques, technologie	**TECH**	technical term, technology
télécommunications	**TEL**	telecommunications
théâtre	**THÉÂT, THEAT**	theatre
télévision	**TV**	television
typographie	**TYP(O)**	typography, printing
anglais des USA	**US**	American English
verbe	**vb**	verb
verbe ou groupe verbal à fonction intransitive	**vi**	verb or phrasal verb used intransitively
verbe ou groupe verbal à fonction transitive	**vt**	verb or phrasal verb used transitively
zoologie	**ZOOL**	zoology
marque déposée	**®**	registered trademark
indique une équivalence culturelle	**≈**	introduces a cultural equivalent
pas de liaison devant h aspiré	**'**	no liaison before aspirate h

TRANSCRIPTION PHONÉTIQUE

Consonnes

NB. p, b, t, d, k, g sont suivis d'une aspiration en anglais.

Consonants

NB. p, b, t, d, k, g are not aspirated in French.

Consonnes		Consonants
_p_ou_p_ée	p	_p_u_pp_y
_b_om_b_e	b	_b_a_b_y
_t_en_t_e _th_ermal	t	_t_en_t_
_d_in_d_e	d	_d_a_dd_y
_c_o_q_ _qu_i _k_épi	k	_c_or_k_ _k_iss _ch_ord
_g_ag ba_gue_	g	_g_ag _g_uess
_s_ale _c_e na_t_ion	s	_s_o ri_c_e ki_ss_
_z_éro ro_se_	z	cou_s_in bu_zz_
ta_che_ _ch_at	ʃ	_sh_eep _s_ugar
gi_l_et _j_uge	ʒ	plea_s_ure bei_ge_
	tʃ	_ch_ur_ch_
	dʒ	_j_udge general
_f_er _ph_are	f	_f_arm ra_ff_le
_v_al_ve_	v	_v_ery re_v_
	θ	_th_in ma_th_s
	ð	_th_at o_th_er
_l_ent sa_ll_e	l	_l_itt_l_e ba_ll_
_r_a_r_e _r_ent_r_er	R	
	r	_r_at _r_a_r_e
_m_a_m_an fe_mm_e	m	_m_u_mm_y co_m_b
_n_on _n_on_n_e	n	_n_o ra_n_
a_gn_eau vi_gne_	ɲ	
	ŋ	si_ng_ing ba_nk_
_h_op!	h	_h_at re_h_eat
_y_eux pai_ll_e _p_ied	j	_y_et
n_ou_er _ou_i	w	_w_all be_w_ail
_h_u_i_le l_u_i	ɥ	
	x	lo_ch_

Divers

pour l'anglais: le r final se prononce en liaison devant une voyelle

*

pour l'anglais: précède la syllabe accentuée

ˈ

Miscellaneous

in French transcription: no liaison before aspirate h

En règle générale, la prononciation est donnée entre crochets après chaque entrée. Toutefois, du côté anglais-français et dans le cas des expressions composées de deux ou plusieurs mots non réunis par un trait d'union et faisant l'objet d'une entrée séparée, la prononciation doit être cherchée sous chacun des mots constitutifs de l'expression en question.

PHONETIC TRANSCRIPTION

Voyelles

NB. La mise en équivalence de certains sons n'indique qu'une ressemblance approximative.

Vowels

NB. The pairing of some vowel sounds only indicates approximate equivalence.

ici vie lyre	i iː	heel bead
	ɪ	hit pity
jouer été	e	
lait jouet merci	ɛ	set tent
plat amour	a æ	bat apple
bas pâte	ɑ ɑː	after car calm
	ʌ	fun cousin
le premier	ə	over above
beurre peur	œ	
peu deux	ø əː	urn fern work
or homme	ɔ	wash pot
mot eau gauche	o ɔː	born cork
genou roue	u	full soot
	uː	boon lewd
rue urne	y	

Diphtongues

Diphthongs

ɪə	beer tier
ɛə	tear fair there
eɪ	date plaice day
aɪ	life buy cry
au	owl foul now
əu	low no
ɔɪ	boil boy oily
uə	poor tour

Nasales

Nasal Vowels

matin plein	ɛ̃
brun	œ̃
sang an dans	ɑ̃
non pont	ɔ̃

In general, we give the pronunciation of each entry in square brackets after the word in question. However, on the English-French side, where the entry is composed of two or more unhyphenated words, each of which is given elsewhere in this dictionary, you will find the pronunciation of each word in its alphabetical position.

LE VERBE ANGLAIS

present	pt	pp	present	pt	pp
arise	arose	arisen	drive	drove	driven
awake	awoke	awoken	dwell	dwelt	dwelt
be (am, is, are; being)	was, were	been	eat	ate	eaten
			fall	fell	fallen
			feed	fed	fed
bear	bore	born(e)	feel	felt	felt
beat	beat	beaten	fight	fought	fought
become	became	become	find	found	found
befall	befell	befallen	flee	fled	fled
begin	began	begun	fling	flung	flung
behold	beheld	beheld	fly	flew	flown
bend	bent	bent	forbid	forbad(e)	forbidden
beset	beset	beset	forecast	forecast	forecast
bet	bet, betted	bet, betted	forget	forgot	forgotten
bid (at auction, cards)	bid	bid	forgive	forgave	forgiven
			forsake	forsook	forsaken
			freeze	froze	frozen
bid (say)	bade	bidden	get	got	got, (US) gotten
bind	bound	bound			
bite	bit	bitten	give	gave	given
bleed	bled	bled	go (goes)	went	gone
blow	blew	blown	grind	ground	ground
break	broke	broken	grow	grew	grown
breed	bred	bred	hang	hung	hung
bring	brought	brought	hang (execute)	hanged	hanged
build	built	built			
burn	burnt, burned	burnt, burned	have	had	had
			hear	heard	heard
burst	burst	burst	hide	hid	hidden
buy	bought	bought	hit	hit	hit
can	could	(been able)	hold	held	held
cast	cast	cast	hurt	hurt	hurt
catch	caught	caught	keep	kept	kept
choose	chose	chosen	kneel	knelt, kneeled	knelt, kneeled
cling	clung	clung			
come	came	come	know	knew	known
cost	cost	cost	lay	laid	laid
cost (work out price of)	costed	costed	lead	led	led
			lean	leant, leaned	leant, leaned
creep	crept	crept	leap	leapt, leaped	leapt, leaped
cut	cut	cut			
deal	dealt	dealt	learn	learnt, learned	learnt, learned
dig	dug	dug			
do (3rd person: he/she/it does)	did	done	leave	left	left
			lend	lent	lent
			let	let	let
			lie (lying)	lay	lain
draw	drew	drawn	light	lit, lighted	lit, lighted
dream	dreamed, dreamt	dreamed, dreamt	lose	lost	lost
			make	made	made
drink	drank	drunk	may	might	—

present	pt	pp	present	pt	pp
mean	meant	meant	speed	sped,	sped,
meet	met	met		speeded	speeded
mistake	mistook	mistaken	spell	spelt,	spelt,
mow	mowed	mown,		spelled	spelled
		mowed	spend	spent	spent
must	(had to)	(had to)	spill	spilt,	spilt,
pay	paid	paid		spilled	spilled
put	put	put	spin	spun	spun
quit	quit,	quit,	spit	spat	spat
	quitted	quitted	spoil	spoiled,	spoiled,
read	read	read		spoilt	spoilt
rid	rid	rid	spread	spread	spread
ride	rode	ridden	spring	sprang	sprung
ring	rang	rung	stand	stood	stood
rise	rose	risen	steal	stole	stolen
run	ran	run	stick	stuck	stuck
saw	sawed	sawed,	sting	stung	stung
		sawn	stink	stank	stunk
say	said	said	stride	strode	stridden
see	saw	seen	strike	struck	struck
seek	sought	sought	strive	strove	striven
sell	sold	sold	swear	swore	sworn
send	sent	sent	sweep	swept	swept
set	set	set	swell	swelled	swollen,
sew	sewed	sewn			swelled
shake	shook	shaken	swim	swam	swum
shear	sheared	shorn,	swing	swung	swung
		sheared	take	took	taken
shed	shed	shed	teach	taught	taught
shine	shone	shone	tear	tore	torn
shoot	shot	shot	tell	told	told
show	showed	shown	think	thought	thought
shrink	shrank	shrunk	throw	threw	thrown
shut	shut	shut	thrust	thrust	thrust
sing	sang	sung	tread	trod	trodden
sink	sank	sunk	wake	woke,	woken,
sit	sat	sat		waked	waked
slay	slew	slain	wear	wore	worn
sleep	slept	slept	weave	wove	woven
slide	slid	slid	weave	weaved	weaved
sling	slung	slung	*(wind)*		
slit	slit	slit	wed	wedded,	wedded,
smell	smelt,	smelt,		wed	wed
	smelled	smelled	weep	wept	wept
sow	sowed	sown,	win	won	won
		sowed	wind	wound	wound
speak	spoke	spoken	wring	wrung	wrung
			write	wrote	written

LES NOMBRES

NUMBERS

un (une)	1	one
deux	2	two
trois	3	three
quatre	4	four
cinq	5	five
six	6	six
sept	7	seven
huit	8	eight
neuf	9	nine
dix	10	ten
onze	11	eleven
douze	12	twelve
treize	13	thirteen
quatorze	14	fourteen
quinze	15	fifteen
seize	16	sixteen
dix-sept	17	seventeen
dix-huit	18	eighteen
dix-neuf	19	nineteen
vingt	20	twenty
vingt et un (une)	21	twenty-one
vingt-deux	22	twenty-two
trente	30	thirty
quarante	40	forty
cinquante	50	fifty
soixante	60	sixty
soixante-dix	70	seventy
soixante et onze	71	seventy-one
soixante-douze	72	seventy-two
quatre-vingts	80	eighty
quatre-vingt-un (-une)	81	eighty-one
quatre-vingt-dix	90	ninety
quatre-vingt-onze	91	ninety-one
cent	100	a hundred
cent un (une)	101	a hundred and one
trois cents	300	three hundred
trois cent un (une)	301	three hundred and one
mille	1 000	a thousand
un million	1 000 000	a million

LES NOMBRES

NUMBERS

premier (première), 1er	first, 1st
deuxième, 2e *or* 2ème	second, 2nd
troisième, 3e *or* 3ème	third, 3rd
quatrième	fourth, 4th
cinquième	fifth, 5th
sixième	sixth, 6th
septième	seventh
huitième	eighth
neuvième	ninth
dixième	tenth
onzième	eleventh
douzième	twelfth
treizième	thirteenth
quatorzième	fourteenth
quinzième	fifteenth
seizième	sixteenth
dix-septième	seventeenth
dix-huitième	eighteenth
dix-neuvième	nineteenth
vingtième	twentieth
vingt-et-unième	twenty-first
vingt-deuxième	twenty-second
trentième	thirtieth
centième	hundredth
cent-unième	hundred-and-first
millième	thousandth

L'HEURE

quelle heure est-il?
il est ...

minuit
une heure (du matin)

une heure cinq
une heure dix
une heure et quart
une heure vingt-cinq

une heure et demie, une heure
  trente
deux heures moins vingt-cinq, une
  heure trente-cinq
deux heures moins vingt, une
  heure quarante
deux heures moins le quart, une
  heure quarante-cinq
deux heures moins dix, une heure
  cinquante
midi
deux heures (de l'après-midi)

sept heures (du soir)

à quelle heure?

à minuit
à sept heures
à une heure

dans vingt minutes
il y a dix minutes

LA DATE

aujourd'hui
demain
après-demain
hier
avant-hier
la veille
le lendemain

THE TIME

what time is it?
it's ...

midnight
one o'clock (in the morning) , one
  (am)
five past one
ten past one
a quarter past one, one fifteen
twenty-five past one, one twenty-
  five
half past one, one thirty

twenty-five to two, one thirty-five

twenty to two, one forty

a quarter to two, one forty-five

ten to two, one fifty

twelve o'clock, midday, noon
two o'clock (in the afternoon), two
  (pm)
seven o'clock (in the evening),
  seven (pm)

at what time?

at midnight
at seven o'clock
at one o'clock

in twenty minutes
ten minutes ago

THE DATE

today
tomorrow
the day after tomorrow
yesterday
the day before yesterday
the day before, the previous day
the next *or* following day

le matin	morning
le soir	evening
ce matin	this morning
ce soir	this evening
cet après-midi	this afternoon
hier matin	yesterday morning
hier soir	yesterday evening
demain matin	tomorrow morning
demain soir	tomorrow evening
dans la nuit du samedi au dimanche	during Saturday night, during the night of Saturday to Sunday
il viendra samedi	he's coming on Saturday
le samedi	on Saturdays
tous les samedis	every Saturday
samedi passé *ou* dernier	last Saturday
samedi prochain	next Saturday
samedi en huit	a week on Saturday
samedi en quinze	a fortnight *or* two weeks on Saturday
du lundi au samedi	from Monday to Saturday
tous les jours	every day
une fois par semaine	once a week
une fois par mois	once a month
deux fois par semaine	twice a week
il y a une semaine *ou* huit jours	a week ago
il y a quinze jours	a fortnight *or* two weeks ago
l'année passée *ou* dernière	last year
dans deux jours	in two days
dans huit jours *ou* une semaine	in a week
dans quinze jours	in a fortnight *or* two weeks
le mois prochain	next month
l'année prochaine	next year
quel jour sommes-nous?	*what day is it?*
le 1er/24 octobre 1996	the 1st/24th of October 1996, October 1st/24th 1996
en 1996	in 1996
mille neuf cent quatre-vingt seize	nineteen ninety-six
44 av. J.-C.	44 BC
14 apr. J.-C.	14 AD
au XIXe (siècle)	in the nineteenth century
dans les années trente	in the thirties
il était une fois ...	once upon a time ...

A a

A, a [ɑ] *nm inv* A, a ♦ *abr* = **anticyclone, are**; (= *ampère*) amp; (= *autoroute*) ≈ M (*BRIT*); **A comme Anatole** A for Andrew (*BRIT*) *ou* Able (*US*); **de a à z** from a to z; **prouver qch par a + b** to prove sth conclusively.
a [a] *vb voir* **avoir**.

=== MOT-CLÉ

à [a] (*à + le* = **au**, *à + les* = **aux**) *prép* **1** (*endroit, situation*) at, in; **être ~ Paris/au Portugal** to be in Paris/Portugal; **être ~ la maison/~ l'école** to be at home/at school; **~ la campagne** in the country; **c'est ~ 10 km/~ 20 minutes (d'ici)** it's 10 km/20 minutes away
2 (*direction*) to; **aller ~ Paris/au Portugal** to go to Paris/Portugal; **aller ~ la maison/~ l'école** to go home/to school; **~ la campagne** to the country
3 (*temps*): **~ 3 heures/minuit** at 3 o'clock/midnight; **au printemps** in the spring; **au mois de juin** in June; **au départ** at the start, at the outset; **~ demain/la semaine prochaine!** see you tomorrow/next week!; **visites de 5 heures ~ 6 heures** visiting from 5 to *ou* till 6 o'clock
4 (*attribution, appartenance*) to; **le livre est ~ Paul/~ lui/~ nous** this book is Paul's/his/ours; **donner qch ~ qn** to give sth to sb; **un ami ~ moi** a friend of mine; **c'est ~ moi de le faire** it's up to me to do it
5 (*moyen*) with; **se chauffer au gaz** to have gas heating; **~ bicyclette** on a *ou* by bicycle; **~ la main/machine** by hand/machine; **~ la télévision/la radio** on television/the radio
6 (*provenance*) from; **boire ~ la bouteille** to drink from the bottle
7 (*caractérisation, manière*): **l'homme aux yeux bleus** the man with the blue eyes; **~ la russe** the Russian way; **glace ~ la framboise** raspberry ice cream
8 (*but, destination*): **tasse ~ café** coffee cup; **maison ~ vendre** house for sale; **problème ~ régler** problem to sort out
9 (*rapport, évaluation, distribution*): **100 km/unités ~ l'heure** 100 km/units per *ou* an hour; **payé ~ l'heure** paid by the hour; **cinq ~ six** five to six

10 (*conséquence, résultat*): **~ ce qu'il prétend** according to him; **~ leur grande surprise** much to their surprise; **~ nous trois nous n'avons pas su le faire** we couldn't do it even between the three of us; **ils sont arrivés ~ 4** 4 of them arrived (together).

Å *abr* (= *Angstrom*) A *ou* Å.
A2 *abr* (= *Antenne 2*) *French TV channel*.
AB *abr* = *assez bien*.
abaissement [abɛsmɑ̃] *nm* lowering; pulling down.
abaisser [abese] *vt* to lower, bring down; (*manette*) to pull down; (*fig*) to debase; to humiliate; **s'~** *vi* to go down; (*fig*) to demean o.s.; **s'~ à faire/à qch** to stoop *ou* descend to doing/to sth.
abandon [abɑ̃dɔ̃] *nm* abandoning; deserting; giving up; withdrawal; surrender, relinquishing; (*fig*) lack of constraint; relaxed pose *ou* mood; **être à l'~** to be in a state of neglect; **laisser à l'~** to abandon.
abandonné, e [abɑ̃dɔne] *adj* (*solitaire*) deserted; (*route, usine*) disused; (*jardin*) abandoned.
abandonner [abɑ̃dɔne] *vt* to leave, abandon, desert; (*projet, activité*) to abandon, give up; (*SPORT*) to retire *ou* withdraw from; (*céder*) to surrender, relinquish; **s'~** *vi* to let o.s. go; **s'~ à** (*paresse, plaisirs*) to give o.s. up to; **~ qch à qn** to give sth up to sb.
abasourdir [abazurdir] *vt* to stun, stagger.
abat [aba] *etc vb voir* **abattre**.
abat-jour [abaʒur] *nm inv* lampshade.
abats [aba] *vb voir* **abattre** ♦ *nmpl* (*de bœuf, porc*) offal *sg* (*BRIT*), entrails (*US*); (*de volaille*) giblets.
abattage [abataʒ] *nm* cutting down, felling.
abattant [abatɑ̃] *vb voir* **abattre** ♦ *nm* leaf, flap.
abattement [abatmɑ̃] *nm* (*physique*) enfeeblement; (*moral*) dejection, despondency; (*déduction*) reduction; **~ fiscal** ≈ tax allowance.
abattis [abati] *vb voir* **abattre** ♦ *nmpl* giblets.
abattoir [abatwar] *nm* abattoir (*BRIT*), slaughterhouse.
abattre [abatʀ(ə)] *vt* (*arbre*) to cut down, fell; (*mur, maison*) to pull down; (*avion, personne*)

to shoot down; (*animal*) to shoot, kill; (*fig: physiquement*) to wear out, tire out; (: *moralement*) to demoralize; **s'~** *vi* to crash down; **s'~ sur** (*suj: pluie*) to beat down on; (: *coups, injures*) to rain down on; **~ ses cartes** (*aussi fig*) to lay one's cards on the table; **~ du travail** *ou* **de la besogne** to get through a lot of work.

abattu, e [abaty] *pp de* **abattre ♦** *adj* (*déprimé*) downcast.

abbatiale [abasjal] *nf* abbey (*church*).

abbaye [abei] *nf* abbey.

abbé [abe] *nm* priest; (*d'une abbaye*) abbot; **M l'~** Father.

abbesse [abɛs] *nf* abbess.

abc, ABC [abese] *nm* alphabet primer; (*fig*) rudiments *pl*.

abcès [apsɛ] *nm* abscess.

abdication [abdikasjɔ̃] *nf* abdication.

abdiquer [abdike] *vi* to abdicate **♦** *vt* to renounce, give up.

abdomen [abdɔmɛn] *nm* abdomen.

abdominal, e, aux [abdɔminal, -o] *adj* abdominal **♦** *nmpl*: **faire des abdominaux** to do exercises for the stomach muscles.

abécédaire [abesedɛʀ] *nm* alphabet primer.

abeille [abɛj] *nf* bee.

aberrant, e [abeʀɑ̃, -ɑ̃t] *adj* absurd.

aberration [abeʀasjɔ̃] *nf* aberration.

abêtir [abetiʀ] *vt* to make morons (*ou* a moron) of.

abêtissant, e [abetisɑ̃, -ɑ̃t] *adj* stultifying.

abhorrer [abɔʀe] *vt* to abhor, loathe.

abîme [abim] *nm* abyss, gulf.

abîmer [abime] *vt* to spoil, damage; **s'~** *vi* to get spoilt *ou* damaged; (*fruits*) to spoil; (*tomber*) to sink, founder; **s'~ les yeux** to ruin one's eyes *ou* eyesight.

abject, e [abʒɛkt] *adj* abject, despicable.

abjurer [abʒyʀe] *vt* to abjure, renounce.

ablatif [ablatif] *nm* ablative.

ablation [ablasjɔ̃] *nf* removal.

ablutions [ablysjɔ̃] *nfpl*: **faire ses ~** to perform one's ablutions.

abnégation [abnegasjɔ̃] *nf* (self-)abnegation.

aboie [abwa] *etc vb voir* **aboyer**.

aboiement [abwamɑ̃] *nm* bark, barking *no pl*.

aboierai [abwajəʀe] *etc vb voir* **aboyer**.

abois [abwa] *nmpl*: **aux ~** at bay.

abolir [abɔliʀ] *vt* to abolish.

abolition [abɔlisjɔ̃] *nf* abolition.

abolitionniste [abɔlisjɔnist(ə)] *adj, nm/f* abolitionist.

abominable [abɔminabl(ə)] *adj* abominable.

abomination [abɔminasjɔ̃] *nf* abomination.

abondamment [abɔ̃damɑ̃] *adv* abundantly.

abondance [abɔ̃dɑ̃s] *nf* abundance; (*richesse*) affluence; **en ~** in abundance.

abondant, e [abɔ̃dɑ̃, -ɑ̃t] *adj* plentiful, abundant, copious.

abonder [abɔ̃de] *vi* to abound, be plentiful; **~ en** to be full of, abound in; **~ dans le sens de**

qn to concur with sb.

abonné, e [abɔne] *nm/f* subscriber; season ticket holder **♦** *adj*: **être ~ à un journal** to subscribe to *ou* have a subscription to a periodical; **être ~ au téléphone** to be on the (tele)phone.

abonnement [abɔnmɑ̃] *nm* subscription; (*pour transports en commun, concerts*) season ticket.

abonner [abɔne] *vt*: **s'~ à** to subscribe to, take out a subscription to.

abord [abɔʀ] *nm*: **être d'un ~ facile** to be approachable; **être d'un ~ difficile** (*personne*) to be unapproachable; (*lieu*) to be hard to reach *ou* difficult to get to; **de prime ~, au premier ~** at first sight; **d'~** *adv* first; **tout d'~** first of all.

abordable [abɔʀdabl(ə)] *adj* (*personne*) approachable; (*marchandise*) reasonably priced; (*prix*) affordable, reasonable.

abordage [abɔʀdaʒ] *nm* boarding.

aborder [abɔʀde] *vi* to land **♦** *vt* (*sujet, difficulté*) to tackle; (*personne*) to approach; (*rivage etc*) to reach; (*NAVIG: attaquer*) to board; (: *heurter*) to collide with.

abords [abɔʀ] *nmpl* surroundings.

aborigène [abɔʀiʒɛn] *nm* aborigine, native.

Abou Dhabî, Abu Dhabî [abudabi] *nm* Abu Dhabi.

aboulique [abulik] *adj* totally lacking in willpower.

aboutir [abutiʀ] *vi* (*négociations etc*) to succeed; (*abcès*) to come to a head; **~ à/dans/sur** to end up at/in/on.

aboutissants [abutisɑ̃] *nmpl voir* **tenants**.

aboutissement [abutismɑ̃] *nm* success; (*de concept, projet*) successful realization; (*d'années de travail*) successful conclusion.

aboyer [abwaje] *vi* to bark.

abracadabrant, e [abʀakadabʀɑ̃, -ɑ̃t] *adj* incredible, preposterous.

abrasif, ive [abʀazif, -iv] *adj, nm* abrasive.

abrégé [abʀeʒe] *nm* summary; **en ~** in a shortened *ou* abbreviated form.

abréger [abʀeʒe] *vt* (*texte*) to shorten, abridge; (*mot*) to shorten, abbreviate; (*réunion, voyage*) to cut short, shorten.

abreuver [abʀœve] *vt* to water; (*fig*): **~ qn de** to shower *ou* swamp sb with; (*injures etc*) to shower sb with; **s'~** *vi* to drink.

abreuvoir [abʀœvwaʀ] *nm* watering place.

abréviation [abʀevjasjɔ̃] *nf* abbreviation.

abri [abʀi] *nm* shelter; **à l'~** under cover; **être/se mettre à l'~** to be/get under cover *ou* shelter; **à l'~ de** sheltered from; (*fig*) safe from.

Abribus [abʀibys] *nm ®* bus shelter.

abricot [abʀiko] *nm* apricot.

abricotier [abʀikɔtje] *nm* apricot tree.

abrité, e [abʀite] *adj* sheltered.

abriter [abʀite] *vt* to shelter; (*loger*) to accommodate; **s'~** to shelter, take cover.

abrogation [abʁɔgasjɔ̃] *nf* (*JUR*) repeal, abrogation.

abroger [abʁɔʒe] *vt* to repeal, abrogate.

abrupt, e [abʁypt] *adj* sheer, steep; (*ton*) abrupt.

abruti, e [abʁyti] *nm/f* (*fam*) idiot, moron.

abrutir [abʁytiʁ] *vt* to daze; (*fatiguer*) to exhaust; (*abêtir*) to stupefy.

abrutissant, e [abʁytisɑ̃, -ɑ̃t] *adj* (*bruit, travail*) stupefying.

abscisse [apsis] *nf* X axis, abscissa.

absence [apsɑ̃s] *nf* absence; (*MÉD*) blackout; (*distraction*) mental blank; **en l'~ de** in the absence of.

absent, e [apsɑ̃, -ɑ̃t] *adj* absent; (*chose*) missing, lacking; (*distrait: air*) vacant, faraway ♦ *nm/f* absentee.

absentéisme [apsɑ̃teism(ə)] *nm* absenteeism.

absenter [apsɑ̃te]: **s'~** *vi* to take time off work; (*sortir*) to leave, go out.

abside [apsid] *nf* (*ARCHIT*) apse.

absinthe [apsɛ̃t] *nf* (*boisson*) absinth(e); (*BOT*) wormwood, absinth(e).

absolu, e [apsɔly] *adj* absolute; (*caractère*) rigid, uncompromising ♦ *nm* (*PHILOSOPHIE*): **l'~** the Absolute; **dans l'~** in the absolute, in a vacuum.

absolument [apsɔlymɑ̃] *adv* absolutely.

absolution [apsɔlysjɔ̃] *nf* absolution; (*JUR*) dismissal (*of case*).

absolutisme [apsɔlytism(ə)] *nm* absolutism.

absolvais [apsɔlvɛ] *etc vb voir* **absoudre**.

absorbant, e [apsɔʁbɑ̃, -ɑ̃t] *adj* absorbent; (*tâche*) absorbing, engrossing.

absorbé, e [apsɔʁbe] *adj* absorbed, engrossed.

absorber [apsɔʁbe] *vt* to absorb; (*gén MÉD: manger, boire*) to take; (*ÉCON: firme*) to take over, absorb.

absorption [apsɔʁpsjɔ̃] *nf* absorption.

absoudre [apsudʁ(ə)] *vt* to absolve; (*JUR*) to dismiss.

absous, oute [apsu, -ut] *pp de* **absoudre**.

abstenir [apstəniʁ]: **s'~** *vi* (*POL*) to abstain; **s'~ de qch/de faire** to refrain from sth/from doing.

abstention [apstɑ̃sjɔ̃] *nf* abstention.

abstentionnisme [apstɑ̃sjɔnism(ə)] *nm* abstaining.

abstentionniste [apstɑ̃sjɔnist(ə)] *nm* abstentionist.

abstenu, e [apstəny] *pp de* **abstenir**.

abstiendrai [apstjɛ̃dʁe], **abstiens** [apstjɛ̃] *etc voir* **abstenir**.

abstinence [apstinɑ̃s] *nf* abstinence; **faire ~** to abstain (*from meat on Fridays*).

abstint [apstɛ̃] *etc vb voir* **abstenir**.

abstraction [apstʁaksjɔ̃] *nf* abstraction; **faire ~ de** to set *ou* leave aside; **~ faite de ...** leaving aside ....

abstraire [apstʁɛʁ] *vt* to abstract; **s'~** *vi*: **s'~ (de)** (*s'isoler*) to cut o.s. off (from).

abstrait, e [apstʁɛ, -ɛt] *pp de* **abstraire** ♦ *adj* abstract ♦ *nm*: **dans l'~** in the abstract.

abstraitement [apstʁɛtmɑ̃] *adv* abstractly.

abstrayais [apstʁɛje] *etc vb voir* **abstraire**.

absurde [apsyʁd(ə)] *adj* absurd ♦ *nm* absurdity; (*PHILOSOPHIE*): **l'~** absurd; **par l'~** ad absurdio.

absurdité [apsyʁdite] *nf* absurdity.

abus [aby] *nm* (*excès*) abuse, misuse; (*injustice*) abuse; **~ de confiance** breach of trust; (*détournement de fonds*) embezzlement; **~ de pouvoir** abuse of power.

abuser [abyze] *vi* to go too far, overstep the mark ♦ *vt* to deceive, mislead; **s'~** *vi* (*se méprendre*) to be mistaken; **~ de** *vt* (*force, droit*) to misuse; (*alcool*) to take to excess; (*violer, duper*) to take advantage of.

abusif, ive [abyzif, -iv] *adj* exorbitant; (*punition*) excessive; (*pratique*) improper.

abusivement [abyzivmɑ̃] *adv* exorbitantly; excessively; improperly.

AC *sigle f* (= *appellation contrôlée*) *guarantee of quality of wine*.

acabit [akabi] *nm*: **du même ~** of the same type.

acacia [akasja] *nm* (*BOT*) acacia.

académicien, ne [akademisjɛ̃, -ɛn] *nm/f* academician.

académie [akademi] *nf* (*société*) learned society; (*école: d'art, de danse*) academy; (*ART: nu*) nude; (*SCOL: circonscription*) ≈ regional education authority; **l'A~ (française)** the French Academy.

> The **Académie française** was founded by Cardinal Richelieu in 1635 during the reign of Louis XIII. It consists of forty elected scholars and writers who are known as "les Quarante" or "les Immortels". One of the Académie's functions is to regulate the development of the French language and its recommendations are frequently the subject of lively public debate. It has produced several editions of its famous dictionary and also awards various literary prizes.

académique [akademik] *adj* academic.

Acadie [akadi] *nf*: **l'~** the Maritime Provinces.

acadien, ne [akadjɛ̃, -ɛn] *adj* Acadian, of *ou* from the Maritime Provinces.

acajou [akaʒu] *nm* mahogany.

acariâtre [akaʁjɑtʁ(ə)] *adj* sour(-tempered) (*BRIT*), cantankerous.

accablant, e [akablɑ̃, -ɑ̃t] *adj* (*témoignage, preuve*) overwhelming.

accablement [akabləmɑ̃] *nm* deep despondency.

accabler [akable] *vt* to overwhelm, overcome; (*suj: témoignage*) to condemn, damn; **~ qn d'injures** to heap *ou* shower abuse on sb; **~ qn de travail** to overburden sb with work; **accablé de dettes/soucis** weighed down with debts/cares.

accalmie [akalmi] *nf* lull.

accaparant, e [akaparɑ̃, -ɑ̃t] *adj* that takes up all one's time *ou* attention.

accaparer [akapaʀe] *vt* to monopolize; *(suj: travail etc)* to take up (all) the time *ou* attention of.

accéder [aksede]: ~ **à** *vt (lieu)* to reach; *(fig: pouvoir)* to accede to; *(: poste)* to attain; *(accorder: requête)* to grant, accede to.

accélérateur [akseleʀatœʀ] *nm* accelerator.

accélération [akseleʀasjɔ̃] *nf* speeding up; acceleration.

accéléré [akseleʀe] *nm:* **en** ~ *(CINÉ)* speeded up.

accélérer [akseleʀe] *vt (mouvement, travaux)* to speed up ♦ *vi (AUTO)* to accelerate.

accent [aksɑ̃] *nm* accent; *(inflexions expressives)* tone (of voice); *(PHONÉTIQUE, fig)* stress; **aux ~s de** *(musique)* to the strains of; **mettre l'~ sur** *(fig)* to stress; ~ **aigu/grave/ circonflexe** acute/grave/ circumflex accent.

accentuation [aksɑ̃tɥasjɔ̃] *nf* accenting; stressing.

accentué, e [aksɑ̃tɥe] *adj* marked, pronounced.

accentuer [aksɑ̃tɥe] *vt (LING: orthographe)* to accent; *(: phonétique)* to stress, accent; *(fig)* to accentuate, emphasize; *(: effort, pression)* to increase; **s'~** *vi* to become more marked *ou* pronounced.

acceptable [aksɛptabl(ə)] *adj* satisfactory, acceptable.

acceptation [aksɛptasjɔ̃] *nf* acceptance.

accepter [aksɛpte] *vt* to accept; *(tolérer):* ~ **que qn fasse** to agree to sb doing; ~ **de faire** to agree to do.

acception [aksɛpsjɔ̃] *nf* meaning, sense; **dans toute l'~ du terme** in the full sense *ou* meaning of the word.

accès [aksɛ] *nm (à un lieu, INFORM)* access; *(MÉD)* attack; *(: de toux)* fit, bout ♦ *nmpl (routes etc)* means of access, approaches; **d'~ facile/malaisé** easily/not easily accessible; **donner** ~ **à** *(lieu)* to give access to; *(carrière)* to open the door to; **avoir** ~ **auprès de qn** to have access to sb; **l'~ aux quais est interdit aux personnes non munies d'un billet** ticket-holders only on platforms, no access to platforms without a ticket; ~ **de colère** fit of anger; ~ **de joie** burst of joy.

accessible [aksesibl(ə)] *adj* accessible; *(personne)* approachable; *(livre, sujet):* ~ **à qn** within the reach of sb; *(sensible):* ~ **à la pitié/l'amour** open to pity/love.

accession [aksɛsjɔ̃] *nf:* ~ **à** accession to; *(à un poste)* attainment of; ~ **à la propriété** homeownership.

accessit [aksesit] *nm (SCOL)* ≈ certificate of merit.

accessoire [akseswaʀ] *adj* secondary, of secondary importance; *(frais)* incidental ♦ *nm*

accessory; *(THÉÂT)* prop.

accessoirement [akseswaʀmɑ̃] *adv* secondarily; incidentally.

accessoiriste [akseswaʀist(ə)] *nm/f (TV, CINÉ)* property man/woman.

accident [aksidɑ̃] *nm* accident; **par** ~ by chance; ~ **de parcours** mishap; ~ **de la route** road accident; ~ **du travail** accident at work; industrial injury *ou* accident; **~s de terrain** unevenness of the ground.

accidenté, e [aksidɑ̃te] *adj* damaged *ou* injured (in an accident); *(relief, terrain)* uneven; hilly.

accidentel, le [aksidɑ̃tɛl] *adj* accidental.

accidentellement [aksidɑ̃tɛlmɑ̃] *adv (par hasard)* accidentally; *(mourir)* in an accident.

accise [aksiz] *nf:* **droit d'~(s)** excise duty.

acclamation [aklamasjɔ̃] *nf:* **par** ~ *(vote)* by acclamation; **~s** *nfpl* cheers, cheering *sg*.

acclamer [aklame] *vt* to cheer, acclaim.

acclimatation [aklimatasjɔ̃] *nf* acclimatization.

acclimater [aklimate] *vt* to acclimatize; **s'~** *vi* to become acclimatized.

accointances [akwɛ̃tɑ̃s] *nfpl:* **avoir des** ~ **avec** to have contacts with.

accolade [akɔlad] *nf (amicale)* embrace; *(signe)* brace; **donner l'~ à qn** to embrace sb.

accoler [akɔle] *vt* to place side by side.

accommodant, e [akɔmɔdɑ̃, -ɑ̃t] *adj* accommodating, easy-going.

accommodement [akɔmɔdmɑ̃] *nm* compromise.

accommoder [akɔmɔde] *vt (CULIN)* to prepare; *(points de vue)* to reconcile; ~ **qch à** *(adapter)* to adapt sth to; **s'~ de** to put up with; *(se contenter de)* to make do with; **s'~ à** *(s'adapter)* to adapt to.

accompagnateur, trice [akɔ̃paɲatœʀ, -tʀis] *nm/f (MUS)* accompanist; *(de voyage)* guide; *(de voyage organisé)* courier; *(d'enfants)* accompanying adult.

accompagnement [akɔ̃paɲmɑ̃] *nm (MUS)* accompaniment; *(MIL)* support.

accompagner [akɔ̃paɲe] *vt* to accompany, be *ou* go *ou* come with; *(MUS)* to accompany; **s'~ de** to bring, be accompanied by.

accompli, e [akɔ̃pli] *adj* accomplished.

accomplir [akɔ̃pliʀ] *vt (tâche, projet)* to carry out; *(souhait)* to fulfil; **s'~** *vi* to be fulfilled.

accomplissement [akɔ̃plismɑ̃] *nm* carrying out; fulfilment *(BRIT)*, fulfillment *(US)*.

accord [akɔʀ] *nm (entente, convention, LING)* agreement; *(entre des styles, tons etc)* harmony; *(consentement)* agreement, consent; *(MUS)* chord; **donner son** ~ to give one's agreement; **mettre 2 personnes d'~** to make 2 people come to an agreement, reconcile 2 people; **se mettre d'~** to come to an agreement (with each other); **être d'~** to agree; **être d'~ avec qn** to agree with sb; **d'~!** OK!, right!; **d'un commun ~** of one accord; **~ parfait** (MUS) tonic chord.

accord-cadre, pl **accords-cadres** [akɔʀkadʀ(ə)] nm framework ou outline agreement.

accordéon [akɔʀdeɔ̃] nm (MUS) accordion.

accordéoniste [akɔʀdeɔnist(ə)] nm/f accordionist.

accorder [akɔʀde] vt (faveur, délai) to grant; (attribuer): **~ de l'importance/de la valeur à qch** to attach importance/value to sth; (harmoniser) to match; (MUS) to tune; **s'~** to get on together; (être d'accord) to agree; (couleurs, caractères) to go together, match; (LING) to agree; **je vous accorde que** ... I grant you that ....

accordeur [akɔʀdœʀ] nm (MUS) tuner.

accoster [akɔste] vt (NAVIG) to draw alongside; (personne) to accost ♦ vi (NAVIG) to berth.

accotement [akɔtmɑ̃] nm (de route) verge (BRIT), shoulder; **~ stabilisé/non stabilisé** hard shoulder/soft verge ou shoulder.

accoter [akɔte] vt: **~ qch contre/à** to lean ou rest sth against/on; **s'~ contre/à** to lean against/on.

accouchement [akuʃmɑ̃] nm delivery, (child)birth; (travail) labour (BRIT), labor (US); **~ à terme** delivery at (full) term; **~ sans douleur** natural childbirth.

accoucher [akuʃe] vi to give birth, have a baby; (être en travail) to be in labour (BRIT) ou labor (US) ♦ vt to deliver; **~ d'un garçon** to give birth to a boy.

accoucheur [akuʃœʀ] nm: **(médecin) ~** obstetrician.

accoucheuse [akuʃøz] nf midwife.

accouder [akude]: **s'~** vi: **s'~ à/contre/sur** to rest one's elbows on/against/on; **accoudé à la fenêtre** leaning on the windowsill.

accoudoir [akudwaʀ] nm armrest.

accouplement [akupləmɑ̃] nm coupling; mating.

accoupler [akuple] vt to couple; (pour la reproduction) to mate; **s'~** to mate.

accourir [akuʀiʀ] vi to rush ou run up.

accoutrement [akutʀəmɑ̃] nm (péj) getup (BRIT), outfit.

accoutrer [akutʀe] (péj) vt to do ou get up; **s'~** to do ou get o.s. up.

accoutumance [akutymɑ̃s] nf (gén) adaptation; (MÉD) addiction.

accoutumé, e [akutyme] adj (habituel) customary, usual; **comme à l'~e** as is customary ou usual.

accoutumer [akutyme] vt: **~ qn à qch/faire** to accustom sb to sth/to doing; **s'~ à** to get accustomed ou used to.

accréditer [akʀedite] vt (nouvelle) to substantiate; **~ qn (auprès de)** to accredit sb (to).

accro [akʀo] nm/f (fam: = accroché(e)) addict.

accroc [akʀo] nm (déchirure) tear; (fig) hitch, snag; **sans ~** without a hitch; **faire un ~ à** (vêtement) to make a tear in, tear; (fig: règle etc) to infringe.

accrochage [akʀɔʃaʒ] nm hanging (up); hitching (up); (AUTO) (minor) collision; (MIL) encounter, engagement; (dispute) clash, brush.

accroche-cœur [akʀɔʃkœʀ] nm kiss-curl.

accrocher [akʀɔʃe] vt (suspendre): **~ qch à** to hang sth (up) on; (attacher: remorque): **~ qch à** to hitch sth (up) to; (heurter) to catch; to hit; (déchirer): **~ qch (à)** to catch sth (on); (MIL) to engage; (fig) to catch, attract ♦ vi to stick, get stuck; (fig: pourparlers etc) to hit a snag; (plaire: disque etc) to catch on; **s'~** (se disputer) to have a clash ou brush; (ne pas céder) to hold one's own, hang on in (fam); **s'~ à** (rester pris à) to catch on; (agripper, fig) to hang on ou cling to.

accrocheur, euse [akʀɔʃœʀ, -øz] adj (vendeur, concurrent) tenacious; (publicité) eye-catching; (titre) catchy, eye-catching.

accroire [akʀwaʀ] vt: **faire ou laisser ~ à qn/que** to give sb to believe sth/that.

accroîs [akʀwa], **accroissais** [akʀwasɛ] etc vb voir **accroître**.

accroissement [akʀwasmɑ̃] nm increase.

accroître [akʀwatʀ(ə)] vt, **s'~** vi to increase.

accroupi, e [akʀupi] adj squatting, crouching (down).

accroupir [akʀupiʀ]: **s'~** vi to squat, crouch (down).

accru, e [akʀy] pp de **accroître**.

accu [aky] nm (fam: = accumulateur) accumulator, battery.

accueil [akœj] nm welcome; (endroit) reception (desk); (: dans une gare) information kiosk; **comité/centre d'~** reception committee/centre.

accueillant, e [akœjɑ̃, -ɑ̃t] adj welcoming, friendly.

accueillir [akœjiʀ] vt to welcome; (loger) to accommodate.

acculer [akyle] vt: **~ qn à ou contre** to drive sb back against; **~ qn dans** to corner sb in; **~ qn à** (faillite) to drive sb to the brink of.

accumulateur [akymylatœʀ] nm accumulator, battery.

accumulation [akymylɑsjɔ̃] nf accumulation; **chauffage/radiateur à ~** (night-)storage heating/heater.

accumuler [akymyle] vt to accumulate, amass; **s'~** vi to accumulate; to pile up.

accusateur, trice [akyzatœʀ, -tʀis] nm/f accuser ♦ adj accusing; (document, preuve) incriminating.

accusatif [akyzatif] nm (LING) accusative.

accusation [akyzɑsjɔ̃] nf (gén) accusation; (JUR) charge; (partie): **l'~** the prosecution; **mettre en ~** to indict; **acte d'~** bill of indictment.

accusé, e [akyze] nm/f accused; (prévenu(e))

defendant ♦ *nm*: ~ **de réception** acknowledgement of receipt.

accuser [akyze] *vt* to accuse; (*fig*) to emphasize, bring out; (: *montrer*) to show; **s'~** *vi* (*s'accentuer*) to become more marked; ~ **qn de** to accuse sb of; (*JUR*) to charge sb with; ~ **qn/qch de qch** (*rendre responsable*) to blame sb/sth for sth; **s'~ de qch/d'avoir fait qch** to admit sth/having done sth; to blame o.s. for sth/for having done sth; ~ **réception de** to acknowledge receipt of; ~ **le coup** (*aussi fig*) to be visibly affected.

acerbe [asɛrb(ə)] *adj* caustic, acid.

acéré, e [asere] *adj* sharp.

acétate [asetat] *nm* acetate.

acétique [asetik] *adj*: **acide** ~ acetic acid.

acétone [asetɔn] *nf* acetone.

acétylène [asetilɛn] *nm* acetylene.

ACF *sigle m* (= *Automobile Club de France*) ≈ AA (*BRIT*), ≈ AAA (*US*).

ach. *abr* = **achète**.

acharné, e [aʃarne] *adj* (*lutte, adversaire*) fierce, bitter; (*travail*) relentless, unremitting.

acharnement [aʃarnəmɑ̃] *nm* fierceness; relentlessness.

acharner [aʃarne]: **s'~** *vi*: **s'~ sur** to go at fiercely, hound; **s'~ contre** to set o.s. against; to dog, pursue; (*suj: malchance*) to hound; **s'~ à faire** to try doggedly to do; to persist in doing.

achat [aʃa] *nm* buying *no pl*; (*article acheté*) purchase; **faire l'~ de** to buy, purchase; **faire des ~s** to do some shopping, buy a few things.

acheminement [aʃminmɑ̃] *nm* conveyance.

acheminer [aʃmine] *vt* (*courrier*) to forward, dispatch; (*troupes*) to convey, transport; (*train*) to route; **s'~ vers** to head for.

acheter [aʃte] *vt* to buy, purchase; (*soudoyer*) to buy, bribe; ~ **qch à** (*marchand*) to buy *ou* purchase sth from; (*ami etc: offrir*) to buy sth for; ~ **à crédit** to buy on credit.

acheteur, euse [aʃtœr, -øz] *nm/f* buyer; shopper; (*COMM*) buyer; (*JUR*) vendee, purchaser.

achevé, e [aʃve] *adj*: **d'un ridicule** ~ thoroughly *ou* absolutely ridiculous; **d'un comique** ~ absolutely hilarious.

achèvement [aʃɛvmɑ̃] *nm* completion, finishing.

achever [aʃve] *vt* to complete, end; (*blessé*) to finish off; **s'~** *vi* to end.

achoppement [aʃɔpmɑ̃] *nm*: **pierre d'~** stumbling block.

acide [asid] *adj* sour, sharp; (*ton*) acid, biting; (*CHIMIE*) acid(ic) ♦ *nm* acid.

acidifier [asidifje] *vt* to acidify.

acidité [asidite] *nf* sharpness; acidity.

acidulé, e [asidyle] *adj* slightly acid; **bonbons ~s** acid drops (*BRIT*), ≈ lemon drops (*US*).

acier [asje] *nm* steel; ~ **inoxydable** stainless steel.

aciérie [asjeri] *nf* steelworks *sg*.

acné [akne] *nf* acne.

acolyte [akɔlit] *nm* (*péj*) associate.

acompte [akɔ̃t] *nm* deposit; (*versement régulier*) instalment; (*sur somme due*) payment on account; (*sur salaire*) advance; **un ~ de 100 F** 100 F on account.

acoquiner [akɔkine]: **s'~ avec** *vt* (*péj*) to team up with.

Açores [asɔr] *nfpl*: **les** ~ the Azores.

à-côté [akote] *nm* side-issue; (*argent*) extra.

à-coup [aku] *nm* (*du moteur*) (hic)cough; (*fig*) jolt; **sans ~s** smoothly; **par ~s** by fits and starts.

acoustique [akustik] *nf* (*d'une salle*) acoustics *pl*; (*science*) acoustics *sg* ♦ *adj* acoustic.

acquéreur [akerœr] *nm* buyer, purchaser; **se porter/se rendre ~ de qch** to announce one's intention to purchase/to purchase sth.

acquérir [akerir] *vt* to acquire; (*par achat*) to purchase, acquire; (*valeur*) to gain; (*résultats*) to achieve; **ce que ses efforts lui ont acquis** what his efforts have won *ou* gained (for) him.

acquiers [akjɛr] *etc vb voir* **acquérir**.

acquiescement [akjɛsmɑ̃] *nm* acquiescence, agreement.

acquiescer [akjese] *vi* (*opiner*) to agree; (*consentir*): ~ **(à qch)** to acquiesce *ou* assent (to sth).

acquis, e [aki, -iz] *pp de* **acquérir** ♦ *nm* (accumulated) experience; (*avantage*) gain ♦ *adj* (*voir acquérir*) acquired; gained; achieved; **être ~ à** (*plan, idée*) to be in full agreement with; **son aide nous est ~e** we can count on *ou* be sure of his help; **tenir qch pour ~** to take sth for granted.

acquisition [akizisjɔ̃] *nf* acquisition; (*achat*) purchase; **faire l'~ de** to acquire; to purchase.

acquit [aki] *vb voir* **acquérir** ♦ *nm* (*quittance*) receipt; **pour ~** received; **par ~ de conscience** to set one's mind at rest.

acquittement [akitmɑ̃] *nm* acquittal; payment, settlement.

acquitter [akite] *vt* (*JUR*) to acquit; (*facture*) to pay, settle; **s'~ de** to discharge; (*promesse, tâche*) to fulfil (*BRIT*), fulfill (*US*), carry out.

âcre [akr(ə)] *adj* acrid, pungent.

âcreté [akrəte] *nf* acridness, pungency.

acrimonie [akrimɔni] *nf* acrimony.

acrobate [akrɔbat] *nm/f* acrobat.

acrobatie [akrɔbasi] *nf* (*art*) acrobatics *sg*; (*exercice*) acrobatic feat; ~ **aérienne** aerobatics *sg*.

acrobatique [akrɔbatik] *adj* acrobatic.

acronyme [akrɔnim] *nm* acronym.

Acropole [akrɔpɔl] *nf*: **l'~** the Acropolis.

acrylique [akrilik] *adj, nm* acrylic.

acte [akt(ə)] *nm* act, action; (*THÉÂT*) act; **~s** *nmpl* (*compte-rendu*) proceedings; **prendre ~**

de to note, take note of; **faire ~ de présence** to put in an appearance; **faire ~ de candidature** to submit an application; **~ d'accusation** charge (*BRIT*), bill of indictment; **~ de baptême** baptismal certificate; **~ de mariage/naissance** marriage/birth certificate; **~ de vente** bill of sale.

acteur [aktœʀ] *nm* actor.

actif, ive [aktif, -iv] *adj* active ♦ *nm* (*COMM*) assets *pl*; (*LING*) active (voice); (*fig*): **avoir à son ~** to have to one's credit; **~s** *nmpl* people in employment; **mettre à son ~** to add to one's list of achievements; **l'~ et le passif** assets and liabilities; **prendre une part active à qch** to take an active part in sth; **population active** working population.

action [aksjɔ̃] *nf* (*gén*) action; (*COMM*) share; **une bonne/mauvaise ~** a good/an unkind deed; **mettre en ~** to put into action; **passer à l'~** to take action; **sous l'~ de** under the effect of; **l'~ syndicale** (the) union action; **un film d'~** an action film *ou* movie; **~ en diffamation** libel action; **~ de grâce(s)** (*REL*) thanksgiving.

actionnaire [aksjɔnɛʀ] *nm/f* shareholder.

actionner [aksjɔne] *vt* to work; to activate; to operate.

active [aktiv] *adj f voir* **actif**.

activement [aktivmɑ̃] *adv* actively.

activer [aktive] *vt* to speed up; (*CHIMIE*) to activate; **s'~** *vi* (*s'affairer*) to bustle about; (*se hâter*) to hurry up.

activisme [aktivism(ə)] *nm* activism.

activiste [aktivist(ə)] *nm/f* activist.

activité [aktivite] *nf* activity; **en ~** (*volcan*) active; (*fonctionnaire*) in active life; (*militaire*) on active service.

actrice [aktʀis] *nf* actress.

actualiser [aktɥalize] *vt* to actualize; (*mettre à jour*) to bring up to date.

actualité [aktɥalite] *nf* (*d'un problème*) topicality; (*événements*): **l'~** current events; **les ~s** (*CINÉ*, *TV*) the news; **l'~ politique/sportive** the political/sports *ou* sporting news; **les ~s télévisées** the television news; **d'~** topical.

actuel, le [aktɥɛl] *adj* (*présent*) present; (*d'actualité*) topical; (*non virtuel*) actual; **à l'heure ~le** at this moment in time, at the moment.

actuellement [aktɥɛlmɑ̃] *adv* at present, at the present time.

acuité [akɥite] *nf* acuteness.

acuponcteur, acupuncteur [akypɔ̃ktœʀ] *nm* acupuncturist.

acuponcture, acupuncture [akypɔ̃ktyʀ] *nf* acupuncture.

adage [adaʒ] *nm* adage.

adagio [ada(d)ʒjo] *adv, nm* adagio.

adaptable [adaptabl(ə)] *adj* adaptable.

adaptateur, trice [adaptatœʀ, -tʀis] *nm/f* adapter.

adaptation [adaptasjɔ̃] *nf* adaptation.

adapter [adapte] *vt* to adapt; **s'~ (à)** (*suj: personne*) to adapt (to); (: *objet, prise etc*) to apply (to); **~ qch à** (*approprier*) to adapt sth to (fit); **~ qch sur/dans/à** (*fixer*) to fit sth on/into/to.

addenda [adɛ̃da] *nm inv* addenda.

Addis-Ababa [adisababa], **Addis-Abeba** [adisababa] *n* Addis Ababa.

additif [aditif] *nm* additional clause; (*substance*) additive; **~ alimentaire** food additive.

addition [adisjɔ̃] *nf* addition; (*au café*) bill.

additionnel, le [adisjɔnɛl] *adj* additional.

additionner [adisjɔne] *vt* to add (up); **s'~** *vi* to add up; **~ un produit d'eau** to add water to a product.

adduction [adyksjɔ̃] *nf* (*de gaz, d'eau*) conveyance.

ADEP *sigle f* (= *Agence nationale pour le développement de l'éducation permanente*) *national body which promotes adult education*.

adepte [adɛpt(ə)] *nm/f* follower.

adéquat, e [adekwa, -at] *adj* appropriate, suitable.

adéquation [adekwasjɔ̃] *nf* appropriateness; (*LING*) adequacy.

adhérence [aderɑ̃s] *nf* adhesion.

adhérent, e [aderɑ̃, -ɑ̃t] *nm/f* (*de club*) member.

adhérer [adere] *vi* (*coller*) to adhere, stick; **~ à** (*coller*) to adhere *ou* stick to; (*se rallier à: parti, club*) to join; to be a member of; (: *opinion, mouvement*) to support.

adhésif, ive [adezif, -iv] *adj* adhesive, sticky ♦ *nm* adhesive.

adhésion [adezjɔ̃] *nf* (*à un club*) joining; membership; (*à une opinion*) support.

ad hoc [adɔk] *adj* ad hoc.

adieu, x [adjø] *excl* goodbye ♦ *nm* farewell; **dire ~ à qn** to say goodbye *ou* farewell to sb; **dire ~ à qch** (*renoncer*) to say *ou* wave goodbye to sth.

adipeux, euse [adipø, -øz] *adj* bloated, fat; (*ANAT*) adipose.

adjacent, e [adʒasɑ̃, -ɑ̃t] *adj*: **~ (à)** adjacent (to).

adjectif [adʒɛktif] *nm* adjective; **~ attribut** adjectival complement; **~ épithète** attributive adjective.

adjectival, e, aux [adʒɛktival, -o] *adj* adjectival.

adjoignais [adʒwaɲɛ] *etc vb voir* **adjoindre**.

adjoindre [adʒwɛ̃dʀ(ə)] *vt*: **~ qch à** to attach sth to; (*ajouter*) to add sth to; **~ qn à** (*personne*) to appoint sb as an assistant to; (*comité*) to appoint sb to, attach sb to; **s'~** *vt* (*collaborateur etc*) to take on, appoint.

adjoint, e [adʒwɛ̃, -wɛ̃t] *pp de* **adjoindre** ♦ *nm/f* assistant; **directeur ~** assistant manager.

adjonction [adʒɔ̃ksjɔ̃] *nf* (*voir adjoindre*) attaching; addition; appointment.

adjudant [adʒydɑ̃] *nm* (*MIL*) warrant officer;

~-chef ≈ warrant officer 1st class (*BRIT*), ≈ chief warrant officer (*US*).

adjudicataire [adʒydikatɛʀ] *nm/f* successful bidder, purchaser; (*pour travaux*) successful tenderer (*BRIT*) *ou* bidder (*US*).

adjudicateur, trice [adʒydikatœʀ, -tʀis] *nm/f* (*aux enchères*) seller.

adjudication [adʒydikɑsjɔ̃] *nf* sale by auction; (*pour travaux*) invitation to tender (*BRIT*) *ou* bid (*US*).

adjuger [adʒyʒe] *vt* (*prix, récompense*) to award; (*lors d'une vente*) to auction (off); **s'~** *vt* to take for o.s.; **adjugé!** (*vendu*) gone!, sold!

adjurer [adʒyʀe] *vt*: **~ qn de faire** to implore *ou* beg sb to do.

adjuvant [adʒyvɑ̃] *nm* (*médicament*) adjuvant; (*additif*) additive; (*stimulant*) stimulant.

admettre [admɛtʀ(ə)] *vt* (*visiteur, nouveau-venu*) to admit, let in; (*candidat: SCOL*) to pass; (*TECH: gaz, eau, air*) to admit; (*tolérer*) to allow, accept; (*reconnaître*) to admit, acknowledge; (*supposer*) to suppose; **j'admets que ...** I admit that ...; **je n'admets pas que tu fasses cela** I won't allow you to do that; **admettons que ...** let's suppose that ...; **admettons** let's suppose so.

administrateur, trice [administʀatœʀ, -tʀis] *nm/f* (*COMM*) director; (*ADMIN*) administrator; **~ délégué** managing director; **~ judiciaire** receiver.

administratif, ive [administʀatif, -iv] *adj* administrative ♦ *nm* person in administration.

administration [administʀɑsjɔ̃] *nf* administration; **l'A~** ≈ the Civil Service.

administré, e [administʀe] *nm/f* ≈ citizen.

administrer [administʀe] *vt* (*firme*) to manage, run; (*biens, remède, sacrement etc*) to administer.

admirable [admiʀabl(ə)] *adj* admirable, wonderful.

admirablement [admiʀabləmɑ̃] *adv* admirably.

admirateur, trice [admiʀatœʀ, -tʀis] *nm/f* admirer.

admiratif, ive [admiʀatif, -iv] *adj* admiring.

admiration [admiʀɑsjɔ̃] *nf* admiration; **être en ~ devant** to be lost in admiration before.

admirativement [admiʀativmɑ̃] *adv* admiringly.

admirer [admiʀe] *vt* to admire.

admis, e [admi, -iz] *pp de* **admettre**.

admissibilité [admisibilite] *nf* eligibility; admissibility, acceptability.

admissible [admisibl(ə)] *adj* (*candidat*) eligible; (*comportement*) admissible, acceptable; (*JUR*) receivable.

admission [admisjɔ̃] *nf* admission; **tuyau d'~** intake pipe; **demande d'~** application for membership; **service des ~s** admissions.

admonester [admɔnɛste] *vt* to admonish.

ADN *sigle m* (= *acide désoxyribonucléique*) DNA.

ado [ado] *nm/f* (*fam*: = *adolescent(e)*) adolescent, teenager.

adolescence [adɔlesɑ̃s] *nf* adolescence.

adolescent, e [adɔlesɑ̃, -ɑ̃t] *nm/f* adolescent, teenager.

adonner [adɔne]: **s'~ à** *vt* (*sport*) to devote o.s. to; (*boisson*) to give o.s. over to.

adopter [adɔpte] *vt* to adopt; (*projet de loi etc*) to pass.

adoptif, ive [adɔptif, -iv] *adj* (*parents*) adoptive; (*fils, patrie*) adopted.

adoption [adɔpsjɔ̃] *nf* adoption; **son pays/sa ville d'~** his adopted country/town.

adorable [adɔʀabl(ə)] *adj* adorable.

adoration [adɔʀɑsjɔ̃] *nf* adoration; (*REL*) worship; **être en ~ devant** to be lost in adoration before.

adorer [adɔʀe] *vt* to adore; (*REL*) to worship.

adosser [adose] *vt*: **~ qch à ou contre** to stand sth against; **s'~ à ou contre** to lean with one's back against; **être adossé à ou contre** to be leaning with one's back against.

adoucir [adusiʀ] *vt* (*goût, température*) to make milder; (*avec du sucre*) to sweeten; (*peau, voix, eau*) to soften; (*caractère, personne*) to mellow; (*peine*) to soothe, allay; **s'~** *vi* to become milder; to soften; to mellow.

adoucissement [adusismɑ̃] *nm* becoming milder; sweetening; softening; mellowing; soothing.

adoucisseur [adusisœʀ] *nm*: **~ (d'eau)** water softener.

adr. *abr* = **adresse, adresser**.

adrénaline [adʀenalin] *nf* adrenaline.

adresse [adʀɛs] *nf* (*voir adroit*) skill, dexterity; (*domicile, INFORM*) address; **à l'~ de** (*pour*) for the benefit of.

adresser [adʀese] *vt* (*lettre: expédier*) to send; (: *écrire l'adresse sur*) to address; (*injure, compliments*) to address; **~ qn à un docteur/bureau** to refer *ou* send sb to a doctor/an office; **~ la parole à qn** to speak to *ou* address sb; **s'~ à** (*parler à*) to speak to, address; (*s'informer auprès de*) to go and see, go and speak to; (: *bureau*) to enquire at; (*suj: livre, conseil*) to be aimed at.

Adriatique [adʀijatik] *nf*: **l'~** the Adriatic.

adroit, e [adʀwa, -wat] *adj* (*joueur, mécanicien*) skilful (*BRIT*), skillful (*US*), dext(e)rous; (*politicien etc*) shrewd, skilled.

adroitement [adʀwatmɑ̃] *adv* skilfully (*BRIT*), skillfully (*US*), dext(e)rously; shrewdly.

AdS *sigle f* = *Académie des Sciences*.

aduler [adyle] *vt* to adulate.

adulte [adylt(ə)] *nm/f* adult, grown-up ♦ *adj* (*personne, attitude*) adult, grown-up; (*chien, arbre*) fully-grown, mature; **l'âge ~** adulthood; **formation/film pour ~s** adult training/film.

adultère [adyltɛʀ] *adj* adulterous ♦ *nm/f* adulterer/adulteress ♦ *nm* (*acte*) adultery.

adultérin, e [adylteʀɛ̃, -in] *adj* born of adultery.

advenir [advəniʀ] vi to happen; **qu'est-il adve-nu de?** what has become of?; **quoi qu'il advienne** whatever befalls ou happens.

adventiste [advɑ̃tist(ə)] nm/f (REL) Adventist.

adverbe [advɛʀb(ə)] nm adverb; ~ **de manière** adverb of manner.

adverbial, e, aux [advɛʀbjal, -o] adj adverbial.

adversaire [advɛʀsɛʀ] nm/f (SPORT, gén) opponent, adversary; (MIL) adversary, enemy.

adverse [advɛʀs(ə)] adj opposing.

adversité [advɛʀsite] nf adversity.

AE sigle m (= adjoint d'enseignement) non-certificated teacher.

AELE sigle f (= Association européenne de libre-échange) EFTA (= European Free Trade Association).

AEN sigle f (= Agence pour l'énergie nucléaire) ≈ AEA (= Atomic Energy Authority).

aérateur [aeʀatœʀ] nm ventilator.

aération [aeʀɑsjɔ̃] nf airing; (circulation de l'air) ventilation; **conduit d'~** ventilation shaft; **bouche d'~** air vent.

aéré, e [aeʀe] adj (pièce, local) airy, well-ventilated; (tissu) loose-woven; **centre ~** outdoor centre.

aérer [aeʀe] vt to air; (fig) to lighten; **s'~** vi to get some (fresh) air.

aérien, ne [aeʀjɛ̃, -ɛn] adj (AVIAT) air cpd, aerial; (câble, métro) overhead; (fig) light; **compagnie ~ne** airline (company); **ligne ~ne** airline.

aérobic [aeʀɔbik] nf aerobics sg.

aérobie [aeʀɔbi] adj aerobic.

aéro-club [aeʀɔklœb] nm flying club.

aérodrome [aeʀɔdʀɔm] nm airfield, aerodrome.

aérodynamique [aeʀɔdinamik] adj aerodynamic, streamlined ♦ nf aerodynamics sg.

aérofrein [aeʀɔfʀɛ̃] nm air brake.

aérogare [aeʀɔgaʀ] nf airport (buildings); (en ville) air terminal.

aéroglisseur [aeʀɔglisœʀ] nm hovercraft.

aérogramme [aeʀɔgʀam] nm air letter, aerogram(me).

aéromodélisme [aeʀɔmɔdelism(ə)] nm model aircraft making.

aéronaute [aeʀɔnot] nm/f aeronaut.

aéronautique [aeʀɔnotik] adj aeronautical ♦ nf aeronautics sg.

aéronaval, e [aeʀɔnaval] adj air and sea cpd ♦ nf: **l'A~e** ≈ the Fleet Air Arm (BRIT), ≈ the Naval Air Force (US).

aéronef [aeʀɔnɛf] nm aircraft.

aérophagie [aeʀɔfaʒi] nf aerophagy.

aéroport [aeʀɔpɔʀ] nm airport; ~ **d'embarquement** departure airport.

aéroporté, e [aeʀɔpɔʀte] adj airborne, airlifted.

aéroportuaire [aeʀɔpɔʀtɥɛʀ] adj of an ou the airport, airport cpd.

aéropostal, e, aux [aeʀɔpɔstal, -o] adj airmail cpd.

aérosol [aeʀɔsɔl] nm aerosol.

aérospatial, e, aux [aeʀɔspasjal, -o] adj aerospace ♦ nf the aerospace industry.

aérostat [aeʀɔsta] nm aerostat.

aérotrain [aeʀɔtʀɛ̃] nm hovertrain.

AF sigle fpl = **allocations familiales** ♦ sigle f (Suisse) = **Assemblée fédérale**.

AFAT [afat] sigle m (= Auxiliaire féminin de l'armée de terre) member of the women's army.

affabilité [afabilite] nf affability.

affable [afabl(ə)] adj affable.

affabulateur, trice [afabylatœʀ, -tʀis] nm/f storyteller.

affabulation [afabylɑsjɔ̃] nf invention, fantasy.

affabuler [afabyle] vi to make up stories.

affacturage [afaktyʀaʒ] nm factoring.

affadir [afadiʀ] vt to make insipid ou tasteless.

affaiblir [afebliʀ] vt to weaken; **s'~** vi to weaken, grow weaker; (vue) to grow dim.

affaiblissement [afeblismɑ̃] nm weakening.

affaire [afɛʀ] nf (problème, question) matter; (criminelle, judiciaire) case; (scandaleuse etc) affair; (entreprise) business; (marché, transaction) (business) deal, (piece of) business no pl; (occasion intéressante) good deal, bargain; **~s** nfpl affairs; (activité commerciale) business sg; (effets personnels) things, belongings; **tirer qn/se tirer d'~** to get sb/o.s. out of trouble; **ceci fera l'~** this will do (nicely); **avoir ~** à (comme adversaire) to be faced with; (en contact) to be dealing with; **tu auras ~ à moi!** (menace) you'll have me to contend with!; **c'est une ~ de goût/d'argent** it's a question ou matter of taste/money; **c'est l'~ d'une minute/heure** it'll only take a minute/an hour; **ce sont mes ~s** (cela me concerne) that's my business; **toutes ~s cessantes** forthwith; **les ~s étrangères** (POL) foreign affairs.

affairé, e [afeʀe] adj busy.

affairer [afeʀe]: **s'~** vi to busy o.s., bustle about.

affairisme [afeʀism(ə)] nm (political) racketeering.

affaissement [afɛsmɑ̃] nm subsidence; collapse.

affaisser [afese]: **s'~** vi (terrain, immeuble) to subside, sink; (personne) to collapse.

affaler [afale]: **s'~** vi: **s'~ dans/sur** to collapse ou slump into/onto.

affamé, e [afame] adj starving, famished.

affamer [afame] vt to starve.

affectation [afɛktɑsjɔ̃] nf (voir affecter) allotment; appointment; posting; (voir affecté) affectedness.

affecté, e [afɛkte] adj affected.

affecter [afɛkte] vt (émouvoir) to affect, move; (feindre) to affect, feign; (telle ou telle forme *etc)* to take on, assume; ~ **qch à** to allocate *ou* allot sth to; ~ **qn à** to appoint sb to; *(diplomate)* to post sb to; ~ **qch de** *(de coefficient)* to modify sth by.

affectif, ive [afɛktif, -iv] *adj* emotional, affective.

affection [afɛksjɔ̃] *nf* affection; *(mal)* ailment; **avoir de l'~ pour** to feel affection for; **prendre en** ~ to become fond of.

affectionner [afɛksjɔne] *vt* to be fond of.

affectueusement [afɛktɥøzmɑ̃] *adv* affectionately.

affectueux, euse [afɛktɥø, -øz] *adj* affectionate.

afférent, e [aferɑ̃, -ɑ̃t] *adj*: ~ **à** pertaining *ou* relating to.

affermir [afɛʀmiʀ] *vt* to consolidate, strengthen.

aff. étr. *abr* (= *Affaires étrangères*) *voir* **affaire.**

affichage [afiʃaʒ] *nm* billposting, billsticking; *(électronique)* display; "~ **interdit**" "stick no bills", "billsticking prohibited"; ~ **à cristaux liquides** liquid crystal display, LCD; ~ **numérique** *ou* **digital** digital display.

affiche [afiʃ] *nf* poster; *(officielle)* (public) notice; *(THÉÂT)* bill; **être à l'~** *(THÉÂT)* to be on; **tenir l'~** to run.

afficher [afiʃe] *vt (affiche)* to put up, post up; *(réunion)* to put up a notice about; *(électroniquement)* to display; *(fig)* to exhibit, display; **s'~** *(péj)* to flaunt o.s.; "**défense d'~**" "stick no bills".

affichette [afiʃɛt] *nf* small poster *ou* notice.

affilé, e [afile] *adj* sharp.

affilée [afile] *: d'~ adv* at a stretch.

affiler [afile] *vt* to sharpen.

affiliation [afiljasjɔ̃] *nf* affiliation.

affilié, e [afilje] *adj*: **être** ~ **à** to be affiliated to ♦ *nm/f* affiliated party *ou* member.

affilier [afilje] *vt*: **s'~ à** to become affiliated to.

affiner [afine] *vt* to refine; **s'~** *vi* to become (more) refined.

affinité [afinite] *nf* affinity.

affirmatif, ive [afiʀmatif, -iv] *adj* affirmative ♦ *nf*: **répondre par l'affirmative** to reply in the affirmative; **dans l'affirmative** *(si oui)* if (the answer is) yes ..., if he does *(ou* you do *etc)* ....

affirmation [afiʀmasjɔ̃] *nf* assertion.

affirmativement [afiʀmativmɑ̃] *adv* affirmatively, in the affirmative.

affirmer [afiʀme] *vt (prétendre)* to maintain, assert; *(autorité etc)* to assert; **s'~** to assert o.s.; to assert itself.

affleurer [aflœʀe] *vi* to show on the surface.

affliction [afliksjɔ̃] *nf* affliction.

affligé, e [afliʒe] *adj* distressed, grieved; ~ **de** *(maladie, tare)* afflicted with.

affligeant, e [afliʒɑ̃, -ɑ̃t] *adj* distressing.

affliger [afliʒe] *vt (peiner)* to distress, grieve.

affluence [aflyɑ̃s] *nf* crowds *pl*; **heures d'~** rush hour *sg*; **jours d'~** busiest days.

affluent [aflyɑ̃] *nm* tributary.

affluer [aflye] *vi (secours, biens)* to flood in, pour in; *(sang)* to rush, flow.

afflux [afly] *nm* flood, influx; rush.

affolant, e [afɔlɑ̃, -ɑ̃t] *adj* terrifying.

affolé, e [afɔle] *adj* panic-stricken, panicky.

affolement [afɔlmɑ̃] *nm* panic.

affoler [afɔle] *vt* to throw into a panic; **s'~** *vi* to panic.

affranchir [afʀɑ̃ʃiʀ] *vt* to put a stamp *ou* stamps on; *(à la machine)* to frank *(BRIT)*, meter *(US)*; *(esclave)* to enfranchise, emancipate; *(fig)* to free, liberate; **s'~ de** to free o.s. from; **machine à** ~ franking machine, postage meter.

affranchissement [afʀɑ̃ʃismɑ̃] *nm* franking *(BRIT)*, metering *(US)*; freeing; *(POSTES: prix payé)* postage; **tarifs d'~** postage rates.

affres [afʀ(ə)] *nfpl*: **dans les** ~ **de** in the throes of.

affréter [afʀete] *vt* to charter.

affreusement [afʀøzmɑ̃] *adv* dreadfully, awfully.

affreux, euse [afʀø, -øz] *adj* dreadful, awful.

affriolant, e [afʀijɔlɑ̃, -ɑ̃t] *adj* tempting, enticing.

affront [afʀɔ̃] *nm* affront.

affrontement [afʀɔ̃tmɑ̃] *nm (MIL, POL)* clash, confrontation.

affronter [afʀɔ̃te] *vt* to confront, face; **s'~** to confront each other.

affubler [afyble] *vt (péj)*: ~ **qn de** to rig *ou* deck sb out in; *(surnom)* to attach to sb.

affût [afy] *nm (de canon)* gun carriage; **à l'~ (de)** *(gibier)* lying in wait (for); *(fig)* on the look-out (for).

affûter [afyte] *vt* to sharpen, grind.

afghan, e [afgɑ̃, -an] *adj* Afghan.

Afghanistan [afganistɑ̃] *nm*: **l'~** Afghanistan.

afin [afɛ̃]: ~ **que** *conj* so that, in order that; ~ **de faire** in order to do, so as to do.

AFNOR [afnɔʀ] *sigle f* (= *Association française de normalisation*) *industrial standards authority.*

a fortiori [afɔʀsjɔʀi] *adv* all the more, a fortiori.

AFP *sigle f* = *Agence France-Presse.*

AFPA *sigle f* = *Association pour la formation professionnelle des adultes.*

africain, e [afʀikɛ̃, -ɛn] *adj* African ♦ *nm/f*: **A~, e** African.

afrikaans [afʀikɑ̃] *nm, adj inv* Afrikaans.

Afrikaner [afʀikanɛʀ] *nm/f* Afrikaner.

Afrique [afʀik] *nf*: **l'~** Africa; **l'~ australe/du Nord/du Sud** southern/North/South Africa.

afro [afʀo] *adj inv*: **coupe** ~ afro hairstyle ♦ *nm/f*: **A~** Afro.

afro-américain, e [afʀoameʀikɛ̃, -ɛn] *adj* Afro-American.

afro-asiatique [afʀoazjatik] *adj* Afro-Asian.

AG *sigle f* = *assemblée générale.*

ag. *abr* = **agence.**

agaçant, e [agasɑ̃, -ɑ̃t] *adj* irritating, aggravating.

agacement [agasmɑ̃] *nm* irritation, aggravation.

agacer [agase] *vt* to pester, tease; (*involontairement*) to irritate, aggravate; (*aguicher*) to excite, lead on.

agapes [agap] *nfpl* (*humoristique: festin*) feast.

agate [agat] *nf* agate.

AGE *sigle f* = assemblée générale extraordinaire.

âge [ɑʒ] *nm* age; **quel ~ as-tu?** how old are you?; **une femme d'un certain ~** a middle-aged woman, a woman who is getting on (in years); **bien porter son ~** to wear well; **prendre de l'~** to be getting on (in years), grow older; **limite d'~** age limit; **dispense d'~** special exemption from age limit; **troisième ~** (*période*) retirement; (*personnes âgées*) senior citizens; **l'~ ingrat** the awkward *ou* difficult age; **~ légal** legal age; **~ mental** mental age; **l'~ mûr** maturity, middle age; **~ de raison** age of reason.

âgé, e [ɑʒe] *adj* old, elderly; **~ de 10 ans** 10 years old.

agence [aʒɑ̃s] *nf* agency, office; (*succursale*) branch; **~ immobilière** estate agent's (office) (*BRIT*), real estate office (*US*); **~ matrimoniale** marriage bureau; **~ de placement** employment agency; **~ de publicité** advertising agency; **~ de voyages** travel agency.

agencé, e [aʒɑ̃se] *adj*: **bien/mal ~** well/badly put together; well/badly laid out *ou* arranged.

agencement [aʒɑ̃smɑ̃] *nm* putting together; arrangement, laying out.

agencer [aʒɑ̃se] *vt* to put together; (*local*) to arrange, lay out.

agenda [aʒɛ̃da] *nm* diary.

agenouiller [aʒnuje]: **s'~** *vi* to kneel (down).

agent [aʒɑ̃] *nm* (*aussi*: **~ de police**) policeman; (*ADMIN*) official, officer; (*fig: élément, facteur*) agent; **~ d'assurances** insurance broker; **~ de change** stockbroker; **~ commercial** sales representative; **~ immobilier** estate agent (*BRIT*), realtor (*US*); **~ (secret)** (secret) agent.

agglo [aglo] *nm* (*fam*) = **aggloméré**.

agglomérat [aglɔmera] *nm* (*GÉO*) agglomerate.

agglomération [aglɔmerasjɔ̃] *nf* town; (*AUTO*) built-up area; **l'~ parisienne** the urban area of Paris.

aggloméré [aglɔmere] *nm* (*bois*) chipboard; (*pierre*) conglomerate.

agglomérer [aglɔmere] *vt* to pile up; (*TECH: bois, pierre*) to compress; **s'~** *vi* to pile up.

agglutiner [aglytine] *vt* to stick together; **s'~** *vi* to congregate.

aggravant, e [agravɑ̃, -ɑ̃t] *adj*: **circonstances ~es** aggravating circumstances.

aggravation [agravasjɔ̃] *nf* worsening, aggravation; increase.

aggraver [agrave] *vt* to worsen, aggravate; (*JUR: peine*) to increase; **s'~** *vi* to worsen; **~ son cas** to make one's case worse.

agile [aʒil] *adj* agile, nimble.

agilement [aʒilmɑ̃] *adv* nimbly.

agilité [aʒilite] *nf* agility, nimbleness.

agio [aʒjo] *nm* (bank) charges *pl*.

agir [aʒiʀ] *vi* (*se comporter*) to behave, act; (*faire quelque chose*) to act, take action; (*avoir de l'effet*) to act; **il s'agit de** it's a matter *ou* question of; it is about; (*il importe que*) **il s'agit de faire** we (*ou* you *etc*) must do; **de quoi s'agit-il?** what is it about?

agissements [aʒismɑ̃] *nmpl* (*gén péj*) schemes, intrigues.

agitateur, trice [aʒitatœʀ, -tʀis] *nm/f* agitator.

agitation [aʒitasjɔ̃] *nf* (hustle and) bustle; (*trouble*) agitation, excitement; (*politique*) unrest, agitation.

agité, e [aʒite] *adj* (*remuant*) fidgety, restless; (*troublé*) agitated, perturbed; (*journée*) hectic; (*mer*) rough; (*sommeil*) disturbed, broken.

agiter [aʒite] *vt* (*bouteille, chiffon*) to shake; (*bras, mains*) to wave; (*préoccuper, exciter*) to trouble, perturb; **s'~** *vi* to bustle about; (*dormeur*) to toss and turn; (*enfant*) to fidget; (*POL*) to grow restless; **"~ avant l'emploi"** "shake before use".

agneau, x [aɲo] *nm* lamb; (*toison*) lambswool.

agnelet [aɲlɛ] *nm* little lamb.

agnostique [agnɔstik] *adj, nm/f* agnostic.

agonie [agɔni] *nf* mortal agony, death pangs *pl*; (*fig*) death throes *pl*.

agonir [agɔniʀ] *vt*: **~ qn d'injures** to hurl abuse at sb.

agoniser [agɔnize] *vi* to be dying; (*fig*) to be in its death throes.

agrafe [agraf] *nf* (*de vêtement*) hook, fastener; (*de bureau*) staple; (*MÉD*) clip.

agrafer [agrafe] *vt* to fasten; to staple.

agrafeuse [agraføz] *nf* stapler.

agraire [agʀɛʀ] *adj* agrarian; (*mesure, surface*) land *cpd*.

agrandir [agʀɑ̃diʀ] *vt* (*magasin, domaine*) to extend, enlarge; (*trou*) to enlarge, make bigger; (*PHOTO*) to enlarge, blow up; **s'~** *vi* to be extended; to be enlarged.

agrandissement [agʀɑ̃dismɑ̃] *nm* extension; enlargement; (*photographie*) enlargement.

agrandisseur [agʀɑ̃disœʀ] *nm* (*PHOTO*) enlarger.

agréable [agʀeabl(ə)] *adj* pleasant, nice.

agréablement [agʀeabləmɑ̃] *adv* pleasantly.

agréé, e [agʀee] *adj*: **concessionnaire ~** registered dealer; **magasin ~** registered dealer('s).

agréer [agʀee] *vt* (*requête*) to accept; **~ à** *vt* to please, suit; **veuillez ~ ...** (*formule épistolaire*) yours faithfully.

agrég [agʀɛg] *nf* (*fam*) = **agrégation**.

agrégat [agʀega] _nm_ aggregate.
agrégation [agʀegasjɔ̃] _nf_ highest teaching diploma in France.

> The **agrégation**, colloquially known as the **agrég**, is a prestigious competitive examination for the recruitment of secondary education teachers in France. The number of candidates always far exceeds the number of posts available. Most teachers of **classes préparatoires** and university lecturers hold the agrégation; see also **CAPES**.

agrégé, e [agʀeʒe] _nm/f_ holder of the _agrégation._
agréger [agʀeʒe]: **s'~** _vi_ to aggregate.
agrément [agʀemɑ̃] _nm_ (_accord_) consent, approval; (_attraits_) charm, attractiveness; (_plaisir_) pleasure; **voyage/jardin d'~** pleasure trip/garden.
agrémenter [agʀemɑ̃te] _vt_: **~ (de)** to embellish (with), adorn (with).
agrès [agʀɛ] _nmpl_ (gymnastics) apparatus _sg._
agresser [agʀese] _vt_ to attack.
agresseur [agʀesœʀ] _nm_ aggressor.
agressif, ive [agʀesif, -iv] _adj_ aggressive.
agression [agʀesjɔ̃] _nf_ attack; (_POL, MIL, PSYCH_) aggression.
agressivement [agʀesivmɑ̃] _adv_ aggressively.
agressivité [agʀesivite] _nf_ aggressiveness.
agreste [agʀɛst(ə)] _adj_ rustic.
agricole [agʀikɔl] _adj_ agricultural, farm _cpd._
agriculteur, trice [agʀikyltœʀ, -tʀis] _nm/f_ farmer.
agriculture [agʀikyltyʀ] _nf_ agriculture; farming.
agripper [agʀipe] _vt_ to grab, clutch; (_pour arracher_) to snatch, grab; **s'~ à** to cling (on) to, clutch, grip.
agro-alimentaire [agʀɔalimɑ̃tɛʀ] _adj_ farming _cpd_ ♦ _nm_: **l'~** agribusiness.
agronome [agʀɔnɔm] _nm/f_ agronomist.
agronomie [agʀɔnɔmi] _nf_ agronomy.
agronomique [agʀɔnɔmik] _adj_ agronomic(al).
agrumes [agʀym] _nmpl_ citrus fruit(s).
aguerrir [ageʀiʀ] _vt_ to harden; **s'~ (contre)** to become hardened (to).
aguets [agɛ]: **aux ~** _adv_: **être aux ~** to be on the look-out.
aguichant, e [agiʃɑ̃, -ɑ̃t] _adj_ enticing.
aguicher [agiʃe] _vt_ to entice.
aguicheur, euse [agiʃœʀ, -øz] _adj_ enticing.
ah [ɑ] _excl_ ah!; **~ bon?** really?, is that so?; **~ mais ...** yes, but ...; **~ non!** oh no!
ahuri, e [ayʀi] _adj_ (_stupéfait_) flabbergasted; (_idiot_) dim-witted.
ahurir [ayʀiʀ] _vt_ to stupefy, stagger.
ahurissant, e [ayʀisɑ̃, -ɑ̃t] _adj_ stupefying, staggering, mind-boggling.
ai [e] _vb voir_ **avoir.**
aide [ɛd] _nm/f_ assistant ♦ _nf_ assistance, help; (_secours financier_) aid; **à l'~ de** with the help

_ou_ aid of; **aller à l'~ de qn** to go to sb's aid, go to help sb; **venir en ~ à qn** to help sb, come to sb's assistance; **appeler (qn) à l'~** to call for help (from sb); **à l'~!** help!; **~ de camp** _nm_ aide-de-camp; **~ comptable** _nm_ accountant's assistant; **~ électricien** _nm_ electrician's mate; **~ familiale** _nf_ mother's help, ≈ home help; **~ judiciaire** _nf_ legal aid; **~ de laboratoire** _nm/f_ laboratory assistant; **~ ménagère** _nf_ ≈ home help; **~ sociale** _nf_ (_assistance_) state aid; **~ soignant, e** _nm/f_ auxiliary nurse; **~ technique** _nf_ ≈ VSO (_BRIT_), ≈ Peace Corps (_US_).
aide-mémoire [ɛdmemwaʀ] _nm inv_ (key facts) handbook.
aider [ede] _vt_ to help; **~ à qch** to help (towards) sth; **~ qn à faire qch** to help sb to do sth; **s'~ de** (_se servir de_) to use, make use of.
aie [ɛ] _etc vb voir_ **avoir.**
aïe [aj] _excl_ ouch!
AIEA _sigle f_ (= _Agence internationale de l'énergie nucléaire_) IAEA (= _International Atomic Energy Agency_).
aïeul, e [ajœl] _nm/f_ grandparent, grandfather/grandmother; (_ancêtre_) forebear.
aïeux [ajø] _nmpl_ grandparents; forebears, forefathers.
aigle [ɛgl(ə)] _nm_ eagle.
aiglefin [ɛgləfɛ̃] _nm_ = **églefin.**
aigre [ɛgʀ(ə)] _adj_ sour, sharp; (_fig_) sharp, cutting; **tourner à l'~** to turn sour.
aigre-doux, -douce [ɛgʀədu, -dus] _adj_ (_fruit_) bitter-sweet; (_sauce_) sweet and sour.
aigrefin [ɛgʀəfɛ̃] _nm_ swindler.
aigrelet, te [ɛgʀəlɛ, -ɛt] _adj_ (_taste_) sourish; (_voix, son_) sharpish.
aigrette [ɛgʀɛt] _nf_ (_plume_) feather.
aigreur [ɛgʀœʀ] _nf_ sourness; sharpness; **~s d'estomac** heartburn _sg._
aigri, e [egʀi] _adj_ embittered.
aigrir [egʀiʀ] _vt_ (_personne_) to embitter; (_caractère_) to sour; **s'~** _vi_ to become embittered; to sour; (_lait etc_) to turn sour.
aigu, ë [egy] _adj_ (_objet, arête_) sharp, pointed; (_son, voix_) high-pitched, shrill; (_note_) high(-pitched); (_douleur, intelligence_) acute, sharp.
aigue-marine, _pl_ **aigues-marines** [ɛgmaʀin] _nf_ aquamarine.
aiguillage [eguijaʒ] _nm_ (_RAIL_) points _pl._
aiguille [eguij] _nf_ needle; (_de montre_) hand; **~ à tricoter** knitting needle.
aiguiller [eguije] _vt_ (_orienter_) to direct; (_RAIL_) to shunt.
aiguillette [eguijɛt] _nf_ (_CULIN_) aiguillette.
aiguilleur [eguijœʀ] _nm_ (_RAIL_) pointsman; **~ du ciel** air traffic controller.
aiguillon [eguijɔ̃] _nm_ (_d'abeille_) sting; (_fig_) spur, stimulus.
aiguillonner [eguijɔne] _vt_ to spur _ou_ goad on.
aiguiser [egize] _vt_ to sharpen, grind; (_fig_) to stimulate; (: _esprit_) to sharpen; (: _sens_) to excite.

aiguisoir [egizwaʀ] *nm* sharpener.
aïkido [ajkido] *nm* aikido.
ail [aj] *nm* garlic.
aile [ɛl] *nf* wing; (*de voiture*) wing (*BRIT*), fender (*US*); **battre de l'~** (*fig*) to be in a sorry state; **voler de ses propres ~s** to stand on one's own two feet; **~ libre** hang-glider.
ailé, e [ele] *adj* winged.
aileron [ɛlʀɔ̃] *nm* (*de requin*) fin; (*d'avion*) aileron.
ailette [ɛlɛt] *nf* (*TECH*) fin; (: *de turbine*) blade.
ailier [elje] *nm* (*SPORT*) winger.
aille [aj] *etc vb voir* **aller**.
ailleurs [ajœʀ] *adv* elsewhere, somewhere else; **partout/nulle part ~** everywhere/nowhere else; **d'~** *adv* (*du reste*) moreover, besides; **par ~** *adv* (*d'autre part*) moreover, furthermore.
ailloli [ajɔli] *nm* garlic mayonnaise.
aimable [ɛmabl(ə)] *adj* kind, nice; **vous êtes bien ~** that's very nice *ou* kind of you, how kind (of you)!
aimablement [ɛmabləmɑ̃] *adv* kindly.
aimant [ɛmɑ̃] *nm* magnet.
aimant, e [ɛmɑ̃, -ɑ̃t] *adj* loving, affectionate.
aimanté, e [ɛmɑ̃te] *adj* magnetic.
aimanter [ɛmɑ̃te] *vt* to magnetize.
aimer [eme] *vt* to love; (*d'amitié, affection, par goût*) to like; (*souhait*): **j'aimerais ...** I would like ...; **s'~** to love each other; to like each other; **je n'aime pas beaucoup Paul** I don't like Paul much, I don't care much for Paul; **~ faire qch** to like doing sth, like to do sth; **aimeriez-vous que je vous accompagne?** would you like me to come with you?; **j'aimerais (bien) m'en aller** I should (really) like to go; **bien ~ qn/qch** to like sb/sth; **j'aime mieux Paul (que Pierre)** I prefer Paul (to Pierre); **j'aime mieux** *ou* **autant vous dire que** I may as well tell you that; **j'aimerais autant** *ou* **mieux y aller maintenant** I'd sooner *ou* rather go now; **j'aime assez aller au cinéma** I quite like going to the cinema.
aine [ɛn] *nf* groin.
aîné, e [ene] *adj* elder, older; (*le plus âgé*) eldest, oldest ♦ *nm/f* oldest child *ou* one, oldest boy *ou* son/girl *ou* daughter; **~s** *nmpl* (*fig: anciens*) elders; **il est mon ~ (de 2 ans)** he's (2 years) older than me, he's 2 years my senior.
aînesse [ɛnɛs] *nf*: **droit d'~** birthright.
ainsi [ɛ̃si] *adv* (*de cette façon*) like this, in this way, thus; (*ce faisant*) thus ♦ *conj* thus, so; **~ que** (*comme*) (just) as; (*et aussi*) as well as; **pour ~ dire** so to speak, as it were; **~ donc** and so; **~ soit-il** (*REL*) so be it; **et ~ de suite** and so on (and so forth).
aïoli [ajɔli] *nm* = **ailloli**.
air [ɛʀ] *nm* air; (*mélodie*) tune; (*expression*) look, air; (*atmosphère, ambiance*): **dans l'~** in the air (*fig*); **prendre de grands ~s (avec qn)** to give o.s. airs (with sb); **en l'~** (up) into

the air; **tirer en l'~** to fire shots in the air; **paroles/menaces en l'~** idle words/threats; **prendre l'~** to get some (fresh) air; (*avion*) to take off; **avoir l'~ triste** to look *ou* seem sad; **avoir l'~ de qch** to look like sth; **avoir l'~ de faire** to look as though one is doing, appear to be doing; **courant d'~** draught (*BRIT*), draft (*US*); **le grand ~** the open air; **mal de l'~** air-sickness; **tête en l'~** scatterbrain; **~ comprimé** compressed air; **~ conditionné** air-conditioning.
airbag [ɛʀbag] *nm* air bag.
aire [ɛʀ] *nf* (*zone, fig, MATH*) area; (*nid*) eyrie (*BRIT*), aerie (*US*); **~ d'atterrissage** landing strip; landing patch; **~ de jeu** play area; **~ de lancement** launching site; **~ de stationnement** parking area.
airelle [ɛʀɛl] *nf* bilberry.
aisance [ɛzɑ̃s] *nf* ease; (*COUTURE*) easing, freedom of movement; (*richesse*) affluence; **être dans l'~** to be well-off *ou* affluent.
aise [ɛz] *nf* comfort ♦ *adj*: **être bien ~ de/que** to be delighted to/that; **~s** *nfpl*: **aimer ses ~s** to like one's (creature) comforts; **prendre ses ~s** to make o.s. comfortable; **frémir d'~** to shudder with pleasure; **être à l'~** *ou* **à son ~** to be comfortable; (*pas embarrassé*) to be at ease; (*financièrement*) to be comfortably off; **se mettre à l'~** to make o.s. comfortable; **être mal à l'~** *ou* **à son ~** to be uncomfortable; (*gêné*) to be ill at ease; **mettre qn à l'~** to put sb at his (*ou* her) ease; **mettre qn mal à l'~** to make sb feel ill at ease; **à votre ~** please yourself, just as you like; **en faire à son ~** to do as one likes; **en prendre à son ~ avec qch** to be free and easy with sth, do as one likes with sth.
aisé, e [eze] *adj* easy; (*assez riche*) well-to-do, well-off.
aisément [ezemɑ̃] *adv* easily.
aisselle [ɛsɛl] *nf* armpit.
ait [ɛ] *vb voir* **avoir**.
ajonc [aʒɔ̃] *nm* gorse *no pl*.
ajouré, e [aʒuʀe] *adj* openwork *cpd*.
ajournement [aʒuʀnəmɑ̃] *nm* adjournment; deferment, postponement.
ajourner [aʒuʀne] *vt* (*réunion*) to adjourn; (*décision*) to defer, postpone; (*candidat*) to refer; (*conscrit*) to defer.
ajout [aʒu] *nm* addition.
ajouter [aʒute] *vt* to add; (*INFORM*) to append; **~ à** *vt* (*accroître*) to add to; **s'~ à** to add to; **~ que** to add that; **~ foi à** to lend *ou* give credence to.
ajustage [aʒystaʒ] *nm* fitting.
ajusté, e [aʒyste] *adj*: **bien ~** (*robe etc*) close-fitting.
ajustement [aʒystəmɑ̃] *nm* adjustment.
ajuster [aʒyste] *vt* (*régler*) to adjust; (*vêtement*) to alter; (*arranger*): **~ sa cravate** to adjust one's tie; (*coup de fusil*) to aim; (*cible*) to aim at; (*adapter*): **~ qch à** to fit sth to.

ajusteur [aʒystœʀ] *nm* metal worker.

al *abr* = **année-lumière.**

alaise [alɛz] *nf* = **alèse.**

alambic [alɑ̃bik] *nm* still.

alambiqué, e [alɑ̃bike] *adj* convoluted, over-complicated.

alangui, e [alɑ̃gi] *adj* languid.

alanguir [alɑ̃giʀ]: **s'~** *vi* to grow languid.

alarmant, e [alaʀmɑ̃, -ɑ̃t] *adj* alarming.

alarme [alaʀm(ə)] *nf* alarm; **donner l'~** to give *ou* raise the alarm; **jeter l'~** to cause alarm.

alarmer [alaʀme] *vt* to alarm; **s'~** *vi* to become alarmed.

alarmiste [alaʀmist(ə)] *adj* alarmist.

Alaska [alaska] *nm*: **l'~** Alaska.

albanais, e [albanɛ, -ɛz] *adj* Albanian ♦ *nm* (*LING*) Albanian ♦ *nmf*: **A~, e** Albanian.

Albanie [albani] *nf*: **l'~** Albania.

albâtre [albɑtʀ(ə)] *nm* alabaster.

albatros [albatʀos] *nm* albatross.

albigeois, e [albiʒwa, -waz] *adj* of *ou* from Albi.

albinos [albinos] *nmf* albino.

album [albɔm] *nm* album; **~ à colorier** colouring book; **~ de timbres** stamp album.

albumen [albymɛn] *nm* albumen.

albumine [albymin] *nf* albumin; **avoir** *ou* **faire de l'~** to suffer from albuminuria.

alcalin, e [alkalɛ̃, -in] *adj* alkaline.

alchimie [alʃimi] *nf* alchemy.

alchimiste [alʃimist(ə)] *nm* alchemist.

alcool [alkɔl] *nm*: **l'~** alcohol; **un ~** a spirit, a brandy; **~ à brûler** methylated spirits (*BRIT*), wood alcohol (*US*); **~ à 90°** surgical spirit; **~ camphré** camphorated alcohol; **~ de prune** *etc* plum *etc* brandy.

alcoolémie [alkɔlemi] *nf* blood alcohol level.

alcoolique [alkɔlik] *adj*, *nmf* alcoholic.

alcoolisé, e [alkɔlize] *adj* alcoholic.

alcoolisme [alkɔlism(ə)] *nm* alcoholism.

alco(o)test [alkɔtɛst] *nm* ® (*objet*) Breath-alyser ®; (*test*) breath-test; **faire subir l'~ à qn** to Breathalyze ® sb.

alcôve [alkov] *nf* alcove, recess.

aléas [alea] *nmpl* hazards.

aléatoire [aleatwaʀ] *adj* uncertain; (*INFORM, STATISTIQUE*) random.

alémanique [alemanik] *adj*: **la Suisse ~** German-speaking Switzerland.

ALENA [alena] *sigle m* (= *Accord de libre-échange nord-américain*) NAFTA (= *North American Free Trade Agreement*).

alentour [alɑ̃tuʀ] *adv* around (about); **~s** *nmpl* surroundings; **aux ~s de** in the vicinity *ou* neighbourhood of, around about; (*temps*) around about.

Aléoutiennes [aleusjɛn] *nfpl*: **les (îles) ~** the Aleutian Islands.

alerte [alɛʀt(ə)] *adj* agile, nimble; (*style*) brisk, lively ♦ *nf* alert; warning; **donner l'~** to give the alert; **à la première ~** at the first sign of trouble *ou* danger; **~ à la bombe** bomb scare.

alerter [alɛʀte] *vt* to alert.

alèse [alɛz] *nf* (*drap*) undersheet, drawsheet.

aléser [aleze] *vt* to ream.

alevin [alvɛ̃] *nm* alevin, young fish.

alevinage [alvinaʒ] *nm* fish farming.

Alexandrie [alɛksɑ̃dʀi] *n* Alexandria.

alexandrin [alɛksɑ̃dʀɛ̃] *nm* alexandrine.

alezan, e [alzɑ̃, -an] *adj* chestnut.

algarade [algaʀad] *nf* row, dispute.

algèbre [alʒɛbʀ(ə)] *nf* algebra.

algébrique [alʒebʀik] *adj* algebraic.

Alger [alʒe] *n* Algiers.

Algérie [alʒeʀi] *nf*: **l'~** Algeria.

algérien, ne [alʒeʀjɛ̃, -ɛn] *adj* Algerian ♦ *nmf*: **A~, ne** Algerian.

algérois, e [alʒeʀwa, -waz] *adj* of *ou* from Algiers ♦ *nm*: **l'A~** (*région*) the Algiers region.

algorithme [algɔʀitm(ə)] *nm* algorithm.

algue [alg(ə)] *nf* (*gén*) seaweed *no pl*; (*BOT*) alga (*pl* -ae).

alias [aljas] *adv* alias.

alibi [alibi] *nm* alibi.

aliénation [aljenasjɔ̃] *nf* alienation.

aliéné, e [aljene] *nmf* insane person, lunatic (*péj*).

aliéner [aljene] *vt* to alienate; (*bien, liberté*) to give up; **s'~** *vt* to alienate.

alignement [alinmɑ̃] *nm* alignment, lining up; **à l'~** in line.

aligner [aline] *vt* to align, line up; (*idées, chiffres*) to string together; (*adapter*): **~ qch sur** to bring sth into alignment with; **s'~** (*soldats etc*) to line up; **s'~ sur** (*POL*) to align o.s. with.

aliment [alimɑ̃] *nm* food; **~ complet** whole food.

alimentaire [alimɑ̃tɛʀ] *adj* food *cpd*; (*péj: besogne*) done merely to earn a living; **produits ~s** foodstuffs, foods.

alimentation [alimɑ̃tasjɔ̃] *nf* feeding; supplying, supply; (*commerce*) food trade; (*produits*) groceries *pl*; (*régime*) diet; (*INFORM*) feed; **~ (générale)** (general) grocer's; **~ de base** staple diet; **~ en feuilles/en continu/en papier** form/stream/sheet feed.

alimenter [alimɑ̃te] *vt* to feed; (*TECH*): **~ (en)** to supply (with), feed (with); (*fig*) to sustain, keep going.

alinéa [alinea] *nm* paragraph; **"nouvel ~"** "new line".

aliter [alite]: **s'~** *vi* to take to one's bed; **infirme alité** bedridden person *ou* invalid.

alizé [alize] *adj*, *nm*: **(vent) ~** trade wind.

allaitement [alɛtmɑ̃] *nm* feeding; **~ maternel/au biberon** breast-/bottle-feeding; **~ mixte** mixed feeding.

allaiter [alete] *vt* (*suj: femme*) to (breast-)feed, nurse; (*suj: animal*) to suckle; **~ au biberon** to bottle-feed.

allant [alɑ̃] *nm* drive, go.

alléchant, e [aleʃɑ̃, -ɑ̃t] *adj* tempting, enticing.

allécher [aleʃe] *vt*: ~ **qn** to make sb's mouth water; to tempt sb, entice sb.

allée [ale] *nf* (*de jardin*) path; (*en ville*) avenue, drive; **~s et venues** comings and goings.

allégation [alegɑsjɔ̃] *nf* allegation.

alléger [aleʒe] *vt* (*voiture*) to make lighter; (*chargement*) to lighten; (*souffrance*) to alleviate, soothe.

allégorie [alegɔʀi] *nf* allegory.

allégorique [alegɔʀik] *adj* allegorical.

allègre [alɛgʀ(ə)] *adj* lively, jaunty (*BRIT*); (*personne*) gay, cheerful.

allégresse [alegʀɛs] *nf* elation, gaiety.

allegretto [al(l)egʀɛt(t)o] *adv, nm* allegretto.

allegro [al(l)egʀo] *adv, nm* allegro.

alléguer [alege] *vt* to put forward (as proof *ou* an excuse).

Allemagne [aləmaɲ] *nf*: **l'~** Germany; **l'~ de l'Est/Ouest** East/West Germany; **l'~ fédérale (RFA)** the Federal Republic of Germany (FRG).

allemand, e [almɑ̃, -ɑ̃d] *adj* German ♦ *nm* (*LING*) German ♦ *nm/f*: **A~, e** German; **A~ de l'Est/l'Ouest** East/West German.

aller [ale] *nm* (*trajet*) outward journey; (*billet*): ~ **(simple)** single (*BRIT*) *ou* one-way ticket; ~ **(et) retour (AR)** (*trajet*) return trip *ou* journey (*BRIT*), round trip (*US*); (*billet*) return (*BRIT*) *ou* round-trip (*US*) ticket ♦ *vi* (*gén*) to go; ~ **à** (*convenir*) to suit; (*suj: forme, pointure etc*) to fit; **cela me va** (*couleur*) that suits me; (*vêtement*) that suits me; that fits me; (*projet, disposition*) that suits me, that's fine *ou* OK by me; ~ **à la chasse/pêche** to go hunting/fishing; ~ **avec** (*couleurs, style etc*) to go (well) with; **je vais le faire/me fâcher** I'm going to do it/to get angry; ~ **voir/chercher qn** to go and see/look for sb; **comment allez-vous?** how are you?; **comment ça va?** how are you?; (*affaires etc*) how are things?; **ça va? — oui (ça va)!** how are things? — fine!; **ça va (comme ça)** that's fine (as it is); **il va bien/mal** he's well/not well, he's fine/ill; **ça va bien/mal** (*affaires etc*) it's going well/not going well; **tout va bien** everything's fine; **ça ne va pas!** (*mauvaise humeur etc*) that's not on!, hey, come on!; **ça ne va pas sans difficultés** it's not without difficulties; ~ **mieux** to be better; **il y va de leur vie** their lives are at stake; **se laisser** ~ to let o.s. go; **s'en** ~ *vi* (*partir*) to be off, go, leave; (*disparaître*) to go away; ~ **jusqu'à** to go as far as; **ça va de soi, ça va sans dire** that goes without saying; **tu y vas un peu fort** you're going a bit (too) far; **allez!** go on!; come on!; **allons-y!** let's go!; **allez, au revoir** right *ou* OK then, bye-bye!

allergène [alɛʀʒɛn] *nm* allergen.

allergie [alɛʀʒi] *nf* allergy.

allergique [alɛʀʒik] *adj* allergic; ~ **à** allergic to.

allez [ale] *vb voir* **aller**.

alliage [aljaʒ] *nm* alloy.

alliance [aljɑ̃s] *nf* (*MIL, POL*) alliance; (*mariage*) marriage; (*bague*) wedding ring; **neveu par** ~ nephew by marriage.

allié, e [alje] *nm/f* ally; **parents et ~s** relatives and relatives by marriage.

allier [alje] *vt* (*métaux*) to alloy; (*POL, gén*) to ally; (*fig*) to combine; **s'~** to become allies; (*éléments, caractéristiques*) to combine; **s'~ à** to become allied to *ou* with.

alligator [aligatɔʀ] *nm* alligator.

allitération [aliteʀɑsjɔ̃] *nf* alliteration.

allô [alo] *excl* hullo, hallo.

allocataire [alɔkatɛʀ] *nm/f* beneficiary.

allocation [alɔkɑsjɔ̃] *nf* allowance; ~ **(de) chômage** unemployment benefit; ~ **(de) logement** rent allowance; **~s familiales** ≈ child benefit *no pl*; **~s de maternité** maternity allowance.

allocution [alɔkysjɔ̃] *nf* short speech.

allongé, e [alɔ̃ʒe] *adj* (*étendu*): **être** ~ to be stretched out *ou* lying down; (*long*) long; (*étiré*) elongated; (*oblong*) oblong; **rester** ~ to be lying down; **mine ~e** long face.

allonger [alɔ̃ʒe] *vt* to lengthen, make longer; (*étendre: bras, jambe*) to stretch (out); (*sauce*) to spin out, make go further; **s'~** *vi* to get longer; (*se coucher*) to lie down, stretch out; ~ **le pas** to hasten one's step(s).

allouer [alwe] *vt*: ~ **qch à** to allocate sth to, allot sth to.

allumage [alymaʒ] *nm* (*AUTO*) ignition.

allume-cigare [alymsigaʀ] *nm inv* cigar lighter.

allume-gaz [alymgɑz] *nm inv* gas lighter.

allumer [alyme] *vt* (*lampe, phare, radio*) to put *ou* switch on; (*pièce*) to put *ou* switch the light(s) on in; (*feu, bougie, cigare, pipe, gaz*) to light; (*chauffage*) to put on; **s'~** *vi* (*lumière, lampe*) to come *ou* go on; ~ **(la lumière *ou* l'électricité)** to put on the light.

allumette [alymɛt] *nf* match; (*morceau de bois*) matchstick; (*CULIN*): ~ **au fromage** cheese straw; ~ **de sûreté** safety match.

allumeuse [alymøz] *nf* (*péj*) tease (*woman*).

allure [alyʀ] *nf* (*vitesse*) speed; (: *à pied*) pace; (*démarche*) walk; (*maintien*) bearing; (*aspect, air*) look; **avoir de l'~** to have style *ou* a certain elegance; **à toute** ~ at top *ou* full speed.

allusion [alyzjɔ̃] *nf* allusion; (*sous-entendu*) hint; **faire** ~ **à** to allude *ou* refer to; to hint at.

alluvions [alyvjɔ̃] *nfpl* alluvial deposits, alluvium *sg*.

almanach [almana] *nm* almanac.

aloès [alɔɛs] *nm* (*BOT*) aloe.

aloi [alwa] *nm*: **de bon/mauvais** ~ of genuine/doubtful worth *ou* quality.

=============================== MOT-CLÉ

alors [alɔʀ] *adv* **1** (*à ce moment-là*) then, at that time; **il habitait ~ à Paris** he lived in Paris at that time; **jusqu'~** up till *ou* until then
2 (*par conséquent*) then; **tu as fini? ~ je m'en vais** have you finished? I'm going then
3 (*expressions*): **~? quoi de neuf?** well *ou* so? what's new?; **et ~?** so (what)?; **ça ~!** (well) really!
~ que *conj* **1** (*au moment où*) when, as; **il est arrivé alors que je partais** he arrived as I was leaving
2 (*pendant que*) while, when; **~ qu'il était à Paris, il a visité ...** while *ou* when he was in Paris, he visited ...
3 (*tandis que*) whereas, while; **~ que son frère travaillait dur, lui se reposait** while his brother was working hard, HE would rest.

alouette [alwɛt] *nf* (sky)lark.
alourdir [aluʀdiʀ] *vt* to weigh down, make heavy; **s'~** *vi* to grow heavy *ou* heavier.
aloyau [alwajo] *nm* sirloin.
alpaga [alpaga] *nm* (*tissu*) alpaca.
alpage [alpaʒ] *nm* high mountain pasture.
Alpes [alp(ə)] *nfpl*: **les ~** the Alps.
alpestre [alpɛstʀ(ə)] *adj* alpine.
alphabet [alfabɛ] *nm* alphabet; (*livre*) ABC (book), primer.
alphabétique [alfabetik] *adj* alphabetic(al); **par ordre ~** in alphabetical order.
alphabétisation [alfabetizasjɔ̃] *nf* literacy teaching.
alphabétiser [alfabetize] *vt* to teach to read and write; (*pays*) to eliminate illiteracy in.
alphanumérique [alfanymeʀik] *adj* alphanumeric.
alpin, e [alpɛ̃, -in] *adj* (*plante etc*) alpine; (*club*) climbing.
alpinisme [alpinism(ə)] *nm* mountaineering, climbing.
alpiniste [alpinist(ə)] *nmf* mountaineer, climber.
Alsace [alzas] *nf*: **l'~** Alsace.
alsacien, ne [alzasjɛ̃, -ɛn] *adj* Alsatian.
altercation [altɛʀkasjɔ̃] *nf* altercation.
alter ego [altɛʀego] *nm* alter ego.
altérer [alteʀe] *vt* (*faits, vérité*) to falsify, distort; (*qualité*) to debase, impair; (*données*) to corrupt; (*donner soif à*) to make thirsty; **s'~** *vi* to deteriorate, spoil.
alternance [altɛʀnɑ̃s] *nf* alternation; **en ~** alternately; **formation en ~** sandwich course.
alternateur [altɛʀnatœʀ] *nm* alternator.
alternatif, ive [altɛʀnatif, -iv] *adj* alternating ♦ *nf* alternative.
alternativement [altɛʀnativmɑ̃] *adv* alternately.
alterner [altɛʀne] *vt* to alternate ♦ *vi*: **~ (avec)** to alternate (with); **(faire) ~ qch avec qch** to alternate sth with sth.

Altesse [altɛs] *nf* Highness.
altier, ière [altje, -jɛʀ] *adj* haughty.
altimètre [altimɛtʀ(ə)] *nm* altimeter.
altiport [altipɔʀ] *nm* mountain airfield.
altiste [altist(ə)] *nmf* viola player, violist.
altitude [altityd] *nf* altitude, height; **à 1 000 m d'~** at a height *ou* an altitude of 1000 m; **en ~** at high altitudes; **perdre/prendre de l'~** to lose/gain height; **voler à haute/basse ~** to fly at a high/low altitude.
alto [alto] *nm* (*instrument*) viola ♦ *nf* (contr)alto.
altruisme [altʀɥism(ə)] *nm* altruism.
altruiste [altʀɥist(ə)] *adj* altruistic.
aluminium [alyminjɔm] *nm* aluminium (*BRIT*), aluminum (*US*).
alun [alœ̃] *nm* alum.
alunir [alyniʀ] *vi* to land on the moon.
alunissage [alynisaʒ] *nm* (moon) landing.
alvéole [alveɔl] *nm ou f* (*de ruche*) alveolus.
alvéolé, e [alveɔle] *adj* honeycombed.
AM *sigle f* = **assurance maladie**.
amabilité [amabilite] *nf* kindness; **il a eu l'~ de** he was kind *ou* good enough to.
amadou [amadu] *nm* touchwood, amadou.
amadouer [amadwe] *vt* to coax, cajole; (*adoucir*) to mollify, soothe.
amaigrir [amegʀiʀ] *vt* to make thin *ou* thinner.
amaigrissant, e [amegʀisɑ̃, -ɑ̃t] *adj*: **régime ~** slimming (*BRIT*) *ou* weight-reduction (*US*) diet.
amalgame [amalgam] *nm* amalgam; (*fig: de gens, d'idées*) hotch-potch, mixture.
amalgamer [amalgame] *vt* to amalgamate.
amande [amɑ̃d] *nf* (*de l'amandier*) almond; (*de noyau de fruit*) kernel; **en ~** (*yeux*) almond *cpd*, almond-shaped.
amandier [amɑ̃dje] *nm* almond (tree).
amanite [amanit] *nf* (*BOT*) mushroom of the genus *Amanita*; **~ tue-mouches** fly agaric.
amant [amɑ̃] *nm* lover.
amarre [amaʀ] *nf* (*NAVIG*) (mooring) rope *ou* line; **~s** *nfpl* moorings.
amarrer [amaʀe] *vt* (*NAVIG*) to moor; (*gén*) to make fast.
amaryllis [amaʀilis] *nf* amaryllis.
amas [ama] *nm* heap, pile.
amasser [amase] *vt* to amass; **s'~** *vi* to pile up, accumulate; (*foule*) to gather.
amateur [amatœʀ] *nm* amateur; **en ~** (*péj*) amateurishly; **musicien/sportif ~** amateur musician/sportsman; **~ de musique/sport** *etc* music/sport *etc* lover.
amateurisme [amatœʀism(ə)] *nm* amateurism; (*péj*) amateurishness.
Amazone [amazon] *nf*: **l'~** the Amazon.
amazone [amazon] *nf* horsewoman; **en ~** side-saddle.
Amazonie [amazɔni] *nf*: **l'~** Amazonia.
ambages [ɑ̃baʒ]: **sans ~** *adv* without beating about the bush, plainly.
ambassade [ɑ̃basad] *nf* embassy; (*mission*): **en**

~ **on** a mission.
ambassadeur, drice [ūbasadœʀ, -dʀis] *nm/f* ambassador/ambassadress.
ambiance [ūbjūs] *nf* atmosphere; **il y a de l'**~ everyone's having a good time.
ambiant, e [ūbjū, -ūt] *adj* (*air, milieu*) surrounding; (*température*) ambient.
ambidextre [ūbidɛkstʀ(ə)] *adj* ambidextrous.
ambigu, ë [ūbigy] *adj* ambiguous.
ambiguïté [ūbiguite] *nf* ambiguousness *no pl*, ambiguity.
ambitieux, euse [ūbisjø, -øz] *adj* ambitious.
ambition [ūbisjɔ̃] *nf* ambition.
ambitionner [ūbisjɔne] *vt* to have as one's aim *ou* ambition.
ambivalent, e [ūbivalū, -ūt] *adj* ambivalent.
amble [ūbl(ə)] *nm*: **aller l'**~ to amble.
ambre [ūbʀ(ə)] *nm*: ~ **(jaune)** amber; ~ **gris** ambergris.
ambré, e [ūbʀe] *adj* (*couleur*) amber; (*parfum*) ambergris-scented.
ambulance [ūbylūs] *nf* ambulance.
ambulancier, ière [ūbylūsje, -jɛʀ] *nm/f* ambulanceman/woman (*BRIT*), paramedic (*US*).
ambulant, e [ūbylū, -ūt] *adj* travelling, itinerant.
âme [ɑm] *nf* soul; **rendre l'**~ to give up the ghost; **bonne** ~ (*aussi ironique*) kind soul; **un joueur/tricheur dans l'**~ a gambler/cheat through and through; ~ **sœur** kindred spirit.
amélioration [ameljɔʀasjɔ̃] *nf* improvement.
améliorer [ameljɔʀe] *vt* to improve; **s'**~ *vi* to improve, get better.
aménagement [amenaʒmū] *nm* fitting out; laying out; development; ~**s** *nmpl* developments; **l'**~ **du territoire** ≈ town and country planning; ~**s fiscaux** tax adjustments.
aménager [amenaʒe] *vt* (*agencer: espace, local*) to fit out; (*: terrain*) to lay out; (*: quartier, territoire*) to develop; (*installer*) to fix up, put in; **ferme aménagée** converted farmhouse.
amende [amūd] *nf* fine; **mettre à l'**~ to penalize; **faire** ~ **honorable** to make amends.
amendement [amūdmū] *nm* (*JUR*) amendment.
amender [amūde] *vt* (*loi*) to amend; (*terre*) to enrich; **s'**~ *vi* to mend one's ways.
amène [amɛn] *adj* affable; **peu** ~ unkind.
amener [amne] *vt* to bring; (*causer*) to bring about; (*baisser: drapeau, voiles*) to strike; **s'**~ *vi* (*fam*) to show up, turn up; ~ **qn à qch/à faire** to lead sb to sth/to do.
amenuiser [amənɥize]: **s'**~ *vi* to dwindle; (*chances*) to grow slimmer, lessen.
amer, amère [amɛʀ] *adj* bitter.
amèrement [amɛʀmū] *adv* bitterly.
américain, e [ameʀikɛ̃, -ɛn] *adj* American ♦ *nm* (*LING*) American (English) ♦ *nm/f*: **A**~, **e** American; **en vedette** ~**e** as a special guest (star).

américaniser [ameʀikanize] *vt* to Americanize.
américanisme [ameʀikanism(ə)] *nm* Americanism.
amérindien, ne [ameʀɛ̃djɛ̃, -ɛn] *adj* Amerindian, American Indian.
Amérique [ameʀik] *nf* America; **l'**~ **centrale** Central America; **l'**~ **latine** Latin America; **l'**~ **du Nord** North America; **l'**~ **du Sud** South America.
Amerloque [amɛʀlɔk] *nm/f* (*fam*) Yank, Yankee.
amerrir [ameʀiʀ] *vi* to land (on the sea); (*capsule spatiale*) to splash down.
amerrissage [ameʀisaʒ] *nm* landing (on the sea); splash-down.
amertume [amɛʀtym] *nf* bitterness.
améthyste [amɛtist(ə)] *nf* amethyst.
ameublement [amœbləmū] *nm* furnishing; (*meubles*) furniture; **articles d'**~ furnishings; **tissus d'**~ soft furnishings, furnishing fabrics.
ameuter [amøte] *vt* (*badauds*) to draw a crowd of; (*peuple*) to rouse, stir up.
ami, e [ami] *nm/f* friend; (*amant/maîtresse*) boyfriend/girlfriend ♦ *adj*: **pays/groupe** ~ friendly country/group; **être (très)** ~ **avec qn** to be (very) friendly with sb; **être** ~ **de l'ordre** to be a lover of order; **un** ~ **des arts** a patron of the arts; **un** ~ **des chiens** a dog lover; **petit** ~/**petite** ~**e** (*fam*) boyfriend/girlfriend.
amiable [amjabl(ə)]: **à l'**~ *adv* (*JUR*) out of court; (*gén*) amicably.
amiante [amjūt] *nm* asbestos.
amibe [amib] *nf* amoeba (*pl* -ae).
amical, e, aux [amikal, -o] *adj* friendly ♦ *nf* (*club*) association.
amicalement [amikalmū] *adv* in a friendly way; (*formule épistolaire*) regards.
amidon [amidɔ̃] *nm* starch.
amidonner [amidɔne] *vt* to starch.
amincir [amɛ̃siʀ] *vt* (*objet*) to thin (down); **s'**~ *vi* to get thinner *ou* slimmer; ~ **qn** to make sb thinner *ou* slimmer.
amincissant, e [amɛ̃sisū, -ūt] *adj* slimming.
aminé, e [amine] *adj*: **acide** ~ amino acid.
amiral, aux [amiʀal, -o] *nm* admiral.
amirauté [amiʀote] *nf* admiralty.
amitié [amitje] *nf* friendship; **prendre en** ~ to take a liking to; **faire** *ou* **présenter ses** ~**s à qn** to send sb one's best regards; ~**s** (*formule épistolaire*) (with) best wishes.
ammoniac [amɔnjak] *nm*: (**gaz**) ~ ammonia.
ammoniaque [amɔnjak] *nf* ammonia (water).
amnésie [amnezi] *nf* amnesia.
amnésique [amnezik] *adj* amnesic.
Amnesty International [amnɛsti-] *n* Amnesty International.
amniocentèse [amnjosɛ̃tɛz] *nf* amniocentesis.
amnistie [amnisti] *nf* amnesty.
amnistier [amnistje] *vt* to amnesty.

amocher [amɔʃe] *vt* (*fam*) to mess up.
amoindrir [amwɛ̃dʀiʀ] *vt* to reduce.
amollir [amɔliʀ] *vt* to soften.
amonceler [amɔ̃sle] *vt*, **s'~** *vi* to pile *ou* heap up; (*fig*) to accumulate.
amoncellement [amɔ̃sɛlmɑ̃] *nm* piling *ou* heaping up; accumulation; (*tas*) pile, heap; accumulation.
amont [amɔ̃]: **en ~** *adv* upstream; (*sur une pente*) uphill; **en ~ de** *prép* upstream from; uphill from, above.
amoral, e, aux [amɔʀal, -o] *adj* amoral.
amorce [amɔʀs(ə)] *nf* (*sur un hameçon*) bait; (*explosif*) cap; (*tube*) primer; (: *contenu*) priming; (*fig: début*) beginning(s), start.
amorcer [amɔʀse] *vt* to bait; to prime; (*commencer*) to begin, start.
amorphe [amɔʀf(ə)] *adj* passive, lifeless.
amortir [amɔʀtiʀ] *vt* (*atténuer: choc*) to absorb, cushion; (*bruit, douleur*) to deaden; (*COMM: dette*) to pay off, amortize; (: *mise de fonds, matériel*) to write off; **~ un abonnement** to make a season ticket pay (for itself).
amortissable [amɔʀtisabl(ə)] *adj* (*COMM*) that can be paid off.
amortissement [amɔʀtismɑ̃] *nm* (*de matériel*) writing off; (*d'une dette*) paying off.
amortisseur [amɔʀtisœʀ] *nm* shock absorber.
amour [amuʀ] *nm* love; (*liaison*) love affair, love; (*statuette etc*) cupid; **un ~ de** a lovely little; **faire l'~** to make love.
amouracher [amuʀaʃe]: **s'~ de** *vt* (*péj*) to become infatuated with.
amourette [amuʀɛt] *nf* passing fancy.
amoureusement [amuʀøzmɑ̃] *adv* lovingly.
amoureux, euse [amuʀø, -øz] *adj* (*regard, tempérament*) amorous; (*vie, problèmes*) love *cpd*; (*personne*): **~ (de qn)** in love (with sb) ♦ *nm/f* lover ♦ *nmpl* courting couple(s); **tomber ~ de qn** to fall in love with sb; **être ~ de qch** to be passionately fond of sth; **un ~ de la nature** a nature lover.
amour-propre, *pl* **amours-propres** [amuʀpʀɔpʀ(ə)] *nm* self-esteem.
amovible [amɔvibl(ə)] *adj* removable, detachable.
ampère [ɑ̃pɛʀ] *nm* amp(ere).
ampèremètre [ɑ̃pɛʀmɛtʀ(ə)] *nm* ammeter.
amphétamine [ɑ̃fetamin] *nf* amphetamine.
amphi [ɑ̃fi] *nm* (*SCOL fam*: = *amphithéâtre*) lecture hall *ou* theatre.
amphibie [ɑ̃fibi] *adj* amphibious.
amphibien [ɑ̃fibjɛ̃] *nm* (*ZOOL*) amphibian.
amphithéâtre [ɑ̃fiteatʀ(ə)] *nm* amphitheatre; (*d'université*) lecture hall *ou* theatre.
amphore [ɑ̃fɔʀ] *nf* amphora.
ample [ɑ̃pl(ə)] *adj* (*vêtement*) roomy, ample; (*gestes, mouvement*) broad; (*ressources*) ample; **jusqu'à plus ~ informé** (*ADMIN*) until further details are available.
amplement [ɑ̃pləmɑ̃] *adv* amply; **~ suffisant** ample, more than enough.

ampleur [ɑ̃plœʀ] *nf* scale, size; extent, magnitude.
ampli [ɑ̃pli] *nm* (*fam*: = *amplificateur*) amplifier, amp.
amplificateur [ɑ̃plifikatœʀ] *nm* amplifier.
amplification [ɑ̃plifikasjɔ̃] *nf* amplification; expansion, increase.
amplifier [ɑ̃plifje] *vt* (*son, oscillation*) to amplify; (*fig*) to expand, increase.
amplitude [ɑ̃plityd] *nf* amplitude; (*des températures*) range.
ampoule [ɑ̃pul] *nf* (*électrique*) bulb; (*de médicament*) phial; (*aux mains, pieds*) blister.
ampoulé, e [ɑ̃pule] *adj* (*péj*) pompous, bombastic.
amputation [ɑ̃pytasjɔ̃] *nf* amputation.
amputer [ɑ̃pyte] *vt* (*MÉD*) to amputate; (*fig*) to cut *ou* reduce drastically; **~ qn d'un bras/pied** to amputate sb's arm/foot.
Amsterdam [amstɛʀdam] *n* Amsterdam.
amulette [amylɛt] *nf* amulet.
amusant, e [amyzɑ̃, -ɑ̃t] *adj* (*divertissant, spirituel*) entertaining, amusing; (*comique*) funny, amusing.
amusé, e [amyze] *adj* amused.
amuse-gueule [amyzgœl] *nm inv* appetizer, snack.
amusement [amyzmɑ̃] *nm* (*voir amusé*) amusement; (*voir amuser*) entertaining, amusing; (*jeu etc*) pastime, diversion.
amuser [amyze] *vt* (*divertir*) to entertain, amuse; (*égayer, faire rire*) to amuse; (*détourner l'attention de*) to distract; **s'~** *vi* (*jouer*) to amuse o.s., play; (*se divertir*) to enjoy o.s., have fun; (*fig*) to mess around; **s'~ de qch** (*trouver comique*) to find sth amusing; **s'~ avec** *ou* **de qn** (*duper*) to make a fool of sb.
amusette [amyzɛt] *nf* idle pleasure, trivial pastime.
amuseur [amyzœʀ] *nm* entertainer; (*péj*) clown.
amygdale [amidal] *nf* tonsil; **opérer qn des ~s** to take sb's tonsils out.
amygdalite [amidalit] *nf* tonsillitis.
AN *sigle f* = **Assemblée nationale**.
an [ɑ̃] *nm* year; **être âgé de** *ou* **avoir 3 ~s** to be 3 (years old); **en l'~ 1980** in the year 1980; **le jour de l'~, le premier de l'~, le nouvel ~** New Year's Day.
anabolisant [anabɔlizɑ̃] *nm* anabolic steroid.
anachronique [anakʀɔnik] *adj* anachronistic.
anachronisme [anakʀɔnism(ə)] *nm* anachronism.
anaconda [anakɔ̃da] *nm* (*ZOOL*) anaconda.
anaérobie [anaeʀɔbi] *adj* anaerobic.
anagramme [anagʀam] *nf* anagram.
ANAH *sigle f* = **Agence nationale pour l'amélioration de l'habitat**.
anal, e, aux [anal, -o] *adj* anal.
analgésique [analʒezik] *nm* analgesic.
anallergique [analɛʀʒik] *adj* hypoallergenic.
analogie [analɔʒi] *nf* analogy.

analogique [analɔʒik] *adj* (*LOGIQUE: raisonnement*) analogical; (*calculateur, montre etc*) analogue; (*INFORM*) analog.

analogue [analɔg] *adj*: ~ **(à)** analogous (to), similar (to).

analphabète [analfabɛt] *nm/f* illiterate.

analphabétisme [analfabetism(ə)] *nm* illiteracy.

analyse [analiz] *nf* analysis; (*MÉD*) test; **faire l'~ de** to analyse; **une ~ approfondie** an in-depth analysis; **en dernière ~** in the last analysis; **avoir l'esprit d'~** to have an analytical turn of mind; ~ **grammaticale** grammatical analysis, parsing (*SCOL*).

analyser [analize] *vt* to analyse; (*MÉD*) to test.

analyste [analist(ə)] *nm/f* analyst; (*psychanalyste*) (psycho)analyst.

analyste-programmeur, euse, *pl* **analystes-programmeurs, euses** [analist-pʀɔgʀamœʀ, -øz] *nm/f* systems analyst.

analytique [analitik] *adj* analytical.

analytiquement [analitikmɑ̃] *adv* analytically.

ananas [anana] *nm* pineapple.

anarchie [anaʀʃi] *nf* anarchy.

anarchique [anaʀʃik] *adj* anarchic.

anarchisme [anaʀʃism(ə)] *nm* anarchism.

anarchiste [anaʀʃist(ə)] *adj* anarchistic ♦ *nm/f* anarchist.

anathème [anatɛm] *nm*: **jeter l'~ sur, lancer l'~ contre** to anathematize, curse.

anatomie [anatɔmi] *nf* anatomy.

anatomique [anatɔmik] *adj* anatomical.

ancestral, e, aux [ɑ̃sɛstʀal, -o] *adj* ancestral.

ancêtre [ɑ̃sɛtʀ(ə)] *nm/f* ancestor; (*fig*): **l'~ de** the forerunner of.

anche [ɑ̃ʃ] *nf* reed.

anchois [ɑ̃ʃwa] *nm* anchovy.

ancien, ne [ɑ̃sjɛ̃, -ɛn] *adj* old; (*de jadis, de l'antiquité*) ancient; (*précédent, ex-*) former, old ♦ *nm* (*mobilier ancien*): **l'~** antiques *pl* ♦ *nm/f* (*dans une tribu etc*) elder; **un ~ ministre** a former minister; **mon ~ne voiture** my previous car; **être plus ~ que qn dans une maison** to have been in a firm longer than sb; (*dans l'hiérarchie*) to be senior to sb in a firm; ~ **combattant** ex-serviceman; ~ **(élève)** (*SCOL*) ex-pupil (*BRIT*), alumnus (*US*).

anciennement [ɑ̃sjɛnmɑ̃] *adv* formerly.

ancienneté [ɑ̃sjɛnte] *nf* oldness; antiquity; (*ADMIN*) (length of) service; seniority.

ancrage [ɑ̃kʀaʒ] *nm* anchoring; (*NAVIG*) anchorage; (*CONSTR*) anchor.

ancre [ɑ̃kʀ(ə)] *nf* anchor; **jeter/lever l'~** to cast/weigh anchor; **à l'~** at anchor.

ancrer [ɑ̃kʀe] *vt* (*CONSTR*) to anchor; (*fig*) to fix firmly; **s'~** *vi* (*NAVIG*) to (cast) anchor.

andalou, ouse [ɑ̃dalu, -uz] *adj* Andalusian.

Andalousie [ɑ̃daluzi] *nf*: **l'~** Andalusia.

andante [ɑ̃dɑ̃t] *adv, nm* andante.

Andes [ɑ̃d] *nfpl*: **les ~** the Andes.

Andorre [ɑ̃dɔʀ] *nf* Andorra.

andouille [ɑ̃duj] *nf* (*CULIN*) sausage made of

chitterlings; (*fam*) clot, nit.

andouillette [ɑ̃dujɛt] *nf* small andouille.

âne [ɑn] *nm* donkey, ass; (*péj*) dunce, fool.

anéantir [aneɑ̃tiʀ] *vt* to annihilate, wipe out; (*fig*) to obliterate, destroy; (*déprimer*) to overwhelm.

anecdote [anɛkdɔt] *nf* anecdote.

anecdotique [anɛkdɔtik] *adj* anecdotal.

anémie [anemi] *nf* anaemia.

anémié, e [anemje] *adj* anaemic; (*fig*) enfeebled.

anémique [anemik] *adj* anaemic.

anémone [anemɔn] *nf* anemone; ~ **de mer** sea anemone.

ânerie [ɑnʀi] *nf* stupidity; (*parole etc*) stupid *ou* idiotic comment *etc*.

anéroïde [aneʀɔid] *adj voir* **baromètre**.

ânesse [ɑnɛs] *nf* she-ass.

anesthésie [anɛstezi] *nf* anaesthesia; **sous ~** under anaesthetic; ~ **générale/locale** general/local anaesthetic; **faire une ~ locale à qn** to give sb a local anaesthetic.

anesthésier [anɛstezje] *vt* to anaesthetize.

anesthésique [anɛstezik] *adj* anaesthetic.

anesthésiste [anɛstezist(ə)] *nm/f* anaesthetist.

anfractuosité [ɑ̃fʀaktɥozite] *nf* crevice.

ange [ɑ̃ʒ] *nm* angel; **être aux ~s** to be over the moon; ~ **gardien** guardian angel.

angélique [ɑ̃ʒelik] *adj* angelic(al) ♦ *nf* angelica.

angelot [ɑ̃ʒlo] *nm* cherub.

angélus [ɑ̃ʒelys] *nm* angelus; (*cloches*) evening bells *pl*.

angevin, e [ɑ̃ʒvɛ̃, -in] *adj* of *ou* from Anjou; of *ou* from Angers.

angine [ɑ̃ʒin] *nf* sore throat, throat infection; ~ **de poitrine** angina (pectoris).

angiome [ɑ̃ʒjom] *nm* angioma.

anglais, e [ɑ̃glɛ, -ɛz] *adj* English ♦ *nm* (*LING*) English ♦ *nm/f*: **A~, e** Englishman/woman; **les A~** the English; **filer à l'~e** to take French leave; **à l'~e** (*CULIN*) boiled.

anglaises [ɑ̃glɛz] *nfpl* (*cheveux*) ringlets.

angle [ɑ̃gl(ə)] *nm* angle; (*coin*) corner; ~ **droit/obtus/aigu/mort** right/obtuse/acute/dead angle.

Angleterre [ɑ̃glətɛʀ] *nf*: **l'~** England.

anglican, e [ɑ̃glikɑ̃, -an] *adj, nm/f* Anglican.

anglicanisme [ɑ̃glikanism(ə)] *nm* Anglicanism.

anglicisme [ɑ̃glisism(ə)] *nm* anglicism.

angliciste [ɑ̃glisist(ə)] *nm/f* English scholar; (*étudiant*) student of English.

anglo... [ɑ̃glɔ] *préfixe* Anglo-, anglo(-).

anglo-américain, e [ɑ̃glɔameʀikɛ̃, -ɛn] *adj* Anglo-American ♦ *nm* (*LING*) American English.

anglo-arabe [ɑ̃glɔaʀab] *adj* Anglo-Arab.

anglo-canadien, ne [ɑ̃glɔkanadjɛ̃, -ɛn] *adj* Anglo-Canadian ♦ *nm* (*LING*) Canadian English.

anglo-normand, e [ɑ̃glɔnɔʀmɑ̃, -ɑ̃d] *adj*

Anglo-Norman; **les îles ~es** the Channel Islands.

anglophile [ɑ̃glɔfil] *adj* anglophilic.

anglophobe [ɑ̃glɔfɔb] *adj* anglophobic.

anglophone [ɑ̃glɔfɔn] *adj* English-speaking.

anglo-saxon, ne [ɑ̃glɔsaksɔ̃, -ɔn] *adj* Anglo-Saxon.

angoissant, e [ɑ̃gwasɑ̃, -ɑ̃t] *adj* harrowing.

angoisse [ɑ̃gwas] *nf:* **l'~** anguish *no pl.*

angoissé, e [ɑ̃gwase] *adj* anguished; (*personne*) full of anxieties *ou* hang-ups (*fam*).

angoisser [ɑ̃gwase] *vt* to harrow, cause anguish to ♦ *vi* to worry, fret.

Angola [ɑ̃gɔla] *nm:* **l'~** Angola.

angolais, e [ɑ̃gɔlɛ, -ɛz] *adj* Angolan.

angora [ɑ̃gɔra] *adj, nm* angora.

anguille [ɑ̃gij] *nf* eel; **~ de mer** conger (eel); **il y a ~ sous roche** (*fig*) there's something going on, there's something beneath all this.

angulaire [ɑ̃gylɛʀ] *adj* angular.

anguleux, euse [ɑ̃gylø, -øz] *adj* angular.

anhydride [anidʀid] *nm* anhydride.

anicroche [anikʀɔʃ] *nf* hitch, snag.

animal, e, aux [animal, -o] *adj, nm* animal; **~ domestique/sauvage** domestic/wild animal.

animalier [animalje] *adj:* **peintre ~** animal painter.

animateur, trice [animatœʀ, -tʀis] *nm/f* (*de télévision*) host; (*de music-hall*) compère; (*de groupe*) leader, organizer; (*CINÉ: technicien*) animator.

animation [animasjɔ̃] *nf* (*voir animé*) busyness; liveliness; (*CINÉ: technique*) animation; (*activité*): **~s** *nfpl* activities; **centre d'~** ≈ community centre.

animé, e [anime] *adj* (*rue, lieu*) busy, lively; (*conversation, réunion*) lively, animated; (*opposé à inanimé, aussi LING*) animate.

animer [anime] *vt* (*ville, soirée*) to liven up, enliven; (*mettre en mouvement*) to drive; (*stimuler*) to drive, impel; **s'~** *vi* to liven up, come to life.

animosité [animozite] *nf* animosity.

anis [ani] *nm* (*CULIN*) aniseed; (*BOT*) anise.

anisette [anizɛt] *nf* anisette.

Ankara [ɑ̃kaʀa] *n* Ankara.

ankyloser [ɑ̃kiloze]: **s'~** *vi* to get stiff, ankylose.

annales [anal] *nfpl* annals.

anneau, x [ano] *nm* ring; (*de chaîne*) link; (*SPORT*): **exercices aux ~x** ring exercises.

année [ane] *nf* year; **souhaiter la bonne ~ à qn** to wish sb a Happy New Year; **tout au long de l'~** all year long; **d'une ~ à l'autre** from one year to the next; **d'~ en ~** from year to year; **l'~ scolaire/fiscale** the school/tax year.

année-lumière, *pl* **années-lumière** [anelymjɛʀ] *nf* light year.

annexe [anɛks(ə)] *adj* (*problème*) related; (*document*) appended; (*salle*) adjoining ♦ *nf* (*bâtiment*) annex(e); (*de document, ouvrage*) annex, appendix; (*jointe à une lettre, un dossier*) enclosure.

annexer [anɛkse] *vt* to annex; **s'~** (*pays*) to annex; **~ qch à** (*joindre*) to append sth to.

annexion [anɛksjɔ̃] *nf* annexation.

annihiler [aniile] *vt* to annihilate.

anniversaire [anivɛʀsɛʀ] *nm* birthday; (*d'un événement, bâtiment*) anniversary ♦ *adj:* **jour ~** anniversary.

annonce [anɔ̃s] *nf* announcement; (*signe, indice*) sign; (*aussi:* **~ publicitaire**) advertisement; (*CARTES*) declaration; **~ personnelle** personal message; **les petites ~s** the small *ou* classified ads.

annoncer [anɔ̃se] *vt* to announce; (*être le signe de*) to herald; (*CARTES*) to declare; **je vous annonce que ...** I wish to tell you that ...; **s'~ bien/difficile** to look promising/difficult; **~ la couleur** (*fig*) to lay one's cards on the table.

annonceur, euse [anɔ̃sœʀ, -øz] *nm/f* (*TV, RADIO: speaker*) announcer; (*publicitaire*) advertiser.

annonciateur, trice [anɔ̃sjatœʀ, -tʀis] *adj:* **~ d'un événement** presaging an event.

Annonciation [anɔ̃sjasjɔ̃] *nf:* **l'~** (*REL*) the Annunciation; (*jour*) Annunciation Day.

annotation [anɔtasjɔ̃] *nf* annotation.

annoter [anɔte] *vt* to annotate.

annuaire [anɥɛʀ] *nm* yearbook, annual; **~ téléphonique** (telephone) directory, phone book.

annuel, le [anɥɛl] *adj* annual, yearly.

annuellement [anɥɛlmɑ̃] *adv* annually, yearly.

annuité [anɥite] *nf* annual instalment.

annulaire [anylɛʀ] *nm* ring *ou* third finger.

annulation [anylasjɔ̃] *nf* cancellation; annulment; quashing, repeal.

annuler [anyle] *vt* (*rendez-vous, voyage*) to cancel, call off; (*mariage*) to annul; (*jugement*) to quash (*BRIT*), repeal (*US*); (*résultats*) to declare void; (*MATH, PHYSIQUE*) to cancel out; **s'~** to cancel each other out.

anoblir [anɔbliʀ] *vt* to ennoble.

anode [anɔd] *nf* anode.

anodin, e [anɔdɛ̃, -in] *adj* harmless; (*sans importance*) insignificant, trivial.

anomalie [anɔmali] *nf* anomaly.

ânon [ɑnɔ̃] *nm* baby donkey; (*petit âne*) little donkey.

ânonner [ɑnɔne] *vi, vt* to read in a drone; (*hésiter*) to read in a fumbling manner.

anonymat [anɔnima] *nm* anonymity; **garder l'~** to remain anonymous.

anonyme [anɔnim] *adj* anonymous; (*fig*) impersonal.

anonymement [anɔnimmɑ̃] *adv* anonymously.

anorak [anɔʀak] *nm* anorak.

anorexie [anɔʀɛksi] *nf* anorexia.

anorexique [anɔʀɛksik] *adj, nm/f* anorexic.

anormal, e, aux [anɔʀmal, -o] *adj* abnormal; (*insolite*) unusual, abnormal.

anormalement [anɔʀmalmɑ̃] *adv* abnormally; unusually.

ANPE *sigle f* (= Agence nationale pour l'emploi) national employment agency (*functions include job creation*).

anse [ɑ̃s] *nf* handle; (*GÉO*) cove.

antagonisme [ɑ̃tagɔnism(ə)] *nm* antagonism.

antagoniste [ɑ̃tagɔnist(ə)] *adj* antagonistic ♦ *nm* antagonist.

antan [ɑ̃tɑ̃]: **d'~** *adj* of yesteryear, of long ago.

antarctique [ɑ̃taʀktik] *adj* Antarctic ♦ *nm*: **l'A~** the Antarctic; **le cercle A~** the Antarctic Circle; **l'océan A~** the Antarctic Ocean.

antécédent [ɑ̃tesedɑ̃] *nm* (*LING*) antecedent; **~s** *nmpl* (*MÉD etc*) past history *sg*; **~s professionnels** record, career to date.

antédiluvien, ne [ɑ̃tedilyvjɛ̃, -ɛn] *adj* (*fig*) ancient, antediluvian.

antenne [ɑ̃tɛn] *nf* (*de radio, télévision*) aerial; (*d'insecte*) antenna (*pl* -ae), feeler; (*poste avancé*) outpost; (*petite succursale*) sub-branch; **sur l'~** on the air; **passer à/avoir l'~** to go/be on the air; **2 heures d'~** 2 hours' broadcasting time; **hors ~** off the air; **~ chirurgicale** (*MIL*) advance surgical unit.

antépénultième [ɑ̃tepenyltjɛm] *adj* antepenultimate.

antérieur, e [ɑ̃teʀjœʀ] *adj* (*d'avant*) previous, earlier; (*de devant*) front; **~ à** prior *ou* previous to; **passé/futur ~** (*LING*) past/future anterior.

antérieurement [ɑ̃teʀjœʀmɑ̃] *adv* earlier; (*précédemment*) previously; **~ à** prior *ou* previous to.

antériorité [ɑ̃teʀjɔʀite] *nf* precedence (*in time*).

anthologie [ɑ̃tɔlɔʒi] *nf* anthology.

anthracite [ɑ̃tʀasit] *nm* anthracite ♦ *adj*: **(gris) ~** charcoal (grey).

anthropologie [ɑ̃tʀɔpɔlɔʒi] *nf* anthropology.

anthropologue [ɑ̃tʀɔpɔlɔg] *nm/f* anthropologist.

anthropomorphisme [ɑ̃tʀɔpɔmɔʀfism(ə)] *nm* anthropomorphism.

anthropophage [ɑ̃tʀɔpɔfaʒ] *adj* cannibalistic.

anthropophagie [ɑ̃tʀɔpɔfaʒi] *nf* cannibalism, anthropophagy.

anti... [ɑ̃ti] *préfixe* anti....

antiaérien, ne [ɑ̃tiaeʀjɛ̃, -ɛn] *adj* anti-aircraft; **abri ~** air-raid shelter.

antialcoolique [ɑ̃tialkɔlik] *adj* anti-alcohol; **ligue ~** temperance league.

antiatomique [ɑ̃tiatɔmik] *adj*: **abri ~** fallout shelter.

antibiotique [ɑ̃tibjɔtik] *nm* antibiotic.

antibrouillard [ɑ̃tibʀujaʀ] *adj*: **phare ~** fog lamp.

antibruit [ɑ̃tibʀɥi] *adj inv*: **mur ~** (*sur autoroute*) sound-muffling wall.

antibuée [ɑ̃tibɥe] *adj inv*: **dispositif ~** demist-er; **bombe ~** demister spray.

anticancéreux, euse [ɑ̃tikɑ̃seʀø, -øz] *adj* cancer *cpd*.

anticasseur(s) [ɑ̃tikasœʀ] *adj*: **loi/mesure ~** law/measure against damage done by demonstrators.

antichambre [ɑ̃tiʃɑ̃bʀ(ə)] *nf* antechamber, anteroom; **faire ~** to wait (for an audience).

antichar [ɑ̃tiʃaʀ] *adj* antitank.

antichoc [ɑ̃tiʃɔk] *adj* shockproof.

anticipation [ɑ̃tisipasjɔ̃] *nf* anticipation; (*COMM*) payment in advance; **par ~** in anticipation, in advance; **livre/film d'~** science fiction book/film.

anticipé, e [ɑ̃tisipe] *adj* (*règlement, paiement*) early, in advance; (*joie etc*) anticipated, early; **avec mes remerciements ~s** thanking you in advance *ou* anticipation.

anticiper [ɑ̃tisipe] *vt* to anticipate, foresee; (*paiement*) to pay *ou* make in advance ♦ *vi* to look *ou* think ahead; (*en racontant*) to jump ahead; (*prévoir*) to anticipate; **~ sur** to anticipate.

anticlérical, e, aux [ɑ̃tikleʀikal, -o] *adj* anticlerical.

anticoagulant, e [ɑ̃tikɔagylɑ̃, -ɑ̃t] *adj, nm* anticoagulant.

anticolonialisme [ɑ̃tikɔlɔnjalism(ə)] *nm* anticolonialism.

anticonceptionnel, le [ɑ̃tikɔ̃sɛpsjɔnɛl] *adj* contraceptive.

anticonformisme [ɑ̃tikɔ̃fɔʀmism(ə)] *nm* nonconformism.

anticonstitutionnel, le [ɑ̃tikɔ̃stitysjɔnɛl] *adj* unconstitutional.

anticorps [ɑ̃tikɔʀ] *nm* antibody.

anticyclone [ɑ̃tisiklɔn] *nm* anticyclone.

antidater [ɑ̃tidate] *vt* to backdate, predate.

antidémocratique [ɑ̃tidemɔkʀatik] *adj* antidemocratic; (*peu démocratique*) undemocratic.

antidérapant, e [ɑ̃tideʀapɑ̃, -ɑ̃t] *adj* nonskid.

antidopage [ɑ̃tidɔpaʒ], **antidoping** [ɑ̃tidɔpiŋ] *adj* (*lutte*) antidoping; (*contrôle*) dope *cpd*.

antidote [ɑ̃tidɔt] *nm* antidote.

antienne [ɑ̃tjɛn] *nf* (*fig*) chant, refrain.

antigang [ɑ̃tigɑ̃g] *adj inv*: **brigade ~** commando unit.

antigel [ɑ̃tiʒɛl] *nm* antifreeze.

antigène [ɑ̃tiʒɛn] *nm* antigen.

antigouvernemental, e, aux [ɑ̃tiguvɛʀnəmɑ̃tal, -o] *adj* antigovernment.

Antigua et Barbude [ɑ̃tigaebaʀbyd] *nf* Antigua and Barbuda.

antihistaminique [ɑ̃tiistaminik] *nm* antihistamine.

anti-inflammatoire [ɑ̃tiɛ̃flamatwaʀ] *adj* anti-inflammatory.

anti-inflationniste [ɑ̃tiɛ̃flasjɔnist(ə)] *adj* anti-inflationary.

antillais, e [ɑ̃tijɛ, -ɛz] *adj* West Indian.

Antilles [ɑ̃tij] *nfpl*: **les ~** the West Indies; **les**

Grandes/Petites ~ the Greater/Lesser Antilles.

antilope [ātilɔp] *nf* antelope.

antimilitarisme [ātimilitaʀism(ə)] *nm* antimilitarism.

antimilitariste [ātimilitaʀist(ə)] *adj* antimilitarist.

antimissile [ātimisil] *adj* antimissile.

antimite(s) [ātimit] *adj, nm*: **(produit)** ~ mothproofer, moth repellent.

antinucléaire [ātinykleɛʀ] *adj* antinuclear.

antioxydant [ātiɔksidā] *nm* antioxidant.

antiparasite [ātipaʀazit] *adj (RADIO, TV)* antiinterference; **dispositif** ~ suppressor.

antipathie [ātipati] *nf* antipathy.

antipathique [ātipatik] *adj* unpleasant, disagreeable.

antipelliculaire [ātipelikylɛʀ] *adj* antidandruff.

antiphrase [ātifʀaz] *nf*: **par** ~ ironically.

antipodes [ātipɔd] *nmpl (GÉO)*: **les** ~ the antipodes; *(fig)*: **être aux** ~ **de** to be the opposite extreme of.

antipoison [ātipwazɔ̃] *adj inv*: **centre** ~ poison centre.

antipoliomyélitique [ātipɔljɔmjelitik] *adj* polio *cpd*.

antiprotectionniste [ātipʀɔtɛksjɔnist(ə)] *adj* free-trade.

antiquaire [ātikɛʀ] *nm/f* antique dealer.

antique [ātik] *adj* antique; *(très vieux)* ancient, antiquated.

antiquité [ātikite] *nf (objet)* antique; **l'A~** Antiquity; **magasin/marchand d'~s** antique shop/dealer.

antirabique [ātiʀabik] *adj* rabies *cpd*.

antiraciste [ātiʀasist(ə)] *adj* antiracist, antiracialist.

antireflet [ātiʀəflɛ] *adj inv (verres)* antireflective.

antirépublicain, e [ātiʀepyblikɛ̃, -ɛn] *adj* antirepublican.

antirides [ātiʀid] *adj (crème)* antiwrinkle.

antirouille [ātiʀuj] *adj inv*: **peinture** ~ antirust paint; **traitement** ~ rustproofing.

antisémite [ātisemit] *adj* anti-Semitic.

antisémitisme [ātisemitism(ə)] *nm* anti-Semitism.

antiseptique [ātisɛptik] *adj, nm* antiseptic.

antisocial, e, aux [ātisɔsjal, -o] *adj* antisocial.

antispasmodique [ātispasmɔdik] *adj, nm* antispasmodic.

antisportif, ive [ātispɔʀtif, -iv] *adj* unsporting; *(hostile au sport)* against sport, antisport.

antitétanique [ātitetanik] *adj* tetanus *cpd*.

antithèse [ātitɛz] *nf* antithesis.

antitrust [ātitʀœst] *adj inv (loi, mesures)* antimonopoly.

antituberculeux, euse [ātitybɛʀkylø, -øz] *adj* tuberculosis *cpd*.

antitussif, ive [ātitysif, -iv] *adj* antitussive, cough *cpd*.

antivariolique [ātivaʀjɔlik] *adj* smallpox *cpd*.

antivol [ātivɔl] *adj, nm*: **(dispositif)** ~ antitheft device; *(pour vélo)* padlock.

antonyme [ātɔnim] *nm* antonym.

antre [ātʀ(ə)] *nm* den, lair.

anus [anys] *nm* anus.

Anvers [āvɛʀ] *n* Antwerp.

anxiété [āksjete] *nf* anxiety.

anxieusement [āksjøzmā] *adv* anxiously.

anxieux, euse [āksjø, -øz] *adj* anxious, worried; **être** ~ **de faire** to be anxious to do.

AOC *sigle f* (= *Appellation d'origine contrôlée*) guarantee of quality of wine.

> *AOC is the highest French wine classification. It indicates that the wine meets strict requirements concerning the vineyard of origin, the type of vine grown, the method of production, and the volume of alcohol present; see also* **VDQS.**

aorte [aɔʀt(ə)] *nf* aorta.

août [u] *nm* August; *voir aussi* **juillet**; **Assomption.**

aoûtien, ne [ausjɛ̃, -ɛn] *nm/f* August holidaymaker.

AP *sigle f* = **Assistance publique.**

apaisant, e [apɛzā, -āt] *adj* soothing.

apaisement [apɛzmā] *nm* calming; soothing; *(aussi POL)* appeasement; ~**s** *nmpl* soothing reassurances; *(pour calmer)* pacifying words.

apaiser [apeze] *vt (colère)* to calm, quell, soothe; *(faim)* to appease, assuage; *(douleur)* to soothe; *(personne)* to calm (down), pacify; **s'**~ *vi (tempête, bruit)* to die down, subside.

apanage [apanaʒ] *nm*: **être l'**~ **de** to be the privilege *ou* prerogative of.

aparté [apaʀte] *nm (THÉÂT)* aside; *(entretien)* private conversation; **en** ~ *adv* in an aside *(BRIT)*; *(entretien)* in private.

apartheid [apaʀtɛd] *nm* apartheid.

apathie [apati] *nf* apathy.

apathique [apatik] *adj* apathetic.

apatride [apatʀid] *nm/f* stateless person.

Apennins [aponɛ̃] *nmpl*: **les** ~ the Apennines.

apercevoir [apɛʀsəvwaʀ] *vt* to see; **s'**~ **de** *vt* to notice; **s'**~ **que** to notice that; **sans s'en** ~ without realizing *ou* noticing.

aperçu, e [apɛʀsy] *pp de* **apercevoir** ♦ *nm (vue d'ensemble)* general survey; *(intuition)* insight.

apéritif, ive [apeʀitif, -iv] *adj* which stimulates the appetite ♦ *nm (boisson)* aperitif; *(réunion)* (pre-lunch *ou* -dinner) drinks *pl*; **prendre l'**~ to have drinks (before lunch *ou* dinner) *ou* an aperitif.

apesanteur [apəzātœʀ] *nf* weightlessness.

à-peu-près [apøpʀɛ] *nm inv (péj)* vague approximation.

apeuré, e [apœʀe] *adj* frightened, scared.

aphasie [afazi] *nm* aphasia.
aphone [afɔn] *adj* voiceless.
aphorisme [afɔrism(ə)] *nm* aphorism.
aphrodisiaque [afrɔdizjak] *adj, nm* aphrodisiac.
aphte [aft(ə)] *nm* mouth ulcer.
aphteuse [aftøz] *adj f*: **fièvre** ~ foot-and-mouth disease.
à-pic [apik] *nm* cliff, drop.
apicole [apikɔl] *adj* beekeeping *cpd*.
apiculteur, trice [apikyltœr, -tris] *nm/f* beekeeper.
apiculture [apikyltyr] *nf* beekeeping, apiculture.
apitoiement [apitwamã] *nm* pity, compassion.
apitoyer [apitwaje] *vt* to move to pity; ~ **qn sur qn/qch** to move sb to pity for sb/over sth; **s'**~ **(sur qn/qch)** to feel pity *ou* compassion (for sb/over sth).
ap. J.-C. *abr* (= *après Jésus-Christ*) AD.
APL *sigle f* (= *aide personnalisée au logement*) *type of loan for house purchase.*
aplanir [aplanir] *vt* to level; (*fig*) to smooth away, iron out.
aplati, e [aplati] *adj* flat, flattened.
aplatir [aplatir] *vt* to flatten; **s'**~ *vi* to become flatter; (*écrasé*) to be flattened; (*fig*) to lie flat on the ground; (: *fam*) to fall flat on one's face; (: *péj*) to grovel.
aplomb [aplɔ̃] *nm* (*équilibre*) balance, equilibrium; (*fig*) self-assurance; (: *péj*) nerve; **d'**~ *adv* steady; (*CONSTR*) plumb.
apocalypse [apɔkalips(ə)] *nf* apocalypse.
apocalyptique [apɔkaliptik] *adj* (*fig*) apocalyptic.
apocryphe [apɔkrif] *adj* apocryphal.
apogée [apɔʒe] *nm* (*fig*) peak, apogee.
apolitique [apɔlitik] *adj* (*indifférent*) apolitical; (*indépendant*) unpolitical, non-political.
apologie [apɔlɔʒi] *nf* praise; (*JUR*) vindication.
apoplexie [apɔplɛksi] *nf* apoplexy.
a posteriori [aposterjɔri] *adv* after the event, with hindsight, a posteriori.
apostolat [apostɔla] *nm* (*REL*) apostolate, discipleship; (*gén*) evangelism.
apostolique [apostɔlik] *adj* apostolic.
apostrophe [apostrɔf] *nf* (*signe*) apostrophe; (*appel*) interpellation.
apostropher [apostrɔfe] *vt* (*interpeller*) to shout at, address sharply.
apothéose [apɔteoz] *nf* pinnacle (of achievement); (*MUS etc*) grand finale.
apothicaire [apɔtikɛr] *nm* apothecary.
apôtre [apotr(ə)] *nm* apostle, disciple.
Appalaches [apalaʃ] *nmpl*: **les** ~ the Appalachian Mountains.
appalachien, ne [apalaʃjɛ̃, -ɛn] *adj* Appalachian.
apparaître [aparɛtr] *vi* to appear ♦ *vb avec attribut* to appear, seem.
apparat [apara] *nm*: **tenue/dîner d'**~ ceremonial dress/dinner.

appareil [aparɛj] *nm* (*outil, machine*) piece of apparatus, device; (*électrique etc*) appliance; (*politique, syndical*) machinery; (*avion*) (aero)plane (*BRIT*), (air)plane (*US*), aircraft *inv*; (*téléphonique*) telephone; (*dentier*) brace (*BRIT*), braces (*US*); ~ **digestif/reproducteur** digestive/reproductive system *ou* apparatus; **l'**~ **productif** the means of production; **qui est à l'**~? who's speaking?; **dans le plus simple** ~ in one's birthday suit; ~ **(photographique)** camera; ~ **24 x 36** *ou* **petit format 35 mm** camera.
appareillage [aparɛjaʒ] *nm* (*appareils*) equipment; (*NAVIG*) casting off, getting under way.
appareiller [apareje] *vi* (*NAVIG*) to cast off, get under way ♦ *vt* (*assortir*) to match up.
appareil-photo, *pl* **appareils-photos** [aparɛjfɔtɔ] *nm* camera.
apparemment [aparamã] *adv* apparently.
apparence [aparãs] *nf* appearance; **malgré les** ~**s** despite appearances; **en** ~ apparently, seemingly.
apparent, e [aparã, -ãt] *adj* visible; (*évident*) obvious; (*superficiel*) apparent; **coutures** ~**es** topstitched seams; **poutres** ~**es** exposed beams.
apparenté, e [aparãte] *adj*: ~ **à** related to; (*fig*) similar to.
apparenter [aparãte]: **s'**~ **à** *vt* to be similar to.
apparier [aparje] *vt* (*gants*) to pair, match.
appariteur [aparitœr] *nm* attendant, porter (*in French universities*).
apparition [aparisjɔ̃] *nf* appearance; (*surnaturelle*) apparition; **faire son** ~ to appear.
appartement [apartəmã] *nm* flat (*BRIT*), apartment (*US*).
appartenance [apartənãs] *nf*: ~ **à** belonging to, membership of.
appartenir [apartənir]: ~ **à** *vt* to belong to; (*faire partie de*) to belong to, be a member of; **il lui appartient de** it is up to him to.
appartiendrai [apartjɛ̃dre], **appartiens** [apartjɛ̃] *etc voir* **appartenir**.
apparu, e [apary] *pp de* **apparaître**.
appas [apa] *nmpl* (*d'une femme*) charms.
appât [apa] *nm* (*PÊCHE*) bait; (*fig*) lure, bait.
appâter [apɑte] *vt* (*hameçon*) to bait; (*poisson, fig*) to lure, entice.
appauvrir [apovrir] *vt* to impoverish; **s'**~ *vi* to grow poorer, become impoverished.
appauvrissement [apovrismã] *nm* impoverishment.
appel [apɛl] *nm* call; (*nominal*) roll call; (: *SCOL*) register; (*MIL: recrutement*) call-up; (*JUR*) appeal; **faire** ~ **à** (*invoquer*) to appeal to; (*avoir recours à*) to call on; (*nécessiter*) to call for, require; **faire** *ou* **interjeter** ~ (*JUR*) to appeal, lodge an appeal; **faire l'**~ to call the roll; to call the register; **indicatif d'**~ call sign; **numéro d'**~ (*TÉL*) number; **produit**

d'~ (COMM) loss leader; **sans ~** (fig) final, irrevocable; **~ d'air** in-draught; **~ d'offres** (COMM) invitation to tender; **faire un ~ de phares** to flash one's headlights; **~ (téléphonique)** (tele)phone call.

appelé [aple] nm (MIL) conscript.

appeler [aple] vt to call; (TÉL) to call, ring; (faire venir: médecin etc) to call, send for; (fig: nécessiter) to call for, demand; **~ au secours** to call for help; **~ qn à l'aide** ou **au secours** to call to sb to help; **~ qn à un poste/des fonctions** to appoint sb to a post/assign duties to sb; **être appelé à** (fig) to be destined to; **~ qn à comparaître** (JUR) to summon sb to appear; **en ~ à** to appeal to; **s'~**: **elle s'appelle Gabrielle** her name is Gabrielle, she's called Gabrielle; **comment ça s'appelle?** what is it ou that called?

appellation [apelɑsjɔ̃] nf designation, appellation; **vin d'~ contrôlée** "appellation contrôlée" wine, wine guaranteed of a certain quality.

appelle [apɛl] etc vb voir **appeler**.

appendice [apɛ̃dis] nm appendix.

appendicite [apɑ̃disit] nf appendicitis.

appentis [apɑ̃ti] nm lean-to.

appert [apɛʀ] vb: **il ~ que** it appears that, it is evident that.

appesantir [apzɑ̃tiʀ]: **s'~** vi to grow heavier; **s'~ sur** (fig) to dwell at length on.

appétissant, e [apetisɑ̃, -ɑ̃t] adj appetizing, mouth-watering.

appétit [apeti] nm appetite; **couper l'~ à qn** to take away sb's appetite; **bon ~!** enjoy your meal!

applaudimètre [aplodimɛtʀ(ə)] nm applause meter.

applaudir [aplodiʀ] vt to applaud ♦ vi to applaud, clap; **~ à** vt (décision) to applaud, commend.

applaudissements [aplodismɑ̃] nmpl applause sg, clapping sg.

applicable [aplikabl(ə)] adj applicable.

applicateur [aplikatœʀ] nm applicator.

application [aplikɑsjɔ̃] nf application; (d'une loi) enforcement; **mettre en ~** to implement.

applique [aplik] nf wall lamp.

appliqué, e [aplike] adj (élève etc) industrious, assiduous; (science) applied.

appliquer [aplike] vt to apply; (loi) to enforce; (donner: gifle, châtiment) to give; **s'~** vi (élève etc) to apply o.s.; **s'~ à** (loi, remarque) to apply to; **s'~ à faire qch** to apply o.s. to doing sth, take pains to do sth; **s'~ sur** (coïncider avec) to fit over.

appoint [apwɛ̃] nm (extra) contribution ou help; **avoir/faire l'~** (en payant) to have/give the right change ou money; **chauffage d'~** extra heating.

appointements [apwɛ̃tmɑ̃] nmpl salary sg, stipend (surtout REL).

appointer [apwɛ̃te] vt: **être appointé à**

l'année/au mois to be paid yearly/monthly.

appontage [apɔ̃taʒ] nm landing (on an aircraft carrier).

appontement [apɔ̃tmɑ̃] nm landing stage, wharf.

apponter [apɔ̃te] vi (avion, hélicoptère) to land.

apport [apɔʀ] nm supply; (argent, biens etc) contribution.

apporter [apɔʀte] vt to bring; (preuve) to give, provide; (modification) to make; (suj: remarque) to contribute, add.

apposer [apoze] vt to append; (sceau etc) to affix.

apposition [apozisjɔ̃] nf appending; affixing; (LING): **en ~** in apposition.

appréciable [apʀesjabl(ə)] adj (important) appreciable, significant.

appréciation [apʀesjɑsjɔ̃] nf appreciation; estimation, assessment; **~s** nfpl (avis) assessment sg, appraisal sg.

apprécier [apʀesje] vt to appreciate; (évaluer) to estimate, assess; **j'apprécierais que tu ...** I should appreciate (it) if you ....

appréhender [apʀeɑ̃de] vt (craindre) to dread; (arrêter) to apprehend; **~ que** to fear that; **~ de faire** to dread doing.

appréhensif, ive [apʀeɑ̃sif, -iv] adj apprehensive.

appréhension [apʀeɑ̃sjɔ̃] nf apprehension.

apprendre [apʀɑ̃dʀ(ə)] vt to learn; (événement, résultats) to learn of, hear of; **~ qch à qn** (informer) to tell sb (of) sth; (enseigner) to teach sb sth; **tu me l'apprends!** that's news to me!; **~ à faire qch** to learn to do sth; **~ à qn à faire qch** to teach sb to do sth.

apprenti, e [apʀɑ̃ti] nm/f apprentice; (fig) novice, beginner.

apprentissage [apʀɑ̃tisaʒ] nm learning; (COMM, SCOL: période) apprenticeship; **école** ou **centre d'~** training school ou centre; **faire l'~ de qch** (fig) to be initiated into sth.

apprêt [apʀɛ] nm (sur un cuir, une étoffe) dressing; (sur un mur) size; (sur un papier) finish; **sans ~** (fig) without artifice, unaffectedly.

apprêté, e [apʀɛte] adj (fig) affected.

apprêter [apʀɛte] vt to dress, finish; **s'~** vi: **s'~ à qch/à faire qch** to prepare for sth/for doing sth.

appris, e [apʀi, -iz] pp de **apprendre**.

apprivoisé, e [apʀivwaze] adj tame, tamed.

apprivoiser [apʀivwaze] vt to tame.

approbateur, trice [apʀɔbatœʀ, -tʀis] adj approving.

approbatif, ive [apʀɔbatif, -iv] adj approving.

approbation [apʀɔbɑsjɔ̃] nf approval; **digne d'~** (conduite, travail) praiseworthy, commendable.

approchant, e [apʀɔʃɑ̃, -ɑ̃t] adj similar, close; **quelque chose d'~** something similar.

approche [apʀɔʃ] nf approaching; (arrivée, attitude) approach; **~s** nfpl (abords) surroundings; **à l'~ du bateau/de l'ennemi** as the ship/enemy approached ou drew near; **l'~ d'un problème** the approach to a problem; **travaux d'~** (fig) manoeuvrings.

approché, e [apRɔʃe] adj approximate.

approcher [apRɔʃe] vi to approach, come near ♦ vt (vedette, artiste) to come close to, approach; (rapprocher): ~ **qch (de qch)** to bring ou put ou move sth near (to sth); ~ **de** vt to draw near to; (quantité, moment) to approach; **s'~ de** vt to approach, go ou come ou move near to; **approchez-vous** come ou go nearer.

approfondi, e [apRɔfɔ̃di] adj thorough, detailed.

approfondir [apRɔfɔ̃diR] vt to deepen; (question) to go further into; **sans ~** without going too deeply into it.

appropriation [apRɔpRijɑsjɔ̃] nf appropriation.

approprié, e [apRɔpRije] adj: ~ **(à)** appropriate (to), suited to.

approprier [apRɔpRije] vt (adapter) adapt; **s'~** vt to appropriate, take over.

approuver [apRuve] vt to agree with; (autoriser: loi, projet) to approve, pass; (trouver louable) to approve of; **je vous approuve entièrement/ne vous approuve pas** I agree with you entirely/don't agree with you; **lu et approuvé** (read and) approved.

approvisionnement [apRɔvizjɔnmɑ̃] nm supplying; (provisions) supply, stock.

approvisionner [apRɔvizjɔne] vt to supply; (compte bancaire) to pay funds into; ~ **qn en** to supply sb with; **s'~** vi: **s'~ dans un certain magasin/au marché** to shop in a certain shop/at the market; **s'~ en** to stock up with.

approximatif, ive [apRɔksimatif, -iv] adj approximate, rough; (imprécis) vague.

approximation [apRɔksimɑsjɔ̃] nf approximation.

approximativement [apRɔksimativmɑ̃] adv approximately, roughly; vaguely.

appt abr = **appartement**.

appui [apɥi] nm support; **prendre ~ sur** to lean on; (objet) to rest on; **point d'~** fulcrum; (fig) something to lean on; **à l'~ de** (pour prouver) in support of; **à l'~** adv to support one's argument; **l'~ de la fenêtre** the windowsill, the window ledge.

appuie [apɥi] etc vb voir **appuyer**.

appui-tête, appuie-tête [apɥitɛt] nm inv headrest.

appuyé, e [apɥije] adj (regard) meaningful; (: insistant) intent, insistent; (excessif: politesse, compliment) exaggerated, overdone.

appuyer [apɥije] vt (poser): ~ **qch sur/contre/à** to lean ou rest sth on/against/on; (soutenir: personne, demande) to support, back (up) ♦ vi: ~ **sur** (bouton, frein) to press, push; (mot, détail) to stress, emphasize; (suj: chose: peser sur) to rest (heavily) on, press against; **s'~ sur** vt to lean on; (compter sur) to rely on;

s'~ sur qn to lean on sb; ~ **contre** (toucher: mur, porte) to lean ou rest against; ~ **à droite** ou **sur sa droite** to bear (to the) right; ~ **sur le champignon** to put one's foot down.

apr. abr = **après**.

âpre [ɑpR(ə)] adj acrid, pungent; (fig) harsh; (lutte) bitter; ~ **au gain** grasping, greedy.

après [apRɛ] prép after ♦ adv afterwards; **2 heures ~** 2 hours later; ~ **qu'il est parti/avoir fait** after he left/having done; **courir ~ qn** to run after sb; **crier ~ qn** to shout at sb; **être toujours ~ qn** (critiquer etc) to be always on at sb; ~ **quoi** after which; **d'~** prép (selon) according to; **d'~ lui** according to him; **d'~ moi** in my opinion; ~ **coup** adv after the event, afterwards; ~ **tout** adv (au fond) after all; **et (puis) ~?** so what?

après-demain [apRɛdmɛ̃] adv the day after tomorrow.

après-guerre [apRɛgɛR] nm post-war years pl; **d'~** adj post-war.

après-midi [apRɛmidi] nm ou nf inv afternoon.

après-rasage [apRɛRazaʒ] nm inv: **(lotion) ~** after-shave (lotion).

après-ski [apRɛski] nm inv (chaussure) snow boot; (moment) après-ski.

après-vente [apRɛvɑ̃t] adj inv after-sales cpd.

âpreté [apRəte] nf (voir âpre) pungency; harshness; bitterness.

à-propos [apRɔpo] nm (d'une remarque) aptness; **faire preuve d'~** to show presence of mind, do the right thing; **avec ~** suitably, aptly.

apte [apt(ə)] adj: ~ **à qch/faire qch** capable of sth/doing sth; ~ **(au service)** (MIL) fit (for service).

aptitude [aptityd] nf ability, aptitude.

apurer [apyRe] vt (COMM) to clear.

aquaculture [akwakyltyR] nf fish farming.

aquaplanage [akwaplanaʒ] nm (AUTO) aquaplaning.

aquaplane [akwaplan] nm (planche) aquaplane; (sport) aquaplaning.

aquaplaning [akwaplaniŋ] nm aquaplaning.

aquarelle [akwaRɛl] nf (tableau) watercolour (BRIT), watercolor (US); (genre) watercolo(u)rs pl, aquarelle.

aquarelliste [akwaRelist(ə)] nm/f painter in watercolo(u)rs.

aquarium [akwaRjɔm] nm aquarium.

aquatique [akwatik] adj aquatic, water cpd.

aqueduc [akdyk] nm aqueduct.

aqueux, euse [akø, -øz] adj aqueous.

aquilin [akilɛ̃] adj m: **nez ~** aquiline nose.

AR sigle m (= accusé de réception): **lettre/paquet avec ~** ≈ recorded delivery letter/parcel; (AVIAT, RAIL etc) = **aller (et) retour** ♦ abr (AUTO) = **arrière**.

arabe [aRab] adj Arabic; (désert, cheval) Arabian; (nation, peuple) Arab ♦ nm (LING) Arabic ♦ nm/f: **A~** Arab.

arabesque [aRabɛsk(ə)] nf arabesque.

Arabie [aʀabi] *nf*: l'~ Arabia; l'~ **Saoudite** *ou* **Séoudite** Saudi Arabia.

arable [aʀabl(ə)] *adj* arable.

arachide [aʀaʃid] *nf* groundnut (plant); (*graine*) peanut, groundnut.

araignée [aʀɛɲe] *nf* spider; ~ **de mer** spider crab.

araser [aʀɑze] *vt* to level; (*en rabotant*) to plane (down).

aratoire [aʀatwaʀ] *adj*: **instrument** ~ ploughing implement.

arbalète [aʀbalɛt] *nf* crossbow.

arbitrage [aʀbitʀaʒ] *nm* refereeing; umpiring; arbitration.

arbitraire [aʀbitʀɛʀ] *adj* arbitrary.

arbitrairement [aʀbitʀɛʀmɑ̃] *adv* arbitrarily.

arbitre [aʀbitʀ(ə)] *nm* (*SPORT*) referee; (: *TENNIS, CRICKET*) umpire; (*fig*) arbiter, judge; (*JUR*) arbitrator.

arbitrer [aʀbitʀe] *vt* to referee; to umpire; to arbitrate.

arborer [aʀbɔʀe] *vt* to bear, display; (*avec ostentation*) to sport.

arborescence [aʀbɔʀesɑ̃s] *nf* tree structure.

arboricole [aʀbɔʀikɔl] *adj* (*animal*) arboreal; (*technique*) arboricultural.

arboriculture [aʀbɔʀikyltyʀ] *nf* arboriculture; ~ **fruitière** fruit (tree) growing.

arbre [aʀbʀ(ə)] *nm* tree; (*TECH*) shaft; ~ **à cames** camshaft; ~ **fruitier** fruit tree; ~ **généalogique** family tree; ~ **de Noël** Christmas tree; ~ **de transmission** (*AUTO*) driveshaft.

arbrisseau, x [aʀbʀiso] *nm* shrub.

arbuste [aʀbyst(ə)] *nm* small shrub, bush.

arc [aʀk] *nm* (*arme*) bow; (*GÉOM*) arc; (*ARCHIT*) arch; ~ **de cercle** arc of a circle; **en** ~ **de cercle** *adj* semi-circular.

arcade [aʀkad] *nf* arch(way); ~s *nfpl* arcade *sg*, arches; ~ **sourcilière** arch of the eyebrows.

arcanes [aʀkan] *nmpl* mysteries.

arc-boutant, *pl* **arcs-boutants** [aʀkbutɑ̃] *nm* flying buttress.

arc-bouter [aʀkbute]: **s'~** *vi*: **s'~ contre** to lean *ou* press against.

arceau, x [aʀso] *nm* (*métallique etc*) hoop.

arc-en-ciel, *pl* **arcs-en-ciel** [aʀkɑ̃sjɛl] *nm* rainbow.

archaïque [aʀkaik] *adj* archaic.

archaïsme [aʀkaism(ə)] *nm* archaism.

archange [aʀkɑ̃ʒ] *nm* archangel.

arche [aʀʃ(ə)] *nf* arch; ~ **de Noé** Noah's Ark.

archéologie [aʀkeɔlɔʒi] *nf* arch(a)eology.

archéologique [aʀkeɔlɔʒik] *adj* arch(a)eological.

archéologue [aʀkeɔlɔg] *nm/f* arch(a)eologist.

archer [aʀʃe] *nm* archer.

archet [aʀʃɛ] *nm* bow.

archétype [aʀketip] *nm* archetype.

archevêché [aʀʃəveʃe] *nm* archbishopric; (*palais*) archbishop's palace.

archevêque [aʀʃəvɛk] *nm* archbishop.

archi... [aʀʃi] *préfixe* (*très*) dead, extra.

archibondé, e [aʀʃibɔ̃de] *adj* chock-a-block (*BRIT*), packed solid.

archiduc [aʀʃidyk] *nm* archduke.

archiduchesse [aʀʃidyʃɛs] *nf* archduchess.

archipel [aʀʃipɛl] *nm* archipelago.

archisimple [aʀʃisɛ̃pl(ə)] *adj* dead easy *ou* simple.

architecte [aʀʃitɛkt(ə)] *nm* architect.

architectural, e, aux [aʀʃitɛktyʀal, -o] *adj* architectural.

architecture [aʀʃitɛktyʀ] *nf* architecture.

archive [aʀʃiv] *nf* file; ~**s** *nfpl* archives.

archiver [aʀʃive] *vt* to file.

archiviste [aʀʃivist(ə)] *nm/f* archivist.

arçon [aʀsɔ̃] *nm voir* **cheval**.

arctique [aʀktik] *adj* Arctic ♦ *nm*: **l'A~** the Arctic; **le cercle A~** the Arctic Circle; **l'océan A~** the Arctic Ocean.

ardemment [aʀdamɑ̃] *adv* ardently, fervently.

ardent, e [aʀdɑ̃, -ɑ̃t] *adj* (*soleil*) blazing; (*fièvre*) raging; (*amour*) ardent, passionate; (*prière*) fervent.

ardeur [aʀdœʀ] *nf* blazing heat; (*fig*) fervour, ardour.

ardoise [aʀdwaz] *nf* slate.

ardu, e [aʀdy] *adj* arduous, difficult; (*pente*) steep, abrupt.

are [aʀ] *nm* are, 100 square metres.

arène [aʀɛn] *nf* arena; (*fig*): l'~ **politique/littéraire** the political/literary arena; ~**s** *nfpl* bull-ring *sg*.

arête [aʀɛt] *nf* (*de poisson*) bone; (*d'une montagne*) ridge; (*GÉOM etc*) edge (*where two faces meet*).

arg. *abr* = **argus**.

argent [aʀʒɑ̃] *nm* (*métal*) silver; (*monnaie*) money; (*couleur*) silver; **en avoir pour son** ~ to get value for money; **gagner beaucoup d'**~ to earn a lot of money; ~ **comptant** (hard) cash; ~ **liquide** ready money, (ready) cash; ~ **de poche** pocket money.

argenté, e [aʀʒɑ̃te] *adj* silver(y); (*métal*) silver-plated.

argenter [aʀʒɑ̃te] *vt* to silver(-plate).

argenterie [aʀʒɑ̃tʀi] *nf* silverware; (*en métal argenté*) silver plate.

argentin, e [aʀʒɑ̃tɛ̃, -in] *adj* (*son*) silvery; (*d'Argentine*) Argentinian, Argentine ♦ *nm/f*: **A~, e** Argentinian, Argentine.

Argentine [aʀʒɑ̃tin] *nf*: l'~ Argentina, the Argentine.

argile [aʀʒil] *nf* clay.

argileux, euse [aʀʒilø, -øz] *adj* clayey.

argot [aʀgo] *nm* slang.

*Initially **argot** was the jargon of the criminal underworld, characterized by colourful images and distinctive intonation and designed to confuse the outsider. Some French authors write in argot and contribute to its diffusion and de-*

velopment. More generally, the special vocabulary used by any social or professional group is also known as argot.

argotique [aʀgɔtik] *adj* slang *cpd*; (*très familier*) slangy.

arguer [aʀgɥe]: ~ **de** *vt* to put forward as a pretext *ou* reason; ~ **que** to argue that.

argument [aʀgymɑ̃] *nm* argument.

argumentaire [aʀgymɑ̃tɛʀ] *nm* list of sales points; (*brochure*) sales leaflet.

argumentation [aʀgymɑ̃tasjɔ̃] *nf* (*fait d'argumenter*) arguing; (*ensemble des arguments*) argument.

argumenter [aʀgymɑ̃te] *vi* to argue.

argus [aʀgys] *nm guide to second-hand car etc prices.*

arguties [aʀgysi] *nfpl* pettifoggery *sg* (*BRIT*), quibbles.

aride [aʀid] *adj* arid.

aridité [aʀidite] *nf* aridity.

arien, ne [aʀjɛ̃, -ɛn] *adj* Arian.

aristocrate [aʀistɔkʀat] *nm/f* aristocrat.

aristocratie [aʀistɔkʀasi] *nf* aristocracy.

aristocratique [aʀistɔkʀatik] *adj* aristocratic.

arithmétique [aʀitmetik] *adj* arithmetic(al) ♦ *nf* arithmetic.

armada [aʀmada] *nf* (*fig*) army.

armagnac [aʀmaɲak] *nm* armagnac.

armateur [aʀmatœʀ] *nm* shipowner.

armature [aʀmatyʀ] *nf* framework; (*de tente etc*) frame; (*de corset*) bone; (*de soutien-gorge*) wiring.

arme [aʀm(ə)] *nf* weapon; (*section de l'armée*) arm; ~**s** *nfpl* weapons, arms; (*blason*) (coat of) arms; **les** ~**s** (*profession*) soldiering *sg*; **à** ~**s égales** on equal terms; **en** ~**s** up in arms; **passer par les** ~**s** to execute (by firing squad); **prendre/présenter les** ~**s** to take up/present arms; **se battre à l'**~ **blanche** to fight with blades; ~ **à feu** firearm.

armé, e [aʀme] *adj* armed; ~ **de** armed with.

armée [aʀme] *nf* army; ~ **de l'air** Air Force; **l'**~ **du Salut** the Salvation Army; ~ **de terre** Army.

armement [aʀməmɑ̃] *nm* (*matériel*) arms *pl*, weapons *pl*; (*: d'un pays*) arms *pl*, armament; (*action d'équiper: d'un navire*) fitting out; ~**s nucléaires** nuclear armaments; **course aux** ~**s** arms race.

Arménie [aʀmeni] *nf*: **l'**~ Armenia.

arménien, ne [aʀmenjɛ̃, -ɛn] *adj* Armenian ♦ *nm* (*LING*) Armenian ♦ *nm/f*: **A**~, **ne** Armenian.

armer [aʀme] *vt* to arm; (*arme à feu*) to cock; (*appareil-photo*) to wind on; ~ **qch de** to fit sth with; (*renforcer*) to reinforce sth with; ~ **qn de** to arm *ou* equip sb with; **s'**~ **de** to arm o.s. with.

armistice [aʀmistis] *nm* armistice; **l'A**~ ≈ Remembrance (*BRIT*) *ou* Veterans (*US*) Day.

armoire [aʀmwaʀ] *nf* (tall) cupboard; (*pende-*

rie) wardrobe (*BRIT*), closet (*US*); ~ **à pharmacie** medicine chest.

armoiries [aʀmwaʀi] *nfpl* coat of arms *sg*.

armure [aʀmyʀ] *nf* armour *no pl*, suit of armour.

armurerie [aʀmyʀʀi] *nf* arms factory; (*magasin*) gunsmith's (shop).

armurier [aʀmyʀje] *nm* gunsmith; (*MIL*, *d'armes blanches*) armourer.

ARN *sigle m* (= *acide ribonucléique*) RNA.

arnaque [aʀnak] *nf*: **de l'**~ daylight robbery.

arnaquer [aʀnake] *vt* to do (*fam*), swindle; **se faire** ~ to be had (*fam*) *ou* done.

arnaqueur [aʀnakœʀ] *nm* swindler.

arnica [aʀnika] *nm*: **(teinture d')**~ arnica.

aromates [aʀɔmat] *nmpl* seasoning *sg*, herbs (and spices).

aromathérapie [aʀɔmateʀapi] *nf* aromatherapy.

aromatique [aʀɔmatik] *adj* aromatic.

aromatiser [aʀɔmatize] *vt* to flavour.

arôme [aʀom] *nm* aroma; (*d'une fleur etc*) fragrance.

arpège [aʀpɛʒ] *nm* arpeggio.

arpentage [aʀpɑ̃taʒ] *nm* (land) surveying.

arpenter [aʀpɑ̃te] *vt* to pace up and down.

arpenteur [aʀpɑ̃tœʀ] *nm* land surveyor.

arqué, e [aʀke] *adj* arched; (*jambes*) bow *cpd*, bandy.

arr. *abr* = **arrondissement**.

arrachage [aʀaʃaʒ] *nm*: ~ **des mauvaises herbes** weeding.

arraché [aʀaʃe] *nm* (*SPORT*) snatch; **obtenir à l'**~ (*fig*) to snatch.

arrache-pied [aʀaʃpje]: **d'**~ *adv* relentlessly.

arracher [aʀaʃe] *vt* to pull out; (*page etc*) to tear off, tear out; (*déplanter: légume*) to lift; (*: herbe, souche*) to pull up; (*bras etc: par explosion*) to blow off; (*: par accident*) to tear off; **s'**~ *vt* (*article très recherché*) to fight over; ~ **qch à qn** to snatch sth from sb; (*fig*) to wring sth out of sb, wrest sth from sb; ~ **qn à** (*solitude, rêverie*) to drag sb out of; (*famille etc*) to tear *ou* wrench sb away from; **se faire** ~ **une dent** to have a tooth out *ou* pulled (*US*); **s'**~ **de** (*lieu*) to tear o.s. away from; (*habitude*) to force o.s. out of.

arraisonner [aʀɛzɔne] *vt* to board and search.

arrangeant, e [aʀɑ̃ʒɑ̃, -ɑ̃t] *adj* accommodating, obliging.

arrangement [aʀɑ̃ʒmɑ̃] *nm* arrangement.

arranger [aʀɑ̃ʒe] *vt* to arrange; (*réparer*) to fix, put right; (*régler*) to settle, sort out; (*convenir à*) to suit, be convenient for; **s'**~ (*se mettre d'accord*) to come to an agreement *ou* arrangement; (*s'améliorer: querelle, situation*) to be sorted out; (*se débrouiller*): **s'**~ **pour que ...** to arrange things so that ...; **je vais m'**~ I'll manage; **ça va s'**~ it'll sort itself out; **s'**~ **pour faire** to make sure that *ou* see to it that one can do.

arrangeur [aʀɑ̃ʒœʀ] *nm* (*MUS*) arranger.

arrestation [aʀɛstɑsjɔ̃] *nf* arrest.

arrêt [aʀɛ] *nm* stopping; (*de bus etc*) stop; (*JUR*) judgment, decision; (*FOOTBALL*) save; **~s** *nmpl* (*MIL*) arrest *sg*; **être à l'~** to be stopped, have come to a halt; **rester** *ou* **tomber en ~ devant** to stop short in front of; **sans ~** without stopping, non-stop; (*fréquemment*) continually; **~ d'autobus** bus stop; **~ facultatif** request stop; **~ de mort** capital sentence; **~ de travail** stoppage (of work).

arrêté, e [aʀete] *adj* (*idées*) firm, fixed ♦ *nm* order, decree; **~ municipal** ≈ bylaw, byelaw.

arrêter [aʀete] *vt* to stop; (*chauffage etc*) to turn off, switch off; (*COMM: compte*) to settle; (*COUTURE: point*) to fasten off; (*fixer: date etc*) to appoint, decide on; (*criminel, suspect*) to arrest; **s'~** *vi* to stop; (*s'interrompre*) to stop o.s.; **~ de faire** to stop doing; **arrête de te plaindre** stop complaining; **ne pas ~ de faire** to keep on doing; **s'~ de faire** to stop doing; **s'~ sur** (*suj: choix, regard*) to fall on.

arrhes [aʀ] *nfpl* deposit *sg*.

arrière [aʀjɛʀ] *nm* back; (*SPORT*) fullback ♦ *adj inv*: **siège/roue ~** back *ou* rear seat/wheel; **~s** *nmpl* (*fig*): **protéger ses ~s** to protect the rear; **à l'~** *adv* behind, at the back; **en ~** *adv* behind; (*regarder*) back, behind; (*tomber, aller*) backwards; **en ~ de** *prép* behind.

arriéré, e [aʀjeʀe] *adj* (*péj*) backward ♦ *nm* (*d'argent*) arrears *pl*.

arrière-boutique [aʀjɛʀbutik] *nf* back shop.

arrière-cour [aʀjɛʀkuʀ] *nf* backyard.

arrière-cuisine [aʀjɛʀkɥizin] *nf* scullery.

arrière-garde [aʀjɛʀgaʀd(ə)] *nf* rearguard.

arrière-goût [aʀjɛʀgu] *nm* aftertaste.

arrière-grand-mère, *pl* **arrière-grand-mères** [aʀjɛʀgʀɑ̃mɛʀ] *nf* great-grandmother.

arrière-grand-père, *pl* **arrière-grands-pères** [aʀjɛʀgʀɑ̃pɛʀ] *nm* great-grandfather.

arrière-grands-parents [aʀjɛʀgʀɑ̃paʀɑ̃] *nmpl* great-grandparents.

arrière-pays [aʀjɛʀpei] *nm inv* hinterland.

arrière-pensée [aʀjɛʀpɑ̃se] *nf* ulterior motive; (*doute*) mental reservation.

arrière-petite-fille, *pl* **arrière-petites-filles** [aʀjɛʀpətitfij] *nf* great-granddaughter.

arrière-petit-fils, *pl* **arrière-petits-fils** [aʀjɛʀpətifis] *nm* great-grandson.

arrière-petits-enfants [aʀjɛʀpətizɑ̃fɑ̃] *nmpl* great-grandchildren.

arrière-plan [aʀjɛʀplɑ̃] *nm* background; **d'~** *adj* (*INFORM*) background *cpd*.

arriérer [aʀjeʀe] **s'~** *vi* (*COMM*) to fall into arrears.

arrière-saison [aʀjɛʀsezɔ̃] *nf* late autumn.

arrière-salle [aʀjɛʀsal] *nf* back room.

arrière-train [aʀjɛʀtʀɛ̃] *nm* hindquarters *pl*.

arrimer [aʀime] *vt* to stow; (*fixer*) to secure, fasten securely.

arrivage [aʀivaʒ] *nm* arrival.

arrivant, e [aʀivɑ̃, -ɑ̃t] *nm/f* newcomer.

arrivée [aʀive] *nf* arrival; (*ligne d'arrivée*)

finish; **~ d'air/de gaz** air/gas inlet; **courrier à l'~** incoming mail; **à mon ~** when I arrived.

arriver [aʀive] *vi* to arrive; (*survenir*) to happen, occur; **j'arrive!** (I'm) just coming!; **il arrive à Paris à 8 h** he gets to *ou* arrives in Paris at 8; **~ à destination** to arrive at one's destination; **~ à** (*atteindre*) to reach; **~ à (faire) qch** (*réussir*) to manage (to do) sth; **~ à échéance** to fall due; **en ~ à faire** to end up doing, get to the point of doing; **il arrive que** it happens that; **il lui arrive de faire** he sometimes does.

arrivisme [aʀivism(ə)] *nm* ambition, ambitiousness.

arriviste [aʀivist(ə)] *nm/f* go-getter.

arrogance [aʀɔgɑ̃s] *nf* arrogance.

arrogant, e [aʀɔgɑ̃, -ɑ̃t] *adj* arrogant.

arroger [aʀɔʒe]: **s'~** *vt* to assume (without right); **s'~ le droit de ...** to assume the right to ....

arrondi, e [aʀɔ̃di] *adj* round ♦ *nm* roundness.

arrondir [aʀɔ̃diʀ] *vt* (*forme, objet*) to round; (*somme*) to round off; **s'~** *vi* to become round(ed); **~ ses fins de mois** to supplement one's pay.

arrondissement [aʀɔ̃dismɑ̃] *nm* (*ADMIN*) ≈ district.

arrosage [aʀozaʒ] *nm* watering; **tuyau d'~** hose(pipe).

arroser [aʀoze] *vt* to water; (*victoire etc*) to celebrate (over a drink); (*CULIN*) to baste.

arroseur [aʀozœʀ] *nm* (*tourniquet*) sprinkler.

arroseuse [aʀozøz] *nf* water cart.

arrosoir [aʀozwaʀ] *nm* watering can.

arrt *abr* = **arrondissement**.

arsenal, aux [aʀsənal, -o] *nm* (*NAVIG*) naval dockyard; (*MIL*) arsenal; (*fig*) gear, paraphernalia.

arsenic [aʀsənik] *nm* arsenic.

art [aʀ] *nm* art; **avoir l'~ de faire** (*fig: personne*) to have a talent for doing; **les ~s** the arts; **livre/critique d'~** art book/critic; **objet d'~** objet d'art; **~ dramatique** dramatic art; **~s martiaux** martial arts; **~s et métiers** applied arts and crafts; **~s ménagers** home economics *sg*; **~s plastiques** plastic arts.

art. *abr* = **article**.

artère [aʀtɛʀ] *nf* (*ANAT*) artery; (*rue*) main road.

artériel, le [aʀteʀjɛl] *adj* arterial.

artériosclérose [aʀteʀjoskleʀoz] *nf* arteriosclerosis.

arthrite [aʀtʀit] *nf* arthritis.

arthrose [aʀtʀoz] *nf* (degenerative) osteoarthritis.

artichaut [aʀtiʃo] *nm* artichoke.

article [aʀtikl(ə)] *nm* article; (*COMM*) item, article; (*INFORM*) record, item; **faire l'~** (*COMM*) to do one's sales spiel; **faire l'~ de** (*fig*) to sing the praises of; **à l'~ de la mort** at the point of death; **~ défini/indéfini** definite/indefinite article; **~ de fond**

(*PRESSE*) feature article; **~s de bureau** office equipment; **~s de voyage** travel goods *ou* items.

articulaire [aʀtikylɛʀ] *adj* of the joints, articular.

articulation [aʀtikylɑsjɔ̃] *nf* articulation; (*ANAT*) joint.

articulé, e [aʀtikyle] *adj* (*membre*) jointed; (*poupée*) with moving joints.

articuler [aʀtikyle] *vt* to articulate; **s'~ (sur)** (*ANAT, TECH*) to articulate (with); **s'~ autour de** (*fig*) to centre around *ou* on, turn on.

artifice [aʀtifis] *nm* device, trick.

artificiel, le [aʀtifisjɛl] *adj* artificial.

artificiellement [aʀtifisjɛlmɑ̃] *adv* artificially.

artificier [aʀtifisje] *nm* pyrotechnist.

artificieux, euse [aʀtifisjø, -øz] *adj* guileful, deceitful.

artillerie [aʀtijʀi] *nf* artillery, ordnance.

artilleur [aʀtijœʀ] *nm* artilleryman, gunner.

artisan [aʀtizɑ̃] *nm* artisan, (self-employed) craftsman; **l'~ de la victoire/du malheur** the architect of victory/of the disaster.

artisanal, e, aux [aʀtizanal, -o] *adj* of *ou* made by craftsmen; (*péj*) cottage industry *cpd*, unsophisticated.

artisanalement [aʀtizanalmɑ̃] *adv* by craftsmen.

artisanat [aʀtizana] *nm* arts and crafts *pl*.

artiste [aʀtist(ə)] *nm/f* artist; (*THÉÂT, MUS*) artist, performer; (: *de variétés*) entertainer.

artistique [aʀtistik] *adj* artistic.

artistiquement [aʀtistikmɑ̃] *adv* artistically.

aryen, ne [aʀjɛ̃, -ɛn] *adj* Aryan.

AS *sigle fpl* (*ADMIN*) = **assurances sociales** ♦ *sigle f* (*SPORT*: = *Association sportive*) ≈ FC (= Football Club).

as *vb* [a] *voir* **avoir** ♦ *nm* [ɑs] ace.

a/s *abr* (= *aux soins de*) c/o.

ASBL *sigle f* (= *association sans but lucratif*) non-profit-making organization.

asc. *abr* = **ascenseur**.

ascendance [asɑ̃dɑ̃s] *nf* (*origine*) ancestry; (*ASTROLOGIE*) ascendant.

ascendant, e [asɑ̃dɑ̃, -ɑ̃t] *adj* upward ♦ *nm* influence; **~s** *nmpl* ascendants.

ascenseur [asɑ̃sœʀ] *nm* lift (*BRIT*), elevator (*US*).

ascension [asɑ̃sjɔ̃] *nf* ascent; climb; **l'A~** (*REL*) the Ascension; (: *jour férié*) Ascension (Day); **(île de) l'A~** Ascension Island.

La fête de l'Ascension is a public holiday in France. Falling on a Thursday, usually in May, the holiday provides the opportunity for many French people also to take Friday off work and enjoy a long weekend; see also faire le **pont**.

---

ascète [asɛt] *nm/f* ascetic.

ascétique [asetik] *adj* ascetic.

ascétisme [asetism(ə)] *nm* asceticism.

ascorbique [askɔʀbik] *adj*: **acide ~** ascorbic acid.

ASE *sigle f* (= *Agence spatiale européenne*) ESA (= *European Space Agency*).

asepsie [asɛpsi] *nf* asepsis.

aseptique [asɛptik] *adj* aseptic.

aseptiser [asɛptize] *vt* to sterilize; (*plaie*) to disinfect.

asexué, e [asɛksɥe] *adj* asexual.

asiatique [azjatik] *adj* Asian, Asiatic ♦ *nm/f*: **A~** Asian.

Asie [azi] *nf*: **l'~** Asia.

asile [azil] *nm* (*refuge*) refuge, sanctuary; (*POL*): **droit d'~** (political) asylum; (*pour malades, vieillards etc*) home; **accorder l'~ politique à qn** to grant *ou* give sb political asylum; **chercher/trouver ~ quelque part** to seek/find refuge somewhere.

asocial, e, aux [asɔsjal, -o] *adj* antisocial.

aspect [aspɛ] *nm* appearance, look; (*fig*) aspect, side; (*LING*) aspect; **à l'~ de** at the sight of.

asperge [aspɛʀʒ(ə)] *nf* asparagus *no pl*.

asperger [aspɛʀʒe] *vt* to spray, sprinkle.

aspérité [aspeʀite] *nf* excrescence, protruding bit (of rock *etc*).

aspersion [aspɛʀsjɔ̃] *nf* spraying, sprinkling.

asphalte [asfalt(ə)] *nm* asphalt.

asphyxiant, e [asfiksjɑ̃, -ɑ̃t] *adj* suffocating; **gaz ~** poison gas.

asphyxie [asfiksi] *nf* suffocation, asphyxia, asphyxiation.

asphyxier [asfiksje] *vt* to suffocate, asphyxiate; (*fig*) to stifle; **mourir asphyxié** to die of suffocation *ou* asphyxiation.

aspic [aspik] *nm* (*ZOOL*) asp; (*CULIN*) aspic.

aspirant, e [aspiʀɑ̃, -ɑ̃t] *adj*: **pompe ~e** suction pump ♦ *nm* (*NAVIG*) midshipman.

aspirateur [aspiʀatœʀ] *nm* vacuum cleaner, hoover ®.

aspiration [aspiʀasjɔ̃] *nf* inhalation; sucking (up); drawing up; **~s** *nfpl* (*ambitions*) aspirations.

aspirer [aspiʀe] *vt* (*air*) to inhale; (*liquide*) to suck (up); (*suj: appareil*) to suck *ou* draw up; **~ à** *vt* to aspire to.

aspirine [aspiʀin] *nf* aspirin.

assagir [asaʒiʀ] *vt*, **s'~** *vi* to quieten down, sober down.

assaillant, e [asajɑ̃, -ɑ̃t] *nm/f* assailant, attacker.

assaillir [asajiʀ] *vt* to assail, attack; **~ qn de** (*questions*) to assail *ou* bombard sb with.

assainir [aseniʀ] *vt* to clean up; (*eau, air*) to purify.

assainissement [asenismɑ̃] *nm* cleaning up; purifying.

assaisonnement [asɛzɔnmɑ̃] *nm* seasoning.

assaisonner [asɛzɔne] *vt* to season; **bien assaisonné** highly seasoned.

assassin [asasɛ̃] *nm* murderer; assassin.

assassinat [asasina] *nm* murder; assassination.

assassiner [asasine] *vt* to murder; (*surtout POL*) to assassinate.

assaut [aso] *nm* assault, attack; **prendre d'~** to (take by) storm, assault; **donner l'~ (à)** to attack; **faire ~ de** (*rivaliser*) to vie with *ou* rival each other in.

assèchement [asɛʃmɑ̃] *nm* draining, drainage.

assécher [aseʃe] *vt* to drain.

ASSEDIC [asedik] *sigle f* (= *Association pour l'emploi dans l'industrie et le commerce*) *unemployment insurance scheme.*

assemblage [asɑ̃blaʒ] *nm* assembling; (*MENUISERIE*) joint; **un ~ de** (*fig*) a collection of; **langage d'~** (*INFORM*) assembly language.

assemblée [asɑ̃ble] *nf* (*réunion*) meeting; (*public, assistance*) gathering; assembled people; (*POL*) assembly; (*REL*): **l'~ des fidèles** the congregation; **l'A~ nationale (AN)** the (French) National Assembly.

---

*The **Assemblée nationale** is the lower house of the French parliament, the upper house being the **Sénat**. It sits at the Palais Bourbon in Paris and consists of about 580 **députés** elected every five years; see also **élection**.*

---

assembler [asɑ̃ble] *vt* (*joindre, monter*) to assemble, put together; (*amasser*) to gather (together), collect (together); **s'~** *vi* to gather, collect.

assembleur [asɑ̃blœʀ] *nm* assembler, fitter; (*INFORM*) assembler.

assener, asséner [asene] *vt*: **~ un coup à qn** to deal sb a blow.

assentiment [asɑ̃timɑ̃] *nm* assent, consent; (*approbation*) approval.

asseoir [aswaʀ] *vt* (*malade, bébé*) to sit up; (*personne debout*) to sit down; (*autorité, réputation*) to establish; **s'~** *vi* to sit (o.s.) up; to sit (o.s.) down; **faire ~ qn** to ask sb to sit down; **~ qch sur** (*appuyer*) to base sth on.

assermenté, e [asɛʀmɑ̃te] *adj* sworn, on oath.

assertion [asɛʀsjɔ̃] *nf* assertion.

asservir [asɛʀviʀ] *vt* to subjugate, enslave.

asservissement [asɛʀvismɑ̃] *nm* (*action*) enslavement; (*état*) slavery.

assesseur [asesœʀ] *nm* (*JUR*) assessor.

asseyais [aseje] *etc vb voir* **asseoir**.

assez [ase] *adv* (*suffisamment*) enough, sufficiently; (*passablement*) rather, quite, fairly; **~! enough!, that'll do!; ~/pas ~ cuit** well enough done/underdone; **est-il ~ fort/rapide?** is he strong/fast enough *ou* sufficiently strong/fast?; **il est passé ~ vite** he went past rather *ou* quite *ou* fairly fast; **~ de pain/livres** enough *ou* sufficient bread/books; **vous en avez ~?** have you got enough?; **en avoir ~ de qch** (*en être fatigué*) to have had enough of sth; **travailler ~** to work sufficiently (hard), work (hard) enough.

assidu, e [asidy] *adj* assiduous, painstaking; (*régulier*) regular; **~ auprès de qn** attentive towards sb.

assiduité [asidɥite] *nf* assiduousness, painstaking; regularity; attentiveness; **~s** *nfpl* assiduous attentions.

assidûment [asidymɑ̃] *adv* assiduously, painstakingly; attentively.

assied [asje] *etc vb voir* **asseoir**.

assiégé, e [asjeʒe] *adj* under siege, besieged.

assiéger [asjeʒe] *vt* to besiege, lay siege to; (*suj: foule, touristes*) to mob, besiege.

assiérai [asjeʀe] *etc vb voir* **asseoir**.

assiette [asjɛt] *nf* plate; (*contenu*) plate(ful); (*équilibre*) seat; (*de colonne*) seating; (*de navire*) trim; **~ anglaise** assorted cold meats; **~ creuse** (soup) dish, soup plate; **~ à dessert** dessert *ou* side plate; **~ de l'impôt** basis of (tax) assessment; **~ plate** (dinner) plate.

assiettée [asjete] *nf* plateful.

assignation [asiɲasjɔ̃] *nf* assignation; (*JUR*) summons; (*: de témoin*) subpoena; **~ à résidence** compulsory order of residence.

assigner [asiɲe] *vt*: **~ qch à** to assign *ou* allot sth to; (*valeur, importance*) to attach sth to; (*somme*) to allocate sth to; (*limites*) to set *ou* fix sth to; (*cause, effet*) to ascribe *ou* attribute sth to; **~ qn à** (*affecter*) to assign sb to; **~ qn à résidence** (*JUR*) to give sb a compulsory order of residence.

assimilable [asimilabl(ə)] *adj* easily assimilated *ou* absorbed.

assimilation [asimilasjɔ̃] *nf* assimilation, absorption.

assimiler [asimile] *vt* to assimilate, absorb; (*comparer*): **~ qch/qn à** to liken *ou* compare sth/sb to; **s'~** *vi* (*s'intégrer*) to be assimilated *ou* absorbed; **ils sont assimilés aux infirmières** (*ADMIN*) they are classed as nurses.

assis, e [asi, -iz] *pp de* **asseoir** ♦ *adj* sitting (down), seated ♦ *nf* (*CONSTR*) course; (*GÉO*) stratum (*pl* -a); (*fig*) basis (*pl* bases), foundation; **~ en tailleur** sitting cross-legged.

assises [asiz] *nfpl* (*JUR*) assizes; (*congrès*) (annual) conference.

assistanat [asistana] *nm* assistantship; (*à l'université*) probationary lectureship.

assistance [asistɑ̃s] *nf* (*public*) audience; (*aide*) assistance; **porter** *ou* **prêter ~ à qn** to give sb assistance; **A~ publique (AP)** *public health service*; **enfant de l'A~ (publique)** (*formerly*) child in care; **~ technique** technical aid.

assistant, e [asistɑ̃, -ɑ̃t] *nm/f* assistant; (*d'université*) probationary lecturer; **les ~s** *nmpl* (*auditeurs etc*) those present; **~e sociale** social worker.

assisté, e [asiste] *adj* (*AUTO*) power assisted ♦ *nm/f* person receiving aid from the State.

assister [asiste] *vt* to assist; **~ à** *vt* (*scène, évé-*

nement) to witness; *(conférence, séminaire)* to attend, be (present) at; *(spectacle, match)* to be at, see.

association [asɔsjɑsjɔ̃] *nf* association; *(COMM)* partnership; ~ **d'idées/images** association of ideas/images.

associé, e [asɔsje] *nm/f* associate; *(COMM)* partner.

associer [asɔsje] *vt* to associate; ~ **qn à** *(profits)* to give sb a share of; *(affaire)* to make sb a partner in; *(joie, triomphe)* to include sb in; ~ **qch à** *(joindre, allier)* to combine sth with; **s'~** *vi* to join together; *(COMM)* to form a partnership ♦ *vt (collaborateur)* to take on (as a partner); **s'~ à** to be combined with; *(opinions, joie de qn)* to share in; **s'~ à** *ou* **avec qn pour faire** to join (forces) *ou* join together with sb to do.

assoie [aswa] *etc vb voir* **asseoir.**

assoiffé, e [aswafe] *adj* thirsty; *(fig)*: ~ **de** *(sang)* thirsting for; *(gloire)* thirsting after.

assoirai [aswaʀe], **assois** [aswa] *etc vb voir* **asseoir.**

assolement [asɔlmɑ̃] *nm* (systematic) rotation of crops.

assombrir [asɔ̃bʀiʀ] *vt* to darken; *(fig)* to fill with gloom; **s'~** *vi* to darken; *(devenir nuageux, fig: visage)* to cloud over; *(fig)* to become gloomy.

assommer [asɔme] *vt (étourdir, abrutir)* to knock out, stun; *(fam: ennuyer)* to bore stiff.

Assomption [asɔ̃psjɔ̃] *nf*: **l'~** the Assumption.

> La fête de l'Assomption, *or more commonly* Le 15 août *on August 15 is a national holiday in France. Traditionally, large numbers of holidaymakers set out on this date, frequently causing chaos on French roads; see also* faire le pont.

assorti, e [asɔʀti] *adj* matched, matching; **fromages/légumes** ~**s** assorted cheeses/vegetables; ~ **à** matching; ~ **de** accompanied with; *(conditions, conseils)* coupled with; **bien/mal** ~ well/ill-matched.

assortiment [asɔʀtimɑ̃] *nm (choix)* assortment, selection; *(harmonie de couleurs, formes)* arrangement; *(COMM: lot, stock)* selection.

assortir [asɔʀtiʀ] *vt* to match; **s'~** to go well together, match; ~ **qch à** to match sth with; ~ **qch de** to accompany sth with; **s'~ de** to be accompanied by.

assoupi, e [asupi] *adj* dozing, sleeping; *(fig)* (be)numbed; *(sens)* dulled.

assoupir [asupiʀ]: **s'~** *vi (personne)* to doze off; *(sens)* to go numb.

assoupissement [asupismɑ̃] *nm (sommeil)* dozing; *(fig: somnolence)* drowsiness.

assouplir [asupliʀ] *vt* to make supple, soften; *(membres, corps)* to limber up, make supple; *(fig)* to relax; *(: caractère)* to soften, make

more flexible; **s'~** *vi* to soften; to limber up; to relax; to become more flexible.

assouplissement [asuplismɑ̃] *nm* softening; limbering up; relaxation; **exercices d'~** limbering up exercises.

assourdir [asuʀdiʀ] *vt (bruit)* to deaden, muffle; *(suj: bruit)* to deafen.

assourdissant, e [asuʀdisɑ̃, -ɑ̃t] *adj (bruit)* deafening.

assouvir [asuviʀ] *vt* to satisfy, appease.

assoyais [aswajɛ] *etc vb voir* **asseoir.**

ASSU [asy] *sigle f =* Association du sport scolaire et universitaire.

assujetti, e [asyʒeti] *adj*: ~ **(à)** subject (to); *(ADMIN)*: ~ **à l'impôt** subject to tax(ation).

assujettir [asyʒetiʀ] *vt* to subject, subjugate; *(fixer: planches, tableau)* to secure, fix securely; ~ **qn à** *(règle, impôt)* to subject sb to.

assujettissement [asyʒetismɑ̃] *nm* subjection, subjugation.

assumer [asyme] *vt (fonction, emploi)* to assume, take on; *(accepter: conséquence, situation)* to accept.

assurance [asyʀɑ̃s] *nf (certitude)* assurance; *(confiance en soi)* (self-)confidence; *(contrat)* insurance (policy); *(secteur commercial)* insurance; **prendre une** ~ **contre** to take out insurance *ou* an insurance policy against; ~ **contre l'incendie** fire insurance; ~ **contre le vol** insurance against theft; **société d'~**, **compagnie d'~s** insurance company; ~ **maladie (AM)** health insurance; ~ **au tiers** third party insurance; ~ **tous risques** *(AUTO)* comprehensive insurance; ~**s sociales (AS)** ≈ National Insurance *(BRIT)*, ≈ Social Security *(US)*.

assurance-vie, *pl* assurances-vie [asyʀɑ̃svi] *nf* life assurance *ou* insurance.

assurance-vol, *pl* assurances-vol [asyʀɑ̃svɔl] *nf* insurance against theft.

assuré, e [asyʀe] *adj (victoire etc)* certain, sure; *(démarche, voix)* assured, (self-)confident; *(certain)*: ~ **de** confident of; *(ASSURANCES)* insured ♦ *nm/f* insured (person); ~ **social** ≈ member of the National Insurance *(BRIT)* ou Social Security *(US)* scheme.

assurément [asyʀemɑ̃] *adv* assuredly, most certainly.

assurer [asyʀe] *vt (COMM)* to insure; *(stabiliser)* to steady, stabilize; *(victoire etc)* to ensure, make certain; *(frontières, pouvoir)* to make secure; *(service, garde)* to provide, operate; ~ **qch à qn** *(garantir)* to secure *ou* guarantee sth for sb; *(certifier)* to assure sb of sth; ~ **à qn que** to assure sb that; **je vous assure que non/si** I assure you that that is not the case/is the case; ~ **qn de** to assure sb of; ~ **ses arrières** *(fig)* to be sure one has something to fall back on; **s'~ (contre)** *(COMM)* to insure o.s. (against); **s'~ de/que** *(vérifier)* to make sure of/that: **s'~ (de)** *(aide* *de qn*) to secure; **s'~ sur la vie** to take out a life insurance; **s'~ le concours/la collaboration de qn** to secure sb's aid/collaboration.

assureur [asyʀœʀ] *nm* insurance agent; (*société*) insurers *pl*.

Assyrie [asiʀi] *nf*: **l'~** Assyria.

assyrien, ne [asiʀjɛ̃, -ɛn] *adj* Assyrian ♦ *nm/f*: **A~, ne** Assyrian.

astérisque [asteʀisk(ə)] *nm* asterisk.

astéroïde [asteʀɔid] *nm* asteroid.

asthmatique [asmatik] *adj* asthmatic.

asthme [asm(ə)] *nm* asthma.

asticot [astiko] *nm* maggot.

asticoter [astikɔte] *vt* (*fam*) to needle, get at.

astigmate [astigmat] *adj* (*MÉD: personne*) astigmatic, having an astigmatism.

astiquer [astike] *vt* to polish, shine.

astrakan [astʀakɑ̃] *nm* astrakhan.

astral, e, aux [astʀal, -o] *adj* astral.

astre [astʀ(ə)] *nm* star.

astreignant, e [astʀɛɲɑ̃, -ɑ̃t] *adj* demanding.

astreindre [astʀɛ̃dʀ(ə)] *vt*: **~ qn à qch** to force sth upon sb; **~ qn à faire** to compel *ou* force sb to do; **s'~ à** to compel *ou* force o.s. to.

astringent, e [astʀɛ̃ʒɑ̃, -ɑ̃t] *adj* astringent.

astrologie [astʀɔlɔʒi] *nf* astrology.

astrologique [astʀɔlɔʒik] *adj* astrological.

astrologue [astʀɔlɔg] *nm/f* astrologer.

astronaute [astʀɔnot] *nm/f* astronaut.

astronautique [astʀɔnotik] *nf* astronautics *sg*.

astronome [astʀɔnɔm] *nm/f* astronomer.

astronomie [astʀɔnɔmi] *nf* astronomy.

astronomique [astʀɔnɔmik] *adj* astronomic(al).

astrophysicien, ne [astʀɔfizisjɛ̃, -ɛn] *nm/f* astrophysicist.

astrophysique [astʀɔfizik] *nf* astrophysics *sg*.

astuce [astys] *nf* shrewdness, astuteness; (*truc*) trick, clever way; (*plaisanterie*) wisecrack.

astucieusement [astysjøzmɑ̃] *adv* shrewdly, cleverly, astutely.

astucieux, euse [astysjø, -øz] *adj* shrewd, clever, astute.

asymétrique [asimetʀik] *adj* asymmetric(al).

AT *sigle m* (= *Ancien Testament*) OT.

atavisme [atavism(ə)] *nm* atavism, heredity.

atelier [atəlje] *nm* workshop; (*de peintre*) studio.

atermoiements [atɛʀmwamɑ̃] *nmpl* procrastination *sg*.

atermoyer [atɛʀmwaje] *vi* to temporize, procrastinate.

athée [ate] *adj* atheistic ♦ *nm/f* atheist.

athéisme [ateism(ə)] *nm* atheism.

Athènes [atɛn] *n* Athens.

athénien, ne [atenjɛ̃, -ɛn] *adj* Athenian.

athlète [atlɛt] *nm/f* (*SPORT*) athlete; (*costaud*) muscleman.

athlétique [atletik] *adj* athletic.

athlétisme [atletism(ə)] *nm* athletics *sg*; **faire de l'~** to do athletics; **tournoi d'~** athletics

meeting.

Atlantide [atlɑ̃tid] *nf*: **l'~** Atlantis.

atlantique [atlɑ̃tik] *adj* Atlantic ♦ *nm*: **l'(océan) A~** the Atlantic (Ocean).

atlantiste [atlɑ̃tist(ə)] *adj*, *nm/f* Atlanticist.

Atlas [atlɑs] *nm*: **l'~** the Atlas Mountains.

atlas [atlɑs] *nm* atlas.

atmosphère [atmɔsfɛʀ] *nf* atmosphere.

atmosphérique [atmɔsfeʀik] *adj* atmospheric.

atoll [atɔl] *nm* atoll.

atome [atom] *nm* atom.

atomique [atɔmik] *adj* atomic, nuclear; (*usine*) nuclear; (*nombre, masse*) atomic.

atomiseur [atɔmizœʀ] *nm* atomizer.

atomiste [atɔmist(ə)] *nm/f* (*aussi*: **savant, ingénieur** *etc* **~**) atomic scientist.

atone [aton] *adj* lifeless; (*LING*) unstressed, unaccented.

atours [atuʀ] *nmpl* attire *sg*, finery *sg*.

atout [atu] *nm* trump; (*fig*) asset; (*: plus fort*) trump card; **"~" pique/trèfle** "spades/clubs are trumps".

ATP *sigle f* (= *Association des tennismen professionnels*) ATP (= *Association of Tennis Professionals*) ♦ *sigle mpl* (= *arts et traditions populaires*): **musée des ~** ≈ folk museum.

âtre [ɑtʀ(ə)] *nm* hearth.

atroce [atʀɔs] *adj* atrocious, horrible.

atrocement [atʀɔsmɑ̃] *adv* atrociously, horribly.

atrocité [atʀɔsite] *nf* atrocity.

atrophie [atʀɔfi] *nf* atrophy.

atrophier [atʀɔfje]: **s'~** *vi* to atrophy.

atropine [atʀɔpin] *nf* (*CHIMIE*) atropine.

attabler [atable]: **s'~** *vi* to sit down at (the) table; **s'~ à la terrasse** to sit down (at a table) on the terrace.

attachant, e [ataʃɑ̃, -ɑ̃t] *adj* engaging, likeable.

attache [ataʃ] *nf* clip, fastener; (*fig*) tie; **~s** *nfpl* (*relations*) connections; **à l'~** (*chien*) tied up.

attaché, e [ataʃe] *adj*: **être ~ à** (*aimer*) to be attached to ♦ *nm* (*ADMIN*) attaché; **~ de presse/d'ambassade** press/embassy attaché; **~ commercial** commercial attaché.

attaché-case [ataʃekɛz] *nm inv* attaché case (*BRIT*), briefcase.

attachement [ataʃmɑ̃] *nm* attachment.

attacher [ataʃe] *vt* to tie up; (*étiquette*) to attach, tie on; (*souliers*) to do up ♦ *vi* (*poêle, riz*) to stick; **s'~** (*robe etc*) to do up; **s'~ à** (*par affection*) to become attached to; **s'~ à faire qch** to endeavour to do sth; **~ qch à** to tie *ou* fasten *ou* attach sth to; **~ qn à** (*fig: lier*) to attach sb to; **~ du prix/de l'importance à** to attach great value/attach importance to.

attaquant [atakɑ̃] *nm* (*MIL*) attacker; (*SPORT*) striker, forward.

attaque [atak] *nf* attack; (*cérébrale*) stroke; (*d'épilepsie*) fit; **être/se sentir d'~** to be/feel on form; **~ à main armée** armed attack.

attaquer [atake] *vt* to attack; (*en justice*) to

bring an action against, sue; (*travail*) to tackle, set about ♦ *vi* to attack; **s'~ à** to attack; (*épidémie, misère*) to tackle, attack.

attardé, e [atarde] *adj* (*passants*) late; (*enfant*) backward; (*conceptions*) old-fashioned.

attarder [atarde]: **s'~** *vi* (*sur qch, en chemin*) to linger; (*chez qn*) to stay on.

atteignais [atɛɲɛ] *etc* vb voir **atteindre**.

atteindre [atɛ̃dʀ(ə)] *vt* to reach; (*blesser*) to hit; (*contacter*) to reach, contact, get in touch with; (*émouvoir*) to affect.

atteint, e [atɛ̃, -ɛ̃t] *pp de* **atteindre** ♦ *adj* (*MÉD*): **être ~ de** to be suffering from ♦ *nf* attack; **hors d'~e** out of reach; **porter ~e à** to strike a blow at, undermine.

attelage [atlaʒ] *nm* (*de remorque etc*) coupling (*BRIT*), (trailer) hitch (*US*); (*animaux*) team; (*harnachement*) harness; (: *de bœufs*) yoke.

atteler [atle] *vt* (*cheval, bœufs*) to hitch up; (*wagons*) to couple; **s'~ à** (*travail*) to buckle down to.

attelle [atɛl] *nf* splint.

attenant, e [atnɑ̃, -ɑ̃t] *adj*: **~ (à)** adjoining.

attendant [atɑ̃dɑ̃]: **en ~** *adv* (*dans l'intervalle*) meanwhile, in the meantime.

attendre [atɑ̃dʀ(ə)] *vt* to wait for; (*être destiné ou réservé à*) to await, be in store for ♦ *vi* to wait; **je n'attends plus rien (de la vie)** I expect nothing more (from life); **attendez que je réfléchisse** wait while I think; **s'~ à (ce que)** (*escompter*) to expect (that); **je ne m'y attendais pas** I didn't expect that; **ce n'est pas ce à quoi je m'attendais** that's not what I expected; **~ un enfant** to be expecting a baby; **~ de pied ferme** to wait determinedly; **~ de faire/d'être** to wait until one does/is; **~ que** to wait until; **~ qch de** to expect sth of; **faire ~ qn** to keep sb waiting; **se faire ~** to keep people (*ou* us *etc*) waiting; **en attendant** *adv voir* **attendant**.

attendri, e [atɑ̃dʀi] *adj* tender.

attendrir [atɑ̃dʀiʀ] *vt* to move (to pity); (*viande*) to tenderize; **s'~ (sur)** to be moved *ou* touched (by).

attendrissant, e [atɑ̃dʀisɑ̃, -ɑ̃t] *adj* moving, touching.

attendrissement [atɑ̃dʀismɑ̃] *nm* (*tendre*) emotion; (*apitoyé*) pity.

attendrisseur [atɑ̃dʀisœʀ] *nm* tenderizer.

attendu, e [atɑ̃dy] *pp de* **attendre** ♦ *adj* long-awaited; (*prévu*) expected ♦ *nm*: **~s** *reasons adduced for a judgment*; **~ que** *conj* considering that, since.

attentat [atɑ̃ta] *nm* (*contre une personne*) assassination attempt; (*contre un bâtiment*) attack; **~ à la bombe** bomb attack; **~ à la pudeur** (*exhibitionnisme*) indecent exposure *no pl*; (*agression*) indecent assault *no pl*.

attente [atɑ̃t] *nf* wait; (*espérance*) expectation; **contre toute ~** contrary to (all) expectations.

attenter [atɑ̃te]: **~ à** *vt* (*liberté*) to violate; **~ à**

la vie de qn to make an attempt on sb's life; **~ à ses jours** to make an attempt on one's life.

attentif, ive [atɑ̃tif, -iv] *adj* (*auditeur*) attentive; (*soin*) scrupulous; (*travail*) careful; **~ à** paying attention to; (*devoir*) mindful of; **~ à faire** careful to do.

attention [atɑ̃sjɔ̃] *nf* attention; (*prévenance*) attention, thoughtfulness *no pl*; **mériter ~** to be worthy of attention; **à l'~ de** for the attention of; **porter qch à l'~ de qn** to bring sth to sb's attention; **attirer l'~ de qn sur qch** to draw sb's attention to sth; **faire ~ (à)** to be careful (of); **faire ~ (à ce) que** to be *ou* make sure that; **~! careful!**, watch!, watch *ou* mind (*BRIT*) out!; **~, si vous ouvrez cette lettre** (*sanction*) just watch out, if you open that letter; **~, respectez les consignes de sécurité** be sure to observe the safety instructions.

attentionné, e [atɑ̃sjɔne] *adj* thoughtful, considerate.

attentisme [atɑ̃tism(ə)] *nm* wait-and-see policy.

attentiste [atɑ̃tist(ə)] *adj* (*politique*) wait-and-see ♦ *nm/f* believer in a wait-and-see policy.

attentivement [atɑ̃tivmɑ̃] *adv* attentively.

atténuant, e [atenɥɑ̃, -ɑ̃t] *adj*: **circonstances ~es** extenuating circumstances.

atténuer [atenɥe] *vt* to alleviate, ease; (*diminuer*) to lessen; (*amoindrir*) to mitigate the effects of; **s'~** *vi* to ease; (*violence etc*) to abate.

atterrer [atere] *vt* to dismay, appal.

atterrir [ateʀiʀ] *vi* to land.

atterrissage [aterisaʒ] *nm* landing; **~ sur le ventre/sans visibilité/forcé** belly/blind/forced landing.

attestation [atɛstɑsjɔ̃] *nf* certificate, testimonial; **~ médicale** doctor's certificate.

attester [atɛste] *vt* to testify to, vouch for; (*démontrer*) to attest, testify to; **~ que** to testify that.

attiédir [atjediʀ]: **s'~** *vi* to become lukewarm; (*fig*) to cool down.

attifé, e [atife] *adj* (*fam*) got up (*BRIT*), decked out.

attifer [atife] *vt* to get up (*BRIT*) *ou* do up, deck out.

attique [atik] *nm*: **appartement en ~** penthouse (flat (*BRIT*) *ou* apartment (*US*)).

attirail [atiʀaj] *nm* gear; (*péj*) paraphernalia.

attirance [atiʀɑ̃s] *nf* attraction; (*séduction*) lure.

attirant, e [atiʀɑ̃, -ɑ̃t] *adj* attractive, appealing.

attirer [atiʀe] *vt* to attract; (*appâter*) to lure, entice; **~ qn dans un coin/vers soi** to draw sb into a corner/towards one; **~ l'attention de qn** to attract sb's attention; **l'attention de qn sur qch** to draw sb's attention to sth; **~ des ennuis à qn** to make trouble for sb;

s'~ des ennuis to bring trouble upon o.s., get into trouble.

attiser [atize] *vt* (*feu*) to poke (up), stir up; (*fig*) to fan the flame of, stir up.

attitré, e [atitʀe] *adj* qualified; (*agréé*) accredited, appointed.

attitude [atityd] *nf* attitude; (*position du corps*) bearing.

attouchements [atuʃmɑ̃] *nmpl* touching *sg*; (*sexuels*) fondling *sg*, stroking *sg*.

attractif, ive [atʀaktif, -iv] *adj* attractive.

attraction [atʀaksjɔ̃] *nf* attraction; (*de cabaret, cirque*) number.

attrait [atʀɛ] *nm* appeal, attraction; (*plus fort*) lure; **~s** *nmpl* attractions; **éprouver de l'~ pour** to be attracted to.

attrape [atʀap] *nf voir* **farce.**

attrape-nigaud [atʀapnigo] *nm* con.

attraper [atʀape] *vt* to catch; (*habitude, amende*) to get, pick up; (*fam: duper*) to take in (*BRIT*), con.

attrayant, e [atʀɛjɑ̃, -ɑ̃t] *adj* attractive.

attribuer [atʀibɥe] *vt* (*prix*) to award; (*rôle, tâche*) to allocate, assign; (*imputer*): **~ qch à** to attribute sth to, ascribe sth to, put sth down to; **s'~** *vt* (*s'approprier*) to claim for o.s.

attribut [atʀiby] *nm* attribute; (*LING*) complement.

attribution [atʀibysjɔ̃] *nf* (*voir attribuer*) awarding; allocation, assignment; attribution; **~s** *nfpl* (*compétence*) attributions; **complément d'~** (*LING*) indirect object.

attristant, e [atʀistɑ̃, -ɑ̃t] *adj* saddening.

attrister [atʀiste] *vt* to sadden; **s'~ de qch** to be saddened by sth.

attroupement [atʀupmɑ̃] *nm* crowd, mob.

attrouper [atʀupe]: **s'~** *vi* to gather.

au [o] *prép + dét voir* **à.**

aubade [obad] *nf* dawn serenade.

aubaine [obɛn] *nf* godsend; (*financière*) windfall; (*COMM*) bonanza.

aube [ob] *nf* dawn, daybreak; (*REL*) alb; **à l'~** at dawn *ou* daybreak; **à l'~ de** (*fig*) at the dawn of.

aubépine [obepin] *nf* hawthorn.

auberge [obɛʀʒ(ə)] *nf* inn; **~ de jeunesse** youth hostel.

aubergine [obɛʀʒin] *nf* aubergine (*BRIT*), eggplant (*US*).

aubergiste [obɛʀʒist(ə)] *nm/f* inn-keeper, hotel-keeper.

auburn [obœʀn] *adj inv* auburn.

aucun, e [okœ̃, -yn] *dét* no, *tournure négative +* any; (*positif*) any ♦ *pron* none, *tournure négative +* any; (*positif*) any(one); **il n'y a ~ livre** there isn't any book, there is no book; **je n'en vois ~ qui** I can't see any which, I (can) see none which; **~ homme** no man; **sans ~ doute** without any doubt; **sans ~e hésitation** without hesitation; **plus qu'~ autre** more than any other; **plus qu'~ de ceux qui ...** more than any of those who ...; **en ~e façon**

in no way at all; **~ des deux** neither of the two; **~ d'entre eux** none of them; **d'~s** (*certains*) some.

aucunement [okynmɑ̃] *adv* in no way, not in the least.

audace [odas] *nf* daring, boldness; (*péj*) audacity; **il a eu l'~ de ...** he had the audacity to ...; **vous ne manquez pas d'~!** you're not lacking in nerve *ou* cheek!

audacieux, euse [odasjø, -øz] *adj* daring, bold.

au-dedans [odədɑ̃] *adv, prép* inside.

au-dehors [odəɔʀ] *adv, prép* outside.

au-delà [odla] *adv* beyond ♦ *nm*: **l'~** the hereafter; **~ de** *prép* beyond.

au-dessous [odsu] *adv* underneath; below; **~ de** *prép* under(neath), below; (*limite, somme etc*) below, under; (*dignité, condition*) below.

au-dessus [odsy] *adv* above; **~ de** *prép* above.

au-devant [odvɑ̃]: **~ de** *prép*: **aller ~ de** to go (out) and meet; (*souhaits de qn*) to anticipate.

audible [odibl(ə)] *adj* audible.

audience [odjɑ̃s] *nf* audience; (*JUR: séance*) hearing; **trouver ~ auprès de** to arouse much interest among, get the (interested) attention of.

audimat [odimat] *nm* (*taux d'écoute*) ratings *pl*.

audiogramme [odjɔgʀam] *nm* audiogramme.

audio-visuel, le [odjovizɥɛl] *adj* audio-visual ♦ *nm* (*équipement*) audio-visual aids *pl*; (*méthodes*) audio-visual methods *pl*; **l'~** radio and television.

auditeur, trice [oditœʀ, -tʀis] *nm/f* (*à la radio*) listener; (*à une conférence*) member of the audience, listener; **~ libre** unregistered student (*attending lectures*), auditor (*US*).

auditif, ive [oditif, -iv] *adj* (*mémoire*) auditory; **appareil ~** hearing aid.

audition [odisjɔ̃] *nf* (*ouïe, écoute*) hearing; (*JUR: de témoins*) examination; (*MUS, THÉÂT: épreuve*) audition.

auditionner [odisjɔne] *vt, vi* to audition.

auditoire [oditwaʀ] *nm* audience.

auditorium [oditɔʀjɔm] *nm* (*public*) studio.

auge [oʒ] *nf* trough.

augmentation [ɔgmɑ̃tasjɔ̃] *nf* (*action*) increasing; raising; (*résultat*) increase; **~ (de salaire)** rise (in salary) (*BRIT*), (pay) raise (*US*).

augmenter [ɔgmɑ̃te] *vt* to increase; (*salaire, prix*) to increase, raise, put up; (*employé*) to increase the salary of, give a (salary) rise (*BRIT*) *ou* (pay) raise (*US*) to ♦ *vi* to increase; **~ de poids/volume** to gain (in) weight/volume.

augure [ɔgyʀ] *nm* soothsayer, oracle; **de bon/mauvais ~** of good/ill omen.

augurer [ɔgyʀe] *vt*: **~ qch de** to foresee sth (coming) from *ou* out of; **~ bien de** to augur well for.

auguste [ɔgyst(ə)] *adj* august, noble, majestic.

aujourd'hui [oʒuʁdɥi] *adv* today; ~ **en huit/ quinze** a week/two weeks today, a week/two weeks from now; **à dater** *ou* **partir d'**~ from today('s date).

aumône [omon] *nf* alms *sg* (*pl inv*); **faire l'**~ (**à qn**) to give alms (to sb); **faire l'**~ **de qch à qn** (*fig*) to favour sb with sth.

aumônerie [omonʁi] *nf* chaplaincy.

aumônier [omonje] *nm* chaplain.

auparavant [opaʁavɑ̃] *adv* before(hand).

auprès [opʁɛ]: ~ **de** *prép* next to, close to; (*recourir, s'adresser*) to; (*en comparaison de*) compared with, next to; (*dans l'opinion de*) in the opinion of.

auquel [okɛl] *prép + pron voir* **lequel**.

aurai [oʁe] *etc vb voir* **avoir**.

auréole [oʁeɔl] *nf* halo; (*tache*) ring.

auréolé, e [oʁeɔle] *adj* (*fig*): ~ **de gloire** crowned with *ou* in glory.

auriculaire [oʁikylɛʁ] *nm* little finger.

aurore [oʁɔʁ] *nf* dawn, daybreak; ~ **boréale** northern lights *pl*.

ausculter [oskylte] *vt* to sound.

auspices [ospis] *nmpl*: **sous les** ~ **de** under the patronage *ou* auspices of; **sous de bons/ mauvais** ~ under favourable/unfavourable auspices.

aussi [osi] *adv* (*également*) also, too; (*de comparaison*) as ♦ *conj* therefore, consequently; ~ **fort que** as strong as; **lui** ~ (*sujet*) he too; (*objet*) him too; ~ **bien que** (*de même que*) as well as.

aussitôt [osito] *adv* straight away, immediately; ~ **que** as soon as; ~ **envoyé** as soon as it is (*ou* was) sent; ~ **fait** no sooner done.

austère [ostɛʁ] *adj* austere; (*sévère*) stern.

austérité [osteʁite] *nf* austerity; **plan/budget d'**~ austerity plan/budget.

austral, e [ostʁal] *adj* southern; **l'océan A**~ the Antarctic Ocean; **les Terres A**~**es** Antarctica.

Australie [ostʁali] *nf*: **l'**~ Australia.

australien, ne [ostʁaljɛ̃, -ɛn] *adj* Australian ♦ *nm/f*: **A**~, **ne** Australian.

autant [otɑ̃] *adv* so much; (*comparatif*): ~ **(que)** as much (as); (*nombre*) as many (as); ~ **(de)** so much (*ou* many); as many (*ou* many); **n'importe qui aurait pu en faire** ~ anyone could have done the same *ou* as much; ~ **partir** we (*ou* you *etc*) may as well leave; ~ **ne rien dire** best not say anything; ~ **dire que ...** one might as well say that ...; **fort** ~ **que courageux** as strong as he is brave; **il n'est pas découragé pour** ~ he isn't discouraged for all that; **pour** ~ **que** *conj* assuming, as long as; **d'**~ *adv* accordingly, in proportion; **d'**~ **plus/mieux (que)** all the more/the better (since).

autarcie [otaʁsi] *nf* autarky, self-sufficiency.

autel [otɛl] *nm* altar.

auteur [otœʁ] *nm* author; **l'**~ **de cette remarque** the person who said that; **droit d'**~

copyright.

auteur-compositeur [otœʁkɔ̃pozitœʁ] *nm/f* composer-songwriter.

authenticité [otɑ̃tisite] *nf* authenticity.

authentifier [otɑ̃tifje] *vt* to authenticate.

authentique [otɑ̃tik] *adj* authentic, genuine.

autiste [otist] *adj* autistic.

auto [oto] *nf* car; ~**s tamponneuses** bumper cars, dodgems.

auto... [oto] *préfixe* auto..., self-.

autobiographie [otɔbjɔgʁafi] *nf* autobiography.

autobiographique [otɔbjɔgʁafik] *adj* autobiographical.

autobus [otɔbys] *nm* bus.

autocar [otɔkaʁ] *nm* coach.

autocensure [otosɑ̃syʁ] *nf* self-censorship.

autochtone [otɔktɔn] *nm/f* native.

autocollant, e [otɔkɔlɑ̃, -ɑ̃t] *adj* self-adhesive; (*enveloppe*) self-seal ♦ *nm* sticker.

auto-couchettes [otokuʃɛt] *adj inv*: **train** ~ car sleeper train, motorail ® train (*BRIT*).

autocratique [otɔkʁatik] *adj* autocratic.

autocritique [otɔkʁitik] *nf* self-criticism.

autocuiseur [otɔkɥizœʁ] *nm* (*CULIN*) pressure cooker.

autodéfense [otodefɑ̃s] *nf* self-defence; **groupe d'**~ vigilante committee.

autodétermination [otodetɛʁminasjɔ̃] *nf* self-determination.

autodidacte [otodidakt(ə)] *nm/f* self-taught person.

autodiscipline [otodisiplin] *nf* self-discipline.

autodrome [otodʁom] *nm* motor-racing stadium.

auto-école [otoekɔl] *nf* driving school.

autofinancement [otofinɑ̃smɑ̃] *nm* self-financing.

autogéré, e [otoʒeʁe] *adj* self-managed, managed internally.

autogestion [otoʒɛstjɔ̃] *nf* joint worker-management control.

autographe [otogʁaf] *nm* autograph.

autoguidé, e [otogide] *adj* self-guided.

auto-immun, e [otoimœ̃, -yn] *adj* auto-immune.

automate [otomat] *nm* (*robot*) automaton; (*machine*) (automatic) machine.

automatique [otomatik] *adj*, *nm* automatic; **l'**~ (*TÉL*) ≈ direct dialling.

automatiquement [otomatikmɑ̃] *adv* automatically.

automatisation [otomatizasjɔ̃] *nf* automation.

automatiser [otomatize] *vt* to automate.

automatisme [otomatism(ə)] *nm* automatism.

automédication [otomedikasjɔ̃] *nf* self-medication.

automitrailleuse [otomitʁajøz] *nf* armoured car.

automnal, e, aux [otɔnal, -o] *adj* autumnal.

automne [otɔn] *nm* autumn (*BRIT*), fall (*US*).

automobile [otomɔbil] *adj* motor *cpd* ♦ *nf* (motor) car; **l'~** motoring; (*industrie*) the car *ou* automobile (*US*) industry.

automobiliste [ɔtɔmɔbilist(ə)] *nm/f* motorist.

autonettoyant, e [ɔtɔnɛtwajɑ̃, -āt] *adj*: **four ~** self-cleaning oven.

autonome [ɔtɔnɔm] *adj* autonomous; (*INFORM*) stand-alone; (**en mode**) **~ off line.**

autonomie [ɔtɔnɔmi] *nf* autonomy; (*POL*) self-government, autonomy; **~ de vol** range.

autonomiste [ɔtɔnɔmist(ə)] *nm/f* separatist.

autoportrait [ɔtɔpɔʀtʀɛ] *nm* self-portrait.

autopsie [ɔtɔpsi] *nf* post-mortem (examination), autopsy.

autopsier [ɔtɔpsje] *vt* to carry out a post-mortem *ou* an autopsy on.

autoradio [ɔtɔʀadjo] *nf* car radio.

autorail [ɔtɔʀaj] *nm* railcar.

autorisation [ɔtɔʀizasjɔ̃] *nf* permission, authorization; (*papiers*) permit; **donner à qn l'~ de** to give sb permission to, authorize sb to; **avoir l'~ de faire** to be allowed *ou* have permission to do, be authorized to do.

autorisé, e [ɔtɔʀize] *adj* (*opinion, sources*) authoritative; (*permis*): **~ à faire** authorized *ou* permitted to do; **dans les milieux ~s** in official circles.

autoriser [ɔtɔʀize] *vt* to give permission for, authorize; (*fig*) to allow (of), sanction; **~ qn à faire** to give permission to sb to do, authorize sb to do.

autoritaire [ɔtɔʀitɛʀ] *adj* authoritarian.

autoritarisme [ɔtɔʀitaʀism(ə)] *nm* authoritarianism.

autorité [ɔtɔʀite] *nf* authority; **faire ~** to be authoritative; **~s constituées** constitutional authorities.

autoroute [ɔtɔʀut] *nf* motorway (*BRIT*), expressway (*US*); **~ de l'information** information superhighway.

autoroutier, ière [ɔtɔʀutje, -jɛʀ] *adj* motorway *cpd* (*BRIT*), expressway *cpd* (*US*).

autosatisfaction [ɔtɔsatisfaksjɔ̃] *nf* self-satisfaction.

auto-stop [ɔtɔstɔp] *nm*: **l'~** hitch-hiking; **faire de l'~** to hitch-hike; **prendre qn en ~** to give sb a lift.

auto-stoppeur, euse [ɔtɔstɔpœʀ, -øz] *nm/f* hitch-hiker, hitcher (*BRIT*).

autosuffisant, e [ɔtɔsyfizɑ̃, -āt] *adj* self-sufficient.

autosuggestion [ɔtɔsygʒɛstjɔ̃] *nf* autosuggestion.

autour [otuʀ] *adv* around; **~ de** *prép* around; (*environ*) around, about; **tout ~** *adv* all around.

═══════════════ *MOT-CLÉ*

autre [otʀ(ə)] *adj* **1** (*différent*) other, different; **je préférerais un ~ verre** I'd prefer another *ou* a different glass; **d'~s verres** different glasses; **se sentir ~** to feel different; **la difficulté est ~** the difficulty is *ou* lies else-

where

2 (*supplémentaire*) other; **je voudrais un ~ verre d'eau** I'd like another glass of water

3: **~ chose** something else; **~ part** somewhere else; **d'~ part** on the other hand

♦ *pron* **1**: **un ~** another (one); **nous/vous ~s** us/you; **d'~s** others; **l'~** the other (one); **les ~s** the others; (*autrui*) others; **l'un et l'~** both of them; **ni l'un ni l'~** neither of them; **se détester l'un l'~/les uns les ~s** to hate each other *ou* one another; **d'une semaine/minute à l'~** from one week/minute *ou* moment to the next; (*incessamment*) any week/minute *ou* moment now; **de temps à ~** from time to time; **entre ~s** among other things

2 (*expressions*): **j'en ai vu d'~s** I've seen worse; **à d'~s!** pull the other one!

autrefois [otʀəfwa] *adv* in the past.

autrement [otʀəmɑ̃] *adv* differently; (*d'une manière différente*) in another way; (*sinon*) otherwise; **je n'ai pas pu faire ~** I couldn't do anything else, I couldn't do otherwise; **~ dit** in other words; (*c'est-à-dire*) that is to say.

Autriche [otʀiʃ] *nf*: **l'~** Austria.

autrichien, ne [otʀiʃjɛ̃, -ɛn] *adj* Austrian ♦ *nm/f*: **A~, ne** Austrian.

autruche [otʀyʃ] *nf* ostrich; **faire l'~** (*fig*) to bury one's head in the sand.

autrui [otʀɥi] *pron* others.

auvent [ovɑ̃] *nm* canopy.

auvergnat, e [ovɛʀɲa, -at] *adj* of *ou* from the Auvergne.

Auvergne [ovɛʀɲ(ə)] *nf*: **l'~** the Auvergne.

aux [o] *prép* + *dét voir* **à**.

auxiliaire [ɔksiljɛʀ] *adj, nm/f* auxiliary.

auxquels, auxquelles [okɛl] *prép* + *pron voir* **lequel**.

AV *sigle m* (*BANQUE*: = *avis de virement*) *advice of bank transfer* ♦ *abr* (*AUTO*) = **avant**.

av. *abr* (= *avenue*) Av(e).

avachi, e [avaʃi] *adj* limp, flabby; (*chaussure, vêtement*) out-of-shape; (*personne*): **~ sur qch** slumped on *ou* across sth.

avais [avɛ] *etc vb voir* **avoir**.

aval [aval] *nm* (*accord*) endorsement, backing; (*GÉO*): **en ~** downstream, downriver; (*sur une pente*) downhill; **en ~ de** downstream *ou* downriver from; downhill from.

avalanche [avalɑ̃ʃ] *nf* avalanche; **~ poudreuse** powder snow avalanche.

avaler [avale] *vt* to swallow.

avaliser [avalize] *vt* (*plan, entreprise*) to back, support; (*COMM, JUR*) to guarantee.

avance [avɑ̃s] *nf* (*de troupes etc*) advance; (*progrès*) progress; (*d'argent*) advance; (*opposé à retard*) lead; being ahead of schedule; **~s** *nfpl* overtures; (*amoureuses*) advances; **une ~ de 300 m/4 h** (*SPORT*) a 300 m/4 hour lead; (**être**) **en ~** (to be) early; (*sur un programme*) (to be) ahead of schedule; **on n'est**

pas en ~! we're kind of late!; **être en** ~ **sur qn** to be ahead of sb; **d'**~, **à l'**~, **par** ~ in advance; ~ **(du) papier** (*INFORM*) paper advance.

avancé, e [avɑ̃se] *adj* advanced; (*travail etc*) well on, well under way; (*fruit, fromage*) overripe ♦ *nf* projection; overhang; **il est** ~ **pour son âge** he is advanced for his age.

avancement [avɑ̃smɑ̃] *nm* (*professionnel*) promotion; (*de travaux*) progress.

avancer [avɑ̃se] *vi* to move forward, advance; (*projet, travail*) to make progress; (*être en saillie*) to overhang; to project; (*montre, réveil*) to be fast; (*: d'habitude*) to gain ♦ *vt* to move forward, advance; (*argent*) to advance; (*montre, pendule*) to put forward; (*faire progresser: travail etc*) to advance, move on; **s'**~ *vi* to move forward, advance; (*fig*) to commit o.s.; (*faire saillie*) to overhang; to project; **j'avance (d'une heure)** I'm (an hour) fast.

avanies [avani] *nfpl* snubs (*BRIT*), insults.

avant [avɑ̃] *prép* before ♦ *adv*: **trop/plus** ~ too far/further forward ♦ *adj inv*: **siège/roue** ~ front seat/wheel ♦ *nm* front; (*SPORT: joueur*) forward; ~ **qu'il parte/de partir** before he leaves/leaving; ~ **qu'il (ne) pleuve** before it rains (*ou* rained); ~ **tout** (*surtout*) above all; **à l'**~ (*dans un véhicule*) in (the) front; **en** ~ *adv* forward(s); **en** ~ **de** *prép* in front of; **aller de l'**~ to steam ahead (*fig*), make good progress.

avantage [avɑ̃taʒ] *nm* advantage; (*TENNIS*): ~ **service/dehors** advantage *ou* van (*BRIT*) *ou* ad (*US*) in/out; **tirer** ~ **de** to take advantage of; **vous auriez** ~ **à faire** you would be well-advised to do, it would be to your advantage to do; **à l'**~ **de qn** to sb's advantage; **être à son** ~ to be at one's best; ~**s en nature** benefits in kind; ~**s sociaux** fringe benefits.

avantager [avɑ̃taʒe] *vt* (*favoriser*) to favour; (*embellir*) to flatter.

avantageux, euse [avɑ̃taʒø, -øz] *adj* attractive; (*intéressant*) attractively priced; (*portrait, coiffure*) flattering; **conditions avantageuses** favourable terms.

avant-bras [avɑ̃bra] *nm inv* forearm.

avant-centre [avɑ̃sɑ̃tʀ(ə)] *nm* centre-forward.

avant-coureur [avɑ̃kuʀœʀ] *adj inv* (*bruit etc*) precursory; **signe** ~ advance indication *ou* sign.

avant-dernier, ière [avɑ̃dɛʀnje, -jɛʀ] *adj, nm/f* next to last, last but one.

avant-garde [avɑ̃gaʀd(ə)] *nf* (*MIL*) vanguard; (*fig*) avant-garde; **d'**~ avant-garde.

avant-goût [avɑ̃gu] *nm* foretaste.

avant-hier [avɑ̃tjɛʀ] *adv* the day before yesterday.

avant-poste [avɑ̃pɔst(ə)] *nm* outpost.

avant-première [avɑ̃pʀəmjɛʀ] *nf* (*de film*) preview; **en** ~ as a preview, in a preview show-

ing.

avant-projet [avɑ̃pʀɔʒɛ] *nm* preliminary draft.

avant-propos [avɑ̃pʀɔpo] *nm* foreword.

avant-veille [avɑ̃vɛj] *nf*: **l'**~ two days before.

avare [avaʀ] *adj* miserly, avaricious ♦ *nm/f* miser; ~ **de compliments** stingy *ou* sparing with one's compliments.

avarice [avaʀis] *nf* avarice, miserliness.

avaricieux, euse [avaʀisjø, -øz] *adj* miserly, niggardly.

avarié, e [avaʀje] *adj* (*viande, fruits*) rotting, going off (*BRIT*); (*NAVIG: navire*) damaged.

avaries [avaʀi] *nfpl* (*NAVIG*) damage *sg*.

avatar [avataʀ] *nm* misadventure; (*transformation*) metamorphosis (*pl* -phoses).

avec [avɛk] *prép* with; (*à l'égard de*) to(wards), with ♦ *adv* (*fam*) with it (*ou* him *etc*); ~ **habileté/lenteur** skilfully/slowly; ~ **eux/ces maladies** with them/these diseases; ~ **ça** (*malgré ça*) for all that; **et** ~ **ça?** (*dans un magasin*) anything *ou* something else?

avenant, e [avnɑ̃, -ɑ̃t] *adj* pleasant ♦ *nm* (*ASSURANCES*) additional clause; **à l'**~ *adv* in keeping.

avènement [avɛnmɑ̃] *nm* (*d'un roi*) accession, succession; (*d'un changement*) advent; (*d'une politique, idée*) coming.

avenir [avniʀ] *nm*: **l'**~ the future; **à l'**~ in future; **sans** ~ with no future, without a future; **carrière/politicien d'**~ career/politician with prospects *ou* a future.

Avent [avɑ̃] *nm*: **l'**~ Advent.

aventure [avɑ̃tyʀ] *nf*: **l'**~ adventure; **une** ~ an adventure; (*amoureuse*) an affair; **partir à l'**~ to go off in search of adventure; (*au hasard*) to go where one's fancy takes one; **roman/film d'**~ adventure story/film.

aventurer [avɑ̃tyʀe] *vt* (*somme, réputation, vie*) to stake; (*remarque, opinion*) to venture; **s'**~ *vi* to venture; **s'**~ **à faire qch** to venture into sth.

aventureux, euse [avɑ̃tyʀø, -øz] *adj* adventurous, venturesome; (*projet*) risky, chancy.

aventurier, ière [avɑ̃tyʀje, -jɛʀ] *nm/f* adventurer ♦ *nf* (*péj*) adventuress.

avenu, e [avny] *adj*: **nul et non** ~ null and void.

avenue [avny] *nf* avenue.

avéré, e [aveʀe] *adj* recognized, acknowledged.

avérer [aveʀe]: **s'**~ *vb avec attribut*: **s'**~ **faux/coûteux** to prove (to be) wrong/expensive.

averse [avɛʀs(ə)] *nf* shower.

aversion [avɛʀsjɔ̃] *nf* aversion, loathing.

averti, e [avɛʀti] *adj* (well-)informed.

avertir [avɛʀtiʀ] *vt*: ~ **qn (de qch/que)** to warn sb (of sth/that); (*renseigner*) to inform sb (of sth/that); ~ **qn de ne pas faire qch** to warn sb not to do sth.

avertissement [avɛʀtismɑ̃] *nm* warning.

avertisseur [avɛʀtisœʀ] *nm* horn, siren; ~

(d'incendie) (fire) alarm.

aveu, x [avø] *nm* confession; **passer aux ~x** to make a confession; **de l'~ de** according to.

aveuglant, e [avœglɑ̃, -ɑ̃t] *adj* blinding.

aveugle [avœgl(ə)] *adj* blind ♦ *nm/f* blind person; **les ~s** the blind; **test en (double) ~** (double) blind test.

aveuglement [avœgləmɑ̃] *nm* blindness.

aveuglément [avœglemɑ̃] *adv* blindly.

aveugler [avœgle] *vt* to blind.

aveuglette [avœglɛt]: **à l'~** groping one's way along; (*fig*) in the dark, blindly.

avez [ave] *vb voir* **avoir.**

aviateur, trice [avjatœr, -tris] *nm/f* aviator, pilot.

aviation [avjasjɔ̃] *nf* (*secteur commercial*) aviation; (*sport, métier de pilote*) flying; (*MIL*) air force; **terrain d'~** airfield; **~ de chasse** fighter force.

aviculteur, trice [avikyltœr, -tris] *nm/f* poultry farmer; bird breeder.

aviculture [avikyltyr] *nf* (*de volailles*) poultry farming.

avide [avid] *adj* eager; (*péj*) greedy, grasping; **~ de** (*sang etc*) thirsting for; **~ d'honneurs/d'argent** greedy for honours/money; **~ de connaître/d'apprendre** eager to know/learn.

avidité [avidite] *nf* eagerness; greed.

avilir [avilir] *vt* to debase.

avilissant, e [avilisɑ̃, -ɑ̃t] *adj* degrading.

aviné, e [avine] *adj* drunken.

avion [avjɔ̃] *nm* (aero)plane (*BRIT*), (air)plane (*US*); **aller (quelque part) en ~** to go (somewhere) by plane, fly (somewhere); **par ~** by airmail; **~ de chasse** fighter; **~ de ligne** airliner; **~ à réaction** jet (plane).

avion-cargo [avjɔ̃kargo] *nm* air freighter.

avion-citerne [avjɔ̃sitɛrn(ə)] *nm* air tanker.

aviron [avirɔ̃] *nm* oar; (*sport*): **l'~** rowing.

avis [avi] *nm* opinion; (*notification*) notice; (*COMM*): **~ de crédit/débit** credit/debit advice; **à mon ~** in my opinion; **je suis de votre ~** I share your opinion, I am of your opinion; **être d'~ que** to be of the opinion that; **changer d'~** to change one's mind; **sauf ~ contraire** unless you hear to the contrary; **sans ~ préalable** without notice; **jusqu'à nouvel ~** until further notice; **~ de décès** death announcement.

avisé, e [avize] *adj* sensible, wise; **être bien/mal ~ de faire** to be well-/ill-advised to do.

aviser [avize] *vt* (*voir*) to notice, catch sight of; (*informer*): **~ qn de/que** to advise *ou* inform *ou* notify sb of/that ♦ *vi* to think about things, assess the situation; **s'~ de qch/que** to become suddenly aware of sth/that; **s'~ de faire** to take it into one's head to do.

aviver [avive] *vt* (*douleur, chagrin*) to intensify; (*intérêt, désir*) to sharpen; (*colère, querelle*) to stir up; (*couleur*) to brighten up.

av. J.-C. *abr* (= *avant Jésus-Christ*) BC.

avocat, e [avɔka, -at] *nm/f* (*JUR*) ≈ barrister (*BRIT*), lawyer; (*fig*) advocate, champion ♦ *nm* (*CULIN*) avocado (pear); **se faire l'~ du diable** to be the devil's advocate; **l'~ de la défense/partie civile** the counsel for the defence/plaintiff; **~ d'affaires** business lawyer; **~ général** assistant public prosecutor.

avocat-conseil, *pl* **avocats-conseils** [avɔkakɔ̃sɛj] *nm* ≈ barrister (*BRIT*).

avocat-stagiaire, *pl* **avocats-stagiaires** [avɔkastaʒjɛr] *nm* ≈ barrister doing his articles (*BRIT*).

avoine [avwan] *nf* oats *pl*.

════════════════════════════ MOT-CLÉ

avoir [avwar] *nm* assets *pl*, resources *pl*; (*COMM*) credit; **~ fiscal** tax credit

♦ *vt* **1** (*posséder*) to have; **elle a 2 enfants/une belle maison** she has (got) 2 children/a lovely house; **il a les yeux bleus** he has (got) blue eyes

2 (*éprouver*): **qu'est-ce que tu as?, qu'as-tu?** what's wrong?, what's the matter?; *voir aussi* **faim, peur** *etc*

3 (*âge, dimensions*) to be; **il a 3 ans** he is 3 (years old); **le mur a 3 mètres de haut** the wall is 3 metres high

4 (*fam: duper*) to do, have; **on vous a eu!** you've been done *ou* had!

5: en ~ contre qn to have a grudge against sb; **en ~ assez** to be fed up; **j'en ai pour une demi-heure** it'll take me half an hour; **n'~ que faire de qch** to have no use for sth

♦ *vb aux* **1** to have; **~ mangé/dormi** to have eaten/slept; **hier je n'ai pas mangé** I didn't eat yesterday

2 (*avoir à +infinitif*): **~ à faire qch** to have to do sth; **vous n'avez qu'à lui demander** you only have to ask him; **tu n'as pas à me poser des questions** it's not for you to ask me questions

♦ *vb impers* **1**: **il y a** (+ *singulier*) there is; (+ *pluriel*) there are; **qu'y a-t-il?, qu'est-ce qu'il y a?** what's the matter?, what is it?; **il doit y avoir une explication** there must be an explanation; **il n'y a qu'à ...** we (*ou* you *etc*) will just have to ...; **il ne peut y en ~ qu'un** there can only be one

2 (*temporel*): **il y a 10 ans** 10 years ago; **il y a 10 ans/longtemps que je le connais** I've known him for 10 years/a long time; **il y a 10 ans qu'il est arrivé** it's 10 years since he arrived.

avoisinant, e [avwazinɑ̃, -ɑ̃t] *adj* neighbouring.

avoisiner [avwazine] *vt* to be near *ou* close to; (*fig*) to border *ou* verge on.

avons [avɔ̃] *vb voir* **avoir.**

avortement [avɔrtəmɑ̃] *nm* abortion.

avorter [avɔrte] *vi* (*MÉD*) to have an abortion; (*fig*) to fail; **faire ~** to abort; **se faire ~** to have an abortion.

avorton [avɔʀtɔ̃] *nm* (*péj*) little runt.
avouable [avwabl(ə)] *adj* respectable; **des pensées non ~s** unrepeatable thoughts.
avoué, e [avwe] *adj* avowed ♦ *nm* (*JUR*) ≈ solicitor (*BRIT*), lawyer.
avouer [avwe] *vt* (*crime, défaut*) to confess (to) ♦ *vi* (*se confesser*) to confess; (*admettre*) to admit; **~ avoir fait/que** to admit *ou* confess to having done/that; **~ que oui/non** to admit that that is so/not so; **s'~ vaincu** to admit defeat.
avril [avʀil] *nm* April; *voir aussi* **juillet**.

The traditional prank on April 1 in France involves placing a cut-out paper fish, known as a **poisson d'avril**, *on the back of one's victim, without being caught.*

---

axe [aks(ə)] *nm* axis (*pl* axes); (*de roue etc*) axle; (*prolongement*): **dans l'~ de** directly in line with; (*fig*) main line; **~ routier** trunk road, main road.
axer [akse] *vt*: **~ qch sur** to centre sth on.
axial, e, aux [aksjal, -o] *adj* axial.
axiome [aksjom] *nm* axiom.
ayant [ɛjɑ̃] *vb voir* **avoir** ♦ *nm*: **~ droit** assignee; **~ droit à** (*pension etc*) person eligible for *ou* entitled to.
ayons [ɛjɔ̃] *etc vb voir* **avoir**.
azalée [azale] *nf* azalea.
Azerbaïdjan [azɛʀbaidʒɑ̃] *nm* Azerbaijan.
azerbaïdjanais, e [azɛʀbaidʒanɛ, -ɛz] *adj* Azerbaijani ♦ *nm* (*LING*) Azerbaijani ♦ *nm/f*: **A~, e** Azerbaijani.
azimut [azimyt] *nm* azimuth; **tous ~s** *adj* (*fig*) omnidirectional.
azote [azɔt] *nm* nitrogen.
azoté, e [azɔte] *adj* nitrogenous.
AZT *sigle m* (= *azidothymidine*) AZT.
aztèque [aztɛk] *adj* Aztec.
azur [azyʀ] *nm* (*couleur*) azure, sky blue; (*ciel*) sky, skies *pl*.
azyme [azim] *adj*: **pain ~** unleavened bread.

B b

B, b [be] *nm inv* B, b ♦ *abr* = **bien**; **B comme Bertha** B for Benjamin (*BRIT*) *ou* Baker (*US*).
BA *sigle f* (= *bonne action*) good deed.
baba [baba] *adj inv*: **en être ~** (*fam*) to be flabbergasted ♦ *nm*: **~ au rhum** rum baba.
babil [babi] *nm* prattle.
babillage [babijaʒ] *nm* chatter.
babiller [babije] *vi* to prattle, chatter; (*bébé*) to babble.

babines [babin] *nfpl* chops.
babiole [babjɔl] *nf* (*bibelot*) trinket; (*vétille*) trifle.
bâbord [babɔʀ] *nm*: **à** *ou* **par ~** to port, on the port side.
babouin [babwɛ̃] *nm* baboon.
baby-foot [babifut] *nm inv* table football.
Babylone [babilɔn] *n* Babylon.
babylonien, ne [babilɔnjɛ̃, -ɛn] *adj* Babylonian.
baby-sitter [babisitœʀ] *nm/f* baby-sitter.
baby-sitting [babisitiŋ] *nm* baby-sitting.
bac [bak] *nm* (*SCOL*) = **baccalauréat**; (*bateau*) ferry; (*récipient*) tub; (: *PHOTO etc*) tray; (: *INDUSTRIE*) tank; **~ à glace** ice-tray; **~ à légumes** vegetable compartment *ou* rack.
baccalauréat [bakalɔʀea] *nm* ≈ GCE A-levels *pl* (*BRIT*), ≈ high school diploma (*US*).

In France the **baccalauréat** *or* **bac** *is the school-leaving certificate taken at a lycée at the age of seventeen or eighteen after seven years of secondary education. A variety of subject combinations is available, although in all cases a broad range of subjects is studied. Holders of the certificate are entitled to go on to university.*

---

bâche [baʃ] *nf* tarpaulin, canvas sheet.
bachelier, ière [baʃəlje, -jɛʀ] *nm/f* holder of the *baccalauréat*.
bâcher [baʃe] *vt* to cover (with a canvas sheet *ou* a tarpaulin).
bachot [baʃo] *nm* = **baccalauréat**.
bachotage [baʃotaʒ] *nm* (*SCOL*) cramming.
bachoter [baʃote] *vi* (*SCOL*) to cram (for an exam).
bacille [basil] *nm* bacillus (*pl* -i).
bâcler [bakle] *vt* to botch (up).
bacon [bekɔn] *nm* bacon.
bactéricide [bakteʀisid] *nm* (*MÉD*) bactericide.
bactérie [bakteʀi] *nf* bacterium (*pl* -ia).
bactérien, ne [bakteʀjɛ̃, -ɛn] *adj* bacterial.
bactériologie [bakteʀjɔlɔʒi] *nf* bacteriology.
bactériologique [bakteʀjɔlɔʒik] *adj* bacteriological.
bactériologiste [bakteʀjɔlɔʒist(ə)] *nm/f* bacteriologist.
badaud, e [bado, -od] *nm/f* idle onlooker, stroller.
baderne [badɛʀn(ə)] *nf* (*péj*): (**vieille**) **~** old fossil.
badge [badʒ(ə)] *nm* badge.
badigeon [badiʒɔ̃] *nm* distemper; colourwash.
badigeonner [badiʒɔne] *vt* to distemper; to colourwash; (*péj: barbouiller*) to daub; (*MÉD*) to paint.
badin, e [badɛ̃, -in] *adj* light-hearted, playful.
badinage [badinaʒ] *nm* banter.
badine [badin] *nf* switch (*stick*).
badiner [badine] *vi*: **~ avec qch** to treat sth lightly; **ne pas ~ avec qch** not to trifle with

sth.
badminton [badmintɔn] *nm* badminton.
BAFA [bafa] *sigle m* (= *Brevet d'aptitude aux fonctions d'animation*) *diploma for youth leaders and workers.*
baffe [baf] *nf (fam)* slap, clout.
Baffin [bafin] *nf*: **terre de ~** Baffin Island.
baffle [bafl(ə)] *nm* baffle (board).
bafouer [bafwe] *vt* to deride, ridicule.
bafouillage [bafujaʒ] *nm (fam: propos incohérents)* jumble of words.
bafouiller [bafuje] *vi, vt* to stammer.
bâfrer [bɑfʀe] *vi, vt (fam)* to guzzle, gobble.
bagage [bagaʒ] *nm*: **~s** luggage *sg*, baggage *sg*; **~ littéraire** (stock of) literary knowledge; **~s à main** hand-luggage.
bagarre [bagaʀ] *nf* fight, brawl; **il aime la ~** he loves a fight, he likes fighting.
bagarrer [bagaʀe]: **se ~** *vi* to (have a) fight.
bagarreur, euse [bagaʀœʀ, -øz] *adj* pugnacious ♦ *nm/f*: **il est ~** he loves a fight.
bagatelle [bagatɛl] *nf* trifle, trifling sum (*ou* matter).
Bagdad, Baghdâd [bagdad] *n* Baghdad.
bagnard [baɲaʀ] *nm* convict.
bagne [baɲ] *nm* penal colony; **c'est le ~** (*fig*) it's forced labour.
bagnole [baɲɔl] *nf (fam)* car, wheels *pl (BRIT)*.
bagout [bagu] *nm* glibness; **avoir du ~** to have the gift of the gab.
bague [bag] *nf* ring; **~ de fiançailles** engagement ring; **~ de serrage** clip.
baguenauder [bagnode]: **se ~** *vi* to trail around, loaf around.
baguer [bage] *vt* to ring.
baguette [bagɛt] *nf* stick; (*cuisine chinoise*) chopstick; (*de chef d'orchestre*) baton; (*pain*) stick of (French) bread; (*CONSTR: moulure*) beading; **mener qn à la ~** to rule sb with a rod of iron; **~ magique** magic wand; **~ de sourcier** divining rod; **~ de tambour** drumstick.
Bahamas [baamas] *nfpl*: **les (îles) ~** the Bahamas.
Bahrein [baʀɛn] *nm* Bahrain *ou* Bahrein.
bahut [bay] *nm* chest.
bai, e [bɛ] *adj (cheval)* bay.
baie [bɛ] *nf (GÉO)* bay; (*fruit*) berry; **~ (vitrée)** picture window.
baignade [bɛɲad] *nf (action)* bathing; (*bain*) bathe; (*endroit*) bathing place.
baigné, e [beɲe] *adj*: **~ de** bathed in; (*trempé*) soaked with; (*inondé*) flooded with.
baigner [beɲe] *vt (bébé)* to bath ♦ *vi*: **~ dans son sang** to lie in a pool of blood; **~ dans la brume** to be shrouded in mist; **se ~** *vi* to go swimming *ou* bathing; (*dans une baignoire*) to have a bath; **ça baigne!** (*fam*) everything's great!
baigneur, euse [bɛɲœʀ, -øz] *nm/f* bather ♦ *nm* (*poupée*) baby doll.
baignoire [bɛɲwaʀ] *nf* bath(tub); (*THÉÂT*)

ground-floor box.
bail, baux [baj, bo] *nm* lease; **donner** *ou* **prendre qch à ~** to lease sth.
bâillement [bɑjmɑ̃] *nm* yawn.
bâiller [bɑje] *vi* to yawn; (*être ouvert*) to gape.
bailleur [bajœʀ] *nm*: **~ de fonds** sponsor, backer; (*COMM*) sleeping *ou* silent partner.
bâillon [bɑjɔ̃] *nm* gag.
bâillonner [bɑjɔne] *vt* to gag.
bain [bɛ̃] *nm (dans une baignoire, PHOTO, TECH)* bath; (*dans la mer, une piscine*) swim; **costume de ~** bathing costume *(BRIT)*, swimsuit; **prendre un ~** to have a bath; **se mettre dans le ~** (*fig*) to get into (the way of) it *ou* things; **~ de bouche** mouthwash; **~ de foule** walkabout; **~ de pieds** footbath; (*au bord de la mer*) paddle; **~ de siège** hip bath; **~ de soleil** sunbathing *no pl*; **prendre un ~ de soleil** to sunbathe; **~s de mer** sea bathing *sg*; **~s(-douches) municipaux** public baths.
bain-marie, *pl* **bains-marie** [bɛ̃maʀi] *nm* double boiler; **faire chauffer au ~** (*boîte etc*) to immerse in boiling water.
baïonnette [bajɔnɛt] *nf* bayonet; (*ÉLEC*): **douille à ~** bayonet socket; **ampoule à ~** bulb with a bayonet fitting.
baisemain [bɛzmɛ̃] *nm* kissing a lady's hand.
baiser [beze] *nm* kiss ♦ *vt (main, front)* to kiss; (*fam!*) to screw (*!*).
baisse [bɛs] *nf* fall, drop; (*COMM*): **"~ sur la viande"** "meat prices down"; **en ~** (*cours, action*) falling; **à la ~** downwards.
baisser [bese] *vt* to lower; (*radio, chauffage*) to turn down; (*AUTO: phares*) to dip *(BRIT)*, lower *(US)* ♦ *vi* to fall, drop, go down; **se ~** *vi* to bend down.
bajoues [baʒu] *nfpl* chaps, chops.
bal [bal] *nm* dance; (*grande soirée*) ball; **~ costumé/masqué** fancy-dress/masked ball; **~ musette** dance (*with accordion accompaniment*).
balade [balad] *nf* walk, stroll; (*en voiture*) drive; **faire une ~** to go for a walk *ou* stroll; to go for a drive.
balader [balade] *vt (traîner)* to trail around; **se ~** *vi* to go for a walk *ou* stroll; to go for a drive.
baladeur [baladœʀ] *nm* personal stereo.
baladeuse [baladøz] *nf* inspection lamp.
baladin [baladɛ̃] *nm* wandering entertainer.
balafre [balafʀ(ə)] *nf* gash, slash; (*cicatrice*) scar.
balafrer [balafʀe] *vt* to gash, slash.
balai [balɛ] *nm* broom, brush; (*AUTO: d'essuie-glace*) blade; (*MUS: de batterie etc*) brush; **donner un coup de ~** to give the floor a sweep; **~ mécanique** carpet sweeper.
balai-brosse, *pl* **balais-brosses** [balɛbʀɔs] *nm* (long-handled) scrubbing brush.
balance [balɑ̃s] *nf (à plateaux)* scales *pl*; (*de précision*) balance; (*COMM, POL*): **~ des comptes** *ou* **paiements** balance of pay-

ments; (signe): **la B**~ Libra, the Scales; **être de la B**~ to be Libra; ~ **commerciale** balance of trade; ~ **des forces** balance of power; ~ **romaine** steelyard.

balancelle [balɑ̃sɛl] *nf* garden hammock-seat.

balancer [balɑ̃se] *vt* to swing; (*lancer*) to fling, chuck; (*renvoyer, jeter*) to chuck out ♦ *vi* to swing; **se** ~ *vi* to swing; (*bateau*) to rock; (*branche*) to sway; **se** ~ **de qch** (*fam*) not to give a toss about sth.

balancier [balɑ̃sje] *nm* (*de pendule*) pendulum; (*de montre*) balance wheel; (*perche*) (balancing) pole.

balançoire [balɑ̃swaʀ] *nf* swing; (*sur pivot*) seesaw.

balayage [balɛjaʒ] *nm* sweeping; scanning.

balayer [baleje] *vt* (*feuilles etc*) to sweep up, brush up; (*pièce, cour*) to sweep; (*chasser*) to sweep away *ou* aside; (*suj: radar*) to scan; (*: phares*) to sweep across.

balayette [balɛjɛt] *nf* small brush.

balayeur, euse [balɛjœʀ, -øz] *nm/f* roadsweeper ♦ *nf* (*engin*) roadsweeper.

balayures [balɛjyʀ] *nfpl* sweepings.

balbutiement [balbysimɑ̃] *nm* (*paroles*) stammering *no pl*; ~**s** *nmpl* (*fig: débuts*) first faltering steps.

balbutier [balbysje] *vi, vt* to stammer.

balcon [balkɔ̃] *nm* balcony; (*THÉÂT*) dress circle.

baldaquin [baldakɛ̃] *nm* canopy.

Bâle [bɑl] *n* Basle *ou* Basel.

Baléares [baleaʀ] *nfpl*: **les** ~ the Balearic Islands.

baleine [balɛn] *nf* whale; (*de parapluie*) rib; (*de corset*) bone.

baleinier [balenje] *nm* (*NAVIG*) whaler.

baleinière [balenjɛʀ] *nf* whaleboat.

balisage [balizaʒ] *nm* (*signaux*) beacons *pl*; buoys *pl*; runway lights *pl*; signs *pl*, markers *pl*.

balise [baliz] *nf* (*NAVIG*) beacon, (marker) buoy; (*AVIAT*) runway light, beacon; (*AUTO, SKI*) sign, marker.

baliser [balize] *vt* to mark out (with beacons *ou* lights *etc*).

balistique [balistik] *adj* (*engin*) ballistic ♦ *nf* ballistics.

balivernes [balivɛʀn(ə)] *nfpl* twaddle *sg* (*BRIT*), nonsense *sg*.

balkanique [balkanik] *adj* Balkan.

Balkans [balkɑ̃] *nmpl*: **les** ~ the Balkans.

ballade [balad] *nf* ballad.

ballant, e [balɑ̃, -ɑ̃t] *adj* dangling.

ballast [balast] *nm* ballast.

balle [bal] *nf* (*de fusil*) bullet; (*de sport*) ball; (*du blé*) chaff; (*paquet*) bale; (*fam: franc*) franc; ~ **perdue** stray bullet.

ballerine [balʀin] *nf* ballet dancer; (*chaussure*) pump, ballerina.

ballet [balɛ] *nm* ballet; (*fig*): ~ **diplomatique** diplomatic to-ings and fro-ings.

ballon [balɔ̃] *nm* (*de sport*) ball; (*jouet, AVIAT, de bande dessinée*) balloon; (*de vin*) glass; ~ **d'essai** (*météorologique*) pilot balloon; (*fig*) feeler(s); ~ **de football** football; ~ **d'oxygène** oxygen bottle.

ballonner [balɔne] *vt*: **j'ai le ventre ballonné** I feel bloated.

ballon-sonde, *pl* **ballons-sondes** [balɔ̃sɔ̃d] *nm* sounding balloon.

ballot [balo] *nm* bundle; (*péj*) nitwit.

ballottage [balɔtaʒ] *nm* (*POL*) second ballot.

ballotter [balɔte] *vi* to roll around; (*bateau etc*) to toss ♦ *vt* to shake *ou* throw about; to toss; **être ballotté entre** (*fig*) to be shunted between; (*: indécis*) to be torn between.

ballottine [balɔtin] *nf* (*CULIN*): ~ **de volaille** meat loaf made with poultry.

ball-trap [baltʀap] *nm* (*appareil*) trap; (*tir*) clay pigeon shooting.

balluchon [balyʃɔ̃] *nm* bundle (of clothes).

balnéaire [balneɛʀ] *adj* seaside *cpd*.

balnéothérapie [balneɔteʀapi] *nf* spa bath therapy.

BALO *sigle m* (= *Bulletin des annonces légales obligatoires*) ≈ Public Notices (*in newspapers etc*).

balourd, e [baluʀ, -uʀd(ə)] *adj* clumsy ♦ *nm/f* clodhopper.

balourdise [baluʀdiz] *nf* clumsiness; (*gaffe*) blunder.

balte [balt] *adj* Baltic ♦ *nm/f*: **B**~ native of the Baltic States.

baltique [baltik] *adj* Baltic ♦ *nf*: **la (mer) B**~ the Baltic (Sea).

baluchon [balyʃɔ̃] *nm* = **balluchon.**

balustrade [balystʀad] *nf* railings *pl*, handrail.

bambin [bɑ̃bɛ̃] *nm* little child.

bambou [bɑ̃bu] *nm* bamboo.

ban [bɑ̃] *nm* round of applause, cheer; **être/mettre au** ~ **de** to be outlawed/to outlaw from; **le** ~ **et l'arrière-**~ **de sa famille** every last one of his relatives; ~**s (de mariage)** banns, bans.

banal, e [banal] *adj* banal, commonplace; (*péj*) trite; **four/moulin** ~ village oven/mill.

banalisé, e [banalize] *adj* (*voiture de police*) unmarked.

banalité [banalite] *nf* banality; (*remarque*) truism, trite remark.

banane [banan] *nf* banana.

bananeraie [bananʀɛ] *nf* banana plantation.

bananier [bananje] *nm* banana tree; (*bateau*) banana boat.

banc [bɑ̃] *nm* seat, bench; (*de poissons*) shoal; ~ **des accusés** dock; ~ **d'essai** (*fig*) testing ground; ~ **de sable** sandbank; ~ **des témoins** witness box; ~ **de touche** dugout.

bancaire [bɑ̃kɛʀ] *adj* banking, bank *cpd*.

bancal, e [bɑ̃kal] *adj* wobbly; (*personne*) bow-legged; (*fig: projet*) shaky.

bandage [bɑ̃daʒ] *nm* bandaging; (*pansement*) bandage; ~ **herniaire** truss.

bande [bɑ̃d] nf (de tissu etc) strip; (MÉD) bandage; (motif, dessin) stripe; (CINÉ) film; (INFORM) tape; (RADIO, groupe) band; (péj): **une ~ de** a bunch ou crowd of; **par la ~** in a roundabout way; **donner de la ~** to list; **faire ~ à part** to keep to o.s.; **~ dessinée (BD)** strip cartoon (BRIT), comic strip; **~ magnétique** magnetic tape; **~ perforée** punched tape; **~ de roulement** (de pneu) tread; **~ sonore** sound track; **~ de terre** strip of land; **~ Velpeau** ® (MÉD) crêpe bandage.

The **bande dessinée** or **BD** enjoys a huge following in France amongst adults as well as children, with the strip cartoon being accorded both literary and artistic status. An international show takes place at Angoulême at the end of January every year. Astérix, Tintin, Lucky Luke and Gaston Lagaffe are among the most famous cartoon characters.

bandé, e [bɑ̃de] adj bandaged; **les yeux ~s** blindfold.
bande-annonce, pl **bandes-annonces** [bɑ̃dɑ̃nɔ̃s] nf (CINÉ) trailer.
bandeau, x [bɑ̃do] nm headband; (sur les yeux) blindfold; (MÉD) head bandage.
bandelette [bɑ̃dlɛt] nf strip of cloth, bandage.
bander [bɑ̃de] vt to bandage; (muscle) to tense; (arc) to bend ♦ vi (fam!) to have a hard on (!); **~ les yeux à qn** to blindfold sb.
banderole [bɑ̃drɔl] nf banderole; (dans un défilé etc) streamer.
bande-son, pl **bandes-son** [bɑ̃dsɔ̃] nf (CINÉ) soundtrack.
bande-vidéo, pl **bandes-vidéo** [bɑ̃dvideo] nf video tape.
bandit [bɑ̃di] nm bandit.
banditisme [bɑ̃ditism(ə)] nm violent crime, armed robberies pl.
bandoulière [bɑ̃duljɛR] nf: **en ~** (slung ou worn) across the shoulder.
Bangkok [bɑ̃ŋkɔk] n Bangkok.
Bangladesh [bɑ̃gladɛʃ] nm: **le ~** Bangladesh.
banjo [bɑ̃(d)ʒo] nm banjo.
banlieue [bɑ̃ljø] nf suburbs pl; **lignes/quartiers de ~** suburban lines/areas; **trains de ~** commuter trains.
banlieusard, e [bɑ̃ljøzaR, -aRd(ə)] nm/f suburbanite.
bannière [banjɛR] nf banner.
bannir [baniR] vt to banish.
banque [bɑ̃k] nf bank; (activités) banking; **~ des yeux/du sang** eye/blood bank; **~ d'affaires** merchant bank; **~ de dépôt** deposit bank; **~ de données** (INFORM) data bank; **~ d'émission** bank of issue.
banqueroute [bɑ̃kRut] nf bankruptcy.
banquet [bɑ̃kɛ] ŋm (de club) dinner; (de noces) reception; (d'apparat) banquet.
banquette [bɑ̃kɛt] nf seat.
banquier [bɑ̃kje] nm banker.

banquise [bɑ̃kiz] nf ice field.
bantou, e [bɑ̃tu] adj Bantu.
baptême [batɛm] nm (sacrement) baptism; (cérémonie) christening, baptism; (d'un navire) launching; (d'une cloche) consecration, dedication; **~ de l'air** first flight.
baptiser [batize] vt to christen; to baptize; to launch; to consecrate, dedicate.
baptismal, e, aux [batismal, -o] adj: **eau ~e** baptismal water.
baptiste [batist(ə)] adj, nm/f Baptist.
baquet [bakɛ] nm tub, bucket.
bar [baR] nm bar; (poisson) bass.
baragouin [baRagwɛ̃] nm gibberish.
baragouiner [baRagwine] vi to gibber, jabber.
baraque [baRak] nf shed; (fam) house; **~ foraine** fairground stand.
baraqué, e [baRake] adj well-built, hefty.
baraquements [baRakmɑ̃] nmpl huts (for refugees, workers etc).
baratin [baRatɛ̃] nm (fam) smooth talk, patter.
baratiner [baRatine] vt to chat up.
baratte [baRat] nf churn.
Barbade [baRbad] nf: **la ~** Barbados.
barbant, e [baRbɑ̃, -ɑ̃t] adj (fam) deadly (boring).
barbare [baRbaR] adj barbaric ♦ nm/f barbarian.
Barbarie [baRbaRi] nf: **la ~** the Barbary Coast.
barbarie [baRbaRi] nf barbarism; (cruauté) barbarity.
barbarisme [baRbaRism(ə)] nm (LING) barbarism.
barbe [baRb(ə)] nf beard; **(au nez et) à la ~ de qn** (fig) under sb's very nose; **quelle ~!** (fam) what a drag ou bore!; **~ à papa** candy-floss (BRIT), cotton candy (US).
barbecue [baRbəkju] nm barbecue.
barbelé [baRbəle] nm barbed wire no pl.
barber [baRbe] vt (fam) to bore stiff.
barbiche [baRbiʃ] nf goatee.
barbichette [baRbiʃɛt] nf small goatee.
barbiturique [baRbityRik] nm barbiturate.
barboter [baRbɔte] vi to paddle, dabble ♦ vt (fam) to filch.
barboteuse [baRbɔtøz] nf rompers pl.
barbouiller [baRbuje] vt to daub; (péj: écrire, dessiner) to scribble; **avoir l'estomac barbouillé** to feel queasy ou sick.
barbu, e [baRby] adj bearded.
barbue [baRby] nf (poisson) brill.
Barcelone [baRsəlɔn] n Barcelona.
barda [baRda] nm (fam) kit, gear.
barde [baRd(ə)] nf (CULIN) piece of fat bacon ♦ nm (poète) bard.
bardé, e [baRde] adj: **~ de médailles etc** bedecked with medals etc.
bardeaux [baRdo] nmpl shingle no pl.
barder [baRde] vt (CULIN: rôti, volaille) to bard ♦ vi (fam): **ça va ~** sparks will fly, things are going to get hot.
barème [baRɛm] nm scale; (liste) table; **~ des**

salaires salary scale.
barge [baʀʒ] *nf* barge.
barguigner [baʀɡiɲe] *vi*: **sans** ~ without (any) humming and hawing *ou* shilly-shallying.
baril [baʀil] *nm* (*tonneau*) barrel; (*de poudre*) keg.
barillet [baʀijɛ] *nm* (*de revolver*) cylinder.
bariolé, e [baʀjɔle] *adj* many-coloured, rainbow-coloured.
barman [baʀman] *nm* barman.
baromètre [baʀɔmɛtʀ(ə)] *nm* barometer; ~ **anéroïde** aneroid barometer.
baron [baʀɔ̃] *nm* baron.
baronne [baʀɔn] *nf* baroness.
baroque [baʀɔk] *adj* (*ART*) baroque; (*fig*) weird.
baroud [baʀud] *nm*: ~ **d'honneur** gallant last stand.
baroudeur [baʀudœʀ] *nm* (*fam*) fighter.
barque [baʀk(ə)] *nf* small boat.
barquette [baʀkɛt] *nf* small boat-shaped tart; (*récipient: en aluminium*) tub; (: *en bois*) basket.
barracuda [baʀakyda] *nm* barracuda.
barrage [baʀaʒ] *nm* dam; (*sur route*) roadblock, barricade; ~ **de police** police roadblock.
barre [baʀ] *nf* (*de fer etc*) rod, bar; (*NAVIG*) helm; (*écrite*) line, stroke; (*DANSE*) barre; (*niveau*): **la livre a franchi la** ~ **des 10 frs** the pound has broken the 10 frs barrier; (*JUR*): **comparaître à la** ~ to appear as a witness; **être à** *ou* **tenir la** ~ (*NAVIG*) to be at the helm; **coup de** ~ (*fig*): **c'est le coup de** ~! it's daylight robbery!; **j'ai le coup de** ~! I'm all in!; ~ **fixe** (*GYM*) horizontal bar; ~ **de mesure** (*MUS*) bar line; ~ **à mine** crowbar; ~**s parallèles/asymétriques** (*GYM*) parallel/asymmetric bars.
barreau, x [baʀo] *nm* bar; (*JUR*): **le** ~ the Bar.
barrer [baʀe] *vt* (*route etc*) to block; (*mot*) to cross out; (*chèque*) to cross (*BRIT*); (*NAVIG*) to steer; **se** ~ *vi* (*fam*) to clear off.
barrette [baʀɛt] *nf* (*pour cheveux*) (hair) slide (*BRIT*) *ou* clip (*US*); (*REL: bonnet*) biretta; (*broche*) brooch.
barreur [baʀœʀ] *nm* helmsman; (*aviron*) coxswain.
barricade [baʀikad] *nf* barricade.
barricader [baʀikade] *vt* to barricade; **se** ~ **chez soi** (*fig*) to lock o.s. in.
barrière [baʀjɛʀ] *nf* fence; (*obstacle*) barrier; (*porte*) gate; **la Grande B**~ the Great Barrier Reef; ~ **de dégel** (*ADMIN: on roadsigns*) no heavy vehicles - road liable to subsidence due to thaw; ~**s douanières** trade barriers.
barrique [baʀik] *nf* barrel, cask.
barrir [baʀiʀ] *vi* to trumpet.
baryton [baʀitɔ̃] *nm* baritone.
BAS *sigle m* (= *bureau d'aide sociale*) ≈ social security office (*BRIT*), ≈ Welfare office (*US*).
bas, basse [ba, bas] *adj* low; (*action*) low, ig-

noble ♦ *nm* (*vêtement*) stocking; (*partie inférieure*): **le** ~ **de** the lower part *ou* foot *ou* bottom of ♦ *nf* (*MUS*) bass ♦ *adv* low; (*parler*) softly; **plus** ~ lower down; more softly; (*dans un texte*) further on, below; **la tête basse** with lowered head; (*fig*) with head hung low; **avoir la vue basse** to be shortsighted; **au** ~ **mot** at the lowest estimate; **enfant en** ~ **âge** infant, young child; **en** ~ down below; at (*ou* to) the bottom; (*dans une maison*) downstairs; **en** ~ **de** at the bottom of; **de** ~ **en haut** upwards; from the bottom to the top; **des hauts et des** ~ ups and downs; **un** ~ **de laine** (*fam: économies*) money under the mattress (*fig*); **mettre** ~ *vi* to give birth; **à** ~ **la dictature!** down with dictatorship!; ~ **morceaux** (*viande*) cheap cuts.
basalte [bazalt(ə)] *nm* basalt.
basané, e [bazane] *adj* tanned, bronzed; (*immigré etc*) swarthy.
bas-côté [bakote] *nm* (*de route*) verge (*BRIT*), shoulder (*US*); (*d'église*) (side) aisle.
bascule [baskyl] *nf*: (*jeu de*) ~ seesaw; (*balance à*) ~ scales *pl*; **fauteuil à** ~ rocking chair; **système à** ~ tip-over device; rocker device.
basculer [baskyle] *vi* to fall over, topple (over); (*benne*) to tip up ♦ *vt* (*aussi*: **faire** ~) to topple over; to tip out, tip up.
base [baz] *nf* base; (*POL*): **la** ~ the rank and file, the grass roots; (*fondement, principe*) basis (*pl* bases); **jeter les** ~**s de** to lay the foundations of; **à la** ~ **de** (*fig*) at the root of; **sur la** ~ **de** (*fig*) on the basis of; **de** ~ basic; **à** ~ **de café** *etc* coffee *etc* -based; ~ **de données** (*INFORM*) database; ~ **de lancement** launching site.
base-ball [bɛzbol] *nm* baseball.
baser [baze] *vt*: ~ **qch sur** to base sth on; **se** ~ **sur** (*données, preuves*) to base one's argument on; **être basé à/dans** (*MIL*) to be based at/in.
bas-fond [bafɔ̃] *nm* (*NAVIG*) shallow; ~**s** *nmpl* (*fig*) dregs.
BASIC [bazik] *nm* BASIC.
basilic [bazilik] *nm* (*CULIN*) basil.
basilique [bazilik] *nf* basilica.
basket(-ball) [baskɛt(bol)] *nm* basketball.
baskets [baskɛt] *nfpl* (*chaussures*) trainers (*BRIT*), sneakers (*US*).
basketteur, euse [baskɛtœʀ, -øz] *nm/f* basketball player.
basquaise [baskɛz] *adj f* Basque ♦ *nf*: **B**~ Basque.
basque [bask(ə)] *adj, nm* (*LING*) Basque ♦ *nm/f*: **B**~ Basque; **le Pays** ~ the Basque country.
basques [bask(ə)] *nfpl* skirts; **pendu aux** ~ **de qn** constantly pestering sb; (*mère etc*) hanging on sb's apron strings.
bas-relief [baʀəljɛf] *nm* bas-relief.
basse [bas] *adj f, nf voir* **bas**.

basse-cour, pl **basses-cours** [bɑskuʀ] nf farmyard; (animaux) farmyard animals.

bassement [bɑsmɑ̃] adv basely.

bassesse [bɑsɛs] nf baseness; (acte) base act.

basset [bɑsɛ] nm (ZOOL) basset (hound).

bassin [bɑsɛ̃] nm (cuvette) bowl; (pièce d'eau) pond, pool; (de fontaine, GÉO) basin; (ANAT) pelvis; (portuaire) dock; ~ **houiller** coalfield.

bassine [bɑsin] nf basin; (contenu) bowl, bowlful.

bassiner [bɑsine] vt (plaie) to bathe; (lit) to warm with a warming pan; (fam: ennuyer) to bore; (: importuner) to bug, pester.

bassiste [bɑsist(ə)] nm/f (double) bass player.

basson [bɑsɔ̃] nm bassoon.

bastide [bastid] nf (maison) country house (in Provence); (ville) walled town (in SW France).

bastingage [bastɛ̃gaʒ] nm (ship's) rail.

bastion [bastjɔ̃] nm (aussi fig, POL) bastion.

bas-ventre [bɑvɑ̃tʀ(ə)] nm (lower part of the) stomach.

bât [bɑ] nm packsaddle.

bataille [bɑtɑj] nf battle; **en** ~ (en travers) at an angle; (en désordre) awry; ~ **rangée** pitched battle.

bataillon [bɑtɑjɔ̃] nm battalion.

bâtard, e [bɑtaʀ, -aʀd(ə)] adj (enfant) illegitimate; (fig) hybrid ♦ nm/f illegitimate child, bastard (péj) ♦ nm (BOULANGERIE) ≈ Vienna loaf; **chien** ~ mongrel.

batavia [bɑtɑvjɑ] nf ≈ Webb lettuce.

bateau, x [bɑto] nm boat; (grand) ship ♦ adj inv (banal, rebattu) hackneyed; ~ **de pêche/à moteur** fishing/motor boat.

bateau-citerne [bɑtositɛʀn(ə)] nm tanker.

bateau-mouche [bɑtomuʃ] nm (passenger) pleasure boat (on the Seine).

bateau-pilote [bɑtopilɔt] nm pilot ship.

bateleur, euse [bɑtlœʀ, -øz] nm/f street performer.

batelier, ière [bɑtəlje, -jɛʀ] nm/f ferryman/woman.

bat-flanc [bɑflɑ̃] nm inv *raised boards for sleeping, in cells, army huts etc.*

bâti, e [bɑti] adj (terrain) developed ♦ nm (armature) frame; (COUTURE) tacking; **bien** ~ (personne) well-built.

batifoler [bɑtifɔle] vi to frolic ou lark about.

batik [bɑtik] nm batik.

bâtiment [bɑtimɑ̃] nm building; (NAVIG) ship, vessel; (industrie): **le** ~ the building trade.

bâtir [bɑtiʀ] vt to build; (COUTURE: jupe, ourlet) to tack; **fil à** ~ (COUTURE) tacking thread.

bâtisse [bɑtis] nf building.

bâtisseur, euse [bɑtisœʀ, -øz] nm/f builder.

batiste [bɑtist(ə)] nf (COUTURE) batiste, cambric.

bâton [bɑtɔ̃] nm stick; **mettre des** ~s **dans les roues à qn** to put a spoke in sb's wheel; **à** ~s **rompus** informally; ~ **de rouge (à lèvres)** lipstick; ~ **de ski** ski stick.

bâtonnet [bɑtɔnɛ] nm short stick ou rod.

bâtonnier [bɑtɔnje] nm (JUR) ≈ President of the Bar.

batraciens [bɑtʀɑsjɛ̃] nmpl amphibians.

battage [bɑtaʒ] nm (publicité) (hard) plugging.

battant, e [bɑtɑ̃, -ɑ̃t] vb voir **battre** ♦ adj: **pluie** ~**e** lashing rain ♦ nm (de cloche) clapper; (de volets) shutter, flap; (de porte) side; (fig: personne) fighter; **porte à double** ~ double door; **tambour** ~ briskly.

batte [bɑt] nf (SPORT) bat.

battement [bɑtmɑ̃] nm (de cœur) beat; (intervalle) interval (between classes, trains etc); ~ **de paupières** blinking no pl (of eyelids); **un** ~ **de 10 minutes, 10 minutes de** ~ 10 minutes to spare.

batterie [bɑtʀi] nf (MIL, ÉLEC) battery; (MUS) drums pl, drum kit; ~ **de cuisine** kitchen utensils pl; (casseroles etc) pots and pans pl; **une** ~ **de tests** a string of tests.

batteur [bɑtœʀ] nm (MUS) drummer; (appareil) whisk.

batteuse [bɑtøz] nf (AGR) threshing machine.

battoir [bɑtwaʀ] nm (à linge) beetle (for laundry); (à tapis) (carpet) beater.

battre [bɑtʀ(ə)] vt to beat; (suj: pluie, vagues) to beat ou lash against; (œufs etc) to beat up, whisk; (blé) to thresh; (cartes) to shuffle; (passer au peigne fin) to scour ♦ vi (cœur) to beat; (volets etc) to bang, rattle; **se** ~ vi to fight; ~ **la mesure** to beat time; ~ **en brèche** (MIL: mur) to batter; (fig: théorie) to demolish; (: institution etc) to attack; ~ **son plein** to be at its height, be going full swing; ~ **pavillon britannique** to fly the British flag; ~ **des mains** to clap one's hands; ~ **des ailes** to flap its wings; ~ **de l'aile** (fig) to be in a bad way ou in bad shape; ~ **la semelle** to stamp one's feet; ~ **en retraite** to beat a retreat.

battu, e [bɑty] pp de **battre** ♦ nf (chasse) beat; (policière etc) search, hunt.

baud [bo(d)] nm baud.

baudruche [bodʀyʃ] nf: **ballon en** ~ (toy) balloon; (fig) windbag.

baume [bom] nm balm.

bauxite [boksit] nf bauxite.

bavard, e [bavaʀ, -aʀd(ə)] adj (very) talkative; gossipy.

bavardage [bavaʀdaʒ] nm chatter no pl; gossip no pl.

bavarder [bavaʀde] vi to chatter; (indiscrètement) to gossip; (: révéler un secret) to blab.

bavarois, e [bavaʀwa, -waz] adj Bavarian ♦ nm ou nf (CULIN) bavarois.

bave [bav] nf dribble; (de chien etc) slobber, slaver (BRIT), drool (US); (d'escargot) slime.

baver [bave] vi to dribble; to slobber, slaver (BRIT), drool (US); (encre, couleur) to run; **en** ~ (fam) to have a hard time (of it).

bavette [bavɛt] nf bib.

baveux, euse [bavø, -øz] adj dribbling; (omelette) runny.

Bavière [bavjɛʀ] *nf:* **la ~** Bavaria.
bavoir [bavwaʀ] *nm (de bébé)* bib.
bavure [bavyʀ] *nf* smudge; *(fig)* hitch; blunder.
bayer [baje] *vi:* **~ aux corneilles** to stand gaping.
bazar [bazaʀ] *nm* general store; *(fam)* jumble.
bazarder [bazaʀde] *vt (fam)* to chuck out.
BCBG *sigle a (= bon chic bon genre)* ≈ preppy.
BCE *sigle f (= Banque centrale européenne)* ECB.
BCG *sigle m (= bacille Calmette-Guérin)* BCG.
bcp *abr* = **beaucoup**.
BD *sigle f* = **bande dessinée**; *(= base de données)* DB.
bd *abr* = **boulevard**.
b.d.c. *abr (TYPO: = bas de casse)* l.c.
béant, e [beɑ̃, -ɑ̃t] *adj* gaping.
béarnais, e [beaʀnɛ, -ɛz] *adj* of *ou* from the Béarn.
béat, e [bea, -at] *adj* showing open-eyed wonder; *(sourire etc)* blissful.
béatitude [beatityd] *nf* bliss.
beau (bel), belle, beaux [bo, bɛl] *adj* beautiful, lovely; *(homme)* handsome ♦ *nf (SPORT)* decider ♦ *adv:* **il fait ~** the weather's fine ♦ *nm:* **avoir le sens du ~** to have an aesthetic sense; **le temps est au ~** the weather is set fair; **un ~ geste** *(fig)* a fine gesture; **un ~ salaire** a good salary; **un ~ gâchis/rhume** a fine mess/nasty cold; **en faire/dire de belles** to do/say (some) stupid things; **le ~ monde** high society; **~ parleur** smooth talker; **un ~ jour** one (fine) day; **de plus belle** more than ever, even more; **bel et bien** well and truly; *(vraiment)* really (and truly); **le plus ~ c'est que ...** the best of it is that ...; **c'est du ~ !** that's great, that is!; **on a ~ essayer** however hard *ou* no matter how hard we try; **il a ~ jeu de protester** it's easy for him to protest; **faire le ~** *(chien)* to sit up and beg.
beauceron, ne [bosʀɔ̃, -ɔn] *adj* of *ou* from the Beauce.

═══════════════════ *MOT-CLÉ*

beaucoup [boku] *adv* **1** a lot; **il boit ~** he drinks a lot; **il ne boit pas ~** he doesn't drink much *ou* a lot
2 *(suivi de plus, trop etc)* much, a lot, far; **il est ~ plus grand** he is much *ou* a lot *ou* far taller
3: **~ de** *(nombre)* many, a lot of; *(quantité)* a lot of; **pas ~ de** *(nombre)* not many, not a lot of; *(quantité)* not much, not a lot of; **~ d'étudiants/de touristes** a lot of *ou* many students/tourists; **~ de courage** a lot of courage; **il n'a pas ~ d'argent** he hasn't got much *ou* a lot of money; **il n'y a pas ~ de touristes** there aren't many *ou* a lot of tourists
4: **de ~** by far
♦ *pron:* **~ le savent** lots of people know that.

beau-fils, *pl* **beaux-fils** [bofis] *nm* son-in-law;

(remariage) stepson.
beau-frère, *pl* **beaux-frères** [bofʀɛʀ] *nm* brother-in-law.
beau-père, *pl* **beaux-pères** [bopɛʀ] *nm* father-in-law; *(remariage)* stepfather.
beauté [bote] *nf* beauty; **de toute ~** beautiful; **en ~** *adv* with a flourish, brilliantly.
beaux-arts [bozaʀ] *nmpl* fine arts.
beaux-parents [bopaʀɑ̃] *nmpl* wife's/husband's family *sg ou pl*, in-laws.
bébé [bebe] *nm* baby.
bébé-éprouvette, *pl* **bébés-éprouvette** [bebeepʀuvɛt] *nm* test-tube baby.
bec [bɛk] *nm* beak, bill; *(de plume)* nib; *(de cafetière etc)* spout; *(de casserole etc)* lip; *(d'une clarinette etc)* mouthpiece; *(fam)* mouth; **clouer le ~ à qn** *(fam)* to shut sb up; **ouvrir le ~** *(fam)* to open one's mouth; **~ de gaz** (street) gaslamp; **~ verseur** pouring lip.
bécane [bekan] *nf (fam)* bike.
bécarre [bekaʀ] *nm (MUS)* natural.
bécasse [bekas] *nf (ZOOL)* woodcock; *(fam)* silly goose.
bec-de-cane, *pl* **becs-de-cane** [bɛkdəkan] *nm (poignée)* door handle.
bec-de-lièvre, *pl* **becs-de-lièvre** [bɛkdəljɛvʀ(ə)] *nm* harelip.
béchamel [beʃamɛl] *nf:* **(sauce) ~** white sauce, bechamel sauce.
bêche [bɛʃ] *nf* spade.
bêcher [beʃe] *vt (terre)* to dig; *(personne: critiquer)* to slate; *(: snober)* to look down on.
bêcheur, euse [beʃœʀ, -øz] *adj (fam)* stuck-up ♦ *nm/f* fault-finder; *(snob)* stuck-up person.
bécoter [bekɔte] *:* **se ~** *vi* to smooch.
becquée [beke] *nf:* **donner la ~ à** to feed.
becqueter [bɛkte] *vt (fam)* to eat.
bedaine [bədɛn] *nf* paunch.
bédé [bede] *nf (fam:* = *bande dessinée)* strip cartoon *(BRIT)*, comic strip.
bedeau, x [bədo] *nm* beadle.
bedonnant, e [bədɔnɑ̃, -ɑ̃t] *adj* paunchy, pot-bellied.
bée [be] *adj:* **bouche ~** gaping.
beffroi [befʀwa] *nm* belfry.
bégaiement [begɛmɑ̃] *nm* stammering, stuttering.
bégayer [begeje] *vt, vi* to stammer.
bégonia [begɔnja] *nm (BOT)* begonia.
bègue [bɛg] *nm/f:* **être ~** to have a stammer.
bégueule [begœl] *adj* prudish.
beige [bɛʒ] *adj* beige.
beignet [bɛɲɛ] *nm* fritter.
bel [bɛl] *adj m voir* **beau**.
bêler [bele] *vi* to bleat.
belette [bəlɛt] *nf* weasel.
belge [bɛlʒ(ə)] *adj* Belgian ♦ *nm/f:* **B~** Belgian.

┌───┐
│ **La fête nationale belge,** on July 21, is the anni-│
│ versary of Leopold of Saxe-Coburg Gotha be-│
│ coming King Leopold I in 1831.   │
└───┘

Belgique [bɛlʒik] *nf*: **la ~** Belgium.

Belgrade [bɛlgʀad] *n* Belgrade.

bélier [belje] *nm* ram; (*engin*) (battering) ram; (*signe*): **le B~** Aries, the Ram; **être du B~** to be Aries.

Bélize [beliz] *nm*: **le ~** Belize.

bellâtre [bɛlɑtʀ(ə)] *nm* dandy.

belle [bɛl] *adj f, nf voir* **beau**.

belle-famille, *pl* **belles-familles** [bɛlfamij] *nf* (*fam*) in-laws *pl*.

belle-fille, *pl* **belles-filles** [bɛlfij] *nf* daughter-in-law; (*remariage*) stepdaughter.

belle-mère, *pl* **belles-mères** [bɛlmɛʀ] *nf* mother-in-law; (*remariage*) stepmother.

belle-sœur, *pl* **belles-sœurs** [bɛlsœʀ] *nf* sister-in-law.

belliciste [belisist(ə)] *adj* warmongering.

belligérance [beliʒeʀɑ̃s] *nf* belligerence.

belligérant, e [beliʒeʀɑ̃, -ɑ̃t] *adj* belligerent.

belliqueux, euse [belikø, -øz] *adj* aggressive, warlike.

belote [bəlɔt] *nf* belote (*card game*).

belvédère [bɛlvedɛʀ] *nm* panoramic viewpoint (*or small building there*).

bémol [bemɔl] *nm* (*MUS*) flat.

ben [bɛ̃] *excl* (*fam*) well.

bénédiction [benediksjɔ̃] *nf* blessing.

bénéfice [benefis] *nm* (*COMM*) profit; (*avantage*) benefit; **au ~ de** in aid of.

bénéficiaire [benefisjɛʀ] *nm/f* beneficiary.

bénéficier [benefisje] *vi*: **~ de** to enjoy; (*profiter*) to benefit by *ou* from; (*obtenir*) to get, be given.

bénéfique [benefik] *adj* beneficial.

Benelux [benelyks] *nm*: **le ~** Benelux, the Benelux countries.

benêt [bənɛ] *nm* simpleton.

bénévolat [benevɔla] *nm* voluntary service *ou* work.

bénévole [benevɔl] *adj* voluntary, unpaid.

bénévolement [benevɔlmɑ̃] *adv* voluntarily.

Bengale [bɛ̃gal] *nm*: **le ~** Bengal; **le golfe du ~** the Bay of Bengal.

bengali [bɛ̃gali] *adj* Bengali, Bengalese ♦ *nm* (*LING*) Bengali.

Bénin [benɛ̃] *nm*: **le ~** Benin.

bénin, igne [benɛ̃, -iɲ] *adj* minor, mild; (*tumeur*) benign.

bénir [beniʀ] *vt* to bless.

bénit, e [beni, -it] *adj* consecrated; **eau ~e** holy water.

bénitier [benitje] *nm* stoup, font (*for holy water*).

benjamin, e [bɛ̃ʒamɛ̃, -in] *nm/f* youngest child; (*SPORT*) under-13.

benne [bɛn] *nf* skip; (*de téléphérique*) (cable) car; **~ basculante** tipper (*BRIT*), dump *ou* dumper truck.

benzine [bɛ̃zin] *nf* benzine.

béotien, ne [beɔsjɛ̃, -ɛn] *nm/f* philistine.

BEP *sigle m* (= *Brevet d'études professionnelles*) *school-leaving diploma, taken at approx. 18 years*.

BEPA [bepa] *sigle m* (= *Brevet d'études professionnelles agricoles*) *school-leaving diploma in agriculture, taken at approx. 18 years*.

BEPC *sigle m* (= *Brevet d'études du premier cycle*) *former school certificate (taken at approx. 16 years*).

béquille [bekij] *nf* crutch; (*de bicyclette*) stand.

berbère [bɛʀbɛʀ] *adj* Berber ♦ *nm* (*LING*) Berber ♦ *nm/f*: **B~** Berber.

bercail [bɛʀkaj] *nm* fold.

berceau, x [bɛʀso] *nm* cradle, crib.

bercer [bɛʀse] *vt* to rock, cradle; (*suj: musique etc*) to lull; **~ qn de** (*promesses etc*) to delude sb with.

berceur, euse [bɛʀsœʀ, -øz] *adj* soothing ♦ *nf* (*chanson*) lullaby.

BERD [bɛʀd] *sigle f* (= *Banque européenne pour la reconstruction et le développement*) EBRD.

béret (basque) [beʀɛ(bask(ə))] *nm* beret.

bergamote [bɛʀgamɔt] *nf* (*BOT*) bergamot.

berge [bɛʀʒ(ə)] *nf* bank.

berger, ère [bɛʀʒe, -ɛʀ] *nm/f* shepherd/ shepherdess; **~ allemand** (*chien*) alsatian (dog) (*BRIT*), German shepherd (dog) (*US*).

bergerie [bɛʀʒəʀi] *nf* sheep pen.

bergeronnette [bɛʀʒəʀɔnɛt] *nf* wagtail.

béribéri [beʀibeʀi] *nm* beriberi.

Berlin [bɛʀlɛ̃] *n* Berlin; **~-Est/-Ouest** East/ West Berlin.

berline [bɛʀlin] *nf* (*AUTO*) saloon (car) (*BRIT*), sedan (*US*).

berlingot [bɛʀlɛ̃go] *nm* (*emballage*) carton (*pyramid shaped*); (*bonbon*) lozenge.

berlinois, e [bɛʀlinwa, -waz] *adj* of *ou* from Berlin ♦ *nm/f*: **B~, e** Berliner.

berlue [bɛʀly] *nf*: **j'ai la ~** I must be seeing things.

bermuda [bɛʀmyda] *nm* (*short*) Bermuda shorts.

Bermudes [bɛʀmyd] *nfpl*: **les (îles) ~** Bermuda.

Berne [bɛʀn(ə)] *n* Bern.

berne [bɛʀn(ə)] *nf*: **en ~** at half-mast; **mettre en ~** to fly at half-mast.

berner [bɛʀne] *vt* to fool.

bernois, e [bɛʀnwa, -waz] *adj* Bernese.

berrichon, ne [beʀiʃɔ̃, -ɔn] *adj* of *ou* from the Berry.

besace [bəzas] *nf* beggar's bag.

besogne [bəzɔɲ] *nf* work *no pl*, job.

besogneux, euse [bəzɔɲø, -øz] *adj* hardworking.

besoin [bəzwɛ̃] *nm* need; (*pauvreté*): **le ~** need, want; **le ~ d'argent/de gloire** the need for money/glory; **~s (naturels)** nature's needs; **faire ses ~s** to relieve o.s.; **avoir ~ de qch/ faire qch** to need sth/to do sth; **il n'y a pas ~ de (faire)** there is no need to (do); **au ~, si ~ est** if need be; **pour les ~s de la cause** for the purpose in hand.

bestial, e, aux [bɛstjal, -o] adj bestial, brutish
♦ nmpl cattle.
bestiole [bɛstjɔl] nf (tiny) creature.
bétail [betaj] nm livestock, cattle pl.
bétaillère [betajɛR] nf livestock truck.
bête [bɛt] nf animal; (bestiole) insect, creature
♦ adj stupid, silly; **les ~s** (the) animals;
chercher la petite ~ to nit-pick; **~ noire** pet
hate, bugbear (BRIT); **~ sauvage** wild beast;
~ de somme beast of burden.
bêtement [bɛtmɑ̃] adv stupidly; **tout ~** quite
simply.
Bethléem [bɛtleɛm] n Bethlehem.
bêtifier [betifje] vi to talk nonsense.
bêtise [betiz] nf stupidity; (action, remarque)
stupid thing (to say ou do); (bonbon) type of
mint sweet (BRIT) ou candy (US); **faire/dire
une ~** to do/say something stupid.
béton [betɔ̃] nm concrete; **(en) ~** (fig: alibi, argument) cast iron; **~ armé** reinforced concrete; **~ précontraint** prestressed concrete.
bétonner [betɔne] vt to concrete (over).
bétonnière [betɔnjɛR] nf cement mixer.
bette [bɛt] nf (BOT) (Swiss) chard.
betterave [bɛtRav] nf (rouge) beetroot (BRIT),
beet (US); **~ fourragère** mangel-wurzel; **~
sucrière** sugar beet.
beugler [bøgle] vi to low; (péj: radio etc) to
blare ♦ vt (péj: chanson etc) to bawl out.
Beur [bœR] adj, nmf second-generation Arab
immigrant.

Beur is the term used to refer to a person born
in France of North African immigrant parents.
It is not a racist term and is often used by the
media, anti-racist groups and second-
generation North Africans themselves. The
word itself comes from verlan.

---

beurre [bœR] nm butter; **mettre du ~ dans les
épinards** (fig) to add a little to the kitty; **~
de cacao** cocoa butter; **~ noir** brown butter
(sauce).
beurrer [bœRe] vt to butter.
beurrier [bœRje] nm butter dish.
beuverie [bœvRi] nf drinking session.
bévue [bevy] nf blunder.
Beyrouth [beRut] n Beirut.
Bhoutan [butɑ̃] nm: **le ~** Bhutan.
bi... [bi] préfixe bi..., two-.
Biafra [bjafRa] nm: **le ~** Biafra.
biafrais, e [bjafRɛ, -ɛz] adj Biafran.
biais [bjɛ] nm (moyen) device, expedient;
(aspect) angle; (bande de tissu) piece of cloth
cut on the bias; **en ~, de ~** (obliquement) at
an angle; (fig) indirectly.
biaiser [bjeze] vi (fig) to sidestep the issue.
biathlon [biatlɔ̃] nm biathlon.
bibelot [biblo] nm trinket, curio.
biberon [bibRɔ̃] nm (feeding) bottle; **nourrir au
~** to bottle-feed.
bible [bibl(ə)] nf bible.

bibliobus [biblijɔbys] nm mobile library van.
bibliographie [biblijɔgRafi] nf bibliography.
bibliophile [biblijɔfil] nm/f book-lover.
bibliothécaire [biblijɔtekɛR] nm/f librarian.
bibliothèque [biblijɔtɛk] nf library; (meuble)
bookcase; **~ municipale** public library.
biblique [biblik] adj biblical.
bicarbonate [bikaRbɔnat] nm: **~ (de soude)** bicarbonate of soda.
bicentenaire [bisɑ̃tnɛR] nm bicentenary.
biceps [bisɛps] nm biceps.
biche [biʃ] nf doe.
bichonner [biʃɔne] vt to groom.
bicolore [bikɔlɔR] adj two-coloured (BRIT),
two-colored (US).
bicoque [bikɔk] nf (péj) shack, dump.
bicorne [bikɔRn(ə)] nm cocked hat.
bicyclette [bisiklɛt] nf bicycle.
bidasse [bidas] nm (fam) squaddie (BRIT).
bide [bid] nm (fam: ventre) belly; (THÉÂT) flop.
bidet [bidɛ] nm bidet.
bidirectionnel, le [bidiRɛksjɔnɛl] adj bidirectional.
bidoche [bidɔʃ] nf (fam) meat.
bidon [bidɔ̃] nm can ♦ adj inv (fam) phoney.
bidonnant, e [bidɔnɑ̃, -ɑ̃t] adj (fam) hilarious.
bidonville [bidɔ̃vil] nm shanty town.
bidule [bidyl] nm (fam) thingamajig.
bielle [bjɛl] nf connecting rod; (AUTO) track
rod.
biélorusse [bjelɔRys] adj Belarussian ♦ nm/f:
B~ Belarussian.
Biélorussie [bjelɔRysi] nf Belorussia.

=============================== *MOT-CLÉ*

bien [bjɛ̃] nm 1 (avantage, profit): **faire le ~** to
do good; **faire du ~ à qn** to do sb good; **ça
fait du ~ de faire** it does you good to do; **dire
du ~ de** to speak well of; **c'est pour son ~**
it's for his own good; **changer en ~** to
change for the better; **le ~ public** the public
good; **vouloir du ~ à qn** (vouloir aider) to
have sb's (best) interests at heart; **je te
veux du ~** (pour mettre en confiance) I don't
wish you any harm
2 (possession, patrimoine) possession, property; **son ~ le plus précieux** his most treas-
ured possession; **avoir du ~** to have property; **~s (de consommation** etc) (consumer
etc) goods; **~s durables** (consumer) durables
3 (moral): **le ~** good; **distinguer le ~ du mal**
to tell good from evil
♦ adv 1 (de façon satisfaisante) well; **elle
travaille/mange ~** she works/eats well; **aller** or **se porter ~** to be well; **croyant ~
faire, je/il ...** thinking I/he was doing the
right thing, I/he ...
2 (valeur intensive) quite; **~ jeune** quite
young; **~ assez** quite enough; **~ mieux**
(very) much better; **~ du temps/des gens**
quite a time/a number of people; **j'espère ~**

y aller I do hope to go; **je veux ~ le faire** (*concession*) I'm quite willing to do it; **il faut ~ le faire** it has to be done; **il y a ~ 2 ans** at least 2 years ago; **il semble ~ que** it really seems that; **peut-être ~** it could well be; **aimer ~** to like; **Paul est ~ venu, n'est-ce pas?** Paul HAS come, hasn't he?; **où peut-il ~ être passé?** where on earth can he have got to?

3 (*conséquence, résultat*): **si ~ que** with the result that; **on verra ~** we'll see; **faire ~ de** ... to be right to ...

♦ *excl* right!, OK!, fine!; **eh ~!** well!; **(c'est)** **~ fait!** it serves you (*ou* him *etc*) right!; **~ sûr!, ~ entendu!** certainly!, of course!

♦ *adj inv* **1** (*en bonne forme, à l'aise*): **je me sens ~, je suis ~** I feel fine; **je ne me sens pas ~, je ne suis pas ~** I don't feel well; **on est ~ dans ce fauteuil** this chair is very comfortable

2 (*joli, beau*) good-looking; **tu es ~ dans cette robe** you look good in that dress

3 (*satisfaisant*) good; **elle est ~, cette maison/secrétaire** it's a good house/she's a good secretary; **c'est très ~ (comme ça)** it's fine (like that); **ce n'est pas si ~ que ça** it's not as good *ou* great as all that; **c'est ~?** is that all right?

4 (*moralement*) right; (: *personne*) good, nice; (*respectable*) respectable; **ce n'est pas ~ de** ... it's not right to ...; **elle est ~, cette femme** she's a good woman, she's a good sort; **des gens ~** respectable people

5 (*en bons termes*): **être ~ avec qn** to be on good terms with sb.

bien-aimé, e [bjɛ̃neme] *adj, nm/f* beloved.
bien-être [bjɛ̃nɛtʀ(ə)] *nm* well-being.
bienfaisance [bjɛ̃fəzɑ̃s] *nf* charity.
bienfaisant, e [bjɛ̃fəzɑ̃, -ɑ̃t] *adj* (*chose*) beneficial.
bienfait [bjɛ̃fɛ] *nm* act of generosity, benefaction; (*de la science etc*) benefit.
bienfaiteur, trice [bjɛ̃fɛtœʀ, -tʀis] *nm/f* benefactor/benefactress.
bien-fondé [bjɛ̃fɔ̃de] *nm* soundness.
bien-fonds [bjɛ̃fɔ̃] *nm* property.
bienheureux, euse [bjɛ̃nœʀø, -øz] *adj* happy; (*REL*) blessed, blest.
biennal, e, aux [bjenal, -o] *adj* biennial.
bien-pensant, e [bjɛ̃pɑ̃sɑ̃, -ɑ̃t] *adj* right-thinking ♦ *nm/f*: **les ~s** right-minded people.
bien que [bjɛ̃k(ə)] *conj* although.
bienséance [bjɛ̃seɑ̃s] *nf* propriety, decorum *no pl*; **les ~s** (*convenances*) the proprieties.
bienséant, e [bjɛ̃seɑ̃, -ɑ̃t] *adj* proper, seemly.
bientôt [bjɛ̃to] *adv* soon; **à ~** see you soon.
bienveillance [bjɛ̃vɛjɑ̃s] *nf* kindness.
bienveillant, e [bjɛ̃vɛjɑ̃, -ɑ̃t] *adj* kindly.
bienvenu, e [bjɛ̃vny] *adj* welcome ♦ *nm/f*: **être le ~/la ~e** to be welcome ♦ *nf*: **souhaiter la ~e à** to welcome; **~e à** welcome to.

bière [bjɛʀ] *nf* (*boisson*) beer; (*cercueil*) bier; **~ blonde** lager; **~ brune** brown ale; **~ (à la) pression** draught beer.
biffer [bife] *vt* to cross out.
bifteck [biftɛk] *nm* steak.
bifurcation [bifyʀkɑsjɔ̃] *nf* fork (*in road*); (*fig*) new direction.
bifurquer [bifyʀke] *vi* (*route*) to fork; (*véhicule*) to turn off.
bigame [bigam] *adj* bigamous.
bigamie [bigami] *nf* bigamy.
bigarré, e [bigaʀe] *adj* multicoloured (*BRIT*), multicolored (*US*); (*disparate*) motley.
bigarreau, x [bigaʀo] *nm* type of cherry.
bigleux, euse [biglø, -øz] *adj* (*fam: qui louche*) cross-eyed; (: *qui voit mal*) short-sighted; **il est complètement ~** he's as blind as a bat.
bigorneau, x [bigɔʀno] *nm* winkle.
bigot, e [bigo, -ɔt] (*péj*) *adj* bigoted ♦ *nm/f* bigot.
bigoterie [bigɔtʀi] *nf* bigotry.
bigoudi [bigudi] *nm* curler.
bigrement [bigʀəmɑ̃] *adv* (*fam*) fantastically.
bijou, x [biʒu] *nm* jewel.
bijouterie [biʒutʀi] *nf* (*magasin*) jeweller's (shop) (*BRIT*), jewelry store (*US*); (*bijoux*) jewellery, jewelry.
bijoutier, ière [biʒutje, -jɛʀ] *nm/f* jeweller (*BRIT*), jeweler (*US*).
bikini [bikini] *nm* bikini.
bilan [bilɑ̃] *nm* (*COMM*) balance sheet(s); (*annuel*) end of year statement; (*fig*) (net) outcome; (: *de victimes*) toll; **faire le ~ de** to assess; to review; **déposer son ~** to file a bankruptcy statement; **~ de santé** (*MÉD*) checkup; **~ social** *statement of a firm's policies towards its employees.*
bilatéral, e, aux [bilateʀal, -o] *adj* bilateral.
bilboquet [bilbɔkɛ] *nm* (*jouet*) cup-and-ball game.
bile [bil] *nf* bile; **se faire de la ~** (*fam*) to worry o.s. sick.
biliaire [biljɛʀ] *adj* biliary.
bilieux, euse [biljø, -øz] *adj* bilious; (*fig: colérique*) testy.
bilingue [bilɛ̃g] *adj* bilingual.
bilinguisme [bilɛ̃gɥism(ə)] *nm* bilingualism.
billard [bijaʀ] *nm* billiards *sg*; (*table*) billiard table; **c'est du ~** (*fam*) it's a cinch; **passer sur le ~** (*fam*) to have an (*ou* one's) operation; **~ électrique** pinball.
bille [bij] *nf* ball; (*du jeu de billes*) marble; (*de bois*) log; **jouer aux ~s** to play marbles.
billet [bijɛ] *nm* (*aussi:* **~ de banque**) (bank)note; (*de cinéma, de bus etc*) ticket; (*courte lettre*) note; **~ à ordre** *ou* **de commerce** (*COMM*) promissory note, IOU; **~ d'avion/de train** plane/train ticket; **~ circulaire** round-trip ticket; **~ doux** love letter; **~ de faveur** complimentary ticket; **~ de loterie** lottery ticket; **~ de quai** platform ticket.
billetterie [bijɛtʀi] *nf* ticket office; (*distribu-*

teur) ticket dispenser; (BANQUE) cash dispenser.

billion [biljɔ̃] nm billion (BRIT), trillion (US).

billot [bijo] nm block.

BIMA sigle m = Bulletin d'information du ministère de l'agriculture.

bimbeloterie [bɛ̃blɔtʀi] nf (objets) fancy goods.

bimensuel, le [bimɑ̃sɥɛl] adj bimonthly, twice-monthly.

bimestriel, le [bimɛstʀijɛl] adj bimonthly, two-monthly.

bimoteur [bimɔtœʀ] adj twin-engined.

binaire [binɛʀ] adj binary.

biner [bine] vt to hoe.

binette [binɛt] nf (outil) hoe.

binoclard, e [binɔklaʀ, -aʀd(ə)] (fam) adj specky ♦ nm/f four-eyes.

binocle [binɔkl(ə)] nm pince-nez.

binoculaire [binɔkylɛʀ] adj binocular.

binôme [binom] nm binomial.

bio... [bjo] préfixe bio....

biochimie [bjoʃimi] nf biochemistry.

biochimique [bjoʃimik] adj biochemical.

biochimiste [bjoʃimist(ə)] nm/f biochemist.

biodégradable [bjodegʀadabl(ə)] adj biodegradable.

biodiversité [bjodivɛʀsite] nf biodiversity.

bioéthique [bjoetik] nf bioethics sg.

biographe [bjɔgʀaf] nm/f biographer.

biographie [bjɔgʀafi] nf biography.

biographique [bjɔgʀafik] adj biographical.

biologie [bjɔlɔʒi] nf biology.

biologique [bjɔlɔʒik] adj biological.

biologiste [bjɔlɔʒist(ə)] nm/f biologist.

biomasse [bjomas] nf biomass.

biopsie [bjɔpsi] nf (MÉD) biopsy.

biosphère [bjosfɛʀ] nf biosphere.

biotope [bjɔtɔp] nm biotope.

bipartisme [bipaʀtism(ə)] nm two-party system.

bipartite [bipaʀtit] adj (POL) two-party, bipartisan.

bipède [bipɛd] nm biped, two-footed creature.

biphasé, e [bifaze] adj (ÉLEC) two-phase.

biplace [biplas] adj, nm (avion) two-seater.

biplan [biplɑ̃] nm biplane.

bique [bik] nf nanny goat; (péj) old hag.

biquet, te [bikɛ, -ɛt] nm/f: **mon ~** (fam) my lamb.

BIRD [biʀd] sigle f (= Banque internationale pour la reconstruction et le développement) IBRD.

biréacteur [biʀeaktœʀ] nm twin-engined jet.

birman, e [biʀmɑ̃, -an] adj Burmese.

Birmanie [biʀmani] nf: **la ~** Burma.

bis, e [bi, biz] adj (couleur) greyish brown ♦ adv [bis]: **12 ~ 12a** ou A ♦ excl, nm [bis] encore ♦ nf (baiser) kiss; (vent) North wind.

bisaïeul, e [bizajœl] nm/f great-grandfather/great-grandmother.

bisannuel, le [bizanɥɛl] adj biennial.

bisbille [bisbij] nf: **être en ~ avec qn** to be at loggerheads with sb.

Biscaye [biskɛ] nf: **le golfe de ~** the Bay of Biscay.

biscornu, e [biskɔʀny] adj crooked; (bizarre) weird(-looking).

biscotte [biskɔt] nf (breakfast) rusk.

biscuit [biskɥi] nm biscuit (BRIT), cookie (US); (gateau) sponge cake; **~ à la cuiller** sponge finger.

biscuiterie [biskɥitʀi] nf biscuit manufacturing.

bise [biz] adj f, nf voir **bis**.

biseau, x [bizo] nm bevelled edge; **en ~** bevelled.

biseauter [bizote] vt to bevel.

bisexué, e [bisɛksɥe] adj bisexual.

bisexuel, le [bisɛksɥɛl] adj, nm/f bisexual.

bismuth [bismyt] nm bismuth.

bison [bizɔ̃] nm bison.

bisou [bizu] nm (fam) kiss.

bisque [bisk(ə)] nf: **~ d'écrevisses** shrimp bisque.

bissectrice [bisɛktʀis] nf bisector.

bisser [bise] vt (faire rejouer: artiste, chanson) to encore; (rejouer: morceau) to give an encore of.

bissextile [bisɛkstil] adj: **année ~** leap year.

bistouri [bisturi] nm lancet.

bistre [bistʀ(ə)] adj (couleur) bistre; (peau, teint) tanned.

bistro(t) [bistʀo] nm bistro, café.

BIT sigle m (= Bureau international du travail) ILO.

bit [bit] nm (INFORM) bit.

biterrois, e [bitɛʀwa, -waz] adj of ou from Béziers.

bitte [bit] nf: **~ d'amarrage** bollard (NAUT).

bitume [bitym] nm asphalt.

bitumer [bityme] vt to asphalt.

bivalent, e [bivalɑ̃, -ɑ̃t] adj bivalent.

bivouac [bivwak] nm bivouac.

bizarre [bizaʀ] adj strange, odd.

bizarrement [bizaʀmɑ̃] adv strangely, oddly.

bizarrerie [bizaʀʀi] nf strangeness, oddness.

blackbouler [blakbule] vt (à une élection) to blackball.

blafard, e [blafaʀ, -aʀd(ə)] adj wan.

blague [blag] nf (propos) joke; (farce) trick; **sans ~!** no kidding!; **~ à tabac** tobacco pouch.

blaguer [blage] vi to joke ♦ vt to tease.

blagueur, euse [blagœʀ, -øz] adj teasing ♦ nm/f joker.

blair [blɛʀ] nm (fam) conk.

blaireau, x [blɛʀo] nm (ZOOL) badger; (brosse) shaving brush.

blairer [blɛʀe] vt: **je ne peux pas le ~** I can't bear ou stand him.

blâmable [blɑmabl(ə)] adj blameworthy.

blâme [blɑm] nm blame; (sanction) reprimand.

blâmer [blɑme] vt (réprouver) to blame; (réprimander) to reprimand.

blanc, blanche [blɑ̃, blɑ̃ʃ] *adj* white; (*non imprimé*) blank; (*innocent*) pure ♦ *nm/f* white, white man/woman ♦ *nm* (*couleur*) white; (*linge*): **le ~** whites *pl*; (*espace non écrit*) blank; (*aussi*: **~ d'œuf**) (egg-)white; (*aussi*: **~ de poulet**) breast, white meat; (*aussi*: **vin ~**) white wine ♦ *nf* (*MUS*) minim (*BRIT*), halfnote (*US*); (*fam*: *drogue*) smack; **d'une voix blanche** in a toneless voice; **aux cheveux ~s** white-haired; **le ~ de l'œil** the white of the eye; **laisser en ~** to leave blank; **chèque en ~** blank cheque; **à ~** *adv* (*chauffer*) white-hot; (*tirer, charger*) with blanks; **saigner à ~** to bleed white; **~ cassé** off-white.

blanc-bec, *pl* **blancs-becs** [blɑ̃bɛk] *nm* greenhorn.

blanchâtre [blɑ̃ʃɑtʀ(ə)] *adj* (*teint, lumière*) whitish.

blancheur [blɑ̃ʃœʀ] *nf* whiteness.

blanchir [blɑ̃ʃiʀ] *vt* (*gén*) to whiten; (*linge, fig*: *argent*) to launder; (*CULIN*) to blanch; (*fig*: *disculper*) to clear ♦ *vi* to grow white; (*cheveux*) to go white; **blanchi à la chaux** whitewashed.

blanchissage [blɑ̃ʃisaʒ] *nm* (*du linge*) laundering.

blanchisserie [blɑ̃ʃisʀi] *nf* laundry.

blanchisseur, euse [blɑ̃ʃisœʀ, -øz] *nm/f* launderer.

blanc-seing, *pl* **blancs-seings** [blɑ̃sɛ̃] *nm* signed blank paper.

blanquette [blɑ̃kɛt] *nf* (*CULIN*): **~ de veau** veal in a white sauce, blanquette de veau.

blasé, e [blaze] *adj* blasé.

blaser [blaze] *vt* to make blasé.

blason [blazɔ̃] *nm* coat of arms.

blasphémateur, trice [blasfematœʀ, -tʀis] *nm/f* blasphemer.

blasphématoire [blasfematwaʀ] *adj* blasphemous.

blasphème [blasfɛm] *nm* blasphemy.

blasphémer [blasfeme] *vi* to blaspheme ♦ *vt* to blaspheme against.

blatte [blat] *nf* cockroach.

blazer [blazɛʀ] *nm* blazer.

blé [ble] *nm* wheat; **~ en herbe** wheat on the ear; **~ noir** buckwheat.

bled [blɛd] *nm* (*péj*) hole; (*en Afrique du Nord*): **le ~** the interior.

blême [blɛm] *adj* pale.

blêmir [blemiʀ] *vi* (*personne*) to (turn) pale; (*lueur*) to grow pale.

blennorragie [blenɔʀaʒi] *nf* blennorrhoea.

blessant, e [blɛsɑ̃, -ɑ̃t] *adj* hurtful.

blessé, e [blese] *adj* injured ♦ *nm/f* injured person, casualty; **un ~ grave, un grand ~** a seriously injured *ou* wounded person.

blesser [blese] *vt* to injure; (*délibérément*: *MIL etc*) to wound; (*suj*: *souliers etc, offenser*) to hurt; **se ~** to injure o.s.; **se ~ au pied** *etc* to injure one's foot *etc*.

blessure [blesyʀ] *nf* injury; wound.

blet, te [blɛ, blɛt] *adj* overripe.

blette [blɛt] *nf* = **bette**.

bleu, e [blø] *adj* blue; (*bifteck*) very rare ♦ *nm* (*couleur*) blue; (*novice*) greenhorn; (*contusion*) bruise; (*vêtement*: *aussi*: **~s**) overalls *pl* (*BRIT*), coveralls *pl* (*US*); **avoir une peur ~e** to be scared stiff; **zone ~e** ≈ restricted parking area; **fromage ~** blue cheese; **au ~** (*CULIN*) au bleu; (*de lessive*) ≈ blue bag; **~ de méthylène** (*MÉD*) methylene blue; **~ marine/nuit/roi** navy/midnight/royal blue.

bleuâtre [bløɑtʀ(ə)] *adj* (*fumée etc*) bluish, blueish.

bleuet [bløɛ] *nm* cornflower.

bleuir [bløiʀ] *vt, vi* to turn blue.

bleuté, e [bløte] *adj* blue-shaded.

blindage [blɛ̃daʒ] *nm* armo(u)r-plating.

blindé, e [blɛ̃de] *adj* armoured (*BRIT*), armored (*US*); (*fig*) hardened ♦ *nm* armoured *ou* armored car; (*char*) tank.

blinder [blɛ̃de] *vt* to armour (*BRIT*), armor (*US*); (*fig*) to harden.

blizzard [blizaʀ] *nm* blizzard.

bloc [blɔk] *nm* (*de pierre etc, INFORM*) block; (*de papier à lettres*) pad; (*ensemble*) group, block; **serré à ~** tightened right down; **en ~** as a whole; wholesale; **faire ~** to unite; **~ opératoire** operating *ou* theatre block; **~ sanitaire** toilet block; **~ sténo** shorthand notebook.

blocage [blɔkaʒ] *nm* (*voir bloquer*) blocking; jamming; freezing; (*PSYCH*) hang-up.

bloc-cuisine, *pl* **blocs-cuisines** [blɔkkɥizin] *nm* kitchen unit.

bloc-cylindres, *pl* **blocs-cylindres** [blɔksilɛ̃dʀ(ə)] *nm* cylinder block.

bloc-évier, *pl* **blocs-éviers** [blɔkevje] *nm* sink unit.

bloc-moteur, *pl* **blocs-moteurs** [blɔkmɔtœʀ] *nm* engine block.

bloc-notes, *pl* **blocs-notes** [blɔknɔt] *nm* note pad.

blocus [blɔkys] *nm* blockade.

blond, e [blɔ̃, -ɔ̃d] *adj* fair; (*plus clair*) blond; (*sable, blés*) golden ♦ *nm/f* fair-haired *ou* blond man/woman; **~ cendré** ash blond.

blondeur [blɔ̃dœʀ] *nf* fairness; blondness.

blondin, e [blɔ̃dɛ̃, -in] *nm/f* fair-haired *ou* blond child *ou* young person.

blondinet, te [blɔ̃dinɛ, -ɛt] *nm/f* blondy.

blondir [blɔ̃diʀ] *vi* (*personne, cheveux*) to go fair *ou* blond.

bloquer [blɔke] *vt* (*passage*) to block; (*pièce mobile*) to jam; (*crédits, compte*) to freeze; (*personne, négociations etc*) to hold up; (*regrouper*) to group; **~ les freins** to jam on the brakes.

blottir [blɔtiʀ]: **se ~** *vi* to huddle up.

blousant, e [bluzɑ̃, ɑ̃t] *adj* blousing out.

blouse [bluz] *nf* overall.

blouser [bluze] *vi* to blouse out.

blouson [bluzɔ̃] *nm* blouson (jacket); **~ noir** (*fig*) ≈ rocker.

blue-jean(s) [bludʒin(s)] *nm* jeans.
blues [bluz] *nm* blues *pl*.
bluet [blyɛ] *nm* = **bleuet**.
bluff [blœf] *nm* bluff.
bluffer [blœfe] *vi*, *vt* to bluff.
BN *sigle f* = Bibliothèque nationale.
BNP *sigle f* = Banque nationale de Paris.
boa [bɔa] *nm* (ZOOL): ~ **(constricteur)** boa (constrictor); (*tour de cou*) (*feather ou fur*) boa.
bobard [bɔbaʀ] *nm* (*fam*) tall story.
bobèche [bɔbɛʃ] *nf* candle-ring.
bobine [bɔbin] *nf* (*de fil*) reel; (*de machine à coudre*) spool; (*de machine à écrire*) ribbon; (ÉLEC) coil; ~ **(d'allumage)** (AUTO) coil; ~ **de pellicule** (PHOTO) roll of film.
bobo [bɔbo] *nm* (*aussi fig*) sore spot.
bob(sleigh) [bɔb(slɛg)] *nm* bob(sleigh).
bocage [bɔkaʒ] *nm* (GÉO) bocage, *farmland criss-crossed by hedges and trees*; (*bois*) grove, copse (BRIT).
bocal, aux [bɔkal, -o] *nm* jar.
bock [bɔk] *nm* (*beer*) glass; (*contenu*) glass of beer.
bœuf [bœf, *pl* bø] *nm* ox (*pl* oxen), steer; (CULIN) beef; (MUS: *fam*) jam session.
bof [bɔf] *excl* (*fam*: *indifférence*) don't care!; (: *pas terrible*) nothing special.
Bogota [bɔgɔta] *n* Bogotá.
bogue [bɔg] *nf* (BOT) husk ♦ *nm* (ORDIN) bug; ~ **de l'an 2000** millennium bug.
Bohème [bɔɛm] *nf*: **la** ~ Bohemia.
bohème [bɔɛm] *adj* happy-go-lucky, unconventional.
bohémien, ne [bɔemjɛ̃, -ɛn] *adj* Bohemian ♦ *nm/f* gipsy.
boire [bwaʀ] *vt* to drink; (*s'imprégner de*) to soak up; ~ **un coup** to have a drink.
bois [bwa] *vb voir* **boire** ♦ *nm* wood; (ZOOL) antler; (MUS): **les** ~ the woodwind; **de** ~, **en** ~ wooden; ~ **vert** green wood; ~ **mort** deadwood; ~ **de lit** bedstead.
boisé, e [bwaze] *adj* woody, wooded.
boiser [bwaze] *vt* (*galerie de mine*) to timber; (*chambre*) to panel; (*terrain*) to plant with trees.
boiseries [bwazʀi] *nfpl* panelling *sg*.
boisson [bwasɔ̃] *nf* drink; **pris de** ~ drunk, intoxicated; ~**s alcoolisées** alcoholic beverages *ou* drinks; ~**s non alcoolisées** soft drinks.
boit [bwa] *vb voir* **boire**.
boîte [bwat] *nf* box; (*fam*: *entreprise*) firm, company; **aliments en** ~ canned *ou* tinned (BRIT) foods; ~ **de sardines/petits pois** can *ou* tin (BRIT) of sardines/peas; **mettre qn en** ~ (*fam*) to have a laugh at sb's expense; ~ **d'allumettes** box of matches; (*vide*) matchbox; ~ **de conserves** can *ou* tin (BRIT) (of food); ~ **crânienne** cranium; ~ **à gants** glove compartment; ~ **aux lettres** letter box, mailbox (US); (INFORM) mailbox; ~ **à musique** musical box; ~ **noire** (AVIAT) black box;

~ **de nuit** night club; ~ **à ordures** dustbin (BRIT), trash can (US); ~ **postale (BP)** PO box; ~ **de vitesses** gear box; ~ **vocale** (*dispositif*) voice mail.
boiter [bwate] *vi* to limp; (*fig*) to wobble; (*raisonnement*) to be shaky.
boiteux, euse [bwatø, -øz] *adj* lame; wobbly; shaky.
boîtier [bwatje] *nm* case; (*d'appareil-photo*) body; ~ **de montre** watch case.
boitiller [bwatije] *vi* to limp slightly, have a slight limp.
boive [bwav] *etc vb voir* **boire**.
bol [bɔl] *nm* bowl; (*contenu*): **un** ~ **de café** *etc* a bowl of coffee *etc*; **un** ~ **d'air** a breath of fresh air; **en avoir ras le** ~ (*fam*) to have had a bellyful.
bolée [bɔle] *nf* bowlful.
boléro [bɔleʀo] *nm* bolero.
bolet [bɔlɛ] *nm* boletus (mushroom).
bolide [bɔlid] *nm* racing car; **comme un** ~ like a rocket.
Bolivie [bɔlivi] *nf*: **la** ~ Bolivia.
bolivien, ne [bɔlivjɛ̃, -ɛn] *adj* Bolivian ♦ *nm/f*: **B~, ne** Bolivian.
bolognais, e [bɔlɔɲɛ, -ɛz] *adj* Bolognese.
Bologne [bɔlɔɲ] *n* Bologna.
bombardement [bɔ̃baʀdəmũ] *nm* bombing.
bombarder [bɔ̃baʀde] *vt* to bomb; ~ **qn de** (*cailloux, lettres*) to bombard sb with; ~ **qn directeur** to thrust sb into the director's seat.
bombardier [bɔ̃baʀdje] *nm* (*avion*) bomber; (*aviateur*) bombardier.
bombe [bɔ̃b] *nf* bomb; (*atomiseur*) (aerosol) spray; (ÉQUITATION) riding cap; **faire la** ~ (*fam*) to go on a binge; ~ **atomique** atomic bomb; ~ **à retardement** time bomb.
bombé, e [bɔ̃be] *adj* rounded; (*mur*) bulging; (*front*) domed; (*route*) steeply cambered.
bomber [bɔ̃be] *vi* to bulge; (*route*) to camber ♦ *vt*: ~ **le torse** to swell out one's chest.

═══════════════════════ *MOT-CLÉ*

bon, bonne [bɔ̃, bɔn] *adj* **1** (*agréable, satisfaisant*) good; **un** ~ **repas/restaurant** a good meal/restaurant; **être** ~ **en maths** to be good at maths
2 (*charitable*): **être** ~ **(envers)** to be good (to), to be kind (to); **vous êtes trop** ~ you're too kind
3 (*correct*) right; **le** ~ **numéro/moment** the right number/moment
4 (*souhaits*): ~ **anniversaire** happy birthday; ~ **voyage** have a good trip; **bonne chance** good luck; **bonne année** happy New Year; **bonne nuit** good night
5 (*approprié*): ~ **à/pour** fit to/for; ~ **à jeter** fit for the bin; **c'est** ~ **à savoir** that's useful to know; **à quoi** ~ (...)? what's the point *ou* use (of ...)?
6 (*intensif*): **ça m'a pris 2 bonnes heures** it

took me a good 2 hours; **un ~ nombre de** a good number of 7: **~ enfant** *adj inv* accommodating, easygoing; **bonne femme** (*péj*) woman; **de bonne heure** early; **~ marché** cheap; **~ mot** witticism; **pour faire ~ poids** ... to make up for it ...; **~ sens** common sense; **~ vivant** jovial chap; **bonnes œuvres** charitable works, charities; **bonne sœur** nun ♦ *nm* **1** (*billet*) voucher; (*aussi*: **~ cadeau**) gift voucher; **~ de caisse** cash voucher; **~ d'essence** petrol coupon; **~ à tirer** pass for press; **~ du Trésor** Treasury bond **2**: **avoir du ~** to have its good points; **il y a du ~ dans ce qu'il dit** there's some sense in what he says; **pour de ~** for good ♦ *nm/f*: **un ~ à rien** a good-for-nothing ♦ *adv*: **il fait ~** it's *ou* the weather is fine; **sentir ~** to smell good; **tenir ~** to stand firm; **juger ~ de faire** ... to think fit to do ... ♦ *excl* right!, good!; **ah ~?** really?; **~, je reste** right, I'll stay; *voir aussi* **bonne**.

bonasse [bɔnas] *adj* soft, meek.
bonbon [bɔ̃bɔ̃] *nm* (boiled) sweet.
bonbonne [bɔ̃bɔn] *nf* demijohn; carboy.
bonbonnière [bɔ̃bɔnjɛʀ] *nf* sweet (*BRIT*) *ou* candy (*US*) box.
bond [bɔ̃] *nm* leap; (*d'une balle*) rebound, ricochet; **faire un ~** to leap in the air; **d'un seul ~** in one bound, with one leap; **~ en avant** (*fig: progrès*) leap forward.
bonde [bɔ̃d] *nf* (*d'évier etc*) plug; (: *trou*) plughole; (*de tonneau*) bung; bunghole.
bondé, e [bɔ̃de] *adj* packed (full).
bondieuserie [bɔ̃djøzʀi] *nf* (*péj: objet*) religious knick-knack.
bondir [bɔ̃diʀ] *vi* to leap; **~ de joie** (*fig*) to jump for joy; **~ de colère** (*fig*) to be hopping mad.
bonheur [bɔnœʀ] *nm* happiness; **avoir le ~ de** to have the good fortune to; **porter ~ (à qn)** to bring (sb) luck; **au petit ~** haphazardly; **par ~** fortunately.
bonhomie [bɔnɔmi] *nf* goodnaturedness.
bonhomme [bɔnɔm], *pl* **bonshommes** [bɔ̃zɔm] *nm* fellow ♦ *adj* good-natured; **un vieux ~** an old chap; **aller son ~ de chemin** to carry on in one's own sweet way; **~ de neige** snowman.
boni [bɔni] *nm* profit.
bonification [bɔnifikasjɔ̃] *nf* bonus.
bonifier [bɔnifje] *vt*, **se ~** *vi* to improve.
boniment [bɔnimɑ̃] *nm* patter *no pl*.
bonjour [bɔ̃ʒuʀ] *excl, nm* hello; (*selon l'heure*) good morning (*ou* afternoon); **donner** *ou* **souhaiter le ~ à qn** to bid sb good morning *ou* afternoon.
Bonn [bɔn] *n* Bonn.
bonne [bɔn] *adj f voir* **bon** ♦ *nf* (*domestique*) maid; **~ à tout faire** general help; **~ d'enfant** nanny.

bonne-maman, *pl* **bonnes-mamans** [bɔnmamɑ̃] granny, grandma, gran.
bonnement [bɔnmɑ̃] *adv*: **tout ~** quite simply.
bonnet [bɔnɛ] *nm* bonnet, hat; (*de soutien-gorge*) cup; **~ d'âne** dunce's cap; **~ de bain** bathing cap; **~ de nuit** nightcap.
bonneterie [bɔnɛtʀi] *nf* hosiery.
bon-papa, *pl* **bons-papas** [bɔ̃papa] *nm* grandpa, grandad.
bonsoir [bɔ̃swaʀ] *excl* good evening.
bonté [bɔ̃te] *nf* kindness *no pl*; **avoir la ~ de** to be kind *ou* good enough to.
bonus [bɔnys] *nm* (*assurances*) no-claims bonus.
bonze [bɔ̃z] *nm* (*REL*) bonze.
boomerang [bumʀɑ̃g] *nm* boomerang.
boots [buts] *nfpl* boots.
borborygme [bɔʀbɔʀigm(ə)] *nm* rumbling noise.
bord [bɔʀ] *nm* (*de table, verre, falaise*) edge; (*de rivière, lac*) bank; (*de route*) side; (*de vêtement*) edge, border; (*de chapeau*) brim; (*monter*) **à ~** (to go) on board; **jeter par-dessus ~** to throw overboard; **le commandant de ~/les hommes du ~** the ship's master/crew; **du même ~** (*fig*) of the same opinion; **au ~ de la mer/route** at the seaside/roadside; **être au ~ des larmes** to be on the verge of tears; **virer de ~** (*NAVIG*) to tack; **sur les ~s** (*fig*) slightly; **de tous ~s** on all sides; **~ du trottoir** kerb (*BRIT*), curb (*US*).
bordage [bɔʀdaʒ] *nm* (*NAVIG*) planking *no pl*; plating *no pl*.
bordeaux [bɔʀdo] *nm* Bordeaux ♦ *adj inv* maroon.
bordée [bɔʀde] *nf* broadside; **une ~ d'injures** a volley of abuse; **tirer une ~** to go on the town.
bordel [bɔʀdɛl] *nm* brothel; (*fam!*) bloody (*BRIT*) *ou* goddamn (*US*) mess (!) ♦ *excl* hell!
bordelais, e [bɔʀdəlɛ, -ɛz] *adj* of *ou* from Bordeaux.
border [bɔʀde] *vt* (*être le long de*) to border, line; (*garnir*): **~ qch de** to line sth with; to trim sth with; (*qn dans son lit*) to tuck up.
bordereau, x [bɔʀdəʀo] *nm* docket, slip.
bordure [bɔʀdyʀ] *nf* border; (*sur un vêtement*) trim(ming), border; **en ~ de** on the edge of.
boréal, e, aux [bɔʀeal, -o] *adj* boreal, northern.
borgne [bɔʀɲ(ə)] *adj* one-eyed; **hôtel ~** shady hotel; **fenêtre ~** obstructed window.
bornage [bɔʀnaʒ] *nm* (*d'un terrain*) demarcation.
borne [bɔʀn(ə)] *nf* boundary stone; (*aussi*: **~ kilométrique**) kilometre-marker, ≈ milestone; **~s** *nfpl* (*fig*) limits; **dépasser les ~s** to go too far; **sans ~s** boundless.
borné, e [bɔʀne] *adj* narrow; (*obtus*) narrow-minded.
Bornéo [bɔʀneo] *nm*: **le ~** Borneo.
borner [bɔʀne] *vt* (*délimiter*) to limit; (*limiter*)

to confine; **se ~ à faire** to content o.s. with doing; to limit o.s. to doing.

bosniaque [bɔznjak] *adj* Bosnian ♦ *nm/f*: **B~** Bosnian.

Bosnie [bɔsni] *nf* Bosnia.

bosnien, ne [bɔznjɛ̃, -ɛn] *adj* Bosnian ♦ *nm/f*: **B~, ne** Bosnian.

Bosphore [bɔsfɔR] *nm*: **le ~** the Bosphorus.

bosquet [bɔskɛ] *nm* copse (*BRIT*), grove.

bosse [bɔs] *nf* (*de terrain etc*) bump; (*enflure*) lump; (*du bossu, du chameau*) hump; **avoir la ~ des maths** *etc* to have a gift for maths *etc*; **il a roulé sa ~** he's been around.

bosseler [bɔsle] *vt* (*ouvrer*) to emboss; (*abîmer*) to dent.

bosser [bɔse] *vi* (*fam*) to work; (*: dur*) to slog (hard) (*BRIT*), slave (away).

bosseur, euse [bɔsœR, -øz] *nm/f* (hard) worker, slogger (*BRIT*).

bossu, e [bɔsy] *nm/f* hunchback.

bot [bo] *adj m*: **pied ~** club foot.

botanique [bɔtanik] *nf* botany ♦ *adj* botanic(al).

botaniste [bɔtanist(ə)] *nm/f* botanist.

Botswana [bɔtswana] *nm*: **le ~** Botswana.

botte [bɔt] *nf* (*soulier*) (high) boot; (*ESCRIME*) thrust; (*gerbe*): **~ de paille** bundle of straw; **~ de radis/d'asperges** bunch of radishes/asparagus; **~s de caoutchouc** wellington boots.

botter [bɔte] *vt* to put boots on; (*donner un coup de pied à*) to kick; (*fam*): **ça me botte** I fancy that.

bottier [bɔtje] *nm* bootmaker.

bottillon [bɔtijɔ̃] *nm* bootee.

bottin [bɔtɛ̃] *nm* ® directory.

bottine [bɔtin] *nf* ankle boot.

botulisme [bɔtylism(ə)] *nm* botulism.

bouc [buk] *nm* goat; (*barbe*) goatee; **~ émissaire** scapegoat.

boucan [bukɑ̃] *nm* din, racket.

bouche [buʃ] *nf* mouth; **une ~ à nourrir** a mouth to feed; **les ~s inutiles** the non-productive members of the population; **faire du ~ à ~ à qn** to give sb the kiss of life (*BRIT*), give sb mouth-to-mouth resuscitation; **de ~ à oreille** confidentially; **pour la bonne ~** (*pour la fin*) till last; **faire venir l'eau à la ~** to make one's mouth water; **~ cousue!** mum's the word!; **~ d'aération** air vent; **~ de chaleur** hot air vent; **~ d'égout** manhole; **~ d'incendie** fire hydrant; **~ de métro** métro entrance.

bouché, e [buʃe] *adj* (*flacon etc*) stoppered; (*temps, ciel*) overcast; (*carrière*) blocked; (*péj: personne*) thick; (*trompette*) muted; **avoir le nez ~** to have a blocked(-up) nose.

bouchée [buʃe] *nf* mouthful; **ne faire qu'une ~ de** (*fig*) to make short work of; **pour une ~ de pain** (*fig*) for next to nothing; **~s à la reine** chicken vol-au-vents.

boucher [buʃe] *nm* butcher ♦ *vt* (*pour colmater*) to stop up; to fill up; (*obstruer*) to block (up); **se ~** (*tuyau etc*) to block up, get blocked up; **se ~ le nez** to hold one's nose.

bouchère [buʃɛR] *nf* butcher; (*femme du boucher*) butcher's wife.

boucherie [buʃRi] *nf* butcher's (shop); (*métier*) butchery; (*fig*) slaughter, butchery.

bouche-trou [buʃtRu] *nm* (*fig*) stop-gap.

bouchon [buʃɔ̃] *nm* (*en liège*) cork; (*autre matière*) stopper; (*fig: embouteillage*) holdup; (*PÊCHE*) float; **~ doseur** measuring cap.

bouchonner [buʃɔne] *vt* to rub down ♦ *vi* to form a traffic jam.

bouchot [buʃo] *nm* mussel bed.

bouclage [buklaʒ] *nm* sealing off.

boucle [bukl(ə)] *nf* (*forme, figure, aussi INFORM*) loop; (*objet*) buckle; **~ (de cheveux)** curl; **~ d'oreilles** earring.

bouclé, e [bukle] *adj* curly; (*tapis*) uncut.

boucler [bukle] *vt* (*fermer: ceinture etc*) to fasten; (*: magasin*) to shut; (*terminer*) to finish off; (*: circuit*) to complete; (*budget*) to balance; (*enfermer*) to shut away; (*: condamné*) to lock up; (*: quartier*) to seal off ♦ *vi* to curl; **faire ~** (*cheveux*) to curl; **~ la boucle** (*AVIAT*) to loop the loop.

bouclette [buklɛt] *nf* small curl.

bouclier [buklije] *nm* shield.

bouddha [buda] *nm* Buddha.

bouddhisme [budism(ə)] *nm* Buddhism.

bouddhiste [budist(ə)] *nm/f* Buddhist.

bouder [bude] *vi* to sulk ♦ *vt* (*chose*) to turn one's nose up at; (*personne*) to refuse to have anything to do with.

bouderie [budRi] *nf* sulking *no pl*.

boudeur, euse [budœR, -øz] *adj* sullen, sulky.

boudin [budɛ̃] *nm* (*CULIN*) black pudding; (*TECH*) roll; **~ blanc** white pudding.

boudiné, e [budine] *adj* (*doigt*) podgy; (*serré*): **~ dans** (*vêtement*) bulging out of.

boudoir [budwaR] *nm* boudoir; (*biscuit*) sponge finger.

boue [bu] *nf* mud.

bouée [bwe] *nf* buoy; (*de baigneur*) rubber ring; **~ (de sauvetage)** lifebuoy; (*fig*) lifeline.

boueux, euse [bwø, -øz] *adj* muddy ♦ *nm* (*fam*) refuse (*BRIT*) *ou* garbage (*US*) collector.

bouffant, e [bufɑ̃, -ɑ̃t] *adj* puffed out.

bouffe [buf] *nf* (*fam*) grub, food.

bouffée [bufe] *nf* puff; **~ de chaleur** (*gén*) blast of hot air; (*MÉD*) hot flush (*BRIT*) *ou* flash (*US*); **~ de fièvre/de honte** flush of fever/shame; **~ d'orgueil** fit of pride.

bouffer [bufe] *vi* (*fam*) to eat; (*COUTURE*) to puff out ♦ *vt* (*fam*) to eat.

bouffi, e [bufi] *adj* swollen.

bouffon, ne [bufɔ̃, -ɔn] *adj* farcical, comical ♦ *nm* jester.

bouge [buʒ] *nm* (*bar louche*) (low) dive; (*taudis*) hovel.

bougeoir [buʒwaR] *nm* candlestick.

bougeotte [buʒɔt] *nf*: **avoir la** ~ to have the fidgets.

bouger [buʒe] *vi* to move; (*dent etc*) to be loose; (*changer*) to alter; (*agir*) to stir ♦ *vt* to move; **se** ~ (*fam*) to move (oneself).

bougie [buʒi] *nf* candle; (*AUTO*) spark(ing) plug.

bougon, ne [bugɔ̃, -ɔn] *adj* grumpy.

bougonner [bugɔne] *vi, vt* to grumble.

bougre [bugʀ(ə)] *nm* chap; (*fam*): **ce** ~ **de** ... that confounded ....

boui-boui [bwibwi] *nm* (*fam*) greasy spoon.

bouillabaisse [bujabɛs] *nf* type of fish soup.

bouillant, e [bujɑ̃, -ɑ̃t] *adj* (*qui bout*) boiling; (*très chaud*) boiling (hot); (*fig: ardent*) hotheaded; ~ **de colère** *etc* seething with anger *etc*.

bouille [buj] *nf* (*fam*) mug.

bouilleur [bujœʀ] *nm*: ~ **de cru** (home) distiller.

bouillie [buji] *nf* gruel; (*de bébé*) cereal; **en** ~ (*fig*) crushed.

bouillir [bujiʀ] *vi* to boil ♦ *vt* (*aussi*: **faire** ~: *CULIN*) to boil; ~ **de colère** *etc* to seethe with anger *etc*.

bouilloire [bujwaʀ] *nf* kettle.

bouillon [bujɔ̃] *nm* (*CULIN*) stock *no pl*; (*bulles, écume*) bubble; ~ **de culture** culture medium.

bouillonnement [bujɔnmɑ̃] *nm* (*d'un liquide*) bubbling; (*des idées*) ferment.

bouillonner [bujɔne] *vi* to bubble; (*fig*) to bubble up; (*torrent*) to foam.

bouillotte [bujɔt] *nf* hot-water bottle.

boulanger, ère [bulɑ̃ʒe, -ɛʀ] *nm/f* baker ♦ *nf* (*femme du boulanger*) baker's wife.

boulangerie [bulɑ̃ʒʀi] *nf* bakery, baker's (shop); (*commerce*) bakery; ~ **industrielle** bakery.

boulangerie-pâtisserie, *pl* **boulangeries-pâtisseries** [bulɑ̃ʒʀipɑtisʀi] *nf* baker's and confectioner's (shop).

boule [bul] *nf* (*gén*) ball; (*pour jouer*) bowl; (*de machine à écrire*) golf ball; **roulé en** ~ curled up in a ball; **se mettre en** ~ (*fig*) to fly off the handle, blow one's top; **perdre la** ~ (*fig: fam*) to go off one's rocker; ~ **de gomme** (*bonbon*) gum(drop), pastille; ~ **de neige** snowball; **faire** ~ **de neige** (*fig*) to snowball.

bouleau, x [bulo] *nm* (silver) birch.

bouledogue [buldɔg] *nm* bulldog.

bouler [bule] *vi* (*fam*): **envoyer** ~ **qn** to send sb packing; **je me suis fait** ~ (*à un examen*) they flunked me.

boulet [bulɛ] *nm* (*aussi*: ~ **de canon**) cannonball; (*de bagnard*) ball and chain; (*charbon*) (coal) nut.

boulette [bulɛt] *nf* ball.

boulevard [bulvaʀ] *nm* boulevard.

bouleversant, e [bulvɛʀsɑ̃, -ɑ̃t] *adj* (*récit*) deeply distressing; (*nouvelle*) shattering.

bouleversé, e [bulvɛʀse] *adj* (*ému*) deeply distressed; shattered.

bouleversement [bulvɛʀsəmɑ̃] *nm* (*politique, social*) upheaval.

bouleverser [bulvɛʀse] *vt* (*émouvoir*) to overwhelm; (*causer du chagrin à*) to distress; (*pays, vie*) to disrupt; (*papiers, objets*) to turn upside down, upset.

boulier [bulje] *nm* abacus; (*de jeu*) scoring board.

boulimie [bulimi] *nf* bulimia; compulsive eating.

boulimique [bulimik] *adj* bulimic.

boulingrin [bulɛ̃gʀɛ̃] *nm* lawn.

bouliste [bulist(ə)] *nm/f* bowler.

boulocher [bulɔʃe] *vi* (*laine etc*) to develop little snarls.

boulodrome [bulɔdʀɔm] *nm* bowling pitch.

boulon [bulɔ̃] *nm* bolt.

boulonner [bulɔne] *vt* to bolt.

boulot [bulo] *nm* (*fam: travail*) work.

boulot, te [bulo, -ɔt] *adj* plump, tubby.

boum [bum] *nm* bang ♦ *nf* party.

bouquet [bukɛ] *nm* (*de fleurs*) bunch (of flowers), bouquet; (*de persil etc*) bunch; (*parfum*) bouquet; (*fig*) crowning piece; **c'est le** ~! that's the last straw!; ~ **garni** (*CULIN*) bouquet garni.

bouquetin [buktɛ̃] *nm* ibex.

bouquin [bukɛ̃] *nm* (*fam*) book.

bouquiner [bukine] *vi* (*fam*) to read.

bouquiniste [bukinist(ə)] *nm/f* bookseller.

bourbeux, euse [buʀbø, -øz] *adj* muddy.

bourbier [buʀbje] *nm* (quag)mire.

bourde [buʀd(ə)] *nf* (*erreur*) howler; (*gaffe*) blunder.

bourdon [buʀdɔ̃] *nm* bumblebee.

bourdonnement [buʀdɔnmɑ̃] *nm* buzzing *no pl*, buzz; **avoir des** ~**s d'oreilles** to have a buzzing (noise) in one's ears.

bourdonner [buʀdɔne] *vi* to buzz; (*moteur*) to hum.

bourg [buʀ] *nm* small market town (*ou* village).

bourgade [buʀgad] *nf* township.

bourgeois, e [buʀʒwa, -waz] *adj* (*péj*) ≈ (upper) middle class; bourgeois; (*maison etc*) very comfortable ♦ *nm/f* (*autrefois*) burgher.

bourgeoisie [buʀʒwazi] *nf* ≈ upper middle classes *pl*; bourgeoisie; **petite** ~ middle classes.

bourgeon [buʀʒɔ̃] *nm* bud.

bourgeonner [buʀʒɔne] *vi* to bud.

Bourgogne [buʀgɔɲ] *nf*: **la** ~ Burgundy ♦ *nm*: **b**~ burgundy (wine).

bourguignon, ne [buʀgiɲɔ̃, -ɔn] *adj* of *ou* from Burgundy, Burgundian; **bœuf** ~ bœuf bourguignon.

bourlinguer [buʀlɛ̃ge] *vi* to knock about a lot, get around a lot.

bourrade [buʀad] *nf* shove, thump.

bourrage [buʀaʒ] *nm* (*papier*) jamming; ~ **de**

crâne brainwashing; (*SCOL*) cramming.

bourrasque [buʀask(ə)] *nf* squall.

bourratif, ive [buʀatif, -iv] *adj* filling, stodgy.

bourre [buʀ] *nf* (*de coussin, matelas etc*) stuffing.

bourré, e [buʀe] *adj* (*rempli*): ~ **de** crammed full of; (*fam: ivre*) pickled, plastered.

bourreau, x [buʀo] *nm* executioner; (*fig*) torturer; ~ **de travail** workaholic, glutton for work.

bourrelé, e [buʀle] *adj*: **être** ~ **de remords** to be racked by remorse.

bourrelet [buʀlɛ] *nm* draught (*BRIT*) *ou* draft (*US*) excluder; (*de peau*) fold *ou* roll (of flesh).

bourrer [buʀe] *vt* (*pipe*) to fill; (*poêle*) to pack; (*valise*) to cram (full); ~ **de** to cram (full) with, stuff with; ~ **de coups** to hammer blows on, pummel; ~ **le crâne à qn** to pull the wool over sb's eyes; (*endoctriner*) to brainwash sb.

bourricot [buʀiko] *nm* small donkey.

bourrique [buʀik] *nf* (*âne*) ass.

bourru, e [buʀy] *adj* surly, gruff.

bourse [buʀs(ə)] *nf* (*subvention*) grant; (*porte-monnaie*) purse; **sans** ~ **délier** without spending a penny; **la B**~ the Stock Exchange; ~ **du travail** ≈ trades union council (regional headquarters).

boursicoter [buʀsikɔte] *vi* (*COMM*) to dabble on the Stock Market.

boursier, ière [buʀsje, -jɛʀ] *adj* (*COMM*) Stock Market *cpd* ♦ *nm/f* (*SCOL*) grant-holder.

boursouflé, e [buʀsufle] *adj* swollen, puffy; (*fig*) bombastic, turgid.

boursoufler [buʀsufle] *vt* to puff up, bloat; **se** ~ *vi* (*visage*) to swell *ou* puff up; (*peinture*) to blister.

boursouflure [buʀsuflyʀ] *nf* (*du visage*) swelling, puffiness; (*de la peinture*) blister; (*fig: du style*) pomposity.

bous [bu] *vb voir* **bouillir**.

bousculade [buskylad] *nf* (*hâte*) rush; (*poussée*) crush.

bousculer [buskyle] *vt* to knock over; to knock into; (*fig*) to push, rush.

bouse [buz] *nf*: ~ (**de vache**) (cow) dung *no pl* (*BRIT*), manure *no pl*.

bousiller [buzije] *vt* (*fam*) to wreck.

boussole [busɔl] *nf* compass.

bout [bu] *vb voir* **bouillir** ♦ *nm* bit; (*extrémité: d'un bâton etc*) tip; (: *d'une ficelle, table, rue, période*) end; **au** ~ **de** at the end of, after; **au** ~ **du compte** at the end of the day; **pousser qn à** ~ to push sb to the limit (of his patience); **venir à** ~ **de** to manage to finish (off) *ou* overcome; ~ **à** ~ end to end; **à tout** ~ **de champ** at every turn; **d'un** ~ **à l'autre, de** ~ **en** ~ from one end to the other; **à** ~ **portant** at point-blank range; **un** ~ **de chou** (*enfant*) a little tot; ~ **d'essai** (*CINÉ etc*) screen test; ~ **filtre** filter tip.

boutade [butad] *nf* quip, sally.

boute-en-train [butɑ̃tʀɛ̃] *nm inv* live wire (*fig*).

bouteille [butɛj] *nf* bottle; (*de gaz butane*) cylinder.

boutiquaire [butikɛʀ] *adj*: **niveau** ~ shopping level.

boutique [butik] *nf* shop (*BRIT*), store (*US*); (*de grand couturier, de mode*) boutique.

boutiquier, ière [butikje, -jɛʀ] *nm/f* shopkeeper (*BRIT*), storekeeper (*US*).

boutoir [butwaʀ] *nm*: **coup de** ~ (*choc*) thrust; (*fig: propos*) barb.

bouton [butɔ̃] *nm* (*de vêtement, électrique etc*) button; (*BOT*) bud; (*sur la peau*) spot; (*de porte*) knob; ~ **de manchette** cuff-link; ~ **d'or** buttercup.

boutonnage [butɔnaʒ] *nm* (*action*) buttoning(-up); **un manteau à double** ~ a coat with two rows of buttons.

boutonner [butɔne] *vt* to button up, do up; **se** ~ to button one's clothes up.

boutonneux, euse [butɔnø, -øz] *adj* spotty.

boutonnière [butɔnjɛʀ] *nf* buttonhole.

bouton-poussoir, *pl* **boutons-poussoirs** [butɔ̃puswaʀ] *nm* pushbutton.

bouton-pression, *pl* **boutons-pression** [butɔ̃pʀesjɔ̃] *nm* press stud, snap fastener.

bouture [butyʀ] *nf* cutting; **faire des** ~**s** to take cuttings.

bouvreuil [buvʀœj] *nm* bullfinch.

bovidé [bɔvide] *nm* bovine.

bovin, e [bɔvɛ̃, -in] *adj* bovine ♦ *nm*: ~**s** cattle.

bowling [boliŋ] *nm* (tenpin) bowling; (*salle*) bowling alley.

box [bɔks] *nm* lock-up (garage); (*de salle, dortoir*) cubicle; (*d'écurie*) loose-box; **le** ~ **des accusés** the dock.

box(-calf) [bɔks(kalf)] *nm inv* box calf.

boxe [bɔks(ə)] *nf* boxing.

boxer [bɔkse] *vi* to box ♦ *nm* [bɔksɛʀ] (*chien*) boxer.

boxeur [bɔksœʀ] *nm* boxer.

boyau, x [bwajo] *nm* (*corde de raquette etc*) (cat) gut; (*galerie*) passage(way); (narrow) gallery; (*pneu de bicyclette*) tubeless tyre ♦ *nmpl* (*viscères*) entrails, guts.

boycottage [bɔjkɔtaʒ] *nm* (*d'un produit*) boycotting.

boycotter [bɔjkɔte] *vt* to boycott.

BP *sigle f* = **boîte postale**.

BPAL *sigle f* (= *base de plein air et de loisir*) open-air leisure centre.

BPF *sigle* (= *bon pour francs*) *printed on cheques before space for amount to be inserted*.

brabançon, ne [bʀabɑ̃sɔ̃, -ɔn] *adj* of *ou* from Brabant.

Brabant [bʀabɑ̃] *nm*: **le** ~ Brabant.

bracelet [bʀaslɛ] *nm* bracelet.

bracelet-montre [bʀaslɛmɔ̃tʀ(ə)] *nm* wristwatch.

braconnage [bʀakɔnaʒ] *nm* poaching.

braconner [bʀakɔne] *vi* to poach.

braconnier [bʀakɔnje] *nm* poacher.

brader [bʀade] *vt* to sell off, sell cheaply.

braderie [bʀadʀi] *nf* clearance sale; (*par des particuliers*) ≈ car boot sale (*BRIT*), ≈ garage sale (*US*); (*magasin*) discount store; (*sur marché*) cut-price (*BRIT*) *ou* cut-rate (*US*) stall.

braguette [bʀagɛt] *nf* fly, flies *pl* (*BRIT*), zipper (*US*).

braillard, e [bʀajaʀ, -aʀd] *adj* (*fam*) bawling, yelling.

braille [bʀaj] *nm* Braille.

braillement [bʀajmɑ̃] *nm* (*cri*) bawling *no pl*, yelling *no pl*.

brailler [bʀaje] *vi* to bawl, yell ♦ *vt* to bawl out, yell out.

braire [bʀɛʀ] *vi* to bray.

braise [bʀɛz] *nf* embers *pl*.

braiser [bʀeze] *vt* to braise; **bœuf braisé** braised steak.

bramer [bʀame] *vi* to bell; (*fig*) to wail.

brancard [bʀɑ̃kaʀ] *nm* (*civière*) stretcher; (*bras, perche*) shaft.

brancardier [bʀɑ̃kaʀdje] *nm* stretcher-bearer.

branchages [bʀɑ̃ʃaʒ] *nmpl* branches, boughs.

branche [bʀɑ̃ʃ] *nf* branch; (*de lunettes*) side(-piece).

branché, e [bʀɑ̃ʃe] *adj* (*fam*) switched-on, trendy ♦ *nm/f* (*fam*) trendy.

branchement [bʀɑ̃ʃmɑ̃] *nm* connection.

brancher [bʀɑ̃ʃe] *vt* to connect (up); (*en mettant la prise*) to plug in; ~ **qn/qch sur** (*fig*) to get sb/sth launched onto.

branchies [bʀɑ̃ʃi] *nfpl* gills.

brandade [bʀɑ̃dad] *nf* brandade (*cod dish*).

brandebourgeois, e [bʀɑ̃dəbuʀʒwa, -waz] *adj* of *ou* from Brandenburg.

brandir [bʀɑ̃diʀ] *vt* (*arme*) to brandish, wield; (*document*) to flourish, wave.

brandon [bʀɑ̃dɔ̃] *nm* firebrand.

branlant, e [bʀɑ̃lɑ̃, -ɑ̃t] *adj* (*mur, meuble*) shaky.

branle [bʀɑ̃l] *nm*: **mettre en** ~ to set swinging; **donner le** ~ **à** to set in motion.

branle-bas [bʀɑ̃lba] *nm inv* commotion.

branler [bʀɑ̃le] *vi* to be shaky, be loose ♦ *vt*: ~ **la tête** to shake one's head.

braquage [bʀakaʒ] *nm* (*fam*) stick-up, hold-up; (*AUTO*): **rayon de** ~ turning circle.

braque [bʀak] *nm* (*ZOOL*) pointer.

braquer [bʀake] *vi* (*AUTO*) to turn (the wheel) ♦ *vt* (*revolver etc*): ~ **qch sur** to aim sth at, point sth at; (*mettre en colère*): ~ **qn** to antagonize sb, put sb's back up; ~ **son regard sur** to fix one's gaze on; **se** ~ *vi*: **se** ~ (**contre**) to take a stand (against).

bras [bʀa] *nm* arm; (*de fleuve*) branch ♦ *nmpl* (*fig*: *travailleurs*) labour *sg* (*BRIT*), labor *sg* (*US*), hands; ~ **dessus** ~ **dessous** arm in arm; **à** ~ **raccourcis** with fists flying; **à tour de** ~ with all one's might; **baisser les** ~ to

give up; ~ **droit** (*fig*) right hand man; ~ **de fer** arm-wrestling; **une partie de** ~ **de fer** (*fig*) a trial of strength; ~ **de levier** lever arm; ~ **de mer** arm of the sea, sound.

brasero [bʀazeʀo] *nm* brazier.

brasier [bʀazje] *nm* blaze, (blazing) inferno; (*fig*) inferno.

Brasilia [bʀazilja] *n* Brasilia.

bras-le-corps [bʀalkɔʀ]: **à** ~ *adv* (a)round the waist.

brassage [bʀasaʒ] *nm* (*de la bière*) brewing; (*fig*) mixing.

brassard [bʀasaʀ] *nm* armband.

brasse [bʀas] *nf* (*nage*) breast-stroke; (*mesure*) fathom; ~ **papillon** butterfly(-stroke).

brassée [bʀase] *nf* armful; **une** ~ **de** (*fig*) a number of.

brasser [bʀase] *vt* (*bière*) to brew; (*remuer: salade*) to toss; (: *cartes*) to shuffle; (*fig*) to mix; ~ **l'argent/les affaires** to handle a lot of money/business.

brasserie [bʀasʀi] *nf* (*restaurant*) bar (*selling food*), brasserie; (*usine*) brewery.

brasseur [bʀasœʀ] *nm* (*de bière*) brewer; ~ **d'affaires** big businessman.

brassière [bʀasjɛʀ] *nf* (*baby's*) vest (*BRIT*) *ou* undershirt (*US*); (*de sauvetage*) life jacket.

bravache [bʀavaʃ] *nm* blusterer, braggart.

bravade [bʀavad] *nf*: **par** ~ out of bravado.

brave [bʀav] *adj* (*courageux*) brave; (*bon, gentil*) good, kind.

bravement [bʀavmɑ̃] *adv* bravely; (*résolument*) boldly.

braver [bʀave] *vt* to defy.

bravo [bʀavo] *excl* bravo! ♦ *nm* cheer.

bravoure [bʀavuʀ] *nf* bravery.

BRB *sigle f* (*POLICE*: = *Brigade de répression du banditisme*) ≈ serious crime squad.

break [bʀɛk] *nm* (*AUTO*) estate car (*BRIT*), station wagon (*US*).

brebis [bʀəbi] *nf* ewe; ~ **galeuse** black sheep.

brèche [bʀɛʃ] *nf* breach, gap; **être sur la** ~ (*fig*) to be on the go.

bredouille [bʀəduj] *adj* empty-handed.

bredouiller [bʀəduje] *vi*, *vt* to mumble, stammer.

bref, brève [bʀɛf, bʀɛv] *adj* short, brief ♦ *adv* in short ♦ *nf* (*voyelle*) short vowel; (*information*) brief news item; **d'un ton** ~ sharply, curtly; **en** ~ in short, in brief; **à** ~ **délai** shortly.

brelan [bʀəlɑ̃] *nm*: **un** ~ three of a kind; **un** ~ **d'as** three aces.

breloque [bʀəlɔk] *nf* charm.

brème [bʀɛm] *nf* bream.

Brésil [bʀezil] *nm*: **le** ~ Brazil.

brésilien, ne [bʀeziljɛ̃, -ɛn] *adj* Brazilian ♦ *nm/ f*: **B**~, **ne** Brazilian.

bressan, e [bʀesɑ̃, -an] *adj* of *ou* from Bresse.

Bretagne [bʀətaɲ] *nf*: **la** ~ Brittany.

bretelle [bʀətɛl] *nf* (*de fusil etc*) sling; (*de vêtement*) strap; (*d'autoroute*) slip road

(*BRIT*), entrance *ou* exit ramp (*US*); ~s *nfpl* (*pour pantalon*) braces (*BRIT*), suspenders (*US*); ~ **de contournement** (*AUTO*) bypass; ~ **de raccordement** (*AUTO*) access road.

breton, ne [brǝtɔ̃, -ɔn] *adj* Breton ♦ *nm* (*LING*) Breton ♦ *nm/f*: **B~, ne** Breton.

breuvage [brœvaʒ] *nm* beverage, drink.

brève [brɛv] *adj f, nf voir* **bref**.

brevet [brǝvɛ] *nm* diploma, certificate; ~ **(d'invention)** patent; ~ **d'apprentissage** certificate of apprenticeship; ~ **(des collèges)** *school certificate, taken at approx. 16 years.*

breveté, e [brǝvte] *adj* patented; (*diplômé*) qualified.

breveter [brǝvte] *vt* to patent.

bréviaire [brevjɛr] *nm* breviary.

BRGM *sigle m* = *Bureau de recherches géologiques et minières.*

briard, e [brijar, -ard(ǝ)] *adj* of *ou* from Brie ♦ *nm* (*chien*) briard.

bribes [brib] *nfpl* bits, scraps; (*d'une conversation*) snatches; **par** ~ piecemeal.

bric [brik]: **de** ~ **et de broc** *adv* with any old thing.

bric-à-brac [brikabrak] *nm inv* bric-a-brac, jumble.

bricolage [brikɔlaʒ] *nm*: **le** ~ do-it-yourself (jobs); (*péj*) patched-up job.

bricole [brikɔl] *nf* (*babiole, chose insignifiante*) trifle; (*petit travail*) small job.

bricoler [brikɔle] *vi* to do odd jobs; (*en amateur*) to do DIY jobs; (*passe-temps*) to potter about ♦ *vt* (*réparer*) to fix up; (*mal réparer*) to tinker with; (*trafiquer: voiture etc*) to doctor, fix.

bricoleur, euse [brikɔlœr, -øz] *nm/f* handyman/woman, DIY enthusiast.

bride [brid] *nf* bridle; (*d'un bonnet*) string, tie; **à** ~ **abattue** flat out, hell for leather; **tenir en** ~ to keep in check; **lâcher la** ~ **à, laisser la** ~ **sur le cou à** to give free rein to.

bridé, e [bride] *adj*: **yeux** ~**s** slit eyes.

brider [bride] *vt* (*réprimer*) to keep in check; (*cheval*) to bridle; (*CULIN: volaille*) to truss.

bridge [bridʒ(ǝ)] *nm* bridge.

brie [bri] *nm* Brie (*cheese*).

brièvement [brijɛvmɑ̃] *adv* briefly.

brièveté [brijɛvte] *nf* brevity.

brigade [brigad] *nf* squad; (*MIL*) brigade.

brigadier [brigadje] *nm* (*POLICE*) ≈ sergeant; (*MIL*) bombardier; corporal.

brigadier-chef, *pl* **brigadiers-chefs** [brigadjeʃɛf] *nm* ≈ lance-sergeant.

brigand [brigɑ̃] *nm* brigand.

brigandage [brigɑ̃daʒ] *nm* robbery.

briguer [brige] *vt* to aspire to; (*suffrages*) to canvass.

brillamment [brijamɑ̃] *adv* brilliantly.

brillant, e [brijɑ̃, -ɑ̃t] *adj* brilliant; bright; (*luisant*) shiny, shining ♦ *nm* (*diamant*) brilliant.

briller [brije] *vi* to shine.

brimade [brimad] *nf* vexation, harassment *no pl*; bullying *no pl.*

brimbaler [brɛ̃bale] *vb* = **bringuebaler.**

brimer [brime] *vt* to harass; to bully.

brin [brɛ̃] *nm* (*de laine, ficelle etc*) strand; (*fig*): **un** ~ **de** a bit of; **un** ~ **mystérieux** *etc* (*fam*) a weeny bit mysterious *etc*; ~ **d'herbe** blade of grass; ~ **de muguet** sprig of lily of the valley; ~ **de paille** wisp of straw.

brindille [brɛ̃dij] *nf* twig.

bringue [brɛ̃g] *nf* (*fam*): **faire la** ~ to go on a binge.

bringuebaler [brɛ̃gbale] *vi* to shake (about) ♦ *vt* to cart about.

brio [brijo] *nm* brilliance; (*MUS*) brio; **avec** ~ brilliantly, with panache.

brioche [brijɔʃ] *nf* brioche (bun); (*fam: ventre*) paunch.

brioché, e [brijɔʃe] *adj* brioche-style.

brique [brik] *nf* brick; (*fam*) 10,000 francs ♦ *adj inv* brick red.

briquer [brike] *vt* (*fam*) to polish up.

briquet [brikɛ] *nm* (*cigarette*) lighter.

briqueterie [briktri] *nf* brickyard.

bris [bri] *nm*: ~ **de clôture** (*JUR*) breaking in; ~ **de glaces** (*AUTO*) breaking of windows.

brisant [brizɑ̃] *nm* reef; (*vague*) breaker.

brise [briz] *nf* breeze.

brisé, e [brize] *adj* broken; ~ **(de fatigue)** exhausted; **d'une voix** ~**e** in a voice broken with emotion; **pâte** ~**e** shortcrust pastry.

brisées [brize] *nfpl*: **aller** *ou* **marcher sur les** ~ **de qn** to compete with sb in his own province.

brise-glace(s) [brizglas] *nm inv* (*navire*) icebreaker.

brise-jet [brizʒɛ] *nm inv* tap swirl.

brise-lames [brizlam] *nm inv* breakwater.

briser [brize] *vt* to break; **se** ~ *vi* to break.

brise-tout [briztu] *nm inv* wrecker.

briseur, euse [brizœr, -øz] *nm/f*: ~ **de grève** strike-breaker.

brise-vent [brizvɑ̃] *nm inv* windbreak.

bristol [bristɔl] *nm* (*carte de visite*) visiting card.

britannique [britanik] *adj* British ♦ *nm/f*: **B~** Briton, British person; **les B~s** the British.

broc [bro] *nm* pitcher.

brocante [brokɑ̃t] *nf* (*objets*) secondhand goods *pl*, junk; (*commerce*) secondhand trade; junk dealing.

brocanteur, euse [brokɑ̃tœr, -øz] *nm/f* junkshop owner; junk dealer.

brocart [brokar] *nm* brocade.

broche [brɔʃ] *nf* brooch; (*CULIN*) spit; (*fiche*) spike, peg; (*MÉD*) pin; **à la** ~ spit-roasted, roasted on a spit.

broché, e [brɔʃe] *adj* (*livre*) paper-backed; (*tissu*) brocaded.

brochet [brɔʃɛ] *nm* pike *inv.*

brochette [brɔʃɛt] *nf* skewer; ~ **de décorations** row of medals.

brochure [bʀɔʃyʀ] *nf* pamphlet, brochure, booklet.
brocoli [bʀɔkɔli] *nm* broccoli.
brodequins [bʀɔdkɛ̃] *nmpl* (*de marche*) (lace-up) boots.
broder [bʀɔde] *vt* to embroider ♦ *vi*: ~ **(sur des faits** *ou* **une histoire)** to embroider the facts.
broderie [bʀɔdʀi] *nf* embroidery.
bromure [bʀɔmyʀ] *nm* bromide.
broncher [bʀɔ̃ʃe] *vi*: **sans** ~ without flinching, without turning a hair.
bronches [bʀɔ̃ʃ] *nfpl* bronchial tubes.
bronchite [bʀɔ̃ʃit] *nf* bronchitis.
broncho-pneumonie [bʀɔ̃kɔpnømɔni] *nf* broncho-pneumonia *no pl.*
bronzage [bʀɔ̃zaʒ] *nm* (*hâle*) (sun)tan.
bronze [bʀɔ̃z] *nm* bronze.
bronzé, e [bʀɔ̃ze] *adj* tanned.
bronzer [bʀɔ̃ze] *vt* to tan ♦ *vi* to get a tan; **se** ~ to sunbathe.
brosse [bʀɔs] *nf* brush; **donner un coup de** ~ **à qch** to give sth a brush; **coiffé en** ~ with a crewcut; ~ **à cheveux** hairbrush; ~ **à dents** toothbrush; ~ **à habits** clothesbrush.
brosser [bʀɔse] *vt* (*nettoyer*) to brush; (*fig: tableau etc*) to paint; to draw; **se** ~ to brush one's clothes; ~ **les dents** to brush one's teeth; **tu peux te** ~! (*fam*) you can sing for it!
brou [bʀu] *nm*: ~ **de noix** (*pour bois*) walnut stain; (*liqueur*) walnut liqueur.
brouette [bʀuɛt] *nf* wheelbarrow.
brouhaha [bʀuaa] *nm* hubbub.
brouillage [bʀujaʒ] *nm* (*d'une émission*) jamming.
brouillard [bʀujaʀ] *nm* fog; **être dans le** ~ (*fig*) to be all at sea.
brouille [bʀuj] *nf* quarrel.
brouillé, e [bʀuje] *adj* (*fâché*): **il est** ~ **avec ses parents** he has fallen out with his parents; (*teint*) muddy.
brouiller [bʀuje] *vt* to mix up; to confuse; (*RADIO*) to cause interference to; (: *délibérément*) to jam; (*rendre trouble*) to cloud; (*désunir: amis*) to set at odds; **se** ~ *vi* (*ciel, vue*) to cloud over; (*détails*) to become confused; **se** ~ **(avec)** to fall out (with); ~ **les pistes** to cover one's tracks; (*fig*) to confuse the issue.
brouillon, ne [bʀujɔ̃, -ɔn] *adj* disorganized, unmethodical ♦ *nm* (first) draft; **cahier de** ~ rough (work) book.
broussailles [bʀusaj] *nfpl* undergrowth *sg.*
broussailleux, euse [bʀusajø, -øz] *adj* bushy.
brousse [bʀus] *nf*: **la** ~ the bush.
brouter [bʀute] *vt* to graze on ♦ *vi* to graze; (*AUTO*) to judder.
broutille [bʀutij] *nf* trifle.
broyer [bʀwaje] *vt* to crush; ~ **du noir** to be down in the dumps.
bru [bʀy] *nf* daughter-in-law.
brucelles [bʀysɛl] *nfpl*: **(pinces)** ~ tweezers.

brugnon [bʀyɲɔ̃] *nm* nectarine.
bruine [bʀɥin] *nf* drizzle.
bruiner [bʀɥine] *vb impers*: **il bruine** it's drizzling, there's a drizzle.
bruire [bʀɥiʀ] *vi* (*eau*) to murmur; (*feuilles, étoffe*) to rustle.
bruissement [bʀɥismɑ̃] *nm* murmuring; rustling.
bruit [bʀɥi] *nm*: **un** ~ a noise, a sound; (*fig: rumeur*) a rumour (*BRIT*), a rumor (*US*); **le** ~ noise; **pas/trop de** ~ no/too much noise; **sans** ~ without a sound, noiselessly; **faire du** ~ to make a noise; ~ **de fond** background noise.
bruitage [bʀɥitaʒ] *nm* sound effects *pl.*
bruiteur, euse [bʀɥitœʀ, -øz] *nm/f* sound-effects engineer.
brûlant, e [bʀylɑ̃, -ɑ̃t] *adj* burning (hot); (*liquide*) boiling (hot); (*regard*) fiery; (*sujet*) red-hot.
brûlé, e [bʀyle] *adj* (*fig: démasqué*) blown; (: *homme politique etc*) discredited ♦ *nm*: **odeur de** ~ smell of burning.
brûle-pourpoint [bʀylpuʀpwɛ̃]: **à** ~ *adv* point-blank.
brûler [bʀyle] *vt* to burn; (*suj: eau bouillante*) to scald; (*consommer: électricité, essence*) to use; (*feu rouge, signal*) to go through (without stopping) ♦ *vi* to burn; (*jeu*): **tu brûles** you're getting warm *ou* hot; **se** ~ to burn o.s.; to scald o.s.; **se** ~ **la cervelle** to blow one's brains out; ~ **les étapes** to make rapid progress; (*aller trop vite*) to cut corners; ~ **(d'impatience) de faire qch** to burn with impatience to do sth, be dying to do sth.
brûleur [bʀylœʀ] *nm* burner.
brûlot [bʀylo] *nm* (*CULIN*) flaming brandy; **un** ~ **de contestation** (*fig*) a hotbed of dissent.
brûlure [bʀylyʀ] *nf* (*lésion*) burn; (*sensation*) burning *no pl*, burning sensation; ~**s d'estomac** heartburn *sg.*
brume [bʀym] *nf* mist.
brumeux, euse [bʀymø, -øz] *adj* misty; (*fig*) hazy.
brumisateur [bʀymizatœʀ] *nm* atomizer.
brun, e [bʀœ̃, -yn] *adj* brown; (*cheveux, personne*) dark ♦ *nm* (*couleur*) brown ♦ *nf* (*cigarette*) cigarette made of dark tobacco; (*bière*) ≈ brown ale, stout.
brunâtre [bʀynɑtʀ(ə)] *adj* brownish.
brunch [bʀœntʃ] *nm* brunch.
Brunei [bʀynei] *nm*: **le** ~ Brunei.
brunir [bʀyniʀ] *vi* (*aussi*: **se** ~) to get a tan ♦ *vt* to tan.
brushing [bʀœʃiŋ] *nm* blow-dry.
brusque [bʀysk(ə)] *adj* (*soudain*) abrupt, sudden; (*rude*) abrupt, brusque.
brusquement [bʀyskəmɑ̃] *adv* (*soudainement*) abruptly, suddenly.
brusquer [bʀyske] *vt* to rush.
brusquerie [bʀyskəʀi] *nf* abruptness, brusqueness.

brut, e [bʀyt] *adj* raw, crude, rough; (*diamant*) uncut; (*soie, minéral, INFORM*: *données*) raw; (*COMM*) gross ♦ *nf* brute; **(champagne)** ~ brut champagne; **(pétrole)** ~ crude (oil).

brutal, e, aux [bʀytal, -o] *adj* brutal.

brutalement [bʀytalmɑ̃] *adv* brutally.

brutaliser [bʀytalize] *vt* to handle roughly, manhandle.

brutalité [bʀytalite] *nf* brutality *no pl*.

brute [bʀyt] *adj f*, *nf voir* **brut**.

Bruxelles [bʀysɛl] *n* Brussels.

bruxellois, e [bʀysɛlwa, -waz] *adj* of *ou* from Brussels ♦ *nm/f*: **B~, e** inhabitant *ou* native of Brussels.

bruyamment [bʀɥijamɑ̃] *adv* noisily.

bruyant, e [bʀɥijɑ̃, -ɑ̃t] *adj* noisy.

bruyère [bʀyjɛʀ] *nf* heather.

BT *sigle m* (= *Brevet de technicien*) *vocational training certificate, taken at approx. 18 years*.

BTA *sigle m* (= *Brevet de technicien agricole*) *agricultural training certificate, taken at approx. 18 years*.

BTP *sigle m* (= *Bâtiments et travaux publics*) *public buildings and works sector*.

BTS *sigle m* (= *Brevet de technicien supérieur*) *vocational training certificate taken at end of 2-year higher education course*.

BU *sigle f* = *Bibliothèque universitaire*.

bu, e [by] *pp de* **boire**.

buanderie [bɥɑ̃dʀi] *nf* laundry.

Bucarest [bykaʀɛst] *n* Bucharest.

buccal, e, aux [bykal, -o] *adj*: **par voie ~e** orally.

bûche [byʃ] *nf* log; **prendre une ~** (*fig*) to come a cropper (*BRIT*), fall flat on one's face; **~ de Noël** Yule log.

bûcher [byʃe] *nm* pyre; bonfire ♦ *vi* (*fam: étudier*) to swot (*BRIT*), grind (*US*) ♦ *vt* to swot up (*BRIT*), cram.

bûcheron [byʃʀɔ̃] *nm* woodcutter.

bûchette [byʃɛt] *nf* (*de bois*) stick, twig; (*pour compter*) rod.

bûcheur, euse [byʃœʀ, -øz] *nm/f* (*fam: étudiant*) swot (*BRIT*), grind (*US*).

bucolique [bykɔlik] *adj* bucolic, pastoral.

Budapest [bydapɛst] *n* Budapest.

budget [bydʒɛ] *nm* budget.

budgétaire [bydʒetɛʀ] *adj* budgetary, budget *cpd*.

budgétiser [bydʒetize] *vt* to budget (for).

buée [bɥe] *nf* (*sur une vitre*) mist; (*de l'haleine*) steam.

Buenos Aires [bwenɔzɛʀ] *n* Buenos Aires.

buffet [byfɛ] *nm* (*meuble*) sideboard; (*de réception*) buffet; **~ (de gare)** (station) buffet, snack bar.

buffle [byfl(ə)] *nm* buffalo.

buis [bɥi] *nm* box tree; (*bois*) box(wood).

buisson [bɥisɔ̃] *nm* bush.

buissonnière [bɥisɔnjɛʀ] *adj f*: **faire l'école ~** to play truant (*BRIT*), skip school.

bulbe [bylb(ə)] *nm* (*BOT, ANAT*) bulb; (*coupole*) onion-shaped dome.

bulgare [bylgaʀ] *adj* Bulgarian ♦ *nm* (*LING*) Bulgarian ♦ *nm/f*: **B~** Bulgarian, Bulgar.

Bulgarie [bylgaʀi] *nf*: **la ~** Bulgaria.

bulldozer [buldozœʀ] *nm* bulldozer.

bulle [byl] *adj*, *nm*: **(papier)** ~ manil(l)a paper ♦ *nf* bubble; (*de bande dessinée*) balloon; (*papale*) bull; **~ de savon** soap bubble.

bulletin [byltɛ̃] *nm* (*communiqué, journal*) bulletin; (*papier*) form; (*: de bagages*) ticket; (*SCOL*) report; **~ d'informations** news bulletin; **~ météorologique** weather report; **~ de naissance** birth certificate; **~ de salaire** pay slip; **~ de santé** medical bulletin; **~ (de vote)** ballot paper.

buraliste [byʀalist(ə)] *nm/f* (*de bureau de tabac*) tobacconist; (*de poste*) clerk.

bure [byʀ] *nf* homespun; (*de moine*) frock.

bureau, x [byʀo] *nm* (*meuble*) desk; (*pièce, service*) office; **~ de change** (foreign) exchange office *ou* bureau; **~ d'embauche** ≈ job centre; **~ d'études** design office; **~ de location** box office; **~ de placement** employment agency; **~ de poste** post office; **~ de tabac** tobacconist's (shop), smoke shop (*US*); **~ de vote** polling station.

bureaucrate [byʀokʀat] *nm* bureaucrat.

bureaucratie [byʀokʀasi] *nf* bureaucracy.

bureaucratique [byʀokʀatik] *adj* bureaucratic.

bureautique [byʀɔtik] *nf* office automation.

burette [byʀɛt] *nf* (*de mécanicien*) oilcan; (*de chimiste*) burette.

burin [byʀɛ̃] *nm* cold chisel; (*ART*) burin.

buriné, e [byʀine] *adj* (*fig: visage*) craggy, seamed.

Burkina(-Faso) [byʀkina(faso)] *nm*: **le ~** Burkina Faso.

burlesque [byʀlɛsk(ə)] *adj* ridiculous; (*LITTÉRATURE*) burlesque.

burnous [byʀnu(s)] *nm* burnous.

Burundi [buʀundi] *nm*: **le ~** Burundi.

BUS *sigle m* = *Bureau universitaire de statistiques*.

bus *vb* [by] *voir* **boire** ♦ *nm* [bys] (*véhicule, aussi INFORM*) bus.

busard [byzaʀ] *nm* harrier.

buse [byz] *nf* buzzard.

busqué, e [byske] *adj*: **nez ~** hook(ed) nose.

buste [byst(ə)] *nm* (*ANAT*) chest; (*: de femme*) bust; (*sculpture*) bust.

bustier [bystje] *nm* (*soutien-gorge*) long-line bra.

but [by] *vb voir* **boire** ♦ *nm* (*cible*) target; (*fig*) goal, aim; (*FOOTBALL etc*) goal; **de ~ en blanc** point-blank; **avoir pour ~ de faire** to aim to do; **dans le ~ de** with the intention of.

butane [bytan] *nm* butane; (*domestique*) calor gas ® (*BRIT*), butane.

buté, e [byte] *adj* stubborn, obstinate ♦ *nf* (*ARCHIT*) abutment; (*TECH*) stop.

buter [byte] *vi:* ~ **contre** *ou* **sur** to bump into; (*trébucher*) to stumble against ♦ *vt* to antagonize; **se** ~ *vi* to get obstinate, dig in one's heels.

buteur [bytœʀ] *nm* striker.

butin [bytɛ̃] *nm* booty, spoils *pl*; (*d'un vol*) loot.

butiner [bytine] *vi* to gather nectar.

butor [bytɔʀ] *nm* (*fig*) lout.

butte [byt] *nf* mound, hillock; **être en** ~ **à** to be exposed to.

buvable [byvabl(ə)] *adj* (*eau, vin*) drinkable; (*MÉD: ampoule etc*) to be taken orally; (*fig: roman etc*) reasonable.

buvais [byvɛ] *etc vb voir* **boire**.

buvard [byvaʀ] *nm* blotter.

buvette [byvɛt] *nf* refreshment room *ou* stall; (*comptoir*) bar.

buveur, euse [byvœʀ, -øz] *nm/f* drinker.

buvons [byvɔ̃] *etc vb voir* **boire**.

BVP *sigle m* (= *Bureau de vérification de la publicité*) *advertising standards authority*.

Byzance [bizɑ̃s] *n* Byzantium.

byzantin, e [bizɑ̃tɛ̃, -in] *adj* Byzantine.

BZH *abr* (= *Breizh*) Brittany.

C c

C, c [se] *nm inv* C, c ♦ *abr* (= *centime*) c; (= *Celsius*) C; **C comme Célestin** C for Charlie.

c' [s] *dét voir* **ce**.

CA *sigle m* = **chiffre d'affaires, conseil d'administration, corps d'armée** ♦ *sigle f* = **chambre d'agriculture**.

ca *abr* (= *centiare*) 1 *m²*.

ça [sa] *pron* (*pour désigner*) this; (*: plus loin*) that; (*comme sujet indéfini*) it; ~ **m'étonne que** it surprises me that; ~ **va?** how are you?; how are things?; (*d'accord?*) OK?, all right?; ~ **alors!** (*désapprobation*) well!, really!; (*étonnement*) heavens!; **c'est** ~ that's right.

çà [sa] *adv:* ~ **et là** here and there.

cabale [kabal] *nf* (*THÉÂT, POL*) cabal, clique.

caban [kabɑ̃] *nm* reefer jacket, donkey jacket.

cabane [kaban] *nf* hut, cabin.

cabanon [kabanɔ̃] *nm* chalet; (*country*) cottage.

cabaret [kabaʀɛ] *nm* night club.

cabas [kabɑ] *nm* shopping bag.

cabestan [kabɛstɑ̃] *nm* capstan.

cabillaud [kabijo] *nm* cod *inv*.

cabine [kabin] *nf* (*de bateau*) cabin; (*de plage*) (beach) hut; (*de piscine etc*) cubicle; (*de camion, train*) cab; (*d'avion*) cockpit; ~ **(d'ascenseur)** lift cage; ~ **d'essayage** fitting room; ~ **de projection** projection room; ~ **spatiale** space capsule; ~ **(téléphonique)** call *ou* (tele)phone box, (tele)phone booth.

cabinet [kabinɛ] *nm* (*petite pièce*) closet; (*de médecin*) surgery (*BRIT*), office (*US*); (*de notaire etc*) office; (*: clientèle*) practice; (*POL*) cabinet; (*d'un ministre*) advisers *pl*; ~**s** *nmpl* (*w.-c.*) toilet *sg*, loo *sg* (*fam BRIT*); ~ **d'affaires** business consultants' (bureau), business partnership; ~ **de toilette** toilet; ~ **de travail** study.

câble [kabl(ə)] *nm* cable; **le** ~ (*TV*) cable television, cablevision (*US*).

câblé, e [kable] *adj* (*fam*) switched on; (*TECH*) linked to cable television.

câbler [kable] *vt* to cable; ~ **un quartier** (*TV*) to put cable television into an area.

câblogramme [kablɔgʀam] *nm* cablegram.

cabosser [kabɔse] *vt* to dent.

cabot [kabo] *nm* (*péj: chien*) mutt.

cabotage [kabɔtaʒ] *nm* coastal navigation.

caboteur [kabɔtœʀ] *nm* coaster.

cabotin, e [kabɔtɛ̃, -in] *nm/f* (*péj: personne maniérée*) poseur; (*: acteur*) ham ♦ *adj* dramatic, theatrical.

cabotinage [kabɔtinaʒ] *nm* playacting; thirdrate acting, ham acting.

cabrer [kabʀe]: **se** ~ *vi* (*cheval*) to rear up; (*avion*) to nose up; (*fig*) to revolt, rebel; to jib.

cabri [kabʀi] *nm* kid.

cabriole [kabʀijɔl] *nf* caper; (*gymnastique etc*) somersault.

cabriolet [kabʀijɔlɛ] *nm* convertible.

CAC [kak] *sigle f* (= *Compagnie des agents de change*): **indice** ~ ≈ FT index (*BRIT*), ≈ Dow Jones average (*US*).

caca [kaka] *nm* (*langage enfantin*) pooh; (*couleur*): ~ **d'oie** greeny-yellow; **faire** ~ (*fam*) to do a pooh.

cacahuète [kakayɛt] *nf* peanut.

cacao [kakao] *nm* cocoa (powder); (*boisson*) cocoa.

cachalot [kaʃalo] *nm* sperm whale.

cache [kaʃ] *nm* mask, card (*for masking*) ♦ *nf* hiding place.

cache-cache [kaʃkaʃ] *nm:* **jouer à** ~ to play hide-and-seek.

cache-col [kaʃkɔl] *nm* scarf (*pl* scarves).

cachemire [kaʃmiʀ] *nm* cashmere ♦ *adj:* **dessin** ~ paisley pattern; **le C~** Kashmir.

cache-nez [kaʃne] *nm inv* scarf (*pl* scarves), muffler.

cache-pot [kaʃpo] *nm inv* flower-pot holder.

cache-prise [kaʃpʀiz] *nm inv* socket cover.

cacher [kaʃe] *vt* to hide, conceal; ~ **qch à qn** to hide *ou* conceal sth from sb; **se** ~ to hide; to be hidden *ou* concealed; **il ne s'en cache pas** he makes no secret of it.

cache-sexe [kaʃsɛks] *nm inv* G-string.

cachet [kaʃɛ] *nm* (*comprimé*) tablet; (*sceau: du roi*) seal; (*: de la poste*) postmark; (*rétribution*)

fee; (*fig*) style, character.
cacheter [kaʃte] *vt* to seal; **vin cacheté** vintage wine.
cachette [kaʃɛt] *nf* hiding place; **en ~ on the sly**, secretly.
cachot [kaʃo] *nm* dungeon.
cachotterie [kaʃɔtʀi] *nf* mystery; **faire des ~s** to be secretive.
cachottier, ière [kaʃɔtje, -jɛʀ] *adj* secretive.
cachou [kaʃu] *nm*: **pastille de ~** cachou (*sweet*).
cacophonie [kakɔfɔni] *nf* cacophony, din.
cacophonique [kakɔfɔnik] *adj* cacophonous.
cactus [kaktys] *nm* cactus.
c-à-d *abr* (= *c'est-à-dire*) i.e.
cadastre [kadastʀ(ə)] *nm* land register.
cadavéreux, euse [kadavøʀø, -øz] *adj* (*teint, visage*) deathly pale.
cadavérique [kadaveʀik] *adj* deathly (pale), deadly pale.
cadavre [kadavʀ(ə)] *nm* corpse, (dead) body.
Caddie [kadi] *nm* ® (supermarket) trolley.
cadeau, x [kado] *nm* present, gift; **faire un ~ à qn** to give sb a present *ou* gift; **faire ~ de qch à qn** to make a present of sth to sb, give sb sth as a present.
cadenas [kadna] *nm* padlock.
cadenasser [kadnase] *vt* to padlock.
cadence [kadãs] *nf* (*MUS*) cadence; (: *rythme*) rhythm; (*de travail*) rate; **~s** *nfpl* (*en usine*) production rate *sg*; **en ~** rhythmically; in time.
cadencé, e [kadãse] *adj* rhythmic(al); **au pas ~** (*MIL*) in quick time.
cadet, te [kadɛ, -ɛt] *adj* younger; (*le plus jeune*) youngest ♦ *nm/f* youngest child *ou* one, youngest boy *ou* son/girl *ou* daughter; **il est mon ~ de deux ans** he's 2 years younger than me, he's 2 years my junior; **les ~s** (*SPORT*) the minors (*15 - 17 years*); **le ~ de mes soucis** the least of my worries.
cadrage [kadʀaʒ] *nm* framing (*of shot*).
cadran [kadʀã] *nm* dial; **~ solaire** sundial.
cadre [kadʀ(ə)] *nm* frame; (*environnement*) surroundings *pl*; (*limites*) scope ♦ *nm/f* (*ADMIN*) managerial employee, executive ♦ *adj*: **loi ~** outline *ou* blueprint law; **~ moyen/supérieur** (*ADMIN*) middle/senior management employee, junior/senior executive; **rayer qn des ~s** to discharge sb; to dismiss sb; **dans le ~ de** (*fig*) within the framework *ou* context of.
cadrer [kadʀe] *vi*: **~ avec** to tally *ou* correspond with ♦ *vt* (*CINÉ, PHOTO*) to frame.
cadreur, euse [kadʀœʀ, -øz] *nm/f* (*CINÉ*) cameraman/woman.
caduc, uque [kadyk] *adj* obsolete; (*BOT*) deciduous.
CAF *sigle f* (= *Caisse d'allocations familiales*) family allowance office.
caf *abr* (= *coût, assurance, fret*) cif.
cafard [kafaʀ] *nm* cockroach; **avoir le ~** to be

down in the dumps, be feeling low.
cafardeux, euse [kafaʀdø, -øz] *adj* (*personne, ambiance*) depressing, melancholy.
café [kafe] *nm* coffee; (*bistro*) café ♦ *adj inv* coffee *cpd*; **~ crème** coffee with cream; **~ au lait** white coffee; **~ noir** black coffee; **~ en grains** coffee beans; **~ en poudre** instant coffee; **~ tabac** tobacconist's *or* newsagent's *also serving coffee and spirits*; **~ liégeois** *coffee ice cream with whipped cream*.
café-concert, *pl* **cafés-concerts** [kafekɔ̃sɛʀ] *nm* (*aussi*: **caf'conc'**) *café with a cabaret.*
caféine [kafein] *nf* caffeine.
cafétéria [kafeteʀja] *nf* cafeteria.
café-théâtre, *pl* **cafés-théâtres** [kafeteatʀ(ə)] *nm café used as a venue by (experimental) theatre groups.*
cafetier, ière [kaftje, -jɛʀ] *nm/f* café-owner ♦ *nf* (*pot*) coffee-pot.
cafouillage [kafujaʒ] *nm* shambles *sg*.
cafouiller [kafuje] *vi* to get in a shambles; (*machine etc*) to work in fits and starts.
cage [kaʒ] *nf* cage; **~ (des buts)** goal; **en ~** in a cage, caged up *ou* in; **~ d'ascenseur** lift shaft; **~ d'escalier** (stair)well; **~ thoracique** rib cage.
cageot [kaʒo] *nm* crate.
cagibi [kaʒibi] *nm* shed.
cagneux, euse [kaɲø, -øz] *adj* knock-kneed.
cagnotte [kaɲɔt] *nf* kitty.
cagoule [kagul] *nf* cowl; hood; (*SKI etc*) cagoule.
cahier [kaje] *nm* notebook; (*TYPO*) signature; (*revue*): **~s** journal; **~ de revendications/doléances** list of claims/grievances; **~ de brouillons** roughbook, jotter; **~ des charges** specification; **~ d'exercices** exercise book.
cahin-caha [kaɛ̃kaa] *adv*: **aller ~** to jog along; (*fig*) to be so-so.
cahot [kao] *nm* jolt, bump.
cahoter [kaɔte] *vi* to bump along, jog along.
cahoteux, euse [kaɔtø, -øz] *adj* bumpy.
cahute [kayt] *nf* shack, hut.
caïd [kaid] *nm* big chief, boss.
caillasse [kajas] *nf* (*pierraille*) loose stones *pl*.
caille [kaj] *nf* quail.
caillé, e [kaje] *adj*: **lait ~** curdled milk, curds *pl*.
caillebotis [kajbɔti] *nm* duckboard.
cailler [kaje] *vi* (*lait*) to curdle; (*sang*) to clot; (*fam*) to be cold.
caillot [kajo] *nm* (blood) clot.
caillou, x [kaju] *nm* (little) stone.
caillouter [kajute] *vt* (*chemin*) to metal.
caillouteux, euse [kajutø, -øz] *adj* stony; pebbly.
cailloutis [kajuti] *nm* (*petits graviers*) gravel.
caïman [kaimã] *nm* cayman.
Caïmans [kaimã] *nfpl*: **les ~** the Cayman Islands.
Caire [kɛʀ] *nm*: **Le ~** Cairo.
caisse [kɛs] *nf* box; (*où l'on met la recette*) cash-

box; (: *machine*) till; (*où l'on paye*) cash desk (*BRIT*), checkout counter; (: *au supermarché*) checkout; (*de banque*) cashier's desk; (*TECH*) case, casing; **faire sa** ~ (*COMM*) to count the takings; ~ **claire** (*MUS*) side *ou* snare drum; ~ **éclair** express checkout; ~ **enregistreuse** cash register; ~ **d'épargne** (*CE*) savings bank; ~ **noire** slush fund; ~ **de retraite** pension fund; ~ **de sortie** checkout; *voir* **grosse.**

caissier, ière [kesje, -jɛʀ] *nm/f* cashier.

caisson [kɛsɔ̃] *nm* box, case.

cajoler [kaʒɔle] *vt* to wheedle, coax; to surround with love and care, make a fuss of.

cajoleries [kaʒɔlʀi] *nfpl* coaxing *sg*, flattery *sg*.

cajou [kaʒu] *nm* cashew nut.

cake [kɛk] *nm* fruit cake.

CAL *sigle m* (= *Comité d'action lycéen*) *pupils' action group seeking to reform school system.*

cal [kal] *nm* callus.

cal. *abr* = **calorie.**

calamar [kalamaʀ] *nm* = **calmar.**

calaminé, e [kalamine] *adj* (*AUTO*) coked up.

calamité [kalamite] *nf* calamity, disaster.

calandre [kalɑ̃dʀ(ə)] *nf* radiator grill; (*machine*) calender, mangle.

calanque [kalɑ̃k] *nf* rocky inlet.

calcaire [kalkɛʀ] *nm* limestone ♦ *adj* (*eau*) hard; (*GÉO*) limestone *cpd*.

calciné, e [kalsine] *adj* burnt to ashes.

calcium [kalsjɔm] *nm* calcium.

calcul [kalkyl] *nm* calculation; **le** ~ (*SCOL*) arithmetic; ~ **différentiel/intégral** differential/integral calculus; ~ **mental** mental arithmetic; ~ (**biliaire**) (gall)stone; ~ (**rénal**) (kidney) stone; **d'après mes** ~**s** by my reckoning.

calculateur [kalkylatœʀ] *nm*, **calculatrice** [kalkylatʀis] *nf* calculator.

calculé, e [kalkyle] *adj*: **risque** ~ calculated risk.

calculer [kalkyle] *vt* to calculate, work out, reckon; (*combiner*) to calculate; ~ **qch de tête** to work sth out in one's head.

calculette [kalkylɛt] *nf* (pocket) calculator.

cale [kal] *nf* (*de bateau*) hold; (*en bois*) wedge, chock; ~ **sèche** *ou* **de radoub** dry dock.

calé, e [kale] *adj* (*fam*) clever, bright.

calebasse [kalbas] *nf* calabash, gourd.

calèche [kalɛʃ] *nf* horse-drawn carriage.

caleçon [kalsɔ̃] *nm* pair of underpants, trunks *pl*; ~ **de bain** bathing trunks *pl*.

calembour [kalɑ̃buʀ] *nm* pun.

calendes [kalɑ̃d] *nfpl*: **renvoyer aux** ~ **grecques** to postpone indefinitely.

calendrier [kalɑ̃dʀije] *nm* calendar; (*fig*) timetable.

cale-pied [kalpje] *nm inv* toe clip.

calepin [kalpɛ̃] *nm* notebook.

caler [kale] *vt* to wedge, chock up; ~ (**son moteur/véhicule**) to stall (one's engine/vehicle); **se** ~ **dans un fauteuil** to make o.s.

comfortable in an armchair.

calfater [kalfate] *vt* to caulk.

calfeutrage [kalføtʀaʒ] *nm* draughtproofing (*BRIT*), draftproofing (*US*).

calfeutrer [kalføtʀe] *vt* to (make) draughtproof (*BRIT*) *ou* draftproof (*US*); **se** ~ to make o.s. snug and comfortable.

calibre [kalibʀ(ə)] *nm* (*d'un fruit*) grade; (*d'une arme*) bore, calibre (*BRIT*), caliber (*US*); (*fig*) calibre, caliber.

calibrer [kalibʀe] *vt* to grade.

calice [kalis] *nm* (*REL*) chalice; (*BOT*) calyx.

calicot [kaliko] *nm* (*tissu*) calico.

calife [kalif] *nm* caliph.

Californie [kalifɔʀni] *nf*: **la** ~ California.

californien, ne [kalifɔʀnjɛ̃, -ɛn] *adj* Californian.

califourchon [kalifuʀʃɔ̃]: **à** ~ *adv* astride; **à** ~ **sur** astride, straddling.

câlin, e [kɑlɛ̃, -in] *adj* cuddly, cuddlesome; tender.

câliner [kɑline] *vt* to fondle, cuddle.

câlineries [kɑlinʀi] *nfpl* cuddles.

calisson [kalisɔ̃] *nm* diamond-shaped sweet or candy made with ground almonds.

calleux, euse [kalø, -øz] *adj* horny, callous.

calligraphie [kaligʀafi] *nf* calligraphy.

callosité [kalozite] *nf* callus.

calmant [kalmɑ̃] *nm* tranquillizer, sedative; (*contre la douleur*) painkiller.

calmar [kalmaʀ] *nm* squid.

calme [kalm(ə)] *adj* calm, quiet ♦ *nm* calm(ness), quietness; **sans perdre son** ~ without losing one's cool *ou* calmness; ~ **plat** (*NAVIG*) dead calm.

calmement [kalməmɑ̃] *adv* calmly, quietly.

calmer [kalme] *vt* to calm (down); (*douleur, inquiétude*) to ease, soothe; **se** ~ to calm down.

calomniateur, trice [kalɔmnjatœʀ, -tʀis] *nm/f* slanderer; libeller.

calomnie [kalɔmni] *nf* slander; (*écrite*) libel.

calomnier [kalɔmnje] *vt* to slander; to libel.

calomnieux, euse [kalɔmnjø, -øz] *adj* slanderous; libellous.

calorie [kalɔʀi] *nf* calorie.

calorifère [kalɔʀifɛʀ] *nm* stove.

calorifique [kalɔʀifik] *adj* calorific.

calorifuge [kalɔʀifyʒ] *adj* (heat-)insulating, heat-retaining.

calot [kalo] *nm* forage cap.

calotte [kalɔt] *nf* (*coiffure*) skullcap; (*gifle*) slap; **la** ~ (*péj: clergé*) the cloth, the clergy; ~ **glaciaire** icecap.

calque [kalk(ə)] *nm* (*aussi: papier* ~) tracing paper; (*dessin*) tracing; (*fig*) carbon copy.

calquer [kalke] *vt* to trace; (*fig*) to copy exactly.

calvados [kalvados] *nm* Calvados (*apple brandy*).

calvaire [kalvɛʀ] *nm* (*croix*) wayside cross, calvary; (*souffrances*) suffering, martyrdom.

calvitie [kalvisi] *nf* baldness.

camaïeu [kamajø] *nm*: **(motif en)** ~ monochrome motif.

camarade [kamaʀad] *nm/f* friend, pal; (*POL*) comrade.

camaraderie [kamaʀadʀi] *nf* friendship.

camarguais, e [kamaʀgɛ, -ɛz] *adj* of *ou* from the Camargue.

Camargue [kamaʀg] *nf*: **la** ~ the Camargue.

cambiste [kɑ̃bist(ə)] *nm* (*COMM*) foreign exchange dealer, exchange agent.

Cambodge [kɑ̃bɔdʒ] *nm*: **le** ~ Cambodia.

cambodgien, ne [kɑ̃bɔdʒjɛ̃, -ɛn] *adj* Cambodian ♦ *nm/f*: **C~, ne** Cambodian.

cambouis [kɑ̃bwi] *nm* dirty oil *ou* grease.

cambré, e [kɑ̃bʀe] *adj*: **avoir les reins ~s** to have an arched back; **avoir le pied très ~** to have very high arches *ou* insteps.

cambrer [kɑ̃bʀe] *vt* to arch; **se ~** to arch one's back; **~ la taille** *ou* **les reins** to arch one's back.

cambriolage [kɑ̃bʀijɔlaʒ] *nm* burglary.

cambrioler [kɑ̃bʀijɔle] *vt* to burgle (*BRIT*), burglarize (*US*).

cambrioleur, euse [kɑ̃bʀijɔlœʀ, -øz] *nm/f* burglar.

cambrure [kɑ̃bʀyʀ] *nf* (*du pied*) arch; (*de la route*) camber; **~ des reins** small of the back.

cambuse [kɑ̃byz] *nf* storeroom.

came [kam] *nf*: **arbre à ~s** camshaft; **arbre à ~s en tête** overhead camshaft.

camée [kame] *nm* cameo.

caméléon [kamele5] *nm* chameleon.

camélia [kamelja] *nm* camellia.

camelot [kamlo] *nm* street pedlar.

camelote [kamlɔt] *nf* rubbish, trash, junk.

camembert [kamɑ̃bɛʀ] *nm* Camembert (*cheese*).

caméra [kameʀa] *nf* (*CINÉ, TV*) camera; (*d'amateur*) cine-camera.

caméraman [kameʀaman] *nm* cameraman/woman.

Cameroun [kamʀun] *nm*: **le** ~ Cameroon.

camerounais, e [kamʀunɛ, -ɛz] *adj* Cameroonian.

caméscope [kameskɔp] ® *nm* camcorder ®.

camion [kamjɔ̃] *nm* lorry (*BRIT*), truck; (*plus petit, fermé*) van; (*charge*): **~ de sable/cailloux** lorry-load (*BRIT*) *ou* truck-load of sand/stones; **~ de dépannage** breakdown (*BRIT*) *ou* tow (*US*) truck.

camion-citerne, *pl* **camions-citernes** [kamjɔ̃sitɛʀn(ə)] *nm* tanker.

camionnage [kamjɔnaʒ] *nm* haulage (*BRIT*), trucking (*US*); **frais/entreprise de ~** haulage costs/business.

camionnette [kamjɔnɛt] *nf* (small) van.

camionneur [kamjɔnœʀ] *nm* (*entrepreneur*) haulage contractor (*BRIT*), trucker (*US*); (*chauffeur*) lorry (*BRIT*) *ou* truck driver; van driver.

camisole [kamizɔl] *nf*: ~ **(de force)** straitjacket.

camomille [kamɔmij] *nf* camomile; (*boisson*) camomile tea.

camouflage [kamuflaʒ] *nm* camouflage.

camoufler [kamufle] *vt* to camouflage; (*fig*) to conceal, cover up.

camouflet [kamufle] *nm* (*fam*) snub.

camp [kɑ̃] *nm* camp; (*fig*) side; ~ **de nudistes/vacances** nudist/holiday camp; ~ **de concentration** concentration camp.

campagnard, e [kɑ̃paɲaʀ, -aʀd(ə)] *adj* country *cpd* ♦ *nm/f* countryman/woman.

campagne [kɑ̃paɲ] *nf* country, countryside; (*MIL, POL, COMM*) campaign; **en** ~ (*MIL*) in the field; **à la** ~ in/to the country; **faire** ~ **pour** to campaign for; ~ **électorale** election campaign; ~ **de publicité** advertising campaign.

campanile [kɑ̃panil] *nm* (*tour*) bell tower.

campé, e [kɑ̃pe] *adj*: **bien** ~ (*personnage, tableau*) well-drawn.

campement [kɑ̃pmɑ̃] *nm* camp, encampment.

camper [kɑ̃pe] *vi* to camp ♦ *vt* (*chapeau etc*) to pull *ou* put on firmly; (*dessin*) to sketch; **se ~ devant** to plant o.s. in front of.

campeur, euse [kɑ̃pœʀ, -øz] *nm/f* camper.

camphre [kɑ̃fʀ(ə)] *nm* camphor.

camphré, e [kɑ̃fʀe] *adj* camphorated.

camping [kɑ̃piŋ] *nm* camping; **(terrain de)** ~ campsite, camping site; **faire du** ~ to go camping; **faire du** ~ **sauvage** to camp rough.

camping-car [kɑ̃piŋkaʀ] *nm* caravanette, camper (*US*).

campus [kɑ̃pys] *nm* campus.

camus, e [kamy, -yz] *adj*: **nez** ~ pug nose.

Canada [kanada] *nm*: **le** ~ Canada.

canadair [kanadɛʀ] *nm* ® fire-fighting plane.

canadien, ne [kanadjɛ̃, -ɛn] *adj* Canadian ♦ *nm/f*: **C~, ne** Canadian ♦ *nf* (*veste*) fur-lined jacket.

canaille [kanaj] *nf* (*péj*) scoundrel; (*populace*) riff-raff ♦ *adj* raffish, rakish.

canal, aux [kanal, -o] *nm* canal; (*naturel*) channel; (*ADMIN*): **par le** ~ **de** through (the medium of), via; ~ **de distribution/télévision** distribution/television channel; ~ **de Panama/Suez** Panama/Suez Canal.

canalisation [kanalizɑsjɔ̃] *nf* (*tuyau*) pipe.

canaliser [kanalize] *vt* to canalize; (*fig*) to channel.

canapé [kanape] *nm* settee, sofa; (*CULIN*) canapé, open sandwich.

canapé-lit, *pl* **canapés-lits** [kanapeli] *nm* sofa bed.

canaque [kanak] *adj* of *ou* from New Caledonia ♦ *nm/f*: **C~** native of New Caledonia.

canard [kanaʀ] *nm* duck.

canari [kanaʀi] *nm* canary.

Canaries [kanaʀi] *nfpl*: **les (îles)** ~ the Canary Islands, the Canaries.

cancaner [kɑ̃kane] *vi* to gossip (maliciously); (*canard*) to quack.

cancanier, ière [kɑ̃kanje, -jɛʀ] *adj* gossiping.

cancans [kɑ̃kɑ̃] *nmpl* (malicious) gossip *sg.*

cancer [kɑ̃sɛʀ] *nm* cancer; (*signe*): **le C~** Cancer, the Crab; **être du C~** to be Cancer; **il a un ~** he has cancer.

cancéreux, euse [kɑ̃seʀø, -øz] *adj* cancerous; (*personne*) suffering from cancer.

cancérigène [kɑ̃seʀiʒɛn] *adj* carcinogenic.

cancérologue [kɑ̃seʀɔlɔg] *nm/f* cancer specialist.

cancre [kɑ̃kʀ(ə)] *nm* dunce.

cancrelat [kɑ̃kʀəla] *nm* cockroach.

candélabre [kɑ̃delɑbʀ(ə)] *nm* candelabrum; (*lampadaire*) street lamp, lamppost.

candeur [kɑ̃dœʀ] *nf* ingenuousness, guilelessness.

candi [kɑ̃di] *adj inv*: **sucre ~** (sugar-)candy.

candidat, e [kɑ̃dida, -at] *nm/f* candidate; (*à un poste*) applicant, candidate.

candidature [kɑ̃didatyʀ] *nf* candidacy; application; **poser sa ~** to submit an application, apply.

candide [kɑ̃did] *adj* ingenuous, guileless, naïve.

cane [kan] *nf* (female) duck.

caneton [kantɔ̃] *nm* duckling.

canette [kanɛt] *nf* (*de bière*) (flip-top) bottle; (*de machine à coudre*) spool.

canevas [kanva] *nm* (*COUTURE*) canvas (for tapestry work); (*fig*) framework, structure.

caniche [kaniʃ] *nm* poodle.

caniculaire [kanikylɛʀ] *adj* (*chaleur, jour*) scorching.

canicule [kanikyl] *nf* scorching heat; midsummer heat, dog days *pl*.

canif [kanif] *nm* penknife, pocket knife.

canin, e [kanɛ̃, -in] *adj* canine ♦ *nf* canine (tooth), eye tooth; **exposition ~e** dog show.

caniveau, x [kanivo] *nm* gutter.

cannabis [kanabis] *nm* cannabis.

canne [kan] *nf* (walking) stick; **~ à pêche** fishing rod; **~ à sucre** sugar cane; **les ~s blanches** (*les aveugles*) the blind.

canné, e [kane] *adj* (*chaise*) cane *cpd*.

cannelé, e [kanle] *adj* fluted.

cannelle [kanɛl] *nf* cinnamon.

cannelure [kanlyʀ] *nf* fluting *no pl*.

canner [kane] *vt* (*chaise*) to make *ou* repair with cane.

cannibale [kanibal] *nm/f* cannibal.

cannibalisme [kanibalism(ə)] *nm* cannibalism.

canoë [kanɔe] *nm* canoe; (*sport*) canoeing; **~ (kayak)** kayak.

canon [kanɔ̃] *nm* (*arme*) gun; (*HIST*) cannon; (*d'une arme: tube*) barrel; (*fig*) model; (*MUS*) canon ♦ *adj*: **droit ~** canon law; **~ rayé** rifled barrel.

cañon [kaɲɔ̃] *nm* canyon.

canonique [kanɔnik] *adj*: **âge ~** respectable age.

canoniser [kanɔnize] *vt* to canonize.

canonnade [kanɔnad] *nf* cannonade.

canonnier [kanɔnje] *nm* gunner.

canonnière [kanɔnjɛʀ] *nf* gunboat.

canot [kano] *nm* boat, ding(h)y; **~ pneumatique** rubber *ou* inflatable ding(h)y; **~ de sauvetage** lifeboat.

canotage [kanɔtaʒ] *nm* rowing.

canoter [kanɔte] *vi* to go rowing.

canoteur, euse [kanɔtœʀ, -øz] *nm/f* rower.

canotier [kanɔtje] *nm* boater.

Cantal [kɑ̃tal] *nm*: **le ~** Cantal.

cantate [kɑ̃tat] *nf* cantata.

cantatrice [kɑ̃tatʀis] *nf* (opera) singer.

cantilène [kɑ̃tilɛn] *nf* (*MUS*) cantilena.

cantine [kɑ̃tin] *nf* canteen; (*réfectoire d'école*) dining hall.

cantique [kɑ̃tik] *nm* hymn.

canton [kɑ̃tɔ̃] *nm* district (*consisting of several communes*); (*en Suisse*) canton.

In France the **canton** *is the administrative division represented by a councillor in the* **Conseil général**. *It comprises a number of* **communes** *and is, in turn, a subdivision of the* **arrondissement**. *In Switzerland the cantons are the 23 sovereign political divisions comprising the Swiss confederation.*

---

cantonade [kɑ̃tɔnad]: **à la ~** *adv* to everyone in general; (*crier*) from the rooftops.

cantonais, e [kɑ̃tɔnɛ, -ɛz] *adj* Cantonese ♦ *nm* (*LING*) Cantonese.

cantonal, e, aux [kɑ̃tɔnal, -o] *adj* cantonal, ≈ district.

cantonnement [kɑ̃tɔnmɑ̃] *nm* (*lieu*) billet; (*action*) billeting.

cantonner [kɑ̃tɔne] *vt* (*MIL*) to billet (*BRIT*), quarter; to station; **se ~ dans** to confine o.s. to.

cantonnier [kɑ̃tɔnje] *nm* roadmender.

canular [kanylaʀ] *nm* hoax.

CAO *sigle f* (= *conception assistée par ordinateur*) CAD.

caoutchouc [kautʃu] *nm* rubber; **~ mousse** foam rubber; **en ~** rubber *cpd*.

caoutchouté, e [kautʃute] *adj* rubberized.

caoutchouteux, euse [kautʃutø, -øz] *adj* rubbery.

CAP *sigle m* (= *Certificat d'aptitude professionnelle*) vocational training certificate taken at secondary school.

cap [kap] *nm* (*GÉO*) cape; headland; (*fig*) hurdle; watershed; (*NAVIG*): **changer de ~** to change course; **mettre le ~ sur** to head *ou* steer for; **doubler** *ou* **passer le ~** (*fig*) to get over the worst; **Le C~** Cape Town; **le ~ de Bonne Espérance** the Cape of Good Hope; **le ~ Horn** Cape Horn; **les îles du C~ Vert** (*aussi*: **le C~-Vert**) the Cape Verde Islands.

capable [kapabl(ə)] *adj* able, capable; **~ de qch/faire** capable of sth/doing; **il est ~ d'oublier** he could easily forget; **spectacle/livre ~ d'intéresser** show/book liable *ou* likely to be of interest.

capacité [kapasite], *nf* (*compétence*) ability; (*JUR, INFORM, d'un récipient*) capacity; ~ **(en droit)** *basic legal qualification*.
caparaçonner [kaparasɔne] *vt* (*fig*) to clad.
cape [kap] *nf* cape, cloak; **rire sous** ~ to laugh up one's sleeve.
capeline [kaplin] *nf* wide-brimmed hat.
CAPES [kapɛs] *sigle m* (= *Certificat d'aptitude au professorat de l'enseignement du second degré*) *secondary teaching diploma*.

The **CAPES** *is a competitive examination for the recruitment of French secondary school teachers. It is taken after the* **licence.** *Successful candidates become fully-qualified teachers (professeurs certifiés); see also* **agrégation.**

capésien, ne [kapesjɛ̃, -ɛn] *nm/f person who holds the CAPES.*
CAPET [kapɛt] *sigle m* (= *Certificat d'aptitude au professorat de l'enseignement technique*) *technical teaching diploma.*
capharnaüm [kafarnaɔm] *nm* shambles *sg.*
capillaire [kapilɛr] *adj* (*soins, lotion*) hair *cpd*; (*vaisseau etc*) capillary; **artiste** ~ hair artist *ou* designer.
capillarité [kapilarite] *nf* capillary action.
capilliculteur [kapilikyltœr] *nm* hair-care specialist.
capilotade [kapilɔtad]: **en** ~ *adv* crushed to a pulp; smashed to pieces.
capitaine [kapitɛn] *nm* captain; ~ **des pompiers** fire chief (*BRIT*), fire marshal (*US*); ~ **au long cours** master mariner.
capitainerie [kapitɛnri] *nf* (*du port*) harbour (*BRIT*) *ou* harbor (*US*) master's (office).
capital, e, aux [kapital, -o] *adj* major; of paramount importance; fundamental; (*JUR*) capital ♦ *nm* capital; (*fig*) stock; asset ♦ *nf* (*ville*) capital; (*lettre*) capital (letter) ♦ *nmpl* (*fonds*) capital *sg*, money *sg*; **les sept péchés capitaux** the seven deadly sins; **peine** ~**e** capital punishment; ~ **(social)** authorized capital; ~ **d'exploitation** working capital.
capitaliser [kapitalize] *vt* to amass, build up; (*COMM*) to capitalize ♦ *vi* to save.
capitalisme [kapitalism(ə)] *nm* capitalism.
capitaliste [kapitalist(ə)] *adj, nm/f* capitalist.
capiteux, euse [kapitø, -øz] *adj* (*vin, parfum*) heady; (*sensuel*) sensuous, alluring.
capitonnage [kapitɔnaʒ] *nm* padding.
capitonné, e [kapitɔne] *adj* padded.
capitonner [kapitɔne] *vt* to pad.
capitulation [kapitylasjɔ̃] *nf* capitulation.
capituler [kapityle] *vi* to capitulate.
caporal, aux [kapɔral, -o] *nm* lance corporal.
caporal-chef, *pl* **caporaux-chefs** [kapɔralʃɛf, kapɔro-] *nm* corporal.
capot [kapo] *nm* (*AUTO*) bonnet (*BRIT*), hood (*US*) ♦ *adj inv* (*CARTES*): **être** ~ to lose without taking a single trick.
capote [kapɔt] *nf* (*de voiture*) hood (*BRIT*), top

(*US*); (*de soldat*) greatcoat; ~ **(anglaise)** (*fam*) rubber, condom.
capoter [kapɔte] *vi* to overturn; (*négociations*) to founder.
câpre [kɑpʀ(ə)] *nf* caper.
caprice [kapʀis] *nm* whim, caprice; passing fancy; ~**s** *nmpl* (*de la mode etc*) vagaries; **faire un** ~ to throw a tantrum; **faire des** ~**s** to be temperamental.
capricieux, euse [kapʀisjø, -øz] *adj* capricious; whimsical; temperamental.
Capricorne [kapʀikɔʀn] *nm*: **le** ~ Capricorn, the Goat; **être du** ~ to be Capricorn.
capsule [kapsyl] *nf* (*de bouteille*) cap; (*amorce*) primer; cap; (*BOT etc, spatiale*) capsule.
captage [kaptaʒ] *nm* (*d'une émission de radio*) picking-up; (*d'énergie, d'eau*) harnessing.
capter [kapte] *vt* (*ondes radio*) to pick up; (*eau*) to harness; (*fig*) to win, capture.
capteur [kaptœr] *nm*: ~ **solaire** solar collector.
captieux, euse [kapsjø, -øz] *adj* specious.
captif, ive [kaptif, -iv] *adj, nm/f* captive.
captivant, e [kaptivɑ̃, -ɑ̃t] *adj* captivating.
captiver [kaptive] *vt* to captivate.
captivité [kaptivite] *nf* captivity; **en** ~ in captivity.
capture [kaptyr] *nf* capture, catching *no pl*; catch.
capturer [kaptyre] *vt* to capture, catch.
capuche [kapyʃ] *nf* hood.
capuchon [kapyʃɔ̃] *nm* hood; (*de stylo*) cap, top.
capucin [kapysɛ̃] *nm* Capuchin monk.
capucine [kapysin] *nf* (*BOT*) nasturtium.
Cap-Vert [kabvɛr] *nm*: **le** ~ Cape Verde.
caquelon [kaklɔ̃] *nm* (*ustensile de cuisson*) fondue pot.
caquet [kakɛ] *nm*: **rabattre le** ~ **à qn** to bring sb down a peg or two.
caqueter [kakte] *vi* (*poule*) to cackle; (*fig*) to prattle.
car [kar] *nm* coach (*BRIT*), bus ♦ *conj* because, for; ~ **de police** police van; ~ **de reportage** broadcasting *ou* radio van.
carabine [karabin] *nf* carbine, rifle; ~ **à air comprimé** airgun.
carabiné, e [karabine] *adj* violent; (*cocktail, amende*) stiff.
Caracas [karakas] *n* Caracas.
caracoler [karakɔle] *vi* to caracole, prance.
caractère [karaktɛr] *nm* (*gén*) character; **en** ~**s gras** in bold type; **en petits** ~**s** in small print; **en** ~**s d'imprimerie** in block capitals; **avoir du** ~ to have character; **avoir bon/ mauvais** ~ to be good-/ill-natured *ou* tempered; ~ **de remplacement** wild card (*INFORM*); ~**s/seconde (cps)** characters per second (cps).
caractériel, le [karakterjɛl] *adj* (*enfant*) (emotionally) disturbed ♦ *nm/f* problem child; **troubles** ~**s** emotional problems.

caractérisé, e [kaʀakteʀize] adj: c'est une grippe/de l'insubordination ~e it is a clear(-cut) case of flu/insubordination.

caractériser [kaʀakteʀize] vt to characterize; se ~ par to be characterized ou distinguished by.

caractéristique [kaʀakteʀistik] adj, nf characteristic.

carafe [kaʀaf] nf decanter; carafe.

carafon [kaʀafɔ̃] nm small carafe.

caraïbe [kaʀaib] adj Caribbean; les C~s nfpl the Caribbean (Islands); la mer des C~s the Caribbean Sea.

carambolage [kaʀɑ̃bɔlaʒ] nm multiple crash, pileup.

caramel [kaʀamɛl] nm (bonbon) caramel, toffee; (substance) caramel.

caraméliser [kaʀamelize] vt to caramelize.

carapace [kaʀapas] nf shell.

carapater [kaʀapate]: se ~ vi to take to one's heels, scram.

carat [kaʀa] nm carat; or à 18 ~s 18-carat gold.

caravane [kaʀavan] nf caravan.

caravanier [kaʀavanje] nm caravanner.

caravaning [kaʀavaniŋ] nm caravanning; (emplacement) caravan site.

caravelle [kaʀavɛl] nf caravel.

carbonate [kaʀbɔnat] nm (CHIMIE): ~ de soude sodium carbonate.

carbone [kaʀbɔn] nm carbon; (feuille) carbon, sheet of carbon paper; (double) carbon (copy).

carbonique [kaʀbɔnik] adj: gaz ~ carbon dioxide; neige ~ dry ice.

carbonisé, e [kaʀbɔnize] adj charred; mourir ~ to be burned to death.

carboniser [kaʀbɔnize] vt to carbonize; (brûler complètement) to burn down, reduce to ashes.

carburant [kaʀbyʀɑ̃] nm (motor) fuel.

carburateur [kaʀbyʀatœʀ] nm carburettor.

carburation [kaʀbyʀasjɔ̃] nf carburation.

carburer [kaʀbyʀe] vi (moteur): bien/mal ~ to be well/badly tuned.

carcan [kaʀkɑ̃] nm (fig) yoke, shackles pl.

carcasse [kaʀkas] nf carcass; (de véhicule etc) shell.

carcéral, e, aux [kaʀseʀal, -o] adj prison cpd.

carcinogène [kaʀsinɔʒɛn] adj carcinogenic.

cardan [kaʀdɑ̃] nm universal joint.

carder [kaʀde] vt to card.

cardiaque [kaʀdjak] adj cardiac, heart cpd ♦ nm/f heart patient; être ~ to have a heart condition.

cardigan [kaʀdigɑ̃] nm cardigan.

cardinal, e, aux [kaʀdinal, -o] adj cardinal ♦ nm (REL) cardinal.

cardiologie [kaʀdjɔlɔʒi] nf cardiology.

cardiologue [kaʀdjɔlɔg] nm/f cardiologist, heart specialist.

cardio-vasculaire [kaʀdjɔvaskylɛʀ] adj cardio-vascular.

cardon [kaʀdɔ̃] nm cardoon.

carême [kaʀɛm] nm: le C~ Lent.

carence [kaʀɑ̃s] nf incompetence, inadequacy; (manque) deficiency; ~ vitaminique vitamin deficiency.

carène [kaʀɛn] nf hull.

caréner [kaʀene] vt (NAVIG) to careen; (carrosserie) to streamline.

caressant, e [kaʀɛsɑ̃, -ɑ̃t] adj affectionate; caressing, tender.

caresse [kaʀɛs] nf caress.

caresser [kaʀese] vt to caress, stroke, fondle; (fig: projet, espoir) to toy with.

cargaison [kaʀgɛzɔ̃] nf cargo, freight.

cargo [kaʀgo] nm cargo boat, freighter; ~ mixte cargo and passenger ship.

cari [kaʀi] nm = curry.

caricatural, e, aux [kaʀikatyʀal, -o] adj caricatural, caricature-like.

caricature [kaʀikatyʀ] nf caricature; (politique etc) (satirical) cartoon.

caricaturer [kaʀikatyʀe] vt (personne) to caricature; (politique etc) to satirize.

caricaturiste [kaʀikatyʀist(ə)] nm/f caricaturist; (satirical) cartoonist.

carie [kaʀi] nf: la ~ (dentaire) tooth decay; une ~ a bad tooth.

carié, e [kaʀje] adj: dent ~e bad ou decayed tooth.

carillon [kaʀijɔ̃] nm (d'église) bells pl; (de pendule) chimes pl; (de porte): ~ (électrique) (electric) door chime ou bell.

carillonner [kaʀijɔne] vi to ring, chime, peal.

caritatif, ive [kaʀitatif, -iv] adj charitable.

carlingue [kaʀlɛ̃g] nf cabin.

carmélite [kaʀmelit] nf Carmelite nun.

carmin [kaʀmɛ̃] adj inv crimson.

carnage [kaʀnaʒ] nm carnage, slaughter.

carnassier, ière [kaʀnasje, -jɛʀ] adj carnivorous ♦ nm carnivore.

carnation [kaʀnɑsjɔ̃] nf complexion; ~s nfpl (PEINTURE) flesh tones.

carnaval [kaʀnaval] nm carnival.

carné, e [kaʀne] adj meat cpd, meat-based.

carnet [kaʀnɛ] nm (calepin) notebook; (de tickets, timbres etc) book; (d'école) school report; (journal intime) diary; ~ d'adresses address book; ~ de chèques cheque book (BRIT), checkbook (US); ~ de commandes order book; ~ de notes (SCOL) (school) report; ~ à souches counterfoil book.

carnier [kaʀnje] nm gamebag.

carnivore [kaʀnivɔʀ] adj carnivorous ♦ nm carnivore.

Carolines [kaʀɔlin] nfpl: les ~ the Caroline Islands.

carotide [kaʀɔtid] nf carotid (artery).

carotte [kaʀɔt] nf (aussi fig) carrot.

Carpates [kaʀpat] nfpl: les ~ the Carpathians, the Carpathian Mountains.

carpe [kaʀp(ə)] nf carp.

carpette [kaʀpɛt] *nf* rug.
carquois [kaʀkwa] *nm* quiver.
carre [kaʀ] *nf* (*de ski*) edge.
carré, e [kaʀe] *adj* square; (*fig: franc*) straight-forward ♦ *nm* (*de terrain, jardin*) patch, plot; (*NAVIG: salle*) wardroom; (*MATH*) square; (*CARTES*): ~ **d'as/de rois** four aces/kings; **élever un nombre au** ~ to square a number; **mètre/kilomètre** ~ square metre/kilometre; ~ **de soie** silk headsquare *ou* headscarf; ~ **d'agneau** loin of lamb.
carreau, x [kaʀo] *nm* (*en faïence etc*) (floor) tile; (*wall*) tile; (*de fenêtre*) (window) pane; (*motif*) check, square; (*CARTES: couleur*) diamonds *pl*; (*: carte*) diamond; **tissu à ~x** checked fabric; **papier à ~x** squared paper.
carrefour [kaʀfuʀ] *nm* crossroads *sg*.
carrelage [kaʀlaʒ] *nm* tiling; (tiled) floor.
carreler [kaʀle] *vt* to tile.
carrelet [kaʀlɛ] *nm* (*poisson*) plaice.
carreleur [kaʀlœʀ] *nm* (floor) tiler.
carrément [kaʀemɑ̃] *adv* (*franchement*) straight out, bluntly; (*sans détours, sans hésiter*) straight; (*nettement*) definitely; **il l'a ~ mis à la porte** he threw him straight out.
carrer [kaʀe]: **se ~** *vi*: **se ~ dans un fauteuil** to settle o.s. comfortably *ou* ensconce o.s. in an armchair.
carrière [kaʀjɛʀ] *nf* (*de roches*) quarry; (*métier*) career; **militaire de ~** professional soldier; **faire ~ dans** to make one's career in.
carriériste [kaʀjeʀist(ə)] *nm/f* careerist.
carriole [kaʀjɔl] *nf* (*péj*) old cart.
carrossable [kaʀɔsabl(ə)] *adj* suitable for (motor) vehicles.
carrosse [kaʀɔs] *nm* (horse-drawn) coach.
carrosserie [kaʀɔsʀi] *nf* body, bodywork *no pl* (*BRIT*); (*activité, commerce*) coachwork (*BRIT*), (car) body manufacturing; **atelier de ~** (*pour réparations*) body shop, panel beaters' (yard) (*BRIT*).
carrossier [kaʀɔsje] *nm* coachbuilder (*BRIT*), (car) body repairer; (*dessinateur*) car designer.
carrousel [kaʀuzɛl] *nm* (*ÉQUITATION*) carousel; (*fig*) merry-go-round.
carrure [kaʀyʀ] *nf* build; (*fig*) stature.
cartable [kaʀtabl(ə)] *nm* (*d'écolier*) satchel, (school)bag.
carte [kaʀt(ə)] *nf* (*de géographie*) map; (*marine, du ciel*) chart; (*de fichier, d'abonnement etc, à jouer*) card; (*au restaurant*) menu; (*aussi: ~ postale*) (post)card; (*aussi: ~ de visite*) (visiting) card; **avoir/donner ~ blanche** to have/give carte blanche *ou* a free hand; **tirer les ~s à qn** to read sb's cards; **jouer aux ~s** to play cards; **jouer ~s sur table** (*fig*) to put one's cards on the table; **à la ~** (*au restaurant*) à la carte; ~ **bancaire** cash card; **à circuit imprimé** printed circuit; ~ **à puce** smartcard; ~ **de crédit** credit card; ~

d'état-major ≈ Ordnance (*BRIT*) *ou* Geological (*US*) Survey map; ~ **de fidélité** loyalty card; **la ~ grise** (*AUTO*) ≈ the (car) registration document; ~ **d'identité** identity card; ~ **jeune** young person's railcard; ~ **perforée** punch(ed) card; ~ **de séjour** residence permit; ~ **routière** road map; **la ~ verte** (*AUTO*) the green card; **la ~ des vins** the wine list.
cartel [kaʀtɛl] *nm* cartel.
carte-lettre, *pl* **cartes-lettres** [kaʀtəlɛtʀ(ə)] *nf* letter-card.
carte-mère, *pl* **cartes-mères** [kaʀtəmɛʀ] *nf* (*INFORM*) mother board.
carter [kaʀtɛʀ] *nm* (*AUTO: d'huile*) sump (*BRIT*), oil pan (*US*); (*: de la boîte de vitesses*) casing; (*de bicyclette*) chain guard.
carte-réponse, *pl* **cartes-réponses** [kaʀt(ə)ʀepɔ̃s] *nf* reply card.
cartésien, ne [kaʀtezjɛ̃, -ɛn] *adj* Cartesian.
Carthage [kaʀtaʒ] *n* Carthage.
carthaginois, e [kaʀtaʒinwa, -waz] *adj* Carthaginian.
cartilage [kaʀtilaʒ] *nm* (*ANAT*) cartilage.
cartilagineux, euse [kaʀtilaʒinø, -øz] *adj* (*viande*) gristly.
cartographe [kaʀtɔgʀaf] *nm/f* cartographer.
cartographie [kaʀtɔgʀafi] *nf* cartography, map-making.
cartomancie [kaʀtɔmɑ̃si] *nf* fortune-telling, card-reading.
cartomancien, ne [kaʀtɔmɑ̃sjɛ̃, -ɛn] *nm/f* fortune-teller (*with cards*).
carton [kaʀtɔ̃] *nm* (*matériau*) cardboard; (*boîte*) (cardboard) box; (*d'invitation*) invitation card; (*ART*) sketch; cartoon; **en ~** cardboard *cpd*; **faire un ~** (*au tir*) to have a go at the rifle range; to score a hit; ~ (**à dessin**) portfolio.
cartonnage [kaʀtɔnaʒ] *nm* cardboard (packing).
cartonné, e [kaʀtɔne] *adj* (*livre*) hardback, cased.
carton-pâte [kaʀtɔ̃pat] *nm* pasteboard; **de ~** (*fig*) cardboard *cpd*.
cartouche [kaʀtuʃ] *nf* cartridge; (*de cigarettes*) carton.
cartouchière [kaʀtuʃjɛʀ] *nf* cartridge belt.
cas [kɑ] *nm* case; **faire peu de ~/grand ~ de** to attach little/great importance to; **le ~ échéant** if need be; **en aucun ~** on no account, under no circumstances (whatsoever); **au ~ où** in case; **dans ce ~** in that case; **en ~ de** in case of, in the event of; **en ~ de besoin** if need be; **en ce ~** in that case; **en tout ~** in any case, at any rate; ~ **de conscience** matter of conscience; ~ **de force majeure** case of absolute necessity; (*ASSURANCES*) act of God; ~ **limite** borderline case; ~ **social** social problem.
Casablanca [kazablɑ̃ka] *n* Casablanca.

casanier, ière [kazanje, -jɛʀ] *adj* stay-at-home.

casaque [kazak] *nf* (*de jockey*) blouse.

cascade [kaskad] *nf* waterfall, cascade; (*fig*) stream, torrent.

cascadeur, euse [kaskadœʀ, -øz] *nm/f* stuntman/girl.

case [kɑz] *nf* (*hutte*) hut; (*compartiment*) compartment; (*pour le courrier*) pigeonhole; (*de mots croisés, d'échiquier*) square; (*sur un formulaire*) box.

casemate [kazmat] *nf* blockhouse.

caser [kɑze] *vt* (*mettre*) to put; (*loger*) to put up; (*péj*) to find a job for; to marry off; **se ~** (*personne*) to settle down.

caserne [kazɛʀn(ə)] *nf* barracks.

casernement [kazɛʀnəmɑ̃] *nm* barrack buildings *pl*.

cash [kaʃ] *adv*: **payer ~** to pay cash down.

casier [kazje] *nm* (*à journaux etc*) rack; (*de bureau*) filing cabinet; (*: à cases*) set of pigeonholes; (*case*) compartment; pigeonhole; (*: à clef*) locker; (*PÊCHE*) lobster pot; **~ à bouteilles** bottle rack; **~ judiciaire** police record.

casino [kazino] *nm* casino.

casque [kask(ə)] *nm* helmet; (*chez le coiffeur*) (hair-)dryer; (*pour audition*) (head-)phones *pl*, headset; **les C~s bleus** the UN peacekeeping force.

casquer [kaske] *vi* (*fam*) to cough up, stump up (*BRIT*).

casquette [kaskɛt] *nf* cap.

cassable [kɑsabl(ə)] *adj* (*fragile*) breakable.

cassant, e [kɑsɑ̃, -ɑ̃t] *adj* brittle; (*fig*) brusque, abrupt.

cassate [kasat] *nf*: **(glace) ~** cassata.

cassation [kɑsasjɔ̃] *nf*: **se pourvoir en ~** to lodge an appeal; **recours en ~** appeal to the Supreme Court.

casse [kas] *nf* (*pour voitures*): **mettre à la ~** to scrap, send to the breakers (*BRIT*); (*dégâts*): **il y a eu de la ~** there were a lot of breakages; (*TYPO*): **haut/bas de ~** upper/lower case.

cassé, e [kɑse] *adj* (*voix*) cracked; (*vieillard*) bent.

casse-cou [kɑsku] *adj inv* daredevil, reckless; **crier ~ à qn** to warn sb (*against a risky undertaking*).

casse-croûte [kɑskʀut] *nm inv* snack.

casse-noisette(s) [kɑsnwazɛt], **casse-noix** [kɑsnwa] *nm inv* nutcrackers *pl*.

casse-pieds [kɑspje] *adj, nm/f inv* (*fam*): **il est ~, c'est un ~** he's a pain (in the neck).

casser [kɑse] *vt* to break; (*ADMIN: gradé*) to demote; (*JUR*) to quash; (*COMM*): **~ les prix** to slash prices; **se ~** *vi* to break; (*fam*) to go, leave ♦ *vt*: **se ~ la jambe/une jambe** to break one's leg/a leg; **à tout ~** fantastic, brilliant; **se ~ net** to break clean off.

casserole [kɑsʀɔl] *nf* saucepan; **à la ~** (*CULIN*) braised.

casse-tête [kɑstɛt] *nm inv* (*fig*) brain teaser; (*difficultés*) headache (*fig*).

cassette [kasɛt] *nf* (*bande magnétique*) cassette; (*coffret*) casket; **~ numérique** digital compact cassette.

casseur [kɑsœʀ] *nm* hooligan; rioter.

cassis [kasis] *nm* blackcurrant; (*de la route*) dip, bump.

cassonade [kasɔnad] *nf* brown sugar.

cassoulet [kasulɛ] *nm* *sausage and bean hotpot*.

cassure [kɑsyʀ] *nf* break, crack.

castagnettes [kastaɲɛt] *nfpl* castanets.

caste [kast(ə)] *nf* caste.

castillan, e [kastijɑ̃, -an] *adj* Castilian ♦ *nm* (*LING*) Castilian.

Castille [kastij] *nf*: **la ~** Castile.

castor [kastɔʀ] *nm* beaver.

castrer [kastʀe] *vt* (*mâle*) to castrate; (*femelle*) to spay; (*cheval*) to geld; (*chat, chien*) to doctor (*BRIT*), fix (*US*).

cataclysme [kataklism(ə)] *nm* cataclysm.

catacombes [katakɔ̃b] *nfpl* catacombs.

catadioptre [katadjɔptʀ(ə)] *nm* = **cataphote**.

catafalque [katafalk(ə)] *nm* catafalque.

catalan, e [katalɑ̃, -an] *adj* Catalan, Catalonian ♦ *nm* (*LING*) Catalan.

Catalogne [katalɔɲ] *nf*: **la ~** Catalonia.

catalogue [katalɔg] *nm* catalogue.

cataloguer [katalɔge] *vt* to catalogue, list; (*péj*) to put a label on.

catalyse [kataliz] *nf* catalysis.

catalyser [katalize] *vt* to catalyze.

catalyseur [katalizœʀ] *nm* catalyst.

catalytique [katalitik] *adj* catalytic.

catamaran [katamaʀɑ̃] *nm* (*voilier*) catamaran.

cataphote [katafɔt] *nm* reflector.

cataplasme [kataplasm(ə)] *nm* poultice.

catapulte [katapylt(ə)] *nf* catapult.

catapulter [katapylte] *vt* to catapult.

cataracte [kataʀakt(ə)] *nf* cataract; **opérer qn de la ~** to operate on sb for a cataract.

catarrhe [kataʀ] *nm* catarrh.

catarrheux, euse [kataʀø, -øz] *adj* catarrhal.

catastrophe [katastʀɔf] *nf* catastrophe, disaster; **atterrir en ~** to make an emergency landing; **partir en ~** to rush away.

catastropher [katastʀɔfe] *vt* (*personne*) to shatter.

catastrophique [katastʀɔfik] *adj* catastrophic, disastrous.

catch [katʃ] *nm* (all-in) wrestling.

catcheur, euse [katʃœʀ, -øz] *nm/f* (all-in) wrestler.

catéchiser [kateʃize] *vt* to indoctrinate; to lecture.

catéchisme [kateʃism(ə)] *nm* catechism.

catéchumène [katekymɛn] *nm/f* catechumen, *person attending religious instruction prior to baptism*.

catégorie [kategɔʀi] *nf* category; (*BOUCHERIE*):

morceaux de première/deuxième ~ prime/ second cuts.

catégorique [kategɔʀik] *adj* categorical.

catégoriquement [kategɔʀikmã] *adv* categorically.

catégoriser [kategɔʀize] *vt* to categorize.

caténaire [katenɛʀ] *nf* (*RAIL*) catenary.

cathédrale [katedʀal] *nf* cathedral.

cathéter [katetɛʀ] *nm* (*MÉD*) catheter.

cathode [katɔd] *nf* cathode.

cathodique [katɔdik] *adj*: **rayons ~s** cathode rays; **tube/écran ~** cathode-ray tube/ screen.

catholicisme [katɔlisism(ə)] *nm* (Roman) Catholicism.

catholique [katɔlik] *adj*, *nm/f* (Roman) Catholic; **pas très ~** a bit shady *ou* fishy.

catimini [katimini]: **en ~** *adv* on the sly, on the quiet.

catogan [katɔgã] *nm* bow (*tying hair on neck*).

Caucase [kokaz] *nm*: **le ~** the Caucasus (Mountains).

caucasien, ne [kokazjɛ̃, -ɛn] *adj* Caucasian.

cauchemar [koʃmaʀ] *nm* nightmare.

cauchemardesque [koʃmaʀdɛsk(ə)] *adj* nightmarish.

caudal, e, aux [kodal, -o] *adj* caudal, tail *cpd*.

causal, e [kozal] *adj* causal.

causalité [kozalite] *nf* causality.

causant, e [kozã, -ãt] *adj* chatty, talkative.

cause [koz] *nf* cause; (*JUR*) lawsuit, case; brief; **faire ~ commune avec qn** to take sides with sb; **être ~ de** to be the cause of; **à ~ de** because of, owing to; **pour ~ de** on account of; owing to; **(et) pour ~** and for (a very) good reason; **être en ~** (*intérêts*) to be at stake; (*personne*) to be involved; (*qualité*) to be in question; **mettre en ~** to implicate; to call into question; **remettre en ~** to challenge, call into question; **c'est hors de ~** it's out of the question; **en tout état de ~** in any case.

causer [koze] *vt* to cause ♦ *vi* to chat, talk.

causerie [kozʀi] *nf* talk.

causette [kozɛt] *nf*: **faire la** *ou* **un brin de ~** to have a chat.

caustique [kostik] *adj* caustic.

cauteleux, euse [kotlø, -øz] *adj* wily.

cautériser [koteʀize] *vt* to cauterize.

caution [kosjõ] *nf* guarantee, security; deposit; (*JUR*) bail (bond); (*fig*) backing, support; **payer la ~ de qn** to stand bail for sb; **se porter ~ pour qn** to stand security for sb; **libéré sous ~** released on bail; **sujet à ~** unconfirmed.

cautionnement [kosjɔnmã] *nm* (*somme*) guarantee, security.

cautionner [kosjɔne] *vt* to guarantee; (*soutenir*) to support.

cavalcade [kavalkad] *nf* (*fig*) stampede.

cavale [kaval] *nf*: **en ~** on the run.

cavalerie [kavalʀi] *nf* cavalry.

cavalier, ière [kavalje, -jɛʀ] *adj* (*désinvolte*) offhand ♦ *nm/f* rider; (*au bal*) partner ♦ *nm* (*ÉCHECS*) knight; **faire ~ seul** to go it alone; **allée** *ou* **piste cavalière** riding path.

cavalièrement [kavaljɛʀmã] *adv* offhandedly.

cave [kav] *nf* cellar; (*cabaret*) (cellar) nightclub ♦ *adj*: **yeux ~s** sunken eyes; **joues ~s** hollow cheeks.

caveau, x [kavo] *nm* vault.

caverne [kavɛʀn(ə)] *nf* cave.

caverneux, euse [kavɛʀnø, -øz] *adj* cavernous.

caviar [kavjaʀ] *nm* caviar(e).

cavité [kavite] *nf* cavity.

Cayenne [kajɛn] *n* Cayenne.

CB [sibi] *sigle f* (= *citizens' band, canaux banalisés*) CB.

CC *sigle m* = **corps consulaire, compte courant**.

CCI *sigle f* = **Chambre de commerce et d'industrie**.

CCP *sigle m* = **compte chèque postal**.

CD *sigle m* (= *chemin départemental*) secondary road, ≈ B road (*BRIT*); (= *compact disc*) CD; (= *comité directeur*) steering committee; (*POL*) = **corps diplomatique**.

CDD *sigle m* (= *contrat à durée déterminée*) fixed-term contract.

CDF, CdF *sigle mpl* (= *Charbonnages de France*) national coal board.

CDI *sigle m* (= *Centre de documentation et d'information*) school library; (= *contrat à durée indéterminée*) permanent *ou* open-ended contract.

CD-I *sigle m* (= *compact disc interactif*) CD-I®.

CD-Rom [sedeʀɔm] *nm inv* (= *Compact Disc Read Only Memory*) CD-Rom.

CDS *sigle m* (= *Centre des démocrates sociaux*) political party.

CE *sigle f* (= *Communauté européenne*) EC; (*COMM*) = **caisse d'épargne** ♦ *sigle m* (*INDUSTRIE*) = **comité d'entreprise**; (*SCOL*) = **cours élémentaire**.

========================= *MOT-CLÉ*

ce, cette [sə, sɛt] (*devant nm* **cet** + *voyelle ou h aspiré, pl* **ces**) *dét* (*proximité*) this; these *pl*; (*non-proximité*) that; those *pl*; **cette maison(-ci/là)** this/that house; **cette nuit** (*qui vient*) tonight; (*passée*) last night

♦ *pron* **1**: **c'est** it's, it is; **c'est petit/grand/un livre** it's *ou* it is small/big/a book; **c'est un peintre** he's *ou* he is a painter; **ce sont des peintres** they're *ou* they are painters; **c'est le facteur** *etc* (*à la porte*) it's the postman *etc*; **qui est-ce?** who is it?; (*en désignant*) who is he/she?; **qu'est-ce?** what is it?; **c'est toi qui lui as parlé** it was you who spoke to him

2: **c'est que**: **c'est qu'il est lent/qu'il n'a pas faim** the fact is, he's slow/he's not hungry

3 (*expressions*): **c'est ça** (*correct*) that's it, that's right; **c'est toi qui le dis!** that's what YOU say!; *voir aussi* **c'est-à-dire**; **-ci**; **est-ce**

que; n'est-ce pas.
4: ~ **qui**, ~ **que** what; (*chose qui*): **il est bête,** ~ **qui me chagrine** he's stupid, which saddens me; **tout** ~ **qui bouge** everything that *ou* which moves; **tout** ~ **que je sais** all I know; ~ **dont j'ai parlé** what I talked about; ~ **que c'est grand!** it's so big!

CEA *sigle m* (= *Commissariat à l'énergie atomique*) ≈ AEA (= *Atomic Energy Authority*) (*BRIT*), ≈ AEC (= *Atomic Energy Commission*) (*US*).

CECA [seka] *sigle f* (= *Communauté européenne du charbon et de l'acier*) ECSC (= *European Coal and Steel Community*).

ceci [səsi] *pron* this.

cécité [sesite] *nf* blindness.

céder [sede] *vt* to give up ♦ *vi* (*pont, barrage*) to give way; (*personne*) to give in; ~ **à** to yield to, give in to.

CEDEX [sedɛks] *sigle m* (= *courrier d'entreprise à distribution exceptionnelle*) *accelerated postal service for bulk users*.

cédille [sedij] *nf* cedilla.

cèdre [sɛdʀ(ə)] *nm* cedar.

CEE *sigle f* (= *Communauté économique européenne*) EEC.

CEG *sigle m* (= *Collège d'enseignement général*) ≈ junior secondary school (*BRIT*), ≈ junior high school (*US*).

CEI *sigle f* (= *Communauté des États indépendants*) CIS.

ceindre [sɛ̃dʀ(ə)] *vt* (*mettre*) to put on, don; (*entourer*): ~ **qch de qch** to put sth round sth.

ceinture [sɛ̃tyʀ] *nf* belt; (*taille*) waist; (*fig*) ring; belt; circle; ~ **de sauvetage** lifebelt (*BRIT*), life preserver (*US*); ~ **de sécurité** safety *ou* seat belt; ~ **(de sécurité) à enrouleur** inertia reel seat belt; ~ **verte** green belt.

ceinturer [sɛ̃tyʀe] *vt* (*saisir*) to grasp (round the waist); (*entourer*) to surround.

ceinturon [sɛ̃tyʀɔ̃] *nm* belt.

cela [səla] *pron* that; (*comme sujet indéfini*) it; ~ **m'étonne que** it surprises me that; **quand/où** ~**?** when/where (was that)?

célébrant [selebʀɑ̃] *nm* (*REL*) celebrant.

célébration [selebʀɑsjɔ̃] *nf* celebration.

célèbre [selɛbʀ(ə)] *adj* famous.

célébrer [selebʀe] *vt* to celebrate; (*louer*) to extol.

célébrité [selebʀite] *nf* fame; (*star*) celebrity.

céleri [sɛlʀi] *nm*: ~**(-rave)** celeriac; ~ **(en branche)** celery.

célérité [seleʀite] *nf* speed, swiftness.

céleste [selɛst(ə)] *adj* celestial; heavenly.

célibat [seliba] *nm* celibacy; bachelor/spinsterhood.

célibataire [selibatɛʀ] *adj* single, unmarried ♦ *nm/f* bachelor/unmarried *ou* single woman; **mère** ~ single *ou* unmarried mother.

celle, celles [sɛl] *pron voir* **celui**.

cellier [selje] *nm* storeroom.

cellophane [selɔfan] *nf* ® cellophane.

cellulaire [selylɛʀ] *adj* (*BIO*) cell *cpd*, cellular; **voiture** *ou* **fourgon** ~ prison *ou* police van; **régime** ~ confinement.

cellule [selyl] *nf* (*gén*) cell; ~ **(photoélectrique)** electronic eye.

cellulite [selylit] *nf* cellulite.

celluloïd [selylɔid] *nm* ® Celluloid.

cellulose [selyloz] *nf* cellulose.

celte [sɛlt(ə)], **celtique** [sɛltik] *adj* Celt, Celtic.

═══════════════════════════ *MOT-CLÉ*

celui, celle [səlɥi, sɛl] (*mpl* **ceux**, *fpl* **celles**) *pron*
1: ~**-ci/là**, **celle-ci/là** this one/that one; **ceux-ci**, **celles-ci** these (ones); **ceux-là**, **celles-là** those (ones); ~ **de mon frère** my brother's; ~ **du salon/du dessous** the one in (*ou* from) the lounge/below
2: ~ **qui bouge** the one which *ou* that moves; (*personne*) the one who moves; ~ **que je vois** the one (which *ou* that) I see; (*personne*) the one (whom) I see; ~ **dont je parle** the one I'm talking about
3 (*valeur indéfinie*): ~ **qui veut** whoever wants.

─────────────────────────────

cénacle [senakl(ə)] *nm* (literary) coterie *ou* set.

cendre [sɑ̃dʀ(ə)] *nf* ash; ~**s** (*d'un foyer*) ash(es), cinders; (*volcaniques*) ash *sg*; (*d'un défunt*) ashes; **sous la** ~ (*CULIN*) in (the) embers.

cendré, e [sɑ̃dʀe] *adj* (*couleur*) ashen; (*piste*) ~**e** cinder track.

cendreux, euse [sɑ̃dʀø, -øz] *adj* (*terrain, substance*) cindery; (*teint*) ashen.

cendrier [sɑ̃dʀije] *nm* ashtray.

cène [sɛn] *nf*: **la** ~ (Holy) Communion; (*ART*) the Last Supper.

censé, e [sɑ̃se] *adj*: **être** ~ **faire** to be supposed to do.

censément [sɑ̃semɑ̃] *adv* supposedly.

censeur [sɑ̃sœʀ] *nm* (*SCOL*) deputy-head (*BRIT*), vice-principal (*US*); (*CINÉ, POL*) censor.

censure [sɑ̃syʀ] *nf* censorship.

censurer [sɑ̃syʀe] *vt* (*CINÉ, PRESSE*) to censor; (*POL*) to censure.

cent [sɑ̃] *num* a hundred, one hundred; **pour** ~ **(%)** per cent (%); **faire les** ~ **pas** to pace up and down.

centaine [sɑ̃tɛn] *nf*: **une** ~ **(de)** about a hundred, a hundred or so; (*COMM*) a hundred; **plusieurs** ~**s (de)** several hundred; **des** ~**s (de)** hundreds (of).

centenaire [sɑ̃tnɛʀ] *adj* hundred-year-old ♦ *nm/f* centenarian ♦ *nm* (*anniversaire*) centenary.

centième [sɑ̃tjɛm] *num* hundredth.

centigrade [sɑ̃tigʀad] *nm* centigrade.

centigramme [sɑ̃tigʀam] *nm* centigramme.
centilitre [sɑ̃tilitʀ(ə)] *nm* centilitre (*BRIT*), centiliter (*US*).
centime [sɑ̃tim] *nm* centime.
centimètre [sɑ̃timɛtʀ(ə)] *nm* centimetre (*BRIT*), centimeter (*US*); (*ruban*) tape measure, measuring tape.
centrafricain, e [sɑ̃tʀafʀikɛ̃, -ɛn] *adj* of *ou* from the Central African Republic.
central, e, aux [sɑ̃tʀal, -o] *adj* central ♦ *nm*: ~ **(téléphonique)** (telephone) exchange ♦ *nf*: ~**e d'achat** (*COMM*) central buying service; ~**e électrique/nucléaire** electric/nuclear power station; ~**e syndicale** group of affiliated trade unions.
centralisation [sɑ̃tʀalizɑsjɔ̃] *nf* centralization.
centraliser [sɑ̃tʀalize] *vt* to centralize.
centralisme [sɑ̃tʀalism(ə)] *nm* centralism.
centraméricain, e [sɑ̃tʀameʀikɛ̃, -ɛn] *adj* Central American.
centre [sɑ̃tʀ(ə)] *nm* centre (*BRIT*), center (*US*); ~ **commercial/sportif/culturel** shopping/sports/arts centre; ~ **aéré** outdoor centre; ~ **d'appels** call centre; ~ **d'apprentissage** training college; ~ **d'attraction** centre of attraction; ~ **de gravité** centre of gravity; ~ **d'enfouissement des déchets** landfill site; ~ **hospitalier** hospital complex; ~ **de tri** (*POSTES*) sorting office; ~**s nerveux** (*ANAT*) nerve centres.
centrer [sɑ̃tʀe] *vt* to centre (*BRIT*), center (*US*) ♦ *vi* (*FOOTBALL*) to centre the ball.
centre-ville, *pl* **centres-villes** [sɑ̃tʀavil] *nm* town centre (*BRIT*) *ou* center (*US*), downtown (area) (*US*).
centrifuge [sɑ̃tʀifyʒ] *adj*: **force** ~ centrifugal force.
centrifuger [sɑ̃tʀifyʒe] *vt* to centrifuge.
centrifugeuse [sɑ̃tʀifyʒøz] *nf* (*pour fruits*) juice extractor.
centripète [sɑ̃tʀipɛt] *adj*: **force** ~ centripetal force.
centrisme [sɑ̃tʀism(ə)] *nm* centrism.
centriste [sɑ̃tʀist(ə)] *adj*, *nm/f* centrist.
centuple [sɑ̃typl(ə)] *nm*: **le** ~ **de qch** a hundred times sth; **au** ~ a hundredfold.
centupler [sɑ̃typle] *vi*, *vt* to increase a hundredfold.
CEP *sigle m* = **Certificat d'études (primaires).**
cépage [sepaʒ] *nm* (type of) vine.
cèpe [sɛp] *nm* (edible) boletus.
cependant [səpɑ̃dɑ̃] *adv* however, nevertheless.
céramique [seʀamik] *adj* ceramic ♦ *nf* ceramic; (*art*) ceramics *sg*.
céramiste [seʀamist(ə)] *nm/f* ceramist.
cerbère [sɛʀbɛʀ] *nm* (*fig*: *péj*) bad-tempered doorkeeper.
cerceau, x [sɛʀso] *nm* (*d'enfant, de tonnelle*) hoop.
cercle [sɛʀkl(ə)] *nm* circle; (*objet*) band, hoop; **décrire un** ~ (*avion*) to circle; (*projectile*) to

describe a circle; ~ **d'amis** circle of friends; ~ **de famille** family circle; ~ **vicieux** vicious circle.
cercler [sɛʀkle] *vt*: **lunettes cerclées d'or** gold-rimmed glasses.
cercueil [sɛʀkœj] *nm* coffin.
céréale [seʀeal] *nf* cereal.
céréalier, ière [seʀealje, -jɛʀ] *adj* (*production, cultures*) cereal *cpd*.
cérébral, e, aux [seʀebʀal, -o] *adj* (*ANAT*) cerebral, brain *cpd*; (*fig*) mental, cerebral.
cérémonial [seʀemɔnjal] *nm* ceremonial.
cérémonie [seʀemɔni] *nf* ceremony; ~**s** *nfpl* (*péj*) fuss *sg*, to-do *sg*.
cérémonieux, euse [seʀemɔnjø, -øz] *adj* ceremonious, formal.
CERES [seʀɛs] *sigle m* (= *Centre d'études, de recherches et d'éducation socialiste*) (*formerly*) *intellectual section of the French Socialist party*.
cerf [sɛʀ] *nm* stag.
cerfeuil [sɛʀfœj] *nm* chervil.
cerf-volant [sɛʀvɔlɑ̃] *nm* kite; **jouer au** ~ to fly a kite.
cerisaie [səʀizɛ] *nf* cherry orchard.
cerise [səʀiz] *nf* cherry.
cerisier [səʀizje] *nm* cherry (tree).
CERN [sɛʀn] *sigle m* (= *Centre européen de recherche nucléaire*) CERN.
cerné, e [sɛʀne] *adj*: **les yeux** ~**s** with dark rings *ou* shadows under the eyes.
cerner [sɛʀne] *vt* (*MIL etc*) to surround; (*fig*: *problème*) to delimit, define.
cernes [sɛʀn(ə)] *nfpl* (dark) rings, shadows (under the eyes).
certain, e [sɛʀtɛ̃, -ɛn] *adj* certain; (*sûr*): ~ **(de/que)** certain *ou* sure (of/ that) ♦ *dét* certain; **d'un** ~ **âge** past one's prime, not so young; **un** ~ **temps** (quite) some time; **sûr et** ~ absolutely certain; ~**s** *pron* some.
certainement [sɛʀtɛnmɑ̃] *adv* (*probablement*) most probably *ou* likely; (*bien sûr*) certainly, of course.
certes [sɛʀt(ə)] *adv* admittedly; of course; indeed (yes).
certificat [sɛʀtifika] *nm* certificate; **C~ d'études (primaires) (CEP)** *former school leaving certificate* (*taken at the end of primary education*); **C~ de fin d'études secondaires (CFES)** school leaving certificate.
certifié, e [sɛʀtifje] *adj*: **professeur** ~ qualified teacher; (*ADMIN*): **copie** ~**e conforme (à l'original)** certified copy (of the original).
certifier [sɛʀtifje] *vt* to certify, guarantee; ~ **à qn que** to assure sb that, guarantee to sb that; ~ **qch à qn** to guarantee sth to sb.
certitude [sɛʀtityd] *nf* certainty.
cérumen [seʀymɛn] *nm* (ear)wax.
cerveau, x [sɛʀvo] *nm* brain; ~ **électronique** electronic brain.
cervelas [sɛʀvəla] *nm* saveloy.
cervelle [sɛʀvɛl] *nf* (*ANAT*) brain; (*CULIN*)

brain(s); **se creuser la ~** to rack one's brains.

cervical, e, aux [sɛʀvikal, -o] *adj* cervical.

cervidés [sɛʀvide] *nmpl* cervidae.

CES *sigle m* (= *Collège d'enseignement secondaire*) ≈ (junior) secondary school (*BRIT*), ≈ junior high school (*US*).

ces [se] *dét voir* **ce.**

césarienne [sezaʀjɛn] *nf* caesarean (*BRIT*) *ou* cesarean (*US*) (section).

cessantes [sɛsɑ̃t] *adj fpl*: **toutes affaires ~** forthwith.

cessation [sɛsɑsjɔ̃] *nf*: **~ des hostilités** cessation of hostilities; **~ de paiements/commerce** suspension of payments/trading.

cesse [sɛs]: **sans ~** *adv* continually, constantly; continuously; **il n'avait de ~ que** he would not rest until.

cesser [sese] *vt* to stop ♦ *vi* to stop, cease; **~ de faire** to stop doing; **faire ~** (*bruit, scandale*) to put a stop to.

cessez-le-feu [seselfø] *nm inv* ceasefire.

cession [sɛsjɔ̃] *nf* transfer.

c'est [sɛ] *pron* + *vb voir* **ce.**

c'est-à-dire [sɛtadiʀ] *adv* that is (to say); (*demander de préciser*): **~?** what does that mean?; **~ que ...** (*en conséquence*) which means that ...; (*manière d'excuse*) well, in fact ....

CET *sigle m* (= *Collège d'enseignement technique*) (*formerly*) technical school.

cet [sɛt] *dét voir* **ce.**

cétacé [setase] *nm* cetacean.

cette [sɛt] *dét voir* **ce.**

ceux [sø] *pron voir* **celui.**

cévenol, e [sevnɔl] *adj* of *ou* from the Cévennes region.

cf. *abr* (= *confer*) cf, cp.

CFAO *sigle f* (= *conception de fabrication assistée par ordinateur*) CAM.

CFC *sigle mpl* (= *chlorofluorocarbures*) CFC.

CFDT *sigle f* (= *Confédération française démocratique du travail*) trade union.

CFES *sigle m* = **Certificat de fin d'études secondaires.**

CFF *sigle m* (= *Chemins de fer fédéraux*) Swiss railways.

CFL *sigle m* (= *Chemins de fer luxembourgeois*) Luxembourg railways.

CFP *sigle m* = *Centre de formation professionnelle* ♦ *sigle f* = *Compagnie française des pétroles.*

CFTC *sigle f* (= *Confédération française des travailleurs chrétiens*) trade union.

CGC *sigle f* (= *Confédération générale des cadres*) management union.

CGPME *sigle f* = *Confédération générale des petites et moyennes entreprises.*

CGT *sigle f* (= *Confédération générale du travail*) trade union.

CH *abr* (= *Confédération helvétique*) CH.

ch. *abr* = **charges, chauffage, cherche.**

chacal [ʃakal] *nm* jackal.

chacun, e [ʃakœ̃, -yn] *pron* each; (*indéfini*) everyone, everybody.

chagrin, e [ʃagʀɛ̃, -in] *adj* morose ♦ *nm* grief, sorrow; **avoir du ~** to be grieved *ou* sorrowful.

chagriner [ʃagʀine] *vt* to grieve, distress; (*contrarier*) to bother, worry.

chahut [ʃay] *nm* uproar.

chahuter [ʃayte] *vt* to rag, bait ♦ *vi* to make an uproar.

chahuteur, euse [ʃaytœʀ, -øz] *nm/f* rowdy.

chai [ʃɛ] *nm* wine and spirit store(house).

chaîne [ʃɛn] *nf* chain; (*RADIO, TV*) channel; (*INFORM*) string; **~s** *nfpl* (*liens, asservissement*) fetters, bonds; **travail à la ~** production line work; **réactions en ~** chain reactions; **faire la ~** to form a (human) chain; **~ alimentaire** food chain; **~ compacte** music centre; **~ d'entraide** mutual aid association; **~ (haute-fidélité** *ou* **hi-fi)** hi-fi system; **~ (de montage** *ou* **de fabrication)** production *ou* assembly line; **~ (de montagnes)** (mountain) range; **~ de solidarité** solidarity network; **~ (stéréo** *ou* **audio)** stereo (system).

chaînette [ʃɛnɛt] *nf* (small) chain.

chaînon [ʃɛnɔ̃] *nm* link.

chair [ʃɛʀ] *nf* flesh ♦ *adj*: (*couleur*) **~** flesh-coloured; **avoir la ~ de poule** to have goose-pimples *ou* gooseflesh; **bien en ~** plump, well-padded; **en ~ et en os** in the flesh; **~ à saucisses** sausage meat.

chaire [ʃɛʀ] *nf* (*d'église*) pulpit; (*d'université*) chair.

chaise [ʃɛz] *nf* chair; **~ de bébé** high chair; **~ électrique** electric chair; **~ longue** deck-chair.

chaland [ʃalɑ̃] *nm* (*bateau*) barge.

châle [ʃal] *nm* shawl.

chalet [ʃalɛ] *nm* chalet.

chaleur [ʃalœʀ] *nf* heat; (*fig*) warmth; fire, fervour (*BRIT*), fervor (*US*); heat; **en ~** (*ZOOL*) on heat.

chaleureusement [ʃalœʀøzmɑ̃] *adv* warmly.

chaleureux, euse [ʃalœʀø, -øz] *adj* warm.

challenge [ʃalɑ̃ʒ] *nm* contest, tournament.

challenger [ʃalɑ̃ʒɛʀ] *nm* (*SPORT*) challenger.

chaloupe [ʃalup] *nf* launch; (*de sauvetage*) lifeboat.

chalumeau, x [ʃalymo] *nm* blowlamp (*BRIT*), blowtorch.

chalut [ʃaly] *nm* trawl (net); **pêcher au ~** to trawl.

chalutier [ʃalytje] *nm* trawler; (*pêcheur*) trawlerman.

chamade [ʃamad] *nf*: **battre la ~** to beat wildly.

chamailler [ʃamaje]: **se ~** *vi* to squabble, bicker.

chamarré, e [ʃamaʀe] *adj* richly brocaded.

chambard [ʃɑ̃baʀ] *nm* rumpus.

chambardement [ʃɑ̃baʀdəmɑ̃] *nm*: **c'est le grand ~** everything has been (*ou* is being) turned upside down.

chambarder [ʃɑ̃baʀde] vt to turn upside down.

chamboulement [ʃɑ̃bulmɑ̃] nm disruption.

chambouler [ʃɑ̃bule] vt to disrupt, turn upside down.

chambranle [ʃɑ̃bʀɑ̃l] nm (door) frame.

chambre [ʃɑ̃bʀ(ə)] nf bedroom; (TECH) chamber; (POL) chamber, house; (JUR) court; (COMM) chamber; federation; **faire ~ à part** to sleep in separate rooms; **stratège/ alpiniste en ~** armchair strategist/ mountaineer; **~ à un lit/deux lits** single/ twin-bedded room; **~ pour une/deux personne(s)** single/double room; **~ d'accusation** court of criminal appeal; **~ d'agriculture** body responsible for the agricultural interests of a département; **~ à air** (de pneu) (inner) tube; **~ d'amis** spare ou guest room; **~ de combustion** combustion chamber; **~ de commerce et d'industrie (CCI)** chamber of commerce and industry; **~ à coucher** bedroom; **la C~ des députés** the Chamber of Deputies, ≈ the House of (Commons) (BRIT), ≈ the House of Rep- resentatives (US); **~ forte** strongroom; **~ froide** ou **frigorifique** cold room; **~ à gaz** gas chamber; **~ d'hôte** ≈ bed and breakfast (in private home); **~ des machines** engine-room; **~ des métiers (CM)** chamber of commerce for trades; **~ meublée** bedsit(ter) (BRIT), furnished room; **~ noire** (PHOTO) dark room.

chambrée [ʃɑ̃bʀe] nf room.

chambrer [ʃɑ̃bʀe] vt (vin) to bring to room temperature.

chameau, x [ʃamo] nm camel.

chamois [ʃamwa] nm chamois ♦ adj: (couleur) ~ fawn, buff.

champ [ʃɑ̃] nm (aussi INFORM) field; (PHOTO): **dans le ~** in the picture; **prendre du ~** to draw back; **laisser le ~ libre à qn** to leave sb a clear field; **~ d'action** sphere of operation(s); **~ de bataille** battlefield; **~ de courses** racecourse; **~ d'honneur** field of honour; **~ de manœvre** (MIL) parade ground; **~ de mines** minefield; **~ de tir** shooting ou rifle range; **~ visuel** field of vision.

Champagne [ʃɑ̃paɲ] nf: **la ~** Champagne, the Champagne region.

champagne [ʃɑ̃paɲ] nm champagne.

champenois, e [ʃɑ̃pənwa, -waz] adj of ou from Champagne; (vin): **méthode ~e** champagne-type.

champêtre [ʃɑ̃pɛtʀ(ə)] adj country cpd, rural.

champignon [ʃɑ̃piɲɔ̃] nm mushroom; (terme générique) fungus (pl -i); (fam: accélérateur) accelerator, gas pedal (US); **~ de couche** ou **de Paris** button mushroom; **~ vénéneux** toadstool, poisonous mushroom.

champion, ne [ʃɑ̃pjɔ̃, -ɔn] adj, nm/f champion.

championnat [ʃɑ̃pjɔna] nm championship.

chance [ʃɑ̃s] nf: **la ~** luck; **une ~** a stroke ou

piece of luck ou good fortune; (occasion) a lucky break; **~s** nfpl (probabilités) chances; **avoir de la ~** to be lucky; **il a des ~s de gagner** he has a chance of winning; **il y a de fortes ~s pour que Paul soit malade** it's highly probable that Paul is ill; **bonne ~!** good luck!; **encore une ~ que tu viennes!** it's lucky you're coming; **je n'ai pas de ~** I'm out of luck; (toujours) I never have any luck; **donner sa ~ à qn** to give sb a chance.

chancelant, e [ʃɑ̃slɑ̃, -ɑ̃t] adj (personne) tottering; (santé) failing.

chanceler [ʃɑ̃sle] vi to totter.

chancelier [ʃɑ̃səlje] nm (allemand) chancellor; (d'ambassade) secretary.

chancellerie [ʃɑ̃sɛlʀi] nf (en France) ministry of justice; (en Allemagne) chancellery; (d'ambassade) chancery.

chanceux, euse [ʃɑ̃sø, -øz] adj lucky, fortunate.

chancre [ʃɑ̃kʀ(ə)] nm canker.

chandail [ʃɑ̃daj] nm (thick) jumper ou sweater.

Chandeleur [ʃɑ̃dlœʀ] nf: **la ~** Candlemas.

chandelier [ʃɑ̃dəlje] nm candlestick; (à plusieurs branches) candelabra.

chandelle [ʃɑ̃dɛl] nf (tallow) candle; (TENNIS): **faire une ~** to lob; (AVIAT): **monter en ~** to climb vertically; **tenir la ~** to play gooseberry; **dîner aux ~s** candlelight dinner.

change [ʃɑ̃ʒ] nm (COMM) exchange; **opérations de ~** (foreign) exchange transactions; **contrôle des ~s** exchange control; **gagner/ perdre au ~** to be better/worse off (for it); **donner le ~ à qn** (fig) to lead sb up the garden path.

changeant, e [ʃɑ̃ʒɑ̃, -ɑ̃t] adj changeable, fickle.

changement [ʃɑ̃ʒmɑ̃] nm change; **~ de vitesse** (dispositif) gears pl; (action) gear change.

changer [ʃɑ̃ʒe] vt (modifier) to change, alter; (remplacer, COMM, rhabiller) to change ♦ vi to change, alter; **se ~** to change (o.s.); **~ de** (remplacer: adresse, nom, voiture etc) to change one's; (échanger, alterner: côté, place, train etc) to change + npl; **~ d'air** to get a change of air; **~ de couleur/direction** to change colour/direction; **~ d'idée** to change one's mind; **~ de place avec qn** to change places with sb; **~ de vitesse** (AUTO) to change gear; **~ qn/qch de place** to move sb/sth to another place; **~ (de train etc)** to change (trains etc); **~ qch en** to change sth into.

changeur [ʃɑ̃ʒœʀ] nm (personne) moneychanger; **~ automatique** change machine; **~ de disques** record changer, autochange.

chanoine [ʃanwan] nm canon.

chanson [ʃɑ̃sɔ̃] nf song.

chansonnette [ʃɑ̃sɔnɛt] nf ditty.

chansonnier [ʃɑ̃sɔnje] nm cabaret artist (specializing in political satire); (recueil) song book.

chant [ʃɑ̃] nm song; (art vocal) singing; (d'église) hymn; (de poème) canto; (TECH): **posé de** ou **sur** ~ placed edgeways; ~ **de Noël** Christmas carol.

chantage [ʃɑ̃taʒ] nm blackmail; **faire du** ~ to use blackmail; **soumettre qn à un** ~ to blackmail sb.

chantant, e [ʃɑ̃tɑ̃, -ɑ̃t] adj (accent, voix) singsong.

chanter [ʃɑ̃te] vt, vi to sing; ~ **juste/faux** to sing in tune/out of tune; **si cela lui chante** (fam) if he feels like it ou fancies it.

chanterelle [ʃɑ̃tʀɛl] nf chanterelle (edible mushroom).

chanteur, euse [ʃɑ̃tœʀ, -øz] nm/f singer; ~ **de charme** crooner.

chantier [ʃɑ̃tje] nm (building) site; (sur une route) roadworks pl; **mettre en** ~ to start work on; ~ **naval** shipyard.

chantilly [ʃɑ̃tiji] nf voir **crème**.

chantonner [ʃɑ̃tɔne] vi, vt to sing to oneself, hum.

chantre [ʃɑ̃tʀ(ə)] nm (fig) eulogist.

chanvre [ʃɑ̃vʀ(ə)] nm hemp.

chaos [kao] nm chaos.

chaotique [kaɔtik] adj chaotic.

chap. abr (= chapitre) ch.

chapardage [ʃapaʀdaʒ] nm pilfering.

chaparder [ʃapaʀde] vt to pinch.

chapeau, x [ʃapo] nm hat; (PRESSE) introductory paragraph; ~! well done!; ~ **melon** bowler hat; ~ **mou** trilby; ~x **de roues** hub caps.

chapeauter [ʃapote] vt (ADMIN) to head, oversee.

chapelain [ʃaplɛ̃] nm (REL) chaplain.

chapelet [ʃaplɛ] nm (REL) rosary; (fig): **un** ~ **de** a string of; **dire son** ~ to tell one's beads.

chapelier, ière [ʃapəlje, -jɛʀ] nm/f hatter; milliner.

chapelle [ʃapɛl] nf chapel; ~ **ardente** chapel of rest.

chapellerie [ʃapɛlʀi] nf (magasin) hat shop; (commerce) hat trade.

chapelure [ʃaplyʀ] nf (dried) breadcrumbs pl.

chaperon [ʃapʀɔ̃] nm chaperon.

chaperonner [ʃapʀɔne] vt to chaperon.

chapiteau, x [ʃapito] nm (ARCHIT) capital; (de cirque) marquee, big top.

chapitre [ʃapitʀ(ə)] nm (fig) chapter; (fig) subject, matter; **avoir voix au** ~ to have a say in the matter.

chapitrer [ʃapitʀe] vt to lecture, reprimand.

chapon [ʃapɔ̃] nm capon.

chaque [ʃak] dét each, every; (indéfini) every.

char [ʃaʀ] nm (à foin etc) cart, waggon; (de carnaval) float; ~ **(d'assaut)** tank.

charabia [ʃaʀabja] nm (péj) gibberish, gobbledygook (BRIT).

charade [ʃaʀad] nf riddle; (mimée) charade.

charbon [ʃaʀbɔ̃] nm coal; ~ **de bois** charcoal.

charbonnage [ʃaʀbɔnaʒ] nm: **les** ~**s de France** the (French) Coal Board sg.

charbonnier [ʃaʀbɔnje] nm coalman.

charcuterie [ʃaʀkytʀi] nf (magasin) pork butcher's shop and delicatessen; (produits) cooked pork meats pl.

charcutier, ière [ʃaʀkytje, -jɛʀ] nm/f pork butcher.

chardon [ʃaʀdɔ̃] nm thistle.

chardonneret [ʃaʀdɔnʀɛ] nm goldfinch.

charentais, e [ʃaʀɑ̃tɛ, -ɛz] adj of ou from Charente ♦ nf (pantoufle) slipper.

charge [ʃaʀʒ(ə)] nf (fardeau) load; (explosif, ÉLEC, MIL, JUR) charge; (rôle, mission) responsibility; ~**s** nfpl (du loyer) service charges; **à la** ~ **de** (dépendant de) dependent upon, supported by; (aux frais de) chargeable to, payable by; **j'accepte, à** ~ **de revanche** I accept, provided I can do the same for you (in return) one day; **prendre en** ~ to take charge of; (suj: véhicule) to take on; (dépenses) to take care of; ~ **utile** (AUTO) live load; (COMM) payload; ~**s sociales** social security contributions.

chargé [ʃaʀʒe] adj (voiture, animal, personne) laden; (fusil, batterie, caméra) loaded; (occupé: emploi du temps, journée) busy, full; (estomac) heavy, full; (langue) furred; (décoration, style) heavy, ornate ♦ nm: ~ **d'affaires** chargé d'affaires; ~ **de cours** ≈ lecturer; ~ **de** (responsable de) responsible for.

chargement [ʃaʀʒəmɑ̃] nm (action) loading; charging; (objets) load.

charger [ʃaʀʒe] vt (voiture, fusil, caméra, INFORM) to load; (batterie) to charge ♦ vi (MIL etc) to charge; **se** ~ **de** vt to see to, take care of; ~ **qn de qch/faire qch** to give sb the responsibility for sth/of doing sth; to put sb in charge of sth/doing sth; **se** ~ **de faire qch** to take it upon o.s. to do sth.

chargeur [ʃaʀʒœʀ] nm (dispositif: d'arme à feu) magazine; (: PHOTO) cartridge; ~ **de batterie** (ÉLEC) battery charger.

chariot [ʃaʀjo] nm trolley; (charrette) waggon; (de machine à écrire) carriage; ~ **élévateur** fork-lift truck.

charisme [kaʀism(ə)] nm charisma.

charitable [ʃaʀitabl(ə)] adj charitable; kind.

charité [ʃaʀite] nf charity; **faire la** ~ to give to charity; to do charitable works; **faire la** ~ **à** to give (something) to; **fête/vente de** ~ fête/sale in aid of charity.

charivari [ʃaʀivaʀi] nm hullabaloo.

charlatan [ʃaʀlatɑ̃] nm charlatan.

charlotte [ʃaʀlɔt] nf (CULIN) charlotte.

charmant, e [ʃaʀmɑ̃, -ɑ̃t] adj charming.

charme [ʃaʀm(ə)] nm charm; ~**s** nmpl (appas) charms; **c'est ce qui en fait le** ~ that is its attraction; **faire du** ~ to be charming, turn on the charm; **aller** ou **se porter comme un** ~ to be in the pink.

charmer [ʃaʀme] vt to charm; **je suis charmé**

de I'm delighted to.

charmeur, euse [ʃaʀmœʀ, -øz] *nm/f* charmer; ~ **de serpents** snake charmer.

charnel, le [ʃaʀnɛl] *adj* carnal.

charnier [ʃaʀnje] *nm* mass grave.

charnière [ʃaʀnjɛʀ] *nf* hinge; *(fig)* turning-point.

charnu, e [ʃaʀny] *adj* fleshy.

charogne [ʃaʀɔɲ] *nf* carrion *no pl*; *(fam!)* bastard *(!)*.

charolais, e [ʃaʀɔlɛ, -ɛz] *adj* of *ou* from the Charolais.

charpente [ʃaʀpɑ̃t] *nf* frame(work); *(fig)* structure, framework; *(carrure)* build, frame.

charpenté, e [ʃaʀpɑ̃te] *adj*: **bien** *ou* **solidement** ~ *(personne)* well-built; *(texte)* well-constructed.

charpenterie [ʃaʀpɑ̃tʀi] *nf* carpentry.

charpentier [ʃaʀpɑ̃tje] *nm* carpenter.

charpie [ʃaʀpi] *nf*: **en** ~ *(fig)* in shreds *ou* ribbons.

charretier [ʃaʀtje] *nm* carter; **de** ~ *(péj: langage, manières)* uncouth.

charrette [ʃaʀɛt] *nf* cart.

charrier [ʃaʀje] *vt* to carry (along); to cart, carry ♦ *vi (fam)* to exaggerate.

charrue [ʃaʀy] *nf* plough *(BRIT)*, plow *(US)*.

charte [ʃaʀt(ə)] *nf* charter.

charter [tʃaʀtœʀ] *nm (vol)* charter flight; *(avion)* charter plane.

chasse [ʃas] *nf* hunting; *(au fusil)* shooting; *(poursuite)* chase; *(aussi:* ~ **d'eau)** flush; **la** ~ **est ouverte** the hunting season is open; **la** ~ **est fermée** it is the close *(BRIT) ou* closed *(US)* season; **aller à la** ~ to go hunting; **prendre en** ~, **donner la** ~ **à** to give chase to; **tirer la** ~ **(d'eau)** to flush the toilet, pull the chain; ~ **aérienne** aerial pursuit; ~ **à courre** hunting; ~ **à l'homme** manhunt; ~ **gardée** private hunting grounds *pl*; ~ **sous-marine** underwater fishing.

châsse [ʃas] *nf* reliquary, shrine.

chassé-croisé,   *pl*   **chassés-croisés** [ʃasekʀwaze] *nm (DANSE)* chassé-croisé; *(fig)* mix-up *(where people miss each other in turn)*.

chasse-neige [ʃasnɛʒ] *nm inv* snowplough *(BRIT)*, snowplow *(US)*.

chasser [ʃase] *vt* to hunt; *(expulser)* to chase away *ou* out, drive away *ou* out; *(dissiper)* to chase *ou* sweep away; to dispel, drive away.

chasseur, euse [ʃasœʀ, -øz] *nm/f* hunter ♦ *nm (avion)* fighter; *(domestique)* page (boy), messenger (boy); ~ **d'images** roving photographer; ~ **de têtes** *(fig)* headhunter; ~**s alpins** mountain infantry.

chassieux, euse [ʃasjø, -øz] *adj* sticky, gummy.

châssis [ʃasi] *nm (AUTO)* chassis; *(cadre)* frame; *(de jardin)* cold frame.

chaste [ʃast(ə)] *adj* chaste.

chasteté [ʃastəte] *nf* chastity.

chasuble [ʃazybl(ə)] *nf* chasuble; **robe** ~ pinafore dress *(BRIT)*, jumper *(US)*.

chat [ʃa] *nm* cat; ~ **sauvage** wildcat.

châtaigne [ʃatɛɲ] *nf* chestnut.

châtaignier [ʃatɛɲe] *nm* chestnut (tree).

châtain [ʃatɛ̃] *adj inv* chestnut (brown); *(personne)* chestnut-haired.

château, x [ʃato] *nm* castle; ~ **d'eau** water tower; ~ **fort** stronghold, fortified castle; ~ **de sable** sandcastle.

châtelain, e [ʃatlɛ̃, -ɛn] *nm/f* lord/lady of the manor ♦ *nf (ceinture)* chatelaine.

châtier [ʃatje] *vt* to punish, castigate; *(fig: style)* to polish, refine.

chatière [ʃatjɛʀ] *nf (porte)* cat flap.

châtiment [ʃatimɑ̃] *nm* punishment, castigation; ~ **corporel** corporal punishment.

chatoiement [ʃatwamɑ̃] *nm* shimmer(ing).

chaton [ʃatɔ̃] *nm (ZOOL)* kitten; *(BOT)* catkin; *(de bague)* bezel; stone.

chatouillement [ʃatujmɑ̃] *nm (gén)* tickling; *(dans le nez, la gorge)* tickle.

chatouiller [ʃatuje] *vt* to tickle; *(l'odorat, le palais)* to titillate.

chatouilleux, euse [ʃatujø, -øz] *adj* ticklish; *(fig)* touchy, over-sensitive.

chatoyant, e [ʃatwajɑ̃, -ɑ̃t] *adj (reflet, étoffe)* shimmering; *(couleurs)* sparkling.

chatoyer [ʃatwaje] *vi* to shimmer.

châtrer [ʃatʀe] *vt (mâle)* to castrate; *(femelle)* to spay; *(cheval)* to geld; *(chat, chien)* to doctor *(BRIT)*, fix *(US)*; *(fig)* to mutilate.

chatte [ʃat] *nf* (she-)cat.

chatterton [ʃatɛʀtɔn] *nm (ruban isolant: ÉLEC)* (adhesive) insulating tape.

chaud, e [ʃo, -od] *adj (gén)* warm; *(très chaud)* hot; *(fig: félicitations)* hearty; *(discussion)* heated; **il fait** ~ it's warm; it's hot; **manger** ~ to have something hot to eat; **avoir** ~ to be warm; to be hot; **tenir** ~ to keep hot; **ça me tient** ~ it keeps me warm; **tenir au** ~ to keep in a warm place; **rester au** ~ to stay in the warm.

chaudement [ʃodmɑ̃] *adv* warmly; *(fig)* hotly.

chaudière [ʃodjɛʀ] *nf* boiler.

chaudron [ʃodʀɔ̃] *nm* cauldron.

chaudronnerie [ʃodʀɔnʀi] *nf (usine)* boilerworks; *(activité)* boilermaking; *(boutique)* coppersmith's workshop.

chauffage [ʃofaʒ] *nm* heating; ~ **au gaz/à l'électricité/au charbon** gas/electric/solid fuel heating; ~ **central** central heating; ~ **par le sol** underfloor heating.

chauffagiste [ʃofaʒist(ə)] *nm (installateur)* heating engineer.

chauffant, e [ʃofɑ̃, -ɑ̃t]: **couverture** ~**e** electric blanket; **plaque** ~**e** hotplate.

chauffard [ʃofaʀ] *nm (péj)* reckless driver; roadhog; *(après un accident)* hit-and-run driver.

chauffe-bain [ʃofbɛ̃] *nm* = **chauffe-eau**.

chauffe-biberon [ʃofbibʀɔ̃] *nm* (baby's) bottle

warmer.
chauffe-eau [ʃofo] *nm inv* water heater.
chauffe-plats [ʃofpla] *nm inv* dish warmer.
chauffer [ʃofe] *vt* to heat ♦ *vi* to heat up, warm up; (*trop chauffer: moteur*) to overheat; **se ~** (*se mettre en train*) to warm up; (*au soleil*) to warm o.s.
chaufferie [ʃofʀi] *nf* boiler room.
chauffeur [ʃofœʀ] *nm* driver; (*privé*) chauffeur; **voiture avec/sans ~** chauffeur-driven/self-drive car.
chauffeuse [ʃoføz] *nf* fireside chair.
chauler [ʃole] *vt* (*mur*) to whitewash.
chaume [ʃom] *nm* (*du toit*) thatch; (*tiges*) stubble.
chaumière [ʃomjɛʀ] *nf* (thatched) cottage.
chaussée [ʃose] *nf* road(way); (*digue*) causeway.
chausse-pied [ʃospje] *nm* shoe-horn.
chausser [ʃose] *vt* (*bottes, skis*) to put on; (*enfant*) to put shoes on; (*suj: soulier*) to fit; **~ du 38/42** to take size 38/42; **~ grand/bien** to be big-/well-fitting; **se ~** to put one's shoes on.
chausse-trappe [ʃostʀap] *nf* trap.
chaussette [ʃosɛt] *nf* sock.
chausseur [ʃosœʀ] *nm* (*marchand*) footwear specialist, shoemaker.
chausson [ʃosɔ̃] *nm* slipper; (*de bébé*) bootee; **~ (aux pommes)** (apple) turnover.
chaussure [ʃosyʀ] *nf* shoe; (*commerce*): **la ~** the shoe industry *ou* trade; **~s basses** flat shoes; **~s montantes** ankle boots; **~s de ski** ski boots.
chaut [ʃo] *vb*: **peu me ~** it matters little to me.
chauve [ʃov] *adj* bald.
chauve-souris, *pl* **chauves-souris** [ʃovsuʀi] *nf* bat.
chauvin, e [ʃovɛ̃, -in] *adj* chauvinistic; jingoistic.
chauvinisme [ʃovinism(ə)] *nm* chauvinism; jingoism.
chaux [ʃo] *nf* lime; **blanchi à la ~** whitewashed.
chavirer [ʃaviʀe] *vi* to capsize, overturn.
chef [ʃɛf] *nm* head, leader; (*patron*) boss; (*de cuisine*) chef; **au premier ~** extremely, to the nth degree; **de son propre ~** on his *ou* her own initiative; **général/commandant en ~** general-/commander-in-chief; **~ d'accusation** (*JUR*) charge, count (of indictment); **~ d'atelier** (shop) foreman; **~ de bureau** head clerk; **~ de clinique** senior hospital lecturer; **~ d'entreprise** company head; **~ d'équipe** team leader; **~ d'état** head of state; **~ de famille** head of the family; **~ de file** (*de parti etc*) leader; **~ de gare** station master; **~ d'orchestre** conductor (*BRIT*), leader (*US*); **~ de rayon** department(al) supervisor; **~ de service** departmental head.
chef-d'œuvre, *pl* **chefs-d'œuvre** [ʃɛdœvʀ(ə)] *nm* masterpiece.

chef-lieu, *pl* **chefs-lieux** [ʃɛfljø] *nm* county town.
cheftaine [ʃɛftɛn] *nf* (guide) captain.
cheik(h) [ʃɛk] *nm* sheik.
chemin [ʃəmɛ̃] *nm* path; (*itinéraire, direction, trajet*) way; **en ~, ~ faisant** on the way; **~ de fer** railway (*BRIT*), railroad (*US*); **par ~ de fer** by rail; **les ~s de fer** the railways (*BRIT*), the railroad (*US*); **~ de terre** dirt track.
cheminée [ʃəmine] *nf* chimney; (*à l'intérieur*) chimney piece, fireplace; (*de bateau*) funnel.
cheminement [ʃəminmɑ̃] *nm* progress; course.
cheminer [ʃəmine] *vi* to walk (along).
cheminot [ʃəmino] *nm* railwayman (*BRIT*), railroad worker (*US*).
chemise [ʃəmiz] *nf* shirt; (*dossier*) folder; **~ de nuit** nightdress.
chemiserie [ʃəmizʀi] *nf* (gentlemen's) outfitters'.
chemisette [ʃəmizɛt] *nf* short-sleeved shirt.
chemisier [ʃəmizje] *nm* blouse.
chenal, aux [ʃənal, -o] *nm* channel.
chenapan [ʃənapɑ̃] *nm* (*garnement*) rascal; (*péj: vaurien*) rogue.
chêne [ʃɛn] *nm* oak (tree); (*bois*) oak.
chenet [ʃənɛ] *nm* fire-dog, andiron.
chenil [ʃənil] *nm* kennels *pl*.
chenille [ʃənij] *nf* (*ZOOL*) caterpillar; (*AUTO*) caterpillar track; **véhicule à ~s** tracked vehicle, caterpillar.
chenillette [ʃənijɛt] *nf* tracked vehicle.
cheptel [ʃɛptɛl] *nm* livestock.
chèque [ʃɛk] *nm* cheque (*BRIT*), check (*US*); **faire/toucher un ~** to write/cash a cheque; **par ~** by cheque; **~ barré/sans provision** crossed (*BRIT*)/bad cheque; **~ en blanc** blank cheque; **~ au porteur** cheque to bearer; **~ postal** post office cheque, ≈ giro cheque (*BRIT*); **~ de voyage** traveller's cheque.
chèque-cadeau, *pl* **chèques-cadeaux** [ʃɛkkado] *nm* gift token.
chèque-repas, *pl* **chèques-repas** [ʃɛkʀəpa], **chèque-restaurant,** *pl* **chèques-restaurant** [ʃɛkʀɛstɔʀɑ̃] *nm* ≈ luncheon voucher.
chéquier [ʃekje] *nm* cheque book (*BRIT*), checkbook (*US*).
cher, ère [ʃɛʀ] *adj* (*aimé*) dear; (*coûteux*) expensive, dear ♦ *adv*: **coûter/payer ~** to cost/pay a lot ♦ *nf*: **la bonne chère** good food; **cela coûte ~** it's expensive, it costs a lot of money; **mon ~, ma chère** my dear.
chercher [ʃɛʀʃe] *vt* to look for; (*gloire etc*) to seek; (*INFORM*) to search; **~ des ennuis/la bagarre** to be looking for trouble/a fight; **aller ~** to go for, go and fetch; **~ à faire** to try to do.
chercheur, euse [ʃɛʀʃœʀ, -øz] *nm/f* researcher, research worker; **~ de** seeker of; hunter of; **~ d'or** gold digger.
chère [ʃɛʀ] *adj f*, *nf voir* **cher.**

chèrement [ʃɛʀmɑ̃] adv dearly.
chéri, e [ʃeʀi] adj beloved, dear; **(mon)** ~ darling.
chérir [ʃeʀiʀ] vt to cherish.
cherté [ʃɛʀte] nf: **la** ~ **de la vie** the high cost of living.
chérubin [ʃeʀybɛ̃] nm cherub.
chétif, ive [ʃetif, -iv] adj puny, stunted.
cheval, aux [ʃəval, -o] nm horse; (AUTO): ~ **(vapeur) (CV)** horsepower no pl; **50 chevaux (au frein)** 50 brake horsepower, 50 b.h.p.; **10 chevaux (fiscaux)** 10 horsepower (for tax purposes); **faire du** ~ to ride; **à** ~ on horseback; **à** ~ **sur** astride, straddling; (fig) overlapping; ~ **d'arçons** vaulting horse; ~ **à bascule** rocking horse; ~ **de bataille** charger; (fig) hobby-horse; ~ **de course** race horse; **chevaux de bois** (des manèges) wooden (fairground) horses; (manège) merry-go-round.
chevaleresque [ʃəvalʀɛsk(ə)] adj chivalrous.
chevalerie [ʃəvalʀi] nf chivalry; knighthood.
chevalet [ʃəvalɛ] nm easel.
chevalier [ʃəvalje] nm knight; ~ **servant** escort.
chevalière [ʃəvaljɛʀ] nf signet ring.
chevalin, e [ʃəvalɛ̃, -in] adj of horses, equine; (péj) horsy; **boucherie** ~**e** horse-meat butcher's.
cheval-vapeur, pl **chevaux-vapeur** [ʃəvalvapœʀ, ʃəvo-] nm voir **cheval.**
chevauchée [ʃəvoʃe] nf ride; cavalcade.
chevauchement [ʃəvoʃmɑ̃] nm overlap.
chevaucher [ʃəvoʃe] vi (aussi: **se** ~) to overlap (each other) ♦ vt to be astride, straddle.
chevaux [ʃəvo] nmpl voir **cheval.**
chevelu, e [ʃəvly] adj with a good head of hair, hairy (péj).
chevelure [ʃəvlyʀ] nf hair no pl.
chevet [ʃəvɛ] nm: **au** ~ **de qn** at sb's bedside; **lampe de** ~ bedside lamp.
cheveu, x [ʃəvø] nm hair ♦ nmpl (chevelure) hair sg; **avoir les** ~**x courts/en brosse** to have short hair/a crew cut; **se faire couper les** ~**x** to get ou have one's hair cut; **tiré par les** ~**x** (histoire) far-fetched.
cheville [ʃəvij] nf (ANAT) ankle; (de bois) peg; (pour enfoncer une vis) plug; **être en** ~ **avec qn** to be in cahoots with sb; ~ **ouvrière** (fig) kingpin.
chèvre [ʃɛvʀ(ə)] nf (she-)goat; **ménager la** ~ **et le chou** to try to please everyone.
chevreau, x [ʃəvʀo] nm kid.
chèvrefeuille [ʃɛvʀəfœj] nm honeysuckle.
chevreuil [ʃəvʀœj] nm roe deer inv; (CULIN) venison.
chevron [ʃəvʀɔ̃] nm (poutre) rafter; (motif) chevron, v(-shape); **à** ~**s** chevron-patterned; (petits) herringbone.
chevronné, e [ʃəvʀɔne] adj seasoned, experienced.
chevrotant, e [ʃəvʀɔtɑ̃, -ɑ̃t] adj quavering.
chevroter [ʃəvʀɔte] vi (personne, voix) to qua-

ver.
chevrotine [ʃəvʀɔtin] nf buckshot no pl.
chewing-gum [ʃwiŋgɔm] nm chewing gum.

═══════════════════════════════ **MOT-CLÉ**

chez [ʃe] prép **1** (à la demeure de) at; (: direction) to; ~ **qn** at/to sb's house ou place; ~ **moi** at home; (direction) home
2 (à l'entreprise de): **il travaille** ~ **Renault** he works for Renault, he works at Renault('s)
3 (+profession) at; (: direction) to; ~ **le boulanger/dentiste** at ou to the baker's/dentist's
4 (dans le caractère, l'œuvre de) in; ~ **les renards/Racine** in foxes/Racine; ~ **les Français** among the French; ~ **lui, c'est un devoir** for him, it's a duty
♦ nm inv: **mon** ~ **moi/ton** ~ **toi** etc my/your etc home ou place.

chez-soi [ʃeswa] nm inv home.
Chf. cent. abr (= chauffage central) c.h.
chiadé, e [ʃjade] adj (fam: fignolé, soigné) wicked.
chialer [ʃjale] vi (fam) to blubber; **arrête de** ~! stop blubbering!
chiant, e [ʃjɑ̃, -ɑ̃t] adj (fam!) bloody annoying (BRIT!), damn annoying; **qu'est-ce qu'il est** ~! he's such a bloody pain! (!).
chic [ʃik] adj inv chic, smart; (généreux) nice, decent ♦ nm stylishness; **avoir le** ~ **de** ou **pour** to have the knack of ou for; **de** ~ adv off the cuff; ~! great!, terrific!
chicane [ʃikan] nf (obstacle) zigzag; (querelle) squabble.
chicaner [ʃikane] vi (ergoter): ~ **sur** to quibble about.
chiche [ʃiʃ] adj (mesquin) niggardly, mean; (pauvre) meagre (BRIT), meager (US) ♦ excl (en réponse à un défi) you're on!; **tu n'es pas** ~ **de lui parler!** you wouldn't (dare) speak to her!
chichement [ʃiʃmɑ̃] adv (pauvrement) meagrely (BRIT), meagerly (US); (mesquinement) meanly.
chichi [ʃiʃi] nm (fam) fuss; **faire des** ~**s** to make a fuss.
chicorée [ʃikɔʀe] nf (café) chicory; (salade) endive; ~ **frisée** curly endive.
chicot [ʃiko] nm stump.
chien [ʃjɛ̃] nm dog; (de pistolet) hammer; **temps de** ~ rotten weather; **vie de** ~ dog's life; **couché en** ~ **de fusil** curled up; ~ **d'aveugle** guide dog; ~ **de chasse** gun dog; ~ **de garde** guard dog; ~ **policier** police dog; ~ **de race** pedigree dog; ~ **de traîneau** husky.
chiendent [ʃjɛ̃dɑ̃] nm couch grass.
chien-loup, pl **chiens-loups** [ʃjɛ̃lu] nm wolfhound.
chienne [ʃjɛn] nf (she-)dog, bitch.
chier [ʃje] vi (fam!) to crap (!), shit (!); **faire** ~

qn (_importuner_) to bug sb; (_causer des ennuis à_) to piss sb around (!); **se faire ~** (_s'ennuyer_) to be bored rigid.

chiffe [ʃif] _nf_: **il est mou comme une ~, c'est une ~ molle** he's spineless _ou_ wet.

chiffon [ʃifɔ̃] _nm_ (piece of) rag.

chiffonné, e [ʃifɔne] _adj_ (_fatigué: visage_) worn-looking.

chiffonner [ʃifɔne] _vt_ to crumple, crease; (_tracasser_) to concern.

chiffonnier [ʃifɔnje] _nm_ ragman, rag-and-bone man; (_meuble_) chiffonier.

chiffrable [ʃifʀabl(ə)] _adj_ numerable.

chiffre [ʃifʀ(ə)] _nm_ (_représentant un nombre_) figure; numeral; (_montant, total_) total, sum; (_d'un code_) code, cipher; **~s romains/arabes** roman/arabic figures _ou_ numerals; **en ~s ronds** in round figures; **écrire un nombre en ~s** to write a number in figures; **~ d'affaires** (CA) turnover; **~ de ventes** sales figures.

chiffrer [ʃifʀe] _vt_ (_dépense_) to put a figure to, assess; (_message_) to (en)code, cipher ♦ _vi_: **~ à, se ~ à** to add up to.

chignole [ʃiɲɔl] _nf_ drill.

chignon [ʃiɲɔ̃] _nm_ chignon, bun.

chiite [ʃiit] _adj_ Shiite ♦ _nm/f_: **C~** Shiite.

Chili [ʃili] _nm_: **le ~** Chile.

chilien, ne [ʃiljɛ̃, -ɛn] _adj_ Chilean ♦ _nm/f_: **C~, ne** Chilean.

chimère [ʃimɛʀ] _nf_ (_wild_) dream; pipe dream, idle fancy.

chimérique [ʃimeʀik] _adj_ (_utopique_) fanciful.

chimie [ʃimi] _nf_ chemistry.

chimio [ʃimjo], **chimiothérapie** [ʃimjoteʀapi] _nf_ chemotherapy.

chimique [ʃimik] _adj_ chemical; **produits ~s** chemicals.

chimiste [ʃimist(ə)] _nm/f_ chemist.

chimpanzé [ʃɛ̃pɑ̃ze] _nm_ chimpanzee.

chinchilla [ʃɛ̃ʃila] _nm_ chinchilla.

Chine [ʃin] _nf_: **la ~** China; **la ~ libre, la république de ~** the Republic of China, Nationalist China (_Taiwan_).

chine [ʃin] _nm_ rice paper; (_porcelaine_) china (vase).

chiné, e [ʃine] _adj_ flecked.

chinois, e [ʃinwa, -waz] _adj_ Chinese; (_fig: péj_) pernickety, fussy ♦ _nm_ (LING) Chinese ♦ _nm/f_: **C~, e** Chinese.

chinoiserie(s) [ʃinwazʀi] _nf(pl)_ (_péj_) red tape, fuss.

chiot [ʃjo] _nm_ pup(py).

chiper [ʃipe] _vt_ (_fam_) to pinch.

chipie [ʃipi] _nf_ shrew.

chipolata [ʃipolata] _nf_ chipolata.

chipoter [ʃipɔte] _vi_ (_manger_) to nibble; (_ergoter_) to quibble, haggle.

chips [ʃips] _nfpl_ (_aussi_: **pommes ~**) crisps (BRIT), (potato) chips (US).

chique [ʃik] _nf_ quid, chew.

chiquenaude [ʃiknod] _nf_ flick, flip.

chiquer [ʃike] _vi_ to chew tobacco.

chiromancie [kiʀɔmɑ̃si] _nf_ palmistry.

chiromancien, ne [kiʀɔmɑ̃sjɛ̃, -ɛn] _nm/f_ palmist.

chiropracteur [kiʀɔpʀaktœʀ] _nm_, **chiropraticien, ne** [kiʀɔpʀatisjɛ̃, -ɛn] _nm/f_ chiropractor.

chirurgical, e, aux [ʃiʀyʀʒikal, -o] _adj_ surgical.

chirurgie [ʃiʀyʀʒi] _nf_ surgery; **~ esthétique** cosmetic _ou_ plastic surgery.

chirurgien [ʃiʀyʀʒjɛ̃] _nm_ surgeon; **~ dentiste** dental surgeon.

chiure [ʃjyʀ] _nf_: **~s de mouche** fly specks.

ch.-l. _abr_ = **chef-lieu**.

chlore [klɔʀ] _nm_ chlorine.

chloroforme [klɔʀɔfɔʀm(ə)] _nm_ chloroform.

chlorophylle [klɔʀɔfil] _nf_ chlorophyll.

chlorure [klɔʀyʀ] _nm_ chloride.

choc [ʃɔk] _nm_ impact; shock; crash; (_moral_) shock; (_affrontement_) clash ♦ _adj_: **prix ~** amazing _ou_ incredible price/prices; **de ~** (_troupe, traitement_) shock _cpd_; (_patron etc_) high-powered; **~ opératoire/nerveux** post-operative/nervous shock; **~ en retour** return shock; (_fig_) backlash.

chocolat [ʃɔkɔla] _nm_ chocolate; (_boisson_) (hot) chocolate; **~ à cuire** cooking chocolate; **~ au lait** milk chocolate; **~ en poudre** drinking chocolate.

chocolaté, e [ʃɔkɔlate] _adj_ chocolate _cpd_, chocolate-flavoured.

chocolaterie [ʃɔkɔlatʀi] _nf_ (_fabrique_) chocolate factory.

chocolatier, ière [ʃɔkɔlatje, -jɛʀ] _nm/f_ chocolate maker.

chœur [kœʀ] _nm_ (_chorale_) choir; (_OPÉRA, THÉÂT_) chorus; (_ARCHIT_) choir, chancel; **en ~** in chorus.

choir [ʃwaʀ] _vi_ to fall.

choisi, e [ʃwazi] _adj_ (_de premier choix_) carefully chosen; select; **textes ~s** selected writings.

choisir [ʃwaziʀ] _vt_ to choose; (_entre plusieurs_) to choose, select; **~ de faire qch** to choose _ou_ opt to do sth.

choix [ʃwa] _nm_ choice; selection; **avoir le ~** to have the choice; **je n'avais pas le ~** I had no choice; **de premier ~** (COMM) class _ou_ grade one; **de ~** choice _cpd_, selected; **au ~** as you wish _ou_ prefer; **de mon/son ~** of my/his _ou_ her choosing.

choléra [kɔleʀa] _nm_ cholera.

cholestérol [kɔlesteʀɔl] _nm_ cholesterol.

chômage [ʃomaʒ] _nm_ unemployment; **mettre au ~** to make redundant, put out of work; **être au ~** to be unemployed _ou_ out of work; **~ partiel** short-time working; **~ structurel** structural unemployment; **~ technique** lay-offs _pl_.

chômer [ʃome] _vi_ to be unemployed, be idle; **jour chômé** public holiday.

chômeur, euse [ʃomœʀ, -øz] _nm/f_ unemployed person, person out of work.

chope [ʃɔp] *nf* tankard.
choquant, e [ʃɔkɑ̃, -ɑ̃t] *adj* shocking.
choquer [ʃɔke] *vt* (*offenser*) to shock; (*commotionner*) to shake (up).
choral, e [kɔRal] *adj* choral ♦ *nf* choral society, choir.
chorégraphe [kɔRegRaf] *nm/f* choreographer.
chorégraphie [kɔRegRafi] *nf* choreography.
choriste [kɔRist(ə)] *nm/f* choir member; (*OPÉRA*) chorus member.
chorus [kɔRys] *nm*: **faire ~ (avec)** to voice one's agreement (with).
chose [ʃoz] *nf* thing ♦ *nm* (*fam*: *machin*) thingamajig ♦ *adj inv*: **être/se sentir tout ~** (*bizarre*) to be/feel a bit odd; (*malade*) to be/feel out of sorts; **dire bien des ~s à qn** to give sb's regards to sb; **parler de ~(s) et d'autre(s)** to talk about one thing and another; **c'est peu de ~** it's nothing much.
chou, x [ʃu] *nm* cabbage ♦ *adj inv* cute; **mon petit ~** (my) sweetheart; **faire ~ blanc** to draw a blank; **feuille de ~** (*fig*: *journal*) rag; **~ à la crème** cream bun (*made of choux pastry*); **~ de Bruxelles** Brussels sprout.
choucas [ʃuka] *nm* jackdaw.
chouchou, te [ʃuʃu, -ut] *nm/f* (*SCOL*) teacher's pet.
chouchouter [ʃuʃute] *vt* to pet.
choucroute [ʃukRut] *nf* sauerkraut; **~ garnie** sauerkraut with cooked meats and potatoes.
chouette [ʃwɛt] *nf* owl ♦ *adj* (*fam*) great, smashing.
chou-fleur, *pl* **choux-fleurs** [ʃuflœR] *nm* cauliflower.
chou-rave, *pl* **choux-raves** [ʃuRav] *nm* kohlrabi.
choyer [ʃwaje] *vt* to cherish; to pamper.
CHR *sigle m* = *Centre hospitalier régional*.
chrétien, ne [kRetjɛ̃, -ɛn] *adj*, *nm/f* Christian.
chrétiennement [kRetjɛnmɑ̃] *adv* in a Christian way *ou* spirit.
chrétienté [kRetjɛ̃te] *nf* Christendom.
Christ [kRist] *nm*: **le ~** Christ; **c~** (*crucifix etc*) figure of Christ; **Jésus ~** Jesus Christ.
christianiser [kRistjanize] *vt* to convert to Christianity.
christianisme [kRistjanism(ə)] *nm* Christianity.
Christmas [kRistmas] *nf*: **(l'île) ~** Christmas Island.
chromatique [kRɔmatik] *adj* chromatic.
chrome [kRom] *nm* chromium; (*revêtement*) chrome, chromium.
chromé, e [kRome] *adj* chrome-plated, chromium-plated.
chromosome [kRɔmozom] *nm* chromosome.
chronique [kRɔnik] *adj* chronic ♦ *nf* (*de journal*) column, page; (*historique*) chronicle; (*RADIO*, *TV*): **la ~ sportive/théâtrale** the sports/theatre review; **la ~ locale** local news and gossip.

chroniqueur [kRɔnikœR] *nm* columnist; chronicler.
chrono [kRɔno] *nm* (*fam*) = **chronomètre**.
chronologie [kRɔnɔlɔʒi] *nf* chronology.
chronologique [kRɔnɔlɔʒik] *adj* chronological.
chronologiquement [kRɔnɔlɔʒikmɑ̃] *adv* chronologically.
chronomètre [kRɔnɔmɛtR(ə)] *nm* stopwatch.
chronométrer [kRɔnɔmetRe] *vt* to time.
chronométreur [kRɔnɔmetRœR] *nm* timekeeper.
chrysalide [kRizalid] *nf* chrysalis.
chrysanthème [kRizɑ̃tɛm] *nm* chrysanthemum.
CHU *sigle m* (= *Centre hospitalo-universitaire*) ≈ (teaching) hospital.
chu, e [ʃy] *pp de* **choir**.
chuchotement [ʃyʃɔtmɑ̃] *nm* whisper.
chuchoter [ʃyʃɔte] *vt*, *vi* to whisper.
chuintement [ʃɥɛ̃tmɑ̃] *nm* hiss.
chuinter [ʃɥɛ̃te] *vi* to hiss.
chut *excl* [ʃyt] sh! ♦ *vb* [ʃy] *voir* **choir**.
chute [ʃyt] *nf* fall; (*de bois, papier*: *déchet*) scrap; **la ~ des cheveux** hair loss; **faire une ~ (de 10 m)** to fall (10 m); **~s de pluie/neige** rain/snowfalls; **~ (d'eau)** waterfall; **~ du jour** nightfall; **~ libre** free fall; **~ des reins** small of the back.
Chypre [ʃipR] *nm*: **le ~** Cyprus.
chypriote [ʃipRiɔt] *adj*, *nm/f* = **cypriote**.
-ci, ci- [si] *adv voir* **par, ci-contre, ci-joint** *etc* ♦ *dét*: **ce garçon-ci/-là** this/that boy; **ces femmes-ci/-là** these/those women.
CIA *sigle f* CIA.
cial *abr* = **commercial**.
ciao [tʃao] *excl* (*fam*) (bye-)bye.
ci-après [siapRɛ] *adv* hereafter.
cibiste [sibist(ə)] *nm* CB enthusiast.
cible [sibl(ə)] *nf* target.
cibler [sible] *vt* to target.
ciboire [sibwaR] *nm* ciborium (*vessel*).
ciboule [sibul] *nf* (large) chive.
ciboulette [sibulɛt] *nf* (small) chive.
ciboulot [sibulo] *nm* (*fam*) head, nut; **il n'a rien dans le ~** he's got nothing between his ears.
cicatrice [sikatRis] *nf* scar.
cicatriser [sikatRize] *vt* to heal; **se ~** to heal (up), form a scar.
ci-contre [sikɔ̃tR(ə)] *adv* opposite.
CICR *sigle m* (= *Comité international de la Croix-Rouge*) ICRC.
ci-dessous [sidəsu] *adv* below.
ci-dessus [sidəsy] *adv* above.
ci-devant [sidəvɑ̃] *nm/f inv* aristocrat who lost his/her title in the French Revolution.
CIDEX *sigle m* (= *Courrier individuel à distribution exceptionnelle*) system which groups letter boxes in country areas, rather than each house having its letter box at its front door.
CIDJ *sigle m* (= *Centre d'information et de documentation de la jeunesse*) careers advisory

service.

cidre [sidʀ(ə)] *nm* cider.

cidrerie [sidʀəʀi] *nf* cider factory.

CIDUNATI [sidynati] *sigle m* (= *Comité interprofessionnel de défense de l'union nationale des artisans et travailleurs indépendants*) union of self-employed craftsmen.

Cie *abr* (= *compagnie*) Co.

ciel [sjɛl] *nm* sky; (*REL*) heaven; ~s *nmpl* (*PEINTURE etc*) skies; **cieux** *nmpl* sky *sg*, skies; (*REL*) heaven *sg*; **à** ~ **ouvert** open-air; (*mine*) opencast; **tomber du** ~ (*arriver à l'improviste*) to appear out of the blue; (*être stupéfait*) to be unable to believe one's eyes; **C~!** good heavens!; ~ **de lit** canopy.

cierge [sjɛʀʒ(ə)] *nm* candle; ~ **pascal** Easter candle.

cieux [sjø] *nmpl voir* **ciel**.

cigale [sigal] *nf* cicada.

cigare [sigaʀ] *nm* cigar.

cigarette [sigaʀɛt] *nf* cigarette; ~ **(à) bout filtre** filter cigarette.

ci-gît [siʒi] *adv* here lies.

cigogne [sigɔɲ] *nf* stork.

ciguë [sigy] *nf* hemlock.

ci-inclus, e [siɛ̃kly, -yz] *adj, adv* enclosed.

ci-joint, e [siʒwɛ̃, -ɛt] *adj, adv* enclosed; **veuillez trouver** ~ please find enclosed.

cil [sil] *nm* (eye)lash.

ciller [sije] *vi* to blink.

cimaise [simɛz] *nf* picture rail.

cime [sim] *nf* top; (*montagne*) peak.

ciment [simɑ̃] *nm* cement; ~ **armé** reinforced concrete.

cimenter [simɑ̃te] *vt* to cement.

cimenterie [simɑ̃tʀi] *nf* cement works *sg*.

cimetière [simtjɛʀ] *nm* cemetery; (*d'église*) churchyard; ~ **de voitures** scrapyard.

cinéaste [sineast(ə)] *nm/f* film-maker.

ciné-club [sineklœb] *nm* film club; film society.

cinéma [sinema] *nm* cinema; **aller au** ~ to go to the cinema *ou* pictures *ou* movies; ~ **d'animation** cartoon (film).

cinémascope [sinemaskɔp] *nm* ® Cinemascope ®.

cinémathèque [sinematɛk] *nf* film archives *pl ou* library.

cinématographie [sinematɔgʀafi] *nf* cinematography.

cinématographique [sinematɔgʀafik] *adj* film *cpd*, cinema *cpd*.

cinéphile [sinefil] *nm/f* film buff.

cinérama [sinerama] *nm* ®: **en** ~ in Cinerama ®.

cinétique [sinetik] *adj* kinetic.

cing(h)alais, e [sɛ̃galɛ, -ɛz] *adj* Sin(g)halese.

cinglant, e [sɛ̃glɑ̃, -ɑ̃t] *adj* (*propos, ironie*) scathing, biting; (*échec*) crushing.

cinglé, e [sɛ̃gle] *adj* (*fam*) crazy.

cingler [sɛ̃gle] *vt* to lash; (*fig*) to sting ♦ *vi* (*NAVIG*): ~ **vers** to make *ou* head for.

cinq [sɛ̃k] *num* five.

cinquantaine [sɛ̃kɑ̃tɛn] *nf*: **une** ~ **(de)** about fifty; **avoir la** ~ (*âge*) to be around fifty.

cinquante [sɛ̃kɑ̃t] *num* fifty.

cinquantenaire [sɛ̃kɑ̃tnɛʀ] *adj*, *nm/f* fifty-year-old.

cinquantième [sɛ̃kɑ̃tjɛm] *num* fiftieth.

cinquième [sɛ̃kjɛm] *num* fifth.

cinquièmement [sɛ̃kjɛmmɑ̃] *adv* fifthly.

cintre [sɛ̃tʀ(ə)] *nm* coat-hanger; (*ARCHIT*) arch; **plein** ~ semicircular arch.

cintré, e [sɛ̃tʀe] *adj* curved; (*chemise*) fitted, slim-fitting.

CIO *sigle m* (= *Comité international olympique*) IOC (= *International Olympic Committee*).

cirage [siʀaʒ] *nm* (shoe) polish.

circoncis, e [siʀkɔ̃si, -iz] *adj* circumcized.

circoncision [siʀkɔ̃sizjɔ̃] *nf* circumcision.

circonférence [siʀkɔ̃feʀɑ̃s] *nf* circumference.

circonflexe [siʀkɔ̃flɛks(ə)] *adj*: **accent** ~ circumflex accent.

circonlocution [siʀkɔ̃lɔkysjɔ̃] *nf* circumlocution.

circonscription [siʀkɔ̃skʀipsjɔ̃] *nf* district; ~ **électorale** (*d'un député*) constituency; ~ **militaire** military area.

circonscrire [siʀkɔ̃skʀiʀ] *vt* to define, delimit; (*incendie*) to contain; (*propriété*) to mark out; (*sujet*) to define.

circonspect, e [siʀkɔ̃spɛkt] *adj* circumspect, cautious.

circonspection [siʀkɔ̃spɛksjɔ̃] *nf* circumspection, caution.

circonstance [siʀkɔ̃stɑ̃s] *nf* circumstance; (*occasion*) occasion; **œuvre de** ~ occasional work; **air de** ~ fitting air; **tête de** ~ appropriate demeanour (*BRIT*) *ou* demeanor (*US*); ~s **atténuantes** mitigating circumstances.

circonstancié, e [siʀkɔ̃stɑ̃sje] *adj* detailed.

circonstanciel, le [siʀkɔ̃stɑ̃sjɛl] *adj*: **complément/proposition** ~**(le)** adverbial phrase/clause.

circonvenir [siʀkɔ̃vniʀ] *vt* to circumvent.

circonvolutions [siʀkɔ̃vɔlysjɔ̃] *nfpl* twists, convolutions.

circuit [siʀkɥi] *nm* (*trajet*) tour, (round) trip; (*ÉLEC, TECH*) circuit; ~ **automobile** motor circuit; ~ **de distribution** distribution network; ~ **fermé** closed circuit; ~ **intégré** integrated circuit.

circulaire [siʀkylɛʀ] *adj*, *nf* circular.

circulation [siʀkylasjɔ̃] *nf* circulation; (*AUTO*): **la** ~ (the) traffic; **bonne/mauvaise** ~ good/bad circulation; **mettre en** ~ to put into circulation.

circulatoire [siʀkylatwaʀ] *adj*: **avoir des troubles** ~**s** to have problems with one's circulation.

circuler [siʀkyle] *vi* to drive (along); to walk along; (*train etc*) to run; (*sang, devises*) to circulate; **faire** ~ (*nouvelle*) to spread (about), circulate; (*badauds*) to move on.

cire [siʀ] *nf* wax; ~ **à cacheter** sealing wax.

ciré [siʀe] *nm* oilskin.

cirer [siʀe] *vt* to wax, polish.

cireur [siʀœʀ] *nm* shoeshine-boy.

cireuse [siʀøz] *nf* floor polisher.

cireux, euse [siʀø, -øz] *adj* (*fig: teint*) sallow, waxen.

cirque [siʀk(ə)] *nm* circus; (*arène*) amphitheatre (*BRIT*), amphitheater (*US*); (*GÉO*) cirque; (*fig: désordre*) chaos, bedlam; (: *chichis*) carry-on.

cirrhose [siʀoz] *nf*: ~ **du foie** cirrhosis of the liver.

cisailler [sizaje] *vt* to clip.

cisaille(s) [sizaj] *nf(pl)* (gardening) shears *pl*.

ciseau, x [sizo] *nm*: ~ **(à bois)** chisel ♦ *nmpl* (pair of) scissors; **sauter en** ~**x** to do a scissors jump; ~ **à froid** cold chisel.

ciseler [sizle] *vt* to chisel, carve.

ciselure [sizlyʀ] *nf* engraving; (*bois*) carving.

Cisjordanie [sisʒɔʀdani] *nf*: **la** ~ the West Bank (of Jordan).

citadelle [sitadɛl] *nf* citadel.

citadin, e [sitadɛ̃, -in] *nm/f* city dweller ♦ *adj* town *cpd*, city *cpd*, urban.

citation [sitasjɔ̃] *nf* (*d'auteur*) quotation; (*JUR*) summons *sg*; (*MIL: récompense*) mention.

cité [site] *nf* town; (*plus grande*) city; ~ **ouvrière** (workers') housing estate; ~ **universitaire** students' residences *pl*.

cité-dortoir, *pl* **cités-dortoirs** [sitedɔʀtwaʀ] *nf* dormitory town.

cité-jardin, *pl* **cités-jardins** [siteʒaʀdɛ̃] *nf* garden city.

citer [site] *vt* (*un auteur*) to quote (from); (*nommer*) to name; (*JUR*) to summon; ~ **(en exemple)** (*personne*) to hold up (as an example); **je ne veux** ~ **personne** I don't want to name names.

citerne [sitɛʀn(ə)] *nf* tank.

cithare [sitaʀ] *nf* zither.

citoyen, ne [sitwajɛ̃, -ɛn] *nm/f* citizen.

citoyenneté [sitwajɛnte] *nf* citizenship.

citrique [sitʀik] *adj*: **acide** ~ citric acid.

citron [sitʀɔ̃] *nm* lemon; ~ **pressé** (fresh) lemon juice; ~ **vert** lime.

citronnade [sitʀɔnad] *nf* lemonade.

citronné, e [sitʀɔne] *adj* (*boisson*) lemon-flavoured (*BRIT*) *ou* -flavored (*US*); (*eau de toilette*) lemon-scented.

citronnelle [sitʀɔnɛl] *nf* citronella.

citronnier [sitʀɔnje] *nm* lemon tree.

citrouille [sitʀuj] *nf* pumpkin.

cive(s) [siv] *nf(pl)* (*BOT*) chive(s); (*CULIN*) chives.

civet [sivɛ] *nm* stew; ~ **de lièvre** jugged hare.

civette [sivɛt] *nf* (*BOT*) chives *pl*; (*ZOOL*) civet (cat).

civière [sivjɛʀ] *nf* stretcher.

civil, e [sivil] *adj* (*JUR, ADMIN, poli*) civil; (*non militaire*) civilian ♦ *nm* civilian; **en** ~ in civil-

ian clothes; **dans le** ~ in civilian life.

civilement [sivilmɑ̃] *adv* (*poliment*) civilly; **se marier** ~ to have a civil wedding.

civilisation [sivilizasjɔ̃] *nf* civilization.

civilisé, e [sivilize] *adj* civilized.

civiliser [sivilize] *vt* to civilize.

civilité [sivilite] *nf* civility; **présenter ses** ~**s to** present one's compliments.

civique [sivik] *adj* civic; **instruction** ~ (*SCOL*) civics *sg*.

civisme [sivism(ə)] *nm* public-spiritedness.

cl. *abr* (= *centilitre*) cl.

clafoutis [klafuti] *nm* batter pudding (*containing fruit*).

claie [klɛ] *nf* grid, riddle.

clair, e [klɛʀ] *adj* light; (*chambre*) light, bright; (*eau, son, fig*) clear ♦ *adv*: **voir** ~ to see clearly ♦ *nm*: **mettre au** ~ (*notes etc*) to tidy up; **tirer qch au** ~ to clear sth up, clarify sth; **bleu** ~ light blue; **pour être** ~ so as to make it plain; **y voir** ~ (*comprendre*) to understand, see; **le plus** ~ **de son temps/argent** the better part of his time/money; **en** ~ (*non codé*) in clear; ~ **de lune** moonlight.

claire [klɛʀ] *nf*: **(huître de)** ~ fattened oyster.

clairement [klɛʀmɑ̃] *adv* clearly.

claire-voie [klɛʀvwa]: **à** ~ *adj* letting the light through; openwork *cpd*.

clairière [klɛʀjɛʀ] *nf* clearing.

clair-obscur, *pl* **clairs-obscurs** [klɛʀɔpskyʀ] *nm* half-light; (*fig*) uncertainty.

clairon [klɛʀɔ̃] *nm* bugle.

claironner [klɛʀɔne] *vt* (*fig*) to trumpet, shout from the rooftops.

clairsemé, e [klɛʀsəme] *adj* sparse.

clairvoyance [klɛʀvwajɑ̃s] *nf* clear-sightedness.

clairvoyant, e [klɛʀvwajɑ̃, -ɑ̃t] *adj* perceptive, clear-sighted.

clam [klam] *nm* (*ZOOL*) clam.

clamer [klame] *vt* to proclaim.

clameur [klamœʀ] *nf* clamour (*BRIT*), clamor (*US*).

clan [klɑ̃] *nm* clan.

clandestin, e [klɑ̃dɛstɛ̃, -in] *adj* clandestine, covert; (*POL*) underground, clandestine; **passager** ~ stowaway.

clandestinement [klɑ̃dɛstinmɑ̃] *adv* secretly; **s'embarquer** ~ to stow away.

clandestinité [klɑ̃dɛstinite] *nf*: **dans la** ~ (*en secret*) under cover; (*en se cachant: vivre*) underground; **entrer dans la** ~ to go underground.

clapet [klapɛ] *nm* (*TECH*) valve.

clapier [klapje] *nm* (rabbit) hutch.

clapotement [klapɔtmɑ̃] *nm* lap(ping).

clapoter [klapɔte] *vi* to lap.

clapotis [klapɔti] *nm* lap(ping).

claquage [klakaʒ] *nm* pulled *ou* strained muscle.

claque [klak] *nf* (*gifle*) slap; (*THÉÂT*) claque ♦ *nm* (*chapeau*) opera hat.

claquement [klakmɑ̃] *nm* (*de porte: bruit répété*) banging; (*: bruit isolé*) slam.
claquemurer [klakmyʀe]: **se ~** *vi* to shut o.s. away, closet o.s.
claquer [klake] *vi* (*drapeau*) to flap; (*porte*) to bang, slam; (*coup de feu*) to ring out ♦ *vt* (*porte*) to slam, bang; (*doigts*) to snap; **elle claquait des dents** her teeth were chattering; **se ~ un muscle** to pull *ou* strain a muscle.
claquettes [klakɛt] *nfpl* tap-dancing *sg*.
clarification [klaʀifikasjɔ̃] *nf* (*fig*) clarification.
clarifier [klaʀifje] *vt* (*fig*) to clarify.
clarinette [klaʀinɛt] *nf* clarinet.
clarinettiste [klaʀinetist(ə)] *nm/f* clarinettist.
clarté [klaʀte] *nf* lightness; brightness; (*d'un son, de l'eau*) clearness; (*d'une explication*) clarity.
classe [klɑs] *nf* class; (*SCOL: local*) class(room); (*: leçon*) class; (*: élèves*) class, form; **1ère/2ème ~** 1st/2nd class; **un** (**soldat de**) **deuxième ~** (*MIL: armée de terre*) ≈ private (soldier); (*: armée de l'air*) ≈ aircraftman (*BRIT*), ≈ airman basic (*US*); **de ~** luxury *cpd*; **faire ses ~s** (*MIL*) to do one's (recruit's) training; **faire la ~** (*SCOL*) to be a *ou* the teacher; to teach; **aller en ~** to go to school; **aller en ~ verte/de neige/de mer** to go to the countryside/skiing/to the seaside with the school; **~ ouvrière** working class; **~ préparatoire** class which prepares students for the *Grandes Écoles* entry exams; **~ sociale** social class; **~ touriste** economy class.

> **Classes préparatoires** *is the term given to the two years of intensive study required to sit the competitive entry examinations to the* **grandes écoles**. *They are extremely demanding post-baccalauréat courses, usually taken in a* **lycée**. *Schools which provide such classes are more highly regarded than those which do not.*

classement [klɑsmɑ̃] *nm* classifying; filing; grading; closing; (*rang: SCOL*) place; (*: SPORT*) placing; (*liste: SCOL*) class list in order of merit; (*: SPORT*) placings *pl*; **premier au ~ général** (*SPORT*) first overall.
classer [klɑse] *vt* (*idées, livres*) to classify; (*papiers*) to file; (*candidat, concurrent*) to grade; (*personne: juger: péj*) to rate; (*JUR: affaire*) to close; **se ~ premier/dernier** to come first/last; (*SPORT*) to finish first/last.
classeur [klɑsœʀ] *nm* (*cahier*) file; (*meuble*) filing cabinet; **~ à feuillets mobiles** ring binder.
classification [klasifikasjɔ̃] *nf* classification.
classifier [klasifje] *vt* to classify.
classique [klasik] *adj* classical; (*sobre: coupe etc*) classic(al); (*habituel*) standard, classic ♦ *nm* classic; classical author; **études ~s** classical studies, classics.

claudication [klodikasjɔ̃] *nf* limp.
clause [kloz] *nf* clause.
claustrer [klostʀe] *vt* to confine.
claustrophobie [klostʀɔfɔbi] *nf* claustrophobia.
clavecin [klavsɛ̃] *nm* harpsichord.
claveciniste [klavsinist(ə)] *nm/f* harpsichordist.
clavicule [klavikyl] *nf* clavicle, collarbone.
clavier [klavje] *nm* keyboard.
clé *ou* **clef** [kle] *nf* key; (*MUS*) clef; (*de mécanicien*) spanner (*BRIT*), wrench (*US*) ♦ *adj*: **problème/position ~** key problem/position; **mettre sous ~** to place under lock and key; **prendre la ~ des champs** to run away, make off; **prix ~s en main** (*d'une voiture*) on-the-road price; (*d'un appartement*) price with immediate entry; **~ de sol/de fa/d'ut** treble/bass/alto clef; **livre/film etc à ~** *book/film etc in which real people are depicted under fictitious names*; **à la ~** (*à la fin*) at the end of it all; **~ anglaise = ~ à molette**; **~ de contact** ignition key; **~ à molette** adjustable spanner (*BRIT*) *ou* wrench, monkey wrench; **~ de voûte** keystone.
clématite [klematit] *nf* clematis.
clémence [klemɑ̃s] *nf* mildness; leniency.
clément, e [klemɑ̃, -ɑ̃t] *adj* (*temps*) mild; (*indulgent*) lenient.
clémentine [klemɑ̃tin] *nf* (*BOT*) clementine.
clenche [klɑ̃ʃ] *nf* latch.
cleptomane [klɛptɔman] *nm/f* = **kleptomane**.
clerc [klɛʀ] *nm*: **~ de notaire** *ou* **d'avoué** lawyer's clerk.
clergé [klɛʀʒe] *nm* clergy.
clérical, e, aux [kleʀikal, -o] *adj* clerical.
cliché [kliʃe] *nm* (*PHOTO*) negative; print; (*TYPO*) (printing) plate; (*LING*) cliché.
client, e [klijɑ̃, -ɑ̃t] *nm/f* (*acheteur*) customer, client; (*d'hôtel*) guest, patron; (*du docteur*) patient; (*de l'avocat*) client.
clientèle [klijɑ̃tɛl] *nf* (*du magasin*) customers *pl*, clientèle; (*du docteur, de l'avocat*) practice; **accorder sa ~ à** to give one's custom to; **retirer sa ~ à** to take one's business away from.
cligner [kliɲe] *vi*: **~ des yeux** to blink (one's eyes); **~ de l'œil** to wink.
clignotant [kliɲɔtɑ̃] *nm* (*AUTO*) indicator.
clignoter [kliɲɔte] *vi* (*étoiles etc*) to twinkle; (*lumière: à intervalles réguliers*) to flash; (*: vaciller*) to flicker; (*yeux*) to blink.
climat [klima] *nm* climate.
climatique [klimatik] *adj* climatic.
climatisation [klimatizasjɔ̃] *nf* air conditioning.
climatisé, e [klimatize] *adj* air-conditioned.
climatiseur [klimatizœʀ] *nm* air conditioner.
clin d'œil [klɛ̃dœj] *nm* wink; **en un ~** in a flash.
clinique [klinik] *adj* clinical ♦ *nf* nursing home, (private) clinic.

clinquant, e [klɛ̃kɑ̃, -ɑ̃t] adj flashy.

clip [klip] nm (pince) clip; (vidéo) pop (ou promotional) video.

clique [klik] nf (péj: bande) clique, set; **prendre ses ~s et ses claques** to pack one's bags.

cliqueter [klikte] vi to clash; (ferraille, clefs, monnaie) to jangle, jingle; (verres) to chink.

cliquetis [klikti] nm jangle, jingle; chink.

clitoris [klitɔʀis] nm clitoris.

clivage [klivaʒ] nm cleavage; (fig) rift, split.

cloaque [klɔak] nm (fig) cesspit.

clochard, e [klɔʃaʀ, -aʀd(ə)] nm/f tramp.

cloche [klɔʃ] nf (d'église) bell; (fam) clot; (chapeau) cloche (hat); ~ **à fromage** cheesecover.

cloche-pied [klɔʃpje]: **à ~** adv on one leg, hopping (along).

clocher [klɔʃe] nm church tower; (en pointe) steeple ♦ vi (fam) to be ou go wrong; **de ~** (péj) parochial.

clocheton [klɔʃtɔ̃] nm pinnacle.

clochette [klɔʃɛt] nf bell.

clodo [klɔdo] nm (fam: = clochard) tramp.

cloison [klwazɔ̃] nf partition (wall); ~ **étanche** (fig) impenetrable barrier, brick wall (fig).

cloisonner [klwazɔne] vt to partition (off); to divide up; (fig) to compartmentalize.

cloître [klwatʀ(ə)] nm cloister.

cloîtrer [klwatʀe] vt: **se ~** to shut o.s. up ou away; (REL) to enter a convent ou monastery.

clone [klɔn] nm clone.

clope [klɔp] nm ou f (fam) fag (BRIT), cigarette.

clopin-clopant [klɔpɛ̃klɔpɑ̃] adv hobbling along; (fig) so-so.

clopiner [klɔpine] vi to hobble along.

cloporte [klɔpɔʀt(ə)] nm woodlouse (pl -lice).

cloque [klɔk] nf blister.

cloqué, e [klɔke] adj: **étoffe ~e** seersucker.

cloquer [klɔke] vi (peau, peinture) to blister.

clore [klɔʀ] vt to close; ~ **une session** (INFORM) to log out.

clos, e [klo, -oz] pp de **clore** ♦ adj voir **maison, huis, vase** ♦ nm (enclosed) field.

clôt [klo] vb voir **clore**.

clôture [klotyʀ] nf closure, closing; (barrière) enclosure, fence.

clôturer [klotyʀe] vt (terrain) to enclose, close off; (festival, débats) to close.

clou [klu] nm nail; (MÉD) boil; ~**s** nmpl = **passage clouté; pneus à ~s** studded tyres; **le ~ du spectacle** the highlight of the show; ~ **de girofle** clove.

clouer [klue] vt to nail down (ou up); (fig): ~ **sur/contre** to pin to/against.

clouté, e [klute] adj studded.

clown [klun] nm clown; **faire le ~** (fig) to clown (about), play the fool.

clownerie [klunʀi] nf clowning no pl; **faire des ~s** to clown around.

CLT sigle f = Compagnie Luxembourgeoise de Télévision.

club [klœb] nm club.

CM sigle f = **chambre des métiers** ♦ sigle m = **conseil municipal**; (SCOL) = **cours moyen**.

cm. abr (= centimètre) cm.

CNAT sigle f (= Commission nationale d'aménagement du territoire) national development agency.

CNC sigle m (= Conseil national de la consommation) national consumers' council.

CNCL sigle f (= Commission nationale de la communication et des libertés) independent broadcasting authority.

CNDP sigle m = Centre national de documentation pédagogique.

CNE sigle f (= Caisse nationale d'épargne) national savings bank.

CNEC sigle m (= Centre national de l'enseignement par correspondance) ≈ Open University.

CNIL sigle f (= Commission nationale de l'informatique et des libertés) board which enforces law on data protection.

CNIT sigle m (= Centre national des industries et des techniques) exhibition centre in Paris.

CNJA sigle m (= Centre national des jeunes agriculteurs) farmers' union.

CNL sigle f (= Confédération nationale du logement) consumer group for housing.

CNP sigle f (= Caisse nationale de prévoyance) savings bank.

CNPF sigle m (= Conseil national du patronat français) national council of French employers.

CNRS sigle m = Centre national de la recherche scientifique.

c/o abr (= care of) c/o.

coagulant [kɔagylɑ̃] nm (MÉD) coagulant.

coaguler [kɔagyle] vi, vt, **se ~** vi to coagulate.

coaliser [kɔalize]: **se ~** vi to unite, join forces.

coalition [kɔalisjɔ̃] nf coalition.

coasser [kɔase] vi to croak.

coauteur [kɔotœʀ] nm co-author.

coaxial, e, aux [kɔaksjal, -o] adj coaxial.

cobalt [kɔbalt] nm cobalt.

cobaye [kɔbaj] nm guinea-pig.

COBOL, Cobol [kɔbɔl] nm COBOL, Cobol.

cobra [kɔbʀa] nm cobra.

coca [kɔka] nm ® Coke ®.

cocagne [kɔkaɲ] nf: **pays de ~** land of plenty; **mât de ~** greasy pole (fig).

cocaïne [kɔkain] nf cocaine.

cocarde [kɔkaʀd(ə)] nf rosette.

cocardier, ière [kɔkaʀdje, -jɛʀ] adj jingoistic, chauvinistic; militaristic.

cocasse [kɔkas] adj comical, funny.

coccinelle [kɔksinɛl] nf ladybird (BRIT), ladybug (US).

coccyx [kɔksis] nm coccyx.

cocher [kɔʃe] nm coachman ♦ vt to tick off; (entailler) to notch.

cochère [kɔʃɛʀ]

cochon, ne [kɔʃɔ̃, -ɔn] nm pig ♦ nm/f (péj: sale)

(filthy) pig; (: *méchant*) swine ♦ *adj* (*fam*) dirty, smutty; ~ **d'Inde** guinea-pig; ~ **de lait** (*CULIN*) sucking pig.

cochonnaille [kɔʃɔnaj] *nf* (*péj*: *charcuterie*) (cold) pork.

cochonnerie [kɔʃɔnʀi] *nf* (*fam*: *saleté*) filth; (: *marchandises*) rubbish, trash.

cochonnet [kɔʃɔnɛ] *nm* (*BOULES*) jack.

cocker [kɔkɛʀ] *nm* cocker spaniel.

cocktail [kɔktɛl] *nm* cocktail; (*réception*) cocktail party.

coco [kɔko] *nm voir* **noix**; (*fam*) bloke (*BRIT*), dude (*US*).

cocon [kɔkɔ̃] *nm* cocoon.

cocorico [kɔkɔʀiko] *excl, nm* cock-a-doodle-do.

cocotier [kɔkɔtje] *nm* coconut palm.

cocotte [kɔkɔt] *nf* (*en fonte*) casserole; **ma** ~ (*fam*) sweetie (pie); ~ (**minute**) ® pressure cooker; ~ **en papier** paper shape.

cocu [kɔky] *nm* cuckold.

code [kɔd] *nm* code; **se mettre en** ~(**s**) to dip (*BRIT*) *ou* dim (*US*) one's (head)lights; ~ **à barres** bar code; ~ **de caractère** (*INFORM*) character code; ~ **civil** Common Law; ~ **machine** machine code; ~ **pénal** penal code; ~ **postal** (*numéro*) postcode (*BRIT*), zip code (*US*); ~ **de la route** highway code; ~ **secret** cipher.

codéine [kɔdein] *nf* codeine.

coder [kɔde] *vt* to (en)code.

codétenu, e [kɔdetny] *nm/f* fellow prisoner *ou* inmate.

codicille [kɔdisil] *nm* codicil.

codifier [kɔdifje] *vt* to codify.

codirecteur, trice [kɔdiʀɛktœʀ, -tʀis] *nm/f* co-director.

coéditeur, trice [kɔeditœʀ, -tʀis] *nm/f* co-publisher; (*rédacteur*) co-editor.

coefficient [kɔefisjɑ̃] *nm* coefficient; ~ **d'erreur** margin of error.

coéquipier, ière [kɔekipje, -jɛʀ] *nm/f* team-mate, partner.

coercition [kɔɛʀsisjɔ̃] *nf* coercion.

cœur [kœʀ] *nm* heart; (*CARTES*: *couleur*) hearts *pl*; (: *carte*) heart; (*CULIN*): ~ **de laitue/d'artichaut** lettuce/artichoke heart; (*fig*): ~ **du débat** heart of the debate; ~ **de l'été** height of summer; ~ **de la forêt** depths *pl* of the forest; **affaire de** ~ love affair; **avoir bon** ~ to be kind-hearted; **avoir mal au** ~ to feel sick; **contre** *ou* **sur son** ~ to one's breast; **opérer qn à** ~ **ouvert** to perform open-heart surgery on sb; **recevoir qn à** ~ **ouvert** to welcome sb with open arms; **parler à** ~ **ouvert** to open one's heart; **de tout son** ~ with all one's heart; **avoir le** ~ **gros** *ou* **serré** to have a heavy heart; **en avoir le** ~ **net** to be clear in one's own mind (about it); **par** ~ by heart; **de bon** ~ willingly; **avoir à** ~ **de faire** to be very keen to do; **cela lui tient à** ~ that's (very) close to his heart; **prendre les choses à** ~ to take things to heart; **à** ~ **joie**

to one's heart's content; **être de tout** ~ **avec qn** to be (completely) in accord with sb.

coexistence [kɔɛgzistɑ̃s] *nf* coexistence.

coexister [kɔɛgziste] *vi* to coexist.

coffrage [kɔfʀaʒ] *nm* (*CONSTR*: *dispositif*) form(work).

coffre [kɔfʀ(ə)] *nm* (*meuble*) chest; (*coffre-fort*) safe; (*d'auto*) boot (*BRIT*), trunk (*US*); **avoir du** ~ (*fam*) to have a lot of puff.

coffre-fort, *pl* **coffres-forts** [kɔfʀəfɔʀ] *nm* safe.

coffrer [kɔfʀe] *vt* (*fam*) to put inside, lock up.

coffret [kɔfʀɛ] *nm* casket; ~ **à bijoux** jewel box.

cogérant, e [kɔʒeʀɑ̃, -ɑ̃t] *nm/f* joint manager/manageress.

cogestion [kɔʒɛstjɔ̃] *nf* joint management.

cogiter [kɔʒite] *vi* to cogitate.

cognac [kɔɲak] *nm* brandy, cognac.

cognement [kɔɲmɑ̃] *nm* knocking.

cogner [kɔɲe] *vi* to knock, bang; **se** ~ to bump o.s.

cohabitation [kɔabitasjɔ̃] *nf* living together; (*POL, JUR*) cohabitation.

cohabiter [kɔabite] *vi* to live together.

cohérence [kɔeʀɑ̃s] *nf* coherence.

cohérent, e [kɔeʀɑ̃, -ɑ̃t] *adj* coherent.

cohésion [kɔezjɔ̃] *nf* cohesion.

cohorte [kɔɔʀt(ə)] *nf* troop.

cohue [kɔy] *nf* crowd.

coi, coite [kwa, kwat] *adj*: **rester** ~ to remain silent.

coiffe [kwaf] *nf* headdress.

coiffé, e [kwafe] *adj*: **bien/mal** ~ with tidy/untidy hair; ~ **d'un béret** wearing a beret; ~ **en arrière** with one's hair brushed *ou* combed back; ~ **en brosse** with a crew cut.

coiffer [kwafe] *vt* (*fig*) to cover, top; ~ **qn** to do sb's hair; ~ **qn d'un béret** to put a beret on sb; **se** ~ to do one's hair; to put on a *ou* one's hat.

coiffeur, euse [kwafœʀ, -øz] *nm/f* hairdresser ♦ *nf* (*table*) dressing table.

coiffure [kwafyʀ] *nf* (*cheveux*) hairstyle, hairdo; (*chapeau*) hat, headgear *no pl*; (*art*): **la** ~ hairdressing.

coin [kwɛ̃] *nm* corner; (*pour graver*) die; (*pour coincer*) wedge; (*poinçon*) hallmark; **l'épicerie du** ~ the local grocer; **dans le** ~ (*aux alentours*) in the area, around about; locally; **au** ~ **du feu** by the fireside; **du** ~ **de l'œil** out of the corner of one's eye; **regard en** ~ side(ways) glance; **sourire en** ~ half-smile.

coincé, e [kwɛ̃se] *adj* stuck, jammed; (*fig*: *inhibé*) inhibited, with hang-ups.

coincer [kwɛ̃se] *vt* to jam; (*fam*) to catch (out); to nab; **se** ~ to get stuck *ou* jammed.

coïncidence [kɔɛ̃sidɑ̃s] *nf* coincidence.

coïncider [kɔɛ̃side] *vi*: ~ (**avec**) to coincide (with); (*correspondre*: *témoignage etc*) to correspond *ou* tally (with).

coin-coin [kwɛ̃kwɛ̃] nm inv quack.
coing [kwɛ̃] nm quince.
coït [kɔit] nm coitus.
coite [kwat] adj f voir **coi**.
coke [kɔk] nm coke.
col [kɔl] nm (de chemise) collar; (encolure, cou) neck; (de montagne) pass; ~ **du fémur** neck of the thighbone; ~ **roulé** polo-neck; ~ **de l'utérus** cervix.
coléoptère [kɔleɔptɛʀ] nm beetle.
colère [kɔlɛʀ] nf anger; **une** ~ a fit of anger; **être en** ~ **(contre qn)** to be angry (with sb); **mettre qn en** ~ to make sb angry; **se mettre en** ~ to get angry.
coléreux, euse [kɔleʀø, -øz] adj, **colérique** [kɔleʀik] adj quick-tempered, irascible.
colibacille [kɔlibasil] nm colon bacillus.
colibacillose [kɔlibasiloz] nf colibacillosis.
colifichet [kɔlifiʃɛ] nm trinket.
colimaçon [kɔlimasɔ̃] nm: **escalier en** ~ spiral staircase.
colin [kɔlɛ̃] nm hake.
colin-maillard [kɔlɛ̃majaʀ] nm (jeu) blind man's buff.
colique [kɔlik] nf diarrhoea (BRIT), diarrhea (US); (douleurs) colic (pains pl); (fam: personne ou chose ennuyeuse) pain.
colis [kɔli] nm parcel; **par** ~ **postal** by parcel post.
colistier, ière [kɔlistje, -jɛʀ] nm/f fellow candidate.
colite [kɔlit] nf colitis.
coll. abr = collection; (= collaborateurs): **et** ~ et al.
collaborateur, trice [kɔlabɔʀatœʀ, -tʀis] nm/f (aussi POL) collaborator; (d'une revue) contributor.
collaboration [kɔlabɔʀasjɔ̃] nf collaboration.
collaborer [kɔlabɔʀe] vi to collaborate; ~ **à** to collaborate on; (revue) to contribute to.
collage [kɔlaʒ] nm (ART) collage.
collagène [kɔlaʒɛn] nm collagen.
collant, e [kɔlɑ̃, -ɑ̃t] adj sticky; (robe etc) clinging, skintight; (péj) clinging ♦ nm (bas) tights pl.
collatéral, e, aux [kɔlateʀal, -o] nm/f collateral.
collation [kɔlɑsjɔ̃] nf light meal.
colle [kɔl] nf glue; (à papiers peints) (wallpaper) paste; (devinette) teaser, riddle; (SCOL fam) detention; ~ **forte** superglue ®.
collecte [kɔlɛkt(ə)] nf collection; **faire une** ~ to take up a collection.
collecter [kɔlɛkte] vt to collect.
collecteur [kɔlɛktœʀ] nm (égout) main sewer.
collectif, ive [kɔlɛktif, -iv] adj collective; (visite, billet etc) group cpd ♦ nm: ~ **budgétaire** mini-budget (BRIT), mid-term budget; **immeuble** ~ block of flats.
collection [kɔlɛksjɔ̃] nf collection; (ÉDITION) series; **pièce de** ~ collector's item; **faire (la)** ~ **de** to collect; **(toute) une** ~ **de ...** (fig) a

(complete) set of ....
collectionner [kɔlɛksjɔne] vt (tableaux, timbres) to collect.
collectionneur, euse [kɔlɛksjɔnœʀ, -øz] nm/f collector.
collectivement [kɔlɛktivmɑ̃] adv collectively.
collectiviser [kɔlɛktivize] vt to collectivize.
collectivisme [kɔlɛktivism(ə)] nm collectivism.
collectiviste [kɔlɛktivist(ə)] adj collectivist.
collectivité [kɔlɛktivite] nf group; **la** ~ the community, the collectivity; **les** ~**s locales** local authorities.
collège [kɔlɛʒ] nm (école) (secondary) school; (assemblée) body; ~ **électoral** electoral college; ~ **d'enseignement secondaire (CES)** ≈ junior secondary school (BRIT), ≈ junior high school (US).

> The **collège** is a state secondary school for children aged between eleven and fifteen. Pupils follow a nationally prescribed curriculum consisting of a common core and various options. Schools are free to arrange their own timetable and choose their own teaching methods. Before leaving the collège, pupils are assessed by examination and course work for their **brevet des collèges**.

collégial, e, aux [kɔleʒjal, -o] adj collegiate.
collégien, ne [kɔleʒjɛ̃, -ɛn] nm/f secondary school pupil (BRIT), high school student (US).
collègue [kɔlɛg] nm/f colleague.
coller [kɔle] vt (papier, timbre) to stick (on); (affiche) to stick up; (appuyer, placer contre): ~ **son front à la vitre** to press one's face to the window; (enveloppe) to stick down; (morceaux) to stick ou glue together; (fam: mettre, fourrer) to stick, shove; (SCOL fam) to keep in, give detention to ♦ vi (être collant) to be sticky; (adhérer) to stick; ~ **qch sur** to stick (ou paste ou glue) sth on(to); ~ **à** to stick to; (fig) to cling to.
collerette [kɔlʀɛt] nf ruff; (TECH) flange.
collet [kɔlɛ] nm (piège) snare, noose; (cou): **prendre qn au** ~ to grab sb by the throat; ~ **monté** adj inv straight-laced.
colleter [kɔlte] vt (adversaire) to collar, grab by the throat; **se** ~ **avec** to wrestle with.
colleur [kɔlœʀ] nm: ~ **d'affiches** bill-poster.
collier [kɔlje] nm (bijou) necklace; (de chien, TECH) collar; ~ **(de barbe), barbe en** ~ narrow beard along the line of the jaw; ~ **de serrage** choke collar.
collimateur [kɔlimatœʀ] nm: **être dans le** ~ (fig) to be in the firing line; **avoir qn/qch dans le** ~ (fig) to have sb/sth in one's sights.
colline [kɔlin] nf hill.
collision [kɔlizjɔ̃] nf collision, crash; **entrer en** ~ **(avec)** to collide (with).
colloque [kɔlɔk] nm colloquium, symposium.

collusion [kɔlyzjɔ̃] *nf* collusion.
collutoire [kɔlytwaʀ] *nm* (*MÉD*) oral medication; (*en bombe*) throat spray.
collyre [kɔliʀ] *nm* (*MÉD*) eye lotion.
colmater [kɔlmate] *vt* (*fuite*) to seal off; (*brèche*) to plug, fill in.
Cologne [kɔlɔɲ] *n* Cologne.
colombage [kɔlɔ̃baʒ] *nm* half-timbering; **une maison à ~s** a half-timbered house.
colombe [kɔlɔ̃b] *nf* dove.
Colombie [kɔlɔ̃bi] *nf*: **la ~** Colombia.
colombien, ne [kɔlɔ̃bjɛ̃, -ɛn] *adj* Colombian ♦ *nm/f*: **C~, ne** Colombian.
colon [kɔlɔ̃] *nm* settler; (*enfant*) boarder (*in children's holiday camp*).
côlon [kolɔ̃] *nm* colon (*MÉD*).
colonel [kɔlɔnɛl] *nm* colonel; (*armée de l'air*) group captain.
colonial, e, aux [kɔlɔnjal, -o] *adj* colonial.
colonialisme [kɔlɔnjalism(ə)] *nm* colonialism.
colonialiste [kɔlɔnjalist(ə)] *adj, nm/f* colonialist.
colonie [kɔlɔni] *nf* colony; **~ (de vacances)** holiday camp (*for children*).
colonisation [kɔlɔnizasjɔ̃] *nf* colonization.
coloniser [kɔlɔnize] *vt* to colonize.
colonnade [kɔlɔnad] *nf* colonnade.
colonne [kɔlɔn] *nf* column; **se mettre en ~ par deux/quatre** to get into twos/fours; **en ~ par deux** in double file; **~ de secours** rescue party; **~ (vertébrale)** spine, spinal column.
colonnette [kɔlɔnɛt] *nf* small column.
colophane [kɔlɔfan] *nf* rosin.
colorant [kɔlɔʀɑ̃] *nm* colo(u)ring.
coloration [kɔlɔʀasjɔ̃] *nf* colour(ing) (*BRIT*), color(ing) (*US*); **se faire faire une ~** (*chez le coiffeur*) to have one's hair dyed.
coloré, e [kɔlɔʀe] *adj* (*fig*) colo(u)rful.
colorer [kɔlɔʀe] *vt* to colour (*BRIT*), color (*US*); **se ~** *vi* to turn red; to blush.
coloriage [kɔlɔʀjaʒ] *nm* colo(u)ring.
colorier [kɔlɔʀje] *vt* to colo(u)r (in); **album à ~** colouring book.
coloris [kɔlɔʀi] *nm* colo(u)r, shade.
coloriste [kɔlɔʀist(ə)] *nm/f* colo(u)rist.
colossal, e, aux [kɔlɔsal, -o] *adj* colossal, huge.
colosse [kɔlɔs] *nm* giant.
colostrum [kɔlɔstʀɔm] *nm* colostrum.
colporter [kɔlpɔʀte] *vt* to hawk, peddle.
colporteur, euse [kɔlpɔʀtœʀ, -øz] *nm/f* hawker, pedlar.
colt [kɔlt] *nm* revolver, Colt ®.
coltiner [kɔltine] *vt* to lug about.
colza [kɔlza] *nm* rape(seed).
coma [kɔma] *nm* coma; **être dans le ~** to be in a coma.
comateux, euse [kɔmatø, -øz] *adj* comatose.
combat [kɔ̃ba] *vb voir* **combattre** ♦ *nm* fight; fighting *no pl*; **~ de boxe** boxing match; **~ de rues** street fighting *no pl*; **~ singulier** single combat.
combatif, ive [kɔ̃batif, -iv] *adj* with a lot of fight.

combativité [kɔ̃bativite] *nf* fighting spirit.
combattant [kɔ̃batɑ̃] *vb voir* **combattre** ♦ *nm* combatant; (*d'une rixe*) brawler; **ancien ~** war veteran.
combattre [kɔ̃batʀ(ə)] *vi* to fight ♦ *vt* to fight; (*épidémie, ignorance*) to combat, fight (against).
combien [kɔ̃bjɛ̃] *adv* (*quantité*) how much; (*nombre*) how many; (*exclamatif*) how; **~ de** how much; how many; **~ de temps** how long, how much time; **~ coûte/pèse ceci?** how much does this cost/weigh?; **vous mesurez ~?** what size are you?; **ça fait ~ en largeur?** how wide is that?
combinaison [kɔ̃binɛzɔ̃] *nf* combination; (*astuce*) device, scheme; (*de femme*) slip; (*d'aviateur*) flying suit; (*d'homme-grenouille*) wetsuit; (*bleu de travail*) boilersuit (*BRIT*), coveralls *pl* (*US*).
combine [kɔ̃bin] *nf* trick; (*péj*) scheme, fiddle (*BRIT*).
combiné [kɔ̃bine] *nm* (*aussi*: **~ téléphonique**) receiver; (*SKI*) combination (event); (*vêtement de femme*) corselet.
combiner [kɔ̃bine] *vt* to combine; (*plan, horaire*) to work out, devise.
comble [kɔ̃bl(ə)] *adj* (*salle*) packed (full) ♦ *nm* (*du bonheur, plaisir*) height; **~s** *nmpl* (*CONSTR*) attic *sg*, loft *sg*; **de fond en ~** from top to bottom; **pour ~ de malchance** to cap it all; **c'est le ~!** that beats everything!, that takes the biscuit! (*BRIT*); **sous les ~s** in the attic.
combler [kɔ̃ble] *vt* (*trou*) to fill in; (*besoin, lacune*) to fill; (*déficit*) to make good; (*satisfaire*) to gratify, fulfil (*BRIT*), fulfill (*US*); **~ qn de joie** to fill sb with joy; **~ qn d'honneurs** to shower sb with honours.
combustible [kɔ̃bystibl(ə)] *adj* combustible ♦ *nm* fuel.
combustion [kɔ̃bystjɔ̃] *nf* combustion.
COMECON [komekon] *sigle m* Comecon.
comédie [kɔmedi] *nf* comedy; (*fig*) playacting *no pl*; **jouer la ~** (*fig*) to put on an act; **~ musicale** musical.

Founded in 1680 by Louis XIV, the **Comédie française** *is the French national theatre. Subsidized by the state, the company performs mainly in the Palais-Royal in Paris and concentrates on staging classical French plays.*

---

comédien, ne [kɔmedjɛ̃, -ɛn] *nm/f* actor/actress; (*comique*) comedy actor/actress, comedian/comedienne; (*fig*) sham.
COMES [kɔmɛs] *sigle m* = Commissariat à l'énergie solaire.
comestible [kɔmɛstibl(ə)] *adj* edible; **~s** *nmpl* foods.
comète [kɔmɛt] *nf* comet.
comice [kɔmis] *nm*: **~ agricole** agricultural show.

comique [kɔmik] *adj* (*drôle*) comical; (*THÉÂT*) comic ♦ *nm* (*artiste*) comic, comedian; **le ~ de qch** the funny *ou* comical side of sth.

comité [kɔmite] *nm* committee; **petit ~** select group; **~ directeur** management committee; **~ d'entreprise (CE)** works council; **~ des fêtes** festival committee.

commandant [kɔmɑ̃dɑ̃] *nm* (*gén*) commander, commandant; (*MIL: grade*) major; (*: armée de l'air*) squadron leader; (*NAVIG*) captain; **~ (de bord)** (*AVIAT*) captain.

commande [kɔmɑ̃d] *nf* (*COMM*) order; (*INFORM*) command; **~s** *nfpl* (*AVIAT etc*) controls; **passer une ~ (de)** to put in an or- der (for); **sur ~** to order; **~ à distance** remote control; **véhicule à double ~** vehicle with dual controls.

commandement [kɔmɑ̃dmɑ̃] *nm* command; (*ordre*) command, order; (*REL*) commandment.

commander [kɔmɑ̃de] *vt* (*COMM*) to order; (*diriger, ordonner*) to command; **~ à** (*MIL*) to command; (*contrôler, maîtriser*) to have control over; **~ à qn de faire** to command *ou* order sb to do.

commanditaire [kɔmɑ̃ditɛʀ] *nm* sleeping (*BRIT*) *ou* silent (*US*) partner.

commandite [kɔmɑ̃dit] *nf*: **(société en) ~** limited partnership.

commanditer [kɔmɑ̃dite] *vt* (*COMM*) to finance, back; to commission.

commando [kɔmɑ̃do] *nm* commando (squad).

========================= MOT-CLÉ

comme [kɔm] *prép* **1** (*comparaison*) like; **tout ~ son père** just like his father; **fort ~ un bœuf** as strong as an ox; **joli ~ tout** ever so pretty

2 (*manière*) like; **faites-le ~ ça** do it like this, do it this way; **~ ça ou cela on n'aura pas d'ennuis** that way we won't have any problems; **~ ci, ~ ça** so-so, middling; **comment ça va? — ~ ça** how are things? — OK; **~ on dit** as they say

3 (*en tant que*) as a; **donner ~ prix** to give as a prize; **travailler ~ secrétaire** to work as a secretary

4: **~ quoi** (*d'où il s'ensuit que*) which shows that; **il a écrit une lettre ~ quoi il ... ** he's written a letter saying that ...

5: **~ il faut** *phr adv* properly; *phr adj* (*correct*) proper, correct

♦ *conj* **1** (*ainsi que*) as; **elle écrit ~ elle parle** she writes as she talks; **~ si** as if

2 (*au moment où, alors que*) as; **il est parti ~ j'arrivais** he left as I arrived

3 (*parce que, puisque*) as, since; **~ il était en retard, il ...** as he was late, he ...

♦ *adv*: **~ il est fort/c'est bon!** he's so strong/ it's so good!; **il est malin ~ c'est pas permis** he's as smart as anything.

commémoratif, ive [kɔmemɔratif, -iv] *adj* commemorative; **un monument ~** a memorial.

commémoration [kɔmemɔʀɑsjɔ̃] *nf* commemoration.

commémorer [kɔmemɔʀe] *vt* to commemorate.

commencement [kɔmɑ̃smɑ̃] *nm* beginning, start, commencement; **~s** *nmpl* (*débuts*) beginnings.

commencer [kɔmɑ̃se] *vt* to begin, start, commence; (*être placé au début de*) to begin ♦ *vi* to begin, start, commence; **~ à ou de faire** to begin *ou* start doing; **~ par qch** to begin with sth; **~ par faire qch** to begin by doing sth.

commensal, e, aux [kɔmɑ̃sal, -o] *nm/f* companion at table.

comment [kɔmɑ̃] *adv* how; **~?** (*que dites-vous*) (I beg your) pardon?; **~! what!** ♦ *nm*: **le ~ et le pourquoi** the whys and wherefores; **et ~!** and how!; **~ donc!** of course!; **~ faire?** how will we do it?; **~ se fait-il que?** how is it that?

commentaire [kɔmɑ̃tɛʀ] *nm* comment; remark; **~ (de texte)** (*SCOL*) commentary; **~ sur image** voice-over.

commentateur, trice [kɔmɑ̃tatœʀ, -tʀis] *nm/f* commentator.

commenter [kɔmɑ̃te] *vt* (*jugement, événement*) to comment (up)on; (*RADIO, TV: match, manifestation*) to cover, give a commentary on.

commérages [kɔmeʀaʒ] *nmpl* gossip *sg*.

commerçant, e [kɔmɛʀsɑ̃, -ɑ̃t] *adj* commercial; trading; (*rue*) shopping *cpd*; (*personne*) commercially shrewd ♦ *nm/f* shopkeeper, trader.

commerce [kɔmɛʀs(ə)] *nm* (*activité*) trade, commerce; (*boutique*) business; **le petit ~** small shopowners *pl*, small traders *pl*; **faire ~ de** to trade in; (*fig: péj*) to trade on; **chambre de ~** Chamber of Commerce; **livres de ~** (account) books; **vendu dans le ~** sold in the shops; **vendu hors-~** sold directly to the public; **~ en ou de gros/détail** wholesale/retail trade; **~ intérieur/ extérieur** home/foreign trade.

commercer [kɔmɛʀse] *vi*: **~ avec** to trade with.

commercial, e, aux [kɔmɛʀsjal, -o] *adj* commercial, trading; (*péj*) commercial ♦ *nm*: **les commerciaux** the commercial people.

commercialisable [kɔmɛʀsjalizabl(ə)] *adj* marketable.

commercialisation [kɔmɛʀsjalizasjɔ̃] *nf* marketing.

commercialiser [kɔmɛʀsjalize] *vt* to market.

commère [kɔmɛʀ] *nf* gossip.

commettant [kɔmetɑ̃] *vb voir* **commettre** ♦ *nm* (*JUR*) principal.

commettre [kɔmetʀ(ə)] *vt* to commit; **se ~** to compromise one's good name.

commis [kɔmi] *vb voir* **commettre** ♦ *nm* (*de magasin*) (shop) assistant (*BRIT*), sales clerk (*US*); (*de banque*) clerk; ~ **voyageur** commercial traveller (*BRIT*) *ou* traveler (*US*).

commis, e [kɔmi, -iz] *pp de* **commettre**.

commisération [kɔmizeʀɑsjɔ̃] *nf* commiseration.

commissaire [kɔmisɛʀ] *nm* (*de police*) ≈ (police) superintendent (*BRIT*), ≈ (police) captain (*US*); (*de rencontre sportive etc*) steward; ~ **du bord** (*NAVIG*) purser; ~ **aux comptes** (*ADMIN*) auditor.

commissaire-priseur, *pl* **commissaires-priseurs** [kɔmisɛʀpʀizœʀ] *nm* (official) auctioneer.

commissariat [kɔmisaʀja] *nm* police station; (*ADMIN*) commissionership.

commission [kɔmisjɔ̃] *nf* (*comité, pourcentage*) commission; (*message*) message; (*course*) errand; ~**s** *nfpl* (*achats*) shopping *sg*; ~ **d'examen** examining board.

commissionnaire [kɔmisjɔnɛʀ] *nm* delivery boy (*ou* man); messenger; (*TRANSPORTS*) (forwarding) agent.

commissure [kɔmisyʀ] *nf*: **les ~s des lèvres** the corners of the mouth.

commode [kɔmɔd] *adj* (*pratique*) convenient, handy; (*facile*) easy; (*air, personne*) easygoing; (*personne*): **pas** ~ awkward (to deal with) ♦ *nf* chest of drawers.

commodité [kɔmɔdite] *nf* convenience.

commotion [kɔmɔsjɔ̃] *nf*: ~ **(cérébrale)** concussion.

commotionné, e [kɔmɔsjɔne] *adj* shocked, shaken.

commuer [kɔmɥe] *vt* to commute.

commun, e [kɔmœ̃, -yn] *adj* common; (*pièce*) communal, shared; (*réunion, effort*) joint ♦ *nf* (*ADMIN*) commune, ≈ district; (: *urbaine*) ≈ borough; ~**s** *nmpl* (*bâtiments*) outbuildings; **cela sort du** ~ it's out of the ordinary; **le** ~ **des mortels** the common run of people; **sans** ~**e mesure** incomparable; **être** ~ **à** (*suj: chose*) to be shared by; **en** ~ (*faire*) jointly; **mettre en** ~ to pool, share; **peu** ~ unusual; **d'un** ~ **accord** of one accord; with one accord.

communal, e, aux [kɔmynal, -o] *adj* (*ADMIN*) of the commune, ≈ (district *ou* borough) council *cpd*.

communard, e [kɔmynaʀ, -aʀd(ə)] *nm/f* (*HIST*) Communard; (*péj: communiste*) commie.

communautaire [kɔmynotɛʀ] *adj* community *cpd*.

communauté [kɔmynote] *nf* community; (*JUR*): **régime de la** ~ communal estate settlement.

commune [kɔmyn] *adj f, nf voir* **commun**.

communément [kɔmynemɑ̃] *adv* commonly.

Communes [kɔmyn] *nfpl* (*BRIT: parlement*) Commons.

communiant, e [kɔmynjɑ̃, -ɑ̃t] *nm/f* communi-

cant; **premier** ~ child taking his first communion.

communicant, e [kɔmynikɑ̃, -ɑ̃t] *adj* communicating.

communicatif, ive [kɔmynikatif, -iv] *adj* (*personne*) communicative; (*rire*) infectious.

communication [kɔmynikɑsjɔ̃] *nf* communication; ~ **(téléphonique)** (telephone) call; **avoir la** ~ **(avec)** to get *ou* be through (to); **vous avez la** ~ you're through; **donnez-moi la** ~ **avec** put me through to; **mettre qn en** ~ **avec qn** (*en contact*) to put sb in touch with sb; (*au téléphone*) to connect sb with sb; ~ **interurbaine** long-distance call; ~ **en PCV** reverse charge (*BRIT*) *ou* collect (*US*) call; ~ **avec préavis** personal call.

communier [kɔmynje] *vi* (*REL*) to receive communion; (*fig*) to be united.

communion [kɔmynjɔ̃] *nf* communion.

communiqué [kɔmynike] *nm* communiqué; ~ **de presse** press release.

communiquer [kɔmynike] *vt* (*nouvelle, dossier*) to pass on, convey; (*maladie*) to pass on; (*peur etc*) to communicate; (*chaleur, mouvement*) to transmit ♦ *vi* to communicate; ~ **avec** (*suj: salle*) to communicate with; **se** ~ **à** (*se propager*) to spread to.

communisant, e [kɔmynizɑ̃, -ɑ̃t] *adj* communistic ♦ *nm/f* communist sympathizer.

communisme [kɔmynism(ə)] *nm* communism.

communiste [kɔmynist(ə)] *adj, nm/f* communist.

commutateur [kɔmytatœʀ] *nm* (*ÉLEC*) (change-over) switch, commutator.

commutation [kɔmytɑsjɔ̃] *nf* (*INFORM*): ~ **de messages** message switching; ~ **de paquets** packet switching.

Comores [kɔmɔʀ] *nfpl*: **les (îles)** ~ the Comoros (Islands).

comorien, ne [kɔmɔʀjɛ̃, -ɛn] *adj* of *ou* from the Comoros.

compact, e [kɔ̃pakt] *adj* dense; compact.

compagne [kɔ̃paɲ] *nf* companion.

compagnie [kɔ̃paɲi] *nf* (*firme, MIL*) company; (*groupe*) gathering; (*présence*): **la** ~ **de qn** sb's company; **homme/femme de** ~ escort; **tenir** ~ **à qn** to keep sb company; **fausser** ~ **à qn** to give sb the slip, slip *ou* sneak away from sb; **en** ~ **de** in the company of; **Dupont et** ~, **Dupont et Cie** Dupont and Company, Dupont and Co; ~ **aérienne** airline (company).

compagnon [kɔ̃paɲɔ̃] *nm* companion; (*autrefois: ouvrier*) craftsman; journeyman.

comparable [kɔ̃paʀabl(ə)] *adj*: ~ **(à)** comparable (to).

comparaison [kɔ̃paʀɛzɔ̃] *nf* comparison; (*métaphore*) simile; **en** ~ **(de)** in comparison (with); **par** ~ **(à)** by comparison (with).

comparaître [kɔ̃paʀɛtʀ(ə)] *vi*: ~ **(devant)** to appear (before).

comparatif, ive [kɔ̃paʀatif, -iv] *adj, nm* comparative.

comparativement [kɔ̃paʀativmɑ̃] *adv* comparatively; ~ à by comparison with.

comparé, e [kɔ̃paʀe] *adj*: **littérature** *etc* ~**e** comparative literature *etc*.

comparer [kɔ̃paʀe] *vt* to compare; ~ **qch/qn à** *ou* **et** (*pour choisir*) to compare sth/sb with *ou* and; (*pour établir une similitude*) to compare sth/sb to *ou* and.

comparse [kɔ̃paʀs(ə)] *nm/f* (*péj*) associate, stooge.

compartiment [kɔ̃paʀtimɑ̃] *nm* compartment.

compartimenté, e [kɔ̃paʀtimɑ̃te] *adj* partitioned; (*fig*) compartmentalized.

comparu, e [kɔ̃paʀy] *pp de* **comparaître**.

comparution [kɔ̃paʀysjɔ̃] *nf* appearance.

compas [kɔ̃pa] *nm* (*GÉOM*) (pair of) compasses *pl*; (*NAVIG*) compass.

compassé, e [kɔ̃pase] *adj* starchy, formal.

compassion [kɔ̃pasjɔ̃] *nf* compassion.

compatibilité [kɔ̃patibilite] *nf* compatibility.

compatible [kɔ̃patibl(ə)] *adj*: ~ (**avec**) compatible (with).

compatir [kɔ̃patiʀ] *vi*: ~ (**à**) to sympathize (with).

compatissant, e [kɔ̃patisɑ̃, -ɑ̃t] *adj* sympathetic.

compatriote [kɔ̃patʀijɔt] *nm/f* compatriot, fellow countryman/woman.

compensateur, trice [kɔ̃pɑ̃satœʀ, -tʀis] *adj* compensatory.

compensation [kɔ̃pɑ̃susjɔ̃] *nf* compensation; (*BANQUE*) clearing; **en** ~ in *ou* as compensation.

compensé, e [kɔ̃pɑ̃se] *adj*: **semelle** ~**e** platform sole.

compenser [kɔ̃pɑ̃se] *vt* to compensate for, make up for.

compère [kɔ̃pɛʀ] *nm* accomplice; fellow musician *ou* comedian *etc*.

compétence [kɔ̃petɑ̃s] *nf* competence.

compétent, e [kɔ̃petɑ̃, -ɑ̃t] *adj* (*apte*) competent, capable; (*JUR*) competent.

compétitif, ive [kɔ̃petitif, -iv] *adj* competitive.

compétition [kɔ̃petisjɔ̃] *nf* (*gén*) competition; (*SPORT*: *épreuve*) event; **la** ~ competitive sport; **être en** ~ **avec** to be competing with; **la** ~ **automobile** motor racing.

compétitivité [kɔ̃petitivite] *nf* competitiveness.

compilateur [kɔ̃pilatœʀ] *nm* (*INFORM*) compiler.

compiler [kɔ̃pile] *vt* to compile.

complainte [kɔ̃plɛ̃t] *nf* lament.

complaire [kɔ̃plɛʀ]: **se** ~ *vi*: **se** ~ **dans/parmi** to take pleasure in/in being among.

complaisais [kɔ̃plɛzɛ] *etc vb voir* **complaire**.

complaisamment [kɔ̃plɛzamɑ̃] *adv* kindly; complacently.

complaisance [kɔ̃plɛzɑ̃s] *nf* kindness; (*péj*) indulgence; (: *fatuité*) complacency; **attestation de** ~ certificate produced to oblige a

patient *etc*; **pavillon de** ~ flag of convenience.

complaisant, e [kɔ̃plɛzɑ̃, -ɑ̃t] *vb voir* **complaire** ♦ *adj* (*aimable*) kind; obliging; (*péj*) accommodating; (: *fat*) complacent.

complaît [kɔ̃plɛ] *vb voir* **complaire**.

complément [kɔ̃plemɑ̃] *nm* complement; (*reste*) remainder; (*LING*) complement; ~ **d'information** (*ADMIN*) supplementary *ou* further information; ~ **d'agent** agent; ~ (**d'objet**) **direct/indirect** direct/indirect object; ~ (**circonstanciel**) **de lieu/temps** adverbial phrase of place/time; ~ **de nom** possessive phrase.

complémentaire [kɔ̃plemɑ̃tɛʀ] *adj* complementary; (*additionnel*) supplementary.

complet, ète [kɔ̃plɛ, -ɛt] *adj* complete; (*plein*: *hôtel etc*) full ♦ *nm* (*aussi*: ~-**veston**) suit; **au** (**grand**) ~ all together.

complètement [kɔ̃plɛtmɑ̃] *adv* (*en entier*) completely; (*absolument*: *fou, faux etc*) absolutely; (*à fond*: *étudier etc*) fully, in depth.

compléter [kɔ̃plete] *vt* (*porter à la quantité voulue*) to complete; (*augmenter*) to complement, supplement; to add to; **se** ~ (*personnes*) to complement one another; (*collection etc*) to become complete.

complexe [kɔ̃plɛks(ə)] *adj* complex ♦ *nm* (*PSYCH*) complex, hang-up; (*bâtiments*): ~ **hospitalier/industriel** hospital/industrial complex.

complexé, e [kɔ̃plɛkse] *adj* mixed-up, hungup.

complexité [kɔ̃plɛksite] *nf* complexity.

complication [kɔ̃plikasjɔ̃] *nf* complexity, intricacy; (*difficulté, ennui*) complication; ~**s** *nfpl* (*MÉD*) complications.

complice [kɔ̃plis] *nm* accomplice.

complicité [kɔ̃plisite] *nf* complicity.

compliment [kɔ̃plimɑ̃] *nm* (*louange*) compliment; ~**s** *nmpl* (*félicitations*) congratulations.

complimenter [kɔ̃plimɑ̃te] *vt*: ~ **qn** (**sur** *ou* **de**) to congratulate *ou* compliment sb (on).

compliqué, e [kɔ̃plike] *adj* complicated, complex, intricate; (*personne*) complicated.

compliquer [kɔ̃plike] *vt* to complicate; **se** ~ *vi* (*situation*) to become complicated; **se** ~ **la vie** to make life difficult *ou* complicated for o.s.

complot [kɔ̃plo] *nm* plot.

comploter [kɔ̃plɔte] *vi, vt* to plot.

complu, e [kɔ̃ply] *pp de* **complaire**.

comportement [kɔ̃pɔʀtəmɑ̃] *nm* behaviour (*BRIT*), behavior (*US*); (*TECH*: *d'une pièce, d'un véhicule*) behavio(u)r, performance.

comporter [kɔ̃pɔʀte] *vt* to be composed of, consist of, comprise; (*être équipé de*) to have; (*impliquer*) to entail, involve; **se** ~ *vi* to behave; (*TECH*) to behave, perform.

composant [kɔ̃pozɑ̃] *nm* component, constituent.

composante [kɔ̃pozɑ̃t] *nf* component.

composé, e [kɔ̃poze] _adj (visage, air)_ studied; _(BIO, CHIMIE, LING)_ compound ♦ _nm (CHIMIE, LING)_ compound; ~ **de** made up of.

composer [kɔ̃poze] _vt (musique, texte)_ to compose; _(mélange, équipe)_ to make up; _(faire partie de)_ to make up, form; _(TYPO)_ to (type)set ♦ _vi (SCOL)_ to sit _ou_ do a test; _(transiger)_ to come to terms; **se** ~ **de** to be composed of, be made up of; ~ **un numéro** _(au téléphone)_ to dial a number.

composite [kɔ̃pozit] _adj_ heterogeneous.

compositeur, trice [kɔ̃pozitœʀ, -tʀis] _nm/f (MUS)_ composer; _(TYPO)_ compositor, typesetter.

composition [kɔ̃pozisjɔ̃] _nf_ composition; _(SCOL)_ test; _(TYPO)_ (type)setting, composition; **de bonne** ~ _(accommodant)_ easy to deal with; **amener qn à** ~ to get sb to come to terms; ~ **française** _(SCOL)_ French essay.

compost [kɔ̃pɔst] _nm_ compost.

composter [kɔ̃pɔste] _vt_ to date-stamp; to punch.

composteur [kɔ̃pɔstœʀ] _nm_ date stamp; punch; _(TYPO)_ composing stick.

compote [kɔ̃pɔt] _nf_ stewed fruit _no pl_; ~ **de pommes** stewed apples.

compotier [kɔ̃pɔtje] _nm_ fruit dish _ou_ bowl.

compréhensible [kɔ̃pʀeɑ̃sibl(ə)] _adj_ comprehensible; _(attitude)_ understandable.

compréhensif, ive [kɔ̃pʀeɑ̃sif, -iv] _adj_ understanding.

compréhension [kɔ̃pʀeɑ̃sjɔ̃] _nf_ understanding; comprehension.

comprendre [kɔ̃pʀɑ̃dʀ(ə)] _vt_ to understand; _(se composer de)_ to comprise, consist of; _(inclure)_ to include; **se faire** ~ to make o.s. understood; to get one's ideas across; **mal** ~ to misunderstand.

compresse [kɔ̃pʀɛs] _nf_ compress.

compresser [kɔ̃pʀese] _vt_ to squash in, crush together.

compresseur [kɔ̃pʀesœʀ] _adj m voir_ **rouleau.**

compressible [kɔ̃pʀesibl(ə)] _adj (PHYSIQUE)_ compressible; _(dépenses)_ reducible.

compression [kɔ̃pʀesjɔ̃] _nf_ compression; _(d'un crédit etc)_ reduction.

comprimé, e [kɔ̃pʀime] _adj:_ **air** ~ compressed air ♦ _nm_ tablet.

comprimer [kɔ̃pʀime] _vt_ to compress; _(fig: crédit etc)_ to reduce, cut down.

compris, e [kɔ̃pʀi, -iz] _pp de_ **comprendre** ♦ _adj (inclus)_ included; ~**?** understood?, is that clear?; ~ **entre** _(situé)_ contained between; **la maison** ~**e/non** ~**e, y/non** ~ **la maison** including/excluding the house; **service** ~ service (charge) included; **100 F tout** ~ 100 F all inclusive _ou_ all-in.

compromettant, e [kɔ̃pʀɔmetɑ̃, -ɑ̃t] _adj_ compromising.

compromettre [kɔ̃pʀɔmetʀ(ə)] _vt_ to compromise.

compromis [kɔ̃pʀɔmi] _vb voir_ **compromettre**

♦ _nm_ compromise.

compromission [kɔ̃pʀɔmisjɔ̃] _nf_ compromise, deal.

comptabiliser [kɔ̃tabilize] _vt (valeur)_ to post; _(fig)_ to evaluate.

comptabilité [kɔ̃tabilite] _nf (activité, technique)_ accounting, accountancy; _(d'une société: comptes)_ accounts _pl,_ books _pl; (: service)_ accounts office _ou_ department; ~ **à partie double** double-entry book-keeping.

comptable [kɔ̃tabl(ə)] _nm/f_ accountant ♦ _adj_ accounts _cpd,_ accounting.

comptant [kɔ̃tɑ̃] _adv:_ **payer** ~ to pay cash; **acheter** ~ to buy for cash.

compte [kɔ̃t] _nm_ count, counting; _(total, montant)_ count, (right) number; _(bancaire, facture)_ account; ~**s** _nmpl_ accounts, books; _(fig)_ explanation _sg;_ **ouvrir un** ~ to open an account; **rendre des** ~**s à qn** _(fig)_ to be answerable to sb; **faire le** ~ **de** to count up, make a count of; **tout** ~ **fait** on the whole; **à ce** ~**-là** _(dans ce cas)_ in that case; _(à ce train-là)_ at that rate; **en fin de** ~ _(fig)_ all things considered, weighing it all up; **au bout du** ~ in the final analysis; **à bon** ~ at a favourable price; _(fig)_ lightly; **avoir son** ~ _(fig: fam)_ to have had it; **pour le** ~ **de** on behalf of; **pour son propre** ~ for one's own benefit; **sur le** ~ **de qn** _(à son sujet)_ about sb; **travailler à son** ~ to work for oneself; **mettre qch sur le** ~ **de qn** _(le rendre responsable)_ to attribute sth to sb; **prendre qch à son** ~ to take responsibility for sth; **trouver son** ~ **à qch** to do well out of sth; **régler un** ~ _(s'acquitter de qch)_ to settle an account; _(se venger)_ to get one's own back; **rendre** ~ **(à qn) de qch** to give (sb) an account of sth; **tenir** ~ **de qch** to take sth into account; ~ **tenu de** taking into account; ~ **chèque(s)** current account; ~ **chèque postal (CCP)** Post Office account; ~ **client** _(sur bilan)_ accounts receivable; ~ **courant (CC)** current account; ~ **de dépôt** deposit account; ~ **d'exploitation** operating ac- count; ~ **fournisseur** _(sur bilan)_ accounts payable; ~ **à rebours** countdown; ~ **rendu** account, report; _(de film, livre)_ review; _voir aussi_ **rendre.**

compte-gouttes [kɔ̃tgut] _nm inv_ dropper.

compter [kɔ̃te] _vt_ to count; _(facturer)_ to charge for; _(avoir à son actif, comporter)_ to have; _(prévoir)_ to allow, reckon; _(tenir compte de, inclure)_ to include; _(penser, espérer):_ ~ **réussir/revenir** to expect to succeed/return ♦ _vi_ to count; _(être économe)_ to economize; _(être non·négligeable)_ to count, matter; _(valoir):_ ~ **pour** to count for; _(figurer):_ ~ **parmi** to be _ou_ rank among; ~ **sur** to count (up)on; ~ **avec qch/qn** to reckon with _ou_ take account of sth/sb; ~ **sans qch/qn** to reckon without sth/sb; **sans** ~ **que** besides which; **à** ~ **du 10 janvier** _(COMM)_ (as) from 10th January.

compte-tours [kɔ̃ttuʀ] *nm inv* rev(olution) counter.

compteur [kɔ̃tœʀ] *nm* meter; ~ **de vitesse** speedometer.

comptine [kɔ̃tin] *nf* nursery rhyme.

comptoir [kɔ̃twaʀ] *nm* (*de magasin*) counter; (*de café*) counter, bar; (*colonial*) trading post.

compulser [kɔ̃pylse] *vt* to consult.

comte, comtesse [kɔ̃t, kɔ̃tɛs] *nm/f* count/ countess.

con, ne [kɔ̃, kɔn] *adj* (*fam!*) bloody (*BRIT*) *ou* damned stupid (*!*).

concasser [kɔ̃kase] *vt* (*pierre, sucre*) to crush; (*poivre*) to grind.

concave [kɔ̃kav] *adj* concave.

concéder [kɔ̃sede] *vt* to grant; (*défaite, point*) to concede; ~ **que** to concede that.

concentration [kɔ̃sɑ̃tʀasjɔ̃] *nf* concentration.

concentrationnaire [kɔ̃sɑ̃tʀasjɔnɛʀ] *adj* of *ou* in concentration camps.

concentré [kɔ̃sɑ̃tʀe] *nm* concentrate; ~ **de tomates** tomato purée.

concentrer [kɔ̃sɑ̃tʀe] *vt* to concentrate; **se** ~ to concentrate.

concentrique [kɔ̃sɑ̃tʀik] *adj* concentric.

concept [kɔ̃sɛpt] *nm* concept.

concepteur, trice [kɔ̃sɛptœʀ, -tʀis] *nm/f* designer.

conception [kɔ̃sɛpsjɔ̃] *nf* conception; (*d'une machine etc*) design.

concernant [kɔ̃sɛʀnɑ̃] *prép* (*se rapportant à*) concerning; (*en ce qui concerne*) as regards.

concerner [kɔ̃sɛʀne] *vt* to concern; **en ce qui me concerne** as far as I am concerned; **en ce qui concerne ceci** as far as this is concerned, with regard to this.

concert [kɔ̃sɛʀ] *nm* concert; **de** ~ *adv* in unison; together.

concertation [kɔ̃sɛʀtasjɔ̃] *nf* (*échange de vues*) dialogue; (*rencontre*) meeting.

concerter [kɔ̃sɛʀte] *vt* to devise; **se** ~ *vi* (*collaborateurs etc*) to put our (*ou* their *etc*) heads together, consult (each other).

concertiste [kɔ̃sɛʀtist(ə)] *nm/f* concert artist.

concerto [kɔ̃sɛʀto] *nm* concerto.

concession [kɔ̃sesjɔ̃] *nf* concession.

concessionnaire [kɔ̃sesjɔnɛʀ] *nm/f* agent, dealer.

concevable [kɔ̃svabl(ə)] *adj* conceivable.

concevoir [kɔ̃svwaʀ] *vt* (*idée, projet*) to conceive (of); (*méthode, plan d'appartement, décoration etc*) to plan, design; (*enfant*) to conceive; **maison bien/mal conçue** well-/badly-designed *ou* -planned house.

concierge [kɔ̃sjɛʀʒ(ə)] *nm/f* caretaker; (*d'hôtel*) head porter.

conciergerie [kɔ̃sjɛʀʒəʀi] *nf* caretaker's lodge.

concile [kɔ̃sil] *nm* council, synod.

conciliable [kɔ̃siljabl(ə)] *adj* (*opinions etc*) reconcilable.

conciliabules [kɔ̃siljabyl] *nmpl* (private) discussions, confabulations (*BRIT*).

conciliant, e [kɔ̃siljɑ̃, -ɑ̃t] *adj* conciliatory.

conciliateur, trice [kɔ̃siljatœʀ, -tʀis] *nm/f* mediator, go-between.

conciliation [kɔ̃siljasjɔ̃] *nf* conciliation.

concilier [kɔ̃silje] *vt* to reconcile; **se** ~ **qn/ l'appui de qn** to win sb over/sb's support.

concis, e [kɔ̃si, -iz] *adj* concise.

concision [kɔ̃sizjɔ̃] *nf* concision, conciseness.

concitoyen, ne [kɔ̃sitwajɛ̃, -ɛn] *nm/f* fellow citizen.

conclave [kɔ̃klav] *nm* conclave.

concluant, e [kɔ̃klyɑ̃, -ɑ̃t] *vb voir* **conclure** ♦ *adj* conclusive.

conclure [kɔ̃klyʀ] *vt* to conclude; (*signer: accord, pacte*) to enter into; (*déduire*): ~ **qch de qch** to deduce sth from sth; ~ **à l'acquittement** to decide in favour of an acquittal; ~ **au suicide** to come to the conclusion (*ou JUR* to pronounce) that it is a case of suicide; ~ **un marché** to clinch a deal; **j'en conclus que** from that I conclude that.

conclusion [kɔ̃klyzjɔ̃] *nf* conclusion; ~**s** *nfpl* (*JUR*) submissions; findings; **en** ~ in conclusion.

concocter [kɔ̃kɔkte] *vt* to concoct.

concois [kɔ̃swa], **conçoive** [kɔ̃swav] *etc vb voir* **concevoir**.

concombre [kɔ̃kɔ̃bʀ(ə)] *nm* cucumber.

concomitant, e [kɔ̃kɔmitɑ̃, -ɑ̃t] *adj* concomitant.

concordance [kɔ̃kɔʀdɑ̃s] *nf* concordance; **la** ~ **des temps** (*LING*) the sequence of tenses.

concordant, e [kɔ̃kɔʀdɑ̃, -ɑ̃t] *adj* (*témoignages, versions*) corroborating.

concorde [kɔ̃kɔʀd(ə)] *nf* concord.

concorder [kɔ̃kɔʀde] *vi* to tally, agree.

concourir [kɔ̃kuʀiʀ] *vi* (*SPORT*) to compete; ~ **à** *vt* (*effet etc*) to work towards.

concours [kɔ̃kuʀ] *vb voir* **concourir** ♦ *nm* competition; (*SCOL*) competitive examination; (*assistance*) aid, help; **recrutement par voie de** ~ recruitment by (competitive) examination; **apporter son** ~ **à** to give one's support to; ~ **de circonstances** combination of circumstances; ~ **hippique** horse show; *voir* **hors**.

concret, ète [kɔ̃kʀɛ, -ɛt] *adj* concrete.

concrètement [kɔ̃kʀɛtmɑ̃] *adv* in concrete terms.

concrétisation [kɔ̃kʀetizasjɔ̃] *nf* realization.

concrétiser [kɔ̃kʀetize] *vt* to realize; **se** ~ *vi* to materialize.

conçu, e [kɔ̃sy] *pp de* **concevoir**.

concubin, e [kɔ̃kybɛ̃, -in] *nm/f* (*JUR*) cohabitant.

concubinage [kɔ̃kybinaʒ] *nm* (*JUR*) cohabitation.

concupiscence [kɔ̃kypisɑ̃s] *nf* concupiscence.

concurremment [kɔ̃kyʀamɑ̃] *adv* concurrently; jointly.

concurrence [kɔkyʀɑ̃s] *nf* competition; **jusqu'à ~ de** up to; **~ déloyale** unfair competition.

concurrencer [kɔkyʀɑ̃se] *vt* to compete with; **ils nous concurrencent dangereusement** they are a serious threat to us.

concurrent, e [kɔkyʀɑ̃, -ɑ̃t] *adj* competing ♦ *nm/f* (*SPORT, ÉCON etc*) competitor; (*SCOL*) candidate.

concurrentiel, le [kɔkyʀɑ̃sjɛl] *adj* competitive.

conçus [kɔsy] *vb voir* **concevoir**.

condamnable [kɔdɑnabl(ə)] *adj* (*action, opinion*) reprehensible.

condamnation [kɔdɑnasjɔ̃] *nf* (*action*) condemnation; sentencing; (*peine*) sentence; conviction; **~ à mort** death sentence.

condamné, e [kɔdɑne] *nm/f* (*JUR*) convict.

condamner [kɔdɑne] *vt* (*blâmer*) to condemn; (*JUR*) to sentence; (*porte, ouverture*) to fill in, block up; (*malade*) to give up (hope for); (*obliger*): **~ qn à qch/à faire** to condemn sb to sth/to do; **~ qn à 2 ans de prison** to sentence sb to 2 years' imprisonment; **~ qn à une amende** to impose a fine on sb.

condensateur [kɔdɑ̃satœʀ] *nm* condenser.

condensation [kɔdɑ̃sɑsjɔ̃] *nf* condensation.

condensé [kɔdɑ̃se] *nm* digest.

condenser [kɔdɑ̃se] *vt*, **se ~** *vi* to condense.

condescendance [kɔdesɑ̃dɑ̃s] *nf* condescension.

condescendant, e [kɔdesɑ̃dɑ̃, -ɑ̃t] *adj* (*personne, attitude*) condescending.

condescendre [kɔdesɑ̃dʀ(ə)] *vi*: **~ à** to condescend to.

condiment [kɔdimɑ̃] *nm* condiment.

condisciple [kɔdisipl(ə)] *nm/f* school fellow, fellow student.

condition [kɔdisjɔ̃] *nf* condition; **~s** *nfpl* (*tarif, prix*) terms; (*circonstances*) conditions; **sans ~** *adj* unconditional ♦ *adv* unconditionally; **sous ~ que** on condition that; **à ~ de ou que** provided that; **en bonne ~** in good condition; **mettre en ~** (*SPORT etc*) to get fit; (*PSYCH*) to condition (mentally); **~s de vie** living conditions.

conditionnel, le [kɔdisjɔnɛl] *adj* conditional ♦ *nm* conditional (tense).

conditionnement [kɔdisjɔnmɑ̃] *nm* (*emballage*) packaging; (*fig*) conditioning.

conditionner [kɔdisjɔne] *vt* (*déterminer*) to determine; (*COMM: produit*) to package; (*fig: personne*) to condition; **air conditionné** air conditioning; **réflexe conditionné** conditioned reflex.

condoléances [kɔdɔleɑ̃s] *nfpl* condolences.

conducteur, trice [kɔdyktœʀ, -tʀis] *adj* (*ÉLEC*) conducting ♦ *nm/f* (*AUTO etc*) driver; (*machine*) operator ♦ *nm* (*ÉLEC etc*) conductor.

conduire [kɔdɥiʀ] *vt* (*véhicule, passager*) to drive; (*délégation, troupeau*) to lead; **se ~** *vi*

to behave; **~ vers/à** to lead towards/to; **~ qn quelque part** to take sb somewhere; to drive sb somewhere.

conduit, e [kɔdɥi, -it] *pp de* **conduire** ♦ *nm* (*TECH*) conduit, pipe; (*ANAT*) duct, canal.

conduite [kɔdɥit] *nf* (*en auto*) driving; (*comportement*) behaviour (*BRIT*), behavior (*US*); (*d'eau, de gaz*) pipe; **sous la ~ de** led by; **~ forcée** pressure pipe; **~ à gauche** left-hand drive; **~ intérieure** saloon (car).

cône [kon] *nm* cone; **en forme de ~** cone-shaped.

conf. *abr* (= *confort*): **tt ~** all mod cons (*BRIT*).

confection [kɔfɛksjɔ̃] *nf* (*fabrication*) making; (*COUTURE*): **la ~** the clothing industry, the rag trade (*fam*); **vêtement de ~** ready-to-wear *ou* off-the-peg garment.

confectionner [kɔfɛksjɔne] *vt* to make.

confédération [kɔfederɑsjɔ̃] *nf* confederation.

conférence [kɔfeʀɑ̃s] *nf* (*exposé*) lecture; (*pourparlers*) conference; **~ de presse** press conference; **~ au sommet** summit (conference).

conférencier, ière [kɔfeʀɑ̃sje, -jɛʀ] *nm/f* lecturer.

conférer [kɔfeʀe] *vt*: **~ à qn** (*titre, grade*) to confer on sb; **~ à qch/qn** (*aspect etc*) to endow sth/sb with, give (to) sth/sb.

confesser [kɔfese] *vt* to confess; **se ~** *vi* (*REL*) to go to confession.

confesseur [kɔfesœʀ] *nm* confessor.

confession [kɔfesjɔ̃] *nf* confession; (*culte*) denomination.

confessionnal, aux [kɔfesjɔnal, -o] *nm* confessional.

confessionnel, le [kɔfesjɔnɛl] *adj* denominational.

confetti [kɔfeti] *nm* confetti *no pl*.

confiance [kɔfjɑ̃s] *nf* confidence, trust; faith; **avoir ~ en** to have confidence *ou* faith in, trust; **faire ~ à** to trust; **en toute ~** with complete confidence; **de ~** trustworthy, reliable; **mettre qn en ~** to win sb's trust; **vote de ~** (*POL*) vote of confidence; **inspirer ~ à** to inspire confidence in; **~ en soi** self-confidence; *voir* **question**.

confiant, e [kɔfjɑ̃, -ɑ̃t] *adj* confident; trusting.

confidence [kɔfidɑ̃s] *nf* confidence.

confident, e [kɔfidɑ̃, -ɑ̃t] *nm/f* confidant/confidante.

confidentiel, le [kɔfidɑ̃sjɛl] *adj* confidential.

confidentiellement [kɔfidɑ̃sjɛlmɑ̃] *adv* in confidence, confidentially.

confier [kɔfje] *vt*: **~ à qn** (*objet en dépôt, travail etc*) to entrust to sb; (*secret, pensée*) to confide to sb; **se ~ à qn** to confide in sb.

configuration [kɔfigyʀɑsjɔ̃] *nf* configuration, layout; (*INFORM*) configuration.

configurer [kɔfigyʀe] *vt* to configure.

confiné, e [kɔfine] *adj* enclosed; (*air*) stale.

confiner [kɔfine] *vt*: **~ à** to confine to;

(*toucher*) to border on; **se ~ dans** *ou* **à** to confine o.s. to.

confins [kɔ̃fɛ̃] *nmpl*: **aux ~ de** on the borders of.

confirmation [kɔ̃fiʀmɑsjɔ̃] *nf* confirmation.

confirmer [kɔ̃fiʀme] *vt* to confirm; **~ qn dans une croyance/ses fonctions** to strengthen sb in a belief/his duties.

confiscation [kɔ̃fiskɑsjɔ̃] *nf* confiscation.

confiserie [kɔ̃fizʀi] *nf* (*magasin*) confectioner's *ou* sweet shop (*BRIT*), candy store (*US*); **~s** *nfpl* (*bonbons*) confectionery *sg*, sweets, candy *no pl*.

confiseur, euse [kɔ̃fizœR, -øz] *nm/f* confectioner.

confisquer [kɔ̃fiske] *vt* to confiscate.

confit, e [kɔ̃fi, -it] *adj*: **fruits ~s** crystallized fruits ♦ *nm*: **~ d'oie** potted goose.

confiture [kɔ̃fityʀ] *nf* jam; **~ d'oranges** (orange) marmalade.

conflagration [kɔ̃flagʀɑsjɔ̃] *nf* cataclysm.

conflictuel, le [kɔ̃fliktɥɛl] *adj* full of clashes *ou* conflicts.

conflit [kɔ̃fli] *nm* conflict.

confluent [kɔ̃flyɑ̃] *nm* confluence.

confondre [kɔ̃fɔ̃dʀ(ə)] *vt* (*jumeaux, faits*) to confuse, mix up; (*témoin, menteur*) to confound; **se ~** *vi* to merge; **se ~ en excuses** to offer profuse apologies, apologize profusely; **~ qch/qn avec qch/qn d'autre** to mistake sth/sb for sth/sb else.

confondu, e [kɔ̃fɔ̃dy] *pp de* **confondre** ♦ *adj* (*stupéfait*) speechless, overcome; **toutes catégories ~es** taking all categories together.

conformation [kɔ̃fɔʀmɑsjɔ̃] *nf* conformation.

conforme [kɔ̃fɔʀm(ə)] *adj*: **~ à** (*en accord avec*) in accordance with, in keeping with; (*identique à*) true to; **copie certifiée ~** (*ADMIN*) certified copy; **~ à la commande** as per order.

conformé, e [kɔ̃fɔʀme] *adj*: **bien ~** well-formed.

conformément [kɔ̃fɔʀmemɑ̃] *adv*: **~ à** in accordance with.

conformer [kɔ̃fɔʀme] *vt*: **~ qch à** to model sth on; **se ~ à** to conform to.

conformisme [kɔ̃fɔʀmism(ə)] *nm* conformity.

conformiste [kɔ̃fɔʀmist(ə)] *adj, nm/f* conformist.

conformité [kɔ̃fɔʀmite] *nf* conformity; agreement; **en ~ avec** in accordance with.

confort [kɔ̃fɔʀ] *nm* comfort; **tout ~** (*COMM*) with all mod cons (*BRIT*) *ou* modern conveniences.

confortable [kɔ̃fɔʀtabl(ə)] *adj* comfortable.

confortablement [kɔ̃fɔʀtabləmɑ̃] *adv* comfortably.

conforter [kɔ̃fɔʀte] *vt* to reinforce, strengthen.

confrère [kɔ̃fʀɛʀ] *nm* colleague; fellow member.

confrérie [kɔ̃fʀeʀi] *nf* brotherhood.

confrontation [kɔ̃fʀɔ̃tɑsjɔ̃] *nf* confrontation.

confronté, e [kɔ̃fʀɔ̃te] *adj*: **~ à** confronted by, facing.

confronter [kɔ̃fʀɔ̃te] *vt* to confront; (*textes*) to compare, collate.

confus, e [kɔ̃fy, -yz] *adj* (*vague*) confused; (*embarrassé*) embarrassed.

confusément [kɔ̃fyzemɑ̃] *adv* (*distinguer, ressentir*) vaguely; (*parler*) confusedly.

confusion [kɔ̃fyzjɔ̃] *nf* (*voir confus*) confusion; embarrassment; (*voir confondre*) confusion; mixing up; (*erreur*) confusion; **~ des peines** (*JUR*) concurrency of sentences.

congé [kɔ̃ʒe] *nm* (*vacances*) holiday; (*arrêt de travail*) time off *no pl*; leave *no pl*; (*MIL*) leave *no pl*; (*avis de départ*) notice; **en ~** on holiday; off (work); on leave; **semaine/jour de ~** week/day off; **prendre ~ de qn** to take one's leave of sb; **donner son ~ à** to hand *ou* give in one's notice to; **~ de maladie** sick leave; **~ de maternité** maternity leave; **~s payés** paid holiday *ou* leave.

congédier [kɔ̃ʒedje] *vt* to dismiss.

congélateur [kɔ̃ʒelatœʀ] *nm* freezer, deep freeze.

congélation [kɔ̃ʒelɑsjɔ̃] *nf* freezing; (*de l'huile*) congealing.

congeler [kɔ̃ʒle] *vt*, **se ~** *vi* to freeze.

congénère [kɔ̃ʒenɛʀ] *nm/f* fellow (bear *ou* lion *etc*), fellow creature.

congénital, e, aux [kɔ̃ʒenital, -o] *adj* congenital.

congère [kɔ̃ʒɛʀ] *nf* snowdrift.

congestion [kɔ̃ʒɛstjɔ̃] *nf* congestion; **~ cérébrale** stroke; **~ pulmonaire** congestion of the lungs.

congestionner [kɔ̃ʒɛstjone] *vt* to congest; (*MÉD*) to flush.

conglomérat [kɔ̃glomeʀa] *nm* conglomerate.

Congo [kɔ̃go] *nm*: **le ~** (*pays, fleuve*) the Congo.

congolais, e [kɔ̃gole, -ɛz] *adj* Congolese ♦ *nm/f*: **C~, e** Congolese.

congratuler [kɔ̃gʀatyle] *vt* to congratulate.

congre [kɔ̃gʀ(ə)] *nm* conger (eel).

congrégation [kɔ̃gʀegɑsjɔ̃] *nf* (*REL*) congregation; (*gén*) assembly; gathering.

congrès [kɔ̃gʀɛ] *nm* congress.

congressiste [kɔ̃gʀesist(ə)] *nm/f* delegate, participant (at a congress).

congru, e [kɔ̃gʀy] *adj*: **la portion ~e** the smallest *ou* meanest share.

conifère [konifɛʀ] *nm* conifer.

conique [konik] *adj* conical.

conjecture [kɔ̃ʒɛktyʀ] *nf* conjecture, speculation *no pl*.

conjecturer [kɔ̃ʒɛktyʀe] *vt*, *vi* to conjecture.

conjoint, e [kɔ̃ʒwɛ̃, -wɛ̃t] *adj* joint ♦ *nm/f* spouse.

conjointement [kɔ̃ʒwɛ̃tmɑ̃] *adv* jointly.

conjonctif, ive [kɔ̃ʒɔ̃ktif, -iv] *adj*: **tissu ~** connective tissue.

conjonction [kɔ̃ʒɔ̃ksjɔ̃] *nf* (*LING*) conjunction.

conjonctivite [kɔ̃ʒɔ̃ktivit] *nf* conjunctivitis.
conjoncture [kɔ̃ʒɔ̃ktyʀ] *nf* circumstances *pl*; **la ~ (économique)** the economic climate *ou* situation.
conjoncturel, le [kɔ̃ʒɔ̃ktyʀɛl] *adj*: **variations/ tendances ~les** economic fluctuations/ trends.
conjugaison [kɔ̃ʒygɛzɔ̃] *nf (LING)* conjugation.
conjugal, e, aux [kɔ̃ʒygal, -o] *adj* conjugal; married.
conjugué, e [kɔ̃ʒyge] *adj* combined.
conjuguer [kɔ̃ʒyge] *vt (LING)* to conjugate; (*efforts etc*) to combine.
conjuration [kɔ̃ʒyʀasjɔ̃] *nf* conspiracy.
conjuré, e [kɔ̃ʒyʀe] *nm/f* conspirator.
conjurer [kɔ̃ʒyʀe] *vt (sort, maladie)* to avert; (*implorer*): **~ qn de faire qch** to beseech *ou* entreat sb to do sth.
connais [kɔnɛ], **connaissais** [kɔnɛsɛ] *etc vb voir* **connaître.**
connaissance [kɔnɛsɑ̃s] *nf (savoir)* knowledge *no pl*; (*personne connue*) acquaintance; (*conscience, perception*) consciousness; **~s** *nfpl* knowledge *no pl*; **être sans ~** to be unconscious; **perdre/reprendre ~** to lose/regain consciousness; **à ma/sa ~** to (the best of) my/his knowledge; **faire ~ avec qn** *ou* **la ~ de qn** (*rencontrer*) to meet sb; (*apprendre à connaître*) to get to know sb; **avoir ~ de** to be aware of; **prendre ~ de** (*document etc*) to peruse; **en ~ de cause** with full knowledge of the facts; **de ~** (*personne, visage*) familiar.
connaissant [kɔnɛsɑ̃] *etc vb voir* **connaître.**
connaissement [kɔnɛsmɑ̃] *nm* bill of lading.
connaisseur, euse [kɔnɛsœʀ, -øz] *nm/f* connoisseur ♦ *adj* expert.
connaître [kɔnɛtʀ(ə)] *vt* to know; (*éprouver*) to experience; (*avoir*) to have; to enjoy; **~ de nom/vue** to know by name/sight; **se ~** to know each other; (*soi-même*) to know o.s.; **ils se sont connus à Genève** they (first) met in Geneva; **s'y ~ en qch** to know about sth.
connasse [kɔnas] *nf (fam!)* stupid bitch (!) *ou* cow (!).
connecté, e [kɔnɛkte] *adj (INFORM)* on line.
connecter [kɔnɛkte] *vt* to connect.
connerie [kɔnʀi] *nf (fam)* (bloody) stupid (*BRIT*) *ou* damn-fool (*US*) thing to do *ou* say.
connexe [kɔnɛks(ə)] *adj* closely related.
connexion [kɔnɛksjɔ̃] *nf* connection.
connivence [kɔnivɑ̃s] *nf* connivance.
connotation [kɔnɔtasjɔ̃] *nf* connotation.
connu, e [kɔny] *pp de* **connaître** ♦ *adj (célèbre)* well-known.
conque [kɔ̃k] *nf (coquille)* conch (shell).
conquérant, e [kɔ̃keʀɑ̃, -ɑ̃t] *nm/f* conqueror.
conquérir [kɔ̃keʀiʀ] *vt* to conquer, win.
conquerrai [kɔ̃kɛʀʀe] *etc vb voir* **conquérir.**
conquête [kɔ̃kɛt] *nf* conquest.
conquière, conquiers [kɔ̃kjɛʀ] *etc vb voir* **conquérir.**

conquis, e [kɔ̃ki, -iz] *pp de* **conquérir.**
consacrer [kɔ̃sakʀe] *vt (REL)*: **~ qch (à)** to consecrate sth (to); (*fig: usage etc*) to sanction, establish; (*employer*): **~ qch à** to devote *ou* dedicate sth to; **se ~ à qch/faire** to dedicate *ou* devote o.s. to sth/to doing.
consanguin, e [kɔ̃sɑ̃gɛ̃, -in] *adj* between blood relations; **frère ~** half-brother (*on father's side*); **mariage ~** intermarriage.
consciemment [kɔ̃sjamɑ̃] *adv* consciously.
conscience [kɔ̃sjɑ̃s] *nf* conscience; (*perception*) consciousness; **avoir/prendre ~ de** to be/become aware of; **perdre/reprendre ~** to lose/regain consciousness; **avoir bonne/ mauvaise ~** to have a clear/guilty conscience; **en (toute) ~** in all conscience; **~ professionnelle** professional conscience.
consciencieux, euse [kɔ̃sjɑ̃sjø, -øz] *adj* conscientious.
conscient, e [kɔ̃sjɑ̃, -ɑ̃t] *adj* conscious; **~ de** aware *ou* conscious of.
conscription [kɔ̃skʀipsjɔ̃] *nf* conscription.
conscrit [kɔ̃skʀi] *nm* conscript.
consécration [kɔ̃sekʀasjɔ̃] *nf* consecration.
consécutif, ive [kɔ̃sekytif, -iv] *adj* consecutive; **~ à** following upon.
consécutivement [kɔ̃sekytivmɑ̃] *adv* consecutively; **~ à** following on.
conseil [kɔ̃sɛj] *nm (avis)* piece of advice, advice *no pl*; (*assemblée*) council; (*expert*): **en recrutement** recruitment consultant ♦ *adj*: **ingénieur-~** consulting engineer, engineering consultant; **tenir ~** to hold a meeting; to deliberate; **donner un ~** *ou* **des ~s à qn** to give sb (a piece of) advice; **demander ~ à qn** to ask sb's advice; **prendre ~ (auprès de qn)** to take advice (from sb); **~ d'administration (CA)** board (of directors); **~ de classe** (*SCOL*) meeting of teachers, parents and class representatives to discuss pupils' progress; **~ de discipline** disciplinary committee; **~ général** regional council; **~ de guerre** court-martial; **le ~ des ministres** ≈ the Cabinet; **~ municipal (CM)** town council; **~ régional** regional board of elected representatives; **~ de révision** recruitment *ou* draft (*US*) board.

Each **département** *has an elected body called a* **Conseil général** *made up of* **conseillers généraux** *each of whom represents a* **canton** *and is elected for a six year term. Half of the council's membership is elected every three years. The remit of the Conseil général is to administer matters affecting the département, including personnel, transport infrastructure, housing, school grants and economic development.*

conseiller¹ [kɔ̃seje] *vt (personne)* to advise; (*méthode, action*) to recommend, advise; **~ qch à qn** to recommend sth to sb; **~ à qn de faire qch** to advise sb to do sth.

conseiller², **ère** [kɔ̃seje, -ɛʀ] *nm/f* adviser; ~ **général** regional councillor; ~ **matrimonial** marriage guidance counsellor; ~ **municipal** town councillor.

consensuel, le [kɔ̃sɑ̃sɥɛl] *adj* consensual.

consensus [kɔ̃sɛ̃sys] *nm* consensus.

consentement [kɔ̃sɑ̃tmɑ̃] *nm* consent.

consentir [kɔ̃sɑ̃tiʀ] *vt*: ~ **(à qch/faire)** to agree *ou* consent (to sth/to doing); ~ **qch à qn** to grant sb sth.

conséquence [kɔ̃sekɑ̃s] *nf* consequence, outcome; ~**s** *nfpl* consequences, repercussions; **en** ~ *(donc)* consequently; *(de façon appropriée)* accordingly; **ne pas tirer à** ~ to be unlikely to have any repercussions; **sans** ~ unimportant; **de** ~ important.

conséquent, e [kɔ̃sekɑ̃, -ɑ̃t] *adj* logical, rational; *(fam: important)* substantial; **par** ~ consequently.

conservateur, trice [kɔ̃sɛʀvatœʀ, -tʀis] *adj* conservative ♦ *nm/f (POL)* conservative; *(de musée)* curator.

conservation [kɔ̃sɛʀvasjɔ̃] *nf* retention; keeping; preserving; preservation.

conservatisme [kɔ̃sɛʀvatism(ə)] *nm* conservatism.

conservatoire [kɔ̃sɛʀvatwaʀ] *nm* academy; *(ÉCOLOGIE)* conservation area.

conserve [kɔ̃sɛʀv(ə)] *nf (gén pl)* canned *ou* tinned *(BRIT)* food; ~**s de poisson** canned *ou* tinned *(BRIT)* fish; **en** ~ canned, tinned *(BRIT)*; **de** ~ *(ensemble)* in concert; *(naviguer)* in convoy.

conservé, e [kɔ̃sɛʀve] *adj*: **bien** ~ *(personne)* well-preserved.

conserver [kɔ̃sɛʀve] *vt (faculté)* to retain, keep; *(habitude)* to keep up; *(amis, livres)* to keep; *(préserver, aussi CULIN)* to preserve; **se** ~ *vi (aliments)* to keep; "~ **au frais**" "store in a cool place".

conserverie [kɔ̃sɛʀvəʀi] *nf* canning factory.

considérable [kɔ̃sideʀabl(ə)] *adj* considerable, significant, extensive.

considération [kɔ̃sideʀasjɔ̃] *nf* consideration; *(estime)* esteem, respect; ~**s** *nfpl (remarques)* reflections; **prendre en** ~ to take into consideration *ou* account; **ceci mérite** ~ this is worth considering; **en** ~ **de** given, because of.

considéré, e [kɔ̃sideʀe] *adj* respected; **tout bien** ~ all things considered.

considérer [kɔ̃sideʀe] *vt* to consider; *(regarder)* to consider, study; ~ **qch comme** to regard sth as.

consigne [kɔ̃siɲ] *nf (COMM)* deposit; *(de gare)* left luggage (office) *(BRIT)*, checkroom *(US)*; *(punition: SCOL)* detention; *(: MIL)* confinement to barracks; *(ordre, instruction)* instructions *pl*; ~ **automatique** left-luggage locker; ~**s de sécurité** safety instructions.

consigné, e [kɔ̃siɲe] *adj (COMM: bouteille, emballage)* returnable; **non** ~ non-returnable.

consigner [kɔ̃siɲe] *vt (note, pensée)* to record; *(marchandises)* to deposit; *(punir: MIL)* to confine to barracks; *(: élève)* to put in detention; *(COMM)* to put a deposit on.

consistance [kɔ̃sistɑ̃s] *nf* consistency.

consistant, e [kɔ̃sistɑ̃, -ɑ̃t] *adj* thick; solid.

consister [kɔ̃siste] *vi*: ~ **en/dans/à faire** to consist of/in/in doing.

consœur [kɔ̃sœʀ] *nf* (lady) colleague; fellow member.

consolation [kɔ̃sɔlasjɔ̃] *nf* consolation *no pl*, comfort *no pl*.

console [kɔ̃sɔl] *nf* console; ~ **graphique** *ou* **de visualisation** *(INFORM)* visual display unit, VDU; ~ **de jeux vidéo** games console.

consoler [kɔ̃sɔle] *vt* to console; **se** ~ **(de qch)** to console o.s. (for sth).

consolider [kɔ̃sɔlide] *vt* to strengthen, reinforce; *(fig)* to consolidate; **bilan consolidé** consolidated balance sheet.

consommateur, trice [kɔ̃sɔmatœʀ, -tʀis] *nm/f (ÉCON)* consumer; *(dans un café)* customer.

consommation [kɔ̃sɔmasjɔ̃] *nf* consumption; *(JUR)* consummation; *(boisson)* drink; ~ **aux 100 km** *(AUTO)* (fuel) consumption per 100 km, ≈ miles per gallon (mpg), ≈ gas mileage *(US)*; **de** ~ *(biens, société)* consumer *cpd*.

consommé, e [kɔ̃sɔme] *adj* consummate ♦ *nm* consommé.

consommer [kɔ̃sɔme] *vt (suj: personne)* to eat *ou* drink, consume; *(suj: voiture, usine, poêle)* to use, consume; *(JUR)* to consummate ♦ *vi (dans un café)* to (have a) drink.

consonance [kɔ̃sɔnɑ̃s] *nf* consonance; **nom à** ~ **étrangère** foreign-sounding name.

consonne [kɔ̃sɔn] *nf* consonant.

consortium [kɔ̃sɔʀsjɔm] *nm* consortium.

consorts [kɔ̃sɔʀ] *nmpl*: **et** ~ *(péj)* and company, and his bunch *ou* like.

conspirateur, trice [kɔ̃spiʀatœʀ, -tʀis] *nm/f* conspirator, plotter.

conspiration [kɔ̃spiʀasjɔ̃] *nf* conspiracy.

conspirer [kɔ̃spiʀe] *vi* to conspire, plot; ~ **à** *(tendre à)* to conspire to.

conspuer [kɔ̃spɥe] *vt* to boo, shout down.

constamment [kɔ̃stamɑ̃] *adv* constantly.

constance [kɔ̃stɑ̃s] *nf* permanence, constancy; *(d'une amitié)* steadfastness; **travailler avec** ~ to work steadily; **il faut de la** ~ **pour la supporter** *(fam)* you need a lot of patience to put up with her.

constant, e [kɔ̃stɑ̃, -ɑ̃t] *adj* constant; *(personne)* steadfast ♦ *nf* constant.

Constantinople [kɔ̃stɑ̃tinɔpl(ə)] *n* Constantinople.

constat [kɔ̃sta] *nm (d'huissier)* certified report *(by bailiff)*; *(de police)* report; *(observation)* (observed) fact, observation; *(affirmation)* statement; ~ **(à l'amiable)** *(jointly agreed)* statement for insurance purposes.

constatation [kɔ̃statasjɔ̃] *nf* noticing, certifying; *(remarque)* observation.

constater [kɔ̃state] *vt* (*remarquer*) to note, notice; (*ADMIN, JUR: attester*) to certify; (*dégâts*) to note; ~ **que** (*dire*) to state that.

constellation [kɔ̃stelasjɔ̃] *nf* constellation.

constellé, e [kɔ̃stele] *adj:* ~ **de** (*étoiles*) studded *ou* spangled with; (*taches*) spotted with.

consternant, e [kɔ̃stɛRnɑ̃ -ɑ̃t] *adj* (*nouvelle*) dismaying; (*attristant, étonnant: bêtise*) appalling.

consternation [kɔ̃stɛRnasjɔ̃] *nf* consternation, dismay.

consterner [kɔ̃stɛRne] *vt* to dismay.

constipation [kɔ̃stipasjɔ̃] *nf* constipation.

constipé, e [kɔ̃stipe] *adj* constipated; (*fig*) stiff.

constituant, e [kɔ̃stityɑ̃, -ɑ̃t] *adj* (*élément*) constituent; **assemblée** ~**e** (*POL*) constituent assembly.

constitué, e [kɔ̃stitye] *adj:* ~ **de** made up *ou* composed of; **bien** ~ of sound constitution; well-formed.

constituer [kɔ̃stitye] *vt* (*comité, équipe*) to set up, form; (*dossier, collection*) to put together, build up; (*suj: éléments, parties: composer*) to make up, constitute; (*représenter, être*) to constitute; **se** ~ **prisonnier** to give o.s. up; **se** ~ **partie civile** *to bring an independent action for damages.*

constitution [kɔ̃stitysjɔ̃] *nf* setting up; building up; (*composition*) composition, make-up; (*santé, POL*) constitution.

constitutionnel, le [kɔ̃stitysjɔnɛl] *adj* constitutional.

constructeur [kɔ̃stRyktœR] *nm* manufacturer, builder.

constructif, ive [kɔ̃stRyktif, -iv] *adj* (*positif*) constructive.

construction [kɔ̃stRyksjɔ̃] *nf* construction, building.

construire [kɔ̃stRᶣiR] *vt* to build, construct; **se** ~: **l'immeuble s'est construit très vite** the building went up *ou* was built very quickly.

consul [kɔ̃syl] *nm* consul.

consulaire [kɔ̃sylɛR] *adj* consular.

consulat [kɔ̃syla] *nm* consulate.

consultant, e [kɔ̃syltɑ̃, -ɑ̃t] *adj* consultant.

consultatif, ive [kɔ̃syltatif, -iv] *adj* advisory.

consultation [kɔ̃syltasjɔ̃] *nf* consultation; ~**s** *nfpl* (*POL*) talks; **être en** ~ (*délibération*) to be in consultation; (*médecin*) to be consulting; **aller à la** ~ (*MÉD*) to go to the surgery (*BRIT*) *ou* doctor's office (*US*); **heures de** ~ (*MÉD*) surgery (*BRIT*) *ou* office (*US*) hours.

consulter [kɔ̃sylte] *vt* to consult ♦ *vi* (*médecin*) to hold surgery (*BRIT*), be in (the office) (*US*); **se** ~ to confer.

consumer [kɔ̃syme] *vt* to consume; **se** ~ *vi* to burn; **se** ~ **de chagrin/douleur** to be consumed with sorrow/grief.

consumérisme [kɔ̃symeRism(ə)] *nm* consumerism.

contact [kɔ̃takt] *nm* contact; **au** ~ **de** (*air, peau*) on contact with; (*gens*) through contact with; **mettre/couper le** ~ (*AUTO*) to switch on/off the ignition; **entrer en** ~ (*fils, objets*) to come into contact, make contact; **se mettre en** ~ **avec** (*RADIO*) to make contact with; **prendre** ~ **avec** (*relation d'affaires, connaissance*) to get in touch *ou* contact with.

contacter [kɔ̃takte] *vt* to contact, get in touch with.

contagieux, euse [kɔ̃taʒjø, -øz] *adj* contagious; infectious.

contagion [kɔ̃taʒjɔ̃] *nf* contagion.

container [kɔ̃tɛnɛR] *nm* container.

contamination [kɔ̃taminasjɔ̃] *nf* infection; contamination.

contaminer [kɔ̃tamine] *vt* (*par un virus*) to infect; (*par des radiations*) to contaminate.

conte [kɔ̃t] *nm* tale; ~ **de fées** fairy tale.

contemplatif, ive [kɔ̃tɑ̃platif, -iv] *adj* contemplative.

contemplation [kɔ̃tɑ̃plasjɔ̃] *nf* contemplation; (*REL, PHILOSOPHIE*) meditation.

contempler [kɔ̃tɑ̃ple] *vt* to contemplate, gaze at.

contemporain, e [kɔ̃tɑ̃pɔRɛ̃, -ɛn] *adj, nm/f* contemporary.

contenance [kɔ̃tnɑ̃s] *nf* (*d'un récipient*) capacity; (*attitude*) bearing, attitude; **perdre** ~ to lose one's composure; **se donner une** ~ to give the impression of composure; **faire bonne** ~ (**devant**) to put on a bold front (in the face of).

conteneur [kɔ̃tnœR] *nm* container; ~ (**de bouteilles**) bottle bank.

conteneurisation [kɔ̃tnœRizasjɔ̃] *nf* containerization.

contenir [kɔ̃tniR] *vt* to contain; (*avoir une capacité de*) to hold; **se** ~ (*se retenir*) to control o.s. *ou* one's emotions, contain o.s.

content, e [kɔ̃tɑ̃, -ɑ̃t] *adj* pleased, glad; ~ **de** pleased with; **je serais** ~ **que tu** ... I would be pleased if you ....

contentement [kɔ̃tɑ̃tmɑ̃] *nm* contentment, satisfaction.

contenter [kɔ̃tɑ̃te] *vt* to satisfy, please; (*envie*) to satisfy; **se** ~ **de** to content o.s. with.

contentieux [kɔ̃tɑ̃sjø] *nm* (*COMM*) litigation; (*: service*) litigation department; (*POL etc*) contentious issues *pl.*

contenu, e [kɔ̃tny] *pp de* **contenir** ♦ *nm* (*d'un bol*) contents *pl;* (*d'un texte*) content.

conter [kɔ̃te] *vt* to recount, relate; **en** ~ **de belles à qn** to tell tall stories to sb.

contestable [kɔ̃tɛstabl(ə)] *adj* questionable.

contestataire [kɔ̃tɛstatɛR] *adj* (*journal, étudiant*) anti-establishment ♦ *nm/f* (anti-establishment) protester.

contestation [kɔ̃tɛstasjɔ̃] *nf* questioning, contesting; (*POL*): **la** ~ anti-establishment activity, protest.

conteste [kɔ̃tɛst(ə)]: **sans** ~ *adv* unquestionably, indisputably.

contesté, e [kɔ̃tɛste] adj (roman, écrivain) controversial.

contester [kɔ̃tɛste] vt to question, contest ♦ vi (POL, gén) to protest, rebel (against established authority).

conteur, euse [kɔ̃tœʀ, -øz] nm/f story-teller.

contexte [kɔ̃tɛkst(ə)] nm context.

contiendrai [kɔ̃tjɛ̃dʀe], **contiens** [kɔ̃tjɛ̃] etc vb voir **contenir**.

contigu, ë [kɔ̃tigy] adj: ~ (à) adjacent (to).

continent [kɔ̃tinɑ̃] nm continent.

continental, e, aux [kɔ̃tinɑ̃tal, -o] adj continental.

contingences [kɔ̃tɛ̃ʒɑ̃s] nfpl contingencies.

contingent [kɔ̃tɛ̃ʒɑ̃] nm (MIL) contingent; (COMM) quota.

contingenter [kɔ̃tɛ̃ʒɑ̃te] vt (COMM) to fix a quota on.

contins [kɔ̃tɛ̃] etc vb voir **contenir**.

continu, e [kɔ̃tiny] adj continuous; **(courant)** ~ direct current, DC.

continuation [kɔ̃tinɥasjɔ̃] nf continuation.

continuel, le [kɔ̃tinɥɛl] adj (qui se répète) constant, continual; (continu) continuous.

continuellement [kɔ̃tinɥɛlmɑ̃] adv continually; continuously.

continuer [kɔ̃tinɥe] vt (travail, voyage etc) to continue (with), carry on (with), go on with; (prolonger: alignement, rue) to continue ♦ vi (pluie, vie, bruit) to continue, go on; (voyageur) to go on; se ~ vi to carry on; ~ à ou de faire to go on ou continue doing.

continuité [kɔ̃tinɥite] nf continuity; continuation.

contondant, e [kɔ̃tɔ̃dɑ̃, -ɑ̃t] adj: **arme** ~**e** blunt instrument.

contorsion [kɔ̃tɔʀsjɔ̃] nf contortion.

contorsionner [kɔ̃tɔʀsjɔne]: **se** ~ vi to contort o.s., writhe about.

contorsionniste [kɔ̃tɔʀsjɔnist(ə)] nm/f contortionist.

contour [kɔ̃tuʀ] nm outline, contour; ~**s** nmpl (d'une rivière etc) windings.

contourner [kɔ̃tuʀne] vt to bypass, walk (ou drive) round.

contraceptif, ive [kɔ̃tʀasɛptif, -iv] adj, nm contraceptive.

contraception [kɔ̃tʀasɛpsjɔ̃] nf contraception.

contracté, e [kɔ̃tʀakte] adj (muscle) tense, contracted; (personne: tendu) tense, tensed up; **article** ~ (LING) contracted article.

contracter [kɔ̃tʀakte] vt (muscle etc) to tense, contract; (maladie, dette, obligation) to contract; (assurance) to take out; **se** ~ vi (métal, muscles) to contract.

contraction [kɔ̃tʀaksjɔ̃] nf contraction.

contractuel, le [kɔ̃tʀaktɥɛl] adj contractual ♦ nm/f (agent) traffic warden; (employé) contract employee.

contradiction [kɔ̃tʀadiksjɔ̃] nf contradiction.

contradictoire [kɔ̃tʀadiktwaʀ] adj contradic-

---

tory, conflicting; **débat** ~ (open) debate.

contraignant, e [kɔ̃tʀɛɲɑ̃, -ɑ̃t] vb voir **contraindre** ♦ adj restricting.

contraindre [kɔ̃tʀɛ̃dʀ(ə)] vt: ~ **qn à faire** to force ou compel sb to do.

contraint, e [kɔ̃tʀɛ̃, -ɛ̃t] pp de **contraindre** ♦ adj (mine, air) constrained, forced ♦ nf constraint; **sans** ~**e** unrestrainedly, unconstrainedly.

contraire [kɔ̃tʀɛʀ] adj, nm opposite; ~ **à** contrary to; **au** ~ adv on the contrary.

contrairement [kɔ̃tʀɛʀmɑ̃] adv: ~ **à** contrary to, unlike.

contralto [kɔ̃tʀalto] nm contralto.

contrariant, e [kɔ̃tʀaʀjɑ̃, -ɑ̃t] adj (personne) contrary, perverse; (incident) annoying.

contrarier [kɔ̃tʀaʀje] vt (personne) to annoy, bother; (fig) to impede; to thwart, frustrate.

contrariété [kɔ̃tʀaʀjete] nf annoyance.

contraste [kɔ̃tʀast(ə)] nm contrast.

contraster [kɔ̃tʀaste] vt, vi to contrast.

contrat [kɔ̃tʀa] nm contract; (fig: accord, pacte) agreement; ~ **de travail** employment contract.

contravention [kɔ̃tʀavɑ̃sjɔ̃] nf (infraction): ~ **à** contravention of; (amende) fine; (PV pour stationnement interdit) parking ticket; **dresser** ~ **à** (automobiliste) to book; to write out a parking ticket for.

contre [kɔ̃tʀ(ə)] prép against; (en échange) (in exchange) for; **par** ~ on the other hand.

contre-amiral, aux [kɔ̃tʀamiʀal, -o] nm rear admiral.

contre-attaque [kɔ̃tʀatak] nf counterattack.

contre-attaquer [kɔ̃tʀatake] vi to counterattack.

contre-balancer [kɔ̃tʀəbalɑ̃se] vt to counterbalance; (fig) to offset.

contrebande [kɔ̃tʀəbɑ̃d] nf (trafic) contraband, smuggling; (marchandise) contraband, smuggled goods pl; **faire la** ~ **de** to smuggle.

contrebandier, ière [kɔ̃tʀəbɑ̃dje, -jɛʀ] nm/f smuggler.

contrebas [kɔ̃tʀəba]: **en** ~ adv (down) below.

contrebasse [kɔ̃tʀəbas] nf (double) bass.

contrebassiste [kɔ̃tʀəbasist(ə)] nm/f (double) bass player.

contre-braquer [kɔ̃tʀəbʀake] vi to steer into a skid.

contrecarrer [kɔ̃tʀəkaʀe] vt to thwart.

contrechamp [kɔ̃tʀəʃɑ̃] nm (CINÉ) reverse shot.

contrecœur [kɔ̃tʀəkœʀ]: **à** ~ adv (be)grudgingly, reluctantly.

contrecoup [kɔ̃tʀəku] nm repercussions pl; **par** ~ as an indirect consequence.

contre-courant [kɔ̃tʀəkuʀɑ̃]: **à** ~ adv against the current.

contredire [kɔ̃tʀədiʀ] vt (personne) to contradict; (témoignage, assertion, faits) to refute; **se** ~ to contradict o.s.

contredit, e [kɔ̃tʀədi, -it] pp de **contredire**

♦ *nm*: **sans** ~ without question.

contrée [kɔ̃tʀe] *nf* region; land.

contre-écrou [kɔ̃tʀekʀu] *nm* lock nut.

contre-enquête [kɔ̃tʀɑ̃kɛt] *nf* counter-inquiry.

contre-espionnage [kɔ̃tʀɛspjɔnaʒ] *nm* counter-espionage.

contre-exemple [kɔ̃tʀɛgzɑ̃pl(ə)] *nf* counter-example.

contre-expertise [kɔ̃tʀɛkspɛʀtiz] *nf* second (expert) assessment.

contrefaçon [kɔ̃tʀəfasɔ̃] *nf* forgery; ~ **de brevet** patent infringement.

contrefaire [kɔ̃tʀəfɛʀ] *vt* (*document, signature*) to forge, counterfeit; (*personne, démarche*) to mimic; (*dénaturer: sa voix etc*) to disguise.

contrefait, e [kɔ̃tʀəfɛ, -ɛt] *pp de* **contrefaire** ♦ *adj* misshapen, deformed.

contrefasse [kɔ̃tʀəfas], **contreferai** [kɔ̃tʀəfʀe] *etc vb voir* **contrefaire.**

contre-filet [kɔ̃tʀəfilɛ] *nm* (*CULIN*) sirloin.

contreforts [kɔ̃tʀəfɔʀ] *nmpl* foothills.

contre-haut [kɔ̃tʀəo]: **en ~** *adv* (up) above.

contre-indication [kɔ̃tʀɛ̃dikasjɔ̃] *nf* contra-indication.

contre-indiqué, e [kɔ̃tʀɛ̃dike] *adj* (*MÉD*) contraindicated.

contre-interrogatoire [kɔ̃tʀɛ̃teʀɔgatwaʀ] *nm*: **faire subir un ~ à qn** to cross-examine sb.

contre-jour [kɔ̃tʀəʒuʀ]: **à ~** *adv* against the light.

contremaître [kɔ̃tʀəmɛtʀ(ə)] *nm* foreman.

contre-manifestant, e [kɔ̃tʀəmanifɛstɑ̃, -ɑ̃t] *nm/f* counter-demonstrator.

contre-manifestation [kɔ̃tʀəmanifɛstasjɔ̃] *nf* counter-demonstration.

contremarque [kɔ̃tʀəmaʀk(ə)] *nf* (*ticket*) pass-out ticket.

contre-offensive [kɔ̃tʀɔfɑ̃siv] *nf* counter-offensive.

contre-ordre [kɔ̃tʀɔʀdʀ(ə)] *nm* = **contrordre.**

contrepartie [kɔ̃tʀəpaʀti] *nf* compensation; **en ~** in compensation; in return.

contre-performance [kɔ̃tʀəpɛʀfɔʀmɑ̃s] *nf* below-average performance.

contrepèterie [kɔ̃tʀəpetʀi] *nf* spoonerism.

contre-pied [kɔ̃tʀəpje] *nm* (*inverse, opposé*): **le ~ de ...** the exact opposite of ...; **prendre le ~ de** to take the opposing view of; to take the opposite course to; **prendre qn à ~** (*SPORT*) to wrong-foot sb.

contre-plaqué [kɔ̃tʀəplake] *nm* plywood.

contre-plongée [kɔ̃tʀəplɔ̃ʒe] *nf* low-angle shot.

contrepoids [kɔ̃tʀəpwa] *nm* counterweight, counterbalance; **faire ~** to act as a counter-balance.

contrepoil [kɔ̃tʀəpwal]: **à ~** *adv* the wrong way.

contrepoint [kɔ̃tʀəpwɛ̃] *nm* counterpoint.

contrepoison [kɔ̃tʀəpwazɔ̃] *nm* antidote.

contrer [kɔ̃tʀe] *vt* to counter.

contre-révolution [kɔ̃tʀəʀevɔlysjɔ̃] *nf* counter-revolution.

contre-révolutionnaire [kɔ̃tʀəʀevɔlysjɔnɛʀ] *nm/f* counter-revolutionary.

contresens [kɔ̃tʀəsɑ̃s] *nm* misinterpretation; (*mauvaise traduction*) mistranslation; (*absurdité*) nonsense *no pl*; **à ~** *adv* the wrong way.

contresigner [kɔ̃tʀəsiɲe] *vt* to countersign.

contretemps [kɔ̃tʀətɑ̃] *nm* hitch, contretemps; **à ~** *adv* (*MUS*) out of time; (*fig*) at an inopportune moment.

contre-terrorisme [kɔ̃tʀəteʀɔʀism(ə)] *nm* counter-terrorism.

contre-terroriste [kɔ̃tʀəteʀɔʀist(ə)] *nm/f* counter-terrorist.

contre-torpilleur [kɔ̃tʀətɔʀpijœʀ] *nm* destroyer.

contrevenant, e [kɔ̃tʀəvnɑ̃, -ɑ̃t] *vb voir* **contrevenir** ♦ *nm/f* offender.

contrevenir [kɔ̃tʀəvniʀ]: ~ **à** *vt* to contravene.

contre-voie [kɔ̃tʀəvwa]: **à ~** *adv* (*en sens inverse*) on the wrong track; (*du mauvais côté*) on the wrong side.

contribuable [kɔ̃tʀibɥabl(ə)] *nm/f* taxpayer.

contribuer [kɔ̃tʀibɥe]: ~ **à** *vt* to contribute towards.

contribution [kɔ̃tʀibysjɔ̃] *nf* contribution; **les ~s** (*bureaux*) the tax office; **mettre à ~** to call upon; **~s directes/indirectes** direct/indirect taxation.

contrit, e [kɔ̃tʀi, -it] *adj* contrite.

contrôlable [kɔ̃tʀolabl(ə)] *adj* (*maîtrisable: situation, débit*) controllable; (*alibi, déclarations*) verifiable.

contrôle [kɔ̃tʀol] *nm* checking *no pl*, check; supervision; monitoring; (*test*) test, examination; **perdre le ~ de son véhicule** to lose control of one's vehicle; **~ des changes** (*COMM*) exchange controls; **~ continu** (*SCOL*) continuous assessment; **~ d'identité** identity check; **~ des naissances** birth control; **~ des prix** price control.

contrôler [kɔ̃tʀole] *vt* (*vérifier*) to check; (*surveiller*) to supervise; to monitor, control; (*maîtriser, COMM: firme*) to control; **se ~** to control o.s.

contrôleur, euse [kɔ̃tʀolœʀ, -øz] *nm/f* (*de train*) (ticket) inspector; (*de bus*) (bus) conductor/tress; **~ de la navigation aérienne, ~ aérien** air traffic controller; **~ financier** financial controller.

contrordre [kɔ̃tʀɔʀdʀ(ə)] *nm* counter-order, countermand; **sauf ~** unless otherwise directed.

controverse [kɔ̃tʀɔvɛʀs(ə)] *nf* controversy.

controversé, e [kɔ̃tʀɔvɛʀse] *adj* (*personnage, question*) controversial.

contumace [kɔ̃tymas]: **par ~** *adv* in absentia.

contusion [kɔ̃tyzjɔ̃] *nf* bruise, contusion.

contusionné, e [kɔ̃tyzjɔne] *adj* bruised.

conurbation [kɔnyʀbasjɔ̃] *nf* conurbation.

convaincant, e [kɔ̃vɛ̃kɑ̃, -ɑ̃t] *vb voir* **convaincre**

♦ adj convincing.

convaincre [kɔ̃vɛ̃kʀ(ə)] vt: ~ qn (de qch) to convince sb (of sth); ~ qn (de faire) to persuade sb (to do); ~ qn de (JUR: délit) to convict sb of.

convaincu, e [kɔ̃vɛ̃ky] pp de **convaincre** ♦ adj: d'un ton ~ with conviction.

convainquais [kɔ̃vɛ̃kɛ] etc vb voir **convaincre**.

convalescence [kɔ̃valesɑ̃s] nf convalescence; **maison de** ~ convalescent home.

convalescent, e [kɔ̃valesɑ̃, -ɑ̃t] adj, nm/f convalescent.

convenable [kɔ̃vnabl(ə)] adj suitable; (décent) acceptable, proper; (assez bon) decent, acceptable; adequate, passable.

convenablement [kɔ̃vnabləmɑ̃] adv (placé, choisi) suitably; (s'habiller, s'exprimer) properly; (payé, logé) decently.

convenance [kɔ̃vnɑ̃s] nf: à ma/votre ~ to my/ your liking; ~s nfpl proprieties.

convenir [kɔ̃vniʀ] vt to be suitable; ~ à to suit; **il convient de** it is advisable to; (bienséant) it is right ou proper to; ~ de (bienfondé de qch) to admit (to), acknowledge; (date, somme etc) to agree upon; ~ que (admettre) to admit that, acknowledge the fact that; ~ de faire qch to agree to do sth; **il a été convenu que** it has been agreed that; **comme convenu** as agreed.

convention [kɔ̃vɑ̃sjɔ̃] nf convention; ~s nfpl (convenances) convention sg, social conventions; **de** ~ conventional; ~ **collective** (ÉCON) collective agreement.

conventionnalisme [kɔ̃vɑ̃sjɔnalism(ə)] nm (des idées) conventionality.

conventionné, e [kɔ̃vɑ̃sjɔne] adj (ADMIN) applying charges laid down by the state.

conventionnel, le [kɔ̃vɑ̃sjɔnɛl] adj conventional.

conventionnellement [kɔ̃vɑ̃sjɔnɛlmɑ̃] adv conventionally.

conventuel, le [kɔ̃vɑ̃tɥɛl] adj monastic; monastery cpd; conventual, convent cpd.

convenu, e [kɔ̃vny] pp de **convenir** ♦ adj agreed.

convergent, e [kɔ̃vɛʀʒɑ̃, -ɑ̃t] adj convergent.

converger [kɔ̃vɛʀʒe] vi to converge; ~ **vers** ou **sur** to converge on.

conversation [kɔ̃vɛʀsasjɔ̃] nf conversation; **avoir de la** ~ to be a good conversationalist.

converser [kɔ̃vɛʀse] vi to converse.

conversion [kɔ̃vɛʀsjɔ̃] nf conversion; (SKI) kick turn.

convertible [kɔ̃vɛʀtibl(ə)] adj (ÉCON) convertible; (canapé) ~ sofa bed.

convertir [kɔ̃vɛʀtiʀ] vt: ~ qn (à) to convert sb (to); ~ qch en to convert sth into; **se** ~ (à) to be converted (to).

convertisseur [kɔ̃vɛʀtisœʀ] nm (ÉLEC) converter.

convexe [kɔ̃vɛks(ə)] adj convex.

conviction [kɔ̃viksjɔ̃] nf conviction.

conviendrai [kɔ̃vjɛ̃dʀe], **conviens** [kɔ̃vjɛ̃] etc vb voir **convenir**.

convier [kɔ̃vje] vt: ~ qn à (dîner etc) to (cordially) invite sb to; ~ qn à faire to urge sb to do.

convint [kɔ̃vɛ̃] etc vb voir **convenir**.

convive [kɔ̃viv] nm/f guest (at table).

convivial, e [kɔ̃vivjal] adj (INFORM) userfriendly.

convocation [kɔ̃vɔkasjɔ̃] nf (voir convoquer) convening, convoking; summoning; invitation; (document) notification to attend; summons sg.

convoi [kɔ̃vwa] nm (de voitures, prisonniers) convoy; (train) train; ~ **(funèbre)** funeral procession.

convoiter [kɔ̃vwate] vt to covet.

convoitise [kɔ̃vwatiz] nf covetousness; (sexuelle) lust, desire.

convoler [kɔ̃vɔle] vi: ~ **(en justes noces)** to be wed.

convoquer [kɔ̃vɔke] vt (assemblée) to convene, convoke; (subordonné, témoin) to summon; (candidat) to ask to attend; ~ qn (à) (réunion) to invite sb (to attend).

convoyer [kɔ̃vwaje] vt to escort.

convoyeur [kɔ̃vwajœʀ] nm (NAVIG) escort ship; ~ **de fonds** security guard.

convulsé, e [kɔ̃vylse] adj (visage) distorted.

convulsif, ive [kɔ̃vylsif, -iv] adj convulsive.

convulsions [kɔ̃vylsjɔ̃] nfpl convulsions.

coopérant [kɔɔpeʀɑ̃] nm ≈ person doing Voluntary Service Overseas (BRIT), ≈ member of the Peace Corps (US).

coopératif, ive [kɔɔpeʀatif, -iv] adj, nf cooperative.

coopération [kɔɔpeʀasjɔ̃] nf co-operation; (ADMIN): **la C~** ≈ Voluntary Service Overseas (BRIT) ou the Peace Corps (US) (done as alternative to military service).

coopérer [kɔɔpeʀe] vi: ~ **(à)** to co-operate (in).

coordination [kɔɔʀdinasjɔ̃] nf coordination.

coordonnateur, trice [kɔɔʀdɔnatœʀ, -tʀis] adj coordinating ♦ nm/f coordinator.

coordonné, e [kɔɔʀdɔne] adj coordinated ♦ nf (LING) coordinate clause; ~s nmpl (vêtements) coordinates; ~**es** nfpl (MATH) coordinates; (détails personnels) address, phone number, schedule etc; whereabouts.

coordonner [kɔɔʀdɔne] vt to coordinate.

copain, copine [kɔpɛ̃, kɔpin] nm/f mate (BRIT), pal ♦ adj: **être** ~ **avec** to be pally with.

copeau, x [kɔpo] nm shaving; (de métal) turning.

Copenhague [kɔpənag] n Copenhagen.

copie [kɔpi] nf copy; (SCOL) script, paper; exercise; ~ **certifiée conforme** certified copy; ~ **papier** (INFORM) hard copy.

copier [kɔpje] vt, vi to copy; ~ **sur** to copy from.

copieur [kɔpjœʀ] nm (photo)copier.

copieusement [kɔpjøzmɑ̃] adv copiously.

copieux, euse [kɔpjø, -øz] *adj* copious, hearty.

copilote [kɔpilɔt] *nm* (*AVIAT*) co-pilot; (*AUTO*) co-driver, navigator.

copinage [kɔpinaʒ] *nm*: **obtenir qch par ~ to** get sth through contacts.

copine [kɔpin] *nf voir* **copain**.

copiste [kɔpist(ə)] *nm/f* copyist, transcriber.

coproduction [kɔpʀɔdyksjɔ̃] *nf* coproduction, joint production.

copropriétaire [kɔpʀɔpʀijetɛʀ] *nm/f* co-owner.

copropriété [kɔpʀɔpʀijete] *nf* co-ownership, joint ownership; **acheter en ~ to** buy on a co-ownership basis.

copulation [kɔpylasjɔ̃] *nf* copulation.

copyright [kɔpiʀajt] *nm* copyright.

coq [kɔk] *nm* cock, rooster ♦ *adj inv* (*BOXE*): **poids ~** bantamweight; **~ de bruyère** grouse; **~ du village** (*fig: péj*) ladykiller.

coq-à-l'âne [kɔkalɑn] *nm inv* abrupt change of subject.

coque [kɔk] *nf* (*de noix, mollusque*) shell; (*de bateau*) hull; **à la ~** (*CULIN*) (soft-)boiled.

coquelet [kɔklɛ] *nm* (*CULIN*) cockerel.

coquelicot [kɔkliko] *nm* poppy.

coqueluche [kɔklyʃ] *nf* whooping-cough; (*fig*): **être la ~ de qn** to be sb's flavour of the month.

coquet, te [kɔkɛ, -ɛt] *adj* appearance-conscious; (*joli*) pretty.

coquetier [kɔktje] *nm* egg-cup.

coquettement [kɔkɛtmɑ̃] *adv* (*s'habiller*) attractively; (*meubler*) prettily.

coquetterie [kɔkɛtʀi] *nf* appearance-consciousness.

coquillage [kɔkijaʒ] *nm* (*mollusque*) shellfish *inv*; (*coquille*) shell.

coquille [kɔkij] *nf* shell; (*TYPO*) misprint; **~ de beurre** pat of butter; **~ d'œuf** *adj* (*couleur*) eggshell; **~ de noix** nutshell; **~ St Jacques** scallop.

coquillettes [kɔkijɛt] *nfpl* pasta shells.

coquin, e [kɔkɛ̃, -in] *adj* mischievous, roguish; (*polisson*) naughty ♦ *nm/f* (*péj*) rascal.

cor [kɔʀ] *nm* (*MUS*) horn; (*MÉD*): **~ (au pied)** corn; **réclamer à ~ et à cri** to clamour for; **~ anglais** cor anglais; **~ de chasse** hunting horn.

corail, aux [kɔʀaj, -o] *nm* coral *no pl*.

Coran [kɔʀɑ̃] *nm*: **le ~** the Koran.

coraux [kɔʀo] *pl de* **corail**.

corbeau, x [kɔʀbo] *nm* crow.

corbeille [kɔʀbɛj] *nf* basket; (*BOURSE*): **la ~** the floor (of the Stock Exchange); **~ de mariage** (*fig*) wedding presents *pl*; **~ à ouvrage** work-basket; **~ à pain** breadbasket; **~ à papier** waste paper basket *ou* bin.

corbillard [kɔʀbijaʀ] *nm* hearse.

cordage [kɔʀdaʒ] *nm* rope; **~s** *nmpl* (*de voilure*) rigging *sg*.

corde [kɔʀd(ə)] *nf* rope; (*de violon, raquette, d'arc*) string; (*trame*): **la ~** the thread; (*ATH-*

LÉTISME, AUTO): **la ~** the rails *pl*; **les ~s** (*BOXE*) the ropes; **les (instruments à) ~s** (*MUS*) the strings, the stringed instruments; **semelles de ~** rope soles; **tenir la ~** (*ATH-LÉTISME, AUTO*) to be in the inside lane; **tomber des ~s** to rain cats and dogs; **tirer sur la ~** to go too far; **la ~ sensible** the right chord; **usé jusqu'à la ~** threadbare; **~ à linge** washing *ou* clothes line; **~ lisse** (climbing) rope; **~ à nœuds** knotted climbing rope; **~ raide** tightrope; **~ à sauter** skipping rope; **~s vocales** vocal cords.

cordeau, x [kɔʀdo] *nm* string, line; **tracé au ~** as straight as a die.

cordée [kɔʀde] *nf* (*d'alpinistes*) rope, roped party.

cordelière [kɔʀdəljɛʀ] *nf* cord (belt).

cordial, e, aux [kɔʀdjal, -o] *adj* warm, cordial ♦ *nm* cordial, pick-me-up.

cordialement [kɔʀdjalmɑ̃] *adv* cordially, heartily; (*formule épistolaire*) (kind) regards.

cordialité [kɔʀdjalite] *nf* warmth, cordiality.

cordillère [kɔʀdijɛʀ] *nf*: **la ~ des Andes** the Andes cordillera *ou* range.

cordon [kɔʀdɔ̃] *nm* cord, string; **~ sanitaire/de police** sanitary/police cordon; **~ littoral** sandbank, sandbar; **~ ombilical** umbilical cord.

cordon-bleu [kɔʀdɔ̃blø] *adj, nm/f* cordon bleu.

cordonnerie [kɔʀdɔnʀi] *nf* shoe repairer's *ou* mender's (shop).

cordonnier [kɔʀdɔnje] *nm* shoe repairer *ou* mender, cobbler.

cordouan, e [kɔʀduɑ̃, -an] *adj* Cordovan.

Cordoue [kɔʀdu] *n* Cordoba.

Corée [kɔʀe] *nf*: **la ~** Korea; **la ~ du Sud/du Nord** South/North Korea; **la République (démocratique populaire) de ~** the (Democratic People's) Republic of Korea.

coréen, ne [kɔʀeɛ̃, -ɛn] *adj* Korean ♦ *nm* (*LING*) Korean ♦ *nm/f*: **C~, ne** Korean.

coreligionnaire [kɔʀəliʒjɔnɛʀ] *nm/f* fellow Christian/Muslim/Jew *etc*.

Corfou [kɔʀfu] *n* Corfu.

coriace [kɔʀjas] *adj* tough.

coriandre [kɔʀjɑ̃dʀ(ə)] *nf* coriander.

Corinthe [kɔʀɛ̃t] *n* Corinth.

cormoran [kɔʀmɔʀɑ̃] *nm* cormorant.

cornac [kɔʀnak] *nm* elephant driver.

corne [kɔʀn(ə)] *nf* horn; (*de cerf*) antler; (*de la peau*) callus; **~ d'abondance** horn of plenty; **~ de brume** (*NAVIG*) foghorn.

cornée [kɔʀne] *nf* cornea.

corneille [kɔʀnɛj] *nf* crow.

cornélien, ne [kɔʀneljɛ̃, -ɛn] *adj* (*débat etc*) where love and duty conflict.

cornemuse [kɔʀnəmyz] *nf* bagpipes *pl*; **joueur de ~** piper.

corner *nm* [kɔʀnɛʀ] (*FOOTBALL*) corner (kick) ♦ *vb* [kɔʀne] *vt* (*pages*) to make dog-eared ♦ *vi* (*klaxonner*) to blare out.

cornet [kɔʀnɛ] *nm* (paper) cone; (*de glace*) cor-

net, cone; ~ **à pistons** cornet.
cornette [kɔʀnɛt] *nf* cornet (*headgear*).
corniaud [kɔʀnjo] *nm* (*chien*) mongrel; (*péj*) twit, clot.
corniche [kɔʀniʃ] *nf* (*de meuble, neigeuse*) cornice; (*route*) coast road.
cornichon [kɔʀniʃɔ̃] *nm* gherkin.
Cornouailles [kɔʀnwaj] *nf(pl)* Cornwall.
cornue [kɔʀny] *nf* retort.
corollaire [kɔʀɔlɛʀ] *nm* corollary.
corolle [kɔʀɔl] *nf* corolla.
coron [kɔʀɔ̃] *nm* mining cottage; mining village.
coronaire [kɔʀɔnɛʀ] *adj* coronary.
corporation [kɔʀpɔʀasjɔ̃] *nf* corporate body; (*au Moyen-Âge*) guild.
corporel, le [kɔʀpɔʀɛl] *adj* bodily; (*punition*) corporal; **soins ~s** care *sg* of the body.
corps [kɔʀ] *nm* (*gén*) body; (*cadavre*) (dead) body; **à son ~ défendant** against one's will; **à ~ perdu** headland; **perdu ~ et biens** lost with all hands; **prendre ~** to take shape; **faire ~ avec** to be joined to; to form one body with; **~ d'armée (CA)** army corps; **~ de ballet** corps de ballet; **~ constitués** (*POL*) constitutional bodies; **le ~ consulaire (CC)** the consular corps; **~ à ~** *adv* hand-to-hand ♦ *nm* clinch; **le ~ du délit** (*JUR*) corpus delicti; **le ~ diplomatique (CD)** the diplomatic corps; **le ~ électoral** the electorate; **le ~ enseignant** the teaching profession; **~ étranger** (*MÉD*) foreign body; **~ expéditionnaire** task force; **~ de garde** guardroom; **~ législatif** legislative body; **le ~ médical** the medical profession.
corpulence [kɔʀpylɑ̃s] *nf* build; (*embonpoint*) stoutness (*BRIT*), corpulence; **de forte ~** of large build.
corpulent, e [kɔʀpylɑ̃, -ɑ̃t] *adj* stout (*BRIT*), corpulent.
corpus [kɔʀpys] *nm* (*LING*) corpus.
correct, e [kɔʀɛkt] *adj* (*exact*) accurate, correct; (*bienséant, honnête*) correct; (*passable*) adequate.
correctement [kɔʀɛktəmɑ̃] *adv* accurately; correctly; adequately.
correcteur, trice [kɔʀɛktœʀ, -tʀis] *nm/f* (*SCOL*) examiner, marker; (*TYPO*) proofreader.
correctif, ive [kɔʀɛktif, -iv] *adj* corrective ♦ *nm* (*mise au point*) rider, qualification.
correction [kɔʀɛksjɔ̃] *nf* (*voir corriger*) correction; marking; (*voir correct*) correctness; (*rature, surcharge*) correction, emendation; (*coups*) thrashing; **~ sur écran** (*INFORM*) screen editing; **~ (des épreuves)** proofreading.
correctionnel, le [kɔʀɛksjɔnɛl] *adj* (*JUR*): **tribunal ~ ≈** criminal court.
corrélation [kɔʀelasjɔ̃] *nf* correlation.
correspondance [kɔʀɛspɔ̃dɑ̃s] *nf* correspondence; (*de train, d'avion*) connection; **ce train assure la ~ avec l'avion de 10 heures** this

train connects with the 10 o'clock plane; **cours par ~** correspondence course; **vente par ~** mail-order business.
correspondancier, ière [kɔʀɛspɔ̃dɑ̃sje, -jɛʀ] *nm/f* correspondence clerk.
correspondant, e [kɔʀɛspɔ̃dɑ̃, -ɑ̃t] *nm/f* correspondent; (*TÉL*) person phoning (*ou* being phoned).
correspondre [kɔʀɛspɔ̃dʀ(ə)] *vi* (*données, témoignages*) to correspond, tally; (*chambres*) to communicate; **~ à** to correspond to; **~ avec qn** to correspond with sb.
Corrèze [kɔʀɛz] *nf*: **la ~** the Corrèze.
corrézien, ne [kɔʀezjɛ̃, -ɛn] *adj* of *ou* from the Corrèze.
corrida [kɔʀida] *nf* bullfight.
corridor [kɔʀidɔʀ] *nm* corridor, passage.
corrigé [kɔʀiʒe] *nm* (*SCOL*) correct version; fair copy.
corriger [kɔʀiʒe] *vt* (*devoir*) to correct, mark; (*texte*) to correct, emend; (*erreur, défaut*) to correct, put right; (*punir*) to thrash; **~ qn de** (*défaut*) to cure sb of; **se ~ de** to cure o.s. of.
corroborer [kɔʀɔbɔʀe] *vt* to corroborate.
corroder [kɔʀɔde] *vt* to corrode.
corrompre [kɔʀɔ̃pʀ(ə)] *vt* (*dépraver*) to corrupt; (*acheter: témoin etc*) to bribe.
corrompu, e [kɔʀɔ̃py] *adj* corrupt.
corrosif, ive [kɔʀɔzif, -iv] *adj* corrosive.
corrosion [kɔʀɔzjɔ̃] *nf* corrosion.
corruption [kɔʀypsjɔ̃] *nf* corruption; bribery.
corsage [kɔʀsaʒ] *nm* (*d'une robe*) bodice; (*chemisier*) blouse.
corsaire [kɔʀsɛʀ] *nm* pirate, corsair; privateer.
corse [kɔʀs(ə)] *adj* Corsican ♦ *nm/f*: **C~** Corsican ♦ *nf*: **la C~** Corsica.
corsé, e [kɔʀse] *adj* vigorous; (*café etc*) full-flavoured (*BRIT*) *ou* -flavored (*US*); (*goût*) full; (*fig*) spicy; tricky.
corselet [kɔʀsəlɛ] *nm* corselet.
corser [kɔʀse] *vt* (*difficulté*) to aggravate; (*intrigue*) to liven up; (*sauce*) to add spice to.
corset [kɔʀsɛ] *nm* corset; (*d'une robe*) bodice; **~ orthopédique** surgical corset.
corso [kɔʀso] *nm*: **~ fleuri** procession of floral floats.
cortège [kɔʀtɛʒ] *nm* procession.
cortisone [kɔʀtizɔn] *nf* (*MÉD*) cortisone.
corvée [kɔʀve] *nf* chore, drudgery *no pl*; (*MIL*) fatigue (duty).
cosaque [kɔzak] *nm* cossack.
cosignataire [kɔsiɲatɛʀ] *adj, nm/f* cosignatory.
cosinus [kɔsinys] *nm* (*MATH*) cosine.
cosmétique [kɔsmetik] *nm* (*pour les cheveux*) hair-oil; (*produit de beauté*) beauty care product.
cosmétologie [kɔsmetɔlɔʒi] *nf* beauty care.
cosmique [kɔsmik] *adj* cosmic.
cosmonaute [kɔsmɔnot] *nm/f* cosmonaut, astronaut.

cosmopolite [kɔsmɔpɔlit] *adj* cosmopolitan.

cosmos [kɔsmɔs] *nm* outer space; cosmos.

cosse [kɔs] *nf (BOT)* pod, hull.

cossu, e [kɔsy] *adj* opulent-looking, well-to-do.

Costa Rica [kɔstaʀika] *nm*: **le** ~ Costa Rica.

costaricien, ne [kɔstaʀisjɛ̃, -ɛn] *adj* Costa Rican ♦ *nm/f*: **C**~, **ne** Costa Rican.

costaud, e [kɔsto, -od] *adj* strong, sturdy.

costume [kɔstym] *nm (d'homme)* suit; *(de théâtre)* costume.

costumé, e [kɔstyme] *adj* dressed up.

costumier, ière [kɔstymje, -jɛʀ] *nm/f (fabricant, loueur)* costumier; *(THÉÂT)* wardrobe master/mistress.

cotangente [kɔtɑ̃ʒɑ̃t] *nf (MATH)* cotangent.

cotation [kɔtasjɔ̃] *nf* quoted value.

cote [kɔt] *nf (en Bourse etc)* quotation; quoted value; *(d'un cheval)*: **la** ~ **de** the odds *pl* on; *(d'un candidat etc)* rating; *(mesure: sur une carte)* spot height; *(: sur un croquis)* dimension; *(de classement)* (classification) mark; reference number; **avoir la** ~ to be very popular; **inscrit à la** ~ quoted on the Stock Exchange; ~ **d'alerte** danger *ou* flood level; ~ **mal taillée** *(fig)* compromise; ~ **de popularité** popularity rating.

coté, e [kɔte] *adj*: **être** ~ to be listed *ou* quoted; **être** ~ **en Bourse** to be quoted on the Stock Exchange; **être bien/mal** ~ to be highly/poorly rated.

côte [kot] *nf (rivage)* coast(line); *(pente)* slope; *(: sur une route)* hill; *(ANAT)* rib; *(d'un tricot, tissu)* rib, ribbing *no pl*; ~ **à** ~ *adv* side by side; **la C**~ **(d'Azur)** the (French) Riviera; **la C**~ **d'Ivoire** the Ivory Coast.

côté [kote] *nm (gén)* side; *(direction)* way, direction; **de chaque** ~ **(de)** on each side of; **de tous les** ~**s** from all directions; **de quel** ~ **est-il parti?** which way *ou* in which direction did he go?; **de ce/de l'autre** ~ this/the other way; **d'un** ~ ... **de l'autre** ~ *(alternative)* on (the) one hand ... on the other (hand); **du** ~ **de** *(provenance)* from; *(direction)* towards; **du** ~ **de Lyon** *(proximité)* near Lyons; **du** ~ **gauche** on the left-hand side; **de** ~ *adv* sideways; on one side; to one side; aside; **laisser de** ~ to leave on one side; **mettre de** ~ to put on one side, put aside; **de mon** ~ *(quant à moi)* for my part; **à** ~ *adv* (right) nearby; beside; next door; *(d'autre part)* besides; **à** ~ **de** beside; next to; *(fig)* in comparison to; **à** ~ **(de la cible)** off target, wide (of the mark); **être aux** ~**s de** to be by the side of.

coteau, x [kɔto] *nm* hill.

côtelé, e [kotle] *adj* ribbed; **pantalon en velours** ~ corduroy trousers *pl*.

côtelette [kotlɛt] *nf* chop.

coter [kɔte] *vt (BOURSE)* to quote.

coterie [kɔtʀi] *nf* set.

côtier, ière [kotje, -jɛʀ] *adj* coastal.

cotisation [kɔtizasjɔ̃] *nf* subscription, dues *pl*;

(pour une pension) contributions *pl*.

cotiser [kɔtize] *vi*: ~ **(à)** to pay contributions (to); *(à une association)* to subscribe (to); **se** ~ to club together.

coton [kɔtɔ̃] *nm* cotton; ~ **hydrophile** cotton wool *(BRIT)*, absorbent cotton *(US)*.

cotonnade [kɔtɔnad] *nf* cotton (fabric).

Coton-Tige [kɔtɔ̃tiʒ] *nm ®* cotton bud ®.

côtoyer [kotwaje] *vt* to be close to; *(rencontrer)* to rub shoulders with; *(longer)* to run alongside; *(fig: friser)* to be bordering *ou* verging on.

cotte [kɔt] *nf*: ~ **de mailles** coat of mail.

cou [ku] *nm* neck.

couac [kwak] *nm (fam)* bum note.

couard, e [kwaʀ, -aʀd(ə)] *adj* cowardly.

couchage [kuʃaʒ] *nm voir* **sac.**

couchant [kuʃɑ̃] *adj*: **soleil** ~ setting sun.

couche [kuʃ] *nf (strate: gén, GÉO)* layer, stratum *(pl -a)*; *(de peinture, vernis)* coat; *(de poussière, crème)* layer; *(de bébé)* nappy *(BRIT)*, diaper *(US)*; ~ **d'ozone** ozone layer; ~**s** *(MÉD)* confinement *sg*; ~**s sociales** social levels *ou* strata.

couché, e [kuʃe] *adj (étendu)* lying down; *(au lit)* in bed.

couche-culotte, *pl* **couches-culottes** [kuʃkylɔt] *nf* (plastic-coated) disposable nappy *(BRIT)* ou diaper *(US)*.

coucher [kuʃe] *nm (du soleil)* setting ♦ *vt (personne)* to put to bed; *(: loger)* to put up; *(objet)* to lay on its side; *(écrire)* to inscribe, couch ♦ *vi (dormir)* to sleep, spend the night; ~ **avec qn** to sleep with sb, go to bed with sb; **se** ~ *vi (pour dormir)* to go to bed; *(pour se reposer)* to lie down; *(soleil)* to set, go down; **à prendre avant le** ~ *(MÉD)* take at night *ou* before going to bed; ~ **de soleil** sunset.

couchette [kuʃɛt] *nf* couchette; *(de marin)* bunk.

coucheur [kuʃœʀ] *nm*: **mauvais** ~ awkward customer.

couci-couça [kusikusa] *adv (fam)* so-so.

coucou [kuku] *nm* cuckoo ♦ *excl* peek-a-boo.

coude [kud] *nm (ANAT)* elbow; *(de tuyau, de la route)* bend; ~ **à** ~ *adv* shoulder to shoulder, side by side.

coudée [kude] *nf*: **avoir ses** ~**s franches** *(fig)* to have a free rein.

cou-de-pied, *pl* **cous-de-pied** [kudpje] *nm* instep.

coudoyer [kudwaje] *vt* to brush past *ou* against; *(fig)* to rub shoulders with.

coudre [kudʀ(ə)] *vt (bouton)* to sew on; *(robe)* to sew (up) ♦ *vi* to sew.

couenne [kwan] *nf (de lard)* rind.

couette [kwɛt] *nf* duvet, (continental) quilt; ~**s** *nfpl (cheveux)* bunches.

couffin [kufɛ̃] *nm* Moses basket; *(straw)* basket.

couilles [kuj] *nfpl (fam!)* balls (!).

couiner [kwine] *vi* to squeal.

coulage [kulaʒ] *nm* (*COMM*) loss of stock (*due to theft or negligence*).

coulant, e [kulā, -āt] *adj* (*indulgent*) easy-going; (*fromage etc*) runny.

coulée [kule] *nf* (*de lave, métal en fusion*) flow; ~ **de neige** snowslide.

couler [kule] *vi* to flow, run; (*fuir: stylo, récipient*) to leak; (*sombrer: bateau*) to sink ♦ *vt* (*cloche, sculpture*) to cast; (*bateau*) to sink; (*fig*) to ruin, bring down; (: *passer*): ~ **une vie heureuse** to enjoy a happy life; **se** ~ **dans** (*interstice etc*) to slip into; **faire** ~ (*eau*) to run; **faire** ~ **un bain** to run a bath; **il a coulé une bielle** (*AUTO*) his big end went; ~ **de source** to follow on naturally; ~ **à pic** to sink *ou* go straight to the bottom.

couleur [kulœʀ] *nf* colour (*BRIT*), color (*US*); (*CARTES*) suit; ~**s** *nfpl* (*du teint*) colo(u)r *sg*; **les** ~**s** (*MIL*) the colo(u)rs; **en** ~**s** (*film*) in colo(u)r; **télévision en** ~**s** colo(u)r television; **de** ~ (*homme, femme*) colo(u)red; **sous** ~ **de** on the pretext of.

couleuvre [kulœvʀ(ə)] *nf* grass snake.

coulisse [kulis] *nf* (*TECH*) runner; ~**s** *nfpl* (*THÉÂT*) wings; (*fig*): **dans les** ~**s** behind the scenes; **porte à** ~ sliding door.

coulisser [kulise] *vi* to slide, run.

couloir [kulwaʀ] *nm* corridor, passage; (*d'avion*) aisle; (*de bus*) gangway; (: *sur la route*) bus lane; (*SPORT: de piste*) lane; (*GÉO*) gully; ~ **aérien** air corridor *ou* lane; ~ **de navigation** shipping lane.

coulpe [kulp(ə)] *nf*: **battre sa** ~ to repent openly.

coup [ku] *nm* (*heurt, choc*) knock; (*affectif*) blow, shock; (*agressif*) blow; (*avec arme à feu*) shot; (*de l'horloge*) chime; stroke; (*SPORT*) stroke; shot; blow; (*fam: fois*) time; (*ÉCHECS*) move; ~ **de coude/genou** nudge (with the elbow)/with the knee; **à** ~**s de hache/marteau** (hitting) with an axe/a hammer; ~ **de tonnerre** clap of thunder; ~ **de sonnette** ring of the bell; ~ **de crayon/pinceau** stroke of the pencil/brush; **donner un** ~ **de balai** to sweep up, give the floor a sweep; **donner un** ~ **de chiffon** to go round with the duster; **avoir le** ~ (*fig*) to have the knack; **être dans le/hors du** ~ to be/not to be in on it; **boire un** ~ to have a drink; **d'un seul** ~ (*subitement*) suddenly; (*à la fois*) at one go; in one blow; **du** ~ so (you see); **du premier** ~ first time *ou* go, at the first attempt; **du même** ~ at the same time; **à** ~ **sûr** definitely, without fail; **après** ~ afterwards; ~ **sur** ~ in quick succession; **être sur un** ~ to be on to something; **sur le** ~ outright; **sous le** ~ **de** (*surprise etc*) under the influence of; **tomber sous le** ~ **de la loi** to constitute a statutory offence; **à tous les** ~**s** every time; **il a raté son** ~ he missed his turn; **pour le** ~ for once; ~ **bas** (*fig*): **donner un** ~ **bas à qn** to hit sb below the belt; ~ **de chance** stroke of luck; ~ **de chapeau** (*fig*) pat on the back; ~ **de couteau** stab (of a knife); ~ **dur** hard blow; ~ **d'éclat** (great) feat; ~ **d'envoi** kick-off; ~ **d'essai** first attempt; ~ **d'état** coup d'état; ~ **de feu** shot; ~ **de filet** (*POLICE*) haul; ~ **de foudre** (*fig*) love at first sight; ~ **fourré** stab in the back; ~ **franc** free kick; ~ **de frein** (sharp) braking *no pl*; ~ **de grâce** coup de grâce; ~ **du lapin** (*AUTO*) whiplash; ~ **de main: donner un** ~ **de main à qn** to give sb a (helping) hand; ~ **de maître** master stroke; ~ **d'œil** glance; ~ **de pied** kick; ~ **de poing** punch; ~ **de soleil** sunburn *no pl*; ~ **de téléphone** phone call; ~ **de tête** (*fig*) (sudden) impulse; ~ **de théâtre** (*fig*) dramatic turn of events; ~ **de vent** gust of wind; **en** ~ **de vent** (*rapidement*) in a tearing hurry.

coupable [kupabl(ə)] *adj* guilty; (*pensée*) guilty, culpable ♦ *nm/f* (*gén*) culprit; (*JUR*) guilty party; ~ **de** guilty of.

coupant, e [kupā, -āt] *adj* (*lame*) sharp; (*fig: voix, ton*) cutting.

coupe [kup] *nf* (*verre*) goblet; (*à fruits*) dish; (*SPORT*) cup; (*de cheveux, de vêtement*) cut; (*graphique, plan*) (cross) section; **être sous la** ~ **de** to be under the control of; **faire des** ~**s sombres dans** to make drastic cuts in.

coupé, e [kupe] *adj* (*communications, route*) cut, blocked; (*vêtement*): **bien/mal** ~ well/badly cut ♦ *nm* (*AUTO*) coupé.

coupe-circuit [kupsiʀkɥi] *nm inv* cutout, circuit breaker.

coupée [kupe] *nf* (*NAVIG*) gangway.

coupe-feu [kupfø] *nm inv* firebreak.

coupe-gorge [kupgɔʀʒ(ə)] *nm inv* cut-throats' den.

coupe-ongles [kupɔ̃gl(ə)] *nm inv* nail clippers; (*ciseaux*) nail scissors.

coupe-papier [kuppapje] *nm inv* paper knife.

couper [kupe] *vt* to cut; (*retrancher*) to cut (out), take out; (*route, courant*) to cut off; (*appétit*) to take away; (*fièvre*) to take down, reduce; (*vin, cidre*) to blend; (: *à table*) to dilute (with water) ♦ *vi* to cut; (*prendre un raccourci*) to take a short-cut; (*CARTES: diviser le paquet*) to cut; (: *avec l'atout*) to trump; **se** ~ (*se blesser*) to cut o.s.; (*en témoignant etc*) to give o.s. away; ~ **l'appétit à qn** to spoil sb's appetite; ~ **la parole à qn** to cut sb short; ~ **les vivres à qn** to cut off sb's vital supplies; ~ **le contact** *ou* **l'allumage** (*AUTO*) to turn off the ignition; ~ **les ponts avec qn** to break with sb; **se faire** ~ **les cheveux** to have *ou* get one's hair cut.

couperet [kupʀɛ] *nm* cleaver, chopper.

couperosé, e [kupʀoze] *adj* blotchy.

couple [kupl(ə)] *nm* couple; ~ **de torsion** torque.

coupler [kuple] *vt* to couple (together).

couplet [kuplɛ] *nm* verse.

coupleur [kuplœʀ] *nm*: ~ **acoustique** acoustic

coupler.

coupole [kupɔl] *nf* dome; cupola.

coupon [kupɔ̃] *nm* (*ticket*) coupon; (*de tissu*) remnant; roll.

coupon-réponse, *pl* **coupons-réponses** [kupɔ̃repɔ̃s] *nm* reply coupon.

coupure [kupyʀ] *nf* cut; (*billet de banque*) note; (*de journal*) cutting; ~ **de courant** power cut.

cour [kuʀ] *nf* (*de ferme, jardin*) (court)yard; (*d'immeuble*) back yard; (*JUR, royale*) court; **faire la** ~ **à qn** to court sb; ~ **d'appel** appeal court (*BRIT*), appellate court (*US*); ~ **d'assises** court of assizes, ≈ Crown Court (*BRIT*); ~ **de cassation** final court of appeal; ~ **des comptes** (*ADMIN*) revenue court; ~ **martiale** court-martial; ~ **de récréation** (*SCOL*) schoolyard, playground.

courage [kuʀaʒ] *nm* courage, bravery.

courageusement [kuʀaʒøzmɑ̃] *adv* bravely, courageously.

courageux, euse [kuʀaʒø, -øz] *adj* brave, courageous.

couramment [kuʀamɑ̃] *adv* commonly; (*parler*) fluently.

courant, e [kuʀɑ̃, -ɑ̃t] *adj* (*fréquent*) common; (*COMM, gén: normal*) standard; (*en cours*) current ♦ *nm* current; (*fig*) movement, trend; **être au** ~ **(de)** (*fait, nouvelle*) to know (about); **mettre qn au** ~ **(de)** (*fait, nouvelle*) to tell sb (about); (*nouveau travail etc*) to teach sb the basics (of), brief sb (about); **se tenir au** ~ **(de)** (*techniques etc*) to keep o.s. up-to-date (on); **dans le** ~ **de** (*pendant*) in the course of; ~ **octobre** *etc* in the course of October *etc*; **le 10** ~ (*COMM*) the 10th inst; ~ **d'air** draught (*BRIT*), draft (*US*); ~ **électrique** (electric) current, power.

courbature [kuʀbatyʀ] *nf* ache.

courbaturé, e [kuʀbatyʀe] *adj* aching.

courbe [kuʀb(ə)] *adj* curved ♦ *nf* curve; ~ **de niveau** contour line.

courber [kuʀbe] *vt* to bend; ~ **la tête** to bow one's head; **se** ~ *vi* (*branche etc*) to bend, curve; (*personne*) to bend (down).

courbette [kuʀbɛt] *nf* low bow.

coure [kuʀ] *etc vb voir* **courir**.

coureur, euse [kuʀœʀ, -øz] *nm/f* (*SPORT*) runner (*ou* driver); (*péj*) womanizer/manhunter; ~ **cycliste/automobile** racing cyclist/driver.

courge [kuʀʒ(ə)] *nf* (*BOT*) gourd; (*CULIN*) marrow.

courgette [kuʀʒɛt] *nf* courgette (*BRIT*), zucchini (*US*).

courir [kuʀiʀ] *vi* (*gén*) to run; (*se dépêcher*) to rush; (*fig: rumeurs*) to go round; (*COMM: intérêt*) to accrue ♦ *vt* (*SPORT: épreuve*) to compete in; (*risque*) to run; (*danger*) to face; ~ **les cafés/bals** to do the rounds of the cafés/dances; **le bruit court que** the rumour is going round that; **par les temps qui courent** at the present time; ~ **après qn** to run after

sb, chase (after) sb; **laisser** ~ to let things alone; **faire** ~ **qn** to make sb run around (all over the place); **tu peux (toujours)** ~! you've got a hope!

couronne [kuʀɔn] *nf* crown; (*de fleurs*) wreath, circlet; ~ **(funéraire ou mortuaire)** (funeral) wreath.

couronnement [kuʀɔnmɑ̃] *nm* coronation, crowning; (*fig*) crowning achievement.

couronner [kuʀɔne] *vt* to crown.

courons [kuʀɔ̃], **courrai** [kuʀe] *etc vb voir* **courir**.

courre [kuʀ] *vb voir* **chasse**.

courrier [kuʀje] *nm* mail, post; (*lettres à écrire*) letters *pl*; (*rubrique*) column; **qualité** ~ letter quality; **long/moyen** ~ *adj* (*AVIAT*) long-/medium-haul; ~ **du cœur** problem page; ~ **électronique** electronic mail, E-mail.

courroie [kuʀwa] *nf* strap; (*TECH*) belt; ~ **de transmission/de ventilateur** driving/fan belt.

courrons [kuʀɔ̃] *etc vb voir* **courir**.

courroucé, e [kuʀuse] *adj* wrathful.

cours [kuʀ] *vb voir* **courir** ♦ *nm* (*leçon*) lesson, class; (*série de leçons*) course; (*cheminement*) course; (*écoulement*) flow; (*avenue*) walk; (*COMM*) rate; price; (*BOURSE*) quotation; **donner libre** ~ **à** to give free expression to; **avoir** ~ (*monnaie*) to be legal tender; (*fig*) to be current; (*SCOL*) to have a class *ou* lecture; **en** ~ (*année*) current; (*travaux*) in progress; **en** ~ **de route** on the way; **au** ~ **de** in the course of, during; **le** ~ **du change** the exchange rate; ~ **d'eau** waterway; ~ **élémentaire (CE)** 2nd and 3rd years of primary school; ~ **moyen (CM)** 4th and 5th years of primary school; ~ **préparatoire** ≈ infants' class (*BRIT*), ≈ 1st grade (*US*); ~ **du soir** night school.

course [kuʀs(ə)] *nf* running; (*SPORT: épreuve*) race; (*trajet: du soleil*) course; (*: d'un projectile*) flight; (*: d'une pièce mécanique*) travel; (*excursion*) outing; climb; (*d'un taxi, autocar*) journey, trip; (*petite mission*) errand; ~**s** *nfpl* (*achats*) shopping *sg*; (*HIPPISME*) races; **faire les ou ses** ~**s** to go shopping; **jouer aux** ~**s** to bet on the races; **à bout de** ~ (*épuisé*) exhausted; ~ **automobile** car race; ~ **de côte** (*AUTO*) hill climb; ~ **par étapes ou d'étapes** race in stages; ~ **d'obstacles** obstacle race; ~ **à pied** walking race; ~ **de vitesse** sprint; ~**s de chevaux** horse racing.

coursier, ière [kuʀsje, -jɛʀ] *nm/f* courier.

court, e [kuʀ, kuʀt(ə)] *adj* short ♦ *adv* short ♦ *nm*: ~ **(de tennis)** (tennis) court; **tourner** ~ to come to a sudden end; **couper** ~ **à** to cut short; **à** ~ **de** short of; **prendre qn de** ~ to catch sb unawares; **pour faire** ~ briefly, to cut a long story short; **ça fait** ~ that's not very long; **tirer à la** ~**e paille** to draw lots; **faire la** ~**e échelle à qn** to give sb a leg up; ~ **métrage** (*CINÉ*) short (film).

court-bouillon, *pl* **courts-bouillons** [kuʀbujɔ̃] *nm* court-bouillon.

court-circuit, *pl* **courts-circuits** [kuʀsiʀkɥi] *nm* short-circuit.

court-circuiter [kuʀsiʀkɥite] *vt* (*fig*) to bypass.

courtier, ière [kuʀtje, -jɛʀ] *nm/f* broker.

courtisan [kuʀtizɑ̃] *nm* courtier.

courtisane [kuʀtizan] *nf* courtesan.

courtiser [kuʀtize] *vt* to court, woo.

courtois, e [kuʀtwa, -waz] *adj* courteous.

courtoisement [kuʀtwazmɑ̃] *adv* courteously.

courtoisie [kuʀtwazi] *nf* courtesy.

couru, e [kuʀy] *pp de* **courir** ♦ *adj* (*spectacle etc*) popular; **c'est ~ (d'avance)!** (*fam*) it's a safe bet!

cousais [kuzɛ] *etc vb voir* **coudre**.

couscous [kuskus] *nm* couscous.

cousin, e [kuzɛ̃, -in] *nm/f* cousin ♦ *nm* (*ZOOL*) mosquito; **~ germain** first cousin.

cousons [kuzɔ̃] *etc vb voir* **coudre**.

coussin [kusɛ̃] *nm* cushion; **~ d'air** (*TECH*) air cushion.

cousu, e [kuzy] *pp de* **coudre** ♦ *adj*: **~ d'or** rolling in riches.

coût [ku] *nm* cost; **le ~ de la vie** the cost of living.

coûtant [kutɑ̃] *adj m*: **au prix ~** at cost price.

couteau, x [kuto] *nm* knife; **~ à cran d'arrêt** flick-knife; **~ de cuisine** kitchen knife; **~ à pain** bread knife; **~ de poche** pocket knife.

couteau-scie, *pl* **couteaux-scies** [kutosi] *nm* serrated(-edged) knife.

coutelier, ière [kutəlje, -jɛʀ] *adj*: **l'industrie ~ière** the cutlery industry ♦ *nm/f* cutler.

coutellerie [kutɛlʀi] *nf* cutlery shop; cutlery.

coûter [kute] *vt* to cost ♦ *vi*: **~ à qn** to cost sb a lot; **~ cher** to be expensive; **~ cher à qn** (*fig*) to cost sb dear *ou* dearly; **combien ça coûte?** how much is it?, what does it cost?; **coûte que coûte** at all costs.

coûteux, euse [kutø, -øz] *adj* costly, expensive.

coutume [kutym] *nf* custom; **de ~** usual, customary.

coutumier, ière [kutymje, -jɛʀ] *adj* customary: **elle est coutumière du fait** that's her usual trick.

couture [kutyʀ] *nf* sewing; dress-making; (*points*) seam.

couturier [kutyʀje] *nm* fashion designer, couturier.

couturière [kutyʀjɛʀ] *nf* dressmaker.

couvée [kuve] *nf* brood, clutch.

couvent [kuvɑ̃] *nm* (*de sœurs*) convent; (*de frères*) monastery; (*établissement scolaire*) convent (school).

couver [kuve] *vt* to hatch; (*maladie*) to be sickening for ♦ *vi* (*feu*) to smoulder (*BRIT*), smolder (*US*); (*révolte*) to be brewing; **~ qn/qch des yeux** to look lovingly at sb/sth; (*convoiter*) to look longingly at sb/sth.

couvercle [kuvɛʀkl(ə)] *nm* lid; (*de bombe aéro-*sol etc, qui se visse*) cap, top.

couvert, e [kuvɛʀ, -ɛʀt(ə)] *pp de* **couvrir** ♦ *adj* (*ciel*) overcast; (*coiffé d'un chapeau*) wearing a hat ♦ *nm* place setting; (*place à table*) place; (*au restaurant*) cover charge; **~s** *nmpl* place settings; cutlery *sg*; **~ de** covered with *ou* in; **bien ~** (*habillé*) well wrapped up; **mettre le ~** to lay the table; **à ~** under cover; **sous le ~ de** under the shelter of; (*fig*) under cover of.

couverture [kuvɛʀtyʀ] *nf* (*de lit*) blanket; (*de bâtiment*) roofing; (*de livre, fig: d'un espion etc, ASSURANCES*) cover; (*PRESSE*) coverage; **de ~** (*lettre etc*) covering; **~ chauffante** electric blanket.

couveuse [kuvøz] *nf* (*à poules*) sitter, brooder; (*de maternité*) incubator.

couvre [kuvʀ(ə)] *etc vb voir* **couvrir**.

couvre-chef [kuvʀəʃɛf] *nm* hat.

couvre-feu, x [kuvʀəfø] *nm* curfew.

couvre-lit [kuvʀəli] *nm* bedspread.

couvre-pieds [kuvʀəpje] *nm inv* quilt.

couvreur [kuvʀœʀ] *nm* roofer.

couvrir [kuvʀiʀ] *vt* to cover; (*dominer, étouffer: voix, pas*) to drown out; (*erreur*) to cover up; (*ZOOL: s'accoupler à*) to cover; **se ~** (*ciel*) to cloud over; (*s'habiller*) to cover up, wrap up; (*se coiffer*) to put on one's hat; (*par une assurance*) to cover o.s.; **se ~ de** (*fleurs, boutons*) to become covered in.

cover-girl [kɔvœʀgœʀl] *nf* model.

cow-boy [kobɔj] *nm* cowboy.

coyote [kɔjɔt] *nm* coyote.

CP *sigle m* = **cours préparatoire**.

CPAM *sigle f* (= *Caisse primaire d'assurances maladie*) *health insurance office*.

cps *abr* (= *caractères par seconde*) cps.

cpt *abr* = **comptant**.

CQFD *abr* (= *ce qu'il fallait démontrer*) QED (= *quod erat demonstrandum*).

CR *sigle m* = **compte rendu**.

crabe [kʀab] *nm* crab.

crachat [kʀaʃa] *nm* spittle *no pl*, spit *no pl*.

craché, e [kʀaʃe] *adj*: **son père tout ~** the spitting image of his (*ou* her) father.

cracher [kʀaʃe] *vi* to spit ♦ *vt* to spit out; (*fig: lave etc*) to belch (out); **~ du sang** to spit blood.

crachin [kʀaʃɛ̃] *nm* drizzle.

crachiner [kʀaʃine] *vi* to drizzle.

crachoir [kʀaʃwaʀ] *nm* spittoon; (*de dentiste*) bowl.

crachotement [kʀaʃɔtmɑ̃] *nm* crackling *no pl*.

crachoter [kʀaʃɔte] *vi* (*haut-parleur, radio*) to crackle.

crack [kʀak] *nm* (*intellectuel*) whizzkid; (*sportif*) ace; (*poulain*) hot favourite (*BRIT*) *ou* favorite (*US*).

Cracovie [kʀakɔvi] *n* Cracow.

cradingue [kʀadɛ̃g] *adj* (*fam*) disgustingly dirty, filthy-dirty.

craie [kʀɛ] *nf* chalk.

craignais [kʀɛɲɛ] *etc vb voir* **craindre**.

craindre [kʀɛ̃dʀ(ə)] *vt* to fear, be afraid of; *(être sensible à: chaleur, froid)* to be easily damaged by; **~ de/que** to be afraid of/that; **je crains qu'il (ne) vienne** I am afraid he may come.

crainte [kʀɛ̃t] *nf* fear; **de ~ de/que** for fear of/that.

craintif, ive [kʀɛ̃tif, -iv] *adj* timid.

craintivement [kʀɛ̃tivmɑ̃] *adv* timidly.

cramer [kʀame] *vi (fam)* to burn.

cramoisi, e [kʀamwazi] *adj* crimson.

crampe [kʀɑ̃p] *nf* cramp; **~ d'estomac** stomach cramp.

crampon [kʀɑ̃põ] *nm (de semelle)* stud; *(ALPINISME)* crampon.

cramponner [kʀɑ̃pɔne]: **se ~** *vi:* **se ~ (à)** to hang *ou* cling on (to).

cran [kʀɑ̃] *nm (entaille)* notch; *(de courroie)* hole; *(courage)* guts *pl;* **~ d'arrêt** safety catch; **~ de mire** bead; **~ de sûreté** safety catch.

crâne [kʀɑn] *nm* skull.

crâner [kʀɑne] *vi (fam)* to swank, show off.

crânien, ne [kʀɑnjɛ̃, -ɛn] *adj* cranial, skull *cpd,* brain *cpd.*

crapaud [kʀapo] *nm* toad.

crapule [kʀapyl] *nf* villain.

crapuleux, euse [kʀapylø, -øz] *adj:* **crime ~** villainous crime.

craquelure [kʀaklyʀ] *nf* crack; crackle *no pl.*

craquement [kʀakmɑ̃] *nm* crack, snap; *(du plancher)* creak, creaking *no pl.*

craquer [kʀake] *vi (bois, plancher)* to creak; *(fil, branche)* to snap; *(couture)* to come apart, burst; *(fig)* to break down, fall apart; *(: être enthousiasmé)* to go wild ♦ *vt:* **~ une allumette** to strike a match.

crasse [kʀas] *nf* grime, filth ♦ *adj (fig: ignorance)* crass.

crasseux, euse [kʀasø, øz] *adj* filthy.

crassier [kʀasje] *nm* slag heap.

cratère [kʀatɛʀ] *nm* crater.

cravache [kʀavaʃ] *nf (riding)* crop.

cravacher [kʀavaʃe] *vt* to use the crop on.

cravate [kʀavat] *nf* tie.

cravater [kʀavate] *vt* to put a tie on; *(fig)* to grab round the neck.

crawl [kʀol] *nm* crawl.

crawlé, e [kʀole] *adj:* **dos ~** backstroke.

crayeux, euse [kʀɛjø, -øz] *adj* chalky.

crayon [kʀɛjõ] *nm* pencil; *(de rouge à lèvres etc)* stick, pencil; **écrire au ~** to write in pencil; **~ à bille** ball-point pen; **~ de couleur** crayon; **~ optique** light pen.

crayon-feutre, *pl* **crayons-feutres** [kʀɛjõføtʀ(ə)] *nm* felt(-tip) pen.

crayonner [kʀɛjɔne] *vt* to scribble, sketch.

CRDP *sigle m (= Centre régional de documentation pédagogique)* teachers' resource centre.

créance [kʀeɑ̃s] *nf (COMM)* (financial) claim, (recoverable) debt; **donner ~ à qch** to lend credence to sth.

créancier, ière [kʀeɑ̃sje, -jɛʀ] *nm/f* creditor.

créateur, trice [kʀeatœʀ, -tʀis] *adj* creative ♦ *nm/f* creator; **le C~** *(REL)* the Creator.

créatif, ive [kʀeatif, -iv] *adj* creative.

création [kʀeasjõ] *nf* creation.

créativité [kʀeativite] *nf* creativity.

créature [kʀeatyʀ] *nf* creature.

crécelle [kʀesɛl] *nf* rattle.

crèche [kʀɛʃ] *nf (de Noël)* crib; *(garderie)* crèche, day nursery.

---

*In France the Christmas crib (**crèche**) usually contains figurines representing a miller, a wood-cutter and other villagers in addition to the Holy Family and the traditional cow, donkey and shepherds. Figurines representing the magi are added to the nativity scene at Epiphany; see also **fête des Rois**.*

---

crédence [kʀedɑ̃s] *nf* (small) sideboard.

crédibilité [kʀedibilite] *nf* credibility.

crédible [kʀedibl(ə)] *adj* credible.

CREDIF [kʀedif] *sigle m (= Centre de recherche et d'étude pour la diffusion du français)* official body promoting use of the French language.

crédit [kʀedi] *nm (gén)* credit; **~s** *nmpl* funds; **payer/acheter à ~** to pay/buy on credit *ou* on easy terms; **faire ~ à qn** to give sb credit; **~ municipal** pawnshop; **~ relais** bridging loan.

crédit-bail, *pl* **crédits-bails** [kʀedibaj] *nm (ÉCON)* leasing.

créditer [kʀedite] *vt:* **~ un compte (de)** to credit an account (with).

créditeur, trice [kʀeditœʀ, -tʀis] *adj* in credit, credit *cpd* ♦ *nm/f* customer in credit.

credo [kʀedo] *nm* credo, creed.

crédule [kʀedyl] *adj* credulous, gullible.

crédulité [kʀedylite] *nf* credulity, gullibility.

créer [kʀee] *vt* to create; *(THÉÂT: pièce)* to produce (for the first time); *(: rôle)* to create.

crémaillère [kʀemajɛʀ] *nf (RAIL)* rack; *(tige crantée)* trammel; **direction à ~** *(AUTO)* rack and pinion steering; **pendre la ~** to have a house-warming party.

crémation [kʀemasjõ] *nf* cremation.

crématoire [kʀematwaʀ] *adj:* **four ~** crematorium.

crématorium [kʀematɔʀjɔm] *nm* crematorium.

crème [kʀɛm] *nf* cream; *(entremets)* cream dessert ♦ *adj inv* cream; **un (café) ~** ≈ a white coffee; **~ chantilly** whipped cream, crème Chantilly; **~ fouettée** whipped cream; **~ glacée** ice cream; **~ à raser** shaving cream.

crémerie [kʀɛmʀi] *nf* dairy; *(tearoom)* teashop.

crémeux, euse [kʀemø, -øz] *adj* creamy.

crémier, ière [kʀemje, -jɛʀ] *nm/f* dairyman/woman.

créneau, x [kʀeno] *nm (de fortification)* crenel(le); (*fig, aussi* COMM) gap, slot; (AUTO): **faire un** ~ to reverse into a parking space (*between cars alongside the kerb*).

créole [kʀeɔl] *adj, nm/f* Creole.

créosote [kʀeozɔt] *nf* creosote.

crêpe [kʀɛp] *nf* (*galette*) pancake ♦ *nm* (*tissu*) crêpe; (*de deuil*) black mourning crêpe; (*ruban*) black armband (*ou* hatband *ou* ribbon); **semelle (de)** ~ crêpe sole; ~ **de Chine** crêpe de Chine.

crêpé, e [kʀepe] *adj* (*cheveux*) backcombed.

crêperie [kʀɛpʀi] *nf* pancake shop *ou* restaurant.

crépi [kʀepi] *nm* roughcast.

crépir [kʀepiʀ] *vt* to roughcast.

crépitement [kʀepitmɑ̃] *nm* (*du feu*) crackling *no pl*; (*d'une arme automatique*) rattle *no pl*.

crépiter [kʀepite] *vi* to sputter, splutter, crackle.

crépon [kʀepɔ̃] *nm* seersucker.

CREPS [kʀɛps] *sigle m* (= *Centre régional d'éducation physique et sportive*) ≈ sports *ou* leisure centre.

crépu, e [kʀepy] *adj* frizzy, fuzzy.

crépuscule [kʀepyskyl] *nm* twilight, dusk.

crescendo [kʀeʃɛndo] *nm, adv* (MUS) crescendo; **aller** ~ (*fig*) to rise higher and higher, grow ever greater.

cresson [kʀesɔ̃] *nm* watercress.

Crète [kʀɛt] *nf*: **la** ~ Crete.

crête [kʀɛt] *nf* (*de coq*) comb; (*de vague, montagne*) crest.

crétin, e [kʀetɛ̃, -in] *nm/f* cretin.

crétois, e [kʀetwa, -waz] *adj* Cretan.

cretonne [kʀətɔn] *nf* cretonne.

creuser [kʀøze] *vt* (*trou, tunnel*) to dig; (*sol*) to dig a hole in; (*bois*) to hollow out; (*fig*) to go (deeply) into; **ça creuse** that gives you a real appetite; **se** ~ (**la cervelle**) to rack one's brains.

creuset [kʀøzɛ] *nm* crucible; (*fig*) melting pot; (*severe*) test.

creux, euse [kʀø, -øz] *adj* hollow ♦ *nm* hollow; (*fig: sur graphique etc*) trough; **heures creuses** slack periods; off-peak periods; **le** ~ **de l'estomac** the pit of the stomach.

crevaison [kʀəvɛzɔ̃] *nf* puncture, flat.

crevant, e [kʀəvɑ̃, -ɑ̃t] *adj* (*fam: fatigant*) knackering; (: *très drôle*) priceless.

crevasse [kʀəvas] *nf* (*dans le sol*) crack, fissure; (*de glacier*) crevasse; (*de la peau*) crack.

crevé, e [kʀəve] *adj* (*fam: fatigué*) worn out, dead beat.

crève-cœur [kʀɛvkœʀ] *nm inv* heartbreak.

crever [kʀəve] *vt* (*papier*) to tear, break; (*tambour, ballon*) to burst ♦ *vi* (*pneu*) to burst; (*automobiliste*) to have a puncture (BRIT) *ou* a flat (tire) (US); (*abcès, outre, nuage*) to burst (open); (*fam*) to die; **cela lui a crevé un œil** it blinded him in one eye; ~ **l'écran** to have real screen presence.

crevette [kʀəvɛt] *nf*: ~ (**rose**) prawn; ~ **grise** shrimp.

CRF *sigle f* (= *Croix-Rouge française*) French Red Cross.

cri [kʀi] *nm* cry, shout; (*d'animal: spécifique*) cry, call; **à grands** ~**s** at the top of one's voice; **c'est le dernier** ~ (*fig*) it's the latest fashion.

criant, e [kʀijɑ̃, -ɑ̃t] *adj* (*injustice*) glaring.

criard, e [kʀijaʀ, -aʀd(ə)] *adj* (*couleur*) garish, loud; (*voix*) yelling.

crible [kʀibl(ə)] *nm* riddle; (*mécanique*) screen, jig; **passer qch au** ~ to put sth through a riddle; (*fig*) to go over sth with a fine-tooth comb.

criblé, e [kʀible] *adj*: ~ **de** riddled with.

cric [kʀik] *nm* (AUTO) jack.

cricket [kʀikɛt] *nm* cricket.

criée [kʀije] *nf*: (**vente à la**) ~ (sale by) auction.

crier [kʀije] *vi* (*pour appeler*) to shout, cry (out); (*de peur, de douleur etc*) to scream, yell; (*fig: grincer*) to squeal, screech ♦ *vt* (*ordre, injure*) to shout (out), yell (out); **sans** ~ **gare** without warning; ~ **grâce** to cry for mercy; ~ **au secours** to shout for help.

crieur, euse [kʀijœʀ, -øz] *nm/f*: ~ **de journaux** newspaper seller.

crime [kʀim] *nm* crime; (*meurtre*) murder.

Crimée [kʀime] *nf*: **la** ~ the Crimea.

criminaliste [kʀiminalist(ə)] *nm/f* specialist in criminal law.

criminalité [kʀiminalite] *nf* criminality, crime.

criminel, le [kʀiminɛl] *adj* criminal ♦ *nm/f* criminal; murderer; ~ **de guerre** war criminal.

criminologie [kʀiminɔlɔʒi] *nf* criminology.

criminologiste [kʀiminɔlɔʒist(ə)] *nm/f* criminologist.

criminologue [kʀiminɔlɔg] *nm/f* criminologist.

crin [kʀɛ̃] *nm* hair *no pl*; (*fibre*) horsehair; **à tous** ~**s, à tout** ~ diehard, out-and-out.

crinière [kʀinjɛʀ] *nf* mane.

crique [kʀik] *nf* creek, inlet.

criquet [kʀikɛ] *nm* grasshopper.

crise [kʀiz] *nf* crisis (*pl* crises); (MÉD) attack; fit; ~ **cardiaque** heart attack; ~ **de foi** crisis of belief; ~ **de foie** bilious attack; ~ **de nerfs** attack of nerves.

crispant, e [kʀispɑ̃, -ɑ̃t] *adj* annoying, irritating.

crispation [kʀispasjɔ̃] *nf* (*spasme*) twitch; (*contraction*) contraction; tenseness.

crispé, e [kʀispe] *adj* tense, nervous.

crisper [kʀispe] *vt* to tense; (*poings*) to clench; **se** ~ to tense; to clench; (*personne*) to get tense.

crissement [kʀismɑ̃] *nm* crunch; rustle; screech.

crisser [kʀise] *vi* (*neige*) to crunch; (*tissu*) to rustle; (*pneu*) to screech.

cristal, aux [kʀistal, -o] *nm* crystal ♦ *nmpl* (*objets*) crystal(ware) *sg*; ~ **de plomb** (lead) crystal; ~ **de roche** rock-crystal; **cristaux de soude** washing soda *sg.*

cristallin, e [kʀistalɛ̃, -in] *adj* crystal-clear ♦ *nm* (*ANAT*) crystalline lens.

cristalliser [kʀistalize] *vi, vt,* **se** ~ *vi* to crystallize.

critère [kʀitɛʀ] *nm* criterion (*pl* -ia).

critiquable [kʀitikabl(ə)] *adj* open to criticism.

critique [kʀitik] *adj* critical ♦ *nm/f* (*de théâtre, musique*) critic ♦ *nf* criticism; (*THÉÂT etc: article*) review; **la** ~ (*activité*) criticism; (*personnes*) the critics *pl.*

critiquer [kʀitike] *vt* (*dénigrer*) to criticize; (*évaluer, juger*) to assess, examine (critically).

croasser [kʀɔase] *vi* to caw.

croate [kʀɔat] *adj* Croatian ♦ *nm* (*LING*) Croat, Croatian.

Croatie [kʀɔasi] *nf:* **la** ~ Croatia.

croc [kʀo] *nm* (*dent*) fang; (*de boucher*) hook.

croc-en-jambe, *pl* **crocs-en-jambe** [kʀɔkɑ̃-ʒɑ̃b] *nm:* **faire un** ~ **à qn** to trip sb up.

croche [kʀɔʃ] *nf* (*MUS*) quaver (*BRIT*), eighth note (*US*); **double** ~ semiquaver (*BRIT*), sixteenth note (*US*).

croche-pied [kʀɔʃpje] *nm* = **croc-en-jambe.**

crochet [kʀɔʃɛ] *nm* hook; (*clef*) picklock; (*détour*) detour; (*BOXE*): ~ **du gauche** left hook; (*TRICOT: aiguille*) crochet hook; (*: technique*) crochet; ~**s** *nmpl* (*TYPO*) square brackets; **vivre aux** ~**s de qn** to live *ou* sponge off sb.

crocheter [kʀɔʃte] *vt* (*serrure*) to pick.

crochu, e [kʀɔʃy] *adj* hooked; claw-like.

crocodile [kʀɔkɔdil] *nm* crocodile.

crocus [kʀɔkys] *nm* crocus.

croire [kʀwaʀ] *vt* to believe; ~ **qn honnête** to believe sb (to be) honest; **se** ~ **fort** to think one is strong; ~ **que** to believe *ou* think that; **vous croyez?** do you think so?; ~ **être/ faire** to think one is/does; ~ **à,** ~ **en** to believe in.

croîs [kʀwa] *etc vb voir* **croître.**

croisade [kʀwazad] *nf* crusade.

croisé, e [kʀwaze] *adj* (*veston*) double-breasted ♦ *nm* (*guerrier*) crusader ♦ *nf* (*fenêtre*) window, casement; ~**e d'ogives** intersecting ribs; **à la** ~**e des chemins** at the crossroads.

croisement [kʀwazmɑ̃] *nm* (*carrefour*) crossroads *sg*; (*BIO*) crossing; crossbreed.

croiser [kʀwaze] *vt* (*personne, voiture*) to pass; (*route*) to cross, cut across; (*BIO*) to cross ♦ *vi* (*NAVIG*) to cruise; ~ **les jambes/bras** to cross one's legs/fold one's arms; **se** ~ (*personnes, véhicules*) to pass each other; (*routes*) to cross, intersect; (*lettres*) to cross (in the post); (*regards*) to meet; **se** ~ **les bras** (*fig*) to twiddle one's thumbs.

croiseur [kʀwazœʀ] *nm* cruiser (*warship*).

croisière [kʀwazjɛʀ] *nf* cruise; **vitesse de** ~ (*AUTO etc*) cruising speed.

croisillon [kʀwazijɔ̃] *nm:* **motif/fenêtre à** ~**s** lattice pattern/window.

croissais [kʀwasɛ] *etc vb voir* **croître.**

croissance [kʀwasɑ̃s] *nf* growing, growth; **troubles de la** ~ growing pains; **maladie de** ~ growth disease; ~ **économique** economic growth.

croissant, e [kʀwasɑ̃, -ɑ̃t] *vb voir* **croître** ♦ *adj* growing; rising ♦ *nm* (*à manger*) croissant; (*motif*) crescent; ~ **de lune** crescent moon.

croître [kʀwatʀ(ə)] *vi* to grow; (*lune*) to wax.

croix [kʀwa] *nf* cross; **en** ~ *adj, adv* in the form of a cross; **la C**~ **Rouge** the Red Cross.

croquant, e [kʀokɑ̃, -ɑ̃t] *adj* crisp, crunchy ♦ *nm/f* (*péj*) yokel, (country) bumpkin.

croque-madame [kʀɔkmadam] *nm inv* toasted cheese sandwich with a fried egg on top.

croque-mitaine [kʀɔkmitɛn] *nm* bog(e)y-man (*pl* -men).

croque-monsieur [kʀɔkməsjø] *nm inv* toasted ham and cheese sandwich.

croque-mort [kʀɔkmɔʀ] *nm* (*péj*) pallbearer.

croquer [kʀoke] *vt* (*manger*) to crunch; to munch; (*dessiner*) to sketch ♦ *vi* to be crisp *ou* crunchy; **chocolat à** ~ plain dessert chocolate.

croquet [kʀoke] *nm* croquet.

croquette [kʀokɛt] *nf* croquette.

croquis [kʀoki] *nm* sketch.

cross(-country), *pl* **cross(-countries)** [kʀos(kuntʀi)] *nm* cross-country race *ou* run; cross-country racing *ou* running.

crosse [kʀos] *nf* (*de fusil*) butt; (*de revolver*) grip; (*d'évêque*) crook, crosier; (*de hockey*) hockey stick.

crotale [kʀɔtal] *nm* rattlesnake.

crotte [kʀɔt] *nf* droppings *pl;* ~! (*fam*) damn!

crotté, e [kʀote] *adj* muddy, mucky.

crottin [kʀɔtɛ̃] *nm:* ~ (**de cheval**) (horse) dung *ou* manure.

croulant, e [kʀulɑ̃, -ɑ̃t] *nm/f* (*fam*) old fogey.

crouler [kʀule] *vi* (*s'effondrer*) to collapse; (*être délabré*) to be crumbling.

croupe [kʀup] *nf* croup, rump; **en** ~ pillion.

croupier [kʀupje] *nm* croupier.

croupion [kʀupjɔ̃] *nm* (*d'un oiseau*) rump; (*CULIN*) parson's nose.

croupir [kʀupiʀ] *vi* to stagnate.

CROUS [kʀus] *sigle m* (= *Centre régional des œuvres universitaires et scolaires*) *students' representative body.*

croustade [kʀustad] *nf* (*CULIN*) croustade.

croustillant, e [kʀustijɑ̃, -ɑ̃t] *adj* crisp; (*fig*) spicy.

croustiller [kʀustije] *vi* to be crisp *ou* crusty.

croûte [kʀut] *nf* crust; (*du fromage*) rind; (*de vol-au-vent*) case; (*MÉD*) scab; **en** ~ (*CULIN*) in pastry, in a pie; ~ **aux champignons** mushrooms on toast; ~ **au fromage** cheese on toast *no pl;* ~ **de pain** (*morceau*) crust (of bread); ~ **terrestre** earth's crust.

croûton [kʀutɔ̃] *nm* (*CULIN*) crouton; (*bout du pain*) crust, heel.

croyable [kʀwajabl(ə)] *adj* believable, credible.

croyais [kʀwajɛ] *etc vb voir* **croire**.

croyance [kʀwajɑ̃s] *nf* belief.

croyant, e [kʀwajɑ̃, -ɑ̃t] *vb voir* **croire** ♦ *adj*: **être/ne pas être** ~ to be/not to be a believer ♦ *nm/f* believer.

Crozet [kʀɔzɛ] *n*: **les îles** ~ the Crozet Islands.

CRS *sigle fpl* (= *Compagnies républicaines de sécurité*) state security police force ♦ *sigle m* member of the CRS.

cru, e [kʀy] *pp de* **croire** ♦ *adj* (*non cuit*) raw; (*lumière, couleur*) harsh; (*description*) crude; (*paroles, langage: franc*) blunt; (: *grossier*) crude ♦ *nm* (*vignoble*) vineyard; (*vin*) wine ♦ *nf* (*d'un cours d'eau*) swelling, rising; **de son (propre)** ~ (*fig*) of his own devising; **monter à** ~ to ride bareback; **du** ~ local; **en** ~**e** in spate.

crû [kʀy] *pp de* **croître**.

cruauté [kʀyote] *nf* cruelty.

cruche [kʀyʃ] *nf* pitcher, (earthenware) jug.

crucial, e, aux [kʀysjal, -o] *adj* crucial.

crucifier [kʀysifje] *vt* to crucify.

crucifix [kʀysifi] *nm* crucifix.

crucifixion [kʀysifiksjɔ̃] *nf* crucifixion.

cruciforme [kʀysifɔʀm(ə)] *adj* cruciform, cross-shaped.

cruciverbiste [kʀysivɛʀbist(ə)] *nm/f* crossword puzzle enthusiast.

crudité [kʀydite] *nf* crudeness *no pl*; harshness *no pl*; ~**s** *nfpl* (*CULIN*) mixed salads (*as hors d'œuvre*).

crue [kʀy] *nf voir* **cru**.

cruel, le [kʀyɛl] *adj* cruel.

cruellement [kʀyɛlmɑ̃] *adv* cruelly.

crûment [kʀymɑ̃] *adv* (*voir cru*) harshly; bluntly; crudely.

crus, crûs [kʀy] *etc vb voir* **croire; croître**.

crustacés [kʀystase] *nmpl* shellfish.

crypte [kʀipt(ə)] *nf* crypt.

CSA *sigle f* (= *Conseil supérieur de l'audiovisuel*) French broadcasting regulatory body, ≈ IBA (*BRIT*), ≈ FCC (*US*).

CSCE *sigle f* = *Conférence sur la sécurité et la coopération en Europe*) CSCE.

cse *abr* = **cause**.

CSEN *sigle f* (= *Confédération des syndicats de l'éducation nationale*) group of teachers' unions.

CSG *sigle f* (= *contribution sociale généralisée*) supplementary social security contribution in aid of the underprivileged.

Cte *abr* = **Comtesse**.

CU *sigle f* = *communauté urbaine*.

Cuba [kyba] *nm*: **le** ~ Cuba.

cubage [kybaʒ] *nm* cubage, cubic content.

cubain, e [kybɛ̃, -ɛn] *adj* Cuban ♦ *nm/f*: **C**~, **e** Cuban.

cube [kyb] *nm* cube; (*jouet*) brick, building block; **gros** ~ powerful motorbike; **mètre** ~ cubic metre; **2 au** ~ = **8** 2 cubed is 8; **élever**

au ~ to cube.

cubique [kybik] *adj* cubic.

cubisme [kybism(ə)] *nm* cubism.

cubiste [kybist(ə)] *adj, nm/f* cubist.

cubitus [kybitys] *nm* ulna.

cueillette [kœjɛt] *nf* picking, gathering; harvest *ou* crop (of fruit).

cueillir [kœjiʀ] *vt* (*fruits, fleurs*) to pick, gather; (*fig*) to catch.

cuiller *ou* **cuillère** [kɥijɛʀ] *nf* spoon; ~ **à café** coffee spoon; (*CULIN*) ≈ teaspoonful; ~ **à soupe** soup spoon; (*CULIN*) ≈ tablespoonful.

cuillerée [kɥijʀe] *nf* spoonful; (*CULIN*): ~ **à soupe/café** tablespoonful/teaspoonful.

cuir [kɥiʀ] *nm* leather; (*avant tannage*) hide; ~ **chevelu** scalp.

cuirasse [kɥiʀas] *nf* breastplate.

cuirassé [kɥiʀase] *nm* (*NAVIG*) battleship.

cuire [kɥiʀ] *vt* (*aliments*) to cook; (*au four*) to bake; (*poterie*) to fire ♦ *vi* to cook; (*picoter*) to smart, sting, burn; **bien cuit** (*viande*) well done; **trop cuit** overdone; **pas assez cuit** underdone; **cuit à point** medium done; done to a turn.

cuisant, e [kɥizɑ̃, -ɑ̃t] *vb voir* **cuire** ♦ *adj* (*douleur*) smarting, burning; (*fig: souvenir, échec*) bitter.

cuisine [kɥizin] *nf* (*pièce*) kitchen; (*art culinaire*) cookery, cooking; (*nourriture*) cooking, food; **faire la** ~ to cook.

cuisiné, e [kɥizine] *adj*: **plat** ~ ready-made meal *ou* dish.

cuisiner [kɥizine] *vt* to cook; (*fam*) to grill ♦ *vi* to cook.

cuisinette [kɥizinɛt] *nf* kitchenette.

cuisinier, ière [kɥizinje, -jɛʀ] *nm/f* cook ♦ *nf* (*poêle*) cooker.

cuisis [kɥizi] *etc vb voir* **cuire**.

cuissardes [kɥisaʀd] *nfpl* (*de pêcheur*) waders; (*de femme*) thigh boots.

cuisse [kɥis] *nf* (*ANAT*) thigh; (*CULIN*) leg.

cuisson [kɥisɔ̃] *nf* cooking; (*de poterie*) firing.

cuissot [kɥiso] *nm* haunch.

cuistre [kɥistʀ(ə)] *nm* prig.

cuit, e [kɥi, -it] *pp de* **cuire** ♦ *nf* (*fam*): **prendre une** ~**e** to get plastered *ou* smashed.

cuivre [kɥivʀ(ə)] *nm* copper; **les** ~**s** (*MUS*) the brass; ~ **rouge** copper; ~ **jaune** brass.

cuivré, e [kɥivʀe] *adj* coppery; (*peau*) bronzed.

cul [ky] *nm* (*fam!*) arse (*BRIT !*), ass (*US !*), bum (*BRIT*); ~ **de bouteille** bottom of a bottle.

culasse [kylas] *nf* (*AUTO*) cylinder-head; (*de fusil*) breech.

culbute [kylbyt] *nf* somersault; (*accidentelle*) tumble, fall.

culbuter [kylbyte] *vi* to (take a) tumble, fall (head over heels).

culbuteur [kylbytœʀ] *nm* (*AUTO*) rocker arm.

cul-de-jatte [kydʒat] *pl* **culs-de-jatte** [kydʒat] *nm/f* legless cripple.

cul-de-sac [kydsak] *pl* **culs-de-sac** [kydsak] *nm* cul-de-sac.

culinaire [kylinɛʀ] *adj* culinary.
culminant, e [kylminã, -ãt] *adj*: **point ~** highest point; (*fig*) height, climax.
culminer [kylmine] *vi* to reach its highest point; to tower.
culot [kylo] *nm* (*d'ampoule*) cap; (*effronterie*) cheek, nerve.
culotte [kylɔt] *nf* (*de femme*) panties *pl*, knickers *pl* (*BRIT*); (*d'homme*) underpants *pl*; (*pantalon*) trousers *pl* (*BRIT*), pants *pl* (*US*); **~ de cheval** riding breeches *pl*.
culotté, e [kylɔte] *adj* (*pipe*) seasoned; (*cuir*) mellowed; (*effronté*) cheeky.
culpabiliser [kylpabilize] *vt*: **~ qn** to make sb feel guilty.
culpabilité [kylpabilite] *nf* guilt.
culte [kylt(ə)] *adj*: **livre/film ~** cult film/book ♦ *nm* (*religion*) religion; (*hommage, vénération*) worship; (*protestant*) service.
cultivable [kyltivabl(ə)] *adj* cultivable.
cultivateur, trice [kyltivatœʀ, -tʀis] *nm/f* farmer.
cultivé, e [kyltive] *adj* (*personne*) cultured, cultivated.
cultiver [kyltive] *vt* to cultivate; (*légumes*) to grow, cultivate.
culture [kyltyʀ] *nf* cultivation; growing; (*connaissances etc*) culture; **(champs de) ~s** land(s) under cultivation; **~ physique** physical training.
culturel, le [kyltyʀɛl] *adj* cultural.
culturisme [kyltyʀism(ə)] *nm* body-building.
culturiste [kyltyʀist(ə)] *nm/f* body-builder.
cumin [kymɛ̃] *nm* (*CULIN*) caraway seeds *pl*; cumin.
cumul [kymyl] *nm* (*voir cumuler*) holding (*ou* drawing) concurrently; **~ de peines** sentences to run consecutively.
cumulable [kymylabl(ə)] *adj* (*fonctions*) which may be held concurrently.
cumuler [kymyle] *vt* (*emplois, honneurs*) to hold concurrently; (*salaires*) to draw concurrently; (*JUR: droits*) to accumulate.
cupide [kypid] *adj* greedy, grasping.
cupidité [kypidite] *nf* greed.
curable [kyʀabl(ə)] *adj* curable.
Curaçao [kyʀaso] *n* Curaçao ♦ *nm*: **c~** curaçao.
curare [kyʀaʀ] *nm* curare.
curatif, ive [kyʀatif, -iv] *adj* curative.
cure [kyʀ] *nf* (*MÉD*) course of treatment; (*REL*) cure, ≈ living; presbytery, ≈ vicarage; **faire une ~ de fruits** to go on a fruit cure *ou* diet; **faire une ~ thermale** to take the waters; **n'avoir ~ de** to pay no attention to; **~ d'amaigrissement** slimming course; **~ de repos** rest cure; **~ de sommeil** sleep therapy *no pl*.
curé [kyʀe] *nm* parish priest; **M le ~** ≈ Vicar.
cure-dent [kyʀdã] *nm* toothpick.
curée [kyʀe] *nf* (*fig*) scramble for the pickings.
cure-ongles [kyʀɔ̃gl(ə)] *nm inv* nail cleaner.

cure-pipe [kyʀpip] *nm* pipe cleaner.
curer [kyʀe] *vt* to clean out; **se ~ les dents** to pick one's teeth.
curetage [kyʀtaʒ] *nm* (*MÉD*) curettage.
curieusement [kyʀjøzmã] *adv* oddly.
curieux, euse [kyʀjø, -øz] *adj* (*étrange*) strange, curious; (*indiscret*) curious, inquisitive; (*intéressé*) inquiring, curious ♦ *nmpl* (*badauds*) onlookers, bystanders.
curiosité [kyʀjozite] *nf* curiosity, inquisitiveness; (*objet*) curio(sity); (*site*) unusual feature *ou* sight.
curiste [kyʀist(ə)] *nm/f person taking the waters at a spa.*
curriculum vitae (CV) [kyʀikylɔmvite] *nm inv* curriculum vitae (CV).
curry [kyʀi] *nm* curry; **poulet au ~** curried chicken, chicken curry.
curseur [kyʀsœʀ] *nm* (*INFORM*) cursor; (*de règle*) slide; (*de fermeture-éclair*) slider.
cursif, ive [kyʀsif, -iv] *adj*: **écriture cursive** cursive script.
cursus [kyʀsys] *nm* degree course.
cutané, e [kytane] *adj* cutaneous, skin *cpd*.
cuti-réaction [kytiʀeaksjɔ̃] *nf* (*MÉD*) skin-test.
cuve [kyv] *nf* vat; (*à mazout etc*) tank.
cuvée [kyve] *nf* vintage.
cuvette [kyvɛt] *nf* (*récipient*) bowl, basin; (*du lavabo*) (wash)basin; (*des w.-c.*) pan; (*GÉO*) basin.
CV *sigle m* (*AUTO*) = **cheval vapeur**; (*ADMIN*) = **curriculum vitae**.
CVS *sigle adj* (= *corrigées des variations saisonnières*) seasonally adjusted.
cx *abr* (= *coefficient de pénétration dans l'air*) drag coefficient.
cyanure [sjanyʀ] *nm* cyanide.
cybercafé [sibɛʀkafe] *nm* cybercafé.
cybernétique [sibɛʀnetik] *nf* cybernetics *sg*.
cyclable [siklabl(ə)] *adj*: **piste ~** cycle track.
cyclamen [siklamɛn] *nm* cyclamen.
cycle [sikl(ə)] *nm* cycle; (*SCOL*): **premier/second ~** ≈ middle/upper school (*BRIT*), ≈ junior/senior high school (*US*).
cyclique [siklik] *adj* cyclic(al).
cyclisme [siklism(ə)] *nm* cycling.
cycliste [siklist(ə)] *nm/f* cyclist ♦ *adj* cycle *cpd*; **coureur ~** racing cyclist.
cyclo-cross [siklokʀɔs] *nm* (*SPORT*) cyclo-cross; (*épreuve*) cyclo-cross race.
cyclomoteur [siklomotœʀ] *nm* moped.
cyclomotoriste [siklomotoʀist(ə)] *nm/f* moped rider.
cyclone [siklon] *nm* hurricane.
cyclotourisme [siklotuʀism(ə)] *nm* (bi)cycle touring.
cygne [siɲ] *nm* swan.
cylindre [silɛ̃dʀ(ə)] *nm* cylinder; **moteur à 4 ~s en ligne** straight-4 engine.
cylindrée [silɛ̃dʀe] *nf* (*AUTO*) (cubic) capacity; **une (voiture de) grosse ~** a big-engined car.
cylindrique [silɛ̃dʀik] *adj* cylindrical.

cymbale [sɛ̃bal] *nf* cymbal.
cynique [sinik] *adj* cynical.
cyniquement [sinikmɑ̃] *adv* cynically.
cynisme [sinism(ə)] *nm* cynicism.
cyprès [sipʀɛ] *nm* cypress.
cypriote [sipʀijɔt] *adj* Cypriot ♦ *nm/f*: **C~** Cypriot.
cyrillique [siʀilik] *adj* Cyrillic.
cystite [sistit] *nf* cystitis.
cytise [sitiz] *nm* laburnum.
cytologie [sitɔlɔʒi] *nf* cytology.

D d

D, d [de] *nm inv* D, d ♦ *abr*: **D** (*MÉTÉO*: = *dépression*) low, depression; **D comme Désiré** D for David (*BRIT*) *ou* Dog (*US*); *voir* **système.**
d' *prép, dét voir* **de.**
Dacca [daka] *n* Dacca.
dactylo [daktilo] *nf* (*aussi*: **~graphe**) typist; (*aussi*: **~graphie**) typing, typewriting.
dactylographier [daktilɔgʀafje] *vt* to type (out).
dada [dada] *nm* hobby-horse.
dadais [dadɛ] *nm* ninny, lump.
dague [dag] *nf* dagger.
dahlia [dalja] *nm* dahlia.
dahoméen, ne [daɔmeɛ̃, -ɛn] *adj* Dahomean.
Dahomey [daɔme] *nm*: **le ~** Dahomey.
daigner [deɲe] *vt* to deign.
daim [dɛ̃] *nm* (*fallow*) deer *inv*; (*peau*) buckskin; (*imitation*) suede.
dais [dɛ] *nm* (*tenture*) canopy.
Dakar [dakaʀ] *n* Dakar.
dal. *abr* (= *décalitre*) dal.
dallage [dalaʒ] *nm* paving.
dalle [dal] *nf* slab; (*au sol*) paving stone, flag(stone); **que ~** nothing at all, damn all (*BRIT*).
daller [dale] *vt* to pave.
dalmate [dalmat] *adj* Dalmatian.
Dalmatie [dalmasi] *nf*: **la ~** Dalmatia.
dalmatien, ne [dalmasjɛ̃, -ɛn] *nm/f* (*chien*) Dalmatian.
daltonien, ne [daltɔnjɛ̃, -ɛn] *adj* colour-blind (*BRIT*), color-blind (*US*).
daltonisme [daltɔnism(ə)] *nm* colour (*BRIT*) *ou* color (*US*) blindness.
dam [dam] *nm*: **au grand ~ de** much to the detriment (*ou* annoyance) of.
Damas [dama] *n* Damascus.
damas [dama] *nm* (*étoffe*) damask.
damassé, e [damase] *adj* damask *cpd*.
dame [dam] *nf* lady; (*CARTES, ÉCHECS*) queen; **~s** *nfpl* (*jeu*) draughts *sg* (*BRIT*), checkers *sg*

(*US*); **les (toilettes des) ~s** the ladies' (toilets); **~ de charité** benefactress; **~ de compagnie** lady's companion.
dame-jeanne, *pl* **dames-jeannes** [damʒɑn] *nf* demijohn.
damer [dame] *vt* to ram *ou* pack down; **~ le pion à** (*fig*) to get the better of.
damier [damje] *nm* draughtboard (*BRIT*), checkerboard (*US*); (*dessin*) check (pattern); **en ~** check.
damner [dane] *vt* to damn.
dancing [dɑ̃siŋ] *nm* dance hall.
dandiner [dɑ̃dine]: **se ~** *vi* to sway about; (*en marchant*) to waddle along.
Danemark [danmaʀk] *nm*: **le ~** Denmark.
danger [dɑ̃ʒe] *nm* danger; **mettre en ~** to endanger, put in danger; **être en ~ de mort** to be in peril of one's life; **être hors de ~** to be out of danger.
dangereusement [dɑ̃ʒʀøzmɑ̃] *adv* dangerously.
dangereux, euse [dɑ̃ʒʀø, -øz] *adj* dangerous.
danois, e [danwa, -waz] *adj* Danish ♦ *nm* (*LING*) Danish ♦ *nm/f*: **D~, e** Dane.

======================= *MOT-CLÉ*

dans [dɑ̃] *prép* **1** (*position*) in; (*à l'intérieur de*) inside; **c'est ~ le tiroir/le salon** it's in the drawer/lounge; **~ la boîte** in *ou* inside the box; **marcher ~ la ville/la rue** to walk about the town/along the street; **je l'ai lu ~ le journal** I read it in the newspaper; **être ~ les meilleurs** to be among *ou* one of the best
2 (*direction*) into; **elle a couru ~ le salon** she ran into the lounge
3 (*provenance*) out of, from; **je l'ai pris ~ le tiroir/salon** I took it out of *ou* from the drawer/lounge; **boire ~ un verre** to drink out of *ou* from a glass
4 (*temps*) in; **~ 2 mois** in 2 months, in 2 months' time
5 (*approximation*) about; **~ les 20 F** about 20 F.

dansant, e [dɑ̃sɑ̃, -ɑ̃t] *adj*: **soirée ~e** evening of dancing; (*bal*) dinner dance.
danse [dɑ̃s] *nf*: **la ~** dancing; (*classique*) (ballet) dancing; **une ~** a dance; **~ du ventre** belly dancing.
danser [dɑ̃se] *vi, vt* to dance.
danseur, euse [dɑ̃sœʀ, -øz] *nm/f* ballet dancer; (*au bal etc*) dancer; (*: cavalier*) partner; **~ de claquettes** tap-dancer; **en danseuse** (*à vélo*) standing on the pedals.
Danube [danyb] *nm*: **le ~** the Danube.
DAO *sigle m* (= *dessin assisté par ordinateur*) CAD.
dard [daʀ] *nm* sting (*organ*).
Dardanelles [daʀdanɛl] *nfpl*: **les ~** the Dardanelles.
darder [daʀde] *vt* to shoot, send forth.
dare-dare [daʀdaʀ] *adv* in double quick time.

Dar-es-Salaam, Dar-es-Salam [daʀɛsalam] n Dar-es-Salaam.

darne [daʀn] nf steak (of fish).

darse [daʀs(ə)] nf sheltered dock (in a Mediterranean port).

dartre [daʀtʀ(ə)] nf (MÉD) sore.

datation [datasjɔ̃] nf dating.

date [dat] nf date; **faire** ~ to mark a milestone; **de longue** ~ adj longstanding; ~ **de naissance** date of birth; ~ **limite** deadline; (d'un aliment: aussi: ~ **limite de vente**) sell-by date.

dater [date] vt, vi to date; ~ **de** to date from, go back to; **à** ~ **de** (as) from.

dateur [datœʀ] nm (de montre) date indicator; **timbre** ~ date stamp.

datif [datif] nm dative.

datte [dat] nf date.

dattier [datje] nm date palm.

daube [dob] nf: **bœuf en** ~ beef casserole.

dauphin [dofɛ̃] nm (ZOOL) dolphin; (du roi) dauphin; (fig) heir apparent.

Dauphiné [dofine] nm: **le** ~ the Dauphiné.

dauphinois, e [dofinwa, -waz] adj of ou from the Dauphiné.

daurade [dɔʀad] nf sea bream.

davantage [davɑ̃taʒ] adv more; (plus longtemps) longer; ~ **de** more; ~ **que** more than.

DB sigle f (MIL) = division blindée.

DCA sigle f (= défense contre avions) anti-aircraft defence.

DCC sigle f ® (= digital compact cassette) DCC ®.

DCT sigle m (= diphtérie coqueluche tétanos) DPT.

DDASS [das] sigle f (= Direction départementale d'action sanitaire et sociale) ≈ DHSS (= Department of Health and Social Security) (BRIT), ≈ SSA (= Social Security Administration) (US).

DDT sigle m (= dichloro-diphénol-trichloréthane) DDT.

================= MOT-CLÉ

de (d') (de +le = **du**, de +les = **des**) prép 1 (appartenance) of; **le toit** ~ **la maison** the roof of the house; **la voiture d'Elisabeth/**~ **mes parents** Elizabeth's/my parents' car

2 (provenance) from; **il vient** ~ **Londres** he comes from London; ~ **Londres à Paris** from London to Paris; **elle est sortie du cinéma** she came out of the cinema

3 (moyen) with; **je l'ai fait** ~ **mes propres mains** I did it with my own two hands

4 (caractérisation, mesure): **un mur** ~ **brique/ bureau d'acajou** a brick wall/mahogany desk; **un billet** ~ **50 F** a 50 F note; **une pièce** ~ **2 m** ~ **large** ou **large** ~ **2 m** a room 2 m wide, a 2m-wide room; **un bébé** ~ **10 mois** a 10-month-old baby; **12 mois** ~ **crédit/travail** 12 months' credit/work; **elle est payée 20 F** ~ **l'heure** she's paid 20 F an hour ou per hour; **augmenter** ~ **10 F** to increase by 10 F;

3 jours ~ **libres** 3 free days, 3 days free; **un verre d'eau** a glass of water; **il mange** ~ **tout** he'll eat anything

5 (rapport) from; ~ **4 à 6** from 4 to 6

6 (de la part de): **estimé** ~ **ses collègues** respected by his colleagues

7 (cause): **mourir** ~ **faim** to die of hunger; **rouge** ~ **colère** red with fury

8 (vb +de +infin) to; **il m'a dit** ~ **rester** he told me to stay

9 (en apposition): **cet imbécile** ~ **Paul** that idiot Paul; **le terme** ~ **franglais** the term "franglais"

♦ dét 1 (phrases affirmatives) some (souvent omis); **du vin,** ~ **l'eau, des pommes** (some) wine, (some) water, (some) apples; **des enfants sont venus** some children came; **pendant des mois** for months

2 (phrases interrogatives et négatives) any; **a-t-il du vin?** has he got any wine?; **il n'a pas** ~ **pommes/d'enfants** he hasn't (got) any apples/children, he has no apples/children.

dé [de] nm (à jouer) die ou dice (pl dice); (aussi: ~ **à coudre**) thimble; ~**s** nmpl (jeu) (game of) dice; **un coup de** ~**s** a throw of the dice; **couper en** ~**s** (CULIN) to dice.

DEA sigle m (= Diplôme d'études approfondies) post-graduate diploma.

dealer [dilœʀ] nm (fam) (drug) pusher.

déambulateur [deɑ̃bylatœʀ] nm zimmer ®.

déambuler [deɑ̃byle] vi to stroll about.

déb. abr = **débutant**; (COMM) = à débattre.

débâcle [debakl(ə)] nf rout.

déballage [debalaʒ] nm (de marchandises) display (of loose goods); (fig: fam) outpourings pl.

déballer [debale] vt to unpack.

débandade [debɑ̃dad] nf scattering; (déroute) rout.

débander [debɑ̃de] vt to unbandage.

débaptiser [debatize] vt (rue) to rename.

débarbouiller [debaʀbuje] vt to wash; **se** ~ to wash (one's face).

débarcadère [debaʀkadɛʀ] nm landing stage (BRIT), wharf.

débardeur [debaʀdœʀ] nm docker, stevedore; (maillot) slipover, tank top.

débarquement [debaʀkəmɑ̃] nm unloading, landing; disembarcation; (MIL) landing; **le D**~ the Normandy landings.

débarquer [debaʀke] vt to unload, land ♦ vi to disembark; (fig) to turn up.

débarras [debaʀa] nm lumber room; (placard) junk cupboard; (remise) outhouse; **bon** ~! good riddance!

débarrasser [debaʀase] vt to clear ♦ vi (enlever le couvert) to clear away; ~ **qn de** (vêtements, paquets) to relieve sb of; (habitude, ennemi) to rid sb of; ~ **qch de** (fouillis etc) to clear sth of; **se** ~ **de** vt to get rid of; to rid o.s. of.

débat [deba] vb voir **débattre** ♦ nm discussion,

debate; ~s *nmpl* (*POL*) proceedings, debates.

débattre [debatʀ(ə)] *vt* to discuss, debate; **se** ~ *vi* to struggle.

débauchage [deboʃaʒ] *nm* (*licenciement*) laying off (of staff); (*par un concurrent*) poaching.

débauche [deboʃ] *nf* debauchery; **une** ~ **de** (*fig*) a profusion of; (: *de couleurs*) a riot of.

débauché, e [deboʃe] *adj* debauched ♦ *nm/f* profligate.

débaucher [deboʃe] *vt* (*licencier*) to lay off, dismiss; (*salarié d'une autre entreprise*) to poach; (*entraîner*) to lead astray, debauch; (*inciter à la grève*) to incite.

débile [debil] *adj* weak, feeble; (*fam*: *idiot*) dim-witted ♦ *nm/f*: ~ **mental, e** mental defective.

débilitant, e [debilitɑ̃, -ɑ̃t] *adj* debilitating.

débilité [debilite] *nf* debility; (*fam*: *idiotie*) stupidity; ~ **mentale** mental debility.

débiner [debine]: **se** ~ *vi* to do a bunk (*BRIT*), clear out.

débit [debi] *nm* (*d'un liquide, fleuve*) (rate of) flow; (*d'un magasin*) turnover (of goods); (*élocution*) delivery; (*bancaire*) debit; **avoir un** ~ **de 10 F** to be 10 F in debit; ~ **de boissons** drinking establishment; ~ **de tabac** tobacconist's (shop) (*BRIT*), tobacco *ou* smoke shop (*US*).

débiter [debite] *vt* (*compte*) to debit; (*liquide, gaz*) to yield, produce, give out; (*couper*: *bois, viande*) to cut up; (*vendre*) to retail; (*péj*: *paroles etc*) to come out with, churn out.

débiteur, trice [debitœʀ, -tʀis] *nm/f* debtor ♦ *adj* in debit; (*compte*) debit *cpd*.

déblai [deblɛ] *nm* (*nettoyage*) clearing; ~s *nmpl* (*terre*) earth; (*décombres*) rubble.

déblaiement [deblɛmɑ̃] *nm* clearing; **travaux de** ~ earth moving *sg*.

déblatérer [deblatere] *vi*: ~ **contre** to go on about.

déblayer [debleje] *vt* to clear; ~ **le terrain** (*fig*) to clear the ground.

déblocage [deblɔkaʒ] *nm* (*des prix, cours*) unfreezing.

débloquer [deblɔke] *vt* (*frein, fonds*) to release; (*prix*) to unfreeze ♦ *vi* (*fam*) to talk rubbish.

débobiner [debɔbine] *vt* to unwind.

déboires [debwaʀ] *nmpl* setbacks.

déboisement [debwazmɑ̃] *nm* deforestation.

déboiser [debwaze] *vt* to clear of trees; (*région*) to deforest; **se** ~ *vi* (*colline, montagne*) to become bare of trees.

déboîter [debwate] *vt* (*AUTO*) to pull out; **se** ~ **le genou** *etc* to dislocate one's knee *etc*.

débonnaire [debɔnɛʀ] *adj* easy-going, good-natured.

débordant, e [debɔʀdɑ̃, -ɑ̃t] *adj* (*joie*) unbounded; (*activité*) exuberant.

débordé, e [debɔʀde] *adj*: **être** ~ **de** (*travail, demandes*) to be snowed under with.

débordement [debɔʀdəmɑ̃] *nm* overflowing.

déborder [debɔʀde] *vi* to overflow; (*lait etc*) to boil over ♦ *vt* (*MIL*, *SPORT*) to outflank; ~ (**de**) **qch** (*dépasser*) to extend beyond sth; ~ **de** (*joie, zèle*) to be brimming over with *ou* bursting with.

débouché [debuʃe] *nm* (*pour vendre*) outlet; (*perspective d'emploi*) opening; (*sortie*): **au** ~ **de la vallée** where the valley opens out (onto the plain).

déboucher [debuʃe] *vt* (*évier, tuyau etc*) to unblock; (*bouteille*) to uncork, open ♦ *vi*: ~ **de** to emerge from, come out of; ~ **sur** to come out onto; to open out onto; (*fig*) to arrive at, lead up to.

débouler [debule] *vi* to go (*ou* come) tumbling down; (*sans tomber*) to come careering down ♦ *vt*: ~ **l'escalier** to belt down the stairs.

déboulonner [debulɔne] *vt* to dismantle; (*fig*: *renvoyer*) to dismiss; (: *détruire le prestige de*) to discredit.

débours [debuʀ] *nmpl* outlay.

débourser [debuʀse] *vt* to pay out, lay out.

déboussoler [debusɔle] *vt* to disorientate, disorient.

debout [dəbu] *adv*: **être** ~ (*personne*) to be standing, stand; (: *levé, éveillé*) to be up (and about); (*chose*) to be upright; **être encore** ~ (*fig*: *en état*) to be still going; to be still standing; to be still up; **mettre qn** ~ to get sb to his feet; **mettre qch** ~ to stand sth up; **se mettre** ~ to get up (on one's feet); **se tenir** ~ to stand; ~! get up!; **cette histoire ne tient pas** ~ this story doesn't hold water.

débouter [debute] *vt* (*JUR*) to dismiss; ~ **qn de sa demande** to dismiss sb's petition.

déboutonner [debutɔne] *vt* to undo, unbutton; **se** ~ *vi* to come undone *ou* unbuttoned.

débraillé, e [debʀaje] *adj* slovenly, untidy.

débrancher [debʀɑ̃ʃe] *vt* (*appareil électrique*) to unplug; (*téléphone, courant électrique*) to disconnect, cut off.

débrayage [debʀɛjaʒ] *nm* (*AUTO*) clutch; (: *action*) disengaging the clutch; (*grève*) stoppage; **faire un double** ~ to double-declutch.

débrayer [debʀeje] *vi* (*AUTO*) to declutch, disengage the clutch; (*cesser le travail*) to stop work.

débridé, e [debʀide] *adj* unbridled, unrestrained.

débrider [debʀide] *vt* (*cheval*) to unbridle; (*CULIN*: *volaille*) to untruss.

débris [debʀi] *nm* (*fragment*) fragment ♦ *nmpl* (*déchets*) pieces, debris *sg*; rubbish *sg* (*BRIT*), garbage *sg* (*US*).

débrouillard, e [debʀujaʀ, -aʀd(ə)] *adj* smart, resourceful.

débrouillardise [debʀujaʀdiz] *nf* smartness, resourcefulness.

débrouiller [debʀuje] *vt* to disentangle, untangle; (*fig*) to sort out, unravel; **se** ~ *vi* to manage.

débroussailler [debʀusaje] *vt* to clear (of brushwood).

débusquer [debyske] *vt* to drive out (from cover).

début [deby] *nm* beginning, start; **~s** *nmpl* beginnings; (*de carrière*) début *sg*; **faire ses ~s** to start out; **au ~** in *ou* at the beginning, at first; **au ~ de** at the beginning *ou* start of; **dès le ~** from the start.

débutant, e [debytɑ̃, -ɑ̃t] *nm/f* beginner, novice.

débuter [debyte] *vi* to begin, start; (*faire ses débuts*) to start out.

deçà [dəsa]: **en ~ de** *prép* this side of; **en ~** *adv* on this side.

décacheter [dekaʃte] *vt* to unseal, open.

décade [dekad] *nf* (*10 jours*) (period of) ten days; (*10 ans*) decade.

décadence [dekadɑ̃s] *nf* decadence; decline.

décadent, e [dekadɑ̃, -ɑ̃t] *adj* decadent.

décaféiné, e [dekafeine] *adj* decaffeinated, caffeine-free.

décalage [dekalaʒ] *nm* move forward *ou* back; shift forward *ou* back; (*écart*) gap; (*désaccord*) discrepancy; **~ horaire** time difference (between time zones), time-lag.

décalaminer [dekalamine] *vt* to decoke.

décalcification [dekalsifikasjɔ̃] *nf* decalcification.

décalcifier [dekalsifje]: **se ~** *vr* to decalcify.

décalcomanie [dekalkɔmani] *nf* transfer.

décaler [dekale] *vt* (*dans le temps: avancer*) to bring forward; (*: retarder*) to put back; (*changer de position*) to shift forward *ou* back; **~ de 10 cm** to move forward *ou* back by 10 cm; **~ de 2 h** to bring *ou* move forward 2 hours; to put back 2 hours.

décalitre [dekalitʀ(ə)] *nm* decalitre (*BRIT*), decaliter (*US*).

décalogue [dekalɔg] *nm* Decalogue.

décalquer [dekalke] *vt* to trace; (*par pression*) to transfer.

décamètre [dekamɛtʀ(ə)] *nm* decametre (*BRIT*), decameter (*US*).

décamper [dekɑ̃pe] *vi* to clear out *ou* off.

décan [dekɑ̃] *nm* (*ASTROLOGIE*) decan.

décanter [dekɑ̃te] *vt* to (allow to) settle (and decant); **se ~** *vi* to settle.

décapage [dekapaʒ] *nm* stripping; scouring; sanding.

décapant [dekapɑ̃] *nm* acid solution; scouring agent; paint stripper.

décaper [dekape] *vt* to strip; (*avec abrasif*) to scour; (*avec papier de verre*) to sand.

décapiter [dekapite] *vt* to behead; (*par accident*) to decapitate; (*fig*) to cut the top off; (*: organisation*) to remove the top people from.

décapotable [dekapɔtabl(ə)] *adj* convertible.

décapoter [dekapɔte] *vt* to put down the top of.

décapsuler [dekapsyle] *vt* to take the cap *ou* top off.

décapsuleur [dekapsylœʀ] *nm* bottle-opener.

décarcasser [dekaʀkase] *vt*: **se ~ pour qn/ pour faire qch** (*fam*) to slog one's guts out for sb/to do sth.

décathlon [dekatlɔ̃] *nm* decathlon.

décati, e [dekati] *adj* faded, aged.

décédé, e [desede] *adj* deceased.

décéder [desede] *vi* to die.

décelable [des(ə)labl(ə)] *adj* discernible.

déceler [desle] *vt* to discover, detect; (*révéler*) to indicate, reveal.

décélération [deseleʀasjɔ̃] *nf* deceleration.

décélérer [deseleʀe] *vi* to decelerate, slow down.

décembre [desɑ̃bʀ(ə)] *nm* December; *voir aussi* **juillet**.

décemment [desamɑ̃] *adv* decently.

décence [desɑ̃s] *nf* decency.

décennal, e, aux [desenal, -o] *adj* (*qui dure dix ans*) having a term of ten years, ten-year; (*qui revient tous les dix ans*) ten-yearly.

décennie [desni] *nf* decade.

décent, e [desɑ̃, -ɑ̃t] *adj* decent.

décentralisation [desɑ̃tʀalizasjɔ̃] *nf* decentralization.

décentraliser [desɑ̃tʀalize] *vt* to decentralize.

décentrer [desɑ̃tʀe] *vt* to decentre; **se ~** to move off-centre.

déception [desɛpsjɔ̃] *nf* disappointment.

décerner [desɛʀne] *vt* to award.

décès [desɛ] *nm* death, decease; **acte de ~** death certificate.

décevant, e [desvɑ̃, -ɑ̃t] *adj* disappointing.

décevoir [desvwaʀ] *vt* to disappoint.

déchaîné, e [deʃene] *adj* unbridled, raging.

déchaînement [deʃɛnmɑ̃] *nm* (*de haine, violence*) outbreak, outburst.

déchaîner [deʃene] *vt* (*passions, colère*) to unleash; (*rires etc*) to give rise to, arouse; **se ~** *vi* to be unleashed; (*rires*) to burst out; (*se mettre en colère*) to fly into a rage; **se ~ contre qn** to unleash one's fury on sb.

déchanter [deʃɑ̃te] *vi* to become disillusioned.

décharge [deʃaʀʒ(ə)] *nf* (*dépôt d'ordures*) rubbish tip *ou* dump; (*électrique*) electrical discharge; (*salve*) volley of shots; **à la ~ de** in defence of.

déchargement [deʃaʀʒəmɑ̃] *nm* unloading.

décharger [deʃaʀʒe] *vt* (*marchandise, véhicule*) to unload; (*ÉLEC*) to discharge; (*arme: neutraliser*) to unload; (*: faire feu*) to discharge, fire; **~ qn de** (*responsabilité*) to relieve sb of, release sb from; **~ sa colère (sur)** to vent one's anger (on); **~ sa conscience** to unburden one's conscience; **se ~ dans** (*se déverser*) to flow into; **se ~ d'une affaire sur qn** to hand a matter over to sb.

décharné, e [deʃaʀne] *adj* bony, emaciated, fleshless.

déchaussé, e [deʃose] *adj* (*dent*) loose.

déchausser [deʃose] vt (personne) to take the shoes off; (skis) to take off; **se** ~ to take off one's shoes; (dent) to come ou work loose.

dèche [dɛʃ] nf (fam): **être dans la** ~ to be flat broke.

déchéance [deʃeɑ̃s] nf (déclin) degeneration, decay, decline; (chute) fall.

déchet [deʃɛ] nm (de bois, tissu etc) scrap; (perte: gén COMM) wastage, waste; ~**s** nmpl (ordures) refuse sg, rubbish sg (BRIT), garbage sg (US); ~**s radioactifs** radioactive waste.

déchiffrage [deʃifʁaʒ] nm sight-reading.

déchiffrer [deʃifʁe] vt to decipher.

déchiqueté, e [deʃikte] adj jagged(-edged), ragged.

déchiqueter [deʃikte] vt to tear ou pull to pieces.

déchirant, e [deʃiʁɑ̃, -ɑ̃t] adj heart-breaking, heart-rending.

déchiré, e [deʃiʁe] adj torn; (fig) heart-broken.

déchirement [deʃiʁmɑ̃] nm (chagrin) wrench, heartbreak; (gén pl: conflit) rift, split.

déchirer [deʃiʁe] vt to tear, rip; (mettre en morceaux) to tear up; (pour ouvrir) to tear off; (arracher) to tear out; (fig) to tear apart; **se** ~ vi to tear, rip; **se** ~ **un muscle/tendon** to tear a muscle/tendon.

déchirure [deʃiʁyʁ] nf (accroc) tear, rip; ~ **musculaire** torn muscle.

déchoir [deʃwaʁ] vi (personne) to lower o.s., demean o.s; ~ **de** to fall from.

déchu, e [deʃy] pp de **déchoir** ♦ adj fallen; (roi) deposed.

décibel [desibɛl] nm decibel.

décidé, e [deside] adj (personne, air) determined; **c'est** ~ it's decided; **être** ~ **à faire** to be determined to do.

décidément [desidemɑ̃] adv undoubtedly; really.

décider [deside] vt: ~ **qch** to decide on sth; ~ **de faire/que** to decide to do/that; ~ **qn** (**à faire qch**) to persuade ou induce sb (to do sth); ~ **de qch** to decide upon sth; (suj: chose) to determine sth; **se** ~ vi (personne) to decide, make up one's mind; (problème, affaire) to be resolved; **se** ~ **à qch** to decide on sth; **se** ~ **à faire** to decide ou make up one's mind to do; **se** ~ **pour qch** to decide on ou in favour of sth.

décideur [desidœʁ] nm decision-maker.

décilitre [desilitʁ(ə)] nm decilitre (BRIT), deciliter (US).

décimal, e, aux [desimal, -o] adj, nf decimal.

décimalisation [desimalizɑsjɔ̃] nf decimalization.

décimaliser [desimalize] vt to decimalize.

décimer [desime] vt to decimate.

décimètre [desimɛtʁ(ə)] nm decimetre (BRIT), decimeter (US); **double** ~ (20 cm) ruler.

décisif, ive [desizif, -iv] adj decisive; (qui l'emporte): **le facteur/l'argument** ~ the de-

ciding factor/argument.

décision [desizjɔ̃] nf decision; (fermeté) decisiveness, decision; **prendre une** ~ to make a decision; **prendre la** ~ **de faire** to take the decision to do; **emporter** ou **faire la** ~ to be decisive.

déclamation [deklamɑsjɔ̃] nf declamation; (péj) ranting, spouting.

déclamatoire [deklamatwaʁ] adj declamatory.

déclamer [deklame] vt to declaim; (péj) to spout ♦ vi: ~ **contre** to rail against.

déclarable [deklaʁabl(ə)] adj (marchandise) dutiable; (revenus) declarable.

déclaration [deklaʁɑsjɔ̃] nf declaration; registration; (discours: POL etc) statement; (compte rendu) report; **fausse** ~ misrepresentation; ~ (**d'amour**) declaration; ~ **de décès** registration of death; ~ **de guerre** declaration of war; ~ (**d'impôts**) statement of income, tax declaration; ≈ tax return; ~ (**de sinistre**) (insurance) claim; ~ **de revenus** statement of income.

déclaré, e [deklaʁe] adj (juré) avowed.

déclarer [deklaʁe] vt to declare, announce; (revenus, employés, marchandises) to declare; (décès, naissance) to register; (vol etc: à la police) to report; **se** ~ vi (feu, maladie) to break out; ~ **la guerre** to declare war.

déclassé, e [deklɑse] adj relegated, downgraded; (matériel) (to be) sold off.

déclassement [deklɑsmɑ̃] nm relegation, downgrading; (RAIL etc) change of class.

déclasser [deklɑse] vt to relegate, downgrade; (déranger: fiches, livres) to get out of order.

déclenchement [deklɑ̃ʃmɑ̃] nm release; setting off.

déclencher [deklɑ̃ʃe] vt (mécanisme etc) to release; (sonnerie) to set off, activate; (attaque, grève) to launch; (provoquer) to trigger off; **se** ~ vi to release itself; to go off.

déclencheur [deklɑ̃ʃœʁ] nm release mechanism.

déclic [deklik] nm trigger mechanism; (bruit) click.

déclin [deklɛ̃] nm decline.

déclinaison [deklinɛzɔ̃] nf declension.

décliner [dekline] vi to decline ♦ vt (invitation) to decline, refuse; (responsabilité) to refuse to accept; (nom, adresse) to state; (LING) to decline; **se** ~ (LING) to decline.

déclivité [deklivite] nf slope, incline; **en** ~ sloping, on the incline.

décloisonner [deklwazɔne] vt to decompartmentalize.

déclouer [deklue] vt to unnail.

décocher [dekɔʃe] vt to hurl; (flèche, regard) to shoot.

décoction [dekɔksjɔ̃] nf decoction.

décodage [dekɔdaʒ] nm deciphering, decoding.

décoder [dekɔde] vt to decipher, decode.

décodeur [dekɔdœʁ] nm decoder.

décoiffé, e [dekwafe] *adj*: **elle est toute ~e** her hair is in a mess.

décoiffer [dekwafe] *vt*: **~ qn** to disarrange *ou* mess up sb's hair; to take sb's hat off; **se ~** to take off one's hat.

décoincer [dekwẽse] *vt* to unjam, loosen.

déçois [deswa] *etc*, **déçoive** [deswav] *etc vb voir* **décevoir**.

décolérer [dekɔleʀe] *vi*: **il ne décolère pas** he's still angry, he hasn't calmed down.

décollage [dekɔlaʒ] *nm* (*AVIAT, ÉCON*) takeoff.

décollé, e [dekɔle] *adj*: **oreilles ~es** sticking-out ears.

décollement [dekɔlmɑ̃] *nm* (*MÉD*): **~ de la rétine** retinal detachment.

décoller [dekɔle] *vt* to unstick ♦ *vi* to take off; (*projet, entreprise*) to take off, get off the ground; **se ~** *vi* to come unstuck.

décolleté, e [dekɔlte] *adj* low-necked, low-cut; (*femme*) wearing a low-cut dress ♦ *nm* low neck(line); (*épaules*) (bare) neck and shoulders; (*plongeant*) cleavage.

décolleter [dekɔlte] *vt* (*vêtement*) to give a low neckline to; (*TECH*) to cut.

décolonisation [dekɔlɔnizasjɔ̃] *nf* decolonization.

décoloniser [dekɔlɔnize] *vt* to decolonize.

décolorant [dekɔlɔʀɑ̃] *nm* decolorant, bleaching agent.

décoloration [dekɔlɔʀasjɔ̃] *nf*: **se faire faire une ~** (*chez le coiffeur*) to have one's hair bleached *ou* lightened.

décoloré, e [dekɔlɔʀe] *adj* (*vêtement*) faded; (*cheveux*) bleached.

décolorer [dekɔlɔʀe] *vt* (*tissu*) to fade; (*cheveux*) to bleach, lighten; **se ~** *vi* to fade.

décombres [dekɔ̃bʀ(ə)] *nmpl* rubble *sg*, debris *sg*.

décommander [dekɔmɑ̃de] *vt* to cancel; (*invités*) to put off; **se ~** to cancel, cry off.

décomposé, e [dekɔ̃poze] *adj* (*pourri*) decomposed; (*visage*) haggard, distorted.

décomposer [dekɔ̃poze] *vt* to break up; (*CHIMIE*) to decompose; (*MATH*) to factorize; **se ~** *vi* to decompose.

décomposition [dekɔ̃pozisjɔ̃] *nf* breaking up; decomposition; factorization; **en ~** (*organisme*) in a state of decay, decomposing.

décompresser [dekɔ̃pʀese] *vi* (*fam: se détendre*) to unwind.

décompresseur [dekɔ̃pʀesœʀ] *nm* decompressor.

décompression [dekɔ̃pʀesjɔ̃] *nf* decompression.

décomprimer [dekɔ̃pʀime] *vt* to decompress.

décompte [dekɔ̃t] *nm* deduction; (*facture*) breakdown (of an account), detailed account.

décompter [dekɔ̃te] *vt* to deduct.

déconcentration [dekɔ̃sɑ̃tʀasjɔ̃] *nf* (*des industries etc*) dispersal; **~ des pouvoirs** devolution.

déconcentré, e [dekɔ̃sɑ̃tʀe] *adj* (*sportif etc*) who has lost (his/her) concentration.

déconcentrer [dekɔ̃sɑ̃tʀe] *vt* (*ADMIN*) to disperse; **se ~** *vi* to lose (one's) concentration.

déconcertant, e [dekɔ̃sɛʀtɑ̃, -ɑ̃t] *adj* disconcerting.

déconcerter [dekɔ̃sɛʀte] *vt* to disconcert, confound.

déconditionner [dekɔ̃disjɔne] *vt*: **~ l'opinion américaine** to change the way the Americans have been forced to think.

déconfit, e [dekɔ̃fi, -it] *adj* crestfallen, downcast.

déconfiture [dekɔ̃fityʀ] *nf* collapse, ruin; (*morale*) defeat.

décongélation [dekɔ̃ʒelasjɔ̃] *nf* defrosting, thawing.

décongeler [dekɔ̃ʒle] *vt* to thaw (out).

décongestionner [dekɔ̃ʒɛstjɔne] *vt* (*MÉD*) to decongest; (*rues*) to relieve congestion in.

déconnecter [dekɔnɛkte] *vt* to disconnect.

déconner [dekɔne] *vi* (*fam!: en parlant*) to talk (a load of). rubbish (*BRIT*) *ou* garbage (*US*); (*: faire des bêtises*) to muck about; **sans ~** no kidding.

déconseiller [dekɔ̃seje] *vt*: **~ qch (à qn)** to advise (sb) against sth; **~ à qn de faire** to advise sb against doing; **c'est déconseillé** it's not advised *ou* advisable.

déconsidérer [dekɔ̃sideʀe] *vt* to discredit.

décontamination [dekɔ̃taminasjɔ̃] *nf* decontamination.

décontaminer [dekɔ̃tamine] *vt* to decontaminate.

décontenancer [dekɔ̃tnɑ̃se] *vt* to disconcert, discountenance.

décontracté, e [dekɔ̃tʀakte] *adj* relaxed.

décontracter [dekɔ̃tʀakte] *vt*, **se ~** *vi* to relax.

décontraction [dekɔ̃tʀaksjɔ̃] *nf* relaxation.

déconvenue [dekɔ̃vny] *nf* disappointment.

décor [dekɔʀ] *nm* décor; (*paysage*) scenery; **~s** *nmpl* (*THÉÂT*) scenery sg, decor sg; (*CINÉ*) set sg; **changement de ~** (*fig*) change of scene; **entrer dans le ~** (*fig*) to run off the road; **en ~ naturel** (*CINÉ*) on location.

décorateur, trice [dekɔʀatœʀ, -tʀis] *nm/f* (interior) decorator; (*CINÉ*) set designer.

décoratif, ive [dekɔʀatif, -iv] *adj* decorative.

décoration [dekɔʀasjɔ̃] *nf* decoration.

décorer [dekɔʀe] *vt* to decorate.

décortiqué, e [dekɔʀtike] *adj* shelled; hulled.

décortiquer [dekɔʀtike] *vt* to shell; (*riz*) to hull; (*fig*) to dissect.

décorum [dekɔʀɔm] *nm* decorum; etiquette.

décote [dekɔt] *nf* tax relief.

découcher [dekuʃe] *vi* to spend the night away.

découdre [dekudʀ(ə)] *vt* (*vêtement, couture*) to unpick, take the stitching out of; (*bouton*) to take off; **se ~** *vi* to come unstitched; (*bouton*) to come off; **en ~** (*fig*) to fight, do battle.

découler [dekule] *vi*: ~ **de** to ensue *ou* follow from.

découpage [dekupaʒ] *nm* cutting up; carving; (*image*) cut-out (figure); ~ **électoral** division into constituencies.

découper [dekupe] *vt* (*papier, tissu etc*) to cut up; (*volaille, viande*) to carve; (*détacher: manche, article*) to cut out; **se** ~ **sur** (*ciel, fond*) to stand out against.

découplé, e [dekuple] *adj*: **bien** ~ well-built, well-proportioned.

découpure [dekupyʀ] *nf*: ~**s** (*morceaux*) cut-out bits; (*d'une côte, arête*) indentations, jagged outline *sg*.

décourageant, e [dekuraʒɑ̃, ɑ̃t] *adj* discouraging; (*personne, attitude*) discouraging, negative.

découragement [dekuraʒmɑ̃] *nm* discouragement, despondency.

décourager [dekuraʒe] *vt* to discourage, dishearten; (*dissuader*) to discourage, put off; **se** ~ *vi* to lose heart, become discouraged; ~ **qn de faire/de qch** to discourage sb from doing/from sth, put sb off doing/sth.

décousu, e [dekuzy] *pp de* **découdre** ♦ *adj* unstitched; (*fig*) disjointed, disconnected.

découvert, e [dekuvɛʀ, -ɛʀt(ə)] *pp de* **découvrir** ♦ *adj* (*tête*) bare, uncovered; (*lieu*) open, exposed ♦ *nm* (*bancaire*) overdraft ♦ *nf* discovery; **à** ~ *adv* (*MIL*) exposed, without cover; (*fig*) openly ♦ *adj* (*COMM*) overdrawn; **à visage** ~ openly; **aller à la** ~**e de** to go in search of.

découvrir [dekuvʀiʀ] *vt* to discover; (*apercevoir*) to see; (*enlever ce qui couvre ou protège*) to uncover; (*montrer, dévoiler*) to reveal; **se** ~ to take off one's hat; (*se déshabiller*) to take something off; (*au lit*) to uncover o.s.; (*ciel*) to clear; **se** ~ **des talents** to find hidden talents in o.s.

décrasser [dekrase] *vt* to clean.

décrêper [dekrepe] *vt* (*cheveux*) to straighten.

décrépi, e [dekrepi] *adj* peeling; with roughcast rendering removed.

décrépit, e [dekrepi, -it] *adj* decrepit.

décrépitude [dekrepityd] *nf* decrepitude; decay.

decrescendo [dekreʃɛndo] *nm* (*MUS*) decrescendo; **aller** ~ (*fig*) to decline, be on the wane.

décret [dekrɛ] *nm* decree.

décréter [dekrete] *vt* to decree; (*ordonner*) to order.

décret-loi [dekrɛlwa] *nm* statutory order.

décrié, e [dekrije] *adj* disparaged.

décrire [dekriʀ] *vt* to describe; (*courbe, cercle*) to follow, describe.

décrisper [dekrispe] *vt* to defuse.

décrit, e [dekri, -it] *pp de* **décrire**.

décrivais [dekrive] *etc vb voir* **décrire**.

décrochement [dekrɔʃmɑ̃] *nm* (*d'un mur etc*) recess.

décrocher [dekrɔʃe] *vt* (*dépendre*) to take down; (*téléphone*) to take off the hook; (*: pour répondre*): ~ **(le téléphone)** to pick up *ou* lift the receiver; (*fig: contrat etc*) to get, land ♦ *vi* to drop out; to switch off; **se** ~ *vi* (*tableau, rideau*) to fall down.

décroîs [dekrwa] *etc vb voir* **décroître**.

décroiser [dekrwaze] *vt* (*bras*) to unfold; (*jambes*) to uncross.

décroissant, e [dekrwasɑ̃, -ɑ̃t] *vb voir* **décroître** ♦ *adj* decreasing, declining, diminishing; **par ordre** ~ in descending order.

décroître [dekrwatʀ(ə)] *vi* to decrease, decline, diminish.

décrotter [dekrɔte] *vt* (*chaussures*) to clean the mud from; **se** ~ **le nez** to pick one's nose.

décru, e [dekry] *pp de* **décroître**.

décrue [dekry] *nf* drop in level (of the waters).

décrypter [dekripte] *vt* to decipher.

déçu, e [desy] *pp de* **décevoir** ♦ *adj* disappointed.

déculotter [dekylɔte] *vt*: ~ **qn** to take off *ou* down sb's trousers; **se** ~ to take off *ou* down one's trousers.

déculpabiliser [dekylpabilize] *vt* (*personne*) to relieve of guilt; (*chose*) to decriminalize.

décuple [dekypl(ə)] *nm*: **le** ~ **de** ten times; **au** ~ tenfold.

décupler [dekyple] *vt, vi* to increase tenfold.

déçut [desy] *etc vb voir* **décevoir**.

dédaignable [dedɛɲabl(ə)] *adj*: **pas** ~ not to be despised.

dédaigner [dedɛɲe] *vt* to despise, scorn; (*négliger*) to disregard, spurn; ~ **de faire** to consider it beneath one to do, not deign to do.

dédaigneusement [dedɛɲøzmɑ̃] *adv* scornfully, disdainfully.

dédaigneux, euse [dedɛɲø, -øz] *adj* scornful, disdainful.

dédain [dedɛ̃] *nm* scorn, disdain.

dédale [dedal] *nm* maze.

dedans [dədɑ̃] *adv* inside; (*pas en plein air*) indoors, inside ♦ *nm* inside; **au** ~ on the inside; inside; **en** ~ (*vers l'intérieur*) inwards; *voir aussi* **là**.

dédicace [dedikas] *nf* (*imprimée*) dedication; (*manuscrite, sur une photo etc*) inscription.

dédicacer [dedikase] *vt*: ~ **(à qn)** to sign (for sb), autograph (for sb), inscribe (to sb).

dédié, e [dedje] *adj*: **ordinateur** ~ dedicated computer.

dédier [dedje] *vt* to dedicate.

dédire [dediʀ]: **se** ~ *vi* to go back on one's word; (*se rétracter*) to retract, recant.

dédit, e [dedi, -it] *pp de* **dédire** ♦ *nm* (*COMM*) forfeit, penalty.

dédommagement [dedɔmaʒmɑ̃] *nm* compensation.

dédommager [dedɔmaʒe] *vt*: ~ **qn (de)** to compensate sb (for); (*fig*) to repay sb (for).

dédouaner [dedwane] *vt* to clear through customs.

dédoublement [dedublǝmɑ̃] *nm* splitting; (*PSYCH*): ~ **de la personnalité** split *ou* dual personality.

dédoubler [deduble] *vt* (*classe, effectifs*) to split (into two); (*couverture etc*) to unfold; (*manteau*) to remove the lining of; ~ **un train/les trains** to run a relief train/ additional trains; **se** ~ *vi* (*PSYCH*) to have a split personality.

dédramatiser [dedʀamatize] *vt* (*situation*) to defuse; (*événement*) to play down.

déductible [dedyktibl(ǝ)] *adj* deductible.

déduction [dedyksjɔ̃] *nf* (*d'argent*) deduction; (*raisonnement*) deduction, inference.

déduire [dedɥiʀ] *vt*: ~ **qch (de)** (*ôter*) to deduct sth (from); (*conclure*) to deduce *ou* infer sth (from).

déesse [dees] *nf* goddess.

DEFA *sigle m* (= *Diplôme d'État relatif aux fonctions d'animation*) diploma for senior youth leaders.

défaillance [defajɑ̃s] *nf* (*syncope*) blackout; (*fatigue*) (sudden) weakness *no pl*; (*technique*) fault, failure; (*morale etc*) weakness; ~ **cardiaque** heart failure.

défaillant, e [defajɑ̃, -ɑ̃t] *adj* defective; (*JUR*: *témoin*) defaulting.

défaillir [defajiʀ] *vi* to faint; to feel faint; (*mémoire etc*) to fail.

défaire [defɛʀ] *vt* (*installation, échafaudage*) to take down, dismantle; (*paquet etc, nœud, vêtement*) to undo; (*bagages*) to unpack; (*ouvrage*) to undo, unpick; (*cheveux*) to take out; **se** ~ *vi* to come undone; **se** ~ **de** *vt* (*se débarrasser de*) to get rid of; (*se séparer de*) to part with; ~ **le lit** (*pour changer les draps*) to strip the bed; (*pour se coucher*) to turn back the bedclothes.

défait, e [defɛ, -ɛt] *pp de* **défaire** ♦ *adj* (*visage*) haggard, ravaged ♦ *nf* defeat.

défaites [defɛt] *vb voir* **défaire**.

défaitisme [defetism(ǝ)] *nm* defeatism.

défaitiste [defetist(ǝ)] *adj, nm/f* defeatist.

défalcation [defalkasjɔ̃] *nf* deduction.

défalquer [defalke] *vt* to deduct.

défasse [defas] *etc vb voir* **défaire**.

défausser [defose] *vt* to get rid of; **se** ~ *vi* (*CARTES*) to discard.

défaut [defo] *nm* (*moral*) fault, failing, defect; (*d'étoffe, métal*) fault, flaw, defect; (*manque, carence*): ~ **de** lack of; shortage of; (*INFORM*) bug; ~ **de la cuirasse** (*fig*) chink in the armour (*BRIT*) *ou* armor (*US*); **en** ~ at fault; in the wrong; **faire** ~ (*manquer*) to be lacking; **à** ~ *adv* failing that; **à** ~ **de** for lack *ou* want of; **par** ~ (*JUR*) in his (*ou* her *etc*) absence.

défaveur [defavœʀ] *nf* disfavour (*BRIT*), disfavor (*US*).

défavorable [defavɔʀabl(ǝ)] *adj* unfavourable (*BRIT*), unfavorable (*US*).

défavoriser [defavɔʀize] *vt* to put at a disadvantage.

défectif, ive [defɛktif, -iv] *adj*: **verbe** ~ defective verb.

défection [defɛksjɔ̃] *nf* defection, failure to give support *ou* assistance; failure to appear; **faire** ~ (*d'un parti etc*) to withdraw one's support, leave.

défectueux, euse [defɛktɥø, -øz] *adj* faulty, defective.

défectuosité [defɛktɥozite] *nf* defectiveness *no pl*; (*défaut*) defect, fault.

défendable [defɑ̃dabl(ǝ)] *adj* defensible.

défendeur, eresse [defɑ̃dœʀ, -dʀɛs] *nm/f* (*JUR*) defendant.

défendre [defɑ̃dʀ(ǝ)] *vt* to defend; (*interdire*) to forbid; ~ **à qn qch/de faire** to forbid sb sth/ to do; **il est défendu de cracher** spitting (is) prohibited *ou* is not allowed; **c'est défendu** it is forbidden; **se** ~ to defend o.s.; **il se défend** (*fig*) he can hold his own; **ça se défend** (*fig*) it holds together; **se** ~ **de/contre** (*se protéger*) to protect o.s. from/against; **se** ~ **de** (*se garder de*) to refrain from; (*nier*): **se** ~ **de vouloir** to deny wanting.

défenestrer [defǝnɛstʀe] *vt* to throw out of the window.

défense [defɑ̃s] *nf* defence (*BRIT*), defense (*US*); (*d'éléphant etc*) tusk; **ministre de la** ~ Minister of Defence (*BRIT*), Defence Secretary; **la** ~ **nationale** defence, the defence of the realm (*BRIT*); **la** ~ **contre avions** anti-aircraft defence; **"** ~ **de fumer/cracher"** "no smoking/spitting", "smoking/spitting prohibited"; **prendre la** ~ **de qn** to stand up for sb; ~ **des consommateurs** consumerism.

défenseur [defɑ̃sœʀ] *nm* defender; (*JUR*) counsel for the defence.

défensif, ive [defɑ̃sif, -iv] *adj, nf* defensive; **être sur la défensive** to be on the defensive.

déféquer [defeke] *vi* to defecate.

déferai [defʀe] *etc vb voir* **défaire**.

déférence [defeʀɑ̃s] *nf* deference.

déférent, e [defeʀɑ̃, -ɑ̃t] *adj* (*poli*) deferential, deferent.

déférer [defeʀe] *vt* (*JUR*) to refer; ~ **à** *vt* (*requête, décision*) to defer to; ~ **qn à la justice** to hand sb over to justice.

déferlant, e [defɛʀlɑ̃, -ɑ̃t] *adj*: **vague** ~**e** breaker.

déferlement [defɛʀlǝmɑ̃] *nm* breaking; surge.

déferler [defɛʀle] *vi* (*vagues*) to break; (*fig*) to surge.

défi [defi] *nm* (*provocation*) challenge; (*bravade*) defiance; **mettre qn au** ~ **de faire qch** to challenge sb to do sth; **relever un** ~ to take up *ou* accept a challenge.

défiance [defjɑ̃s] *nf* mistrust, distrust.

déficeler [defisle] *vt* (*paquet*) to undo, untie.

déficience [defisjɑ̃s] *nf* deficiency.

déficient, e [defisjɑ̃, -ɑ̃t] *adj* deficient.

déficit [defisit] *nm* (*COMM*) deficit; (*PSYCH etc*:

manque) defect; ~ **budgétaire** budget deficit; **être en** ~ to be in deficit.

déficitaire [defisitɛʀ] adj (année, récolte) bad; **entreprise/budget** ~ business/budget in deficit.

défier [defje] vt (provoquer) to challenge; (fig) to defy, brave; **se** ~ **de** (se méfier de) to distrust, mistrust; ~ **qn de faire** to challenge ou defy sb to do; ~ **qn à** to challenge sb to; ~ **toute comparaison/concurrence** to be incomparable/unbeatable.

défigurer [defigyʀe] vt to disfigure; (suj: boutons etc) to mar ou spoil (the looks of); (fig: œuvre) to mutilate, deface.

défilé [defile] nm (GÉO) (narrow) gorge ou pass; (soldats) parade; (manifestants) procession, march; **un** ~ **de** (voitures, visiteurs etc) a stream of.

défiler [defile] vi (troupes) to march past; (sportifs) to parade; (manifestants) to march; (visiteurs) to pour, stream; **se** ~ vi (se dérober) to slip away, sneak off; **faire** ~ (bande, film) to put on; (INFORM) to scroll.

défini, e [defini] adj definite.

définir [definiʀ] vt to define.

définissable [definisabl(ə)] adj definable.

définitif, ive [definitif, -iv] adj (final) final, definitive; (pour longtemps) permanent, definitive; (sans appel) final, definite ♦ nf: **en définitive** eventually; (somme toute) when all is said and done.

définition [definisjɔ̃] nf definition; (de mots croisés) clue; (TV) (picture) resolution.

définitivement [definitivmã] adv definitively; permanently; definitely.

défit [defi] etc vb voir **défaire**.

déflagration [deflagʀasjɔ̃] nf explosion.

déflation [deflasjɔ̃] nf deflation.

déflationniste [deflasjɔnist(ə)] adj deflationist, deflationary.

déflecteur [deflɛktœʀ] nm (AUTO) quarterlight (BRIT), deflector (US).

déflorer [deflɔʀe] vt (jeune fille) to deflower; (fig) to spoil the charm of.

défoncé, e [defɔ̃se] adj smashed in; broken down; (route) full of potholes ♦ nm/f addict.

défoncer [defɔ̃se] vt (caisse) to stave in; (porte) to smash in ou down; (lit, fauteuil) to burst (the springs of); (terrain, route) to rip ou plough up; **se** ~ vi (se donner à fond) to give it all one's got.

défont [defɔ̃] vb voir **défaire**.

déformant, e [defɔʀmã, -ãt] adj: **glace** ~**e** ou **miroir** ~ distorting mirror.

déformation [defɔʀmasjɔ̃] nf loss of shape; deformation; distortion; ~ **professionnelle** conditioning by one's job.

déformer [defɔʀme] vt to put out of shape; (corps) to deform; (pensée, fait) to distort; **se** ~ vi to lose its shape.

défoulement [defulmã] nm release of tension; unwinding.

défouler [defule]: **se** ~ vi (PSYCH) to work off one's tensions, release one's pent-up feelings; (gén) to unwind, let off steam.

défraîchi, e [defʀeʃi] adj faded; (article à vendre) shop-soiled.

défraîchir [defʀeʃiʀ]: **se** ~ vi to fade; to become shop-soiled.

défrayer [defʀeje] vt: ~ **qn** to pay sb's expenses; ~ **la chronique** to be in the news; ~ **la conversation** to be the main topic of conversation.

défrichement [defʀiʃmã] nm clearance.

défricher [defʀiʃe] vt to clear (for cultivation).

défriser [defʀize] vt (cheveux) to straighten; (fig) to annoy.

défroisser [defʀwase] vt to smooth out.

défroque [defʀɔk] nf cast-off.

défroqué [defʀɔke] nm former monk (ou priest).

défroquer [defʀɔke] vi (aussi: **se** ~) to give up the cloth, renounce one's vows.

défunt, e [defœ̃, -œ̃t] adj: **son** ~ **père** his late father ♦ nm/f deceased.

dégagé, e [degaʒe] adj clear; (ton, air) casual, jaunty.

dégagement [degaʒmã] nm emission; freeing; clearing; (espace libre) clearing; passage; clearance; (FOOTBALL) clearance; **voie de** ~ slip road; **itinéraire de** ~ alternative route (to relieve traffic congestion).

dégager [degaʒe] vt (exhaler) to give off, emit; (délivrer) to free, extricate; (MIL: troupes) to relieve; (désencombrer) to clear; (isoler, mettre en valeur) to bring out; (crédits) to release; **se** ~ vi (odeur) to emanate, be given off; (passage, ciel) to clear; ~ **qn de** (engagement, parole etc) to release ou free sb from; **se** ~ **de** (fig: engagement etc) to get out of; (: promesse) to go back on.

dégaine [degɛn] nf awkward way of walking.

dégainer [degene] vt to draw.

dégarni, e [degaʀni] adj bald.

dégarnir [degaʀniʀ] vt (vider) to empty, clear; **se** ~ vi to empty; to be cleaned out ou cleared; (tempes, crâne) to go bald.

dégâts [dega] nmpl damage sg; **faire des** ~ to damage.

dégauchir [degoʃiʀ] vt (TECH) to surface.

dégazer [degaze] vi (pétrolier) to clean its tanks.

dégel [deʒɛl] nm thaw; (fig: des prix etc) unfreezing.

dégeler [deʒle] vt to thaw (out); (fig) to unfreeze ♦ vi to thaw (out); **se** ~ vi (fig) to thaw out.

dégénéré, e [deʒeneʀe] adj, nm/f degenerate.

dégénérer [deʒeneʀe] vi to degenerate; (empirer) to go from bad to worse; (devenir): ~ **en** to degenerate into.

dégénérescence [deʒeneʀesɑ̃s] nf degeneration.

dégingandé, e [deʒɛ̃gɑ̃de] *adj* gangling, lanky.

dégivrage [deʒivʀaʒ] *nm* defrosting; de-icing.

dégivrer [deʒivʀe] *vt* (*frigo*) to defrost; (*vitres*) to de-ice.

dégivreur [deʒivʀœʀ] *nm* defroster; de-icer.

déglinguer [deglɛ̃ge] *vt* to bust.

déglutir [deglytiʀ] *vt, vi* to swallow.

déglutition [deglytisjɔ̃] *nf* swallowing.

dégonflé, e [degɔ̃fle] *adj* (*pneu*) flat; (*fam*) chicken ♦ *nm/f* (*fam*) chicken.

dégonfler [degɔ̃fle] *vt* (*pneu, ballon*) to let down, deflate ♦ *vi* (*désenfler*) to go down; **se ~** *vi* (*fam*) to chicken out.

dégorger [degɔʀʒe] *vi* (*CULIN*): **faire ~** to leave to sweat; (*aussi*) **se ~**: *rivière*): **~ dans** to flow into ♦ *vt* to disgorge.

dégoter [degɔte] *vt* (*fam*) to dig up, find.

dégouliner [deguline] *vi* to trickle, drip; **~ de** to be dripping with.

dégoupiller [degupije] *vt* (*grenade*) to take the pin out of.

dégourdi, e [deguʀdi] *adj* smart, resourceful.

dégourdir [deguʀdiʀ] *vt* to warm (up); **se ~ (les jambes)** to stretch one's legs.

dégoût [degu] *nm* disgust, distaste.

dégoûtant, e [degutɑ̃, -ɑ̃t] *adj* disgusting.

dégoûté, e [degute] *adj* disgusted; **~ de** sick of.

dégoûter [degute] *vt* to disgust; **cela me dégoûte** I find this disgusting *ou* revolting; **~ qn de qch** to put sb off sth; **se ~ de** to get *ou* become sick of.

dégoutter [degute] *vi* to drip; **~ de** to be dripping with.

dégradant, e [degʀadɑ̃, -ɑ̃t] *adj* degrading.

dégradation [degʀadasjɔ̃] *nf* reduction in rank; defacement; degradation, debasement; deterioration; (*aussi*: **~s**: *dégâts*) damage *no pl*.

dégradé, e [degʀade] *adj* (*couleur*) shaded off; (*teintes*) faded; (*cheveux*) layered ♦ *nm* (*PEINTURE*) gradation.

dégrader [degʀade] *vt* (*MIL*: *officier*) to degrade; (*abîmer*) to damage, deface; (*avilir*) to degrade, debase; **se ~** *vi* (*relations, situation*) to deteriorate.

dégrafer [degʀafe] *vt* to unclip, unhook, unfasten.

dégraissage [degʀɛsaʒ] *nm* (*ÉCON*) cutbacks *pl*; **~ et nettoyage à sec** dry cleaning.

dégraissant [degʀɛsɑ̃] *nm* spot-remover.

dégraisser [degʀese] *vt* (*soupe*) to skim; (*vêtement*) to take the grease marks out of; (*ÉCON*) to cut back; (: *entreprise*) to slim down.

degré [dəgʀe] *nm* degree; (*d'escalier*) step; **brûlure au 1er/2ème ~** 1st/2nd degree burn; **équation du 1er/2ème ~** linear/quadratic equation; **le premier ~** (*SCOL*) primary level; **alcool à 90 ~s** surgical spirit; **vin de 10 ~s** 10° wine (*on Gay-Lussac scale*); **par ~(s)** *adv* by degrees, gradually.

dégressif, ive [degʀesif, -iv] *adj* on a decreasing scale, degressive; **tarif ~** decreasing rate of charge.

dégrèvement [degʀɛvmɑ̃] *nm* tax relief.

dégrever [degʀəve] *vt* to grant tax relief to; to reduce the tax burden on.

dégriffé, e [degʀife] *adj* (*vêtement*) sold without the designer's label.

dégringolade [degʀɛ̃gɔlad] *nf* tumble; (*fig*) collapse.

dégringoler [degʀɛ̃gɔle] *vi* to tumble (down); (*fig*: *prix, monnaie etc*) to collapse.

dégriser [degʀize] *vt* to sober up.

dégrossir [degʀosiʀ] *vt* (*bois*) to trim; (*fig*) to work out roughly; (: *personne*) to knock the rough edges off.

déguenillé, e [dəgnije] *adj* ragged, tattered.

déguerpir [degɛʀpiʀ] *vi* to clear off.

dégueulasse [degœlas] *adj* (*fam*) disgusting.

dégueuler [degœle] *vi* (*fam*) to puke, throw up.

déguisé, e [degize] *adj* disguised; dressed up; **~ en** disguised (*ou* dressed up) as.

déguisement [degizmɑ̃] *nm* disguise; (*habits*: *pour s'amuser*) dressing-up clothes; (: *pour tromper*) disguise.

déguiser [degize] *vt* to disguise; **se ~ (en)** (*se costumer*) to dress up (as); (*pour tromper*) to disguise o.s. (as).

dégustation [degystasjɔ̃] *nf* tasting; sampling; savouring (*BRIT*), savoring (*US*); (*séance*): **~ de vin(s)** wine-tasting.

déguster [degyste] *vt* (*vins*) to taste; (*fromages etc*) to sample; (*savourer*) to enjoy, savour (*BRIT*), savor (*US*).

déhancher [deɑ̃ʃe]: **se ~** *vi* to sway one's hips; to lean (one's weight) on one hip.

dehors [dəɔʀ] *adv* outside; (*en plein air*) outdoors, outside ♦ *nm* outside ♦ *nmpl* (*apparences*) appearances, exterior *sg*; **mettre** *ou* **jeter ~** to throw out; **au ~** outside; (*en apparence*) outwardly; **au ~ de** outside; **de ~** from outside; **en ~** outside; outwards; **en ~ de** apart from.

déifier [deifje] *vt* to deify.

déjà [deʒa] *adv* already; (*auparavant*) before, already; **as-tu ~ été en France?** have you been to France before?; **c'est ~ pas mal** that's not too bad (at all); **c'est ~ quelque chose** (at least) it's better than nothing; **quel nom, ~?** what was the name again?

déjanter [deʒɑ̃te]: **se ~** *vi* (*pneu*) to come off the rim.

déjà-vu [deʒavy] *nm*: **c'est du ~** there's nothing new in that.

déjeté, e [deʒte] *adj* lop-sided, crooked.

déjeuner [deʒœne] *vi* to (have) lunch; (*le matin*) to have breakfast ♦ *nm* lunch; (*petit déjeuner*) breakfast; **~ d'affaires** business lunch.

déjouer [deʒwe] *vt* to elude; to foil, thwart.

déjuger [deʒyʒe]: **se** ~ *vi* to go back on one's opinion.

delà [dəla] *adv*: **par** ~, **en** ~ **(de)**, **au** ~ **(de)** beyond.

délabré, e [delɑbʀe] *adj* dilapidated, broken-down.

délabrement [delɑbʀəmɑ̃] *nm* decay, dilapidation.

délabrer [delɑbʀe]: **se** ~ *vi* to fall into decay, become dilapidated.

délacer [delase] *vt* to unlace, undo.

délai [delɛ] *nm* (*attente*) waiting period; (*sursis*) extension (of time); (*temps accordé: aussi:* ~s) time limit; **sans** ~ without delay; **à bref** ~ shortly, very soon; at short notice; **dans les** ~s within the time limit; **un** ~ **de 30 jours** a period of 30 days; **comptez un** ~ **de livraison de 10 jours** allow 10 days for delivery.

délaissé, e [delese] *adj* abandoned, deserted; neglected.

délaisser [delese] *vt* (*abandonner*) to abandon, desert; (*négliger*) to neglect.

délassant, e [delasɑ̃, -ɑ̃t] *adj* relaxing.

délassement [delasmɑ̃] *nm* relaxation.

délasser [delase] *vt* (*reposer*) to relax; (*divertir*) to divert, entertain; **se** ~ *vi* to relax.

délateur, trice [delatœʀ, -tʀis] *nm/f* informer.

délation [delasjɔ̃] *nf* denouncement, informing.

délavé, e [delave] *adj* faded.

délayage [delejaʒ] *nm* mixing; thinning down.

délayer [deleje] *vt* (*CULIN*) to mix (with water *etc*); (*peinture*) to thin down; (*fig*) to pad out, spin out.

delco [dɛlko] *nm* ® (*AUTO*) distributor; **tête de** ~ distributor cap.

délectation [delɛktasjɔ̃] *nf* delight.

délecter [delɛkte]: **se** ~ *vi*: **se** ~ **de** to revel *ou* delight in.

délégation [delegasjɔ̃] *nf* delegation; ~ **de pouvoir** delegation of power.

délégué, e [delege] *adj* delegated ♦ *nm/f* delegate; representative; **ministre** ~ **à** minister with special responsibility for.

déléguer [delege] *vt* to delegate.

délestage [delɛstaʒ] *nm*: **itinéraire de** ~ alternative route (*to relieve traffic congestion*).

délester [delɛste] *vt* (*navire*) to unballast; ~ **une route** to relieve traffic congestion on a road by diverting traffic.

Delhi [dɛli] *n* Delhi.

délibérant, e [delibeʀɑ̃, -ɑ̃t] *adj*: **assemblée** ~**e** deliberative assembly.

délibératif, ive [delibeʀatif, -iv] *adj*: **avoir voix délibérative** to have voting rights.

délibération [delibeʀasjɔ̃] *nf* deliberation.

délibéré, e [delibeʀe] *adj* (*conscient*) deliberate; (*déterminé*) determined, resolute; **de propos** ~ (*à dessein, exprès*) intentionally.

délibérément [delibeʀemɑ̃] *adv* deliberately; (*résolument*) resolutely.

délibérer [delibeʀe] *vi* to deliberate.

délicat, e [delika, -at] *adj* delicate; (*plein de tact*) tactful; (*attentionné*) thoughtful; (*exigeant*) fussy, particular; **procédés peu** ~s unscrupulous methods.

délicatement [delikatmɑ̃] *adv* delicately; (*avec douceur*) gently.

délicatesse [delikatɛs] *nf* delicacy; tactfulness; thoughtfulness; ~**s** *nfpl* attentions, consideration *sg*.

délice [delis] *nm* delight.

délicieusement [delisjøzmɑ̃] *adv* deliciously; delightfully.

délicieux, euse [delisjø, -øz] *adj* (*au goût*) delicious; (*sensation, impression*) delightful.

délictueux, euse [deliktɥø, -øz] *adj* criminal.

délié, e [delje] *adj* nimble, agile; (*mince*) slender, fine ♦ *nm*: **les** ~**s** the upstrokes (*in handwriting*).

délier [delje] *vt* to untie; ~ **qn de** (*serment etc*) to free *ou* release sb from.

délimitation [delimitasjɔ̃] *nf* delimitation.

délimiter [delimite] *vt* to delimit.

délinquance [delɛ̃kɑ̃s] *nf* criminality; ~ **juvénile** juvenile delinquency.

délinquant, e [delɛ̃kɑ̃, -ɑ̃t] *adj, nm/f* delinquent.

déliquescence [delikesɑ̃s] *nf*: **en** ~ in a state of decay.

déliquescent, e [delikesɑ̃, -ɑ̃t] *adj* decaying.

délirant, e [deliʀɑ̃, -ɑ̃t] *adj* (*MÉD: fièvre*) delirious; (*imagination*) frenzied; (*fam: déraisonnable*) crazy.

délire [deliʀ] *nm* (*fièvre*) delirium; (*fig*) frenzy; (: *folie*) lunacy.

délirer [deliʀe] *vi* to be delirious; (*fig*) to be raving.

délit [deli] *nm* (criminal) offence; ~ **de droit commun** violation of common law; ~ **de fuite** failure to stop after an accident; ~ **d'initiés** insider dealing *ou* trading; ~ **de presse** violation of the press laws.

délivrance [delivʀɑ̃s] *nf* freeing, release; (*sentiment*) relief.

délivrer [delivʀe] *vt* (*prisonnier*) to (set) free, release; (*passeport, certificat*) to issue; ~ **qn de** (*ennemis*) to set sb free from, deliver *ou* free sb from; (*fig*) to rid sb of.

déloger [delɔʒe] *vt* (*locataire*) to turn out; (*objet coincé, ennemi*) to dislodge.

déloyal, e, aux [delwajal, -o] *adj* (*personne, conduite*) disloyal; (*procédé*) unfair.

Delphes [dɛlf] *n* Delphi.

delta [dɛlta] *nm* (*GÉO*) delta.

deltaplane [dɛltaplan] *nm* ® hang-glider.

déluge [delyʒ] *nm* (*biblique*) Flood, Deluge; (*grosse pluie*) downpour, deluge; (*grand nombre*): ~ **de** flood of.

déluré, e [delyʀe] *adj* smart, resourceful; (*péj*) forward, pert.

démagnétiser [demaɲetize] *vt* to demagnetize.

démagogie [demagɔʒi] *nf* demagogy.

démagogique [demagɔʒik] *adj* demagogic, popularity-seeking; (*POL*) vote-catching.

démagogue [demagɔg] *adj* demagogic ♦ *nm* demagogue.

démaillé, e [demaje] *adj* (*bas*) laddered (*BRIT*), with a run (*ou* runs).

demain [dəmɛ̃] *adv* tomorrow; ~ **matin/soir** tomorrow morning/evening; ~ **midi** tomorrow at midday; à ~! see you tomorrow!

demande [dəmɑ̃d] *nf* (*requête*) request; (*revendication*) demand; (*ADMIN, formulaire*) application; (*ÉCON*): **la** ~ demand; "~**s d'emploi**" "situations wanted"; **à la** ~ **générale** by popular request; ~ **en mariage** (marriage) proposal; **faire sa** ~ **(en mariage)** to propose (marriage); ~ **de naturalisation** application for naturalization; ~ **de poste** job application.

demandé, e [dəmɑ̃de] *adj* (*article etc*): **très** ~ (very) much in demand.

demander [dəmɑ̃de] *vt* to ask for; (*question: date, heure, chemin*) to ask; (*requérir, nécessiter*) to require, demand; ~ **qch à qn** to ask sb for sth, ask sb sth; **ils demandent 2 secrétaires et un ingénieur** they're looking for 2 secretaries and an engineer; ~ **la main de qn** to ask for sb's hand (in marriage); ~ **pardon à qn** to apologize to sb; ~ **à ou de voir/faire** to ask to see/ask if one can do; ~ **à qn de faire** to ask sb to do; ~ **que/pourquoi** to ask that/why; **se** ~ **si/pourquoi** *etc* to wonder if/why *etc*; (*sens purement réfléchi*) to ask o.s. if/why *etc*; **on vous demande au téléphone** you're wanted on the phone, there's someone for you on the phone; **il ne demande que ça** that's all he wants; **je ne demande pas mieux** I'm asking nothing more; **il ne demande qu'à faire** all he wants is to do.

demandeur, euse [dəmɑ̃dœʀ, -øz] *nm/f*: ~ **d'emploi** job-seeker.

démangeaison [demɑ̃ʒɛzɔ̃] *nf* itching.

démanger [demɑ̃ʒe] *vi* to itch; **la main me démange** my hand is itching; **l'envie** *ou* **ça me démange de faire** I'm itching to do.

démantèlement [demɑ̃tɛlmɑ̃] *nm* breaking up.

démanteler [demɑ̃tle] *vt* to break up; to demolish.

démaquillant [demakijɑ̃] *nm* make-up remover.

démaquiller [demakije] *vt*: **se** ~ to remove one's make-up.

démarcage [demaʀkaʒ] *nm* = **démarquage**.

démarcation [demaʀkasjɔ̃] *nf* demarcation.

démarchage [demaʀʃaʒ] *nm* (*COMM*) door-to-door selling.

démarche [demaʀʃ(ə)] *nf* (*allure*) gait, walk; (*intervention*) step; approach; (*fig: intellectuelle*) thought processes *pl*; approach; **faire** *ou* **entreprendre des** ~s to take action; **faire**

des ~s **auprès de qn** to approach sb.

démarcheur, euse [demaʀʃœʀ, -øz] *nm/f* (*COMM*) door-to-door salesman/woman; (*POL etc*) canvasser.

démarquage [demaʀkaʒ] *nm* marking down.

démarque [demaʀk(ə)] *nf* (*COMM: d'un article*) mark-down.

démarqué, e [demaʀke] *adj* (*FOOTBALL*) unmarked; (*COMM*) reduced; **prix** ~s markeddown prices.

démarquer [demaʀke] *vt* (*prix*) to mark down; (*joueur*) to stop marking; **se** ~ *vi* (*SPORT*) to shake off one's marker.

démarrage [demaʀaʒ] *nm* starting *no pl*, start; ~ **en côte** hill start.

démarrer [demaʀe] *vt* to start up ♦ *vi* (*conducteur*) to start (up); (*véhicule*) to move off; (*travaux, affaire*) to get moving; (*coureur: accélérer*) to pull away.

démarreur [demaʀœʀ] *nm* (*AUTO*) starter.

démasquer [demaske] *vt* to unmask; **se** ~ to unmask; (*fig*) to drop one's mask.

démâter [demɑte] *vt* to dismast ♦ *vi* to be dismasted.

démêlant, e [demelɑ̃, -ɑ̃t] *adj*: **baume** ~, **crème** ~**e** (hair) conditioner.

démêler [demele] *vt* to untangle, disentangle.

démêlés [demele] *nmpl* problems.

démembrement [demɑ̃bʀəmɑ̃] *nm* dismemberment.

démembrer [demɑ̃bʀe] *vt* to dismember.

déménagement [demenaʒmɑ̃] *nm* (*du point de vue du locataire etc*) move; (: *du déménageur*) removal (*BRIT*), moving (*US*); **entreprise/camion de** ~ removal (*BRIT*) *ou* moving (*US*) firm/van.

déménager [demenaʒe] *vt* (*meubles*) to (re)move ♦ *vi* to move (house).

déménageur [demenaʒœʀ] *nm* removal man (*BRIT*), (furniture) mover (*US*); (*entrepreneur*) furniture remover.

démence [demɑ̃s] *nf* madness, insanity; (*MÉD*) dementia.

démener [demne]: **se** ~ *vi* to thrash about; (*fig*) to exert o.s.

dément, e [demɑ̃, -ɑ̃t] *vb voir* **démentir** ♦ *adj* (*fou*) mad (*BRIT*), crazy; (*fam*) brilliant, fantastic.

démenti [demɑ̃ti] *nm* refutation.

démentiel, le [demɑ̃sjɛl] *adj* insane.

démentir [demɑ̃tiʀ] *vt* (*nouvelle, témoin*) to refute; (*suj: faits etc*) to belie, refute; ~ **que** to deny that; **ne pas se** ~ not to fail, keep up.

démerder [demɛʀde]: **se** ~ *vi* (*fam!*) to bloody well manage for o.s.

démériter [demeʀite] *vi*: ~ **auprès de qn** to come down in sb's esteem.

démesure [deməzyʀ] *nf* immoderation, immoderateness.

démesuré, e [deməzyʀe] *adj* immoderate, disproportionate.

démesurément [deməzyʀemɑ̃] *adv* disproportionately.

démettre [demεtʀ(ə)] vt: ~ **qn de** (fonction, poste) to dismiss sb from; **se ~ (de ses fonctions)** to resign (from) one's duties; **se ~ l'épaule** etc to dislocate one's shoulder etc.

demeurant [dəmœʀɑ̃]: **au ~** adv for all that.

demeure [dəmœʀ] nf residence; **dernière ~** (fig) last resting place; **mettre qn en ~ de faire** to enjoin ou order sb to do; **à ~** adv permanently.

demeuré, e [dəmœʀe] adj backward ♦ nm/f backward person.

demeurer [dəmœʀe] vi (habiter) to live; (séjourner) to stay; (rester) to remain; **en ~ là** (suj: personne) to leave it at that; (: choses) to be left at that.

demi, e [dəmi] adj: **et ~: trois heures/ bouteilles et ~e** three and a half hours/ bottles, three hours/bottles and a half ♦ nm (bière: = 0.25 litre) ≈ half-pint; (FOOTBALL) half-back; **il est 2 heures et ~e** it's half past 2; **il est midi et ~** it's half past 12; **~ de mêlée/d'ouverture** (RUGBY) scrum/fly half; **à ~** adv half-; **ouvrir à ~** to half-open; **faire les choses à ~** to do things by halves; **à la ~e** (heure) on the half-hour.

demi... [dəmi] préfixe half-, semi..., demi-.

demi-bas [dəmibɑ] nm inv (chaussette) kneesock.

demi-bouteille [dəmibutεj] nf half-bottle.

demi-cercle [dəmisεʀkl(ə)] nm semicircle; **en ~** adj semicircular ♦ adv in a semicircle.

demi-douzaine [dəmiduzεn] nf half-dozen, half a dozen.

demi-finale [dəmifinal] nf semifinal.

demi-finaliste [dəmifinalist(ə)] nm/f semifinalist.

demi-fond [dəmifɔ̃] nm (SPORT) mediumdistance running.

demi-frère [dəmifʀεʀ] nm half-brother.

demi-gros [dəmigʀo] nm inv wholesale trade.

demi-heure [dəmijœʀ] nf: **une ~** a half-hour, half an hour.

demi-jour [dəmiʒuʀ] nm half-light.

demi-journée [dəmiʒuʀne] nf half-day, half a day.

démilitariser [demilitaʀize] vt to demilitarize.

demi-litre [dəmilitʀ(ə)] nm half-litre (BRIT), half-liter (US), half a litre ou liter.

demi-livre [dəmilivʀ(ə)] nf half-pound, half a pound.

demi-longueur [dəmilɔ̃gœʀ] nf (SPORT) halflength, half a length.

demi-lune [dəmilyn]: **en ~** adj inv semicircular.

demi-mal [dəmimal] nm: **il n'y a que ~** there's not much harm done.

demi-mesure [dəmiməzyʀ] nf half-measure.

demi-mot [dəmimo]: **à ~** adv without having to spell things out.

déminer [demine] vt to clear of mines.

démineur [deminœʀ] nm bomb disposal expert.

demi-pension [dəmipɑ̃sjɔ̃] nf half-board; **être en ~** (SCOL) to take school meals.

demi-pensionnaire [dəmipɑ̃sjɔnεʀ] nm/f (SCOL) half-boarder.

demi-place [dəmiplas] nf half-price; (TRANSPORTS) half-fare.

démis, e [demi, -iz] pp de **démettre** ♦ adj (épaule etc) dislocated.

demi-saison [dəmisεzɔ̃] nf: **vêtements de ~** spring ou autumn clothing.

demi-sel [dəmisεl] adj inv slightly salted.

demi-sœur [dəmisœʀ] nf half-sister.

demi-sommeil [dəmisɔmεj] nm doze.

demi-soupir [dəmisupiʀ] nm (MUS) quaver (BRIT) ou eighth note (US) rest.

démission [demisjɔ̃] nf resignation; **donner sa ~** to give ou hand in one's notice, hand in one's resignation.

démissionnaire [demisjɔnεʀ] adj outgoing ♦ nm/f person resigning.

démissionner [demisjɔne] vi (de son poste) to resign, give ou hand in one's notice.

demi-tarif [dəmitaʀif] nm half-price; (TRANSPORTS) half-fare.

demi-ton [dəmitɔ̃] nm (MUS) semitone.

demi-tour [dəmituʀ] nm about-turn; **faire un ~** (MIL etc) to make an about-turn; **faire ~** to turn (and go) back; (AUTO) to do a U-turn.

démobilisation [demɔbilizasjɔ̃] nf demobilization; (fig) demotivation, demoralization.

démobiliser [demɔbilize] vt to demobilize; (fig) to demotivate, demoralize.

démocrate [demɔkʀat] adj democratic ♦ nm/f democrat.

démocrate-chrétien, ne [demɔkʀatkʀetjɛ̃, -εn] nm/f Christian Democrat.

démocratie [demɔkʀasi] nf democracy; **~ populaire/libérale** people's/liberal democracy.

démocratique [demɔkʀatik] adj democratic.

démocratiquement [demɔkʀatikmɑ̃] adv democratically.

démocratisation [demɔkʀatizasjɔ̃] nf democratization.

démocratiser [demɔkʀatize] vt to democratize.

démodé, e [demɔde] adj old-fashioned.

démoder [demɔde]: **se ~** vi to go out of fashion.

démographe [demɔgʀaf] nm/f demographer.

démographie [demɔgʀafi] nf demography.

démographique [demɔgʀafik] adj demographic; **poussée ~** increase in population.

demoiselle [dəmwazεl] nf (jeune fille) young lady; (célibataire) single lady, maiden lady; **~ d'honneur** bridesmaid.

démolir [demɔliʀ] vt to demolish; (fig: personne) to do for.

démolisseur [demɔlisœʀ] nm demolition worker.

démolition [demɔlisjɔ̃] nf demolition.

démon [demɔ̃] *nm* demon, fiend; evil spirit; (*enfant turbulent*) devil, demon; **le ~ du jeu/ des femmes** a mania for gambling/women; **le D~** the Devil.

démonétiser [demɔnetize] *vt* to demonetize.

démoniaque [demɔnjak] *adj* fiendish.

démonstrateur, trice [demɔ̃stratœr, -tris] *nm/f* demonstrator.

démonstratif, ive [demɔ̃stratif, -iv] *adj, nm* (*aussi LING*) demonstrative.

démonstration [demɔ̃strasjɔ̃] *nf* demonstration; (*aérienne, navale*) display.

démontable [demɔ̃tabl(ə)] *adj* folding.

démontage [demɔ̃taʒ] *nm* dismantling.

démonté, e [demɔ̃te] *adj* (*fig*) raging, wild.

démonte-pneu [demɔ̃təpnø] *nm* tyre lever (*BRIT*), tire iron (*US*).

démonter [demɔ̃te] *vt* (*machine etc*) to take down, dismantle; (*pneu, porte*) to take off; (*cavalier*) to throw, unseat; (*fig: personne*) to disconcert; **se ~** *vi* (*personne*) to lose countenance.

démontrable [demɔ̃trabl(ə)] *adj* demonstrable.

démontrer [demɔ̃tre] *vt* to demonstrate, show.

démoralisant, e [demɔralizɑ̃, -ɑ̃t] *adj* demoralizing.

démoralisateur, trice [demɔralizatœr, -tris] *adj* demoralizing.

démoraliser [demɔralize] *vt* to demoralize.

démordre [demɔrdr(ə)] *vi*: **ne pas ~ de** to refuse to give up, stick to.

démouler [demule] *vt* (*gâteau*) to turn out.

démoustiquer [demustike] *vt* to clear of mosquitoes.

démultiplication [demyltiplikasjɔ̃] *nf* reduction; reduction ratio.

démuni, e [demyni] *adj* (*sans argent*) impoverished; **~ de** without, lacking in.

démunir [demynir] *vt*: **~ qn de** to deprive sb of; **se ~ de** to part with, give up.

démuseler [demyzle] *vt* to unmuzzle.

démystifier [demistifje] *vt* to demystify.

démythifier [demitifje] *vt* to demythologize.

dénatalité [denatalite] *nf* fall in the birth rate.

dénationalisation [denasjɔnalizasjɔ̃] *nf* denationalization.

dénationaliser [denasjɔnalize] *vt* to denationalize.

dénaturé, e [denatyre] *adj* (*alcool*) denaturized; (*goûts*) unnatural.

dénaturer [denatyre] *vt* (*goût*) to alter (completely); (*pensée, fait*) to distort, misrepresent.

dénégations [denegasjɔ̃] *nfpl* denials.

déneigement [denɛʒmɑ̃] *nm* snow clearance.

déneiger [denɛʒe] *vt* to clear snow from.

déni [deni] *nm*: **~ (de justice)** denial of justice.

déniaiser [denjeze] *vt*: **~ qn** to teach sb about life.

dénicher [deniʃe] *vt* to unearth.

dénicotinisé, e [denikɔtinize] *adj* nicotine-free.

denier [dənje] *nm* (*monnaie*) *formerly, a coin of small value*; (*de bas*) denier; **~ du culte** contribution to parish upkeep; **~s publics** public money; **de ses (propres) ~s** out of one's own pocket.

dénier [denje] *vt* to deny; **~ qch à qn** to deny sb sth.

dénigrement [denigrəmɑ̃] *nm* denigration; **campagne de ~** smear campaign.

dénigrer [denigre] *vt* to denigrate, run down.

dénivelé, e [denivle] *adj* (*chaussée*) on a lower level ♦ *nm* difference in height.

déniveler [denivle] *vt* to make uneven; to put on a lower level.

dénivellation [denivɛlasjɔ̃] *nf*, **dénivellement** [denivɛlmɑ̃] *nm* difference in level; (*pente*) ramp; (*creux*) dip.

dénombrer [denɔ̃bre] *vt* (*compter*) to count; (*énumérer*) to enumerate, list.

dénominateur [denɔminatœr] *nm* denominator; **~ commun** common denominator.

dénomination [denɔminasjɔ̃] *nf* designation, appellation.

dénommé, e [denɔme] *adj*: **le ~ Dupont** the man by the name of Dupont.

dénommer [denɔme] *vt* to name.

dénoncer [denɔ̃se] *vt* to denounce; **se ~** to give o.s. up, come forward.

dénonciation [denɔ̃sjasjɔ̃] *nf* denunciation.

dénoter [denɔte] *vt* to denote.

dénouement [denumɑ̃] *nm* outcome, conclusion; (*THÉÂT*) dénouement.

dénouer [denwe] *vt* to unknot, undo.

dénoyauter [denwajote] *vt* to stone; **appareil à ~** stoner.

dénoyauteur [denwajotœr] *nm* stoner.

denrée [dɑ̃re] *nf* commodity; (*aussi:* **~ alimentaire**) food(stuff).

dense [dɑ̃s] *adj* dense.

densité [dɑ̃site] *nf* denseness; (*PHYSIQUE*) density.

dent [dɑ̃] *nf* tooth (*pl* teeth); **avoir/garder une ~ contre qn** to have/hold a grudge against sb; **se mettre qch sous la ~** to eat sth; **être sur les ~s** to be on one's last legs; **faire ses ~s** to teethe, cut (one's) teeth; **en ~s de scie** serrated; (*irrégulier*) jagged; **avoir les ~s longues** (*fig*) to be ruthlessly ambitious; **~ de lait/sagesse** milk/wisdom tooth.

dentaire [dɑ̃tɛr] *adj* dental; **cabinet ~** dental surgery; **école ~** dental school.

denté, e [dɑ̃te] *adj*: **roue ~e** cog wheel.

dentelé, e [dɑ̃tle] *adj* jagged, indented.

dentelle [dɑ̃tɛl] *nf* lace *no pl*.

dentelure [dɑ̃tlyr] *nf* (*aussi:* **~s**) jagged outline.

dentier [dɑ̃tje] *nm* denture.

dentifrice [dɑ̃tifris] *adj, nm*: **(pâte) ~** toothpaste; **eau ~** mouthwash.

dentiste [dɑ̃tist(ə)] *nm/f* dentist.

dentition [dɑ̃tisjɔ̃] *nf* teeth *pl*, dentition.
dénucléariser [denyklearize] *vt* to make nuclear-free.
dénudé, e [denyde] *adj* bare.
dénuder [denyde] *vt* to bare; **se ~** (*personne*) to strip.
dénué, e [denɥe] *adj*: **~ de** lacking in; (*intérêt*) devoid of.
dénuement [denymɑ̃] *nm* destitution.
dénutrition [denytrisjɔ̃] *nf* undernourishment.
déodorant [deɔdɔrɑ̃] *nm* deodorant.
déodoriser [deɔdɔrize] *vt* to deodorize.
déontologie [deɔ̃tɔlɔʒi] *nf* code of ethics; (*professionnelle*) (professional) code of practice.
dép. *abr* (*ADMIN*: = *département*) dept; (= *départ*) dep.
dépannage [depanaʒ] *nm*: **service/camion de ~** (*AUTO*) breakdown service/truck.
dépanner [depane] *vt* (*voiture, télévision*) to fix, repair; (*fig*) to bail out, help out.
dépanneur [depanœr] *nm* (*AUTO*) breakdown mechanic; (*TV*) television engineer.
dépanneuse [depanøz] *nf* breakdown lorry (*BRIT*), tow truck (*US*).
dépareillé, e [depareje] *adj* (*collection, service*) incomplete; (*gant, volume, objet*) odd.
déparer [depare] *vt* to spoil, mar.
départ [depar] *nm* leaving *no pl*, departure; (*SPORT*) start; (*sur un horaire*) departure; **à son ~** when he left; **au ~** (*au début*) initially, at the start; **courrier au ~** outgoing mail.
départager [departaʒe] *vt* to decide between.
département [departəmɑ̃] *nm* department.

> France is divided into 96 administrative units called **départements**. These local government divisions are headed by a state-appointed **préfet**, and administered by an elected **Conseil général**. Départements are usually named after prominent geographical features such as rivers or mountain ranges; see also **DOM-TOM**.

départemental, e, aux [departəmɑ̃tal, -o] *adj* departmental.
départementaliser [departəmɑ̃talize] *vt* to devolve authority to.
départir [departir]: **se ~ de** *vt* to abandon, depart from.
dépassé, e [depase] *adj* superseded, outmoded; (*fig*) out of one's depth.
dépassement [depasmɑ̃] *nm* (*AUTO*) overtaking *no pl*.
dépasser [depase] *vt* (*véhicule, concurrent*) to overtake; (*endroit*) to pass, go past; (*somme, limite*) to exceed; (*fig: en beauté etc*) to surpass, outshine; (*être en saillie sur*) to jut out above (*ou* in front of); (*dérouter*): **cela me dépasse** it's beyond me ♦ *vi* (*AUTO*) to overtake; (*jupon*) to show; **se ~** to excel o.s.
dépassionner [depasjɔne] *vt* (*débat etc*) to

take the heat out of.
dépaver [depave] *vt* to remove the cobblestones from.
dépaysé, e [depeize] *adj* disorientated.
dépaysement [depeizmɑ̃] *nm* disorientation; change of scenery.
dépayser [depeize] *vt* (*désorienter*) to disorientate; (*changer agréablement*) to provide with a change of scenery.
dépecer [depəse] *vt* (*suj: boucher*) to joint, cut up; (*suj: animal*) to dismember.
dépêche [depɛʃ] *nf* dispatch; **~ (télégraphique)** telegram, wire.
dépêcher [depeʃe] *vt* to dispatch; **se ~** *vi* to hurry; **se ~ de faire qch** to hasten to do sth, hurry (in order) to do sth.
dépeindre [depɛ̃dr(ə)] *vt* to depict.
dépénalisation [depenalizasjɔ̃] *nf* decriminalization.
dépendance [depɑ̃dɑ̃s] *nf* (*interdépendance*) dependence *no pl*, dependency; (*bâtiment*) outbuilding.
dépendant, e [depɑ̃dɑ̃, -ɑ̃t] *vb voir* **dépendre** ♦ *adj* (*financièrement*) dependent.
dépendre [depɑ̃dr(ə)] *vt* (*tableau*) to take down; **~ de** *vt* to depend on; (*financièrement etc*) to be dependent on; (*appartenir*) to belong to.
dépens [depɑ̃] *nmpl*: **aux ~ de** at the expense of.
dépense [depɑ̃s] *nf* spending *no pl*, expense, expenditure *no pl*; (*fig*) consumption; (*: de temps, de forces*) expenditure; **pousser qn à la ~** to make sb incur an expense; **~ physique** (physical) exertion; **~ de temps** investment of time; **~s de fonctionnement** revenue expenditure; **~s d'investissement** capital expenditure; **~s publiques** public expenditure.
dépenser [depɑ̃se] *vt* to spend; (*gaz, eau*) to use; (*fig*) to expend, use up; **se ~** (*se fatiguer*) to exert o.s.
dépensier, ière [depɑ̃sje, -jɛr] *adj*: **il est ~** he's a spendthrift.
déperdition [deperdisjɔ̃] *nf* loss.
dépérir [deperir] *vi* (*personne*) to waste away; (*plante*) to wither.
dépersonnaliser [depersɔnalize] *vt* to depersonalize.
dépêtrer [depetre] *vt*: **se ~ de** (*situation*) to extricate o.s. from.
dépeuplé, e [depœple] *adj* depopulated.
dépeuplement [depœpləmɑ̃] *nm* depopulation.
dépeupler [depœple] *vt* to depopulate; **se ~** to be depopulated.
déphasage [defazaʒ] *nm* (*fig*) being out of touch.
déphasé, e [defaze] *adj* (*ÉLEC*) out of phase; (*fig*) out of touch.
déphaser [defaze] *vt* (*fig*) to put out of touch.
dépilation [depilasjɔ̃] *nf* hair loss; hair re-

moval.

dépilatoire [depilatwaʀ] *adj* depilatory, hair-removing.

dépiler [depile] *vt* (*épiler*) to depilate, remove hair from.

dépistage [depistaʒ] *nm* (*MÉD*) screening.

dépister [depiste] *vt* to detect; (*MÉD*) to screen; (*voleur*) to track down; (*poursuivants*) to throw off the scent.

dépit [depi] *nm* vexation, frustration; **en ~ de** *prép* in spite of; **en ~ du bon sens** contrary to all good sense.

dépité, e [depite] *adj* vexed, frustrated.

dépiter [depite] *vt* to vex, frustrate.

déplacé, e [deplase] *adj* (*propos*) out of place, uncalled-for; **personne ~e** displaced person.

déplacement [deplasmɑ̃] *nm* moving; shifting; transfer; (*voyage*) trip, travelling *no pl* (*BRIT*), traveling *no pl* (*US*); **en ~** away (on a trip); **~ d'air** displacement of air; **~ de vertèbre** slipped disc.

déplacer [deplase] *vt* (*table, voiture*) to move, shift; (*employé*) to transfer, move; **se ~** *vi* (*objet*) to move; (*organe*) to become displaced; (*personne: bouger*) to move, walk; (: *voyager*) to travel ♦ *vt* (*vertèbre etc*) to displace.

déplaire [deplɛʀ] *vi*: **ceci me déplaît** I don't like this, I dislike this; **il cherche à nous ~** he's trying to displease us *ou* be disagreeable to us; **se ~ quelque part** to dislike it *ou* be unhappy somewhere.

déplaisant, e [deplɛzɑ̃, -ɑ̃t] *vb voir* **déplaire** ♦ *adj* disagreeable, unpleasant.

déplaisir [deplɛziʀ] *nm* displeasure, annoyance.

déplaît [deplɛ] *vb voir* **déplaire**.

dépliant [deplijɑ̃] *nm* leaflet.

déplier [deplije] *vt* to unfold; **se ~** (*parachute*) to open.

déplisser [deplise] *vt* to smooth out.

déploiement [deplwamɑ̃] *nm* (*voir déployer*) deployment; display.

déplomber [deplɔ̃be] *vt* (*caisse, compteur*) to break (open) the seal of.

déplorable [deplɔrabl(ə)] *adj* deplorable; lamentable.

déplorer [deplɔre] *vt* (*regretter*) to deplore; (*pleurer sur*) to lament.

déployer [deplwaje] *vt* to open out, spread; (*MIL*) to deploy; (*montrer*) to display, exhibit.

déplu [deply] *pp de* **déplaire**.

dépointer [depwɛ̃te] *vi* to clock out.

dépoli, e [depɔli] *adj*: **verre ~** frosted glass.

dépolitiser [depɔlitize] *vt* to depoliticize.

dépopulation [depɔpylasjɔ̃] *nf* depopulation.

déportation [depɔrtasjɔ̃] *nf* deportation.

déporté, e [depɔrte] *nm/f* deportee; (*1939-45*) concentration camp prisoner.

déporter [depɔrte] *vt* (*POL*) to deport; (*dévier*) to carry off course; **se ~** *vi* (*voiture*) to swerve.

déposant, e [depozɑ̃, -ɑ̃t] *nm/f* (*épargnant*) depositor.

dépose [depoz] *nf* taking out; taking down.

déposé, e [depoze] *adj* registered; *voir aussi* **marque**.

déposer [depoze] *vt* (*gén: mettre, poser*) to lay down, put down, set down; (*à la banque, à la consigne*) to deposit; (*caution*) to put down; (*passager*) to drop (off), set down; (*démonter: serrure, moteur*) to take out; (: *rideau*) to take down; (*roi*) to depose; (*ADMIN: faire enregistrer*) to file; to register ♦ *vi* to form a sediment *ou* deposit; (*JUR*): **~** (**contre**) to testify *ou* give evidence (against); **se ~** *vi* to settle; **~ son bilan** (*COMM*) to go into (voluntary) liquidation.

dépositaire [depozitɛr] *nm/f* (*JUR*) depository; (*COMM*) agent; **~ agréé** authorized agent.

déposition [depozisjɔ̃] *nf* (*JUR*) deposition.

déposséder [depɔsede] *vt* to dispossess.

dépôt [depo] *nm* (*à la banque, sédiment*) deposit; (*entrepôt, réserve*) warehouse, store; (*gare*) depot; (*prison*) cells *pl*; **~ d'ordures** rubbish (*BRIT*) *ou* garbage (*US*) dump, tip (*BRIT*); **~ de bilan** (voluntary) liquidation; **~ légal** registration of copyright.

dépoter [depɔte] *vt* (*plante*) to take from the pot, transplant.

dépotoir [depɔtwaʀ] *nm* dumping ground, rubbish (*BRIT*) *ou* garbage (*US*) dump; **~ nucléaire** nuclear (waste) dump.

dépouille [depuj] *nf* (*d'animal*) skin, hide; (*humaine*): **~** (**mortelle**) mortal remains *pl*.

dépouillé, e [depuje] *adj* (*fig*) bare, bald; **~ de** stripped of; lacking in.

dépouillement [depujmɑ̃] *nm* (*de scrutin*) count, counting *no pl*.

dépouiller [depuje] *vt* (*animal*) to skin; (*spolier*) to deprive of one's possessions; (*documents*) to go through, peruse; **~ qn/qch de** to strip sb/sth of; **~ le scrutin** to count the votes.

dépourvu, e [depurvy] *adj*: **~ de** lacking in, without; **au ~** *adv*: **prendre qn au ~** to catch sb unawares.

dépoussiérer [depusjere] *vt* to remove dust from.

dépravation [depravasjɔ̃] *nf* depravity.

dépravé, e [deprave] *adj* depraved.

dépraver [deprave] *vt* to deprave.

dépréciation [depresjasjɔ̃] *nf* depreciation.

déprécier [depresje] *vt*, **se ~** *vi* to depreciate.

déprédations [depredasjɔ̃] *nfpl* damage *sg*.

dépressif, ive [depresif, -iv] *adj* depressive.

dépression [depresjɔ̃] *nf* depression; **~** (**nerveuse**) (nervous) breakdown.

déprimant, e [deprimɑ̃, -ɑ̃t] *adj* depressing.

déprime [deprim] *nf* (*fam*): **la ~** depression.

déprimé, e [deprime] *adj* (*découragé*) depressed.

déprimer [deprime] *vt* to depress.

déprogrammer [depʀɔgʀame] vt (supprimer) to cancel.

DEPS sigle (= dernier entré premier sorti) LIFO (= last in first out).

dépt abr (= département) dept.

dépuceler [depysle] vt (fam) to take the virginity of.

═══════════════════════════════ MOT-CLÉ

depuis [dəpɥi] prép 1 (point de départ dans le temps) since; **il habite Paris ~ 1983/l'an dernier** he has been living in Paris since 1983/last year; **~ quand?** since when? **~ quand le connaissez-vous?** how long have you known him?; **~ lors** since then
2 (temps écoulé) for; **il habite Paris ~ 5 ans** he has been living in Paris for 5 years; **je le connais ~ 3 ans** I've known him for 3 years; **~ combien de temps êtes-vous ici?** how long have you been here?
3 (lieu): **il a plu ~ Metz** it's been raining since Metz; **elle a téléphoné ~ Valence** she rang from Valence
4 (quantité, rang) from; **~ les plus petits jusqu'aux plus grands** from the youngest to the oldest
♦ adv (temps) since (then); **je ne lui ai pas parlé ~** I haven't spoken to him since (then); **~ que** conj (ever) since; **~ qu'il m'a dit ça** (ever) since he said that to me

───

dépuratif, ive [depyʀatif, -iv] adj depurative, purgative.

députation [depytɑsjɔ̃] nf deputation; (fonction) position of deputy, ≈ parliamentary seat (BRIT), ≈ seat in Congress (US).

député, e [depyte] nm/f (POL) deputy, ≈ Member of Parliament (BRIT), ≈ Congressman/woman (US).

députer [depyte] vt to delegate; **~ qn auprès de** to send sb (as a representative) to.

déracinement [deʀasinmɑ̃] nm (gén) uprooting; (d'un préjugé) eradication.

déraciner [deʀasine] vt to uproot.

déraillement [deʀajmɑ̃] nm derailment.

dérailler [deʀaje] vi (train) to be derailed, go off ou jump the rails; (fam) to be completely off the track; **faire ~** to derail.

dérailleur [deʀajœʀ] nm (de vélo) dérailleur gears pl.

déraison [deʀɛzɔ̃] nf unreasonableness.

déraisonnable [deʀɛzɔnabl(ə)] adj unreasonable.

déraisonner [deʀɛzɔne] vi to talk nonsense, rave.

dérangement [deʀɑ̃ʒmɑ̃] nm (gêne, déplacement) trouble; (gastrique etc) disorder; (mécanique) breakdown; **en ~** (téléphone) out of order.

déranger [deʀɑ̃ʒe] vt (personne) to trouble, bother, disturb; (projets) to disrupt, upset; (objets, vêtements) to disarrange; **se ~** to put

o.s. out; (se déplacer) to (take the trouble to) come (ou go) out; **est-ce que cela vous dérange si ...?** do you mind if ...?; **ça te dérangerait de faire ...?** would you mind doing ...?; **ne vous dérangez pas** don't go to any trouble; don't disturb yourself.

dérapage [deʀapaʒ] nm skid, skidding no pl; going out of control.

déraper [deʀape] vi (voiture) to skid; (personne, semelles, couteau) to slip; (fig: économie etc) to go out of control.

dératé, e [deʀate] nm/f: **courir comme un ~** to run like the clappers.

dératiser [deʀatize] vt to rid of rats.

déréglé, e [deʀegle] adj (mœurs) dissolute.

dérèglement [deʀɛgləmɑ̃] nm upsetting no pl, upset.

déréglementation [deʀɛgləmɑ̃tasjɔ̃] nf deregulation.

dérégler [deʀegle] vt (mécanisme) to put out of order, cause to break down; (estomac) to upset; **se ~** vi to break down, go wrong.

dérider [deʀide] vt, **se ~** vi to brighten ou cheer up.

dérision [deʀizjɔ̃] nf derision; **tourner en ~** to deride; **par ~** in mockery.

dérisoire [deʀizwaʀ] adj derisory.

dérivatif [deʀivatif] nm distraction.

dérivation [deʀivasjɔ̃] nf derivation; diversion.

dérive [deʀiv] nf (de dériveur) centre-board; **aller à la ~** (NAVIG, fig) to drift; **~ des continents** (GÉO) continental drift.

dérivé, e [deʀive] adj derived ♦ nm (LING) derivative; (TECH) by-product ♦ nf (MATH) derivative.

dériver [deʀive] vt (MATH) to derive; (cours d'eau etc) to divert ♦ vi (bateau) to drift; **~ de** to derive from.

dériveur [deʀivœʀ] nm sailing dinghy.

dermatite [dɛʀmatit] nf dermatitis.

dermato [dɛʀmato] nm/f (fam: = dermatologue) dermatologist.

dermatologie [dɛʀmatɔlɔʒi] nf dermatology.

dermatologue [dɛʀmatɔlɔg] nm/f dermatologist.

dermatose [dɛʀmatoz] nf dermatosis.

dermite [dɛʀmit] nf = **dermatite**.

dernier, ière [dɛʀnje, -jɛʀ] adj (dans le temps, l'espace) last; (le plus récent: gén avant n) latest, last; (final, ultime: effort) final; (échelon, grade) top, highest ♦ nm (étage) top floor; **lundi/le mois ~** last Monday/month; **du ~ chic** extremely smart; **le ~ cri** the last word (in fashion); **les ~s honneurs** the last tribute; **le ~ soupir: rendre le ~ soupir** to breathe one's last; **en ~** adv last; **ce ~, cette dernière** the latter.

dernièrement [dɛʀnjɛʀmɑ̃] adv recently.

dernier-né, dernière-née [dɛʀnjene, dɛʀnjɛʀne] nm/f (enfant) last-born.

dérobade [deʀɔbad] nf side-stepping no pl.

dérobé, e [deʁɔbe] *adj* (*porte*) secret, hidden; **à la ~e** surreptitiously.

dérober [deʁɔbe] *vt* to steal; (*cacher*): **~ qch à (la vue de) qn** to conceal *ou* hide sth from sb('s view); **se ~** *vi* (*s'esquiver*) to slip away; (*fig*) to shy away; **se ~ sous** (*s'effondrer*) to give way beneath; **se ~ à** (*justice, regards*) to hide from; (*obligation*) to shirk.

dérogation [deʁɔgasjɔ̃] *nf* (special) dispensation.

déroger [deʁɔʒe]: **~ à** *vt* to go against, depart from.

dérouiller [deʁuje] *vt*: **se ~ les jambes** to stretch one's legs.

déroulement [deʁulmɑ̃] *nm* (*d'une opération etc*) progress.

dérouler [deʁule] *vt* (*ficelle*) to unwind; (*papier*) to unroll; **se ~** *vi* to unwind; to unroll, come unrolled; (*avoir lieu*) to take place; (*se passer*) to go.

déroutant, e [deʁutɑ̃, -ɑ̃t] *adj* disconcerting.

déroute [deʁut] *nf* (*MIL*) rout; (*fig*) total collapse; **mettre en ~** to rout; **en ~** routed.

dérouter [deʁute] *vt* (*avion, train*) to reroute, divert; (*étonner*) to disconcert, throw (out).

derrick [deʁik] *nm* derrick (*over oil well*).

derrière [dɛʁjɛʁ] *adv, prép* behind ♦ *nm* (*d'une maison*) back; (*postérieur*) behind, bottom; **les pattes de ~** the back legs, the hind legs; **par ~** from behind; (*fig*) in an underhand way, behind one's back.

derviche [dɛʁviʃ] *nm* dervish.

DES *sigle m* (= *diplôme d'études supérieures*) university post-graduate degree.

des [de] *dét, prép* + *dét voir* **de**.

dès [de] *prép* from; **~ que** *conj* as soon as; **~ à présent** here and now; **~ son retour** as soon as he was (*ou* is) back; **~ réception** upon receipt; **~ lors** *adv* from then on; **~ lors que** *conj* from the moment (that).

désabusé, e [dezabyze] *adj* disillusioned.

désaccord [dezakɔʁ] *nm* disagreement.

désaccordé, e [dezakɔʁde] *adj* (*MUS*) out of tune.

désacraliser [desakʁalize] *vt* to deconsecrate; (*fig: profession, institution*) to take the mystique out of.

désaffecté, e [dezafɛkte] *adj* disused.

désaffection [dezafɛksjɔ̃] *nf*: **~ pour** estrangement from.

désagréable [dezagʁeable(ə)] *adj* unpleasant, disagreeable.

désagréablement [dezagʁeabləmɑ̃] *adv* disagreeably, unpleasantly.

désagrégation [dezagʁegasjɔ̃] *nf* disintegration.

désagréger [dezagʁeʒe]: **se ~** *vi* to disintegrate, break up.

désagrément [dezagʁemɑ̃] *nm* annoyance, trouble *no pl*.

désaltérant, e [dezalteʁɑ̃, -ɑ̃t] *adj* thirst-quenching.

désaltérer [dezalteʁe] *vt*: **se ~** to quench one's thirst; **ça désaltère** it's thirst-quenching, it quenches your thirst.

désamorcer [dezamɔʁse] *vt* to remove the primer from; (*fig*) to defuse; (: *prévenir*) to forestall.

désappointé, e [dezapwɛ̃te] *adj* disappointed.

désapprobateur, trice [dezapʁɔbatœʁ, -tʁis] *adj* disapproving.

désapprobation [dezapʁɔbasjɔ̃] *nf* disapproval.

désapprouver [dezapʁuve] *vt* to disapprove of.

désarçonner [dezaʁsɔne] *vt* to unseat, throw; (*fig*) to throw, nonplus (*BRIT*), disconcert.

désargenté, e [dezaʁʒɑ̃te] *adj* impoverished.

désarmant, e [dezaʁmɑ̃, -ɑ̃t] *adj* disarming.

désarmé, e [dezaʁme] *adj* (*fig*) disarmed.

désarmement [dezaʁməmɑ̃] *nm* disarmament.

désarmer [dezaʁme] *vt* (*MIL, aussi fig*) to disarm; (*NAVIG*) to lay up; (*fusil*) to unload; (: *mettre le cran de sûreté*) to put the safety catch on ♦ *vi* (*pays*) to disarm; (*haine*) to wane; (*personne*) to give up.

désarrimer [dezaʁime] *vt* to shift.

désarroi [dezaʁwa] *nm* helplessness, disarray.

désarticulé, e [dezaʁtikyle] *adj* (*pantin, corps*) dislocated.

désarticuler [dezaʁtikyle] *vt*: **se ~** to contort (o.s.).

désassorti, e [dezasɔʁti] *adj* unmatching, unmatched; (*magasin, marchand*) sold out.

désastre [dezastʁ(ə)] *nm* disaster.

désastreux, euse [dezastʁø, -øz] *adj* disastrous.

désavantage [dezavɑ̃taʒ] *nm* disadvantage; (*inconvénient*) drawback, disadvantage.

désavantager [dezavɑ̃taʒe] *vt* to put at a disadvantage.

désavantageux, euse [dezavɑ̃taʒø, -øz] *adj* unfavourable, disadvantageous.

désaveu [dezavø] *nm* repudiation; (*déni*) disclaimer.

désavouer [dezavwe] *vt* to disown, repudiate, disclaim.

désaxé, e [dezakse] *adj* (*fig*) unbalanced.

désaxer [dezakse] *vt* (*roue*) to put out of true; (*personne*) to throw off balance.

desceller [desele] *vt* (*pierre*) to pull free.

descendance [desɑ̃dɑ̃s] *nf* (*famille*) descendants *pl*, issue; (*origine*) descent.

descendant, e [desɑ̃dɑ̃, -ɑ̃t] *vb voir* **descendre** ♦ *nm/f* descendant.

descendeur, euse [desɑ̃dœʁ, -øz] *nm/f* (*SPORT*) downhiller.

descendre [desɑ̃dʁ(ə)] *vt* (*escalier, montagne*) to go (*ou* come) down; (*valise, paquet*) to take *ou* get down; (*étagère etc*) to lower; (*fam: abattre*) to shoot down; (: *boire*) to knock back ♦ *vi* to go (*ou* come) down; (*passager: s'arrêter*) to get out, alight; (*niveau, tempéra-*

ture) to go *ou* come down, fall, drop; (*marée*) to go out; ~ **à pied/en voiture** to walk/drive down, go down on foot/by car; ~ **de** (*famille*) to be descended from; ~ **du train** to get out of *ou* off the train; ~ **d'un arbre** to climb down from a tree; ~ **de cheval** to dismount, get off one's horse; ~ **à l'hôtel** to stay at a hotel; ~ **dans la rue** (*manifester*) to take to the streets; ~ **en ville** to go into town, go down town.

descente [desɑ̃t] *nf* descent, going down; (*chemin*) way down; (*SKI*) downhill (race); **au milieu de la** ~ halfway down; **freinez dans les ~s** use the brakes going downhill; ~ **de lit** bedside rug; ~ **(de police)** (police) raid.

descriptif, ive [dɛskʀiptif, -iv] *adj* descriptive ♦ *nm* explanatory leaflet.

description [dɛskʀipsjɔ̃] *nf* description.

désembourber [dezɑ̃buʀbe] *vt* to pull out of the mud.

désembourgeoiser [dezɑ̃buʀʒwaze] *vt*: ~ **qn** to get sb out of his (*ou* her) middle-class attitudes.

désembuer [dezɑ̃bɥe] *vt* to demist.

désemparé, e [dezɑ̃paʀe] *adj* bewildered, distraught; (*bateau, avion*) crippled.

désemparer [dezɑ̃paʀe] *vi*: **sans** ~ without stopping.

désemplir [dezɑ̃pliʀ] *vi*: **ne pas** ~ to be always full.

désenchanté, e [dezɑ̃ʃɑ̃te] *adj* disenchanted, disillusioned.

désenchantement [dezɑ̃ʃɑ̃tmɑ̃] *nm* disenchantment, disillusion.

désenclaver [dezɑ̃klave] *vt* to open up.

désencombrer [dezɑ̃kɔ̃bʀe] *vt* to clear.

désenfler [dezɑ̃fle] *vi* to become less swollen.

désengagement [dezɑ̃gaʒmɑ̃] *nm* (*POL*) disengagement.

désensabler [dezɑ̃sable] *vt* to pull out of the sand.

désensibiliser [desɑ̃sibilize] *vt* (*MÉD*) to desensitize.

désenvenimer [dezɑ̃vnime] *vt* (*plaie*) to remove the poison from; (*fig*) to take the sting out of.

désépaissir [dezepesiʀ] *vt* to thin (out).

déséquilibre [dezekilibʀ(ə)] *nm* (*position*): **être en** ~ to be unsteady; (*fig: des forces, du budget*) imbalance; (*PSYCH*) unbalance.

déséquilibré, e [dezekilibʀe] *nm/f* (*PSYCH*) unbalanced person.

déséquilibrer [dezekilibʀe] *vt* to throw off balance.

désert, e [dezɛʀ, -ɛʀt(ə)] *adj* deserted ♦ *nm* desert.

déserter [dezɛʀte] *vi, vt* to desert.

déserteur [dezɛʀtœʀ] *nm* deserter.

désertion [dezɛʀsjɔ̃] *nf* desertion.

désertique [dezɛʀtik] *adj* desert *cpd*; (*inculte*) barren, empty.

désescalade [dezɛskalad] *nf* (*MIL*) de-

escalation.

désespérant, e [dezɛspeʀɑ̃, -ɑ̃t] *adj* hopeless, despairing.

désespéré, e [dezɛspeʀe] *adj* desperate; (*regard*) despairing; **état** ~ (*MÉD*) hopeless condition.

désespérément [dezɛspeʀemɑ̃] *adv* desperately.

désespérer [dezɛspeʀe] *vt* to drive to despair ♦ *vi*, **se** ~ *vi* to despair; ~ **de** to despair of.

désespoir [dezɛspwaʀ] *nm* despair; **être** *ou* **faire le** ~ **de qn** to be the despair of sb; **en** ~ **de cause** in desperation.

déshabillé, e [dezabije] *adj* undressed ♦ *nm* négligée.

déshabiller [dezabije] *vt* to undress; **se** ~ to undress (o.s.).

déshabituer [dezabitɥe] *vt*: **se** ~ **de** to get out of the habit of.

désherbant [dezɛʀbɑ̃] *nm* weed-killer.

désherber [dezɛʀbe] *vt* to weed.

déshérité, e [dezeʀite] *adj* disinherited ♦ *nm/f*: **les** ~**s** (*pauvres*) the underprivileged, the deprived.

déshériter [dezeʀite] *vt* to disinherit.

déshonneur [dezɔnœʀ] *nm* dishonour (*BRIT*), dishonor (*US*), disgrace.

déshonorer [dezɔnɔʀe] *vt* to dishonour (*BRIT*), dishonor (*US*), bring disgrace upon; **se** ~ to bring dishono(u)r on o.s.

déshumaniser [dezymanize] *vt* to dehumanize.

déshydratation [dezidʀatasjɔ̃] *nf* dehydration.

déshydraté, e [dezidʀate] *adj* dehydrated.

déshydrater [dezidʀate] *vt* to dehydrate.

desiderata [deziderata] *nmpl* requirements.

design [dizajn] *adj* (*mobilier*) designer *cpd* ♦ *nm* (industrial) design.

désignation [deziɲasjɔ̃] *nf* naming, appointment; (*signe, mot*) name, designation.

designer [dizajnɛʀ] *nm* designer.

désigner [deziɲe] *vt* (*montrer*) to point out, indicate; (*dénommer*) to denote, refer to; (*nommer: candidat etc*) to name, appoint.

désillusion [dezilyzjɔ̃] *nf* disillusion(ment).

désillusionner [dezilyzjɔne] *vt* to disillusion.

désincarné, e [dezɛ̃kaʀne] *adj* disembodied.

désinence [dezinɑ̃s] *nf* ending, inflexion.

désinfectant, e [dezɛ̃fɛktɑ̃, -ɑ̃t] *adj*, *nm* disinfectant.

désinfecter [dezɛ̃fɛkte] *vt* to disinfect.

désinfection [dezɛ̃fɛksjɔ̃] *nf* disinfection.

désinformation [dezɛ̃fɔʀmasjɔ̃] *nf* disinformation.

désintégration [dezɛ̃tegʀasjɔ̃] *nf* disintegration.

désintégrer [dezɛ̃tegʀe] *vt*, **se** ~ *vi* to disintegrate.

désintéressé, e [dezɛ̃teʀese] *adj* (*généreux, bénévole*) disinterested, unselfish.

désintéressement [dezɛ̃teʀɛsmɑ̃] *nm* (*géné-*

rosité) disinterestedness.

désintéresser [dezɛ̃terese] *vt*: **se ~ (de)** to lose interest (in).

désintérêt [dezɛ̃terɛ] *nm* (*indifférence*) disinterest.

désintoxication [dezɛ̃tɔksikasjɔ̃] *nf* treatment for alcoholism (*ou* drug addiction); **faire une cure de ~** to have *ou* undergo treatment for alcoholism (*ou* drug addiction).

désintoxiquer [dezɛ̃tɔksike] *vt* to treat for alcoholism (*ou* drug addiction).

désinvolte [dezɛ̃vɔlt(ə)] *adj* casual, off-hand.

désinvolture [dezɛ̃vɔltyʀ] *nf* casualness.

désir [deziʀ] *nm* wish; (*fort, sensuel*) desire.

désirable [deziʀabl(ə)] *adj* desirable.

désirer [deziʀe] *vt* to want, wish for; (*sexuellement*) to desire; **je désire** ... (*formule de politesse*) I would like ...; **il désire que tu l'aides** he would like *ou* he wants you to help him; **~ faire** to want *ou* wish to do; **ça laisse à ~** it leaves something to be desired.

désireux, euse [deziʀø, -øz] *adj*: **~ de faire** anxious to do.

désistement [dezistəmɑ̃] *nm* withdrawal.

désister [deziste]: **se ~** *vi* to stand down, withdraw.

désobéir [dezɔbeiʀ] *vi*: **~ (à qn/qch)** to disobey (sb/sth).

désobéissance [dezɔbeisɑ̃s] *nf* disobedience.

désobéissant, e [dezɔbeisɑ̃, -ɑ̃t] *adj* disobedient.

désobligeant, e [dezɔbliʒɑ̃, -ɑ̃t] *adj* disagreeable, unpleasant.

désobliger [dezɔbliʒe] *vt* to offend.

désodorisant [dezɔdɔʀizɑ̃] *nm* air freshener, deodorizer.

désodoriser [dezɔdɔʀize] *vt* to deodorize.

désœuvré, e [dezœvʀe] *adj* idle.

désœuvrement [dezœvʀəmɑ̃] *nm* idleness.

désolant, e [dezɔlɑ̃, -ɑ̃t] *adj* distressing.

désolation [dezɔlasjɔ̃] *nf* (*affliction*) distress, grief; (*d'un paysage etc*) desolation, devastation.

désolé, e [dezɔle] *adj* (*paysage*) desolate; **je suis ~** I'm sorry.

désoler [dezɔle] *vt* to distress, grieve; **se ~** to be upset.

désolidariser [dezɔlidaʀize] *vt*: **se ~ de** *ou* **d'avec** to dissociate o.s. from.

désopilant, e [dezɔpilɑ̃, -ɑ̃t] *adj* screamingly funny, hilarious.

désordonné, e [dezɔʀdɔne] *adj* untidy, disorderly.

désordre [dezɔʀdʀ(ə)] *nm* disorder(liness), untidiness; (*anarchie*) disorder; **~s** *nmpl* (*POL*) disturbances, disorder *sg*; **en ~** in a mess, untidy.

désorganiser [dezɔʀɡanize] *vt* to disorganize.

désorienté, e [dezɔʀjɑ̃te] *adj* disorientated; (*fig*) bewildered.

désorienter [dezɔʀjɑ̃te] *vt* (*fig*) to confuse.

désormais [dezɔʀmɛ] *adv* in future, from now on.

désosser [dezose] *vt* to bone.

despote [dɛspɔt] *nm* despot; (*fig*) tyrant.

despotique [dɛspɔtik] *adj* despotic.

despotisme [dɛspɔtism(ə)] *nm* despotism.

desquamer [dɛskwame]: **se ~** *vi* to flake off.

desquels, desquelles [dekɛl] *prép + pron voir* **lequel**.

DESS *sigle m* (= *Diplôme d'études supérieures spécialisées*) post-graduate diploma.

dessaisir [deseziʀ] *vt*: **~ un tribunal d'une affaire** to remove a case from a court; **se ~ de** *vt* to give up, part with.

dessaler [desale] *vt* (*eau de mer*) to desalinate; (*CULIN: morue etc*) to soak; (*fig fam: délurer*): **~ qn** to teach sb a thing or two ♦ *vi* (*voilier*) to capsize.

Desse *abr* = **duchesse**.

desséché, e [deseʃe] *adj* dried up.

dessèchement [desɛʃmɑ̃] *nm* drying out; dryness; hardness.

dessécher [deseʃe] *vt* (*terre, plante*) to dry out, parch; (*peau*) to dry out; (*volontairement: aliments etc*) to dry, dehydrate; (*fig: cœur*) to harden; **se ~** *vi* to dry out; (*peau, lèvres*) to go dry.

dessein [desɛ̃] *nm* design; **dans le ~ de** with the intention of; **à ~** intentionally, deliberately.

desseller [desele] *vt* to unsaddle.

desserrer [deseʀe] *vt* to loosen; (*frein*) to release; (*poing, dents*) to unclench; (*objets alignés*) to space out; **ne pas ~ les dents** not to open one's mouth.

dessert [desɛʀ] *vb voir* **desservir** ♦ *nm* dessert, pudding.

desserte [desɛʀt(ə)] *nf* (*table*) side table; (*transport*): **la ~ du village est assurée par autocar** there is a coach service to the village; **chemin** *ou* **voie de ~** service road.

desservir [desɛʀviʀ] *vt* (*ville, quartier*) to serve; (: *suj: voie de communication*) to lead into; (*suj: vicaire: paroisse*) to serve; (*nuire à: personne*) to do a disservice to; (*débarrasser*): **~ (la table)** to clear the table.

dessiller [desije] *vt* (*fig*): **~ les yeux à qn** to open sb's eyes.

dessin [desɛ̃] *nm* (*œuvre, art*) drawing; (*motif*) pattern, design; (*contour*) (out)line; **le ~ industriel** draughtsmanship (*BRIT*), draftsmanship (*US*); **~ animé** cartoon (film); **~ humoristique** cartoon.

dessinateur, trice [desinatœʀ, -tʀis] *nm/f* drawer; (*de bandes dessinées*) cartoonist; (*industriel*) draughtsman (*BRIT*), draftsman (*US*); **dessinatrice de mode** fashion designer.

dessiner [desine] *vt* to draw; (*concevoir: carrosserie, maison*) to design; (*suj: robe: taille*) to show off; **se ~** *vi* (*forme*) to be outlined; (*fig: solution*) to emerge.

dessoûler [desule] *vt, vi* to sober up.

dessous [dəsu] *adv* underneath, beneath ♦ *nm* underside; (*étage inférieur*): **les voisins du ~** the downstairs neighbours ♦ *nmpl* (*sous-vêtements*) underwear *sg*; (*fig*) hidden aspects; **en ~** underneath; below; (*fig: en catimini*) slyly, on the sly; **par ~** underneath; below; **le ~** le lit from under the bed; **au-~** *adv* below; **au-~ de** *prép* below; (*peu digne de*) beneath; **au-~ de tout** the (absolute) limit; **avoir le ~** to get the worst of it.

dessous-de-bouteille [dəsudbutɛj] *nm* bottle mat.

dessous-de-plat [dəsudpla] *nm inv* tablemat.

dessous-de-table [dəsudtabl(ə)] *nm* (*fig*) bribe, under-the-counter payment.

dessus [dəsy] *adv* on top; (*collé, écrit*) on it ♦ *nm* top; (*étage supérieur*): **les voisins/ l'appartement du ~** the upstairs neighbours/flat; **en ~** above; **par ~** *adv* over it ♦ *prép* over; **au-~** above; **au-~ de** above; **avoir/prendre le ~** to have/get the upper hand; **reprendre le ~** to get over it; **bras ~ bras dessous** arm in arm; **sens ~ dessous** upside down; *voir* **ci-**; **là-**.

dessus-de-lit [dəsydli] *nm inv* bedspread.

déstabiliser [destabilize] *vt* (*POL*) to destabilize.

destin [dɛstɛ̃] *nm* fate; (*avenir*) destiny.

destinataire [dɛstinatɛʀ] *nm/f* (*POSTES*) addressee; (*d'un colis*) consignee; (*d'un mandat*) payee; **aux risques et périls du ~** at owner's risk.

destination [dɛstinasjɔ̃] *nf* (*lieu*) destination; (*usage*) purpose; **à ~ de** (*avion etc*) bound for; (*voyageur*) bound for, travelling to.

destinée [dɛstine] *nf* fate; (*existence, avenir*) destiny.

destiner [dɛstine] *vt*: **~ qn à** (*poste, sort*) to destine sb for, intend sb to + *verbe*; **~ qn/qch à** (*prédestiner*) to mark sb/sth out for, destine sb/sth to + *verbe*; **~ qch à** (*envisager d'affecter*) to intend to use sth for; **~ qch à qn** (*envisager de donner*) to intend to give sth to sb, intend sb to have sth; (*adresser*) to intend sth for sb; **se ~ à l'enseignement** to intend to become a teacher; **être destiné à** (*sort*) to be destined to + *verbe*; (*usage*) to be intended *ou* meant for; (*suj: sort*) to be in store for.

destituer [dɛstitɥe] *vt* to depose; **~ qn de ses fonctions** to relieve sb of his duties.

destitution [dɛstitysjɔ̃] *nf* deposition.

destructeur, trice [dɛstryktœʀ, -tʀis] *adj* destructive.

destructif, ive [dɛstryktif, -iv] *adj* destructive.

destruction [dɛstryksjɔ̃] *nf* destruction.

déstructuré, e [destryktyre] *adj*: **vêtements ~s** casual clothes.

déstructurer [destryktyre] *vt* to break down, take to pieces.

désuet, ète [desɥɛ, -ɛt] *adj* outdated, out-moded.

désuétude [desɥetyd] *nf*: **tomber en ~** to fall into disuse, become obsolete.

désuni, e [dezyni] *adj* divided, disunited.

désunion [dezynjɔ̃] *nf* disunity.

désunir [dezyniʀ] *vt* to disunite; **se ~** *vi* (*athlète*) to get out of one's stride.

détachable [detaʃabl(ə)] *adj* (*coupon etc*) tear-off *cpd*; (*capuche etc*) detachable.

détachant [detaʃɑ̃] *nm* stain remover.

détaché, e [detaʃe] *adj* (*fig*) detached ♦ *nm/f* (*représentant*) person on secondment (*BRIT*) *ou* a posting.

détachement [detaʃmɑ̃] *nm* detachment; (*fonctionnaire, employé*): **être en ~** to be on secondment (*BRIT*) *ou* a posting.

détacher [detaʃe] *vt* (*enlever*) to detach, remove; (*délier*) to untie; (*ADMIN*): **~ qn (auprès de ou à)** to send sb on secondment (to) (*BRIT*), post sb (to); (*MIL*) to detail; (*vêtement: nettoyer*) to remove the stains from; **se ~** *vi* (*tomber*) to come off; to come out; (*se défaire*) to come undone; (*SPORT*) to pull *ou* break away; (*se délier: chien, prisonnier*) to break loose; **se ~ sur** to stand out against; **se ~ de** (*se désintéresser*) to grow away from.

détail [detaj] *nm* detail; (*COMM*): **le ~** retail; **prix de ~** retail price; **au ~** *adv* (*COMM*) retail; (*: individuellement*) separately; **donner le ~ de** to give a detailed account of; (*compte*) to give a breakdown of; **en ~** in detail.

détaillant, e [detajɑ̃, -ɑ̃t] *nm/f* retailer.

détaillé, e [detaje] *adj* (*récit*) detailed.

détailler [detaje] *vt* (*COMM*) to sell retail; to sell separately; (*expliquer*) to explain in detail; to detail; (*examiner*) to look over, examine.

détaler [detale] *vi* (*lapin*) to scamper off; (*fam: personne*) to make off, scarper (*fam*).

détartrant [detartrɑ̃] *nm* descaling agent (*BRIT*), scale remover.

détartrer [detartre] *vt* to descale; (*dents*) to scale.

détaxe [detaks(ə)] *nf* (*réduction*) reduction in tax; (*suppression*) removal of tax; (*remboursement*) tax refund.

détaxer [detakse] *vt* (*réduire*) to reduce the tax on; (*ôter*) to remove the tax on.

détecter [detɛkte] *vt* to detect.

détecteur [detɛktœʀ] *nm* detector, sensor; **~ de mensonges** lie detector; **~ (de mines)** mine detector.

détection [detɛksjɔ̃] *nf* detection.

détective [detɛktiv] *nm* (*BRIT: policier*) detective; **~ (privé)** private detective *ou* investigator.

déteindre [detɛ̃dʀ(ə)] *vi* to fade; (*fig*): **~ sur** to rub off on.

déteint, e [detɛ̃, -ɛt] *pp de* **déteindre**.

dételer [dɛtle] *vt* to unharness; (*voiture, wagon*) to unhitch ♦ *vi* (*fig: s'arrêter*) to leave off

(working).
détendeur [detɑ̃dœʀ] *nm* (*de bouteille à gaz*) regulator.
détendre [detɑ̃dʀ(ə)] *vt* (*fil*) to slacken, loosen; (*relaxer: personne, atmosphère*) to relax; (: *situation*) to relieve; **se ~** to lose its tension; to relax.
détendu, e [detɑ̃dy] *adj* relaxed.
détenir [detniʀ] *vt* (*fortune, objet, secret*) to be in possession of, have (in one's possession); (*prisonnier*) to detain, hold; (*record*) to hold; **~ le pouvoir** to be in power.
détente [detɑ̃t] *nf* relaxation; (*POL*) détente; (*d'une arme*) trigger; (*d'un athlète qui saute*) spring.
détenteur, trice [detɑ̃tœʀ, -tʀis] *nm/f* holder.
détention [detɑ̃sjɔ̃] *nf* (*voir détenir*) possession; detention; holding; **~ préventive** (pretrial) custody.
détenu, e [detny] *pp de* **détenir** ♦ *nm/f* prisoner.
détergent [detɛʀʒɑ̃] *nm* detergent.
détérioration [deteʀjɔʀasjɔ̃] *nf* damaging; deterioration.
détériorer [deteʀjɔʀe] *vt* to damage; **se ~** *vi* to deteriorate.
déterminant, e [detɛʀminɑ̃, -ɑ̃t] *adj*: **un facteur ~** a determining factor ♦ *nm* (*LING*) determiner.
détermination [detɛʀminasjɔ̃] *nf* determining; (*résolution*) decision; (*fermeté*) determination.
déterminé, e [detɛʀmine] *adj* (*résolu*) determined; (*précis*) specific, definite.
déterminer [detɛʀmine] *vt* (*fixer*) to determine; (*décider*): **~ qn à faire** to decide sb to do; **se ~ à faire** to make up one's mind to do.
déterminisme [detɛʀminism(ə)] *nm* determinism.
déterré, e [deteʀe] *nm/f*: **avoir une mine de ~** to look like death warmed up (*BRIT*) *ou* warmed over (*US*).
déterrer [deteʀe] *vt* to dig up.
détersif, ive [detɛʀsif, -iv] *adj, nm* detergent.
détestable [detɛstabl(ə)] *adj* foul, detestable.
détester [detɛste] *vt* to hate, detest.
détiendrai [detjɛ̃dʀe], **détiens** [detjɛ̃] *etc vb voir* **détenir**.
détonant, e [detɔnɑ̃, -ɑ̃t] *adj*: **mélange ~** explosive mixture.
détonateur [detɔnatœʀ] *nm* detonator.
détonation [detɔnasjɔ̃] *nf* detonation, bang, report (of a gun).
détoner [detɔne] *vi* to detonate, explode.
détonner [detɔne] *vi* (*MUS*) to go out of tune; (*fig*) to clash.
détordre [detɔʀdʀ(ə)] *vt* to untwist, unwind.
détour [detuʀ] *nm* detour; (*tournant*) bend, curve; (*fig: subterfuge*) roundabout means; **au ~ de chemin** at the bend in the path; **sans ~** (*fig*) plainly.
détourné, e [detuʀne] *adj* (*sentier, chemin, moyen*) roundabout.

détournement [detuʀnəmɑ̃] *nm* diversion, rerouting; **~ d'avion** hijacking; **~ (de fonds)** embezzlement *ou* misappropriation (of funds); **~ de mineur** corruption of a minor.
détourner [detuʀne] *vt* to divert; (*avion*) to divert, reroute; (: *par la force*) to hijack; (*yeux, tête*) to turn away; (*de l'argent*) to embezzle, misappropriate; **se ~** to turn away; **~ la conversation** to change the subject; **~ qn de son devoir** to divert sb from his duty; **~ l'attention (de qn)** to distract *ou* divert (sb's) attention.
détracteur, trice [detʀaktœʀ, -tʀis] *nm/f* disparager, critic.
détraqué, e [detʀake] *adj* (*machine, santé*) broken-down ♦ *nm/f* (*fam*): **c'est un ~** he's unhinged.
détraquer [detʀake] *vt* to put out of order; (*estomac*) to upset; **se ~** *vi* to go wrong.
détrempe [detʀɑ̃p] *nf* (*ART*) tempera.
détrempé, e [detʀɑ̃pe] *adj* (*sol*) sodden, waterlogged.
détremper [detʀɑ̃pe] *vt* (*peinture*) to water down.
détresse [detʀɛs] *nf* distress; **en ~** (*avion etc*) in distress; **appel/signal de ~** distress call/signal.
détriment [detʀimɑ̃] *nm*: **au ~ de** to the detriment of.
détritus [detʀitys] *nmpl* rubbish *sg*, refuse *sg*, garbage *sg* (*US*).
détroit [detʀwa] *nm* strait; **le ~ de Bering** *ou* **Behring** the Bering Strait; **le ~ de Gibraltar** the Straits of Gibraltar; **le ~ du Bosphore** the Bosphorus; **le ~ de Magellan** the Strait of Magellan, the Magellan Strait.
détromper [detʀɔ̃pe] *vt* to disabuse; **se ~**: **détrompez-vous** don't believe it.
détrôner [detʀone] *vt* to dethrone, depose; (*fig*) to oust, dethrone.
détrousser [detʀuse] *vt* to rob.
détruire [detʀɥiʀ] *vt* to destroy; (*fig: santé, réputation*) to ruin; (*documents*) to shred.
détruit, e [detʀɥi, -it] *pp de* **détruire**.
dette [dɛt] *nf* debt; **~ publique** *ou* **de l'État** national debt.
DEUG [dœg] *sigle m* = *Diplôme d'études universitaires générales.*

> *French students sit their **DEUG** after two years of university study. Students can leave university after the DEUG, which may be awarded with distinction, or proceed to the **licence**. The certificate obtained specifies the principal subject area studied.*

deuil [dœj] *nm* (*perte*) bereavement; (*période*) mourning; (*chagrin*) grief; **porter le ~** to wear mourning; **prendre le/être en ~** to go into/be in mourning.
DEUST [dœst] *sigle m* = *Diplôme d'études universitaires scientifiques et techniques.*

deux [dø] *num* two; **les** ~ both; **ses** ~ **mains** both his hands, his two hands; **à** ~ **pas** a short distance away; **tous les** ~ **mois** every two months, every other month; ~ **points** colon *sg.*

deuxième [døzjɛm] *num* second.

deuxièmement [døzjɛmmɑ̃] *adv* secondly, in the second place.

deux-pièces [døpjɛs] *nm inv* (*tailleur*) two-piece (suit); (*de bain*) two-piece (swimsuit); (*appartement*) two-roomed flat (*BRIT*) *ou* apartment (*US*).

deux-roues [døʀu] *nm* two-wheeled vehicle.

deux-temps [døtɑ̃] *adj* two-stroke.

devais [dəvɛ] *etc vb voir* **devoir.**

dévaler [devale] *vt* to hurtle down.

dévaliser [devalize] *vt* to rob, burgle.

dévalorisant, e [devalɔʀizɑ̃, -ɑ̃t] *adj* depreciatory.

dévalorisation [devalɔʀizɑsjɔ̃] *nf* depreciation.

dévaloriser [devalɔʀize] *vt*, **se** ~ *vi* to depreciate.

dévaluation [devalɥɑsjɔ̃] *nf* depreciation; (*ÉCON: mesure*) devaluation.

dévaluer [devalɥe] *vt*, **se** ~ *vi* to devalue.

devancer [dəvɑ̃se] *vt* to be ahead of; (*distancer*) to get ahead of; (*arriver avant*) to arrive before; (*prévenir*) to anticipate; ~ **l'appel** (*MIL*) to enlist before call-up.

devancier, ière [dəvɑ̃sje, -jɛʀ] *nm/f* precursor.

devant [dəvɑ̃] *vb voir* **devoir** ♦ *adv* in front; (*à distance: en avant*) ahead ♦ *prép* in front of; ahead of; (*avec mouvement: passer*) past; (*fig*) before, in front of; (*: face à*) faced with, in the face of; (*: vu*) in view of ♦ *nm* front; **prendre les** ~**s** to make the first move; **de** ~ (*roue, porte*) front; **les pattes de** ~ the front legs, the forelegs; **par** ~ (*boutonner*) at the front; (*entrer*) the front way; **par-**~ **notaire** in the presence of a notary; **aller au-**~ **de qn** to go out to meet sb; **aller au-**~ **de** (*désirs de qn*) to anticipate; **aller au-**~ **des ennuis** *ou* **difficultés** to be asking for trouble.

devanture [dəvɑ̃tyʀ] *nf* (*façade*) (shop) front; (*étalage*) display; (shop) window.

dévastateur, trice [devastatœʀ, -tʀis] *adj* devastating.

dévastation [devastɑsjɔ̃] *nf* devastation.

dévaster [devaste] *vt* to devastate.

déveine [devɛn] *nf* rotten luck *no pl.*

développement [devlɔpmɑ̃] *nm* development.

développer [devlɔpe] *vt*, **se** ~ *vi* to develop.

devenir [dəvniʀ] *vb avec attribut* to become; ~ **instituteur** to become a teacher; **que sont-ils devenus?** what has become of them?

devenu, e [dəvny] *pp de* **devenir.**

dévergondé, e [devɛʀgɔ̃de] *adj* wild, shameless.

dévergonder [devɛʀgɔ̃de] *vt*, **se** ~ *vi* to get into bad ways.

déverrouiller [devɛʀuje] *vt* to unbolt.

devers [dəvɛʀ] *adv*: **par** ~ **soi** to oneself.

déverser [devɛʀse] *vt* (*liquide*) to pour (out); (*ordures*) to tip (out); **se** ~ **dans** (*fleuve, mer*) to flow into.

déversoir [devɛʀswaʀ] *nm* overflow.

dévêtir [devetiʀ] *vt*, **se** ~ *vi* to undress.

devez [dəve] *vb voir* **devoir.**

déviation [devjɑsjɔ̃] *nf* deviation; (*AUTO*) diversion (*BRIT*), detour (*US*); ~ **de la colonne (vertébrale)** curvature of the spine.

dévider [devide] *vt* to unwind.

dévidoir [devidwaʀ] *nm* reel.

deviendrai [dəvjɛ̃dʀe], **deviens** [dəvjɛ̃] *etc vb voir* **devenir.**

dévier [devje] *vt* (*fleuve, circulation*) to divert; (*coup*) to deflect ♦ *vi* to veer (off course); **(faire)** ~ (*projectile*) to deflect; (*véhicule*) to push off course.

devin [dəvɛ̃] *nm* soothsayer, seer.

deviner [dəvine] *vt* to guess; (*prévoir*) to foretell, foresee; (*apercevoir*) to distinguish.

devinette [dəvinɛt] *nf* riddle.

devint [dəvɛ̃] *etc vb voir* **devenir.**

devis [dəvi] *nm* estimate, quotation; ~ **descriptif/estimatif** detailed/preliminary estimate.

dévisager [devizaʒe] *vt* to stare at.

devise [dəviz] *nf* (*formule*) motto, watchword; (*ÉCON: monnaie*) currency; ~**s** *nfpl* (*argent*) currency *sg.*

deviser [dəvize] *vi* to converse.

dévisser [devise] *vt* to unscrew, undo; **se** ~ *vi* to come unscrewed.

de visu [devizy] *adv*: **se rendre compte de qch** ~ to see sth for o.s.

dévitaliser [devitalize] *vt* (*dent*) to remove the nerve from.

dévoiler [devwale] *vt* to unveil.

devoir [dəvwaʀ] *nm* duty; (*SCOL*) piece of homework, homework *no pl*; (*: en classe*) exercise ♦ *vt* (*argent, respect*): ~ **qch (à qn)** to owe (sb) sth; (*suivi de l'infinitif: obligation*): **il doit le faire** he has to do it, he must do it; (*: fatalité*): **cela devait arriver un jour** it was bound to happen; (*: intention*): **il doit partir demain** he is (due) to leave tomorrow; (*: probabilité*): **il doit être tard** it must be late; **se faire un** ~ **de faire qch** to make it one's duty to do sth; ~**s de vacances** homework set for the holidays; **se** ~ **de faire qch** to be duty bound to do sth; **je devrais faire** I ought to *ou* should do; **tu n'aurais pas dû** you ought not to have *ou* shouldn't have; **comme il se doit** (*comme il faut*) as is right and proper.

dévolu, e [devɔly] *adj*: ~ **à** allotted to ♦ *nm*: **jeter son** ~ **sur** to fix one's choice on.

devons [dəvɔ̃] *vb voir* **devoir.**

dévorant, e [devɔʀɑ̃, -ɑ̃t] *adj* (*faim, passion*) raging.

dévorer [devɔʀe] *vt* to devour; (*suj: feu, soucis*) to consume; ~ **qn/qch des yeux** *ou* **du re-**

gard (*fig*) to eye sb/sth intently; (: *convoitise*) to eye sb/sth greedily.

dévot, e [devo, -ɔt] *adj* devout, pious ♦ *nm/f* devout person; **un faux ~** a falsely pious person.

dévotion [devosjɔ̃] *nf* devoutness; **être à la ~ de qn** to be totally devoted to sb; **avoir une ~ pour qn** to worship sb.

dévoué, e [devwe] *adj* devoted.

dévouement [devumɑ̃] *nm* devotion, dedication.

dévouer [devwe]: **se ~** *vi* (*se sacrifier*): **se ~ (pour)** to sacrifice o.s. (for); (*se consacrer*): **se ~ à** to devote *ou* dedicate o.s. to.

dévoyé, e [devwaje] *adj* delinquent.

dévoyer [devwaje] *vt* to lead astray; **se ~** *vi* to go off the rails; **~ l'opinion publique** to influence public opinion.

devrai [dəvʁe] *etc vb voir* **devoir**.

dextérité [dɛksteʁite] *nf* skill, dexterity.

dfc *abr* (= *désire faire connaissance*) *in personal column of newspaper*.

DG *sigle m* = **directeur général**.

dg. *abr* (= *décigramme*) dg.

DGE *sigle f* (= *Dotation globale d'équipement*) *state contribution to local government budget*.

DGSE *sigle f* (= *Direction générale des services extérieurs*) ≈ MI6 (*BRIT*), ≈ CIA (*US*).

DI *sigle f* (*MIL*) = **division d'infanterie**.

dia [dja] *abr* = **diapositive**.

diabète [djabɛt] *nm* diabetes *sg*.

diabétique [djabetik] *nm/f* diabetic.

diable [djɑbl(ə)] *nm* devil; **une musique du ~** an unholy racket; **il fait une chaleur du ~** it's fiendishly hot; **avoir le ~ au corps** to be the very devil.

diablement [djɑbləmɑ̃] *adv* fiendishly.

diableries [djɑbləʁi] *nfpl* (*d'enfant*) devilment *sg*, mischief *sg*.

diablesse [djɑblɛs] *nf* (*petite fille*) little devil.

diablotin [djɑblɔtɛ̃] *nm* imp; (*pétard*) cracker.

diabolique [djɑbɔlik] *adj* diabolical.

diabolo [djɑbɔlo] *nm* (*jeu*) diabolo; (*boisson*) lemonade and fruit cordial; **~(-menthe)** lemonade and mint cordial.

diacre [djakʁ(ə)] *nm* deacon.

diadème [djadɛm] *nm* diadem.

diagnostic [djagnɔstik] *nm* diagnosis *sg*.

diagnostiquer [djagnɔstike] *vt* to diagnose.

diagonal, e, aux [djagɔnal, -o] *adj, nf* diagonal; **en ~e** diagonally; **lire en ~e** (*fig*) to skim through.

diagramme [djagʁam] *nm* chart, graph.

dialecte [djalɛkt(ə)] *nm* dialect.

dialectique [djalɛktik] *adj* dialectic(al).

dialogue [djalɔg] *nm* dialogue; **~ de sourds** dialogue of the deaf.

dialoguer [djalɔge] *vi* to converse; (*POL*) to have a dialogue.

dialoguiste [djalɔgist(ə)] *nm/f* dialogue writer.

dialyse [djaliz] *nf* dialysis.

diamant [djamɑ̃] *nm* diamond.

diamantaire [djamɑ̃tɛʁ] *nm* diamond dealer.

diamétralement [djametʁalmɑ̃] *adv* diametrically; **~ opposés** (*opinions*) diametrically opposed.

diamètre [djamɛtʁ(ə)] *nm* diameter.

diapason [djapazɔ̃] *nm* tuning fork; (*fig*): **être/se mettre au ~ (de)** to be/get in tune (with).

diaphane [djafan] *adj* diaphanous.

diaphragme [djafʁagm(ə)] *nm* (*ANAT, PHOTO*) diaphragm; (*contraceptif*) diaphragm, cap; **ouverture du ~** (*PHOTO*) aperture.

diapo [djapo], **diapositive** [djapozitiv] *nf* transparency, slide.

diaporama [djapɔʁama] *nm* slide show.

diapré, e [djapʁe] *adj* many-coloured (*BRIT*), many-colored (*US*).

diarrhée [djaʁe] *nf* diarrhoea (*BRIT*), diarrhea (*US*).

diatribe [djatʁib] *nf* diatribe.

dichotomie [dikɔtɔmi] *nf* dichotomy.

Dictaphone [diktafɔn] *nm* Dictaphone ®.

dictateur [diktatœʁ] *nm* dictator.

dictatorial, e, aux [diktatɔʁjal, -o] *adj* dictatorial.

dictature [diktatyʁ] *nf* dictatorship.

dictée [dikte] *nf* dictation; **prendre sous ~** to take down (*sth dictated*).

dicter [dikte] *vt* to dictate.

diction [diksjɔ̃] *nf* diction, delivery; **cours de ~** speech production lesson(s).

dictionnaire [diksjɔnɛʁ] *nm* dictionary; **~ géographique** gazetteer.

dicton [diktɔ̃] *nm* saying, dictum.

didacticiel [didaktisjɛl] *nm* educational software.

didactique [didaktik] *adj* didactic.

dièse [djɛz] *nm* (*MUS*) sharp.

diesel [djezɛl] *nm, adj inv* diesel.

diète [djɛt] *nf* diet; **être à la ~** to be on a diet.

diététicien, ne [djetetisjɛ̃, -ɛn] *nm/f* dietician.

diététique [djetetik] *nf* dietetics *sg* ♦ *adj*: **magasin ~** health food shop (*BRIT*) *ou* store (*US*).

dieu, x [djø] *nm* god; **D~** God; **le bon D~** the good Lord; **mon D~!** good heavens!

diffamant, e [difamɑ̃, -ɑ̃t] *adj* slanderous, defamatory; libellous.

diffamation [difamasjɔ̃] *nf* slander; (*écrite*) libel; **attaquer qn en ~** to sue sb for slander (*ou* libel).

diffamatoire [difamatwaʁ] *adj* slanderous, defamatory; libellous.

diffamer [difame] *vt* to slander, defame; to libel.

différé [difeʁe] *adj* (*INFORM*): **traitement ~** batch processing; **crédit ~** deferred credit ♦ *nm* (*TV*): **en ~** (pre-)recorded.

différemment [difeʁamɑ̃] *adv* differently.

différence [difeʁɑ̃s] *nf* difference; **à la ~ de** unlike.

différenciation [diferãsjɑsjɔ̃] nf differentiation.

différencier [diferãsje] vt to differentiate; **se ~ de** to become differentiated; **se ~ de** to differentiate o.s. from; (être différent) to differ from.

différend [diferã] nm difference (of opinion), disagreement.

différent, e [diferã, -ãt] adj: **~ (de)** different (from); **~s objets** different ou various objects; **à ~es reprises** on various occasions.

différentiel, le [diferãsjɛl] adj, nm differential.

différer [difere] vt to postpone, put off ♦ vi: **~ (de)** to differ (from); **~ de faire** (tarder) to delay doing.

difficile [difisil] adj difficult; (exigeant) hard to please, difficult (to please); **faire le** ou **la ~** to be hard to please, be difficult.

difficilement [difisilmã] adv (marcher, s'expliquer etc) with difficulty; **~ lisible/ compréhensible** difficult ou hard to read/ understand.

difficulté [difikylte] nf difficulty; **en ~** (bateau, alpiniste) in trouble ou difficulties; **avoir de la ~ à faire** to have difficulty (in) doing.

difforme [difɔʀm(ə)] adj deformed, misshapen.

difformité [difɔʀmite] nf deformity.

diffracter [difʀakte] vt to diffract.

diffus, e [dify, -yz] adj diffuse.

diffuser [difyze] vt (chaleur, bruit, lumière) to diffuse; (émission, musique) to broadcast; (nouvelle, idée) to circulate; (COMM: livres, journaux) to distribute.

diffuseur [difyzœʀ] nm diffuser; distributor.

diffusion [difyzjɔ̃] nf diffusion; broadcast(ing); circulation; distribution.

digérer [diʒere] vt (suj: personne) to digest; (: machine) to process; (fig: accepter) to stomach, put up with.

digeste [diʒɛst(ə)] adj easily digestible.

digestible [diʒɛstibl(ə)] adj digestible.

digestif, ive [diʒɛstif, -iv] adj digestive ♦ nm (after-dinner) liqueur.

digestion [diʒɛstjɔ̃] nf digestion.

digit [didʒit] nm: **~ binaire** binary digit.

digital, e, aux [diʒital, -o] adj digital.

digitale [diʒital] nf digitalis, foxglove.

digne [diɲ] adj dignified; **~ de** worthy of; **~ de foi** trustworthy.

dignitaire [diɲitɛʀ] nm dignitary.

dignité [diɲite] nf dignity.

digression [digʀesjɔ̃] nf digression.

digue [dig] nf dike, dyke; (pour protéger la côte) sea wall.

dijonnais, e [diʒɔnɛ, -ɛz] adj of ou from Dijon ♦ nm/f: **D~, e** inhabitant ou native of Dijon.

diktat [diktat] nm diktat.

dilapidation [dilapidasjɔ̃] nf (voir vb) squandering; embezzlement, misappropriation.

dilapider [dilapide] vt to squander, waste; (dé-

tourner: biens, fonds publics) to embezzle, misappropriate.

dilater [dilate] vt to dilate; (gaz, métal) to cause to expand; (ballon) to distend; **se ~** vi to expand.

dilemme [dilɛm] nm dilemma.

dilettante [diletãt] nm/f dilettante; **en ~** in a dilettantish way.

dilettantisme [diletãtism(ə)] nm dilettant(e)ism.

diligence [diliʒãs] nf stagecoach, diligence; (empressement) despatch; **faire ~** to make haste.

diligent, e [diliʒã, -ãt] adj prompt and efficient; diligent.

diluant [dilɥã] nm thinner(s).

diluer [dilɥe] vt to dilute.

dilution [dilysjɔ̃] nf dilution.

diluvien, ne [dilyvjɛ̃, -ɛn] adj: **pluie ~ne** torrential rain.

dimanche [dimãʃ] nm Sunday; **le ~ des Rameaux/de Pâques** Palm/Easter Sunday; voir aussi **lundi**.

dîme [dim] nf tithe.

dimension [dimãsjɔ̃] nf (grandeur) size; (gén pl: cotes, MATH: de l'espace) dimension.

diminué, e [diminɥe] adj (personne: physiquement) run-down; (: mentalement) less alert.

diminuer [diminɥe] vt to reduce, decrease; (ardeur etc) to lessen; (personne: physiquement) to undermine; (dénigrer) to belittle ♦ vi to decrease, diminish.

diminutif [diminytif] nm (LING) diminutive; (surnom) pet name.

diminution [diminysjɔ̃] nf decreasing, diminishing.

dînatoire [dinatwaʀ] adj: **goûter ~** ≈ high tea (BRIT); **apéritif ~** ≈ evening buffet.

dinde [dɛ̃d] nf turkey; (femme stupide) goose.

dindon [dɛ̃dɔ̃] nm turkey.

dindonneau, x [dɛ̃dɔno] nm turkey poult.

dîner [dine] nm dinner ♦ vi to have dinner; **~ d'affaires/de famille** business/family dinner.

dînette [dinɛt] nf (jeu): **jouer à la ~** to play at tea parties.

dingue [dɛ̃g] adj (fam) crazy.

dinosaure [dinozɔʀ] nm dinosaur.

diocèse [djɔsɛz] nm diocese.

diode [djɔd] nf diode.

diphasé, e [difaze] adj (ÉLEC) two-phase.

diphtérie [difteʀi] nf diphtheria.

diphtongue [diftɔ̃g] nf diphthong.

diplomate [diplɔmat] adj diplomatic ♦ nm diplomat; (fig: personne habile) diplomatist; (CULIN: gâteau) dessert made of sponge cake, candied fruit and custard, ≈ trifle (BRIT).

diplomatie [diplɔmasi] nf diplomacy.

diplomatique [diplɔmatik] adj diplomatic.

diplôme [diplom] nm diploma certificate; (examen) (diploma) examination.

diplômé, e [diplome] adj qualified.

dire [diʀ] *nm*: **au ~ de** according to; **leurs ~s** what they say ♦ *vt* to say; (*secret, mensonge*) to tell; **~ l'heure/la vérité** to tell the time/the truth; **dis pardon/merci** say sorry/thank you; **~ qch à qn** to tell sb sth; **~ à qn qu'il fasse** *ou* **de faire** to tell sb to do; **~ que** to say that; **on dit que** they say that; **comme on dit** as they say; **on dirait que** it looks (*ou* sounds *etc*) as though; **on dirait du vin** you'd *ou* one would think it was wine; **que dites-vous de** (*penser*) what do you think of; **si cela lui dit** if he feels like it, if he fancies it; **cela ne me dit rien** that doesn't appeal to me; **à vrai ~** truth to tell; **pour ainsi ~** so to speak; **cela va sans ~** that goes without saying; **dis donc!, dites donc!** (*pour attirer l'attention*) hey!; (*au fait*) by the way; **et ~ que ...** and to think that ...; **ceci** *ou* **cela dit** that being said; (*à ces mots*) whereupon; **c'est dit, voilà qui est dit** so that's settled; **il n'y a pas à ~** there's no getting away from it; **c'est ~ si ...** that just shows that ...; **c'est beaucoup/peu ~** that's saying a lot/not saying much; **se ~** (*à soi-même*) to say to oneself; (*se prétendre*): **se ~ malade** *etc* to say (that) one is ill *etc*; **ça se dit ... en anglais** that is ... in English; **cela ne se dit pas comme ça** you don't say it like that; **se ~ au revoir** to say goodbye (to each other).

direct, e [diʀɛkt] *adj* direct ♦ *nm* (*train*) through train; **en ~** (*émission*) live; **train/bus ~** express train/bus.

directement [diʀɛktəmã] *adv* directly.

directeur, trice [diʀɛktœʀ, -tʀis] *nm/f* (*d'entreprise*) director; (*de service*) manager/eress; (*d'école*) head(teacher) (*BRIT*), principal (*US*); **comité ~** management *ou* steering committee; **~ général** general manager; **~ de thèse** ≈ PhD supervisor.

direction [diʀɛksjõ] *nf* management; conducting; supervision; (*AUTO*) steering; (*sens*) direction; **sous la ~ de** (*MUS*) conducted by; **en ~ de** (*avion, train, bateau*) for; **"toutes ~s"** (*AUTO*) "all routes".

directive [diʀɛktiv] *nf* directive, instruction.

directorial, e, aux [diʀɛktɔʀjal, -o] *adj* (*bureau*) director's; manager's; head teacher's.

directrice [diʀɛktʀis] *adj f, nf voir* **directeur**.

dirent [diʀ] *vb voir* **dire**.

dirigeable [diʀiʒabl(ə)] *adj, nm*: **(ballon) ~** dirigible.

dirigeant, e [diʀiʒã, -ãt] *adj* managerial; (*classes*) ruling ♦ *nm/f* (*d'un parti etc*) leader; (*d'entreprise*) manager, member of the management.

diriger [diʀiʒe] *vt* (*entreprise*) to manage, run; (*véhicule*) to steer; (*orchestre*) to conduct; (*recherches, travaux*) to supervise, be in charge of; (*braquer: regard, arme*): **~ sur** to point *ou* level *ou* aim at; (*fig: critiques*): **~ contre** to aim at; **se ~** (*s'orienter*) to find one's way; **se ~ vers** *ou* **sur** to make *ou* head for.

dirigisme [diʀiʒism(ə)] *nm* (*ÉCON*) state intervention, interventionism.

dirigiste [diʀiʒist(ə)] *adj* interventionist.

dis [di], **disais** [dizɛ] *etc vb voir* **dire**.

discal, e, aux [diskal, -o] *adj* (*MÉD*): **hernie ~e** slipped disc.

discernement [disɛʀnəmã] *nm* discernment, judgment.

discerner [disɛʀne] *vt* to discern, make out.

disciple [disipl(ə)] *nm/f* disciple.

disciplinaire [disiplinɛʀ] *adj* disciplinary.

discipline [disiplin] *nf* discipline.

discipliné, e [discipline] *adj* (well-)disciplined.

discipliner [discipline] *vt* to discipline; (*cheveux*) to control.

discobole [diskɔbɔl] *nm/f* discus thrower.

discographie [diskɔgʀafi] *nf* discography.

discontinu, e [diskõtiny] *adj* intermittent; (*bande: sur la route*) broken.

discontinuer [diskõtinɥe] *vi*: **sans ~** without stopping, without a break.

disconvenir [diskõvniʀ] *vi*: **ne pas ~ de qch/que** not to deny sth/that.

discophile [diskɔfil] *nm/f* record enthusiast.

discordance [diskɔʀdãs] *nf* discordance; conflict.

discordant, e [diskɔʀdã, -ãt] *adj* discordant, conflicting.

discorde [diskɔʀd(ə)] *nf* discord, dissension.

discothèque [diskɔtɛk] *nf* (*disques*) record collection; (: *dans une bibliothèque*): **~ (de prêt)** record library; (*boîte de nuit*) disco(thèque).

discourais [diskuʀɛ] *etc vb voir* **discourir**.

discourir [diskuʀiʀ] *vi* to discourse, hold forth.

discours [diskuʀ] *vb voir* **discourir** ♦ *nm* speech; **~ direct/indirect** (*LING*) direct/indirect *ou* reported speech.

discourtois, e [diskuʀtwa, waz] *adj* discourteous.

discrédit [diskʀedi] *nm*: **jeter le ~ sur** to discredit.

discréditer [diskʀedite] *vt* to discredit.

discret, ète [diskʀɛ, -ɛt] *adj* discreet; (*fig: musique, style*) unobtrusive; (: *endroit*) quiet.

discrètement [diskʀɛtmã] *adv* discreetly.

discrétion [diskʀesjõ] *nf* discretion; **à la ~ de qn** at sb's discretion; in sb's hands; **à ~** (*boisson etc*) unlimited, as much as one wants.

discrétionnaire [diskʀesjɔnɛʀ] *adj* discretionary.

discrimination [diskʀiminasjõ] *nf* discrimination; **sans ~** indiscriminately.

discriminatoire [diskʀiminatwaʀ] *adj* discriminatory.

disculper [diskylpe] *vt* to exonerate.

discussion [diskysjõ] *nf* discussion.

discutable [diskytabl(ə)] *adj* (*contestable*) doubtful; (*à débattre*) debatable.

discuté, e [diskyte] *adj* controversial.

discuter [diskyte] *vt* (*contester*) to question, dispute; (*débattre: prix*) to discuss ♦ *vi* to talk; (*ergoter*) to argue; ~ **de** to discuss.

dise [diz] *etc vb voir* **dire.**

disert, e [dizɛR, -ɛRt(ə)] *adj* loquacious.

disette [dizɛt] *nf* food shortage.

diseuse [dizøz] *nf*: ~ **de bonne aventure** fortuneteller.

disgrâce [disgRɑs] *nf* disgrace; **être en** ~ to be in disgrace.

disgracié, e [disgRasje] *adj* (*en disgrâce*) disgraced.

disgracieux, euse [disgRasjø, -øz] *adj* ungainly, awkward.

disjoindre [disʒwɛ̃dR(ə)] *vt* to take apart; **se** ~ *vi* to come apart.

disjoint, e [disʒwɛ̃, -wɛ̃t] *pp de* **disjoindre** ♦ *adj* loose.

disjoncteur [disʒɔ̃ktœR] *nm* (*ÉLEC*) circuit breaker.

dislocation [dislɔkasjɔ̃] *nf* dislocation.

disloquer [dislɔke] *vt* (*membre*) to dislocate; (*chaise*) to dismantle; (*troupe*) to disperse; **se** ~ *vi* (*parti, empire*) to break up; **se** ~ **l'épaule** to dislocate one's shoulder.

disons [dizɔ̃] *etc vb voir* **dire.**

disparaître [disparɛtR(ə)] *vi* to disappear; (*à la vue*) to vanish, disappear; to be hidden *ou* concealed; (*être manquant*) to go missing, disappear; (*se perdre: traditions etc*) to die out; (*personne: mourir*) to die; **faire** ~ (*objet, tache, trace*) to remove; (*personne*) to get rid of.

disparate [disparat] *adj* disparate; (*couleurs*) ill-assorted.

disparité [disparite] *nf* disparity.

disparition [disparisjɔ̃] *nf* disappearance.

disparu, e [dispary] *pp de* **disparaître** ♦ *nm/f* missing person; (*défunt*) departed; **être porté** ~ to be reported missing.

dispendieux, euse [dispɑ̃djø, -øz] *adj* extravagant, expensive.

dispensaire [dispɑ̃sɛR] *nm* community clinic.

dispense [dispɑ̃s] *nf* exemption; (*permission*) special permission; ~ **d'âge** special exemption from age limit.

dispenser [dispɑ̃se] *vt* (*donner*) to lavish, bestow; (*exempter*): ~ **qn de** to exempt sb from; **se** ~ **de** *vt* to avoid, get out of.

disperser [dispɛRse] *vt* to scatter; (*fig: son attention*) to dissipate; **se** ~ *vi* to scatter; (*fig*) to dissipate one's efforts.

dispersion [dispɛRsjɔ̃] *nf* scattering; (*des efforts*) dissipation.

disponibilité [disponibilite] *nf* availability; (*ADMIN*): **être en** ~ to be on leave of absence; ~**s** *nfpl* (*COMM*) liquid assets.

disponible [disponibl(ə)] *adj* available.

dispos [dispo] *adj m*: **(frais et)** ~ fresh (as a daisy).

disposé, e [dispoze] *adj* (*d'une certaine manière*) arranged, laid-out; **bien/mal** ~ (*hu-*

meur) in a good/bad mood; **bien/mal** ~ **pour** *ou* **envers qn** well/badly disposed towards sb; ~ **à** (*prêt à*) willing *ou* prepared to.

disposer [dispoze] *vt* (*arranger, placer*) to arrange; (*inciter*): ~ **qn à qch/faire qch** to dispose *ou* incline sb towards sth/to do sth ♦ *vi*: **vous pouvez** ~ you may leave; ~ **de** *vt* to have (at one's disposal); **se** ~ **à faire** to prepare to do, be about to do.

dispositif [dispozitif] *nm* device; (*fig*) system, plan of action; set-up; (*d'un texte de loi*) operative part; ~ **de sûreté** safety device.

disposition [dispozisjɔ̃] *nf* (*arrangement*) arrangement, layout; (*humeur*) mood; (*tendance*) tendency; ~**s** *nfpl* (*mesures*) steps, measures; (*préparatifs*) arrangements; (*de loi, testament*) provisions; (*aptitudes*) bent *sg*, aptitude *sg*; **à la** ~ **de qn** at sb's disposal.

disproportion [dispRɔpɔRsjɔ̃] *nf* disproportion.

disproportionné, e [dispRɔpɔRsjɔne] *adj* disproportionate, out of all proportion.

dispute [dispyt] *nf* quarrel, argument.

disputer [dispyte] *vt* (*match*) to play; (*combat*) to fight; (*course*) to run; **se** ~ *vi* to quarrel, have a quarrel; (*match, combat, course*) to take place; ~ **qch à qn** to fight with sb for *ou* over sth.

disquaire [diskɛR] *nm/f* record dealer.

disqualification [diskalifikasjɔ̃] *nf* disqualification.

disqualifier [diskalifje] *vt* to disqualify; **se** ~ *vi* to bring discredit on o.s.

disque [disk(ə)] *nm* (*MUS*) record; (*INFORM*) disk, disc; (*forme, pièce*) disc; (*SPORT*) discus; ~ **compact** compact disc; ~ **compact interactif** CD-I ®; ~ **dur** hard disk; ~ **d'embrayage** (*AUTO*) clutch plate; ~ **laser** compact disc; ~ **de stationnement** parking disc; ~ **système** system disk.

disquette [diskɛt] *nf* diskette, floppy (disk); ~ **(à) simple/double densité** single/double density disk; ~ **une face/double face** single-/double-sided disk.

dissection [disɛksjɔ̃] *nf* dissection.

dissemblable [disɑ̃blabl(ə)] *adj* dissimilar.

dissemblance [disɑ̃blɑ̃s] *nf* dissimilarity, difference.

dissémination [diseminasjɔ̃] *nf* (*voir vb*) scattering; dispersal; (*des armes*) proliferation.

disséminer [disemine] *vt* to scatter; (*troupes: sur un territoire*) to disperse.

dissension [disɑ̃sjɔ̃] *nf* dissension; ~**s** *nfpl* dissension.

disséquer [diseke] *vt* to dissect.

dissertation [disɛRtasjɔ̃] *nf* (*SCOL*) essay.

disserter [disɛRte] *vi*: ~ **sur** to discourse upon.

dissidence [disidɑ̃s] *nf* (*concept*) dissidence; **rejoindre la** ~ to join the dissidents.

dissident, e [disidɑ̃, -ɑ̃t] *adj*, *nm/f* dissident.

dissimilitude [disimilityd] *nf* dissimilarity.

dissimulateur, trice [disimyltœR, -tRis] *adj*

dissembling ♦ *nm/f* dissembler.

dissimulation [disimylɑsjɔ̃] *nf* concealing; (*duplicité*) dissimulation; ~ **de bénéfices/de revenus** concealment of profits/income.

dissimulé, e [disimyle] (*personne: secret*) secretive; (*: fourbe, hypocrite*) deceitful.

dissimuler [disimyle] *vt* to conceal; **se** ~ to conceal o.s.; to be concealed.

dissipation [disipɑsjɔ̃] *nf* squandering; unruliness; (*débauche*) dissipation.

dissipé, e [disipe] *adj* (*indiscipliné*) unruly.

dissiper [disipe] *vt* to dissipate; (*fortune*) to squander, fritter away; **se** ~ *vi* (*brouillard*) to clear, disperse; (*doutes*) to disappear, melt away; (*élève*) to become undisciplined *ou* unruly.

dissociable [disɔsjabl(ə)] *adj* separable.

dissocier [disɔsje] *vt* to dissociate; **se** ~ *vi* (*éléments, groupe*) to break up, split up; **se** ~ **de** (*groupe, point de vue*) to dissociate o.s. from.

dissolu, e [disɔly] *adj* dissolute.

dissoluble [disɔlybl(ə)] *adj* (*POL: assemblée*) dissolvable.

dissolution [disɔlysjɔ̃] *nf* dissolving; (*POL, JUR*) dissolution.

dissolvant, e [disɔlvɑ̃, -ɑ̃t] *vb voir* **dissoudre** ♦ *nm* (*CHIMIE*) solvent; ~ (**gras**) nail polish remover.

dissonant, e [disɔnɑ̃, -ɑ̃t] *adj* discordant.

dissoudre [disudʀ] *vt*, **se** ~ *vi* to dissolve.

dissous, oute [disu, -ut] *pp de* **dissoudre**.

dissuader [disɥade] *vt*: ~ **qn de faire/de qch** to dissuade sb from doing/from sth.

dissuasif, ive [disɥazif, iv] *adj* dissuasive.

dissuasion [disɥazjɔ̃] *nf* dissuasion; **force de** ~ deterrent power.

distance [distɑ̃s] *nf* distance; (*fig: écart*) gap; **à** ~ at *ou* from a distance; (*mettre en marche, commander*) by remote control; (**situé**) **à** ~ (*INFORM*) remote; **tenir qn à** ~ to keep sb at a distance; **se tenir à** ~ to keep one's distance; **à une** ~ **de 10 km, à 10 km de** ~ 10 km away, at a distance of 10 km; **à 2 ans de** ~ with a gap of 2 years; **prendre ses** ~**s** to space out; **garder ses** ~**s** to keep one's distance; **tenir la** ~ (*SPORT*) to cover the distance, last the course; ~ **focale** (*PHOTO*) focal length.

distancer [distɑ̃se] *vt* to outdistance, leave behind.

distancier [distɑ̃sje]: **se** ~ *vi* to distance o.s.

distant, e [distɑ̃, -ɑ̃t] *adj* (*réservé*) distant, aloof; (*éloigné*) distant, far away; ~ **de** (*lieu*) far away *ou* a long way from; ~ **de 5 km** (*d'un lieu*) 5 km away (from a place).

distendre [distɑ̃dʀ(ə)] *vt*, **se** ~ *vi* to distend.

distillation [distilɑsjɔ̃] *nf* distillation, distilling.

distillé, e [distile] *adj*: **eau** ~**e** distilled water.

distiller [distile] *vt* to distil; (*fig*) to exude; to elaborate.

distillerie [distilʀi] *nf* distillery.

distinct, e [distɛ̃(kt), distɛ̃kt(ə)] *adj* distinct.

distinctement [distɛ̃ktəmɑ̃] *adv* distinctly.

distinctif, ive [distɛ̃ktif, -iv] *adj* distinctive.

distinction [distɛ̃ksjɔ̃] *nf* distinction.

distingué, e [distɛ̃ge] *adj* distinguished.

distinguer [distɛ̃ge] *vt* to distinguish; **se** ~ *vi* (*s'illustrer*) to distinguish o.s.; (*différer*): **se** ~ (**de**) to distinguish o.s. *ou* be distinguished (from).

distinguo [distɛ̃go] *nm* distinction.

distorsion [distɔʀsjɔ̃] *nf* (*gén*) distorsion; (*fig: déséquilibre*) disparity, imbalance.

distraction [distʀaksjɔ̃] *nf* (*manque d'attention*) absent-mindedness; (*oubli*) lapse (in concentration *ou* attention); (*détente*) diversion, recreation; (*passe-temps*) distraction, entertainment.

distraire [distʀɛʀ] *vt* (*déranger*) to distract; (*divertir*) to entertain, divert; (*détourner: somme d'argent*) to divert, misappropriate; **se** ~ to amuse *ou* enjoy o.s.

distrait, e [distʀɛ, -ɛt] *pp de* **distraire** ♦ *adj* absent-minded.

distraitement [distʀɛtmɑ̃] *adv* absent-mindedly.

distrayant, e [distʀɛjɑ̃, -ɑ̃t] *vb voir* **distraire** ♦ *adj* entertaining.

distribanque [distʀibɑ̃k] *nm* cash dispenser.

distribuer [distʀibɥe] *vt* to distribute; to hand out; (*CARTES*) to deal (out); (*courrier*) to deliver.

distributeur [distʀibytœʀ] *nm* (*AUTO, COMM*) distributor; (*automatique*) (vending) machine; ~ **de billets** (*RAIL*) ticket machine; (*BANQUE*) cash dispenser.

distribution [distʀibysjɔ̃] *nf* distribution; (*postale*) delivery; (*choix d'acteurs*) casting; **circuits de** ~ (*COMM*) distribution network; ~ **des prix** (*SCOL*) prize giving.

district [distʀik(t)] *nm* district.

dit, e [di, dit] *pp de* **dire** ♦ *adj* (*fixé*): **le jour** ~ the arranged day; (*surnommé*): **X,** ~ **Pierrot** X, known as *ou* called Pierrot.

dites [dit] *vb voir* **dire**.

dithyrambique [ditiʀɑ̃bik] *adj* eulogistic.

DIU *sigle m* (= *dispositif intra-utérin*) IUD.

diurétique [djyʀetik] *adj, nm* diuretic.

diurne [djyʀn(ə)] *adj* diurnal, daytime *cpd*.

divagations [divagɑsjɔ̃] *nfpl* ramblings; ravings.

divaguer [divage] *vi* to ramble; (*malade*) to rave.

divan [divɑ̃] *nm* divan.

divan-lit [divɑ̃li] *nm* divan (bed).

divergence [divɛʀʒɑ̃s] *nf* divergence; **des** ~**s d'opinion au sein de ...** differences of opinion within ....

divergent, e [divɛʀʒɑ̃, -ɑ̃t] *adj* divergent.

diverger [divɛʀʒe] *vi* to diverge.

divers, e [divɛʀ, -ɛʀs(ə)] *adj* (*varié*) diverse, varied; (*différent*) different, various ♦ *dét* (*plusieurs*) various, several; (**frais**) ~ (*COMM*)

diversement – DOM

sundries, miscellaneous (expenses); "~" (*rubrique*) "miscellaneous".
diversement [divɛʀsəmɑ̃] *adv* in various *ou* diverse ways.
diversification [divɛʀsifikasjɔ̃] *nf* diversification.
diversifier [divɛʀsifje] *vt*, **se** ~ *vi* to diversify.
diversion [divɛʀsjɔ̃] *nf* diversion; **faire** ~ to create a diversion.
diversité [divɛʀsite] *nf* diversity, variety.
divertir [divɛʀtiʀ] *vt* to amuse, entertain; **se** ~ to amuse *ou* enjoy o.s.
divertissant, e [divɛʀtisɑ̃, -ɑ̃t] *adj* entertaining.
divertissement [divɛʀtismɑ̃] *nm* entertainment; (*MUS*) divertimento, divertissement.
dividende [dividɑ̃d] *nm* (*MATH*, *COMM*) dividend.
divin, e [divɛ̃, -in] *adj* divine; (*fig: excellent*) heavenly, divine.
divinateur, trice [divinatœʀ, -tʀis] *adj* perspicacious.
divinatoire [divinatwaʀ] *adj* (*art, science*) divinatory; **baguette** ~ divining rod.
diviniser [divinize] *vt* to deify.
divinité [divinite] *nf* divinity.
divisé, e [divize] *adj* divided.
diviser [divize] *vt* (*gén, MATH*) to divide; (*morceler, subdiviser*) to divide (up), split (up); **se** ~ **en** to divide into; ~ **par** to divide by.
diviseur [divizœʀ] *nm* (*MATH*) divisor.
divisible [divizibl(ə)] *adj* divisible.
division [divizjɔ̃] *nf* (*gén*) division; ~ **du travail** (*ÉCON*) division of labour.
divisionnaire [divizjɔnɛʀ] *adj*: **commissaire** ~ ≈ chief superintendent (*BRIT*), ≈ police chief (*US*).
divorce [divɔʀs(ə)] *nm* divorce.
divorcé, e [divɔʀse] *nm/f* divorcee.
divorcer [divɔʀse] *vi* to get a divorce, get divorced; ~ **de** *ou* **d'avec qn** to divorce sb.
divulgation [divylgasjɔ̃] *nf* disclosure.
divulguer [divylge] *vt* to divulge, disclose.
dix [di, dis, diz] *num* ten.
dix-huit [dizɥit] *num* eighteen.
dix-huitième [dizɥitjɛm] *num* eighteenth.
dixième [dizjɛm] *num* tenth.
dix-neuf [diznœf] *num* nineteen.
dix-neuvième [diznœvjɛm] *num* nineteenth.
dix-sept [disɛt] *num* seventeen.
dix-septième [disɛtjɛm] *num* seventeenth.
dizaine [dizɛn] *nf* (*10*) ten; (*environ 10*): **une** ~ (**de**) about ten, ten or so.
Djakarta [dʒakaʀta] *n* Djakarta.
Djibouti [dʒibuti] *n* Djibouti.
dl *abr* (= *décilitre*) dl.
DM *abr* (= *Deutschmark*) DM.
dm. *abr* (= *décimètre*) dm.
do [do] *nm* (*note*) C; (*en chantant la gamme*) do(h).

docile [dɔsil] *adj* docile.
docilement [dɔsilmɑ̃] *adv* docilely.
docilité [dɔsilite] *nf* docility.
dock [dɔk] *nm* dock; (*hangar, bâtiment*) warehouse.
docker [dɔkɛʀ] *nm* docker.
docte [dɔkt(ə)] *adj* (*péj*) learned.
docteur [dɔktœʀ] *nm* doctor; ~ **en médecine** doctor of medicine.
doctoral, e, aux [dɔktɔʀal, -o] *adj* pompous, bombastic.
doctorat [dɔktɔʀa] *nm*: ~ (**d'Université**) ≈ doctorate; ~ **d'État** ≈ PhD; ~ **de troisième cycle** ≈ doctorate.
doctoresse [dɔktɔʀɛs] *nf* lady doctor.
doctrinaire [dɔktʀinɛʀ] *adj* doctrinaire; (*sententieux*) pompous, sententious.
doctrinal, e, aux [dɔktʀinal, o] *adj* doctrinal.
doctrine [dɔktʀin] *nf* doctrine.
document [dɔkymɑ̃] *nm* document.
documentaire [dɔkymɑ̃tɛʀ] *adj*, *nm* documentary.
documentaliste [dɔkymɑ̃talist(ə)] *nm/f* archivist; (*PRESSE, TV*) researcher.
documentation [dɔkymɑ̃tasjɔ̃] *nf* documentation, literature; (*PRESSE, TV: service*) research.
documenté, e [dɔkymɑ̃te] *adj* well-informed, well-documented; well-researched.
documenter [dɔkymɑ̃te] *vt*: **se** ~ (**sur**) to gather information *ou* material (on *ou* about).
Dodécanèse [dɔdekanɛz] *nm* Dodecanese (Islands).
dodeliner [dɔdline] *vi*: ~ **de la tête** to nod one's head gently.
dodo [dɔdo] *nm*: **aller faire** ~ to go to beddybyes.
dodu, e [dɔdy] *adj* plump.
dogmatique [dɔgmatik] *adj* dogmatic.
dogmatisme [dɔgmatism(ə)] *nm* dogmatism.
dogme [dɔgm(ə)] *nm* dogma.
dogue [dɔg] *nm* mastiff.
doigt [dwa] *nm* finger; **à deux** ~**s de** within an ace (*BRIT*) *ou* an inch of; **un** ~ **de lait/whisky** a drop of milk/whisky; **désigner** *ou* **montrer du** ~ to point at; **au** ~ **et à l'œil** to the letter; **connaître qch sur le bout du** ~ to know sth backwards; **mettre le** ~ **sur la plaie** (*fig*) to find the sensitive spot; ~ **de pied** toe.
doigté [dwate] *nm* (*MUS*) fingering; (*fig: habileté*) diplomacy, tact.
doigtier [dwatje] *nm* fingerstall.
dois [dwa] *etc vb voir* **devoir**.
doive [dwav] *etc vb voir* **devoir**.
doléances [dɔleɑ̃s] *nfpl* complaints; (*réclamations*) grievances.
dolent, e [dɔlɑ̃, -ɑ̃t] *adj* doleful, mournful.
dollar [dɔlaʀ] *nm* dollar.
dolmen [dɔlmɛn] *nm* dolmen.
DOM [deɔm, dɔm] *sigle m ou mpl* = *Département(s) d'outre-mer*.

France has four overseas départements or **DOMs**: *French Guiana, Guadeloupe, Martinique and Réunion. Since 1982 each of these has also had regional status. France also has five overseas territories or* **TOMs**: *Austral and Antarctic French territories, French Polynesia, Mayotte, New Caledonia and Wallis and Futuna. Citizens of both DOMs and TOMs have French nationality.*

---

domaine [dɔmɛn] *nm* estate, property; (*fig*) domain, field; **tomber dans le ~ public** (*livre etc*) to be out of copyright; **dans tous les ~s** in all areas.

domanial, e, aux [dɔmanjal, -o] *adj* national, state *cpd*.

dôme [dom] *nm* dome.

domestication [dɔmɛstikasjɔ̃] *nf* (*voir domestiquer*) domestication; harnessing.

domesticité [dɔmɛstisite] *nf* (*domestic*) staff.

domestique [dɔmɛstik] *adj* domestic ♦ *nm/f* servant, domestic.

domestiquer [dɔmɛstike] *vt* to domesticate; (*vent, marées*) to harness.

domicile [dɔmisil] *nm* home, place of residence; **à ~** at home; **élire ~ à** to take up residence in; **sans ~ fixe** of no fixed abode; **~ conjugal** marital home; **~ légal** domicile.

domicilié, e [dɔmisilje] *adj*: **être ~ à** to have one's home in *ou* at.

dominant, e [dɔminɑ̃, -ɑ̃t] *adj* dominant; (*plus important*) predominant ♦ *nf* (*caractéristique*) dominant characteristic; (*couleur*) dominant colour.

dominateur, trice [dɔminatœʀ, -tʀis] *adj* dominating; (*qui aime à dominer*) domineering.

domination [dɔminasjɔ̃] *nf* domination.

dominer [dɔmine] *vt* to dominate; (*passions etc*) to master; (*surpasser*) to outclass, surpass; (*surplomber*) to tower above, dominate ♦ *vi* to be in the dominant position; **se ~** to control o.s.

dominicain, e [dɔminikɛ̃, -ɛn] *adj* Dominican.

dominical, e, aux [dɔminikal, -o] *adj* Sunday *cpd*, dominical.

Dominique [dɔminik] *nf*: **la ~** Dominica.

domino [dɔmino] *nm* domino; **~s** *nmpl* (*jeu*) dominoes *sg*.

dommage [dɔmaʒ] *nm* (*préjudice*) harm, injury; (*dégâts, pertes*) damage *no pl*; **c'est ~ de faire/que** it's a shame *ou* pity to do/that; **~s corporels** physical injury.

dommages-intérêts [dɔmaʒ(əz)ɛ̃teʀɛ] *nmpl* damages.

dompter [dɔ̃te] *vt* to tame.

dompteur, euse [dɔ̃tœʀ, -øz] *nm/f* trainer; (*de lion*) liontamer.

DOM-TOM [dɔmtɔm] *sigle m ou mpl* = *Département(s) d'outre-mer/Territoire(s) d'outre-mer.*

don [dɔ̃] *nm* (*cadeau*) gift; (*charité*) donation; (*aptitude*) gift, talent; **avoir des ~s pour** to

have a gift *ou* talent for; **faire ~ de** to make a gift of; **~ en argent** cash donation.

donateur, trice [dɔnatœʀ, -tʀis] *nm/f* donor.

donation [dɔnasjɔ̃] *nf* donation.

donc [dɔ̃k] *conj* therefore, so; (*après une digression*) so, then; (*intensif*): **voilà ~ la solution** so there's the solution; **je disais ~ que** ... as I was saying, ...; **venez ~ dîner à la maison** do come for dinner; **allons ~!** come now!; **faites ~** go ahead.

donjon [dɔ̃ʒɔ̃] *nm* keep.

don Juan [dɔ̃ʒɥɑ̃] *nm* Don Juan.

donnant, e [dɔnɑ̃, -ɑ̃t] *adj*: **~, ~** fair's fair.

donne [dɔn] *nf* (*CARTES*): **il y a mauvaise** *ou* **fausse ~** there's been a misdeal.

donné, e [dɔne] *adj* (*convenu*) given; (*pas cher*) dirt cheap, very cheap ♦ *nf* (*MATH, INFORM, gén*) datum (*pl* data); **c'est ~** it's a gift; **étant ~ ...** given ....

donner [dɔne] *vt* to give; (*vieux habits etc*) to give away; (*spectacle*) to put on; (*film*) to show; **~ qch à qn** to give sb sth, give sth to sb; **~ sur** (*suj: fenêtre, chambre*) to look (out) onto; (*piège etc*) to fall into; **faire ~ l'infanterie** (*MIL*) to send in the infantry; **~ l'heure à qn** to tell sb the time; **~ le ton** (*fig*) to set the tone; **~ à penser/entendre que ...** to make one think/give one to understand that ...; **se ~ à fond (à son travail)** to give one's all (to one's work), devote o.s. heart and soul (to one's work); **se ~ du mal** *ou* **de la peine (pour faire qch)** to go to a lot of trouble (to do sth); **s'en ~ à cœur joie** (*fam*) to have a great time (of it).

donneur, euse [dɔnœʀ, -øz] *nm/f* (*MÉD*) donor; (*CARTES*) dealer; **~ de sang** blood donor.

=============================== *MOT-CLÉ*

dont [dɔ̃] *pron relatif* **1** (*appartenance: objets*) whose, of which; (: *êtres animés*) whose; **la maison ~ le toit est rouge** the house the roof of which is red, the house whose roof is red; **l'homme ~ je connais la sœur** the man whose sister I know

2 (*parmi lesquel(le)s*): **2 livres, ~ l'un est ...** 2 books, one of which is ...; **il y avait plusieurs personnes, ~ Gabrielle** there were several people, among them Gabrielle; **10 blessés, ~ 2 grièvement** 10 injured, 2 of them seriously

3 (*complément d'adjectif, de verbe*): **le fils ~ il est si fier** the son he's so proud of; **ce ~ je parle** what I'm talking about; **la façon ~ il l'a fait** the way (in which) he did it.

---

donzelle [dɔ̃zɛl] *nf* (*péj*) young madam.

dopage [dɔpaʒ] *nm* doping.

dopant [dɔpɑ̃] *nm* dope.

doper [dɔpe] *vt* to dope; **se ~** to take dope.

doping [dɔpiŋ] *nm* doping; (*excitant*) dope.

dorade [dɔʀad] *nf* = daurade.

doré, e [dɔʀe] *adj* golden; (*avec dorure*) gilt,

dorénavant – douter

gilded.

dorénavant [dɔʀenavɑ̃] *adv* from now on, henceforth.

dorer [dɔʀe] *vt (cadre)* to gild; **(faire)** ~ *(CULIN)* to brown; *(: gâteau)* to glaze; **se ~ au soleil** to sunbathe; ~ **la pilule à qn** to sugar the pill for sb.

dorloter [dɔʀlɔte] *vt* to pamper, cosset *(BRIT)*; **se faire** ~ to be pampered *ou* cosseted.

dormant, e [dɔʀmɑ̃, -ɑ̃t] *adj:* **eau ~e** still water.

dorme [dɔʀm(ə)] *etc vb voir* **dormir**.

dormeur, euse [dɔʀmœʀ, -øz] *nm/f* sleeper.

dormir [dɔʀmiʀ] *vi* to sleep; *(être endormi)* to be asleep; ~ **à poings fermés** to sleep very soundly.

dorsal, e, aux [dɔʀsal, -o] *adj* dorsal; *voir* **rouleau**.

dortoir [dɔʀtwaʀ] *nm* dormitory.

dorure [dɔʀyʀ] *nf* gilding.

doryphore [dɔʀifɔʀ] *nm* Colorado beetle.

dos [do] *nm* back; *(de livre)* spine; **"voir au ~"** "see over"; **robe décolletée dans le ~** low-backed dress; **de ~** from the back, from behind; ~ **à ~** back to back; **sur le ~** on one's back; **à ~ de chameau** riding on a camel; **avoir bon ~** to be a good excuse; **se mettre qn à ~** to turn sb against one.

dosage [doza3] *nm* mixture.

dos-d'âne [dodɑn] *nm* humpback; **pont en ~** humpbacked bridge.

dose [doz] *nf (MÉD)* dose; **forcer la ~** *(fig)* to overstep the mark.

doser [doze] *vt* to measure out; *(mélanger)* to mix in the correct proportions; *(fig)* to expend in the right amounts *ou* proportions; to strike a balance between.

doseur [dozœʀ] *nm* measure; **bouchon ~** measuring cap.

dossard [dosaʀ] *nm* number *(worn by competitor)*.

dossier [dosje] *nm (renseignements, fichier)* file; *(enveloppe)* folder, file; *(de chaise)* back; *(PRESSE)* feature; **le ~ social/monétaire** *(fig)* the social/financial question; ~ **suspendu** suspension file.

dot [dɔt] *nf* dowry.

dotation [dɔtasjɔ̃] *nf* block grant; endowment.

doté, e [dɔte] *adj:* ~ **de** equipped with.

doter [dɔte] *vt:* ~ **qn/qch de** to equip sb/sth with.

douairière [dwɛʀjɛʀ] *nf* dowager.

douane [dwan] *nf (poste, bureau)* customs *pl*; *(taxes)* (customs) duty; **passer la ~** to go through customs; **en ~** *(marchandises, entrepôt)* bonded.

douanier, ière [dwanje, -jɛʀ] *adj* customs *cpd* ♦ *nm* customs officer.

doublage [dubla3] *nm (CINÉ)* dubbing.

double [dubl(ə)] *adj, adv* double ♦ *nm (2 fois plus):* **le ~ (de)** twice as much *(ou* many)

(as), double the amount *(ou* number) (of); *(autre exemplaire)* duplicate, copy; *(sosie)* double; *(TENNIS)* doubles *sg*; **voir ~** to see double; **en ~ (exemplaire)** in duplicate; **faire ~ emploi** to be redundant; **à ~ sens** with a double meaning; **à ~ tranchant** two-edged; ~ **carburateur** twin carburettor; **à ~s commandes** dual-control; ~ **messieurs/mixte** men's/mixed doubles *sg*; ~ **toit** *(de tente)* fly sheet; ~ **vue** second sight.

doublé, e [duble] *adj (vêtement):* ~ **(de)** lined (with).

doublement [dubləmɑ̃] *nm* doubling; twofold increase ♦ *adv* doubly; *(pour deux raisons)* in two ways, on two counts.

doubler [duble] *vt (multiplier par 2)* to double; *(vêtement)* to line; *(dépasser)* to overtake, pass; *(film)* to dub; *(acteur)* to stand in for ♦ *vi* to double, increase twofold; **se ~ de** to be coupled with; ~ **(la classe)** *(SCOL)* to repeat a year; ~ **un cap** *(NAVIG)* to round a cape; *(fig)* to get over a hurdle.

doublure [dublyʀ] *nf* lining; *(CINÉ)* stand-in.

douce [dus] *adj f voir* **doux**.

douceâtre [dusɑtʀ(ə)] *adj* sickly sweet.

doucement [dusmɑ̃] *adv* gently; *(à voix basse)* softly; *(lentement)* slowly.

doucereux, euse [dusʀø, -øz] *adj (péj)* sugary.

douceur [dusœʀ] *nf* softness; sweetness; mildness; gentleness; ~**s** *nfpl (friandises)* sweets *(BRIT)*, candy *sg (US)*; **en ~** gently.

douche [duʃ] *nf* shower; ~**s** *nfpl* shower room *sg*; **prendre une ~** to have *ou* take a shower; ~ **écossaise** *(fig)*, ~ **froide** *(fig)* let-down.

doucher [duʃe] *vt:* ~ **qn** to give sb a shower; *(mouiller)* to drench sb; *(fig)* to give sb a telling-off; **se ~** to have *ou* take a shower.

doudoune [dudun] *nf* padded jacket; *(fam)* boob.

doué, e [dwe] *adj* gifted, talented; ~ **de** endowed with; **être ~ pour** to have a gift for.

douille [duj] *nf (ÉLEC)* socket; *(de projectile)* case.

douillet, te [dujɛ, -ɛt] *adj* cosy; *(péj)* soft.

douleur [dulœʀ] *nf* pain; *(chagrin)* grief, distress; **ressentir des ~s** to feel pain; **il a eu la ~ de perdre son père** he suffered the grief of losing his father.

douloureux, euse [duluʀø, -øz] *adj* painful.

doute [dut] *nm* doubt; **sans ~** *adv* no doubt; *(probablement)* probably; **sans nul** *ou* **aucun** ~ without (a) doubt; **hors de ~** beyond doubt; **nul ~ que** there's no doubt that; **mettre en ~** to call into question; **mettre en ~ que** to question whether.

douter [dute] *vt* to doubt; ~ **de** *vt (allié)* to doubt, have (one's) doubts about; *(résultat)* to be doubtful of; ~ **que** to doubt whether *ou* if; **j'en doute** I have my doubts; **se ~ de qch/que** to suspect sth/that; **je m'en doutais** I suspected as much; **il ne se doutait de rien**

he didn't suspect a thing.

douteux, euse [dutø, -øz] *adj* (*incertain*) doubtful; (*discutable*) dubious, questionable; (*péj*) dubious-looking.

douve [duv] *nf* (*de château*) moat; (*de tonneau*) stave.

Douvres [duvʀ(ə)] *n* Dover.

doux, douce [du, dus] *adj* (*lisse, moelleux, pas vif: couleur, non calcaire: eau*) soft; (*sucré, agréable*) sweet; (*peu fort: moutarde etc, clément: climat*) mild; (*pas brusque*) gentle; **en douce** (*partir etc*) on the quiet.

douzaine [duzɛn] *nf* (*12*) dozen; (*environ 12*): **une ~ (de)** a dozen or so, twelve or so.

douze [duz] *num* twelve; **les D~** (*membres de la CEE*) the Twelve.

douzième [duzjɛm] *num* twelfth.

doyen, ne [dwajɛ̃, -ɛn] *nm/f* (*en âge, ancienneté*) most senior member; (*de faculté*) dean.

DPLG *sigle* (= *diplômé par le gouvernement*) *extra certificate for architects, engineers etc.*

Dr *abr* (= *docteur*) Dr.

dr. *abr* (= *droit(e)*) R, r.

draconien, ne [dʀakɔnjɛ̃, -ɛn] *adj* draconian, stringent.

dragage [dʀagaʒ] *nm* dredging.

dragée [dʀaʒe] *nf* sugared almond; (*MÉD*) (sugar-coated) pill.

dragéifié, e [dʀaʒeifje] *adj* (*MÉD*) sugar-coated.

dragon [dʀagɔ̃] *nm* dragon.

drague [dʀag] *nf* (*filet*) dragnet; (*bateau*) dredger.

draguer [dʀage] *vt* (*rivière: pour nettoyer*) to dredge; (*: pour trouver qch*) to drag; (*fam*) to try and pick up, chat up (*BRIT*) ♦ *vi* (*fam*) to try and pick sb up, chat sb up (*BRIT*).

dragueur [dʀagœʀ] *nm* (*aussi: ~ de mines*) minesweeper; (*fam*): **quel ~!** he's a great one for picking up girls!

drain [dʀɛ̃] *nm* (*MÉD*) drain.

drainage [dʀɛnaʒ] *nm* drainage.

drainer [dʀene] *vt* to drain; (*fig: visiteurs, région*) to drain off.

dramatique [dʀamatik] *adj* dramatic; (*tragique*) tragic ♦ *nf* (*TV*) (television) drama.

dramatisation [dʀamatizasjɔ̃] *nf* dramatization.

dramatiser [dʀamatize] *vt* to dramatize.

dramaturge [dʀamatyʀʒ(ə)] *nm* dramatist, playwright.

drame [dʀam] *nm* (*THÉÂT*) drama; (*catastrophe*) drama, tragedy; **~ familial** family drama.

drap [dʀa] *nm* (*de lit*) sheet; (*tissu*) woollen fabric; **~ de plage** beach towel.

drapé [dʀape] *nm* (*d'un vêtement*) hang.

drapeau, x [dʀapo] *nm* flag; **sous les ~x** with the colours (*BRIT*) *ou* colors (*US*), in the army.

draper [dʀape] *vt* to drape; (*robe, jupe*) to arrange.

draperies [dʀapʀi] *nfpl* hangings.

drap-housse, *pl* **draps-housses** [dʀaus] *nm* fitted sheet.

drapier [dʀapje] *nm* (*woollen*) cloth manufacturer; (*marchand*) clothier.

drastique [dʀastik] *adj* drastic.

dressage [dʀesaʒ] *nm* training.

dresser [dʀese] *vt* (*mettre vertical, monter: tente*) to put up, erect; (*fig: liste, bilan, contrat*) to draw up; (*animal*) to train; **se ~** *vi* (*falaise, obstacle*) to stand; (*avec grandeur, menace*) to tower (up); (*personne*) to draw o.s. up; **~ l'oreille** to prick up one's ears; **~ la table** to set *ou* lay the table; **~ qn contre qn d'autre** to set sb against sb else; **~ un procès-verbal** *ou* **une contravention à qn** to book sb.

dresseur, euse [dʀesœʀ, -øz] *nm/f* trainer.

dressoir [dʀeswaʀ] *nm* dresser.

dribbler [dʀible] *vt, vi* (*SPORT*) to dribble.

drille [dʀij] *nm*: **joyeux ~** cheerful sort.

drogue [dʀɔg] *nf* drug; **la ~** drugs *pl*; **~ dure/douce** hard/soft drugs *pl*.

drogué, e [dʀɔge] *nm/f* drug addict.

droguer [dʀɔge] *vt* (*victime*) to drug; (*malade*) to give drugs to; **se ~** (*aux stupéfiants*) to take drugs; (*péj: de médicaments*) to dose o.s. up.

droguerie [dʀɔgʀi] *nf* ≈ hardware shop (*BRIT*) *ou* store (*US*).

droguiste [dʀɔgist(ə)] *nm* ≈ keeper (*ou* owner) of a hardware shop *ou* store.

droit, e [dʀwa, dʀwat] *adj* (*non courbe*) straight; (*vertical*) upright, straight; (*fig: loyal, franc*) upright, straight(forward); (*opposé à gauche*) right, right-hand ♦ *adv* straight ♦ *nm* (*prérogative, BOXE*) right; (*taxe*) duty, tax; (*: d'inscription*) fee; (*lois, branche*): **le ~** law ♦ *nf* (*POL*) right (wing); (*ligne*) straight line; **~ au but** *ou* **au fait/cœur** straight to the point/heart; **avoir le ~ de** to be allowed to; **avoir ~ à** to be entitled to; **être en ~ de** to have a *ou* the right to; **faire ~ à** to grant, accede to; **être dans son ~** to be within one's rights; **à bon ~** (*justement*) with good reason; **de quel ~?** by what right?; **à qui de ~** to whom it may concern; **à ~e** on the right; (*direction*) (to the) right; **à ~e de** to the right of; **de ~e** (*POL*) rightwing; **~ d'auteur** copyright; **avoir ~ de cité** (**dans**) (*fig*) to belong (to); **~ coutumier** common law; **~ de regard** right of access *ou* inspection; **~ de réponse** right to reply; **~ de visite** (right of) access; **~ de vote** (right to) vote; **~s d'auteur** royalties; **~s de douane** customs duties; **~s de l'homme** human rights; **~s d'inscription** enrolment *ou* registration fees.

droitement [dʀwatmɑ̃] *adv* (*agir*) uprightly.

droitier, ière [dʀwatje, -jɛʀ] *nm/f* right-handed person.

droiture [dʀwatyʀ] *nf* uprightness, straightness.

drôle [dʀol] *adj* (*amusant*) funny, amusing; (*bizarre*) funny, peculiar; **un ~ de ...** (*bizarre*) a strange *ou* funny ...; (*intensif*) an incredible ..., a terrific ....

drôlement [dʀolmɑ̃] *adv* funnily; peculiarly; (*très*) terribly, awfully; **il fait ~ froid** it's awfully cold.

drôlerie [dʀolʀi] *nf* funniness; funny thing.

dromadaire [dʀomadɛʀ] *nm* dromedary.

dru, e [dʀy] *adj* (*cheveux*) thick, bushy; (*pluie*) heavy ♦ *adv* (*pousser*) thickly; (*tomber*) heavily.

drugstore [dʀœgstɔʀ] *nm* drugstore.

druide [dʀyid] *nm* Druid.

ds *abr* = **dans**.

DST *sigle f* (= *Direction de la surveillance du territoire*) *internal security service*, ≈ MI5 (*BRIT*).

DT *sigle m* (= *diphtérie tétanos*) *vaccine*.

DTCP *sigle m* (= *diphtérie tétanos coqueluche polio*) *vaccine*.

DTP *sigle m* (= *diphtérie tétanos polio*) *vaccine*.

DTTAB *sigle m* (= *diphtérie tétanos typhoïde A et B*) *vaccine*.

du [dy] *prép + dét, dét voir* **de**.

dû, due [dy] *pp de* **devoir** ♦ *adj* (*somme*) owing, owed; (: *venant à échéance*) due; (*causé par*): **~ à** due to ♦ *nm* due; (*somme*) dues *pl*.

dualisme [dɥalism(ə)] *nm* dualism.

Dubaï, Dubay [dybaj] *n* Dubai.

dubitatif, ive [dybitatif, -iv] *adj* doubtful, dubious.

Dublin [dyblɛ̃] *n* Dublin.

duc [dyk] *nm* duke.

duché [dyʃe] *nm* dukedom, duchy.

duchesse [dyʃɛs] *nf* duchess.

DUEL [dɥɛl] *sigle m* = *Diplôme universitaire d'études littéraires*.

duel [dɥɛl] *nm* duel.

DUES [dɥɛs] *sigle m* = *Diplôme universitaire d'études scientifiques*.

duettiste [dɥetist(ə)] *nm/f* duettist.

duffel-coat [dœfœlkot] *nm* duffelcoat.

dûment [dymɑ̃] *adv* duly.

dumping [dœmpiŋ] *nm* dumping.

dune [dyn] *nf* dune.

Dunkerque [dœ̃kɛʀk] *n* Dunkirk.

duo [dɥo] *nm* (*MUS*) duet; (*fig: couple*) duo, pair.

dupe [dyp] *nf* dupe ♦ *adj*: **(ne pas) être ~ de** (not) to be taken in by.

duper [dype] *vt* to dupe, deceive.

duperie [dypʀi] *nf* deception, dupery.

duplex [dyplɛks] *nm* (*appartement*) split-level apartment, duplex; (*TV*): **émission en ~** link-up.

duplicata [dyplikata] *nm* duplicate.

duplicateur [dyplikatœʀ] *nm* duplicator; **~ à alcool** spirit duplicator.

duplicité [dyplisite] *nf* duplicity.

duquel [dykɛl] *prép + pron voir* **lequel**.

dur, e [dyʀ] *adj* (*pierre, siège, travail, problème*) hard; (*lumière, voix, climat*) harsh; (*sévère*) hard, harsh; (*cruel*) hard(-hearted); (*porte, col*) stiff; (*viande*) tough ♦ *adv* hard ♦ *nf*: **à la ~e** rough; **mener la vie ~e à qn** to give sb a hard time; **~ d'oreille** hard of hearing.

durabilité [dyʀabilite] *nf* durability.

durable [dyʀabl(ə)] *adj* lasting.

durablement [dyʀabləmɑ̃] *adv* for the long term.

durant [dyʀɑ̃] *prép* (*au cours de*) during; (*pendant*) for; **~ des mois, des mois ~** for months.

durcir [dyʀsiʀ] *vt, vi,* **se ~** *vi* to harden.

durcissement [dyʀsismɑ̃] *nm* hardening.

durée [dyʀe] *nf* length; (*d'une pile etc*) life; (*déroulement: des opérations etc*) duration; **pour une ~ illimitée** for an unlimited length of time; **de courte ~** (*séjour, répit*) brief, short-term; **de longue ~** (*effet*) long-term; **pile de longue ~** long-life battery.

durement [dyʀmɑ̃] *adv* harshly.

durent [dyʀ] *vb voir* **devoir**.

durer [dyʀe] *vi* to last.

dureté [dyʀte] *nf* (*voir dur*) hardness; harshness; stiffness; toughness.

durillon [dyʀijɔ̃] *nm* callus.

durit [dyʀit] *nf* ® (*car radiator*) hose.

DUT *sigle m* = *Diplôme universitaire de technologie*.

dut [dy] *etc vb voir* **devoir**.

duvet [dyvɛ] *nm* down; **(sac de couchage en) ~** down-filled sleeping bag.

duveteux, euse [dyvtø, -øz] *adj* downy.

dynamique [dinamik] *adj* dynamic.

dynamiser [dinamize] *vt* to pep up, enliven; (*équipe, service*) to inject some dynamism into.

dynamisme [dinamism(ə)] *nm* dynamism.

dynamite [dinamit] *nf* dynamite.

dynamiter [dinamite] *vt* to (blow up with) dynamite.

dynamo [dinamo] *nf* dynamo.

dynastie [dinasti] *nf* dynasty.

dysenterie [disɑ̃tʀi] *nf* dysentery.

dyslexie [dislɛksi] *nf* dyslexia, word blindness.

dyslexique [dislɛksik] *adj* dyslexic.

dyspepsie [dispɛpsi] *nf* dyspepsia.

E e

E, e [ə] *nm inv* E, e ♦ *abr* (= *Est*) E; **E comme Eugène** E for Edward (*BRIT*) *ou* Easy (*US*).

EAO *sigle m* (= *enseignement assisté par ordinateur*) CAL (= *computer-aided learning*).

EAU *sigle mpl* (= *Émirats arabes unis*) UAE (= *United Arab Emirates*).

eau, x [o] *nf* water ♦ *nfpl* waters; **prendre l'~** (*chaussure etc*) to leak, let in water; **prendre les ~x** to take the waters; **faire ~** to leak; **tomber à l'~** (*fig*) to fall through; **à l'~ de rose** slushy, sentimental; **~ bénite** holy water; **~ de Cologne** eau de Cologne; **~ courante** running water; **~ distillée** distilled water; **~ douce** fresh water; **~ de Javel** bleach; **~ lourde** heavy water; **~ minérale** mineral water; **~ oxygénée** hydrogen peroxide; **~ de pluie** rainwater; **~ salée** salt water; **~ de toilette** toilet water; **~x ménagères** dirty water (*from washing up etc*); **~x territoriales** territorial waters; **~x usées** liquid waste.

eau-de-vie, *pl* **eaux-de-vie** [odvi] *nf* brandy.

eau-forte, *pl* **eaux-fortes** [ofɔʀt(ə)] *nf* etching.

ébahi, e [ebai] *adj* dumbfounded, flabbergasted.

ébahir [ebaiʀ] *vt* to astonish, astound.

ébats [eba] *vb voir* **ébattre** ♦ *nmpl* frolics, gambols.

ébattre [ebatʀ(ə)]: **s'~** *vi* to frolic.

ébauche [eboʃ] *nf* (rough) outline, sketch.

ébaucher [eboʃe] *vt* to sketch out, outline; (*fig*): **~ un sourire/geste** to give a hint of a smile/make a slight gesture; **s'~** *vi* to take shape.

ébène [ebɛn] *nf* ebony.

ébéniste [ebenist(ə)] *nm* cabinetmaker.

ébénisterie [ebenistʀi] *nf* cabinetmaking; (*bâti*) cabinetwork.

éberlué, e [ebɛʀlɥe] *adj* astounded, flabbergasted.

éblouir [ebluiʀ] *vt* to dazzle.

éblouissant, e [ebluisɑ̃, -ɑ̃t] *adj* dazzling.

éblouissement [ebluismɑ̃] *nm* dazzle; (*faiblesse*) dizzy turn.

ébonite [ebɔnit] *nf* vulcanite.

éborgner [ebɔʀɲe] *vt*: **~ qn** to blind sb in one eye.

éboueur [ebwœʀ] *nm* dustman (*BRIT*), garbageman (*US*).

ébouillanter [ebujɑ̃te] *vt* to scald; (*CULIN*) to blanch; **s'~** to scald o.s.

éboulement [ebulmɑ̃] *nm* falling rocks *pl*, rock fall; (*amas*) heap of boulders *etc*.

ébouler [ebule]: **s'~** *vi* to crumble, collapse.

éboulis [ebuli] *nmpl* fallen rocks.

ébouriffé, e [ebuʀife] *adj* tousled, ruffled.

ébouriffer [ebuʀife] *vt* to tousle, ruffle.

ébranlement [ebʀɑ̃lmɑ̃] *nm* shaking.

ébranler [ebʀɑ̃le] *vt* to shake; (*rendre instable: mur, santé*) to weaken; **s'~** *vi* (*partir*) to move off.

ébrécher [ebʀeʃe] *vt* to chip.

ébriété [ebʀijete] *nf*: **en état d'~** in a state of intoxication.

ébrouer [ebʀue]: **s'~** *vi* (*souffler*) to snort; (*s'agiter*) to shake o.s.

ébruiter [ebʀɥite] *vt*, **s'~** *vi* to spread.

ébullition [ebylisjɔ̃] *nf* boiling point; **en ~** boiling; (*fig*) in an uproar.

écaille [ekɑj] *nf* (*de poisson*) scale; (*de coquillage*) shell; (*matière*) tortoiseshell; (*de roc etc*) flake.

écaillé, e [ekɑje] *adj* (*peinture*) flaking.

écailler [ekɑje] *vt* (*poisson*) to scale; (*huître*) to open; **s'~** *vi* to flake *ou* peel (off).

écarlate [ekaʀlat] *adj* scarlet.

écarquiller [ekaʀkije] *vt*: **~ les yeux** to stare wide-eyed.

écart [ekaʀ] *nm* gap; (*embardée*) swerve; (*saut*) sideways leap; (*fig*) departure, deviation; **à l'~** *adv* out of the way; **à l'~ de** *prép* away from; (*fig*) out of; **faire le grand ~** (*DANSE, GYMNASTIQUE*) to do the splits; **~ de conduite** misdemeanour.

écarté, e [ekaʀte] *adj* (*lieu*) out-of-the-way, remote; (*ouvert*): **les jambes ~es** legs apart; **les bras ~s** arms outstretched.

écarteler [ekaʀtəle] *vt* to quarter; (*fig*) to tear.

écartement [ekaʀtəmɑ̃] *nm* space, gap; (*RAIL*) gauge.

écarter [ekaʀte] *vt* (*séparer*) to move apart, separate; (*éloigner*) to push back, move away; (*ouvrir: bras, jambes*) to spread, open; (*: rideau*) to draw (back); (*éliminer: candidat, possibilité*) to dismiss; (*CARTES*) to discard; **s'~** *vi* to part; (*personne*) to move away; **s'~ de** to wander from.

ecchymose [ekimoz] *nf* bruise.

ecclésiastique [eklezjastik] *adj* ecclesiastical ♦ *nm* ecclesiastic.

écervelé, e [esɛʀvəle] *adj* scatterbrained, featherbrained.

ECG *sigle m* (= *électrocardiogramme*) ECG.

échafaud [eʃafo] *nm* scaffold.

échafaudage [eʃafodaʒ] *nm* scaffolding; (*fig*) heap, pile.

échafauder [eʃafode] *vt* (*plan*) to construct.

échalas [eʃala] *nm* stake, pole; (*personne*) beanpole.

échalote [eʃalɔt] *nf* shallot.

échancré, e [eʃɑ̃kʀe] *adj* (*robe, corsage*) low-necked; (*côte*) indented.

échancrure [eʃɑ̃kʀyʀ] *nf* (*de robe*) scoop neckline; (de côte, arête rocheuse) indentation.

échange [eʃɑ̃ʒ] nm exchange; **en ~** in exchange; **en ~ de** in exchange ou return for; **libre ~** free trade; **~ de lettres/politesses/ vues** exchange of letters/civilities/views; **~s commerciaux** trade; **~s culturels** cultural exchanges.

échangeable [eʃɑ̃ʒabl(ə)] adj exchangeable.

échanger [eʃɑ̃ʒe] vt: **~ qch (contre)** to exchange sth (for).

échangeur [eʃɑ̃ʒœʀ] nm (AUTO) interchange.

échantillon [eʃɑ̃tijɔ̃] nm sample.

échantillonnage [eʃɑ̃tijɔnaʒ] nm selection of samples.

échappatoire [eʃapatwaʀ] nf way out.

échappée [eʃape] nf (vue) vista; (CYCLISME) breakaway.

échappement [eʃapmɑ̃] nm (AUTO) exhaust; **~ libre** cutout.

échapper [eʃape]: **~ à** vt (gardien) to escape (from); (punition, péril) to escape; **~ à qn** (détail, sens) to escape sb; (objet qu'on tient: aussi: **~ des mains de qn**) to slip out of sb's hands; **laisser ~** to let fall; (cri etc) to let out; **s'~** vi to escape; **l'~ belle** to have a narrow escape.

écharde [eʃaʀd(ə)] nf splinter (of wood).

écharpe [eʃaʀp(ə)] nf scarf (pl scarves); (de maire) sash; (MÉD) sling; **prendre en ~** (dans une collision) to hit sideways on.

écharper [eʃaʀpe] vt to tear to pieces.

échasse [eʃas] nf stilt.

échassier [eʃasje] nm wader.

échauder [eʃode] vt: **se faire ~** (fig) to get one's fingers burnt.

échauffement [eʃofmɑ̃] nm overheating; (SPORT) warm-up.

échauffer [eʃofe] vt (métal, moteur) to overheat; (fig: exciter) to fire, excite; **s'~** vi (SPORT) to warm up; (discussion) to become heated.

échauffourée [eʃofuʀe] nf clash, brawl; (MIL) skirmish.

échéance [eʃeɑ̃s] nf (d'un paiement: date) settlement date; (: somme due) financial commitment(s); (fig) deadline; **à brève/longue ~** adj short-/long-term ♦ adv in the short/long term.

échéancier [eʃeɑ̃sje] nm schedule.

échéant [eʃeɑ̃]: **le cas ~** adv if the case arises.

échec [eʃɛk] nm failure; (ÉCHECS): **~ et mat/au roi** checkmate/check; **~s** nmpl (jeu) chess sg; **mettre en ~** to put in check; **tenir en ~** to hold in check; **faire ~ à** to foil, thwart.

échelle [eʃɛl] nf ladder; (fig, d'une carte) scale; **à l'~ de** on the scale of; **sur une grande/ petite ~** on a large/small scale; **faire la courte ~ à qn** to give sb a leg up; **~ de corde** rope ladder.

échelon [eʃlɔ̃] nm (d'échelle) rung; (ADMIN) grade.

échelonner [eʃlɔne] vt to space out, spread

out; (versement) **échelonné** (payment) by instalments.

écheveau, x [eʃvo] nm skein, hank.

échevelé, e [eʃəvle] adj tousled, dishevelled; (fig) wild, frenzied.

échine [eʃin] nf backbone, spine.

échiner [eʃine]: **s'~** vi (se fatiguer) to work o.s. to the bone.

échiquier [eʃikje] nm chessboard.

écho [eko] nm echo; **~s** nmpl (potins) gossip sg, rumours; (PRESSE: rubrique) "news in brief"; **rester sans ~** (suggestion etc) to come to nothing; **se faire l'~ de** to repeat, spread about.

échographie [ekɔgʀafi] nf ultrasound (scan).

échoir [eʃwaʀ] vi (dette) to fall due; (délais) to expire; **~ à** vt to fall to.

échoppe [eʃɔp] nf stall, booth.

échouer [eʃwe] vi to fail; (débris etc : sur la plage) to be washed up; (aboutir: personne dans un café etc) to arrive ♦ vt (bateau) to ground; **s'~** vi to run aground.

échu, e [eʃy] pp de **échoir** ♦ adj due, mature.

échut [eʃy] etc vb voir **échoir**.

éclabousser [eklabuse] vt to splash; (fig) to tarnish.

éclaboussure [eklabusyʀ] nf splash; (fig) stain.

éclair [eklɛʀ] nm (d'orage) flash of lightning, lightning no pl; (PHOTO: de flash) flash; (fig) flash, spark; (gâteau) éclair.

éclairage [eklɛʀaʒ] nm lighting.

éclairagiste [eklɛʀaʒist(ə)] nm/f lighting engineer.

éclaircie [eklɛʀsi] nf bright ou sunny interval.

éclaircir [eklɛʀsiʀ] vt to lighten; (fig) to clear up, clarify; (CULIN) to thin (down); **s'~** vi (ciel) to brighten up, clear; (cheveux) to go thin; (situation etc) to become clearer; **s'~ la voix** to clear one's throat.

éclaircissement [eklɛʀsismɑ̃] nm clearing up, clarification.

éclairer [eklɛʀe] vt (lieu) to light (up); (personne: avec une lampe de poche etc) to light the way for; (fig: instruire) to enlighten; (: rendre compréhensible) to shed light on ♦ vi: **~ mal/bien** to give a poor/good light; **s'~** vi (phare, rue) to light up; (situation etc) to become clearer; **s'~ à la bougie/l'électricité** to use candlelight/have electric lighting.

éclaireur, euse [eklɛʀœʀ, -øz] nm/f (scout) (boy) scout/(girl) guide ♦ nm (MIL) scout; **partir en ~** to go off to reconnoitre.

éclat [ekla] nm (de bombe, de verre) fragment; (du soleil, d'une couleur etc) brightness, brilliance; (d'une cérémonie) splendour; (scandale): **faire un ~** to cause a commotion; **action d'~** outstanding action; **voler en ~s** to shatter; **des ~s de verre** broken glass; flying glass; **~ de rire** burst ou roar of laughter; **~ de voix** shout.

éclatant, e [eklatɑ̃, -ɑ̃t] adj brilliant, bright;

(*succès*) resounding; (*revanche*) devastating.

éclater [eklate] *vi* (*pneu*) to burst; (*bombe*) to explode; (*guerre, épidémie*) to break out; (*groupe, parti*) to break up; ~ **de rire/en sanglots** to burst out laughing/sobbing.

éclectique [eklɛktik] *adj* eclectic.

éclipse [eklips(ə)] *nf* eclipse.

éclipser [eklipse] *vt* to eclipse; **s'**~ *vi* to slip away.

éclopé, e [eklɔpe] *adj* lame.

éclore [eklɔʀ] *vi* (*œuf*) to hatch; (*fleur*) to open (out).

éclosion [eklozjɔ̃] *nf* blossoming.

écluse [eklyz] *nf* lock.

éclusier [eklyzje] *nm* lock keeper.

éco- [eko] *préfixe* eco-.

écœurant, e [ekœʀɑ̃, -ɑ̃t] *adj* sickening; (*gâteau etc*) sickly.

écœurement [ekœʀmɑ̃] *nm* disgust.

écœurer [ekœʀe] *vt*: ~ **qn** to make sb feel sick; (*fig: démoraliser*) to disgust sb.

école [ekɔl] *nf* school; **aller à l'**~ to go to school; **faire** ~ to collect a following; **les grandes** ~**s** *prestige university-level colleges with competitive entrance examinations*; ~ **maternelle** nursery school; ~ **primaire** primary (*BRIT*) *ou* grade (*US*) school; ~ **secondaire** secondary (*BRIT*) *ou* high (*US*) school; ~ **privée/publique/élementaire** private/state/elementary school; ~ **de dessin/danse/musique** art/dancing/music school; ~ **hôtelière** catering college; ~ **normale (d'instituteurs) (ENI)** *primary school teachers' training college*; ~ **normale supérieure (ENS)** *grande école for training secondary school teachers*; ~ **de secrétariat** secretarial college.

> *Nursery school* (**l'école maternelle**) *is publicly funded in France and, though not compulsory, is attended by most children between the ages of two and six. Statutory education begins with primary school* (**l'école primaire**) *from the age of six to ten or eleven; see also* **collège, lycée**.

écolier, ière [ekɔlje, -jɛʀ] *nm/f* schoolboy/girl.

écolo [ekɔlo] *nm/f* (*fam*) ecologist ♦ *adj* ecological.

écologie [ekɔlɔʒi] *nf* ecology; (*sujet scolaire*) environmental studies *pl*.

écologique [ekɔlɔʒik] *adj* ecological; environmental.

écologiste [ekɔlɔʒist(ə)] *nm/f* ecologist; environmentalist.

éconduire [ekɔ̃dɥiʀ] *vt* to dismiss.

économat [ekɔnɔma] *nm* (*fonction*) bursarship (*BRIT*), treasurership (*US*); (*bureau*) bursar's office (*BRIT*), treasury (*US*).

économe [ekɔnɔm] *adj* thrifty ♦ *nm/f* (*de lycée etc*) bursar (*BRIT*), treasurer (*US*).

économie [ekɔnɔmi] *nf* (*vertu*) economy, thrift; (*gain: d'argent, de temps etc*) saving;

(*science*) economics *sg*; (*situation économique*) economy; ~**s** *nfpl* (*pécule*) savings; **une** ~ **de temps/d'argent** a saving in time/of money; ~ **dirigée** planned economy; ~ **de marché** market economy.

économique [ekɔnɔmik] *adj* (*avantageux*) economical; (*ÉCON*) economic.

économiquement [ekɔnɔmikmɑ̃] *adv* economically; **les** ~ **faibles** (*ADMIN*) the low-paid, people on low incomes.

économiser [ekɔnɔmize] *vt, vi* to save.

économiseur [ekɔnɔmizœʀ] *nm* (*INFORM*): ~ **d'écran** screen saver.

économiste [ekɔnɔmist(ə)] *nm/f* economist.

écoper [ekɔpe] *vi* to bale out; (*fig*) to cop it; ~ (**de**) *vt* to get.

écorce [ekɔʀs(ə)] *nf* bark; (*de fruit*) peel.

écorché, e [ekɔʀʃe] *adj*: ~ **vif** flayed alive ♦ *nm* cut-away drawing.

écorcher [ekɔʀʃe] *vt* (*animal*) to skin; (*égratigner*) to graze; ~ **une langue** to speak a language brokenly; **s'**~ **le genou** *etc* to scrape *ou* graze one's knee *etc*.

écorchure [ekɔʀʃyʀ] *nf* graze.

écorner [ekɔʀne] *vt* (*taureau*) to dehorn; (*livre*) to make dog-eared.

écossais, e [ekɔsɛ, -ɛz] *adj* (*lacs, tempérament*) Scottish, Scots; (*whisky, confiture*) Scotch; (*écharpe, tissu*) tartan ♦ *nm* (*LING*) Scots; (: *gaélique*) Gaelic; (*tissu*) tartan (cloth) ♦ *nm/f*: É~, **e** Scot, Scotsman/woman; **les** É~ the Scots.

écosser [ekɔse] *vt* to shell.

écosystème [ekɔsistɛm] *nm* ecosystem.

écot [eko] *nm*: **payer son** ~ to pay one's share.

écoulement [ekulmɑ̃] *nm* (*de faux billets*) circulation; (*de stock*) selling.

écouler [ekule] *vt* to dispose of; **s'**~ *vi* (*eau*) to flow (out); (*foule*) to drift away; (*jours, temps*) to pass (by).

écourter [ekuʀte] *vt* to curtail, cut short.

écoute [ekut] *nf* (*NAVIG: cordage*) sheet; (*RADIO, TV*): **temps/heure d'**~ (listening *ou* viewing) time/ hour; **heure de grande** ~ peak listening *ou* viewing time; **prendre l'**~ to tune in; **rester à l'**~ (**de**) to stay listening (to) *ou* tuned in (to); ~**s téléphoniques** phone tapping *sg*.

écouter [ekute] *vt* to listen to.

écouteur [ekutœʀ] *nm* (*TÉL*) (additional) earpiece; ~**s** *nmpl* (*RADIO*) headphones, headset *sg*.

écoutille [ekutij] *nf* hatch.

écr. *abr* = **écrire**.

écrabouiller [ekʀabuje] *vt* to squash, crush.

écran [ekʀɑ̃] *nm* screen; (*INFORM*) VDU, screen; ~ **de fumée/d'eau** curtain of smoke/water; **porter à l'**~ (*CINÉ*) to adapt for the screen; **le petit** ~ television, the small screen.

écrasant, e [ekʀazɑ̃, -ɑ̃t] *adj* overwhelming.

écraser [ekʀaze] *vt* to crush; (*piéton*) to run

over; (*INFORM*) to overwrite; **se faire** ~ to be run over; **écrase(-toi)!** shut up!; **s'~ (au sol)** to crash; **s'~ contre** to crash into.

écrémer [ekReme] *vt* to skim.

écrevisse [ekRəvis] *nf* crayfish *inv*.

écrier [ekRije]: **s'~** *vi* to exclaim.

écrin [ekRɛ̃] *nm* case, box.

écrire [ekRiR] *vt*, *vi* to write ♦ *vi*: **ça s'écrit comment?** how is it spelt?; ~ **à qn que** to write and tell sb that; **s'~** to write to one another.

écrit, e [ekRi, -it] *pp de* **écrire** ♦ *adj*: **bien/mal** ~ well/badly written ♦ *nm* document; (*examen*) written paper; **par** ~ in writing.

écriteau, x [ekRito] *nm* notice, sign.

écritoire [ekRitwaR] *nf* writing case.

écriture [ekRityR] *nf* writing; (*COMM*) entry; **~s** *nfpl* (*COMM*) accounts, books; **l'É~ (sainte), les É~s** the Scriptures.

écrivain [ekRivɛ̃] *nm* writer.

écrivais [ekRivɛ] *etc vb voir* **écrire**.

écrou [ekRu] *nm* nut.

écrouer [ekRue] *vt* to imprison; (*provisoirement*) to remand in custody.

écroulé, e [ekRule] *adj* (*de fatigue*) exhausted; (*par un malheur*) overwhelmed; ~ **(de rire)** in stitches.

écroulement [ekRulmɑ̃] *nm* collapse.

écrouler [ekRule]: **s'~** *vi* to collapse.

écru, e [ekRy] *adj* (*toile*) raw, unbleached; (*couleur*) off-white, écru.

écu [eky] *nm* (*bouclier*) shield; (*monnaie: ancienne*) crown; (*: de la CEE*) ecu.

écueil [ekœj] *nm* reef; (*fig*) pitfall; stumbling block.

écuelle [ekɥɛl] *nf* bowl.

éculé, e [ekyle] *adj* (*chaussure*) down-at-heel; (*fig: péj*) hackneyed.

écume [ekym] *nf* foam; (*CULIN*) scum; ~ **de mer** meerschaum.

écumer [ekyme] *vt* (*CULIN*) to skim; (*fig*) to plunder ♦ *vi* (*mer*) to foam; (*fig*) to boil with rage.

écumoire [ekymwaR] *nf* skimmer.

écureuil [ekyRœj] *nm* squirrel.

écurie [ekyRi] *nf* stable.

écusson [ekysɔ̃] *nm* badge.

écuyer, ère [ekɥije, -ɛR] *nm/f* rider.

eczéma [egzema] *nm* eczema.

éd. *abr* = **édition**.

édam [edam] *nm* (*fromage*) edam.

edelweiss [edelvajs] *nm inv* edelweiss.

éden [edɛn] *nm* Eden.

édenté, e [edɑ̃te] *adj* toothless.

EDF *sigle f* (= *Électricité de France*) national electricity company.

édifiant, e [edifjɑ̃, -ɑ̃t] *adj* edifying.

édification [edifikasjɔ̃] (*d'un bâtiment*) building, erection.

édifice [edifis] *nm* building, edifice.

édifier [edifje] *vt* to build, erect; (*fig*) to edify.

édiles [edil] *nmpl* city fathers.

Édimbourg [edɛ̃buR] *n* Edinburgh.

édit [edi] *nm* edict.

édit. *abr* = **éditeur**.

éditer [edite] *vt* (*publier*) to publish; (*: disque*) to produce; (*préparer: texte, INFORM*) to edit.

éditeur, trice [editœR, -tRis] *nm/f* publisher; editor.

édition [edisjɔ̃] *nf* editing *no pl*; (*série d'exemplaires*) edition; (*industrie du livre*): **l'~** publishing; ~ **sur écran** (*INFORM*) screen editing.

édito [edito] *nm* (*fam: éditorial*) editorial, leader.

éditorial, aux [editoRjal, -o] *nm* editorial, leader.

éditorialiste [editoRjalist(ə)] *nm/f* editorial *ou* leader writer.

édredon [edRədɔ̃] *nm* eiderdown, comforter (*US*).

éducateur, trice [edykatœR, -tRis] *nm/f* teacher; ~ **spécialisé** specialist teacher.

éducatif, ive [edykatif, -iv] *adj* educational.

éducation [edykasjɔ̃] *nf* education; (*familiale*) upbringing; (*manières*) (good) manners *pl*; **bonne/mauvaise** ~ good/bad upbringing; **sans** ~ bad-mannered, ill-bred; **l'É~ (nationale)** ≈ the Department for Education; ~ **permanente** continuing education; ~ **physique** physical education.

édulcorer [edylkoRe] *vt* to sweeten; (*fig*) to tone down.

éduquer [edyke] *vt* to educate; (*élever*) to bring up; (*faculté*) to train; **bien/mal éduqué** well/badly brought up.

EEG *sigle m* (= *électroencéphalogramme*) EEG.

effacé, e [efase] *adj* (*fig*) retiring, unassuming.

effacer [efase] *vt* to erase, rub out; (*bande magnétique*) to erase; (*INFORM: fichier, fiche*) to delete, erase; **s'~** *vi* (*inscription etc*) to wear off; (*pour laisser passer*) to step aside; ~ **le ventre** to pull one's stomach in.

effarant, e [efaRɑ̃, -ɑ̃t] *adj* alarming.

effaré, e [efaRe] *adj* alarmed.

effarement [efaRmɑ̃] *nm* alarm.

effarer [efaRe] *vt* to alarm.

effarouchement [efaRuʃmɑ̃] *nm* alarm.

effaroucher [efaRuʃe] *vt* to frighten *ou* scare away; (*personne*) to alarm.

effectif, ive [efɛktif, -iv] *adj* real; effective ♦ *nm* (*MIL*) strength; (*SCOL*) total number of pupils, size; **~s** numbers, strength *sg*; (*COMM*) manpower *sg*; **réduire l'~ de** to downsize.

effectivement [efɛktivmɑ̃] *adv* effectively; (*réellement*) actually, really; (*en effet*) indeed.

effectuer [efɛktɥe] *vt* (*opération, mission*) to carry out; (*déplacement, trajet*) to make, complete; (*mouvement*) to execute, make; **s'~** to be carried out.

efféminé, e [efemine] *adj* effeminate.

effervescence [efɛRvesɑ̃s] *nf* (*fig*): **en** ~ in a turmoil.

effervescent, e [efɛʀvesã, -ãt] *adj* (*cachet, boisson*) effervescent; (*fig*) agitated, in a turmoil.

effet [efɛ] *nm* (*résultat, artifice*) effect; (*impression*) impression; (*COMM*) bill; (*JUR: d'une loi, d'un jugement*): **avec ~ rétroactif** applied retrospectively; **~s** *nmpl* (*vêtements etc*) things; **~ de style/couleur/lumière** stylistic/colour/lighting effect; **~s de voix** dramatic effects with one's voice; **faire de l'~** (*médicament, menace*) to have an effect, be effective; **sous l'~ de** under the effect of; **donner de l'~ à une balle** (*TENNIS*) to put some spin on a ball; **à cet ~** to that end; **en ~** *adv* indeed; **~ (de commerce)** bill of exchange; **~ de serre** greenhouse effect; **~s spéciaux** (*CINÉ*) special effects.

effeuiller [efœje] *vt* to remove the leaves (*ou* petals) from.

efficace [efikas] *adj* (*personne*) efficient; (*action, médicament*) effective.

efficacité [efikasite] *nf* efficiency; effectiveness.

effigie [efiʒi] *nf* effigy; **brûler qn en ~** to burn an effigy of sb.

effilé, e [efile] *adj* slender; (*pointe*) sharp; (*carrosserie*) streamlined.

effiler [efile] *vt* (*cheveux*) to thin (out); (*tissu*) to fray.

effilocher [efilɔʃe]: **s'~** *vi* to fray.

efflanqué, e [eflãke] *adj* emaciated.

effleurement [eflœrmã] *nm*: **touche à ~** touch-sensitive control *ou* key.

effleurer [eflœre] *vt* to brush (against); (*sujet*) to touch upon; (*suj: idée, pensée*): **~ qn** to cross sb's mind.

effluves [eflyv] *nmpl* exhalation(s).

effondré, e [efɔ̃dre] *adj* (*abattu: par un malheur, échec*) overwhelmed.

effondrement [efɔ̃drəmã] *nm* collapse.

effondrer [efɔ̃dre]: **s'~** *vi* to collapse.

efforcer [efɔrse]: **s'~ de** *vt*: **s'~ de faire** to try hard to do.

effort [efɔr] *nm* effort; **faire un ~** to make an effort; **faire tous ses ~s** to try one's hardest; **faire l'~ de ...** to make the effort to ...; **sans ~** *adj* effortless ◆ *adv* effortlessly; **~ de mémoire** attempt to remember; **~ de volonté** effort of will.

effraction [efraksjɔ̃] *nf* breaking-in; **s'introduire par ~ dans** to break into.

effrangé, e [efrãʒe] *adj* fringed; (*effiloché*) frayed.

effrayant, e [efrɛjã, -ãt] *adj* frightening, fearsome; (*sens affaibli*) dreadful.

effrayer [efreje] *vt* to frighten, scare; (*rebuter*) to put off; **s'~ (de)** to be frightened *ou* scared (by).

effréné, e [efrene] *adj* wild.

effritement [efritmã] *nm* crumbling; erosion; slackening off.

effriter [efrite]: **s'~** *vi* to crumble; (*monnaie*) to be eroded; (*valeurs*) to slacken off.

effroi [efrwa] *nm* terror, dread *no pl*.

effronté, e [efrɔ̃te] *adj* insolent.

effrontément [efrɔ̃temã] *adv* insolently.

effronterie [efrɔ̃tri] *nf* insolence.

effroyable [efrwajabl(ə)] *adj* horrifying, appalling.

effusion [efyzjɔ̃] *nf* effusion; **sans ~ de sang** without bloodshed.

égailler [egaje]: **s'~** *vi* to scatter, disperse.

égal, e, aux [egal, -o] *adj* (*identique, ayant les mêmes droits*) equal; (*plan: surface*) even, level; (*constant: vitesse*) steady; (*équitable*) even ◆ *nm/f* equal; **être ~ à** (*prix, nombre*) to be equal to; **ça lui est ~** it's all the same to him, it doesn't matter to him, he doesn't mind; **c'est ~, ...** all the same, ...; **sans ~** matchless, unequalled; **à l'~ de** (*comme*) just like; **d'~ à ~** as equals.

également [egalmã] *adv* equally; evenly; steadily; (*aussi*) too, as well.

égaler [egale] *vt* to equal.

égalisateur, trice [egalizatœr, -tris] *adj* (*SPORT*): **but ~** equalizing goal, equalizer.

égalisation [egalizasjɔ̃] *nf* (*SPORT*) equalization.

égaliser [egalize] *vt* (*sol, salaires*) to level (out); (*chances*) to equalize ◆ *vi* (*SPORT*) to equalize.

égalitaire [egalitɛr] *adj* egalitarian.

égalitarisme [egalitarism(ə)] *nm* egalitarianism.

égalité [egalite] *nf* equality; evenness; steadiness; (*MATH*) identity; **être à ~ (de points)** to be level; **~ de droits** equality of rights; **~ d'humeur** evenness of temper.

égard [egar] *nm*: **~s** *nmpl* consideration *sg*; **à cet ~** in this respect; **à certains ~s/tous ~s** in certain respects/all respects; **eu ~ à** in view of; **par ~ pour** out of consideration for; **sans ~ pour** without regard for; **à l'~ de** *prép* towards; (*en ce qui concerne*) concerning, as regards.

égaré, e [egare] *adj* lost.

égarement [egarmã] *nm* distraction; aberration.

égarer [egare] *vt* (*objet*) to mislay; (*moralement*) to lead astray; **s'~** *vi* to get lost, lose one's way; (*objet*) to go astray; (*fig: dans une discussion*) to wander.

égayer [egeje] *vt* (*personne*) to amuse; (: *remonter*) to cheer up; (*récit, endroit*) to brighten up, liven up.

Égée [eʒe] *adj*: **la mer ~** the Aegean (Sea).

égéen, ne [eʒeɛ̃, -ɛn] *adj* Aegean.

égérie [eʒeri] *nf*: **l'~ de qn/qch** the brains behind sb/sth.

égide [eʒid] *nf*: **sous l'~ de** under the aegis of.

églantier [eglãtje] *nm* wild *ou* dog rose(-bush).

églantine [eglãtin] *nf* wild *ou* dog rose.

églefin [egləfɛ̃] *nm* haddock.

église [egliz] *nf* church.

égocentrique [egɔsɑ̃tʀik] *adj* egocentric, self-centred.

égocentrisme [egɔsɑ̃tʀism(ə)] *nm* egocentricity.

égoïne [egɔin] *nf* handsaw.

égoïsme [egɔism(ə)] *nm* selfishness, egoism.

égoïste [egɔist(ə)] *adj* selfish, egoistic ♦ *nm/f* egoist.

égoïstement [egɔistəmɑ̃] *adv* selfishly.

égorger [egɔʀʒe] *vt* to cut the throat of.

égosiller [egozije]: **s'~** *vi* to shout o.s. hoarse.

égotisme [egɔtism(ə)] *nm* egotism, egoism.

égout [egu] *nm* sewer; **eaux d'~** sewage.

égoutier [egutje] *nm* sewer worker.

égoutter [egute] *vt* (*linge*) to wring out; (*vaisselle, fromage*) to drain ♦ *vi*, **s'~** *vi* to drip.

égouttoir [egutwaʀ] *nm* draining board; (*mobile*) draining rack.

égratigner [egʀatiɲe] *vt* to scratch; **s'~** to scratch o.s.

égratignure [egʀatiɲyʀ] *nf* scratch.

égrener [egʀəne] *vt:* **~ une grappe**, **~ des raisins** to pick grapes off a bunch; **s'~** *vi* (*fig: heures etc*) to pass by; (: *notes*) to chime out.

égrillard, e [egʀijaʀ, -aʀd(ə)] *adj* ribald, bawdy.

Égypte [eʒipt] *nf:* **l'~** Egypt.

égyptien, ne [eʒipsjɛ̃, -ɛn] *adj* Egyptian ♦ *nm/f:* **E~, ne** Egyptian.

égyptologue [eʒiptɔlɔg] *nm/f* Egyptologist.

eh [e] *excl* hey!; **~ bien** well.

éhonté, e [eɔ̃te] *adj* shameless, brazen (*BRIT*).

éjaculation [eʒakylasjɔ̃] *nf* ejaculation.

éjaculer [eʒakyle] *vi* to ejaculate.

éjectable [eʒɛktabl(ə)] *adj:* **siège ~** ejector seat.

éjecter [eʒɛkte] *vt* (*TECH*) to eject; (*fam*) to kick *ou* chuck out.

éjection [eʒɛksjɔ̃] *nf* ejection.

élaboration [elabɔʀasjɔ̃] *nf* elaboration.

élaboré, e [elabɔʀe] *adj* (*complexe*) elaborate.

élaborer [elabɔʀe] *vt* to elaborate; (*projet, stratégie*) to work out; (*rapport*) to draft.

élagage [elagaʒ] *nm* pruning.

élaguer [elage] *vt* to prune.

élan [elɑ̃] *nm* (*ZOOL*) elk, moose; (*SPORT: avant le saut*) run up; (*de véhicule ou objet en mouvement*) momentum; (*fig: de tendresse etc*) surge; **prendre son ~/de l'~** to take a run up/gather speed; **perdre son ~** to lose one's momentum.

élancé, e [elɑ̃se] *adj* slender.

élancement [elɑ̃smɑ̃] *nm* shooting pain.

élancer [elɑ̃se]: **s'~** *vi* to dash, hurl o.s.; (*fig: arbre, clocher*) to soar (upwards).

élargir [elaʀʒiʀ] *vt* to widen; (*vêtement*) to let out; (*JUR*) to release; **s'~** *vi* to widen; (*vêtement*) to stretch.

élargissement [elaʀʒismɑ̃] *nm* widening; letting out.

élasticité [elastisite] *nf* (*aussi ÉCON*) elasticity;

~ de l'offre/de la demande flexibility of supply/demand.

élastique [elastik] *adj* elastic ♦ *nm* (*de bureau*) rubber band; (*pour la couture*) elastic *no pl.*

élastomère [elastɔmɛʀ] *nm* elastomer.

Elbe [ɛlb] *nf:* **l'île d'~** (the Island of) Elba; (*fleuve*): **l'~** the Elbe.

eldorado [ɛldɔʀado] *nm* Eldorado.

électeur, trice [elɛktœʀ, -tʀis] *nm/f* elector, voter.

électif, ive [elɛktif, -iv] *adj* elective.

élection [elɛksjɔ̃] *nf* election; **~s** *nfpl* (*POL*) election(s); **sa terre/patrie d'~** one's chosen land/country, the land/country of one's choice; **~ partielle** ≈ by-election; **~s législatives/présidentielles** general/presidential election *sg.*

> Élections législatives *are held in France every five years to elect* députés *to the* Assemblée nationale. *The president is elected in the* élection présidentielle, *held every seven years. Elections are by universal direct suffrage and two rounds of voting take place. Elections take place on a Sunday.*

électoral, e, aux [elɛktɔʀal, -o] *adj* electoral, election *cpd.*

électoralisme [elɛktɔʀalism(ə)] *nm* electioneering.

électorat [elɛktɔʀa] *nm* electorate.

électricien, ne [elɛktʀisjɛ̃, -ɛn] *nm/f* electrician.

électricité [elɛktʀisite] *nf* electricity; **allumer/éteindre l'~** to put on/off the light; **~ statique** static electricity.

électrification [elɛktʀifikasjɔ̃] *nf* (*RAIL*) electrification; (*d'un village etc*) laying on of electricity.

électrifier [elɛktʀifje] *vt* (*RAIL*) to electrify.

électrique [elɛktʀik] *adj* electric(al).

électriser [elɛktʀize] *vt* to electrify.

électro... [elɛktʀɔ] *préfixe* electro....

électro-aimant [elɛktʀɔɛmɑ̃] *nm* electromagnet.

électrocardiogramme [elɛktʀɔkaʀdjɔgʀam] *nm* electrocardiogram.

électrocardiographe [elɛktʀɔkaʀdjɔgʀaf] *nm* electrocardiograph.

électrochoc [elɛktʀɔʃɔk] *nm* electric shock treatment.

électrocuter [elɛktʀɔkyte] *vt* to electrocute.

électrocution [elɛktʀɔkysjɔ̃] *nf* electrocution.

électrode [elɛktʀɔd] *nf* electrode.

électro-encéphalogramme [elɛktʀɔɑ̃sefalɔgʀam] *nm* electroencephalogram.

électrogène [elɛktʀɔʒɛn] *adj:* **groupe ~** generating set.

électrolyse [elɛktʀɔliz] *nf* electrolysis *sg.*

électromagnétique [elɛktʀɔmaɲetik] *adj* electromagnetic.

électroménager [elɛktʀɔmenaʒe] *adj:* **appa-**

reils ~s domestic (electrical) appliances ♦ *nm*: l'~ household appliances.

électron [elɛktRɔ̃] *nm* electron.

électronicien, ne [elɛktRɔnisjɛ̃, -ɛn] *nm/f* electronics (*BRIT*) *ou* electrical (*US*) engineer.

électronique [elɛktRɔnik] *adj* electronic ♦ *nf* (*science*) electronics *sg*.

électronucléaire [elɛktRɔnykleɛR] *adj* nuclear power *cpd* ♦ *nm*: l'~ nuclear power.

électrophone [elɛktRɔfɔn] *nm* record player.

électrostatique [elɛktRɔstatik] *adj* electrostatic ♦ *nf* electrostatics *sg*.

élégamment [elegamɑ̃] *adv* elegantly.

élégance [elegɑ̃s] *nf* elegance.

élégant, e [elegɑ̃, -ɑ̃t] *adj* elegant; (*solution*) neat, elegant; (*attitude, procédé*) courteous, civilized.

élément [elemɑ̃] *nm* element; (*pièce*) component, part; ~s *nmpl* (*aussi: rudiments*) elements.

élémentaire [elemɑ̃tɛR] *adj* elementary; (*CHIMIE*) elemental.

éléphant [elefɑ̃] *nm* elephant; ~ de mer elephant seal.

éléphanteau, x [elefɑ̃to] *nm* baby elephant.

éléphantesque [elefɑ̃tɛsk(ə)] *adj* elephantine.

élevage [ɛlvaʒ] *nm* breeding; (*de bovins*) cattle breeding *ou* rearing; (*ferme*) cattle farm.

élévateur [elevatœR] *nm* elevator.

élévation [elevasjɔ̃] *nf* (*gén*) elevation; (*voir élever*) raising; (*voir s'élever*) rise.

élevé, e [ɛlve] *adj* (*prix, sommet*) high; (*fig: noble*) elevated; **bien/mal** ~ well-/ill-mannered.

élève [elɛv] *nm/f* pupil; ~ **infirmière** student nurse.

élever [ɛlve] *vt* (*enfant*) to bring up, raise; (*bétail, volaille*) to breed; (*abeilles*) to keep; (*hausser: taux, niveau*) to raise; (*fig: âme, esprit*) to elevate; (*édifier: monument*) to put up, erect; **s'**~ *vi* (*avion, alpiniste*) to go up; (*niveau, température, aussi: cri etc*) to rise; (*survenir: difficultés*) to arise; **s'**~ **à** (*suj: frais, dégâts*) to amount to, add up to; **s'**~ **contre** to rise up against; ~ **une protestation/critique** to raise a protest/make a criticism; ~ **la voix** to raise one's voice; ~ **qn au rang de** to raise *ou* elevate sb to the rank of; ~ **un nombre au carré/au cube** to square/cube a number.

éleveur, euse [elvœR, -øz] *nm/f* stock breeder.

elfe [ɛlf(ə)] *nm* elf.

élidé, e [elide] *adj* elided.

élider [elide] *vt* to elide.

éligibilité [eliʒibilite] *nf* eligibility.

éligible [eliʒibl(ə)] *adj* eligible.

élimé, e [elime] *adj* worn (thin), threadbare.

élimination [eliminasjɔ̃] *nf* elimination.

éliminatoire [eliminatwaR] *adj* eliminatory; (*SPORT*) disqualifying ♦ *nf* (*SPORT*) heat.

éliminer [elimine] *vt* to eliminate.

élire [eliR] *vt* to elect; ~ **domicile à** to take up

residence in *ou* at.

élision [elizjɔ̃] *nf* elision.

élite [elit] *nf* elite; **tireur d'**~ crack rifleman; **chercheur d'**~ top-notch researcher.

élitisme [elitism(ə)] *nm* elitism.

élitiste [elitist(ə)] *adj* elitist.

élixir [eliksiR] *nm* elixir.

elle [ɛl] *pron* (*sujet*) she; (*: chose*) it; (*complément*) her; it; ~s (*sujet*) they; (*complément*) them; ~-**même** herself; itself; ~s-**mêmes** themselves; *voir* **il**.

ellipse [elips(ə)] *nf* ellipse; (*LING*) ellipsis *sg*.

elliptique [eliptik] *adj* elliptical.

élocution [elɔkysjɔ̃] *nf* delivery; **défaut d'**~ speech impediment.

éloge [elɔʒ] *nm* praise (*gén no pl*); **faire l'**~ **de** to praise.

élogieusement [elɔʒjøzmɑ̃] *adv* very favourably.

élogieux, euse [elɔʒjø, -øz] *adj* laudatory, full of praise.

éloigné, e [elwaɲe] *adj* distant, far-off.

éloignement [elwaɲmɑ̃] *nm* removal; putting off; estrangement; (*fig: distance*) distance.

éloigner [elwaɲe] *vt* (*objet*): ~ **qch (de)** to move *ou* take sth away (from); (*personne*): ~ **qn (de)** to take sb away *ou* remove sb (from); (*échéance*) to put off, postpone; (*soupçons, danger*) to ward off; **s'**~ **(de)** (*personne*) to go away (from); (*véhicule*) to move away (from); (*affectivement*) to become estranged (from).

élongation [elɔ̃gasjɔ̃] *nf* strained muscle.

éloquence [elɔkɑ̃s] *nf* eloquence.

éloquent, e [elɔkɑ̃, -ɑ̃t] *adj* eloquent.

élu, e [ely] *pp de* **élire** ♦ *nm/f* (*POL*) elected representative.

élucider [elyside] *vt* to elucidate.

élucubrations [elykybRasjɔ̃] *nfpl* wild imaginings.

éluder [elyde] *vt* to evade.

élus [ely] *etc vb voir* **élire**.

élusif, ive [elyzif, -iv] *adj* elusive.

Élysée [elize] *nm*: **(le palais de) l'**~ the Élysée palace; **les Champs** ~s the Champs Élysées.

The **palais de l'Élysée**, *situated in the heart of Paris off the Champs-Élysées, is the official residence of the French President. Built in the eighteenth century, it has been used in its present role since 1876.* **L'Élysée** *is frequently used to mean the presidency itself.*

émacié, e [emasje] *adj* emaciated.

émail, aux [emaj, -o] *nm* enamel.

émaillé, e [emaje] *adj* enamelled; (*fig*): ~ **de** dotted with.

émailler [emaje] *vt* to enamel.

émanation [emanasjɔ̃] *nf* emanation; **être l'**~ **de** to emanate from; to proceed from.

émancipation [emɑ̃sipasjɔ̃] *nf* emancipation.

émancipé, e [emɑ̃sipe] *adj* emancipated.

émanciper [emɑ̃sipe] *vt* to emancipate; **s'~** (*fig*) to become emancipated *ou* liberated.

émaner [emane]: **~ de** *vt* to emanate from; (*ADMIN*) to proceed from.

émarger [emaʀʒe] *vt* to sign; **~ de 1 000 F à un budget** to receive 1000 F out of a budget.

émasculer [emaskyle] *vt* to emasculate.

emballage [ɑ̃balaʒ] *nm* wrapping; packing; (*papier*) wrapping; (*carton*) packaging.

emballer [ɑ̃bale] *vt* to wrap (up); (*dans un carton*) to pack (up); (*fig: fam*) to thrill (to bits); **s'~** *vi* (*moteur*) to race; (*cheval*) to bolt; (*fig: personne*) to get carried away.

emballeur, euse [ɑ̃balœʀ, -øz] *nm/f* packer.

embarcadère [ɑ̃baʀkadɛʀ] *nm* landing stage (*BRIT*), pier.

embarcation [ɑ̃baʀkɑsjɔ̃] *nf* (small) boat, (small) craft *inv*.

embardée [ɑ̃baʀde] *nf* swerve; **faire une ~** to swerve.

embargo [ɑ̃baʀɡo] *nm* embargo; **mettre l'~ sur** to put an embargo on, embargo.

embarquement [ɑ̃baʀkəmɑ̃] *nm* embarkation; loading; boarding.

embarquer [ɑ̃baʀke] *vt* (*personne*) to embark; (*marchandise*) to load; (*fam*) to cart off; (*: arrêter*) to nick ♦ *vi* (*passager*) to board; (*NAVIG*) to ship water; **s'~** *vi* to board; **s'~ dans** (*affaire, aventure*) to embark upon.

embarras [ɑ̃baʀa] *nm* (*obstacle*) hindrance; (*confusion*) embarrassment; (*ennuis*): **être dans l'~** to be in a predicament *ou* an awkward position; (*gêne financière*) to be in difficulties; **~ gastrique** stomach upset.

embarrassant, e [ɑ̃baʀasɑ̃, -ɑ̃t] *adj* cumbersome; embarrassing; awkward.

embarrassé, e [ɑ̃baʀase] *adj* (*encombré*) encumbered; (*gêné*) embarrassed; (*explications etc*) awkward.

embarrasser [ɑ̃baʀase] *vt* (*encombrer*) to clutter (up); (*gêner*) to hinder, hamper; (*fig*) to cause embarrassment to; to put in an awkward position; **s'~ de** to burden o.s. with.

embauche [ɑ̃boʃ] *nf* hiring; **bureau d'~** labour office.

embaucher [ɑ̃boʃe] *vt* to take on, hire; **s'~ comme** to get (o.s.) a job as.

embauchoir [ɑ̃boʃwaʀ] *nm* shoetree.

embaumer [ɑ̃bome] *vt* to embalm; (*parfumer*) to fill with its fragrance; **~ la lavande** to be fragrant with (the scent of) lavender.

embellie [ɑ̃beli] *nf* bright spell, brighter period.

embellir [ɑ̃beliʀ] *vt* to make more attractive; (*une histoire*) to embellish ♦ *vi* to grow lovelier *ou* more attractive.

embellissement [ɑ̃belismɑ̃] *nm* embellishment.

embêtant, e [ɑ̃betɑ̃, -ɑ̃t] *adj* annoying.

embêtement [ɑ̃betmɑ̃] *nm* problem, difficulty; **~s** *nmpl* trouble *sg*.

embêter [ɑ̃bete] *vt* to bother; **s'~** *vi* (*s'ennuyer*) to be bored; **il ne s'embête pas!** (*ironique*) he does all right for himself!

emblée [ɑ̃ble]: **d'~** *adv* straightaway.

emblème [ɑ̃blɛm] *nm* emblem.

embobiner [ɑ̃bɔbine] *vt* (*enjôler*): **~ qn** to get round sb.

emboîtable [ɑ̃bwatabl(ə)] *adj* interlocking.

emboîter [ɑ̃bwate] *vt* to fit together; **s'~ dans** to fit into; **s'~** (**l'un dans l'autre**) to fit together; **~ le pas à qn** to follow in sb's footsteps.

embolie [ɑ̃bɔli] *nf* embolism.

embonpoint [ɑ̃bɔ̃pwɛ̃] *nm* stoutness (*BRIT*), corpulence; **prendre de l'~** to grow stout (*BRIT*) *ou* corpulent.

embouché, e [ɑ̃buʃe] *adj*: **mal ~** foul-mouthed.

embouchure [ɑ̃buʃyʀ] *nf* (*GÉO*) mouth; (*MUS*) mouthpiece.

embourber [ɑ̃buʀbe]: **s'~** *vi* to get stuck in the mud; (*fig*): **s'~ dans** to sink into.

embourgeoiser [ɑ̃buʀʒwaze]: **s'~** *vi* to adopt a middle-class outlook.

embout [ɑ̃bu] *nm* (*de canne*) tip; (*de tuyau*) nozzle.

embouteillage [ɑ̃buteja ʒ] *nm* traffic jam, (traffic) holdup (*BRIT*).

embouteiller [ɑ̃buteje] *vt* (*suj: véhicules etc*) to block.

emboutir [ɑ̃butiʀ] *vt* (*TECH*) to stamp; (*heurter*) to crash into, ram.

embranchement [ɑ̃bʀɑ̃ʃmɑ̃] *nm* (*routier*) junction; (*classification*) branch.

embrancher [ɑ̃bʀɑ̃ʃe] *vt* (*tuyaux*) to join; **~ qch sur** to join sth to.

embraser [ɑ̃bʀaze]: **s'~** *vi* to flare up.

embrassade [ɑ̃bʀasad] *nf* (*gén pl*) hugging and kissing *no pl*.

embrasse [ɑ̃bʀas] *nf* (*de rideau*) tie-back, loop.

embrasser [ɑ̃bʀase] *vt* to kiss; (*sujet, période*) to embrace, encompass; (*carrière*) to embark on; (*métier*) to go in for, take up; **~ du regard** to take in (with eyes); **s'~** to kiss (each other).

embrasure [ɑ̃bʀazyʀ] *nf*: **dans l'~ de la porte** in the door(way).

embrayage [ɑ̃bʀejaʒ] *nm* clutch.

embrayer [ɑ̃bʀeje] *vi* (*AUTO*) to let in the clutch ♦ *vt* (*fig: affaire*) to set in motion; **~ sur qch** to begin on sth.

embrigader [ɑ̃bʀigade] *vt* to recruit.

embrocher [ɑ̃bʀɔʃe] *vt* to (put on a) spit (*ou* skewer).

embrouillamini [ɑ̃bʀujamini] *nm* (*fam*) muddle.

embrouillé, e [ɑ̃bʀuje] *adj* (*affaire*) confused, muddled.

embrouiller [ɑ̃bʀuje] *vt* (*fils*) to tangle (up); (*fiches, idées, personne*) to muddle up; **s'~** *vi* to get in a muddle.

embroussaillé, e [ɑ̃bʀusaje] *adj* overgrown, scrubby; (*cheveux*) bushy, shaggy.

embruns [ɑ̃bʀœ̃] *nmpl* sea spray *sg.*
embryologie [ɑ̃bʀijɔlɔʒi] *nf* embryology.
embryon [ɑ̃bʀijɔ̃] *nm* embryo.
embryonnaire [ɑ̃bʀijɔnɛʀ] *adj* embryonic.
embûches [ɑ̃byʃ] *nfpl* pitfalls, traps.
embué, e [ɑ̃bɥe] *adj* misted up; **yeux ~s de larmes** eyes misty with tears.
embuscade [ɑ̃byskad] *nf* ambush; **tendre une ~ à** to lay an ambush for.
embusqué, e [ɑ̃byske] *adj* in ambush ♦ *nm* (*péj*) shirker, skiver (*BRIT*).
embusquer [ɑ̃byske] **s'~** *vi* to take up position (for an ambush).
éméché, e [emeʃe] *adj* tipsy, merry.
émeraude [ɛmʀod] *nf* emerald ♦ *adj inv* emerald-green.
émergence [emɛʀʒɑ̃s] *nf* (*fig*) emergence.
émerger [emɛʀʒe] *vi* to emerge; (*faire saillie, aussi fig*) to stand out.
émeri [ɛmʀi] *nm*: **toile** *ou* **papier ~** emery paper.
émérite [emeʀit] *adj* highly skilled.
émerveillement [emɛʀvɛjmɑ̃] *nm* wonderment.
émerveiller [emɛʀveje] *vt* to fill with wonder; **s'~ de** to marvel at.
émet [emɛ] *etc vb voir* **émettre.**
émétique [emetik] *nm* emetic.
émetteur, trice [emɛtœʀ, -tʀis] *adj* transmitting; **(poste) ~** transmitter.
émetteur-récepteur, *pl* **émetteurs-récepteurs** [emetœʀʀesɛptœʀ] *nm* transceiver.
émettre [emɛtʀ(ə)] *vt* (*son, lumière*) to give out, emit; (*message etc: RADIO*) to transmit; (*billet, timbre, emprunt, chèque*) to issue; (*hypothèse, avis*) to voice, put forward; (*vœu*) to express ♦ *vi*: **~ sur ondes courtes** to broadcast on short wave.
émeus [emø] *etc vb voir* **émouvoir.**
émeute [emøt] *nf* riot.
émeutier, ière [emøtje, -jɛʀ] *nm/f* rioter.
émeuve [emœv] *etc vb voir* **émouvoir.**
émietter [emjete] *vt* ➤(*pain, terre*) to crumble; (*fig*) to split up, disperse; **s'~** *vi* (*pain, terre*) to crumble.
émigrant, e [emigʀɑ̃, -ɑ̃t] *nm/f* emigrant.
émigration [emigʀɑsjɔ̃] *nf* emigration.
émigré, e [emigʀe] *nm/f* expatriate.
émigrer [emigʀe] *vi* to emigrate.
émincer [emɛ̃se] *vt* (*CULIN*) to slice thinly.
éminemment [eminamɑ̃] *adv* eminently.
éminence [eminɑ̃s] *nf* distinction; (*colline*) knoll, hill; **Son É~** His Eminence; **~ grise** éminence grise.
éminent, e [eminɑ̃, -ɑ̃t] *adj* distinguished.
émir [emiʀ] *nm* emir.
émirat [emiʀa] *nm* emirate; **les É~s arabes unis (EAU)** the United Arab Emirates (UAE).
émis, e [emi, -iz] *pp de* **émettre.**
émissaire [emisɛʀ] *nm* emissary.

émission [emisjɔ̃] *nf* (*voir émettre*) emission; transmission; issue; (*RADIO, TV*) programme, broadcast.
émit [emi] *etc vb voir* **émettre.**
emmagasinage [ɑ̃magazinaʒ] *nm* storage; storing away.
emmagasiner [ɑ̃magazine] *vt* to (put into) store; (*fig*) to store up.
emmailloter [ɑ̃majɔte] *vt* to wrap up.
emmanchure [ɑ̃mɑ̃ʃyʀ] *nf* armhole.
emmêlement [ɑ̃mɛlmɑ̃] *nm* (*état*) tangle.
emmêler [ɑ̃mele] *vt* to tangle (up); (*fig*) to muddle up; **s'~** to get into a tangle.
emménagement [ɑ̃menaʒmɑ̃] *nm* settling in.
emménager [ɑ̃menaʒe] *vi* to move in; **~ dans** to move into.
emmener [ɑ̃mne] *vt* to take (with one); (*comme otage, capture*) to take away; **~ qn au concert** to take sb to a concert.
emment(h)al [emɛtal] *nm* (*fromage*) Emmenthal.
emmerder [ɑ̃mɛʀde] (*fam!*) *vt* to bug, bother; **s'~** *vi* (*s'ennuyer*) to be bored stiff; **je t'emmerde!** to hell with you!
emmitoufler [ɑ̃mitufle] *vt* to wrap up (warmly); **s'~** to wrap (o.s.) up (warmly).
emmurer [ɑ̃myʀe] *vt* to wall up, immure.
émoi [emwa] *nm* (*agitation, effervescence*) commotion; (*trouble*) agitation; **en ~** (*sens*) excited, stirred.
émollient, e [emɔljɑ̃, -ɑ̃t] *adj* (*MÉD*) emollient.
émoluments [emɔlymɑ̃] *nmpl* remuneration *sg*, fee *sg*.
émonder [emɔ̃de] *vt* (*arbre etc*) to prune; (*amande etc*) to blanch.
émotif, ive [emɔtif, -iv] *adj* emotional.
émotion [emɔsjɔ̃] *nf* emotion; **avoir des ~s** (*fig*) to get a fright; **donner des ~s à** to give a fright to; **sans ~** without emotion, coldly.
émotionnant, e [emɔsjɔnɑ̃, -ɑ̃t] *adj* upsetting.
émotionnel, le [emɔsjɔnɛl] *adj* emotional.
émotionner [emɔsjɔne] *vt* to upset.
émoulu, e [emuly] *adj*: **frais ~ de** fresh from, just out of.
émoussé, e [emuse] *adj* blunt.
émousser [emuse] *vt* to blunt; (*fig*) to dull.
émoustiller [emustije] *vt* to titillate, arouse.
émouvant, e [emuvɑ̃, -ɑ̃t] *adj* moving.
émouvoir [emuvwaʀ] *vt* (*troubler*) to stir, affect; (*toucher, attendrir*) to move; (*indigner*) to rouse; (*effrayer*) to disturb, worry; **s'~** *vi* to be affected; to be moved; to be roused; to be disturbed *ou* worried.
empailler [ɑ̃paje] *vt* to stuff.
empailleur, euse [ɑ̃pajœʀ, -øz] *nm/f* (*d'animaux*) taxidermist.
empaler [ɑ̃pale] *vt* to impale.
empaquetage [ɑ̃paktaʒ] *nm* packing, packaging.
empaqueter [ɑ̃pakte] *vt* to pack up.
emparer [ɑ̃paʀe]: **s'~ de** *vt* (*objet*) to seize, grab; (*comme otage, MIL*) to seize; (*suj: peur*

etc) to take hold of.

empâter [ɑ̃pɑte]: **s'~** *vi* to thicken out.

empattement [ɑ̃patmɑ̃] *nm* (*AUTO*) wheelbase; (*TYPO*) serif.

empêché, e [ɑ̃peʃe] *adj* detained.

empêchement [ɑ̃pɛʃmɑ̃] *nm* (unexpected) obstacle, hitch.

empêcher [ɑ̃peʃe] *vt* to prevent; **~ qn de faire** to prevent *ou* stop sb (from) doing; **~ que qch (n')arrive/qn (ne) fasse** to prevent sth from happening/sb from doing; **il n'empêche que** nevertheless, be that as it may; **il n'a pas pu s'~ de rire** he couldn't help laughing.

empêcheur [ɑ̃pɛʃœʀ] *nm*: **~ de danser en rond** spoilsport, killjoy (*BRIT*).

empeigne [ɑ̃pɛɲ] *nf* upper (*of shoe*).

empennage [ɑ̃penaʒ] *nm* (*AVIAT*) tailplane.

empereur [ɑ̃pʀœʀ] *nm* emperor.

empesé, e [ɑ̃pəze] *adj* (*fig*) stiff, starchy.

empeser [ɑ̃pəze] *vt* to starch.

empester [ɑ̃peste] *vt* (*lieu*) to stink out ♦ *vi* to stink, reek; **~ le tabac/le vin** to stink *ou* reek of tobacco/wine.

empêtrer [ɑ̃petʀe] *vt*: **s'~ dans** (*fils etc, aussi fig*) to get tangled up in.

emphase [ɑ̃faz] *nf* pomposity, bombast; **avec ~** pompously.

emphatique [ɑ̃fatik] *adj* emphatic.

empiècement [ɑ̃pjɛsmɑ̃] *nm* (*COUTURE*) yoke.

empierrer [ɑ̃pjeʀe] *vt* (*route*) to metal.

empiéter [ɑ̃pjete]: **~ sur** *vt* to encroach upon.

empiffrer [ɑ̃pifʀe]: **s'~** *vi* (*péj*) to stuff o.s.

empiler [ɑ̃pile] *vt* to pile (up), stack (up); **s'~** *vi* to pile up.

empire [ɑ̃piʀ] *nm* empire; (*fig*) influence; **style E~** Empire style; **sous l'~ de** in the grip of.

empirer [ɑ̃piʀe] *vi* to worsen, deteriorate.

empirique [ɑ̃piʀik] *adj* empirical.

empirisme [ɑ̃piʀism(ə)] *nm* empiricism.

emplacement [ɑ̃plasmɑ̃] *nm* site; **sur l'~ de** on the site of.

emplâtre [ɑ̃plɑtʀ(ə)] *nm* plaster; (*fam*) twit.

emplette [ɑ̃plɛt] *nf*: **faire l'~ de** to purchase; **~s** shopping *sg*; **faire des ~s** to go shopping.

emplir [ɑ̃pliʀ] *vt* to fill; **s'~ (de)** to fill (with).

emploi [ɑ̃plwa] *nm* use; (*COMM, ÉCON*): **l'~** employment; (*poste*) job, situation; **d'~ facile** easy to use; **le plein ~** full employment; **~ du temps** timetable, schedule.

emploie [ɑ̃plwa] *etc vb voir* **employer.**

employé, e [ɑ̃plwaje] *nm/f* employee; **~ de bureau/banque** office/bank employee *ou* clerk; **~ de maison** domestic (servant).

employer [ɑ̃plwaje] *vt* (*outil, moyen, méthode, mot*) to use; (*ouvrier, main-d'œuvre*) to employ; **s'~ à qch/à faire** to apply *ou* devote o.s. to sth/to doing.

employeur, euse [ɑ̃plwajœʀ, -øz] *nm/f* employer.

empocher [ɑ̃pɔʃe] *vt* to pocket.

empoignade [ɑ̃pwaɲad] *nf* row, set-to.

empoigne [ɑ̃pwaɲ] *nf*: **foire d'~** free-for-all.

empoigner [ɑ̃pwaɲe] *vt* to grab; **s'~** (*fig*) to have a row *ou* set-to.

empois [ɑ̃pwa] *nm* starch.

empoisonnement [ɑ̃pwazɔnmɑ̃] *nm* poisoning; (*fam: ennui*) annoyance, irritation.

empoisonner [ɑ̃pwazɔne] *vt* to poison; (*empester: air, pièce*) to stink out; (*fam*): **~ qn** to drive sb mad; **s'~** to poison o.s.; **~ l'atmosphère** (*aussi fig*) to poison the atmosphere; **il nous empoisonne l'existence** he's the bane of our life.

empoissonner [ɑ̃pwasɔne] *vt* (*étang, rivière*) to stock with fish.

emporté, e [ɑ̃pɔʀte] *adj* (*personne, caractère*) fiery.

emportement [ɑ̃pɔʀtəmɑ̃] *nm* fit of rage, anger *no pl.*

emporte-pièce [ɑ̃pɔʀtəpjɛs] *nm inv* (*TECH*) punch; **à l'~** *adj* (*fig*) incisive.

emporter [ɑ̃pɔʀte] *vt* to take (with one); (*en dérobant ou enlevant, emmener: blessés, voyageurs*) to take away; (*entraîner*) to carry away *ou* along; (*arracher*) to tear off; (*suj: rivière, vent*) to carry away; (*MIL: position*) to take; (*avantage, approbation*) to win; **s'~** *vi* (*de colère*) to fly into a rage, lose one's temper; **la maladie qui l'a emporté** the illness which caused his death; **l'~** to gain victory; **l'~ (sur)** to get the upper hand (of); (*méthode etc*) to prevail (over); **boissons à ~** take-away drinks.

empoté, e [ɑ̃pɔte] *adj* (*maladroit*) clumsy.

empourpré, e [ɑ̃puʀpʀe] *adj* crimson.

empreint, e [ɑ̃pʀɛ̃, -ɛ̃t] *adj*: **~ de** marked with; tinged with ♦ *nf* (*de pied, main*) print; (*fig*) stamp, mark; **~e (digitale)** fingerprint.

empressé, e [ɑ̃pʀese] *adj* attentive; (*péj*) overanxious to please, overattentive.

empressement [ɑ̃pʀɛsmɑ̃] *nm* eagerness.

empresser [ɑ̃pʀese]: **s'~** *vi*: **s'~ auprès de qn** to surround sb with attentions; **s'~ de faire** to hasten to do.

emprise [ɑ̃pʀiz] *nf* hold, ascendancy; **sous l'~ de** under the influence of.

emprisonnement [ɑ̃pʀizɔnmɑ̃] *nm* imprisonment.

emprisonner [ɑ̃pʀizɔne] *vt* to imprison, jail.

emprunt [ɑ̃pʀœ̃] *nm* borrowing *no pl*, loan (*from debtor's point of view*); (*LING etc*) borrowing; **nom d'~** assumed name; **~ d'État** government *ou* state loan; **~ public à 5%** 5% public loan.

emprunté, e [ɑ̃pʀœ̃te] *adj* (*fig*) ill-at-ease, awkward.

emprunter [ɑ̃pʀœ̃te] *vt* to borrow; (*itinéraire*) to take, follow; (*style, manière*) to adopt, assume.

emprunteur, euse [ɑ̃pʀœ̃tœʀ, -øz] *nm/f* borrower.

empuantir [ɑ̃pɥɑ̃tiʀ] *vt* to stink out.

EMT *sigle f* (= *éducation manuelle et technique*)

handwork as a school subject.

ému, e [emy] *pp de* **émouvoir ♦** *adj* excited; touched; moved.

émulation [emylɑsjɔ̃] *nf* emulation.

émule [emyl] *nm/f* imitator.

émulsion [emylsjɔ̃] *nf* emulsion; (*cosmétique*) (water-based) lotion.

émut [emy] *etc vb voir* **émouvoir**.

EN *sigle f* (= *Éducation nationale*) *voir* **éducation**.

========================= *MOT-CLÉ*

en [ɑ̃] *prép* **1** (*endroit, pays*) in; (*direction*) to; **habiter ~ France/ville** to live in France/town; **aller ~ France/ville** to go to France/town

2 (*moment, temps*) in; **~ été/juin** in summer/June; **~ 3 jours/20 ans** in 3 days/20 years

3 (*moyen*) by; **~ avion/taxi** by plane/taxi

4 (*composition*) made of; **c'est ~ verre** it's (made of) glass; **un collier ~ argent** a silver necklace; **~ 2 volumes/une pièce** in 2 volumes/one piece

5 (*description, état*): **une femme (habillée) ~ rouge** a woman (dressed) in red; **peindre qch ~ rouge** to paint sth red; **~ T/étoile** T-/star-shaped; **~ chemise/chaussettes** in one's shirt sleeves/socks; **~ soldat** as a soldier; **~ civil** in civilian clothes; **cassé ~ plusieurs morceaux** broken into several pieces; **~ réparation** being repaired, under repair; **~ vacances** on holiday; **~ bonne santé** healthy, in good health; **~ deuil** in mourning; **le même ~ plus grand** the same but *ou* only bigger

6 (*avec gérondif*) while; on; **~ dormant** while sleeping, as one sleeps; **~ sortant** on going out, as he *etc* went out; **sortir ~ courant** to run out; **~ apprenant la nouvelle, il s'est évanoui** he fainted at the news *ou* when he heard the news

7 (*matière*): **fort ~ math** good at maths; **expert ~** expert in

8 (*conformité*): **~ tant que** as; **~ bon politicien, il ...** good politician that he is, he ..., like a good *ou* true politician, he ...; **je te parle ~ ami** I'm talking to you as a friend

♦ *pron* **1** (*indéfini*): **j'~ ai/veux** I have/want some; **~ as-tu?** have you got any?; **je n'~ veux pas** I don't want any; **j'~ ai 2** I've got 2; **combien y ~ a-t-il?** how many (of them) are there?; **j'~ ai assez** I've got enough (of it *ou* them); (*j'en ai marre*) I've had enough; **où ~ étais-je?** where was I?

2 (*provenance*) from there; **j'~ viens** I've come from there

3 (*cause*): **il ~ est malade/perd le sommeil** he is ill/can't sleep because of it

4 (*de la part de*): **elle ~ est aimée** she is loved by him (*ou* them *etc*)

5 (*complément de nom, d'adjectif, de verbe*): **j'~ connais les dangers** I know its *ou* the dangers; **j'~ suis fier/ai besoin** I am proud

of it/need it; **il ~ est ainsi** *ou* **de même pour moi** it's the same for me, same here.

ENA [ena] *sigle f* (= *École nationale d'administration*) *grande école* for training civil servants.

énarque [enaʀk(ə)] *nm/f* former ENA student.

encablure [ɑ̃kablyʀ] *nf* (*NAVIG*) cable's length.

encadrement [ɑ̃kadʀəmɑ̃] *nm* framing; training; (*de porte*) frame; **~ du crédit** credit restrictions.

encadrer [ɑ̃kadʀe] *vt* (*tableau, image*) to frame; (*fig: entourer*) to surround; (*personnel, soldats etc*) to train; (*COMM: crédit*) to restrict.

encadreur [ɑ̃kadʀœʀ] *nm* (picture) framer.

encaisse [ɑ̃kɛs] *nf* cash in hand; **~ or/métallique** gold/gold and silver reserves.

encaissé, e [ɑ̃kese] *adj* (*vallée*) steep-sided; (*rivière*) with steep banks.

encaisser [ɑ̃kese] *vt* (*chèque*) to cash; (*argent*) to collect; (*fig: coup, défaite*) to take.

encaisseur [ɑ̃kesœʀ] *nm* collector (*of debts etc*).

encan [ɑ̃kɑ̃]: **à l'~** *adv* by auction.

encanailler [ɑ̃kanaje]: **s'~** *vi* to become vulgar *ou* common; to mix with the riffraff.

encart [ɑ̃kaʀ] *nm* insert; **~ publicitaire** publicity insert.

encarter [ɑ̃kaʀte] *vt* to insert.

en-cas [ɑ̃ka] *nm inv* snack.

encastrable [ɑ̃kastʀabl(ə)] *adj* (*four, élément*) that can be built in.

encastré, e [ɑ̃kastʀe] *adj* (*four, baignoire*) built-in.

encastrer [ɑ̃kastʀe] *vt*: **~ qch dans** (*mur*) to embed sth in(to); (*boîtier*) to fit sth into; **s'~ dans** to fit into; (*heurter*) to crash into.

encaustiquage [ɑ̃kɔstikaʒ] *nm* polishing, waxing.

encaustique [ɑ̃kɔstik] *nf* polish, wax.

encaustiquer [ɑ̃kɔstike] *vt* to polish, wax.

enceinte [ɑ̃sɛ̃t] *adj f*: **~ (de 6 mois)** (6 months) pregnant **♦** *nf* (*mur*) wall; (*espace*) enclosure; **~ (acoustique)** speaker.

encens [ɑ̃sɑ̃] *nm* incense.

encenser [ɑ̃sɑ̃se] *vt* to (in)cense; (*fig*) to praise to the skies.

encensoir [ɑ̃sɑ̃swaʀ] *nm* thurible (*BRIT*), censer.

encéphalogramme [ɑ̃sefalɔgʀam] *nm* encephalogram.

encercler [ɑ̃sɛʀkle] *vt* to surround.

enchaîné [ɑ̃ʃene] *nm* (*CINÉ*) link shot.

enchaînement [ɑ̃ʃɛnmɑ̃] *nm* (*fig*) linking.

enchaîner [ɑ̃ʃene] *vt* to chain up; (*mouvements, séquences*) to link (together) **♦** *vi* to carry on.

enchanté, e [ɑ̃ʃɑ̃te] *adj* (*ravi*) delighted; (*ensorcelé*) enchanted; **~ (de faire votre connaissance)** pleased to meet you, how do you do?

enchantement [ãʃãtmã] *nm* delight; (*magie*) enchantment; **comme par** ~ as if by magic.

enchanter [ãʃãte] *vt* to delight.

enchanteur, teresse [ãʃãtœr, -trɛs] *adj* enchanting.

enchâsser [ãʃase] *vt*: ~ **qch (dans)** to set sth (in).

enchère [ãʃɛr] *nf* bid; **faire une** ~ to (make a) bid; **mettre/vendre aux** ~**s** to put up for (sale by)/sell by auction; **les** ~**s montent** the bids are rising; **faire monter les** ~**s** (*fig*) to raise the bidding.

enchérir [ãʃerir] *vi*: ~ **sur qn** (*aux enchères, aussi fig*) to outbid sb.

enchérisseur, euse [ãʃerisœr, -øz] *nm/f* bidder.

enchevêtrement [ãʃvɛtrəmã] *nm* tangle.

enchevêtrer [ãʃvetre] *vt* to tangle (up).

enclave [ãklav] *nf* enclave.

enclaver [ãklave] *vt* to enclose, hem in.

enclencher [ãklãʃe] *vt* (*mécanisme*) to engage; (*fig: affaire*) to set in motion; **s'**~ *vi* to engage.

enclin, e [ãklɛ̃, -in] *adj*: ~ **à qch/à faire** inclined *ou* prone to sth/to do.

enclore [ãklɔr] *vt* to enclose.

enclos [ãklo] *nm* enclosure; (*clôture*) fence.

enclume [ãklym] *nf* anvil.

encoche [ãkɔʃ] *nf* notch.

encoder [ãkɔde] *vt* to encode.

encodeur [ãkɔdœr] *nm* encoder.

encoignure [ãkɔɲyr] *nf* corner.

encoller [ãkɔle] *vt* to paste.

encolure [ãkɔlyr] *nf* (*tour de cou*) collar size; (*col, cou*) neck.

encombrant, e [ãkɔ̃brã, -ãt] *adj* cumbersome, bulky.

encombre [ãkɔ̃br(ə)]: **sans** ~ *adv* without mishap *ou* incident.

encombré, e [ãkɔ̃bre] *adj* (*pièce, passage*) cluttered; (*lignes téléphoniques*) engaged; (*marché*) saturated.

encombrement [ãkɔ̃brəmã] *nm* (*d'un lieu*) cluttering (up); (*d'un objet: dimensions*) bulk.

encombrer [ãkɔ̃bre] *vt* to clutter (up); (*gêner*) to hamper; **s'**~ **de** (*bagages etc*) to load *ou* burden o.s. with; ~ **le passage** to block *ou* obstruct the way.

encontre [ãkɔ̃tr(ə)]: **à l'**~ **de** *prép* against, counter to.

encorbellement [ãkɔrbɛlmã] *nm*: **fenêtre en** ~ oriel window.

encorder [ãkɔrde] *vt*: **s'**~ (*ALPINISME*) to rope up.

=========== *MOT-CLÉ* ===========

encore [ãkɔr] *adv* **1** (*continuation*) still; **il y travaille** ~ he's still working on it; **pas** ~ not yet

2 (*de nouveau*) again; **j'irai** ~ **demain** I'll go again tomorrow; ~ **une fois** (once) again; ~ **un effort** one last effort; ~ **deux jours** two more days

3 (*intensif*) even, still; ~ **plus fort/mieux** even louder/better, louder/better still; **hier** ~ even yesterday; **non seulement ..., mais** ~ ... not only ..., but also ...; ~**!** (*insatisfaction*) not again!; **quoi** ~**?** what now?

4 (*restriction*) even so *ou* then, only; ~ **pourrais-je le faire si ...** even so, I might be able to do it if ...; **si** ~ if only

encore que *conj* although.

_____

encourageant, e [ãkuraʒã, -ãt] *adj* encouraging.

encouragement [ãkuraʒmã] *nm* encouragement; (*récompense*) incentive.

encourager [ãkuraʒe] *vt* to encourage; ~ **qn à faire qch** to encourage sb to do sth.

encourir [ãkurir] *vt* to incur.

encrasser [ãkrase] *vt* to foul up; (*AUTO etc*) to soot up.

encre [ãkr(ə)] *nf* ink; ~ **de Chine** Indian ink; ~ **indélébile** indelible ink; ~ **sympathique** invisible ink.

encrer [ãkre] *vt* to ink.

encreur [ãkrœr] *adj m*: **rouleau** ~ inking roller.

encrier [ãkrije] *nm* inkwell.

encroûter [ãkrute]: **s'**~ *vi* (*fig*) to get into a rut, get set in one's ways.

encyclique [ãsiklik] *nf* encyclical.

encyclopédie [ãsiklɔpedi] *nf* encyclopaedia (*BRIT*), encyclopedia (*US*).

encyclopédique [ãsiklɔpedik] *adj* encyclopaedic (*BRIT*), encyclopedic (*US*).

endémique [ãdemik] *adj* endemic.

endetté, e [ãdete] *adj* in debt; (*fig*): **très** ~ **envers qn** deeply indebted to sb.

endettement [ãdɛtmã] *nm* debts *pl*.

endetter [ãdete] *vt*, **s'**~ *vi* to get into debt.

endeuiller [ãdœje] *vt* to plunge into mourning; **manifestation endeuillée par** event over which a tragic shadow was cast by.

endiablé, e [ãdjable] *adj* furious; (*enfant*) boisterous.

endiguer [ãdige] *vt* to dyke (up); (*fig*) to check, hold back.

endimancher [ãdimãʃe] *vt*: **s'**~ to put on one's Sunday best; **avoir l'air endimanché** to be all done up to the nines (*fam*).

endive [ãdiv] *nf* chicory *no pl*.

endocrine [ãdɔkrin] *adj f*: **glande** ~ endocrine (gland).

endoctrinement [ãdɔktrinmã] *nm* indoctrination.

endoctriner [ãdɔktrine] *vt* to indoctrinate.

endolori, e [ãdɔlɔri] *adj* painful.

endommager [ãdɔmaʒe] *vt* to damage.

endormant, e [ãdɔrmã, -ãt] *adj* dull, boring.

endormi, e [ãdɔrmi] *pp de* **endormir** ♦ *adj* (*personne*) asleep; (*fig: indolent, lent*) sluggish; (*engourdi: main, pied*) numb.

endormir [ãdɔrmir] *vt* to put to sleep; (*suj: chaleur etc*) to send to sleep; (*MÉD: dent, nerf*) to anaesthetize; (*fig: soupçons*) to allay; **s'~** *vi* to fall asleep, go to sleep.

endoscope [ãdɔskɔp] *nm* (*MÉD*) endoscope.

endoscopie [ãdɔskɔpi] *nf* endoscopy.

endosser [ãdose] *vt* (*responsabilité*) to take, shoulder; (*chèque*) to endorse; (*uniforme, tenue*) to put on, don.

endroit [ãdʀwa] *nm* place; (*localité*): **les gens de l'~** the local people; (*opposé à l'envers*) right side; **à cet ~** in this place; **à l'~** right side out; the right way up; (*vêtement*) the right way out; **à l'~ de** *prép* regarding, with regard to; **par ~s** in places.

enduire [ãdɥiʀ] *vt* to coat; **~ qch de** to coat sth with.

enduit, e [ãdɥi, -it] *pp de* **enduire** ♦ *nm* coating.

endurance [ãdyʀãs] *nf* endurance.

endurant, e [ãdyʀã, -ãt] *adj* tough, hardy.

endurcir [ãdyʀsiʀ] *vt* (*physiquement*) to toughen; (*moralement*) to harden; **s'~** *vi* to become tougher; to become hardened.

endurer [ãdyʀe] *vt* to endure, bear.

énergétique [enɛʀʒetik] *adj* (*ressources etc*) energy *cpd*; (*aliment*) energizing.

énergie [enɛʀʒi] *nf* (*PHYSIQUE*) energy; (*TECH*) power; (*fig: physique*) energy; (*: morale*) vigour, spirit; **~ éolienne/solaire** wind/solar power.

énergique [enɛʀʒik] *adj* energetic; vigorous; (*mesures*) drastic, stringent.

énergiquement [enɛʀʒikmã] *adv* energetically; drastically.

énergisant, e [enɛʀʒizã, -ãt] *adj* energizing.

énergumène [enɛʀgymɛn] *nm* rowdy character *ou* customer.

énervant, e [enɛʀvã, -ãt] *adj* irritating.

énervé, e [enɛʀve] *adj* nervy, on edge; (*agacé*) irritated.

énervement [enɛʀvəmã] *nm* nerviness; irritation.

énerver [enɛʀve] *vt* to irritate, annoy; **s'~** *vi* to get excited, get worked up.

enfance [ãfãs] *nf* (*âge*) childhood; (*fig*) infancy; (*enfants*) children *pl*; **c'est l'~ de l'art** it's child's play; **petite ~** infancy; **souvenir/ami d'~** childhood memory/friend; **retomber en ~** to lapse into one's second childhood.

enfant [ãfã] *nm/f* child (*pl* children); **~ adoptif/naturel** adopted/natural child; **bon ~** *adj* good-natured, easy-going; **~ de chœur** *nm* (*REL*) altar boy; **~ prodige** child prodigy; **~ unique** only child.

enfanter [ãfãte] *vi* to give birth ♦ *vt* to give birth to.

enfantillage [ãfãtijaʒ] *nm* (*péj*) childish behaviour *no pl*.

enfantin, e [ãfãtɛ̃, -in] *adj* childlike; (*péj*) childish; (*langage*) child *cpd*.

enfer [ãfɛʀ] *nm* hell; **allure/bruit d'~** horrendous speed/noise.

enfermer [ãfɛʀme] *vt* to shut up; (*à clef, inter-*

ner) to lock up; **s'~** to shut o.s. away; **s'~ à clé** to lock o.s. in; **s'~ dans la solitude/le mutisme** to retreat into solitude/silence.

enferrer [ãfeʀe]: **s'~** *vi*: **s'~ dans** to tangle o.s. up in.

enfiévré, e [ãfjevʀe] *adj* (*fig*) feverish.

enfilade [ãfilad] *nf*: **une ~ de** a series *ou* line of; **prendre des rues en ~** to cross directly from one street into the next.

enfiler [ãfile] *vt* (*vêtement*): **~ qch** to slip sth on, slip into sth; (*insérer*): **~ qch dans** to stick sth into; (*rue, couloir*) to take; (*perles*) to string; (*aiguille*) to thread; **s'~ dans** to disappear into.

enfin [ãfɛ̃] *adv* at last; (*en énumérant*) lastly; (*de restriction, résignation*) still; (*eh bien*) well; (*pour conclure*) in a word.

enflammé, e [ãflame] *adj* (*torche, allumette*) burning; (*MÉD: plaie*) inflamed; (*fig: nature, discours, déclaration*) fiery.

enflammer [ãflame] *vt* to set fire to; (*MÉD*) to inflame; **s'~** *vi* to catch fire; to become inflamed.

enflé, e [ãfle] *adj* swollen; (*péj: style*) bombastic, turgid.

enfler [ãfle] *vi* to swell (up); **s'~** *vi* to swell.

enflure [ãflyʀ] *nf* swelling.

enfoncé, e [ãfɔ̃se] *adj* staved-in, smashed-in; (*yeux*) deep-set.

enfoncement [ãfɔ̃smã] *nm* (*recoin*) nook.

enfoncer [ãfɔ̃se] *vt* (*clou*) to drive in; (*faire pénétrer*): **~ qch dans** to push (*ou* drive) sth into; (*forcer: porte*) to break open; (*: plancher*) to cause to cave in; (*défoncer: côtes etc*) to smash; (*fam: surpasser*) to lick, beat (hollow) ♦ *vi* (*dans la vase etc*) to sink in; (*sol, surface porteuse*) to give way; **s'~** *vi* to sink; **s'~ dans** to sink into; (*forêt, ville*) to disappear into; **~ un chapeau sur la tête** to cram *ou* jam a hat on one's head; **~ qn dans la dette** to drag sb into debt.

enfouir [ãfwiʀ] *vt* (*dans le sol*) to bury; (*dans un tiroir etc*) to tuck away; **s'~ dans/sous** to bury o.s. in/under.

enfourcher [ãfuʀʃe] *vt* to mount; **~ son dada** (*fig*) to get on one's hobby-horse.

enfourner [ãfuʀne] *vt* to put in the oven; (*poterie*) to put in the kiln; **~ qch dans** to shove *ou* stuff sth into; **s'~ dans** (*suj: personne*) to dive into.

enfreignais [ãfʀɛɲɛ] *etc vb voir* **enfreindre**.

enfreindre [ãfʀɛ̃dʀ(ə)] *vt* to infringe, break.

enfuir [ãfɥiʀ]: **s'~** *vi* to run away *ou* off.

enfumer [ãfyme] *vt* to smoke out.

enfuyais [ãfɥijɛ] *etc vb voir* **enfuir**.

engagé, e [ãgaʒe] *adj* (*littérature etc*) engagé, committed.

engageant, e [ãgaʒã, -ãt] *adj* attractive, appealing.

engagement [ãgaʒmã] *nm* taking on, engaging; starting; investing; (*promesse*) commitment; (*MIL: combat*) engagement; (*: recrute-*

ment) enlistment; (*SPORT*) entry; **prendre l'~ de faire** to undertake to do; **sans** ~ (*COMM*) without obligation.

engager [ãgaʒe] *vt* (*embaucher*) to take on, engage; (*commencer*) to start; (*lier*) to bind, commit; (*impliquer, entraîner*) to involve; (*investir*) to invest, lay out; (*faire intervenir*) to engage; (*SPORT: concurrents, chevaux*) to enter; (*inciter*): ~ **qn à faire** to urge sb to do; (*faire pénétrer*): ~ **qch dans** to insert sth into; ~ **qn à qch** to urge sth on sb; **s'~** to get taken on; (*MIL*) to enlist; (*promettre, politiquement*) to commit o.s.; (*débuter*) to start (up); **s'~ à faire** to undertake to do; **s'~ dans** (*rue, passage*) to enter, turn into; (*s'emboîter*) to engage *ou* fit into; (*fig: affaire, discussion*) to enter into, embark on.

engazonner [ãgazɔne] *vt* to turf.

engeance [ãʒãs] *nf* mob.

engelure [ãʒlyʀ] *nf* chilblain.

engendrer [ãʒãdʀe] *vt* to father; (*fig*) to create, breed.

engin [ãʒɛ̃] *nm* machine; instrument; vehicle; (*péj*) gadget; (*AVIAT: avion*) aircraft *inv*; (: *missile*) missile; ~ **blindé** armoured vehicle; ~ (**explosif**) (explosive) device; ~**s** (**spéciaux**) missiles.

englober [ãglɔbe] *vt* to include.

engloutir [ãglutiʀ] *vt* to swallow up; (*fig: dépenses*) to devour; **s'~** to be engulfed.

englué, e [ãglye] sticky.

engoncé, e [ãgɔ̃se] *adj*: ~ **dans** cramped in.

engorgement [ãgɔʀʒəmã] *nm* blocking; (*MÉD*) engorgement.

engorger [ãgɔʀʒe] *vt* to obstruct, block; **s'~** *vi* to become blocked.

engouement [ãgumã] *nm* (sudden) passion.

engouffrer [ãgufʀe] *vt* to swallow up, devour; **s'~ dans** to rush into.

engourdi, e [ãgurdi] *adj* numb.

engourdir [ãgurdiʀ] *vt* to numb; (*fig*) to dull, blunt; **s'~** *vi* to go numb.

engrais [ãgʀɛ] *nm* manure; ~ (**chimique**) (chemical) fertilizer; ~ **organique/inorganique** organic/inorganic fertilizer.

engraisser [ãgʀɛse] *vt* to fatten (up); (*terre: fertiliser*) to fertilize ♦ *vi* (*péj*) to get fat(ter).

engranger [ãgʀãʒe] *vt* (*foin*) to bring in; (*fig*) to store away.

engrenage [ãgʀənaʒ] *nm* gears *pl*, gearing; (*fig*) chain.

engueuler [ãgœle] *vt* (*fam*) to bawl at *ou* out.

enguirlander [ãgiʀlãde] *vt* (*fam*) to give sb a bawling out, bawl at.

enhardir [ãardiʀ]: **s'~** *vi* to grow bolder.

ENI [eni] *sigle f* = **école normale (d'instituteurs)**.

énième [ɛnjɛm] *adj* = **nième**.

énigmatique [enigmatik] *adj* enigmatic.

énigmatiquement [enigmatikmã] *adv* enigmatically.

énigme [enigm(ə)] *nf* riddle.

enivrant, e [ãnivʀã, -ãt] *adj* intoxicating.

enivrer [ãnivʀe] *vt*: **s'~** to get drunk; **s'~ de** (*fig*) to become intoxicated with.

enjambée [ãʒãbe] *nf* stride; **d'une** ~ with one stride.

enjamber [ãʒãbe] *vt* to stride over; (*suj: pont etc*) to span, straddle.

enjeu, x [ãʒø] *nm* stakes *pl*.

enjoindre [ãʒwɛ̃dʀ(ə)] *vt*: ~ **à qn de faire** to enjoin *ou* order sb to do.

enjôler [ãʒole] *vt* to coax, wheedle.

enjôleur, euse [ãʒolœʀ, -øz] *adj* (*sourire, paroles*) winning.

enjolivement [ãʒɔlivmã] *nm* embellishment.

enjoliver [ãʒɔlive] *vt* to embellish.

enjoliveur [ãʒɔlivœʀ] *nm* (*AUTO*) hub cap.

enjoué, e [ãʒwe] *adj* playful.

enlacer [ãlase] *vt* (*étreindre*) to embrace, hug; (*suj: lianes*) to wind round, entwine.

enlaidir [ãlediʀ] *vt* to make ugly ♦ *vi* to become ugly.

enlevé, e [ãlve] *adj* (*morceau de musique*) played brightly.

enlèvement [ãlɛvmã] *nm* removal; (*rapt*) abduction, kidnapping; **l'~ des ordures ménagères** refuse collection.

enlever [ãlve] *vt* (*ôter: gén*) to remove; (: *vêtement, lunettes*) to take off; (: *MÉD: organe*) to remove; (*emporter: ordures etc*) to collect, take away; (*kidnapper*) to abduct, kidnap; (*obtenir: prix, contrat*) to win; (*MIL: position*) to take; (*morceau de piano etc*) to execute with spirit *ou* brio; (*prendre*): ~ **qch à qn** to take sth (away) from sb; **s'~** *vi* (*tache*) to come out *ou* off; **la maladie qui nous l'a enlevé** (*euphémisme*) the illness which took him from us.

enliser [ãlize]: **s'~** *vi* to sink, get stuck; (*dialogue etc*) to get bogged down.

enluminure [ãlyminyʀ] *nf* illumination.

ENM *sigle f* (= *École nationale de la magistrature*) *grande école* for law students.

enneigé, e [ãneʒe] *adj* snowy; (*col*) snowed-up; (*maison*) snowed-in.

enneigement [ãnɛʒmã] *nm* depth of snow, snowfall; **bulletin d'~** snow report.

ennemi, e [ɛnmi] *adj* hostile; (*MIL*) enemy *cpd* ♦ *nm/f* enemy; **être** ~ **de** to be strongly averse *ou* opposed to.

ennième [ɛnjɛm] *adj* = **nième**.

ennoblir [ãnɔbliʀ] *vt* to ennoble.

ennui [ãnyi] *nm* (*lassitude*) boredom; (*difficulté*) trouble *no pl*; **avoir des ~s** to have problems; **s'attirer des ~s** to cause problems for o.s.

ennuie [ãnyi] *etc vb voir* **ennuyer**.

ennuyé, e [ãnyije] *adj* (*air, personne*) preoccupied, worried.

ennuyer [ãnyije] *vt* to bother; (*lasser*) to bore; **s'~** *vi* to be bored; **s'~ de** (*regretter*) to miss; **si cela ne vous ennuie pas** if it's no trouble to you.

ennuyeux, euse [ãnyijø, -øz] *adj* boring, tedious; (*agaçant*) annoying.

énoncé [enɔ̃se] *nm* terms *pl*; wording; (*LING*) utterance.

énoncer [enɔ̃se] *vt* to say, express; (*conditions*) to set out, lay down, state.

énonciation [enɔ̃sjasjɔ̃] *nf* statement.

enorgueillir [ɑ̃nɔʀgœjiʀ]: **s'~ de** *vt* to pride o.s. on; to boast.

énorme [enɔʀm(ə)] *adj* enormous, huge.

énormément [enɔʀmemɑ̃] *adv* enormously, tremendously; **~ de neige/gens** an enormous amount of snow/number of people.

énormité [enɔʀmite] *nf* enormity, hugeness; (*propos*) outrageous remark.

en part. *abr* (= *en particulier*) esp.

enquérir [ɑ̃keʀiʀ]: **s'~ de** *vt* to inquire about.

enquête [ɑ̃kɛt] *nf* (*de journaliste, de police*) investigation; (*judiciaire, administrative*) inquiry; (*sondage d'opinion*) survey.

enquêter [ɑ̃kete] *vi* to investigate; to hold an inquiry; (*faire un sondage*): **~ (sur)** to do a survey (on), carry out an opinion poll (on).

enquêteur, euse *ou* **trice** [ɑ̃kɛtœʀ, -øz, -tʀis] *nm/f* officer in charge of an investigation; person conducting a survey; pollster.

enquiers, enquière [ɑ̃kjɛʀ] *etc vb voir* **enquérir.**

enquiquiner [ɑ̃kikine] *vt* to rile, irritate.

enquis, e [ɑ̃ki, -iz] *pp de* **enquérir.**

enraciné, e [ɑ̃ʀasine] *adj* deep-rooted.

enragé, e [ɑ̃ʀaʒe] *adj* (*MÉD*) rabid, with rabies; (*furieux*) furiously angry; (*fig*) fanatical; **~ de** wild about.

enrageant, e [ɑ̃ʀaʒɑ̃, -ɑ̃t] *adj* infuriating.

enrager [ɑ̃ʀaʒe] *vi* to be furious, be in a rage; **faire ~ qn** to make sb wild with anger.

enrayer [ɑ̃ʀeje] *vt* to check, stop; **s'~** *vi* (*arme à feu*) to jam.

enrégimenter [ɑ̃ʀeʒimɑ̃te] *vt* (*péj*) to enlist.

enregistrement [ɑ̃ʀʒistʀəmɑ̃] *nm* recording; (*ADMIN*) registration; **~ des bagages** (*à l'aéroport*) baggage check-in; **~ magnétique** tape-recording.

enregistrer [ɑ̃ʀʒistʀe] *vt* (*MUS, INFORM etc*) to record; (*remarquer, noter*) to note, record; (*COMM: commande*) to note, enter; (*fig: mémoriser*) to make a mental note of; (*ADMIN*) to register; (*aussi:* **faire ~**: *bagages: par train*) to register; (*: à l'aéroport*) to check in.

enregistreur, euse [ɑ̃ʀʒistʀœʀ, -øz] *adj* (*machine*) recording *cpd* ♦ *nm* (*appareil*): **~ de vol** (*AVIAT*) flight recorder.

enrhumé, e [ɑ̃ʀyme] *adj*: **il est ~** he has a cold.

enrhumer [ɑ̃ʀyme]: **s'~** *vi* to catch a cold.

enrichir [ɑ̃ʀiʃiʀ] *vt* to make rich(er); (*fig*) to enrich; **s'~** *vi* to get rich(er).

enrichissant, e [ɑ̃ʀiʃisɑ̃, -ɑ̃t] *adj* instructive.

enrichissement [ɑ̃ʀiʃismɑ̃] *nm* enrichment.

enrober [ɑ̃ʀɔbe] *vt*: **~ qch de** to coat sth with; (*fig*) to wrap sth up in.

enrôlement [ɑ̃ʀolmɑ̃] *nm* enlistment.

enrôler [ɑ̃ʀole] *vt* to enlist; **s'~ (dans)** to enlist (in).

enroué, e [ɑ̃ʀwe] *adj* hoarse.

enrouer [ɑ̃ʀwe]: **s'~** *vi* to go hoarse.

enrouler [ɑ̃ʀule] *vt* (*fil, corde*) to wind (up); **s'~** to coil up; **~ qch autour de** to wind sth (a)round.

enrouleur, euse [ɑ̃ʀulœʀ, -øz] *adj* (*TECH*) winding ♦ *nm voir* **ceinture.**

enrubanné, e [ɑ̃ʀybane] *adj* trimmed with ribbon.

ENS *sigle f* = **école normale supérieure.**

ensabler [ɑ̃sɑble] *vt* (*port, canal*) to silt up, sand up; (*embarcation*) to strand (on a sandbank); **s'~** *vi* to silt up; to get stranded.

ensacher [ɑ̃saʃe] *vt* to pack into bags.

ENSAM *sigle f* (= *École nationale supérieure des arts et métiers*) *grande école for engineering students.*

ensanglanté, e [ɑ̃sɑ̃glɑ̃te] *adj* covered with blood.

enseignant, e [ɑ̃sɛɲɑ̃, -ɑ̃t] *adj* teaching ♦ *nm/f* teacher.

enseigne [ɑ̃sɛɲ] *nf* sign ♦ *nm*: **~ de vaisseau** lieutenant; **à telle ~ que** so much so that; **être logés à la même ~** (*fig*) to be in the same boat; **~ lumineuse** neon sign.

enseignement [ɑ̃sɛɲmɑ̃] *nm* teaching; **~ ménager** home economics; **~ primaire** primary (*BRIT*) *ou* grade school (*US*) education; **~ secondaire** secondary (*BRIT*) *ou* high school (*US*) education.

enseigner [ɑ̃seɲe] *vt, vi* to teach; **~ qch à qn/ à qn que** to teach sb sth/sb that.

ensemble [ɑ̃sɑ̃bl(ə)] *adv* together ♦ *nm* (*assemblage, MATH*) set; (*totalité*): **l'~ du/de la** the whole *ou* entire; (*vêtement féminin*) ensemble, suit; (*unité, harmonie*) unity; (*résidentiel*) housing development; **aller ~** to go together; **impression/idée d'~** overall *ou* general impression/idea; **dans l'~** (*en gros*) on the whole; **dans son ~** overall, in general; **~ vocal/musical** vocal/musical ensemble.

ensemblier [ɑ̃sɑ̃blije] *nm* interior designer.

ensemencer [ɑ̃smɑ̃se] *vt* to sow.

enserrer [ɑ̃seʀe] *vt* to hug (tightly).

ENSET [ɑ̃sɛt] *sigle f* (= *École normale supérieure de l'enseignement technique*) *grande école for training technical teachers.*

ensevelir [ɑ̃səvliʀ] *vt* to bury.

ensilage [ɑ̃silaʒ] *nm* (*aliment*) silage.

ensoleillé, e [ɑ̃sɔleje] *adj* sunny.

ensoleillement [ɑ̃sɔlejmɑ̃] *nm* period *ou* hours *pl* of sunshine.

ensommeillé, e [ɑ̃sɔmeje] *adj* sleepy, drowsy.

ensorceler [ɑ̃sɔʀsəle] *vt* to enchant, bewitch.

ensuite [ɑ̃sɥit] *adv* then, next; (*plus tard*) afterwards, later; **~ de quoi** after which.

ensuivre [ɑ̃sɥivʀ(ə)]: **s'~** *vi* to follow, ensue; **il s'ensuit que ...** it follows that ...; **et tout ce qui s'ensuit** and all that goes with it.

entaché, e [ɑ̃taʃe] *adj*: **~ de** marred by; **~ de nullité** null and void.

entacher [ãtaʃe] *vt* to soil.

entaille [ãtaj] *nf* (*encoche*) notch; (*blessure*) cut; **se faire une ~** to cut o.s.

entailler [ãtaje] *vt* to notch; to cut; **s'~ le doigt** to cut one's finger.

entamer [ãtame] *vt* to start; (*hostilités, pourparlers*) to open; (*fig: altérer*) to make a dent in; to damage.

entartrer [ãtaʀtʀe]: **s'~** *vi* to fur up; (*dents*) to become covered with plaque.

entassement [ãtɑsmã] *nm* (*tas*) pile, heap.

entasser [ãtɑse] *vt* (*empiler*) to pile up, heap up; (*tenir à l'étroit*) to cram together; **s'~** *vi* to pile up; to cram; **s'~ dans** to cram into.

entendement [ãtãdmã] *nm* understanding.

entendre [ãtãdʀ(ə)] *vt* to hear; (*comprendre*) to understand; (*vouloir dire*) to mean; (*vouloir*): **~ être obéi/que** to intend *ou* mean to be obeyed/that; **j'ai entendu dire que** I've heard (it said) that; **je suis heureux de vous l'~ dire** I'm pleased to hear you say it; **~ parler de** to hear of; **laisser ~ que, donner à ~ que** to let it be understood that; **~ raison** to see sense, listen to reason; **qu'est- ce qu'il ne faut pas ~!** whatever next!; **j'ai mal entendu** I didn't catch what was said; **je vous entends très mal** I can hardly hear you; **s'~** *vi* (*sympathiser*) to get on; (*se mettre d'accord*) to agree; **s'~ à qch/à faire** (*être compétent*) to be good at sth/doing; **ça s'entend** (*est audible*) it's audible; **je m'entends** I mean; **entendons-nous!** let's be clear what we mean.

entendu, e [ãtãdy] *pp de* **entendre** ♦ *adj* (*réglé*) agreed; (*au courant: air*) knowing; **étant ~ que** since (it's understood *ou* agreed that); **(c'est) ~** all right, agreed; **c'est ~** (*concession*) all right, granted; **bien ~** of course.

entente [ãtãt] *nf* (*entre amis, pays*) understanding, harmony; (*accord, traité*) agreement, understanding; **à double ~** (*sens*) with a double meaning.

entériner [ãteʀine] *vt* to ratify, confirm.

entérite [ãteʀit] *nf* enteritis *no pl.*

enterrement [ãtɛʀmã] *nm* burying; (*cérémonie*) funeral, burial; (*cortège funèbre*) funeral procession.

enterrer [ãteʀe] *vt* to bury.

entêtant, e [ãtɛtã, -ãt] *adj* heady.

entêté, e [ãtete] *adj* stubborn.

en-tête [ãtɛt] *nm* heading; (*de papier à lettres*) letterhead; **papier à ~** headed notepaper.

entêtement [ãtɛtmã] *nm* stubbornness.

entêter [ãtete]: **s'~** *vi*: **s'~ (à faire)** to persist (in doing).

enthousiasmant, e [ãtuzjasmã, -ãt] *adj* exciting.

enthousiasme [ãtuzjasm(ə)] *nm* enthusiasm; **avec ~** enthusiastically.

enthousiasmé, e [ãtuzjasme] *adj* filled with enthusiasm.

enthousiasmer [ãtuzjasme] *vt* to fill with enthusiasm; **s'~ (pour qch)** to get enthusiastic (about sth).

enthousiaste [ãtuzjast(ə)] *adj* enthusiastic.

enticher [ãtiʃe]: **s'~ de** *vt* to become infatuated with.

entier, ière [ãtje, -jɛʀ] *adj* (*non entamé, en totalité*) whole; (*total, complet*) complete; (*fig: caractère*) unbending, averse to compromise ♦ *nm* (*MATH*) whole; **en ~** totally; **in its entirety**; **se donner tout ~ à qch** to devote o.s. completely to sth; **lait ~** full-cream milk; **pain ~** wholemeal bread; **nombre ~** whole number.

entièrement [ãtjɛʀmã] *adv* entirely, completely, wholly.

entité [ãtite] *nf* entity.

entomologie [ãtɔmɔlɔʒi] *nf* entomology.

entonner [ãtɔne] *vt* (*chanson*) to strike up.

entonnoir [ãtɔnwaʀ] *nm* (*ustensile*) funnel; (*trou*) shell-hole, crater.

entorse [ãtɔʀs(ə)] *nf* (*MÉD*) sprain; (*fig*): **~ à la loi/au règlement** infringement of the law/rule; **se faire une ~ à la cheville/au poignet** to sprain one's ankle/wrist.

entortiller [ãtɔʀtije] *vt* (*envelopper*): **~ qch dans/avec** to wrap sth in/with; (*enrouler*): **~ qch autour de** to twist *ou* wind sth (a)round; (*fam*): **~ qn** to get (a)round sb; (*: duper*) to hoodwink sb (*BRIT*), trick sb; **s'~ dans** (*draps*) to roll o.s. up in; (*fig: réponses*) to get tangled up in.

entourage [ãtuʀaʒ] *nm* circle; family (circle); (*d'une vedette etc*) entourage; (*ce qui enclôt*) surround.

entouré, e [ãtuʀe] *adj* (*recherché, admiré*) popular; **~ de** surrounded by.

entourer [ãtuʀe] *vt* to surround; (*apporter son soutien à*) to rally round; **~ de** to surround with; (*trait*) to encircle with; **s'~ de** to surround o.s. with; **s'~ de précautions** to take all possible precautions.

entourloupette [ãtuʀlupɛt] *nf* mean trick.

entournures [ãtuʀnyʀ] *nfpl*: **gêné aux ~** in financial difficulties; (*fig*) a bit awkward.

entracte [ãtʀakt(ə)] *nm* interval.

entraide [ãtʀɛd] *nf* mutual aid *ou* assistance.

entraider [ãtʀede]: **s'~** *vi* to help each other.

entrailles [ãtʀaj] *nfpl* entrails; (*humaines*) bowels.

entrain [ãtʀɛ̃] *nm* spirit; **avec ~** (*répondre, travailler*) energetically; **faire qch sans ~** to do sth half-heartedly *ou* without enthusiasm.

entraînant, e [ãtʀɛnã, -ãt] *adj* (*musique*) stirring, rousing.

entraînement [ãtʀɛnmã] *nm* training; (*TECH*): **~ à chaîne/galet** chain/wheel drive; **manquer d'~** to be unfit; **~ par ergots/friction** (*INFORM*) tractor/friction feed.

entraîner [ãtʀene] *vt* (*tirer: wagons*) to pull; (*charrier*) to carry *ou* drag along; (*TECH*) to drive; (*emmener: personne*) to take (off); (*mener à l'assaut, influencer*) to lead; (*SPORT*)

to train; (*impliquer*) to entail; (*causer*) to lead to, bring about; ~ **qn à faire** (*inciter*) to lead sb to do; **s'~** (*SPORT*) to train; **s'~ à qch/à faire** to train o.s. for sth/to do.
entraîneur [ɑ̃tʀɛnœʀ] *nm* (*SPORT*) coach, trainer; (*HIPPISME*) trainer.
entraîneuse [ɑ̃tʀɛnøz] *nf* (*de bar*) hostess.
entrapercevoir [ɑ̃tʀapɛʀsəvwaʀ] *vt* to catch a glimpse of.
entrave [ɑ̃tʀav] *nf* hindrance.
entraver [ɑ̃tʀave] *vt* (*circulation*) to hold up; (*action, progrès*) to hinder, hamper.
entre [ɑ̃tʀ(ə)] *prép* between; (*parmi*) among(st); **l'un d'~ eux/nous** one of them/us; **le meilleur d'~ eux/nous** the best of them/us; **ils préfèrent rester ~ eux** they prefer to keep to themselves; **~ autres (choses)** among other things; **~ nous, ...** between ourselves ..., between you and me ...; **ils se battent ~ eux** they are fighting among(st) themselves.
entrebâillé, e [ɑ̃tʀəbaje] *adj* half-open, ajar.
entrebâillement [ɑ̃tʀəbajmɑ̃] *nm*: **dans l'~ (de la porte)** in the half-open door.
entrebâiller [ɑ̃tʀəbaje] *vt* to half open.
entrechat [ɑ̃tʀəʃa] *nm* leap.
entrechoquer [ɑ̃tʀəʃɔke]: **s'~** *vi* to knock *ou* bang together.
entrecôte [ɑ̃tʀəkot] *nf* entrecôte *ou* rib steak.
entrecoupé, e [ɑ̃tʀəkupe] *adj* (*paroles, voix*) broken.
entrecouper [ɑ̃tʀəkupe] *vt*: **~ qch de** to intersperse sth with; **~ un récit/voyage de** to interrupt a story/journey with; **s'~** (*traits, lignes*) to cut across each other.
entrecroiser [ɑ̃tʀəkʀwaze] *vt*, **s'~** *vi* to intertwine.
entrée [ɑ̃tʀe] *nf* entrance; (*accès: au cinéma etc*) admission; (*billet*) (admission) ticket; (*CULIN*) first course; (*COMM: de marchandises*) entry; (*INFORM*) entry, input; **~s** *nfpl*: **avoir ses ~s chez** *ou* **auprès de** to be a welcome visitor to; **d'~** *adv* from the outset; **erreur d'~** input error; **"~ interdite"** "no admittance *ou* entry"; **~ des artistes** stage door; **~ en matière** introduction; **~ en scène** entrance; **~ de service** service entrance.
entrefaites [ɑ̃tʀəfɛt]: **sur ces ~** *adv* at this juncture.
entrefilet [ɑ̃tʀəfilɛ] *nm* (*article*) paragraph, short report.
entregent [ɑ̃tʀəʒɑ̃] *nm*: **avoir de l'~** to have an easy manner.
entre-jambes [ɑ̃tʀəʒɑ̃b] *nm inv* crotch.
entrelacement [ɑ̃tʀəlasmɑ̃] *nm*: **un ~ de ...** a network of ....
entrelacer [ɑ̃tʀəlase] *vt*, **s'~** *vi* to intertwine.
entrelarder [ɑ̃tʀəlaʀde] *vt* to lard; (*fig*): **entrelardé de** interspersed with.
entremêler [ɑ̃tʀəmele] *vt*: **~ qch de** to (inter)mingle sth with.
entremets [ɑ̃tʀəmɛ] *nm* (cream) dessert.

entremetteur, euse [ɑ̃tʀəmɛtœʀ, -øz] *nm/f* go-between.
entremettre [ɑ̃tʀəmɛtʀ(ə)]: **s'~** *vi* to intervene.
entremise [ɑ̃tʀəmiz] *nf* intervention; **par l'~ de** through.
entrepont [ɑ̃tʀəpɔ̃] *nm* steerage; **dans l'~** in steerage.
entreposer [ɑ̃tʀəpoze] *vt* to store, put into storage.
entrepôt [ɑ̃tʀəpo] *nm* warehouse.
entreprenant, e [ɑ̃tʀəpʀənɑ̃, -ɑ̃t] *vb voir* **entreprendre** ♦ *adj* (*actif*) enterprising; (*trop galant*) forward.
entreprendre [ɑ̃tʀəpʀɑ̃dʀ(ə)] *vt* (*se lancer dans*) to undertake; (*commencer*) to begin *ou* start (upon); (*personne*) to buttonhole; **~ qn sur un sujet** to tackle sb on a subject; **~ de faire** to undertake to do.
entrepreneur [ɑ̃tʀəpʀənœʀ] *nm*: **~ (en bâtiment)** (building) contractor; **~ de pompes funèbres** funeral director, undertaker.
entreprenne [ɑ̃tʀəpʀɛn] *etc vb voir* **entreprendre**.
entrepris, e [ɑ̃tʀəpʀi, -iz] *pp de* **entreprendre** ♦ *nf* (*société*) firm, business; (*action*) undertaking, venture.
entrer [ɑ̃tʀe] *vi* to go (*ou* come) in, enter ♦ *vt* (*INFORM*) to input, enter; **(faire) ~ qch dans** to get sth in; **~ dans** (*gén*) to enter; (*pièce*) to go (*ou* come) into, enter; (*club*) to join; (*heurter*) to run into; (*partager: vues, craintes de qn*) to share; (*être une composante de*) to go into; (*faire partie de*) to form part of; **~ au couvent** to enter a convent; **~ à l'hôpital** to go into hospital; **~ dans le système** (*INFORM*) to log in; **~ en fureur** to become angry; **~ en ébullition** to start to boil; **~ en scène** to come on stage; **laisser ~ qn/qch** to let sb/sth in; **faire ~** (*visiteur*) to show in.
entresol [ɑ̃tʀəsɔl] *nm* entresol, mezzanine.
entre-temps [ɑ̃tʀətɑ̃] *adv* meanwhile, (in the) meantime.
entretenir [ɑ̃tʀətniʀ] *vt* to maintain; (*amitié*) to keep alive; (*famille, maîtresse*) to support, keep; **~ qn (de)** to speak to sb (about); **s'~ (de)** to converse (about); **~ qn dans l'erreur** to let sb remain in ignorance.
entretenu, e [ɑ̃tʀətny] *pp de* **entretenir** ♦ *adj* (*femme*) kept; **bien/mal ~** (*maison, jardin*) well/badly kept.
entretien [ɑ̃tʀətjɛ̃] *nm* maintenance; (*discussion*) discussion, talk; (*audience*) interview; **frais d'~** maintenance charges.
entretiendrai [ɑ̃tʀətjɛ̃dʀe], **entretiens** [ɑ̃tʀətjɛ̃] *etc vb voir* **entretenir**.
entretuer [ɑ̃tʀətɥe]: **s'~** *vi* to kill one another.
entreverrai [ɑ̃tʀəveʀe], **entrevit** [ɑ̃tʀəvi] *etc vb voir* **entrevoir**.
entrevoir [ɑ̃tʀəvwaʀ] *vt* (*à peine*) to make out; (*brièvement*) to catch a glimpse of.

entrevu, e [ātRəvy] *pp de* **entrevoir ♦** *nf* meeting; (*audience*) interview.
entrouvert, e [ātRuvɛR, -ɛRt(ə)] *pp de* **entrouvrir ♦** *adj* half-open.
entrouvrir [ātRuvRiR] *vt*, **s'~** *vi* to half open.
énumération [enymeRɑsjɔ̃] *nf* enumeration.
énumérer [enymeRe] *vt* to list, enumerate.
énurésie [enyRezi] *nf* enuresis.
envahir [āvaiR] *vt* to invade; (*suj: inquiétude, peur*) to come over.
envahissant, e [āvaisā, -āt] *adj* (*péj: personne*) interfering, intrusive.
envahissement [āvaismā] *nm* invasion.
envahisseur [āvaisœR] *nm* (*MIL*) invader.
envasement [ānvazmā] *nm* silting up.
envaser [āvaze]: **s'~** *vi* to get bogged down (in the mud).
enveloppe [āvlɔp] *nf* (*de lettre*) envelope; (*TECH*) casing; outer layer; **mettre sous ~** to put in an envelope; **~ autocollante** self-seal envelope; **~ budgétaire** budget; **~ à fenêtre** window envelope.
envelopper [āvlɔpe] *vt* to wrap; (*fig*) to envelop, shroud; **s'~ dans un châle/une couverture** to wrap o.s. in a shawl/blanket.
envenimer [āvnime] *vt* to aggravate; **s'~** *vi* (*plaie*) to fester; (*situation, relations*) to worsen.
envergure [āvɛRgyR] *nf* (*d'un oiseau, avion*) wingspan; (*fig: étendue*) scope; (*: valeur*) calibre.
enverrai [āvɛRe] *etc vb voir* **envoyer.**
envers [āvɛR] *prép* towards, to ♦ *nm* other side; (*d'une étoffe*) wrong side; **à l'~** upside down; back to front; (*vêtement*) inside out; **~ et contre tous** *ou* **tout** against all opposition.
enviable [āvjabl(ə)] *adj* enviable; **peu ~** unenviable.
envie [āvi] *nf* (*sentiment*) envy; (*souhait*) desire, wish; (*tache sur la peau*) birthmark; (*filet de peau*) hangnail; **avoir ~ de** to feel like; (*désir plus fort*) to want; **avoir ~ de faire** to feel like doing; to want to do; **avoir ~ que** to wish that; **donner à qn l'~ de faire** to make sb want to do; **ça lui fait ~** he would like that.
envier [āvje] *vt* to envy; **~ qch à qn** to envy sb sth; **n'avoir rien à ~ à** to have no cause to be envious of.
envieux, euse [āvjø, -øz] *adj* envious.
environ [āviRɔ̃] *adv*: **~ 3 h/2 km, 3 h/2 km ~** (around) about 3 o'clock/2 km, 3 o'clock/2 km or so.
environnant, e [āviRɔnā, -āt] *adj* surrounding.
environnement [āviRɔnmā] *nm* environment.
environnementaliste [āviRɔnmātalist(ə)] *nm/f* environmentalist.
environner [āviRɔne] *vt* to surround.
environs [āviRɔ̃] *nmpl* surroundings; **aux ~ de** around.
envisageable [āvizaʒabl(ə)] *adj* conceivable.

envisager [āvizaʒe] *vt* (*examiner, considérer*) to view, contemplate; (*avoir en vue*) to envisage; **~ de faire** to consider *ou* contemplate doing.
envoi [āvwa] *nm* sending; (*paquet*) parcel, consignment; **~ contre remboursement** (*COMM*) cash on delivery.
envoie [āvwa] *etc vb voir* **envoyer.**
envol [āvɔl] *nm* takeoff.
envolée [āvɔle] *nf* (*fig*) flight.
envoler [āvɔle]: **s'~** *vi* (*oiseau*) to fly away *ou* off; (*avion*) to take off; (*papier, feuille*) to blow away; (*fig*) to vanish (into thin air).
envoûtant, e [āvutā, -āt] *adj* enchanting.
envoûtement [āvutmā] *nm* bewitchment.
envoûter [āvute] *vt* to bewitch.
envoyé, e [āvwaje] *nm/f* (*POL*) envoy; (*PRESSE*) correspondent ♦ *adj*: **bien ~** (*remarque, réponse*) well-aimed.
envoyer [āvwaje] *vt* to send; (*lancer*) to hurl, throw; **~ une gifle/un sourire à qn** to aim a blow/flash a smile at sb; **~ les couleurs** to run up the colours; **~ chercher** to send for; **~ par le fond** (*bateau*) to send to the bottom.
envoyeur, euse [āvwajœR, -øz] *nm/f* sender.
enzyme [āzim] *nf ou m* enzyme.
éolien, ne [eɔljɛ̃, -ɛn] *adj* wind *cpd*; **pompe ~ne** windpump.
EOR *sigle m* (= élève officier de réserve) ≈ military cadet.
éosine [eɔzin] *nf* eosin (*antiseptic used in France to treat skin ailments*).
épagneul, e [epaɲœl] *nm/f* spaniel.
épais, se [epɛ, -ɛs] *adj* thick.
épaisseur [epɛsœR] *nf* thickness.
épaissir [epesiR] *vt*, **s'~** *vi* to thicken.
épaississement [epesismā] *nm* thickening.
épanchement [epāʃmā] *nm*: **un ~ de sinovie** water on the knee; **~s** *nmpl* (*fig*) (sentimental) outpourings.
épancher [epāʃe] *vt* to give vent to; **s'~** *vi* to open one's heart; (*liquide*) to pour out.
épandage [epādaʒ] *nm* manure spreading.
épanoui, e [epanwi] *adj* (*éclos, ouvert, développé*) blooming; (*radieux*) radiant.
épanouir [epanwiR]: **s'~** *vi* (*fleur*) to bloom, open out; (*visage*) to light up; (*fig: se développer*) to blossom (out); (*: mentalement*) to open up.
épanouissement [epanwismā] *nm* blossoming; opening up.
épargnant, e [epaRɲā, -āt] *nm/f* saver, investor.
épargne [epaRɲ(ə)] *nf* saving; **l'~-logement** property investment.
épargner [epaRɲe] *vt* to save; (*ne pas tuer ou endommager*) to spare ♦ *vi* to save; **~ qch à qn** to spare sb sth.
éparpillement [epaRpijmā] *nm* (*de papier*) scattering; (*des efforts*) dissipation.
éparpiller [epaRpije] *vt* to scatter; (*pour répartir*) to disperse; (*fig: efforts*) to dissipate; **s'~**

vi to scatter; (*fig*) to dissipate one's efforts.

épars, e [epaʀ, -aʀs(ə)] *adj* (*maisons*) scattered; (*cheveux*) sparse.

épatant, e [epatɑ̃, -ɑ̃t] *adj* (*fam*) super, splendid.

épaté, e [epate] *adj*: **nez** ~ flat nose (with wide nostrils).

épater [epate] *vt* to amaze; (*impressionner*) to impress.

épaule [epol] *nf* shoulder.

épaulé-jeté, *pl* **épaulés-jetés** [epoleʒəte] *nm* (*SPORT*) clean-and-jerk.

épaulement [epolmɑ̃] *nm* escarpment; (*mur*) retaining wall.

épauler [epole] *vt* (*aider*) to back up, support; (*arme*) to raise (to one's shoulder) ♦ *vi* to (take) aim.

épaulette [epolɛt] *nf* (*MIL*, *d'un veston*) epaulette; (*de combinaison*) shoulder strap.

épave [epav] *nf* wreck.

épée [epe] *nf* sword.

épeler [eple] *vt* to spell.

éperdu, e [epɛʀdy] *adj* (*personne*) overcome; (*sentiment*) passionate; (*fuite*) frantic.

éperdument [epɛʀdymɑ̃] *adv* (*aimer*) wildly; (*espérer*) fervently.

éperlan [epɛʀlɑ̃] *nm* (*ZOOL*) smelt.

éperon [epʀɔ̃] *nm* spur.

éperonner [epʀɔne] *vt* to spur (on); (*navire*) to ram.

épervier [epɛʀvje] *nm* (*ZOOL*) sparrowhawk; (*PÊCHE*) casting net.

éphèbe [efɛb] *nm* beautiful young man.

éphémère [efemɛʀ] *adj* ephemeral, fleeting.

éphéméride [efemeʀid] *nf* block *ou* tear-off calendar.

épi [epi] *nm* (*de blé, d'orge*) ear; ~ **de cheveux** tuft of hair; **stationne/se garer en** ~ parking/to park at an angle to the kerb.

épice [epis] *nf* spice.

épicé, e [epise] *adj* highly spiced, spicy; (*fig*) spicy.

épicéa [episea] *nm* spruce.

épicentre [episɑ̃tʀ(ə)] *nm* epicentre.

épicer [epise] *vt* to spice; (*fig*) to add spice to.

épicerie [episʀi] *nf* (*magasin*) grocer's shop; (*denrées*) groceries *pl*; ~ **fine** delicatessen (shop).

épicier, ière [episje, -jɛʀ] *nm/f* grocer.

épicurien, ne [epikyʀjɛ̃, -ɛn] *adj* epicurean.

épidémie [epidemi] *nf* epidemic.

épidémique [epidemik] *adj* epidemic.

épiderme [epidɛʀm(ə)] *nm* skin, epidermis.

épidermique [epidɛʀmik] *adj* skin *cpd*, epidermic.

épier [epje] *vt* to spy on, watch closely; (*occasion*) to look out for.

épieu, x [epjø] *nm* (hunting-)spear.

épigramme [epigʀam] *nf* epigram.

épigraphe [epigʀaf] *nf* epigraph.

épilation [epilasjɔ̃] *nf* removal of unwanted hair.

épilatoire [epilatwaʀ] *adj* depilatory, hair-removing.

épilepsie [epilɛpsi] *nf* epilepsy.

épileptique [epilɛptik] *adj, nm/f* epileptic.

épiler [epile] *vt* (*jambes*) to remove the hair from; (*sourcils*) to pluck; **s'**~ **les jambes** to remove the hair from one's legs; **s'**~ **les sourcils** to pluck one's eyebrows; **se faire** ~ to get unwanted hair removed; **crème à** ~ hair-removing *ou* depilatory cream; **pince à** ~ eyebrow tweezers.

épilogue [epilɔg] *nm* (*fig*) conclusion, dénouement.

épiloguer [epilɔge] *vi*: ~ **sur** to hold forth on.

épinard [epinaʀ] *nm* (*aussi*: ~**s**) spinach *sg*.

épine [epin] *nf* thorn, prickle; (*d'oursin etc*) spine, prickle; ~ **dorsale** backbone.

épineux, euse [epinø, -øz] *adj* thorny, prickly.

épinglage [epɛ̃glaʒ] *nm* pinning.

épingle [epɛ̃gl(ə)] *nf* pin; **tirer son** ~ **du jeu** to play one's game well; **tiré à quatre** ~**s** well turned-out; **monter qch en** ~ to build sth up, make a thing of sth (*fam*); ~ **à chapeau** hatpin; ~ **à cheveux** hairpin; **virage en** ~ **à cheveux** hairpin bend; ~ **de cravate** tie pin; ~ **de nourrice** *ou* **de sûreté** *ou* **double** safety pin, nappy (*BRIT*) *ou* diaper (*US*) pin.

épingler [epɛ̃gle] *vt* (*badge, décoration*): ~ **qch sur** to pin sth on(to); (*COUTURE: tissu, robe*) to pin together; (*fam*) to catch, nick.

épinière [epinjɛʀ] *adj f voir* **moelle**.

Épiphanie [epifani] *nf* Epiphany.

épique [epik] *adj* epic.

épiscopal, e, aux [episkɔpal, -o] *adj* episcopal.

épiscopat [episkɔpa] *nm* bishopric, episcopate.

épisiotomie [epizjɔtomi] *nf* (*MÉD*) episiotomy.

épisode [epizɔd] *nm* episode; **film/roman à** ~**s** serialized film/novel, serial.

épisodique [epizɔdik] *adj* occasional.

épisodiquement [epizɔdikmɑ̃] *adv* occasionally.

épissure [episyʀ] *nf* splice.

épistémologie [epistemɔlɔʒi] *nf* epistemology.

épistolaire [epistɔlɛʀ] *adj* epistolary; **être en relations** ~**s avec qn** to correspond with sb.

épitaphe [epitaf] *nf* epitaph.

épithète [epitɛt] *nf* (*nom, surnom*) epithet; **adjectif** ~ attributive adjective.

épître [epitʀ(ə)] *nf* epistle.

éploré, e [eplɔʀe] *adj* in tears, tearful.

épluchage [eplyʃaʒ] *nm* peeling; (*de dossier etc*) careful reading *ou* analysis.

épluche-légumes [eplyʃlegym] *nm inv* potato peeler.

éplucher [eplyʃe] *vt* (*fruit, légumes*) to peel; (*comptes, dossier*) to go over with a fine-tooth comb.

éplucheur [eplyʃœʀ] *nm* (automatic) peeler.

épluchures [eplyʃyʀ] *nfpl* peelings.

épointer [epwɛ̃te] *vt* to blunt.

éponge [epɔ̃ʒ] *nf* sponge; **passer l'~ (sur)** (*fig*) to let bygones be bygones (with regard to); **jeter l'~** (*fig*) to throw in the towel; ~ **métallique** scourer.

éponger [epɔ̃ʒe] *vt* (*liquide*) to mop *ou* sponge up; (*surface*) to sponge; (*fig: déficit*) to soak up, absorb; **s'~ le front** to mop one's brow.

épopée [epɔpe] *nf* epic.

époque [epɔk] *nf* (*de l'histoire*) age, era; (*de l'année, la vie*) time; **d'~** *adj* (*meuble*) period *cpd*; **à cette ~** at this (*ou* that) time *ou* period; **faire ~** to make history.

épouiller [epuje] *vt* to pick lice off; (*avec un produit*) to delouse.

époumoner [epumɔne]: **s'~** *vi* to shout (*ou* sing) o.s. hoarse.

épouse [epuz] *nf* wife (*pl* wives).

épouser [epuze] *vt* to marry; (*fig: idées*) to espouse; (: *forme*) to fit.

époussetage [epustaʒ] *nm* dusting.

épousseter [epuste] *vt* to dust.

époustouflant, e [epustuflɑ̃, -ɑ̃t] *adj* staggering, mind-boggling.

époustoufler [epustufle] *vt* to flabbergast, astound.

épouvantable [epuvɑ̃tabl(ə)] *adj* appalling, dreadful.

épouvantablement [epuvɑ̃tabləmɑ̃] *adj* terribly, dreadfully.

épouvantail [epuvɑ̃taj] *nm* (*à moineaux*) scarecrow; (*fig*) bog(e)y; bugbear.

épouvante [epuvɑ̃t] *nf* terror; **film d'~** horror film.

épouvanter [epuvɑ̃te] *vt* to terrify.

époux [epu] *nm* husband ♦ *nmpl*: **les ~** the (married) couple, the husband and wife.

éprendre [eprɑ̃dr(ə)]: **s'~ de** *vt* to fall in love with.

épreuve [eprœv] *nf* (*d'examen*) test; (*malheur, difficulté*) trial, ordeal; (*PHOTO*) print; (*TYPO*) proof; (*SPORT*) event; **à l'~ des balles/du feu** (*vêtement*) bulletproof/fireproof; **à toute ~** unfailing; **mettre à l'~** to put to the test; ~ **de force** trial of strength; (*fig*) showdown; ~ **de résistance** test of resistance; ~ **de sélection** (*SPORT*) heat.

épris, e [epri, -iz] *vb voir* **éprendre** ♦ *adj*: ~ **de** in love with.

éprouvant, e [epruvɑ̃, -ɑ̃t] *adj* trying.

éprouvé, e [epruve] *adj* tested, proven.

éprouver [epruve] *vt* (*tester*) to test; (*mettre à l'épreuve*) to put to the test; (*marquer, faire souffrir*) to afflict, distress; (*ressentir*) to experience.

éprouvette [epruvɛt] *nf* test tube.

EPS *sigle f* (= *Éducation physique et sportive*) ≈ PE.

épuisant, e [epɥizɑ̃, -ɑ̃t] *adj* exhausting.

épuisé, e [epɥize] *adj* exhausted; (*livre*) out of print.

épuisement [epɥizmɑ̃] *nm* exhaustion; **jusqu'à**

~ **des stocks** while stocks last.

épuiser [epɥize] *vt* (*fatiguer*) to exhaust, wear *ou* tire out; (*stock, sujet*) to exhaust; **s'~** *vi* to wear *ou* tire o.s. out, exhaust o.s.; (*stock*) to run out.

épuisette [epɥizɛt] *nf* landing net; shrimping net.

épuration [epyRasjɔ̃] *nf* purification; purging; refinement.

épure [epyR] *nf* working drawing.

épurer [epyRe] *vt* (*liquide*) to purify; (*parti, administration*) to purge; (*langue, texte*) to refine.

équarrir [ekaRiR] *vt* (*pierre, arbre*) to square (off); (*animal*) to quarter.

équateur [ekwatœR] *nm* equator; **(la république de) l'E~** Ecuador.

équation [ekwasjɔ̃] *nf* equation; **mettre en ~** to equate; ~ **du premier/second degré** simple/quadratic equation.

équatorial, e, aux [ekwatɔRjal, -o] *adj* equatorial.

équatorien, ne [ekwatɔRjɛ̃, -ɛn] *adj* Ecuadorian ♦ *nm/f*: **É~, ne** Ecuadorian.

équerre [ekɛR] *nf* (*à dessin*) (set) square; (*pour fixer*) brace; **en ~** at right angles; **à l'~, d'~** straight; **double ~** T-square.

équestre [ekɛstR(ə)] *adj* equestrian.

équeuter [ekøte] *vt* (*CULIN*) to remove the stalk(s) from.

équidé [ekide] *nm* (*ZOOL*) member of the horse family.

équidistance [ekɥidistɑ̃s] *nf*: **à ~ (de)** equidistant (from).

équidistant, e [ekɥidistɑ̃, -ɑ̃t] *adj*: ~ **(de)** equidistant (from).

équilatéral, e, aux [ekɥilateRal, -o] *adj* equilateral.

équilibrage [ekilibRaʒ] *nm* (*AUTO*): ~ **des roues** wheel balancing.

équilibre [ekilibR(ə)] *nm* balance; (*d'une balance*) equilibrium; ~ **budgétaire** balanced budget; **garder/perdre l'~** to keep/lose one's balance; **être en ~** to be balanced; **mettre en ~** to make steady; **avoir le sens de l'~** to be well-balanced.

équilibré, e [ekilibRe] *adj* (*fig*) well-balanced, stable.

équilibrer [ekilibRe] *vt* to balance; **s'~** (*poids*) to balance; (*fig: défauts etc*) to balance each other out.

équilibriste [ekilibRist(ə)] *nm/f* tightrope walker.

équinoxe [ekinɔks] *nm* equinox.

équipage [ekipaʒ] *nm* crew; **en grand ~** in great array.

équipe [ekip] *nf* team; (*bande: parfois péj*) bunch; **travailler par ~s** to work in shifts; **travailler en ~** to work as a team; **faire ~ avec** to team up with; ~ **de chercheurs** research team; ~ **de secours** *ou* **de sauvetage** rescue team.

équipé, e [ekipe] *adj (cuisine etc)* equipped, fitted(-out) ♦ *nf* escapade.

équipement [ekipmɑ̃] *nm* equipment; ~**s** *nmpl* amenities, facilities; installations; **biens/ dépenses d'~** capital goods/expenditure; **ministère de l'É~** department of public works; ~**s sportifs/collectifs** sports/ community facilities *ou* resources.

équiper [ekipe] *vt* to equip; *(voiture, cuisine)* to equip, fit out; ~ **qn/qch de** to equip sb/sth with; **s'~** *(sportif)* to equip o.s., kit o.s. out.

équipier, ière [ekipje, -jɛʀ] *nm/f* team member.

équitable [ekitabl(ə)] *adj* fair.

équitablement [ekitabləmɑ̃] *adv* fairly, equitably.

équitation [ekitasjɔ̃] *nf* (horse-)riding; **faire de l'~** to go (horse-)riding.

équité [ekite] *nf* equity.

équivaille [ekivaj] *etc vb voir* **équivaloir.**

équivalence [ekivalɑ̃s] *nf* equivalence.

équivalent, e [ekivalɑ̃, -ɑ̃t] *adj, nm* equivalent.

équivaloir [ekivalwaʀ]: ~ **à** *vt* to be equivalent to; *(représenter)* to amount to.

équivaut [ekivo] *etc vb voir* **équivaloir.**

équivoque [ekivɔk] *adj* equivocal, ambiguous; *(louche)* dubious ♦ *nf* ambiguity.

érable [eʀabl(ə)] *nm* maple.

éradication [eʀadikasjɔ̃] *nf* eradication.

éradiquer [eʀadike] *vt* to eradicate.

érafler [eʀafle] *vt* to scratch; **s'~ la main/les jambes** to scrape *ou* scratch one's hand/ legs.

éraflure [eʀaflyʀ] *nf* scratch.

éraillé, e [eʀaje] *adj (voix)* rasping, hoarse.

ère [ɛʀ] *nf* era; **en l'an 1050 de notre ~** in the year 1050 A.D.

érection [eʀeksjɔ̃] *nf* erection.

éreintant, e [eʀɛ̃tɑ̃, -ɑ̃t] *adj* exhausting.

éreinté, e [eʀɛ̃te] *adj* exhausted.

éreintement [eʀɛ̃tmɑ̃] *nm* exhaustion.

éreinter [eʀɛ̃te] *vt* to exhaust, wear out; *(fig: critiquer)* to slate; **s'~ (à faire qch/à qch)** to wear o.s. out (doing sth/with sth).

ergonomie [ɛʀgɔnɔmi] *nf* ergonomics *sg.*

ergonomique [ɛʀgɔnɔmik] *adj* ergonomic.

ergot [ɛʀgo] *nm (de coq)* spur; *(TECH)* lug.

ergoter [ɛʀgɔte] *vi* to split hairs, argue over details.

ergoteur, euse [ɛʀgɔtœʀ, -øz] *nm/f* hairsplitter.

ériger [eʀiʒe] *vt (monument)* to erect; ~ **qch en principe/loi** to make sth a principle/law; **s'~ en critique (de)** to set o.s. up as a critic (of).

ermitage [ɛʀmitaʒ] *nm* retreat.

ermite [ɛʀmit] *nm* hermit.

éroder [eʀɔde] *vt* to erode.

érogène [eʀɔʒɛn] *adj* erogenous.

érosion [eʀozjɔ̃] *nf* erosion.

érotique [eʀɔtik] *adj* erotic.

érotiquement [eʀɔtikmɑ̃] *adv* erotically.

érotisme [eʀɔtism(ə)] *nm* eroticism.

errance [eʀɑ̃s] *nf* wandering.

errant, e [eʀɑ̃, -ɑ̃t] *adj*: **un chien** ~ a stray dog.

erratum, a [eʀatɔm, -a] *nm* erratum *(pl* -a).

errements [eʀmɑ̃] *nmpl* misguided ways.

errer [eʀe] *vi* to wander.

erreur [eʀœʀ] *nf* mistake, error; *(INFORM: de programme)* bug; *(morale)*: ~**s** *nfpl* errors; **être dans l'~** to be wrong; **induire qn en** ~ to mislead sb; **par** ~ by mistake; **sauf** ~ unless I'm mistaken; **faire** ~ to be mistaken; ~ **de date** mistake in the date; ~ **de fait** error of fact; ~ **d'impression** *(TYPO)* misprint; ~ **judiciaire** miscarriage of justice; ~ **de jugement** error of judgment; ~ **matérielle** *ou* **d'écriture** clerical error; ~ **tactique** tactical error.

erroné, e [eʀɔne] *adj* wrong, erroneous.

ersatz [ɛʀzats] *nm* substitute, ersatz; ~ **de café** coffee substitute.

éructer [eʀykte] *vi* to belch.

érudit, e [eʀydi, -it] *adj* erudite, learned ♦ *nm/f* scholar.

érudition [eʀydisjɔ̃] *nf* erudition, scholarship.

éruptif, ive [eʀyptif, -iv] *adj* eruptive.

éruption [eʀypsjɔ̃] *nf* eruption; *(cutanée)* outbreak; *(: boutons)* rash; *(fig: de joie, colère, folie)* outburst.

es [ɛ] *vb voir* **être.**

ès [ɛs] *prép*: **licencié** ~ **lettres/sciences** ≈ Bachelor of Arts/Science; **docteur** ~ **lettres** ≈ doctor of philosophy, PhD.

E/S *abr* (= *entrée/sortie)* I/O (= *in/out).*

esbroufe [ɛsbʀuf] *nf*: **faire de l'~** to have people on.

escabeau, x [ɛskabo] *nm (tabouret)* stool; *(échelle)* stepladder.

escadre [ɛskadʀ(ə)] *nf (NAVIG)* squadron; *(AVIAT)* wing.

escadrille [ɛskadʀij] *nf (AVIAT)* flight.

escadron [ɛskadʀɔ̃] *nm* squadron.

escalade [ɛskalad] *nf* climbing *no pl*; *(POL etc)* escalation.

escalader [ɛskalade] *vt* to climb, scale.

escalator [ɛskalatɔʀ] *nm* escalator.

escale [ɛskal] *nf (NAVIG)* call; *(: port)* port of call; *(AVIAT)* stop(over); **faire** ~ **à** to put in at, call in at; to stop over at; ~ **technique** *(AVIAT)* refuelling stop.

escalier [ɛskalje] *nm* stairs *pl*; **dans l'~** *ou* **les** ~**s** on the stairs; **descendre l'~** *ou* **les** ~**s** to go downstairs; ~ **mécanique** *ou* **roulant** escalator; ~ **de secours** fire escape; ~ **de service** backstairs; ~ **à vis** *ou* **en colimaçon** spiral staircase.

escalope [ɛskalɔp] *nf* escalope.

escamotable [ɛskamɔtabl(ə)] *adj (train d'atterrissage, antenne)* retractable; *(table, lit)* fold-away.

escamoter [ɛskamɔte] *vt (esquiver)* to get round, evade; *(faire disparaître)* to conjure away; *(dérober: portefeuille etc)* to snatch; *(train d'atterrissage)* to retract; *(mots)* to miss out.

escapade [ɛskapad] *nf*: **faire une ~** to go on a jaunt; (*s'enfuir*) to run away *ou* off.

escarbille [ɛskaʀbij] *nf* bit of grit.

escarcelle [ɛskaʀsɛl] *nf*: **faire tomber dans l'~** (*argent*) to bring in.

escargot [ɛskaʀgo] *nm* snail.

escarmouche [ɛskaʀmuʃ] *nf* (*MIL*) skirmish; (*fig: propos hostiles*) angry exchange.

escarpé, e [ɛskaʀpe] *adj* steep.

escarpement [ɛskaʀpəmɑ̃] *nm* steep slope.

escarpin [ɛskaʀpɛ̃] *nm* flat(-heeled) shoe.

escarre [ɛskaʀ] *nf* bedsore.

Escaut [ɛsko] *nm*: **l'~** the Scheldt.

escient [ɛsjɑ̃] *nm*: **à bon ~** advisedly.

esclaffer [ɛsklafe]: **s'~** *vi* to guffaw.

esclandre [ɛsklɑ̃dʀ(ə)] *nm* scene, fracas.

esclavage [ɛsklavaʒ] *nm* slavery.

esclavagiste [ɛsklavaʒist(ə)] *adj* pro-slavery ♦ *nm/f* supporter of slavery.

esclave [ɛsklav] *nm/f* slave; **être ~ de** (*fig*) to be a slave of.

escogriffe [ɛskɔgʀif] *nm* (*péj*) beanpole.

escompte [ɛskɔ̃t] *nm* discount.

escompter [ɛskɔ̃te] *vt* (*COMM*) to discount; (*espérer*) to expect, reckon upon; **~ que** to reckon *ou* expect that.

escorte [ɛskɔʀt(ə)] *nf* escort; **faire ~ à** to escort.

escorter [ɛskɔʀte] *vt* to escort.

escorteur [ɛskɔʀtœʀ] *nm* (*NAVIG*) escort (ship).

escouade [ɛskwad] *nf* squad; (*fig: groupe de personnes*) group.

escrime [ɛskʀim] *nf* fencing; **faire de l'~** to fence.

escrimer [ɛskʀime]: **s'~** *vi*: **s'~ à faire** to wear o.s. out doing.

escrimeur, euse [ɛskʀimœʀ, -øz] *nm/f* fencer.

escroc [ɛskʀo] *nm* swindler, con-man.

escroquer [ɛskʀɔke] *vt*: **~ qn (de qch)/qch à qn** to swindle sb (out of sth)/sth out of sb.

escroquerie [ɛskʀɔkʀi] *nf* swindle.

ésotérique [ezɔteʀik] *adj* esoteric.

espace [ɛspas] *nm* space; **~ publicitaire** advertising space; **~ vital** living space.

espacé, e [ɛspase] *adj* spaced out.

espacement [ɛspasmɑ̃] *nm*: **~ proportionnel** proportional spacing (*on printer*).

espacer [ɛspase] *vt* to space out; **s'~** *vi* (*visites etc*) to become less frequent.

espadon [ɛspadɔ̃] *nm* swordfish *inv*.

espadrille [ɛspadʀij] *nf* rope-soled sandal.

Espagne [ɛspaɲ(ə)] *nf*: **l'~** Spain.

espagnol, e [ɛspaɲɔl] *adj* Spanish ♦ *nm* (*LING*) Spanish ♦ *nm/f*: **E~, e** Spaniard.

espagnolette [ɛspaɲɔlɛt] *nf* (window) catch; **fermé à l'~** resting on the catch.

espalier [ɛspalje] *nm* (*arbre fruitier*) espalier.

espèce [ɛspɛs] *nf* (*BIO, BOT, ZOOL*) species *inv*; (*gén: sorte*) sort, kind, type; (*péj*): **~ de maladroit/de brute!** you clumsy oaf/you

brute!; **~s** *nfpl* (*COMM*) cash *sg*; (*REL*) species; **de toute ~** of all kinds *ou* sorts; **en l'~** *adv* in the case in point; **payer en ~s** to pay (in) cash; **cas d'~** individual case; **l'~ humaine** humankind.

espérance [ɛspeʀɑ̃s] *nf* hope; **~ de vie** life expectancy.

espéranto [ɛspeʀɑ̃to] *nm* esperanto.

espérer [ɛspeʀe] *vt* to hope for; **j'espère (bien)** I hope so; **~ que/faire** to hope that/to do; **~ en** to trust in.

espiègle [ɛspjɛgl(ə)] *adj* mischievous.

espièglerie [ɛspjɛgləʀi] *nf* mischievousness; (*tour, farce*) piece of mischief, prank.

espion, ne [ɛspjɔ̃, -ɔn] *nm/f* spy; **avion ~** spy plane.

espionnage [ɛspjɔnaʒ] *nm* espionage, spying; **film/roman d'~** spy film/novel.

espionner [ɛspjɔne] *vt* to spy (up)on.

espionnite [ɛspjɔnit] *nf* spy mania.

esplanade [ɛsplanad] *nf* esplanade.

espoir [ɛspwaʀ] *nm* hope; **l'~ de qch/de faire qch** the hope of sth/of doing sth; **avoir bon ~ que ...** to have high hopes that ...; **garder l'~ que ...** to remain hopeful that ...; **un ~ de la boxe/du ski** one of boxing's/skiing's hopefuls, one of the hopes of boxing/skiing; **sans ~** *adj* hopeless.

esprit [ɛspʀi] *nm* (*pensée, intellect*) mind; (*humour, ironie*) wit; (*mentalité, d'une loi etc, fantôme etc*) spirit; **l'~ d'équipe/de compétition** team/competitive spirit; **faire de l'~** to try to be witty; **reprendre ses ~s** to come to; **perdre l'~** to lose one's mind; **avoir bon/mauvais ~** to be of a good/bad disposition; **avoir l'~ à faire qch** to have a mind to do sth; **avoir l'~ critique** to be critical; **~ de contradiction** contrariness; **~ de corps** esprit de corps; **~ de famille** family loyalty; **l'~ malin** (*le diable*) the Evil One; **~s chagrins** faultfinders.

esquif [ɛskif] *nm* skiff.

esquimau, de, x [ɛskimo, -od] *adj* Eskimo ♦ *nm* (*LING*) Eskimo; (*glace*): **E~** ® ice lolly (*BRIT*), popsicle (*US*) ♦ *nm/f*: **E~, de** Eskimo; **chien ~** husky.

esquinter [ɛskɛ̃te] *vt* (*fam*) to mess up; **s'~** *vi*: **s'~ à faire qch** to knock o.s. out doing sth.

esquisse [ɛskis] *nf* sketch; **l'~ d'un sourire/changement** a hint of a smile/of change.

esquisser [ɛskise] *vt* to sketch; **s'~** *vi* (*amélioration*) to begin to be detectable; **~ un sourire** to give a hint of a smile.

esquive [ɛskiv] *nf* (*BOXE*) dodging; (*fig*) sidestepping.

esquiver [ɛskive] *vt* to dodge; **s'~** *vi* to slip away.

essai [ɛsɛ] *nm* trying; (*tentative*) attempt, try; (*RUGBY*) try; (*LITTÉRATURE*) essay; **~s** *nmpl* (*AUTO*) trials; **à l'~** on a trial basis; **~ gratuit** (*COMM*) free trial.

essaim [ɛsɛ̃] *nm* swarm.

essaimer [eseme] *vi* to swarm; (*fig*) to spread, expand.

essayage [esɛjaʒ] *nm* (*d'un vêtement*) trying on, fitting; **salon d'~** fitting room; **cabine d'~** fitting room (*cubicle*).

essayer [eseje] *vt* (*gén*) to try; (*vêtement, chaussures*) to try (on); (*restaurant, méthode, voiture*) to try (out) ♦ *vi* to try; **~ de faire** to try *ou* attempt to do; **s'~ à faire** to try one's hand at doing; **essayez un peu!** (*menace*) just you try!

essayeur, euse [esɛjœr, -øz] *nm/f* (*chez un tailleur etc*) fitter.

essayiste [esejist(ə)] *nm/f* essayist.

ESSEC [esɛk] *sigle f* (= *École supérieure des sciences économiques et sociales*) *grande école for management and business studies.*

essence [esɑ̃s] *nf* (*de voiture*) petrol (*BRIT*), gas(oline) (*US*); (*extrait de plante, PHILOSOPHIE*) essence; (*espèce: d'arbre*) species *inv*; **prendre de l'~** to get (some) petrol *ou* gas; **par ~** (*essentiellement*) essentially; **~ de citron/rose** lemon/rose oil; **~ de térébenthine** turpentine.

essentiel, le [esɑ̃sjɛl] *adj* essential ♦ *nm*: **l'~ d'un discours/d'une œuvre** the essence of a speech/work of art; **emporter l'~** to take the essentials; **c'est l'~** (*ce qui importe*) that's the main thing; **l'~ de** (*la majeure partie*) the main part of.

essentiellement [esɑ̃sjɛlmɑ̃] *adv* essentially.

esseulé, e [esœle] *adj* forlorn.

essieu, x [esjø] *nm* axle.

essor [esɔr] *nm* (*de l'économie etc*) rapid expansion; **prendre son ~** (*oiseau*) to fly off.

essorage [esɔraʒ] *nm* wringing out; spindrying; spinning; shaking.

essorer [esɔre] *vt* (*en tordant*) to wring (out); (*par la force centrifuge*) to spin-dry; (*salade*) to spin; (: *en secouant*) to shake dry.

essoreuse [esɔrøz] *nf* mangle, wringer; (*à tambour*) spin-dryer.

essouffler [esufle] *vt* to make breathless; **s'~** *vi* to get out of breath; (*fig: économie*) to run out of steam.

essuie [esɥi] *etc vb voir* **essuyer**.

essuie-glace [esɥiglas] *nm* windscreen (*BRIT*) *ou* windshield (*US*) wiper.

essuie-mains [esɥimɛ̃] *nm inv* hand towel.

essuierai [esɥire] *etc vb voir* **essuyer**.

essuie-tout [esɥitu] *nm inv* kitchen paper.

essuyer [esɥije] *vt* to wipe; (*fig: subir*) to suffer; **s'~** (*après le bain*) to dry o.s.; **~ la vaisselle** to dry up, dry the dishes.

est [ɛ] *vb voir* **être** ♦ *nm* [ɛst]: **l'~** the east ♦ *adj inv* east; (*région*) east(ern); **à l'~** in the east; (*direction*) to the east, east(wards); **à l'~ de** (to the) east of; **les pays de l'E~** the eastern countries.

estafette [ɛstafɛt] *nf* (*MIL*) dispatch rider.

estafilade [ɛstafilad] *nf* gash, slash.

est-allemand, e [ɛstalmɑ̃, -ɑ̃d] *adj* East German.

estaminet [ɛstaminɛ] *nm* tavern.

estampe [ɛstɑ̃p] *nf* print, engraving.

estamper [ɛstɑ̃pe] *vt* (*monnaies etc*) to stamp; (*fam: escroquer*) to swindle.

estampille [ɛstɑ̃pij] *nf* stamp.

est-ce que [ɛskə] *adv*: **~ c'est cher/c'était bon?** is it expensive/was it good?; **quand est-ce qu'il part?** when does he leave?, when is he leaving?; **où est-ce qu'il va?** where's he going?; **qui est-ce qui le connaît/a fait ça?** who knows him/did that?; *voir aussi* **que.**

este [ɛst(ə)] *adj* Estonian ♦ *nm/f*: **E~** Estonian.

esthète [ɛstɛt] *nm/f* aesthete.

esthéticienne [ɛstetisjɛn] *nf* beautician.

esthétique [ɛstetik] *adj* (*sens, jugement*) aesthetic; (*beau*) attractive, aesthetically pleasing ♦ *nf* aesthetics *sg*; **l'~ industrielle** industrial design.

esthétiquement [ɛstetikmɑ̃] *adv* aesthetically.

estimable [ɛstimabl(ə)] *adj* respected.

estimatif, ive [ɛstimatif, -iv] *adj* estimated.

estimation [ɛstimasjɔ̃] *nf* valuation; assessment; **d'après mes ~s** according to my calculations.

estime [ɛstim] *nf* esteem, regard; **avoir de l'~ pour qn** to think highly of sb.

estimer [ɛstime] *vt* (*respecter*) to esteem, hold in high regard; (*expertiser*) to value; (*évaluer*) to assess, estimate; (*penser*): **~ que/être** to consider that/o.s. to be; **s'~ satisfait/heureux** to feel satisfied/happy; **j'estime la distance à 10 km** I reckon the distance to be 10 km.

estival, e, aux [ɛstival, -o] *adj* summer *cpd*; **station ~e** (summer) holiday resort.

estivant, e [ɛstivɑ̃, -ɑ̃t] *nm/f* (summer) holiday-maker.

estoc [ɛstɔk] *nm*: **frapper d'~ et de taille** to cut and thrust.

estocade [ɛstɔkad] *nf* death-blow.

estomac [ɛstɔma] *nm* stomach; **avoir mal à l'~** to have stomach ache; **avoir l'~ creux** to have an empty stomach.

estomaqué, e [ɛstɔmake] *adj* flabbergasted.

estompe [ɛstɔ̃p] *nf* stump; (*dessin*) stump drawing.

estompé, e [ɛstɔ̃pe] *adj* blurred.

estomper [ɛstɔ̃pe] *vt* (*ART*) to shade off; (*fig*) to blur, dim; **s'~** *vi* (*sentiments*) to soften; (*contour*) to become blurred.

Estonie [ɛstɔni] *nf*: **l'~** Estonia.

estonien, ne [ɛstɔnjɛ̃, -ɛn] *adj* Estonian ♦ *nm* (*LING*) Estonian ♦ *nm/f*: **E~, ne** Estonian.

estrade [ɛstrad] *nf* platform, rostrum.

estragon [ɛstragɔ̃] *nm* tarragon.

estropié, e [ɛstrɔpje] *nm/f* cripple.

estropier [ɛstrɔpje] *vt* to cripple, maim; (*fig*) to twist, distort.

estuaire [ɛstɥɛr] *nm* estuary.

estudiantin, e [ɛstydjɑ̃tɛ̃, -in] *adj* student *cpd*.

esturgeon [ɛstyʀʒɔ̃] *nm* sturgeon.
et [e] *conj* and; ~ **lui?** what about him?; ~ **alors?,** ~ **(puis) après?** so what?; (*ensuite*) and then?
ét. *abr* = **étage.**
ETA [eta] *sigle m* (*POL*) ETA.
étable [etabl(ə)] *nf* cowshed.
établi, e [etabli] *adj* established ♦ *nm* (work)bench.
établir [etabliʀ] *vt* (*papiers d'identité, facture*) to make out; (*liste, programme*) to draw up; (*gouvernement, artisan etc: aider à s'installer*) to set up, establish; (*entreprise, atelier, camp*) to set up; (*réputation, usage, fait, culpabilité, relations*) to establish; (*SPORT: record*) to set; **s'~** *vi* (*se faire: entente etc*) to be established; **s'~** **(à son compte)** to set up in business; **s'~** **à/près de** to settle in/near.
établissement [etablismɑ̃] *nm* making out; drawing up; setting up, establishing; (*entreprise, institution*) establishment; ~ **de crédit** credit . institution; ~ **hospitalier** hospital complex; ~ **industriel** industrial plant, factory; ~ **scolaire** school, educational establishment.
étage [etaʒ] *nm* (*d'immeuble*) storey (*BRIT*), story (*US*), floor; (*de fusée*) stage; (*GÉO: de culture, végétation*) level; **au 2ème** ~ on the 2nd (*BRIT*) *ou* 3rd (*US*) floor; **à l'**~ upstairs; **maison à deux** ~**s** two-storey *ou* -story house; **de bas** ~. *adj* low-born; (*médiocre*) inferior.
étager [etaʒe] *vt* (*cultures*) to lay out in tiers; **s'~** *vi* (*prix*) to range; (*zones, cultures*) to lie on different levels.
étagère [etaʒɛʀ] *nf* (*rayon*) shelf; (*meuble*) shelves *pl*, set of shelves.
étai [etɛ] *nm* stay, prop.
étain [etɛ̃] *nm* tin; (*ORFÈVRERIE*) pewter *no pl*.
étais [etɛ] *etc vb voir* **être.**
étal [etal] *nm* stall.
étalage [etalaʒ] *nm* display; (*vitrine*) display window; **faire** ~ **de** to show off, parade.
étalagiste [etalaʒist(ə)] *nm/f* window-dresser.
étale [etal] *adj* (*mer*) slack.
étalement [etalmɑ̃] *nm* spreading; (*échelonnement*) staggering.
étaler [etale] *vt* (*carte, nappe*) to spread (out); (*peinture, liquide*) to spread; (*échelonner: paiements, dates, vacances*) to spread, stagger; (*exposer: marchandises*) to display; (*richesses, connaissances*) to parade; **s'~** *vi* (*liquide*) to spread out; (*fam*) to come a cropper (*BRIT*), fall flat on one's face; **s'~ sur** (*suj: paiements etc*) to be spread over.
étalon [etalɔ̃] *nm* (*mesure*) standard; (*cheval*) stallion; **l'~-or** the gold standard.
étalonner [etalɔne] *vt* to calibrate.
étamer [etame] *vt* (*casserole*) to tin(plate); (*glace*) to silver.
étamine [etamin] *nf* (*BOT*) stamen; (*tissu*) butter muslin.

étanche [etɑ̃ʃ] *adj* (*récipient; aussi fig*) watertight; (*montre, vêtement*) waterproof; ~ **à l'air** airtight.
étanchéité [etɑ̃ʃeite] *nf* watertightness; airtightness.
étancher [etɑ̃ʃe] *vt* (*liquide*) to stop (flowing); ~ **sa soif** to quench *ou* slake one's thirst.
étançon [etɑ̃sɔ̃] *nm* (*TECH*) prop.
étançonner [etɑ̃sɔne] *vt* to prop up.
étang [etɑ̃] *nm* pond.
étant [etɑ̃] *vb voir* **être, donné.**
étape [etap] *nf* stage; (*lieu d'arrivée*) stopping place; (*: CYCLISME*) staging point; **faire** ~ **à** to stop off at; **brûler les** ~**s** (*fig*) to cut corners.
état [eta] *nm* (*POL, condition*) state; (*d'un article d'occasion etc*) condition, state; (*liste*) inventory, statement; (*condition: professionnelle*) profession, trade; (*: sociale*) status; **en mauvais** ~ in poor condition; **en** ~ **(de marche)** in (working) order; **remettre en** ~ to repair; **hors d'**~ out of order; **être en** ~**/hors d'**~ **de faire** to be in a state/in no fit state to do; **en tout** ~ **de cause** in any event; **être dans tous ses** ~**s** to be in a state; **faire** ~ **de** (*alléguer*) to put forward; **en** ~ **d'arrestation** under arrest; ~ **de grâce** (*REL*) state of grace; (*fig*) honeymoon period; **en** ~ **de grâce** (*fig*) inspired; **en** ~ **d'ivresse** under the influence of drink; ~ **de choses** (*situation*) state of affairs; ~ **civil** civil status; (*bureau*) registry office (*BRIT*); ~ **d'esprit** frame of mind; ~ **des lieux** inventory of fixtures; ~ **de santé** state of health; ~ **de siège/d'urgence** state of siege/emergency; ~ **de veille** (*PSYCH*) waking state; ~**s d'âme** moods; **les É**~**s barbaresques** the Barbary States; **les É**~**s du Golfe** the Gulf States; ~**s de service** service record *sg*.
étatique [etatik] *adj* state *cpd*, State *cpd*.
étatisation [etatizɑsjɔ̃] *nf* nationalization.
étatiser [etatize] *vt* to bring under state control.
étatisme [etatism(ə)] *nm* state control.
étatiste [etatist(ə)] *adj* (*doctrine etc*) of state control ♦ *nm/f* partisan of state control.
état-major, *pl* **états-majors** [etamaʒɔʀ] *nm* (*MIL*) staff; (*d'un parti etc*) top advisers *pl*; (*d'une entreprise*) top management.
État-providence [etapʀɔvidɑ̃s] *nm* welfare state.
États-Unis [etazyni] *nmpl:* **les** ~ **(d'Amérique)** the United States (of America).
étau, x [eto] *nm* vice (*BRIT*), vise (*US*).
étayer [eteje] *vt* to prop *ou* shore up; (*fig*) to back up.
et c(a)etera [ɛtseteʀa], **etc.** *adv* et cetera, and so on, etc.
été [ete] *pp de* **être** ♦ *nm* summer; **en** ~ in summer.
éteignais [etɛɲɛ] *etc vb voir* **éteindre.**
éteignoir [etɛɲwaʀ] *nm* (candle) snuffer; (*péj*) killjoy, wet blanket.

éteindre [etɛ̃dʀ(ə)] *vt* (*lampe, lumière, radio, chauffage*) to turn *ou* switch off; (*cigarette, incendie, bougie*) to put out, extinguish; (*JUR: dette*) to extinguish; **s'~** *vi* to go off; to go out; (*mourir*) to pass away.

éteint, e [etɛ̃, -ɛ̃t] *pp de* **éteindre** ♦ *adj* (*fig*) lacklustre, dull; (*volcan*) extinct; **tous feux ~s** (*AUTO: rouler*) without lights.

étendard [etɑ̃daʀ] *nm* standard.

étendre [etɑ̃dʀ(ə)] *vt* (*appliquer: pâte, liquide*) to spread; (*déployer: carte etc*) to spread out; (*sur un fil: lessive, linge*) to hang up *ou* out; (*bras, jambes, par terre: blessé*) to stretch out; (*diluer*) to dilute, thin; (*fig: agrandir*) to extend; (*fam: adversaire*) to floor; **s'~** *vi* (*augmenter, se propager*) to spread; (*terrain, forêt etc*): **s'~ jusqu'à/de ... à** to stretch as far as/ from ... to; **s'~ (sur)** (*s'allonger*) to stretch out (upon); (*se coucher*) to lie down (on); (*fig: expliquer*) to elaborate *ou* enlarge (upon).

étendu, e [etɑ̃dy] *adj* extensive ♦ *nf* (*d'eau, de sable*) stretch, expanse; (*importance*) extent.

éternel, le [etɛʀnɛl] *adj* eternal; **les neiges ~les** perpetual snow.

éternellement [etɛʀnɛlmɑ̃] *adv* eternally.

éterniser [etɛʀnize]: **s'~** *vi* to last for ages; (*personne*) to stay for ages.

éternité [etɛʀnite] *nf* eternity; **il y a** *ou* **ça fait une ~ que** it's ages since; **de toute ~** from time immemorial.

éternuement [etɛʀnymɑ̃] *nm* sneeze.

éternuer [etɛʀnɥe] *vi* to sneeze.

êtes [ɛt] *vb voir* **être**.

étêter [etete] *vt* (*arbre*) to poll(ard); (*clou, poisson*) to cut the head off.

éther [etɛʀ] *nm* ether.

éthéré, e [etere] *adj* ethereal.

Ethiopie [etjɔpi] *nf*: **l'~** Ethiopia.

éthiopien, ne [etjɔpjɛ̃, -ɛn] *adj* Ethiopian.

éthique [etik] *adj* ethical ♦ *nf* ethics *sg*.

ethnie [ɛtni] *nf* ethnic group.

ethnique [ɛtnik] *adj* ethnic.

ethnographe [ɛtnɔgʀaf] *nm/f* ethnographer.

ethnographie [ɛtnɔgʀafi] *nf* ethnography.

ethnographique [ɛtnɔgʀafik] *adj* ethnographic(al).

ethnologie [ɛtnɔlɔʒi] *nf* ethnology.

ethnologique [ɛtnɔlɔʒik] *adj* ethnological.

ethnologue [ɛtnɔlɔg] *nm/f* ethnologist.

éthylique [etilik] *adj* alcoholic.

éthylisme [etilism(ə)] *nm* alcoholism.

étiage [etjaʒ] *nm* low water.

étiez [etje] *vb voir* **être**.

étincelant, e [etɛ̃slɑ̃, -ɑ̃t] *adj* sparkling.

étinceler [etɛ̃sle] *vi* to sparkle.

étincelle [etɛ̃sɛl] *nf* spark.

étioler [etjɔle]: **s'~** *vi* to wilt.

étions [etjɔ̃] *vb voir* **être**.

étique [etik] *adj* skinny, bony.

étiquetage [etiktaʒ] *nm* labelling.

étiqueter [etikte] *vt* to label.

étiquette [etikɛt] *vb voir* **étiqueter** ♦ *nf* label;

(*protocole*): **l'~** etiquette.

étirer [etire] *vt* to stretch; (*ressort*) to stretch out; **s'~** *vi* (*personne*) to stretch; (*convoi, route*): **s'~ sur** to stretch out over.

étoffe [etɔf] *nf* material, fabric; **avoir l'~ d'un chef** *etc* to be cut out to be a leader *etc*; **avoir de l'~** to be a forceful personality.

étoffer [etɔfe] *vt*, **s'~** *vi* to fill out.

étoile [etwal] *nf* star ♦ *adj*: **danseuse** *ou* **danceur ~** leading dancer; **la bonne/mauvaise ~ de qn** sb's lucky/unlucky star; **à la belle ~** (out) in the open; **~ filante** shooting star; **~ de mer** starfish; **~ polaire** pole star.

étoilé, e [etwale] *adj* starry.

étole [etɔl] *nf* stole.

étonnamment [etɔnamɑ̃] *adv* amazingly.

étonnant, e [etɔnɑ̃, -ɑ̃t] *adj* surprising.

étonné, e [etɔne] *adj* surprised.

étonnement [etɔnmɑ̃] *nm* surprise; **à mon grand ~ ...** to my great surprise *ou* amazement ....

étonner [etɔne] *vt* to surprise; **s'~ que/de** to be surprised that/at; **cela m'étonnerait (que)** (*j'en doute*) I'd be (very) surprised (if).

étouffant, e [etufɑ̃, -ɑ̃t] *adj* stifling.

étouffé, e [etufe] *adj* (*asphyxié*) suffocated; (*assourdi: cris, rires*) smothered ♦ *nf*: **à l'~e** (*CULIN: poisson, légumes*) steamed; (*: viande*) braised.

étouffement [etufmɑ̃] *nm* suffocation.

étouffer [etufe] *vt* to suffocate; (*bruit*) to muffle; (*scandale*) to hush up ♦ *vi* to suffocate; (*avoir trop chaud; aussi fig*) to feel stifled; **s'~** *vi* (*en mangeant etc*) to choke.

étouffoir [etufwaʀ] *nm* (*MUS*) damper.

étourderie [etuʀdəʀi] *nf* heedlessness *no pl*; thoughtless blunder; **faute d'~** careless mistake.

étourdi, e [etuʀdi] *adj* (*distrait*) scatterbrained, heedless.

étourdiment [etuʀdimɑ̃] *adv* rashly.

étourdir [etuʀdiʀ] *vt* (*assommer*) to stun, daze; (*griser*) to make dizzy *ou* giddy.

étourdissant, e [etuʀdisɑ̃, -ɑ̃t] *adj* staggering.

étourdissement [etuʀdismɑ̃] *nm* dizzy spell.

étourneau, x [etuʀno] *nm* starling.

étrange [etʀɑ̃ʒ] *adj* strange.

étrangement [etʀɑ̃ʒmɑ̃] *adv* strangely.

étranger, ère [etʀɑ̃ʒe, -ɛʀ] *adj* foreign; (*pas de la famille, non familier*) strange ♦ *nm/f* foreigner; stranger ♦ *nm*: **l'~** foreign countries; **à l'~** abroad; **de l'~** from abroad; **~ à** (*mal connu*) unfamiliar to; (*sans rapport*) irrelevant to.

étrangeté [etʀɑ̃ʒte] *nf* strangeness.

étranglé, e [etʀɑ̃gle] *adj*: **d'une voix ~e** in a strangled voice.

étranglement [etʀɑ̃gləmɑ̃] *nm* (*d'une vallée etc*) constriction, narrow passage.

étrangler [etʀɑ̃gle] *vt* to strangle; (*fig: presse, libertés*) to stifle; **s'~** *vi* (*en mangeant etc*) to choke; (*se resserrer*) to make a bottleneck.

étrave [etʀav] *nf* stem.

═══════════════════════ MOT-CLÉ

être [ɛtʀ(ə)] *nm* being; ~ **humain** human being
♦ *vb +attrib* **1** (*état, description*) to be; **il est instituteur** he is *ou* he's a teacher; **vous êtes grand/intelligent/fatigué** you are *ou* you're tall/clever/tired
2 (*+à: appartenir*) to be; **le livre est à Paul** the book is Paul's *ou* belongs to Paul; **c'est à moi/eux** it is *ou* it's mine/theirs
3 (*+de: provenance*): **il est de Paris** he is from Paris; (: *appartenance*): **il est des nôtres** he is one of us
4 (*date*): **nous sommes le 10 janvier** it's the 10th of January (today)
♦ *vi* to be; **je ne serai pas ici demain** I won't be here tomorrow
♦ *vb aux* **1** to have; to be; ~ **arrivé/allé** to have arrived/gone; **il est parti** he has left, he has gone
2 (*forme passive*) to be; ~ **fait par** to be made by; **il a été promu** he has been promoted
3 (*+à +inf: obligation, but*): **c'est à réparer** it needs repairing; **c'est à essayer** it should be tried; **il est à espérer que ...** it is *ou* it's to be hoped that ...
♦ *vb impers* **1**: **il est** +*adjectif* it is +*adjective*; **il est impossible de le faire** it's impossible to do it
2 (*heure, date*): **il est 10 heures** it is *ou* it's 10 o'clock
3 (*emphatique*): **c'est moi** it's me; **c'est à lui de le faire** it's up to him to do it; *voir aussi* **est-ce que, n'est-ce pas, c'est-à-dire, ce.**

étreindre [etʀɛ̃dʀ(ə)] *vt* to clutch, grip; (*amoureusement, amicalement*) to embrace; **s'~** to embrace.

étreinte [etʀɛ̃t] *nf* clutch, grip; embrace; **resserrer son ~ autour de** (*fig*) to tighten one's grip on *ou* around.

étrenner [etʀene] *vt* to use (*ou* wear) for the first time.

étrennes [etʀɛn] *nfpl* (*cadeaux*) New Year's present; (*gratifications*) ≈ Christmas box *sg*, ≈ Christmas bonus.

étrier [etʀije] *nm* stirrup.

étriller [etʀije] *vt* (*cheval*) to curry; (*fam: battre*) to slaughter (*fig*).

étriper [etʀipe] *vt* to gut; (*fam*) ~ **qn** to tear sb's guts out.

étriqué, e [etʀike] *adj* skimpy.

étroit, e [etʀwa, -wat] *adj* narrow; (*vêtement*) tight; (*fig: serré*) close, tight; **à l'~** cramped; ~ **d'esprit** narrow-minded.

étroitement [etʀwatmɑ̃] *adv* closely.

étroitesse [etʀwatɛs] *nf* narrowness; ~ **d'esprit** narrow-mindedness.

Étrurie [etʀyʀi] *nf*: **l'~** Etruria.

étrusque [etʀysk(ə)] *adj* Etruscan.

étude [etyd] *nf* studying; (*ouvrage, rapport,*

MUS) study; (*de notaire: bureau*) office; (: *charge*) practice; (*SCOL: salle de travail*) study room; ~**s** *nfpl* (*SCOL*) studies; **être à l'~** (*projet etc*) to be under consideration; **faire des ~s** (**de droit/médecine**) to study (law/medicine); ~**s secondaires/supérieures** secondary/higher education; ~ **de cas** case study; ~ **de faisabilité** feasibility study; ~ **de marché** (*ÉCON*) market research.

étudiant, e [etydjɑ̃, -ɑ̃t] *adj, nm/f* student.

étudié, e [etydje] *adj* (*démarche*) studied; (*système*) carefully designed; (*prix*) keen.

étudier [etydje] *vt, vi* to study.

étui [etɥi] *nm* case.

étuve [etyv] *nf* steamroom; (*appareil*) sterilizer.

étuvée [etyve]: **à l'~** *adv* braised.

étymologie [etimɔlɔʒi] *nf* etymology.

étymologique [etimɔlɔʒik] *adj* etymological.

eu, eue [y] *pp de* avoir.

EU(A) *sigle mpl* (= *États-Unis* (*d'Amérique*)) US(A).

eucalyptus [økaliptys] *nm* eucalyptus.

Eucharistie [økaʀisti] *nf*: **l'~** the Eucharist, the Lord's Supper.

eucharistique [økaʀistik] *adj* eucharistic.

euclidien, ne [øklidjɛ̃, -ɛn] *adj* Euclidian.

eugénique [øʒenik] *adj* eugenic ♦ *nf* eugenics *sg.*

eugénisme [øʒenism(ə)] *nm* eugenics *sg.*

euh [ø] *excl* er.

eunuque [ønyk] *nm* eunuch.

euphémique [øfemik] *adj* euphemistic.

euphémisme [øfemism(ə)] *nm* euphemism.

euphonie [øfɔni] *nf* euphony.

euphorbe [øfɔʀb(ə)] *nf* (*BOT*) spurge.

euphorie [øfɔʀi] *nf* euphoria.

euphorique [øfɔʀik] *adj* euphoric.

euphorisant, e [øfɔʀizɑ̃, -ɑ̃t] *adj* exhilarating.

Euphrate [øfʀat] *nm*: **l'~** the Euphrates *sg.*

eurafricain, e [øʀafʀikɛ̃, -ɛn] *adj* Eurafrican.

Eurasie [øʀazi] *nf*: **l'~** Eurasia.

eurasiatique [øʀazjatik] *adj* Eurasiatic.

eurasien, ne [øʀazjɛ̃, -ɛn] *adj* Eurasian.

EURATOM [øʀatɔm] *sigle f* Euratom.

eurent [yʀ(ə)] *vb voir* avoir.

euro [øʀo] *nm* (*monnaie*) euro.

euro- [øʀo] *préfixe* Euro-.

eurocrate [øʀɔkʀat] *nm/f* (*péj*) Eurocrat.

eurodevise [øʀɔdəviz] *nf* Eurocurrency.

eurodollar [øʀodɔlaʀ] *nm* Eurodollar.

Euroland [øʀolɑ̃d] *nm* Euroland.

Europe [øʀɔp] *nf*: **l'~** Europe; **l'~ centrale** Central Europe; **l'~ verte** European agriculture.

européanisation [øʀɔpeanizasjɔ̃] *nf* Europeanization.

européaniser [øʀɔpeanize] *vt* to Europeanize.

européen, ne [øʀɔpeɛ̃, -ɛn] *adj* European ♦ *nm/f*: **E~, ne** European.

eurosceptique [øʀɔsɛptik] *nm/f* Eurosceptic.

Eurovision [øʀovizjɔ̃] *nf* Eurovision.

eus [y] *etc vb voir* **avoir**.
euthanasie [øtanazi] *nf* euthanasia.
eux [ø] *pron* (*sujet*) they; (*objet*) them; ~, **ils ont fait** ... THEY did ....
EV *abr* (= *en ville*) *used on mail to be delivered by hand, courier etc within the same town.*
évacuation [evakɥasjɔ̃] *nf* evacuation.
évacué, e [evakɥe] *nm/f* evacuee.
évacuer [evakɥe] *vt* (*salle, région*) to evacuate, clear; (*occupants, population*) to evacuate; (*toxine etc*) to evacuate, discharge.
évadé, e [evade] *adj* escaped ♦ *nm/f* escapee.
évader [evade]: **s'**~ *vi* to escape.
évaluation [evalɥasjɔ̃] *nf* assessment, evaluation.
évaluer [evalɥe] *vt* to assess, evaluate.
évanescent, e [evanesɑ̃, -ɑ̃t] *adj* evanescent.
évangélique [evɑ̃ʒelik] *adj* evangelical.
évangélisation [evɑ̃ʒelizasjɔ̃] *nf* evangelization.
évangéliser [evɑ̃ʒelize] *vt* to evangelize.
évangéliste [evɑ̃ʒelist(ə)] *nm* evangelist.
évangile [evɑ̃ʒil] *nm* gospel; (*texte de la Bible*): **É**~ Gospel; **ce n'est pas l'É**~ (*fig*) it's not gospel.
évanoui, e [evanwi] *adj* in a faint; **tomber** ~ to faint.
évanouir [evanwiʀ]: **s'**~ *vi* to faint, pass out; (*disparaître*) to vanish, disappear.
évanouissement [evanwismɑ̃] *nm* (*syncope*) fainting fit; (*MÉD*) loss of consciousness.
évaporation [evapɔʀasjɔ̃] *nf* evaporation.
évaporé, e [evapɔʀe] *adj* giddy, scatterbrained.
évaporer [evapɔʀe]: **s'**~ *vi* to evaporate.
évasé, e [evɑze] *adj* (*jupe etc*) flared.
évaser [evɑze] *vt* (*tuyau*) to widen, open out; (*jupe, pantalon*) to flare; **s'**~ *vi* to widen, open out.
évasif, ive [evazif, -iv] *adj* evasive.
évasion [evazjɔ̃] *nf* escape; **littérature d'**~ escapist literature; ~ **des capitaux** (*ÉCON*) flight of capital; ~ **fiscale** tax avoidance.
évasivement [evazivmɑ̃] *adv* evasively.
évêché [eveʃe] *nm* (*fonction*) bishopric; (*palais*) bishop's palace.
éveil [evɛj] *nm* awakening; **être en** ~ to be alert; **mettre qn en** ~, **donner l'**~ **à qn** to arouse sb's suspicions; **activités d'**~ early-learning activities.
éveillé, e [eveje] *adj* awake; (*vif*) alert, sharp.
éveiller [eveje] *vt* to (a)waken; **s'**~ *vi* to (a)waken; (*fig*) to be aroused.
événement [evɛnmɑ̃] *nm* event.
éventail [evɑ̃taj] *nm* fan; (*choix*) range; **en** ~ fanned out; fan-shaped.
éventaire [evɑ̃tɛʀ] *nm* stall, stand.
éventé, e [evɑ̃te] *adj* (*parfum, vin*) stale.
éventer [evɑ̃te] *vt* (*secret, complot*) to uncover; (*avec un éventail*) to fan; **s'**~ *vi* (*parfum, vin*) to go stale.
éventrer [evɑ̃tʀe] *vt* to disembowel; (*fig*) to

tear *ou* rip open.
éventualité [evɑ̃tɥalite] *nf* eventuality; possibility; **dans l'**~ **de** in the event of; **parer à toute** ~ to guard against all eventualities.
éventuel, le [evɑ̃tɥɛl] *adj* possible.
éventuellement [evɑ̃tɥɛlmɑ̃] *adv* possibly.
évêque [evɛk] *nm* bishop.
Everest [ɛvʀɛst] *nm:* (**mont**) ~ (Mount) Everest.
évertuer [evɛʀtɥe]: **s'**~ *vi:* **s'**~ **à faire** to try very hard to do.
éviction [eviksjɔ̃] *nf* ousting, supplanting; (*de locataire*) eviction.
évidemment [evidamɑ̃] *adv* obviously.
évidence [evidɑ̃s] *nf* obviousness; (*fait*) obvious fact; **se rendre à l'**~ to bow before the evidence; **nier l'**~ to deny the evidence; **à l'**~ evidently; **de toute** ~ quite obviously *ou* evidently; **en** ~ conspicuous; **mettre en** ~ to bring to the fore.
évident, e [evidɑ̃, -ɑ̃t] *adj* obvious, evident; **ce n'est pas** ~ (*cela pose des problèmes*) it's not (all that) straightforward, it's not as simple as all that.
évider [evide] *vt* to scoop out.
évier [evje] *nm* (kitchen) sink.
évincement [evɛ̃smɑ̃] *nm* ousting.
évincer [evɛ̃se] *vt* to oust, supplant.
évitable [evitabl(ə)] *adj* avoidable.
évitement [evitmɑ̃] *nm:* **place d'**~ (*AUTO*) passing place.
éviter [evite] *vt* to avoid; ~ **de faire/que qch ne se passe** to avoid doing/sth happening; ~ **qch à qn** to spare sb sth.
évocateur, trice [evɔkatœʀ, -tʀis] *adj* evocative, suggestive.
évocation [evɔkasjɔ̃] *nf* evocation.
évolué, e [evɔlɥe] *adj* advanced; (*personne*) broad-minded.
évoluer [evɔlɥe] *vi* (*enfant, maladie*) to develop; (*situation, moralement*) to evolve, develop; (*aller et venir: danseur etc*) to move about, circle.
évolutif, ive [evɔlytif, -iv] *adj* evolving.
évolution [evɔlysjɔ̃] *nf* development; evolution; ~**s** *nfpl* movements.
évolutionnisme [evɔlysjɔnism(ə)] *nm* evolutionism.
évoquer [evɔke] *vt* to call to mind, evoke; (*mentionner*) to mention.
ex. *abr* (= *exemple*) ex.
ex- [ɛks] *préfixe* ex-.
exacerbé, e [ɛgzasɛʀbe] *adj* (*orgueil, sensibilité*) exaggerated.
exacerber [ɛgzasɛʀbe] *vt* to exacerbate.
exact, e [ɛgzakt] *adj* (*précis*) exact, accurate, precise; (*correct*) correct; (*ponctuel*) punctual; **l'heure** ~**e** the right *ou* exact time.
exactement [ɛgzaktəmɑ̃] *adv* exactly, accurately, precisely; correctly; (*c'est cela même*) exactly.
exaction [ɛgzaksjɔ̃] *nf* (*d'argent*) exaction; (*gén*

pl: actes de violence) abuse(s).
exactitude [ɛgzaktityd] *nf* exactitude, accurateness, precision.
ex aequo [ɛgzeko] *adj* equally placed; **classé 1er** ~ placed equal first.
exagération [ɛgzaʒerasjɔ̃] *nf* exaggeration.
exagéré, e [ɛgzaʒeʀe] *adj (prix etc)* excessive.
exagérément [ɛgzaʒeʀemɑ̃] *adv* excessively.
exagérer [ɛgzaʒeʀe] *vt* to exaggerate ♦ *vi (abuser)* to go too far; *(dépasser les bornes)* to overstep the mark; *(déformer les faits)* to exaggerate; **s'~ qch** to exaggerate sth.
exaltant, e [ɛgzaltɑ̃, -ɑ̃t] *adj* exhilarating.
exaltation [ɛgzaltasjɔ̃] *nf* exaltation.
exalté, e [ɛgzalte] *adj* (over)excited ♦ *nm/f (péj)* fanatic.
exalter [ɛgzalte] *vt (enthousiasmer)* to excite, elate; *(glorifier)* to exalt.
examen [ɛgzamɛ̃] *nm* examination; *(SCOL)* exam, examination; **à l'~** *(dossier, projet)* under consideration; *(COMM)* on approval; ~ **blanc** mock exam(ination); ~ **de la vue** sight test.
examinateur, trice [ɛgzaminatœʀ, -tʀis] *nm/f* examiner.
examiner [ɛgzamine] *vt* to examine.
exaspérant, e [ɛgzaspeʀɑ̃, -ɑ̃t] *adj* exasperating.
exaspération [ɛgzaspeʀasjɔ̃] *nf* exasperation.
exaspéré, e [ɛgzaspeʀe] *adj* exasperated.
exaspérer [ɛgzaspeʀe] *vt* to exasperate; *(aggraver)* to exacerbate.
exaucer [ɛgzose] *vt (vœu)* to grant, fulfil; ~ **qn** to grant sb's wishes.
ex cathedra [ɛkskatedʀa] *adj, adv* ex cathedra.
excavateur [ɛkskavatœʀ] *nm* excavator, mechanical digger.
excavation [ɛkskavasjɔ̃] *nf* excavation.
excavatrice [ɛkskavatʀis] *nf* = **excavateur**.
excédent [ɛksedɑ̃] *nm* surplus; **en** ~ surplus; **payer 600 F d'~** *(de bagages)* to pay 600 francs excess luggage; ~ **de bagages** excess luggage; ~ **commercial** trade surplus.
excédentaire [ɛksedɑ̃tɛʀ] *adj* surplus, excess.
excéder [ɛksede] *vt (dépasser)* to exceed; *(agacer)* to exasperate; **excédé de fatigue** exhausted; **excédé de travail** worn out with work.
excellence [ɛksɛlɑ̃s] *nf* excellence; *(titre)* Excellency; **par** ~ par excellence.
excellent, e [ɛksɛlɑ̃, -ɑ̃t] *adj* excellent.
exceller [ɛksele] *vi:* ~ **(dans)** to excel (in).
excentricité [ɛksɑ̃tʀisite] *nf* eccentricity.
excentrique [ɛksɑ̃tʀik] *adj* eccentric; *(quartier)* outlying ♦ *nm/f* eccentric.
excentriquement [ɛksɑ̃tʀikmɑ̃] *adv* eccentrically.
excepté, e [ɛksɛpte] *adj, prép:* **les élèves ~s,** ~ **les élèves** except for *ou* apart from the pupils; ~ **si/quand** except if/when; ~ **que** except that.
excepter [ɛksɛpte] *vt* to except.

exception [ɛksɛpsjɔ̃] *nf* exception; **faire** ~ to be an exception; **faire une** ~ to make an exception; **sans** ~ without exception; **à l'~ de** except for, with the exception of; **d'~** *(mesure, loi)* special, exceptional.
exceptionnel, le [ɛksɛpsjɔnɛl] *adj* exceptional; *(prix)* special.
exceptionnellement [ɛksɛpsjɔnɛlmɑ̃] *adv* exceptionally; *(par exception)* by way of an exception, on this occasion.
excès [ɛksɛ] *nm* surplus ♦ *nmpl* excesses; **à l'~** *(méticuleux, généreux)* to excess; **avec** ~ to excess; **sans** ~ in moderation; **tomber dans l'~ inverse** to go to the opposite extreme; ~ **de langage** immoderate language; ~ **de pouvoir** abuse of power; ~ **de vitesse** speeding *no pl*, exceeding the speed limit; ~ **de zèle** overzealousness *no pl*.
excessif, ive [ɛksesif, -iv] *adj* excessive.
excessivement [ɛksesivmɑ̃] *adv (trop: cher)* excessively, inordinately; *(très: riche, laid)* extremely, incredibly; **manger/boire** ~ to eat/drink to excess.
exciper [ɛksipe]: ~ **de** *vt* to plead.
excipient [ɛksipjɑ̃] *nm (MÉD)* inert base, excipient.
exciser [ɛksize] *vt (MÉD)* to excise.
excision [ɛksizjɔ̃] *nf (MÉD)* excision; *(rituelle)* circumcision.
excitant, e [ɛksitɑ̃, -ɑ̃t] *adj* exciting ♦ *nm* stimulant.
excitation [ɛksitasjɔ̃] *nf (état)* excitement.
excité, e [ɛksite] *adj* excited.
exciter [ɛksite] *vt* to excite; *(suj: café etc)* to stimulate; **s'~** *vi* to get excited; ~ **qn à** *(révolte etc)* to incite sb to.
exclamation [ɛksklamasjɔ̃] *nf* exclamation.
exclamer [ɛksklame]: **s'~** *vi* to exclaim.
exclu, e [ɛkskly] *pp de* **exclure** ♦ *adj:* **il est/n'est pas** ~ **que** ... it's out of the question/not impossible that ...; **ce n'est pas exclu** it's not impossible, I don't rule that out.
exclure [ɛksklyʀ] *vt (faire sortir)* to expel; *(ne pas compter)* to exclude, leave out; *(rendre impossible)* to exclude, rule out.
exclusif, ive [ɛksklyzif, -iv] *adj* exclusive; **avec la mission exclusive/dans le but** ~ **de** ... with the sole mission/aim of ...; **agent** ~ sole agent.
exclusion [ɛksklyzjɔ̃] *nf* expulsion; **à l'~ de** with the exclusion *ou* exception of.
exclusivement [ɛksklyzivmɑ̃] *adv* exclusively.
exclusivité [ɛksklyzivite] *nf* exclusiveness; *(COMM)* exclusive rights *pl*; **passer en** ~ *(film)* to go on general release.
excommunier [ɛkskɔmynje] *vt* to excommunicate.
excréments [ɛkskʀemɑ̃] *nmpl* excrement *sg*, faeces.
excréter [ɛkskʀete] *vt* to excrete.
excroissance [ɛkskʀwasɑ̃s] *nf* excrescence, outgrowth.

excursion [εkskyʀsjɔ̃] nf (en autocar) excursion, trip; (à pied) walk, hike; **faire une** ~ to go on an excursion ou a trip; to go on a walk ou hike.

excursionniste [εkskyʀsjɔnist(ə)] nm/f tripper; hiker.

excusable [εkskyzabl(ə)] adj excusable.

excuse [εkskyz] nf excuse; ~**s** nfpl apology sg, apologies; **faire des** ~**s** to apologize; **faire ses** ~**s** to offer one's apologies; **mot d'**~ (SCOL) note from one's parent(s) (to explain absence etc); **lettre d'**~**s** letter of apology.

excuser [εkskyze] vt to excuse; ~ **qn de qch** (dispenser) to excuse sb from sth; **s'**~ **(de)** to apologize (for); **"excusez-moi"** "I'm sorry"; (pour attirer l'attention) "excuse me"; **se faire** ~ to ask to be excused.

exécrable [εgzεkʀabl(ə)] adj atrocious.

exécrer [εgzεkʀe] vt to loathe, abhor.

exécutant, e [εgzekytɑ̃, -ɑ̃t] nm/f performer.

exécuter [εgzekyte] vt (prisonnier) to execute; (tâche etc) to execute, carry out; (MUS: jouer) to perform, execute; (INFORM) to run; **s'**~ vi to comply.

exécuteur, trice [εgzekytœʀ, -tʀis] nm/f (testamentaire) executor ♦ nm (bourreau) executioner.

exécutif, ive [εgzekytif, -iv] adj, nm (POL) executive.

exécution [εgzekysjɔ̃] nf execution; carrying out; **mettre à** ~ to carry out.

exécutoire [εgzekytwaʀ] adj (JUR) (legally) binding.

exégèse [εgzeʒεz] nf exegesis.

exégète [εgzeʒεt] nm exegete.

exemplaire [εgzɑ̃plεʀ] adj exemplary ♦ nm copy.

exemple [εgzɑ̃pl(ə)] nm example; **par** ~ for instance, for example; (valeur intensive) really!; **sans** ~ (bêtise, gourmandise etc) unparalleled; **donner l'**~ to set an example; **prendre** ~ **sur** to take as a model; **à l'**~ **de** just like; **pour l'**~ (punir) as an example.

exempt, e [εgzɑ̃, -ɑ̃t] adj: ~ **de** (dispensé de) exempt from; (sans) free from; ~ **de taxes** tax-free.

exempter [εgzɑ̃te] vt: ~ **de** to exempt from.

exercé, e [εgzεʀse] adj trained.

exercer [εgzεʀse] vt (pratiquer) to exercise, practise; (faire usage de: prérogative) to exercise; (effectuer: influence, contrôle, pression) to exert; (former) to exercise, train ♦ vi (médecin) to be in practice; **s'**~ (sportif, musicien) to practise; (se faire sentir: pression etc): **s'**~ **(sur ou contre)** to be exerted (on); **s'**~ **à faire qch** to train o.s. to do sth.

exercice [εgzεʀsis] nm practice; exercising; (tâche, travail) exercise; (COMM, ADMIN: période) accounting period; **l'**~ (sportive etc) exercise; (MIL) drill; **en** ~ (juge) in office; (médecin) practising; **dans l'**~ **de ses fonctions** in the discharge of his duties; ~**s**

d'assouplissement limbering-up (exercises).

exergue [εgzεʀg(ə)] nm: **mettre en** ~ (inscription) to inscribe; **porter en** ~ to be inscribed with.

exhalaison [εgzalεzɔ̃] nf exhalation.

exhaler [εgzale] vt (parfum) to exhale; (souffle, son, soupir) to utter, breathe; **s'**~ vi to rise (up).

exhausser [εgzose] vt to raise (up).

exhausteur [εgzostœʀ] nm extractor fan.

exhaustif, ive [εgzostif, -iv] adj exhaustive.

exhiber [εgzibe] vt (montrer: papiers, certificat) to present, produce; (péj) to display, flaunt; **s'**~ (personne) to parade; (suj: exhibitionniste) to expose o.s.

exhibitionnisme [εgzibisjɔnism(ə)] nm exhibitionism.

exhibitionniste [εgzibisjɔnist(ə)] nm/f exhibitionist.

exhortation [εgzɔʀtɑsjɔ̃] nf exhortation.

exhorter [εgzɔʀte] vt: ~ **qn à faire** to urge sb to do.

exhumer [εgzyme] vt to exhume.

exigeant, e [εgziʒɑ̃, -ɑ̃t] adj demanding; (péj) hard to please.

exigence [εgziʒɑ̃s] nf demand, requirement.

exiger [εgziʒe] vt to demand, require.

exigible [εgziʒibl(ə)] adj (COMM, JUR) payable.

exigu, ë [εgzigy] adj cramped, tiny.

exigüité [εgziɡɥite] nf (d'un lieu) cramped nature.

exil [εgzil] nm exile; **en** ~ in exile.

exilé, e [εgzile] nm/f exile.

exiler [εgzile] vt to exile; **s'**~ to go into exile.

existant, e [εgzistɑ̃, -ɑ̃t] adj (actuel, présent) existing.

existence [εgzistɑ̃s] nf existence; **dans l'**~ in life.

existentialisme [εgzistɑ̃sjalism(ə)] nm existentialism.

existentiel, le [εgzistɑ̃sjεl] adj existential.

exister [εgziste] vi to exist; **il existe un/des** there is a/are (some).

exode [εgzɔd] nm exodus.

exonération [εgzɔneʀɑsjɔ̃] nf exemption.

exonéré, e [εgzɔneʀe] adj: ~ **de TVA** zero-rated (for VAT).

exonérer [εgzɔneʀe] vt: ~ **de** to exempt from.

exorbitant, e [εgzɔʀbitɑ̃, -ɑ̃t] adj exorbitant.

exorbité, e [εgzɔʀbite] adj: **yeux** ~**s** bulging eyes.

exorciser [εgzɔʀsize] vt to exorcize.

exorde [εgzɔʀd(ə)] nm introduction.

exotique [εgzɔtik] adj exotic.

exotisme [εgzɔtism(ə)] nm exoticism.

expansif, ive [εkspɑ̃sif, -iv] adj expansive, communicative.

expansion [εkspɑ̃sjɔ̃] nf expansion.

expansionniste [εkspɑ̃sjɔnist(ə)] adj expansionist.

expansivité [εkspɑ̃sivite] nf expansiveness.

expatrié, e [ɛkspatrije] *nm/f* expatriate.

expatrier [ɛkspatrije] *vt* (*argent*) to take *ou* send out of the country; **s'~** to leave one's country.

expectative [ɛkspɛktativ] *nf*: **être dans l'~** to be waiting to see.

expectorant, e [ɛkspɛktɔrɑ̃, -ɑ̃t] *adj*: **sirop ~** expectorant (syrup).

expectorer [ɛkspɛktɔre] *vi* to expectorate.

expédient [ɛkspedjɑ̃] *nm* (*parfois péj*) expedient; **vivre d'~s** to live by one's wits.

expédier [ɛkspedje] *vt* (*lettre, paquet*) to send; (*troupes, renfort*) to dispatch; (*péj: travail etc*) to dispose of, dispatch.

expéditeur, trice [ɛkspeditœr, -tris] *nm/f* (*POSTES*) sender.

expéditif, ive [ɛkspeditif, -iv] *adj* quick, expeditious.

expédition [ɛkspedisjɔ̃] *nf* sending; (*scientifique, sportive, MIL*) expedition; **~ punitive** punitive raid.

expéditionnaire [ɛkspedisjɔnɛr] *adj*: **corps ~** (*MIL*) task force.

expérience [ɛksperjɑ̃s] *nf* (*de la vie, des choses*) experience; (*scientifique*) experiment; **avoir de l'~** to have experience, be experienced; **avoir l'~ de** to have experience of; **faire l'~ de qch** to experience sth; **~ de chimie/d'électricité** chemical/electrical experiment.

expérimental, e, aux [ɛksperimɑ̃tal, -o] *adj* experimental.

expérimentalement [ɛksperimɑ̃talmɑ̃] *adv* experimentally.

expérimenté, e [ɛksperimɑ̃te] *adj* experienced.

expérimenter [ɛksperimɑ̃te] *vt* (*machine, technique*) to test out, experiment with.

expert, e [ɛkspɛr, -ɛrt(ə)] *adj*: **~ en** expert in ♦ *nm* (*spécialiste*) expert; **~ en assurances** insurance valuer.

expert-comptable, *pl* **experts-comptables** [ɛkspɛrkɔ̃tabl(ə)] *nm* ≈ chartered (*BRIT*) *ou* certified public (*US*) accountant.

expertise [ɛkspɛrtiz] *nf* valuation; assessment; valuer's (*ou* assessor's) report; (*JUR*) (forensic) examination.

expertiser [ɛkspɛrtize] *vt* (*objet de valeur*) to value; (*voiture accidentée etc*) to assess damage to.

expier [ɛkspje] *vt* to expiate, atone for.

expiration [ɛkspirasjɔ̃] *nf* expiry (*BRIT*), expiration; breathing out *no pl.*

expirer [ɛkspire] *vi* (*prendre fin, littéraire: mourir*) to expire; (*respirer*) to breathe out.

explétif, ive [ɛkspletif, -iv] *adj* (*LING*) expletive.

explicable [ɛksplikabl(ə)] *adj*: **pas ~** inexplicable.

explicatif, ive [ɛksplikatif, -iv] *adj* (*mot, texte, note*) explanatory.

explication [ɛksplikasjɔ̃] *nf* explanation; (*discussion*) discussion; **~ de texte** (*SCOL*) critical analysis (of a text).

explicite [ɛksplisit] *adj* explicit.

explicitement [ɛksplisitmɑ̃] *adv* explicitly.

expliciter [ɛksplisite] *vt* to make explicit.

expliquer [ɛksplike] *vt* to explain; **~ (à qn) comment/que** to point out *ou* explain (to sb) how/that; **s'~** (*se faire comprendre: personne*) to explain o.s.; (*discuter*) to discuss things; (*se disputer*) to have it out; (*comprendre*): **je m'explique son retard/absence** I understand his lateness/absence; **son erreur s'explique** one can understand his mistake.

exploit [ɛksplwa] *nm* exploit, feat.

exploitable [ɛksplwatabl(ə)] *adj* (*gisement etc*) that can be exploited; **~ par une machine** machine-readable.

exploitant [ɛksplwatɑ̃] *nm* farmer.

exploitation [ɛksplwatasjɔ̃] *nf* exploitation; running; (*entreprise*): **~ agricole** farming concern.

exploiter [ɛksplwate] *vt* to exploit; (*entreprise, ferme*) to run, operate.

exploiteur, euse [ɛksplwatœr, -øz] *nm/f* (*péj*) exploiter.

explorateur, trice [ɛksplɔratœr, -tris] *nm/f* explorer.

exploration [ɛksplɔrasjɔ̃] *nf* exploration.

explorer [ɛksplɔre] *vt* to explore.

exploser [ɛksploze] *vi* to explode, blow up; (*engin explosif*) to go off; (*fig: joie, colère*) to burst out, explode; (*: personne: de colère*) to explode, flare up; **faire ~** (*bombe*) to explode, detonate; (*bâtiment, véhicule*) to blow up.

explosif, ive [ɛksplozif, -iv] *adj, nm* explosive.

explosion [ɛksplozjɔ̃] *nf* explosion; **~ de joie/colère** outburst of joy/rage; **~ démographique** population explosion.

exponentiel, le [ɛkspɔnɑ̃sjɛl] *adj* exponential.

exportateur, trice [ɛkspɔrtatœr, -tris] *adj* exporting ♦ *nm* exporter.

exportation [ɛkspɔrtasjɔ̃] *nf* export.

exporter [ɛkspɔrte] *vt* to export.

exposant [ɛkspozɑ̃] *nm* exhibitor; (*MATH*) exponent.

exposé, e [ɛkspoze] *nm* (*écrit*) exposé; (*oral*) talk ♦ *adj*: **~ au sud** facing south, with a southern aspect; **bien ~** well situated; **très ~** very exposed.

exposer [ɛkspoze] *vt* (*montrer: marchandise*) to display; (*: peinture*) to exhibit, show; (*parler de: problème, situation*) to explain, expose, set out; (*mettre en danger, orienter: maison etc*) to expose; **~ qn/qch à** to expose sb/sth to; **~ sa vie** to risk one's life; **s'~ à** (*soleil, danger*) to expose o.s. to; (*critiques, punition*) to lay o.s. open to.

exposition [ɛkspozisjɔ̃] *nf* (*voir exposer*) displaying; exhibiting; explanation, exposition; exposure; (*voir exposé*) aspect, situation; (*manifestation*) exhibition; (*PHOTO*) exposure;

(*introduction*) exposition.

exprès [ɛkspʀɛ] *adv* (*délibérément*) on purpose; (*spécialement*) specially; **faire ~ de faire qch** to do sth on purpose.

exprès, esse [ɛkspʀɛs] *adj* (*ordre, défense*) express, formal ♦ *adj inv, adv* (*POSTES*) express; **envoyer qch en ~** to send sth express.

express [ɛkspʀɛs] *adj, nm:* (**café**) **~** espresso; (**train**) **~** fast train.

expressément [ɛkspʀɛsemã] *adv* expressly, specifically.

expressif, ive [ɛkspʀɛsif, -iv] *adj* expressive.

expression [ɛkspʀɛsjɔ̃] *nf* expression; **réduit à sa plus simple ~** reduced to its simplest terms; **liberté/moyens d'~** freedom/means of expression; **~ toute faite** set phrase.

expressionnisme [ɛkspʀɛsjɔnism(ə)] *nm* expressionism.

expressivité [ɛkspʀɛsivite] *nf* expressiveness.

exprimer [ɛkspʀime] *vt* (*sentiment, idée*) to express; (*faire sortir: jus, liquide*) to press out; **s'~** *vi* (*personne*) to express o.s.

expropriation [ɛkspʀɔpʀijɑsjɔ̃] *nf* expropriation; **frapper d'~** to put a compulsory purchase order on.

exproprier [ɛkspʀɔpʀije] *vt* to buy up (*ou* buy the property of) by compulsory purchase, expropriate.

expulser [ɛkspylse] *vt* (*d'une salle, d'un groupe*) to expel; (*locataire*) to evict; (*FOOTBALL*) to send off.

expulsion [ɛkspylsjɔ̃] *nf* expulsion; eviction; sending off.

expurger [ɛkspyʀʒe] *vt* to expurgate, bowdlerize.

exquis, e [ɛkski, -iz] *adj* (*gâteau, parfum, élégance*) exquisite; (*personne, temps*) delightful.

exsangue [ɛksãg] *adj* bloodless, drained of blood.

exsuder [ɛksyde] *vt* to exude.

extase [ɛkstaz] *nf* ecstasy; **être en ~** to be in raptures.

extasier [ɛkstazje]: **s'~** *vi:* **s'~ sur** to go into raptures over.

extatique [ɛkstatik] *adj* ecstatic.

extenseur [ɛkstãsœʀ] *nm* (*SPORT*) chest expander.

extensible [ɛkstãsibl(ə)] *adj* extensible.

extensif, ive [ɛkstãsif, -iv] *adj* extensive.

extension [ɛkstãsjɔ̃] *nf* (*d'un muscle, ressort*) stretching; (*MÉD*): **à l'~** in traction; (*fig*) extension; expansion.

exténuant [ɛkstenyã, -ãt] *adj* exhausting.

exténuer [ɛkstenɥe] *vt* to exhaust.

extérieur, e [ɛksteʀjœʀ] *adj* (*de dehors: porte, mur etc*) outer, outside; (*: commerce, politique*) foreign; (*: influences, pressions*) external; (*au dehors: escalier, w.-c.*) outside; (*apparent: calme, gaieté etc*) outer ♦ *nm* (*d'une maison, d'un récipient etc*) outside, exterior; (*d'une personne: apparence*) exterior; (*d'un*

pays, d'un groupe social): **l'~** the outside world; **à l'~** (*dehors*) outside; (*fig: à l'étranger*) abroad.

extérieurement [ɛksteʀjœʀmã] *adv* (*de dehors*) on the outside; (*en apparence*) on the surface.

extérioriser [ɛksteʀjɔʀize] *vt* to exteriorize.

extermination [ɛkstɛʀminasjɔ̃] *nf* extermination, wiping out.

exterminer [ɛkstɛʀmine] *vt* to exterminate, wipe out.

externat [ɛkstɛʀna] *nm* day school.

externe [ɛkstɛʀn(ə)] *adj* external, outer ♦ *nm/f* (*MÉD*) non-resident medical student, extern (*US*); (*SCOL*) day pupil.

extincteur [ɛkstɛ̃ktœʀ] *nm* (fire) extinguisher.

extinction [ɛkstɛ̃ksjɔ̃] *nf* extinction; (*JUR: d'une dette*) extinguishment; **~ de voix** (*MÉD*) loss of voice.

extirper [ɛkstiʀpe] *vt* (*tumeur*) to extirpate; (*plante*) to root out, pull up; (*préjugés*) to eradicate.

extorquer [ɛkstɔʀke] *vt* (*de l'argent, un renseignement*): **~ qch à qn** to extort sth from sb.

extorsion [ɛkstɔʀsjɔ̃] *nf:* **~ de fonds** extortion of money.

extra [ɛkstʀa] *adj inv* first-rate; (*marchandises*) top-quality ♦ *nm inv* extra help ♦ *préfixe* extra(-).

extraction [ɛkstʀaksjɔ̃] *nf* extraction.

extrader [ɛkstʀade] *vt* to extradite.

extradition [ɛkstʀadisjɔ̃] *nf* extradition.

extra-fin, e [ɛkstʀafɛ̃, -in] *adj* extra-fine.

extra-fort, e [ɛkstʀafɔʀ] *adj* extra strong.

extraire [ɛkstʀɛʀ] *vt* to extract.

extrait, e [ɛkstʀɛ, -ɛt] *pp de* **extraire** ♦ *nm* (*de plante*) extract; (*de film, livre*) extract, excerpt; **~ de naissance** birth certificate.

extra-lucide [ɛkstʀalysid] *adj:* **voyante ~** clairvoyant.

extraordinaire [ɛkstʀaɔʀdinɛʀ] *adj* extraordinary; (*POL, ADMIN*) special; **ambassadeur ~** ambassador extraordinary; **assemblée ~** extraordinary meeting; **par ~** by some unlikely chance.

extraordinairement [ɛksʀaɔʀdinɛʀmã] *adv* extraordinarily.

extrapoler [ɛkstʀapɔle] *vt, vi* to extrapolate.

extra-sensoriel, le [ɛkstʀasãsɔʀjɛl] *adj* extrasensory.

extra-terrestre [ɛkstʀatɛʀɛstʀ(ə)] *nm/f* extraterrestrial.

extra-utérin, e [ɛkstʀayteʀɛ̃, -in] *adj* extrauterine.

extravagance [ɛkstʀavagãs] *nf* extravagance *no pl*; extravagant behaviour *no pl*.

extravagant, e [ɛkstʀavagã, -ãt] *adj* (*personne, attitude*) extravagant; (*idée*) wild.

extraverti, e [ɛkstʀavɛʀti] *adj* extrovert.

extrayais [ɛkstʀɛje] *etc vb voir* **extraire**.

extrême [ɛkstʀɛm] *adj, nm* extreme; (*intensif*): **d'une ~ simplicité/brutalité** extremely simple/brutal; **d'un** ~ **à l'autre** from one extreme to another; **à l'**~ in the extreme; **à l'**~ **rigueur** in the absolute extreme.

extrêmement [ɛkstʀɛmmɑ̃] *adv* extremely.

extrême-onction, *pl* **extrêmes-onctions** [ɛkstʀɛmɔ̃ksjɔ̃] *nf* (REL) last rites *pl*, Extreme Unction.

Extrême-Orient [ɛkstʀɛmɔʀjɑ̃] *nm:* **l'**~ the Far East.

extrême-oriental, e, aux [ɛkstʀɛmɔʀjɑ̃tal, -o] *adj* Far Eastern.

extrémisme [ɛkstʀemism(ə)] *nm* extremism.

extrémiste [ɛkstʀemist(ə)] *adj, nm/f* extremist.

extrémité [ɛkstʀemite] *nf* (bout) end; (situation) straits *pl*, plight; (geste désespéré) extreme action; ~**s** *nfpl* (pieds et mains) extremities; **à la dernière** ~ (à l'agonie) on the point of death.

extroverti, e [ɛkstʀɔvɛʀti] *adj* = **extraverti.**

exubérance [ɛgzybeʀɑ̃] *nf* exuberance.

exubérant, e [ɛgzybeʀɑ̃, -ɑ̃t] *adj* exuberant.

exulter [ɛgzylte] *vi* to exult.

exutoire [ɛgzytwaʀ] *nm* outlet, release.

ex-voto [ɛksvɔto] *nm inv* ex-voto.

eye-liner [ajlajnœʀ] *nm* eyeliner.

F f

F, f [ɛf] *nm inv* F, f ♦ *abr* = **féminin;** (= franc) fr.; (= Fahrenheit) F; (= frère) Br(o).; (= femme) W; (appartement): **un F2/F3** a 2-/3-roomed flat (BRIT) ou apartment (US); **F comme François** F for Frederick (BRIT) ou Fox (US).

fa [fɑ] *nm inv* (MUS) F; (en chantant la gamme) fa.

fable [fɑbl(ə)] *nf* fable; (mensonge) story, tale.

fabricant [fabʀikɑ̃] *nm* manufacturer, maker.

fabrication [fabʀikasjɔ̃] *nf* manufacture, making.

fabrique [fabʀik] *nf* factory.

fabriquer [fabʀike] *vt* to make; (industriellement) to manufacture, make; (construire: voiture) to manufacture, build; (: maison) to build; (fig: inventer: histoire, alibi) to make up; (fam): **qu'est-ce qu'il fabrique?** what is he up to?; ~ **en série** to mass-produce.

fabulateur, trice [fabylatœʀ, -tʀis] *nm/f:* **c'est un** ~ he fantasizes, he makes up stories.

fabulation [fabylasjɔ̃] *nf* (PSYCH) fantasizing.

fabuleusement [fabyløzmɑ̃] *adv* fabulously, fantastically.

fabuleux, euse [fabylø, -øz] *adj* fabulous, fantastic.

fac [fak] *abr f* (fam: = faculté) Uni (BRIT fam), ≈ college (US).

façade [fasad] *nf* front, façade; (fig) façade.

face [fas] *nf* face; (fig: aspect) side ♦ *adj:* **le côté** ~ heads; **perdre/sauver la** ~ to lose/save face; **regarder qn en** ~ to look sb in the face; **la maison/le trottoir d'en** ~ the house/pavement opposite; **en** ~ **de** prép opposite; (fig) in front of; **de** ~ *adv* from the front; **face on;** ~ **à** prép facing; (fig) faced with, in the face of; **faire** ~ **à** to face; **faire** ~ **à la demande** (COMM) to meet the demand; ~ **à** ~ *adv* facing each other ♦ *nm inv* encounter.

face-à-main, *pl* **faces-à-main** [fasamɛ̃] *nm* lorgnette.

facéties [fasesi] *nfpl* jokes, pranks.

facétieux, euse [fasesjø, -øz] *adj* mischievous.

facette [fasɛt] *nf* facet.

fâché, e [fɑʃe] *adj* angry; (désolé) sorry.

fâcher [fɑʃe] *vt* to anger; **se** ~ *vi* to get angry; **se** ~ **avec** (se brouiller) to fall out with.

fâcherie [fɑʃʀi] *nf* quarrel.

fâcheusement [fɑʃøzmɑ̃] *adv* unpleasantly; (impressionné etc) badly; **avoir** ~ **tendance à** to have an irritating tendency to.

fâcheux, euse [fɑʃø, -øz] *adj* unfortunate, regrettable.

facho [faʃo] *adj, nm/f* (fam: = fasciste) fascist.

facial, e, aux [fasjal, -o] *adj* facial.

faciès [fasjɛs] *nm* (visage) features *pl*.

facile [fasil] *adj* easy; (accommodant) easygoing; ~ **d'emploi** (INFORM) user-friendly.

facilement [fasilmɑ̃] *adv* easily.

facilité [fasilite] *nf* easiness; (disposition, don) aptitude; (moyen, occasion, possibilité): **il a la** ~ **de rencontrer les gens** he has every opportunity to meet people; ~**s** *nfpl* facilities; (COMM) terms; ~**s de crédit** credit terms; ~**s de paiement** easy terms.

faciliter [fasilite] *vt* to make easier.

façon [fasɔ̃] *nf* (manière) way; (d'une robe etc) making-up; cut; (: main-d'œuvre) labour (BRIT), labor (US); (: imitation): **châle** ~ **cachemire** cashmere-style shawl; ~**s** *nfpl* (péj) fuss *sg*; **faire des** ~**s** (péj: être affecté) to be affected; (: faire des histoires) to make a fuss; **de quelle** ~? (in) what way?; **sans** ~ *adv* without fuss ♦ *adj* unaffected; **d'une autre** ~ in another way; **en aucune** ~ in no way; **de** ~ **à so as to; de** ~ **à ce que, de (telle)** ~ **que** so that; **de toute** ~ anyway, in any case; **(c'est une)** ~ **de parler** it's a way of putting it; **travail à** ~ tailoring.

façonner [fasɔne] *vt* (fabriquer) to manufacture; (travailler: matière) to shape, fashion; (fig) to mould, shape.

fac-similé [faksimile] *nm* facsimile.

facteur, trice [faktœʀ, -tʀis] *nm/f* postman/woman (BRIT), mailman/woman (US) ♦ *nm* (MATH, gén) factor; ~ **d'orgues** organ builder; ~ **de pianos** piano maker; ~ **rhésus** rhesus factor.

factice [faktis] *adj* artificial.

faction [faksjɔ̃] *nf* (*groupe*) faction; (*MIL*) guard *ou* sentry (duty); watch; **en** ~ on guard; standing watch.
factionnaire [faksjɔnɛʀ] *nm* guard, sentry.
factoriel, le [faktɔʀjɛl] *adj, nf* factorial.
factotum [faktɔtɔm] *nm* odd-job man, dogsbody (*BRIT*).
factuel, le [faktɥɛl] *adj* factual.
facturation [faktyʀasjɔ̃] *nf* invoicing; (*bureau*) invoicing (office).
facture [faktyʀ] *nf* (*à payer: gén*) bill; (: *COMM*) invoice; (*d'un artisan, artiste*) technique, workmanship.
facturer [faktyʀe] *vt* to invoice.
facturier, ière [faktyʀje, -jɛʀ] *nm/f* invoice clerk.
facultatif, ive [fakyltatif, -iv] *adj* optional; (*arrêt de bus*) request *cpd*.
faculté [fakylte] *nf* (*intellectuelle, d'université*) faculty; (*pouvoir, possibilité*) power.
fadaises [fadɛz] *nfpl* twaddle *sg*.
fade [fad] *adj* insipid.
fading [fadiŋ] *nm* (*RADIO*) fading.
fagot [fago] *nm* (*de bois*) bundle of sticks.
fagoté, e [fagɔte] *adj* (*fam*): **drôlement** ~ oddly dressed.
faible [fɛbl(ə)] *adj* weak; (*voix, lumière, vent*) faint; (*élève, copie*) poor; (*rendement, intensité, revenu etc*) low ♦ *nm* weak point; (*pour quelqu'un*) weakness, soft spot; ~ **d'esprit** feeble-minded.
faiblement [fɛbləmã] *adv* weakly; (*peu: éclairer etc*) faintly.
faiblesse [fɛblɛs] *nf* weakness.
faiblir [febliʀ] *vi* to weaken; (*lumière*) to dim; (*vent*) to drop.
faïence [fajãs] *nf* earthenware *no pl*; (*objet*) piece of earthenware.
faignant, e [fɛɲɑ̃, -ãt] *nm/f* = **fainéant, e.**
faille [faj] *vb voir* **falloir** ♦ *nf* (*GÉO*) fault; (*fig*) flaw, weakness.
failli, e [faji] *adj, nm/f* bankrupt.
faillible [fajibl(ə)] *adj* fallible.
faillir [fajiʀ] *vi*: **j'ai failli tomber/lui dire** I almost *ou* nearly fell/told him; ~ **à une promesse/un engagement** to break a promise/an agreement.
faillite [fajit] *nf* bankruptcy; (*échec: d'une politique etc*) collapse; **être en** ~ to be bankrupt; **faire** ~ to go bankrupt.
faim [fɛ̃] *nf* hunger; (*fig*): ~ **d'amour/de richesse** hunger *ou* yearning for love/wealth; **avoir** ~ to be hungry; **rester sur sa** ~ (*aussi fig*) to be left wanting more.
fainéant, e [fɛneã, -ãt] *nm/f* idler, loafer.
fainéantise [feneãtiz] *nf* idleness, laziness.

═══════════════════════════ *MOT-CLÉ*

faire [fɛʀ] *vt* **1** (*fabriquer, être l'auteur de*) to make; (*produire*) to produce; (*construire: maison, bateau*) to build; ~ **du vin/une offre/un film** to make wine/an offer/a film; ~ **du bruit** to make a noise

2 (*effectuer: travail, opération*) to do; **que faites-vous?** (*quel métier etc*) what do you do?; (*quelle activité: au moment de la question*) what are you doing?; **que** ~? what are we going to do?, what can be done (about it)?; ~ **la lessive/le ménage** to do the washing/ the housework

3 (*études*) to do; (*sport, musique*) to play; ~ **du droit/du français** to do law/French; ~ **du rugby/piano** to play rugby/the piano; ~ **du cheval/du ski** to go riding/skiing

4 (*visiter*): ~ **les magasins** to go shopping; ~ **l'Europe** to tour *ou* do Europe

5 (*simuler*): ~ **le malade/l'ignorant** to act the invalid/the fool

6 (*transformer, avoir un effet sur*): ~ **de qn un frustré/avocat** to make sb frustrated/a lawyer; **ça ne me fait rien** (*m'est égal*) I don't care *ou* mind; (*me laisse froid*) it has no effect on me; **ça ne fait rien** it doesn't matter; ~ **que** (*impliquer*) to mean that

7 (*calculs, prix, mesures*): **2 et 2 font 4** 2 and 2 are *ou* make 4; **ça fait 10 m/15 F** it's 10 m/ 15 F; **je vous le fais 10 F** I'll let you have it for 10 F

8 (*vb +de*): **qu'a-t-il fait de sa valise/de sa sœur?** what has he done with his case/his sister?

9: **ne** ~ **que**: **il ne fait que critiquer** (*sans cesse*) all he (ever) does is criticize; (*seulement*) he's only criticizing

10 (*dire*) to say; **vraiment? fit-il** really? he said

11 (*maladie*) to have; ~ **du diabète/de la tension** to have diabetes *sg*/high blood pressure

♦ *vi* **1** (*agir, s'y prendre*) to act, do; **il faut** ~ **vite** we (*ou* you *etc*) must act quickly; **comment a-t-il fait pour?** how did he manage to?; **faites comme chez vous** make yourself at home; **je n'ai pas pu** ~ **autrement** there was nothing else I could do

2 (*paraître*) to look; ~ **vieux/démodé** to look old/old-fashioned; **ça fait bien** it looks good; **tu fais jeune dans cette robe** that dress makes you look young(er)

♦ *vb substitut* to do; **ne le casse pas comme je l'ai fait** don't break it as I did; **je peux le voir? — faites!** can I see it? — please do!; **remets-le en place — je viens de le** ~ put it back in its place — I just have (done)

♦ *vb impers* **1**: **il fait beau** *etc* the weather is fine *etc*; *voir aussi* **jour**; **froid** *etc*

2 (*temps écoulé, durée*): **ça fait 2 ans qu'il est parti** it's 2 years since he left; **ça fait 2 ans qu'il y est** he's been there for 2 years

♦ *vb semi-aux* **1**: ~ **+infinitif** (*action directe*) to make; ~ **tomber/bouger qch** to make sth fall/move; ~ **démarrer un moteur/chauffer de l'eau** to start up an engine/heat some water; **cela fait dormir** it makes you sleep; ~

travailler les enfants to make the children work *ou* get the children to work; **il m'a fait traverser la rue** he helped me to cross the road
2 *(indirectement, par un intermédiaire)*: ~ **réparer qch** to get *ou* have sth repaired; ~ **punir les enfants** to have the children punished; **il m'a fait ouvrir la porte** he got me to open the door
se ~ *vi* 1 *(vin, fromage)* to mature
2: **cela se fait beaucoup/ne se fait pas** it's done a lot/not done
3 *(+nom ou pron)*: **se ~ une jupe** to make o.s. a skirt; **se ~ des amis** to make friends; **se ~ du souci** to worry; **se ~ des illusions** to delude o.s.; **se ~ beaucoup d'argent** to make a lot of money; **il ne s'en fait pas** he doesn't worry
4 *(+adj)* *(devenir)*: **se ~ vieux** to be getting old; *(délibérément)*: **se ~ beau** to do o.s. up
5: **se ~ à** *(s'habituer)* to get used to; **je n'arrive pas à me ~ à la nourriture/au climat** I can't get used to the food/climate
6 *(+infinitif)*: **se ~ examiner la vue/opérer** to have one's eyes tested/have an operation; **se ~ couper les cheveux** to get one's hair cut; **il va se ~ tuer/punir** he's going to get himself killed/get (himself) punished; **il s'est fait aider** he got somebody to help him; **il s'est fait aider par Simon** he got Simon to help him; **se ~ ~ un vêtement** to get a garment made for o.s.
7 *(impersonnel)*: **comment se fait-il/faisait-il que?** how is it/was it that?; **il peut se ~ que nous utilisions ...** it's possible that we could use ...

faire-part [fɛʀpaʀ] *nm inv* announcement *(of birth, marriage etc)*.
fair-play [fɛʀplɛ] *adj inv* fair.
fais [fɛ] *vb voir* faire.
faisabilité [fəzabilite] *nf* feasibility.
faisable [fəzabl(ə)] *adj* feasible.
faisais [fəzɛ] *etc vb voir* faire.
faisan, e [fəzɑ̃, -an] *nm/f* pheasant.
faisandé, e [fəzɑ̃de] *adj* high *(bad)*; *(fig péj)* corrupt, decadent.
faisceau, x [fɛso] *nm (de lumière etc)* beam; *(de branches etc)* bundle.
faiseur, euse [fəzœʀ, -øz] *nm/f (gén: péj)*: ~ **de maker** of ♦ *nm (bespoke)* tailor; ~ **d'embarras** fusspot; ~ **de projets** schemer.
faisons [fəzɔ̃] *etc vb voir* faire.
faisselle [fɛsɛl] *nf* cheese strainer.
fait [fɛ] *vb voir* faire ♦ *nm (événement)* event, occurrence; *(réalité, donnée)* fact; **le ~ que/de manger** the fact that/of eating; **être le ~ de** *(causé par)* to be the work of; **être au ~ (de)** to be informed (of); **mettre qn au ~** to inform sb, put sb in the picture; **au ~** *(à propos)* by the way; **en venir au ~** to get to the point; **de ~** *adj (opposé à: de droit)* de facto

♦ *adv* in fact; **du ~ de ceci/qu'il a menti** because of *ou* on account of this/his having lied; **de ce ~** therefore, for this reason; **en ~** in fact; **en ~ de repas** by way of a meal; **prendre ~ et cause pour qn** to support sb, side with sb; **prendre qn sur le ~** to catch sb in the act; **dire à qn son ~** to give sb a piece of one's mind; **hauts ~s** *(exploits)* exploits; ~ **d'armes** feat of arms; ~ **divers** (short) news item; **les ~s et gestes de qn** sb's actions *ou* doings.
fait, e [fɛ, fɛt] *pp de* faire ♦ *adj (mûr: fromage, melon)* ripe; *(maquillé: yeux)* made-up; *(vernis: ongles)* painted, polished; **un homme ~** a grown man; **tout(e) ~(e)** *(préparé à l'avance)* ready-made; **c'en est ~ de notre tranquillité** that's the end of our peace; **c'est bien ~ (pour lui ou eux etc)** it serves him *(ou* them *etc)* right.
faîte [fɛt] *nm* top; *(fig)* pinnacle, height.
faites [fɛt] *vb voir* faire.
faîtière [fɛtjɛʀ] *nf (de tente)* ridge pole.
fait-tout *nm inv*, **faitout** [fɛtu] *nm* stewpot.
fakir [fakiʀ] *nm (THÉÂT)* wizard.
falaise [falɛz] *nf* cliff.
falbalas [falbala] *nmpl* fripperies, frills.
fallacieux, euse [falasjø, -øz] *adj (raisonnement)* fallacious; *(apparences)* deceptive; *(espoir)* illusory.
falloir [falwaʀ] *vb impers*: **il faut faire les lits** we *(ou* you *etc)* have to *ou* must make the beds; **il faut que je fasse les lits** I have to *ou* must make the beds; **il a fallu qu'il parte** he had to leave; **il faudrait qu'elle rentre** she ought to go home; **il va ~ 100 F** we'll *(ou* I'll *etc)* need 100 F; **il doit ~ du temps** that must take time; **il vous faut tourner à gauche après l'église** you have to turn left past the church; **nous avons ce qu'il (nous) faut** we have what we need; **il faut qu'il ait oublié** he must have forgotten; **il a fallu qu'il l'apprenne** he would have to hear about it; **il ne fallait pas** *(pour remercier)* you shouldn't have (done); **faut le faire!** (it) takes some doing! ♦ *vi*: **s'en ~**: **il s'en est fallu de 100 F/5 minutes** we *(ou* they *etc)* were 100 F short/5 minutes late *(ou* early); **il s'en faut de beaucoup qu'il soit ...** he is far from being ...; **il s'en est fallu de peu que cela n'arrive** it very nearly happened; **ou peu s'en faut** or just about, or as good as; **comme il faut** *adj* proper ♦ *adv* properly.
fallu [faly] *pp de* falloir.
falot, e [falo, -ɔt] *adj* dreary, colourless *(BRIT)*, colorless *(US)* ♦ *nm* lantern.
falsification [falsifikasjɔ̃] *nf* falsification.
falsifier [falsifje] *vt* to falsify.
famé, e [fame] *adj*: **mal ~** disreputable, of ill repute.
famélique [famelik] *adj* half-starved.
fameux, euse [famø, -øz] *adj (illustre: parfois péj)* famous; *(bon: repas, plat etc)* first-rate,

first-class; (*intensif*): un ~ problème *etc* a real problem *etc*; pas ~ not great, not much good.

familial, e, aux [familjal, -o] *adj* family *cpd* ♦ *nf* (*AUTO*) family estate car (*BRIT*), station wagon (*US*).

familiariser [familjaʀize] *vt*: ~ qn avec to familiarize sb with; se ~ avec to familiarize o.s. with.

familiarité [familjaʀite] *nf* familiarity; informality; ~s *nfpl* familiarities; ~ avec (*sujet, science*) familiarity with.

familier, ière [familje, -jɛʀ] *adj* (*connu, impertinent*) familiar; (*dénotant une certaine intimité*) informal, friendly; (*LING*) informal, colloquial ♦ *nm* regular (visitor).

familièrement [familjɛʀmɑ̃] *adv* (*sans façon: s'entretenir*) informally; (*cavalièrement*) familiarly.

famille [famij] *nf* family; il a de la ~ à Paris he has relatives in Paris.

famine [famin] *nf* famine.

fan [fan] *nm/f* fan.

fana [fana] *adj, nm/f* (*fam*) = fanatique.

fanal, aux [fanal, -o] *nm* beacon; lantern.

fanatique [fanatik] *adj*: ~ (de) fanatical (about) ♦ *nm/f* fanatic.

fanatisme [fanatism(ə)] *nm* fanaticism.

fane [fan] *nf* top.

fané, e [fane] *adj* faded.

faner [fane]: se ~ *vi* to fade.

faneur, euse [fanœʀ, -øz] *nm/f* haymaker ♦ *nf* (*TECH*) tedder.

fanfare [fɑ̃faʀ] *nf* (*orchestre*) brass band; (*musique*) fanfare; en ~ (*avec bruit*) noisily.

fanfaron, ne [fɑ̃faʀɔ̃, -ɔn] *nm/f* braggart.

fanfaronnades [fɑ̃faʀɔnad] *nfpl* bragging *no pl*.

fanfreluches [fɑ̃fʀəlyʃ] *nfpl* trimming *no pl*.

fange [fɑ̃ʒ] *nf* mire.

fanion [fanjɔ̃] *nm* pennant.

fanon [fanɔ̃] *nm* (*de baleine*) plate of baleen; (*repli de peau*) dewlap, wattle.

fantaisie [fɑ̃tezi] *nf* (*spontanéité*) fancy, imagination; (*caprice*) whim; extravagance; (*MUS*) fantasia ♦ *adj*: bijou (de) ~ (piece of) costume jewellery (*BRIT*) ou jewelry (*US*); pain (de) ~ fancy bread.

fantaisiste [fɑ̃tezist(ə)] *adj* (*péj*) unorthodox, eccentric ♦ *nm/f* (*de music-hall*) variety artist ou entertainer.

fantasmagorique [fɑ̃tasmagɔʀik] *adj* phantasmagorical.

fantasme [fɑ̃tasm(ə)] *nm* fantasy.

fantasmer [fɑ̃tasme] *vi* to fantasize.

fantasque [fɑ̃task(ə)] *adj* whimsical, capricious; fantastic.

fantassin [fɑ̃tasɛ̃] *nm* infantryman.

fantastique [fɑ̃tastik] *adj* fantastic.

fantoche [fɑ̃tɔʃ] *nm* (*péj*) puppet.

fantomatique [fɑ̃tɔmatik] *adj* ghostly.

fantôme [fɑ̃tom] *nm* ghost, phantom.

FAO *sigle f* (= *Food and Agricultural Organization*) FAO.

faon [fɑ̃] *nm* fawn (*deer*).

faramineux, euse [faʀaminø, -øz] *adj* (*fam*) fantastic.

farandole [faʀɑ̃dɔl] *nf* farandole.

farce [faʀs(ə)] *nf* (*viande*) stuffing; (*blague*) (practical) joke; (*THÉÂT*) farce; faire une ~ à qn to play a (practical) joke on sb; ~s et attrapes jokes and novelties.

farceur, euse [faʀsœʀ, -øz] *nm/f* practical joker; (*fumiste*) clown.

farci, e [faʀsi] *adj* (*CULIN*) stuffed.

farcir [faʀsiʀ] *vt* (*viande*) to stuff; (*fig*): ~ qch de to stuff sth with; se ~ (*fam*): je me suis farci la vaisselle I've got stuck ou landed with the washing-up.

fard [faʀ] *nm* make-up; ~ à joues blusher.

fardeau, x [faʀdo] *nm* burden.

farder [faʀde] *vt* to make up; (*vérité*) to disguise; se ~ to make o.s. up.

farfelu, e [faʀfəly] *adj* wacky (*fam*), harebrained.

farfouiller [faʀfuje] *vi* (*péj*) to rummage around.

fariboles [faʀibɔl] *nfpl* nonsense *no pl*.

farine [faʀin] *nf* flour; ~ de blé wheatflour; ~ de maïs cornflour (*BRIT*), cornstarch (*US*); ~ lactée (*pour bouillie*) gruel.

fariner [faʀine] *vt* to flour.

farineux, euse [faʀinø, -øz] *adj* (*sauce, pomme*) floury ♦ *nmpl* (*aliments*) starchy foods.

farniente [faʀnjɛnte] *nm* idleness.

farouche [faʀuʃ] *adj* shy, timid; (*sauvage*) savage, wild; (*violent*) fierce.

farouchement [faʀuʃmɑ̃] *adv* fiercely.

fart [faʀ(t)] *nm* (ski) wax.

farter [faʀte] *vt* to wax.

fascicule [fasikyl] *nm* volume.

fascinant, e [fasinɑ̃, -ɑ̃t] *adj* fascinating.

fascination [fasinɑsjɔ̃] *nf* fascination.

fasciner [fasine] *vt* to fascinate.

fascisant, e [faʃizɑ̃, -ɑ̃t] *adj* fascistic.

fascisme [faʃism(ə)] *nm* fascism.

fasciste [faʃist(ə)] *adj, nm/f* fascist.

fasse [fas] *etc vb voir* faire.

faste [fast(ə)] *nm* splendour (*BRIT*), splendor (*US*) ♦ *adj*: c'est un jour ~ it's his (ou our *etc*) lucky day.

fastidieux, euse [fastidjø, -øz] *adj* tedious, tiresome.

fastueux, euse [fastɥø, -øz] *adj* sumptuous, luxurious.

fat [fa] *adj m* conceited, smug.

fatal, e [fatal] *adj* fatal; (*inévitable*) inevitable.

fatalement [fatalmɑ̃] *adv* inevitably.

fatalisme [fatalism(ə)] *nm* fatalism.

fataliste [fatalist(ə)] *adj* fatalistic.

fatalité [fatalite] *nf* (*destin*) fate; (*coïncidence*) fateful coincidence; (*caractère inévitable*) inevitability.

fatidique [fatidik] *adj* fateful.

fatigant, e [fatigɑ̃, -ɑ̃t] *adj* tiring; (*agaçant*) tiresome.

fatigue [fatig] *nf* tiredness, fatigue; (*détérioration*) fatigue; **les ~s du voyage** the wear and tear of the journey.

fatigué, e [fatige] *adj* tired.

fatiguer [fatige] *vt* to tire, make tired; (*TECH*) to put a strain on, strain; (*fig: importuner*) to wear out ♦ *vi* (*moteur*) to labour (*BRIT*), labor (*US*), strain; **se ~** *vi* to get tired; to tire o.s. (out); **se ~ à faire qch** to tire o.s. out doing sth.

fatras [fatʀa] *nm* jumble, hotchpotch.

fatuité [fatɥite] *nf* conceitedness, smugness.

faubourg [fobuʀ] *nm* suburb.

faubourien, ne [fobuʀjɛ̃, -ɛn] *adj* (*accent*) working-class.

fauché, e [foʃe] *adj* (*fam*) broke.

faucher [foʃe] *vt* (*herbe*) to cut; (*champs, blés*) to reap; (*fig*) to cut down; to mow down; (*fam: voler*) to pinch, nick.

faucheur, euse [foʃœʀ, -øz] *nm/f* reaper, mower.

faucille [fosij] *nf* sickle.

faucon [fokɔ̃] *nm* falcon, hawk.

faudra [fodʀa] *etc vb voir* **falloir**.

faufil [fofil] *nm* (*COUTURE*) tacking thread.

faufilage [fofilaʒ] *nm* (*COUTURE*) tacking.

faufiler [fofile] *vt* to tack, baste; **se ~** *vi*: **se ~ dans** to edge one's way into; **se ~ parmi/entre** to thread one's way among/between.

faune [fon] *nf* (*ZOOL*) wildlife, fauna; (*fig péj*) set, crowd ♦ *nm* faun; **~ marine** marine (animal) life.

faussaire [fosɛʀ] *nm/f* forger.

fausse [fos] *adj f voir* **faux**.

faussement [fosmɑ̃] *adv* (*accuser*) wrongly, wrongfully; (*croire*) falsely, erroneously.

fausser [fose] *vt* (*objet*) to bend, buckle; (*fig*) to distort; **~ compagnie à qn** to give sb the slip.

fausset [fosɛ] *nm*: **voix de ~** falsetto voice.

fausseté [foste] *nf* wrongness; falseness.

faut [fo] *vb voir* **falloir**.

faute [fot] *nf* (*erreur*) mistake, error; (*péché, manquement*) misdemeanour; (*FOOTBALL etc*) offence; (*TENNIS*) fault; (*responsabilité*): **par la ~ de** through the fault of, because of; **c'est de sa/ma ~** it's his/my fault; **être en ~** to be in the wrong; **prendre qn en ~** to catch sb out; **~ de** (*temps, argent*) for *ou* through lack of; **~ de mieux** for want of anything *ou* something better; **sans ~** *adv* without fail; **~ de frappe** typing error; **~ d'inattention** careless mistake; **~ d'orthographe** spelling mistake; **~ professionnelle** professional misconduct *no pl*.

fauteuil [fotœj] *nm* armchair; **~ à bascule** rocking chair; **~ club** (big) easy chair; **~ d'orchestre** seat in the front stalls (*BRIT*) *ou* the orchestra (*US*); **~ roulant** wheelchair.

fauteur [fotœʀ] *nm*: **~ de troubles** trouble-

maker.

fautif, ive [fotif, -iv] *adj* (*incorrect*) incorrect, inaccurate; (*responsable*) at fault, in the wrong; (*coupable*) guilty ♦ *nm/f* culprit.

fauve [fov] *nm* wildcat; (*peintre*) Fauve ♦ *adj* (*couleur*) fawn.

fauvette [fovɛt] *nf* warbler.

fauvisme [fovism(ə)] *nm* (*ART*) Fauvism.

faux¹ [fo] *nf* scythe.

faux², fausse [fo, fos] *adj* (*inexact*) wrong; (*piano, voix*) out of tune; (*falsifié*) fake, forged; (*sournois, postiche*) false ♦ *adv* (*MUS*) out of tune ♦ *nm* (*copie*) fake, forgery; (*opposé au vrai*): **le ~** falsehood; **le ~ numéro/la fausse clé** the wrong number/key; **faire ~ bond à qn** to let sb down; **~ ami** (*LING*) faux ami; **~ col** detachable collar; **~ départ** (*SPORT, fig*) false start; **~ frais** *nmpl* extras, incidental expenses; **~ frère** (*fig péj*) false friend; **~ mouvement** awkward movement; **~ nez** false nose; **~ nom** assumed name; **~ pas** tripping *no pl*; (*fig*) faux pas; **~ témoignage** (*délit*) perjury; **fausse alerte** false alarm; **fausse clé** skeleton key; **fausse couche** (*MÉD*) miscarriage; **fausse joie** vain joy; **fausse note** wrong note.

faux-filet [fofilɛ] *nm* sirloin.

faux-fuyant [fofɥijɑ̃] *nm* equivocation.

faux-monnayeur [fomɔnɛjœʀ] *nm* counterfeiter, forger.

faux-semblant [fosɑ̃blɑ̃] *nm* pretence (*BRIT*), pretense (*US*).

faux-sens [fosɑ̃s] *nm* mistranslation.

faveur [favœʀ] *nf* favour (*BRIT*), favor (*US*); **traitement de ~** preferential treatment; **à la ~ de** under cover of; (*grâce à*) thanks to; **en ~ de** in favo(u)r of.

favorable [favɔʀabl(ə)] *adj* favo(u)rable.

favori, te [favɔʀi, -it] *adj, nm/f* favo(u)rite.

favoris [favɔʀi] *nmpl* (*barbe*) sideboards (*BRIT*), sideburns.

favoriser [favɔʀize] *vt* to favour (*BRIT*), favor (*US*).

favoritisme [favɔʀitism(ə)] *nm* (*péj*) favo(u)ritism.

fayot [fajo] *nm* (*fam*) crawler.

FB *abr* (= *franc belge*) BF, FB.

FBI *sigle m* FBI.

FC *sigle m* (= *Football Club*) FC.

fébrile [febʀil] *adj* feverish, febrile; **capitaux ~s** (*ÉCON*) hot money.

fébrilement [febʀilmɑ̃] *adv* feverishly.

fécal, e, aux [fekal, -o] *adj voir* **matière**.

FECOM [fekɔm] *sigle m* (= *Fonds européen de coopération militaire*) EMCF.

fécond, e [fekɔ̃, -ɔ̃d] *adj* fertile.

fécondation [fekɔ̃dasjɔ̃] *nf* fertilization.

féconder [fekɔ̃de] *vt* to fertilize.

fécondité [fekɔ̃dite] *nf* fertility.

fécule [fekyl] *nf* potato flour.

féculent [fekylɑ̃] *nm* starchy food.

fédéral, e, aux [fedeʀal, -o] *adj* federal.
fédéralisme [federalism(ə)] *nm* federalism.
fédéraliste [federalist(ə)] *adj* federalist.
fédération [federasjɔ̃] *nf* federation.
fée [fe] *nf* fairy.
féerie [feʀi] *nf* enchantment.
féerique [feʀik] *adj* magical, fairytale *cpd*.
feignant, e [fɛɲɑ̃, -ɑ̃t] *nm/f* = **fainéant, e.**
feindre [fɛ̃dʀ(ə)] *vt* to feign ♦ *vi* to dissemble; **~ de faire** to pretend to do.
feint, e [fɛ̃, fɛ̃t] *pp de* **feindre** ♦ *adj* feigned ♦ *nf* (*SPORT: escrime*) feint; (*: football, rugby*) dummy (*BRIT*), fake (*US*): (*fam: ruse*) sham.
feinter [fɛ̃te] *vi* (*SPORT: escrime*) to feint; (*: football, rugby*) to dummy (*BRIT*), fake (*US*) ♦ *vt* (*fam: tromper*) to fool.
fêlé, e [fele] *adj* (*aussi fig*) cracked.
fêler [fele] *vt* to crack.
félicitations [felisitasjɔ̃] *nfpl* congratulations.
félicité [felisite] *nf* bliss.
féliciter [felisite] *vt*: **~ qn (de)** to congratulate sb (on).
félin, e [felɛ̃, -in] *adj* feline ♦ *nm* (big) cat.
félon, ne [felɔ̃, -ɔn] *adj* perfidious, treacherous.
félonie [feloni] *nf* treachery.
fêlure [felyʀ] *nf* crack.
femelle [fəmɛl] *adj* (*aussi ÉLEC, TECH*) female ♦ *nf* female.
féminin, e [feminɛ̃, -in] *adj* feminine; (*sexe*) female; (*équipe, vêtements etc*) women's; (*parfois péj: homme*) effeminate ♦ *nm* (*LING*) feminine.
féminiser [feminize] *vt* to feminize; (*rendre efféminé*) to make effeminate; **se ~** *vi*: **cette profession se féminise** this profession is attracting more women.
féminisme [feminism(ə)] *nm* feminism.
féministe [feminist(ə)] *adj, nf* feminist.
féminité [feminite] *nf* femininity.
femme [fam] *nf* woman; (*épouse*) wife (*pl* wives); **être très ~** to be very much a woman; **devenir ~** to attain womanhood; **~ d'affaires** businesswoman; **~ de chambre** chambermaid; **~ fatale** femme fatale; **~ au foyer** housewife; **~ d'intérieur** (real) homemaker; **~ de ménage** domestic help, cleaning lady; **~ du monde** society woman; **~-objet** sex object; **~ de tête** determined, intellectual woman.
fémoral, e, aux [femɔʀal, -o] *adj* femoral.
fémur [femyʀ] *nm* femur, thighbone.
FEN [fɛn] *sigle f* (= *Fédération de l'Éducation nationale*) *teachers' trades union*.
fenaison [fənɛzɔ̃] *nf* haymaking.
fendillé, e [fɑ̃dije] *adj* (*terre etc*) crazed.
fendre [fɑ̃dʀ(ə)] *vt* (*couper en deux*) to split; (*fissurer*) to crack; (*fig: traverser*) to cut through; to push one's way through; **se ~** *vi* to crack.
fendu, e [fɑ̃dy] *adj* (*sol, mur*) cracked; (*jupe*) slit.

fenêtre [fənɛtʀ(ə)] *nf* window; **~ à guillotine** sash window.
fennec [fenɛk] *nm* fennec.
fenouil [fənuj] *nm* fennel.
fente [fɑ̃t] *nf* slit; (*fissure*) crack.
féodal, e, aux [feɔdal, -o] *adj* feudal.
féodalisme [feɔdalism(ə)] *nm* feudalism.
feodalité [feɔdalite] *nf* feudalism.
fer [fɛʀ] *nm* iron; (*de cheval*) shoe; **~s** *pl* (*MÉD*) forceps; **mettre aux ~s** (*enchaîner*) to put in chains; **au ~ rouge** with a red-hot iron; **santé/main de ~** iron constitution/hand; **~ à cheval** horseshoe; **en ~ à cheval** (*fig*) horseshoe-shaped; **~ forgé** wrought iron; **~ à friser** curling tongs; **~ de lance** spearhead; **~ (à repasser)** iron; **~ à souder** soldering iron.
ferai [fəʀe] *etc vb voir* **faire.**
fer-blanc [fɛʀblɑ̃] *nm* tin(plate).
ferblanterie [fɛʀblɑ̃tʀi] *nf* tinplate making; (*produit*) tinware.
ferblantier [fɛʀblɑ̃tje] *nm* tinsmith.
férié, e [feʀje] *adj*: **jour ~** public holiday.
férir [feʀiʀ]: **sans coup ~** *adv* without meeting any opposition.
fermage [fɛʀmaʒ] *nm* tenant farming.
ferme [fɛʀm(ə)] *adj* firm ♦ *adv* (*travailler etc*) hard; (*discuter*) ardently ♦ *nf* (*exploitation*) farm; (*maison*) farmhouse; **tenir ~** to stand firm.
fermé, e [fɛʀme] *adj* closed, shut; (*gaz, eau etc*) off; (*fig: personne*) uncommunicative; (*: milieu*) exclusive.
fermement [fɛʀməmɑ̃] *adv* firmly.
ferment [fɛʀmɑ̃] *nm* ferment.
fermentation [fɛʀmɑ̃tasjɔ̃] *nf* fermentation.
fermenter [fɛʀmɑ̃te] *vi* to ferment.
fermer [fɛʀme] *vt* to close, shut; (*cesser l'exploitation de*) to close down, shut down; (*eau, lumière, électricité, robinet*) to put off, turn off; (*aéroport, route*) to close ♦ *vi* to close, shut; to close down, shut down; **se ~** *vi* (*yeux*) to close, shut; (*fleur, blessure*) to close up; **~ à clef** to lock; **~ au verrou** to bolt; **~ les yeux (sur qch)** (*fig*) to close one's eyes (to sth); **se ~ à** (*pitié, amour*) to close one's heart *ou* mind to.
fermeté [fɛʀməte] *nf* firmness.
fermette [fɛʀmɛt] *nf* farmhouse.
fermeture [fɛʀmətyʀ] *nf* (*voir fermer*) closing; shutting; closing *ou* shutting down; putting *ou* turning off; (*dispositif*) catch; fastening, fastener; **heure de ~** (*COMM*) closing time; **jour de ~** (*COMM*) day on which the shop (*etc*) is closed; **~ éclair** ® *ou* **à glissière** zip (fastener) (*BRIT*), zipper.
fermier, ière [fɛʀmje, -jɛʀ] *nm/f* farmer ♦ *nf* (*femme de fermier*) farmer's wife ♦ *adj*: **beurre/cidre ~** farm butter/cider.
fermoir [fɛʀmwaʀ] *nm* clasp.
féroce [feʀɔs] *adj* ferocious, fierce.
férocement [feʀɔsmɑ̃] *adv* ferociously.

férocité [ferɔsite] *nf* ferocity, ferociousness.
ferons [fərɔ̃] *etc vb voir* **faire**.
ferraille [feraj] *nf* scrap iron; **mettre à la ~** to scrap; **bruit de ~** clanking.
ferrailler [feraje] *vi* to clank.
ferrailleur [ferajœr] *nm* scrap merchant.
ferrant [ferã] *adj m voir* **maréchal-ferrant**.
ferré, e [fere] *adj* (*chaussure*) hobnailed; (*canne*) steel-tipped; **~ sur** (*fam: savant*) well up on.
ferrer [fere] *vt* (*cheval*) to shoe; (*chaussure*) to nail; (*canne*) to tip; (*poisson*) to strike.
ferreux, euse [ferø, -øz] *adj* ferrous.
ferronnerie [ferɔnri] *nf* ironwork; **~ d'art** wrought iron work.
ferronnier [ferɔnje] *nm* craftsman in wrought iron; (*marchand*) ironware merchant.
ferroviaire [ferɔvjer] *adj* rail *cpd*, railway *cpd* (*BRIT*), railroad *cpd* (*US*).
ferrugineux, euse [feryʒinø, -øz] *adj* ferruginous.
ferrure [feryr] *nf* (*ornamental*) hinge.
ferry(-boat) [fere(bot)] *nm* ferry.
fertile [fertil] *adj* fertile; **~ en incidents** eventful, packed with incidents.
fertilisant [fertilizã] *nm* fertilizer.
fertilisation [fertilizasjɔ̃] *nf* fertilization.
fertiliser [fertilize] *vt* to fertilize.
fertilité [fertilite] *nf* fertility.
féru, e [fery] *adj:* **~ de** with a keen interest in.
férule [feryl] *nf:* **être sous la ~ de qn** to be under sb's (iron) rule.
fervent, e [fervã, -ãt] *adj* fervent.
ferveur [fervœr] *nf* fervour (*BRIT*), fervor (*US*).
fesse [fes] *nf* buttock; **les ~s** the bottom *sg*, the buttocks.
fessée [fese] *nf* spanking.
fessier [fesje] *nm* (*fam*) behind.
festin [festɛ̃] *nm* feast.
festival [festival] *nm* festival.
festivalier [festivalje] *nm* festival-goer.
festivités [festivite] *nfpl* festivities, merry-making *sg*.
feston [festɔ̃] *nm* (*ARCHIT*) festoon; (*COUTURE*) scallop.
festoyer [festwaje] *vi* to feast.
fêtard [fetar] *nm* (*péj*) high liver, merry-maker.
fête [fet] *nf* (*religieuse*) feast; (*publique*) holiday; (*en famille etc*) celebration; (*kermesse*) fête, fair, festival; (*du nom*) feast day, name day; **faire la ~** to live it up; **faire ~ à qn** to give sb a warm welcome; **se faire une ~ de** to look forward to; to enjoy; **ça va être sa ~!** (*fam*) he's going to get it!; **jour de ~** holiday; **les ~s (de fin d'année)** the festive season; **la salle/le comité des ~s** the village hall/festival committee; **la ~ des Mères/Pères** Mother's/Father's Day; **~ de charité** charity fair *ou* fête; **~ foraine** (fun)fair; **~ mobile** movable feast (day); **la F~ Nationale** the national holiday.

Fête-Dieu [fetdjø] *nf:* **la ~** Corpus Christi.
fêter [fete] *vt* to celebrate; (*personne*) to have a celebration for.
fétiche [fetiʃ] *nm* fetish; **animal ~, objet ~** mascot.
fétichisme [fetiʃism(ə)] *nm* fetishism.
fétichiste [fetiʃist(ə)] *adj* fetishist.
fétide [fetid] *adj* fetid.
fétu [fety] *nm:* **~ de paille** wisp of straw.
feu¹ [fø] *adj inv:* **~ son père** his late father.
feu², x [fø] *nm* (*gén*) fire; (*signal lumineux*) light; (*de cuisinière*) ring; (*sensation de brûlure*) burning (sensation); **~x** *nmpl* fire *sg*; (*AUTO*) (traffic) lights; **tous ~x éteints** (*NAVIG, AUTO*) without lights; **au ~!** (*incendie*) fire!; **à ~ doux/vif** over a slow/brisk heat; **à petit ~** (*CULIN*) over a gentle heat; (*fig*) slowly; **faire ~** to fire; **ne pas faire long ~** (*fig*) not to last long; **commander le ~** (*MIL*) to give the order to (open) fire; **tué au ~** (*MIL*) killed in action; **mettre à ~** (*fusée*) to fire off; **pris entre deux ~x** caught in the crossfire; **en ~** on fire; **être tout ~ tout flamme (pour)** (*passion*) to be aflame with passion (for); (*enthousiasme*) to be fired with enthusiasm (for); **prendre ~** to catch fire; **mettre le ~ à** to set fire to, set on fire; **faire du ~** to make a fire; **avez-vous du ~?** (*pour cigarette*) have you (got) a light?; **~ rouge/vert/orange** (*AUTO*) red/green/amber (*BRIT*) *ou* yellow (*US*) light; **donner le ~ vert à qch/qn** (*fig*) to give sth/sb the go-ahead *ou* green light; **~ arrière** (*AUTO*) rear light; **~ d'artifice** firework; (*spectacle*) fireworks *pl*; **~ de camp** campfire; **~ de cheminée** chimney fire; **~ de joie** bonfire; **~ de paille** (*fig*) flash in the pan; **~x de brouillard** (*AUTO*) fog lights *ou* lamps; **~x de croisement** (*AUTO*) dipped (*BRIT*) *ou* dimmed (*US*) headlights; **~x de position** (*AUTO*) sidelights; **~x de route** (*AUTO*) headlights on full (*BRIT*) *ou* high (*US*) beam); **~x de stationnement** parking lights.
feuillage [fœjaʒ] *nm* foliage, leaves *pl*.
feuille [fœj] *nf* (*d'arbre*) leaf (*pl* leaves); **~ (de papier)** sheet (of paper); **rendre ~ blanche** (*SCOL*) to give in a blank paper; **~ d'or/de métal** gold/metal leaf; **~ de chou** (*péj: journal*) rag; **~ d'impôts** tax form; **~ de maladie** medical expenses claim form; **~ morte** dead leaf; **~ de paye** pay slip; **~ de présence** attendance sheet; **~ de température** temperature chart; **~ de vigne** (*BOT*) vine leaf; (*sur statue*) fig leaf; **~ volante** loose sheet.

feuillet [fœjɛ] *nm* leaf (*pl* leaves), page.
feuilletage [fœjtaʒ] *nm* (*aspect feuilleté*) flakiness.
feuilleté, e [fœjte] *adj* (*CULIN*) flaky; (*verre*) laminated.
feuilleter [fœjte] *vt* (*livre*) to leaf through.
feuilleton [fœjtɔ̃] *nm* serial.
feuillette [fœjɛt] *etc vb voir* **feuilleter**.
feuillu, e [fœjy] *adj* leafy ♦ *nm* broad-leaved tree.
feulement [følmɑ̃] *nm* growl.
feutre [føtʀ(ə)] *nm* felt; (*chapeau*) felt hat; (*stylo*) felt-tip(ped pen).
feutré, e [føtʀe] *adj* feltlike; (*pas, voix*) muffled.
feutrer [føtʀe] *vt* to felt; (*fig: bruits*) to muffle ♦ *vi*, **se ~** *vi* (*tissu*) to felt.
feutrine [føtʀin] *nf* (lightweight) felt.
fève [fɛv] *nf* broad bean; (*dans la galette des Rois*) charm (*hidden in cake eaten on Twelfth Night*).
février [fevʀije] *nm* February; *voir aussi* **juillet**.
fez [fɛz] *nm* fez.
FF *abr* (= franc français) FF.
FFA *sigle fpl* (= Forces françaises en Allemagne) French forces in Germany.
FFI *sigle fpl* = Forces françaises de l'intérieur (1942-45) ♦ *sigle m* member of the FFI.
FFL *sigle fpl* (= Forces françaises libres) Free French Army.
Fg *abr* = faubourg.
FGA *sigle m* (= Fonds de garantie automobile) fund financed through insurance premiums, to compensate victims of uninsured losses.
FGEN *sigle f* (= Fédération générale de l'éducation nationale) teachers' trade union.
fi [fi] *excl*: **faire ~ de** to snap one's fingers at.
fiabilité [fjabilite] *nf* reliability.
fiable [fjabl(ə)] *adj* reliable.
fiacre [fjakʀ(ə)] *nm* (hackney) cab *ou* carriage.
fiançailles [fjɑ̃sɑj] *nfpl* engagement *sg*.
fiancé, e [fjɑ̃se] *nm/f* fiancé/fiancée ♦ *adj*: **être ~ (à)** to be engaged (to).
fiancer [fjɑ̃se]: **se ~** *vi*: **se ~ (avec)** to become engaged (to).
fiasco [fjasko] *nm* fiasco.
fibranne [fibʀan] *nf* bonded fibre *ou* fiber (*US*).
fibre [fibʀ(ə)] *nf* fibre, fiber (*US*); **avoir la ~ paternelle/militaire** to be a born father/soldier; **~ optique** optical fibre *ou* fiber; **~ de verre** fibreglass (*BRIT*), fiberglass (*US*), glass fibre *ou* fiber.
fibreux, euse [fibʀø, -øz] *adj* fibrous; (*viande*) stringy.
fibrome [fibʀom] *nm* (*MÉD*) fibroma.
ficelage [fislaʒ] *nm* tying (up).
ficelé, e [fisle] *adj* (*fam*): **être mal ~** (*habillé*) to be badly got up; **bien/mal ~** (*conçu: roman, projet*) well/badly put together.
ficeler [fisle] *vt* to tie up.
ficelle [fisɛl] *nf* string *no pl*; (*morceau*) piece *ou*

length of string; (*pain*) stick of French bread; **~s** *pl* (*fig*) strings; **tirer sur la ~** (*fig*) to go too far.
fiche [fiʃ] *nf* (*carte*) (index) card; (*INFORM*) record; (*formulaire*) form; (*ÉLEC*) plug; **~ de paye** pay slip; **~ signalétique** (*POLICE*) identification card; **~ technique** data sheet, specification *ou* spec sheet.
ficher [fiʃe] *vt* (*dans un fichier*) to file; (*: POLICE*) to put on file; (*fam*) to do; (*: donner*) to give; (*: mettre*) to stick *ou* shove; (*planter*): **~ qch dans** to stick *ou* drive sth into; **~ qn à la porte** (*fam*) to chuck sb out; **fiche(-moi) le camp** (*fam*) clear off; **fiche-moi la paix** (*fam*) leave me alone; **se ~ dans** (*s'enfoncer*) to get stuck in, embed itself in; **se ~ de** (*fam*) to make fun of; not to care about.
fichier [fiʃje] *nm* (*gén*, *INFORM*) file; (*à cartes*) card index; **~ actif** *ou* **en cours d'utilisation** (*INFORM*) active file; **~ d'adresses** mailing list; **~ d'archives** (*INFORM*) archive file.
fichu, e [fiʃy] *pp de* **ficher** (*fam*) ♦ *adj* (*fam: fini, inutilisable*) bust, done for; (*: intensif*) wretched, darned ♦ *nm* (*foulard*) (head)scarf (*pl* -scarves); **être ~ de** to be capable of; **mal ~** feeling lousy; useless; **bien ~** great.
fictif, ive [fiktif, -iv] *adj* fictitious.
fiction [fiksjɔ̃] *nf* fiction; (*fait imaginé*) invention.
fictivement [fiktivmɑ̃] *adv* fictitiously.
fidèle [fidɛl] *adj*: **~ (à)** faithful (to) ♦ *nm/f* (*REL*): **les ~s** the faithful; (*à l'église*) the congregation.
fidèlement [fidɛlmɑ̃] *adv* faithfully.
fidélité [fidelite] *nf* faithfulness.
Fidji [fidʒi] *nfpl*: (**les îles**) **~** Fiji.
fiduciaire [fidysjɛʀ] *adj* fiduciary; **héritier ~** heir, trustee; **monnaie ~** fiat money.
fief [fjɛf] *nm* fief; (*fig*) preserve; stronghold.
fieffé, e [fjefe] *adj* (*ivrogne, menteur*) arrant, out-and-out.
fiel [fjɛl] *nm* gall.
fiente [fjɑ̃t] *nf* (bird) droppings *pl*.
fier¹ [fje]: **se ~ à** *vt* to trust.
fier², fière [fjɛʀ] *adj* proud; **~ de** proud of; **avoir fière allure** to cut a fine figure.
fièrement [fjɛʀmɑ̃] *adv* proudly.
fierté [fjɛʀte] *nf* pride.
fièvre [fjɛvʀ(ə)] *nf* fever; **avoir de la ~/39 de ~** to have a high temperature/a temperature of 39°C; **~ typhoïde** typhoid fever.
fiévreusement [fjevʀøzmɑ̃] *adv* (*fig*) feverishly.
fiévreux, euse [fjevʀø, -øz] *adj* feverish.
FIFA [fifa] *sigle f* (= Fédération internationale de Football association) FIFA.
fifre [fifʀ(ə)] *nm* fife; (*personne*) fife-player.
fig *abr* (= figure) fig.
figer [fiʒe] *vt* to congeal; (*fig: personne*) to freeze, root to the spot; **se ~** *vi* to congeal; to freeze; (*institutions etc*) to become set, stop evolving.

fignoler [fiɲɔle] *vt* to put the finishing touches to.

figue [fig] *nf* fig.

figuier [figje] *nm* fig tree.

figurant, e [figyʀɑ̃, -ɑ̃t] *nm/f* (*THÉÂT*) walk-on; (*CINÉ*) extra.

figuratif, ive [figyʀatif, -iv] *adj* representational, figurative.

figuration [figyʀɑsjɔ̃] *nf* walk-on parts *pl*; extras *pl*.

figure [figyʀ] *nf* (*visage*) face; (*image, tracé, forme, personnage*) figure; (*illustration*) picture, diagram; **faire ~ de** to look like; **faire bonne ~** to put up a good show; **faire triste ~** to be a sorry sight; **~ de rhétorique** figure of speech.

figuré, e [figyʀe] *adj* (*sens*) figurative.

figurer [figyʀe] *vi* to appear ♦ *vt* to represent; **se ~ que** to imagine that; **figurez-vous que ... would you believe that ...?**

figurine [figyʀin] *nf* figurine.

fil [fil] *nm* (*brin, fig: d'une histoire*) thread; (*du téléphone*) cable, wire; (*textile de lin*) linen; (*d'un couteau: tranchant*) edge; **au ~ des années** with the passing of the years; **au ~ de l'eau** with the stream *ou* current; **de ~ en aiguille** one thing leading to another; **ne tenir qu'à un ~** (*vie, réussite etc*) to hang by a thread; **donner du ~ à retordre à qn** to make life difficult for sb; **donner/recevoir un coup de ~** to make/get a phone call; (**à coudre** (sewing) thread *ou* yarn; **~ dentaire** dental floss; **~ électrique** electric wire; **~ de fer** wire; **~ de fer barbelé** barbed wire; **~ à pêche** fishing line; **~ à plomb** plumbline; **~ à souder** soldering wire.

filament [filamɑ̃] *nm* (*ÉLEC*) filament; (*de liquide*) trickle, thread.

filandreux, euse [filɑ̃dʀø, -øz] *adj* stringy.

filant, e [filɑ̃, -ɑ̃t] *adj*: **étoile ~e** shooting star.

filasse [filas] *adj inv* white blond.

filature [filatyʀ] *nf* (*fabrique*) mill; (*policière*) shadowing *no pl*, tailing *no pl*; **prendre qn en ~** to shadow *ou* tail sb.

fil-de-fériste [fildəfeʀist(ə)] *nm/f* high-wire artist.

file [fil] *nf* line; **~ (d'attente)** queue (*BRIT*), line (*US*); **prendre la ~** to join the (end of the) queue *ou* line; **prendre la ~ de droite** (*AUTO*) to move into the right-hand lane; **se mettre en ~** to form a line; (*AUTO*) to get into lane; **stationner en double ~** (*AUTO*) to double-park; **à la ~** *adv* (*d'affilée*) in succession; (*à la suite*) one after another; **à la** *ou* **en ~ indienne** in single file.

filer [file] *vt* (*tissu, toile, verre*) to spin; (*dérouler: câble etc*) to pay *ou* let out; (*prendre en filature*) to shadow, tail; (*fam: donner*): **~ qch à qn** to slip sb sth ♦ *vi* (*bas, maille, liquide, pâte*) to run; (*aller vite*) to fly past *ou* by; (*fam: partir*) to make off; **~ à l'anglaise** to take French leave; **~ doux** to behave o.s., toe the

line; **~ un mauvais coton** to be in a bad way.

filet [filɛ] *nm* net; (*CULIN*) fillet; (*d'eau, de sang*) trickle; **tendre un ~** (*suj: police*) to set a trap; **~ (à bagages)** (*RAIL*) luggage rack; **~ (à provisions)** string bag.

filetage [filtaʒ] *nm* threading; thread.

fileter [filte] *vt* to thread.

filial, e, aux [filjal, -o] *adj* filial ♦ *nf* (*COMM*) subsidiary; affiliate.

filiation [filjɑsjɔ̃] *nf* filiation.

filière [filjɛʀ] *nf*: **passer par la ~** to go through the (administrative) channels; **suivre la ~** to work one's way up (through the hierarchy).

filiforme [filifɔʀm(ə)] *adj* spindly; threadlike.

filigrane [filigʀan] *nm* (*d'un billet, timbre*) watermark; **en ~** (*fig*) showing just beneath the surface.

filin [filɛ̃] *nm* (*NAVIG*) rope.

fille [fij] *nf* girl; (*opposé à fils*) daughter; **vieille ~** old maid; **~ de joie** prostitute; **~ de salle** waitress.

fille-mère, *pl* filles-mères [fijmɛʀ] *nf* unmarried mother.

fillette [fijɛt] *nf* (little) girl.

filleul, e [fijœl] *nm/f* godchild, godson/daughter.

film [film] *nm* (*pour photo*) (roll of) film; (*œuvre*) film, picture, movie; (*couche*) film; **~ muet/parlant** silent/talking picture *ou* movie; **~ alimentaire** clingfilm; **~ d'animation** animated film; **~ policier** thriller.

filmer [filme] *vt* to film.

filon [filɔ̃] *nm* vein, lode; (*fig*) lucrative line, moneyspinner.

filou [filu] *nm* (*escroc*) swindler.

fils [fis] *nm* son; **~ de famille** moneyed young man; **~ à papa** (*péj*) daddy's boy.

filtrage [filtʀaʒ] *nm* filtering.

filtrant, e [filtʀɑ̃, -ɑ̃t] *adj* (*huile solaire etc*) filtering.

filtre [filtʀ(ə)] *nm* filter; "**~ ou sans ~?**" (*cigarettes*) "tipped or plain?"; **~ à air** air filter.

filtrer [filtʀe] *vt* to filter; (*fig: candidats, visiteurs*) to screen ♦ *vi* to filter (through).

fin¹ [fɛ̃] *nf* end; **~s** *nfpl* (*but*) ends; **(la) ~ mai, ~ mai** at the end of May; **en ~ de semaine** at the end of the week; **prendre ~** to come to an end; **toucher à sa ~** to be drawing to a close; **mettre ~ à** to put an end to; **mener à bonne ~** to bring to a successful conclusion; **à cette ~** to this end; **à toutes ~s utiles** for your information; **à la ~** in the end, eventually; **sans ~** *adj* endless ♦ *adv* endlessly; **~ de non-recevoir** (*JUR, ADMIN*) objection; **~ de section** (*de ligne d'autobus*) (fare) stage.

fin², e [fɛ̃, fin] *adj* (*papier, couche, fil*) thin; (*cheveux, poudre, pointe, visage*) fine; (*taille*) neat, slim; (*esprit, remarque*) subtle; shrewd ♦ *adv* (*moudre, couper*) finely ♦ *nm*: **vouloir jouer au plus ~ (avec qn)** to try to outsmart sb ♦ *nf* (*alcool*) liqueur brandy; **c'est** ~! (*ironique*) how clever!; ~ **prêt/soûl** quite ready/drunk; **un** ~ **gourmet** a gourmet; **un** ~ **tireur** a crack shot; **avoir la vue/l'ouïe** ~**e** to have sharp eyes/ears, have keen eyesight/hearing; **or/linge/vin** ~ fine gold/linen/wine; **le** ~ **fond de** the very depths of; **le** ~ **mot de** the real story behind; **la** ~**e fleur de** the flower of; **une** ~**e mouche** (*fig*) a sharp customer; ~**es herbes** mixed herbs.

final, e [final] *adj*, *nf* final ♦ *nm* (*MUS*) finale; **quarts de** ~**e** quarter finals; **8èmes/16èmes de** ~**e** 2nd/1st round (*in 5 round knock-out competition*).

finalement [finalmɑ̃] *adv* finally, in the end; (*après tout*) after all.

finaliste [finalist(ə)] *nm/f* finalist.

finalité [finalite] *nf* (*but*) aim, goal; (*fonction*) purpose.

finance [finɑ̃s] *nf* finance; ~**s** *nfpl* (*situation financière*) finances; (*activités financières*) finance *sg*; **moyennant** ~ for a fee *ou* consideration.

financement [finɑ̃smɑ̃] *nm* financing.

financer [finɑ̃se] *vt* to finance.

financier, ière [finɑ̃sje, -jɛʀ] *adj* financial ♦ *nm* financier.

financièrement [finɑ̃sjɛʀmɑ̃] *adv* financially.

finasser [finase] *vi* (*péj*) to wheel and deal.

finaud, e [fino, -od] *adj* wily.

fine [fin] *adj f*, *nf voir* **fin, e**.

finement [finmɑ̃] *adv* thinly; finely; neatly, slimly; subtly; shrewdly.

finesse [finɛs] *nf* thinness; fineness; neatness, slimness; subtlety; shrewdness; ~**s** *nfpl* (*subtilités*) niceties; finer points.

fini, e [fini] *adj* finished; (*MATH*) finite; (*intensif*): **un menteur** ~ a liar through and through ♦ *nm* (*d'un objet manufacturé*) finish.

finir [finiʀ] *vt* to finish ♦ *vi* to finish, end; ~ **quelque part** to end *ou* finish up somewhere; ~ **de faire** to finish doing; (*cesser*) to stop doing; ~ **par faire** to end *ou* finish up doing; **il finit par m'agacer** he's beginning to get on my nerves; ~ **en pointe/tragédie** to end in a point/in tragedy; **en** ~ **avec** to be *ou* have done with; **à n'en plus** ~ (*route, discussions*) never-ending; **il va mal** ~ he will come to a bad end; **c'est bientôt fini?** (*reproche*) have you quite finished?

finish [finiʃ] *nm* (*SPORT*) finish.

finissage [finisaʒ] *nm* finishing.

finisseur, euse [finisœʀ, -øz] *nm/f* (*SPORT*) strong finisher.

finition [finisjɔ̃] *nf* finishing; finish.

finlandais, e [fɛ̃lɑ̃dɛ, -ɛz] *adj* Finnish ♦ *nm/f*: **F**~, **e** Finn.

Finlande [fɛ̃lɑ̃d] *nf*: **la** ~ Finland.

finnois, e [finwa, -waz] *adj* Finnish ♦ *nm* (*LING*) Finnish.

fiole [fjɔl] *nf* phial.

fiord [fjɔʀ(d)] *nm* = **fjord**.

fioriture [fjɔʀityʀ] *nf* embellishment, flourish.

fioul [fjul] *nm* fuel oil.

firent [fiʀ] *vb voir* **faire**.

firmament [fiʀmamɑ̃] *nm* firmament, skies *pl*.

firme [fiʀm(ə)] *nf* firm.

fis [fi] *vb voir* **faire**.

fisc [fisk] *nm* tax authorities *pl*, ≈ Inland Revenue (*BRIT*), ≈ Internal Revenue Service (*US*).

fiscal, e, aux [fiskal, -o] *adj* tax *cpd*, fiscal.

fiscaliser [fiskalize] *vt* to subject to tax.

fiscaliste [fiskalist(ə)] *nm/f* tax specialist.

fiscalité [fiskalite] *nf* tax system; (*charges*) taxation.

fissible [fisibl(ə)] *adj* fissile.

fission [fisjɔ̃] *nf* fission.

fissure [fisyʀ] *nf* crack.

fissurer [fisyʀe] *vt*, **se** ~ *vi* to crack.

fiston [fistɔ̃] *nm* (*fam*) son, lad.

fit [fi] *vb voir* **faire**.

FIV *sigle f* (= *fécondation in vitro*) IVF.

fixage [fiksaʒ] *nm* (*PHOTO*) fixing.

fixateur [fiksatœʀ] *nm* (*PHOTO*) fixer; (*pour cheveux*) hair cream.

fixatif [fiksatif] *nm* fixative.

fixation [fiksasjɔ̃] *nf* fixing; fastening; setting; (*de ski*) binding; (*PSYCH*) fixation.

fixe [fiks(ə)] *adj* fixed; (*emploi*) steady, regular ♦ *nm* (*salaire*) basic salary; **à heure** ~ at a set time; **menu à prix** ~ set menu.

fixé, e [fikse] *adj* (*heure, jour*) appointed; **être** ~ (**sur**) to have made up one's mind (about); to know for certain (about).

fixement [fiksmɑ̃] *adv* fixedly, steadily.

fixer [fikse] *vt* (*attacher*): ~ **qch (à/sur)** to fix *ou* fasten sth (to/onto); (*déterminer*) to fix, set; (*CHIMIE, PHOTO*) to fix; (*poser son regard sur*) to look hard at, stare at; **se** ~ (*s'établir*) to settle down; ~ **son choix sur qch** to decide on sth; **se** ~ **sur** (*suj: attention*) to focus on.

fixité [fiksite] *nf* fixedness.

fjord [fjɔʀ(d)] *nm* fjord, fiord.

fl. *abr* (= *fleuve*) r, R; (= *florin*) fl.

flacon [flakɔ̃] *nm* bottle.

flagada [flagada] *adj inv* (*fam: fatigué*) shattered.

flagellation [flaʒɛlasjɔ̃] *nf* flogging.

flageller [flaʒele] *vt* to flog, scourge.

flageoler [flaʒɔle] *vi* to have knees like jelly.

flageolet [flaʒɔlɛ] *nm* (*MUS*) flageolet; (*CULIN*) dwarf kidney bean.

flagornerie [flagɔʀnəʀi] *nf* toadying, fawning.

flagorneur, euse [flagɔʀnœʀ, -øz] *nm/f* toady, fawner.

flagrant, e [flagʀɑ̃, -ɑ̃t] *adj* flagrant, blatant; **en** ~ **délit** in the act, in flagrante delicto.

flair [flɛʀ] *nm* sense of smell; (*fig*) intuition.

flairer [flɛʀe] *vt* (*humer*) to sniff (at); (*détecter*) to scent.

flamand, e [flamɑ̃, -ɑ̃d] *adj* Flemish ♦ *nm* (*LING*) Flemish ♦ *nm/f*: **F**~, **e** Fleming; **les F**~**s** the Flemish.

flamant [flamɑ̃] *nm* flamingo.
flambant [flɑ̃bɑ̃] *adv*: ~ **neuf** brand new.
flambé, e [flɑ̃be] *adj* (*CULIN*) flambé ♦ *nf* blaze; (*fig*) flaring-up, explosion.
flambeau, x [flɑ̃bo] *nm* (flaming) torch; **se passer le** ~ (*fig*) to hand down the (*ou* a) tradition.
flambée [flɑ̃be] *nf* (*feu*) blaze; (*COMM*): ~ **des prix** (sudden) shooting up of prices.
flamber [flɑ̃be] *vi* to blaze (up) ♦ *vt* (*poulet*) to singe; (*aiguille*) to sterilize.
flambeur, euse [flɑ̃bœʀ, -øz] *nm/f* big-time gambler.
flamboyant, e [flɑ̃bwajɑ̃, -ɑ̃t] *adj* blazing; flaming.
flamboyer [flɑ̃bwaje] *vi* to blaze (up); (*fig*) to flame.
flamenco [flamɛnko] *nm* flamenco.
flamingant, e [flamɛ̃gɑ̃, -ɑ̃t] *adj* Flemish-speaking ♦ *nm/f*: **F~, e** Flemish speaker; (*POL*) Flemish nationalist.
flamme [flam] *nf* flame; (*fig*) fire, fervour; **en ~s** on fire, ablaze.
flammèche [flamɛʃ] *nf* (flying) spark.
flammerole [flamʀɔl] *nf* will-o'-the-wisp.
flan [flɑ̃] *nm* (*CULIN*) custard tart *ou* pie.
flanc [flɑ̃] *nm* side; (*MIL*) flank; **à ~ de colline** on the hillside; **prêter le ~ à** (*fig*) to lay o.s. open to.
flancher [flɑ̃ʃe] *vi* (*cesser de fonctionner*) to fail, pack up; (*ARMÉE*) to quit.
Flandre [flɑ̃dʀ(ə)] *nf*: **la** ~ (*aussi*: **les ~s**) Flanders.
flanelle [flanɛl] *nf* flannel.
flâner [flɑne] *vi* to stroll.
flânerie [flɑnʀi] *nf* stroll.
flâneur, euse [flɑnœʀ, -øz] *adj* idle ♦ *nm/f* stroller.
flanquer [flɑ̃ke] *vt* to flank; (*fam: jeter*): ~ **par terre/à la porte** to fling to the ground/chuck out; (*: donner*): ~ **la frousse à qn** to put the wind up sb, give sb an awful fright.
flapi, e [flapi] *adj* dog-tired.
flaque [flak] *nf* (*d'eau*) puddle; (*d'huile, de sang etc*) pool.
flash, *pl* **flashes** [flaʃ] *nm* (*PHOTO*) flash; ~ **(d'information)** newsflash.
flasque [flask(ə)] *adj* flabby ♦ *nf* (*flacon*) flask.
flatter [flate] *vt* to flatter; (*caresser*) to stroke; **se ~ de qch** to pride o.s. on sth.
flatterie [flatʀi] *nf* flattery.
flatteur, euse [flatœʀ, -øz] *adj* flattering ♦ *nm/f* flatterer.
flatulence [flatylɑ̃s], **flatuosité** [flatɥozite] *nf* (*MÉD*) flatulence, wind.
FLB *abr* (= *franco long du bord*) FAS ♦ *sigle m* (*POL*) = *Front de libération de la Bretagne*.
FLC *sigle m* = *Front de libération de la Corse*.
fléau, x [fleo] *nm* scourge, curse; (*de balance*) beam; (*pour le blé*) flail.
fléchage [fleʃaʒ] *nm* (*d'un itinéraire*) signposting.

flèche [flɛʃ] *nf* arrow; (*de clocher*) spire; (*de grue*) jib; (*trait d'esprit, critique*) shaft; **monter en** ~ (*fig*) to soar, rocket; **partir en** ~ (*fig*) to be off like a shot; **à** ~ **variable** (*avion*) swing-wing *cpd*.
flécher [fleʃe] *vt* to arrow, mark with arrows.
fléchette [fleʃɛt] *nf* dart; **~s** *nfpl* (*jeu*) darts *sg*.
fléchir [fleʃiʀ] *vt* (*corps, genou*) to bend; (*fig*) to sway, weaken ♦ *vi* (*poutre*) to sag, bend; (*fig*) to weaken, flag; (*: baisser: prix*) to fall off.
fléchissement [fleʃismɑ̃] *nm* bending; sagging; flagging; (*de l'économie*) dullness.
flegmatique [flɛgmatik] *adj* phlegmatic.
flegme [flɛgm(ə)] *nm* composure.
flemmard, e [flemaʀ, -aʀd(ə)] *nm/f* lazybones *sg*, loafer.
flemme [flɛm] *nf* (*fam*): **j'ai la** ~ **de faire** I can't be bothered to do.
flétan [fletɑ̃] *nm* (*ZOOL*) halibut.
flétrir [fletʀiʀ] *vt* to wither; (*stigmatiser*) to condemn (in the most severe terms); **se** ~ *vi* to wither.
fleur [flœʀ] *nf* flower; (*d'un arbre*) blossom; **être en** ~ (*arbre*) to be in blossom; **tissu à ~s** flowered *ou* flowery fabric; **la (fine)** ~ **de** (*fig*) the flower of; **être** ~ **bleue** to be soppy *ou* sentimental; **à** ~ **de terre** just above the ground; **faire une** ~ **à qn** to do sb a favour (*BRIT*) *ou* favor (*US*); ~ **de lis** fleur-de-lis.
fleurer [flœʀe] *vt*: ~ **la lavande** to have the scent of lavender.
fleuret [flœʀɛ] *nm* (*arme*) foil; (*sport*) fencing.
fleurette [flœʀɛt] *nf*: **conter** ~ **à qn** to whisper sweet nothings to sb.
fleuri, e [flœʀi] *adj* in flower *ou* bloom; surrounded by flowers; (*fig: style*) flowery; (*: teint*) glowing.
fleurir [flœʀiʀ] *vi* (*rose*) to flower; (*arbre*) to blossom; (*fig*) to flourish ♦ *vt* (*tombe*) to put flowers on; (*chambre*) to decorate with flowers.
fleuriste [flœʀist(ə)] *nm/f* florist.
fleuron [flœʀɔ̃] *nm* jewel (*fig*).
fleuve [flœv] *nm* river; **roman-~** saga; **discours-~** interminable speech.
flexibilité [flɛksibilite] *nf* flexibility.
flexible [flɛksibl(ə)] *adj* flexible.
flexion [flɛksjɔ̃] *nf* flexing, bending; (*LING*) inflection.
flibustier [flibystje] *nm* buccaneer.
flic [flik] *nm* (*fam: péj*) cop.
flingue [flɛ̃g] *nm* (*fam*) shooter.
flipper *nm* [flipœʀ] pinball (machine) ♦ *vi* [flipe] (*fam: être déprimé*) to feel down, be on a downer; (*: être exalté*) to freak out.
flirt [flœʀt] *nm* flirting; (*personne*) boyfriend, girlfriend.
flirter [flœʀte] *vi* to flirt.
FLN *sigle m* = *Front de libération nationale (during the Algerian war).*
FLNKS *sigle m* (= *Front de libération nationale kanak et socialiste*) *political movement in New*

Caledonia.
flocon [flɔkɔ̃] *nm* flake; (*de laine etc: boule:te*) flock; **~s d'avoine** oatflakes, porridge oats.
floconneux, euse [flɔkɔnø, -øz] *adj* fluffy, fleecy.
flonflons [flɔ̃flɔ̃] *nmpl* blare *sg*.
flopée [flɔpe] *nf*: **une ~ de** loads of.
floraison [flɔʀɛzɔ̃] *nf* (*voir fleurir*) flowering; blossoming; flourishing.
floral, e, aux [flɔʀal, -o] *adj* floral, flower *cpd*.
floralies [flɔʀali] *nfpl* flower show *sg*.
flore [flɔʀ] *nf* flora.
Florence [flɔʀɑ̃s] *n* (*ville*) Florence.
florentin, e [flɔʀɑ̃tɛ̃, -in] *adj* Florentine.
floriculture [flɔʀikyltyʀ] *nf* flower-growing.
florissant, e [flɔʀisɑ̃, -ɑ̃t] *vb voir* **fleurir** ♦ *adj* flourishing; (*santé, teint, mine*) blooming.
flot [flo] *nm* flood, stream; (*marée*) flood tide; **~s** *nmpl* (*de la mer*) waves; **être à ~** (*NAVIG*) to be afloat; (*fig*) to be on an even keel; **à ~s** (*couler*) in torrents; **entrer à ~s** to stream *ou* pour in.
flottage [flɔtaʒ] *nm* (*du bois*) floating.
flottaison [flɔtɛzɔ̃] *nf*: **ligne de ~** waterline.
flottant, e [flɔtɑ̃, -ɑ̃t] *adj* (*vêtement*) loose(-fitting); (*cours, barème*) floating.
flotte [flɔt] *nf* (*NAVIG*) fleet; (*fam*) water; rain.
flottement [flɔtmɑ̃] *nm* (*fig*) wavering, hesitation; (*ÉCON*) floating.
flotter [flɔte] *vi* to float; (*nuage, odeur*) to drift; (*drapeau*) to fly; (*vêtements*) to hang loose ♦ *vb impers* (*fam: pleuvoir*): **il flotte** it's raining ♦ *vt* to float; **faire ~** to float.
flotteur [flɔtœʀ] *nm* float.
flottille [flɔtij] *nf* flotilla.
flou, e [flu] *adj* fuzzy, blurred; (*fig*) woolly (*BRIT*), vague; (*non ajusté: robe*) loose(-fitting).
flouer [flue] *vt* to swindle.
FLQ *abr* (= *franco long du quai*) FAQ.
fluctuant, e [flyktɥɑ̃, -ɑ̃t] *adj* (*prix, cours*) fluctuating; (*opinions*) changing.
fluctuation [flyktɥasjɔ̃] *nf* fluctuation.
fluctuer [flyktɥe] *vi* to fluctuate.
fluet, te [flyɛ, -ɛt] *adj* thin, slight; (*voix*) thin.
fluide [flyid] *adj* fluid; (*circulation etc*) flowing freely ♦ *nm* fluid; (*force*) (mysterious) power.
fluidifier [flyidifje] *vt* to make fluid.
fluidité [flyidite] *nf* fluidity; free flow.
fluor [flyɔʀ] *nm* fluorine.
fluoré, e [flyɔʀe] *adj* fluoridated.
fluorescent, e [flyɔʀesɑ̃, -ɑ̃t] *adj* fluorescent.
flûte [flyt] *nf* (*aussi*: **~ traversière**) flute; (*verre*) flute glass; (*pain*) long loaf (*pl* loaves); **petite ~** piccolo (*pl* -s); **~!** drat it!; **~ (à bec)** recorder; **~ de Pan** panpipes *pl*.
flûtiste [flytist(ə)] *nm/f* flautist, flute player.
fluvial, e, aux [flyvjal, -o] *adj* river *cpd*, fluvial.
flux [fly] *nm* incoming tide; (*écoulement*) flow; **le ~ et le reflux** the ebb and flow.

fluxion [flyksjɔ̃] *nf*: **~ de poitrine** pneumonia.
FM *sigle f* (= *frequency modulation*) FM.
Fme *abr* (= *femme*) W.
FMI *sigle m* (= *Fonds monétaire international*) IMF.
FN *sigle m* (= *Front national*) ≈ NF (= *National Front*).
FNAC [fnak] *sigle f* (= *Fédération nationale des achats des cadres*) chain of discount shops (*hi-fi, photo etc*).
FNAH *sigle m* = *Fonds national d'amélioration de l'habitat*.
FNEF [fnɛf] *sigle f* (= *Fédération nationale des étudiants de France*) student union.
FNSEA *sigle f* (= *Fédération nationale des syndicats d'exploitants agricoles*) farmers' union.
FO *sigle f* (= *Force ouvrière*) trades union.
foc [fɔk] *nm* jib.
focal, e, aux [fɔkal, -o] *adj* focal ♦ *nf* focal length.
focaliser [fɔkalize] *vt* to focus.
foehn [føn] *nm* foehn, föhn.
fœtal, e, aux [fetal, -o] *adj* fetal, foetal (*BRIT*).
fœtus [fetys] *nm* fetus, foetus (*BRIT*).
foi [fwa] *nf* faith; **sous la ~ du serment** under *ou* on oath; **ajouter ~ à** to lend credence to; **faire ~** (*prouver*) to be evidence; **digne de ~** reliable; **sur la ~ de** on the word *ou* strength of; **être de bonne/mauvaise ~** to be in good faith/not to be in good faith; **ma ~!** well!
foie [fwa] *nm* liver; **~ gras** foie gras.
foin [fwɛ̃] *nm* hay; **faire les ~s** to make hay; **faire du ~** (*fam*) to kick up a row.
foire [fwaʀ] *nf* fair; (*fête foraine*) (fun) fair; (*fig: désordre, confusion*) bear garden; **faire la ~** to whoop it up; **~ (exposition)** trade fair.
fois [fwa] *nf* time; **une/deux ~** once/twice; **trois/vingt ~** three/twenty times; **2 ~ 2 2** times 2; **deux/quatre ~ plus grand (que)** twice/four times as big (as); **une ~** (*passé*) once; (*futur*) sometime; **une (bonne) ~ pour toutes** once and for all; **encore une ~** again, once more; **il était une ~** once upon a time; **une ~ que c'est fait** once it's done; **une ~ parti** once he (*ou* I etc) had left; **des ~** (*parfois*) sometimes; **si des ~ ...** (*fam*) if ever ...; **non mais des ~!** (*fam*) (now) look here!; **à la ~** (*ensemble*) (all) at once; **à la ~ grand et beau** both tall and handsome.
foison [fwazɔ̃] *nf*: **une ~ de** an abundance of; **à ~** *adv* in plenty.
foisonnant, e [fwazɔnɑ̃, -ɑ̃t] *adj* teeming.
foisonnement [fwazɔnmɑ̃] *nm* profusion, abundance.
foisonner [fwazɔne] *vi* to abound; **~ en ou de** to abound in.
fol [fɔl] *adj m voir* **fou**.
folâtre [fɔlɑtʀ(ə)] *adj* playful.
folâtrer [fɔlɑtʀe] *vi* to frolic (about).
folichon, ne [fɔliʃɔ̃, -ɔn] *adj*: **ça n'a rien de ~** it's not a lot of fun.

folie [fɔli] *nf* (*d'une décision, d'un acte*) madness, folly; (*état*) madness, insanity; (*acte*) folly; **la ~ des grandeurs** delusions of grandeur; **faire des ~s** (*en dépenses*) to be extravagant.

folklore [fɔlklɔʀ] *nm* folklore.

folklorique [fɔlklɔʀik] *adj* folk *cpd*; (*fam*) weird.

folle [fɔl] *adj f, nf voir* **fou**.

follement [fɔlmɑ̃] *adv* (*très*) madly, wildly.

follet [fɔlɛ] *adj m*: **feu ~** will-o'-the-wisp.

fomentateur, trice [fɔmɑ̃tatœʀ, -tʀis] *nm/f* agitator.

fomenter [fɔmɑ̃te] *vt* to stir up, foment.

foncé, e [fɔ̃se] *adj* dark; **bleu ~** dark blue.

foncer [fɔ̃se] *vt* to make darker; (*CULIN: moule etc*) to line ♦ *vi* to go darker; (*fam: aller vite*) to tear *ou* belt along; **~ sur** to charge at.

fonceur, euse [fɔ̃sœʀ, -øz] *nm/f* whizz kid.

foncier, ière [fɔ̃sje, -jɛʀ] *adj* (*honnêteté etc*) basic, fundamental; (*malhonnêteté*) deep-rooted; (*COMM*) real estate *cpd*.

foncièrement [fɔ̃sjɛʀmɑ̃] *adv* basically; (*absolument*) thoroughly.

fonction [fɔ̃ksjɔ̃] *nf* (*rôle, MATH, LING*) function; (*emploi, poste*) post, position; **~s** (*professionnelles*) duties; **entrer en ~s** to take up one's post *ou* duties; to take up office; **voiture de ~** company car; **être ~ de** (*dépendre de*) to depend on; **en ~ de** (*par rapport à*) according to; **faire ~ de** to serve as; **la ~ publique** the state *ou* civil (*BRIT*) service.

fonctionnaire [fɔ̃ksjɔnɛʀ] *nm/f* state employee *ou* official; (*dans l'administration*) ≈ civil servant (*BRIT*).

fonctionnariser [fɔ̃ksjɔnaʀize] *vt* (*ADMIN: personne*) to give the status of a state employee to.

fonctionnel, le [fɔ̃ksjɔnɛl] *adj* functional.

fonctionnellement [fɔ̃ksjɔnɛlmɑ̃] *adv* functionally.

fonctionnement [fɔ̃ksjɔnmɑ̃] *nm* working; functioning; operation.

fonctionner [fɔ̃ksjɔne] *vi* to work, function; (*entreprise*) to operate, function; **faire ~** to work, operate.

fond [fɔ̃] *nm voir aussi* **fonds**; (*d'un récipient, trou*) bottom; (*d'une salle, scène*) back; (*d'un tableau, décor*) background; (*opposé à la forme*) content; (*petite quantité*): **un ~ de verre** a drop; (*SPORT*): **le ~** long distance (running); **course/épreuve de ~** long-distance race/trial; **au ~ de** at the bottom of; at the back of; **aller au ~ des choses** to get to the root of things; **le ~ de sa pensée** his (*ou* her) true thoughts *ou* feelings; **sans ~** *adj* bottomless; **envoyer par le ~** (*NAVIG: couler*) to sink, scuttle; **à ~** *adv* (*connaître, soutenir*) thoroughly; (*appuyer, visser*) right down *ou* home; **à ~** (*de train*) *adv* (*fam*) full tilt; **dans le ~, au ~** *adv* (*en somme*) basically, really; **de ~ en comble** *adv* from top to bottom; **~**

sonore background noise; background music; **~ de teint** (*make-up*) foundation.

fondamental, e, aux [fɔ̃damɑ̃tal, -o] *adj* fundamental.

fondamentalement [fɔ̃damɑ̃talmɑ̃] *adv* fundamentally.

fondamentalisme [fɔ̃damɑ̃talism(ə)] *nm* fundamentalism.

fondamentaliste [fɔ̃damɑ̃talist(ə)] *adj, nm/f* fundamentalist.

fondant, e [fɔ̃dɑ̃, -ɑ̃t] *adj* (*neige*) melting; (*poire*) that melts in the mouth; (*chocolat*) fondant.

fondateur, trice [fɔ̃datœʀ, -tʀis] *nm/f* founder; **membre ~** founder (*BRIT*) *ou* founding (*US*) member.

fondation [fɔ̃dasjɔ̃] *nf* founding; (*établissement*) foundation; **~s** *nfpl* (*d'une maison*) foundations; **travail de ~** foundation works *pl*.

fondé, e [fɔ̃de] *adj* (*accusation etc*) well-founded ♦ *nm*: **~ de pouvoir** authorized representative; **mal ~** unfounded; **être ~ à croire** to have grounds for believing *ou* good reason to believe.

fondement [fɔ̃dmɑ̃] *nm* (*derrière*) behind; **~s** *nmpl* foundations; **sans ~** *adj* (*rumeur etc*) groundless, unfounded.

fonder [fɔ̃de] *vt* to found; (*fig*): **~ qch sur** to base sth on; **se ~ sur** (*suj: personne*) to base o.s. on; **~ un foyer** (*se marier*) to set up home.

fonderie [fɔ̃dʀi] *nf* smelting works *sg*.

fondeur, euse [fɔ̃dœʀ, -øz] *nm/f* (*skieur*) long-distance skier ♦ *nm*: (**ouvrier**) ~ caster.

fondre [fɔ̃dʀ(ə)] *vt* to melt; (*dans l'eau: sucre, sel*) to dissolve; (*fig: mélanger*) to merge, blend ♦ *vi* to melt; to dissolve; (*fig*) to melt away; (*se précipiter*): **~ sur** to swoop down on; **se ~** *vi* (*se combiner, se confondre*) to merge into each other; to dissolve; **~ en larmes** to dissolve into tears.

fondrière [fɔ̃dʀijɛʀ] *nf* rut.

fonds [fɔ̃] *nm* (*de bibliothèque*) collection; (*COMM*): **~ (de commerce)** business; (*fig*): **~ de probité** *etc* fund of integrity *etc* ♦ *nmpl* (*argent*) funds; **à ~ perdus** *adv* with little or no hope of getting the money back; **être en ~** to be in funds; **mise de ~** investment, (capital) outlay; **F~ monétaire international (FMI)** International Monetary Fund (IMF); **~ de roulement** *nm* float.

fondu, e [fɔ̃dy] *adj* (*beurre, neige*) melted; (*métal*) molten ♦ *nm* (*CINÉ*): **~ (enchaîné)** dissolve ♦ *nf* (*CULIN*) fondue.

fongicide [fɔ̃ʒisid] *nm* fungicide.

font [fɔ̃] *vb voir* **faire**.

fontaine [fɔ̃tɛn] *nf* fountain; (*source*) spring.

fontanelle [fɔ̃tanɛl] *nf* fontanelle.

fonte [fɔ̃t] *nf* melting; (*métal*) cast iron; **la ~ des neiges** the (spring) thaw.

fonts baptismaux [fɔ̃batismo] *nmpl* (baptismal) font *sg.*

foot(ball) [fut(bol)] *nm* football, soccer.

footballeur, euse [futbolœR, -øz] *nm/f* footballer (*BRIT*), football *ou* soccer player.

footing [futiŋ] *nm* jogging; **faire du** ~ **to go jogging.**

for [fɔR] *nm:* **dans** *ou* **en son** ~ **intérieur** in one's heart of hearts.

forage [fɔRaʒ] *nm* drilling, boring.

forain, e [fɔRɛ̃, -ɛn] *adj* fairground *cpd* ♦ *nm* (*marchand*) stallholder; (*acteur etc*) fairground entertainer.

forban [fɔRbɑ̃] *nm* (*pirate*) pirate; (*escroc*) crook.

forçat [fɔRsa] *nm* convict.

force [fɔRs(ə)] *nf* strength; (*puissance: surnaturelle etc*) power; (*PHYSIQUE, MÉCANIQUE*) force; ~**s** *nfpl* (*physiques*) strength *sg;* (*MIL*) forces; (*effectifs*): **d'importantes** ~**s de police** large contingents of police; **avoir de la** ~ to be strong; **être à bout de** ~ to have no strength left; **à la** ~ **du poignet** (*fig*) by the sweat of one's brow; **à** ~ **de faire** by dint of doing; **arriver en** ~ (*nombreux*) to arrive in force; **cas de** ~ **majeure** case of absolute necessity; (*ASSURANCES*) act of God; ~ **de la nature** natural force; **de** ~ *adv* forcibly, by force; **de toutes mes/ses** ~**s** with all my/his strength; **par la** ~ using force; **par la** ~ **des choses/d'habitude** by force of circumstances/habit; **à toute** ~ (*absolument*) at all costs; **faire** ~ **de rames/voiles** to ply the oars/cram on sail; **être de** ~ **à faire** to be up to doing; **de première** ~ first class; **la** ~ **armée** (*les troupes*) the army; ~ **d'âme** fortitude; ~ **de frappe** strike force; ~ **d'inertie** force of inertia; **la** ~ **publique** the authorities responsible for public order; ~**s d'intervention** (*MIL, POLICE*) peace-keeping force *sg;* **les** ~**s de l'ordre** the police.

forcé, e [fɔRse] *adj* forced; (*bain*) unintended; (*inevitable*): **c'est** ~! it's inevitable!, it HAS to be!

forcément [fɔRsemɑ̃] *adv* necessarily; inevitably; (*bien sûr*) of course.

forcené, e [fɔRsəne] *adj* frenzied ♦ *nm/f* maniac.

forceps [fɔRsɛps] *nm* forceps *pl.*

forcer [fɔRse] *vt* (*contraindre*): ~ **qn à faire** to force sb to do; (*porte, serrure, plante*) to force; (*moteur, voix*) to strain ♦ *vi* (*SPORT*) to overtax o.s.; **se** ~ **à faire qch** to force o.s. to do sth; ~ **la dose/l'allure** to overdo it/ increase the pace; ~ **l'attention/le respect** to command attention/respect; ~ **la consigne** to bypass orders.

forcing [fɔRsiŋ] *nm* (*SPORT*): **faire le** ~ to pile on the pressure.

forcir [fɔRsiR] *vi* (*grossir*) to broaden out; (*vent*) to freshen.

forclore [fɔRklɔR] *vt* (*JUR: personne*) to debar.

forclusion [fɔRklyzjɔ̃] *nf* (*JUR*) debarment.

forer [fɔRe] *vt* to drill, bore.

forestier, ière [fɔRɛstje, -jɛR] *adj* forest *cpd.*

foret [fɔRɛ] *nm* drill.

forêt [fɔRɛ] *nf* forest; **Office National des F**~**s** (*ADMIN*) ≈ Forestry Commission (*BRIT*), ≈ National Forest Service (*US*); **la F**~ **Noire** the Black Forest.

foreuse [fɔRøz] *nf* (electric) drill.

forfait [fɔRfɛ] *nm* (*COMM*) fixed *ou* set price; all-in deal *ou* price; (*crime*) infamy; **déclarer** ~ to withdraw; **gagner par** ~ to win by a walkover; **travailler à** ~ to work for a lump sum.

forfaitaire [fɔRfɛtɛR] *adj* set; inclusive.

forfait-vacances, *pl* **forfaits-vacances** [fɔRfɛvakɑ̃s] *nm* package holiday.

forfanterie [fɔRfɑ̃tRi] *nf* boastfulness *no pl.*

forge [fɔRʒ(ə)] *nf* forge, smithy.

forgé, e [fɔRʒe] *adj:* ~ **de toutes pièces** (*histoire*) completely fabricated.

forger [fɔRʒe] *vt* to forge; (*fig: personnalité*) to form; (*: prétexte*) to contrive, make up.

forgeron [fɔRʒərɔ̃] *nm* (black)smith.

formaliser [fɔRmalize] *vt:* **se** ~ *vi:* **se** ~ **(de)** to take offence (at).

formalisme [fɔRmalism(ə)] *nm* formality.

formalité [fɔRmalite] *nf* formality.

format [fɔRma] *nm* size; **petit** ~ small size; (*PHOTO*) 35 mm (film).

formater [fɔRmate] *vt* (*disque*) to format; **non formaté** unformatted.

formateur, trice [fɔRmatœR, -tRis] *adj* formative.

formation [fɔRmasjɔ̃] *nf* forming; (*éducation*) training; (*MUS*) group; (*MIL, AVIAT, GÉO*) formation; **la** ~ **permanente** *ou* **continue** continuing education; **la** ~ **professionnelle** vocational training.

forme [fɔRm(ə)] *nf* (*gén*) form; (*d'un objet*) shape, form; ~**s** *nfpl* (*bonnes manières*) proprieties; (*d'une femme*) figure *sg;* **en** ~ **de poire** pear-shaped, in the shape of a pear; **sous** ~ **de** in the form of; in the guise of; **sous** ~ **de cachets** in the form of tablets; **être en** (**bonne** *ou* **pleine**) ~, **avoir la** ~ (*SPORT etc*) to be on form; **en bonne et due** ~ in due form; **pour la** ~ for the sake of form; **sans autre** ~ **de procès** (*fig*) without further ado; **prendre** ~ to take shape.

formel, le [fɔRmɛl] *adj* (*preuve, décision*) definite, positive; (*logique*) formal.

formellement [fɔRmɛlmɑ̃] *adv* (*interdit*) strictly.

former [fɔRme] *vt* (*gén*) to form; (*éduquer: soldat, ingénieur etc*) to train; **se** ~ *to* form; to train.

formidable [fɔRmidabl(ə)] *adj* tremendous.

formidablement [fɔRmidabləmɑ̃] *adv* tremendously.

formol [fɔRmɔl] *nm* formalin, formol.

formosan, e [fɔRmozɑ̃, -an] *adj* Formosan.

Formose [fɔRmoz] *nm* Formosa.

formulaire [fɔʀmylɛʀ] *nm* form.
formulation [fɔʀmylɑsjɔ̃] *nf* (*voir vb*) formulation; expression.
formule [fɔʀmyl] *nf* (*gén*) formula; (*formulaire*) form; **selon la ~ consacrée** as one says; **~ de politesse** polite phrase; (*en fin de lettre*) letter ending.
formuler [fɔʀmyle] *vt* (*émettre: réponse, vœux*) to formulate; (*expliciter: sa pensée*) to express.
forniquer [fɔʀnike] *vi* to fornicate.
FORPRONU [fɔʀpʀɔny] *sigle f* (= *Force de protection des Nations unies*) UNPROFOR.
fort, e [fɔʀ, fɔʀt(ə)] *adj* strong; (*intensité, rendement*) high, great; (*corpulent*) large; (*doué*): **être ~ (en)** to be good (at) ♦ *adv* (*serrer, frapper*) hard; (*sonner*) loud(ly); (*beaucoup*) greatly, very much; (*très*) very ♦ *nm* (*édifice*) fort; (*point fort*) strong point, forte; (*gén pl: personne, pays*): **le ~, les ~s** the strong; **c'est un peu ~!** it's a bit much!; **à plus ~e raison** even more so, all the more reason; **avoir ~ à faire avec qn** to have a hard job with sb; **se faire ~ de faire** to claim one can do; **~ bien/peu** very well/few; **au plus ~ de** (*au milieu de*) in the thick of, at the height of; **~e tête** rebel.
fortement [fɔʀtəmɑ̃] *adv* strongly; (*s'intéresser*) deeply.
forteresse [fɔʀtəʀɛs] *nf* fortress.
fortifiant [fɔʀtifjɑ̃] *nm* tonic.
fortifications [fɔʀtifikasjɔ̃] *nfpl* fortifications.
fortifier [fɔʀtifje] *vt* to strengthen, fortify; (*MIL*) to fortify; **se ~** *vi* (*personne, santé*) to grow stronger.
fortin [fɔʀtɛ̃] *nm* (small) fort.
fortiori [fɔʀtjɔʀi]: **à ~** *adv* all the more so.
FORTRAN [fɔʀtʀɑ̃] *nm* FORTRAN.
fortuit, e [fɔʀtɥi, -it] *adj* fortuitous, chance *cpd*.
fortuitement [fɔʀtɥitmɑ̃] *adv* fortuitously.
fortune [fɔʀtyn] *nf* fortune; **faire ~** to make one's fortune; **de ~** *adj* makeshift; (*compagnon*) chance *cpd*.
fortuné, e [fɔʀtyne] *adj* wealthy, well-off.
forum [fɔʀɔm] *nm* forum.
fosse [fos] *nf* (*grand trou*) pit; (*tombe*) grave; **la ~ aux lions/ours** the lions' den/bear pit; **~ commune** common *ou* communal grave; **~ (d'orchestre)** (orchestra) pit; **~ à purin** cesspit; **~ septique** septic tank; **~s nasales** nasal fossae.
fossé [fose] *nm* ditch; (*fig*) gulf, gap.
fossette [fosɛt] *nf* dimple.
fossile [fosil] *nm* fossil ♦ *adj* fossilized, fossil *cpd*.
fossilisé, e [fosilize] *adj* fossilized.
fossoyeur [foswajœʀ] *nm* gravedigger.
fou (fol), folle [fu, fɔl] *adj* mad, crazy; (*déréglé etc*) wild, erratic; (*mèche*) stray; (*herbe*) wild; (*fam: extrême, très grand*) terrific, tremendous ♦ *nm/f* madman/woman ♦ *nm* (*du roi*)

jester, fool; (*ÉCHECS*) bishop; **~ à lier, ~ furieux (folle furieuse)** raving mad; **être ~ de** to be mad *ou* crazy about; (*chagrin, joie, colère*) to be wild with; **faire le ~** to play *ou* act the fool; **avoir le ~ rire** to have the giggles.
foucade [fukad] *nf* caprice.
foudre [fudʀ(ə)] *nf* lightning; **~s** *nfpl* (*fig: colère*) wrath *sg*.
foudroyant, e [fudʀwajɑ̃, -ɑ̃t] *adj* devastating; (*maladie, poison*) violent.
foudroyer [fudʀwaje] *vt* to strike down; **~ qn du regard** to look daggers at sb; **il a été foudroyé** he was struck by lightning.
fouet [fwɛ] *nm* whip; (*CULIN*) whisk; **de plein ~** *adv* head on.
fouettement [fwɛtmɑ̃] *nm* lashing *no pl*.
fouetter [fwete] *vt* to whip; to whisk.
fougasse [fugas] *nf* type of flat pastry.
fougère [fuʒɛʀ] *nf* fern.
fougue [fug] *nf* ardour (*BRIT*), ardor (*US*), spirit.
fougueusement [fugøzmɑ̃] *adv* ardently.
fougueux, euse [fugø, -øz] *adj* fiery, ardent.
fouille [fuj] *nf* search; **~s** *nfpl* (*archéologiques*) excavations; **passer à la ~** to be searched.
fouillé, e [fuje] *adj* detailed.
fouiller [fuje] *vt* to search; (*creuser*) to dig; (*: suj: archéologue*) to excavate; (*approfondir: étude etc*) to go into ♦ *vi* (*archéologue*) to excavate; **~ dans/parmi** to rummage in/among.
fouillis [fuji] *nm* jumble, muddle.
fouine [fwin] *nf* stone marten.
fouiner [fwine] *vi* (*péj*): **~ dans** to nose around *ou* about in.
fouineur, euse [fwinœʀ, -øz] *adj* nosey ♦ *nm/f* nosey parker, snooper.
fouir [fwiʀ] *vt* to dig.
fouisseur, euse [fwisœʀ, -øz] *adj* burrowing.
foulage [fulaʒ] *nm* pressing.
foulante [fulɑ̃t] *adj f*: **pompe ~** force pump.
foulard [fulaʀ] *nm* scarf (*pl* scarves).
foule [ful] *nf* crowd; **une ~ de** masses of; **venir en ~** to come in droves.
foulée [fule] *nf* stride; **dans la ~ de** on the heels of.
fouler [fule] *vt* to press; (*sol*) to tread upon; **se ~** *vi* (*fam*) to overexert o.s.; **se ~ la cheville** to sprain one's ankle; **~ aux pieds** to trample underfoot.
foulure [fulyʀ] *nf* sprain.
four [fuʀ] *nm* oven; (*de potier*) kiln; (*THÉÂT: échec*) flop; **allant au ~** ovenproof.
fourbe [fuʀb(ə)] *adj* deceitful.
fourberie [fuʀbəʀi] *nf* deceit.
fourbi [fuʀbi] *nm* (*fam*) gear, junk.
fourbir [fuʀbiʀ] *vt*: **~ ses armes** (*fig*) to get ready for the fray.
fourbu, e [fuʀby] *adj* exhausted.
fourche [fuʀʃ(ə)] *nf* pitchfork; (*de bicyclette*) fork.
fourcher [fuʀʃe] *vi*: **ma langue a fourché** it

was a slip of the tongue.

fourchette [fuʁʃɛt] *nf* fork; (*STATISTIQUE*) bracket, margin.

fourchu, e [fuʁʃy] *adj* split; (*arbre etc*) forked.

fourgon [fuʁgɔ̃] *nm* van; (*RAIL*) wag(g)on; ~ **mortuaire** hearse.

fourgonnette [fuʁgɔnɛt] *nf* (delivery) van.

fourmi [fuʁmi] *nf* ant; **avoir des** ~**s** (*fig*) to have pins and needles.

fourmilière [fuʁmiljɛʁ] *nf* ant-hill; (*fig*) hive of activity.

fourmillement [fuʁmijmɑ̃] *nm* (*démangeaison*) pins and needles *pl*; (*grouillement*) swarming *no pl*.

fourmiller [fuʁmije] *vi* to swarm; ~ **de** to be teeming with, be swarming with.

fournaise [fuʁnɛz] *nf* blaze; (*fig*) furnace, oven.

fourneau, x [fuʁno] *nm* stove.

fournée [fuʁne] *nf* batch.

fourni, e [fuʁni] *adj* (*barbe, cheveux*) thick; (*magasin*): **bien** ~ **(en)** well stocked (with).

fournil [fuʁni] *nm* bakehouse.

fournir [fuʁniʁ] *vt* to supply; (*preuve, exemple*) to provide, supply; (*effort*) to put in; ~ **qch à qn** to supply sth to sb, supply *ou* provide sb with sth; ~ **qn en** (*COMM*) to supply sb with; **se** ~ **chez** to shop at.

fournisseur, euse [fuʁnisœʁ, -øz] *nm/f* supplier.

fourniture [fuʁnityʁ] *nf* supply(ing); ~**s** *nfpl* supplies; ~**s de bureau** office supplies, stationery; ~**s scolaires** school stationery.

fourrage [fuʁaʒ] *nm* fodder.

fourrager [fuʁaʒe] *vi*: ~ **dans/parmi** to rummage through/among.

fourrager, ère [fuʁaʒe, -ɛʁ] *adj* fodder *cpd* ♦ *nf* (*MIL*) fourragère.

fourré, e [fuʁe] *adj* (*bonbon, chocolat*) filled; (*manteau, botte*) fur-lined ♦ *nm* thicket.

fourreau, x [fuʁo] *nm* sheath; (*de parapluie*) cover; **robe/jupe** ~ figure-hugging dress/skirt.

fourrer [fuʁe] *vt* (*fam*): ~ **qch dans** to stick *ou* shove sth into; **se** ~ **dans/sous** to get into/under; **se** ~ **dans** (*une mauvaise situation*) to land o.s. in.

fourre-tout [fuʁtu] *nm inv* (*sac*) holdall; (*péj*) junk room (*ou* cupboard); (*fig*) rag-bag.

fourreur [fuʁœʁ] *nm* furrier.

fourrière [fuʁjɛʁ] *nf* pound.

fourrure [fuʁyʁ] *nf* fur; (*sur l'animal*) coat; **manteau/col de** ~ fur coat/collar.

fourvoyer [fuʁvwaje]: **se** ~ *vi* to go astray, stray; **se** ~ **dans** to stray into.

foutre [futʁ(ə)] *vt* (*fam!*) = **ficher** (*fam*).

foutu, e [futy] *adj* (*fam!*) = **fichu**.

foyer [fwaje] *nm* (*de cheminée*) hearth; (*fig*) seat, centre; (*famille*) family; (*domicile*) home; (*local de réunion*) (social) club; (*résidence*) hostel; (*salon*) foyer; (*OPTIQUE, PHOTO*) focus; **lunettes à double** ~ bi-focal glasses.

FP *sigle f* (= *franchise postale*) *exemption from postage*.

FPA *sigle f* (= *Formation professionnelle pour adultes*) adult education.

FPLP *sigle m* (= *Front populaire de la libération de la Palestine*) PFLP (= *Popular Front for the Liberation of Palestine*).

FR3 [ɛfɛʁtʁwa] *sigle f* (= *France Régions 3*) TV channel.

fracas [fʁaka] *nm* din; crash.

fracassant, e [fʁakasɑ̃, -ɑ̃t] *adj* sensational, staggering.

fracasser [fʁakase] *vt* to smash; **se** ~ **contre** *ou* **sur** to crash against.

fraction [fʁaksjɔ̃] *nf* fraction.

fractionnement [fʁaksjɔnmɑ̃] *nm* division.

fractionner [fʁaksjɔne] *vt* to divide (up), split (up).

fracture [fʁaktyʁ] *nf* fracture; ~ **du crâne** fractured skull; ~ **de la jambe** broken leg.

fracturer [fʁaktyʁe] *vt* (*coffre, serrure*) to break open; (*os, membre*) to fracture.

fragile [fʁaʒil] *adj* fragile, delicate; (*fig*) frail.

fragiliser [fʁaʒilize] *vt* to weaken, make fragile.

fragilité [fʁaʒilite] *nf* fragility.

fragment [fʁagmɑ̃] *nm* (*d'un objet*) fragment, piece; (*d'un texte*) passage, extract.

fragmentaire [fʁagmɑ̃tɛʁ] *adj* sketchy.

fragmenter [fʁagmɑ̃te] *vt* to split up.

frai [fʁɛ] *nm* spawn; (*ponte*) spawning.

fraîche [fʁɛʃ] *adj f voir* **frais**.

fraîchement [fʁɛʃmɑ̃] *adv* (*sans enthousiasme*) coolly; (*récemment*) freshly, newly.

fraîcheur [fʁɛʃœʁ] *nf* (*voir frais*) coolness; freshness.

fraîchir [fʁɛʃiʁ] *vi* to get cooler; (*vent*) to freshen.

frais, fraîche [fʁɛ, fʁɛʃ] *adj* (*air, eau, accueil*) cool; (*petit pois, œufs, nouvelles, couleur, troupes*) fresh; **le voilà** ~! he's in a (right) mess! ♦ *adv* (*récemment*) newly, fresh(ly); **il fait** ~ it's cool; **servir** ~ chill before serving, serve chilled ♦ *nm*: **mettre au** ~ to put in a cool place; **prendre le** ~ to take a breath of cool air ♦ *nmpl* (*débours*) expenses; (*COMM*) costs; charges; **faire des** ~ to spend; to go to a lot of expense; **faire les** ~ **de** to bear the brunt of; **faire les** ~ **de la conversation** (*parler*) to do most of the talking; (*en être le sujet*) to be the topic of conversation; **il en a été pour ses** ~ he could have spared himself the trouble; **rentrer dans ses** ~ to recover one's expenses; ~ **de déplacement** travel(ling) expenses; ~ **d'entretien** upkeep; ~ **généraux** overheads; ~ **de scolarité** school fees, tuition (*US*).

fraise [fʁɛz] *nf* strawberry; (*TECH*) countersink (bit); (*de dentiste*) drill; ~ **des bois** wild strawberry.

fraiser [fʁeze] *vt* to countersink; (*CULIN: pâte*)

to knead.
fraiseuse [fʀɛzøz] nf (TECH) milling machine.
fraisier [fʀezje] nm strawberry plant.
framboise [fʀɑ̃bwaz] nf raspberry.
framboisier [fʀɑ̃bwazje] nm raspberry bush.
franc, franche [fʀɑ̃, fʀɑ̃ʃ] adj (personne) frank, straightforward; (visage) open; (net: refus, couleur) clear; (: coupure) clean; (intensif) downright; (exempt): ~ **de port** post free, postage paid; (zone, port) free; (boutique) duty-free ♦ adv: **parler** ~ to be frank ou candid ♦ nm franc.
français, e [fʀɑ̃sɛ, -ɛz] adj French ♦ nm (LING) French ♦ nm/f: **F~, e** Frenchman/woman; **les F~** the French.
franc-comtois, e, mpl **francs-comtois** [fʀɑ̃kɔ̃twa, -waz] adj of ou from (the) Franche-Comté.
France [fʀɑ̃s] nf: **la** ~ France; **en** ~ in France.
Francfort [fʀɑ̃kfɔʀ] n Frankfurt.
franche [fʀɑ̃ʃ] adj f voir **franc**.
Franche-Comté [fʀɑ̃ʃkɔ̃te] nf Franche-Comté.
franchement [fʀɑ̃ʃmɑ̃] adv (voir franc) frankly; clearly; (tout à fait) downright ♦ excl well, really!
franchir [fʀɑ̃ʃiʀ] vt (obstacle) to clear, get over; (seuil, ligne, rivière) to cross; (distance) to cover.
franchisage [fʀɑ̃ʃizaʒ] nm (COMM) franchising.
franchise [fʀɑ̃ʃiz] nf frankness; (douanière, d'impôt) exemption; (ASSURANCES) excess; (COMM) franchise; ~ **de bagages** baggage allowance.
franchissable [fʀɑ̃ʃisabl(ə)] adj (obstacle) surmountable.
francilien, ne [fʀɑ̃siljɛ̃, -ɛn] adj of ou from the Île-de-France region ♦ nm/f: **F~, ne** person from the Île-de-France region.
franciscain, e [fʀɑ̃siskɛ̃, -ɛn] adj Franciscan.
franciser [fʀɑ̃size] vt to gallicize, Frenchify.
franc-jeu [fʀɑ̃ʒø] nm: **jouer** ~ to play fair.
franc-maçon, pl **francs-maçons** [fʀɑ̃masɔ̃] nm Freemason.
franc-maçonnerie [fʀɑ̃masɔnʀi] nf Freemasonry.
franco [fʀɑ̃ko] adv (COMM): ~ **(de port)** postage paid.
franco... [fʀɑ̃ko] préfixe franco-.
franco-canadien [fʀɑ̃kɔkanadjɛ̃] nm (LING) Canadian French.
francophile [fʀɑ̃kɔfil] adj Francophile.
francophobe [fʀɑ̃kɔfɔb] adj Francophobe.
francophone [fʀɑ̃kɔfɔn] adj French-speaking ♦ nm/f French speaker.
francophonie [fʀɑ̃kɔfɔni] nf French-speaking communities pl.
franco-québécois [fʀɑ̃kɔkebekwa] nm (LING) Quebec French.
franc-parler [fʀɑ̃paʀle] nm inv outspokenness.
franc-tireur [fʀɑ̃tiʀœʀ] nm (MIL) irregular; (fig) freelance.

frange [fʀɑ̃ʒ] nf fringe; (cheveux) fringe (BRIT), bangs (US).
frangé, e [fʀɑ̃ʒe] adj (tapis, nappe): ~ **de** trimmed with.
frangin [fʀɑ̃ʒɛ̃] nm (fam) brother.
frangine [fʀɑ̃ʒin] nf (fam) sis, sister.
frangipane [fʀɑ̃ʒipan] nf almond paste.
franglais [fʀɑ̃glɛ] nm Franglais.
franquette [fʀɑ̃ket]: **à la bonne** ~ adv without any fuss.
frappant, e [fʀapɑ̃, -ɑ̃t] adj striking.
frappe [fʀap] nf (d'une dactylo, pianiste, machine à écrire) touch; (BOXE) punch; (péj) hood, thug.
frappé, e [fʀape] adj (CULIN) iced; ~ **de panique** panic-stricken; ~ **de stupeur** thunderstruck, dumbfounded.
frapper [fʀape] vt to hit, strike; (étonner) to strike; (monnaie) to strike, stamp; **se** ~ vi (s'inquiéter) to get worked up; ~ **à la porte** to knock at the door; ~ **dans ses mains** to clap one's hands; ~ **du poing sur** to bang one's fist on; ~ **un grand coup** (fig) to strike a blow.
frasques [fʀask(ə)] nfpl escapades; **faire des** ~**s** to get up to mischief.
fraternel, le [fʀatɛʀnɛl] adj brotherly, fraternal.
fraternellement [fʀatɛʀnɛlmɑ̃] adv in a brotherly way.
fraterniser [fʀatɛʀnize] vi to fraternize.
fraternité [fʀatɛʀnite] nf brotherhood.
fratricide [fʀatʀisid] adj fratricidal.
fraude [fʀod] nf fraud; (SCOL) cheating; **passer qch en** ~ to smuggle sth in (ou out); ~ **fiscale** tax evasion.
frauder [fʀode] vi, vt to cheat; ~ **le fisc** to evade paying tax(es).
fraudeur, euse [fʀodœʀ, -øz] nm/f person guilty of fraud; (candidat) candidate who cheats; (au fisc) tax evader.
frauduleux, euse [fʀodylø, -øz] adj fraudulent.
frauduleusement [fʀodyløzmɑ̃] adv fraudulently.
frayer [fʀeje] vt to open up, clear ♦ vi to spawn; (fréquenter): ~ **avec** to mix ou associate with; **se** ~ **un passage dans** to clear o.s. a path through, force one's way through.
frayeur [fʀejœʀ] nf fright.
fredaines [fʀədɛn] nfpl mischief sg, escapades.
fredonner [fʀədɔne] vt to hum.
freezer [fʀizœʀ] nm freezing compartment.
frégate [fʀegat] nf frigate.
frein [fʀɛ̃] nm brake; **mettre un** ~ **à** (fig) to put a brake on, check; **sans** ~ (sans limites) unchecked; ~ **à main** handbrake; ~ **moteur** engine braking; ~**s à disques** disc brakes; ~**s à tambour** drum brakes.
freinage [fʀɛnaʒ] nm braking; **distance de** ~ braking distance; **traces de** ~ tyre (BRIT) ou tire (US) marks.

freiner [fʀene] *vi* to brake ♦ *vt* (*progrès etc*) to check.

frelaté, e [fʀəlate] *adj* adulterated; (*fig*) tainted.

frêle [fʀɛl] *adj* frail, fragile.

frelon [fʀəlɔ̃] *nm* hornet.

freluquet [fʀəlykɛ] *nm* (*péj*) whippersnapper.

frémir [fʀemiʀ] *vi* (*de froid, de peur*) to tremble, shiver; (*de joie*) to quiver; (*eau*) to (begin to) bubble.

frémissement [fʀemismɑ̃] *nm* shiver; quiver; bubbling *no pl*.

frêne [fʀɛn] *nm* ash (tree).

frénésie [fʀenezi] *nf* frenzy.

frénétique [fʀenetik] *adj* frenzied, frenetic.

frénétiquement [fʀenetikmɑ̃] *adv* frenetically.

fréon [fʀeɔ̃] *nm* ® Freon ®.

fréquemment [fʀekamɑ̃] *adv* frequently.

fréquence [fʀekɑ̃s] *nf* frequency.

fréquent, e [fʀekɑ̃, -ɑ̃t] *adj* frequent.

fréquentable [fʀekɑ̃tabl(ə)] *adj*: **il est peu** ~ he's not the type one can associate oneself with.

fréquentation [fʀekɑ̃tasjɔ̃] *nf* frequenting; seeing; ~**s** *nfpl* company *sg*.

fréquenté, e [fʀekɑ̃te] *adj*: **très** ~ (very) busy; **mal** ~ patronized by disreputable elements.

fréquenter [fʀekɑ̃te] *vt* (*lieu*) to frequent; (*personne*) to see; **se** ~ to see a lot of each other.

frère [fʀɛʀ] *nm* brother ♦ *adj*: **partis/pays** ~**s** sister parties/countries.

fresque [fʀɛsk(ə)] *nf* (*ART*) fresco.

fret [fʀɛ] *nm* freight.

fréter [fʀete] *vt* to charter.

frétiller [fʀetije] *vi* to wriggle; to quiver; ~ **de la queue** to wag its tail.

fretin [fʀətɛ̃] *nm*: **le menu** ~ the small fry.

freudien, ne [fʀødjɛ̃, -ɛn] *adj* Freudian.

freux [fʀø] *nm* (*ZOOL*) rook.

friable [fʀijabl(ə)] *adj* crumbly.

friand, e [fʀijɑ̃, -ɑ̃d] *adj*: ~ **de** very fond of ♦ *nm* (*CULIN*) small minced-meat (*BRIT*) *ou* ground-meat (*US*) pie; (*: sucré*) small almond cake.

friandise [fʀijɑ̃diz] *nf* sweet.

fric [fʀik] *nm* (*fam*) cash, bread.

fricassée [fʀikase] *nf* fricassee.

fric-frac [fʀikfʀak] *nm* break-in.

friche [fʀiʃ] *nf*: **en** ~ *adj, adv* (lying) fallow.

friction [fʀiksjɔ̃] *nf* (*massage*) rub, rub-down; (*chez le coiffeur*) scalp massage; (*TECH, fig*) friction.

frictionner [fʀiksjɔne] *vt* to rub (down); to massage.

frigidaire [fʀiʒidɛʀ] *nm* ® refrigerator.

frigide [fʀiʒid] *adj* frigid.

frigidité [fʀiʒidite] *nf* frigidity.

frigo [fʀigo] *nm* (= *frigidaire*) fridge.

frigorifier [fʀigɔʀifje] *vt* to refrigerate; (*fig: personne*) to freeze.

frigorifique [fʀigɔʀifik] *adj* refrigerating.

frileusement [fʀiløzmɑ̃] *adv* with a shiver.

frileux, euse [fʀilø, -øz] *adj* sensitive to (the) cold; (*fig*) overcautious.

frimas [fʀima] *nmpl* wintry weather *sg*.

frime [fʀim] *nf* (*fam*): **c'est de la** ~ it's all put on; **pour la** ~ just for show.

frimer [fʀime] *vi* to put on an act.

frimeur, euse [fʀimœʀ, -øz] *nm/f* poser.

frimousse [fʀimus] *nf* (sweet) little face.

fringale [fʀɛ̃gal] *nf*: **avoir la** ~ to be ravenous.

fringant, e [fʀɛ̃gɑ̃, -ɑ̃t] *adj* dashing.

fringues [fʀɛ̃g] *nfpl* (*fam*) clothes, gear *no pl*.

fripé, e [fʀipe] *adj* crumpled.

friperie [fʀipʀi] *nf* (*commerce*) secondhand clothes shop; (*vêtements*) secondhand clothes.

fripes [fʀip] *nfpl* secondhand clothes.

fripier, ière [fʀipje, -jɛʀ] *nm/f* secondhand clothes dealer.

fripon, ne [fʀipɔ̃, -ɔn] *adj* roguish, mischievous ♦ *nm/f* rascal, rogue.

fripouille [fʀipuj] *nf* scoundrel.

frire [fʀiʀ] *vt* (*aussi*: **faire** ~), *vi* to fry.

Frisbee [fʀizbi] *nm* ® Frisbee ®.

frise [fʀiz] *nf* frieze.

frisé, e [fʀize] *adj* curly, curly-haired ♦ *nf*: (**chicorée**) ~**e** curly endive.

friser [fʀize] *vt* to curl; (*fig: surface*) to skim, graze; (*: mort*) to come within a hair's breadth of; (*: hérésie*) to verge on ♦ *vi* (*cheveux*) to curl; (*personne*) to have curly hair; **se faire** ~ to have one's hair curled.

frisette [fʀizɛt] *nf* little curl.

frisotter [fʀizɔte] *vt* (*cheveux*) to curl tightly.

frisquet [fʀiskɛ] *adj* chilly.

frisson [fʀisɔ̃], **frissonnement** [fʀisɔnmɑ̃] *nm* shudder, shiver; quiver.

frissonner [fʀisɔne] *vi* (*personne*) to shudder, shiver; (*feuilles*) to quiver.

frit, e [fʀi, fʀit] *pp de* **frire** ♦ *adj* fried ♦ *nf*: (**pommes**) ~**es** chips (*BRIT*), French fries.

friterie [fʀitʀi] *nf* ≈ chip shop (*BRIT*), ≈ hamburger stand (*US*).

friteuse [fʀitøz] *nf* chip pan (*BRIT*), deep (fat) fryer.

friture [fʀityʀ] *nf* (*huile*) (deep) fat; (*plat*): ~ (**de poissons**) fried fish; (*RADIO*) crackle, crackling *no pl*; ~**s** *nfpl* (*aliments frits*) fried food *sg*.

frivole [fʀivɔl] *adj* frivolous.

frivolité [fʀivɔlite] *nf* frivolity.

froc [fʀɔk] *nm* (*REL*) habit; (*fam: pantalon*) trousers *pl*, pants *pl*.

froid, e [fʀwa, fʀwad] *adj* cold ♦ *nm* cold; (*absence de sympathie*) coolness *no pl*; **il fait** ~ it's cold; **avoir** ~ to be cold; **prendre** ~ to catch a chill *ou* cold; **à** ~ *adv* (*démarrer*) (from) cold; (**pendant**) **les grands** ~**s** (in) the depths of winter, (during) the cold season; **jeter un** ~ (*fig*) to cast a chill; **être en** ~ **avec** to be on bad terms with; **battre** ~ **à qn** to give sb the cold shoulder.

froidement [fʀwadmɑ̃] adv (accueillir) coldly; (décider) coolly.

froideur [fʀwadœʀ] nf coolness no pl.

froisser [fʀwase] vt to crumple (up), crease; (fig) to hurt, offend; **se** ~ vi to crumple, crease; to take offence (BRIT) ou offense (US); **se** ~ **un muscle** to strain a muscle.

frôlement [fʀolmɑ̃] nm (contact) light touch.

frôler [fʀole] vt to brush against; (suj: projectile) to skim past; (fig) to come within a hair's breadth of, come very close to.

fromage [fʀɔmaʒ] nm cheese; ~ **blanc** soft white cheese; ~ **de tête** pork brawn.

fromager, ère [fʀɔmaʒe, -ɛʀ] nm/f cheese merchant ♦ adj (industrie) cheese cpd.

fromagerie [fʀɔmaʒʀi] nf cheese dairy.

froment [fʀɔmɑ̃] nm wheat.

fronce [fʀɔ̃s] nf (de tissu) gather.

froncement [fʀɔ̃smɑ̃] nm: ~ **de sourcils** frown.

froncer [fʀɔ̃se] vt to gather; ~ **les sourcils** to frown.

frondaison [fʀɔ̃dɛzɔ̃] nf foliage.

fronde [fʀɔ̃d] nf sling; (fig) rebellion, rebelliousness.

frondeur, euse [fʀɔ̃dœʀ, -øz] adj rebellious.

front [fʀɔ̃] nm forehead, brow; (MIL, MÉTÉOROLOGIE, POL) front; **avoir le** ~ **de faire** to have the effrontery ou front to do; **de** ~ adv (se heurter) head-on; (rouler) together (i.e. 2 ou 3 abreast); (simultanément) at once; **faire** ~ **à** to face up to; ~ **de mer** (sea) front.

frontal, e, aux [fʀɔ̃tal, -o] adj frontal.

frontalier, ière [fʀɔ̃talje, -jɛʀ] adj border cpd, frontier cpd ♦ nm/f: (travailleurs) ~s workers who cross the border to go to work, commuters from across the border.

frontière [fʀɔ̃tjɛʀ] nf (GÉO, POL) frontier, border; (fig) frontier, boundary.

frontispice [fʀɔ̃tispis] nm frontispiece.

fronton [fʀɔ̃tɔ̃] nm pediment; (de pelote basque) (front) wall.

frottement [fʀɔtmɑ̃] nm rubbing, scraping; ~s nmpl (fig: difficultés) friction sg.

frotter [fʀɔte] vi to rub, scrape ♦ vt to rub; (pour nettoyer) to rub (up); (: avec une brosse) to scrub; ~ **une allumette** to strike a match; **se** ~ **à qn** to cross swords with sb; **se** ~ **à qch** to come up against sth; **se** ~ **les mains** (fig) to rub one's hands (gleefully).

frottis [fʀɔti] nm (MÉD) smear.

frottoir [fʀɔtwaʀ] nm (d'allumettes) friction strip; (pour encaustiquer) (long-handled) brush.

frou-frou, pl **frous-frous** [fʀufʀu] nm rustle.

frousse [fʀus] nf (fam: peur): **avoir la** ~ to be in a blue funk.

fructifier [fʀyktifje] vi to yield a profit; **faire** ~ to turn to good account.

fructueux, euse [fʀyktɥø, -øz] adj fruitful; profitable.

frugal, e, aux [fʀygal, -o] adj frugal.

frugalement [fʀygalmɑ̃] adv frugally.

frugalité [fʀygalite] nf frugality.

fruit [fʀɥi] nm fruit gén no pl; ~s **de mer** (CULIN) seafood(s); ~s **secs** dried fruit sg.

fruité, e [fʀɥite] adj (vin) fruity.

fruiterie [fʀɥitʀi] nf (boutique) greengrocer's (BRIT), fruit (and vegetable) store (US).

fruitier, ière [fʀɥitje, -jɛʀ] adj: **arbre** ~ fruit tree ♦ nm/f fruiterer (BRIT), fruit merchant (US).

fruste [fʀyst(ə)] adj unpolished, uncultivated.

frustrant, e [fʀystʀɑ̃, -ɑ̃t] adj frustrating.

frustration [fʀystʀasjɔ̃] nf frustration.

frustré, e [fʀystʀe] adj frustrated.

frustrer [fʀystʀe] vt to frustrate; (priver): ~ **qn de qch** to deprive sb of sth.

FS abr (= franc suisse) FS, SF.

FSE sigle m (= foyer socio-éducatif) community home.

FTP sigle mpl (= Francs-tireurs et partisans) Communist Resistance in 1940-45.

fuchsia [fyʃja] nm fuchsia.

fuel(-oil) [fjul(ɔjl)] nm fuel oil; (pour chauffer) heating oil.

fugace [fygas] adj fleeting.

fugitif, ive [fyʒitif, -iv] adj (lueur, amour) fleeting; (prisonnier etc) runaway ♦ nm/f fugitive, runaway.

fugue [fyg] nf (d'un enfant) running away no pl; (MUS) fugue; **faire une** ~ to run away, abscond.

fuir [fɥiʀ] vt to flee from; (éviter) to shun ♦ vi to run away; (gaz, robinet) to leak.

fuite [fɥit] nf flight; (écoulement) leak, leakage; (divulgation) leak; **être en** ~ to be on the run; **mettre en** ~ to put to flight; **prendre la** ~ to take flight.

fulgurant, e [fylgyʀɑ̃, -ɑ̃t] adj lightning cpd, dazzling.

fulminant, e [fylminɑ̃, -ɑ̃t] adj (lettre, regard) furious; ~ **de colère** raging with anger.

fulminer [fylmine] vi: ~ **(contre)** to thunder forth (against).

fumant, e [fymɑ̃, -ɑ̃t] adj smoking; (liquide) steaming; **un coup** ~ (fam) a master stroke.

fumé, e [fyme] adj (CULIN) smoked; (verre) tinted ♦ nf smoke; **partir en** ~e to go up in smoke.

fume-cigarette [fymsigaʀɛt] nm inv cigarette holder.

fumer [fyme] vi to smoke; (liquide) to steam ♦ vt to smoke; (terre, champ) to manure.

fumerie [fymʀi] nf: ~ **d'opium** opium den.

fumerolles [fymʀɔl] nfpl gas and smoke (from volcano).

fûmes [fym] vb voir **être**.

fumet [fymɛ] nm aroma.

fumeur, euse [fymœʀ, -øz] nm/f smoker; (compartiment) ~s smoking compartment.

fumeux, euse [fymø, -øz] adj (péj) woolly (BRIT), hazy.

fumier [fymje] nm manure.

fumigation [fymigasjɔ̃] nf fumigation.

fumigène [fymiʒɛn] *adj* smoke *cpd*.
fumiste [fymist(ə)] *nm* (*ramoneur*) chimney sweep ♦ *nm/f* (*péj*: *paresseux*) shirker; (*charlatan*) phoney.
fumisterie [fymistəʀi] *nf* (*péj*) fraud, con.
fumoir [fymwaʀ] *nm* smoking room.
funambule [fynɑ̃byl] *nm* tightrope walker.
funèbre [fynɛbʀ(ə)] *adj* funeral *cpd*; (*fig*) doleful; funereal.
funérailles [fyneʀɑj] *nfpl* funeral *sg*.
funéraire [fyneʀɛʀ] *adj* funeral *cpd*, funerary.
funeste [fynɛst(ə)] *adj* disastrous; deathly.
funiculaire [fynikylɛʀ] *nm* funicular (railway).
FUNU [fyny] *sigle f* (= *Force d'urgence des Nations unies*) UNEF (= *United Nations Emergency Forces*).
fur [fyʀ]: **au ~ et à mesure** *adv* as one goes along; **au ~ et à mesure que** as; **au ~ et à mesure de leur progression** as they advance (*ou* advanced).
furax [fyʀaks] *adj inv* (*fam*) livid.
furent [fyʀ] *vb voir* **être**.
furet [fyʀɛ] *nm* ferret.
fureter [fyʀte] *vi* (*péj*) to nose about.
fureur [fyʀœʀ] *nf* fury; (*passion*): **~ de** passion for; **faire ~** to be all the rage.
furibard, e [fyʀibaʀ, -aʀd(ə)] *adj* (*fam*) livid, absolutely furious.
furibond, e [fyʀibɔ̃, -ɔ̃d] *adj* livid, absolutely furious.
furie [fyʀi] *nf* fury; (*femme*) shrew, vixen; **en ~** (*mer*) raging.
furieusement [fyʀjøzmɑ̃] *adv* furiously.
furieux, euse [fyʀjø, -øz] *adj* furious.
furoncle [fyʀɔ̃kl(ə)] *nm* boil.
furtif, ive [fyʀtif, -iv] *adj* furtive.
furtivement [fyʀtivmɑ̃] *adv* furtively.
fus [fy] *vb voir* **être**.
fusain [fyzɛ̃] *nm* (*BOT*) spindle-tree; (*ART*) charcoal.
fuseau, x [fyzo] *nm* (*pantalon*) (ski-)pants *pl*; (*pour filer*) spindle; **en ~** (*jambes*) tapering; (*colonne*) bulging; **~ horaire** time zone.
fusée [fyze] *nf* rocket; **~ éclairante** flare.
fuselage [fyzlaʒ] *nm* fuselage.
fuselé, e [fyzle] *adj* slender; (*galbé*) tapering.
fuser [fyze] *vi* (*rires etc*) to burst forth.
fusible [fyzibl(ə)] *nm* (*ÉLEC*: *fil*) fuse wire; (*: fiche*) fuse.
fusil [fyzi] *nm* (*de guerre, à canon rayé*) rifle, gun; (*de chasse, à canon lisse*) shotgun, gun; **~ à deux coups** double-barrelled rifle *ou* shotgun; **~ sous-marin** spear-gun.
fusilier [fyzilje] *nm* (*MIL*) rifleman.
fusillade [fyzijad] *nf* gunfire *no pl*, shooting *no pl*; (*combat*) gun battle.
fusiller [fyzije] *vt* to shoot; **~ qn du regard** to look daggers at sb.
fusil-mitrailleur [fyzimitʀajœʀ] *nm* machine gun.
fusion [fyzjɔ̃] *nf* fusion, melting; (*fig*) merging; (*COMM*) merger; **en ~** (*métal, roches*) molten.
fusionnement [fyzjɔnmɑ̃] *nm* merger.
fusionner [fyzjɔne] *vi* to merge.
fustiger [fystiʒe] *vt* to denounce.
fut [fy] *vb voir* **être**.
fût [fy] *vb voir* **être** ♦ *nm* (*tonneau*) barrel, cask; (*de canon*) stock; (*d'arbre*) bole, trunk; (*de colonne*) shaft.
futaie [fytɛ] *nf* forest, plantation.
futé, e [fyte] *adj* crafty.
fûtes [fyt] *vb voir* **être**.
futile [fytil] *adj* (*inutile*) futile; (*frivole*) frivolous.
futilement [fytilmɑ̃] *adv* frivolously.
futilité [fytilite] *nf* futility; frivolousness; (*chose futile*) futile pursuit (*ou* thing *etc*).
futon [fytɔ̃] *nm* futon.
futur, e [fytyʀ] *adj, nm* future; **son ~ époux** her husband-to-be; **au ~** (*LING*) in the future.
futuriste [fytyʀist(ə)] *adj* futuristic.
futurologie [fytyʀɔlɔʒi] *nf* futurology.
fuyant, e [fɥijɑ̃, -ɑ̃t] *vb voir* **fuir** ♦ *adj* (*regard etc*) evasive; (*lignes etc*) receding; (*perspective*) vanishing.
fuyard, e [fɥijaʀ, -aʀd(ə)] *nm/f* runaway.
fuyons [fɥijɔ̃] *etc vb voir* **fuir**.

G g

G, g [ʒe] *nm inv* G, g ♦ *abr* (= *gramme*) g; (= *gauche*) L, l; **G comme Gaston** G for George; **le G7** (*POL*) the G7 nations, the Group of Seven.
gabardine [gabaʀdin] *nf* gabardine.
gabarit [gabaʀi] *nm* (*fig: dimension, taille*) size; (*: valeur*) calibre; (*TECH*) template; **du même ~** (*fig*) of the same type, of that ilk.
gabegie [gabʒi] *nf* (*péj*) chaos.
Gabon [gabɔ̃] *nm*: **le ~** Gabon.
gabonais, e [gabɔnɛ, -ɛz] *adj* Gabonese.
gâcher [gɑʃe] *vt* (*gâter*) to spoil, ruin; (*gaspiller*) to waste; (*plâtre*) to temper; (*mortier*) to mix.
gâchette [gɑʃɛt] *nf* trigger.
gâchis [gɑʃi] *nm* (*désordre*) mess; (*gaspillage*) waste *no pl*.
gadget [gadʒɛt] *nm* thingumajig; (*nouveauté*) gimmick.
gadin [gadɛ̃] *nm* (*fam*): **prendre un ~** to come a cropper (*BRIT*).
gadoue [gadu] *nf* sludge.
gaélique [gaelik] *adj* Gaelic ♦ *nm* (*LING*) Gaelic.
gaffe [gaf] *nf* (*instrument*) boat hook; (*fam*: *er-*

reur) blunder; **faire ~** (*fam*) to watch out.

gaffer [gafe] *vi* to blunder.

gaffeur, euse [gafœʀ, -øz] *nm/f* blunderer.

gag [gag] *nm* gag.

gaga [gaga] *adj* (*fam*) gaga.

gage [gaʒ] *nm* (*dans un jeu*) forfeit; (*fig: de fidélité*) token; **~s** *nmpl* (*salaire*) wages; (*garantie*) guarantee *sg*; **mettre en ~** to pawn; **laisser en ~** to leave as security.

gager [gaʒe] *vt*: **~ que** to bet *ou* wager that.

gageure [gaʒyʀ] *nf*: **c'est une ~** it's attempting the impossible.

gagnant, e [gaɲɑ̃, -ɑ̃t] *adj*: **billet/numéro ~** winning ticket/number ♦ *adv*: **jouer ~** (*aux courses*) to be bound to win ♦ *nm/f* winner.

gagne-pain [gaɲpɛ̃] *nm inv* job.

gagne-petit [gaɲpəti] *nm inv* low wage earner.

gagner [gaɲe] *vt* (*concours, procès, pari*) to win; (*somme d'argent, revenu*) to earn; (*aller vers, atteindre*) to reach; (*s'emparer de*) to overcome; (*envahir*) to spread to; (*se concilier*): **~ qn** to win sb over ♦ *vi* to win; (*fig*) to gain; **~ du temps/de la place** to gain time/save space; **~ sa vie** to earn one's living; **~ du terrain** (*aussi fig*) to gain ground; **~ qn de vitesse** (*aussi fig*) to outstrip sb; **~ à faire** (*s'en trouver bien*) to be better off doing; **il y gagne** it's in his interest, it's to his advantage.

gagneur [gaɲœʀ] *nm* winner.

gai, e [ge] *adj* cheerful; (*livre, pièce de théâtre*) light-hearted; (*un peu ivre*) merry.

gaiement [gemɑ̃] *adv* cheerfully.

gaieté [gete] *nf* cheerfulness; **~s** *nfpl* (*souvent ironique*) delights; **de ~ de cœur** with a light heart.

gaillard, e [gajaʀ, -aʀd(ə)] *adj* (*robuste*) sprightly; (*grivois*) bawdy, ribald ♦ *nm/f* (*strapping*) fellow/wench.

gaillardement [gajaʀdəmɑ̃] *adv* cheerfully.

gain [gɛ̃] *nm* (*revenu*) earnings *pl*; (*bénéfice: gén pl*) profits *pl*; (*au jeu: gén pl*) winnings *pl*; (*fig: de temps, place*) saving; (*: avantage*) benefit; (*: lucre*) gain; **avoir ~ de cause** to win the case; (*fig*) to be proved right; **obtenir ~ de cause** (*fig*) to win out.

gaine [gɛn] *nf* (*corset*) girdle; (*fourreau*) sheath; (*de fil électrique etc*) outer covering.

gaine-culotte, *pl* **gaines-culottes** [gɛnkylɔt] *nf* pantie girdle.

gainer [gene] *vt* to cover.

gala [gala] *nm* official reception; **soirée de ~** gala evening.

galamment [galamɑ̃] *adv* courteously.

galant, e [galɑ̃, -ɑ̃t] *adj* (*courtois*) courteous, gentlemanly; (*entreprenant*) flirtatious, gallant; (*aventure, poésie*) amorous; **en ~e compagnie** (*homme*) with a lady friend; (*femme*) with a gentleman friend.

galanterie [galɑ̃tʀi] *nf* gallantry.

galantine [galɑ̃tin] *nf* galantine.

Galapagos [galapagɔs] *nfpl*: **les (îles) ~** the Galapagos Islands.

galaxie [galaksi] *nf* galaxy.

galbe [galb(ə)] *nm* curve(s); shapeliness.

galbé, e [galbe] *adj* (*jambes*) (well-)rounded; **bien ~** shapely.

gale [gal] *nf* (*MÉD*) scabies *sg*; (*de chien*) mange.

galéjade [galeʒad] *nf* tall story.

galère [galɛʀ] *nf* galley.

galérer [galeʀe] *vi* (*fam*) to work hard, slave (away).

galerie [galʀi] *nf* gallery; (*THÉÂT*) circle; (*de voiture*) roof rack; (*fig: spectateurs*) audience; **~ marchande** shopping mall; **~ de peinture** (*private*) art gallery.

galérien [galeʀjɛ̃] *nm* galley slave.

galet [galɛ] *nm* pebble; (*TECH*) wheel; **~s** *nmpl* pebbles, shingle *sg*.

galette [galɛt] *nf* (*gâteau*) flat pastry cake; (*crêpe*) savoury pancake; **la ~ des Rois** *cake traditionally eaten on Twelfth Night*.

galeux, euse [galø, -øz] *adj*: **un chien ~** a mangy dog.

Galice [galis] *nf*: **la ~** Galicia (*in Spain*).

Galicie [galisi] *nf*: **la ~** Galicia (*in Central Europe*).

galiléen, ne [galileɛ̃, -ɛn] *adj* Galilean.

galimatias [galimatja] *nm* (*péj*) gibberish.

galipette [galipɛt] *nf*: **faire des ~s** to turn somersaults.

Galles [gal] *nfpl*: **le pays de ~** Wales.

gallicisme [galisism(ə)] *nm* French idiom; (*tournure fautive*) gallicism.

gallois, e [galwa, -waz] *adj* Welsh ♦ *nm* (*LING*) Welsh ♦ *nm/f*: **G~, e** Welshman/woman.

gallo-romain, e [galoʀɔmɛ̃, -ɛn] *adj* Gallo-Roman.

galoche [galɔʃ] *nf* clog.

galon [galɔ̃] *nm* (*MIL*) stripe; (*décoratif*) piece of braid; **prendre du ~** to be promoted.

galop [galo] *nm* gallop; **au ~** at a gallop; **~ d'essai** (*fig*) trial run.

galopade [galɔpad] *nf* stampede.

galopant, e [galɔpɑ̃, -ɑ̃t] *adj*: **inflation ~e** galloping inflation; **démographie ~e** exploding population.

galoper [galɔpe] *vi* to gallop.

galopin [galɔpɛ̃] *nm* urchin, ragamuffin.

galvaniser [galvanize] *vt* to galvanize.

galvaudé, e [galvode] *adj* (*expression*) hackneyed; (*mot*) clichéd.

galvauder [galvode] *vt* to debase.

gambade [gɑ̃bad] *nf*: **faire des ~s** to skip *ou* frisk about.

gambader [gɑ̃bade] *vi* to skip *ou* frisk about.

gamberger [gɑ̃bɛʀʒe] (*fam*) *vi* to (have a) think ♦ *vt* to dream up.

Gambie [gɑ̃bi] *nf*: **la ~** (*pays*) Gambia; (*fleuve*) the Gambia.

gamelle [gamɛl] *nf* mess tin; billy can; (*fam*): **ramasser une ~** to fall flat on one's face.

gamin, e [gamɛ̃, -in] *nm/f* kid ♦ *adj* mischie-

vous, playful.
gaminerie [gaminʀi] *nf* mischievousness, playfulness.
gamme [gam] *nf (MUS)* scale; *(fig)* range.
gammé, e [game] *adj*: **croix ~e** swastika.
Gand [gɑ̃] *n* Ghent.
gang [gɑ̃g] *nm* gang.
Gange [gɑ̃ʒ] *nm*: **le ~** the Ganges.
ganglion [gɑ̃glijɔ̃] *nm* ganglion; *(lymphatique)* gland; **avoir des ~s** to have swollen glands.
gangrène [gɑ̃gʀɛn] *nf* gangrene; *(fig)* corruption; corrupting influence.
gangster [gɑ̃gstɛʀ] *nm* gangster.
gangstérisme [gɑ̃gsteʀism(ə)] *nm* gangsterism.
gangue [gɑ̃g] *nf* coating.
ganse [gɑ̃s] *nf* braid.
gant [gɑ̃] *nm* glove; **prendre des ~s** *(fig)* to handle the situation with kid gloves; **relever le ~** *(fig)* to take up the gauntlet; **~ de crin** massage glove; **~ de toilette** (face) flannel *(BRIT)*, face cloth; **~s de boxe** boxing gloves; **~s de caoutchouc** rubber gloves.
ganté, e [gɑ̃te] *adj*: **~ de blanc** wearing white gloves.
ganterie [gɑ̃tʀi] *nf* glove trade; *(magasin)* glove shop.
garage [gaʀaʒ] *nm* garage; **~ à vélos** bicycle shed.
garagiste [gaʀaʒist(ə)] *nm/f (propriétaire)* garage owner; *(mécanicien)* garage mechanic.
garant, e [gaʀɑ̃, -ɑ̃t] *nm/f* guarantor ♦ *nm* guarantee; **se porter ~ de** to vouch for; to be answerable for.
garantie [gaʀɑ̃ti] *nf* guarantee, warranty; *(gage)* security, surety; **(bon de) ~** guarantee *ou* warranty slip; **~ de bonne exécution** performance bond.
garantir [gaʀɑ̃tiʀ] *vt* to guarantee; *(protéger)*: **~ de** to protect from; **je vous garantis que** I can assure you that; **garanti pure laine/2 ans** guaranteed pure wool/for 2 years.
garce [gaʀs(ə)] *nf (péj)* bitch.
garçon [gaʀsɔ̃] *nm* boy; *(célibataire)* bachelor; *(jeune homme)* boy, lad; *(aussi*: **~ de café**) waiter; **~ boucher/coiffeur** butcher's/hairdresser's assistant; **~ de courses** messenger; **~ d'écurie** stable lad; **~ manqué** tomboy.
garçonnet [gaʀsɔnɛ] *nm* small boy.
garçonnière [gaʀsɔnjɛʀ] *nf* bachelor flat.
garde [gaʀd(ə)] *nm (de prisonnier)* guard; *(de domaine etc)* warden; *(soldat, sentinelle)* guardsman ♦ *nf* guarding; looking after; *(soldats, BOXE, ESCRIME)* guard; *(faction)* watch; *(d'une arme)* hilt; *(TYPO: aussi*: **page** *ou* **feuille de ~**) flyleaf; *(: collée)* endpaper; **de ~** *adj, adv* on duty; **monter la ~** to stand guard; **être sur ses ~s** to be on one's guard; **mettre en ~** to warn; **mise en ~** warning; **prendre ~ (à)** to be careful (of); **avoir la ~ des enfants** *(après divorce)* to have custody

of the children; **~ champêtre** *nm* rural policeman; **~ du corps** *nm* bodyguard; **~ d'enfants** *nf* child minder; **~ forestier** *nm* forest warden; **~ mobile** *nm, nf* mobile guard; **~ des Sceaux** *nm* ≈ Lord Chancellor *(BRIT)*, ≈ Attorney General *(US)*; **~ à vue** *nf (JUR)* ≈ police custody.
garde-à-vous [gaʀdavu] *nm inv*: **être/se mettre au ~** to be at/stand to attention; **~ (fixe)!** *(MIL)* attention!
garde-barrière, *pl* **gardes-barrière(s)** [gaʀdəbaʀjɛʀ] *nm/f* level-crossing keeper.
garde-boue [gaʀdəbu] *nm inv* mudguard.
garde-chasse, *pl* **gardes-chasse(s)** [gaʀdəʃas] *nm* gamekeeper.
garde-côte [gaʀdəkot] *nm (vaisseau)* coastguard boat.
garde-feu [gaʀdəfø] *nm inv* fender.
garde-fou [gaʀdəfu] *nm* railing, parapet.
garde-malade, *pl* **gardes-malade(s)** [gaʀdəmalad] *nf* home nurse.
garde-manger [gaʀdəmɑ̃ʒe] *nm inv (boîte)* meat safe; *(placard)* pantry, larder.
garde-meuble [gaʀdəmœbl(ə)] *nm* furniture depository.
garde-pêche [gaʀdəpɛʃ] *nm inv (personne)* water bailiff; *(navire)* fisheries protection ship.
garder [gaʀde] *vt (conserver)* to keep; *(: sur soi: vêtement, chapeau)* to keep on; *(surveiller: enfants)* to look after; *(: immeuble, lieu, prisonnier)* to guard; **se ~** *vi (aliment: se conserver)* to keep; **se ~ de faire** to be careful not to do; **~ le lit/la chambre** to stay in bed/indoors; **~ le silence** to keep silent *ou* quiet; **~ la ligne** to keep one's figure; **~ à vue** to keep in custody; **pêche/chasse gardée** private fishing/hunting (ground).
garderie [gaʀdəʀi] *nf* day nursery, crèche.
garde-robe [gaʀdəʀɔb] *nf* wardrobe.
gardeur, euse [gaʀdœʀ, -øz] *nm/f (de vaches)* cowherd; *(de chèvres)* goatherd.
gardian [gaʀdjɑ̃] *nm* cowboy *(in the Camargue)*.
gardien, ne [gaʀdjɛ̃, -ɛn] *nm/f (garde)* guard; *(de prison)* warder; *(de domaine, réserve)* warden; *(de musée etc)* attendant; *(de phare, cimetière)* keeper; *(d'immeuble)* caretaker; *(fig)* guardian; **~ de but** goalkeeper; **~ de nuit** night watchman; **~ de la paix** policeman.
gardiennage [gaʀdjɛnaʒ] *nm (emploi)* caretaking; **société de ~** security firm.
gardon [gaʀdɔ̃] *nm* roach.
gare [gaʀ] *nf* (railway) station, train station *(US)* ♦ *excl*: **~ à ... mind ...!**, watch out for ...!; **~ à ne pas ...** mind you don't ...; **~ à toi!** watch out!; **sans crier ~** without warning; **~ maritime** harbour station; **~ routière** coach *(BRIT) ou* bus station; *(camions)* haulage *(BRIT) ou* trucking *(US)* depot; **~ de triage** marshalling yard.
garenne [gaʀɛn] *nf voir* lapin.
garer [gaʀe] *vt* to park; **se ~** to park; *(pour lais-*

ser passer) to draw into the side.

gargantuesque [gaʀgɑ̃tɥɛsk(ə)] *adj* gargantuan.

gargariser [gaʀgaʀize]: **se** ~ *vi* to gargle; **se** ~ **de** (*fig*) to revel in.

gargarisme [gaʀgaʀism(ə)] *nm* gargling *no pl*; (*produit*) gargle.

gargote [gaʀgɔt] *nf* cheap restaurant, greasy spoon (*fam*).

gargouille [gaʀguj] *nf* gargoyle.

gargouillement [gaʀgujmɑ̃] *nm* = **gargouillis**.

gargouiller [gaʀguje] *vi* (*estomac*) to rumble; (*eau*) to gurgle.

gargouillis [gaʀguji] *nm* (*gén pl: voir vb*) rumbling; gurgling.

garnement [gaʀnəmɑ̃] *nm* rascal, scallywag.

garni, e [gaʀni] *adj* (*plat*) served with vegetables (*and chips or pasta or rice*) ♦ *nm* (*appartement*) furnished accommodation *no pl* (*BRIT*) *ou* accommodations *pl* (*US*).

garnir [gaʀniʀ] *vt* to decorate; (*remplir*) to fill; (*recouvrir*) to cover; **se** ~ *vi* (*pièce, salle*) to fill up; ~ **qch de** (*orner*) to decorate sth with; to trim sth with; (*approvisionner*) to fill *ou* stock sth with; (*protéger*) to fit sth with; (*CULIN*) to garnish sth with.

garnison [gaʀnizɔ̃] *nf* garrison.

garniture [gaʀnityʀ] *nf* (*CULIN: légumes*) vegetables *pl*; (: *persil etc*) garnish; (: *farce*) filling; (*décoration*) trimming; (*protection*) fittings *pl*; ~ **de cheminée** mantelpiece ornaments *pl*; ~ **de frein** (*AUTO*) brake lining; ~ **intérieure** (*AUTO*) interior trim; ~ **périodique** sanitary towel (*BRIT*) *ou* napkin (*US*).

garrigue [gaʀig] *nf* scrubland.

garrot [gaʀo] *nm* (*MÉD*) tourniquet; (*torture*) garrotte.

garrotter [gaʀɔte] *vt* to tie up; (*fig*) to muzzle.

gars [gɑ] *nm* lad; (*type*) guy.

Gascogne [gaskɔɲ] *nf*: **la** ~ Gascony.

gascon, ne [gaskɔ̃, -ɔn] *adj* Gascon ♦ *nm*: G~ (*hâbleur*) braggart.

gas-oil [gazɔjl] *nm* diesel oil.

gaspillage [gaspijaʒ] *nm* waste.

gaspiller [gaspije] *vt* to waste.

gaspilleur, euse [gaspijœʀ, -øz] *adj* wasteful.

gastrique [gastʀik] *adj* gastric, stomach *cpd*.

gastro-entérite [gastʀɔɑ̃teʀit] *nf* (*MÉD*) gastro-enteritis.

gastro-intestinal, e, aux [gastʀoɛ̃tɛstinal, -o] *adj* gastrointestinal.

gastronome [gastʀɔnɔm] *nm/f* gourmet.

gastronomie [gastʀɔnɔmi] *nf* gastronomy.

gastronomique [gastʀɔnɔmik] *adj*: **menu** ~ gourmet menu.

gâteau, x [gɑto] *nm* cake ♦ *adj inv* (*fam: trop indulgent*): **papa-/maman-**~ doting father/mother; ~ **d'anniversaire** birthday cake; ~ **de riz** ≈ rice pudding; ~ **sec** biscuit.

gâter [gɑte] *vt* to spoil; **se** ~ *vi* (*dent, fruit*) to go bad; (*temps, situation*) to change for the worse.

gâterie [gɑtʀi] *nf* little treat.

gâteux, euse [gɑtø, -øz] *adj* senile.

gâtisme [gɑtism(ə)] *nm* senility.

GATT [gat] *sigle m* (= *General Agreement on Tariffs and Trade*) GATT.

gauche [goʃ] *adj* left, left-hand; (*maladroit*) awkward, clumsy ♦ *nf* (*POL*) left (wing); (*BOXE*) left; **à** ~ on the left; (*direction*) (to the) left; **à** ~ **de** (on *ou* to the) left of; **à la** ~ **de** to the left of; **de** ~ (*POL*) left-wing.

gauchement [goʃmɑ̃] *adv* awkwardly, clumsily.

gaucher, ère [goʃe, -ɛʀ] *adj* left-handed.

gaucherie [goʃʀi] *nf* awkwardness, clumsiness.

gauchir [goʃiʀ] *vt* (*planche, objet*) to warp; (*fig: fait, idée*) to distort.

gauchisant, e [goʃizɑ̃, -ɑ̃t] *adj* with left-wing tendencies.

gauchisme [goʃism(ə)] *nm* leftism.

gauchiste [goʃist(ə)] *adj, nm/f* leftist.

gaufre [gofʀ(ə)] *nf* (*pâtisserie*) waffle; (*de cire*) honeycomb.

gaufrer [gofʀe] *vt* (*papier*) to emboss; (*tissu*) to goffer.

gaufrette [gofʀɛt] *nf* wafer.

gaufrier [gofʀije] *nm* (*moule*) waffle iron.

Gaule [gol] *nf*: **la** ~ Gaul.

gaule [gol] *nf* (*perche*) (long) pole; (*canne à pêche*) fishing rod.

gauler [gole] *vt* (*arbre*) to beat (*using a long pole to bring down fruit etc*); (*fruits*) to beat down (*with a pole*).

gaullisme [golism(ə)] *nm* Gaullism.

gaulliste [golist(ə)] *adj, nm/f* Gaullist.

gaulois, e [golwa, -waz] *adj* Gallic; (*grivois*) bawdy ♦ *nm/f*: G~, **e** Gaul.

gauloiserie [golwazʀi] *nf* bawdiness.

gausser [gose]: **se** ~ **de** *vt* to deride.

gaver [gave] *vt* to force-feed; (*fig*): ~ **de** to cram with, fill up with; (*personne*): **se** ~ **de** to stuff o.s. with.

gay [gɛ] *adj, nm* (*fam*) gay.

gaz [gaz] *nm inv* gas; **mettre les** ~ (*AUTO*) to put one's foot down; **chambre/masque à** ~ gas chamber/mask; ~ **en bouteille** bottled gas; ~ **butane** Calor gas ® (*BRIT*), butane gas; ~ **carbonique** carbon dioxide; ~ **hilarant** laughing gas; ~ **lacrymogène** tear gas; ~ **naturel** natural gas; ~ **de ville** town gas (*BRIT*), manufactured domestic gas.

gaze [gaz] *nf* gauze.

gazéifié, e [gazeifje] *adj* carbonated, aerated.

gazelle [gazɛl] *nf* gazelle.

gazer [gaze] *vt* to gas ♦ *vi* (*fam*) to be going *ou* working well.

gazette [gazɛt] *nf* news sheet.

gazeux, euse [gazø, -øz] *adj* gaseous; (*eau*) sparkling; (*boisson*) fizzy.

gazoduc [gazɔdyk] *nm* gas pipeline.

gazole [gazɔl] *nm* = **gas-oil**.

gazomètre [gazɔmɛtʀ(ə)] *nm* gasometer.

gazon [gazõ] *nm* (*herbe*) turf, grass; (*pelouse*) lawn.

gazonner [gazɔne] *vt* (*terrain*) to grass over.

gazouillement [gazujmã] *nm* (*voir vb*) chirping; babbling.

gazouiller [gazuje] *vi* (*oiseau*) to chirp; (*enfant*) to babble.

gazouillis [gazuji] *nmpl* chirp *sg*.

GB *sigle f* (= *Grande Bretagne*) GB.

gd *abr* (= *grand*) L.

GDF *sigle m* (= *Gaz de France*) *national gas company.*

geai [ʒɛ] *nm* jay.

géant, e [ʒeã, -ãt] *adj* gigantic, giant; (*COMM*) giant-size ♦ *nm/f* giant.

geignement [ʒɛɲmã] *nm* groaning, moaning.

geindre [ʒɛ̃dʀ(ə)] *vi* to groan, moan.

gel [ʒɛl] *nm* frost; (*de l'eau*) freezing; (*fig: des salaires, prix*) freeze; freezing; (*produit de beauté*) gel.

gélatine [ʒelatin] *nf* gelatine.

gélatineux, euse [ʒelatinø, -øz] *adj* jelly-like, gelatinous.

gelé, e [ʒəle] *adj* frozen ♦ *nf* jelly; (*gel*) frost; ~ **blanche** hoarfrost, white frost.

geler [ʒəle] *vt, vi* to freeze; **il gèle** it's freezing.

gélule [ʒelyl] *nf* capsule.

gelures [ʒəlyʀ] *nfpl* frostbite *sg*.

Gémeaux [ʒemo] *nmpl*: **les** ~ Gemini, the Twins; **être des** ~ to be Gemini.

gémir [ʒemiʀ] *vi* to groan, moan.

gémissement [ʒemismã] *nm* groan, moan.

gemme [ʒɛm] *nf* gem(stone).

gémonies [ʒemɔni] *nfpl*: **vouer qn aux** ~ to subject sb to public scorn.

gén. *abr* (= *généralement*) gen.

gênant, e [ʒɛnã, -ãt] *adj* (*objet*) awkward, in the way; (*histoire, personne*) embarrassing.

gencive [ʒãsiv] *nf* gum.

gendarme [ʒãdaʀm(ə)] *nm* gendarme.

gendarmer [ʒãdaʀme]: **se** ~ *vi* to kick up a fuss.

gendarmerie [ʒãdaʀməʀi] *nf military police force in countryside and small towns; their police station or barracks.*

gendre [ʒãdʀ(ə)] *nm* son-in-law.

gène [ʒɛn] *nm* (*BIO*) gene.

gêne [ʒɛn] *nf* (*à respirer, bouger*) discomfort, difficulty; (*dérangement*) bother, trouble; (*manque d'argent*) financial difficulties *pl ou* straits *pl*; (*confusion*) embarrassment; **sans** ~ *adj* inconsiderate.

gêné, e [ʒɛne] *adj* embarrassed; (*dépourvu d'argent*) short (of money).

généalogie [ʒenealɔʒi] *nf* genealogy.

généalogique [ʒenealɔʒik] *adj* genealogical.

gêner [ʒɛne] *vt* (*incommoder*) to bother; (*encombrer*) to hamper; (*bloquer le passage*) to be in the way of; (*déranger*) to bother; (*embarrasser*): ~ **qn** to make sb feel ill-at-ease; **se** ~ to put o.s. out; **ne vous gênez pas!** (*ironique*) go right ahead!, don't mind me!; **je**

vais me ~! (*ironique*) why should I care?

général, e, aux [ʒeneʀal, -o] *adj, nm* general ♦ *nf*: (*répétition*) ~**e** final dress rehearsal; **en** ~ usually, in general; **à la satisfaction** ~**e** to everyone's satisfaction.

généralement [ʒeneʀalmã] *adv* generally.

généralisable [ʒeneʀalizabl(ə)] *adj* generally applicable.

généralisation [ʒeneʀalizasjõ] *nf* generalization.

généraliser [ʒeneʀalize] *vt, vi* to generalize; **se** ~ *vi* to become widespread.

généraliste [ʒeneʀalist(ə)] *nm/f* (*MÉD*) general practitioner, GP.

généralité [ʒeneʀalite] *nf*: **la** ~ **des** ... the majority of ...; ~**s** *nfpl* generalities; (*introduction*) general points.

générateur, trice [ʒeneʀatœʀ, -tʀis] *adj*: ~ **de** which causes *ou* brings about ♦ *nf* (*ÉLEC*) generator.

génération [ʒeneʀasjõ] *nf* (*aussi INFORM*) generation.

généreusement [ʒeneʀøzmã] *adv* generously.

généreux, euse [ʒeneʀø, -øz] *adj* generous.

générique [ʒeneʀik] *adj* generic ♦ *nm* (*CINÉ, TV*) credits *pl*, credit titles *pl*.

générosité [ʒeneʀozite] *nf* generosity.

Gênes [ʒɛn] *n* Genoa.

genèse [ʒɔnɛz] *nf* genesis.

genêt [ʒɔnɛ] *nm* (*BOT*) broom *no pl*.

généticien, ne [ʒenetisjɛ̃, -ɛn] *nm/f* geneticist.

génétique [ʒenetik] *adj* genetic ♦ *nf* genetics *sg*.

génétiquement [ʒenetikmã] *adv* genetically.

gêneur, euse [ʒɛnœʀ, -øz] *nm/f* (*personne qui gêne*) obstacle; (*importun*) intruder.

Genève [ʒɔnɛv] *n* Geneva.

genevois, e [ʒɔnəvwa, -waz] *adj* Genevan.

genévrier [ʒɔnevʀije] *nm* juniper.

génial, e, aux [ʒenjal, -o] *adj* of genius; (*fam*) fantastic, brilliant.

génie [ʒeni] *nm* genius; (*MIL*): **le** ~ ≈ the Engineers *pl*; **avoir du** ~ to have genius; ~ **civil** civil engineering; ~ **génétique** genetic engineering.

genièvre [ʒɔnjɛvʀ(ə)] *nm* (*BOT*) juniper (tree); (*boisson*) geneva; **grain de** ~ juniper berry.

génisse [ʒenis] *nf* heifer; **foie de** ~ ox liver.

génital, e, aux [ʒenital, -o] *adj* genital.

génitif [ʒenitif] *nm* genitive.

génocide [ʒenɔsid] *nm* genocide.

génois, e [ʒenwa, -waz] *adj* Genoese ♦ *nf* (*gâteau*) ≈ sponge cake.

genou, x [ʒnu] *nm* knee; **à** ~**x** on one's knees; **se mettre à** ~**x** to kneel down.

genouillère [ʒɔnujɛʀ] *nf* (*SPORT*) kneepad.

genre [ʒãʀ] *nm* (*espèce, sorte*) kind, type, sort; (*allure*) manner; (*LING*) gender; (*ART*) genre; (*ZOOL etc*) genus; **se donner du** ~ to give o.s. airs; **avoir bon** ~ to have style; **avoir mauvais** ~ to be ill-mannered.

gens [ʒã] *nmpl* (*f in some phrases*) people *pl*; **les**

~ **d'Église** the clergy; **les** ~ **du monde** society people; ~ **de maison** domestics.
gentiane [ʒɑ̃sjɑn] nf gentian.
gentil, le [ʒɑ̃ti, -ij] adj kind; (enfant: sage) good; (sympa: endroit etc) nice; **c'est très** ~ **à vous** it's very kind ou good ou nice of you.
gentilhommière [ʒɑ̃tijɔmjɛʀ] nf (small) manor house ou country seat.
gentillesse [ʒɑ̃tijɛs] nf kindness.
gentillet, te [ʒɑ̃tijɛ, -ɛt] adj nice little.
gentiment [ʒɑ̃timɑ̃] adv kindly.
génuflexion [ʒenyflɛksjɔ̃] nf genuflexion.
géodésique [ʒeɔdezik] adj geodesic.
géographe [ʒeɔɡʀaf] nm/f geographer.
géographie [ʒeɔɡʀafi] nf geography.
géographique [ʒeɔɡʀafik] adj geographical.
geôlier [ʒolje] nm jailer.
géologie [ʒeɔlɔʒi] nf geology.
géologique [ʒeɔlɔʒik] adj geological.
géologiquement [ʒeɔlɔʒikmɑ̃] adv geologically.
géologue [ʒeɔlɔɡ] nm/f geologist.
géomètre [ʒeɔmɛtʀ(ə)] nm: **(arpenteur-)**~ (land) surveyor.
géométrie [ʒeɔmetʀi] nf geometry; **à** ~ **variable** (AVIAT) swing-wing.
géométrique [ʒeɔmetʀik] adj geometric.
géophysique [ʒeɔfizik] nf geophysics sg.
géopolitique [ʒeɔpɔlitik] nf geopolitics sg.
Géorgie [ʒeɔʀʒi] nf: **la** ~ (URSS, USA) Georgia; **la** ~ **du Sud** South Georgia.
géorgien, ne [ʒeɔʀʒjɛ̃, -ɛn] adj Georgian.
géostationnaire [ʒeɔstasjɔnɛʀ] adj geostationary.
géothermique [ʒeɔtɛʀmik] adj: **énergie** ~ geothermal energy.
gérance [ʒeʀɑ̃s] nf management; **mettre en** ~ to appoint a manager for; **prendre en** ~ to take over (the management of).
géranium [ʒeʀanjɔm] nm geranium.
gérant, e [ʒeʀɑ̃, -ɑ̃t] nm/f manager/manageress; ~ **d'immeuble** managing agent.
gerbe [ʒɛʀb(ə)] nf (de fleurs, d'eau) spray; (de blé) sheaf (pl sheaves); (fig) shower, burst.
gercé, e [ʒɛʀse] adj chapped.
gercer [ʒɛʀse] vi, **se** ~ vi to chap.
gerçure [ʒɛʀsyʀ] nf crack.
gérer [ʒeʀe] vt to manage.
gériatrie [ʒeʀjatʀi] nf geriatrics sg.
gériatrique [ʒeʀjatʀik] adj geriatric.
germain, e [ʒɛʀmɛ̃, -ɛn] adj: **cousin** ~ first cousin.
germanique [ʒɛʀmanik] adj Germanic.
germaniste [ʒɛʀmanist(ə)] nm/f German scholar.
germe [ʒɛʀm(ə)] nm germ.
germer [ʒɛʀme] vi to sprout; (semence, aussi fig) to germinate.
gérondif [ʒeʀɔ̃dif] nm gerund; (en latin) gerundive.
gérontologie [ʒeʀɔ̃tɔlɔʒi] nf gerontology.

gérontologue [ʒeʀɔ̃tɔlɔɡ] nm/f gerontologist.
gésier [ʒezje] nm gizzard.
gésir [ʒeziʀ] vi to be lying (down); voir aussi **ci-gît**.
gestation [ʒɛstasjɔ̃] nf gestation.
geste [ʒɛst(ə)] nm gesture; move; motion; **il fit un** ~ **de la main pour m'appeler** he signed to me to come over, he waved me over; **ne faites pas un** ~ (ne bougez pas) don't move.
gesticuler [ʒɛstikyle] vi to gesticulate.
gestion [ʒɛstjɔ̃] nf management; ~ **des disques** (INFORM) housekeeping; ~ **de fichier(s)** (INFORM) file management.
gestionnaire [ʒɛstjɔnɛʀ] nm/f administrator; ~ **de fichier** (INFORM) file manager.
geyser [ʒɛzɛʀ] nm geyser.
Ghana [gana] nm: **le** ~ Ghana.
ghanéen, ne [ganeɛ̃, -ɛn] adj Ghanaian.
ghetto [gɛto] nm ghetto.
gibecière [ʒibsjɛʀ] nf (de chasseur) gamebag; (sac en bandoulière) shoulder bag.
gibelotte [ʒiblɔt] nf rabbit fricassee in white wine.
gibet [ʒibɛ] nm gallows pl.
gibier [ʒibje] nm (animaux) game; (fig) prey.
giboulée [ʒibule] nf sudden shower.
giboyeux, euse [ʒibwajø, -øz] adj well-stocked with game.
Gibraltar [ʒibʀaltaʀ] nm Gibraltar.
gibus [ʒibys] nm opera hat.
giclée [ʒikle] nf spurt, squirt.
gicler [ʒikle] vi to spurt, squirt.
gicleur [ʒiklœʀ] nm (AUTO) jet.
GIE sigle m = **groupement d'intérêt économique**.
gifle [ʒifl(ə)] nf slap (in the face).
gifler [ʒifle] vt to slap (in the face).
gigantesque [ʒigɑ̃tɛsk(ə)] adj gigantic.
gigantisme [ʒigɑ̃tism(ə)] nm (MÉD) gigantism; (des mégalopoles) vastness.
gigaoctet [ʒigaɔktɛ] nm gigabyte.
GIGN sigle m (= Groupe d'intervention de la gendarmerie nationale) special crack force of the gendarmerie, ≈ SAS (BRIT).
gigogne [ʒigɔɲ] adj: **lits** ~s truckle (BRIT) ou trundle (US) beds; **tables/poupées** ~s nest of tables/dolls.
gigolo [ʒigɔlo] nm gigolo.
gigot [ʒigo] nm leg (of mutton ou lamb).
gigoter [ʒigɔte] vi to wriggle (about).
gilet [ʒilɛ] nm waistcoat; (pull) cardigan; (de corps) vest; ~ **pare-balles** bulletproof jacket; ~ **de sauvetage** life jacket.
gin [dʒin] nm gin.
gingembre [ʒɛ̃ʒɑ̃bʀ(ə)] nm ginger.
gingivite [ʒɛ̃ʒivit] nf inflammation of the gums, gingivitis.
ginseng [ʒinsɛŋ] nm ginseng.
girafe [ʒiʀaf] nf giraffe.
giratoire [ʒiʀatwaʀ] adj: **sens** ~ roundabout.
girofle [ʒiʀɔfl(ə)] nm: **clou de** ~ clove.
giroflée [ʒiʀɔfle] nf wallflower.

girolle [ʒiʀɔl] *nf* chanterelle.

giron [ʒiʀɔ̃] *nm* (*genoux*) lap; (*fig: sein*) bosom.

Gironde [ʒiʀɔ̃d] *nf*: **la** ~ the Gironde.

girophare [ʒiʀɔfaʀ] *nm* revolving (flashing) light.

girouette [ʒiʀwɛt] *nf* weather vane *ou* cock.

gis [ʒi], **gisais** [ʒizɛ] *etc vb voir* **gésir.**

gisement [ʒizmɑ̃] *nm* deposit.

gît [ʒi] *vb voir* **gésir.**

gitan, e [ʒitɑ̃, -an] *nm/f* gipsy.

gîte [ʒit] *nm* home; shelter; (*du lièvre*) form; ~ **(rural)** (*country*) holiday cottage *ou* apartment.

gîter [ʒite] *vi* (*NAVIG*) to list.

givrage [ʒivʀaʒ] *nm* icing.

givrant, e [ʒivʀɑ̃, -ɑ̃t] *adj*: **brouillard** ~ freezing fog.

givre [ʒivʀ(ə)] *nm* (hoar)frost.

givré, e [ʒivʀe] *adj*: **citron** ~/**orange** ~**e** lemon/orange sorbet (*served in fruit skin*).

glabre [glabʀ(ə)] *adj* hairless; (*menton*) clean-shaven.

glaçage [glasaʒ] *nm* (*au sucre*) icing; (*au blanc d'œuf, de la viande*) glazing.

glace [glas] *nf* ice; (*crème glacée*) ice cream; (*verre*) sheet of glass; (*miroir*) mirror; (*de voiture*) window; ~**s** *nfpl* (*GÉO*) ice sheets, ice *sg*; **de** ~ (*fig: accueil, visage*) frosty, icy; **rester de** ~ to remain unmoved.

glacé, e [glase] *adj* icy; (*boisson*) iced.

glacer [glase] *vt* to freeze; (*boisson*) to chill, ice; (*gâteau*) to ice (*BRIT*), frost (*US*); (*papier, tissu*) to glaze; (*fig*): ~ **qn** to chill sb; (*fig*) to make sb's blood run cold.

glaciaire [glasjɛʀ] *adj* (*période*) ice *cpd*; (*relief*) glacial.

glacial, e [glasjal] *adj* icy.

glacier [glasje] *nm* (*GÉO*) glacier; (*marchand*) ice-cream maker.

glacière [glasjɛʀ] *nf* icebox.

glaçon [glasɔ̃] *nm* icicle; (*pour boisson*) ice cube.

gladiateur [gladjatœʀ] *nm* gladiator.

glaïeul [glajœl] *nm* gladiola.

glaire [glɛʀ] *nf* (*MÉD*) phlegm *no pl*.

glaise [glɛz] *nf* clay.

glaive [glɛv] *nm* two-edged sword.

gland [glɑ̃] *nm* (*de chêne*) acorn; (*décoration*) tassel; (*ANAT*) glans.

glande [glɑ̃d] *nf* gland.

glander [glɑ̃de] *vi* (*fam*) to fart around (*BRIT !*), screw around (*US !*).

glaner [glane] *vt, vi* to glean.

glapir [glapiʀ] *vi* to yelp.

glapissement [glapismɑ̃] *nm* yelping.

glas [glɑ] *nm* knell, toll.

glauque [glok] *adj* dull blue-green.

glissade [glisad] *nf* (*par jeu*) slide; (*chute*) slip; (*dérapage*) skid; **faire des** ~**s** to slide.

glissant, e [glisɑ̃, -ɑ̃t] *adj* slippery.

glisse [glis] *nf*: **sports de** ~ sports involving sliding or gliding (*eg skiing, surfing, windsurfing*).

glissement [glismɑ̃] *nm* sliding; (*fig*) shift; ~ **de terrain** landslide.

glisser [glise] *vi* (*avancer*) to glide *ou* slide along; (*coulisser, tomber*) to slide; (*déraper*) to slip; (*être glissant*) to be slippery ♦ *vt*: ~ **qch sous/dans/à** to slip sth under/into/to; ~ **sur** (*fig: détail etc*) to skate over; **se** ~ **dans/entre** to slip into/between.

glissière [glisjɛʀ] *nf* slide channel; **à** ~ (*porte, fenêtre*) sliding; ~ **de sécurité** (*AUTO*) crash barrier.

glissoire [gliswaʀ] *nf* slide.

global, e, aux [glɔbal, -o] *adj* overall.

globalement [glɔbalmɑ̃] *adv* taken as a whole.

globe [glɔb] *nm* globe; **sous** ~ under glass; ~ **oculaire** eyeball; **le** ~ **terrestre** the globe.

globe-trotter [glɔbtʀɔtœʀ] *nm* globe-trotter.

globule [glɔbyl] *nm* (*du sang*): ~ **blanc/rouge** white/red corpuscle.

globuleux, euse [glɔbylø, -øz] *adj*: **yeux** ~ protruding eyes.

gloire [glwaʀ] *nf* glory; (*mérite*) distinction, credit; (*personne*) celebrity.

glorieux, euse [glɔʀjø, -øz] *adj* glorious.

glorifier [glɔʀifje] *vt* to glorify, extol; **se** ~ **de** to glory in.

gloriole [glɔʀjɔl] *nf* vainglory.

glose [gloz] *nf* gloss.

glossaire [glɔsɛʀ] *nm* glossary.

glotte [glɔt] *nf* (*ANAT*) glottis.

glouglouter [gluglute] *vi* to gurgle.

gloussement [glusmɑ̃] *nm* (*de poule*) cluck; (*rire*) chuckle.

glousser [gluse] *vi* to cluck; (*rire*) to chuckle.

glouton, ne [glutɔ̃, -ɔn] *adj* gluttonous, greedy.

gloutonnerie [glutɔnʀi] *nf* gluttony.

glu [gly] *nf* birdlime.

gluant, e [glyɑ̃, -ɑ̃t] *adj* sticky, gummy.

glucide [glysid] *nm* carbohydrate.

glucose [glykoz] *nm* glucose.

gluten [glytɛn] *nm* gluten.

glycérine [gliseʀin] *nf* glycerine.

glycine [glisin] *nf* wisteria.

GMT *sigle adj* (= *Greenwich Mean Time*) GMT.

gnangnan [ɲɑ̃ɲɑ̃] *adj inv* (*fam: livre, film*) soppy.

GNL *sigle m* (= *gaz naturel liquéfié*) LNG (= *liquefied natural gas*).

gnôle [ɲol] *nf* (*fam*) booze *no pl*; **un petit verre de** ~ a drop of the hard stuff.

gnome [gnom] *nm* gnome.

gnon [ɲɔ̃] *nm* (*fam: coup de poing*) bash; (: *marque*) dent.

GO *sigle fpl* (= *grandes ondes*) LW ♦ *sigle m* (= *gentil organisateur*) title given to leaders on *Club Méditerranée* holidays; *extended to refer to easy-going leader of any group.*

go [go]: **tout de** ~ *adv* straight out.

goal [gol] *nm* goalkeeper.

gobelet [gɔblɛ] *nm* (*en métal*) tumbler; (*en*

plastique) beaker; *(à dés)* cup.

gober [gɔbe] *vt* to swallow.

goberger [gɔbɛRʒe]: **se ~** *vi* to cosset o.s.

Gobi [gɔbi] *n*: **désert de ~** Gobi Desert.

godasse [gɔdas] *nf (fam)* shoe.

godet [gɔdɛ] *nm* pot; *(COUTURE)* unpressed pleat.

godiller [gɔdije] *vi (NAVIG)* to scull; *(SKI)* to wedeln.

goéland [gɔelɑ̃] *nm* (sea)gull.

goélette [gɔelɛt] *nf* schooner.

goémon [gɔemɔ̃] *nm* wrack.

gogo [gɔgo] *nm (péj)* mug, sucker; **à ~** *adv* galore.

goguenard, e [gɔgnaR, -aRd(ə)] *adj* mocking.

goguette [gɔgɛt] *nf*: **en ~** on the binge.

goinfre [gwɛ̃fR(ə)] *nm* glutton.

goinfrer [gwɛ̃fRe]: **se ~** *vi* to make a pig of o.s.; **se ~ de** to guzzle.

goitre [gwatR(ə)] *nm* goitre.

golf [gɔlf] *nm (jeu)* golf; *(terrain)* golf course; **~ miniature** crazy *ou* miniature golf.

golfe [gɔlf(ə)] *nm* gulf; bay; **le ~ d'Aden** the Gulf of Aden; **le ~ de Gascogne** the Bay of Biscay; **le ~ du Lion** the Gulf of Lions; **le ~ Persique** the Persian Gulf.

golfeur, euse [gɔlfœR, -øz] *nm/f* golfer.

gominé, e [gɔmine] *adj* slicked down.

gomme [gɔm] *nf (à effacer)* rubber *(BRIT)*, eraser; *(résine)* gum; **boule** *ou* **pastille de ~** throat pastille.

gommé, e [gɔme] *adj*: **papier ~** gummed paper.

gommer [gɔme] *vt (effacer)* to rub out *(BRIT)*, erase; *(enduire de gomme)* to gum.

gond [gɔ̃] *nm* hinge; **sortir de ses ~s** *(fig)* to fly off the handle.

gondole [gɔ̃dɔl] *nf* gondola; *(pour l'étalage)* shelves *pl*, gondola.

gondoler [gɔ̃dɔle]: **se ~** *vi* to warp, buckle; *(fam: rire)* to hoot with laughter; to be in stitches.

gondolier [gɔ̃dɔlje] *nm* gondolier.

gonflable [gɔ̃flabl(ə)] *adj* inflatable.

gonflage [gɔ̃flaʒ] *nm* inflating, blowing up.

gonflé, e [gɔ̃fle] *adj* swollen; *(ventre)* bloated; *(fam: culotté)*: **être ~** to have a nerve.

gonflement [gɔ̃fləmɑ̃] *nm* inflation; *(MÉD)* swelling.

gonfler [gɔ̃fle] *vt (pneu, ballon)* to inflate, blow up; *(nombre, importance)* to inflate ♦ *vi (pied etc)* to swell (up); *(CULIN: pâte)* to rise.

gonfleur [gɔ̃flœR] *nm* air pump.

gong [gɔ̃g] *nm* gong.

gonzesse [gɔ̃zɛs] *nf (fam)* chick, bird *(BRIT)*.

goret [gɔRɛ] *nm* piglet.

gorge [gɔRʒ(ə)] *nf (ANAT)* throat; *(poitrine)* breast; *(GÉO)* gorge; *(rainure)* groove; **avoir mal à la ~** to have a sore throat; **avoir la ~ serrée** to have a lump in one's throat.

gorgé, e [gɔRʒe] *adj*: **~ de** filled with; *(eau)* saturated with ♦ *nf* mouthful; sip; gulp;

boire à petites/grandes ~es to take little sips/big gulps.

gorille [gɔRij] *nm* gorilla; *(fam)* bodyguard.

gosier [gozje] *nm* throat.

gosse [gɔs] *nm/f* kid.

gothique [gɔtik] *adj* gothic.

gouache [gwaʃ] *nf* gouache.

gouaille [gwaj] *nf* street wit, cocky humour *(BRIT)* ou humor *(US)*.

goudron [gudRɔ̃] *nm (asphalte)* tar(mac) *(BRIT)*, asphalt; *(du tabac)* tar.

goudronner [gudRɔne] *vt* to tar(mac) *(BRIT)*, asphalt.

gouffre [gufR(ə)] *nm* abyss, gulf.

goujat [guʒa] *nm* boor.

goujon [guʒɔ̃] *nm* gudgeon.

goulée [gule] *nf* gulp.

goulet [gulɛ] *nm* bottleneck.

goulot [gulo] *nm* neck; **boire au ~** to drink from the bottle.

goulu, e [guly] *adj* greedy.

goulûment [gulymɑ̃] *adv* greedily.

goupille [gupij] *nf* (metal) pin.

goupiller [gupije] *vt* to pin (together).

goupillon [gupijɔ̃] *nm (REL)* sprinkler; *(brosse)* bottle brush; **le ~** *(fig)* the cloth, the clergy.

gourd, e [guR, guRd(ə)] *adj* numb (with cold); *(fam)* oafish.

gourde [guRd(ə)] *nf (récipient)* flask; *(fam)* (clumsy) clot *ou* oaf.

gourdin [guRdɛ̃] *nm* club, bludgeon.

gourmand, e [guRmɑ̃, -ɑ̃d] *adj* greedy.

gourmandise [guRmɑ̃diz] *nf* greed; *(bonbon)* sweet *(BRIT)*, piece of candy *(US)*.

gourmet [guRmɛ] *nm* epicure.

gourmette [guRmɛt] *nf* chain bracelet.

gourou [guRu] *nm* guru.

gousse [gus] *nf (de vanille etc)* pod; **~ d'ail** clove of garlic.

gousset [gusɛ] *nm (de gilet)* fob.

goût [gu] *nm* taste; *(fig: appréciation)* taste, liking; **le (bon) ~** good taste; **de bon ~** in good taste, tasteful; **de mauvais ~** in bad taste, tasteless; **avoir bon/mauvais ~** *(aliment)* to taste nice/nasty; *(personne)* to have good/bad taste; **avoir du/manquer de ~** to have/lack taste; **avoir du ~ pour** to have a liking for; **prendre ~ à** to develop a taste *ou* a liking for.

goûter [gute] *vt (essayer)* to taste; *(apprécier)* to enjoy ♦ *vi* to have (afternoon) tea ♦ *nm* (afternoon) tea; **~ à** to taste, sample; **~ de** to have a taste of; **~ d'enfants/d'anniversaire** children's tea/birthday party.

goutte [gut] *nf* drop; *(MÉD)* gout; *(alcool)* nip *(BRIT)*, tot *(BRIT)*, drop *(US)*; **~s** *nfpl (MÉD)* drops; **~ à ~** *adv* a drop at a time; **tomber à ~** to drip.

goutte-à-goutte [gutagut] *nm inv (MÉD)* drip; **alimenter au ~** to drip-feed.

gouttelette [gutlɛt] *nf* droplet.

goutter [gute] *vi* to drip.

gouttière [gutjɛʀ] *nf* gutter.

gouvernail [guvɛʀnaj] *nm* rudder; (*barre*) helm, tiller.

gouvernant, e [guvɛʀnɑ̃, -ɑ̃t] *adj* ruling *cpd* ♦ *nf* housekeeper; (*d'un enfant*) governess.

gouverne [guvɛʀn(ə)] *nf*: **pour sa ~** for his guidance.

gouvernement [guvɛʀnəmɑ̃] *nm* government.

gouvernemental, e, aux [guvɛʀnəmɑ̃tal, -o] *adj* (*politique*) government *cpd*; (*journal, parti*) pro-government.

gouverner [guvɛʀne] *vt* to govern; (*diriger*) to steer; (*fig*) to control.

gouverneur [guvɛʀnœʀ] *nm* governor; (*MIL*) commanding officer.

goyave [gɔjav] *nf* guava.

GPL *sigle m* (= *gaz de pétrole liquéfié*) LPG (= liquefied petroleum gas).

GQG *sigle m* (= *grand quartier général*) GHQ.

grabataire [gʀabatɛʀ] *adj* bedridden ♦ *nm/f* bedridden invalid.

grâce [gʀɑs] *nf* grace; (*faveur*) favour; (*JUR*) pardon; **~s** *nfpl* (*REL*) grace *sg*; **de bonne/ mauvaise ~** with (a) good/bad grace; **dans les bonnes ~s de qn** in favour with sb; **faire ~ à qn de qch** to spare sb sth; **rendre ~(s) à** to give thanks to; **demander ~** to beg for mercy; **droit de ~** right of reprieve; **recours en ~** plea for pardon; **~ à** *prép* thanks to.

gracier [gʀasje] *vt* to pardon.

gracieusement [gʀasjøzmɑ̃] *adv* graciously, kindly; (*gratuitement*) freely; (*avec grâce*) gracefully.

gracieux, euse [gʀasjø, -øz] *adj* (*charmant, élégant*) graceful; (*aimable*) gracious, kind; **à titre ~** free of charge.

gracile [gʀasil] *adj* slender.

gradation [gʀadɑsjɔ̃] *nf* gradation.

grade [gʀad] *nm* (*MIL*) rank; (*SCOL*) degree; **monter en ~** to be promoted.

gradé [gʀade] *nm* (*MIL*) officer.

gradin [gʀadɛ̃] *nm* (*dans un théâtre*) tier; (*de stade*) step; **~s** *nmpl* (*de stade*) terracing *no pl* (*BRIT*), standing area; **en ~s** terraced.

graduation [gʀadɥasjɔ̃] *nf* graduation.

gradué, e [gʀadɥe] *adj* (*exercices*) graded (for difficulty); (*thermomètre, verre*) graduated.

graduel, le [gʀadɥɛl] *adj* gradual; progressive.

graduer [gʀadɥe] *vt* (*effort etc*) to increase gradually; (*règle, verre*) to graduate; (*exercices*) to increase in difficulty.

graffiti [gʀafiti] *nmpl* graffiti.

grain [gʀɛ̃] *nm* (*gén*) grain; (*de chapelet*) bead; (*NAVIG*) squall; (*averse*) heavy shower; (*fig: petite quantité*): **un ~ de** a touch of; **~ de beauté** beauty spot; **~ de café** coffee bean; **~ de poivre** peppercorn; **~ de poussière** speck of dust; **~ de raisin** grape.

graine [gʀɛn] *nf* seed; **mauvaise ~** (*mauvais sujet*) bad lot; **une ~ de voyou** a hooligan in the making.

graineterie [gʀɛntʀi] *nf* seed merchant's (shop).

grainetier, -ière [gʀɛntje, -jɛʀ] *nm/f* seed merchant.

graissage [gʀɛsaʒ] *nm* lubrication, greasing.

graisse [gʀɛs] *nf* fat; (*lubrifiant*) grease; **~ saturée** saturated fat.

graisser [gʀese] *vt* to lubricate, grease; (*tacher*) to make greasy.

graisseux, euse [gʀesø, -øz] *adj* greasy; (*ANAT*) fatty.

grammaire [gʀamɛʀ] *nf* grammar.

grammatical, e, aux [gʀamatikal, -o] *adj* grammatical.

gramme [gʀam] *nm* gramme.

grand, e [gʀɑ̃, gʀɑ̃d] *adj* (*haut*) tall; (*gros, vaste, large*) big, large; (*long*) long; (*sens abstraits*) great ♦ *adv*: **~ ouvert** wide open; **un ~ buveur** a heavy drinker; **un ~ homme** a great man; **son ~ frère** his big *ou* older brother; **avoir ~ besoin de** to be in dire *ou* desperate need of; **il est ~ temps de** it's high time to; **il est assez ~ pour** he's big *ou* old enough to; **voir ~** to think big; **en ~** on a large scale; **au ~ air** in the open (air); **les ~s blessés/brûlés** the severely injured/burned; **de ~ matin** at the crack of dawn; **~ écart** splits *pl*; **~ ensemble** housing scheme; **~ jour** broad daylight; **~ livre** (*COMM*) ledger; **~ magasin** department store; **~ malade** very sick person; **~ public** general public; **~e personne** grown-up; **~e surface** hypermarket, superstore; **~es écoles** prestige university-level colleges with competitive entrance examinations; **~es lignes** (*RAIL*) main lines; **~es vacances** summer holidays.

> The **grandes écoles** are prestigious French establishments of tertiary education preparing students for specific careers. Students who have undertaken two years study after the **baccalauréat** in the **classes préparatoires** are recruited by competitive entry examination. The grandes écoles have a strong corporate identity and provide the intellectual, administrative and political elite of the country.

grand-angle, pl grands-angles [gʀɑ̃tɑ̃gl(ə)] *nm* (*PHOTO*) wide-angle lens.

grand-angulaire, pl grands-angulaires [gʀɑ̃tɑ̃gylɛʀ] *nm* (*PHOTO*) wide-angle lens.

grand-chose [gʀɑ̃ʃoz] *nm/f inv*: **pas ~** not much.

Grande-Bretagne [gʀɑ̃dbʀətaɲ] *nf*: **la ~** (Great) Britain; **en ~** in (Great) Britain.

grandement [gʀɑ̃dmɑ̃] *adv* (*tout à fait*) greatly; (*largement*) easily; (*généreusement*) lavishly.

grandeur [gʀɑ̃dœʀ] *nf* (*dimension*) size; (*fig: ampleur, importance*) magnitude; (: *gloire, puissance*) greatness; **~ nature** *adj* life-size.

grand-guignolesque [gʀɑ̃giɲɔlɛsk(ə)] *adj* gruesome.

grandiloquent, e [gʀɑ̃dilɔkɑ̃, -ɑ̃t] *adj* bombastic, grandiloquent.

grandiose [gʀɑ̃djoz] *adj* (*paysage, spectacle*) imposing.

grandir [gʀɑ̃diʀ] *vi* (*enfant, arbre*) to grow; (*bruit, hostilité*) to increase, grow ♦ *vt:* ~ **qn** (*suj: vêtement, chaussure*) to make sb look taller; (*fig*) to make sb grow in stature.

grandissant, e [gʀɑ̃disɑ̃, -ɑ̃t] growing.

grand-mère, *pl* **grand(s)-mères** [gʀɑ̃mɛʀ] *nf* grandmother.

grand-messe [gʀɑ̃mɛs] *nf* high mass.

grand-oncle, *pl* **grands-oncles** [gʀɑ̃tɔ̃kl(ə), gʀɑ̃zɔ̃kl(ə)] *nm* great-uncle.

grand-peine [gʀɑ̃pɛn]: **à** ~ *adv* with (great) difficulty.

grand-père, *pl* **grands-pères** [gʀɑ̃pɛʀ] *nm* grandfather.

grand-route [gʀɑ̃ʀut] *nf* main road.

grand-rue [gʀɑ̃ʀy] *nf* high street.

grands-parents [gʀɑ̃paʀɑ̃] *nmpl* grandparents.

grand-tante, *pl* **grand(s)-tantes** [gʀɑ̃tɑ̃t] *nf* great-aunt.

grand-voile [gʀɑ̃vwal] *nf* mainsail.

grange [gʀɑ̃ʒ] *nf* barn.

granit(e) [gʀanit] *nm* granite.

granitique [gʀanitik] *adj* granite; (*terrain*) granitic.

granule [gʀanyl] *nm* small pill.

granulé [gʀanyle] *nm* granule.

granuleux, euse [gʀanylø, -øz] *adj* granular.

graphe [gʀaf] *nm* graph.

graphie [gʀafi] *nf* written form.

graphique [gʀafik] *adj* graphic ♦ *nm* graph.

graphisme [gʀafism(ə)] *nm* graphic arts *pl*; graphics *sg*; (*écriture*) handwriting.

graphiste [gʀafist(ə)] *nm/f* graphic designer.

graphologie [gʀafɔlɔʒi] *nf* graphology.

graphologue [gʀafɔlɔg] *nm/f* graphologist.

grappe [gʀap] *nf* cluster; ~ **de raisin** bunch of grapes.

grappiller [gʀapije] *vt* to glean.

grappin [gʀapɛ̃] *nm* grapnel; **mettre le** ~ **sur** (*fig*) to get one's claws on.

gras, se [gʀɑ, gʀɑs] *adj* (*viande, soupe*) fatty; (*personne*) fat; (*surface, main, cheveux*) greasy; (*terre*) sticky; (*toux*) loose, phlegmy; (*rire*) throaty; (*plaisanterie*) coarse; (*crayon*) soft-lead; (*TYPO*) bold ♦ *nm* (*CULIN*) fat; **faire la** ~**se matinée** to have a lie-in (*BRIT*), sleep late; **matière** ~**se** fat (content).

gras-double [gʀɑdubl(ə)] *nm* (*CULIN*) tripe.

grassement [gʀɑsmɑ̃] *adv* (*généreusement*): ~ **payé** handsomely paid; (*grossièrement: rire*) coarsely.

grassouillet, te [gʀasujɛ, -ɛt] *adj* podgy, plump.

gratifiant, e [gʀatifjɑ̃, -ɑ̃t] *adj* gratifying, rewarding.

gratification [gʀatifikasjɔ̃] *nf* bonus.

gratifier [gʀatifje] *vt:* ~ **qn de** to favour (*BRIT*)

ou favor (*US*) sb with; to reward sb with; (*sourire etc*) to favo(u)r sb with.

gratin [gʀatɛ̃] *nm* (*CULIN*) cheese- (*ou* crumb-) topped dish; (: *croûte*) topping; **au** ~ au gratin; **tout le** ~ **parisien** all the best people of Paris.

gratiné, e [gʀatine] *adj* (*CULIN*) au gratin; (*fam*) hellish ♦ *nf* (*soupe*) onion soup au gratin.

gratis [gʀatis] *adv, adj* free.

gratitude [gʀatityd] *nf* gratitude.

gratte-ciel [gʀatsjɛl] *nm inv* skyscraper.

grattement [gʀatmɑ̃] *nm* (*bruit*) scratching (noise).

gratte-papier [gʀatpapje] *nm inv* (*péj*) penpusher.

gratter [gʀate] *vt* (*frotter*) to scrape; (*enlever*) to scrape off; (*bras, bouton*) to scratch; **se** ~ to scratch o.s.

grattoir [gʀatwaʀ] *nm* scraper.

gratuit, e [gʀatɥi, -ɥit] *adj* (*entrée*) free; (*billet*) free, complimentary; (*fig*) gratuitous.

gratuité [gʀatɥite] *nf* being free (of charge); gratuitousness.

gratuitement [gʀatɥitmɑ̃] *adv* (*sans payer*) free; (*sans preuve, motif*) gratuitously.

gravats [gʀava] *nmpl* rubble *sg*.

grave [gʀav] *adj* (*dangereux: maladie, accident*) serious, bad; (*sérieux: sujet, problème*) serious, grave; (*personne, air*) grave, solemn; (*voix, son*) deep, low-pitched ♦ *nm* (*MUS*) low register; **ce n'est pas** ~! it's all right, don't worry; **blessé** ~ seriously injured person.

graveleux, euse [gʀavlø, -øz] *adj* (*terre*) gravelly; (*fruit*) gritty; (*contes, propos*) smutty.

gravement [gʀavmɑ̃] *adv* seriously; badly; gravely.

graver [gʀave] *vt* (*plaque, nom*) to engrave; (*fig*): ~ **qch dans son esprit/sa mémoire** to etch sth in one's mind/memory.

graveur [gʀavœʀ] *nm* engraver.

gravier [gʀavje] *nm* (*loose*) gravel *no pl*.

gravillons [gʀavijɔ̃] *nmpl* gravel *sg*, loose chippings *ou* gravel.

gravir [gʀaviʀ] *vt* to climb (up).

gravitation [gʀavitasjɔ̃] *nf* gravitation.

gravité [gʀavite] *nf* (*voir grave*) seriousness; gravity; (*PHYSIQUE*) gravity.

graviter [gʀavite] *vi:* ~ **autour de** to revolve around.

gravure [gʀavyʀ] *nf* engraving; (*reproduction*) print; plate.

GRE *sigle f* (= *garantie contre les risques à l'exportation*) ≈ service provided by ECGD (= *Export Credit Guarantees Department*).

gré [gʀe] *nm:* **à son** ~ *adj* to his liking ♦ *adv* as he pleases; **au** ~ **de** according to, following; **contre le** ~ **de qn** against sb's will; **de son (plein)** ~ of one's own free will; **de** ~ **ou de force** whether one likes it or not; **de bon** ~ willingly; **bon** ~ **mal** ~ like it or not; willy-nilly; **de** ~ **à** ~ (*COMM*) by mutual agreement; **savoir (bien)** ~ **à qn de qch** to be (most) grateful to sb for sth.

grec, grecque [gʀɛk] *adj* Greek; (*classique: vase etc*) Grecian ♦ *nm* (*LING*) Greek ♦ *nm/f:* **G~, Grecque** Greek.

Grèce [gʀɛs] *nf:* **la** ~ Greece.

gredin, e [gʀədɛ̃, -in] *nm/f* rogue, rascal.

gréement [gʀemɑ̃] *nm* rigging.

greffe [gʀɛf] *nf* graft; transplant ♦ *nm* (*JUR*) office.

greffer [gʀefe] *vt* (*BOT, MÉD: tissu*) to graft; (*MÉD: organe*) to transplant.

greffier [gʀefje] *nm* clerk of the court.

grégaire [gʀegɛʀ] *adj* gregarious.

grège [gʀɛʒ] *adj:* **soie** ~ raw silk.

grêle [gʀɛl] *adj* (very) thin ♦ *nf* hail.

grêlé, e [gʀele] *adj* pockmarked.

grêler [gʀele] *vb impers:* **il grêle** it's hailing ♦ *vt:* **la région a été grêlée** the region was damaged by hail.

grêlon [gʀɛlɔ̃] *nm* hailstone.

grelot [gʀəlo] *nm* little bell.

grelottant, e [gʀəlɔtɑ̃, -ɑ̃t] *adj* shivering, shivery.

grelotter [gʀəlɔte] *vi* (*trembler*) to shiver.

Grenade [gʀənad] *n* Granada ♦ *nf* (*île*) Grenada.

grenade [gʀənad] *nf* (*explosive*) grenade; (*BOT*) pomegranate; ~ **lacrymogène** teargas grenade.

grenadier [gʀənadje] *nm* (*MIL*) grenadier; (*BOT*) pomegranate tree.

grenadine [gʀənadin] *nf* grenadine.

grenat [gʀəna] *adj inv* dark red.

grenier [gʀənje] *nm* (*de maison*) attic; (*de ferme*) loft.

grenouille [gʀənuj] *nf* frog.

grenouillère [gʀənujɛʀ] *nf* (*de bébé*) leggings; (*: combinaison*) sleepsuit.

grenu, e [gʀəny] *adj* grainy, grained.

grès [gʀɛ] *nm* (*roche*) sandstone; (*poterie*) stoneware.

grésil [gʀezi] *nm* (fine) hail.

grésillement [gʀezijmɑ̃] *nm* sizzling; crackling.

grésiller [gʀezije] *vi* to sizzle; (*RADIO*) to crackle.

grève [gʀɛv] *nf* (*d'ouvriers*) strike; (*plage*) shore; **se mettre en/faire** ~ to go on/be on strike; ~ **bouchon** partial strike (*in key areas of a company*); ~ **de la faim** hunger strike; ~ **perlée** go-slow (*BRIT*), slowdown (*US*); ~ **sauvage** wildcat strike; ~ **de solidarité** sympathy strike; ~ **surprise** lightning strike; ~ **sur le tas** sit down strike; ~ **tournante** strike by rota; ~ **du zèle** work-to-rule (*BRIT*), slowdown (*US*).

grever [gʀəve] *vt* (*budget, économie*) to put a strain on; **grevé d'impôts** crippled by taxes; **grevé d'hypothèques** heavily mortgaged.

gréviste [gʀevist(ə)] *nm/f* striker.

gribouillage [gʀibujaʒ] *nm* scribble, scrawl.

gribouiller [gʀibuje] *vt* to scribble, scrawl ♦ *vi* to doodle.

gribouillis [gʀibuji] *nm* (*dessin*) doodle; (*action*) doodling *no pl*; (*écriture*) scribble.

grief [gʀijɛf] *nm* grievance; **faire** ~ **à qn de** to reproach sb for.

grièvement [gʀijɛvmɑ̃] *adv* seriously.

griffe [gʀif] *nf* claw; (*fig*) signature; (*: d'un couturier, parfumeur*) label, signature.

griffé, e [gʀife] *adj* designer(-label) *cpd*.

griffer [gʀife] *vt* to scratch.

griffon [gʀifɔ̃] *nm* (*chien*) griffon.

griffonnage [gʀifɔnaʒ] *nm* scribble.

griffonner [gʀifɔne] *vt* to scribble.

griffure [gʀifyʀ] *nf* scratch.

grignoter [gʀiɲɔte] *vt, vi* to nibble.

gril [gʀil] *nm* steak *ou* grill pan.

grillade [gʀijad] *nf* grill.

grillage [gʀijaʒ] *nm* (*treillis*) wire netting; (*clôture*) wire fencing.

grillager [gʀijaʒe] *vt* (*objet*) to put wire netting on; (*périmètre, jardin*) to put wire fencing around.

grille [gʀij] *nf* (*portail*) (metal) gate; (*clôture*) railings *pl*; (*d'égout*) (metal) grate; (*fig*) grid.

grille-pain [gʀijpɛ̃] *nm inv* toaster.

griller [gʀije] *vt* (*aussi:* **faire** ~: *pain*) to toast; (*: viande*) to grill (*BRIT*), broil (*US*); (*: café*) to roast; (*fig: ampoule etc*) to burn out, blow; ~ **un feu rouge** to jump the lights (*BRIT*), run a stoplight (*US*) ♦ *vi* (*brûler*) to be roasting.

grillon [gʀijɔ̃] *nm* (*ZOOL*) cricket.

grimace [gʀimas] *nf* grimace; (*pour faire rire*): **faire des** ~**s** to pull *ou* make faces.

grimacer [gʀimase] *vi* to grimace.

grimacier, ière [gʀimasje, -jɛʀ] *adj:* **c'est un enfant** ~ that child is always pulling faces.

grimer [gʀime] *vt* to make up.

grimoire [gʀimwaʀ] *nm* (*illisible*) unreadable scribble; (*livre de magie*) book of magic spells.

grimpant, e [gʀɛ̃pɑ̃, -ɑ̃t] *adj:* **plante** ~**e** climbing plant, climber.

grimper [gʀɛ̃pe] *vi, vt* to climb ♦ *nm:* **le** ~ (*SPORT*) rope-climbing; ~ **à/sur** to climb (up)/climb onto.

grimpeur, euse [gʀɛ̃pœʀ, -øz] *nm/f* climber.

grinçant, e [gʀɛ̃sɑ̃, -ɑ̃t] *adj* grating.

grincement [gʀɛ̃smɑ̃] *nm* grating (noise); creaking (noise).

grincer [gʀɛ̃se] *vi* (*porte, roue*) to grate; (*plancher*) to creak; ~ **des dents** to grind one's teeth.

grincheux, euse [gʀɛ̃ʃø, -øz] *adj* grumpy.

gringalet [gʀɛ̃galɛ] *adj m* puny ♦ *nm* weakling.

griotte [gʀijɔt] *nf* Morello cherry.

grippal, e, aux [gʀipal, -o] *adj* (*état*) flu-like.

grippe [gʀip] *nf* flu, influenza; **avoir la** ~ to have (the) flu; **prendre qn/qch en** ~ (*fig*) to take a sudden dislike to sb/sth.

grippé, e [gʀipe] *adj:* **être** ~ to have (the) flu; (*moteur*) to have seized up (*BRIT*) *ou* jammed.

gripper [gʀipe] vt, vi to jam.

grippe-sou [gʀipsu] nm/f penny pincher.

gris, e [gʀi, gʀiz] adj grey (BRIT), gray (US); (ivre) tipsy ♦ nm (couleur) grey (BRIT), gray (US); **il fait ~** it's a dull ou grey day; **faire ~e mine** to look miserable ou morose; **faire ~e mine à** qn to give sb a cool reception.

grisaille [gʀizaj] nf greyness (BRIT), grayness (US), dullness.

grisant, e [gʀizɑ̃, -ɑ̃t] adj intoxicating, exhilarating.

grisâtre [gʀizɑtʀ(ə)] adj greyish (BRIT), grayish (US).

griser [gʀize] vt to intoxicate; **se ~ de** (fig) to become intoxicated with.

griserie [gʀizʀi] nf intoxication.

grisonnant, e [gʀizɔnɑ̃, -ɑ̃t] adj greying (BRIT), graying (US).

grisonner [gʀizɔne] vi to be going grey (BRIT) ou gray (US).

Grisons [gʀizɔ̃] nmpl: **les ~** Graubünden.

grisou [gʀizu] nm firedamp.

gris-vert [gʀivɛʀ] adj grey-green.

grive [gʀiv] nf (ZOOL) thrush.

grivois, e [gʀivwa, -waz] adj saucy.

grivoiserie [gʀivwazʀi] nf sauciness.

Groenland [gʀɔɛnlɑ̃d] nm: **le ~** Greenland.

groenlandais, e [gʀɔɛnlɑ̃dɛ, -ɛz] adj of ou from Greenland ♦ nm/f: **G~, e** Greenlander.

grog [gʀɔg] nm grog.

groggy [gʀɔgi] adj inv dazed.

grogne [gʀɔɲ] nf grumble.

grognement [gʀɔɲmɑ̃] nm grunt; growl.

grogner [gʀɔɲe] vi to growl; (fig) to grumble.

grognon, ne [gʀɔɲɔ̃, -ɔn] adj grumpy, grouchy.

groin [gʀwɛ̃] nm snout.

grommeler [gʀɔmle] vi to mutter to o.s.

grondement [gʀɔ̃dmɑ̃] nm rumble; growl.

gronder [gʀɔ̃de] vi (canon, moteur, tonnerre) to rumble; (animal) to growl; (fig: révolte) to be brewing ♦ vt to scold.

groom [gʀum] nm page, bellhop (US).

gros, se [gʀo, gʀos] adj big, large; (obèse) fat; (problème, quantité) great; (travaux, dégâts) extensive; (large: trait, fil) thick, heavy ♦ adv: **risquer/gagner ~** to risk/win a lot ♦ nm (COMM): **le ~** the wholesale business; **écrire ~** to write in big letters; **prix de ~** wholesale price; **par ~ temps/~se mer** in rough weather/heavy seas; **le ~ de** the main body of; (du travail etc) the bulk of; **en avoir ~ sur le cœur** to be upset; **en ~** roughly; (COMM) wholesale; **~ intestin** large intestine; **~ lot** jackpot; **~ mot** coarse word, vulgarity; **~ œuvre** shell (of building); **~ plan** (PHOTO) close-up; **~ porteur** wide-bodied aircraft, jumbo (jet); **~ sel** cooking salt; **~ titre** headline; **~se caisse** big drum.

groseille [gʀozɛj] nf: **~ (rouge)/(blanche)** red/white currant; **~ à maquereau** gooseberry.

groseillier [gʀozeje] nm red ou white currant bush; gooseberry bush.

grosse [gʀos] adj f voir **gros** ♦ nf (COMM) gross.

grossesse [gʀosɛs] nf pregnancy; **~ nerveuse** phantom pregnancy.

grosseur [gʀosœʀ] nf size; fatness; (tumeur) lump.

grossier, ière [gʀosje, -jɛʀ] adj coarse; (travail) rough; crude; (évident: erreur) gross.

grossièrement [gʀosjɛʀmɑ̃] adv coarsely; roughly; crudely; (en gros) roughly.

grossièreté [gʀosjɛʀte] nf coarseness; rudeness.

grossir [gʀosiʀ] vi (personne) to put on weight; (fig) to grow, get bigger; (rivière) to swell ♦ vt to increase; (exagérer) to exaggerate; (au microscope) to magnify, enlarge; (suj: vêtement): **~ qn** to make sb look fatter.

grossissant, e [gʀosisɑ̃, -ɑ̃t] adj magnifying, enlarging.

grossissement [gʀosisɑ̃] nm (optique) magnification.

grossiste [gʀosist(ə)] nm/f wholesaler.

grosso modo [gʀosomɔdo] adv roughly.

grotesque [gʀɔtɛsk(ə)] adj grotesque.

grotte [gʀɔt] nf cave.

grouiller [gʀuje] vi (foule) to mill about; (fourmis) to swarm about; **~ de** to be swarming with.

groupe [gʀup] nm group; **cabinet de ~** group practice; **médecine de ~** group practice; **~ électrogène** generator; **~ de pression** pressure group; **~ sanguin** blood group; **~ scolaire** school complex.

groupement [gʀupmɑ̃] nm grouping; (groupe) group; **~ d'intérêt économique (GIE)** ≈ trade association.

grouper [gʀupe] vt to group; (ressources, moyens) to pool; **se ~** to get together.

groupuscule [gʀupyskyl] nm clique.

gruau [gʀyo] nm: **pain de ~** wheaten bread.

grue [gʀy] nf crane; **faire le pied de ~** (fam) to hang around (waiting), kick one's heels (BRIT).

gruger [gʀyʒe] vt to cheat, dupe.

grumeaux [gʀymo] nmpl (CULIN) lumps.

grumeleux, euse [gʀymlø, -øz] adj (sauce etc) lumpy; (peau etc) bumpy.

grutier [gʀytje] nm crane driver.

gruyère [gʀyjɛʀ] nm gruyère (BRIT) ou Swiss cheese.

Guadeloupe [gwadlup] nf: **la ~** Guadeloupe.

guadeloupéen, ne [gwadlupeɛ̃, -ɛn] adj Guadelupian.

Guatémala [gwatemala] nm: **le ~** Guatemala.

guatémalien, ne [gwatemaljɛ̃, -ɛn] adj Guatemalan.

guatémaltèque [gwatemaltɛk] adj Guatemalan.

GUD [gyd] sigle m (= Groupe Union Défense) student union.

gué [ge] nm ford; **passer à ~** to ford.

guenilles [gənij] *nfpl* rags.

guenon [gənɔ̃] *nf* female monkey.

guépard [gepaʀ] *nm* cheetah.

guêpe [gɛp] *nf* wasp.

guêpier [gepje] *nm* (*fig*) trap.

guère [gɛʀ] *adv* (*avec adjectif, adverbe*): **ne ... ~** hardly; (*avec verbe*): **ne ... ~** *tournure négative* + much; hardly ever; *tournure négative* + (very) long; **il n'y a ~ que/de** there's hardly anybody (*ou* anything) but/hardly any.

guéridon [geʀidɔ̃] *nm* pedestal table.

guérilla [geʀija] *nf* guerrilla warfare.

guérillero [geʀijeʀo] *nm* guerrilla.

guérir [geʀiʀ] *vt* (*personne, maladie*) to cure; (*membre, plaie*) to heal ♦ *vi* (*personne*) to recover, be cured; (*plaie, chagrin*) to heal; **~ de** to be cured of, recover from; **~ qn de** to cure sb of.

guérison [geʀizɔ̃] *nf* curing; healing; recovery.

guérissable [geʀisabl(ə)] *adj* curable.

guérisseur, euse [geʀisœʀ, -øz] *nm/f* healer.

guérite [geʀit] *nf* (*MIL*) sentry box; (*sur un chantier*) (workman's) hut.

Guernesey [gɛʀnəzɛ] *nf* Guernsey.

guernesiais, e [gɛʀnəzjɛ, -ɛz] *adj* of *ou* from Guernsey.

guerre [gɛʀ] *nf* war; (*méthode*): **~ atomique/ de tranchées** atomic/trench warfare *no pl*; **en ~** at war; **faire la ~ à** to wage war against; **de ~ lasse** (*fig*) tired of fighting *ou* resisting; **de bonne ~** fair and square; **~ civile/ mondiale** civil/world war; **~ froide/sainte** cold/holy war; **~ d'usure** war of attrition.

guerrier, ière [gɛʀje, -jɛʀ] *adj* warlike ♦ *nm/f* warrior.

guerroyer [gɛʀwaje] *vi* to wage war.

guet [gɛ] *nm*: **faire le ~** to be on the watch *ou* look-out.

guet-apens, *pl* **guets-apens** [gɛtapɑ̃] *nm* ambush.

guêtre [gɛtʀ(ə)] *nf* gaiter.

guetter [gete] *vt* (*épier*) to watch (intently); (*attendre*) to watch (out) for; (*: pour surprendre*) to be lying in wait for.

guetteur [getœʀ] *nm* look-out.

gueule [gœl] *nf* mouth; (*fam: visage*) mug; (*: bouche*) gob (*!*), mouth; **ta ~!** (*fam*) shut up!; **~ de bois** (*fam*) hangover.

gueule-de-loup, *pl* **gueules-de-loup** [gœldə-lu] *nf* snapdragon.

gueuler [gœle] *vi* (*fam*) to bawl.

gueuleton [gœltɔ̃] *nm* (*fam*) blowout (*BRIT*), big meal.

gueux [gø] *nm* beggar; (*coquin*) rogue.

gui [gi] *nm* mistletoe.

guibole [gibɔl] *nf* (*fam*) leg.

guichet [giʃɛ] *nm* (*de bureau, banque*) counter, window; (*d'une porte*) wicket, hatch; **les ~s** (*à la gare, au théâtre*) the ticket office; **jouer à ~s fermés** to play to a full house.

guichetier, ière [giʃtje, -jɛʀ] *nm/f* counter clerk.

guide [gid] *nm* guide; (*livre*) guide(book) ♦ *nf* (*fille scout*) (girl) guide (*BRIT*), girl scout (*US*); **~s** *nfpl* (*d'un cheval*) reins.

guider [gide] *vt* to guide.

guidon [gidɔ̃] *nm* handlebars *pl*.

guigne [giɲ] *nf* (*fam*): **avoir la ~** to be jinxed.

guignol [giɲɔl] *nm* ≈ Punch and Judy show; (*fig*) clown.

guillemets [gijmɛ] *nmpl*: **entre ~** in inverted commas *ou* quotation marks; **~ de répétition** ditto marks.

guilleret, te [gijʀɛ, -ɛt] *adj* perky, bright.

guillotine [gijɔtin] *nf* guillotine.

guillotiner [gijɔtine] *vt* to guillotine.

guimauve [gimov] *nf* (*BOT*) marshmallow; (*fig*) sentimentality, sloppiness.

guimbarde [gɛ̃baʀd(ə)] *nf* old banger (*BRIT*), jalopy.

guindé, e [gɛ̃de] *adj* stiff, starchy.

Guinée [gine] *nf*: **la (République de) ~** (the Republic of) Guinea; **la ~ équatoriale** Equatorial Guinea.

Guinée-Bissau [ginebiso] *nf*: **la ~** Guinea-Bissau.

guinéen, ne [gineɛ̃, -ɛn] *adj* Guinean.

guingois [gɛ̃gwa]: **de ~** *adv* askew.

guinguette [gɛ̃gɛt] *nf* open-air café or dance hall.

guirlande [giʀlɑ̃d] *nf* garland; (*de papier*) paper chain; **~ lumineuse** (fairy (*BRIT*)) lights *pl*; **~ de Noël** tinsel *no pl*.

guise [giz] *nf*: **à votre ~** as you wish *ou* please; **en ~ de** by way of.

guitare [gitaʀ] *nf* guitar.

guitariste [gitaʀist(ə)] *nm/f* guitarist, guitar player.

gustatif, ive [gystatif, -iv] *adj* gustatory; *voir* **papille**.

guttural, e, aux [gytyʀal, -o] *adj* guttural.

guyanais, e [gɥijanɛ, -ɛz] *adj* Guyanese, Guyanan; (*français*) Guianese, Guianan.

Guyane [gɥijan] *nf*: **la ~** Guyana; **la ~ (française)** (French) Guiana.

gvt *abr* (= *gouvernement*) govt.

gymkhana [ʒimkana] *nm* rally; **~ motocycliste** (motorbike) scramble (*BRIT*), motocross.

gymnase [ʒimnɑz] *nm* gym(nasium).

gymnaste [ʒimnast(ə)] *nm/f* gymnast.

gymnastique [ʒimnastik] *nf* gymnastics *sg*; (*au réveil etc*) keep-fit exercises *pl*; **~ corrective** remedial gymnastics.

gynécologie [ʒinekɔlɔʒi] *nf* gynaecology (*BRIT*), gynecology (*US*).

gynécologique [ʒinekɔlɔʒik] *adj* gynaecological (*BRIT*), gynecological (*US*).

gynécologue [ʒinekɔlɔg] *nm/f* gynaecologist (*BRIT*), gynecologist (*US*).

gypse [ʒips(ə)] *nm* gypsum.

gyrophare [ʒiʀofaʀ] *nm* (*sur une voiture*) revolving (flashing) light.

H h

H, h [aʃ] *nm inv* H, h ♦ *abr* (= *homme*) M; (= *hydrogène*) H; (= *heure*): **à l'heure** ~ at zero hour; **bombe** ~ H bomb; **H comme Henri** H for Harry (*BRIT*) *ou* How (*US*).

ha. *abr* (= *hectare*) ha.

hab. *abr* = **habitant**.

habile [abil] *adj* skilful; (*malin*) clever.

habilement [abilmɑ̃] *adv* skilfully; cleverly.

habileté [abilte] *nf* skill, skilfulness; cleverness.

habilité, e [abilite] *adj*: ~ **à faire** entitled to do, empowered to do.

habiliter [abilite] *vt* empower, entitle.

habillage [abijaʒ] *nm* dressing.

habillé, e [abije] *adj* dressed; (*chic*) dressy; (*TECH*): ~ **de** covered with; encased in.

habillement [abijmɑ̃] *nm* clothes *pl*; (*profession*) clothing industry.

habiller [abije] *vt* to dress; (*fournir en vêtements*) to clothe; **s'**~ to dress (o.s.); (*se déguiser, mettre des vêtements chic*) to dress up; **s'**~ **de/en** to dress in/dress up as; **s'**~ **chez/à** to buy one's clothes from/at.

habilleuse [abijøz] *nf* (*CINÉ, THÉÂT*) dresser.

habit [abi] *nm* outfit; ~**s** *nmpl* (*vêtements*) clothes; ~ **(de soirée)** tails *pl*; evening dress; **prendre l'**~ (*REL: entrer en religion*) to enter (holy) orders.

habitable [abitabl(ə)] *adj* (in)habitable.

habitacle [abitakl(ə)] *nm* cockpit; (*AUTO*) passenger cell.

habitant, e [abitɑ̃, -ɑ̃t] *nm/f* inhabitant; (*d'une maison*) occupant, occupier; **loger chez l'**~ to stay with the locals.

habitat [abita] *nm* housing conditions *pl*; (*BOT, ZOOL*) habitat.

habitation [abitasjɔ̃] *nf* living; (*demeure*) residence, home; (*maison*) house; ~**s à loyer modéré (HLM)** low-rent, state-owned housing, ≈ council housing *sg* (*BRIT*), ≈ public housing units (*US*).

habité, e [abite] *adj* inhabited; lived in.

habiter [abite] *vt* to live in; (*suj: sentiment*) to dwell in ♦ *vi*: ~ **à/dans** to live in *ou* at/in; ~ **chez** *ou* **avec qn** to live with sb; ~ **16 rue Montmartre** to live at number 16 rue Montmartre; ~ **rue Montmartre** to live in rue Montmartre.

habitude [abityd] *nf* habit; **avoir l'**~ **de faire** to be in the habit of doing; **avoir l'**~ **des enfants** to be used to children; **prendre l'**~ **de faire qch** to get into the habit of doing sth;

perdre une ~ to get out of a habit; **d'**~ usually; **comme d'**~ as usual; **par** ~ out of habit.

habitué, e [abitɥe] *adj*: **être** ~ **à** to be used *ou* accustomed to ♦ *nm/f* regular visitor; (*client*) regular (customer).

habituel, le [abitɥɛl] *adj* usual.

habituellement [abitɥɛlmɑ̃] *adv* usually.

habituer [abitɥe] *vt*: ~ **qn à** to get sb used to; **s'**~ **à** to get used to.

'hâbleur, euse [ˈɑblœʀ, -øz] *adj* boastful.

'hache [ˈaʃ] *nf* axe.

'haché, e [ˈaʃe] *adj* minced (*BRIT*), ground (*US*); (*persil*) chopped; (*fig*) jerky.

'hache-légumes [ˈaʃlegym] *nm inv* vegetable chopper.

'hacher [ˈaʃe] *vt* (*viande*) to mince (*BRIT*), grind (*US*); (*persil*) to chop; ~ **menu** to mince *ou* grind finely; to chop finely.

'hachette [ˈaʃɛt] *nf* hatchet.

'hache-viande [ˈaʃvjɑ̃d] *nm inv* (*meat*) mincer (*BRIT*) *ou* grinder (*US*); (*couteau*) (*meat*) cleaver.

'hachis [ˈaʃi] *nm* mince *no pl* (*BRIT*), hamburger meat (*US*); ~ **de viande** minced (*BRIT*) *ou* ground (*US*) meat.

'hachisch [ˈaʃiʃ] *nm* hashish.

'hachoir [ˈaʃwaʀ] *nm* chopper; (*meat*) mincer (*BRIT*) *ou* grinder (*US*); (*planche*) chopping board.

'hachurer [ˈaʃyʀe] *vt* to hatch.

'hachures [ˈaʃyʀ] *nfpl* hatching *sg*.

'hagard, e [ˈagaʀ, -aʀd(ə)] *adj* wild, distraught.

'haie [ˈɛ] *nf* hedge; (*SPORT*) hurdle; (*fig: rang*) line, row; **200 m** ~ 200 m hurdles; ~ **d'honneur** guard of honour.

'haillons [ˈɑjɔ̃] *nmpl* rags.

'haine [ˈɛn] *nf* hatred.

'haineux, euse [ˈɛnø, -øz] *adj* full of hatred.

'haïr [ˈaiʀ] *vt* to detest, hate; **se** ~ to hate each other.

'hais [ˈɛ], **'haïs** [ˈai] *etc vb voir* **haïr**.

'haïssable [ˈaisabl(ə)] *adj* detestable.

Haïti [aiti] *n* Haiti.

haïtien, ne [aisjɛ̃, -ɛn] *adj* Haitian.

'halage [ˈalaʒ] *nm*: **chemin de** ~ towpath.

'hâle [ˈɑl] *nm* (sun)tan.

'hâlé, e [ˈɑle] *adj* (sun)tanned, sunburnt.

haleine [alɛn] *nf* breath; **perdre** ~ to get out of breath; **à perdre** ~ until one is gasping for breath; **avoir mauvaise** ~ to have bad breath; **reprendre** ~ to get one's breath back; **hors d'**~ out of breath; **tenir en** ~ to hold spellbound; (*en attente*) to keep in suspense; **de longue** ~ *adj* long-term.

'haler [ˈale] *vt* to haul in; (*remorquer*) to tow.

'haleter [ˈalte] *vi* to pant.

'hall [ˈol] *nm* hall.

hallali [alali] *nm* kill.

'halle [ˈal] *nf* (covered) market; ~**s** *nfpl* central food market *sg*.

'hallebarde [ˈalbaʀd] *nf* halberd; **il pleut des**

~s (*fam*) it's bucketing down.
hallucinant, e [alysinɑ̃, -ɑ̃t] *adj* staggering.
hallucination [alysinɑsjɔ̃] *nf* hallucination.
hallucinatoire [alysinatwaʀ] *adj* hallucinatory.
halluciné, e [alysine] *nm/f* person suffering from hallucinations; (*fou*) (raving) lunatic.
hallucinogène [a(l)lysinɔʒɛn] *adj* hallucinogenic ♦ *nm* hallucinogen.
'**halo** ['alo] *nm* halo.
halogène [alɔʒɛn] *nm*: **lampe (à)** ~ halogen lamp.
'**halte** ['alt(ə)] *nf* stop, break; (*escale*) stopping place; (*RAIL*) halt ♦ *excl* stop!; **faire** ~ to stop.
'**halte-garderie,** *pl* '**haltes-garderies** ['altgaʀdəʀi] *nf* crèche.
haltère [altɛʀ] *nm* (*à boules, disques*) dumbbell, barbell; (**poids et**) ~s weightlifting.
haltérophile [alteʀɔfil] *nm/f* weightlifter.
haltérophilie [alteʀɔfili] *nf* weightlifting.
'**hamac** ['amak] *nm* hammock.
'**Hambourg** ['ɑ̃buʀ] *n* Hamburg.
'**hamburger** ['ɑ̃buʀgœʀ] *nm* hamburger.
'**hameau, x** ['amo] *nm* hamlet.
hameçon [amsɔ̃] *nm* (fish) hook.
'**hampe** ['ɑ̃p] *nf* (*de drapeau etc*) pole; (*de lance*) shaft.
'**hamster** ['amstɛʀ] *nm* hamster.
'**hanche** ['ɑ̃ʃ] *nf* hip.
'**hand-ball** ['ɑ̃dbal] *nm* handball.
'**handballeur, euse** ['ɑ̃dbalœʀ, -øz] *nm/f* handball player.
'**handicap** ['ɑ̃dikap] *nm* handicap.
'**handicapé, e** ['ɑ̃dikape] *adj* handicapped ♦ *nm/f* physically (*ou* mentally) handicapped person; ~ **moteur** spastic.
'**handicaper** ['ɑ̃dikape] *vt* to handicap.
'**hangar** ['ɑ̃gaʀ] *nm* shed; (*AVIAT*) hangar.
'**hanneton** ['antɔ̃] *nm* cockchafer.
'**Hanovre** ['anɔvʀ(ə)] *n* Hanover.
'**hanovrien, ne** ['anɔvʀjɛ̃, -ɛn] *adj* Hanoverian.
'**hanter** ['ɑ̃te] *vt* to haunt.
'**hantise** ['ɑ̃tiz] *nf* obsessive fear.
'**happer** ['ape] *vt* to snatch; (*suj: train etc*) to hit.
'**harangue** ['aʀɑ̃g] *nf* harangue.
'**haranguer** ['aʀɑ̃ge] *vt* to harangue.
'**haras** ['aʀɑ] *nm* stud farm.
'**harassant, e** ['aʀasɑ̃, -ɑ̃t] *adj* exhausting.
'**harcèlement** ['aʀsɛlmɑ̃] *nm* harassment; ~ **sexuel** sexual harassment.
'**harceler** ['aʀsəle] *vt* (*MIL, CHASSE*) to harass, harry; (*importuner*) to plague.
'**hardes** ['aʀd(ə)] *nfpl* rags.
'**hardi, e** ['aʀdi] *adj* bold, daring.
'**hardiesse** ['aʀdjɛs] *nf* audacity; **avoir la** ~ **de** to have the audacity *ou* effrontery to.
'**harem** ['aʀɛm] *nm* harem.
'**hareng** ['aʀɑ̃] *nm* herring.
'**hargne** ['aʀɲ(ə)] *nf* aggressivity, aggressiveness.

'**hargneusement** ['aʀɲøzmɑ̃] *adv* belligerently, aggressively.
'**hargneux, -euse** ['aʀɲø, -øz] *adj* (*propos, personne*) belligerent, aggressive; (*chien*) fierce.
'**haricot** ['aʀiko] *nm* bean; ~ **blanc/rouge** haricot/kidney bean; ~ **vert** French (*BRIT*) *ou* green bean.
harmonica [aʀmɔnika] *nm* mouth organ.
harmonie [aʀmɔni] *nf* harmony.
harmonieux, euse [aʀmɔnjø, -øz] *adj* harmonious.
harmonique [aʀmɔnik] *adj, nm ou nf* harmonic.
harmoniser [aʀmɔnize] *vt* to harmonize; **s'**~ (*couleurs, teintes*) to go well together.
harmonium [aʀmɔnjɔm] *nm* harmonium.
'**harnaché, e** ['aʀnaʃe] *adj* (*fig*) rigged out.
'**harnachement** ['aʀnaʃmɑ̃] *nm* (*habillement*) rig-out; (*équipement*) harness, equipment.
'**harnacher** ['aʀnaʃe] *vt* to harness.
'**harnais** ['aʀnɛ] *nm* harness.
'**haro** ['aʀo] *nm*: **crier** ~ **sur qn/qch** to inveigh against sb/sth.
'**harpe** ['aʀp(ə)] *nf* harp.
'**harpie** ['aʀpi] *nf* harpy.
'**harpiste** ['aʀpist(ə)] *nm/f* harpist.
'**harpon** ['aʀpɔ̃] *nm* harpoon.
'**harponner** ['aʀpɔne] *vt* to harpoon; (*fam*) to collar.
'**hasard** ['azaʀ] *nm*: **le** ~ chance, fate; **un** ~ a coincidence; (*aubaine, chance*) a stroke of luck; **au** ~ (*sans but*) aimlessly; (*à l'aveuglette*) at random, haphazardly; **par** ~ by chance; **comme par** ~ as if by chance; **à tout** ~ on the off chance; (*en cas de besoin*) just in case.
'**hasarder** ['azaʀde] *vt* (*mot*) to venture; (*fortune*) to risk; **se** ~ **à faire** to risk doing, venture to do.
'**hasardeux, euse** ['azaʀdø, -øz] *adj* hazardous, risky; (*hypothèse*) rash.
'**haschisch** ['aʃiʃ] *nm* hashish.
'**hâte** ['ɑt] *nf* haste; **à la** ~ hurriedly, hastily; **en** ~ posthaste, with all possible speed; **avoir** ~ **de** to be eager *ou* anxious to.
'**hâter** ['ɑte] *vt* to hasten; **se** ~ to hurry; **se** ~ **de** to hurry *ou* hasten to.
'**hâtif, ive** ['ɑtif, -iv] *adj* (*travail*) hurried; (*décision*) hasty; (*légume*) early.
'**hâtivement** ['ɑtivmɑ̃] *adv* hurriedly; hastily.
'**hauban** ['obɑ̃] *nm* (*NAVIG*) shroud.
'**hausse** ['os] *nf* rise, increase; (*de fusil*) backsight adjuster; **à la** ~ upwards; **en** ~ rising.
'**hausser** ['ose] *vt* to raise; ~ **les épaules** to shrug (one's shoulders); **se** ~ **sur la pointe des pieds** to stand (up) on tiptoe *ou* tippytoe (*US*).
'**haut, e** ['o, 'ot] *adj* high; (*grand*) tall; (*son, voix*) high(-pitched) ♦ *adv* high ♦ *nm* top (part); **de 3 m de** ~, ~ **de 3 m** 3 m high, 3 m in height; **en** ~**e montagne** high up in the mountains; **en** ~ **lieu** in high places; **à** ~**e**

voix, (tout) ~ aloud, out loud; **des ~s et des bas** ups and downs; **du ~ de** from the top of; **tomber de ~** to fall from a height; (fig) to have one's hopes dashed; **dire qch bien ~** to say sth plainly; **prendre qch de (très) ~** to react haughtily to sth; **traiter qn de ~** to treat sb with disdain; **de ~ en bas** from top to bottom; downwards; **~ en couleur** (chose) highly coloured; (personne): **un personnage ~ en couleur** a colourful character; **plus ~** higher up, further up; (dans un texte) above; (parler) louder; **en ~** up above; at (ou to) the top; (dans une maison) upstairs; **en ~ de** at the top of; **~ les mains!** hands up!, stick 'em up!; **la ~e couture/coiffure** haute couture/coiffure; **~e fidélité** hi-fi, high fidelity; **la ~e finance** high finance; **~e trahison** high treason.

'**hautain, e** ['otɛ̃, -ɛn] adj (personne, regard) haughty.

'**hautbois** ['obwa] nm oboe.

'**hautboïste** [ob>ist(ə)] nm/f oboist.

'**haut-de-forme**, pl '**hauts-de-forme** ['od-fɔrm(ə)] nm top hat.

'**haute-contre**, pl '**hautes-contre** ['otkɔ̃tr(ə)] nf counter-tenor.

'**hautement** ['otmɑ̃] adv (ouvertement) openly; (supérieurement): **~ qualifié** highly qualified.

'**hauteur** ['otœr] nf height; (GÉO) height, hill; (fig) loftiness; haughtiness; **à ~ de** up to (the level of); **à ~ des yeux** at eye level; **à la ~ de** (sur la même ligne) level with; by; (fig) equal to; **à la ~** (fig) up to it, equal to the task.

'**Haute-Volta** ['otvɔlta] nf: **la ~** Upper Volta.

'**haut-fond**, pl '**hauts-fonds** ['ofɔ̃] nm shallow.

'**haut-fourneau**, pl '**hauts-fourneaux** ['ofur-no] nm blast ou smelting furnace.

'**haut-le-cœur** ['olkœr] nm inv retch, heave.

'**haut-le-corps** ['olkɔr] nm inv start, jump.

'**haut-parleur**, pl '**haut-parleurs** ['oparlœr] nm (loud)speaker.

'**hauturier, ière** ['otyrje, -jɛr] adj (NAVIG) deep-sea.

'**havanais, e** ['avanɛ, -ɛz] adj of ou from Havana.

'**Havane** ['avan] nf: **la ~** Havana ♦ nm: '**h~** (cigare) Havana.

'**hâve** ['av] adj gaunt.

'**havrais, e** ['avrɛ, -ɛz] adj of ou from Le Havre.

'**havre** ['avr(ə)] nm haven.

'**havresac** ['avrəsak] nm haversack.

Hawaï [awai] n Hawaii; **les îles ~** the Hawaiian Islands.

hawaïen, ne [awajɛ̃, -ɛn] adj Hawaiian ♦ nm (LING) Hawaiian.

'**Haye** ['ɛ] n: **la ~** the Hague.

'**hayon** ['ɛjɔ̃] nm tailgate.

HCR sigle m (= Haut-Commissariat des Nations unies pour les réfugiés) UNHCR.

hdb. abr (= heures de bureau) o.h. (= office hours).

'**hé** ['e] excl hey!

hebdo [ɛbdo] nm (fam) weekly.

hebdomadaire [ɛbdɔmadɛr] adj, nm weekly.

hébergement [ebɛrʒəmɑ̃] nm accommodation, lodging; taking in.

héberger [ebɛrʒe] vt to accommodate, lodge; (réfugiés) to take in.

hébété, e [ebete] adj dazed.

hébétude [ebetyd] nf stupor.

hébraïque [ebraik] adj Hebrew, Hebraic.

hébreu, x [ebrø] adj m, nm Hebrew.

Hébrides [ebrid] nf: **les ~** the Hebrides.

HEC sigle fpl (= École des hautes études commerciales) grande école for management and business studies.

hécatombe [ekatɔ̃b] nf slaughter.

hectare [ɛktar] nm hectare, 10,000 square metres.

hecto... [ɛkto] préfixe hecto....

hectolitre [ɛktɔlitr(ə)] nm hectolitre.

hédoniste [edɔnist(ə)] adj hedonistic.

hégémonie [eʒemɔni] nf hegemony.

'**hein** ['ɛ̃] excl eh?; (sollicitant l'approbation): **tu m'approuves, ~?** so I did the right thing then?; **Paul est venu, ~?** Paul came, did he?; **que fais-tu, ~?** hey! what are you doing?

'**hélas** ['elas] excl alas! ♦ adv unfortunately.

'**héler** ['ele] vt to hail.

hélice [elis] nf propeller.

hélicoïdal, e, aux [elikɔidal, -o] adj helical; helicoid.

hélicoptère [elikɔptɛr] nm helicopter.

hélio(gravure) [eljɔgravyr] nf heliogravure.

héliomarin, e [eljɔmarɛ̃, -in] adj: **centre ~** centre offering sea and sun therapy.

héliotrope [eljɔtrɔp] nm (BOT) heliotrope.

héliport [elipɔr] nm heliport.

héliporté, e [elipɔrte] adj transported by helicopter.

hélium [eljɔm] nm helium.

hellénique [elenik] adj Hellenic.

hellénisant, e [elenizɑ̃, -ɑ̃t], **helléniste** [elenist(ə)] nm/f hellenist.

Helsinki [ɛlzinki] n Helsinki.

helvète [ɛlvɛt] adj Helvetian ♦ nm/f: **H~** Helvetian.

Helvétie [ɛlvesi] nf: **la ~** Helvetia.

helvétique [ɛlvetik] adj Swiss.

hématologie [ematɔlɔʒi] nf (MÉD) haematology.

hématome [ematom] nm haematoma.

hémicycle [emisikl(ə)] nm semicircle; (POL): **l'~** the benches (in French parliament).

hémiplégie [emipleʒi] nf paralysis of one side, hemiplegia.

hémisphère [emisfɛr] nf: **~ nord/sud** northern/southern hemisphere.

hémisphérique [emisferik] adj hemispherical.

hémoglobine [emɔglɔbin] nf haemoglobin

(*BRIT*), hemoglobin (*US*).

hémophile [emɔfil] *adj* haemophiliac (*BRIT*), hemophiliac (*US*).

hémophilie [emɔfili] *nf* haemophilia (*BRIT*), hemophilia (*US*).

hémorragie [emɔraʒi] *nf* bleeding *no pl*, haemorrhage (*BRIT*), hemorrhage (*US*); ~ **cérébrale** cerebral haemorrhage; ~ **interne** internal bleeding *ou* haemorrhage.

hémorroïdes [emɔrɔid] *nfpl* piles, haemorrhoids (*BRIT*), hemorrhoids (*US*).

hémostatique [emɔstatik] *adj* haemostatic (*BRIT*), hemostatic (*US*).

'**henné** ['ene] *nm* henna.

'**hennir** ['eniʀ] *vi* to neigh, whinny.

'**hennissement** ['enismɑ̃] *nm* neighing, whinnying.

'**hep** ['ɛp] *excl* hey!

hépatite [epatit] *nf* hepatitis, liver infection.

héraldique [eʀaldik] *adj* heraldry.

herbacé, e [ɛʀbase] *adj* herbaceous.

herbage [ɛʀbaʒ] *nm* pasture.

herbe [ɛʀb(ə)] *nf* grass; (*CULIN, MÉD*) herb; **en** ~ unripe; (*fig*) budding; **touffe/brin** d'~ clump/blade of grass.

herbeux, euse [ɛʀbø, -øz] *adj* grassy.

herbicide [ɛʀbisid] *nm* weed-killer.

herbier [ɛʀbje] *nm* herbarium.

herbivore [ɛʀbivɔʀ] *nm* herbivore.

herboriser [ɛʀbɔʀize] *vi* to collect plants.

herboriste [ɛʀbɔʀist(ə)] *nm/f* herbalist.

herboristerie [ɛʀbɔʀistʀi] *nf* (*magasin*) herbalist's shop; (*commerce*) herb trade.

herculéen, ne [ɛʀkyleɛ̃, -ɛn] *adj* (*fig*) herculean.

'**hère** ['ɛʀ] *nm*: **pauvre** ~ poor wretch.

héréditaire [eʀeditɛʀ] *adj* hereditary.

hérédité [eʀedite] *nf* heredity.

hérésie [eʀezi] *nf* heresy.

hérétique [eʀetik] *nm/f* heretic.

'**hérissé, e** [e'ʀise] *adj* bristling; ~ **de** spiked with; (*fig*) bristling with.

'**hérisser** ['eʀise] *vt*: ~ **qn** (*fig*) to ruffle sb; **se** ~ *vi* to bristle, bristle up.

'**hérisson** ['eʀisɔ̃] *nm* hedgehog.

héritage [eʀitaʒ] *nm* inheritance; (*fig*) heritage; (: *legs*) legacy; **faire un (petit)** ~ to come into (a little) money.

hériter [eʀite] *vi*: ~ **de qch (de qn)** to inherit sth (from sb); ~ **de qn** to inherit sb's property.

héritier, ière [eʀitje, -jɛʀ] *nm/f* heir/heiress.

hermaphrodite [ɛʀmafʀɔdit] *adj* (*BOT, ZOOL*) hermaphrodite.

hermétique [ɛʀmetik] *adj* (*à l'air*) airtight; (*à l'eau*) watertight; (*fig*: *écrivain, style*) abstruse; (: *visage*) impenetrable.

hermétiquement [ɛʀmetikmɑ̃] *adv* hermetically.

hermine [ɛʀmin] *nf* ermine.

'**hernie** ['ɛʀni] *nf* hernia.

héroïne [eʀɔin] *nf* heroine; (*drogue*) heroin.

héroïnomane [eʀɔinɔman] *nm/f* heroin addict.

héroïque [eʀɔik] *adj* heroic.

héroïquement [eʀɔikmɑ̃] *adv* heroically.

héroïsme [eʀɔism(ə)] *nm* heroism.

'**héron** ['eʀɔ̃] *nm* heron.

'**héros** ['eʀo] *nm* hero.

herpès [ɛʀpɛs] *nm* herpes.

'**herse** ['ɛʀs(ə)] *nf* harrow; (*de château*) portcullis.

hertz [ɛʀts] *nm* (*ÉLEC*) hertz.

hertzien, ne [ɛʀtsjɛ̃, -ɛn] *adj* (*ÉLEC*) Hertzian.

hésitant, e [ezitɑ̃, -ɑ̃t] *adj* hesitant.

hésitation [ezitɑsjɔ̃] *nf* hesitation.

hésiter [ezite] *vi*: ~ **(à faire)** to hesitate (to do); ~ **sur qch** to hesitate over sth.

hétéro [eteʀo] *adj inv* (= *hétérosexuel(le)*) hetero.

hétéroclite [eteʀɔklit] *adj* heterogeneous; (*objets*) sundry.

hétérogène [eteʀɔʒɛn] *adj* heterogeneous.

hétérosexuel, le [eteʀɔsɛkɥɛl] *adj* heterosexual.

'**hêtre** ['ɛtʀ(ə)] *nm* beech.

heure [œʀ] *nf* hour; (*SCOL*) period; (*moment, moment fixé*) time; **c'est l'**~ it's time; **pourriez-vous me donner l'**~, **s'il vous plaît?** could you tell me the time, please?; **quelle** ~ **est-il?** what time is it?; **2** ~**s (du matin)** 2 o'clock (in the morning); **à la bonne** ~! (*parfois ironique*) splendid!; **être à l'**~ to be on time; (*montre*) to be right; **le bus passe à l'**~ the bus runs on the hour; **mettre à l'**~ to set right; **100 km à l'**~ ≈ 60 miles an *ou* per hour; **à toute** ~ at any time; **24** ~**s sur 24** round the clock, 24 hours a day; **à l'**~ **qu'il est** at this time (of day); (*fig*) now; **à l'**~ **actuelle** at the present time; **sur l'**~ at once; **pour l'**~ for the time being; **d'**~ **en** ~ from one hour to the next; (*régulièrement*) hourly; **d'une** ~ **à l'autre** from hour to hour; **de bonne** ~ early; **2** ~**s de marche/travail** 2 hours' walking/work; **une** ~ **d'arrêt** an hour's break *ou* stop; ~ **d'été** summer time (*BRIT*), daylight saving time (*US*); ~ **de pointe** rush hour; ~**s de bureau** office hours; ~**s supplémentaires** overtime *sg*.

heureusement [œʀøzmɑ̃] *adv* (*par bonheur*) fortunately, luckily; ~ **que** ... it's a good job that ..., fortunately ....

heureux, euse [œʀø, -øz] *adj* happy; (*chanceux*) lucky, fortunate; (*judicieux*) felicitous, fortunate; **être** ~ **de qch** to be pleased *ou* happy about sth; **être** ~ **de faire/que** to be pleased *ou* happy to do/that; **s'estimer** ~ **de qch/que** to consider o.s. fortunate with/that; **encore** ~ **que** ... just as well that ....

'**heurt** ['œʀ] *nm* (*choc*) collision; ~**s** *nmpl* (*fig*) clashes.

'**heurté, e** ['œʀte] *adj* (*fig*) jerky, uneven; (: *couleurs*) clashing.

'**heurter** ['œʀte] *vt* (*mur*) to strike, hit; (*personne*) to collide with; (*fig*) to go against, upset; **se** ~ (*couleurs, tons*) to clash; **se** ~ **à** to collide with; (*fig*) to come up against; ~ **qn de front** to clash head-on with sb.

'heurtoir ['œʀtwaʀ] *nm* door knocker.

hévéa [evea] *nm* rubber tree.

hexagonal, e, aux [ɛgzagɔnal, -o] *adj* hexagonal; (*français*) French (*see note at hexagone*).

hexagone [ɛgzagɔn] *nm* hexagon; (*la France*) France (*because of its roughly hexagonal shape*).

HF *sigle f* (= *haute fréquence*) HF.

hiatus [jatys] *nm* hiatus.

hibernation [ibɛʀnasjɔ̃] *nf* hibernation.

hiberner [ibɛʀne] *vi* to hibernate.

hibiscus [ibiskys] *nm* hibiscus.

'hibou, x ['ibu] *nm* owl.

'hic ['ik] *nm* (*fam*) snag.

'hideusement ['idøzmɑ̃] *adv* hideously.

'hideux, euse ['idø, -øz] *adj* hideous.

hier [jɛʀ] *adv* yesterday; ~ **matin/soir/midi** yesterday morning/evening/at midday; **toute la journée d'**~ all day yesterday; **toute la matinée d'**~ all yesterday morning.

'hiérarchie ['jeʀaʀʃi] *nf* hierarchy.

'hiérarchique ['jeʀaʀʃik] *adj* hierarchic.

'hiérarchiquement ['jeʀaʀʃikmɑ̃] *adv* hierarchically.

'hiérarchiser ['jeʀaʀʃize] *vt* to organize into a hierarchy.

'hiéroglyphe ['jeʀɔglif] *nm* hieroglyphic.

'hiéroglyphique ['jeʀɔglifik] *adj* hieroglyphic.

'hi-fi ['ifi] *nf inv* hi-fi.

hilarant, e [ilaʀɑ̃, -ɑ̃t] *adj* hilarious.

hilare [ilaʀ] *adj* mirthful.

hilarité [ilaʀite] *nf* hilarity, mirth.

Himalaya [imalaja] *nm*: **l'**~ the Himalayas *pl*.

himalayen, ne [imalajɛ̃, -ɛn] *adj* Himalayan.

hindou, e [ɛ̃du] *adj, nm/f* Hindu; (*Indien*) Indian.

hindouisme [ɛ̃duism(ə)] *nm* Hinduism.

Hindoustan [ɛ̃dustɑ̃] *nm*: **l'**~ Hindustan.

'hippie ['ipi] *nm/f* hippy.

hippique [ipik] *adj* equestrian, horse *cpd*.

hippisme [ipism(ə)] *nm* (horse-)riding.

hippocampe [ipokɑ̃p] *nm* sea horse.

hippodrome [ipodʀom] *nm* racecourse.

hippophagique [ipofaʒik] *adj*: **boucherie** ~ horse butcher's.

hippopotame [ipopotam] *nm* hippopotamus.

hirondelle [iʀɔ̃dɛl] *nf* swallow.

hirsute [iʀsyt] *adj* (*personne*) hairy; (*barbe*) shaggy; (*tête*) tousled.

hispanique [ispanik] *adj* Hispanic.

hispanisant, e [ispanizɑ̃, -ɑ̃t] *adj*, **hispaniste** [ispanist(ə)] *nm/f* Hispanist.

hispano-américain, e [ispanoameʀikɛ̃, -ɛn] *adj* Spanish-American.

hispano-arabe [ispanoaʀab] *adj* Hispano-Moresque.

'hisser ['ise] *vt* to hoist, haul up; **se** ~ **sur** to haul o.s. up onto.

histoire [istwaʀ] *nf* (*science, événements*) his-

tory; (*anecdote, récit, mensonge*) story; (*affaire*) business *no pl*; (*chichis: gén pl*) fuss *no pl*; ~**s** *nfpl* (*ennuis*) trouble *sg*; **l'**~ **de France** French history, the history of France; **l'**~ **sainte** biblical history; **une** ~ **de** (*fig*) a question of.

histologie [istɔlɔʒi] *nf* histology.

historien, ne [istɔʀjɛ̃, -ɛn] *nm/f* historian.

historique [istɔʀik] *adj* historical; (*important*) historic ♦ *nm* (*exposé, récit*): **faire l'**~ **de** to give the background to.

historiquement [istɔʀikmɑ̃] *adv* historically.

'hit-parade ['itpaʀad] *nm*: **le** ~ the charts.

HIV *sigle m* (= *human immunodeficiency virus*) HIV.

hiver [ivɛʀ] *nm* winter; **en** ~ in winter.

hivernal, e, aux [ivɛʀnal, -o] *adj* (*de l'hiver*) winter *cpd*; (*comme en hiver*) wintry.

hivernant, e [ivɛʀnɑ̃, -ɑ̃t] *n* winter holiday-maker.

hiverner [ivɛʀne] *vi* to winter.

HLM *sigle m ou f* (= *habitations à loyer modéré*) low-rent, state-owned housing; **un(e)** ~ ≈ a council flat (*ou* house) (*BRIT*), ≈ a public housing unit (*US*).

Hme *abr* (= *homme*) M.

HO *abr* (= *hors œuvre*) labour not included (*on invoices*).

'hobby ['ɔbi] *nm* hobby.

'hochement ['ɔʃmɑ̃] *nm*: ~ **de tête** nod; shake of the head.

'hocher ['ɔʃe] *vt*: ~ **la tête** to nod; (*signe négatif ou dubitatif*) to shake one's head.

'hochet ['ɔʃe] *nm* rattle.

'hockey ['ɔkɛ] *nm*: ~ (**sur glace/gazon**) (ice/field) hockey.

'hockeyeur, euse ['ɔkɛjœʀ, -øz] *nm/f* hockey player.

'holà ['ɔla] *nm*: **mettre le** ~ **à qch** to put a stop to sth.

'holding ['ɔldiŋ] *nm* holding company.

'hold-up ['ɔldœp] *nm inv* hold-up.

'hollandais, e ['ɔlɑ̃dɛ, -ɛz] *adj* Dutch ♦ *nm* (*LING*) Dutch ♦ *nm/f*: **H**~, **e** Dutchman/woman; **les H**~ the Dutch.

'Hollande ['ɔlɑ̃d] *nf*: **la** ~ Holland ♦ *nm*: **h**~ (*fromage*) Dutch cheese.

holocauste [ɔlɔkost(ə)] *nm* holocaust.

hologramme [ɔlɔgʀam] *nm* hologram.

homard ['ɔmaʀ] *nm* lobster.

homéopathe [ɔmeɔpat] *n* homoeopath.

homéopathie [ɔmeɔpati] *nf* homoeopathy.

homéopathique [ɔmeɔpatik] *adj* homoeopathic.

homérique [ɔmeʀik] *adj* Homeric.

homicide [ɔmisid] *nm* murder ♦ *nm/f* murderer/eress; ~ **involontaire** manslaughter.

hommage [ɔmaʒ] *nm* tribute; ~**s** *nmpl*: **présenter ses** ~**s** to pay one's respects; **rendre** ~ **à** to pay tribute *ou* homage to; **en** ~ **de** as a token of; **faire** ~ **de qch à qn** to present sb with sth.

homme [ɔm] *nm* man; (*espèce humaine*): **l'~** man, mankind; **~ d'affaires** businessman; **~ des cavernes** caveman; **~ d'Église** churchman, clergyman; **~ d'État** statesman; **~ de loi** lawyer; **~ de main** hired man; **~ de paille** stooge; **l'~ de la rue** the man in the street; **~ à tout faire** odd-job man.

homme-grenouille, *pl* **hommes-grenouilles** [ɔmgrənuj] *nm* frogman.

homme-orchestre, *pl* **hommes-orchestres** [ɔmɔʀkɛstʀ(ə)] *nm* one-man band.

homme-sandwich, *pl* **hommes-sandwichs** [ɔmsɑ̃dwitʃ] *nm* sandwich (board) man.

homo [ɔmo] *adj, nm/f* = **homosexuel.**

homogène [ɔmɔʒɛn] *adj* homogeneous.

homogénéisé, e [ɔmɔʒeneize] *adj*: **lait ~** homogenized milk.

homogénéité [ɔmɔʒeneite] *nf* homogeneity.

homologation [ɔmɔlɔgasjɔ̃] *nf* ratification; official recognition.

homologue [ɔmɔlɔg] *nm/f* counterpart, opposite number.

homologué, e [ɔmɔlɔge] *adj* (*SPORT*) officially recognized, ratified; (*tarif*) authorized.

homologuer [ɔmɔlɔge] *vt* (*JUR*) to ratify; (*SPORT*) to recognize officially, ratify.

homonyme [ɔmɔnim] *nm* (*LING*) homonym; (*d'une personne*) namesake.

homosexualité [ɔmɔsɛksɥalite] *nf* homosexuality.

homosexuel, le [ɔmɔsɛksɥɛl] *adj* homosexual.

'Honduras ['ɔdyʀas] *nm*: **le ~** Honduras.

'hondurien, ne ['ɔdyʀjɛ̃, -ɛn] *adj* Honduran.

'Hong-Kong ['ɔ̃gkɔ̃g] *n* Hong Kong.

'hongre ['ɔ̃gʀ(ə)] *adj* (*cheval*) gelded ♦ *nm* gelding.

'Hongrie ['ɔ̃gʀi] *nf*: **la ~** Hungary.

'hongrois, e ['ɔ̃gʀwa, -waz] *adj* Hungarian ♦ *nm* (*LING*) Hungarian ♦ *nm/f*: **'H~, e** Hungarian.

honnête [ɔnɛt] *adj* (*intègre*) honest; (*juste, satisfaisant*) fair.

honnêtement [ɔnɛtmɑ̃] *adv* honestly.

honnêteté [ɔnɛtte] *nf* honesty.

honneur [ɔnœʀ] *nm* honour; (*mérite*): **l'~ lui revient** the credit is his; **à qui ai-je l'~?** to whom have I the pleasure of speaking?; **"j'ai l'~ de ..."** "I have the honour of ..."; **en l'~ de** (*personne*) in honour of; (*événement*) on the occasion of; **faire ~ à** (*engagements*) to honour; (*famille, professeur*) to be a credit to; (*fig: repas etc*) to do justice to; **être à l'~** to be in the place of honour; **être en ~** to be in favour; **membre d'~** honorary member; **table d'~** top table.

Honolulu [ɔnɔlyly] *n* Honolulu.

honorable [ɔnɔʀabl(ə)] *adj* worthy, honourable; (*suffisant*) decent.

honorablement [ɔnɔʀabləmɑ̃] *adv* honourably; decently.

honoraire [ɔnɔʀɛʀ] *adj* honorary; **~s** *nmpl*

fees; **professeur ~** professor emeritus.

honorer [ɔnɔʀe] *vt* to honour; (*estimer*) to hold in high regard; (*faire honneur à*) to do credit to; **~ qn de** to honour sb with; **s'~ de** to pride o.s. upon.

honorifique [ɔnɔʀifik] *adj* honorary.

'honte ['ɔ̃t] *nf* shame; **avoir ~ de** to be ashamed of; **faire ~ à qn** to make sb (feel) ashamed.

'honteusement ['ɔ̃tøzmɑ̃] *adv* ashamedly; shamefully.

'honteux, euse ['ɔ̃tø, -øz] *adj* ashamed; (*conduite, acte*) shameful, disgraceful.

hôpital, aux [ɔpital, -o] *nm* hospital.

'hoquet ['ɔkɛ] *nm* hiccough; **avoir le ~** to have (the) hiccoughs.

'hoqueter ['ɔkte] *vi* to hiccough.

horaire [ɔʀɛʀ] *adj* hourly ♦ *nm* timetable, schedule; **~s** *nmpl* (*heures de travail*) hours; **~ flexible** *ou* **mobile** *ou* **à la carte** *ou* **souple** flex(i)time.

'horde ['ɔʀd(ə)] *nf* horde.

'horions ['ɔʀjɔ̃] *nmpl* blows.

horizon [ɔʀizɔ̃] *nm* horizon; (*paysage*) landscape, view; **sur l'~** on the skyline *ou* horizon.

horizontal, e, aux [ɔʀizɔ̃tal, -o] *adj* horizontal ♦ *nf*: **à l'~e** on the horizontal.

horizontalement [ɔʀizɔ̃talmɑ̃] *adv* horizontally.

horloge [ɔʀlɔʒ] *nf* clock; **l'~ parlante** the speaking clock; **~ normande** grandfather clock; **~ physiologique** biological clock.

horloger, ère [ɔʀlɔʒe, -ɛʀ] *nm/f* watchmaker; clockmaker.

horlogerie [ɔʀlɔʒʀi] *nf* watchmaking; watchmaker's (shop); clockmaker's (shop); **pièces d'~** watch parts *ou* components.

'hormis ['ɔʀmi] *prép* save.

hormonal, e, aux [ɔʀmɔnal, -o] *adj* hormonal.

hormone [ɔʀmɔn] *nf* hormone.

horodaté, e [ɔʀɔdate] *adj* (*ticket*) time- and date-stamped; (*stationnement*) pay and display.

horodateur, trice [ɔʀɔdatœʀ, -tʀis] *adj* (*appareil*) for stamping the time and date ♦ *nm/f* (parking) ticket machine.

horoscope [ɔʀɔskɔp] *nm* horoscope.

horreur [ɔʀœʀ] *nf* horror; **avoir ~ de** to loathe, detest; **quelle ~!** how awful!; **cela me fait ~** I find that awful.

horrible [ɔʀibl(ə)] *adj* horrible.

horriblement [ɔʀibləmɑ̃] *adv* horribly.

horrifiant, e [ɔʀifjɑ̃, -ɑ̃t] *adj* horrifying.

horrifier [ɔʀifje] *vt* to horrify.

horrifique [ɔʀifik] *adj* horrific.

horripilant, e [ɔʀipilɑ̃, -ɑ̃t] *adj* exasperating.

horripiler [ɔʀipile] *vt* to exasperate.

'hors ['ɔʀ] *prép* except (for); **~ de** out of; **~ ligne, ~ pair** outstanding; **~ de propos** inopportune; **~ série** (*sur mesure*) made-to-order; (*exceptionnel*) exceptional; **~ service (HS), ~**

d'usage out of service; **être ~ de soi** to be beside o.s.

'**hors-bord** ['ɔʀbɔʀ] *nm inv* outboard motor; (*canot*) speedboat (with outboard motor).

'**hors-concours** ['ɔʀkɔ̃kuʀ] *adj inv* ineligible to compete; (*fig*) in a class of one's own.

'**hors-d'œuvre** ['ɔʀdœvʀ(ə)] *nm inv* hors d'œuvre.

'**hors-jeu** ['ɔʀʒø] *nm inv* being offside *no pl*.

'**hors-la-loi** ['ɔʀlalwa] *nm inv* outlaw.

'**hors-piste(s)** ['ɔʀpist] *nm inv* (*SKI*) cross-country.

hors-taxe [ɔʀtaks] *adj* (*sur une facture, prix*) excluding VAT; (*boutique, marchandises*) duty-free.

'**hors-texte** ['ɔʀtɛkst(ə)] *nm inv* plate.

hortensia [ɔʀtɑ̃sja] *nm* hydrangea.

horticole [ɔʀtikɔl] *adj* horticultural.

horticulteur, trice [ɔʀtikyltœʀ, -tʀis] *nm/f* horticulturalist (*BRIT*), horticulturist (*US*).

horticulture [ɔʀtikyltyʀ] *nf* horticulture.

hospice [ɔspis] *nm* (*de vieillards*) home; (*asile*) hospice.

hospitalier, ière [ɔspitalje, -jɛʀ] *adj* (*accueillant*) hospitable; (*MÉD: service, centre*) hospital *cpd*.

hospitalisation [ɔspitalizɑsjɔ̃] *nf* hospitalization.

hospitaliser [ɔspitalize] *vt* to take (*ou* send) to hospital, hospitalize.

hospitalité [ɔspitalite] *nf* hospitality.

hospitalo-universitaire [ɔspitaloynivɛʀsitɛʀ] *adj*: **centre ~ (CHU)** ≈ (teaching) hospital.

hostie [ɔsti] *nf* host (*REL*).

hostile [ɔstil] *adj* hostile.

hostilité [ɔstilite] *nf* hostility; **~s** *nfpl* hostilities.

hôte [ot] *nm* (*maître de maison*) host; (*client*) patron; (*fig*) inhabitant, occupant ♦ *nm/f* (*invité*) guest; **~ payant** paying guest.

hôtel [otɛl] *nm* hotel; **aller à l'~** to stay in a hotel; **~ (particulier)** (private) mansion; **~ de ville** town hall.

hôtelier, ière [otəlje, -jɛʀ] *adj* hotel *cpd* ♦ *nm/f* hotelier, hotel-keeper.

hôtellerie [otɛlʀi] *nf* (*profession*) hotel business; (*auberge*) inn.

hôtesse [otɛs] *nf* hostess; **~ de l'air** air hostess (*BRIT*) *ou* stewardess; **~ (d'accueil)** receptionist.

'**hotte** ['ɔt] *nf* (*panier*) basket (*carried on the back*); (*de cheminée*) hood; **~ aspirante** cooker hood.

'**houblon** ['ublɔ̃] *nm* (*BOT*) hop; (*pour la bière*) hops *pl*.

'**houe** ['u] *nf* hoe.

'**houille** ['uj] *nf* coal; **~ blanche** hydroelectric power.

'**houiller, ère** ['uje, -ɛʀ] *adj* coal *cpd*; (*terrain*) coal-bearing ♦ *nf* coal mine.

'**houle** ['ul] *nf* swell.

'**houlette** ['ulɛt] *nf*: **sous la ~ de** under the guidance of.

'**houleux, euse** ['ulø, -øz] *adj* heavy, swelling; (*fig*) stormy, turbulent.

'**houppe** ['up] *nf*, '**houppette** ['upɛt] *nf* powder puff; (*cheveux*) tuft.

'**hourra** ['uʀa] *nm* cheer ♦ *excl* hurrah!

'**houspiller** ['uspije] *vt* to scold.

'**housse** ['us] *nf* cover; (*pour protégér provisoirement*) dust cover; (*pour recouvrir à neuf*) loose *ou* stretch cover; **~ (penderie)** hanging wardrobe.

'**houx** ['u] *nm* holly.

HS *abr* = **hors service**.

HT *abr* = **hors taxe**.

'**hublot** ['yblo] *nm* porthole.

'**huche** ['yʃ] *nf*: **~ à pain** bread bin.

'**huées** ['ɥe] *nfpl* boos.

'**huer** ['ɥe] *vt* to boo; (*hibou, chouette*) to hoot.

huile [ɥil] *nf* oil; (*ART*) oil painting; (*fam*) bigwig; **mer d'~** (*très calme*) glassy sea, sea of glass; **faire tache d'~** (*fig*) to spread; **~ d'arachide** groundnut oil; **~ essentielle** essential oil; **~ de foie de morue** cod-liver oil; **~ de ricin** castor oil; **~ solaire** suntan oil; **~ de table** salad oil.

huiler [ɥile] *vt* to oil.

huilerie [ɥilʀi] *nf* (*usine*) oil-works.

huileux, euse [ɥilø, -øz] *adj* oily.

huilier [ɥilje] *nm* (oil and vinegar) cruet.

huis [ɥi] *nm*: **à ~ clos** in camera.

huissier [ɥisje] *nm* usher; (*JUR*) ≈ bailiff.

'**huit** ['ɥi(t)] *num* eight; **samedi en ~** a week on Saturday; **dans ~ jours** in a week('s time).

'**huitaine** ['ɥitɛn] *nf*: **une ~ de** about eight, eight or so; **une ~ de jours** a week or so.

'**huitante** ['ɥitɑ̃t] *num* (*Suisse*) eighty.

'**huitième** ['ɥitjɛm] *num* eighth.

huître [ɥitʀ(ə)] *nf* oyster.

'**hululement** ['ylylmɑ̃] *nm* hooting.

'**hululer** ['ylyle] *vi* to hoot.

humain, e ['ymɛ̃, -ɛn] *adj* human; (*compatissant*) humane ♦ *nm* human (being).

humainement [ymɛnmɑ̃] *adv* humanly; humanely.

humanisation [ymanizɑsjɑ̃] *nf* humanization.

humaniser [ymanize] *vt* to humanize.

humaniste [ymanist(ə)] *nm/f* (*LING*) classicist; humanist.

humanitaire [ymanitɛʀ] *adj* humanitarian.

humanitarisme [ymanitaʀism(ə)] *nm* humanitarianism.

humanité [ymanite] *nf* humanity.

humanoïde [ymanɔid] *nm/f* humanoid.

humble [œ̃bl(ə)] *adj* humble.

humblement [œ̃bləmɑ̃] *adv* humbly.

humecter [ymɛkte] *vt* to dampen; **s'~ les lèvres** to moisten one's lips.

'**humer** ['yme] *vt* to inhale; (*pour sentir*) to smell.

humérus [ymeʀys] *nm* (*ANAT*) humerus.

humeur [ymœʀ] *nf* mood; (*tempérament*) temper; (*irritation*) bad temper; **de bonne/**

mauvaise ~ in a good/bad mood; **être d'**~ **à faire qch** to be in the mood for doing sth.
humide [ymid] *adj* (*linge*) damp; (*main, yeux*) moist; (*climat, chaleur*) humid; (*saison, route*) wet.
humidificateur [ymidifikatœʀ] *nm* humidifier.
humidifier [ymidifje] *vt* to humidify.
humidité [ymidite] *nf* humidity; dampness; **traces d'**~ traces of moisture *ou* damp.
humiliant, e [ymiljɑ̃, -ɑ̃t] *adj* humiliating.
humiliation [ymiljasjɔ̃] *nf* humiliation.
humilier [ymilje] *vt* to humiliate; **s'**~ **devant qn** to humble o.s. before sb.
humilité [ymilite] *nf* humility.
humoriste [ymɔʀist(ə)] *nm/f* humorist.
humoristique [ymɔʀistik] *adj* humorous; humoristic.
humour [ymuʀ] *nm* humour; **avoir de l'**~ to have a sense of humour; ~ **noir** sick humour.
humus [ymys] *nm* humus.
'huppé, e ['ype] *adj* crested; (*fam*) posh.
'hurlement ['yʀləmɑ̃] *nm* howling *no pl*, howl; yelling *no pl*, yell.
'hurler ['yʀle] *vi* to howl, yell; (*fig: vent*) to howl; (*: couleurs etc*) to clash; ~ **à la mort** (*suj: chien*) to bay at the moon.
hurluberlu [yʀlybɛʀly] *nm* (*péj*) crank ♦ *adj* cranky.
'hutte ['yt] *nf* hut.
hybride [ibʀid] *adj* hybrid.
hydratant, e [idʀatɑ̃, -ɑ̃t] *adj* (*crème*) moisturizing.
hydrate [idʀat] *nm*: ~**s de carbone** carbohydrates.
hydrater [idʀate] *vt* to hydrate.
hydraulique [idʀolik] *adj* hydraulic.
hydravion [idʀavjɔ̃] *nm* seaplane, hydroplane.
hydro... [idʀo] *préfixe* hydro....
hydrocarbure [idʀɔkaʀbyʀ] *nm* hydrocarbon.
hydrocution [idʀɔkysjɔ̃] *nf* immersion syncope.
hydro-électrique [idʀɔelɛktʀik] *adj* hydroelectric.
hydrogène [idʀɔʒɛn] *nm* hydrogen.
hydroglisseur [idʀɔglisœʀ] *nm* hydroplane.
hydrographie [idʀɔgʀafi] *nf* (*fleuves*) hydrography.
hydrophile [idʀɔfil] *adj voir* **coton.**
hyène [jɛn] *nf* hyena.
hygiène [iʒjɛn] *nf* hygiene; ~ **intime** personal hygiene.
hygiénique [iʒenik] *adj* hygienic.
hymne [imn(ə)] *nm* hymn; ~ **national** national anthem.
hyper... [ipɛʀ] *préfixe* hyper....
hypermarché [ipɛʀmaʀʃe] *nm* hypermarket.
hypermétrope [ipɛʀmetʀɔp] *adj* long-sighted.
hypernerveux, euse [ipɛʀnɛʀvø, -øz] *adj* highly-strung.
hypersensible [ipɛʀsɑ̃sibl(ə)] *adj* hypersensitive.

hypertendu, e [ipɛʀtɑ̃dy] *adj* having high blood pressure, hypertensive.
hypertension [ipɛʀtɑ̃sjɔ̃] *nf* high blood pressure, hypertension.
hypertexte [ipɛʀtɛkst] *nm* (*INFORM*) hypertext.
hypnose [ipnoz] *nf* hypnosis.
hypnotique [ipnɔtik] *adj* hypnotic.
hypnotiser [ipnɔtize] *vt* to hypnotize.
hypnotiseur [ipnɔtizœʀ] *nm* hypnotist.
hypnotisme [ipnɔtism(ə)] *nm* hypnotism.
hypocondriaque [ipɔkɔ̃dʀijak] *adj* hypochondriac.
hypocrisie [ipɔkʀizi] *nf* hypocrisy.
hypocrite [ipɔkʀit] *adj* hypocritical ♦ *nm/f* hypocrite.
hypocritement [ipɔkʀitmɑ̃] *adv* hypocritically.
hypotendu, e [ipɔtɑ̃dy] *adj* having low blood pressure, hypotensive.
hypotension [ipɔtɑ̃sjɔ̃] *nf* low blood pressure, hypotension.
hypoténuse [ipɔtenyz] *nf* hypotenuse.
hypothécaire [ipɔtekɛʀ] *adj* hypothecary; **garantie/prêt** ~ mortgage security/loan.
hypothèque [ipɔtɛk] *nf* mortgage.
hypothéquer [ipɔteke] *vt* to mortgage.
hypothermie [ipɔtɛʀmi] *nf* hypothermia.
hypothèse [ipɔtɛz] *nf* hypothesis; **dans l'**~ **où** assuming that.
hypothétique [ipɔtetik] *adj* hypothetical.
hypothétiquement [ipɔtetikmɑ̃] *adv* hypothetically.
hystérectomie [isteʀɛktɔmi] *nf* hysterectomy.
hystérie [isteʀi] *nf* hysteria; ~ **collective** mass hysteria.
hystérique [isteʀik] *adj* hysterical.
Hz *abr* (= *Hertz*) Hz.

I i

I, i [i] *nm inv* I, i; **I comme Irma** I for Isaac (*BRIT*) *ou* Item (*US*).
IAC *sigle f* (= *insémination artificielle entre conjoints*) AIH.
IAD *sigle f* (= *insémination artificielle par donneur extérieur*) AID.
ibère [ibɛʀ] *adj* Iberian ♦ *nm/f*: **I**~ Iberian.
ibérique [ibeʀik] *adj*: **la péninsule** ~ the Iberian peninsula.
ibid. [ibid] *abr* (= *ibidem*) ibid., ib.
iceberg [isbɛʀg] *nm* iceberg.
ici [isi] *adv* here; **jusqu'**~ as far as this; (*temporel*) until now; **d'**~ **là** by then; (*en atten-*

dant) in the meantime; **d'~ peu** before long.

icône [ikon] *nf (aussi INFORM)* icon.

iconoclaste [ikɔnɔklast(ə)] *nm/f* iconoclast.

iconographie [ikɔnɔgʀafi] *nf* iconography; *(illustrations)* (collection of) illustrations.

id. [id] *abr (= idem)* id.

idéal, e, aux [ideal, -o] *adj* ideal ♦ *nm* ideal; *(système de valeurs)* ideals *pl.*

idéalement [idealmã] *adv* ideally.

idéalisation [idealizasjɔ̃] *nf* idealization.

idéaliser [idealize] *vt* to idealize.

idéalisme [idealism(ə)] *nm* idealism.

idéaliste [idealist(ə)] *adj* idealistic ♦ *nm/f* idealist.

idée [ide] *nf* idea; *(illusion):* **se faire des ~s** to imagine things, get ideas into one's head; **avoir dans l'~ que** to have an idea that; **mon ~, c'est que ...** I suggest that ..., I think that ...; **à l'~ de/que** at the idea of/that, at the thought of/that; **je n'ai pas la moindre ~** I haven't the faintest idea; **avoir ~ que** to have an idea that; **avoir des ~s larges/étroites** to be broad-/narrow-minded; **venir à l'~ de qn** to occur to sb; **en voilà des ~s!** the very idea!; **~ fixe** idée fixe, obsession; **~s noires** black *ou* dark thoughts; **~s reçues** accepted ideas *ou* wisdom.

identifiable [idãtifjabl(ə)] *adj* identifiable.

identification [idãtifikasjɔ̃] *nf* identification.

identifier [idãtifje] *vt* to identify; **~ qch/qn à** to identify sth/sb with; **s'~ avec** *ou* **à qn/qch** *(héros etc)* to identify with sb/sth.

identique [idãtik] *adj:* **~ (à)** identical (to).

identité [idãtite] *nf* identity; **~ judiciaire** *(POLICE)* ≈ Criminal Records Office.

idéogramme [ideɔgʀam] *nm* ideogram.

idéologie [ideɔlɔʒi] *nf* ideology.

idéologique [ideɔlɔʒik] *adj* ideological.

idiomatique [idjɔmatik] *adj:* **expression ~** idiom, idiomatic expression.

idiome [idjɔm] *nm (LING)* idiom.

idiot, e [idjo, idjɔt] *adj* idiotic ♦ *nm/f* idiot.

idiotie [idjɔsi] *nf* idiocy; *(propos)* idiotic remark *etc.*

idiotisme [idjɔtism(ə)] *nm* idiom, idiomatic phrase.

idoine [idwan] *adj* fitting.

idolâtrer [idɔlɑtʀe] *vt* to idolize.

idolâtrie [idɔlɑtʀi] *nf* idolatry.

idole [idɔl] *nf* idol.

IDS *sigle f (= Initiative de défense stratégique)* SDI.

idylle [idil] *nf* idyll.

idyllique [idilik] *adj* idyllic.

if [if] *nm* yew.

IFOP [ifɔp] *sigle m (= Institut français d'opinion publique)* French market research institute.

IGF *sigle m (= impôt sur les grandes fortunes)* wealth tax.

IGH *sigle m = immeuble de grande hauteur.*

igloo [iglu] *nm* igloo.

IGN *sigle m = Institut géographique national.*

ignare [iɲaʀ] *adj* ignorant.

ignifuge [iɲifyʒ] *adj* fireproofing ♦ *nm* fireproofing (substance).

ignifuger [iɲifyʒe] *vt* to fireproof.

ignoble [iɲɔbl(ə)] *adj* vile.

ignominie [iɲɔmini] *nf* ignominy; *(acte)* ignominious *ou* base act.

ignominieux, euse [iɲɔminjø, øz] *adj* ignominious.

ignorance [iɲɔʀɑ̃s] *nf* ignorance; **dans l'~ de** in ignorance of, ignorant of.

ignorant, e [iɲɔʀɑ̃, -ɑ̃t] *adj* ignorant ♦ *nm/f:* **faire l'~** to pretend one doesn't know; **~ de** ignorant of, not aware of; **~ en** ignorant of, knowing nothing of.

ignoré, e [iɲɔʀe] *adj* unknown.

ignorer [iɲɔʀe] *vt (ne pas connaître)* not to know, be unaware *ou* ignorant of; *(être sans expérience de: plaisir, guerre etc)* not to know about, have no experience of; *(bouder: personne)* to ignore; **j'ignore comment/si** I do not know how/if; **~ que** to be unaware that, not to know that; **je n'ignore pas que ...** I'm not forgetting that ..., I'm not unaware that ...; **je l'ignore** I don't know.

IGPN *sigle f (= Inspection générale de la police nationale) police disciplinary body.*

IGS *sigle f (= Inspection générale des services) police disciplinary body for Paris.*

iguane [igwan] *nm* iguana.

il [il] *pron* he; *(animal, chose, en tournure impersonnelle)* it; *NB: en anglais les navires et les pays sont en général assimilés aux femelles, et les bébés aux choses, si le sexe n'est pas spécifié;* **~s** they; **~ neige** it's snowing; *voir aussi* **avoir.**

île [il] *nf* island; **les Î~s** the West Indies; **l'~ de Beauté** Corsica; **l'~ Maurice** Mauritius; **les ~s anglo-normandes** the Channel Islands; **les ~s Britanniques** the British Isles; **les ~s Cocos** *ou* **Keeling** the Cocos *ou* Keeling Islands; **les ~s Cook** the Cook Islands; **les ~s Scilly** the Scilly Isles, the Scillies; **les ~s Shetland** the Shetland Islands, Shetland; **les ~s Sorlingues = les ~s Scilly; les ~s Vierges** the Virgin Islands.

iliaque [iljak] *adj (ANAT):* **os/artère ~** iliac bone/artery.

illégal, e, aux [ilegal, -o] *adj* illegal, unlawful *(ADMIN).*

illégalement [ilegalmã] *adv* illegally.

illégalité [ilegalite] *nf* illegality; unlawfulness; **être dans l'~** to be outside the law.

illégitime [ileʒitim] *adj* illegitimate; *(optimisme, sévérité)* unjustified, unwarranted.

illégitimement [ileʒitimmã] *adv* illegitimately.

illégitimité [ileʒitimite] *nf* illegitimacy; **gouverner dans l'~** to rule illegally.

illettré, e [iletʀe] *adj, nm/f* illiterate.

illicite [ilisit] *adj* illicit.

illicitement [ilisitmã] *adv* illicitly.

illico [iliko] *adv* (*fam*) pronto.

illimité, e [ilimite] *adj* (*immense*) boundless, unlimited; (*congé, durée*) indefinite, unlimited.

illisible [ilizibl(ə)] *adj* illegible; (*roman*) unreadable.

illisiblement [ilizibləmɑ̃] *adv* illegibly.

illogique [iləʒik] *adj* illogical.

illogisme [iləʒism(ə)] *nm* illogicality.

illumination [ilyminasjɔ̃] *nf* illumination, floodlighting; (*inspiration*) flash of inspiration; ~s *nfpl* illuminations, lights.

illuminé, e [ilymine] *adj* lit up; illuminated, floodlit ♦ *nm/f* (*fig: péj*) crank.

illuminer [ilymine] *vt* to light up; (*monument, rue: pour une fête*) to illuminate, floodlight; **s'~** *vi* to light up.

illusion [ilyzjɔ̃] *nf* illusion; **se faire des** ~**s** to delude o.s.; **faire** ~ to delude *ou* fool people; ~ **d'optique** optical illusion.

illusionner [ilyzjɔne] *vt* to delude; **s'~** **(sur qn/qch)** to delude o.s. (about sb/sth).

illusionnisme [ilyzjɔnism(ə)] *nm* conjuring.

illusionniste [ilyzjɔnist(ə)] *nm/f* conjuror.

illusoire [ilyzwaʀ] *adj* illusory, illusive.

illustrateur [ilystʀatœʀ] *nm* illustrator.

illustratif, ive [ilystʀatif, -iv] *adj* illustrative.

illustration [ilystʀasjɔ̃] *nf* illustration; (*d'un ouvrage: photos*) illustrations *pl*.

illustre [ilystʀ(ə)] *adj* illustrious, renowned.

illustré, e [ilystʀe] *adj* illustrated ♦ *nm* illustrated magazine; (*pour enfants*) comic.

illustrer [ilystʀe] *vt* to illustrate; **s'~** to become famous, win fame.

îlot [ilo] *nm* small island, islet; (*de maisons*) block; (*petite zone*): **un** ~ **de verdure** an island of greenery, a patch of green.

ils [il] *pron voir* **il**.

image [imaʒ] *nf* (*gén*) picture; (*comparaison, ressemblance, OPTIQUE*) image; ~ **de** picture *ou* image of; ~ **d'Épinal** (*social*) stereotype; ~ **de marque** brand image; (*d'une personne*) (*public*) image; (*d'une entreprise*) corporate image; ~ **pieuse** holy picture.

imagé, e [imaʒe] *adj* full of imagery.

imaginable [imaʒinabl(ə)] *adj* imaginable; **difficilement** ~ hard to imagine.

imaginaire [imaʒinɛʀ] *adj* imaginary.

imaginatif, ive [imaʒinatif, -iv] *adj* imaginative.

imagination [imaʒinasjɔ̃] *nf* imagination; (*chimère*) fancy, imagining; **avoir de l'~** to be imaginative, have a good imagination.

imaginer [imaʒine] *vt* to imagine; (*croire*): **qu'allez-vous** ~ **là?** what on earth are you thinking of?; (*inventer: expédient, mesure*) to devise, think up; **s'~** *vt* (*se figurer: scène etc*) to imagine, picture; **s'~** **à 60 ans** to picture *ou* imagine o.s. at 60; **s'~** **que** to imagine that; **s'~** **pouvoir faire qch** to think one can do sth; **j'imagine qu'il a voulu plaisanter** I suppose he was joking; ~ **de faire** (*se mettre*

dans l'idée de) to dream up the idea of doing.

imbattable [ɛ̃batabl(ə)] *adj* unbeatable.

imbécile [ɛ̃besil] *adj* idiotic ♦ *nm/f* idiot; (*MÉD*) imbecile.

imbécillité [ɛ̃besilite] *nf* idiocy; imbecility; idiotic action (*ou* remark *etc*).

imberbe [ɛ̃bɛʀb(ə)] *adj* beardless.

imbiber [ɛ̃bibe] *vt*: ~ **qch de** to moisten *ou* wet sth with; **s'~ de** to become saturated with; **imbibé(e) d'eau** (*chaussures, étoffe*) saturated; (*terre*) waterlogged.

imbriqué, e [ɛ̃bʀike] *adj* overlapping.

imbriquer [ɛ̃bʀike]: **s'~** *vi* to overlap (each other); (*fig*) to become interlinked *ou* interwoven.

imbroglio [ɛ̃bʀɔljo] *nm* imbroglio.

imbu, e [ɛ̃by] *adj*: ~ **de** full of; ~ **de soi-même/sa supériorité** full of oneself/one's superiority.

imbuvable [ɛ̃byvabl(ə)] *adj* undrinkable.

imitable [imitabl(ə)] *adj* imitable; **facilement** ~ easily imitated.

imitateur, trice [imitatœʀ, -tʀis] *nm/f* (*gén*) imitator; (*MUSIC-HALL: d'une personnalité*) impersonator.

imitation [imitasjɔ̃] *nf* imitation; impersonation; **sac** ~ **cuir** bag in imitation *ou* simulated leather; **à l'~ de** in imitation of.

imiter [imite] *vt* to imitate; (*personne*) to imitate, impersonate; (*contrefaire: signature, document*) to forge, copy; (*ressembler à*) to look like; **il se leva et je l'imitai** he got up and I did likewise.

imm. *abr* = **immeuble**.

immaculé, e [imakyle] *adj* spotless, immaculate; **l'I~e Conception** (*REL*) the Immaculate Conception.

immanent, e [imanɑ̃, -ɑ̃t] *adj* immanent.

immangeable [ɛ̃mɑ̃ʒabl(ə)] *adj* inedible, uneatable.

immanquable [ɛ̃mɑ̃kabl(ə)] *adj* (*cible*) impossible to miss; (*fatal, inévitable*) bound to happen, inevitable.

immanquablement [ɛ̃mɑ̃kabləmɑ̃] *adv* inevitably.

immatériel, le [imateʀjɛl] *adj* ethereal; (*PHILOSOPHIE*) immaterial.

immatriculation [imatʀikylasjɔ̃] *nf* registration.

immatriculer [imatʀikyle] *vt* to register; **faire/se faire** ~ to register; **voiture immatriculée dans la Seine** car with a Seine registration (number).

immature [imatyʀ] *adj* immature.

immaturité [imatyʀite] *nf* immaturity.

immédiat, e [imedja, -at] *adj* immediate ♦ *nm*: **dans l'**~ for the time being; **dans le voisinage** ~ **de** in the immediate vicinity of.

immédiatement [imedjatmɑ̃] *adv* immediately.

immémorial, e, aux [imemɔʀjal, -o] *adj* ancient, age-old.

immense [imɑ̃s] *adj* immense.
immensément [imɑ̃semɑ̃] *adv* immensely.
immensité [imɑ̃site] *nf* immensity.
immerger [imɛRʒe] *vt* to immerse, submerge; (*câble etc*) to lay under water; (*déchets*) to dump at sea; **s'~** *vi* (*sous-marin*) to dive, submerge.
immérité, e [imeRite] *adj* undeserved.
immersion [imɛRsjɔ̃] *nf* immersion.
immettable [ɛ̃metabl(ə)] *adj* unwearable.
immeuble [imœbl(ə)] *nm* building ♦ *adj* (*JUR*) immovable, real; **~ locatif** block of rented flats (*BRIT*), rental building (*US*); **~ de rapport** investment property.
immigrant, e [imigRɑ̃, -ɑ̃t] *nm/f* immigrant.
immigration [imigRasjɔ̃] *nf* immigration.
immigré, e [imigRe] *nm/f* immigrant.
immigrer [imigRe] *vi* to immigrate.
imminence [iminɑ̃s] *nf* imminence.
imminent, e [iminɑ̃, -ɑ̃t] *adj* imminent, impending.
immiscer [imise]: **s'~** *vi*: **s'~ dans** to interfere in *ou* with.
immixtion [imiksjɔ̃] *nf* interference.
immobile [imɔbil] *adj* still, motionless; (*pièce de machine*) fixed; (*fig*) unchanging; **rester/ se tenir ~** to stay/keep still.
immobilier, ière [imɔbilje, -jɛR] *adj* property *cpd*, in real property ♦ *nm*: **l'~** the property *ou* the real estate business.
immobilisation [imɔbilizasjɔ̃] *nf* immobilization; **~s** *nfpl* (*JUR*) fixed assets.
immobiliser [imɔbilize] *vt* (*gén*) to immobilize; (*circulation, véhicule, affaires*) to bring to a standstill; **s'~** (*personne*) to stand still; (*machine, véhicule*) to come to a halt *ou* a standstill.
immobilisme [imɔbilism(ə)] *nm* strong resistance *ou* opposition to change.
immobilité [imɔbilite] *nf* immobility.
immodéré, e [imɔdeRe] *adj* immoderate, inordinate.
immodérément [imɔdeRemɑ̃] *adv* immoderately.
immoler [imɔle] *vt* to sacrifice.
immonde [imɔ̃d] *adj* foul; (*sale: ruelle, taudis*) squalid.
immondices [imɔ̃dis] *nfpl* (*ordures*) refuse *sg*; (*saletés*) filth *sg*.
immoral, e, aux [imɔRal, -o] *adj* immoral.
immoralisme [imɔRalism(ə)] *nm* immoralism.
immoralité [imɔRalite] *nf* immorality.
immortaliser [imɔRtalize] *vt* to immortalize.
immortel, le [imɔRtɛl] *adj* immortal ♦ *nf* (*BOT*) everlasting (flower).
immuable [imɥabl(ə)] *adj* (*inébranlable*) immutable; (*qui ne change pas*) unchanging; (*personne*): **~ dans ses convictions** immovable (in one's convictions).
immunisation [imynizasjɔ̃] *nf* immunization.
immuniser [imynize] *vt* (*MÉD*) to immunize; **~ qn contre** to immunize sb against; (*fig*) to make sb immune to.
immunitaire [imynitɛR] *adj* immune.
immunité [imynite] *nf* immunity; **~ diplomatique** diplomatic immunity; **~ parlementaire** parliamentary privilege.
immunologie [imynɔlɔʒi] *nf* immunology.
immutabilité [imytabilite] *nf* immutability.
impact [ɛ̃pakt] *nm* impact; **point d'~** point of impact.
impair, e [ɛ̃pɛR] *adj* odd ♦ *nm* faux pas, blunder; **numéros ~s** odd numbers.
impalpable [ɛ̃palpabl(ə)] *adj* impalpable.
impaludation [ɛ̃palydɑsjɔ̃] *nf* inoculation against malaria.
imparable [ɛ̃paRabl(ə)] *adj* unstoppable.
impardonnable [ɛ̃paRdɔnabl(ə)] *adj* unpardonable, unforgivable; **vous êtes ~ d'avoir fait cela** it's unforgivable of you to have done that.
imparfait, e [ɛ̃paRfɛ, -ɛt] *adj* imperfect ♦ *nm* (*LING*) imperfect (tense).
imparfaitement [ɛ̃paRfɛtmɑ̃] *adv* imperfectly.
impartial, e, aux [ɛ̃paRsjal, -o] *adj* impartial, unbiased.
impartialité [ɛ̃paRsjalite] *nf* impartiality.
impartir [ɛ̃paRtiR] *vt*: **~ qch à qn** to assign sth to sb; (*dons*) to bestow sth upon sb; **dans les délais impartis** in the time allowed.
impasse [ɛ̃pɑs] *nf* dead-end, cul-de-sac; (*fig*) deadlock; **être dans l'~** (*négociations*) to have reached deadlock; **~ budgétaire** budget deficit.
impassibilité [ɛ̃pasibilite] *nf* impassiveness.
impassible [ɛ̃pasibl(ə)] *adj* impassive.
impassiblement [ɛ̃pasibləmɑ̃] *adv* impassively.
impatiemment [ɛ̃pasjamɑ̃] *adv* impatiently.
impatience [ɛ̃pasjɑ̃s] *nf* impatience.
impatient, e [ɛ̃pasjɑ̃, -ɑ̃t] *adj* impatient; **~ de faire qch** keen *ou* impatient to do sth.
impatienter [ɛ̃pasjɑ̃te] *vt* to irritate, annoy; **s'~** *vi* to get impatient; **s'~ de/contre** to lose patience at/with, grow impatient at/with.
impayable [ɛ̃pɛjabl(ə)] *adj* (*drôle*) priceless.
impayé, e [ɛ̃peje] *adj* unpaid, outstanding.
impeccable [ɛ̃pekabl(ə)] *adj* faultless, impeccable; (*propre*) spotlessly clean; (*chic*) impeccably dressed; (*fam*) smashing.
impeccablement [ɛ̃pekabləmɑ̃] *adv* impeccably.
impénétrable [ɛ̃penetRabl(ə)] *adj* impenetrable.
impénitent, e [ɛ̃penitɑ̃, -ɑ̃t] *adj* unrepentant.
impensable [ɛ̃pɑ̃sabl(ə)] *adj* unthinkable, unbelievable.
imper [ɛ̃pɛR] *nm* (= *imperméable*) mac.
impératif, ive [ɛ̃peRatif, -iv] *adj* imperative; (*JUR*) mandatory ♦ *nm* (*LING*) imperative; **~s** *nmpl* requirements; demands.
impérativement [ɛ̃peRativmɑ̃] *adv* imperatively.
impératrice [ɛ̃peRatRis] *nf* empress.

imperceptible [ɛpɛʀsɛptibl(ə)] *adj* imperceptible.

imperceptiblement [ɛpɛʀsɛptibləmɑ̃] *adv* imperceptibly.

imperdable [ɛpɛʀdabl(ə)] *adj* that cannot be lost.

imperfectible [ɛpɛʀfɛktibl(ə)] *adj* which cannot be perfected.

imperfection [ɛpɛʀfɛksjɔ̃] *nf* imperfection.

impérial, e, aux [ɛpeʀjal, -o] *adj* imperial ♦ *nf* upper deck; **autobus à ~e** double-decker bus.

impérialisme [ɛpeʀjalism(ə)] *nm* imperialism.

impérialiste [ɛpeʀjalist(ə)] *adj* imperialist.

impérieusement [ɛpeʀjøzmɑ̃] *adv*: **avoir ~ besoin de qch** to have urgent need of sth.

impérieux, euse [ɛpeʀjø, -øz] *adj* (*caractère, ton*) imperious; (*obligation, besoin*) pressing, urgent.

impérissable [ɛpeʀisabl(ə)] *adj* undying, imperishable.

imperméabilisation [ɛpɛʀmeabilizɑsjɔ̃] *nf* waterproofing.

imperméabiliser [ɛpɛʀmeabilize] *vt* to waterproof.

imperméable [ɛpɛʀmeabl(ə)] *adj* waterproof; (*GÉO*) impermeable; (*fig*): **~ à** impervious to ♦ *nm* raincoat; **~ à l'air** airtight.

impersonnel, le [ɛpɛʀsɔnɛl] *adj* impersonal.

impertinemment [ɛpɛʀtinamɑ̃] *adv* impertinently.

impertinence [ɛpɛʀtinɑ̃s] *nf* impertinence.

impertinent, e [ɛpɛʀtinɑ̃, -ɑ̃t] *adj* impertinent.

imperturbable [ɛpɛʀtyʀbabl(ə)] *adj* (*personne*) imperturbable; (*sang-froid*) unshakeable; **rester ~** to remain unruffled.

imperturbablement [ɛpɛʀtyʀbabləmɑ̃] *adv* imperturbably; unshakeably.

impétrant, e [ɛpetʀɑ̃, -ɑ̃t] *nm/f* (*JUR*) applicant.

impétueux, euse [ɛpetɥø, -øz] *adj* fiery.

impétuosité [ɛpetɥozite] *nf* fieriness.

impie [ɛpi] *adj* impious, ungodly.

impiété [ɛpjete] *nf* impiety.

impitoyable [ɛpitwajabl(ə)] *adj* pitiless, merciless.

impitoyablement [ɛpitwajabləmɑ̃] *adv* mercilessly.

implacable [ɛplakabl(ə)] *adj* implacable.

implacablement [ɛplakabləmɑ̃] *adv* implacably.

implant [ɛplɑ̃] *nm* (*MÉD*) implant.

implantation [ɛplɑ̃tɑsjɔ̃] *nf* establishment; settling; implantation.

implanter [ɛplɑ̃te] *vt* (*usine, industrie, usage*) to establish; (*colons etc*) to settle; (*idée, préjugé*) to implant; **s'~ dans** to be established in; to settle in; to become implanted in.

implémenter [ɛplemɑ̃te] *vt* to implement.

implication [ɛplikasjɔ̃] *nf* implication.

implicite [ɛplisit] *adj* implicit.

implicitement [ɛplisitmɑ̃] *adv* implicitly.

impliquer [ɛplike] *vt* to imply; **~ qn (dans)** to implicate sb (in).

implorant, e [ɛplɔʀɑ̃, -ɑ̃t] *adj* imploring.

implorer [ɛplɔʀe] *vt* to implore.

imploser [ɛploze] *vi* to implode.

implosion [ɛplozjɔ̃] *nf* implosion.

impoli, e [ɛpɔli] *adj* impolite, rude.

impoliment [ɛpɔlimɑ̃] *adv* impolitely.

impolitesse [ɛpɔlitɛs] *nf* impoliteness, rudeness; (*propos*) impolite *ou* rude remark.

impondérable [ɛpɔ̃deʀabl(ə)] *nm* imponderable.

impopulaire [ɛpɔpylɛʀ] *adj* unpopular.

impopularité [ɛpɔpylaʀite] *nf* unpopularity.

importable [ɛpɔʀtabl(ə)] *adj* (*COMM: marchandise*) importable; (*vêtement: immettable*) unwearable.

importance [ɛpɔʀtɑ̃s] *nf* importance; **avoir de l'~** to be important; **sans ~** unimportant; **d'~** important, considerable; **quelle ~?** what does it matter?

important, e [ɛpɔʀtɑ̃, -ɑ̃t] *adj* important; (*en quantité*) considerable, sizeable; (*: gamme, dégâts*) extensive; (*péj: airs, ton*) self-important ♦ *nm*: **l'~** the important thing.

importateur, trice [ɛpɔʀtatœʀ, -tʀis] *adj* importing ♦ *nm/f* importer; **pays ~ de blé** wheat-importing country.

importation [ɛpɔʀtɑsjɔ̃] *nf* import; introduction; (*produit*) import.

importer [ɛpɔʀte] *vt* (*COMM*) to import; (*maladies, plantes*) to introduce ♦ *vi* (*être important*) to matter; **~ à qn** to matter to sb; **il importe qu'il fasse** he must do, it is important that he should do; **peu m'importe** I don't mind, I don't care; **peu importe** it doesn't matter; **peu importe (que)** it doesn't matter (if); **peu importe le prix** never mind the price; *voir aussi* **n'importe**.

import-export [ɛpɔʀɛkspɔʀ] *nm* import-export business.

importun, e [ɛpɔʀtœ̃, -yn] *adj* irksome, importunate; (*arrivée, visite*) inopportune, ill-timed ♦ *nm* intruder.

importuner [ɛpɔʀtyne] *vt* to bother.

imposable [ɛpozabl(ə)] *adj* taxable.

imposant, e [ɛpozɑ̃, -ɑ̃t] *adj* imposing.

imposé, e [ɛpoze] *adj* (*soumis à l'impôt*) taxed; (*GYM etc: figures*) set.

imposer [ɛpoze] *vt* (*taxer*) to tax; (*REL*): **~ les mains** to lay on hands; **~ qch à qn** to impose sth on sb; **s'~** (*être nécessaire*) to be imperative; (*montrer sa proéminence*) to stand out, emerge; (*artiste: se faire connaître*) to win recognition, come to the fore; **en ~** to be imposing; **en ~ à** to impress; **ça s'impose** it's essential, it's vital.

imposition [ɛpozisjɔ̃] *nf* (*ADMIN*) taxation.

impossibilité [ɛpɔsibilite] *nf* impossibility; **être dans l'~ de faire** to be unable to do, find it impossible to do.

impossible [ɛpɔsibl(ə)] *adj* impossible ♦ *nm*: **l'~** the impossible; **~ à faire** impossible to do; **il m'est ~ de le faire** it is impossible for me to do it, I can't possibly do it; **faire l'~ (pour que)** to do one's utmost (so that); **si, par ~ ...** if, by some miracle ....

imposteur [ɛpɔstœʀ] *nm* impostor.

imposture [ɛpɔstyʀ] *nf* imposture, deception.

impôt [ɛpo] *nm* tax; *(taxes)* taxation, taxes *pl*; **~s** *nmpl* *(contributions)* (income) tax *sg*; **payer 1 000 F d'~s** to pay 1,000 F in tax; **~ direct/indirect** direct/indirect tax; **~ sur le chiffre d'affaires** tax on turnover; **~ foncier** land tax; **~ sur la fortune** wealth tax; **~ sur les plus-values** capital gains tax; **~ sur le revenu** income tax; **~ sur le RPP** personal income tax; **~ sur les sociétés** tax on companies; **~s locaux** rates, local taxes *(US)*, ≈ council tax *(BRIT)*.

impotence [ɛpɔtɑ̃s] *nf* disability.

impotent, e [ɛpɔtɑ̃, -ɑ̃t] *adj* disabled.

impraticable [ɛpʀatikabl(ə)] *adj* *(projet)* impracticable, unworkable; *(piste)* impassable.

imprécation [ɛpʀekasjɔ̃] *nf* imprecation.

imprécis, e [ɛpʀesi, -iz] *adj* *(contours, souvenir)* imprecise, vague; *(tir)* inaccurate, imprecise.

imprécision [ɛpʀesizjɔ̃] *nf* imprecision.

imprégner [ɛpʀeɲe] *vt* *(tissu, tampon)*: **~ (de)** to soak *ou* impregnate (with); *(lieu, air)*: **~ (de)** to fill (with); *(suj: amertume, ironie)* to pervade; **s'~ de** to become impregnated with; to be filled with; *(fig)* to absorb.

imprenable [ɛpʀənabl(ə)] *adj* *(forteresse)* impregnable; **vue ~** unimpeded outlook.

impresario [ɛpʀesaʀjo] *nm* manager, impresario.

impression [ɛpʀesjɔ̃] *nf* impression; *(d'un ouvrage, tissu)* printing; *(PHOTO)* exposure; **faire bonne ~** to make a good impression; **donner une ~ de/l'~ que** to give the impression of/that; **avoir l'~ de/que** to have the impression of/that; **faire ~** to make an impression; **~s de voyage** impressions of one's journey.

impressionnable [ɛpʀesjɔnabl(ə)] *adj* impressionable.

impressionnant, e [ɛpʀesjɔnɑ̃, -ɑ̃t] *adj* impressive; upsetting.

impressionner [ɛpʀesjɔne] *vt* *(frapper)* to impress; *(troubler)* to upset; *(PHOTO)* to expose.

impressionnisme [ɛpʀesjɔnism(ə)] *nm* impressionism.

impressionniste [ɛpʀesjɔnist(ə)] *adj, nm/f* impressionist.

imprévisible [ɛpʀevizibl(ə)] *adj* unforeseeable; *(réaction, personne)* unpredictable.

imprévoyance [ɛpʀevwajɑ̃s] *nf* lack of foresight.

imprévoyant, e [ɛpʀevwajɑ̃, -ɑ̃t] *adj* lacking in foresight; *(en matière d'argent)* improvident.

imprévu, e [ɛpʀevy] *adj* unforeseen, unexpected ♦ *nm* unexpected incident; **l'~** the unexpected; **en cas d'~** if anything unexpected happens; **sauf ~** barring anything unexpected.

imprimante [ɛpʀimɑ̃t] *nf* *(INFORM)* printer; **~ à bulle d'encre** bubblejet printer; **~ à jet d'encre** ink-jet printer; **~ à laser** laser printer; **~ (ligne par) ligne** line printer; **~ à marguerite** daisy-wheel printer; **~ matricielle** dot-matrix printer; **~ thermique** thermal printer.

imprimé [ɛpʀime] *nm* *(formulaire)* printed form; *(POSTES)* printed matter *no pl*; *(tissu)* printed fabric; **un ~ à fleurs/pois** *(tissu)* a floral/polka-dot print.

imprimer [ɛpʀime] *vt* to print; *(INFORM)* to print (out); *(apposer: visa, cachet)* to stamp; *(empreinte etc)* to imprint; *(publier)* to publish; *(communiquer: mouvement, impulsion)* to impart, transmit.

imprimerie [ɛpʀimʀi] *nf* printing; *(établissement)* printing works *sg*; *(atelier)* printing house, printery.

imprimeur [ɛpʀimœʀ] *nm* printer; **imprimeur-éditeur/-libraire** printer and publisher/ bookseller.

improbable [ɛpʀɔbabl(ə)] *adj* unlikely, improbable.

improductif, ive [ɛpʀɔdyktif, -iv] *adj* unproductive.

impromptu, e [ɛpʀɔ̃pty] *adj* impromptu; *(départ)* sudden.

imprononçable [ɛpʀɔnɔ̃sabl(ə)] *adj* unpronounceable.

impropre [ɛpʀɔpʀ(ə)] *adj* inappropriate; **~ à** unsuitable for.

improprement [ɛpʀɔpʀəmɑ̃] *adv* improperly.

impropriété [ɛpʀɔpʀijete] *nf*: **~ (de langage)** incorrect usage *no pl*.

improvisation [ɛpʀɔvizasjɔ̃] *nf* improvization.

improvisé, e [ɛpʀɔvize] *adj* makeshift, improvized; *(jeu etc)* scratch, improvized; **avec des moyens ~s** using whatever comes to hand.

improviser [ɛpʀɔvize] *vt, vi* to improvize; **s'~** *(secours, réunion)* to be improvized; **s'~ cuisinier** to (decide to) act as cook; **~ qn cuisinier** to get sb to act as cook.

improviste [ɛpʀɔvist(ə)]: **à l'~** *adv* unexpectedly, without warning.

imprudemment [ɛpʀydamɑ̃] *adv* carelessly; unwisely, imprudently.

imprudence [ɛpʀydɑ̃s] *nf* carelessness *no pl*; imprudence *no pl*; act of carelessness; foolish *ou* unwise action.

imprudent, e [ɛpʀydɑ̃, -ɑ̃t] *adj* *(conducteur, geste, action)* careless; *(remarque)* unwise, imprudent; *(projet)* foolhardy.

impubère [ɛpybɛʀ] *adj* below the age of puberty.

impubliable [ɛpyblijabl(ə)] *adj* unpublishable.

impudemment [ɛpydamɑ̃] *adv* impudently.
impudence [ɛpydɑ̃s] *nf* impudence.
impudent, e [ɛpydɑ̃, -ɑ̃t] *adj* impudent.
impudeur [ɛpydœʀ] *nf* shamelessness.
impudique [ɛpydik] *adj* shameless.
impuissance [ɛpɥisɑ̃s] *nf* helplessness; ineffectualness; impotence.
impuissant, e [ɛpɥisɑ̃, -ɑ̃t] *adj* helpless; (*sans effet*) ineffectual; (*sexuellement*) impotent ♦ *nm* impotent man; ~ **à faire qch** powerless to do sth.
impulsif, ive [ɛpylsif, -iv] *adj* impulsive.
impulsion [ɛpylsjɔ̃] *nf* (*ÉLEC, instinct*) impulse; (*élan, influence*) impetus.
impulsivement [ɛpylsivmɑ̃] *adv* impulsively.
impulsivité [ɛpylsivite] *nf* impulsiveness.
impunément [ɛpynemɑ̃] *adv* with impunity.
impuni, e [ɛpyni] *adj* unpunished.
impunité [ɛpynite] *nf* impunity.
impur, e [ɛpyʀ] *adj* impure.
impureté [ɛpyʀte] *nf* impurity.
imputable [ɛpytabl(ə)] *adj* (*attribuable*): ~ **à** imputable to, ascribable to; (*COMM: somme*): ~ **sur** chargeable to.
imputation [ɛpytasjɔ̃] *nf* imputation, charge.
imputer [ɛpyte] *vt* (*attribuer*): ~ **qch à** to ascribe *ou* impute sth to; (*COMM*): ~ **qch à** *ou* **sur** to charge sth to.
imputrescible [ɛpytʀesibl(ə)] *adj* rotproof.
in [in] *adj inv* in, trendy.
INA [ina] *sigle m* (= *Institut national de l'audiovisuel*) *library of television archives.*
inabordable [inabɔʀdabl(ə)] *adj* (*lieu*) inaccessible; (*cher*) prohibitive.
inaccentué, e [inaksɑ̃tɥe] *adj* (*LING*) unstressed.
inacceptable [inaksɛptabl(ə)] *adj* unacceptable.
inaccessible [inaksesibl(ə)] *adj* inaccessible; (*objectif*) unattainable; (*insensible*): ~ **à** impervious to.
inaccoutumé, e [inakutyme] *adj* unaccustomed.
inachevé, e [inaʃve] *adj* unfinished.
inactif, ive [inaktif, -iv] *adj* inactive, idle.
inaction [inaksjɔ̃] *nf* inactivity.
inactivité [inaktivite] *nf* (*ADMIN*): **en** ~ out of active service.
inadaptation [inadaptasjɔ̃] *nf* (*PSYCH*) maladjustment.
inadapté, e [inadapte] *adj* (*PSYCH: adulte, enfant*) maladjusted ♦ *nm/f* (*péj: adulte: asocial*) misfit; ~ **à** not adapted to, unsuited to.
inadéquat, e [inadekwa, wat] *adj* inadequate.
inadéquation [inadekwasjɔ̃] *nf* inadequacy.
inadmissible [inadmisibl(ə)] *adj* inadmissible.
inadvertance [inadvɛʀtɑ̃s]: **par** ~ *adv* inadvertently.
inaliénable [inaljenabl(ə)] *adj* inalienable.
inaltérable [inaltɛʀabl(ə)] *adj* (*matière*) stable; (*fig*) unchanging; ~ **à** unaffected by; **couleur** ~ (*au lavage/à la lumière*) fast colour/

fade-resistant colour.
inamovible [inamɔvibl(ə)] *adj* fixed; (*JUR*) irremovable.
inanimé, e [inanime] *adj* (*matière*) inanimate; (*évanoui*) unconscious; (*sans vie*) lifeless.
inanité [inanite] *nf* futility.
inanition [inanisjɔ̃] *nf*: **tomber d'** ~ to faint with hunger (and exhaustion).
inaperçu, e [inapɛʀsy] *adj*: **passer** ~ to go unnoticed.
inappétence [inapetɑ̃s] *nf* lack of appetite.
inapplicable [inaplikabl(ə)] *adj* inapplicable.
inapplication [inaplikasjɔ̃] *nf* lack of application.
inappliqué, e [inaplike] *adj* lacking in application.
inappréciable [inapʀesjabl(ə)] *adj* (*service*) invaluable; (*différence, nuance*) inappreciable.
inapte [inapt(ə)] *adj*: ~ **à** incapable of; (*MIL*) unfit for.
inaptitude [inaptityd] *nf* inaptitude; unfitness.
inarticulé, e [inaʀtikyle] *adj* inarticulate.
inassimilable [inasimilabl(ə)] *adj* that cannot be assimilated.
inassouvi, e [inasuvi] *adj* unsatisfied, unfulfilled.
inattaquable [inatakabl(ə)] *adj* (*MIL*) unassailable; (*texte, preuve*) irrefutable.
inattendu, e [inatɑ̃dy] *adj* unexpected ♦ *nm*: **l'**~ the unexpected.
inattentif, ive [inatɑ̃tif, -iv] *adj* inattentive; ~ **à** (*dangers, détails*) heedless of.
inattention [inatɑ̃sjɔ̃] *nf* inattention; (*inadvertance*): **une minute d'**~ a minute of inattention, a minute's carelessness; **par** ~ inadvertently; **faute d'**~ careless mistake.
inaudible [inodibl(ə)] *adj* inaudible.
inaugural, e, aux [inoɡyʀal, -o] *adj* (*cérémonie*) inaugural, opening; (*vol, voyage*) maiden.
inauguration [inoɡyʀasjɔ̃] *nf* unveiling; opening; **discours/cérémonie d'**~ inaugural speech/ceremony.
inaugurer [inoɡyʀe] *vt* (*monument*) to unveil; (*exposition, usine*) to open; (*fig*) to inaugurate.
inauthenticité [inotɑ̃tisite] *nf* inauthenticity.
inavouable [inavwabl(ə)] *adj* undisclosable; (*honteux*) shameful.
inavoué, e [inavwe] *adj* unavowed.
INC *sigle m* (= *Institut national de la consommation*) *consumer research organization.*
inca [ɛ̃ka] *adj inv* Inca ♦ *nm/f*: **I**~ Inca.
incalculable [ɛ̃kalkylabl(ə)] *adj* incalculable; **un nombre** ~ **de** countless numbers of.
incandescence [ɛ̃kɑ̃desɑ̃s] *nf* incandescence; **en** ~ incandescent, white-hot; **porter à** ~ to heat white-hot; **lampe/manchon à** ~ incandescent lamp/(gas) mantle.
incandescent, e [ɛ̃kɑ̃desɑ̃, -ɑ̃t] *adj* incandescent, white-hot.
incantation [ɛ̃kɑ̃tasjɔ̃] *nf* incantation.

incantatoire [ɛ̃kɑ̃tatwaʀ] *adj*: **formule** ~ incantation.

incapable [ɛ̃kapabl(ə)] *adj* incapable; ~ **de faire** incapable of doing; (*empêché*) unable to do.

incapacitant, e [ɛ̃kapasitɑ̃, -ɑ̃t] *adj* (*MIL*) incapacitating.

incapacité [ɛ̃kapasite] *nf* incapability; (*JUR*) incapacity; **être dans l'**~ **de faire** to be unable to do; ~ **permanente/de travail** permanent/industrial disablement; ~ **électorale** ineligibility to vote.

incarcération [ɛ̃kaʀseʀɑsjɔ̃] *nf* incarceration.

incarcérer [ɛ̃kaʀseʀe] *vt* to incarcerate.

incarnat, e [ɛ̃kaʀna, -at] *adj* (rosy) pink.

incarnation [ɛ̃kaʀnɑsjɔ̃] *nf* incarnation.

incarné, e [ɛ̃kaʀne] *adj* incarnate; (*ongle*) ingrown.

incarner [ɛ̃kaʀne] *vt* to embody, personify; (*THÉÂT*) to play; (*REL*) to incarnate; **s'**~ **dans** (*REL*) to be incarnate in.

incartade [ɛ̃kaʀtad] *nf* prank, escapade.

incassable [ɛ̃kɑsabl(ə)] *adj* unbreakable.

incendiaire [ɛ̃sɑ̃djɛʀ] *adj* incendiary; (*fig: discours*) inflammatory ♦ *nm/f* fire-raiser, arsonist.

incendie [ɛ̃sɑ̃di] *nm* fire; ~ **criminel** arson *no pl*; ~ **de forêt** forest fire.

incendier [ɛ̃sɑ̃dje] *vt* (*mettre le feu à*) to set fire to, set alight; (*brûler complètement*) to burn down.

incertain, e [ɛ̃sɛʀtɛ̃, -ɛn] *adj* uncertain; (*temps*) uncertain, unsettled; (*imprécis: contours*) indistinct, blurred.

incertitude [ɛ̃sɛʀtityd] *nf* uncertainty.

incessamment [ɛ̃sɛsamɑ̃] *adv* very shortly.

incessant, e [ɛ̃sɛsɑ̃, -ɑ̃t] *adj* incessant, unceasing.

incessible [ɛ̃sesibl(ə)] *adj* (*JUR*) nontransferable.

inceste [ɛ̃sɛst(ə)] *nm* incest.

incestueux, euse [ɛ̃sɛstɥø, -øz] *adj* incestuous.

inchangé, e [ɛ̃ʃɑ̃ʒe] *adj* unchanged, unaltered.

inchantable [ɛ̃ʃɑ̃tabl(ə)] *adj* unsingable.

inchauffable [ɛ̃ʃofabl(ə)] *adj* impossible to heat.

incidemment [ɛ̃sidamɑ̃] *adv* in passing.

incidence [ɛ̃sidɑ̃s] *nf* (*effet, influence*) effect; (*PHYSIQUE*) incidence.

incident [ɛ̃sidɑ̃] *nm* incident; ~ **de frontière** border incident; ~ **de parcours** minor hitch *ou* setback; ~ **technique** technical difficulties *pl*, technical hitch.

incinérateur [ɛ̃sineʀatœʀ] *nm* incinerator.

incinération [ɛ̃sineʀɑsjɔ̃] *nf* (*d'ordures*) incineration; (*crémation*) cremation.

incinérer [ɛ̃sineʀe] *vt* (*ordures*) to incinerate; (*mort*) to cremate.

incise [ɛ̃siz] *nf* (*LING*) interpolated clause.

inciser [ɛ̃size] *vt* to make an incision in;

(*abcès*) to lance.

incisif, ive [ɛ̃sizif, -iv] *adj* incisive, cutting ♦ *nf* incisor.

incision [ɛ̃sizjɔ̃] *nf* incision; (*d'un abcès*) lancing.

incitation [ɛ̃sitɑsjɔ̃] *nf* (*encouragement*) incentive; (*provocation*) incitement.

inciter [ɛ̃site] *vt*: ~ **qn à (faire) qch** to prompt *ou* encourage sb to do sth; (*à la révolte etc*) to incite sb to do sth.

incivil, e [ɛ̃sivil] *adj* uncivil.

incivilité [ɛ̃sivilite] *nf* incivility.

inclinable [ɛ̃klinabl(ə)] *adj* (*dossier etc*) tilting; **siège à dossier** ~ reclining seat.

inclinaison [ɛ̃klinɛzɔ̃] *nf* (*déclivité: d'une route etc*) incline; (: *d'un toit*) slope; (*état penché: d'un mur*) lean; (: *de la tête*) tilt; (: *d'un navire*) list.

inclination [ɛ̃klinɑsjɔ̃] *nf* (*penchant*) inclination, tendency; **montrer de l'**~ **pour les sciences** *etc* to show an inclination for the sciences *etc*; ~**s égoïstes/altruistes** egoistic/altruistic tendencies; ~ **de (la) tête** nod (of the head); ~ **(de buste)** bow.

incliner [ɛ̃kline] *vt* (*bouteille*) to tilt; (*tête*) to incline; (*inciter*): ~ **qn à qch/à faire** to encourage sb towards sth/to do ♦ *vi*: ~ **à qch/à faire** (*tendre à, pencher pour*) to incline towards sth/doing, tend towards sth/to do; **s'**~ (*route*) to slope; (*toit*) to be sloping; **s'**~ **(devant)** to bow (before).

inclure [ɛ̃klyʀ] *vt* to include; (*joindre à un envoi*) to enclose; **jusqu'au 10 mars inclus** until 10th March inclusive.

inclus, e [ɛ̃kly, -yz] *pp de* **inclure** ♦ *adj* (*joint à un envoi*) enclosed; (*compris: frais, dépense*) included; (*MATH: ensemble*): ~ **dans** included in; **jusqu'au troisième chapitre** ~ up to and including the third chapter.

inclusion [ɛ̃klyzjɔ̃] *nf* (*voir* **inclure**) inclusion; enclosing.

inclusivement [ɛ̃klyzivmɑ̃] *adv* inclusively.

inclut [ɛ̃kly] *vb voir* **inclure**.

incoercible [ɛ̃kɔɛʀsibl(ə)] *adj* uncontrollable.

incognito [ɛ̃kɔɲito] *adv* incognito ♦ *nm*: **garder l'**~ to remain incognito.

incohérence [ɛ̃kɔeʀɑ̃s] *nf* inconsistency; incoherence.

incohérent, e [ɛ̃kɔeʀɑ̃, -ɑ̃t] *adj* inconsistent; incoherent.

incollable [ɛ̃kɔlabl(ə)] *adj* (*riz*) that does not stick; (*fam: personne*): **il est** ~ he's got all the answers.

incolore [ɛ̃kɔlɔʀ] *adj* colourless.

incomber [ɛ̃kɔbe]: ~ **à** *vt* (*suj: devoirs, responsabilité*) to rest *ou* be incumbent upon; (: *frais, travail*) to be the responsibility of.

incombustible [ɛ̃kɔ̃bystibl(ə)] *adj* incombustible.

incommensurable [ɛ̃kɔmɑ̃syʀabl(ə)] *adj* immeasurable.

incommodant, e [ɛ̃kɔmɔdɑ̃, -ɑ̃t] *adj* (*bruit*) an-

noying; (*chaleur*) uncomfortable.
incommode [ɛ̃kɔmɔd] *adj* inconvenient; (*posture, siège*) uncomfortable.
incommodément [ɛ̃kɔmɔdemɑ̃] *adv* (*installé, assis*) uncomfortably; (*logé, situé*) inconveniently.
incommoder [ɛ̃kɔmɔde] *vt*: ~ **qn** to bother *ou* inconvenience sb; (*embarrasser*) to make sb feel uncomfortable *ou* ill at ease.
incommodité [ɛ̃kɔmɔdite] *nf* inconvenience.
incommunicable [ɛ̃kɔmynikabl(ə)] *adj* (*JUR: droits, privilèges*) non-transferable; (*pensée*) incommunicable.
incomparable [ɛ̃kɔ̃paʀabl(ə)] *adj* not comparable; (*inégalable*) incomparable, matchless.
incomparablement [ɛ̃kɔ̃paʀabləmɑ̃] *adv* incomparably.
incompatibilité [ɛ̃kɔ̃patibilite] *nf* incompatibility; ~ **d'humeur** (mutual) incompatibility.
incompatible [ɛ̃kɔ̃patibl(ə)] *adj* incompatible.
incompétence [ɛ̃kɔ̃petɑ̃s] *nf* lack of expertise; incompetence.
incompétent, e [ɛ̃kɔ̃petɑ̃, -ɑ̃t] *adj* (*ignorant*) inexpert; (*incapable*) incompetent, not competent.
incomplet, ète [ɛ̃kɔ̃plɛ, -ɛt] *adj* incomplete.
incomplètement [ɛ̃kɔ̃plɛtmɑ̃] *adv* not completely, incompletely.
incompréhensible [ɛ̃kɔ̃pʀeɑ̃sibl(ə)] *adj* incomprehensible.
incompréhensif, ive [ɛ̃kɔ̃pʀeɑ̃sif, -iv] *adj* lacking in understanding, unsympathetic.
incompréhension [ɛ̃kɔ̃pʀeɑ̃sjɔ̃] *nf* lack of understanding.
incompressible [ɛ̃kɔ̃pʀesibl(ə)] *adj* (*PHYSIQUE*) incompressible; (*fig: dépenses*) that cannot be reduced; (*JUR: peine*) irreducible.
incompris, e [ɛ̃kɔ̃pʀi, -iz] *adj* misunderstood.
inconcevable [ɛ̃kɔ̃svabl(ə)] *adj* (*conduite etc*) inconceivable; (*mystère*) incredible.
inconciliable [ɛ̃kɔ̃siljabl(ə)] *adj* irreconcilable.
inconditionnel, le [ɛ̃kɔ̃disjɔnɛl] *adj* unconditional; (*partisan*) unquestioning ♦ *nm/f* (*partisan*) unquestioning supporter.
inconditionnellement [ɛ̃kɔ̃disjɔnɛlmɑ̃] *adv* unconditionally.
inconduite [ɛ̃kɔ̃dɥit] *nf* bad *ou* unsuitable behaviour *no pl*.
inconfort [ɛ̃kɔ̃fɔʀ] *nm* lack of comfort, discomfort.
inconfortable [ɛ̃kɔ̃fɔʀtabl(ə)] *adj* uncomfortable.
inconfortablement [ɛ̃kɔ̃fɔʀtabləmɑ̃] *adv* uncomfortably.
incongru, e [ɛ̃kɔ̃gʀy] *adj* unseemly; (*remarque*) ill-chosen, incongruous.
incongruité [ɛ̃kɔ̃gʀyite] *nf* unseemliness; incongruity; (*parole incongrue*) ill-chosen remark.
inconnu, e [ɛ̃kɔny] *adj* unknown; (*sentiment, plaisir*) new, strange ♦ *nm/f* stranger; un-

known person (*ou* artist *etc*) ♦ *nm*: **l'~** the unknown ♦ *nf* (*MATH*) unknown; (*fig*) unknown factor.
inconsciemment [ɛ̃kɔ̃sjamɑ̃] *adv* unconsciously.
inconscience [ɛ̃kɔ̃sjɑ̃s] *nf* unconsciousness; recklessness.
inconscient, e [ɛ̃kɔ̃sjɑ̃, -ɑ̃t] *adj* unconscious; (*irréfléchi*) reckless ♦ *nm* (*PSYCH*): **l'~** the subconscious, the unconscious; ~ **de** unaware of.
inconséquence [ɛ̃kɔ̃sekɑ̃s] *nf* inconsistency; thoughtlessness; (*action, parole*) thoughtless thing to do (*ou* say).
inconséquent, e [ɛ̃kɔ̃sekɑ̃, -ɑ̃t] *adj* (*illogique*) inconsistent; (*irréfléchi*) thoughtless.
inconsidéré, e [ɛ̃kɔ̃sideʀe] *adj* ill-considered.
inconsidérément [ɛ̃kɔ̃sideʀemɑ̃] *adv* thoughtlessly.
inconsistant, e [ɛ̃kɔ̃sistɑ̃, -ɑ̃t] *adj* flimsy, weak; (*crème etc*) runny.
inconsolable [ɛ̃kɔ̃sɔlabl(ə)] *adj* inconsolable.
inconstance [ɛ̃kɔ̃stɑ̃s] *nf* inconstancy, fickleness.
inconstant, e [ɛ̃kɔ̃stɑ̃, -ɑ̃t] *adj* inconstant, fickle.
inconstitutionnel, le [ɛ̃kɔ̃stitysjɔnɛl] *adj* unconstitutional.
incontestable [ɛ̃kɔ̃tɛstabl(ə)] *adj* unquestionable, indisputable.
incontestablement [ɛ̃kɔ̃tɛstabləmɑ̃] *adv* unquestionably, indisputably.
incontesté, e [ɛ̃kɔ̃tɛste] *adj* undisputed.
incontinence [ɛ̃kɔ̃tinɑ̃s] *nf* (*MÉD*) incontinence.
incontinent, e [ɛ̃kɔ̃tinɑ̃, -ɑ̃t] *adj* (*MÉD*) incontinent ♦ *adv* (*tout de suite*) forthwith.
incontournable [ɛ̃kɔ̃tuʀnabl(ə)] *adj* unavoidable.
incontrôlable [ɛ̃kɔ̃tʀolabl(ə)] *adj* unverifiable.
incontrôlé, e [ɛ̃kɔ̃tʀole] *adj* uncontrolled.
inconvenance [ɛ̃kɔ̃vnɑ̃s] *nf* (*parole, action*) impropriety.
inconvenant, e [ɛ̃kɔ̃vnɑ̃, -ɑ̃t] *adj* unseemly, improper.
inconvénient [ɛ̃kɔ̃venjɑ̃] *nm* (*d'une situation, d'un projet*) disadvantage, drawback; (*d'un remède, changement etc*) risk, inconvenience; **si vous n'y voyez pas d'~** if you have no objections; **y a-t-il un ~ à ...?** (*risque*) isn't there a risk in ...?; (*objection*) is there any objection to ...?
inconvertible [ɛ̃kɔ̃vɛʀtibl(ə)] *adj* inconvertible.
incorporation [ɛ̃kɔʀpɔʀasjɔ̃] *nf* (*MIL*) call-up.
incorporé, e [ɛ̃kɔʀpɔʀe] *adj* (*micro etc*) built-in.
incorporel, le [ɛ̃kɔʀpɔʀɛl] *adj* (*JUR*): **biens ~s** intangible property.
incorporer [ɛ̃kɔʀpɔʀe] *vt*: ~ **(à)** to mix in (with); (*paragraphe etc*): ~ **(dans)** to incorporate (in); (*territoire, immigrants*): ~ **(dans)**

to incorporate (into); (*MIL: appeler*) to recruit, call up; (: *affecter*): ~ **qn dans** to enlist sb into.

incorrect, e [ɛ̃kɔRɛkt] *adj* (*impropre, inconvenant*) improper; (*défectueux*) faulty; (*inexact*) incorrect; (*impoli*) impolite; (*déloyal*) underhand.

incorrectement [ɛ̃kɔRɛktəmɑ̃] *adv* improperly; faultily; incorrectly; impolitely; in an underhand way.

incorrection [ɛ̃kɔRɛksjɔ̃] *nf* impropriety; incorrectness; underhand nature; (*terme impropre*) impropriety; (*action, remarque*) improper behaviour (*ou* remark).

incorrigible [ɛ̃kɔRiʒibl(ə)] *adj* incorrigible.

incorruptible [ɛ̃kɔRyptibl(ə)] *adj* incorruptible.

incrédibilité [ɛ̃kRedibilite] *nf* incredibility.

incrédule [ɛ̃kRedyl] *adj* incredulous; (*REL*) unbelieving.

incrédulité [ɛ̃kRedylite] *nf* incredulity; **avec** ~ incredulously.

increvable [ɛ̃kRəvabl(ə)] *adj* (*pneu*) punctureproof; (*fam*) tireless.

incriminer [ɛ̃kRimine] *vt* (*personne*) to incriminate; (*action, conduite*) to bring under attack; (*bonne foi, honnêteté*) to call into question; **livre/article incriminé** offending book/article.

incrochetable [ɛ̃kRɔʃtabl(ə)] *adj* (*serrure*) that can't be picked, burglarproof.

incroyable [ɛ̃kRwajabl(ə)] *adj* incredible, unbelievable.

incroyablement [ɛ̃kRwajabləmɑ̃] *adv* incredibly, unbelievably.

incroyant, e [ɛ̃kRwajɑ̃, -ɑ̃t] *nm/f* non-believer.

incrustation [ɛ̃kRystasjɔ̃] *nf* inlaying *no pl*; inlay; (*dans une chaudière etc*) fur *no pl*, scale *no pl*.

incruster [ɛ̃kRyste] *vt* (*ART*): ~ **qch dans/qch de** to inlay sth into/sth with; (*radiateur etc*) to coat with scale *ou* fur; **s'**~ *vi* (*invité*) to take root; (*radiateur etc*) to become coated with fur *ou* scale; **s'**~ **dans** (*suj: corps étranger, caillou*) to become embedded in.

incubateur [ɛ̃kybatœR] *nm* incubator.

incubation [ɛ̃kybasjɔ̃] *nf* incubation.

inculpation [ɛ̃kylpasjɔ̃] *nf* charging *no pl*; charge; **sous l'**~ **de** on a charge of.

inculpé, e [ɛ̃kylpe] *nm/f* accused.

inculper [ɛ̃kylpe] *vt*: ~ **(de)** to charge (with).

inculquer [ɛ̃kylke] *vt*: ~ **qch à** to inculcate sth in, instil sth into.

inculte [ɛ̃kylt(ə)] *adj* uncultivated; (*esprit, peuple*) uncultured; (*barbe*) unkempt.

incultivable [ɛ̃kyltivabl(ə)] *adj* (*terrain*) unworkable.

inculture [ɛ̃kyltyR] *nf* lack of education.

incurable [ɛ̃kyRabl(ə)] *adj* incurable.

incurie [ɛ̃kyRi] *nf* carelessness.

incursion [ɛ̃kyRsjɔ̃] *nf* incursion, foray.

incurvé, e [ɛ̃kyRve] *adj* curved.

incurver [ɛ̃kyRve] *vt* (*barre de fer*) to bend into a curve; **s'**~ *vi* (*planche, route*) to bend.

Inde [ɛ̃d] *nf*: **l'**~ India.

indécemment [ɛ̃desamɑ̃] *adv* indecently.

indécence [ɛ̃desɑ̃s] *nf* indecency; (*propos, acte*) indecent remark (*ou* act *etc*).

indécent, e [ɛ̃desɑ̃, -ɑ̃t] *adj* indecent.

indéchiffrable [ɛ̃deʃifRabl(ə)] *adj* indecipherable.

indéchirable [ɛ̃deʃiRabl(ə)] *adj* tearproof.

indécis, e [ɛ̃desi, -iz] *adj* indecisive; (*perplexe*) undecided.

indécision [ɛ̃desizjɔ̃] *nf* indecision, indecisiveness.

indéclinable [ɛ̃deklinabl(ə)] *adj* (*LING: mot*) indeclinable.

indécomposable [ɛ̃dekɔ̃pozabl(ə)] *adj* that cannot be broken down.

indécrottable [ɛ̃dekRɔtabl(ə)] *adj* (*fam*) hopeless.

indéfectible [ɛ̃defɛktibl(ə)] *adj* (*attachement*) indestructible.

indéfendable [ɛ̃defɑ̃dabl(ə)] *adj* indefensible.

indéfini, e [ɛ̃defini] *adj* (*imprécis, incertain*) undefined; (*illimité, LING*) indefinite.

indéfiniment [ɛ̃definimɑ̃] *adv* indefinitely.

indéfinissable [ɛ̃definisabl(ə)] *adj* indefinable.

indéformable [ɛ̃defɔRmabl(ə)] *adj* that keeps its shape.

indélébile [ɛ̃delebil] *adj* indelible.

indélicat, e [ɛ̃delika, -at] *adj* tactless; (*malhonnête*) dishonest.

indélicatesse [ɛ̃delikatɛs] *nf* tactlessness; dishonesty.

indémaillable [ɛ̃demajabl(ə)] *adj* run-resist.

indemne [ɛ̃dɛmn(ə)] *adj* unharmed.

indemnisable [ɛ̃dɛmnizabl(ə)] *adj* entitled to compensation.

indemnisation [ɛ̃dɛmnizasjɔ̃] *nf* (*somme*) indemnity, compensation.

indemniser [ɛ̃dɛmnize] *vt*: ~ **qn (de)** to compensate sb (for); **se faire** ~ to get compensation.

indemnité [ɛ̃dɛmnite] *nf* (*dédommagement*) compensation *no pl*; (*allocation*) allowance; ~ **de licenciement** redundancy payment; ~ **de logement** housing allowance; ~ **parlementaire** ≈ M.P.'s (*BRIT*) *ou* Congressman's (*US*) salary.

indémontable [ɛ̃demɔ̃tabl(ə)] *adj* (*meuble etc*) that cannot be dismantled, in one piece.

indéniable [ɛ̃denjabl(ə)] *adj* undeniable, indisputable.

indéniablement [ɛ̃denjabləmɑ̃] *adv* undeniably.

indépendamment [ɛ̃depɑ̃damɑ̃] *adv* independently; ~ **de** independently of; (*abstraction faite de*) irrespective of; (*en plus de*) over and above.

indépendance [ɛ̃depɑ̃dɑ̃s] *nf* independence; ~ **matérielle** financial independence.

indépendant, e [ɛ̃depɑ̃dɑ̃, -ɑ̃t] *adj* independent; ~ **de** independent of; **chambre** ~**e** room with private entrance; **travailleur** ~ self-employed worker.

indépendantiste [ɛ̃depɑ̃dɑ̃tist(ə)] *adj*, *nm/f* separatist.

indéracinable [ɛ̃deʀasinabl(ə)] *adj* (*fig:* *croyance etc*) ineradicable.

indéréglable [ɛ̃deʀeglabl(ə)] *adj* which will not break down.

indescriptible [ɛ̃dɛskʀiptibl(ə)] *adj* indescribable.

indésirable [ɛ̃deziʀabl(ə)] *adj* undesirable.

indestructible [ɛ̃dɛstʀyktibl(ə)] *adj* indestructible; (*marque, impression*) indelible.

indéterminable [ɛ̃detɛʀminabl(ə)] *adj* indeterminable.

indétermination [ɛ̃detɛʀminɑsjɔ̃] *nf* indecision, indecisiveness.

indéterminé, e [ɛ̃detɛʀmine] *adj* unspecified; indeterminate; indeterminable.

index [ɛ̃dɛks] *nm* (*doigt*) index finger; (*d'un livre etc*) index; **mettre à l'**~ to blacklist.

indexation [ɛ̃dɛksasjɔ̃] *nf* indexing.

indexé, e [ɛ̃dɛkse] *adj* (*ÉCON*): ~ **(sur)** index-linked (to).

indexer [ɛ̃dɛkse] *vt* (*salaire, emprunt*): ~ **(sur)** to index (on).

indicateur [ɛ̃dikatœʀ] *nm* (*POLICE*) informer; (*livre*) guide; (*: liste*) directory; (*TECH*) gauge; indicator; (*ÉCON*) indicator ♦ *adj:* **poteau** ~ signpost; **tableau** ~ indicator (board); ~ **des chemins de fer** railway timetable; ~ **de direction** (*AUTO*) indicator; ~ **immobilier** property gazette; ~ **de niveau** level, gauge; ~ **de pression** pressure gauge; ~ **de rues** street directory; ~ **de vitesse** speedometer.

indicatif, ive [ɛ̃dikatif, -iv] *adj:* **à titre** ~ for (your) information ♦ *nm* (*LING*) indicative; (*d'une émission*) theme *ou* signature tune; (*TÉL*) dialling code; ~ **d'appel** (*RADIO*) call sign.

indication [ɛ̃dikasjɔ̃] *nf* indication; (*renseignement*) information *no pl*; ~**s** *nfpl* (*directives*) instructions; ~ **d'origine** (*COMM*) place of origin.

indice [ɛ̃dis] *nm* (*marque, signe*) indication, sign; (*POLICE: lors d'une enquête*) clue; (*JUR: présomption*) piece of evidence; (*SCIENCE, ÉCON, TECH*) index; (*ADMIN*) grading; rating; ~ **du coût de la vie** cost-of-living index; ~ **inférieur** subscript; ~ **d'octane** octane rating; ~ **des prix** price index; ~ **de traitement** salary grading.

indicible [ɛ̃disibl(ə)] *adj* inexpressible.

indien, ne [ɛ̃djɛ̃, -ɛn] *adj* Indian ♦ *nm/f:* **I**~, **ne** (*d'Amérique*) (American *ou* Red) Indian; (*d'Inde*) Indian.

indifféremment [ɛ̃difeʀamɑ̃] *adv* (*sans distinction*) equally; indiscriminately.

indifférence [ɛ̃difeʀɑ̃s] *nf* indifference.

indifférencié, e [ɛ̃difeʀɑ̃sje] *adj* undifferentiated.

indifférent, e [ɛ̃difeʀɑ̃, -ɑ̃t] *adj* (*peu intéressé*) indifferent; ~ **à** (*insensible à*) indifferent to, unconcerned about; (*peu intéressant pour*) indifferent to; immaterial to; **ça m'est** ~ **(que** ...**)** it doesn't matter to me (whether ...).

indifférer [ɛ̃difeʀe] *vt:* **cela m'indiffère** I'm indifferent about it.

indigence [ɛ̃diʒɑ̃s] *nf* poverty; **être dans l'**~ to be destitute.

indigène [ɛ̃diʒɛn] *adj* native, indigenous; (*de la région*) local ♦ *nm/f* native.

indigent, e [ɛ̃diʒɑ̃, -ɑ̃t] *adj* destitute, poverty-stricken; (*fig*) poor.

indigeste [ɛ̃diʒɛst(ə)] *adj* indigestible.

indigestion [ɛ̃diʒɛstjɔ̃] *nf* indigestion *no pl*; **avoir une** ~ to have indigestion.

indignation [ɛ̃diɲasjɔ̃] *nf* indignation; **avec** ~ indignantly.

indigne [ɛ̃diɲ] *adj:* ~ **(de)** unworthy (of).

indigné, e [ɛ̃diɲe] *adj* indignant.

indignement [ɛ̃diɲmɑ̃] *adv* shamefully.

indigner [ɛ̃diɲe] *vt* to make indignant; **s'**~ **(de/contre)** to be (*ou* become) indignant (at).

indignité [ɛ̃diɲite] *nf* unworthiness *no pl*; (*acte*) shameful act.

indigo [ɛ̃digo] *nm* indigo.

indiqué, e [ɛ̃dike] *adj* (*date, lieu*) given, appointed; (*adéquat*) appropriate, suitable; (*conseillé*) advisable; (*remède, traitement*) appropriate.

indiquer [ɛ̃dike] *vt* (*désigner*): ~ **qch/qn à qn** to point sth/sb out to sb; (*suj: pendule, aiguille*) to show; (*suj: étiquette, plan*) to show, indicate; (*faire connaître: médecin, restaurant*): ~ **qch/qn à qn** to tell sb of sth/sb; (*renseigner sur*) to point out, tell; (*déterminer: date, lieu*) to give, state; (*dénoter*) to indicate, point to; ~ **du doigt** to point out; ~ **de la main** to indicate with one's hand; ~ **du regard** to glance towards *ou* in the direction of; **pourriez-vous m'**~ **les toilettes/l'heure?** could you direct me to the toilets/tell me the time?

indirect, e [ɛ̃diʀɛkt] *adj* indirect.

indirectement [ɛ̃diʀɛktəmɑ̃] *adv* indirectly; (*apprendre*) in a roundabout way.

indiscernable [ɛ̃disɛʀnabl(ə)] *adj* indiscernible.

indiscipline [ɛ̃disiplin] *nf* lack of discipline.

indiscipliné, e [ɛ̃disipline] *adj* undisciplined; (*fig*) unmanageable.

indiscret, ète [ɛ̃diskʀɛ, -ɛt] *adj* indiscreet.

indiscrétion [ɛ̃diskʀesjɔ̃] *nf* indiscretion; **sans** ~, ... without wishing to be indiscreet, ...

indiscutable [ɛ̃diskytabl(ə)] *adj* indisputable.

indiscutablement [ɛ̃diskytabləmɑ̃] *adv* indisputably.

indiscuté, e [ɛ̃dispyte] *adj* (*incontesté: droit, chef*) undisputed.

indispensable [ɛ̃dispɑ̃sabl(ə)] *adj* indispensable, essential; ~ **à qn/pour faire qch** essential for sb/to do sth.

indisponibilité [ɛdispɔnibilite] *nf* unavailability.

indisponible [ɛdispɔnibl(ə)] *adj* unavailable.

indisposé, e [ɛdispoze] *adj* indisposed, unwell.

indisposer [ɛdispoze] *vt* (*incommoder*) to upset; (*déplaire à*) to antagonize.

indisposition [ɛdispozisjɔ̃] *nf* (slight) illness, indisposition.

indissociable [ɛdisɔsjabl(ə)] *adj* indissociable.

indissoluble [ɛdisɔlybl(ə)] *adj* indissoluble.

indissolublement [ɛdisɔlybləmɑ̃] *adv* indissolubly.

indistinct, e [ɛdistɛ̃, -ɛkt(ə)] *adj* indistinct.

indistinctement [ɛdistɛ̃ktəmɑ̃] *adv* (*voir, prononcer*) indistinctly; (*sans distinction*) without distinction, indiscriminately.

individu [ɛdividy] *nm* individual.

individualiser [ɛdividɥalize] *vt* to individualize; (*personnaliser*) to tailor to individual requirements; **s'~** to develop one's own identity.

individualisme [ɛdividɥalism(ə)] *nm* individualism.

individualiste [ɛdividɥalist(ə)] *nmf* individualist.

individualité [ɛdividɥalite] *nf* individuality.

individuel, le [ɛdividɥɛl] *adj* (*gén*) individual; (*opinion, livret, contrôle, avantages*) personal; **chambre ~le** single room; **maison ~le** detached house; **propriété ~le** personal *ou* private property.

individuellement [ɛdividɥɛlmɑ̃] *adv* individually.

indivis, e [ɛdivi, -iz] *adj* (*JUR: bien, propriété, succession*) indivisible; (*: cohéritiers, propriétaires*) joint.

indivisible [ɛdivizibl(ə)] *adj* indivisible.

Indochine [ɛdɔʃin] *nf*: **l'~** Indochina.

indochinois, e [ɛdɔʃinwa, -waz] *adj* Indochinese.

indocile [ɛdɔsil] *adj* unruly.

indo-européen, ne [ɛdɔøʀɔpeɛ̃, -ɛn] *adj* Indo-European ♦ *nm* (*LING*) Indo-European.

indolence [ɛdɔlɑ̃s] *nf* indolence.

indolent, e [ɛdɔlɑ̃, -ɑ̃t] *adj* indolent.

indolore [ɛdɔlɔʀ] *adj* painless.

indomptable [ɛdɔ̃tabl(ə)] *adj* untameable; (*fig*) invincible, indomitable.

indompté, e [ɛdɔ̃te] *adj* (*cheval*) unbroken.

Indonésie [ɛdɔnezi] *nf*: **l'~** Indonesia.

indonésien, ne [ɛdɔnezjɛ̃, -ɛn] *adj* Indonesian ♦ *nmf*: **I~, ne** Indonesian.

indu, e [ɛdy] *adj*: **à des heures ~es** at an ungodly hour.

indubitable [ɛdybitabl(ə)] *adj* indubitable.

indubitablement [ɛdybitabləmɑ̃] *adv* indubitably.

induction [ɛdyksjɔ̃] *nf* induction.

induire [ɛdɥiʀ] *vt*: **~ qch de** to induce sth from; **~ qn en erreur** to lead sb astray, mis-

lead sb.

indulgence [ɛdylʒɑ̃s] *nf* indulgence; leniency; **avec ~** indulgently; leniently.

indulgent, e [ɛdylʒɑ̃, -ɑ̃t] *adj* (*parent, regard*) indulgent; (*juge, examinateur*) lenient.

indûment [ɛdymɑ̃] *adv* without due cause; (*illégitimement*) wrongfully.

industrialisation [ɛdystʀijalizɑsjɔ̃] *nf* industrialization.

industrialiser [ɛdystʀijalize] *vt* to industrialize; **s'~** to become industrialized.

industrie [ɛdystʀi] *nf* industry; **~ automobile/textile** car/textile industry; **~ du spectacle** entertainment business.

industriel, le [ɛdystʀijɛl] *adj* industrial; (*produit industriellement: pain etc*) mass-produced, factory-produced ♦ *nm* industrialist; (*fabricant*) manufacturer.

industriellement [ɛdystʀijɛlmɑ̃] *adv* industrially.

industrieux, euse [ɛdystʀijø, -øz] *adj* industrious.

inébranlable [inebʀɑ̃labl(ə)] *adj* (*masse, colonne*) solid; (*personne, certitude, foi*) steadfast, unwavering.

inédit, e [inedi, -it] *adj* (*correspondance etc*) (hitherto) unpublished; (*spectacle, moyen*) novel, original.

ineffable [inefabl(ə)] *adj* inexpressible, ineffable.

ineffaçable [inefasabl(ə)] *adj* indelible.

inefficace [inefikas] *adj* (*remède, moyen*) ineffective; (*machine, employé*) inefficient.

inefficacité [inefikasite] *nf* ineffectiveness; inefficiency.

inégal, e, aux [inegal, -o] *adj* unequal; (*irrégulier*) uneven.

inégalable [inegalabl(e)] *adj* matchless.

inégalé, e [inegale] *adj* unmatched, unequalled.

inégalement [inegalmɑ̃] *adv* unequally.

inégalité [inegalite] *nf* inequality; unevenness *no pl*; **~ de 2 hauteurs** difference *ou* disparity between 2 heights; **~s de terrain** uneven ground.

inélégance [inelegɑ̃s] *nf* inelegance.

inélégant, e [inelegɑ̃, -ɑ̃t] *adj* inelegant; (*indélicat*) discourteous.

inéligible [ineliʒibl(ə)] *adj* ineligible.

inéluctable [inelyktabl(ə)] *adj* inescapable.

inéluctablement [inelyktabləmɑ̃] *adv* inescapably.

inemployable [inɑ̃plwajabl(ə)] *adj* unusable.

inemployé, e [inɑ̃plwaje] *adj* unused.

inénarrable [inenaʀabl(ə)] *adj* hilarious.

inepte [inɛpt(ə)] *adj* inept.

ineptie [inɛpsi] *nf* ineptitude; (*propos*) nonsense *no pl*.

inépuisable [inepɥizabl(ə)] *adj* inexhaustible.

inéquitable [inekitabl(ə)] *adj* inequitable.

inerte [inɛʀt(ə)] *adj* lifeless; (*apathique*) passive, inert; (*PHYSIQUE, CHIMIE*) inert.

inertie [inɛʀsi] *nf* inertia.
inescompté, e [inɛskɔ̃te] *adj* unexpected, unhoped-for.
inespéré, e [inɛspeʀe] *adj* unhoped-for, unexpected.
inesthétique [inɛstetik] *adj* unsightly.
inestimable [inɛstimabl(e)] *adj* priceless; (*fig: bienfait*) invaluable.
inévitable [inevitabl(ə)] *adj* unavoidable; (*fatal, habituel*) inevitable.
inévitablement [inevitabləmɑ̃] *adv* inevitably.
inexact, e [inɛgzakt] *adj* inaccurate, inexact; (*non ponctuel*) unpunctual.
inexactement [inɛgzaktəmɑ̃] *adv* inaccurately.
inexactitude [inɛgzaktityd] *nf* inaccuracy.
inexcusable [inɛkskyzabl(ə)] *adj* inexcusable, unforgivable.
inexécutable [inɛgzekytabl(ə)] *adj* impracticable, unworkable; (*MUS*) unplayable.
inexistant, e [inɛgzistɑ̃, -ɑ̃t] *adj* non-existent.
inexorable [inɛgzɔʀabl(ə)] *adj* inexorable; (*personne: dur*): ~ **(à)** unmoved (by).
inexorablement [inɛgzɔʀabləmɑ̃] *adv* inexorably.
inexpérience [inɛkspeʀjɑ̃s] *nf* inexperience, lack of experience.
inexpérimenté, e [inɛkspeʀimɑ̃te] *adj* inexperienced; (*arme, procédé*) untested.
inexplicable [inɛksplikabl(ə)] *adj* inexplicable.
inexplicablement [inɛksplikabləmɑ̃] *adv* inexplicably.
inexpliqué, e [inɛksplike] *adj* unexplained.
inexploitable [inɛksplwatabl(ə)] *adj* (*gisement, richesse*) unexploitable; (*données, renseignements*) unusable.
inexploité, e [inɛksplwate] *adj* unexploited, untapped.
inexploré, e [inɛksplɔʀe] *adj* unexplored.
inexpressif, ive [inɛkspʀesif, -iv] *adj* inexpressive; (*regard etc*) expressionless.
inexpressivité [inɛkspʀesivite] *nf* expressionlessness.
inexprimable [inɛkspʀimabl(ə)] *adj* inexpressible.
inexprimé, e [inɛkspʀime] *adj* unspoken, unexpressed.
inexpugnable [inɛkspygnabl(ə)] *adj* impregnable.
inextensible [inɛkstɑ̃sibl(ə)] *adj* (*tissu*) non-stretch.
in extenso [inɛkstɛ̃so] *adv* in full.
inextinguible [inɛkstɛ̃gibl(ə)] *adj* (*soif*) unquenchable; (*rire*) uncontrollable.
in extremis [inɛkstʀemis] *adv* at the last minute ♦ *adj* last-minute; (*testament*) death bed *cpd*.
inextricable [inɛkstʀikabl(ə)] *adj* inextricable.
inextricablement [inɛkstʀikabləmɑ̃] *adv* inextricably.
infaillibilité [ɛ̃fajibilite] *nf* infallibility.
infaillible [ɛ̃fajibl(ə)] *adj* infallible; (*instinct*) in-

fallible, unerring.
infailliblement [ɛ̃fajibləmɑ̃] *adv* (*certainement*) without fail.
infaisable [ɛ̃fəzabl(ə)] *adj* (*travail etc*) impossible, impractical.
infamant, e [ɛ̃famɑ̃, -ɑ̃t] *adj* libellous, defamatory.
infâme [ɛ̃fɑm] *adj* vile.
infamie [ɛ̃fami] *nf* infamy.
infanterie [ɛ̃fɑ̃tʀi] *nf* infantry.
infanticide [ɛ̃fɑ̃tisid] *nm/f* child-murderer/eress ♦ *nm* (*meurtre*) infanticide.
infantile [ɛ̃fɑ̃til] *adj* (*MÉD*) infantile, child *cpd*; (*péj: ton, réaction*) infantile, childish.
infantilisme [ɛ̃fɑ̃tilism(ə)] *nm* infantilism.
infarctus [ɛ̃faʀktys] *nm*: ~ **(du myocarde)** coronary (thrombosis).
infatigable [ɛ̃fatigabl(ə)] *adj* tireless, indefatigable.
infatigablement [ɛ̃fatigabləmɑ̃] *adv* tirelessly, indefatigably.
infatué, e [ɛ̃fatɥe] *adj* conceited; ~ **de** full of.
infécond, e [ɛ̃fekɔ̃, -ɔ̃d] *adj* infertile, barren.
infect, e [ɛ̃fɛkt] *adj* vile, foul; (*repas, vin*) revolting, foul.
infecter [ɛ̃fɛkte] *vt* (*atmosphère, eau*) to contaminate; (*MÉD*) to infect; **s'**~ to become infected *ou* septic.
infectieux, euse [ɛ̃fɛksjø, -øz] *adj* infectious.
infection [ɛ̃fɛksjɔ̃] *nf* infection.
inféoder [ɛ̃feɔde] *vt*: **s'**~ **à** to pledge allegiance to.
inférer [ɛ̃feʀe] *vt*: ~ **qch de** to infer sth from.
inférieur, e [ɛ̃feʀjœʀ] *adj* lower; (*en qualité, intelligence*) inferior ♦ *nm/f* inferior; ~ **à** (*somme, quantité*) less *ou* smaller than; (*moins bon que*) inferior to; (*tâche: pas à la hauteur de*) unequal to.
infériorité [ɛ̃feʀjɔʀite] *nf* inferiority; ~ **en nombre** inferiority in numbers.
infernal, e, aux [ɛ̃fɛʀnal, -o] *adj* (*chaleur, rythme*) infernal; (*méchanceté, complot*) diabolical.
infester [ɛ̃fɛste] *vt* to infest; **infesté de moustiques** infested with mosquitoes, mosquito-ridden.
infidèle [ɛ̃fidɛl] *adj* unfaithful; (*REL*) infidel.
infidélité [ɛ̃fidelite] *nf* unfaithfulness *no pl*.
infiltration [ɛ̃filtʀasjɔ̃] *nf* infiltration.
infiltrer [ɛ̃filtʀe]: **s'**~ *vi*: **s'**~ **dans** to penetrate into; (*liquide*) to seep into; (*fig: noyauter*) to infiltrate.
infime [ɛ̃fim] *adj* minute, tiny; (*inférieur*) lowly.
infini, e [ɛ̃fini] *adj* infinite ♦ *nm* infinity; **à l'**~ (*MATH*) to infinity; (*discourir*) ad infinitum, endlessly; (*agrandir, varier*) infinitely; (*à perte de vue*) endlessly (into the distance).
infiniment [ɛ̃finimɑ̃] *adv* infinitely; ~ **grand/petit** (*MATH*) infinitely great/infinitesimal.
infinité [ɛ̃finite] *nf*: **une** ~ **de** an infinite number of.

infinitésimal, e, aux [ɛfinitezimal, -o] *adj* infinitessimal.

infinitif, ive [ɛfinitif, -iv] *adj, nm* infinitive.

infirme [ɛfiʀm(ə)] *adj* disabled ♦ *nm/f* disabled person; ~ **mental** mentally-handicapped person; ~ **moteur** spastic; ~ **de guerre** war cripple; ~ **du travail** industrially disabled person.

infirmer [ɛfiʀme] *vt* to invalidate.

infirmerie [ɛfiʀməʀi] *nf* sick bay.

infirmier, ière [ɛfiʀmje, -jɛʀ] *nm/f* nurse ♦ *adj*: **élève** ~ student nurse; **infirmière chef** sister; **infirmière diplômée** registered nurse; **infirmière visiteuse** visiting nurse, ≈ district nurse (*BRIT*).

infirmité [ɛfiʀmite] *nf* disability.

inflammable [ɛflamabl(ə)] *adj* (in)flammable.

inflammation [ɛflamasjɔ̃] *nf* inflammation.

inflammatoire [ɛflamatwaʀ] *adj* (*MÉD*) inflammatory.

inflation [ɛflasjɔ̃] *nf* inflation; ~ **rampante/galopante** creeping/galloping inflation.

inflationniste [ɛflasjɔnist(ə)] *adj* inflationist.

infléchir [ɛfleʃiʀ] *vt* (*fig: politique*) to reorientate, redirect; **s'~** *vi* (*poutre, tringle*) to bend, sag.

inflexibilité [ɛflɛksibilite] *nf* inflexibility.

inflexible [ɛflɛksibl(ə)] *adj* inflexible.

inflexion [ɛflɛksjɔ̃] *nf* inflexion; ~ **de la tête** slight nod (of the head).

infliger [ɛfliʒe] *vt*: ~ **qch (à qn)** to inflict sth (on sb); (*amende, sanction*) to impose sth (on sb).

influençable [ɛflyɑ̃sabl(ə)] *adj* easily influenced.

influence [ɛflyɑ̃s] *nf* influence; (*d'un médicament*) effect.

influencer [ɛflyɑ̃se] *vt* to influence.

influent, e [ɛflyɑ̃, -ɑ̃t] *adj* influential.

influer [ɛflye]: ~ **sur** *vt* to have an influence upon.

influx [ɛfly] *nm*: ~ **nerveux** (nervous) impulse.

infographie [ɛfɔgʀafi] *nf* computer graphics *sg*.

informateur, trice [ɛfɔʀmatœʀ, -tʀis] *nm/f* informant.

informaticien, ne [ɛfɔʀmatisjɛ̃, -ɛn] *nm/f* computer scientist.

informatif, ive [ɛfɔʀmatif, -iv] *adj* informative.

information [ɛfɔʀmasjɔ̃] *nf* (*renseignement*) piece of information; (*PRESSE, TV: nouvelle*) item of news; (*diffusion de renseignements, INFORM*) information; (*JUR*) inquiry, investigation; ~**s** *nfpl* (*TV*) news *sg*; **voyage d'~** fact-finding trip; **agence d'~** news agency; **journal d'~** quality (*BRIT*) *ou* serious newspaper.

informatique [ɛfɔʀmatik] *nf* (*technique*) data processing; (*science*) computer science ♦ *adj* computer *cpd*.

informatisation [ɛfɔʀmatizasjɔ̃] *nf* computer-

ization.

informatiser [ɛfɔʀmatize] *vt* to computerize.

informe [ɛfɔʀm(ə)] *adj* shapeless.

informé, e [ɛfɔʀme] *adj*: **jusqu'à plus ample** ~ until further information is available.

informel, le [ɛfɔʀmɛl] *adj* informal.

informer [ɛfɔʀme] *vt*: ~ **qn (de)** to inform sb (of) ♦ *vi* (*JUR*): ~ **contre qn/sur qch** to initiate inquiries about sb/sth; **s'~ (sur)** to inform o.s. (about); **s'~ (de qch/si)** to inquire *ou* find out (about sth/whether *ou* if).

informulé, e [ɛfɔʀmyle] *adj* unformulated.

infortune [ɛfɔʀtyn] *nf* misfortune.

infos [ɛfo] *nfpl* (= *informations*) news.

infraction [ɛfʀaksjɔ̃] *nf* offence; ~ **à** violation *ou* breach of; **être en** ~ to be in breach of the law.

infranchissable [ɛfʀɑ̃ʃisabl(ə)] *adj* impassable; (*fig*) insuperable.

infrarouge [ɛfʀaʀuʒ] *adj, nm* infrared.

infrason [ɛfʀasɔ̃] *nm* infrasonic vibration.

infrastructure [ɛfʀastʀyktyʀ] *nf* (*d'une route etc*) substructure; (*AVIAT, MIL*) ground installations *pl*; (*touristique etc*) facilities.

infréquentable [ɛfʀekɑ̃tabl(ə)] *adj* not to be associated with.

infroissable [ɛfʀwasabl(ə)] *adj* crease-resistant.

infructueux, euse [ɛfʀyktɥø, -øz] *adj* fruitless, unfruitful.

infus, e [ɛfy, -yz] *adj*: **avoir la science** ~**e** to have innate knowledge.

infuser [ɛfyze] *vt* (*aussi: faire* ~: *thé*) to brew; (: *tisane*) to infuse ♦ *vi* to brew; to infuse; **laisser** ~ (to leave) to brew.

infusion [ɛfyzjɔ̃] *nf* (*tisane*) infusion, herb tea.

ingambe [ɛ̃gɑ̃b] *adj* spry, nimble.

ingénier [ɛ̃ʒenje]: **s'~** *vi*: **s'~ à faire** to strive to do.

ingénierie [ɛ̃ʒeniʀi] *nf* engineering.

ingénieur [ɛ̃ʒenjœʀ] *nm* engineer; ~ **agronome/chimiste** agricultural/chemical engineer; ~ **conseil** consulting engineer; ~ **du son** sound engineer.

ingénieusement [ɛ̃ʒenjøzmɑ̃] *adv* ingeniously.

ingénieux, euse [ɛ̃ʒenjø, -øz] *adj* ingenious, clever.

ingéniosité [ɛ̃ʒenjozite] *nf* ingenuity.

ingénu, e [ɛ̃ʒeny] *adj* ingenuous, artless ♦ *nf* (*THÉÂT*) ingénue.

ingénuité [ɛ̃ʒenɥite] *nf* ingenuousness.

ingénument [ɛ̃ʒenymɑ̃] *adv* ingenuously.

ingérence [ɛ̃ʒeʀɑ̃s] *nf* interference.

ingérer [ɛ̃ʒeʀe]: **s'~** *vi*: **s'~ dans** to interfere in.

ingouvernable [ɛ̃guvɛʀnabl(ə)] *adj* ungovernable.

ingrat, e [ɛ̃gʀa, -at] *adj* (*personne*) ungrateful; (*sol*) poor; (*travail, sujet*) arid, thankless; (*visage*) unprepossessing.

ingratitude [ɛ̃gʀatityd] *nf* ingratitude.

ingrédient [ɛ̃gʀedjɑ̃] *nm* ingredient.
inguérissable [ɛ̃geʀisabl(ə)] *adj* incurable.
ingurgiter [ɛ̃gyʀʒite] *vt* to swallow; **faire ~ qch à qn** to make sb swallow sth; (*fig: connaissances*) to force sth into sb.
inhabile [inabil] *adj* clumsy; (*fig*) inept.
inhabitable [inabitabl(ə)] *adj* uninhabitable.
inhabité, e [inabite] *adj* (*régions*) uninhabited; (*maison*) unoccupied.
inhabituel, le [inabitɥɛl] *adj* unusual.
inhalateur [inalatœʀ] *nm* inhaler; **~ d'oxygène** oxygen mask.
inhalation [inalɑsjɔ̃] *nf* (*MÉD*) inhalation; **faire des ~s** to use an inhalation bath.
inhaler [inale] *vt* to inhale.
inhérent, e [ineʀɑ̃, -ɑ̃t] *adj*: **~ à** inherent in.
inhiber [inibe] *vt* to inhibit.
inhibition [inibisjɔ̃] *nf* inhibition.
inhospitalier, ière [inɔspitalje, -jɛʀ] *adj* inhospitable.
inhumain, e [inymɛ̃, -ɛn] *adj* inhuman.
inhumation [inymɑsjɔ̃] *nf* interment, burial.
inhumer [inyme] *vt* to inter, bury.
inimaginable [inimaʒinabl(ə)] *adj* unimaginable.
inimitable [inimitabl(ə)] *adj* inimitable.
inimitié [inimitje] *nf* enmity.
ininflammable [inɛ̃flamabl(ə)] *adj* nonflammable.
inintelligent, e [inɛ̃teliʒɑ̃, -ɑ̃t] *adj* unintelligent.
inintelligible [inɛ̃teliʒibl(ə)] *adj* unintelligible.
inintelligiblement [inɛ̃teliʒibləmɑ̃] *adv* unintelligibly.
inintéressant, e [inɛ̃teʀɛsɑ̃, -ɑ̃t] *adj* uninteresting.
ininterrompu, e [inɛ̃teʀɔ̃py] *adj* (*file, série*) unbroken; (*flot, vacarme*) uninterrupted, nonstop; (*effort*) unremitting, continuous.
iniquité [inikite] *nf* iniquity.
initial, e, aux [inisjal, -o] *adj, nf* initial; **~es** *nfpl* initials.
initialement [inisjalmɑ̃] *adv* initially.
initialiser [inisjalize] *vt* to initialize.
initiateur, trice [inisjatœʀ, -tʀis] *nm/f* initiator; (*d'une mode, technique*) innovator, pioneer.
initiation [inisjɑsjɔ̃] *nf* initiation.
initiatique [inisjatik] *adj* (*rites, épreuves*) initiatory.
initiative [inisjativ] *nf* initiative; **prendre l'~ de qch/de faire** to take the initiative for sth/of doing; **avoir de l'~** to have initiative, show enterprise; **esprit/qualités d'~** spirit/qualities of initiative; **à** *ou* **sur l'~ de qn** on sb's initiative; **de sa propre ~** on one's own initiative.
initié, e [inisje] *adj* initiated ♦ *nm/f* initiate.
initier [inisje] *vt* to initiate; **~ qn à** to initiate sb into; (*faire découvrir: art, jeu*) to introduce sb to; **s'~ à** (*métier, profession, technique*) to become initiated into.
injectable [ɛ̃ʒɛktabl(ə)] *adj* injectable.

injecté, e [ɛ̃ʒɛkte] *adj*: **yeux ~s de sang** bloodshot eyes.
injecter [ɛ̃ʒɛkte] *vt* to inject.
injection [ɛ̃ʒɛksjɔ̃] *nf* injection; **à ~** (*AUTO*) fuel injection *cpd*.
injonction [ɛ̃ʒɔ̃ksjɔ̃] *nf* injunction, order; **~ de payer** (*JUR*) order to pay.
injouable [ɛ̃ʒwabl(ə)] *adj* unplayable.
injure [ɛ̃ʒyʀ] *nf* insult, abuse *no pl*.
injurier [ɛ̃ʒyʀje] *vt* to insult, abuse.
injurieux, euse [ɛ̃ʒyʀjø, -øz] *adj* abusive, insulting.
injuste [ɛ̃ʒyst(ə)] *adj* unjust, unfair.
injustement [ɛ̃ʒystəmɑ̃] *adv* unjustly, unfairly.
injustice [ɛ̃ʒystis] *nf* injustice.
injustifiable [ɛ̃ʒystifjabl(ə)] *adj* unjustifiable.
injustifié, e [ɛ̃ʒystifje] *adj* unjustified, unwarranted.
inlassable [ɛ̃lɑsabl(ə)] *adj* tireless, indefatigable.
inlassablement [ɛ̃lɑsabləmɑ̃] *adv* tirelessly.
inné, e [ine] *adj* innate, inborn.
innocemment [inɔsamɑ̃] *adv* innocently.
innocence [inɔsɑ̃s] *nf* innocence.
innocent, e [inɔsɑ̃, -ɑ̃t] *adj* innocent ♦ *nm/f* innocent person; **faire l'~** to play *ou* come the innocent.
innocenter [inɔsɑ̃te] *vt* to clear, prove innocent.
innocuité [inɔkɥite] *nf* innocuousness.
innombrable [inɔ̃bʀabl(ə)] *adj* innumerable.
innommable [inɔmabl(ə)] *adj* unspeakable.
innovateur, trice [inɔvatœʀ, -tʀis] *adj* innovatory.
innovation [inɔvɑsjɔ̃] *nf* innovation.
innover [inɔve] *vi*: **~ en matière d'art** to break new ground in the field of art.
inobservance [inɔpsɛʀvɑ̃s] *nf* nonobservance.
inobservation [inɔpsɛʀvɑsjɔ̃] *nf* nonobservation, inobservance.
inoccupé, e [inɔkype] *adj* unoccupied.
inoculer [inɔkyle] *vt*: **~ qch à qn** (*volontairement*) to inoculate sb with sth; (*accidentellement*) to infect sb with sth; **~ qn contre** to inoculate sb against.
inodore [inɔdɔʀ] *adj* (*gaz*) odourless; (*fleur*) scentless.
inoffensif, ive [inɔfɑ̃sif, -iv] *adj* harmless, innocuous.
inondable [inɔ̃dabl(ə)] *adj* (*zone etc*) liable to flooding.
inondation [inɔ̃dɑsjɔ̃] *nf* flooding *no pl*; (*torrent, eau*) flood.
inonder [inɔ̃de] *vt* to flood; (*fig*) to inundate, overrun; **~ de** (*fig*) to flood *ou* swamp with.
inopérable [inɔpeʀabl(ə)] *adj* inoperable.
inopérant, e [inɔpeʀɑ̃, -ɑ̃t] *adj* inoperative, ineffective.
inopiné, e [inɔpine] *adj* unexpected, sudden.
inopinément [inɔpinemɑ̃] *adv* unexpectedly.

inopportun, e [inɔpɔʀtœ̃, -yn] *adj* ill-timed, untimely; inappropriate; (*moment*) inopportune.

inorganisation [inɔʀganizasjɔ̃] *nf* lack of organization.

inorganisé, e [inɔʀganize] *adj* (*travailleurs*) non-organized.

inoubliable [inublijabl(ə)] *adj* unforgettable.

inouï, e [inwi] *adj* unheard-of, extraordinary.

inox [inɔks] *adj*, *nm* (= *inoxydable*) stainless (steel).

inoxydable [inɔksidabl(ə)] *adj* stainless; (*couverts*) stainless steel *cpd*.

inqualifiable [ĕkalifjabl(ə)] *adj* unspeakable.

inquiet, ète [ĕkjɛ, -ɛt] *adj* (*par nature*) anxious; (*momentanément*) worried; ~ **de qch/au sujet de qn** worried about sth/sb.

inquiétant, e [ĕkjetɑ̃, -ɑ̃t] *adj* worrying, disturbing.

inquiéter [ĕkjete] *vt* to worry, disturb; (*harceler*) to harass; **s'**~ to worry, become anxious; **s'**~ **de** to worry about; (*s'enquérir de*) to inquire about.

inquiétude [ĕkjetyd] *nf* anxiety; **donner de l'**~ *ou* **des** ~**s à** to worry; **avoir de l'**~ *ou* **des** ~**s au sujet de** to feel anxious *ou* worried about.

inquisiteur, trice [ĕkizitœʀ, -tʀis] *adj* (*regards, questions*) inquisitive, prying.

inquisition [ĕkizisjɔ̃] *nf* inquisition.

INR *sigle m* = *Institut national (belge) de radiodiffusion.*

INRA [inʀa] *sigle m* = *Institut national de la recherche agronomique.*

inracontable [ĕʀakɔ̃tabl(ə)] *adj* (*trop osé*) unrepeatable; (*trop compliqué*): **l'histoire est** ~ the story is too complicated to relate.

insaisissable [ĕsezizabl(ə)] *adj* elusive.

insalubre [ĕsalybʀ(ə)] *adj* unhealthy, insalubrious.

insalubrité [ĕsalybʀite] *nf* unhealthiness, insalubrity.

insanité [ĕsanite] *nf* madness *no pl*, insanity *no pl*.

insatiable [ĕsasjabl(ə)] *adj* insatiable.

insatisfaction [ĕsatisfaksjɔ̃] *nf* dissatisfaction.

insatisfait, e [ĕsatisfɛ, -ɛt] *adj* (*non comblé*) unsatisfied; (*: passion, envie*) unfulfilled; (*mécontent*) dissatisfied.

inscription [ĕskʀipsjɔ̃] *nf* (*sur un mur, écriteau etc*) inscription; (*à une institution: voir s'inscrire*) enrolment; registration.

inscrire [ĕskʀiʀ] *vt* (*marquer: sur son calepin etc*) to note *ou* write down; (*: sur un mur, une affiche etc*) to write; (*: dans la pierre, le métal*) to inscribe; (*mettre: sur une liste, un budget etc*) to put down; (*enrôler: soldat*) to enlist; ~ **qn à** (*club, école etc*) to enrol sb at; **s'**~ (*pour une excursion etc*) to put one's name down; **s'**~ **(à)** (*club, parti*) to join; (*université*) to register at; (*examen, concours*) to register *ou* enter (for); **s'**~ **dans** (*se situer: négociations etc*) to come within the scope of; **s'**~ **en faux contre** to deny (strongly); (*JUR*) to challenge.

inscrit, e [ĕskʀi, it] *pp de* **inscrire** ♦ *adj* (*étudiant, électeur etc*) registered.

insécable [ĕsekabl(ə)] *adj* (*INFORM*) indivisible.

insecte [ĕsɛkt(ə)] *nm* insect.

insecticide [ĕsɛktisid] *nm* insecticide.

insécurité [ĕsekyʀite] *nf* insecurity, lack of security.

INSEE [inse] *sigle m* (= *Institut national de la statistique et des études économiques*) *national institute of statistical and economic information.*

insémination [ĕseminasjɔ̃] *nf* insemination.

insensé, e [ĕsɑ̃se] *adj* insane, mad.

insensibiliser [ĕsɑ̃sibilize] *vt* to anaesthetize; (*à une allergie*) to desensitize; ~ **à qch** (*fig*) to cause to become insensitive to sth.

insensibilité [ĕsɑ̃sibilite] *nf* insensitivity.

insensible [ĕsɑ̃sibl(ə)] *adj* (*nerf, membre*) numb; (*dur, indifférent*) insensitive; (*imperceptible*) imperceptible.

insensiblement [ĕsɑ̃siblǝmɑ̃] *adv* (*doucement, peu à peu*) imperceptibly.

inséparable [ĕsepaʀabl(ə)] *adj*: ~ **(de)** inseparable (from) ♦ *nmpl*: ~**s** (*oiseaux*) lovebirds.

insérer [ĕseʀe] *vt* to insert; **s'**~ **dans** to fit into; (*fig*) to come within.

INSERM [ĕsɛʀm] *sigle m* (= *Institut national de la santé et de la recherche médicale*) *national institute for medical research.*

insert [ĕsɛʀ] *nm* enclosed fireplace burning solid fuel.

insertion [ĕsɛʀsjɔ̃] *nf* (*d'une personne*) integration.

insidieusement [ĕsidjøzmɑ̃] *adv* insidiously.

insidieux, euse [ĕsidjø, -øz] *adj* insidious.

insigne [ĕsiɲ] *nm* (*d'un parti, club*) badge ♦ *adj* distinguished; ~**s** *nmpl* (*d'une fonction*) insignia *pl*.

insignifiant, e [ĕsiɲifjɑ̃, -ɑ̃t] *adj* insignificant; (*somme, affaire, détail*) trivial, insignificant.

insinuant, e [ĕsinɥɑ̃, -ɑ̃t] *adj* ingratiating.

insinuation [ĕsinɥasjɔ̃] *nf* innuendo, insinuation.

insinuer [ĕsinɥe] *vt* to insinuate, imply; **s'**~ **dans** to seep into; (*fig*) to worm one's way into, creep into.

insipide [ĕsipid] *adj* insipid.

insistance [ĕsistɑ̃s] *nf* insistence; **avec** ~ insistently.

insistant, e [ĕsistɑ̃, -ɑ̃t] *adj* insistent.

insister [ĕsiste] *vi* to insist; (*s'obstiner*) to keep on; ~ **sur** (*détail, note*) to stress; ~ **pour qch/pour faire qch** to be insistent about sth/about doing sth.

insociable [ĕsɔsjabl(ə)] *adj* unsociable.

insolation [ĕsɔlasjɔ̃] *nf* (*MÉD*) sunstroke *no pl*; (*ensoleillement*) period of sunshine.

insolence [ĕsɔlɑ̃s] *nf* insolence *no pl*; **avec** ~ insolently.

insolent, e [ɛ̃sɔlɑ̃, -ɑ̃t] *adj* insolent.

insolite [ɛ̃sɔlit] *adj* strange, unusual.

insoluble [ɛ̃sɔlybl(ə)] *adj* insoluble.

insolvable [ɛ̃sɔlvabl(ə)] *adj* insolvent.

insomniaque [ɛ̃sɔmnjak] *adj, nm/f* insomniac.

insomnie [ɛ̃sɔmni] *nf* insomnia *no pl*, sleeplessness *no pl*; **avoir des ~s** to suffer from insomnia.

insondable [ɛ̃sɔ̃dabl(ə)] *adj* unfathomable.

insonore [ɛ̃sɔnɔʀ] *adj* soundproof.

insonorisation [ɛ̃sɔnɔʀizɑsjɔ̃] *nf* soundproofing.

insonoriser [ɛ̃sɔnɔʀize] *vt* to soundproof.

insouciance [ɛ̃susjɑ̃s] *nf* carefree attitude; heedless attitude.

insouciant, e [ɛ̃susjɑ̃, -ɑ̃t] *adj* carefree; (*imprévoyant*) heedless.

insoumis, e [ɛ̃sumi, -iz] *adj* (*caractère, enfant*) rebellious, refractory; (*contrée, tribu*) unsubdued; (*MIL: soldat*) absent without leave ♦ *nm* (*MIL: soldat*) absentee.

insoumission [ɛ̃sumisjɔ̃] *nf* rebelliousness; (*MIL*) absence without leave.

insoupçonnable [ɛ̃supsɔnabl(ə)] *adj* above suspicion.

insoupçonné, e [ɛ̃supsɔne] *adj* unsuspected.

insoutenable [ɛ̃sutnabl(ə)] *adj* (*argument*) untenable; (*chaleur*) unbearable.

inspecter [ɛ̃spɛkte] *vt* to inspect.

inspecteur, trice [ɛ̃spɛktœʀ, -tʀis] *nm/f* inspector; (*des assurances*) assessor; ~ **d'Académie** (regional) director of education; ~ **(de l'enseignement) primaire** primary school inspector; ~ **des finances** ≈ tax inspector (*BRIT*), ≈ Internal Revenue Service agent (*US*); ~ **(de police)** (police) inspector.

inspection [ɛ̃spɛksjɔ̃] *nf* inspection.

inspirateur, trice [ɛ̃spiʀatœʀ, -tʀis] *nm/f* (*instigateur*) instigator; (*animateur*) inspirer.

inspiration [ɛ̃spiʀɑsjɔ̃] *nf* inspiration; breathing in *no pl*; (*idée*) flash of inspiration, brainwave; **sous l'~ de** prompted by.

inspiré, e [ɛ̃spiʀe] *adj*: **être bien/mal ~ de faire qch** to be well-advised/ill-advised to do sth.

inspirer [ɛ̃spiʀe] *vt* (*gén*) to inspire ♦ *vi* (*aspirer*) to breathe in; **s'~ de** (*suj: artiste*) to draw one's inspiration from; (*suj: tableau*) to be inspired by; ~ **qch à qn** (*œuvre, project, action*) to inspire sb with sth; (*dégoût, crainte, horreur*) to fill sb with sth; **ça ne m'inspire pas** I'm not keen on the idea.

instabilité [ɛ̃stabilite] *nf* instability.

instable [ɛ̃stabl(ə)] *adj* (*meuble, équilibre*) unsteady; (*population, temps*) unsettled; (*paix, régime, caractère*) unstable.

installateur [ɛ̃stalatœʀ] *nm* fitter.

installation [ɛ̃stalɑsjɔ̃] *nf* installation; putting in *ou* up; fitting out; settling in; (*appareils etc*) fittings *pl*, installations *pl*; ~s *nfpl* installations; (*industrielles*) plant *sg*; (*de loisirs*) fa-

cilities.

installé, e [ɛ̃stale] *adj*: **bien/mal ~** well/poorly equipped; (*personne*) well/not very well set up *ou* organized.

installer [ɛ̃stale] *vt* (*loger*): ~ **qn** to get sb settled, install sb; (*asseoir, coucher*) to settle (down); (*placer*) to put, place; (*meuble*) to put in; (*rideau, étagère, tente*) to put up; (*gaz, électricité etc*) to put in, install; (*appartement*) to fit out; (*aménager*): ~ **une salle de bains dans une pièce** to fit out a room with a bathroom suite; **s'~** (*s'établir: artisan, dentiste etc*) to set o.s. up; (*se loger*): **s'~ à l'hôtel/chez qn** to move into a hotel/in with sb; (*emménager*) to settle in; (*sur un siège, à un emplacement*) to settle (down); (*fig: maladie, grève*) to take a firm hold *ou* grip.

instamment [ɛ̃stamɑ̃] *adv* urgently.

instance [ɛ̃stɑ̃s] *nf* (*JUR: procédure*) (legal) proceedings *pl*; (*ADMIN: autorité*) authority; ~s *nfpl* (*prières*) entreaties; **affaire en ~** matter pending; **courrier en ~** mail ready for posting; **être en ~ de divorce** to be awaiting a divorce; **train en ~ de départ** train on the point of departure; **tribunal de première ~** court of first instance; **en seconde ~** on appeal.

instant [ɛ̃stɑ̃] *nm* moment, instant; **dans un ~** in a moment; **à l'~** this instant; **je l'ai vu à l'~** I've just this minute seen him, I saw him a moment ago; **à l'~ (même) où** at the (very) moment that *ou* when, (just) as; **à chaque ~, à tout ~** at any moment; constantly; **pour l'~** for the moment, for the time being; **par ~s** at times; **de tous les ~s** perpetual; **dès l'~ où** *ou* **que ...** from the moment when ..., since that moment when ....

instantané, e [ɛ̃stɑ̃tane] *adj* (*lait, café*) instant; (*explosion, mort*) instantaneous ♦ *nm* snapshot.

instantanément [ɛ̃stɑ̃tanemɑ̃] *adv* instantaneously.

instar [ɛ̃staʀ]: **à l'~ de** *prép* following the example of, like.

instaurer [ɛ̃stɔʀe] *vt* to institute; **s'~** *vi* to set o.s. up; (*collaboration etc*) to be established.

instigateur, trice [ɛ̃stigatœʀ, -tʀis] *nm/f* instigator.

instigation [ɛ̃stigɑsjɔ̃] *nf*: **à l'~ de qn** at sb's instigation.

instiller [ɛ̃stile] *vt* to instil, apply.

instinct [ɛ̃stɛ̃] *nm* instinct; **d'~** (*spontanément*) instinctively; ~ **grégaire** herd instinct; ~ **de conservation** instinct of self-preservation.

instinctif, ive [ɛ̃stɛ̃ktif, -iv] *adj* instinctive.

instinctivement [ɛ̃stɛ̃ktivmɑ̃] *adv* instinctively.

instituer [ɛ̃stitɥe] *vt* to institute, set up; **s'~ défenseur d'une cause** to set o.s up as defender of a cause.

institut [ɛ̃stity] *nm* institute; ~ **de beauté** beauty salon; ~ **médico-légal** mortuary; **I~**

universitaire de technologie (IUT) technical college.

instituteur, trice [ɛ̃stitytœʀ, -tʀis] *nm/f* (primary (*BRIT*) *ou* grade (*US*) school) teacher.

institution [ɛ̃stitysjɔ̃] *nf* institution; (*collège*) private school.

institutionnaliser [ɛ̃stitysjɔnalize] *vt* to institutionalize.

instructeur, trice [ɛ̃stʀyktœʀ, -tʀis] *adj* (*MIL*): **sergent** ~ drill sergeant; (*JUR*): **juge** ~ examining (*BRIT*) *ou* committing (*US*) magistrate ♦ *nm/f* instructor.

instructif, ive [ɛ̃stʀyktif, -iv] *adj* instructive.

instruction [ɛ̃stʀyksjɔ̃] *nf* (*enseignement, savoir*) education; (*JUR*) (preliminary) investigation and hearing; (*directive*) instruction; (*ADMIN: document*) directive; ~**s** *nfpl* instructions; (*mode d'emploi*) directions, instructions; ~ **civique** civics *sg*; ~ **primaire/publique** primary/public education; ~ **religieuse** religious instruction; ~ **professionnelle** vocational training.

instruire [ɛ̃stʀɥiʀ] *vt* (*élèves*) to teach; (*recrues*) to train; (*JUR: affaire*) to conduct the investigation for; **s'**~ to educate o.s.; **s'**~ **auprès de qn de qch** (*s'informer*) to find sth out from sb; ~ **qn de qch** (*informer*) to inform *ou* advise sb of sth; ~ **contre qn** (*JUR*) to investigate sb.

instruit, e [ɛ̃stʀɥi, -it] *pp de* **instruire** ♦ *adj* educated.

instrument [ɛ̃stʀymɑ̃] *nm* instrument; ~ **à cordes/vent** stringed/wind instrument; ~ **de mesure** measuring instrument; ~ **de musique** musical instrument; ~ **de travail** (working) tool.

instrumental, e, aux [ɛ̃stʀymɑ̃tal, -o] *adj* instrumental.

instrumentation [ɛ̃stʀymɑ̃tasjɔ̃] *nf* instrumentation.

instrumentiste [ɛ̃stʀymɑ̃tist(ə)] *nm/f* instrumentalist.

insu [ɛ̃sy] *nm*: **à l'**~ **de qn** without sb knowing.

insubmersible [ɛ̃sybmɛʀsibl(ə)] *adj* unsinkable.

insubordination [ɛ̃sybɔʀdinasjɔ̃] *nf* rebelliousness; (*MIL*) insubordination.

insubordonné, e [ɛ̃sybɔʀdɔne] *adj* insubordinate.

insuccès [ɛ̃syksɛ] *nm* failure.

insuffisamment [ɛ̃syfizamɑ̃] *adv* insufficiently.

insuffisance [ɛ̃syfizɑ̃s] *nf* insufficiency; inadequacy; ~**s** *nfpl* (*lacunes*) inadequacies; ~ **cardiaque** cardiac insufficiency *no pl*; ~ **hépatique** liver deficiency.

insuffisant, e [ɛ̃syfizɑ̃, -ɑ̃t] *adj* insufficient; (*élève, travail*) inadequate.

insuffler [ɛ̃syfle] *vt*: ~ **qch dans** to blow sth into; ~ **qch à qn** to inspire sb with sth.

insulaire [ɛ̃sylɛʀ] *adj* island *cpd*; (*attitude*) insular.

insularité [ɛ̃sylaʀite] *nf* insularity.

insuline [ɛ̃sylin] *nf* insulin.

insultant, e [ɛ̃syltɑ̃, -ɑ̃t] *adj* insulting.

insulte [ɛ̃sylt(ə)] *nf* insult.

insulter [ɛ̃sylte] *vt* to insult.

insupportable [ɛ̃sypɔʀtabl(ə)] *adj* unbearable.

insurgé, e [ɛ̃syʀʒe] *adj, nm/f* insurgent, rebel.

insurger [ɛ̃syʀʒe]: **s'**~ *vi*: **s'**~ **(contre)** to rise up *ou* rebel (against).

insurmontable [ɛ̃syʀmɔ̃tabl(ə)] *adj* (*difficulté*) insuperable; (*aversion*) unconquerable.

insurpassable [ɛ̃syʀpɑsabl(ə)] *adj* unsurpassable, unsurpassed.

insurrection [ɛ̃syʀɛksjɔ̃] *nf* insurrection, revolt.

insurrectionnel, le [ɛ̃syʀɛksjɔnɛl] *adj* insurrectionary.

intact, e [ɛ̃takt] *adj* intact.

intangible [ɛ̃tɑ̃ʒibl(ə)] *adj* intangible; (*principe*) inviolable.

intarissable [ɛ̃taʀisabl(ə)] *adj* inexhaustible.

intégral, e, aux [ɛ̃tegʀal, -o] *adj* complete ♦ *nf* (*MATH*) integral; (*œuvres complètes*) complete works.

intégralement [ɛ̃tegʀalmɑ̃] *adv* in full, fully.

intégralité [ɛ̃tegʀalite] *nf* (*d'une somme, d'un revenu*) whole (*ou* full) amount; **dans son** ~ in its entirety.

intégrant, e [ɛ̃tegʀɑ̃, -ɑ̃t] *adj*: **faire partie** ~**e de** to be an integral part of, be part and parcel of.

intégration [ɛ̃tegʀasjɔ̃] *nf* integration.

intégrationniste [ɛ̃tegʀasjɔnist(ə)] *adj, nm/f* integrationist.

intègre [ɛ̃tɛgʀ(ə)] *adj* perfectly honest, upright.

intégré, e [ɛ̃tegʀe] *adj*: **circuit** ~ integrated circuit.

intégrer [ɛ̃tegʀe] *vt*: ~ **qch à** *ou* **dans** to integrate sth into; **s'**~ **à** *ou* **dans** to become integrated into.

intégrisme [ɛ̃tegʀism(ə)] *nm* fundamentalism.

intégriste [ɛ̃tegʀist(ə)] *adj, nm/f* fundamentalist.

intégrité [ɛ̃tegʀite] *nf* integrity.

intellect [ɛ̃telɛkt] *nm* intellect.

intellectualisme [ɛ̃telɛkɥalism(ə)] *nm* intellectualism.

intellectuel, le [ɛ̃telɛktɥɛl] *adj, nm/f* intellectual; (*péj*) highbrow.

intellectuellement [ɛ̃telɛktɥɛlmɑ̃] *adv* intellectually.

intelligemment [ɛ̃teliʒamɑ̃] *adv* intelligently.

intelligence [ɛ̃teliʒɑ̃s] *nf* intelligence; (*compréhension*): **l'**~ **de** the understanding of; (*complicité*): **regard d'**~ glance of complicity, meaningful *ou* knowing look; (*accord*): **vivre en bonne** ~ **avec qn** to be on good terms with sb; ~**s** *nfpl* (*MIL, fig*) secret contacts; **être d'**~ to have an understanding; ~ **artificielle** artificial intelligence (A.I.).

intelligent, e [ɛ̃teliʒɑ̃, -ɑ̃t] *adj* intelligent; (*ca-*

pable): ~ **en affaires** competent in business.

intelligentsia [ɛ̃telidʒɛnsja] _nf_ intelligentsia.

intelligible [ɛ̃teliʒibl(ə)] _adj_ intelligible.

intello [ɛ̃telo] _adj, nm/f (fam)_ highbrow.

intempérance [ɛ̃tɑ̃peRɑ̃s] _nf_ overindulgence _no pl_; intemperance _no pl._

intempérant, e [ɛ̃tɑ̃peRɑ̃, -ɑ̃t] _adj_ overindulgent; _(moralement)_ intemperate.

intempéries [ɛ̃tɑ̃peRi] _nfpl_ bad weather _sg._

intempestif, ive [ɛ̃tɑ̃pɛstif, -iv] _adj_ untimely.

intenable [ɛ̃tnabl(ə)] _adj_ unbearable.

intendance [ɛ̃tɑ̃dɑ̃s] _nf_ (_MIL_) supply corps; (: _bureau_) supplies office; (_SCOL_) bursar's office.

intendant, e [ɛ̃tɑ̃dɑ̃, -ɑ̃t] _nm/f_ (_MIL_) quartermaster; (_SCOL_) bursar; (_d'une propriété_) steward.

intense [ɛ̃tɑ̃s] _adj_ intense.

intensément [ɛ̃tɑ̃semɑ̃] _adv_ intensely.

intensif, ive [ɛ̃tɑ̃sif, -iv] _adj_ intensive; **cours ~** crash course; **~ en main-d'œuvre** labour-intensive; **~ en capital** capital-intensive.

intensification [ɛ̃tɑ̃sifikɑsjɔ̃] _nf_ intensification.

intensifier [ɛ̃tɑ̃sifje] _vt_, **s'~** _vi_ to intensify.

intensité [ɛ̃tɑ̃site] _nf_ intensity.

intensivement [ɛ̃tɑ̃sivmɑ̃] _adv_ intensively.

intenter [ɛ̃tɑ̃te] _vt:_ ~ **un procès contre** _ou_ **à qn** to start proceedings against sb.

intention [ɛ̃tɑ̃sjɔ̃] _nf_ intention; (_JUR_) intent; **avoir l'~ de faire** to intend to do, have the intention of doing; **dans l'~ de faire qch** with a view to doing sth; **à l'~ de** _prép_ for; (_renseignement_) for the benefit _ou_ information of; (_film, ouvrage_) aimed at; **à cette ~** with this aim in view; **sans ~** unintentionally; **faire qch sans mauvaise ~** to do sth without ill intent; **agir dans une bonne ~** to act with good intentions.

intentionné, e [ɛ̃tɑ̃sjɔne] _adj:_ **bien ~** well-meaning _ou_ -intentioned; **mal ~** ill-intentioned.

intentionnel, le [ɛ̃tɑ̃sjɔnɛl] _adj_ intentional, deliberate.

intentionnellement [ɛ̃tɑ̃sjɔnɛlmɑ̃] _adv_ intentionally, deliberately.

inter [ɛ̃tɛR] _nm_ (_TÉL:_ = _interurbain_) long-distance call service; (_SPORT_): **~ gauche/droit** inside-left/-right.

interactif, ive [ɛ̃tɛRaktif, -iv] _adj_ (_aussi IN-FORM_) interactive.

interaction [ɛ̃tɛRaksjɔ̃] _nf_ interaction.

interarmées [ɛ̃tɛRaRme] _adj inv_ inter-army, combined.

interbancaire [ɛ̃tɛRbɑ̃kɛR] _adj_ interbank.

intercalaire [ɛ̃tɛRkalɛR] _adj, nm:_ (**feuillet**) ~ insert; (**fiche**) ~ divider.

intercaler [ɛ̃tɛRkale] _vt_ to insert; **s'~ entre** to come in between; to slip in between.

intercéder [ɛ̃tɛRsede] _vi:_ ~ (**pour qn**) to intercede (on behalf of sb).

intercepter [ɛ̃tɛRsɛpte] _vt_ to intercept; (_lu-_

mière, chaleur) to cut off.

intercepteur [ɛ̃tɛRsɛptœR] _nm_ (_AVIAT_) interceptor.

interception [ɛ̃tɛRsɛpsjɔ̃] _nf_ interception; **avion d'~** interceptor.

intercession [ɛ̃tɛRsesjɔ̃] _nf_ intercession.

interchangeable [ɛ̃tɛRʃɑ̃ʒabl(ə)] _adj_ interchangeable.

interclasse [ɛ̃tɛRklas] _nm_ (_SCOL_) break (between classes).

interclubs [ɛ̃tɛRklœb] _adj inv_ interclub.

intercommunal, e, aux [ɛ̃tɛRkɔmynal, -o] _adj_ intervillage, intercommunity.

intercommunautaire [ɛ̃tɛRkɔmynotɛR] _adj_ intercommunity.

interconnexion [ɛ̃tɛRkɔnɛksjɔ̃] _nf_ (_INFORM_) networking.

intercontinental, e, aux [ɛ̃tɛRkɔ̃tinɑtal, -o] _adj_ intercontinental.

intercostal, e, aux [ɛ̃tɛRkɔstal, -o] _adj_ intercostal, between the ribs.

interdépartemental, e, aux [ɛ̃tɛRdepaRtə-mɑtal, -o] _adj_ interdepartmental.

interdépendance [ɛ̃tɛRdepɑ̃dɑ̃s] _nf_ interdependence.

interdépendant, e [ɛ̃tɛRdepɑ̃dɑ̃, -ɑ̃t] _adj_ interdependent.

interdiction [ɛ̃tɛRdiksjɔ̃] _nf_ ban; ~ **de faire qch** ban on doing sth; ~ **de séjour** (_JUR_) order banning ex-prisoner from frequenting specified places.

interdire [ɛ̃tɛRdiR] _vt_ to forbid; (_ADMIN: stationnement, meeting, passage_) to ban, prohibit; (: _journal, livre_) to ban; ~ **qch à qn** to forbid sb sth; ~ **à qn de faire** to forbid sb to do, prohibit sb from doing; (_suj: empêchement_) to prevent _ou_ preclude sb from doing; **s'~ qch** (_éviter_) to refrain _ou_ abstain from sth; (_se refuser_): **il s'interdit d'y penser** he doesn't allow himself to think about it.

interdisciplinaire [ɛ̃tɛRdisiplinɛR] _adj_ interdisciplinary.

interdit, e [ɛ̃tɛRdi, -it] _pp de_ **interdire** ♦ _adj_ (_stupéfait_) taken aback; (_défendu_) forbidden, prohibited ♦ _nm_ interdict, prohibition; **film ~ aux moins de 18/13 ans** ≈ 18-/PG-rated film; **sens ~** one way; **stationnement ~** no parking; ~ **de chéquier** having cheque book facilities suspended; ~ **de séjour** subject to an _interdiction de séjour._

intéressant, e [ɛ̃teresɑ̃, -ɑ̃t] _adj_ interesting; **faire l'~** to draw attention to o.s.

intéressé, e [ɛ̃terese] _adj_ (_parties_) involved, concerned; (_amitié, motifs_) self-interested ♦ _nm:_ **l'~** the interested party; **les ~s** those concerned _ou_ involved.

intéressement [ɛ̃teresmɑ̃] _nm_ (_COMM_) profit-sharing.

intéresser [ɛ̃terese] _vt_ to interest; (_toucher_) to be of interest _ou_ concern to; (_ADMIN: concerner_) to affect, concern; (_COMM: travailleur_) to give a share in the profits to; (: _partenaire_) to interest (in the business); **s'~ à** to take an interest in, be interested in; **~ qn à qch** to get sb interested in sth.

intérêt [ɛ̃teRɛ] *nm (aussi COMM)* interest; (*égoïsme*) self-interest; **porter de l'~ à qn** to take an interest in sb; **agir par ~** to act out of self-interest; **avoir des ~s dans** (*COMM*) to have a financial interest *ou* a stake in; **avoir ~ à faire** to do well to do; **il y a ~ à ...** it would be a good thing to ...; **~ composé** compound interest.

interface [ɛ̃teRfas] *nf (INFORM)* interface.

interférence [ɛ̃teRfeRɑ̃s] *nf* interference.

interférer [ɛ̃teRfeRe] *vi:* **~ (avec)** to interfere (with).

intergouvernemental, e, aux [ɛ̃teRguvɛRnəmɑ̃tal, -o] *adj* intergovernmental.

intérieur, e [ɛ̃teRjœR] *adj (mur, escalier, poche)* inside; (*commerce, politique*) domestic; (*cour, calme, vie*) inner; (*navigation*) inland ♦ *nm* (*d'une maison, d'un récipient etc*) inside; (*d'un pays, aussi: décor, mobilier*) interior; (*POL*): **l'l~** (the Department of) the Interior, ≈ the Home Office (*BRIT*); **à l'~ (de)** inside; (*fig*) within; **de l'~** (*fig*) from the inside; **en ~** (*CINÉ*) in the studio; **vêtement d'~** indoor garment.

intérieurement [ɛ̃teRjœRmɑ̃] *adv* inwardly.

intérim [ɛ̃teRim] *nm* interim period; **assurer l'~ (de)** to deputize (for); **par ~** *adj* interim ♦ *adv* in a temporary capacity.

intérimaire [ɛ̃teRimɛR] *adj* temporary, interim ♦ *nm/f (secrétaire etc)* temporary, temp (*BRIT*); (*suppléant*) deputy.

intérioriser [ɛ̃teRjɔRize] *vt* to internalize.

interjection [ɛ̃teRʒɛksjɔ̃] *nf* interjection.

interjeter [ɛ̃teRʒəte] *vt (JUR):* **~ appel** to lodge an appeal.

interligne [ɛ̃teRliɲ] *nm* inter-line space ♦ *nf* (*TYPO*) lead, leading; **simple/double ~** single/double spacing.

interlocuteur, trice [ɛ̃teRlɔkytœR, -tRis] *nm/f* speaker; (*POL*): **~ valable** valid representative; **son ~** the person he *ou* she was speaking to.

interlope [ɛ̃teRlɔp] *adj* illicit; (*milieu, bar*) shady.

interloquer [ɛ̃teRlɔke] *vt* to take aback.

interlude [ɛ̃teRlyd] *nm* interlude.

intermède [ɛ̃teRmɛd] *nm* interlude.

intermédiaire [ɛ̃teRmedjɛR] *adj* intermediate; middle; half-way ♦ *nm/f* intermediary; (*COMM*) middleman; **sans ~** directly; **par l'~ de** through.

interminable [ɛ̃teRminabl(ə)] *adj* never-ending.

interminablement [ɛ̃teRminabləmɑ̃] *adv* interminably.

interministériel, le [ɛ̃teRministeRjɛl] *adj:* **comité ~** interdepartmental committee.

intermittence [ɛ̃teRmitɑ̃s] *nf:* **par ~** intermittently, sporadically.

intermittent, e [ɛ̃teRmitɑ̃, -ɑ̃t] *adj* intermittent, sporadic.

internat [ɛ̃teRna] *nm (SCOL)* boarding school.

international, e, aux [ɛ̃teRnasjɔnal, -o] *adj, nm/f* international.

internationalisation [ɛ̃teRnasjɔnalizasjɔ̃] *nf* internationalization.

internationaliser [ɛ̃teRnasjɔnalize] *vt* to internationalize.

internationalisme [ɛ̃teRnasjɔnalism(ə)] *nm* internationalism.

interne [ɛ̃teRn(ə)] *adj* internal ♦ *nm/f (SCOL)* boarder; (*MÉD*) houseman (*BRIT*), intern (*US*).

internement [ɛ̃teRnəmɑ̃] *nm (POL)* internment; (*MÉD*) confinement.

interner [ɛ̃teRne] *vt (POL)* to intern; (*MÉD*) to confine to a mental institution.

Internet [ɛ̃teRnɛt] *nm:* **l'~** the Internet.

interparlementaire [ɛ̃teRpaRləmɑ̃tɛR] *adj* interparliamentary.

interpellation [ɛ̃teRpelasjɔ̃] *nf* interpellation; (*POL*) question.

interpeller [ɛ̃teRpele] *vt (appeler)* to call out to; (*apostropher*) to shout at; (*POLICE*) to take in for questioning; (*POL*) to question; **s'~** to exchange insults.

interphone [ɛ̃teRfɔn] *nm* intercom.

interplanétaire [ɛ̃teRplanetɛR] *adj* interplanetary.

Interpol [ɛ̃teRpɔl] *sigle m* Interpol.

interposer [ɛ̃teRpoze] *vt* to interpose; **s'~** *vi* to intervene; **par personnes interposées** through a third party.

interprétariat [ɛ̃teRpretaRja] *nm* interpreting.

interprétation [ɛ̃teRpretasjɔ̃] *nf* interpretation.

interprète [ɛ̃teRpRɛt] *nm/f* interpreter; (*porte-parole*) spokesman.

interpréter [ɛ̃teRpRete] *vt* to interpret.

interprofessionnel, le [ɛ̃teRpRɔfesjɔnɛl] *adj* interprofessional.

interrogateur, trice [ɛ̃teRɔgatœR, -tRis] *adj* questioning, inquiring ♦ *nm/f (SCOL)* (oral) examiner.

interrogatif, ive [ɛ̃teRɔgatif, -iv] *adj (LING)* interrogative.

interrogation [ɛ̃teRɔgasjɔ̃] *nf* question; (*SCOL*) (written *ou* oral) test.

interrogatoire [ɛ̃teRɔgatwaR] *nm (POLICE)* questioning *no pl*; (*JUR*) cross-examination, interrogation.

interroger [ɛ̃teRɔʒe] *vt* to question; (*INFORM*) to interrogate; (*SCOL: candidat*) to test; **~ qn (sur qch)** to question sb (about sth); **~ qn du regard** to look questioningly at sb, give sb a questioning look; **s'~ sur qch** to ask o.s. about sth, ponder (about) sth.

interrompre [ɛ̃teRɔ̃pR(ə)] *vt (gén)* to interrupt; (*travail, voyage*) to break off, interrupt; **s'~** to break off.

interrupteur [ɛ̃teRyptœR] *nm* switch; **~ à bas-**

cule (*INFORM*) toggle switch.
interruption [ɛ̃teʀypsjɔ̃] *nf* interruption; **sans ~** without a break; **~ de grossesse** termination of pregnancy; **~ volontaire de grossesse** voluntary termination of pregnancy, abortion.
interscolaire [ɛ̃teʀskɔlɛʀ] *adj* interschool(s).
intersection [ɛ̃teʀseksjɔ̃] *nf* intersection.
intersidéral, e, aux [ɛ̃teʀsideʀal, -o] *adj* intersidereal, interstellar.
interstice [ɛ̃teʀstis] *nm* crack, slit.
intersyndical, e, aux [ɛ̃teʀsɛ̃dikal, -o] *adj* interunion.
interurbain [ɛ̃teʀyʀbɛ̃] (*TÉL*) *nm* long-distance call service ♦ *adj* long-distance.
intervalle [ɛ̃teʀval] *nm* (*espace*) space; (*de temps*) interval; **dans l'~** in the meantime; **à 2 mois d'~** after a space of 2 months; **à ~s rapprochés** at close intervals; **par ~s** at intervals.
intervenant, e [ɛ̃teʀvənɑ̃, -ɑ̃t] *vb voir* **intervenir** ♦ *nm/f* speaker (*at conference*).
intervenir [ɛ̃teʀvəniʀ] *vi* (*gén*) to intervene; (*survenir*) to take place; (*faire une conférence*) to give a talk *ou* lecture; **~ auprès de/en faveur de qn** to intervene with/on behalf of sb; **la police a dû ~** police had to step in *ou* intervene; **les médecins ont dû ~** the doctors had to operate.
intervention [ɛ̃teʀvɑ̃sjɔ̃] *nf* intervention; (*conférence*) talk, paper; **~ (chirurgicale)** operation.
interventionnisme [ɛ̃teʀvɑ̃sjɔnism(ə)] *nm* interventionism.
interventionniste [ɛ̃teʀvɑ̃sjɔnist(ə)] *adj* interventionist.
intervenu, e [ɛ̃teʀv(ə)ny] *pp de* **intervenir**.
intervertible [ɛ̃teʀveʀtibl(ə)] *adj* interchangeable.
intervertir [ɛ̃teʀveʀtiʀ] *vt* to invert (the order of), reverse.
interviendrai [ɛ̃teʀvjɛ̃dʀe], **interviens** [ɛ̃teʀvjɛ̃] *etc vb voir* **intervenir**.
interview [ɛ̃teʀvju] *nf* interview.
interviewer [ɛ̃teʀvjuve] *vt* to interview ♦ *nm* [ɛ̃teʀvjuvœʀ] (*journaliste*) interviewer.
intervins [ɛ̃teʀvɛ̃] *etc vb voir* **intervenir**.
intestat [ɛ̃testa] *adj* (*JUR*): **décéder ~** to die intestate.
intestin, e [ɛ̃testɛ̃, -in] *adj* internal ♦ *nm* intestine; **~ grêle** small intestine.
intestinal, e, aux [ɛ̃testinal, -o] *adj* intestinal.
intime [ɛ̃tim] *adj* intimate; (*vie, journal*) private; (*convictions*) inmost; (*dîner, cérémonie*) held among friends, quiet ♦ *nm/f* close friend.
intimement [ɛ̃timmɑ̃] *adv* (*profondément*) deeply, firmly; (*étroitement*) intimately.
intimer [ɛ̃time] *vt* (*JUR*) to notify; **~ à qn l'ordre de faire** to order sb to do.
intimidant, e [ɛ̃timidɑ̃, -ɑ̃t] *adj* intimidating.
intimidation [ɛ̃timidasjɔ̃] intimidation; **ma-**

nœuvres d'~ (*action*) acts of intimidation; (*stratégie*) intimidatory tactics.
intimider [ɛ̃timide] *vt* to intimidate.
intimité [ɛ̃timite] *nf* intimacy; (*vie privée*) privacy; private life; **dans l'~** in private; (*sans formalités*) with only a few friends, quietly.
intitulé [ɛ̃tityle] *nm* title.
intituler [ɛ̃tityle] *vt*: **comment a-t-il intitulé son livre?** what title did he give his book?; **s'~** to be entitled; (*personne*) to call o.s.
intolérable [ɛ̃tɔleʀabl(ə)] *adj* intolerable.
intolérance [ɛ̃tɔleʀɑ̃s] *nf* intolerance; **~ aux antibiotiques** intolerance to antibiotics.
intolérant, e [ɛ̃tɔleʀɑ̃, -ɑ̃t] *adj* intolerant.
intonation [ɛ̃tɔnasjɔ̃] *nf* intonation.
intouchable [ɛ̃tuʃabl(ə)] *adj* (*fig*) above the law, sacrosanct; (*REL*) untouchable.
intoxication [ɛ̃tɔksikasjɔ̃] *nf* poisoning *no pl*; (*toxicomanie*) drug addiction; (*fig*) brainwashing; **~ alimentaire** food poisoning.
intoxiqué, e [ɛ̃tɔksike] *nm/f* addict.
intoxiquer [ɛ̃tɔksike] *vt* to poison; (*fig*) to brainwash; **s'~** to poison o.s.
intradermique [ɛ̃tʀadeʀmik] *adj*, *nf*: **(injection) ~** intradermal *ou* intracutaneous injection.
intraduisible [ɛ̃tʀadɥizibl(ə)] *adj* untranslatable; (*fig*) inexpressible.
intraitable [ɛ̃tʀɛtabl(ə)] *adj* inflexible, uncompromising.
intramusculaire [ɛ̃tʀamyskylɛʀ] *adj*, *nf*: **(injection) ~** intramuscular injection.
intranet [ɛ̃tʀanɛt] *nm* intranet.
intransigeance [ɛ̃tʀɑ̃ziʒɑ̃s] *nf* intransigence.
intransigeant, e [ɛ̃tʀɑ̃ziʒɑ̃, -ɑ̃t] *adj* intransigent; (*morale, passion*) uncompromising.
intransitif, ive [ɛ̃tʀɑ̃zitif, -iv] *adj* (*LING*) intransitive.
intransportable [ɛ̃tʀɑ̃spɔʀtabl(ə)] *adj* (*blessé*) unable to travel.
intraveineux, euse [ɛ̃tʀavɛnø, -øz] *adj* intravenous.
intrépide [ɛ̃tʀepid] *adj* dauntless, intrepid.
intrépidité [ɛ̃tʀepidite] *nf* dauntlessness.
intrigant, e [ɛ̃tʀigɑ̃, -ɑ̃t] *nm/f* schemer.
intrigue [ɛ̃tʀig] *nf* intrigue; (*scénario*) plot.
intriguer [ɛ̃tʀige] *vi* to scheme ♦ *vt* to puzzle, intrigue.
intrinsèque [ɛ̃tʀɛ̃sɛk] *adj* intrinsic.
introductif, ive [ɛ̃tʀɔdyktif, -iv] *adj* introductory.
introduction [ɛ̃tʀɔdyksjɔ̃] *nf* introduction; **paroles/chapitre d'~** introductory words/chapter; **lettre d'~** letter of introduction.
introduire [ɛ̃tʀɔdɥiʀ] *vt* to introduce; (*visiteur*) to show in; (*aiguille, clef*): **~ qch dans** to insert *ou* introduce sth into; (*personne*): **~ à qch** to introduce to sth; (*: présenter*): **~ qn à qn/dans un club** to introduce sb to sb/to a club; (*INFORM*) to input, enter; **s'~** (*techniques, usages*) to be introduced; **s'~ dans** to gain entry into; to get o.s. accepted into; (*eau, fumée*) to get into; **~ au clavier** to key

in.
introduit, e [ɛ̃tʀɔdɥi, -it] *pp de* **introduire** ♦ *adj*: **bien ~** (*personne*) well-received.
introniser [ɛ̃tʀɔnize] *vt* to enthrone.
introspection [ɛ̃tʀɔspɛksjɔ̃] *nf* introspection.
introuvable [ɛ̃tʀuvabl(ə)] *adj* which cannot be found; (*COMM*) unobtainable.
introverti, e [ɛ̃tʀɔvɛʀti] *nm/f* introvert.
intrus, e [ɛ̃tʀy, -yz] *nm/f* intruder.
intrusion [ɛ̃tʀyzjɔ̃] *nf* intrusion; (*ingérence*) interference.
intuitif, ive [ɛ̃tɥitif, -iv] *adj* intuitive.
intuition [ɛ̃tɥisjɔ̃] *nf* intuition; **avoir une ~** to have a feeling; **avoir l'~ de qch** to have an intuition of sth; **avoir de l'~** to have intuition.
intuitivement [ɛ̃tɥitivmɑ̃] *adv* intuitively.
inusable [inyzabl(ə)] *adj* hard-wearing.
inusité, e [inyzite] *adj* rarely used.
inutile [inytil] *adj* useless; (*superflu*) unnecessary.
inutilement [inytilmɑ̃] *adv* needlessly.
inutilisable [inytilizabl(ə)] *adj* unusable.
inutilisé, e [inytilize] *adj* unused.
inutilité [inytilite] *nf* uselessness.
invaincu, e [ɛ̃vɛ̃ky] *adj* unbeaten; (*armée, peuple*) unconquered.
invalide [ɛ̃valid] *adj* disabled ♦ *nm/f*: **~ de guerre** disabled ex-serviceman; **~ du travail** industrially disabled person.
invalider [ɛ̃valide] *vt* to invalidate.
invalidité [ɛ̃validite] *nf* disability.
invariable [ɛ̃vaʀjabl(ə)] *adj* invariable.
invariablement [ɛ̃vaʀjabləmɑ̃] *adv* invariably.
invasion [ɛ̃vazjɔ̃] *nf* invasion.
invective [ɛ̃vɛktiv] *nf* invective.
invectiver [ɛ̃vɛktive] *vt* to hurl abuse at ♦ *vi*: **~ contre** to rail against.
invendable [ɛ̃vɑ̃dabl(ə)] *adj* unsaleable, unmarketable.
invendu, e [ɛ̃vɑ̃dy] *adj* unsold ♦ *nm* return; **~s** *nmpl* unsold goods.
inventaire [ɛ̃vɑ̃tɛʀ] *nm* inventory; (*COMM*: *liste*) stocklist; (: *opération*) stocktaking *no pl*; (*fig*) survey; **faire un ~** to make an inventory; (*COMM*) to take stock; **faire ou procéder à l'~** to take stock.
inventer [ɛ̃vɑ̃te] *vt* to invent; (*subterfuge*) to devise, invent; (*histoire, excuse*) to make up, invent; **~ de faire** to hit on the idea of doing.
inventeur, trice [ɛ̃vɑ̃tœʀ, -tʀis] *nm/f* inventor.
inventif, ive [ɛ̃vɑ̃tif, -iv] *adj* inventive.
invention [ɛ̃vɑ̃sjɔ̃] *nf* invention; (*imagination, inspiration*) inventiveness.
inventivité [ɛ̃vɑ̃tivite] *nf* inventiveness.
inventorier [ɛ̃vɑ̃tɔʀje] *vt* to make an inventory of.
invérifiable [ɛ̃veʀifjabl(ə)] *adj* unverifiable.
inverse [ɛ̃vɛʀs(ə)] *adj* (*ordre*) reverse; (*sens*) opposite; (*rapport*) inverse ♦ *nm* reverse; inversion; **en proportion ~** in inverse proportion; **dans le sens ~ des aiguilles d'une mon-**

tre anti-clockwise; **en sens ~** in (*ou* from) the opposite direction; **à l'~** conversely.
inversement [ɛ̃vɛʀsəmɑ̃] *adv* conversely.
inverser [ɛ̃vɛʀse] *vt* to reverse, invert; (*ÉLEC*) to reverse.
inversion [ɛ̃vɛʀsjɔ̃] *nf* reversal; inversion.
invertébré, e [ɛ̃vɛʀtebʀe] *adj, nm* invertebrate.
inverti, e [ɛ̃vɛʀti] *nm/f* homosexual.
investigation [ɛ̃vɛstigasjɔ̃] *nf* investigation, inquiry.
investir [ɛ̃vɛstiʀ] *vt* to invest; **s'~** *vi* (*PSYCH*) to involve o.s.; **~ qn de** to vest *ou* invest sb with.
investissement [ɛ̃vɛstismɑ̃] *nm* investment; (*PSYCH*) involvement.
investisseur [ɛ̃vɛstisœʀ] *nm* investor.
investiture [ɛ̃vɛstityʀ] *nf* investiture; (*à une élection*) nomination.
invétéré, e [ɛ̃veteʀe] *adj* (*habitude*) ingrained; (*bavard, buveur*) inveterate.
invincible [ɛ̃vɛ̃sibl(ə)] *adj* invincible, unconquerable.
invinciblement [ɛ̃vɛ̃sibləmɑ̃] *adv* (*fig*) invincibly.
inviolabilité [ɛ̃vjɔlabilite] *nf*: **~ parlementaire** parliamentary immunity.
inviolable [ɛ̃vjɔlabl(ə)] *adj* inviolable.
invisible [ɛ̃vizibl(ə)] *adj* invisible; (*fig: personne*) not available.
invitation [ɛ̃vitasjɔ̃] *nf* invitation; **à/sur l'~ de qn** at/on sb's invitation; **carte/lettre d'~** invitation card/letter.
invite [ɛ̃vit] *nf* invitation.
invité, e [ɛ̃vite] *nm/f* guest.
inviter [ɛ̃vite] *vt* to invite; **~ qn à faire qch** to invite sb to do sth; (*suj: chose*) to induce *ou* tempt sb to do sth.
invivable [ɛ̃vivabl(ə)] *adj* unbearable, impossible.
involontaire [ɛ̃vɔlɔ̃tɛʀ] *adj* (*mouvement*) involuntary; (*insulte*) unintentional; (*complice*) unwitting.
involontairement [ɛ̃vɔlɔ̃tɛʀmɑ̃] *adv* involuntarily.
invoquer [ɛ̃vɔke] *vt* (*Dieu, muse*) to call upon, invoke; (*prétexte*) to put forward (as an excuse); (*témoignage*) to call upon; (*loi, texte*) to refer to; **~ la clémence de qn** to beg sb *ou* appeal to sb for clemency.
invraisemblable [ɛ̃vʀɛsɑ̃blabl(ə)] *adj* unlikely, improbable; (*bizarre*) incredible.
invraisemblance [ɛ̃vʀɛsɑ̃blɑ̃s] *nf* unlikelihood *no pl*, improbability.
invulnérable [ɛ̃vylneʀabl(ə)] *adj* invulnerable.
iode [jɔd] *nm* iodine.
iodé, e [jɔde] *adj* iodized.
ion [jɔ̃] *nm* ion.
ionique [jɔnik] *adj* (*ARCHIT*) Ionic; (*SCIENCE*) ionic.
ioniseur [jɔnizœʀ] *nm* ionizer.
iota [jɔta] *nm*: **sans changer un ~** without

changing one iota *ou* the tiniest bit.
IPC *sigle m* (= *Indice des prix à la consommation*) CPI.
IR. *abr* = **infrarouge.**
IRA *sigle f* (= *Irish Republican Army*) IRA.
irai [iʀe] *etc vb voir* **aller.**
Irak [iʀak] *nm*: **l'~** Iraq *ou* Irak.
irakien, ne [iʀakjɛ̃, -ɛn] *adj* Iraqi ♦ *nm/f*: **I~, ne** Iraqi.
Iran [iʀɑ̃] *nm*: **l'~** Iran.
iranien, ne [iʀanjɛ̃, -ɛn] *adj* Iranian ♦ *nm* (*LING*) Iranian ♦ *nm/f*: **I~, ne** Iranian.
Iraq [iʀak] = **Irak.**
iraquien, ne [iʀakjɛ̃, -ɛn] = **irakien, ne.**
irascible [iʀasibl(ə)] *adj* short-tempered, irascible.
irions [iʀjɔ̃] *etc vb voir* **aller.**
iris [iʀis] *nm* iris.
irisé, e [iʀize] *adj* iridescent.
irlandais, e [iʀlɑ̃dɛ, -ɛz] *adj, nm* (*LING*) Irish ♦ *nm/f*: **I~, e** Irishman/woman; **les I~** the Irish.
Irlande [iʀlɑ̃d] *nf*: **l'~** (*pays*) Ireland; (*état*) the Irish Republic, the Republic of Ireland, Eire; **~ du Nord** Northern Ireland, Ulster; **~ du Sud** Southern Ireland, Irish Republic, Eire; **la mer d'~** the Irish Sea.
ironie [iʀɔni] *nf* irony.
ironique [iʀɔnik] *adj* ironical.
ironiquement [iʀɔnikmɑ̃] *adv* ironically.
ironiser [iʀɔnize] *vi* to be ironical.
irons [iʀɔ̃] *etc vb voir* **aller.**
IRPP *sigle m* (= *impôt sur le revenu des personnes physiques*) income tax.
irradiation [iʀadjasjɔ̃] *nf* irradiation.
irradier [iʀadje] *vi* to radiate ♦ *vt* to irradiate.
irraisonné, e [iʀezɔne] *adj* irrational, unreasoned.
irrationnel, le [iʀasjɔnɛl] *adj* irrational.
irrattrapable [iʀatʀapabl(ə)] *adj* (*retard*) that cannot be made up; (*bévue*) that cannot be made good.
irréalisable [iʀealizabl(ə)] *adj* unrealizable; (*projet*) impracticable.
irréalisme [iʀealism(ə)] *nm* lack of realism.
irréaliste [iʀealist(ə)] *adj* unrealistic.
irréalité [iʀealite] *nf* unreality.
irrecevable [iʀsəvabl(ə)] *adj* unacceptable.
irréconciliable [iʀekɔ̃siljabl(ə)] *adj* irreconcilable.
irrécouvrable [iʀekuvʀabl(ə)] *adj* irrecoverable.
irrécupérable [iʀekypeʀabl(ə)] *adj* unreclaimable, beyond repair; (*personne*) beyond redemption *ou* recall.
irrécusable [iʀekyzabl(ə)] *adj* (*témoignage*) unimpeachable; (*preuve*) incontestable, indisputable.
irréductible [iʀedyktibl(ə)] *adj* indomitable, implacable; (*MATH: fraction, équation*) irreducible.
irréductiblement [iʀedyktibləmɑ̃] *adv* implacably.

irréel, le [iʀeɛl] *adj* unreal.
irréfléchi, e [iʀefleʃi] *adj* thoughtless.
irréfutable [iʀefytabl(ə)] *adj* irrefutable.
irréfutablement [iʀefytabləmɑ̃] *adv* irrefutably.
irrégularité [iʀegylaʀite] *nf* irregularity; unevenness *no pl.*
irrégulier, ière [iʀegylje, -jɛʀ] *adj* irregular; (*surface, rythme, écriture*) uneven, irregular; (*élève, athlète*) erratic.
irrégulièrement [iʀegyljɛʀmɑ̃] *adv* irregularly.
irrémédiable [iʀemedjabl(ə)] *adj* irreparable.
irrémédiablement [iʀemedjabləmɑ̃] *adv* irreparably.
irremplaçable [iʀɑ̃plasabl(ə)] *adj* irreplaceable.
irréparable [iʀepaʀabl(ə)] *adj* beyond repair, irreparable; (*fig*) irreparable.
irrépréhensible [iʀepʀeɑ̃sibl(ə)] *adj* irreprehensible.
irrépressible [iʀepʀesibl(ə)] *adj* irrepressible.
irréprochable [iʀepʀɔʃabl(ə)] *adj* irreproachable, beyond reproach; (*tenue, toilette*) impeccable.
irrésistible [iʀezistibl(ə)] *adj* irresistible; (*preuve, logique*) compelling.
irrésistiblement [iʀezistibləmɑ̃] *adv* irresistibly.
irrésolu, e [iʀezɔly] *adj* irresolute.
irrésolution [iʀezɔlysjɔ̃] *nf* irresoluteness.
irrespectueux, euse [iʀɛspɛktɥø, -øz] *adj* disrespectful.
irrespirable [iʀɛspiʀabl(ə)] *adj* unbreathable; (*fig*) oppressive, stifling.
irresponsabilité [iʀɛspɔ̃sabilite] *nf* irresponsibility.
irresponsable [iʀɛspɔ̃sabl(ə)] *adj* irresponsible.
irrévérencieux, euse [iʀeveʀɑ̃sjø, -øz] *adj* irreverent.
irréversible [iʀevɛʀsibl(ə)] *adj* irreversible.
irréversiblement [iʀevɛʀsibləmɑ̃] *adv* irreversibly.
irrévocable [iʀevɔkabl(ə)] *adj* irrevocable.
irrévocablement [iʀevɔkábləmɑ̃] *adv* irrevocably.
irrigation [iʀigasjɔ̃] *nf* irrigation.
irriguer [iʀige] *vt* to irrigate.
irritabilité [iʀitabilite] *nf* irritability.
irritable [iʀitabl(ə)] *adj* irritable.
irritant, e [iʀitɑ̃, -ɑ̃t] *adj* irritating; (*MÉD*) irritant.
irritation [iʀitasjɔ̃] *nf* irritation.
irrité, e [iʀite] *adj* irritated.
irriter [iʀite] *vt* (*agacer*) to irritate, annoy; (*MÉD: enflammer*) to irritate; **s'~ contre qn/ de qch** to get annoyed *ou* irritated with sb/ at sth.
irruption [iʀypsjɔ̃] *nf* irruption *no pl*; **faire ~ dans** to burst into.
ISBN *sigle m* (= *International Standard Book*

Number) ISBN.
Islam [islam] *nm* Islam.
islamique [islamik] *adj* Islamic.
islamiste [islamist(ə)] *adj, nm/f* Islamic.
islandais, e [islɑ̃dɛ, -ɛz] *adj* Icelandic ♦ *nm* (*LING*) Icelandic ♦ *nm/f*: **I~, e** Icelander.
Islande [islɑ̃d] *nf*: **I'~** Iceland.
ISMH *sigle m* (= *Inventaire supplémentaire des monuments historiques*): **monument inscrit à I'~** ≈ listed building.
isocèle [izɔsɛl] *adj* isoceles.
isolant, e [izɔlɑ̃, -ɑ̃t] *adj* insulating; (*insonorisant*) soundproofing ♦ *nm* insulator.
isolateur [izɔlatœR] *nm* (*ÉLEC*) insulator.
isolation [izɔlasjɔ̃] *nf* insulation; **~ acoustique/thermique** sound/thermal insulation.
isolationnisme [izɔlasjɔnism(ə)] *nm* isolationism.
isolé, e [izɔle] *adj* isolated; (*ÉLEC*) insulated.
isolement [izɔlmɑ̃] *nm* isolation; solitary confinement.
isolément [izɔlemɑ̃] *adv* in isolation.
isoler [izɔle] *vt* to isolate; (*prisonnier*) to put in solitary confinement; (*ville*) to cut off, isolate; (*ÉLEC*) to insulate.
isoloir [izɔlwaR] *nm* polling booth.
isorel [izɔRɛl] *nm* ® hardboard.
isotherme [izɔtɛRm(ə)] *adj* (*camion*) refrigerated.
Israël [israɛl] *nm*: **I'~** Israel.
israélien, ne [israeljɛ̃, -ɛn] *adj* Israeli ♦ *nm/f*: **I~, ne** Israeli.
israélite [israelit] *adj* Jewish; (*dans l'Ancien Testament*) Israelite ♦ *nm/f*: **I~** Jew/Jewess; Israelite.
issu, e [isy] *adj*: **~ de** descended from; (*fig*) stemming from ♦ *nf* (*ouverture, sortie*) exit; (*solution*) way out, solution; (*dénouement*) outcome; **à l'~e de** at the conclusion *ou* close of; **rue sans ~e** dead end, no through road (*BRIT*), no outlet (*US*); **~e de secours** emergency exit.
Istamboul *ou* **Istanbul** [istɑ̃bul] *n* Istanbul.
isthme [ism(ə)] *nm* isthmus.
Italie [itali] *nf*: **I'~** Italy.
italien, ne [italjɛ̃, -ɛn] *adj* Italian ♦ *nm* (*LING*) Italian ♦ *nm/f*: **I~, ne** Italian.
italique [italik] *nm*: **en ~(s)** in italics.
item [itɛm] *nm* item; (*question*) question, test.
itinéraire [itineRɛR] *nm* itinerary, route.
itinérant, e [itineRɑ̃, -ɑ̃t] *adj* itinerant, travelling.
ITP *sigle m* (= *ingénieur des travaux publics*) civil engineer.
IUT *sigle m* = **Institut universitaire de technologie**.
IVG *sigle f* (= *interruption volontaire de grossesse*) abortion.
ivoire [ivwaR] *nm* ivory.
ivoirien, ne [ivwaRjɛ̃, -ɛn] *adj* of *ou* from the Ivory Coast.

ivraie [ivRɛ] *nf*: **séparer le bon grain de l'~** (*fig*) to separate the wheat from the chaff.
ivre [ivR(ə)] *adj* drunk; **~ de** (*colère*) wild with; (*bonheur*) drunk *ou* intoxicated with; **~ mort** dead drunk.
ivresse [ivRɛs] *nf* drunkenness; (*euphorie*) intoxication.
ivrogne [ivRɔɲ] *nm/f* drunkard.

J j

J, j [ʒi] *nm inv* J, j ♦ *abr* (= *jour*): **jour ~** D-day; (= *Joule*) J; **J comme Joseph** J for Jack (*BRIT*) *ou* Jig (*US*).
j' [ʒ] *pron voir* **je**.
jabot [ʒabo] *nm* (*ZOOL*) crop; (*de vêtement*) jabot.
JAC [ʒak] *sigle f* (= *Jeunesse agricole catholique*) youth organization.
jacasser [ʒakase] *vi* to chatter.
jachère [ʒaʃɛR] *nf*: **(être) en ~** (to lie) fallow.
jacinthe [ʒasɛ̃t] *nf* hyacinth; **~ des bois** bluebell.
jack [dʒak] *nm* jack plug.
jacquard [ʒakaR] *adj inv* Fair Isle.
jacquerie [ʒakRi] *nf* riot.
jade [ʒad] *nm* jade.
jadis [ʒadis] *adv* in times past, formerly.
jaguar [ʒagwaR] *nm* (*ZOOL*) jaguar.
jaillir [ʒajiR] *vi* (*liquide*) to spurt out, gush out; (*lumière*) to flood out; (*fig*) to rear up; to burst out.
jaillissement [ʒajismɑ̃] *nm* spurt, gush.
jais [ʒɛ] *nm* jet; (**d'un noir**) **de ~** jet-black.
jalon [ʒalɔ̃] *nm* range pole; (*fig*) milestone; **poser des ~s** (*fig*) to pave the way.
jalonner [ʒalɔne] *vt* to mark out; (*fig*) to mark, punctuate.
jalousement [ʒaluzmɑ̃] *adv* jealously.
jalouser [ʒaluze] *vt* to be jealous of.
jalousie [ʒaluzi] *nf* jealousy; (*store*) (venetian) blind.
jaloux, ouse [ʒalu, -uz] *adj* jealous; **être ~ de qn/qch** to be jealous of sb/sth.
jamaïquain, e [ʒamaikɛ̃, -ɛn] *adj* Jamaican.
Jamaïque [ʒamaik] *nf*: **la ~** Jamaica.
jamais [ʒamɛ] *adv* never; (*sans négation*) ever; **ne ... ~** never; **~ de la vie!** never!; **si ~ ...** if ever ...; **à (tout) ~, pour ~** for ever, for ever and ever.
jambage [ʒɑ̃baʒ] *nm* (*de lettre*) downstroke; (*de porte*) jamb.
jambe [ʒɑ̃b] *nf* leg; **à toutes ~s** as fast as one's legs can carry one.
jambières [ʒɑ̃bjɛR] *nfpl* legwarmers; (*SPORT*)

shin pads.
jambon [ʒɑ̃bɔ̃] *nm* ham.
jambonneau, x [ʒɑ̃bɔno] *nm* knuckle of ham.
jante [ʒɑ̃t] *nf* (wheel) rim.
janvier [ʒɑ̃vje] *nm* January; *voir aussi* **juillet**.
Japon [ʒapɔ̃] *nm*: **le ~** Japan.
japonais, e [ʒapɔnɛ, -ɛz] *adj* Japanese ♦ *nm* (LING) Japanese ♦ *nm/f*: **J~, e** Japanese.
japonaiserie [ʒapɔnɛzʀi] *nf* (bibelot) Japanese curio.
jappement [ʒapmɑ̃] *nm* yap, yelp.
japper [ʒape] *vi* to yap, yelp.
jaquette [ʒakɛt] *nf* (de cérémonie) morning coat; (de femme) jacket; (de livre) dust cover, (dust) jacket.
jardin [ʒaʀdɛ̃] *nm* garden; **~ d'acclimatation** zoological gardens *pl*; **~ botanique** botanical gardens *pl*; **~ d'enfants** nursery school; **~ potager** vegetable garden; **~ public** (public) park, public gardens *pl*; **~s suspendus** hanging gardens.
jardinage [ʒaʀdinaʒ] *nm* gardening.
jardiner [ʒaʀdine] *vi* to garden, do some gardening.
jardinet [ʒaʀdinɛ] *nm* little garden.
jardinier, ière [ʒaʀdinje, -jɛʀ] *nm/f* gardener ♦ *nf* (de fenêtre) window box; **jardinière d'enfants** nursery school teacher; **jardinière (de légumes)** (CULIN) mixed vegetables.
jargon [ʒaʀgɔ̃] *nm* (charabia) gibberish; (publicitaire, scientifique etc) jargon.
jarre [ʒaʀ] *nf* (earthenware) jar.
jarret [ʒaʀɛ] *nm* back of knee; (CULIN) knuckle, shin.
jarretelle [ʒaʀtɛl] *nf* suspender (BRIT), garter (US).
jarretière [ʒaʀtjɛʀ] *nf* garter.
jars [ʒaʀ] *nm* (ZOOL) gander.
jaser [ʒaze] *vi* to chatter, prattle; (indiscrètement) to gossip.
jasmin [ʒasmɛ̃] *nm* jasmin.
jaspe [ʒasp(ə)] *nm* jasper.
jaspé, e [ʒaspe] *adj* marbled, mottled.
jatte [ʒat] *nf* basin, bowl.
jauge [ʒoʒ] *nf* (capacité) capacity, tonnage; (instrument) gauge; **~ (de niveau) d'huile** dipstick.
jauger [ʒoʒe] *vt* to gauge the capacity of; (fig) to size up; **~ 3 000 tonneaux** to measure 3,000 tons.
jaunâtre [ʒonɑtʀ(ə)] *adj* (couleur, teint) yellowish.
jaune [ʒon] *adj, nm* yellow ♦ *nm/f* Asiatic; (briseur de grève) blackleg ♦ *adv* (fam): **rire ~** to laugh on the other side of one's face; **~ d'œuf** (egg) yolk.
jaunir [ʒoniʀ] *vi, vt* to turn yellow.
jaunisse [ʒonis] *nf* jaundice.
Java [ʒava] *nf* Java.
java [ʒava] *nf* (fam): **faire la ~** to live it up, have a real party.
javanais, e [ʒavanɛ, -ɛz] *adj* Javanese.

Javel [ʒavɛl] *nf voir* **eau**.
javelliser [ʒavelize] *vt* (eau) to chlorinate.
javelot [ʒavlo] *nm* javelin; (SPORT): **faire du ~** to throw the javelin.
jazz [dʒaz] *nm* jazz.
J.-C. *abr* = **Jésus-Christ**.
JCR *sigle f* (= Jeunesse communiste révolutionnaire) communist youth movement.
je, j' [ʒ(ə)] *pron* I.
jean [dʒin] *nm* jeans *pl*.
jeannette [ʒanɛt] *nf* (planchette) sleeveboard; (petite fille scout) Brownie.
JEC [ʒɛk] *sigle f* (= Jeunesse étudiante chrétienne) youth organization.
jeep [(d)ʒip] *nf* ® (AUTO) jeep ®.
jérémiades [ʒeʀemjad] *nfpl* moaning *sg*.
jerrycan [ʒeʀikan] *nm* jerrycan.
Jersey [ʒɛʀzɛ] *nf* Jersey.
jersey [ʒɛʀzɛ] *nm* jersey; (TRICOT): **pointe de ~** stocking stitch.
jersiais, e [ʒɛʀzjɛ, -ɛz] *adj* Jersey *cpd*, of *ou* from Jersey.
Jérusalem [ʒeʀyzalɛm] *n* Jerusalem.
jésuite [ʒezɥit] *nm* Jesuit.
Jésus-Christ [ʒezykʀi(st)] *n* Jesus Christ; **600 avant/après ~** *ou* **J.-C.** 600 B.C./A.D.
jet¹ [ʒɛ] *nm* (lancer) throwing *no pl*, throw; (jaillissement) jet; spurt; (de tuyau) nozzle; (fig): **premier ~** (ébauche) rough outline; **arroser au ~** to hose; **d'un (seul) ~** (d'un seul coup) at (*ou* in) one go; **du premier ~** at the first attempt *ou* shot; **~ d'eau** spray; (fontaine) fountain.
jet² [dʒɛt] *nm* (avion) jet.
jetable [ʒətabl(ə)] *adj* disposable.
jeté [ʒəte] *nm* (TRICOT): **un ~** make one; **~ de table** (table) runner; **~ de lit** bedspread.
jetée [ʒəte] *nf* jetty; pier.
jeter [ʒəte] *vt* (gén) to throw; (se défaire de) to throw away *ou* out; (son, lueur etc) to give out; **~ qch à qn** to throw sth to sb; (de façon agressive) to throw sth at sb; (NAVIG): **~ l'ancre** to cast anchor; **~ un coup d'œil (à)** to take a look (at); **~ les bras en avant/la tête en arrière** to throw one's arms forward/one's head back(ward); **~ l'effroi parmi** to spread fear among; **~ un sort à qn** to cast a spell on sb; **~ qn dans la misère** to reduce sb to poverty; **~ qn dehors/en prison** to throw sb out/into prison; **~ l'éponge** (fig) to throw in the towel; **~ des fleurs à qn** (fig) to say lovely things to sb; **~ la pierre à qn** (accuser, blâmer) to accuse sb; **se ~ sur** to throw o.s. onto; **se ~ dans** (suj: fleuve) to flow into; **se ~ par la fenêtre** to throw o.s. out of the window; **se ~ à l'eau** (fig) to take the plunge.
jeton [ʒətɔ̃] *nm* (au jeu) counter; (de téléphone) token; **~s de présence** (director's) fees.
jette [ʒɛt] etc *vb voir* **jeter**.
jeu, x [ʒø] *nm* (divertissement, TECH: d'une pièce) play; (défini par des règles, TENNIS: partie,

FOOTBALL etc: façon de jouer) game; (THÉÂT etc) acting; (fonctionnement) working, interplay; (série d'objets, jouet) set; (CARTES) hand; (au casino): **le ~** gambling; **cacher son ~** (fig) to keep one's cards hidden, conceal one's hand; **c'est un ~ d'enfant!** (fig) it's child's play!; **en ~** at stake; at work; (FOOTBALL) in play; **remettre en ~** to throw in; **entrer/mettre en ~** to come/bring into play; **par ~** (pour s'amuser) for fun; **d'entrée de ~** (tout de suite, dès le début) from the outset; **entrer dans le ~/le ~ de qn** (fig) to play the game/sb's game; **jouer gros ~** to play for high stakes; **se piquer/se prendre au ~** to get excited over/get caught up in ou involved in the game; **~ de boules** game of bowls; (endroit) bowling pitch; (boules) set of bowls; **~ de cartes** card game; (paquet) pack of cards; **~ de construction** building set; **~ d'échecs** chess set; **~ d'écritures** (COMM) paper transaction; **~ de hasard** game of chance; **~ de mots** pun; **le ~ de l'oie** snakes and ladders sg; **~ d'orgue(s)** organ stop; **~ de patience** puzzle; **~ de physionomie** facial expressions pl; **~ de société** parlour game; **~ vidéo** computer game; **~x de lumière** lighting effects; **J~x olympiques (JO)** Olympic Games.

jeu-concours, pl **jeux-concours** [ʒøkɔ̃kuʀ] nm competition.

jeudi [ʒødi] nm Thursday; **~ saint** Maundy Thursday; voir aussi **lundi**.

jeun [ʒœ̃]: **à ~** adv on an empty stomach.

jeune [ʒœn] adj young ♦ adv: **faire/s'habiller ~** to look/dress young; **les ~s** young people, the young; **~ fille** nf girl; **~ homme** nm young man; **~ loup** nm (POL, ÉCON) young go-getter; **~ premier** leading man; **~s gens** nmpl young people; **~s mariés** nmpl newly weds.

jeûne [ʒøn] nm fast.

jeûner [ʒøne] vi to fast, go without food.

jeunesse [ʒœnɛs] nf youth; (aspect) youthfulness; (jeunes) young people pl, youth.

jf sigle f = **jeune fille.**

jh sigle m = **jeune homme.**

JI sigle m = **juge d'instruction.**

jiu-jitsu [ʒyʒitsy] nm inv (SPORT) jujitsu.

JMF sigle f (= Jeunesses musicales de France) association to promote music among the young.

JO sigle m = **Journal officiel** ♦ sigle mpl = **Jeux olympiques.**

joaillerie [ʒɔɑjʀi] nf jewel trade; jewellery (BRIT), jewelry (US).

joaillier, ière [ʒɔɑje, -jɛʀ] nm/f jeweller (BRIT), jeweler (US).

job [dʒɔb] nm job.

jobard [ʒɔbaʀ] nm (péj) sucker, mug.

JOC [ʒɔk] sigle f (= Jeunesse ouvrière chrétienne) youth organization.

jockey [ʒɔkɛ] nm jockey.

jodler [ʒɔdle] vi to yodel.

jogging [dʒɔgiŋ] nm tracksuit (BRIT), sweatsuit (US); **faire du ~** to jog, go jogging.

joie [ʒwa] nf joy.

joignais [ʒwaɲɛ] etc vb voir **joindre.**

joindre [ʒwɛ̃dʀ(ə)] vt to join; (à une lettre): **~ qch à** to enclose sth with; (contacter) to contact, get in touch with; **~ les mains/talons** to put one's hands/heels together; **~ les deux bouts** (fig: du mois) to make ends meet; **se ~** (mains etc) to come together; **se ~ à qn** to join sb; **se ~ à qch** to join in sth.

joint, e [ʒwɛ̃, -ɛ̃t] pp de **joindre** ♦ adj: **~ (à)** (lettre, paquet) attached (to), enclosed (with); **pièce ~e** enclosure ♦ nm joint; (ligne) join; (de ciment etc) pointing no pl; **chercher/ trouver le ~** (fig) to look for/come up with the answer; **~ de cardan** cardan joint; **~ de culasse** cylinder head gasket; **~ de robinet** washer; **~ universel** universal joint.

jointure [ʒwɛ̃tyʀ] nf (ANAT: articulation) joint; (TECH: assemblage) joint; (: ligne) join.

joker [ʒɔkɛʀ] nm (CARTES) joker.

joli, e [ʒɔli] adj pretty, attractive; **une ~e somme/situation** a nice little sum/situation; **un ~ gâchis** etc a nice mess etc; **c'est du ~!** that's very nice!; **tout ça, c'est bien ~ mais** ... that's all very well but ....

joliment [ʒɔlimɑ̃] adv prettily, attractively; (fam: très) pretty.

jonc [ʒɔ̃] nm (bul)rush; (bague, bracelet) band.

joncher [ʒɔ̃ʃe] vt (suj: choses) to be strewed on; **jonché de** strewn with.

jonction [ʒɔ̃ksjɔ̃] nf joining; (point de) **~** (de routes) junction; (de fleuves) confluence; **opérer une ~** (MIL etc) to rendez-vous.

jongler [ʒɔ̃gle] vi to juggle; (fig): **~ avec** to juggle with, play with.

jongleur, euse [ʒɔ̃glœʀ, -øz] nm/f juggler.

jonquille [ʒɔ̃kij] nf daffodil.

Jordanie [ʒɔʀdani] nf: **la ~** Jordan.

jordanien, ne [ʒɔʀdanjɛ̃, -ɛn] adj Jordanian ♦ nm/f: **J~, ne** Jordanian.

jouable [ʒwabl(ə)] adj playable.

joue [ʒu] nf cheek; **mettre en ~** to take aim at.

jouer [ʒwe] vt (partie, carte, coup, MUS: morceau) to play; (somme d'argent, réputation) to stake, wager; (pièce, rôle) to perform; (film) to show; (simuler: sentiment) to affect, feign ♦ vi to play; (THÉÂT, CINÉ) to act, perform; (bois, porte: se voiler) to warp; (clef, pièce: avoir du jeu) to be loose; (entrer ou être en jeu) to come into play, come into it; **~ sur** (miser) to gamble on; **~ de** (MUS) to play; **~ du couteau/des coudes** to use knives/one's elbows; **~ à** (jeu, sport, roulette) to play; **~ au héros** to act ou play the hero; **~ avec** (risquer) to gamble with; **se ~ de** (difficultés) to make light of; **se ~ de qn** to deceive ou dupe sb; **~ un tour à qn** to play a trick on sb; **~ la comédie** (fig) to put on an act, put it on; **~ aux courses** to back horses, bet on horses; **~ à la baisse/hausse** (BOURSE) to play for a fall/rise; ~ **serré** to play a close game; ~ **de malchance** to be dogged with ill-luck; ~ **sur les mots** to play with words; **à toi/nous de** ~ it's your/our go *ou* turn.

jouet [ʒwɛ] *nm* toy; **être le** ~ **de** (*illusion etc*) to be the victim of.

joueur, euse [ʒwœʀ, -øz] *nm/f* player ♦ *adj* (*enfant, chat*) playful; **être beau/mauvais** ~ to be a good/bad loser.

joufflu, e [ʒufly] *adj* chubby(-cheeked).

joug [ʒu] *nm* yoke.

jouir [ʒwiʀ]: ~ **de** *vt* to enjoy.

jouissance [ʒwisɑ̃s] *nf* pleasure; (*JUR*) use.

jouisseur, euse [ʒwisœʀ, -øz] *nm/f* sensualist.

joujou [ʒuʒu] *nm* (*fam*) toy.

jour [ʒuʀ] *nm* day; (*opposé à la nuit*) day, daytime; (*clarté*) daylight; (*fig: aspect*): **sous un** ~ **favourable/nouveau** in a favourable/new light; (*ouverture*) opening; (*COUTURE*) openwork *no pl*; **au** ~ **le** ~ from day to day; **de nos** ~**s** these days, nowadays; **tous les** ~**s** every day; **de** ~ **en** ~ day by day; **d'un** ~ **à l'autre** from one day to the next; **du** ~ **au lendemain** overnight; **il fait** ~ it's daylight; **en plein** ~ in broad daylight; **au** ~ in daylight; **au petit** ~ at daybreak; **au grand** ~ (*fig*) in the open; **mettre au** ~ to uncover, disclose; **être à** ~ to be up to date; **mettre à** ~ to bring up to date, update; **mise à** ~ updating; **donner le** ~ **à** to give birth to; **voir le** ~ to be born; **se faire** ~ (*fig*) to become clear; ~ **férié** public holiday; **le** ~ **J** D-day.

Jourdain [ʒuʀdɛ̃] *nm*: **le** ~ the (River) Jordan.

journal, aux [ʒuʀnal, -o] *nm* (news)paper; (*personnel*) journal, diary; ~ **de bord** log; ~ **de mode** fashion magazine; **le J**~ **officiel (de la République française) (JO)** *bulletin giving details of laws and official announcements*; ~ **parlé/télévisé** radio/television news *sg*.

journalier, ière [ʒuʀnalje, -jɛʀ] *adj* daily; (*banal*) everyday ♦ *nm* day labourer.

journalisme [ʒuʀnalism(ə)] *nm* journalism.

journaliste [ʒuʀnalist(ə)] *nm/f* journalist.

journalistique [ʒuʀnalistik] *adj* journalistic.

journée [ʒuʀne] *nf* day; **la** ~ **continue** the 9 to 5 working day (*with short lunch break*).

journellement [ʒuʀnɛlmɑ̃] *adv* (*tous les jours*) daily; (*souvent*) every day.

joute [ʒut] *nf* (*tournoi*) duel; (*verbale*) duel, battle of words.

jouvence [ʒuvɑ̃s] *nf*: **bain de** ~ rejuvenating experience.

jouxter [ʒukste] *vt* to adjoin.

jovial [ʒɔvjal] *adj* jovial, jolly.

jovialité [ʒɔvjalite] *nf* joviality.

joyau, x [ʒwajo] *nm* gem, jewel.

joyeusement [ʒwajøzmɑ̃] *adv* joyfully, gladly.

joyeux, euse [ʒwajø, -øz] *adj* joyful, merry; ~ **Noël!** merry *ou* happy Christmas!; ~ **anniversaire!** many happy returns!

JT *sigle m* = **journal télévisé**.

jubilation [ʒybilɑsjɔ̃] *nf* jubilation.

jubilé [ʒybile] *nm* jubilee.

jubiler [ʒybile] *vi* to be jubilant, exult.

jucher [ʒyʃe] *vt*: ~ **qch sur** to perch sth (up)on ♦ *vi* (*oiseau*): ~ **sur** to perch (up)on; **se** ~ **sur** to perch o.s. (up)on.

judaïque [ʒydaik] *adj* (*loi*) Judaic; (*religion*) Jewish.

judaïsme [ʒydaism(ə)] *nm* Judaism.

judas [ʒyda] *nm* (*trou*) spy-hole.

Judée [ʒyde] *nf*: **la** ~ Jud(a)ea.

judéo- [ʒydeɔ] *préfixe* Judeo-.

judéo-allemand, e [ʒydeɔalmɑ̃, -ɑ̃d] *adj*, *nm* Yiddish.

judéo-chrétien, ne [ʒydeɔkʀetjɛ̃, -ɛn] *adj* Judeo-Christian.

judiciaire [ʒydisjɛʀ] *adj* judicial.

judicieusement [ʒydisjøzmɑ̃] *adv* judiciously.

judicieux, euse [ʒydisjø, -øz] *adj* judicious.

judo [ʒydo] *nm* judo.

judoka [ʒydɔka] *nm/f* judoka.

juge [ʒyʒ] *nm* judge; ~ **des enfants** children's judge, ≈ juvenile magistrate; ~ **d'instruction** examining (*BRIT*) *ou* committing (*US*) magistrate; ~ **de paix** justice of the peace; ~ **de touche** linesman.

jugé [ʒyʒe]: **au** ~ *adv* by guesswork.

jugement [ʒyʒmɑ̃] *nm* judgment; (*JUR*: *au pénal*) sentence; (: *au civil*) decision; ~ **de valeur** value judgment.

jugeote [ʒyʒɔt] *nf* (*fam*) gumption.

juger [ʒyʒe] *vt* to judge ♦ *nm*: **au** ~ by guesswork; ~ **qn/qch satisfaisant** to consider sb/sth (to be) satisfactory; ~ **que** to think *ou* consider that; ~ **bon de faire** to consider it a good idea to do, see fit to do; ~ **de** *vt* to judge; **jugez de ma surprise** imagine my surprise.

jugulaire [ʒygylɛʀ] *adj* jugular ♦ *nf* (*MIL*) chinstrap.

juguler [ʒygyle] *vt* (*maladie*) to halt; (*révolte*) to suppress, put down; (*inflation etc*) to control, curb.

juif, ive [ʒɥif, -iv] *adj* Jewish ♦ *nm/f*: **J**~, **ive** Jew/Jewess *ou* Jewish woman.

juillet [ʒɥijɛ] *nm* July; **le premier** ~ the first of July (*BRIT*), July first (*US*); **le deux/onze** ~ the second/eleventh of July, July second/eleventh; **il est venu le 5** ~ he came on 5th July *ou* July 5th; **en** ~ in July; **début/fin** ~ at the beginning/end of July.

---

*In France, **le 14 juillet** is a national holiday commemorating the storming of the Bastille during the French Revolution. Throughout the country there are celebrations, parades, music, dancing and firework displays. In Paris, there is a military parade, along the Champs-Élysées, attended by the President.*

---

juin [ʒɥɛ̃] *nm* June; *voir aussi* **juillet**.

juive [ʒɥiv] *voir* **juif**.

jumeau, elle, x [ʒymo, -ɛl] *adj, nm/f* twin; **maisons jumelles** semidetached houses.
jumelage [ʒymlaʒ] *nm* twinning.
jumeler [ʒymle] *vt* to twin; **roues jumelées** double wheels; **billets de loterie jumelés** double series lottery tickets; **pari jumelé** double bet.
jumelle [ʒymɛl] *adj f, nf voir* **jumeau** ♦ *vb voir* **jumeler.**
jumelles [ʒymɛl] *nfpl* binoculars.
jument [ʒymɑ̃] *nf* mare.
jungle [ʒɔ̃gl(ə)] *nf* jungle.
junior [ʒynjɔʀ] *adj* junior.
junte [ʒœ̃t] *nf* junta.
jupe [ʒyp] *nf* skirt.
jupe-culotte, *pl* **jupes-culottes** [ʒypkylɔt] *nf* divided skirt, culotte(s).
jupette [ʒypɛt] *nf* short skirt.
jupon [ʒypɔ̃] *nm* waist slip *ou* petticoat.
Jura [ʒyʀa] *nm:* **le ~** the Jura (Mountains).
jurassien, ne [ʒyʀasjɛ̃, -ɛn] *adj* of *ou* from the Jura Mountains.
juré, e [ʒyʀe] *nm/f* juror ♦ *adj:* **ennemi ~** sworn *ou* avowed enemy.
jurer [ʒyʀe] *vt (obéissance etc)* to swear, vow ♦ *vi (dire des jurons)* to swear, curse; *(dissoner):* ~ **(avec)** to clash (with); *(s'engager):* ~ **de faire/que** to swear *ou* vow to do/that; *(affirmer):* ~ **que** to swear *ou* vouch that; ~ **de qch** *(s'en porter garant)* to swear to sth; **ils ne jurent que par lui** they swear by him; **je vous jure!** honestly!
juridiction [ʒyʀidiksjɔ̃] *nf* jurisdiction; *(tribunal, tribunaux)* court(s) of law.
juridique [ʒyʀidik] *adj* legal.
juridiquement [ʒyʀidikmɑ̃] *adv (devant la justice)* juridically; *(du point de vue du droit)* legally.
jurisconsulte [ʒyʀikɔ̃sylt(ə)] *nm* jurisconsult.
jurisprudence [ʒyʀispʀydɑ̃s] *nf (JUR: décisions)* (legal) precedents; *(principes juridiques)* jurisprudence; **faire ~** *(faire autorité)* to set a precedent.
juriste [ʒyʀist(ə)] *nm/f* jurist; lawyer.
juron [ʒyʀɔ̃] *nm* curse, swearword.
jury [ʒyʀi] *nm (JUR)* jury; *(SCOL)* board (of examiners), jury.
jus [ʒy] *nm* juice; *(de viande)* gravy, (meat) juice; ~ **de fruits** fruit juice; ~ **de raisin/tomates** grape/tomato juice.
jusant [ʒyzɑ̃] *nm* ebb (tide).
jusqu'au-boutiste [ʒyskobutist(ə)] *nm/f* extremist, hardliner.
jusque [ʒysk(ə)]: **jusqu'à** *prép (endroit)* as far as, (up) to; *(moment)* until, till; *(limite)* up to; ~ **sur/dans** up to, as far as; *(y compris)* even on/in; **jusque vers** until about; **jusqu'à ce que** *conj* until; **jusque-là** *(temps)* until then; *(espace)* up to there; **jusqu'ici** *(temps)* until now; *(espace)* up to here; **jusqu'à présent** until now, so far.
justaucorps [ʒystokɔʀ] *nm inv (DANSE, SPORT)* leotard.

juste [ʒyst(ə)] *adj (équitable)* just, fair; *(légitime)* just, justified; *(exact, vrai)* right; *(étroit, insuffisant)* tight ♦ *adv* right; tight; *(chanter)* in tune; *(seulement)* just; ~ **assez/au-dessus** just enough/above; **pouvoir tout ~ faire** to be only just able to do; **au ~** exactly, actually; **comme de ~** of course, naturally; **le ~ milieu** the happy medium; **à ~ titre** rightfully.
justement [ʒystəmɑ̃] *adv* rightly; justly; *(précisément):* **c'est ~ ce qu'il fallait faire** that's just *ou* precisely what needed doing.
justesse [ʒystɛs] *nf (précision)* accuracy; *(d'une remarque)* aptness; *(d'une opinion)* soundness; **de ~** just, by a narrow margin.
justice [ʒystis] *nf (équité)* fairness, justice; *(ADMIN)* justice; **rendre la ~** to dispense justice; **traduire en ~** to bring before the courts; **obtenir ~** to obtain justice; **rendre ~ à qn** to do sb justice; **se faire ~** to take the law into one's own hands; *(se suicider)* to take one's life.
justiciable [ʒystisjabl(ə)] *adj:* ~ **de** *(JUR)* answerable to.
justicier, ière [ʒystisje, -jɛʀ] *nm/f* judge, righter of wrongs.
justifiable [ʒystifjabl(ə)] *adj* justifiable.
justificatif, ive [ʒystifikatif, -iv] *adj (document etc)* supporting ♦ *nm* supporting proof.
justification [ʒystifikɑsjɔ̃] *nf* justification.
justifier [ʒystifje] *vt* to justify; ~ **de** *vt* to prove; **non justifié** unjustified; **justifié à droite/gauche** ranged right/left.
jute [ʒyt] *nm* jute.
juteux, euse [ʒytø, -øz] *adj* juicy.
juvénile [ʒyvenil] *adj* young, youthful.
juxtaposer [ʒykstapoze] *vt* to juxtapose.
juxtaposition [ʒykstapozisjɔ̃] *nf* juxtaposition.

K k

K, k [ka] *nm inv* K, k ♦ *abr (= kilo)* kg; *(= kilooctet)* K; **K comme Kléber** K for King.
Kaboul, Kabul [kabul] *n* Kabul.
kabyle [kabil] *adj* Kabyle ♦ *nm (LING)* Kabyle ♦ *nm/f:* **K~** Kabyle.
Kabylie [kabili] *nf:* **la ~** Kabylia.
kafkaïen, ne [kafkajɛ̃, -ɛn] *adj* Kafkaesque.
kaki [kaki] *adj inv* khaki.
Kalahari [kalaaʀi] *n:* **désert de ~** Kalahari Desert.
kaléidoscope [kaleidɔskɔp] *nm* kaleidoscope.
Kampala [kɑ̃pala] *n* Kampala.
Kampuchéa [kɑ̃putʃea] *nm:* **le ~ (démocrati-**

que) (the People's Republic of) Kampuchea.
kangourou [kãguʀu] *nm* kangaroo.
kaolin [kaɔlɛ̃] *nm* kaolin.
kapok [kapɔk] *nm* kapok.
karaoke [kaʀaoke] *nm* karaoke.
karaté [kaʀate] *nm* karate.
kart [kaʀt] *nm* go-cart.
karting [kaʀtiŋ] *nm* go-carting, karting.
kascher [kaʃɛʀ] *adj inv* kosher.
kayac, kayak [kajak] *nm* kayak.
Kazakhstan [kaʒakstɑ̃] *nm* Kazakhstan.
Kenya [kenja] *nm*: **le ~** Kenya.
kenyan, e [kenjɑ̃, -an] *adj* Kenyan ♦ *nm/f*: **K~, ne** Kenyan.
képi [kepi] *nm* kepi.
Kerguelen [kɛʀgelɛn]: **les (îles) ~** Kerguelen.
kermesse [kɛʀmɛs] *nf* bazaar, (charity) fête; village fair.
kérosène [keʀozɛn] *nm* jet fuel; rocket fuel.
kg *abr* (= *kilogramme*) kg.
KGB *sigle m* KGB.
khmer, ère [kmɛʀ] *adj* Khmer ♦ *nm* (*LING*) Khmer.
khôl [kol] *nm* khol.
kibboutz [kibuts] *nm* kibbutz.
kidnapper [kidnape] *vt* to kidnap.
kidnappeur, euse [kidnapœʀ, -øz] *nm/f* kidnapper.
kidnapping [kidnapiŋ] *nm* kidnapping.
Kilimandjaro [kilimɑ̃dʒaʀo] *nm*: **le ~** Mount Kilimanjaro.
kilo [kilo] *nm* kilo.
kilogramme [kilɔgʀam] *nm* kilogramme (*BRIT*), kilogram (*US*).
kilométrage [kilɔmetʀaʒ] *nm* number of kilometres travelled, ≈ mileage.
kilomètre [kilɔmɛtʀ(ə)] *nm* kilometre (*BRIT*), kilometer (*US*); **~s-heure** kilometres per hour.
kilométrique [kilɔmetʀik] *adj* (*distance*) in kilometres; **compteur ~** ≈ mileage indicator.
kilooctet [kilɔɔktɛ] *nm* kilobyte.
kilowatt [kilɔwat] *nm* kilowatt.
kinésithérapeute [kineziteʀapøt] *nm/f* physiotherapist.
kinésithérapie [kineziteʀapi] *nf* physiotherapy.
kiosque [kjɔsk(ə)] *nm* kiosk, stall; (*TÉL etc*) *telephone and/or videotext information service.*
Kirghizistan [kiʀgizistɑ̃] *nm* Kirghizia.
kirsch [kiʀʃ] *nm* kirsch.
kitchenette [kitʃ(ə)nɛt] *nf* kitchenette.
kiwi [kiwi] *nm* (*ZOOL*) kiwi; (*BOT*) kiwi (fruit).
klaxon [klaksɔn] *nm* horn.
klaxonner [klaksɔne] *vi, vt* to hoot (*BRIT*), honk (one's horn) (*US*).
kleptomane [klɛptɔman] *nm/f* kleptomaniac.
km *abr* (= *kilomètre*) km.
km/h *abr* (= *kilomètres/heure*) km/h.
knock-out [nɔkawt] *nm* knock-out.
Ko *abr* (*INFORM*: = *kilooctet*) K.

K.-O. [kao] *adj inv* (knocked) out, out for the count.
koala [kɔala] *nm* koala (bear).
kolkhoze [kɔlkoz] *nm* kolkhoz.
Koweit *ou* **Kuweit** [kɔwɛt] *nm*: **le ~** Kuwait, Koweit.
koweïtien, ne [kɔwɛtjɛ̃, -ɛn] *adj* Kuwaiti ♦ *nm/f*: **K~, ne** Kuwaiti.
krach [kʀak] *nm* (*ÉCON*) crash.
kraft [kʀaft] *nm* brown *ou* kraft paper.
Kremlin [kʀɛmlɛ̃] *nm*: **le ~** the Kremlin.
Kuala Lumpur [kwalalympuʀ] *n* Kuala Lumpur.
kurde [kyʀd(ə)] *adj* Kurdish ♦ *nm* (*LING*) Kurdish ♦ *nm/f*: **K~** Kurd.
Kurdistan [kyʀdistɑ̃] *nm*: **le ~** Kurdistan.
Kuweit [kɔwɛt] = **Koweit**.
kW *abr* (= *kilowatt*) kW.
kW/h *abr* (= *kilowatt/heure*) kW/h.
kyrielle [kiʀjɛl] *nf*: **une ~ de** a stream of.
kyste [kist(ə)] *nm* cyst.

L l

L, l [ɛl] *nm inv* L, l ♦ *abr* (= *litre*) l; (*SCOL*): **L ès L** = Licence ès Lettres; **L en D** = Licence en Droit; **L comme Louis** L for Lucy (*BRIT*) *ou* Love (*US*).
l' [l] *art déf voir* le.
la [la] *art déf, pron voir* le ♦ *nm* (*MUS*) A; (*en chantant la gamme*) la.
là [la] *adv* (*voir aussi* **-ci, celui**) there; (*ici*) here; (*dans le temps*) then; **est-ce que Catherine est ~?** is Catherine there (*ou* here)?; **c'est ~ que** this is where; **~ où** where; **de ~** (*fig*) hence; **par ~** (*fig*) by that; **tout est ~** (*fig*) that's what it's all about.
là-bas [labɑ] *adv* there.
label [label] *nm* stamp, seal.
labeur [labœʀ] *nm* toil *no pl*, toiling *no pl*.
labo [labo] *nm* (= *laboratoire*) lab.
laborantin, e [labɔʀɑ̃tɛ̃, -in] *nm/f* laboratory assistant.
laboratoire [labɔʀatwaʀ] *nm* laboratory; **~ de langues/d'analyses** language/(medical) analysis laboratory.
laborieux, euse [labɔʀjø, -øz] *adj* (*tâche*) laborious; **classes ~euses** working classes.
laborieusement [labɔʀjøzmɑ̃] *adv* laboriously.
labour [labuʀ] *nm* ploughing *no pl* (*BRIT*), plowing *no pl* (*US*); **~s** *nmpl* (*champs*) ploughed fields; **cheval de ~** plough- *ou* cart-horse; **bœuf de ~** ox (*pl* oxen).
labourage [labuʀaʒ] *nm* ploughing (*BRIT*),

plowing (*US*).
labourer [labuʀe] *vt* to plough (*BRIT*), plow (*US*); (*fig*) to make deep gashes *ou* furrows in.
laboureur [labuʀœʀ] *nm* ploughman (*BRIT*), plowman (*US*).
labrador [labʀadɔʀ] *nm* (*chien*) labrador; (*GÉO*): **le L~** Labrador.
labyrinthe [labiʀɛ̃t] *nm* labyrinth, maze.
lac [lak] *nm* lake; **le ~ Léman** Lake Geneva; **les Grands L~s** the Great Lakes; *voir aussi* **lacs.**
lacer [lase] *vt* to lace up do up.
lacérer [laseʀe] *vt* to tear to shreds.
lacet [lasɛ] *nm* (*de chaussure*) lace; (*de route*) sharp bend; (*piège*) snare; **chaussures à ~s** lace-up *ou* lacing shoes.
lâche [lɑʃ] *adj* (*poltron*) cowardly; (*desserré*) loose, slack; (*morale, mœurs*) lax ♦ *nm/f* coward.
lâchement [lɑʃmɑ̃] *adv* (*par peur*) like a coward; (*par bassesse*) despicably.
lâcher [lɑʃe] *nm* (*de ballons, oiseaux*) release ♦ *vt* to let go of; (*ce qui tombe, abandonner*) to drop; (*oiseau, animal: libérer*) to release, set free; (*fig: mot, remarque*) to let slip, come out with; (*SPORT: distancer*) to leave behind ♦ *vi* (*fil, amarres*) to break, give way; (*freins*) to fail; **~ les amarres** (*NAVIG*) to cast off (the moorings); **~ prise** to let go.
lâcheté [lɑʃte] *nf* cowardice; (*bassesse*) lowness.
lacis [lasi] *nm* (*de ruelles*) maze.
laconique [lakɔnik] *adj* laconic.
laconiquement [lakɔnikmɑ̃] *adv* laconically.
lacrymal, e, aux [lakʀimal, -o] *adj* (*canal, glande*) tear *cpd*.
lacrymogène [lakʀimɔʒɛn] *adj*: **grenade/gaz ~** tear gas grenade/tear gas.
lacs [lɑ] *nm* (*piège*) snare.
lactation [laktasjɔ̃] *nf* lactation.
lacté, e [lakte] *adj* milk *cpd*.
lactique [laktik] *adj*: **acide/ferment ~** lactic acid/ferment.
lactose [laktoz] *nm* lactose, milk sugar.
lacune [lakyn] *nf* gap.
lacustre [lakystʀ(ə)] *adj* lake *cpd*, lakeside *cpd*.
lad [lad] *nm* stable-lad.
là-dedans [ladədɑ̃] *adv* inside (there), in it; (*fig*) in that.
là-dehors [ladəɔʀ] *adv* out there.
là-derrière [ladɛʀjɛʀ] *adv* behind there; (*fig*) behind that.
là-dessous [ladsu] *adv* underneath, under there; (*fig*) behind that.
là-dessus [ladsy] *adv* on there; (*fig*) at that point; (*: à ce sujet*) about that.
là-devant [ladvɑ̃] *adv* there (in front).
ladite [ladit] *dét voir* **ledit.**
ladre [ladʀ(ə)] *adj* miserly.
lagon [lagɔ̃] *nm* lagoon.
Lagos [lagɔs] *n* Lagos.
lagune [lagyn] *nf* lagoon.

là-haut [lao] *adv* up there.
laïc [laik] *adj, nm/f* = **laïque.**
laïciser [laisize] *vt* to secularize.
laïcité [laisite] *nf* secularity, secularism.
laid, e [lɛ, lɛd] *adj* ugly; (*fig: acte*) mean, cheap.
laideron [lɛdʀɔ̃] *nm* ugly girl.
laideur [lɛdœʀ] *nf* ugliness *no pl*; meanness *no pl*.
laie [lɛ] *nf* wild sow.
lainage [lɛnaʒ] *nm* woollen garment; (*étoffe*) woollen material.
laine [lɛn] *nf* wool; **~ peignée** worsted (wool); **~ à tricoter** knitting wool; **~ de verre** glass wool; **~ vierge** new wool.
laineux, euse [lɛnø, -øz] *adj* woolly.
lainier, ière [lenje, -jɛʀ] *adj* (*industrie etc*) woollen.
laïque [laik] *adj* lay, civil; (*SCOL*) state *cpd* (*as opposed to private and Roman Catholic*) ♦ *nm/f* layman/woman.
laisse [lɛs] *nf* (*de chien*) lead, leash; **tenir en ~** to keep on a lead *ou* leash.
laissé-pour-compte, laissée-, laissés- [lesepuʀkɔ̃t] *adj* (*COMM*) unsold; (*: refusé*) returned ♦ *nm/f* (*fig*) reject; **les laissés-pour-compte de la reprise économique** those who are left out of the economic upturn.
laisser [lese] *vt* to leave ♦ *vb aux*: **~ qn faire** to let sb do; **se ~ exploiter** to let o.s. be exploited; **se ~ aller** to let o.s. go; **~ qn tranquille** to leave sb alone; **laisse-toi faire** let me (*ou* him) do it; **rien ne laisse penser que ...** there is no reason to think that ...; **cela ne laisse pas de surprendre** nonetheless it is surprising.
laisser-aller [leseale] *nm* carelessness, slovenliness.
laisser-faire [lesefɛʀ] *nm* laissez-faire.
laissez-passer [lesepɑse] *nm inv* pass.
lait [lɛ] *nm* milk; **frère/sœur de ~** foster brother/sister; **~ écrémé/concentré/condensé** skimmed/condensed/evaporated milk; **~ en poudre** powdered milk, milk powder; **~ de chèvre/vache** goat's/cow's milk; **~ maternel** mother's milk; **~ démaquillant/de beauté** cleansing/beauty lotion.
laitage [lɛtaʒ] *nm* milk product.
laiterie [lɛtʀi] *nf* dairy.
laiteux, euse [lɛtø, -øz] *adj* milky.
laitier, ière [letje, -jɛʀ] *adj* dairy ♦ *nm/f* milkman/dairywoman.
laiton [lɛtɔ̃] *nm* brass.
laitue [lety] *nf* lettuce.
laïus [lajys] *nm* (*péj*) spiel.
lama [lama] *nm* llama.
lambeau, x [lɑ̃bo] *nm* scrap; **en ~x** in tatters, tattered.
lambin, e [lɑ̃bɛ̃, -in] *adj* (*péj*) slow.
lambiner [lɑ̃bine] *vi* (*péj*) to dawdle.
lambris [lɑ̃bʀi] *nm* panelling *no pl*.
lambrissé, e [lɑ̃bʀise] *adj* panelled.

lame [lam] *nf* blade; (*vague*) wave; (*lamelle*) strip; ~ **de fond** ground swell *no pl*; ~ **de rasoir** razor blade.

lamé [lame] *nm* lamé.

lamelle [lamɛl] *nf* (*lame*) small blade; (*morceau*) sliver; (*de champignon*) gill; **couper en** ~**s** to slice thinly.

lamentable [lamɑ̃tabl(ə)] *adj* (*déplorable*) appalling; (*pitoyable*) pitiful.

lamentablement [lamɑ̃tabləmɑ̃] *adv* (*échouer*) miserably; (*se conduire*) appallingly.

lamentation [lamɑ̃tasjɔ̃] *nf* wailing *no pl*, lamentation; moaning *no pl*.

lamenter [lamɑ̃te]: **se** ~ *vi*: **se** ~ (**sur**) to moan (over).

laminage [laminaʒ] *nm* lamination.

laminer [lamine] *vt* to laminate; (*fig: écraser*) to wipe out.

laminoir [laminwaR] *nm* rolling mill; **passer au** ~ (*fig*) to go (*ou* put) through the mill.

lampadaire [lɑ̃padɛR] *nm* (*de salon*) standard lamp; (*dans la rue*) street lamp.

lampe [lɑ̃p(ə)] *nf* lamp; (*TECH*) valve; ~ **à alcool** spirit lamp; ~ **à bronzer** sunlamp; ~ **de poche** torch (*BRIT*), flashlight (*US*); ~ **à souder** blowlamp; ~ **témoin** warning light.

lampée [lɑ̃pe] *nf* gulp, swig.

lampe-tempête, *pl* **lampes-tempête** [lɑ̃ptɑ̃pɛt] *nf* storm lantern.

lampion [lɑ̃pjɔ̃] *nm* Chinese lantern.

lampiste [lɑ̃pist(ə)] *nm* light (maintenance) man; (*fig*) underling.

lamproie [lɑ̃pRwa] *nf* lamprey.

lance [lɑ̃s] *nf* spear; ~ **d'arrosage** garden hose; ~ **à eau** water hose; ~ **d'incendie** fire hose.

lancée [lɑ̃se] *nf*: **être/continuer sur sa** ~ to be under way/keep going.

lance-flammes [lɑ̃sflam] *nm inv* flamethrower.

lance-fusées [lɑ̃sfyze] *nm inv* rocket launcher.

lance-grenades [lɑ̃sgRənad] *nm inv* grenade launcher.

lancement [lɑ̃smɑ̃] *nm* launching *no pl*, launch; **offre de** ~ introductory offer.

lance-missiles [lɑ̃smisil] *nm inv* missile launcher.

lance-pierres [lɑ̃spjɛR] *nm inv* catapult.

lancer [lɑ̃se] *nm* (*SPORT*) throwing *no pl*, throw; (*PÊCHE*) rod and reel fishing ♦ *vt* to throw; (*émettre, projeter*) to throw out, send out; (*produit, fusée, bateau, artiste*) to launch; (*injure*) to hurl, fling; (*proclamation, mandat d'arrêt*) to issue; (*emprunt*) to float; (*moteur*) to send roaring away; ~ **qch à qn** to throw sth to sb; (*de façon agressive*) to throw sth at sb; ~ **un cri** *ou* **un appel** to shout *ou* call out; **se** ~ *vi* (*prendre de l'élan*) to build up speed; (*se précipiter*): **se** ~ **sur** *ou* **contre** to rush at; **se** ~ **dans** (*discussion*) to launch into; (*aventure*) to embark on; (*les affaires, la politique*) to go into; ~ **du poids** *nm* putting the shot.

lance-roquettes [lɑ̃sRɔkɛt] *nm inv* rocket launcher.

lance-torpilles [lɑ̃stɔRpij] *nm inv* torpedo tube.

lanceur, euse [lɑ̃sœR, -øz] *nm/f* bowler; (*BASEBALL*) pitcher ♦ *nm* (*ESPACE*) launcher.

lancinant, e [lɑ̃sinɑ̃, -ɑ̃t] *adj* (*regrets etc*) haunting; (*douleur*) shooting.

lanciner [lɑ̃sine] *vi* to throb; (*fig*) to nag.

landais, e [lɑ̃dɛ, -ɛz] *adj* of *ou* from the Landes.

landau [lɑ̃do] *nm* pram (*BRIT*), baby carriage (*US*).

lande [lɑ̃d] *nf* moor.

Landes [lɑ̃d] *nfpl*: **les** ~ the Landes.

langage [lɑ̃gaʒ] *nm* language; ~ **d'assemblage** (*INFORM*) assembly language; ~ **du corps** body language; ~ **évolué/machine** (*INFORM*) high-level/machine language; ~ **de programmation** (*INFORM*) programming language.

lange [lɑ̃ʒ] *nm* flannel blanket; ~**s** *nmpl* swaddling clothes.

langer [lɑ̃ʒe] *vt* to change (the nappy (*BRIT*) *ou* diaper (*US*) of); **table à** ~ changing table.

langoureux, euse [lɑ̃guRø, -øz] *adj* languorous.

langoureusement [lɑ̃guRøzmɑ̃] *adv* languorously.

langouste [lɑ̃gust(ə)] *nf* crayfish *inv*.

langoustine [lɑ̃gustin] *nf* Dublin Bay prawn.

langue [lɑ̃g] *nf* (*ANAT, CULIN*) tongue; (*LING*) language; (*bande*): ~ **de terre** spit of land; **tirer la** ~ (**à**) to stick out one's tongue (at); **donner sa** ~ **au chat** to give up, give in; **de** ~ **française** French-speaking; ~ **de bois** officialese; ~ **maternelle** native language, mother tongue; ~ **verte** slang; ~ **vivante** modern language.

langue-de-chat [lɑ̃gdəʃa] *nf* finger biscuit.

languedocien, ne [lɑ̃gdɔsjɛ̃, -ɛn] *adj* of *ou* from the Languedoc.

languette [lɑ̃gɛt] *nf* tongue.

langueur [lɑ̃gœR] *nf* languidness.

languir [lɑ̃giR] *vi* to languish; (*conversation*) to flag; **se** ~ *vi* to be languishing; **faire** ~ **qn** to keep sb waiting.

languissant, e [lɑ̃gisɑ̃, -ɑ̃t] *adj* languid.

lanière [lanjɛR] *nf* (*de fouet*) lash; (*de valise, bretelle*) strap.

lanoline [lanɔlin] *nf* lanolin.

lanterne [lɑ̃tɛRn(ə)] *nf* (*portable*) lantern; (*électrique*) light, lamp; (*de voiture*) (side)light; ~ **rouge** (*fig*) tail-ender; ~ **vénitienne** Chinese lantern.

lanterneau, x [lɑ̃tɛRno] *nm* skylight.

lanterner [lɑ̃tɛRne] *vi*: **faire** ~ **qn** to keep sb hanging around.

Laos [laɔs] *nm*: **le** ~ Laos.

laotien, ne [laɔsjɛ̃, -ɛn] *adj* Laotian.

lapalissade [lapalisad] *nf* statement of the obvious.

La Paz [lapaz] *n* La Paz.

laper [lape] *vt* to lap up.

lapereau, x [lapʀo] *nm* young rabbit.
lapidaire [lapidɛʀ] *adj* stone *cpd*; (*fig*) terse.
lapider [lapide] *vt* to stone.
lapin [lapɛ̃] *nm* rabbit; (*fourrure*) cony; **coup du** ~ rabbit punch; **poser un** ~ **à qn** to stand sb up; ~ **de garenne** wild rabbit.
lapis(-lazuli) [lapis(lazyli)] *nm inv* lapis lazuli.
lapon, e [lapɔ̃, -ɔn] *adj* Lapp, Lappish ♦ *nm* (*LING*) Lapp, Lappish ♦ *nm/f*: **L~, e** Lapp, Laplander.
Laponie [laponi] *nf*: **la** ~ Lapland.
laps [laps] *nm*: ~ **de temps** space of time, time *no pl*.
lapsus [lapsys] *nm* slip.
laquais [lakɛ] *nm* lackey.
laque [lak] *nf* lacquer; (*brute*) shellac; (*pour cheveux*) hair spray ♦ *nm* lacquer; piece of lacquer ware.
laqué, e [lake] *adj* lacquered.
laquelle [lakɛl] *pron voir* **lequel**.
larbin [laʀbɛ̃] *nm* (*péj*) flunkey.
larcin [laʀsɛ̃] *nm* theft.
lard [laʀ] *nm* (*graisse*) fat; (*bacon*) (streaky) bacon.
larder [laʀde] *vt* (*CULIN*) to lard.
lardon [laʀdɔ̃] *nm* (*CULIN*) piece of chopped bacon; (*fam: enfant*) kid.
large [laʀʒ(ə)] *adj* wide; broad; (*fig*) generous ♦ *adv*: **calculer/voir** ~ to allow extra/think big ♦ *nm* (*largeur*): **5 m de** ~ 5 m wide *ou* in width; (*mer*): **le** ~ the open sea; **en** ~ *adv* sideways; **au** ~ **de** off; ~ **d'esprit** broad-minded; **ne pas en mener** ~ to have one's heart in one's boots.
largement [laʀʒəmɑ̃] *adv* widely; (*de loin*) greatly; (*amplement, au minimum*) easily; (*sans compter: donner etc*) generously.
largesse [laʀʒɛs] *nf* generosity; ~**s** *nfpl* liberalities.
largeur [laʀʒœʀ] *nf* (*qu'on mesure*) width; (*impression visuelle*) wideness, width; breadth; broadness.
larguer [laʀge] *vt* to drop; (*fam: se débarrasser de*) to get rid of; ~ **les amarres** to cast off (the moorings).
larme [laʀm(ə)] *nf* tear; (*fig*): **une** ~ **de** a drop of; **en** ~**s** in tears; **pleurer à chaudes** ~**s** to cry one's eyes out, cry bitterly.
larmoyant, e [laʀmwajɑ̃, -ɑ̃t] *adj* tearful.
larmoyer [laʀmwaje] *vi* (*yeux*) to water; (*se plaindre*) to whimper.
larron [laʀɔ̃] *nm* thief (*pl* thieves).
larve [laʀv(ə)] *nf* (*ZOOL*) larva (*pl* -ae); (*fig*) worm.
larvé, e [laʀve] *adj* (*fig*) latent.
laryngite [laʀɛ̃ʒit] *nf* laryngitis.
laryngologiste [laʀɛ̃gɔlɔʒist(ə)] *nm/f* throat specialist.
larynx [laʀɛ̃ks] *nm* larynx.
las, lasse [lɑ, lɑs] *adj* weary.
lasagne [lazaɲ] *nf* lasagne.
lascar [laskaʀ] *nm* character; (*malin*) rogue.

lascif, ive [lasif, -iv] *adj* lascivious.
laser [lazɛʀ] *nm*: (**rayon**) ~ laser (beam); **chaîne** *ou* **platine** ~ compact disc (player); **disque** ~ compact disc.
lassant, e [lɑsɑ̃, -ɑ̃t] *adj* tiresome, wearisome.
lasse [lɑs] *adj f voir* **las**.
lasser [lɑse] *vt* to weary, tire; **se** ~ **de** to grow weary *ou* tired of.
lassitude [lɑsityd] *nf* lassitude, weariness.
lasso [laso] *nm* lasso; **prendre au** ~ to lasso.
latent, e [latɑ̃, -ɑ̃t] *adj* latent.
latéral, e, aux [lateʀal, -o] *adj* side *cpd*, lateral.
latéralement [lateʀalmɑ̃] *adv* edgeways; (*arriver, souffler*) from the side.
latex [latɛks] *nm inv* latex.
latin, e [latɛ̃, -in] *adj* Latin ♦ *nm* (*LING*) Latin ♦ *nm/f*: **L~, e** Latin; **j'y perds mon** ~ it's all Greek to me.
latiniste [latinist(ə)] *nm/f* Latin scholar (*ou* student).
latino-américain, e [latinoameʀikɛ̃, -ɛn] *adj* Latin-American.
latitude [latityd] *nf* latitude; (*fig*): **avoir la** ~ **de faire** to be left free *ou* be at liberty to do; **à 48° de** ~ **Nord** at latitude 48° North; **sous toutes les** ~**s** (*fig*) world-wide, throughout the world.
latrines [latʀin] *nfpl* latrines.
latte [lat] *nf* lath, slat; (*de plancher*) board.
lattis [lati] *nm* lathwork.
laudanum [lodanɔm] *nm* laudanum.
laudatif, ive [lodatif, -iv] *adj* laudatory.
lauréat, e [lɔʀea, -at] *nm/f* winner.
laurier [lɔʀje] *nm* (*BOT*) laurel; (*CULIN*) bay leaves *pl*; ~**s** *nmpl* (*fig*) laurels.
laurier-rose, *pl* **lauriers-roses** [lɔʀjeʀoz] *nm* oleander.
laurier-tin, *pl* **lauriers-tins** [lɔʀjetɛ̃] *nm* laurustinus.
lavable [lavabl(ə)] *adj* washable.
lavabo [lavabo] *nm* washbasin; ~**s** *nmpl* toilet *sg*.
lavage [lavaʒ] *nm* washing *no pl*, wash; ~ **d'estomac/d'intestin** stomach/intestinal wash; ~ **de cerveau** brainwashing *no pl*.
lavande [lavɑ̃d] *nf* lavender.
lavandière [lavɑ̃djɛʀ] *nf* washerwoman.
lave [lav] *nf* lava *no pl*.
lave-glace [lavglas] *nm* (*AUTO*) windscreen (*BRIT*) *ou* windshield (*US*) washer.
lave-linge [lavlɛ̃ʒ] *nm inv* washing machine.
lavement [lavmɑ̃] *nm* (*MÉD*) enema.
laver [lave] *vt* to wash; (*tache*) to wash off; (*fig: affront*) to avenge; **se** ~ to have a wash, wash; **se** ~ **les mains/dents** to wash one's hands/clean one's teeth; ~ **la vaisselle/le linge** to wash the dishes/clothes; ~ **qn de** (*accusation*) to clear sb of.
laverie [lavʀi] *nf*: ~ (**automatique**) launderette.
lavette [lavɛt] *nf* (*chiffon*) dish cloth; (*brosse*) dish mop; (*fam: homme*) wimp, drip.

laveur, euse [lavœʀ, -øz] *nm/f* cleaner.
lave-vaisselle [lavvɛsɛl] *nm inv* dishwasher.
lavis [lavi] *nm* (*technique*) washing; (*dessin*) wash drawing.
lavoir [lavwaʀ] *nm* wash house; (*bac*) washtub.
laxatif, ive [laksatif, -iv] *adj, nm* laxative.
laxisme [laksism(ə)] *nm* laxity.
laxiste [laksist(ə)] *adj* lax.
layette [lɛjɛt] *nf* layette.
layon [lɛjɔ̃] *nm* trail.
lazaret [lazaʀɛ] *nm* quarantine area.
lazzi [ladzi] *nm* gibe.
LCR *sigle f* (= *Ligue communiste révolutionnaire*) political party.

=============================== MOT-CLÉ

le (l'), la [l(ə)] (*pl* **les**) *art déf* **1** the; ~ **livre/la pomme/l'arbre** the book/the apple/the tree; **les étudiants** the students
2 (*noms abstraits*): ~ **courage/l'amour/la jeunesse** courage/love/youth
3 (*indiquant la possession*): **se casser la jambe** *etc* to break one's leg *etc*; **levez la main** put your hand up; **avoir les yeux gris/** ~ **nez rouge** to have grey eyes/a red nose
4 (*temps*): **le matin/soir** in the morning/ evening; mornings/evenings; ~ **jeudi** *etc* (*d'habitude*) on Thursdays *etc*; (*ce jeudi-là etc*) on (the) Thursday; **nous venons** ~ **3 décembre** (*parlé*) we're coming on the 3rd of December *ou* on December the 3rd; (*écrit*) we're coming (on) 3rd *ou* 3 December
5 (*distribution, évaluation*) a, an; **10 F** ~ **mètre/kilo** 10 F a *ou* per metre/kilo; ~ **tiers/quart de** a third/quarter of
♦ *pron* **1** (*personne: mâle*) him; (: *femelle*) her; (: *pluriel*) them; **je** ~**/la/les vois** I can see him/her/them
2 (*animal, chose: singulier*) it; (: *pluriel*) them; **je** ~ (*ou* **la**) **vois** I can see it; **je les vois** I can see them
3 (*remplaçant une phrase*): **je ne** ~ **savais pas** I didn't know (about it); **il était riche et ne l'est plus** he was once rich but no longer is.

lé [le] *nm* (*de tissu*) width; (*de papier peint*) strip, length.
leader [lidœʀ] *nm* leader.
leadership [lidœʀʃip] *nm* (*POL*) leadership.
leasing [liziŋ] *nm* leasing.
lèche-bottes [lɛʃbɔt] *nm inv* bootlicker.
lèchefrite [lɛʃfʀit] *nf* dripping pan *ou* tray.
lécher [leʃe] *vt* to lick; (*laper: lait, eau*) to lick *ou* lap up; (*finir, polir*) to over-refine; ~ **les vitrines** to go window-shopping; **se** ~ **les doigts/lèvres** to lick one's fingers/lips.
lèche-vitrines [lɛʃvitʀin] *nm inv*: **faire du** ~ to go window-shopping.
leçon [ləsɔ̃] *nf* lesson; **faire la** ~ to teach; **faire la** ~ **à** (*fig*) to give a lecture to; ~**s de conduite** driving lessons; ~**s particulières** private lessons *ou* tuition *sg* (*BRIT*).

lecteur, trice [lɛktœʀ, -tʀis] *nm/f* reader; (*d'université*) (foreign language) assistant (*BRIT*), (foreign) teaching assistant (*US*) ♦ *nm* (*TECH*): ~ **de cassettes** cassette player; (*INFORM*): ~ **de disquette(s)** *ou* **de disque** disk drive; ~ **compact-disc** *ou* **CD** compact disc (player).
lectorat [lɛktɔʀa] *nm* (foreign language *ou* teaching) assistantship.
lecture [lɛktyʀ] *nf* reading.
LED [lɛd] *sigle f* (= *light emitting diode*) LED; **affichage** ~ LED display.
ledit [lədi], **ladite** [ladit], *mpl* **lesdits** [ledi], *fpl* **lesdites** [ledit] *dét* the aforesaid.
légal, e, aux [legal, -o] *adj* legal.
légalement [legalmɑ̃] *adv* legally.
légalisation [legalizasjɔ̃] *nf* legalization.
légaliser [legalize] *vt* to legalize.
légalité [legalite] *nf* legality, lawfulness; **être dans/sortir de la** ~ to be within/step outside the law.
légat [lega] *nm* (*REL*) legate.
légataire [legatɛʀ] *nm* legatee.
légendaire [leʒɑ̃dɛʀ] *adj* legendary.
légende [leʒɑ̃d] *nf* (*mythe*) legend; (*de carte, plan*) key, legend; (*de dessin*) caption, legend.
léger, ère [leʒe, -ɛʀ] *adj* light; (*bruit, retard*) slight; (*boisson, parfum*) weak; (*couche, étoffe*) thin; (*superficiel*) thoughtless; (*volage*) free and easy; flighty; (*peu sérieux*) lightweight; **blessé** ~ slightly injured person; **à la légère** *adv* (*parler, agir*) rashly, thoughtlessly.
légèrement [leʒɛʀmɑ̃] *adv* lightly; thoughtlessly, rashly; ~ **plus grand** slightly bigger.
légèreté [leʒɛʀte] *nf* lightness; thoughtlessness.
légiférer [leʒifeʀe] *vi* to legislate.
légion [leʒjɔ̃] *nf* legion; **la L**~ **étrangère** the Foreign Legion; **la L**~ **d'honneur** the Legion of Honour.

> *Created by Napoleon in 1802 to reward service to the state,* **la Légion d'honneur** *is a prestigious French order headed by the President of the Republic, the Grand Maître. Members receive a nominal tax-free payment each year.*

légionnaire [leʒjɔnɛʀ] *nm* (*MIL*) legionnaire; (*de la Légion d'honneur*) holder of the Legion of Honour.
législateur [leʒislatœʀ] *nm* legislator, lawmaker.
législatif, ive [leʒislatif, -iv] *adj* legislative; **législatives** *nfpl* general election *sg*.
législation [leʒislasjɔ̃] *nf* legislation.
législature [leʒislatyʀ] *nf* legislature; (*période*) term (of office).
légiste [leʒist(ə)] *nm* jurist ♦ *adj*: **médecin** ~ forensic scientist (*BRIT*), medical examiner (*US*).

légitime [leʒitim] *adj* (*JUR*) lawful, legitimate; (*enfant*) legitimate; (*fig*) rightful, legitimate; **en état de ~ défense** in self-defence.

légitimement [leʒitimmɑ̃] *adv* lawfully; legitimately; rightfully.

légitimer [leʒitime] *vt* (*enfant*) to legitimize; (*justifier: conduite etc*) to justify.

légitimité [leʒitimite] *nf* (*JUR*) legitimacy.

legs [lɛg] *nm* legacy.

léguer [lege] *vt*: **~ qch à qn** (*JUR*) to bequeath sth to sb; (*fig*) to hand sth down *ou* pass sth on to sb.

légume [legym] *nm* vegetable; **~s verts** green vegetables; **~s secs** pulses.

légumier [legymje] *nm* vegetable dish.

leitmotiv [lejtmotiv] *nm* leitmotiv, leitmotif.

Léman [lemɑ̃] *nm voir* **lac**.

lendemain [lɑ̃dmɛ̃] *nm*: **le ~** the next *ou* following day; **le ~ matin/soir** the next *ou* following morning/evening; **le ~ de** the day after; **au ~ de** in the days following; in the wake of; **penser au ~** to think of the future; **sans ~** short-lived; **de beaux ~s** bright prospects; **des ~s qui chantent** a rosy future.

lénifiant, e [lenifjɑ̃, -ɑ̃t] *adj* soothing.

léniniste [leninist(ə)] *adj, nm/f* Leninist.

lent, e [lɑ̃, lɑ̃t] *adj* slow.

lente [lɑ̃t] *nf* nit.

lentement [lɑ̃tmɑ̃] *adv* slowly.

lenteur [lɑ̃tœʀ] *nf* slowness *no pl*; **~s** *nfpl* (*actions, décisions lentes*) slowness *sg*.

lentille [lɑ̃tij] *nf* (*OPTIQUE*) lens *sg*; (*BOT*) lentil; **~ d'eau** duckweed; **~s de contact** contact lenses.

léonin, e [leɔnɛ̃, -in] *adj* (*fig: contrat etc*) one-sided.

léopard [leɔpaʀ] *nm* leopard.

LEP [lɛp] *sigle m* (= *lycée d'enseignement professionnel*) *secondary school for vocational training, pre-1986.*

lèpre [lɛpʀ(ə)] *nf* leprosy.

lépreux, euse [lepʀø, -øz] *nm/f* leper ♦ *adj* (*fig*) flaking, peeling.

═══════════════════ *MOT-CLÉ*

lequel, laquelle [ləkɛl, lakɛl] (*mpl* **lesquels**, *fpl* **lesquelles**; *à* + *lequel* = **auquel**, *de* + *lequel* = **duquel**) *pron* **1** (*interrogatif*) which, which one **2** (*relatif: personne: sujet*) who; (*: objet, après préposition*) whom; (*sujet: possessif*) whose; (*: chose*) which; **je l'ai proposé au directeur, ~ est d'accord** I suggested it to the director, who agrees; **la femme à laquelle j'ai acheté mon chien** the woman from whom I bought my dog; **le pont sur ~ nous sommes passés** the bridge (over) which we crossed; **un homme sur la compétence duquel on peut compter** a man whose competence one can count on

♦ *adj*: **auquel cas** in which case.

les [le] *voir* **le**.

lesbienne [lɛsbjɛn] *nf* lesbian.

lesdits [ledi], **lesdites** [ledit] *dét voir* **ledit**.

lèse-majesté [lɛzmaʒɛste] *nf inv*: **crime de ~** crime of lese-majesty.

léser [leze] *vt* to wrong; (*MÉD*) to injure.

lésiner [lezine] *vt*: **~ (sur)** to skimp (on).

lésion [lezjɔ̃] *nf* lesion, damage *no pl*; **~s cérébrales** brain damage.

Lesotho [lezɔto] *nm*: **le ~** Lesotho.

lesquels, lesquelles [lekɛl] *pron voir* **lequel**.

lessivable [lesivabl(ə)] *adj* washable.

lessive [lesiv] *nf* (*poudre*) washing powder; (*linge*) washing *no pl*, wash; (*opération*) washing *no pl*; **faire la ~** to do the washing.

lessivé, e [lesive] *adj* (*fam*) washed out.

lessiver [lesive] *vt* to wash.

lessiveuse [lesivøz] *nf* (*récipient*) washtub.

lessiviel [lesivjɛl] *adj* detergent.

lest [lɛst] *nm* ballast; **jeter** *ou* **lâcher du ~** (*fig*) to make concessions.

leste [lɛst(ə)] *adj* (*personne, mouvement*) sprightly, nimble; (*désinvolte: manières*) offhand; (*osé: plaisanterie*) risqué.

lestement [lɛstəmɑ̃] *adv* nimbly.

lester [lɛste] *vt* to ballast.

letchi [lɛtʃi] *nm* = **litchi**.

léthargie [letaʀʒi] *nf* lethargy.

léthargique [letaʀʒik] *adj* lethargic.

letton, ne [lɛtɔ̃, -ɔn] *adj* Latvian, Lett.

Lettonie [lɛtɔni] *nf*: **la ~** Latvia.

lettre [lɛtʀ(ə)] *nf* letter; **~s** *nfpl* (*étude, culture*) literature *sg*; (*SCOL*) arts (subjects); **à la ~** (*au sens propre*) literally; (*ponctuellement*) to the letter; **en ~s majuscules** *ou* **capitales** in capital letters, in capitals; **en toutes ~s** in words, in full; **~ de change** bill of exchange; **~ piégée** letter bomb; **~ de voiture (aérienne)** (air) waybill, (air) bill of lading; **~s de noblesse** pedigree.

lettré, e [letʀe] *adj* well-read, scholarly.

lettre-transfert, *pl* **lettres-transferts** [letʀatʀɑ̃sfɛʀ] *nf* (*pressure*) transfer.

leu [lø] *voir* **queue**.

leucémie [løsemi] *nf* leukaemia.

═══════════════════ *MOT-CLÉ*

leur [lœʀ] *adj possessif* their; **~ maison** their house; **~s amis** their friends; **à ~ approche** as they came near; **à ~ vue** at the sight of them

♦ *pron* **1** (*objet indirect*) (to) them; **je ~ ai dit la vérité** I told them the truth; **je le ~ ai donné** I gave it to them, I gave them it **2** (*possessif*): **le(la) ~, les ~s** theirs.

leurre [lœʀ] *nm* (*appât*) lure; (*fig*) delusion; (*: piège*) snare.

leurrer [lœʀe] *vt* to delude, deceive.

levain [ləvɛ̃] *nm* leaven; **sans ~** unleavened.

levant, e [ləvɑ̃, -ɑ̃t] *adj*: **soleil ~** rising sun ♦ *nm*: **le L~** the Levant; **au soleil ~** at sunrise.

levantin, e [ləvɑ̃tɛ̃, -in] *adj* Levantine ♦ *nm/f*:

L~, e Levantine.

levé, e [ləve] *adj*: **être ~** to be up ♦ *nm*: **~ de terrain** land survey; **à mains ~es** (*vote*) by a show of hands; **au pied ~** at a moment's notice.

levée [ləve] *nf* (*POSTES*) collection; (*CARTES*) trick; **~ de boucliers** general outcry; **~ du corps** collection of the body from house of the deceased, before funeral; **~ d'écrou** release from custody; **~ de terre** levee; **~ de troupes** levy.

lever [ləve] *vt* (*vitre, bras etc*) to raise; (*soulever de terre, supprimer: interdiction, siège*) to lift; (: *difficulté*) to remove; (*séance*) to close; (*impôts, armée*) to levy; (*CHASSE: lièvre*) to start; (: *perdrix*) to flush; (*fam: fille*) to pick up ♦ *vi* (*CULIN*) to rise ♦ *nm*: **au ~** on getting up; **se ~** *vi* to get up; (*soleil*) to rise; (*jour*) to break; (*brouillard*) to lift; **ça va se ~** the weather will clear; **~ du jour** daybreak; **~ du rideau** (*THÉÂT*) curtain; **~ de rideau** (*pièce*) curtain raiser; **~ de soleil** sunrise.

lève-tard [lɛvtar] *nm/f inv* late riser.

lève-tôt [lɛvto] *nm/f inv* early riser, early bird.

levier [ləvje] *nm* lever; **faire ~ sur** to lever up (*ou* off); **~ de changement de vitesse** gear lever.

lévitation [levitasjɔ̃] *nf* levitation.

levraut [ləvro] *nm* (*ZOOL*) leveret.

lèvre [lɛvʀ(ə)] *nf* lip (*d'une plaie*) edges; **petites/grandes ~s** labia minora/majora; **du bout des ~s** half-heartedly.

lévrier [levʀije] *nm* greyhound.

levure [ləvyr] *nf* yeast; **~ chimique** baking powder.

lexical, e, aux [lɛksikal, -o] *adj* lexical.

lexicographe [lɛksikɔgʀaf] *nm/f* lexicographer.

lexicographie [lɛksikɔgʀafi] *nf* lexicography, dictionary writing.

lexicologie [lɛksikɔlɔʒi] *nf* lexicology.

lexique [lɛksik] *nm* vocabulary, lexicon; (*glossaire*) vocabulary.

lézard [lezar] *nm* lizard; (*peau*) lizardskin.

lézarde [lezard(ə)] *nf* crack.

lézarder [lezarde]: **se ~** *vi* to crack.

liaison [ljezɔ̃] *nf* (*rapport*) connection, link; (*RAIL, AVIAT etc*) link; (*relation: d'amitié*) friendship; (: *d'affaires*) relationship; (: *amoureuse*) affair; (*CULIN, PHONÉTIQUE*) liaison; **entrer/être en ~ avec** to get/be in contact with; **~ radio** radio contact; **~ (de transmission de données)** (*INFORM*) data link.

liane [ljan] *nf* creeper.

liant, e [ljã, -ãt] *adj* sociable.

liasse [ljas] *nf* wad, bundle.

Liban [libã] *nm*: **le ~** (the) Lebanon.

libanais, e [libanɛ, -ɛz] *adj* Lebanese ♦ *nm/f*: **L~, e** Lebanese.

libations [libasjɔ̃] *nfpl* libations.

libelle [libɛl] *nm* lampoon.

libellé [libele] *nm* wording.

libeller [libele] *vt* (*chèque, mandat*): **~ (au nom de)** to make out (to); (*lettre*) to word.

libellule [libelyl] *nf* dragonfly.

libéral, e, aux [liberal, -o] *adj, nm/f* liberal; **les professions ~es** the professions.

libéralement [liberalmã] *adv* liberally.

libéralisation [liberalizasjɔ̃] *nf* liberalization; **~ du commerce** easing of trade restrictions.

libéraliser [liberalize] *vt* to liberalize.

libéralisme [liberalism(ə)] *nm* liberalism.

libéralité [liberalite] *nf* liberality *no pl*, generosity *no pl*.

libérateur, trice [liberatœr, -tris] *adj* liberating ♦ *nm/f* liberator.

libération [liberasjɔ̃] *nf* liberation, freeing; release; discharge; **~ conditionnelle** release on parole.

libéré, e [libere] *adj* liberated; **~ de** freed from; **être ~ sous caution/sur parole** to be released on bail/on parole.

libérer [libere] *vt* (*délivrer*) to free, liberate; (: *moralement, PSYCH*) to liberate; (*relâcher: prisonnier*) to release; (: *soldat*) to discharge; (*dégager: gaz, cran d'arrêt*) to release; (*ÉCON: échanges commerciaux*) to ease restrictions on; **se ~** (*de rendez-vous*) to try and be free, get out of previous engagements; **~ qn de** (*liens, dette*) to free sb from; (*promesse*) to release sb from.

Libéria [liberja] *nm*: **le ~** Liberia.

libérien, ne [liberjɛ̃, -ɛn] *adj* Liberian ♦ *nm/f*: **L~, ne** Liberian.

libéro [libero] *nm* (*FOOTBALL*) sweeper.

libertaire [libertɛr] *adj* libertarian.

liberté [libɛrte] *nf* freedom; (*loisir*) free time; **~s** *nfpl* (*privautés*) liberties; **mettre/être en ~** to set/be free; **en ~ provisoire/surveillée/conditionnelle** on bail/probation/parole; **~ d'association** right of association; **~ de conscience** freedom of conscience; **~ du culte** freedom of worship; **~ d'esprit** independence of mind; **~ d'opinion** freedom of thought; **~ de la presse** freedom of the press; **~ de réunion** right to hold meetings; **~ syndicale** union rights *pl*; **~s individuelles** personal freedom *sg*; **~s publiques** civil rights.

libertin, e [libɛrtɛ̃, -in] *adj* libertine, licentious.

libertinage [libɛrtinaʒ] *nm* licentiousness.

libidineux, euse [libidinø, -øz] *adj* libidinous, lustful.

libido [libido] *nf* libido.

libraire [librɛr] *nm/f* bookseller.

libraire-éditeur, *pl* **libraires-éditeurs** [librɛreditœr] *nm* publisher and bookseller.

librairie [librɛri] *nf* bookshop.

librairie-papeterie, *pl* **librairies-papeteries** [librɛripapetri] bookseller's and stationer's.

libre [libʀ(ə)] *adj* free; (*route*) clear; (*place etc*) vacant, free; (*fig: propos, manières*) open;

(*SCOL*) private and Roman Catholic (*as opposed to "laïque"*); **de ~** (*place*) free; **~ de qch/de faire** free from sth/to do; **vente ~** (*COMM*) unrestricted sale; **~ arbitre** free will; **~ concurrence** free-market economy; **~ entreprise** free enterprise.

libre-échange [libʀeʃɑ̃ʒ] *nm* free trade.

librement [libʀəmɑ̃] *adv* freely.

libre-penseur, euse [libʀəpɑ̃sœʀ, -øz] *nm/f* free thinker.

libre-service [libʀəsɛʀvis] *nm inv* (*magasin*) self-service store; (*restaurant*) self-service restaurant.

librettiste [libʀetist(ə)] *nm/f* librettist.

Libye [libi] *nf*: **la ~** Libya.

libyen, ne [libjɛ̃, -ɛn] *adj* Libyan ♦ *nm/f*: **L~, ne** Libyan.

lice [lis] *nf*: **entrer en ~** (*fig*) to enter the lists.

licence [lisɑ̃s] *nf* (*permis*) permit; (*diplôme*) (first) degree; (*liberté*) liberty; (*poétique, orthographique*) licence (*BRIT*), license (*US*); (*des mœurs*) licentiousness; **~ ès lettres/en droit** arts/law degree.

After gaining their **DEUG**, *French university students take their* **licence** *after a third year of study. It is roughly equivalent to a Bachelor's Degree in Britain.*

licencié, e [lisɑ̃sje] *nm/f* (*SCOL*): **~ ès lettres/en droit** ≈ Bachelor of Arts/Law, arts/law graduate; (*SPORT*) permit-holder.

licenciement [lisɑ̃simɑ̃] *nm* dismissal; redundancy; laying off *no pl*.

licencier [lisɑ̃sje] *vt* (*renvoyer*) to dismiss; (*débaucher*) to make redundant; to lay off.

licencieux, euse [lisɑ̃sjø, -øz] *adj* licentious.

lichen [likɛn] *nm* lichen.

licite [lisit] *adj* lawful.

licorne [likɔʀn(ə)] *nf* unicorn.

licou [liku] *nm* halter.

lie [li] *nf* dregs *pl*, sediment.

lié, e [lje] *adj*: **très ~ avec** (*fig*) very friendly with *ou* close to; **~ par** (*serment, promesse*) bound by; **avoir partie ~e (avec qn)** to be involved (with sb).

Liechtenstein [liʃtɛnʃtajn] *nm*: **le ~** Liechtenstein.

lie-de-vin [lidvɛ̃] *adj inv* wine(-coloured).

liège [ljɛʒ] *nm* cork.

liégeois, e [ljeʒwa, -waz] *adj* of *ou* from Liège ♦ *nm/f*: **L~, e** inhabitant *ou* native of Liège; **café/chocolat ~** coffee/chocolate ice cream topped with whipped cream.

lien [ljɛ̃] *nm* (*corde, fig: affectif, culturel*) bond; (*rapport*) link, connection; (*analogie*) link; **~ de parenté** family tie.

lier [lje] *vt* (*attacher*) to tie up; (*joindre*) to link up; (*fig: unir, engager*) to bind; (*CULIN*) to thicken; **~ qch à** (*attacher*) to tie sth to; (*associer*) to link sth to; **~ amitié/ conversation (avec)** to strike up a friendship/

conversation (with); **se ~ avec** to make friends with.

lierre [ljɛʀ] *nm* ivy.

liesse [ljɛs] *nf*: **être en ~** to be jubilant.

lieu, x [ljø] *nm* place; **~x** *nmpl* (*locaux*) premises; (*endroit: d'un accident etc*) scene *sg*; **en ~ sûr** in a safe place; **en haut ~** in high places; **vider** *ou* **quitter les ~x** to leave the premises; **arriver/être sur les ~x** to arrive/be on the scene; **en premier ~** in the first place; **en dernier ~** lastly; **avoir ~** to take place; **avoir ~ de faire** to have grounds *ou* good reason for doing; **tenir ~ de** to take the place of; (*servir de*) to serve as; **donner ~ à** to give rise to, give cause for; **au ~ de** instead of; **au ~ qu'il y aille** instead of him going; **~ commun** commonplace; **~ géométrique** locus; **~ de naissance** place of birth; **~ de rendez-vous** venue, meeting place.

lieu-dit, *pl* **lieux-dits** [ljødi] *nm* locality.

lieue [ljø] *nf* league.

lieutenant [ljøtnɑ̃] *nm* lieutenant; **~ de vaisseau** (*NAVIG*) lieutenant.

lieutenant-colonel, *pl* **lieutenants-colonels** [ljøtnɑ̃kɔlɔnɛl] *nm* (*armée de terre*) lieutenant colonel; (*armée de l'air*) wing commander (*BRIT*), lieutenant colonel (*US*).

lièvre [ljɛvʀ(ə)] *nm* hare; (*coureur*) pacemaker; **lever un ~** (*fig*) to bring up a prickly subject.

liftier, ière [liftje, -jɛʀ] lift (*BRIT*) *ou* elevator (*US*) attendant.

lifting [liftiŋ] *nm* face lift.

ligament [ligamɑ̃] *nm* ligament.

ligature [ligatyʀ] *nf* ligature.

lige [liʒ] *adj*: **homme ~** (*péj*) henchman.

ligne [liɲ] *nf* (*gén*) line; (*TRANSPORTS: liaison*) service; (: *trajet*) route; (*silhouette*): **garder la ~** to keep one's figure; **en ~** (*INFORM*) on line; **en ~ droite** as the crow flies; **"à la ~"** "new paragraph"; **entrer en ~ de compte** to be taken into account; to come into it; **~ de but/médiane** goal/halfway line; **~ d'arrivée/ de départ** finishing/starting line; **~ de conduite** course of action; **~ directrice** guiding line; **~ d'horizon** skyline; **~ de mire** line of sight; **~ de touche** touchline.

ligné, e [liɲe] *adj*: **papier ~** ruled paper ♦ *nf* (*race, famille*) line, lineage; (*postérité*) descendants *pl*.

ligneux, euse [liɲø, -øz] *adj* ligneous, woody.

lignite [liɲit] *nm* lignite.

ligoter [ligɔte] *vt* to tie up.

ligue [lig] *nf* league.

liguer [lige]: **se ~** *vi* to form a league; **se ~ contre** (*fig*) to combine against.

lilas [lila] *nm* lilac.

lillois, e [lilwa, -waz] *adj* of *ou* from Lille.

Lima [lima] *n* Lima.

limace [limas] *nf* slug.

limaille [limaj] *nf*: **~ de fer** iron filings *pl*.

limande [limɑ̃d] *nf* dab.

limande-sole [limãdsɔl] *nf* lemon sole.

limbes [lɛ̃b] *nmpl* limbo *sg*; **être dans les ~** (*fig: projet etc*) to be up in the air.

lime [lim] *nf* (*TECH*) file; (*BOT*) lime; **~ à ongles** nail file.

limer [lime] *vt* (*bois, métal*) to file (down); (*ongles*) to file; (*fig: prix*) to pare down.

limier [limje] *nm* (*ZOOL*) bloodhound; (*détective*) sleuth.

liminaire [liminɛʀ] *adj* (*propos*) introductory.

limitatif, ive [limitatif, -iv] *adj* restrictive.

limitation [limitasjɔ̃] *nf* limitation, restriction; **sans ~ de temps** with no time limit; **~ des naissances** birth control; **~ de vitesse** speed limit.

limite [limit] *nf* (*de terrain*) boundary; (*partie ou point extrême*) limit; **dans la ~ de** within the limits of; **à la ~** (*au pire*) if the worst comes (*ou* came) to the worst; **sans ~s** (*bêtise, richesse, pouvoir*) limitless, boundless; **vitesse/charge ~** maximum speed/load; **cas ~** borderline case; **date ~** deadline; **date ~ de vente/consommation** sell-by/best-before date; **prix ~** upper price limit; **~ d'âge** maximum age, age limit.

limiter [limite] *vt* (*restreindre*) to limit, restrict; (*délimiter*) to border, form the boundary of; **se ~ (à qch/à faire)** (*personne*) to limit *ou* confine o.s. (to sth/to doing sth); **se ~ à** (*chose*) to be limited to.

limitrophe [limitʀɔf] *adj* border *cpd*; **~ de** bordering on.

limogeage [limɔʒaʒ] *nm* dismissal.

limoger [limɔʒe] *vt* to dismiss.

limon [limɔ̃] *nm* silt.

limonade [limɔnad] *nf* lemonade (*BRIT*), (lemon) soda (*US*).

limonadier, ière [limɔnadje, -jɛʀ] *nm/f* (*commerçant*) café owner; (*fabricant de limonade*) soft drinks manufacturer.

limoneux, euse [limɔnø, -øz] *adj* muddy.

limousin, e [limuzɛ̃, -in] *adj* of *ou* from Limousin ♦ *nm* (*région*): **le L~** the Limousin ♦ *nf* limousine.

limpide [lɛ̃pid] *adj* limpid.

lin [lɛ̃] *nm* (*BOT*) flax; (*tissu, toile*) linen.

linceul [lɛ̃sœl] *nm* shroud.

linéaire [lineɛʀ] *adj* linear ♦ *nm*: **~ (de vente)** shelves *pl*.

linéament [lineamɑ̃] *nm* outline.

linge [lɛ̃ʒ] *nm* (*serviettes etc*) linen; (*pièce de tissu*) cloth; (*aussi*: **~ de corps**) underwear; (*aussi*: **~ de toilette**) towel; (*lessive*) washing; **~ sale** dirty linen.

lingère [lɛ̃ʒɛʀ] *nf* linen maid.

lingerie [lɛ̃ʒʀi] *nf* lingerie, underwear.

lingot [lɛ̃go] *nm* ingot.

linguiste [lɛ̃ɡɥist(ə)] *nm/f* linguist.

linguistique [lɛ̃ɡɥistik] *adj* linguistic ♦ *nf* linguistics *sg*.

lino(léum) [lino(leɔm)] *nm* lino(leum).

linotte [linɔt] *nf*: **tête de ~** bird brain.

linteau, x [lɛ̃to] *nm* lintel.

lion, ne [ljɔ̃, ljɔn] *nm/f* lion/lioness; (*signe*): **le L~** Leo, the Lion; **être du L~** to be Leo; **~ de mer** sealion.

lionceau, x [ljɔ̃so] *nm* lion cub.

liposuccion [liposyksjɔ̃] *nf* liposuction.

lippu, e [lipy] *adj* thick-lipped.

liquéfier [likefje] *vt* to liquefy; **se ~** *vi* (*gaz etc*) to liquefy; (*fig: personne*) to succumb.

liqueur [likœʀ] *nf* liqueur.

liquidateur, trice [likidatœʀ, -tʀis] *nm/f* (*JUR*) receiver; **~ judiciaire** official liquidator.

liquidation [likidasjɔ̃] *nf* liquidation; (*COMM*) clearance (sale); **~ judiciaire** compulsory liquidation.

liquide [likid] *adj* liquid ♦ *nm* liquid; (*COMM*): **en ~** in ready money *ou* cash.

liquider [likide] *vt* (*société, biens, témoin gênant*) to liquidate; (*compte, problème*) to settle; (*COMM: articles*) to clear, sell off.

liquidités [likidite] *nfpl* (*COMM*) liquid assets.

liquoreux, euse [likɔʀø, -øz] *adj* syrupy.

lire [liʀ] *nf* (*monnaie*) lira ♦ *vt, vi* to read; **~ qch à qn** to read sth (out) to sb.

lis *vb* [li] *voir* **lire** ♦ *nm* [lis] = **lys**.

lisais [lizɛ] *etc vb voir* **lire**.

Lisbonne [lizbɔn] *n* Lisbon.

lise [liz] *etc vb voir* **lire**.

liseré [lizʀe] *nm* border, edging.

liseron [lizʀɔ̃] *nm* bindweed.

liseuse [lizøz] *nf* book-cover; (*veste*) bedjacket.

lisible [lizibl(ə)] *adj* legible; (*digne d'être lu*) readable.

lisiblement [lizibləmɑ̃] *adv* legibly.

lisière [lizjɛʀ] *nf* (*de forêt*) edge; (*de tissu*) selvage.

lisons [lizɔ̃] *vb voir* **lire**.

lisse [lis] *adj* smooth.

lisser [lise] *vt* to smooth.

listage [listaʒ] *nm* (*INFORM*) listing.

liste [list(ə)] *nf* list; (*INFORM*) listing; **faire la ~ de** to list, make out a list of; **~ d'attente** waiting list; **~ civile** civil list; **~ électorale** electoral roll; **~ de mariage** wedding (present) list; **~ noire** hit list.

lister [liste] *vt* (*aussi INFORM*) to list; **~ la mémoire** to dump.

listéria [listeʀja] *nf* listeria.

listing [listiŋ] *nm* (*INFORM*) listing; **qualité ~** draft quality.

lit [li] *nm* (*gén*) bed; **faire son ~** to make one's bed; **aller/se mettre au ~** to go to/get into bed; **prendre le ~** to take to one's bed; **d'un premier ~** (*JUR*) of a first marriage; **~ de camp** campbed (*BRIT*), cot (*US*); **~ d'enfant** cot (*BRIT*), crib (*US*).

litanie [litani] *nf* litany.

lit-cage, *pl* **lits-cages** [likaʒ] *nm* folding bed.

litchi [litʃi] *nm* lychee.

literie [litʀi] *nf* bedding; (*linge*) bedding, bedclothes *pl*.

litho [lito], **lithographie** [litɔɡʀafi] *nf*

litho(graphy); (*épreuve*) litho(graph).
litière [litjɛʀ] *nf* litter.
litige [litiʒ] *nm* dispute; **en** ~ in contention.
litigieux, euse [litiʒjø, -øz] *adj* litigious, contentious.
litote [litɔt] *nf* understatement.
litre [litʀ(ə)] *nm* litre; (*récipient*) litre measure.
littéraire [liteʀɛʀ] *adj* literary.
littéral, e, aux [liteʀal, -o] *adj* literal.
littéralement [liteʀalmɑ̃] *adv* literally.
littérature [liteʀatyʀ] *nf* literature.
littoral, e, aux [litɔʀal, -o] *adj* coastal ♦ *nm* coast.
Lituanie [lityani] *nf*: **la** ~ Lithuania.
lituanien, ne [lityanjɛ̃, -ɛn] *adj* Lithuanian ♦ *nm* (*LING*) Lithuanian ♦ *nm/f*: **L~, ne** Lithuanian.
liturgie [lityʀʒi] *nf* liturgy.
liturgique [lityʀʒik] *adj* liturgical.
livide [livid] *adj* livid, pallid.
living(-room) [liviŋ(ʀum)] *nm* living room.
livrable [livʀabl(ə)] *adj* (*COMM*) that can be delivered.
livraison [livʀɛzɔ̃] *nf* delivery; ~ **à domicile** home delivery (service).
livre [livʀ(ə)] *nm* book; (*imprimerie etc*): **le** ~ the book industry ♦ *nf* (*poids, monnaie*) pound; **traduire qch à** ~ **ouvert** to translate sth off the cuff *ou* at sight; ~ **blanc** official report (*prepared by independent body, following war, natural disaster etc*); ~ **de bord** (*NAVIG*) logbook; ~ **de comptes** account(s) book; ~ **de cuisine** cookery book (*BRIT*), cookbook; ~ **de messe** mass *ou* prayer book; ~ **d'or** visitors' book; ~ **de poche** paperback (*cheap and pocket size*); ~ **verte** green pound.
livré, e [livʀe] *nf* livery ♦ *adj*: ~ **à** (*l'anarchie etc*) given over to; ~ **à soi-même** left to oneself *ou* one's own devices.
livrer [livʀe] *vt* (*COMM*) to deliver; (*otage, coupable*) to hand over; (*secret, information*) to give away; **se** ~ **à** (*se confier*) to confide in; (*se rendre*) to give o.s. up to; (*s'abandonner à: débauche etc*) to give o.s. up *ou* over to; (*faire: pratiques, actes*) to indulge in; (*travail*) to be engaged in, engage in; (*: sport*) to practise; (*: enquête*) to carry out; ~ **bataille** to give battle.
livresque [livʀɛsk(ə)] *adj* (*péj*) bookish.
livret [livʀɛ] *nm* booklet; (*d'opéra*) libretto (*pl* -s); ~ **de caisse d'épargne** (savings) bankbook; ~ **de famille** (official) family record book; ~ **scolaire** (school) report book.
livreur, euse [livʀœʀ, -øz] *nm/f* delivery boy *ou* man/girl *ou* woman.
LO *sigle f* (= Lutte ouvrière) political party.
lob [lɔb] *nm* lob.
lobe [lɔb] *nm*: ~ **de l'oreille** ear lobe.
lobé, e [lɔbe] *adj* (*ARCHIT*) foiled.
lober [lɔbe] *vt* to lob.
local, e, aux [lɔkal, -o] *adj* local ♦ *nm* (*salle*) premises *pl* ♦ *nmpl* premises.

localement [lɔkalmɑ̃] *adv* locally.
localisé, e [lɔkalize] *adj* localized.
localiser [lɔkalize] *vt* (*repérer*) to locate, place; (*limiter*) to localize, confine.
localité [lɔkalite] *nf* locality.
locataire [lɔkatɛʀ] *nm/f* tenant; (*de chambre*) lodger.
locatif, ive [lɔkatif, -iv] *adj* (*charges, réparations*) incumbent upon the tenant; (*valeur*) rental; (*immeuble*) with rented flats, used as a letting *ou* rental (*US*) concern.
location [lɔkasjɔ̃] *nf* (*par le locataire*) renting; (*par l'usager: de voiture etc*) hiring (*BRIT*), renting (*US*); (*par le propriétaire*) renting out, letting; hiring out (*BRIT*); (*de billets, places*) booking; (*bureau*) booking office; "~ **de voitures**" "car hire (*BRIT*) *ou* rental (*US*)".
location-vente [lɔkasjɔ̃vɑ̃t] *nf* form of hire purchase (*BRIT*) *ou* instalment plan (*US*).
lock-out [lɔkawt] *nm inv* lockout.
locomoteur, trice [lɔkɔmɔtœʀ, -tʀis] *adj, nf* locomotive.
locomotion [lɔkɔmosjɔ̃] *nf* locomotion.
locomotive [lɔkɔmɔtiv] *nf* locomotive, engine; (*fig*) pacesetter, pacemaker.
locuteur, trice [lɔkytœʀ, -tʀis] *nm/f* (*LING*) speaker.
locution [lɔkysjɔ̃] *nf* phrase.
loden [lɔdɛn] *nm* loden.
lofer [lɔfe] *vi* (*NAVIG*) to luff.
logarithme [lɔgaʀitm(ə)] *nm* logarithm.
loge [lɔʒ] *nf* (*THÉÂT: d'artiste*) dressing room; (*: de spectateurs*) box; (*de concierge, franc-maçon*) lodge.
logeable [lɔʒabl(ə)] *adj* habitable; (*spacieux*) roomy.
logement [lɔʒmɑ̃] *nm* flat (*BRIT*), apartment (*US*); accommodation *no pl* (*BRIT*), accommodations *pl* (*US*); **le** ~ housing; **chercher un** ~ to look for a flat *ou* apartment, look for accommodation(s); **construire des** ~**s bon marché** to build cheap housing *sg*; **crise du** ~ housing shortage; ~ **de fonction** (*ADMIN*) company flat *ou* apartment, accommodation(s) provided with one's job.
loger [lɔʒe] *vt* to accommodate ♦ *vi* to live; **se** ~: **trouver à se** ~ to find accommodation; **se** ~ **dans** (*suj: balle, flèche*) to lodge itself in.
logeur, euse [lɔʒœʀ, -øz] *nm/f* landlord/landlady.
loggia [lɔdʒja] *nf* loggia.
logiciel [lɔʒisjɛl] *nm* software.
logicien, ne [lɔʒisjɛ̃, -ɛn] *nm/f* logician.
logique [lɔʒik] *adj* logical ♦ *nf* logic; **c'est** ~ it stands to reason.
logiquement [lɔʒikmɑ̃] *adv* logically.
logis [lɔʒi] *nm* home; abode, dwelling.
logisticien, ne [lɔʒistisjɛ̃, -ɛn] *nm/f* logistician.
logistique [lɔʒistik] *nf* logistics *sg* ♦ *adj* logistic.
logo [lɔgo], **logotype** [lɔgotip] *nm* logo.
loi [lwa] *nf* law; **faire la** ~ to lay down the law;

les ~s de la mode (*fig*) the dictates of fashion; **proposition de** ~ (private member's) bill; **projet de** ~ (government) bill.

loi-cadre, *pl* **lois-cadres** [lwakadʀ(ə)] *nf* (*POL*) blueprint law.

loin [lwɛ̃] *adv* far; (*dans le temps: futur*) a long way off; (: *passé*) a long time ago; **plus** ~ further; **moins** ~ (**que**) not as far (as); ~ **de** far from; **pas** ~ **de 1 000 F** not far off 1000 F; **au** ~ far off; **de** ~ *adv* from a distance; (*fig: de beaucoup*) by far; **il vient de** ~ he's come a long way; he comes from a long way away; **de** ~ **en** ~ here and there; (*de temps en temps*) (every) now and then; ~ **de là** (*au contraire*) far from it.

lointain, e [lwɛ̃tɛ̃, -ɛn] *adj* faraway, distant; (*dans le futur, passé*) distant, far-off; (*cause, parent*) remote, distant ♦ *nm:* **dans le** ~ in the distance.

loi-programme, *pl* **lois-programmes** [lwapʀɔgʀam] *nf* (*POL*) act providing framework for government programme.

loir [lwaʀ] *nm* dormouse (*pl* -mice).

Loire [lwaʀ] *nf:* **la** ~ the Loire.

loisible [lwazibl(ə)] *adj:* **il vous est** ~ **de ...** you are free to ....

loisir [lwaziʀ] *nm:* **heures de** ~ spare time; ~**s** *nmpl* leisure *sg;* (*activités*) leisure activities; **avoir le** ~ **de faire** to have the time *ou* opportunity to do; (**tout**) **à** ~ (*en prenant son temps*) at leisure; (*autant qu'on le désire*) at one's pleasure.

lombaire [lɔ̃bɛʀ] *adj* lumbar.

lombalgie [lɔ̃balʒi] *nf* back pain.

lombard, e [lɔ̃baʀ, -aʀd(ə)] *adj* Lombard.

Lombardie [lɔ̃baʀdi] *nf:* **la** ~ Lombardy.

londonien, ne [lɔ̃dɔnjɛ̃, -ɛn] *adj* London *cpd*, of London ♦ *nm/f:* **L~, ne** Londoner.

Londres [lɔ̃dʀ(ə)] *n* London.

long, longue [lɔ̃, lɔ̃g] *adj* long ♦ *adv:* **en savoir** ~ to know a great deal ♦ *nm:* **de 3 m de** ~ 3 m long, 3 m in length ♦ *nf:* **à la longue** in the end; **faire** ~ **feu** to fizzle out; **ne pas faire** ~ **feu** not to last long; **au** ~ **cours** (*NAVIG*) ocean *cpd*, ocean-going; **de longue date** *adj* long-standing; **longue durée** *adj* long-term; **de longue haleine** *adj* long-term; **être** ~ **à faire** to take a long time to do; **en** ~ *adv* lengthwise, lengthways; (**tout**) **le** ~ **de** (all) along; **tout au** ~ **de** (*année, vie*) throughout; **de** ~ **en large** (*marcher*) to and fro, up and down; **en** ~ **et en large** (*fig*) in every detail.

longanimité [lɔ̃ganimite] *nf* forbearance.

long-courrier [lɔ̃kuʀje] *nm* (*AVIAT*) long-haul aircraft.

longe [lɔ̃ʒ] *nf* (*corde: pour attacher*) tether; (*pour mener*) lead; (*CULIN*) loin.

longer [lɔ̃ʒe] *vt* to go (*ou* walk *ou* drive) along(side); (*suj: mur, route*) to border.

longévité [lɔ̃ʒevite] *nf* longevity.

longiligne [lɔ̃ʒiliɲ] *adj* long-limbed.

longitude [lɔ̃ʒityd] *nf* longitude; **à 45° de** ~ **ouest** at 45° longitude west.

longitudinal, e, aux [lɔ̃ʒitydinal, -o] *adj* longitudinal, lengthways; (*entaille, vallée*) running lengthways.

longtemps [lɔ̃tɑ̃] *adv* (for) a long time, (for) long; **ça ne va pas durer** ~ it won't last long; **avant** ~ before long; **pour/pendant** ~ for a long time; **je n'en ai pas pour** ~ I shan't be long; **mettre** ~ **à faire** to take a long time to do; **il en a pour** ~ he'll be a long time; **il y a** ~ **que je travaille** I have been working (for) a long time; **il n'y a pas** ~ **que je l'ai rencontré** it's not long since I met him.

longue [lɔ̃g] *adj f voir* **long.**

longuement [lɔ̃gmɑ̃] *adv* (*longtemps: parler, regarder*) for a long time; (*en détail: expliquer, raconter*) at length.

longueur [lɔ̃gœʀ] *nf* length; ~**s** *nfpl* (*fig: d'un film etc*) tedious parts; **sur une** ~ **de 10 km** for *ou* over 10 km; **en** ~ *adv* lengthwise, lengthways; **tirer en** ~ to drag on; **à** ~ **de journée** all day long; **d'une** ~ (*gagner*) by a length; ~ **d'onde** wavelength.

longue-vue [lɔ̃gvy] *nf* telescope.

looping [lupiŋ] *nm* (*AVIAT*): **faire des** ~**s** to loop the loop.

lopin [lɔpɛ̃] *nm:* ~ **de terre** patch of land.

loquace [lɔkas] *adj* talkative, loquacious.

loque [lɔk] *nf* (*personne*) wreck; ~**s** *nfpl* (*habits*) rags; **être** *ou* **tomber en** ~**s** to be in rags.

loquet [lɔkɛ] *nm* latch.

lorgner [lɔʀɲe] *vt* to eye; (*convoiter*) to have one's eye on.

lorgnette [lɔʀɲɛt] *nf* opera glasses *pl*.

lorgnon [lɔʀɲɔ̃] *nm* (*face-à-main*) lorgnette; (*pince-nez*) pince-nez.

loriot [lɔʀjo] *nm* (golden) oriole.

lorrain, e [lɔʀɛ̃, -ɛn] *adj* of *ou* from Lorraine; **quiche** ~**e** quiche lorraine.

lors [lɔʀ]: ~ **de** *prép* (*au moment de*) at the time of; (*pendant*) during; ~ **même que** even though.

lorsque [lɔʀsk(ə)] *conj* when, as.

losange [lɔzɑ̃ʒ] *nm* diamond; (*GÉOM*) lozenge; **en** ~ diamond-shaped.

lot [lo] *nm* (*part*) share; (*de loterie*) prize; (*fig: destin*) fate, lot; (*COMM, INFORM*) batch; ~ **de consolation** consolation prize.

loterie [lɔtʀi] *nf* lottery; (*tombola*) raffle; **L~ nationale** (*formerly*) French national lottery.

loti, e [lɔti] *adj:* **bien/mal** ~ well-/badly off, lucky/unlucky.

lotion [losjɔ̃] *nf* lotion; ~ **après rasage** aftershave (lotion); ~ **capillaire** hair lotion.

lotir [lɔtiʀ] *vt* (*terrain: diviser*) to divide into plots; (: *vendre*) to sell by lots.

lotissement [lɔtismɑ̃] *nm* (*groupe de maisons, d'immeubles*) housing development; (*parcelle*) (building) plot, lot.

loto [lɔto] *nm* lotto.

Le **Loto** *is a state-run national lottery with large cash prizes. Participants select 7 numbers out of 49. There is a sliding scale of winnings: all 7 numbers correct wins the top prize, 6 correct wins a smaller sum and so on. The draw is televised twice weekly.*

lotte [lɔt] *nf* (*ZOOL: de rivière*) burbot; (*: de mer*) monkfish.

louable [lwabl(ə)] *adj* (*appartement, garage*) rentable; (*action, personne*) praiseworthy, commendable.

louage [lwaʒ] *nm*: **voiture de** ~ hired (*BRIT*) *ou* rented (*US*) car; (*à louer*) hire (*BRIT*) *ou* rental (*US*) car.

louange [lwɑ̃ʒ] *nf*: **à la** ~ **de** in praise of; ~**s** *nfpl* praise *sg*.

loubar(d) [lubaʀ] *nm* (*fam*) lout.

louche [luʃ] *adj* shady, fishy, dubious ♦ *nf* ladle.

loucher [luʃe] *vi* to squint; (*fig*): ~ **sur** to have one's (beady) eye on.

louer [lwe] *vt* (*maison: suj: propriétaire*) to let, rent (*out*); (*: locataire*) to rent; (*voiture etc*) to hire out (*BRIT*), rent (*out*); to hire (*BRIT*), rent; (*réserver*) to book; (*faire l'éloge de*) to praise; **"à** ~**"** "to let" (*BRIT*), "for rent" (*US*); ~ **qn de** to praise sb for; **se** ~ **de** to congratulate o.s. on.

loufoque [lufɔk] *adj* (*fam*) crazy, zany.

loukoum [lukum] *nm* Turkish delight.

loulou [lulu] *nm* (*chien*) spitz; ~ **de Poméranie** Pomeranian (dog).

loup [lu] *nm* wolf (*pl* wolves); (*poisson*) bass; (*masque*) (eye) mask; **jeune** ~ young go-getter; ~ **de mer** (*marin*) old seadog.

loupe [lup] *nf* magnifying glass; ~ **de noyer** burr walnut; **à la** ~ (*fig*) in minute detail.

louper [lupe] *vt* (*fam: manquer*) to miss; (*: gâcher*) to mess up, bungle.

lourd, e [luʀ, luʀd(ə)] *adj* heavy; (*chaleur, temps*) sultry; (*fig: personne, style*) heavy-handed ♦ *adv*: **peser** ~ to be heavy; ~ **de** (*menaces*) charged with; (*conséquences*) fraught with; **artillerie/industrie** ~**e** heavy artillery/industry.

lourdaud, e [luʀdo, -od] *adj* oafish.

lourdement [luʀdəmɑ̃] *adv* heavily; **se tromper** ~ to make a big mistake.

lourdeur [luʀdœʀ] *nf* heaviness; ~ **d'estomac** indigestion *no pl*.

loustic [lustik] *nm* (*fam péj*) joker.

loutre [lutʀ(ə)] *nf* otter; (*fourrure*) otter skin.

louve [luv] *nf* she-wolf.

louveteau, x [luvto] *nm* (*ZOOL*) wolf-cub; (*scout*) cub (scout).

louvoyer [luvwaje] *vi* (*NAVIG*) to tack; (*fig*) to hedge, evade the issue.

lover [lɔve]: **se** ~ *vi* to coil up.

loyal, e, aux [lwajal, -o] *adj* (*fidèle*) loyal, faithful; (*fair-play*) fair.

loyalement [lwajalmɑ̃] *adv* loyally, faithfully; fairly.

loyalisme [lwajalism(ə)] *nm* loyalty.

loyauté [lwajote] *nf* loyalty, faithfulness; fairness.

loyer [lwaje] *nm* rent; ~ **de l'argent** interest rate.

LP *sigle m* (= *lycée professionnel*) *secondary school for vocational training.*

LPO *sigle f* (= *Ligue pour la protection des oiseaux*) *bird protection society.*

LSD *sigle m* (= *Lyserg Säure Diäthylamid*) LSD.

lu, e [ly] *pp de* **lire.**

lubie [lybi] *nf* whim, craze.

lubricité [lybʀisite] *nf* lust.

lubrifiant [lybʀifjɑ̃] *nm* lubricant.

lubrifier [lybʀifje] *vt* to lubricate.

lubrique [lybʀik] *adj* lecherous.

lucarne [lykaʀn(ə)] *nf* skylight.

lucide [lysid] *adj* (*conscient*) lucid, conscious; (*perspicace*) clear-headed.

lucidité [lysidite] *nf* lucidity.

luciole [lysjɔl] *nf* firefly.

lucratif, ive [lykʀatif, -iv] *adj* lucrative; profitable; **à but non** ~ non profit-making.

ludique [lydik] *adj* play *cpd*, playing.

ludothèque [lydɔtɛk] *nf* toy library.

luette [lɥɛt] *nf* uvula.

lueur [lɥœʀ] *nf* (*chatoyante*) glimmer *no pl*; (*métallique, mouillée*) gleam *no pl*; (*rougeoyante, chaude*) glow *no pl*; (*pâle*) (faint) light; (*fig*) spark; (*: d'espérance*) glimmer, gleam.

luge [lyʒ] *nf* sledge (*BRIT*), sled (*US*); **faire de la** ~ to sledge (*BRIT*), sled (*US*), toboggan.

lugubre [lygybʀ(ə)] *adj* gloomy; dismal.

━━━━━━━━━━━━━━━━━━━━━━━ *MOT-CLÉ*

lui [lɥi] *pp de* **luire**
♦ *pron* **1** (*objet indirect: mâle*) (to) him; (*: femelle*) (to) her; (*: chose, animal*) (to) it; **je** ~ **ai parlé** I have spoken to him (*ou* to her); **il** ~ **a offert un cadeau** he gave him (*ou* her) a present; **je le** ~ **ai donné** I gave it to him (*ou* her)

2 (*après préposition, comparatif: personne*) him; (*: chose, animal*) it; **elle est contente de** ~ she is pleased with him; **je la connais mieux que** ~ I know her better than he does; I know her better than him; **cette voiture est à** ~ this car belongs to him, this is HIS car

3 (*sujet, forme emphatique*) he; ~**, il est à Paris** HE is in Paris; **c'est** ~ **qui l'a fait** HE did it.

━━━━━━━━━━━━━━━━━━━━━━━

lui-même [lɥimɛm] *pron* (*personne*) himself; (*chose*) itself.

luire [lɥiʀ] *vi* (*gén*) to shine, gleam; (*surface mouillée*) to glisten; (*reflets chauds, cuivrés*) to glow.

luisant, e [lɥizɑ̃, -ɑ̃t] *vb voir* **luire** ♦ *adj* shining, gleaming.

lumbago [lɔ̃bago] *nm* lumbago.

lumière [lymjɛʀ] *nf* light; **~s** *nfpl* (*d'une personne*) knowledge *sg*, wisdom *sg*; **à la ~ de** by the light of; (*fig: événements*) in the light of; **fais de la ~** let's have some light, give us some light; **faire (toute) la ~ sur** (*fig*) to clarify (completely); **mettre en ~** (*fig*) to highlight; **~ du jour/soleil** day/sunlight.

luminaire [lyminɛʀ] *nm* lamp, light.

lumineux, euse [lyminø, -øz] *adj* (*émettant de la lumière*) luminous; (*éclairé*) illuminated; (*ciel, journée, couleur*) bright; (*relatif à la lumière: rayon etc*) of light, light *cpd*; (*fig: regard*) radiant.

luminosité [lyminozite] *nf* (*TECH*) luminosity.

lump [lœp] *nm*: **œufs de ~** lump-fish roe.

lunaire [lynɛʀ] *adj* lunar, moon *cpd*.

lunatique [lynatik] *adj* whimsical, temperamental.

lunch [lœntʃ] *nm* (*réception*) buffet lunch.

lundi [lœdi] *nm* Monday; **on est ~** it's Monday; **le ~ 20 août** Monday 20th August; **il est venu ~** he came on Monday; **le(s) ~(s)** on Mondays; **à ~!** see you (on) Monday!; **~ de Pâques** Easter Monday; **~ de Pentecôte** Whit Monday (*BRIT*).

lune [lyn] *nf* moon; **pleine/nouvelle ~** full/new moon; **être dans la ~** (*distrait*) to have one's head in the clouds; **~ de miel** honeymoon.

luné, e [lyne] *adj*: **bien/mal ~** in a good/bad mood.

lunette [lynɛt] *nf*: **~s** *nfpl* glasses, spectacles; (*protectrices*) goggles; **~ d'approche** telescope; **~ arrière** (*AUTO*) rear window; **~s noires** dark glasses; **~s de soleil** sunglasses.

lurent [lyʀ] *vb voir* **lire.**

lurette [lyʀɛt] *nf*: **il y a belle ~** ages ago.

luron, ne [lyʀɔ̃, -ɔn] *nm/f* lad/lass; **joyeux** *ou* **gai ~** gay dog.

lus [ly] *etc vb voir* **lire.**

lustre [lystʀ(ə)] *nm* (*de plafond*) chandelier; (*fig: éclat*) lustre.

lustrer [lystʀe] *vt*: **~ qch** (*faire briller*) to make sth shine; (*user*) to make sth shiny.

lut [ly] *vb voir* **lire.**

luth [lyt] *nm* lute.

luthier [lytje] *nm* (stringed-)instrument maker.

lutin [lytɛ̃] *nm* imp, goblin.

lutrin [lytʀɛ̃] *nm* lectern.

lutte [lyt] *nf* (*conflit*) struggle; (*SPORT*): **la ~** wrestling; **de haute ~** after a hard-fought struggle; **~ des classes** class struggle; **~ libre** (*SPORT*) all-in wrestling.

lutter [lyte] *vi* to fight, struggle; (*SPORT*) to wrestle.

lutteur, euse [lytœʀ, -øz] *nm/f* (*SPORT*) wrestler; (*fig*) battler, fighter.

luxation [lyksasjɔ̃] *nf* dislocation.

luxe [lyks(ə)] *nm* luxury; **un ~ de** (*détails, précautions*) a wealth of; **de ~** *adj* luxury *cpd*.

Luxembourg [lyksɑ̃buʀ] *nm*: **le ~** Luxembourg.

luxembourgeois, e [lyksɑ̃buʀʒwa, -waz] *adj* of *ou* from Luxembourg ♦ *nm/f*: **L~, e** inhabitant *ou* native of Luxembourg.

luxer [lykse] *vt*: **se ~ l'épaule** to dislocate one's shoulder.

luxueusement [lyksɥøzmɑ̃] *adv* luxuriously.

luxueux, euse [lyksɥø, -øz] *adj* luxurious.

luxure [lyksyʀ] *nf* lust.

luxuriant, e [lyksyʀjɑ̃, -ɑ̃t] *adj* luxuriant, lush.

luzerne [lyzɛʀn(ə)] *nf* lucerne, alfalfa.

lycée [lise] *nm* (state) secondary (*BRIT*) *ou* high (*US*) school; **~ technique** technical secondary *ou* high school.

French pupils spend the last three years of their secondary education at a **lycée**, *where they sit their* **baccalauréat** *before leaving school or going on to higher education. There are various types of lycée, including the "lycées d'enseignement technologique" providing technical courses and the "lycées d'enseignement professionnel" providing vocational courses. Some lycées, particularly those with a wide catchment area or those providing specialist courses, have boarding facilities; see also* **école maternelle/primaire, collège**.

---

lycéen, ne [liseɛ̃, -ɛn] *nm/f* secondary school pupil.

Lycra [likʀa] *nm* ® Lycra ®.

lymphatique [lɛ̃fatik] *adj* (*fig*) lethargic, sluggish.

lymphe [lɛ̃f] *nf* lymph.

lyncher [lɛ̃ʃe] *vt* to lynch.

lynx [lɛ̃ks] *nm* lynx.

Lyon [ljɔ̃] *n* Lyons.

lyonnais, e [ljɔnɛ, -ɛz] *adj* of *ou* from Lyons; (*CULIN*) Lyonnaise.

lyophilisé, e [ljɔfilize] *adj* freeze-dried.

lyre [liʀ] *nf* lyre.

lyrique [liʀik] *adj* lyrical; (*OPÉRA*) lyric; **artiste ~** opera singer; **comédie ~** comic opera; **théâtre ~** opera house (*for light opera*).

lyrisme [liʀism(ə)] *nm* lyricism.

lys [lis] *nm* lily.

M m

M, m [ɛm] *nm inv* M, m ♦ *abr* = **majeur, masculin, mètre, Monsieur;** (= *million*) M; **M comme Marcel** M for Mike.
m' [m] *pron voir* **me.**
MA *sigle m* = **maître auxiliaire.**
ma [ma] *adj possessif voir* **mon.**
maboul, e [mabul] *adj (fam)* loony.
macabre [makɑbʀ(ə)] *adj* macabre, gruesome.
macadam [makadam] *nm* tarmac (*BRIT*), asphalt.
Macao [makao] *nf* Macao.
macaron [makaʀɔ̃] *nm (gâteau)* macaroon; (*insigne*) (round) badge.
macaroni(s) [makaʀɔni] *nm(pl)* macaroni *sg;* ~ **au fromage** *ou* **au gratin** macaroni cheese (*BRIT*), macaroni and cheese (*US*).
Macédoine [masedwan] *nf* Macedonia.
macédoine [masedwan] *nf:* ~ **de fruits** fruit salad; ~ **de légumes** mixed vegetables *pl.*
macédonien, ne [masedɔnjɛ̃, -ɛn] *adj* Macedonian ♦ *nm/f:* **M~, ne** Macedonian.
macérer [maseʀe] *vi, vt* to macerate; (*dans du vinaigre*) to pickle.
mâchefer [mɑʃfɛʀ] *nm* clinker, cinders *pl.*
mâcher [mɑʃe] *vt* to chew; **ne pas** ~ **ses mots** not to mince one's words; ~ **le travail à qn** (*fig*) to spoonfeed sb, do half sb's work for him.
machiavélique [makjavelik] *adj* Machiavellian.
machin [maʃɛ̃] *nm (fam)* thingamajig, thing; (*personne*): **M~** what's-his(*ou*-her)-name.
machinal, e, aux [maʃinal, -o] *adj* mechanical, automatic.
machination [maʃinasjɔ̃] *nf* scheming, frame-up.
machine [maʃin] *nf* machine; (*locomotive; de navire etc*) engine; (*fig: rouages*) machinery; (*fam: personne*): **M~** what's-her-name; **faire** ~ **arrière** (*NAVIG*) to go astern; (*fig*) to backpedal; ~ **à laver/coudre/tricoter** washing/sewing/knitting machine; ~ **à écrire** typewriter; ~ **à sous** fruit machine; ~ **à vapeur** steam engine.
machine-outil, *pl* **machines-outils** [maʃinuti] *nf* machine tool.
machinerie [maʃinʀi] *nf* machinery, plant; (*d'un navire*) engine room.
machinisme [maʃinism(ə)] *nm* mechanization.
machiniste [maʃinist(ə)] *nm* (*THÉÂT*) scene shifter; (*de bus, métro*) driver.
mâchoire [mɑʃwaʀ] *nf* jaw; ~ **de frein** brake

shoe.
mâchonner [mɑʃɔne] *vt* to chew (at).
mâcon [makɔ̃] *nm* Mâcon wine.
maçon [masɔ̃] *nm* bricklayer; (*constructeur*) builder.
maçonner [masɔne] *vt* (*revêtir*) to face, render (with cement); (*boucher*) to brick up.
maçonnerie [masɔnʀi] *nf* (*murs: de brique*) brickwork; (*: de pierre*) masonry, stonework; (*activité*) bricklaying; building; ~ **de béton** concrete.
maçonnique [masɔnik] *adj* masonic.
macramé [makʀame] *nm* macramé.
macrobiotique [makʀɔbjɔtik] *adj* macrobiotic.
macrocosme [makʀɔkɔsm(ə)] *nm* macrocosm.
macro-économie [makʀɔekɔnɔmi] *nf* macroeconomics *sg.*
macrophotographie [makʀofɔtɔgʀafi] *nf* macrophotography.
maculer [makyle] *vt* to stain; (*TYPO*) to mackle.
Madagascar [madagaskaʀ] *nf* Madagascar.
Madame [madam], *pl* **Mesdames** [medam] *nf:* ~ **X** Mrs X ['mɪsɪz]; **occupez-vous de** ~/ **Monsieur/Mademoiselle** please serve this lady/gentleman/(young) lady; **bonjour** ~/ **Monsieur/Mademoiselle** good morning; (*ton déférent*) good morning Madam/Sir/Madam; (*le nom est connu*) good morning Mrs X/Mr X/Miss X; ~/**Monsieur/Mademoiselle!** (*pour appeler*) excuse me!; (*ton déférent*) Madam/ Sir/Miss!; ~/**Monsieur/Mademoiselle** (*sur lettre*) Dear Madam/Sir/Madam; **chère** ~/ **cher Monsieur/chère Mademoiselle** Dear Mrs X/Mr X/Miss X; ~ **la Directrice** the director; the manageress; the headteacher; **Mesdames** Ladies.
Madeleine [madlɛn]: **îles de la** ~ *nfpl* Magdalen Islands.
madeleine [madlɛn] *nf* madeleine, ≈ sponge finger cake.
Madelinot, e [madlino, -ɔt] *nm/f* inhabitant *ou* native of the Magdalen Islands.
Mademoiselle [madmwazɛl], *pl* **Mesdemoiselles** [medmwazɛl] *nf* Miss; *voir aussi* **Madame.**
Madère [madɛʀ] *nf* Madeira ♦ *nm:* **m~** Madeira (wine).
madone [madɔn] *nf* madonna.
madré, e [madʀe] *adj* crafty, wily.
Madrid [madʀid] *n* Madrid.
madrier [madʀije] *nm* beam.
madrigal, aux [madʀigal, -o] *nm* madrigal.
madrilène [madʀilɛn] *adj* of *ou* from Madrid.
maestria [maɛstʀija] *nf* (*masterly*) skill.
maestro [maɛstʀo] *nm* maestro.
maf(f)ia [mafja] *nf* Maf(f)ia.
magasin [magazɛ̃] *nm* (*boutique*) shop; (*entrepôt*) warehouse; (*d'arme, appareil-photo*) magazine; **en** ~ (*COMM*) in stock; **faire les** ~**s** to go (a)round the shops, do the shops; ~

d'alimentation grocer's shop (*BRIT*), grocery store (*US*).

magasinier [magazinje] *nm* warehouseman.

magazine [magazin] *nm* magazine.

mage [maʒ] *nm*: **les Rois M~s** the Magi, the (Three) Wise Men.

Maghreb [magʀɛb] *nm*: **le ~** the Maghreb, North(-West) Africa.

maghrébin, e [magʀebɛ̃, -in] *adj* of *ou* from the Maghreb ♦ *nm/f*: **M~, e** North African, Maghrebi.

magicien, ne [maʒisjɛ̃, -ɛn] *nm/f* magician.

magie [maʒi] *nf* magic; **~ noire** black magic.

magique [maʒik] *adj* (*occulte*) magic; (*fig*) magical.

magistral, e, aux [maʒistʀal, -o] *adj* (*œuvre, adresse*) masterly; (*ton*) authoritative; (*gifle etc*) sound, resounding; (*ex cathedra*): **enseignement ~** lecturing, lectures *pl*; **cours ~** lecture.

magistrat [maʒistʀa] *nm* magistrate.

magistrature [maʒistʀatyʀ] *nf* magistracy, magistrature; **~ assise** judges *pl*, bench; **~ debout** state prosecutors *pl*.

magma [magma] *nm* (*GÉO*) magma; (*fig*) jumble.

magnanerie [maɲanʀi] *nf* silk farm.

magnanime [maɲanim] *adj* magnanimous.

magnanimité [maɲanimite] *nf* magnanimity.

magnat [magna] *nm* tycoon, magnate; **~ de la presse** press baron.

magner [maɲe]: **se ~** *vi* (*fam*) to get a move on.

magnésie [maɲezi] *nf* magnesia.

magnésium [maɲezjɔm] *nm* magnesium.

magnétique [maɲetik] *adj* magnetic.

magnétiser [maɲetize] *vt* to magnetize; (*fig*) to mesmerize, hypnotize.

magnétiseur, euse [maɲetizœʀ, -øz] *nm/f* hypnotist.

magnétisme [maɲetism(ə)] *nm* magnetism.

magnéto [maɲeto] *nm* (= *magnétocassette*) cassette deck; (= *magnétophone*) tape recorder.

magnétocassette [maɲetokasɛt] *nm* cassette deck.

magnétophone [maɲetofɔn] *nm* tape recorder; **~ à cassettes** cassette recorder.

magnétoscope [maɲetoskɔp] *nm*: **~ (à cassette)** video (recorder).

magnificence [maɲifisɑ̃s] *nf* (*faste*) magnificence, splendour (*BRIT*), splendor (*US*); (*générosité, prodigalité*) munificence, lavishness.

magnifier [maɲifje] *vt* (*glorifier*) to glorify; (*idéaliser*) to idealize.

magnifique [maɲifik] *adj* magnificent.

magnifiquement [maɲifikmɑ̃] *adv* magnificently.

magnolia [maɲɔlja] *nm* magnolia.

magnum [magnɔm] *nm* magnum.

magot [mago] *nm* (*argent*) pile (of money); (*économies*) nest egg.

magouille [maguj] *nf* (*fam*) scheming.

mahométan, e [maɔmetɑ̃, -an] *adj* Mohammedan, Mahometan.

mai [mɛ] *nm* May; *voir aussi* **juillet**.

Le premier mai is a public holiday in France commemorating demonstrations by the unions in the United States in 1886 to secure the eight-hour working day. It is traditional in France to exchange sprigs of lily of the valley. Le 8 mai is a public holiday in France commemorating the surrender of the German army to Eisenhower on May 7, 1945. There are parades of ex-servicemen in most towns. The social upheavals of May and June 1968, marked by student demonstrations, workers' strikes and general rioting, are generally referred to as "les événements de mai 68". De Gaulle's government survived the onslaught, but reforms in education and a move towards decentralization ensued.

---

maigre [mɛgʀ(ə)] *adj* (very) thin, skinny; (*viande*) lean; (*fromage*) low-fat; (*végétation*) thin, sparse; (*fig*) poor, meagre, skimpy ♦ *adv*: **faire ~** not to eat meat; **jours ~s** days of abstinence, fish days.

maigrelet, te [mɛgʀəlɛ, -ɛt] *adj* skinny, scrawny.

maigreur [mɛgʀœʀ] *nf* thinness.

maigrichon, ne [megʀiʃɔ̃, -ɔn] *adj* = **maigrelet, te**.

maigrir [megʀiʀ] *vi* to get thinner, lose weight ♦ *vt*: **~ qn** (*suj: vêtement*) to make sb look slim(mer).

mailing [mɛliŋ] *nm* direct mail *no pl*; **un ~** a mailshot.

maille [maj] *nf* (*boucle*) stitch; (*ouverture*) hole (in the mesh); **avoir ~ à partir avec qn** to have a brush with sb; **~ à l'endroit/à l'envers** knit one/purl one; (*boucle*) plain/purl stitch.

maillechort [majʃɔʀ] *nm* nickel silver.

maillet [majɛ] *nm* mallet.

maillon [majɔ̃] *nm* link.

maillot [majo] *nm* (*aussi*: **~ de corps**) vest; (*de danseur*) leotard; (*de sportif*) jersey; **~ de bain** bathing costume (*BRIT*), swimsuit; (*d'homme*) bathing trunks *pl*; **~ une pièce** one-piece swimsuit; **~ deux pièces** two-piece swimsuit, bikini.

main [mɛ̃] *nf* hand; **la ~ dans la ~** hand in hand; **à deux ~s** with both hands; **à une ~** with one hand; **à la ~ (tenir, avoir)** in one's hand; **(faire, tricoter etc)** by hand; **se donner la ~** to hold hands; **donner ou tendre la ~ à qn** to hold out one's hand to sb; **se serrer la ~** to shake hands; **serrer la ~ à qn** to shake hands with sb; **sous la ~** to *ou* at hand; **haut les ~s!** hands up!; **à ~ levée** (*ART*) freehand;

à ~s levées (*voter*) with a show of hands; **attaque à ~ armée** armed attack; **à ~ droite/gauche** to the right/left; **à remettre en ~s propres** to be delivered personally; **de première ~** (*renseignement*) first-hand; (*COMM: voiture etc*) with only one previous owner; **faire ~ basse sur** to help o.s. to; **mettre la dernière ~ à** to put the finishing touches to; **mettre la ~ à la pâte** (*fig*) to lend a hand; **prendre qch en ~** (*fig*) to take sth in hand; **avoir/passer la ~** (*CARTES*) to lead/hand over the lead; **s'en laver les ~s** (*fig*) to wash one's hands of it; **se faire/perdre la ~** to get one's hand in/lose one's touch; **avoir qch bien en ~** to have got the hang of sth; **en un tour de ~** (*fig*) in the twinkling of an eye; **~ courante** handrail.

mainate [mɛnat] *nm* myna(h) bird.

main-d'œuvre [mɛ̃dœvʀ(ə)] *nf* manpower, labour (*BRIT*), labor (*US*).

main-forte [mɛ̃fɔʀt(ə)] *nf*: **prêter ~ à qn** to come to sb's assistance.

mainmise [mɛ̃miz] *nf* seizure; (*fig*): **avoir la ~ sur** to have a complete hold on.

maint, e [mɛ̃, mɛ̃t] *adj* many a; **~s** many; **à ~es reprises** time and (time) again.

maintenance [mɛ̃tnɑ̃s] *nf* maintenance.

maintenant [mɛ̃tnɑ̃] *adv* now; (*actuellement*) nowadays.

maintenir [mɛ̃tniʀ] *vt* (*retenir, soutenir*) to support; (*contenir: foule etc*) to keep in check, hold back; (*conserver*) to maintain, uphold; (*affirmer*) to maintain; **se ~** *vi* (*paix, temps*) to hold; (*préjugé*) to persist; (*malade*) to remain stable.

maintien [mɛ̃tjɛ̃] *nm* maintaining, upholding; (*attitude*) bearing; **~ de l'ordre** maintenance of law and order.

maintiendrai [mɛ̃tjɛ̃dʀe], **maintiens** [mɛ̃tjɛ̃] *etc vb voir* **maintenir**.

maire [mɛʀ] *nm* mayor.

mairie [meʀi] *nf* (*endroit*) town hall; (*administration*) town council.

mais [mɛ] *conj* but; **~ non!** of course not!; **~ enfin** but after all; (*indignation*) look here!; **~ encore?** is that all?

maïs [mais] *nm* maize (*BRIT*), corn (*US*).

maison [mɛzɔ̃] *nf* (*bâtiment*) house; (*chez-soi*) home; (*COMM*) firm; (*famille*): **ami de la ~** friend of the family ♦ *adj inv* (*CULIN*) home-made; (: *au restaurant*) made by the chef; (*COMM*) in-house, own; (*fam*) first-rate; **à la ~** at home; (*direction*) home; **~ d'arrêt** (short-stay) prison; **~ de campagne** country cottage; **~ centrale** prison; **~ close** brothel; **~ de correction** ≈ remand home (*BRIT*), reformatory (*US*); **~ de la culture** ≈ arts centre; **~ des jeunes** ≈ youth club; **~ mère** parent company; **~ de passe** = **~ close**; **~ de repos** convalescent home; **~ de retraite** old people's home; **~ de santé** mental home.

Maisons des jeunes et de la culture *are centres for young people which combine the functions of youth club and community arts centre. They organize a wide range of sporting and cultural activities (theatre, music, exhibitions), and are also engaged in welfare work. The centres are, in part, publicly financed.*

Maison-Blanche [mɛzɔ̃blɑ̃ʃ] *nf*: **la ~** the White House.

maisonnée [mɛzɔne] *nf* household, family.

maisonnette [mɛzɔnɛt] *nf* small house, cottage.

maître, esse [mɛtʀ(ə), mɛtʀɛs] *nm/f* master/mistress; (*SCOL*) teacher, schoolmaster/mistress ♦ *nm* (*peintre etc*) master; (*titre*): **M~** (**Me**) Maître, *term of address for lawyers etc* ♦ *nf* (*amante*) mistress ♦ *adj* (*principal, essentiel*) main; **maison de ~** family seat; **être ~ de** (*soi-même, situation*) to be in control of; **se rendre ~ de** (*pays, ville*) to gain control of; (*situation, incendie*) to bring under control; **être passé ~ dans l'art de** to be a (past) master in the art of; **une maîtresse femme** a forceful woman; **~ d'armes** fencing master; **~ auxiliaire (MA)** (*SCOL*) temporary teacher; **~ chanteur** blackmailer; **~ de chapelle** choirmaster; **~ de conférences** ≈ senior lecturer (*BRIT*), ≈ assistant professor (*US*); **~/maîtresse d'école** teacher, schoolmaster/mistress; **~ d'hôtel** (*domestique*) butler; (*d'hôtel*) head waiter; **~ de maison** host; **~ nageur** lifeguard; **~ d'œuvre** (*CONSTR*) project manager; **~ d'ouvrage** (*CONSTR*) client; **~ à penser** intellectual leader; **~ queux** chef; **maîtresse de maison** hostess; (*ménagère*) housewife (*pl* -wives).

maître-assistant, e, *pl* **maîtres-assistants, es** [mɛtʀasistɑ̃, -ɑ̃t] *nm/f* ≈ lecturer.

maître-autel, *pl* **maîtres-autels** [mɛtʀotɛl] *nm* high altar.

maîtrise [mɛtʀiz] *nf* (*aussi:* **~ de soi**) self-control, self-possession; (*habileté*) skill, mastery; (*suprématie*) mastery, command; (*diplôme*) ≈ master's degree; (*chefs d'équipe*) supervisory staff.

The **maîtrise** *is a French university degree awarded following two years successful study after the* **DEUG**. *Students wishing to undertake research and prepare a doctorate must hold a* **maîtrise**.

---

maîtriser [mɛtʀize] *vt* (*cheval, incendie*) to (bring under) control; (*sujet*) to master; (*émotion*) to control; **se ~** to control o.s.

majesté [maʒɛste] *nf* majesty.

majestueux, euse [maʒɛstɥø, -øz] *adj* majestic.

majeur, e [maʒœʀ] *adj* (*important*) major; (*JUR*) of age; (*fig*) adult ♦ *nm/f* (*JUR*) person who has come of age *ou* attained his (*ou* her) majority ♦ *nm* (*doigt*) middle finger; **en ~e partie** for the most part; **la ~e partie de** the major part of.

major [maʒɔʀ] *nm* adjutant; (*SCOL*): **~ de la promotion** first in one's year.

majoration [maʒɔʀasjɔ̃] *nf* increase.

majordome [maʒɔʀdom] *nm* major-domo.

majorer [maʒɔʀe] *vt* to increase.

majorette [maʒɔʀɛt] *nf* majorette.

majoritaire [maʒɔʀitɛʀ] *adj* majority *cpd*; **système/scrutin ~** majority system/ballot.

majorité [maʒɔʀite] *nf* (*gén*) majority; (*parti*) party in power; **en ~** (*composé etc*) mainly.

Majorque [maʒɔʀk(ə)] *nf* Majorca.

majorquin, e [maʒɔʀkɛ̃, -in] *adj* Majorcan ♦ *nm/f*: **M~, e** Majorcan.

majuscule [maʒyskyl] *adj*, *nf*: (**lettre**) **~** capital (letter).

MAL [mal] *sigle f* (= *Maison d'animation et des loisirs*) cultural centre.

mal, maux [mal, mo] *nm* (*opposé au bien*) evil; (*tort, dommage*) harm; (*douleur physique*) pain, ache; (*maladie*) illness, sickness *no pl*; (*difficulté, peine*) trouble; (*souffrance morale*) pain ♦ *adv* badly ♦ *adj*: **c'est ~ (de faire)** it's bad *ou* wrong (to do); **être ~** to be uncomfortable; **être ~ avec qn** to be on bad terms with sb; **être au plus ~** (*malade*) to be very bad; (*brouillé*) to be at daggers drawn; **il comprend ~** he has difficulty in understanding; **il a ~ compris** he misunderstood; **~ tourner** to go wrong; **dire/penser du ~ de** to speak/think ill of; **ne vouloir de ~ à personne** to wish nobody any ill; **il n'a rien fait de ~** he has done nothing wrong; **avoir du ~ à faire qch** to have trouble doing sth; **se donner du ~ pour faire qch** to go to a lot of trouble to do sth; **ne voir aucun ~ à** to see no harm in, see nothing wrong in; **craignant ~ faire** fearing he *etc* was doing the wrong thing; **sans penser** *ou* **songer à ~** without meaning any harm; **faire du ~ à qn** to hurt sb; to harm sb; **se faire ~** to hurt o.s.; **se faire ~ au pied** to hurt one's foot; **ça fait ~** it hurts; **j'ai ~ (ici)** it hurts (here); **j'ai ~ au dos** my back aches, I've got a pain in my back; **avoir ~ à la tête/à la gorge/aux dents** to have a headache/a sore throat/toothache; **avoir le ~ de l'air** to be airsick; **avoir le ~ du pays** to be homesick; **~ de mer** seasickness; **~ de la route** carsickness; **~ en point** *adj inv* in a bad state; **maux de ventre** stomach ache *sg*; *voir* **cœur**.

Malabar [malabaʀ] *nm*: **le ~, la côte de ~** the Malabar (Coast).

malabar [malabaʀ] *nm* (*fam*) muscle man.

malade [malad] *adj* ill, sick; (*poitrine, jambe*) bad; (*plante*) diseased; (*fig: entreprise, monde*) ailing ♦ *nm/f* invalid, sick person; (*à l'hôpital etc*) patient; **tomber ~** to fall ill; **être ~ du cœur** to have heart trouble *ou* a bad heart;

grand ~ seriously ill person; **~ mental** mentally sick *ou* ill person.

maladie [maladi] *nf* (*spécifique*) disease, illness; (*mauvaise santé*) illness, sickness; (*fig: manie*) mania; **être rongé par la ~** to be wasting away (through illness); **~ d'Alzheimer** Alzheimer's disease; **~ de peau** skin disease.

maladif, ive [maladif, -iv] *adj* sickly; (*curiosité, besoin*) pathological.

maladresse [maladʀɛs] *nf* clumsiness *no pl*; (*gaffe*) blunder.

maladroit, e [maladʀwa, -wat] *adj* clumsy.

maladroitement [maladʀwatmã] *adv* clumsily.

mal-aimé, e [maleme] *nm/f* unpopular person; (*de la scène politique, de la société*) persona non grata; **le ~ du bureau** the unpopular one in the office.

malais, e [malɛ, -ɛz] *adj* Malay, Malayan ♦ *nm* (*LING*) Malay ♦ *nm/f*: **M~, e** Malay, Malayan.

malaise [malɛz] *nm* (*MÉD*) feeling of faintness; feeling of discomfort; (*fig*) uneasiness, malaise; **avoir un ~** to feel faint *ou* dizzy.

malaisé, e [maleze] *adj* difficult.

Malaisie [malɛzi] *nf*: **la ~** Malaya, West Malaysia; **la péninsule de ~** the Malay Peninsula.

malappris, e [malapʀi, -iz] *nm/f* ill-mannered *ou* boorish person.

malaria [malaʀja] *nf* malaria.

malavisé, e [malavize] *adj* ill-advised, unwise.

Malawi [malawi] *nm*: **le ~** Malawi.

malaxer [malakse] *vt* (*pétrir*) to knead; (*mêler*) to mix.

Malaysia [malɛzja] *nf*: **la ~** Malaysia.

malchance [malʃãs] *nf* misfortune, ill luck *no pl*; **par ~** unfortunately; **quelle ~!** what bad luck!

malchanceux, euse [malʃãsø, -øz] *adj* unlucky.

malcommode [malkɔmɔd] *adj* impractical, inconvenient.

Maldives [maldiv] *nfpl*: **les ~** the Maldive Islands.

maldonne [maldɔn] *nf* (*CARTES*) misdeal; **il y a ~** (*fig*) there's been a misunderstanding.

mâle [mɑl] *adj* (*aussi ÉLEC, TECH*) male; (*viril: voix, traits*) manly ♦ *nm* male.

malédiction [malediksjɔ̃] *nf* curse.

maléfice [malefis] *nm* evil spell.

maléfique [malefik] *adj* evil, baleful.

malencontreusement [malãkɔ̃tʀøzmã] *adv* (*arriver*) at the wrong moment; (*rappeler, mentionner*) inopportunely.

malencontreux, euse [malãkɔ̃tʀø, -øz] *adj* unfortunate, untoward.

malentendant, e [malãtãdã, -ãt] *nm/f*: **les ~s** the hard of hearing.

malentendu [malãtãdy] *nm* misunderstanding.

malfaçon [malfasɔ̃] *nf* fault.

malfaisant, e [malfəzɑ̃, -ɑ̃t] *adj* evil, harmful.
malfaiteur [malfɛtœr] *nm* lawbreaker, criminal; (*voleur*) thief (*pl* thieves).
malfamé, e [malfame] *adj* disreputable, of ill repute.
malfrat [malfrɑ] *nm* villain, crook.
malgache [malgaʃ] *adj* Malagasy, Madagascan ♦ *nm* (*LING*) Malagasy ♦ *nm/f*: **M~** Malagasy, Madagascan.
malgré [malgre] *prép* in spite of, despite; ~ **tout** *adv* in spite of everything.
malhabile [malabil] *adj* clumsy.
malheur [malœr] *nm* (*situation*) adversity, misfortune; (*événement*) misfortune; (: *plus fort*) disaster, tragedy; **par** ~ unfortunately; **quel ~!** what a shame *ou* pity!; **faire un** ~ (*fam*: *un éclat*) to do something desperate; (: *avoir du succès*) to be a smash hit.
malheureusement [malœrøzmɑ̃] *adv* unfortunately.
malheureux, euse [malœrø, -øz] *adj* (*triste*) unhappy, miserable; (*infortuné, regrettable*) unfortunate; (*malchanceux*) unlucky; (*insignifiant*) wretched ♦ *nm/f* (*infortuné, misérable*) poor soul; (*indigent, miséreux*) unfortunate creature; **les** ~ the destitute; **avoir la main malheureuse** (*au jeu*) to be unlucky; (*tout casser*) to be ham-fisted.
malhonnête [malɔnɛt] *adj* dishonest; (*impoli*) rude.
malhonnêtement [malɔnɛtmɑ̃] *adv* dishonestly.
malhonnêteté [malɔnɛtte] *nf* dishonesty; rudeness *no pl*.
Mali [mali] *nm*: **le** ~ Mali.
malice [malis] *nf* mischievousness; (*méchanceté*) par ~ out of malice *ou* spite; **sans** ~ guileless.
malicieusement [malisjøzmɑ̃] *adv* mischievously.
malicieux, euse [malisjø, -øz] *adj* mischievous.
malien, ne [maljɛ̃, -ɛn] *adj* Malian.
malignité [maliɲite] *nf* (*d'une tumeur, d'un mal*) malignancy.
malin, igne [malɛ̃, -iɲ] *adj* (*futé: f gén*: **maline**) smart, shrewd; (: *sourire*) knowing; (*MÉD, influence*) malignant; **faire le** ~ to show off; **éprouver un** ~ **plaisir à** to take malicious pleasure in.
malingre [malɛ̃gr(ə)] *adj* puny.
malintentionné, e [malɛ̃tɑ̃sjɔne] *adj* ill-intentioned, malicious.
malle [mal] *nf* trunk; (*AUTO*): ~ (**arrière**) boot (*BRIT*), trunk (*US*).
malléable [maleabl(ə)] *adj* malleable.
malle-poste *pl* **malles-poste** [malpɔst(ə)] *nf* mail coach.
mallette [malɛt] *nf* (*valise*) (small) suitcase; (*aussi*: ~ **de voyage**) overnight case; (*pour documents*) attaché case.
malmener [malməne] *vt* to manhandle; (*fig*) to

give a rough ride to.
malnutrition [malnytrisjɔ̃] *nf* malnutrition.
malodorant, e [malɔdɔrɑ̃, -ɑ̃t] *adj* foulsmelling.
malotru [malɔtry] *nm* lout, boor.
malouin, e [malwɛ̃, -in] *adj* of *ou* from Saint Malo.
Malouines [malwin] *nfpl*: **les** ~ the Falklands, the Falkland Islands.
malpoli, e [malpɔli] *nm/f* rude individual.
malpropre [malprɔpr(ə)] *adj* (*personne, vêtement*) dirty; (*travail*) slovenly; (*histoire, plaisanterie*) unsavoury (*BRIT*), unsavory (*US*), smutty; (*malhonnête*) dishonest.
malpropreté [malprɔprəte] *nf* dirtiness.
malsain, e [malsɛ̃, -ɛn] *adj* unhealthy.
malséant, e [malseɑ̃, -ɑ̃t] *adj* unseemly, unbecoming.
malsonnant, e [malsɔnɑ̃, -ɑ̃t] *adj* offensive.
malt [malt] *nm* malt; **pur** ~ (*whisky*) malt (whisky).
maltais, e [maltɛ, -ɛz] *adj* Maltese.
Malte [malt(ə)] *nf* Malta.
malté, e [malte] *adj* (*lait etc*) malted.
maltraiter [maltrete] *vt* (*brutaliser*) to manhandle, ill-treat; (*critiquer, éreinter*) to slate (*BRIT*), roast.
malus [malys] *nm* (*ASSURANCES*) car insurance weighting, penalty.
malveillance [malvɛjɑ̃s] *nf* (*animosité*) ill will; (*intention de nuire*) malevolence; (*JUR*) malicious intent *no pl*.
malveillant, e [malvɛjɑ̃, -ɑ̃t] *adj* malevolent, malicious.
malvenu, e [malvəny] *adj*: **être** ~ **de** *ou* **à faire qch** not to be in a position to do sth.
malversation [malvɛrsasjɔ̃] *nf* embezzlement, misappropriation (of funds).
maman [mamɑ̃] *nf* mum(my) (*BRIT*), mom (*US*).
mamelle [mamɛl] *nf* teat.
mamelon [maml5] *nm* (*ANAT*) nipple; (*colline*) knoll, hillock.
mamie [mami] *nf* (*fam*) granny.
mammifère [mamifɛr] *nm* mammal.
mammouth [mamut] *nm* mammoth.
manager [manadʒɛr] *nm* (*SPORT*) manager; (*COMM*): ~ **commercial** commercial director.
manceau, elle, x [mɑ̃so, -ɛl] *adj* of *ou* from Le Mans.
manche [mɑ̃ʃ] *nf* (*de vêtement*) sleeve; (*d'un jeu, tournoi*) round; (*GÉO*): **la M~** the (English) Channel ♦ *nm* (*d'outil, casserole*) handle; (*de pelle, pioche etc*) shaft; (*de violon, guitare*) neck; (*fam*) clumsy oaf; **faire la** ~ to pass the hat; ~ **à air** *nf* (*AVIAT*) wind-sock; ~ **à balai** *nm* broomstick; (*AVIAT, INFORM*) joystick.
manchette [mɑ̃ʃɛt] *nf* (*de chemise*) cuff; (*coup*) forearm blow; (*titre*) headline.
manchon [mɑ̃ʃ5] *nm* (*de fourrure*) muff; ~ **à incandescence** incandescent (gas) mantle.

manchot [mɑ̃ʃo] *nm* one-armed man; armless man; (*ZOOL*) penguin.

mandarine [mɑ̃daʀin] *nf* mandarin (orange), tangerine.

mandat [mɑ̃da] *nm* (*postal*) postal *ou* money order; (*d'un député etc*) mandate; (*procuration*) power of attorney, proxy; (*POLICE*) warrant; ~ **d'amener** summons *sg*; ~ **d'arrêt** warrant for arrest; ~ **de dépôt** committal order; ~ **de perquisition** (*POLICE*) search warrant.

mandataire [mɑ̃datɛʀ] *nm/f* (*représentant, délégué*) representative; (*JUR*) proxy.

mandat-carte, *pl* **mandats-cartes** [mɑ̃dakaʀt(ə)] *nm* money order (*in postcard form*).

mandater [mɑ̃date] *vt* (*personne*) to appoint; (*POL: député*) to elect.

mandat-lettre, *pl* **mandats-lettres** [mɑ̃dalɛtʀ(ə)] *nm* money order (*with space for correspondence*).

mandchou, e [mɑ̃tʃu] *adj* Manchu, Manchurian ♦ *nm* (*LING*) Manchu ♦ *nm/f:* **M~, e** Manchu.

Mandchourie [mɑ̃tʃuʀi] *nf:* **la** ~ Manchuria.

mander [mɑ̃de] *vt* to summon.

mandibule [mɑ̃dibyl] *nf* mandible.

mandoline [mɑ̃dɔlin] *nf* mandolin(e).

manège [manɛʒ] *nm* riding school; (*à la foire*) roundabout (*BRIT*), merry-go-round; (*fig*) game, ploy; **faire un tour de** ~ to go for a ride on a *ou* the roundabout *etc*; ~ (**de chevaux de bois**) roundabout (*BRIT*), merry-go-round.

manette [manɛt] *nf* lever, tap; ~ **de jeu** (*INFORM*) joystick.

manganèse [mɑ̃ganɛz] *nm* manganese.

mangeable [mɑ̃ʒabl(ə)] *adj* edible, eatable.

mangeaille [mɑ̃ʒaj] *nf* (*péj*) grub.

mangeoire [mɑ̃ʒwaʀ] *nf* trough, manger.

manger [mɑ̃ʒe] *vt* to eat; (*ronger: suj: rouille etc*) to eat into *ou* away; (*utiliser, consommer*) to eat up ♦ *vi* to eat.

mange-tout [mɑ̃ʒtu] *nm inv* mange-tout.

mangeur, euse [mɑ̃ʒœʀ, -øz] *nm/f* eater.

mangouste [mɑ̃gust(ə)] *nf* mongoose.

mangue [mɑ̃g] *nf* mango.

maniabilité [manjabilite] *nf* (*d'un outil*) handiness; (*d'un véhicule, voilier*) manoeuvrability.

maniable [manjabl(ə)] *adj* (*outil*) handy; (*voiture, voilier*) easy to handle, manoeuvrable (*BRIT*), maneuverable (*US*); (*fig: personne*) easily influenced, manipulable.

maniaque [manjak] *adj* (*pointilleux, méticuleux*) finicky, fussy; (*atteint de manie*) suffering from a mania ♦ *nm/f* maniac.

manie [mani] *nf* mania; (*tic*) odd habit.

maniement [manimɑ̃] *nm* handling; ~ **d'armes** arms drill.

manier [manje] *vt* to handle; **se** ~ *vi* (*fam*) to get a move on.

manière [manjɛʀ] *nf* (*façon*) way, manner; (*genre, style*) style; ~**s** *nfpl* (*attitude*) manners; (*chichis*) fuss *sg*; **de** ~ **à** so as to; **de telle** ~ **que** in such a way that; **de cette** ~ in this way *ou* manner; **d'une** ~ **générale** generally speaking, as a general rule; **de toute** ~ in any case; **d'une certaine** ~ in a (certain) way; **faire des** ~**s** to put on airs; **employer la** ~ **forte** to use strong-arm tactics; **adverbe de** ~ adverb of manner.

maniéré, e [manjeʀe] *adj* affected.

manif [manif] *nf* (= *manifestation*) demo (*pl* -s).

manifestant, e [manifɛstɑ̃, -ɑ̃t] *nm/f* demonstrator.

manifestation [manifɛstasjɔ̃] *nf* (*de joie, mécontentement*) expression, demonstration; (*symptôme*) outward sign; (*fête etc*) event; (*POL*) demonstration.

manifeste [manifɛst(ə)] *adj* obvious, evident ♦ *nm* manifesto (*pl* -s).

manifestement [manifɛstəmɑ̃] *adv* obviously.

manifester [manifɛste] *vt* (*volonté, intentions*) to show, indicate; (*joie, peur*) to express, show ♦ *vi* (*POL*) to demonstrate; **se** ~ *vi* (*émotion*) to show *ou* express itself; (*difficultés*) to arise; (*symptômes*) to appear; (*témoin etc*) to come forward.

manigance [manigɑ̃s] *nf* scheme.

manigancer [manigɑ̃se] *vt* to plot, devise.

Manille [manij] *n* Manila.

manioc [manjɔk] *nm* cassava, manioc.

manipulateur, trice [manipylatœʀ, -tʀis] *adj* (*technicien*) technician, operator; (*prestidigitateur*) conjurer; (*péj*) manipulator.

manipulation [manipylasjɔ̃] *nf* handling; manipulation.

manipuler [manipyle] *vt* to handle; (*fig*) to manipulate.

manivelle [manivɛl] *nf* crank.

manne [man] *nf* (*REL*) manna; (*fig*) godsend.

mannequin [mankɛ̃] *nm* (*COUTURE*) dummy; (*MODE*) model.

manœuvrable [manœvʀabl(ə)] *adj* (*bateau, véhicule*) manoeuvrable (*BRIT*), maneuverable (*US*).

manœuvre [manœvʀ(ə)] *nf* (*gén*) manoeuvre (*BRIT*), maneuver (*US*) ♦ *nm* (*ouvrier*) labourer (*BRIT*), laborer (*US*).

manœuvrer [manœvʀe] *vt* to manoeuvre (*BRIT*), maneuver (*US*); (*levier, machine*) to operate; (*personne*) to manipulate ♦ *vi* to manoeuvre *ou* maneuver.

manoir [manwaʀ] *nm* manor *ou* country house.

manomètre [manɔmɛtʀ(ə)] *nm* gauge, manometer.

manquant, e [mɑ̃kɑ̃, -ɑ̃t] *adj* missing.

manque [mɑ̃k] *nm* (*insuffisance*): ~ **de** lack of; (*vide*) emptiness, gap; (*MÉD*) withdrawal; ~**s** *nmpl* (*lacunes*) faults, defects; **par** ~ **de** for want of; ~ **à gagner** loss of profit *ou* earnings.

manqué, e [mɑ̃ke] adj failed; **garçon** ~ tomboy.

manquement [mɑ̃kmɑ̃] nm: ~ **à** (discipline, règle) breach of.

manquer [mɑ̃ke] vi (faire défaut) to be lacking; (être absent) to be missing; (échouer) to fail ♦ vt to miss ♦ vb impers: **il (nous) manque encore 100 F** we are still 100 F short; **il manque des pages (au livre)** there are some pages missing ou some pages are missing (from the book); **l'argent qui leur manque** the money they need ou are short of; **le pied/la voix lui manqua** he missed his footing/his voice failed him; ~ **à qn** (absent etc): **il/cela me manque** I miss him/that; ~ **à** vt (règles etc) to be in breach of, fail to observe; ~ **de** vt to lack; (COMM) to be out of (stock of); **ne pas** ~ **de faire: il n'a pas manqué de le dire** he certainly said it; ~ **(de) faire: il a manqué (de) se tuer** he very nearly got killed; **il ne manquerait plus qu'il fasse** all we need now is for him to do; **je n'y manquerai pas** leave it to me, I'll definitely do it.

mansarde [mɑ̃saʀd(ə)] nf attic.

mansardé, e [mɑ̃saʀde] adj attic cpd.

mansuétude [mɑ̃sɥetyd] nf leniency.

mante [mɑ̃t] nf: ~ **religieuse** praying mantis.

manteau, x [mɑ̃to] nm coat; ~ **de cheminée** mantelpiece; **sous le** ~ (fig) under cover.

mantille [mɑ̃tij] nf mantilla.

Mantoue [mɑ̃tu] n Mantua.

manucure [manykyʀ] nf manicurist.

manuel, le [manɥɛl] adj manual ♦ nm/f manually gifted pupil etc (as opposed to intellectually gifted) ♦ nm (ouvrage) manual, handbook.

manuellement [manɥɛlmɑ̃] adv manually.

manufacture [manyfaktyʀ] nf (établissement) factory; (fabrication) manufacture.

manufacturé, e [manyfaktyʀe] adj manufactured.

manufacturier, ière [manyfaktyʀje, -jɛʀ] nm/f factory owner.

manuscrit, e [manyskʀi, -it] adj handwritten ♦ nm manuscript.

manutention [manytɑ̃sjɔ̃] nf (COMM) handling; (local) storehouse.

manutentionnaire [manytɑ̃sjɔnɛʀ] nm/f warehouseman/woman, packer.

manutentionner [manytɑ̃sjɔne] vt to handle.

MAP sigle f (PHOTO: = mise au point) focusing.

mappemonde [mapmɔ̃d] nf (plane) map of the world; (sphère) globe.

maquereau, x [makʀo] nm mackerel inv; (fam: proxénète) pimp.

maquerelle [makʀɛl] nf (fam) madam.

maquette [makɛt] nf (d'un décor, bâtiment, véhicule) (scale) model; (TYPO) mockup; (: d'une page illustrée, affiche) paste-up; (: prêt à la réproduction) artwork.

maquignon [makiɲɔ̃] nm horse-dealer.

maquillage [makijaʒ] nm making up; faking; (produits) make-up.

maquiller [makije] vt (personne, visage) to make up; (truquer: passeport, statistique) to fake; (: voiture volée) to do over (respray etc); **se** ~ to make o.s. up.

maquilleur, euse [makijœʀ, -øz] nm/f make-up artist.

maquis [maki] nm (GÉO) scrub; (fig) tangle; (MIL) maquis, underground fighting no pl.

maquisard, e [makizaʀ, -aʀd(ə)] nm/f maquis, member of the Resistance.

marabout [maʀabu] nm (ZOOL) marabou(t).

maraîcher, ère [maʀeʃe, maʀeʃɛʀ] adj: **cultures maraîchères** market gardening sg ♦ nm/f market gardener.

marais [maʀɛ] nm marsh, swamp; ~ **salant** saltworks.

marasme [maʀasm(ə)] nm (POL, ÉCON) stagnation, sluggishness; (accablement) dejection, depression.

marathon [maʀatɔ̃] nm marathon.

marâtre [maʀɑtʀ(ə)] nf cruel mother.

maraude [maʀod] nf pilfering, thieving (of poultry, crops); (dans un verger) scrumping; (vagabondage) prowling; **en** ~ on the prowl; (taxi) cruising.

maraudeur, euse [maʀodœʀ, -øz] nm/f marauder; prowler.

marbre [maʀbʀ(ə)] nm (pierre, statue) marble; (d'une table, commode) marble top; (TYPO) stone, bed; **rester de** ~ to remain stonily indifferent.

marbrer [maʀbʀe] vt to mottle, blotch; (TECH: papier) to marble.

marbrerie [maʀbʀəʀi] nf (atelier) marble mason's workshop; (industrie) marble industry.

marbrier [maʀbʀije] nm monumental mason.

marbrière [maʀbʀijɛʀ] nf marble quarry.

marbrures [maʀbʀyʀ] nfpl blotches pl; (TECH) marbling sg.

marc [maʀ] nm (de raisin, pommes) marc; ~ **de café** coffee grounds pl ou dregs pl.

marcassin [maʀkasɛ̃] nm young wild boar.

marchand, e [maʀʃɑ̃, -ɑ̃d] nm/f shopkeeper, tradesman/woman; (au marché) stallholder; (spécifique): ~ **de cycles/tapis** bicycle/carpet dealer; ~ **de charbon/vins** coal/wine merchant ♦ adj: **prix/valeur** ~(e) market price/value; **qualité** ~e standard quality; ~ **en gros/au détail** wholesaler/retailer; ~ **de biens** real estate agent; ~ **de canons** (péj) arms dealer; ~ **de couleurs** ironmonger (BRIT), hardware dealer (US); ~/e **de fruits** fruiterer (BRIT), fruit seller (US); ~/e **de journaux** newsagent (BRIT), newsdealer (US); ~/e **de légumes** greengrocer (BRIT), produce dealer (US); ~/e **de poisson** fishmonger (BRIT), fish seller (US); ~/e **de(s) quatre-saisons** costermonger (BRIT), street vendor (selling fresh fruit and vegetables); ~ **de sable** (fig) sandman; ~ **de tableaux** art dealer.

marchandage [maʁʃɑ̃daʒ] *nm* bargaining; (*péj: électoral*) bargaining, manoeuvring.

marchander [maʁʃɑ̃de] *vt* (*article*) to bargain *ou* haggle over; (*éloges*) to be sparing with ♦ *vi* to bargain, haggle.

marchandisage [maʁʃɑ̃dizaʒ] *nm* merchandizing.

marchandise [maʁʃɑ̃diz] *nf* goods *pl*, merchandise *no pl*.

marche [maʁʃ(ə)] *nf* (*d'escalier*) step; (*activité*) walking; (*promenade, trajet, allure*) walk; (*démarche*) walk, gait; (*MIL etc, MUS*) march; (*fonctionnement*) running; (*progression*) progress; course; **à une heure de ~** an hour's walk (away); **ouvrir/fermer la ~** to lead the way/bring up the rear; **dans le sens de la ~** (*RAIL*) facing the engine; **en ~** (*monter etc*) while the vehicle is moving *ou* in motion; **mettre en ~** to start; **remettre qch en ~** to set *ou* start sth going again; **se mettre en ~** (*personne*) to get moving; (*machine*) to start; **~ arrière** (*AUTO*) reverse (gear); **faire ~ arrière** (*AUTO*) to reverse; (*fig*) to backtrack, back-pedal; **~ à suivre** (*correct*) procedure; (*sur notice*) (step by step) instructions *pl*.

marché [maʁʃe] *nm* (*lieu, COMM, ÉCON*) market; (*ville*) trading centre; (*transaction*) bargain, deal; **par-dessus le ~** into the bargain; **faire son ~** to do one's shopping; **mettre le ~ en main à qn** to tell sb to take it or leave it; **~ au comptant** (*BOURSE*) spot market; **M~ commun** Common Market; **~ aux fleurs** flower market; **~ noir** black market; **faire du ~ noir** to buy and sell on the black market; **~ aux puces** flea market; **~ à terme** (*BOURSE*) forward market; **~ du travail** labour market.

marchepied [maʁʃəpje] *nm* (*RAIL*) step; (*AUTO*) running board; (*fig*) stepping stone.

marcher [maʁʃe] *vi* to walk; (*MIL*) to march; (*aller: voiture, train, affaires*) to go; (*prospérer*) to go well; (*fonctionner*) to work, run; (*fam*) to go along, agree; (: *croire naïvement*) to be taken in; **~ sur** to walk on; (*mettre le pied sur*) to step on *ou* in; (*MIL*) to march upon; **~ dans** (*herbe etc*) to walk in *ou* on; (*flaque*) to step in; **faire ~ qn** (*pour rire*) to pull sb's leg; (*pour tromper*) to lead sb up the garden path.

marcheur, euse [maʁʃœʁ, -øz] *nm/f* walker.

marcotter [maʁkɔte] *vt* to layer.

mardi [maʁdi] *nm* Tuesday; **M~ gras** Shrove Tuesday; *voir aussi* **lundi**.

mare [maʁ] *nf* pond; **~ de sang** pool of blood.

marécage [maʁekaʒ] *nm* marsh, swamp.

marécageux, euse [maʁekaʒø, -øz] *adj* marshy, swampy.

maréchal, aux [maʁeʃal, -o] *nm* marshal; **~ des logis** (*MIL*) sergeant.

maréchal-ferrant, *pl* **maréchaux-ferrants** [maʁeʃalfɛʁɑ̃, maʁeʃo-] *nm* blacksmith, farrier (*BRIT*).

maréchaussée [maʁeʃose] *nf* (*humoristique: gendarmes*) constabulary (*BRIT*), police.

marée [maʁe] *nf* tide; (*poissons*) fresh (sea) fish; **~ haute/basse** high/low tide; **~ montante/descendante** rising/ebb tide; **~ noire** oil slick.

marelle [maʁɛl] *nf*: **(jouer à) la ~** (to play) hopscotch.

marémotrice [maʁemɔtʁis] *adj f* tidal.

mareyeur, euse [maʁɛjœʁ, -øz] *nm/f* wholesale (sea) fish merchant.

margarine [maʁgaʁin] *nf* margarine.

marge [maʁʒ(ə)] *nf* margin; **en ~** in the margin; **en ~ de** (*fig*) on the fringe of; (*en dehors de*) cut off from; (*qui se rapporte à*) connected with; **~ bénéficiaire** profit margin, mark-up; **~ de sécurité** safety margin.

margelle [maʁʒɛl] *nf* coping.

margeur [maʁʒœʁ] *nm* margin stop.

marginal, e, aux [maʁʒinal, -o] *adj* marginal ♦ *nm/f* dropout.

marguerite [maʁgəʁit] *nf* marguerite, (oxeye) daisy; (*INFORM*) daisy wheel.

marguillier [maʁgije] *nm* churchwarden.

mari [maʁi] *nm* husband.

mariage [maʁjaʒ] *nm* (*union, état, fig*) marriage; (*noce*) wedding; **~ civil/religieux** registry office (*BRIT*) *ou* civil/church wedding; **un ~ de raison/d'amour** a marriage of convenience/a love match; **~ blanc** unconsummated marriage; **~ en blanc** white wedding.

marié, e [maʁje] *adj* married ♦ *nm/f* (*bride*)groom/bride; **les ~s** the bride and groom; **les (jeunes) ~s** the newly-weds.

marier [maʁje] *vt* to marry; (*fig*) to blend; **se ~ (avec)** to marry, get married (to); (*fig*) to blend (with).

marijuana [maʁiʒwana] *nf* marijuana.

marin, e [maʁɛ̃, -in] *adj* sea *cpd*, marine ♦ *nm* sailor ♦ *nf* navy; (*ART*) seascape; (*couleur*) navy (blue); **avoir le pied ~** to be a good sailor; (*garder son équilibre*) to have one's sea legs; **~e de guerre** navy; **~e marchande** merchant navy; **~e à voiles** sailing ships *pl*.

marina [maʁina] *nf* marina.

marinade [maʁinad] *nf* marinade.

marine [maʁin] *adj f, nf voir* **marin** ♦ *adj inv* navy (blue) ♦ *nm* (*MIL*) marine.

mariner [maʁine] *vi, vt* to marinate, marinade.

marinier [maʁinje] *nm* bargee.

marinière [maʁinjɛʁ] *nf* (*blouse*) smock ♦ *adj inv*: **moules ~** (*CULIN*) mussels in white wine.

marionnette [maʁjɔnɛt] *nf* puppet.

marital, e, aux [maʁital, -o] *adj*: **autorisation ~e** husband's permission.

maritalement [maʁitalmɑ̃] *adv*: **vivre ~** to live together (as husband and wife).

maritime [maʁitim] *adj* sea *cpd*, maritime; (*ville*) coastal, seaside; (*droit*) shipping, maritime.

marjolaine [maʁʒɔlɛn] *nf* marjoram.

mark [maʀk] nm (monnaie) mark.
marketing [maʀkətiŋ] nm (COMM) marketing.
marmaille [maʀmɑj] nf (péj) (gang of) brats pl.
marmelade [maʀməlad] nf (compote) stewed fruit, compote; ~ **d'oranges** (orange) marmalade; **en** ~ (fig) crushed (to a pulp).
marmite [maʀmit] nf (cooking-)pot.
marmiton [maʀmitɔ̃] nm kitchen boy.
marmonner [maʀmɔne] vt, vi to mumble, mutter.
marmot [maʀmo] nm (fam) brat.
marmotte [maʀmɔt] nf marmot.
marmotter [maʀmɔte] vt (prière) to mumble, mutter.
marne [maʀn(ə)] nf (GÉO) marl.
Maroc [maʀɔk] nm: **le** ~ Morocco.
marocain, e [maʀɔkɛ̃, -ɛn] adj Moroccan ♦ nm/f: **M~, e** Moroccan.
maroquin [maʀɔkɛ̃] nm (peau) morocco (leather); (fig) (minister's) portfolio.
maroquinerie [maʀɔkinʀi] nf (industrie) leather craft; (commerce) leather shop; (articles) fine leather goods pl.
maroquinier [maʀɔkinje] nm (fabricant) leather craftsman; (marchand) leather dealer.
marotte [maʀɔt] nf fad.
marquant, e [maʀkɑ̃, -ɑ̃t] adj outstanding.
marque [maʀk(ə)] nf mark; (SPORT, JEU: décompte des points) score; (COMM: de produits) brand, make; (: de disques) label; (insigne: d'une fonction) badge; (fig): ~ **d'affection** token of affection; ~ **de joie** sign of joy; **à vos ~s!** (SPORT) on your marks!; **de** ~ adj (COMM) brand-name cpd; proprietary; (fig) high-class; (: personnage, hôte) distinguished; **produit de** ~ (COMM) quality product; ~ **déposée** registered trademark; ~ **de fabrique** trademark.
marqué, e [maʀke] adj marked.
marquer [maʀke] vt to mark; (inscrire) to write down; (bétail) to brand; (SPORT: but etc) to score; (: joueur) to mark; (accentuer: taille etc) to emphasize; (manifester: refus, intérêt) to show ♦ vi (événement, personnalité) to stand out, be outstanding; (SPORT) to score; ~ **qn de son influence/empreinte** to have an influence/leave its impression on sb; ~ **un temps d'arrêt** to pause momentarily; ~ **le pas** (fig) to mark time; **il a marqué ce jour-là d'une pierre blanche** that was a red-letter day for him; ~ **les points** (tenir la marque) to keep the score.
marqueté, e [maʀkəte] adj inlaid.
marqueterie [maʀkətʀi] nf inlaid work, marquetry.
marqueur, euse [maʀkœʀ, -øz] nm/f (SPORT: de but) scorer ♦ nm (crayon feutre) marker pen.
marquis, e [maʀki, -iz] nm/f marquis ou marquess/marchioness ♦ nf (auvent) glass

canopy ou awning.
Marquises [maʀkiz] nfpl: **les (îles)** ~ the Marquesas Islands.
marraine [maʀɛn] nf godmother; (d'un navire, d'une rose etc) namer.
Marrakech [maʀakɛʃ] n Marrakech ou Marrakesh.
marrant, e [maʀɑ̃, -ɑ̃t] adj (fam) funny.
marre [maʀ] adv (fam): **en avoir** ~ **de** to be fed up with.
marrer [maʀe]: **se** ~ vi (fam) to have a (good) laugh.
marron, ne [maʀɔ̃, -ɔn] nm (fruit) chestnut ♦ adj inv brown ♦ adj (péj) crooked; (: faux) bogus; ~**s glacés** marrons glacés.
marronnier [maʀɔnje] nm chestnut (tree).
Mars [maʀs] nm ou f Mars.
mars [maʀs] nm March; voir aussi **juillet**.
marseillais, e [maʀsɛjɛ, -ɛz] adj of ou from Marseilles ♦ nf: **la M~e** the French national anthem.

La **Marseillaise** has been France's national anthem since 1879. The words of the "Chant de guerre de l'armée du Rhin", as the song was originally called, were written to an anonymous tune by the army captain Rouget de Lisle in 1792. Adopted as a marching song by the battalion of Marseille, it was finally popularized as the Marseillaise.

Marseille [maʀsɛj] n Marseilles.
marsouin [maʀswɛ̃] nm porpoise.
marsupiaux [maʀsypjo] nmpl marsupials.
marteau, x [maʀto] nm hammer; (de porte) knocker; ~ **pneumatique** pneumatic drill.
marteau-pilon, pl marteaux-pilons [maʀto-pilɔ̃] nm power hammer.
marteau-piqueur, pl marteaux-piqueurs [maʀtopikœʀ] nm pneumatic drill.
martel [maʀtɛl] nm: **se mettre** ~ **en tête** to worry o.s.
martèlement [maʀtɛlmɑ̃] nm hammering.
marteler [maʀtəle] vt to hammer; (mots, phrases) to rap out.
martial, e, aux [maʀsjal, -o] adj martial; **cour** ~**e** court-martial.
martien, ne [maʀsjɛ̃, -ɛn] adj Martian, of ou from Mars.
martinet [maʀtinɛ] nm (fouet) small whip; (ZOOL) swift.
martingale [maʀtɛ̃gal] nf (COUTURE) half-belt; (JEU) winning formula.
martiniquais, e [maʀtinikɛ, -ɛz] adj of ou from Martinique.
Martinique [maʀtinik] nf: **la** ~ Martinique.
martin-pêcheur, pl martins-pêcheurs [maʀtɛ̃pɛʃœʀ] nm kingfisher.
martre [maʀtʀ(ə)] nf marten; ~ **zibeline** sable.
martyr, e [maʀtiʀ] nm/f martyr ♦ adj martyred; **enfants** ~**s** battered children.
martyre [maʀtiʀ] nm martyrdom; (fig: sens af-

faibli) agony, torture; **souffrir le** ~ to suffer agonies.

martyriser [maʀtiʀize] *vt* (*REL*) to martyr; (*fig*) to bully; (: *enfant*) to batter.

marxisme [maʀksism(ə)] *nm* Marxism.

marxiste [maʀksist(ə)] *adj, nm/f* Marxist.

mas [mɑ(s)] *nm traditional house or farm in Provence.*

mascara [maskaʀa] *nm* mascara.

mascarade [maskaʀad] *nf* masquerade.

mascotte [maskɔt] *nf* mascot.

masculin, e [maskylɛ̃, -in] *adj* masculine; (*sexe, population*) male; (*équipe, vêtements*) men's; (*viril*) manly ♦ *nm* masculine.

masochisme [mazɔʃism(ə)] *nm* masochism.

masochiste [mazɔʃist(ə)] *adj* masochistic ♦ *nm/f* masochist.

masque [mask(ə)] *nm* mask; ~ **de beauté** face pack; ~ **à gaz** gas mask; ~ **de plongée** diving mask.

masqué, e [maske] *adj* masked.

masquer [maske] *vt* (*cacher: porte, goût*) to hide, conceal; (*dissimuler: vérité, projet*) to mask, obscure.

massacrant, e [masakʀɑ̃, -ɑ̃t] *adj*: **humeur** ~e foul temper.

massacre [masakʀ(ə)] *nm* massacre, slaughter; **jeu de** ~ (*fig*) wholesale slaughter.

massacrer [masakʀe] *vt* to massacre, slaughter; (*fig: adversaire*) to slaughter; (: *texte etc*) to murder.

massage [masaʒ] *nm* massage.

masse [mas] *nf* mass; (*péj*): **la** ~ the masses *pl*; (*ÉLEC*) earth; (*maillet*) sledgehammer; ~**s** *nfpl* masses; **une** ~ **de**, **des** ~**s de** (*fam*) masses *ou* loads of; **en** ~ *adv* (*en bloc*) in bulk; (*en foule*) en masse ♦ *adj* (*exécutions, production*) mass *cpd*; ~ **monétaire** (*ÉCON*) money supply; ~ **salariale** (*COMM*) wage(s) bill.

massepain [maspɛ̃] *nm* marzipan.

masser [mase] *vt* (*assembler*) to gather; (*pétrir*) to massage; **se** ~ *vi* to gather.

masseur, euse [masœʀ, -øz] *nm/f* (*personne*) masseur/masseuse ♦ *nm* (*appareil*) massager.

massicot [masiko] *nm* (*TYPO*) guillotine.

massif, ive [masif, -iv] *adj* (*porte*) solid, massive; (*visage*) heavy, large; (*bois, or*) solid; (*dose*) massive; (*déportations etc*) mass *cpd* ♦ *nm* (*montagneux*) massif; (*de fleurs*) clump, bank.

massivement [masivmɑ̃] *adv* (*répondre*) en masse; (*administrer, injecter*) in massive doses.

mass media [masmedja] *nmpl* mass media.

massue [masy] *nf* club, bludgeon ♦ *adj inv*: **argument** ~ sledgehammer argument.

mastectomie [mastɛktɔmi] *nf* mastectomy.

mastic [mastik] *nm* (*pour vitres*) putty; (*pour fentes*) filler.

masticage [mastikaʒ] *nm* (*d'une fente*) filling; (*d'une vitre*) puttying.

mastication [mastikɑsjɔ̃] *nf* chewing, mastication.

mastiquer [mastike] *vt* (*aliment*) to chew, masticate; (*fente*) to fill; (*vitre*) to putty.

mastoc [mastɔk] *adj inv* hefty.

mastodonte [mastɔdɔ̃t] *nm* monster (*fig*).

masturbation [mastyʀbɑsjɔ̃] *nf* masturbation.

masturber [mastyʀbe] *vt*: **se** ~ to masturbate.

m'as-tu-vu [matyvy] *nm/f inv* show-off.

masure [mazyʀ] *nf* tumbledown cottage.

mat, e [mat] *adj* (*couleur, métal*) mat(t); (*bruit, son*) dull ♦ *adj inv* (*ÉCHECS*): **être** ~ to be checkmate.

mât [mɑ] *nm* (*NAVIG*) mast; (*poteau*) pole, post.

matamore [matamɔʀ] *nm* braggart, blusterer.

match [matʃ] *nm* match; ~ **nul** draw, tie (*US*); **faire** ~ **nul** to draw (*BRIT*), tie (*US*); ~ **aller** first leg; ~ **retour** second leg, return match.

matelas [matla] *nm* mattress; ~ **pneumatique** air bed *ou* mattress; ~ **à ressorts** spring *ou* interior-sprung mattress.

matelasser [matlase] *vt* to pad.

matelot [matlo] *nm* sailor, seaman.

mater [mate] *vt* (*personne*) to bring to heel, subdue; (*révolte*) to put down; (*fam*) to watch, look at.

matérialisation [mateʀjalizɑsjɔ̃] *nf* materialization.

matérialiser [mateʀjalize]: **se** ~ *vi* to materialize.

matérialisme [mateʀjalism(ə)] *nm* materialism.

matérialiste [mateʀjalist(ə)] *adj* materialistic ♦ *nm/f* materialist.

matériau, x [mateʀjo] *nm* material; ~**x** *nmpl* material(s); ~**x de construction** building materials.

matériel, le [mateʀjɛl] *adj* material; (*organisation, aide, obstacle*) practical; (*fig: péj: personne*) materialistic ♦ *nm* equipment *no pl*; (*de camping etc*) gear *no pl*; **il n'a pas le temps** ~ **de le faire** he doesn't have the time (needed) to do it; ~ **d'exploitation** (*COMM*) plant; ~ **roulant** rolling stock.

matériellement [mateʀjɛlmɑ̃] *adv* (*financièrement*) materially; ~ **à l'aise** comfortably off; **je n'en ai** ~ **pas le temps** I simply do not have the time.

maternel, le [matɛʀnɛl] *adj* (*amour, geste*) motherly, maternal; (*grand-père, oncle*) maternal ♦ *nf* (*aussi*: **école** ~**le**) (state) nursery school.

materner [matɛʀne] *vt* (*personne*) to mother.

maternisé, e [matɛʀnize] *adj*: **lait** ~ (infant) formula.

maternité [matɛʀnite] *nf* (*établissement*) maternity hospital; (*état de mère*) motherhood, maternity; (*grossesse*) pregnancy.

math [mat] *nfpl* maths (*BRIT*), math (*US*).

mathématicien, ne [matematisjɛ̃, -ɛn] *nm/f* mathematician.

mathématique [matematik] *adj* mathematical.

mathématiques [matematik] *nfpl* mathematics *sg*.

matheux, euse [matø, -øz] *nm/f* (*fam*) maths (*BRIT*) *ou* math (*US*) student; (*fort en math*) mathematical genius.

maths [mat] *nfpl* maths (*BRIT*), math (*US*).

matière [matjɛʀ] *nf* (*PHYSIQUE*) matter; (*COMM, TECH*) material, matter *no pl*; (*fig: d'un livre etc*) subject matter; (*SCOL*) subject; **en ~ de** as regards; **donner ~ à** to give cause to; **~ grise** grey matter; **~ plastique** plastic; **~s fécales** faeces; **~s grasses** fat (content) *sg*; **~s premières** raw materials.

MATIF [matif] *sigle m* (= *Marché à terme des instruments financiers*) *body which regulates the activities of the French Stock Exchange.*

L'hôtel Matignon *is the Paris office and residence of the French Prime Minister. By extension, the term "Matignon" is often used to refer to the Prime Minister or his staff.*

matin [matɛ̃] *nm, adv* morning; **le ~** (*pendant le ~*) in the morning; **demain ~** tomorrow morning; **le lendemain ~** (the) next morning; **du ~ au soir** from morning till night; **une heure du ~** one o'clock in the morning; **de grand** *ou* **bon ~** early in the morning.

matinal, e, aux [matinal, -o] *adj* (*toilette, gymnastique*) morning *cpd*; (*de bonne heure*) early; **être ~** (*personne*) to be up early; (*: habituellement*) to be an early riser.

mâtiné, e [matine] *adj* crossbred, mixed race *cpd*.

matinée [matine] *nf* morning; (*spectacle*) matinée, afternoon performance.

matois, e [matwa, -waz] *adj* wily.

matou [matu] *nm* tom(cat).

matraquage [matʀakaʒ] *nm* beating up; **~ publicitaire** plug, plugging.

matraque [matʀak] *nf* (*de malfaiteur*) cosh (*BRIT*), club; (*de policier*) truncheon (*BRIT*), billy (*US*).

matraquer [matʀake] *vt* to beat up (with a truncheon *ou* billy); to cosh (*BRIT*), club; (*fig: touristes etc*) to rip off; (*: disque*) to plug.

matriarcal, e, aux [matʀijaʀkal, -o] *adj* matriarchal.

matrice [matʀis] *nf* (*ANAT*) womb; (*TECH*) mould; (*MATH etc*) matrix.

matricule [matʀikyl] *nf* (*aussi*: **registre ~**) roll, register ♦ *nm* (*aussi*: **numéro ~**: *MIL*) regimental number; (*: ADMIN*) reference number.

matrimonial, e, aux [matʀimɔnjal, -o] *adj* marital, marriage *cpd*.

matrone [matʀɔn] *nf* matron.

mâture [mɑtyʀ] *nf* masts *pl*.

maturité [matyʀite] *nf* maturity; (*d'un fruit*) ripeness, maturity.

maudire [modiʀ] *vt* to curse.

maudit, e [modi, -it] *adj* (*fam: satané*) blasted, confounded.

maugréer [mogʀee] *vi* to grumble.

mauresque [mɔʀɛsk(ə)] *adj* Moorish.

Maurice [mɔʀis] *nf*: (**l'île**) **~** Mauritius.

mauricien, ne [mɔʀisjɛ̃, -ɛn] *adj* Mauritian.

Mauritanie [mɔʀitani] *nf*: **la ~** Mauritania.

mauritanien, ne [mɔʀitanjɛ̃, -ɛn] *adj* Mauritanian.

mausolée [mozɔle] *nm* mausoleum.

maussade [mosad] *adj* (*air, personne*) sullen; (*ciel, temps*) dismal.

mauvais, e [mɔvɛ, -ɛz] *adj* bad; (*faux*): **le ~ numéro/moment** the wrong number/moment; (*méchant, malveillant*) malicious, spiteful ♦ *nm*: **le ~** the bad side ♦ *adv*: **il fait ~** the weather is bad; **sentir ~** to have a nasty smell, smell bad *ou* nasty; **la mer est ~e** the sea is rough; **~ coucheur** awkward customer; **~ coup** (*fig*) criminal venture; **~ garçon** tough; **~ pas** tight spot; **~ plaisant** hoaxer; **~ traitements** ill treatment *sg*; **~e herbe** weed; **~e langue** gossip, scandalmonger (*BRIT*); **~e passe** difficult situation; (*période*) bad patch; **~e tête** rebellious *ou* headstrong customer.

mauve [mov] *adj* (*couleur*) mauve ♦ *nf* (*BOT*) mallow.

mauviette [movjɛt] *nf* (*péj*) weakling.

maux [mo] *nmpl voir* **mal.**

max. *abr* (= *maximum*) max.

maximal, e, aux [maksimal, -o] *adj* maximal.

maxime [maksim] *nf* maxim.

maximum [maksimɔm] *adj, nm* maximum; **atteindre un/son ~** to reach a/his peak; **au ~** *adv* (*le plus possible*) to the full; as much as one can; (*tout au plus*) at the (very) most *ou* maximum.

Mayence [majɑ̃s] *n* Mainz.

mayonnaise [majɔnɛz] *nf* mayonnaise.

Mayotte [majɔt] *nf* Mayotte.

mazout [mazut] *nm* (fuel) oil; **chaudière/poêle à ~** oil-fired boiler/stove.

mazouté, e [mazute] *adj* oil-polluted.

MDM *sigle mpl* (= *Médecins du Monde*) *medical association for aid to Third World countries.*

Me *abr* = **Maître.**

me, m' [m(ə)] *pron* me; (*réfléchi*) myself.

méandres [meɑ̃dʀ(ə)] *nmpl* meanderings.

mec [mɛk] *nm* (*fam*) guy, bloke (*BRIT*).

mécanicien, ne [mekanisjɛ̃, -ɛn] *nm/f* mechanic; (*RAIL*) (train *ou* engine) driver; **~ navigant** *ou* **de bord** (*AVIAT*) flight engineer.

mécanicien-dentiste [mekanisjɛ̃dɑ̃tist(ə)], **mécanicienne-dentiste** [mekanisjɛn-] (*pl* **~s-~s**) *nm/f* dental technician.

mécanique [mekanik] *adj* mechanical ♦ *nf* (*science*) mechanics *sg*; (*technologie*) mechanical engineering; (*mécanisme*) mechanism; engineering; works *pl*; **ennui ~** engine trouble *no pl*; **s'y connaître en ~** to be mechanically minded; ~ **hydraulique** hydraulics *sg*; ~ **ondulataire** wave mechanics *sg*.

mécaniquement [mekanikmɑ̃] *adv* mechanically.

mécanisation [mekanizɑsjɔ̃] *nf* mechanization.

mécaniser [mekanize] *vt* to mechanize.

mécanisme [mekanism(ə)] *nm* mechanism; ~ **du taux de change** exchange rate mechanism.

mécano [mekano] *nm* (*fam*) mechanic.

mécanographie [mekanɔgʀafi] *nf* (mechanical) data processing.

mécène [mesɛn] *nm* patron.

méchamment [meʃamɑ̃] *adv* nastily, maliciously, spitefully; viciously.

méchanceté [meʃɑ̃ste] *nf* (*d'une personne, d'une parole*) nastiness, maliciousness, spitefulness; (*parole, action*) nasty *ou* spiteful *ou* malicious remark (*ou* action).

méchant, e [meʃɑ̃, -ɑ̃t] *adj* nasty, malicious, spiteful; (*enfant: pas sage*) naughty; (*animal*) vicious; (*avant le nom: valeur péjorative*) nasty; miserable; (*: intensive*) terrific.

mèche [mɛʃ] *nf* (*de lampe, bougie*) wick; (*d'un explosif*) fuse; (*MÉD*) pack, dressing; (*de vilebrequin, perceuse*) bit; (*de dentiste*) drill; (*de fouet*) lash; (*de cheveux*) lock; **se faire faire des ~s** (*chez le coiffeur*) to have one's hair streaked, have highlights put in one's hair; **vendre la ~** to give the game away; **de ~ avec** in league with.

méchoui [meʃwi] *nm whole sheep barbecue*.

mécompte [mekɔ̃t] *nm* (*erreur*) miscalculation; (*déception*) disappointment.

méconnais [mekɔnɛ] *etc vb voir* **méconnaître**.

méconnaissable [mekɔnɛsabl(ə)] *adj* unrecognizable.

méconnaissais [mekɔnɛsɛ] *etc vb voir* **méconnaître**.

méconnaissance [mekɔnɛsɑ̃s] *nf* ignorance.

méconnaître [mekɔnɛtʀ(ə)] *vt* (*ignorer*) to be unaware of; (*mésestimer*) to misjudge.

méconnu, e [mekɔny] *pp de* **méconnaître ♦** *adj* (*génie etc*) unrecognized.

mécontent, e [mekɔ̃tɑ̃, -ɑ̃t] *adj*: ~ (**de**) (*insatisfait*) discontented *ou* dissatisfied *ou* displeased (with); (*contrarié*) annoyed (at) **♦** *nm/f* malcontent, dissatisfied person.

mécontentement [mekɔ̃tɑ̃tmɑ̃] *nm* dissatisfaction, discontent, displeasure; annoyance.

mécontenter [mekɔ̃tɑ̃te] *vt* to displease.

Mecque [mɛk] *nf*: **la ~** Mecca.

mécréant, e [mekʀeɑ̃, -ɑ̃t] *adj* (*peuple*) infidel; (*personne*) atheistic.

méd. *abr* = **médecin**.

médaille [medaj] *nf* medal.

médaillé, e [medaje] *nm/f* (*SPORT*) medalholder.

médaillon [medajɔ̃] *nm* (*portrait*) medallion; (*bijou*) locket; (*CULIN*) médaillon; **en ~** *adj* (*carte etc*) inset.

médecin [medsɛ̃] *nm* doctor; ~ **du bord** (*NAVIG*) ship's doctor; ~ **généraliste** general practitioner, GP; ~ **légiste** forensic scientist (*BRIT*), medical examiner (*US*); ~ **traitant** family doctor, GP.

médecine [medsin] *nf* medicine; ~ **générale** general medicine; ~ **infantile** paediatrics *sg* (*BRIT*), pediatrics *sg* (*US*); ~ **légale** forensic medicine; ~ **préventive** preventive medicine; ~ **du travail** occupational *ou* industrial medicine; ~**s parallèles** *ou* **douces** alternative medicine.

médian, e [medjɑ̃, -an] *adj* median.

médias [medja] *nmpl*: **les ~** the media.

médiateur, trice [medjatœʀ, -tʀis] *nm/f* (*voir médiation*) mediator; arbitrator.

médiathèque [medjatɛk] *nf* media library.

médiation [medjɑsjɔ̃] *nf* mediation; (*dans conflit social etc*) arbitration.

médiatique [medjatik] *adj* media *cpd*.

médiatisé, e [medjatize] *adj* reported in the media; **ce procès a été très ~** (*péj*) this trial was turned into a media event.

médiator [medjatɔʀ] *nm* plectrum.

médical, e, aux [medikal, -o] *adj* medical; **visiteur** *ou* **délégué ~** medical rep *ou* representative.

médicalement [medikalmɑ̃] *adv* medically.

médicament [medikamɑ̃] *nm* medicine, drug.

médicamenteux, euse [medikamɑ̃tø, -øz] *adj* medicinal.

médication [medikɑsjɔ̃] *nf* medication.

médicinal, e, aux [medisinal, -o] *adj* medicinal.

médico-légal, e, aux [medikɔlegal, -o] *adj* forensic.

médico-social, e, aux [medikɔsɔsjal, -o] *adj*: **assistance ~e** medical and social assistance.

médiéval, e, aux [medjeval, -o] *adj* medieval.

médiocre [medjɔkʀ(ə)] *adj* mediocre, poor.

médiocrité [medjɔkʀite] *nf* mediocrity.

médire [mediʀ] *vi*: ~ **de** to speak ill of.

médisance [medizɑ̃s] *nf* scandalmongering *no pl* (*BRIT*), mud-slinging *no pl*; (*propos*) piece of scandal *ou* malicious gossip.

médisant, e [medizɑ̃, -ɑ̃t] *vb voir* **médire ♦** *adj* slanderous, malicious.

médit, e [medi, -it] *pp de* **médire**.

méditatif, ive [meditatif, -iv] *adj* thoughtful.

méditation [meditɑsjɔ̃] *nf* meditation.

méditer [medite] *vt* (*approfondir*) to meditate on, ponder (over); (*combiner*) to meditate **♦** *vi* to meditate; ~ **de faire** to contemplate doing, plan to do.

Méditerranée [mediterane] *nf*: **la (mer) ~** the Mediterranean (Sea).

méditerranéen, ne [mediteraneɛ̃, -ɛn] *adj* Mediterranean **♦** *nm/f*: **M~, ne** Mediterranean.

médium [medjɔm] *nm* medium (*spiritualist*).

médius [medjys] *nm* middle finger.

méduse [medyz] *nf* jellyfish.
méduser [medyze] *vt* to dumbfound.
meeting [mitiŋ] *nm* (POL, SPORT) rally, meeting; ~ **d'aviation** air show.
méfait [mefɛ] *nm* (*faute*) misdemeanour, wrongdoing; ~**s** *nmpl* (*ravages*) ravages.
méfiance [mefjɑ̃s] *nf* mistrust, distrust.
méfiant, e [mefjɑ̃, -ɑ̃t] *adj* mistrustful, distrustful.
méfier [mefje]: **se** ~ *vi* to be wary; (*faire attention*) to be careful; **se** ~ **de** *vt* to mistrust, distrust, be wary of; to be careful about.
mégalomane [megalɔman] *adj* megalomaniac.
mégalomanie [megalɔmani] *nf* megalomania.
mégalopole [megalɔpɔl] *nf* megalopolis.
méga-octet [megaɔktɛ] *nm* megabyte.
mégarde [megaRd(ə)] *nf*: **par** ~ accidentally; (*par erreur*) by mistake.
mégatonne [megatɔn] *nf* megaton.
mégère [meʒɛR] *nf* (*péj: femme*) shrew.
mégot [mego] *nm* cigarette end *ou* butt.
mégoter [megɔte] *vi* to nitpick.
meilleur, e [mɛjœR] *adj*, *adv* better; (*valeur superlative*) best ♦ *nm*: **le** ~ (*celui qui ...*) the best (one); (*ce qui ...*) the best ♦ *nf*: **la** ~**e** the best (one); **le** ~ **des deux** the better of the two; **de** ~**e heure** earlier; ~ **marché** cheaper.
méjuger [meʒyʒe] *vt* to misjudge.
mélancolie [melɑ̃kɔli] *nf* melancholy, gloom.
mélancolique [melɑ̃kɔlik] *adj* melancholy, gloomy.
Mélanésie [melanezi] *nf*: **la** ~ Melanesia.
mélange [melɑ̃ʒ] *nm* (*opération*) mixing; blending; (*résultat*) mixture; blend; **sans** ~ unadulterated.
mélanger [melɑ̃ʒe] *vt* (*substances*) to mix; (*vins, couleurs*) to blend; (*mettre en désordre, confondre*) to mix up, muddle (up); **se** ~ (*liquides, couleurs*) to blend, mix.
mélanine [melanin] *nf* melanin.
mélasse [melas] *nf* treacle, molasses *sg*.
mêlée [mele] *nf* (*bataille, cohue*) mêlée, scramble; (*lutte, conflit*) tussle, scuffle; (RUGBY) scrum(mage).
mêler [mele] *vt* (*substances, odeurs, races*) to mix; (*embrouiller*) to muddle (up), mix up; **se** ~ to mix; (*se joindre, s'allier*) to mingle; **se** ~ **à** (*suj: personne*) to join; to mix with; (*: odeurs etc*) to mingle with; **se** ~ **de** (*suj: personne*) to meddle with, interfere in; **mêle-toi de tes affaires!** mind your own business!; ~ **à** *ou* **avec** *ou* **de** to mix with; to mingle with; ~ **qn à** (*affaire*) to get sb mixed up *ou* involved in.
mélo [melo] *nm*, *adj* = **mélodrame, mélodramatique**.
mélodie [melɔdi] *nf* melody.
mélodieux, euse [melɔdjø, -øz] *adj* melodious, tuneful.
mélodique [melɔdik] *adj* melodic.
mélodramatique [melɔdRamatik] *adj* melodramatic.
mélodrame [melɔdRam] *nm* melodrama.
mélomane [melɔman] *nm/f* music lover.
melon [məlɔ̃] *nm* (BOT) (honeydew) melon; (*aussi*: **chapeau** ~) bowler (hat); ~ **d'eau** watermelon.
mélopée [melɔpe] *nf* monotonous chant.
membrane [mɑ̃bRan] *nf* membrane.
membre [mɑ̃bR(ə)] *nm* (ANAT) limb; (*personne, pays, élément*) member ♦ *adj* member; **être** ~ **de** to be a member of; ~ (**viril**) (male) organ.
mémé [meme] *nf* (*fam*) granny; (*: vieille femme*) old dear.

════════════════════════════ MOT-CLÉ

même [mɛm] *adj* **1** (*avant le nom*) same; **en** ~ **temps** at the same time; **ils ont les** ~**s goûts** they have the same *ou* similar tastes
2 (*après le nom: renforcement*): **il est la loyauté** ~ he is loyalty itself; **ce sont ses paroles/celles-là** ~ they are his very words/the very ones
♦ *pron*: **le(la)** ~ the same one
♦ *adv* **1** (*renforcement*): **il n'a** ~ **pas pleuré** he didn't even cry; ~ **lui l'a dit** even *HE* said it; **ici** ~ at this very place; ~ **si** even if
2: **à** ~: **à** ~ **la bouteille** straight from the bottle; **à** ~ **la peau** next to the skin; **être à** ~ **de faire** to be in a position to do, be able to do; **mettre qn à** ~ **de faire** to enable sb to do
3: **de** ~: likewise; **faire de** ~ to do likewise *ou* the same; **lui de** ~ so does (*ou* did *ou* is) he; **de** ~ **que** just as; **il en va de** ~ **pour** the same goes for.

mémento [memɛ̃to] *nm* (*agenda*) appointments diary; (*ouvrage*) summary.
mémoire [memwaR] *nf* memory ♦ *nm* (ADMIN, JUR) memorandum (*pl* -a); (SCOL) dissertation, paper; **avoir la** ~ **des visages/chiffres** to have a (good) memory for faces/figures; **n'avoir aucune** ~ to have a terrible memory; **avoir de la** ~ to have a good memory; **à la** ~ **de** to the *ou* in memory of; **pour** ~ *adv* for the record; **de** ~ *adv* from memory; **de** ~ **d'homme** in living memory; **mettre en** ~ (INFORM) to store; ~ **morte** ROM; ~ **rémanente** *ou* **non volatile** non-volatile memory; ~ **vive** RAM.
mémoires [memwaR] *nmpl* memoirs.
mémorable [memɔRabl(ə)] *adj* memorable.
mémorandum [memɔRɑ̃dɔm] *nm* memorandum (*pl* -a); (*carnet*) notebook.
mémorial, aux [memɔRjal, -o] *nm* memorial.
mémoriser [memɔRize] *vt* to memorize; (INFORM) to store.
menaçant, e [mənasɑ̃, -ɑ̃t] *adj* threatening, menacing.
menace [mənas] *nf* threat; ~ **en l'air** empty threat.
menacer [mənase] *vt* to threaten; ~ **qn de qch/de faire qch** to threaten sb with sth/to

do sth.

ménage [menaʒ] *nm* (*travail*) housekeeping, housework; (*couple*) (married) couple; (*famille*, ADMIN) household; **faire le** ~ to do the housework; **faire des** ~s to work as a cleaner (*in people's homes*); **monter son** ~ to set up house; **se mettre en** ~ (avec) to set up house (with); **heureux en** ~ happily married; **faire bon** ~ **avec** to get on well with; ~ **de poupée** doll's kitchen set; ~ **à trois** love triangle.

ménagement [menaʒmã] *nm* care and attention; ~s *nmpl* (*égards*) consideration *sg*, attention *sg*.

ménager [menaʒe] *vt* (*traiter avec mesure*) to handle with tact; to treat considerately; (*utiliser*) to use with care; (*: avec économie*) to use sparingly; (*prendre soin de*) to take (great) care of, look after; (*organiser*) to arrange; (*installer*) to put in; to make; **se** ~ to look after o.s.; ~ **qch à qn** (*réserver*) to have sth in store for sb.

ménager, ère [menaʒe, -ɛʀ] *adj* household *cpd*, domestic ♦ *nf* (*femme*) housewife (*pl* -wives); (*couverts*) canteen (of cutlery).

ménagerie [menaʒʀi] *nf* menagerie.

mendiant, e [mãdjã, -ãt] *nm/f* beggar.

mendicité [mãdisite] *nf* begging.

mendier [mãdje] *vi* to beg ♦ *vt* to beg (for); (*fig: éloges, compliments*) to fish for.

menées [məne] *nfpl* intrigues, manœuvres (BRIT), maneuvers (US); (COMM) activities.

mener [məne] *vt* to lead; (*enquête*) to conduct; (*affaires*) to manage, conduct, run ♦ *vi*: ~ (à la marque) to lead, be in the lead; ~ **à/dans** (*emmener*) to take to/into; ~ **qch à bonne fin** *ou* **à terme** *ou* **à bien** to see sth through (to a successful conclusion), complete sth successfully.

meneur, euse [mənœʀ, -øz] *nm/f* leader; (*péj: agitateur*) ringleader; ~ **d'hommes** born leader; ~ **de jeu** host, quizmaster (BRIT).

menhir [meniʀ] *nm* standing stone.

méningite [menɛ̃ʒit] *nf* meningitis *no pl.*

ménisque [menisk] *nm* (ANAT) meniscus.

ménopause [menopoz] *nf* menopause.

menotte [mənɔt] *nf* (*langage enfantin*) handie; ~s *nfpl* handcuffs; **passer les** ~s **à** to handcuff.

mens [mã] *vb voir* **mentir**.

mensonge [mãsɔ̃ʒ] *nm*: **le** ~ lying *no pl*; **un** ~ a lie.

mensonger, ère [mãsɔ̃ʒe, -ɛʀ] *adj* false.

menstruation [mãstʀyasjɔ̃] *nf* menstruation.

menstruel, le [mãstʀyɛl] *adj* menstrual.

mensualiser [mãsɥalize] *vt* to pay monthly.

mensualité [mãsɥalite] *nf* (*somme payée*) monthly payment; (*somme perçue*) monthly salary.

mensuel, le [mãsɥɛl] *adj* monthly ♦ *nm/f* (*employé*) employee paid monthly ♦ *nm* (PRESSE) monthly.

mensuellement [mãsɥɛlmã] *adv* monthly.

mensurations [mãsyʀasjɔ̃] *nfpl* measurements.

mentais [mãtɛ] *etc vb voir* **mentir**.

mental, e, aux [mãtal, -o] *adj* mental.

mentalement [mãtalmã] *adv* in one's head, mentally.

mentalité [mãtalite] *nf* mentality.

menteur, euse [mãtœʀ, -øz] *nm/f* liar.

menthe [mãt] *nf* mint; ~ (à l'eau) peppermint cordial.

mentholé, e [mãtɔle] *adj* menthol *cpd*, mentholated.

mention [mãsjɔ̃] *nf* (*note*) note, comment; (SCOL): ~ (**très**) **bien/passable** (*very*) good/ satisfactory pass; **faire** ~ **de** to mention; "**rayer la** ~ **inutile**" "delete as appropriate".

mentionner [mãsjɔne] *vt* to mention.

mentir [mãtiʀ] *vi* to lie.

menton [mãtɔ̃] *nm* chin.

mentonnière [mãtɔnjɛʀ] *nf* chin strap.

menu, e [məny] *adj* (*mince*) thin; (*petit*) tiny; (*frais, difficulté*) minor ♦ *adv* (*couper, hacher*) very fine ♦ *nm* menu; **par le** ~ (*raconter*) in minute detail; ~ **touristique** popular *ou* tourist menu; ~e **monnaie** small change.

menuet [mənɥɛ] *nm* minuet.

menuiserie [mənɥizʀi] *nf* (*travail*) joinery, carpentry; (*d'amateur*) woodwork; (*local*) joiner's workshop; (*ouvrages*) woodwork *no pl.*

menuisier [mənɥizje] *nm* joiner, carpenter.

méprendre [mepʀãdʀ(ə)]: **se** ~ *vi*: **se** ~ **sur** to be mistaken about.

mépris, e [mepʀi, -iz] *pp de* **méprendre** ♦ *nm* (*dédain*) contempt, scorn; (*indifférence*): **le** ~ **de** contempt *ou* disregard for; **au** ~ **de** regardless of, in defiance of.

méprisable [mepʀizabl(ə)] *adj* contemptible, despicable.

méprisant, e [mepʀizã, -ãt] *adj* contemptuous, scornful.

méprise [mepʀiz] *nf* mistake, error; (*malentendu*) misunderstanding.

mépriser [mepʀize] *vt* to scorn, despise; (*gloire, danger*) to scorn, spurn.

mer [mɛʀ] *nf* sea; (*marée*) tide; ~ **fermée** inland sea; **en** ~ at sea; **prendre la** ~ to put out to sea; **en haute** *ou* **pleine** ~ off shore, on the open sea; **la** ~ **Adriatique** the Adriatic (Sea); **la** ~ **des Antilles** *ou* **des Caraïbes** the Caribbean (Sea); **la** ~ **Baltique** the Baltic (Sea); **la** ~ **Caspienne** the Caspian Sea; **la** ~ **de Corail** the Coral Sea; **la** ~ **Égée** the Aegean (Sea); **la** ~ **Ionienne** the Ionian Sea; **la** ~ **Morte** the Dead Sea; **la** ~ **Noire** the Black Sea; **la** ~ **du Nord** the North Sea; **la** ~ **Rouge** the Red Sea; **la** ~ **des Sargasses** the Sargasso Sea, the Sargasso Sea; **les** ~s **du Sud** the South Seas; **la** ~ **Tyrrhénienne** the Tyrrhenian Sea.

mercantile [mɛʀkãtil] *adj* (*péj*) mercenary.

mercantilisme [mɛʀkãtilism(ə)] *nm* (*esprit*

mercantile) mercenary attitude.
mercenaire [mɛʀsənɛʀ] *nm* mercenary.
mercerie [mɛʀsəʀi] *nf* (*COUTURE*) haberdashery (*BRIT*), notions *pl* (*US*); (*boutique*) haberdasher's shop (*BRIT*), notions store (*US*).
merci [mɛʀsi] *excl* thank you ♦ *nf*: **à la ~ de qn/qch** at sb's mercy/the mercy of sth; **~ beaucoup** thank you very much; **~ de** *ou* **pour** thank you for; **sans ~** *adj* merciless ♦ *adv* mercilessly.
mercier, ière [mɛʀsje, -jɛʀ] *nm/f* haberdasher.
mercredi [mɛʀkʀədi] *nm* Wednesday; **~ des Cendres** Ash Wednesday; *voir aussi* **lundi**.
mercure [mɛʀkyʀ] *nm* mercury.
merde [mɛʀd(ə)] (*fam!*) *nf* shit (*!*) ♦ *excl* (bloody) hell (*!*).
merdeux, euse [mɛʀdø, -øz] *nm/f* (*fam!*) little bugger (*BRIT !*), little devil.
mère [mɛʀ] *nf* mother ♦ *adj inv* mother *cpd*; **~ célibataire** single parent, unmarried mother.
merguez [mɛʀgɛz] *nf* spicy North African sausage.
méridien [meʀidjɛ̃] *nm* meridian.
méridional, e, aux [meʀidjɔnal, -o] *adj* southern; (*du midi de la France*) Southern (French) ♦ *nm/f* Southerner.
meringue [məʀɛ̃g] *nf* meringue.
mérinos [meʀinos] *nm* merino.
merisier [məʀizje] *nm* wild cherry (tree).
méritant, e [meʀitɑ̃, -ɑ̃t] *adj* deserving.
mérite [meʀit] *nm* merit; **le ~ (de ceci) lui revient** the credit (for this) is his.
mériter [meʀite] *vt* to deserve; **~ de réussir** to deserve to succeed; **il mérite qu'on fasse ...** he deserves people to do ....
méritocratie [meʀitɔkʀasi] *nf* meritocracy.
méritoire [meʀitwaʀ] *adj* praiseworthy, commendable.
merlan [mɛʀlɑ̃] *nm* whiting.
merle [mɛʀl(ə)] *nm* blackbird.
mérou [meʀu] *nm* grouper (*fish*).
merveille [mɛʀvɛj] *nf* marvel, wonder; **faire ~** *ou* **des ~s** to work wonders; **à ~** perfectly, wonderfully.
merveilleux, euse [mɛʀvɛjø, -øz] *adj* marvellous, wonderful.
mes [me] *adj possessif voir* **mon**.
mésalliance [mezaljɑ̃s] *nf* misalliance, mismatch.
mésallier [mezalje]: **se ~** *vi* to marry beneath (*ou* above) o.s.
mésange [mezɑ̃ʒ] *nf* tit(mouse) (*pl* -mice); **~ bleue** bluetit.
mésaventure [mezavɑ̃tyʀ] *nf* misadventure, misfortune.
Mesdames [medam] *nfpl voir* **Madame**.
Mesdemoiselles [medmwazɛl] *nfpl voir* **Mademoiselle**.
mésentente [mezɑ̃tɑ̃t] *nf* dissension, disagreement.
mésestimer [mezɛstime] *vt* to underestimate, underrate.
Mésopotamie [mezɔpɔtami] *nf*: **la ~** Mesopotamia.
mésopotamien, ne [mezɔpɔtamjɛ̃, -ɛn] *adj* Mesopotamian.
mesquin, e [mɛskɛ̃, -in] *adj* mean, petty.
mesquinerie [mɛskinʀi] *nf* meanness *no pl*, pettiness *no pl*.
mess [mɛs] *nm* mess.
message [mesaʒ] *nm* message; **~ d'erreur** (*INFORM*) error message; **~ (de guidage)** (*INFORM*) prompt; **~ publicitaire** ad, advertisement; **~ téléphoné** telegram dictated by telephone.
messager, ère [mesaʒe, -ɛʀ] *nm/f* messenger.
messagerie [mesaʒʀi] *nf*: **~ (électronique)** (electronic) bulletin board; **~ rose** lonely hearts and contact service on videotext; **~ vocale** (*service*) voice mail; **~s aériennes/maritimes** air freight/shipping service *sg*; **~s de presse** press distribution service.
messe [mɛs] *nf* mass; **aller à la ~** to go to mass; **~ de minuit** midnight mass; **faire des ~s basses** (*fig, péj*) to mutter.
messie [mesi] *nm*: **le M~** the Messiah.
Messieurs [mesjø] *nmpl voir* **Monsieur**.
mesure [məzyʀ] *nf* (*évaluation, dimension*) measurement; (*étalon, récipient, contenu*) measure; (*MUS: cadence*) time, tempo; (*: division*) bar; (*retenue*) moderation; (*disposition*) measure, step; **unité/système de ~** unit/system of measurement; **sur ~** (*costume*) made-to-measure; (*fig*) personally adapted; **à la ~ de** (*fig: personne*) worthy of; (*chambre etc*) on the same scale as; **dans la ~ où** insofar as, inasmuch as; **dans une certaine ~** to some *ou* a certain extent; **à ~ que** as; **en ~** (*MUS*) in time *ou* tempo; **être en ~ de** to be in a position to; **dépasser la ~** (*fig*) to overstep the mark.
mesuré, e [məzyʀe] *adj* (*ton, effort*) measured; (*personne*) restrained.
mesurer [məzyʀe] *vt* to measure; (*juger*) to weigh up, assess; (*limiter*) to limit, ration; (*modérer*) to moderate; (*proportionner*): **~ qch à** to match sth to, gear sth to; **se ~ avec** to have a confrontation with; to tackle; **il mesure 1 m 80** he's 1 m 80 tall.
met [mɛ] *vb voir* **mettre**.
métabolisme [metabɔlism(ə)] *nm* metabolism.
métairie [meteʀi] *nf* smallholding.
métal, aux [metal, -o] *nm* metal.
métalangage [metalɑ̃gaʒ] *nm* metalanguage.
métallique [metalik] *adj* metallic.
métallisé, e [metalize] *adj* metallic.
métallurgie [metalyʀʒi] *nf* metallurgy.
métallurgique [metalyʀʒik] *adj* steel *cpd*, metal *cpd*.
métallurgiste [metalyʀʒist(ə)] *nm/f* (*ouvrier*) steel *ou* metal worker; (*industriel*) metallurgist.
métamorphose [metamɔʀfoz] *nf* metamor-

phosis (*pl* -oses).

métamorphoser [metamɔʀfoze] *vt* to transform.

métaphore [metafɔʀ] *nf* metaphor.

métaphorique [metafɔʀik] *adj* metaphorical, figurative.

métaphoriquement [metafɔʀikmɑ̃] *adv* metaphorically.

métaphysique [metafizik] *nf* metaphysics *sg* ♦ *adj* metaphysical.

métapsychique [metapsiʃik] *adj* psychic, parapsychological.

métayer, ère [meteje, metejɛʀ] *nm/f* (tenant) farmer.

météo [meteo] *nf* (*bulletin*) (weather) forecast; (*service*) ≈ Met Office (*BRIT*), ≈ National Weather Service (*US*).

météore [meteɔʀ] *nm* meteor.

météorite [meteɔʀit] *nm ou f* meteorite.

météorologie [meteɔʀɔlɔʒi] *nf* (*étude*) meteorology; (*service*) ≈ Meteorological Office (*BRIT*), ≈ National Weather Service (*US*).

météorologique [meteɔʀɔlɔʒik] *adj* meteorological, weather *cpd*.

météorologue [meteɔʀɔlɔg] *nm/f*, **météorologiste** [meteɔʀɔlɔʒist(ə)] *nm/f* meteorologist, weather forecaster.

métèque [metɛk] *nm* (*péj*) wop (!).

méthane [metan] *nm* methane.

méthanier [metanje] *nm* (*bateau*) (liquefied) gas carrier *ou* tanker.

méthode [metɔd] *nf* method; (*livre, ouvrage*) manual, tutor.

méthodique [metɔdik] *adj* methodical.

méthodiquement [metɔdikmɑ̃] *adv* methodically.

méthodiste [metɔdist(ə)] *adj*, *nm/f* (*REL*) Methodist.

méthylène [metilɛn] *nm*: **bleu de** ~ *nm* methylene blue.

méticuleux, euse [metikylø, -øz] *adj* meticulous.

métier [metje] *nm* (*profession: gén*) job; (: *manuel*) trade; (: *artisanal*) craft; (*technique, expérience*) (acquired) skill *ou* technique; (*aussi*: ~ **à tisser**) (weaving) loom; **être du** ~ to be in the trade *ou* profession.

métis, se [metis] *adj*, *nm/f* half-caste, half-breed.

métisser [metise] *vt* to cross(breed).

métrage [metʀaʒ] *nm* (*de tissu*) length; (*CINÉ*) footage, length; **long/moyen/court** ~ feature *ou* full-length/medium-length/short film.

mètre [mɛtʀ(ə)] *nm* metre (*BRIT*), meter (*US*); (*règle*) (metre *ou* meter) rule; (*ruban*) tape measure; ~ **carré/cube** square/cubic metre *ou* meter.

métrer [metʀe] *vt* (*TECH*) to measure (in metres *ou* meters); (*CONSTR*) to survey.

métreur, euse [metʀœʀ, -øz] *nm/f*: ~ (**vérificateur**), **métreuse (vérificatrice)** (quantity)

surveyor.

métrique [metʀik] *adj* metric ♦ *nf* metrics *sg*.

métro [metʀo] *nm* underground (*BRIT*), subway (*US*).

métronome [metʀɔnɔm] *nm* metronome.

métropole [metʀɔpɔl] *nf* (*capitale*) metropolis; (*pays*) home country.

métropolitain, e [metʀɔpɔlitɛ̃, -ɛn] *adj* metropolitan.

mets [mɛ] *nm* dish ♦ *vb voir* **mettre**.

mettable [mɛtabl(ə)] *adj* fit to be worn, decent.

metteur [mɛtœʀ] *nm*: ~ **en scène** (*THÉÂT*) producer; (*CINÉ*) director; ~ **en ondes** (*RADIO*) producer.

=================================== *MOT-CLÉ*

mettre [mɛtʀ(ə)] *vt* **1** (*placer*) to put; ~ **en bouteille/en sac** to bottle/put in bags *ou* sacks; ~ **qch à la poste** to post sth (*BRIT*), mail sth; ~ **un examen (pour)** to charge (with) (*BRIT*), indict (for) (*US*); ~ **une note gaie/amusante** to inject a cheerful/an amusing note; ~ **qn debout/assis** to help sb up *ou* to their feet/help sb to sit down

2 (*vêtements: revêtir*) to put on; (: *porter*) to wear; **mets ton gilet** put your cardigan on; **je ne mets plus mon manteau** I no longer wear my coat

3 (*faire fonctionner: chauffage, électricité*) to put on; (: *reveil, minuteur*) to set; (*installer: gaz, eau*) to put in, lay on; ~ **en marche** to start up

4 (*consacrer*): ~ **du temps/2 heures à faire qch** to take time/2 hours to do sth *ou* over sth; **y** ~ **du sien** to pull one's weight

5 (*noter, écrire*) to say, put (down); **qu'est-ce qu'il a mis sur la carte?** what did he say *ou* write on the card?; **mettez au pluriel ...** put ... into the plural

6 (*supposer*): **mettons que ...** let's suppose *ou* say that ...

7 (*faire +vb*): **faire** ~ **le gaz/l'électricité** to have gas/electricity put in *ou* installed

se ~ *vi* **1** (*se placer*): **vous pouvez vous** ~ **là** you can sit (*ou* stand) there; **où ça se met?** where does it go?; **se** ~ **au lit** to get into bed; **se** ~ **au piano** to sit down at the piano; **se** ~ **à l'eau** to get into the water; **se** ~ **de l'encre sur les doigts** to get ink on one's fingers

2 (*s'habiller*): **se** ~ **en maillot de bain** to get into *ou* put on a swimsuit; **n'avoir rien à se** ~ to have nothing to wear

3 (*dans rapports*): **se** ~ **bien/mal avec qn** to get on the right/wrong side of sb; **se** ~ **qn à dos** to get on sb's bad side; **se** ~ **avec qn** (*prendre parti*) to side with sb; (*faire équipe*) to team up with sb; (*en ménage*) to move in with sb

4: **se** ~ **à** to begin, start; **se** ~ **à faire** to begin *ou* start doing *ou* to do; **se** ~ **au piano** to start learning the piano; **se ~ au régime** to go on a diet; **se ~ au travail/à l'étude** to get down to work/one's studies; **il est temps de s'y ~** it's time we got down to it *ou* got on with it.

meublant, e [mœblɑ̃, -ɑ̃t] *adj* (*tissus etc*) effective (in the room).

meuble [mœbl(ə)] *nm* (*objet*) piece of furniture; (*ameublement*) furniture *no pl* ♦ *adj* (*terre*) loose, friable; (*JUR*): **biens ~s** movables.

meublé [mœble] *nm* (*pièce*) furnished room; (*appartement*) furnished flat (*BRIT*) *ou* apartment (*US*).

meubler [mœble] *vt* to furnish; (*fig*): **~ qch (de)** to fill sth (with); **se ~** to furnish one's house.

meugler [møgle] *vi* to low, moo.

meule [møl] *nf* (*à broyer*) millstone; (*à aiguiser*) grindstone; (*à polir*) buffwheel; (*de foin, blé*) stack; (*de fromage*) round.

meunerie [mønʀi] *nf* (*industrie*) flour trade; (*métier*) milling.

meunier, ière [mønje, -jɛʀ] *nm* miller ♦ *nf* miller's wife ♦ *adj f* (*CULIN*) meunière.

meurs [mœʀ] *etc vb voir* **mourir**.

meurtre [mœʀtʀ(ə)] *nm* murder.

meurtrier, ière [mœʀtʀije, -jɛʀ] *adj* (*arme, épidémie, combat*) deadly; (*accident*) fatal; (*carrefour, route*) lethal; (*fureur, instincts*) murderous ♦ *nm/f* murderer/murderess ♦ *nf* (*ouverture*) loophole.

meurtrir [mœʀtʀiʀ] *vt* to bruise; (*fig*) to wound.

meurtrissure [mœʀtʀisyʀ] *nf* bruise; (*fig*) scar.

meus [mœ] *etc vb voir* **mouvoir**.

Meuse [møz] *nf*: **la ~** the Meuse.

meute [møt] *nf* pack.

meuve [mœv] *etc vb voir* **mouvoir**.

mévente [mevɑ̃t] *nf* slump (in sales).

mexicain, e [mɛksikɛ̃, -ɛn] *adj* Mexican ♦ *nm/f*: **M~, e** Mexican.

Mexico [mɛksiko] *n* Mexico City.

Mexique [mɛksik] *nm*: **le ~** Mexico.

mezzanine [mɛdzanin] *nf* mezzanine (floor).

MF *sigle mpl* = millions de francs ♦ *sigle f* (*RADIO*: = modulation de fréquence*) FM.

Mgr *abr* = **Monseigneur**.

mi [mi] *nm* (*MUS*) E; (*en chantant la gamme*) mi.

mi... [mi] *préfixe* half(-); mid-; **à la ~-janvier** in mid-January; **~-bureau, ~-chambre** half office, half bedroom; **à ~-jambes/-corps** (up *ou* down) to the knees/waist; **à ~-hauteur/-pente** halfway up (*ou* down)/up (*ou* down) the hill.

miaou [mjau] *nm* miaow.

miaulement [mjolmɑ̃] *nm* (*cri*) miaow; (*continu*) miaowing *no pl*.

miauler [mjole] *vi* to miaow.

mi-bas [miba] *nm inv* knee-length sock.

mica [mika] *nm* mica.

mi-carême [mikaʀɛm] *nf*: **la ~** the third Thursday in Lent.

miche [miʃ] *nf* round *ou* cob loaf.

mi-chemin [miʃmɛ̃]: **à ~** *adv* halfway, midway.

mi-clos, e [miklo, -kloz] *adj* half-closed.

micmac [mikmak] *nm* (*péj*) carry-on.

mi-côte [mikot]: **à ~** *adv* halfway up (*ou* down) the hill.

mi-course [mikuʀs]: **à ~** *adv* halfway through the race.

micro [mikʀo] *nm* mike, microphone; (*INFORM*) micro; **~ cravate** lapel mike.

microbe [mikʀɔb] *nm* germ, microbe.

microbiologie [mikʀɔbjɔlɔʒi] *nf* microbiology.

microchirurgie [mikʀoʃiʀyʀʒi] *nf* microsurgery.

microclimat [mikʀoklima] *nm* microclimate.

microcosme [mikʀɔkɔsm(ə)] *nm* microcosm.

micro-édition [mikʀoedisjɔ̃] *nf* desk-top publishing.

micro-électronique [mikʀoelɛktʀɔnik] *nf* microelectronics *sg*.

microfiche [mikʀofiʃ] *nf* microfiche.

microfilm [mikʀofilm] *nm* microfilm.

micro-onde [mikʀoɔ̃d] *nf*: **four à ~s** microwave oven.

micro-ordinateur [mikʀoɔʀdinatœʀ] *nm* microcomputer.

micro-organisme [mikʀoɔʀganism(ə)] *nm* micro-organism.

microphone [mikʀofɔn] *nm* microphone.

microplaquette [mikʀoplakɛt] *nf* microchip.

microprocesseur [mikʀopʀɔsɛsœʀ] *nm* microprocessor.

microscope [mikʀɔskɔp] *nm* microscope; **au ~** under *ou* through the microscope.

microscopique [mikʀɔskɔpik] *adj* microscopic.

microsillon [mikʀosijɔ̃] *nm* long-playing record.

MIDEM [midɛm] *sigle m* (= Marché international du disque et de l'édition musicale) music industry trade fair.

midi [midi] *nm* (*milieu du jour*) midday, noon; (*moment du déjeuner*) lunchtime; (*sud*) south; (: *de la France*): **le M~** the South (of France), the Midi; **à ~** at 12 (o'clock) *ou* midday *ou* noon; **tous les ~s** every lunchtime; **le repas de ~** lunch; **en plein ~** (right) in the middle of the day; (*sud*) facing south.

midinette [midinɛt] *nf* silly young townie.

mie [mi] *nf* inside (of the loaf).

miel [mjɛl] *nm* honey; **être tout ~** (*fig*) to be all sweetness and light.

mielleux, euse [mjɛlø, -øz] *adj* (*péj*) sugary, honeyed.

mien, ne [mjɛ̃, mjɛn] *adj, pron*: **le (la) ~(ne), les ~s mine; les ~s** (*ma famille*) my family.

miette [mjɛt] *nf* (*de pain, gâteau*) crumb; (*fig: de la conversation etc*) scrap; **en ~s** (*fig*) in pieces *ou* bits.

========================= MOT-CLÉ

mieux [mjø] *adv* **1** (*d'une meilleure façon*): ~ **(que)** better (than); **elle travaille/mange ~** she works/eats better; **aimer ~** to prefer; **j'attendais ~ de vous** I expected better of you; **elle va ~** she is better; **de ~ en ~** better and better

2 (*de la meilleure façon*) best; **ce que je sais le ~** what I know best; **les livres les ~ faits** the best made books

3 (*intensif*): **vous feriez ~ de faire ...** you would be better to do ...; **crier à qui ~ ~** to try to shout each other down

♦ *adj* **1** (*plus à l'aise, en meilleure forme*) better; **se sentir ~** to feel better

2 (*plus satisfaisant*) better; **c'est ~ ainsi** it's better like this; **c'est le ~ des deux** it's the better of the two; **le(la) ~, les ~** the best; **demandez-lui, c'est le ~** ask him, it's the best thing

3 (*plus joli*) better-looking; (*plus gentil*) nicer; **il est ~ que son frère** (*plus beau*) he's better-looking than his brother; (*plus gentil*) he's nicer than his brother; **il est ~ sans moustache** he looks better without a moustache

4: **au ~** at best; **au ~ avec** on the best of terms with; **pour le ~** for the best; **qui ~ est** even better, better still

♦ *nm* **1** (*progrès*) improvement

2: **de mon/ton ~** as best I/you can (*ou* could); **faire de son ~** to do one's best; **du ~ qu'il peut** the best he can; **faute de ~** for want of anything better, failing anything better.

mieux-être [mjøzɛtʀ(ə)] *nm* greater well-being; (*financier*) improved standard of living.

mièvre [mjɛvʀ(ə)] *adj* sickly sentimental.

mignon, ne [miɲɔ̃, -ɔn] *adj* sweet, cute.

migraine [migʀɛn] *nf* headache; migraine.

migrant, e [migʀɑ̃, -ɑ̃t] *adj, nm/f* migrant.

migrateur, trice [migʀatœʀ, -tʀis] *adj* migratory.

migration [migʀasjɔ̃] *nf* migration.

mijaurée [miʒɔʀe] *nf* pretentious (young) madam.

mijoter [miʒɔte] *vt* to simmer; (*préparer avec soin*) to cook lovingly; (*affaire, projet*) to plot, cook up ♦ *vi* to simmer.

mil [mil] *num* = **mille**.

Milan [milɑ̃] *n* Milan.

milanais, e [milanɛ, -ɛz] *adj* Milanese.

mildiou [mildju] *nm* mildew.

milice [milis] *nf* militia.

milicien, ne [milisjɛ̃, -ɛn] *nm/f* militiaman/woman.

milieu, x [miljø] *nm* (*centre*) middle; (*fig*) middle course *ou* way; (*aussi:* **juste ~**) happy medium; (*BIO, GÉO*) environment; (*entourage social*) milieu; (*familial*) background; circle; (*pègre*): **le ~** the underworld; **au ~ de** in the middle of; **au beau *ou* en plein ~ (de)** right in the middle (of); **~ de terrain** (*FOOTBALL*: *joueur*) midfield player; (: *joueurs*) midfield.

militaire [militɛʀ] *adj* military ♦ *nm* serviceman; **service ~** military service.

militant, e [militɑ̃, -ɑ̃t] *adj, nm/f* militant.

militantisme [militɑ̃tism(ə)] *nm* militancy.

militariser [militaʀize] *vt* to militarize.

militarisme [militaʀism(ə)] *nm* (*péj*) militarism.

militer [milite] *vi* to be a militant; **~ pour/contre** to militate in favour of/against.

milk-shake [milkʃɛk] *nm* milk shake.

mille [mil] *num* a *ou* one thousand ♦ *nm* (*mesure*): **~ (marin)** nautical mile; **mettre dans le ~** to hit the bull's-eye; (*fig*) to be bang on (target).

millefeuille [milfœj] *nm* cream *ou* vanilla slice.

millénaire [milenɛʀ] *nm* millennium ♦ *adj* thousand-year-old; (*fig*) ancient.

mille-pattes [milpat] *nm inv* centipede.

millésime [milezim] *nm* year.

millésimé, e [milezime] *adj* vintage *cpd*.

millet [mijɛ] *nm* millet.

milliard [miljaʀ] *nm* milliard, thousand million (*BRIT*), billion (*US*).

milliardaire [miljaʀdɛʀ] *nm/f* multimillionaire (*BRIT*), billionaire (*US*).

millième [miljɛm] *num* thousandth.

millier [milje] *nm* thousand; **un ~ (de)** a thousand or so, about a thousand; **par ~s** in (their) thousands, by the thousand.

milligramme [miligʀam] *nm* milligramme (*BRIT*), milligram (*US*).

millimètre [milimɛtʀ(ə)] *nm* millimetre (*BRIT*), millimeter (*US*).

millimétré, e [milimetʀe] *adj*: **papier ~** graph paper.

million [miljɔ̃] *nm* million; **deux ~s de** two million; **riche à ~s** worth millions.

millionième [miljɔnjɛm] *num* millionth.

millionnaire [miljɔnɛʀ] *nm/f* millionaire.

mi-lourd [miluʀ] *adj m, nm* light heavyweight.

mime [mim] *nm/f* (*acteur*) mime(r); (*imitateur*) mimic ♦ *nm* (*art*) mime, miming.

mimer [mime] *vt* to mime; (*singer*) to mimic, take off.

mimétisme [mimetism(ə)] *nm* (*BIO*) mimicry.

mimique [mimik] *nf* (*funny*) face; (*signes*) gesticulations *pl*, sign language *no pl*.

mimosa [mimoza] *nm* mimosa.

mi-moyen [mimwajɛ̃] *adj m, nm* welterweight.

MIN *sigle m* (= *Marché d'intérêt national*) whole-sale market for fruit, vegetables and agricultural produce.

min. *abr* (= *minimum*) min.

minable [minabl(ə)] *adj* (*personne*) shabby(-looking); (*travail*) pathetic.

minaret [minaʀɛ] nm minaret.
minauder [minode] vi to mince, simper.
minauderies [minodʀi] nfpl simperings.
mince [mɛ̃s] adj thin; (personne, taille) slim, slender; (fig: profit, connaissances) slight, small; (: prétexte) weak ♦ excl: ~ (alors)! darn it!
minceur [mɛ̃sœʀ] nf thinness; slimness, slenderness.
mincir [mɛ̃siʀ] vi to get slimmer ou thinner.
mine [min] nf (physionomie) expression, look; (extérieur) exterior, appearance; (de crayon) lead; (gisement, exploitation, explosif) mine; ~s nfpl (péj) simpering airs; **les M~s** (ADMIN) the national mining and geological service; the government vehicle testing department; **avoir bonne** ~ (personne) to look well; (ironique) to look an utter idiot; **avoir mauvaise** ~ to look unwell ou poorly; **faire** ~ **de faire** to make a pretence of doing; to make as if to do; **ne pas payer de** ~ to be not much to look at; ~ **de rien** adv with a casual air; although you wouldn't think so; ~ **de charbon** coalmine; ~ **à ciel ouvert** opencast (BRIT) ou open-air (US) mine.
miner [mine] vt (saper) to undermine, erode; (MIL) to mine.
minerai [minʀɛ] nm ore.
minéral, e, aux [mineʀal, -o] adj mineral; (CHIMIE) inorganic ♦ nm mineral.
minéralier [mineʀalje] nm (bateau) ore tanker.
minéralisé, e [mineʀalize] adj mineralized.
minéralogie [mineʀalɔʒi] nf mineralogy.
minéralogique [mineʀalɔʒik] adj mineralogical; **plaque** ~ number (BRIT) ou license (US) plate; **numéro** ~ registration (BRIT) ou license (US) number.
minet, te [minɛ, -ɛt] nm/f (chat) pussy-cat; (péj) young trendy.
mineur, e [minœʀ] adj minor ♦ nm/f (JUR) minor ♦ nm (travailleur) miner; (MIL) sapper; ~ **de fond** face worker.
miniature [minjatyʀ] adj, nf miniature.
miniaturisation [minjatyʀizɑsjɔ̃] nf miniaturization.
miniaturiser [minjatyʀize] vt to miniaturize.
minibus [minibys] nm minibus.
mini-cassette [minikasɛt] nf cassette (recorder).
minichaîne [miniʃɛn] nf mini system.
minier, ière [minje, -jɛʀ] adj mining.
mini-jupe [miniʒyp] nf mini-skirt.
minimal, e, aux [minimal, -o] adj minimum.
minimaliste [minimalist(ə)] adj (ART) minimalist.
minime [minim] adj minor ♦ nm/f (SPORT) junior.
minimiser [minimize] vt to minimize; (fig) to play down.
minimum [minimɔm] adj, nm minimum; **au** ~ at the very least; ~ **vital** (salaire) living wage; (niveau de vie) subsistance level.

mini-ordinateur [miniɔʀdinatœʀ] nm mini-computer.
ministère [ministɛʀ] nm (cabinet) government; (département) ministry (BRIT), department; (REL) ministry; ~ **public** (JUR) Prosecution, State Prosecutor.
ministériel, le [ministeʀjɛl] adj government cpd; ministerial, departmental; (partisan) pro-government.
ministrable [ministʀabl(ə)] adj (POL): **il est** ~ he's a potential minister.
ministre [ministʀ(ə)] nm minister (BRIT), secretary; (REL) minister; ~ **d'État** senior minister ou secretary.
Minitel [minitɛl] nm ® videotext terminal and service.

Minitel is a personal computer terminal supplied by France-Télécom to telephone subscribers. It serves as a computerized telephone directory as well as giving access to a wide variety of services, including information on train timetables, the stock market and situations vacant. Services are accessed by dialling the relevant number on the telephone, and services used are included in the subscriber's phone bill.

---

minium [minjɔm] nm red lead paint.
minois [minwa] nm little face.
minorer [minɔʀe] vt to cut, reduce.
minoritaire [minɔʀitɛʀ] adj minority cpd.
minorité [minɔʀite] nf minority; **être en** ~ to be in the ou a minority; **mettre en** ~ (POL) to defeat.
Minorque [minɔʀk] nf Minorca.
minorquin, e [minɔʀkɛ̃, -in] adj Minorcan.
minoterie [minɔtʀi] nf flour-mill.
minuit [minɥi] nm midnight.
minuscule [minyskyl] adj minute, tiny ♦ nf: **(lettre)** ~ small letter.
minutage [minytaʒ] nm timing.
minute [minyt] nf minute; (JUR: original) minute, draft ♦ excl just a minute!, hang on!; **à la** ~ (présent) (just) this instant; (passé) there and then; **entrecôte** ou **steak** ~ minute steak.
minuter [minyte] vt to time.
minuterie [minytʀi] nf time switch.
minuteur [minytœʀ] nm timer.
minutie [minysi] nf meticulousness; minute detail; **avec** ~ meticulously; in minute detail.
minutieusement [minysjøzmɑ̃] adv (organiser, travailler) meticulously; (examiner) minutely.
minutieux, euse [minysjø, -øz] adj (personne) meticulous; (inspection) minutely detailed; (travail) requiring painstaking attention to detail.
mioche [mjɔʃ] nm (fam) nipper, brat.
mirabelle [miʀabɛl] nf (fruit) (cherry) plum; (eau-de-vie) plum brandy.

miracle [miʀakl(ə)] *nm* miracle.
miraculé, e [miʀakyle] *adj* who has been miraculously cured (*ou* rescued).
miraculeux, euse [miʀakylø, -øz] *adj* miraculous.
mirador [miʀadɔʀ] *nm* (*MIL*) watchtower.
mirage [miʀaʒ] *nm* mirage.
mire [miʀ] *nf* (*d'un fusil*) sight; (*TV*) test card; **point de ~** target; (*fig*) focal point; **ligne de ~** line of sight.
mirent [miʀ] *vb voir* **mettre**.
mirer [miʀe] *vt* (*œufs*) to candle; **se ~** *vi*: **se ~ dans** (*suj: personne*) to gaze at one's reflection in; (*: chose*) to be mirrored in.
mirifique [miʀifik] *adj* wonderful.
mirobolant, e [miʀɔbɔlɑ̃, -ɑ̃t] *adj* fantastic.
miroir [miʀwaʀ] *nm* mirror.
miroiter [miʀwate] *vi* to sparkle, shimmer; **faire ~ qch à qn** to paint sth in glowing colours for sb, dangle sth in front of sb's eyes.
miroiterie [miʀwatʀi] *nf* (*usine*) mirror factory; (*magasin*) mirror dealer's (shop).
Mis *abr* = **marquis**.
mis, e [mi, miz] *pp de* **mettre ♦** *adj* (*couvert, table*) set, laid; (*personne*): **bien ~** well dressed ♦ *nf* (*argent: au jeu*) stake; (*tenue*) clothing; attire; **être de ~e** to be acceptable *ou* in season; **~e en bouteilles** bottling; **~e en examen** charging, indictment; **~e à feu** blast-off; **~e de fonds** capital outlay; **~e à jour** updating; **~e à mort** kill; **~e à pied** (*d'un employé*) suspension; lay-off; **~e sur pied** (*d'une affaire, entreprise*) setting up; **~e en plis** set; **~e au point** (*PHOTO*) focusing; (*fig*) clarification; **~e à prix** reserve (*BRIT*) *ou* upset price; **~e en scène** production.
misaine [mizɛn] *nf*: **mât de ~** foremast.
misanthrope [mizɑ̃tʀɔp] *nm/f* misanthropist.
Mise *abr* = **marquise**.
mise [miz] *adj f, nf voir* **mis**.
miser [mize] *vt* (*enjeu*) to stake, bet; **~ sur** *vt* (*cheval, numéro*) to bet on; (*fig*) to bank *ou* count on.
misérable [mizeʀabl(ə)] *adj* (*lamentable, malheureux*) pitiful, wretched; (*pauvre*) poverty-stricken; (*insignifiant, mesquin*) miserable ♦ *nm/f* wretch; (*miséreux*) poor wretch.
misère [mizɛʀ] *nf* (*pauvreté*) (extreme) poverty, destitution; **~s** *nfpl* (*malheurs*) woes, miseries; (*ennuis*) little troubles; **être dans la ~** to be destitute *ou* poverty-stricken; **salaire de ~** starvation wage; **faire des ~s à qn** to torment sb; **~ noire** utter destitution, abject poverty.
miséreux, euse [mizeʀø, -øz] *adj* poverty-stricken ♦ *nm/f* down-and-out.
miséricorde [mizeʀikɔʀd(ə)] *nf* mercy, forgiveness.
miséricordieux, euse [mizeʀikɔʀdjø, -øz] *adj* merciful, forgiving.

misogyne [mizɔʒin] *adj* misogynous ♦ *nm/f* misogynist.
missel [misɛl] *nm* missal.
missile [misil] *nm* missile.
mission [misjɔ̃] *nf* mission; **partir en ~** (*ADMIN, POL*) to go on an assignment.
missionnaire [misjɔnɛʀ] *nm/f* missionary.
missive [misiv] *nf* missive.
mistral [mistʀal] *nm* mistral (wind).
mit [mi] *vb voir* **mettre**.
mitaine [mitɛn] *nf* mitt(en).
mite [mit] *nf* clothes moth.
mité, e [mite] *adj* moth-eaten.
mi-temps [mitɑ̃] *nf inv* (*SPORT: période*) half (*pl* halves); (*: pause*) half-time; **à ~** *adj, adv* part-time.
miteux, euse [mitø, -øz] *adj* seedy, shabby.
mitigé, e [mitiʒe] *adj* (*conviction, ardeur*) lukewarm; (*sentiments*) mixed.
mitonner [mitɔne] *vt* (*préparer*) to cook with loving care; (*fig*) to cook up quietly.
mitoyen, ne [mitwajɛ̃, -ɛn] *adj* common, party *cpd*; **maisons ~nes** semi-detached houses; (*plus de deux*) terraced (*BRIT*) *ou* row (*US*) houses.
mitraille [mitʀaj] *nf* (*balles de fonte*) grapeshot; (*décharge d'obus*) shellfire.
mitrailler [mitʀaje] *vt* to machine-gun; (*fig: photographier*) to snap away at; **~ qn de** to pelt *ou* bombard sb with.
mitraillette [mitʀajɛt] *nf* submachine gun.
mitrailleur [mitʀajœʀ] *nm* machine gunner ♦ *adj m*: **fusil ~** machine gun.
mitrailleuse [mitʀajøz] *nf* machine gun.
mitre [mitʀ(ə)] *nf* mitre.
mitron [mitʀɔ̃] *nm* baker's boy.
mi-voix [mivwa]: **à ~** *adv* in a low *ou* hushed voice.
mixage [miksaʒ] *nm* (*CINÉ*) (sound) mixing.
mixer, mixeur [miksœʀ] *nm* (*CULIN*) (food) mixer.
mixité [miksite] *nf* (*SCOL*) coeducation.
mixte [mikst(ə)] *adj* (*gén*) mixed; (*SCOL*) mixed, coeducational; **à usage ~** dual-purpose; **cuisinière ~** combined gas and electric cooker; **équipe ~** combined team.
mixture [mikstyʀ] *nf* mixture; (*fig*) concoction.
MJC *sigle f* (= *maison des jeunes et de la culture*) *community arts centre and youth club*.
ml *abr* (= *millilitre*) ml.
MLF *sigle m* (= *Mouvement de libération de la femme*) Women's Movement.
Mlle, *pl* **Mlles** *abr* = **Mademoiselle**.
MM *abr* = **Messieurs**; *voir* **Monsieur**.
Mme, *pl* **Mmes** *abr* = **Madame**.
mn. *abr* (= *minute*) min.
mnémotechnique [mnemɔtɛknik] *adj* mnemonic.
MNS *sigle m* (= *maître nageur sauveteur*) ≈ lifeguard.
MO *sigle f* (= *main-d'œuvre*) *labour costs* (on in-

voices).
Mo *abr* = **méga-octet, métro.**
mobile [mɔbil] *adj* mobile; (*amovible*) loose, removable; (*pièce de machine*) moving; (*élément de meuble etc*) movable ♦ *nm* (*motif*) motive; (*œuvre d'art*) mobile; (*PHYSIQUE*) moving object *ou* body.
mobilier, ière [mɔbilje, -jɛʀ] *adj* (*JUR*) personal ♦ *nm* (*meubles*) furniture; **valeurs mobilières** transferable securities; **vente mobilière** sale of personal property *ou* chattels.
mobilisation [mɔbilizasjɔ̃] *nf* mobilization.
mobiliser [mɔbilize] *vt* (*MIL, gén*) to mobilize.
mobilité [mɔbilite] *nf* mobility.
mobylette [mɔbilɛt] *nf*® moped.
mocassin [mɔkasɛ̃] *nm* moccasin.
moche [mɔʃ] *adj* (*fam: laid*) ugly; (: *mauvais, méprisable*) rotten.
modalité [mɔdalite] *nf* form, mode; **~s** *nfpl* (*d'un accord etc*) clauses, terms; **~s de paiement** methods of payment.
mode [mɔd] *nf* fashion; (*commerce*) fashion trade *ou* industry ♦ *nm* (*manière*) form, mode, method; (*LING*) mood; (*INFORM, MUS*) mode; **travailler dans la ~** to be in the fashion business; **à la ~** fashionable, in fashion; **~ dialogué** (*INFORM*) interactive *ou* conversational mode; **~ d'emploi** directions *pl* (for use); **~ de vie** way of life.
modelage [mɔdlaʒ] *nm* modelling.
modelé [mɔdle] *nm* (*GÉO*) relief; (*du corps etc*) contours *pl*.
modèle [mɔdɛl] *adj* model ♦ *nm* model; (*qui pose: de peintre*) sitter; (*type*) type; (*gabarit, patron*) pattern; **~ courant** *ou* **de série** (*COMM*) production model; **~ déposé** registered design; **~ réduit** small-scale model.
modeler [mɔdle] *vt* (*ART*) to model, mould; (*suj: vêtement, érosion*) to mould, shape; **~ qch sur/d'après** to model sth on.
modélisation [mɔdelizasjɔ̃] *nf* (*MATH*) modelling.
modéliste [mɔdelist(ə)] *nm/f* (*COUTURE*) designer; (*de modèles réduits*) model maker.
modem [mɔdɛm] *nm* modem.
Modène [mɔdɛn] *n* Modena.
modérateur, trice [mɔdeʀatœʀ, -tʀis] *adj* moderating ♦ *nm/f* moderator.
modération [mɔdeʀasjɔ̃] *nf* moderation; **~ de peine** reduction of sentence.
modéré, e [mɔdeʀe] *adj, nm/f* moderate.
modérément [mɔdeʀemɑ̃] *adv* moderately, in moderation.
modérer [mɔdeʀe] *vt* to moderate; **se ~** *vi* to restrain o.s.
moderne [mɔdɛʀn(ə)] *adj* modern ♦ *nm* (*ART*) modern style; (*ameublement*) modern furniture.
modernisation [mɔdɛʀnizasjɔ̃] *nf* modernization.
moderniser [mɔdɛʀnize] *vt* to modernize.
modernisme [mɔdɛʀnism(ə)] *nm* modernism.

modernité [mɔdɛʀnite] *nf* modernity.
modeste [mɔdɛst(ə)] *adj* modest; (*origine*) humble, lowly.
modestement [mɔdɛstəmɑ̃] *adv* modestly.
modestie [mɔdɛsti] *nf* modesty; **fausse ~** false modesty.
modicité [mɔdisite] *nf*: **la ~ des prix** *etc* the low prices *etc*.
modificatif, ive [mɔdifikatif, -iv] *adj* modifying.
modification [mɔdifikasjɔ̃] *nf* modification.
modifier [mɔdifje] *vt* to modify, alter; (*LING*) to modify; **se ~** *vi* to alter.
modique [mɔdik] *adj* (*salaire, somme*) modest.
modiste [mɔdist(ə)] *nf* milliner.
modulaire [mɔdylɛʀ] *adj* modular.
modulation [mɔdylasjɔ̃] *nf* modulation; **~ de fréquence (FM** *ou* **MF)** frequency modulation (FM).
module [mɔdyl] *nm* module.
moduler [mɔdyle] *vt* to modulate; (*air*) to warble.
moelle [mwal] *nf* marrow; (*fig*) pith, core; **~ épinière** spinal chord.
moelleux, euse [mwalø, -øz] *adj* soft; (*au goût, à l'ouïe*) mellow; (*gracieux, souple*) smooth.
moellon [mwalɔ̃] *nm* rubble stone.
mœurs [mœʀ] *nfpl* (*conduite*) morals; (*manières*) manners; (*pratiques sociales*) habits; (*mode de vie*) life style *sg*; (*d'une espèce animale*) behaviour *sg* (*BRIT*), behavior *sg* (*US*); **femme de mauvaises ~** loose woman; **passer dans les ~** to become the custom; **contraire aux bonnes ~** contrary to proprieties.
mohair [mɔɛʀ] *nm* mohair.
moi [mwa] *pron* me; (*emphatique*): **~, je ...** for my part, I ..., I myself ... ♦ *nm inv* (*PSYCH*) ego, self; **à ~!** (*à l'aide*) help (me)!
moignon [mwaɲɔ̃] *nm* stump.
moi-même [mwamɛm] *pron* myself; (*emphatique*) I myself.
moindre [mwɛ̃dʀ(ə)] *adj* lesser; lower; **le(la) ~, les ~s** the least; the slightest; **le(la) ~ de** the least of; **c'est la ~ des choses** it's nothing at all.
moindrement [mwɛ̃dʀəmɑ̃] *adv*: **pas le ~** not in the least.
moine [mwan] *nm* monk, friar.
moineau, x [mwano] *nm* sparrow.

═══════════════════ — *MOT-CLÉ*

moins [mwɛ̃] *adv* **1** (*comparatif*): **~ (que)** less (than); **~ grand que** less tall than, not as tall as; **il a 3 ans de ~ que moi** he's 3 years younger than me; **il est ~ intelligent que moi** he's not as clever as me, he's less clever than me; **~ je travaille, mieux je me porte** the less I work, the better I feel
2 (*superlatif*): **le ~** (the) least; **c'est ce que j'aime le ~** it's what I like (the) least; **le(la) ~ doué(e)** the least gifted; **au ~, du ~** at least; **pour le ~** at the very least

3: ~ **de** (_quantité_) less (than); (_nombre_) fewer (than); ~ **de sable/d'eau** less sand/water; ~ **de livres/gens** fewer books/people; ~ **de 2 ans** less than 2 years; ~ **de midi** not yet midday
4: de ~, en ~: **100 F/3 jours de** ~ 100 F/3 days less; **3 livres en** ~ 3 books fewer; 3 books too few; **de l'argent en** ~ less money; **le soleil en** ~ but for the sun, minus the sun; **de** ~ **en** ~ less and less; **en** ~ **de deux** in a flash _ou_ a trice
5: à ~ **de, à** ~ **que** unless; **à** ~ **de faire** unless we do (_ou_ he does _etc_); **à** ~ **que tu ne fasses** unless you do; **à** ~ **d'un accident** barring any accident
♦ _prép:_ **4** ~ **2** 4 minus 2; **10 heures** ~ **5** 5 to 10; **il fait** ~ **5** it's 5 (degrees) below (freezing), it's minus 5; **il est** ~ **5** it's 5 to
♦ _nm_ (_signe_) minus sign.

moins-value [mwɛvaly] _nf_ (_ÉCON, COMM_) depreciation.
moire [mwaʀ] _nf_ moiré.
moiré, e [mware] _adj_ (_tissu, papier_) moiré, watered; (_reflets_) shimmering.
mois [mwa] _nm_ month; (_salaire, somme dû_) (monthly) pay _ou_ salary; **treizième** ~, **double** ~ extra month's salary.
moïse [mɔiz] _nm_ Moses basket.
moisi, e [mwazi] _adj_ mouldy (_BRIT_), moldy (_US_), mildewed ♦ _nm_ mould, mold, mildew; **odeur de** ~ musty smell.
moisir [mwaziʀ] _vi_ to go mouldy (_BRIT_) _ou_ moldy (_US_); (_fig_) to rot; (_personne_) to hang about ♦ _vt_ to make mouldy _ou_ moldy.
moisissure [mwazisyʀ] _nf_ mould _no pl_ (_BRIT_), mold _no pl_ (_US_).
moisson [mwasɔ̃] _nf_ harvest; (_époque_) harvest (time); (_fig_): **faire une** ~ **de** to gather a wealth of.
moissonner [mwasɔne] _vt_ to harvest, reap; (_fig_) to collect.
moissonneur, euse [mwasɔnœʀ, -øz] _nm/f_ harvester, reaper ♦ _nf_ (_machine_) harvester.
moissonneuse-batteuse, _pl_ **moissonneuses-batteuses** [mwasɔnøzbatøz] _nf_ combine harvester.
moite [mwat] _adj_ (_peau, mains_) sweaty, sticky; (_atmosphère_) muggy.
moitié [mwatje] _nf_ half (_pl_ halves); (_épouse_): **sa** ~ his better half; **la** ~ half; **la** ~ **de** half (of), half the amount (_ou_ number) of; **la** ~ **du temps/des gens** half the time/the people; **à la** ~ **de** halfway through; ~ **moins grand** half as tall; ~ **plus long** half as long again, longer by half; **à** ~ half (_avant le verbe_), half- (_avant l'adjectif_); **à** ~ **prix** (at) half price, half-price; **de** ~ by half; ~ ~ half-and-half.
moka [mɔka] _nm_ (_café_) mocha coffee; (_gâteau_) mocha cake.
mol [mɔl] _adj m voir_ **mou.**
molaire [mɔlɛʀ] _nf_ molar.

moldave [mɔldav] _adj_ Moldavian.
Moldavie [mɔldavi] _nf:_ **la** ~ Moldavia.
môle [mol] _nm_ jetty.
moléculaire [mɔlekylɛʀ] _adj_ molecular.
molécule [mɔlekyl] _nf_ molecule.
moleskine [mɔlɛskin] _nf_ imitation leather.
molester [mɔlɛste] _vt_ to manhandle, maul (about).
molette [mɔlɛt] _nf_ toothed _ou_ cutting wheel.
mollasse [mɔlas] _adj_ (_péj: sans énergie_) sluggish; (_: flasque_) flabby.
molle [mɔl] _adj f voir_ **mou.**
mollement [mɔlmɑ̃] _adv_ softly; (_péj_) sluggishly; (_protester_) feebly.
mollesse [mɔlɛs] _nf_ (_voir mou_) softness; flabbiness; limpness; sluggishness; feebleness.
mollet [mɔlɛ] _nm_ calf (_pl_ calves) ♦ _adj m:_ **œuf** ~ soft-boiled egg.
molletière [mɔltjɛʀ] _adj f:_ **bande** ~ puttee.
molleton [mɔltɔ̃] _nm_ (_TEXTILES_) felt.
molletonné, e [mɔltɔne] _adj_ (_gants etc_) fleece-lined.
mollir [mɔliʀ] _vi_ (_jambes_) to give way; (_NAVIG: vent_) to drop, die down; (_fig: personne_) to relent; (_: courage_) to fail, flag.
mollusque [mɔlysk(ə)] _nm_ (_ZOOL_) mollusc; (_fig: personne_) lazy lump.
molosse [mɔlɔs] _nm_ big ferocious dog.
môme [mom] _nm/f_ (_fam: enfant_) brat; (_: fille_) bird (_BRIT_), chick.
moment [mɔmɑ̃] _nm_ moment; (_occasion_): **profiter du** ~ to take (advantage of) the opportunity; **ce n'est pas le** ~ this is not the right time; **à un certain** ~ at some point; **à un** ~ **donné** at a certain point; **à quel** ~? when exactly?; **au même** ~ at the same time; (_instant_) at the same moment; **pour un bon** ~ for a good while; **pour le** ~ for the moment, for the time being; **au** ~ **de** at the time of; **au** ~ **où** as; at a time when; **à tout** ~ at any time _ou_ moment; (_continuellement_) constantly, continually; **en ce** ~ at the moment; (_aujourd'hui_) at present; **sur le** ~ at the time; **par** ~s now and then, at times; **d'un** ~ **à l'autre** any time (now); **du** ~ **où** _ou_ **que** seeing that, since; **n'avoir pas un** ~ **à soi** not to have a minute to oneself.
momentané, e [mɔmɑ̃tane] _adj_ temporary, momentary.
momentanément [mɔmɑ̃tanemɑ̃] _adv_ for a moment, for a while.
momie [mɔmi] _nf_ mummy.
mon [mɔ̃], **ma** [ma], _pl_ **mes** [me] _adj possessif_ my.
monacal, e, aux [mɔnakal, -o] _adj_ monastic.
Monaco [mɔnako] _nm:_ **le** ~ Monaco.
monarchie [mɔnaʀʃi] _nf_ monarchy.
monarchiste [mɔnaʀʃist(ə)] _adj, nm/f_ monarchist.
monarque [mɔnaʀk(ə)] _nm_ monarch.
monastère [mɔnastɛʀ] _nm_ monastery.
monastique [mɔnastik] _adj_ monastic.

monceau, x [mɔ̃so] *nm* heap.

mondain, e [mɔ̃dɛ̃, -ɛn] *adj* (*soirée, vie*) society *cpd*; (*obligations*) social; (*peintre, écrivain*) fashionable; (*personne*) society *cpd* ♦ *nm/f* society man/woman, socialite ♦ *nf*: **la M~e, la police ~e** ≈ the vice squad.

mondanités [mɔ̃danite] *nfpl* (*vie mondaine*) society life *sg*; (*paroles*) (society) small talk *sg*; (*PRESSE*) (society) gossip column *sg*.

monde [mɔ̃d] *nm* world; (*personnes mondaines*): **le** ~ (high) society; (*milieu*): **être du même** ~ to move in the same circles; (*gens*): **il y a du** ~ (*beaucoup de gens*) there are a lot of people; (*quelques personnes*) there are some people; **y a-t-il du** ~ **dans le salon?** is there anybody in the lounge?; **beaucoup/peu de** ~ many/few people; **le meilleur** *etc* **du** ~ the best *etc* in the world *ou* on earth; **mettre au** ~ to bring into the world; **pas le moins du** ~ not in the least; **se faire un** ~ **de qch** to make a great deal of fuss about sth; **tour du** ~ round-the-world trip; **homme/femme du** ~ society man/woman.

mondial, e, aux [mɔ̃djal, -o] *adj* (*population*) world *cpd*; (*influence*) world-wide.

mondialement [mɔ̃djalmɑ̃] *adv* throughout the world.

mondialisation [mɔ̃djalizasjɔ̃] *nf* (*d'une technique*) global application; (*d'un conflit*) global spread.

mondovision [mɔ̃dɔvizjɔ̃] *nf* (world coverage by) satellite television.

monégasque [mɔnegask(ə)] *adj* Monegasque, of *ou* from Monaco ♦ *nm/f*: **M~** Monegasque.

monétaire [mɔnetɛʀ] *adj* monetary.

monétarisme [mɔnetaʀism(ə)] *nm* monetarism.

monétique [mɔnetik] *nf* electronic money.

mongol, e [mɔ̃gɔl] *adj* Mongol, Mongolian ♦ *nm* (*LING*) Mongolian ♦ *nm/f*: **M~, e** (*de la Mongolie*) Mongolian.

Mongolie [mɔ̃gɔli] *nf*: **la** ~ Mongolia.

mongolien, ne [mɔ̃gɔljɛ̃, -ɛn] *adj, nm/f* mongol.

mongolisme [mɔ̃gɔlism(ə)] *nm* mongolism, Down's syndrome.

moniteur, trice [mɔnitœʀ, -tʀis] *nm/f* (*SPORT*) instructor/instructress; (*de colonie de vacances*) supervisor ♦ *nm* (*écran*) monitor; ~ **cardiaque** cardiac monitor; ~ **d'auto-école** driving instructor.

monitorage [mɔnitɔʀaʒ] *nm* monitoring.

monitorat [mɔnitɔʀa] *nm* (*formation*) instructor's training (course); (*fonction*) instructorship.

monnaie [mɔnɛ] *nf* (*pièce*) coin; (*ÉCON, gén: moyen d'échange*) currency; (*petites pièces*): **avoir de la** ~ to have (some) change; **faire de la** ~ to get (some) change; **avoir/faire la** ~ **de 20 F** to have change of/get change for 20 F; **faire** *ou* **donner à qn la** ~ **de 20 F** to give sb change for 20 F, change 20 F for sb;

rendre à qn la ~ (**sur 20 F**) to give sb the change (from *ou* out of 20 F); **servir de** ~ **d'échange** (*fig*) to be used as a bargaining counter *ou* as bargaining counters; **payer en** ~ **de singe** to fob (sb) off with empty promises; **c'est** ~ **courante** it's a common occurrence; ~ **légale** legal tender.

monnayable [mɔnɛjabl(ə)] *adj* (*vendable*) convertible into cash; **mes services sont ~s** my services are worth money.

monnayer [mɔnɛje] *vt* to convert into cash; (*talent*) to capitalize on.

monnayeur [mɔnɛjœʀ] *nm voir* **faux**.

mono [mɔno] *nf* (= *monophonie*) mono ♦ *nm* (= *monoski*) monoski.

monochrome [mɔnɔkʀom] *adj* monochrome.

monocle [mɔnɔkl(ə)] *nm* monocle, eyeglass.

monocoque [mɔnɔkɔk] *adj* (*voiture*) monocoque ♦ *nm* (*voilier*) monohull.

monocorde [mɔnɔkɔʀd(ə)] *adj* monotonous.

monoculture [mɔnɔkyltyʀ] *nf* single-crop farming, monoculture.

monogamie [mɔnɔgami] *nf* monogamy.

monogramme [mɔnɔgʀam] *nm* monogram.

monokini [mɔnɔkini] *nm* one-piece bikini, bikini pants *pl*.

monolingue [mɔnɔlɛ̃g] *adj* monolingual.

monolithique [mɔnɔlitik] *adj* (*lit, fig*) monolithic.

monologue [mɔnɔlɔg] *nm* monologue, soliloquy; ~ **intérieur** stream of consciousness.

monologuer [mɔnɔlɔge] *vi* to soliloquize.

monôme [mɔnom] *nm* (*MATH*) monomial; (*d'étudiants*) students' rag procession.

monoparental, e, aux [mɔnɔpaʀɑ̃tal, -o] *adj*: **famille ~e** single-parent *ou* one-parent family.

monophasé, e [mɔnɔfaze] *adj* single-phase *cpd*.

monophonie [mɔnɔfɔni] *nf* monophony.

monoplace [mɔnɔplas] *adj, nm, nf* single-seater, one-seater.

monoplan [mɔnɔplɑ̃] *nm* monoplane.

monopole [mɔnɔpɔl] *nm* monopoly.

monopolisation [mɔnɔpɔlizasjɔ̃] *nf* monopolization.

monopoliser [mɔnɔpɔlize] *vt* to monopolize.

monorail [mɔnɔʀaj] *nm* monorail; monorail train.

monoski [mɔnɔski] *nm* monoski.

monosyllabe [mɔnɔsilab] *nm* monosyllable, word of one syllable.

monosyllabique [mɔnɔsilabik] *adj* monosyllabic.

monotone [mɔnɔtɔn] *adj* monotonous.

monotonie [mɔnɔtɔni] *nf* monotony.

monseigneur [mɔ̃sɛɲœʀ] *nm* (*archevêque, évêque*) Your (*ou* His) Grace; (*cardinal*) Your (*ou* His) Eminence; **Mgr Thomas** Bishop Thomas; Cardinal Thomas.

Monsieur [məsjø], *pl* **Messieurs** [mesjø] *titre* Mr ['mɪstə*] ♦ *nm* (*homme quelconque*): **un/le**

m~ a/the gentleman; *voir aussi* **Madame**.

monstre [mɔ̃stʀ(ə)] *nm* monster ♦ *adj* (*fam: effet, publicité*) massive; **un travail** ~ a fantastic amount of work; an enormous job; ~ **sacré** superstar.

monstrueux, euse [mɔ̃stʀyø, -øz] *adj* monstrous.

monstruosité [mɔ̃stʀyozite] *nf* monstrosity.

mont [mɔ̃] *nm*: **par** ~**s et par vaux** up hill and down dale; **le M**~ **Blanc** Mont Blanc; ~ **de Vénus** mons veneris.

montage [mɔ̃taʒ] *nm* putting up; (*d'un bijou*) mounting, setting; (*d'une machine etc*) assembly; (*PHOTO*) photomontage; (*CINÉ*) editing; ~ **sonore** sound editing.

montagnard, e [mɔ̃taɲaʀ, -aʀd(ə)] *adj* mountain *cpd* ♦ *nm/f* mountain-dweller.

montagne [mɔ̃taɲ] *nf* (*cime*) mountain; (*région*): **la** ~ the mountains *pl*; **la haute** ~ the high mountains; **les** ~**s Rocheuses** the Rocky Mountains, the Rockies; ~**s russes** big dipper *sg*, switchback *sg*.

montagneux, euse [mɔ̃taɲø, -øz] *adj* mountainous; hilly.

montant, e [mɔ̃tɑ̃, -ɑ̃t] *adj* (*mouvement, marée*) rising; (*chemin*) uphill; (*robe, corsage*) high-necked ♦ *nm* (*somme, total*) (sum) total, (total) amount; (*de fenêtre*) upright; (*de lit*) post.

mont-de-piété, *pl* **monts-de-piété** [mɔ̃dpjete] *nm* pawnshop.

monte [mɔ̃t] *nf* (*accouplement*): **la** ~ stud; (*d'un jockey*) seat.

monté, e [mɔ̃te] *adj*: **être** ~ **contre qn** to be angry with sb; (*fourni, équipé*): ~ **en** equipped with.

monte-charge [mɔ̃tʃaʀʒ(ə)] *nm inv* goods lift, hoist.

montée [mɔ̃te] *nf* rising, rise; (*escalade*) ascent, climb; (*chemin*) way up; (*côte*) hill; **au milieu de la** ~ halfway up; **le moteur chauffe dans les** ~**s** the engine overheats going uphill.

monte-plats [mɔ̃tpla] *nm inv* service lift.

monter [mɔ̃te] *vt* (*escalier, côte*) to go (*ou* come) up; (*valise, paquet*) to take (*ou* bring) up; (*cheval*) to mount; (*femelle*) to cover, serve; (*tente, échafaudage*) to put up; (*machine*) to assemble; (*bijou*) to mount, set; (*COUTURE*) to sew on; (: *manche*) to set in; (*CINÉ*) to edit; (*THÉÂT*) to put on, stage; (*société, coup etc*) to set up; (*fournir, équiper*) to equip ♦ *vi* to go (*ou* come) up; (*avion, voiture*) to climb, go up; (*chemin, niveau, température, voix, prix*) to go up, rise; (*brouillard, bruit*) to rise, come up; (*passager*) to get on; (*à cheval*): ~ **bien/mal** to ride well/badly; ~ **à cheval/bicyclette** to get on *ou* mount a horse/bicycle; (*faire du cheval etc*) to ride (a horse); to (ride a) bicycle; ~ **à pied/en voiture** to walk/drive up, go up on foot/by car; ~ **dans le train/l'avion** to get into the train/plane, board the train/plane; ~ **sur** to climb

up onto; ~ **sur** *ou* **à un arbre/une échelle** to climb (up) a tree/ladder; ~ **à bord** to (get on) board; ~ **à la tête de qn** to go to sb's head; ~ **sur les planches** to go on the stage; ~ **en grade** to be promoted; **se** ~ (*s'équiper*) to equip o.s., get kitted out (*BRIT*); **se** ~ **à** (*frais etc*) to add up to, come to; ~ **qn contre qn** to set sb against sb; ~ **la tête à qn** to give sb ideas.

monteur, euse [mɔ̃tœʀ, -øz] *nm/f* (*TECH*) fitter; (*CINÉ*) (film) editor.

monticule [mɔ̃tikyl] *nm* mound.

montmartrois, e [mɔ̃maʀtʀwa, -waz] *adj* of *ou* from Montmartre.

montre [mɔ̃tʀ(ə)] *nf* watch; (*ostentation*): **pour la** ~ for show; ~ **en main** exactly, to the minute; **faire** ~ **de** to show, display; **contre la** ~ (*SPORT*) against the clock; ~ **de plongée** diver's watch.

Montréal [mɔ̃real] *n* Montreal.

montréalais, e [mɔ̃reale, -ez] *adj* of *ou* from Montreal ♦ *nm/f*: **M**~, **e** Montrealer.

montre-bracelet, *pl* **montres-bracelets** [mɔ̃tʀəbʀaslɛ] *nf* wrist watch.

montrer [mɔ̃tʀe] *vt* to show; **se** ~ to appear; ~ **qch à qn** to show sb sth; ~ **qch du doigt** to point to sth, point one's finger at sth; **se** ~ **intelligent** to prove (to be) intelligent.

montreur, euse [mɔ̃tʀœʀ, -øz] *nm/f*: ~ **de marionnettes** puppeteer.

monture [mɔ̃tyʀ] *nf* (*bête*) mount; (*d'une bague*) setting; (*de lunettes*) frame.

monument [mɔnymɑ̃] *nm* monument; ~ **aux morts** war memorial.

monumental, e, aux [mɔnymɑ̃tal, -o] *adj* monumental.

moquer [mɔke]: **se** ~ **de** *vt* to make fun of, laugh at; (*fam: se désintéresser de*) not to care about; (*tromper*): **se** ~ **de qn** to take sb for a ride.

moquerie [mɔkʀi] *nf* mockery *no pl*.

moquette [mɔkɛt] *nf* fitted carpet, wall-to-wall carpeting *no pl*.

moqueter [mɔkete] *vt* to carpet.

moqueur, euse [mɔkœʀ, -øz] *adj* mocking.

moral, e, aux [mɔʀal, -o] *adj* moral ♦ *nm* morale ♦ *nf* (*conduite*) morals *pl*; (*règles*) moral code, ethic; (*valeurs*) moral standards *pl*, morality; (*science*) ethics *sg*, moral philosophy; (*conclusion: d'une fable etc*) moral; **au** ~, **sur le plan** ~ morally; **avoir le** ~ **à zéro** to be really down; **faire la** ~**e à** to lecture, preach at.

moralement [mɔʀalmɑ̃] *adv* morally.

moralisateur, trice [mɔʀalizatœʀ, -tʀis] *adj* moralizing, sanctimonious ♦ *nm/f* moralizer.

moraliser [mɔʀalize] *vt* (*sermonner*) to lecture, preach at.

moraliste [mɔʀalist(ə)] *nm/f* moralist ♦ *adj* moralistic.

moralité [mɔʀalite] *nf* (*d'une action, attitude*) morality; (*conduite*) morals *pl*; (*conclusion,* *enseignement*) moral.

moratoire [mɔratwaʀ] *adj m*: **intérêts ~s**
(*ÉCON*) interest on arrears.

morave [mɔʀav] *adj* Moravian.

Moravie [mɔʀavi] *nf*: **la ~** Moravia.

morbide [mɔʀbid] *adj* morbid.

morceau, x [mɔʀso] *nm* piece, bit; (*d'une œuvre*) passage, extract; (*MUS*) piece; (*CULIN: de viande*) cut; **mettre en ~x** to pull to pieces *ou* bits.

morceler [mɔʀsəle] *vt* to break up, divide up.

morcellement [mɔʀsɛlmɑ̃] *nm* breaking up.

mordant, e [mɔʀdɑ̃, -ɑ̃t] *adj* scathing, cutting; (*froid*) biting ♦ *nm* (*dynamisme, énergie*) spirit; (*fougue*) bite, punch.

mordicus [mɔʀdikys] *adv* (*fam*) obstinately, stubbornly.

mordiller [mɔʀdije] *vt* to nibble at, chew at.

mordoré, e [mɔʀdɔʀe] *adj* lustrous bronze.

mordre [mɔʀdʀ(ə)] *vt* to bite; (*suj: lime, vis*) to bite into ♦ *vi* (*poisson*) to bite; **~ dans** to bite into; **~ sur** (*fig*) to go over into, overlap into; **~ à qch** (*comprendre, aimer*) to take to; **~ à l'hameçon** to bite, rise to the bait.

mordu, e [mɔʀdy] *pp de* **mordre** ♦ *adj* (*amoureux*) smitten ♦ *nm/f*: **un ~ de jazz/de voile** a jazz/sailing fanatic *ou* buff.

morfondre [mɔʀfɔ̃dʀ(ə)]: **se ~** *vi* to mope.

morgue [mɔʀg(ə)] *nf* (*arrogance*) haughtiness; (*lieu: de la police*) morgue; (: *à l'hôpital*) mortuary.

moribond, e [mɔʀibɔ̃, -ɔ̃d] *adj* dying, moribund.

morille [mɔʀij] *nf* morel (*mushroom*).

mormon, e [mɔʀmɔ̃, -ɔn] *adj, nm/f* Mormon.

morne [mɔʀn(ə)] *adj* (*personne, visage*) glum, gloomy; (*temps, vie*) dismal, dreary.

morose [mɔʀoz] *adj* sullen, morose; (*marché*) sluggish.

morphine [mɔʀfin] *nf* morphine.

morphinomane [mɔʀfinɔman] *nm/f* morphine addict.

morphologie [mɔʀfɔlɔʒi] *nf* morphology.

morphologique [mɔʀfɔlɔʒik] *adj* morphological.

mors [mɔʀ] *nm* bit.

morse [mɔʀs(ə)] *nm* (*ZOOL*) walrus; (*TÉL*) Morse (code).

morsure [mɔʀsyʀ] *nf* bite.

mort¹ [mɔʀ] *nf* death; **se donner la ~** to take one's own life; **de ~** (*silence, pâleur*) deathly; **blessé à ~** fatally wounded *ou* injured; **à la vie, à la ~** for better, for worse; **~ clinique** brain death; **~ subite du nourrisson, ~ au berceau** cot death.

mort², e [mɔʀ, mɔʀt(ə)] *pp de* **mourir** ♦ *adj* dead ♦ *nm/f* (*défunt*) dead man/woman; (*victime*): **il y a eu plusieurs ~s** several people were killed, there were several killed ♦ *nm* (*CARTES*) dummy; **~ ou vif** dead or alive; **~ de peur/fatigue** frightened to death/dead tired; **~s et blessés** casualties; **faire le ~** to

play dead; (*fig*) to lie low.

mortadelle [mɔʀtadɛl] *nf* mortadella (*type of luncheon meat*).

mortalité [mɔʀtalite] *nf* mortality, death rate.

mort-aux-rats [mɔʀtoʀa] *nf inv* rat poison.

mortel, le [mɔʀtɛl] *adj* (*poison etc*) deadly, lethal; (*accident, blessure*) fatal; (*REL, danger, frayeur*) mortal; (*fig: froid*) deathly; (: *ennui, soirée*) deadly (boring) ♦ *nm/f* mortal.

mortellement [mɔʀtɛlmɑ̃] *adv* (*blessé etc*) fatally, mortally; (*pâle etc*) deathly; (*fig: ennuyeux etc*) deadly.

morte-saison, pl mortes-saisons [mɔʀtəsɛzɔ̃] *nf* slack *ou* off season.

mortier [mɔʀtje] *nm* (*gén*) mortar.

mortifier [mɔʀtifje] *vt* to mortify.

mort-né, e [mɔʀne] *adj* (*enfant*) stillborn; (*fig*) abortive.

mortuaire [mɔʀtɥɛʀ] *adj* funeral *cpd*; **avis ~s** death announcements, intimations; **chapelle ~** mortuary chapel; **couronne ~** (*funeral*) wreath; **domicile ~** house of the deceased; **drap ~** pall.

morue [mɔʀy] *nf* (*ZOOL*) cod *inv*; (*CULIN: salée*) salt-cod.

morutier [mɔʀytje] *nm* (*pêcheur*) cod fisherman; (*bateau*) cod fishing boat.

morvandeau, elle, x [mɔʀvɑ̃do, -ɛl] *adj* of *ou* from the Morvan region.

morveux, euse [mɔʀvø, -øz] *adj* (*fam*) snotty-nosed.

mosaïque [mɔzaik] *nf* (*ART*) mosaic; (*fig*) patchwork.

Moscou [mɔsku] *n* Moscow.

moscovite [mɔskɔvit] *adj* of *ou* from Moscow, Moscow *cpd* ♦ *nm/f*: **M~** Muscovite.

mosquée [mɔske] *nf* mosque.

mot [mo] *nm* word; (*message*) line, note; (*bon mot etc*) saying; **le ~ de la fin** the last word; **~ à ~** *adj, adv* word for word; **~ pour ~** word for word, verbatim; **sur ou à ces ~s** with these words; **en un ~** in a word; **à ~s couverts** in veiled terms; **prendre qn au ~** to take sb at his word; **se donner le ~** to send the word round; **avoir son ~ à dire** to have a say; **~ d'ordre** watchword; **~ de passe** password; **~s croisés** crossword (puzzle) *sg*.

motard [mɔtaʀ] *nm* biker; (*policier*) motorcycle cop.

motel [mɔtɛl] *nm* motel.

moteur, trice [mɔtœʀ, -tʀis] *adj* (*ANAT, PHYSIOL*) motor; (*TECH*) driving; (*AUTO*): **à 4 roues motrices** 4-wheel drive ♦ *nm* engine, motor; (*fig*) mover, mainspring; **à ~** power-driven, motor *cpd*; **~ à deux temps** two-stroke engine; **~ à explosion** internal combustion engine; **~ à réaction** jet engine; **~ thermique** heat engine.

motif [mɔtif] *nm* (*cause*) motive; (*décoratif*) design, pattern, motif; (*d'un tableau*) subject, motif; (*MUS*) figure, motif; **~s** *nmpl* (*JUR*) grounds *pl*; **sans ~** *adj* groundless.

motion [mosjɔ̃] *nf* motion; ~ **de censure** motion of censure, vote of no confidence.

motivation [mɔtivasjɔ̃] *nf* motivation.

motivé, e [mɔtive] *adj* (*acte*) justified; (*personne*) motivated.

motiver [mɔtive] *vt* (*justifier*) to justify, account for; (*ADMIN, JUR, PSYCH*) to motivate.

moto [mɔto] *nf* (*motor*)bike; ~ **verte** *ou* **de trial** trail (*BRIT*) *ou* dirt (*US*) bike.

moto-cross [mɔtɔkrɔs] *nm* motocross.

motoculteur [mɔtɔkyltœr] *nm* (motorized) cultivator.

motocyclette [mɔtɔsiklɛt] *nf* motorbike, motorcycle.

motocyclisme [mɔtɔsiklism(ə)] *nm* motorcycle racing.

motocycliste [mɔtɔsiklist(ə)] *nm/f* motorcyclist.

motoneige [mɔtɔnɛʒ] *nf* snow bike.

motorisé, e [mɔtɔrize] *adj* (*troupe*) motorized; (*personne*) having one's own transport.

motrice [mɔtris] *adj f voir* **moteur**.

motte [mɔt] *nf:* ~ **de terre** lump of earth, clod (of earth); ~ **de gazon** turf, sod; ~ **de beurre** lump of butter.

motus [mɔtys] *excl:* ~ **(et bouche cousue)!** mum's the word!

mou (mol), molle [mu, mɔl] *adj* soft; (*péj: visage, traits*) flabby; (: *geste*) limp; (: *personne*) sluggish; (: *résistance, protestations*) feeble ♦ *nm* (*homme mou*) wimp; (*abats*) lights *pl*, lungs *pl*; (*de la corde*): **avoir du** ~ to be slack; **donner du** ~ to slacken, loosen; **avoir les jambes molles** to be weak at the knees.

mouchard, e [muʃar, -ard(ə)] *nm/f* (*péj: SCOL*) sneak; (: *POLICE*) stool pigeon, grass (*BRIT*) ♦ *nm* (*appareil*) control device; (: *de camion*) tachograph.

mouche [muʃ] *nf* fly; (*ESCRIME*) button; (*de taffetas*) patch; **prendre la** ~ to go into a huff; **faire** ~ to score a bull's-eye.

moucher [muʃe] *vt* (*enfant*) to blow the nose of; (*chandelle*) to snuff (out); **se** ~ to blow one's nose.

moucheron [muʃrɔ̃] *nm* midge.

moucheté, e [muʃte] *adj* (*cheval*) dappled; (*laine*) flecked; (*ESCRIME*) buttoned.

mouchoir [muʃwar] *nm* handkerchief, hanky; ~ **en papier** tissue, paper hanky.

moudre [mudr(ə)] *vt* to grind.

moue [mu] *nf* pout; **faire la** ~ to pout; (*fig*) to pull a face.

mouette [mwɛt] *nf* (sea)gull.

mouf(f)ette [mufɛt] *nf* skunk.

moufle [mufl(ə)] *nf* (*gant*) mitt(en); (*TECH*) pulley block.

mouflon [muflɔ̃] *nm* mouf(f)lon.

mouillage [mujaʒ] *nm* (*NAVIG: lieu*) anchorage, moorings *pl*.

mouillé, e [muje] *adj* wet.

mouiller [muje] *vt* (*humecter*) to wet, moisten; (*tremper*): ~ **qn/qch** to make sb/sth wet; (*CU-*

LIN: ragoût) to add stock *ou* wine to; (*couper, diluer*) to water down; (*mine etc*) to lay ♦ *vi* (*NAVIG*) to lie *ou* be at anchor; **se** ~ to get wet; (*fam*) to commit o.s.; to get (o.s.) involved; ~ **l'ancre** to drop *ou* cast anchor.

mouillette [mujɛt] *nf* (bread) finger.

mouillure [mujyr] *nf* wet *no pl*; (*tache*) wet patch.

moulage [mulaʒ] *nm* moulding (*BRIT*), molding (*US*); casting; (*objet*) cast.

moulais [mulɛ] *etc vb voir* **moudre**.

moulant, e [mulɑ̃, -ɑ̃t] *adj* figure-hugging.

moule [mul] *vb voir* **moudre** ♦ *nf* (*mollusque*) mussel ♦ *nm* (*creux, CULIN*) mould (*BRIT*), mold (*US*); (*modèle plein*) cast; ~ **à gâteau** *nm* cake tin (*BRIT*) *ou* pan (*US*); ~ **à gaufre** *nm* waffle iron; ~ **à tarte** *nm* pie *ou* flan dish.

moulent [mul] *vb voir* **moudre, mouler**.

mouler [mule] *vt* (*brique*) to mould (*BRIT*), mold (*US*); (*statue*) to cast; (*visage, bas-relief*) to make a cast of; (*lettre*) to shape with care; (*suj: vêtement*) to hug, fit closely round; ~ **qch sur** (*fig*) to model sth on.

moulin [mulɛ̃] *nm* mill; (*fam*) engine; ~ **à café** coffee mill; ~ **à eau** watermill; ~ **à légumes** (vegetable) shredder; ~ **à paroles** (*fig*) chatterbox; ~ **à poivre** pepper mill; ~ **à prières** prayer wheel; ~ **à vent** windmill.

mouliner [muline] *vt* to shred.

moulinet [mulinɛ] *nm* (*de treuil*) winch; (*de canne à pêche*) reel; (*mouvement*): **faire des** ~**s avec qch** to whirl sth around.

moulinette [mulinɛt] *nf* ® (vegetable) shredder.

moulons [mulɔ̃] *etc vb voir* **moudre**.

moulu, e [muly] *pp de* **moudre** ♦ *adj* (*café*) ground.

moulure [mulyr] *nf* (*ornement*) moulding (*BRIT*), molding (*US*).

mourant, e [murɑ̃, -ɑ̃t] *vb voir* **mourir** ♦ *adj* dying ♦ *nm/f* dying man/woman.

mourir [murir] *vi* to die; (*civilisation*) to die out; ~ **assassiné** to be murdered; ~ **de froid/faim/vieillesse** to die of exposure/hunger/old age; ~ **de faim/d'ennui** (*fig*) to be starving/be bored to death; ~ **d'envie de faire** to be dying to do; **s'ennuyer à** ~ to be bored to death.

mousquetaire [muskətɛr] *nm* musketeer.

mousqueton [muskətɔ̃] *nm* (*fusil*) carbine; (*anneau*) snap-link, karabiner.

moussant, e [musɑ̃, -ɑ̃t] *adj* foaming; **bain** ~ foam *ou* bubble bath, bath foam.

mousse [mus] *nf* (*BOT*) moss; (*écume: sur eau, bière*) froth, foam; (: *shampooing*) lather; (*de champagne*) bubbles *pl*; (*CULIN*) mousse; (*en caoutchouc etc*) foam ♦ *nm* (*NAVIG*) ship's boy; **bain de** ~ bubble bath; **bas** ~ stretch stockings; **balle** ~ rubber ball; ~ **carbonique** (fire-fighting) foam; ~ **de nylon** nylon foam; (*tissu*) stretch nylon; ~ **à raser** shaving foam.

mousseline [muslin̩] *nf* (*TEXTILES*) muslin; chiffon; **pommes** ~ (*CULIN*) creamed potatoes.

mousser [muse] *vi* to foam; to lather.

mousseux, euse [musø, -øz] *adj* (*chocolat*) frothy; (*eau*) foamy, frothy; (*vin*) sparkling ♦ *nm*: (**vin**) ~ sparkling wine.

mousson [musɔ̃] *nf* monsoon.

moussu, e [musy] *adj* mossy.

moustache [mustaʃ] *nf* moustache; ~**s** *nfpl* (*d'animal*) whiskers *pl*.

moustachu, e [mustaʃy] *adj* wearing a moustache.

moustiquaire [mustikɛʀ] *nf* (*rideau*) mosquito net; (*chassis*) mosquito screen.

moustique [mustik] *nm* mosquito.

moutarde [mutaʀd(ə)] *nf* mustard ♦ *adj inv* mustard(-coloured).

moutardier [mutaʀdje] *nm* mustard jar.

mouton [mutɔ̃] *nm* (*ZOOL*, *péj*) sheep *inv*; (*peau*) sheepskin; (*CULIN*) mutton.

mouture [mutyʀ] *nf* grinding; (*péj*) rehash.

mouvant, e [muvɑ̃, -ɑ̃t] *adj* unsettled; changing; shifting.

mouvement [muvmɑ̃] *nm* (*gén*, *aussi: mécanisme*) movement; (*ligne courbe*) contours *pl*; (*fig: tumulte, agitation*) activity, bustle; (*: impulsion*) impulse; reaction; (*geste*) gesture; (*MUS: rythme*) tempo (*pl* -s *ou* tempi); **en** ~ in motion; on the move; **mettre qch en** ~ to set sth in motion, set sth going; ~ **d'humeur** fit *ou* burst of temper; ~ **d'opinion** trend of (public) opinion; **le** ~ **perpétuel** perpetual motion.

mouvementé, e [muvmɑ̃te] *adj* (*vie, poursuite*) eventful; (*réunion*) turbulent.

mouvoir [muvwaʀ] *vt* (*levier, membre*) to move; (*machine*) to move; **se** ~ to move.

moyen, ne [mwajɛ̃, -ɛn] *adj* average; (*tailles, prix*) medium; (*de grandeur moyenne*) medium-sized ♦ *nf* average; (*STATISTIQUE*) mean; (*SCOL: à l'examen*) pass mark; (*AUTO*) average speed; ~**s** *nmpl* (*capacités*) means; **au** ~ **de** by means of; **y a-t-il** ~ **de** ...? is it possible to ...?, can one ...?; **par quel** ~? how?, which way?, by which means?; **par tous les** ~**s** by every possible means, every possible way; **avec les** ~**s du bord** (*fig*) with what's available *ou* what comes to hand; **employer les grands** ~**s** to resort to drastic measures; **par ses propres** ~**s** all by oneself; **en** ~**ne** (on (an) average; **faire la** ~**ne** to work out the average; ~ **de locomotion/d'expression** means of transport/expression; ~ **âge** Middle Ages; ~ **de transport** means of transport; ~**ne d'âge** average age; ~**ne entreprise** (*COMM*) medium-sized firm.

moyenâgeux, euse [mwajɛnaʒø, -øz] *adj* medieval.

moyen-courrier [mwajɛ̃kuʀje] *nm* (*AVIAT*) medium-haul aircraft.

moyennant [mwajɛnɑ̃] *prép* (*somme*) for; (*service, conditions*) in return for; (*travail, effort*) with.

moyennement [mwajɛnmɑ̃] *adv* fairly, moderately; (*faire qch*) fairly *ou* moderately well.

Moyen-Orient [mwajɛnɔʀjɑ̃] *nm*: **le** ~ the Middle East.

moyeu, x [mwajø] *nm* hub.

mozambicain, e [mɔzɑ̃bikɛ̃, -ɛn] *adj* Mozambican.

Mozambique [mɔzɑ̃bik] *nm*: **le** ~ Mozambique.

MRAP *sigle m* = *Mouvement contre le racisme, l'antisémitisme et pour la paix.*

MRP *sigle m* (= *Mouvement républicain populaire*) *political party.*

ms *abr* (= *manuscrit*) MS., ms.

MST *sigle f* (= *maladie sexuellement transmissible*) STD (= *sexually transmitted disease*).

MTC *sigle m* (= *mécanisme du taux de change*) ERM.

mû, mue [my] *pp de* **mouvoir.**

mucosité [mykozite] *nf* mucus *no pl.*

mucus [mykys] *nm* mucus *no pl.*

mue [my] *pp de* **mouvoir** ♦ *nf* moulting (*BRIT*), molting (*US*); sloughing; breaking of the voice.

muer [mɥe] *vi* (*oiseau, mammifère*) to moult (*BRIT*), molt (*US*); (*serpent*) to slough; (*jeune garçon*): **il mue** his voice is breaking; **se** ~ **en** to transform into.

muet, te [mɥɛ, -ɛt] *adj* dumb; (*fig*): ~ **d'admiration** *etc* speechless with admiration *etc*; (*joie, douleur, CINÉ*) silent; (*LING: lettre*) silent, mute; (*carte*) blank ♦ *nm/f* mute ♦ *nm*: **le** ~ (*CINÉ*) the silent cinema *ou* movies (*esp US*).

mufle [myfl(ə)] *nm* muzzle; (*goujat*) boor ♦ *adj* boorish.

mugir [myʒiʀ] *vi* (*bœuf*) to bellow; (*vache*) to low, moo; (*fig*) to howl.

mugissement [myʒismɑ̃] *nm* (*voir mugir*) bellowing; lowing, mooing; howling.

muguet [mygɛ] *nm* (*BOT*) lily of the valley; (*MÉD*) thrush.

mulâtre, tresse [mylɑtʀ(ə), -tʀɛs] *nm/f* mulatto.

mule [myl] *nf* (*ZOOL*) (she-)mule.

mules [myl] *nfpl* (*pantoufles*) mules.

mulet [mylɛ] *nm* (*ZOOL*) (he-)mule; (*poisson*) mullet.

muletier, ière [myltje, -jɛʀ] *adj*: **sentier** *ou* **chemin** ~ mule track.

mulot [mylo] *nm* fieldmouse (*pl* -mice).

multicolore [myltikɔlɔʀ] *adj* multicoloured (*BRIT*), multicolored (*US*).

multicoque [myltikɔk] *nm* multihull.

multidisciplinaire [myltidisiplinɛʀ] *adj* multidisciplinary.

multiforme [myltifɔʀm(ə)] *adj* many-sided.

multilatéral, e, aux [myltilateʀal, -o] *adj*

multilateral.

multimilliardaire [myltimiljaʀdɛʀ], **multimillionnaire** [myltimiljɔnɛʀ] *adj*, *nm/f* multimillionaire.

multinational, e, aux [myltinasjɔnal, -o] *adj*, *nf* multinational.

multiple [myltipl(ə)] *adj* multiple, numerous; (*varié*) many, manifold ♦ *nm* (*MATH*) multiple.

multiplex [myltiplɛks] *nm* (*RADIO*) live link-up.

multiplicateur [myltiplikatœʀ] *nm* multiplier.

multiplication [myltiplikasjɔ̃] *nf* multiplication.

multiplicité [myltiplisite] *nf* multiplicity.

multiplier [myltiplije] *vt* to multiply; **se ~** *vi* to multiply; (*fig: personne*) to be everywhere at once.

multiprogrammation [myltipʀɔgʀamasjɔ̃] *nf* (*INFORM*) multiprogramming.

multipropriété [myltipʀɔpʀijete] *nf* time-sharing *no pl*.

multirisque [myltiʀisk] *adj*: **assurance ~** multiple-risk insurance.

multisalles [myltisal] *adj*: (**cinéma**) **~** multiplex (cinema).

multitraitement [myltitʀɛtmɑ̃] *nm* (*INFORM*) multiprocessing.

multitude [myltityd] *nf* multitude; mass; **une ~ de** a vast number of, a multitude of.

Munich [mynik] *n* Munich.

munichois, e [mynikwa, -waz] *adj ou* from Munich.

municipal, e, aux [mynisipal, -o] *adj* municipal; town *cpd*.

municipalité [mynisipalite] *nf* (*corps municipal*) town council, corporation; (*commune*) town, municipality.

munificence [mynifisɑ̃s] *nf* munificence.

munir [myniʀ] *vt*: **~ qn/qch de** to equip sb/sth with; **se ~ de** to provide o.s. with.

munitions [mynisjɔ̃] *nfpl* ammunition *sg*.

muqueuse [mykøz] *nf* mucous membrane.

mur [myʀ] *nm* wall; (*fig*) stone *ou* brick wall; **faire le ~** (*interne, soldat*) to jump the wall; **~ du son** sound barrier.

mûr, e [myʀ] *adj* ripe; (*personne*) mature ♦ *nf* (*de la ronce*) blackberry; (*du mûrier*) mulberry.

muraille [myʀɑj] *nf* (high) wall.

mural, e, aux [myʀal, -o] *adj* wall *cpd* ♦ *nm* (*ART*) mural.

mûre [myʀ] *nf voir* **mûr**.

mûrement [myʀmɑ̃] *adv*: **ayant ~ réfléchi** having given the matter much thought.

murène [myʀɛn] *nf* moray (eel).

murer [myʀe] *vt* (*enclos*) to wall (in); (*porte, issue*) to wall up; (*personne*) to wall up *ou* in.

muret [myʀɛ] *nm* low wall.

mûrier [myʀje] *nm* mulberry tree; (*ronce*) blackberry bush.

mûrir [myʀiʀ] *vi* (*fruit, blé*) to ripen; (*abcès, furoncle*) to come to a head; (*fig: idée, personne*)

to mature; (*projet*) to develop ♦ *vt* (*fruit, blé*) to ripen; (*personne*) to (make) mature; (*pensée, projet*) to nurture.

murmure [myʀmyʀ] *nm* murmur; **~s** *nmpl* (*plaintes*) murmurings, mutterings.

murmurer [myʀmyʀe] *vi* to murmur; (*se plaindre*) to mutter, grumble.

mus [my] *etc vb voir* **mouvoir**.

musaraigne [myzaʀɛɲ] *nf* shrew.

musarder [myzaʀde] *vi* to idle (about); (*en marchant*) to dawdle (along).

musc [mysk] *nm* musk.

muscade [myskad] *nf* (*aussi*: **noix ~**) nutmeg.

muscat [myska] *nm* (*raisin*) muscat grape; (*vin*) muscatel (wine).

muscle [myskl(ə)] *nm* muscle.

musclé, e [myskle] *adj* (*personne, corps*) muscular; (*fig: politique, régime etc*) strong-arm *cpd*.

muscler [myskle] *vt* to develop the muscles of.

musculaire [myskylɛʀ] *adj* muscular.

musculation [myskylasjɔ̃] *nf*: **exercices de ~** muscle-developing exercises.

musculature [myskylatyʀ] *nf* muscle structure, muscles *pl*, musculature.

muse [myz] *nf* muse.

museau, x [myzo] *nm* muzzle.

musée [myze] *nm* museum; (*de peinture*) art gallery.

museler [myzle] *vt* to muzzle.

muselière [myzəljɛʀ] *nf* muzzle.

musette [myzɛt] *nf* (*sac*) lunchbag ♦ *adj inv* (*orchestre etc*) accordion *cpd*.

muséum [myzeɔm] *nm* museum.

musical, e, aux [myzikal, -o] *adj* musical.

music-hall [myzikol] *nm* variety theatre; (*genre*) variety.

musicien, ne [myzisjɛ̃, -ɛn] *adj* musical ♦ *nm/f* musician.

musique [myzik] *nf* music; (*fanfare*) band; **faire de la ~** to make music; (*jouer d'un instrument*) to play an instrument; **~ de chambre** chamber music; **~ de fond** background music.

musqué, e [myske] *adj* musky.

must [mœst] *nm* must.

musulman, e [myzylmɑ̃, -an] *adj*, *nm/f* Moslem, Muslim.

mutant, e [mytɑ̃, -ɑ̃t] *nm/f* mutant.

mutation [mytasjɔ̃] *nf* (*ADMIN*) transfer; (*BIO*) mutation.

muter [myte] *vt* (*ADMIN*) to transfer.

mutilation [mytilasjɔ̃] *nf* mutilation.

mutilé, e [mytile] *nm/f* disabled person (*through loss of limbs*); **~ de guerre** disabled ex-serviceman; **grand ~** severely disabled person.

mutiler [mytile] *vt* to mutilate, maim; (*fig*) to mutilate, deface.

mutin, e [mytɛ̃, -in] *adj* (*enfant, air, ton*) mischievous, impish ♦ *nm/f* (*MIL, NAVIG*) muti-

neer.
mutiner [mytine]: **se** ~ *vi* to mutiny.
mutinerie [mytinʀi] *nf* mutiny.
mutisme [mytism(ə)] *nm* silence.
mutualiste [mytɥalist(ə)] *adj*: **société** ~ mutual benefit society, ≈ Friendly Society.
mutualité [mytɥalite] *nf* (*assurance*) mutual (benefit) insurance scheme.
mutuel, le [mytɥɛl] *adj* mutual ♦ *nf* mutual benefit society.
mutuellement [mytɥɛlmã] *adv* each other, one another.
Myanmar [mjanmaʀ] *nm* Myanmar.
myocarde [mjɔkaʀd(ə)] *nm voir* **infarctus.**
myope [mjɔp] *adj* short-sighted.
myopie [mjɔpi] *nf* short-sightedness, myopia.
myosotis [mjozɔtis] *nm* forget-me-not.
myriade [miʀjad] *nf* myriad.
myrtille [miʀtij] *nf* bilberry (*BRIT*), blueberry (*US*), whortleberry.
mystère [mistɛʀ] *nm* mystery.
mystérieusement [misteʀjøzmã] *adv* mysteriously.
mystérieux, euse [misteʀjø, -øz] *adj* mysterious.
mysticisme [mistisism(ə)] *nm* mysticism.
mystificateur, trice [mistifikatœʀ, -tʀis] *nm/f* hoaxer, practical joker.
mystification [mistifikasjɔ̃] *nf* (*tromperie, mensonge*) hoax; (*mythe*) mystification.
mystifier [mistifje] *vt* to fool, take in; (*tromper*) to mystify.
mystique [mistik] *adj* mystic, mystical ♦ *nm/f* mystic.
mythe [mit] *nm* myth.
mythifier [mitifje] *vt* to turn into a myth, mythologize.
mythique [mitik] *adj* mythical.
mythologie [mitɔlɔʒi] *nf* mythology.
mythologique [mitɔlɔʒik] *adj* mythological.
mythomane [mitɔman] *adj, nm/f* mythomaniac.

N n

N, n [ɛn] *nm inv* N, n ♦ *abr* (= *nord*) N; **N comme Nicolas** N for Nelly (*BRIT*) *ou* Nan (*US*).
n' [n] *adv voir* **ne.**
nabot [nabo] *nm* dwarf.
nacelle [nasɛl] *nf* (*de ballon*) basket.
nacre [nakʀ(ə)] *nf* mother-of-pearl.
nacré, e [nakʀe] *adj* pearly.
nage [naʒ] *nf* swimming; (*manière*) style of swimming, stroke; **traverser/s'éloigner à la** ~ to swim across/away; **en** ~ bathed in perspiration; ~ **indienne** sidestroke; ~ **libre** freestyle; ~ **papillon** butterfly.
nageoire [naʒwaʀ] *nf* fin.
nager [naʒe] *vi* to swim; (*fig: ne rien comprendre*) to be all at sea; ~ **dans** to be swimming in; (*vêtements*) to be lost in; ~ **dans le bonheur** to be overjoyed.
nageur, euse [naʒœʀ, -øz] *nm/f* swimmer.
naguère [nagɛʀ] *adv* (*il y a peu de temps*) not long ago; (*autrefois*) formerly.
naïf, ïve [naif, naiv] *adj* naïve.
nain, e [nɛ̃, nɛn] *adj, nm/f* dwarf.
Nairobi [naiʀɔbi] *n* Nairobi.
nais [nɛ], **naissais** [nɛsɛ] *etc vb voir* **naître.**
naissance [nɛsãs] *nf* birth; **donner** ~ **à** to give birth to; (*fig*) to give rise to; **prendre** ~ to originate; **aveugle de** ~ born blind; **Français de** ~ French by birth; **à la** ~ **des cheveux** at the roots of the hair; **lieu de** ~ place of birth.
naissant, e [nɛsã, -ãt] *vb voir* **naître** ♦ *adj* budding, incipient; (*jour*) dawning.
naît [nɛ] *vb voir* **naître.**
naître [nɛtʀ(ə)] *vi* to be born; (*conflit, complications*): ~ **de** to arise from, be born out of; ~ **à** (*amour, poésie*) to awaken to; **il est né en 1960** he was born in 1960; **il naît plus de filles que de garçons** there are more girls born than boys; **faire** ~ (*fig*) to give rise to, arouse.
naïvement [naivmã] *adv* naïvely.
naïveté [naivte] *nf* naïvety.
Namibie [namibi] *nf*: **la** ~ Namibia.
nana [nana] *nf* (*fam: fille*) bird (*BRIT*), chick.
nancéien, ne [nãsejɛ̃, -ɛn] *adj* of *ou* from Nancy.
nantais, e [nãtɛ, -ɛz] *adj* of *ou* from Nantes.
nantir [nãtiʀ] *vt*: ~ **qn de** to provide sb with; **les nantis** (*péj*) the well-to-do.
NAP *sigle a* (= *Neuilly Auteuil Passy*) ≈ preppy, ≈ Sloane Ranger *cpd* (*BRIT*).
napalm [napalm] *nm* napalm.
naphtaline [naftalin] *nf*: **boules de** ~ mothballs.
Naples [napl(ə)] *n* Naples.
napolitain, e [napɔlitɛ̃, -ɛn] *adj* Neapolitan; **tranche** ~**e** Neapolitan ice cream.
nappe [nap] *nf* tablecloth; (*fig*) sheet; layer; ~ **de mazout** oil slick; ~ (**phréatique**) water table.
napper [nape] *vt*: ~ **qch de** to coat sth with.
napperon [napʀɔ̃] *nm* table-mat; ~ **individuel** place mat.
naquis [naki] *etc vb voir* **naître.**
narcisse [narsis] *nm* narcissus.
narcissique [narsisik] *adj* narcissistic.
narcissisme [narsisism(ə)] *nm* narcissism.
narcodollars [narkodɔlaʀ] *nmpl* drug money *no pl*.
narcotique [narkɔtik] *adj, nm* narcotic.
narguer [narge] *vt* to taunt.
narine [naʀin] *nf* nostril.

narquois, e [naʀkwa, -waz] *adj* derisive, mocking.

narrateur, trice [naʀatœʀ, -tʀis] *nm/f* narrator.

narration [naʀɑsjɔ̃] *nf* narration, narrative; (*SCOL*) essay.

narrer [naʀe] *vt* to tell the story of, recount.

NASA [nasa] *sigle f* (= *National Aeronautics and Space Administration*) NASA.

nasal, e, aux [nazal, -o] *adj* nasal.

naseau, x [nazo] *nm* nostril.

nasillard, e [nazijaʀ, -aʀd(ə)] *adj* nasal.

nasiller [nazije] *vi* to speak with a (nasal) twang.

Nassau [naso] *n* Nassau.

nasse [nas] *nf* fish-trap.

natal, e [natal] *adj* native.

nataliste [natalist(ə)] *adj* supporting a rising birth rate.

natalité [natalite] *nf* birth rate.

natation [natɑsjɔ̃] *nf* swimming; **faire de la ~** to go swimming (*regularly*); **~ synchronisée** synchronized swimming.

natif, ive [natif, -iv] *adj* native.

nation [nɑsjɔ̃] *nf* nation; **les N~s unies (NU)** the United Nations (UN).

national, e, aux [nasjɔnal, -o] *adj* national ♦ *nf:* **(route) ~e** ≈ A road (*BRIT*), ≈ state highway (*US*); **obsèques ~es** state funeral.

nationalisation [nasjɔnalizɑsjɔ̃] *nf* nationalization.

nationaliser [nasjɔnalize] *vt* to nationalize.

nationalisme [nasjɔnalism(ə)] *nm* nationalism.

nationaliste [nasjɔnalist(ə)] *adj, nm/f* nationalist.

nationalité [nasjɔnalite] *nf* nationality; **de ~ française** of French nationality.

natte [nat] *nf* (*tapis*) mat; (*cheveux*) plait.

natter [nate] *vt* (*cheveux*) to plait.

naturalisation [natyʀalizɑsjɔ̃] *nf* naturalization.

naturaliser [natyʀalize] *vt* to naturalize; (*empailler*) to stuff.

naturaliste [natyʀalist(ə)] *nm/f* naturalist; (*empailleur*) taxidermist.

nature [natyʀ] *nf* nature ♦ *adj, adv* (*CULIN*) plain, without seasoning or sweetening; (*café, thé: sans lait*) black; (: *sans sucre*) without sugar; **payer en ~** to pay in kind; **peint d'après ~** painted from life; **être de ~ à faire qch** (*propre à*) to be the sort of thing (*ou* person) to do sth; **~ morte** still-life.

naturel, le [natyʀɛl] *adj* (*gén, aussi: enfant*) natural ♦ *nm* naturalness; (*caractère*) disposition, nature; (*autochtone*) native; **au ~** (*CULIN*) in water; in its own juices.

naturellement [natyʀɛlmɑ̃] *adv* naturally; (*bien sûr*) of course.

naturisme [natyʀism(ə)] *nm* naturism.

naturiste [natyʀist(ə)] *nm/f* naturist.

naufrage [nofʀaʒ] *nm* (ship)wreck; (*fig*) wreck; **faire ~** to be shipwrecked.

naufragé, e [nofʀaʒe] *nm/f* shipwreck victim, castaway.

Nauru [nɔʀy] *nm* Nauru.

nauséabond, e [nozeabɔ̃, -ɔ̃d] *adj* foul, nauseous.

nausée [noze] *nf* nausea; **avoir la ~** to feel sick; **avoir des ~s** to have waves of nausea, feel nauseous *ou* sick.

nautique [notik] *adj* nautical, water *cpd*; **sports ~s** water sports.

nautisme [notism(ə)] *nm* water sports *pl*.

naval, e [naval] *adj* naval.

navarrais, e [navaʀɛ, -ɛz] *adj* Navarrian.

navet [navɛ] *nm* turnip; (*péj*) third-rate film.

navette [navɛt] *nf* shuttle; (*en car etc*) shuttle (service); **faire la ~ (entre)** to go to and fro (between), shuttle (between); **~ spatiale** space shuttle.

navigabilité [navigabilite] *nf* (*d'un navire*) seaworthiness; (*d'un avion*) airworthiness.

navigable [navigabl(ə)] *adj* navigable.

navigant, e [navigɑ̃, -ɑ̃t] *adj* (*AVIAT: personnel*) flying ♦ *nm/f:* **les ~s** the flying staff *ou* personnel.

navigateur [navigatœʀ] *nm* (*NAVIG*) seafarer, sailor; (*AVIAT*) navigator; (*INFORM*) browser.

navigation [navigɑsjɔ̃] *nf* navigation, sailing; (*COMM*) shipping; **compagnie de ~** shipping company; **~ spatiale** space navigation.

naviguer [navige] *vi* to navigate, sail.

navire [naviʀ] *nm* ship; **~ de guerre** warship; **~ marchand** merchantman.

navire-citerne, *pl* **navires-citernes** [naviʀsitɛʀn(ə)] *nm* tanker.

navire-hôpital, *pl* **navires-hôpitaux** [naviʀɔpital, -to] *nm* hospital ship.

navrant, e [navʀɑ̃, -ɑ̃t] *adj* (*affligeant*) upsetting; (*consternant*) annoying.

navrer [navʀe] *vt* to upset, distress; **je suis navré (de/de faire/que)** I'm so sorry (for/for doing/that).

nazaréen, ne [nazaʀeɛ̃, -ɛn] *adj* Nazarene.

Nazareth [nazaʀɛt] *n* Nazareth.

NB *abr* (= *nota bene*) NB.

nbr. *abr* = **nombreux.**

nbses *abr* = **nombreuses.**

n.c. *abr* = **non communiqué, non coté.**

ND *sigle f* = **Notre Dame.**

n.d. *abr* = **non daté, non disponible.**

NDA *sigle f* = **note de l'auteur.**

NDE *sigle f* = **note de l'éditeur.**

NDLR *sigle f* = **note de la rédaction.**

ne, n' [n(ə)] *adv voir* **pas, plus, jamais** *etc*; (*explétif*) *non traduit*.

né, e [ne] *pp de* **naître;** **~ en 1960** born in 1960; **~e Scott** née Scott; **~(e) de ... et de ... son/daughter of ... and of ...;** **~ d'une mère française** having a French mother; **~ pour commander** born to lead ♦ *adj:* **un comédien ~** a born comedian.

néanmoins [neɑ̃mwɛ̃] *adv* nevertheless, yet.

néant [neɑ̃] *nm* nothingness; **réduire à ~** to bring to nought; (*espoir*) to dash.

nébuleux, euse [nebylø, -øz] *adj* (*ciel*) cloudy; (*fig*) nebulous ♦ *nf* (*ASTRONOMIE*) nebula.

nébuliser [nebylize] *vt* (*liquide*) to spray.

nébulosité [nebylozite] *nf* cloud cover; ~ **variable** cloudy in places.

nécessaire [neseser] *adj* necessary ♦ *nm* necessary; (*sac*) kit; **faire le** ~ to do the necessary; **n'emporter que le strict** ~ to take only what is strictly necessary; ~ **de couture** sewing kit; ~ **de toilette** toilet bag; ~ **de voyage** overnight bag.

nécessairement [nesesermɑ̃] *adv* necessarily.

nécessité [nesesite] *nf* necessity; **se trouver dans la** ~ **de faire qch** to find it necessary to do sth; **par** ~ out of necessity.

nécessiter [nesesite] *vt* to require.

nécessiteux, euse [nesesitø, -øz] *adj* needy.

nec plus ultra [nekplysyltra] *nm*: **le** ~ **de** the last word in.

nécrologie [nekrɔlɔʒi] *nf* obituary.

nécrologique [nekrɔlɔʒik] *adj*: **article** ~ obituary; **rubrique** ~ obituary column.

nécromancie [nekrɔmɑ̃si] *nf* necromancy.

nécromancien, ne [nekrɔmɑ̃sjɛ̃, -ɛn] *nm/f* necromancer.

nécrose [nekroz] *nf* necrosis.

nectar [nektar] *nm* nectar.

nectarine [nɛktarin] *nf* nectarine.

néerlandais, e [neɛrlɑ̃dɛ, -ɛz] *adj* Dutch, of the Netherlands ♦ *nm* (*LING*) Dutch ♦ *nm/f*: **N~, e** Dutchman/woman; **les N~** the Dutch.

nef [nɛf] *nf* (*d'église*) nave.

néfaste [nefast(ə)] *adj* baneful; ill-fated.

négatif, ive [negatif, iv] *adj* negative ♦ *nm* (*PHOTO*) negative.

négation [negasjɔ̃] *nf* denial; (*LING*) negation.

négativement [negativmɑ̃] *adv*: **répondre** ~ to give a negative response.

négligé, e [negliʒe] *adj* (*en désordre*) slovenly ♦ *nm* (*tenue*) negligee.

négligeable [negliʒabl(ə)] *adj* insignificant, negligible.

négligemment [negliʒamɑ̃] *adv* carelessly.

négligence [negliʒɑ̃s] *nf* carelessness *no pl*; (*faute*) careless omission.

négligent, e [negliʒɑ̃, -ɑ̃t] *adj* careless; (*JUR etc*) negligent.

négliger [negliʒe] *vt* (*épouse, jardin*) to neglect; (*tenue*) to be careless about; (*avis, précautions*) to disregard, overlook; ~ **de faire** to fail to do, not bother to do; **se** ~ to neglect o.s.

négoce [negɔs] *nm* trade.

négociable [negɔsjabl(ə)] *adj* negotiable.

négociant [negɔsjɑ̃] *nm* merchant.

négociateur [negɔsjatœr] *nm* negotiator.

négociation [negɔsjasjɔ̃] *nf* negotiation; ~**s collectives** collective bargaining *sg*.

négocier [negɔsje] *vi, vt* to negotiate.

nègre [negr(ə)] *nm* (*péj*) Negro; (*péj: écrivain*) ghost writer ♦ *adj* Negro.

négresse [negres] *nf* (*péj*) Negress.

négrier [negrije] *nm* (*fig*) slave driver.

neige [nɛʒ] *nf* snow; **battre les œufs en** ~ (*CULIN*) to whip *ou* beat the egg whites until stiff; ~ **carbonique** dry ice; ~ **fondue** (*par terre*) slush; (*qui tombe*) sleet; ~ **poudreuse** powder snow.

neiger [neʒe] *vi* to snow.

neigeux, euse [nɛʒø, -øz] *adj* snowy, snow-covered.

nénuphar [nenyfar] *nm* water-lily.

néo-calédonien, ne [neɔkaledɔnjɛ̃, -ɛn] *adj* New Caledonian ♦ *nm/f*: **N~, ne** native of New Caledonia.

néocapitalisme [neokapitalism(ə)] *nm* neocapitalism.

néo-colonialisme [neokɔlɔnjalism(ə)] *nm* neocolonialism.

néologisme [neɔlɔʒism(ə)] *nm* neologism.

néon [neɔ̃] *nm* neon.

néo-natal, e [neɔnatal] *adj* neonatal.

néophyte [neɔfit] *nm/f* novice.

néo-zélandais, e [neɔzelɑ̃dɛ, -ɛz] *adj* New Zealand *cpd* ♦ *nm/f*: **N~, e** New Zealander.

Népal [nepal] *nm*: **le** ~ Nepal.

népalais, e [nepalɛ, -ɛz] *adj* Nepalese, Nepali ♦ *nm* (*LING*) Nepalese, Nepali ♦ *nm/f*: **N~, e** Nepalese, Nepali.

néphrétique [nefretik] *adj* (*MÉD: colique*) nephritic.

néphrite [nefrit] *nf* (*MÉD*) nephritis.

népotisme [nepotism(ə)] *nm* nepotism.

nerf [nɛr] *nm* nerve; (*fig*) spirit; (: *forces*) stamina; ~**s** *nmpl* nerves; **être** *ou* **vivre sur les** ~**s** to live on one's nerves; **être à bout de** ~**s** to be at the end of one's tether; **passer ses** ~**s sur qn** to take it out on sb.

nerveusement [nɛrvøzmɑ̃] *adv* nervously.

nerveux, euse [nɛrvø, -øz] *adj* nervous; (*cheval*) highly-strung; (*voiture*) nippy, responsive; (*tendineux*) sinewy.

nervosité [nɛrvozite] *nf* nervousness; (*émotivité*) excitability.

nervure [nɛrvyr] *nf* (*de feuille*) vein; (*ARCHIT, TECH*) rib.

n'est-ce pas [nɛspa] *adv* isn't it?, won't you? *etc, selon le verbe qui précède*; **c'est bon,** ~? it's good, isn't it?; **il a peur,** ~? he's afraid, isn't he?; ~ **que c'est bon?** don't you think it's good?; **lui,** ~, **il peut se le permettre** he, of course, can afford to do that, can't he?

Net [nɛt] *nm* (*Internet*): **le** ~ the Net.

net, nette [nɛt] *adj* (*sans équivoque, distinct*) clear; (*photo*) sharp; (*évident*) definite; (*propre*) neat, clean; (*COMM: prix, salaire, poids*) net ♦ *adv* (*refuser*) flatly ♦ *nm*: **mettre au** ~ to copy out; **s'arrêter** ~ to stop dead; **la lame a cassé** ~ the blade snapped clean through; **faire place nette** to make a clean sweep; ~ **d'impôt** tax free.

nettement [nɛtmɑ̃] *adv* (*distinctement*) clearly; (*évidemment*) definitely; (*avec comparatif, superlatif*): ~ **mieux** definitely *ou* clearly better.

netteté [nɛtte] *nf* clearness.

nettoie [nɛtwa] *etc vb voir* **nettoyer**.

nettoiement [netwamɑ̃] *nm* (*ADMIN*) cleaning; **service du** ~ refuse collection.

nettoierai [nɛtwaRE] *etc vb voir* **nettoyer**.

nettoyage [nɛtwajaʒ] *nm* cleaning; ~ **à sec** dry cleaning.

nettoyant [netwajɑ̃] *nm* (*produit*) cleaning agent.

nettoyer [nɛtwaje] *vt* to clean; (*fig*) to clean out.

neuf [nœf] *num* nine.

neuf, neuve [nœf, nœv] *adj* new ♦ *nm*: **repeindre à** ~ to redecorate; **remettre à** ~ to do up (as good as new), refurbish; **n'acheter que du** ~ to buy everything new; **quoi de** ~? what's new?

neurasthénique [nøRastenik] *adj* neurasthenic.

neurochirurgie [nøRoʃiRyRʒi] *nf* neurosurgery.

neurochirurgien [nøRoʃiRyRʒjɛ̃] *nm* neurosurgeon.

neuroleptique [nøRɔlɛptik] *adj* neuroleptic.

neurologie [nøRɔlɔʒi] *nf* neurology.

neurologique [nøRɔlɔʒik] *adj* neurological.

neurologue [nøRɔlɔg] *nm/f* neurologist.

neurone [nøRɔn] *nm* neuron(e).

neuropsychiatre [nøRopsikjatR(ə)] *nm/f* neuropsychiatrist.

neutralisation [nøtRalizɑsjɔ̃] *nf* neutralization.

neutraliser [nøtRalize] *vt* to neutralize.

neutralisme [nøtRalism(ə)] *nm* neutralism.

neutraliste [nøtRalist(ə)] *adj* neutralist.

neutralité [nøtRalite] *nf* neutrality.

neutre [nøtR(ə)] *adj*, *nm* (*aussi LING*) neutral.

neutron [nøtRɔ̃] *nm* neutron.

neuve [nœv] *adj f voir* **neuf**.

neuvième [nœvjɛm] *num* ninth.

névé [neve] *nm* permanent snowpatch.

neveu, x [nəvø] *nm* nephew.

névralgie [nevralʒi] *nf* neuralgia.

névralgique [nevralʒik] *adj* (*fig: sensible*) sensitive; **centre** ~ nerve centre.

névrite [nevRit] *nf* neuritis.

névrose [nevRoz] *nf* neurosis.

névrosé, e [nevRoze] *adj*, *nm/f* neurotic.

névrotique [nevRɔtik] *adj* neurotic.

New York [njujɔRk] *n* New York.

new-yorkais, e [njujɔRkɛ, -ɛz] *adj* of *ou* from New York, New York *cpd* ♦ *nm/f*: **New-Yorkais, e** New Yorker.

nez [ne] *nm* nose; **rire au** ~ **de qn** to laugh in sb's face; **avoir du** ~ to have flair; **avoir le** ~ **fin** to have foresight; ~ **à** ~ **avec** face to face with; **à vue de** ~ roughly.

NF *sigle mpl* = *nouveaux francs* ♦ *sigle f* (*INDUSTRIE*: = *norme française*) industrial standard.

ni [ni] *conj*: ~ **l'un** ~ **l'autre ne sont** *ou* **n'est** neither one nor the other is; **il n'a rien dit** ~

fait he hasn't said or done anything.

Niagara [njagaRa] *nm*: **les chutes du** ~ the Niagara Falls.

niais, e [njɛ, -ɛz] *adj* silly, thick.

niaiserie [njɛzRi] *nf* gullibility; (*action, propos, futilité*) silliness.

Nicaragua [nikaRagwa] *nm*: **le** ~ Nicaragua.

nicaraguayen, ne [nikaRagwajɛ̃, -ɛn] *adj* Nicaraguan ♦ *nm/f*: **N~, ne** Nicaraguan.

Nice [nis] *n* Nice.

niche [niʃ] *nf* (*du chien*) kennel; (*de mur*) recess, niche; (*farce*) trick.

nichée [niʃe] *nf* brood, nest.

nicher [niʃe] *vi* to nest; **se** ~ **dans** (*personne: se blottir*) to snuggle into; (: *se cacher*) to hide in; (*objet*) to lodge itself in.

nichon [niʃɔ̃] *nm* (*fam*) boob, tit.

nickel [nikɛl] *nm* nickel.

niçois, e [niswa, -waz] *adj* of *ou* from Nice; (*CULIN*) Niçoise.

Nicosie [nikɔsi] *n* Nicosia.

nicotine [nikɔtin] *nf* nicotine.

nid [ni] *nm* nest; (*fig: repaire etc*) den, lair; ~ **d'abeilles** (*COUTURE, TEXTILE*) honeycomb stitch; ~ **de poule** pothole.

nièce [njɛs] *nf* niece.

nième [ɛnjɛm] *adj*: **la** ~ **fois** the nth *ou* umpteenth time.

nier [nje] *vt* to deny.

nigaud, e [nigo, -od] *nm/f* booby, fool.

Niger [niʒɛR] *nm*: **le** ~ Niger; (*fleuve*) the Niger.

Nigéria [niʒeRja] *nm ou nf* Nigeria.

nigérian, e [niʒeRjɑ̃, -an] *adj* Nigerian ♦ *nm/f*: **N~, e** Nigerian.

nigérien, ne [niʒeRjɛ̃, -ɛn] *adj* of *ou* from Niger.

night-club [najtklœb] *nm* nightclub.

nihilisme [niilism(ə)] *nm* nihilism.

nihiliste [niilist(ə)] *adj* nihilist, nihilistic.

Nil [nil] *nm*: **le** ~ the Nile.

n'importe [nɛ̃pɔRt(ə)] *adv*: ~! no matter!; ~ **qui/quoi/où** anybody/anything/anywhere; ~ **quoi!** (*fam: désapprobation*) what rubbish!; ~ **quand** any time; ~ **quel/quelle** any; ~ **lequel/laquelle** any (one); ~ **comment** (*sans soin*) carelessly; ~ **comment, il part ce soir** he's leaving tonight in any case.

nippes [nip] *nfpl* (*fam*) togs.

nippon, e *ou* **ne** [nipɔ̃, -ɔn] *adj* Japanese.

nique [nik] *nf*: **faire la** ~ **à** to thumb one's nose at (*fig*).

nitouche [nituʃ] *nf* (*péj*): **c'est une sainte** ~ she looks as if butter wouldn't melt in her mouth.

nitrate [nitRat] *nm* nitrate.

nitrique [nitRik] *adj*: **acide** ~ nitric acid.

nitroglycérine [nitRɔgliseRin] *nf* nitroglycerin(e).

niveau, x [nivo] *nm* level; (*des élèves, études*) standard; **au** ~ **de** at the level of; (*personne*) on a level with; **de** ~ **(avec)** level (with); **le**

~ **de la mer** sea level; ~ **(à bulle)** spirit level; ~ **(d'eau)** water level; ~ **de vie** standard of living.

niveler [nivle] *vt* to level.

niveleuse [nivløz] *nf* (*TECH*) grader.

nivellement [nivɛlmɑ̃] *nm* levelling.

nivernais, e [nivɛrnɛ, -ɛz] *adj* of *ou* from Nevers (and region) ♦ *nm/f*: **N~, e** inhabitant *ou* native of Nevers (and region).

NL *sigle f* = **nouvelle lune.**

NN *abr* (= *nouvelle norme*) *revised standard of hotel classification.*

nº *abr* (= *numéro*) no.

nobiliaire [nɔbiljɛr] *adj f voir* **particule.**

noble [nɔbl(ə)] *adj* noble; (*de qualité: métal etc*) precious ♦ *nm/f* noble(man/woman).

noblesse [nɔblɛs] *nf* (*classe sociale*) nobility; (*d'une action etc*) nobleness.

noce [nɔs] *nf* wedding; (*gens*) wedding party (*ou* guests *pl*); **il l'a épousée en secondes ~s** she was his second wife; **faire la ~** (*fam*) to go on a binge; **~s d'or/d'argent/de diamant** golden/silver/diamond wedding.

noceur [nɔsœr] *nm* (*fam*): **c'est un sacré ~** he's a real party animal.

nocif, ive [nɔsif, -iv] *adj* harmful, noxious.

noctambule [nɔktɑ̃byl] *nm* night-bird.

nocturne [nɔktyrn(ə)] *adj* nocturnal ♦ *nf* (*SPORT*) floodlit fixture; (*d'un magasin*) late opening.

Noël [nɔɛl] *nm* Christmas; **la (fête de) ~** Christmas time.

nœud [nø] *nm* (*de corde, du bois, NAVIG*) knot; (*ruban*) bow; (*fig: liens*) bond, tie; (: *d'une question*) crux; (*THÉÂT etc*): **le ~ de l'action** the web of events; ~ **coulant** noose; ~ **gordien** Gordian knot; ~ **papillon** bow tie.

noie [nwa] *etc vb voir* **noyer.**

noir, e [nwar] *adj* black; (*obscur, sombre*) dark ♦ *nm/f* black man/woman, Negro/Negro woman ♦ *nm*: **dans le ~** in the dark ♦ *nf* (*MUS*) crotchet (*BRIT*), quarter note (*US*); **il fait ~** it is dark; **au ~** *adv* (*acheter, vendre*) on the black market; **travail au ~** moonlighting.

noirâtre [nwarɑtr(ə)] *adj* (*teinte*) blackish.

noirceur [nwarsœr] *nf* blackness; darkness.

noircir [nwarsir] *vt, vi* to blacken.

noise [nwaz] *nf*: **chercher ~ à** to try and pick a quarrel with.

noisetier [nwaztje] *nm* hazel (tree).

noisette [nwazɛt] *nf* hazelnut; (*morceau: de beurre etc*) small knob ♦ *adj* (*yeux*) hazel.

noix [nwa] *nf* walnut; (*fam*) twit; (*CULIN*): **une ~ de beurre** a knob of butter; **à la ~** (*fam*) worthless; ~ **de cajou** cashew nut; ~ **de coco** coconut; ~ **muscade** nutmeg; ~ **de veau** (*CULIN*) round fillet of veal.

nom [nɔ̃] *nm* name; (*LING*) noun; **connaître qn de ~** to know sb by name; **au ~ de** in the name of; ~ **d'une pipe** *ou* **d'un chien!** (*fam*) for goodness' sake!; ~ **de Dieu!** (*fam!*) bloody hell! (*BRIT*), my God! (*BRIT*); ~ **commun/**

propre common/proper noun; ~ **composé** (*LING*) compound noun; ~ **déposé** trade name; ~ **d'emprunt** assumed name; ~ **de famille** surname; ~ **de fichier** file name; ~ **de jeune fille** maiden name.

nomade [nɔmad] *adj* nomadic ♦ *nm/f* nomad.

nombre [nɔ̃br(ə)] *nm* number; **venir en ~** to come in large numbers; **depuis ~ d'années** for many years; **ils sont au ~ de 3** there are 3 of them; **au ~ de mes amis** among my friends; **sans ~** countless; **(bon) ~ de** (*beaucoup, plusieurs*) a (large) number of; ~ **premier/entier** prime/whole number.

nombreux, euse [nɔ̃brø, -øz] *adj* many, numerous; (*avec nom sg: foule etc*) large; **peu ~** few; small; **de ~ cas** many cases.

nombril [nɔ̃bri] *nm* navel.

nomenclature [nɔmɑ̃klatyr] *nf* wordlist; list of items.

nominal, e, aux [nɔminal, -o] *adj* nominal; (*appel, liste*) of names.

nominatif, ive [nɔminatif, -iv] *nm* (*LING*) nominative ♦ *adj*: **liste ~ive** list of names; **carte ~ive** calling card; **titre ~** registered name.

nomination [nɔminasjɔ̃] *nf* nomination.

nommément [nɔmemɑ̃] *adv* (*désigner*) by name.

nommer [nɔme] *vt* (*baptiser*) to name, give a name to; (*qualifier*) to call; (*mentionner*) to name, give the name of; (*élire*) to appoint, nominate; **se ~**: **il se nomme Pascal** his name's Pascal, he's called Pascal.

non [nɔ̃] *adv* (*réponse*) no; (*suivi d'un adjectif, adverbe*) not; **Paul est venu, ~?** Paul came, didn't he?; **répondre** *ou* **dire que ~** to say no; ~ **pas que** not that; ~ **plus**: **moi ~ plus** neither do I, I don't either; **je préférerais que ~** I would prefer not; **il se trouve que ~** perhaps not; **je pense que ~** I don't think so; ~ **mais!** well really!; ~ **mais des fois!** you must be joking!; ~ **alcoolisé** non-alcoholic; ~ **loin/seulement** not far/only.

nonagénaire [nɔnaʒenɛr] *nm/f* nonagenarian.

non-agression [nɔnagresjɔ̃] *nf*: **pacte de ~** non-aggression pact.

non aligné, e [nɔnaliɲe] *adj* (*POL*) non-aligned.

nonante [nɔnɑ̃t] *num* (*Belgique, Suisse*) ninety.

non-assistance [nɔnasistɑ̃s] *nf* (*JUR*): ~ **à personne en danger** *failure to render assistance to a person in danger.*

nonce [nɔ̃s] *nm* (*REL*) nuncio.

nonchalamment [nɔ̃ʃalamɑ̃] *adv* nonchalantly.

nonchalance [nɔ̃ʃalɑ̃s] *nf* nonchalance, casualness.

nonchalant, e [nɔ̃ʃalɑ̃, -ɑ̃t] *adj* nonchalant, casual.

non-conformisme [nɔ̃kɔ̃fɔrmism(ə)] *nm* non-conformism.

non-conformiste [nɔ̃kɔ̃fɔrmist(ə)] *adj, nm/f* non-conformist.

non-conformité [nɔ̃kɔ̃fɔrmite] *nf* nonconformity.

non-croyant, e [nɔ̃kʀwajɑ̃, -ɑ̃t] *nm/f* (*REL*) non-believer.

non(-)engagé, e [nɔnɑ̃gaʒe] *adj* non-aligned.

non-fumeur [nɔ̃fymœʀ] *nm* non-smoker.

non-ingérence [nɔnɛ̃ʒeʀɑ̃s] *nf* non-interference.

non-initié, e [nɔninisje] *nm/f* lay person; **les ~s** the uninitiated.

non-inscrit, e [nɔnɛ̃skʀi, -it] *nm/f* (*POL: député*) independent.

non-intervention [nɔnɛ̃tɛʀvɑ̃sjɔ̃] *nf* non-intervention.

non-lieu [nɔ̃ljø] *nm*: **il y a eu ~** the case was dismissed.

nonne [nɔn] *nf* nun.

nonobstant [nɔnɔpstɑ̃] *prép* notwithstanding.

non-paiement [nɔ̃pɛmɑ̃] *nm* non-payment.

non-prolifération [nɔ̃pʀɔlifeʀɑsjɔ̃] *nf* non-proliferation.

non-résident [nɔ̃ʀesidɑ̃] *nm* (*ÉCON*) non-resident.

non-retour [nɔ̃ʀətuʀ] *nm*: **point de ~** point of no return.

non-sens [nɔ̃sɑ̃s] *nm* absurdity.

non-spécialiste [nɔ̃spesjalist(ə)] *nm/f* non-specialist.

non-stop [nɔnstɔp] *adj inv* nonstop.

non-syndiqué, e [nɔ̃sɛ̃dike] *nm/f* non-union member.

non-violence [nɔ̃vjɔlɑ̃s] *nf* nonviolence.

non-violent, e [nɔ̃vjɔlɑ̃, -ɑ̃t] *adj* non-violent.

nord [nɔʀ] *nm* North ♦ *adj* northern; north; **au ~** (*situation*) in the north; (*direction*) to the north; **au ~ de** north of, to the north of; **perdre le ~** to lose the place (*fig*).

nord-africain, e [nɔʀafʀikɛ̃, -ɛn] *adj* North-African ♦ *nm/f*: **Nord-Africain, e** North African.

nord-américain, e [nɔʀameʀikɛ̃, -ɛn] *adj* North American ♦ *nm/f*: **Nord-Américain, e** North American.

nord-coréen, ne [nɔʀkɔʀeɛ̃, -ɛn] *adj* North Korean ♦ *nm/f*: **Nord-Coréen, ne** North Korean.

nord-est [nɔʀɛst] *nm* North-East.

nordique [nɔʀdik] *adj* (*pays, race*) Nordic; (*langues*) Scandinavian, Nordic ♦ *nm/f*: **N~** Scandinavian.

nord-ouest [nɔʀwɛst] *nm* North-West.

nord-vietnamien, ne [nɔʀvjɛtnamjɛ̃, -ɛn] *adj* North Vietnamese ♦ *nm/f*: **Nord-Vietnamien, ne** North Vietnamese.

normal, e, aux [nɔʀmal, -o] *adj* normal ♦ *nf*: **la ~e** the norm, the average.

normalement [nɔʀmalmɑ̃] *adv* (*en général*) normally; (*comme prévu*): **~, il le fera demain** he should be doing it tomorrow, he's supposed to do it tomorrow.

normalien, ne [nɔʀmaljɛ̃, -ɛn] *nm/f* student of *École normale supérieure*.

normalisation [nɔʀmalizɑsjɔ̃] *nf* standardiza-

tion; normalization.

normaliser [nɔʀmalize] *vt* (*COMM, TECH*) to standardize; (*POL*) to normalize.

normand, e [nɔʀmɑ̃, -ɑ̃d] *adj* (*de Normandie*) Norman ♦ *nm/f*: **N~, e** (*de Normandie*) Norman.

Normandie [nɔʀmɑ̃di] *nf*: **la ~** Normandy.

norme [nɔʀm(ə)] *nf* norm; (*TECH*) standard.

Norvège [nɔʀvɛʒ] *nf*: **la ~** Norway.

norvégien, ne [nɔʀveʒjɛ̃, -ɛn] *adj* Norwegian ♦ *nm* (*LING*) Norwegian ♦ *nm/f*: **N~, ne** Norwegian.

nos [no] *adj possessif voir* **notre**.

nostalgie [nɔstalʒi] *nf* nostalgia.

nostalgique [nɔstalʒik] *adj* nostalgic.

notabilité [nɔtabilite] *nf* notability.

notable [nɔtabl(ə)] *adj* notable, noteworthy; (*marqué*) noticeable, marked ♦ *nm* prominent citizen.

notablement [nɔtabləmɑ̃] *adv* notably; (*sensiblement*) noticeably.

notaire [nɔtɛʀ] *nm* notary; solicitor.

notamment [nɔtamɑ̃] *adv* in particular, among others.

notariat [nɔtaʀja] *nm* profession of notary (*ou* solicitor).

notarié, e [nɔtaʀje] *adj*: **acte ~** deed drawn up by a notary (*ou* solicitor).

notation [nɔtasjɔ̃] *nf* notation.

note [nɔt] *nf* (*écrite, MUS*) note; (*SCOL*) mark (*BRIT*), grade; (*facture*) bill; **prendre des ~s** to take notes; **prendre ~ de** to note; (*par écrit*) to note, write down; **dans la ~** exactly right; **forcer la ~** to exaggerate; **une ~ de tristesse/de gaieté** a sad/happy note; **~ de service** memorandum.

noté, e [nɔte] *adj*: **être bien/mal ~** (*employé etc*) to have a good/bad record.

noter [nɔte] *vt* (*écrire*) to write down, note; (*remarquer*) to note, notice; (*SCOL, ADMIN: donner une appréciation*) to mark, give a grade to; **notez bien que ...** (please) note that ....

notice [nɔtis] *nf* summary, short article; (*brochure*): **~ explicative** explanatory leaflet, instruction booklet.

notification [nɔtifikasjɔ̃] *nf* notification.

notifier [nɔtifje] *vt*: **~ qch à qn** to notify sb of sth, notify sth to sb.

notion [nosjɔ̃] *nf* notion, idea; **~s** *nfpl* (*rudiments*) rudiments.

notoire [nɔtwaʀ] *adj* widely known; (*en mal*) notorious; **le fait est ~** the fact is common knowledge.

notoriété [nɔtɔʀjete] *nf*: **c'est de ~ publique** it's common knowledge.

notre, nos [nɔtʀ(ə), no] *adj possessif* our.

nôtre, nos [notʀ(ə)] *adj ours* ♦ *pron*: **le/la ~** ours; **les ~s** ours; (*alliés etc*) our own people; **soyez des ~s** join us.

nouba [nuba] *nf* (*fam*): **faire la ~** to live it up.

nouer [nwe] *vt* to tie, knot; (*fig: alliance etc*) to strike up; **~ la conversation** to start a con-

versation; **se ~** *vi*: **c'est là où l'intrigue se
noue** it's at that point that the strands of
the plot come together; **ma gorge se noua** a
lump came to my throat.

noueux, euse [nwø, -øz] *adj* gnarled.

nougat [nuga] *nm* nougat.

nougatine [nugatin] *nf* kind of nougat.

nouille [nuj] *nf* (*pâtes*): **~s** noodles; pasta *sg*;
(*fam*) noodle (*BRIT*), fathead.

nounou [nunu] *nf* nanny.

nounours [nunuʀs] *nm* teddy (bear).

nourri, e [nuʀi] *adj* (*feu etc*) sustained.

nourrice [nuʀis] *nf* ≈ baby-minder; (*autrefois*)
wet-nurse.

nourrir [nuʀiʀ] *vt* to feed; (*fig: espoir*) to harbour, nurse; **logé nourri** with board and
lodging; **~ au sein** to breast-feed; **se ~ de
légumes/rêves** to live on vegetables/
dreams.

nourrissant, e [nuʀisɑ̃, -ɑ̃t] *adj* nourishing,
nutritious.

nourrisson [nuʀisɔ̃] *nm* (unweaned) infant.

nourriture [nuʀityʀ] *nf* food.

nous [nu] *pron* (*sujet*) we; (*objet*) us.

nous-mêmes [numɛm] *pron* ourselves.

nouveau (nouvel), elle, x [nuvo, -ɛl] *adj* new;
(*original*) novel ♦ *nm/f* new pupil (*ou* employee) ♦ *nm*: **il y a du ~** there's something
new ♦ *nf* (piece of) news *sg*; (*LITTÉRATURE*)
short story; **nouvelles** *nfpl* (*PRESSE, TV*) news;
de ~, à ~ again; **je suis sans nouvelles de lui**
I haven't heard from him; **Nouvel An** New
Year; **~ riche** nouveau riche; **~ venu, nouvelle venue** newcomer; **~x mariés** newly-
weds; **nouvelle vague** new wave.

nouveau-né, e [nuvone] *nm/f* newborn (baby).

nouveauté [nuvote] *nf* novelty; (*chose nouvelle*) innovation, something new; (*COMM*)
new film (*ou* book *ou* creation *etc*).

nouvel *adj m*, **nouvelle** *adj f*, *nf* [nuvɛl] *voir* **nouveau.**

Nouvelle-Angleterre [nuvɛlɑ̃glətɛʀ] *nf*: **la ~**
New England.

Nouvelle-Calédonie [nuvɛlkaledɔni] *nf*: **la ~**
New Caledonia.

Nouvelle-Écosse [nuvɛlekɔs] *nf*: **la ~** Nova
Scotia.

Nouvelle-Galles du Sud [nuvɛlgaldysyd] *nf*:
la ~ New South Wales.

Nouvelle-Guinée [nuvɛlgine] *nf*: **la ~** New
Guinea.

nouvellement [nuvɛlmɑ̃] *adv* (*arrivé etc*) recently, newly.

Nouvelle-Orléans [nuvɛlɔʀleɑ̃] *nf*: **la ~** New
Orleans.

Nouvelles-Hébrides [nuvɛlsebʀid] *nfpl*: **les ~**
the New Hebrides.

Nouvelle-Zélande [nuvɛlzelɑ̃d] *nf*: **la ~** New
Zealand.

nouvelliste [nuvelist(ə)] *nm/f* editor *ou* writer
of short stories.

novateur, trice [nɔvatœʀ, -tʀis] *adj* innovative

♦ *nm/f* innovator.

novembre [nɔvɑ̃bʀ(ə)] *nm* November; *voir aussi*
juillet.

---

*Le 11 novembre is a public holiday in France
commemorating the signing of the armistice,
near Compiègne, at the end of World War I.*

---

novice [nɔvis] *adj* inexperienced ♦ *nm/f* novice.

noviciat [nɔvisja] *nm* (*REL*) noviciate.

noyade [nwajad] *nf* drowning *no pl.*

noyau, x [nwajo] *nm* (*de fruit*) stone; (*BIO, PHY-
SIQUE*) nucleus; (*ÉLEC, GÉO, fig: centre*) core;
(*fig: d'artistes etc*) group; (*: de résistants etc*)
cell.

noyautage [nwajotaʒ] *nm* (*POL*) infiltration.

noyauter [nwajote] *vt* (*POL*) to infiltrate.

noyé, e [nwaje] *nm/f* drowning (*ou* drowned)
man/woman ♦ *adj* (*fig: dépassé*) out of one's
depth.

noyer [nwaje] *nm* walnut (tree); (*bois*) walnut
♦ *vt* to drown; (*fig*) to flood; to submerge;
(*AUTO: moteur*) to flood; **se ~** to be drowned,
drown; (*suicide*) to drown o.s; **~ son chagrin**
to drown one's sorrows; **~ le poisson** to
duck the issue.

NSP *sigle m* (*REL*) = *Notre Saint Père*; (*dans les
sondages*: = *ne sais pas*) don't know.

NT *sigle m* (= *Nouveau Testament*) NT.

NU *sigle fpl* (= *Nations unies*) UN.

nu, e [ny] *adj* naked; (*membres*) naked, bare;
(*chambre, fil, plaine*) bare ♦ *nm* (*ART*) nude; **le
~ intégral** total nudity; **à mains ~es** with
one's bare hands; **se mettre ~** to strip;
mettre à ~ to bare.

nuage [nɥaʒ] *nm* cloud; **être dans les ~s** (*distrait*) to have one's head in the clouds; **~ de
lait** drop of milk.

nuageux, euse [nɥaʒø, -øz] *adj* cloudy.

nuance [nɥɑ̃s] *nf* (*de couleur, sens*) shade; **il y a
une ~ (entre)** there's a slight difference
(between); **une ~ de tristesse** a tinge of sadness.

nuancé, e [nɥɑ̃se] *adj* (*opinion*) finely-shaded,
subtly differing; **être ~ dans ses opinions** to
have finely-shaded opinions.

nuancer [nɥɑ̃se] *vt* (*pensée, opinion*) to qualify.

nubile [nybil] *adj* nubile.

nucléaire [nykleɛʀ] *adj* nuclear ♦ *nm* nuclear
power.

nudisme [nydism(ə)] *nm* nudism.

nudiste [nydist(ə)] *adj, nm/f* nudist.

nudité [nydite] *nf* (*voir nu*) nudity, nakedness;
bareness.

nuée [nɥe] *nf*: **une ~ de** a cloud *ou* host *ou*
swarm of.

nues [ny] *nfpl*: **tomber des ~** to be taken
aback; **porter qn aux ~** to praise sb to the
skies.

nui [nɥi] *pp de* **nuire.**

nuire [nɥiʀ] *vi* to be harmful; **~ à** to harm, do
damage to.

nuisance [nɥizɑ̃s] *nf* nuisance; **~s** *nfpl* pollution *sg*.
nuisible [nɥizibl(ə)] *adj* harmful; **(animal)** ~ pest.
nuisis [nɥizi] *etc vb voir* **nuire**.
nuit [nɥi] *nf* night; **payer sa** ~ **to** pay for one's overnight accommodation; **il fait** ~ it's dark; **cette** ~ *(hier)* last night; *(aujourd'hui)* tonight; **de** ~ *(vol, service)* night *cpd*; ~ **blanche** sleepless night; ~ **de noces** wedding night; ~ **de Noël** Christmas Eve.
nuitamment [nɥitamɑ̃] *adv* by night.
nuitées [nɥite] *nfpl* overnight stays, beds occupied *(in statistics)*.
nul, nulle [nyl] *adj (aucun)* no; *(minime)* nil, non-existent; *(non valable)* null; *(péj)* useless, hopeless ♦ *pron* none, no one; **résultat** ~, **match** ~ draw; **nulle part** *adv* nowhere.
nullement [nylmɑ̃] *adv* by no means.
nullité [nylite] *nf* nullity; *(péj)* hopelessness; *(: personne)* hopeless individual, nonentity.
numéraire [nymeʀɛʀ] *nm* cash; metal currency.
numéral, e, aux [nymeʀal, -o] *adj* numeral.
numérateur [nymeʀatœʀ] *nm* numerator.
numération [nymeʀasjɔ̃] *nf*: ~ **décimale/ binaire** decimal/binary notation; ~ **globulaire** blood count.
numérique [nymeʀik] *adj* numerical; *(INFORM)* digital.
numériquement [nymeʀikmɑ̃] *adv* numerically.
numériser [nymeʀize] *vt (INFORM)* to digitize.
numéro [nymeʀo] *nm* number; *(spectacle)* act, turn; **faire** *ou* **composer un** ~ **to** dial a number; ~ **d'identification personnel** personal identification number (PIN); ~ **d'immatriculation** *ou* **minéralogique** *ou* **de police** registration *(BRIT)* *ou* license *(US)* number; ~ **de téléphone** (tele)phone number; ~ **vert** ≈ Freefone ® number *(BRIT)*, ≈ toll-free number *(US)*.
numérotage [nymeʀɔtaʒ] *nm* numbering.
numérotation [nymeʀɔtasjɔ̃] *nf* numeration.
numéroter [nymeʀɔte] *vt* to number.
numerus clausus [nymeʀysklozys] *nm inv* restriction *ou* limitation of numbers.
numismate [nymismat] *nm/f* numismatist, coin collector.
nu-pieds [nypje] *nm inv* sandal ♦ *adj inv* barefoot.
nuptial, e, aux [nypsjal, -o] *adj* nuptial; wedding *cpd*.
nuptialité [nypsjalite] *nf*: **taux de** ~ marriage rate.
nuque [nyk] *nf* nape of the neck.
nu-tête [nytɛt] *adj inv* bareheaded.
nutritif, ive [nytʀitif, -iv] *adj* nutritional; *(aliment)* nutritious, nourishing.
nutrition [nytʀisjɔ̃] *nf* nutrition.
nutritionnel, le [nytʀisjɔnɛl] *adj* nutritional.
nutritionniste [nytʀisjɔnist(ə)] *nm/f* nutritionist.
nylon [nilɔ̃] *nm* nylon.
nymphomane [nɛ̃fɔman] *adj*, *nf* nymphomaniac.

O o

O, o [o] *nm inv* O, o ♦ *abr* (= *ouest*) W; **O comme Oscar** ≈ O for Oliver *(BRIT)* *ou* Oboe *(US)*.
OAS *sigle f* (= *Organisation de l'armée secrète*) *organization opposed to Algerian independence (1961-63)*.
oasis [ɔazis] *nf ou m* oasis *(pl* oases*)*.
obédience [ɔbedjɑ̃s] *nf* allegiance.
obéir [ɔbeiʀ] *vi* to obey; ~ **à** to obey; *(suj: moteur, véhicule)* to respond to.
obéissance [ɔbeisɑ̃s] *nf* obedience.
obéissant, e [ɔbeisɑ̃, -ɑ̃t] *adj* obedient.
obélisque [ɔbelisk(ə)] *nm* obelisk.
obèse [ɔbɛz] *adj* obese.
obésité [ɔbezite] *nf* obesity.
objecter [ɔbʒɛkte] *vt (prétexter)* to plead, put forward as an excuse; ~ **qch à** *(argument)* to put forward sth against; ~ **(à qn) que** to object (to sb) that.
objecteur [ɔbʒɛktœʀ] *nm*: ~ **de conscience** conscientious objector.
objectif, ive [ɔbʒɛktif, -iv] *adj* objective ♦ *nm (OPTIQUE, PHOTO)* lens *sg*; *(MIL, fig)* objective; ~ **grand angulaire/à focale variable** wide-angle/zoom lens.
objection [ɔbʒɛksjɔ̃] *nf* objection; ~ **de conscience** conscientious objection.
objectivement [ɔbʒɛktivmɑ̃] *adv* objectively.
objectivité [ɔbʒɛktivite] *nf* objectivity.
objet [ɔbʒɛ] *nm (chose)* object; *(d'une discussion, recherche)* subject; **être** *ou* **faire l'~ de** *(discussion)* to be the subject of; *(soins)* to be given *ou* shown; **sans** ~ *adj* purposeless; *(sans fondement)* groundless; ~ **d'art** objet d'art; **~s personnels** personal items; **~s de toilette** toiletries; **~s trouvés** lost property *sg (BRIT)*, lost-and-found *sg (US)*.
objurgations [ɔbʒyʀɡasjɔ̃] *nfpl* objurgations; *(prières)* entreaties.
obligataire [ɔbliɡatɛʀ] *adj* bond *cpd* ♦ *nm/f* bondholder, debenture holder.
obligation [ɔbliɡasjɔ̃] *nf* obligation; *(gén pl: devoir)* duty; *(COMM)* bond, debenture; **sans** ~ **d'achat** with no obligation (to buy); **être dans l'~ de faire** to be obliged to do; **avoir l'~ de faire** to be under an obligation to do; **~s familiales** family obligations *ou* responsibilities; **~s militaires** military obligations *ou* duties.

obligatoire [ɔbligatwaʀ] *adj* compulsory, obligatory.

obligatoirement [ɔbligatwaʀmɑ̃] *adv* compulsorily; (*fatalement*) necessarily.

obligé, e [ɔbliʒe] *adj* (*redevable*): être très ~ à qn to be most obliged to sb; (*contraint*): je suis (bien) ~ (de le faire) I have to (do it); (*nécessaire: conséquence*) necessary; c'est ~! it's inevitable!

obligeamment [ɔbliʒamɑ̃] *adv* obligingly.

obligeance [ɔbliʒɑ̃s] *nf*: avoir l'~ de to be kind *ou* good enough to.

obligeant, e [ɔbliʒɑ̃, -ɑ̃t] *adj* obliging; kind.

obliger [ɔbliʒe] *vt* (*contraindre*): ~ qn à faire to force *ou* oblige sb to do; (*JUR: engager*) to bind; (*rendre service à*) to oblige.

oblique [ɔblik] *adj* oblique; **regard** ~ sidelong glance; **en** ~ *adv* diagonally.

obliquer [ɔblike] *vi*: ~ **vers** to turn off towards.

oblitération [ɔbliteʀasjɔ̃] *nf* cancelling *no pl*, cancellation; obstruction.

oblitérer [ɔblitere] *vt* (*timbre-poste*) to cancel; (*MÉD: canal, vaisseau*) to obstruct.

oblong, oblongue [ɔblɔ̃, ɔblɔ̃g] *adj* oblong.

obnubiler [ɔbnybile] *vt* to obsess.

obole [ɔbɔl] *nf* offering.

obscène [ɔpsɛn] *adj* obscene.

obscénité [ɔpsenite] *nf* obscenity.

obscur, e [ɔpskyʀ] *adj* (*sombre*) dark; (*fig: raisons*) obscure; (*: sentiment, malaise*) vague; (*: personne, vie*) humble, lowly.

obscurcir [ɔpskyʀsiʀ] *vt* to darken; (*fig*) to obscure; s'~ *vi* to grow dark.

obscurité [ɔpskyʀite] *nf* darkness; **dans l'~** in the dark, in darkness; (*anonymat, médiocrité*) in obscurity.

obsédant, e [ɔpsedɑ̃, -ɑ̃t] *adj* obsessive.

obsédé, e [ɔpsede] *nm/f* fanatic; ~(e) **sexuel(le)** sex maniac.

obséder [ɔpsede] *vt* to obsess, haunt.

obsèques [ɔpsɛk] *nfpl* funeral *sg*.

obséquieux, euse [ɔpsekjø, -øz] *adj* obsequious.

observance [ɔpsɛʀvɑ̃s] *nf* observance.

observateur, trice [ɔpsɛʀvatœʀ, -tʀis] *adj* observant, perceptive ♦ *nm/f* observer.

observation [ɔpsɛʀvasjɔ̃] *nf* observation; (*d'un règlement etc*) observance; (*commentaire*) observation, remark; (*reproche*) reproof; **en** ~ (*MÉD*) under observation.

observatoire [ɔpsɛʀvatwaʀ] *nm* observatory; (*lieu élevé*) observation post, vantage point.

observer [ɔpsɛʀve] *vt* (*regarder*) to observe, watch; (*examiner*) to examine; (*scientifiquement, aussi: règlement, jeûne etc*) to observe; (*surveiller*) to watch; (*remarquer*) to observe, notice; **faire** ~ **qch à qn** (*dire*) to point out sth to sb; s'~ (*se surveiller*) to keep a check on o.s.

obsession [ɔpsesjɔ̃] *nf* obsession; **avoir l'~ de** to have an obsession with.

obsessionnel, le [ɔpsesjɔnɛl] *adj* obsessive.

obsolescent, e [ɔpsɔlesɑ̃, -ɑ̃t] *adj* obsolescent.

obstacle [ɔpstakl(ə)] *nm* obstacle; (*ÉQUITATION*) jump, hurdle; **faire** ~ **à** (*lumière*) to block out; (*projet*) to hinder, put obstacles in the path of; ~s **antichars** tank defences.

obstétricien, ne [ɔpstetʀisjɛ̃, -ɛn] *nm/f* obstetrician.

obstétrique [ɔpstetʀik] *nf* obstetrics *sg*.

obstination [ɔpstinasjɔ̃] *nf* obstinacy.

obstiné, e [ɔpstine] *adj* obstinate.

obstinément [ɔpstinemɑ̃] *adv* obstinately.

obstiner [ɔpstine]: s'~ *vi* to insist, dig one's heels in; s'~ **à faire** to persist (obstinately) in doing; s'~ **sur qch** to keep working at sth, labour away at sth.

obstruction [ɔpstʀyksjɔ̃] *nf* obstruction, blockage; (*SPORT*) obstruction; **faire de l'~** (*fig*) to be obstructive.

obstruer [ɔpstʀye] *vt* to block, obstruct; s'~ *vi* to become blocked.

obtempérer [ɔptɑ̃peʀe] *vi* to obey; ~ **à** to obey, comply with.

obtenir [ɔptəniʀ] *vt* to obtain, get; (*total*) to arrive at, reach; (*résultat*) to achieve, obtain; ~ **de pouvoir faire** to obtain permission to do; ~ **qch à qn** to obtain sth for sb; ~ **de qn qu'il fasse** to get sb to agree to do(ing).

obtention [ɔptɑ̃sjɔ̃] *nf* obtaining.

obtenu, e [ɔpt(ə)ny] *pp de* obtenir.

obtiendrai [ɔptjɛ̃dʀe], **obtiens** [ɔptjɛ̃], **obtint** [ɔptɛ̃] *etc vb voir* obtenir.

obturateur [ɔptyʀatœʀ] *nm* (*PHOTO*) shutter; ~ **à rideau** focal plane shutter.

obturation [ɔptyʀasjɔ̃] *nf* closing (up); ~ (**dentaire**) filling; **vitesse d'~** (*PHOTO*) shutter speed.

obturer [ɔptyʀe] *vt* to close (up); (*dent*) to fill.

obtus, e [ɔpty, -yz] *adj* obtuse.

obus [ɔby] *nm* shell; ~ **explosif** high-explosive shell; ~ **incendiaire** incendiary device, fire bomb.

obvier [ɔbvje]: ~ **à** *vt* to obviate.

OC *sigle fpl* (= *ondes courtes*) SW.

occasion [ɔkazjɔ̃] *nf* (*aubaine, possibilité*) opportunity; (*circonstance*) occasion; (*COMM: article non neuf*) secondhand buy; (*: acquisition avantageuse*) bargain; **à plusieurs** ~s on several occasions; **à la première** ~ at the first *ou* earliest opportunity; **avoir l'~ de faire** to have the opportunity to do; **être l'~ de** to occasion, give rise to; **à l'~** *adv* sometimes, on occasions; (*un jour*) some time; **à l'~ de** on the occasion of; **d'~** *adj, adv* secondhand.

occasionnel, le [ɔkazjɔnɛl] *adj* (*fortuit*) chance *cpd*; (*non régulier*) occasional; (*: travail*) casual.

occasionner [ɔkazjɔne] *vt* to cause, bring about; ~ **qch à qn** to cause sb sth.

occident [ɔksidɑ̃] *nm*: l'O~ the West.

occidental, e, aux [ɔksidɑ̃tal, -o] *adj* western;

(*POL*) Western ♦ *nm/f* Westerner.

occidentaliser [ɔksidɑ̃talize] *vt* (*coutumes, mœurs*) to westernize.

occiput [ɔksipyt] *nm* back of the head, occiput.

occire [ɔksiʀ] *vt* to slay.

occitan, e [ɔksitɑ̃, -an] *adj* of the langue d'oc, of Provençal French.

occlusion [ɔklyzjɔ̃] *nf*: ~ **intestinale** obstruction of the bowel.

occulte [ɔkylt(ə)] *adj* occult, supernatural.

occulter [ɔkylte] *vt* (*fig*) to overshadow.

occupant, e [ɔkypɑ̃, -ɑ̃t] *adj* occupying ♦ *nm/f* (*d'un appartement*) occupier, occupant; (*d'un véhicule*) occupant ♦ *nm* (*MIL*) occupying forces *pl*; (*POL: d'usine etc*) occupier.

occupation [ɔkypasjɔ̃] *nf* occupation; l'O~ the Occupation (of France).

occupationnel, le [ɔkypasjɔnɛl] *adj*: **thérapie** ~**le** occupational therapy.

occupé, e [ɔkype] *adj* (*MIL, POL*) occupied; (*personne: affairé, pris*) busy; (*esprit: absorbé*) occupied; (*place, sièges*) taken; (*toilettes, ligne*) engaged.

occuper [ɔkype] *vt* to occupy; (*poste, fonction*) to hold; (*main-d'œuvre*) to employ; s'~ (*à qch*) to occupy o.s. *ou* keep o.s. busy (with sth); s'~ **de** (*être responsable de*) to be in charge of; (*se charger de: affaire*) to take charge of, deal with; (*: clients etc*) to attend to; (*s'intéresser à, pratiquer: politique etc*) to be involved in; **ça occupe trop de place** it takes up too much room.

occurrence [ɔkyʀɑ̃s] *nf*: **en l'**~ in this case.

OCDE *sigle f* (= *Organisation de coopération et de développement économique*) OECD.

océan [ɔseɑ̃] *nm* ocean; l'~ **Indien** the Indian Ocean.

Océanie [ɔseani] *nf*: l'~ Oceania, South Sea Islands.

océanique [ɔseanik] *adj* oceanic.

océanographe [ɔseanɔgʀaf] *nm/f* oceanographer.

océanographie [ɔseanɔgʀafi] *nf* oceanography.

océanologie [ɔseanɔlɔʒi] *nf* oceanology.

ocelot [ɔslo] *nm* (*ZOOL*) ocelot; (*fourrure*) ocelot fur.

ocre [ɔkʀ(ə)] *adj inv* ochre.

octane [ɔktan] *nm* octane.

octante [ɔktɑ̃t] *num* (*Belgique, Suisse*) eighty.

octave [ɔktav] *nf* octave.

octet [ɔktɛ] *nm* byte.

octobre [ɔktɔbʀ(ə)] *nm* October; *voir aussi* **juillet**.

octogénaire [ɔktɔʒenɛʀ] *adj, nm/f* octogenarian.

octogonal, e, aux [ɔktɔgɔnal, -o] *adj* octogonal.

octogone [ɔktɔgɔn] *nm* octagon.

octroi [ɔktʀwa] *nm* granting.

octroyer [ɔktʀwaje] *vt*: ~ **qch à qn** to grant

sth to sb, grant sb sth.

oculaire [ɔkylɛʀ] *adj* ocular, eye *cpd* ♦ *nm* (*de microscope*) eyepiece.

oculiste [ɔkylist(ə)] *nm/f* eye specialist, oculist.

ode [ɔd] *nf* ode.

odeur [ɔdœʀ] *nf* smell.

odieusement [ɔdjøzmɑ̃] *adv* odiously.

odieux, euse [ɔdjø, -øz] *adj* odious, hateful.

odontologie [ɔdɔ̃tɔlɔʒi] *nf* odontology.

odorant, e [ɔdɔʀɑ̃, -ɑ̃t] *adj* sweet-smelling, fragrant.

odorat [ɔdɔʀa] *nm* (sense of) smell; **avoir l'**~ **fin** to have a keen sense of smell.

odoriférant, e [ɔdɔʀifeʀɑ̃, -ɑ̃t] *adj* sweet-smelling, fragrant.

odyssée [ɔdise] *nf* odyssey.

OEA *sigle f* (= *Organisation des États américains*) OAS.

œcuménique [ekymenik] *adj* ecumenical.

œdème [edɛm] *nm* oedema (*BRIT*), edema (*US*).

œil [œj], *pl* **yeux** [jø] *nm* eye; **avoir un** ~ **poché** *ou* **au beurre noir** to have a black eye; **à l'**~ (*fam*) for free; **à l'**~ **nu** with the naked eye; **tenir qn à l'**~ to keep an eye *ou* a watch on sb; **avoir l'**~ **à** to keep an eye on; **faire de l'**~ **à qn** to make eyes at sb; **voir qch d'un bon/ mauvais** ~ to view sth in a favourable/an unfavourable light; **à l'**~ **vif** with a lively expression; **à mes/ses yeux** in my/his eyes; **de ses propres yeux** with his own eyes; **fermer les yeux (sur)** (*fig*) to turn a blind eye (to); **les yeux fermés** (*aussi fig*) with one's eyes shut; **fermer l'**~ to get a moment's sleep; ~ **pour** ~, **dent pour dent** an eye for an eye, a tooth for a tooth; **pour les beaux yeux de qn** (*fig*) for love of sb; ~ **de verre** glass eye.

œil-de-bœuf, *pl* **œils-de-bœuf** [œjdəbœf] *nm* bull's-eye (window).

œillade [œjad] *nf*: **lancer une** ~ **à qn** to wink at sb, give sb a wink; **faire des** ~**s à** to make eyes at.

œillères [œjɛʀ] *nfpl* blinkers (*BRIT*), blinders (*US*); **avoir des** ~ (*fig*) to be blinkered, wear blinders.

œillet [œjɛ] *nm* (*BOT*) carnation; (*trou*) eyelet.

œnologue [enɔlɔg] *nm/f* wine expert.

œsophage [ezɔfaʒ] *nm* oesophagus (*BRIT*), esophagus (*US*).

œstrogène [ɛstʀɔʒɛn] *adj* oestrogen (*BRIT*), estrogen (*US*).

œuf [œf, *pl* ø] *nm* egg; **étouffer dans l'**~ to nip in the bud; ~ **à la coque/dur/mollet** boiled/ hard-boiled/soft-boiled egg; ~ **au plat/poché** fried/poached egg; ~**s brouillés** scrambled eggs; ~ **de Pâques** Easter egg; ~ **à repriser** darning egg.

œuvre [œvʀ(ə)] *nf* (*tâche*) task, undertaking; (*ouvrage achevé, livre, tableau etc*) work; (*ensemble de la production artistique*) works *pl*;

(*organisation charitable*) charity ♦ *nm* (*d'un artiste*) works *pl*; (*CONSTR*): **le gros** ~ the shell; **~s** *nfpl* (*actes*) deeds, works; **être/se mettre à l'**~ to be at/get (down) to work; **mettre en** ~ (*moyens*) to make use of; (*plan, loi, projet etc*) to implement; ~ **d'art** work of art; **bonnes ~s** good works *ou* deeds; **~s de bienfaisance** charitable works.

OFCE *sigle m* (= *Observatoire français des conjonctures économiques*) *economic research institute.*

offensant, e [ɔfɑ̃sɑ̃, -ɑ̃t] *adj* offensive, insulting.

offense [ɔfɑ̃s] *nf* (*affront*) insult; (*REL*): **péché** transgression, trespass.

offenser [ɔfɑ̃se] *vt* to offend, hurt; (*principes, Dieu*) to offend against; **s'**~ **de** to take offence (*BRIT*) *ou* offense (*US*) at.

offensif, ive [ɔfɑ̃sif, -iv] *adj* (*armes, guerre*) offensive ♦ *nf* offensive; (*fig: du froid, de l'hiver*) onslaught; **passer à l'offensive** to go into the attack *ou* offensive.

offert, e [ɔfɛʀ, -ɛʀt(ə)] *pp de* **offrir**.

offertoire [ɔfɛʀtwaʀ] *nm* offertory.

office [ɔfis] *nm* (*charge*) office; (*agence*) bureau, agency; (*REL*) service ♦ *nm ou nf* (*pièce*) pantry; **faire** ~ to act as; to do duty as; **d'**~ *adv* automatically; **bons ~s** (*POL*) good offices; ~ **du tourisme** tourist bureau.

officialiser [ɔfisjalize] *vt* to make official.

officiel, le [ɔfisjɛl] *adj*, *nm/f* official.

officiellement [ɔfisjɛlmɑ̃] *adv* officially.

officier [ɔfisje] *nm* officer ♦ *vi* (*REL*) to officiate; ~ **de l'état-civil** registrar; ~ **ministériel** member of the legal profession; ~ **de police** ≈ police officer.

officieusement [ɔfisjøzmɑ̃] *adv* unofficially.

officieux, euse [ɔfisjø, -øz] *adj* unofficial.

officinal, e, aux [ɔfisinal, -o] *adj*: **plantes ~es** medicinal plants.

officine [ɔfisin] *nf* (*de pharmacie*) dispensary; (*ADMIN: pharmacie*) pharmacy; (*gén péj: bureau*) agency, office.

offrais [ɔfʀɛ] *etc vb voir* **offrir**.

offrande [ɔfʀɑ̃d] *nf* offering.

offrant [ɔfʀɑ̃] *nm*: **au plus** ~ to the highest bidder.

offre [ɔfʀ(ə)] *vb voir* **offrir** ♦ *nf* offer; (*aux enchères*) bid; (*ADMIN: soumission*) tender; (*ÉCON*): **l'**~ supply; ~ **d'emploi** job advertised; **"~s d'emploi"** "situations vacant"; ~ **publique d'achat (OPA)** takeover bid; **~s de service** offer of service.

offrir [ɔfʀiʀ] *vt*: ~ (**à qn**) to offer (to sb); (*faire cadeau*) to give to (sb); **s'**~ *vi* (*se présenter: occasion, paysage*) to present itself ♦ *vt* (*se payer: vacances, voiture*) to treat o.s. to; ~ (**à qn**) **de faire qch** to offer to do sth (for sb); ~ **à boire à qn** to offer sb a drink; **s'**~ **à faire qch** to offer *ou* volunteer to do sth; **s'**~ **comme guide/en otage** to offer one's services as (a) guide/offer o.s. as (a) hostage;

s'~ **aux regards** (*suj: personne*) to expose o.s. to the public gaze.

offset [ɔfsɛt] *nm* offset (printing).

offusquer [ɔfyske] *vt* to offend; **s'**~ **de** to take offence (*BRIT*) *ou* offense (*US*) at, be offended by.

ogive [ɔʒiv] *nf* (*ARCHIT*) diagonal rib; (*d'obus, de missile*) nose cone; **voûte en** ~ rib vault; **arc en** ~ lancet arch; ~ **nucléaire** nuclear warhead.

OGM *sigle m* (= *organisme génétiquement modifié*) GM organism.

ogre [ɔgʀ(ə)] *nm* ogre.

oh [o] *excl* oh!; ~ **la la!** oh (dear)!; **pousser des ~!** **et des ah!** to gasp with admiration.

oie [wa] *nf* (*ZOOL*) goose (*pl* geese); ~ **blanche** (*fig*) young innocent.

oignon [ɔɲɔ̃] *nm* (*CULIN*) onion; (*de tulipe etc: bulbe*) bulb; (*MÉD*) bunion; **ce ne sont pas tes ~s** (*fam*) that's none of your business.

oindre [wɛ̃dʀ(ə)] *vt* to anoint.

oiseau, x [wazo] *nm* bird; ~ **de proie** bird of prey.

oiseau-mouche, *pl* **oiseaux-mouches** [wazomuʃ] *nm* hummingbird.

oiseleur [wazlœʀ] *nm* bird-catcher.

oiselier, ière [wazəlje, -jɛʀ] *nm/f* bird-seller.

oisellerie [wazɛlʀi] *nf* bird shop.

oiseux, euse [wazø, -øz] *adj* pointless, idle; (*sans valeur, importance*) trivial.

oisif, ive [wazif, -iv] *adj* idle ♦ *nm/f* (*péj*) man/lady of leisure.

oisillon [wazijɔ̃] *nm* little *ou* baby bird.

oisiveté [wazivte] *nf* idleness.

OIT *sigle f* (= *Organisation internationale du travail*) ILO.

OK [oke] *excl* OK!, all right!

OL *sigle fpl* (= *ondes longues*) LW.

oléagineux, euse [ɔleaʒinø, -øz] *adj* oleaginous, oil-producing.

oléiculture [ɔleikyltyʀ] *nm* olive growing.

oléoduc [ɔleɔdyk] *nm* (oil) pipeline.

olfactif, ive [ɔlfaktif, -iv] *adj* olfactory.

olibrius [ɔlibʀijys] *nm* oddball.

oligarchie [ɔligaʀʃi] *nf* oligarchy.

oligo-élément [ɔligɔelemɑ̃] *nm* trace element.

oligopole [ɔligɔpɔl] *nm* oligopoly.

olivâtre [ɔlivɑtʀ(ə)] *adj* olive-greenish; (*teint*) sallow.

olive [ɔliv] *nf* (*BOT*) olive ♦ *adj inv* olive(-green).

oliveraie [ɔlivʀɛ] *nf* olive grove.

olivier [ɔlivje] *nm* olive (tree); (*bois*) olive (wood).

olographe [ɔlɔgʀaf] *adj*: **testament** ~ *will written, dated and signed by the testator.*

OLP *sigle f* (= *Organisation de libération de la Palestine*) PLO.

olympiade [ɔlɛ̃pjad] *nf* (*période*) Olympiad; **les ~s** (*jeux*) the Olympiad *sg*.

olympique [ɔlɛ̃pik] *adj* Olympic.

OM *sigle fpl* (= *ondes moyennes*) MW.

Oman [ɔman] *nm*: l'~, **le sultanat d'~** (the Sultanate of) Oman.

ombilical, e, aux [ɔbilikal, -o] *adj* umbilical.

ombrage [ɔbʀaʒ] *nm* (*ombre*) (leafy) shade; (*fig*): **prendre ~ de** to take umbrage at; **faire** *ou* **porter ~ à qn** to offend sb.

ombragé, e [ɔbʀaʒe] *adj* shaded, shady.

ombrageux, euse [ɔbʀaʒø, -øz] *adj* (*cheval*) skittish, nervous; (*personne*) touchy, easily offended.

ombre [ɔbʀ(ə)] *nf* (*espace non ensoleillé*) shade; (*ombre portée, tache*) shadow; **à l'~** in the shade; (*fam*: *en prison*) behind bars; **à l'~ de** in the shade of; (*tout près de, fig*) in the shadow of; **tu me fais de l'~** you're in my light; **ça nous donne de l'~** it gives us (some) shade; **il n'y a pas l'~ d'un doute** there's not the shadow of a doubt; **dans l'~** in the shade; **vivre dans l'~** (*fig*) to live in obscurity; **laisser dans l'~** (*fig*) to leave in the dark; **~ à paupières** eyeshadow; **~ portée** shadow; **~s chinoises** (*spectacle*) shadow show *sg*.

ombrelle [ɔbʀɛl] *nf* parasol, sunshade.

ombrer [ɔbʀe] *vt* to shade.

omelette [ɔmlɛt] *nf* omelette; **~ baveuse** runny omelette; **~ au fromage/au jambon** cheese/ham omelette; **~ aux herbes** omelette with herbs; **~ norvégienne** baked Alaska.

omettre [ɔmɛtʀ(ə)] *vt* to omit, leave out; **~ de faire** to fail *ou* omit to do.

omis, e [ɔmi, -iz] *pp de* **omettre.**

omission [ɔmisjɔ] *nf* omission.

omnibus [ɔmnibys] *nm* slow *ou* stopping train.

omnipotent, e [ɔmnipɔtɑ, -ɑt] *adj* omnipotent.

omnipraticien, ne [ɔmnipʀatisjɛ, -ɛn] *nm/f* (*MÉD*) general practitioner.

omniprésent, e [ɔmnipʀezɑ, -ɑt] *adj* omnipresent.

omniscient, e [ɔmnisjɑ, -ɑt] *adj* omniscient.

omnisports [ɔmnispɔʀ] *adj inv* (*club*) general sports *cpd*; (*salle*) multi-purpose *cpd*; (*terrain*) all-purpose *cpd*.

omnium [ɔmnjɔm] *nm* (*COMM*) corporation; (*CYCLISME*) omnium; (*COURSES*) open handicap.

omnivore [ɔmnivɔʀ] *adj* omnivorous.

omoplate [ɔmɔplat] *nf* shoulder blade.

OMS *sigle f* (= *Organisation mondiale de la santé*) WHO.

═══════════════ *MOT-CLÉ*

on [ɔ] *pron* **1** (*indéterminé*) you, one; **~ peut le faire ainsi** you *ou* one can do it like this, it can be done like this; **~ dit que** ... they say that ..., it is said that ...

2 (*quelqu'un*): **~ les a attaqués** they were attacked; **~ vous demande au téléphone** there's a phone call for you, you're wanted on the phone; **~ frappe à la porte** someone's knocking at the door

once [ɔs] *nf*: **une ~ de** an ounce of.

oncle [ɔkl(ə)] *nm* uncle.

onction [ɔksjɔ] *nf voir* **extrême-onction.**

onctueux, euse [ɔktɥø, -øz] *adj* creamy, smooth; (*fig*) smooth, unctuous.

onde [ɔd] *nf* (*PHYSIQUE*) wave; **sur l'~** on the waters; **sur les ~s** on the radio; **mettre en ~s** to produce for the radio; **~ de choc** shock wave; **~s courtes (OC)** short wave *sg*; **petites ~s (PO)**, **~s moyennes (OM)** medium wave *sg*; **grandes ~s (GO)**, **~s longues (OL)** long wave *sg*; **~s sonores** sound waves.

ondée [ɔde] *nf* shower.

on-dit [ɔdi] *nm inv* rumour.

ondoyer [ɔdwaje] *vi* to ripple, wave ♦ *vt* (*REL*) to baptize (*in an emergency*).

ondulant, e [ɔdylɑ, -ɑt] *adj* (*démarche*) swaying; (*ligne*) undulating.

ondulation [ɔdylasjɔ] *nf* undulation; wave.

ondulé, e [ɔdyle] *adj* undulating; wavy.

onduler [ɔdyle] *vi* to undulate; (*cheveux*) to wave.

onéreux, euse [ɔneʀø, -øz] *adj* costly; **à titre ~** in return for payment.

ONF *sigle m* (= *Office national des forêts*) ≈ Forestry Commission (*BRIT*), ≈ National Forest Service (*US*).

ongle [ɔgl(ə)] *nm* (*ANAT*) nail; **manger** *ou* **ronger ses ~s** to bite one's nails; **se faire les ~s** to do one's nails.

onglet [ɔglɛ] *nm* (*rainure*) (thumbnail) groove; (*bande de papier*) tab.

onguent [ɔgɑ] *nm* ointment.

onirique [ɔniʀik] *adj* dreamlike, dream *cpd*.

onirisme [ɔniʀism(ə)] *nm* dreams *pl*.

onomatopée [ɔnɔmatɔpe] *nf* onomatopoeia.

ont [ɔ] *vb voir* **avoir.**

ontarien, ne [ɔtaʀjɛ, -ɛn] *adj* Ontarian.

ONU [ɔny] *sigle f* (= *Organisation des Nations unies*) UN(O).

onusien, ne [ɔnyzjɛ, -ɛn] *adj* of the UN(O), of the United Nations (Organization).

onyx [ɔniks] *nm* onyx.

onze [ɔz] *num* eleven.

onzième [ɔzjɛm] *num* eleventh.

op [ɔp] *nf* (= *opération*): **salle d'~** (operating) theatre.

OPA *sigle f* = **offre publique d'achat.**

opacité [ɔpasite] *nf* opaqueness.

opale [ɔpal] *nf* opal.

opalescent, e [ɔpalesɑ, -ɑt] *adj* opalescent.

opalin, e [ɔpalɛ, -in] *adj, nf* opaline.

opaque [ɔpak] *adj* (*vitre, verre*) opaque; (*brouillard, nuit*) impenetrable.

OPE *sigle f* (= *offre publique d'échange*) takeover bid where bidder offers shares in his company in exchange for shares in target company.

OPEP [ɔpɛp] sigle f (= Organisation des pays exportateurs de pétrole) OPEC.

opéra [ɔpeʀa] nm opera; (édifice) opera house.

opérable [ɔpeʀabl(ə)] adj operable.

opéra-comique, pl **opéras-comiques** [ɔpeʀakɔmik] nm light opera, opéra comique.

opérant, e [ɔpeʀɑ̃, -ɑ̃t] adj (mesure) effective.

opérateur, trice [ɔpeʀatœʀ, -tʀis] nm/f operator; ~ **(de prise de vues)** cameraman.

opération [ɔpeʀasjɔ̃] nf operation; (COMM) dealing; **salle/table d'**~ operating theatre/table; ~ **de sauvetage** rescue operation; ~ **à cœur ouvert** open-heart surgery no pl.

opérationnel, le [ɔpeʀasjɔnɛl] adj operational.

opératoire [ɔpeʀatwaʀ] adj (manœuvre, méthode) operating; (choc etc) postoperative.

opéré, e [ɔpeʀe] nm/f post-operative patient.

opérer [ɔpeʀe] vt (MÉD) to operate on; (faire, exécuter) to carry out, make ♦ vi (remède: faire effet) to act, work; (procéder) to proceed; (MÉD) to operate; **s'**~ vi (avoir lieu) to occur, take place; **se faire** ~ to have an operation; **se faire** ~ **des amygdales/du cœur** to have one's tonsils out/have a heart operation.

opérette [ɔpeʀɛt] nf operetta, light opera.

ophtalmique [ɔftalmik] adj ophthalmic.

ophtalmologie [ɔftalmɔlɔʒi] nf ophthalmology.

ophtalmologue [ɔftalmɔlɔg] nm/f ophthalmologist.

opiacé, e [ɔpjase] adj opiate.

opiner [ɔpine] vi: ~ **de la tête** to nod assent ♦ vt: ~ **à** to consent to.

opiniâtre [ɔpinjatʀ(ə)] adj stubborn.

opiniâtreté [ɔpinjatʀəte] nf stubbornness.

opinion [ɔpinjɔ̃] nf opinion; l'~ **(publique)** public opinion; **avoir bonne/mauvaise** ~ **de** to have a high/low opinion of.

opiomane [ɔpjɔman] nm/f opium addict.

opium [ɔpjɔm] nm opium.

OPJ sigle m (= officier de police judiciaire) ≈ DC (= Detective Constable).

opportun, e [ɔpɔʀtœ̃, -yn] adj timely, opportune; **en temps** ~ at the appropriate time.

opportunément [ɔpɔʀtynemɑ̃] adv opportunely.

opportunisme [ɔpɔʀtynism(ə)] nm opportunism.

opportuniste [ɔpɔʀtynist(ə)] adj, nm/f opportunist.

opportunité [ɔpɔʀtynite] nf timeliness, opportuneness.

opposant, e [ɔpozɑ̃, -ɑ̃t] adj opposing ♦ nm/f opponent.

opposé, e [ɔpoze] adj (direction, rive) opposite; (faction) opposing; (couleurs) contrasting; (opinions, intérêts) conflicting; (contre): ~ **à** opposed to, against ♦ nm: **l'**~ the other ou opposite side (ou direction); (contraire) the opposite; **être** ~ **à** to be opposed to; **à l'**~ (fig) on the other hand; **à l'**~ **de** on the other ou opposite side from; (fig) contrary to, unlike.

opposer [ɔpoze] vt (meubles, objets) to place opposite each other; (personnes, armées, équipes) to oppose; (couleurs, termes, tons) to contrast; (comparer: livres, avantages) to contrast; ~ **qch à** (comme obstacle, défense) to set sth against; (comme objection) to put sth forward against; (en contraste) to set sth opposite; to match sth with; **s'**~ (sens réciproque) to conflict; to clash; to face each other; to contrast; **s'**~ **à** (interdire, empêcher) to oppose; (tenir tête à) to rebel against; **sa religion s'y oppose** it's against his religion; **s'**~ **à ce que qn fasse** to be opposed to sb's doing.

opposition [ɔpozisjɔ̃] nf opposition; **par** ~ in contrast; **par** ~ **à** as opposed to, in contrast with; **entrer en** ~ **avec** to come into conflict with; **être en** ~ **avec** (idées, conduite) to be at variance with; **faire** ~ **à un chèque** to stop a cheque.

oppressant, e [ɔpʀesɑ̃, -ɑ̃t] adj oppressive.

oppresser [ɔpʀese] vt to oppress; **se sentir oppressé** to feel breathless.

oppresseur [ɔpʀesœʀ] nm oppressor.

oppressif, ive [ɔpʀesif, -iv] adj oppressive.

oppression [ɔpʀesjɔ̃] nf oppression; (malaise) feeling of suffocation.

opprimer [ɔpʀime] vt (asservir: peuple, faibles) to oppress; (étouffer: liberté, opinion) to suppress, stifle; (suj: chaleur etc) to suffocate, oppress.

opprobre [ɔpʀɔbʀ(ə)] nm disgrace.

opter [ɔpte] vi: ~ **pour** to opt for; ~ **entre** to choose between.

opticien, ne [ɔptisjɛ̃, -ɛn] nm/f optician.

optimal, e, aux [ɔptimal, -o] adj optimal.

optimisation [ɔptimizasjɔ̃] nf optimization.

optimiser [ɔptimize] vt to optimize.

optimisme [ɔptimism(ə)] nm optimism.

optimiste [ɔptimist(ə)] adj optimistic ♦ nm/f optimist.

optimum [ɔptimɔm] adj, nm optimum.

option [ɔpsjɔ̃] nf option; (AUTO: supplément) optional extra; **matière à** ~ (SCOL) optional subject (BRIT), elective (US); **prendre une** ~ **sur** to take (out) an option on; ~ **par défaut** (INFORM) default (option).

optionnel, le [ɔpsjɔnɛl] adj optional.

optique [ɔptik] adj (nerf) optic; (verres) optical ♦ nf (PHOTO: lentilles etc) optics pl; (science, industrie) optics sg; (fig: manière de voir) perspective.

opulence [ɔpylɑ̃s] nf wealth, opulence.

opulent, e [ɔpylɑ̃, -ɑ̃t] adj wealthy, opulent; (formes, poitrine) ample, generous.

OPV *sigle f* (= *offre publique de vente*) public offer of sale.

or [ɔʀ] *nm* gold ♦ *conj* now, but; **d'~** (*fig*) golden; **en** ~ gold *cpd*; (*occasion*) golden; **un mari/enfant en** ~ a treasure; **une affaire en** ~ (*achat*) a real bargain; (*commerce*) a gold mine; **plaqué** ~ gold-plated; ~ **noir** black gold.

oracle [ɔʀakl(ə)] *nm* oracle.

orage [ɔʀaʒ] *nm* (thunder)storm.

orageux, euse [ɔʀaʒø, -øz] *adj* stormy.

oraison [ɔʀɛzɔ̃] *nf* orison, prayer; ~ **funèbre** funeral oration.

oral, e, aux [ɔʀal, -o] *adj* (*déposition, promesse*) oral, verbal; (*MÉD*): **par voie ~e** by mouth, orally ♦ *nm* (*SCOL*) oral.

oralement [ɔʀalmɑ̃] *adv* orally.

orange [ɔʀɑ̃ʒ] *adj inv, nf* orange; ~ **sanguine** blood orange; ~ **pressée** freshly-squeezed orange juice.

orangé, e [ɔʀɑ̃ʒe] *adj* orangey, orange-coloured.

orangeade [ɔʀɑ̃ʒad] *nf* orangeade.

oranger [ɔʀɑ̃ʒe] *nm* orange tree.

orangeraie [ɔʀɑ̃ʒʀɛ] *nf* orange grove.

orangerie [ɔʀɑ̃ʒʀi] *nf* orangery.

orang-outan(g) [ɔʀɑ̃utɑ̃] *nm* orangutan.

orateur [ɔʀatœʀ] *nm* speaker; orator.

oratoire [ɔʀatwaʀ] *nm* (*lieu, chapelle*) oratory; (*au bord du chemin*) wayside shrine ♦ *adj* oratorical.

oratorio [ɔʀatɔʀjo] *nm* oratorio.

orbital, e, aux [ɔʀbital, -o] *adj* orbital; **station ~e** space station.

orbite [ɔʀbit] *nf* (*ANAT*) (eye-)socket; (*PHYSIQUE*) orbit; **mettre sur** ~ to put into orbit; (*fig*) to launch; **dans l'~ de** (*fig*) within the sphere of influence of.

Orcades [ɔʀkad] *nfpl*: **les** ~ the Orkneys, the Orkney Islands.

orchestral, e, aux [ɔʀkɛstʀal, -o] *adj* orchestral.

orchestrateur, trice [ɔʀkɛstʀatœʀ, -tʀis] *nm/f* orchestrator.

orchestration [ɔʀkɛstʀasjɔ̃] *nf* orchestration.

orchestre [ɔʀkɛstʀ(ə)] *nm* orchestra; (*de jazz, danse*) band; (*places*) stalls *pl* (*BRIT*), orchestra (*US*).

orchestrer [ɔʀkɛstʀe] *vt* (*MUS*) to orchestrate; (*fig*) to mount, stage-manage.

orchidée [ɔʀkide] *nf* orchid.

ordinaire [ɔʀdinɛʀ] *adj* ordinary; (*coutumier: maladresse etc*) usual; (*de tous les jours*) everyday; (*modèle, qualité*) standard ♦ *nm* ordinary; (*menus*) everyday fare ♦ *nf* (*essence*) ≈ two-star (petrol) (*BRIT*), ≈ regular (gas) (*US*); **d'~** usually, normally; **à l'~** usually, ordinarily.

ordinairement [ɔʀdinɛʀmɑ̃] *adv* ordinarily, usually.

ordinal, e, aux [ɔʀdinal, -o] *adj* ordinal.

ordinateur [ɔʀdinatœʀ] *nm* computer; **mettre sur** ~ to computerize, put on computer; ~ **de bureau** desktop computer; ~ **domestique** home computer; ~ **individuel** *ou* **personnel** personal computer; ~ **portatif** laptop (computer).

ordination [ɔʀdinasjɔ̃] *nf* ordination.

ordonnance [ɔʀdɔnɑ̃s] *nf* organization; (*groupement, disposition*) layout; (*MÉD*) prescription; (*JUR*) order; (*MIL*) orderly, batman (*BRIT*); **d'~** (*MIL*) regulation *cpd*; **officier d'~** aide-de-camp.

ordonnateur, trice [ɔʀdɔnatœʀ, -tʀis] *nm/f* (*d'une cérémonie, fête*) organizer; ~ **des pompes funèbres** funeral director.

ordonné, e [ɔʀdɔne] *adj* tidy, orderly; (*MATH*) ordered ♦ *nf* (*MATH*) Y-axis, ordinate.

ordonner [ɔʀdɔne] *vt* (*agencer*) to organize, arrange; (*: meubles, appartement*) to lay out, arrange; (*donner un ordre*): ~ **à qn de faire** to order sb to do; (*MATH*) (to arrange in) order; (*REL*) to ordain; (*MÉD*) to prescribe; (*JUR*) to order; **s'~** (*faits*) to organize themselves.

ordre [ɔʀdʀ(ə)] *nm* (*gén*) order; (*propreté et soin*) orderliness, tidiness; (*association professionnelle, honorifique*) association; (*COMM*): **à l'~ de** payable to; (*nature*): **d'~ pratique** of a practical nature; ~**s** *nmpl* (*REL*) holy orders; **avoir de l'~** to be tidy *ou* orderly; **mettre en** ~ to tidy (up), put in order; **mettre bon** ~ **à** to put to rights, sort out; **procéder par** ~ to take things one at a time; **être aux ~s de qn/sous les ~s de qn** to be at sb's disposal/under sb's command; **rappeler qn à l'~** to call sb to order; **jusqu'à nouvel** ~ until further notice; **dans le même** ~ **d'idées** in this connection; **par** ~ **d'entrée en scène** in order of appearance; **un** ~ **de grandeur** some idea of the size (*ou* amount); **de premier** ~ first-rate; ~ **de grève** strike call; ~ **du jour** (*d'une réunion*) agenda; (*MIL*) order of the day; **à l'~ du jour** on the agenda; (*fig*) topical; (*MIL: citer*) in dispatches; ~ **de mission** (*MIL*) orders *pl*; ~ **public** law and order; ~ **de route** marching orders *pl*.

ordure [ɔʀdyʀ] *nf* filth *no pl*; (*propos, écrit*) obscenity, (piece of) filth; ~**s** *nfpl* (*balayures, déchets*) rubbish *sg*, refuse *sg*; ~**s ménagères** household refuse.

ordurier, ière [ɔʀdyʀje, -jɛʀ] *adj* lewd, filthy.

oreille [ɔʀɛj] *nf* (*ANAT*) ear; (*de marmite, tasse*) handle; (*TECH: d'un écrou*) wing; **avoir de l'~** to have a good ear (for music); **avoir l'~ fine** to have good *ou* sharp ears; **l'~ basse** crestfallen, dejected; **se faire tirer l'~** to take a lot of persuading; **dire qch à l'~ de qn** to have a word in sb's ear (about sth).

oreiller [ɔʀeje] *nm* pillow.

oreillette [ɔʀejɛt] *nf* (*ANAT*) auricle.

oreillons [ɔʀejɔ̃] *nmpl* mumps *sg*.

ores [ɔʀ]: **d'~ et déjà** *adv* already.

orfèvre [ɔʀfɛvʀ(ə)] *nm* goldsmith; silversmith.

orfèvrerie [ɔʀfɛvʀəʀi] *nf* (*art, métier*) goldsmith's (*ou* silversmith's) trade; (*ouvrage*) (silver *ou* gold) plate.

orfraie [ɔʀfʀɛ] *nm* white-tailed eagle; **pousser des cris d'~** to yell at the top of one's voice.

organe [ɔʀgan] *nm* organ; (*véhicule, instrument*) instrument; (*voix*) voice; (*porte-parole*) representative, mouthpiece; **~s de commande** (*TECH*) controls; **~s de transmission** (*TECH*) transmission system *sg*.

organigramme [ɔʀganigʀam] *nm* (*hiérarchique, structurel*) organization chart; (*des opérations*) flow chart.

organique [ɔʀganik] *adj* organic.

organisateur, trice [ɔʀganizatœʀ, -tʀis] *nm/f* organizer.

organisation [ɔʀganizasjɔ̃] *nf* organization; **O~ des Nations unies (ONU)** United Nations (Organization) (UN, UNO); **O~ mondiale de la santé (OMS)** World Health Organization (WHO); **O~ du traité de l'Atlantique Nord (OTAN)** North Atlantic Treaty Organization (NATO).

organisationnel, le [ɔʀganizasjɔnɛl] *adj* organizational.

organiser [ɔʀganize] *vt* to organize; (*mettre sur pied: service etc*) to set up; **s'~** to get organized.

organisme [ɔʀganism(ə)] *nm* (*BIO*) organism; (*corps humain*) body; (*ADMIN, POL etc*) body, organism.

organiste [ɔʀganist(ə)] *nm/f* organist.

orgasme [ɔʀgasm(ə)] *nm* orgasm, climax.

orge [ɔʀʒ(ə)] *nf* barley.

orgeat [ɔʀʒa] *nm*: **sirop d'~** barley water.

orgelet [ɔʀʒəlɛ] *nm* sty(e).

orgie [ɔʀʒi] *nf* orgy.

orgue [ɔʀg(ə)] *nm* organ; **~s** *nfpl* organ *sg*; **~ de Barbarie** barrel *ou* street organ.

orgueil [ɔʀgœj] *nm* pride.

orgueilleux, euse [ɔʀgœjø, -øz] *adj* proud.

Orient [ɔʀjɑ̃] *nm*: **l'~** the East, the Orient.

orientable [ɔʀjɑ̃tabl(ə)] *adj* (*phare, lampe etc*) adjustable.

oriental, e, aux [ɔʀjɑ̃tal, -o] *adj* oriental, eastern; (*frontière*) eastern ♦ *nm/f*: **O~, e** Oriental.

orientation [ɔʀjɑ̃tasjɔ̃] *nf* positioning; adjustment; orientation; direction; (*d'une maison etc*) aspect; (*d'un journal*) leanings *pl*; **avoir le sens de l'~** to have a (good) sense of direction; **course d'~** orienteering exercise; **~ professionnelle** careers advice *ou* guidance; (*service*) careers advisory service.

orienté, e [ɔʀjɑ̃te] *adj* (*fig: article, journal*) slanted; **bien/mal ~** (*appartement*) well/badly positioned; **~ au sud** facing south, with a southern aspect.

orienter [ɔʀjɑ̃te] *vt* (*situer*) to position; (*placer, disposer: pièce mobile*) to adjust, position; (*tourner*) to direct, turn; (*voyageur, touriste, recherches*) to direct; (*fig: élève*) to orientate; **s'~** (*se repérer*) to find one's bearings; **s'~ vers** (*fig*) to turn towards.

orienteur, euse [ɔʀjɑ̃tœʀ, -øz] *nm/f* (*SCOL*) careers adviser.

orifice [ɔʀifis] *nm* opening, orifice.

oriflamme [ɔʀiflam] *nf* banner, standard.

origan [ɔʀigɑ̃] *nm* oregano.

originaire [ɔʀiʒinɛʀ] *adj* original; **être ~ de** (*pays, lieu*) to be a native of; (*provenir de*) to originate from; to be native to.

original, e, aux [ɔʀiʒinal, -o] *adj* original; (*bizarre*) eccentric ♦ *nm/f* (*fam: excentrique*) eccentric; (: *fantaisiste*) joker ♦ *nm* (*document etc, ART*) original; (*dactylographie*) top copy.

originalité [ɔʀiʒinalite] *nf* (*d'un nouveau modèle*) originality *no pl*; (*excentricité, bizarrerie*) eccentricity.

origine [ɔʀiʒin] *nf* origin; (*d'un message, appel téléphonique*) source; (*d'une révolution, réussite*) root; **~s** *nfpl* (*d'une personne*) origins; **d'~** of origin; (*pneus etc*) original; (*bureau postal*) dispatching; **d'~ française** of French origin; **dès l'~** at *ou* from the outset; **à l'~** originally; **avoir son ~ dans** to have its origins in, originate in.

originel, le [ɔʀiʒinɛl] *adj* original.

originellement [ɔʀiʒinɛlmɑ̃] *adv* (*à l'origine*) originally; (*dès l'origine*) from the beginning.

oripeaux [ɔʀipo] *nmpl* rags.

ORL *sigle f* (= *oto-rhino-laryngologie*) ENT ♦ *sigle m/f* (= *oto-rhino-laryngologiste*) ENT specialist; **être en ~** (*malade*) to be in the ENT hospital *ou* department.

orme [ɔʀm(ə)] *nm* elm.

orné, e [ɔʀne] *adj* ornate; **~ de** adorned *ou* decorated with.

ornement [ɔʀnəmɑ̃] *nm* ornament; (*fig*) embellishment, adornment; **~s sacerdotaux** vestments.

ornemental, e, aux [ɔʀnəmɑ̃tal, -o] *adj* ornamental.

ornementer [ɔʀnəmɑ̃te] *vt* to ornament.

orner [ɔʀne] *vt* to decorate, adorn; **~ qch de** to decorate sth with.

ornière [ɔʀnjɛʀ] *nf* rut; (*fig*): **sortir de l'~** (*routine*) to get out of the rut; (*impasse*) to get out of a spot.

ornithologie [ɔʀnitɔlɔʒi] *nf* ornithology.

ornithologue [ɔʀnitɔlɔg] *nm/f* ornithologist; **~ amateur** birdwatcher.

orphelin, e [ɔʀfəlɛ̃, -in] *adj* orphan(ed) ♦ *nm/f* orphan; **~ de père/mère** fatherless/motherless.

orphelinat [ɔʀfəlina] *nm* orphanage.

ORSEC [ɔʀsɛk] *sigle f* (= *Organisation des secours*): **le plan ~** disaster contingency plan.

ORSECRAD [ɔʀsɛkʀad] *sigle m* = *ORSEC en cas d'accident nucléaire*.

orteil [ɔʀtɛj] *nm* toe; **gros ~** big toe.

ORTF *sigle m* (= *Office de radio-diffusion télévision française*) (*former*) *French broadcasting corporation*.

orthodontiste [ɔʀtɔdɔ̃tist(ə)] *nm/f* orthodon-

tist.
orthodoxe [ɔʀtɔdɔks(ə)] *adj* orthodox.
orthodoxie [ɔʀtɔdɔksi] *nf* orthodoxy.
orthogénie [ɔʀtɔʒeni] *nf* family planning.
orthographe [ɔʀtɔgʀaf] *nf* spelling.
orthographier [ɔʀtɔgʀafje] *vt* to spell; **mal orthographié** misspelt.
orthopédie [ɔʀtɔpedi] *nf* orthopaedics *sg* (*BRIT*), orthopedics *sg* (*US*).
orthopédique [ɔʀtɔpedik] *adj* orthopaedic (*BRIT*), orthopedic (*US*).
orthopédiste [ɔʀtɔpedist(ə)] *nm/f* orthopaedic (*BRIT*) *ou* orthopedic (*US*) specialist.
orthophonie [ɔʀtɔfɔni] *nf* (*MÉD*) speech therapy; (*LING*) correct pronunciation.
orthophoniste [ɔʀtɔfɔnist(ə)] *nm/f* speech therapist.
ortie [ɔʀti] *nf* (stinging) nettle; ~ **blanche** white dead-nettle.
OS *sigle m* = **ouvrier spécialisé**.
os [ɔs, *pl* o] *nm* bone; **sans** ~ (*BOUCHERIE*) off the bone, boned; ~ **à moelle** marrowbone.
oscillation [ɔsilasjɔ̃] *nf* oscillation; ~**s** *nfpl* (*fig*) fluctuations.
osciller [ɔsile] *vi* (*pendule*) to swing; (*au vent etc*) to rock; (*TECH*) to oscillate; (*fig*): ~ **entre** to waver *ou* fluctuate between.
osé, e [oze] *adj* daring, bold.
oseille [ozɛj] *nf* sorrel.
oser [oze] *vi, vt* to dare; ~ **faire** to dare (to) do.
osier [ozje] *nm* (*BOT*) willow; **d'**~, **en** ~ wicker(work) *cpd*.
Oslo [ɔslo] *n* Oslo.
osmose [ɔsmoz] *nf* osmosis.
ossature [ɔsatyʀ] *nf* (*ANAT: squelette*) frame, skeletal structure; (*: du visage*) bone structure; (*fig*) framework.
osselet [ɔslɛ] *nm* (*ANAT*) ossicle; **jouer aux** ~**s** to play jacks.
ossements [ɔsmɑ̃] *nmpl* bones.
osseux, euse [ɔsø, -øz] *adj* bony; (*tissu, maladie, greffe*) bone *cpd*.
ossifier [ɔsifje]: **s'**~ *vi* to ossify.
ossuaire [ɔsɥɛʀ] *nm* ossuary.
Ostende [ɔstɑ̃d] *n* Ostend.
ostensible [ɔstɑ̃sibl(ə)] *adj* conspicuous.
ostensiblement [ɔstɑ̃sibləmɑ̃] *adv* conspicuously.
ostensoir [ɔstɑ̃swaʀ] *nm* monstrance.
ostentation [ɔstɑ̃tasjɔ̃] *nf* ostentation; **faire** ~ **de** to parade, make a display of.
ostentatoir [ɔstɑ̃tatwaʀ] *adj* ostentatious.
ostracisme [ɔstʀasism(ə)] *nm* ostracism; **frapper d'**~ to ostracize.
ostréicole [ɔstʀeikɔl] *adj* oyster *cpd*.
ostréiculture [ɔstʀeikyltyʀ] *nf* oyster-farming.
otage [ɔtaʒ] *nm* hostage; **prendre qn comme** ~ to take sb hostage.
OTAN [ɔtɑ̃] *sigle f* (= *Organisation du traité de l'Atlantique Nord*) NATO.
otarie [ɔtaʀi] *nf* sea-lion.

OTASE [ɔtaz] *sigle f* (= *Organisation du traité de l'Asie du Sud-Est*) SEATO (= *Southeast Asia Treaty Organization*).
ôter [ote] *vt* to remove; (*soustraire*) to take away; ~ **qch à qn** to take sth (away) from sb; ~ **qch de** to remove sth from; **6 ôté de 10 égale 4** 6 from 10 equals *ou* is 4.
otite [ɔtit] *nf* ear infection.
oto-rhino(-laryngologiste) [ɔtɔʀinɔ(-laʀɛ̃gɔlɔʒist(ə))] *nm/f* ear, nose and throat specialist.
ottomane [ɔtɔman] *nf* ottoman.
ou [u] *conj* or; ~ ... ~ either ... or; ~ **bien** or (else).

═══════════════════ *MOT-CLÉ*

où [u] *pron relatif* **1** (*position, situation*) where, that (*souvent omis*); **la chambre** ~ **il était** the room (that) he was in, the room where he was; **la ville** ~ **je l'ai rencontré** the town where I met him; **la pièce d'**~ **il est sorti** the room he came out of; **le village d'**~ **je viens** the village I come from; **les villes par** ~ **il est passé** the towns he went through
2 (*temps, état*) that (*souvent omis*); **le jour** ~ **il est parti** the day (that) he left; **au prix** ~ **c'est** at the price it is
♦ *adv* **1** (*interrogation*) where; ~ **est-il/va-t-il?** where is he/is he going?; **par** ~? which way?; **d'**~ **vient que ...?** how come ...?
2 (*position*) where; **je sais** ~ **il est** I know where he is; ~ **que l'on aille** wherever you go.

OUA *sigle f* (= *Organisation de l'unité africaine*) OAU (= *Organization of African Unity*).
ouais [wɛ] *excl* yeah.
ouate [wat] *nf* cotton wool (*BRIT*), cotton (*US*); (*bourre*) padding, wadding; ~ (**hydrophile**) cotton wool (*BRIT*), (absorbent) cotton (*US*).
ouaté, e [wate] *adj* cotton-wool; (*doublé*) padded; (*fig: atmosphère*) cocoon-like; (*: pas, bruit*) muffled.
oubli [ubli] *nm* (*acte*): **l'**~ **de** forgetting; (*étourderie*) forgetfulness *no pl*; (*négligence*) omission, oversight; (*absence de souvenirs*) oblivion; ~ **de soi** self-effacement, self-negation.
oublier [ublije] *vt* (*gén*) to forget; (*ne pas voir: erreurs etc*) to miss; (*ne pas mettre: virgule, nom*) to leave out, forget; (*laisser quelque part: chapeau etc*) to leave behind; **s'**~ to forget o.s; (*enfant, animal*) to have an accident (*euphemism*); ~ **l'heure** to forget (about) the time.
oubliettes [ublijɛt] *nfpl* dungeon *sg*; (**jeter**) **aux** ~ (*fig*) (to put) completely out of mind.
oublieux, euse [ublijø, -øz] *adj* forgetful.
oued [wɛd] *nm* wadi.
ouest [wɛst] *nm* west ♦ *adj inv* west; (*région*) western; **à l'**~ in the west; (to the) west, westwards; **à l'**~ **de** (to the) west of; **vent d'**~ westerly wind.

ouest-allemand, e [wɛstalmɑ̃, -ɑ̃d] *adj* West German.

ouf [uf] *excl* phew!

Ouganda [ugɑ̃da] *nm*: **l'~** Uganda.

ougandais, e [ugɑ̃dɛ, -ɛz] *adj* Ugandan.

oui [wi] *adv* yes; **répondre (par)** ~ to answer yes; **mais ~, bien sûr** yes, of course; **je pense que** ~ I think so; **pour un** ~ **ou pour un non** for no apparent reason.

oui-dire [widiʀ]: **par** ~ *adv* by hearsay.

ouïe [wi] *nf* hearing; **~s** *nfpl* (*de poisson*) gills; (*de violon*) sound-hole *sg*.

ouïr [wiʀ] *vt* to hear; **avoir ouï dire que** to have heard it said that.

ouistiti [wistiti] *nm* marmoset.

ouragan [uʀagɑ̃] *nm* hurricane; (*fig*) storm.

Oural [uʀal] *nm*: **l'~** (*fleuve*) the Ural; (*aussi*: **les monts** ~) the Urals, the Ural Mountains.

ouralo-altaïque [uʀaloaltaik] *adj*, *nm* Ural-Altaic.

ourdir [uʀdiʀ] *vt* (*complot*) to hatch.

ourdou [uʀdu] *adj inv* Urdu ♦ *nm* (*LING*) Urdu.

ourlé, e [uʀle] *adj* hemmed; (*fig*) rimmed.

ourler [uʀle] *vt* to hem.

ourlet [uʀlɛ] *nm* hem; (*de l'oreille*) rim; **faire un** ~ **à** to hem.

ours [uʀs] *nm* bear; ~ **brun/blanc** brown/polar bear; ~ **marin** fur seal; ~ **mal léché** uncouth fellow; ~ **(en peluche)** teddy (bear).

ourse [uʀs(ə)] *nf* (*ZOOL*) she-bear; **la Grande/ Petite O~** the Great/Little Bear, Ursa Major/Minor.

oursin [uʀsɛ̃] *nm* sea urchin.

ourson [uʀsɔ̃] *nm* (bear-)cub.

ouste [ust(ə)] *excl* hop it!

outil [uti] *nm* tool.

outillage [utijaʒ] *nm* set of tools; (*d'atelier*) equipment *no pl*.

outiller [utije] *vt* (*ouvrier, usine*) to equip.

outrage [utʀaʒ] *nm* insult; **faire subir les derniers ~s à** (*femme*) to ravish; ~ **aux bonnes mœurs** (*JUR*) outrage to public decency; ~ **à magistrat** (*JUR*) contempt of court; ~ **à la pudeur** (*JUR*) indecent behaviour *no pl*.

outragé, e [utʀaʒe] *adj* offended; outraged.

outrageant, e [utʀaʒɑ̃, -ɑ̃t] *adj* offensive.

outrager [utʀaʒe] *vt* to offend gravely; (*fig: contrevenir à*) to outrage, insult.

outrageusement [utʀaʒøzmɑ̃] *adv* outrageously.

outrance [utʀɑ̃s] *nf* excessiveness *no pl*, excess; **à** ~ *adv* excessively, to excess.

outrancier, ière [utʀɑ̃sje, -jɛʀ] *adj* extreme.

outre [utʀ(ə)] *nf* goatskin, water skin ♦ *prép* besides ♦ *adv*: **passer** ~ to carry on regardless; **passer** ~ **à** to disregard, take no notice of; **en** ~ besides, moreover; ~ **que** apart from the fact that; ~ **mesure** immoderately; unduly.

outré, e [utʀe] *adj* (*flatterie, éloge*) excessive, exaggerated; (*indigné, scandalisé*) outraged.

outre-Atlantique [utʀatlɑ̃tik] *adv* across the Atlantic.

outrecuidance [utʀəkɥidɑ̃s] *nf* presumptuousness *no pl*.

outre-Manche [utʀəmɑ̃ʃ] *adv* across the Channel.

outremer [utʀəmɛʀ] *adj inv* ultramarine.

outre-mer [utʀəmɛʀ] *adv* overseas; **d'~** overseas.

outrepasser [utʀəpɑse] *vt* to go beyond, exceed.

outrer [utʀe] *vt* (*pensée, attitude*) to exaggerate; (*indigner: personne*) to outrage.

outre-Rhin [utʀəʀɛ̃] *adv* across the Rhine, in Germany.

outsider [awtsajdœʀ] *nm* outsider.

ouvert, e [uvɛʀ, -ɛʀt(ə)] *pp de* **ouvrir** ♦ *adj* open; (*robinet, gaz etc*) on; **à bras ~s** with open arms.

ouvertement [uvɛʀtəmɑ̃] *adv* openly.

ouverture [uvɛʀtyʀ] *nf* opening; (*MUS*) overture; (*POL*): **l'~** the widening of the political spectrum; (*PHOTO*): ~ **(du diaphragme)** aperture; **~s** *nfpl* (*propositions*) overtures; ~ **d'esprit** open-mindedness; **heures d'~** (*COMM*) opening hours; **jours d'~** (*COMM*) days of opening.

ouvrable [uvʀabl(ə)] *adj*: **jour** ~ working day, weekday; **heures ~s** business hours.

ouvrage [uvʀaʒ] *nm* (*tâche, de tricot etc, MIL*) work *no pl*; (*objet: COUTURE, ART*) (piece of) work; (*texte, livre*) work; **panier** *ou* **corbeille à** ~ work basket; ~ **d'art** (*GÉNIE CIVIL*) bridge or tunnel etc.

ouvragé, e [uvʀaʒe] *adj* finely embroidered (*ou* worked *ou* carved).

ouvrant, e [uvʀɑ̃, -ɑ̃t] *vb voir* **ouvrir** ♦ *adj*: **toit** ~ sunroof.

ouvré, e [uvʀe] *adj* finely-worked; **jour** ~ working day.

ouvre-boîte(s) [uvʀəbwat] *nm inv* tin (*BRIT*) *ou* can opener.

ouvre-bouteille(s) [uvʀəbutɛj] *nm inv* bottle-opener.

ouvreuse [uvʀøz] *nf* usherette.

ouvrier, ière [uvʀije, -jɛʀ] *nm/f* worker ♦ *nf* (*ZOOL*) worker (bee) ♦ *adj* working-class; (*problèmes, conflit*) industrial, labour *cpd* (*BRIT*), labor *cpd* (*US*); (*revendications*) workers'; **classe ouvrière** working class; ~ **agricole** farmworker; ~ **qualifié** skilled worker; ~ **spécialisé (OS)** semiskilled worker; ~ **d'usine** factory worker.

ouvrir [uvʀiʀ] *vt* (*gén*) to open; (*brèche, passage*) to open up; (*commencer l'exploitation de, créer*) to open (up); (*eau, électricité, chauffage, robinet*) to turn on; (*MÉD: abcès*) to open up, cut open ♦ *vi* to open; to open up; (*CARTES*): ~ **à trèfle** to open in clubs; **s'~** *vi* to open; **s'~ à** (*art etc*) to open one's mind to; **s'~ à qn (de qch)** to open one's heart to sb (about sth); **s'~ les veines** to slash *ou* cut one's wrists; ~ **sur** to open onto; ~ **l'appétit**

à qn to whet sb's appetite; ~ **des horizons** to open up new horizons; ~ **l'esprit** to broaden one's horizons; ~ **une session** (*INFORM*) to log in.

ouvroir [uvʀwaʀ] *nm* workroom, sewing room.

ovaire [ɔvɛʀ] *nm* ovary.

ovale [ɔval] *adj* oval.

ovation [ɔvasjɔ̃] *nf* ovation.

ovationner [ɔvasjɔne] *vt:* ~ **qn** to give sb an ovation.

ovin, e [ɔvɛ̃, -in] *adj* ovine.

OVNI [ɔvni] *sigle m* (= *objet volant non identifié*) UFO.

ovoïde [ɔvɔid] *adj* egg-shaped.

ovulation [ɔvylasjɔ̃] *nf* (*PHYSIOL*) ovulation.

ovule [ɔvyl] *nm* (*PHYSIOL*) ovum (*pl* ova); (*MÉD*) pessary.

oxfordien, ne [ɔksfɔʀdjɛ̃, -ɛn] *adj* Oxonian ♦ *nm/f:* **O~, ne** Oxonian.

oxydable [ɔksidabl(ə)] *adj* liable to rust.

oxyde [ɔksid] *nm* oxide; ~ **de carbone** carbon monoxide.

oxyder [ɔkside]: **s'~** *vi* to become oxidized.

oxygène [ɔksiʒɛn] *nm* oxygen; (*fig*): **cure d'~** fresh air cure.

oxygéné, e [ɔksiʒene] *adj:* **eau ~e** hydrogen peroxide; **cheveux ~s** bleached hair.

ozone [ozon] *nm* ozone; **trou dans la couche d'~** ozone hole.

P p

P, p [pe] *nm inv* P, p ♦ *abr* (= *Père*) Fr; (= *page*) p; **P comme Pierre** P for Peter.

PA *sigle f* = **petites annonces**.

PAC *sigle f* (= *Politique agricole commune*) CAP.

pacage [pakaʒ] *nm* grazing, pasture.

pace-maker [pɛsmɛkœʀ] *nm* pacemaker.

pachyderme [paʃidɛʀm(ə)] *nm* pachyderm; elephant.

pacificateur, trice [pasifikatœʀ, -tʀis] *adj* pacificatory.

pacification [pasifikasjɔ̃] *nf* pacification.

pacifier [pasifje] *vt* to pacify.

pacifique [pasifik] *adj* (*personne*) peaceable; (*intentions, coexistence*) peaceful ♦ *nm:* **le P~, l'océan P~** the Pacific (Ocean).

pacifiquement [pasifikmɑ̃] *adv* peaceably; peacefully.

pacifisme [pasifism(ə)] *nm* pacifism.

pacifiste [pasifist(ə)] *nm/f* pacifist.

pack [pak] *nm* pack.

pacotille [pakɔtij] *nf* (*péj*) cheap goods *pl*; **de ~** cheap.

pacte [pakt(ə)] *nm* pact, treaty.

pactiser [paktize] *vi:* ~ **avec** to come to terms with.

pactole [paktɔl] *nm* gold mine (*fig*).

paddock [padɔk] *nm* paddock.

Padoue [padu] *n* Padua.

PAF *sigle f* (= *Police de l'air et des frontières*) police authority responsible for civil aviation, border control etc ♦ *sigle m* (= *paysage audiovisuel français*) French broadcasting scene.

pagaie [pagɛ] *nf* paddle.

pagaille [pagaj] *nf* mess, shambles *sg*; **il y en a en ~** there are loads *ou* heaps of them.

paganisme [paganism(ə)] *nm* paganism.

pagayer [pageje] *vi* to paddle.

page [paʒ] *nf* page; (*passage: d'un roman*) passage ♦ *nm* page (boy); **mise en ~** layout; **à la ~** (*fig*) up-to-date; ~ **d'accueil** (*INFORM*) home page; ~ **blanche** blank page; ~ **de garde** endpaper.

page-écran, *pl* **pages-écrans** [paʒekʀɑ̃] *nf* (*INFORM*) screen page.

pagination [paʒinasjɔ̃] *nf* pagination.

paginer [paʒine] *vt* to paginate.

pagne [paɲ] *nm* loincloth.

pagode [pagɔd] *nf* pagoda.

paie [pɛ] *nf* = **paye**.

paiement [pɛmɑ̃] *nm* = **payement**.

païen, ne [pajɛ̃, -ɛn] *adj*, *nm/f* pagan, heathen.

paillard, e [pajaʀ, -aʀd(ə)] *adj* bawdy.

paillasse [pajas] *nf* (*matelas*) straw mattress; (*d'un évier*) draining board.

paillasson [pajasɔ̃] *nm* doormat.

paille [paj] *nf* straw; (*défaut*) flaw; **être sur la ~** to be ruined; ~ **de fer** steel wool.

paillé, e [paje] *adj* with a straw seat.

pailleté, e [pajte] *adj* sequined.

paillette [pajɛt] *nf* speck, flake; **~s** *nfpl* (*décoratives*) sequins, spangles; **lessive en ~s** soapflakes *pl*.

pain [pɛ̃] *nm* (*substance*) bread; (*unité*) loaf (*pl* loaves); (*of bread*); (*morceau*): ~ **de cire** *etc* bar of wax *etc*; (*CULIN*): ~ **de poisson/légumes** fish/vegetable loaf; **petit ~** (bread) roll; ~ **bis/complet** brown/wholemeal (*BRIT*) *ou* wholewheat (*US*) bread; ~ **de campagne** farmhouse bread; ~ **d'épice** ≈ gingerbread; ~ **grillé** toast; ~ **de mie** sandwich loaf; ~ **perdu** French toast; ~ **de seigle** rye bread; ~ **de sucre** sugar loaf.

pair, e [pɛʀ] *adj* (*nombre*) even ♦ *nm* peer; **aller de ~ (avec)** to go hand in hand *ou* together (with); **au ~** (*FINANCE*) at par; **valeur au ~** par value; **jeune fille au ~** au pair.

paire [pɛʀ] *nf* pair; **une ~ de lunettes/tenailles** a pair of glasses/pincers; **faire la ~: les deux font la ~** they are two of a kind.

pais [pɛ] *vb voir* **paître**.

paisible [pezibl(ə)] *adj* peaceful, quiet.

paisiblement [peziblmɑ̃] *adv* peacefully, quietly.

paître [pɛtʀ(ə)] *vi* to graze.

paix [pɛ] *nf* peace; *(fig)* peacefulness, peace; **faire la ~ avec** to make peace with; **avoir la ~** to have peace (and quiet).

Pakistan [pakistã] *nm:* **le ~** Pakistan.

pakistanais, e [pakistanɛ, -ɛz] *adj* Pakistani.

PAL *sigle m* (= *Phase Alternation Line*) PAL.

palabrer [palabʀe] *vi* to argue endlessly.

palabres [palabʀ(ə)] *nfpl ou mpl* endless discussions.

palace [palas] *nm* luxury hotel.

palais [palɛ] *nm* palace; *(ANAT)* palate; **le P~ Bourbon** *the seat of the French National Assembly;* **le P~ de l'Élysée** the Élysée Palace; **~ des expositions** exhibition centre; **le P~ de Justice** the Law Courts *pl.*

palan [palã] *nm* hoist.

Palatin [palatɛ̃]: **le (mont) ~** the Palatine (Hill).

pale [pal] *nf* (*d'hélice, de rame*) blade; *(de roue)* paddle.

pâle [pɑl] *adj* pale; *(fig):* **une ~ imitation** a pale imitation; **bleu ~** pale blue; **~ de colère** white *ou* pale with anger.

palefrenier [palfʀənje] *nm* groom *(for horses).*

paléontologie [paleɔ̃tɔlɔʒi] *nf* paleontology.

paléontologiste [paleɔ̃tɔlɔʒist(ə)], **paléontologue** [paleɔ̃tɔlɔg] *nm/f* paleontologist.

Palerme [palɛʀm(ə)] *n* Palermo.

Palestine [palɛstin] *nf:* **la ~** Palestine.

palestinien, ne [palɛstinjɛ̃, -ɛn] *adj* Palestinian ♦ *nm/f:* **P~, ne** Palestinian.

palet [palɛ] *nm* disc; *(HOCKEY)* puck.

paletot [palto] *nm* (short) coat.

palette [palɛt] *nf* palette; *(produits)* range.

palétuvier [paletyvje] *nm* mangrove.

pâleur [pɑlœʀ] *nf* paleness.

palier [palje] *nm* (*d'escalier*) landing; *(fig)* level, plateau; *(: phase stable)* levelling *(BRIT) ou* leveling *(US)* off, new level; *(TECH)* bearing; **nos voisins de ~** our neighbo(u)rs across the landing *(BRIT) ou* the hall *(US)*; **en ~** *adv* level; **par ~s** in stages.

palière [paljɛʀ] *adj f* landing *cpd.*

pâlir [pɑliʀ] *vi* to turn *ou* go pale; *(couleur)* to fade; **faire ~ qn** *(de jalousie)* to make sb green (with envy).

palissade [palisad] *nf* fence.

palissandre [palisɑ̃dʀ(ə)] *nm* rosewood.

palliatif [paljatif] *nm* palliative; *(expédient)* stopgap measure.

pallier [palje] *vt,* **~ à** *vt* to offset, make up for.

palmarès [palmaʀɛs] *nm* record (of achievements); *(SCOL)* prize list; *(SPORT)* list of winners.

palme [palm(ə)] *nf* *(BOT)* palm leaf *(pl* leaves); *(symbole)* palm; *(de plongeur)* flipper; **~s (académiques)** *decoration for services to education.*

palmé, e [palme] *adj (pattes)* webbed.

palmeraie [palməʀɛ] *nf* palm grove.

palmier [palmje] *nm* palm tree.

palmipède [palmipɛd] *nm* palmiped, web-footed bird.

palois, e [palwa, -waz] *adj* of *ou* from Pau ♦ *nm/f:* **P~, e** inhabitant *ou* native of Pau.

palombe [palɔ̃b] *nf* woodpigeon, ringdove.

pâlot, te [pɑlo, -ɔt] *adj* pale, peaky.

palourde [paluʀd(ə)] *nf* clam.

palpable [palpabl(ə)] *adj* tangible, palpable.

palper [palpe] *vt* to feel, finger.

palpitant, e [palpitã, -ãt] *adj* thrilling, gripping.

palpitation [palpitasjɔ̃] *nf* palpitation.

palpiter [palpite] *vi (cœur, pouls)* to beat; *(: plus fort)* to pound, throb; *(narines, chair)* to quiver.

paludisme [palydism(ə)] *nm* malaria.

palustre [palystʀ(ə)] *adj (coquillage etc)* marsh *cpd; (fièvre)* malarial.

pâmer [pame]: **se ~** *vi* to swoon; *(fig):* **se ~ devant** to go into raptures over.

pâmoison [pamwazɔ̃] *nf:* **tomber en ~** to swoon.

pampa [pãpa] *nf* pampas *pl.*

pamphlet [pãflɛ] *nm* lampoon, satirical tract.

pamphlétaire [pãfletɛʀ] *nm/f* lampoonist.

pamplemousse [pãpləmus] *nm* grapefruit.

pan [pã] *nm* section, piece; *(côté: d'un prisme, d'une tour)* side, face ♦ *excl* bang!; **~ de chemise** shirt tail; **~ de mur** section of wall.

panacée [panase] *nf* panacea.

panachage [panaʃaʒ] *nm* blend, mix; *(POL)* voting for candidates from different parties instead of for the set list of one party.

panache [panaʃ] *nm* plume; *(fig)* spirit, panache.

panaché, e [panaʃe] *adj:* **œillet ~** variegated carnation; **glace ~e** mixed ice cream; **salade ~e** mixed salad; **bière ~e** shandy.

panais [panɛ] *nm* parsnip.

Panama [panama] *nm:* **le ~** Panama.

panaméen, ne [panameɛ̃, -ɛn] *adj* Panamanian ♦ *nm/f:* **P~, ne** Panamanian.

panaris [panaʀi] *nm* whitlow.

pancarte [pãkaʀt(ə)] *nf* sign, notice; *(dans un défilé)* placard.

pancréas [pãkʀeas] *nm* pancreas.

panda [pãda] *nm* panda.

pané, e [pane] *adj* fried in breadcrumbs.

panégyrique [paneʒiʀik] *nm:* **faire le ~ de qn** to extol sb's merits *ou* virtues.

panier [panje] *nm* basket; *(à diapositives)* magazine; **mettre au ~** to chuck away; **~ de crabes: c'est un ~ de crabes** *(fig)* they're constantly at one another's throats; **~ percé** *(fig)* spendthrift; **~ à provisions** shopping basket; **~ à salade** *(CULIN)* salad shaker; *(POLICE)* paddy wagon, police van.

panier-repas, *pl* **paniers-repas** [panjeʀ(ə)pa] *nm* packed lunch.

panification [panifikasjɔ̃] *nf* bread-making.

panique [panik] *adj* panicky ♦ *nf* panic.

paniquer [panike] *vi* to panic.

panne [pan] *nf* *(d'un mécanisme, moteur)*

panneau – paquet

breakdown; **être/tomber en** ~ to have broken down/break down; **être en** ~ **d'essence** *ou* **en** ~ **sèche** to have run out of petrol (*BRIT*) *ou* gas (*US*); **mettre en** ~ (*NAVIG*) to bring to; ~ **d'électricité** *ou* **de courant** power *ou* electrical failure.

panneau, x [pano] *nm* (*écriteau*) sign, notice; (*de boiserie, de tapisserie etc*) panel; **tomber dans le** ~ (*fig*) to walk into the trap; ~ **d'affichage** notice (*BRIT*) *ou* bulletin (*US*) board; ~ **électoral** board for election poster; ~ **indicateur** signpost; ~ **publicitaire** hoarding (*BRIT*), billboard (*US*); ~ **de signalisation** roadsign; ~ **solaire** solar panel.

panneau-réclame, *pl* **panneaux-réclame** [panoʀeklam] *nm* hoarding (*BRIT*), billboard (*US*).

panonceau, x [panɔso] *nm* (*de magasin etc*) sign; (*de médecin etc*) plaque.

panoplie [panɔpli] *nf* (*jouet*) outfit; (*d'armes*) display; (*fig*) array.

panorama [panɔʀama] *nm* (*vue*) all-round view, panorama; (*peinture*) panorama; (*fig: étude complète*) complete overview.

panoramique [panɔʀamik] *adj* panoramic; (*carrosserie*) with panoramic windows ♦ *nm* (*CINÉ, TV*) panoramic shot.

panse [pɑ̃s] *nf* paunch.

pansement [pɑ̃smɑ̃] *nm* dressing, bandage; ~ **adhésif** sticking plaster (*BRIT*), bandaid ® (*US*).

panser [pɑ̃se] *vt* (*plaie*) to dress, bandage; (*bras*) to put a dressing on, bandage; (*cheval*) to groom.

pantalon [pɑ̃talɔ̃] *nm* (*aussi:* ~**s, paire de** ~**s**) trousers *pl* (*BRIT*), pants *pl* (*US*), pair of trousers *ou* pants; ~ **de ski** ski pants *pl*.

pantalonnade [pɑ̃talɔnad] *nf* slapstick (comedy).

pantelant, e [pɑ̃tlɑ̃, -ɑ̃t] *adj* gasping for breath, panting.

panthère [pɑ̃tɛʀ] *nf* panther.

pantin [pɑ̃tɛ̃] *nm* (*jouet*) jumping jack; (*péj: personne*) puppet.

pantois [pɑ̃twa] *adj m*: **rester** ~ to be flabbergasted.

pantomime [pɑ̃tɔmim] *nf* mime; (*pièce*) mime show; (*péj*) fuss, carry-on.

pantouflard, e [pɑ̃tuflaʀ, -aʀd(ə)] *adj* (*péj*) stay-at-home.

pantoufle [pɑ̃tufl(ə)] *nf* slipper.

panure [panyʀ] *nf* breadcrumbs *pl*.

PAO *sigle f* (= *publication assistée par ordinateur*) desk-top publishing.

paon [pɑ̃] *nm* peacock.

papa [papa] *nm* dad(dy).

papauté [papote] *nf* papacy.

papaye [papaj] *nf* pawpaw.

pape [pap] *nm* pope.

paperasse [papʀas] *nf* (*péj*) bumf *no pl*, papers *pl*; forms *pl*.

paperasserie [papʀasʀi] *nf* (*péj*) red tape *no pl*;

paperwork *no pl*.

papeterie [papɛtʀi] *nf* (*fabrication du papier*) paper-making (industry); (*usine*) paper mill; (*magasin*) stationer's (shop (*BRIT*)); (*articles*) stationery.

papetier, ière [paptje, -jɛʀ] *nm/f* paper-maker; stationer.

papetier-libraire, *pl* **papetiers-libraires** [paptjelibʀɛʀ] *nm* bookseller and stationer.

papier [papje] *nm* paper; (*feuille*) sheet *ou* piece of paper; (*article*) article; (*écrit officiel*) document; ~**s** *nmpl* (*aussi:* ~**s d'identité**) (identity) papers; **sur le** ~ (*théoriquement*) on paper; **noircir du** ~ to write page after page; ~ **couché/glacé** art/glazed paper; ~ **(d')aluminium** aluminium (*BRIT*) *ou* aluminum (*US*) foil, tinfoil; ~ **d'Arménie** incense paper; ~ **bible** India *ou* bible paper; ~ **de brouillon** rough *ou* scrap paper; ~ **bulle** manil(l)a paper; ~ **buvard** blotting paper; ~ **calque** tracing paper; ~ **carbone** carbon paper; ~ **collant** Sellotape ® (*BRIT*), Scotch ® (*US*) *ou* sticky tape; ~ **en continu** continuous stationery; ~ **à dessin** drawing paper; ~ **d'emballage** wrapping paper; ~ **gommé** gummed paper; ~ **hygiénique** toilet paper; ~ **journal** newsprint; (*pour emballer*) newspaper; ~ **à lettres** writing paper, notepaper; ~ **mâché** papier-mâché; ~ **machine** typing paper; ~ **peint** wallpaper; ~ **pelure** India paper; ~ **à pliage accordéon** fanfold paper; ~ **de soie** tissue paper; ~ **thermique** thermal paper; ~ **de tournesol** litmus paper; ~ **de verre** sandpaper.

papier-filtre, *pl* **papiers-filtres** [papjefiltʀ(ə)] *nm* filter paper.

papier-monnaie, *pl* **papiers-monnaies** [papjemɔnɛ] *nm* paper money.

papille [papij] *nf*: ~**s gustatives** taste buds.

papillon [papijɔ̃] *nm* butterfly; (*fam: contravention*) (parking) ticket; (*TECH: écrou*) wing *ou* butterfly nut; ~ **de nuit** moth.

papillonner [papijɔne] *vi* to flit from one thing (*ou* person) to another.

papillote [papijɔt] *nf* (*pour cheveux*) curl-paper; (*de gigot*) (paper) frill.

papilloter [papijɔte] *vi* (*yeux*) to blink; (*paupières*) to flutter; (*lumière*) to flicker.

papotage [papɔtaʒ] *nm* chitchat.

papoter [papɔte] *vi* to chatter.

papou, e [papu] *adj* Papuan.

Papouasie-Nouvelle-Guinée [papwazinuvɛlgine] *nf*: **la** ~ Papua-New-Guinea.

paprika [paprika] *nm* paprika.

papyrus [papiʀys] *nm* papyrus.

pâque [pak] *nf*: **la** ~ Passover; *voir aussi* **Pâques**.

paquebot [pakbo] *nm* liner.

pâquerette [pakʀɛt] *nf* daisy.

Pâques [pak] *nm, nfpl* Easter; **faire ses** ~ to do one's Easter duties; **l'île de** ~ Easter Island.

paquet [pakɛ] *nm* packet; (*colis*) parcel; (*bal-*

lot) bundle; (*dans négociations*) package (deal); (*fig: tas*): ~ **de** pile *ou* heap of; **~s** *nmpl* (*bagages*) bags; **mettre le** ~ (*fam*) to give one's all; ~ **de mer** big wave.

paquetage [pakta3] *nm* (*MIL*) kit, pack.

paquet-cadeau, *pl* **paquets-cadeaux** [pakɛkado] *nm* gift-wrapped parcel.

par [paʀ] *prép* by; **finir** *etc* ~ to end *etc* with; ~ **amour** out of love; **passer** ~ **Lyon/la côte** to go via *ou* through Lyons/along by the coast; ~ **la fenêtre** (*jeter, regarder*) out of the window; **3** ~ **jour/personne** 3 a *ou* per day/head; **deux** ~ **deux** two at a time; (*marcher etc*) in twos; ~ **où?** which way?; ~ **ici** this way; (*dans le coin*) round here; **~-ci, ~-là** here and there.

para [paʀa] *nm* (= *parachutiste*) para.

parabole [paʀabɔl] *nf* (*REL*) parable; (*GÉOM*) parabola.

parabolique [paʀabɔlik] *adj* parabolic; **antenne** ~ satellite dish.

parachever [paʀaʃve] *vt* to perfect.

parachutage [paʀaʃyta3] *nm* (*de soldats, vivres*) parachuting-in; **nous sommes contre le** ~ **d'un candidat parisien dans notre circonscription** (*POL, fig*) we are against a Parisian candidate being landed on us.

parachute [paʀaʃyt] *nm* parachute.

parachuter [paʀaʃyte] *vt* (*soldat etc*) to parachute; (*fig*) to pitchfork; **il a été parachuté à la tête de l'entreprise** he was brought in from outside as head of the company.

parachutisme [paʀaʃytism(ə)] *nm* parachuting.

parachutiste [paʀaʃytist(ə)] *nm/f* parachutist; (*MIL*) paratrooper.

parade [paʀad] *nf* (*spectacle, défilé*) parade; (*ESCRIME, BOXE*) parry; (*ostentation*): **faire** ~ **de** to display, show off; (*défense, riposte*): **trouver la** ~ **à une attaque** to find the answer to an attack; **de** ~ *adj* ceremonial; (*superficiel*) superficial, outward.

parader [paʀade] *vi* to swagger (around), show off.

paradis [paʀadi] *nm* heaven, paradise; **P~ terrestre** (*REL*) Garden of Eden; (*fig*) heaven on earth.

paradisiaque [paʀadizjak] *adj* heavenly, divine.

paradoxal, e, aux [paʀadɔksal, -o] *adj* paradoxical.

paradoxalement [paʀadɔksalmɑ̃] *adv* paradoxically.

paradoxe [paʀadɔks(ə)] *nm* paradox.

parafe [paʀaf] *nm*, **parafer** [paʀafe] *vt* = **paraphe, parapher**.

paraffine [paʀafin] *nf* paraffin; paraffin wax.

paraffiné, e [paʀafine] *adj*: **papier** ~ wax(ed) paper.

parafoudre [paʀafudʀ(ə)] *nm* (*ÉLEC*) lightning conductor.

parages [paʀa3] *nmpl* (*NAVIG*) waters; **dans les** ~ **(de)** in the area *ou* vicinity (of).

paragraphe [paʀagʀaf] *nm* paragraph.

Paraguay [paʀagwɛ] *nm*: **le** ~ Paraguay.

paraguayen, ne [paʀagwajɛ̃, -ɛn] *adj* Paraguayan ♦ *nm/f*: **P~, ne** Paraguayan.

paraître [paʀɛtʀ(ə)] *vb avec attribut* to seem, look, appear ♦ *vi* to appear; (*être visible*) to show; (*PRESSE, ÉDITION*) to be published, come out, appear; (*briller*) to show off; **laisser** ~ **qch** to let (sth) show ♦ *vb impers*: **il paraît que** it seems *ou* appears that; **il me paraît que** it seems to me that; **il paraît absurde de** it seems absurd to; **il ne paraît pas son âge** he doesn't look his age; ~ **en justice** to appear before the court(s); ~ **en scène/en public/à l'écran** to appear on stage/in public/on the screen.

parallèle [paʀalɛl] *adj* parallel; (*police, marché*) unofficial; (*société, énergie*) alternative ♦ *nm* (*comparaison*): **faire un** ~ **entre** to draw a parallel between; (*GÉO*) parallel ♦ *nf* parallel (line); **en** ~ in parallel; **mettre en** ~ (*choses opposées*) to compare; (*choses semblables*) to parallel.

parallèlement [paʀalɛlmɑ̃] *adv* in parallel; (*fig: en même temps*) at the same time.

parallélépipède [paʀalelepiped] *nm* parallelepiped.

parallélisme [paʀalelism(ə)] *nm* parallelism; (*AUTO*) wheel alignment.

parallélogramme [paʀalelɔgʀam] *nm* parallelogram.

paralyser [paʀalize] *vt* to paralyze.

paralysie [paʀalizi] *nf* paralysis.

paralytique [paʀalitik] *adj*, *nm/f* paralytic.

paramédical, e, aux [paʀamedikal, -o] *adj* paramedical.

paramètre [paʀamɛtʀ(ə)] *nm* parameter.

paramilitaire [paʀamilitɛʀ] *adj* paramilitary.

paranoïa [paʀanɔja] *nf* paranoia.

paranoïaque [paʀanɔjak] *nm/f* paranoiac.

paranormal, e, aux [paʀanɔʀmal, -o] *adj* paranormal.

parapet [paʀapɛ] *nm* parapet.

paraphe [paʀaf] *nm* (*trait*) flourish; (*signature*) initials *pl*; signature.

parapher [paʀafe] *vt* to initial; to sign.

paraphrase [paʀafʀɑz] *nf* paraphrase.

paraphraser [paʀafʀɑze] *vt* to paraphrase.

paraplégie [paʀaple3i] *nf* paraplegia.

paraplégique [paʀaple3ik] *adj*, *nm/f* paraplegic.

parapluie [paʀaplɥi] *nm* umbrella; ~ **atomique** *ou* **nucléaire** nuclear umbrella; ~ **pliant** telescopic umbrella.

parapsychique [paʀapsiʃik] *adj* parapsychological.

parapsychologie [paʀapsikɔlɔ3i] *nf* parapsychology.

parapublic, ique [paʀapyblik] *adj* partly state-controlled.

parascolaire [paʀaskɔlɛʀ] *adj* extracurricular.

parasitaire [paʀazitɛʀ] *adj* parasitic(al).
parasite [paʀazit] *nm* parasite ♦ *adj* (*BOT, BIO*) parasitic(al); ~**s** *nmpl* (*TÉL*) interference *sg*.
parasitisme [paʀazitism(ə)] *nm* parasitism.
parasol [paʀasɔl] *nm* parasol, sunshade.
paratonnerre [paʀatɔnɛʀ] *nm* lightning conductor.
paravent [paʀavɑ̃] *nm* folding screen; (*fig*) screen.
parc [paʀk] *nm* (public) park, gardens *pl*; (*de château etc*) grounds *pl*; (*pour le bétail*) pen, enclosure; (*d'enfant*) playpen; (*MIL: entrepôt*) depot; (*ensemble d'unités*) stock; (*de voitures etc*) fleet; ~ **d'attractions** amusement park; ~ **automobile** (*d'un pays*) number of cars on the roads; ~ **à huîtres** oyster bed; ~ **à thème** theme park; ~ **national** national park; ~ **naturel** nature reserve; ~ **de stationnement** car park; ~ **zoologique** zoological gardens *pl*.
parcelle [paʀsɛl] *nf* fragment, scrap; (*de terrain*) plot, parcel.
parcelliser [paʀselize] *vt* to divide *ou* split up.
parce que [paʀsk(ə)] *conj* because.
parchemin [paʀʃəmɛ̃] *nm* parchment.
parcheminé, e [paʀʃəmine] *adj* wrinkled; (*papier*) with a parchment finish.
parcimonie [paʀsimɔni] *nf* parsimony, parsimoniousness.
parcimonieux, euse [paʀsimɔnjø, -øz] *adj* parsimonious, miserly.
parc(o)mètre [paʀk(ɔ)mɛtʀ(ə)] *nm* parking meter.
parcotrain [paʀkɔtʀɛ̃] *nm* station car park (*BRIT*) *ou* parking lot (*US*), park-and-ride car park (*BRIT*).
parcourir [paʀkuʀiʀ] *vt* (*trajet, distance*) to cover; (*article, livre*) to skim *ou* glance through; (*lieu*) to go all over, travel up and down; (*suj: frisson, vibration*) to run through; ~ **des yeux** to run one's eye over.
parcours [paʀkuʀ] *vb voir* **parcourir** ♦ *nm* (*trajet*) journey; (*itinéraire*) route; (*SPORT: terrain*) course; (*: tour*) round; run; lap; ~ **du combattant** assault course.
parcouru, e [paʀkuʀy] *pp de* **parcourir**.
par-delà [paʀdəla] *prép* beyond.
par-dessous [paʀdəsu] *prép, adv* under(neath).
pardessus [paʀdəsy] *nm* overcoat.
par-dessus [paʀdəsy] *prép* over (the top of) ♦ *adv* over (the top); ~ **le marché** on top of it all.
par-devant [paʀdəvɑ̃] *prép* in the presence of, before ♦ *adv* at the front; round the front.
pardon [paʀdɔ̃] *nm* forgiveness *no pl* ♦ *excl* (*excuses*) (I'm) sorry; (*pour interpeller etc*) excuse me; (*demander de répéter*) (I beg your) pardon? (*BRIT*), pardon me? (*US*).
pardonnable [paʀdɔnabl(ə)] *adj* forgivable, excusable.
pardonner [paʀdɔne] *vt* to forgive; ~ **qch à qn** to forgive sb for sth; **qui ne pardonne**

pas (*maladie, erreur*) fatal.
paré, e [paʀe] *adj* ready, prepared.
pare-balles [paʀbal] *adj inv* bulletproof.
pare-boue [paʀbu] *nm inv* mudflap.
pare-brise [paʀbʀiz] *nm inv* windscreen (*BRIT*), windshield (*US*).
pare-chocs [paʀʃɔk] *nm inv* bumper (*BRIT*), fender (*US*).
pare-étincelles [paʀetɛ̃sɛl] *nm inv* fireguard.
pare-feu [paʀfø] *nm inv* firebreak ♦ *adj inv*: **portes** ~ fire (resistant) doors.
pareil, le [paʀɛj] *adj* (*identique*) the same, alike; (*similaire*) similar; (*tel*): **un courage/livre** ~ such courage/a book, courage/a book like this; **de** ~**s livres** such books ♦ *adv*: **habillés** ~ dressed the same (way), dressed alike; **faire** ~ to do the same (thing); **j'en veux un** ~ I'd like one just like it; **rien de** ~ no (*ou* any) such thing, nothing (*ou* anything) like it; **ses** ~**s** one's fellow men; one's peers; **ne pas avoir son (sa)** ~**(le)** to be second to none; ~ **à** the same as; similar to; **sans** ~ unparalleled, unequalled; **c'est du** ~ **au même** it comes to the same thing, it's six (of one) and half-a-dozen (of the other); **en** ~ **cas** in such a case; **rendre la** ~**le à qn** to pay sb back in his own coin.
pareillement [paʀɛjmɑ̃] *adv* the same, alike; in such a way; (*également*) likewise.
parement [paʀmɑ̃] *nm* (*CONSTR, revers d'un col, d'une manche*) facing; (*REL*): ~ **d'autel** antependium.
parent, e [paʀɑ̃, -ɑ̃t] *nm/f*: **un/une** ~**/e** a relative *ou* relation ♦ *adj*: **être** ~ **de** to be related to; ~**s** *nmpl* (*père et mère*) parents; (*famille, proches*) relatives, relations; ~ **unique** lone parent; ~**s par alliance** relatives *ou* relations by marriage; ~**s en ligne directe** blood relations.
parental, e, aux [paʀɑ̃tal, -o] *adj* parental.
parenté [paʀɑ̃te] *nf* (*lien*) relationship; (*personnes*) relatives *pl*, relations *pl*.
parenthèse [paʀɑ̃tɛz] *nf* (*ponctuation*) bracket, parenthesis; (*MATH*) bracket; (*digression*) parenthesis, digression; **ouvrir/fermer la** ~ to open/close the brackets; **entre** ~**s** in brackets; (*fig*) incidentally.
parer [paʀe] *vt* to adorn; (*CULIN*) to dress, trim; (*éviter*) to ward off; ~ **à** (*danger*) to ward off; (*inconvénient*) to deal with; **se** ~ **de** (*fig: qualité, titre*) to assume; ~ **à toute éventualité** to be ready for every eventuality; ~ **au plus pressé** to attend to what's most urgent.
pare-soleil [paʀsɔlɛj] *nm inv* sun visor.
paresse [paʀɛs] *nf* laziness.
paresser [paʀese] *vi* to laze around.
paresseusement [paʀɛsøzmɑ̃] *adv* lazily; sluggishly.
paresseux, euse [paʀɛsø, -øz] *adj* lazy; (*fig*) slow, sluggish ♦ *nm* (*ZOOL*) sloth.
parfaire [paʀfɛʀ] *vt* to perfect, complete.

parfait, e [paʀfɛ, -ɛt] *pp de* **parfaire** ♦ *adj* perfect ♦ *nm* (*LING*) perfect (tense); (*CULIN*) parfait ♦ *excl* fine, excellent.
parfaitement [paʀfɛtmɑ̃] *adv* perfectly ♦ *excl* (most) certainly.
parfaites [paʀfɛt], **parfasse** [paʀfas], **parferai** [paʀfʀe] *etc vb voir* **parfaire**.
parfois [paʀfwa] *adv* sometimes.
parfum [paʀfœ̃] *nm* (*produit*) perfume, scent; (*odeur: de fleur*) scent, fragrance; (: *de tabac, vin*) aroma; (*goût: de glace, milk-shake*) flavour (*BRIT*), flavor (*US*).
parfumé, e [paʀfyme] *adj* (*fleur, fruit*) fragrant; (*papier à lettres etc*) scented; (*femme*) wearing perfume *ou* scent, perfumed; (*aromatisé*): ~ **au café** coffee-flavoured (*BRIT*) *ou* -flavored (*US*).
parfumer [paʀfyme] *vt* (*suj: odeur, bouquet*) to perfume; (*mouchoir*) to put scent *ou* perfume on; (*crème, gâteau*) to flavour (*BRIT*), flavor (*US*); **se** ~ to put on (some) perfume *ou* scent; (*d'habitude*) to use perfume *ou* scent.
parfumerie [paʀfymʀi] *nf* (*commerce*) perfumery; (*produits*) perfumes *pl*; (*boutique*) perfume shop (*BRIT*) *ou* store (*US*).
pari [paʀi] *nm* bet, wager; (*SPORT*) bet; ~ **mutuel urbain (PMU)** *system of betting on horses*.
paria [paʀja] *nm* outcast.
parier [paʀje] *vt* to bet; **j'aurais parié que si/non** I'd have said he (*ou* you *etc*) would/wouldn't.
parieur [paʀjœʀ] *nm* (*turfiste etc*) punter.
Paris [paʀi] *n* Paris.
parisien, ne [paʀizjɛ̃, -ɛn] *adj* Parisian; (*GÉO, ADMIN*) Paris *cpd* ♦ *nm/f*: **P~, ne** Parisian.
paritaire [paʀitɛʀ] *adj*: **commission** ~ joint commission.
parité [paʀite] *nf* parity; ~ **de change** (*ÉCON*) exchange parity.
parjure [paʀʒyʀ] *nm* (*faux serment*) false oath, perjury; (*violation de serment*) breach of oath, perjury ♦ *nm/f* perjurer.
parjurer [paʀʒyʀe]: **se** ~ *vi* to perjure o.s.
parka [paʀka] *nf* parka.
parking [paʀkiŋ] *nm* (*lieu*) car park (*BRIT*), parking lot (*US*).
parlant, e [paʀlɑ̃, -ɑ̃t] *adj* (*fig*) graphic, vivid; (: *comparaison, preuve*) eloquent; (*CINÉ*) talking ♦ *adv*: **généralement** ~ generally speaking.
parlé, e [paʀle] *adj*: **langue** ~**e** spoken language.
parlement [paʀləmɑ̃] *nm* parliament; **le P**~ **européen** the European Parliament.
parlementaire [paʀləmɑ̃tɛʀ] *adj* parliamentary ♦ *nm/f* (*député*) ≈ Member of Parliament (*BRIT*) *ou* Congress (*US*); parliamentarian; (*négociateur*) negotiator, mediator.
parlementarisme [paʀləmɑ̃taʀism(ə)] *nm* parliamentary government.

parlementer [paʀləmɑ̃te] *vi* (*ennemis*) to negotiate, parley; (*s'entretenir, discuter*) to argue at length, have lengthy talks.
parler [paʀle] *nm* speech; dialect ♦ *vi* to speak, talk; (*avouer*) to talk; ~ (**à qn) de** to talk *ou* speak (to sb) about; ~ **pour qn** (*intercéder*) to speak for sb; ~ **en l'air** to say the first thing that comes into one's head; ~ **le/en français** to speak French/in French; ~ **affaires** to talk business; ~ **en dormant/du nez** to talk in one's sleep/through one's nose; **sans** ~ **de** (*fig*) not to mention, to say nothing of; **tu parles!** you must be joking!; **n'en parlons plus!** let's forget it!
parleur [paʀlœʀ] *nm*: **beau** ~ fine talker.
parloir [paʀlwaʀ] *nm* (*d'une prison, d'un hôpital*) visiting room; (*REL*) parlour (*BRIT*), parlor (*US*).
parlote [paʀlɔt] *nf* chitchat.
Parme [paʀm(ə)] *n* Parma.
parme [paʀm(ə)] *adj* violet (blue).
parmesan [paʀməzɑ̃] *nm* Parmesan (cheese).
parmi [paʀmi] *prép* among(st).
parodie [paʀɔdi] *nf* parody.
parodier [paʀɔdje] *vt* (*œuvre, auteur*) to parody.
paroi [paʀwa] *nf* wall; (*cloison*) partition; ~ **rocheuse** rock face.
paroisse [paʀwas] *nf* parish.
paroissial, e, aux [paʀwasjal, -o] *adj* parish *cpd*.
paroissien, ne [paʀwasjɛ̃, -ɛn] *nm/f* parishioner ♦ *nm* prayer book.
parole [paʀɔl] *nf* (*faculté*): **la** ~ speech; (*mot, promesse*) word; (*REL*): **la bonne** ~ the word of God; ~**s** *nfpl* (*MUS*) words, lyrics; **tenir** ~ to keep one's word; **avoir la** ~ to have the floor; **n'avoir qu'une** ~ to be true to one's word; **donner la** ~ **à qn** to hand over to sb; **prendre la** ~ to speak; **demander la** ~ to ask for permission to speak; **perdre la** ~ to lose the power of speech; (*fig*) to lose one's tongue; **je le crois sur** ~ I'll take his word for it, I'll take him at his word; **temps de** ~ (*TV, RADIO etc*) discussion time; **ma** ~! my word!, good heavens!; ~ **d'honneur** word of honour (*BRIT*) *ou* honor (*US*).
parolier, ière [paʀɔlje, -jɛʀ] *nm/f* lyricist; (*OPÉRA*) librettist.
paroxysme [paʀɔksism(ə)] *nm* height, paroxysm.
parpaing [paʀpɛ̃] *nm* bond-stone, parpen.
parquer [paʀke] *vt* (*voiture, matériel*) to park; (*bestiaux*) to pen (in *ou* up); (*prisonniers*) to pack in.
parquet [paʀkɛ] *nm* (*parquet*) floor; (*JUR: bureau*) public prosecutor's office; **le** ~ (**général**) (*magistrats*) ≈ the Bench.
parqueter [paʀkəte] *vt* to lay a parquet floor in.
parrain [paʀɛ̃] *nm* godfather; (*d'un navire*) namer; (*d'un nouvel adhérent*) sponsor, pro-

poser.

parrainage [parɛnaʒ] *nm* sponsorship.

parrainer [parene] *vt* (*nouvel adhérent*) to sponsor, propose; (*entreprise*) to promote, sponsor.

parricide [parisid] *nm, nf* parricide.

pars [par] *vb voir* **partir**.

parsemer [parsəme] *vt* (*suj: feuilles, papiers*) to be scattered over; ~ **qch de** to scatter sth with.

parsi, e [parsi] *adj* Parsee.

part [par] *vb voir* **partir** ♦ *nf* (*qui revient à qn*) share; (*fraction, partie*) part; (*de gâteau, fromage*) portion; (*FINANCE*) (non-voting) share; **prendre** ~ **à** (*débat etc*) to take part in; (*soucis, douleur de qn*) to share in; **faire** ~ **de qch à qn** to announce sth to sb, inform sb of sth; **pour ma** ~ as for me, as far as I'm concerned; **à** ~ **entière** *adj* full; **de la** ~ **de** (*au nom de*) on behalf of; (*donné par*) from; **c'est de la** ~ **de qui?** (*au téléphone*) who's calling *ou* speaking (please)?; **de toute(s)** ~**(s)** from all sides *ou* quarters; **de** ~ **et d'autre** on both sides, on either side; **de** ~ **en** ~ right through; **d'une** ~ ... **d'autre** ~ on the one hand ... on the other hand; **nulle/autre/quelque** ~ nowhere/elsewhere/somewhere; **à** ~ *adv* separately; (*de côté*) aside ♦ *prép* apart from, except for ♦ *adj* exceptional, special; **pour une large** *ou* **bonne** ~ to a great extent; **prendre qch en bonne/mauvaise** ~ to take sth well/badly; **faire la** ~ **des choses** to make allowances; **faire la** ~ **du feu** (*fig*) to cut one's losses; **faire la** ~ **(trop) belle à qn** to give sb more than his (*ou* her) share.

part. *abr* = **particulier**.

partage [partaʒ] *nm* (*voir partager*) sharing (out) *no pl*, share-out; sharing; dividing up; (*POL: de suffrages*) share; **recevoir qch en** ~ to receive sth as one's share (*ou* lot); **sans** ~ undivided.

partagé, e [partaʒe] *adj* (*opinions etc*) divided; (*amour*) shared; **temps** ~ (*INFORM*) time sharing; **être** ~ **entre** to be shared between; **être** ~ **sur** to be divided about.

partager [partaʒe] *vt* to share; (*distribuer, répartir*) to share (out); (*morceler, diviser*) to divide (up); **se** ~ *vt* (*héritage etc*) to share between themselves (*ou* ourselves *etc*).

partance [partɑ̃s]: **en** ~ *adv* outbound, due to leave; **en** ~ **pour** (bound) for.

partant, e [partɑ̃, -ɑ̃t] *vb voir* **partir** ♦ *adj:* **être** ~ **pour qch** (*d'accord pour*) to be quite ready for sth ♦ *nm* (*SPORT*) starter; (*HIPPISME*) runner.

partenaire [partənɛr] *nm/f* partner; ~**s sociaux** management and workforce.

parterre [partɛr] *nm* (*de fleurs*) (flower) bed, border; (*THÉÂT*) stalls *pl*.

parti [parti] *nm* (*POL*) party; (*décision*) course of action; (*personne à marier*) match; **tirer** ~

de to take advantage of, turn to good account; **prendre le** ~ **de faire** to make up one's mind to do, resolve to do; **prendre le** ~ **de qn** to stand up for sb, side with sb; **prendre** ~ **(pour/contre)** to take sides *ou* a stand (for/against); **prendre son** ~ **de** to come to terms with; ~ **pris** bias.

partial, e, aux [parsjal, -o] *adj* biased, partial.

partialement [parsjalmɑ̃] *adv* in a biased way.

partialité [parsjalite] *nf* bias, partiality.

participant, e [partisipɑ̃, -ɑ̃t] *nm/f* participant; (*à un concours*) entrant; (*d'une société*) member.

participation [partisipasjɔ̃] *nf* participation; sharing; (*COMM*) interest; **la** ~ **aux bénéfices** profit-sharing; **la** ~ **ouvrière** worker participation; **"avec la** ~ **de ...**" "featuring ...".

participe [partisip] *nm* participle; ~ **passé/présent** past/present participle.

participer [partisipe]: ~ **à** *vt* (*course, réunion*) to take part in; (*profits etc*) to share in; (*frais etc*) to contribute to; (*entreprise: financièrement*) to cooperate in; (*chagrin, succès de qn*) to share (in); ~ **de** *vt* to partake of.

particulariser [partikylarize] *vt:* **se** ~ to mark o.s. (*ou* itself) out.

particularisme [partikylarism(ə)] *nm* sense of identity.

particularité [partikylarite] *nf* particularity; (*distinctive*) characteristic, feature.

particule [partikyl] *nf* particle; ~ **(nobiliaire)** nobiliary particle.

particulier, ière [partikylje, -jɛr] *adj* (*personnel, privé*) private; (*spécial*) special, particular; (*caractéristique*) characteristic, distinctive; (*spécifique*) particular ♦ *nm* (*individu: ADMIN*) private individual; "~ **vend ...**" (*COMM*) "for sale privately ...", "for sale by owner ..." (*US*); ~ **à** peculiar to; **en** ~ *adv* (*surtout*) in particular, particularly; (*à part*) separately; (*en privé*) in private.

particulièrement [partikyljɛrmɑ̃] *adv* particularly.

partie [parti] *nf* (*gén*) part; (*profession, spécialité*) field, subject; (*JUR etc: protagonistes*) party; (*de cartes, tennis etc*) game; (*fig: lutte, combat*) struggle, fight; **une** ~ **de campagne/de pêche** an outing in the country/a fishing party *ou* trip; **en** ~ *adv* partly, in part; **faire** ~ **de** to belong to; (*suj: chose*) to be part of; **prendre qn à** ~ to take sb to task; (*malmener*) to set on sb; **en grande** ~ largely, in the main; **ce n'est que** ~ **remise** it will be for another time *ou* the next time; **avoir** ~ **liée avec qn** to be in league with sb; ~ **civile** (*JUR*) party claiming damages in a criminal case.

partiel, le [parsjɛl] *adj* partial ♦ *nm* (*SCOL*) class exam.

partiellement [parsjɛlmɑ̃] *adv* partially, partly.

partir [partir] *vi* (*gén*) to go; (*quitter*) to go,

leave; (s'éloigner) to go (ou drive etc) away ou off; (moteur) to start; (pétard) to go off; (bouchon) to come out; (bouton) to come off; ~ **de** (lieu: quitter) to leave; (: commencer à) to start from; (date) to run ou start from; ~ **pour/à** (lieu, pays etc) to leave for/go off to; **à** ~ **de** from.

partisan, e [paʀtizɑ̃, -an] nm/f partisan; (d'un parti, régime etc) supporter ♦ adj (lutte, querelle) partisan, one-sided; **être** ~ **de qch/faire** to be in favour (BRIT) ou favor (US) of sth/doing.

partitif, ive [paʀtitif, -iv] adj: **article** ~ partitive article.

partition [paʀtisjɔ̃] nf (MUS) score; (POL) partition.

partout [paʀtu] adv everywhere; ~ **où il allait** everywhere ou wherever he went; **trente** ~ (TENNIS) thirty all.

paru [paʀy] pp de **paraître**.

parure [paʀyʀ] nf (bijoux etc) finery no pl; jewellery no pl (BRIT), jewelry no pl (US); (assortiment) set.

parus [paʀy] etc vb voir **paraître**.

parution [paʀysjɔ̃] nf publication, appearance.

parvenir [paʀvəniʀ]: ~ **à** vt (atteindre) to reach; (obtenir, arriver à) to attain; (réussir): ~ **à faire** to manage to do, succeed in doing; **faire** ~ **qch à qn** to have sth sent to sb.

parvenu, e [paʀvəny] pp de **parvenir** ♦ nm/f (péj) parvenu, upstart.

parviendrai [paʀvjɛ̃dʀe], **parviens** [paʀvjɛ̃] etc voir **parvenir**.

parvis [paʀvi] nm square (in front of a church).

======================= MOT-CLÉ

pas¹ [pɑ] adv **1** (en corrélation avec ne, non etc) not; **il ne pleure** ~ (habituellement) he does not ou doesn't cry; (maintenant) he's not ou isn't crying; **je ne mange** ~ **de viande** I don't ou do not eat meat; **il n'a** ~ **pleuré/ne pleurera** ~ he did not ou didn't/will not ou won't cry; **ils n'ont** ~ **de voiture/d'enfants** they haven't got a car/any children, they have no car/children; **il m'a dit de ne** ~ **le faire** he told me not to do it; **non** ~ **que** ... not that ...

2 (employé sans ne etc): ~ **moi** not me, not I, I don't (ou can't etc); **elle travaille, (mais) lui** ~ **ou** ~ **lui** she works but he doesn't ou does not; **une pomme** ~ **mûre** an apple which isn't ripe; ~ **plus tard qu'hier** only yesterday; ~ **du tout** not at all; ~ **de sucre, merci** no sugar, thanks; **ceci est à vous ou** ~? is this yours or not?, is this yours or isn't it?

3: ~ **mal** (joli: personne, maison) not bad; ~ **mal fait** not badly done ou made; **comment ça va?** — ~ **mal** how are things? — not bad; ~ **mal de** quite a lot of.

pas² [pɑ] nm (allure, mesure) pace; (démarche)

tread; (enjambée, DANSE, fig: étape) step; (bruit) (foot)step; (trace) footprint; (allure) pace; (d'un cheval) walk; (mesure) pace; (TECH: de vis, d'écrou) thread; ~ **à** ~ step by step; **au** ~ at walking pace; **de ce** ~ (à l'instant même) straightaway, at once; **marcher à grands** ~ to stride along; **mettre qn au** ~ to bring sb to heel; **au** ~ **de gymnastique/de course** at a jog trot/at a run; **à** ~ **de loup** stealthily; **faire les cent** ~ to pace up and down; **faire les premiers** ~ to make the first move; **retourner** ou **revenir sur ses** ~ to retrace one's steps; **se tirer d'un mauvais** ~ to get o.s. out of a tight spot; **sur le** ~ **de la porte** on the doorstep; **le** ~ **de Calais** (détroit) the Straits pl of Dover; ~ **de porte** (fig) key money.

pascal, e, aux [paskal, -o] adj Easter cpd.

passable [pɑsabl(ə)] adj passable, tolerable.

passablement [pɑsabləmɑ̃] adv (pas trop mal) reasonably well; (beaucoup) quite a lot.

passade [pɑsad] nf passing fancy, whim.

passage [pɑsaʒ] nm (fait de passer) voir **passer**; (lieu, prix de la traversée, extrait de livre etc) passage; (chemin) way; (itinéraire): **sur le** ~ **du cortège** along the route of the procession; **"laissez/n'obstruez pas le** ~" "keep clear/do not obstruct"; **au** ~ (en passant) as I (ou he etc) went by; **de** ~ (touristes) passing through; (amants etc) casual; ~ **clouté** pedestrian crossing; "~ **interdit**" "no entry"; ~ **à niveau** level (BRIT) ou grade (US) crossing; "~ **protégé**" right of way over secondary road(s) on your right; ~ **souterrain** subway (BRIT), underpass; ~ **à tabac** beating-up; ~ **à vide** (fig) bad patch.

passager, ère [pɑsaʒe, -ɛʀ] adj passing; (hôte) short-stay cpd; (oiseau) migratory ♦ nm/f passenger; ~ **clandestin** stowaway.

passagèrement [pɑsaʒɛʀmɑ̃] adv temporarily, for a short time.

passant, e [pɑsɑ̃, -ɑ̃t] adj (rue, endroit) busy ♦ nm/f passer-by ♦ nm (pour ceinture etc) loop; **en** ~: **remarquer qch en** ~ to notice sth in passing.

passation [pɑsasjɔ̃] nf (JUR: d'un acte) signing; ~ **des pouvoirs** transfer ou handover of power.

passe [pɑs] nf (SPORT, magnétique) pass; (NAVIG) channel ♦ nm (passe-partout) master ou skeleton key; **être en** ~ **de faire** to be on the way to doing; **être dans une bonne/mauvaise** ~ (fig) to be going through a good/bad patch; ~ **d'armes** (fig) heated exchange.

passé, e [pɑse] adj (événement, temps) past; (couleur, tapisserie) faded; (précédent): **dimanche** ~ last Sunday ♦ prép after ♦ nm past; (LING) past (tense); **il est** ~ **midi** ou **midi** ~ it's gone (BRIT) ou past twelve; ~ **de mode** out of fashion; ~ **composé** perfect (tense); ~ **simple** past historic.

passe-droit [pɑsdʀwa] *nm* special privilege.
passéiste [pɑseist(ə)] *adj* backward-looking.
passementerie [pɑsmɑ̃tʀi] *nf* trimmings *pl*.
passe-montagne [pɑsmɔ̃taɲ] *nm* balaclava.
passe-partout [pɑspaʀtu] *nm inv* master *ou* skeleton key ♦ *adj inv* all-purpose.
passe-passe [pɑspas] *nm*: **tour de** ~ trick, sleight of hand *no pl*.
passe-plat [pɑspla] *nm* serving hatch.
passeport [pɑspɔʀ] *nm* passport.
passer [pɑse] *vi* (*se rendre, aller*) to go; (*voiture, piétons: défiler*) to pass (by), go by; (*faire une halte rapide: facteur, laitier etc*) to come, call; (*: pour rendre visite*) to call *ou* drop in; (*courant, air, lumière, franchir un obstacle etc*) to get through; (*accusé, projet de loi*): ~ **devant** to come before; (*film, émission*) to be on; (*temps, jours*) to pass, go by; (*liquide, café*) to go through; (*être digéré, avalé*) to go down; (*couleur, papier*) to fade; (*mode*) to die out; (*douleur*) to pass, go away; (*CARTES*) to pass; (*SCOL*) to go up (to the next class); (*devenir*): ~ **président** to be appointed *ou* become president ♦ *vt* (*frontière, rivière etc*) to cross; (*douane*) to go through; (*examen*) to sit, take; (*visite médicale etc*) to have; (*journée, temps*) to spend; (*donner*): ~ **qch à qn** to pass sth to sb; to give sb sth; (*transmettre*): ~ **qch à qn** to pass sth on to sb; (*enfiler: vêtement*) to slip on; (*faire entrer, mettre*): **(faire)** ~ **qch dans/par** to get sth into/through; (*café*) to pour the water on; (*thé, soupe*) to strain; (*film, pièce*) to show, put on; (*disque*) to play, put on; (*marché, accord*) to agree on; (*tolérer*): ~ **qch à qn** to let sb get away with sth; **se** ~ *vi* (*avoir lieu: scène, action*) to take place; (*se dérouler: entretien etc*) to go; (*arriver*): **que s'est-il passé?** what happened?; (*s'écouler: semaine etc*) to pass, go by; **se** ~ **de** to go *ou* do without; **se** ~ **les mains sous l'eau/de l'eau sur le visage** to put one's hands under the tap/run water over one's face; **en passant** in passing; ~ **par** to go through; **passez devant/par ici** go in front/this way; ~ **sur** *vt* (*faute, détail inutile*) to pass over; ~ **dans les mœurs/l'usage** to become the custom/normal usage; ~ **avant qch/qn** (*fig*) to come before sth/sb; **laisser** ~ (*air, lumière, personne*) to let through; (*occasion*) to let slip, miss; (*erreur*) to overlook; **faire** ~ (*message*) to get over *ou* across; **faire** ~ **à qn le goût de qch** to cure sb of his (*ou* her) taste for sth; ~ **à la radio/ fouille** to be X-rayed/searched; ~ **à la radio/télévision** to be on the radio/on television; ~ **à table** to sit down to eat; ~ **au salon** to go into the sitting room; ~ **à l'opposition** to go over to the opposition; ~ **aux aveux** to confess, make a confession; ~ **à l'action** to go into action; ~ **pour riche** to be taken for a rich man; **il passait pour avoir** he was said to have; **faire** ~ **qn/qch pour** to make sb/sth out to be; **passe encore de le**

penser, **mais de le dire!** it's one thing to think it, but to say it!; **passons!** let's say no more (about it); **et j'en passe!** and that's not all!; ~ **en seconde**, ~ **la seconde** (*AUTO*) to change into second; ~ **qch en fraude** to smuggle sth in (*ou* out); ~ **la main par la portière** to stick one's hand out of the door; ~ **le balai/l'aspirateur** to sweep up/hoover; ~ **commande/la parole à qn** to hand over to sb; **je vous passe M X** (*je vous mets en communication avec lui*) I'm putting you through to Mr X; (*je lui passe l'appareil*) here is Mr X, I'll hand you over to Mr X; ~ **prendre** to (come and) collect.
passereau, x [pɑsʀo] *nm* sparrow.
passerelle [pɑsʀɛl] *nf* footbridge; (*de navire, avion*) gangway; (*NAVIG*): ~ **(de commandement)** bridge.
passe-temps [pɑstɑ̃] *nm inv* pastime.
passette [pɑsɛt] *nf* (tea-)strainer.
passeur, euse [pɑsœʀ, -øz] *nm/f* smuggler.
passible [pasibl(ə)] *adj*: ~ **de** liable to.
passif, ive [pasif, -iv] *adj* passive ♦ *nm* (*LING*) passive; (*COMM*) liabilities *pl*.
passion [pɑsjɔ̃] *nf* passion; **avoir la** ~ **de** to have a passion for; **fruit de la** ~ passion fruit.
passionnant, e [pɑsjɔnɑ̃, -ɑ̃t] *adj* fascinating.
passionné, e [pɑsjɔne] *adj* (*personne, tempérament*) passionate; (*description*) impassioned ♦ *nm/f*: **c'est un** ~ **d'échecs** he's a chess fanatic; **être** ~ **de** *ou* **pour qch** to have a passion for sth.
passionnel, le [pɑsjɔnɛl] *adj* of passion.
passionnément [pɑsjɔnemɑ̃] *adv* passionately.
passionner [pɑsjɔne] *vt* (*personne*) to fascinate, grip; (*débat, discussion*) to inflame; **se** ~ **pour** to take an avid interest in; to have a passion for.
passivement [pasivmɑ̃] *adv* passively.
passivité [pasivite] *nf* passivity, passiveness.
passoire [pɑswaʀ] *nf* sieve; (*à légumes*) colander; (*à thé*) strainer.
pastel [pastɛl] *nm*, *adj inv* (*ART*) pastel.
pastèque [pastɛk] *nf* watermelon.
pasteur [pastœʀ] *nm* (*protestant*) minister, pastor.
pasteurisation [pastœʀizasjɔ̃] *nf* pasteurization.
pasteuriser [pastœʀize] *vt* to pasteurize.
pastiche [pastiʃ] *nm* pastiche.
pastille [pastij] *nf* (*à sucer*) lozenge, pastille; (*de papier etc*) (small) disc; ~**s pour la toux** cough drops *ou* lozenges.
pastis [pastis] *nm* anise-flavoured alcoholic drink.
pastoral, e, aux [pastɔʀal, -o] *adj* pastoral.
patagon, ne [patagɔ̃, -ɔn] *adj* Patagonian.
Patagonie [patagɔni] *nf*: **la** ~ Patagonia.
patate [patat] *nf* spud; ~ **douce** sweet potato.
pataud, e [pato, -od] *adj* lumbering.

patauger [pɑtoʒe] *vi* (*pour s'amuser*) to splash about; (*avec effort*) to wade about; (*fig*) to flounder; ~ **dans** (*en marchant*) to wade through.

patch [patʃ] *nm* nicotine patch.

patchouli [patʃuli] *nm* patchouli.

patchwork [patʃwœrk] *nm* patchwork.

pâte [pɑt] *nf* (*à tarte*) pastry; (*à pain*) dough; (*à frire*) batter; (*substance molle*) paste; cream; ~**s** *nfpl* (*macaroni etc*) pasta *sg*; **fromage à ~ dure/molle** hard/soft cheese; ~ **d'amandes** almond paste; ~ **brisée** shortcrust (*BRIT*) *ou* pie crust (*US*) pastry; ~ **à choux/feuilletée** choux/puff *ou* flaky (*BRIT*) pastry; ~ **de fruits** crystallized fruit *no pl*; ~ **à modeler** modelling clay, Plasticine ® (*BRIT*); ~ **à papier** paper pulp.

pâté [pɑte] *nm* (*charcuterie: terrine*) pâté; (*tache*) ink blot; (*de sable*) sandpie; ~ **(en croûte)** ≈ meat pie; ~ **de foie** liver pâté; ~ **de maisons** block (of houses).

pâtée [pɑte] *nf* mash, feed.

patelin [patlɛ̃] *nm* little place.

patente [patɑ̃t] *nf* (*COMM*) trading licence (*BRIT*) *ou* license (*US*).

patenté, e [patɑ̃te] *adj* (*COMM*) licensed; (*fig: attitré*) registered, (officially) recognized.

patère [patɛr] *nf* (coat-)peg.

paternalisme [patɛrnalism(ə)] *nm* paternalism.

paternaliste [patɛrnalist(ə)] *adj* paternalistic.

paternel, le [patɛrnɛl] *adj* (*amour, soins*) fatherly; (*ligne, autorité*) paternal.

paternité [patɛrnite] *nf* paternity, fatherhood.

pâteux, euse [pɑtø, -øz] *adj* thick; pasty; **avoir la bouche** *ou* **langue pâteuse** to have a furred (*BRIT*) *ou* coated tongue.

pathétique [patetik] *adj* pathetic, moving.

pathologie [patɔlɔʒi] *nf* pathology.

pathologique [patɔlɔʒik] *adj* pathological.

patibulaire [patibylɛr] *adj* sinister.

patiemment [pasjamɑ̃] *adv* patiently.

patience [pasjɑ̃s] *nf* patience; **être à bout de ~** to have run out of patience; **perdre/prendre ~** to lose (one's)/have patience.

patient, e [pasjɑ̃, -ɑ̃t] *adj, nm/f* patient.

patienter [pasjɑ̃te] *vi* to wait.

patin [patɛ̃] *nm* skate; (*sport*) skating; (*de traîneau, luge*) runner; (*pièce de tissu*) cloth pad (*used as slippers to protect polished floor*); ~ **(de frein)** brake block; ~**s (à glace)** (ice) skates; ~**s à roulettes** roller skates.

patinage [patinaʒ] *nm* skating; ~ **artistique/de vitesse** figure/speed skating.

patine [patin] *nf* sheen.

patiner [patine] *vi* to skate; (*embrayage*) to slip; (*roue, voiture*) to spin; **se ~** *vi* (*meuble, cuir*) to acquire a sheen, become polished.

patineur, euse [patinœr, -øz] *nm/f* skater.

patinoire [patinwar] *nf* skating rink, (ice) rink.

patio [patjo] *nm* patio.

pâtir [pɑtir]: ~ **de** *vt* to suffer because of.

pâtisserie [pɑtisri] *nf* (*boutique*) cake shop; (*métier*) confectionery; (*à la maison*) pastry- *ou* cake-making, baking; ~**s** *nfpl* (*gâteaux*) pastries, cakes.

pâtissier, ière [pɑtisje, -jɛr] *nm/f* pastrycook; confectioner.

patois [patwa] *nm* dialect, patois.

patriarche [patrijarʃ(ə)] *nm* patriarch.

patrie [patri] *nf* homeland.

patrimoine [patrimwan] *nm* inheritance, patrimony; (*culture*) heritage; ~ **génétique** *ou* **héréditaire** genetic inheritance.

patriote [patrijot] *adj* patriotic ♦ *nm/f* patriot.

patriotique [patrijotik] *adj* patriotic.

patriotisme [patrijotism(ə)] *nm* patriotism.

patron, ne [patrɔ̃, -ɔn] *nm/f* (*chef*) boss, manager/eress; (*propriétaire*) owner, proprietor/tress; (*employeur*) employer; (*MÉD*) ≈ senior consultant; (*REL*) patron saint ♦ *nm* (*COUTURE*) pattern; ~ **de thèse** supervisor (of postgraduate thesis).

patronage [patrɔnaʒ] *nm* patronage; (*organisation, club*) (parish) youth club; (parish) children's club.

patronal, e, aux [patrɔnal, -o] *adj* (*syndicat, intérêts*) employers'.

patronat [patrɔna] *nm* employers *pl*.

patronner [patrɔne] *vt* to sponsor, support.

patronnesse [patrɔnɛs] *adj f*: **dame ~** patroness.

patronyme [patrɔnim] *nm* name.

patronymique [patrɔnimik] *adj*: **nom ~** patronymic (name).

patrouille [patruj] *nf* patrol.

patrouiller [patruje] *vi* to patrol, be on patrol.

patrouilleur [patrujœr] *nm* (*AVIAT*) scout (plane); (*NAVIG*) patrol boat.

patte [pat] *nf* (*jambe*) leg; (*pied: de chien, chat*) paw; (: *d'oiseau*) foot; (*languette*) strap; (: *de poche*) flap; (*favoris*): ~**s (de lapin)** (short) sideburns; **à ~s d'éléphant** *adj* (*pantalon*) flared; ~**s de mouche** (*fig*) spidery scrawl *sg*; ~**s d'oie** (*fig*) crow's feet.

pattemouille [patmuj] *nf* damp cloth (*for ironing*).

pâturage [pɑtyraʒ] *nm* pasture.

pâture [pɑtyr] *nf* food.

paume [pom] *nf* palm.

paumé, e [pome] *nm/f* (*fam*) drop-out.

paumer [pome] *vt* (*fam*) to lose.

paupérisation [poperizasjɔ̃] *nf* pauperization.

paupérisme [poperism(ə)] *nm* pauperism.

paupière [popjɛr] *nf* eyelid.

paupiette [popjɛt] *nf*: ~**s de veau** veal olives.

pause [poz] *nf* (*arrêt*) break; (*en parlant, MUS*) pause.

pause-café, *pl* **pauses-café** [pozkafe] *nf* coffee-break.

pauvre [povr(ə)] *adj* poor ♦ *nm/f* poor man/woman; **les ~s** the poor; ~ **en calcium** low in calcium.

pauvrement [povrəmɑ̃] *adv* poorly.
pauvreté [povrəte] *nf* (*état*) poverty.
pavage [pavaʒ] *nm* paving; cobbles *pl*.
pavaner [pavane]: **se ~** *vi* to strut about.
pavé, e [pave] *adj* (*cour*) paved; (*rue*) cobbled ♦ *nm* (*bloc*) paving stone; cobblestone; (*pavage*) paving; (*bifteck*) slab of steak; (*fam: livre*) hefty tome; **être sur le ~** (*sans domicile*) to be on the streets; (*sans emploi*) to be out of a job; **~ numérique** (*INFORM*) keypad.
pavillon [pavijɔ̃] *nm* (*de banlieue*) small (detached) house; (*kiosque*) lodge; pavilion; (*d'hôpital*) ward; (*MUS: de cor etc*) bell; (*ANAT: de l'oreille*) pavilion, pinna; (*NAVIG*) flag; **~ de complaisance** flag of convenience.
pavoiser [pavwaze] *vt* to deck with flags ♦ *vi* to put out flags; (*fig*) to rejoice, exult.
pavot [pavo] *nm* poppy.
payable [pɛjabl(ə)] *adj* payable.
payant, e [pɛjɑ̃, -ɑ̃t] *adj* (*spectateurs etc*) paying; (*billet*) that you pay for, to be paid for; (*fig: entreprise*) profitable; **c'est ~** you have to pay, there is a charge.
paye [pɛj] *nf* pay, wages *pl*.
payement [pɛjmɑ̃] *nm* payment.
payer [peje] *vt* (*créancier, employé, loyer*) to pay; (*achat, réparations, fig: faute*) to pay for ♦ *vi* to pay; (*métier*) to pay, be well-paid; (*effort, tactique etc*) to pay off; **il me l'a fait ~ 10 F** he charged me 10 F for it; **~ qn de** (*ses efforts, peines*) to reward sb for; **~ qch à qn** to buy sth for sb, buy sb sth; **ils nous ont payé le voyage** they paid for our trip; **~ de sa personne** to give of oneself; **~ d'audace** to act with great daring; **~ cher qch** to pay dear(ly) for sth; **cela ne paie pas de mine** it doesn't look much; **se ~ qch** to buy o.s. sth; **se ~ de mots** to shoot one's mouth off; **se ~ la tête de qn** to take the mickey out of sb (*BRIT*), make a fool of sb; (*duper*) to take sb for a ride.
payeur, euse [pɛjœr, -øz] *adj* (*organisme, bureau*) payments *cpd* ♦ *nm/f* payer.
pays [pei] *nm* (*territoire, habitants*) country, land; (*région*) region; (*village*) village; **du ~** *adj* local; **le ~ de Galles** Wales.
paysage [peizaʒ] *nm* landscape.
paysager, ère [peizaʒe, -ɛr] *adj* (*jardin, parc*) landscaped.
paysagiste [peizaʒist(ə)] *nm/f* (*de jardin*) landscape gardener; (*ART*) landscapist, landscape painter.
paysan, ne [peizɑ̃, -an] *nm/f* countryman/woman; farmer; (*péj*) peasant ♦ *adj* country *cpd*, farming; farmers'.
paysannat [peizana] *nm* peasantry.
Pays-Bas [peiba] *nmpl*: **les ~** the Netherlands.
PC *sigle m* (*POL*) = *parti communiste*; (*INFORM: = personal computer*) PC; (*= prêt conventionné*) *type of loan for house purchase*; (*CONSTR*) = **permis de construire**; (*MIL*) = **poste de commandement**.

pcc *abr* (= *pour copie conforme*) c.c.
Pce *abr* = **prince**.
Pcesse *abr* = **princesse**.
PCV *abr* (= *percevoir*) *voir* **communication**.
p de p *abr* = **pas de porte**.
PDG *sigle m* = **président directeur général**.
p.ê. *abr* = **peut-être**.
PEA *sigle m* (= *plan d'épargne en actions*) *building society savings plan*.
péage [peaʒ] *nm* toll; (*endroit*) tollgate; **pont à ~** toll bridge.
peau, x [po] *nf* skin; (*cuir*): **gants de ~** leather gloves; **être bien/mal dans sa ~** to be at ease/odds with oneself; **se mettre dans la ~ de qn** to put o.s. in sb's place *ou* shoes; **faire ~ neuve** (*se renouveler*) to change one's image; **~ de chamois** (*chiffon*) chamois leather, shammy; **~ d'orange** orange peel.
peaufiner [pofine] *vt* to polish (up).
Peau-Rouge [poruʒ] *nm/f* Red Indian, red skin.
peccadille [pekadij] *nf* trifle, peccadillo.
péché [peʃe] *nm* sin; **~ mignon** weakness.
pêche [pɛʃ] *nf* (*sport, activité*) fishing; (*poissons pêchés*) catch; (*fruit*) peach; **aller à la ~** to go fishing; **avoir la ~** (*fam*) to be on (top) form; **~ à la ligne** (*en rivière*) angling; **~ sous-marine** deep-sea fishing.
pêche-abricot, *pl* **pêches-abricots** [pɛʃabriko] *nf* yellow peach.
pécher [peʃe] *vi* (*REL*) to sin; (*fig: personne*) to err; (: *chose*) to be flawed; **~ contre la bienséance** to break the rules of good behaviour.
pêcher [peʃe] *nm* peach tree ♦ *vi* to go fishing; (*en rivière*) to go angling ♦ *vt* (*attraper*) to catch, land; (*chercher*) to fish for; **~ au chalut** to trawl.
pécheur, eresse [peʃœr, peʃrɛs] *nm/f* sinner.
pêcheur [peʃœr] *nm* (*voir pêcher*) fisherman; angler; **~ de perles** pearl diver.
pectine [pɛktin] *nf* pectin.
pectoral, e, aux [pɛktɔral, -o] *adj* (*ANAT*) pectoral; (*sirop*) throat *cpd*, cough *cpd* ♦ *nmpl* pectoral muscles.
pécule [pekyl] *nm* savings *pl*, nest egg; (*d'un détenu*) earnings *pl* (*paid on release*).
pécuniaire [pekynjɛr] *adj* financial.
pédagogie [pedagɔʒi] *nf* educational methods *pl*, pedagogy.
pédagogique [pedagɔʒik] *adj* educational; **formation ~** teacher training.
pédagogue [pedagɔg] *nm/f* teacher; educatio(al)ist.
pédale [pedal] *nf* pedal; **mettre la ~ douce** to soft-pedal.
pédaler [pedale] *vi* to pedal.
pédalier [pedalje] *nm* pedal and gear mechanism.
pédalo [pedalo] *nm* pedalo, pedal-boat.
pédant, e [pedɑ̃, -ɑ̃t] *adj* (*péj*) pedantic ♦ *nm/f* pedant.

pédantisme [pedɑ̃tism(ə)] nm pedantry.
pédéraste [pedeʀast(ə)] nm homosexual, pederast.
pédérastie [pedeʀasti] nf homosexuality, pederasty.
pédestre [pedɛstʀ(ə)] adj: **tourisme** ~ hiking; **randonnée** ~ (activité) rambling; (excursion) ramble.
pédiatre [pedjatʀ(ə)] nm/f paediatrician (BRIT), pediatrician ou pediatrist (US), child specialist.
pédiatrie [pedjatʀi] nf paediatrics sg (BRIT), pediatrics sg (US).
pédicure [pedikyʀ] nm/f chiropodist.
pedigree [pedigʀe] nm pedigree.
peeling [piliŋ] nm exfoliation treatment.
PEEP sigle f = Fédération des parents d'élèves de l'enseignement public.
pègre [pɛgʀ(ə)] nf underworld.
peignais [peɲɛ] etc vb voir **peindre**.
peigne [pɛɲ] vb voir **peindre, peigner** ♦ nm comb.
peigné, e [peɲe] adj: **laine** ~e wool worsted; combed wool.
peigner [peɲe] vt to comb (the hair of); **se** ~ to comb one's hair.
peignez [peɲe] etc vb voir **peindre**.
peignoir [peɲwaʀ] nm dressing gown; ~ **de bain** bathrobe; ~ **de plage** beach robe.
peignons [peɲɔ̃] vb voir **peindre**.
peinard, e [penaʀ, -aʀd(ə)] adj (emploi) cushy (BRIT), easy; (personne): **on est** ~ **ici** we're left in peace here.
peindre [pɛ̃dʀ(ə)] vt to paint; (fig) to portray, depict.
peine [pɛn] nf (affliction) sorrow, sadness no pl; (mal, effort) trouble no pl, effort; (difficulté) difficulty; (punition, châtiment) punishment; (JUR) sentence; **faire de la** ~ **à qn** to distress ou upset sb; **prendre la** ~ **de faire** to go to the trouble of doing; **se donner de la** ~ to make an effort; **ce n'est pas la** ~ **de faire** there's no point in doing, it's not worth doing; **ce n'est pas la** ~ **que vous vous fassiez** there's no point (in) you doing; **avoir de la** ~ **à faire** to have difficulty doing; **donnez-vous** ou **veuillez-vous donner la** ~ **d'entrer** please do come in; **c'est** ~ ~ **perdue** it's a waste of time (and effort); **à** ~ adv scarcely, hardly, barely; **à** ~ ... **que** hardly ... than; **c'est à** ~ **si** ... it's (ou it was) a job to ...; **sous** ~: **sous** ~ **d'être puni** for fear of being punished; **défense d'afficher sous** ~ **d'amende** billposters will be fined; ~ **capitale** capital punishment; ~ **de mort** death sentence ou penalty.
peiner [pene] vi to work hard; to struggle; (moteur, voiture) to labour (BRIT), labor (US) ♦ vt to grieve, sadden.
peint, e [pɛ̃, pɛ̃t] pp de **peindre**.
peintre [pɛ̃tʀ(ə)] nm painter; ~ **en bâtiment** house painter, painter and decorator; ~ **d'enseignes** signwriter.

peinture [pɛ̃tyʀ] nf painting; (couche de couleur, couleur) paint; (surfaces peintes: aussi: ~s) paintwork; **je ne peux pas le voir en** ~ I can't stand the sight of him; ~ **mate/brillante** matt/gloss paint; "~ **fraîche**" "wet paint".
péjoratif, ive [peʒɔʀatif, -iv] adj pejorative, derogatory.
Pékin [pekɛ̃] n Peking.
pékinois, e [pekinwa, -waz] adj Pekin(g)ese ♦ nm (chien) peke, pekin(g)ese; (LING) Mandarin, Pekin(g)ese ♦ nm/f: **P**~, **e** Pekin(g)ese.
PEL sigle m (= plan d'épargne logement) savings scheme providing lower-interest mortgages.
pelade [pəlad] nf alopecia.
pelage [pəlaʒ] nm coat, fur.
pelé, e [pəle] adj (chien) hairless; (vêtement) threadbare; (terrain) bare.
pêle-mêle [pɛlmɛl] adv higgledy-piggledy.
peler [pəle] vt, vi to peel.
pèlerin [pɛlʀɛ̃] nm pilgrim.
pèlerinage [pɛlʀinaʒ] nm (voyage) pilgrimage; (lieu) place of pilgrimage, shrine.
pèlerine [pɛlʀin] nf cape.
pélican [pelikɑ̃] nm pelican.
pelisse [pəlis] nf fur-lined cloak.
pelle [pɛl] nf shovel; (d'enfant, de terrassier) spade; ~ **à gâteau** cake slice; ~ **mécanique** mechanical digger.
pelletée [pɛlte] nf shovelful; spadeful.
pelleter [pɛlte] vt to shovel (up).
pelleteuse [pɛltøz] nf mechanical digger, excavator.
pelletier [pɛltje] nm furrier.
pellicule [pelikyl] nf film; ~s nfpl (MÉD) dandruff sg.
Péloponnèse [pelɔpɔnɛz] nm: **le** ~ the Peloponnese.
pelote [pəlɔt] nf (de fil, laine) ball; (d'épingles) pin cushion; ~ **basque** pelota.
peloter [pəlɔte] vt (fam) to feel (up); **se** ~ to pet.
peloton [pəlɔtɔ̃] nm (groupe: personnes) group; (: pompiers, gendarmes) squad; (: SPORT) pack; (de laine) ball; ~ **d'exécution** firing squad.
pelotonner [pəlɔtɔne]: **se** ~ vi to curl (o.s.) up.
pelouse [pəluz] nf lawn; (HIPPISME) spectating area inside racetrack.
peluche [pəlyʃ] nf (bit of) fluff; **animal en** ~ soft toy, fluffy animal.
pelucher [p(ə)lyʃe] vi to become fluffy, fluff up.
pelucheux, euse [p(ə)lyʃø, -øz] adj fluffy.
pelure [pəlyʀ] nf peeling, peel no pl; ~ **d'oignon** onion skin.
pénal, e, aux [penal, -o] adj penal.
pénalisation [penalizasjɔ̃] nf (SPORT) sanction, penalty.
pénaliser [penalize] vt to penalize.
pénalité [penalite] nf penalty.

penalty, ies [penalti, -z] *nm* (*SPORT*) penalty (kick).

pénard, e [penaʀ, -aʀd(ə)] *adj* = **peinard**.

pénates [penat] *nmpl*: **regagner ses ~** to return to the bosom of one's family.

penaud, e [pəno, -od] *adj* sheepish, contrite.

penchant [pɑ̃ʃɑ̃] *nm*: **un ~ à faire/à qch** a tendency to do/to sth; **un ~ pour qch** a liking *ou* fondness for sth.

penché, e [pɑ̃ʃe] *adj* slanting.

pencher [pɑ̃ʃe] *vi* to tilt, lean over ♦ *vt* to tilt; **se ~** *vi* to lean over; (*se baisser*) to bend down; **se ~ sur** to bend over; (*fig: problème*) to look into; **se ~ au dehors** to lean out; **~ pour** to be inclined to favour (*BRIT*) *ou* favor (*US*).

pendable [pɑ̃dabl(ə)] *adj*: **tour ~** rotten trick; **c'est un cas ~!** he (*ou* she) deserves to be shot!

pendaison [pɑ̃dɛzɔ̃] *nf* hanging.

pendant, e [pɑ̃dɑ̃, -ɑ̃t] *adj* hanging (out); (*ADMIN, JUR*) pending ♦ *nm* counterpart; matching piece ♦ *prép* during; **faire ~ à** to match; **to be the counterpart of**; **~ que** while; **~s d'oreilles** drop *ou* pendant earrings.

pendeloque [pɑ̃dlɔk] *nf* pendant.

pendentif [pɑ̃dɑ̃tif] *nm* pendant.

penderie [pɑ̃dʀi] *nf* wardrobe; (*placard*) walk-in cupboard.

pendiller [pɑ̃dije] *vi* to flap (about).

pendre [pɑ̃dʀ(ə)] *vt, vi* to hang; **se ~ (à)** (*se suicider*) to hang o.s. (on); **se ~ à** (*se suspendre*) to hang from; **~ à** to hang (down) from; **~ qch à** (*mur*) to hang sth (up) on; (*plafond*) to hang sth (up) from.

pendu, e [pɑ̃dy] *pp de* **pendre** ♦ *nm/f* hanged man (*ou* woman).

pendulaire [pɑ̃dylɛʀ] *adj* pendular, of a pendulum.

pendule [pɑ̃dyl] *nf* clock ♦ *nm* pendulum.

pendulette [pɑ̃dylɛt] *nf* small clock.

pêne [pɛn] *nm* bolt.

pénétrant, e [penetʀɑ̃, -ɑ̃t] *adj* (*air, froid*) biting; (*pluie*) that soaks right through you; (*fig: odeur*) noticeable; (*œil, regard*) piercing; (*clairvoyant, perspicace*) perceptive ♦ *nf* (*route*) expressway.

pénétration [penetʀɑsjɔ̃] *nf* (*fig: d'idées etc*) penetration; (*perspicacité*) perception.

pénétré, e [penetʀe] *adj* (*air, ton*) earnest; **être ~ de soi-même/son importance** to be full of oneself/one's own importance.

pénétrer [penetʀe] *vi* to come *ou* get in ♦ *vt* to penetrate; **~ dans** to enter; (*suj: froid, projectile*) to penetrate; (*: air, eau*) to come into, get into; (*mystère, secret*) to fathom; **se ~ de qch** to get sth firmly set in one's mind.

pénible [penibl(ə)] *adj* (*astreignant*) hard; (*affligeant*) painful; (*personne, caractère*) tiresome; **il m'est ~ de ...** I'm sorry to ....

péniblement [penibləmɑ̃] *adv* with difficulty.

péniche [peniʃ] *nf* barge; **~ de débarquement** landing craft *inv*.

pénicilline [penisilin] *nf* penicillin.

péninsulaire [penɛ̃sylɛʀ] *adj* peninsular.

péninsule [penɛ̃syl] *nf* peninsula.

pénis [penis] *nm* penis.

pénitence [penitɑ̃s] *nf* (*repentir*) penitence; (*peine*) penance; (*punition, châtiment*) punishment; **mettre un enfant en ~** ≈ to make a child stand in the corner; **faire ~** to do a penance.

pénitencier [penitɑ̃sje] *nm* prison, penitentiary (*US*).

pénitent, e [penitɑ̃, -ɑ̃t] *adj* penitent.

pénitentiaire [penitɑ̃sjɛʀ] *adj* prison *cpd*, penitentiary (*US*).

pénombre [penɔ̃bʀ(ə)] *nf* half-light.

pensable [pɑ̃sabl(ə)] *adj*: **ce n'est pas ~** it's unthinkable.

pensant, e [pɑ̃sɑ̃, -ɑ̃t] *adj*: **bien ~** right-thinking.

pense-bête [pɑ̃sbɛt] *nm* aide-mémoire, mnemonic device.

pensée [pɑ̃se] *nf* thought; (*démarche, doctrine*) thinking *no pl*; (*BOT*) pansy; **se représenter qch par la ~** to conjure up a mental picture of sth; **en ~** in one's mind.

penser [pɑ̃se] *vi* to think ♦ *vt* to think; (*concevoir: problème, machine*) to think out; **~ à** to think of; (*songer à: ami, vacances*) to think of *ou* about; (*réfléchir à: problème, offre*): **~ à qch** to think about sth, think sth over; **~ à faire qch** to think of doing sth; **~ faire qch** to be thinking of doing sth, intend to do sth; **faire ~ à** to remind one of; **n'y pensons plus** let's forget it; **vous n'y pensez pas!** don't let it bother you!; **sans ~ à mal** without meaning any harm; **je le pense aussi** I think so too; **je pense que oui/non** I think so/don't think so.

penseur [pɑ̃sœʀ] *nm* thinker; **libre ~** free-thinker.

pensif, ive [pɑ̃sif, -iv] *adj* pensive, thoughtful.

pension [pɑ̃sjɔ̃] *nf* (*allocation*) pension; (*prix du logement*) board and lodging, bed and board; (*maison particulière*) boarding house; (*hôtel*) guesthouse, hotel; (*école*) boarding school; **prendre ~ chez** to take board and lodging at; **prendre qn en ~** to take sb (in) as a lodger; **mettre en ~** to send to boarding school; **~ alimentaire** (*d'étudiant*) living allowance; (*de divorcée*) maintenance allowance; alimony; **~ complète** full board; **~ de famille** boarding house, guesthouse; **~ de guerre/d'invalidité** war/disablement pension.

pensionnaire [pɑ̃sjɔnɛʀ] *nm/f* boarder; guest.

pensionnat [pɑ̃sjɔna] *nm* boarding school.

pensionné, e [pɑ̃sjɔne] *nm/f* pensioner.

pensivement [pɑ̃sivmɑ̃] *adv* pensively, thoughtfully.

pensum [pɛ̃sɔm] *nm* (*SCOL*) punishment exercise; (*fig*) chore.

pentagone [pɛ̃tagɔn] *nm* pentagon; **le P~** the

Pentagon.
pentathlon [pɛtatlɔ̃] *nm* pentathlon.
pente [pɑ̃t] *nf* slope; **en ~** *adj* sloping.
Pentecôte [pɑ̃tkot] *nf*: **la ~** Whitsun (*BRIT*), Pentecost; (*dimanche*) Whitsunday (*BRIT*); **lundi de ~** Whit Monday (*BRIT*).
pénurie [penyʀi] *nf* shortage; **~ de main-d'œuvre** undermanning.
PEP [pɛp] *sigle m* (= *plan d'épargne populaire*) *individual savings plan*.
pépé [pepe] *nm* (*fam*) grandad.
pépère [pepɛʀ] *adj* (*fam*) cushy (*fam*), quiet ♦ *nm* (*fam*) grandad.
pépier [pepje] *vi* to chirp, tweet.
pépin [pepɛ̃] *nm* (*BOT*: *graine*) pip; (*fam*: *ennui*) snag, hitch; (*: parapluie*) brolly (*BRIT*), umbrella.
pépinière [pepinjɛʀ] *nf* nursery; (*fig*) nest, breeding-ground.
pépiniériste [pepinjeʀist(ə)] *nm* nurseryman.
pépite [pepit] *nf* nugget.
PEPS *abr* (= *premier entré premier sorti*) first in first out.
PER [pɛʀ] *sigle m* (= *plan d'épargne retraite*) *type of personal pension plan*.
perçant, e [pɛʀsɑ̃, -ɑ̃t] *adj* (*vue, regard, yeux*) sharp, keen; (*cri, voix*) piercing, shrill.
percée [pɛʀse] *nf* (*trouée*) opening; (*MIL, COMM, fig*) breakthrough; (*SPORT*) break.
perce-neige [pɛʀsənɛʒ] *nm ou f inv* snowdrop.
perce-oreille [pɛʀsɔʀɛj] *nm* earwig.
percepteur [pɛʀsɛptœʀ] *nm* tax collector.
perceptible [pɛʀsɛptibl(ə)] *adj* (*son, différence*) perceptible; (*impôt*) payable, collectable.
perception [pɛʀsɛpsjɔ̃] *nf* perception; (*d'impôts etc*) collection; (*bureau*) tax (collector's) office.
percer [pɛʀse] *vt* to pierce; (*ouverture etc*) to make; (*mystère, énigme*) to penetrate ♦ *vi* to come through; (*réussir*) to break through; **~ une dent** to cut a tooth.
perceuse [pɛʀsøz] *nf* drill; **~ à percussion** hammer drill.
percevable [pɛʀsəvabl(ə)] *adj* collectable, payable.
percevoir [pɛʀsəvwaʀ] *vt* (*distinguer*) to perceive, detect; (*taxe, impôt*) to collect; (*revenu, indemnité*) to receive.
perche [pɛʀʃ(ə)] *nf* (*ZOOL*) perch; (*bâton*) pole; **~ à son** (sound) boom.
percher [pɛʀʃe] *vt*: **~ qch sur** to perch sth on ♦ *vi*, **se ~** *vi* (*oiseau*) to perch.
perchiste [pɛʀʃist(ə)] *nm/f* (*SPORT*) pole vaulter; (*TV etc*) boom operator.
perchoir [pɛʀʃwaʀ] *nm* perch; (*fig*) *presidency of the French National Assembly.*
perclus, e [pɛʀkly, -yz] *adj*: **~ de** (*rhumatismes*) crippled with.
perçois [pɛʀswa] *etc vb voir* **percevoir**.
percolateur [pɛʀkɔlatœʀ] *nm* percolator.
perçu, e [pɛʀsy] *pp de* **percevoir**.
percussion [pɛʀkysjɔ̃] *nf* percussion.

percussionniste [pɛʀkysjɔnist(ə)] *nm/f* percussionist.
percutant, e [pɛʀkytɑ̃, -ɑ̃t] *adj* (*article etc*) resounding, forceful.
percuter [pɛʀkyte] *vt* to strike; (*suj: véhicule*) to crash into ♦ *vi*: **~ contre** to crash into.
percuteur [pɛʀkytœʀ] *nm* firing pin, hammer.
perdant, e [pɛʀdɑ̃, -ɑ̃t] *nm/f* loser ♦ *adj* losing.
perdition [pɛʀdisjɔ̃] *nf* (*morale*) ruin; **en ~** (*NAVIG*) in distress; **lieu de ~** den of vice.
perdre [pɛʀdʀ(ə)] *vt* to lose; (*gaspiller: temps, argent*) to waste; (*: occasion*) to waste, miss; (*personne: moralement etc*) to ruin ♦ *vi* to lose; (*sur une vente etc*) to lose out; (*récipient*) to leak; **se ~** *vi* (*s'égarer*) to get lost, lose one's way; (*fig: se gâter*) to go to waste; (*disparaître*) to disappear, vanish; **il ne perd rien pour attendre** it can wait, it'll keep.
perdreau, x [pɛʀdʀo] *nm* (young) partridge.
perdrix [pɛʀdʀi] *nf* partridge.
perdu, e [pɛʀdy] *pp de* **perdre** ♦ *adj* (*enfant, cause, objet*) lost; (*isolé*) out-of-the-way; (*COMM: emballage*) non-returnable; (*récolte etc*) ruined; (*malade*): **il est ~** there's no hope left for him; **à vos moments ~s** in your spare time.
père [pɛʀ] *nm* father; **~s** *nmpl* (*ancêtres*) forefathers; **de ~ en fils** from father to son; **~ de famille** father; family man; **mon ~** (*REL*) Father; **le ~ Noël** Father Christmas.
pérégrinations [peʀegʀinasjɔ̃] *nfpl* travels.
péremption [peʀɑ̃psjɔ̃] *nf*: **date de ~** expiry date.
péremptoire [peʀɑ̃ptwaʀ] *adj* peremptory.
pérennité [peʀenite] *nf* durability, lasting quality.
péréquation [peʀekwasjɔ̃] *nf* (*des salaires*) realignment; (*des prix, impôts*) equalization.
perfectible [pɛʀfɛktibl(ə)] *adj* perfectible.
perfection [pɛʀfɛksjɔ̃] *nf* perfection; **à la ~** *adv* to perfection.
perfectionné, e [pɛʀfɛksjɔne] *adj* sophisticated.
perfectionnement [pɛʀfɛksjɔnmɑ̃] *nm* improvement.
perfectionner [pɛʀfɛksjɔne] *vt* to improve, perfect; **se ~ en anglais** to improve one's English.
perfectionniste [pɛʀfɛksjɔnist(ə)] *nm/f* perfectionist.
perfide [pɛʀfid] *adj* perfidious, treacherous.
perfidie [pɛʀfidi] *nf* treachery.
perforant, e [pɛʀfɔʀɑ̃, -ɑ̃t] *adj* (*balle*) armour-piercing (*BRIT*), armor-piercing (*US*).
perforateur, trice [pɛʀfɔʀatœʀ, -tʀis] *nm/f* punch-card operator ♦ *nm* (*perceuse*) borer; drill ♦ *nf* (*perceuse*) borer; drill; (*pour cartes*) card-punch; (*de bureau*) punch.
perforation [pɛʀfɔʀasjɔ̃] *nf* perforation; punching; (*trou*) hole.
perforatrice [pɛʀfɔʀatʀis] *nf voir* **perforateur**.
perforé, e [pɛʀfɔʀe] *adj*: **bande ~** punched

tape; **carte** ~ punch card.
perforer [pɛRfɔRe] *vt* to perforate, punch a hole (*ou* holes) in; (*ticket, bande, carte*) to punch.
perforeuse [pɛRfɔRøz] *nf* (*machine*) (card) punch; (*personne*) card punch operator.
performance [pɛRfɔRmãs] *nf* performance.
performant, e [pɛRfɔRmã, -ãt] *adj* (*ÉCON:* produit, entreprise) high-return *cpd*; (*TECH:* appareil, machine*) high-performance *cpd*.
perfusion [pɛRfyzjɔ̃] *nf* perfusion; **faire une** ~ **à qn** to put sb on a drip.
péricliter [peRiklite] *vi* to go downhill.
péridurale [peRidyRal] *nf* epidural.
périgourdin, e [peRiguRdɛ̃, -in] *adj* of *ou* from the Perigord.
péril [peRil] *nm* peril; **au** ~ **de sa vie** at the risk of his life; **à ses risques et** ~**s** at his (*ou* her) own risk.
périlleux, euse [peRijø, -øz] *adj* perilous.
périmé, e [peRime] *adj* (out)dated; (*ADMIN*) out-of-date, expired.
périmètre [peRimɛtR(ə)] *nm* perimeter.
périnatal, e [peRinatal] *adj* perinatal.
période [peRjɔd] *nf* period.
périodique [peRjɔdik] *adj* (*phases*) periodic; (*publication*) periodical; (*MATH:* fraction) recurring ♦ *nm* periodical; **garniture** *ou* **serviette** ~ sanitary towel (*BRIT*) *ou* napkin (*US*).
périodiquement [peRjɔdikmã] *adv* periodically.
péripéties [peRipesi] *nfpl* events, episodes.
périphérie [peRifeRi] *nf* periphery; (*d'une ville*) outskirts *pl*.
périphérique [peRifeRik] *adj* (*quartiers*) outlying; (*ANAT, TECH*) peripheral; (*station de radio*) operating from a neighbouring country ♦ *nm* (*INFORM*) peripheral; (*AUTO*): **(boulevard)** ~ ring road (*BRIT*), circular route (*US*).
périphrase [peRifRaz] *nf* circumlocution.
périple [peRipl(ə)] *nm* journey.
périr [peRiR] *vi* to die, perish.
périscolaire [peRiskɔlɛR] *adj* extracurricular.
périscope [peRiskɔp] *nm* periscope.
périssable [peRisabl(ə)] *adj* perishable.
péristyle [peRistil] *nm* peristyle.
péritonite [peRitɔnit] *nf* peritonitis.
perle [pɛRl(ə)] *nf* pearl; (*de plastique, métal, sueur*) bead; (*personne, chose*) gem, treasure; (*erreur*) gem, howler.
perlé, e [pɛRle] *adj* (*rire*) rippling, tinkling; (*travail*) exquisite; (*orge*) pearl *cpd*; **grève** ~**e** go-slow, selective strike (action).
perler [pɛRle] *vi* to form in droplets.
perlier, ière [pɛRlje, -jɛR] *adj* pearl *cpd*.
permanence [pɛRmanãs] *nf* permanence; (*local*) (duty) office; strike headquarters; (*service des urgences*) emergency service; (*SCOL*) study room; **assurer une** ~ (*service public, bureaux*) to operate *ou* maintain a basic service; **être de** ~ to be on call *ou* duty;

en ~ *adv* (*toujours*) permanently; (*continûment*) continuously.
permanent, e [pɛRmanã, -ãt] *adj* permanent; (*spectacle*) continuous; (*armée, comité*) standing ♦ *nf* perm ♦ *nm/f* (*d'un syndicat, parti*) paid official.
perméable [pɛRmeabl(ə)] *adj* (*terrain*) permeable; ~ **à** (*fig*) receptive *ou* open to.
permettre [pɛRmɛtR(ə)] *vt* to allow, permit; ~ **à qn de faire/qch** to allow sb to do/sth; **se** ~ **de faire qch** to take the liberty of doing sth; **permettez!** excuse me!
permis, e [pɛRmi, -iz] *pp de* **permettre** ♦ *nm* permit, licence (*BRIT*), license (*US*); ~ **de chasse** hunting permit; ~ **(de conduire)** (driving) licence (*BRIT*), (driver's) license (*US*); ~ **de construire** planning permission (*BRIT*), building permit (*US*); ~ **d'inhumer** burial certificate; ~ **poids lourds** ≈ HGV (driving) licence (*BRIT*), ≈ class E (driver's) license (*US*); ~ **de séjour** residence permit; ~ **de travail** work permit.
permissif, ive [pɛRmisif, -iv] *adj* permissive.
permission [pɛRmisjɔ̃] *nf* permission; (*MIL*) leave; (*: papier*) pass; **en** ~ on leave; **avoir la** ~ **de faire** to have permission to do, be allowed to do.
permissionnaire [pɛRmisjɔnɛR] *nm* soldier on leave.
permutable [pɛRmytabl(ə)] *adj* which can be changed *ou* switched around.
permuter [pɛRmyte] *vt* to change around, permutate ♦ *vi* to change, swap.
pernicieux, euse [pɛRnisjø, -øz] *adj* pernicious.
péroné [peRɔne] *nm* fibula.
pérorer [peRɔRe] *vi* to hold forth.
Pérou [peRu] *nm:* **le** ~ Peru.
perpendiculaire [pɛRpãdikylɛR] *adj, nf* perpendicular.
perpendiculairement [pɛRpãdikylɛRmã] *adv* perpendicularly.
perpète [pɛRpɛt] *nf:* **à** ~ (*fam: loin*) miles away; (*: longtemps*) forever.
perpétrer [pɛRpetRe] *vt* to perpetrate.
perpétuel, le [pɛRpetɥɛl] *adj* perpetual; (*ADMIN etc*) permanent; for life.
perpétuellement [pɛRpetɥɛlmã] *adv* perpetually, constantly.
perpétuer [pɛRpetɥe] *vt* to perpetuate; **se** ~ (*usage, injustice*) to be perpetuated; (*espèces*) to survive.
perpétuité [pɛRpetɥite] *nf:* **à** ~ *adj, adv* for life; **être condamné à** ~ to be sentenced to life imprisonment, receive a life sentence.
perplexe [pɛRplɛks(ə)] *adj* perplexed, puzzled.
perplexité [pɛRplɛksite] *nf* perplexity.
perquisition [pɛRkizisjɔ̃] *nf* (police) search.
perquisitionner [pɛRkizisjɔne] *vi* to carry out a search.
perron [pɛRɔ̃] *nm* steps *pl* (in front of mansion etc).

perroquet [pɛʀɔkɛ] *nm* parrot.
perruche [pɛʀyʃ] *nf* budgerigar (*BRIT*), budgie (*BRIT*), parakeet (*US*).
perruque [pɛʀyk] *nf* wig.
persan, e [pɛʀsã, -an] *adj* Persian ♦ *nm* (*LING*) Persian.
perse [pɛʀs(ə)] *adj* Persian ♦ *nm* (*LING*) Persian ♦ *nm/f*: **P~** Persian ♦ *nf*: **la P~** Persia.
persécuter [pɛʀsekyte] *vt* to persecute.
persécution [pɛʀsekysjɔ̃] *nf* persecution.
persévérance [pɛʀseveʀãs] *nf* perseverance.
persévérant, e [pɛʀseveʀã, -ãt] *adj* persevering.
persévérer [pɛʀseveʀe] *vi* to persevere; **~ à croire que** to continue to believe that.
persiennes [pɛʀsjɛn] *nfpl* (slatted) shutters.
persiflage [pɛʀsiflaʒ] *nm* mockery *no pl*.
persifleur, euse [pɛʀsiflœʀ, -øz] *adj* mocking.
persil [pɛʀsi] *nm* parsley.
persillé, e [pɛʀsije] *adj* (sprinkled) with parsley; (*fromage*) veined; (*viande*) marbled, with fat running through.
Persique [pɛʀsik] *adj*: **le golfe ~** the (Persian) Gulf.
persistance [pɛʀsistãs] *nf* persistence.
persistant, e [pɛʀsistã, -ãt] *adj* persistent; (*feuilles*) evergreen; **à feuillage ~** evergreen.
persister [pɛʀsiste] *vi* to persist; **~ à faire qch** to persist in doing sth.
personnage [pɛʀsɔnaʒ] *nm* (*notable*) personality; figure; (*individu*) character, individual; (*THÉÂT*) character; (*PEINTURE*) figure.
personnaliser [pɛʀsɔnalize] *vt* to personalize; (*appartement*) to give a personal touch to.
personnalité [pɛʀsɔnalite] *nf* personality; (*personnage*) prominent figure.
personne [pɛʀsɔn] *nf* person ♦ *pron* nobody, no one; (*quelqu'un*) anybody, anyone; **~s** *nfpl* people *pl*; **il n'y a ~** there's nobody in *ou* there, there isn't anybody in *ou* there; **10 F par ~** 10 F per person *ou* a head; **en ~** personally, in person; **~ âgée** elderly person; **~ à charge** (*JUR*) dependent; **~ morale** *ou* **civile** (*JUR*) legal entity.
personnel, le [pɛʀsɔnɛl] *adj* personal; (*égoïste*: *personne*) selfish, self-centred; (*idée, opinion*): **j'ai des idées ~les à ce sujet** I have my own ideas about that ♦ *nm* personnel, staff; **service du ~** personnel department.
personnellement [pɛʀsɔnɛlmã] *adv* personally.
personnification [pɛʀsɔnifikasjɔ̃] *nf* personification; **c'est la ~ de la cruauté** he's cruelty personified.
personnifier [pɛʀsɔnifje] *vt* to personify; to typify; **c'est l'honnêteté personnifiée** he (*ou* she *etc*) is honesty personified.
perspective [pɛʀspɛktiv] *nf* (*ART*) perspective; (*vue, coup d'œil*) view; (*point de vue*) viewpoint, angle; (*chose escomptée, envisagée*) prospect; **en ~** in prospect.

perspicace [pɛʀspikas] *adj* clear-sighted, gifted with (*ou* showing) insight.
perspicacité [pɛʀspikasite] *nf* insight, perspicacity.
persuader [pɛʀsɥade] *vt*: **~ qn (de/de faire)** to persuade sb (of/to do); **j'en suis persuadé** I'm quite sure *ou* convinced (of it).
persuasif, ive [pɛʀsɥazif, -iv] *adj* persuasive.
persuasion [pɛʀsɥazjɔ̃] *nf* persuasion.
perte [pɛʀt(ə)] *nf* loss; (*de temps*) waste; (*fig: morale*) ruin; **~s** *nfpl* losses; **à ~** (*COMM*) at a loss; **à ~ de vue** as far as the eye can (*ou* could) see; (*fig*) interminably; **en pure ~** for absolutely nothing; **courir à sa ~** to be on the road to ruin; **être en ~ de vitesse** (*fig*) to be losing momentum; **avec ~ et fracas** forcibly; **~ de chaleur** heat loss; **~ sèche** dead loss; **~s blanches** (vaginal) discharge *sg*.
pertinemment [pɛʀtinamã] *adv* to the point; (*savoir*) perfectly well, full well.
pertinence [pɛʀtinãs] *nf* pertinence, relevance; discernment.
pertinent, e [pɛʀtinã, -ãt] *adj* (*remarque*) apt, pertinent, relevant; (*analyse*) discerning, judicious.
perturbateur, trice [pɛʀtyʀbatœʀ, -tʀis] *adj* disruptive.
perturbation [pɛʀtyʀbasjɔ̃] *nf* (*dans un service public*) disruption; (*agitation, trouble*) perturbation; **~ (atmosphérique)** atmospheric disturbance.
perturber [pɛʀtyʀbe] *vt* to disrupt; (*PSYCH*) to perturb, disturb.
péruvien, ne [peʀyvjɛ̃, -ɛn] *adj* Peruvian ♦ *nm/f*: **P~, ne** Peruvian.
pervenche [pɛʀvãʃ] *nf* periwinkle; (*fam*) traffic warden (*BRIT*), meter maid (*US*).
pervers, e [pɛʀvɛʀ, -ɛʀs(ə)] *adj* perverted, depraved; (*malfaisant*) perverse.
perversion [pɛʀvɛʀsjɔ̃] *nf* perversion.
perversité [pɛʀvɛʀsite] *nf* depravity; perversity.
perverti, e [pɛʀvɛʀti] *nm/f* pervert.
pervertir [pɛʀvɛʀtiʀ] *vt* to pervert.
pesage [pəzaʒ] *nm* weighing; (*HIPPISME*: *action*) weigh-in; (: *salle*) weighing room; (: *enceinte*) enclosure.
pesamment [pəzamã] *adv* heavily.
pesant, e [pəzã, -ãt] *adj* heavy; (*fig*) burdensome ♦ *nm*: **valoir son ~ de** to be worth one's weight in.
pesanteur [pəzãtœʀ] *nf* gravity.
pèse-bébé [pɛzbebe] *nm* (baby) scales *pl*.
pesée [pəze] *nf* weighing; (*BOXE*) weigh-in; (*pression*) pressure.
pèse-lettre [pɛzlɛtʀ(ə)] *nm* letter scales *pl*.
pèse-personne [pɛzpɛʀsɔn] *nm* (bathroom) scales *pl*.
peser [pəze] *vt, vb avec attribut* to weigh; (*considérer, comparer*) to weigh up ♦ *vi* to be heavy; (*fig*) to carry weight; **~ sur** (*levier, bouton*) to press, push; (*fig: accabler*) to lie heavy on;

(*: influencer*) to influence; ~ **à qn** to weigh heavy on sb.

pessaire [pesɛʀ] *nm* pessary.

pessimisme [pesimism(ə)] *nm* pessimism.

pessimiste [pesimist(ə)] *adj* pessimistic ♦ *nm/f* pessimist.

peste [pɛst(ə)] *nf* plague; (*fig*) pest, nuisance.

pester [pɛste] *vi*: ~ **contre** to curse.

pesticide [pɛstisid] *nm* pesticide.

pestiféré, e [pɛstifeʀe] *nm/f* plague victim.

pestilentiel, le [pɛstilɑ̃sjɛl] *adj* foul.

pet [pɛ] *nm* (*fam!*) fart (*!*).

pétale [petal] *nm* petal.

pétanque [petɑ̃k] *nf* type of bowls.

Pétanque *is a version of the game of* **boules**, *played on a variety of hard surfaces. Standing with their feet together, players throw steel bowls towards a wooden jack. Pétanque originated in the south of France and is still very much associated with that area.*

---

pétarade [petaʀad] *nf* backfiring *no pl.*

pétarader [petaʀade] *vi* to backfire.

pétard [petaʀ] *nm* (*feu d'artifice*) banger (*BRIT*), firecracker; (*de cotillon*) cracker; (*RAIL*) detonator.

pet-de-nonne, *pl* **pets-de-nonne** [pɛdnɔn] *nm* ≈ choux bun.

péter [pete] *vi* (*fam: casser, sauter*) to burst; to bust; (*fam!*) to fart (*!*).

pète-sec [pɛtsɛk] *adj inv* abrupt, sharp(-tongued).

pétillant, e [petijɑ̃, -ɑ̃t] *adj* sparkling.

pétiller [petije] *vi* (*flamme, bois*) to crackle; (*mousse, champagne*) to bubble; (*pierre, métal*) to glisten; (*yeux*) to sparkle; (*fig*): ~ **d'esprit** to sparkle with wit.

petit, e [pəti, -it] *adj* (*gén*) small; (*main, objet, colline, en âge: enfant*) small, little; (*mince, fin: personne, taille, pluie*) slight; (*voyage*) short, little; (*bruit etc*) faint, slight; (*mesquin*) mean; (*peu important*) minor ♦ *nm/f* (*petit enfant*) little one, child ♦ *nmpl* (*d'un animal*) young *pl*; **faire des ~s** to have kittens (*ou* puppies *etc*); **en ~** in miniature; **mon ~** son; little one; **ma ~e** dear; little one; **pauvre ~** poor little thing; **la classe des ~s** the infant class; **pour ~s et grands** for children and adults; **les tout-~s** the little ones, the tiny tots; ~ **à** ~ bit by bit, gradually; ~**(e) ami/e** boyfriend/girlfriend; **les ~es annonces** the small ads; ~ **déjeuner** breakfast; ~ **doigt** little finger; **le** ~ **écran** the small screen; ~ **four** petit four; ~ **pain** (bread) roll; ~**e monnaie** small change; ~**e vérole** smallpox; ~**s pois** petit pois *pl*, garden peas; ~**es gens** people of modest means.

petit-beurre, *pl* **petits-beurre** [pətibœʀ] *nm* sweet butter biscuit (*BRIT*) *ou* cookie (*US*).

petit(e)-bourgeois(e), *pl* **petit(e)s-bourgeois(es)** [pəti(t)buʀʒwa(z)] *adj* (*péj*)

petit-bourgeois, middle-class.

petite-fille, *pl* **petites-filles** [pətitfij] *nf* granddaughter.

petitement [pətitmɑ̃] *adv* poorly; meanly; **être logé** ~ to be in cramped accommodation.

petitesse [pətitɛs] *nf* smallness; (*d'un salaire, de revenus*) modestness; (*mesquinerie*) meanness.

petit-fils, *pl* **petits-fils** [pətifis] *nm* grandson.

pétition [petisjɔ̃] *nf* petition; **faire signer une** ~ to get up a petition.

pétitionnaire [petisjɔnɛʀ] *nm/f* petitioner.

pétitionner [petisjɔne] *vi* to petition.

petit-lait, *pl* **petits-laits** [pətilɛ] *nm* whey *no pl.*

petit-nègre [pətinɛgʀ(ə)] *nm* (*péj*) pidgin French.

petits-enfants [pətizɑ̃fɑ̃] *nmpl* grandchildren.

petit-suisse, *pl* **petits-suisses** [pətisɥis] *nm* small individual pot of cream cheese.

pétoche [petɔʃ] *nf* (*fam*): **avoir la** ~ to be scared out of one's wits.

pétri, e [petʀi] *adj*: ~ **d'orgueil** filled with pride.

pétrifier [petʀifje] *vt* to petrify; (*fig*) to paralyze, transfix.

pétrin [petʀɛ̃] *nm* kneading-trough; (*fig*): **dans le** ~ in a jam *ou* fix.

pétrir [petʀiʀ] *vt* to knead.

pétrochimie [petʀoʃimi] *nf* petrochemistry.

pétrochimique [petʀoʃimik] *adj* petrochemical.

pétrodollar [petʀodɔlaʀ] *nm* petrodollar.

pétrole [petʀɔl] *nm* oil; (*aussi*: ~ **lampant**) paraffin (*BRIT*), kerosene (*US*).

pétrolier, ière [petʀolje, -jɛʀ] *adj* oil *cpd*; (*pays*) oil-producing ♦ *nm* (*navire*) oil tanker; (*financier*) oilman; (*technicien*) petroleum engineer.

pétrolifère [petʀolifɛʀ] *adj* oil(-bearing).

P et T *sigle fpl* = postes et télécommunications.

pétulant, e [petylɑ̃, -ɑ̃t] *adj* exuberant.

pétunia [petynja] *nm* petunia.

═══════════════════════════ *MOT-CLÉ*

peu [pø] *adv* **1** (*modifiant verbe, adjectif, adverbe*): **il boit** ~ he doesn't drink (very) much; **il est** ~ **bavard** he's not very talkative; ~ **avant/après** shortly before/afterwards; **pour** ~ **qu'il fasse** if he should do, if by any chance he does

2 (*modifiant nom*): ~ **de**: ~ **de gens/d'arbres** few *ou* not (very) many people/trees; **il a** ~ **d'espoir** he hasn't (got) much hope, he has little hope; **pour** ~ **de temps** for (only) a short while; **à** ~ **de frais** for very little cost

3: ~ **à** ~ little by little; **à** ~ **près** just about, more or less; **à** ~ **près 10 kg/10 F** approximately 10 kg/10 F

♦ *nm* **1**: **le** ~ **de gens qui** the few people who; **le** ~ **de sable qui** what little sand, the little sand which

2: **un** ~ a little; **un petit** ~ a little bit; **un** ~

d'espoir a little hope; **elle est un ~ bavarde** she's rather talkative; **un ~ plus/moins de** slightly more/less (ou fewer) than; **pour un ~ il ...**, **un ~ plus et il ...** he very nearly ou all but ...; **essayez un ~!** have a go!, just try it!

♦ pron: **~ le savent** few know (it); **avant** ou **sous ~** shortly, before long; **depuis ~** fɔr a short ou little while; (au passé) a short ou little while ago; **de ~** (only) just; **c'est ~ de chose** it's nothing; **il est de ~ mon cadet** he's just a little ou bit younger than me.

peuplade [pœplad] nf (horde, tribu) tribe, people.

peuple [pœpl(ə)] nm people; (masse indifférenciée): **un ~ de vacanciers** a crowd of holiday-makers; **il y a du ~** there are a lot of people.

peuplé, e [pœple] adj: **très/peu ~** densely/sparsely populated.

peupler [pœple] vt (pays, région) to populate; (étang) to stock; (suj: hommes, poissons) to inhabit; (fig: imagination, rêves) to fill; **se ~** vi (ville, région) to become populated; (fig: s'animer) to fill (up), be filled.

peuplier [pøplije] nm poplar (tree).

peur [pœʀ] nf fear; **avoir ~ (de/de faire/que)** to be frightened ou afraid (of/of doing/that); **prendre ~** to take fright; **faire ~ à** to frighten; **de ~ de/que** for fear of/that; **j'ai ~ qu'il ne soit trop tard** I'm afraid it might be too late; **j'ai ~ qu'il (ne) vienne (pas)** I'm afraid he may (not) come.

peureux, euse [pœʀø, -øz] adj fearful, timorous.

peut [pø] vb voir **pouvoir.**

peut-être [pøtɛtʀ(ə)] adv perhaps, maybe; **~ que** perhaps, maybe; **~ bien qu'il fera/est** he may well do/be.

peuvent [pœv], **peux** [pø] etc vb voir **pouvoir.**

p. ex. abr (= par exemple) e.g.

phalange [falɑ̃ʒ] nf (ANAT) phalanx (pl phalanges); (MIL, fig) phalanx (pl -es).

phallique [falik] adj phallic.

phallocrate [falɔkʀat] nm male chauvinist.

phallocratie [falɔkʀasi] nf male chauvinism.

phallus [falys] nm phallus.

pharaon [faʀaɔ̃] nm Pharaoh.

phare [faʀ] nm (en mer) lighthouse; (d'aéroport) beacon; (de véhicule) headlight, headlamp (BRIT) ♦ adj: **produit ~** leading product; **se mettre en ~s, mettre ses ~s** to put on one's headlights; **~s de recul** reversing (BRIT) ou back-up (US) lights.

pharmaceutique [faʀmasøtik] adj pharmaceutic(al).

pharmacie [faʀmasi] nf (science) pharmacology; (magasin) chemist's (BRIT), pharmacy; (officine) dispensary; (produits) pharmaceuticals pl; (armoire) medicine chest ou cupboard, first-aid cupboard.

pharmacien, ne [faʀmasjɛ̃, -ɛn] nm/f pharmacist, chemist (BRIT).

pharmacologie [faʀmakɔlɔʒi] nf pharmacology.

pharyngite [faʀɛ̃ʒit] nf pharyngitis no pl.

pharynx [faʀɛ̃ks] nm pharynx.

phase [faz] nf phase.

phénoménal, e, aux [fenɔmenal, -o] phenomenal.

phénomène [fenɔmɛn] nm phenomenon (pl -a); (monstre) freak.

philanthrope [filɑ̃tʀɔp] nm/f philanthropist.

philanthropie [filɑ̃tʀɔpi] nf philanthropy.

philanthropique [filɑ̃tʀɔpik] adj philanthropic.

philatélie [filateli] nf philately, stamp collecting.

philatélique [filatelik] adj philatelic.

philatéliste [filatelist(ə)] nm/f philatelist, stamp collector.

philharmonique [filaʀmɔnik] adj philharmonic.

philippin, e [filipɛ̃, -in] adj Filipino.

Philippines [filipin] nfpl: **les ~** the Philippines.

philistin [filistɛ̃] nm philistine.

philo [filo] nf (fam: = philosophie) philosophy.

philosophe [filɔzɔf] nm/f philosopher ♦ adj philosophical.

philosopher [filɔzɔfe] vi to philosophize.

philosophie [filɔzɔfi] nf philosophy.

philosophique [filɔzɔfik] adj philosophical.

philosophiquement [filɔzɔfikmɑ̃] adv philosophically.

philtre [filtʀ(ə)] nm philtre, love potion.

phlébite [flebit] nf phlebitis.

phlébologue [flebɔlɔg] nm/f vein specialist.

phobie [fɔbi] nf phobia.

phonétique [fɔnetik] adj phonetic ♦ nf phonetics sg.

phonétiquement [fɔnetikmɑ̃] adv phonetically.

phonographe [fɔnɔgʀaf] nm (wind-up) gramophone.

phoque [fɔk] nm seal; (fourrure) sealskin.

phosphate [fɔsfat] nm phosphate.

phosphaté, e [fɔsfate] adj phosphate-enriched.

phosphore [fɔsfɔʀ] nm phosphorus.

phosphoré, e [fɔsfɔʀe] adj phosphorous.

phosphorescent, e [fɔsfɔʀesɑ̃, -ɑ̃t] adj luminous.

phosphorique [fɔsfɔʀik] adj: **acide ~** phosphoric acid.

photo [fɔto] nf (= photographie) photo ♦ adj: **appareil/pellicule ~** camera/film; **en ~** in ou on a photo; **prendre en ~** to take a photo of; **aimer la/faire de la ~** to like taking/take photos; **~ en couleurs** colour photo; **~ d'identité** passport photo.

photo... [fɔtɔ] préfixe photo....

photocopie [fɔtɔkɔpi] nf (procédé) photocopying; (document) photocopy.

photocopier [fɔtɔkɔpje] *vt* to photocopy.

photocopieur [fɔtɔkɔpjœʀ] *nm*, **photocopieuse** [fɔtɔkɔpjøz] *nf* (photo)copier.

photo-électrique [fɔtɔelɛktʀik] *adj* photo-electric.

photo-finish, *pl* **photos-finish** [fɔtofiniʃ] *nf* (*appareil*) photo finish camera; (*photo*) photo finish picture; **il y a eu ~ pour la troisième place** there was a photo finish for third place.

photogénique [fɔtɔʒenik] *adj* photogenic.

photographe [fɔtɔgʀaf] *nmf* photographer.

photographie [fɔtɔgʀafi] *nf* (*procédé, technique*) photography; (*cliché*) photograph; **faire de la ~** to have photography as a hobby; (*comme métier*) to be a photographer.

photographier [fɔtɔgʀafje] *vt* to photograph, take.

photographique [fɔtɔgʀafik] *adj* photographic.

photogravure [fɔtɔgʀavyʀ] *nf* photoengraving.

photomaton [fɔtɔmatɔ̃] *nm* photo-booth, photomat.

photomontage [fɔtɔmɔ̃taʒ] *nm* photomontage.

photo-robot [fɔtɔʀɔbo] *nf* Identikit ® (picture).

photosensible [fɔtɔsɑ̃sibl(ə)] *adj* photosensitive.

photostat [fɔtɔsta] *nm* photostat.

phrase [fʀaz] *nf* (*LING*) sentence; (*propos, MUS*) phrase; **~s** *nfpl* (*péj*) flowery language *sg*.

phraséologie [fʀazeɔlɔʒi] *nf* phraseology; (*rhétorique*) flowery language.

phraseur, euse [fʀazœʀ, -øz] *nm/f*: **c'est un ~** he uses such flowery language.

phrygien, ne [fʀiʒjɛ̃, -ɛn] *adj*: **bonnet ~** Phrygian cap.

phtisie [ftizi] *nf* consumption.

phylloxéra [filɔkseʀa] *nm* phylloxera.

physicien, ne [fizisjɛ̃, -ɛn] *nm/f* physicist.

physiologie [fizjɔlɔʒi] *nf* physiology.

physiologique [fizjɔlɔʒik] *adj* physiological.

physiologiquement [fizjɔlɔʒikmɑ̃] *adv* physiologically.

physionomie [fizjɔnɔmi] *nf* face; (*d'un paysage etc*) physiognomy.

physionomiste [fizjɔnɔmist(ə)] *nm/f* good judge of faces; person who has a good memory for faces.

physiothérapie [fizjɔteʀapi] *nf* natural medicine, alternative medicine.

physique [fizik] *adj* physical ♦ *nm* physique ♦ *nf* physics *sg*; **au ~** physically.

physiquement [fizikmɑ̃] *adv* physically.

phytothérapie [fitɔteʀapi] *nf* herbal medicine.

p.i. *abr* = **par intérim**; *voir* **intérim**.

piaffer [pjafe] *vi* to stamp.

piaillement [pjɑjmɑ̃] *nm* squawking *no pl*.

piailler [pjaje] *vi* to squawk.

pianiste [pjanist(ə)] *nm/f* pianist.

piano [pjano] *nm* piano; **~ à queue** grand piano.

pianoter [pjanɔte] *vi* to tinkle away (at the piano); (*tapoter*): **~ sur** to drum one's fingers on.

piaule [pjol] *nf* (*fam*) pad.

piauler [pjole] *vi* (*enfant*) to whimper; (*oiseau*) to cheep.

PIB *sigle m* (= *produit intérieur brut*) GDP.

pic [pik] *nm* (*instrument*) pick(axe); (*montagne*) peak; (*ZOOL*) woodpecker; **à ~** *adv* vertically; (*fig*) just at the right time; **couler à ~** (*bateau*) to go straight down; **~ à glace** ice pick.

picard, e [pikaʀ, -aʀd(ə)] *adj of ou* from Picardy.

Picardie [pikaʀdi] *nf*: **la ~** Picardy.

picaresque [pikaʀɛsk(ə)] *adj* picaresque.

piccolo [pikɔlo] *nm* piccolo.

pichenette [piʃnɛt] *nf* flick.

pichet [piʃɛ] *nm* jug.

pickpocket [pikpɔkɛt] *nm* pickpocket.

pick-up [pikœp] *nm inv* record player.

picorer [pikɔʀe] *vt* to peck.

picot [piko] *nm* sprocket; **entraînement par roue à ~s** sprocket feed.

picotement [pikɔtmɑ̃] *nm* smarting *no pl*, prickling *no pl*.

picoter [pikɔte] *vt* (*suj: oiseau*) to peck ♦ *vi* (*irriter*) to smart, prickle.

pictural, e, aux [piktyʀal, -o] *adj* pictorial.

pie [pi] *nf* magpie; (*fig*) chatterbox ♦ *adj inv*: **cheval ~** piebald; **vache ~** black and white cow.

pièce [pjɛs] *nf* (*d'un logement*) room; (*THÉÂT*) play; (*de mécanisme, machine*) part; (*de monnaie*) coin; (*COUTURE*) patch; (*document*) document; (*de drap, fragment, d'une collection*) piece; (*de bétail*) head; **mettre en ~s** to smash to pieces; **dix francs ~** ten francs each; **vendre à la ~** to sell separately *ou* individually; **travailler/payer à la ~** to do piecework/pay piece rate; **de toutes ~s**: **c'est inventé de toutes ~s** it's a complete fabrication; **un maillot une ~** a one-piece swimsuit; **un deux-~s cuisine** a two-room(ed) flat (*BRIT*) *ou* apartment (*US*) with kitchen; **tout d'une ~** (*personne: franc*) blunt; (*: sans souplesse*) inflexible; **~ à conviction** exhibit; **~ d'eau** ornamental lake *ou* pond; **~ d'identité**: **avez-vous une ~ d'identité?** have you got any (means of) identification?; **~ montée** tiered cake; **~ de rechange** spare (part); **~ de résistance** pièce de résistance; (*plat*) main dish; **~s détachées** spares, (spare) parts; **en ~s détachées** (*à monter*) in kit form; **~s justificatives** supporting documents.

pied [pje] *nm* foot (*pl* feet); (*de verre*) stem; (*de table*) leg; (*de lampe*) base; (*plante*) plant; **~s**

nus barefoot; **à ~ on** foot; **à ~ sec** without getting one's feet wet; **à ~ d'œuvre** ready to start (work); **au ~ de la lettre** literally; **au ~ levé** at a moment's notice; **de ~ en cap** from head to foot; **en ~** (*portrait*) full-length; **avoir ~** to be able to touch the bottom, not to be out of one's depth; **avoir le ~ marin** to be a good sailor; **perdre ~** to lose one's footing; (*fig*) to get out of one's depth; **sur ~** (*AGR*) on the stalk, uncut; (*debout, rétabli*) up and about; **mettre sur ~** (*entreprise*) to set up; **mettre à ~** to suspend; to lay off; **mettre qn au ~ du mur** to get sb with his (*ou* her) back to the wall; **sur le ~ de guerre** ready for action; **sur un ~ d'égalité** on an equal footing; **sur ~ d'intervention** on stand-by; **faire du ~ à qn** (*prévenir*) to give sb a (warning) kick; (*galamment*) to play footsie with sb; **mettre les ~s quelque part** to set foot somewhere; **faire des ~s et des mains** (*fig*) to move heaven and earth, pull out all the stops; **c'est le ~!** (*fam*) it's terrific!; **se lever du bon ~/du ~ gauche** to get out of bed on the right/wrong side; **~ de lit** footboard; **~ de nez: faire un ~ de nez à** to thumb one's nose at; **~ de vigne** vine.

pied-à-terre [pjetatɛʀ] *nm inv* pied-à-terre.

pied-bot, *pl* **pieds-bots** [pjebo] *nm* person with a club foot.

pied-de-biche, *pl* **pieds-de-biche** [pjedbiʃ] *nm* claw; (*COUTURE*) presser foot.

pied-de-poule [pjedpul] *adj inv* hound's-tooth.

piédestal, aux [pjedɛstal, -o] *nm* pedestal.

pied-noir, *pl* **pieds-noirs** [pjenwaʀ] *nm* Algerian-born Frenchman.

piège [pjɛʒ] *nm* trap; **prendre au ~** to trap.

piéger [pjeʒe] *vt* (*animal, fig*) to trap; (*avec une bombe*) to booby-trap; **lettre/voiture piégée** letter-/car-bomb.

pierraille [pjɛʀaj] *nf* loose stones *pl*.

pierre [pjɛʀ] *nf* stone; **première ~** (*d'un édifice*) foundation stone; **mur de ~s sèches** drystone wall; **faire d'une ~ deux coups** to kill two birds with one stone; **~ à briquet** flint; **~ fine** semiprecious stone; **~ ponce** pumice stone; **~ de taille** freestone *no pl*; **~ tombale** tombstone, gravestone; **~ de touche** touchstone.

pierreries [pjɛʀʀi] *nfpl* gems, precious stones.

pierreux, euse [pjɛʀø, -øz] *adj* stony.

piété [pjete] *nf* piety.

piétinement [pjetinmɑ̃] *nm* stamping *no pl*.

piétiner [pjetine] *vi* (*trépigner*) to stamp (one's foot); (*marquer le pas*) to stand about; (*fig*) to be at a standstill ♦ *vt* to trample on.

piéton, ne [pjetɔ̃, -ɔn] *nm/f* pedestrian ♦ *adj* pedestrian *cpd*.

piétonnier, ière [pjetɔnje, -jɛʀ] *adj* pedestrian *cpd*.

piètre [pjɛtʀ(ə)] *adj* poor, mediocre.

pieu, x [pjø] *nm* (*piquet*) post; (*pointu*) stake; (*fam: lit*) bed.

pieusement [pjøzmɑ̃] *adv* piously.

pieuvre [pjœvʀ(ə)] *nf* octopus.

pieux, euse [pjø, -øz] *adj* pious.

pif [pif] *nm* (*fam*) conk (*BRIT*), beak; **au ~ = au pifomètre**.

piffer [pife] *vt* (*fam*): **je ne peux pas le ~** I can't stand him.

pifomètre [pifɔmɛtʀ(ə)] *nm* (*fam*): **choisir** *etc* **au ~** to follow one's nose when choosing *etc*.

pige [piʒ] *nf* piecework rate.

pigeon [piʒɔ̃] *nm* pigeon; **~ voyageur** homing pigeon.

pigeonnant, e [piʒɔnɑ̃, -ɑ̃t] *adj* full, well-developed.

pigeonneau, x [piʒɔno] *nm* young pigeon.

pigeonnier [piʒɔnje] *nm* pigeon loft, dovecot(e).

piger [piʒe] *vi* (*fam*) to get it ♦ *vt* (*fam*) to get, understand.

pigiste [piʒist(ə)] *nm/f* (*typographe*) typesetter on piecework; (*journaliste*) freelance journalist (*paid by the line*).

pigment [pigmɑ̃] *nm* pigment.

pignon [piɲɔ̃] *nm* (*de mur*) gable; (*d'engrenage*) cog(wheel), gearwheel; (*graine*) pine kernel; **avoir ~ sur rue** (*fig*) to have a prosperous business.

pile [pil] *nf* (*tas, pilier*) pile; (*ÉLEC*) battery ♦ *adj*: **le côté ~ tails** ♦ *adv* (*net, brusquement*) dead; (*à temps, à point nommé*) just at the right time; **à deux heures ~** at two on the dot; **jouer à ~ ou face** to toss up (for it); **~ ou face?** heads or tails?

piler [pile] *vt* to crush, pound.

pileux, euse [pilø, -øz] *adj*: **système ~** (body) hair.

pilier [pilje] *nm* (*colonne, support*) pillar; (*personne*) mainstay; (*RUGBY*) prop (forward).

pillage [pijaʒ] *nm* pillaging, plundering, looting.

pillard, e [pijaʀ, -aʀd(ə)] *nm/f* looter; plunderer.

piller [pije] *vt* to pillage, plunder, loot.

pilleur, euse [pijœʀ, -øz] *nm/f* looter.

pilon [pilɔ̃] *nm* (*instrument*) pestle; (*de volaille*) drumstick; **mettre un livre au ~** to pulp a book.

pilonner [pilɔne] *vt* to pound.

pilori [pilɔʀi] *nm*: **mettre** *ou* **clouer au ~** to pillory.

pilotage [pilɔtaʒ] *nm* piloting; flying; **~ automatique** automatic piloting; **~ sans visibilité** blind flying.

pilote [pilɔt] *nm* pilot; (*de char, voiture*) driver ♦ *adj* pilot *cpd*; **usine/ferme ~** experimental factory/farm; **~ de chasse/d'essai/de ligne** fighter/test/airline pilot; **~ de course** racing driver.

piloter [pilɔte] *vt* (*navire*) to pilot; (*avion*) to fly; (*automobile*) to drive; (*fig*): **~ qn** to guide sb round; **piloté par menu** (*INFORM*) menu-driven.

pilotis [pilɔti] *nm* pile; stilt.

pilule [pilyl] *nf* pill; **prendre la** ~ to be on the pill; ~ **du lendemain** morning-after pill.

pimbêche [pɛ̃bɛʃ] *nf (péj)* stuck-up girl.

piment [pimã] *nm (BOT)* pepper, capsicum; *(fig)* spice, piquancy; ~ **rouge** *(CULIN)* chilli.

pimenté, e [pimãte] *adj* hot and spicy.

pimenter [pimãte] *vt (plat)* to season (with peppers *ou* chillis); *(fig)* to add *ou* give spice to.

pimpant, e [pɛ̃pã, -ãt] *adj* spruce.

pin [pɛ̃] *nm* pine (tree); *(bois)* pine(wood).

pinacle [pinakl(ə)] *nm*: **porter qn au** ~ *(fig)* to praise sb to the skies.

pinard [pinaʀ] *nm (fam)* (cheap) wine, plonk *(BRIT)*.

pince [pɛ̃s] *nf (outil)* pliers *pl*; *(de homard, crabe)* pincer, claw; *(COUTURE)* dart; ~ **à sucre/glace** sugar/ice tongs *pl*; ~ **à épiler** tweezers *pl*; ~ **à linge** clothes peg *(BRIT)* ou pin *(US)*; ~ **universelle** (universal) pliers *pl*; ~**s de cycliste** bicycle clips.

pincé, e [pɛ̃se] *adj (air)* stiff; *(mince: bouche)* pinched ♦ *nf*: **une** ~**e de** a pinch of.

pinceau, x [pɛ̃so] *nm* (paint)brush.

pincement [pɛ̃smã] *nm*: ~ **au cœur** twinge of regret.

pince-monseigneur, *pl* **pinces-monseigneur** [pɛ̃smɔ̃sɛɲœʀ] *nf* crowbar.

pince-nez [pɛ̃sne] *nm inv* pince-nez.

pincer [pɛ̃se] *vt* to pinch; *(MUS: cordes)* to pluck; *(COUTURE)* to dart, put darts in; *(fam)* to nab; **se** ~ **le doigt** to squeeze *ou* nip one's finger; **se** ~ **le nez** to hold one's nose.

pince-sans-rire [pɛ̃ssɑ̃ʀiʀ] *adj inv* deadpan.

pincettes [pɛ̃sɛt] *nfpl* tweezers; *(pour le feu)* (fire) tongs.

pinçon [pɛ̃sɔ̃] *nm* pinch mark.

pinède [pinɛd] *nf* pinewood, pine forest.

pingouin [pɛ̃gwɛ̃] *nm* penguin.

ping-pong [piŋpɔ̃g] *nm* table tennis.

pingre [pɛ̃gʀ(ə)] *adj* niggardly.

pinson [pɛ̃sɔ̃] *nm* chaffinch.

pintade [pɛ̃tad] *nf* guinea-fowl.

pin up [pinœp] *nf inv* pin-up (girl).

pioche [pjɔʃ] *nf* pickaxe.

piocher [pjɔʃe] *vt* to dig up (with a pickaxe); *(fam)* to swot *(BRIT)* ou grind *(US)* at; ~ **dans** to dig into.

piolet [pjɔlɛ] *nm* ice axe.

pion, ne [pjɔ̃, pjɔn] *nm/f (SCOL: péj)* student paid to supervise schoolchildren ♦ *nm (ÉCHECS)* pawn; *(DAMES)* piece, draught *(BRIT)*, checker *(US)*.

pionnier [pjɔnje] *nm* pioneer.

pipe [pip] *nf* pipe; **fumer la** *ou* **une** ~ to smoke a pipe; ~ **de bruyère** briar pipe.

pipeau, x [pipo] *nm* (reed-)pipe.

pipe-line [piplin] *nm* pipeline.

piper [pipe] *vt (dé)* to load; *(carte)* to mark; **sans** ~ **mot** *(fam)* without a squeak; **les dés** **sont pipés** *(fig)* the dice are loaded.

pipette [pipɛt] *nf* pipette.

pipi [pipi] *nm (fam)*: **faire** ~ to have a wee.

piquant, e [pikã, -ãt] *adj (barbe, rosier etc)* prickly; *(saveur, sauce)* hot, pungent; *(fig: description, style)* racy; *(: mordant, caustique)* biting ♦ *nm (épine)* thorn, prickle; *(de hérisson)* quill, spine; *(fig)* spiciness, spice.

pique [pik] *nf (arme)* pike; *(fig)*: **envoyer** *ou* **lancer des** ~**s à qn** to make cutting remarks to sb ♦ *nm (CARTES: couleur)* spades *pl*; *(: carte)* spade.

piqué, e [pike] *adj (COUTURE)* (machine-) stitched; quilted; *(livre, glace)* mildewed; *(vin)* sour; *(MUS: note)* staccato; *(fam: personne)* nuts ♦ *nm (AVIAT)* dive; *(TEXTILE)* piqué.

pique-assiette [pikasjɛt] *nm/f inv (péj)* scrounger, sponger.

pique-fleurs [pikflœʀ] *nm inv* flower holder.

pique-nique [piknik] *nm* picnic.

pique-niquer [piknike] *vi* to (have a) picnic.

pique-niqueur, euse [piknikœʀ, -øz] *nm/f* picnicker.

piquer [pike] *vt (percer)* to prick; *(planter)*: ~ **qch dans** to stick sth into; *(fixer)*: ~ **qch à** *ou* **sur** to pin sth onto; *(MÉD)* to give an injection to; *(: animal blessé etc)* to put to sleep; *(suj: insecte, fumée, ortie)* to sting; *(: poivre)* to burn; *(: froid)* to bite; *(COUTURE)* to machine (stitch); *(intérêt etc)* to arouse; *(fam: prendre)* to pick up; *(: voler)* to pinch; *(: arrêter)* to nab ♦ *vi (oiseau, avion)* to go into a dive; *(saveur)* to be pungent; *(sauce)* to be sour; **se** ~ *(avec une aiguille)* to prick o.s.; *(se faire une piqûre)* to inject o.s.; *(se vexer)* to get annoyed; **se** ~ **de faire** to pride o.s. on doing; ~ **sur** to swoop down on; to head straight for; ~ **du nez** *(avion)* to go into a nose-dive; ~ **une tête** *(plonger)* to dive headfirst; ~ **un galop/un cent mètres** to break into a gallop/put on a sprint; ~ **une crise** to throw a fit; ~ **au vif** *(fig)* to sting.

piquet [pikɛ] *nm (pieu)* post, stake; *(de tente)* peg; **mettre un élève au** ~ to make a pupil stand in the corner; ~ **de grève** (strike) picket; ~ **d'incendie** fire-fighting squad.

piqueté, e [pikte] *adj*: ~ **de** dotted with.

piquette [pikɛt] *nf (fam)* cheap wine, plonk *(BRIT)*.

piqûre [pikyʀ] *nf (d'épingle)* prick; *(d'ortie)* sting; *(de moustique)* bite; *(MÉD)* injection, shot *(US)*; *(COUTURE)* (straight) stitch; straight stitching; *(de ver)* hole; *(tache)* (spot of) mildew; **faire une** ~ **à qn** to give sb an injection.

piranha [piʀana] *nm* piranha.

piratage [piʀataʒ] *nm* piracy.

pirate [piʀat] *adj* pirate *cpd* ♦ *nm* pirate; *(fig: escroc)* crook, shark; ~ **de l'air** hijacker.

pirater [piʀate] *vt* to pirate.

piraterie [piʀatʀi] *nf* (act of) piracy; ~

aérienne hijacking.
pire [piR] *adj* (*comparatif*) worse; (*superlatif*): **le (la)** ~ ... the worst ... ♦ *nm:* **le** ~ **(de)** the worst (of).
Pirée [piRe] *n* Piraeus.
pirogue [piRɔg] *nf* dugout (canoe).
pirouette [piRwɛt] *nf* pirouette; (*fig: volte-face*) about-turn.
pis [pi] *nm* (*de vache*) udder; (*pire*): **le** ~ the worst ♦ *adj, adv* worse; **qui** ~ **est** what is worse; **au** ~ **aller** if the worst comes to the worst, at worst.
pis-aller [pizale] *nm inv* stopgap.
pisciculture [pisikyltyR] *nf* fish farming.
piscine [pisin] *nf* (swimming) pool; ~ **couverte** indoor (swimming) pool.
Pise [piz] *n* Pisa.
pissenlit [pisɑ̃li] *nm* dandelion.
pisser [pise] *vi* (*fam!*) to pee.
pissotière [pisɔtjɛR] *nf* (*fam*) public urinal.
pistache [pistaʃ] *nf* pistachio (nut).
pistard [pistaR] *nm* (*CYCLISME*) track cyclist.
piste [pist(ə)] *nf* (*d'un animal, sentier*) track, trail; (*indice*) lead; (*de stade, de magnéto-phone, INFORM*) track; (*de cirque*) ring; (*de danse*) floor; (*de patinage*) rink; (*de ski*) run; (*AVIAT*) runway; ~ **cavalière** bridle path; ~ **cyclable** cycle track, bikeway (*US*); ~ **sonore** sound track.
pister [piste] *vt* to track, trail.
pisteur [pistœR] *nm* (*SKI*) member of the ski patrol.
pistil [pistil] *nm* pistil.
pistolet [pistɔlɛ] *nm* (*arme*) pistol, gun; (*à peinture*) spray gun; ~ **à bouchon/air comprimé** popgun/airgun; ~ **à eau** water pistol.
pistolet-mitrailleur, *pl* **pistolets-mitrailleurs** [pistɔlɛmitRajœR] *nm* sub-machine gun.
piston [pistɔ̃] *nm* (*TECH*) piston; (*MUS*) valve; (*fig: appui*) string-pulling.
pistonner [pistɔne] *vt* (*candidat*) to pull strings for.
pitance [pitɑ̃s] *nf* (*péj*) (means of) sustenance.
piteusement [pitøzmɑ̃] *adv* (*échouer*) miserably.
piteux, euse [pitø, -øz] *adj* pitiful, sorry (*avant le nom*); **en** ~ **état** in a sorry state.
pitié [pitje] *nf* pity; **sans** ~ *adj* pitiless, merciless; **faire** ~ to inspire pity; **il me fait** ~ I pity him, I feel sorry for him; **avoir** ~ **de** (*compassion*) to pity, feel sorry for; (*merci*) to have pity ou mercy on; **par** ~! for pity's sake!
piton [pitɔ̃] *nm* (*clou*) peg, bolt; ~ **rocheux** rocky outcrop.
pitoyable [pitwajabl(ə)] *adj* pitiful.
pitre [pitR(ə)] *nm* clown.
pitrerie [pitRəRi] *nf* tomfoolery no pl.
pittoresque [pitɔRɛsk(ə)] *adj* picturesque; (*expression, détail*) colourful (*BRIT*), colorful (*US*).

pivert [pivɛR] *nm* green woodpecker.
pivoine [pivwan] *nf* peony.
pivot [pivo] *nm* pivot; (*d'une dent*) post.
pivoter [pivɔte] *vi* (*fauteuil*) to swivel; (*porte*) to revolve; ~ **sur ses talons** to swing round.
pixel [piksɛl] *nm* pixel.
pizza [pidza] *nf* pizza.
PJ *sigle f* = **police judiciaire** ♦ *sigle fpl* (= *pièces jointes*) encl.
PL *sigle m* (*AUTO*) = **poids lourd**.
Pl. *abr* = **place**.
placage [plakaʒ] *nm* (*bois*) veneer.
placard [plakaR] *nm* (*armoire*) cupboard; (*affiche*) poster, notice; (*TYPO*) galley; ~ **publicitaire** display advertisement.
placarder [plakaRde] *vt* (*affiche*) to put up; (*mur*) to stick posters on.
place [plas] *nf* (*emplacement, situation, classement*) place; (*de ville, village*) square; (*ÉCON*): ~ **financière/boursière** money/stock market; (*espace libre*) room, space; (*de parking*) space; (*siège: de train, cinéma, voiture*) seat; (*prix: au cinéma etc*) price; (*: dans un bus, taxi*) fare; (*emploi*) job; **en** ~ (*mettre*) in its place; **de** ~ **en** ~, **par** ~s here and there, in places; **sur** ~ on the spot; **faire** ~ **à** to give way to; **faire de la** ~ **à** to make room for; **ça prend de la** ~ it takes up a lot of room ou space; **prendre** ~ to take one's place; **remettre qn à sa** ~ to put sb in his (ou her) place; **ne pas rester** ou **tenir en** ~ to be always on the go; **à la** ~ **de** in place of, instead of; **une quatre** ~**s** (*AUTO*) a four-seater; **il y a 20** ~**s assises/debout** there are 20 seats/there is standing room for 20; ~ **forte** fortified town; ~ **d'honneur** place (ou seat) of honour (*BRIT*) ou honor (*US*).
placé, e [plase] *adj* (*HIPPISME*) placed; **haut** ~ (*fig*) high-ranking; **être bien/mal** ~ to be well/badly placed; (*spectateur*) to have a good/bad seat; **être bien/mal** ~ **pour faire** to be in/not to be in a position to do.
placebo [plasebo] *nm* placebo.
placement [plasmɑ̃] *nm* placing; (*FINANCE*) investment; **agence** ou **bureau de** ~ employment agency.
placenta [plasɑ̃ta] *nm* placenta.
placer [plase] *vt* to place, put; (*convive, spectateur*) to seat; (*capital, argent*) to place, invest; (*dans la conversation*) to put ou get in; ~ **qn chez** to get sb a job at (ou with); **se** ~ **au premier rang** to go and stand (ou sit) in the first row.
placide [plasid] *adj* placid.
placidité [plasidite] *nf* placidity.
placier, ière [plasje, -jɛR] *nm/f* commercial rep(resentative), salesman/woman.
Placoplâtre [plakoplatR] *nm* ® plasterboard.
plafond [plafɔ̃] *nm* ceiling.
plafonner [plafɔne] *vt* (*pièce*) to put a ceiling (up) in ♦ *vi* to reach one's (ou a) ceiling.
plafonnier [plafɔnje] *nm* ceiling light; (*AUTO*)

interior light.

plage [plaʒ] *nf* beach; (*station*) (seaside) resort; (*fig*) band, bracket; (*de disque*) track, band; ~ **arrière** (*AUTO*) parcel *ou* back shelf.

plagiaire [plaʒjɛʀ] *nm/f* plagiarist.

plagiat [plaʒja] *nm* plagiarism.

plagier [plaʒje] *vt* to plagiarize.

plagiste [plaʒist(ə)] *nm/f* beach attendant.

plaid [plɛd] *nm* (tartan) car rug, lap robe (*US*).

plaidant, e [plɛdɑ̃, -ɑ̃t] *adj* litigant.

plaider [plede] *vi* (*avocat*) to plead; (*plaignant*) to go to court, litigate ♦ *vt* to plead; ~ **pour** (*fig*) to speak for.

plaideur, euse [plɛdœʀ, -øz] *nm/f* litigant.

plaidoirie [plɛdwaʀi] *nf* (*JUR*) speech for the defence (*BRIT*) *ou* defense (*US*).

plaidoyer [plɛdwaje] *nm* (*JUR*) speech for the defence (*BRIT*) *ou* defense (*US*); (*fig*) plea.

plaie [plɛ] *nf* wound.

plaignant, e [plɛɲɑ̃, -ɑ̃t] *vb voir* **plaindre** ♦ *nm/f* plaintiff.

plaindre [plɛ̃dʀ(ə)] *vt* to pity, feel sorry for; **se** ~ *vi* (*gémir*) to moan; (*protester, rouspéter*): **se** ~ **(à qn) (de)** to complain (to sb) (about); (*souffrir*): **se** ~ **de** to complain of.

plaine [plɛn] *nf* plain.

plain-pied [plɛ̃pje]: **de** ~ *adv* at street-level; (*fig*) straight; **de** ~ **(avec)** on the same level (as).

plaint, e [plɛ̃, -ɛ̃t] *pp de* **plaindre** ♦ *nf* (*gémissement*) moan, groan; (*doléance*) complaint; **porter** ~**e** to lodge a complaint.

plaintif, ive [plɛ̃tif, -iv] *adj* plaintive.

plaire [plɛʀ] *vi* to be a success, be successful; to please; ~ **à**: **cela me plaît** I like it; **essayer de** ~ **à qn** (*en étant serviable etc*) to try and please sb; **elle plaît aux hommes** she's a success with men, men like her; **se** ~ **quelque part** to like being somewhere, like it somewhere; **se** ~ **à faire** to take pleasure in doing; **ce qu'il vous plaira** what(ever) you like *ou* wish; **s'il vous plaît** please.

plaisamment [plɛzamɑ̃] *adv* pleasantly.

plaisance [plɛzɑ̃s] *nf* (*aussi:* **navigation de** ~) (pleasure) sailing, yachting.

plaisancier [plɛzɑ̃sje] *nm* amateur sailor, yachting enthusiast.

plaisant, e [plɛzɑ̃, -ɑ̃t] *adj* pleasant; (*histoire, anecdote*) amusing.

plaisanter [plɛzɑ̃te] *vi* to joke ♦ *vt* (*personne*) to tease, make fun of; **pour** ~ for a joke; **on ne plaisante pas avec cela** that's no joking matter; **tu plaisantes!** you're joking *ou* kidding!

plaisanterie [plɛzɑ̃tʀi] *nf* joke; joking *no pl*.

plaisantin [plɛzɑ̃tɛ̃] *nm* joker; (*fumiste*) fly-by-night.

plaise [plɛz] *etc vb voir* **plaire**.

plaisir [pleziʀ] *nm* pleasure; **faire** ~ **à qn** (*délibérément*) to be nice to sb, please sb; (*suj: cadeau, nouvelle etc*): **ceci me fait** ~ I'm delighted *ou* very pleased with this; **prendre** ~

à/à faire to take pleasure in/in doing; **j'ai le** ~ **de** ... it is with great pleasure that I ...; **M. et Mme X ont le** ~ **de vous faire part de** ... M. and Mme X are pleased to announce ...; **se faire un** ~ **de faire qch** to be (only too) pleased to do sth; **faites-moi le** ~ **de** ... would you mind ..., would you be kind enough to ...; **à** ~ freely; for the sake of it; **au** ~ **(de vous revoir)** (I hope to) see you again; **pour le** *ou* **pour son** *ou* **par** ~ for pleasure.

plaît [plɛ] *vb voir* **plaire.**

plan, e [plɑ̃, -an] *adj* flat ♦ *nm* plan; (*GÉOM*) plane; (*fig*) level, plane; (*CINÉ*) shot; **au premier/second** ~ in the foreground/middle distance; **à l'arrière** ~ in the background; **mettre qch au premier** ~ (*fig*) to consider sth to be of primary importance; **sur le** ~ **sexuel** sexually, as far as sex is concerned; **laisser/rester en** ~ to abandon/be abandoned; ~ **d'action** plan of action; ~ **directeur** (*ÉCON*) master plan; ~ **d'eau** lake; pond; ~ **de travail** work-top, work surface; ~ **de vol** (*AVIAT*) flight plan.

planche [plɑ̃ʃ] *nf* (*pièce de bois*) plank, (wooden) board; (*illustration*) plate; (*de salades, radis, poireaux*) bed; (*d'un plongeoir*) (diving) board; **les** ~**s** (*THÉÂT*) the boards; **en** ~**s** *adj* wooden; **faire la** ~ (*dans l'eau*) to float on one's back; **avoir du pain sur la** ~ to have one's work cut out; ~ **à découper** chopping board; ~ **à dessin** drawing board; ~ **à pain** breadboard; ~ **à repasser** ironing board; ~ **(à roulettes)** (*planche*) skateboard; (*sport*) skateboarding; ~ **de salut** (*fig*) sheet anchor; ~ **à voile** (*planche*) windsurfer, sailboard; (*sport*) windsurfing.

plancher [plɑ̃ʃe] *nm* floor; (*planches*) floorboards *pl*; (*fig*) minimum level ♦ *vi* to work hard.

planchiste [plɑ̃ʃist(ə)] *nm/f* windsurfer.

plancton [plɑ̃ktɔ̃] *nm* plankton.

planer [plane] *vi* (*oiseau, avion*) to glide; (*fumée, vapeur*) to float, hover; (*drogué*) to be (on a) high; ~ **sur** (*fig*) to hang over; to hover above.

planétaire [planetɛʀ] *adj* planetary.

planétarium [planetaʀjɔm] *nm* planetarium.

planète [planɛt] *nf* planet.

planeur [planœʀ] *nm* glider.

planification [planifikasjɔ̃] *nf* (economic) planning.

planifier [planifje] *vt* to plan.

planisphère [planisfɛʀ] *nm* planisphere.

planning [planiŋ] *nm* programme (*BRIT*), program (*US*), schedule; ~ **familial** family planning.

planque [plɑ̃k] *nf* (*fam: combine, filon*) cushy (*BRIT*) *ou* easy number; (: *cachette*) hideout.

planquer [plɑ̃ke] *vt* (*fam*) to hide (away), stash away; **se** ~ to hide.

plant [plɑ̃] *nm* seedling, young plant.

plantaire [plɑ̃tɛʀ] *adj voir* **voûte.**

plantation [plɑ̃tasjɔ̃] *nf* planting; (*de fleurs, légumes*) bed; (*exploitation*) plantation.

plante [plɑ̃t] *nf* plant; ~ **d'appartement** house *ou* pot plant; ~ **du pied** sole (of the foot); ~ **verte** house plant.

planter [plɑ̃te] *vt* (*plante*) to plant; (*enfoncer*) to hammer *ou* drive in; (*tente*) to put up, pitch; (*drapeau, échelle, décors*) to put up; (*fam: mettre*) to dump; (: *abandonner*): ~ **là** to ditch; **se** ~ *vi* (*fam: se tromper*) to get it wrong; ~ **qch dans** to hammer *ou* drive sth into; to stick sth into; **se** ~ **dans** to sink into; to get stuck in; **se** ~ **devant** to plant o.s. in front of.

planteur [plɑ̃tœʀ] *nm* planter.

planton [plɑ̃tɔ̃] *nm* orderly.

plantureux, euse [plɑ̃tyʀø, -øz] *adj* (*repas*) copious, lavish; (*femme*) buxom.

plaquage [plaka3] *nm* (*RUGBY*) tackle.

plaque [plak] *nf* plate; (*de verre*) sheet; (*de verglas, d'eczéma*) patch; (*dentaire*) plaque; (*avec inscription*) plaque; ~ (**minéralogique** *ou* **de police** *ou* **d'immatriculation**) number (*BRIT*) *ou* license (*US*) plate; ~ **de beurre** slab of butter; ~ **chauffante** hotplate; ~ **de chocolat** bar of chocolate; ~ **de cuisson** hob; ~ **d'identité** identity disc; ~ **tournante** (*fig*) centre (*BRIT*), center (*US*).

plaqué, e [plake] *adj*: ~ **or/argent** gold-/silver-plated ♦ *nm*: ~ **or/argent** gold/silver plate; ~ **acajou** with a mahogany veneer.

plaquer [plake] *vt* (*bijou*) to plate; (*bois*) to veneer; (*aplatir*): ~ **qch sur/contre** to make sth stick *ou* cling to; (*RUGBY*) to bring down; (*fam: laisser tomber*) to drop, ditch; **se** ~ **contre** to flatten o.s. against; ~ **qn contre** to pin sb to.

plaquette [plakɛt] *nf* tablet; (*de chocolat*) bar; (*de beurre*) slab, packet; (*livre*) small volume; (*MÉD: de pilules, gélules*) pack, packet; (*INFORM*) circuit board; ~ **de frein** (*AUTO*) brake pad.

plasma [plasma] *nm* plasma.

plastic [plastik] *nm* plastic explosive.

plastifié, e [plastifje] *adj* plastic-coated.

plastifier [plastifje] *vt* (*document, photo*) to laminate.

plastiquage [plastika3] *nm* bombing, bomb attack.

plastique [plastik] *adj* plastic ♦ *nm* plastic ♦ *nf* plastic arts *pl*; (*d'une statue*) modelling.

plastiquer [plastike] *vt* to blow up.

plastiqueur [plastikœʀ] *nm* terrorist (*planting a plastic bomb*).

plastron [plastʀɔ̃] *nm* shirt front.

plastronner [plastʀɔne] *vi* to swagger.

plat, e [pla, -at] *adj* flat; (*fade: vin*) flat-tasting, insipid; (*personne, livre*) dull ♦ *nm* (*récipient, CULIN*) dish; (*d'un repas*): **le premier** ~ the first course; (*partie plate*): **le** ~ **de la main** the flat of the hand; (: *d'une route*) flat (part); **à** ~ **ventre** *adv* face down; (*tomber*) flat on one's

face; **à** ~ *adj* (*pneu, batterie*) flat; (*fam: fatigué*) dead beat, tired out; ~ **cuisiné** pre-cooked meal (*ou* dish); ~ **du jour** dish of the day; ~ **de résistance** main course; ~**s préparés** convenience food(s).

platane [platan] *nm* plane tree.

plateau, x [plato] *nm* (*support*) tray; (*d'une table*) top; (*d'une balance*) pan; (*GÉO*) plateau; (*de tourne-disques*) turntable; (*CINÉ*) set; (*TV*): **nous avons 2 journalistes sur le** ~ **ce soir** we have 2 journalists with us tonight; ~ **à fromages** cheeseboard.

plateau-repas, *pl* **plateaux-repas** [platoʀəpa] *nm* tray meal, TV dinner (*US*).

plate-bande, *pl* **plates-bandes** [platbɑ̃d] *nf* flower bed.

platée [plate] *nf* dish(ful).

plate-forme, *pl* **plates-formes** [platfɔrm(ə)] *nf* platform; ~ **de forage/pétrolière** drilling/oil rig.

platine [platin] *nm* platinum ♦ *nf* (*d'un tourne-disque*) turntable; ~ **disque/cassette** record/cassette deck; ~ **laser** *ou* **compact-disc** compact disc (player).

platitude [platityd] *nf* platitude.

platonique [platɔnik] *adj* platonic.

plâtras [platʀa] *nm* rubble *no pl*.

plâtre [platʀ(ə)] *nm* (*matériau*) plaster; (*statue*) plaster statue; (*MÉD*) (plaster) cast; ~**s** *nmpl* plasterwork *sg*; **avoir un bras dans le** ~ to have an arm in plaster.

plâtrer [platʀe] *vt* to plaster; (*MÉD*) to set *ou* put in a plaster (cast).

plâtrier [platʀije] *nm* plasterer.

plausible [plozibl(ə)] *adj* plausible.

play-back [plɛbak] *nm* miming.

play-boy [plɛbɔj] *nm* playboy.

plébiscite [plebisit] *nm* plebiscite.

plébisciter [plebisite] *vt* (*approuver*) to give overwhelming support to; (*élire*) to elect by an overwhelming majority.

plectre [plɛktʀ(ə)] *nm* plectrum.

plein, e [plɛ̃, -ɛn] *adj* full; (*porte, roue*) solid; (*chienne, jument*) big (with young) ♦ *nm*: **faire le** ~ (**d'essence**) to fill up (with petrol (*BRIT*) *ou* gas (*US*)) ♦ *prép*: **avoir de l'argent** ~ **les poches** to have loads of money; ~ **de** full of; **avoir les mains** ~**es** to have one's hands full; **à** ~**es mains** (*ramasser*) in handfuls; (*empoigner*) firmly; **à** ~ **régime** at maximum revs; (*fig*) at full speed; **à** ~ **temps** full-time; **en** ~ **air** in the open air; **jeux en** ~ **air** outdoor games; **en** ~**e mer** on the open sea; **en** ~ **soleil** in direct sunlight; **en** ~**e nuit/rue** in the middle of the night/street; **en** ~ **milieu** right in the middle; **en** ~ **jour** in broad daylight; **les** ~**s** the downstrokes (*in handwriting*); **faire le** ~ **des voix** to get the maximum number of votes possible; **en** ~ **sur** right on; **en avoir** ~ **le dos** (*fam*) to have had it up to here.

pleinement [plɛnmɑ̃] *adv* fully; to the full.

plein-emploi [plɛnɑ̃plwa] *nm* full employment.

plénière [plenjɛʀ] *adj f:* **assemblée ~** plenary assembly.

plénipotentiaire [plenipɔtɑ̃sjɛʀ] *nm* plenipotentiary.

plénitude [plenityd] *nf* fullness.

pléthore [pletɔʀ] *nf:* **~ de** overabundance *ou* plethora of.

pléthorique [pletɔʀik] *adj* (*classes*) overcrowded; (*documentation*) excessive.

pleurer [plœʀe] *vi* to cry; (*yeux*) to water ♦ *vt* to mourn (for); **~ sur** *vt* to lament (over), bemoan; **~ de rire** to laugh till one cries.

pleurésie [plœʀezi] *nf* pleurisy.

pleureuse [plœʀøz] *nf* professional mourner.

pleurnicher [plœʀniʃe] *vi* to snivel, whine.

pleurs [plœʀ] *nmpl:* **en ~** in tears.

pleut [plø] *vb voir* **pleuvoir**.

pleutre [pløtʀ(ə)] *adj* cowardly.

pleuvait [pløvɛ] *etc vb voir* **pleuvoir**.

pleuviner [pløvine] *vb impers* to drizzle.

pleuvoir [pløvwaʀ] *vb impers* to rain ♦ *vi* (*fig*): **~ (sur)** to shower down (upon), be showered upon; **il pleut** it's raining; **il pleut des cordes** *ou* **à verse** *ou* **à torrents** it's pouring (down), it's raining cats and dogs.

pleuvra [pløvʀa] *etc vb voir* **pleuvoir**.

Plexiglas [plɛksiglɑs] *nm* ® Plexiglas ® (*US*).

pli [pli] *nm* fold; (*de jupe*) pleat; (*de pantalon*) crease; (*aussi:* **faux ~**) crease; (*enveloppe*) envelope; (*lettre*) letter; (*CARTES*) trick; **prendre le ~ de faire** to get into the habit of doing; **ça ne fait pas un ~!** don't you worry!; **~ d'aisance** inverted pleat.

pliable [plijabl(ə)] *adj* pliable, flexible.

pliage [plijaʒ] *nm* folding; (*ART*) origami.

pliant, e [plijɑ̃, -ɑ̃t] *adj* folding ♦ *nm* folding stool, campstool.

plier [plije] *vt* to fold; (*pour ranger*) to fold up; (*table pliante*) to fold down; (*genou, bras*) to bend ♦ *vi* to bend; (*fig*) to yield; **se ~ à** to submit to; **~ bagages** (*fig*) to pack up (and go).

plinthe [plɛ̃t] *nf* skirting board.

plissé, e [plise] *adj* (*jupe, robe*) pleated; (*peau*) wrinkled; (*GÉO*) folded ♦ *nm* (*COUTURE*) pleats *pl*.

plissement [plismɑ̃] *nm* (*GÉO*) fold.

plisser [plise] *vt* (*chiffonner: papier, étoffe*) to crease; (*rider: front*) to furrow, wrinkle; (*: bouche*) to pucker; (*jupe*) to put pleats in; **se ~** *vi* (*vêtement, étoffe*) to crease.

pliure [plijyʀ] *nf* (*du bras, genou*) bend; (*d'un ourlet*) fold.

plomb [plɔ̃] *nm* (*métal*) lead; (*d'une cartouche*) (lead) shot; (*PÊCHE*) sinker; (*sceau*) (lead) seal; (*ÉLEC*) fuse; **de ~** (*soleil*) blazing; **sans ~** (*essence*) unleaded; **sommeil de ~** heavy *ou* very deep sleep; **mettre à ~** to plumb.

plombage [plɔ̃baʒ] *nm* (*de dent*) filling.

plomber [plɔ̃be] *vt* (*canne, ligne*) to weight (with lead); (*colis, wagon*) to put a lead seal on; (*TECH: mur*) to plumb; (*dent*) to fill (*BRIT*), stop (*US*); (*INFORM*) to protect.

plomberie [plɔ̃bʀi] *nf* plumbing.

plombier [plɔ̃bje] *nm* plumber.

plonge [plɔ̃ʒ] *nf:* **faire la ~** to be a washer-up (*BRIT*) *ou* dishwasher (*person*).

plongeant, e [plɔ̃ʒɑ̃, -ɑ̃t] *adj* (*vue*) from above; (*tir, décolleté*) plunging.

plongée [plɔ̃ʒe] *nf* (*SPORT*) diving *no pl*; (*: sans scaphandre*) skin diving; (*de sous-marin*) submersion, dive; **en ~** (*sous-marin*) submerged; (*prise de vue*) high angle.

plongeoir [plɔ̃ʒwaʀ] *nm* diving board.

plongeon [plɔ̃ʒɔ̃] *nm* dive.

plonger [plɔ̃ʒe] *vi* to dive ♦ *vt:* **~ qch dans** to plunge sth into; **~ dans un sommeil profond** to sink straight into a deep sleep; **~ qn dans l'embarras** to throw sb into a state of confusion.

plongeur, euse [plɔ̃ʒœʀ, -øz] *nm/f* diver; (*de café*) washer-up (*BRIT*), dishwasher (*person*).

plot [plo] *nm* (*ÉLEC*) contact.

ploutocratie [plutɔkʀasi] *nf* plutocracy.

ploutocratique [plutɔkʀatik] *adj* plutocratic.

ployer [plwaje] *vt* to bend ♦ *vi* to bend; (*plancher*) to sag.

plu [ply] *pp de* **plaire, pleuvoir**.

pluie [plɥi] *nf* rain; (*averse, ondée*): **une ~ brève** a shower; (*fig*): **~ de** shower of; **une ~ fine** fine rain; **retomber en ~** to shower down; **sous la ~** in the rain.

plumage [plymaʒ] *nm* plumage *no pl*, feathers *pl*.

plume [plym] *nf* feather; (*pour écrire*) (pen) nib; (*fig*) pen; **dessin à la ~** pen and ink drawing.

plumeau, x [plymo] *nm* feather duster.

plumer [plyme] *vt* to pluck.

plumet [plymɛ] *nm* plume.

plumier [plymje] *nm* pencil box.

plupart [plypaʀ]: **la ~** *pron* the majority, most (of them); **la ~ des** most, the majority of; **la ~ du temps/d'entre nous** most of the time/ of us; **pour la ~** *adv* for the most part, mostly.

pluralisme [plyʀalism(ə)] *nm* pluralism.

pluralité [plyʀalite] *nf* plurality.

pluridisciplinaire [plyʀidisiplinɛʀ] *adj* multidisciplinary.

pluriel [plyʀjɛl] *nm* plural; **au ~** in the plural.

plus¹ [ply] *vb voir* **plaire**.

═══════════════════ *MOT-CLÉ*

plus² [ply] *adv* **1** (*forme négative*): **ne ... ~** no more, no longer; **je n'ai ~ d'argent** I've got no more money *ou* no money left; **il ne travaille ~** he's no longer working, he doesn't work any more

2 (*comparatif*) more, ...+er; (*superlatif*): **le ~** the most, the ...+est; **~ grand/intelligent (que)** bigger/more intelligent (than); **le ~ grand/intelligent** the biggest/most intelligent; **tout au ~** at the very most

3 [plys] (*davantage*) more; **il travaille ~ (que)** he works more (than); **~ il travaille, ~ il est heureux** the more he works, the happier he is; **~ de pain** more bread; **~ de 10 personnes/3 heures/4 kilos** more than *ou* over 10 people/3 hours/4 kilos; **3 heures de ~ que** 3 hours more than; **~ de minuit** after *ou* past midnight; **de ~** what's more, moreover; **il a 3 ans de ~ que moi** he's 3 years older than me; **3 kilos en ~** 3 kilos more; **en ~ de** in addition to; **de ~ en ~** more and more; **en ~ de cela ...** what is more ...; **~ ou moins** more or less; **ni ~ ni moins** no more, no less; **sans ~** (but) no more than that, (but) that's all; **qui ~ est** what is more
♦ *prép* [plys]: **4 ~ 2** 4 plus 2.

plusieurs [plyzjœʀ] *dét, pron* several; **ils sont ~** there are several of them.

plus-que-parfait [plyskəpaʀfɛ] *nm* pluperfect, past perfect.

plus-value [plyvaly] *nf* (*d'un bien*) appreciation; (*bénéfice*) capital gain; (*budgétaire*) surplus.

plut [ply] *vb voir* **plaire, pleuvoir**.

plutonium [plytɔnjɔm] *nm* plutonium.

plutôt [plyto] *adv* rather; **je ferais ~ ceci** I'd rather *ou* sooner do this; **fais ~ comme ça** try this way instead, you'd better try this way; **~ que (de) faire** rather than *ou* instead of doing.

pluvial, e, aux [plyvjal, -o] *adj* (*eaux*) rain *cpd*.

pluvieux, euse [plyvjø, -øz] *adj* rainy, wet.

pluviosité [plyvjozite] *nf* rainfall.

PM *sigle f* = **Police militaire**.

p.m. *abr* (= *pour mémoire*) for the record.

PME *sigle fpl* = **petites et moyennes entreprises**.

PMI *sigle fpl* = **petites et moyennes industries** ♦ *sigle f* = **protection maternelle et infantile**.

PMU *sigle m* = **pari mutuel urbain**; (*café*) betting agency.

The **PMU** is a government-regulated network of horse-race betting counters run from bars displaying the PMU sign. Punters buy fixed-price tickets predicting winners or finishing positions. The traditional bet is the **tiercé**, a triple forecast, although other multiple forecasts (**quarté** etc) are becoming increasingly popular.

PNB *sigle m* (= *produit national brut*) GNP.

pneu [pnø] *nm* (*de roue*) tyre (*BRIT*), tire (*US*); (*message*) letter sent by pneumatic tube.

pneumatique [pnømatik] *adj* pneumatic; (*gonflable*) inflatable ♦ *nm* tyre (*BRIT*), tire (*US*).

pneumonie [pnømɔni] *nf* pneumonia.

PO *sigle fpl* (= *petites ondes*) MW.

po [po] *abr voir* **science**.

Pô [po] *nm*: **le ~** the Po.

p.o. *abr* (= *par ordre*) p.p. (*on letters etc*).

poche [pɔʃ] *nf* pocket; (*déformation*): **faire une/des ~(s)** to bag; (*sous les yeux*) bag, pouch; (*ZOOL*) pouch ♦ *nm* (= *livre de ~*) (pocket-size) paperback; **de ~** pocket *cpd*; **en être de sa ~** to be out of pocket; **c'est dans la ~** it's in the bag.

poché, e [pɔʃe] *adj*: **œuf ~** poached egg; **œil ~** black eye.

pocher [pɔʃe] *vt* (*CULIN*) to poach; (*ART*) to sketch ♦ *vi* (*vêtement*) to bag.

poche-revolver,   *pl*   **poches-revolver** [pɔʃʀəvɔlvɛʀ] *nf* hip pocket.

pochette [pɔʃɛt] *nf* (*de timbres*) wallet, envelope; (*d'aiguilles etc*) case; (*sac: de femme*) clutch bag, purse; (*: d'homme*) bag; (*sur veston*) breast pocket; (*mouchoir*) breast pocket handkerchief; **~ d'allumettes** book of matches; **~ de disque** record sleeve; **~ surprise** lucky bag.

pochoir [pɔʃwaʀ] *nm* (*ART: cache*) stencil; (*: tampon*) transfer.

podium [pɔdjɔm] *nm* podium (*pl* -ia).

poêle [pwal] *nm* stove ♦ *nf*: **~ (à frire)** frying pan.

poêlon [pwalɔ̃] *nm* casserole.

poème [pɔɛm] *nm* poem.

poésie [pɔezi] *nf* (*poème*) poem; (*art*): **la ~** poetry.

poète [pɔɛt] *nm* poet; (*fig*) dreamer ♦ *adj* poetic.

poétique [pɔetik] *adj* poetic.

pognon [pɔɲɔ̃] *nm* (*fam: argent*) dough.

poids [pwa] *nm* weight; (*SPORT*) shot; **vendre au ~** to sell by weight; **de ~** *adj* (*argument etc*) weighty; **prendre du ~** to put on weight; **faire le ~** (*fig*) to measure up; **~ plume/mouche/coq/moyen** (*BOXE*) feather/fly/bantam/middleweight; **~ et haltères** *nmpl* weight lifting *sg*; **~ lourd** (*BOXE*) heavyweight; (*camion: aussi*: **PL**) (big) lorry (*BRIT*), truck (*US*); (*: ADMIN*) large goods vehicle (*BRIT*), truck (*US*); **~ mort** dead weight; **~ utile** net weight.

poignant, e [pwaɲɑ̃, -ɑ̃t] *adj* poignant, harrowing.

poignard [pwaɲaʀ] *nm* dagger.

poignarder [pwaɲaʀde] *vt* to stab, knife.

poigne [pwaɲ] *nf* grip; (*fig*) firm-handedness; **à ~** firm-handed.

poignée [pwaɲe] *nf* (*de sel etc, fig*) handful; (*de couvercle, porte*) handle; **~ de main** handshake.

poignet [pwaɲɛ] *nm* (*ANAT*) wrist; (*de chemise*) cuff.

poil [pwal] *nm* (*ANAT*) hair; (*de pinceau, brosse*) bristle; (*de tapis, tissu*) strand; (*pelage*) coat; (*ensemble des poils*): **avoir du ~ sur la poitrine** to have hair(s) on one's chest, have a hairy chest; **à ~** *adj* (*fam*) starkers; **au ~** *adj* (*fam*) hunky-dory; **de tout** ~ of all kinds; **être de bon/mauvais** ~ to be in a good/bad mood; ~ **à gratter** itching powder.

poilu, e [pwaly] *adj* hairy.

poinçon [pwɛ̃sɔ̃] *nm* awl; bodkin; (*marque*) hallmark.

poinçonner [pwɛ̃sɔne] *vt* (*marchandise*) to stamp; (*bijou etc*) to hallmark; (*billet, ticket*) to clip, punch.

poinçonneuse [pwɛ̃sɔnøz] *nf* (*outil*) punch.

poindre [pwɛ̃dʀ(ə)] *vi* (*fleur*) to come up; (*aube*) to break; (*jour*) to dawn.

poing [pwɛ̃] *nm* fist; **dormir à** ~**s fermés** to sleep soundly.

point [pwɛ̃] *vb voir* **poindre ♦** *nm* (*marque, signe*) dot; (*: de ponctuation*) full stop, period (*US*); (*moment, de score etc, fig: question*) point; (*endroit*) spot; (*COUTURE, TRICOT*) stitch ♦ *adv* = **pas; ne ...** ~ not (at all); **faire le** ~ (*NAVIG*) to take a bearing; (*fig*) to take stock (of the situation); **faire le** ~ **sur** to review; **en tout** ~ in every respect; **sur le** ~ **de faire** (just) about to do; **au** ~ **que, à tel** ~ **que** so much so that; **mettre au** ~ (*mécanisme, procédé*) to develop; (*appareil-photo*) to focus; (*affaire*) to settle; (*: CULIN*) just right; (*: viande*) medium; **à** ~ (*nommé*) just at the right time; ~ **de croix/tige/chaînette** (*COUTURE*) cross/stem/chain stitch; ~ **mousse/jersey** (*TRICOT*) garter/stocking stitch; ~ **de départ/d'arrivée/d'arrêt** departure/arrival/stopping point; ~ **chaud** (*MIL, POL*) hot spot; ~ **de chute** landing place; (*fig*) stopping-off point; ~ (**de côté**) stitch (*pain*); ~ **culminant** summit; (*fig*) height, climax; ~ **d'eau** spring; water point; ~ **d'exclamation** exclamation mark; ~ **faible** weak spot; ~ **final** full stop, period (*US*); ~ **d'interrogation** question mark; ~ **mort** (*FINANCE*) break-even point; **au** ~ **mort** (*AUTO*) in neutral; (*affaire, entreprise*) at a standstill; ~ **noir** (*sur le visage*) blackhead; (*AUTO*) accident black spot; ~ **de non-retour** point of no return; ~ **de repère** landmark; (*dans le temps*) point of reference; ~ **de vente** retail outlet; ~ **de vue** viewpoint; (*fig: opinion*) point of view; **du** ~ **de vue de** from the point of view of; ~**s cardinaux** points of the compass, cardinal points; ~**s de suspension** suspension points.

pointage [pwɛ̃taʒ] *nm* ticking off; checking in.

pointe [pwɛ̃t] *nf* point; (*de la côte*) headland; (*allusion*) dig, sally; (*fig*): **une** ~ **d'ail/d'accent** a touch *ou* hint of garlic/of an accent; ~**s** *nfpl* (*DANSE*) points, point shoes; **être à la** ~ **de** (*fig*) to be in the forefront of; **faire** *ou* **pousser une** ~ **jusqu'à ...** to press on as far as ...; **sur la** ~ **des pieds** on tiptoe; **en** ~ *adv* (*tailler*) into a point ♦ *adj* pointed, tapered; **de** ~ *adj* (*technique etc*) leading; (*vitesse*) maximum, top; **heures/jours de** ~ peak hours/days; **faire du 180 en** ~ (*AUTO*) to

have a top *ou* maximum speed of 180; **faire des** ~**s** (*DANSE*) to dance on points; ~ **d'asperge** asparagus tip; ~ **de courant** surge (of current); ~ **de tension** (*INFORM*) spike; ~ **de vitesse** burst of speed.

pointer [pwɛ̃te] *vt* (*cocher*) to tick off; (*employés etc*) to check in; (*diriger: canon, longue-vue, doigt*): ~ **vers qch** to point at sth; (*MUS: note*) to dot ♦ *vi* (*employé*) to clock in; (*pousses*) to come through; (*jour*) to break; ~ **les oreilles** (*chien*) to prick up its ears.

pointeur, euse [pwɛ̃tœʀ, -øz] *nm/f* time-keeper ♦ *nf* timeclock.

pointillé [pwɛ̃tije] *nm* (*trait*) dotted line; (*ART*) stippling *no pl*.

pointilleux, euse [pwɛ̃tijø, -øz] *adj* particular, pernickety.

pointu, e [pwɛ̃ty] *adj* pointed; (*clou*) sharp; (*voix*) shrill; (*analyse*) precise.

pointure [pwɛ̃tyʀ] *nf* size.

point-virgule, *pl* **points-virgules** [pwɛ̃viʀgyl] *nm* semi-colon.

poire [pwaʀ] *nf* pear; (*fam: péj*) mug; ~ **électrique** (*pear-shaped*) switch; ~ **à injections** syringe.

poireau, x [pwaʀo] *nm* leek.

poireauter [pwaʀote] *vi* (*fam*) to hang about (waiting).

poirier [pwaʀje] *nm* pear tree; (*GYMNASTIQUE*): **faire le** ~ to do a headstand.

pois [pwa] *nm* (*BOT*) pea; (*sur une étoffe*) dot, spot; **à** ~ (*cravate etc*) spotted, polka-dot *cpd*; ~ **chiche** chickpea; ~ **de senteur** sweet pea; ~ **cassés** split peas.

poison [pwazɔ̃] *nm* poison.

poisse [pwas] *nf* rotten luck.

poisser [pwase] *vt* to make sticky.

poisseux, euse [pwasø, -øz] *adj* sticky.

poisson [pwasɔ̃] *nm* fish *gén inv*; **les P**~**s** (*signe*) Pisces, the Fish; **être des P**~**s** to be Pisces; **pêcher** *ou* **prendre du** ~ *ou* **des** ~**s** to fish; ~ **d'avril** April fool; (*blague*) April fool's day trick; ~ **rouge** goldfish.

> The traditional prank in France on April 1 involves placing a cut-out paper fish, known as a **poisson d'avril**, on the back of one's victim, without being caught.

poisson-chat, *pl* **poissons-chats** [pwasɔ̃ʃa] *nm* catfish.

poissonnerie [pwasɔnʀi] *nf* fishmonger's (*BRIT*), fish store (*US*).

poissonneux, euse [pwasɔnø, -øz] *adj* abounding in fish.

poissonnier, ière [pwasɔnje, -jɛʀ] *nm/f* fishmonger (*BRIT*), fish merchant (*US*) ♦ *nf* (*ustensile*) fish kettle.

poisson-scie, *pl* **poissons-scies** [pwasɔ̃si] *nm* sawfish.

poitevin, e [pwatvɛ̃, -in] *adj* (*région*) of *ou* from Poitou; (*ville*) of *ou* from Poitiers.

poitrail [pwatʀaj] nm (d'un cheval etc) breast.
poitrine [pwatʀin] nf (ANAT) chest; (seins) bust, bosom; (CULIN) breast; ~ **de bœuf** brisket.
poivre [pwavʀ(ə)] nm pepper; ~ **en grains/moulu** whole/ground pepper; ~ **de cayenne** cayenne (pepper); ~ **et sel** adj (cheveux) pepper-and-salt.
poivré, e [pwavʀe] adj peppery.
poivrer [pwavʀe] vt to pepper.
poivrier [pwavʀije] nm (BOT) pepper plant.
poivrière [pwavʀijɛʀ] nf pepperpot, pepper shaker (US).
poivron [pwavʀɔ̃] nm pepper, capsicum; ~ **vert/rouge** green/red pepper.
poix [pwa] nf pitch (tar).
poker [pɔkɛʀ] nm: **le** ~ poker; **partie de** ~ (fig) gamble; ~ **d'as** four aces.
polaire [pɔlɛʀ] adj polar.
polarisation [pɔlaʀizasjɔ̃] nf (PHYSIQUE, ÉLEC) polarization; (fig) focusing.
polariser [pɔlaʀize] vt to polarize; (fig: attirer) to attract; (: réunir, concentrer) to focus; **être polarisé sur** (personne) to be completely bound up with ou absorbed by.
pôle [pol] nm (GÉO, ÉLEC) pole; **le** ~ **Nord/Sud** the North/South Pole; ~ **d'attraction** (fig) centre of attraction.
polémique [pɔlemik] adj controversial, polemic(al) ♦ nf controversy.
polémiquer [pɔlemike] vi to be involved in controversy.
polémiste [pɔlemist(ə)] nm/f polemist, polemicist.
poli, e [pɔli] adj polite; (lisse) smooth, polished.
police [pɔlis] nf police; (discipline): **assurer la** ~ **de** ou **dans** to keep order in; **peine de simple** ~ **sentence given by a magistrates' or police court**; ~ (**d'assurance**) (insurance) policy; ~ (**de caractères**) (TYPO, INFORM) typeface; ~ **judiciaire (PJ)** ≈ Criminal Investigation Department (CID) (BRIT), ≈ Federal Bureau of Investigation (FBI) (US); ~ **des mœurs** ≈ vice squad; ~ **secours** ≈ emergency services pl.
polichinelle [pɔliʃinɛl] nm Punch; (péj) buffoon; **secret de** ~ open secret.
policier, ière [pɔlisje, -jɛʀ] adj police cpd ♦ nm policeman; (aussi: **roman** ~) detective novel.
policlinique [pɔliklinik] nf ≈ outpatients sg (clinic).
poliment [pɔlimɑ̃] adv politely.
polio(myélite) [pɔljɔ(mjelit)] nf polio(-myelitis).
polio(myélitique) [pɔljɔ(mjelitik)] nm/f polio patient ou case.
polir [pɔliʀ] vt to polish.
polisson, ne [pɔlisɔ̃, -ɔn] adj naughty.
politesse [pɔlitɛs] nf politeness; ~**s** nfpl (exchange of) courtesies; **rendre une** ~ **à qn** to

return sb's favour (BRIT) ou favor (US).
politicard [pɔlitikaʀ] nm (péj) politico, political schemer.
politicien, ne [pɔlitisjɛ̃, -ɛn] adj political ♦ nm/f politician.
politique [pɔlitik] adj political ♦ nf (science, activité) politics sg; (principes, tactique) policy, policies pl ♦ nm (politicien) politician; ~ **étrangère/intérieure** foreign/domestic policy.
politique-fiction [pɔlitikfiksjɔ̃] nf political fiction.
politiquement [pɔlitikmɑ̃] adv politically.
politisation [pɔlitizasjɔ̃] nf politicization.
politiser [pɔlitize] vt to politicize; ~ **qn** to make sb politically aware.
pollen [pɔlɛn] nm pollen.
polluant, e [pɔlɥɑ̃, -ɑ̃t] adj polluting ♦ nm polluting agent, pollutant.
polluer [pɔlɥe] vt to pollute.
pollueur, euse [pɔlɥœʀ, -øz] nm/f polluter.
pollution [pɔlysjɔ̃] nf pollution.
polo [pɔlo] nm (sport) polo; (tricot) polo shirt.
Pologne [pɔlɔɲ] nf: **la** ~ Poland.
polonais, e [pɔlɔnɛ, -ɛz] adj Polish ♦ nm (LING) Polish ♦ nm/f: P~, e Pole.
poltron, ne [pɔltʀɔ̃, -ɔn] adj cowardly.
poly... [pɔli] préfixe poly....
polyamide [pɔliamid] nf polyamide.
polychrome [pɔlikʀom] adj polychrome, polychromatic.
polyclinique [pɔliklinik] nf (private) clinic (treating different illnesses).
polycopie [pɔlikɔpi] nf (procédé) duplicating; (reproduction) duplicated copy.
polycopié, e [pɔlikɔpje] adj duplicated ♦ nm handout, duplicated notes pl.
polycopier [pɔlikɔpje] vt to duplicate.
polyculture [pɔlikyltyʀ] nf mixed farming.
polyester [pɔliɛstɛʀ] nm polyester.
polyéthylène [pɔlietilɛn] nm polyethylene.
polygame [pɔligam] adj polygamous.
polygamie [pɔligami] nf polygamy.
polyglotte [pɔliglɔt] adj polyglot.
polygone [pɔligɔn] nm polygon.
Polynésie [pɔlinezi] nf: **la** ~ Polynesia; **la** ~ **française** French Polynesia.
polynésien, ne [pɔlinezjɛ̃, -ɛn] adj Polynesian.
polynôme [pɔlinom] nm polynomial.
polype [pɔlip] nm polyp.
polystyrène [pɔlistiʀɛn] nm polystyrene.
polytechnicien, ne [pɔliteknisjɛ̃, -ɛn] nm/f student or former student of the École polytechnique.
Polytechnique [pɔliteknik] nf: (**École**) p~ prestigious military academy producing high-ranking officers and engineers.
polyvalent, e [pɔlivalɑ̃, -ɑ̃t] adj (vaccin) polyvalent; (personne) versatile; (salle) multipurpose ♦ nm ≈ tax inspector.
pomélo [pɔmelo] nm pomelo, grapefruit.
Poméranie [pɔmeʀani] nf: **la** ~ Pomerania.

pommade [pɔmad] *nf* ointment, cream.

pomme [pɔm] *nf* (*BOT*) apple; (*boule décorative*) knob; (*pomme de terre*): **steak ~s (frites)** steak and chips (*BRIT*) *ou* (French) fries (*US*); **tomber dans les ~s** (*fam*) to pass out; ~ **d'Adam** Adam's apple; **~s allumettes** French fries (*thin-cut*); ~ **d'arrosoir** (sprinkler) rose; ~ **de pin** pine *ou* fir cone; ~ **de terre** potato; **~s vapeur** boiled potatoes.

pommé, e [pɔme] *adj* (*chou etc*) firm, with a firm heart.

pommeau, x [pɔmo] *nm* (*boule*) knob; (*de selle*) pommel.

pommelé, e [pɔmle] *adj*: **gris ~** dapple grey.

pommette [pɔmɛt] *nf* cheekbone.

pommier [pɔmje] *nm* apple tree.

pompe [pɔ̃p] *nf* pump; (*faste*) pomp (and ceremony); ~ **de bicyclette** bicycle pump; ~ **à eau/essence** water/petrol pump; ~ **à huile** oil pump; ~ **à incendie** fire engine (*apparatus*); **~s funèbres** undertaker's *sg*, funeral parlour *sg* (*BRIT*), mortician's *sg* (*US*).

Pompéi [pɔ̃pei] *n* Pompeii.

pompéien, ne [pɔ̃pejɛ̃, -ɛn] *adj* Pompeiian.

pomper [pɔ̃pe] *vt* to pump; (*évacuer*) to pump out; (*aspirer*) to pump up; (*absorber*) to soak up ♦ *vi* to pump.

pompeusement [pɔ̃pøzmɑ̃] *adv* pompously.

pompeux, euse [pɔ̃pø, -øz] *adj* pompous.

pompier [pɔ̃pje] *nm* fireman ♦ *adj m* (*style*) pretentious, pompous.

pompiste [pɔ̃pist(ə)] *nm/f* petrol (*BRIT*) *ou* gas (*US*) pump attendant.

pompon [pɔ̃pɔ̃] *nm* pompom, bobble.

pomponner [pɔ̃pɔne] *vt* to titivate (*BRIT*), dress up.

ponce [pɔ̃s] *nf*: **pierre ~** pumice stone.

poncer [pɔ̃se] *vt* to sand (down).

ponceuse [pɔ̃søz] *nf* sander.

poncif [pɔ̃sif] *nm* cliché.

ponction [pɔ̃ksjɔ̃] *nf* (*d'argent etc*) withdrawal; ~ **lombaire** lumbar puncture.

ponctualité [pɔ̃ktɥalite] *nf* punctuality.

ponctuation [pɔ̃ktɥasjɔ̃] *nf* punctuation.

ponctuel, le [pɔ̃ktɥɛl] *adj* (*à l'heure, aussi TECH*) punctual; (*fig: opération etc*) one-off, single; (*scrupuleux*) punctilious, meticulous.

ponctuellement [pɔ̃ktɥɛlmɑ̃] *adv* punctually; punctiliously, meticulously.

ponctuer [pɔ̃ktɥe] *vt* to punctuate; (*MUS*) to phrase.

pondéré, e [pɔ̃dere] *adj* level-headed, composed.

pondérer [pɔ̃dere] *vt* to balance.

pondeuse [pɔ̃døz] *nf* layer, laying hen.

pondre [pɔ̃dʀ(ə)] *vt* to lay; (*fig*) to produce ♦ *vi* to lay.

poney [pɔnɛ] *nm* pony.

pongiste [pɔ̃ʒist(ə)] *nm/f* table tennis player.

pont [pɔ̃] *nm* bridge; (*AUTO*): ~ **arrière/avant** rear/front axle; (*NAVIG*) deck; **faire le ~** to take the extra day off; **faire un ~ d'or à qn**

to offer sb a fortune to take a job; ~ **aérien** airlift; ~ **basculant** bascule bridge; ~ **d'envol** flight deck; ~ **élévateur** hydraulic ramp; ~ **de graissage** ramp (*in garage*); ~ **à péage** tollbridge; ~ **roulant** travelling crane; ~ **suspendu** suspension bridge; ~ **tournant** swing bridge; **P~s et Chaussées** highways department.

The expression "**faire le pont**" *refers to the practice of taking a Monday or Friday off to make a long weekend if a public holiday falls on a Tuesday or Thursday. The French commonly take an extra day off to give four consecutive days holiday at* **l'Ascension, le 14 juillet** *and* **le 15 août**.

ponte [pɔ̃t] *nf* laying; (*œufs pondus*) clutch ♦ *nm* (*fam*) big shot.

pontife [pɔ̃tif] *nm* pontiff.

pontifier [pɔ̃tifje] *vi* to pontificate.

pont-levis, *pl* **ponts-levis** [pɔ̃lvi] *nm* drawbridge.

ponton [pɔ̃tɔ̃] *nm* pontoon (*on water*).

pop [pɔp] *adj inv* pop ♦ *nm*: **le ~** pop (music).

pop-corn [pɔpkɔʀn] *nm* popcorn.

popeline [pɔplin] *nf* poplin.

populace [pɔpylas] *nf* (*péj*) rabble.

populaire [pɔpylɛʀ] *adj* popular; (*manifestation*) mass *cpd*, of the people; (*milieux, clientèle*) working-class; (*LING: mot etc*) used by the lower classes (of society).

populariser [pɔpylaʀize] *vt* to popularize.

popularité [pɔpylaʀite] *nf* popularity.

population [pɔpylasjɔ̃] *nf* population; ~ **active/agricole** working/farming population.

populeux, euse [pɔpylø, -øz] *adj* densely populated.

porc [pɔʀ] *nm* (*ZOOL*) pig; (*CULIN*) pork; (*peau*) pigskin.

porcelaine [pɔʀsəlɛn] *nf* (*substance*) porcelain, china; (*objet*) piece of china(ware).

porcelet [pɔʀsəlɛ] *nm* piglet.

porc-épic, *pl* **porcs-épics** [pɔʀkepik] *nm* porcupine.

porche [pɔʀʃ(ə)] *nm* porch.

porcher, ère [pɔʀʃe, -ɛʀ] *nm/f* pig-keeper.

porcherie [pɔʀʃəʀi] *nf* pigsty.

porcin, e [pɔʀsɛ̃, -in] *adj* (*race*) porcine; (*élevage*) pig *cpd*; (*fig*) piglike.

pore [pɔʀ] *nm* pore.

poreux, euse [pɔʀø, -øz] *adj* porous.

porno [pɔʀno] *adj* porno ♦ *nm* porn.

pornographie [pɔʀnɔgʀafi] *nf* pornography.

pornographique [pɔʀnɔgʀafik] *adj* pornographic.

port [pɔʀ] *nm* (*NAVIG*) harbour (*BRIT*), harbor (*US*), port; (*ville, aussi INFORM*) port; (*de l'uniforme etc*) wearing; (*pour lettre*) postage; (*pour colis, aussi: posture*) carriage; ~ **de commerce/de pêche** commercial/fishing port; **arriver à bon ~** to arrive safe and sound; ~ **d'arme** (*JUR*) carrying of a firearm; ~ **d'attache** (*NAVIG*) port of registry; (*fig*) home base; ~ **d'escale** port of call; ~ **franc** free port.

portable [pɔʀtabl(ə)] *adj* (*vêtement*) wearable; (*portatif*) transportable.

portail [pɔʀtaj] *nm* gate; (*de cathédrale*) portal.

portant, e [pɔʀtɑ̃, -ɑ̃t] *adj* (*murs*) structural, supporting; (*roues*) running; **bien/mal** ~ in good/poor health.

portatif, ive [pɔʀtatif, -iv] *adj* portable.

porte [pɔʀt(ə)] *nf* door; (*de ville, forteresse, SKI*) gate; **mettre à la** ~ to throw out; **prendre la** ~ to leave, go away; **à ma/sa** ~ (*tout près*) on my/his (*ou* her) doorstep; ~ **(d'embarquement)** (*AVIAT*) (departure) gate; ~ **d'entrée** front door; ~ **à** ~ *nm* door-to-door selling; ~ **de secours** emergency exit; ~ **de service** service entrance.

porté, e [pɔʀte] *adj*: **être** ~ **à faire qch** to be apt to do sth, tend to do sth; **être** ~ **sur qch** to be partial to sth.

porte-à-faux [pɔʀtafo] *nm*: **en** ~ cantilevered; (*fig*) in an awkward position.

porte-aiguilles [pɔʀtegɥij] *nm inv* needle case.

porte-avions [pɔʀtavjɔ̃] *nm inv* aircraft carrier.

porte-bagages [pɔʀtbagaʒ] *nm inv* luggage rack (*ou* basket *etc*).

porte-bébé [pɔʀtbebe] *nm* baby sling *ou* carrier.

porte-bonheur [pɔʀtbɔnœʀ] *nm inv* lucky charm.

porte-bouteilles [pɔʀtbutɛj] *nm inv* bottle carrier; (*à casiers*) wine rack.

porte-cartes [pɔʀtəkaʀt(ə)] *nm inv* (*de cartes d'identité*) card holder; (*de cartes géographiques*) map wallet.

porte-cigarettes [pɔʀtsigaʀɛt] *nm inv* cigarette case.

porte-clefs [pɔʀtəkle] *nm inv* key ring.

porte-conteneurs [pɔʀtəkɔ̃tnœʀ] *nm inv* container ship.

porte-couteau, x [pɔʀtkuto] *nm* knife rest.

porte-crayon [pɔʀtkʀɛjɔ̃] *nm* pencil holder.

porte-documents [pɔʀtdɔkymɑ̃] *nm inv* attaché *ou* document case.

porte-drapeau, x [pɔʀtdʀapo] *nm* standard bearer.

portée [pɔʀte] *nf* (*d'une arme*) range; (*fig: importance*) impact, import; (*: capacités*) scope, capability; (*de chatte etc*) litter; (*MUS*) stave, staff (*pl* staves); **à/hors de** ~ **(de)** within/out of reach (of); **à** ~ **de (la) main** within (arm's) reach; **à** ~ **de voix** within earshot; **à la** ~ **de qn** (*fig*) at sb's level, within sb's capabilities; **à la** ~ **de toutes les bourses** to suit every pocket, within everyone's means.

portefaix [pɔʀtəfɛ] *nm inv* porter.

porte-fenêtre, *pl* **portes-fenêtres** [pɔʀtfənɛtʀ(ə)] *nf* French window.

portefeuille [pɔʀtəfœj] *nm* wallet; (*POL, BOURSE*) portfolio; **faire un lit en** ~ to make an apple-pie bed.

porte-jarretelles [pɔʀtʒaʀtɛl] *nm inv* suspender belt (*BRIT*), garter belt (*US*).

porte-jupe [pɔʀtəʒyp] *nm* skirt hanger.

portemanteau, x [pɔʀtmɑ̃to] *nm* coat rack.

porte-mine [pɔʀtəmin] *nm* propelling (*BRIT*) *ou* mechanical (*US*) pencil.

porte-monnaie [pɔʀtmɔnɛ] *nm inv* purse.

porte-parapluies [pɔʀtpaʀaplɥi] *nm inv* umbrella stand.

porte-parole [pɔʀtpaʀɔl] *nm inv* spokesperson.

porte-plume [pɔʀtəplym] *nm inv* penholder.

porter [pɔʀte] *vt* (*charge ou sac etc, aussi: fœtus*) to carry; (*sur soi: vêtement, barbe, bague*) to wear; (*fig: responsabilité etc*) to bear, carry; (*inscription, marque, titre, patronyme, suj: arbre: fruits, fleurs*) to bear; (*jugement*) to pass; (*apporter*): ~ **qch quelque part/à qn** to take sth somewhere/to sb; (*inscrire*): ~ **qch sur** to put sth down on; to enter sth in ♦ *vi* (*voix, regard, canon*) to carry; (*coup, argument*) to hit home; **se** ~ *vi* (*se sentir*): **se** ~ **bien/mal** to be well/unwell; (*aller*): **se** ~ **vers** to go towards; ~ **sur** (*peser*) to rest on; (*accent*) to fall on; (*conférence etc*) to concern; (*heurter*) to strike; **être porté à faire** to be apt *ou* inclined to do; **elle portait le nom de Rosalie** she was called Rosalie; ~ **qn au pouvoir** to bring sb to power; ~ **bonheur à qn** to bring sb luck; ~ **qn à croire** to lead sb to believe; ~ **son âge** to look one's age; ~ **un toast** to drink a toast; ~ **de l'argent au crédit d'un compte** to credit an account with some money; **se** ~ **partie civile** *to associate in a court action with the public prosecutor*; **se** ~ **garant de qch** to guarantee sth, vouch for sth; **se** ~ **candidat à la députation** ≈ **to stand for Parliament** (*BRIT*), ≈ run for Congress (*US*); **se faire** ~ **malade** to report sick; ~ **la main à son chapeau** to raise one's hand to one's hat; ~ **son effort sur** to direct one's efforts towards; ~ **un fait à la connaissance de qn** to bring a fact to sb's attention *ou* notice.

porte-savon [pɔʀtsavɔ̃] *nm* soap dish.

porte-serviettes [pɔʀtsɛʀvjɛt] *nm inv* towel rail.

portes-ouvertes [pɔʀtuvɛʀt(ə)] *adj inv*: **journée** ~ open day.

porteur, euse [pɔʀtœʀ, -øz] *adj* (*COMM*) strong, promising; (*nouvelle, chèque etc*): **être** ~ **de** to be the bearer of ♦ *nm/f* (*de messages*) bearer ♦ *nm* (*de bagages*) porter; (*COMM: de chèque*) bearer; (*: d'actions*) holder; **(avion) gros** ~ wide-bodied aircraft, jumbo (jet).

porte-voix [pɔʀtəvwa] *nm inv* megaphone, loudhailer (*BRIT*).

portier [pɔʀtje] *nm* doorman, commissionaire (*BRIT*).

portière [pɔʀtjɛʀ] *nf* door.
portillon [pɔʀtijɔ̃] *nm* gate.
portion [pɔʀsjɔ̃] *nf* (*part*) portion, share; (*partie*) portion, section.
portique [pɔʀtik] *nm* (*GYMNASTIQUE*) crossbar; (*ARCHIT*) portico; (*RAIL*) gantry.
porto [pɔʀto] *nm* port (wine).
portoricain, e [pɔʀtɔʀikɛ̃, -ɛn] *adj* Puerto Rican.
Porto Rico [pɔʀtɔʀiko] *nf* Puerto Rico.
portrait [pɔʀtʀɛ] *nm* portrait; (*photographie*) photograph; (*fig*): **elle est le ~ de sa mère** she's the image of her mother.
portraitiste [pɔʀtʀetist(ə)] *nm/f* portrait painter.
portrait-robot [pɔʀtʀeʀɔbo] *nm* Identikit ® *ou* Photo-fit ® (*BRIT*) picture.
portuaire [pɔʀtɥɛʀ] *adj* port *cpd*, harbour *cpd* (*BRIT*), harbor *cpd* (*US*).
portugais, e [pɔʀtygɛ, -ɛz] *adj* Portuguese ♦ *nm* (*LING*) Portuguese ♦ *nm/f*: **P~, e** Portuguese.
Portugal [pɔʀtygal] *nm*: **le ~** Portugal.
POS *sigle m* (= *plan d'occupation des sols*) zoning ordinances *ou* regulations.
pose [poz] *nf* (*de moquette*) laying; (*de rideaux, papier peint*) hanging; (*attitude, d'un modèle*) pose; (*PHOTO*) exposure.
posé, e [poze] *adj* calm, unruffled.
posément [pozemɑ̃] *adv* calmly.
posemètre [pozmɛtʀ(ə)] *nm* exposure meter.
poser [poze] *vt* (*déposer*): **~ qch (sur)/qn à** to put sth down (on)/drop sb at; (*placer*): **~ qch sur/quelque part** to put sth on/somewhere; (*installer: moquette, carrelage*) to lay; (*rideaux, papier peint*) to hang; (*MATH: chiffre*) to put (down); (*question*) to ask; (*principe, conditions*) to lay *ou* set down; (*problème*) to formulate; (*difficulté*) to pose; (*personne: mettre en valeur*) to give standing to ♦ *vi* (*modèle*) to pose; to sit; **se ~** (*oiseau, avion*) to land; (*question*) to arise; **se ~ en** to pass o.s. off as, pose as; **~ son** *ou* **un regard sur qn/qch** to turn one's gaze on sb/sth; **~ sa candidature** to apply; (*POL*) to put o.s. up for election.
poseur, euse [pozœʀ, -øz] *nm/f* (*péj*) show-off, poseur; **~ de parquets/carrelages** floor/tile layer.
positif, ive [pozitif, -iv] *adj* positive.
position [pozisjɔ̃] *nf* position; **prendre ~** (*fig*) to take a stand.
positionner [pozisjɔne] *vt* to position; (*compte en banque*) to calculate the balance of.
positivement [pozitivmɑ̃] *adv* positively.
posologie [pozɔlɔʒi] *nf* directions *pl* for use, dosage.
possédant, e [pɔsedɑ̃, -ɑ̃t] *adj* (*classe*) wealthy ♦ *nm/f*: **les ~s** the haves, the wealthy.
possédé, e [pɔsede] *nm/f* person possessed.
posséder [pɔsede] *vt* to own, possess; (*qualité, talent*) to have, possess; (*bien connaître: mé-*

tier, langue) to have mastered, have a thorough knowledge of; (*sexuellement, aussi: suj: colère etc*) to possess; (*fam: duper*) to take in.
possesseur [pɔsesœʀ] *nm* owner.
possessif, ive [pɔsesif, -iv] *adj, nm* (*aussi LING*) possessive.
possession [pɔsesjɔ̃] *nf* ownership *no pl*; possession; **être/entrer en ~ de qch** to be in/take possession of sth.
possibilité [pɔsibilite] *nf* possibility; **~s** *nfpl* (*moyens*) means; (*potentiel*) potential *sg*; **avoir la ~ de faire** to be in a position to do; to have the opportunity to do.
possible [pɔsibl(ə)] *adj* possible; (*projet, entreprise*) feasible ♦ *nm*: **faire son ~** to do all one can, do one's utmost; (**ce n'est**) **pas ~!** impossible!; **le plus/moins de livres ~** as many/few books as possible; **dès que ~** as soon as possible; **gentil** *etc* **au ~** as nice *etc* as it is possible to be.
postal, e, aux [pɔstal, -o] *adj* postal, post office *cpd*; **sac ~** mailbag, postbag.
postdater [pɔstdate] *vt* to postdate.
poste [pɔst(ə)] *nf* (*service*) post, postal service; (*administration, bureau*) post office ♦ *nm* (*fonction, MIL*) post; (*TÉL*) extension; (*de radio etc*) set; (*de budget*) item; **~s** *nfpl* post office *sg*; **P~s télécommunications et télédiffusion (PTT)** *postal and telecommunications service*; **agent** *ou* **employé des ~s** post office worker; **mettre à la ~** to post; **~ de commandement (PC)** *nm* (*MIL etc*) headquarters; **~ de contrôle** *nm* checkpoint; **~ de douane** *nm* customs post; **~ émetteur** *nm* transmitting set; **~ d'essence** *nm* filling station; **~ d'incendie** *nm* fire point; **~ de péage** *nm* tollgate; **~ de pilotage** *nm* cockpit; **~ (de police)** *nm* police station; **~ de radio** *nm* radio set; **~ restante (PR)** *nf* poste restante (*BRIT*), general delivery (*US*); **~ de secours** *nm* first-aid post; **~ de télévision** *nm* television set; **~ de travail** *nm* work station.
poster *vt* [pɔste] to post ♦ *nm* [pɔstɛʀ] poster; **se ~** to position o.s.
postérieur, e [pɔsteʀjœʀ] *adj* (*date*) later; (*partie*) back ♦ *nm* (*fam*) behind.
postérieurement [pɔsteʀjœʀmɑ̃] *adv* later, subsequently; **~ à** after.
posteriori [pɔsteʀjɔʀi]: **a ~** *adv* with hindsight, a posteriori.
postérité [pɔsteʀite] *nf* posterity.
postface [pɔstfas] *nf* appendix.
posthume [pɔstym] *adj* posthumous.
postiche [pɔstiʃ] *adj* false ♦ *nm* hairpiece.
postier, ière [pɔstje, -jɛʀ] *nm/f* post office worker.
postillon [pɔstijɔ̃] *nm*: **envoyer des ~s** to splutter.
postillonner [pɔstijɔne] *vi* to splutter.
post-natal, e [pɔstnatal] *adj* postnatal.
postopératoire [pɔstɔpeʀatwaʀ] *adj* postoperative.

postscolaire [pɔstskɔlɛʀ] *adj* further, continuing.

post-scriptum [pɔstskʀiptɔm] *nm inv* postscript.

postsynchronisation [pɔstsɛ̃kʀɔnizasjɔ̃] *nf* dubbing.

postsynchroniser [pɔstsɛ̃kʀɔnize] *vt* to dub.

postulant, e [pɔstylɑ̃, -ɑ̃t] *nm/f* (*candidat*) applicant; (*REL*) postulant.

postulat [pɔstyla] *nm* postulate.

postuler [pɔstyle] *vt* (*emploi*) to apply for, put in for.

posture [pɔstyʀ] *nf* posture, position; (*fig*) position.

pot [po] *nm* jar, pot; (*en plastique, carton*) carton; (*en métal*) tin; (*fam*): **avoir du ~** to be lucky; **boire** *ou* **prendre un ~** (*fam*) to have a drink; **découvrir le ~ aux roses** to find out what's been going on; **~ catalytique** catalytic converter; **~** (**de chambre**) (chamber)pot; **~ d'échappement** exhaust pipe; **~ de fleurs** plant pot, flowerpot; (*plante*) pot plant; **~ à tabac** tobacco jar.

potable [pɔtabl(ə)] *adj* (*fig: boisson*) drinkable; (: *travail, devoir*) decent; **eau** (**non**) **~** (not) drinking water.

potache [pɔtaʃ] *nm* schoolboy.

potage [pɔtaʒ] *nm* soup.

potager, ère [pɔtaʒe, -ɛʀ] *adj* (*plante*) edible, vegetable *cpd*; (**jardin**) **~** kitchen *ou* vegetable garden.

potasse [pɔtas] *nf* potassium hydroxide; (*engrais*) potash.

potasser [pɔtase] *vt* (*fam*) to swot up (*BRIT*), cram.

potassium [pɔtasjɔm] *nm* potassium.

pot-au-feu [pɔtofø] *nm inv* (beef) stew; (*viande*) stewing beef ♦ *adj* (*fam: personne*) stay-at-home.

pot-de-vin, *pl* **pots-de-vin** [podvɛ̃] *nm* bribe.

pote [pɔt] *nm* (*fam*) mate (*BRIT*), pal.

poteau, x [pɔto] *nm* post; **~ de départ/arrivée** starting/finishing post; **~** (**d'exécution**) execution post, stake; **~ indicateur** signpost; **~ télégraphique** telegraph pole; **~x** (**de but**) goal-posts.

potée [pɔte] *nf* hotpot (*of pork and cabbage*).

potelé, e [pɔtle] *adj* plump, chubby.

potence [pɔtɑ̃s] *nf* gallows *sg*; **en ~** T-shaped.

potentat [pɔtɑ̃ta] *nm* potentate; (*fig: péj*) despot.

potentiel, le [pɔtɑ̃sjɛl] *adj, nm* potential.

potentiellement [pɔtɑ̃sjɛlmɑ̃] *adv* potentially.

poterie [pɔtʀi] *nf* (*fabrication*) pottery; (*objet*) piece of pottery.

potiche [pɔtiʃ] *nf* large vase.

potier [pɔtje] *nm* potter.

potins [pɔtɛ̃] *nmpl* gossip *sg*.

potion [posjɔ̃] *nf* potion.

potiron [pɔtiʀɔ̃] *nm* pumpkin.

pot-pourri, *pl* **pots-pourris** [popuʀi] *nm* (*MUS*) potpourri, medley.

pou, x [pu] *nm* louse (*pl* lice).

pouah [pwa] *excl* ugh!, yuk!

poubelle [pubɛl] *nf* (dust)bin.

pouce [pus] *nm* thumb; **se tourner** *ou* **se rouler les ~s** (*fig*) to twiddle one's thumbs; **manger sur le ~** to eat on the run, snatch something to eat.

poudre [pudʀ(ə)] *nf* powder; (*fard*) (face) powder; (*explosif*) gunpowder; **en ~: café en ~** instant coffee; **savon en ~** soap powder; **lait en ~** dried *ou* powdered milk; **~ à canon** gunpowder; **~ à éternuer** sneezing powder; **~ à récurer** scouring powder; **~ de riz** face powder.

poudrer [pudʀe] *vt* to powder.

poudrerie [pudʀəʀi] *nf* gunpowder factory.

poudreux, euse [pudʀø, -øz] *adj* dusty; (*neige*) powdery, powder *cpd*.

poudrier [pudʀije] *nm* (powder) compact.

poudrière [pudʀijɛʀ] *nf* powder magazine; (*fig*) powder keg.

poudroyer [pudʀwaje] *vi* to rise in clouds *ou* a flurry.

pouf [puf] *nm* pouffe.

pouffer [pufe] *vi*: **~** (**de rire**) to snigger; to giggle.

pouffiasse [pufjas] *nf* (*fam*) fat cow; (*prostituée*) tart.

pouilleux, euse [pujø, -øz] *adj* flea-ridden; (*fig*) seedy.

poulailler [pulaje] *nm* henhouse; (*THÉÂT*): **le ~** the gods *sg*.

poulain [pulɛ̃] *nm* foal; (*fig*) protégé.

poularde [pulaʀd(ə)] *nf* fatted chicken.

poule [pul] *nf* (*ZOOL*) hen; (*CULIN*) (boiling) fowl; (*SPORT*) (round-robin) tournament; (*RUGBY*) group; (*fam*) bird (*BRIT*), chick, broad (*US*); (*prostituée*) tart; **~ d'eau** moorhen; **~ mouillée** coward; **~ pondeuse** laying hen, layer; **~ au riz** chicken and rice.

poulet [pulɛ] *nm* chicken; (*fam*) cop.

poulette [pulɛt] *nf* (*jeune poule*) pullet.

pouliche [puliʃ] *nf* filly.

poulie [puli] *nf* pulley.

poulpe [pulp(ə)] *nm* octopus.

pouls [pu] *nm* pulse (*ANAT*); **prendre le ~ de qn** to feel sb's pulse.

poumon [pumɔ̃] *nm* lung; **~ d'acier** *ou* **artificiel** iron *ou* artificial lung.

poupe [pup] *nf* stern; **en ~** astern.

poupée [pupe] *nf* doll; **jouer à la ~** to play with one's doll (*ou* dolls); **de ~** (*très petit*): **jardin de ~** doll's garden, pocket-handkerchief-sized garden.

poupin, e [pupɛ̃, -in] *adj* chubby.

poupon [pupɔ̃] *nm* babe-in-arms.

pouponner [pupɔne] *vi* to fuss (around).

pouponnière [pupɔnjɛʀ] *nf* crèche, day nursery.

pour [puʀ] *prép* for ♦ *nm*: **le ~ et le contre** the pros and cons; **~ faire** (so as) to do, in order to do; **~ avoir fait** for having done; **~ que so**

that, in order that; ~ **moi** (*à mon avis, pour ma part*) for my part, personally; ~ **riche qu'il soit** rich though he may be; ~ **100 francs d'essence** 100 francs' worth of petrol; ~ **cent** per cent; ~ **ce qui est de** as for; **y être ~ quelque chose** to have something to do with it.

pourboire [puʀbwaʀ] *nm* tip.

pourcentage [puʀsɑ̃taʒ] *nm* percentage; **travailler au** ~ to work on commission.

pourchasser [puʀʃase] *vt* to pursue.

pourfendeur [puʀfɑ̃dœʀ] *nm* sworn opponent.

pourfendre [puʀfɑ̃dʀ(ə)] *vt* to assail.

pourlécher [puʀleʃe]: **se** ~ *vi* to lick one's lips.

pourparlers [puʀpaʀle] *nmpl* talks, negotiations; **être en** ~ **avec** to be having talks with.

pourpre [puʀpʀ(ə)] *adj* crimson.

pourquoi [puʀkwa] *adv, conj* why ♦ *nm inv:* **le** ~ **(de)** the reason (for).

pourrai [puʀe] *etc vb voir* **pouvoir.**

pourri, e [puʀi] *adj* rotten; (*roche, pierre*) crumbling; (*temps, climat*) filthy, foul ♦ *nm:* **sentir le** ~ to smell rotten.

pourrir [puʀiʀ] *vi* to rot; (*fruit*) to go rotten *ou* bad; (*fig: situation*) to deteriorate ♦ *vt* to rot; (*fig: corrompre: personne*) to corrupt; (: *gâter: enfant*) to spoil thoroughly.

pourrissement [puʀismɑ̃] *nm* deterioration.

pourriture [puʀityʀ] *nf* rot.

pourrons [puʀɔ̃] *etc vb voir* **pouvoir.**

poursuis [puʀsɥi] *etc vb voir* **poursuivre.**

poursuite [puʀsɥit] *nf* pursuit, chase; ~**s** *nfpl* (*JUR*) legal proceedings; **(course)** ~ track race; (*fig*) chase.

poursuivant, e [puʀsɥivɑ̃, -ɑ̃t] *vb voir* **poursuivre** ♦ *nm/f* pursuer; (*JUR*) plaintiff.

poursuivre [puʀsɥivʀ(ə)] *vt* to pursue, chase (after); (*relancer*) to hound, harry; (*obséder*) to haunt; (*JUR*) to bring proceedings against, prosecute; (: *au civil*) to sue; (*but*) to strive towards; (*voyage, études*) to carry on with, continue ♦ *vi* to carry on, go on; **se** ~ *vi* to go on, continue.

pourtant [puʀtɑ̃] *adv* yet; **mais** ~ but nevertheless, but even so; **c'est** ~ **facile** (and) yet it's easy.

pourtour [puʀtuʀ] *nm* perimeter.

pourvoi [puʀvwa] *nm* appeal.

pourvoir [puʀvwaʀ] *nm* (*COMM*) supply ♦ *vt:* ~ **qch/qn de** to equip sth/sb with ♦ *vi:* ~ **à** to provide for; (*emploi*) to fill; **se** ~ (*JUR*): **se** ~ **en cassation** to take one's case to the Court of Appeal.

pourvoyeur, euse [puʀvwajœʀ, -øz] *nm/f* supplier.

pourvu, e [puʀvy] *pp de* **pourvoir** ♦ *adj:* ~ **de** equipped with; ~ **que** *conj* (*si*) provided that, so long as; (*espérons que*) let's hope (that).

pousse [pus] *nf* growth; (*bourgeon*) shoot.

poussé, e [puse] *adj* sophisticated, advanced; (*moteur*) souped-up.

pousse-café [puskafe] *nm inv* (after-dinner) liqueur.

poussée [puse] *nf* thrust; (*coup*) push; (*MÉD*) eruption; (*fig*) upsurge.

pousse-pousse [puspus] *nm inv* rickshaw.

pousser [puse] *vt* to push; (*inciter*): ~ **qn à** to urge *ou* press sb to + *infinitif*; (*acculer*): ~ **qn à** to drive sb to; (*moteur, voiture*) to drive hard; (*émettre: cri etc*) to give; (*stimuler*) to urge on; to drive hard; (*poursuivre*) to carry on ♦ *vi* to push; (*croître*) to grow; (*aller*): ~ **plus loin** to push on a bit further; **se** ~ *vi* to move over; **faire** ~ (*plante*) to grow; ~ **le dévouement** *etc* **jusqu'à** ... to take devotion *etc* as far as ....

poussette [puset] *nf* (*voiture d'enfant*) pushchair (*BRIT*), stroller (*US*).

poussette-canne, *pl* **poussettes-cannes** [pusetkan] *nf* baby buggy (*BRIT*), (folding) stroller (*US*).

poussier [pusje] *nm* coaldust.

poussière [pusjɛʀ] *nf* dust; (*grain*) speck of dust; **et des** ~**s** (*fig*) and a bit; ~ **de charbon** coaldust.

poussiéreux, euse [pusjeʀø, -øz] *adj* dusty.

poussif, ive [pusif, -iv] *adj* wheezy, wheezing.

poussin [pusɛ̃] *nm* chick.

poussoir [puswaʀ] *nm* button.

poutre [putʀ(ə)] *nf* beam; (*en fer, ciment armé*) girder; ~**s apparentes** exposed beams.

poutrelle [putʀɛl] *nf* (*petite poutre*) small beam; (*barre d'acier*) girder.

================================== *MOT-CLÉ*

pouvoir [puvwaʀ] *nm* power; (*POL: dirigeants*): **le** ~ those in power; **les** ~**s publics** the authorities; **avoir** ~ **de faire** (*autorisation*) to have (the) authority to do; (*droit*) to have the right to do; ~ **absolu** absolute power; ~ **absorbant** absorbency; ~ **d'achat** purchasing power; ~ **calorifique** calorific value

♦ *vb semi-aux* **1** (*être en état de*) can, be able to; **je ne peux pas le réparer** I can't *ou* I am not able to repair it; **déçu de ne pas** ~ **le faire** disappointed at not being able to do it

2 (*avoir la permission*) can, may, be allowed to; **vous pouvez aller au cinéma** you can *ou* may go to the pictures

3 (*probabilité, hypothèse*) may, might, could; **il a pu avoir un accident** he may *ou* might *ou* could have had an accident; **il aurait pu le dire!** he might *ou* could have said (so)!

4 (*expressions*): **tu ne peux pas savoir!** you have no idea!; **tu peux le dire!** you can say that again!

♦ *vb impers* may, might, could; **il peut arriver que** it may *ou* might *ou* could happen that; **il pourrait pleuvoir** it might rain

♦ *vt* **1** can, be able to; **j'ai fait tout ce que j'ai pu** I did all I could; **je n'en peux plus** (*épuisé*) I'm exhausted; (*à bout*) I can't take any more

2 (*vb +adj ou adv comparatif*): **je me porte on ne peut mieux** I'm absolutely fine, I couldn't be better; **elle est on ne peut plus gentille** she couldn't be nicer, she's as nice as can be

se ~ *vi*: **il se peut que** it may *ou* might be that; **cela se pourrait** that's quite possible.

PP *sigle f* (= *préventive de la pellagre: vitamine*) niacin ♦ *abr* (= *pages*) pp.

p.p. *abr* (= *par procuration*) p.p.

p.p.c.m. *sigle m* (*MATH*: = *plus petit commun multiple*) LCM (= *lowest common multiple*).

PQ *sigle f* (*Canada*: = *province de Québec*) PQ.

PR *sigle m* = *parti républicain* ♦ *sigle f* = **poste restante.**

pr *abr* = **pour.**

pragmatique [pʀagmatik] *adj* pragmatic.

pragmatisme [pʀagmatism(ə)] *nm* pragmatism.

Prague [pʀag] *n* Prague.

prairie [pʀeʀi] *nf* meadow.

praline [pʀalin] *nf* (*bonbon*) sugared almond; (*au chocolat*) praline.

praliné, e [pʀaline] *adj* (*amande*) sugared; (*chocolat, glace*) praline *cpd*.

praticable [pʀatikabl(ə)] *adj* (*route etc*) passable, practicable; (*projet*) practicable.

praticien, ne [pʀatisjɛ̃, -ɛn] *nm/f* practitioner.

pratiquant, e [pʀatikɑ̃, -ɑ̃t] *adj* practising (*BRIT*), practicing (*US*).

pratique [pʀatik] *nf* practice ♦ *adj* practical; (*commode: horaire etc*) convenient; (*: outil*) handy, useful; **dans la** ~ in (actual) practice; **mettre en** ~ to put into practice.

pratiquement [pʀatikmɑ̃] *adv* (*dans la pratique*) in practice; (*pour ainsi dire*) practically, virtually.

pratiquer [pʀatike] *vt* to practise (*BRIT*), practice (*US*); (*SPORT etc*) to go in for, play; (*appliquer: méthode, théorie*) to apply; (*intervention, opération*) to carry out; (*ouverture, abri*) to make ♦ *vi* (*REL*) to be a churchgoer.

pré [pʀe] *nm* meadow.

préalable [pʀealabl(ə)] *adj* preliminary; **condition** ~ (**de**) precondition (for), prerequisite (for); **sans avis** ~ without prior *ou* previous notice; **au** ~ first, beforehand.

préalablement [pʀealabləmɑ̃] *adv* first, beforehand.

Préalpes [pʀealp(ə)] *nfpl*: **les** ~ the Pre-Alps.

préalpin, e [pʀealpɛ̃, -in] *adj* of the Pre-Alps.

préambule [pʀeɑ̃byl] *nm* preamble; (*fig*) prelude; **sans** ~ straight away.

préau, x [pʀeo] *nm* (*d'une cour d'école*) covered playground; (*d'un monastère, d'une prison*) inner courtyard.

préavis [pʀeavi] *nm* notice; ~ **de congé** notice; **communication avec** ~ (*TÉL*) personal *ou* person-to-person call.

prébende [pʀebɑ̃d] *nf* (*péj*) remuneration.

précaire [pʀekɛʀ] *adj* precarious.

précaution [pʀekosjɔ̃] *nf* precaution; **avec** ~ cautiously; **prendre des** *ou* **ses** ~**s** to take precautions; **par** ~ as a precaution; **pour plus de** ~ to be on the safe side; ~**s oratoires** carefully phrased remarks.

précautionneux, euse [pʀekosjɔnø, -øz] *adj* cautious, careful.

précédemment [pʀesedamɑ̃] *adv* before, previously.

précédent, e [pʀesedɑ̃, -ɑ̃t] *adj* previous ♦ *nm* precedent; **sans** ~ unprecedented; **le jour** ~ the day before, the previous day.

précéder [pʀesede] *vt* to precede; (*marcher ou rouler devant*) to be in front of; (*arriver avant*) to get ahead of.

précepte [pʀesɛpt(ə)] *nm* precept.

précepteur, trice [pʀesɛptœʀ, -tʀis] *nm/f* (private) tutor.

préchauffer [pʀeʃofe] *vt* to preheat.

prêcher [pʀeʃe] *vt, vi* to preach.

prêcheur, euse [pʀeʃœʀ, -øz] *adj* moralizing ♦ *nm/f* (*REL*) preacher; (*fig*) moralizer.

précieusement [pʀesjøzmɑ̃] *adv* (*avec soin*) carefully; (*avec préciosité*) preciously.

précieux, euse [pʀesjø, -øz] *adj* precious; (*collaborateur, conseils*) invaluable; (*style, écrivain*) précieux, precious.

préciosité [pʀesjozite] *nf* preciosity, preciousness.

précipice [pʀesipis] *nm* drop, chasm; (*fig*) abyss; **au bord du** ~ at the edge of the precipice.

précipitamment [pʀesipitamɑ̃] *adv* hurriedly, hastily.

précipitation [pʀesipitasjɔ̃] *nf* (*hâte*) haste; ~**s** (*atmosphériques*) *nfpl* precipitation *sg*.

précipité, e [pʀesipite] *adj* (*respiration*) fast; (*pas*) hurried; (*départ*) hasty.

précipiter [pʀesipite] *vt* (*faire tomber*): ~ **qn/ qch du haut de** to throw *ou* hurl sb/sth off *ou* from; (*hâter: marche*) to quicken; (*: départ*) to hasten; **se** ~ *vi* (*événements*) to move faster; (*respiration*) to speed up; **se** ~ **sur/ vers** to rush at/towards; **se** ~ **au-devant de qn** to throw o.s. before sb.

précis, e [pʀesi, -iz] *adj* precise; (*tir, mesures*) accurate, precise ♦ *nm* handbook.

précisément [pʀesizemɑ̃] *adv* precisely; **ma vie n'est pas** ~ **distrayante** my life is not exactly entertaining.

préciser [pʀesize] *vt* (*expliquer*) to be more specific about, clarify; (*spécifier*) to state, specify; **se** ~ *vi* to become clear(er).

précision [pʀesizjɔ̃] *nf* precision; accuracy; (*détail*) point *ou* detail (*made clear or to be clarified*); ~**s** *nfpl* further details.

précoce [pʀekɔs] *adj* early; (*enfant*) precocious; (*calvitie*) premature.

précocité [pʀekɔsite] *nf* earliness; precociousness.

préconçu, e [pʀekɔ̃sy] *adj* preconceived.

préconiser [pʀekɔnize] *vt* to advocate.

précontraint, e [pʀekɔ̃tʀɛ̃, -ɛ̃t] *adj*: **béton ~** prestressed concrete.

précuit, e [pʀekɥi, -it] *adj* precooked.

précurseur [pʀekyʀsœʀ] *adj m* precursory ♦ *nm* forerunner, precursor.

prédateur [pʀedatœʀ] *nm* predator.

prédécesseur [pʀedesesœʀ] *nm* predecessor.

prédécoupé, e [pʀedekupe] *adj* pre-cut.

prédestiner [pʀedɛstine] *vt*: **~ qn à qch/à faire** to predestine sb for sth/to do.

prédicateur [pʀedikatœʀ] *nm* preacher.

prédiction [pʀediksjɔ̃] *nf* prediction.

prédilection [pʀedilɛksjɔ̃] *nf*: **avoir une ~ pour** to be partial to; **de ~** favourite (*BRIT*), favorite (*US*).

prédire [pʀediʀ] *vt* to predict.

prédisposer [pʀedispoze] *vt*: **~ qn à qch/à faire** to predispose sb to sth/to do.

prédisposition [pʀedispozisjɔ̃] *nf* predisposition.

prédit, e [pʀedi, -it] *pp de* **prédire**.

prédominance [pʀedɔminɑ̃s] *nf* predominance.

prédominant, e [pʀedɔminɑ̃, -ɑ̃t] *adj* predominant; prevailing.

prédominer [pʀedɔmine] *vi* to predominate; (*avis*) to prevail.

pré-électoral, e, aux [pʀeelɛktɔʀal, -o] *adj* pre-election *cpd*.

pré-emballé, e [pʀeɑ̃bale] *adj* pre-packed.

prééminent, e [pʀeeminɑ̃, -ɑ̃t] *adj* pre-eminent.

préemption [pʀeɑ̃psjɔ̃] *nf*: **droit de ~** (*JUR*) pre-emptive right.

pré-encollé, e [pʀeɑ̃kɔle] *adj* pre-pasted.

préétabli, e [pʀeetabli] *adj* pre-established.

préexistant, e [pʀeɛgzistɑ̃, -ɑ̃t] *adj* pre-existing.

préfabriqué, e [pʀefabʀike] *adj* prefabricated; (*péj*: *sourire*) artificial ♦ *nm* prefabricated material.

préface [pʀefas] *nf* preface.

préfacer [pʀefase] *vt* to write a preface for.

préfectoral, e, aux [pʀefɛktɔʀal, -o] *adj* prefectorial.

préfecture [pʀefɛktyʀ] *nf* prefecture; **~ de police** police headquarters *pl*.

> *The* **préfecture** *is the administrative headquarters of the* **département**. *The* **préfet**, *a senior civil servant appointed by the government, is responsible for executing government decisions. France's 22 regions, each comprising a number of départements, also have a préfet, the préfet de région.*

préférable [pʀefeʀabl(ə)] *adj* preferable.

préféré, e [pʀefeʀe] *adj, nm/f* favourite (*BRIT*), favorite (*US*).

préférence [pʀefeʀɑ̃s] *nf* preference; **de ~** preferably; **de** *ou* **par ~ à** in preference to,

rather than; **donner la ~ à qn** to give preference to sb; **par ordre de ~** in order of preference; **obtenir la ~ sur** to have preference over.

préférentiel, le [pʀefeʀɑ̃sjɛl] *adj* preferential.

préférer [pʀefeʀe] *vt*: **~ qn/qch (à)** to prefer sb/sth (to), like sb/sth better (than); **~ faire** to prefer to do; **je préférerais du thé** I would rather have tea, I'd prefer tea.

préfet [pʀefɛ] *nm* prefect; **~ de police** ≈ Chief Constable (*BRIT*), ≈ Police Commissioner (*US*).

préfigurer [pʀefigyʀe] *vt* to prefigure.

préfixe [pʀefiks(ə)] *nm* prefix.

préhistoire [pʀeistwaʀ] *nf* prehistory.

préhistorique [pʀeistɔʀik] *adj* prehistoric.

préjudice [pʀeʒydis] *nm* (*matériel*) loss; (*moral*) harm *no pl*; **porter ~ à** to harm, be detrimental to; **au ~ de** at the expense of.

préjudiciable [pʀeʒydisjabl(ə)] *adj*: **~ à** prejudicial *ou* harmful to.

préjugé [pʀeʒyʒe] *nm* prejudice; **avoir un ~ contre** to be prejudiced *ou* biased against; **bénéficier d'un ~ favorable** to be viewed favourably.

préjuger [pʀeʒyʒe]: **~ de** *vt* to prejudge.

prélasser [pʀelase]: **se ~** *vi* to lounge.

prélat [pʀela] *nm* prelate.

prélavage [pʀelavaʒ] *nm* pre-wash.

prélèvement [pʀelɛvmɑ̃] *nm* deduction; withdrawal; **faire un ~ de sang** to take a blood sample.

prélever [pʀelve] *vt* (*échantillon*) to take; (*argent*): **~ (sur)** to deduct (from); (: *sur son compte*): **~ (sur)** to withdraw (from).

préliminaire [pʀeliminɛʀ] *adj* preliminary; **~s** *nmpl* preliminaries; (*négociations*) preliminary talks.

prélude [pʀelyd] *nm* prelude; (*avant le concert*) warm-up.

prématuré, e [pʀematyʀe] *adj* premature; (*retraite*) early ♦ *nm* premature baby.

prématurément [pʀematyʀemɑ̃] *adv* prematurely.

préméditation [pʀemeditasjɔ̃] *nf*: **avec ~** *adj* premeditated ♦ *adv* with intent.

préméditer [pʀemedite] *vt* to premeditate, plan.

prémices [pʀemis] *nfpl* beginnings.

premier, ière [pʀəmje, -jɛʀ] *adj* first; (*branche, marche, grade*) bottom; (*fig: fondamental*) basic; prime; (*en importance*) first, foremost ♦ *nm* (**~ étage**) first (*BRIT*) *ou* second (*US*) floor ♦ *nf* (*AUTO*) first (gear); (*RAIL, AVIAT etc*) first class; (*SCOL: classe*) penultimate school year (age 16-17); (*THÉÂT*) first night; (*CINÉ*) première; (*exploit*) first; **au ~ abord** at first sight; **au** *ou* **du ~ coup** at the first attempt *ou* go; **de ~ ordre** first-class, first-rate; **de première qualité, de ~ choix** best *ou* top quality; **de première importance** of the highest importance; **de première nécessité** absolutely essential; **le ~ venu** the first person to come along; **jeune ~** leading man; **le ~ de l'an** New Year's Day; **enfant du ~** lit child of a first marriage; **en ~ lieu** in the first place; **~ âge** (*d'un enfant*) the first 3 months (of life); **P~ Ministre** Prime Minister.

premièrement [pʀəmjɛʀmɑ̃] *adv* firstly.

première-née, *pl* **premières-nées** [pʀəmjɛʀne] *nf* first-born.

premier-né, *pl* **premiers-nés** [pʀəmjene] *nm* first-born.

prémisse [pʀemis] *nf* premise.

prémolaire [pʀemɔlɛʀ] *nf* premolar.

prémonition [pʀemɔnisjɔ̃] *nf* premonition.

prémonitoire [pʀemɔnitwaʀ] *adj* premonitory.

prémunir [pʀemyniʀ]: **se ~** *vi*: **se ~ contre** to protect o.s. from, guard against.

prenant, e [pʀənɑ̃, -ɑ̃t] *vb voir* **prendre** ♦ *adj* absorbing, engrossing.

prénatal, e [pʀenatal] *adj* (*MÉD*) antenatal; (*allocation*) maternity *cpd*.

prendre [pʀɑ̃dʀ(ə)] *vt* to take; (*ôter*): **~ qch à** to take sth from; (*aller chercher*) to get, fetch; (*se procurer*) to get; (*réserver: place*) to book; (*acquérir: du poids, de la valeur*) to put on, gain; (*malfaiteur, poisson*) to catch; (*passager*) to pick up; (*personnel, aussi: couleur, goût*) to take on; (*locataire*) to take in; (*traiter: enfant, problème*) to handle; (*voix, ton*) to put on; (*prélever: pourcentage, argent*) to take off; (*coincer*): **se ~ les doigts dans** to get one's fingers caught in ♦ *vi* (*liquide, ciment*) to set; (*greffe, vaccin*) to take; (*mensonge*) to be successful; (*feu: foyer*) to go; (: *incendie*) to start; (*allumette*) to light; (*se diriger*): **~ à gauche** to turn (to the) left; **~ son origine** *ou* **sa source** (*mot, rivière*) to have its source; **~ qn pour** to take sb for; **se ~ pour** to think one is; **~ sur soi de faire qch** to take it upon o.s. to do sth; **~ qn en sympathie/horreur** to get to like/loathe sb; **à tout ~** all things considered; **s'en ~ à** (*agresser*) to set about; (*passer sa colère sur*) to take it out on; (*critiquer*) to attack; (*remettre en question*) to challenge; **se ~ d'amitié/d'affection pour** to befriend/become fond of; **s'y ~** (*procéder*) to set about it; **s'y ~ à l'avance** to see to it in advance; **s'y ~ à deux fois** to try twice, make two attempts.

preneur [pʀənœʀ] *nm*: **être ~** to be willing to buy; **trouver ~** to find a buyer.

prénom [pʀenɔ̃] *nm* first name.

prénommer [pʀenɔme] *vt*: **elle se prénomme Claude** her (first) name is Claude.

prénuptial, e, aux [pʀenypsjal, -o] *adj* premarital.

préoccupant, e [pʀeɔkypɑ̃, -ɑ̃t] *adj* worrying.

préoccupation [pʀeɔkypasjɔ̃] *nf* (*souci*) concern; (*idée fixe*) preoccupation.

préoccupé, e [pʀeɔkype] *adj* concerned; preoccupied.

préoccuper [pʀeɔkype] *vt* (*tourmenter, tracas-*

ser) to concern; (*absorber, obséder*) to preoccupy; **se ~ de qch** to be concerned about sth; to show concern about sth.

préparateur, trice [pʀepaʀatœʀ, -tʀis] *nm/f* assistant.

préparatifs [pʀepaʀatif] *nmpl* preparations.

préparation [pʀepaʀasjɔ̃] *nf* preparation; (*SCOL*) piece of homework.

préparatoire [pʀepaʀatwaʀ] *adj* preparatory.

préparer [pʀepaʀe] *vt* to prepare; (*café, repas*) to make; (*examen*) to prepare for; (*voyage, entreprise*) to plan; **se ~** *vi* (*orage, tragédie*) to brew, be in the air; **se ~ (à qch/à faire)** to prepare (o.s.) *ou* get ready (for sth/to do); **~ qch à qn** (*surprise etc*) to have sth in store for sb; **~ qn à qch** (*nouvelle etc*) to prepare sb for sth.

prépondérance [pʀepɔ̃deʀɑ̃s] *nf*: **~ (sur)** predominance (over).

prépondérant, e [pʀepɔ̃deʀɑ̃, -ɑ̃t] *adj* major, dominating; **voix ~e** casting vote.

préposé, e [pʀepoze] *adj*: **~ à** in charge of ♦ *nm/f* (*gén: employé*) employee; (*ADMIN: facteur*) postman/woman (*BRIT*), mailman/woman (*US*); (*de la douane etc*) official; (*de vestiaire*) attendant.

préposer [pʀepoze] *vt*: **~ qn à qch** to appoint sb to sth.

préposition [pʀepozisjɔ̃] *nf* preposition.

prérentrée [pʀeʀɑ̃tʀe] *nf* in-service training period before start of school term.

préretraite [pʀeʀətʀɛt] *nf* early retirement.

prérogative [pʀeʀɔgativ] *nf* prerogative.

près [pʀɛ] *adv* near, close; **~ de** *prép* near (to), close to; (*environ*) nearly, almost; **de ~** *adv* closely; **à 5 kg ~** to within about 5 kg; **à cela ~ que** apart from the fact that; **je ne suis pas ~ de lui pardonner** I'm nowhere near ready to forgive him; **on n'est pas à un jour ~** one day (either way) won't make any difference, we're not going to quibble over the odd day.

présage [pʀezaʒ] *nm* omen.

présager [pʀezaʒe] *vt* (*prévoir*) to foresee; (*annoncer*) to portend.

pré-salé, *pl* **prés-salés** [pʀesale] *nm* (*CULIN*) salt-meadow lamb.

presbyte [pʀɛsbit] *adj* long-sighted (*BRIT*), far-sighted (*US*).

presbytère [pʀɛsbitɛʀ] *nm* presbytery.

presbytérien, ne [pʀɛsbiteʀjɛ̃, -ɛn] *adj, nm/f* Presbyterian.

presbytie [pʀɛsbisi] *nf* long-sightedness (*BRIT*), far-sightedness (*US*).

prescience [pʀesjɑ̃s] *nf* prescience, foresight.

préscolaire [pʀeskɔlɛʀ] *adj* preschool *cpd*.

prescription [pʀɛskʀipsjɔ̃] *nf* (*instruction*) order, instruction; (*MÉD, JUR*) prescription.

prescrire [pʀɛskʀiʀ] *vt* to prescribe; **se ~** *vi* (*JUR*) to lapse.

prescrit, e [pʀɛskʀi, -it] *pp de* **prescrire** ♦ *adj* (*date etc*) stipulated.

préséance [pʀeseɑ̃s] *nf* precedence *no pl.*

présélection [pʀeseleksjɔ̃] *nf* (*de candidats*) short-listing; **effectuer une** ~ to draw up a shortlist.

présélectionner [pʀeseleksjɔne] *vt* to preselect; (*dispositif*) to preset; (*candidats*) to make an initial selection from among, short-list (*BRIT*).

présence [pʀezɑ̃s] *nf* presence; (*au bureau etc*) attendance; **en** ~ face to face; **en** ~ **de** in (the) presence of; (*fig*) in the face of; **faire acte de** ~ to put in a token appearance; ~ **d'esprit** presence of mind.

présent, e [pʀezɑ̃, -ɑ̃t] *adj, nm* present; (*AD-MIN, COMM*): **la** ~**e lettre/loi** this letter/law ♦ *nm/f*: **les** ~**s** (*personnes*) those present ♦ *nf* (*COMM: lettre*): **la** ~**e** this letter; **à** ~ now, at present; **dès à** ~ here and now; **jusqu'à** ~ up till now, until now; **à** ~ **que** now that.

présentable [pʀezɑ̃tabl(ə)] *adj* presentable.

présentateur, trice [pʀezɑ̃tatœʀ, -tʀis] *nm/f* presenter.

présentation [pʀezɑ̃tasjɔ̃] *nf* presentation; introduction; (*allure*) appearance.

présenter [pʀezɑ̃te] *vt* to present; (*invité, candidat*) to introduce; (*félicitations, condoléances*) to offer; (*montrer: billet, pièce d'identité*) to show, produce; (*faire inscrire: candidat*) to put forward; (*soumettre*) to submit ♦ *vi*: ~ **mal/bien** to have an unattractive/a pleasing appearance; **se** ~ *vi* (*sur convocation*) to report, come; (*se faire connaître*) to come forward; (*à une élection*) to stand; (*occasion*) to arise; **se** ~ **à un examen** to sit an exam; **se** ~ **bien/mal** to look good/not too good.

présentoir [pʀezɑ̃twaʀ] *nm* (*étagère*) display shelf (*pl* shelves); (*vitrine*) showcase; (*étal*) display stand.

préservatif [pʀezɛʀvatif] *nm* condom, sheath.

préservation [pʀezɛʀvasjɔ̃] *nf* protection, preservation.

préserver [pʀezɛʀve] *vt*: ~ **de** (*protéger*) to protect from; (*sauver*) to save from.

présidence [pʀezidɑ̃s] *nf* presidency; chairmanship.

président [pʀezidɑ̃] *nm* (*POL*) president; (*d'une assemblée, COMM*) chairman; ~ **directeur général (PDG)** chairman and managing director (*BRIT*), chairman and president (*US*); ~ **du jury** (*JUR*) foreman of the jury; (*d'examen*) chief examiner.

présidente [pʀezidɑ̃t] *nf* president; (*femme du président*) president's wife; (*d'une réunion*) chairwoman.

présidentiable [pʀezidɑ̃sjabl(ə)] *adj, nm/f* potential president.

présidentiel, le [pʀezidɑ̃sjɛl] *adj* presidential; ~**les** *nfpl* presidential election(s).

présider [pʀezide] *vt* to preside over; (*dîner*) to be the guest of honour (*BRIT*) *ou* honor (*US*) at; ~ **à** *vt* to direct; to govern.

présomption [pʀezɔ̃psjɔ̃] *nf* presumption.

présomptueux, euse [pʀezɔ̃ptɥø, -øz] *adj* presumptuous.

presque [pʀɛsk(ə)] *adv* almost, nearly; ~ **rien** hardly anything; ~ **pas** hardly (at all); ~ **pas de** hardly any; **personne, ou** ~ next to nobody, hardly anyone; **la** ~ **totalité (de)** almost *ou* nearly all.

presqu'île [pʀɛskil] *nf* peninsula.

pressant, e [pʀesɑ̃, -ɑ̃t] *adj* urgent; (*personne*) insistent; **se faire** ~ to become insistent.

presse [pʀɛs] *nf* press; (*affluence*): **heures de** ~ busy times; **sous** ~ gone to press; **mettre sous** ~ to send to press; **avoir une bonne/ mauvaise** ~ to have a good/bad press; ~ **féminine** women's magazines *pl*; ~ **d'information** quality newspapers *pl*.

pressé, e [pʀese] *adj* in a hurry; (*air*) hurried; (*besogne*) urgent ♦ *nm*: **aller au plus** ~ to see to first things first; **être** ~ **de faire qch** to be in a hurry to do sth; **orange** ~**e** freshly squeezed orange juice.

presse-citron [pʀɛsitʀɔ̃] *nm inv* lemon squeezer.

presse-fruits [pʀɛsfʀɥi] *nm inv* lemon squeezer.

pressentiment [pʀesɑ̃timɑ̃] *nm* foreboding, premonition.

pressentir [pʀesɑ̃tiʀ] *vt* to sense; (*prendre contact avec*) to approach.

presse-papiers [pʀɛspapje] *nm inv* paperweight.

presse-purée [pʀɛspyʀe] *nm inv* potato masher.

presser [pʀese] *vt* (*fruit, éponge*) to squeeze; (*interrupteur, bouton*) to press, push; (*allure, affaire*) to speed up; (*débiteur etc*) to press; (*inciter*): ~ **qn de faire** to urge *ou* press sb to do ♦ *vi* to be urgent; **se** ~ (*se hâter*) to hurry (up); (*se grouper*) to crowd; **rien ne presse** there's no hurry; **se** ~ **contre qn** to squeeze up against sb; ~ **le pas** to quicken one's step; ~ **qn entre ses bras** to squeeze sb tight.

pressing [pʀesiŋ] *nm* (*repassage*) steam-pressing; (*magasin*) dry-cleaner's.

pression [pʀesjɔ̃] *nf* pressure; (*bouton*) press stud (*BRIT*), snap fastener; **faire** ~ **sur** to put pressure on; **sous** ~ pressurized, under pressure; (*fig*) keyed up; ~ **artérielle** blood pressure.

pressoir [pʀeswaʀ] *nm* (*wine ou oil etc*) press.

pressurer [pʀesyʀe] *vt* (*fig*) to squeeze.

pressurisé, e [pʀesyʀize] *adj* pressurized.

prestance [pʀɛstɑ̃s] *nf* presence, imposing bearing.

prestataire [pʀɛstatɛʀ] *nm/f* person receiving benefits; (*COMM*): ~ **de services** provider of services.

prestation [pʀɛstasjɔ̃] *nf* (*allocation*) benefit; (*d'une assurance*) cover *no pl*; (*d'une entreprise*) service provided; (*d'un joueur, artiste*) performance; ~ **de serment** taking the oath; ~ **de service** provision of a service; ~s **familiales** ≈ child benefit.

preste [pʀɛst(ə)] *adj* nimble.

prestement [pʀɛstəmɑ̃] *adv* nimbly.

prestidigitateur, trice [pʀɛstidiʒitatœʀ, -tʀis] *nm/f* conjurer.

prestidigitation [pʀɛstidiʒitasjɔ̃] *nf* conjuring.

prestige [pʀɛstiʒ] *nm* prestige.

prestigieux, euse [pʀɛstiʒjø, -øz] *adj* prestigious.

présumer [pʀezyme] *vt:* ~ **que** to presume *ou* assume that; ~ **de** to overrate; ~ **qn coupable** to presume sb guilty.

présupposé [pʀesypoze] *nm* presupposition.

présupposer [pʀesypoze] *vt* to presuppose.

présupposition [pʀesypozisjɔ̃] *nf* presupposition.

présure [pʀezyʀ] *nf* rennet.

prêt, e [pʀɛ, pʀɛt] *adj* ready ♦ *nm* lending *no pl*; (*somme prêtée*) loan; ~ **à faire** ready to do; ~ **à tout** ready for anything; ~ **sur gages** pawnbroking *no pl*.

prêt-à-porter, *pl* **prêts-à-porter** [pʀɛtapɔʀte] *nm* ready-to-wear *ou* off-the-peg (*BRIT*) clothes *pl*.

prétendant [pʀetɑ̃dɑ̃] *nm* pretender; (*d'une femme*) suitor.

prétendre [pʀetɑ̃dʀ(ə)] *vt* (*affirmer*): ~ **que** to claim that; (*avoir l'intention de*): ~ **à** *vt* (*droit, titre*) to lay claim to.

prétendu, e [pʀetɑ̃dy] *adj* (*supposé*) so-called.

prétendument [pʀetɑ̃dymɑ̃] *adv* allegedly.

prête-nom [pʀɛtnɔ̃] *nm* (*péj*) figurehead; (*COMM etc*) dummy.

prétentieux, euse [pʀetɑ̃sjø, -øz] *adj* pretentious.

prétention [pʀetɑ̃sjɔ̃] *nf* pretentiousness; (*exigence, ambition*) claim; **sans** ~ unpretentious.

prêter [pʀete] *vt* (*livres, argent*): ~ **qch (à)** to lend sth (to); (*supposer*): ~ **à qn** (*caractère, propos*) to attribute to sb ♦ *vi* (*aussi:* **se** ~: *tissu, cuir*) to give; ~ **à** (*commentaires etc*) to be open to, give rise to; **se** ~ **à** to lend o.s. (*ou* itself) to; (*manigances etc*) to go along with; ~ **assistance à** to give help to; ~ **attention** to pay attention; ~ **serment** to take the oath; ~ **l'oreille** to listen.

prêteur, euse [pʀɛtœʀ, -øz] *nm/f* moneylender; ~ **sur gages** pawnbroker.

prétexte [pʀetɛkst(ə)] *nm* pretext, excuse; **sous aucun** ~ on no account; **sous (le)** ~ **que/de** on the pretext that/of.

prétexter [pʀetɛkste] *vt* to give as a pretext *ou* an excuse.

prêtre [pʀɛtʀ(ə)] *nm* priest.

prêtre-ouvrier, *pl* **prêtres-ouvriers** [pʀɛtʀuvʀije] *nm* worker-priest.

prêtrise [pʀɛtʀiz] *nf* priesthood.

preuve [pʀœv] *nf* proof; (*indice*) proof, evidence *no pl*; **jusqu'à** ~ **du contraire** until proved otherwise; **faire** ~ **de** to show; **faire ses** ~s to prove o.s. (*ou* itself); ~ **matérielle** material evidence.

prévaloir [pʀevalwaʀ] *vi* to prevail; **se** ~ **de** *vt* to take advantage of; (*tirer vanité de*) to pride o.s. on.

prévarication [pʀevaʀikasjɔ̃] *nf* maladministration.

prévaut [pʀevo] *etc vb voir* **prévaloir**.

prévenances [pʀevnɑ̃s] *nfpl* thoughtfulness *sg*, kindness *sg*.

prévenant, e [pʀevnɑ̃, -ɑ̃t] *adj* thoughtful, kind.

prévenir [pʀevniʀ] *vt* (*avertir*): ~ **qn (de)** to warn sb (about); (*informer*): ~ **qn (de)** to tell *ou* inform sb (about); (*éviter*) to avoid, prevent; (*anticiper*) to anticipate; (*influencer*): ~ **qn contre** to prejudice sb against.

préventif, ive [pʀevɑ̃tif, -iv] *adj* preventive.

prévention [pʀevɑ̃sjɔ̃] *nf* prevention; (*préjugé*) prejudice; (*JUR*) custody, detention; ~ **routière** road safety.

prévenu, e [pʀevny] *nm/f* (*JUR*) defendant, accused.

prévisible [pʀevizibl(ə)] *adj* foreseeable.

prévision [pʀevizjɔ̃] *nf:* ~s predictions; (*météorologiques, économiques*) forecast *sg*; **en** ~ **de** in anticipation of; ~s **météorologiques** *ou* **du temps** weather forecast *sg*.

prévisionnel, le [pʀevizjɔnɛl] *adj* concerned with future requirements.

prévit [pʀevi] *etc vb voir* **prévoir**.

prévoir [pʀevwaʀ] *vt* (*deviner*) to foresee; (*s'attendre à*) to expect, reckon on; (*prévenir*) to anticipate; (*organiser*) to plan; (*préparer, réserver*) to allow; **prévu pour 4 personnes** designed for 4 people; **prévu pour 10 h** scheduled for 10 o'clock.

prévoyance [pʀevwajɑ̃s] *nf* foresight; **société/caisse de** ~ provident society/ contingency fund.

prévoyant, e [pʀevwajɑ̃, -ɑ̃t] *vb voir* **prévoir** ♦ *adj* gifted with (*ou* showing) foresight, far-sighted.

prévu, e [pʀevy] *pp de* **prévoir**.

prier [pʀije] *vi* to pray ♦ *vt* (*Dieu*) to pray to; (*implorer*) to beg; (*demander*): ~ **qn de faire** to ask sb to do; (*inviter*): ~ **qn à dîner** to invite sb to dinner; **se faire** ~ to need coaxing *ou* persuading; **je vous en prie** (*allez-y*) please do; (*de rien*) don't mention it; **je vous prie de faire** please (would you) do.

prière [pʀijɛʀ] *nf* prayer; (*demande instante*) plea, entreaty; "~ **de faire ...**" "please do ...".

primaire [pʀimɛʀ] *adj* primary; (*péj: personne*) simple-minded; (: *idées*) simplistic ♦ *nm* (*SCOL*) primary education.

primauté [pʀimote] *nf* (*fig*) primacy.

prime [pʀim] *nf* (*bonification*) bonus; (*subside*) allowance; (*COMM: cadeau*) free gift; (*ASSU-*

RANCES, BOURSE) premium ♦ adj: de ~ abord at first glance; ~ de risque danger money no pl; ~ de transport travel allowance.

primer [pʀime] vt (l'emporter sur) to prevail over; (récompenser) to award a prize to ♦ vi to dominate, prevail.

primesautier, ière [pʀimsotje, -jɛʀ] adj impulsive.

primeur [pʀimœʀ] nf: avoir la ~ de to be the first to hear (ou see etc); ~s nfpl (fruits, légumes) early fruits and vegetables; **marchand de** ~ greengrocer (BRIT), produce dealer (US).

primevère [pʀimvɛʀ] nf primrose.

primitif, ive [pʀimitif, -iv] adj primitive; (original) original ♦ nm/f primitive.

primo [pʀimo] adv first (of all), firstly.

primordial, e, aux [pʀimɔʀdjal, -o] adj essential, primordial.

prince [pʀɛ̃s] nm prince; ~ **charmant** Prince Charming; ~ **de Galles** nm inv (tissu) check cloth; ~ **héritier** crown prince.

princesse [pʀɛ̃sɛs] nf princess.

princier, ière [pʀɛ̃sje, -jɛʀ] adj princely.

principal, e, aux [pʀɛ̃sipal, -o] adj principal, main ♦ nm (SCOL) head(teacher) (BRIT), principal (US); (essentiel) main thing ♦ nf (LING): (proposition) ~e main clause.

principalement [pʀɛ̃sipalmɑ̃] adv principally, mainly.

principauté [pʀɛ̃sipote] nf principality.

principe [pʀɛ̃sip] nm principle; **partir du** ~ **que** to work on the principle ou assumption that; **pour le** ~ on principle, for the sake of it; **de** ~ adj (hostilité) automatic; (accord) in principle; **par** ~ on principle; **en** ~ (habituellement) as a rule; (théoriquement) in principle.

printanier, ière [pʀɛ̃tanje, -jɛʀ] adj spring cpd; spring-like.

printemps [pʀɛ̃tɑ̃] nm spring; **au** ~ in spring.

priori [pʀijɔʀi]: **a** ~ adv at first glance; initially; a priori.

prioritaire [pʀijɔʀitɛʀ] adj having priority; (AUTO) having right of way; (INFORM) foreground.

priorité [pʀijɔʀite] nf (AUTO): **avoir la** ~ (sur) to have right of way (over); ~ **à droite** right of way to vehicles coming from the right; **en** ~ as a (matter of) priority.

pris, e [pʀi, pʀiz] pp de **prendre** ♦ adj (place) taken; (billets) sold; (journée, mains) full; (personne) busy; (crème, ciment) set; (MÉD: enflammé): **avoir le nez/la gorge** ~(e) to have a stuffy nose/a bad throat; (saisi): **être** ~ **de peur/de fatigue** to be stricken with fear/ overcome with fatigue.

prise [pʀiz] nf (d'une ville) capture; (PÊCHE, CHASSE) catch; (de judo ou catch, point d'appui ou pour empoigner) hold; (ÉLEC: fiche) plug; (: femelle) socket; (: au mur) point; **en** ~ (AUTO) in gear; **être aux** ~s avec to be grap-

pling with; to be battling with; **lâcher** ~ to let go; **donner** ~ **à** (fig) to give rise to; **avoir** ~ **sur qn** to have a hold over sb; ~ **en charge** (taxe) pick-up charge; (par la sécurité sociale) undertaking to reimburse costs; ~ **de contact** initial meeting, first contact; ~ **de courant** power point; ~ **d'eau** water (supply) point; tap; ~ **multiple** adaptor; ~ **d'otages** hostage-taking; ~ **à partie** (JUR) action against a judge; ~ **péritel** SCART socket; ~ **de sang** blood test; ~ **de son** sound recording; ~ **de tabac** pinch of snuff; ~ **de terre** earth; ~ **de vue** (photo) shot; (action): ~ **de vue(s)** filming, shooting.

priser [pʀize] vt (tabac, héroïne) to take; (estimer) to prize, value ♦ vi to take snuff.

prisme [pʀism(ə)] nm prism.

prison [pʀizɔ̃] nf prison; **aller/être en** ~ to go to/be in prison ou jail; **faire de la** ~ to serve time; **être condamné à 5 ans de** ~ to be sentenced to 5 years' imprisonment ou 5 years in prison.

prisonnier, ière [pʀizɔnje, -jɛʀ] nm/f prisoner ♦ adj captive; **faire qn** ~ to take sb prisoner.

prit [pʀi] vb voir **prendre**.

privatif, ive [pʀivatif, -iv] adj (jardin etc) private; (peine) which deprives one of one's liberties.

privations [pʀivasjɔ̃] nfpl privations, hardships.

privatisation [pʀivatizasjɔ̃] nf privatization.

privatiser [pʀivatize] vt to privatize.

privautés [pʀivote] nfpl liberties.

privé, e [pʀive] adj private; (dépourvu): ~ **de** without, lacking; **en** ~, **dans le** ~ in private.

priver [pʀive] vt: ~ **qn de** to deprive sb of; **se** ~ **de** to go ou do without; **ne pas se** ~ **de faire** not to refrain from doing.

privilège [pʀivilɛʒ] nm privilege.

privilégié, e [pʀivileʒje] adj privileged.

privilégier [pʀivileʒje] vt to favour (BRIT), favor (US).

prix [pʀi] nm (valeur) price; (récompense, SCOL) prize; **mettre à** ~ to set a reserve (BRIT) ou an upset (US) price on; **au** ~ **fort** at a very high price; **acheter qch à** ~ **d'or** to pay a (small) fortune for sth; **hors de** ~ exorbitantly priced; **à aucun** ~ not at any price; **à tout** ~ at all costs; **grand** ~ (SPORT) Grand Prix; ~ **d'achat/de vente/de revient** purchasing/selling/cost price; ~ **conseillé** manufacturer's recommended price (MRP).

pro [pʀo] nm (= professionnel) pro.

probabilité [pʀɔbabilite] nf probability; **selon toute** ~ in all probability.

probable [pʀɔbabl(ə)] adj likely, probable.

probablement [pʀɔbabləmɑ̃] adv probably.

probant, e [pʀɔbɑ̃, -ɑ̃t] adj convincing.

probatoire [pʀɔbatwaʀ] adj (examen, test) preliminary; (stage) probationary, trial cpd.

probité [pʀɔbite] nf integrity, probity.

problématique [pʀɔblematik] adj problematic(al) ♦ *nf* problematics *sg*; (*problème*) problem.

problème [pʀɔblɛm] *nm* problem.

procédé [pʀɔsede] *nm* (*méthode*) process; (*comportement*) behaviour *no pl* (*BRIT*), behavior *no pl* (*US*).

procéder [pʀɔsede] *vi* to proceed; to behave; ~ **à** *vt* to carry out.

procédure [pʀɔsedyʀ] *nf* (*ADMIN*, *JUR*) procedure.

procès [pʀɔsɛ] *nm* (*JUR*) trial; (*: poursuites*) proceedings *pl*; **être en** ~ **avec** to be involved in a lawsuit with; **faire le** ~ **de qn/qch** (*fig*) to put sb/sth on trial; **sans autre forme de** ~ without further ado.

processeur [pʀɔsɛsœʀ] *nm* processor.

procession [pʀɔsesjɔ̃] *nf* procession.

processus [pʀɔsesys] *nm* process.

procès-verbal, aux [pʀɔsɛvɛʀbal, -o] *nm* (*constat*) statement; (*aussi*: **PV**): **avoir un** ~ to get a parking ticket; to be booked; (*de réunion*) minutes *pl*.

prochain, e [pʀɔʃɛ̃, -ɛn] *adj* next; (*proche*) impending; near ♦ *nm* fellow man; **la** ~**e fois/semaine** ~**e** next time/week; **à la** ~**e!** (*fam*), **à la** ~**e fois** see you!, till the next time!; **un** ~ **jour** (some day) soon.

prochainement [pʀɔʃɛnmɑ̃] *adv* soon, shortly.

proche [pʀɔʃ] *adj* nearby; (*dans le temps*) imminent; close at hand; (*parent, ami*) close; ~**s** *nmpl* (*parents*) close relatives, next of kin; (*amis*): **l'un de ses** ~**s** one of those close to him (*ou* her); **être** ~ (**de**) to be near, be close (to); **de** ~ **en** ~ gradually.

Proche-Orient [pʀɔʃɔʀjɑ̃] *nm*: **le** ~ the Near East.

proclamation [pʀɔklamasjɔ̃] *nf* proclamation.

proclamer [pʀɔklame] *vt* to proclaim; (*résultat d'un examen*) to announce.

procréer [pʀɔkʀee] *vt* to procreate.

procuration [pʀɔkyʀasjɔ̃] *nf* proxy; power of attorney; **voter par** ~ to vote by proxy.

procurer [pʀɔkyʀe] *vt* (*fournir*): ~ **qch à qn** to get *ou* obtain sth for sb; (*causer: plaisir etc*): ~ **qch à qn** to bring *ou* give sb sth; **se** ~ *vt* to get.

procureur [pʀɔkyʀœʀ] *nm* public prosecutor; ~ **général** public prosecutor (*in appeal court*).

prodigalité [pʀɔdigalite] *nf* (*générosité*) generosity; (*extravagance*) extravagance, wastefulness.

prodige [pʀɔdiʒ] *nm* (*miracle, merveille*) marvel, wonder; (*personne*) prodigy.

prodigieusement [pʀɔdiʒjøzmɑ̃] *adv* tremendously.

prodigieux, euse [pʀɔdiʒjø, -øz] *adj* prodigious; phenomenal.

prodigue [pʀɔdig] *adj* (*généreux*) generous; (*dépensier*) extravagant, wasteful; **fils** ~ prodigal son.

prodiguer [pʀɔdige] *vt* (*argent, biens*) to be lavish with; (*soins, attentions*): ~ **qch à qn** to lavish sth on sb.

producteur, trice [pʀɔdyktœʀ, -tʀis] *adj*: ~ **de blé** wheat-producing; (*CINÉ*): **société productrice** film *ou* movie company ♦ *nm/f* producer.

productif, ive [pʀɔdyktif, -iv] *adj* productive.

production [pʀɔdyksjɔ̃] *nf* (*gén*) production; (*rendement*) output; (*produits*) products *pl*, goods *pl*; (*œuvres*): **la** ~ **dramatique du XVIIe siècle** the plays of the 17th century.

productivité [pʀɔdyktivite] *nf* productivity.

produire [pʀɔdɥiʀ] *vt*, *vi* to produce; **se** ~ *vi* (*acteur*) to perform, appear; (*événement*) to happen, occur.

produit, e [pʀɔdɥi, -it] *pp de* **produire** ♦ *nm* (*gén*) product; ~ **d'entretien** cleaning product; ~ **national brut (PNB)** gross national product (GNP); ~ **net** net profit; ~ **pour la vaisselle** washing-up (*BRIT*) *ou* dish-washing (*US*) liquid; ~ **des ventes** income from sales; ~**s agricoles** farm produce *sg*; ~**s alimentaires** foodstuffs; ~**s de beauté** beauty products, cosmetics.

proéminent, e [pʀɔeminɑ̃, -ɑ̃t] *adj* prominent.

prof [pʀɔf] *nm* (*fam*: = **professeur**) teacher; professor; lecturer.

prof. [pʀɔf] *abr* = **professeur, professionnel**.

profane [pʀɔfan] *adj* (*REL*) secular; (*ignorant, non initié*) uninitiated ♦ *nm/f* layman.

profaner [pʀɔfane] *vt* to desecrate; (*fig: sentiment*) to defile; (*: talent*) to debase.

proférer [pʀɔfeʀe] *vt* to utter.

professer [pʀɔfese] *vt* to profess.

professeur [pʀɔfesœʀ] *nm* teacher; (*titulaire d'une chaire*) professor; ~ (**de faculté**) (university) lecturer.

profession [pʀɔfesjɔ̃] *nf* (*libérale*) profession; (*gén*) occupation; **faire** ~ **de** (*opinion, religion*) to profess; **de** ~ by profession; **"sans** ~**"** "unemployed"; (*femme mariée*) "housewife".

professionnel, le [pʀɔfesjɔnɛl] *adj* professional ♦ *nm/f* professional; (*ouvrier qualifié*) skilled worker.

professoral, e, aux [pʀɔfesɔʀal, -o] *adj* professorial; **le corps** ~ the teaching profession.

professorat [pʀɔfesɔʀa] *nm*: **le** ~ the teaching profession.

profil [pʀɔfil] *nm* profile; (*d'une voiture*) line, contour; **de** ~ in profile.

profilé, e [pʀɔfile] *adj* shaped; (*aile etc*) streamlined.

profiler [pʀɔfile] *vt* to streamline; **se** ~ *vi* (*arbre, tour*) to stand out, be silhouetted.

profit [pʀɔfi] *nm* (*avantage*) benefit, advantage; (*COMM, FINANCE*) profit; **au** ~ **de** in aid of; **tirer** *ou* **retirer** ~ **de** to profit from; **mettre à** ~ to take advantage of; to turn to good account; ~**s et pertes** (*COMM*) profit and loss(es).

profitable [pʀɔfitabl(ə)] *adj* beneficial; profitable.

profiter [pʀɔfite] *vi:* ~ **de** to take advantage of; to make the most of; ~ **de ce que** ... to take advantage of the fact that ...; ~ **à** to be of benefit to, benefit; to be profitable to.

profiteur, euse [pʀɔfitœʀ, -øz] *nm/f (péj)* profiteer.

profond, e [pʀɔfɔ̃, -ɔ̃d] *adj* deep; (*méditation, mépris*) profound; **au plus** ~ **de** in the depths of, at the (very) bottom of; **la France** ~**e** the heartlands of France.

profondément [pʀɔfɔ̃demɑ̃] *adv* deeply; profoundly.

profondeur [pʀɔfɔ̃dœʀ] *nf* depth.

profusément [pʀɔfyzemɑ̃] *adv* profusely.

profusion [pʀɔfyzjɔ̃] *nf* profusion; **à** ~ in plenty.

progéniture [pʀɔʒenityʀ] *nf* offspring *inv*.

progiciel [pʀɔʒisjɛl] *nm* (*INFORM*) (software) package; ~ **d'application** applications package, applications software *no pl*.

progouvernemental, e, aux [pʀɔguvɛʀnəmɑ̃tal, -o] *adj* pro-government *cpd*.

programmable [pʀɔgʀamabl(ə)] *adj* programmable.

programmateur, trice [pʀɔgʀamatœʀ, -tʀis] *nm/f* (*CINÉ, TV*) programme (*BRIT*) *ou* program (*US*) planner ♦ *nm* (*de machine à laver etc*) timer.

programmation [pʀɔgʀamasjɔ̃] *nf* programming.

programme [pʀɔgʀam] *nm* programme (*BRIT*), program (*US*); (*TV, RADIO*) program(me)s *pl*; (*SCOL*) syllabus, curriculum; (*INFORM*) program; **au** ~ **de ce soir** (*TV*) among tonight's program(me)s.

programmé, e [pʀɔgʀame] *adj*: **enseignement** ~ programmed learning.

programmer [pʀɔgʀame] *vt* (*TV, RADIO*) to put on, show; (*organiser, prévoir*) to schedule; (*INFORM*) to program.

programmeur, euse [pʀɔgʀamœʀ, -øz] *nm/f* (computer) programmer.

progrès [pʀɔgʀɛ] *nm* progress *no pl*; **faire des/être en** ~ to make/be making progress.

progresser [pʀɔgʀese] *vi* to progress; (*troupes etc*) to make headway *ou* progress.

progressif, ive [pʀɔgʀesif, -iv] *adj* progressive.

progression [pʀɔgʀesjɔ̃] *nf* progression; (*d'une troupe etc*) advance, progress.

progressiste [pʀɔgʀesist(ə)] *adj* progressive.

progressivement [pʀɔgʀesivmɑ̃] *adv* progressively.

prohiber [pʀɔibe] *vt* to prohibit, ban.

prohibitif, ive [pʀɔibitif, -iv] *adj* prohibitive.

prohibition [pʀɔibisjɔ̃] *nf* ban, prohibition; (*HIST*) Prohibition.

proie [pʀwa] *nf* prey *no pl*; **être la** ~ **de** to fall prey to; **être en** ~ **à** (*doutes, sentiment*) to be

prey to; (*douleur, mal*) to be suffering.

projecteur [pʀɔʒɛktœʀ] *nm* projector; (*de théâtre, cirque*) spotlight.

projectile [pʀɔʒɛktil] *nm* missile; (*d'arme*) projectile, bullet (*ou* shell *etc*).

projection [pʀɔʒɛksjɔ̃] *nf* projection; showing; **conférence avec** ~**s** lecture with slides (*ou a* film).

projectionniste [pʀɔʒɛksjɔnist(ə)] *nm/f* (*CINÉ*) projectionist.

projet [pʀɔʒɛ] *nm* plan; (*ébauche*) draft; **faire des** ~**s** to make plans; ~ **de loi** bill.

projeter [pʀɔʒte] *vt* (*envisager*) to plan; (*film, photos*) to project; (*passer*) to show; (*ombre, lueur*) to throw, cast, project; (*jeter*) to throw up (*ou* off *ou* out); ~ **de faire qch** to plan to do sth.

prolétaire [pʀɔletɛʀ] *adj, nm/f* proletarian.

prolétariat [pʀɔletaʀja] *nm* proletariat.

prolétarien, -ne [pʀɔletaʀjɛ̃, -ɛn] *adj* proletarian.

prolifération [pʀɔlifeʀasjɔ̃] *nf* proliferation.

proliférer [pʀɔlifeʀe] *vi* to proliferate.

prolifique [pʀɔlifik] *adj* prolific.

prolixe [pʀɔliks(ə)] *adj* verbose.

prolo [pʀɔlo] *nm/f* (*fam*: = *prolétaire*) prole (*péj*).

prologue [pʀɔlɔg] *nm* prologue.

prolongateur [pʀɔlɔ̃gatœʀ] *nm* (*ÉLEC*) extension cable.

prolongation [pʀɔlɔ̃gasjɔ̃] *nf* prolongation; extension; ~**s** *nfpl* (*FOOTBALL*) extra time *sg*.

prolongement [pʀɔlɔ̃ʒmɑ̃] *nm* extension; ~**s** *nmpl* (*fig*) repercussions, effects; **dans le** ~ **de** running on from.

prolonger [pʀɔlɔ̃ʒe] *vt* (*débat, séjour*) to prolong; (*délai, billet, rue*) to extend; (*suj: chose*) to be a continuation *ou* an extension of; **se** ~ *vi* to go on.

promenade [pʀɔmnad] *nf* walk (*ou* drive *ou* ride); **faire une** ~ to go for a walk; **une** ~ (à **pied)/en voiture/à vélo** a walk/drive/ (bicycle) ride.

promener [pʀɔmne] *vt* (*personne, chien*) to take out for a walk; (*fig*) to carry around; to trail round; (*doigts, regard*): ~ **qch sur** to run sth over; **se** ~ *vi* (à *pied*) to go for (*ou* be out for) a walk; (*en voiture*) to go for (*ou* be out for) a drive; (*fig*): **se** ~ **sur** to wander over.

promeneur, euse [pʀɔmnœʀ, -øz] *nm/f* walker, stroller.

promenoir [pʀɔmənwaʀ] *nm* gallery, (covered) walkway.

promesse [pʀɔmɛs] *nf* promise; ~ **d'achat** commitment to buy.

prometteur, euse [pʀɔmɛtœʀ, -øz] *adj* promising.

promettre [pʀɔmɛtʀ(ə)] *vt* to promise ♦ *vi* (*récolte, arbre*) to look promising; (*enfant, musicien*) to be promising; **se** ~ **de faire** to resolve *ou* mean to do; ~ **à qn de faire** to promise sb that one will do.

promeus [pʀɔmø] *etc vb voir* **promouvoir**.

promis, e [pʀɔmi, -iz] *pp de* **promettre** ♦ *adj:* **être ~ à qch** (*destiné*) to be destined for sth.

promiscuité [pʀɔmiskɥite] *nf* crowding; lack of privacy.

promit [pʀɔmi] *vb voir* **promettre**.

promontoire [pʀɔmɔ̃twaʀ] *nm* headland.

promoteur, trice [pʀɔmɔtœʀ, -tʀis] *nm/f* (*instigateur*) instigator, promoter; ~ **(immobilier)** property developer (*BRIT*), real estate promoter (*US*).

promotion [pʀɔmɔsjɔ̃] *nf* (*avancement*) promotion; (*SCOL*) year (*BRIT*), class; **en ~** (*COMM*) on promotion, on (special) offer.

promotionnel, le [pʀɔmɔsjɔnɛl] *adj* (*article*) on promotion, on (special) offer; (*vente*) promotional.

promouvoir [pʀɔmuvwaʀ] *vt* to promote.

prompt, e [pʀɔ̃, pʀɔ̃t] *adj* swift, rapid; (*intervention, changement*) sudden; ~ **à faire qch** quick to do sth.

promptement [pʀɔ̃ptəmɑ̃] *adv* swiftly.

prompteur [pʀɔ̃tœʀ] *nm* ® Autocue ® (*BRIT*), Teleprompter ® (*US*).

promptitude [pʀɔ̃tityd] *nf* swiftness, rapidity.

promu, e [pʀɔmy] *pp de* **promouvoir**.

promulguer [pʀɔmylge] *vt* to promulgate.

prôner [pʀone] *vt* (*louer*) to laud, extol; (*préconiser*) to advocate, commend.

pronom [pʀɔnɔ̃] *nm* pronoun.

pronominal, e, aux [pʀɔnɔminal, -o] *adj* pronominal; (*verbe*) reflexive, pronominal.

prononcé, e [pʀɔnɔ̃se] *adj* pronounced, marked.

prononcer [pʀɔnɔ̃se] *vt* (*son, mot, jugement*) to pronounce; (*dire*) to utter; (*allocution*) to deliver ♦ *vi* (*JUR*) to deliver *ou* give a verdict; ~ **bien/mal** to have a good/poor pronunciation; **se ~** *vi* to reach a decision, give a verdict; **se ~ sur** to give an opinion on; **se ~ contre** to come down against; **ça se prononce comment?** how do you pronounce this?

prononciation [pʀɔnɔ̃sjasjɔ̃] *nf* pronunciation.

pronostic [pʀɔnɔstik] *nm* (*MÉD*) prognosis (*pl* -oses); (*fig: aussi:* **~s**) forecast.

pronostiquer [pʀɔnɔstike] *vt* (*MÉD*) to prognosticate; (*annoncer, prévoir*) to forecast, foretell.

pronostiqueur, euse [pʀɔnɔstikœʀ, -øz] *nm/f* forecaster.

propagande [pʀɔpagɑ̃d] *nf* propaganda; **faire de la ~ pour qch** to plug *ou* push sth.

propagandiste [pʀɔpagɑ̃dist(ə)] *nm/f* propagandist.

propagation [pʀɔpagasjɔ̃] *nf* propagation.

propager [pʀɔpaʒe] *vt* to spread; **se ~** *vi* to spread; (*PHYSIQUE*) to be propagated.

propane [pʀɔpan] *nm* propane.

propension [pʀɔpɑ̃sjɔ̃] *nf:* ~ **à (faire) qch** propensity to (do) sth.

prophète [pʀɔfɛt], **prophétesse** [pʀɔfetɛs] *nm/f* prophet(ess).

prophétie [pʀɔfesi] *nf* prophecy.

prophétique [pʀɔfetik] *adj* prophetic.

prophétiser [pʀɔfetize] *vt* to prophesy.

prophylactique [pʀɔfilaktik] *adj* prophylactic.

propice [pʀɔpis] *adj* favourable (*BRIT*), favorable (*US*).

proportion [pʀɔpɔʀsjɔ̃] *nf* proportion; **il n'y a aucune ~ entre le prix demandé et le prix réel** the asking price bears no relation to the real price; **à ~ de** proportionally to, in proportion to; **en ~ (de)** in proportion (to); **hors de ~** out of proportion; **toute(s) ~(s) gardée(s)** making due allowance(s).

proportionné, e [pʀɔpɔʀsjɔne] *adj:* **bien ~** well-proportioned; ~ **à** proportionate to.

proportionnel, le [pʀɔpɔʀsjɔnɛl] *adj* proportional; ~ **à** proportional to ♦ *nf* proportional representation.

proportionnellement [pʀɔpɔʀsjɔnɛlmɑ̃] *adv* proportionally, proportionately.

proportionner [pʀɔpɔʀsjɔne] *vt:* ~ **qch à** to proportion *ou* adjust sth to.

propos [pʀɔpo] *nm* (*paroles*) talk *no pl*, remark; (*intention, but*) intention, aim; (*sujet*): **à quel ~?** what about?; **à ~ de** about, regarding; **à tout ~** for no reason at all; **à ce ~** on that subject, in this connection; **à ~** *adv* by the way; (*opportunément*) (just) at the right moment; **hors de ~, mal à ~** *adv* at the wrong moment.

proposer [pʀɔpoze] *vt* (*suggérer*): ~ **qch (à qn)/de faire** to suggest sth (to sb)/doing, propose sth (to sb)/to do; (*offrir*): ~ **qch à qn/de faire** to offer sb sth/to do; (*candidat*) to nominate, put forward; (*loi, motion*) to propose; **se ~ (pour faire)** to offer one's services (to do); **se ~ de faire** to intend *ou* propose to do.

proposition [pʀɔpozisjɔ̃] *nf* suggestion; proposal; offer; (*LING*) clause; **sur la ~ de** at the suggestion of; ~ **de loi** private bill.

propre [pʀɔpʀ(ə)] *adj* clean; (*net*) neat, tidy; (*qui ne salit pas: chien, chat*) house-trained; (*: enfant*) toilet-trained; (*fig: honnête*) honest; (*possessif*) own; (*sens*) literal; (*particulier*): ~ **à** peculiar to, characteristic of; (*approprié*): ~ **à** suitable *ou* appropriate for; (*de nature à*): ~ **à faire** likely to do, that will do ♦ *nm:* **recopier au ~** to make a fair copy of; (*particularité*): **le ~ de** the peculiarity of, the distinctive feature of; **au ~** (*LING*) literally; **appartenir à qn en ~** to belong to sb (exclusively); ~ **à rien** *nm/f* (*péj*) good-for-nothing.

proprement [pʀɔpʀəmɑ̃] *adv* cleanly; neatly, tidily; **à ~ parler** strictly speaking; **le village ~ dit** the actual village, the village itself.

propret, te [pʀɔpʀɛ, -ɛt] *adj* neat and tidy, spick-and-span.

propreté [pʀɔpʀəte] *nf* cleanliness, cleanness; neatness, tidiness.

propriétaire [prɔprijetɛr] *nm/f* owner; (*d'hôtel etc*) proprietor/tress, owner; (*pour le locataire*) landlord/lady; ~ **(immobilier)** houseowner; householder; ~ **récoltant** grower; ~ **(terrien)** landowner.

propriété [prɔprijete] *nf* (*droit*) ownership; (*objet, immeuble etc*) property *gén no pl*; (*villa*) residence, property; (*terres*) property *gén no pl*, land *gén no pl*; (*qualité, CHIMIE, MATH*) property; (*correction*) appropriateness, suitability; ~ **artistique et littéraire** artistic and literary copyright; ~ **industrielle** patent rights *pl*.

propulser [prɔpylse] *vt* (*missile*) to propel; (*projeter*) to hurl, fling.

propulsion [prɔpylsjɔ̃] *nf* propulsion.

prorata [prɔrata] *nm inv*: **au ~ de** in proportion to, on the basis of.

prorogation [prɔrɔgasjɔ̃] *nf* deferment; extension; adjournment.

proroger [prɔrɔʒe] *vt* to put back, defer; (*prolonger*) to extend; (*assemblée*) to adjourn, prorogue.

prosaïque [prɔzaik] *adj* mundane, prosaic.

proscription [prɔskripsjɔ̃] *nf* banishment; (*interdiction*) banning; prohibition.

proscrire [prɔskrir] *vt* (*bannir*) to banish; (*interdire*) to ban, prohibit.

prose [proz] *nf* prose (*style*).

prosélyte [prɔzelit] *nm/f* proselyte, convert.

prospecter [prɔspɛkte] *vt* to prospect; (*COMM*) to canvass.

prospecteur-placier, *pl* **prospecteurs-placiers** [prɔspɛktœrplasje] *nm* placement officer.

prospectif, ive [prɔspɛktif, -iv] *adj* prospective.

prospectus [prɔspɛktys] *nm* (*feuille*) leaflet; (*dépliant*) brochure, leaflet.

prospère [prɔspɛr] *adj* prosperous; (*santé, entreprise*) thriving, flourishing.

prospérer [prɔspere] *vi* to thrive.

prospérité [prɔsperite] *nf* prosperity.

prostate [prɔstat] *nf* prostate (gland).

prosterner [prɔstɛrne]: **se ~** *vi* to bow low, prostrate o.s.

prostituée [prɔstitɥe] *nf* prostitute.

prostitution [prɔstitysjɔ̃] *nf* prostitution.

prostré, e [prɔstre] *adj* prostrate.

protagoniste [prɔtagɔnist(ə)] *nm* protagonist.

protecteur, trice [prɔtɛktœr, -tris] *adj* protective; (*air, ton: péj*) patronizing ♦ *nm/f* (*défenseur*) protector; (*des arts*) patron.

protection [prɔtɛksjɔ̃] *nf* protection; (*d'un personnage influent: aide*) patronage; **écran de ~** protective screen; ~ **civile** state-financed civilian rescue service; ~ **maternelle et infantile (PMI)** social service concerned with child welfare.

protectionnisme [prɔtɛksjɔnism(ə)] *nm* protectionism.

protectionniste [prɔtɛksjɔnist(ə)] *adj* protectionist.

protégé, e [prɔteʒe] *nm/f* protégé/e.

protège-cahier [prɔtɛʒkaje] *nm* exercise book cover.

protéger [prɔteʒe] *vt* to protect; (*aider, patronner: personne, arts*) to be a patron of; (*: carrière*) to further; **se ~ de/contre** to protect o.s. from.

protéine [prɔtein] *nf* protein.

protestant, e [prɔtɛstɑ̃, -ɑ̃t] *adj, nm/f* Protestant.

protestantisme [prɔtɛstɑ̃tism(ə)] *nm* Protestantism.

protestataire [prɔtɛstatɛr] *nm/f* protestor.

protestation [prɔtɛstasjɔ̃] *nf* (*plainte*) protest; (*déclaration*) protestation, profession.

protester [prɔtɛste] *vi*: ~ **(contre)** to protest (against *ou* about); ~ **de** (*son innocence, sa loyauté*) to protest.

prothèse [prɔtɛz] *nf* artificial limb, prosthesis (*pl* -ses); ~ **dentaire** (*appareil*) denture; (*science*) dental engineering.

protocolaire [prɔtɔkɔlɛr] *adj* formal; (*questions, règles*) of protocol.

protocole [prɔtɔkɔl] *nm* protocol; (*fig*) etiquette; ~ **d'accord** draft treaty; ~ **opératoire** (*MÉD*) operating procedure.

prototype [prɔtɔtip] *nm* prototype.

protubérance [prɔtyberɑ̃s] *nf* bulge, protuberance.

protubérant, e [prɔtyberɑ̃, -ɑ̃t] *adj* protruding, bulging, protuberant.

proue [pru] *nf* bow(s *pl*), prow.

prouesse [prues] *nf* feat.

prouver [pruve] *vt* to prove.

provenance [prɔvnɑ̃s] *nf* origin; (*de mot, coutume*) source; **avion en ~ de** plane (arriving) from.

provençal, e, aux [prɔvɑ̃sal, -o] *adj* Provençal ♦ *nm* (*LING*) Provençal.

Provence [prɔvɑ̃s] *nf*: **la ~** Provence.

provenir [prɔvnir]: ~ **de** *vt* to come from; (*résulter de*) to be due to, be the result of.

proverbe [prɔvɛrb(ə)] *nm* proverb.

proverbial, e, aux [prɔvɛrbjal, -o] *adj* proverbial.

providence [prɔvidɑ̃s] *nf*: **la ~** providence.

providentiel, le [prɔvidɑ̃sjɛl] *adj* providential.

province [prɔvɛ̃s] *nf* province.

provincial, e, aux [prɔvɛ̃sjal, -o] *adj, nm/f* provincial.

proviseur [prɔvizœr] *nm* ≈ head(teacher) (*BRIT*), ≈ principal (*US*).

provision [prɔvizjɔ̃] *nf* (*réserve*) stock, supply; (*avance: à un avocat, avoué*) retainer, retaining fee; (*COMM*) funds *pl* (in account); reserve; ~**s** *nfpl* (*vivres*) provisions, food *no pl*; **faire ~ de** to stock up with; **placard** *ou* **armoire à ~s** food cupboard.

provisoire [prɔvizwar] *adj* temporary; (*JUR*) provisional; **mise en liberté ~** release on bail.

provisoirement [pʀɔvizwaʀmɑ̃] *adv* temporarily, for the time being.

provocant, e [pʀɔvɔkɑ̃, -ɑ̃t] *adj* provocative.

provocateur, trice [pʀɔvɔkatœʀ, -tʀis] *adj* provocative ♦ *nm* (*meneur*) agitator.

provocation [pʀɔvɔkɑsjɔ̃] *nf* provocation.

provoquer [pʀɔvɔke] *vt* (*défier*) to provoke; (*causer*) to cause, bring about; (: *curiosité*) to arouse, give rise to; (: *aveux*) to prompt, elicit; (*inciter*): ~ **qn à** to incite sb to.

prox. *abr* = **proximité.**

proxénète [pʀɔksenɛt] *nm* procurer.

proxénétisme [pʀɔksenetism(ə)] *nm* procuring.

proximité [pʀɔksimite] *nf* nearness, closeness, proximity; (*dans le temps*) imminence, closeness; **à** ~ near *ou* close by; **à** ~ **de** near (to), close to.

prude [pʀyd] *adj* prudish.

prudemment [pʀydamɑ̃] *adv* (*voir prudent*) carefully; cautiously; prudently; wisely, sensibly.

prudence [pʀydɑ̃s] *nf* carefulness; caution; prudence; **avec** ~ carefully; cautiously; wisely; **par (mesure de)** ~ as a precaution.

prudent, e [pʀydɑ̃, -ɑ̃t] *adj* (*pas~ téméraire*) careful, cautious, prudent; (: *en général*) safety-conscious; (*sage, conseillé*) wise, sensible; (*réservé*) cautious; **ce n'est pas** ~ it's risky; it's not sensible; **soyez** ~ take care, be careful.

prune [pʀyn] *nf* plum.

pruneau, x [pʀyno] *nm* prune.

prunelle [pʀynɛl] *nf* pupil; (*œil*) eye; (*BOT*) sloe; (*eau de vie*) sloe gin.

prunier [pʀynje] *nm* plum tree.

Prusse [pʀys] *nf*: **la** ~ Prussia.

PS *sigle m* = **parti socialiste**; (= *post-scriptum*) PS.

psalmodier [psalmɔdje] *vt* to chant; (*fig*) to drone out.

psaume [psom] *nm* psalm.

pseudonyme [psødɔnim] *nm* (*gén*) fictitious name; (*d'écrivain*) pseudonym, pen name; (*de comédien*) stage name.

PSIG *sigle m* (= *Peloton de surveillance et d'intervention de gendarmerie*) type of police commando squad.

PSU *sigle m* = **parti socialiste unifié.**

psy [psi] *nm/f* (*fam, péj*: = *psychiatre, psychologue*) shrink.

psychanalyse [psikanaliz] *nf* psychoanalysis.

psychanalyser [psikanalize] *vt* to psychoanalyze; **se faire** ~ to undergo (psycho-) analysis.

psychanalyste [psikanalist(ə)] *nm/f* psychoanalyst.

psychanalytique [psikanalitik] *adj* psychoanalytical.

psychédélique [psikedelik] *adj* psychedelic.

psychiatre [psikjatʀ(ə)] *nm/f* psychiatrist.

psychiatrie [psikjatʀi] *nf* psychiatry.

psychiatrique [psikjatʀik] *adj* psychiatric;

(*hôpital*) mental, psychiatric.

psychique [psiʃik] *adj* psychological.

psychisme [psiʃism(ə)] *nm* psyche.

psychologie [psikɔlɔʒi] *nf* psychology.

psychologique [psikɔlɔʒik] *adj* psychological.

psychologiquement [psikɔlɔʒikmɑ̃] *adv* psychologically.

psychologue [psikɔlɔg] *nm/f* psychologist; **être** ~ (*fig*) to be a good psychologist.

psychomoteur, trice [psikɔmɔtœʀ, -tʀis] *adj* psychomotor.

psychopathe [psikɔpat] *nm/f* psychopath.

psychopédagogie [psikɔpedagɔʒi] *nf* educational psychology.

psychose [psikoz] *nf* (*MÉD*) psychosis (*pl* -ses); (*obsession, idée fixe*) obsessive fear.

psychosomatique [psikɔsɔmatik] *adj* psychosomatic.

psychothérapie [psikɔteʀapi] *nf* psychotherapy.

psychotique [psikɔtik] *adj* psychotic.

PTCA *sigle m* = *poids total en charge autorisé.*

Pte *abr* = **Porte.**

pte *abr* (= *pointe*) pt.

PTMA *sigle m* (= *poids total maximum autorisé*) maximum loaded weight.

PTT *sigle fpl voir* **poste.**

pu [py] *pp de* **pouvoir.**

puanteur [pɥɑ̃tœʀ] *nf* stink, stench.

pub [pyb] *nf* (*fam*: = *publicité*): **la** ~ advertising.

pubère [pybɛʀ] *adj* pubescent.

puberté [pybɛʀte] *nf* puberty.

pubis [pybis] *nm* (*bas-ventre*) pubes *pl*; (*os*) pubis.

public, ique [pyblik] *adj* public; (*école, instruction*) state *cpd*; (*scrutin*) open ♦ *nm* public; (*assistance*) audience; **en** ~ in public; **le grand** ~ the general public.

publication [pyblikɑsjɔ̃] *nf* publication.

publiciste [pyblisist(ə)] *nm/f* adman.

publicitaire [pyblisitɛʀ] *adj* advertising *cpd*; (*film, voiture*) publicity *cpd*; (*vente*) promotional ♦ *nm* adman; **rédacteur** ~ copywriter.

publicité [pyblisite] *nf* (*méthode, profession*) advertising; (*annonce*) advertisement; (*révélations*) publicity.

publier [pyblije] *vt* to publish; (*nouvelle*) to publicize, make public.

publipostage [pyblipɔstaʒ] *nm* mailshot, (mass) mailing.

publique [pyblik] *adj f voir* **public.**

publiquement [pyblikmɑ̃] *adv* publicly.

puce [pys] *nf* flea; (*INFORM*) chip; (**marché aux**) ~**s** flea market *sg*; **mettre la** ~ **à l'oreille de qn** to give sb something to think about.

puceau, x [pyso] *adj m*: **être** ~ to be a virgin.

pucelle [pysɛl] *adj f*: **être** ~ to be a virgin.

puceron [pysʀɔ̃] *nm* aphid.

pudeur [pydœʀ] *nf* modesty.

pudibond, e [pydibɔ̃, -ɔ̃d] *adj* prudish.

pudique [pydik] *adj* (*chaste*) modest; (*discret*)

discreet.

pudiquement [pydikmɑ̃] *adv* modestly.

puer [pɥe] *(péj) vi* to stink ♦ *vt* to stink of, reek of.

puéricultrice [pɥerikyltris] *nf* ≈ nursery nurse.

puériculture [pɥerikyltyr] *nf* infant care.

puéril, e [pɥeril] *adj* childish.

puérilement [pɥerilmɑ̃] *adv* childishly.

puérilité [pɥerilite] *nf* childishness; (*acte, idée*) childish thing.

pugilat [pyʒila] *nm* (fist) fight.

puis [pɥi] *vb voir* **pouvoir** ♦ *adv* (*ensuite*) then; (*dans une énumération*) next; (*en outre*): **et ~ and (then); et ~ (après ou quoi)?** so (what?)

puisard [pɥizar] *nm* (*égout*) cesspool.

puiser [pɥize] *vt*: **~ (dans)** to draw (from); **~ dans qch** to dip into sth.

puisque [pɥisk(ə)] *conj* since; (*valeur intensive*): **~ je te le dis!** I'm telling you!

puissamment [pɥisamɑ̃] *adv* powerfully.

puissance [pɥisɑ̃s] *nf* power; **en ~** *adj* potential; **2 (à la) ~ 5** 2 to the power (of) 5.

puissant, e [pɥisɑ̃, -ɑ̃t] *adj* powerful.

puisse [pɥis] *etc vb voir* **pouvoir**.

puits [pɥi] *nm* well; **~ artésien** artesian well; **~ de mine** mine shaft; **~ de science** fount of knowledge.

pull(-over) [pyl(ɔvœr)] *nm* sweater, jumper (*BRIT*).

pulluler [pylyle] *vi* to swarm; (*fig: erreurs*) to abound, proliferate.

pulmonaire [pylmɔnɛr] *adj* lung *cpd*; (*artère*) pulmonary.

pulpe [pylp(ə)] *nf* pulp.

pulsation [pylsasjɔ̃] *nf* (*MÉD*) beat.

pulsé [pylse] *adj m*: **chauffage à air ~** warm air heating.

pulsion [pylsjɔ̃] *nf* (*PSYCH*) drive, urge.

pulvérisateur [pylverizatœr] *nm* spray.

pulvérisation [pylverizasjɔ̃] *nf* spraying.

pulvériser [pylverize] *vt* (*solide*) to pulverize; (*liquide*) to spray; (*fig: anéantir: adversaire*) to pulverize; (*: record*) to smash, shatter; (*: argument*) to demolish.

puma [pyma] *nm* puma, cougar.

punaise [pynɛz] *nf* (*ZOOL*) bug; (*clou*) drawing pin (*BRIT*), thumb tack (*US*).

punch [pɔ̃ʃ] *nm* (*boisson*) punch; [pœnʃ] (*BOXE*) punching ability; (*fig*) punch.

punching-ball [pœnʃiŋbol] *nm* punchball.

punir [pynir] *vt* to punish; **~ qn de qch** to punish sb for sth.

punitif, ive [pynitif, -iv] *adj* punitive.

punition [pynisjɔ̃] *nf* punishment.

pupille [pypij] *nf* (*ANAT*) pupil ♦ *nm/f* (*enfant*) ward; **~ de l'État** child in care; **~ de la Nation** war orphan.

pupitre [pypitr(ə)] *nm* (*SCOL*) desk; (*REL*) lectern; (*de chef d'orchestre*) rostrum; (*INFORM*) console; **~ de commande** control panel.

pupitreur, euse [pypitrœr, -øz] *nm/f* (*INFORM*)

(computer) operator, keyboarder.

pur, e [pyr] *adj* pure; (*vin*) undiluted; (*whisky*) neat; (*intentions*) honourable (*BRIT*), honorable (*US*) ♦ *nm* (*personne*) hard-liner; **en ~e perte** fruitlessly, to no avail.

purée [pyre] *nf*: **~ (de pommes de terre)** ≈ mashed potatoes *pl*; **~ de marrons** chestnut purée; **~ de pois** (*fig*) peasoup(er).

purement [pyrmɑ̃] *adv* purely.

pureté [pyrte] *nf* purity.

purgatif [pyrgatif] *nm* purgative, purge.

purgatoire [pyrgatwar] *nm* purgatory.

purge [pyrʒ(ə)] *nf* (*POL*) purge; (*MÉD*) purging *no pl*; purge.

purger [pyrʒe] *vt* (*radiateur*) to flush (out), drain; (*circuit hydraulique*) to bleed; (*MÉD, POL*) to purge; (*JUR: peine*) to serve.

purification [pyrifikasjɔ̃] *nf* (*de l'eau*) purification; **~ ethnique** ethnic cleansing.

purifier [pyrifje] *vt* to purify; (*TECH: métal*) to refine.

purin [pyrɛ̃] *nm* liquid manure.

puriste [pyrist(ə)] *nm/f* purist.

puritain, e [pyritɛ̃, -ɛn] *adj*, *nm/f* Puritan.

puritanisme [pyritanism(ə)] *nm* Puritanism.

pur-sang [pyrsɑ̃] *nm inv* thoroughbred, purebred.

purulent, e [pyrylɑ̃, -ɑ̃t] *adj* purulent.

pus [py] *vb voir* **pouvoir** ♦ *nm* pus.

pusillanime [pyzilanim] *adj* fainthearted.

pustule [pystyl] *nf* pustule.

putain [pytɛ̃] *nf* (*fam!*) whore (*!*); **ce/cette ~ de ...** this bloody (*BRIT*) *ou* goddamn (*US*) ... (*!*).

putois [pytwa] *nm* polecat; **crier comme un ~** to yell one's head off.

putréfaction [pytrefaksjɔ̃] *nf* putrefaction.

putréfier [pytrefje] *vt*, **se ~** *vi* to putrefy, rot.

putride [pytrid] *adj* putrid.

putsch [putʃ] *nm* (*POL*) putsch.

puzzle [pœzl(ə)] *nm* jigsaw (puzzle).

PV *sigle m* = **procès-verbal**.

PVC *sigle f* (= *polychlorure de vinyle*) PVC.

PVD *sigle mpl* (= *pays en voie de développement*) developing countries.

Px *abr* = **prix**.

pygmée [pigme] *nm* pygmy.

pyjama [piʒama] *nm* pyjamas *pl*, pair of pyjamas.

pylône [pilon] *nm* pylon.

pyramide [piramid] *nf* pyramid.

pyrénéen, ne [pireneɛ̃, -ɛn] *adj* Pyrenean.

Pyrénées [pirene] *nfpl*: **les ~** the Pyrenees.

pyrex [pirɛks] *nm* ® Pyrex ®.

pyrogravure [pirɔgravyr] *nf* poker-work.

pyromane [pirɔman] *nm/f* arsonist.

python [pitɔ̃] *nm* python.

Q q

Q, q [ky] *nm inv* Q, q ♦ *abr* (= *quintal*) q; **Q comme Quintal** Q for Queen.

Qatar [kataʀ] *nm*: **le ~** Qatar.

qcm *sigle m* (= *questionnaire à choix multiple*) multiple choice question paper.

QG *sigle m* (= *quartier général*) HQ.

QHS *sigle m* (= *quartier de haute sécurité*) high-security wing *ou* prison.

QI *sigle m* (= *quotient intellectuel*) IQ.

qqch. *abr* (= *quelque chose*) sth.

qqe(s) *abr* = **quelque(s)**.

qqn *abr* (= *quelqu'un*) sb, s.o.

quadragénaire [kadʀaʒenɛʀ] *nm/f* (*de quarante ai.s*) forty-year-old; (*de quarante à cinquante ans*) man/woman in his/her forties.

quadrangulaire [kwadʀɑ̃gylɛʀ] *adj* quadrangular.

quadrature [kwadʀatyʀ] *nf*: **c'est la ~ du cercle** it's like trying to square the circle.

quadrichromie [kwadʀikʀɔmi] *nf* four-colour (*BRIT*) *ou* -color (*US*) printing.

quadrilatère [k(w)adʀilatɛʀ] *nm* (*GÉOM, MIL*) quadrilateral; (*terrain*) four-sided area.

quadrillage [kadʀijaʒ] *nm* (*lignes etc*) square pattern, criss-cross pattern.

quadrillé, e [kadʀije] *adj* (*papier*) squared.

quadriller [kadʀije] *vt* (*papier*) to mark out in squares; (*POLICE: ville, région etc*) to keep under tight control, be positioned throughout.

quadrimoteur [k(w)adʀimɔtœʀ] *nm* four-engined plane.

quadripartite [kwadʀipaʀtit] *adj* (*entre pays*) four-power; (*entre partis*) four-party.

quadriphonie [kadʀifɔni] *nf* quadraphony.

quadriréacteur [k(w)adʀiʀeaktœʀ] *nm* four-engined jet.

quadrupède [k(w)adʀypɛd] *nm* quadruped.

quadruple [k(w)adʀypl(ə)] *nm*: **le ~ de** four times as much as.

quadrupler [k(w)adʀyple] *vt, vi* to quadruple, increase fourfold.

quadruplés, ées [k(w)adʀyple] *nm/fpl* quadruplets, quads.

quai [ke] *nm* (*de port*) quay; (*de gare*) platform; (*de cours d'eau, canal*) embankment; **être à ~** (*navire*) to be alongside; (*train*) to be in the station; **le Q~ d'Orsay** *offices of the French Ministry for Foreign Affairs*; **le Q~ des Orfèvres** *central police headquarters*.

qualifiable [kalifjabl(ə)] *adj*: **ce n'est pas ~** it defies description.

qualificatif, ive [kalifikatif, -iv] *adj* (*LING*) qualifying ♦ *nm* (*terme*) term; (*LING*) qualifier.

qualification [kalifikasjɔ̃] *nf* qualification.

qualifier [kalifje] *vt* to qualify; (*appeler*): **~ qch/qn de** to describe sth/sb as; **se ~** *vi* (*SPORT*) to qualify; **être qualifié pour** to be qualified for.

qualitatif, ive [kalitatif, -iv] *adj* qualitative.

qualité [kalite] *nf* quality; (*titre, fonction*) position; **en ~ de** in one's capacity as; **ès ~s** in an official capacity; **avoir ~ pour** to have authority to; **de ~** *adj* quality *cpd*; **rapport ~-prix** value (for money).

quand [kɑ̃] *conj, adv* when; **~ je serai riche** when I'm rich; **~ même** (*cependant, pourtant*) nevertheless; (*tout de même*) all the same; really; **~ bien même** even though.

quant [kɑ̃]: **~ à** *prép* (*pour ce qui est de*) as for, as to; (*au sujet de*) regarding.

quant-à-soi [kɑ̃taswa] *nm*: **rester sur son ~** to remain aloof.

quantième [kɑ̃tjɛm] *nm* date, day (of the month).

quantifiable [kɑ̃tifjabl(ə)] *adj* quantifiable.

quantifier [kɑ̃tifje] *vt* to quantify.

quantitatif, ive [kɑ̃titatif, -iv] *adj* quantitative.

quantitativement [kɑ̃titativmɑ̃] *adv* quantitatively.

quantité [kɑ̃tite] *nf* quantity, amount; (*SCIENCE*) quantity; (*grand nombre*): **une ou des ~(s) de** a great deal of; a lot of; **en grande ~** in large quantities; **en ~s industrielles** in vast amounts; **du travail en ~** a great deal of work; **~ de** many.

quarantaine [kaʀɑ̃tɛn] *nf* (*isolement*) quarantine; (*âge*): **avoir la ~** to be around forty; (*nombre*): **une ~ (de)** forty or so, about forty; **mettre en ~** to put into quarantine; (*fig*) to send to Coventry (*BRIT*), ostracize.

quarante [kaʀɑ̃t] *num* forty.

quarantième [kaʀɑ̃tjɛm] *num* fortieth.

quark [kwaʀk] *nm* quark.

quart [kaʀ] *nm* (*fraction*) quarter; (*surveillance*) watch; (*partie*): **un ~ de poulet/fromage** a chicken quarter/a quarter of a cheese; **un ~ de beurre** a quarter kilo of butter, ≈ a half pound of butter; **un ~ de vin** a quarter litre of wine; **une livre un ~** *ou* **et ~** one and a quarter pounds; **le ~ de** a quarter of; **~ d'heure** quarter of an hour; **2 h et** *ou* **un ~** (a) quarter past 2, (a) quarter after 2 (*US*); **il est le ~** it's (a) quarter past *ou* after (*US*); **une heure moins le ~** (a) quarter to one, (a) quarter of one (*US*); **il est moins le ~** it's (a) quarter to; **être de/prendre le ~** to keep/ take the watch; **~ de tour** quarter turn; **au ~ de tour** (*fig*) straight off; **~s de finale** (*SPORT*) quarter finals.

quarté [kaʀte] *nm* (*COURSES*) system of forecast betting giving first four horses.

quarteron [kaʀtəʀɔ̃] *nm* (*péj*) small bunch, handful.

quartette [kwartɛt] *nm* quartet(te).
quartier [kartje] *nm* (*de ville*) district, area; (*de bœuf, de la lune*) quarter; (*de fruit, fromage*) piece; **~s** *nmpl* (*MIL, BLASON*) quarters; **cinéma/salle de ~** local cinema/hall; **avoir ~ libre** to be free; (*MIL*) to have leave from barracks; **ne pas faire de ~** to spare no one, give no quarter; **~ commerçant/résidentiel** shopping/residential area; **~ général (QG)** headquarters (HQ).
quartier-maître [kartjemɛtr(ə)] *nm* ≈ leading seaman.
quasi [kazi] *adv* almost, nearly ♦ *préfixe*: **~-certitude** near certainty.
quasiment [kazimɑ̃] *adv* almost, very nearly.
quaternaire [kwatɛrnɛr] *adj* (*GÉO*) Quaternary.
quatorze [katɔrz(ə)] *num* fourteen.
quatorzième [katɔrzjɛm] *num* fourteenth.
quatrain [katrɛ̃] *nm* quatrain.
quatre [katr(ə)] *num* four; **à ~ pattes** on all fours; **tiré à ~ épingles** dressed up to the nines; **faire les ~ cent coups** to be a bit wild; **se mettre en ~ pour qn** to go out of one's way for sb; **à ~** (*monter, descendre*) four at a time; **à ~ mains** (*jouer*) four-handed.
quatre-vingt-dix [katrəvɛ̃dis] *num* ninety.
quatre-vingts [katrəvɛ̃] *num* eighty.
quatrième [katrijɛm] *num* fourth.
quatuor [kwatyɔr] *nm* quartet(te).

================ *MOT-CLÉ*

que [kə] *conj* **1** (*introduisant complétive*) that; **il sait ~ tu es là** he knows (that) you're here; **je veux ~ tu acceptes** I want you to accept; **il a dit ~ oui** he said he would (*ou* it was *etc*)
2 (*reprise d'autres conjonctions*): **quand il rentrera et qu'il aura mangé** when he gets back and (when) he has eaten; **si vous y allez ou ~ vous** ... if you go there or if you ...
3 (*en tête de phrase: hypothèse, souhait etc*): **qu'il le veuille ou non** whether he likes it or not; **qu'il fasse ce qu'il voudra!** let him do as he pleases!
4 (*but*): **tenez-le qu'il ne tombe pas** hold it so (that) it doesn't fall
5 (*après comparatif*) than; as; *voir aussi* **plus; aussi; autant** *etc*
6 (*seulement*): **ne ... ~** only; **il ne boit ~ de l'eau** he only drinks water
7 (*temps*): **elle venait à peine de sortir qu'il se mit à pleuvoir** she had just gone out when it started to rain, no sooner had she gone out than it started to rain; **il y a 4 ans qu'il est parti** it is 4 years since he left, he left 4 years ago
♦ *adv* (*exclamation*): **qu'il** *ou* **qu'est-ce qu'il est bête/court vite!** he's so silly!/he runs so fast!; **~ de livres!** what a lot of books!
♦ *pron* **1** (*relatif: personne*) whom; (: *chose*) that, which; **l'homme ~ je vois** the man (whom) I see; **le livre ~ tu vois** the book

(that *ou* which) you see; **un jour ~ j'étais** ... a day when I was ...
2 (*interrogatif*) what; **~ fais-tu?, qu'est-ce ~ tu fais?** what are you doing?; **qu'est-ce c'est?** what is it?, what's that?; **~ faire?** what can one do?; **~ préfères-tu, celui-ci ou celui-là?** which (one) do you prefer, this one or that one?

Québec [kebɛk] *n* (*ville*) Quebec ♦ *nm*: **le ~** Quebec (Province).
québécois, e [kebekwa, -waz] *adj* Quebec *cpd* ♦ *nm* (*LING*) Quebec French ♦ *nm/f*: **Q~, e** Quebecois, Quebec(k)er.

================ *MOT-CLÉ*

quel, quelle [kɛl] *adj* **1** (*interrogatif: personne*) who; (: *chose*) what; which; **~ est cet homme?** who is this man?; **~ est ce livre?** what is this book?; **~ livre/homme?** what book/man?; (*parmi un certain choix*) which book/man?; **~s acteurs préférez-vous?** which actors do you prefer?; **dans ~s pays êtes-vous allé?** which *ou* what countries did you go to?
2 (*exclamatif*): **quelle surprise/coïncidence!** what a surprise/coincidence!
3: **~ que soit le coupable** whoever is guilty; **~ que soit votre avis** whatever your opinion (may be).

quelconque [kɛlkɔ̃k] *adj* (*médiocre*) indifferent, poor; (*sans attrait*) ordinary, plain; (*indéfini*) **un ami/prétexte ~** some friend/pretext or other; **un livre ~ suffira** any book will do; **pour une raison ~** for some reason (or other).

================ *MOT-CLÉ*

quelque [kɛlkə] *adj* **1** some; a few; (*tournure interrogative*) any; **~ espoir** some hope; **il a ~s amis** he has a few *ou* some friends; **a-t-il ~s amis?** has he any friends?; **les ~s livres qui** the few books which; **20 kg et ~(s)** a bit over 20 kg; **il habite à ~ distance d'ici** he lives some distance *ou* way (away) from here
2: **~ ... que** whatever, whichever; **~ livre qu'il choisisse** whatever (*ou* whichever) book he chooses; **par ~ temps qu'il fasse** whatever the weather
3: **~ chose** something; (*tournure interrogative*) anything; **~ chose d'autre** something else; anything else; **y être pour ~ chose** to have something to do with it; **faire ~ chose à qn** to have an effect on sb, do something to sb; **~ part** somewhere; anywhere; **en ~ sorte** as it were
♦ *adv* **1** (*environ*): **~ 100 mètres** some 100 metres
2: **~ peu** rather, somewhat.

quelquefois [kɛlkəfwa] *adv* sometimes.

quelques-uns, -unes [kɛlkəzœ̃, -yn] *pron* some, a few; ~ **des lecteurs** some of the readers.

quelqu'un [kɛlkœ̃] *pron* someone, somebody, *tournure interrogative ou négative* + anyone *ou* anybody; ~ **d'autre** someone *ou* somebody else; anybody else.

quémander [kemɑ̃de] *vt* to beg for.

qu'en dira-t-on [kɑ̃diʀatɔ̃] *nm inv:* **le** ~ gossip, what people say.

quenelle [kənɛl] *nf* quenelle.

quenouille [kənuj] *nf* distaff.

querelle [kəʀɛl] *nf* quarrel; **chercher** ~ **à qn** to pick a quarrel with sb.

quereller [kəʀele]: **se** ~ *vi* to quarrel.

querelleur, euse [kəʀelœʀ, -øz] *adj* quarrelsome.

qu'est-ce que *(ou* **qui)** [kɛskə(ki)] *voir* **que, qui.**

question [kɛstjɔ̃] *nf* (*gén*) question; (*fig*) matter; issue; **il a été** ~ **de** we (*ou* they) spoke about; **il est** ~ **de les emprisonner** there's talk of them being jailed; **c'est une** ~ **de temps** it's a matter *ou* question of time; **de quoi est-il** ~? what is it about?; **il n'en est pas** ~ there's no question of it; **en** ~ in question; **hors de** ~ out of the question; **je ne me suis jamais posé la** ~ I've never thought about it; **(re)mettre en** ~ (*autorité, science*) to question; **poser la** ~ **de confiance** (*POL*) to ask for a vote of confidence; ~ **piège** (*d'apparence facile*) trick question; (*pour nuire*) loaded question; ~ **subsidiaire** tiebreaker.

questionnaire [kɛstjɔnɛʀ] *nm* questionnaire.

questionner [kɛstjɔne] *vt* to question.

quête [kɛt] *nf* (*collecte*) collection; (*recherche*) quest, search; **faire la** ~ (*à l'église*) to take the collection; (*artiste*) to pass the hat round; **se mettre en** ~ **de qch** to go in search of sth.

quêter [kete] *vi* (*à l'église*) to take the collection; (*dans la rue*) to collect money (for charity) ♦ *vt* to seek.

quetsche [kwɛtʃ(ə)] *nf* damson.

queue [kø] *nf* tail; (*fig: du classement*) bottom; (: *de poêle*) handle; (: *de fruit, feuille*) stalk; (: *de train, colonne, file*) rear; (*file: de personnes*) queue (*BRIT*), line (*US*); **en** ~ (**de train**) at the rear (of the train); **faire la** ~ to queue (up) (*BRIT*), line up (*US*); **se mettre à la** ~ to join the queue *ou* line; **histoire sans** ~ **ni tête** cock and bull story; **à la** ~ **leu leu** in single file; (*fig*) one after the other; ~ **de cheval** ponytail; ~ **de poisson: faire une** ~ **de poisson à qn** (*AUTO*) to cut in front of sb; **finir en** ~ **de poisson** (*film*) to come to an abrupt end.

queue-de-pie, *pl* **queues-de-pie** [kødpi] *nf* (*habit*) tails *pl*, tail coat.

queux [kø] *adj m voir* **maître.**

qui [ki] *pron* (*personne*) who, *prép* + whom; (*chose, animal*) which, that; (*interrogatif indirect: sujet*): **je me demande** ~ **est là?** I wonder who is there?; (: *objet*): **elle ne sait à** ~ **se plaindre** she doesn't know who to complain to *ou* to whom to complain; **qu'est-ce** ~ **est sur la table?** what is on the table?; **à** ~ **est ce sac?** whose bag is this?; **à** ~ **parlais-tu?** who were you talking to?, to whom were you talking?; **chez** ~ **allez-vous?** whose house are you going to?; **amenez** ~ **vous voulez** bring who(ever) you like; ~ **est-ce** ~ **...?** who?; ~ **est-ce que ...?** who?; whom?; ~ **que ce soit** whoever it may be.

quiche [kiʃ] *nf* quiche; ~ **lorraine** quiche Lorraine.

quiconque [kikɔ̃k] *pron* (*celui qui*) whoever, anyone who; (*n'importe qui, personne*) anyone, anybody.

quidam [kɥidam] *nm* (*hum*) fellow.

quiétude [kjetyd] *nf* (*d'un lieu*) quiet, tranquillity; (*d'une personne*) peace (of mind), serenity; **en toute** ~ in complete peace; (*mentale*) with complete peace of mind.

quignon [kiɲɔ̃] *nm:* ~ **de pain** (*croûton*) crust of bread; (*morceau*) hunk of bread.

quille [kij] *nf* ninepin, skittle (*BRIT*); (*NAVIG: d'un bateau*) keel; (**jeu de**) ~**s** ninepins *sg*, skittles *sg* (*BRIT*).

quincaillerie [kɛ̃kajʀi] *nf* (*ustensiles, métier*) hardware, ironmongery (*BRIT*); (*magasin*) hardware shop *ou* store (*US*), ironmonger's (*BRIT*).

quincaillier, ière [kɛ̃kaje, -jɛʀ] *nm/f* hardware dealer, ironmonger (*BRIT*).

quinconce [kɛ̃kɔ̃s] *nm:* **en** ~ in staggered rows.

quinine [kinin] *nf* quinine.

quinquagénaire [kɛ̃kaʒenɛʀ] *nm/f* (*de cinquante ans*) fifty-year old; (*de cinquante à soixante ans*) man/woman in his/her fifties.

quinquennal, e, aux [kɛ̃kenal, -o] *adj* five-year, quinquennial.

quintal, aux [kɛ̃tal, -o] *nm* quintal (*100 kg*).

quinte [kɛ̃t] *nf:* ~ (**de toux**) coughing fit.

quintessence [kɛ̃tesɑ̃s] *nf* quintessence, very essence.

quintette [kɛ̃tɛt] *nm* quintet(te).

quintuple [kɛ̃typl(ə)] *nm:* **le** ~ **de** five times as much as.

quintupler [kɛ̃typle] *vt, vi* to increase fivefold.

quintuplés, ées [kɛ̃typle] *nm/fpl* quintuplets, quins.

quinzaine [kɛ̃zɛn] *nf:* **une** ~ (**de**) about fifteen, fifteen or so; **une** ~ (**de jours**) (*deux semaines*) a fortnight (*BRIT*), two weeks; ~ **publicitaire** *ou* **commerciale** (two-week) sale.

quinze [kɛ̃z] *num* fifteen; **demain en** ~ a fortnight (*BRIT*) *ou* two weeks tomorrow; **dans** ~ **jours** in a fortnight('s time) (*BRIT*), in two weeks(' time).

quinzième [kɛ̃zjɛm] *num* fifteenth.

quiproquo [kipʀɔko] *nm* (*méprise sur une personne*) mistake; (*malentendu sur un sujet*) misunderstanding; (*THÉÂT*) (case of) mistaken identity.

Quito [kito] *n* Quito.

quittance [kitɑ̃s] *nf* (*reçu*) receipt; (*facture*) bill.

quitte [kit] *adj*: **être ~ envers qn** to be no longer in sb's debt; (*fig*) to be quits with sb; **être ~ de** (*obligation*) to be clear of; **en être ~ à bon compte** to have got off lightly; **~ à faire** even if it means doing; **~ ou double** (*jeu*) double or quits; (*fig*): **c'est du ~ ou double** it's a big risk.

quitter [kite] *vt* to leave; (*espoir, illusion*) to give up; (*vêtement*) to take off; **se ~** (*couples, interlocuteurs*) to part; **ne quittez pas** (*au téléphone*) hold the line; **ne pas ~ qn d'une semelle** to stick to sb like glue.

quitus [kitys] *nm* final discharge; **donner ~ à** to discharge.

qui-vive [kiviv] *nm inv*: **être sur le ~** to be on the alert.

quoi [kwa] *pron* (*interrogatif*) what; **~ de neuf** *ou* **de nouveau?** what's new *ou* the news?; **as-tu de ~ écrire?** have you anything to write with?; **il n'a pas de ~ se l'acheter** he can't afford it, he hasn't got the money to buy it; **il y a de ~ être fier** that's something to be proud of; **"il n'y a pas de ~"** "(please) don't mention it", "not at all"; **~ qu'il arrive** whatever happens; **~ qu'il en soit** be that as it may; **~ que ce soit** anything at all; **en ~ puis-je vous aider?** how can I help you?; **à ~ bon?** what's the use *ou* point?; **et puis ~ encore!** what(ever) next!; **~ faire?** what's to be done?; **sans ~** (*ou sinon*) otherwise.

quoique [kwak(ə)] *conj* (al)though.

quolibet [kɔlibɛ] *nm* gibe, jeer.

quorum [kɔʀɔm] *nm* quorum.

quota [kwɔta] *nm* quota.

quote-part [kɔtpaʀ] *nf* share.

quotidien, ne [kɔtidjɛ̃, -ɛn] *adj* (*journalier*) daily; (*banal*) ordinary, everyday ♦ *nm* (*journal*) daily (paper); (*vie quotidienne*) daily life, day-to-day existence; **les grands ~s** the big (national) dailies.

quotidiennement [kɔtidjɛnmɑ̃] *adv* daily, every day.

quotient [kɔsjɑ̃] *nm* (*MATH*) quotient; **~ intellectuel (QI)** intelligence quotient (IQ).

quotité [kɔtite] *nf* (*FINANCE*) quota.

R r

R, r [ɛʀ] *nm inv* R, r ♦ *abr* = **route, rue; R comme Raoul** R for Robert (*BRIT*) *ou* Roger (*US*).

rab [ʀab] (*fam*), **rabiot** [ʀabjo] *nm* extra, more.

rabâcher [ʀabɑʃe] *vi* to harp on ♦ *vt* keep on repeating.

rabais [ʀabɛ] *nm* reduction, discount; **au ~** at a reduction *ou* discount.

rabaisser [ʀabese] *vt* (*rabattre*) to reduce; (*dénigrer*) to belittle.

rabane [ʀaban] *nf* raffia (matting).

Rabat [ʀaba(t)] *n* Rabat.

rabat [ʀaba] *vb voir* **rabattre** ♦ *nm* flap.

rabat-joie [ʀabaʒwa] *nm/f inv* killjoy (*BRIT*), spoilsport.

rabatteur, euse [ʀabatœʀ, -øz] *nm/f* (*de gibier*) beater; (*péj*) tout.

rabattre [ʀabatʀ(ə)] *vt* (*couvercle, siège*) to pull down; (*col*) to turn down; (*couture*) to stitch down; (*gibier*) to drive; (*somme d'un prix*) to deduct, take off; (*orgueil, prétentions*) to humble; (*TRICOT*) to decrease; **se ~** *vi* (*bords, couvercle*) to fall shut; (*véhicule, coureur*) to cut in; **se ~ sur** (*accepter*) to fall back on.

rabattu, e [ʀabaty] *pp de* **rabattre** ♦ *adj* turned down.

rabbin [ʀabɛ̃] *nm* rabbi.

rabique [ʀabik] *adj* rabies *cpd*.

râble [ʀɑbl(ə)] *nm* back; (*CULIN*) saddle.

râblé, e [ʀɑble] *adj* broad-backed, stocky.

rabot [ʀabo] *nm* plane.

raboter [ʀabɔte] *vt* to plane (down).

raboteux, euse [ʀabɔtø, -øz] *adj* uneven, rough.

rabougri, e [ʀabugri] *adj* stunted.

rabrouer [ʀabʀue] *vt* to snub, rebuff.

racaille [ʀakaj] *nf* (*péj*) rabble, riffraff.

raccommodage [ʀakɔmɔdaʒ] *nm* mending *no pl*, repairing *no pl*; darning *no pl*.

raccommoder [ʀakɔmɔde] *vt* to mend, repair; (*chaussette etc*) to darn; (*fam: réconcilier: amis, ménage*) to bring together again; **se ~ (avec)** (*fam*) to patch it up (with).

raccompagner [ʀakɔ̃paɲe] *vt* to take *ou* see back.

raccord [ʀakɔʀ] *nm* link; **~ de maçonnerie** pointing *no pl*; **~ de peinture** join; touch-up.

raccordement [ʀakɔʀdəmɑ̃] *nm* joining up; connection.

raccorder [ʀakɔʀde] *vt* to join (up), link up; (*suj: pont etc*) to connect, link; **se ~ à** to join up with; (*fig: se rattacher à*) to tie in with; **~ au réseau du téléphone** to connect to the

telephone service.
raccourci [rakursi] *nm* short cut; **en** ~ in brief.
raccourcir [rakursir] *vt* to shorten ♦ *vi* (*vêtement*) to shrink.
raccroc [rakro]: **par** ~ *adv* by chance.
raccrocher [rakrɔʃe] *vt* (*tableau, vêtement*) to hang back up; (*récepteur*) to put down; (*fig: affaire*) to save ♦ *vi* (*TÉL*) to hang up, ring off; **se** ~ **à** *vt* to cling to, hang on to; **ne raccrochez pas** (*TÉL*) hold on, don't hang up.
race [ras] *nf* race; (*d'animaux, fig: espèce*) breed; (*ascendance, origine*) stock, race; **de** ~ *adj* purebred, pedigree.
racé, e [rase] *adj* thoroughbred.
rachat [raʃa] *nm* buying; buying back; redemption; atonement.
racheter [raʃte] *vt* (*article perdu*) to buy another; (*davantage*): ~ **du lait/3 œufs** to buy more milk/another 3 eggs *ou* 3 more eggs; (*après avoir vendu*) to buy back; (*d'occasion*) to buy; (*COMM: part, firme*) to buy up; (: *pension, rente*) to redeem; (*REL: pécheur*) to redeem; (: *péché*) to atone for, expiate; (*mauvaise conduite, oubli, défaut*) to make up for; **se** ~ (*REL*) to redeem o.s.; (*gén*) to make amends, make up for it.
rachidien, ne [raʃidjɛ̃, -ɛn] *adj* rachidian, of the spine.
rachitique [raʃitik] *adj* suffering from rickets; (*fig*) scraggy, scrawny.
rachitisme [raʃitism(ə)] *nm* rickets *sg.*
racial, e, aux [rasjal, -o] *adj* racial.
racine [rasin] *nf* root; (*fig: figure*) roots *pl*; ~ **carrée/cubique** square/cube root; **prendre** ~ (*fig*) to take root; to put down roots.
racisme [rasism(ə)] *nm* racism, racialism.
raciste [rasist(ə)] *adj, nm/f* racist, racialist.
racket [rakɛt] *nm* racketeering *no pl.*
racketteur [rakɛtœr] *nm* racketeer.
raclée [rakle] *nf* (*fam*) hiding, thrashing.
raclement [rakləmɑ̃] *nm* (*bruit*) scraping (noise).
racler [rakle] *vt* (*os, plat*) to scrape; (*tache, boue*) to scrape off; (*fig: instrument*) to scrape on; (*suj: chose: frotter contre*) to scrape (against).
raclette [raklɛt] *nf* (*CULIN*) raclette (*Swiss cheese dish*).
racloir [raklwar] *nm* (*outil*) scraper.
racolage [rakɔlaʒ] *nm* soliciting; touting.
racoler [rakɔle] *vt* (*attirer: suj: prostituée*) to solicit; (: *parti, marchand*) to tout for; (*attraper*) to pick up.
racoleur, euse [rakɔlœr, -øz] *adj* (*péj: publicité*) cheap and alluring ♦ *nm* (*péj: de clients etc*) tout ♦ *nf* streetwalker.
racontars [rakɔ̃tar] *nmpl* stories, gossip *sg.*
raconter [rakɔ̃te] *vt*: ~ (**à qn**) (*décrire*) to relate (to sb), tell (sb) about; (*dire*) to tell (sb).
racorni, e [rakɔrni] *adj* hard(ened).
racornir [rakɔrnir] *vt* to harden.

radar [radar] *nm* radar; **système** ~ radar system; **écran** ~ radar screen.
rade [rad] *nf* (natural) harbour; **en** ~ **de Toulon** in Toulon harbour; **rester en** ~ (*fig*) to be left stranded.
radeau, x [rado] *nm* raft; ~ **de sauvetage** life raft.
radial, e, aux [radjal, -o] *adj* radial; **pneu à carcasse** ~**e** radial tyre.
radiant, e [radjɑ̃, -ɑ̃t] *adj* radiant.
radiateur [radjatœr] *nm* radiator, heater; (*AUTO*) radiator; ~ **électrique/à gaz** electric/gas heater *ou* fire.
radiation [radjasjɔ̃] *nf* (*d'un nom etc*) striking off *no pl*; (*PHYSIQUE*) radiation.
radical, e, aux [radikal, -o] *adj* radical ♦ *nm* (*LING*) stem; (*MATH*) root sign; (*POL*) radical.
radicalement [radikalmɑ̃] *adv* radically, completely.
radicaliser [radikalize] *vt* (*durcir: opinions etc*) to harden; **se** ~ *vi* (*mouvement etc*) to become more radical.
radicalisme [radikalism(ə)] *nm* (*POL*) radicalism.
radier [radje] *vt* to strike off.
radiesthésie [radjɛstezi] *nf* divination (by radiation).
radiesthésiste [radjɛstezist(ə)] *nm/f* diviner.
radieux, euse [radjø, -øz] *adj* (*visage, personne*) radiant; (*journée, soleil*) brilliant, glorious.
radin, e [radɛ̃, -in] *adj* (*fam*) stingy.
radio [radjo] *nf* radio; (*MÉD*) X-ray ♦ *nm* (*personne*) radio operator; **à la** ~ on the radio; **avoir la** ~ to have a radio; **passer à la** ~ to be on the radio; **se faire faire une** ~/**une** ~ **des poumons** to have an X-ray/a chest X-ray.
radio... [radjo] *préfixe* radio....
radioactif, ive [radjoaktif, -iv] *adj* radioactive.
radioactivité [radjoaktivite] *nf* radioactivity.
radioamateur [radjoamatœr] *nm* (radio) ham.
radiobalise [radjobaliz] *nf* radio beacon.
radiocassette [radjokasɛt] *nf* cassette radio.
radiodiffuser [radjodifyze] *vt* to broadcast.
radiodiffusion [radjodifyzjɔ̃] *nf* (radio) broadcasting.
radioélectrique [radjoelɛktrik] *adj* radio *cpd.*
radiogoniomètre [radjogɔnjɔmɛtr(ə)] *nm* direction finder, radiogoniometer.
radiographie [radjografi] *nf* radiography; (*photo*) X-ray photograph, radiograph.
radiographier [radjografje] *vt* to X-ray; **se faire** ~ to have an X-ray.
radioguidage [radjogidaʒ] *nm* (*NAVIG, AVIAT*) radio control; (*AUTO*) (broadcast of) traffic information.
radioguider [radjogide] *vt* (*NAVIG, AVIAT*) to guide by radio, control by radio.
radiologie [radjolɔʒi] *nf* radiology.
radiologique [radjolɔʒik] *adj* radiological.
radiologue [radjolɔg] *nm/f* radiologist.

radionavigant [ʀadjɔnavigɑ̃] *nm* radio officer.
radiophare [ʀadjɔfaʀ] *nm* radio beacon.
radiophonique [ʀadjɔfɔnik] *adj*: **programme/ émission/jeu** ~ radio programme/ broadcast/game.
radioreportage [ʀadjɔʀəpɔʀtaʒ] *nm* radio report.
radio(-)réveil [ʀadjɔʀevɛj] *nm* clock radio.
radioscopie [ʀadjɔskɔpi] *nf* radioscopy.
radio-taxi [ʀadjɔtaksi] *nm* radiotaxi.
radiotélégraphie [ʀadjɔtelegʀafi] *nf* radiotelegraphy.
radiotéléphone [ʀadjɔtelefɔn] *nm* radiotelephone.
radiotélescope [ʀadjɔteleskɔp] *nm* radiotelescope.
radiotélévisé, e [ʀadjɔtelevize] *adj* broadcast on radio and television.
radiothérapie [ʀadjɔteʀapi] *nf* radiotherapy.
radis [ʀadi] *nm* radish; ~ **noir** horseradish *no pl*.
radium [ʀadjɔm] *nm* radium.
radoter [ʀadɔte] *vi* to ramble on.
radoub [ʀadu] *nm*: **bassin** *ou* **cale de** ~ dry dock.
radouber [ʀadube] *vt* to repair, refit.
radoucir [ʀadusiʀ]: **se** ~ *vi* (*se réchauffer*) to become milder; (*se calmer*) to calm down; to soften.
radoucissement [ʀadusismɑ̃] *nm* milder period, better weather.
rafale [ʀafal] *nf* (*vent*) gust (of wind); (*de balles, d'applaudissements*) burst; ~ **de mitrailleuse** burst of machine-gun fire.
raffermir [ʀafɛʀmiʀ] *vt*, **se** ~ *vi* (*tissus, muscle*) to firm up; (*fig*) to strengthen.
raffermissement [ʀafɛʀmismɑ̃] *nm* (*fig*) strengthening.
raffinage [ʀafinaʒ] *nm* refining.
raffiné, e [ʀafine] *adj* refined.
raffinement [ʀafinmɑ̃] *nm* refinement.
raffiner [ʀafine] *vt* to refine.
raffinerie [ʀafinʀi] *nf* refinery.
raffoler [ʀafɔle]: ~ **de** *vt* to be very keen on.
raffut [ʀafy] *nm* (*fam*) row, racket.
rafiot [ʀafjo] *nm* tub.
rafistoler [ʀafistɔle] *vt* (*fam*) to patch up.
rafle [ʀafl(ə)] *nf* (*de police*) roundup, raid.
rafler [ʀafle] *vt* (*fam*) to swipe, nick.
rafraîchir [ʀafʀeʃiʀ] *vt* (*atmosphère, température*) to cool (down); (*aussi*: **mettre à** ~) to chill; (*suj*: *air, eau*) to freshen up; (: *boisson*) to refresh; (*fig*: *rénover*) to brighten up ♦ *vi*: **mettre du vin/une boisson à** ~ to chill wine/a drink; **se** ~ to grow cooler; to freshen up; (*personne*: *en buvant etc*) to refresh o.s.; ~ **la mémoire** *ou* **les idées à qn** to refresh sb's memory.
rafraîchissant, e [ʀafʀeʃisɑ̃, -ɑ̃t] *adj* refreshing.
rafraîchissement [ʀafʀeʃismɑ̃] *nm* cooling; (*boisson*) cool drink; ~**s** *nmpl* (*boissons, fruits etc*) refreshments.

ragaillardir [ʀagajaʀdiʀ] *vt* (*fam*) to perk *ou* buck up.
rage [ʀaʒ] *nf* (*MÉD*): **la** ~ rabies; (*fureur*) rage, fury; **faire** ~ to rage; ~ **de dents** (raging) toothache.
rager [ʀaʒe] *vi* to fume (with rage); **faire** ~ **qn** to enrage sb, get sb mad.
rageur, euse [ʀaʒœʀ, -øz] *adj* snarling; ill-tempered.
raglan [ʀaglɑ̃] *adj inv* raglan.
ragot [ʀago] *nm* (*fam*) malicious gossip *no pl*.
ragoût [ʀagu] *nm* (*plat*) stew.
ragoûtant, e [ʀagutɑ̃, -ɑ̃t] *adj*: **peu** ~ unpalatable.
rai [ʀɛ] *nm*: **un** ~ **de soleil/lumière** a shaft of sunshine/light.
raid [ʀɛd] *nm* (*MIL*) raid; (*attaque aérienne*) air raid; (*SPORT*) long-distance trek.
raide [ʀɛd] *adj* (*tendu*) taut, tight; (*escarpé*) steep; (*droit*: *cheveux*) straight; (*ankylosé, dur, guindé*) stiff; (*fam*: *cher*) steep, stiff; (: *sans argent*) flat broke; (*osé, licencieux*) daring ♦ *adv* (*en pente*) steeply; ~ **mort** stone dead.
raideur [ʀɛdœʀ] *nf* steepness; stiffness.
raidir [ʀediʀ] *vt* (*muscles*) to stiffen; (*câble*) to pull taut, tighten; **se** ~ *vi* to stiffen; to become taut; (*personne*: *se crisper*) to tense up; (: *devenir intransigeant*) to harden.
raidissement [ʀedismɑ̃] *nm* stiffening; tightening; hardening.
raie [ʀɛ] *nf* (*ZOOL*) skate, ray; (*rayure*) stripe; (*des cheveux*) parting.
raifort [ʀɛfɔʀ] *nm* horseradish.
rail [ʀɑj] *nm* (*barre d'acier*) rail; (*chemins de fer*) railways *pl* (*BRIT*), railroads *pl* (*US*); **les** ~**s** (*la voie ferrée*) the rails, the track *sg*; **par** ~ by rail; ~ **conducteur** live *ou* conductor rail.
railler [ʀɑje] *vt* to scoff at, jeer at.
raillerie [ʀɑjʀi] *nf* mockery.
railleur, euse [ʀɑjœʀ, -øz] *adj* mocking.
rail-route [ʀɑjʀut] *nm* road-rail.
rainurage [ʀenyʀaʒ] *nm* (*AUTO*) uneven road surface.
rainure [ʀenyʀ] *nf* groove; slot.
rais [ʀɛ] *nm inv* = **rai**.
raisin [ʀɛzɛ̃] *nm* (*aussi*: ~**s**) grapes *pl*; (*variété*): ~ **blanc/noir** white (*ou* green)/ black grape; ~ **muscat** muscat grape; ~**s secs** raisins.
raison [ʀɛzɔ̃] *nf* reason; **avoir** ~ to be right; **donner** ~ **à qn** (*personne*) to agree with sb; (*fait*) to prove sb right; **avoir** ~ **de qn/qch** to get the better of sb/sth; **se faire une** ~ to learn to live with it; **perdre la** ~ to become insane; (*fig*) to take leave of one's senses; **recouvrer la** ~ to come to one's senses; **ramener qn à la** ~ to make sb see sense; **demander** ~ **à qn de** (*affront etc*) to demand satisfaction from sb for; **entendre** ~ to listen to reason, see reason; **plus que de** ~ too much, more than is reasonable; ~ **de plus** all the more reason; **à plus forte** ~ all the

more so; **en** ~ **de** (*à cause de*) because of; (*à proportion de*) in proportion to; **à** ~ **de** at the rate of; ~ **d'État** reason of state; ~ **d'être** raison d'être; ~ **sociale** corporate name.

raisonnable [rɛzɔnabl(ə)] *adj* reasonable, sensible.

raisonnablement [rɛzɔnabləmɑ̃] *adv* reasonably.

raisonné, e [rɛzɔne] *adj* reasoned.

raisonnement [rɛzɔnmɑ̃] *nm* reasoning; arguing; argument.

raisonner [rɛzɔne] *vi* (*penser*) to reason; (*argumenter, discuter*) to argue ♦ *vt* (*personne*) to reason with; (*attitude: justifier*) to reason out; **se** ~ to reason with oneself.

raisonneur, euse [rɛzɔnœr, -øz] *adj* (*péj*) quibbling.

rajeunir [raʒœnir] *vt* (*suj: coiffure, robe*): ~ **qn** to make sb look younger; (*suj: cure etc*) to rejuvenate; (*fig: rafraîchir*) to brighten up; (: *moderniser*) to give a new look to; (: *en recrutant*) to inject new blood into ♦ *vi* (*personne*) to become (*ou* look) younger; (*entreprise, quartier*) to be modernized.

rajout [raʒu] *nm* addition.

rajouter [raʒute] *vt* (*commentaire*) to add; ~ **du sel/un œuf** to add some more salt/another egg; ~ **que** to add that; **en** ~ to lay it on thick.

rajustement [raʒystəmɑ̃] *nm* adjustment.

rajuster [raʒyste] *vt* (*vêtement*) to straighten, tidy; (*salaires*) to adjust; (*machine*) to readjust; **se** ~ to tidy *ou* straighten o.s. up.

râle [rɑl] *nm* groan; ~ **d'agonie** death rattle.

ralenti [ralɑ̃ti] *nm*: **au** ~ (*CINÉ*) in slow motion; (*fig*) at a slower pace; **tourner au** ~ (*AUTO*) to tick over, idle.

ralentir [ralɑ̃tir] *vt, vi*, **se** ~ *vi* to slow down.

ralentissement [ralɑ̃tismɑ̃] *nm* slowing down.

râler [rɑle] *vi* to groan; (*fam*) to grouse, moan (and groan).

ralliement [ralimɑ̃] *nm* (*rassemblement*) rallying; (*adhésion: à une cause, une opinion*) winning over; **point/signe de** ~ rallying point/sign.

rallier [ralje] *vt* (*rassembler*) to rally; (*rejoindre*) to rejoin; (*gagner à sa cause*) to win over; **se** ~ **à** (*avis*) to come over *ou* round to.

rallonge [ralɔ̃ʒ] *nf* (*de table*) (extra) leaf (*pl* leaves); (*argent etc*) extra *no pl*; (*ÉLEC*) extension (cable *ou* flex); (*fig: de crédit etc*) extension.

rallonger [ralɔ̃ʒe] *vt* to lengthen.

rallumer [ralyme] *vt* to light up again, relight; (*fig*) to revive; **se** ~ *vi* (*lumière*) to come on again.

rallye [rali] *nm* rally; (*POL*) march.

ramages [ramaʒ] *nmpl* (*dessin*) leaf pattern *sg*; (*chants*) songs.

ramassage [ramasaʒ] *nm*: ~ **scolaire** school bus service.

ramassé, e [ramase] *adj* (*trapu*) squat, stocky; (*concis: expression etc*) compact.

ramasse-miettes [ramasmjɛt] *nm inv* tabletidy.

ramasse-monnaie [ramasmɔnɛ] *nm inv* change-tray.

ramasser [ramase] *vt* (*objet tombé ou par terre, fam*) to pick up; (*recueillir*) to collect; (*récolter*) to gather; (: *pommes de terre*) to lift; **se** ~ *vi* (*sur soi-même*) to huddle up; to crouch.

ramasseur, euse [ramasœr, -øz] *nm/f*: ~ **de balles** ballboy/girl.

ramassis [ramasi] *nm* (*péj: de gens*) bunch; (: *de choses*) jumble.

rambarde [rɑ̃bard(ə)] *nf* guardrail.

rame [ram] *nf* (*aviron*) oar; (*de métro*) train; (*de papier*) ream; ~ **de haricots** bean support; **faire force de** ~**s** to row hard.

rameau, x [ramo] *nm* (small) branch; (*fig*) branch; **les R**~**x** (*REL*) Palm Sunday *sg*.

ramener [ramne] *vt* to bring back; (*reconduire*) to take back; (*rabattre: couverture, visière*): ~ **qch sur** to pull sth back over; ~ **qch à** (*réduire à, aussi MATH*) to reduce sth to; ~ **qn à la vie/raison** to bring sb back to life/bring sb to his (*ou* her) senses; **se** ~ *vi* (*fam*) to roll *ou* turn up; **se** ~ **à** (*se réduire à*) to come *ou* boil down to.

ramequin [ramkɛ̃] *nm* ramekin.

ramer [rame] *vi* to row.

rameur, euse [ramœr, -øz] *nm/f* rower.

rameuter [ramøte] *vt* to gather together.

ramier [ramje] *nm*: (**pigeon**) ~ woodpigeon.

ramification [ramifikasjɔ̃] *nf* ramification.

ramifier [ramifje]: **se** ~ *vi* (*tige, secte, réseau*): **se** ~ (**en**) to branch out (into); (*veines, nerfs*) to ramify.

ramolli, e [ramɔli] *adj* soft.

ramollir [ramɔlir] *vt* to soften; **se** ~ *vi* (*os, tissus*) to get (*ou* go) soft; (*beurre, asphalte*) to soften.

ramonage [ramɔnaʒ] *nm* (chimney-) sweeping.

ramoner [ramɔne] *vt* (*cheminée*) to sweep; (*pipe*) to clean.

ramoneur [ramɔnœr] *nm* (chimney) sweep.

rampe [rɑ̃p] *nf* (*d'escalier*) banister(s *pl*); (*dans un garage, d'un terrain*) ramp; (*THÉÂT*): **la** ~ the footlights *pl*; (*lampes: lumineuse, de balisage*) floodlights *pl*; **passer la** ~ (*toucher le public*) to get across to the audience; ~ **de lancement** launching pad.

ramper [rɑ̃pe] *vi* (*reptile, animal*) to crawl; (*plante*) to creep.

rancard [rɑ̃kar] *nm* (*fam*) date; tip.

rancart [rɑ̃kar] *nm*: **mettre au** ~ (*article, projet*) to scrap; (*personne*) to put on the scrapheap.

rance [rɑ̃s] *adj* rancid.

rancir [rɑ̃sir] *vi* to go off, go rancid.

rancœur [rɑ̃kœr] *nf* rancour (*BRIT*), rancor (*US*), resentment.

rançon [rɑ̃sɔ̃] *nf* ransom; (*fig*): **la** ~ **du succès**

etc the price of success *etc.*

rançonner [Rɑ̃sɔne] *vt* to hold to ransom.

rancune [Rɑ̃kyn] *nf* grudge, rancour (*BRIT*), rancor (*US*); **garder ~ à qn (de qch)** to bear sb a grudge (for sth); **sans ~!** no hard feelings!

rancunier, ière [Rɑ̃kynje, -jɛR] *adj* vindictive, spiteful.

randonnée [Rɑ̃dɔne] *nf* ride; (*à pied*) walk, ramble; hike, hiking *no pl.*

randonneur, euse [Rɑ̃dɔnœR, -øz] *nm/f* hiker.

rang [Rɑ̃] *nm* (*rangée*) row; (*de perles*) row, string, rope; (*grade, condition sociale, classement*) rank; **~s** *nmpl* (*MIL*) ranks; **se mettre en ~s/sur un ~** to get into *ou* form rows/a line; **sur 3 ~s** (lined up) 3 deep; **se mettre en ~s par 4** to form fours *ou* rows of 4; **se mettre sur les ~s** (*fig*) to get into the running; **au premier ~** in the first row; (*fig*) ranking first; **rentrer dans le ~** to get into line; **au ~ de** (*au nombre de*) among (the ranks of); **avoir ~ de** to hold the rank of.

rangé, e [Rɑ̃ʒe] *adj* (*sérieux*) orderly, steady.

rangée [Rɑ̃ʒe] *nf* row.

rangement [Rɑ̃ʒmɑ̃] *nm* tidying-up, putting-away; **faire des ~s** to tidy up.

ranger [Rɑ̃ʒe] *vt* (*classer, grouper*) to order, arrange; (*mettre à sa place*) to put away; (*voiture dans la rue*) to park; (*mettre de l'ordre dans*) to tidy up; (*arranger, disposer: en cercle etc*) to arrange; (*fig: classer*): **~ qn/qch parmi** to rank sb/sth among; **se ~** *vi* (*se placer, se disposer: autour d'une table etc*) to take one's place, sit round; (*véhicule, conducteur: s'écarter*) to pull over; (*: s'arrêter*) to pull in; (*piéton*) to step aside; (*s'assagir*) to settle down; **se ~ à** (*avis*) to come round to, fall in with.

ranimer [Ranime] *vt* (*personne évanouie*) to bring round; (*revigorer: forces, courage*) to restore; (*réconforter: troupes etc*) to kindle new life in; (*douleur, souvenir*) to revive; (*feu*) to rekindle.

rapace [Rapas] *nm* bird of prey ♦ *adj* (*péj*) rapacious, grasping; **~ diurne/nocturne** diurnal/nocturnal bird of prey.

rapatrié, e [Rapatrije] *nm/f* repatriate (*esp French North African settler*).

rapatriement [Rapatrimɑ̃] *nm* repatriation.

rapatrier [Rapatrije] *vt* to repatriate; (*capitaux*) to bring (back) into the country.

râpe [Rɑp] *nf* (*CULIN*) grater; (*à bois*) rasp.

râpé, e [Rɑpe] *adj* (*tissu*) threadbare; (*CULIN*) grated.

râper [Rɑpe] *vt* (*CULIN*) to grate; (*gratter, râcler*) to rasp.

rapetasser [Raptase] *vt* (*fam*) to patch up.

rapetisser [Raptise] *vt*: **~ qch** to shorten sth; to make sth look smaller ♦ *vi*, **se ~** *vi* to shrink.

râpeux, euse [Rɑpø, -øz] *adj* rough.

raphia [Rafja] *nm* raffia.

rapide [Rapid] *adj* fast; (*prompt*) quick; (*intelligence*) quick ♦ *nm* express (train); (*de cours d'eau*) rapid.

rapidement [Rapidmɑ̃] *adv* fast; quickly.

rapidité [Rapidite] *nf* speed; quickness.

rapiécer [Rapjese] *vt* to patch.

rappel [Rapɛl] *nm* (*d'un ambassadeur, MIL*) recall; (*THÉÂT*) curtain call; (*MÉD: vaccination*) booster; (*ADMIN: de salaire*) back pay *no pl*; (*d'une aventure, d'un nom*) reminder; (*de limitation de vitesse: sur écriteau*) speed limit sign (*reminder*); (*TECH*) return; (*NAVIG*) sitting out; (*ALPINISME: aussi*: **~ de corde**) abseiling *no pl*, roping down *no pl*; abseil; **~ à l'ordre** call to order.

rappeler [Raple] *vt* (*pour faire revenir, retéléphoner*) to call back; (*ambassadeur, MIL, INFORM*) to recall; (*acteur*) to call back (onto the stage); (*faire se souvenir*): **~ qch à qn** to remind sb of sth; **se ~** *vt* (*se souvenir de*) to remember, recall; **~ qn à la vie** to bring sb back to life; **~ qn à la décence** to recall sb to a sense of decency; **ça rappelle la Provence** it's reminiscent of Provence, it reminds you of Provence; **se ~ que...** to remember that....

rappelle [Rapɛl] *etc vb voir* **rappeler**.

rappliquer [Raplike] *vi* (*fam*) to turn up.

rapport [RapɔR] *nm* (*compte rendu*) report; (*profit*) yield, return; revenue; (*lien, analogie*) relationship; (*corrélation*) connection; (*proportion: MATH, TECH*) ratio (*pl* -s); **~s** *nmpl* (*entre personnes, pays*) relations; **avoir ~ à** to have something to do with, concern; **être en ~ avec** (*idée de corrélation*) to be related to; **être/se mettre en ~ avec qn** to be/get in touch with sb; **par ~ à** (*comparé à*) in relation to; (*à propos de*) with regard to; **sous le ~ de** from the point of view of; **sous tous (les) ~s** in all respects; **~s (sexuels)** (sexual) intercourse *sg*; **~ qualité-prix** value (for money).

rapporté, e [RapɔRte] *adj*: **pièce ~e** (*COUTURE*) patch.

rapporter [RapɔRte] *vt* (*rendre, ramener*) to bring back; (*apporter davantage*) to bring more; (*COUTURE*) to sew on; (*suj: investissement*) to yield; (*: activité*) to bring in; (*relater*) to report; (*JUR: annuler*) to revoke ♦ *vi* (*investissement*) to give a good return *ou* yield; (*activité*) to be very profitable; (*péj: moucharder*) to tell; **~ qch à** (*fig: rattacher*) to relate sth to; **se ~ à** (*correspondre à*) to relate to; **s'en ~ à** to rely on.

rapporteur, euse [RapɔRtœR, -øz] *nm/f* (*de procès, commission*) reporter; (*péj*) telltale ♦ *nm* (*GÉOM*) protractor.

rapproché, e [RapRɔʃe] *adj* (*proche*) near, close at hand; **~s** (*l'un de l'autre*) at close intervals.

rapprochement [RapRɔʃmɑ̃] *nm* (*réconciliation: de nations, familles*) reconciliation; (*analogie,* *rapport*) parallel.

rapprocher [ʀapʀɔʃe] *vt* (*chaise d'une table*): ~ **qch (de)** to bring sth closer (to); (*deux objets*) to bring closer together; (*réunir*) to bring together; (*comparer*) to establish a parallel between; **se** ~ *vi* to draw closer *ou* nearer; (*fig: familles, pays*) to come together; to come closer together; **se** ~ **de** to come closer to; (*présenter une analogie avec*) to be close to.

rapt [ʀapt] *nm* abduction.

raquette [ʀakɛt] *nf* (*de tennis*) racket; (*de ping-pong*) bat; (*à neige*) snowshoe.

rare [ʀaʀ] *adj* rare; (*main-d'œuvre, denrées*) scarce; (*cheveux, herbe*) sparse; **il est** ~ **que** it's rare that, it's unusual that; **se faire** ~ to become scarce; (*fig: personne*) to make oneself scarce.

raréfaction [ʀaʀefaksjɔ̃] *nf* scarcity; (*de l'air*) rarefaction.

raréfier [ʀaʀefje]: **se** ~ *vi* to grow scarce; (*air*) to rarefy.

rarement [ʀaʀmɑ̃] *adv* rarely, seldom.

rareté [ʀaʀte] *nf* (*voir rare*) rarity; scarcity.

rarissime [ʀaʀisim] *adj* extremely rare.

RAS *abr = rien à signaler.*

ras, e [ʀa, ʀaz] *adj* (*tête, cheveux*) close-cropped; (*poil, herbe*) short; (*mesure, cuillère*) level ♦ *adv* short; **faire table** ~**e** to make a clean sweep; **en** ~**e campagne** in open country; **à** ~ **bords** to the brim; **au** ~ **de** level with; **en avoir** ~ **le bol** (*fam*) to be fed up; ~ **du cou** *adj* (*pull, robe*) crew-neck.

rasade [ʀazad] *nf* glassful.

rasant, e [ʀazɑ̃, ɑ̃t] *adj* (*MIL: balle, tir*) grazing; (*fam*) boring.

rascasse [ʀaskas] *nf* (*ZOOL*) scorpion fish.

rasé, e [ʀaze] *adj*: ~ **de frais** freshly shaven; ~ **de près** close-shaven.

rase-mottes [ʀazmɔt] *nm inv*: **faire du** ~ to hedgehop; **vol en** ~ hedgehopping.

raser [ʀaze] *vt* (*barbe, cheveux*) to shave off; (*menton, personne*) to shave; (*fam: ennuyer*) to bore; (*démolir*) to raze (to the ground); (*frôler*) to graze, skim; **se** ~ to shave; (*fam*) to be bored (to tears).

rasoir [ʀazwaʀ] *nm* razor; ~ **électrique** electric shaver *ou* razor; ~ **mécanique** *ou* **de sûreté** safety razor.

rassasier [ʀasazje] *vt* to satisfy; **être rassasié** (*dégoûté*) to be sated; to have had more than enough.

rassemblement [ʀasɑ̃bləmɑ̃] *nm* (*groupe*) gathering; (*POL*) union; association; (*MIL*): **le** ~ parade.

rassembler [ʀasɑ̃ble] *vt* (*réunir*) to assemble, gather; (*regrouper, amasser*) to gather together, collect; **se** ~ *vi* to gather; ~ **ses idées/ses esprits/son courage** to collect one's thoughts/gather one's wits/screw up one's courage.

rasseoir [ʀaswaʀ]: **se** ~ *vi* to sit down again.

rasséréner [ʀaseʀene] *vt*: **se** ~ *vi* to recover one's serenity.

rassir [ʀasiʀ] *vi* to go stale.

rassis, e [ʀasi, -iz] *adj* (*pain*) stale.

rassurant, e [ʀasyʀɑ̃, -ɑ̃t] *adj* (*nouvelles etc*) reassuring.

rassuré, e [ʀasyʀe] *adj*: **ne pas être très** ~ to be rather ill at ease.

rassurer [ʀasyʀe] *vt* to reassure; **se** ~ to be reassured; **rassure-toi** don't worry.

rat [ʀa] *nm* rat; ~ **d'hôtel** hotel thief (*pl* thieves); ~ **musqué** muskrat.

ratatiné, e [ʀatatine] *adj* shrivelled (up), wrinkled.

ratatiner [ʀatatine] *vt* to shrivel; (*peau*) to wrinkle; **se** ~ *vi* to shrivel; to become wrinkled.

ratatouille [ʀatatuj] *nf* (*CULIN*) ratatouille.

rate [ʀat] *nf* female rat; (*ANAT*) spleen.

raté, e [ʀate] *adj* (*tentative*) unsuccessful, failed ♦ *nm/f* failure ♦ *nm* misfiring *no pl.*

râteau, x [ʀato] *nm* rake.

râtelier [ʀatəlje] *nm* rack; (*fam*) false teeth *pl.*

rater [ʀate] *vi* (*ne pas partir: coup de feu*) to fail to go off; (*affaire, projet etc*) to go wrong, fail ♦ *vt* (*cible, train, occasion*) to miss; (*démonstration, plat*) to spoil; (*examen*) to fail; ~ **son coup** to fail, not to bring it off.

raticide [ʀatisid] *nm* rat poison.

ratification [ʀatifikasjɔ̃] *nf* ratification.

ratifier [ʀatifje] *vt* to ratify.

ratio [ʀasjo] *nm* ratio (*pl* -s).

ration [ʀasjɔ̃] *nf* ration; (*fig*) share; ~ **alimentaire** food intake.

rationalisation [ʀasjɔnalizasjɔ̃] *nf* rationalization.

rationaliser [ʀasjɔnalize] *vt* to rationalize.

rationnel, le [ʀasjɔnɛl] *adj* rational.

rationnellement [ʀasjɔnɛlmɑ̃] *adv* rationally.

rationnement [ʀasjɔnmɑ̃] *nm* rationing; **ticket de** ~ ration coupon.

rationner [ʀasjɔne] *vt* to ration; (*personne*) to put on rations; **se** ~ to ration o.s.

ratisser [ʀatise] *vt* (*allée*) to rake; (*feuilles*) to rake up; (*suj: armée, police*) to comb; ~ **large** to cast one's nets wide.

raton [ʀatɔ̃] *nm*: ~ **laveur** raccoon.

RATP *sigle f* (= *Régie autonome des transports parisiens*) Paris transport authority.

rattacher [ʀataʃe] *vt* (*animal, cheveux*) to tie up again; (*incorporer: ADMIN etc*): ~ **qch à** to join sth to, unite sth with; (*fig: relier*): ~ **qch à** to link sth with, relate sth to; (: *lier*): ~ **qn à** to bind *ou* tie sb to; **se** ~ **à** (*fig: avoir un lien avec*) to be linked (*ou* connected) with.

rattrapage [ʀatʀapaʒ] *nm* (*SCOL*) remedial classes *pl*; (*ÉCON*) catching up.

rattraper [ʀatʀape] *vt* (*fugitif*) to recapture; (*retenir, empêcher de tomber*) to catch (hold of); (*atteindre, rejoindre*) to catch up with; (*réparer: imprudence, erreur*) to make up for; **se** ~ *vi* (*regagner: du temps*) to make up for lost time; (: *de l'argent etc*) to make good one's losses; (*réparer une gaffe etc*) to make up for it; **se ~ (à)** (*se raccrocher*) to stop o.s. falling (by catching hold of); **~ son retard/le temps perdu** to make up (for) lost time.

rature [ʀatyʀ] *nf* deletion, erasure.

raturer [ʀatyʀe] *vt* to cross out, delete, erase.

rauque [ʀok] *adj* raucous; hoarse.

ravagé, e [ʀavaʒe] *adj* (*visage*) harrowed.

ravager [ʀavaʒe] *vt* to devastate, ravage.

ravages [ʀavaʒ] *nmpl* ravages; **faire des ~** to wreak havoc; (*fig: séducteur*) to break hearts.

ravalement [ʀavalmɑ̃] *nm* restoration.

ravaler [ʀavale] *vt* (*mur, façade*) to restore; (*déprécier*) to lower; (*avaler de nouveau*) to swallow again; **~ sa colère/son dégoût** to stifle one's anger/distaste.

ravaudage [ʀavodaʒ] *nm* repairing, mending.

ravauder [ʀavode] *vt* to repair, mend.

rave [ʀav] *nf* (*BOT*) rape.

R avec AR *abr* (= *recommandé avec accusé de réception*) recorded delivery.

ravi, e [ʀavi] *adj* delighted; **être ~ de/que** to be delighted with/that.

ravier [ʀavje] *nm* hors d'œuvre dish.

ravigote [ʀavigɔt] *adj*: **sauce ~** oil and vinegar dressing with shallots.

ravigoter [ʀavigɔte] *vt* (*fam*) to buck up.

ravin [ʀavɛ̃] *nm* gully, ravine.

raviner [ʀavine] *vt* to furrow, gully.

ravioli [ʀavjɔli] *nmpl* ravioli *sg*.

ravir [ʀaviʀ] *vt* (*enchanter*) to delight; (*enlever*) **~ qch à qn** to rob sb of sth; **à ~** *adv* delightfully, beautifully; **être beau à ~** to be ravishingly beautiful.

raviser [ʀavize]: **se ~** *vi* to change one's mind.

ravissant, e [ʀavisɑ̃, -ɑ̃t] *adj* delightful.

ravissement [ʀavismɑ̃] *nm* (*enchantement, délice*) rapture.

ravisseur, euse [ʀavisœʀ, -øz] *nm/f* abductor, kidnapper.

ravitaillement [ʀavitajmɑ̃] *nm* resupplying; refuelling; (*provisions*) supplies *pl*; **aller au ~** to go for fresh supplies; **~ en vol** (*AVIAT*) in-flight refuelling.

ravitailler [ʀavitaje] *vt* to resupply; (*véhicule*) to refuel; **se ~** *vi* to get fresh supplies.

raviver [ʀavive] *vt* (*feu, douleur*) to revive; (*couleurs*) to brighten up.

ravoir [ʀavwaʀ] *vt* to get back.

rayé, e [ʀeje] *adj* (*à rayures*) striped; (*éraflé*) scratched.

rayer [ʀeje] *vt* (*érafler*) to scratch; (*barrer*) to cross *ou* score out; (*d'une liste: radier*) to cross *ou* strike off.

rayon [ʀejɔ̃] *nm* (*de soleil etc*) ray; (*GÉOM*) radius; (*de roue*) spoke; (*étagère*) shelf (*pl* shelves); (*de grand magasin*) department; (*fig: domaine*) concern; (*de ruche*) (honey)comb; **dans un ~ de** within a radius of; **~s** *nmpl* (*radiothérapie*) radiation;

~ d'action range; **~ de braquage** (*AUTO*) turning circle; **~ laser** laser beam; **~ de soleil** sunbeam, ray of sunshine; **~s X** X-rays.

rayonnage [ʀejɔnaʒ] *nm* set of shelves.

rayonnant, e [ʀejɔnɑ̃, -ɑ̃t] *adj* radiant.

rayonne [ʀejɔn] *nf* rayon.

rayonnement [ʀejɔnmɑ̃] *nm* radiation; (*fig: éclat*) radiance; (: *influence*) influence.

rayonner [ʀejɔne] *vi* (*chaleur, énergie*) to radiate; (*fig: émotion*) to shine forth; (: *visage*) to be radiant; (*avenues, axes etc*) to radiate; (*touriste*) to go touring (*from one base*).

rayure [ʀejyʀ] *nf* (*motif*) stripe; (*éraflure*) scratch; (*rainure, d'un fusil*) groove; **à ~s** striped.

raz-de-marée [ʀɑdmaʀe] *nm inv* tidal wave.

razzia [ʀazja] *nf* raid, foray.

RBE *sigle m* (= *revenu brut d'exploitation*) gross profit (*of a farm*).

R-D *sigle f* (= *Recherche-Développement*) R & D.

RDA *sigle f* (= *République démocratique allemande*) GDR.

RDB *sigle m* (*STATISTIQUES*: = *revenu disponible brut*) total income (*of a family etc*).

rdc *abr* = **rez-de-chaussée**.

ré [ʀe] *nm* (*MUS*) D; (*en chantant la gamme*) re.

réabonnement [ʀeabɔnmɑ̃] *nm* renewal of subscription.

réabonner [ʀeabɔne] *vt*: **~ qn à** to renew sb's subscription to; **se ~ (à)** to renew one's subscription (to).

réac [ʀeak] *adj, nm/f* (*fam*: = *réactionnaire*) reactionary.

réacteur [ʀeaktœʀ] *nm* jet engine; **~ nucléaire** nuclear reactor.

réactif [ʀeaktif] *nm* reagent.

réaction [ʀeaksjɔ̃] *nf* reaction; **par ~** jet-propelled; **avion/moteur à ~** jet (plane)/jet engine; **~ en chaîne** chain reaction.

réactionnaire [ʀeaksjɔnɛʀ] *adj, nm/f* reactionary.

réactualiser [ʀeaktɥalize] *vt* to update, bring up to date.

réadaptation [ʀeadaptasjɔ̃] *nf* readjustment; rehabilitation.

réadapter [ʀeadapte] *vt* to readjust; (*MÉD*) to rehabilitate; **se ~ (à)** to readjust (to).

réaffirmer [ʀeafiʀme] *vt* to reaffirm, reassert.

réagir [ʀeaʒiʀ] *vi* to react.

réajuster [ʀeaʒyste] *vt* = **rajuster**.

réalisable [ʀealizabl(ə)] *adj* (*projet, plan*) feasible; (*COMM*: *valeur*) realizable.

réalisateur, trice [ʀealizatœʀ, -tʀis] *nm/f* (*TV, CINÉ*) director.

réalisation [ʀealizasjɔ̃] *nf* carrying out; realization; fulfilment; achievement; production; (*œuvre*) production, work; (*création*) creation.

réaliser [ʀealize] *vt* (*projet, opération*) to carry out, realize; (*rêve, souhait*) to realize, fulfil; (*exploit*) to achieve; (*achat, vente*) to make; (*film*) to produce; (*se rendre compte de,*

COMM: *bien, capital)* to realize; **se** ~ *vi* to be realized.

réalisme [Realism(ə)] *nm* realism.

réaliste [Realist(ə)] *adj* realistic; *(peintre, roman)* realist ♦ *nm/f* realist.

réalité [Realite] *nf* reality; **en** ~ in (actual) fact; **dans la** ~ in reality; ~ **virtuelle** virtual reality.

réanimation [Reanimɑsjɔ̃] *nf* resuscitation; **service de** ~ intensive care unit.

réanimer [Reanime] *vt (MÉD)* to resuscitate.

réapparaître [ReapaRɛtR(ə)] *vi* to reappear.

réapparition [ReapaRisjɔ̃] *nf* reappearance.

réapprovisionner [ReapRɔvizjɔne] *vt (magasin)* to restock; **se** ~ **(en)** to restock (with).

réarmement [ReaRməmɑ̃] *nm* rearmament.

réarmer [ReaRme] *vt (arme)* to reload ♦ *vi (état)* to rearm.

réassortiment [ReasɔRtimɑ̃] *nm (COMM)* restocking.

réassortir [ReasɔRtiR] *vt* to match up.

réassurance [ReasyRɑ̃s] *nf* reinsurance.

réassurer [ReasyRe] *vt* to reinsure.

réassureur [ReasyRe] *nm* reinsurer.

rebaptiser [Rəbatize] *vt (rue)* to rename.

rébarbatif, ive [RebaRbatif, -iv] *adj* forbidding; *(style)* off-putting *(BRIT)*, crabbed.

rebattre [RəbatR(ə)] *vt*: ~ **les oreilles à qn de qch** to keep harping on to sb about sth.

rebattu, e [Rəbaty] *pp de* **rebattre** ♦ *adj* hackneyed.

rebelle [Rəbɛl] *nm/f* rebel ♦ *adj (troupes)* rebel; *(enfant)* rebellious; *(mèche etc)* unruly; ~ **à qch** unamenable to sth; ~ **à faire** unwilling to do.

rebeller [Rəbele]: **se** ~ *vi* to rebel.

rébellion [Rebeljɔ̃] *nf* rebellion; *(rebelles)* rebel forces *pl*.

rebiffer [Rəbife]: **se** ~ *vr* to fight back.

reboisement [Rəbwazmɑ̃] *nm* reafforestation.

reboiser [Rəbwaze] *vt* to replant with trees, reafforest.

rebond [Rəbɔ̃] *nm (voir rebondir)* bounce; rebound.

rebondi, e [Rəbɔ̃di] *adj (ventre)* rounded; *(joues)* chubby, well-rounded.

rebondir [Rəbɔ̃diR] *vi (ballon: au sol)* to bounce; *(: contre un mur)* to rebound; *(fig: procès, action, conversation)* to get moving again, be suddenly revived.

rebondissement [Rəbɔ̃dismɑ̃] *nm* new development.

rebord [RəbɔR] *nm* edge.

reboucher [Rəbuʃe] *vt (flacon)* to put the stopper *(ou* top) back on, recork; *(trou)* to stop up.

rebours [RəbuR]: **à** ~ *adv* the wrong way.

rebouteux, euse [Rəbutø, -øz] *nm/f (péj)* bonesetter.

reboutonner [Rəbutɔne] *vt (vêtement)* to button up (again).

rebrousse-poil [Rəbruspwal]: **à** ~ *adv* the wrong way.

rebrousser [Rəbruse] *vt (cheveux, poils)* to brush back, brush up; ~ **chemin** to turn back.

rebuffade [Rəbyfad] *nf* rebuff.

rébus [Rebys] *nm inv (jeu d'esprit)* rebus; *(fig)* puzzle.

rebut [Rəby] *nm*: **mettre au** ~ to scrap, discard.

rebutant, e [Rəbytɑ̃, -ɑ̃t] *adj (travail, démarche)* off-putting, disagreeable.

rebuter [Rəbyte] *vt* to put off.

récalcitrant, e [Rekalsitrɑ̃, -ɑ̃t] *adj* refractory, recalcitrant.

recaler [Rəkale] *vt (SCOL)* to fail.

récapitulatif, ive [Rekapitylatif, -iv] *adj (liste, tableau)* summary *cpd*, that sums up.

récapituler [Rekapityle] *vt* to recapitulate; *(résumer)* to sum up.

recel [Rəsɛl] *nm* receiving (stolen goods).

receler [Rəsəle] *vt (produit d'un vol)* to receive; *(malfaiteur)* to harbour; *(fig)* to conceal.

receleur, euse [Rəsəlœr, -øz] *nm/f* receiver.

récemment [Resamɑ̃] *adv* recently.

recensement [Rəsɑ̃smɑ̃] *nm* census; inventory.

recenser [Rəsɑ̃se] *vt (population)* to take a census of; *(inventorier)* to make an inventory of; *(dénombrer)* to list.

récent, e [Resɑ̃, -ɑ̃t] *adj* recent.

recentrer [Rəsɑ̃tRe] *vt (POL)* to move towards the centre.

récépissé [Resepise] *nm* receipt.

réceptacle [Resɛptakl(ə)] *nm (où les choses aboutissent)* recipient; *(où les choses sont stockées)* repository; *(BOT)* receptacle.

récepteur, trice [Resɛptœr, -tris] *adj* receiving ♦ *nm* receiver; ~ **(de papier)** *(INFORM)* stacker; ~ **(de radio)** radio set *ou* receiver.

réceptif, ive [Resɛptif, -iv] *adj*: ~ **(à)** receptive (to).

réception [Resɛpsjɔ̃] *nf* receiving *no pl*; *(d'une marchandise, commande)* receipt; *(accueil)* reception, welcome; *(bureau)* reception (desk); *(réunion mondaine)* reception, party; *(pièces)* reception rooms *pl*; *(SPORT: après un saut)* landing; *(du ballon)* catching *no pl*; **jour/heures de** ~ day/hours for receiving visitors *(ou* students *etc)*.

réceptionnaire [ResɛpsjɔnɛR] *nm/f* receiving clerk.

réceptionner [Resɛpsjɔne] *vt (COMM)* to take delivery of; *(SPORT: ballon)* to catch (and control).

réceptionniste [Resɛpsjɔnist(ə)] *nm/f* receptionist.

réceptivité [Resɛptivite] *nf (à une influence)* receptiveness; *(à une maladie)* susceptibility.

récessif, ive [Resesif, -iv] *adj (BIOL)* recessive.

récession [Resesjɔ̃] *nf* recession.

recette [Rəsɛt] *nf (CULIN)* recipe; *(fig)* formula, recipe; *(COMM)* takings *pl*; *(ADMIN: bureau)* tax *ou* revenue office; ~s *nfpl* (*COMM*: rentrées) receipts; **faire** ~ (*spectacle, exposition*) to be a winner.

receveur, euse [ʀəsvœʀ, -øz] *nm/f* (*des contributions*) tax collector; (*des postes*) postmaster/mistress; (*d'autobus*) conductor/conductress; (*MÉD*: *de sang, organe*) recipient.

recevoir [ʀəsvwaʀ] *vt* to receive; (*lettre, prime*) to receive, get; (*client, patient, représentant*) to see; (*jour, soleil*: *suj*: *pièce*) to get; (*SCOL*: *candidat*) to pass ♦ *vi* to receive visitors; to give parties; to see patients *etc*; **se** ~ *vi* (*athlète*) to land; ~ **qn à dîner** to invite sb to dinner; **il reçoit de 8 à 10** he's at home from 8 to 10, he will see visitors from 8 to 10; (*docteur, dentiste etc*) he sees patients from 8 to 10; **être reçu** (*à un examen*) to pass; **être bien/mal reçu** to be well/badly received.

rechange [ʀəʃɑ̃ʒ]: **de** ~ *adj* (*pièces, roue*) spare; (*fig*: *solution*) alternative; **des vêtements de** ~ a change of clothes.

rechaper [ʀəʃape] *vt* to remould (*BRIT*), remold (*US*), retread.

réchapper [ʀeʃape]: ~ **de** *ou* **à** *vt* (*accident, maladie*) to come through; **va-t-il en** ~? is he going to get over it?, is he going to come through (it)?

recharge [ʀəʃaʀʒ(ə)] *nf* refill.

rechargeable [ʀəʃaʀʒabl(ə)] *adj* refillable; rechargeable.

recharger [ʀəʃaʀʒe] *vt* (*camion, fusil, appareil-photo*) to reload; (*briquet, stylo*) to refill; (*batterie*) to recharge.

réchaud [ʀeʃo] *nm* (*portable*) stove; plate-warmer.

réchauffé [ʀeʃofe] *nm* (*nourriture*) reheated food; (*fig*) stale news (*ou* joke *etc*).

réchauffement [ʀeʃofmɑ̃] *nm* warming (up); **le** ~ **de la planète** global warming.

réchauffer [ʀeʃofe] *vt* (*plat*) to reheat; (*mains, personne*) to warm; **se** ~ *vi* to get warmer; **se** ~ **les doigts** to warm (up) one's fingers.

rêche [ʀɛʃ] *adj* rough.

recherche [ʀəʃɛʀʃ(ə)] *nf* (*action*): **la** ~ **de** the search for; (*raffinement*) affectedness, studied elegance; (*scientifique etc*): **la** ~ research; ~s *nfpl* (*de la police*) investigations; (*scientifiques*) research *sg*; **être/se mettre à la** ~ **de** to be/go in search of.

recherché, e [ʀəʃɛʀʃe] *adj* (*rare, demandé*) much sought-after; (*entouré: acteur, femme*) in demand; (*raffiné*) studied, affected.

rechercher [ʀəʃɛʀʃe] *vt* (*objet égaré, personne*) to look for, search for; (*témoins, coupable, main-d'œuvre*) to look for; (*causes d'un phénomène, nouveau procédé*) to try to find; (*bonheur etc, l'amitié de qn*) to seek; "~ **et remplacer**" (*INFORM*) "search and replace".

rechigner [ʀəʃiɲe] *vi*: ~ (**à**) to balk (at).

rechute [ʀəʃyt] *nf* (*MÉD*) relapse; (*dans le péché, le vice*) lapse; **faire une** ~ to have a relapse.

rechuter [ʀəʃyte] *vi* (*MÉD*) to relapse.

récidive [ʀesidiv] *nf* (*JUR*) second (*ou* subsequent) offence; (*fig*) repetition; (*MÉD*) recurrence.

récidiver [ʀesidive] *vi* to commit a second (*ou* subsequent) offence; (*fig*) to do it again.

récidiviste [ʀesidivist(ə)] *nm/f* second (*ou* habitual) offender, recidivist.

récif [ʀesif] *nm* reef.

récipiendaire [ʀesipjɑ̃dɛʀ] *nm* recipient (*of diploma etc*); (*d'une société*) newly elected member.

récipient [ʀesipjɑ̃] *nm* container.

réciproque [ʀesipʀɔk] *adj* reciprocal ♦ *nf*: **la** ~ (*l'inverse*) the converse.

réciproquement [ʀesipʀɔkmɑ̃] *adv* reciprocally; **et** ~ and vice versa.

récit [ʀesi] *nm* (*action de narrer*) telling; (*conte, histoire*) story.

récital [ʀesital] *nm* recital.

récitant, e [ʀesitɑ̃, -ɑ̃t] *nm/f* narrator.

récitation [ʀesitasjɔ̃] *nf* recitation.

réciter [ʀesite] *vt* to recite.

réclamation [ʀeklamasjɔ̃] *nf* complaint; ~s *nfpl* (*bureau*) complaints department *sg*.

réclame [ʀeklam] *nf*: **la** ~ advertising; **une** ~ an ad(vertisement), an advert (*BRIT*); **faire de la** ~ (**pour qch/qn**) to advertise (sth/sb); **article en** ~ special offer.

réclamer [ʀeklame] *vt* (*aide, nourriture etc*) to ask for; (*revendiquer: dû, part, indemnité*) to claim, demand; (*nécessiter*) to demand, require ♦ *vi* to complain; **se** ~ **de** to give as one's authority; to claim filiation with.

reclassement [ʀəklasmɑ̃] *nm* reclassifying; regrading; rehabilitation.

reclasser [ʀəklase] *vt* (*fiches, dossiers*) to reclassify; (*fig: fonctionnaire etc*) to regrade; (: *ouvrier licencié*) to place, rehabilitate.

reclus, e [ʀəkly, -yz] *nm/f* recluse.

réclusion [ʀeklyzjɔ̃] *nf* imprisonment; ~ **à perpétuité** life imprisonment.

recoiffer [ʀəkwafe] *vt*: ~ **un enfant** to do a child's hair again; **se** ~ to do one's hair again.

recoin [ʀəkwɛ̃] *nm* nook, corner; (*fig*) hidden recess.

reçois [ʀəswa] *etc vb voir* **recevoir**.

reçoive [ʀəswav] *etc vb voir* **recevoir**.

recoller [ʀəkɔle] *vt* (*enveloppe*) to stick back down.

récolte [ʀekɔlt(ə)] *nf* harvesting, gathering; (*produits*) harvest, crop; (*fig*) crop, collection; (: *d'observations*) findings.

récolter [ʀekɔlte] *vt* to harvest, gather (in); (*fig*) to get.

recommandable [ʀəkɔmɑ̃dabl(ə)] *adj* commendable; **peu** ~ not very commendable.

recommandation [ʀəkɔmɑ̃dasjɔ̃] *nf* recommendation.

recommandé [ʀəkɔmɑ̃de] *nm* (*méthode etc*)

---

lapse.

rechuter [ʀəʃyte] *vi* (*MÉD*) to relapse.

recommended; (*POSTES*): en ~ by registered mail.
recommander [Rəkɔmɑ̃de] *vt* to recommend; (*suj: qualités etc*) to commend; (*POSTES*) to register; ~ **qch à qn** to recommend sth to sb; ~ **à qn de faire** to recommend sb to do; ~ **qn auprès de qn** *ou* **à qn** to recommend sb to sb; **il est recommandé de faire** ... it is recommended that one does ...; **se ~ à qn** to commend o.s. to sb; **se ~ de qn** to give sb's name as a reference.
recommencer [Rəkɔmɑ̃se] *vt* (*reprendre: lutte, séance*) to resume, start again; (*refaire: travail, explications*) to start afresh, start (over) again; (*récidiver: erreur*) to make again ♦ *vi* to start again; (*récidiver*) to do it again; ~ **à faire** to start doing again; **ne recommence pas!** don't do that again!
récompense [Rekɔ̃pɑ̃s] *nf* reward; (*prix*) award; **recevoir qch en ~** to get sth as a reward, be rewarded with sth.
récompenser [Rekɔ̃pɑ̃se] *vt*: ~ **qn (de** *ou* **pour)** to reward sb (for).
réconciliation [Rekɔ̃siljɑsjɔ̃] *nf* reconciliation.
réconcilier [Rekɔ̃silje] *vt* to reconcile; ~ **qn avec qn** to reconcile sb with sb; ~ **qn avec qch** to reconcile sb to sth; **se ~ (avec)** to be reconciled (with).
reconductible [Rəkɔ̃dyktibl(ə)] *adj* (*JUR: contrat, bail*) renewable.
reconduction [Rəkɔ̃dyksjɔ̃] *nf* renewal; (*POL: d'une politique*) continuation.
reconduire [Rəkɔ̃dɥiR] *vt* (*raccompagner*) to take *ou* see back; (: à *la porte*) to show out; (: à *son domicile*) to see home, take home; (*JUR, POL: renouveler*) to renew.
réconfort [Rekɔ̃fɔR] *nm* comfort.
réconfortant, e [Rekɔ̃fɔRtɑ̃, -ɑ̃t] *adj* (*idée, paroles*) comforting; (*boisson*) fortifying.
réconforter [Rekɔ̃fɔRte] *vt* (*consoler*) to comfort; (*revigorer*) to fortify.
reconnais [R(ə)kɔnɛ] *etc vb voir* **reconnaître.**
reconnaissable [Rəkɔnɛsabl(ə)] *adj* recognizable.
reconnaissais [R(ə)kɔnɛsɛ] *etc vb voir* **reconnaître.**
reconnaissance [Rəkɔnɛsɑ̃s] *nf* recognition; acknowledgement; (*gratitude*) gratitude, gratefulness; (*MIL*) reconnaissance, recce; **en ~** (*MIL*) on reconnaissance; ~ **de dette** acknowledgement of a debt, IOU.
reconnaissant, e [Rəkɔnɛsɑ̃, -ɑ̃t] *vb voir* **reconnaître** ♦ *adj* grateful; **je vous serais ~ de bien vouloir** I should be most grateful if you would (kindly).
reconnaître [RəkɔnɛtR(ə)] *vt* to recognize; (*MIL: lieu*) to reconnoitre; (*JUR: enfant, dette, droit*) to acknowledge; ~ **que** to admit *ou* acknowledge that; ~ **qn/qch à** (*l'identifier grâce à*) to recognize sb/sth by; ~ **à qn: je lui reconnais certaines qualités** I recognize certain qualities in him; **se ~ quelque part** (*s'y

retrouver*) to find one's way around (a place).
reconnu, e [R(ə)kɔny] *pp de* **reconnaître** ♦ *adj* (*indiscuté, connu*) recognized.
reconquérir [Rəkɔ̃keRiR] *vt* (*aussi fig*) to reconquer, recapture; (*sa dignité etc*) to recover.
reconquête [Rəkɔ̃kɛt] *nf* recapture; recovery.
reconsidérer [Rəkɔ̃sideRe] *vt* to reconsider.
reconstituant, e [Rəkɔ̃stitɥɑ̃, -ɑ̃t] *adj* (*régime*) strength-building ♦ *nm* tonic, pick-me-up.
reconstituer [Rəkɔ̃stitɥe] *vt* (*monument ancien*) to recreate, build a replica of; (*fresque, vase brisé*) to piece together, reconstitute; (*événement, accident*) to reconstruct; (*fortune, patrimoine*) to rebuild; (*BIO: tissus etc*) to regenerate.
reconstitution [Rəkɔ̃stitysjɔ̃] *nf* (*d'un accident etc*) reconstruction.
reconstruction [Rəkɔ̃stRyksjɔ̃] *nf* rebuilding, reconstruction.
reconstruire [Rəkɔ̃stRɥiR] *vt* to rebuild, reconstruct.
reconversion [Rəkɔ̃vɛRsjɔ̃] *nf* (*du personnel*) redeployment.
reconvertir [Rəkɔ̃vɛRtiR] *vt* (*usine*) to reconvert; (*personnel, troupes etc*) to redeploy; **se ~ dans** (*un métier, une branche*) to move into, be redeployed into.
recopier [Rəkɔpje] *vt* (*transcrire*) to copy out again, write out again; (*mettre au propre: devoir*) to make a clean *ou* fair copy of.
record [RəkɔR] *nm, adj* record; ~ **du monde** world record.
recoucher [Rəkuʃe] *vt* (*enfant*) to put back to bed.
recoudre [RəkudR(ə)] *vt* (*bouton*) to sew back on; (*plaie, incision*) to sew (back) up, stitch up.
recoupement [Rəkupmɑ̃] *nm*: **faire un ~** *ou* **des ~s** to cross-check; **par ~** by cross-checking.
recouper [Rəkupe] *vt* (*tranche*) to cut again; (*vêtement*) to recut ♦ *vi* (*CARTES*) to cut again; **se ~** *vi* (*témoignages*) to tie *ou* match up.
recourais [RəkuRɛ] *etc vb voir* **recourir.**
recourbé, e [RəkuRbe] *adj* curved; hooked; bent.
recourber [RəkuRbe] *vt* (*branche, tige de métal*) to bend.
recourir [RəkuRiR] *vi* (*courir de nouveau*) to run again; (*refaire une course*) to race again; ~ **à** *vt* (*ami, agence*) to turn *ou* appeal to; (*force, ruse, emprunt*) to resort to, have recourse to.
recours [RəkuR] *vb voir* **recourir** ♦ *nm* (*JUR*) appeal; **avoir ~ à** = **recourir à**; **en dernier ~** as a last resort; **sans ~** final; with no way out; ~ **en grâce** plea for clemency (*ou* pardon).
recouru, e [RəkuRy] *pp de* **recourir.**
recousu, e [Rəkuzy] *pp de* **recoudre.**
recouvert, e [RəkuvɛR, -ɛRt(ə)] *pp de* **recouvrir.**
recouvrable [RəkuvRabl(ə)] *adj* (*somme*) recoverable.

recouvrais [ʀəkuvʀɛ] *etc vb voir* **recouvrer, recouvrir.**

recouvrement [ʀəkuvʀəmɑ̃] *nm* recovery.

recouvrer [ʀəkuvʀe] *vt* (*vue, santé etc*) to recover, regain; (*impôts*) to collect; (*créance*) to recover.

recouvrir [ʀəkuvʀiʀ] *vt* (*couvrir à nouveau*) to re-cover; (*couvrir entièrement, aussi fig*) to cover; (*cacher, masquer*) to conceal, hide; **se** ~ (*se superposer*) to overlap.

recracher [ʀəkʀaʃe] *vt* to spit out.

récréatif, ive [ʀekʀeatif, -iv] *adj* of entertainment; recreational.

récréation [ʀekʀeasjɔ̃] *nf* recreation, entertainment; (*SCOL*) break.

recréer [ʀəkʀee] *vt* to recreate.

récrier [ʀekʀije]: **se** ~ *vi* to exclaim.

récriminations [ʀekʀiminasjɔ̃] *nfpl* remonstrations, complaints.

récriminer [ʀekʀimine] *vi*: ~ **contre qn/qch** to remonstrate against sb/sth.

recroqueviller [ʀəkʀɔkvije]: **se** ~ *vi* (*feuilles*) to curl *ou* shrivel up; (*personne*) to huddle up.

recru, e [ʀəkʀy] *adj*: ~ **de fatigue** exhausted ♦ *nf* recruit.

recrudescence [ʀəkʀydesɑ̃s] *nf* fresh outbreak.

recrutement [ʀəkʀytmɑ̃] *nm* recruiting, recruitment.

recruter [ʀəkʀyte] *vt* to recruit.

rectal, e, aux [ʀɛktal, -o] *adj*: **par voie** ~**e** rectally.

rectangle [ʀɛktɑ̃gl(ə)] *nm* rectangle; ~ **blanc** (*TV*) "adults only" symbol.

rectangulaire [ʀɛktɑ̃gylɛʀ] *adj* rectangular.

recteur [ʀɛktœʀ] *nm* ≈ (regional) director of education (*BRIT*), ≈ state superintendent of education (*US*).

rectificatif, ive [ʀɛktifikatif, -iv] *adj* corrected ♦ *nm* correction.

rectification [ʀɛktifikasjɔ̃] *nf* correction.

rectifier [ʀɛktifje] *vt* (*tracé, virage*) to straighten; (*calcul, adresse*) to correct; (*erreur, faute*) to rectify, put right.

rectiligne [ʀɛktiliɲ] *adj* straight; (*GÉOM*) rectilinear.

rectitude [ʀɛktityd] *nf* rectitude, uprightness.

recto [ʀɛkto] *nm* front (*of a sheet of paper*).

rectorat [ʀɛktɔʀa] *nm* (*fonction*) position of *recteur*; (*bureau*) *recteur's office*; *see also* **recteur.**

rectum [ʀɛktɔm] *nm* rectum.

reçu, e [ʀəsy] *pp de* **recevoir** ♦ *adj* (*admis, consacré*) accepted ♦ *nm* (*COMM*) receipt.

recueil [ʀəkœj] *nm* collection.

recueillement [ʀəkœjmɑ̃] *nm* meditation, contemplation.

recueilli, e [ʀəkœji] *adj* contemplative.

recueillir [ʀəkœjiʀ] *vt* to collect; (*voix, suffrages*) to win; (*accueillir: réfugiés, chat*) to take in; **se** ~ *vi* to gather one's thoughts; to meditate.

recuire [ʀəkɥiʀ] *vi*: **faire** ~ to recook.

recul [ʀəkyl] *nm* retreat; recession; decline; (*d'arme à feu*) recoil, kick; **avoir un mouvement de** ~ to recoil, start back; **prendre du** ~ to stand back; **avec le** ~ with the passing of time, in retrospect.

reculade [ʀəkylad] *nf* (*péj*) climb-down.

reculé, e [ʀəkyle] *adj* remote.

reculer [ʀəkyle] *vi* to move back, back away; (*AUTO*) to reverse, back up; (*fig: civilisation, épidémie*) to (be on the) decline; (*: se dérober*) to shrink back ♦ *vt* to move back; to reverse, back (up); (*fig: possibilités, limites*) to extend; (*: date, décision*) to postpone; ~ **devant** (*danger, difficulté*) to shrink from; ~ **pour mieux sauter** (*fig*) to postpone the evil day.

reculons [ʀəkylɔ̃]: **à** ~ *adv* backwards.

récupérable [ʀekypeʀabl(ə)] *adj* (*créance*) recoverable; (*heures*) which can be made up; (*ferraille*) salvageable.

récupération [ʀekypeʀasjɔ̃] *nf* (*de vieux métaux etc*) salvage, reprocessing; (*POL*) bringing into line.

récupérer [ʀekypeʀe] *vt* (*rentrer en possession de*) to recover, get back; (*: forces*) to recover; (*déchets etc*) to salvage (for reprocessing); (*remplacer: journée, heures de travail*) to make up; (*délinquant etc*) to rehabilitate; (*POL*) to bring into line ♦ *vi* to recover.

récurer [ʀekyʀe] *vt* to scour; **poudre à** ~ scouring powder.

reçus [ʀəsy] *etc vb voir* **recevoir.**

récusable [ʀekyzabl(ə)] *adj* (*témoin*) challengeable; (*témoignage*) impugnable.

récuser [ʀekyze] *vt* to challenge; **se** ~ to decline to give an opinion.

recyclage [ʀəsiklaʒ] *nm* reorientation; retraining; recycling; **cours de** ~ retraining course.

recycler [ʀəsikle] *vt* (*SCOL*) to reorientate; (*employés*) to retrain; (*matériau*) to recycle; **se** ~ to retrain; to go on a retraining course.

rédacteur, trice [ʀedaktœʀ, -tʀis] *nm/f* (*journaliste*) writer; subeditor; (*d'ouvrage de référence*) editor, compiler; ~ **en chef** chief editor; ~ **publicitaire** copywriter.

rédaction [ʀedaksjɔ̃] *nf* writing; (*rédacteurs*) editorial staff; (*bureau*) editorial office(s); (*SCOL: devoir*) essay, composition.

reddition [ʀedisjɔ̃] *nf* surrender.

redéfinir [ʀədefiniʀ] *vt* to redefine.

redemander [ʀədmɑ̃de] *vt* (*renseignement*) to ask again for; (*nourriture*): ~ **de** to ask for more (*ou* another); (*objet prêté*): ~ **qch** to ask for sth back.

redémarrer [ʀədemaʀe] *vi* (*véhicule*) to start again, get going again; (*fig: industrie etc*) to get going again.

rédemption [ʀedɑ̃psjɔ̃] *nf* redemption.

redéploiement [Rədeplwamã] *nm* redeployment.

redescendre [RədesãdR(ə)] *vi* (*è nouveau*) to go back down; (*après la montée*) to go down (again) ♦ *vt* (*pente etc*) to go down.

redevable [Rədəvabl(ə)] *adj*: **être ~ de qch à qn** (*somme*) to owe sb sth; (*fig*) to be indebted to sb for sth.

redevance [Rədvãs] *nf* (*TÉL*) rental charge; (*TV*) licence (*BRIT*) *ou* license (*US*) fee.

redevenir [Rədvəniʀ] *vi* to become again.

rédhibitoire [Redibitwaʀ] *adj*: **vice ~** (*JUR*) *latent defect in merchandise that renders the sales contract void*; (*fig*: *défaut*) crippling.

rediffuser [Rədifyze] *vt* (*RADIO*, *TV*) to repeat, broadcast again.

rediffusion [Rədifyzjɔ̃] *nf* repeat (programme).

rédiger [Rediʒe] *vt* to write; (*contrat*) to draw up.

redire [Rədiʀ] *vt* to repeat; **trouver à ~ à** to find fault with.

redistribuer [Rədistʀibÿe] *vt* (*cartes etc*) to deal again; (*richesses, tâches, revenus*) to redistribute.

redite [Rədit] *nf* (*needless*) repetition.

redondance [Rədɔ̃dãs] *nf* redundancy.

redonner [Rədɔne] *vt* (*restituer*) to give back, return; (*du courage, des forces*) to restore.

redoublé, e [Rəduble] *adj*: **à coups ~s** even harder, twice as hard.

redoubler [Rəduble] *vi* (*tempête, violence*) to intensify, get even stronger *ou* fiercer *etc*; (*SCOL*) to repeat a year ♦ *vt* (*SCOL*: *classe*) to repeat; (*LING*: *lettre*) to double; **~ de** *vt* to be twice as + *adjectif*; **le vent redouble de violence** the wind is blowing twice as hard.

redoutable [Rədutabl(ə)] *adj* formidable, fearsome.

redouter [Rədute] *vt* to fear; (*appréhender*) to dread; **~ de faire** to dread doing.

redoux [Rədu] *nm* milder spell.

redressement [RədʀɛsmÃ] *nm* (*de l'économie etc*) putting right; **maison de ~** reformatory; **~ fiscal** repayment of back taxes.

redresser [Rədʀese] *vt* (*arbre, mât*) to set upright, right; (*pièce tordue*) to straighten out; (*AVIAT, AUTO*) to straighten up; (*situation, économie*) to put right; **se ~** *vi* (*objet penché*) to right itself; to straighten up; (*personne*) to sit (*ou* stand) up; to sit (*ou* stand) up straight; (*fig*: *pays, situation*) to recover; **~ (les roues)** (*AUTO*) to straighten up.

redresseur [RədʀɛsœʀR] *nm*: **~ de torts** righter of wrongs.

réducteur, trice [RedyktœʀR, -tʀis] *adj* simplistic.

réduction [Redyksjɔ̃] *nf* reduction; **en ~** *adv* in miniature, scaled-down.

réduire [RedÿiʀR] *vt* (*gén, aussi CULIN, MATH*) to reduce; (*prix, dépenses*) to cut, reduce; (*carte*) to scale down, reduce; (*MÉD*: *fracture*)

to set; **~ qn/qch à** to reduce sb/sth to; **se ~ à** (*revenir à*) to boil down to; **se ~ en** (*se transformer en*) to be reduced to; **en être réduit à** to be reduced to.

réduit, e [Redÿi, -it] *pp de* **réduire** ♦ *adj* (*prix, tarif, échelle*) reduced; (*mécanisme*) scaled-down; (*vitesse*) reduced ♦ *nm* tiny room; recess.

rééchelonner [Reeʃlɔne] *vt* to reschedule.

rééditer [Reedite] *vt* to republish.

réédition [Reedisjɔ̃] *nf* new edition.

rééducation [Reedykasjɔ̃] *nf* (*d'un membre*) re-education; (*de délinquants, d'un blessé*) rehabilitation; **~ de la parole** speech therapy; **centre de ~** physiotherapy *ou* physical therapy (*US*) centre.

rééduquer [Reedyke] *vt* to reeducate; to rehabilitate.

réel, le [Reɛl] *adj* real ♦ *nm*: **le ~** reality.

réélection [Reelɛksjɔ̃] *nf* re-election.

rééligible [Reeliʒibl(ə)] *adj* re-eligible.

réélire [Reeliʀ] *vt* to re-elect.

réellement [Reɛlmã] *adv* really.

réembaucher [Reãboʃe] *vt* to take on again.

réemploi [Reãplwa] *nm* = **remploi**.

réemployer [Reãplwaje] *vt* (*méthode, produit*) to re-use; (*argent*) to reinvest; (*personnel, employé*) to re-employ.

rééquilibrer [Reekilibʀe] *vt* (*budget*) to balance (again).

réescompte [Reɛskɔ̃t] *nm* rediscount.

réessayer [Reɛseje] *vt* to try on again.

réévaluation [Reevalÿasjɔ̃] *nf* revaluation.

réévaluer [Reevalÿe] *vt* to revalue.

réexaminer [Reɛgzamine] *vt* to re-examine.

réexpédier [Reɛkspedje] *vt* (*à l'envoyeur*) to return, send back; (*au destinataire*) to send on, forward.

réexporter [Reɛkspɔʀte] *vt* to re-export.

réf. *abr* (= *référence(s)*): **V/~** Your ref.

refaire [RəfɛʀR] *vt* (*faire de nouveau, recommencer*) to do again; (*réparer, restaurer*) to do up; **se ~** *vi* (*en argent*) to make up one's losses; **se ~ une santé** to recuperate; **se ~ à qch** (*se réhabituer à*) to get used to sth again.

refasse [Rəfas] *etc vb voir* **refaire**.

réfection [Refɛksjɔ̃] *nf* repair; **en ~** under repair.

réfectoire [RefɛktwaʀR] *nm* refectory.

referai [R(ə)fʀe] *etc vb voir* **refaire**.

référé [Refere] *nm* (*JUR*) emergency interim proceedings *ou* ruling.

référence [Referãs] *nf* reference; **~s** *nfpl* (*recommandations*) reference *sg*; **faire ~ à** to refer to; **ouvrage de ~** reference work; **ce n'est pas une ~** (*fig*) that's no recommendation.

référendum [Referãdɔm] *nm* referendum.

référer [Refere]: **se ~ à** *vt* to refer to; **en ~ à qn** to refer the matter to sb.

refermer [Rəfɛʀme] *vt* to close again, shut again.

refiler [ʀəfile] *vt* (*fam*): ~ **qch à qn** to palm (*BRIT*) *ou* fob sth off on sb; to pass sth on to sb.

refit [ʀəfi] *etc vb voir* **refaire**.

réfléchi, e [ʀefleʃi] *adj* (*caractère*) thoughtful; (*action*) well-thought-out; (*LING*) reflexive.

réfléchir [ʀefleʃiʀ] *vt* to reflect ♦ *vi* to think; ~ **à** *ou* **sur** to think about; **c'est tout réfléchi** my mind's made up.

réflecteur [ʀeflɛktœʀ] *nm* (*AUTO*) reflector.

reflet [ʀəflɛ] *nm* reflection; (*sur l'eau etc*) sheen *no pl*, glint; ~**s** *nmpl* gleam *sg*.

refléter [ʀəflete] *vt* to reflect; **se** ~ *vi* to be reflected.

réflex [ʀeflɛks] *adj inv* (*PHOTO*) reflex.

réflexe [ʀeflɛks(ə)] *adj, nm* reflex; ~ **conditionné** conditioned reflex.

réflexion [ʀeflɛksjɔ̃] *nf* (*de la lumière etc, pensée*) reflection; (*fait de penser*) thought; (*remarque*) remark; ~**s** *nfpl* (*méditations*) thought *sg*, reflection *sg*; **sans** ~ without thinking; ~ **faite, à la** ~, **après** ~ on reflection; **délai de** ~ cooling-off period; **groupe de** ~ think tank.

refluer [ʀəflye] *vi* to flow back; (*foule*) to surge back.

reflux [ʀəfly] *nm* (*de la mer*) ebb; (*fig*) backward surge.

refondre [ʀəfɔ̃dʀ(ə)] *vt* (*texte*) to recast.

refont [ʀ(ə)fɔ̃] *vb voir* **refaire**.

reformater [ʀəfɔʀmate] *vt* to reformat.

réformateur, trice [ʀefɔʀmatœʀ, -tʀis] *nm/f* reformer ♦ *adj* (*mesures*) reforming.

Réformation [ʀefɔʀmasjɔ̃] *nf*: **la** ~ the Reformation.

réforme [ʀefɔʀm(ə)] *nf* reform; (*MIL*) declaration of unfitness for service; discharge (*on health grounds*); (*REL*): **la R**~ the Reformation.

réformé, e [ʀefɔʀme] *adj, nm/f* (*REL*) Protestant.

reformer [ʀəfɔʀme] *vt*, **se** ~ *vi* to reform; ~ **les rangs** (*MIL*) to fall in again.

réformer [ʀefɔʀme] *vt* to reform; (*MIL: recrue*) to declare unfit for service; (*: soldat*) to discharge, invalid out; (*matériel*) to scrap.

réformisme [ʀefɔʀmism(ə)] *nm* reformism, policy of reform.

réformiste [ʀefɔʀmist(ə)] *adj, nm/f* (*POL*) reformist.

refoulé, e [ʀəfule] *adj* (*PSYCH*) repressed.

refoulement [ʀəfulmɑ̃] *nm* (*d'une armée*) driving back; (*PSYCH*) repression.

refouler [ʀəfule] *vt* (*envahisseurs*) to drive back, repulse; (*liquide*) to force back; (*fig*) to suppress; (*PSYCH*) to repress.

réfractaire [ʀefʀaktɛʀ] *adj* (*minerai*) refractory; (*brique*) fire *cpd*; (*maladie*) which is resistant to treatment; (*prêtre*) non-juring; **soldat** ~ draft evader; **être** ~ **à** to resist.

réfracter [ʀefʀakte] *vt* to refract.

réfraction [ʀefʀaksjɔ̃] *nf* refraction.

refrain [ʀəfʀɛ̃] *nm* (*MUS*) refrain, chorus; (*air, fig*) tune.

refréner, réfréner [ʀəfʀene, ʀefʀene] *vt* to curb, check.

réfrigérant, e [ʀefʀiʒeʀɑ̃, -ɑ̃t] *adj* refrigerant, cooling.

réfrigérateur [ʀefʀiʒeʀatœʀ] *nm* refrigerator; ~-**congélateur** fridge-freezer.

réfrigération [ʀefʀiʒeʀɑsjɔ̃] *nf* refrigeration.

réfrigéré, e [ʀefʀiʒeʀe] *adj* (*camion, wagon*) refrigerated.

réfrigérer [ʀefʀiʒeʀe] *vt* to refrigerate; (*fam: glacer, aussi fig*) to cool.

refroidir [ʀəfʀwadiʀ] *vt* to cool; (*fig*) to have a cooling effect on ♦ *vi* to cool (down); **se** ~ *vi* (*prendre froid*) to catch a chill; (*temps*) to get cooler *ou* colder; (*fig*) to cool (off).

refroidissement [ʀəfʀwadismɑ̃] *nm* cooling; (*grippe etc*) chill.

refuge [ʀəfyʒ] *nm* refuge; (*pour piétons*) (traffic) island; **demander** ~ **à qn** to ask sb for refuge.

réfugié, e [ʀefyʒje] *adj, nm/f* refugee.

réfugier [ʀefyʒje]: **se** ~ *vi* to take refuge.

refus [ʀəfy] *nm* refusal; **ce n'est pas de** ~ I won't say no, it's very welcome.

refuser [ʀəfyze] *vt* to refuse; (*SCOL: candidat*) to fail ♦ *vi* to refuse; ~ **qch à qn/de faire** to refuse sb sth/to do; ~ **du monde** to have to turn people away; **se** ~ **à qch** *ou* **à faire qch** to refuse to do sth; **il ne se refuse rien** he doesn't stint himself; **se** ~ **à qn** to refuse sb.

réfutable [ʀefytabl(ə)] *adj* refutable.

réfuter [ʀefyte] *vt* to refute.

regagner [ʀəgaɲe] *vt* (*argent, faveur*) to win back; (*lieu*) to get back to; ~ **le temps perdu** to make up (for) lost time; ~ **du terrain** to regain ground.

regain [ʀəgɛ̃] *nm* (*herbe*) second crop of hay; (*renouveau*): **un** ~ **de** renewed + *nom*.

régal [ʀegal] *nm* treat; **un** ~ **pour les yeux** a pleasure *ou* delight to look at.

régalade [ʀegalad] *adv*: **à la** ~ from the bottle (held away from the lips).

régaler [ʀegale] *vt*: ~ **qn** to treat sb to a delicious meal; ~ **qn de** to treat sb to; **se** ~ *vi* to have a delicious meal; (*fig*) to enjoy o.s.

regard [ʀəgaʀ] *nm* (*coup d'œil*) look, glance; (*expression*) look (in one's eye); **parcourir/menacer du** ~ to cast an eye over/look threateningly at; **au** ~ **de** (*loi, morale*) from the point of view of; **en** ~ (*vis à vis*) opposite; **en** ~ **de** in comparison with.

regardant, e [ʀəgaʀdɑ̃, -ɑ̃t] *adj*: **très/peu** ~ (**sur**) quite fussy/very free (about); (*économe*) very tight-fisted/quite generous (with).

regarder [ʀəgaʀde] *vt* (*examiner, observer, lire*) to look at; (*film, télévision, match*) to watch; (*envisager: situation, avenir*) to view; (*considérer: son intérêt etc*) to be concerned with; (*être orienté vers*): ~ (**vers**) to face; (*concer-*

ner) to concern ♦ *vi* to look; ~ **à** *vt* (*dépense, qualité, détails*) to be fussy with *ou* over; ~ **à faire** to hesitate to do; **dépenser sans ~** to spend freely; **qn/qch comme** to regard sb/sth as; ~ **(qch) dans le dictionnaire/ l'annuaire** to look (sth up) in the dictionary/ directory; ~ **par la fenêtre** to look out of the window; **cela me regarde** it concerns me, it's my business.

régate(s) [ʀegat] *nf(pl)* regatta.

régénérer [ʀeʒeneʀe] *vt* to regenerate; (*fig*) to revive.

régent [ʀeʒɑ̃] *nm* regent.

régenter [ʀeʒɑ̃te] *vt* to rule over; to dictate to.

régie [ʀeʒi] *nf* (*COMM, INDUSTRIE*) state-owned company; (*THÉÂT, CINÉ*) production; (*RADIO, TV*) control room; **la ~ de l'État** state control.

regimber [ʀəʒɛ̃be] *vi* to balk, jib.

régime [ʀeʒim] *nm* (*POL, GÉO*) régime; (*ADMIN: carcéral, fiscal etc*) system; (*MÉD*) diet; (*TECH*) (engine) speed; (*fig*) rate, pace; (*de bananes, dattes*) bunch; **se mettre au/suivre un ~** to go on/be on a diet; ~ **sans sel** salt-free diet; **à bas/haut ~** (*AUTO*) at low/high revs; **à plein ~** flat out, at full speed; ~ **matrimonial** marriage settlement.

régiment [ʀeʒimɑ̃] *nm* (*MIL: unité*) regiment; (*fig: fam*): **un ~ de** an army of; **un copain de ~** a pal from military service *ou* (one's) army days.

région [ʀeʒjɔ̃] *nf* region; **la ~ parisienne** the Paris area.

régional, e, aux [ʀeʒjɔnal, -o] *adj* regional.

régionalisation [ʀeʒjɔnalizasjɔ̃] *nf* regionalization.

régionalisme [ʀeʒjɔnalism(ə)] *nm* regionalism.

régir [ʀeʒiʀ] *vt* to govern.

régisseur [ʀeʒisœʀ] *nm* (*d'un domaine*) steward; (*CINÉ, TV*) assistant director; (*THÉÂT*) stage manager.

registre [ʀəʒistʀ(ə)] *nm* (*livre*) register; logbook; ledger; (*MUS, LING*) register; (*d'orgue*) stop; ~ **de comptabilité** ledger; ~ **de l'état civil** register of births, marriages and deaths.

réglable [ʀeglabl(ə)] *adj* (*siège, flamme etc*) adjustable; (*achat*) payable.

réglage [ʀeglaʒ] *nm* (*d'une machine*) adjustment; (*d'un moteur*) tuning.

règle [ʀegl(ə)] *nf* (*instrument*) ruler; (*loi, prescription*) rule; ~**s** *nfpl* (*PHYSIOL*) period *sg*; **avoir pour ~ de** to make it a rule that *ou* to; **en ~** (*papiers d'identité*) in order; **être/se mettre en ~** to be/put o.s. straight with the authorities; **en ~ générale** as a (general) rule; **être la ~** to be the rule; **être de ~** to be usual; ~ **à calcul** slide rule; ~ **de trois** (*MATH*) rule of three.

réglé, e [ʀegle] *adj* well-ordered; stable, steady; (*papier*) ruled; (*arrangé*) settled; (*fem-*

me): **bien ~e** whose periods are regular.

règlement [ʀegləmɑ̃] *nm* settling; (*paiement*) settlement; (*arrêté*) regulation; (*règles, statuts*) regulations *pl*, rules *pl*; ~ **à la commande** cash with order; ~ **de compte(s)** settling of scores; ~ **en espèces/par chèque** payment in cash/by cheque; ~ **intérieur** (*SCOL*) school rules *pl*; (*ADMIN*) by-laws *pl*; ~ **judiciaire** compulsory liquidation.

réglementaire [ʀegləmɑ̃tɛʀ] *adj* conforming to the regulations; (*tenue, uniforme*) regulation *cpd*.

réglementation [ʀegləmɑ̃tasjɔ̃] *nf* regulation, control; (*règlements*) regulations *pl*.

réglementer [ʀegləmɑ̃te] *vt* to regulate, control.

régler [ʀegle] *vt* (*mécanisme, machine*) to regulate, adjust; (*moteur*) to tune; (*thermostat etc*) to set, adjust; (*emploi du temps etc*) to organize, plan; (*question, conflit, facture, dette*) to settle; (*fournisseur*) to settle up with, pay; (*papier*) to rule; ~ **qch sur** to model sth on; ~ **son compte à qn** to sort sb out, settle sb; ~ **un compte avec qn** to settle a score with sb.

réglisse [ʀeglis] *nf ou m* liquorice; **bâton de ~** liquorice stick.

règne [ʀɛɲ] *nm* (*d'un roi etc, fig*) reign; (*BIO*): **le ~ végétal/animal** the vegetable/animal kingdom.

régner [ʀeɲe] *vi* (*roi*) to rule, reign; (*fig*) to reign.

regonfler [ʀ(ə)gɔ̃fle] *vt* (*ballon, pneu*) to re-inflate, blow up again.

regorger [ʀəgɔʀʒe] *vi* to overflow; ~ **de** to overflow with, be bursting with.

régresser [ʀegʀese] *vi* (*phénomène*) to decline; (*enfant, malade*) to regress.

régressif, ive [ʀegʀesif, -iv] *adj* regressive.

régression [ʀegʀesjɔ̃] *nf* decline; regression; **être en ~** to be on the decline.

regret [ʀəgʀɛ] *nm* regret; **à ~** with regret; **avec ~** regretfully; **être au ~ de devoir/ne pas pouvoir faire** to regret to have to/that one is unable to do; **j'ai le ~ de vous informer que ...** I regret to inform you that ....

regrettable [ʀəgʀɛtabl(ə)] *adj* regrettable.

regretter [ʀəgʀete] *vt* to regret; (*personne*) to miss; ~ **d'avoir fait** to regret doing; ~ **que** to regret that, be sorry that; **non, je regrette** no, I'm sorry.

regroupement [ʀ(ə)gʀupmɑ̃] *nm* grouping together; (*groupe*) group.

regrouper [ʀəgʀupe] *vt* (*grouper*) to group together; (*contenir*) to include, comprise; **se ~** *vi* to gather (together).

régularisation [ʀegylaʀizasjɔ̃] *nf* (*de papiers, passeport*) putting in order; (*de sa situation: par le mariage*) regularization; (*d'un mécanisme*) regulation.

régulariser [ʀegylaʀize] *vt* (*fonctionnement, trafic*) to regulate; (*passeport, papiers*) to put in order; (*sa situation*) to straighten out, regularize.

régularité [Regylarite] *nf* regularity.

régulateur, trice [Regylatœr, -tris] *adj* regulating ♦ *nm* (*TECH*): ~ **de vitesse/de température** speed/temperature regulator.

régulation [Regylɑsjɔ̃] *nf* (*du trafic*) regulation; ~ **des naissances** birth control.

régulier, ière [Regylje, -jɛR] *adj* (*gén*) regular; (*vitesse, qualité*) steady; (*répartition, pression, paysage*) even; (*TRANSPORTS: ligne, service*) scheduled, regular; (*légal, réglementaire*) lawful, in order; (*fam: correct*) straight, on the level.

régulièrement [Regyljɛrmɑ̃] *adv* regularly; steadily; evenly; normally.

régurgiter [Regyrʒite] *vt* to regurgitate.

réhabiliter [Reabilite] *vt* to rehabilitate; (*fig*) to restore to favour (*BRIT*) *ou* favor (*US*).

réhabituer [Reabitɥe] *vt*: **se** ~ **à qch/à faire qch** to get used to sth again/to doing sth again.

rehausser [Rɔose] *vt* to heighten, raise; (*fig*) to set off, enhance.

réimporter [Reɛ̃pɔrte] *vt* to reimport.

réimposer [Reɛ̃poze] *vt* (*FINANCE*) to reimpose; to tax again.

réimpression [Reɛ̃prɛsjɔ̃] *nf* reprinting; (*ouvrage*) reprint.

réimprimer [Reɛ̃prime] *vt* to reprint.

Reims [Rɛ̃s] *n* Rheims.

rein [Rɛ̃] *nm* kidney; ~**s** *nmpl* (*dos*) back *sg*; **avoir mal aux** ~**s** to have backache; ~ **artificiel** kidney machine.

réincarnation [Reɛ̃karnɑsjɔ̃] *nf* reincarnation.

réincarner [Reɛ̃karne]: **se** ~ *vr* to be reincarnated.

reine [Rɛn] *nf* queen.

reine-claude [Rɛnklod] *nf* greengage.

reinette [Rɛnɛt] *nf* rennet, pippin.

réinitialisation [Reinisjalizɑsjɔ̃] *nf* (*INFORM*) reset.

réinsérer [Reɛ̃sere] *vt* (*délinquant, handicapé etc*) to rehabilitate.

réinsertion [Reɛ̃sɛrsjɔ̃] *nf* rehabilitation.

réintégrer [Reɛ̃tegre] *vt* (*lieu*) to return to; (*fonctionnaire*) to reinstate.

réitérer [Reitere] *vt* to repeat, reiterate.

rejaillir [Rɔʒajir] *vi* to splash up; ~ **sur** to splash up onto; (*fig*) to rebound on; to fall upon.

rejet [Rɔʒɛ] *nm* (*action, aussi MÉD*) rejection; (*POÉSIE*) enjambement, rejet; (*BOT*) shoot.

rejeter [Rɔʒte] *vt* (*relancer*) to throw back; (*vomir*) to bring *ou* throw up; (*écarter*) to reject; (*déverser*) to throw out, discharge; (*reporter*): ~ **un mot à la fin d'une phrase** to transpose a word to the end of a sentence; **se** ~ **sur qch** (*accepter faute de mieux*) to fall back on sth; ~ **la tête/les épaules en arrière** to throw one's head/pull one's shoulders back; ~ **la responsabilité de qch sur qn** to lay the responsibility for sth at sb's door.

rejeton [Rɔʒtɔ̃] *nm* offspring.

rejette [R(ɔ)ʒɛt] *etc vb voir* **rejeter**.

rejoignais [R(ɔ)ʒwaɲɛ] *etc vb voir* **rejoindre**.

rejoindre [Rɔʒwɛ̃dR(ɔ)] *vt* (*famille, régiment*) to rejoin, return to; (*lieu*) to get (back) to; (*suj: route etc*) to meet, join; (*rattraper*) to catch up (with); **se** ~ *vi* to meet; **je te rejoins au café** I'll see *ou* meet you at the café.

réjoui, e [Reʒwi] *adj* joyous.

réjouir [Reʒwir] *vt* to delight; **se** ~ *vi* to be delighted; **se** ~ **de qch/de faire** to be delighted about sth/to do; **se** ~ **que** to be delighted that.

réjouissances [Reʒwisɑ̃s] *nfpl* (*joie*) rejoicing *sg*; (*fête*) festivities, merry-making *sg*.

réjouissant, e [Reʒwisɑ̃, -ɑ̃t] *adj* heartening, delightful.

relâche [Rɔlɑʃ]: **faire** ~ *vi* (*navire*) to put into port; (*CINÉ*) to be closed; **c'est le jour de** ~ (*CINÉ*) it's closed today; **sans** ~ *adv* without respite *ou* a break.

relâché, e [Rɔlɑʃe] *adj* loose, lax.

relâchement [Rɔlɑʃmɑ̃] *nm* (*d'un prisonnier*) release; (*de la discipline, musculaire*) relaxation.

relâcher [Rɔlɑʃe] *vt* (*ressort, prisonnier*) to release; (*étreinte, cordes*) to loosen; (*discipline*) to relax ♦ *vi* (*NAVIG*) to put into port; **se** ~ *vi* to loosen; (*discipline*) to become slack *ou* lax; (*élève etc*) to slacken off.

relais [Rɔlɛ] *nm* (*SPORT*): (**course de**) ~ relay (race); (*RADIO, TV*) relay; (*intermédiaire*) go-between; **équipe de** ~ shift team; (*SPORT*) relay team; **prendre le** ~ **(de)** to take over (from); ~ **de poste** post house, coaching inn; ~ **routier** ≈ transport café (*BRIT*), ≈ truck stop (*US*).

relance [Rɔlɑ̃s] *nf* boosting, revival; (*ÉCON*) reflation.

relancer [Rɔlɑ̃se] *vt* (*balle*) to throw back (again); (*moteur*) to restart; (*fig*) to boost, revive; (*personne*): ~ **qn** to pester sb; to get on to sb again.

relater [Rɔlate] *vt* to relate, recount.

relatif, ive [Rɔlatif, -iv] *adj* relative.

relation [Rɔlɑsjɔ̃] *nf* (*récit*) account, report; (*rapport*) relation(ship); ~**s** *nfpl* (*rapports*) relations; relationship; (*connaissances*) connections; **être/entrer en** ~**(s) avec** to be in contact *ou* be dealing/get in contact with; **mettre qn en** ~**(s) avec** to put sb in touch with; ~**s internationales** international relations; ~**s publiques (RP)** public relations (PR); ~**s (sexuelles)** sexual relations, (sexual) intercourse *sg*.

relativement [Rɔlativmɑ̃] *adv* relatively; ~ **à** in relation to.

relativiser [Rɔlativize] *vt* to see in relation to; to put into context.

relativité [Rɔlativite] *nf* relativity.

relax [Rɔlaks] *adj inv*, **relaxe** [Rɔlaks(ɔ)] *adj* relaxed, informal, casual; easy-going;

(fauteuil-)~ *nm* reclining chair.
relaxant, e [Rəlaksɑ̃, -ɑ̃t] *adj* (*cure, médicament*) relaxant; (*ambiance*) relaxing.
relaxation [R(ə)laksɑsjɔ̃] *nf* relaxation.
relaxer [Rəlakse] *vt* to relax; (*JUR*) to discharge; **se ~** *vi* to relax.
relayer [Rəleje] *vt* (*collaborateur, coureur etc*) to relieve, take over from; (*RADIO, TV*) to relay; **se ~** (*dans une activité*) to take it in turns.
relecture [R(ə)lɛktyR] *nf* rereading.
relégation [Rəlegasjɔ̃] *nf* (*SPORT*) relegation.
reléguer [Rəlege] *vt* to relegate; **~ au second plan** to push into the background.
relent(s) [Rəlɑ̃] *nm(pl)* stench *sg*.
relevé, e [Rəlve] *adj* (*bord de chapeau*) turned-up; (*manches*) rolled-up; (*fig: style*) elevated; (*: sauce*) highly-seasoned ♦ *nm* (*lecture*) reading; (*de cotes*) plotting; (*liste*) statement; list; (*facture*) account; **~ de compte bank statement**; **~ d'identité bancaire (RIB)** (bank) account number.
relève [Rəlɛv] *nf* relief; (*équipe*) relief team (*ou* troops *pl*); **prendre la ~** to take over.
relèvement [Rəlɛvmɑ̃] *nm* (*d'un taux, niveau*) raising.
relever [Rəlve] *vt* (*statue, meuble*) to stand up again; (*personne tombée*) to help up; (*vitre, plafond, niveau de vie*) to raise; (*pays, économie, entreprise*) to put back on its feet; (*col*) to turn up; (*style, conversation*) to elevate; (*plat, sauce*) to season; (*sentinelle, équipe*) to relieve; (*souligner: fautes, points*) to pick out; (*constater: traces etc*) to find, pick up; (*répliquer à: remarque*) to react to, reply to; (*: défi*) to accept, take up; (*noter: adresse etc*) to take down, note; (*: plan*) to sketch; (*: cotes etc*) to plot; (*compteur*) to read; (*ramasser: cahiers, copies*) to collect, take in ♦ *vi* (*jupe, bord*) to ride up; **~ de** *vt* (*maladie*) to be recovering from; (*être du ressort de*) to be a matter for; (*ADMIN: dépendre de*) to come under; (*fig*) to pertain to; **se ~** *vi* (*se remettre debout*) to get up; (*fig*): **se ~ (de)** to recover (from); **~ qn de** (*vœux*) to release sb from; (*fonctions*) to relieve sb of; **~ la tête** to look up; to hold up one's head.
relief [Rəljɛf] *nm* relief; (*de pneu*) tread pattern; **~s** *nmpl* (*restes*) remains; **en ~** in relief; (*photographie*) three-dimensional; **mettre en ~** (*fig*) to bring out, highlight.
relier [Rəlje] *vt* to link up; (*livre*) to bind; **~ qch à** to link sth to; **livre relié cuir** leather-bound book.
relieur, euse [RəljœR, -øz] *nm/f* (book)binder.
religieusement [R(ə)liʒjøzmɑ̃] *adv* religiously; (*enterré, mariés*) in church; **vivre ~** to lead a religious life.
religieux, euse [Rəliʒjø, -øz] *adj* religious ♦ *nm* monk ♦ *nf* nun; (*gâteau*) cream bun.
religion [Rəliʒjɔ̃] *nf* religion; (*piété, dévotion*) faith; **entrer en ~** to take one's vows.
reliquaire [RəlikɛR] *nm* reliquary.

reliquat [Rəlika] *nm* (*d'une somme*) balance; (*JUR: de succession*) residue.
relique [Rəlik] *nf* relic.
relire [RəliR] *vt* (*à nouveau*) to reread, read again; (*vérifier*) to read over; **se ~** to read through what one has written.
reliure [RəljyR] *nf* binding; (*art, métier*): **la ~** book-binding.
reloger [R(ə)lɔʒe] *vt* (*locataires, sinistrés*) to rehouse.
relu, e [Rəly] *pp de* **relire**.
reluire [RəlɥiR] *vi* to gleam.
reluisant, e [Rəlɥizɑ̃, -ɑ̃t] *vb voir* **reluire** ♦ *adj* gleaming; **peu ~** (*fig*) unattractive; unsavoury (*BRIT*), unsavory (*US*).
reluquer [R(ə)lyke] *vt* (*fam*) to eye (up), ogle.
remâcher [Rəmɑʃe] *vt* to chew *ou* ruminate over.
remailler [Rəmaje] *vt* (*tricot*) to darn; (*filet*) to mend.
remaniement [Rəmanimɑ̃] *nm*: **~ ministériel** Cabinet reshuffle.
remanier [Rəmanje] *vt* to reshape, recast; (*POL*) to reshuffle.
remarier [R(ə)maRje]: **se ~** *vi* to remarry, get married again.
remarquable [RəmaRkabl(ə)] *adj* remarkable.
remarquablement [R(ə)maRkabləmɑ̃] *adv* remarkably.
remarque [RəmaRk(ə)] *nf* remark; (*écrite*) note.
remarquer [RəmaRke] *vt* (*voir*) to notice; (*dire*): **~ que** to remark that; **se ~** to be noticeable; **se faire ~** to draw attention to o.s.; **faire ~ (à qn) que** to point out (to sb) that; **faire ~ qch (à qn)** to point sth out (to sb); **remarquez, ...** mark you, ..., mind you, ...
remballer [Rɑ̃bale] *vt* to wrap up (again); (*dans un carton*) to pack up (again).
rembarrer [Rɑ̃baRe] *vt*: **~ qn** (*repousser*) to rebuff sb; (*remettre à sa place*) to put sb in his (*ou* her) place.
remblai [Rɑ̃blɛ] *nm* embankment.
remblayer [Rɑ̃bleje] *vt* to bank up; (*fossé*) to fill in.
rembobiner [Rɑ̃bɔbine] *vt* to rewind.
rembourrage [Rɑ̃buRaʒ] *nm* stuffing; padding.
rembourré, e [Rɑ̃buRe] *adj* padded.
rembourrer [Rɑ̃buRe] *vt* to stuff; (*dossier, vêtement, souliers*) to pad.
remboursable [Rɑ̃buRsabl(ə)] *adj* repayable.
remboursement [Rɑ̃buRsəmɑ̃] *nm* repayment; **envoi contre ~** cash on delivery.
rembourser [Rɑ̃buRse] *vt* to pay back, repay.
rembrunir [Rɑ̃bRyniR]: **se ~** *vi* to grow sombre (*BRIT*) *ou* somber (*US*).
remède [Rəmɛd] *nm* (*médicament*) medicine; (*traitement, fig*) remedy, cure; **trouver un ~ à** (*MÉD, fig*) to find a cure for.
remédier [Rəmedje]: **~ à** *vt* to remedy.
remembrement [Rəmɑ̃bRəmɑ̃] *nm* (*AGR*) regrouping of lands.
remémorer [RəmemɔRe]: **se ~** *vt* to recall,

recollect.

remerciements [RəmɛRsimɑ̃] *nmpl* thanks; **(avec) tous mes ~** (with) grateful *ou* many thanks.

remercier [RəmɛRsje] *vt* to thank; (*congédier*) to dismiss; **~ qn de/d'avoir fait** to thank sb for/for having done; **non, je vous remercie** no thank you.

remettre [Rəmɛtʀ(ə)] *vt* (*vêtement*): **~ qch** to put sth back on, put sth on again; (*replacer*): **~ qch quelque part** to put sth back somewhere; (*ajouter*): **~ du sel/un sucre** to add more salt/another lump of sugar; (*rétablir: personne*): **~ qn** to set sb back on his (*ou* her) feet; (*rendre, restituer*): **~ qch à qn** to give sth back to sb, return sth to sb; (*donner, confier: paquet, argent*): **~ qch à qn** to hand sth over to sb, deliver sth to sb; (*prix, décoration*): **~ qch à qn** to present sb with sth; (*ajourner*): **~ qch (à)** to postpone sth *ou* put sth off (until); **se ~** *vi* to get better, recover; **se ~ de** to recover from, get over; **s'en ~ à** to leave it (up) to; **se ~ à faire/qch** to start doing/sth again; **~ une pendule à l'heure** to put a clock right; **~ un moteur/une machine en marche** to get an engine/a machine going again; **~ en état/en ordre** to repair/sort out; **~ en cause/question** to challenge/question again; **~ sa démission** to hand in one's notice; **~ qch à neuf** to make sth as good as new; **~ qn à sa place** (*fig*) to put sb in his (*ou* her) place.

réminiscence [Reminisɑ̃s] *nf* reminiscence.

remis, e [Rəmi, -iz] *pp de* remettre ♦ *nf* delivery; presentation; (*rabais*) discount; (*local*) shed; **~ en marche/en ordre** starting up again/sorting out; **~ en cause/question** calling into question/challenging; **~ de fonds** remittance; **~ en jeu** (*FOOTBALL*) throw-in; **~ à neuf** restoration; **~ de peine** remission of sentence.

remiser [Rəmize] *vt* to put away.

rémission [Remisjɔ̃] *nf*: **sans ~** *adj* irremediable ♦ *adv* unremittingly.

remodeler [Rəmɔdle] *vt* to remodel; (*fig: restructurer*) to restructure.

rémois, e [Remwa, -waz] *adj* of *ou* from Rheims ♦ *nm/f*: **R~, e** inhabitant *ou* native of Rheims.

remontant [Rəmɔ̃tɑ̃] *nm* tonic, pick-me-up.

remontée [Rəmɔ̃te] *nf* rising; ascent; **~s mécaniques** (*SKI*) ski lifts, ski tows.

remonte-pente [Rəmɔ̃tpɑ̃t] *nm* ski lift, (ski) tow.

remonter [Rəmɔ̃te] *vi* (*à nouveau*) to go back up; (*sur un cheval*) to remount; (*après une descente*) to go up (again); (*dans une voiture*) to get back in; (*jupe*) to ride up ♦ *vt* (*pente*) to go up; (*fleuve*) to sail (*ou* swim *etc*) up; (*manches, pantalon*) to roll up; (*col*) to turn up; (*niveau, limite*) to raise; (*fig: personne*) to buck up; (*moteur, meuble*) to put back to-

gether, reassemble; (*garde-robe etc*) to renew, replenish; (*montre, mécanisme*) to wind up; **~ le moral à qn** to raise sb's spirits; **~ à** (*date de*) to date *ou* go back to; **~ en voiture** to get back into the car.

remontoir [Rəmɔ̃twaR] *nm* winding mechanism, winder.

remontrance [Rəmɔ̃tRɑ̃s] *nf* reproof, reprimand.

remontrer [Rəmɔ̃tRe] *vt* (*montrer de nouveau*): **~ qch** to show sth again (to sb); (*fig*): **en ~ à** to prove one's superiority over.

remords [Rəmɔʀ] *nm* remorse *no pl*; **avoir des ~** to feel remorse, be conscience-stricken.

remorque [Rəmɔrk(ə)] *nf* trailer; **prendre/être en ~** to tow/be on tow; **être à la ~** (*fig*) to tag along (behind).

remorquer [Rəmɔrke] *vt* to tow.

remorqueur [Rəmɔrkœr] *nm* tug(boat).

rémoulade [Remulad] *nf* dressing with mustard and herbs.

rémouleur [Remulœr] *nm* (knife- *ou* scissor-) grinder.

remous [Rəmu] *nm* (*d'un navire*) (back)wash *no pl*; (*de rivière*) swirl, eddy ♦ *nmpl* (*fig*) stir *sg*.

rempailler [Rɑ̃pɑje] *vt* to reseat (*with straw*).

rempart [Rɑ̃paR] *nm* rampart; **faire à qn un ~ de son corps** to shield sb with one's (own) body.

rempiler [Rɑ̃pile] *vt* (*dossiers, livres etc*) to pile up again ♦ *vi* (*MIL: fam*) to join up again.

remplaçant, e [Rɑ̃plasɑ̃, -ɑ̃t] *nm/f* replacement, substitute, stand-in; (*THÉÂT*) understudy; (*SCOL*) supply (*BRIT*) *ou* substitute (*US*) teacher.

remplacement [Rɑ̃plasmɑ̃] *nm* replacement; (*job*) replacement work *no pl*; (*suppléance: SCOL*) supply (*BRIT*) *ou* substitute (*US*) teacher; **assurer le ~ de qn** (*suj: remplaçant*) to stand in *ou* substitute for sb; **faire des ~s** (*professeur*) to do supply *ou* substitute teaching; (*médecin*) to do locum work.

remplacer [Rɑ̃plase] *vt* to replace; (*prendre temporairement la place de*) to stand in for; (*tenir lieu de*) to take the place of, act as a substitute for; **~ qch/qn par** to replace sth/sb with.

rempli, e [Rɑ̃pli] *adj* (*emploi du temps*) full, busy; **~ de** full of, filled with.

remplir [Rɑ̃pliR] *vt* to fill (up); (*questionnaire*) to fill out *ou* up; (*obligations, fonction, condition*) to fulfil; **se ~** *vi* to fill up; **~ qch de** to fill sth with.

remplissage [Rɑ̃plisaʒ] *nm* (*fig: péj*) padding.

remploi [Rɑ̃plwa] *nm* re-use.

rempocher [Rɑ̃pɔʃe] *vt* to put back into one's pocket.

remporter [Rɑ̃pɔrte] *vt* (*marchandise*) to take away; (*fig*) to win, achieve.

rempoter [Rɑ̃pɔte] *vt* to repot.

remuant, e [Rəmɥɑ̃, -ɑ̃t] *adj* restless.

remue-ménage [Rəmymenaʒ] *nm inv* commotion.

remuer [Rəmɥe] *vt* to move; (*café, sauce*) to stir ♦ *vi* to move; (*fig: opposants*) to show signs of unrest; **se** ~ *vi* to move; (*se démener*) to stir o.s.; (*fam*) to get a move on.

rémunérateur, trice [Remyneratœr, -tris] *adj* remunerative, lucrative.

rémunération [Remynerasjɔ̃] *nf* remuneration.

rémunérer [Remynere] *vt* to remunerate, pay.

renâcler [Rənakle] *vi* to snort; (*fig*) to grumble, balk.

renaissance [Rənɛsɑ̃s] *nf* rebirth, revival; **la R~** the Renaissance.

renaître [RənɛtR(ə)] *vi* to be revived; ~ **à la vie** to take on a new lease of life; ~ **à l'espoir** to find fresh hope.

rénal, e, aux [Renal, -o] *adj* renal, kidney *cpd*.

renard [Rənar] *nm* fox.

renardeau [Rənardo] *nm* fox cub.

rencard [Rãkar] *nm* = **rancard**.

rencart [Rãkar] *nm* = **rancart**.

renchérir [Rãʃerir] *vi* to become more expensive; (*fig*): ~ **(sur)** to add something (to).

renchérissement [Rãʃerismã] *nm* increase (in the cost *ou* price of).

rencontre [Rãkɔ̃tR(ə)] *nf* (*de cours d'eau*) confluence; (*véhicules*) collision; (*entrevue, congrès, match etc*) meeting; (*imprévue*) encounter; **faire la** ~ **de qn** to meet sb; **aller à la** ~ **de qn** to go and meet sb; **amours de** ~ casual love affairs.

rencontrer [Rãkɔ̃tRe] *vt* to meet; (*mot, expression*) to come across; (*difficultés*) to meet with; **se** ~ to meet; (*véhicules*) to collide.

rendement [Rãdmã] *nm* (*d'un travailleur, d'une machine*) output; (*d'une culture*) yield; (*d'un investissement*) return; **à plein** ~ at full capacity.

rendez-vous [Rãdevu] *nm* (*rencontre*) appointment; (: *d'amoureux*) date; (*lieu*) meeting place; **donner** ~ **à qn** to arrange to meet sb; **recevoir sur** ~ to have an appointment system; **fixer un** ~ **à qn** to give sb an appointment; **avoir/prendre** ~ **(avec)** to have/make an appointment (with); **prendre** ~ **chez le médecin** to make an appointment with the doctor; ~ **spatial** *ou* **orbital** docking (in space).

rendormir [Rãdormir]: **se** ~ *vr* to go back to sleep.

rendre [RãdR(ə)] *vt* (*livre, argent etc*) to give back, return; (*otages, politesse, JUR: verdict*) to return; (*honneurs*) to pay; (*sang, aliments*) to bring up; (*sons: suj: instrument*) to produce, make; (*exprimer, traduire*) to render; (*jugement*) to pronounce, render; (*faire devenir*): ~ **qn célèbre/qch possible** to make sb famous/sth possible; **se** ~ *vi* (*capituler*) to surrender, give o.s. up; (*aller*): **se** ~ **quelque part** to go somewhere; **se** ~ **à** (*arguments etc*) to bow to; (*ordres*) to comply with; **se** ~

compte de qch to realize sth; ~ **la vue/la santé à qn** to restore sb's sight/health; ~ **la liberté à qn** to set sb free; ~ **la monnaie** to give change; **se** ~ **insupportable/malade** to become unbearable/make o.s. ill.

rendu, e [Rãdy] *pp* **de rendre** ♦ *adj* (*fatigué*) exhausted.

renégat, e [Rənega, -at] *nm/f* renegade.

renégocier [Rənegɔsje] *vt* to renegociate.

rênes [Rɛn] *nfpl* reins.

renfermé, e [Rãfɛrme] *adj* (*fig*) withdrawn ♦ *nm*: **sentir le** ~ to smell stuffy.

renfermer [Rãfɛrme] *vt* to contain; **se** ~ **(sur soi-même)** to withdraw into o.s.

renfiler [Rãfile] *vt* (*collier*) to rethread; (*pull*) to slip on.

renflé, e [Rãfle] *adj* bulging, bulbous.

renflement [Rãfləmã] *nm* bulge.

renflouer [Rãflue] *vt* to refloat; (*fig*) to set back on its (*ou* his/her *etc*) feet (again).

renfoncement [Rãfɔ̃smã] *nm* recess.

renforcer [Rãfɔrse] *vt* to reinforce; ~ **qn dans ses opinions** to confirm sb's opinion.

renfort [Rãfɔr]: ~**s** *nmpl* reinforcements; **en** ~ as a back-up; **à grand** ~ **de** with a great deal of.

renfrogné, e [RãfRɔɲe] *adj* sullen, scowling.

renfrogner [RãfRɔɲe]: **se** ~ *vi* to scowl.

rengager [Rãgaʒe] *vt* (*personnel*) to take on again; **se** ~ (*MIL*) to re-enlist.

rengaine [Rãgɛn] *nf* (*péj*) old tune.

rengainer [Rãgene] *vt* (*revolver*) to put back in its holster; (*épée*) to sheathe; (*fam: compliment, discours*) to save, withhold.

rengorger [Rãgɔrʒe]: **se** ~ *vi* (*fig*) to puff o.s. up.

renier [Rənje] *vt* (*parents*) to disown, repudiate; (*engagements*) to go back on; (*foi*) to renounce.

renifler [Rənifle] *vi* to sniff ♦ *vt* (*tabac*) to sniff up; (*odeur*) to sniff.

rennais, e [Rɛnɛ, -ɛz] *adj* of *ou* from Rennes ♦ *nm/f*: **R~, e** inhabitant *ou* native of Rennes.

renne [Rɛn] *nm* reindeer *inv*.

renom [Rənɔ̃] *nm* reputation; (*célébrité*) renown; **vin de grand** ~ celebrated *ou* highly renowned wine.

renommé, e [R(ə)nɔme] *adj* celebrated, renowned ♦ *nf* fame.

renoncement [Rənɔ̃smã] *nm* abnegation, renunciation.

renoncer [Rənɔ̃se] *vi*: ~ **à** *vt* to give up; ~ **à faire** to give up the idea of doing; **j'y renonce!** I give up!

renouer [Rənwe] *vt* (*cravate etc*) to retie; (*fig: conversation, liaison*) to renew, resume; ~ **avec** (*tradition*) to revive; (*habitude*) to take up again; ~ **avec qn** to take up with sb again.

renouveau, x [Rənuvo] *nm* revival; ~ **de succès** renewed success.

renouvelable [R(ə)nuvlabl(ə)] *adj* (*contrat, bail*)

renewable; (*expérience*) which can be renewed.

renouveler [Rǝnuvle] *vt* to renew; (*exploit, méfait*) to repeat; **se ~** *vi* (*incident*) to recur,
happen again, be repeated; (*cellules etc*) to
be renewed *ou* replaced; (*artiste, écrivain*) to
try something new.

renouvellement [R(ǝ)nuvɛlmɑ̃] *nm* renewal;
recurrence.

rénovation [Renɔvasjɔ̃] *nf* renovation; restoration; reform(ing); redevelopment.

rénover [Renɔve] *vt* (*immeuble*) to renovate,
do up; (*meuble*) to restore; (*enseignement*) to
reform; (*quartier*) to redevelop.

renseignement [Rɑ̃sɛɲmɑ̃] *nm* information *no
pl*, piece of information; (*MIL*) intelligence *no
pl*; **prendre des ~s sur** to make inquiries
about, ask for information about; **(guichet
des) ~s** information desk; **(service des) ~s**
(*TÉL*) directory inquiries (*BRIT*), information
(*US*); **service/agent de ~s** (*MIL*) intelligence
service/agent; **les ~s généraux** ≈ the secret
police.

renseigner [Rɑ̃seɲe] *vt*: **~ qn (sur)** to give information to sb (about); **se ~** *vi* to ask for information, make inquiries.

rentabiliser [Rɑ̃tabilize] *vt* (*capitaux, production*) to make profitable.

rentabilité [Rɑ̃tabilite] *nf* profitability; cost-
effectiveness; (*d'un investissement*) return;
seuil de ~ break-even point.

rentable [Rɑ̃tabl(ǝ)] *adj* profitable; cost-
effective.

rente [Rɑ̃t] *nf* income; (*pension*) pension; (*titre*)
government stock *ou* bond; **~ viagère** life
annuity.

rentier, ière [Rɑ̃tje, -jɛR] *nm/f* person of private *ou* independent means.

rentrée [Rɑ̃tRe] *nf*: **~ (d'argent)** cash *no pl* coming in; **la ~ (des classes)** the start of the new
school year; **la ~ (parlementaire)** the reopening *ou* reassembly of parliament; **faire
sa ~** (*artiste, acteur*) to make a comeback.

La rentrée (des classes) *in September each year
is more than going back to school for children
and teachers. It is also the time when political
and social life begin again after the long summer break, and it thus marks an important
point in the French year.*

---

rentrer [Rɑ̃tRe] *vi* (*entrer de nouveau*) to go (*ou*
come) back in; (*entrer*) to go (*ou* come) in;
(*revenir chez soi*) to go (*ou* come) (back)
home; (*air, clou: pénétrer*) to go in; (*revenu, argent*) to come in ♦ *vt* (*foins*) to bring in; (*véhicule*) to put away; (*chemise dans pantalon etc*)
to tuck in; (*griffes*) to draw in; (*train
d'atterrissage*) to raise; (*fig: larmes, colère etc*)
to hold back; **~ le ventre** to pull in one's
stomach; **~ dans** to go (*ou* come) back into;
to go (*ou* come) into; (*famille, patrie*) to go

back *ou* return to; (*heurter*) to crash into;
(*appartenir à*) to be included in; (*: catégorie
etc*) to fall into; **~ dans l'ordre** to get back to
normal; **~ dans ses frais** to recover one's
expenses (*ou* initial outlay).

renverrai [Rɑ̃veRe] *etc vb voir* **renvoyer**.

renversant, e [Rɑ̃vɛRsɑ̃, -ɑ̃t] *adj* amazing,
astounding.

renverse [Rɑ̃vɛRs(ǝ)]: **à la ~** *adv* backwards.

renversé, e [Rɑ̃vɛRse] *adj* (*écriture*) backhand;
(*image*) reversed; (*stupéfait*) staggered.

renversement [Rɑ̃vɛRsǝmɑ̃] *nm* (*d'un régime,
des traditions*) overthrow; **~ de la situation**
reversal of the situation.

renverser [Rɑ̃vɛRse] *vt* (*faire tomber: chaise,
verre*) to knock over, overturn; (*piéton*) to
knock down; (*liquide, contenu*) to spill, upset;
(*retourner: verre, image*) to turn upside down,
invert; (*: ordre des mots etc*) to reverse; (*fig:
gouvernement etc*) to overthrow; (*stupéfier*) to
bowl over, stagger; **se ~** *vi* to fall over; to
overturn; to spill; **se ~ (en arrière)** to lean
back; **~ la tête/le corps (en arrière)** to tip
one's head back/throw oneself back; **~ la
vapeur** (*fig*) to change course.

renvoi [Rɑ̃vwa] *nm* dismissal; return; reflection; postponement; (*référence*) cross-
reference; (*éructation*) belch.

renvoyer [Rɑ̃vwaje] *vt* to send back; (*congédier*) to dismiss; (*TENNIS*) to return; (*lumière*)
to reflect; (*son*) to echo; (*ajourner*): **~ qch (à)**
to put sth off *ou* postpone sth (until); **~ qch
à qn** (*rendre*) to return sth to sb; **~ qn à** (*fig*)
to refer sb to.

réorganisation [ReɔRganizasjɔ̃] *nf* reorganiza-
tion.

réorganiser [ReɔRganize] *vt* to reorganize.

réorienter [ReɔRjɑ̃te] *vt* to reorient(ate), redirect.

réouverture [ReuvɛRtyR] *nf* reopening.

repaire [RǝpɛR] *nm* den.

repaître [RǝpɛtR(ǝ)] *vt* to feast; to feed; **se ~
de** *vt* (*animal*) to feed on; (*fig*) to wallow *ou*
revel in.

répandre [Repɑ̃dR(ǝ)] *vt* (*renverser*) to spill;
(*étaler, diffuser*) to spread; (*lumière*) to shed;
(*chaleur, odeur*) to give off; **se ~** *vi* to spill; to
spread; **se ~ en** (*injures etc*) to pour out.

répandu, e [Repɑ̃dy] *pp de* **répandre** ♦ *adj* (*opinion, usage*) widespread.

réparable [Reparabl(ǝ)] *adj* (*montre etc*) repair-
able; (*perte etc*) which can be made up for.

reparaître [RǝparɛtR(ǝ)] *vi* to reappear.

réparateur, trice [Reparatœr, -tRis] *nm/f* repairer.

réparation [Reparasjɔ̃] *nf* repairing *no pl*, repair; **en ~** (*machine etc*) under repair; **demander à qn ~ de** (*offense etc*) to ask sb to
make amends for.

réparer [Repare] *vt* to repair; (*fig: offense*) to
make up for, atone for; (*: oubli, erreur*) to put
right.

reparler [ʀəpaʀle] *vi:* ~ **de qn/qch** to talk about sb/sth again; ~ **à qn** to speak to sb again.

repars [ʀəpaʀ] *etc vb voir* **repartir**.

repartie [ʀəpaʀti] *nf* retort; **avoir de la** ~ to be quick at repartee.

repartir [ʀəpaʀtiʀ] *vi* to set off again; to leave again; (*fig*) to get going again, pick up again; ~ **à zéro** to start from scratch (again).

répartir [ʀepaʀtiʀ] *vt* (*pour attribuer*) to share out; (*pour disperser, disposer*) to divide up; (*poids, chaleur*) to distribute; (*étaler: dans le temps*): ~ **sur** to spread over; (*classer, diviser*): ~ **en** to divide into, split up into; **se** ~ *vt* (*travail, rôles*) to share out between themselves.

répartition [ʀepaʀtisjɔ̃] *nf* sharing out; dividing up; distribution.

repas [ʀəpɑ] *nm* meal; **à l'heure des** ~ at mealtimes.

repassage [ʀəpɑsaʒ] *nm* ironing.

repasser [ʀəpɑse] *vi* to come (*ou* go) back ♦ *vt* (*vêtement, tissu*) to iron; (*examen*) to retake, resit; (*film*) to show again; (*lame*) to sharpen; (*leçon, rôle: revoir*) to go over (again); (*plat, pain*): ~ **qch à qn** to pass sth back to sb.

repasseuse [ʀəpɑsøz] *nf* (*machine*) ironing machine.

repayer [ʀəpeje] *vt* to pay again.

repêchage [ʀəpɛʃaʒ] *nm* (*SCOL*): **question de** ~ question to give candidates a second chance.

repêcher [ʀəpeʃe] *vt* (*noyé*) to recover the body of, fish out; (*fam: candidat*) to pass (*by inflating marks*); to give a second chance to.

repeindre [ʀəpɛ̃dʀ(ə)] *vt* to repaint.

repentir [ʀəpɑ̃tiʀ] *nm* repentance; **se** ~ *vi:* **se** ~ **(de)** to repent (of).

répercussions [ʀepɛʀkysjɔ̃] *nfpl* repercussions.

répercuter [ʀepɛʀkyte] *vt* (*réfléchir, renvoyer: son, voix*) to reflect; (*faire transmettre: consignes, charges etc*) to pass on; **se** ~ *vi* (*bruit*) to reverberate; (*fig*): **se** ~ **sur** to have repercussions on.

repère [ʀəpɛʀ] *nm* mark; (*monument etc*) landmark; (**point de**) ~ point of reference.

repérer [ʀəpeʀe] *vt* (*erreur, connaissance*) to spot; (*abri, ennemi*) to locate; **se** ~ *vi* to get one's bearings; **se faire** ~ to be spotted.

répertoire [ʀepɛʀtwaʀ] *nm* (*liste*) (alphabetical) list; (*carnet*) index notebook; (*INFORM*) directory; (*de carnet*) thumb index; (*indicateur*) directory, index; (*d'un théâtre, artiste*) repertoire.

répertorier [ʀepɛʀtɔʀje] *vt* to itemize, list.

répéter [ʀepete] *vt* to repeat; (*préparer: leçon: aussi vi*) to learn, go over; (*THÉÂT*) to rehearse; **se** ~ (*redire*) to repeat o.s.; (*se reproduire*) to be repeated, recur.

répéteur [ʀepetœʀ] *nm* (*TÉL*) repeater.

répétitif, ive [ʀepetitif, -iv] *adj* repetitive.

répétition [ʀepetisjɔ̃] *nf* repetition; (*THÉÂT*) rehearsal; ~**s** *nfpl* (*leçons*) private coaching *sg*; **armes à** ~ repeater weapons; ~ **générale** final dress rehearsal.

repeupler [ʀəpœple] *vt* to repopulate; (*forêt, rivière*) to restock.

repiquage [ʀəpikaʒ] *nm* pricking out, planting out; re-recording.

repiquer [ʀəpike] *vt* (*plants*) to prick out, plant out; (*enregistrement*) to re-record.

répit [ʀepi] *nm* respite; **sans** ~ without letting up.

replacer [ʀəplase] *vt* to replace, put back.

replanter [ʀəplɑ̃te] *vt* to replant.

replat [ʀəpla] *nm* ledge.

replâtrer [ʀəplɑtʀe] *vt* (*mur*) to replaster; (*fig*) to patch up.

replet, ète [ʀəplɛ, -ɛt] *adj* chubby, fat.

repli [ʀəpli] *nm* (*d'une étoffe*) fold; (*MIL, fig*) withdrawal.

replier [ʀəplije] *vt* (*rabattre*) to fold down *ou* over; **se** ~ *vi* (*troupes, armée*) to withdraw, fall back; **se** ~ **sur soi-même** to withdraw into oneself.

réplique [ʀeplik] *nf* (*repartie, fig*) reply; (*objection*) retort; (*THÉÂT*) line; (*copie*) replica; **donner la** ~ **à** to play opposite; **sans** ~ *adj* no-nonsense; irrefutable.

répliquer [ʀeplike] *vi* to reply; (*avec impertinence*) to answer back; (*riposter*) to retaliate.

replonger [ʀəplɔ̃ʒe] *vt:* ~ **qch dans** to plunge sth back into; **se** ~ **dans** (*journal etc*) to immerse o.s. in again.

répondant, e [ʀepɔ̃dɑ̃, -ɑ̃t] *nm/f* (*garant*) guarantor, surety.

répondeur [ʀepɔ̃dœʀ] *nm:* ~ **(automatique)** (*TÉL*) (telephone) answering machine.

répondre [ʀepɔ̃dʀ(ə)] *vi* to answer, reply; (*freins, mécanisme*) to respond; ~ **à** *vt* to reply to, answer; (*avec impertinence*): ~ **à qn** to answer sb back; (*invitation, convocation*) to reply to; (*affection, salut*) to return; (*provocation, suj: mécanisme etc*) to respond to; (*correspondre à: besoin*) to answer; (: *conditions*) to meet; (: *description*) to match; ~ **que** to answer *ou* reply that; ~ **de** to answer for.

réponse [ʀepɔ̃s] *nf* answer, reply; **avec** ~ **payée** (*POSTES*) reply-paid, post-paid (*US*); **avoir** ~ **à tout** to have an answer for everything; **en** ~ **à** in reply to; **carte-/bulletin-**~ reply card/slip.

report [ʀəpɔʀ] *nm* postponement; transfer; ~ **d'incorporation** (*MIL*) deferment.

reportage [ʀəpɔʀtaʒ] *nm* (*bref*) report; (*écrit: documentaire*) story; article; (*en direct*) commentary; (*genre, activité*): **le** ~ reporting.

reporter *nm* [ʀəpɔʀtɛʀ] reporter ♦ *vt* [ʀəpɔʀte] (*total*): ~ **qch sur** to carry sth forward *ou* over to; (*ajourner*): ~ **qch (à)** to postpone sth (until); (*transférer*): ~ **qch sur** to transfer sth to; **se** ~ **à** (*époque*) to think back to; (*document*) to refer to.

repos [ʀəpo] *nm* rest; (*fig*) peace (and quiet); (*mental*) peace of mind; (*MIL*): ~! (stand) at ease!; **en** ~ at rest; **au** ~ at rest; (*soldat*) at ease; **de tout** ~ safe.

reposant, e [ʀ(ə)pozɑ̃, -ɑ̃t] *adj* restful; (*sommeil*) refreshing.

repose [ʀəpoz] *nf* refitting.

reposé, e [ʀəpoze] *adj* fresh, rested; **à tête** ~**e** in a leisurely way, taking time to think.

repose-pied [ʀəpozpje] *nm inv* footrest.

reposer [ʀəpoze] *vt* (*verre, livre*) to put down; (*rideaux, carreaux*) to put back; (*délasser*) to rest; (*problème*) to reformulate ♦ *vi* (*liquide, pâte*) to settle, rest; (*personne*): **ici repose ...** here lies ...; ~ **sur** to be built on; (*fig*) to rest on; **se** ~ *vi* to rest; **se** ~ **sur qn** to rely on sb.

repoussant, e [ʀəpusɑ̃, -ɑ̃t] *adj* repulsive.

repoussé, e [ʀəpuse] *adj* (*cuir*) embossed (by hand).

repousser [ʀəpuse] *vi* to grow again ♦ *vt* to repel, repulse; (*offre*) to turn down, reject; (*tiroir, personne*) to push back; (*différer*) to put back.

répréhensible [ʀepʀeɑ̃sibl(ə)] *adj* reprehensible.

reprendre [ʀəpʀɑ̃dʀ(ə)] *vt* (*prisonnier, ville*) to recapture; (*objet prêté, donné*) to take back; (*chercher*): **je viendrai te** ~ **à 4 h** I'll come and fetch you *ou* I'll come back for you at 4; (*se resservir de*): ~ **du pain/un œuf** to take (*ou* eat) more bread/another egg; (*COMM: article usagé*) to take back; to take in part exchange; (*firme, entreprise*) to take over; (*travail, promenade*) to resume; (*emprunter: argument, idée*) to take up, use; (*refaire: article etc*) to go over again; (*jupe etc*) to alter; (*émission, pièce*) to put on again; (*réprimander*) to tell off; (*corriger*) to correct ♦ *vi* (*classes, pluie*) to start (up) again; (*activités, travaux, combats*) to resume, start (up) again; (*affaires, industrie*) to pick up; (*dire*): **reprit-il** he went on; **se** ~ (*se ressaisir*) to recover, pull o.s. together; **s'y** ~ to make another attempt; ~ **des forces** to recover one's strength; ~ **courage** to take new heart; ~ **ses habitudes/sa liberté** to get back into one's old habits/regain one's freedom; ~ **la route** to resume one's journey, set off again; ~ **connaissance** to come to, regain consciousness; ~ **haleine** *ou* **son souffle** to get one's breath back; ~ **la parole** to speak again.

repreneur [ʀəpʀənœʀ] *nm* company fixer *ou* doctor.

reprenne [ʀəpʀɛn] *etc vb voir* **reprendre**.

représailles [ʀəpʀezɑj] *nfpl* reprisals, retaliation *sg*.

représentant, e [ʀəpʀezɑ̃tɑ̃, -ɑ̃t] *nm/f* representative.

représentatif, ive [ʀəpʀezɑ̃tatif, -iv] *adj* representative.

représentation [ʀəpʀezɑ̃tasjɔ̃] *nf* representation; performing; (*symbole, image*) representation; (*spectacle*) performance; (*COMM*): **la** ~ commercial travelling; sales representation; **frais de** ~ (*d'un diplomate*) entertainment allowance.

représenter [ʀəpʀezɑ̃te] *vt* to represent; (*donner: pièce, opéra*) to perform; **se** ~ *vt* (*se figurer*) to imagine; to visualize ♦ *vi*: **se** ~ **à** (*POL*) to stand *ou* run again at; (*SCOL*) to resit.

répressif, ive [ʀepʀesif, -iv] *adj* repressive.

répression [ʀepʀesjɔ̃] *nf* (*voir réprimer*) suppression; repression; (*POL*): **la** ~ repression; **mesures de** ~ repressive measures.

réprimande [ʀepʀimɑ̃d] *nf* reprimand, rebuke.

réprimander [ʀepʀimɑ̃de] *vt* to reprimand, rebuke.

réprimer [ʀepʀime] *vt* (*émotions*) to suppress; (*peuple etc*) repress.

repris, e [ʀəpʀi, -iz] *pp de* **reprendre** ♦ *nm*: ~ **de justice** ex-prisoner, ex-convict.

reprise [ʀəpʀiz] *nf* (*recommencement*) resumption; (*économique*) recovery; (*TV*) repeat; (*CINÉ*) rerun; (*BOXE etc*) round; (*AUTO*) acceleration *no pl*; (*COMM*) trade-in, part exchange; (*de location*) *sum asked for any extras or improvements made to the property*; (*raccommodage*) darn; mend; **la** ~ **des hostilités** the resumption of hostilities; **à plusieurs** ~**s** on several occasions, several times.

repriser [ʀəpʀize] *vt* to darn; to mend; **aiguille/coton à** ~ darning needle/thread.

réprobateur, trice [ʀepʀɔbatœʀ, -tʀis] *adj* reproving.

réprobation [ʀepʀɔbasjɔ̃] *nf* reprobation.

reproche [ʀəpʀɔʃ] *nm* (*remontrance*) reproach; **ton/air de** ~ reproachful tone/look; **faire des** ~**s à qn** to reproach sb; **faire** ~ **à qn de qch** to reproach sb for sth; **sans** ~**(s)** beyond *ou* above reproach.

reprocher [ʀəpʀɔʃe] *vt*: ~ **qch à qn** to reproach *ou* blame sb for sth; ~ **qch à** (*machine, théorie*) to have sth against; **se** ~ **qch/d'avoir fait qch** to blame o.s. for sth/for doing sth.

reproducteur, trice [ʀəpʀɔdyktœʀ, -tʀis] *adj* reproductive.

reproduction [ʀəpʀɔdyksjɔ̃] *nf* reproduction; ~ **interdite** all rights (of reproduction) reserved.

reproduire [ʀəpʀɔdɥiʀ] *vt* to reproduce; **se** ~ *vi* (*BIO*) to reproduce; (*recommencer*) to recur, re-occur.

reprographie [ʀəpʀɔgʀafi] *nf* (photo)copying.

réprouvé, e [ʀepʀuve] *nm/f* reprobate.

réprouver [ʀepʀuve] *vt* to reprove.

reptation [ʀɛptɑsjɔ̃] *nf* crawling.

reptile [ʀɛptil] *nm* reptile.

repu, e [ʀəpy] *pp de* **repaître** ♦ *adj* satisfied,

sated.

républicain, e [Repyblikɛ̃, -ɛn] *adj, nm/f* republican.

république [Repyblik] *nf* republic; **R~ arabe du Yémen** Yemen Arab Republic; **R~ Centrafricaine** Central African Republic; **R~ de Corée** South Korea; **R~ démocratique allemande (RDA)** German Democratic Republic (GDR); **R~ dominicaine** Dominican Republic; **R~ fédérale d'Allemagne (RFA)** Federal Republic of Germany (FRG); **R~ d'Irlande** Irish Republic, Eire; **R~ populaire de Chine** People's Republic of China; **R~ populaire démocratique de Corée** Democratic People's Republic of Korea; **R~ populaire du Yémen** People's Democratic Republic of Yemen.

répudier [Repydje] *vt* (*femme*) to repudiate; (*doctrine*) to renounce.

répugnance [Repyñɑ̃s] *nf* repugnance, loathing; **avoir** *ou* **éprouver de la ~ pour** (*médicament, comportement, travail etc*) to have an aversion to; **avoir** *ou* **éprouver de la ~ à faire qch** to be reluctant to do sth.

répugnant, e [Repyñɑ̃, -ɑ̃t] *adj* repulsive, loathsome.

répugner [Repyñe]: **~ à** *vt*: **~ à qn** to repel *ou* disgust sb; **~ à faire** to be loath *ou* reluctant to do.

répulsion [Repylsjɔ̃] *nf* repulsion.

réputation [Repytɑsjɔ̃] *nf* reputation; **avoir la ~ d'être ...** to have a reputation for being ...; **connaître qn/qch de ~** to know sb/sth by repute; **de ~ mondiale** world-renowned.

réputé, e [Repyte] *adj* renowned; **être ~ pour** to have a reputation for, be renowned for.

requérir [RəkeRiR] *vt* (*nécessiter*) to require, call for; (*au nom de la loi*) to call upon; (*JUR: peine*) to call for, demand.

requête [Rəkɛt] *nf* request, petition; (*JUR*) petition.

requiem [Rekɥijɛm] *nm* requiem.

requiers [RəkjɛR] *etc vb voir* **requérir**.

requin [Rəkɛ̃] *nm* shark.

requinquer [Rəkɛ̃ke] *vt* to set up, pep up.

requis, e [Rəki, -iz] *pp de* **requérir** ♦ *adj* required.

réquisition [Rekizisjɔ̃] *nf* requisition.

réquisitionner [Rekizisjɔne] *vt* to requisition.

réquisitoire [RekizitwaR] *nm* (*JUR*) closing speech for the prosecution; (*fig*): **~ contre** indictment of.

RER *sigle m* (= *Réseau express régional*) Greater Paris high speed train service.

rescapé, e [Rɛskape] *nm/f* survivor.

rescousse [Rɛskus] *nf*: **aller à la ~ de qn** to go to sb's aid *ou* rescue; **appeler qn à la ~** to call on sb for help.

réseau, x [Rezo] *nm* network.

réséda [Rezeda] *nm* (*BOT*) reseda, mignonette.

réservation [RezɛRvɑsjɔ̃] *nf* reservation; booking.

réserve [RezɛRv(ə)] *nf* (*retenue*) reserve; (*entrepôt*) storeroom; (*restriction, aussi: d'Indiens*) reservation; (*de pêche, chasse*) preserve; (*restrictions*): **faire des ~s** to have reservations; **officier de ~** reserve officer; **sous toutes ~s** with all reserve; (*dire*) with reservations; **sous ~ de** subject to; **sans ~** *adv* unreservedly; **en ~** in reserve; **de ~** (*provisions etc*) in reserve.

réservé, e [RezɛRve] *adj* (*discret*) reserved; (*chasse, pêche*) private; **~ à** *ou* **pour** reserved for.

réserver [RezɛRve] *vt* (*gén*) to reserve; (*chambre, billet etc*) to book, reserve; (*mettre de côté, garder*): **~ qch pour** *ou* **à** to keep *ou* save sth for; **~ qch à qn** to reserve (*ou* book) sth for sb; (*fig: destiner*) to have sth in store for sb; **se ~ le droit de faire** to reserve the right to do.

réserviste [RezɛRvist(ə)] *nm* reservist.

réservoir [RezɛRvwaR] *nm* tank.

résidence [Rezidɑ̃s] *nf* residence; **~ principale/secondaire** main/second home; **~ universitaire** hall of residence; **(en) ~ surveillée** (under) house arrest.

résident, e [Rezidɑ̃, -ɑ̃t] *nm/f* (*ressortissant*) foreign resident; (*d'un immeuble*) resident ♦ *adj* (*INFORM*) resident.

résidentiel, le [Rezidɑ̃sjɛl] *adj* residential.

résider [Rezide] *vi*: **~ à** *ou* **dans** *ou* **en** to reside in; **~ dans** (*fig*) to lie in.

résidu [Rezidy] *nm* residue *no pl*.

résiduel, le [Rezidɥɛl] *adj* residual.

résignation [Reziñɑsjɔ̃] *nf* resignation.

résigné, e [Reziñe] *adj* resigned.

résigner [Reziñe] *vt* to relinquish, resign; **se ~** *vi*: **se ~ (à qch/à faire)** to resign o.s. (to sth/to doing).

résiliable [Reziljabl(ə)] *adj* which can be terminated.

résilier [Rezilje] *vt* to terminate.

résille [Rezij] *nf* (hair)net.

résine [Rezin] *nf* resin.

résiné, e [Rezine] *adj*: **vin ~** retsina.

résineux, euse [Rezinø, -øz] *adj* resinous ♦ *nm* coniferous tree.

résistance [Rezistɑ̃s] *nf* resistance; (*de réchaud, bouilloire: fil*) element.

résistant, e [Rezistɑ̃, -ɑ̃t] *adj* (*personne*) robust, tough; (*matériau*) strong, hard-wearing ♦ *nm/f* (*patriote*) Resistance worker *ou* fighter.

résister [Reziste] *vi* to resist; **~ à** *vt* (*assaut, tentation*) to resist; (*effort, souffrance*) to withstand; (*suj: matériau, plante*) to stand up to, withstand; (*personne: désobéir à*) to stand up to, oppose.

résolu, e [Rezɔly] *pp de* **résoudre** ♦ *adj* (*ferme*) resolute; **être ~ à qch/faire** to be set upon sth/doing.

résolument [Rezɔlymɑ̃] *adv* resolutely, steadfastly; **~ contre qch** firmly against sth.

résolution [ʀezɔlysjɔ̃] *nf* solving; (*fermeté, décision, INFORM*) resolution; **prendre la** ~ **de** to make a resolution to.

résolvais [ʀezɔlvɛ] *etc vb voir* **résoudre.**

résonance [ʀezɔnɑ̃s] *nf* resonance.

résonner [ʀezɔne] *vi* (*cloche, pas*) to reverberate, resound; (*salle*) to be resonant; ~ **de** to resound with.

résorber [ʀezɔʀbe]: **se** ~ *vi* (*MÉD*) to be resorbed; (*fig*) to be absorbed.

résoudre [ʀezudʀ(ə)] *vt* to solve; ~ **qn à faire qch** to get sb to make up his (*ou* her) mind to do sth; ~ **de faire** to resolve to do; **se** ~ **à faire** to bring o.s. to do.

respect [ʀɛspɛ] *nm* respect; **tenir en** ~ to keep at bay.

respectabilité [ʀɛspɛktabilite] *nf* respectability.

respectable [ʀɛspɛktabl(ə)] *adj* respectable.

respecter [ʀɛspɛkte] *vt* to respect; **faire** ~ to enforce; **le lexicographe qui se respecte** (*fig*) any self-respecting lexicographer.

respectif, ive [ʀɛspɛktif, -iv] *adj* respective.

respectivement [ʀɛspɛktivmɑ̃] *adv* respectively.

respectueusement [ʀɛspɛktɥøzmɑ̃] *adv* respectfully.

respectueux, euse [ʀɛspɛktɥø, -øz] *adj* respectful; ~ **de** respectful of.

respirable [ʀɛspiʀabl(ə)] *adj*: **peu** ~ unbreathable.

respiration [ʀɛspiʀasjɔ̃] *nf* breathing *no pl*; **faire une** ~ **complète** to breathe in and out; **retenir sa** ~ to hold one's breath; ~ **artificielle** artificial respiration.

respiratoire [ʀɛspiʀatwaʀ] *adj* respiratory.

respirer [ʀɛspiʀe] *vi* to breathe; (*fig: se reposer*) to get one's breath, have a break; (*: être soulagé*) to breathe again ♦ *vt* to breathe (in), inhale; (*manifester: santé, calme etc*) to exude.

resplendir [ʀɛsplɑ̃diʀ] *vi* to shine; (*fig*): ~ **(de)** to be radiant (with).

resplendissant, e [ʀɛsplɑ̃disɑ̃, -ɑ̃t] *adj* radiant.

responsabilité [ʀɛspɔ̃sabilite] *nf* responsibility; (*légale*) liability; **refuser la** ~ **de** to deny responsibility (*ou* liability) for; **prendre ses** ~**s** to assume responsibility for one's actions; ~ **civile** civil liability; ~ **pénale/morale/collective** criminal/moral/collective responsibility.

responsable [ʀɛspɔ̃sabl(ə)] *adj* responsible ♦ *nm/f* (*du ravitaillement etc*) person in charge; (*de parti, syndicat*) official; ~ **de** responsible for; (*légalement: de dégâts etc*) liable for; (*chargé de*) in charge of, responsible for.

resquiller [ʀɛskije] *vi* (*au cinéma, au stade*) to get in on the sly; (*dans le train*) to fiddle a free ride.

resquilleur, euse [ʀɛskijœʀ, -øz] *nm/f* (*qui n'est pas invité*) gatecrasher; (*qui ne paie pas*) fare dodger.

ressac [ʀəsak] *nm* backwash.

ressaisir [ʀəseziʀ]: **se** ~ *vi* to regain one's self-control; (*équipe sportive*) to rally.

ressasser [ʀəsase] *vt* (*remâcher*) to keep turning over; (*redire*) to keep trotting out.

ressemblance [ʀəsɑ̃blɑ̃s] *nf* (*visuelle*) resemblance, similarity, likeness; (*: ART*) likeness; (*analogie, trait commun*) similarity.

ressemblant, e [ʀəsɑ̃blɑ̃, -ɑ̃t] *adj* (*portrait*) lifelike, true to life.

ressembler [ʀəsɑ̃ble]: ~ **à** *vt* to be like, resemble; (*visuellement*) to look like; **se** ~ to be (*ou* look) alike.

ressemeler [ʀəsəmle] *vt* to (re)sole.

ressens [ʀ(ə)sɑ̃] *etc vb voir* **ressentir.**

ressentiment [ʀəsɑ̃timɑ̃] *nm* resentment.

ressentir [ʀəsɑ̃tiʀ] *vt* to feel; **se** ~ **de** to feel (*ou* show) the effects of.

resserre [ʀəsɛʀ] *nf* shed.

resserrement [ʀ(ə)sɛʀmɑ̃] *nm* narrowing; strengthening; (*goulet*) narrow part.

resserrer [ʀəseʀe] *vt* (*pores*) to close; (*nœud, boulon*) to tighten (up); (*fig: liens*) to strengthen; **se** ~ *vi* (*route, vallée*) to narrow; (*liens*) to strengthen; **se** ~ **(autour de)** to draw closer (around); to close in (on).

ressers [ʀ(ə)sɛʀ] *etc vb voir* **resservir.**

resservir [ʀəsɛʀviʀ] *vi* to do *ou* serve again ♦ *vt*: ~ **qch (à qn)** to serve sth up again (to sb); ~ **de qch (à qn)** to give (sb) a second helping of sth; ~ **qn (d'un plat)** to give sb a second helping (of a dish); **se** ~ **de** (*plat*) to take a second helping of; (*outil etc*) to use again.

ressort [ʀəsɔʀ] *vb voir* **ressortir** ♦ *nm* (*pièce*) spring; (*force morale*) spirit; (*recours*): **en dernier** ~ as a last resort; (*compétence*): **être du** ~ **de** to fall within the competence of.

ressortir [ʀəsɔʀtiʀ] *vi* to go (*ou* come) out (again); (*contraster*) to stand out; ~ **de** (*résulter de*): **il ressort de ceci que** it emerges from this that; ~ **à** (*JUR*) to come under the jurisdiction of; (*ADMIN*) to be the concern of; **faire** ~ (*fig: souligner*) to bring out.

ressortissant, e [ʀəsɔʀtisɑ̃, -ɑ̃t] *nm/f* national.

ressouder [ʀəsude] *vt* to solder together again.

ressource [ʀəsuʀs(ə)] *nf*: **avoir la** ~ **de** to have the possibility of; ~**s** *nfpl* resources; (*fig*) possibilities; **leur seule** ~ **était de** the only course open to them was to; ~**s d'énergie** energy resources.

ressusciter [ʀesysite] *vt* to resuscitate, restore to life; (*fig*) to revive, bring back ♦ *vi* to rise (from the dead); (*fig: pays*) to come back to life.

restant, e [ʀɛstɑ̃, -ɑ̃t] *adj* remaining ♦ *nm*: **le** ~ **(de)** the remainder (of); **un** ~ **de** (*de trop*) some leftover; (*fig: vestige*) a remnant *ou* last trace of.

restaurant [ʀɛstɔʀɑ̃] *nm* restaurant; **manger au** ~ to eat out; ~ **d'entreprise** staff canteen *ou* cafeteria (*US*); ~ **universitaire (RU)** university refectory *ou* cafeteria (*US*).

restaurateur, trice [RɛstɔRatœR, -tRis] *nm/f* restaurant owner, restaurateur; (*de tableaux*) restorer.

restauration [RɛstɔRɑsjɔ̃] *nf* restoration; (*hôtellerie*) catering; ~ **rapide** fast food.

restaurer [RɛstɔRe] *vt* to restore; **se** ~ *vi* to have something to eat.

restauroute [RɛstɔRut] *nm* = **restoroute**.

reste [Rɛst(ə)] *nm* (*restant*): **le** ~ **(de)** the rest (of); (*de trop*): **un** ~ **(de)** some leftover; (*vestige*): **un** ~ **de** a remnant *ou* last trace of; (*MATH*) remainder; ~**s** *nmpl* leftovers; (*d'une cité etc, dépouille mortelle*) remains; **avoir du temps de** ~ to have time to spare; **ne voulant pas être en** ~ not wishing to be outdone; **partir sans attendre** *ou* **demander son** ~ (*fig*) to leave without waiting to hear more; **du** ~**, au** ~ *adv* besides, moreover; **pour le reste, quant au** ~ *adv* as for the rest.

rester [Rɛste] *vi* (*dans un lieu, une état, une position*) to stay, remain; (*subsister*) to remain, be left; (*durer*) to last, live on ♦ *vb impers*: **il reste du pain/2 œufs** there's some bread/ there are 2 eggs left (over); **il reste du temps/10 minutes** there's some time/there are 10 minutes left; **il me reste assez de temps** I have enough time left; **voilà tout ce qui (me) reste** that's all I've got left; **ce qui reste à faire** what remains to be done; **ce qui me reste à faire** what remains for me to do; **(il) reste à savoir/établir si ...** it remains to be seen/established if *ou* whether ...; **il n'en reste pas moins que ...** the fact remains that ..., it's nevertheless a fact that ...; **en** ~ **à** (*stade, menaces*) to go no further than, only go as far as; **restons-en là** let's leave it at that; ~ **sur une impression** to retain an impression; **y** ~: **il a failli y** ~ he nearly met his end.

restituer [Rɛstitɥe] *vt* (*objet, somme*): ~ **qch (à qn)** to return *ou* restore sth (to sb); (*énergie*) to release; (*son*) to reproduce.

restitution [Rɛstitysjɔ̃] *nf* restoration.

restoroute [RɛstɔRut] *nm* motorway (*BRIT*) *ou* highway (*US*) restaurant.

restreindre [RɛstRɛ̃dR(ə)] *vt* to restrict, limit; **se** ~ (*dans ses dépenses etc*) to cut down; (*champ de recherches*) to narrow.

restreint, e [RɛstRɛ̃, -ɛ̃t] *pp de* **restreindre** ♦ *adj* restricted, limited.

restrictif, ive [RɛstRiktif, -iv] *adj* restrictive, limiting.

restriction [RɛstRiksjɔ̃] *nf* restriction; (*condition*) qualification; ~**s** *nfpl* (*mentales*) reservations; **sans** ~ *adv* unreservedly.

restructuration [RəstRyktyRɑsjɔ̃] *nf* restructuring.

restructurer [RəstRyktyRe] *vt* to restructure.

résultante [Rezyltɑ̃t] *nf* (*conséquence*) result, consequence.

résultat [Rezylta] *nm* result; (*conséquence*) outcome *no pl*, result; (*d'élection etc*) results *pl*; ~**s** *nmpl* (*d'une enquête*) findings; ~**s sportifs** sports results.

résulter [Rezylte]: ~ **de** *vt* to result from, be the result of; **il résulte de ceci que ...** the result of this is that ....

résumé [Rezyme] *nm* summary, résumé; **faire le** ~ **de** to summarize; **en** ~ *adv* in brief; (*pour conclure*) to sum up.

résumer [Rezyme] *vt* (*texte*) to summarize; (*récapituler*) to sum up; (*fig*) to epitomize, typify; **se** ~ *vi* (*personne*) to sum up (one's ideas); **se** ~ **à** to come down to.

resurgir [RəsyRʒiR] *vi* to reappear, re-emerge.

résurrection [RezyRɛksjɔ̃] *nf* resurrection; (*fig*) revival.

rétablir [RetabliR] *vt* to restore, re-establish; (*personne: suj: traitement*): ~ **qn** to restore sb to health, help sb recover; (*ADMIN*): ~ **qn dans son emploi/ses droits** to reinstate sb in his post/restore sb's rights; **se** ~ *vi* (*guérir*) to recover; (*silence, calme*) to return, be restored; (*GYM etc*): **se** ~ **(sur)** to pull o.s. up (onto).

rétablissement [Retablismɑ̃] *nm* restoring; recovery; pull-up.

rétamer [Retame] *vt* to re-coat, re-tin.

rétameur [RetamœR] *nm* tinker.

retaper [Rətape] *vt* (*maison, voiture etc*) to do up; (*fam: revigorer*) to buck up; (*redactylographier*) to retype.

retard [RətaR] *nm* (*d'une personne attendue*) lateness *no pl*; (*sur l'horaire, un programme, une échéance*) delay; (*fig: scolaire, mental etc*) backwardness; **être en** ~ (*pays*) to be backward; (*dans paiement, travail*) to be behind; **en** ~ **(de 2 heures)** (2 hours) late; **avoir un** ~ **de 2 km** (*SPORT*) to be 2 km behind; **rattraper son** ~ to catch up; **avoir du** ~ to be late; (*sur un programme*) to be behind (schedule); **prendre du** ~ (*train, avion*) to be delayed; (*montre*) to lose (time); **sans** ~ *adv* without delay; ~ **à l'allumage** (*AUTO*) retarded spark; ~ **scolaire** backwardness at school.

retardataire [RətaRdatɛR] *adj* late; (*enfant, idées*) backward ♦ *nm/f* latecomer; backward child.

retardé, e [RətaRde] *adj* backward.

retardement [RətaRdəmɑ̃]: **à** ~ *adj* delayed action *cpd*; **bombe à** ~ time bomb.

retarder [RətaRde] *vt* (*sur un horaire*): ~ **qn (d'une heure)** to delay sb (an hour); (*sur un programme*): ~ **qn (de 3 mois)** to set sb back *ou* delay sb 3 months); (*départ, date*): ~ **qch (de 2 jours)** to put sth back (2 days), delay sth (for *ou* by 2 days); (*horloge*) to put back ♦ *vi* (*montre*) to be slow; (*: habituellement*) to lose (time); **je retarde (d'une heure)** I'm (an hour) slow.

retendre [Rətɑ̃dR(ə)] *vt* (*câble etc*) to stretch again; (*MUS: cordes*) to retighten.

retenir [RətniR] *vt* (*garder, retarder*) to keep, detain; (*maintenir: objet qui glisse, fig: colère, larmes, rire*) to hold back; (: *objet suspendu*) to hold; (: *chaleur, odeur*) to retain; (*fig: empêcher d'agir*): ~ **qn (de faire)** to hold sb back (from doing); (*se rappeler*) to retain; (*réserver*) to reserve; (*accepter*) to accept; (*prélever*): ~ **qch (sur)** to deduct sth (from); **se** ~ (*euphémisme*) to hold on; (*se raccrocher*): **se** ~ **à** to hold onto; (*se contenir*): **se** ~ **de faire** to restrain o.s. from doing; ~ **son souffle** *ou* **haleine** to hold one's breath; ~ **qn à dîner** to ask sb to stay for dinner; **je pose 3 et je retiens 2** put down 3 and carry 2.

rétention [Retɑ̃sjɔ̃] *nf*: ~ **d'urine** urine retention.

retentir [Rətɑ̃tiR] *vi* to ring out; (*salle*): ~ **de** to ring *ou* resound with; ~ **sur** *vt* (*fig*) to have an effect upon.

retentissant, e [Rətɑ̃tisɑ̃, -ɑ̃t] *adj* resounding; (*fig*) impact-making.

retentissement [Rətɑ̃tismɑ̃] *nm* (*retombées*) repercussions *pl*; effect, impact.

retenu, e [Rətny] *pp de* **retenir** ♦ *adj* (*place*) reserved; (*personne: empêché*) held up; (*propos: contenu, discret*) restrained ♦ *nf* (*prélèvement*) deduction; (*MATH*) number to carry over; (*SCOL*) detention; (*modération*) (self-)restraint; (*réserve*) reserve, reticence; (*AUTO*) tailback.

réticence [Retisɑ̃s] *nf* reticence *no pl*, reluctance *no pl*; **sans** ~ without hesitation.

réticent, e [Retisɑ̃, -ɑ̃t] *adj* reticent, reluctant.

retiendrai [Rətjɛ̃dRe], **retiens** [Rətjɛ̃] *etc vb voir* **retenir**.

rétif, ive [Retif, -iv] *adj* restive.

rétine [Retin] *nf* retina.

retint [Rətɛ̃] *etc vb voir* **retenir**.

retiré, e [RətiRe] *adj* (*solitaire*) secluded; (*éloigné*) remote.

retirer [RətiRe] *vt* to withdraw; (*vêtement, lunettes*) to take off, remove; (*enlever*): ~ **qch à qn** to take sth from sb; (*extraire*): ~ **qn/qch de** to take sb away from/sth out of, remove sb/sth from; (*reprendre: bagages, billets*) to collect, pick up; ~ **des avantages de** to derive advantages from; **se** ~ *vi* (*partir, reculer*) to withdraw; (*prendre sa retraite*) to retire; **se** ~ **de** to withdraw from; to retire from.

retombées [Rətɔ̃be] *nfpl* (*radioactives*) fallout *sg*; (*fig*) fallout; spin-offs.

retomber [Rətɔ̃be] *vi* (*à nouveau*) to fall again; (*rechuter*): ~ **malade/dans l'erreur** to fall ill again/fall back into error; (*atterrir: après un saut etc*) to land; (*tomber, redescendre*) to fall back; (*pendre*) to fall, hang (down); (*échoir*): ~ **sur qn** to fall on sb.

retordre [RətɔRdR(ə)] *vt*: **donner du fil à** ~ **à qn** to make life difficult for sb.

rétorquer [RetɔRke] *vt*: ~ (**à qn**) **que** to retort (to sb) that.

retors, e [RətɔR, -ɔRs(ə)] *adj* wily.

rétorsion [RetɔRsjɔ̃] *nf*: **mesures de** ~ reprisals.

retouche [Rətuʃ] *nf* touching up *no pl*; alteration; **faire une** ~ *ou* **des** ~**s à** to touch up.

retoucher [Rətuʃe] *vt* (*photographie, tableau*) to touch up; (*texte, vêtement*) to alter.

retour [RətuR] *nm* return; **au** ~ (*en arrivant*) when we (*ou* they *etc*) get (*ou* got) back; (*en route*) on the way back; **pendant le** ~ on the way *ou* journey back; **à mon/ton** ~ on my/your return; **au** ~ **de** on the return of; **être de** ~ (**de**) to be back (from); **de** ~ **à** .../**chez moi** back at .../back home; **en** ~ *adv* in return; **par** ~ **du courrier** by return of post; **par un juste** ~ **des choses** by a favourable twist of fate; **match** ~ return match; ~ **en arrière** (*CINÉ*) flashback; (*mesure*) backward step; ~ **de bâton** kickback; ~ **de chariot** carriage return; ~ **à l'envoyeur** (*POSTES*) return to sender; ~ **de flamme** backfire; ~ (**automatique**) **à la ligne** (*INFORM*) wordwrap; ~ **de manivelle** (*fig*) backfire; ~ **offensif** renewed attack; ~ **aux sources** (*fig*) return to basics.

retournement [RətuRnəmɑ̃] *nm* (*d'une personne: revirement*) turning (round); ~ **de la situation** reversal of the situation.

retourner [RətuRne] *vt* (*dans l'autre sens: matelas, crêpe*) to turn (over); (: *caisse*) to turn upside down; (: *sac, vêtement*) to turn inside out; (*fig: argument*) to turn back; (*en remuant: terre, sol, foin*) to turn over; (*émouvoir: personne*) to shake; (*renvoyer, restituer*): ~ **qch à qn** to return sth to sb ♦ *vi* (*aller, revenir*): ~ **quelque part/à** to go back *ou* return somewhere/to; ~ **à** (*état, activité*) to return to, go back to; **se** ~ *vi* to turn over; (*tourner la tête*) to turn round; **s'en** ~ to go back; **se** ~ **contre** (*fig*) to turn against; **savoir de quoi il retourne** to know what it is all about; ~ **sa veste** (*fig*) to turn one's coat; ~ **en arrière** *ou* **sur ses pas** to turn back, retrace one's steps; ~ **aux sources** to go back to basics.

retracer [RətRase] *vt* to relate, recount.

rétracter [RetRakte] *vt*, **se** ~ *vi* to retract.

retraduire [RətRadµiR] *vt* to translate again; (*dans la langue de départ*) to translate back.

retrait [RətRɛ] *nm* (*voir retirer*) withdrawal; collection; (*voir se retirer*) withdrawal; (*rétrécissement*) shrinkage; **en** ~ *adj* set back; **écrire en** ~ to indent; ~ **du permis (de conduire)** disqualification from driving (*BRIT*), revocation of driver's license (*US*).

retraite [RətRɛt] *nf* (*d'une armée, REL, refuge*) retreat; (*d'un employé*) retirement; (*revenu*) (retirement) pension; **être/mettre à la** ~ to be retired/pension off *ou* retire; **prendre sa** ~ to retire; ~ **anticipée** early retirement; ~ **aux flambeaux** torchlight tattoo.

retraité, e [RətRete] *adj* retired ♦ *nm/f* (old age) pensioner.

retraitement [RətRɛtmɑ̃] *nm* reprocessing.

retraiter [RǝtRɛte] *vt* to reprocess.

retranchement [RǝtRɑ̃ʃmɑ̃] *nm* entrenchment; **poursuivre qn dans ses derniers ~s** to drive sb into a corner.

retrancher [RǝtRɑ̃ʃe] *vt* (*passage, détails*) to take out, remove; (*nombre, somme*): **~ qch de** to take *ou* deduct sth from; (*couper*) to cut off; **se ~ derrière/dans** to entrench o.s. behind/in; (*fig*) to take refuge behind/in.

retranscrire [RǝtRɑ̃skRiR] *vt* to retranscribe.

retransmettre [RǝtRɑ̃smɛtR(ǝ)] *vt* (*RADIO*) to broadcast, relay; (*TV*) to show.

retransmission [RǝtRɑ̃smisjɔ̃] *nf* broadcast; showing.

retravailler [RǝtRavaje] *vi* to start work again ♦ *vt* to work on again.

retraverser [RǝtRavɛRse] *vt* (*dans l'autre sens*) to cross back over.

rétréci, e [RetResi] *adj* (*idées, esprit*) narrow.

rétrécir [RetResiR] *vt* (*vêtement*) to take in ♦ *vi* to shrink; **se ~** *vi* to narrow.

rétrécissement [RetResismɑ̃] *nm* narrowing.

retremper [RǝtRɑ̃pe] *vt*: **se ~ dans** (*fig*) to re-immerse o.s. in.

rétribuer [RetRibɥe] *vt* (*travail*) to pay for; (*personne*) to pay.

rétribution [RetRibysjɔ̃] *nf* payment.

rétro [RetRo] *adj inv* old-style ♦ *nm* (= *rétroviseur*) (rear-view) mirror; **la mode ~** the nostalgia vogue.

rétroactif, ive [RetRɔaktif, -iv] *adj* retroactive.

rétrocéder [RetRɔsede] *vt* to retrocede.

rétrocession [RetRɔsesjɔ̃] *nf* retrocession.

rétrofusée [RetRɔfyze] *nf* retrorocket.

rétrograde [RetRɔgRad] *adj* reactionary, backward-looking.

rétrograder [RetRɔgRade] *vi* (*élève*) to fall back; (*économie*) to regress; (*AUTO*) to change down.

rétroprojecteur [RetRɔpRɔʒɛktœR] *nm* overhead projector.

rétrospectif, ive [RetRɔspɛktif, -iv] *adj, nf* retrospective.

rétrospectivement [RetRɔspɛktivmɑ̃] *adv* in retrospect.

retroussé, e [RǝtRuse] *adj*: **nez ~** turned-up nose.

retrousser [RǝtRuse] *vt* to roll up; (*fig: nez*) to wrinkle; (*: lèvres*) to curl up.

retrouvailles [RǝtRuvɑj] *nfpl* reunion *sg*.

retrouver [RǝtRuve] *vt* (*fugitif, objet perdu*) to find; (*occasion*) to find again; (*calme, santé*) to regain; (*reconnaître: expression, style*) to recognize; (*revoir*) to see again; (*rejoindre*) to meet (again), join; **se ~** *vi* to meet; (*s'orienter*) to find one's way; **se ~ quelque part** to find o.s. somewhere; to end up somewhere; **se ~ seul/sans argent** to find o.s. alone/with no money; **se ~ dans** (*calculs, dossiers, désordre*) to make sense of; **s'y ~** (*rentrer dans ses frais*) to break even.

rétroviseur [RetRɔvizœR] *nm* (rear-view) mirror.

réunifier [Reynifje] *vt* to reunify.

Réunion [Reynjɔ̃] *nf*: **la ~, l'île de la ~** Réunion.

réunion [Reynjɔ̃] *nf* bringing together; joining; (*séance*) meeting.

réunionnais, e [Reynjɔnɛ, -ɛz] *adj* of *ou* from Réunion.

réunir [ReyniR] *vt* (*convoquer*) to call together; (*rassembler*) to gather together; (*cumuler*) to combine; (*rapprocher*) to bring together (again), reunite; (*rattacher*) to join (together); **se ~** *vi* (*se rencontrer*) to meet; (*s'allier*) to unite.

réussi, e [Reysi] *adj* successful.

réussir [ReysiR] *vi* to succeed, be successful; (*à un examen*) to pass; (*plante, culture*) to thrive, do well ♦ *vt* to make a success of; to bring off; **~ à faire** to succeed in doing; **~ à qn** to go right for sb; (*aliment*) to agree with sb; **le travail/le mariage lui réussit** work/married life agrees with him.

réussite [Reysit] *nf* success; (*CARTES*) patience.

réutiliser [Reytilize] *vt* to re-use.

revaloir [RǝvalwaR] *vt*: **je vous revaudrai cela** I'll repay you some day; (*en mal*) I'll pay you back for this.

revalorisation [RǝvalɔRizasjɔ̃] *nf* revaluation; raising.

revaloriser [RǝvalɔRize] *vt* (*monnaie*) to revalue; (*salaires, pensions*) to raise the level of; (*institution, tradition*) to reassert the value of.

revanche [Rǝvɑ̃ʃ] *nf* revenge; **prendre sa ~ (sur)** to take one's revenge (on); **en ~** (*par contre*) on the other hand; (*en compensation*) in return.

rêvasser [Rɛvase] *vi* to daydream.

rêve [Rɛv] *nm* dream; (*activité psychique*): **le ~** dreaming; **paysage/silence de ~** dreamlike landscape/silence; **~ éveillé** daydreaming *no pl*, daydream.

rêvé, e [Reve] *adj* (*endroit, mari etc*) ideal.

revêche [Rǝvɛʃ] *adj* surly, sour-tempered.

réveil [Revɛj] *nm* (*d'un dormeur*) waking up *no pl*; (*fig*) awakening; (*pendule*) alarm (clock); **au ~** when I (*ou* you *etc*) wake (*ou* woke) up, on waking (up); **sonner le ~** (*MIL*) to sound the reveille.

réveille-matin [Revɛjmatɛ̃] *nm inv* alarm clock.

réveiller [Revɛje] *vt* (*personne*) to wake up; (*fig*) to awaken, revive; **se ~** *vi* to wake up; (*fig*) to be revived, reawaken.

réveillon [Revɛjɔ̃] *nm* Christmas Eve; (*de la Saint-Sylvestre*) New Year's Eve; Christmas Eve (*ou* New Year's Eve) party *ou* dinner.

réveillonner [Revɛjɔne] *vi* to celebrate Christmas Eve (*ou* New Year's Eve).

révélateur, trice [RevelatœR, -tRis] *adj*: **~ (de qch)** revealing (sth) ♦ *nm* (*PHOTO*) developer.

révélation [Revelɑsjɔ̃] *nf* revelation.

révéler [ʀevele] *vt* (*gén*) to reveal; (*divulguer*) to disclose, reveal; (*dénoter*) to reveal, show; (*faire connaître au public*): ~ **qn/qch** to make sb/sth widely known, bring sb/sth to the public's notice; **se** ~ *vi* to be revealed, reveal itself ♦ *vb avec attribut:* **se** ~ **facile/faux** to prove (to be) easy/false; **se** ~ **cruel/un allié sûr** to show o.s. to be cruel/a trustworthy ally.

revenant, e [ʀəvnɑ̃, -ɑ̃t] *nm/f* ghost.

revendeur, euse [ʀəvɑ̃dœʀ, -øz] *nm/f* (*détaillant*) retailer; (*d'occasions*) secondhand dealer.

revendicatif, ive [ʀəvɑ̃dikatif, -iv] *adj* (*mouvement*) of protest.

revendication [ʀəvɑ̃dikɑsjɔ̃] *nf* claim, demand; **journée de** ~ day of action (in support of one's claims).

revendiquer [ʀəvɑ̃dike] *vt* to claim, demand; (*responsabilité*) to claim ♦ *vi* to agitate in favour of one's claims.

revendre [ʀəvɑ̃dʀ(ə)] *vt* (*d'occasion*) to resell; (*détailler*) to sell; (*vendre davantage de*): ~ **du sucre/un foulard/deux bagues** to sell more sugar/another scarf/another two rings; **à** ~ *adv* (*en abondance*) to spare.

revenir [ʀəvniʀ] *vi* to come back; (*CULIN*): **faire** ~ to brown; (*coûter*): ~ **cher/à 100 F (à qn)** to cost (sb) a lot/100 F; ~ **à** (*études, projet*) to return to, go back to; (*équivaloir à*) to amount to; ~ **à qn** (*rumeur, nouvelle*) to get back to sb, reach sb's ears; (*part, honneur*) to go to sb, be sb's; (*souvenir, nom*) to come back to sb; ~ **de** (*fig: maladie, étonnement*) to recover from; ~ **sur** (*question, sujet*) to go back over; (*engagement*) to go back on; ~ **à la charge** to return to the attack; ~ **à soi** to come round; **n'en pas** ~: **je n'en reviens pas** I can't get over it; ~ **sur ses pas** to retrace one's steps; **cela revient à dire que/au même** it amounts to saying that/to the same thing; ~ **de loin** (*fig*) to have been at death's door.

revente [ʀəvɑ̃t] *nf* resale.

revenu [ʀəvny] *pp de* **revenir** ♦ *nm* income; (*de l'État*) revenue; (*d'un capital*) yield; ~**s** *nmpl* income *sg*; ~ **national brut** gross national income.

rêver [ʀeve] *vi, vt* to dream; (*rêvasser*) to (day)dream; ~ **de** (*voir en rêve*) to dream of *ou* about; ~ **de qch/de faire** to dream of sth/of doing; ~ **à** to dream of.

réverbération [ʀevɛʀbeʀɑsjɔ̃] *nf* reflection.

réverbère [ʀevɛʀbɛʀ] *nm* street lamp *ou* light.

réverbérer [ʀevɛʀbeʀe] *vt* to reflect.

reverdir [ʀəvɛʀdiʀ] *vi* (*arbre etc*) to turn green again.

révérence [ʀeveʀɑ̃s] *nf* (*vénération*) reverence; (*salut: d'homme*) bow; (: *de femme*) curtsey.

révérencieux, euse [ʀeveʀɑ̃sjø, -øz] *adj* reverent.

révérend, e [ʀeveʀɑ̃, -ɑ̃d] *adj:* **le** ~ **père Pascal** the Reverend Father Pascal.

révérer [ʀeveʀe] *vt* to revere.

rêverie [ʀɛvʀi] *nf* daydreaming *no pl*, daydream.

reverrai [ʀəveʀe] *etc vb voir* **revoir**.

revers [ʀəvɛʀ] *nm* (*de feuille, main*) back; (*d'étoffe*) wrong side; (*de pièce, médaille*) back, reverse; (*TENNIS, PING-PONG*) backhand; (*de veston*) lapel; (*de pantalon*) turn-up; (*fig: échec*) setback; ~ **de fortune** reverse of fortune; **d'un** ~ **de main** with the back of one's hand; **le** ~ **de la médaille** (*fig*) the other side of the coin; **prendre à** ~ (*MIL*) to take from the rear.

reverser [ʀəvɛʀse] *vt* (*reporter: somme etc*): ~ **sur** to put back into; (*liquide*): ~ (**dans**) to pour some more (into).

réversible [ʀevɛʀsibl(ə)] *adj* reversible.

revêtement [ʀəvɛtmɑ̃] *nm* (*de paroi*) facing; (*des sols*) flooring; (*de chaussée*) surface; (*de tuyau etc: enduit*) coating.

revêtir [ʀəvetiʀ] *vt* (*habit*) to don, put on; (*fig*) to take on; ~ **qn de** to dress sb in; (*fig*) to endow *ou* invest sb with; ~ **qch de** to cover sth with; (*fig*) to cloak sth in; ~ **d'un visa** to append a visa to.

rêveur, euse [ʀɛvœʀ, -øz] *adj* dreamy ♦ *nm/f* dreamer.

reviendrai [ʀəvjɛ̃dʀe] *etc vb voir* **revenir**.

revienne [ʀəvjɛn] *etc vb voir* **revenir**.

revient [ʀəvjɛ̃] *vb voir* **revenir** ♦ *nm:* **prix de** ~ cost price.

revigorer [ʀəvigɔʀe] *vt* to invigorate, revive, buck up.

revint [ʀəvɛ̃] *etc vb voir* **revenir**.

revirement [ʀəviʀmɑ̃] *nm* change of mind; (*d'une situation*) reversal.

revis [ʀəvi] *etc vb voir* **revoir**.

révisable [ʀevizabl(ə)] *adj* (*procès, taux etc*) reviewable, subject to review.

réviser [ʀevize] *vt* (*texte, SCOL: matière*) to revise; (*comptes*) to audit; (*machine, installation, moteur*) to overhaul, service; (*JUR: procès*) to review.

révision [ʀevizjɔ̃] *nf* revision; auditing *no pl*; overhaul, servicing *no pl*; review; **conseil de** ~ (*MIL*) recruiting board; **faire ses** ~**s** (*SCOL*) to do one's revision (*BRIT*), revise (*BRIT*), review (*US*); **la** ~ **des 10 000 km** (*AUTO*) the 10,000 km service.

révisionnisme [ʀevizjɔnism(ə)] *nm* revisionism.

revisser [ʀəvise] *vt* to screw back again.

revit [ʀəvi] *vb voir* **revoir**.

revitaliser [ʀəvitalize] *vt* to revitalize.

revivifier [ʀəvivifje] *vt* to revitalize.

revivre [ʀəvivʀ(ə)] *vi* (*reprendre des forces*) to come alive again; (*traditions*) to be revived ♦ *vt* (*épreuve, moment*) to relive; **faire** ~ (*mode, institution, usage*) to bring back to life.

révocable [ʀevɔkabl(ə)] *adj* (*délégué*) dismissible; (*contrat*) revocable.

révocation [ʀevɔkɑsjɔ̃] *nf* dismissal; revocation.

revoir [ʀəvwaʀ] *vt* to see again; *(réviser)* to revise *(BRIT)*, review *(US)* ♦ *nm:* **au ~ goodbye;**
dire au ~ à qn to say goodbye to sb; **se ~**
(amis) to meet (again), see each other again.
révoltant, e [ʀevɔltɑ̃, -ɑ̃t] *adj* revolting.
révolte [ʀevɔlt(ə)] *nf* rebellion, revolt.
révolter [ʀevɔlte] *vt* to revolt, outrage; **se ~** *vi:*
se ~ (contre) to rebel (against); **se ~ (à)** to
be outraged (by).
révolu, e [ʀevɔly] *adj* past; *(ADMIN):* **âgé de 18**
ans ~s over 18 years of age; **après 3 ans ~s**
when 3 full years have passed.
révolution [ʀevɔlysjɔ̃] *nf* revolution; **être en ~**
(pays etc) to be in revolt; **la ~ industrielle**
the industrial revolution.
révolutionnaire [ʀevɔlysjɔnɛʀ] *adj, nm/f* revolutionary.
révolutionner [ʀevɔlysjɔne] *vt* to revolutionize; *(fig)* to stir up.
revolver [ʀevɔlvɛʀ] *nm* gun; *(à barillet)* revolver.
révoquer [ʀevɔke] *vt* *(fonctionnaire)* to dismiss, remove from office; *(arrêt, contrat)* to
revoke.
revoyais [ʀəvwajɛ] *etc vb voir* **revoir.**
revu, e [ʀəvy] *pp de* **revoir** ♦ *nf* *(inventaire, exa-*
men) review; *(MIL: défilé)* review, march
past; *(: inspection)* inspection, review; *(pé-*
riodique) review, magazine; *(pièce satirique)*
revue; *(de music-hall)* variety show; **passer**
en ~ to review, inspect; *(fig)* to review; **~**
de (la) presse press review.
révulsé, e [ʀevylse] *adj* *(yeux)* rolled upwards;
(visage) contorted.
Reykjavik [ʀekjavik] *n* Reykjavik.
rez-de-chaussée [ʀedʃose] *nm inv* ground
floor.
rez-de-jardin [ʀedʒaʀdɛ̃] *nm inv* garden level.
RF *sigle f* = *République française.*
RFA *sigle f* (= *République fédérale d'Allemagne)*
FRG.
RFO *sigle f* (= *Radio-Télévision Française*
d'Outre-mer) French overseas broadcasting
service.
RG *sigle mpl* (= *renseignements généraux)* security section of the police force.
rhabiller [ʀabije] *vt:* **se ~** to get dressed
again, put one's clothes on again.
rhapsodie [ʀapsɔdi] *nf* rhapsody.
rhénan, e [ʀenɑ̃, -an] *adj* Rhine *cpd,* of the
Rhine.
Rhénanie [ʀenani] *nf:* **la ~** the Rhineland.
rhéostat [ʀeɔsta] *nm* rheostat.
rhésus [ʀezys] *adj, nm* rhesus; **~ positif/ néga-**
tif rhesus positive/negative.
rhétorique [ʀetɔʀik] *nf* rhetoric ♦ *adj* rhetorical.
rhéto-roman, e [ʀetɔʀɔmɑ̃, -an] *adj* Rhaeto-
Romanic.
Rhin [ʀɛ̃] *nm:* **le ~** the Rhine.
rhinite [ʀinit] *nf* rhinitis.

rhinocéros [ʀinɔseʀɔs] *nm* rhinoceros.
rhinopharyngite [ʀinɔfaʀɛ̃ʒit] *nf* throat infection.
rhodanien, ne [ʀɔdanjɛ̃, -ɛn] *adj* Rhône *cpd,* of
the Rhône.
Rhodes [ʀɔd] *n:* **(l'île de) ~** (the island of)
Rhodes.
Rhodésie [ʀɔdezi] *nf:* **la ~** Rhodesia.
rhodésien, ne [ʀɔdezjɛ̃, -ɛn] *adj* Rhodesian.
rhododendron [ʀɔdɔdɛ̃dʀɔ̃] *nm* rhododendron.
Rhône [ʀon] *nm:* **le ~** the Rhone.
rhubarbe [ʀybaʀb(ə)] *nf* rhubarb.
rhum [ʀɔm] *nm* rum.
rhumatisant, e [ʀymatizɑ̃, -ɑ̃t] *adj, nm/f* rheumatic.
rhumatismal, e, aux [ʀymatismal, -o] *adj*
rheumatic.
rhumatisme [ʀymatism(ə)] *nm* rheumatism *no*
pl.
rhumatologie [ʀymatɔlɔʒi] *nf* rheumatology.
rhumatologue [ʀymatɔlɔg] *nm/f* rheuma-
tologist.
rhume [ʀym] *nm* cold; **~ de cerveau** head
cold; **le ~ des foins** hay fever.
rhumerie [ʀɔmʀi] *nf* *(distillerie)* rum distillery.
RI *sigle m* (*MIL*) = *régiment d'infanterie* ♦ *sigle mpl*
(= *Républicains indépendants) political party.*
ri [ʀi] *pp de* **rire.**
riant, e [ʀjɑ̃, -ɑ̃t] *vb voir* **rire** ♦ *adj* smiling,
cheerful; *(campagne, paysage)* pleasant.
RIB *sigle m* = **relevé d'identité bancaire.**
ribambelle [ʀibɑ̃bɛl] *nf:* **une ~ de** a herd *ou*
swarm of.
ricain, e [ʀikɛ̃, -ɛn] *adj* *(fam)* Yank, Yankee.
ricanement [ʀikanmɑ̃] *nm* snigger; giggle.
ricaner [ʀikane] *vi* *(avec méchanceté)* to snigger; *(bêtement, avec gêne)* to giggle.
riche [ʀiʃ] *adj* *(gén)* rich; *(personne, pays)* rich,
wealthy; **~ en** rich in; **~ de** full of; rich in.
richement [ʀiʃmɑ̃] *adv* richly.
richesse [ʀiʃɛs] *nf* wealth; *(fig)* richness; **~s**
nfpl wealth *sg;* treasures; **~ en vitamines**
high vitamin content.
richissime [ʀiʃisim] *adj* extremely rich *ou*
wealthy.
ricin [ʀisɛ̃] *nm:* **huile de ~** castor oil.
ricocher [ʀikɔʃe] *vi:* **~ (sur)** to rebound (off);
(sur l'eau) to bounce (on *ou* off); **faire ~** *(ga-*
let) to skim.
ricochet [ʀikɔʃɛ] *nm* rebound; bounce; **faire ~**
to rebound, bounce; *(fig)* to rebound; **faire**
des ~s to skip stones; **par ~** *adv* on the rebound; *(fig)* as an indirect result.
rictus [ʀiktys] *nm* grin; *(snarling)* grimace.
ride [ʀid] *nf* wrinkle; *(fig)* ripple.
ridé, e [ʀide] *adj* wrinkled.
rideau, x [ʀido] *nm* curtain; **tirer/ouvrir les ~x**
to draw/open the curtains; **~ de fer** metal
shutter; *(POL):* **le ~ de fer** the Iron Curtain.
ridelle [ʀidɛl] *nf* slatted side *(of truck).*
rider [ʀide] *vt* to wrinkle; *(fig)* to ripple, ruffle

the surface of; **se ~** *vi* to become wrinkled.
ridicule [ʀidikyl] *adj* ridiculous ♦ *nm* ridiculousness *no pl*; **le ~** ridicule; *(travers: gén pl)* absurdities *pl*; **tourner en ~** to ridicule.
ridiculement [ʀidikylmɑ̃] *adv* ridiculously.
ridiculiser [ʀidikylize] *vt* to ridicule; **se ~** to make a fool of o.s.
ridule [ʀidyl] *nf (euph: ride)* little wrinkle.
rie [ʀi] *etc vb voir* **rire.**

═══════════════════════ *MOT-CLÉ*

rien [ʀjɛ̃] *pron* **1: (ne)** ... **~** nothing; *tournure negative* + anything; **qu'est-ce que vous avez? - ~** what have you got? — nothing; **il n'a ~ dit/fait** he said/did nothing; he hasn't said/done anything; **il n'a ~** *(n'est pas blessé)* he's all right; **ça ne fait ~** it doesn't matter; **il n'y est pour ~** he's got nothing to do with it
2 *(quelque chose)*: **a-t-il jamais ~ fait pour nous?** has he ever done anything for us?
3: ~ de: ~ d'intéressant nothing interesting; **~ d'autre** nothing else; **~ du tout** nothing at all; **il n'a ~ d'un champion** he's no champion, there's nothing of the champion about him
4: ~ que just, only; nothing but; **~ que pour lui faire plaisir** only *ou* just to please him; **~ que la vérité** nothing but the truth; **~ que cela** that alone
♦ *excl*: **de ~!** not at all!, don't mention it!; **il n'en est ~!** it's nothing of the sort!; **~ à faire!** it's no good!, it's no use!
♦ *nm*: **un petit ~** *(cadeau)* a little something; **des ~s** trivia *pl*; **un ~ de** a hint of; **en un ~ de temps** in no time at all; **avoir peur d'un ~** to be frightened of the slightest thing.

rieur, euse [ʀjœʀ, -øz] *adj* cheerful.
rigide [ʀiʒid] *adj* stiff; *(fig)* rigid; *(moralement)* strict.
rigidité [ʀiʒidite] *nf* stiffness; **la ~ cadavérique** rigor mortis.
rigolade [ʀigɔlad] *nf*: **la ~** fun; *(fig)*: **c'est de la ~** it's a big farce; *(c'est facile)* it's a cinch.
rigole [ʀigɔl] *nf (conduit)* channel; *(filet d'eau)* rivulet.
rigoler [ʀigɔle] *vi (rire)* to laugh; *(s'amuser)* to have (some) fun; *(plaisanter)* to be joking *ou* kidding.
rigolo, ote [ʀigɔlo, -ɔt] *adj (fam)* funny ♦ *nm/f* comic; *(péj)* fraud, phoney.
rigorisme [ʀigɔʀism(ə)] *nm (moral)* rigorism.
rigoriste [ʀigɔʀist(ə)] *adj* rigorist.
rigoureusement [ʀiguʀøzmɑ̃] *adv* rigorously; **~ vrai/interdit** strictly true/forbidden.
rigoureux, euse [ʀiguʀø, -øz] *adj (morale)* rigorous, strict; *(personne)* stern, strict; *(climat, châtiment)* rigorous, harsh, severe; *(interdiction, neutralité)* strict; *(preuves, analyse, méthode)* rigorous.
rigueur [ʀigœʀ] *nf* rigour *(BRIT)*, rigor *(US)*; strictness; harshness; **"tenue de soirée de**

~" "evening dress (to be worn)"; **être de ~** to be the usual thing, be the rule; **à la ~** at a pinch; possibly; **tenir ~ à qn de qch** to hold sth against sb.
riions [ʀijɔ̃] *etc vb voir* **rire.**
rillettes [ʀijɛt] *nfpl* ≈ potted meat *sg*.
rime [ʀim] *nf* rhyme; **n'avoir ni ~ ni raison** to have neither rhyme nor reason.
rimer [ʀime] *vi*: **~ (avec)** to rhyme (with); **ne ~ à rien** not to make sense.
Rimmel [ʀimɛl] *nm* ® mascara.
rinçage [ʀɛ̃saʒ] *nm* rinsing (out); *(opération)* rinse.
rince-doigts [ʀɛ̃sdwa] *nm inv* finger-bowl.
rincer [ʀɛ̃se] *vt* to rinse; *(récipient)* to rinse out; **se ~ la bouche** to rinse out one's mouth.
ring [ʀiŋ] *nm* (boxing) ring; **monter sur le ~** *(aussi fig)* to enter the ring; *(: faire carrière de boxeur)* to take up boxing.
ringard, e [ʀɛ̃gaʀ, -aʀd(ə)] *adj (péj)* old-fashioned.
Rio de Janeiro [ʀiodʒanɛʀ(o)] *n* Rio de Janeiro.
rions [ʀjɔ̃] *vb voir* **rire.**
ripaille [ʀipaj] *nf*: **faire ~** to feast.
riper [ʀipe] *vi* to slip, slide.
ripoliné, e [ʀipoline] *adj* enamel-painted.
riposte [ʀipɔst(ə)] *nf* retort, riposte; *(fig)* counter-attack, reprisal.
riposter [ʀipɔste] *vi* to retaliate ♦ *vt*: **~ que** to retort that; **~ à** *vt* to counter; to reply to.
rire [ʀiʀ] *vi* to laugh; *(se divertir)* to have fun; *(plaisanter)* to joke ♦ *nm* laughter; *(fig)*: **~ de** *vt* to laugh at; **se ~ de** to make light of; **tu veux ~!** you must be joking!; **~ aux éclats/aux larmes** to roar with laughter/laugh until one cries; **~ jaune** to force oneself to laugh; **~ sous cape** to laugh up one's sleeve; **~ au nez de qn** to laugh in sb's face; **pour ~** *(pas sérieusement)* for a joke *ou* a laugh.
ris [ʀi] *vb voir* **rire** ♦ *nm*: **~ de veau** (calf) sweetbread.
risée [ʀize] *nf*: **être la ~ de** to be the laughing stock of.
risette [ʀizɛt] *nf*: **faire ~ (à)** to give a nice little smile (to).
risible [ʀizibl(ə)] *adj* laughable, ridiculous.
risque [ʀisk(ə)] *nm* risk; **l'attrait du ~** the lure of danger; **prendre des ~s** to take risks; **à ses ~s et périls** at his own risk; **au ~ de** at the risk of; **~ d'incendie** fire risk; **~ calculé** calculated risk.
risqué, e [ʀiske] *adj* risky; *(plaisanterie)* risqué, daring.
risquer [ʀiske] *vt* to risk; *(allusion, question)* to venture, hazard; **tu risques qu'on te renvoie** you risk being dismissed; **ça ne risque rien** it's quite safe; **~ de: il risque de se tuer** he could get *ou* risks getting himself killed; **il a risqué de se tuer** he almost got himself

killed; **ce qui risque de se produire** what might *ou* could well happen; **il ne risque pas de recommencer** there's no chance of him doing that again; **se ~ dans** (*s'aventurer*) to venture into; **se ~ à faire** (*tenter*) to venture *ou* dare to do; **~ le tout pour le tout** to risk the lot.

risque-tout [Riskətu] *nm/f inv* daredevil.

rissoler [Risɔle] *vi*, *vt*: **(faire)** ~ to brown.

ristourne [Risturn(ə)] *nf* rebate; discount.

rit [Ri] *etc vb voir* **rire.**

rite [Rit] *nm* rite; (*fig*) ritual; **~s d'initiation** initiation rites.

ritournelle [Riturnɛl] *nf* (*fig*) tune; **c'est toujours la même ~** (*fam*) it's always the same old story.

rituel, le [Rityɛl] *adj, nm* ritual.

rituellement [Rityɛlmɑ̃] *adv* religiously.

riv. *abr* (= *rivière*) R.

rivage [Rivaʒ] *nm* shore.

rival, e, aux [Rival, -o] *adj, nm/f* rival; **sans ~** *adj* unrivalled.

rivaliser [Rivalize] *vi*: ~ **avec** to rival, vie with; (*être comparable*) to hold its own against, compare with; ~ **avec qn de** (*élégance etc*) to vie with *ou* rival sb in.

rivalité [Rivalite] *nf* rivalry.

rive [Riv] *nf* shore; (*de fleuve*) bank.

river [Rive] *vt* (*clou, pointe*) to clinch; (*plaques*) to rivet together.

riverain, e [Rivrɛ̃, -ɛn] *adj* riverside *cpd*; lakeside *cpd*; roadside *cpd* ♦ *nm/f* riverside (*ou* lakeside) resident; local *ou* roadside resident.

rivet [Rivɛ] *nm* rivet.

riveter [Rivte] *vt* to rivet (together).

Riviera [Rivjɛra] *nf*: **la ~ (italienne)** the Italian Riviera.

rivière [Rivjɛr] *nf* river; ~ **de diamants** diamond rivière.

rixe [Riks(ə)] *nf* brawl, scuffle.

riz [Ri] *nm* rice; ~ **au lait** ~ rice pudding.

rizière [Rizjɛr] *nf* paddy field.

RMI *sigle m* (= *revenu minimum d'insertion*) ≈ income support (*BRIT*), ≈ welfare (*US*).

RN *sigle f* = **route nationale.**

RNIS *sigle m* (= *Réseau numérique à intégration de service*) ISDN.

robe [Rɔb] *nf* dress; (*de juge, d'ecclésiastique*) robe; (*de professeur*) gown; (*pelage*) coat; ~ **de soirée/de mariée** evening/wedding dress; ~ **de baptême** christening robe; ~ **de chambre** dressing gown; ~ **de grossesse** maternity dress.

robinet [Rɔbinɛ] *nm* tap, faucet (*US*); ~ **du gaz** gas tap; ~ **mélangeur** mixer tap.

robinetterie [RɔbinɛtRi] *nf* taps *pl*, plumbing.

roboratif, ive [Rɔbɔratif, -iv] *adj* bracing, invigorating.

robot [Rɔbo] *nm* robot; ~ **de cuisine** food processor.

robotique [Rɔbɔtik] *nf* robotics *sg*.

robotiser [Rɔbɔtize] *vt* (*personne, travailleur*) to turn into a robot; (*monde, vie*) to automate.

robuste [Rɔbyst(ə)] *adj* robust, sturdy.

robustesse [Rɔbystɛs] *nf* robustness, sturdiness.

roc [Rɔk] *nm* rock.

rocade [Rɔkad] *nf* (*AUTO*) bypass.

rocaille [Rɔkaj] *nf* (*pierres*) loose stones *pl*; (*terrain*) rocky *ou* stony ground; (*jardin*) rockery, rock garden ♦ *adj* (*style*) rocaille.

rocailleux, euse [Rɔkajø, -øz] *adj* rocky, stony; (*voix*) harsh.

rocambolesque [Rɔkɑ̃bɔlɛsk(ə)] *adj* fantastic, incredible.

roche [Rɔʃ] *nf* rock.

rocher [Rɔʃe] *nm* rock; (*ANAT*) petrosal bone.

rochet [Rɔʃɛ] *nm*: **roue à ~** ratchet wheel.

rocheux, euse [Rɔʃø, -øz] *adj* rocky; **les (montagnes) Rocheuses** the Rockies, the Rocky Mountains.

rock (and roll) [Rɔk(ɛnRɔl)] *nm* (*musique*) rock(-'n'-roll); (*danse*) rock.

rocker [Rɔkœr] *nm* (*chanteur*) rock musician; (*adepte*) rock fan.

rocking-chair [Rɔkiŋ(t)ʃɛr] *nm* rocking chair.

rodage [Rɔdaʒ] *nm* running in (*BRIT*), breaking in (*US*); **en ~** (*AUTO*) running *ou* breaking in.

rodé, e [Rɔde] *adj* run in (*BRIT*), broken in (*US*); (*personne*): ~ **à qch** having got the hang of sth.

rodéo [Rɔdeo] *nm* rodeo (*pl* -s).

roder [Rɔde] *vt* (*moteur, voiture*) to run in (*BRIT*), break in (*US*); ~ **un spectacle/service** to iron out the initial problems of a show/service.

rôder [Rɔde] *vi* to roam *ou* wander about; (*de façon suspecte*) to lurk (about *ou* around).

rôdeur, euse [Rɔdœr, -øz] *nm/f* prowler.

rodomontades [Rɔdɔmɔ̃tad] *nfpl* bragging *sg*; sabre rattling *sg*.

rogatoire [Rɔgatwar] *adj*: **commission ~** letters rogatory.

rogne [Rɔɲ] *nf*: **être en ~** to be mad *ou* in a temper; **se mettre en ~** to get mad *ou* in a temper.

rogner [Rɔɲe] *vt* to trim; (*fig*) to whittle down; ~ **sur** (*fig*) to cut down *ou* back on.

rognons [Rɔɲɔ̃] *nmpl* kidneys.

rognures [Rɔɲyr] *nfpl* trimmings.

rogue [Rɔg] *adj* arrogant.

roi [Rwa] *nm* king; **les R~s mages** the Three Wise Men, the Magi; **le jour** *ou* **la fête des R~s, les R~s** Twelfth Night.

La fête des Rois *is celebrated on January 6. Figurines representing the magi are traditionally added to the Christmas crib and people eat* **la galette des Rois**, *a plain, flat cake in which a porcelain charm* (**la fève**) *is hidden. Whoever finds the charm is king or queen for the day and chooses a partner.*

roitelet [ʀwatlɛ] *nm* wren; *(péj)* kinglet.
rôle [ʀol] *nm* role; *(contribution)* part.
rollmops [ʀɔlmɔps] *nm* rollmop.
romain, e [ʀɔmɛ̃, -ɛn] *adj* Roman ♦ *nm/f:* **R~, e** Roman ♦ *nf (CULIN)* cos (lettuce).
roman, e [ʀɔmɑ̃, -an] *adj (ARCHIT)* Romanesque; *(LING)* Romance *cpd*, Romanic ♦ *nm* novel; *(LING)* **policier** detective novel; **~ d'espionnage** spy novel *ou* story; **~ noir** thriller.
romance [ʀɔmɑ̃s] *nf* ballad.
romancer [ʀɔmɑ̃se] *vt* to romanticize.
romanche [ʀɔmɑ̃ʃ] *adj, nm* Romansh.
romancier, ière [ʀɔmɑ̃sje, -jɛʀ] *nm/f* novelist.
romand, e [ʀɔmɑ̃, -ɑ̃d] *adj* of *ou* from French-speaking Switzerland ♦ *nm/f:* **R~, e** French-speaking Swiss.
romanesque [ʀɔmanɛsk(ə)] *adj (fantastique)* fantastic; storybook *cpd;* *(sentimental)* romantic; *(LITTÉRATURE)* novelistic.
roman-feuilleton, *pl* **romans-feuilletons** [ʀɔmɑ̃fœjtɔ̃] *nm* serialized novel.
roman-fleuve, *pl* **romans-fleuves** [ʀɔmɑ̃flœv] *nm* saga, roman-fleuve.
romanichel, le [ʀɔmaniʃɛl] *nm/f* gipsy.
roman-photo, *pl* **romans-photos** [ʀɔmɑ̃fɔto] *nm* (romantic) picture story.
romantique [ʀɔmɑ̃tik] *adj* romantic.
romantisme [ʀɔmɑ̃tism(ə)] *nm* romanticism.
romarin [ʀɔmaʀɛ̃] *nm* rosemary.
rombière [ʀɔ̃bjɛʀ] *nf (péj)* old bag.
Rome [ʀɔm] *n* Rome.
rompre [ʀɔ̃pʀ(ə)] *vt* to break; *(entretien, fiançailles)* to break off ♦ *vi (fiancés)* to break it off; **se ~** *vi* to break; *(MÉD)* to burst, rupture; **se ~ les os** *ou* **le cou** to break one's neck; **~ avec** to break with; **à tout ~** *adv* wildly; **applaudir à tout ~** to bring down the house, applaud wildly; **~ la glace** *(fig)* to break the ice; **rompez (les rangs)!** *(MIL)* dismiss!, fall out!
rompu, e [ʀɔ̃py] *pp de* **rompre** ♦ *adj (fourbu)* exhausted, worn out; **~ à** with wide experience of; inured to.
romsteck [ʀɔ̃mstɛk] *nm* rump steak *no pl.*
ronce [ʀɔ̃s] *nf (BOT)* bramble branch; *(MENUISERIE):* **~ de noyer** burr walnut; **~s** *nfpl* brambles, thorns.
ronchonner [ʀɔ̃ʃɔne] *vi (fam)* to grouse, grouch.
rond, e [ʀɔ̃, ʀɔ̃d] *adj* round; *(joues, mollets)* well-rounded; *(fam: ivre)* tight; *(sincère, décidé):* **être ~ en affaires** to be on the level in business, do an honest deal ♦ *nm (cercle)* ring; *(fam: sou):* **je n'ai plus un ~** I haven't a penny left ♦ *nf (gén: de surveillance)* rounds *pl*, patrol; *(danse)* round (dance); *(MUS)* semibreve *(BRIT)*, whole note *(US)* ♦ *adv:* **tourner ~** *(moteur)* to run smoothly; **ça ne tourne pas ~** *(fig)* there's something not quite right about it; **pour faire un compte ~** to make (it) a round figure, to round (it) off;

avoir le dos ~ to be round-shouldered; **en ~** *(s'asseoir, danser)* in a ring; **à la ~e** *(alentour):* **à 10 km à la ~e** for 10 km round; *(à chacun son tour):* **passer qch à la ~e** to pass sth (a)round; **faire des ~s de jambe** to bow and scrape; **~ de serviette** napkin ring.
rond-de-cuir, *pl* **ronds-de-cuir** [ʀɔ̃dkɥiʀ] *nm (péj)* penpusher.
rondelet, te [ʀɔ̃dlɛ, -ɛt] *adj* plump; *(fig: somme)* tidy; *(: bourse)* well-lined, fat.
rondelle [ʀɔ̃dɛl] *nf (TECH)* washer; *(tranche)* slice, round.
rondement [ʀɔ̃dmɑ̃] *adv (avec décision)* briskly; *(loyalement)* frankly.
rondeur [ʀɔ̃dœʀ] *nf (d'un bras, des formes)* plumpness; *(bonhomie)* friendly straightforwardness; **~s** *nfpl (d'une femme)* curves.
rondin [ʀɔ̃dɛ̃] *nm* log.
rond-point, *pl* **ronds-points** [ʀɔ̃pwɛ̃] *nm* roundabout *(BRIT)*, traffic circle *(US)*.
ronéotyper [ʀɔneɔtipe] *vt* to duplicate, roneo.
ronflant, e [ʀɔ̃flɑ̃, -ɑ̃t] *adj (péj)* high-flown, grand.
ronflement [ʀɔ̃fləmɑ̃] *nm* snore, snoring *no pl.*
ronfler [ʀɔ̃fle] *vi* to snore; *(moteur, poêle)* to hum; *(: plus fort)* to roar.
ronger [ʀɔ̃ʒe] *vt* to gnaw (at); *(suj: vers, rouille)* to eat into; **~ son frein** to champ (at) the bit *(fig)*; **se ~ de souci, se ~ les sangs** to worry o.s. sick, fret; **se ~ les ongles** to bite one's nails.
rongeur, euse [ʀɔ̃ʒœʀ, -øz] *nm/f* rodent.
ronronnement [ʀɔ̃ʀɔnmɑ̃] *nm* purring; *(bruit)* purr.
ronronner [ʀɔ̃ʀɔne] *vi* to purr.
roque [ʀɔk] *nm (ÉCHECS)* castling.
roquefort [ʀɔkfɔʀ] *nm* Roquefort.
roquer [ʀɔke] *vi* to castle.
roquet [ʀɔkɛ] *nm* nasty little lap-dog.
roquette [ʀɔkɛt] *nf* rocket; **~ antichar** anti-tank rocket.
rosace [ʀozas] *nf (vitrail)* rose window, rosace; *(motif: de plafond etc)* rose.
rosaire [ʀozɛʀ] *nm* rosary.
rosbif [ʀɔsbif] *nm:* **du ~** roasting beef; *(cuit)* roast beef; **un ~** a joint of (roasting) beef.
rose [ʀoz] *nf* rose; *(vitrail)* rose window ♦ *adj* pink; **~ bonbon** *adj inv* candy pink; **~ des vents** compass card.
rosé, e [ʀoze] *adj* pinkish; **(vin) ~** rosé (wine).
roseau, x [ʀozo] *nm* reed.
rosée [ʀoze] *adj f voir* **rosé** ♦ *nf:* **goutte de ~** dewdrop.
roseraie [ʀozʀɛ] *nf* rose garden; *(plantation)* rose nursery.
rosette [ʀozɛt] *nf* rosette *(gen of the Légion d'honneur)*.
rosier [ʀozje] *nm* rosebush, rose tree.
rosir [ʀoziʀ] *vi* to go pink.
rosse [ʀɔs] *nf (péj: cheval)* nag ♦ *adj* nasty, vicious.

rosser [ʀɔse] vt (fam) to thrash.
rossignol [ʀɔsiɲɔl] nm (ZOOL) nightingale; (crochet) picklock.
rot [ʀo] nm belch; (de bébé) burp.
rotatif, ive [ʀɔtatif, -iv] adj rotary ♦ nf rotary press.
rotation [ʀɔtasjɔ̃] nf rotation; (fig) rotation, swap-around; (renouvellement) turnover; par ~ on a rota (BRIT) ou rotation (US); ~ des cultures rotation of crops; ~ des stocks stock turnover.
rotatoire [ʀɔtatwaʀ] adj: mouvement ~ rotary movement.
roter [ʀɔte] vi (fam) to burp, belch.
rôti [ʀoti] nm: du ~ roasting meat; (cuit) roast meat; un ~ de bœuf/porc a joint of (roasting) beef/pork.
rotin [ʀɔtɛ̃] nm rattan (cane); fauteuil en ~ cane (arm)chair.
rôtir [ʀotiʀ] vt (aussi: faire ~) to roast ♦ vi to roast; se ~ au soleil to bask in the sun.
rôtisserie [ʀotisʀi] nf (restaurant) steakhouse; (comptoir, magasin) roast meat counter (ou shop).
rôtissoire [ʀotiswaʀ] nf (roasting) spit.
rotonde [ʀɔtɔ̃d] nf (ARCHIT) rotunda; (RAIL) engine shed.
rotondité [ʀɔtɔ̃dite] nf roundness.
rotor [ʀɔtɔʀ] nm rotor.
Rotterdam [ʀɔtɛʀdam] n Rotterdam.
rotule [ʀɔtyl] nf kneecap, patella.
roturier, ière [ʀɔtyʀje, -jɛʀ] nm/f commoner.
rouage [ʀwaʒ] nm cog(wheel), gearwheel; (de montre) part; (fig) cog; ~s nmpl (fig) internal structure sg.
Rouanda [ʀwɑ̃da] nm: le ~ Rwanda.
roubaisien, ne [ʀubezjɛ̃, -ɛn] adj of ou from Roubaix.
roublard, e [ʀublaʀ, -aʀd(ə)] adj (péj) crafty, wily.
rouble [ʀubl(ə)] nm rouble.
roucoulement [ʀukulmɑ̃] nm (de pigeons, fig) coo, cooing.
roucouler [ʀukule] vi to coo; (fig: péj) to warble; (: amoureux) to bill and coo.
roue [ʀu] nf wheel; faire la ~ (paon) to spread ou fan its tail; (GYM) to do a cartwheel; descendre en ~ libre to freewheel ou coast down; pousser à la ~ to put one's shoulder to the wheel; grande ~ (à la foire) big wheel; ~ à aubes paddle wheel; ~ dentée cogwheel; ~ de secours spare wheel.
roué, e [ʀwe] adj wily.
rouennais, e [ʀwanɛ, -ɛz] adj of ou from Rouen.
rouer [ʀwe] vt: ~ qn de coups to give sb a thrashing.
rouet [ʀwɛ] nm spinning wheel.
rouge [ʀuʒ] adj, nm/f red ♦ nm red; (fard) rouge; (vin) ~ red wine; passer au ~ (signal) to go red; (automobiliste) to go through a red light; porter au ~ (métal) to bring to red

heat; sur la liste ~ (TÉL) ex-directory (BRIT), unlisted (US); ~ de honte/colère red with shame/anger; se fâcher tout/voir ~ to blow one's top/see red; ~ (à lèvres) lipstick.
rougeâtre [ʀuʒɑtʀ(ə)] adj reddish.
rougeaud, e [ʀuʒo, -od] adj (teint) red; (personne) red-faced.
rouge-gorge [ʀuʒgɔʀʒ(ə)] nm robin (redbreast).
rougeoiement [ʀuʒwamɑ̃] nm reddish glow.
rougeole [ʀuʒɔl] nf measles sg.
rougeoyant, e [ʀuʒwajɑ̃, -ɑ̃t] adj (ciel, braises) glowing; (aube, reflets) glowing red.
rougeoyer [ʀuʒwaje] vi to glow red.
rouget [ʀuʒɛ] nm mullet.
rougeur [ʀuʒœʀ] nf redness; (du visage) red face; ~s nfpl (MÉD) red blotches.
rougir [ʀuʒiʀ] vi (de honte, timidité) to blush, flush; (de plaisir, colère) to flush; (fraise, tomate) to go ou turn red; (ciel) to redden.
rouille [ʀuj] adj inv rust-coloured, rusty ♦ nf rust; (CULIN) spicy (Provençal) sauce served with fish dishes.
rouillé, e [ʀuje] adj rusty.
rouiller [ʀuje] vt to rust ♦ vi to rust, go rusty; se ~ vi to rust; (fig: mentalement) to become rusty; (: physiquement) to grow stiff.
roulade [ʀulad] nf (GYM) roll; (CULIN) rolled meat no pl; (MUS) roulade, run.
roulage [ʀulaʒ] nm (transport) haulage.
roulant, e [ʀulɑ̃, -ɑ̃t] adj (meuble) on wheels; (surface, trottoir) moving; matériel ~ (RAIL) rolling stock; personnel ~ (RAIL) train crews pl.
roulé, e [ʀule] adj: bien ~e (fam: femme) shapely, curvy.
rouleau, x [ʀulo] nm (de papier, tissu, pièces de monnaie, SPORT) roll; (de machine à écrire) roller, platen; (à mise en plis, à peinture, vague) roller; être au bout du ~ (fig) to be at the end of the line; ~ compresseur steamroller; ~ à pâtisserie rolling pin; ~ de pellicule roll of film.
roulé-boulé, pl **roulés-boulés** [ʀulebule] (SPORT) roll.
roulement [ʀulmɑ̃] nm (bruit) rumbling no pl, rumble; (rotation) rotation; turnover; (: de capitaux) circulation; par ~ on a rota (BRIT) ou rotation (US) basis; ~ (à billes) ball bearings pl; ~ de tambour drum roll; ~ d'yeux roll(ing) of the eyes.
rouler [ʀule] vt to roll; (papier, tapis) to roll up; (CULIN: pâte) to roll out; (fam) to do, con ♦ vi (bille, boule) to roll; (voiture, train) to go, run; (automobiliste) to drive; (cycliste) to ride; (bateau) to roll; (tonnerre) to rumble, roll; (dégringoler): ~ en bas de to roll down; ~ sur (suj: conversation) to turn on; se ~ dans (boue) to roll in; (couverture) to roll o.s. (up) in; ~ dans la farine (fam) to con; ~ les épaules/hanches to sway one's shoulders/wiggle one's hips; ~ les "r" to roll one's r's;

~ **sur l'or** to be rolling in money, be rolling in it; ~ **(sa bosse)** to go places.

roulette [rulɛt] *nf (de table, fauteuil)* castor; *(de pâtissier)* pastry wheel; *(jeu)*: **la** ~ roulette; **à** ~**s** on castors; **la** ~ **russe** Russian roulette.

roulis [ruli] *nm* roll(ing).

roulotte [rulɔt] *nf* caravan.

roumain, e [rumɛ̃, -ɛn] *adj* Rumanian, Romanian ♦ *nm (LING)* Rumanian, Romanian ♦ *nm/f*: **R**~, **e** Rumanian, Romanian.

Roumanie [rumani] *nf*: **la** ~ Rumania, Romania.

roupiller [rupije] *vi (fam)* to sleep.

rouquin, e [rukɛ̃, -in] *nm/f (péj)* redhead.

rouspéter [ruspete] *vi (fam)* to moan, grouse.

rousse [rus] *adj f voir* roux.

rousseur [rusœr] *nf*: **tache de** ~ freckle.

roussi [rusi] *nm*: **ça sent le** ~ there's a smell of burning; *(fig)* I can smell trouble.

roussir [rusir] *vt* to scorch ♦ *vi (feuilles)* to go *ou* turn brown; *(CULIN)*: **faire** ~ to brown.

routage [rutaʒ] *nm* (collective) mailing.

routard, e [rutar, -ard(ə)] *nm/f* traveller.

route [rut] *nf* road; *(fig: chemin)* way; *(itinéraire, parcours)* route; *(fig: voie)* road, path; **par (la)** ~ by road; **il y a 3 heures de** ~ it's a 3-hour ride *ou* journey; **en** ~ *adv* on the way; **en** ~**!** let's go!; **en cours de** ~ en route; **mettre en** ~ to start up; **se mettre en** ~ to set off; **faire** ~ **vers** to head towards; **faire fausse** ~ *(fig)* to be on the wrong track; ~ **nationale (RN)** ≈ A-road *(BRIT)*, ≈ state highway *(US)*.

routier, ière [rutje, -jɛr] *adj* road *cpd* ♦ *nm (camionneur)* (long-distance) lorry *(BRIT)* ou truck driver; *(restaurant)* ≈ transport café *(BRIT)*, ≈ truck stop *(US)*; *(scout)* ≈ rover; *(cycliste)* road racer ♦ *nf (voiture)* touring car; **vieux** ~ old stager; **carte routière** road map.

routine [rutin] *nf* routine; **visite/contrôle de** ~ routine visit/check.

routinier, ière [rutinje, -jɛr] *adj (péj: travail)* humdrum, routine; *(: personne)* addicted to routine.

rouvert, e [ruvɛr, -ɛrt(ə)] *pp de* rouvrir.

rouvrir [ruvrir] *vt, vi* to reopen, open again; **se** ~ *vi (blessure)* to open up again.

roux, rousse [ru, rus] *adj* red; *(personne)* red-haired ♦ *nm/f* redhead ♦ *nm (CULIN)* roux.

royal, e, aux [rwajal, -o] *adj* royal; *(fig)* fit for a king, princely; blissful; thorough.

royalement [rwajalmã] *adv* royally.

royaliste [rwajalist(ə)] *adj, nm/f* royalist.

royaume [rwajom] *nm* kingdom; *(fig)* realm; **le** ~ **des cieux** the kingdom of heaven.

Royaume-Uni [rwajomyni] *nm*: **le** ~ the United Kingdom.

royauté [rwajote] *nf (dignité)* kingship; *(régime)* monarchy.

RP *sigle f* (= *recette principale*) ≈ main post office; = *région parisienne* ♦ *sigle fpl* (= *relations publiques)* PR.

RPR *sigle m* (= *Rassemblement pour la République*) *political party.*

R.S.V.P. *abr* (= *répondez s'il vous plaît*) R.S.V.P.

RTB *sigle f* = *Radio-Télévision belge.*

Rte *abr* = *route.*

RTL *sigle f* = *Radio-Télévision Luxembourg.*

RTVE *sigle f* = *Radio-Télévision espagnole.*

RU [ry] *sigle m* = **restaurant universitaire.**

ruade [ryad] *nf* kick.

Ruanda [rwãda] *nm*: **le** ~ Rwanda.

ruban [rybã] *nm (gén)* ribbon; *(pour ourlet, couture)* binding; *(de téléscripteur etc)* tape; *(d'acier)* strip; ~ **adhésif** adhesive tape; ~ **carbone** carbon ribbon.

rubéole [rybeɔl] *nf* German measles *sg*, rubella.

rubicond, e [rybikɔ̃, -ɔ̃d] *adj* rubicund, ruddy.

rubis [rybi] *nm* ruby; *(HORLOGERIE)* jewel; **payer** ~ **sur l'ongle** to pay cash on the nail.

rubrique [rybrik] *nf (titre, catégorie)* heading, rubric; *(PRESSE: article)* column.

ruche [ryʃ] *nf* hive.

rucher [ryʃe] *nm* apiary.

rude [ryd] *adj (barbe, toile)* rough; *(métier, tâche)* hard, tough; *(climat)* severe, harsh; *(bourru)* harsh, rough; *(fruste)* rugged, tough; *(fam)* jolly good; **être mis à** ~ **épreuve** to be put through the mill.

rudement [rydmã] *adv (tomber, frapper)* hard; *(traiter, reprocher)* harshly; *(fam: très)* terribly; *(: beaucoup)* terribly hard.

rudesse [rydɛs] *nf* roughness; toughness; severity; harshness.

rudimentaire [rydimãtɛr] *adj* rudimentary, basic.

rudiments [rydimã] *nmpl* rudiments; basic knowledge *sg*; basic principles.

rudoyer [rydwaje] *vt* to treat harshly.

rue [ry] *nf* street; **être/jeter qn à la** ~ to be on the streets/throw sb out onto the street.

ruée [rye] *nf* rush; **la** ~ **vers l'or** the gold rush.

ruelle [rɥɛl] *nf* alley(way).

ruer [rɥe] *vi (cheval)* to kick out; **se** ~ *vi*: **se** ~ **sur** to pounce on; **se** ~ **vers/dans/hors de** to rush *ou* dash towards/into/out of; ~ **dans les brancards** to become rebellious.

rugby [rygbi] *nm* rugby (football); ~ **à treize/quinze** rugby league/union.

rugir [ryʒir] *vi* to roar.

rugissement [ryʒismã] *nm* roar, roaring *no pl*.

rugosité [rygozite] *nf* roughness; *(aspérité)* rough patch.

rugueux, euse [rygø, -øz] *adj* rough.

ruine [rɥin] *nf* ruin; ~**s** *nfpl* ruins; **tomber en** ~ to fall into ruin(s).

ruiner [rɥine] *vt* to ruin.

ruineux, euse [rɥinø, -øz] *adj* terribly expensive to buy (*ou* run), ruinous; extravagant.

ruisseau, x [rɥiso] *nm* stream, brook; *(caniveau)* gutter; *(fig)*: ~**x de larmes/sang** floods of tears/streams of blood.

ruisselant, e [ʀ ɥislɑ̃, -ɑ̃t] *adj* streaming.
ruisseler [ʀɥisle] *vi* to stream; ~ **(d'eau)** to be streaming (with water); ~ **de lumière** to stream with light.
ruissellement [ʀɥisɛlmɑ̃] *nm* streaming; ~ **de lumière** stream of light.
rumeur [ʀymœʀ] *nf* (*bruit confus*) rumbling; hubbub *no pl*; (*protestation*) murmur(ing); (*nouvelle*) rumour (*BRIT*), rumor (*US*).
ruminer [ʀymine] *vt* (*herbe*) to ruminate; (*fig*) to ruminate on *ou* over, chew over ♦ *vi* (*vache*) to chew the cud, ruminate.
rumsteck [ʀɔ̃mstɛk] *nm* = **romsteck**.
rupestre [ʀypɛstʀ(ə)] *adj* (*plante*) rock *cpd*; (*art*) wall *cpd*.
rupture [ʀyptyʀ] *nf* (*de câble, digue*) breaking; (*de tendon*) rupture, tearing; (*de négociations etc*) breakdown; (*de contrat*) breach; (*séparation, désunion*) break-up, split; **en ~ de ban** at odds with authority; **en ~ de stock** (*COMM*) out of stock.
rural, e, aux [ʀyʀal, -o] *adj* rural, country *cpd* ♦ *nmpl*: **les ruraux** country people.
ruse [ʀyz] *nf*: **la ~** cunning, craftiness; trickery; **une ~** a trick, a ruse; **par ~** by trickery.
rusé, e [ʀyze] *adj* cunning, crafty.
russe [ʀys] *adj* Russian ♦ *nm* (*LING*) Russian ♦ *nm/f*: **R~** Russian.
Russie [ʀysi] *nf*: **la ~** Russia; **la ~ blanche** White Russia; **la ~ soviétique** Soviet Russia.
rustine [ʀystin] *nf* repair patch (*for bicycle inner tube*).
rustique [ʀystik] *adj* rustic; (*plante*) hardy.
rustre [ʀystʀ(ə)] *nm* boor.
rut [ʀyt] *nm*: **être en ~** (*animal domestique*) to be in *ou* on heat; (*animal sauvage*) to be rutting.
rutabaga [ʀytabaga] *nm* swede.
rutilant, e [ʀytilɑ̃, -ɑ̃t] *adj* gleaming.
RV *sigle m* = **rendez-vous**.
Rwanda [ʀwɑ̃da] *nm*: **le ~** Rwanda.
rythme [ʀitm(ə)] *nm* rhythm; (*vitesse*) rate; (*: de la vie*) pace, tempo; **au ~ de 10 par jour** at the rate of 10 a day.
rythmé, e [ʀitme] *adj* rhythmic(al).
rythmer [ʀitme] *vt* to give rhythm to.
rythmique [ʀitmik] *adj* rhythmic(al) ♦ *nf* rhythmics *sg*.

S s

S, s [ɛs] *nm inv* S, s ♦ *abr* (= *sud*) S; (= *seconde*) sec; (= *siècle*) c., century; **S comme Suzanne** S for Sugar.
s' [s] *pron voir* **se**.
s/ *abr* = **sur**.
SA *sigle f* = **société anonyme**; (= *Son Altesse*) HH.
sa [sa] *adj possessif voir* **son**.
sabbatique [sabatik] *adj*: **année ~** sabbatical year.
sable [sɑbl(ə)] *nm* sand; **~s mouvants** quicksand(s).
sablé [sɑble] *adj* (*allée*) sandy ♦ *nm* shortbread biscuit; **pâte ~e** (*CULIN*) shortbread dough.
sabler [sɑble] *vt* to sand; (*contre le verglas*) to grit; **~ le champagne** to drink champagne.
sableux, euse [sɑblø, -øz] *adj* sandy.
sablier [sɑblije] *nm* hourglass; (*de cuisine*) egg timer.
sablière [sɑblijɛʀ] *nf* sand quarry.
sablonneux, euse [sɑblɔnø, -øz] *adj* sandy.
saborder [sabɔʀde] *vt* (*navire*) to scuttle; (*fig*) to wind up, shut down.
sabot [sabo] *nm* clog; (*de cheval, bœuf*) hoof; ~ **(de Denver)** (wheel) clamp; ~ **de frein** brake shoe.
sabotage [sabɔtaʒ] *nm* sabotage.
saboter [sabɔte] *vt* (*travail, morceau de musique*) to botch, make a mess of; (*machine, installation, négociation etc*) to sabotage.
saboteur, euse [sabɔtœʀ, -øz] *nm/f* saboteur.
sabre [sɑbʀ(ə)] *nm* sabre; **le ~** (*fig*) the sword, the army.
sabrer [sɑbʀe] *vt* to cut down.
SAC [sak] *sigle m* (= *Service d'action civique*) former Gaullist parapolice.
sac [sak] *nm* bag; (*à charbon etc*) sack; (*pillage*) sack(ing); **mettre à ~** to sack; ~ **à provisions/de voyage** shopping/travelling bag; ~ **de couchage** sleeping bag; ~ **à dos** rucksack; ~ **à main** handbag; ~ **de plage** beach bag.
saccade [sakad] *nf* jerk; **par ~s** jerkily; haltingly.
saccadé, e [sakade] *adj* jerky.
saccage [sakaʒ] *nm* havoc.
saccager [sakaʒe] *vt* (*piller*) to sack, lay waste; (*dévaster*) to create havoc in, wreck.
saccharine [sakaʀin] *nf* saccharin(e).
saccharose [sakaʀoz] *nm* sucrose.
SACEM [sasɛm] *sigle f* (= *Société des auteurs, compositeurs et éditeurs de musique*) body re-

sponsible for collecting and distributing royalties.

sacerdoce [sasɛʀdɔs] *nm* priesthood; (*fig*) calling, vocation.

sacerdotal, e, aux [sasɛʀdɔtal, -o] *adj* priestly, sacerdotal.

sachant [saʃɑ̃] *etc vb voir* **savoir.**

sache [saʃ] *etc vb voir* **savoir.**

sachet [saʃɛ] *nm* (small) bag; (*de lavande, poudre, shampooing*) sachet; **thé en** ~**s** tea bags; ~ **de thé** tea bag.

sacoche [sakɔʃ] *nf* (*gén*) bag; (*de bicyclette*) saddlebag; (*du facteur*) (post-)bag; (*d'outils*) toolbag.

sacquer [sake] *vt* (*fam: candidat, employé*) to sack; (*: réprimander, mal noter*) to plough.

sacraliser [sakʀalize] *vt* to make sacred.

sacre [sakʀ(ə)] *nm* coronation; consecration.

sacré, e [sakʀe] *adj* sacred; (*fam: satané*) blasted; (*: fameux*): **un** ~ ... a heck of a ...; (*ANAT*) sacral.

sacrement [sakʀəmɑ̃] *nm* sacrament; **les derniers** ~**s** the last rites.

sacrer [sakʀe] *vt* (*roi*) to crown; (*évêque*) to consecrate ♦ *vi* to curse, swear.

sacrifice [sakʀifis] *nm* sacrifice; **faire le** ~ **de** to sacrifice.

sacrificiel, le [sakʀifisjɛl] *adj* sacrificial.

sacrifier [sakʀifje] *vt* to sacrifice; ~ **à** *vt* to conform to; **se** ~ to sacrifice o.s.; **articles sacrifiés** (*COMM*) items sold at rock-bottom *ou* give-away prices.

sacrilège [sakʀilɛʒ] *nm* sacrilege ♦ *adj* sacrilegious.

sacristain [sakʀistɛ̃] *nm* sexton; sacristan.

sacristie [sakʀisti] *nf* sacristy; (*culte protestant*) vestry.

sacro-saint, e [sakʀɔsɛ̃, -ɛ̃t] *adj* sacrosanct.

sadique [sadik] *adj* sadistic ♦ *nmf* sadist.

sadisme [sadism(ə)] *nm* sadism.

sadomasochisme [sadɔmazoʃism(ə)] *nm* sadomasochism.

sadomasochiste [sadɔmazoʃist(ə)] *nmf* sadomasochist.

safari [safaʀi] *nm* safari; **faire un** ~ to go on safari.

safari-photo [safaʀifoto] *nm* photographic safari.

SAFER [safɛʀ] *sigle f* (= *Société d'aménagement foncier et d'établissement rural*) *organization with the right to buy land in order to retain it for agricultural use.*

safran [safʀɑ̃] *nm* saffron.

saga [saga] *nf* saga.

sagace [sagas] *adj* sagacious, shrewd.

sagacité [sagasite] *nf* sagacity, shrewdness.

sagaie [sagɛ] *nf* assegai.

sage [saʒ] *adj* wise; (*enfant*) good ♦ *nm* wise man; sage.

sage-femme [saʒfam] *nf* midwife (*pl* -wives).

sagement [saʒmɑ̃] *adv* (*raisonnablement*) wisely, sensibly; (*tranquillement*) quietly.

sagesse [saʒɛs] *nf* wisdom.

Sagittaire [saʒitɛʀ] *nm*: **le** ~ Sagittarius, the Archer; **être du** ~ to be Sagittarius.

Sahara [saaʀa] *nm*: **le** ~ the Sahara (Desert); **le** ~ **occidental** (*pays*) Western Sahara.

saharien, ne [saaʀjɛ̃, -ɛn] *adj* Saharan ♦ *nf* safari jacket.

Sahel [sael] *nm*: **le** ~ the Sahel.

sahélien, ne [saeljɛ̃, -ɛn] *adj* Sahelian.

saignant, e [sɛɲɑ̃, -ɑ̃t] *adj* (*viande*) rare; (*blessure, plaie*) bleeding.

saignée [seɲe] *nf* (*MÉD*) bleeding *no pl*, bloodletting *no pl*; (*ANAT*): **la** ~ **du bras** the bend of the arm; (*fig: MIL*) heavy losses *pl*; (*: prélèvement*) savage cut.

saignement [sɛɲmɑ̃] *nm* bleeding; ~ **de nez** nosebleed.

saigner [seɲe] *vi* to bleed ♦ *vt* to bleed; (*animal*) to bleed to death; ~ **qn à blanc** (*fig*) to bleed sb white; ~ **du nez** to have a nosebleed.

Saigon [saigɔ̃] *n* Saigon.

saillant, e [sajɑ̃, -ɑ̃t] *adj* (*pommettes, menton*) prominent; (*corniche etc*) projecting; (*fig*) salient, outstanding.

saillie [saji] *nf* (*sur un mur etc*) projection; (*trait d'esprit*) witticism; (*accouplement*) covering, serving; **faire** ~ to project, stick out; **en** ~, **formant** ~ projecting, overhanging.

saillir [sajiʀ] *vi* to project, stick out; (*veine, muscle*) to bulge ♦ *vt* (*ÉLEVAGE*) to cover, serve.

sain, e [sɛ̃, sɛn] *adj* healthy; (*dents, constitution*) healthy, sound; (*lectures*) wholesome; ~ **et sauf** safe and sound, unharmed; ~ **d'esprit** sound in mind, sane.

saindoux [sɛ̃du] *nm* lard.

sainement [sɛnmɑ̃] *adv* (*vivre*) healthily; (*raisonner*) soundly.

saint, e [sɛ̃, sɛ̃t] *adj* holy; (*fig*) saintly ♦ *nmf* saint; **la S~e Vierge** the Blessed Virgin.

saint-bernard [sɛ̃bɛʀnaʀ] *nm inv* (*chien*) St Bernard.

Sainte-Hélène [sɛ̃telɛn] *nf* St Helena.

Sainte-Lucie [sɛ̃tlysi] *nf* Saint Lucia.

Saint-Esprit [sɛ̃tɛspʀi] *nm*: **le** ~ the Holy Spirit *ou* Ghost.

sainteté [sɛ̃te] *nf* holiness; saintliness.

Saint-Laurent [sɛ̃lɔʀɑ̃] *nm*: **le** ~ the St Lawrence.

Saint-Marin [sɛ̃maʀɛ̃] *nm*: **le** ~ San Marino.

Saint-Père [sɛ̃pɛʀ] *nm*: **le** ~ the Holy Father, the Pontiff.

Saint-Pierre [sɛ̃pjɛʀ] *nm* Saint Peter; (*église*) Saint Peter's.

Saint-Pierre-et-Miquelon [sɛ̃pjɛʀemiklɔ̃] *nm* Saint Pierre and Miquelon.

Saint-Siège [sɛ̃sjɛʒ] *nm*: **le** ~ the Holy See.

Saint-Sylvestre [sɛ̃silvɛstʀ(ə)] *nf*: **la** ~ New Year's Eve.

Saint-Thomas [sɛ̃tɔma] *nf* Saint Thomas.

Saint-Vincent et les Grenadines

[sɛ̃vɛ̃sɑ̃elegʀənadin] *nm* St Vincent and the Grenadines.

sais [sɛ] *etc vb voir* **savoir**.

saisie [sezi] *nf* seizure; **à la** ~ (*texte*) being keyed; ~ **(de données)** (data) capture.

saisine [sezin] *nf* (*JUR*) *submission of a case to the court.*

saisir [seziʀ] *vt* to take hold of, grab; (*fig: occasion*) to seize; (*comprendre*) to grasp; (*entendre*) to get, catch; (*suj: émotions*) to take hold of, come over; (*INFORM*) to capture, keyboard; (*CULIN*) to fry quickly; (*JUR: biens, publication*) to seize; (*: juridiction*): ~ **un tribunal d'une affaire** to submit *ou* refer a case to a court; **se** ~ **de** *vt* to seize; **être saisi** (*frappé de*) to be overcome.

saisissant, e [sezisɑ̃, -ɑ̃t] *adj* startling, striking; (*froid*) biting.

saisissement [sezismɑ̃] *nm*: **muet/figé de** ~ speechless/frozen with emotion.

saison [sɛzɔ̃] *nf* season; **la belle/mauvaise** ~ the summer/winter months; **être de** ~ to be in season; **en/hors** ~ in/out of season; **haute/basse/morte** ~ high/low/slack season; **la** ~ **des pluies/des amours** the rainy/mating season.

saisonnier, ière [sɛzɔnje, -jɛʀ] *adj* seasonal ♦ *nm* (*travailleur*) seasonal worker; (*vacancier*) seasonal holidaymaker.

sait [sɛ] *vb voir* **savoir**.

salace [salas] *adj* salacious.

salade [salad] *nf* (*BOT*) lettuce *etc* (*generic term*); (*CULIN*) (green) salad; (*fam*) tangle, muddle; ~**s** *nfpl* (*fam*): **raconter des** ~**s** to tell tales (*fam*); **haricots en** ~ bean salad; ~ **de concombres** cucumber salad; ~ **de fruits** fruit salad; ~ **niçoise** salade niçoise; ~ **russe** Russian salad.

saladier [saladje] *nm* (salad) bowl.

salaire [salɛʀ] *nm* (*annuel, mensuel*) salary; (*hebdomadaire, journalier*) pay, wages *pl*; (*fig*) reward; ~ **de base** basic salary (*ou* wage); ~ **de misère** starvation wage; ~ **minimum interprofessionnel de croissance (SMIC)** *index-linked guaranteed minimum wage.*

salaison [salɛzɔ̃] *nf* salting; ~**s** *nfpl* salt meat *sg.*

salamandre [salamɑ̃dʀ(ə)] *nf* salamander.

salami [salami] *nm* salami *no pl*, salami sausage.

salant [salɑ̃] *adj m*: **marais** ~ salt pan.

salarial, e, aux [salaʀjal, -o] *adj* salary *cpd*, wage(s) *cpd*.

salariat [salaʀja] *nm* salaried staff.

salarié, e [salaʀje] *adj* salaried; wage-earning ♦ *nm/f* salaried employee; wage-earner.

salaud [salo] *nm* (*fam!*) sod (*!*), bastard (*!*).

sale [sal] *adj* dirty; (*fig: avant le nom*) nasty.

salé, e [sale] *adj* (*liquide, saveur*) salty; (*CULIN*) salted, salt *cpd*; (*fig*) spicy, juicy; (*: note, facture*) steep, stiff ♦ *nm* (*porc salé*) salt pork; **petit** ~ ≈ boiling bacon.

salement [salmɑ̃] *adv* (*manger etc*) dirtily, messily.

saler [sale] *vt* to salt.

saleté [salte] *nf* (*état*) dirtiness; (*crasse*) dirt, filth; (*tache etc*) dirt *no pl*, something dirty, dirty mark; (*fig: tour*) filthy trick; (*: chose sans valeur*) rubbish *no pl*; (*: obscénité*) filth *no pl*; (*: microbe etc*) bug; **vivre dans la** ~ to live in squalor.

salière [saljɛʀ] *nf* saltcellar.

saligaud [saligo] *nm* (*fam!*) bastard (*!*), sod (*!*).

salin, e [salɛ̃, -in] *adj* saline ♦ *nf* saltworks *sg.*

salinité [salinite] *nf* salinity, salt-content.

salir [saliʀ] *vt* to (make) dirty; (*fig*) to soil the reputation of; **se** ~ to get dirty.

salissant, e [salisɑ̃, -ɑ̃t] *adj* (*tissu*) which shows the dirt; (*métier*) dirty, messy.

salissure [salisyʀ] *nf* dirt *no pl*; (*tache*) dirty mark.

salive [saliv] *nf* saliva.

saliver [salive] *vi* to salivate.

salle [sal] *nf* room; (*d'hôpital*) ward; (*de restaurant*) dining room; (*d'un cinéma*) auditorium; (*: public*) audience; **faire** ~ **comble** to have a full house; ~ **d'armes** (*pour l'escrime*) arms room; ~ **d'attente** waiting room; ~ **de bain(s)** bathroom; ~ **de bal** ballroom; ~ **de cinéma** cinema; ~ **de classe** classroom; ~ **commune** (*d'hôpital*) ward; ~ **de concert** concert hall; ~ **de consultation** consulting room (*BRIT*), office (*US*); ~ **de danse** dance hall; ~ **de douches** shower-room; ~ **d'eau** shower-room; ~ **d'embarquement** (*à l'aéroport*) departure lounge; ~ **d'exposition** showroom; ~ **de jeux** games room; playroom; ~ **des machines** engine room; ~ **à manger** dining room; (*mobilier*) dining room suite; ~ **obscure** cinema (*BRIT*), movie theater (*US*); ~ **d'opération** (*d'hôpital*) operating theatre; ~ **de projection** film theatre; ~ **de séjour** living room; ~ **de spectacle** theatre; cinema; ~ **des ventes** saleroom.

salmonellose [salmɔneloz] *nf* (*MÉD*) salmonella poisoning.

Salomon [salɔmɔ̃]: **les îles** ~ the Solomon Islands.

salon [salɔ̃] *nm* lounge, sitting room; (*mobilier*) lounge suite; (*exposition*) exhibition, show; (*mondain, littéraire*) salon; ~ **de coiffure** hairdressing salon; ~ **de thé** tearoom.

salopard [salɔpaʀ] *nm* (*fam!*) bastard (*!*).

salope [salɔp] *nf* (*fam!*) bitch (*!*).

saloper [salɔpe] *vt* (*fam!*) to muck up, mess up.

saloperie [salɔpʀi] *nf* (*fam!*) filth *no pl*; dirty trick; rubbish *no pl*.

salopette [salɔpɛt] *nf* dungarees *pl*; (*d'ouvrier*) overall(s).

salpêtre [salpɛtʀ(ə)] *nm* saltpetre.

salsifis [salsifi] *nm* salsify, oyster plant.

SALT [salt] *sigle* (= *Strategic Arms Limitation Talks ou Treaty*) SALT.

saltimbanque [saltɛ̃bɑ̃k] *nm/f* (travelling) acrobat.

salubre [salybʀ(ə)] *adj* healthy, salubrious.

salubrité [salybʀite] *nf* healthiness, salubrity; ~ **publique** public health.

saluer [salɥe] *vt* (*pour dire bonjour, fig*) to greet; (*pour dire au revoir*) to take one's leave; (*MIL*) to salute.

salut [saly] *nm* (*sauvegarde*) safety; (*REL*) salvation; (*geste*) wave; (*parole*) greeting; (*MIL*) salute ♦ *excl* (*fam: pour dire bonjour*) hi (there); (: *pour dire au revoir*) see you!, bye!; (*style relevé*) (all) hail.

salutaire [salytɛʀ] *adj* (*remède*) beneficial; (*conseils*) salutary.

salutations [salytɑsjɔ̃] *nfpl* greetings; **recevez mes ~ distinguées** *ou* **respectueuses** yours faithfully.

salutiste [salytist(ə)] *nm/f* Salvationist.

Salvador [salvadɔʀ] *nm*: **le ~** El Salvador.

salve [salv(ə)] *nf* salvo; volley of shots; ~ **d'applaudissements** burst of applause.

Samarie [samaʀi] *nf*: **la ~** Samaria.

samaritain [samaʀitɛ̃] *nm*: **le bon S~** the Good Samaritan.

samedi [samdi] *nm* Saturday; *voir aussi* **lundi**.

Samoa [samɔa] *nfpl*: **les (îles) ~** Samoa, the Samoa Islands.

SAMU [samy] *sigle m* (= *service d'assistance médicale d'urgence*) ≈ ambulance (service) (*BRIT*), ≈ paramedics (*US*).

sanatorium [sanatɔʀjɔm] *nm* sanatorium (*pl* -a).

sanctifier [sɑ̃ktifje] *vt* to sanctify.

sanction [sɑ̃ksjɔ̃] *nf* sanction; (*fig*) penalty; **prendre des ~s contre** to impose sanctions on.

sanctionner [sɑ̃ksjɔne] *vt* (*loi, usage*) to sanction; (*punir*) to punish.

sanctuaire [sɑ̃ktɥɛʀ] *nm* sanctuary.

sandale [sɑ̃dal] *nf* sandal.

sandalette [sɑ̃dalɛt] *nf* sandal.

sandow [sɑ̃do] *nm* ® luggage elastic.

sandwich [sɑ̃dwitʃ] *nm* sandwich; **pris en ~** sandwiched.

sang [sɑ̃] *nm* blood; **en ~** covered in blood; **jusqu'au ~** (*mordre, pincer*) till the blood comes; **se faire du mauvais ~** to fret, get in a state.

sang-froid [sɑ̃fʀwa] *nm* calm, sangfroid; **garder/perdre/reprendre son ~** to keep/lose/regain one's cool; **de ~** in cold blood.

sanglant, e [sɑ̃glɑ̃, -ɑ̃t] *adj* bloody, covered in blood; (*combat*) bloody; (*fig: reproche, affront*) cruel.

sangle [sɑ̃gl(ə)] *nf* strap; ~**s** *nfpl* (*pour lit etc*) webbing *sg*.

sangler [sɑ̃gle] *vt* to strap up; (*animal*) to girth.

sanglier [sɑ̃glije] *nm* (wild) boar.

sanglot [sɑ̃glo] *nm* sob.

sangloter [sɑ̃glɔte] *vi* to sob.

sangsue [sɑ̃sy] *nf* leech.

sanguin, e [sɑ̃gɛ̃, -in] *adj* blood *cpd*; (*fig*) fiery ♦ *nf* blood orange; (*ART*) red pencil drawing.

sanguinaire [sɑ̃ginɛʀ] *adj* (*animal, personne*) bloodthirsty; (*lutte*) bloody.

sanguinolent, e [sɑ̃ginɔlɑ̃, -ɑ̃t] *adj* streaked with blood.

Sanisette [sanizɛt] *nf* ® coin-operated public lavatory.

sanitaire [sanitɛʀ] *adj* health *cpd*; ~**s** *nmpl* (*salle de bain et w.-c.*) bathroom *sg*; **installation/appareil ~** bathroom plumbing/appliance.

sans [sɑ̃] *prép* without; ~ **qu'il s'en aperçoive** without him *ou* his noticing; ~ **scrupules** unscrupulous; ~ **manches** sleeveless.

sans-abri [sɑ̃zabʀi] *nmpl* homeless.

sans-emploi [sɑ̃zɑ̃plwa] *nmpl* jobless.

sans-façon [sɑ̃fasɔ̃] *adj inv* fuss-free; free and easy.

sans-gêne [sɑ̃ʒɛn] *adj inv* inconsiderate ♦ *nm inv* (*attitude*) lack of consideration.

sans-logis [sɑ̃lɔʒi] *nmpl* homeless.

sans-souci [sɑ̃susi] *adj inv* carefree.

sans-travail [sɑ̃tʀavaj] *nmpl* unemployed, jobless.

santal [sɑ̃tal] *nm* sandal(wood).

santé [sɑ̃te] *nf* health; **avoir une ~ de fer** to be bursting with health; **être en bonne ~** to be in good health, be healthy; **boire à la ~ de qn** to drink (to) sb's health; **"à la ~ de"** "here's to"; **à ta** *ou* **votre ~!** cheers!; **service de ~** (*dans un port etc*) quarantine service; **la ~ publique** public health.

Santiago (du Chili) [sɑ̃tjago(dyʃili)] *n* Santiago (de Chile).

santon [sɑ̃tɔ̃] *nm* ornamental figure at a Christmas crib.

saoudien, ne [saudjɛ̃, -ɛn] *adj* Saudi (Arabian) ♦ *nm/f*: **S~, ne** Saudi (Arabian).

saoul, e [su, sul] *adj* = **soûl, e**.

sape [sap] *nf*: **travail de ~** (*MIL*) sap; (*fig*) insidious undermining process *ou* work; ~**s** *nfpl* (*fam*) gear *sg*, togs.

saper [sape] *vt* to undermine, sap; **se ~** *vi* (*fam*) to dress.

sapeur [sapœʀ] *nm* sapper.

sapeur-pompier [sapœʀpɔ̃pje] *nm* fireman.

saphir [safiʀ] *nm* sapphire; (*d'électrophone*) needle, sapphire.

sapin [sapɛ̃] *nm* fir (tree); (*bois*) fir; ~ **de Noël** Christmas tree.

sapinière [sapinjɛʀ] *nf* fir plantation *ou* forest.

SAR *sigle f* (= *Son Altesse Royale*) HRH.

sarabande [saʀabɑ̃d] *nf* saraband; (*fig*) hullabaloo; whirl.

sarbacane [saʀbakan] *nf* blowpipe, blowgun; (*jouet*) peashooter.

sarcasme [saʀkasm(ə)] *nm* sarcasm no *pl*; (*propos*) piece of sarcasm.

sarcastique [saʀkastik] *adj* sarcastic.

sarcastiquement [saʀkastikmɑ̃] *adv* sarcastically.

sarclage [saʀklaʒ] nm weeding.
sarcler [saʀkle] vt to weed.
sarcloir [saʀklwaʀ] nm (weeding) hoe, spud.
sarcophage [saʀkɔfaʒ] nm sarcophagus (pl -i).
Sardaigne [saʀdɛɲ] nf: **la ~** Sardinia.
sarde [saʀd(ə)] adj Sardinian.
sardine [saʀdin] nf sardine; **~s à l'huile** sardines in oil.
sardinerie [saʀdinʀi] nf sardine cannery.
sardinier, ière [saʀdinje, -jɛʀ] adj (pêche, industrie) sardine cpd ♦ nm (bateau) sardine boat.
sardonique [saʀdɔnik] adj sardonic.
sari [saʀi] nm sari.
SARL [saʀl] sigle f = **société à responsabilité limitée**.
sarment [saʀmɑ̃] nm: **~ (de vigne)** vine shoot.
sarrasin [saʀazɛ̃] nm buckwheat.
sarrau [saʀo] nm smock.
Sarre [saʀ] nf: **la ~** the Saar.
sarriette [saʀjɛt] nf savory.
sarrois, e [saʀwa, -waz] adj Saar cpd ♦ nm/f: **S~, e** inhabitant ou native of the Saar.
sas [sas] nm (de sous-marin, d'engin spatial) airlock; (d'écluse) lock.
satané, e [satane] adj (fam) confounded.
satanique [satanik] adj satanic, fiendish.
satelliser [satelize] vt (fusée) to put into orbit; (fig: pays) to make into a satellite.
satellite [satelit] nm satellite; **pays ~** satellite country.
satellite-espion, pl **satellites-espions** [satelitɛspjɔ̃] nm spy satellite.
satellite-observatoire, pl **satellites-observatoires** [satelitɔpsɛʀvatwaʀ] nm observation satellite.
satellite-relais, pl **satellites-relais** [satelitʀəlɛ] nm (TV) relay satellite.
satiété [sasjete] nf: **à ~** adv to satiety ou satiation; (répéter) ad nauseam.
satin [satɛ̃] nm satin.
satiné, e [satine] adj satiny; (peau) satin-smooth.
satinette [satinɛt] nf satinet, sateen.
satire [satiʀ] nf satire; **faire la ~** to satirize.
satirique [satiʀik] adj satirical.
satiriser [satiʀize] vt to satirize.
satiriste [satiʀist(ə)] nm/f satirist.
satisfaction [satisfaksjɔ̃] nf satisfaction; **à ma grande ~** to my great satisfaction; **obtenir ~** to obtain ou get satisfaction; **donner ~ (à)** to give satisfaction (to).
satisfaire [satisfɛʀ] vt to satisfy; **se ~ de** to be satisfied ou content with; **~ à** vt (engagement) to fulfil; (revendications, conditions) to satisfy, meet.
satisfaisant, e [satisfəzɑ̃, -ɑ̃t] vb voir **satisfaire** ♦ adj satisfactory; (qui fait plaisir) satisfying.
satisfait, e [satisfɛ, -ɛt] pp de **satisfaire** ♦ adj satisfied; **~ de** happy ou satisfied with.
satisfasse [satisfas], **satisferai** [satisfʀe] etc vb voir **satisfaire**.
saturation [satyʀasjɔ̃] nf saturation; **arriver à ~** to reach saturation point.
saturer [satyʀe] vt to saturate; **~ qn/qch de** to saturate sb/sth with.
saturnisme [satyʀnism(ə)] nm (MÉD) lead poisoning.
satyre [satiʀ] nm satyr; (péj) lecher.
sauce [sos] nf sauce; (avec un rôti) gravy; **en ~** in a sauce; **~ blanche** white sauce; **~ chasseur** sauce chasseur; **~ tomate** tomato sauce.
saucer [sose] vt (assiette) to soak up the sauce from.
saucière [sosjɛʀ] nf sauceboat; gravy boat.
saucisse [sosis] nf sausage.
saucisson [sosisɔ̃] nm (slicing) sausage; **~ à l'ail** garlic sausage.
saucissonner [sosisɔne] vt to cut up, slice ♦ vi to picnic.
sauf [sof] prép except; **~ si** (à moins que) unless; **~ avis contraire** unless you hear to the contrary; **~ empêchement** barring (any) problems; **~ erreur** if I'm not mistaken; **~ imprévu** unless anything unforeseen arises, barring accidents.
sauf, sauve [sof, sov] adj unharmed, unhurt; (fig: honneur) intact, saved; **laisser la vie sauve à qn** to spare sb's life.
sauf-conduit [sofkɔ̃dɥi] nm safe-conduct.
sauge [soʒ] nf sage.
saugrenu, e [sogʀəny] adj preposterous, ludicrous.
saule [sol] nm willow (tree); **~ pleureur** weeping willow.
saumâtre [somɑtʀ(ə)] adj briny; (désagréable: plaisanterie) unsavoury (BRIT), unsavory (US).
saumon [somɔ̃] nm salmon inv ♦ adj inv salmon (pink).
saumoné, e [somɔne] adj: **truite ~e** salmon trout.
saumure [somyʀ] nf brine.
sauna [sona] nm sauna.
saupoudrer [sopudʀe] vt: **~ qch de** to sprinkle sth with.
saupoudreuse [sopudʀøz] nf dredger.
saur [sɔʀ] adj m: **hareng ~** smoked ou red herring, kipper.
saurai [sɔʀe] etc vb voir **savoir**.
saut [so] nm jump; (discipline sportive) jumping; **faire un ~** to (make a) jump ou leap; **faire un ~ chez qn** to pop over to sb's (place); **au ~ du lit** on getting out of bed; **~ en hauteur/longueur** high/long jump; **~ à la corde** skipping; **~ de page** (INFORM) page break; **~ en parachute** parachuting no pl; **~ à la perche** pole vaulting; **~ à l'élastique** bungee jumping; **~ périlleux** somersault.
saute [sot] nf: **~ de vent/température** sudden change of wind direction/in the temperature; **avoir des ~s d'humeur** to have sudden changes of mood.
sauté, e [sote] adj (CULIN) sauté ♦ nm: **~ de**

veau sauté of veal.

saute-mouton [sotmutɔ̃] *nm*: **jouer à** ~ to play leapfrog.

sauter [sote] *vi* to jump, leap; (*exploser*) to blow up, explode; (: *fusibles*) to blow; (*se rompre*) to snap, burst; (*se détacher*) to pop out (*ou* off) ♦ *vt* to jump (over), leap (over); (*fig: omettre*) to skip, miss (out); **faire** ~ to blow up; to burst open; (*CULIN*) to sauté; ~ **à pieds joints/à cloche-pied** to make a standing jump/to hop; ~ **en parachute** to make a parachute jump; ~ **à la corde** to skip; ~ **de joie** to jump for joy; ~ **de colère** to be hopping with rage *ou* hopping mad; ~ **au cou de qn** to fly into sb's arms; ~ **aux yeux** to be quite obvious; ~ **au plafond** (*fig*) to hit the roof.

sauterelle [sotʀɛl] *nf* grasshopper.

sauterie [sotʀi] *nf* party, hop.

sauteur, euse [sotœʀ, -øz] *nm/f* (*athlète*) jumper ♦ *nf* (*casserole*) shallow pan, frying pan; ~ **à la perche** pole vaulter; ~ **à skis** skijumper.

sautillement [sotijmɑ̃] *nm* hopping; skipping.

sautiller [sotije] *vi* to hop; to skip.

sautoir [sotwaʀ] *nm* chain; (*SPORT: emplacement*) jumping pit; ~ **(de perles)** string of pearls.

sauvage [sovaʒ] *adj* (*gén*) wild; (*peuplade*) savage; (*farouche*) unsociable; (*barbare*) wild, savage; (*non officiel*) unauthorized, unofficial ♦ *nm/f* savage; (*timide*) unsociable type, recluse.

sauvagement [sovaʒmɑ̃] *adv* savagely.

sauvageon, ne [sovaʒɔ̃, -ɔn] *nm/f* little savage.

sauvagerie [sovaʒʀi] *nf* wildness; savagery; unsociability.

sauve [sov] *adj f voir* **sauf**.

sauvegarde [sovgaʀd(ə)] *nf* safeguard; **sous la** ~ **de** under the protection of; **disquette/ fichier de** ~ (*INFORM*) backup disk/file.

sauvegarder [sovgaʀde] *vt* to safeguard; (*IN-FORM: enregistrer*) to save; (: *copier*) to back up.

sauve-qui-peut [sovkipø] *nm inv* stampede, mad rush ♦ *excl* run for your life!

sauver [sove] *vt* to save; (*porter secours à*) to rescue; (*récupérer*) to salvage, rescue; **se** ~ *vi* (*s'enfuir*) to run away; (*fam: partir*) to be off; ~ **qn de** to save sb from; ~ **la vie à qn** to save sb's life; ~ **les apparences** to keep up appearances.

sauvetage [sovtaʒ] *nm* rescue; ~ **en montagne** mountain rescue; **ceinture de** ~ lifebelt (*BRIT*), life preserver (*US*); **brassière** *ou* **gilet de** ~ lifejacket (*BRIT*), life preserver (*US*).

sauveteur [sovtœʀ] *nm* rescuer.

sauvette [sovɛt]: **à la** ~ *adv* (*vendre*) without authorization; (*se marier etc*) hastily, hurriedly; **vente à la** ~ (unauthorized) street trading, (street) peddling.

sauveur [sovœʀ] *nm* saviour (*BRIT*), savior (*US*).

SAV *sigle m* = **service après-vente**.

savais [save] *etc vb voir* **savoir**.

savamment [savamɑ̃] *adv* (*avec érudition*) learnedly; (*habilement*) skilfully, cleverly.

savane [savan] *nf* savannah.

savant, e [savɑ̃, -ɑ̃t] *adj* scholarly, learned; (*calé*) clever ♦ *nm* scientist; **animal** ~ performing animal.

savate [savat] *nf* worn-out shoe; (*SPORT*) French boxing.

saveur [savœʀ] *nf* flavour (*BRIT*), flavor (*US*); (*fig*) savour (*BRIT*), savor (*US*).

Savoie [savwa] *nf*: **la** ~ Savoy.

savoir [savwaʀ] *vt* to know; (*être capable de*): **il sait nager** he knows how to swim, he can swim ♦ *nm* knowledge; **se** ~ (*être connu*) to be known; **se** ~ **malade/incurable** to know that one is ill/incurably ill; **il est petit: tu ne peux pas** ~! you won't believe how small he is!; **vous n'êtes pas sans** ~ **que** you are not *ou* will not be unaware of the fact that; **je crois** ~ **que** ... I believe that ..., I think I know that ...; **je n'en sais rien** I (really) don't know; **à** ~ **(que)** that is, namely; **faire** ~ **qch à qn** to inform sb about sth, let sb know sth; **pas que je sache** not as far as I know; **sans le** ~ *adv* unknowingly, unwittingly; **en** ~ **long** to know a lot.

savoir-faire [savwaʀfɛʀ] *nm inv* savoir-faire, know-how.

savoir-vivre [savwaʀvivʀ(ə)] *nm inv*: **le** ~ savoir-faire, good manners *pl*.

savon [savɔ̃] *nm* (*produit*) soap; (*morceau*) bar *ou* tablet of soap; (*fam*): **passer un** ~ **à qn** to give sb a good dressing-down.

savonner [savone] *vt* to soap.

savonnerie [savonʀi] *nf* soap factory.

savonnette [savonɛt] *nf* bar *ou* tablet of soap.

savonneux, euse [savonø, -øz] *adj* soapy.

savons [savɔ̃] *vb voir* **savoir**.

savourer [savuʀe] *vt* to savour (*BRIT*), savor (*US*).

savoureux, euse [savuʀø, -øz] *adj* tasty; (*fig*) spicy, juicy.

savoyard, e [savwajaʀ, -aʀd(ə)] *adj* Savoyard.

Saxe [saks(ə)] *nf*: **la** ~ Saxony.

saxo(phone) [saksɔ(fɔn)] *nm* sax(ophone).

saxophoniste [saksɔfɔnist(ə)] *nm/f* saxophonist, sax(ophone) player.

saynète [sɛnɛt] *nf* playlet.

SBB *sigle f* (= *Schweizerische Bundesbahn*) *Swiss federal railways*.

sbire [sbiʀ] *nm* (*péj*) henchman.

sc. *abr* = **scène**.

s/c *abr* (= *sous couvert de*) ≈ c/o.

scabreux, euse [skabʀø, -øz] *adj* risky; (*indécent*) improper, shocking.

scalpel [skalpɛl] *nm* scalpel.

scalper [skalpe] *vt* to scalp.

scampi [skɑ̃pi] *nmpl* scampi.
scandale [skɑ̃dal] *nm* scandal; (*tapage*): **faire du ~** to make a scene, create a disturbance; **faire ~** to scandalize people; **au grand ~ de** ... to the great indignation of ....
scandaleusement [skɑ̃daløzmɑ̃] *adv* scandalously, outrageously.
scandaleux, euse [skɑ̃dalø, -øz] *adj* scandalous, outrageous.
scandaliser [skɑ̃dalize] *vt* to scandalize; **se ~ (de)** to be scandalized (by).
scander [skɑ̃de] *vt* (*vers*) to scan; (*mots, syllabes*) to stress separately; (*slogans*) to chant.
scandinave [skɑ̃dinav] *adj* Scandinavian ♦ *nm/f*: **S~** Scandinavian.
Scandinavie [skɑ̃dinavi] *nf*: **la ~** Scandinavia.
scanner [skanɛʀ] *nm* (*MÉD*) scanner.
scanographie [skanɔgʀafi] *nf* (*MÉD*) scanning; (*image*) scan.
scaphandre [skafɑ̃dʀ(ə)] *nm* (*de plongeur*) diving suit; (*de cosmonaute*) space-suit; **~ autonome** aqualung.
scaphandrier [skafɑ̃dʀije] *nm* diver.
scarabée [skaʀabe] *nm* beetle.
scarlatine [skaʀlatin] *nf* scarlet fever.
scarole [skaʀɔl] *nf* endive.
scatologique [skatɔlɔʒik] *adj* scatological, lavatorial.
sceau, x [so] *nm* seal; (*fig*) stamp, mark; **sous le ~ du secret** under the seal of secrecy.
scélérat, e [seleʀa, -at] *nm/f* villain, blackguard ♦ *adj* villainous, blackguardly.
sceller [sele] *vt* to seal.
scellés [sele] *nmpl* seals.
scénario [senaʀjo] *nm* (*CINÉ*) screenplay, script; (*: idée, plan*) scenario; (*fig*) pattern; scenario.
scénariste [senaʀist(ə)] *nm/f* scriptwriter.
scène [sɛn] *nf* (*gén*) scene; (*estrade, fig: théâtre*) stage; **entrer en ~** to come on stage; **mettre en ~** (*THÉÂT*) to stage; (*CINÉ*) to direct; (*fig*) to present, introduce; **sur le devant de la ~** (*en pleine actualité*) in the forefront; **porter à la ~** to adapt for the stage; **faire une ~ (à qn)** to make a scene (with sb); **~ de ménage** domestic fight *ou* scene.
scénique [senik] *adj* (*effets*) theatrical; (*art*) scenic.
scepticisme [sɛptisism(ə)] *nm* scepticism.
sceptique [sɛptik] *adj* sceptical ♦ *nm/f* sceptic.
sceptre [sɛptʀ(ə)] *nm* sceptre.
schéma [ʃema] *nm* (*diagramme*) diagram, sketch; (*fig*) outline.
schématique [ʃematik] *adj* diagrammatic(al), schematic; (*fig*) oversimplified.
schématiquement [ʃematikmɑ̃] *adv* schematically, diagrammatically.
schématisation [ʃematizasjɔ̃] *nf* schematization; oversimplification.
schématiser [ʃematize] *vt* to schematize; to (over)simplify.

schismatique [ʃismatik] *adj* schismatic.
schisme [ʃism(ə)] *nm* schism; rift, split.
schiste [ʃist(ə)] *nm* schist.
schizophrène [skizɔfʀɛn] *nm/f* schizophrenic.
schizophrénie [skizɔfʀeni] *nf* schizophrenia.
sciatique [sjatik] *adj*: **nerf ~** sciatic nerve ♦ *nf* sciatica.
scie [si] *nf* saw; (*fam: rengaine*) catch-tune; (*: personne*) bore; **~ à bois** wood saw; **~ circulaire** circular saw; **~ à découper** fretsaw; **~ à métaux** hacksaw; **~ sauteuse** jigsaw.
sciemment [sjamɑ̃] *adv* knowingly, wittingly.
science [sjɑ̃s] *nf* science; (*savoir*) knowledge; (*savoir-faire*) art, skill; **~s humaines/sociales** social sciences; **~s naturelles** natural science *sg*, biology *sg*; **~s po** political studies.
science-fiction [sjɑ̃sfiksjɔ̃] *nf* science fiction.
scientifique [sjɑ̃tifik] *adj* scientific ♦ *nm/f* (*savant*) scientist; (*étudiant*) science student.
scientifiquement [sjɑ̃tifikmɑ̃] *adv* scientifically.
scier [sje] *vt* to saw; (*retrancher*) to saw off.
scierie [siʀi] *nf* sawmill.
scieur [sjœʀ] *nm*: **~ de long** pit sawyer.
Scilly [sili]: **les îles ~** the Scilly Isles, the Scillies, the Isles of Scilly.
scinder [sɛ̃de] *vt*, **se ~** *vi* to split (up).
scintillant, e [sɛ̃tijɑ̃, -ɑ̃t] *adj* sparkling.
scintillement [sɛ̃tijmɑ̃] *nm* sparkling *no pl*.
scintiller [sɛ̃tije] *vi* to sparkle.
scission [sisjɔ̃] *nf* split.
sciure [sjyʀ] *nf*: **~ (de bois)** sawdust.
sclérose [skleʀoz] *nf* sclerosis; (*fig*) ossification; **~ en plaques (SEP)** multiple sclerosis (MS).
sclérosé, e [skleʀoze] *adj* sclerosed, sclerotic; ossified.
scléroser [skleʀoze]: **se ~** *vi* to become sclerosed; (*fig*) to become ossified.
scolaire [skɔlɛʀ] *adj* school *cpd*; (*péj*) schoolish; **l'année ~** the school year; (*à l'université*) the academic year; **en âge ~** of school age.
scolarisation [skɔlaʀizasjɔ̃] *nf* (*d'un enfant*) schooling; **la ~ d'une région** the provision of schooling in a region; **le taux de ~** the proportion of children in full-time education.
scolariser [skɔlaʀize] *vt* to provide with schooling (*ou* schools).
scolarité [skɔlaʀite] *nf* schooling; **frais de ~** school fees (*BRIT*), tuition (*US*).
scolastique [skɔlastik] *adj* (*péj*) scholastic.
scoliose [skɔljoz] *nf* curvature of the spine, scoliosis.
scoop [skup] *nm* (*PRESSE*) scoop, exclusive.
scooter [skutœʀ] *nm* (motor) scooter.
scorbut [skɔʀbyt] *nm* scurvy.
score [skɔʀ] *nm* score; (*électoral etc*) result.
scories [skɔʀi] *nfpl* scoria *pl*.
scorpion [skɔʀpjɔ̃] *nm* (*signe*): **le S~** Scorpio, the Scorpion; **être du S~** to be Scorpio.
scotch [skɔtʃ] *nm* (*whisky*) scotch, whisky; (*ad-*

hésif) Sellotape ® (*BRIT*), Scotch tape ® (*US*).

scotcher [skɔtʃe] *vt* to sellotape ® (*BRIT*), scotchtape ® (*US*).

scout, e [skut] *adj, nm* scout.

scoutisme [skutism(ə)] *nm* (boy) scout movement; (*activités*) scouting.

scribe [skʀib] *nm* scribe; (*péj*) penpusher.

scribouillard [skʀibujaʀ] *nm* penpusher.

script [skʀipt(ə)] *nm* printing; (*CINÉ*) (shooting) script.

scripte [skʀipt(ə)] *nf* continuity girl.

script-girl [skʀiptgœʀl] *nf* continuity girl.

scriptural, e, aux [skʀiptyʀal, -o] *adj*: monnaie ~e bank money.

scrupule [skʀypyl] *nm* scruple; être sans ~s to be unscrupulous; se faire un ~ de qch to have scruples *ou* qualms about doing sth.

scrupuleusement [skʀypyløzmɑ̃] *adv* scrupulously.

scrupuleux, euse [skʀypylø, -øz] *adj* scrupulous.

scrutateur, trice [skʀytatœʀ, -tʀis] *adj* searching ♦ *nm/f* scrutineer.

scruter [skʀyte] *vt* to search, scrutinize; (*l'obscurité*) to peer into; (*motifs, comportement*) to examine, scrutinize.

scrutin [skʀytɛ̃] *nm* (*vote*) ballot; (*ensemble des opérations*) poll; ~ **proportionnel/majoritaire** election on a proportional/majority basis; ~ **à deux tours** poll with two ballots *ou* rounds; ~ **de liste** list system.

sculpter [skylte] *vt* to sculpt; (*suj: érosion*) to carve.

sculpteur [skyltœʀ] *nm* sculptor.

sculptural, e, aux [skyltyʀal, -o] *adj* sculptural; (*fig*) statuesque.

sculpture [skyltyʀ] *nf* sculpture; ~ **sur bois** wood carving.

sdb. *abr* = **salle de bain**.

S.D.F. *sigle m* (= *sans domicile fixe*) homeless person; les ~ the homeless.

SDN *sigle f* (= *Société des Nations*) League of Nations.

SE *sigle f* (= *Son Excellence*) HE.

═══════════════════════ *MOT-CLÉ*

se (s') [s(ə)] *pron* **1** (*emploi réfléchi*) oneself; (: *masc*) himself; (: *fém*) herself; (: *sujet non humain*) itself; (: *pl*) themselves; **se voir comme l'on est** to see o.s. as one is

2 (*réciproque*) one another, each other; **ils s'aiment** they love one another *ou* each other

3 (*passif*): **cela se répare facilement** it is easily repaired

4 (*possessif*): **se casser la jambe/laver les mains** to break one's leg/wash one's hands.

séance [seɑ̃s] *nf* (*d'assemblée, récréative*) meeting, session; (*de tribunal*) sitting, session; (*musicale, CINÉ, THÉÂT*) performance; **ouvrir/lever la** ~ to open/close the meeting; ~ **te-**

nante forthwith.

séant, e [seɑ̃, -ɑ̃t] *adj* seemly, fitting ♦ *nm* posterior.

seau, x [so] *nm* bucket, pail; ~ **à glace** ice bucket.

sébum [sebɔm] *nm* sebum.

sec, sèche [sɛk, sɛʃ] *adj* dry; (*raisins, figues*) dried; (*cœur, personne: insensible*) hard, cold; (*maigre, décharné*) spare, lean; (*réponse, ton*) sharp, curt; (*démarrage*) sharp, sudden ♦ *nm*: **tenir au** ~ to keep in a dry place ♦ *adv* hard; (*démarrer*) sharply; **boire** ~ to be a heavy drinker; **je le bois** ~ I drink it straight *ou* neat; **à pied** ~ without getting one's feet wet; **à** ~ *adj* dried up; (*à court d'argent*) broke.

SECAM [sekam] *sigle m* (= *procédé séquentiel à mémoire*) SECAM.

sécante [sekɑ̃t] *nf* secant.

sécateur [sekatœʀ] *nm* secateurs *pl* (*BRIT*), shears *pl*, pair of secateurs *ou* shears.

sécession [sesesjɔ̃] *nf*: **faire** ~ to secede; **la guerre de S**~ the American Civil War.

séchage [seʃaʒ] *nm* drying; (*de bois*) seasoning.

sèche [sɛʃ] *adj f voir* **sec** ♦ *nf* (*fam*) cigarette, fag (*BRIT*).

sèche-cheveux [sɛʃʃəvø] *nm inv* hair-drier.

sèche-linge [sɛʃlɛ̃ʒ] *nm inv* drying cabinet.

sèche-mains [sɛʃmɛ̃] *nm inv* hand drier.

sèchement [sɛʃmɑ̃] *adv* (*frapper etc*) sharply; (*répliquer etc*) drily, sharply.

sécher [seʃe] *vt* to dry; (*dessécher: peau, blé*) to dry (out); (: *étang*) to dry up; (*bois*) to season; (*fam: classe, cours*) to skip, miss ♦ *vi* to dry; to dry out; to dry up; (*fam: candidat*) to be stumped; **se** ~ (*après le bain*) to dry o.s.

sécheresse [seʃʀɛs] *nf* dryness; (*absence de pluie*) drought.

séchoir [seʃwaʀ] *nm* drier.

second, e [s(ə)gɔ̃, -ɔ̃d] *adj* second ♦ *nm* (*assistant*) second in command; (*étage*) second floor (*BRIT*), third floor (*US*); (*NAVIG*) first mate ♦ *nf* second; (*SCOL*) ≈ fifth form (*BRIT*), ≈ tenth grade (*US*); **en** ~ (*en second rang*) in second place; **voyager en** ~e to travel second-class; **doué de** ~e **vue** having (the gift of) second sight; **trouver son** ~ **souffle** (*SPORT, fig*) to get one's second wind; **être dans un état** ~ to be in a daze (*ou* trance); **de** ~e **main** second-hand.

secondaire [s(ə)gɔ̃dɛʀ] *adj* secondary.

seconder [s(ə)gɔ̃de] *vt* to assist; (*favoriser*) to back.

secouer [s(ə)kwe] *vt* to shake; (*passagers*) to rock; (*traumatiser*) to shake (up); **se** ~ (*chien*) to shake itself; (*fam: se démener*) to shake o.s. up; ~ **la poussière d'un tapis** to shake the dust off a carpet; ~ **la tête** to shake one's head.

secourable [s(ə)kuʀabl(ə)] *adj* helpful.

secourir [s(ə)kuʀiʀ] *vt* (*aller sauver*) to (go and)

rescue; (*prodiguer des soins à*) to help, assist; (*venir en aide à*) to assist, aid.

secourisme [səkuʀism(ə)] *nm* (*premiers soins*) first aid; (*sauvetage*) life saving.

secouriste [səkuʀist(ə)] *nm/f* first-aid worker.

secourons [səkuʀɔ̃] *etc vb voir* **secourir**.

secours [səkuʀ] *vb voir* **secourir** ♦ *nm* help, aid, assistance ♦ *nmpl* aid *sg*; **cela lui a été d'un grand** ~ this was a great help to him; **au** ~! help!; **appeler au** ~ to shout *ou* call for help; **appeler qn à son** ~ to call sb to one's assistance; **porter** ~ **à qn** to give sb assistance, help sb; **les premiers** ~ first aid *sg*; **le** ~ **en montagne** mountain rescue.

secouru, e [səkuʀy] *pp de* **secourir**.

secousse [səkus] *nf* jolt, bump; (*électrique*) shock; (*fig: psychologique*) jolt, shock; ~ **sismique** *ou* **tellurique** earth tremor.

secret, ète [səkʀɛ, -ɛt] *adj* secret; (*fig: renfermé*) reticent, reserved ♦ *nm* secret; (*discrétion absolue*): **le** ~ secrecy; **en** ~ in secret, secretly; **au** ~ in solitary confinement; ~ **de fabrication** trade secret; ~ **professionnel** professional secrecy.

secrétaire [səkʀetɛʀ] *nm/f* secretary ♦ *nm* (*meuble*) writing desk, secretaire; ~ **d'ambassade** embassy secretary; ~ **de direction** private *ou* personal secretary; ~ **d'État** ≈ junior minister; ~ **général (SG)** Secretary-General; (*COMM*) company secretary; ~ **de mairie** town clerk; ~ **médicale** medical secretary; ~ **de rédaction** subeditor.

secrétariat [s(ə)kʀetaʀja] *nm* (*profession*) secretarial work; (*bureau: d'entreprise, d'école*) (secretary's) office; (*: d'organisation internationale*) secretariat; (*POL etc: fonction*) secretaryship, office of Secretary.

secrètement [səkʀɛtmɑ̃] *adv* secretly.

sécréter [sekʀete] *vt* to secrete.

sécrétion [sekʀesjɔ̃] *nf* secretion.

sectaire [sɛktɛʀ] *adj* sectarian, bigoted.

sectarisme [sɛktaʀism(ə)] *nm* sectarianism.

secte [sɛkt(ə)] *nf* sect.

secteur [sɛktœʀ] *nm* sector; (*ADMIN*) district; (*ÉLEC*): **branché sur le** ~ plugged into the mains (supply); **fonctionne sur pile et** ~ battery or mains operated; **le** ~ **privé/public** (*ÉCON*) the private/public sector; **le** ~ **primaire/tertiaire** the primary/tertiary sector.

section [sɛksjɔ̃] *nf* section; (*de parcours d'autobus*) fare stage; (*MIL: unité*) platoon; ~ **rythmique** rhythm section.

sectionner [sɛksjɔne] *vt* to sever; **se** ~ *vi* to be severed.

sectionneur [sɛksjɔnœʀ] *nm* (*ÉLEC*) isolation switch.

sectoriel, le [sɛktɔʀjɛl] *adj* sector-based.

sectorisation [sɛktɔʀizasjɔ̃] *nf* division into sectors.

sectoriser [sɛktɔʀize] *vt* to divide into sectors.

sécu [seky] *nf* (*fam: = sécurité sociale*) ≈ dole (*BRIT*), ≈ Welfare (*US*).

séculaire [sekylɛʀ] *adj* secular; (*très vieux*) age-old.

séculariser [sekylaʀize] *vt* to secularize.

séculier, ière [sekylje, -jɛʀ] *adj* secular.

sécurisant, e [sekyʀizɑ̃, -ɑ̃t] *adj* secure, giving a sense of security.

sécuriser [sekyʀize] *vt* to give a sense of security to.

sécurité [sekyʀite] *nf* security; (*absence de danger*) safety; **impression de** ~ sense of security; **la** ~ **internationale** international security; **système de** ~ security (*ou* safety) system; **être en** ~ to be safe; **la** ~ **de l'emploi** job security; **la** ~ **routière** road safety; **la** ~ **sociale** ≈ (the) Social Security (*BRIT*), ≈ (the) Welfare (*US*).

sédatif, ive [sedatif, -iv] *adj*, *nm* sedative.

sédentaire [sedɑ̃tɛʀ] *adj* sedentary.

sédiment [sedimɑ̃] *nm* sediment; ~**s** *nmpl* (*alluvions*) sediment *sg*.

sédimentaire [sedimɑ̃tɛʀ] *adj* sedimentary.

sédimentation [sedimɑ̃tasjɔ̃] *nf* sedimentation.

séditieux, euse [sedisjø, -øz] *adj* insurgent; seditious.

sédition [sedisjɔ̃] *nf* insurrection; sedition.

séducteur, trice [sedyktœʀ, -tʀis] *adj* seductive ♦ *nm/f* seducer/seductress.

séduction [sedyksjɔ̃] *nf* seduction; (*charme, attrait*) appeal, charm.

séduire [seduiʀ] *vt* to charm; (*femme: abuser de*) to seduce; (*suj: chose*) to appeal to.

séduisant, e [seduizɑ̃, -ɑ̃t] *vb voir* **séduire** ♦ *adj* (*femme*) seductive; (*homme, offre*) very attractive.

séduit, e [sedui, -it] *pp de* **séduire**.

segment [sɛgmɑ̃] *nm* segment; (*AUTO*): ~ **(de piston)** piston ring; ~ **de frein** brake shoe.

segmenter [sɛgmɑ̃te] *vt*, **se** ~ *vi* to segment.

ségrégation [segʀegasjɔ̃] *nf* segregation.

ségrégationnisme [segʀegasjɔnism(ə)] *nm* segregationism.

ségrégationniste [segʀegasjɔnist(ə)] *adj* segregationist.

seiche [sɛʃ] *nf* cuttlefish.

séide [seid] *nm* (*péj*) henchman.

seigle [sɛgl(ə)] *nm* rye.

seigneur [sɛɲœʀ] *nm* lord; **le S**~ the Lord.

seigneurial, e, aux [sɛɲœʀjal, -o] *adj* lordly, stately.

sein [sɛ̃] *nm* breast; (*entrailles*) womb; **au** ~ **de** *prép* (*équipe, institution*) within; (*flots, bonheur*) in the midst of; **donner le** ~ **à** (*bébé*) to feed (at the breast); to breast-feed; **nourrir au** ~ to breast-feed.

Seine [sɛn] *nf*: **la** ~ the Seine.

séisme [seism(ə)] *nm* earthquake.

séismique *etc* [seismik] *voir* **sismique** *etc*.

SEITA [seita] *sigle f = Société d'exploitation indus-*

trielle des tabacs et allumettes.

seize [sɛz] *num* sixteen.

seizième [sɛzjɛm] *num* sixteenth.

séjour [seʒuʀ] *nm* stay; (*pièce*) living room.

séjourner [seʒuʀne] *vi* to stay.

sel [sɛl] *nm* salt; (*fig*) wit; spice; ~ **de cuisine/ de table** cooking/table salt; ~ **gemme** rock salt; ~**s de bain** bathsalts.

sélect, e [selɛkt] *adj* select.

sélectif, ive [selɛktif, -iv] *adj* selective.

sélection [selɛksjɔ̃] *nf* selection; **faire/opérer une** ~ **parmi** to make a selection from among; **épreuve de** ~ (*SPORT*) trial (for selection); ~ **naturelle** natural selection; ~ **professionnelle** professional recruitment.

sélectionné, e [selɛksjɔne] *adj* (*joueur*) selected; (*produit*) specially selected.

sélectionner [selɛksjɔne] *vt* to select.

sélectionneur, euse [selɛksjɔnœʀ, -øz] *nm/f* selector.

sélectivement [selɛktivmɑ̃] *adv* selectively.

sélectivité [selɛktivite] *nf* selectivity.

sélénologie [selenɔlɔʒi] *nf* study of the moon, selenology.

self [sɛlf] *nm* (*fam*) self-service.

self-service [sɛlfsɛʀvis] *adj* self-service ♦ *nm* self-service (restaurant); (*magasin*) self-service shop.

selle [sɛl] *nf* saddle; ~**s** *nfpl* (*MÉD*) stools; **aller à la** ~ (*MÉD*) to have a bowel movement; **se mettre en** ~ to mount, get into the saddle.

seller [sele] *vt* to saddle.

sellette [sɛlɛt] *nf*: **être sur la** ~ to be on the carpet (*fig*).

sellier [selje] *nm* saddler.

selon [səlɔ̃] *prép* according to; (*en se conformant à*) in accordance with; ~ **moi** as I see it; ~ **que** according to, depending on whether.

SEm *sigle f* (= *Son Éminence*) HE.

semailles [səmaj] *nfpl* sowing *sg*.

semaine [səmɛn] *nf* week; (*salaire*) week's wages *ou* pay, weekly wages *ou* pay; **en** ~ during the week, on weekdays; **à la petite** ~ from day to day; **la** ~ **sainte** Holy Week.

semainier [səmenje] *nm* (*bracelet*) bracelet made up of seven bands; (*calendrier*) desk diary; (*meuble*) chest of (seven) drawers.

sémantique [semɑ̃tik] *adj* semantic ♦ *nf* semantics *sg*.

sémaphore [semafɔʀ] *nm* (*RAIL*) semaphore signal.

semblable [sɑ̃blabl(ə)] *adj* similar; (*de ce genre*): **de** ~**s mésaventures** such mishaps ♦ *nm* fellow creature *ou* man; ~ **à** similar to, like.

semblant [sɑ̃blɑ̃] *nm*: **un** ~ **de vérité** a semblance of truth; **faire** ~ (**de faire**) to pretend (to do).

sembler [sɑ̃ble] *vb avec attribut* to seem ♦ *vb impers*: **il semble (bien) que/inutile de** it (really) seems *ou* appears that/useless to; **il me**

semble (bien) que it (really) seems to me that, I (really) think (that); **il me semble le connaître** I think *ou* I've a feeling I know him; ~ **être** to seem to be; **comme bon lui semble** as he sees fit; **me semble-t-il, à ce qu'il me semble** it seems to me, to my mind.

semelle [səmɛl] *nf* sole; (*intérieure*) insole, inner sole; **battre la** ~ to stamp one's feet (to keep them warm); (*fig*) to hang around (waiting); ~**s compensées** platform soles.

semence [səmɑ̃s] *nf* (*graine*) seed; (*clou*) tack.

semer [səme] *vt* to sow; (*fig: éparpiller*) to scatter; (*confusion*) to spread; (*: poursui- vants*) to lose, shake off; ~ **la discorde/terreur parmi** to sow discord/terror among; **semé de** (*difficultés*) riddled with.

semestre [səmɛstʀ(ə)] *nm* half-year; (*SCOL*) semester.

semestriel, le [səmɛstʀijɛl] *adj* half-yearly; semestral.

semeur, euse [səmœʀ, -øz] *nm/f* sower.

semi-automatique [səmiɔtɔmatik] *adj* semi-automatic.

semiconducteur [səmikɔ̃dyktœʀ] *nm* (*INFORM*) semiconductor.

semi-conserve [səmikɔ̃sɛʀv(ə)] *nf* semi-perishable foodstuff.

semi-fini [səmifini] *adj m* (*produit*) semi-finished.

semi-liberté [səmilibɛʀte] *nf* (*JUR*) partial release from prison (*in order to follow a profession or undergo medical treatment*).

sémillant, e [semijɑ̃, -ɑ̃t] *adj* vivacious; dashing.

séminaire [seminɛʀ] *nm* seminar; (*REL*) seminary.

séminariste [seminaʀist(ə)] *nm* seminarist.

sémiologie [semjɔlɔʒi] *nf* semiology.

semi-public, ique [səmipyblik] *adj* (*JUR*) semi-public.

semi-remorque [səmiʀəmɔʀk(ə)] *nf* trailer ♦ *nm* articulated lorry (*BRIT*), semi(trailer) (*US*).

semis [səmi] *nm* (*terrain*) seedbed, seed plot; (*plante*) seedling.

sémite [semit] *adj* Semitic.

sémitique [semitik] *adj* Semitic.

semoir [səmwaʀ] *nm* seed-bag; seeder.

semonce [səmɔ̃s] *nf*: **un coup de** ~ a shot across the bows.

semoule [səmul] *nf* semolina; ~ **de riz** ground rice.

sempiternel, le [sɛ̃pitɛʀnɛl] *adj* eternal, never-ending.

sénat [sena] *nm* senate.

The Sénat is the upper house of the French parliament, sitting in the Palais du Luxembourg in Paris. One third of sénateurs are elected for a nine-year term every three years by an electoral college consisting of députés and other elected representatives. The Sénat has a wide range of powers but is overridden by the **Assemblée nationale** in cases of disagreement.

sénateur [senatœʀ] nm senator.
sénatorial, e, aux [senatɔʀjal, -o] adj senatorial, Senate cpd.
Sénégal [senegal] nm: **le** ~ Senegal.
sénégalais, e [senegalɛ, -ɛz] adj Senegalese.
sénevé [sɛnve] nm (BOT) mustard; (graine) mustard seed.
sénile [senil] adj senile.
sénilité [senilite] nf senility.
senior [senjɔʀ] nm/f (SPORT) senior.
sens [sɑ̃] vb voir **sentir** ♦ nm [sɑ̃s] (PHYSIOL, instinct) sense; (signification) meaning, sense; (direction) direction, way ♦ nmpl (sensualité) senses; **reprendre ses** ~ to regain consciousness; **avoir le** ~ **des affaires/de la mesure** to have business sense/a sense of moderation; **ça n'a pas de** ~ that doesn't make (any) sense; **en dépit du bon** ~ contrary to all good sense; **tomber sous le** ~ to stand to reason, be perfectly obvious; **en un** ~, **dans un** ~ in a way; **en ce** ~ **que** in the sense that; **à mon** ~ to my mind; **dans le** ~ **des aiguilles d'une montre** clockwise; **dans le** ~ **de la longeur/largeur** lengthways/widthways; **dans le mauvais** ~ the wrong way; **in the wrong direction; **bon** ~ good sense; ~ **commun** common sense; ~ **dessus dessous** upside down; ~ **interdit,** ~ **unique** one-way street.
sensass [sɑ̃sas] adj (fam) fantastic.
sensation [sɑ̃sasjɔ̃] nf sensation; **faire** ~ to cause a sensation, create a stir; **à** ~ (péj) sensational.
sensationnel, le [sɑ̃sasjɔnɛl] adj sensational.
sensé, e [sɑ̃se] adj sensible.
sensibilisation [sɑ̃sibilizasjɔ̃] nf consciousness-raising: **une campagne de** ~ **de l'opinion** a campaign to raise public awareness.
sensibiliser [sɑ̃sibilize] vt to sensitize; ~ **qn (à)** to make sb sensitive (to).
sensibilité [sɑ̃sibilite] nf sensitivity; (affectivité, émotivité) sensitivity, sensibility.
sensible [sɑ̃sibl(ə)] adj sensitive; (aux sens) perceptible; (appréciable: différence, progrès) appreciable, noticeable; ~ **à** sensitive to.
sensiblement [sɑ̃sibləmɑ̃] adv (notablement) appreciably, noticeably; (à peu près): **ils ont** ~ **le même poids** they weigh approximately the same.
sensiblerie [sɑ̃sibləri] nf sentimentality; squeamishness.
sensitif, ive [sɑ̃sitif, -iv] adj (nerf) sensory; (personne) oversensitive.
sensoriel, le [sɑ̃sɔʀjɛl] adj sensory, sensorial.
sensualité [sɑ̃syalite] nf sensuality, sensuousness.
sensuel, le [sɑ̃syɛl] adj sensual; sensuous.
sent [sɑ̃] vb voir **sentir**.
sente [sɑ̃t] nf path.

sentence [sɑ̃tɑ̃s] nf (jugement) sentence; (adage) maxim.
sentencieusement [sɑ̃tɑ̃sjøzmɑ̃] adv sententiously.
sentencieux, euse [sɑ̃tɑ̃sjø, -øz] adj sententious.
senteur [sɑ̃tœʀ] nf scent, perfume.
senti, e [sɑ̃ti] adj: **bien** ~ (mots etc) well-chosen.
sentier [sɑ̃tje] nm path.
sentiment [sɑ̃timɑ̃] nm feeling; (conscience, impression): **avoir le** ~ **de/que** to be aware of/have the feeling that; **recevez mes** ~**s respectueux** yours faithfully; **faire du** ~ (péj) to be sentimental; **si vous me prenez par les** ~**s** if you appeal to my feelings.
sentimental, e, aux [sɑ̃timɑ̃tal, -o] adj sentimental; (vie, aventure) love cpd.
sentimentalisme [sɑ̃timɑ̃talism(ə)] nm sentimentalism.
sentimentalité [sɑ̃timɑ̃talite] nf sentimentality.
sentinelle [sɑ̃tinɛl] nf sentry; **en** ~ standing guard; (soldat: en faction) on sentry duty.
sentir [sɑ̃tiʀ] vt (par l'odorat) to smell; (par le goût) to taste; (au toucher, fig) to feel; (répandre une odeur de) to smell of; (: ressemblance) to smell like; (avoir la saveur de) to taste of; to taste like; (fig: dénoter, annoncer) to be indicative of; to smack of; to foreshadow ♦ vi to smell; ~ **mauvais** to smell bad; **se** ~ **bien** to feel good; **se** ~ **mal** (être indisposé) to feel unwell ou ill; **se** ~ **le courage/la force de faire** to feel brave/strong enough to do; **ne plus se** ~ **de joie** to be beside o.s. with joy; **il ne peut pas le** ~ (fam) he can't stand him.
seoir [swaʀ]: ~ **à** vt to become, befit; **comme il (leur) sied** as it is fitting (to them).
Seoul [seul] n Seoul.
SEP sigle f (= sclérose en plaques) MS.
séparation [separasjɔ̃] nf separation; (cloison) division, partition; ~ **de biens** division of property (in marriage settlement); ~ **de corps** legal separation.
séparatisme [separatism(ə)] nm separatism.
séparatiste [separatist(ə)] adj, nm/f (POL) separatist.
séparé, e [separe] adj (appartements, pouvoirs) separate; (époux) separated; ~ **de** separate from; separated from.
séparément [separemɑ̃] adv separately.
séparer [separe] vt (gén) to separate; (suj: divergences etc) to divide; to drive apart; (: différences, obstacles) to stand between; (détacher): ~ **qch de** to pull sth (off) from; (dissocier): to distinguish between; (diviser): ~ **qch par** to divide sth (up) with; ~ **une pièce en deux** to divide a room into two; **se** ~ (époux) to separate, part; (prendre congé: amis etc) to part, leave each other; (adversaires) to separate; (se diviser: route, tige etc)

to divide; *(se détacher):* **se ~ (de)** to split off (from); to come off; **se ~ de** *(époux)* to separate *ou* part from; *(employé, objet personnel)* to part with.

sépia [sepja] *nf* sepia.

sept [sɛt] *num* seven.

septante [sɛptɑ̃t] *num (Belgique, Suisse)* seventy.

septembre [sɛptɑ̃bʀ(ə)] *nm* September; *voir aussi* **juillet.**

septennal, e, aux [sɛptenal, -o] *adj* seven-year; *(festival)* seven-year, septennial.

septennat [sɛptena] *nm* seven-year term (of office); seven-year reign.

septentrional, e, aux [sɛptɑ̃tʀijɔnal, -o] *adj* northern.

septicémie [sɛptisemi] *nf* blood poisoning, septicaemia.

septième [sɛtjɛm] *num* seventh; **être au ~ ciel** to be on cloud nine.

septique [sɛptik] *adj:* **fosse ~** septic tank.

septuagénaire [sɛptɥaʒenɛʀ] *adj, nm/f* septuagenarian.

sépulcral, e, aux [sepylkʀal, -o] *adj (voix)* sepulchral.

sépulcre [sepylkʀ(ə)] *nm* sepulchre.

sépulture [sepyltyʀ] *nf* burial; *(tombeau)* burial place, grave.

séquelles [sekɛl] *nfpl* after-effects; *(fig)* aftermath *sg;* consequences.

séquence [sekɑ̃s] *nf* sequence.

séquentiel, le [sekɑ̃sjɛl] *adj* sequential.

séquestration [sekɛstʀasjɔ̃] *nf* illegal confinement; impounding.

séquestre [sekɛstʀ(ə)] *nm* impoundment; **mettre sous ~** to impound.

séquestrer [sekɛstʀe] *vt (personne)* to confine illegally; *(biens)* to impound.

serai [səʀe] *etc vb voir* **être.**

sérail [seʀaj] *nm* seraglio; harem; **rentrer au ~** to return to the fold.

serbe [sɛʀb(ə)] *adj* Serbian ♦ *nm (LING)* Serbian ♦ *nm/f:* **S~** Serb.

Serbie [sɛʀbi] *nf:* **la ~** Serbia.

serbo-croate [sɛʀbokʀɔat] *adj* Serbo-Croat, Serbo-Croatian ♦ *nm (LING)* Serbo-Croat.

serein, e [səʀɛ̃, -ɛn] *adj* serene; *(jugement)* dispassionate.

sereinement [səʀɛnmɑ̃] *adv* serenely.

sérénade [seʀenad] *nf* serenade; *(fam)* hullabaloo.

sérénité [seʀenite] *nf* serenity.

serez [səʀe] *vb voir* **être.**

serf, serve [sɛʀ, sɛʀv(ə)] *nm/f* serf.

serfouette [sɛʀfwɛt] *nf* weeding hoe.

serge [sɛʀʒ(ə)] *nf* serge.

sergent [sɛʀʒɑ̃] *nm* sergeant.

sergent-chef [sɛʀʒɑ̃ʃɛf] *nm* staff sergeant.

sergent-major [sɛʀʒɑ̃maʒɔʀ] *nm* ≈ quartermaster sergeant.

sériciculture [seʀisikyltyʀ] *nf* silkworm breeding, sericulture.

série [seʀi] *nf (de questions, d'accidents, TV)* series *inv;* *(de clés, casseroles, outils)* set; *(catégorie: SPORT)* rank; class; **en ~** in quick succession; *(COMM)* mass *cpd;* **de ~** *adj* standard; **hors ~** *(COMM)* custom-built; *(fig)* outstanding; **imprimante ~** *(INFORM)* serial printer; **soldes de fin de ~s** end of line special offers; **~ noire** *nm (crime)* thriller ♦ *nf (suite de malheurs)* run of bad luck.

sérier [seʀje] *vt* to classify, sort out.

sérieusement [seʀjøzmɑ̃] *adv* seriously; reliably; responsibly; **il parle ~** he's serious, he means it; **~?** are you serious?, do you mean it?

sérieux, euse [seʀjø, -øz] *adj* serious; *(élève, employé)* reliable, responsible; *(client, maison)* reliable, dependable; *(offre, proposition)* genuine, serious; *(grave, sévère)* serious, solemn; *(maladie, situation)* serious, grave; *(important)* considerable ♦ *nm* seriousness; reliability; **ce n'est pas ~** *(raisonnable)* that's not on; **garder son ~** to keep a straight face; **manquer de ~** not to be very responsible *(ou* reliable); **prendre qch/qn au ~** to take sth/sb seriously.

sérigraphie [seʀigʀafi] *nf* silk screen printing.

serin [səʀɛ̃] *nm* canary.

seriner [səʀine] *vt:* **~ qch à qn** to drum sth into sb.

seringue [səʀɛ̃g] *nf* syringe.

serions [səʀjɔ̃] *etc vb voir* **être.**

serment [sɛʀmɑ̃] *nm (juré)* oath; *(promesse)* pledge, vow; **prêter ~** to take the *ou* an oath; **faire le ~ de** to take a vow to, swear to; **sous ~** on *ou* under oath.

sermon [sɛʀmɔ̃] *nm* sermon; *(péj)* sermon, lecture.

sermonner [sɛʀmɔne] *vt* to lecture.

SERNAM [sɛʀnam] *sigle m* (= *Service national de messageries) rail delivery service.*

sérologie [seʀɔlɔʒi] *nf* serology.

séronégatif, ive [seʀonegatif, -iv] *adj* HIV negative.

séropositif, ive [seʀopozitif, -iv] *adj* HIV positive.

serpe [sɛʀp(ə)] *nf* billhook.

serpent [sɛʀpɑ̃] *nm* snake; **~ à sonnettes** rattlesnake; **~ monétaire (européen)** (European) monetary snake.

serpenter [sɛʀpɑ̃te] *vi* to wind.

serpentin [sɛʀpɑ̃tɛ̃] *nm (tube)* coil; *(ruban)* streamer.

serpillière [sɛʀpijɛʀ] *nf* floorcloth.

serrage [seʀaʒ] *nm* tightening; **collier de ~** clamp.

serre [sɛʀ] *nf (AGR)* greenhouse; **~ chaude** hothouse; **~ froide** unheated greenhouse.

serré, e [seʀe] *adj (tissu)* closely woven; *(réseau)* dense; *(écriture)* close; *(habits)* tight; *(fig: lutte, match)* tight, close-fought; *(passagers etc)* (tightly) packed; *(café)* strong ♦ *adv:* **jouer ~** to play it close, play a close game;

écrire ~ to write a cramped hand; **avoir la gorge** ~**e** to have a lump in one's throat.

serre-livres [sɛʀlivʀ(ə)] nm inv book ends pl.

serrement [sɛʀmɑ̃] nm: ~ **de main** handshake; ~ **de cœur** pang of anguish.

serrer [seʀe] vt (tenir) to grip ou hold tight; (comprimer, coincer) to squeeze; (poings, mâchoires) to clench; (suj: vêtement) to be too tight for; to fit tightly; (rapprocher) to close up, move closer together; (ceinture, nœud, frein, vis) to tighten ♦ vi: ~ **à droite** to keep to the right; to move into the right-hand lane; **se** ~ (se rapprocher) to squeeze up; **se** ~ **contre qn** to huddle up to sb; **se** ~ **les coudes** to stick together, back one another up; **se** ~ **la ceinture** to tighten one's belt; ~ **la main à qn** to shake sb's hand; ~ **qn dans ses bras** to hug sb, clasp sb in one's arms; ~ **la gorge à qn** (suj: chagrin) to bring a lump to sb's throat; ~ **les dents** to clench ou grit one's teeth; ~ **qn de près** to follow close behind sb; ~ **le trottoir** to hug the kerb; ~ **sa droite** to keep well to the right; ~ **la vis à qn** to crack down harder on sb; ~ **les rangs** to close ranks.

serres [sɛʀ] nfpl (griffes) claws, talons.

serre-tête [sɛʀtɛt] nm inv (bandeau) headband; (bonnet) skullcap.

serrure [seʀyʀ] nf lock.

serrurerie [seʀyʀʀi] nf (métier) locksmith's trade; (ferronnerie) ironwork; ~ **d'art** ornamental ironwork.

serrurier [seʀyʀje] nm locksmith.

sers, sert [sɛʀ] vb voir **servir**.

sertir [sɛʀtiʀ] vt (pierre) to set; (pièces métalliques) to crimp.

sérum [seʀɔm] nm serum; ~ **antivenimeux** snakebite serum; ~ **sanguin** (blood) serum; ~ **de vérité** truth drug.

servage [sɛʀvaʒ] nm serfdom.

servant [sɛʀvɑ̃] nm server.

servante [sɛʀvɑ̃t] nf (maid)servant.

serve [sɛʀv] nf voir **serf** ♦ vb voir **servir**.

serveur, euse [sɛʀvœʀ, -øz] nm/f waiter/waitress ♦ adj: **centre** ~ (INFORM) service centre.

servi, e [sɛʀvi] adj: **être bien** ~ to get a large helping (ou helpings); **vous êtes** ~**?** are you being served?

serviable [sɛʀvjabl(ə)] adj obliging, willing to help.

service [sɛʀvis] nm (gén) service; (série de repas): **premier** ~ first sitting; (pourboire) service (charge); (assortiment de vaisselle) set, service; (linge de table) set; (bureau: de la vente etc) department, section; (travail): **pendant le** ~ on duty; ~**s** nmpl (travail, ÉCON) services, inclusive/exclusive of service; **faire le** ~ to serve; **être en** ~ **chez qn** (domestique) to be in sb's service; **être au** ~ **de** (patron, patrie) to be in the service of; **être au** ~ **de qn** (collaborateur, voiture) to be at sb's ser-

vice; **porte de** ~ tradesman's entrance; **rendre** ~ **à** to help; **il aime rendre** ~ he likes to help; **rendre un** ~ **à qn** to do sb a favour; **heures de** ~ hours of duty; **être de** ~ to be on duty; **reprendre du** ~ to get back into action; **avoir 25 ans de** ~ to have completed 25 years' service; **être/mettre en** ~ to be in/put into service ou operation; **hors** ~ not in use; out of order; ~ **à thé/café** tea/ coffee set ou service; ~ **après-vente (SAV)** after-sales service; **en** ~ **commandé** on an official assignment; ~ **funèbre** funeral service; ~ **militaire** military service; ~ **d'ordre** police (ou stewards) in charge of maintaining order; ~**s publics** public services, (public) utilities; ~**s secrets** secret service sg; ~**s sociaux** social services.

> *French men over eighteen years of age are required to do ten months' **service militaire** if passed fit. The call-up can be delayed if the conscript is a full-time student in higher education. Conscientious objectors are required to do two years' public service. Since 1970, women have been able to do military service, though few do.*

serviette [sɛʀvjɛt] nf (de table) (table) napkin, serviette; (de toilette) towel; (porte-documents) briefcase; ~ **éponge** terry towel; ~ **hygiénique** sanitary towel.

servile [sɛʀvil] adj servile.

servir [sɛʀviʀ] vt (gén) to serve; (dîneur: au restaurant) to wait on; (client: au magasin) to serve, attend to; (fig: aider): ~ **qn** to aid sb; to serve sb's interests; to stand sb in good stead; (COMM: rente) to pay ♦ vi (TENNIS) to serve; (CARTES) to deal; (être militaire) to serve; ~ **qch à qn** to serve sb with sth, help sb to sth; **qu'est-ce que je vous sers?** what can I get you?; **se** ~ (prendre d'un plat) to help o.s.; (s'approvisionner): **se** ~ **chez** to shop at; **se** ~ **de** (plat) to help o.s. to; (voiture, outil, relations) to use; ~ **à qn** (diplôme, livre) to be of use to sb; **ça m'a servi pour faire** it was useful to me when I did; I used it to do; ~ **à qch/à faire** (outil etc) to be used for sth/for doing; **ça peut** ~ it may come in handy; **ça peut encore** ~ it can still be used (ou of use); **à quoi cela sert-il (de faire)?** what's the use (of doing)?; **cela ne sert à rien** it's no use; ~ **(à qn) de ...** to serve as ... (for sb); ~ **à dîner (à qn)** to serve dinner (to sb).

serviteur [sɛʀvitœʀ] nm servant.

servitude [sɛʀvityd] nf servitude; (fig) constraint; (JUR) easement.

servofrein [sɛʀvɔfʀɛ̃] nm servo(-assisted) brake.

servomécanisme [sɛʀvɔmekanism(ə)] nm servo system.

ses [se] adj possessif voir **son**.

sésame [sezam] *nm* (*BOT*) sesame; (*graine*) sesame seed.

session [sesjɔ̃] *nf* session.

set [sɛt] *nm* set; (*napperon*) placemat; ~ **de table** set of placemats.

seuil [sœj] *nm* doorstep; (*fig*) threshold; **sur le ~ de sa maison** in the doorway of his house, on his doorstep; **au ~ de** (*fig*) on the threshold *ou* brink *ou* edge of; ~ **de rentabilité** (*COMM*) breakeven point.

seul, e [sœl] *adj* (*sans compagnie*) alone; (*avec nuance affective: isolé*) lonely; (*unique*): **un ~ livre** only one book, a single book; **le ~ livre** the only book; ~ **ce livre, ce livre ~** this book alone, only this book; **d'un ~ coup** (*soudainement*) all at once; (*à la fois*) at one blow ♦ *adv* (*vivre*) alone, on one's own; **parler tout ~** to talk to oneself; **faire qch (tout) ~** to do sth (all) on one's own *ou* (all) by oneself ♦ *nm, nf*: **il en reste un(e) ~(e)** there's only one left; **pas un(e) ~(e)** not a single; **à lui (tout) ~** single-handed, on his own; ~ **à ~** in private.

seulement [sœlmɑ̃] *adv* (*pas davantage*): ~ **5, 5 ~** only 5; (*exclusivement*): ~ **eux** only them, them alone; (*pas avant*): ~ **hier/à 10h** only yesterday/at 10 o'clock; (*mais, toutefois*): **il consent, ~ il demande des garanties** he agrees, only he wants guarantees; **non ~ ... mais aussi** *ou* **encore** not only ... but also.

sève [sɛv] *nf* sap.

sévère [sevɛʀ] *adj* severe.

sévèrement [sevɛʀmɑ̃] *adv* severely.

sévérité [severite] *nf* severity.

sévices [sevis] *nmpl* (physical) cruelty *sg*, ill treatment *sg*.

Séville [sevil] *n* Seville.

sévir [seviʀ] *vi* (*punir*) to use harsh measures, crack down; (*suj: fléau*) to rage, be rampant; ~ **contre** (*abus*) to deal ruthlessly with, crack down on.

sevrage [səvʀaʒ] *nm* weaning; deprivation; (*d'un toxicomane*) withdrawal.

sevrer [səvʀe] *vt* to wean; (*fig*): ~ **qn de** to deprive sb of.

sexagénaire [sɛgzaʒenɛʀ] *adj, nmf* sexagenarian.

SExc *sigle f* (= *Son Excellence*) HE.

sexe [sɛks(ə)] *nm* sex; (*organe mâle*) member.

sexisme [sɛksism(ə)] *nm* sexism.

sexiste [sɛksist(ə)] *adj, nm* sexist.

sexologie [sɛksɔlɔʒi] *nf* sexology.

sexologue [sɛksɔlɔg] *nmf* sexologist, sex specialist.

sextant [sɛkstɑ̃] *nm* sextant.

sexualité [sɛksɥalite] *nf* sexuality.

sexué, e [sɛksɥe] *adj* sexual.

sexuel, le [sɛksɥɛl] *adj* sexual; **acte ~** sex act.

sexuellement [sɛksɥɛlmɑ̃] *adv* sexually.

seyait [sejɛ] *vb voir* **seoir**.

seyant, e [sejɑ̃, -ɑ̃t] *vb voir* **seoir** ♦ *adj* becoming.

Seychelles [seʃɛl] *nfpl*: **les ~** the Seychelles.

SFIO *sigle f* (= *Section française de l'internationale ouvrière*) *former name of French Socialist Party*.

SG *sigle m* = **secrétaire général**.

SGEN *sigle m* (= *Syndicat général de l'éducation nationale*) *trades union*.

shaker [ʃɛkœʀ] *nm* (cocktail) shaker.

shampooiner [ʃɑ̃pwine] *vt* to shampoo.

shampooineur, euse [ʃɑ̃pwinœʀ, -øz] *nmf* (*personne*) junior (*who does the shampooing*).

shampooing [ʃɑ̃pwɛ̃] *nm* shampoo; **se faire un ~** to shampoo one's hair; ~ **colorant** (colour) rinse; ~ **traitant** medicated shampoo.

Shetland [ʃɛtlɑ̃d] *n*: **les îles ~** the Shetland Islands, Shetland.

shoot [ʃut] *nm* (*FOOTBALL*) shot.

shooter [ʃute] *vi* (*FOOTBALL*) to shoot; **se ~** (*drogué*) to mainline.

shopping [ʃɔpiŋ] *nm*: **faire du ~** to go shopping.

short [ʃɔʀt] *nm* (pair of) shorts *pl*.

SI *sigle m* = **syndicat d'initiative**.

───────── *MOT-CLÉ*

si [si] *nm* (*MUS*) B; (*en chantant la gamme*) ti
♦ *adv* **1** (*oui*) yes; "**Paul n'est pas venu**" — "**~!**" "Paul hasn't come" — "Yes he has!"; **je vous assure que ~** I assure you he did/she is *etc*
2 (*tellement*) so; ~ **gentil/rapidement** so kind/fast; (**tant et**) ~ **bien que** so much so that; ~ **rapide qu'il soit** however fast he may be
♦ *conj* if; ~ **tu veux** if you want; **je me demande ~** I wonder if *ou* whether; ~ **j'étais toi** if I were you; ~ **seulement** if only; ~ **ce n'est que** apart from; **une des plus belles**, ~ **ce n'est la plus belle** one of the most beautiful, if not THE most beautiful; **s'il est aimable, eux par contre ...** while *ou* whereas he's nice, they (on the other hand) ...

siamois, e [sjamwa, -waz] *adj* Siamese; **frères/sœurs ~(es)** Siamese twins.

Sibérie [siberi] *nf*: **la ~** Siberia.

sibérien, ne [siberjɛ̃, -ɛn] *adj* Siberian ♦ *nmf*: **S~, ne** Siberian.

sibyllin, e [sibilɛ̃, -in] *adj* sibylline.

SICAV [sikav] *sigle f* (= *société d'investissement à capital variable*) open-ended investment trust; share in such a trust.

Sicile [sisil] *nf*: **la ~** Sicily.

sicilien, ne [sisiljɛ̃, -ɛn] *adj* Sicilian.

SIDA, sida [sida] *nm* (= *syndrome immuno-déficitaire acquis*) AIDS *sg*.

sidéral, e, aux [sideral, -o] *adj* sideral.

sidérant, e [siderɑ̃, -ɑ̃t] *adj* staggering.

sidéré, e [sidere] *adj* staggered.

sidérurgie [sideryrʒi] *nf* steel industry.

sidérurgique [sideryrʒik] *adj* steel *cpd*.

sidérurgiste [sideryrʒist(ə)] *nmf* steel worker.

siècle [sjɛkl(ə)] *nm* century; (*époque*): **le ~ des lumières/de l'atome** the age of enlightenment/atomic age; (*REL*): **le ~** the world.

sied [sje] *vb voir* seoir.

siège [sjɛʒ] *nm* seat; (*d'entreprise*) head office; (*d'organisation*) headquarters *pl*; (*MIL*) siege; **lever le ~** to raise the siege; **mettre le ~ devant** to besiege; **présentation par le ~** (*MÉD*) breech presentation; **~ avant/arrière** (*AUTO*) front/back seat; **~ baquet** bucket seat; **~ social** registered office.

siéger [sjeʒe] *vi* (*assemblée, tribunal*) to sit; (*résider, se trouver*) to lie, be located.

sien, ne [sjɛ̃, sjɛn] *pron*: **le(la) ~(ne), les ~s(~nes)** *m* his; *f* hers; *non humain* its; **y mettre du ~** to pull one's weight; **faire des ~nes** (*fam*) to be up to one's (usual) tricks; **les ~s** (*sa famille*) one's family.

siérait [sjeʀɛ] *etc vb voir* seoir.

Sierra Leone [sjɛʀaleɔne] *nf*: **la ~** Sierra Leone.

sieste [sjɛst(ə)] *nf* (afternoon) snooze *ou* nap, siesta; **faire la ~** to have a snooze *ou* nap.

sieur [sjœʀ] *nm*: **le ~ Thomas** Mr Thomas; (*en plaisantant*) Master Thomas.

sifflant, e [siflɑ̃, -ɑ̃t] *adj* (*bruit*) whistling; (*toux*) wheezing; (**consonne**) **~e** sibilant.

sifflement [sifləmɑ̃] *nm* whistle, whistling *no pl*; wheezing *no pl*; hissing *no pl*.

siffler [sifle] *vi* (*gén*) to whistle; (*avec un sifflet*) to blow (on) one's whistle; (*en respirant*) to wheeze; (*serpent, vapeur*) to hiss ♦ *vt* (*chanson*) to whistle; (*chien etc*) to whistle for; (*fille*) to whistle at; (*pièce, orateur*) to hiss, boo; (*faute*) to blow one's whistle at; (*fin du match, départ*) to blow one's whistle for; (*fam: verre, bouteille*) to guzzle, knock back (*BRIT*).

sifflet [siflɛ] *nm* whistle; **~s** *nmpl* (*de mécontentement*) whistles, boos; **coup de ~** whistle.

siffloter [siflɔte] *vi, vt* to whistle.

sigle [sigl(ə)] *nm* acronym, (set of) initials *pl*.

signal, aux [siɲal, -o] *nm* (*signe convenu, appareil*) signal; (*indice, écriteau*) sign; **donner le ~ de** to give the signal for; **~ d'alarme** alarm signal; **~ d'alerte/de détresse** warning/distress signal; **~ horaire** time signal; **~ optique/sonore** warning light/sound; visual/acoustic signal; **signaux (lumineux)** (*AUTO*) traffic signals; **signaux routiers** road signs; (*lumineux*) traffic lights.

signalement [siɲalmɑ̃] *nm* description, particulars *pl*.

signaler [siɲale] *vt* to indicate; to announce; to report; (*être l'indice de*) to indicate; (*faire remarquer*): **~ qch à qn/à qn que** to point out sth to sb/to sb that; (*appeler l'attention sur*): **~ qn à la police** to bring sb to the notice of the police; **se ~ par** to distinguish o.s. by; **se ~ à l'attention de qn** to attract sb's attention.

signalétique [siɲaletik] *adj*: **fiche ~** identification sheet.

signalisation [siɲalizasjɔ̃] *nf* signalling, signposting; signals *pl*; roadsigns *pl*; **panneau de ~** roadsign.

signaliser [siɲalize] *vt* to put up roadsigns on; to put signals on.

signataire [siɲatɛʀ] *nm/f* signatory.

signature [siɲatyʀ] *nf* signature; (*action*) signing.

signe [siɲ] *nm* sign; (*TYPO*) mark; **ne pas donner ~ de vie** to give no sign of life; **c'est bon ~** it's a good sign; **c'est ~ que** it's a sign that; **faire un ~ de la main/tête** to give a sign with one's hand/shake one's head; **faire ~ à qn** (*fig*) to get in touch with sb; **faire ~ à qn d'entrer** to motion (to) sb to come in; **en ~ de** as a sign *ou* mark of; **le ~ de la croix** the sign of the Cross; **~ de ponctuation** punctuation mark; **~ du zodiaque** sign of the zodiac; **~s particuliers** distinguishing marks.

signer [siɲe] *vt* to sign; **se ~** *vi* to cross o.s.

signet [siɲe] *nm* bookmark.

significatif, ive [siɲifikatif, -iv] *adj* significant.

signification [siɲifikasjɔ̃] *nf* meaning.

signifier [siɲifje] *vt* (*vouloir dire*) to mean, signify; (*faire connaître*): **~ qch (à qn)** to make sth known (to sb); (*JUR*): **~ qch à qn** to serve notice of sth on sb.

silence [silɑ̃s] *nm* silence; (*MUS*) rest; **garder le ~ (sur qch)** to keep silent (about sth), say nothing (about sth); **passer sous ~** to pass over (in silence); **réduire au ~** to silence.

silencieusement [silɑ̃sjøzmɑ̃] *adv* silently.

silencieux, euse [silɑ̃sjø, -øz] *adj* quiet, silent ♦ *nm* silencer (*BRIT*), muffler (*US*).

silex [silɛks] *nm* flint.

silhouette [silwɛt] *nf* outline, silhouette; (*lignes, contour*) outline; (*figure*) figure.

silice [silis] *nf* silica.

siliceux, euse [silisø, -øz] *adj* (*terrain*) chalky.

silicium [silisjɔm] *nm* silicon; **plaquette de ~** silicon chip.

silicone [silikon] *nf* silicone.

silicose [silikoz] *nf* silicosis, dust disease.

sillage [sijaʒ] *nm* wake; (*fig*) trail; **dans le ~ de** (*fig*) in the wake of.

sillon [sijɔ̃] *nm* (*d'un champ*) furrow; (*de disque*) groove.

sillonner [sijɔne] *vt* (*creuser*) to furrow; (*traverser*) to cross, criss-cross.

silo [silo] *nm* silo.

simagrées [simagʀe] *nfpl* fuss *sg*; airs and graces.

simiesque [simjɛsk(ə)] *adj* monkey-like, apelike.

similaire [similɛʀ] *adj* similar.

similarité [similaʀite] *nf* similarity.

simili [simili] *nm* imitation; (*TYPO*) half-tone ♦ *nf* half-tone engraving.

simili... [simili] *préfixe* imitation *cpd*, artificial.

similicuir [similikɥiʀ] *nm* imitation leather.

similigravure [similigʀavyʀ] *nf* half-tone engraving.

similitude [similityd] *nf* similarity.

simple [sɛ̃pl(ə)] *adj* (*gén*) simple; (*non multiple*) single; ~**s** *nmpl* (*MÉD*) medicinal plants; ~ **messieurs** *nm* (*TENNIS*) men's singles *sg*; **un** ~ **particulier** an ordinary citizen; **une** ~ **formalité** a mere formality; **cela varie du** ~ **au double** it can double, it can double the price *etc*; **dans le plus** ~ **appareil** in one's birthday suit; ~ **course** *adj* single; ~ **d'esprit** *nm/f* simpleton; ~ **soldat** private.

simplement [sɛ̃pləmɑ̃] *adv* simply.

simplet, te [sɛ̃plɛ, -ɛt] *adj* (*personne*) simpleminded.

simplicité [sɛ̃plisite] *nf* simplicity; **en toute** ~ quite simply.

simplification [sɛ̃plifikɑsjɔ̃] *nf* simplification.

simplifier [sɛ̃plifje] *vt* to simplify.

simpliste [sɛ̃plist(ə)] *adj* simplistic.

simulacre [simylakʀ(ə)] *nm* enactment; (*péj*): **un** ~ **de** a pretence of, a sham.

simulateur, trice [simylatœʀ, -tʀis] *nm/f* shammer, pretender; (*qui se prétend malade*) malingerer ♦ *nm*: ~ **de vol** flight simulator.

simulation [simylɑsjɔ̃] *nf* shamming, simulation; malingering.

simuler [simyle] *vt* to sham, simulate.

simultané, e [simyltane] *adj* simultaneous.

simultanéité [simyltaneite] *nf* simultaneity.

simultanément [simyltanemɑ̃] *adv* simultaneously.

Sinaï [sinai] *nm*: **le** ~ Sinai.

sinapisme [sinapism(ə)] *nm* (*MÉD*) mustard poultice.

sincère [sɛ̃sɛʀ] *adj* sincere; genuine; heartfelt; **mes** ~**s condoléances** my deepest sympathy.

sincèrement [sɛ̃sɛʀmɑ̃] *adv* sincerely; genuinely.

sincérité [sɛ̃seʀite] *nf* sincerity; **en toute** ~ in all sincerity.

sinécure [sinekyʀ] *nf* sinecure.

sine die [sinedje] *adv* sine die, indefinitely.

sine qua non [sinekwanɔn] *adj*: **condition** ~ indispensable condition.

Singapour [sɛ̃gapuʀ] *nm*: **le** ~ Singapore.

singe [sɛ̃ʒ] *nm* monkey; (*de grande taille*) ape.

singer [sɛ̃ʒe] *vt* to ape, mimic.

singeries [sɛ̃ʒʀi] *nfpl* antics; (*simagrées*) airs and graces.

singulariser [sɛ̃gylaʀize] *vt* to mark out; **se** ~ to call attention to o.s.

singularité [sɛ̃gylaʀite] *nf* peculiarity.

singulier, ière [sɛ̃gylje, -jɛʀ] *adj* remarkable, singular; (*LING*) singular ♦ *nm* singular.

singulièrement [sɛ̃gyljɛʀmɑ̃] *adv* singularly, remarkably.

sinistre [sinistʀ(ə)] *adj* sinister; (*intensif*): **un** ~ **imbécile** an incredible idiot ♦ *nm* (*incendie*) blaze; (*catastrophe*) disaster; (*ASSURANCES*) damage (*giving rise to a claim*).

sinistré, e [sinistʀe] *adj* disaster-stricken ♦ *nm/f* disaster victim.

sinistrose [sinistʀoz] *nf* pessimism.

sino... [sino] *préfixe*: ~**-indien** Sino-Indian, Chinese-Indian.

sinon [sinɔ̃] *conj* (*autrement, sans quoi*) otherwise, or else; (*sauf*) except, other than; (*si ce n'est*) if not.

sinueux, euse [sinɥø, -øz] *adj* winding; (*fig*) tortuous.

sinuosités [sinɥozite] *nfpl* winding *sg*, curves.

sinus [sinys] *nm* (*ANAT*) sinus; (*GÉOM*) sine.

sinusite [sinyzit] *nf* sinusitis, sinus infection.

sinusoïdal, e, aux [sinyzɔidal, -o] *adj* sinusoidal.

sinusoïde [sinyzɔid] *nf* sinusoid.

sionisme [sjɔnism(ə)] *nm* Zionism.

sioniste [sjɔnist(ə)] *adj*, *nm/f* Zionist.

siphon [sifɔ̃] *nm* (*tube, d'eau gazeuse*) siphon; (*d'évier etc*) U-bend.

siphonner [sifɔne] *vt* to siphon.

sire [siʀ] *nm* (*titre*): **S~** Sire; **un triste** ~ an unsavoury individual.

sirène [siʀɛn] *nf* siren; ~ **d'alarme** fire alarm; (*pendant la guerre*) air-raid siren.

sirop [siʀo] *nm* (*à diluer: de fruit etc*) syrup, cordial (*BRIT*); (*boisson*) fruit drink; (*pharmaceutique*) syrup, mixture; ~ **de menthe** mint syrup *ou* cordial; ~ **contre la toux** cough syrup *ou* mixture.

siroter [siʀɔte] *vt* to sip.

sirupeux, euse [siʀypø, -øz] *adj* syrupy.

sis, e [si, siz] *adj*: ~ **rue de la Paix** located in the rue de la Paix.

sisal [sizal] *nm* (*BOT*) sisal.

sismique [sismik] *adj* seismic.

sismographe [sismɔgʀaf] *nm* seismograph.

sismologie [sismɔlɔʒi] *nf* seismology.

site [sit] *nm* (*paysage, environnement*) setting; (*d'une ville etc: emplacement*) site; ~ (**pittoresque**) beauty spot; ~ **Web** (*INFORM*) website; ~**s touristiques** places of interest; ~**s naturels/historiques** natural/historic sites.

sitôt [sito] *adv*: ~ **parti** as soon as he *etc* had left; ~ **après** straight after; **pas de** ~ not for a long time; ~ (**après**) **que** as soon as.

situation [sitɥasjɔ̃] *nf* (*gén*) situation; (*d'un édifice, d'une ville*) situation, position; (*emplacement*) location; **être en** ~ **de faire qch** to be in a position to do sth; ~ **de famille** marital status.

situé, e [sitɥe] *adj*: **bien** ~ well situated, in a good location; **à/près de** situated at/near.

situer [sitɥe] *vt* to site, situate; (*en pensée*) to set, place; **se** ~ *vi*: **se** ~ **à/près de** to be situated at/near.

SIVOM [sivɔm] *sigle m* (= *Syndicat intercommunal à vocation multiple*) *association of* "*communes*".

six [sis] *num* six.

sixième [sizjɛm] *num* sixth.

skaï [skaj] *nm* ® ≈ Leatherette ®.

skate(-board) [sket(bɔʀd)] nm (sport) skateboarding; (planche) skateboard.

sketch [skɛtʃ] nm (variety) sketch.

ski [ski] nm (objet) ski; (sport) skiing; **faire du** ~ to ski; ~ **alpin** Alpine skiing; ~ **court** short ski; ~ **évolutif** short ski method; ~ **de fond** cross-country skiing; ~ **nautique** water-skiing; ~ **de piste** downhill skiing; ~ **de randonnée** cross-country skiing.

ski-bob [skibɔb] nm skibob.

skier [skje] vi to ski.

skieur, euse [skjœʀ, -øz] nm/f skier.

skif(f) [skif] nm skiff.

slalom [slalɔm] nm slalom; **faire du** ~ **entre** to slalom between; ~ **géant/spécial** giant/special slalom.

slalomer [slalɔme] vi (entre des obstacles) to weave in and out; (SKI) to slalom.

slalomeur, euse [slalɔmœʀ, -øz] nm/f (SKI) slalom skier.

slave [slav] adj Slav(onic), Slavic ♦ nm (LING) Slavonic ♦ nm/f: **S**~ Slav.

slip [slip] nm (sous-vêtement) underpants pl, pants pl (BRIT), briefs pl; (de bain: d'homme) (bathing ou swimming) trunks pl; (: du bikini) (bikini) briefs pl ou bottoms pl.

slogan [slɔgɑ̃] nm slogan.

slovaque [slɔvak] adj Slovak ♦ nm (LING) Slovak ♦ nm/f: **S**~ Slovak.

Slovaquie [slɔvaki] nf: **la** ~ Slovakia.

slovène [slɔvɛn] adj Slovene ♦ nm (LING) Slovene ♦ nm/f: **S**~ Slovene.

Slovénie [slɔveni] nf: **la** ~ Slovenia.

slow [slo] nm (danse) slow number.

SM sigle f (= Sa Majesté) HM.

SMAG [smag] sigle m = salaire minimum agricole garanti.

smasher [smaʃe] vi to smash the ball ♦ vt (balle) to smash.

SME sigle m (= Système monétaire européen) EMS.

SMIC [smik] sigle m = salaire minimum interprofessionnel de croissance.

> In France, the **SMIC** is the minimum hourly rate below which it is illegal to pay workers over the age of eighteen. The SMIC is index-linked and is raised each time the cost of living rises by 2%.

smicard, e [smikaʀ, -aʀd(ə)] nm/f minimum wage earner.

smocks [smɔk] nmpl (COUTURE) smocking no pl.

smoking [smɔkiŋ] nm dinner ou evening suit.

SMUR [smyʀ] sigle m (= service médical d'urgence et de réanimation) specialist mobile emergency unit.

snack [snak] nm snack bar.

SNC abr = service non compris.

SNCB sigle f (= Société nationale des chemins de fer belges) Belgian railways.

SNCF sigle f (= Société nationale des chemins de fer français) French railways.

SNES [snɛs] sigle m (= Syndicat national de l'enseignement secondaire) secondary teachers' union.

SNE-sup [ɛsɛnəsyp] sigle m (= Syndicat national de l'enseignement supérieur) university teachers' union.

SNI sigle m (= Syndicat national des instituteurs) primary teachers' union.

SNJ sigle m (= Syndicat national des journalistes) journalists' union.

snob [snɔb] adj snobbish ♦ nm/f snob.

snober [snɔbe] vt: ~ **qn** to give sb the cold shoulder, treat sb with disdain.

snobinard, e [snɔbinaʀ, -aʀd(ə)] nm/f snooty ou stuck-up person.

snobisme [snɔbism(ə)] nm snobbery.

SNSM sigle f (= Société nationale de sauvetage en mer) national sea-rescue association.

s.o. abr (= sans objet) no longer applicable.

sobre [sɔbʀ(ə)] adj temperate, abstemious; (élégance, style) restrained, sober; ~ **de** (gestes, compliments) sparing of.

sobrement [sɔbʀəmɑ̃] adv in moderation, abstemiously; soberly.

sobriété [sɔbʀijete] nf temperance, abstemiousness; sobriety.

sobriquet [sɔbʀikɛ] nm nickname.

soc [sɔk] nm ploughshare.

sociabilité [sɔsjabilite] nf sociability.

sociable [sɔsjabl(ə)] adj sociable.

social, e, aux [sɔsjal, -o] adj social.

socialement [sɔsjalmɑ̃] adv socially.

socialisant, e [sɔsjalizɑ̃, -ɑ̃t] adj with socialist tendencies.

socialisation [sɔsjalizasjɔ̃] nf socialisation.

socialiser [sɔsjalize] vt to socialize.

socialisme [sɔsjalism(ə)] nm socialism.

socialiste [sɔsjalist(ə)] adj, nm/f socialist.

sociétaire [sɔsjetɛʀ] nm/f member.

société [sɔsjete] nf society; (d'abeilles, de fourmis) colony; (sportive) club; (COMM) company; **la bonne** ~ polite society; **se plaire dans la** ~ **de** to enjoy the society of; **l'archipel de la S**~ the Society Islands; **la** ~ **d'abondance/de consommation** the affluent/consumer society; ~ **par actions** joint stock company; ~ **anonyme (SA)** ≈ limited company (Ltd) (BRIT), ≈ incorporated company (Inc.) (US); ~ **d'investissement à capital variable (SICAV)** ≈ investment trust (BRIT), ≈ mutual fund (US); ~ **à responsabilité limitée (SARL)** type of limited liability company (with non-negotiable shares); ~ **savante** learned society; ~ **de services** service company.

socioculturel, le [sɔsjokyltyʀɛl] adj sociocultural.

socio-économique [sɔsjoekɔnɔmik] adj socioeconomic.

socio-éducatif, -ive [sɔsjoedykatif, -iv] adj socioeducational.

sociolinguistique [sɔsjolɛ̃gɥistik] *adj* sociolinguistic.

sociologie [sɔsjɔlɔʒi] *nf* sociology.

sociologique [sɔsjɔlɔʒik] *adj* sociological.

sociologue [sɔsjɔlɔg] *nm/f* sociologist.

socio-professionnel, le [sɔsjoprɔfɛsjɔnɛl] *adj* socioprofessional.

socle [sɔkl(ə)] *nm* (*de colonne, statue*) plinth, pedestal; (*de lampe*) base.

socquette [sɔkɛt] *nf* ankle sock.

soda [sɔda] *nm* (*boisson*) fizzy drink, soda (*US*).

sodium [sɔdjɔm] *nm* sodium.

sodomie [sɔdɔmi] *nf* sodomy; buggery.

sodomiser [sɔdɔmize] *vt* to sodomize; to bugger.

sœur [sœr] *nf* sister; (*religieuse*) nun, sister; ~ **Élisabeth** (*REL*) Sister Elizabeth; ~ **de lait** foster sister.

sofa [sɔfa] *nm* sofa.

Sofia [sɔfja] *n* Sofia.

SOFRES [sɔfrɛs] *sigle f* (= *Société française d'enquête par sondage*) *company which conducts opinion polls.*

soi [swa] *pron* oneself; **cela va de** ~ that *ou* it goes without saying, it stands to reason.

soi-disant [swadizɑ̃] *adj inv* so-called ♦ *adv* supposedly.

soie [swa] *nf* silk; (*de porc, sanglier: poil*) bristle.

soient [swa] *vb voir* **être**.

soierie [swari] *nf* (*industrie*) silk trade; (*tissu*) silk.

soif [swaf] *nf* thirst; (*fig*): ~ **de** thirst *ou* craving for; **avoir** ~ to be thirsty; **donner** ~ **à qn** to make sb thirsty.

soigné, e [swaɲe] *adj* (*tenue*) well-groomed, neat; (*travail*) careful, meticulous; (*fam*) whopping; stiff.

soigner [swaɲe] *vt* (*malade, maladie: suj: docteur*) to treat; (*: suj: infirmière, mère*) to nurse, look after; (*blessé*) to tend; (*travail, détails*) to take care over; (*jardin, chevelure, invités*) to look after.

soigneur [swaɲœr] *nm* (*CYCLISME, FOOTBALL*) trainer; (*BOXE*) second.

soigneusement [swaɲøzmɑ̃] *adv* carefully.

soigneux, euse [swaɲø, -øz] *adj* (*propre*) tidy, neat; (*méticuleux*) painstaking, careful; ~ **de** careful with.

soi-même [swamɛm] *pron* oneself.

soin [swɛ̃] *nm* (*application*) care; (*propreté, ordre*) tidiness, neatness; (*responsabilité*): **le** ~ **de qch** the care of sth; ~**s** *nmpl* (*à un malade, blessé*) treatment *sg*, medical attention *sg*; (*attentions, prévenance*) care and attention *sg*; (*hygiène*) care *sg*; ~**s de la chevelure/de beauté** hair/beauty care; ~**s du corps/ménage** care of one's body/the home; **avoir** *ou* **prendre** ~ **de** to take care of, look after; **avoir** *ou* **prendre** ~ **de faire** to take care to

do; **sans** ~ *adj* careless; untidy; **les premiers** ~**s** first aid *sg*; **aux bons** ~**s de** c/o, care of; **être aux petits** ~**s pour qn** to wait on sb hand and foot, see to sb's every need; **confier qn aux** ~**s de qn** to hand sb over to sb's care.

soir [swar] *nm, adv* evening; **le** ~ in the evening(s); **ce** ~ this evening, tonight; **à ce** ~! see you this evening (*ou* tonight)!; **la veille au** ~ the previous evening; **sept/dix heures du** ~ seven in the evening/ten at night; **le repas/journal du** ~ the evening meal/newspaper: **dimanche** ~ Sunday evening; **hier** ~ yesterday evening; **demain** ~ tomorrow evening, tomorrow night.

soirée [sware] *nf* evening; (*réception*) party; **donner en** ~ (*film, pièce*) to give an evening performance of.

soit [swa] *vb voir* **être** ♦ *conj* (*à savoir*) namely, to wit; (*ou*): ~ ... ~ either ... or ♦ *adv* so be it, very well; ~ **un triangle ABC** let ABC be a triangle; ~ **que** ... ~ **que** *ou* **ou que** whether ... or whether.

soixantaine [swasɑ̃tɛn] *nf*: **une** ~ **(de)** sixty or so, about sixty; **avoir la** ~ to be around sixty.

soixante [swasɑ̃t] *num* sixty.

soixante-dix [swasɑ̃tdis] *num* seventy.

soixante-dixième [swasɑ̃tdizjɛm] *num* seventieth.

soixante-huitard, e [swazɑ̃tɥitar, -ard(ə)] *adj* relating to the demonstrations of May 1968 ♦ *nm/f* participant in the demonstrations of May 1968.

soixantième [swasɑ̃tjɛm] *num* sixtieth.

soja [sɔʒa] *nm* soya; (*graines*) soya beans *pl*; **germes de** ~ beansprouts.

sol [sɔl] *nm* ground; (*de logement*) floor; (*revêtement*) flooring *no pl*; (*territoire, AGR, GÉO*) soil; (*MUS*) G; (*: en chantant la gamme*) so(h).

solaire [sɔlɛr] *adj* solar, sun *cpd*.

solarium [sɔlarjɔm] *nm* solarium.

soldat [sɔlda] *nm* soldier; **S~ inconnu** Unknown Warrior *ou* Soldier; ~ **de plomb** tin *ou* toy soldier.

solde [sɔld(ə)] *nf* pay ♦ *nm* (*COMM*) balance; ~**s** *nmpl* *ou* *nfpl* (*COMM*) sales; (*articles*) sale goods; **à la** ~ **de qn** (*péj*) in sb's pay; ~ **créditeur/débiteur** credit/debit balance; ~ **à payer** balance outstanding; **en** ~ at sale price; **aux** ~**s** at the sales.

solder [sɔlde] *vt* (*compte*) to settle; (*marchandise*) to sell at sale price, sell off; **se** ~ **par** (*fig*) to end in; **article soldé (à) 10 F** item reduced to 10 F.

soldeur, euse [sɔldœr, -øz] *nm/f* (*COMM*) discounter.

sole [sɔl] *nf* sole *inv* (*fish*).

soleil [sɔlɛj] *nm* sun; (*lumière*) sun(light); (*temps ensoleillé*) sun(shine); (*feu d'artifice*) Catherine wheel; (*ACROBATIE*) grand circle; (*BOT*) sunflower; **il y a** *ou* **il fait du** ~ it's sunny; **au** ~ in the sun; **en plein** ~ in full sun; **le** ~ **levant/couchant** the rising/setting sun; **le** ~ **de minuit** the midnight sun.

solennel, le [sɔlanɛl] *adj* solemn; ceremonial.

solennellement [sɔlanɛlmɑ̃] *adv* solemnly.

solenniser [sɔlanize] *vt* to solemnize.

solennité [sɔlanite] *nf* (*d'une fête*) solemnity; ~**s** *nfpl* (*formalités*) formalities.

solénoïde [sɔlenɔid] *nm* (*ÉLEC*) solenoid.

solfège [sɔlfɛʒ] *nm* rudiments *pl* of music; (*exercices*) ear training *no pl*.

solfier [sɔlfje] *vt*: ~ **un morceau** to sing a piece using the sol-fa.

soli [sɔli] *pl de* **solo**.

solidaire [sɔlidɛʀ] *adj* (*personnes*) who stand together, who show solidarity; (*pièces mécaniques*) interdependent; (*JUR: engagement*) binding on all parties; (*: débiteurs*) jointly liable; **être** ~ **de** (*collègues*) to stand by; (*mécanisme*) to be bound up with, be dependent on.

solidairement [sɔlidɛʀmɑ̃] *adv* jointly.

solidariser [sɔlidaʀize]: **se** ~ **avec** *vt* to show solidarity with.

solidarité [sɔlidaʀite] *nf* (*entre personnes*) solidarity; (*de mécanisme, phénomènes*) interdependence; **par** ~ (**avec**) (*cesser le travail etc*) in sympathy (with).

solide [sɔlid] *adj* solid; (*mur, maison, meuble*) solid, sturdy; (*connaissances, argument*) sound; (*personne*) robust, sturdy; (*estomac*) strong ♦ *nm* solid; **avoir les reins** ~**s** (*fig*) to be in a good financial position; to have sound financial backing.

solidement [sɔlidmɑ̃] *adv* solidly; (*fermement*) firmly.

solidifier [sɔlidifje] *vt*, **se** ~ *vi* to solidify.

solidité [sɔlidite] *nf* solidity; sturdiness.

soliloque [sɔlilɔk] *nm* soliloquy.

soliste [sɔlist(ə)] *nm/f* soloist.

solitaire [sɔlitɛʀ] *adj* (*sans compagnie*) solitary, lonely; (*isolé*) solitary, isolated, lone; (*lieu*) lonely ♦ *nm/f* recluse; loner ♦ *nm* (*diamant, jeu*) solitaire.

solitude [sɔlityd] *nf* loneliness; (*paix*) solitude.

solive [sɔliv] *nf* joist.

sollicitations [sɔlisitasjɔ̃] *nfpl* (*requêtes*) entreaties, appeals; (*attractions*) enticements; (*TECH*) stress *sg*.

solliciter [sɔlisite] *vt* (*personne*) to appeal to; (*emploi, faveur*) to seek; (*moteur*) to prompt; (*suj: occupations, attractions etc*): ~ **qn** to appeal to sb's curiosity *etc*; to entice sb; to make demands on sb's time; ~ **qn de faire** to appeal to sb *ou* request sb to do.

sollicitude [sɔlisityd] *nf* concern.

solo [sɔlo] *nm*, *pl* **soli** [sɔli] (*MUS*) solo (*pl* -s *ou* soli).

sol-sol [sɔlsɔl] *adj inv* surface-to-surface.

solstice [sɔlstis] *nm* solstice; ~ **d'hiver/d'été** winter/summer solstice.

solubilisé, e [sɔlybilize] *adj* soluble.

solubilité [sɔlybilite] *nf* solubility.

soluble [sɔlybl(ə)] *adj* (*sucre, cachet*) soluble; (*problème etc*) soluble, solvable.

soluté [sɔlyte] *nm* solution.

solution [sɔlysjɔ̃] *nf* solution; ~ **de continuité** gap, break; ~ **de facilité** easy way out.

solutionner [sɔlysjɔne] *vt* to solve, find a solution for.

solvabilité [sɔlvabilite] *nf* solvency.

solvable [sɔlvabl(ə)] *adj* solvent.

solvant [sɔlvɑ̃] *nm* solvent.

Somalie [sɔmali] *nf*: **la** ~ Somalia.

somalien, ne [sɔmaljɛ̃, -ɛn] *adj* Somalian.

Somaliland [sɔmalilɑ̃d] *nm* Somaliland.

somatique [sɔmatik] *adj* somatic.

sombre [sɔ̃bʀ(ə)] *adj* dark; (*fig*) sombre, gloomy; (*sinistre*) awful, dreadful.

sombrer [sɔ̃bʀe] *vi* (*bateau*) to sink, go down; ~ **corps et biens** to go down with all hands; ~ **dans** (*misère, désespoir*) to sink into.

sommaire [sɔmɛʀ] *adj* (*simple*) basic; (*expéditif*) summary ♦ *nm* summary; **faire le** ~ **de** to make a summary of, summarize; **exécution** ~ summary execution.

sommairement [sɔmɛʀmɑ̃] *adv* basically; summarily.

sommation [sɔmasjɔ̃] *nf* (*JUR*) summons *sg*; (*avant de faire feu*) warning.

somme [sɔm] *nf* (*MATH*) sum; (*fig*) amount; (*argent*) sum, amount ♦ *nm*: **faire un** ~ to have a (short) nap; **faire la** ~ **de** to add up; **en** ~, ~ **toute** *adv* all in all.

sommeil [sɔmɛj] *nm* sleep; **avoir** ~ to be sleepy; **avoir le** ~ **léger** to be a light sleeper; **en** ~ (*fig*) dormant.

sommeiller [sɔmeje] *vi* to doze; (*fig*) to lie dormant.

sommelier [sɔməlje] *nm* wine waiter.

sommer [sɔme] *vt*: ~ **qn de faire** to command *ou* order sb to do; (*JUR*) to summon sb to do.

sommes [sɔm] *vb voir* **être**; *voir aussi* **somme**.

sommet [sɔmɛ] *nm* top; (*d'une montagne*) summit, top; (*fig: de la perfection, gloire*) height; (*GÉOM: d'angle*) vertex (*pl* vertices); (*conférence*) summit (conference).

sommier [sɔmje] *nm* bed base, bedspring (*US*); (*ADMIN: registre*) register; ~ **à ressorts** (interior sprung) divan base (*BRIT*), box spring (*US*); ~ **à lattes** slatted bed base.

sommité [sɔmite] *nf* prominent person, leading light.

somnambule [sɔmnɑ̃byl] *nm/f* sleepwalker.

somnambulisme [sɔmnɑ̃bylism(ə)] *nm* sleepwalking.

somnifère [sɔmnifɛʀ] *nm* sleeping drug; (*comprimé*) sleeping pill *ou* tablet.

somnolence [sɔmnɔlɑ̃s] *nf* drowsiness.

somnolent, e [sɔmnɔlɑ̃, -ɑ̃t] *adj* sleepy, drowsy.

somnoler [sɔmnɔle] *vi* to doze.

somptuaire [sɔ̃ptɥɛʀ] *adj*: **lois** ~**s** sumptuary laws; **dépenses** ~**s** extravagant expenditure *sg.*

somptueusement [sɔ̃ptɥøzmɑ̃] *adv* sumptuously.

somptueux, euse [sɔ̃ptɥø, -øz] *adj* sumptuous; (*cadeau*) lavish.

somptuosité [sɔ̃ptɥozite] *nf* sumptuousness; (*d'un cadeau*) lavishness.

son [sɔ̃], **sa** [sa], *pl* **ses** [se] *adj possessif* (*antécédent humain mâle*) his; (*: femelle*) her; (*: valeur indéfinie*) one's, his/her; (*: non humain*) its; *voir note sous* **il**.

son [sɔ̃] *nm* sound; (*de blé etc*) bran; ~ **et lumière** *adj inv* son et lumière.

sonar [sɔnaʀ] *nm* (*NAVIG*) sonar.

sonate [sɔnat] *nf* sonata.

sondage [sɔ̃daʒ] *nm* (*de terrain*) boring, drilling; (*mer, atmosphère*) sounding; probe; (*enquête*) survey, sounding out of opinion; ~ (**d'opinion**) (opinion) poll.

sonde [sɔ̃d] *nf* (*NAVIG*) lead *ou* sounding line; (*MÉTÉOROLOGIE*) sonde; (*MÉD*) probe; catheter; (*d'alimentation*) feeding tube; (*TECH*) borer, driller; (*de forage, sondage*) drill; (*pour fouiller etc*) probe; ~ **à avalanche** pole (*for probing snow and locating victims*); ~ **spatiale** probe.

sonder [sɔ̃de] *vt* (*NAVIG*) to sound; (*atmosphère, plaie, bagages etc*) to probe; (*TECH*) to bore, drill; (*fig: personne*) to sound out; (*: opinion*) to probe; ~ **le terrain** (*fig*) to see how the land lies.

songe [sɔ̃ʒ] *nm* dream.

songer [sɔ̃ʒe] *vi* to dream; ~ **à** (*rêver à*) to muse over, think over; (*penser à*) to think of; (*envisager*) to contemplate, think of, consider; ~ **que** to consider that; to think that.

songerie [sɔ̃ʒʀi] *nf* reverie.

songeur, euse [sɔ̃ʒœʀ, -øz] *adj* pensive; **ça me laisse** ~ that makes me wonder.

sonnailles [sɔnaj] *nfpl* jingle of bells.

sonnant, e [sɔnɑ̃, -ɑ̃t] *adj*: **en espèces** ~**es et trébuchantes** in coin of the realm; **à 8 heures** ~**es** on the stroke of 8.

sonné, e [sɔne] *adj* (*fam*) cracked; (*passé*): **il est midi** ~ it's gone twelve; **il a quarante ans bien** ~**s** he's well into his forties.

sonner [sɔne] *vi* (*retentir*) to ring; (*donner une impression*) to sound ♦ *vt* (*cloche*) to ring; (*glas, tocsin*) to sound; (*portier, infirmière*) to ring for; (*messe*) to ring the bell for; (*fam: suj: choc, coup*) to knock out; ~ **du clairon** to sound the bugle; ~ **bien/mal/creux** to sound good/bad/hollow; ~ **faux** (*instrument*) to sound out of tune; (*rire*) to ring false; ~ **les heures** to strike the hours; **minuit vient de** ~ midnight has just struck; ~ **chez qn** to ring sb's doorbell, ring at sb's door.

sonnerie [sɔnʀi] *nf* (*son*) ringing; (*sonnette*) bell; (*mécanisme d'horloge*) striking mechanism; ~ **d'alarme** alarm bell; ~ **de clairon** bugle call.

sonnet [sɔnɛ] *nm* sonnet.

sonnette [sɔnɛt] *nf* bell; ~ **d'alarme** alarm bell; ~ **de nuit** night-bell.

sono [sɔno] *nf* (= *sonorisation*) PA (system); (*d'une discothèque*) sound system.

sonore [sɔnɔʀ] *adj* (*voix*) sonorous, ringing; (*salle, métal*) resonant; (*ondes, film, signal*) sound *cpd*; (*LING*) voiced; **effets** ~**s** sound effects.

sonorisation [sɔnɔʀizasjɔ̃] *nf* (*installations*) public address system; (*d'une discothèque*) sound system.

sonoriser [sɔnɔʀize] *vt* (*film, spectacle*) to add the sound track to; (*salle*) to fit with a public address system.

sonorité [sɔnɔʀite] *nf* (*de piano, violon*) tone; (*de voix, mot*) sonority; (*d'une salle*) resonance; acoustics *pl*.

sonothèque [sɔnɔtɛk] *nf* sound library.

sont [sɔ̃] *vb voir* **être**.

sophisme [sɔfism(ə)] *nm* sophism.

sophiste [sɔfist(ə)] *nm/f* sophist.

sophistication [sɔfistikasjɔ̃] *nf* sophistication.

sophistiqué, e [sɔfistike] *adj* sophisticated.

soporifique [sɔpɔʀifik] *adj* soporific.

soprano [sɔpʀano] *nm/f* soprano (*pl* -s).

sorbet [sɔʀbɛ] *nm* water ice, sorbet.

sorbetière [sɔʀbətjɛʀ] *nf* ice-cream maker.

sorbier [sɔʀbje] *nm* service tree.

sorcellerie [sɔʀsɛlʀi] *nf* witchcraft *no pl*, sorcery *no pl*.

sorcier, ière [sɔʀsje, -jɛʀ] *nm/f* sorcerer/witch *ou* sorceress ♦ *adj*: **ce n'est pas** ~ (*fam*) it's as easy as pie.

sordide [sɔʀdid] *adj* sordid; squalid.

Sorlingues [sɔʀlɛ̃g] *nfpl*: **les (îles)** ~ the Scilly Isles, the Isles of Scilly, the Scillies.

sornettes [sɔʀnɛt] *nfpl* twaddle *sg*.

sort [sɔʀ] *vb voir* **sortir** ♦ *nm* (*fortune, destinée*) fate; (*condition, situation*) lot; (*magique*): **jeter un** ~ to cast a spell; **un coup du** ~ a blow dealt by fate; **le** ~ **en est jeté** the die is cast; **tirer au** ~ to draw lots; **tirer qch au** ~ to draw lots for sth.

sortable [sɔʀtabl(ə)] *adj*: **il n'est pas** ~ you can't take him anywhere.

sortant, e [sɔʀtɑ̃, -ɑ̃t] *vb voir* **sortir** ♦ *adj* (*numéro*) which comes up (*in a draw etc*); (*député, président*) outgoing.

sorte [sɔʀt(ə)] *vb voir* **sortir** ♦ *nf* sort, kind; **de la** ~ *adv* in that way; **en quelque** ~ in a way; **de** ~ **à** so as to, in order to; **de (telle)** ~ **que, en** ~ **que** (*de manière que*) so that; (*si bien que*) so much so that; **faire en** ~ **que** to see to it that.

sortie [sɔʀti] *nf* (*issue*) way out, exit; (*MIL*) sortie; (*fig: verbale*) outburst; sally; (*: parole incongrue*) odd remark; (*d'un gaz, de l'eau*) outlet; (*promenade*) outing; (*le soir: au restaurant etc*) night out; (*de produits*) export; (*de capitaux*) outflow; (*COMM: somme*): ~**s** items of expenditure; outgoings *sans sg*; (*INFORM*) output; (*d'imprimante*) printout; **à sa** ~ as he went out *ou* left; **à la ~ de l'école/l'usine** (*moment*) after school/work; when school/ the factory comes out; (*lieu*) at the school/ factory gates; **à la ~ de ce nouveau modèle** when this new model comes (*ou* came) out, when they bring (*ou* brought) out this new model; **~ de bain** (*vêtement*) bathrobe; **"~ de camions"** "vehicle exit"; **~ papier** hard copy; **~ de secours** emergency exit.

sortilège [sɔʀtilɛʒ] *nm* (magic) spell.

sortir [sɔʀtiʀ] *vi* (*gén*) to come out; (*partir, se promener, aller au spectacle etc*) to go out; (*bourgeon, plante, numéro gagnant*) to come up ♦ *vt* (*gén*) to take out; (*produit, ouvrage, modèle*) to bring out; (*boniments, incongruités*) to come out with; (*INFORM*) to output; (: *sur papier*) to print out; (*fam: expulser*) to throw out ♦ *nm*: **au ~ de l'hiver/l'enfance** as winter/childhood nears its end; **~ qch de** to take sth out of; **~ qn d'embarras** to get sb out of trouble; **~ de** (*gén*) to leave; (*endroit*) to go (*ou* come) out of, leave; (*rainure etc*) to come out of; (*maladie*) to get over; (*époque*) to get through; (*cadre, compétence*) to be outside; (*provenir de: famille etc*) to come from; **~ de table** to leave the table; **~ du système** (*INFORM*) to log out; **~ de ses gonds** (*fig*) to fly off the handle; **se ~ de** (*affaire, situation*) to get out of; **s'en ~** (*malade*) to pull through; (*d'une difficulté etc*) to come through all right; to get through, be able to manage.

SOS *sigle m* mayday, SOS.

sosie [sɔzi] *nm* double.

sot, sotte [so, sɔt] *adj* silly, foolish ♦ *nm/f* fool.

sottement [sɔtmɑ̃] *adv* foolishly.

sottise [sɔtiz] *nf* silliness *no pl*, foolishness *no pl*; (*propos, acte*) silly *ou* foolish thing (to do *ou* say).

sou [su] *nm*: **près de ses ~s** tight-fisted; **sans le ~** penniless; **~ à ~** penny by penny; **pas un ~ de bon sens** not a scrap *ou* an ounce of good sense; **de quatre ~s** worthless.

souahéli, e [swaeli] *adj* Swahili ♦ *nm* (*LING*) Swahili.

soubassement [subasmɑ̃] *nm* base.

soubresaut [subʀəso] *nm* (*de peur etc*) start; (*cahot: d'un véhicule*) jolt.

soubrette [subʀɛt] *nf* soubrette, maidservant.

souche [suʃ] *nf* (*d'arbre*) stump; (*de carnet*) counterfoil (*BRIT*), stub; **dormir comme une ~** to sleep like a log; **de vieille ~** of old stock.

souci [susi] *nm* (*inquiétude*) worry; (*préoccupation*) concern; (*BOT*) marigold; **se faire du ~** to worry; **avoir (le) ~ de** to have concern for; **par ~ de** for the sake of, out of concern for.

soucier [susje]: **se ~ de** *vt* to care about.

soucieux, euse [susjø, -øz] *adj* concerned, worried; **~ de** concerned about; **peu ~ de/ que** caring little about/whether.

soucoupe [sukup] *nf* saucer; **~ volante** flying saucer.

soudain, e [sudɛ̃, -ɛn] *adj* (*douleur, mort*) sudden ♦ *adv* suddenly, all of a sudden.

soudainement [sudɛnmɑ̃] *adv* suddenly.

soudaineté [sudɛnte] *nf* suddenness.

Soudan [sudɑ̃] *nm*: **le ~** the Sudan.

soudanais, e [sudanɛ, -ɛz] *adj* Sudanese.

soude [sud] *nf* soda.

soudé, e [sude] *adj* (*fig: pétales, organes*) joined (together).

souder [sude] *vt* (*avec fil à souder*) to solder; (*par soudure autogène*) to weld; (*fig*) to bind *ou* knit together; to fuse (together); **se ~** *vi* (*os*) to knit (together).

soudeur, euse [sudœʀ, -øz] *nm/f* (*ouvrier*) welder.

soudoyer [sudwaje] *vt* (*péj*) to bribe, buy over.

soudure [sudyʀ] *nf* soldering; welding; (*joint*) soldered joint; weld; **faire la ~** (*COMM*) to fill a gap; (*fig: assurer une transition*) to bridge the gap.

souffert, e [sufɛʀ, -ɛʀt(ə)] *pp de* **souffrir**.

soufflage [suflaʒ] *nm* (*du verre*) glass-blowing.

souffle [sufl(ə)] *nm* (*en expirant*) breath; (*en soufflant*) puff, blow; (*respiration*) breathing; (*d'explosion, de ventilateur*) blast; (*du vent*) blowing; (*fig*) inspiration; **retenir son ~** to hold one's breath; **avoir du/manquer de ~** to have a lot of puff/be short of breath; **être à bout de ~** to be out of breath; **avoir le ~ court** to be short-winded; **un ~ d'air** *ou* **de vent** a breath of air, a puff of wind; **~ au cœur** (*MÉD*) heart murmur.

soufflé, e [sufle] *adj* (*CULIN*) soufflé; (*fam: ahuri, stupéfié*) staggered ♦ *nm* (*CULIN*) soufflé.

souffler [sufle] *vi* (*gén*) to blow; (*haleter*) to puff (and blow) ♦ *vt* (*feu, bougie*) to blow out; (*chasser: poussière etc*) to blow away; (*TECH: verre*) to blow; (*suj: explosion*) to destroy (with its blast); (*dire*): **~ qch à qn** to whisper sth to sb; (*fam: voler*): **~ qch à qn** to pinch sth from sb; **~ son rôle à qn** to prompt sb; **ne pas ~ mot** not to breathe a word; **laisser ~ qn** (*fig*) to give sb a breather.

soufflet [suflɛ] *nm* (*instrument*) bellows *pl*; (*entre wagons*) vestibule; (*COUTURE*) gusset; (*gifle*) slap (in the face).

souffleur, euse [suflœʀ, -øz] *nm/f* (*THÉÂT*) prompter; (*TECH*) glass-blower.

souffrance [sufʀɑ̃s] *nf* suffering; **en ~** (*marchandise*) awaiting delivery; (*affaire*) pending.

souffrant, e [sufʀɑ̃, -ɑ̃t] *adj* unwell.

souffre-douleur [sufʀədulœʀ] *nm inv* whipping boy (*BRIT*), butt, underdog.

souffreteux, euse [sufʀətø, -øz] *adj* sickly.

souffrir [sufʀiʀ] *vi* to suffer; (*éprouver des douleurs*) to be in pain ♦ *vt* to suffer, endure; (*supporter*) to bear, stand; (*admettre: excep-*

tion etc) to allow *ou* admit of; ~ **de** (*maladie, froid*) to suffer from; ~ **des dents** to have trouble with one's teeth; **ne pas pouvoir** ~ **qch/que** ... not to be able to endure *ou* bear sth/that ...; **faire** ~ **qn** (*suj: personne*) to make sb suffer; (: *dents, blessure etc*) to hurt sb.

soufre [sufʀ(ə)] *nm* sulphur (*BRIT*), sulfur (*US*).

soufrer [sufʀe] *vt* (*vignes*) to treat with sulphur *ou* sulfur.

souhait [swɛ] *nm* wish; **tous nos ~s de** good wishes *ou* our best wishes for; **riche** *etc* **à** ~ as rich *etc* as one could wish; **à vos ~s!** bless you!

souhaitable [swɛtabl(ə)] *adj* desirable.

souhaiter [swete] *vt* to wish for; ~ **le bonjour à qn** to bid sb good day; ~ **la bonne année à qn** to wish sb a happy New Year; **il est à ~ que** it is to be hoped that.

souiller [suje] *vt* to dirty, soil; (*fig*) to sully, tarnish.

souillure [sujyʀ] *nf* stain.

soûl, e [su, sul] *adj* drunk; (*fig*): ~ **de musique/plaisirs** drunk with music/pleasure ♦ *nm*: **tout son** ~ to one's heart's content.

soulagement [sulaʒmɑ̃] *nm* relief.

soulager [sulaʒe] *vt* to relieve; ~ **qn de** to relieve sb of.

soûler [sule] *vt*: ~ **qn** to get sb drunk; (*suj: boisson*) to make sb drunk; (*fig*) to make sb's head spin *ou* reel; **se** ~ to get drunk; **se** ~ **de** (*fig*) to intoxicate o.s. with.

soûlerie [sulʀi] *nf* (*péj*) drunken binge.

soulèvement [sulɛvmɑ̃] *nm* uprising; (*GÉO*) upthrust.

soulever [sulve] *vt* to lift; (*vagues, poussière*) to send up; (*peuple*) to stir up (to revolt); (*enthousiasme*) to arouse; (*question, débat, protestations, difficultés*) to raise; **se** ~ *vi* (*peuple*) to rise up; (*personne couchée*) to lift o.s. up; (*couvercle etc*) to lift; **cela me soulève le cœur** it makes me feel sick.

soulier [sulje] *nm* shoe; **~s bas** low-heeled shoes; **~s plats/à talons** flat/heeled shoes.

souligner [suliɲe] *vt* to underline; (*fig*) to emphasize, stress.

soumettre [sumɛtʀ(ə)] *vt* (*pays*) to subject, subjugate; (*rebelles*) to put down, subdue; ~ **qn/qch à** to subject sb/sth to; ~ **qch à qn** (*projet etc*) to submit sth to sb; **se** ~ (**à**) (*se rendre, obéir*) to submit (to); **se** ~ **à** (*formalités etc*) to submit to; (*régime etc*) to submit o.s. to.

soumis, e [sumi, -iz] *pp de* **soumettre** ♦ *adj* submissive; **revenus** ~ **à l'impôt** taxable income.

soumission [sumisjɔ̃] *nf* (*voir se soumettre*) submission; (*docilité*) submissiveness; (*COMM*) tender.

soumissionner [sumisjɔne] *vt* (*COMM: travaux*) to bid for, tender for.

soupape [supap] *nf* valve; ~ **de sûreté** safety valve.

soupçon [supsɔ̃] *nm* suspicion; (*petite quantité*): **un** ~ **de** a hint *ou* touch of; **avoir** ~ **de** to suspect; **au dessus de tout** ~ above (all) suspicion.

soupçonner [supsɔne] *vt* to suspect; ~ **qn de qch/d'être** to suspect sb of sth/of being.

soupçonneux, euse [supsɔnø, -øz] *adj* suspicious.

soupe [sup] *nf* soup; ~ **au lait** *adj inv* quick-tempered; ~ **à l'oignon/de poisson** onion/fish soup; ~ **populaire** soup kitchen.

soupente [supɑ̃t] *nf* (*mansarde*) attic; (*placard*) cupboard (*BRIT*) *ou* closet (*US*) under the stairs.

souper [supe] *vi* to have supper ♦ *nm* supper; **avoir soupé de** (*fam*) to be sick and tired of.

soupeser [supəze] *vt* to weigh in one's hand(s), feel the weight of; (*fig*) to weigh up.

soupière [supjɛʀ] *nf* (*soup*) tureen.

soupir [supiʀ] *nm* sigh; (*MUS*) crotchet rest (*BRIT*), quarter note rest (*US*); **rendre le dernier** ~ to breathe one's last.

soupirail, aux [supiʀaj, -o] *nm* (small) basement window.

soupirant [supiʀɑ̃] *nm* (*péj*) suitor, wooer.

soupirer [supiʀe] *vi* to sigh; ~ **après qch** to yearn for sth.

souple [supl(ə)] *adj* supple; (*col*) soft; (*fig: règlement, caractère*) flexible; (: *démarche, taille*) lithe, supple; **disque(tte)** ~ (*INFORM*) floppy disk, diskette.

souplesse [suplɛs] *nf* suppleness; flexibility.

source [suʀs(ə)] *nf* (*point d'eau*) spring; (*d'un cours d'eau, fig*) source; **prendre sa** ~ **à/dans** (*suj: cours d'eau*) to have its source at/in; **tenir qch de bonne** ~/**de** ~ **sûre** to have sth on good authority/from a reliable source; ~ **thermale/d'eau minérale** hot *ou* thermal/mineral spring.

sourcier, ière [suʀsje, -jɛʀ] *nm* water diviner.

sourcil [suʀsij] *nm* (eye)brow.

sourcilière [suʀsiljɛʀ] *adj f voir* **arcade**.

sourciller [suʀsije] *vi*: **sans** ~ without turning a hair *ou* batting an eyelid.

sourcilleux, euse [suʀsijø, -øz] *adj* (*hautain, sévère*) haughty, supercilious; (*pointilleux*) finicky, pernickety.

sourd, e [suʀ, suʀd(ə)] *adj* deaf; (*bruit, voix*) muffled; (*couleur*) muted; (*douleur*) dull; (*lutte*) silent, hidden; (*LING*) voiceless ♦ *nm/f* deaf person; **être** ~ **à** to be deaf to.

sourdement [suʀdəmɑ̃] *adv* (*avec un bruit sourd*) dully; (*secrètement*) silently.

sourdine [suʀdin] *nf* (*MUS*) mute; **en** ~ *adv* softly, quietly; **mettre une** ~ **à** (*fig*) to tone down.

sourd-muet, sourde-muette [suʀmɛ, suʀdmɛt] *adj* deaf-and-dumb ♦ *nm/f* deaf-mute.

sourdre [suʀdʀ(ə)] *vi* (*eau*) to spring up; (*fig*) to rise.

souriant, e [suʀjɑ̃, -ɑ̃t] *vb voir* **sourire** ♦ *adj* cheerful.

souricière [suʀisjɛʀ] *nf* mousetrap; (*fig*) trap.

sourie [suʀi] *etc vb voir* **sourire**.

sourire [suʀiʀ] *nm* smile ♦ *vi* to smile; ~ **à qn** to smile at sb; (*fig*) to appeal to sb; (: *chance*) to smile on sb; **faire un** ~ **à qn** to give sb a smile; **garder le** ~ to keep smiling.

souris [suʀi] *nf* mouse (*pl* mice); (*INFORM*) mouse.

sournois, e [suʀnwa, -waz] *adj* deceitful, underhand.

sournoisement [suʀnwazmɑ̃] *adv* deceitfully.

sournoiserie [suʀnwazʀi] *nf* deceitfulness, underhandedness.

sous [su] *prép* (*gén*) under; ~ **la pluie/le soleil** in the rain/sunshine; ~ **mes yeux** before my eyes; ~ **terre** *adj, adv* underground; ~ **vide** *adj, adv* vacuum-packed; ~ **l'influence/ l'action de** under the influence of/by the action of; ~ **antibiotiques/perfusion** on antibiotics/a drip; ~ **cet angle/ce rapport** from this angle/in this respect; ~ **peu** *adv* shortly, before long.

sous... [su, suz + *vowel*] *préfixe* sub-; under....

sous-alimentation [suzalimɑ̃tasjɔ̃] *nf* undernourishment.

sous-alimenté, e [suzalimɑ̃te] *adj* undernourished.

sous-bois [subwa] *nm inv* undergrowth.

sous-catégorie [sukategɔʀi] *nf* subcategory.

sous-chef [suʃɛf] *nm* deputy chief, second in command; ~ **de bureau** deputy head clerk.

sous-comité [sukɔmite] *nm* subcommittee.

sous-commission [sukɔmisjɔ̃] *nf* subcommittee.

sous-continent [sukɔ̃tinɑ̃] *nm* subcontinent.

sous-couche [sukuʃ] *nf* (*de peinture*) undercoat.

souscripteur, trice [suskʀiptœʀ, -tʀis] *nm/f* subscriber.

souscription [suskʀipsjɔ̃] *nf* subscription; **offert en** ~ available on subscription.

souscrire [suskʀiʀ] ~ **à** *vt* to subscribe to.

sous-cutané, e [sukytane] *adj* subcutaneous.

sous-développé, e [sudevlɔpe] *adj* underdeveloped.

sous-développement [sudevlɔpmɑ̃] *nm* underdevelopment.

sous-directeur, trice [sudiʀɛktœʀ, -tʀis] *nm/f* assistant manager/manageress, submanager/manageress.

sous-emploi [suzɑ̃plwa] *nm* underemployment.

sous-employé, e [suzɑ̃plwaje] *adj* underemployed.

sous-ensemble [suzɑ̃sɑ̃bl(ə)] *nm* subset.

sous-entendre [suzɑ̃tɑ̃dʀ(ə)] *vt* to imply, infer.

sous-entendu, e [suzɑ̃tɑ̃dy] *adj* implied; (*LING*) understood ♦ *nm* innuendo, insinuation.

sous-équipé, e [suzekipe] *adj* under-equipped; ~ **en infrastructures industrielles** (*ÉCON: pays, région*) with an insufficient industrial infrastructure.

sous-estimer [suzɛstime] *vt* to underestimate.

sous-exploiter [suzɛksplwate] *vt* to underexploit.

sous-exposer [suzɛkspoze] *vt* to underexpose.

sous-fifre [sufifʀ(ə)] *nm* (*péj*) underling.

sous-groupe [sugʀup] *nm* subgroup.

sous-homme [suzɔm] *nm* sub-human.

sous-jacent, e [suʒasɑ̃, -ɑ̃t] *adj* underlying.

sous-lieutenant [suljøtnɑ̃] *nm* sub-lieutenant.

sous-locataire [sulɔkatɛʀ] *nm/f* subtenant.

sous-location [sulɔkasjɔ̃] *nf* subletting.

sous-louer [sulwe] *vt* to sublet.

sous-main [sumɛ̃] *nm inv* desk blotter; **en** ~ *adv* secretly.

sous-marin, e [sumaʀɛ̃, -in] *adj* (*flore, volcan*) submarine; (*navigation, pêche, explosif*) underwater ♦ *nm* submarine.

sous-médicalisé, e [sumedikalize] *adj* lacking adequate medical care.

sous-nappe [sunap] *nf* undercloth.

sous-officier [suzɔfisje] *nm* ≈ non-commissioned officer (NCO).

sous-ordre [suzɔʀdʀ(ə)] *nm* subordinate; **créancier en** ~ creditor's creditor.

sous-payé, e [supeje] *adj* underpaid.

sous-préfecture [supʀefɛktyʀ] *nf* subprefecture.

sous-préfet [supʀefɛ] *nm* sub-prefect.

sous-production [supʀɔdyksjɔ̃] *nf* underproduction.

sous-produit [supʀɔdɥi] *nm* by-product; (*fig: péj*) pale imitation.

sous-programme [supʀɔgʀam] *nm* (*INFORM*) subroutine.

sous-pull [supul] *nm* thin poloneck sweater.

sous-secrétaire [susəkʀetɛʀ] *nm*: ~ **d'État** Under-Secretary of State.

soussigné, e [susiɲe] *adj*: **je** ~ I the undersigned.

sous-sol [susɔl] *nm* basement; (*GÉO*) subsoil.

sous-tasse [sutas] *nf* saucer.

sous-tendre [sutɑ̃dʀ(ə)] *vt* to underlie.

sous-titre [sutitʀ(ə)] *nm* subtitle.

sous-titré, e [sutitʀe] *adj* with subtitles.

soustraction [sustʀaksjɔ̃] *nf* subtraction.

soustraire [sustʀɛʀ] *vt* to subtract, take away; (*dérober*): ~ **qch à qn** to remove sth from sb; ~ **qn à** (*danger*) to shield sb from; **se** ~ **à** (*autorité, obligation, devoir*) to elude, escape from.

sous-traitance [sutʀɛtɑ̃s(ə)] *nf* subcontracting.

sous-traitant [sutʀɛtɑ̃] *nm* subcontractor.

sous-traiter [sutʀɛte] *vt, vi* to subcontract.

soustrayais [sustʀɛjɛ] *etc vb voir* **soustraire**.

sous-verre [suvɛʀ] *nm inv* glass mount.

sous-vêtement [suvɛtmɑ̃] *nm* undergarment, item of underwear; **~s** *nmpl* underwear *sg*.
soutane [sutan] *nf* cassock, soutane.
soute [sut] *nf* hold; **~ à bagages** baggage hold.
soutenable [sutnabl(ə)] *adj* (*opinion*) tenable, defensible.
soutenance [sutnɑ̃s] *nf*: **~ de thèse** ≈ viva (voce).
soutènement [sutɛnmɑ̃] *nm*: **mur de ~** retaining wall.
souteneur [sutnœʀ] *nm* procurer.
soutenir [sutniʀ] *vt* to support; (*assaut, choc, regard*) to stand up to, withstand; (*intérêt, effort*) to keep up; (*assurer*): **~ que** to maintain that; **se ~** (*dans l'eau etc*) to hold o.s. up; (*être soutenable: point de vue*) to be tenable; (*s'aider mutuellement*) to stand by each other; **~ la comparaison avec** *ou* stand comparison with; **~ le regard de qn** to be able to look sb in the face.
soutenu, e [sutny] *pp de* **soutenir** ♦ *adj* (*efforts*) sustained, unflagging; (*style*) elevated; (*couleur*) strong.
souterrain, e [sutɛʀɛ̃, -ɛn] *adj* underground; (*fig*) subterranean ♦ *nm* underground passage.
soutien [sutjɛ̃] *nm* support; **apporter son ~ à** to lend one's support to; **~ de famille** breadwinner.
soutiendrai [sutjɛ̃dʀe] *etc vb voir* **soutenir**.
soutien-gorge, *pl* **soutiens-gorge** [sutjɛ̃gɔʀʒ(ə)] *nm* bra; (*de maillot de bain*) top.
soutiens [sutjɛ̃], **soutint** [sutɛ̃] *etc vb voir* **soutenir**.
soutirer [sutiʀe] *vt*: **~ qch à qn** to squeeze *ou* get sth out of sb.
souvenance [suvnɑ̃s] *nf*: **avoir ~ de** to recollect.
souvenir [suvniʀ] *nm* (*réminiscence*) memory; (*cadeau*) souvenir, keepsake; (*de voyage*) souvenir ♦ *vb*: **se ~ de** *vt* to remember; **se ~ que** to remember that; **garder le ~ de** to retain the memory of; **en ~ de** in memory *ou* remembrance of; **avec mes affectueux/meilleurs ~s, ...** with love from, .../ regards, ...
souvent [suvɑ̃] *adv* often; **peu ~** seldom, infrequently; **le plus ~** more often than not, most often.
souvenu, e [suvəny] *pp de* **se souvenir**.
souverain, e [suvʀɛ̃, -ɛn] *adj* sovereign; (*fig: mépris*) supreme ♦ *nm/f* sovereign, monarch.
souverainement [suvʀɛnmɑ̃] *adv* (*sans appel*) with sovereign power; (*extrêmement*) supremely, intensely.
souveraineté [suvʀɛnte] *nf* sovereignty.
souviendrai [suvjɛ̃dʀe], **souviens** [suvjɛ̃], **souvint** [suvɛ̃] *etc vb voir* **se souvenir**.
soviétique [sɔvjetik] *adj* Soviet ♦ *nm/f*: **S~** Soviet citizen.
soviétiser [sɔvjetize] *vt* to sovietize.

soviétologue [sɔvjetɔlɔg] *nm/f* Kremlinologist.
soyeux, euse [swajø, -øz] *adj* silky.
soyez [swaje] *etc vb voir* **être**.
SPA *sigle f* (= *Société protectrice des animaux*) ≈ RSPCA (*BRIT*), ≈ SPCA (*US*).
spacieux, euse [spasjø, -øz] *adj* spacious; roomy.
spaciosité [spasjozite] *nf* spaciousness.
spaghettis [spageti] *nmpl* spaghetti *sg*.
sparadrap [spaʀadʀa] *nm* adhesive *ou* sticking (*BRIT*) plaster, bandaid ® (*US*).
Sparte [spaʀt(ə)] *nf* Sparta.
spartiate [spaʀsjat] *adj* Spartan; **~s** *nfpl* (*sandales*) Roman sandals.
spasme [spazm(ə)] *nm* spasm.
spasmodique [spazmɔdik] *adj* spasmodic.
spatial, e, aux [spasjal, -o] *adj* (*AVIAT*) space *cpd*; (*PSYCH*) spatial.
spatule [spatyl] *nf* (*ustensile*) slice; spatula; (*bout*) tip.
speaker, ine [spikœʀ, -kʀin] *nm/f* announcer.
spécial, e, aux [spesjal, -o] *adj* special; (*bizarre*) peculiar.
spécialement [spesjalmɑ̃] *adv* especially, particularly; (*tout exprès*) specially; **pas ~** not particularly.
spécialisation [spesjalizɑsjɔ̃] *nf* specialization.
spécialisé, e [spesjalize] *adj* specialised; **ordinateur ~** dedicated computer.
spécialiser [spesjalize]: **se ~** *vi* to specialize.
spécialiste [spesjalist(ə)] *nm/f* specialist.
spécialité [spesjalite] *nf* speciality; (*SCOL*) special field; **~ pharmaceutique** patent medicine.
spécieux, euse [spesjø, -øz] *adj* specious.
spécification [spesifikɑsjɔ̃] *nf* specification.
spécificité [spesifisite] *nf* specificity.
spécifier [spesifje] *vt* to specify, state.
spécifique [spesifik] *adj* specific.
spécifiquement [spesifikmɑ̃] *adv* (*typiquement*) typically; (*tout exprès*) specifically.
spécimen [spesimɛn] *nm* specimen; (*revue etc*) specimen *ou* sample copy.
spectacle [spɛktakl(ə)] *nm* (*tableau, scène*) sight; (*représentation*) show; (*industrie*) show business, entertainment; **se donner en ~** (*péj*) to make a spectacle *ou* an exhibition of o.s; **pièce/revue à grand ~** spectacular (play/revue); **au ~ de ...** at the sight of ....
spectaculaire [spɛktakylɛʀ] *adj* spectacular.
spectateur, trice [spɛktatœʀ, -tʀis] *nm/f* (*CINÉ etc*) member of the audience; (*SPORT*) spectator; (*d'un événement*) onlooker, witness.
spectre [spɛktʀ(ə)] *nm* (*fantôme, fig*) spectre; (*PHYSIQUE*) spectrum (*pl* -a); **~ solaire** solar spectrum.
spéculateur, trice [spekylatœʀ, -tʀis] *nm/f* speculator.
spéculatif, ive [spekylatif, -iv] *adj* speculative.

spéculation [spekylasjɔ̃] *nf* speculation.

spéculer [spekyle] *vi* to speculate; ~ **sur** (*COMM*) to speculate in; (*réfléchir*) to speculate on; (*tabler sur*) to bank ou rely on.

spéléologie [speleɔlɔʒi] *nf* (*étude*) speleology; (*activité*) potholing.

spéléologue [speleɔlɔg] *nm/f* speleologist; potholer.

spermatozoïde [spɛrmatozɔid] *nm* sperm, spermatozoon (*pl* -zoa).

sperme [spɛrm(ə)] *nm* semen, sperm.

spermicide [spɛrmisid] *adj, nm* spermicide.

sphère [sfɛr] *nf* sphere.

sphérique [sferik] *adj* spherical.

sphincter [sfɛ̃ktɛr] *nm* sphincter.

sphinx [sfɛ̃ks] *nm inv* sphinx; (*ZOOL*) hawk-moth.

spiral, aux [spiral, -o] *nm* hairspring.

spirale [spiral] *nf* spiral; **en** ~ in a spiral.

spire [spir] *nf* (*d'une spirale*) turn; (*d'une coquille*) whorl.

spiritisme [spiritism(ə)] *nm* spiritualism, spiritism.

spirituel, le [spirityɛl] *adj* spiritual; (*fin, piquant*) witty; **musique** ~**le** sacred music; **concert** ~ concert of sacred music.

spirituellement [spirityɛlmɑ̃] *adv* spiritually; wittily.

spiritueux [spirityø] *nm* spirit.

splendeur [splɑ̃dœr] *nf* splendour (*BRIT*), splendor (*US*).

splendide [splɑ̃did] *adj* splendid, magnificent.

spolier [spɔlje] *vt*: ~ **qn** (**de**) to despoil sb (of).

spongieux, euse [spɔ̃ʒjø, -øz] *adj* spongy.

sponsor [spɔ̃sɔr] *nm* sponsor.

sponsoriser [spɔ̃sɔrize] *vt* to sponsor.

spontané, e [spɔ̃tane] *adj* spontaneous.

spontanéité [spɔ̃taneite] *nf* spontaneity.

spontanément [spɔ̃tanemɑ̃] *adv* spontaneously.

sporadique [spɔradik] *adj* sporadic.

sporadiquement [spɔradikmɑ̃] *adv* sporadically.

sport [spɔr] *nm* sport ♦ *adj inv* (*vêtement*) casual; (*fair-play*) sporting; **faire du** ~ to do sport; ~ **individuel/d'équipe** individual/team sport; ~ **de combat** combative sport; ~**s d'hiver** winter sports.

sportif, ive [spɔrtif, -iv] *adj* (*journal, association, épreuve*) sports *cpd*; (*allure, démarche*) athletic; (*attitude, esprit*) sporting; **les résultats** ~**s** the sports results.

sportivement [spɔrtivmɑ̃] *adv* sportingly.

sportivité [spɔrtivite] *nf* sportsmanship.

spot [spɔt] *nm* (*lampe*) spot(light); (*annonce*): ~ (**publicitaire**) commercial (break).

spray [sprɛ] *nm* spray, aerosol.

sprint [sprint] *nm* sprint; **piquer un** ~ to put on a (final) spurt.

sprinter *nm* [sprintœr] sprinter ♦ *vi* [sprinte] to sprint.

squale [skwal] *nm* (*type of*) shark.

square [skwar] *nm* public garden(s).

squash [skwaʃ] *nm* squash.

squat [skwat] *nm* (*lieu*) squat.

squatter *nm* [skwatœr] squatter ♦ *vt* [skwate] to squat.

squelette [skəlɛt] *nm* skeleton.

squelettique [skəletik] *adj* scrawny; (*fig*) skimpy.

Sri Lanka [srilɑ̃ka] *nm* Sri Lanka.

sri-lankais, e [srilɑ̃kɛ, -ɛz] *adj* Sri-Lankan.

SS *sigle f* = **sécurité sociale**; (= *Sa Sainteté*) HH.

ss *abr* = **sous**.

S/S *sigle m* (= *steamship*) SS.

SSR *sigle f* (= *Société suisse romande*) the Swiss French-language broadcasting company.

stabilisateur, trice [stabilizatœr, -tris] *adj* stabilizing ♦ *nm* stabilizer; (*véhicule*) anti-roll device; (*avion*) tailplane.

stabiliser [stabilize] *vt* to stabilize; (*terrain*) to consolidate.

stabilité [stabilite] *nf* stability.

stable [stabl(ə)] *adj* stable, steady.

stade [stad] *nm* (*SPORT*) stadium; (*phase, niveau*) stage.

stage [staʒ] *nm* training period; training course; (*d'avocat stagiaire*) articles *pl*.

stagiaire [staʒjɛr] *nm/f, adj* trainee (*cpd*).

stagnant, e [stagnɑ̃, -ɑ̃t] *adj* stagnant.

stagnation [stagnasjɔ̃] *nf* stagnation.

stagner [stagne] *vi* to stagnate.

stalactite [stalaktit] *nf* stalactite.

stalagmite [stalagmit] *nf* stalagmite.

stalle [stal] *nf* stall, box.

stand [stɑ̃d] *nm* (*d'exposition*) stand; (*de foire*) stall; ~ **de tir** (*à la foire, SPORT*) shooting range; ~ **de ravitaillement** pit.

standard [stɑ̃dar] *adj inv* standard ♦ *nm* (*type, norme*) standard; (*téléphonique*) switchboard.

standardisation [stɑ̃dardizasjɔ̃] *nf* standardization.

standardiser [stɑ̃dardize] *vt* to standardize.

standardiste [stɑ̃dardist(ə)] *nm/f* switchboard operator.

standing [stɑ̃diŋ] *nm* standing; **immeuble de grand** ~ block of luxury flats (*BRIT*), condo(minium) (*US*).

star [star] *nf* star.

starlette [starlɛt] *nf* starlet.

starter [startɛr] *nm* (*AUTO*) choke; (*SPORT: personne*) starter; **mettre le** ~ to pull out the choke.

station [stasjɔ̃] *nf* station; (*de bus*) stop; (*de villégiature*) resort; (*posture*): **la** ~ **debout** standing, an upright posture; ~ **balnéaire** seaside resort; ~ **de graissage** lubrication bay; ~ **de lavage** carwash; ~ **de ski** ski resort; ~ **de sports d'hiver** winter sports resort; ~ **de taxis** taxi rank (*BRIT*) *ou* stand (*US*); ~ **thermale** thermal spa; ~ **de travail** workstation.

stationnaire [stasjɔnɛr] *adj* stationary.

stationnement [stasjɔnmɑ̃] *nm* parking; **zone de ~ interdit** no parking area; **~ alterné** parking on alternate sides.

stationner [stasjɔne] *vi* to park.

station-service [stasjɔ̃sɛrvis] *nf* service station.

statique [statik] *adj* static.

statisticien, ne [statistisjɛ̃, -ɛn] *nm/f* statistician.

statistique [statistik] *nf* (*science*) statistics *sg*; (*rapport, étude*) statistic ♦ *adj* statistical; **~s** *nfpl* (*données*) statistics *pl*.

statistiquement [statistikmɑ̃] *adv* statistically.

statue [staty] *nf* statue.

statuer [statɥe] *vi:* **~ sur** to rule on, give a ruling on.

statuette [statɥɛt] *nf* statuette.

statu quo [statykwo] *nm* status quo.

stature [statyr] *nf* stature; **de haute ~** of great stature.

statut [staty] *nm* status; **~s** *nmpl* (*JUR, ADMIN*) statutes.

statutaire [statytɛr] *adj* statutory.

St(e) *abr* (= *Saint(e)*) St.

Sté *abr* (= *société*) soc.

steak [stɛk] *nm* steak.

stèle [stɛl] *nf* stela, stele.

stellaire [stelɛr] *adj* stellar.

stencil [stɛnsil] *nm* stencil.

sténodactylo [stenɔdaktilo] *nm/f* shorthand typist (*BRIT*), stenographer (*US*).

sténodactylographie [stenɔdaktilɔgrafi] *nf* shorthand typing (*BRIT*), stenography (*US*).

sténo(graphe) [stenɔ(graf)] *nm/f* shorthand typist (*BRIT*), stenographer (*US*).

sténo(graphie) [stenɔ(grafi)] *nf* shorthand; **prendre en ~** to take down in shorthand.

sténographier [stenɔgrafje] *vt* to take down in shorthand.

sténographique [stenɔgrafik] *adj* shorthand *cpd*.

stentor [stɑ̃tɔr] *nm:* **voix de ~** stentorian voice.

step [stɛp] *nm* ® step aerobics *sg* ®, step Reebok ®.

stéphanois, e [stefanwa, -waz] *adj* of *ou* from Saint-Étienne.

steppe [stɛp] *nf* steppe.

stère [stɛr] *nm* stere.

stéréo(phonie) [stereɔ(fɔni)] *nf* stereo(phony); **émission en ~** stereo broadcast.

stéréo(phonique) [stereɔ(fɔnik)] *adj* stereo(phonic).

stéréoscope [stereɔskɔp] *nm* stereoscope.

stéréoscopique [stereɔskɔpik] *adj* stereoscopic.

stéréotype [stereɔtip] *nm* stereotype.

stéréotypé, e [stereɔtipe] *adj* stereotyped.

stérile [steril] *adj* sterile; (*terre*) barren; (*fig*) fruitless, futile.

stérilement [sterilmɑ̃] *adv* fruitlessly.

stérilet [sterilɛ] *nm* coil, loop.

stérilisateur [sterilizatœr] *nm* sterilizer.

stérilisation [sterilizasjɔ̃] *nf* sterilization.

stériliser [sterilize] *vt* to sterilize.

stérilité [sterilite] *nf* sterility.

sternum [stɛrnɔm] *nm* breastbone, sternum.

stéthoscope [stetɔskɔp] *nm* stethoscope.

stick [stik] *nm* stick.

stigmates [stigmat] *nmpl* scars, marks; (*REL*) stigmata *pl*.

stigmatiser [stigmatize] *vt* to denounce, stigmatize.

stimulant, e [stimylɑ̃, -ɑ̃t] *adj* stimulating ♦ *nm* (*MÉD*) stimulant; (*fig*) stimulus (*pl* -i), incentive.

stimulateur [stimylatœr] *nm:* **~ cardiaque** pacemaker.

stimulation [stimylasjɔ̃] *nf* stimulation.

stimuler [stimyle] *vt* to stimulate.

stimulus, i [stimylys, -i] *nm* stimulus (*pl* -i).

stipulation [stipylasjɔ̃] *nf* stipulation.

stipuler [stipyle] *vt* to stipulate, specify.

stock [stɔk] *nm* stock; **en ~** in stock.

stockage [stɔkaʒ] *nm* stocking; storage.

stocker [stɔke] *vt* to stock; (*déchets*) to store.

Stockholm [stɔkɔlm] *n* Stockholm.

stockiste [stɔkist(ə)] *nm* stockist.

stoïcisme [stɔisism(ə)] *nm* stoicism.

stoïque [stɔik] *adj* stoic, stoical.

stoïquement [stɔikmɑ̃] *adv* stoically.

stomacal, e, aux [stɔmakal, -o] *adj* gastric, stomach *cpd*.

stomatologie [stɔmatɔlɔʒi] *nf* stomatology.

stomatologue [stɔmatɔlɔg] *nm/f* stomatologist.

stop [stɔp] *nm* (*AUTO: écriteau*) stop sign; (*: signal*) brake-light; (*dans un télégramme*) stop ♦ *excl* stop!

stoppage [stɔpaʒ] *nm* invisible mending.

stopper [stɔpe] *vt* to stop, halt; (*COUTURE*) to mend ♦ *vi* to stop, halt.

store [stɔr] *nm* blind; (*de magasin*) shade, awning.

strabisme [strabism(ə)] *nm* squint(ing).

strangulation [strɑ̃gylasjɔ̃] *nf* strangulation.

strapontin [strapɔ̃tɛ̃] *nm* jump *ou* foldaway seat.

Strasbourg [strazbur] *n* Strasbourg.

strass [stras] *nm* paste, strass.

stratagème [strataʒɛm] *nm* stratagem.

strate [strat] *nf* (*GÉO*) stratum, layer.

stratège [stratɛʒ] *nm* strategist.

stratégie [strateʒi] *nf* strategy.

stratégique [strateʒik] *adj* strategic.

stratégiquement [strateʒikmɑ̃] *adv* strategically.

stratifié, e [stratifje] *adj* (*GÉO*) stratified; (*TECH*) laminated.

stratosphère [stratɔsfɛr] *nf* stratosphere.

stress [strɛs] *nm inv* stress.

stressant, e [strɛsɑ̃, -ɑ̃t] *adj* stressful.

stresser [stʀɛse] vt to stress, cause stress in.
strict, e [stʀikt(ə)] adj strict; (tenue, décor) severe, plain; **son droit le plus** ~ his most basic right; **dans la plus** ~e intimité strictly in private; **le** ~ **nécessaire/minimum** the bare essentials/minimum.
strictement [stʀiktəmã] adv strictly; plainly.
strident, e [stʀidã, -ãt] adj shrill, strident.
stridulations [stʀidylasjɔ̃] nfpl stridulations, chirrings.
strie [stʀi] nf streak; (ANAT, GÉO) stria (pl -ae).
strier [stʀije] vt to streak; to striate.
strip-tease [stʀiptiz] nm striptease.
strip-teaseuse [stʀiptizøz] nf stripper, striptease artist.
striures [stʀijyʀ] nfpl streaking sg.
stroboscope [stʀɔbɔskɔp] nm strobe (light).
strophe [stʀɔf] nf verse, stanza.
structure [stʀyktyʀ] nf structure; ~s **d'accueil/touristiques** reception/tourist facilities.
structurer [stʀyktyʀe] vt to structure.
strychnine [stʀiknin] nf strychnine.
stuc [styk] nm stucco.
studieusement [stydjøzmã] adv studiously.
studieux, euse [stydjø, -øz] adj (élève) studious; (vacances) study cpd.
studio [stydjo] nm (logement) studio flat (BRIT) ou apartment (US); (d'artiste, TV etc) studio (pl -s).
stupéfaction [stypefaksjɔ̃] nf stupefaction, astonishment.
stupéfait, e [stypefɛ, -ɛt] adj astonished.
stupéfiant, e [stypefjã, -ãt] adj stunning, astonishing ♦ nm (MÉD) drug, narcotic.
stupéfier [stypefje] vt to stupefy; (étonner) to stun, astonish.
stupeur [stypœʀ] nf (inertie, insensibilité) stupor; (étonnement) astonishment, amazement.
stupide [stypid] adj stupid; (hébété) stunned.
stupidement [stypidmã] adv stupidly.
stupidité [stypidite] nf stupidity no pl; (propos, action) stupid thing (to say ou do).
stups [styp] nmpl (= stupéfiants): **brigade des** ~ narcotics bureau ou squad.
style [stil] nm style; **meuble/robe de** ~ piece of period furniture/period dress; ~ **de vie** lifestyle.
stylé, e [stile] adj well-trained.
stylet [stilɛ] nm (poignard) stiletto; (CHIRURGIE) stylet.
stylisé, e [stilize] adj stylized.
styliste [stilist(ə)] nm/f designer; stylist.
stylistique [stilistik] nf stylistics sg ♦ adj stylistic.
stylo [stilo] nm: ~ **(à encre)** (fountain) pen; ~ **(à) bille** ballpoint pen.
stylo-feutre [stiloføtʀ(ə)] nm felt-tip pen.
su, e [sy] pp de **savoir** ♦ nm: **au** ~ **de** with the knowledge of.
suaire [sɥɛʀ] nm shroud.

suant, e [sɥã, -ãt] adj sweaty.
suave [sɥav] adj (odeur) sweet; (voix) suave, smooth; (coloris) soft, mellow.
subalterne [sybaltɛʀn(ə)] adj (employé, officier) junior; (rôle) subordinate, subsidiary ♦ nm/f subordinate, inferior.
subconscient [sypkɔ̃sjã] nm subconscious.
subdiviser [sybdivize] vt to subdivide.
subdivision [sybdivizjɔ̃] nf subdivision.
subir [sybiʀ] vt (affront, dégâts, mauvais traitements) to suffer; (influence, charme) to be under, be subjected to; (traitement, opération, châtiment) to undergo; (personne) to suffer, be subjected to.
subit, e [sybi, -it] adj sudden.
subitement [sybitmã] adv suddenly, all of a sudden.
subjectif, ive [sybʒɛktif, -iv] adj subjective.
subjectivement [sybʒɛktivmã] adv subjectively.
subjectivité [sybʒɛktivite] nf subjectivity.
subjonctif [sybʒɔ̃ktif] nm subjunctive.
subjuguer [sybʒyge] vt to subjugate.
sublime [syblim] adj sublime.
sublimer [syblime] vt to sublimate.
submergé, e [sybmɛʀʒe] adj submerged; (fig): ~ **de** snowed under with; overwhelmed with.
submerger [sybmɛʀʒe] vt to submerge; (suj: foule) to engulf; (fig) to overwhelm.
submersible [sybmɛʀsibl(ə)] nm submarine.
subordination [sybɔʀdinasjɔ̃] nf subordination.
subordonné, e [sybɔʀdɔne] adj, nm/f subordinate; ~ **à** (personne) subordinate to; (résultats etc) subject to, depending on.
subordonner [sybɔʀdɔne] vt: ~ **qn/qch à** to subordinate sb/sth to.
subornation [sybɔʀnasjɔ̃] nf bribing.
suborner [sybɔʀne] vt to bribe.
subrepticement [sybʀɛptismã] adv surreptitiously.
subroger [sybʀɔʒe] vt (JUR) to subrogate.
subside [sypsid] nm grant.
subsidiaire [sypsidjɛʀ] adj subsidiary; **question** ~ deciding question.
subsistance [sybzistãs] nf subsistence; **pourvoir à la** ~ **de qn** to keep sb, provide for sb's subsistence ou keep.
subsister [sybziste] vi (rester) to remain, subsist; (vivre) to live; (survivre) to live on.
subsonique [sybsɔnik] adj subsonic.
substance [sypstãs] nf substance; **en** ~ in substance.
substantiel, le [sypstãsjɛl] adj substantial.
substantif [sypstãtif] nm noun, substantive.
substantiver [sypstãtive] vt to nominalize.
substituer [sypstitɥe] vt: ~ **qn/qch à** to substitute sb/sth for; **se** ~ **à qn** (représenter) to substitute for sb; (évincer) to substitute o.s. for sb.
substitut [sypstity] nm (JUR) deputy public

prosecutor; (*succédané*) substitute.
substitution [sypstitysjɔ̃] *nf* substitution.
subterfuge [syptɛʀfyʒ] *nm* subterfuge.
subtil, e [syptil] *adj* subtle.
subtilement [syptilmɑ̃] *adv* subtly.
subtiliser [syptilize] *vt*: ~ **qch (à qn)** to spirit sth away (from sb).
subtilité [syptilite] *nf* subtlety.
subtropical, e, aux [sybtʀɔpikal, -o] *adj* subtropical.
suburbain, e [sybyʀbɛ̃, -ɛn] *adj* suburban.
subvenir [sybvəniʀ]: ~ **à** *vt* to meet.
subvention [sybvɑ̃sjɔ̃] *nf* subsidy, grant.
subventionner [sybvɑ̃sjɔne] *vt* to subsidize.
subversif, ive [sybvɛʀsif, -iv] *adj* subversive.
subversion [sybvɛʀsjɔ̃] *nf* subversion.
suc [syk] *nm* (*BOT*) sap; (*de viande, fruit*) juice; ~**s gastriques** gastric juices.
succédané [syksedane] *nm* substitute.
succéder [syksede]: ~ **à** *vt* (*directeur, roi etc*) to succeed; (*venir après: dans une série*) to follow, succeed; **se** ~ *vi* (*accidents, années*) to follow one another.
succès [syksɛ] *nm* success; **avec** ~ successfully; **sans** ~ unsuccessfully; **avoir du** ~ to be a success, be successful; **à** ~ successful; **livre à** ~ bestseller; ~ **de librairie** bestseller; ~ (**féminins**) conquests.
successeur [syksesœʀ] *nm* successor.
successif, ive [syksesif, -iv] *adj* successive.
succession [syksesjɔ̃] *nf* (*série, POL*) succession; (*JUR: patrimoine*) estate, inheritance; **prendre la** ~ **de** (*directeur*) to succeed, take over from; (*entreprise*) to take over.
successivement [syksesivmɑ̃] *adv* successively.
succinct, e [syksɛ̃, -ɛ̃t] *adj* succinct.
succinctement [syksɛ̃tmɑ̃] *adv* succinctly.
succion [syksjɔ̃] *nf*: **bruit de** ~ sucking noise.
succomber [sykɔ̃be] *vi* to die, succumb; (*fig*): ~ **à** to give way to, succumb to.
succulent, e [sykylɑ̃, -ɑ̃t] *adj* succulent.
succursale [sykyʀsal] *nf* branch; **magasin à** ~**s multiples** chain *ou* multiple store.
sucer [syse] *vt* to suck.
sucette [sysɛt] *nf* (*bonbon*) lollipop; (*de bébé*) dummy (*BRIT*), comforter, pacifier (*US*).
suçoter [sysɔte] *vt* to suck.
sucre [sykʀ(ə)] *nm* (*substance*) sugar; (*morceau*) lump of sugar, sugar lump *ou* cube; ~ **de canne/betterave** cane/beet sugar; ~ **en morceaux/cristallisé/en poudre** lump *ou* cube/granulated/caster sugar; ~ **glace** icing sugar; ~ **d'orge** barley sugar.
sucré, e [sykʀe] *adj* (*produit alimentaire*) sweetened; (*au goût*) sweet; (*péj*) sugary, honeyed.
sucrer [sykʀe] *vt* (*thé, café*) to sweeten, put sugar in; ~ **qn** to put sugar in sb's tea (*ou* coffee *etc*); **se** ~ to help o.s. to sugar, have some sugar; (*fam*) to line one's pocket(s).
sucrerie [sykʀəʀi] *nf* (*usine*) sugar refinery; ~**s** *nfpl* (*bonbons*) sweets, sweet things.

sucrier, ière [sykʀije, -jɛʀ] *adj* (*industrie*) sugar *cpd*; (*région*) sugar-producing ♦ *nm* (*fabricant*) sugar producer; (*récipient*) sugar bowl *ou* basin.
sud [syd] *nm*: **le** ~ the south ♦ *adj inv* south; (*côte*) south, southern; **au** ~ (*situation*) in the south; (*direction*) to the south; **au** ~ **de** (to the) south of.
sud-africain, e [sydafʀikɛ̃, -ɛn] *adj* South African ♦ *nm/f*: **Sud-Africain, e** South African.
sud-américain, e [sydameʀikɛ̃, -ɛn] *adj* South American ♦ *nm/f*: **Sud-Américain, e** South American.
sudation [sydasjɔ̃] *nf* sweating, sudation.
sud-coréen, ne [sydkɔʀeɛ̃, -ɛn] *adj* South Korean ♦ *nm/f*: **Sud-Coréen, ne** South Korean.
sud-est [sydɛst] *nm, adj inv* south-east.
sud-ouest [sydwɛst] *nm, adj inv* south-west.
sud-vietnamien, ne [sydvjɛtnamjɛ̃, -ɛn] *adj* South Vietnamese ♦ *nm/f*: **Sud-Vietnamien, ne** South Vietnamese.
Suède [sɥɛd] *nf*: **la** ~ Sweden.
suédois, e [sɥedwa, -waz] *adj* Swedish ♦ *nm* (*LING*) Swedish ♦ *nm/f*: **S~, e** Swede.
suer [sɥe] *vi* to sweat; (*suinter*) to ooze ♦ *vt* (*fig*) to exude; ~ **à grosses gouttes** to sweat profusely.
sueur [sɥœʀ] *nf* sweat; **en** ~ sweating, in a sweat; **avoir des** ~**s froides** to be in a cold sweat.
suffire [syfiʀ] *vi* (*être assez*): ~ (**à qn/pour qch/pour faire**) to be enough *ou* sufficient (for sb/for sth/to do); (*satisfaire*): **cela lui suffit** he's content with this, this is enough for him; **se** ~ *vi* to be self-sufficient; **cela suffit pour les irriter/qu'ils se fâchent** it's enough to annoy them/for them to get angry; **il suffit d'une négligence/qu'on oublie pour que ...** it only takes one act of carelessness/one only needs to forget for ...; **ça suffit!** that's enough!, that'll do!
suffisamment [syfizamɑ̃] *adv* sufficiently, enough; ~ **de** sufficient, enough.
suffisance [syfizɑ̃s] *nf* (*vanité*) self-importance, bumptiousness; (*quantité*): **en** ~ in plenty.
suffisant, e [syfizɑ̃, -ɑ̃t] *adj* (*temps, ressources*) sufficient; (*résultats*) satisfactory; (*vaniteux*) self-important, bumptious.
suffisons [syfizɔ̃] *etc vb voir* **suffire**.
suffixe [syfiks(ə)] *nm* suffix.
suffocant, e [syfɔkɑ̃, -ɑ̃t] *adj* (*étouffant*) suffocating; (*stupéfiant*) staggering.
suffocation [syfɔkasjɔ̃] *nf* suffocation.
suffoquer [syfɔke] *vt* to choke, suffocate; (*stupéfier*) to stagger, astound ♦ *vi* to choke, suffocate; ~ **de colère/d'indignation** to choke with anger/indignation.
suffrage [syfʀaʒ] *nm* (*POL: voix*) vote; (*: méthode*): ~ **universel/direct/indirect** universal/direct/indirect suffrage; (*du public etc*) approval *no pl*; ~**s exprimés** valid

votes.
suggérer [syg3eʀe] *vt* to suggest; ~ **que/de faire** to suggest that/doing.
suggestif, ive [syg3estif, -iv] *adj* suggestive.
suggestion [syg3estjɔ̃] *nf* suggestion.
suggestivité [syg3estivite] *nf* suggestiveness, suggestive nature.
suicidaire [sɥisidɛʀ] *adj* suicidal.
suicide [sɥisid] *nm* suicide ♦ *adj*: **opération** ~ suicide mission.
suicidé, e [sɥiside] *nm/f* suicide.
suicider [sɥiside]: **se** ~ *vi* to commit suicide.
suie [sɥi] *nf* soot.
suif [sɥif] *nm* tallow.
suinter [sɥɛ̃te] *vi* to ooze.
suis [sɥi] *vb voir* **être, suivre**.
suisse [sɥis] *adj* Swiss ♦ *nm* (*bedeau*) ≈ verger ♦ *nm/f*: **S**~ Swiss *pl inv* ♦ *nf*: **la S**~ Switzerland; **la S**~ **romande/allemande** French-speaking/German-speaking Switzerland; ~ **romand** Swiss French.
suisse-allemand, e [sɥisalmɑ̃, -ɑ̃d] *adj*, *nm/f* Swiss German.
Suissesse [sɥisɛs] *nf* Swiss (woman *ou* girl).
suit [sɥi] *vb voir* **suivre**.
suite [sɥit] *nf* (*continuation: d'énumération etc*) rest, remainder; (: *de feuilleton*) continuation; (: *second film etc sur le même thème*) sequel; (*série: de maisons, succès*): **une** ~ **de** a series *ou* succession of; (*MATH*) series *sg*; (*conséquence*) result; (*ordre, liaison logique*) coherence; (*appartement, MUS*) suite; (*escorte*) retinue, suite; ~**s** *nfpl* (*d'une maladie etc*) effects; **prendre la** ~ **de** (*directeur etc*) to succeed, take over from; **donner** ~ **à** (*requête, projet*) to follow up; **faire** ~ **à** to follow; (*faisant*) ~ **à votre lettre du** further to your letter of the; **sans** ~ *adj* incoherent, disjointed ♦ *adv* incoherently, disjointedly; **de** ~ *adv* (*d'affilée*) in succession; (*immédiatement*) at once; **par la** ~ afterwards, subsequently; **à la** ~ *adv* one after the other; **à la** ~ **de** (*derrière*) behind; (*en conséquence de*) following; **par** ~ **de** owing to, as a result of; **avoir de la** ~ **dans les idées** to show great singleness of purpose; **attendre la** ~ **des événements** to (wait and see) what happens.
suivant, e [sɥivɑ̃, -ɑ̃t] *vb voir* **suivre** ♦ *adj* next, following; (*ci-après*): **l'exercice** ~ the following exercise ♦ *prép* (*selon*) according to; ~ **que** according to whether; **au** ~! next!
suive [sɥiv] *etc vb voir* **suivre**.
suiveur [sɥivœʀ] *nm* (*CYCLISME*) (official) follower; (*péj*) (camp) follower.
suivi, e [sɥivi] *pp de* **suivre** ♦ *adj* (*régulier*) regular; (*COMM: article*) in general production; (*cohérent*) consistent; coherent ♦ *nm* follow-up; **très/peu** ~ (*cours*) well-/poorly-attended; (*mode*) widely/not widely adopted; (*feuilleton etc*) widely/not widely followed.
suivre [sɥivʀ(ə)] *vt* (*gén*) to follow; (*SCOL:*

cours) to attend; (: *leçon*) to follow, attend to; (: *programme*) to keep up with; (*COMM: article*) to continue to stock ♦ *vi* to follow; (*élève: écouter*) to attend, pay attention; (: *assimiler le programme*) to keep up, follow; **se** ~ (*accidents, personnes, voitures etc*) to follow one after the other; (*raisonnement*) to be coherent; ~ **des yeux** to follow with one's eyes; **faire** ~ (*lettre*) to forward; ~ **son cours** (*suj: enquête etc*) to run *ou* take its course; "**à** ~" "to be continued".
sujet, te [sy3ɛ, -ɛt] *adj*: **être** ~ **à** (*accidents*) to be prone to; (*vertige etc*) to be liable *ou* subject to ♦ *nm/f* (*d'un souverain*) subject ♦ *nm* subject; **un** ~ **de dispute/discorde/ mécontentement** a cause for argument/ dissension/dissatisfaction; **c'est à quel** ~? what is it about?; **avoir** ~ **de se plaindre** to have cause for complaint; **au** ~ **de** *prép* about; ~ **à caution** *adj* questionable; ~ **de conversation** topic *ou* subject of conversation; ~ **d'examen** (*SCOL*) examination question; examination paper; ~ **d'expérience** (*BIO etc*) experimental subject.
sujétion [sy3esjɔ̃] *nf* subjection; (*fig*) constraint.
sulfater [sylfate] *vt* to spray with copper sulphate.
sulfureux, euse [sylfyʀø, -øz] *adj* sulphurous (*BRIT*), sulfurous (*US*).
sulfurique [sylfyʀik] *adj*: **acide** ~ sulphuric (*BRIT*) *ou* sulfuric (*US*) acid.
sulfurisé, e [sylfyʀize] *adj*: **papier** ~ greaseproof (*BRIT*) *ou* wax (*US*) paper.
Sumatra [symatʀa] *nf* Sumatra.
summum [sɔmɔm] *nm*: **le** ~ **de** the height of.
sumo [symo] *nm inv* sumo (wrestling).
super [sypɛʀ] *adj inv* great, fantastic ♦ *nm* (= *supercarburant*) ≈ 4-star (*BRIT*), ≈ premium (*US*).
superbe [sypɛʀb(ə)] *adj* magnificent, superb ♦ *nf* arrogance.
superbement [sypɛʀbəmɑ̃] *adv* superbly.
supercarburant [sypɛʀkaʀbyʀɑ̃] *nm* ≈ 4-star petrol (*BRIT*), ≈ premium gas (*US*).
supercherie [sypɛʀʃəʀi] *nf* trick, trickery *no pl*; (*fraude*) fraud.
supérette [sypeʀɛt] *nf* minimarket.
superfétatoire [sypeʀfetatwaʀ] *adj* superfluous.
superficie [sypɛʀfisi] *nf* (*surface*) area; (*fig*) surface.
superficiel, le [sypɛʀfisjɛl] *adj* superficial.
superficiellement [sypɛʀfisjɛlmɑ̃] *adv* superficially.
superflu, e [sypɛʀfly] *adj* superfluous ♦ *nm*: **le** ~ the superfluous.
superforme [sypɛʀfɔʀm(ə)] *nf* (*fam*) top form, excellent shape.
super-grand [sypɛʀgʀɑ̃] *nm* superpower.
super-huit [sypɛʀɥit] *adj*: **camera/film** ~ super-eight camera/film.

supérieur, e [sypeʀjœʀ] *adj* (*lèvre, étages, classes*) upper; (*plus élevé: température, niveau*): ~ **(à)** higher (than); (*meilleur: qualité, produit*): ~ **(à)** superior (to); (*excellent, hautain*) superior ♦ *nm/f* superior; **Mère** ~**e** Mother Superior; **à l'étage** ~ on the next floor up; ~ **en nombre** superior in number.

supérieurement [sypeʀjœʀmɑ̃] *adv* exceptionally well, exceptionally + *adj*.

supériorité [sypeʀjɔʀite] *nf* superiority.

superlatif [sypeʀlatif] *nm* superlative.

supermarché [sypeʀmaʀʃe] *nm* supermarket.

supernova [sypeʀnɔva] *nf* supernova.

superposable [sypeʀpozabl(ə)] *adj* (*figures*) that may be superimposed; (*lits*) stackable.

superposer [sypeʀpoze] *vt* to superpose; (*meubles, caisses*) to stack; (*faire chevaucher*) to superimpose; **se** ~ (*images, souvenirs*) to be superimposed; **lits superposés** bunk beds.

superposition [sypeʀpozisjɔ̃] *nf* superposition; superimposition.

superpréfet [sypeʀpʀefɛ] *nm* prefect in charge of a region.

superproduction [sypeʀpʀɔdyksjɔ̃] *nf* (*film*) spectacular.

superpuissance [sypeʀpɥisɑ̃s] *nf* superpower.

supersonique [sypeʀsɔnik] *adj* supersonic.

superstitieux, euse [sypeʀstisjø, -øz] *adj* superstitious.

superstition [sypeʀstisjɔ̃] *nf* superstition.

superstructure [sypeʀstʀyktyʀ] *nf* superstructure.

supertanker [sypeʀtɑ̃kœʀ] *nm* supertanker.

superviser [sypeʀvize] *vt* to supervise.

supervision [sypeʀvizjɔ̃] *nf* supervision.

suppl. *abr* = **supplément**.

supplanter [syplɑ̃te] *vt* to supplant.

suppléance [sypleɑ̃s] *nf* (*poste*) supply post (*BRIT*), substitute teacher's post (*US*).

suppléant, e [sypleɑ̃, -ɑ̃t] *adj* (*juge, fonctionnaire*) deputy *cpd*; (*professeur*) supply *cpd* (*BRIT*), substitute *cpd* (*US*) ♦ *nm/f* deputy; supply *ou* substitute teacher; **médecin** ~ locum.

suppléer [syplee] *vt* (*ajouter: mot manquant etc*) to supply, provide; (*compenser: lacune*) to fill in; (*: défaut*) to make up for; (*remplacer: professeur*) to stand in for; (*: juge*) to deputize for; ~ **à** *vt* to make up for; to substitute for.

supplément [syplemɑ̃] *nm* supplement; **un** ~ **de travail** extra *ou* additional work; **un** ~ **de frites** *etc* an extra portion of chips *etc*; **un** ~ **de 100 F** a supplement of 100 F, an extra *ou* additional 100 F; **ceci est en** ~ (*au menu etc*) this is extra, there is an extra charge for this; ~ **d'information** additional information.

supplémentaire [syplemɑ̃tɛʀ] *adj* additional, further; (*train, bus*) relief *cpd*, extra.

supplétif, ive [sypletif, -iv] *adj* (*MIL*) auxiliary.

suppliant, e [syplijɑ̃, -ɑ̃t] *adj* imploring.

supplication [syplikasjɔ̃] *nf* (*REL*) supplication; ~**s** *nfpl* (*adjurations*) pleas, entreaties.

supplice [syplis] *nm* (*peine corporelle*) torture *no pl*; form of torture; (*douleur physique, morale*) torture, agony; **être au** ~ to be in agony.

supplier [syplije] *vt* to implore, beseech.

supplique [syplik] *nf* petition.

support [sypɔʀ] *nm* support; (*pour livre, outils*) stand; ~ **audio-visuel** audio-visual aid; ~ **publicitaire** advertising medium.

supportable [sypɔʀtabl(ə)] *adj* (*douleur, température*) bearable; (*procédé, conduite*) tolerable.

supporter *nm* [sypɔʀtɛʀ] supporter, fan ♦ *vt* [sypɔʀte] (*poids, poussée, SPORT: concurrent, équipe*) to support; (*conséquences, épreuve*) to bear, endure; (*défauts, personne*) to tolerate, put up with; (*suj: chose: chaleur etc*) to withstand; (*suj: personne: chaleur, vin*) to take.

supposé, e [sypoze] *adj* (*nombre*) estimated; (*auteur*) supposed.

supposer [sypoze] *vt* to suppose; (*impliquer*) to presuppose; **en supposant** *ou* **à** ~ **que** supposing (that).

supposition [sypozisjɔ̃] *nf* supposition.

suppositoire [sypozitwaʀ] *nm* suppository.

suppôt [sypo] *nm* (*péj*) henchman.

suppression [sypʀesjɔ̃] *nf* (*voir supprimer*) removal; deletion; cancellation; suppression.

supprimer [sypʀime] *vt* (*cloison, cause, anxiété*) to remove; (*clause, mot*) to delete; (*congés, service d'autobus etc*) to cancel; (*publication, article*) to suppress; (*emplois, privilèges, témoin gênant*) to do away with; ~ **qch à qn** to deprive sb of sth.

suppurer [sypyʀe] *vi* to suppurate.

supputations [sypytasjɔ̃] *nfpl* calculations, reckonings.

supputer [sypyte] *vt* to calculate, reckon.

supranational, e, aux [sypʀanasjɔnal, -o] *adj* supranational.

suprématie [sypʀemasi] *nf* supremacy.

suprême [sypʀɛm] *adj* supreme.

suprêmement [sypʀɛmmɑ̃] *adv* supremely.

================= *MOT-CLÉ*

sur [syʀ] *prép* **1** (*position*) on; (*pardessus*) over; (*au-dessus*) above; **pose-le** ~ **la table** put it on the table; **je n'ai pas d'argent** ~ **moi** I haven't any money on me

2 (*direction*) towards; **en allant** ~ **Paris** going towards Paris; ~ **votre droite** on *ou* to your right

3 (*à propos de*) on, about; **un livre/une conférence** ~ **Balzac** a book/lecture on *ou* about Balzac

4 (*proportion, mesures*) out of; by; **un** ~ **10** one in 10; (*SCOL*) one out of 10; ~ **20, 2 sont venus** out of 20, 2 came; **4 m** ~ **2** 4 m by 2; **avoir accident** ~ **accident** to have one accident after another

5 (*cause*): ~ **sa recommandation** on *ou* at his recommendation; ~ **son invitation** at his invitation

sur ce *adv* whereupon; ~ **ce, il faut que je vous quitte** and now I must leave you.

sur, e [syʀ] *adj* sour.

sûr, e [syʀ] *adj* sure, certain; (*digne de confiance*) reliable; (*sans danger*) safe; **peu** ~ unreliable; ~ **de qch** sure *ou* certain of sth; **être** ~ **de qn** to be sure of sb; ~ **et certain** absolutely certain; ~ **de soi** self-assured, self-confident; **le plus** ~ **est de** the safest thing is to.

surabondance [syʀabɔ̃dɑ̃s] *nf* overabundance.

surabondant, e [syʀabɔ̃dɑ̃, -ɑ̃t] *adj* overabundant.

surabonder [syʀabɔ̃de] *vi* to be overabundant; ~ **de** to abound with, have an overabundance of.

suractivité [syʀaktivite] *nf* hyperactivity.

suraigu, ë [syʀegy] *adj* very shrill.

surajouter [syʀaʒute] *vt*: ~ **qch à** to add sth to.

suralimentation [syʀalimɑ̃tasjɔ̃] *nf* overfeeding; (*TECH: d'un moteur*) supercharging.

suralimenté, e [syʀalimɑ̃te] *adj* (*personne*) overfed; (*moteur*) supercharged.

suranné, e [syʀane] *adj* outdated, outmoded.

surarmement [syʀaʀməmɑ̃] *nm* (excess) stockpiling of arms (*ou* weapons).

surbaissé, e [syʀbese] *adj* lowered, low.

surcapacité [syʀkapasite] *nf* overcapacity.

surcharge [syʀʃaʀʒ(ə)] *nf* (*de passagers, marchandises*) excess load; (*de détails, d'ornements*) overabundance, excess; (*correction*) alteration; (*POSTES*) surcharge; **prendre des passagers en** ~ to take on excess *ou* extra passengers; ~ **de bagages** excess luggage; ~ **de travail** extra work.

surchargé, e [syʀʃaʀʒe] *adj* (*décoration, style*) over-elaborate, overfussy; (*voiture, emploi du temps*) overloaded.

surcharger [syʀʃaʀʒe] *vt* to overload; (*timbre-poste*) to surcharge; (*décoration*) to overdo.

surchauffe [syʀʃof] *nf* overheating.

surchauffé, e [syʀʃofe] *adj* overheated; (*fig: imagination*) overactive.

surchoix [syʀʃwa] *adj inv* top-quality.

surclasser [syʀklase] *vt* to outclass.

surconsommation [syʀkɔ̃sɔmasjɔ̃] *nf* (*ÉCON*) overconsumption.

surcoté, e [syʀkɔte] *adj* overpriced.

surcouper [syʀkupe] *vt* to overtrump.

surcroît [syʀkʀwa] *nm*: **un** ~ **de** additional + *nom*; **par** *ou* **de** ~ moreover; **en** ~ in addition.

surdi-mutité [syʀdimytite] *nf*: **atteint de** ~ deaf and dumb.

surdité [syʀdite] *nf* deafness; **atteint de** ~ **totale** profoundly deaf.

surdoué, e [syʀdwe] *adj* gifted.

sureau, x [syʀo] *nm* elder (tree).

sureffectif [syʀefɛktif] *nm* overmanning.

surélever [syʀelve] *vt* to raise, heighten.

sûrement [syʀmɑ̃] *adv* reliably; safely, securely; (*certainement*) certainly; ~ **pas** certainly not.

suremploi [syʀɑ̃plwa] *nm* (*ÉCON*) overemployment.

surenchère [syʀɑ̃ʃɛʀ] *nf* (*aux enchères*) higher bid; (*sur prix fixe*) overbid; (*fig*) overstatement; outbidding tactics *pl*; ~ **de violence** build-up of violence; ~ **électorale** political (*ou* electoral) one-upmanship.

surenchérir [syʀɑ̃ʃeʀiʀ] *vi* to bid higher; to raise one's bid; (*fig*) to try and outbid each other.

surendettement [syʀɑ̃dɛtmɑ̃] *nm* excessive debt.

surent [syʀ] *vb voir* **savoir**.

surentraîné, e [syʀɑ̃tʀene] *adj* overtrained.

suréquipé, e [syʀekipe] *adj* overequipped.

surestimer [syʀɛstime] *vt* (*tableau*) to overvalue; (*possibilité, personne*) to overestimate.

sûreté [syʀte] *nf* (*voir* **sûr**) reliability; safety; (*JUR*) guaranty; surety; **mettre en** ~ to put in a safe place; **pour plus de** ~ as an extra precaution; to be on the safe side; **la** ~ **de l'État** State security; **la S**~ **(nationale)** division of the Ministère de l'Intérieur heading all police forces except the gendarmerie and the Paris préfecture de police.

surexcité, e [syʀɛksite] *adj* overexcited.

surexciter [syʀɛksite] *vt* (*personne*) to overexcite; **cela surexcite ma curiosité** it really rouses my curiosity.

surexploiter [syʀɛksplwate] *vt* to overexploit.

surexposer [syʀɛkspoze] *vt* to overexpose.

surf [sœʀf] *nm* surfing; **faire du** ~ to go surfing.

surface [syʀfas] *nf* surface; (*superficie*) surface area; **faire** ~ to surface; **en** ~ *adv* near the surface; (*fig*) superficially; **la pièce fait 100 m² de** ~ the room has a surface area of 100m²; ~ **de réparation** (*SPORT*) penalty area; ~ **porteuse** *ou* **de sustentation** (*AVIAT*) aerofoil.

surfait, e [syʀfɛ, -ɛt] *adj* overrated.

surfeur, euse [sœʀfœʀ, -øz] *nm/f* surfer.

surfiler [syʀfile] *vt* (*COUTURE*) to oversew.

surfin, e [syʀfɛ̃, -in] *adj* superfine.

surgélateur [syʀʒelatœʀ] *nm* deep freeze.

surgélation [syʀʒelasjɔ̃] *nf* deep-freezing.

surgelé, e [syʀʒəle] *adj* (deep-)frozen.

surgeler [syʀʒəle] *vt* to (deep-)freeze.

surgir [syʀʒiʀ] *vi* (*personne, véhicule*) to appear suddenly; (*jaillir*) to shoot up; (*montagne etc*) to rise up, loom up; (*fig: problème, conflit*) to arise.

surhomme [syʀɔm] *nm* superman.

surhumain, e [syʀymɛ̃, -ɛn] *adj* superhuman.

surimposer [syʀɛ̃poze] *vt* to overtax.

surimpression [syʀɛ̃pʀesjɔ̃] *nf* (*PHOTO*) double exposure; **en** ~ superimposed.
surimprimer [syʀɛ̃pʀime] *vt* to overstrike, overprint.
Surinam [syʀinam] *nm*: **le** ~ Surinam.
surinfection [syʀɛ̃fɛksjɔ̃] *nf* (*MÉD*) secondary infection.
surjet [syʀʒɛ] *nm* (*COUTURE*) overcast seam.
sur-le-champ [syʀləʃɑ̃] *adv* immediately.
surlendemain [syʀlɑ̃dmɛ̃] *nm*: **le** ~ (**soir**) two days later (in the evening); **le** ~ **de** two days after.
surligneur [syʀliɲœʀ] *nm* (*feutre*) highlighter (pen).
surmenage [syʀmənaʒ] *nm* overwork; **le** ~ **intellectuel** mental fatigue.
surmené, e [syʀməne] *adj* overworked.
surmener [syʀməne] *vt*, **se** ~ *vi* to overwork.
surmonter [syʀmɔ̃te] *vt* (*suj: coupole etc*) to surmount, top; (*vaincre*) to overcome, surmount.
surmultiplié, e [syʀmyltiplije] *adj, nf*: (**vitesse**) ~**e** overdrive.
surnager [syʀnaʒe] *vi* to float.
surnaturel, le [syʀnatyʀɛl] *adj, nm* supernatural.
surnom [syʀnɔ̃] *nm* nickname.
surnombre [syʀnɔ̃bʀ(ə)] *nm*: **être en** ~ to be too many (*ou* one too many).
surnommer [syʀnɔme] *vt* to nickname.
surnuméraire [syʀnymeʀɛʀ] *nmf* supernumerary.
suroît [syʀwa] *nm* sou'wester.
surpasser [syʀpɑse] *vt* to surpass; **se** ~ to surpass o.s., excel o.s.
surpayer [syʀpeje] *vt* (*personne*) to overpay; (*article etc*) to pay too much for.
surpeuplé, e [syʀpœple] *adj* overpopulated.
surpeuplement [syʀpœpləmɑ̃] *nm* overpopulation.
surpiquer [syʀpike] *vt* (*COUTURE*) to overstitch.
surpiqûre [syʀpikyʀ] *nf* (*COUTURE*) overstitching.
surplace [syʀplas] *nm*: **faire du** ~ to mark time.
surplis [syʀpli] *nm* surplice.
surplomb [syʀplɔ̃] *nm* overhang; **en** ~ overhanging.
surplomber [syʀplɔ̃be] *vi* to be overhanging ♦ *vt* to overhang; (*dominer*) to tower above.
surplus [syʀply] *nm* (*COMM*) surplus; (*reste*): ~ **de bois** wood left over; **au** ~ moreover; ~ **américains** American army surplus *sg*.
surpopulation [syʀpɔpylasjɔ̃] *nf* overpopulation.
surprenant, e [syʀpʀənɑ̃, -ɑ̃t] *vb voir* **surprendre** ♦ *adj* amazing.
surprendre [syʀpʀɑ̃dʀ(ə)] *vt* (*étonner, prendre à l'improviste*) to amaze, surprise; (*secret*) to discover; (*tomber sur: intrus etc*) to catch; (*fig*) to detect; to chance *ou* happen upon;

(*clin d'œil*) to intercept; (*conversation*) to overhear; (*suj: orage, nuit etc*) to catch out, take by surprise; ~ **la vigilance/bonne foi de qn** to catch sb out/betray sb's good faith; **se** ~ **à faire** to catch *ou* find o.s. doing.
surprime [syʀpʀim] *nf* additional premium.
surpris, e [syʀpʀi, -iz] *pp de* **surprendre** ♦ *adj*: ~ (**de/que**) amazed *ou* surprised (at/that).
surprise [syʀpʀiz] *nf* surprise; **faire une** ~ **à qn** to give sb a surprise; **voyage sans** ~**s** uneventful journey; **par** ~ *adv* by surprise.
surprise-partie [syʀpʀizpaʀti] *nf* party.
surprit [syʀpʀi] *vb voir* **surprendre**.
surproduction [syʀpʀɔdyksjɔ̃] *nf* overproduction.
surréaliste [syʀʀealist(ə)] *adj, nmf* surrealist.
sursaut [syʀso] *nm* start, jump; ~ **de** (*énergie, indignation*) sudden fit *ou* burst of; **en** ~ *adv* with a start.
sursauter [syʀsote] *vi* to (give a) start, jump.
surseoir [syʀswaʀ]: ~ **à** *vt* to defer; (*JUR*) to stay.
sursis [syʀsi] *nm* (*JUR: gén*) suspended sentence; (*à l'exécution capitale, aussi fig*) reprieve; (*MIL*): ~ (**d'appel** *ou* **d'incorporation**) deferment; **condamné à 5 mois (de prison) avec** ~ given a 5-month suspended (prison) sentence.
sursitaire [syʀsiteʀ] *nm* (*MIL*) deferred conscript.
sursois [syʀswa], **sursoyais** [syʀswaje] *etc vb voir* **surseoir**.
surtaxe [syʀtaks(ə)] *nf* surcharge.
surtension [syʀtɑ̃sjɔ̃] *nf* (*ÉLEC*) overvoltage.
surtout [syʀtu] *adv* (*avant tout, d'abord*) above all; (*spécialement, particulièrement*) especially; **il aime le sport,** ~ **le football** he likes sport, especially football; **cet été, il a** ~ **fait de la pêche** this summer he went fishing more than anything (else); ~ **pas d'histoires!** no fuss now!; ~, **ne dites rien!** whatever you do - don't say anything!; ~ **pas!** certainly *ou* definitely not!; ~ **que ...** especially as ....
survécu, e [syʀveky] *pp de* **survivre**.
surveillance [syʀvɛjɑ̃s] *nf* watch; (*POLICE, MIL*) surveillance; **sous** ~ **médicale** under medical supervision; **la** ~ **du territoire** internal security; *voir aussi* **DST**.
surveillant, e [syʀvejɑ̃, -ɑ̃t] *nmf* (*de prison*) warder; (*SCOL*) monitor; (*de travaux*) supervisor, overseer.
surveiller [syʀveje] *vt* (*enfant, élèves, bagages*) to watch, keep an eye on; (*malade*) to watch over; (*prisonnier, suspect*) to keep (a) watch on; (*territoire, bâtiment*) to (keep) watch over; (*travaux, cuisson*) to supervise; (*SCOL: examen*) to invigilate; **se** ~ to keep a check *ou* watch on o.s.; ~ **son langage/sa ligne** to watch one's language/figure.
survenir [syʀvəniʀ] *vi* (*incident, retards*) to occur, arise; (*événement*) to take place; (*per-*

sonne) to appear, arrive.

survenu, e [syʀv(ə)ny] *pp de* **survenir**.

survêt(ement) [syʀvɛt(mɑ̃)] *nm* tracksuit (*BRIT*), sweat suit (*US*).

survie [syʀvi] *nf* survival; (*REL*) afterlife; **équipement de** ~ survival equipment; **une** ~ **de quelques mois** a few more months of life.

surviens [syʀvjɛ̃], **survint** [syʀvɛ̃] *etc vb voir* **survenir**.

survit [syʀvi] *etc vb voir* **survivre**.

survitrage [syʀvitʀaʒ] *nm* double-glazing.

survivance [syʀvivɑ̃s] *nf* relic.

survivant, e [syʀvivɑ̃, -ɑ̃t] *vb voir* **survivre** ♦ *nm/f* survivor.

survivre [syʀvivʀ(ə)] *vi* to survive; ~ **à** *vt* (*accident etc*) to survive; (*personne*) to outlive; **la victime a peu de chance de** ~ the victim has little hope of survival.

survol [syʀvɔl] *nm* flying over.

survoler [syʀvɔle] *vt* to fly over; (*fig: livre*) to skim through; (*: question, problèmes*) to skim over.

survolté, e [syʀvɔlte] *adj* (*ÉLEC*) stepped up, boosted; (*fig*) worked up.

sus [sy(s)]: **en** ~ **de** *prép* in addition to, over and above; **en** ~ *adv* in addition; ~ **à** *excl:* ~ **au tyran!** at the tyrant! ♦ *vb* [sy] *voir* **savoir**.

susceptibilité [syseptibilite] *nf* sensitivity *no pl.*

susceptible [syseptibl(ə)] *adj* touchy, sensitive; ~ **d'amélioration** *ou* **d'être amélioré** that can be improved, open to improvement; ~ **de faire** (*capacité*) able to do; (*probabilité*) liable to do.

susciter [sysite] *vt* (*admiration*) to arouse; (*obstacles, ennuis*): ~ (**à qn**) to create (for sb).

susdit, e [sysdi, -dit] *adj* foresaid.

susmentionné, e [sysmɑ̃sjɔne] *adj* abovementioned.

susnommé, e [sysnɔme] *adj* above-named.

suspect, e [syspɛ(kt), -ɛkt(ə)] *adj* suspicious; (*témoignage, opinions, vin etc*) suspect ♦ *nm/f* suspect; **peu** ~ **de** most unlikely to be suspected of.

suspecter [syspɛkte] *vt* to suspect; (*honnêteté de qn*) to question, have one's suspicions about; ~ **qn d'être/d'avoir fait qch** to suspect sb of being/having done sth.

suspendre [syspɑ̃dʀ(ə)] *vt* (*accrocher: vêtement*): ~ **qch (à)** to hang sth up (on); (*fixer: lustre etc*): ~ **qch à** to hang sth from; (*interrompre, démettre*) to suspend; (*remettre*) to defer; **se** ~ **à** to hang from.

suspendu, e [syspɑ̃dy] *pp de* **suspendre** ♦ *adj* (*accroché*): ~ **à** hanging on (*ou* from); (*perché*): ~ **au-dessus de** suspended over; (*AUTO*): **bien/mal** ~ with good/poor suspension; **être** ~ **aux lèvres de qn** to hang upon sb's every word.

suspens [syspɑ̃]: **en** ~ *adv* (*affaire*) in abeyance; **tenir en** ~ to keep in suspense.

suspense [syspɑ̃s] *nm* suspense.

suspension [syspɑ̃sjɔ̃] *nf* suspension; deferment; (*AUTO*) suspension; (*lustre*) pendant light fitting; **en** ~ in suspension, suspended; ~ **d'audience** adjournment.

suspicieux, euse [syspisjø, -øz] *adj* suspicious.

suspicion [syspisjɔ̃] *nf* suspicion.

sustentation [systɑ̃tasjɔ̃] *nf* (*AVIAT*) lift; **base** *ou* **polygone de** ~ support polygon.

sustenter [systɑ̃te]: **se** ~ *vi* to take sustenance.

susurrer [sysyʀe] *vt* to whisper.

sut [sy] *vb voir* **savoir**.

suture [sytyʀ] *nf:* **point de** ~ stitch.

suturer [sytyʀe] *vt* to stitch up, suture.

suzeraineté [syzʀɛnte] *nf* suzerainty.

svelte [svɛlt(ə)] *adj* slender, svelte.

SVP *sigle* (= *s'il vous plaît*) please.

Swaziland [swazilɑ̃d] *nm:* **le** ~ Swaziland.

syllabe [silab] *nf* syllable.

sylphide [silfid] *nf* (*fig*): **sa taille de** ~ her sylph-like figure.

sylvestre [silvɛstʀ(ə)] *adj:* **pin** ~ Scots pine, Scotch fir.

sylvicole [silvikɔl] *adj* forestry *cpd.*

sylviculteur [silvikyltœʀ] *nm* forester.

sylviculture [silvikyltyʀ] *nf* forestry, sylviculture.

symbole [sɛ̃bɔl] *nm* symbol; ~ **graphique** (*INFORM*) icon.

symbolique [sɛ̃bɔlik] *adj* symbolic; (*geste, offrande*) token *cpd*; (*salaire, dommages-intérêts*) nominal.

symboliquement [sɛ̃bɔlikmɑ̃] *adv* symbolically.

symboliser [sɛ̃bɔlize] *vt* to symbolize.

symétrie [simetʀi] *nf* symmetry.

symétrique [simetʀik] *adj* symmetrical.

symétriquement [simetʀikmɑ̃] *adv* symmetrically.

sympa [sɛ̃pa] *adj inv* (= *sympathique*) nice; friendly; good.

sympathie [sɛ̃pati] *nf* (*inclination*) liking; (*affinité*) fellow feeling; (*condoléances*) sympathy; **accueillir avec** ~ (*projet*) to receive favourably; **avoir de la** ~ **pour qn** to like sb, have a liking for sb; **témoignages de** ~ expressions of sympathy; **croyez à toute ma** ~ you have my deepest sympathy.

sympathique [sɛ̃patik] *adj* (*personne, figure*) nice, friendly, likeable; (*geste*) friendly; (*livre*) good; (*déjeuner*) nice; (*réunion, endroit*) pleasant, nice.

sympathisant, e [sɛ̃patizɑ̃, -ɑ̃t] *nm/f* sympathizer.

sympathiser [sɛ̃patize] *vi* (*voisins etc: s'entendre*) to get on (*BRIT*) *ou* along (*US*) (well); (*: se fréquenter*) to socialize, see each other; ~ **avec** to get on *ou* along (well) with; to see, socialize with.

symphonie [sɛ̃fɔni] *nf* symphony.

symphonique [sɛ̃fɔnik] *adj* (*orchestre, concert*) symphony *cpd*; (*musique*) symphonic.
symposium [sɛ̃pozjɔm] *nm* symposium.
symptomatique [sɛ̃ptɔmatik] *adj* symptomatic.
symptôme [sɛ̃ptom] *nm* symptom.
synagogue [sinagɔg] *nf* synagogue.
synchrone [sɛ̃kRɔn] *adj* synchronous.
synchronique [sɛ̃kRɔnik] *adj*: **tableau ~** synchronic table of events.
synchronisation [sɛ̃kRɔnizasjɔ̃] *nf* synchronization; (*AUTO*) ~ **des vitesses** synchromesh.
synchronisé, e [sɛ̃kRɔnize] *adj* synchronized.
synchroniser [sɛ̃kRɔnize] *vt* to synchronize.
syncope [sɛ̃kɔp] *nf* (*MÉD*) blackout; (*MUS*) syncopation; **tomber en ~** to faint, pass out.
syncopé, e [sɛ̃kɔpe] *adj* syncopated.
syndic [sɛ̃dik] *nm* managing agent.
syndical, e, aux [sɛ̃dikal, -o] *adj* (trade-)union *cpd*; **centrale ~e** group of affiliated trade unions.
syndicalisme [sɛ̃dikalism(ə)] *nm* (*mouvement*) trade unionism; (*activités*) union(ist) activities *pl*.
syndicaliste [sɛ̃dikalist(ə)] *nm/f* trade unionist.
syndicat [sɛ̃dika] *nm* (*d'ouvriers, employés*) (*trade(s)*) union; (*autre association d'intérêts*) union, association; ~ **d'initiative (SI)** tourist office *ou* bureau; ~ **patronal** employers' syndicate, federation of employers; ~ **de propriétaires** association of property owners.
syndiqué, e [sɛ̃dike] *adj* belonging to a (trade) union; **non ~** non-union.
syndiquer [sɛ̃dike]: **se ~** *vi* to form a trade union; (*adhérer*) to join a trade union.
syndrome [sɛ̃dRɔm] *nm* syndrome; ~ **prémenstruel** premenstrual syndrome (PMS).
synergie [sinɛRʒi] *nf* synergy.
synode [sinɔd] *nm* synod.
synonyme [sinɔnim] *adj* synonymous ♦ *nm* synonym; ~ **de** synonymous with.
synopsis [sinɔpsis] *nm ou nf* synopsis.
synoptique [sinɔptik] *adj*: **tableau ~** synoptic table.
synovie [sinɔvi] *nf* synovia; **épanchement de ~** water on the knee.
syntaxe [sɛ̃taks(ə)] *nf* syntax.
synthèse [sɛ̃tɛz] *nf* synthesis (*pl* -es); **faire la ~ de** to synthesize.
synthétique [sɛ̃tetik] *adj* synthetic.
synthétiser [sɛ̃tetize] *vt* to synthesize.
synthétiseur [sɛ̃tetizœR] *nm* (*MUS*) synthesizer.
syphilis [sifilis] *nf* syphilis.
Syrie [siRi] *nf*: **la ~** Syria.
syrien, ne [siRjɛ̃, -ɛn] *adj* Syrian ♦ *nm/f*: **S~, ne** Syrian.
systématique [sistematik] *adj* systematic.
systématiquement [sistematikmɑ̃] *adv* systematically.
systématiser [sistematize] *vt* to systematize.

système [sistɛm] *nm* system; **le ~ D** resourcefulness; ~ **décimal** decimal system; ~ **expert** expert system; ~ **d'exploitation à disques** (*INFORM*) disk operating system; ~ **immunitaire** immune system; ~ **métrique** metric system; ~ **solaire** solar system.

T t

T, t [te] *nm inv* T, t ♦ *abr* (= *tonne*) t; **T comme Thérèse** T for Tommy.
t' [t(ə)] *pron voir* **te**.
ta [ta] *adj possessif voir* **ton**.
tabac [taba] *nm* tobacco; (*aussi*: **débit** *ou* **bureau de ~**) tobacconist's (shop) ♦ *adj inv*: (*couleur*) ~ buff, tobacco *cpd*; **passer qn à ~** to beat sb up; **faire un ~** (*fam*) to be a big hit; ~ **blond/brun** light/dark tobacco; ~ **gris** shag; ~ **à priser** snuff.
tabagie [tabaʒi] *nf* smoke den.
tabagisme [tabaʒism(ə)] *nm* nicotine addiction; ~ **passif** passive smoking.
tabasser [tabase] *vt* to beat up.
tabatière [tabatjɛR] *nf* snuffbox.
tabernacle [tabɛRnakl(ə)] *nm* tabernacle.
table [tabl(ə)] *nf* table; **avoir une bonne ~** to keep a good table; **à ~!** dinner *etc* is ready!; **se mettre à ~** to sit down to eat; (*fig: fam*) to come clean; **mettre** *ou* **dresser/desservir la ~** to lay *ou* set/clear the table; **faire ~ rase de** to make a clean sweep of; ~ **basse** coffee table; ~ **de cuisson** (*à l'électricité*) hotplate; (*au gas*) gas ring; ~ **d'écoute** wiretapping set; ~ **d'harmonie** sounding board; ~ **d'hôte** set menu; ~ **de lecture** turntable; ~ **des matières** (table of) contents *pl*; ~ **de multiplication** multiplication table; ~ **des négociations** negotiating table; ~ **de nuit** *ou* **de chevet** bedside table; ~ **ronde** (*débat*) round table; ~ **roulante** (tea) trolley; ~ **de toilette** washstand; ~ **traçante** (*INFORM*) plotter.
tableau, x [tablo] *nm* (*ART*) painting; (*reproduction, fig*) picture; (*panneau*) board; (*schéma*) table, chart; ~ **d'affichage** notice board; ~ **de bord** dashboard; (*AVIAT*) instrument panel; ~ **de chasse** tally; ~ **de contrôle** console, control panel; ~ **de maître** masterpiece; ~ **noir** blackboard.
tablée [table] *nf* (*personnes*) table.
tabler [table] *vi*: ~ **sur** to count *ou* bank on.
tablette [tablɛt] *nf* (*planche*) shelf (*pl* shelves); ~ **de chocolat** bar of chocolate.
tableur [tablœR] *nm* (*INFORM*) spreadsheet.
tablier [tablije] *nm* apron; (*de pont*) roadway;

(de cheminée) (flue-)shutter.

tabou, e [tabu] adj, nm taboo.

tabouret [taburɛ] nm stool.

tabulateur [tabylatœʀ] nm (TECH) tabulator.

TAC sigle m (= train autos-couchettes) car-sleeper train, ≈ Motorail ® (BRIT).

tac [tak] nm: **du ~ au ~** tit for tat.

tache [taʃ] nf (saleté) stain, mark; (ART, de couleur, lumière) spot; splash, patch; **faire ~ d'huile** to spread, gain ground; **~ de rousseur** ou **de son** freckle; **~ de vin** (sur la peau) strawberry mark.

tâche [taʃ] nf task; **travailler à la ~** to do piecework.

tacher [taʃe] vt to stain, mark; (fig) to sully, stain; **se ~** vi (fruits) to become marked.

tâcher [taʃe] vi: **~ de faire** to try to do, endeavour (BRIT) ou endeavor (US) to do.

tâcheron [taʃʀɔ̃] nm (fig) drudge.

tacheté, e [taʃte] adj: **~ de** speckled ou spotted with.

tachisme [taʃism(ə)] nm (PEINTURE) tachisme.

tachygraphe [takigʀaf] nm tachograph.

tachymètre [takimɛtʀ(ə)] nm tachometer.

tacite [tasit] adj tacit.

tacitement [tasitmɑ̃] adv tacitly.

taciturne [tasityʀn(ə)] adj taciturn.

tacot [tako] nm (péj: voiture) banger (BRIT), clunker (US).

tact [takt] nm tact; **avoir du ~** to be tactful, have tact.

tacticien, ne [taktisjɛ̃, -ɛn] nm/f tactician.

tactile [taktil] adj tactile.

tactique [taktik] adj tactical ♦ nf (technique) tactics sg; (plan) tactic.

Tadjikistan [tadʒikistɑ̃] nm Tajikistan.

taffetas [tafta] nm taffeta.

Tage [taʒ] nm: **le ~** the (river) Tagus.

Tahiti [taiti] nf Tahiti.

tahitien, ne [taisjɛ̃, -ɛn] adj Tahitian.

taie [tɛ] nf: **~ (d'oreiller)** pillowslip, pillow-case.

taillader [tajade] vt to gash.

taille [taj] nf cutting; pruning; (milieu du corps) waist; (hauteur) height; (grandeur) size; **de ~ à faire** capable of doing; **de ~** adj sizeable; **quelle ~ faites- vous?** what size are you?

taillé, e [taje] adj (moustache, ongles, arbre) trimmed; **~ pour** (fait pour, apte à) cut out for; tailor-made for; **~ en pointe** sharpened to a point.

taille-crayon(s) [tajkʀɛjɔ̃] nm inv pencil sharpener.

tailler [taje] vt (pierre, diamant) to cut; (arbre, plante) to prune; (vêtement) to cut out; (crayon) to sharpen; **se ~** vt (ongles, barbe) to trim, cut; (fig: réputation) to gain, win ♦ vi (fam: s'enfuir) to beat it; **~ dans** (chair, bois) to cut into; **~ grand/petit** to be on the large/small side.

tailleur [tajœʀ] nm (couturier) tailor;

(vêtement) suit, costume; **en ~** (assis) cross-legged; **~ de diamants** diamond-cutter.

tailleur-pantalon [tajœʀpɑ̃talɔ̃] nm trouser (BRIT) ou pant(s) suit.

taillis [taji] nm copse.

tain [tɛ̃] nm silvering; **glace sans ~** two-way mirror.

taire [tɛʀ] vt to keep to o.s., conceal ♦ vi: **faire ~ qn** to make sb be quiet; (fig) to silence sb; **se ~** vi (s'arrêter de parler) to fall silent, stop talking; (ne pas parler) to be silent ou quiet; (s'abstenir de s'exprimer) to keep quiet; (bruit, voix) to disappear; **tais-toi!, taisez-vous!** be quiet!

Taiwan [tajwan] nf Taiwan.

talc [talk] nm talc, talcum powder.

talé, e [tale] adj (fruit) bruised.

talent [talɑ̃] nm talent; **avoir du ~** to be talented, have talent.

talentueux, euse [talɑ̃tɥø, -øz] adj talented.

talion [taljɔ̃] nm: **la loi du ~** an eye for an eye.

talisman [talismɑ̃] nm talisman.

talkie-walkie [tɔkiwɔki] nm walkie-talkie.

taloche [talɔʃ] nf (fam: claque) slap; (TECH) plaster float.

talon [talɔ̃] nm heel; (de chèque, billet) stub, counterfoil (BRIT); **~s plats/aiguilles** flat/stiletto heels; **être sur les ~s de qn** to be on sb's heels; **tourner les ~s** to turn on one's heel; **montrer les ~s** (fig) to show a clean pair of heels.

talonner [talɔne] vt to follow hard behind; (fig) to hound; (RUGBY) to heel.

talonnette [talɔnɛt] nf (de chaussure) heel-piece; (de pantalon) stirrup.

talquer [talke] vt to put talc(um powder) on.

talus [taly] nm embankment; **~ de remblai/déblai** embankment/excavation slope.

tamarin [tamaʀɛ̃] nm (BOT) tamarind.

tambour [tɑ̃buʀ] nm (MUS, aussi TECH) drum; (musicien) drummer; (porte) revolving door(s pl); **sans ~ ni trompette** unobtrusively.

tambourin [tɑ̃buʀɛ̃] nm tambourine.

tambouriner [tɑ̃buʀine] vi: **~ contre** to drum against ou on.

tambour-major, pl **tambours-majors** [tɑ̃buʀmaʒɔʀ] nm drum major.

tamis [tami] nm sieve.

Tamise [tamiz] nf: **la ~** the Thames.

tamisé, e [tamize] adj (fig) subdued, soft.

tamiser [tamize] vt to sieve, sift.

tampon [tɑ̃pɔ̃] nm (de coton, d'ouate) pad; (aussi: **~ hygiénique** ou **périodique**) tampon; (amortisseur, INFORM: aussi: **mémoire ~**) buffer; (bouchon) plug, stopper; (cachet, timbre) stamp; (CHIMIE) buffer; **~ buvard** blotter; **~ encreur** inking pad; **~ (à récurer)** scouring pad.

tamponné, e [tɑ̃pɔne] adj: **solution ~e** buffer solution.

tamponner [tɑ̃pɔne] vt (timbres) to stamp;

(*heurter*) to crash *ou* ram into; (*essuyer*) to mop up; **se** ~ (*voitures*) to crash (into each other).

tamponneuse [tɑ̃pɔnøz] *adj f:* **autos** ~**s** dodgems, bumper cars.

tam-tam [tamtam] *nm* tomtom.

tancer [tɑ̃se] *vt* to scold.

tanche [tɑ̃ʃ] *nf* tench.

tandem [tɑ̃dɛm] *nm* tandem; (*fig*) duo, pair.

tandis [tɑ̃di]: ~ **que** *conj* while.

tangage [tɑ̃gaʒ] *nm* pitching (and tossing).

tangent, e [tɑ̃ʒɑ̃, -ɑ̃t] *adj* (*MATH*): ~ **à** tangential to; (*fam: de justesse*) close ♦ *nf* (*MATH*) tangent.

Tanger [tɑ̃ʒe] *n* Tangier.

tangible [tɑ̃ʒibl(ə)] *adj* tangible, concrete.

tango [tɑ̃go] *nm* (*MUS*) tango ♦ *adj inv* (*couleur*) dark orange.

tanguer [tɑ̃ge] *vi* to pitch (and toss).

tanière [tanjɛʁ] *nf* lair, den.

tanin [tanɛ̃] *nm* tannin.

tank [tɑ̃k] *nm* tank.

tanker [tɑ̃kɛʁ] *nm* tanker.

tanné, e [tane] *adj* weather-beaten.

tanner [tane] *vt* to tan.

tannerie [tanʁi] *nf* tannery.

tanneur [tanœʁ] *nm* tanner.

tant [tɑ̃] *adv* so much; ~ **de** (*sable, eau*) so much; (*gens, livres*) so many; ~ **que** *conj* as long as; ~ **que** (*comparatif*) as much as; ~ **mieux** that's great; so much the better; ~ **mieux pour lui** good for him; ~ **pis** too bad; **un** ~ **soit peu** (*un peu*) a little bit; (*même un peu*) (even) remotely; ~ **bien que mal** as well as can be expected; ~ **s'en faut** far from it, not by a long way.

tante [tɑ̃t] *nf* aunt.

tantinet [tɑ̃tinɛ]: **un** ~ *adv* a tiny bit.

tantôt [tɑ̃to] *adv* (*parfois*): ~ ... ~ now ... now; (*cet après-midi*) this afternoon.

Tanzanie [tɑ̃zani] *nf:* **la** ~ Tanzania.

tanzanien, ne [tɑ̃zanjɛ̃, -ɛn] *adj* Tanzanian.

TAO *sigle f* (= *traduction assistée par ordinateur*) MAT (= *machine-aided translation*).

taon [tɑ̃] *nm* horsefly, gadfly.

tapage [tapaʒ] *nm* uproar, din; (*fig*) fuss, row; ~ **nocturne** (*JUR*) disturbance of the peace (*at night*).

tapageur, euse [tapaʒœʁ, -øz] *adj* (*bruyant: enfants etc*) noisy; (*toilette*) loud, flashy; (*publicité*) obtrusive.

tape [tap] *nf* slap.

tape-à-l'œil [tapalœj] *adj inv* flashy, showy.

taper [tape] *vt* (*personne*) to clout; (*porte*) to bang, slam; (*dactylographier*) to type (out); (*INFORM*) to key(board); (*fam: emprunter*): ~ **qn de 10 F** to touch sb for 10 F, cadge 10 F off sb ♦ *vi* (*soleil*) to beat down; **se** ~ *vt* (*fam: travail*) to get landed with; (*: boire, manger*) to down; ~ **sur qn** to thump sb; (*fig*) to run sb down; ~ **sur qch** (*clou etc*) to hit sth; (*table etc*) to bang on sth; ~ **à** (*porte etc*) to knock

on; ~ **dans** (*se servir*) to dig into; ~ **des mains/pieds** to clap one's hands/stamp one's feet; ~ (**à la machine**) to type.

tapi, e [tapi] *adj:* ~ **dans/derrière** (*blotti*) crouching *ou* cowering in/behind; (*caché*) hidden away in/behind.

tapinois [tapinwa]: **en** ~ *adv* stealthily.

tapioca [tapjɔka] *nm* tapioca.

tapir [tapiʁ]: **se** ~ *vi* to hide away.

tapis [tapi] *nm* carpet; (*de table*) cloth; **mettre sur le** ~ (*fig*) to bring up for discussion; **aller au** ~ (*BOXE*) to go down; **envoyer au** ~ (*BOXE*) to floor; ~ **roulant** conveyor belt; ~ **de sol** (*de tente*) groundsheet.

tapis-brosse [tapibʁɔs] *nm* doormat.

tapisser [tapise] *vt* (*avec du papier peint*) to paper; (*recouvrir*): ~ **qch (de)** to cover sth (with).

tapisserie [tapisʁi] *nf* (*tenture, broderie*) tapestry; (*: travail*) tapestry-making; (*: ouvrage*) tapestry work; (*papier peint*) wallpaper; (*fig*): **faire** ~ to sit out, be a wallflower.

tapissier, ière [tapisje, -jɛʁ] *nm/f:* ~**(-décorateur)** upholsterer (and decorator).

tapoter [tapɔte] *vt* to pat, tap.

taquet [takɛ] *nm* (*cale*) wedge; (*cheville*) peg.

taquin, e [takɛ̃, -in] *adj* teasing.

taquiner [takine] *vt* to tease.

taquinerie [takinʁi] *nf* teasing *no pl*.

tarabiscoté, e [tarabiskɔte] *adj* over-ornate, fussy.

tarabuster [tarabyste] *vt* to bother, worry.

tarama [tarama] *nm* (*CULIN*) taramasalata.

tarauder [tarode] *vt* (*TECH*) to tap; to thread; (*fig*) to pierce.

tard [taʁ] *adv* late; **au plus** ~ at the latest; **plus** ~ later (on) ♦ *nm:* **sur le** ~ (*à une heure avancée*) late in the day; (*vers la fin de la vie*) late in life.

tarder [taʁde] *vi* (*chose*) to be a long time coming; (*personne*): ~ **à faire** to delay doing; **il me tarde d'être** I am longing to be; **sans (plus)** ~ without (further) delay.

tardif, ive [taʁdif, -iv] *adj* (*heure, repas, fruit*) late; (*talent, goût*) late in developing.

tardivement [taʁdivmɑ̃] *adv* late.

tare [taʁ] *nf* (*COMM*) tare; (*fig*) defect; taint, blemish.

targette [taʁʒɛt] *nf* (*verrou*) bolt.

targuer [taʁge]: **se** ~ **de** *vt* to boast about.

tarif [taʁif] *nm* (*liste*) price list, tariff (*BRIT*); (*barème*) rate, rates *pl*, tariff (*BRIT*); (*: de taxis etc*) fares *pl*; **voyager à plein** ~/**à** ~ **réduit** to travel at full/reduced fare.

tarifaire [taʁifɛʁ] *adj* (*voir tarif*) relating to price lists *etc*.

tarifé, e [taʁife] *adj:* ~ **10 F** priced at 10 F.

tarifer [taʁife] *vt* to fix the price *ou* rate for.

tarification [taʁifikasjɔ̃] *nf* fixing of a price scale.

tarir [taʁiʁ] *vi* to dry up, run dry ♦ *vt* to dry up.

tarot(s) [taʀo] *nm(pl)* tarot cards.

tartare [taʀtaʀ] *adj* (*CULIN*) tartar(e).

tarte [taʀt(ə)] *nf* tart; ~ **aux pommes/à la crème** apple/custard tart.

tartelette [taʀtəlɛt] *nf* tartlet.

tartine [taʀtin] *nf* slice of bread (and butter (*ou* jam)); ~ **de miel** slice of bread and honey; ~ **beurrée** slice of bread and butter.

tartiner [taʀtine] *vt* to spread; **fromage à** ~ cheese spread.

tartre [taʀtʀ(ə)] *nm* (*des dents*) tartar; (*de chaudière*) fur, scale.

tas [tɑ] *nm* heap, pile; (*fig*): **un** ~ **de** heaps of, lots of; **en** ~ in a heap *ou* pile; **dans le** ~ (*fig*) in the crowd; among them; **formé sur le** ~ trained on the job.

Tasmanie [tasmani] *nf*: **la** ~ Tasmania.

tasmanien, ne [tasmanjɛ̃, -ɛn] *adj* Tasmanian.

tasse [tɑs] *nf* cup; **boire la** ~ (*en se baignant*) to swallow a mouthful; ~ **à café/thé** coffee/teacup.

tassé, e [tɑse] *adj*: **bien** ~ (*café etc*) strong.

tasseau, x [tɑso] *nm* length of wood.

tassement [tɑsmɑ̃] *nm* (*de vertèbres*) compression; (*ÉCON, POL*: *ralentissement*) fall-off, slowdown; (*BOURSE*) dullness.

tasser [tɑse] *vt* (*terre, neige*) to pack down; (*entasser*): ~ **qch dans** to cram sth into; (*INFORM*) to pack; **se** ~ *vi* (*terrain*) to settle; (*personne: avec l'âge*) to shrink; (*fig*) to sort itself out, settle down.

tâter [tate] *vt* to feel; (*fig*) to sound out; ~ **de** (*prison etc*) to have a taste of; **se** ~ (*hésiter*) to be in two minds; ~ **le terrain** (*fig*) to test the ground.

tatillon, ne [tatijɔ̃, -ɔn] *adj* pernickety.

tâtonnement [tatɔnmɑ̃] *nm*: **par** ~**s** (*fig*) by trial and error.

tâtonner [tatɔne] *vi* to grope one's way along; (*fig*) to grope around (in the dark).

tâtons [tatɔ̃]: **à** ~ *adv*: **chercher/avancer à** ~ to grope around for/grope one's way forward.

tatouage [tatwaʒ] *nm* tattooing; (*dessin*) tattoo.

tatouer [tatwe] *vt* to tattoo.

taudis [todi] *nm* hovel, slum.

taule [tol] *nf* (*fam*) nick (*BRIT*), jail.

taupe [top] *nf* mole; (*peau*) moleskin.

taupinière [topinjɛʀ] *nf* molehill.

taureau, x [tɔʀo] *nm* bull; (*signe*): **le T**~ Taurus, the Bull; **être du T**~ to be Taurus.

taurillon [tɔʀijɔ̃] *nm* bull-calf.

tauromachie [tɔʀɔmaʃi] *nf* bullfighting.

taux [to] *nm* rate; (*d'alcool*) level; ~ **d'escompte** discount rate; ~ **d'intérêt** interest rate; ~ **de mortalité** mortality rate.

tavelé, e [tavle] *adj* marked.

taverne [tavɛʀn(ə)] *nf* inn, tavern.

taxable [taksabl(ə)] *adj* taxable.

taxation [taksasjɔ̃] *nf* taxation; (*TÉL*) charges *pl*.

taxe [taks(ə)] *nf* tax; (*douanière*) duty; **toutes** ~**s comprises (TTC)** inclusive of tax; ~ **de base** (*TÉL*) unit charge; ~ **de séjour** tourist tax; ~ **à** *ou* **sur la valeur ajoutée (TVA)** value added tax (VAT) (*BRIT*).

taxer [takse] *vt* (*personne*) to tax; (*produit*) to put a tax on, tax; (*fig*): ~ **qn de** (*qualifier de*) to call sb + *attribut*; (*accuser de*) to accuse sb of, tax sb with.

taxi [taksi] *nm* taxi.

taxidermie [taksidɛʀmi] *nf* taxidermy.

taxidermiste [taksidɛʀmist(ə)] *nm/f* taxidermist.

taximètre [taksimɛtʀ(ə)] *nm* (taxi)meter.

taxiphone [taksifɔn] *nm* pay phone.

TB *abr* = **très bien, très bon.**

tbe *abr* (= *très bon état*) VGC, vgc.

TCA *sigle f* (= *taxe sur le chiffre d'affaires*) tax on turnover.

TCF *sigle m* (= *Touring Club de France*) ≈ AA *ou* RAC (*BRIT*), ≈ AAA (*US*).

Tchad [tʃad] *nm*: **le** ~ Chad.

tchadien, ne [tʃadjɛ̃, -ɛn] *adj* Chad(ian), of *ou* from Chad.

tchao [tʃao] *excl* (*fam*) bye(-bye)!

tchécoslovaque [tʃekɔslɔvak] *adj* Czechoslovak(ian) ♦ *nm/f*: **T**~ Czechoslovak(ian).

Tchécoslovaquie [tʃekɔslɔvaki] *nf*: **la** ~ Czechoslovakia.

tchèque [tʃɛk] *adj* Czech ♦ *nm* (*LING*) Czech ♦ *nm/f*: **T**~ Czech.

TCS *sigle m* (= *Touring Club de Suisse*) ≈ AA *ou* RAC (*BRIT*), ≈ AAA (*US*).

TD *sigle mpl* = **travaux dirigés.**

TDF *sigle f* (= *Télévision de France*) French broadcasting authority.

te, t' [t(ə)] *pron* you; (*réfléchi*) yourself.

té [te] *nm* T-square.

technicien, ne [tɛknisjɛ̃, -ɛn] *nm/f* technician.

technicité [tɛknisite] *nf* technical nature.

technico-commercial, e, aux [tɛknikokɔmɛʀsjal, -o] *adj*: **agent** ~ sales technician.

technique [tɛknik] *adj* technical ♦ *nf* technique.

techniquement [tɛknikmɑ̃] *adv* technically.

techno [tɛkno] *nf* (*MUS*) techno.

technocrate [tɛknɔkʀat] *nm/f* technocrat.

technocratie [tɛknɔkʀasi] *nf* technocracy.

technologie [tɛknɔlɔʒi] *nf* technology.

technologique [tɛknɔlɔʒik] *adj* technological.

technologue [tɛknɔlɔg] *nm/f* technologist.

teck [tɛk] *nm* teak.

teckel [tekɛl] *nm* dachshund.

TEE *sigle m* = **Trans-Europ-Express.**

tee-shirt [tiʃœʀt] *nm* T-shirt, tee-shirt.

Téhéran [teeʀɑ̃] *n* Teheran.

teigne [tɛɲ] *vb voir* **teindre** ♦ *nf* (*ZOOL*) moth; (*MÉD*) ringworm.

teigneux, euse [tɛɲø, -øz] *adj* (*péj*) nasty, scabby.

teindre [tɛ̃dʀ(ə)] *vt* to dye; **se** ~ **(les cheveux)**

to dye one's hair.

teint, e [tɛ̃, tɛ̃t] *pp de* **teindre** ♦ *adj* dyed ♦ *nm* (*du visage: permanent*) complexion, colouring (*BRIT*), coloring (*US*); (*momentané*) colour (*BRIT*), color (*US*) ♦ *nf* shade, colour, color; (*fig: petite dose*): **une ~e de** a hint of; **grand ~** *adj inv* colourfast; **bon ~** *adj inv* (*couleur*) fast; (*tissu*) colourfast; (*personne*) staunch, firm.

teinté, e [tɛ̃te] *adj* (*verres*) tinted; (*bois*) stained; **~ acajou** mahogany-stained; **~ de** (*fig*) tinged with.

teinter [tɛ̃te] *vt* to tint; (*bois*) to stain; (*fig: d'ironie etc*) to tinge.

teinture [tɛ̃tyR] *nf* dyeing; (*substance*) dye; (*MÉD*): **~ d'iode** tincture of iodine.

teinturerie [tɛ̃tyRRi] *nf* dry cleaner's.

teinturier, ière [tɛ̃tyRje, -jɛR] *nm/f* dry cleaner.

tel, telle [tɛl] *adj* (*pareil*) such; (*comme*): **~ un/des** ... like a/like ...; (*indéfini*) such-and-such a, a given; (*intensif*): **un ~/de ~s** ... such (a)/such ...; **rien de ~** nothing like it, no such thing; **~ que** *conj* like, such as; **~ quel** as it is *ou* stands (*ou* was *etc*).

tél. *abr* = **téléphone**.

Tel Aviv [tɛlaviv] *n* Tel Aviv.

télé [tele] *nf* (= *télévision*) TV, telly (*BRIT*); **à la ~** on TV *ou* telly.

télébenne [teleben] *nm, nf* telecabine, gondola.

télécabine [telekabin] *nm, nf* telecabine, gondola.

télécarte [telekaRt(ə)] *nf* phonecard.

télécharger [teleʃaRʒe] *vt* (*INFORM*) to download.

TELECOM [telekɔm] *abr* (= *Télécommunications*) ≈ Telecom.

télécommande [telekɔmɑ̃d] *nf* remote control.

télécommander [telekɔmɑ̃de] *vt* to operate by remote control, radio-control.

télécommunications [telekɔmynikɑsjɔ̃] *nfpl* telecommunications.

téléconférence [telekɔ̃feRɑ̃s] *nf* (*méthode*) teleconferencing; (*discussion*) conference call.

télécopie [telekɔpi] *nf* fax, telefax.

télécopieur [telekɔpjœR] *nm* fax (machine).

télédétection [teledetɛksjɔ̃] *nf* remote sensing.

télédiffuser [teledifyze] *vt* to broadcast (on television).

télédiffusion [teledifyzjɔ̃] *nf* television broadcasting.

télédistribution [teledistRibysjɔ̃] *nf* cable TV.

téléenseignement [teleɑ̃sɛɲmɑ̃] *nm* distance teaching (*ou* learning).

téléférique [telefeRik] *nm* = **téléphérique**.

téléfilm [telefilm] *nm* film made for TV, TV film.

télégramme [telegRam] *nm* telegram.

télégraphe [telegRaf] *nm* telegraph.

télégraphier [telegRafje] *vt* to telegraph, cable.

télégraphique [telegRafik] *adj* telegraph *cpd*, telegraphic; (*fig*) telegraphic.

téléguider [telegide] *vt* to operate by remote control, radio-control.

téléinformatique [teleɛ̃fɔRmatik] *nf* remote access computing.

téléjournal, aux [teleʒuRnal, -o] *nm* television news magazine programme.

télématique [telematik] *nf* telematics *sg* ♦ *adj* telematic.

téléobjectif [teleɔbʒɛktif] *nm* telephoto lens *sg*.

télépathie [telepati] *nf* telepathy.

téléphérique [telefeRik] *nm* cable-car.

téléphone [telefɔn] *nm* telephone; **avoir le ~** to be on the (tele)phone; **au ~** on the phone; **les T~s** the (tele)phone service *sg*; **~ arabe** bush telegraph; **~ à carte (magnétique)** cardphone; **~ cellulaire** cellphone, cellular phone; **~ rouge** hotline.

téléphoner [telefɔne] *vt* to telephone ♦ *vi* to telephone; to make a phone call; **~ à** to phone up, ring up, call up.

téléphonie [telefɔni] *nf* telephony.

téléphonique [telefɔnik] *adj* telephone *cpd*, phone *cpd*; **cabine ~** call box (*BRIT*), (tele)phone box (*BRIT*) *ou* booth; **conversation/appel ~** (tele)phone conversation/call.

téléphoniste [telefɔnist(ə)] *nm/f* telephonist, telephone operator; (*d'entreprise*) switchboard operator.

téléport [telepɔR] *nm* teleport.

téléprospection [telepRɔspɛksjɔ̃] *nf* telephone selling.

télescopage [telɛskɔpaʒ] *nm* crash.

télescope [telɛskɔp] *nm* telescope.

télescoper [telɛskɔpe] *vt* to smash up; **se ~** (*véhicules*) to collide, crash into each other.

télescopique [telɛskɔpik] *adj* telescopic.

téléscripteur [teleskRiptœR] *nm* teleprinter.

télésiège [telesjɛʒ] *nm* chairlift.

téléski [teleski] *nm* ski-tow; **~ à archets** T-bar tow; **~ à perche** button lift.

téléspectateur, trice [telespɛktatœR, -tRis] *nm/f* (television) viewer.

télétexte [teletɛkst] *nm* ® Teletext ®.

téléthon [teletɔ̃] *nm* telethon.

télétraitement [teletRɛtmɑ̃] *nm* remote processing.

télétransmission [teletRɑ̃smisjɔ̃] *nf* remote transmission.

télétravail [teletRavaj] *nm* teleworking.

télétype [teletip] *nm* teleprinter.

télévente [televɑ̃t] *nf* telesales.

téléviser [televize] *vt* to televise.

téléviseur [televizœR] *nm* television set.

télévision [televizjɔ̃] *nf* television; **(poste de) ~** television (set); **avoir la ~** to have a television; **à la** ~ on television; ~ **par câble/satellite** cable/satellite television; ~ **en circuit fermé** closed-circuit television; ~ **numérique** digital TV.

télex [telɛks] *nm* telex.

télexer [telɛkse] *vt* to telex.

telle [tɛl] *adj f voir* **tel**.

tellement [tɛlmɑ̃] *adv* (*tant*) so much; (*si*) so; ~ **plus grand (que)** so much bigger (than); ~ **de** (*sable, eau*) so much; (*gens, livres*) so many; **il s'est endormi** ~ **il était fatigué** he was so tired (that) he fell asleep; **pas** ~ not really; **pas** ~ **fort/lentement** not (all) that strong/slowly; **il ne mange pas** ~ he doesn't eat (all that) much.

tellurique [telyʀik] *adj*: **secousse** ~ earth tremor.

téméraire [temeʀɛʀ] *adj* reckless, rash.

témérité [temeʀite] *nf* recklessness, rashness.

témoignage [temwaɲaʒ] *nm* (*JUR: déclaration*) testimony *no pl*, evidence *no pl*; (: *faits*) evidence·*no pl*; (*gén: rapport, récit*) account; (*fig: d'affection etc*) token, mark; expression.

témoigner [temwaɲe] *vt* (*manifester: intérêt, gratitude*) to show ♦ *vi* (*JUR*) to testify, give evidence; ~ **que** to testify that; (*fig: démontrer*) to reveal that, testify to the fact that; ~ **de** *vt* (*confirmer*) to bear witness to.

témoin [temwɛ̃] *nm* witness; (*fig*) testimony; (*SPORT*) baton; (*CONSTR*) telltale ♦ *adj* control *cpd*, test *cpd*; ~ **le fait que** ... (as) witness the fact that ...; **appartement-**~ show flat (*BRIT*), model apartment (*US*); **être** ~ **de** (*voir*) to witness; **prendre à** ~ to call to witness; ~ **à charge** witness for the prosecution; **T**~ **de Jehovah** Jehovah's Witness; ~ **de moralité** character reference; ~ **oculaire** eyewitness.

tempe [tɑ̃p] *nf* (*ANAT*) temple.

tempérament [tɑ̃peʀamɑ̃] *nm* temperament, disposition; (*santé*) constitution; **à** ~ (*vente*) on deferred (payment) terms; (*achat*) by instalments, hire purchase *cpd*; **avoir du** ~ to be hot-blooded.

tempérance [tɑ̃peʀɑ̃s] *nf* temperance; **société de** ~ temperance society.

tempérant, e [tɑ̃peʀɑ̃, -ɑ̃t] *adj* temperate.

température [tɑ̃peʀatyʀ] *nf* temperature; **prendre la** ~ **de** to take the temperature of; (*fig*) to gauge the feeling of; **avoir** *ou* **faire de la** ~ to be running *ou* have a temperature.

tempéré, e [tɑ̃peʀe] *adj* temperate.

tempérer [tɑ̃peʀe] *vt* to temper.

tempête [tɑ̃pɛt] *nf* storm; ~ **de sable/neige** sand/snowstorm; **vent de** ~ gale.

tempêter [tɑ̃pete] *vi* to rant and rave.

temple [tɑ̃pl(ə)] *nm* temple; (*protestant*) church.

tempo [tɛmpo] *nm* tempo (*pl* -s).

temporaire [tɑ̃pɔʀɛʀ] *adj* temporary.

temporairement [tɑ̃pɔʀɛʀmɑ̃] *adv* temporarily.

temporel, le [tɑ̃pɔʀɛl] *adj* temporal.

temporisateur, trice [tɑ̃pɔʀizatœʀ, -tʀis] *adj* temporizing, delaying.

temporisation [tɑ̃pɔʀizɑsjɔ̃] *nf* temporizing, playing for time.

temporiser [tɑ̃pɔʀize] *vi* to temporize, play for time.

temps [tɑ̃] *nm* (*atmosphérique*) weather; (*durée*) time; (*époque*) time, times *pl*; (*LING*) tense; (*MUS*) beat; (*TECH*) stroke; **les** ~ **changent/sont durs** times are changing/hard; **il fait beau/mauvais** ~ the weather is fine/bad; **avoir le** ~/**tout le** ~/**juste le** ~ to have time/plenty of time/just enough time; **avoir fait son** ~ (*fig*) to have had its (*ou* his *etc*) day; **en** ~ **de paix/guerre** in peacetime/wartime; **en** ~ **utile** *ou* **voulu** in due time *ou* course; **de** ~ **en** ~, **de** ~ **à autre** from time to time, now and again; **en même** ~ at the same time; **à** ~ (*partir, arriver*) in time; **à plein/mi-**~ *adv, adj* full-/part-time; **à** ~ **partiel** *adv, adj* part-time; **dans le** ~ at one time; **de tout** ~ always; **du** ~ **que** at the time when, in the days when; **dans le** *ou* **du** *ou* **au** ~ **où** at the time when; **pendant ce** ~ in the meantime; ~ **d'accès** (*INFORM*) access time; ~ **d'arrêt** pause, halt; ~ **mort** (*SPORT*) stoppage (time); (*COMM*) slack period; ~ **partagé** (*INFORM*) time-sharing; ~ **réel** (*INFORM*) real time.

tenable [tənabl(ə)] *adj* bearable.

tenace [tənas] *adj* tenacious, persistent.

ténacité [tenasite] *nf* tenacity, persistence.

tenailler [tənaje] *vt* (*fig*) to torment, torture.

tenailles [tənaj] *nfpl* pincers.

tenais [t(ə)nɛ] *etc vb voir* **tenir**.

tenancier, ière [tənɑ̃sje, -jɛʀ] *nm/f* (*d'hôtel, de bistro*) manager/manageress.

tenant, e [tənɑ̃, -ɑ̃t] *adj f voir* **séance** ♦ *nm/f* (*SPORT*): ~ **du titre** title-holder ♦ *nm*: **d'un seul** ~ in one piece; **les** ~**s et les aboutissants** (*fig*) the ins and outs.

tendance [tɑ̃dɑ̃s] *nf* (*opinions*) leanings *pl*, sympathies *pl*; (*inclination*) tendency; (*évolution*) trend; ~ **à la hausse/baisse** upward/downward trend; **avoir** ~ **à** to have a tendency to, tend to.

tendancieux, euse [tɑ̃dɑ̃sjø, -øz] *adj* tendentious.

tendeur [tɑ̃dœʀ] *nm* (*de vélo*) chain-adjuster; (*de câble*) wire-strainer; (*de tente*) runner; (*attache*) elastic strap.

tendinite [tɑ̃dinit] *nf* tendinitis, tendonitis.

tendon [tɑ̃dɔ̃] *nm* tendon, sinew; ~ **d'Achille** Achilles' tendon.

tendre [tɑ̃dʀ(ə)] *adj* (*viande, légumes*) tender; (*bois, roche, couleur*) soft; (*affectueux*) tender, loving ♦ *vt* (*élastique, peau*) to stretch, draw tight; (*muscle*) to tense; (*donner*): ~ **qch à qn** to hold sth out to sb; to offer sb sth; (*fig: piège*) to set, lay; (*tapisserie*): **tendu de soie** hung with silk, with silk hangings; **se** ~ *vi* (*corde*) to tighten; (*relations*) to become strained; ~ **à qch/à faire** to tend towards sth/to do; ~ **l'oreille** to prick up one's ears; ~ **la main/le bras** to hold out one's hand/stretch out one's arm; ~ **la perche à qn** (*fig*) to throw sb a line.

tendrement [tãdʀəmã] *adv* tenderly, lovingly.

tendresse [tãdʀɛs] *nf* tenderness; ~**s** *nfpl* (*caresses etc*) tenderness *no pl*, caresses.

tendu, e [tãdy] *pp de* **tendre** ♦ *adj* tight; tensed; strained.

ténèbres [tenɛbʀ(ə)] *nfpl* darkness *sg*.

ténébreux, euse [tenebʀø, -øz] *adj* obscure, mysterious; (*personne*) saturnine.

Ténérife [tenerif] *nf* Tenerife.

teneur [tənœʀ] *nf* content, substance; (*d'une lettre*) terms *pl*, content; ~ **en cuivre** copper content.

ténia [tenja] *nm* tapeworm.

tenir [təniʀ] *vt* to hold; (*magasin, hôtel*) to run; (*promesse*) to keep ♦ *vi* to hold; (*neige, gel*) to last; (*survivre*) to survive; **se** ~ *vi* (*avoir lieu*) to be held, take place; (*être: personne*) to stand; **se** ~ **droit** to stand up (*ou* sit up) straight; **bien se** ~ to behave well; **se** ~ **à qch** to hold on to sth; **s'en** ~ **à qch** to confine o.s. to sth; to stick to sth; ~ **à** *vt* to be attached to, care about (*ou* for); (*avoir pour cause*) to be due to, stem from; ~ **à faire** to want to do, be keen to do; ~ **à ce que qn fasse qch** to be anxious that sb should do sth; ~ **de** *vt* to partake of; (*ressembler à*) to take after; **ça ne tient qu'à lui** it is entirely up to him; ~ **qn pour** to take sb for; ~ **qch de qn** (*histoire*) to have heard *ou* learnt sth from sb; (*qualité, défaut*) to have inherited *ou* got sth from sb; ~ **les comptes** to keep the books; ~ **un rôle** to play a part; ~ **de la place** to take up space *ou* room; ~ **l'alcool** to be able to hold a drink; ~ **le coup** to hold out; ~ **bon** to stand *ou* hold fast; ~ **3 jours/2 mois** (*résister*) to hold out *ou* last 3 days/2 months; ~ **au chaud/à l'abri** to keep hot/under shelter *ou* cover; ~ **prêt** to have ready; ~ **sa langue** (*fig*) to hold one's tongue; **tiens** (*ou* **tenez**)**, voilà le stylo** there's the pen!; **tiens, Alain!** look, here's Alain!; **tiens?** (*surprise*) really?; **tiens-toi bien!** (*pour informer*) brace yourself!, take a deep breath!

tennis [tenis] *nm* tennis; (*aussi:* **court de** ~) tennis court ♦ *nmpl ou fpl* (*aussi:* **chaussures de** ~) tennis *ou* gym shoes; ~ **de table** table tennis.

tennisman [tenisman] *nm* tennis player.

ténor [tenɔʀ] *nm* tenor.

tension [tãsjɔ̃] *nf* tension; (*fig: des relations, de la situation*) tension; (*: concentration, effort*) strain; (*MÉD*) blood pressure; **faire** *ou* **avoir de la** ~ to have high blood pressure; ~ **nerveuse/raciale** nervous/racial tension.

tentaculaire [tãtakylɛʀ] *adj* (*fig*) sprawling.

tentacule [tãtakyl] *nm* tentacle.

tentant, e [tãtã, -ãt] *adj* tempting.

tentateur, trice [tãtatœʀ, -tʀis] *adj* tempting ♦ *nm* (*REL*) tempter.

tentation [tãtasjɔ̃] *nf* temptation.

tentative [tãtativ] *nf* attempt, bid; ~ **d'évasion** escape bid; ~ **de suicide** suicide attempt.

tente [tãt] *nf* tent; ~ **à oxygène** oxygen tent.

tenter [tãte] *vt* (*éprouver, attirer*) to tempt; (*essayer*): ~ **qch/de faire** to attempt *ou* try sth/to do; **être tenté de** to be tempted to; ~ **sa chance** to try one's luck.

tenture [tãtyʀ] *nf* hanging.

tenu, e [təny] *pp de* **tenir** ♦ *adj* (*maison, comptes*): **bien** ~ well-kept; (*obligé*): ~ **de faire** under an obligation to do ♦ *nf* (*action de tenir*) running; keeping; holding; (*vêtements*) clothes *pl*, gear; (*allure*) dress *no pl*, appearance; (*comportement*) manners *pl*, behaviour (*BRIT*), behavior (*US*); **être en** ~**e** to be dressed (up); **se mettre en** ~**e** to dress (up); **en grande** ~**e** in full dress; **en petite** ~**e** scantily dressed *ou* clad; **avoir de la** ~**e** to have good manners; (*journal*) to have a high standard; ~**e de combat** combat gear *ou* dress; ~**e de pompier** fireman's uniform; ~**e de route** (*AUTO*) road-holding; ~**e de soirée** evening dress; ~**e de sport/voyage** sports/travelling clothes *pl ou* gear *no pl*.

ténu, e [teny] *adj* (*indice, nuance*) tenuous, subtle; (*fil, objet*) fine; (*voix*) thin.

ter [tɛʀ] *adj*: **16** ~ **16b** *ou* B.

térébenthine [terebãtin] *nf*: (**essence de**) ~ (oil of) turpentine.

tergal [tɛʀgal] *nm* ® Terylene ®.

tergiversations [tɛʀʒiveʀsasjɔ̃] *nfpl* shilly-shallying *no pl*.

tergiverser [tɛʀʒiveʀse] *vi* to shilly-shally.

terme [tɛʀm(ə)] *nm* term; (*fin*) end; **être en bons/mauvais** ~**s avec qn** to be on good/bad terms with sb; **vente/achat à** ~ (*COMM*) forward sale/purchase; **au** ~ **de** at the end of; **en d'autres** ~**s** in other words; **moyen** ~ (*solution intermédiaire*) middle course; **à court/long** ~ *adj* short-/long-term *ou* -range ♦ *adv* in the short/long term; **à** ~ *adj* (*MÉD*) full-term ♦ *adv* sooner or later, eventually; (*MÉD*) at term; **avant** ~ (*MÉD*) *adj* premature ♦ *adv* prematurely; **mettre un** ~ **à** to put an end *ou* a stop to; **toucher à son** ~ to be nearing its end.

terminaison [tɛʀminɛzɔ̃] *nf* (*LING*) ending.

terminal, e, aux [tɛʀminal, -o] *adj* (*partie, phase*) final; (*MÉD*) terminal ♦ *nm* terminal ♦ *nf* (*SCOL*) ≈ sixth form *ou* year (*BRIT*), ≈ twelfth grade (*US*).

terminer [tɛʀmine] *vt* to end; (*travail, repas*) to finish; **se** ~ *vi* to end; **se** ~ **par** to end with.

terminologie [tɛʀminɔlɔʒi] *nf* terminology.

terminus [tɛʀminys] *nm* terminus (*pl* -i); ~**!** all change!

termite [tɛʀmit] *nm* termite, white ant.

termitière [tɛʀmitjɛʀ] *nf* ant-hill.
ternaire [tɛʀnɛʀ] *adj* compound.
terne [tɛʀn(ə)] *adj* dull.
ternir [tɛʀniʀ] *vt* to dull; (*fig*) to sully, tarnish; **se ~** *vi* to become dull.
terrain [tɛʀɛ̃] *nm* (*sol, fig*) ground; (*COMM*) land *no pl*, plot (of land); (*: à bâtir*) site; **sur le ~** (*fig*) on the field; **~ de football/rugby** football/rugby pitch (*BRIT*) *ou* field (*US*); **~ d'atterrissage** landing strip; **~ d'aviation** airfield; **~ de camping** campsite; **un ~ d'entente** an area of agreement; **~ de golf** golf course; **~ de jeu** playground; (*SPORT*) games field; **~ de sport** sports ground; **~ vague** waste ground *no pl*.
terrasse [tɛʀas] *nf* terrace; (*de café*) pavement area, terrasse; **à la ~** (*café*) outside.
terrassement [tɛʀasmɑ̃] *nm* earth-moving, earthworks *pl*; embankment.
terrasser [tɛʀase] *vt* (*adversaire*) to floor, bring down; (*suj: maladie etc*) to lay low.
terrassier [tɛʀasje] *nm* navvy, roadworker.
terre [tɛʀ] *nf* (*gén, aussi ÉLEC*) earth; (*substance*) soil, earth; (*opposé à mer*) land *no pl*; (*contrée*) land; **~s** *nfpl* (*terrains*) lands, land *sg*; **travail de la ~** work on the land; **en ~** (*pipe, poterie*) clay *cpd*; **mettre en ~** (*plante etc*) to plant; (*personne: enterrer*) to bury; **à** *ou* **par ~** (*mettre, être*) on the ground (*ou* floor); (*jeter, tomber*) to the ground, down; **~ à ~** *adj inv* down-to-earth, matter-of-fact; **la T~ Adélie** Adélie Coast *ou* Land; **~ de bruyère** (heath-)peat; **~ cuite** earthenware; terracotta; **la ~ ferme** dry land, terra firma; **la T~ de Feu** Tierra del Fuego; **~ glaise** clay; **la T~ promise** the Promised Land; **la T~ Sainte** the Holy Land.
terreau [tɛʀo] *nm* compost.
Terre-Neuve [tɛʀnœv] *nf*: **la ~** (*aussi*: **l'île de ~**) Newfoundland.
terre-plein [tɛʀplɛ̃] *nm* platform.
terrer [tɛʀe]: **se ~** *vi* to hide away; to go to ground.
terrestre [tɛʀɛstʀ(ə)] *adj* (*surface*) earth's, of the earth; (*BOT, ZOOL, MIL*) land *cpd*; (*REL*) earthly, worldly.
terreur [tɛʀœʀ] *nf* terror *no pl*, fear.
terreux, euse [tɛʀø, -øz] *adj* muddy; (*goût*) earthy.
terrible [tɛʀibl(ə)] *adj* terrible, dreadful; (*fam: fantastique*) terrific.
terriblement [tɛʀibləmɑ̃] *adv* (*très*) terribly, awfully.
terrien, ne [tɛʀjɛ̃, -ɛn] *adj*: **propriétaire ~** landowner ♦ *nm/f* countryman/woman, man/woman of the soil; (*non martien etc*) earthling; (*non marin*) landsman.
terrier [tɛʀje] *nm* burrow, hole; (*chien*) terrier.
terrifiant, e [tɛʀifjɑ̃, -ɑ̃t] *adj* (*effrayant*) terrifying; (*extraordinaire*) terrible, awful.
terrifier [tɛʀifje] *vt* to terrify.
terril [tɛʀil] *nm* slag heap.

terrine [tɛʀin] *nf* (*récipient*) terrine; (*CULIN*) pâté.
territoire [tɛʀitwaʀ] *nm* territory; **T~ des Afars et des Issas** French Territory of Afars and Issas.
territorial, e, aux [tɛʀitɔʀjal, -o] *adj* territorial; **eaux ~es** territorial waters; **armée ~e** regional defence force, ≈ Territorial Army (*BRIT*); **collectivités ~es** local and regional authorities.
terroir [tɛʀwaʀ] *nm* (*AGR*) soil; (*région*) region; **accent du ~** country *ou* rural accent.
terroriser [tɛʀɔʀize] *vt* to terrorize.
terrorisme [tɛʀɔʀism(ə)] *nm* terrorism.
terroriste [tɛʀɔʀist(ə)] *nm/f* terrorist.
tertiaire [tɛʀsjɛʀ] *adj* tertiary ♦ *nm* (*ÉCON*) tertiary sector, service industries *pl*.
tertiarisation [tɛʀsjaʀizɑsjɔ̃] *nf* expansion or development of the service sector.
tertre [tɛʀtʀ(ə)] *nm* hillock, mound.
tes [te] *adj possessif voir* **ton**.
tesson [tesɔ̃] *nm*: **~ de bouteille** piece of broken bottle.
test [tɛst] *nm* test; **~ de grossesse** pregnancy test.
testament [tɛstamɑ̃] *nm* (*JUR*) will; (*fig*) legacy; (*REL*): **T~** Testament; **faire son ~** to make one's will.
testamentaire [tɛstamɑ̃tɛʀ] *adj* of a will.
tester [tɛste] *vt* to test.
testicule [tɛstikyl] *nm* testicle.
tétanie [tetani] *nf* tetany.
tétanos [tetanos] *nm* tetanus.
têtard [tɛtaʀ] *nm* tadpole.
tête [tɛt] *nf* head; (*cheveux*) hair *no pl*; (*visage*) face; (*longueur*): **gagner d'une (courte) ~** to win by a (short) head; (*FOOTBALL*) header; **de ~** *adj* (*wagon etc*) front *cpd*; (*concurrent*) leading ♦ *adv* (*calculer*) in one's head, mentally; **par ~** (*par personne*) per head; **se mettre en ~ que** to get it into one's head that; **se mettre en ~ de faire** to take it into one's head to do; **prendre la ~ de qch** to take the lead in sth; **perdre la ~** (*fig: s'affoler*) to lose one's head; (*: devenir fou*) to go off one's head; **ça ne va pas, la ~?** (*fam*) are you crazy?; **tenir ~ à qn** to stand up to *ou* defy sb; **la ~ en bas** with one's head down; **la ~ la première** (*tomber*) headfirst; **la ~ basse** hanging one's head; **avoir la ~ dure** (*fig*) to be thickheaded; **faire une ~** (*FOOTBALL*) to head the ball; **faire la ~** (*fig*) to sulk; **en ~** (*SPORT*) in the lead; at the front *ou* head; **de la ~ aux pieds** from head to toe; **~ d'affiche** (*THÉÂT etc*) top of the bill; **~ de bétail** head *inv* of cattle; **~ brulée** desperado; **~ chercheuse** homing device; **~ d'enregistrement** recording head; **~ d'impression** printhead; **~ de lecture** (playback) head; **~ de ligne** (*TRANSPORTS*) start of the line; **~ de liste** (*POL*) chief candidate; **~ de mort** skull and crossbones; **~ de pont**

(*MIL*) bridge- *ou* beachhead; ~ **de série** (*TEN-NIS*) seeded player, seed; ~ **de Turc** (*fig*) whipping boy (*BRIT*), butt; ~ **de veau** (*CULIN*) calf's head.

tête-à-queue [tɛtakø] *nm inv*: **faire un** ~ to spin round.

tête-à-tête [tɛtatɛt] *nm inv* tête-à-tête; (*service*) breakfast set for two; **en** ~ in private, alone together.

tête-bêche [tɛtbɛʃ] *adv* head to tail.

tétée [tete] *nf* (*action*) sucking; (*repas*) feed.

téter [tete] *vt*: ~ (**sa mère**) to suck at one's mother's breast, feed.

tétine [tetin] *nf* teat; (*sucette*) dummy (*BRIT*), pacifier (*US*).

téton [tetɔ̃] *nm* breast.

têtu, e [tety] *adj* stubborn, pigheaded.

texte [tɛkst(ə)] *nm* text; (*SCOL: d'un devoir*) subject, topic; **apprendre son** ~ (*THÉÂT*) to learn one's lines; **un** ~ **de loi** the wording of a law.

textile [tɛkstil] *adj* textile *cpd* ♦ *nm* textile; (*industrie*) textile industry.

textuel, le [tɛkstɥɛl] *adj* literal, word for word.

textuellement [tɛkstɥɛlmɑ̃] *adv* literally.

texture [tɛkstyʀ] *nf* texture; (*fig: d'un texte, livre*) feel.

TF1 *sigle f* (= *Télévision française 1*) TV channel.

TG *sigle f* = **Trésorerie générale**.

TGI *sigle m* = **tribunal de grande instance**.

TGV *sigle m* = **train à grande vitesse**.

thaï, e [tai] *adj* Thai ♦ *nm* (*LING*) Thai.

thaïlandais, e [tailɑ̃dɛ, -ɛz] *adj* Thai.

Thaïlande [tailɑ̃d] *nf*: **la** ~ Thailand.

thalassothérapie [talasɔteʀapi] *nf* sea-water therapy.

thé [te] *nm* tea; (*réunion*) tea party; **prendre le** ~ to have tea; ~ **au lait/citron** tea with milk/lemon.

théâtral, e, aux [teatʀal, -o] *adj* theatrical.

théâtre [teatʀ(ə)] *nm* theatre; (*techniques, genre*) drama, theatre; (*activité*) stage, theatre; (*œuvres*) plays *pl*, dramatic works *pl*; (*fig: lieu*): **le** ~ **de** the scene of; (*péj*) histrionics *pl*, playacting; **faire du** ~ (*en professionnel*) to be on the stage; (*en amateur*) to do some acting; ~ **filmé** filmed stage productions *pl*.

thébain, e [tebɛ̃, -ɛn] *adj* Theban.

Thèbes [tɛb] *n* Thebes.

théière [tejɛʀ] *nf* teapot.

théine [tein] *nf* theine.

théisme [teism(ə)] *nm* theism.

thématique [tematik] *adj* thematic.

thème [tɛm] *nm* theme; (*SCOL: traduction*) prose (composition); ~ **astral** birth chart.

théocratie [teɔkʀasi] *nf* theocracy.

théologie [teɔlɔʒi] *nf* theology.

théologien, ne [teɔlɔʒjɛ̃, -ɛn] *nm* theologian.

théologique [teɔlɔʒik] *adj* theological.

théorème [teɔʀɛm] *nm* theorem.

théoricien, ne [teɔʀisjɛ̃, -ɛn] *nm/f* theoretician, theorist.

théorie [teɔʀi] *nf* theory; **en** ~ in theory.

théorique [teɔʀik] *adj* theoretical.

théoriquement [teɔʀikmɑ̃] *adv* theoretically.

théoriser [teɔʀize] *vi* to theorize.

thérapeutique [teʀapøtik] *adj* therapeutic ♦ *nf* (*MÉD: branche*) therapeutics *sg*; (: *traitement*) therapy.

thérapie [teʀapi] *nf* therapy; ~ **de groupe** group therapy.

thermal, e, aux [tɛʀmal, -o] *adj* thermal; **station** ~**e** spa; **cure** ~**e** water cure.

thermes [tɛʀm(ə)] *nmpl* thermal baths; (*romains*) thermae *pl*.

thermique [tɛʀmik] *adj* (*énergie*) thermic; (*unité*) thermal.

thermodynamique [tɛʀmɔdinamik] *nf* thermodynamics *sg*.

thermoélectrique [tɛʀmoelɛktʀik] *adj* thermoelectric.

thermomètre [tɛʀmɔmɛtʀ(ə)] *nm* thermometer.

thermonucléaire [tɛʀmɔnykleɛʀ] *adj* thermonuclear.

thermos [tɛʀmos] *nm ou nf* ®: **(bouteille)** ~ vacuum *ou* Thermos ® flask (*BRIT*) *ou* bottle (*US*).

thermostat [tɛʀmɔsta] *nm* thermostat.

thésauriser [tezɔʀize] *vi* to hoard money.

thèse [tɛz] *nf* thesis (*pl* theses).

Thessalie [tesali] *nf*: **la** ~ Thessaly.

thessalien, ne [tesaljɛ̃, -ɛn] *adj* Thessalian.

thibaude [tibod] *nf* carpet underlay.

thon [tɔ̃] *nm* tuna (fish).

thonier [tɔnje] *nm* tuna boat.

thoracique [tɔʀasik] *adj* thoracic.

thorax [tɔʀaks] *nm* thorax.

thrombose [tʀɔ̃boz] *nf* thrombosis.

thym [tɛ̃] *nm* thyme.

thyroïde [tiʀɔid] *nf* thyroid (gland).

TI *sigle m* = **tribunal d'instance**.

tiare [tjaʀ] *nf* tiara.

Tibet [tibɛ] *nm*: **le** ~ Tibet.

tibétain, e [tibetɛ̃, -ɛn] *adj* Tibetan.

tibia [tibja] *nm* shin; (*os*) shinbone, tibia.

Tibre [tibʀ(ə)] *nm*: **le** ~ the Tiber.

tic [tik] *nm* tic, (nervous) twitch; (*de langage etc*) mannerism.

ticket [tikɛ] *nm* ticket; ~ **de caisse** till receipt; ~ **modérateur** patient's contribution towards medical costs; ~ **de quai** platform ticket; ~ **repas** luncheon voucher.

tic-tac [tiktak] *nm inv* tick-tock.

tictaquer [tiktake] *vi* to tick (away).

tiède [tjɛd] *adj* (*bière etc*) lukewarm; (*thé, café etc*) tepid; (*bain, accueil, sentiment*) lukewarm; (*vent, air*) mild, warm ♦ *adv*: **boire** ~ to drink things lukewarm.

tièdement [tjɛdmɑ̃] *adv* coolly, half-heartedly.

tiédeur [tjedœʀ] *nf* lukewarmness; (*du vent, de*

l'air) mildness.

tiédir [tjediʀ] *vi* (*se réchauffer*) to grow warmer; (*refroidir*) to cool.

tien, tienne [tjɛ̃, tjɛn] *pron*: **le** ~ (**la tienne**), **les** ~**s** (**tiennes**) yours; **à la tienne!** cheers!

tiendrai [tjɛ̃dʀe] *etc vb voir* **tenir**.

tienne [tjɛn] *vb voir* **tenir** ♦ *pron voir* **tien**.

tiens [tjɛ̃] *vb, excl voir* **tenir**.

tierce [tjɛʀs(ə)] *adj f, nf voir* **tiers**.

tiercé [tjɛʀse] *nm system of forecast betting giving first three horses*.

tiers, tierce [tjɛʀ, tjɛʀs(ə)] *adj* third ♦ *nm* (*JUR*) third party; (*fraction*) third ♦ *nf* (*MUS*) third; (*CARTES*) tierce; **une tierce personne** a third party; **assurance au** ~ third-party insurance; **le** ~ **monde** the third world; ~ **payant** *direct payment by insurers of medical expenses*; ~ **provisionnel** *interim payment of tax*.

tiersmondisme [tjɛʀmɔ̃dism(ə)] *nm* support for the Third World.

TIG *sigle m* = **travail d'intérêt général**.

tige [tiʒ] *nf* stem; (*baguette*) rod.

tignasse [tiɲas] *nf* (*péj*) shock *ou* mop of hair.

Tigre [tigʀ(ə)] *nm*: **le** ~ the Tigris.

tigre [tigʀ(ə)] *nm* tiger.

tigré, e [tigʀe] *adj* (*rayé*) striped; (*tacheté*) spotted.

tigresse [tigʀɛs] *nf* tigress.

tilleul [tijœl] *nm* lime (tree), linden (tree); (*boisson*) lime(-blossom) tea.

tilt [tilt(ə)] *nm*: **faire** ~ (*fig: échouer*) to miss the target; (*: inspirer*) to ring a bell.

timbale [tɛ̃bal] *nf* (metal) tumbler; ~**s** *nfpl* (*MUS*) timpani, kettledrums.

timbrage [tɛ̃bʀaʒ] *nm*: **dispensé de** ~ post(age) paid.

timbre [tɛ̃bʀ(ə)] *nm* (*tampon*) stamp; (*aussi*: ~-**poste**) (postage) stamp; (*cachet de la poste*) postmark; (*sonnette*) bell; (*MUS: de voix, instrument*) timbre, tone; ~ **anti-tabac** nicotine patch; ~ **dateur** date stamp.

timbré, e [tɛ̃bʀe] *adj* (*enveloppe*) stamped; (*voix*) resonant; (*fam: fou*) cracked, nuts.

timbrer [tɛ̃bʀe] *vt* to stamp.

timide [timid] *adj* (*emprunté*) shy, timid; (*timoré*) timid, timorous.

timidement [timidmɑ̃] *adv* shyly; timidly.

timidité [timidite] *nf* shyness; timidity.

timonerie [timɔnʀi] *nf* wheelhouse.

timonier [timɔnje] *nm* helmsman.

timoré, e [timɔʀe] *adj* timorous.

tint [tɛ̃] *etc vb voir* **tenir**.

tintamarre [tɛ̃tamaʀ] *nm* din, uproar.

tintement [tɛ̃tmɑ̃] *nm* ringing, chiming; ~**s d'oreilles** ringing in the ears.

tinter [tɛ̃te] *vi* to ring, chime; (*argent, clefs*) to jingle.

Tipp-Ex [tipɛks] *nm* ® Tipp-Ex ®.

tique [tik] *nf* tick (*insect*).

tiquer [tike] *vi* (*personne*) to make a face.

TIR *sigle mpl* (= *Transports internationaux rou-*

tiers) TIR.

tir [tiʀ] *nm* (*sport*) shooting; (*fait ou manière de tirer*) firing *no pl*; (*FOOTBALL*) shot; (*stand*) shooting gallery; ~ **d'obus/de mitraillette** shell/machine gun fire; ~ **à l'arc** archery; ~ **de barrage** barrage fire; ~ **au fusil** (*rifle*) shooting; ~ **au pigeon** (*d'argile*) clay pigeon shooting.

tirade [tiʀad] *nf* tirade.

tirage [tiʀaʒ] *nm* (*action*) printing; (*PHOTO*) print; (*INFORM*) printout; (*de journal*) circulation; (*de livre*) (print-)run; edition; (*de cheminée*) draught (*BRIT*), draft (*US*); (*de loterie*) draw; (*fig: désaccord*) friction; ~ **au sort** drawing lots.

tiraillement [tiʀajmɑ̃] *nm* (*douleur*) sharp pain; (*fig: doutes*) agony *no pl* of indecision; (*conflits*) friction *no pl*.

tirailler [tiʀaje] *vt* to pull at, tug at; (*fig*) to gnaw at ♦ *vi* to fire at random.

tirailleur [tiʀajœʀ] *nm* skirmisher.

tirant [tiʀɑ̃] *nm*: ~ **d'eau** draught (*BRIT*), draft (*US*).

tire [tiʀ] *nf*: **vol à la** ~ pickpocketing.

tiré [tiʀe] *adj* (*visage, traits*) drawn ♦ *nm* (*COMM*) drawee; ~ **par les cheveux** far-fetched; ~ **à part** off-print.

tire-au-flanc [tiʀoflɑ̃] *nm inv* (*péj*) skiver.

tire-bouchon [tiʀbuʃɔ̃] *nm* corkscrew.

tire-bouchonner [tiʀbuʃɔne] *vt* to twirl.

tire-d'aile [tiʀdɛl]: **à** ~ *adv* swiftly.

tire-fesses [tiʀfɛs] *nm inv* ski-tow.

tire-lait [tiʀlɛ] *nm inv* breast-pump.

tire-larigot [tiʀlaʀigo]: **à** ~ *adv* as much as one likes, to one's heart's content.

tirelire [tiʀliʀ] *nf* moneybox.

tirer [tiʀe] *vt* (*gén*) to pull; (*extraire*): ~ **qch de** to take *ou* pull sth out of; to get sth out of; to extract sth from; (*tracer: ligne, trait*) to draw, trace; (*fermer: volet, porte, trappe*) to pull to, close; (*: rideau*) to draw; (*choisir: carte, conclusion, aussi COMM: chèque*) to draw; (*en faisant feu: balle, coup*) to fire; (*: animal*) to shoot; (*journal, livre, photo*) to print; (*FOOTBALL: corner etc*) to take ♦ *vi* (*faire feu*) to fire; (*faire du tir, FOOTBALL*) to shoot; (*cheminée*) to draw; **se** ~ *vi* (*fam*) to push off; **s'en** ~ to pull through; ~ **sur** (*corde, poignée*) to pull on *ou* at; (*faire feu sur*) to shoot *ou* fire at; (*pipe*) to draw on; (*fig: avoisiner*) to verge *ou* border on; ~ **6 mètres** (*NAVIG*) to draw 6 metres of water; ~ **son nom de** to take *ou* get its name from; ~ **la langue** to stick out one's tongue; ~ **qn de** (*embarras etc*) to help *ou* get sb out of; ~ **à l'arc/la carabine** to shoot with a bow and arrow/with a rifle; ~ **en longueur** to drag on; ~ **à sa fin** to be drawing to an end; ~ **les cartes** to read *ou* tell the cards.

tiret [tiʀɛ] *nm* dash; (*en fin de ligne*) hyphen.

tireur [tiʀœʀ] *nm* gunman; (*COMM*) drawer; **bon** ~ good shot; ~ **d'élite** marksman; ~ **de**

cartes fortuneteller.
tiroir [tiʀwaʀ] *nm* drawer.
tiroir-caisse [tiʀwaʀkɛs] *nm* till.
tisane [tizan] *nf* herb tea.
tison [tizɔ̃] *nm* brand.
tisonner [tizɔne] *vt* to poke.
tisonnier [tizɔnje] *nm* poker.
tissage [tisaʒ] *nm* weaving *no pl.*
tisser [tise] *vt* to weave.
tisserand, e [tisʀɑ̃, -ɑ̃d] *nm/f* weaver.
tissu [tisy] *nm* fabric, material, cloth *no pl*; (*fig*) fabric; (*ANAT, BIO*) tissue; ~ **de mensonges** web of lies.
tissu, e [tisy] *adj*: ~ **de** woven through with.
tissu-éponge [tisyepɔ̃ʒ] *nm* (terry) towelling *no pl.*
titane [titan] *nm* titanium.
titanesque [titanɛsk(ə)] *adj* titanic.
titiller [titile] *vt* to titillate.
titrage [titʀaʒ] *nm* (*d'un film*) titling; (*d'un alcool*) determination of alcohol content.
titre [titʀ(ə)] *nm* (*gén*) title; (*de journal*) headline; (*diplôme*) qualification; (*COMM*) security; (*CHIMIE*) titre; **en** ~ (*champion, responsable*) official, recognized; **à juste** ~ with just cause, rightly; **à quel** ~? on what grounds?; **à aucun** ~ on no account; **au même** ~ **(que)** in the same way (as); **au** ~ **de la coopération** *etc* in the name of cooperation *etc*; **à** ~ **d'exemple** as an *ou* by way of an example; **à** ~ **exceptionnel** exceptionally; **à** ~ **d'information** for (your) information; **à** ~ **gracieux** free of charge; **à** ~ **d'essai** on a trial basis; **à** ~ **privé** in a private capacity; ~ **courant** running head; ~ **de propriété** title deed; ~ **de transport** ticket.
titré, e [titʀe] *adj* (*livre, film*) entitled; (*personne*) titled.
titrer [titʀe] *vt* (*CHIMIE*) to titrate; to assay; (*PRESSE*) to run as a headline; (*suj: vin*): ~ **10°** to be 10° proof.
titubant, e [titybɑ̃, -ɑ̃t] *adj* staggering, reeling.
tituber [titybe] *vi* to stagger *ou* reel (along).
titulaire [titylɛʀ] *adj* (*ADMIN*) appointed, with tenure ♦ *nm* (*ADMIN*) incumbent; **être** ~ **de** to hold.
titularisation [titylaʀizasjɔ̃] *nf* granting of tenure.
titulariser [titylaʀize] *vt* to give tenure to.
TNP *sigle m* (= *Théâtre national populaire*).
TNT *sigle m* (= *Trinitrotoluène*) TNT.
toast [tost] *nm* slice *ou* piece of toast; (*de bienvenue*) (welcoming) toast; **porter un** ~ **à qn** to propose *ou* drink a toast to sb.
toboggan [tɔbɔgɑ̃] *nm* toboggan; (*jeu*) slide; (*AUTO*) temporary flyover (*BRIT*) *ou* overpass (*US*); ~ **de secours** (*AVIAT*) escape chute.
toc [tɔk] *nm*: **en** ~ imitation *cpd.*
tocsin [tɔksɛ̃] *nm* alarm (bell).
toge [tɔʒ] *nf* toga; (*de juge*) gown.

Togo [tɔgo] *nm*: **le** ~ Togo.
togolais, e [tɔgɔlɛ, -ɛz] *adj* Togolese.
tohu-bohu [tɔybɔy] *nm* (*désordre*) confusion; (*tumulte*) commotion.
toi [twa] *pron* you; ~, **tu l'as fait?** did YOU do it?
toile [twal] *nf* (*matériau*) cloth *no pl*; (*bâche*) piece of canvas; (*tableau*) canvas; **grosse** ~ canvas; **tisser sa** ~ (*araignée*) to spin its web; ~ **d'araignée** spider's web; (*au plafond etc: à enlever*) cobweb; ~ **cirée** oilcloth; ~ **émeri** emery cloth; ~ **de fond** (*fig*) backdrop; ~ **de jute** hessian; ~ **de lin** linen; ~ **de tente** canvas.
toilettage [twalɛtaʒ] *nm* grooming *no pl*; (*d'un texte*) tidying up.
toilette [twalɛt] *nf* wash; (*s'habiller et se préparer*) getting ready, washing and dressing; (*habits*) outfit; dress *no pl*; ~**s** *nfpl* toilet *sg*; **les** ~**s des dames/messieurs** the ladies'/gents' (toilets) (*BRIT*), the ladies'/mens' (rest)room (*US*); **faire sa** ~ to have a wash, get washed; **faire la** ~ **de** (*animal*) to groom; (*voiture etc*) to clean, wash; (*texte*) to tidy up; **articles de** ~ toiletries; ~ **intime** personal hygiene.
toi-même [twamɛm] *pron* yourself.
toise [twaz] *nf*: **passer à la** ~ to have one's height measured.
toiser [twaze] *vt* to eye up and down.
toison [twazɔ̃] *nf* (*de mouton*) fleece; (*cheveux*) mane.
toit [twa] *nm* roof; ~ **ouvrant** sun roof.
toiture [twatyʀ] *nf* roof.
Tokyo [tɔkjo] *n* Tokyo.
tôle [tol] *nf* sheet metal *no pl*; (*plaque*) steel (*ou* iron) sheet; ~**s** *nfpl* (*carrosserie*) bodywork *sg* (*BRIT*), body *sg*; panels; ~ **d'acier** sheet steel *no pl*; ~ **ondulée** corrugated iron.
Tolède [tɔlɛd] *n* Toledo.
tolérable [tɔleʀabl(ə)] *adj* tolerable, bearable.
tolérance [tɔleʀɑ̃s] *nf* tolerance; (*hors taxe*) allowance.
tolérant, e [tɔleʀɑ̃, -ɑ̃t] *adj* tolerant.
tolérer [tɔleʀe] *vt* to tolerate; (*ADMIN: hors taxe etc*) to allow.
tôlerie [tolʀi] *nf* sheet metal manufacture; (*atelier*) sheet metal workshop; (*ensemble des tôles*) panels *pl.*
tollé [tɔle] *nm*: **un** ~ **(de protestations)** a general outcry.
TOM [*parfois:* tɔm] *sigle m(pl)* (= *territoire(s) d'outre-mer*).
tomate [tɔmat] *nf* tomato.
tombal, e [tɔ̃bal] *adj*: **pierre** ~**e** tombstone, gravestone.
tombant, e [tɔ̃bɑ̃, -ɑ̃t] *adj* (*fig*) drooping, sloping.
tombe [tɔ̃b] *nf* (*sépulture*) grave; (*avec monument*) tomb.
tombeau, x [tɔ̃bo] *nm* tomb; **à** ~ **ouvert** at breakneck speed.
tombée [tɔ̃be] *nf*: **à la** ~ **du jour** *ou* **de la nuit**

at the close of day, at nightfall.

tomber [tɔ̃be] *vi* to fall ♦ *vt:* ~ **la veste** to slip off one's jacket; **laisser** ~ to drop; ~ **sur** *vt* (*rencontrer*) to come across; (*attaquer*) to set about; ~ **de fatigue/sommeil** to drop from exhaustion/be falling asleep on one's feet; ~ **à l'eau** (*fig: projet etc*) to fall through; ~ **en panne** to break down; ~ **juste** (*opération, calcul*) to come out right; ~ **en ruine** to fall into ruins; **ça tombe bien/mal** (*fig*) that's come at the right/wrong time; **si vous le prenez sur ce** ~ if you're going to take it like that; ~ **sur** ~ in matching shades.

tombereau, x [tɔ̃bʀo] *nm* tipcart.

tombeur [tɔ̃bœʀ] *nm* (*péj*) Casanova.

tombola [tɔ̃bɔla] *nf* tombola.

Tombouctou [tɔ̃buktu] *n* Timbuktu.

tome [tɔm] *nm* volume.

tommette [tɔmɛt] *nf* hexagonal floor tile.

ton, ta, *pl* **tes** [tɔ̃, ta, te] *adj possessif* your.

ton [tɔ̃] *nm* (*gén*) tone; (*MUS*) key; (*couleur*) shade, tone; (*de la voix: hauteur*) pitch; **donner le** ~ to set the tone; **élever** *ou* **hausser le** ~ to raise one's voice; **de bon** ~ in good taste; **si vous le prenez sur ce** ~ if you're going to take it like that; ~ **sur** ~ in matching shades.

tonal, e [tɔnal] *adj* tonal.

tonalité [tɔnalite] *nf* (*au téléphone*) dialling tone; (*MUS*) key; (: *ton*) key; (*fig*) tone.

tondeuse [tɔ̃døz] *nf* (*à gazon*) (lawn)mower; (*du coiffeur*) clippers *pl*; (*pour la tonte*) shears *pl*.

tondre [tɔ̃dʀ(ə)] *vt* (*pelouse, herbe*) to mow; (*haie*) to cut, clip; (*mouton, toison*) to shear; (*cheveux*) to crop.

tondu, e [tɔ̃dy] *pp de* **tondre** ♦ *adj* (*cheveux*) cropped; (*mouton, crâne*) shorn.

Tonga [tɔ̃ga] *nf*: **les îles** ~ Tonga.

tonicité [tɔnisite] *nf* (*MÉD: des tissus*) tone; (*fig: de l'air, la mer*) bracing effect.

tonifiant, e [tɔnifjɑ̃, -ɑ̃t] *adj* invigorating, revivifying.

tonifier [tɔnifje] *vt* (*air, eau*) to invigorate; (*peau, organisme*) to tone up.

tonique [tɔnik] *adj* fortifying; (*personne*) dynamic ♦ *nm, nf* tonic.

tonitruant, e [tɔnitʀɥɑ̃, -ɑ̃t] *adj*: **voix** ~**e** thundering voice.

Tonkin [tɔ̃kɛ̃] *nm*: **le** ~ Tonkin, Tongking.

tonkinois, e [tɔ̃kinwa, -waz] *adj* Tonkinese.

tonnage [tɔnaʒ] *nm* tonnage.

tonnant, e [tɔnɑ̃, -ɑ̃t] *adj* thunderous.

tonne [tɔn] *nf* metric ton, tonne.

tonneau, x [tɔno] *nm* (*à vin, cidre*) barrel; (*NAVIG*) ton; **faire des** ~**x** (*voiture, avion*) to roll over.

tonnelet [tɔnlɛ] *nm* keg.

tonnelier [tɔnəlje] *nm* cooper.

tonnelle [tɔnɛl] *nf* bower, arbour (*BRIT*), arbor (*US*).

tonner [tɔne] *vi* to thunder; (*parler avec véhémence*): ~ **contre qn/qch** to inveigh against sb/sth; **il tonne** it is thundering, there's some thunder.

tonnerre [tɔnɛʀ] *nm* thunder; **coup de** ~ (*fig*) thunderbolt, bolt from the blue; **un** ~ **d'applaudissements** thunderous applause; **du** ~ *adj* (*fam*) terrific.

tonsure [tɔ̃syʀ] *nf* bald patch; (*de moine*) tonsure.

tonte [tɔ̃t] *nf* shearing.

tonus [tɔnys] *nm* (*des muscles*) tone; (*d'une personne*) dynamism.

top [tɔp] *nm*: **au 3ème** ~ at the 3rd stroke ♦ *adj*: ~ **secret** top secret ♦ *excl* go!

topaze [tɔpaz] *nf* topaz.

toper [tɔpe] *vi*: **tope-/topez-là** it's a deal!, you're on!

topinambour [tɔpinɑ̃buʀ] *nm* Jerusalem artichoke.

topo [tɔpo] *nm* (*discours, exposé*) talk; (*fam*) spiel.

topographie [tɔpɔgʀafi] *nf* topography.

topographique [tɔpɔgʀafik] *adj* topographical.

toponymie [tɔpɔnimi] *nf* study of place names, toponymy.

toquade [tɔkad] *nf* fad, craze.

toque [tɔk] *nf* (*de fourrure*) fur hat; ~ **de jockey/juge** jockey's/judge's cap; ~ **de cuisinier** chef's hat.

toqué, e [tɔke] *adj* (*fam*) touched, cracked.

torche [tɔʀʃ(ə)] *nf* torch; **se mettre en** ~ (*parachute*) to candle.

torcher [tɔʀʃe] *vt* (*fam*) to wipe.

torchère [tɔʀʃɛʀ] *nf* flare.

torchon [tɔʀʃɔ̃] *nm* cloth, duster; (*à vaisselle*) tea towel *ou* cloth.

tordre [tɔʀdʀ(ə)] *vt* (*chiffon*) to wring; (*barre, fig: visage*) to twist; **se** ~ *vi* (*barre*) to bend; (*roue*) to twist, buckle; (*ver, serpent*) to writhe; **se** ~ **le pied/bras** to twist one's foot/arm; **se** ~ **de douleur/rire** to writhe in pain/be doubled up with laughter.

tordu, e [tɔʀdy] *pp de* **tordre** ♦ *adj* (*fig*) warped, twisted.

torero [tɔʀeʀo] *nm* bullfighter.

tornade [tɔʀnad] *nf* tornado.

toron [tɔʀɔ̃] *nm* strand (of rope).

Toronto [tɔʀɔ̃to] *n* Toronto.

torontois, e [tɔʀɔ̃twa, -waz] *adj* Torontonian ♦ *nm/f*: **T**~, **e** Torontonian.

torpeur [tɔʀpœʀ] *nf* torpor, drowsiness.

torpille [tɔʀpij] *nf* torpedo.

torpiller [tɔʀpije] *vt* to torpedo.

torpilleur [tɔʀpijœʀ] *nm* torpedo boat.

torréfaction [tɔʀefaksjɔ̃] *nf* roasting.

torréfier [tɔʀefje] *vt* to roast.

torrent [tɔʀɑ̃] *nm* torrent, mountain stream; (*fig*): **un** ~ **de** a torrent *ou* flood of; **il pleut à** ~**s** the rain is lashing down.

torrentiel, le [tɔʀɑ̃sjɛl] *adj* torrential.

torride [tɔʀid] *adj* torrid.

tors, torse *ou* **torte** [tɔʀ, tɔʀs(ə) *ou* tɔʀt(ə)]

adj twisted.

torsade [tɔʀsad] *nf* twist; (*ARCHIT*) cable moulding (*BRIT*) *ou* molding (*US*).

torsader [tɔʀsade] *vt* to twist.

torse [tɔʀs(ə)] *nm* torso; (*poitrine*) chest.

torsion [tɔʀsjɔ̃] *nf* (*action*) twisting; (*TECH, PHYSIQUE*) torsion.

tort [tɔʀ] *nm* (*défaut*) fault; (*préjudice*) wrong *no pl*; **~s** *nmpl* (*JUR*) fault *sg*; **avoir ~** to be wrong; **être dans son ~** to be in the wrong; **donner ~ à qn** to lay the blame on sb; (*fig*) to prove sb wrong; **causer du ~ à** to harm; to be harmful *ou* detrimental to; **en ~** in the wrong, at fault; **à ~** wrongly; **à ~ ou à raison** rightly or wrongly; **à ~ et à travers** wildly.

torte [tɔʀt(ə)] *adj f voir* **tors**.

torticolis [tɔʀtikɔli] *nm* stiff neck.

tortiller [tɔʀtije] *vt* (*corde, mouchoir*) to twist; (*doigts*) to twiddle; **se ~** *vi* to wriggle, squirm.

tortionnaire [tɔʀsjɔnɛʀ] *nm* torturer.

tortue [tɔʀty] *nf* tortoise; (*fig*) slowcoach (*BRIT*), slowpoke (*US*).

tortueux, euse [tɔʀtɥø, -øz] *adj* (*rue*) twisting; (*fig*) tortuous.

torture [tɔʀtyʀ] *nf* torture.

torturer [tɔʀtyʀe] *vt* to torture; (*fig*) to torment.

torve [tɔʀv(ə)] *adj*: **regard ~** menacing *ou* grim look.

toscan, e [tɔskã, -an] *adj* Tuscan.

Toscane [tɔskan] *nf*: **la ~** Tuscany.

tôt [to] *adv* early; **~ ou tard** sooner or later; **si ~** so early; (*déjà*) so soon; **au plus ~** at the earliest, as soon as possible; **plus ~** earlier; **il eut ~ fait de faire ...** he soon did ....

total, e, aux [tɔtal, -o] *adj, nm* total; **au ~** in total *ou* all; (*fig*) all in all; **faire le ~** to work out the total.

totalement [tɔtalmã] *adv* totally, completely.

totalisateur [tɔtalizatœʀ] *nm* adding machine.

totaliser [tɔtalize] *vt* to total (up).

totalitaire [tɔtalitɛʀ] *adj* totalitarian.

totalitarisme [tɔtalitaʀism(ə)] *nm* totalitarianism.

totalité [tɔtalite] *nf*: **la ~ de**: **la ~ des élèves** all (of) the pupils; **la ~ de la population/classe** the whole population/class; **en ~** entirely.

totem [tɔtɛm] *nm* totem.

toubib [tubib] *nm* (*fam*) doctor.

touchant, e [tuʃã, -ãt] *adj* touching.

touche [tuʃ] *nf* (*de piano, de machine à écrire*) key; (*de violon*) fingerboard; (*de télécommande etc*) key, button; (*PEINTURE etc*) stroke, touch; (*fig: de couleur, nostalgie*) touch, hint; (*RUGBY*) line-out; (*FOOTBALL: aussi*: **remise en ~**) throw-in; (*aussi*: **ligne de ~**) touch-line; (*ESCRIME*) hit; **en ~** in (*ou* into) touch; **avoir une drôle de ~** to look a sight; **~ de commande/de fonction/de retour** (*IN-*

FORM) control/function/return key; **~ à effleurement** *ou* **sensitive** touch-sensitive control *ou* key.

touche-à-tout [tuʃatu] *nm inv* (*péj*: *gén*: *enfant*) meddler; (: *fig*: *inventeur etc*) dabbler.

toucher [tuʃe] *nm* touch ♦ *vt* to touch; (*palper*) to feel; (*atteindre: d'un coup de feu etc*) to hit; (*affecter*) to touch, affect; (*concerner*) to concern, affect; (*contacter*) to reach, contact; (*recevoir: récompense*) to receive, get; (: *salaire*) to draw, get; (*chèque*) to cash; (*aborder: problème, sujet*) to touch on; **au ~** to the touch; by the feel; **se ~** (*être en contact*) to touch; **~ à** to touch; (*modifier*) to touch, tamper *ou* meddle with; (*traiter de, concerner*) to have to do with, concern; **je vais lui en ~ un mot** I'll have a word with him about it; **~ au but** (*fig*) to near one's goal; **~ à sa fin** to be drawing to a close.

touffe [tuf] *nf* tuft.

touffu, e [tufy] *adj* thick, dense; (*fig*) complex, involved.

toujours [tuʒuʀ] *adv* always; (*encore*) still; (*constamment*) forever; **depuis ~** always; **essaie ~** (you can) try anyway; **pour ~** forever; **~ est-il que** the fact remains that; **~ plus** more and more.

toulonnais, e [tulɔnɛ, -ɛz] of *ou* from Toulon.

toulousain, e [tuluzɛ̃, -ɛn] *adj* of *ou* from Toulouse.

toupet [tupɛ] *nm* quiff (*BRIT*), tuft; (*fam*) nerve, cheek (*BRIT*).

toupie [tupi] *nf* (spinning) top.

tour [tuʀ] *nf* tower; (*immeuble*) high-rise block (*BRIT*) *ou* building (*US*), tower block (*BRIT*); (*ÉCHECS*) castle, rook ♦ *nm* (*excursion: à pied*) stroll, walk; (: *en voiture etc*) run, ride; (: *plus long*) trip; (*SPORT: aussi*: **~ de piste**) lap; (*d'être servi ou de jouer etc, tournure, de vis ou clef*) turn; (*de roue etc*) revolution; (*circonférence*): **de 3 m de ~** 3 m round, with a circumference *ou* girth of 3 m; (*POL: aussi*: **~ de scrutin**) ballot; (*ruse, de prestidigitation, de cartes*) trick; (*de potier*) wheel; (*à bois, métaux*) lathe; **faire le ~ de** to go (a)round; (*à pied*) to walk (a)round; (*fig*) to review; **faire le ~ de l'Europe** to tour Europe; **faire un ~** to go for a walk; (*en voiture etc*) to go for a ride; **faire 2 ~s** to go (a)round twice; (*hélice etc*) to turn *ou* revolve twice; **fermer à double ~** *vi* to double-lock the door; **c'est au ~ de Renée** it's Renée's turn; **à ~ de rôle**, **à ~ in turn; **à ~ de bras** with all one's strength; (*fig*) non-stop, relentlessly; **~ de taille/tête** waist/head measurement; **~ de chant** song recital; **~ de contrôle** *nf* control tower; **~ de garde** spell of duty; **~ d'horizon** (*fig*) general survey; **~ de lit** valance; **~ de main** dexterity, knack; **en un ~ de main** (as) quick as a flash; **~ de passe-passe** trick, sleight of hand; **~ de reins** sprained back.

The **Tour de France** is an annual road race for professional cyclists taking about three weeks to complete in daily stages or "*étapes*" of approximately 110 miles over terrain of varying difficulty. The leading cyclist wears a yellow jersey, the **maillot jaune**. There are a number of time trials. The route varies and is not usually confined only to France, but the race always ends in Paris.

tourangeau, elle, x [tuʀɑ̃ʒo, -ɛl] adj (*de la région*) of ou from Touraine; (*de la ville*) of ou from Tours.

tourbe [tuʀb(ə)] nf peat.

tourbière [tuʀbjɛʀ] nf peat-bog.

tourbillon [tuʀbijɔ̃] nm whirlwind; (*d'eau*) whirlpool; (*fig*) whirl, swirl.

tourbillonner [tuʀbijɔne] vi to whirl, swirl; (*objet, personne*) to whirl ou twirl round.

tourelle [tuʀɛl] nf turret.

tourisme [tuʀism(ə)] nm tourism; **agence de ~** tourist agency; **avion/voiture de ~** private plane/car; **faire du ~** to do some sightseeing, go touring.

touriste [tuʀist] nm/f tourist.

touristique [tuʀistik] adj tourist cpd; (*région*) touristic (*péj*), with tourist appeal.

tourment [tuʀmɑ̃] nm torment.

tourmente [tuʀmɑ̃t] nf storm.

tourmenté, e [tuʀmɑ̃te] adj tormented, tortured; (*mer, période*) turbulent, tempestuous.

tourmenter [tuʀmɑ̃te] vt to torment; **se ~** vi to fret, worry o.s.

tournage [tuʀnaʒ] nm (*d'un film*) shooting.

tournant, e [tuʀnɑ̃, -ɑ̃t] adj (*feu, scène*) revolving; (*chemin*) winding; (*escalier*) spiral cpd; (*mouvement*) circling ♦ nm (*de route*) bend (BRIT), curve (US); (*fig*) turning point; *voir* **plaque, grève**.

tourné, e [tuʀne] adj (*lait, vin*) sour, off; (*MENUISERIE: bois*) turned; (*fig: compliment*) well-phrased; **bien ~** (*personne*) shapely; **mal ~** (*lettre*) badly expressed; **avoir l'esprit mal ~** to have a dirty mind.

tournebroche [tuʀnəbʀɔʃ] nm roasting spit.

tourne-disque [tuʀnədisk(ə)] nm record player.

tournedos [tuʀnədo] nm tournedos.

tournée [tuʀne] nf (*du facteur etc*) round; (*d'artiste, politicien*) tour; (*au café*) round (of drinks); **~ électorale/musicale** election/concert tour; **faire la ~ de** to go (a)round.

tournemain [tuʀnəmɛ̃]: **en un ~** adv in a flash.

tourner [tuʀne] vt to turn; (*sauce, mélange*) to stir; (*contourner*) to get (a)round; (*CINÉ*) to shoot; to make ♦ vi to turn; (*moteur*) to run; (*compteur*) to tick away; (*lait etc*) to turn (sour); (*fig: chance, vie*) to turn out; **se ~** vi to turn (a)round; **se ~ vers** to turn to; to turn towards; **bien ~** to turn out well; **~ autour**

de to go (a)round; (*planète*) to revolve (a)round; (*péj*) to hang (a)round; **~ autour du pot** (*fig*) to go (a)round in circles; **~ à/en** to turn into; **~ à la pluie/au rouge** to turn rainy/red; **~ en ridicule** to ridicule; **~ le dos à** (*mouvement*) to turn one's back on; (*position*) to have one's back to; **~ court** to come to a sudden end; **se ~ les pouces** to twiddle one's thumbs; **~ la tête** to look away; **~ la tête à qn** (*fig*) to go to sb's head; **~ de l'œil** to pass out; **~ la page** (*fig*) to turn the page.

tournesol [tuʀnəsɔl] nm sunflower.

tourneur [tuʀnœʀ] nm turner; lathe-operator.

tournevis [tuʀnəvis] nm screwdriver.

tourniquer [tuʀnike] vi to go (a)round in circles.

tourniquet [tuʀnikɛ] nm (*pour arroser*) sprinkler; (*portillon*) turnstile; (*présentoir*) revolving stand, spinner; (*CHIRURGIE*) tourniquet.

tournis [tuʀni] nm: **avoir/donner le ~** to feel/make dizzy.

tournoi [tuʀnwa] nm tournament.

tournoyer [tuʀnwaje] vi (*oiseau*) to wheel (a)round; (*fumée*) to swirl (a)round.

tournure [tuʀnyʀ] nf (LING: *syntaxe*) turn of phrase; form; (*: d'une phrase*) phrasing; (*évolution*): **la ~ de qch** the way sth is developing; (*aspect*): **la ~ de** the look of; **la ~ des événements** the turn of events; **prendre ~** to take shape; **~ d'esprit** turn ou cast of mind.

tour-opérateur [tuʀɔpeʀatœʀ] nm tour operator.

tourte [tuʀt(ə)] nf pie.

tourteau, x [tuʀto] nm (AGR) oilcake, cattlecake; (ZOOL) edible crab.

tourtereaux [tuʀtəʀo] nmpl lovebirds.

tourterelle [tuʀtəʀɛl] nf turtledove.

tourtière [tuʀtjɛʀ] nf pie dish ou plate.

tous dét [tu] , pron [tus] *voir* **tout**.

Toussaint [tusɛ̃] nf: **la ~** All Saints' Day.

La Toussaint, November 1, is a public holiday in France. People traditionally visit the graves of friends and relatives and decorate them with chrysanthemums.

tousser [tuse] vi to cough.

toussoter [tusɔte] vi to have a slight cough; to cough a little; (*pour avertir*) to give a slight cough.

=========================== MOT-CLÉ

tout, e [tu, tut] (*mpl* **tous**, *fpl* **toutes**) adj 1 (*avec article singulier*) all; **~ le lait** all the milk; **~e la nuit** all night, the whole night; **~ le livre** the whole book; **~ un pain** a whole loaf; **~ le temps** all the time, the whole time; **c'est le contraire** it's quite the opposite; **c'est ~e une affaire** ou **histoire** it's quite a business, it's a whole rigmarole

2 (*avec article pluriel*) every; all; **tous les**

livres all the books; ~**es les nuits** every night; ~**es les fois** every time; ~**es les trois/deux semaines** every third/other *ou* second week, every three/two weeks; **tous les deux** both *ou* each of us (*ou* them *ou* you); ~**es les trois** all three of us (*ou* them *ou* you)

3 (*sans article*): **à** ~ **âge** at any age; **pour** ~**e nourriture, il avait ...** his only food was ...; **de tous côtés, de** ~**es parts** from everywhere, from every side

♦ *pron* everything, all; **il a** ~ **fait** he's done everything; **je les vois tous** I can see them all *ou* all of them; **nous y sommes tous allés** all of us went, we all went; **c'est** ~ that's all; **en** ~ in all; **en** ~ **et pour** ~ all in all; ~ **ce qu'il sait** all he knows; **c'était** ~ **ce qu'il y a de chic** it was the last word *ou* the ultimate in chic

♦ *nm* whole; **le** ~ all of it (*ou* them); **le** ~ **est de ...** the main thing is to ...; **pas du** ~ not at all; **elle a** ~ **d'une mère/d'une intrigante** she's a real *ou* true mother/schemer; **du** ~ **au** ~ utterly

♦ *adv* **1** (*très, complètement*) very; ~ **près** *ou* **à côté** very near; **le** ~ **premier** the very first; ~ **seul** all alone; **il était** ~ **rouge** he was really *ou* all red; **parler** ~ **bas** to speak very quietly; **le livre** ~ **entier** the whole book; ~ **en haut** right at the top; ~ **droit** straight ahead

2: ~ **en** while; ~ **en travaillant** while working, as he *etc* works

3: ~ **d'abord** first of all; ~ **à coup** suddenly; ~ **à fait** absolutely; ~ **à fait!** exactly!; ~ **à l'heure** a short while ago; (*futur*) in a short while, shortly; **à** ~ **à l'heure!** see you later!; **il répondit** ~ **court que non** he just answered no (and that was all); ~ **de même** all the same; ~ **le monde** everybody; ~ **ou rien** all or nothing; ~ **simplement** quite simply; ~ **de suite** immediately, straight away

tout-à-l'égout [tutalegu] *nm inv* mains drainage.
toutefois [tutfwa] *adv* however.
toutou [tutu] *nm* (*fam*) doggie.
tout-petit [tup(ə)ti] *nm* toddler.
tout-puissant, toute-puissante [tupɥisɑ̃, tutpɥisɑ̃t] *adj* all-powerful, omnipotent.
tout-venant [tuvnɑ̃] *nm*: **le** ~ everyday stuff.
toux [tu] *nf* cough.
toxémie [tɔksemi] *nf* toxaemia (*BRIT*), toxemia (*US*).
toxicité [tɔksisite] *nf* toxicity.
toxicologie [tɔksikɔlɔʒi] *nf* toxicology.
toxicomane [tɔksikɔman] *nmf* drug addict.
toxicomanie [tɔksikɔmani] *nf* drug addiction.
toxine [tɔksin] *nf* toxin.
toxique [tɔksik] *adj* toxic, poisonous.
toxoplasmose [tɔksoplasmoz] *nf* toxoplasmosis.

TP *sigle mpl* = **travaux pratiques, travaux publics** ♦ *sigle m* = **trésor public**.
TPG *sigle m* = **Trésorier-payeur général**.
tps *abr* = **temps**.
trac [trak] *nm* nerves *pl*; (*THÉÂT*) stage fright; **avoir le** ~ to get an attack of nerves; to have stage fright; **tout à** ~ all of a sudden.
traçant, e [trasɑ̃, -ɑ̃t] *adj*: **table** ~**e** (*INFORM*) (graph) plotter.
tracas [traka] *nm* bother *no pl*, worry *no pl*.
tracasser [trakase] *vt* to worry, bother; (*harceler*) to harass; **se** ~ *vi* to worry o.s., fret.
tracasserie [trakasri] *nf* annoyance *no pl*; harassment *no pl*.
tracassier, ière [trakasje, -jɛr] *adj* irksome.
trace [tras] *nf* (*empreintes*) tracks *pl*; (*marques, aussi fig*) mark; (*restes, vestige*) trace; (*indice*) sign; **suivre à la** ~ to track; ~**s de pas** footprints.
tracé [trase] *nm* (*contour*) line; (*plan*) layout.
tracer [trase] *vt* to draw; (*mot*) to trace; (*piste*) to open up; (*fig: chemin*) to show.
traceur [trasœr] *nm* (*INFORM*) plotter.
trachée(-artère) [trafe(artɛr)] *nf* windpipe, trachea.
trachéite [trakeit] *nf* tracheitis.
tract [trakt] *nm* tract, pamphlet; (*publicitaire*) handout.
tractations [traktasjɔ̃] *nfpl* dealings, bargaining *sg*.
tracter [trakte] *vt* to tow.
tracteur [traktœr] *nm* tractor.
traction [traksjɔ̃] *nf* traction; (*GYM*) pull-up; ~ **avant/arrière** front-wheel/rear-wheel drive; ~ **électrique** electric(al) traction *ou* haulage.
trad. *abr* (= *traduit*) translated; (= *traduction*) translation; (= *traducteur*) translator.
tradition [tradisjɔ̃] *nf* tradition.
traditionalisme [tradisjɔnalism(ə)] *nm* traditionalism.
traditionaliste [tradisjɔnalist(ə)] *adj, nmf* traditionalist.
traditionnel, le [tradisjɔnɛl] *adj* traditional.
traditionnellement [tradisjɔnɛlmɑ̃] *adv* traditionally.
traducteur, trice [tradyktœr, -tris] *nmf* translator.
traduction [tradyksjɔ̃] *nf* translation.
traduire [tradɥir] *vt* to translate; (*exprimer*) to render, convey; **se** ~ **par** to find expression in; ~ **en français** to translate into French; ~ **en justice** to bring before the courts.
traduis [tradɥi] *etc vb voir* **traduire**.
traduisible [tradɥizibl(ə)] *adj* translatable.
traduit, e [tradɥi, -it] *pp de* **traduire**.
trafic [trafik] *nm* traffic; ~ **d'armes** arms dealing; ~ **de drogue** drug peddling.
trafiquant, e [trafikɑ̃, -ɑ̃t] *nmf* trafficker; dealer.
trafiquer [trafike] *vt* (*péj*) to doctor, tamper with ♦ *vi* to traffic, be engaged in traffick-

ing.

tragédie [tʀaʒedi] *nf* tragedy.

tragédien, ne [tʀaʒedjɛ̃, -ɛn] *nm/f* tragedian/tragedienne.

tragi-comique [tʀaʒikɔmik] *adj* tragi-comic.

tragique [tʀaʒik] *adj* tragic ♦ *nm*: **prendre qch au** ~ to make a tragedy out of sth.

tragiquement [tʀaʒikmɑ̃] *adv* tragically.

trahir [tʀaiʀ] *vt* to betray; (*fig*) to give away, reveal; **se** ~ to betray o.s., give o.s. away.

trahison [tʀaizɔ̃] *nf* betrayal; (*JUR*) treason.

traie [tʀɛ] *etc vb voir* **traire**.

train [tʀɛ̃] *nm* (*RAIL*) train; (*allure*) pace; (*fig: ensemble*) set; **être en** ~ **de faire qch** to be doing sth; **mettre qch en** ~ to get sth under way; **mettre qn en** ~ to put sb in good spirits; **se mettre en** ~ (*commencer*) to get started; (*faire de la gymnastique*) to warm up; **se sentir en** ~ to feel in good form; **aller bon** ~ to make good progress; ~ **avant/arrière** front-wheel/rear-wheel axle unit; ~ **à grande vitesse (TGV)** high-speed train; ~ **d'atterrissage** undercarriage; ~ **autos-couchettes** car-sleeper train; ~ **électrique** (*jouet*) (electric) train set; ~ **de pneus** set of tyres *ou* tires; ~ **de vie** style of living.

traînailler [tʀɛnɑje] *vi* = **traînasser**.

traînant, e [tʀɛnɑ̃, -ɑ̃t] *adj* (*voix, ton*) drawling.

traînard, e [tʀɛnaʀ, -aʀd(ə)] *nm/f* (*péj*) slow-coach (*BRIT*), slowpoke (*US*).

traînasser [tʀɛnase] *vi* to dawdle.

traîne [tʀɛn] *nf* (*de robe*) train; **être à la** ~ to be in tow; (*en arrière*) to lag behind; (*en désordre*) to be lying around.

traîneau, x [tʀɛno] *nm* sleigh, sledge.

traînée [tʀɛne] *nf* streak, trail; (*péj*) slut.

traîner [tʀɛne] *vt* (*remorque*) to pull; (*enfant, chien*) to drag *ou* trail along; (*maladie*): **il traîne un rhume depuis l'hiver** he has a cold which has been dragging on since winter ♦ *vi* (*être en désordre*) to lie around; (*marcher lentement*) to dawdle (along); (*vagabonder*) to hang about; (*agir lentement*) to idle about; (*durer*) to drag on; **se** ~ *vi* (*ramper*) to crawl along; (*marcher avec difficulté*) to drag o.s. along; (*durer*) to drag on; **se** ~ **par terre** to crawl (on the ground); ~ **qn au cinéma** to drag sb to the cinema; ~ **les pieds** to drag one's feet; ~ **par terre** to trail on the ground; ~ **en longueur** to drag out.

training [tʀɛniŋ] *nm* (*pull*) tracksuit top; (*chaussure*) trainer (*BRIT*), sneaker (*US*).

train-train [tʀɛ̃tʀɛ̃] *nm* humdrum routine.

traire [tʀɛʀ] *vt* to milk.

trait, e [tʀɛ, -ɛt] *pp de* **traire** ♦ *nm* (*ligne*) line; (*de dessin*) stroke; (*caractéristique*) feature, trait; (*flèche*) dart, arrow; shaft; ~**s** *nmpl* (*du visage*) features; **d'un** ~ (*boire*) in one gulp; **de** ~ *adj* (*animal*) draught (*BRIT*), draft (*US*); **avoir** ~ **à** to concern; ~ **pour** ~ line for line; ~ **de caractère** characteristic, trait; ~ **d'esprit** flash of wit; ~ **de génie** brainwave;

~ **d'union** hyphen; (*fig*) link.

traitable [tʀɛtabl(ə)] *adj* (*personne*) accommodating; (*sujet*) manageable.

traitant, e [tʀɛtɑ̃, -ɑ̃t] *adj*: **votre médecin** ~ your usual *ou* family doctor; **shampooing** ~ medicated shampoo; **crème** ~**e** conditioning cream, conditioner.

traite [tʀɛt] *nf* (*COMM*) draft; (*AGR*) milking; (*trajet*) stretch; **d'une (seule)** ~ without stopping (once); **la** ~ **des noirs** the slave trade; **la** ~ **des blanches** the white slave trade.

traité [tʀɛte] *nm* treaty.

traitement [tʀɛtmɑ̃] *nm* treatment; processing; (*salaire*) salary; **suivre un** ~ to undergo treatment; **mauvais** ~ ill-treatment; ~ **de données** *ou* **de l'information** (*INFORM*) data processing; ~ **hormono-supplétif** hormone replacement therapy; ~ **par lots** (*INFORM*) batch processing; ~ **de texte** (*INFORM*) word processing.

traiter [tʀɛte] *vt* (*gén*) to treat; (*TECH: matériaux*) to process, treat; (*INFORM*) to process; (*affaire*) to deal with, handle; (*qualifier*): ~ **qn d'idiot** to call sb a fool ♦ *vi* to deal; ~ **de** *vt* to deal with; **bien/mal** ~ to treat well/ill-treat.

traiteur [tʀɛtœʀ] *nm* caterer.

traître, esse [tʀɛtʀ(ə), -tʀɛs] *adj* (*dangereux*) treacherous ♦ *nm* traitor; **prendre qn en** ~ to take sb off-guard.

traîtrise [tʀɛtʀiz] *nf* treachery.

trajectoire [tʀaʒɛktwaʀ] *nf* trajectory, path.

trajet [tʀaʒɛ] *nm* journey; (*itinéraire*) route; (*fig*) path, course.

tralala [tʀalala] *nm* (*péj*) fuss.

tram [tʀam] *nm* tram (*BRIT*), streetcar (*US*).

trame [tʀam] *nf* (*de tissu*) weft; (*fig*) framework; texture; (*TYPO*) screen.

tramer [tʀame] *vt* to plot, hatch.

trampoline [tʀɑ̃pɔlin], **trampolino** [tʀɑ̃pɔlino] *nm* trampoline; (*SPORT*) trampolining.

tramway [tʀamwɛ] *nm* tram(way); (*voiture*) tram(car) (*BRIT*), streetcar (*US*).

tranchant, e [tʀɑ̃ʃɑ̃, -ɑ̃t] *adj* sharp; (*fig: personne*) peremptory; (*: couleurs*) striking ♦ *nm* (*d'un couteau*) cutting edge; (*de la main*) edge; **à double** ~ (*argument, procédé*) double-edged.

tranche [tʀɑ̃ʃ] *nf* (*morceau*) slice; (*arête*) edge; (*partie*) section; (*série*) block; (*d'impôts, revenus etc*) bracket; (*loterie*) issue; ~ **d'âge** age bracket; ~ **(de silicium)** wafer.

tranché, e [tʀɑ̃ʃe] *adj* (*couleurs*) distinct, sharply contrasted; (*opinions*) clear-cut, definite ♦ *nf* trench.

trancher [tʀɑ̃ʃe] *vt* to cut, sever; (*fig: résoudre*) to settle ♦ *vi* to be decisive; (*entre deux choses*) to settle the argument; ~ **avec** to contrast sharply with.

tranchet [tʀɑ̃ʃɛ] *nm* knife.

tranchoir [tʀɑ̃ʃwaʀ] *nm* chopper.

tranquille [tʀɑ̃kil] *adj* calm, quiet; (*enfant,*

élève) quiet; (*rassuré*) easy in one's mind, with one's mind at rest; **se tenir** ~ (*enfant*) to be quiet; **avoir la conscience** ~ to have an easy conscience; **laisse-moi/laisse-ça** ~ leave me/it alone.

tranquillement [tʀɑ̃kilmɑ̃] *adv* calmly.

tranquillisant, e [tʀɑ̃kilizɑ̃, -ɑ̃t] *adj* (*nouvelle*) reassuring ♦ *nm* tranquillizer.

tranquilliser [tʀɑ̃kilize] *vt* to reassure; **se** ~ to calm (o.s.) down.

tranquillité [tʀɑ̃kilite] *nf* quietness; peace (and quiet); **en toute** ~ with complete peace of mind; ~ **d'esprit** peace of mind.

transaction [tʀɑ̃zaksjɔ̃] *nf* (*COMM*) transaction, deal.

transafricain, e [tʀɑ̃safʀikɛ̃, -ɛn] *adj* transafrican.

transalpin, e [tʀɑ̃zalpɛ̃, -in] *adj* transalpine.

transaméricain, e [tʀɑ̃zameʀikɛ̃, -ɛn] *adj* transamerican.

transat [tʀɑ̃zat] *nm* deckchair ♦ *nf* = *course transatlantique*.

transatlantique [tʀɑ̃zatlɑ̃tik] *adj* transatlantic ♦ *nm* transatlantic liner.

transborder [tʀɑ̃sbɔʀde] *vt* to tran(s)ship.

transcendant, e [tʀɑ̃sɑ̃dɑ̃, -ɑ̃t] *adj* (*PHILOSOPHIE, MATH*) transcendental; (*supérieur*) transcendent.

transcodeur [tʀɑ̃skɔdœʀ] *nm* compiler.

transcontinental, e, aux [tʀɑ̃skɔ̃tinɑ̃tal, -o] *adj* transcontinental.

transcription [tʀɑ̃skʀipsjɔ̃] *nf* transcription.

transcrire [tʀɑ̃skʀiʀ] *vt* to transcribe.

transe [tʀɑ̃s] *nf*: **entrer en** ~ to go into a trance; ~**s** *nfpl* agony *sg*.

transférable [tʀɑ̃sfeʀabl(ə)] *adj* transferable.

transfèrement [tʀɑ̃sfɛʀmɑ̃] *nm* transfer.

transférer [tʀɑ̃sfeʀe] *vt* to transfer.

transfert [tʀɑ̃sfɛʀ] *nm* transfer.

transfiguration [tʀɑ̃sfigyʀasjɔ̃] *nf* transformation, transfiguration.

transfigurer [tʀɑ̃sfigyʀe] *vt* to transform.

transfo [tʀɑ̃sfo] *nm* (= *transformateur*) transformer.

transformable [tʀɑ̃sfɔʀmabl(ə)] *adj* convertible.

transformateur [tʀɑ̃sfɔʀmatœʀ] *nm* transformer.

transformation [tʀɑ̃sfɔʀmasjɔ̃] *nf* transformation; (*RUGBY*) conversion; **industries de** ~ processing industries.

transformer [tʀɑ̃sfɔʀme] *vt* to transform, alter (*"alter" implique un changement moins radical*); (*matière première, appartement, RUGBY*) to convert; ~ **en** to transform into; to turn into; to convert into; **se** ~ *vi* to be transformed; to alter.

transfuge [tʀɑ̃sfyʒ] *nm* renegade.

transfuser [tʀɑ̃sfyze] *vt* to transfuse.

transfusion [tʀɑ̃sfyzjɔ̃] *nf*: ~ **sanguine** blood transfusion.

transgresser [tʀɑ̃sgʀese] *vt* to contravene, disobey.

transhumance [tʀɑ̃zymɑ̃s] *nf* transhumance, seasonal move to new pastures.

transi, e [tʀɑ̃zi] *adj* numb (with cold), chilled to the bone.

transiger [tʀɑ̃ziʒe] *vi* to compromise, come to an agreement; ~ **sur** *ou* **avec qch** to compromise on sth.

transistor [tʀɑ̃zistɔʀ] *nm* transistor.

transistorisé, e [tʀɑ̃zistɔʀize] *adj* transistorized.

transit [tʀɑ̃zit] *nm* transit; **de** ~ transit *cpd*; **en** ~ in transit.

transitaire [tʀɑ̃zitɛʀ] *nm/f* forwarding agent.

transiter [tʀɑ̃zite] *vi* to pass in transit.

transitif, ive [tʀɑ̃zitif, -iv] *adj* transitive.

transition [tʀɑ̃zisjɔ̃] *nf* transition; **de** ~ transitional.

transitoire [tʀɑ̃zitwaʀ] *adj* (*mesure, gouvernement*) transitional, provisional; (*fugitif*) transient.

translucide [tʀɑ̃slysid] *adj* translucent.

transmet [tʀɑ̃smɛ] *etc vb voir* **transmettre**.

transmettais [tʀɑ̃smɛtɛ] *etc vb voir* **transmettre**.

transmetteur [tʀɑ̃smɛtœʀ] *nm* transmitter.

transmettre [tʀɑ̃smɛtʀ(ə)] *vt* (*passer*): ~ **qch à qn** to pass sth on to sb; (*TECH, TÉL, MÉD*) to transmit; (*TV, RADIO: retransmettre*) to broadcast.

transmis, e [tʀɑ̃smi, -iz] *pp de* **transmettre**.

transmissible [tʀɑ̃smisibl(ə)] *adj* transmissible.

transmission [tʀɑ̃smisjɔ̃] *nf* transmission, passing on; (*AUTO*) transmission; ~**s** *nfpl* (*MIL*) ≈ signals corps *sg*; ~ **de données** (*INFORM*) data transmission; ~ **de pensée** thought transmission.

transocéanien, ne [tʀɑ̃zɔseanjɛ̃, -ɛn] *adj*, **transocéanique** [tʀɑ̃zɔseanik] *adj* transoceanic.

transparaître [tʀɑ̃spaʀɛtʀ(ə)] *vi* to show (through).

transparence [tʀɑ̃spaʀɑ̃s] *nf* transparence; **par** ~ (*regarder*) against the light; (*voir*) showing through.

transparent, e [tʀɑ̃spaʀɑ̃, -ɑ̃t] *adj* transparent.

transpercer [tʀɑ̃spɛʀse] *vt* to go through, pierce.

transpiration [tʀɑ̃spiʀasjɔ̃] *nf* perspiration.

transpirer [tʀɑ̃spiʀe] *vi* to perspire; (*information, nouvelle*) to come to light.

transplant [tʀɑ̃splɑ̃] *nm* transplant.

transplantation [tʀɑ̃splɑ̃tasjɔ̃] *nf* transplant.

transplanter [tʀɑ̃splɑ̃te] *vt* (*MÉD, BOT*) to transplant; (*personne*) to uproot, move.

transport [tʀɑ̃spɔʀ] *nm* transport; (*émotions*): ~ **de colère** fit of rage; ~ **de joie** transport of delight; ~ **de voyageurs/marchandises** passenger/goods transportation; ~**s en commun** public transport *sg*; ~**s routiers**

haulage (*BRIT*), trucking (*US*).

transportable [tʀɑ̃spɔʀtabl(ə)] *adj* (*marchandises*) transportable; (*malade*) fit (enough) to be moved.

transporter [tʀɑ̃spɔʀte] *vt* to carry, move; (*COMM*) to transport, convey; (*fig*): ~ **qn (de joie)** to send sb into raptures; **se** ~ **quelque part** (*fig*) to let one's imagination carry one away (somewhere); ~ **qn à l'hôpital** to take sb to hospital.

transporteur [tʀɑ̃spɔʀtœʀ] *nm* haulage contractor (*BRIT*), trucker (*US*).

transposer [tʀɑ̃spoze] *vt* to transpose.

transposition [tʀɑ̃spozisjɔ̃] *nf* transposition.

transrhénan, e [tʀɑ̃sʀenɑ̃, -an] *adj* transrhenane.

transsaharien, ne [tʀɑ̃ssaaʀjɛ̃, -ɛn] *adj* trans-Saharan.

transsexuel, le [tʀɑ̃ssɛksɥɛl] *adj*, *nm/f* transsexual.

transsibérien, ne [tʀɑ̃ssibeʀjɛ̃, -ɛn] *adj* trans-Siberian.

transvaser [tʀɑ̃svaze] *vt* to decant.

transversal, e, aux [tʀɑ̃svɛʀsal, -o] *adj* transverse, cross(-); (*route etc*) cross-country; (*mur, chemin, rue*) running at right angles; (*AUTO*): **axe** ~ main cross-country road (*BRIT*) *ou* highway (*US*).

transversalement [tʀɑ̃svɛʀsalmɑ̃] *adv* crosswise.

trapèze [tʀapɛz] *nm* (*GÉOM*) trapezium; (*au cirque*) trapeze.

trapéziste [tʀapezist(ə)] *nm/f* trapeze artist.

trappe [tʀap] *nf* (*de cave, grenier*) trap door; (*piège*) trap.

trappeur [tʀapœʀ] *nm* trapper, fur trader.

trapu, e [tʀapy] *adj* squat, stocky.

traquenard [tʀaknaʀ] *nm* trap.

traquer [tʀake] *vt* to track down; (*harceler*) to hound.

traumatisant, e [tʀomatizɑ̃, -ɑ̃t] *traumatic.

traumatiser [tʀomatize] *vt* to traumatize.

traumatisme [tʀomatism(ə)] *nm* traumatism; ~ **crânien** cranial traumatism.

traumatologie [tʀomatɔlɔʒi] *nf* branch of medicine concerned with accidents.

travail, aux [tʀavaj, -o] *nm* (*gén*) work; (*tâche, métier*) work *no pl*, job; (*ÉCON, MÉD*) labour (*BRIT*), labor (*US*); (*INFORM*) job ♦ *nmpl* (*de réparation, agricoles etc*) work *sg*; (*sur route*) roadworks; (*de construction*) building (work) *sg*; **être/entrer en** ~ (*MÉD*) to be in/go into labour; **être sans** ~ (*employé*) to be out of work, be unemployed; ~ **d'intérêt général (TIG)** ≈ community service; ~ **(au) noir** moonlighting; ~ **posté** shiftwork; **travaux des champs** farmwork *sg*; **travaux dirigés (TD)** (*SCOL*) supervised practical work *sg*; **travaux forcés** hard labour *sg*; **travaux manuels** (*SCOL*) handicrafts; **travaux ménagers** housework *sg*; **travaux pratiques (TP)** (*gén*) practical work; (*en laboratoire*) lab work

(*BRIT*), lab (*US*); **travaux publics (TP)** ≈ public works *sg*.

travaillé, e [tʀavaje] *adj* (*style*) polished.

travailler [tʀavaje] *vi* to work; (*bois*) to warp ♦ *vt* (*bois, métal*) to work; (*pâte*) to knead; (*objet d'art, discipline, fig: influencer*) to work on; **cela le travaille** it is on his mind; ~ **la terre** to work the land; ~ **son piano** to do one's piano practice; ~ **à** to work on; (*fig: contribuer à*) to work towards; ~ **à faire** to endeavour (*BRIT*) *ou* endeavor (*US*) to do.

travailleur, euse [tʀavajœʀ, -øz] *adj* hardworking ♦ *nm/f* worker; ~ **de force** labourer (*BRIT*), laborer (*US*); ~ **intellectuel** non-manual worker; ~ **social** social worker; **travailleuse familiale** home help.

travailliste [tʀavajist(ə)] *adj* ≈ Labour *cpd* ♦ *nm/f* member of the Labour party.

travée [tʀave] *nf* row; (*ARCHIT*) bay; span.

traveller's (chèque) [tʀavlœʀs(ʃɛk)] *nm* traveller's cheque.

travelling [tʀavliŋ] *nm* (*chariot*) dolly; (*technique*) tracking; ~ **optique** zoom shots *pl*.

travelo [tʀavlo] *nm* (*fam*) drag queen.

travers [tʀavɛʀ] *nm* fault, failing; **en** ~ **(de)** across; **au** ~ **(de)** through; **de** ~ *adj* askew ♦ *adv* sideways; (*fig*) the wrong way; **à** ~ through; **regarder de** ~ (*fig*) to look askance at.

traverse [tʀavɛʀs(ə)] *nf* (*de voie ferrée*) sleeper; **chemin de** ~ shortcut.

traversée [tʀavɛʀse] *nf* crossing.

traverser [tʀavɛʀse] *vt* (*gén*) to cross; (*ville, tunnel, aussi: percer, fig*) to go through; (*suj: ligne, trait*) to run across.

traversin [tʀavɛʀsɛ̃] *nm* bolster.

travesti [tʀavɛsti] *nm* (*costume*) fancy dress; (*artiste de cabaret*) female impersonator, drag artist; (*pervers*) transvestite.

travestir [tʀavɛstiʀ] *vt* (*vérité*) to misrepresent; **se** ~ (*se costumer*) to dress up; (*artiste*) to put on drag; (*PSYCH*) to dress as a woman.

trayais [tʀɛjɛ] *etc vb voir* **traire**.

trayeuse [tʀɛjøz] *nf* milking machine.

trébucher [tʀebyʃe] *vi*: ~ **(sur)** to stumble (over), trip (over).

trèfle [tʀɛfl(ə)] *nm* (*BOT*) clover; (*CARTES: couleur*) clubs *pl*; (: *carte*) club; ~ **à quatre feuilles** four-leaf clover.

treillage [tʀɛjaʒ] *nm* lattice work.

treille [tʀɛj] *nf* (*tonnelle*) vine arbour (*BRIT*) *ou* arbor (*US*); (*vigne*) climbing vine.

treillis [tʀɛji] *nm* (*métallique*) wire-mesh; (*toile*) canvas; (*uniforme*) battle-dress.

treize [tʀɛz] *num* thirteen.

treizième [tʀɛzjɛm] *num* thirteenth.

Le treizième mois is an end-of-year bonus corresponding roughly to one month's salary. For many employees it is a standard part of their salary package.

tréma [tRema] *nm* diaeresis.

tremblant, e [tRãblã, -ãt] *adj* trembling, shaking.

tremble [tRãbl(ə)] *nm* (*BOT*) aspen.

tremblé, e [tRãble] *adj* shaky.

tremblement [tRãbləmã] *nm* trembling *no pl*, shaking *no pl*, shivering *no pl*; ~ **de terre** earthquake.

trembler [tRãble] *vi* to tremble, shake; ~ **de** (*froid, fièvre*) to shiver *ou* tremble with; (*peur*) to shake *ou* tremble with; ~ **pour qn** to fear for sb.

tremblotant, e [tRãblɔtã, -ãt] *adj* trembling.

trembloter [tRãblɔte] *vi* to tremble *ou* shake slightly.

trémolo [tRemɔlo] *nm* (*d'un instrument*) tremolo; (*de la voix*) quaver.

trémousser [tRemuse]: **se** ~ *vi* to jig about, wriggle about.

trempe [tRãp] *nf* (*fig*): **de cette/sa** ~ of this/his calibre (*BRIT*) *ou* caliber (*US*).

trempé, e [tRãpe] *adj* soaking (wet), drenched; (*TECH*): **acier** ~ tempered steel.

tremper [tRãpe] *vt* to soak, drench; (*aussi*: **faire** ~, **mettre à** ~) to soak; (*plonger*): ~ **qch dans** to dip sth in(to) ♦ *vi* to soak; (*fig*): ~ **dans** to be involved *ou* have a hand in; **se** ~ *vi* to have a quick dip; **se faire** ~ to get soaked *ou* drenched.

trempette [tRãpɛt] *nf*: **faire** ~ to go paddling.

tremplin [tRãplẽ] *nm* springboard; (*SKI*) ski jump.

trentaine [tRãtɛn] *nf* (*âge*): **avoir la** ~ to be around thirty; **une** ~ **(de)** thirty or so, about thirty.

trente [tRãt] *num* thirty; **voir** ~**-six chandelles** (*fig*) to see stars; **être/se mettre sur son** ~ **et un** to be/get dressed to kill; ~**-trois tours** *nm* long-playing record, LP.

trentième [tRãtjɛm] *num* thirtieth.

trépanation [tRepanasjɔ̃] *nf* trepan.

trépaner [tRepane] *vt* to trepan, trephine.

trépasser [tRepase] *vi* to pass away.

trépidant, e [tRepidã, -ãt] *adj* (*fig*: *rythme*) pulsating; (: *vie*) hectic.

trépidation [tRepidasjɔ̃] *nf* (*d'une machine, d'un moteur*) vibration; (*fig*: *de la vie*) whirl.

trépider [tRepide] *vi* to vibrate.

trépied [tRepje] *nm* (*d'appareil*) tripod; (*meuble*) trivet.

trépignement [tRepiɲmã] *nm* stamping (of feet).

trépigner [tRepiɲe] *vi* to stamp (one's feet).

très [tRɛ] *adv* very; much + *pp*, highly + *pp*; ~ **beau/bien** very beautiful/well; ~ **critiqué** much criticized; ~ **industrialisé** highly industrialized; **j'ai** ~ **faim** I'm very hungry.

trésor [tRezɔR] *nm* treasure; (*ADMIN*) finances *pl*; (*d'un organisation*) funds *pl*; ~ **(public) (TP)** public revenue; (*service*) public revenue office.

trésorerie [tRezɔRRi] *nf* (*fonds*) funds *pl*; (*gestion*) accounts *pl*; (*bureaux*) accounts department; (*poste*) treasurership; **difficultés de** ~ cash problems, shortage of cash *ou* funds; ~ **générale (TG)** *local government finance office*.

trésorier, ière [tRezɔRje, -jɛR] *nm/f* treasurer.

Trésorier-payeur [tRezɔRjepɛjœR] *nm*: ~ **général (TPG)** paymaster.

tressaillement [tResajmã] *nm* shiver, shudder; quiver.

tressaillir [tResajiR] *vi* (*de peur etc*) to shiver, shudder; (*de joie*) to quiver.

tressauter [tResote] *vi* to start, jump.

tresse [tRɛs] *nf* (*de cheveux*) braid, plait; (*cordon, galon*) braid.

tresser [tRese] *vt* (*cheveux*) to braid, plait; (*fil, jonc*) to plait; (*corbeille*) to weave; (*corde*) to twist.

tréteau, x [tReto] *nm* trestle; **les** ~**x** (*fig*: *THÉÂT*) the boards.

treuil [tRœj] *nm* winch.

trêve [tRɛv] *nf* (*MIL, POL*) truce; (*fig*) respite; **sans** ~ unremittingly; ~ **de** ... enough of this ...; **les États de la T**~ the Trucial States.

tri [tRi] *nm* (*voir trier*) sorting (out) *no pl*; selection; screening; (*INFORM*) sort; (*POSTES*: *action*) sorting; (: *bureau*) sorting office.

triage [tRija3] *nm* (*RAIL*) shunting; (*gare*) marshalling yard.

trial [tRijal] *nm* (*SPORT*) scrambling.

triangle [tRijãgl(ə)] *nm* triangle; ~ **isocèle/équilatéral** isosceles/equilateral triangle; ~ **rectangle** right-angled triangle.

triangulaire [tRijãgylɛR] *adj* triangular.

triathlon [tRi(j)atlɔ̃] *nm* triathlon.

tribal, e, aux [tRibal, -o] *adj* tribal.

tribord [tRibɔR] *nm*: **à** ~ to starboard, on the starboard side.

tribu [tRiby] *nf* tribe.

tribulations [tRibylasjɔ̃] *nfpl* tribulations, trials.

tribunal, aux [tRibynal, -o] *nm* (*JUR*) court; (*MIL*) tribunal; ~ **de police/pour enfants** police/juvenile court; ~ **d'instance (TI)** ≈ magistrates' court (*BRIT*), ≈ district court (*US*); ~ **de grande instance (TGI)** ≈ High Court (*BRIT*), ≈ Supreme Court (*US*).

tribune [tRibyn] *nf* (*estrade*) platform, rostrum; (*débat*) forum; (*d'église, de tribunal*) gallery; (*de stade*) stand; ~ **libre** (*PRESSE*) opinion column.

tribut [tRiby] *nm* tribute.

tributaire [tRibytɛR] *adj*: **être** ~ **de** to be dependent on; (*GÉO*) to be a tributary of.

tricentenaire [tRisãtnɛR] *nm* tercentenary, tricentennial.

tricher [tRiʃe] *vi* to cheat.

tricherie [tRiʃRi] *nf* cheating *no pl*.

tricheur, euse [tRiʃœR, -øz] *nm/f* cheat.

trichromie [tRikRɔmi] *nf* three-colour (*BRIT*) *ou* -color (*US*) printing.

tricolore [tRikɔlɔR] *adj* three-coloured (*BRIT*),

three-colored (*US*); (*français: drapeau*) red, white and blue; (*: équipe etc*) French.

tricot [tʀiko] *nm* (*technique, ouvrage*) knitting *no pl*; (*tissu*) knitted fabric; (*vêtement*) jersey, sweater; ~ **de corps** vest (*BRIT*), undershirt (*US*).

tricoter [tʀikɔte] *vt* to knit; **machine/aiguille à** ~ knitting machine/needle (*BRIT*) *ou* pin (*US*).

trictrac [tʀiktʀak] *nm* backgammon.

tricycle [tʀisikl(ə)] *nm* tricycle.

tridimensionnel, le [tʀidimɑ̃sjɔnɛl] *adj* three-dimensional.

triennal, e, aux [tʀiɛnal, -o] *adj* (*prix, foire, élection*) three-yearly; (*charge, mandat, plan*) three-year.

trier [tʀije] *vt* (*classer*) to sort (out); (*choisir*) to select; (*visiteurs*) to screen; (*POSTES, INFORM*) to sort.

trieur, euse [tʀijœʀ, -øz] *nm/f* sorter.

trigonométrie [tʀigɔnɔmetʀi] *nf* trigonometry.

trigonométrique [tʀigɔnɔmetʀik] *adj* trigonometric.

trilingue [tʀilɛ̃g] *adj* trilingual.

trilogie [tʀilɔʒi] *nf* trilogy.

trimaran [tʀimaʀɑ̃] *nm* trimaran.

trimbaler [tʀɛ̃bale] *vt* to cart around, trail along.

trimer [tʀime] *vi* to slave away.

trimestre [tʀimɛstʀ(ə)] *nm* (*SCOL*) term; (*COMM*) quarter.

trimestriel, le [tʀimɛstʀijɛl] *adj* quarterly; (*SCOL*) end-of-term.

trimoteur [tʀimɔtœʀ] *nm* three-engined aircraft.

tringle [tʀɛ̃gl(ə)] *nf* rod.

Trinité [tʀinite] *nf* Trinity.

Trinité et Tobago [tʀiniteetɔbago] *nf* Trinidad and Tobago.

trinquer [tʀɛ̃ke] *vi* to clink glasses; (*fam*) to cop it; ~ **à qch/la santé de qn** to drink to sth/sb.

trio [tʀijo] *nm* trio.

triolet [tʀijɔlɛ] *nm* (*MUS*) triplet.

triomphal, e, aux [tʀijɔ̃fal, -o] *adj* triumphal, triumphal.

triomphalement [tʀijɔ̃falmɑ̃] *adv* triumphantly.

triomphant, e [tʀijɔ̃fɑ̃, -ɑ̃t] *adj* triumphant.

triomphateur, trice [tʀijɔ̃fatœʀ, -tʀis] *nm/f* (triumphant) victor.

triomphe [tʀijɔ̃f] *nm* triumph; **être reçu/porté en** ~ to be given a triumphant welcome/be carried shoulder-high in triumph.

triompher [tʀijɔ̃fe] *vi* to triumph; ~ **de** to triumph over, overcome.

triparti, e [tʀipaʀti] *adj* (*aussi:* **tripartite**: *réunion, assemblée*) tripartite, three-party.

triperie [tʀipʀi] *nf* tripe shop.

tripes [tʀip] *nfpl* (*CULIN*) tripe *sg*; (*fam*) guts.

triplace [tʀiplas] *adj* three-seater *cpd*.

triple [tʀipl(ə)] *adj* (*à trois éléments*) triple; (*trois fois plus grand*) treble ♦ *nm*: **le** ~ **(de)** (*comparaison*) three times as much (as); **en** ~ **exemplaire** in triplicate; ~ **saut** (*SPORT*) triple jump.

triplé [tʀiple] *nm* hat-trick (*BRIT*), triple success.

triplement [tʀipləmɑ̃] *adv* (*à un degré triple*) three times over; (*de trois façons*) in three ways; (*pour trois raisons*) on three counts ♦ *nm* trebling, threefold increase.

tripler [tʀiple] *vi, vt* to triple, treble, increase threefold.

triplés, ées [tʀiple] *nm/fpl* triplets.

Tripoli [tʀipɔli] *n* Tripoli.

triporteur [tʀipɔʀtœʀ] *nm* delivery tricycle.

tripot [tʀipo] *nm* (*péj*) dive.

tripotage [tʀipɔtaʒ] *nm* (*péj*) jiggery-pokery.

tripoter [tʀipɔte] *vt* to fiddle with, finger ♦ *vi* (*fam*) to rummage about.

trique [tʀik] *nf* cudgel.

trisannuel, le [tʀizanɥɛl] *adj* triennial.

trisomie [tʀizɔmi] *nf* Down's syndrome.

triste [tʀist(ə)] *adj* sad; (*péj*): ~ **personnage/affaire** sorry individual/affair; **c'est pas** ~! (*fam*) it's something else!

tristement [tʀistəmɑ̃] *adv* sadly.

tristesse [tʀistɛs] *nf* sadness.

triton [tʀitɔ̃] *nm* triton.

triturer [tʀityʀe] *vt* (*pâte*) to knead; (*objets*) to manipulate.

trivial, e, aux [tʀivjal, -o] *adj* coarse, crude; (*commun*) mundane.

trivialité [tʀivjalite] *nf* coarseness, crudeness; mundaneness.

troc [tʀɔk] *nm* (*ÉCON*) barter; (*transaction*) exchange, swap.

troène [tʀɔɛn] *nm* privet.

troglodyte [tʀɔglɔdit] *nm/f* cave dweller, troglodyte.

trognon [tʀɔɲɔ̃] *nm* (*de fruit*) core; (*de légume*) stalk.

trois [tʀwa] *num* three.

trois-huit [tʀwaɥit] *nmpl*: **faire les** ~ to work eight-hour shifts (round the clock).

troisième [tʀwazjɛm] *num* third; **le** ~ **âge** years of retirement.

troisièmement [tʀwazjɛmmɑ̃] *adv* thirdly.

trois quarts [tʀwakaʀ] *nmpl*: **les** ~ **de** three-quarters of.

trolleybus [tʀɔlɛbys] *nm* trolley bus.

trombe [tʀɔ̃b] *nf* waterspout; **des** ~**s d'eau** a downpour; **en** ~ (*arriver, passer*) like a whirlwind.

trombone [tʀɔ̃bɔn] *nm* (*MUS*) trombone; (*de bureau*) paper clip; ~ **à coulisse** slide trombone.

tromboniste [tʀɔ̃bɔnist(ə)] *nm/f* trombonist.

trompe [tʀɔ̃p] *nf* (*d'éléphant*) trunk; (*MUS*) trumpet, horn; ~ **d'Eustache** Eustachian tube; ~**s utérines** Fallopian tubes.

trompe-l'œil [tʀɔ̃plœj] *nm*: **en** ~ in trompe-l'œil style.

tromper [tʀɔ̃pe] *vt* to deceive; (*fig: espoir, attente*) to disappoint; (*vigilance, poursuivants*) to elude; **se ~** *vi* to make a mistake, be mistaken; **se ~ de voiture/jour** to take the wrong car/get the day wrong; **se ~ de 3 cm/20 F** to be out by 3 cm/20 F.

tromperie [tʀɔ̃pʀi] *nf* deception, trickery *no pl*.

trompette [tʀɔ̃pɛt] *nf* trumpet; **en ~** (*nez*) turned-up.

trompettiste [tʀɔ̃petist(ə)] *nm/f* trumpet player.

trompeur, euse [tʀɔ̃pœʀ, -øz] *adj* deceptive, misleading.

tronc [tʀɔ̃] *nm* (*BOT, ANAT*) trunk; (*d'église*) collection box; **~ d'arbre** tree trunk; **~ commun** (*SCOL*) common-core syllabus; **~ de cône** truncated cone.

tronche [tʀɔ̃ʃ] *nf* (*fam*) mug, face.

tronçon [tʀɔ̃sɔ̃] *nm* section.

tronçonner [tʀɔ̃sɔne] *vt* (*arbre*) to saw up; (*pierre*) to cut up.

tronçonneuse [tʀɔ̃sɔnøz] *nf* chain saw.

trône [tʀon] *nm* throne; **monter sur le ~** to ascend the throne.

trôner [tʀone] *vi* (*fig*) to have (*ou* take) pride of place (*BRIT*) *ou* honor (*US*), have the place of honour (*BRIT*) *ou* honor (*US*).

tronquer [tʀɔ̃ke] *vt* to truncate; (*fig*) to curtail.

trop [tʀo] *adv vb* + too much; too + *adjectif, adverbe*; **~ (nombreux)** too many; **~ peu (nombreux)** too few; **~ (souvent)** too often; **~ (longtemps)** (for) too long; **~ de** (*nombre*) too many; (*quantité*) too much; **de ~, en ~**: **des livres en ~** a few books too many, a few extra books; **du lait en ~** too much milk; **3 livres/5 F de ~** 3 books too many/5 F too much.

trophée [tʀɔfe] *nm* trophy.

tropical, e, aux [tʀɔpikal, -o] *adj* tropical.

tropique [tʀɔpik] *nm* tropic; **~s** *nmpl* tropics; **~ du Cancer/Capricorne** Tropic of Cancer/Capricorn.

trop-plein [tʀoplɛ̃] *nm* (*tuyau*) overflow *ou* outlet (pipe); (*liquide*) overflow.

troquer [tʀɔke] *vt*: **~ qch contre** to barter *ou* trade sth for; (*fig*) to swap sth for.

trot [tʀo] *nm* trot; **aller au ~** to trot along; **partir au ~** to set off at a trot.

trotter [tʀɔte] *vi* to trot; (*fig*) to scamper along (*ou* about).

trotteuse [tʀɔtøz] *nf* (*de montre*) second hand.

trottiner [tʀɔtine] *vi* (*fig*) to scamper along (*ou* about).

trottinette [tʀɔtinɛt] *nf* (child's) scooter.

trottoir [tʀɔtwaʀ] *nm* pavement (*BRIT*), sidewalk (*US*); **faire le ~** (*péj*) to walk the streets; **~ roulant** moving pavement (*BRIT*) *ou* walkway.

trou [tʀu] *nm* hole; (*fig*) gap; (*COMM*) deficit; **~ d'aération** (air) vent; **~**

de mémoire blank, lapse of memory; **~ noir** black hole; **~ de la serrure** keyhole.

troublant, e [tʀublɑ̃, -ɑ̃t] *adj* disturbing.

trouble [tʀubl(ə)] *adj* (*liquide*) cloudy; (*image, mémoire*) indistinct, hazy; (*affaire*) shady, murky ♦ *adv* indistinctly ♦ *nm* (*désarroi*) distress, agitation; (*émoi sensuel*) turmoil, agitation; (*embarras*) confusion; (*zizanie*) unrest, discord; **~s** *nmpl* (*POL*) disturbances, troubles, unrest *sg*; (*MÉD*) trouble *sg*, disorders; **~s de la personnalité** personality problems; **~s de la vision** eye trouble.

trouble-fête [tʀubləfɛt] *nm/f inv* spoilsport.

troubler [tʀuble] *vt* (*embarrasser*) to confuse, disconcert; (*émouvoir*) to agitate; to disturb; to perturb; (*perturber: ordre etc*) to disrupt, disturb; (*liquide*) to make cloudy; **se ~** *vi* (*personne*) to become flustered *ou* confused; **~ l'ordre public** to cause a breach of the peace.

troué, e [tʀue] *adj* with a hole (*ou* holes) in it ♦ *nf* gap; (*MIL*) breach.

trouer [tʀue] *vt* to make a hole (*ou* holes) in; (*fig*) to pierce.

trouille [tʀuj] *nf* (*fam*): **avoir la ~** to be scared stiff, be scared out of one's wits.

troupe [tʀup] *nf* (*MIL*) troop; (*groupe*) troop, group; **la ~** (*MIL: l'armée*) the army; (*: les simples soldats*) the troops *pl*; **~ (de théâtre)** (theatrical) company; **~s de choc** shock troops.

troupeau, x [tʀupo] *nm* (*de moutons*) flock; (*de vaches*) herd.

trousse [tʀus] *nf* case, kit; (*d'écolier*) pencil case; (*de docteur*) instrument case; **aux ~s de** (*fig*) on the heels *ou* tail of; **~ à outils** toolkit; **~ de toilette** toilet *ou* sponge (*BRIT*) bag.

trousseau, x [tʀuso] *nm* (*de mariée*) trousseau; **~ de clefs** bunch of keys.

trouvaille [tʀuvaj] *nf* find; (*fig: idée, expression etc*) brainwave.

trouvé, e [tʀuve] *adj*: **tout ~** ready-made.

trouver [tʀuve] *vt* to find; (*rendre visite*): **aller/venir ~ qn** to go/come and see sb; **je trouve que** I find *ou* think that; **~ à boire/critiquer** to find something to drink/criticize; **~ asile/refuge** to find refuge/shelter; **se ~** *vi* (*être*) to be; (*être soudain*) to find o.s.; **se ~ être/avoir** to happen to be/have; **il se trouve que** it happens that, it turns out that; **se ~ bien** to feel well; **se ~ mal** to pass out.

truand [tʀyɑ̃] *nm* villain, crook.

truander [tʀyɑ̃de] *vi* (*fam*) to cheat, do.

trublion [tʀyblijɔ̃] *nm* troublemaker.

truc [tʀyk] *nm* (*astuce*) way, device; (*de cinéma, prestidigitateur*) trick effect; (*chose*) thing; (*machin*) thingumajig, whatsit (*BRIT*); **avoir le ~** to have the knack; **c'est pas son** (*ou* mon *etc*) **~** (*fam*) it's not really his (*ou* my *etc*) thing.

truchement [tʀyʃmɑ̃] *nm*: **par le ~ de qn**

through (the intervention of) sb.

trucider [tʀyside] *vt (fam)* to do in, bump off.

truculence [tʀykylɑ̃s] *nf* colourfulness (*BRIT*), colorfulness (*US*).

truculent, e [tʀykylɑ̃, -ɑ̃t] *adj* colourful (*BRIT*), colorful (*US*).

truelle [tʀyɛl] *nf* trowel.

truffe [tʀyf] *nf* truffle; (*nez*) nose.

truffer [tʀyfe] *vt (CULIN)* to garnish with truffles; **truffé de** (*fig: citations*) peppered with; (: *pièges*) bristling with.

truie [tʀyi] *nf* sow.

truite [tʀyit] *nf* trout *inv*.

truquage [tʀykaʒ] *nm* fixing; (*CINÉ*) special effects *pl*.

truquer [tʀyke] *vt (élections, serrure, dés)* to fix; (*CINÉ*) to use special effects in.

trust [tʀœst] *nm (COMM)* trust.

truster [tʀœste] *vt (COMM)* to monopolize.

ts *abr* = **tous**.

tsar [dzaʀ] *nm* tsar.

tsé-tsé [tsetse] *nf:* **mouche ~** tsetse fly.

TSF *sigle f* (= *télégraphie sans fil*) wireless.

tsigane [tsigan] *adj, nm/f* = **tzigane**.

TSVP *abr* (= *tournez s'il vous plaît*) PTO.

tt *abr* = **tout**.

TT(A) *sigle m* (= *transit temporaire (autorisé)*) vehicle registration for cars etc bought in France for export tax-free by non-residents.

TTC *abr* = **toutes taxes comprises**.

ttes *abr* = **toutes**.

TU *sigle m* = *temps universel*.

tu [ty] *pron* you ♦ *nm:* **employer le ~** to use the "tu" form.

tu, e [ty] *pp de* **taire**.

tuant, e [tɥɑ̃, -ɑ̃t] *adj (épuisant)* killing; (*énervant*) infuriating.

tuba [tyba] *nm (MUS)* tuba; (*SPORT*) snorkel.

tubage [tybaʒ] *nm (MÉD)* intubation.

tube [tyb] *nm* tube; (*de canalisation, métallique etc*) pipe; (*chanson, disque*) hit song *ou* record; **~ digestif** alimentary canal, digestive tract; **~ à essai** test tube.

tuberculeux, euse [tybɛʀkylø, -øz] *adj* tubercular ♦ *nm/f* tuberculosis ou TB patient.

tuberculose [tybɛʀkyloz] *nf* tuberculosis, TB.

tubulaire [tybylɛʀ] *adj* tubular.

tubulure [tybylyʀ] *nf* pipe; piping *no pl*; (*AUTO*): **~ d'échappement/d'admission** exhaust/inlet manifold.

TUC [tyk] *sigle m* (= *travail d'utilité collective*) community work scheme for the young unemployed.

tuciste [tysist(ə)] *nm/f* young person on a community work scheme.

tué, e [tɥe] *nm/f:* **5 ~s 5** killed *ou* dead.

tue-mouche [tymuʃ] *adj:* **papier ~(s)** flypaper.

tuer [tɥe] *vt* to kill; **se ~** (*se suicider*) to kill o.s.; (*dans un accident*) to be killed; **se ~ au travail** (*fig*) to work o.s. to death.

tuerie [tyʀi] *nf* slaughter *no pl*, massacre.

tue-tête [tytɛt]: **à ~** *adv* at the top of one's voice.

tueur [tɥœʀ] *nm* killer; **~ à gages** hired killer.

tuile [tɥil] *nf* tile; (*fam*) spot of bad luck, blow.

tulipe [tylip] *nf* tulip.

tulle [tyl] *nm* tulle.

tuméfié, e [tymefje] *adj* puffy, swollen.

tumeur [tymœʀ] *nf* growth, tumour (*BRIT*), tumor (*US*).

tumulte [tymylt(ə)] *nm* commotion, hubbub.

tumultueux, euse [tymyltɥø, -øz] *adj* stormy, turbulent.

tuner [tynɛʀ] *nm* tuner.

tungstène [tœ̃kstɛn] *nm* tungsten.

tunique [tynik] *nf* tunic; (*de femme*) smock, tunic.

Tunis [tynis] *n* Tunis.

Tunisie [tynizi] *nf:* **la ~** Tunisia.

tunisien, ne [tynizjɛ̃, -ɛn] *adj* Tunisian ♦ *nm/f:* **T~, ne** Tunisian.

tunisois, e [tynizwa, -waz] *adj* of *ou* from Tunis.

tunnel [tynɛl] *nm* tunnel; **le ~ sous la Manche** the Channel Tunnel, the Chunnel.

TUP *sigle m* (= *titre universel de paiement*) ≈ payment slip.

turban [tyʀbɑ̃] *nm* turban.

turbin [tyʀbɛ̃] *nm (fam)* work *no pl*.

turbine [tyʀbin] *nf* turbine.

turbo [tyʀbo] *nm* turbo; **un moteur ~** a turbo(-charged) engine.

turbomoteur [tyʀbɔmɔtœʀ] *nm* turbo(-boosted) engine.

turbopropulseur [tyʀbɔpʀɔpylsœʀ] *nm* turboprop.

turboréacteur [tyʀbɔʀeaktœʀ] *nm* turbojet.

turbot [tyʀbo] *nm* turbot.

turbotrain [tyʀbɔtʀɛ̃] *nm* turbotrain.

turbulences [tyʀbylɑ̃s] *nfpl (AVIAT)* turbulence *sg*.

turbulent, e [tyʀbylɑ̃, -ɑ̃t] *adj* boisterous, unruly.

turc, turque [tyʀk(ə)] *adj* Turkish; (*w.-c.*) seatless ♦ *nm (LING)* Turkish ♦ *nm/f:* **T~, Turque** Turk/Turkish woman; **à la turque** *adv (assis)* cross-legged.

turf [tyʀf] *nm* racing.

turfiste [tyʀfist(ə)] *nm/f* racegoer.

Turks et Caïques *ou* **Caicos** [tyʀkekaik(ɔs)] *nfpl* Turks and Caicos Islands.

turpitude [tyʀpityd] *nf* base act, baseness *no pl*.

turque [tyʀk(ə)] *adj f, nf voir* **turc**.

Turquie [tyʀki] *nf:* **la ~** Turkey.

turquoise [tyʀkwaz] *nf, adj inv* turquoise.

tut [ty] *etc vb voir* **taire**.

tutelle [tytɛl] *nf (JUR)* guardianship; (*POL*) trusteeship; **sous la ~ de** (*fig*) under the supervision of.

tuteur, trice [tytœʀ, -tʀis] *nm/f (JUR)* guardian; (*de plante*) stake, support.

tutoiement [tytwamɑ̃] *nm* use of familiar "tu" form.

tutoyer [tytwaje] *vt*: ~ **qn** to address sb as "tu".

tutti quanti [tutikwãti] *nmpl*: **et** ~ and all the rest (of them).

tutu [tyty] *nm* (*DANSE*) tutu.

Tuvalu [tyvaly] *nm*: **le** ~ Tuvalu.

tuyau, x [tɥijo] *nm* pipe; (*flexible*) tube; (*fam: conseil*) tip; (*: mise au courant*) gen *no pl*; ~ **d'arrosage** hosepipe; ~ **d'échappement** exhaust pipe; ~ **d'incendie** fire hose.

tuyauté, e [tɥijote] *adj* fluted.

tuyauterie [tɥijotʀi] *nf* piping *no pl*.

tuyère [tɥijɛʀ] *nf* nozzle.

TV [teve] *nf* TV, telly (*BRIT*).

TVA *sigle f* = **taxe à** *ou* **sur la valeur ajoutée**.

tweed [twid] *nm* tweed.

tympan [tɛ̃pɑ̃] *nm* (*ANAT*) eardrum.

type [tip] *nm* type; (*personne, chose: représentant*) classic example, epitome; (*fam*) chap, guy ♦ *adj* typical, standard; **avoir le ~ nordique** to be Nordic-looking.

typé, e [tipe] *adj* ethnic (*euph*).

typhoïde [tifɔid] *nf* typhoid (fever).

typhon [tifɔ̃] *nm* typhoon.

typhus [tifys] *nm* typhus (fever).

typique [tipik] *adj* typical.

typiquement [tipikmã] *adv* typically.

typographe [tipɔgʀaf] *nm/f* typographer.

typographie [tipɔgʀafi] *nf* typography; (*procédé*) letterpress (printing).

typographique [tipɔgʀafik] *adj* typographical; letterpress *cpd*.

typologie [tipɔlɔʒi] *nf* typology.

tyran [tiʀɑ̃] *nm* tyrant.

tyrannie [tiʀani] *nf* tyranny.

tyrannique [tiʀanik] *adj* tyrannical.

tyranniser [tiʀanize] *vt* to tyrannize.

Tyrol [tiʀɔl] *nm*: **le** ~ the Tyrol.

tyrolien, ne [tiʀɔljɛ̃, -ɛn] *adj* Tyrolean.

tzar [dzaʀ] *nm* = **tsar**.

tzigane [dzigan] *adj* gipsy, tzigane ♦ *nm/f* (Hungarian) gipsy, Tzigane.

U u

U, u [y] *nm inv* U, u ♦ *abr* (= *unité*) 10,000 *francs*; **maison à vendre 50 U** house for sale: 500,000 francs; **U comme Ursule** U for Uncle.

ubiquité [ybikɥite] *nf*: **avoir le don d'**~ to be everywhere at once, be ubiquitous.

UDF *sigle f* (= *Union pour la démocratie française*) political party.

UE *sigle f* (= *Union européenne*) EU.

UEFA [yefa] *sigle f* (= *Union of European Football Associations*) UEFA.

UEM *sigle f* (= *Union économique et monétaire*) EMU.

UER *sigle f* (= *unité d'enseignement et de recherche*) old title of UFR; (= *Union européenne de radiodiffusion*) EBU (= *European Broadcasting Union*).

UFC *sigle f* (= *Union fédérale des consommateurs*) national consumer group.

UFR *sigle f* (= *unité de formation et de recherche*) ≈ university department.

UHF *sigle f* (= *ultra-haute fréquence*) UHF.

UHT *sigle* (= *ultra-haute température*) UHT.

UIT *sigle f* (= *Union internationale des télécommunications*) ITU (= *International Telecommunications Union*).

UJP *sigle f* (= *Union des jeunes pour le progrès*) political party.

Ukraine [ykʀɛn] *nf*: **l'**~ the Ukraine.

ukrainien, ne [ykʀɛnjɛ̃, -ɛn] *adj* Ukrainian ♦ *nm* (*LING*) Ukrainian ♦ *nm/f*: **U**~, **ne** Ukrainian.

ulcère [ylsɛʀ] *nm* ulcer; ~ **à l'estomac** stomach ulcer.

ulcérer [ylseʀe] *vt* (*MÉD*) to ulcerate; (*fig*) to sicken, appal. .

ulcéreux, euse [ylseʀø, -øz] *adj* (*plaie, lésion*) ulcerous; (*membre*) ulcerated.

ULM *sigle m* (= *ultra léger motorisé*) microlight.

ultérieur, e [ylteʀjœʀ] *adj* later, subsequent; **remis à une date** ~**e** postponed to a later date.

ultérieurement [ylteʀjœʀmã] *adv* later.

ultimatum [yltimatɔm] *nm* ultimatum.

ultime [yltim] *adj* final.

ultra... [yltʀa] *préfixe* ultra....

ultramoderne [yltʀamɔdɛʀn(ə)] *adj* ultramodern.

ultra-rapide [yltʀaʀapid] *adj* ultra-fast.

ultra-sensible [yltʀasãsibl(ə)] *adj* (*PHOTO*) high-speed.

ultra(-)son [yltʀasɔ̃] *nm* ultrasound *no pl*; ~**s** *nmpl* ultrasonics.

ultra(-)violet, te [yltʀavjɔlɛ, -ɛt] *adj* ultraviolet ♦ *nm*: **les** ~**s** ultraviolet rays.

ululer [ylyle] *vi* = **hululer**.

UME *sigle f* (= *Union monétaire européenne*) EMU.

════════════ MOT-CLÉ

un, une [œ̃, yn] *art indéf* a; (*devant voyelle*) an; ~ **garçon/vieillard** a boy/an old man; **une fille** a girl

♦ *pron* one; **l'**~ **des meilleurs** one of the best; **l'**~ ..., **l'autre** (the) one ..., the other; **les** ~**s** ..., **les autres** some ..., others; **l'**~ **et l'autre** both (of them); **l'**~ **ou l'autre** either (of them); **l'**~ **l'autre, les** ~**s les autres** each other, one another; **pas** ~ **seul** not a single one; ~ **par** ~ one by one

♦ *num* one; **une pomme seulement** one apple

only
♦ *nf*: **la une** (*PRESSE*) the front page.

unanime [ynanim] *adj* unanimous; **ils sont ~s (à penser que)** they are unanimous (in thinking that).

unanimement [ynanimmɑ̃] *adv* (*par tous*) unanimously; (*d'un commun accord*) with one accord.

unanimité [ynanimite] *nf* unanimity; **à l'~** unanimously; **faire l'~** to be approved unanimously.

UNEF [ynɛf] *sigle f* = Union nationale des étudiants de France.

UNESCO [ynɛsko] *sigle f* (= United Nations Educational, Scientific and Cultural Organization) UNESCO.

Unetelle [yntɛl] *nf voir* **Untel**.

UNI *sigle f* = Union nationale interuniversitaire.

uni, e [yni] *adj* (*ton, tissu*) plain; (*surface*) smooth, even; (*famille*) close(-knit); (*pays*) united.

UNICEF [ynisɛf] *sigle m ou f* (= United Nations International Children's Emergency Fund) UNICEF.

unidirectionnel, le [ynidirɛksjɔnɛl] *adj* unidirectional, one-way.

unième [ynjɛm] *num*: **vingt/trente et ~** twenty-/thirty-first; **cent ~** (one) hundred and first.

unificateur, trice [ynifikatœr, -tris] *adj* unifying.

unification [ynifikasjɔ̃] *nf* uniting; unification; standardization.

unifier [ynifje] *vt* to unite, unify; (*systèmes*) to standardize, unify; **s'~** to become united.

uniforme [ynifɔrm(ə)] *adj* (*mouvement*) regular, uniform; (*surface, ton*) even; (*objets, maisons*) uniform; (*fig: vie, conduite*) unchanging ♦ *nm* uniform; **être sous l'~** (*MIL*) to be serving.

uniformément [ynifɔrmemɑ̃] *adv* uniformly.

uniformisation [ynifɔrmizasjɔ̃] *nf* standardization.

uniformiser [ynifɔrmize] *vt* to make uniform; (*systèmes*) to standardize.

uniformité [ynifɔrmite] *nf* regularity; uniformity; evenness.

unijambiste [yniʒɑ̃bist(ə)] *nm/f* one-legged man/woman.

unilatéral, e, aux [ynilateral, -o] *adj* unilateral; **stationnement ~** parking on one side only.

unilatéralement [ynilateralmɑ̃] *adv* unilaterally.

uninominal, e, aux [yninɔminal, -o] *adj* uncontested.

union [ynjɔ̃] *nf* union; **~ conjugale** union of marriage; **~ de consommateurs** consumers' association; **~ libre** free love; **l'U~ des Républiques socialistes soviétiques (URSS)** the Union of Soviet Socialist Republics (USSR);

l'U~ soviétique the Soviet Union.

unique [ynik] *adj* (*seul*) only; (*le même*): **un prix/système ~** a single price/system; (*exceptionnel*) unique; **ménage à salaire ~** one-salary family; **route à voie ~** single-lane road; **fils/fille ~** only son/daughter, only child; **~ en France** the only one of its kind in France.

uniquement [ynikmɑ̃] *adv* only, solely; (*juste*) only, merely.

unir [ynir] *vt* (*nations*) to unite; (*éléments, couleurs*) to combine; (*en mariage*) to unite, join together; **~ qch à** to unite sth with; to combine sth with; **s'~** to unite; (*en mariage*) to be joined together; **s'~ à** *ou* **avec** to unite with.

unisexe [ynisɛks] *adj* unisex.

unisson [ynisɔ̃] **à l'~** *adv* in unison.

unitaire [ynitɛr] *adj* unitary; (*POL*) unitarian; **prix ~** unit price.

unité [ynite] *nf* (*harmonie, cohésion*) unity; (*COMM, MIL, de mesure, MATH*) unit; **~ centrale (de traitement)** central processing unit; **~ de valeur** (university) course, credit.

univers [ynivɛr] *nm* universe.

universalisation [ynivɛrsalizasjɔ̃] *nf* universalization.

universaliser [ynivɛrsalize] *vt* to universalize.

universalité [ynivɛrsalite] *nf* universality.

universel, le [ynivɛrsɛl] *adj* universal; (*esprit*) all-embracing.

universellement [ynivɛrsɛlmɑ̃] *adv* universally.

universitaire [ynivɛrsitɛr] *adj* university *cpd* (*diplôme, études*) academic, university *cpd* ♦ *nm/f* academic.

université [ynivɛrsite] *nf* university.

univoque [ynivɔk] *adj* unambiguous; (*MATH*) one-to-one.

UNR *sigle f* (= Union pour la nouvelle république) former political party.

UNSS *sigle f* = Union nationale de sport scolaire.

Untel, Unetelle [œ̃tɛl, yntɛl] *nm/f*: **Monsieur ~** Mr so-and-so.

uranium [yranjɔm] *nm* uranium.

urbain, e [yrbɛ̃, -ɛn] *adj* urban, city *cpd*, town *cpd*; (*poli*) urbane.

urbanisation [yrbanizasjɔ̃] *nf* urbanization.

urbaniser [yrbanize] *vt* to urbanize.

urbanisme [yrbanism(ə)] *nm* town planning.

urbaniste [yrbanist(ə)] *nm/f* town planner.

urbanité [yrbanite] *nf* urbanity.

urée [yre] *nf* urea.

urémie [yremi] *nf* uraemia (*BRIT*), uremia (*US*).

urgence [yrʒɑ̃s] *nf* urgency; (*MÉD etc*) emergency; **d'~** *adj* emergency *cpd* ♦ *adv* as a matter of urgency; **en cas d'~** in case of emergency; **service des ~s** emergency service.

urgent, e [yrʒɑ̃, -ɑ̃t] *adj* urgent.

urinaire [yrinɛr] *adj* urinary.

urinal, aux [yrinal, -o] *nm* (bed) urinal.

urine [yʀin] *nf* urine.
uriner [yʀine] *vi* to urinate.
urinoir [yʀinwaʀ] *nm* (*public*) urinal.
urne [yʀn(ə)] *nf* (*électorale*) ballot box; (*vase*) urn; **aller aux** ~**s** (*voter*) to go to the polls.
urologie [yʀɔlɔʒi] *nf* urology.
URSS [*parfois:* yʀs] *sigle f* (= *Union des Républiques Socialistes Soviétiques*) USSR.
URSSAF [yʀsaf] *sigle f* (= *Union pour le recouvrement de la sécurité sociale et des allocations familiales*) *administrative body responsible for social security funds and payments.*
urticaire [yʀtikɛʀ] *nf* nettle rash, urticaria.
Uruguay [yʀygwɛ] *nm:* **l'**~ Uruguay.
uruguayen, ne [yʀygwajɛ̃, -ɛn] *adj* Uruguayan ♦ *nm/f:* **U**~**, ne** Uruguayan.
us [ys] *nmpl:* ~ **et coutumes** (habits and) customs.
US(A) *sigle mpl* (= *United States* (*of America*)) US(A).
usage [yzaʒ] *nm* (*emploi, utilisation*) use; (*coutume*) custom; (*éducation*) (good) manners *pl*, (good) breeding; (*LING*): **l'**~ usage; **faire** ~ **de** (*pouvoir, droit*) to exercise; **avoir l'**~ **de** to have the use of; **à l'**~ *adv* with use; **à l'**~ **de** (*pour*) for (use of); **en** ~ in use; **hors d'**~ out of service; **à** ~ **interne** to be taken; **à** ~ **externe** for external use only.
usagé, e [yzaʒe] *adj* (*usé*) worn; (*d'occasion*) used.
usager, ère [yzaʒe, -ɛʀ] *nm/f* user.
usé, e [yze] *adj* worn (down *ou* out *ou* away); ruined; (*banal*) hackneyed.
user [yze] *vt* (*outil*) to wear down; (*vêtement*) to wear out; (*matière*) to wear away; (*consommer: charbon etc*) to use; (*fig: santé*) to ruin; (*: personne*) to wear out; **s'**~ *vi* to wear; to wear out; (*fig*) to decline; **s'**~ **à la tâche** to wear o.s. out with work; ~ **de** *vt* (*moyen, procédé*) to use, employ; (*droit*) to exercise.
usine [yzin] *nf* factory; ~ **atomique** nuclear power plant; ~ **à gaz** gasworks *sg*; ~ **marémotrice** tidal power station.
usiner [yzine] *vt* (*TECH*) to machine; (*fabriquer*) to manufacture.
usité, e [yzite] *adj* in common use, common; **peu** ~ rarely used.
ustensile [ystɑ̃sil] *nm* implement; ~ **de cuisine** kitchen utensil.
usuel, le [yzɥɛl] *adj* everyday, common.
usufruit [yzyfʀɥi] *nm* usufruct.
usuraire [yzyʀɛʀ] *adj* usurious.
usure [yzyʀ] *nf* wear; worn state; (*de l'usurier*) usury; **avoir qn à l'**~ to wear sb down; ~ **normale** fair wear and tear.
usurier, ière [yzyʀje, -jɛʀ] *nm/f* usurer.
usurpateur, trice [yzyʀpatœʀ, -tʀis] *nm/f* usurper.
usurpation [yzyʀpasjɔ̃] *nf* usurpation.
usurper [yzyʀpe] *vt* to usurp.
ut [yt] *nm* (*MUS*) C.
UTA *sigle f* = *Union des transporteurs aériens.*

utérin, e [yteʀɛ̃, -in] *adj* uterine.
utérus [yteʀys] *nm* uterus, womb.
utile [ytil] *adj* useful; ~ **à qn/qch** of use to sb/sth.
utilement [ytilmɑ̃] *adv* usefully.
utilisable [ytilizabl(ə)] *adj* usable.
utilisateur, trice [ytilizatœʀ, -tʀis] *nm/f* user.
utilisation [ytilizasjɔ̃] *nf* use.
utiliser [ytilize] *vt* to use.
utilitaire [ytilitɛʀ] *adj* utilitarian; (*objets*) practical ♦ *nm* (*INFORM*) utility.
utilité [ytilite] *nf* usefulness *no pl*; use; **jouer les** ~**s** (*THÉÂT*) to play bit parts; **reconnu d'**~ **publique** state-approved; **c'est d'une grande** ~ it's extremely useful; **il n'y a aucune** ~ **à** ... there's no use in ....
utopie [ytɔpi] *nf* (*idée, conception*) utopian idea *ou* view; (*société etc idéale*) utopia.
utopique [ytɔpik] *adj* utopian.
utopiste [ytɔpist(ə)] *nm/f* utopian.
UV *sigle f* (*SCOL*) = **unité de valeur**.
uvule [yvyl] *nf* uvula.

V v

V, v [ve] *nm inv* V, v ♦ *abr* (= *voir, verset*) v.; (= *vers: de poésie*) l.; (: *en direction de*) toward(s); **V comme Victor** V for Victor; **en** ~ V-shaped; **encolure en** ~ V-neck; **décolleté en** ~ plunging neckline.
va [va] *vb voir* **aller**.
vacance [vakɑ̃s] *nf* (*ADMIN*) vacancy; ~**s** *nfpl* holiday(s *pl*) (*BRIT*), vacation *sg* (*US*); **les grandes** ~**s** the summer holidays *ou* vacation; **prendre des/ses** ~**s** to take a holiday *ou* vacation/one's holiday(s) *ou* vacation; **aller en** ~**s** to go on holiday *ou* vacation.
vacancier, ière [vakɑ̃sje, -jɛʀ] *nm/f* holidaymaker (*BRIT*), vacationer (*US*).
vacant, e [vakɑ̃, -ɑ̃t] *adj* vacant.
vacarme [vakaʀm(ə)] *nm* row, din.
vacataire [vakatɛʀ] *nm/f* temporary (employee); (*enseignement*) supply (*BRIT*) *ou* substitute (*US*) teacher; (*UNIVERSITÉ*) part-time temporary lecturer.
vaccin [vaksɛ̃] *nm* vaccine; (*opération*) vaccination.
vaccination [vaksinasjɔ̃] *nf* vaccination.
vacciner [vaksine] *vt* to vaccinate; (*fig*) to make immune; **être vacciné** (*fig*) to be immune.
vache [vaʃ] *nf* (*ZOOL*) cow; (*cuir*) cowhide ♦ *adj* (*fam*) rotten, mean; ~ **à eau** (canvas) water bag; (**manger de la**) ~ **enragée** (to go through) hard times; ~ **à lait** (*péj*) mug,

sucker; ~ **laitière** dairy cow; **période des ~s maigres** lean times pl, lean period.

vachement [vaʃmɑ̃] adv (fam) damned, fantastically.

vacher, ère [vaʃe, -ɛʀ] nm/f cowherd.

vacherie [vaʃʀi] nf (fam) meanness no pl; (action) dirty trick; (propos) nasty remark.

vacherin [vaʃʀɛ̃] nm (fromage): vacherin cheese; (gâteau): ~ **glacé** vacherin (type of cream gâteau).

vachette [vaʃɛt] nf calfskin.

vacillant, e [vasijɑ̃, -ɑ̃t] adj wobbly; flickering; failing, faltering.

vaciller [vasije] vi to sway, wobble; (bougie, lumière) to flicker; (fig) to be failing, falter; ~ **dans ses réponses** to falter in one's replies; ~ **dans ses résolutions** to waver in one's resolutions.

vacuité [vakɥite] nf emptiness, vacuity.

vade-mecum [vademekɔm] nm inv pocketbook.

vadrouille [vadʀuj] nf: **être/partir en ~** to be on/go for a wander.

vadrouiller [vadʀuje] vi to wander around ou about.

va-et-vient [vaevjɛ̃] nm inv (de pièce mobile) to and fro (ou up and down) movement; (de personnes, véhicules) comings and goings pl, to-ings and fro-ings pl; (ÉLEC) two-way switch.

vagabond, e [vagabɔ̃, -ɔ̃d] adj wandering; (imagination) roaming, roving ◆ nm (rôdeur) tramp, vagrant; (voyageur) wanderer.

vagabondage [vagabɔ̃daʒ] nm roaming, wandering; (JUR) vagrancy.

vagabonder [vagabɔ̃de] vi to roam, wander.

vagin [vaʒɛ̃] nm vagina.

vaginal, e, aux [vaʒinal, -o] adj vaginal.

vagissement [vaʒismɑ̃] nm cry (of newborn baby).

vague [vag] nf wave ◆ adj vague; (regard) faraway; (manteau, robe) loose(-fitting); (quelconque): **un ~ bureau/cousin** some office/cousin or other ◆ nm: **être dans le ~** to be rather in the dark; **rester dans le ~** to keep things rather vague; **regarder dans le ~** to gaze into space; ~ **à l'âme** nm vague melancholy; ~ **d'assaut** nf (MIL) wave of assault; ~ **de chaleur** nf heatwave; ~ **de fond** nf ground swell; ~ **de froid** nf cold spell.

vaguelette [vaglɛt] nf ripple.

vaguement [vagmɑ̃] adv vaguely.

vaillamment [vajamɑ̃] adv bravely, gallantly.

vaillant, e [vajɑ̃, -ɑ̃t] adj (courageux) brave, gallant; (robuste) vigorous, hale and hearty; **n'avoir plus un sou ~** to be penniless.

vaille [vaj] vb voir **valoir**.

vain, e [vɛ̃, vɛn] adj vain; **en ~** adv in vain.

vaincre [vɛ̃kʀ(ə)] vt to defeat; (fig) to conquer, overcome.

vaincu, e [vɛ̃ky] pp de **vaincre** ◆ nm/f defeated party.

vainement [vɛnmɑ̃] adv vainly.

vainquais [vɛ̃kɛ] etc vb voir **vaincre**.

vainqueur [vɛ̃kœʀ] nm victor; (SPORT) winner ◆ adj m victorious.

vais [vɛ] vb voir **aller**.

vaisseau, x [vɛso] nm (ANAT) vessel; (NAVIG) ship, vessel; ~ **spatial** spaceship.

vaisselier [vɛsəlje] nm dresser.

vaisselle [vɛsɛl] nf (service) crockery; (plats etc à laver) (dirty) dishes pl; **faire la ~** to do the washing-up (BRIT) ou the dishes.

val, vaux ou **vals** [val, vo] nm valley.

valable [valabl(ə)] adj valid; (acceptable) decent, worthwhile.

valablement [valabləmɑ̃] adv legitimately; (de façon satisfaisante) satisfactorily.

Valence [valɑ̃s] n (en Espagne) Valencia; (en France) Valence.

valent [val] etc vb voir **valoir**.

valet [valɛ] nm valet; (péj) lackey; (CARTES) jack, knave (BRIT); ~ **de chambre** manservant, valet; ~ **de ferme** farmhand; ~ **de pied** footman.

valeur [valœʀ] nf (gén) value; (mérite) worth, merit; (COMM: titre) security; **mettre en ~** (bien) to exploit; (terrain, région) to develop; (fig) to highlight; to show off to advantage; **avoir de la ~** to be valuable; **prendre de la ~** to go up ou gain in value; **sans ~** worthless; ~ **absolue** absolute value; ~ **d'échange** exchange value; ~ **nominale** face value; ~**s mobilières** transferable securities.

valeureux, euse [valœʀø, -øz] adj valorous.

validation [validasjɔ̃] nf validation.

valide [valid] adj (en bonne santé) fit, well; (indemne) able-bodied, fit; (valable) valid.

valider [valide] vt to validate.

validité [validite] nf validity.

valions [valjɔ̃] etc vb voir **valoir**.

valise [valiz] nf (suit)case; **faire sa ~** to pack one's (suit)case; **la ~ (diplomatique)** the diplomatic bag.

vallée [vale] nf valley.

vallon [valɔ̃] nm small valley.

vallonné, e [valɔne] adj undulating.

vallonnement [valɔnmɑ̃] nm undulation.

valoir [valwaʀ] vi (être valable) to hold, apply ◆ vt (prix, valeur, effort) to be worth; (causer): ~ **qch à qn** to earn sb sth; **se ~** to be of equal merit; (péj) to be two of a kind; **faire ~** (droits, prérogatives) to assert; (domaine, capitaux) to exploit; **faire ~ que** to point out that; **se faire ~** to make the most of o.s.; **à ~ on** account; **à ~ sur** to be deducted from; **vaille que vaille** somehow or other; **cela me dit rien qui vaille** I don't like the look of it at all; **ce climat ne me vaut rien** this climate doesn't suit me; ~ **la peine** to be worth the trouble, be worth it; ~ **mieux: il vaut mieux se taire** it's better to say nothing; **il vaut mieux que je fasse/comme ceci** it's better if

I do/like this; **ça ne vaut rien** it's worthless; **que vaut ce candidat?** how good is this applicant?

valorisation [valɔʀizasjɔ̃] *nf* (economic) development; increased standing.

valoriser [valɔʀize] *vt* (*ÉCON*) to develop (the economy of); (*produit*) to increase the value of; (*PSYCH*) to increase the standing of; (*fig*) to highlight, bring out.

valse [vals(ə)] *nf* waltz; **c'est la ~ des étiquettes** the prices don't stay the same from one moment to the next.

valser [valse] *vi* to waltz; (*fig*): **aller ~** to go flying.

valu, e [valy] *pp de* **valoir**.

valve [valv(ə)] *nf* valve.

vamp [vãp] *nf* vamp.

vampire [vãpiʀ] *nm* vampire.

van [vã] *nm* horse box (*BRIT*) *ou* trailer (*US*).

vandale [vãdal] *nm/f* vandal.

vandalisme [vãdalism(ə)] *nm* vandalism.

vanille [vanij] *nf* vanilla; **glace à la ~** vanilla ice cream.

vanillé, e [vanije] *adj* vanilla *cpd*.

vanité [vanite] *nf* vanity.

vaniteux, euse [vanitø, -øz] *adj* vain, conceited.

vanity-case [vaniti(e)kɛz] *nm* vanity case.

vanne [van] *nf* gate; (*fam: remarque*) dig, (nasty) crack; **lancer une ~ à qn** to have a go at sb (*BRIT*), knock sb.

vanneau, x [vano] *nm* lapwing.

vanner [vane] *vt* to winnow.

vannerie [vanʀi] *nf* basketwork.

vantail, aux [vãtaj, -o] *nm* door, leaf (*pl* leaves).

vantard, e [vãtaʀ, -aʀd(ə)] *adj* boastful.

vantardise [vãtaʀdiz] *nf* boastfulness *no pl*; boast.

vanter [vãte] *vt* to speak highly of, vaunt; **se ~** *vi* to boast, brag; **se ~ de** to pride o.s. on; (*péj*) to boast of.

Vanuatu [vanwatu] *nm*: **le ~** Vanuatu.

va-nu-pieds [vanypje] *nm/f inv* tramp, beggar.

vapeur [vapœʀ] *nf* steam; (*émanation*) vapour (*BRIT*), vapor (*US*), fumes *pl*; (*brouillard, buée*) haze; **~s** *nfpl* (*bouffées*) vapours, vapors; **à ~** steam-powered, steam *cpd*; **à toute ~** full steam ahead; (*fig*) at full tilt; **renverser la ~** to reverse engines; (*fig*) to backtrack, backpedal; **cuit à la ~** steamed.

vapocuiseur [vapɔkyizœʀ] *nm* pressure cooker.

vaporeux, euse [vapɔʀø, -øz] *adj* (*flou*) hazy, misty; (*léger*) filmy, gossamer *cpd*.

vaporisateur [vapɔʀizatœʀ] *nm* spray.

vaporiser [vapɔʀize] *vt* (*CHIMIE*) to vaporize; (*parfum etc*) to spray.

vaquer [vake] *vi* (*ADMIN*) to be on vacation; **~ à ses occupations** to attend to one's affairs, go about one's business.

varappe [vaʀap] *nf* rock climbing.

varappeur, euse [vaʀapœʀ, -øz] *nm/f* (rock) climber.

varech [vaʀɛk] *nm* wrack, varec.

vareuse [vaʀøz] *nf* (*blouson*) pea jacket; (*d'uniforme*) tunic.

variable [vaʀjabl(ə)] *adj* variable; (*temps, humeur*) changeable; (*TECH: à plusieurs positions etc*) adaptable; (*LING*) inflectional; (*divers: résultats*) varied, various ♦ *nf* (*INFORM, MATH*) variable.

variante [vaʀjãt] *nf* variant.

variation [vaʀjasjɔ̃] *nf* variation; changing *no pl*, change; (*MUS*) variation.

varice [vaʀis] *nf* varicose vein.

varicelle [vaʀisɛl] *nf* chickenpox.

varié, e [vaʀje] *adj* varied; (*divers*) various; **hors-d'œuvre ~s** selection of hors d'œuvres.

varier [vaʀje] *vi* to vary; (*temps, humeur*) to change ♦ *vt* to vary.

variété [vaʀjete] *nf* variety; **spectacle de ~s** variety show.

variole [vaʀjɔl] *nf* smallpox.

variqueux, euse [vaʀikø, -øz] *adj* varicose.

Varsovie [vaʀsɔvi] *n* Warsaw.

vas [va] *vb voir* **aller**; **~-y!** [vazi] go on!

vasculaire [vaskylɛʀ] *adj* vascular.

vase [vɑz] *nm* vase ♦ *nf* silt, mud; **en ~ clos** in isolation; **~ de nuit** chamberpot; **~s communicants** communicating vessels.

vasectomie [vazɛktɔmi] *nf* vasectomy.

vaseline [vazlin] *nf* Vaseline ®.

vaseux, euse [vɑzø, -øz] *adj* silty, muddy; (*fig: confus*) woolly, hazy; (*: fatigué*) peaky; (*: étourdi*) woozy.

vasistas [vazistas] *nm* fanlight.

vasque [vask(ə)] *nf* (*bassin*) basin; (*coupe*) bowl.

vassal, e, aux [vasal, -o] *nm/f* vassal.

vaste [vast(ə)] *adj* vast, immense.

Vatican [vatikã] *nm*: **le ~** the Vatican.

vaticiner [vatisine] *vi* (*péj*) to make pompous predictions.

va-tout [vatu] *nm*: **jouer son ~** to stake one's all.

vaudeville [vodvil] *nm* vaudeville, light comedy.

vaudrai [vodʀe] *etc vb voir* **valoir**.

vau-l'eau [volo]: **à ~** *adv* with the current; **s'en aller à ~** (*fig: projets*) to be adrift.

vaurien, ne [voʀjɛ̃, -ɛn] *nm/f* good-for-nothing, guttersnipe.

vaut [vo] *vb voir* **valoir**.

vautour [votuʀ] *nm* vulture.

vautrer [votʀe]: **se ~** *vi*: **se ~ dans** to wallow in; **se ~ sur** to sprawl on.

vaux [vo] *pl de* **val** ♦ *vb voir* **valoir**.

va-vite [vavit]: **à la ~** *adv* in a rush.

vd *abr* = **vend**.

VDQS *abr* (= *vin délimité de qualité supérieure*) *label guaranteeing quality of wine*.

VDQS, *on a bottle of French wine, indicates that it contains high-quality wine from an approved regional vineyard. It is the second highest French wine classification after* **AOC** *and is followed by* **vin de pays.** *Unlike the previous categories,* **vin de table** *or* **vin ordinaire** *is table wine of unspecified origin, often blended.*

vds *abr* = **vends.**

veau, x [vo] *nm* (*ZOOL*) calf (*pl* calves); (*CULIN*) veal; (*peau*) calfskin; **tuer le ~ gras** to kill the fatted calf.

vecteur [vɛktœʀ] *nm* vector; (*MIL, BIO*) carrier.

vécu, e [veky] *pp de* **vivre ♦** *adj* (*aventure*) real(-life).

vedettariat [vədɛtaʀja] *nm* stardom; (*attitude*) acting like a star.

vedette [vədɛt] *nf* (*artiste etc*) star; (*canot*) patrol boat; launch; **avoir la ~** to top the bill, get star billing; **mettre qn en ~** (*CINÉ etc*) to give sb the starring role; (*fig*) to push sb into the limelight; **voler la ~ à qn** to steal the show from sb.

végétal, e, aux [veʒetal, -o] *adj* vegetable ♦ *nm* vegetable, plant.

végétalien, ne [veʒetaljɛ̃, -ɛn] *adj, nm/f* vegan.

végétalisme [veʒetalism(ə)] *nm* veganism.

végétarien, ne [veʒetaʀjɛ̃, -ɛn] *adj, nm/f* vegetarian.

végétarisme [veʒetaʀism(ə)] *nm* vegetarianism.

végétatif, ive [veʒetatif, -iv] *adj*: **une vie ~ive** a vegetable existence.

végétation [veʒetasjɔ̃] *nf* vegetation; **~s** *nfpl* (*MÉD*) adenoids.

végéter [veʒete] *vi* (*fig*) to vegetate; to stagnate.

véhémence [veemɑ̃s] *nf* vehemence.

véhément, e [veemɑ̃, -ɑ̃t] *adj* vehement.

véhicule [veikyl] *nm* vehicle; **~ utilitaire** commercial vehicle.

véhiculer [veikyle] *vt* (*personnes, marchandises*) to transport, convey; (*fig: idées, substances*) to convey, serve as a vehicle for.

veille [vɛj] *nf* (*garde*) watch; (*PSYCH*) wakefulness; (*jour*): **la ~** the day before, the previous day; **la ~ au soir** the previous evening; **la ~ de** the day before; **à la ~ de** on the eve of; **l'état de ~** the waking state.

veillée [veje] *nf* (*soirée*) evening; (*réunion*) evening gathering; **~ d'armes** night before combat; (*fig*) vigil; **~ (mortuaire)** watch.

veiller [veje] *vi* (*rester debout*) to stay *ou* sit up; (*ne pas dormir*) to be awake; (*être de garde*) to be on watch; (*être vigilant*) to be watchful ♦ *vt* (*malade, mort*) to watch over, sit up with; **~ à** *vt* to attend to, see to; **~ à ce que** to make sure that, see to it that; **~ sur** *vt* to keep a watch *ou* an eye on.

veilleur [vɛjœʀ] *nm*: **~ de nuit** night watchman.

veilleuse [vɛjøz] *nf* (*lampe*) night light; (*AUTO*) sidelight; (*flamme*) pilot light; **en ~** *adj* (*lampe*) dimmed; (*fig: affaire*) shelved, set aside.

veinard, e [vɛnaʀ, -aʀd(ə)] *nm/f* (*fam*) lucky devil.

veine [vɛn] *nf* (*ANAT, du bois etc*) vein; (*filon*) vein, seam; (*fam: chance*): **avoir de la ~** to be lucky; (*inspiration*) inspiration.

veiné, e [vene] *adj* veined; (*bois*) grained.

veineux, euse [venø, -øz] *adj* venous.

Velcro [vɛlkʀo] *nm ®* Velcro ®.

vêler [vele] *vi* to calve.

vélin [velɛ̃] *nm*: **(papier) ~** vellum (paper).

véliplanchiste [veliplɑ̃ʃist(ə)] *nm/f* windsurfer.

velléitaire [veleitɛʀ] *adj* irresolute, indecisive.

velléités [veleite] *nfpl* vague impulses.

vélo [velo] *nm* bike, cycle; **faire du ~** to go cycling.

véloce [velɔs] *adj* swift.

vélocité [velɔsite] *nf* (*MUS*) nimbleness, swiftness; (*vitesse*) velocity.

vélodrome [velɔdʀom] *nm* velodrome.

vélomoteur [velɔmɔtœʀ] *nm* moped.

véloski [veloski] *nm* skibob.

velours [vəluʀ] *nm* velvet; **~ côtelé** corduroy.

velouté, e [vəlute] *adj* (*au toucher*) velvety; (*à la vue*) soft, mellow; (*au goût*) smooth, mellow ♦ *nm*: **~ d'asperges/de tomates** cream of asparagus/tomato soup.

velouteux, euse [vəlutø, -øz] *adj* velvety.

velu, e [vəly] *adj* hairy.

venais [vənɛ] *etc vb voir* **venir.**

venaison [vənɛzɔ̃] *nf* venison.

vénal, e, aux [venal, -o] *adj* venal.

vénalité [venalite] *nf* venality.

venant [vənɑ̃]: **à tout ~** *adv* to all and sundry.

vendable [vɑ̃dabl(ə)] *adj* saleable, marketable.

vendange [vɑ̃dɑ̃ʒ] *nf* (*opération, période: aussi:* **~s**) grape harvest; (*raisins*) grape crop, grapes *pl*.

vendanger [vɑ̃dɑ̃ʒe] *vi* to harvest the grapes.

vendangeur, euse [vɑ̃dɑ̃ʒœʀ, -øz] *nm/f* grape-picker.

vendéen, ne [vɑ̃deɛ̃, -ɛn] *adj* of *ou* from the Vendée.

vendeur, euse [vɑ̃dœʀ, -øz] *nm/f* (*de magasin*) shop *ou* sales assistant (*BRIT*), sales clerk (*US*); (*COMM*) salesman/woman ♦ *nm* (*JUR*) vendor, seller; **~ de journaux** newspaper seller.

vendre [vɑ̃dʀ(ə)] *vt* to sell; **~ qch à qn** to sell sb sth; **cela se vend à la douzaine** these are sold by the dozen; **cela se vend bien** it's selling well; **"à ~"** "for sale".

vendredi [vɑ̃dʀədi] *nm* Friday; **V~ saint** Good Friday; *voir aussi* **lundi.**

vendu, e [vɑ̃dy] *pp de* **vendre ♦** *adj* (*péj*) corrupt.

venelle [vənɛl] *nf* alley.

vénéneux, euse [venenø, -øz] *adj* poisonous.

vénérable [veneʀabl(ə)] *adj* venerable.

vénération [venerɑsjɔ̃] *nf* veneration.

vénérer [venere] *vt* to venerate.

vénerie [vɛnʀi] *nf* hunting.

vénérien, ne [venerjɛ̃, -ɛn] *adj* venereal.

Venezuela [venezɥela] *nm*: **le** ~ Venezuela.

vénézuélien, ne [venezɥeljɛ̃, -ɛn] *adj* Venezuelan ♦ *nm/f*: **V~, ne** Venezuelan.

vengeance [vɑ̃ʒɑ̃s] *nf* vengeance *no pl*, revenge *no pl*; (*acte*) act of vengeance *ou* revenge.

venger [vɑ̃ʒe] *vt* to avenge; **se** ~ *vi* to avenge o.s.; (*par rancune*) to take revenge; **se** ~ **de qch** to avenge o.s. for sth; to take one's revenge for sth; **se** ~ **de qn** to take revenge on sb; **se** ~ **sur** to wreak vengeance upon; to take revenge on *ou* through; to take it out on.

vengeur, eresse [vɑ̃ʒœʀ, -ʒʀɛs] *adj* vengeful ♦ *nm/f* avenger.

véniel, le [venjɛl] *adj* venial.

venimeux, euse [vənimø, -øz] *adj* poisonous, venomous; (*fig: haineux*) venomous, vicious.

venin [vənɛ̃] *nm* venom, poison; (*fig*) venom.

venir [vəniʀ] *vi* to come; ~ **de** to come from; ~ **de faire: je viens d'y aller/de le voir** I've just been there/seen him; **s'il vient à pleuvoir** if it should rain, if it happens to rain; **en** ~ **à faire: j'en viens à croire que** I am coming to believe that; **où veux-tu en** ~? what are you getting at?; **il en est venu à mendier** he has been reduced to begging; **en** ~ **aux mains** to come to blows; **les années/générations à** ~ the years/generations to come; **il me vient une idée** an idea has just occurred to me; **il me vient des soupçons** I'm beginning to be suspicious; **je te vois** ~ I know what you're after; **faire** ~ (*docteur, plombier*) to call (out); **d'où vient que ...?** how is it that ...?; ~ **au monde** to come into the world.

Venise [vəniz] *n* Venice.

vénitien, ne [venisjɛ̃, -ɛn] *adj* Venetian.

vent [vɑ̃] *nm* wind; **il y a du** ~ it's windy; **c'est du** ~ it's all hot air; **au** ~ to windward; **sous le** ~ to leeward; **avoir le** ~ **debout/arrière** to head into the wind/have the wind astern; **dans le** ~ (*fam*) trendy; **prendre le** ~ (*fig*) to see which way the wind blows; **avoir** ~ **de** to get wind of; **contre** ~**s et marées** come hell or high water.

vente [vɑ̃t] *nf* sale; **la** ~ (*activité*) selling; (*secteur*) sales *pl*; **mettre en** ~ to put on sale; (*objets personnels*) to put up for sale; ~ **de charité** jumble (*BRIT*) *ou* rummage (*US*) sale; ~ **par correspondance (VPC)** mail-order selling; ~ **aux enchères** auction sale.

venté, e [vɑ̃te] *adj* windswept, windy.

venter [vɑ̃te] *vb impers*: **il vente** the wind is blowing.

venteux, euse [vɑ̃tø, -øz] *adj* windswept, windy.

ventilateur [vɑ̃tilatœʀ] *nm* fan.

ventilation [vɑ̃tilasjɔ̃] *nf* ventilation.

ventiler [vɑ̃tile] *vt* to ventilate; (*total, statistiques*) to break down.

ventouse [vɑ̃tuz] *nf* (*ampoule*) cupping glass; (*de caoutchouc*) suction pad; (*ZOOL*) sucker.

ventre [vɑ̃tʀ(ə)] *nm* (*ANAT*) stomach; (*fig*) belly; **prendre du** ~ to be getting a paunch; **avoir mal au** ~ to have (a) stomach ache.

ventricule [vɑ̃tʀikyl] *nm* ventricle.

ventriloque [vɑ̃tʀilɔk] *nm/f* ventriloquist.

ventripotent, e [vɑ̃tʀipɔtɑ̃, -ɑ̃t] *adj* potbellied.

ventru, e [vɑ̃tʀy] *adj* potbellied.

venu, e [vəny] *pp de* **venir** ♦ *adj*: **être mal** ~ **à** *ou* **de faire** to have no grounds for doing, be in no position to do; **mal** ~ ill-timed, unwelcome; **bien** ~ timely, welcome ♦ *nf* coming.

vêpres [vɛpʀ(ə)] *nfpl* vespers.

ver [vɛʀ] *nm voir aussi* **vers**; worm; (*des fruits etc*) maggot; (*du bois*) woodworm *no pl*; ~ **blanc** May beetle grub; ~ **luisant** glowworm; ~ **à soie** silkworm; ~ **solitaire** tapeworm; ~ **de terre** earthworm.

véracité [verasite] *nf* veracity.

véranda [verɑ̃da] *nf* veranda(h).

verbal, e, aux [vɛʀbal, -o] *adj* verbal.

verbalement [vɛʀbalmɑ̃] *adv* verbally.

verbaliser [vɛʀbalize] *vi* (*POLICE*) to book *ou* report an offender; (*PSYCH*) to verbalize.

verbe [vɛʀb(ə)] *nm* (*LING*) verb; (*voix*): **avoir le** ~ **sonore** to have a sonorous tone (of voice); (*expression*): **la magie du** ~ the magic of language *ou* the word; (*REL*): **le V~** the Word.

verbeux, euse [vɛʀbø, -øz] *adj* verbose, wordy.

verbiage [vɛʀbjaʒ] *nm* verbiage.

verbosité [vɛʀbozite] *nf* verbosity.

verdâtre [vɛʀdɑtʀ(ə)] *adj* greenish.

verdeur [vɛʀdœʀ] *nf* (*vigueur*) vigour (*BRIT*), vigor (*US*), vitality; (*crudité*) forthrightness; (*défaut de maturité*) tartness, sharpness.

verdict [vɛʀdik(t)] *nm* verdict.

verdir [vɛʀdiʀ] *vi, vt* to turn green.

verdoyant, e [vɛʀdwajɑ̃, -ɑ̃t] *adj* green, verdant.

verdure [vɛʀdyʀ] *nf* (*arbres, feuillages*) greenery; (*légumes verts*) green vegetables *pl*, greens *pl*.

véreux, euse [verø, -øz] *adj* worm-eaten; (*malhonnête*) shady, corrupt.

verge [vɛʀʒ(ə)] *nf* (*ANAT*) penis; (*baguette*) stick, cane.

verger [vɛʀʒe] *nm* orchard.

vergeture [vɛʀʒətyʀ] *nf gén pl* stretch mark.

verglacé, e [vɛʀglase] *adj* icy, iced-over.

verglas [vɛʀgla] *nm* (black) ice.

vergogne [vɛʀgɔɲ]: **sans** ~ *adv* shamelessly.

véridique [veridik] *adj* truthful.

vérificateur, trice [verifikatœʀ, -tʀis] *nm/f* controller, checker ♦ *nf* (*machine*) verifier; ~ **des comptes** (*FINANCE*) auditor.

vérification [verifikasjɔ̃] *nf* checking *no pl*, check; ~ **d'identité** identity check.

vérifier [verifje] *vt* to check; (*corroborer*) to

confirm, bear out; (*INFORM*) to verify; **se ~** *vi* to be confirmed *ou* verified.

vérin [veʀɛ̃] *nm* jack.

véritable [veʀitabl(ə)] *adj* real; (*ami, amour*) true; **un ~ désastre** an absolute disaster; **que le ~ X sorte du rang!** ≈ will the real X (please) stand up!

véritablement [veʀitabləmɑ̃] *adv* (*effectivement*) really; (*absolument*) absolutely.

vérité [veʀite] *nf* truth; (*d'un portrait*) lifelikeness; (*sincérité*) truthfulness, sincerity; **en ~, à la ~** to tell the truth.

verlan [veʀlɑ̃] *nm* (back) slang.

Verlan *is a form of slang popularized in the fifties by Auguste Le Breton. It consists in inverting the syllables of words, verlan itself coming from* l'envers (à l'envers = *back to front*). *Typical examples are* féca (café), ripou (pourri), meuf (femme), beur (Arabe).

---

vermeil, le [veʀmɛj] *adj* bright red, ruby red ♦ *nm* (*substance*) vermeil.

vermicelles [veʀmisɛl] *nmpl* vermicelli *sg*.

vermifuge [veʀmifyʒ] *nm*: **poudre ~** worm powder.

vermillon [veʀmijɔ̃] *adj inv* vermilion, scarlet.

vermine [veʀmin] *nf* vermin *pl*.

vermoulu, e [veʀmuly] *adj* worm-eaten, with woodworm.

vermout(h) [veʀmut] *nm* vermouth.

verni, e [veʀni] *adj* varnished; glazed; (*fam*) lucky; **cuir ~** patent leather; **souliers ~s** patent (leather) shoes.

vernir [veʀniʀ] *vt* (*bois, tableau, ongles*) to varnish; (*poterie*) to glaze.

vernis [veʀni] *nm* (*enduit*) varnish; glaze; (*fig*) veneer; **~ à ongles** nail varnish (*BRIT*) *ou* polish.

vernissage [veʀnisaʒ] *nm* varnishing; glazing; (*d'une exposition*) preview.

vernisser [veʀnise] *vt* to glaze.

vérole [veʀɔl] *nf* (*variole*) smallpox; (*fam: syphilis*) pox.

Vérone [veʀɔn] *n* Verona.

verrai [veʀe] *etc vb voir* **voir**.

verre [veʀ] *nm* glass; (*de lunettes*) lens *sg*; **~s** *nmpl* (*lunettes*) glasses; **boire** *ou* **prendre un ~** to have a drink; **~ à vin/à liqueur** wine/ liqueur glass; **~ à dents** tooth mug; **~ dépoli** frosted glass; **~ de lampe** lamp glass *ou* chimney; **~ de montre** watch glass; **~ à pied** stemmed glass; **~s de contact** contact lenses; **~s fumés** tinted lenses.

verrerie [veʀʀi] *nf* (*fabrique*) glassworks *sg*; (*activité*) glass-making, glass-working; (*objets*) glassware.

verrier [veʀje] *nm* glass-blower.

verrière [veʀjɛʀ] *nf* (*grand vitrage*) window; (*toit vitré*) glass roof.

verrons [veʀɔ̃] *etc vb voir* **voir**.

verroterie [veʀɔtʀi] *nf* glass beads *pl*, glass

jewellery (*BRIT*) *ou* jewelry (*US*).

verrou [veʀu] *nm* (*targette*) bolt; (*fig*) constriction; **mettre le ~** to bolt the door; **mettre qn sous les ~s** to put sb behind bars.

verrouillage [veʀujaʒ] *nm* (*dispositif*) locking mechanism; (*AUTO*): **~ central** *ou* **centralisé** central locking.

verrouiller [veʀuje] *vt* to bolt; to lock; (*MIL*: *brèche*) to close.

verrue [veʀy] *nf* wart; (*plantaire*) verruca; (*fig*) eyesore.

vers [veʀ] *nm* line ♦ *nmpl* (*poésie*) verse *sg* ♦ *prép* (*en direction de*) toward(s); (*près de*) around (about); (*temporel*) about, around.

versant [veʀsɑ̃] *nm* slopes *pl*, side.

versatile [veʀsatil] *adj* fickle, changeable.

verse [veʀs(ə)]: **à ~** *adv*: **il pleut à ~** it's pouring (with rain).

versé, e [veʀse] *adj*: **être ~ dans** (*science*) to be (well-)versed in.

Verseau [veʀso] *nm*: **le ~** Aquarius, the water-carrier; **être du ~** to be Aquarius.

versement [veʀsəmɑ̃] *nm* payment; (*sur un compte*) deposit, remittance; **en 3 ~s** in 3 instalments.

verser [veʀse] *vt* (*liquide, grains*) to pour; (*larmes, sang*) to shed; (*argent*) to pay; (*soldat: affecter*): **~ qn dans** to assign sb to ♦ *vi* (*véhicule*) to overturn; (*fig*): **~ dans** to lapse into; **~ à un compte** to pay into an account.

verset [veʀsɛ] *nm* verse; versicle.

verseur [veʀsœʀ] *adj m voir* **bec, bouchon**.

versification [veʀsifikasjɔ̃] *nf* versification.

versifier [veʀsifje] *vt* to put into verse ♦ *vi* to versify, write verse.

version [veʀsjɔ̃] *nf* version; (*SCOL*) translation (*into the mother tongue*); **film en ~ originale** film in the original language.

verso [veʀso] *nm* back; **voir au ~** see over(leaf).

vert, e [veʀ, veʀt(ə)] *adj* green; (*vin*) young; (*vigoureux*) sprightly; (*cru*) forthright ♦ *nm* green; **dire des ~es (et des pas mûres)** to say some pretty spicy things; **il en a vu des ~es** he's seen a thing or two; **~ bouteille** *adj inv* bottle-green; **~ d'eau** *adj inv* sea-green; **~ pomme** *adj inv* apple-green.

vert-de-gris [veʀdəgʀi] *nm* verdigris ♦ *adj inv* grey(ish)-green.

vertébral, e, aux [veʀtebʀal, -o] *adj* back *cpd*; *voir* **colonne**.

vertèbre [veʀtɛbʀ(ə)] *nf* vertebra (*pl* -ae).

vertébré, e [veʀtebʀe] *adj*, *nm* vertebrate.

vertement [veʀtəmɑ̃] *adv* (*réprimander*) sharply.

vertical, e, aux [veʀtikal, -o] *adj*, *nf* vertical; **à la ~e** *adv* vertically.

verticalement [veʀtikalmɑ̃] *adv* vertically.

verticalité [veʀtikalite] *nf* verticalness, verticality.

vertige [veʀtiʒ] *nm* (*peur du vide*) vertigo; (*étourdissement*) dizzy spell; (*fig*) fever; **ça**

me donne le ~ it makes me dizzy; (*fig*) it makes my head spin *ou* reel.

vertigineux, euse [vɛʀtiʒinø, -øz] *adj* (*hausse, vitesse*) breathtaking; (*altitude, gorge*) breathtakingly high (*ou* deep).

vertu [vɛʀty] *nf* virtue; **une ~** a saint, a paragon of virtue; **avoir la ~ de faire** to have the virtue of doing; **en ~ de** *prép* in accordance with.

vertueusement [vɛʀtɥøzmɑ̃] *adv* virtuously.

vertueux, euse [vɛʀtɥø, -øz] *adj* virtuous.

verve [vɛʀv(ə)] *nf* witty eloquence; **être en ~** to be in brilliant form.

verveine [vɛʀvɛn] *nf* (*BOT*) verbena, vervain; (*infusion*) verbena tea.

vésicule [vezikyl] *nf* vesicle; **~ biliaire** gallbladder.

vespasienne [vɛspazjɛn] *nf* urinal.

vespéral, e, aux [vɛspeʀal, -o] *adj* vespertine, evening *cpd*.

vessie [vesi] *nf* bladder.

veste [vɛst(ə)] *nf* jacket; **~ droite/croisée** single-/double-breasted jacket; **retourner sa ~** (*fig*) to change one's colours.

vestiaire [vɛstjɛʀ] *nm* (*au théâtre etc*) cloakroom; (*de stade etc*) changing-room (*BRIT*), locker-room (*US*); (*métallique*): **(armoire) ~** locker.

vestibule [vɛstibyl] *nm* hall.

vestige [vɛstiʒ] *nm* (*objet*) relic; (*fragment*) trace; (*fig*) remnant, vestige; **~s** *nmpl* (*d'une ville*) remains; (*d'une civilisation, du passé*) remnants, relics.

vestimentaire [vɛstimɑ̃tɛʀ] *adj* (*dépenses*) clothing; (*détail*) of dress; (*élégance*) sartorial.

veston [vɛstɔ̃] *nm* jacket.

Vésuve [vezyv] *nm*: **le ~** Vesuvius.

vêtais [vɛtɛ] *etc vb voir* **vêtir**.

vêtement [vɛtmɑ̃] *nm* garment, item of clothing; (*COMM*): **le ~** the clothing industry; **~s** *nmpl* clothes; **~s de sport** sportswear *sg*, sports clothes.

vétéran [veteʀɑ̃] *nm* veteran.

vétérinaire [veteʀinɛʀ] *adj* veterinary ♦ *nm/f* vet, veterinary surgeon (*BRIT*), veterinarian (*US*).

vétille [vetij] *nf* trifle, triviality.

vétilleux, euse [vetijø, -øz] *adj* punctilious.

vêtir [vetiʀ] *vt* to clothe, dress; **se ~** to dress (o.s.).

vêtit [veti] *etc vb voir* **vêtir**.

vétiver [vetivɛʀ] *nm* (*BOT*) vetiver.

veto [veto] *nm* veto; **droit de ~** right of veto; **mettre** *ou* **opposer un ~ à** to veto.

vêtu, e [vɛty] *pp de* **vêtir** ♦ *adj*: **~ de** dressed in, wearing; **chaudement ~** warmly dressed.

vétuste [vetyst(ə)] *adj* ancient, timeworn.

vétusté [vetyste] *nf* age, delapidation.

veuf, veuve [vœf, vœv] *adj* widowed ♦ *nm* widower ♦ *nf* widow.

veuille [vœj], **veuillez** [vœje] *etc vb voir* **vouloir**.

veule [vøl] *adj* spineless.

veulent [vœl] *etc vb voir* **vouloir**.

veulerie [vølʀi] *nf* spinelessness.

veut [vø] *vb voir* **vouloir**.

veuvage [vœvaʒ] *nm* widowhood.

veuve [vœv] *adj f*, *nf voir* **veuf**.

veux [vø] *vb voir* **vouloir**.

vexant, e [vɛksɑ̃, -ɑ̃t] *adj* (*contrariant*) annoying; (*blessant*) upsetting.

vexations [vɛksasjɔ̃] *nfpl* humiliations.

vexatoire [vɛksatwaʀ] *adj*: **mesures ~s** harassment *sg*.

vexer [vɛkse] *vt* to hurt, upset; **se ~** *vi* to be hurt, get upset.

VF *sigle f* (*CINÉ*) = *version française.*

VHF *sigle f* (= *Very High Frequency*) VHF.

via [vja] *prép* via.

viabiliser [vjabilize] *vt* to provide with services (*water etc*).

viabilité [vjabilite] *nf* viability; (*d'un chemin*) practicability.

viable [vjabl(ə)] *adj* viable.

viaduc [vjadyk] *nm* viaduct.

viager, ère [vjaʒe, -ɛʀ] *adj*: **rente ~ère** life annuity ♦ *nm*: **mettre en ~** to sell in return for a life annuity.

viande [vjɑ̃d] *nf* meat.

viatique [vjatik] *nm* (*REL*) viaticum; (*fig*) provisions *pl ou* money for the journey.

vibrant, e [vibʀɑ̃, -ɑ̃t] *adj* vibrating; (*voix*) vibrant; (*émouvant*) emotive.

vibraphone [vibʀafɔn] *nm* vibraphone, vibes *pl*.

vibraphoniste [vibʀafɔnist(ə)] *nm/f* vibraphone player.

vibration [vibʀasjɔ̃] *nf* vibration.

vibratoire [vibʀatwaʀ] *adj* vibratory.

vibrer [vibʀe] *vi* to vibrate; (*son, voix*) to be vibrant; (*fig*) to be stirred; **faire ~** to (cause to) vibrate; to stir, thrill.

vibromasseur [vibʀomasœʀ] *nm* vibrator.

vicaire [vikɛʀ] *nm* curate.

vice... [vis] *préfixe* vice-.

vice [vis] *nm* vice; (*défaut*) fault; **~ caché** (*COMM*) latent *ou* inherent defect; **~ de forme** legal flaw *ou* irregularity.

vice-consul [viskɔ̃syl] *nm* vice-consul.

vice-présidence [vispʀezidɑ̃s] *nf* (*d'un pays*) vice-presidency; (*d'une société*) vice-presidency, vice-chairmanship (*BRIT*).

vice-président, e [vispʀezidɑ̃, -ɑ̃t] *nm/f* vice-president; vice-chairman.

vice-roi [visʀwa] *nm* viceroy.

vice-versa [visevɛʀsa] *adv* vice versa.

vichy [viʃi] *nm* (*toile*) gingham; (*eau*) Vichy water; **carottes V~** boiled carrots.

vichyssois, e [viʃiswa, -waz] *adj* of *ou* from Vichy, Vichy *cpd* ♦ *nf* (*soupe*) vichyssoise (soup), *cream of leek and potato soup* ♦ *nm/f*: **V~, e** native *ou* inhabitant of Vichy.

vicié, e [visje] *adj* (*air*) polluted, tainted; (*JUR*) invalidated.

vicier [visje] *vt* (*JUR*) to invalidate.

vicieux, euse [visjø, -øz] *adj* (*pervers*) dirty(-minded); (*méchant*) nasty; (*fautif*) incorrect, wrong.

vicinal, e, aux [visinal, -o] *adj*: **chemin ~** byroad, byway.

vicissitudes [visisityd] *nfpl* (trials and) tribulations.

vicomte [vikɔ̃t] *nm* viscount.

vicomtesse [vikɔ̃tɛs] *nf* viscountess.

victime [viktim] *nf* victim; (*d'accident*) casualty; **être (la) ~ de** to be the victim of; **être ~ d'une attaque/d'un accident** to suffer a stroke/be involved in an accident.

victoire [viktwaʀ] *nf* victory.

victorieusement [viktɔʀjøzmɑ̃] *adv* triumphantly, victoriously.

victorieux, euse [viktɔʀjø, -øz] *adj* victorious; (*sourire, attitude*) triumphant.

victuailles [viktɥɑj] *nfpl* provisions.

vidange [vidɑ̃ʒ] *nf* (*d'un fossé, réservoir*) emptying; (*AUTO*) oil change; (*de lavabo: bonde*) waste outlet; **~s** *nfpl* (*matières*) sewage *sg*; **faire la ~** (*AUTO*) to change the oil, do an oil change; **tuyau de ~** drainage pipe.

vidanger [vidɑ̃ʒe] *vt* to empty; **faire ~ la voiture** to have the oil changed in one's car.

vide [vid] *adj* empty ♦ *nm* (*PHYSIQUE*) vacuum; (*espace*) (empty) space, gap; (*sous soi: dans une falaise etc*) drop; (*futilité, néant*) void; **~ de** empty of; (*de sens etc*) devoid of; **sous ~** *adv* in a vacuum; **emballé sous ~** vacuum-packed; **regarder dans le ~** to stare into space; **avoir peur du ~** to be afraid of heights; **parler dans le ~** to waste one's breath; **faire le ~** (*dans son esprit*) to make one's mind go blank; **faire le ~ autour de qn** to isolate sb; **à ~** *adv* (*sans occupants*) empty; (*sans charge*) unladen; (*TECH*) without gripping *ou* being in gear.

vidé, e [vide] *adj* (*épuisé*) done in, all in.

vidéo [video] *nf, adj inv* video; **~ inverse** reverse video.

vidéocassette [videokasɛt] *nf* video cassette.

vidéoclub [videoklœb] *nm* video club.

vidéodisque [videodisk] *nm* videodisc.

vide-ordures [vidɔʀdyʀ] *nm inv* (rubbish) chute.

vidéotex [videotɛks] *nm* ® teletext.

vide-poches [vidpɔʃ] *nm inv* tidy; (*AUTO*) glove compartment.

vide-pomme [vidpɔm] *nm inv* apple-corer.

vider [vide] *vt* to empty; (*CULIN: volaille, poisson*) to gut, clean out; (*régler: querelle*) to settle; (*fatiguer*) to wear out; (*fam: expulser*) to throw out, chuck out; **se ~** *vi* to empty; **~ les lieux** to quit *ou* vacate the premises.

videur [vidœʀ] *nm* (*de boîte de nuit*) bouncer.

vie [vi] *nf* life (*pl* lives); **être en ~** to be alive; **sans ~** lifeless; **à ~** for life; **membre à ~** life member; **dans la ~ courante** in every-

day life; **avoir la ~ dure** to have nine lives; to die hard; **mener la ~ dure à qn** to make life a misery for sb.

vieil [vjɛj] *adj m voir* **vieux**.

vieillard [vjɛjaʀ] *nm* old man; **les ~s** old people, the elderly.

vieille [vjɛj] *adj f, nf voir* **vieux**.

vieilleries [vjɛjʀi] *nfpl* old things *ou* stuff *sg*.

vieillesse [vjɛjɛs] *nf* old age; (*vieillards*): **la ~** the old *pl*, the elderly *pl*.

vieilli, e [vjeji] *adj* (*marqué par l'âge*) aged; (*suranné*) dated.

vieillir [vjejiʀ] *vi* (*prendre de l'âge*) to grow old; (*population, vin*) to age; (*doctrine, auteur*) to become dated ♦ *vt* to age; **il a beaucoup vieilli** he has aged a lot; **se ~** to make o.s. older.

vieillissement [vjejismɑ̃] *nm* growing old; ageing.

vieillot, te [vjɛjo, -ɔt] *adj* antiquated, quaint.

vielle [vjɛl] *nf* hurdy-gurdy.

viendrai [vjɛ̃dʀe] *etc vb voir* **venir**.

Vienne [vjɛn] *n* (*en Autriche*) Vienna.

vienne [vjɛn], **viens** [vjɛ̃] *etc vb voir* **venir**.

viennois, e [vjɛnwa, -waz] *adj* Viennese.

vierge [vjɛʀʒ(ə)] *adj* virgin; (*film*) blank; (*page*) clean, blank; (*jeune fille*): **être ~** to be a virgin ♦ *nf* virgin; (*signe*): **la V~** Virgo, the Virgin; **être de la V~** to be Virgo; **~ de** (*sans*) free from, unsullied by.

Viêt-nam, Vietnam [vjɛtnam] *nm*: **le ~** Vietnam; **le ~ du Nord/du Sud** North/South Vietnam.

vietnamien, ne [vjɛtnamjɛ̃, -ɛn] *adj* Vietnamese ♦ *nm* (*LING*) Vietnamese ♦ *nm/f*: **V~, ne** Vietnamese; **V~, ne du Nord/Sud** North/South Vietnamese.

vieux (vieil), vieille [vjø, vjɛj] *adj* old ♦ *nm/f* old man/woman ♦ *nmpl*: **les ~** the old, old people; (*fam: parents*) the old folk *ou* ones; **un petit ~** a little old man; **mon ~/ma vieille** (*fam*) old man/girl; **pauvre ~** poor old soul; **prendre un coup de ~** to put years on; **se faire ~** to make o.s. look older; **un ~ de la vieille** one of the old brigade; **~ garçon** *nm* bachelor; **~ jeu** *adj inv* old-fashioned; **~ rose** *adj inv* old rose; **vieil or** *adj inv* old gold; **vieille fille** *nf* spinster.

vif, vive [vif, viv] *adj* (*animé*) lively; (*alerte*) sharp, quick; (*brusque*) sharp, brusque; (*aigu*) sharp; (*lumière, couleur*) brilliant; (*air*) crisp; (*vent, émotion*) keen; (*froid*) bitter; (*fort: regret, déception*) great, deep; (*vivant*): **brûlé ~** burnt alive; **eau vive** running water; **de vive voix** personally; **piquer qn au ~** to cut sb to the quick; **tailler dans le ~** to cut into the living flesh; **à ~** (*plaie*) open; **avoir les nerfs à ~** to be on edge; **sur le ~** (*ART*) from life; **entrer dans le ~ du sujet** to get to the very heart of the matter.

vif-argent [vifaʀʒɑ̃] *nm inv* quicksilver.

vigie [viʒi] *nf* (*matelot*) look-out; (*poste*) look-out post, crow's nest.

vigilance [viʒilɑ̃s] *nf* vigilance.
vigilant, e [viʒilɑ̃, -ɑ̃t] *adj* vigilant.
vigile [viʒil] *nm* (*veilleur de nuit*) (night) watchman; (*police privée*) vigilante.
vigne [viɲ] *nf* (*plante*) vine; (*plantation*) vineyard; ~ **vierge** Virginia creeper.
vigneron [viɲʀɔ̃] *nm* wine grower.
vignette [viɲɛt] *nf* (*motif*) vignette; (*de marque*) manufacturer's label *ou* seal; (*petite illustration*) (small) illustration; (*ADMIN*) ≈ (road) tax disc (*BRIT*), ≈ license plate sticker (*US*); (: *sur médicament*) price label (*on medicines for reimbursement by Social Security*).
vignoble [viɲɔbl(ə)] *nm* (*plantation*) vineyard; (*vignes d'une région*) vineyards *pl*.
vigoureusement [viguʀøzmɑ̃] *adv* vigorously.
vigoureux, euse [viguʀø, -øz] *adj* vigorous, robust.
vigueur [vigœʀ] *nf* vigour (*BRIT*), vigor (*US*); **être/entrer en** ~ to be in/come into force; **en** ~ current.
vil, e [vil] *adj* vile, base; **à** ~ **prix** at a very low price.
vilain, e [vilɛ̃, -ɛn] *adj* (*laid*) ugly; (*affaire, blessure*) nasty; (*pas sage: enfant*) naughty ♦ *nm* (*paysan*) villein, villain; **ça va tourner au** ~ things are going to turn nasty; ~ **mot** bad word.
vilainement [vilɛnmɑ̃] *adv* badly.
vilebrequin [vilbʀəkɛ̃] *nm* (*outil*) (bit-)brace; (*AUTO*) crankshaft.
vilenie [vilni] *nf* vileness *no pl*, baseness *no pl*.
vilipender [vilipɑ̃de] *vt* to revile, vilify.
villa [vila] *nf* (detached) house.
village [vilaʒ] *nm* village; ~ **de toile** tent village; ~ **de vacances** holiday village.
villageois, e [vilaʒwa, -waz] *adj* village *cpd* ♦ *nm/f* villager.
ville [vil] *nf* town; (*importante*) city; (*administration*): **la** ~ ≈ the Corporation; ≈ the (town) council; **aller en** ~ to go to town; **habiter en** ~ to live in town; ~ **nouvelle** new town.
ville-champignon, *pl* **villes-champignons** [vilʃɑ̃piɲɔ̃] *nf* boom town.
ville-dortoir, *pl* **villes-dortoirs** [vildɔʀtwaʀ] *nf* dormitory town.
villégiature [vileʒjatyʀ] *nf* (*séjour*) holiday; (*lieu*) (holiday) resort.
vin [vɛ̃] *nm* wine; **avoir le** ~ **gai/triste** to get happy/miserable after a few drinks; ~ **blanc/rosé/rouge** white/rosé/red wine; ~ **d'honneur** reception (*with wine and snacks*); ~ **de messe** altar wine; ~ **ordinaire** *ou* **de table** table wine; ~ **de pays** local wine; *voir aussi* **AOC; VDQS.**
vinaigre [vinɛgʀ(ə)] *nm* vinegar; **tourner au** ~ (*fig*) to turn sour; ~ **de vin/d'alcool** wine/spirit vinegar.
vinaigrette [vinɛgʀɛt] *nf* vinaigrette, French dressing.
vinaigrier [vinɛgʀije] *nm* (*fabricant*) vinegar-

maker; (*flacon*) vinegar cruet *ou* bottle.
vinasse [vinas] *nf* (*péj*) cheap wine, plonk (*BRIT*).
vindicatif, ive [vɛ̃dikatif, -iv] *adj* vindictive.
vindicte [vɛ̃dikt(ə)] *nf*: **désigner qn à la** ~ **publique** to expose sb to public condemnation.
vineux, euse [vinø, -øz] *adj* win(e)y.
vingt [vɛ̃, vɛ̃t + vowel and in 22, 23 etc] *num* twenty; ~**-quatre heures sur** ~**-quatre** twenty-four hours a day, round the clock.
vingtaine [vɛ̃tɛn] *nf*: **une** ~ **(de)** around twenty, twenty or so.
vingtième [vɛ̃tjɛm] *num* twentieth.
vinicole [vinikɔl] *adj* (*production*) wine *cpd*; (*région*) wine-growing.
vinification [vinifikasjɔ̃] *nf* wine-making, wine production; (*des sucres*) vinification.
vinyle [vinil] *nm* vinyl.
viol [vjɔl] *nm* (*d'une femme*) rape; (*d'un lieu sacré*) violation.
violacé, e [vjɔlase] *adj* purplish, mauvish.
violation [vjɔlasjɔ̃] *nf* desecration; violation; (*d'un droit*) breach.
violemment [vjɔlamɑ̃] *adv* violently.
violence [vjɔlɑ̃s] *nf* violence; ~**s** *nfpl* acts of violence; **faire** ~ **à qn** to do violence to sb; **se faire** ~ to force o.s.
violent, e [vjɔlɑ̃, -ɑ̃t] *adj* violent; (*remède*) drastic; (*besoin, désir*) intense, urgent.
violenter [vjɔlɑ̃te] *vt* to assault (sexually).
violer [vjɔle] *vt* (*femme*) to rape; (*sépulture*) to desecrate, violate; (*loi, traité*) to violate.
violet, te [vjɔlɛ, -ɛt] *adj, nm* purple, mauve ♦ *nf* (*fleur*) violet.
violeur [vjɔlœʀ] *nm* rapist.
violine [vjɔlin] *nf* deep purple.
violon [vjɔlɔ̃] *nm* violin; (*dans la musique folklorique etc*) fiddle; (*fam: prison*) lock-up; **premier** ~ first violin; ~ **d'Ingres** (artistic) hobby.
violoncelle [vjɔlɔ̃sɛl] *nm* cello.
violoncelliste [vjɔlɔ̃selist(ə)] *nm/f* cellist.
violoniste [vjɔlɔnist(ə)] *nm/f* violinist, violin-player; (*folklorique etc*) fiddler.
VIP *sigle m* (= *Very Important Person*) VIP.
vipère [vipɛʀ] *nf* viper, adder.
virage [viʀaʒ] *nm* (*d'un véhicule*) turn; (*d'une route, piste*) bend; (*CHIMIE*) change in colour (*BRIT*) *ou* color (*US*); (*de cuti-réaction*) positive reaction; (*PHOTO*) toning; (*fig: POL*) about-turn; **prendre un** ~ to go into a bend, take a bend; ~ **sans visibilité** blind bend.
viral, e, aux [viʀal, -o] *adj* viral.
virée [viʀe] *nf* (*courte*) run; (: *à pied*) walk; (*longue*) trip; hike, walking tour.
virement [viʀmɑ̃] *nm* (*COMM*) transfer; ~ **bancaire** (bank) credit transfer, ≈ (bank) giro transfer (*BRIT*); ~ **postal** Post office credit transfer, ≈ Girobank ® transfer (*BRIT*).
virent [viʀ] *vb voir* **voir.**
virer [viʀe] *vt* (*COMM*): ~ **qch (sur)** to transfer sth (into); (*PHOTO*) to tone; (*fam: renvoyer*) to

sack, boot out ♦ *vi* to turn; (*CHIMIE*) to change colour (*BRIT*) *ou* color (*US*); (*cutiréaction*) to come up positive; (*PHOTO*) to tone; ~ **au bleu** to turn blue; ~ **de bord** to tack; (*fig*) to change tack; ~ **sur l'aile** to bank.

virevolte [viʀvɔlt(ə)] *nf* twirl; (*d'avis, d'opinion*) about-turn.

virevolter [viʀvɔlte] *vi* to twirl around.

virginal, e, aux [viʀʒinal, -o] *adj* virginal.

virginité [viʀʒinite] *nf* virginity; (*fig*) purity.

virgule [viʀgyl] *nf* comma; (*MATH*) point; **4 ~ 2** 4 point 2; ~ **flottante** floating decimal.

viril, e [viʀil] *adj* (*propre à l'homme*) masculine; (*énergique, courageux*) manly, virile.

viriliser [viʀilize] *vt* to make (more) manly *ou* masculine.

virilité [viʀilite] *nf* (*attributs masculins*) masculinity; (*fermeté, courage*) manliness; (*sexuelle*) virility.

virologie [viʀɔlɔʒi] *nf* virology.

virtualité [viʀtɥalite] *nf* virtuality; potentiality.

virtuel, le [viʀtɥɛl] *adj* potential; (*théorique*) virtual.

virtuellement [viʀtɥɛlmɑ̃] *adj* potentially; (*presque*) virtually.

virtuose [viʀtɥoz] *nm/f* (*MUS*) virtuoso; (*gén*) master.

virtuosité [viʀtɥozite] *nf* virtuosity; masterliness, masterful skills *pl*.

virulence [viʀylɑ̃s] *nf* virulence.

virulent, e [viʀylɑ̃, -ɑ̃t] *adj* virulent.

virus [viʀys] *nm* virus.

vis *vb* [vi] *voir* **voir, vivre** ♦ *nf* [vis] screw; ~ **à tête plate/ronde** flat-headed/round-headed screw; ~ **platinées** (*AUTO*) (contact) points; ~ **sans fin** worm, endless screw.

visa [viza] *nm* (*sceau*) stamp; (*validation de passeport*) visa; ~ **de censure** (censor's) certificate.

visage [vizaʒ] *nm* face; **à ~ découvert** (*franchement*) openly.

visagiste [vizaʒist(ə)] *nm/f* beautician.

vis-à-vis [vizavi] *adv* face to face ♦ *nm* person opposite; house *etc* opposite; ~ **de** *prép* opposite; (*fig*) towards, vis-à-vis; **en ~** facing *ou* opposite each other; **sans ~** (*immeuble*) with an open outlook.

viscéral, e, aux [viseʀal, -o] *adj* (*fig*) deep-seated, deep-rooted.

viscères [viseʀ] *nmpl* intestines, entrails.

viscose [viskoz] *nf* viscose.

viscosité [viskozite] *nf* viscosity.

visée [vize] *nf* (*avec une arme*) aiming; (*ARPENTAGE*) sighting; ~**s** *nfpl* (*intentions*) designs; **avoir des ~s sur qn/qch** to have designs on sb/sth.

viser [vize] *vi* to aim ♦ *vt* to aim at; (*concerner*) to be aimed *ou* directed at; (*apposer un visa sur*) to stamp, visa; ~ **à qch/faire** to aim at sth/at doing *ou* to do.

viseur [vizœʀ] *nm* (*d'arme*) sights *pl*; (*PHOTO*) viewfinder.

visibilité [vizibilite] *nf* visibility; **sans ~** (*pilotage, virage*) blind *cpd*.

visible [vizibl(ə)] *adj* visible; (*disponible*): **est-il ~?** can he see me?, will he see visitors?

visiblement [vizibləmɑ̃] *adv* visibly, obviously.

visière [vizjɛʀ] *nf* (*de casquette*) peak; (*qui s'attache*) eyeshade.

vision [vizjɔ̃] *nf* vision; (*sens*) (eye)sight, vision; (*fait de voir*): **la ~ de** the sight of; **première ~** (*CINÉ*) first showing.

visionnaire [vizjɔnɛʀ] *adj, nm/f* visionary.

visionner [vizjɔne] *vt* to view.

visionneuse [vizjɔnøz] *nf* viewer.

visiophone [vizjɔfɔn] *nm* videophone.

visite [vizit] *nf* visit; (*visiteur*) visitor; (*touristique: d'un musée etc*) tour; (*COMM: de représentant*) call; (*expertise, d'inspection*) inspection; (*médicale, à domicile*) visit, call; **la ~** (*MÉD*) medical examination; (*MIL: d'entrée*) medicals *pl*; (: *quotidienne*) sick parade; **faire une ~ à qn** to call on sb, pay sb a visit; **rendre ~ à qn** to visit sb, pay sb a visit; **être en ~ (chez qn)** to be visiting (sb); **heures de ~** (*hôpital, prison*) visiting hours; **le droit de ~** (*JUR: aux enfants*) right of access, access; ~ **de douane** customs inspection *ou* examination.

visiter [vizite] *vt* to visit; (*musée, ville*) to visit, go round.

visiteur, euse [vizitœʀ, -øz] *nm/f* visitor; ~ **des douanes** customs inspector; ~ **médical** medical rep(resentative); ~ **de prison** prison visitor.

vison [vizɔ̃] *nm* mink.

visqueux, euse [viskø, -øz] *adj* viscous; (*péj*) gooey; (: *manières*) slimy.

visser [vise] *vt*: ~ **qch** (*fixer, serrer*) to screw sth on.

visu [vizy]: **de ~** *adv* with one's own eyes.

visualisation [vizɥalizasjɔ̃] *nf* (*INFORM*) display; **écran de ~** visual display unit (VDU).

visualiser [vizɥalize] *vt* to visualize; (*INFORM*) to display, bring up on screen.

visuel, le [vizɥɛl] *adj* visual ♦ *nm* (visual) display; (*INFORM*) visual display unit (VDU).

visuellement [vizɥɛlmɑ̃] *adv* visually.

vit [vi] *vb voir* **vivre, voir**.

vital, e, aux [vital, -o] *adj* vital.

vitalité [vitalite] *nf* vitality.

vitamine [vitamin] *nf* vitamin.

vitaminé, e [vitamine] *adj* with (added) vitamins.

vitaminique [vitaminik] *adj* vitamin *cpd*.

vite [vit] *adv* (*rapidement*) quickly, fast; (*sans délai*) quickly; soon; **faire ~** (*agir rapidement*) to act fast; (*se dépêcher*) to be quick; **ce sera ~ fini** this will soon be finished; **viens ~** come quick(ly).

vitesse [vitɛs] *nf* speed; (*AUTO: dispositif*) gear;

faire de la ~ to drive fast *ou* at speed; **prendre qn de ~** to outstrip sb, get ahead of sb; **prendre de la ~** to pick up *ou* gather speed; **à toute ~** at full *ou* top speed; **en perte de ~** (*avion*) losing lift; (*fig*) losing momentum; **changer de ~** (*AUTO*) to change gear; **~ acquise** momentum; **~ de croisière** cruising speed; **~ de pointe** top speed; **~ du son** speed of sound.

viticole [vitikɔl] *adj* (*industrie*) wine *cpd*; (*région*) wine-growing.

viticulteur [vitikyltœʀ] *nm* wine grower.

viticulture [vitikyltyʀ] *nf* wine growing.

vitrage [vitʀaʒ] *nm* (*cloison*) glass partition; (*toit*) glass roof; (*rideau*) net curtain.

vitrail, aux [vitʀaj, -o] *nm* stained-glass window.

vitre [vitʀ(ə)] *nf* (window) pane; (*de portière, voiture*) window.

vitré, e [vitʀe] *adj* glass *cpd*.

vitrer [vitʀe] *vt* to glaze.

vitreux, euse [vitʀø, -øz] *adj* vitreous; (*terne*) glassy.

vitrier [vitʀije] *nm* glazier.

vitrifier [vitʀifje] *vt* to vitrify; (*parquet*) to glaze.

vitrine [vitʀin] *nf* (*devanture*) (shop) window; (*étalage*) display; (*petite armoire*) display cabinet; **en ~** in the window, on display; **~ publicitaire** display case, showcase.

vitriol [vitʀijɔl] *nm* vitriol; **au ~** (*fig*) vitriolic.

vitupérations [vityperasjɔ̃] *nfpl* invective *sg*.

vitupérer [vitypere] *vi* to rant and rave; **~ contre** to rail against.

vivable [vivabl(ə)] *adj* (*personne*) livable-with; (*endroit*) fit to live in.

vivace *adj* [vivas] (*arbre, plante*) hardy; (*fig*) enduring ♦ [vivatʃe] (*MUS*) vivace.

vivacité [vivasite] *nf* (*voir vif*) liveliness, vivacity; sharpness; brilliance.

vivant, e [vivã, -ãt] *vb voir* **vivre** ♦ *adj* (*qui vit*) living, alive; (*animé*) lively; (*preuve, exemple*) living; (*langue*) modern ♦ *nm*: **du ~ de qn** in sb's lifetime; **les ~s et les morts** the living and the dead.

vivarium [vivaʀjɔm] *nm* vivarium.

vivats [viva] *nmpl* cheers.

vive [viv] *adj f voir* **vif** ♦ *vb voir* **vivre** ♦ *excl*: **~ le roi!** long live the king!; **~ les vacances!** hurrah for the holidays!

vivement [vivmã] *adv* vivaciously; sharply ♦ *excl*: **~ les vacances!** I can't wait for the holidays!, roll on the holidays!

viveur [vivœʀ] *nm* (*péj*) high liver, pleasure-seeker.

vivier [vivje] *nm* (*au restaurant etc*) fish tank; (*étang*) fishpond.

vivifiant, e [vivifjã, -ãt] *adj* invigorating.

vivifier [vivifje] *vt* to invigorate; (*fig: souvenirs, sentiments*) to liven up, enliven.

vivipare [vivipaʀ] *adj* viviparous.

vivisection [vivisɛksjɔ̃] *nf* vivisection.

vivoter [vivɔte] *vi* (*personne*) to scrape a living, get by; (*fig: affaire etc*) to struggle along.

vivre [vivʀ(ə)] *vi, vt* to live ♦ *nm*: **le ~ et le logement** board and lodging ♦ **~s** *nmpl* provisions, food supplies; **il vit encore** he is still alive; **se laisser ~** to take life as it comes; **ne plus ~** (*être anxieux*) to live on one's nerves; **il a vécu** (*eu une vie aventureuse*) he has seen life; **ce régime a vécu** this regime has had its day; **être facile à ~** to be easy to get on with; **faire ~ qn** (*pourvoir à sa subsistance*) to provide (a living) for sb; **~ mal** (*chichement*) to have a meagre existence; **~ de** (*salaire etc*) to live on.

vivrier, ière [vivʀije, -jɛʀ] *adj* food-producing *cpd*.

vlan [vlɑ̃] *excl* wham!, bang!

VO *sigle f* (*CINÉ*: = *version originale*): **voir un film en ~** to see a film in its original language.

vᵒ *abr* = **verso**.

vocable [vɔkabl(ə)] *nm* term.

vocabulaire [vɔkabylɛʀ] *nm* vocabulary.

vocal, e, aux [vɔkal, -o] *adj* vocal.

vocalique [vɔkalik] *adj* vocalic, vowel *cpd*.

vocalise [vɔkaliz] *nf* singing exercise.

vocaliser [vɔkalize] *vi* (*LING*) to vocalize; (*MUS*) to do one's singing exercises.

vocation [vɔkasjɔ̃] *nf* vocation, calling; **avoir la ~** to have a vocation.

vociférations [vɔsiferasjɔ̃] *nfpl* cries of rage, screams.

vociférer [vɔsifere] *vi, vt* to scream.

vodka [vɔdka] *nf* vodka.

vœu, x [vø] *nm* wish; (*à Dieu*) vow; **faire ~ de** to take a vow of; **avec tous nos ~x** with every good wish *ou* our best wishes; **~x de bonheur** best wishes for your future happiness; **~x de bonne année** best wishes for the New Year.

vogue [vɔg] *nf* fashion, vogue; **en ~** in fashion, in vogue.

voguer [vɔge] *vi* to sail.

voici [vwasi] *prép* (*pour introduire, désigner*) here is + *sg*, here are + *pl*; **et ~ que ...** and now it (*ou* he) ...; **il est parti ~ 3 ans** he left 3 years ago; **~ une semaine que je l'ai vue** it's a week since I've seen her; **me ~** here I am; *voir aussi* **voilà**.

voie [vwa] *vb voir* **voir** ♦ *nf* way; (*RAIL*) track, line; (*AUTO*) lane; **par ~ buccale** *ou* **orale** orally; **par ~ rectale** rectally; **suivre la ~ hiérarchique** to go through official channels; **ouvrir/montrer la ~** to open up/show the way; **être en bonne ~** to be shaping *ou* going well; **mettre qn sur la ~** to put sb on the right track; **être en ~ d'achèvement/de rénovation** to be nearing completion/in the process of renovation; **à ~ étroite** narrow-gauge; **à ~ unique** single-track; **route à 2/3 ~s** 2-/3-lane road; **par la ~ aérienne/maritime** by air/sea; **~ d'eau** (*NAVIG*) leak; **~ express** expressway; **~ de fait** (*JUR*) assault (and battery); ~ **ferrée** track; railway line (*BRIT*), railroad (*US*); **par ~ ferrée** by rail, by railroad; **~ de garage** (*RAIL*) siding; **la ~ lactée** the Milky Way; **~ navigable** waterway; **~ prioritaire** (*AUTO*) road with right of way; **~ privée** private road; **la ~ publique** the public highway.

voilà [vwala] *prép* (*en désignant*) there is + *sg*, there are + *pl*; **les ~ ou voici** here *ou* there they are; **en ~ ou voici un** here's one, there's one; **~ ou voici deux ans** two years ago; **~ ou voici deux ans que** it's two years since; **et ~!** there we are!; **~ tout** that's all; "**~ ou voici**" (*en offrant etc*) "there *ou* here you are".

voilage [vwalaʒ] *nm* (*rideau*) net curtain; (*tissu*) net.

voile [vwal] *nm* veil; (*tissu léger*) net ♦ *nf* sail; (*sport*) sailing; **prendre le ~** to take the veil; **mettre à la ~** to make way under sail; **~ du palais** *nm* soft palate, velum; **~ au poumon** *nm* shadow on the lung.

voiler [vwale] *vt* to veil; (*PHOTO*) to fog; (*fausser: roue*) to buckle; (: *bois*) to warp; **se ~** *vi* (*lune, regard*) to mist over; (*ciel*) to grow hazy; (*voix*) to become husky; (*roue, disque*) to buckle; (*planche*) to warp; **se ~ la face** to hide one's face.

voilette [vwalɛt] *nf* (*hat*) veil.

voilier [vwalje] *nm* sailing ship; (*de plaisance*) sailing boat.

voilure [vwalyR] *nf* (*de voilier*) sails *pl*; (*d'avion*) aerofoils *pl* (*BRIT*), airfoils *pl* (*US*); (*de parachute*) canopy.

voir [vwaR] *vi, vt* to see; **se ~**: **se ~ critiquer/transformer** to be criticized/transformed; **cela se voit** (*cela arrive*) it happens; (*c'est visible*) that's obvious, it shows; **~ à faire qch** to see to it that sth is done; **~ loin** (*fig*) to be far-sighted; **~ venir** (*fig*) to wait and see; **faire ~ qch à qn** to show sb sth; **en faire ~ à qn** (*fig*) to give sb a hard time; **ne pas pouvoir ~ qn** (*fig*) not to be able to stand sb; **regardez ~** just look; **montrez ~** show (me); **dites ~** tell me; **voyons!** let's see now; (*indignation etc*) come (along) now!; **c'est à ~!** we'll see!; **c'est ce qu'on va ~!** we'll see about that!; **avoir quelque chose à ~ avec** to have something to do with; **ça n'a rien à ~ avec lui** that has nothing to do with him.

voire [vwaR] *adv* indeed; nay; or even.

voirie [vwaRi] *nf* highway maintenance; (*administration*) highways department; (*enlèvement des ordures*) refuse (*BRIT*) *ou* garbage (*US*) collection.

vois [vwa] *vb voir* **voir**.

voisin, e [vwazɛ̃, -in] *adj* (*proche*) neighbouring (*BRIT*), neighboring (*US*); (*contigu*) next; (*ressemblant*) connected ♦ *nm/f* neighbo(u)r; (*de table, de dortoir etc*) person next to me (*ou* him *etc*); **~ de palier** neighbo(u)r across the landing (*BRIT*) *ou* hall (*US*).

voisinage [vwazinaʒ] *nm* (*proximité*) proximity; (*environs*) vicinity; (*quartier, voisins*) neighbourhood (*BRIT*), neighborhood (*US*); **relations de bon ~** neighbo(u)rly terms.

voisiner [vwazine] *vi*: **~ avec** to be side by side with.

voit [vwa] *vb voir* **voir**.

voiture [vwatyR] *nf* car; (*wagon*) coach, carriage; **en ~!** all aboard!; **~ à bras** handcart; **~ d'enfant** pram (*BRIT*), baby carriage (*US*); **~ d'infirme** invalid carriage; **~ de sport** sports car.

voiture-lit, *pl* **voitures-lits** [vwatyRli] *nf* sleeper.

voiture-restaurant, *pl* **voitures-restaurants** [vwatyRRɛstɔRɑ̃] *nf* dining car.

voix [vwa] *nf* voice; (*POL*) vote; **la ~ de la conscience/raison** the voice of conscience/reason; **à haute ~** aloud; **à ~ basse** in a low voice; **faire la grosse ~** to speak gruffly; **avoir de la ~** to have a good voice; **rester sans ~** to be speechless; **~ de basse/ténor** *etc* bass/tenor *etc* voice; **à 2/4 ~** (*MUS*) in 2/4 parts; **avoir ~ au chapitre** to have a say in the matter; **mettre aux ~** to put to the vote; **~ off** voice-over.

vol [vɔl] *nm* (*mode de locomotion*) flying; (*trajet, voyage, groupe d'oiseaux*) flight; (*mode d'appropriation*) theft, stealing; (*larcin*) theft; **à ~ d'oiseau** as the crow flies; **au ~: attraper qch au ~** to catch sth as it flies past; **saisir une remarque au ~** to pick up a passing remark; **prendre son ~** to take flight; **de haut ~** (*fig*) of the highest order; **en ~** in flight; **~ avec effraction** breaking and entering *no pl*, break-in; **~ à l'étalage** shoplifting *no pl*; **~ libre** hang-gliding; **~ à main armée** armed robbery; **~ de nuit** night flight; **~ plané** (*AVIAT*) glide, gliding *no pl*; **~ à la tire** pick-pocketing *no pl*; **~ à voile** gliding.

vol. *abr* (= *volume*) vol.

volage [vɔlaʒ] *adj* fickle.

volaille [vɔlaj] *nf* (*oiseaux*) poultry *pl*; (*viande*) poultry *no pl*; (*oiseau*) fowl.

volailler [vɔlaje] *nm* poulterer.

volant, e [vɔlɑ̃, -ɑ̃t] *adj voir* **feuille** *etc* ♦ *nm* (*d'automobile*) (steering) wheel; (*de commande*) wheel; (*objet lancé*) shuttlecock; (*jeu*) battledore and shuttlecock; (*bande de tissu*) flounce; (*feuillet détachable*) tear-off portion; **le personnel ~, les ~s** (*AVIAT*) the flight staff; **~ de sécurité** (*fig*) reserve, margin, safeguard.

volatil, e [vɔlatil] *adj* volatile.

volatile [vɔlatil] *nm* (*volaille*) bird; (*tout oiseau*) winged creature.

volatiliser [vɔlatilize]: **se ~** *vi* (*CHIMIE*) to volatilize; (*fig*) to vanish into thin air.

vol-au-vent [vɔlovɑ̃] *nm inv* vol-au-vent.

volcan [vɔlkɑ̃] *nm* volcano; (*fig: personne*) hothead.

volcanique [vɔlkanik] *adj* volcanic; (*fig: tem-*

pérament) volatile.

volcanologie [vɔlkanɔlɔʒi] *nf* vulcanology.

volcanologue [vɔlkanɔlɔg] *nm/f* vulcanologist.

volée [vɔle] *nf* (*groupe d'oiseaux*) flight, flock; (*TENNIS*) volley; ~ **de coups/de flèches** volley of blows/arrows; **à la** ~: **rattraper à la** ~ to catch in midair; **lancer à la** ~ to fling about; **semer à la** ~ to (sow) broadcast; **à toute** ~ (*sonner les cloches*) vigorously; (*lancer un projectile*) with full force; **de haute** ~ (*fig*) of the highest order.

voler [vɔle] *vi* (*avion, oiseau, fig*) to fly; (*voleur*) to steal ♦ *vt* (*objet*) to steal; (*personne*) to rob; ~ **en éclats** to smash to smithereens; ~ **de ses propres ailes** (*fig*) to stand on one's own two feet; ~ **au vent** to fly in the wind; ~ **qch à qn** to steal sth from sb.

volet [vɔlɛ] *nm* (*de fenêtre*) shutter; (*AVIAT*) flap; (*de feuillet, document*) section; (*fig: d'un plan*) facet; **trié sur le** ~ hand-picked.

voleter [vɔlte] *vi* to flutter (about).

voleur, euse [vɔlœʀ, -øz] *nm/f* thief (*pl* thieves) ♦ *adj* thieving.

volière [vɔljɛʀ] *nf* aviary.

volley(-ball) [vɔlɛ(bɔl)] *nm* volleyball.

volleyeur, euse [vɔlɛjœʀ, -øz] *nm/f* volleyball player.

volontaire [vɔlɔ̃tɛʀ] *adj* (*acte, activité*) voluntary; (*délibéré*) deliberate; (*caractère, personne: décidé*) self-willed ♦ *nm/f* volunteer.

volontairement [vɔlɔ̃tɛʀmɑ̃] *adv* voluntarily; deliberately.

volontariat [vɔlɔ̃taʀja] *nm* voluntary service.

volontarisme [vɔlɔ̃taʀism] *nm* voluntarism.

volontariste [vɔlɔ̃taʀist(ə)] *adj, nm/f* voluntarist.

volonté [vɔlɔ̃te] *nf* (*faculté de vouloir*) will; (*énergie, fermeté*) will(power); (*souhait, désir*) wish; **se servir/boire à** ~ to take/drink as much as one likes; **bonne** ~ goodwill, willingness; **mauvaise** ~ lack of goodwill, unwillingness.

volontiers [vɔlɔ̃tje] *adv* (*de bonne grâce*) willingly; (*avec plaisir*) willingly, gladly; (*habituellement, souvent*) readily, willingly; "~" "with pleasure", "I'd be glad to".

volt [vɔlt] *nm* volt.

voltage [vɔltaʒ] *nm* voltage.

volte-face [vɔltəfas] *nf inv* about-turn; (*fig*) about-turn, U-turn; **faire** ~ to do an about-turn; to do a U-turn.

voltige [vɔltiʒ] *nf* (*ÉQUITATION*) trick riding; (*au cirque*) acrobatics *sg*; (*AVIAT*) (aerial) acrobatics *sg*; **numéro de haute** ~ acrobatic act.

voltiger [vɔltiʒe] *vi* to flutter (about).

voltigeur [vɔltiʒœʀ] *nm* (*au cirque*) acrobat; (*MIL*) light infantryman.

voltmètre [vɔltmɛtʀ(ə)] *nm* voltmeter.

volubile [vɔlybil] *adj* voluble.

volubilis [vɔlybilis] *nm* convolvulus.

volume [vɔlym] *nm* volume; (*GÉOM: solide*)

solid.

volumineux, euse [vɔlyminø, -øz] *adj* voluminous, bulky.

volupté [vɔlypte] *nf* sensual delight *ou* pleasure.

voluptueusement [vɔlyptɥøzmɑ̃] *adv* voluptuously.

voluptueux, euse [vɔlyptɥø, -øz] *adj* voluptuous.

volute [vɔlyt] *nf* (*ARCHIT*) volute; ~ **de fumée** curl of smoke.

vomi [vɔmi] *nm* vomit.

vomir [vɔmiʀ] *vi* to vomit, be sick ♦ *vt* to vomit, bring up; (*fig*) to belch out, spew out; (*exécrer*) to loathe, abhor.

vomissement [vɔmismɑ̃] *nm* (*action*) vomiting *no pl*; **des** ~**s** vomit *sg*.

vomissure [vɔmisyʀ] *nf* vomit *no pl*.

vomitif [vɔmitif] *nm* emetic.

vont [vɔ̃] *vb voir* **aller**.

vorace [vɔʀas] *adj* voracious.

voracement [vɔʀasmɑ̃] *adv* voraciously.

voracité [vɔʀasite] *nf* voracity.

vos [vo] *adj possessif voir* **votre**.

Vosges [voʒ] *nfpl*: **les** ~ the Vosges.

vosgien, ne [voʒjɛ̃, -ɛn] *adj of ou* from the Vosges ♦ *nm/f* inhabitant *ou* native of the Vosges.

VOST *sigle f* (*CINÉ*: = *version originale sous-titrée*) sub-titled version.

votant, e [vɔtɑ̃, -ɑ̃t] *nm/f* voter.

vote [vɔt] *nm* vote; ~ **par correspondance/ procuration** postal/proxy vote; ~ **à main levée** vote by show of hands; ~ **secret**, ~ **à bulletins secrets** secret ballot.

voter [vɔte] *vi* to vote ♦ *vt* (*loi, décision*) to vote for.

votre [vɔtʀ(ə)], *pl* **vos** [vo] *adj possessif* your.

vôtre [votʀ(ə)] *pron*: **le** ~, **la** ~, **les** ~**s** yours; **les** ~**s** (*fig*) your family *ou* folks; **à la** ~ (*toast*) your (good) health!

voudrai [vudʀe] *etc vb voir* **vouloir**.

voué, e [vwe] *adj*: ~ **à** doomed to, destined for.

vouer [vwe] *vt*: ~ **qch à** (*Dieu/un saint*) to dedicate sth to; ~ **sa vie/son temps à** (*étude, cause etc*) to devote one's life/time to; ~ **une haine/amitié éternelle à qn** to vow undying hatred/friendship to sb.

════════════════════════ *MOT-CLÉ*

vouloir [vulwaʀ] *nm*: **le bon** ~ **de qn** sb's goodwill; sb's pleasure

♦ *vt* **1** (*exiger, désirer*) to want; ~ **faire/que qn fasse** to want to do/sb to do; **voulez-vous du thé?** would you like *ou* do you want some tea?; ~ **qch à qn** to wish sth for sb; **que me veut-il?** what does he want with me?; **que veux-tu que je te dise?** what do you want me to say?; **sans le** ~ (*involontairement*) without meaning to, unintentionally; **je voudrais ceci/faire** I would *ou* I'd like this/to do; **le**

hasard a voulu que ... as fate would have it, ...; **la tradition veut que** ... tradition demands that ...; ... **qui se veut moderne** ... which purports to be modern
2 (*consentir*): **je veux bien** (*bonne volonté*) I'll be happy to; (*concession*) fair enough, that's fine; **oui, si on veut** (*en quelque sorte*) yes, if you like; **comme tu veux** as you wish; (*en quelque sorte*) if you like; **veuillez attendre** please wait; **veuillez agréer** ... (*formule épistolaire*) yours faithfully
3: **en ~** (*être ambitieux*) to be out to win; **en ~ à qn** to bear sb a grudge; **je lui en veux d'avoir fait ça** I resent his having done that; **s'en ~ (de)** to be annoyed with o.s. (for); **il en veut à mon argent** he's after my money
4: **~ de** to want; **la compagnie ne veut plus de lui** the firm doesn't want him any more; **elle ne veut pas de son aide** she doesn't want his help
5: **~ dire** to mean.

voulu, e [vuly] *pp de* **vouloir ♦** *adj* (*requis*) required, requisite; (*délibéré*) deliberate, intentional.
voulus [vuly] *etc vb voir* **vouloir.**
vous [vu] *pron* you; (*objet indirect*) (to) you; (*réfléchi*) yourself (*pl* yourselves); (*réciproque*) each other **♦** *nm*: **employer le ~** (*vouvoyer*) to use the "vous" form; **~-même** yourself; **~-mêmes** yourselves.
voûte [vut] *nf* vault; **la ~ céleste** the vault of heaven; **~ du palais** (*ANAT*) roof of the mouth; **~ plantaire** arch (of the foot).
voûté, e [vute] *adj* vaulted, arched; (*dos, personne*) bent, stooped.
voûter [vute] *vt* (*ARCHIT*) to arch, vault; **se ~** *vi* (*dos, personne*) to become stooped.
vouvoiement [vuvwamɑ̃] *nm* use of formal "vous" form.
vouvoyer [vuvwaje] *vt*: **~ qn** to address sb as "vous".
voyage [vwajaʒ] *nm* journey, trip; (*fait de voyager*): **le ~** travel(ling); **partir/être en ~** to go off/be away on a journey *ou* trip; **faire un ~** to go on *ou* make a trip *ou* journey; **faire bon ~** to have a good journey; **les gens du ~** travelling people; **~ d'agrément/d'affaires** pleasure/business trip; **~ de noces** honeymoon; **~ organisé** package tour.
voyager [vwajaʒe] *vi* to travel.
voyageur, euse [vwajaʒœʀ, -øz] *nm/f* traveller; (*passager*) passenger **♦** *adj* (*tempérament*) nomadic, wayfaring; **~ (de commerce)** commercial traveller.
voyagiste [vwajaʒist(ə)] *nm* tour operator.
voyais [vwajɛ] *etc vb voir* **voir.**
voyance [vwajɑ̃s] *nf* clairvoyance.
voyant, e [vwajɑ̃, -ɑ̃t] *adj* (*couleur*) loud, gaudy **♦** *nm/f* (*personne qui voit*) sighted person **♦** *nm* (*signal*) (warning) light **♦** *nf* clairvoyant.
voyelle [vwajɛl] *nf* vowel.

voyeur, euse [vwajœʀ, -øz] *nm/f* voyeur; peeping Tom.
voyeurisme [vwajœʀism(ə)] *nm* voyeurism.
voyons [vwajɔ̃] *etc vb voir* **voir.**
voyou [vwaju] *nm* lout, hoodlum; (*enfant*) guttersnipe.
VPC *sigle f* (= *vente par correspondance*) mail order selling.
vrac [vʀak]: **en ~** *adv* higgledy-piggledy; (*COMM*) in bulk.
vrai, e [vʀɛ] *adj* (*véridique: récit, faits*) true; (*non factice, authentique*) real **♦** *nm*: **le ~** the truth; **à ~ dire** to tell the truth; **il est ~ que** it is true that; **être dans le ~** to be right.
vraiment [vʀɛmɑ̃] *adv* really.
vraisemblable [vʀɛsɑ̃blabl(ə)] *adj* (*plausible*) likely, plausible; (*probable*) likely, probable.
vraisemblablement [vʀɛsɑ̃blabləmɑ̃] *adv* in all likelihood, very likely.
vraisemblance [vʀɛsɑ̃blɑ̃s] *nf* likelihood, plausibility; (*romanesque*) verisimilitude; **selon toute ~** in all likelihood.
vraquier [vʀakje] *nm* freighter.
vrille [vʀij] *nf* (*de plante*) tendril; (*outil*) gimlet; (*spirale*) spiral; (*AVIAT*) spin.
vriller [vʀije] *vt* to bore into, pierce.
vrombir [vʀɔ̃biʀ] *vi* to hum.
vrombissant, e [vʀɔ̃bisɑ̃, -ɑ̃t] *adj* humming.
vrombissement [vʀɔ̃bismɑ̃] *nm* hum(ming).
VRP *sigle m* (= *voyageur, représentant, placier*) (sales) rep.
VTT *sigle m* (= *vélo tout-terrain*) mountain bike.
vu [vy] *prép* (*en raison de*) in view of; **~ que** in view of the fact that.
vu, e [vy] *pp de* **voir ♦** *adj*: **bien/mal ~** (*personne*) well/poorly thought of; (*conduite*) good/bad form **♦** *nm*: **au ~ et au su de tous** openly and publicly; **ni ~ ni connu** what the eye doesn't see ...!, no one will be any the wiser; **c'est tout ~** it's a foregone conclusion.
vue [vy] *nf* (*fait de voir*): **la ~ de** the sight of; (*sens, faculté*) (eye)sight; (*panorama, image, photo*) view; (*spectacle*) sight; **~s** *nfpl* (*idées*) views; (*dessein*) designs; **perdre la ~** to lose one's (eye)sight; **perdre de ~** to lose sight of; **à la ~ de tous** in full view of everybody; **hors de ~** out of sight; **à première ~** at first sight; **connaître de ~** to know by sight; **à ~** (*COMM*) at sight; **tirer à ~** to shoot on sight; **à ~ d'œil** *adv* visibly; (*à première vue*) at a quick glance; **avoir ~ sur** to have a view of; **en ~** (*visible*) in sight; (*COMM*) in the public eye; **avoir qch en ~** (*intentions*) to have one's sights on sth; **en ~ de faire** with the intention of doing, with a view to doing; **~ d'ensemble** overall view; **~ de l'esprit** theoretical view.
vulcanisation [vylkanizɑsjɔ̃] *nf* vulcanization.
vulcaniser [vylkanize] *vt* to vulcanize.
vulcanologie [vylkanɔlɔʒi] *nf* = **volcanologie.**
vulcanologue [vylkanɔlɔg] *nm/f* = **volcanolo-**

gue.

vulgaire [vylgɛʀ] *adj* (*grossier*) vulgar, coarse; (*trivial*) commonplace, mundane; (*péj*: *quelconque*): **de ~s touristes/chaises de cuisine** common tourists/kitchen chairs; (*BOT, ZOOL*: *non latin*) common.

vulgairement [vylgɛʀmɑ̃] *adv* vulgarly, coarsely; (*communément*) commonly.

vulgarisation [vylgaʀizasjɔ̃] *nf*: **ouvrage de ~** popularizing work, popularization.

vulgariser [vylgaʀize] *vt* to popularize.

vulgarité [vylgaʀite] *nf* vulgarity, coarseness.

vulnérabilité [vylneʀabilite] *nf* vulnerability.

vulnérable [vylneʀabl(ə)] *adj* vulnerable.

vulve [vylv(ə)] *nf* vulva.

vumètre [vymɛtʀ(ə)] *nm* recording level gauge.

Vve *abr* = **veuve**.

VVF *sigle m* (= *village vacances famille*) state-subsidized holiday village.

vx *abr* = **vieux**.

W w

W, w [dubləve] *nm inv* W, w ♦ *abr* (= *watt*) W; **W comme William** W for William.

wagon [vagɔ̃] *nm* (*de voyageurs*) carriage; (*de marchandises*) truck, wagon.

wagon-citerne, *pl* **wagons-citernes** [vagɔ̃sitɛʀn(ə)] *nm* tanker.

wagon-lit, *pl* **wagons-lits** [vagɔ̃li] *nm* sleeper, sleeping car.

wagonnet [vagɔnɛ] *nm* small truck.

wagon-poste, *pl* **wagons-postes** [vagɔ̃pɔst(ə)] *nm* mail van.

wagon-restaurant, *pl* **wagons-restaurants** [vagɔ̃ʀɛstɔʀɑ̃] *nm* restaurant *ou* dining car.

Walkman [wɔkman] *nm* ® Walkman ®, personal stereo.

Wallis et Futuna [walisefytyna]: **les îles ~** the Wallis and Futuna Islands.

wallon, ne [walɔ̃, -ɔn] *adj* Walloon ♦ *nm* (*LING*) Walloon ♦ *nm/f*: **W~, ne** Walloon.

Wallonie [walɔni] *nf*: **la ~** French-speaking (part of) Belgium.

water-polo [watɛʀpɔlo] *nm* water polo.

waters [watɛʀ] *nmpl* toilet *sg*, loo *sg* (*BRIT*).

watt [wat] *nm* watt.

w.-c. [vese] *nmpl* toilet *sg*, lavatory *sg*.

Web [wɛb] *nm inv*: **le ~** the (Worldwide) Web.

week-end [wikɛnd] *nm* weekend.

western [wɛstɛʀn] *nm* western.

Westphalie [vɛsfali] *nf*: **la ~** Westphalia.

whisky, *pl* **whiskies** [wiski] *nm* whisky.

white-spirit [wajtspiʀit] *nm* white spirit.

Winchester [wintʃɛstɛʀ]: **disque ~** Winchester disk.

wok [wɔk] *nm* wok.

X x

X, x [iks] *nm inv* X, x ♦ *sigle m* = (**École**) polytechnique; **plainte contre X** (*JUR*) action against person or persons unknown; **X comme Xavier** X for Xmas.

xénophobe [gzenɔfɔb] *adj* xenophobic ♦ *nm/f* xenophobe.

xénophobie [gzenɔfɔbi] *nf* xenophobia.

xérès [gzeʀɛs] *nm* sherry.

xylographie [ksilɔgʀafi] *nf* xylography; (*image*) xylograph.

xylophone [ksilɔfɔn] *nm* xylophone.

Y y

Y, y [igʀɛk] *nm inv* Y, y; **Y comme Yvonne** Y for Yellow (*BRIT*) *ou* Yoke (*US*).

y [i] *adv* (*à cet endroit*) there; (*dessus*) on it (*ou* them); (*dedans*) in it (*ou* them) ♦ *pron* (*about ou* on *ou* of) it : *vérifier la syntaxe du verbe employé*; **j'~** pense I'm thinking about it; *voir aussi* **aller, avoir**.

yacht [jɔt] *nm* yacht.

yaourt [jauʀt] *nm* yoghurt.

yaourtière [jauʀtjɛʀ] *nf* yoghurt-maker.

Yémen [jemɛn] *nm*: **le ~** Yemen.

yéménite [jemenit] *adj* Yemeni.

yeux [jø] *pl de* **œil**.

yoga [jɔga] *nm* yoga.

yoghourt [jɔguʀt] *nm* = **yaourt**.

yole [jɔl] *nf* skiff.

yougoslave [jugoslav] *adj* Yugoslav(ian) ♦ *nm/f*: **Y~** Yugoslav(ian).

Yougoslavie [jugoslavi] *nf*: **la ~** Yugoslavia.

youyou [juju] *nm* dinghy.

yo-yo [jojo] *nm inv* yo-yo.

yucca [juka] *nm* yucca (tree *ou* plant).

Z z

Z, z [zɛd] *nm inv* Z, z; **Z comme Zoé** Z for Zebra.

ZAC [zak] *sigle f* (= *zone d'aménagement concerté*) urban development zone.

ZAD [zad] *sigle f* (= *zone d'aménagement différé*) future development zone.

Zaïre [zɑːˈʀə*] *nm*: **le ~** Zaïre.

zaïrois, e [zaiʀwa, -waz] *adj* Zaïrese.

Zambèze [zɑ̃bɛz] *nm*: **le ~** the Zambezi.

Zambie [zɑ̃bi] *nf*: **la ~** Zambia.

zambien, ne [zɑ̃bjɛ̃, -ɛn] *adj* Zambian.

zapping [zapiŋ] *nm*: **faire du ~** to flick through the channels.

zèbre [zɛbʀ(ə)] *nm* (*ZOOL*) zebra.

zébré, e [zebʀe] *adj* striped, streaked.

zébrure [zebʀyʀ] *nf* stripe, streak.

zélateur, trice [zelatœʀ, -tʀis] *nm/f* partisan, zealot.

zèle [zɛl] *nm* diligence, assiduousness; **faire du ~** (*péj*) to be over-zealous.

zélé, e [zele] *adj* zealous.

zénith [zenit] *nm* zenith.

ZEP [zɛp] *sigle f* (= *zone d'éducation prioritaire*) *area targeted for special help in education.*

zéro [zeʀo] *nm* zero, nought (*BRIT*); **au-dessous de ~** below zero (Centigrade), below freezing; **partir de ~** to start from scratch; **réduire à ~** to reduce to nothing; **trois (buts) à ~ 3** (goals) to nil.

zeste [zɛst(ə)] *nm* peel, zest; **un ~ de citron** a piece of lemon peel.

zézaiement [zezɛmɑ̃] *nm* lisp.

zézayer [zezeje] *vi* to have a lisp.

ZI *sigle f* = **zone industrielle**.

zibeline [ziblin] *nf* sable.

ZIF [zif] *sigle f* (= *zone d'intervention foncière*) intervention zone.

zigouiller [ziguje] *vt* (*fam*) to do in.

zigzag [zigzag] *nm* zigzag.

zigzaguer [zigzage] *vi* to zigzag (along).

Zimbabwe [zimbabwe] *nm*: **le ~** Zimbabwe.

zimbabwéen, ne [zimbabweɛ̃, -ɛn] *adj* Zimbabwean.

zinc [zɛ̃g] *nm* (*CHIMIE*) zinc; (*comptoir*) bar, counter.

zinguer [zɛ̃ge] *vt* to cover with zinc.

zircon [ziʀkɔ̃] *nm* zircon.

zizanie [zizani] *nf*: **semer la ~** to stir up ill-feeling.

zizi [zizi] *nm* (*fam*) willy (*BRIT*), peter (*US*).

zodiacal, e, aux [zɔdjakal, -o] *adj* (*signe*) of the zodiac.

zodiaque [zɔdjak] *nm* zodiac.

zona [zona] *nm* shingles *sg*.

zonage [zonaʒ] *nm* (*ADMIN*) zoning.

zonard, e [zonaʀ, -aʀd] *nm/f* (*fam*) (young) hooligan *ou* thug.

zone [zon] *nf* zone, area; (*INFORM*) field; (*quartiers*): **la ~** the slum belt; **de seconde ~** (*fig*) second-rate; **~ d'action** (*MIL*) sphere of activity; **~ bleue** ≈ restricted parking area; **~ d'extension** *ou* **d'urbanisation** urban development area; **~ franche** free zone; **~ industrielle (ZI)** industrial estate; **~ résidentielle** residential area; **~ tampon** buffer zone.

zoner [zone] *vi* (*fam*) to hang around.

zoo [zoo] *nm* zoo.

zoologie [zɔɔlɔʒi] *nf* zoology.

zoologique [zɔɔlɔʒik] *adj* zoological.

zoologiste [zɔɔlɔʒist(ə)] *nm/f* zoologist.

zoom [zum] *nm* (*PHOTO*) zoom (lens).

ZUP [zyp] *sigle f* (= *zone à urbaniser en priorité*) = **ZAC**.

Zurich [zyʀik] *n* Zürich.

zut [zyt] *excl* dash (it)! (*BRIT*), nuts! (*US*).

Aa

A, a [eɪ] n (letter) A, a m; (SCOL: mark) A; (MUS): A la m; **A for Andrew**, (US) **A for Able** A comme Anatole; **A road** n (BRIT AUT) route nationale; **A shares** npl (BRIT STOCK EXCHANGE) actions fpl prioritaires.

═══════════════════ KEYWORD

a [eɪ, ə] (before vowel or silent h: **an**) indef art **1** un(e); ~ **book** un livre; **an apple** une pomme; **she's** ~ **doctor** elle est médecin
2 (instead of the number "one") un(e); ~ **year ago** il y a un an; ~ **hundred/thousand** etc **pounds** cent/mille etc livres
3 (in expressing ratios, prices etc): **3** ~ **day/ week** 3 par jour/semaine; **10 km an hour** 10 km à l'heure; **30p** ~ **kilo** 30p le kilo.

a. abbr = **acre**.
AA n abbr (BRIT: = Automobile Association) ≈ ACF m; (US: = Associate in/of Arts) diplôme universitaire; (= Alcoholics Anonymous) AA; (= anti-aircraft) AA.
AAA n abbr (= American Automobile Association) ≈ ACF m; (BRIT) = Amateur Athletics Association.
A & R n abbr (MUS: = artists and repertoire): ~ **man** découvreur m de talent.
AAUP n abbr (= American Association of University Professors) syndicat universitaire.
AB abbr (BRIT) = **able-bodied seaman**; (Canada) = **Alberta**.
aback [ə'bæk] adv: **to be taken** ~ être décontenancé(e).
abacus, pl **abaci** ['æbəkəs, -saɪ] n boulier m.
abandon [ə'bændən] vt abandonner ♦ n abandon m; **to** ~ **ship** évacuer le navire.
abandoned [ə'bændənd] adj (child, house etc) abandonné(e); (unrestrained) sans retenue.
abase [ə'beɪs] vt: **to** ~ **o.s. (so far as to do)** s'abaisser (à faire).
abashed [ə'bæʃt] adj confus(e), embarrassé(e).

abate [ə'beɪt] vi s'apaiser, se calmer.
abatement [ə'beɪtmənt] n: **noise** ~ lutte f contre le bruit.
abattoir ['æbətwɑː*] n (BRIT) abattoir m.
abbey ['æbɪ] n abbaye f.
abbot ['æbət] n père supérieur.
abbreviate [ə'briːvɪeɪt] vt abréger.
abbreviation [əbriːvɪ'eɪʃən] n abréviation f.
ABC n abbr (= American Broadcasting Company) chaîne de télévision.
abdicate ['æbdɪkeɪt] vt, vi abdiquer.
abdication [æbdɪ'keɪʃən] n abdication f.
abdomen ['æbdəmən] n abdomen m.
abdominal [æb'dɔmɪnl] adj abdominal(e).
abduct [æb'dʌkt] vt enlever.
abduction [æb'dʌkʃən] n enlèvement m.
Aberdonian [æbə'dəʊnɪən] adj d'Aberdeen ♦ n habitant/e d'Aberdeen; natif/ive d'Aberdeen.
aberration [æbə'reɪʃən] n anomalie f; **in a moment of mental** ~ dans un moment d'égarement.
abet [ə'bet] vt see **aid**.
abeyance [ə'beɪəns] n: **in** ~ (law) en désuétude; (matter) en suspens.
abhor [əb'hɔː*] vt abhorrer, exécrer.
abhorrent [əb'hɔrənt] adj odieux(euse), exécrable.
abide [ə'baɪd] vt souffrir, supporter.
▶**abide by** vt fus observer, respecter.
abiding [ə'baɪdɪŋ] adj (memory etc) durable.
ability [ə'bɪlɪtɪ] n compétence f; capacité f; (skill) talent m; **to the best of my** ~ de mon mieux.
abject ['æbdʒekt] adj (poverty) sordide; (coward) méprisable; **an** ~ **apology** les excuses les plus plates.
ablaze [ə'bleɪz] adj en feu, en flammes; ~ **with light** resplendissant de lumière.
able ['eɪbl] adj compétent(e); **to be** ~ **to do sth** pouvoir faire qch, être capable de faire qch.

able-bodied ['eɪbl'bɔdɪd] *adj* robuste; ~ **seaman** (*BRIT*) matelot breveté.

ably ['eɪblɪ] *adv* avec compétence *or* talent, habilement.

ABM *n abbr* = anti-ballistic missile.

abnormal [æb'nɔːməl] *adj* anormal(e).

abnormality [æbnɔː'mælɪtɪ] *n* (*condition*) caractère anormal; (*instance*) anomalie *f*.

aboard [ə'bɔːd] *adv* à bord ♦ *prep* à bord de; (*train*) dans.

abode [ə'bəud] *n* (*old*) demeure *f*; (*LAW*): **of no fixed** ~ sans domicile fixe.

abolish [ə'bɔlɪʃ] *vt* abolir.

abolition [æbə'lɪʃən] *n* abolition *f*.

abominable [ə'bɔmɪnəbl] *adj* abominable.

aborigine [æbə'rɪdʒɪnɪ] *n* aborigène *m/f*.

abort [ə'bɔːt] *vt* (*MED*, *fig*) faire avorter; (*COMPUT*) abandonner.

abortion [ə'bɔːʃən] *n* avortement *m*; **to have an** ~ se faire avorter.

abortionist [ə'bɔːʃənɪst] *n* avorteur/euse.

abortive [ə'bɔːtɪv] *adj* manqué(e).

abound [ə'baund] *vi* abonder; **to** ~ **in** abonder en, regorger de.

═══════════════════════════ *KEYWORD*

about [ə'baut] *adv* **1** (*approximately*) environ, à peu près; ~ **a hundred/thousand** *etc* environ cent/mille *etc*, une centaine (de)/un millier (de) *etc*; **it takes** ~ **10 hours** ça prend environ *or* à peu près 10 heures; **at** ~ **2 o'clock** vers 2 heures; **I've just** ~ **finished** j'ai presque fini

2 (*referring to place*) çà et là, deci delà; **to run** ~ courir çà et là; **to walk** ~ se promener, aller et venir; **is Paul** ~? (*BRIT*) est-ce que Paul est là?; **it's** ~ **here** c'est par ici, c'est dans les parages; **they left all their things lying** ~ ils ont laissé traîner toutes leurs affaires

3: **to be** ~ **to do sth** être sur le point de faire qch; **I'm not** ~ **to do all that for nothing** (*col*) je ne vais quand même pas faire tout ça pour rien

4 (*opposite*): **it's the other way** ~ (*BRIT*) c'est l'inverse

♦ *prep* **1** (*relating to*) au sujet de, à propos de; **a book** ~ **London** un livre sur Londres; **what is it** ~? de quoi s'agit-il?; **we talked** ~ **it** nous en avons parlé; **do something** ~ **it!** faites quelque chose!; **what** *or* **how** ~ **doing this?** et si nous faisions ceci?

2 (*referring to place*) dans; **to walk** ~ **the town** se promener dans la ville.

about face, about turn *n* (*MIL*) demi-tour *m*; (*fig*) volte-face *f*.

above [ə'bʌv] *adv* au-dessus ♦ *prep* au-dessus de; **mentioned** ~ mentionné ci-dessus; **costing** ~ **£10** coûtant plus de 10 livres; ~ **all** par-dessus tout, surtout.

aboveboard [ə'bʌv'bɔːd] *adj* franc(franche),

loyal(e); honnête.

abrasion [ə'breɪʒən] *n* frottement *m*; (*on skin*) écorchure *f*.

abrasive [ə'breɪzɪv] *adj* abrasif(ive); (*fig*) caustique, agressif(ive).

abreast [ə'brest] *adv* de front; **to keep** ~ **of** se tenir au courant de.

abridge [ə'brɪdʒ] *vt* abréger.

abroad [ə'brɔːd] *adv* à l'étranger; **there is a rumour** ~ **that** ... (*fig*) le bruit court que ....

abrupt [ə'brʌpt] *adj* (*steep, blunt*) abrupt(e); (*sudden, gruff*) brusque.

abscess ['æbsɪs] *n* abcès *m*.

abscond [əb'skɔnd] *vi* disparaître, s'enfuir.

absence ['æbsəns] *n* absence *f*; **in the** ~ **of** (*person*) en l'absence de; (*thing*) faute de.

absent ['æbsənt] *adj* absent(e); ~ **without leave (AWOL)** (*MIL*) en absence irrégulière.

absentee [æbsən'tiː] *n* absent/e.

absenteeism [æbsən'tiːɪzəm] *n* absentéisme *m*.

absent-minded ['æbsənt'maɪndɪd] *adj* distrait(e).

absent-mindedness ['æbsənt'maɪndɪdnɪs] *n* distraction *f*.

absolute ['æbsəluːt] *adj* absolu(e).

absolutely [æbsə'luːtlɪ] *adv* absolument.

absolve [əb'zɔlv] *vt*: **to** ~ **sb (from)** (*sin etc*) absoudre qn (de); **to** ~ **sb from** (*oath*) délier qn de.

absorb [əb'zɔːb] *vt* absorber; **to be** ~**ed in a book** être plongé(e) dans un livre.

absorbent [əb'zɔːbənt] *adj* absorbant(e).

absorbent cotton *n* (*US*) coton *m* hydrophile.

absorbing [əb'zɔːbɪŋ] *adj* absorbant(e); (*book, film etc*) captivant(e).

absorption [əb'sɔːpʃən] *n* absorption *f*.

abstain [əb'steɪn] *vi*: **to** ~ **(from)** s'abstenir (de).

abstemious [əb'stiːmɪəs] *adj* sobre, frugal(e).

abstention [əb'stenʃən] *n* abstention *f*.

abstinence ['æbstɪnəns] *n* abstinence *f*.

abstract *adj, n* ['æbstrækt] *adj* abstrait(e) ♦ *n* (*summary*) résumé *m* ♦ *vt* [æb'strækt] extraire.

absurd [əb'sɔːd] *adj* absurde.

absurdity [əb'sɔːdɪtɪ] *n* absurdité *f*.

ABTA ['æbtə] *n abbr* = Association of British Travel Agents.

Abu Dhabi ['æbuː'dɑːbɪ] *n* Ab(o)u Dhabî *m*.

abundance [ə'bʌndəns] *n* abondance *f*.

abundant [ə'bʌndənt] *adj* abondant(e).

abuse *n* [ə'bjuːs] insultes *fpl*, injures *fpl*; (*of power etc*) abus *m* ♦ *vt* [ə'bjuːz] abuser de; **to be open to** ~ se prêter à des abus.

abusive [ə'bjuːsɪv] *adj* grossier(ière), injurieux(euse).

abysmal [ə'bɪzməl] *adj* exécrable; (*ignorance etc*) sans bornes.

abyss [ə'bɪs] *n* abîme *m*, gouffre *m*.

AC *n abbr* (*US*) = athletic club.

a/c *abbr* (*BANKING etc*) = account, account current.

academic [ækə'dɛmɪk] adj universitaire; (pej: issue) oiseux(euse), purement théorique ♦ n universitaire m/f; ~ **freedom** liberté f académique.

academic year n année f universitaire.

academy [ə'kædəmɪ] n (learned body) académie f; (school) collège m; **military/naval** ~ école militaire/navale; ~ **of music** conservatoire m.

ACAS ['eɪkæs] n abbr (BRIT: = Advisory, Conciliation and Arbitration Service) organisme de conciliation et d'arbitrage des conflits du travail.

accede [æk'siːd] vi: **to** ~ **to** (request, throne) accéder à.

accelerate [æk'sɛləreɪt] vt, vi accélérer.

acceleration [æksɛlə'reɪʃən] n accélération f.

accelerator [æk'sɛləreɪtə*] n accélérateur m.

accent ['æksɛnt] n accent m.

accentuate [æk'sɛntjueɪt] vt (syllable) accentuer; (need, difference etc) souligner.

accept [ək'sɛpt] vt accepter.

acceptable [ək'sɛptəbl] adj acceptable.

acceptance [ək'sɛptəns] n acceptation f; **to meet with general** ~ être favorablement accueilli par tous.

access ['æksɛs] n accès m ♦ vt (COMPUT) accéder à; **to have** ~ **to** (information, library etc) avoir accès à, pouvoir utiliser ou consulter; (person) avoir accès auprès de; **the burglars gained** ~ **through a window** les cambrioleurs sont entrés par une fenêtre.

accessible [æk'sɛsəbl] adj accessible.

accession [æk'sɛʃən] n accession f; (of king) avènement m; (to library) acquisition f.

accessory [æk'sɛsərɪ] n accessoire m; **toilet accessories** (BRIT) articles mpl de toilette.

access road n voie f d'accès; (to motorway) bretelle f de raccordement.

access time n (COMPUT) temps m d'accès.

accident ['æksɪdənt] n accident m; (chance) hasard m; **to meet with** or **to have an** ~ avoir un accident; ~**s at work** accidents du travail; **by** ~ par hasard; (not deliberately) accidentellement.

accidental [æksɪ'dɛntl] adj accidentel(le).

accidentally [æksɪ'dɛntəlɪ] adv accidentellement.

accident insurance n assurance f accident.

accident-prone ['æksɪdənt'prəun] adj sujet(te) aux accidents.

acclaim [ə'kleɪm] vt acclamer ♦ n acclamation f.

acclamation [æklə'meɪʃən] n (approval) acclamation f; (applause) ovation f.

acclimatize [ə'klaɪmətaɪz], (US) **acclimate** [ə'klaɪmət] vt: **to become** ~**d** s'acclimater.

accolade ['ækəleɪd] n accolade f; (fig) marque f d'honneur.

accommodate [ə'kɔmədeɪt] vt loger, recevoir; (oblige, help) obliger; (adapt): **to** ~

one's plans to adapter ses projets à; **this car** ~**s 4 people comfortably** on tient confortablement à 4 dans cette voiture.

accommodating [ə'kɔmədeɪtɪŋ] adj obligeant(e), arrangeant(e).

accommodation, (US) **accommodations** [əkɔmə'deɪʃən(z)] n(pl) logement m; **he's found** ~ il a trouvé à se loger; "~ **to let**" (BRIT) "appartement (or studio etc) à louer"; **they have** ~ **for 500** ils peuvent recevoir 500 personnes, il y a de la place pour 500 personnes; **the hall has seating** ~ **for 600** (BRIT) la salle contient 600 places assises.

accompaniment [ə'kʌmpənɪmənt] n accompagnement m.

accompanist [ə'kʌmpənɪst] n accompagnateur/trice.

accompany [ə'kʌmpənɪ] vt accompagner.

accomplice [ə'kʌmplɪs] n complice m/f.

accomplish [ə'kʌmplɪʃ] vt accomplir.

accomplished [ə'kʌmplɪʃt] adj accompli(e).

accomplishment [ə'kʌmplɪʃmənt] n accomplissement m; (achievement) réussite f; ~**s** npl (skills) talents mpl.

accord [ə'kɔːd] n accord m ♦ vt accorder; **of his own** ~ de son plein gré; **with one** ~ d'un commun accord.

accordance [ə'kɔːdəns] n: **in** ~ **with** conformément à.

according [ə'kɔːdɪŋ]: ~ **to** prep selon; ~ **to plan** comme prévu.

accordingly [ə'kɔːdɪŋlɪ] adv en conséquence.

accordion [ə'kɔːdɪən] n accordéon m.

accost [ə'kɔst] vt accoster, aborder.

account [ə'kaunt] n (COMM) compte m; (report) compte rendu, récit m; ~**s** npl (BOOK-KEEPING) comptabilité f, comptes; "~ **payee only**" (BRIT) "chèque non endossable"; **to keep an** ~ **of** noter; **to bring sb to** ~ **for sth/ for having done sth** amener qn à rendre compte de qch/d'avoir fait qch; **by all** ~**s** au dire de tous; **of little** ~ de peu d'importance; **to pay £5 on** ~ verser un acompte de 5 livres; **to buy sth on** ~ acheter qch à crédit; **on no** ~ en aucun cas; **on** ~ **of** à cause de; **to take into** ~, **take** ~ **of** tenir compte de.

▶ **account for** vt fus expliquer, rendre compte de; **all the children were** ~**ed for** aucun enfant ne manquait; **4 people are still not** ~**ed for** on n'a toujours pas retrouvé 4 personnes.

accountability [əkauntə'bɪlɪtɪ] n responsabilité f; (financial, political) transparence f.

accountable [ə'kauntəbl] adj: **(for)** responsable (de).

accountancy [ə'kauntənsɪ] n comptabilité f.

accountant [ə'kauntənt] n comptable m/f.

accounting [ə'kauntɪŋ] n comptabilité f.

accounting period n exercice financier, période f comptable.

account number n numéro m de compte.

account payable n compte m fournisseurs.

account receivable *n* compte *m* clients.
accredited [ə'krɛdɪtɪd] *adj* (*person*) accrédité(e).
accretion [ə'kriːʃən] *n* accroissement *m*.
accrue [ə'kruː] *vi* s'accroître; (*mount up*) s'accumuler; **to ~ to** s'ajouter à; **~d interest** intérêt couru.
accumulate [ə'kjuːmjuleɪt] *vt* accumuler, amasser ♦ *vi* s'accumuler, s'amasser.
accumulation [əkjuːmju'leɪʃən] *n* accumulation *f*.
accuracy ['ækjurəsɪ] *n* exactitude *f*, précision *f*.
accurate ['ækjurɪt] *adj* exact(e), précis(e).
accurately ['ækjurɪtlɪ] *adv* avec précision.
accusation [ækju'zeɪʃən] *n* accusation *f*.
accusative [ə'kjuːzətɪv] *n* (*LING*) accusatif *m*.
accuse [ə'kjuːz] *vt* accuser.
accused [ə'kjuːzd] *n* accusé/e.
accuser [ə'kjuːzə*] *n* accusateur/trice.
accustom [ə'kʌstəm] *vt* accoutumer, habituer; **to ~ o.s. to sth** s'habituer à qch.
accustomed [ə'kʌstəmd] *adj* (*usual*) habituel(le); **~ to** habitué(e) *or* accoutumé(e) à.
AC/DC *abbr* = **alternating current/direct current.**
ACE [eɪs] *n abbr* = **American Council on Education.**
ace [eɪs] *n* as *m*; **within an ~ of** (*BRIT*) à deux doigts *or* un cheveu de.
acerbic [ə'səːbɪk] *adj* (*also fig*) acerbe.
acetate ['æsɪteɪt] *n* acétate *m*.
ache [eɪk] *n* mal *m*, douleur *f* ♦ *vi* (*be sore*) faire mal, être douloureux(euse); (*yearn*): **to ~ to do sth** mourir d'envie de faire qch; **I've got stomach ~** *or* (*US*) **a stomach ~** j'ai mal à l'estomac; **my head ~s** j'ai mal à la tête; **I'm aching all over** j'ai mal partout.
achieve [ə'tʃiːv] *vt* (*aim*) atteindre; (*victory, success*) remporter, obtenir; (*task*) accomplir.
achievement [ə'tʃiːvmənt] *n* exploit *m*, réussite *f*; (*of aims*) réalisation *f*.
Achilles heel [ə'kɪliːz-] *n* talon *m* d'Achille.
acid ['æsɪd] *adj, n* acide (*m*).
acidity [ə'sɪdɪtɪ] *n* acidité *f*.
acid rain *n* pluies *fpl* acides.
acid test *n* (*fig*) épreuve décisive.
acknowledge [ək'nɔlɪdʒ] *vt* (*also:* **~ receipt of**) accuser réception de; (*fact*) reconnaître.
acknowledgement [ək'nɔlɪdʒmənt] *n* accusé *m* de réception; **~s** (*in book*) remerciements *mpl*.
ACLU *n abbr* (= *American Civil Liberties Union*) *ligue des droits de l'homme.*
acme ['ækmɪ] *n* point culminant.
acne ['æknɪ] *n* acné *m*.
acorn ['eɪkɔːn] *n* gland *m*.
acoustic [ə'kuːstɪk] *adj* acoustique.
acoustic coupler *n* (*COMPUT*) coupleur *m* acoustique.
acoustics [ə'kuːstɪks] *n, npl* acoustique *f*.

acquaint [ə'kweɪnt] *vt*: **to ~ sb with sth** mettre qn au courant de qch; **to be ~ed with** (*person*) connaître; (*fact*) savoir.
acquaintance [ə'kweɪntəns] *n* connaissance *f*; **to make sb's ~** faire la connaissance de qn.
acquiesce [ækwɪ'ɛs] *vi* (*agree*): **to ~ (in)** acquiescer (à).
acquire [ə'kwaɪə*] *vt* acquérir.
acquired [ə'kwaɪəd] *adj* acquis(e); **an ~ taste** un goût acquis.
acquisition [ækwɪ'zɪʃən] *n* acquisition *f*.
acquisitive [ə'kwɪzɪtɪv] *adj* qui a l'instinct de possession *or* le goût de la propriété.
acquit [ə'kwɪt] *vt* acquitter; **to ~ o.s. well** s'en tirer très honorablement.
acquittal [ə'kwɪtl] *n* acquittement *m*.
acre ['eɪkə*] *n* acre *f* (= 4047 *m²*).
acreage ['eɪkərɪdʒ] *n* superficie *f*.
acrid ['ækrɪd] *adj* (*smell*) âcre; (*fig*) mordant(e).
acrimonious [ækrɪ'məunɪəs] *adj* acrimonieux(euse), aigre.
acrobat ['ækrəbæt] *n* acrobate *m/f*.
acrobatic [ækrə'bætɪk] *adj* acrobatique.
acrobatics [ækrə'bætɪks] *n, npl* acrobatie *f*.
Acropolis [ə'krɔpəlɪs] *n*: **the ~** l'Acropole *f*.
across [ə'krɔs] *prep* (*on the other side*) de l'autre côté de; (*crosswise*) en travers de ♦ *adv* de l'autre côté; en travers; **to walk ~ (the road)** traverser (la route); **to take sb ~ the road** faire traverser la route à qn; **a road ~ the wood** une route qui traverse le bois; **the lake is 12 km ~** le lac fait 12 km de large; **~ from** en face de; **to get sth ~ (to sb)** faire comprendre qch (à qn).
acrylic [ə'krɪlɪk] *adj, n* acrylique (*m*).
ACT *n abbr* (= *American College Test*) *examen de fin d'études secondaires.*
act [ækt] *n* acte *m*, action *f*; (*THEAT: part of play*) acte; (: *of performer*) numéro *m*; (*LAW*) loi *f* ♦ *vi* agir; (*THEAT*) jouer; (*pretend*) jouer la comédie ♦ *vt* (*role*) jouer, tenir; **~ of God** (*LAW*) catastrophe naturelle; **to catch sb in the ~** prendre qn sur le fait *or* en flagrant délit; **it's only an ~** c'est du cinéma; **to ~ Hamlet** (*BRIT*) tenir *or* jouer le rôle d'Hamlet; **to ~ the fool** (*BRIT*) faire l'idiot; **to ~ as** servir de; **it ~s as a deterrent** cela a un effet dissuasif; **~ing in my capacity as chairman, I ...** en ma qualité de président, je ...
▶**act on** *vt*: **to ~ on sth** agir sur la base de qch.
▶**act out** *vt* (*event*) raconter en mimant; (*fantasies*) réaliser.
acting ['æktɪŋ] *adj* suppléant(e), par intérim ♦ *n* (*of actor*) jeu *m*; (*activity*): **to do some ~** faire du théâtre (*or* du cinéma); **he is the ~ manager** il remplace (provisoirement) le directeur.
action ['ækʃən] *n* action *f*; (*MIL*) combat(s) *m(pl)*; (*LAW*) procès *m*, action en justice; **to bring an ~ against sb** (*LAW*) poursuivre qn

en justice, intenter un procès contre qn;
killed in ~ (MIL) tué au champ d'honneur;
out of ~ hors de combat; (machine etc) hors
d'usage; **to take** ~ agir, prendre des mesures; **to put a plan into** ~ mettre un projet
à exécution.
action replay n (BRIT TV) retour m sur une séquence.
activate ['æktıveıt] vt (mechanism) actionner,
faire fonctionner; (CHEM, PHYSICS) activer.
active ['æktıv] adj actif(ive); (volcano) en activité; **to play an** ~ **part in** jouer un rôle actif
dans.
active duty (AD) n (US MIL) campagne f.
actively ['æktıvlı] adv activement.
active partner n (COMM) associé/e.
active service n (BRIT MIL) campagne f.
activist ['æktıvıst] n activiste m/f.
activity [æk'tıvıtı] n activité f.
actor ['æktə*] n acteur m.
actress ['æktrıs] n actrice f.
actual ['æktjuəl] adj réel(le), véritable.
actually ['æktjuəlı] adv réellement, véritablement; (in fact) en fait.
actuary ['æktjuərı] n actuaire m.
actuate ['æktjueıt] vt déclencher, actionner.
acuity [ə'kju:ıtı] n acuité f.
acumen ['ækjumən] n perspicacité f; **business**
~ sens m des affaires.
acupuncture ['ækjupʌŋktʃə*] n acuponcture f.
acute [ə'kju:t] adj aigu(ë); (mind, observer) pé-
nétrant(e).
AD adv abbr (= Anno Domini) ap. J.-C. ♦ n abbr
(US MIL) = **active duty**.
ad [æd] n abbr = **advertisement**.
adamant ['ædəmənt] adj inflexible.
Adam's apple ['ædəmz-] n pomme f d'Adam.
adapt [ə'dæpt] vt adapter ♦ vi: **to** ~ **(to)**
s'adapter (à).
adaptability [ədæptə'bılıtı] n faculté f
d'adaptation.
adaptable [ə'dæptəbl] adj (device) adaptable;
(person) qui s'adapte facilement.
adaptation [ædæp'teıʃən] n adaptation f.
adapter [ə'dæptə*] n (ELEC) adaptateur m.
ADC n abbr (MIL) = aide-de-camp; (US: = Aid to
Dependent Children) aide pour enfants assistés.
add [æd] vt ajouter; (figures) additionner ♦ vi:
to ~ **to** (increase) ajouter à, accroître.
▶**add on** vt ajouter.
▶**add up** vt (figures) additionner ♦ vi (fig): **it
doesn't** ~ **up** cela ne rime à rien; **it doesn't**
~ **up to much** ça n'est pas grand'chose.
adder ['ædə*] n vipère f.
addict ['ædıkt] n toxicomane m/f; (fig) fanatique m/f; **heroin** ~ héroïnomane m/f; **drug** ~
drogué/e m/f.
addicted [ə'dıktıd] adj: **to be** ~ **to** (drink etc)
être adonné(e) à; (fig: football etc) être un(e)
fanatique de.
addiction [ə'dıkʃən] n (MED) dépendance f.

adding machine ['ædıŋ-] n machine f à calculer.
Addis Ababa ['ædıs'æbəbə] n Addis Abeba,
Addis Ababa.
addition [ə'dıʃən] n addition f; **in** ~ de plus, de
surcroît; **in** ~ **to** en plus de.
additional [ə'dıʃənl] adj supplémentaire.
additive ['ædıtıv] n additif m.
addled ['ædld] adj (BRIT: egg) pourri(e).
address [ə'drɛs] n adresse f; (talk) discours m,
allocution f ♦ vt adresser; (speak to)
s'adresser à; **form of** ~ titre m; **what form of**
~ **do you use for ...?** comment s'adresse-t-
on à ...?; **to** ~ **(o.s. to)** sth (problem, issue)
aborder qch; **absolute/relative** ~ (COMPUT)
adresse absolue/relative.
address book n carnet m d'adresses.
addressee [ædrɛ'si:] n destinataire m/f.
Aden ['eıdən] n: **Gulf of** ~ Golfe m d'Aden.
adenoids ['ædınɔıdz] npl végétations fpl.
adept ['ædɛpt] adj: ~ **at** expert(e) à or en.
adequate ['ædıkwıt] adj (enough) suffisant(e);
to feel ~ **to the task** se sentir à la hauteur
de la tâche.
adequately ['ædıkwıtlı] adv de façon adé-
quate.
adhere [əd'hıə*] vi: **to** ~ **to** adhérer à; (fig:
rule, decision) se tenir à.
adhesion [əd'hi:ʒən] n adhésion f.
adhesive [əd'hi:zıv] adj adhésif(ive) ♦ n adhésif m; ~ **tape** (BRIT) ruban adhésif; (US)
sparadrap m.
ad hoc [æd'hɔk] adj (decision) de circonstance;
(committee) ad hoc.
ad infinitum ['ædınfı'naıtəm] adv à l'infini.
adjacent [ə'dʒeısənt] adj adjacent(e), conti-
gu(ë); ~ **to** adjacent à.
adjective ['ædʒɛktıv] n adjectif m.
adjoin [ə'dʒɔın] vt jouxter.
adjoining [ə'dʒɔınıŋ] adj voisin(e), adja-
cent(e), attenant(e) ♦ prep voisin de, adjacent à.
adjourn [ə'dʒə:n] vt ajourner ♦ vi suspendre la
séance; lever la séance; clore la session;
(go) se retirer; **to** ~ **a meeting till the following week** reporter une réunion à la semaine suivante; **they** ~**ed to the pub** (BRIT
col) ils ont filé au pub.
adjournment [ə'dʒə:nmənt] n (period) ajournement m.
Adjt abbr (MIL: = adjutant) Adj.
adjudicate [ə'dʒu:dıkeıt] vt (contest) juger;
(claim) statuer (sur) ♦ vi se prononcer.
adjudication [ədʒu:dı'keıʃən] n (LAW) jugement m.
adjust [ə'dʒʌst] vt ajuster, régler; rajuster
♦ vi: **to** ~ **(to)** s'adapter (à).
adjustable [ə'dʒʌstəbl] adj réglable.
adjuster [ə'dʒʌstə*] adj n see **loss**.
adjustment [ə'dʒʌstmənt] n ajustage m, réglage m; (of prices, wages) rajustement m; (of
person) adaptation f.

adjutant ['ædʒətənt] *n* adjudant *m*.
ad-lib [æd'lɪb] *vt, vi* improviser ♦ *n* improvisation *f* ♦ *adv*: **ad lib** à volonté, à discrétion.
adman ['ædmæn] *n* (*col*) publicitaire *m*.
admin ['ædmɪn] *n abbr* (*col*) = **administration**.
administer [əd'mɪnɪstə*] *vt* administrer; (*justice*) rendre.
administration [ədmɪnɪs'treɪʃən] *n* administration *f*; **the A~** (*US*) le gouvernement.
administrative [əd'mɪnɪstrətɪv] *adj* administratif(ive).
administrator [əd'mɪnɪstreɪtə*] *n* administrateur/trice.
admirable ['ædmərəbl] *adj* admirable.
admiral ['ædmərəl] *n* amiral *m*.
Admiralty ['ædmərəltɪ] *n* (*BRIT: also*: ~ **Board**) ministère *m* de la Marine.
admiration [ædmə'reɪʃən] *n* admiration *f*.
admire [əd'maɪə*] *vt* admirer.
admirer [əd'maɪərə*] *n* admirateur/trice.
admiring [əd'maɪərɪŋ] *adj* admiratif(ive).
admissible [əd'mɪsəbl] *adj* acceptable, admissible; (*evidence*) recevable.
admission [əd'mɪʃən] *n* admission *f*; (*to exhibition, night club etc*) entrée *f*; (*confession*) aveu *m*; "~ **free**", "**free** ~" "entrée libre"; **by his own** ~ de son propre aveu.
admit [əd'mɪt] *vt* laisser entrer; admettre; (*agree*) reconnaître, admettre; "**children not ~ted**" "entrée interdite aux enfants"; **this ticket ~s two** ce billet est valable pour deux personnes; **I must ~ that** ... je dois admettre *or* reconnaître que ....
▶**admit of** *vt fus* admettre, permettre.
▶**admit to** *vt fus* reconnaître, avouer.
admittance [əd'mɪtəns] *n* admission *f*, (droit *m* d')entrée *f*; "**no ~**" "défense d'entrer".
admittedly [əd'mɪtɪdlɪ] *adv* il faut en convenir.
admonish [əd'mɔnɪʃ] *vt* donner un avertissement à; réprimander.
ad nauseam [æd'nɔːsɪæm] *adv* à satiété.
ado [ə'duː] *n*: **without (any) more** ~ sans plus de cérémonies.
adolescence [ædəu'lɛsns] *n* adolescence *f*.
adolescent [ædəu'lɛsnt] *adj, n* adolescent(e).
adopt [ə'dɔpt] *vt* adopter.
adopted [ə'dɔptɪd] *adj* adoptif(ive), adopté(e).
adoption [ə'dɔpʃən] *n* adoption *f*.
adore [ə'dɔː*] *vt* adorer.
adoring [ə'dɔːrɪŋ] *adj*: **his** ~ **wife** sa femme qui est en adoration devant lui.
adoringly [ə'dɔːrɪŋlɪ] *adv* avec adoration.
adorn [ə'dɔːn] *vt* orner.
adornment [ə'dɔːnmənt] *n* ornement *m*.
ADP *n abbr* = **automatic data processing**.
adrenalin [ə'drɛnəlɪn] *n* adrénaline *f*; **to get the** ~ **going** faire monter le taux d'adrénaline.
Adriatic (Sea) [eɪdrɪ'ætɪk-] *n* Adriatique *f*.
adrift [ə'drɪft] *adv* à la dérive; **to come** ~ (*boat*) aller à la dérive; (*wire, rope, fastening*

etc) se défaire.
adroit [ə'drɔɪt] *adj* adroit(e), habile.
ADT *abbr* (*US*: = *Atlantic Daylight Time*) *heure d'été de New York*.
adult ['ædʌlt] *n* adulte *m/f*.
adult education *n* éducation *f* des adultes.
adulterate [ə'dʌltəreɪt] *vt* frelater, falsifier.
adulterer [ə'dʌltərə*] *n* homme *m* adultère.
adulteress [ə'dʌltərɪs] *n* femme *f* adultère.
adultery [ə'dʌltərɪ] *n* adultère *m*.
adulthood ['ædʌlthud] *n* âge *m* adulte.
advance [əd'vɑːns] *n* avance *f* ♦ *vt* avancer ♦ *vi* s'avancer; **in** ~ en avance, d'avance; **to make ~s to sb** (*gen*) faire des propositions à qn; (*amorously*) faire des avances à qn.
advanced [əd'vɑːnst] *adj* avancé(e); (*SCOL: studies*) supérieur(e); ~ **in years** d'un âge avancé.
advancement [əd'vɑːnsmənt] *n* avancement *m*.
advance notice *n* préavis *m*.
advantage [əd'vɑːntɪdʒ] *n* (*also TENNIS*) avantage *m*; **to take** ~ **of** profiter de; **it's to our** ~ c'est notre intérêt; **it's to our** ~ **to ...** nous avons intérêt à ....
advantageous [ædvən'teɪdʒəs] *adj* avantageux(euse).
advent ['ædvənt] *n* avènement *m*, venue *f*; **A~** (*REL*) avent *m*.
Advent calendar *n* calendrier *m* de l'avent.
adventure [əd'vɛntʃə*] *n* aventure *f*.
adventure playground *n* aire *f* de jeux.
adventurous [əd'vɛntʃərəs] *adj* aventureux(euse).
adverb ['ædvəːb] *n* adverbe *m*.
adversary ['ædvəsərɪ] *n* adversaire *m/f*.
adverse ['ædvəːs] *adj* contraire, adverse; ~ **to** hostile à; **in** ~ **circumstances** dans l'adversité.
adversity [əd'vəːsɪtɪ] *n* adversité *f*.
advert ['ædvəːt] *n abbr* (*BRIT*) = **advertisement**.
advertise ['ædvətaɪz] *vi(vt)* faire de la publicité *or* de la réclame (pour); (*in classified ads etc*) mettre une annonce (pour vendre); **to** ~ **for** (*staff*) recruter par (voie d')annonce.
advertisement [əd'vəːtɪsmənt] *n* (*COMM*) réclame *f*, publicité *f*; (*in classified ads etc*) annonce *f*.
advertiser ['ædvətaɪzə*] *n* annonceur *m*.
advertising ['ædvətaɪzɪŋ] *n* publicité *f*.
advertising agency *n* agence *f* de publicité.
advertising campaign *n* campagne *f* de publicité.
advice [əd'vaɪs] *n* conseils *mpl*; (*notification*) avis *m*; **piece of** ~ conseil; **to ask (sb) for** ~ demander conseil (à qn); **to take legal** ~ consulter un avocat.
advice note *n* (*BRIT*) avis *m* d'expédition.
advisable [əd'vaɪzəbl] *adj* recommandable, indiqué(e).
advise [əd'vaɪz] *vt* conseiller; **to** ~ **sb of sth** aviser *or* informer qn de qch; **to** ~ **sb**

against sth déconseiller qch à qn; **to ~ sb against doing sth** conseiller à qn de ne pas faire qch; **you would be well/ill ~d to go** vous feriez mieux d'y aller/de ne pas y aller, vous auriez intérêt à y aller/à ne pas y aller.

advisedly [əd'vaɪzɪdlɪ] adv (deliberately) délibérément.

adviser, advisor [əd'vaɪzə*] n conseiller/ère.

advisory [əd'vaɪzərɪ] adj consultatif(ive); **in an ~ capacity** à titre consultatif.

advocate n ['ædvəkɪt] (upholder) défenseur m, avocat/e ♦ vt ['ædvəkeɪt] recommander, prôner; **to be an ~ of** être partisan/e de.

advt. abbr = **advertisement.**

AEA n abbr (BRIT: = Atomic Energy Authority) ≈ AEN f (= Agence pour l'énergie nucléaire).

AEC n abbr (US: = Atomic Energy Commission) CEA m (= Commissariat à l'énergie atomique).

AEEU n abbr (BRIT: = Amalgamated Engineering and Electrical Union) syndicat de techniciens et d'électriciens.

Aegean (Sea) [iː'dʒiːən-] n mer f Égée.

aegis ['iːdʒɪs] n: **under the ~ of** sous l'égide de.

aeon ['iːən] n éternité f.

aerial ['ɛərɪəl] n antenne f ♦ adj aérien(ne).

aerie ['ɛərɪ] n (US) aire f.

aerobatics ['ɛərəʊ'bætɪks] npl acrobaties aériennes.

aerobics [ɛə'rəʊbɪks] n aérobic m.

aerodrome ['ɛərədrəʊm] n (BRIT) aérodrome m.

aerodynamic ['ɛərəʊdaɪ'næmɪk] adj aérodynamique.

aeronautics [ɛərə'nɔːtɪks] n aéronautique f.

aeroplane ['ɛərəpleɪn] n (BRIT) avion m.

aerosol ['ɛərəsɔl] n aérosol m.

aerospace industry ['ɛərəʊspeɪs-] n (industrie) aérospatiale f.

aesthetic [ɪs'θɛtɪk] adj esthétique.

afar [ə'faː*] adv: **from ~** de loin.

AFB n abbr (US) = **Air Force Base.**

AFDC n abbr (US: = Aid to Families with Dependent Children) aide pour enfants assistés.

affable ['æfəbl] adj affable.

affair [ə'fɛə*] n affaire f; (also: **love ~**) liaison f; aventure f; **~s** (business) affaires.

affect [ə'fɛkt] vt affecter.

affectation [æfɛk'teɪʃən] n affectation f.

affected [ə'fɛktɪd] adj affecté(e).

affection [ə'fɛkʃən] n affection f.

affectionate [ə'fɛkʃənɪt] adj affectueux(euse).

affectionately [ə'fɛkʃənɪtlɪ] adv affectueusement.

affidavit [æfɪ'deɪvɪt] n (LAW) déclaration écrite sous serment.

affiliated [ə'fɪlɪeɪtɪd] adj affilié(e); **~ company** filiale f.

affinity [ə'fɪnɪtɪ] n affinité f.

affirm [ə'fəːm] vt affirmer.

affirmation [æfə'meɪʃən] n affirmation f, as-

sertion f.

affirmative [ə'fəːmətɪv] adj affirmatif(ive) ♦ n: **in the ~** dans or par l'affirmative.

affix [ə'fɪks] vt apposer, ajouter.

afflict [ə'flɪkt] vt affliger.

affliction [ə'flɪkʃən] n affliction f.

affluence ['æfluəns] n aisance f, opulence f.

affluent ['æfluənt] adj opulent(e); (person) dans l'aisance, riche; **the ~ society** la société d'abondance.

afford [ə'fɔːd] vt (goods etc) avoir les moyens d'acheter or d'entretenir; (behaviour) se permettre; (provide) fournir, procurer; **can we ~ a car?** avons-nous de quoi acheter or les moyens d'acheter une voiture?; **I can't ~ the time** je n'ai vraiment pas le temps.

affordable [ə'fɔːdəbl] adj abordable.

affray [ə'freɪ] n (BRIT LAW) échauffourée f, rixe f.

affront [ə'frʌnt] n affront m.

affronted [ə'frʌntɪd] adj insulté(e).

Afghan ['æfgæn] adj afghan(e) ♦ n Afghan/e.

Afghanistan [æf'gænɪstæn] n Afghanistan m.

afield [ə'fiːld] adv: **far ~** loin.

AFL-CIO n abbr (= American Federation of Labor and Congress of Industrial Organizations) confédération syndicale.

afloat [ə'fləʊt] adj à flot ♦ adv: **to stay ~** surnager; **to keep/get a business ~** maintenir à flot/lancer une affaire.

afoot [ə'fʊt] adv: **there is something ~** il se prépare quelque chose.

aforementioned [ə'fɔːmɛnʃənd] adj, **aforesaid** [ə'fɔːsɛd] adj susdit(e), susmentionné(e).

afraid [ə'freɪd] adj effrayé(e); **to be ~ of** or **to** avoir peur de; **I am ~ that** je crains que + sub; **I'm ~ so/not** oui/non, malheureusement.

afresh [ə'frɛʃ] adv de nouveau.

Africa ['æfrɪkə] n Afrique f.

African ['æfrɪkən] adj africain(e) ♦ n Africain/e.

Afrikaans [æfrɪ'kɑːns] n afrikaans m.

Afrikaner [æfrɪ'kɑːnə*] n Afrikaner m/f.

Afro-American ['æfrəʊə'mɛrɪkən] adj afro-américain(e).

AFT n abbr (= American Federation of Teachers) syndicat enseignant.

aft [ɑːft] adv à l'arrière, vers l'arrière.

after ['ɑːftə*] prep, adv après ♦ conj après que, après avoir or être + pp; **~ dinner** après (le) dîner; **the day ~ tomorrow** après demain; **quarter ~ two** (US) deux heures et quart; **what/who are you ~?** que/qui cherchez-vous?; **the police are ~ him** la police est à ses trousses; **~ you!** après vous!; **~ all** après tout.

afterbirth ['ɑːftəbəːθ] n placenta m.

aftercare ['ɑːftəkɛə*] n (BRIT MED) post-cure f.

after-effects ['ɑːftərɪfɛkts] npl répercussions fpl; (of illness) séquelles fpl, suites fpl.

afterlife ['ɑːftəlaɪf] n vie future.

aftermath ['ɑːftəmɑːθ] *n* conséquences *fpl*; **in the ~ of** dans les mois *or* années *etc* qui suivirent, au lendemain de.

afternoon ['ɑːftə'nuːn] *n* après-midi *m or f*; **good ~!** bonjour!; (*goodbye*) au revoir!

afters ['ɑːftəz] *n* (*BRIT col*: *dessert*) dessert *m*.

after-sales service [ɑːftə'seɪlz-] *n* service *m* après-vente, SAV *m*.

after-shave (lotion) ['ɑːftəʃeɪv-] *n* lotion *f* après-rasage.

aftershock ['ɑːftəʃɔk] *n* réplique *f* (sismique).

aftertaste ['ɑːftəteɪst] *n* arrière-goût *m*.

afterthought ['ɑːftəθɔːt] *n*: **I had an ~** il m'est venu une idée après coup.

afterwards ['ɑːftəwədz] *adv* après.

again [ə'gɛn] *adv* de nouveau, encore une fois; **to begin/see ~** recommencer/revoir; **not ... ~** ne ... plus; **~ and ~** à plusieurs reprises; **he's opened it ~** il l'a rouvert, il l'a de nouveau *or* l'a encore ouvert; **now and ~** de temps à autre.

against [ə'gɛnst] *prep* contre; **~ a blue background** sur un fond bleu; **(as) ~** (*BRIT*) contre.

age [eɪdʒ] *n* âge *m* ♦ *vt, vi* vieillir; **what ~ is he?** quel âge a-t-il?; **he is 20 years of ~** il a 20 ans; **under ~** mineur(e); **to come of ~** atteindre sa majorité; **it's been ~s since** ça fait une éternité que ... ne.

aged [eɪdʒd] *adj* âgé(e); **~ 10** âgé de 10 ans; **the ~** ['eɪdʒɪd] *npl* les personnes âgées.

age group *n* tranche *f* d'âge; **the 40 to 50 ~** la tranche d'âge des 40 à 50 ans.

ageing ['eɪdʒɪŋ] *adj* vieillissant(e).

ageless ['eɪdʒlɪs] *adj* sans âge.

age limit *n* limite *f* d'âge.

agency ['eɪdʒənsɪ] *n* agence *f*; **through *or* by the ~ of** par l'entremise *or* l'action de.

agenda [ə'dʒɛndə] *n* ordre *m* du jour; **on the ~** à l'ordre du jour.

agent ['eɪdʒənt] *n* agent *m*.

aggravate ['ægrəveɪt] *vt* aggraver; (*annoy*) exaspérer, agacer.

aggravation [ægrə'veɪʃən] *n* agacements *mpl*.

aggregate ['ægrɪgɪt] *n* ensemble *m*, total *m*; **on ~** (*SPORT*) au total des points.

aggression [ə'grɛʃən] *n* agression *f*.

aggressive [ə'grɛsɪv] *adj* agressif(ive).

aggressiveness [ə'grɛsɪvnɪs] *n* agressivité *f*.

aggressor [ə'grɛsə*] *n* agresseur *m*.

aggrieved [ə'griːvd] *adj* chagriné(e), affligé(e).

aggro ['ægrəu] *n* (*col*: *physical*) grabuge *m*; (: *hassle*) embêtements *mpl*.

aghast [ə'gɑːst] *adj* consterné(e), atterré(e).

agile ['ædʒaɪl] *adj* agile.

agility [ə'dʒɪlɪtɪ] *n* agilité *f*, souplesse *f*.

agitate ['ædʒɪteɪt] *vt* rendre inquiet(ète) *or* agité(e) ♦ *vi* faire de l'agitation (politique); **to ~ for** faire campagne pour.

agitator ['ædʒɪteɪtə*] *n* agitateur/trice (politique).

AGM *n abbr* = **annual general meeting**.

ago [ə'gəu] *adv*: **2 days ~** il y a 2 jours; **not long ~** il n'y a pas longtemps; **as long ~ as 1960** déjà en 1960; **how long ~?** il y a combien de temps (de cela)?

agog [ə'gɔg] *adj*: **(all) ~** en émoi.

agonize ['ægənaɪz] *vi*: **he ~d over the problem** ce problème lui a causé bien du tourment.

agonizing ['ægənaɪzɪŋ] *adj* angoissant(e); (*cry*) déchirant(e).

agony ['ægənɪ] *n* grande souffrance *or* angoisse; **to be in ~** souffrir le martyre.

agony aunt *n* (*BRIT col*) journaliste *qui tient la rubrique du courrier du cœur*.

agony column *n* courrier *m* du cœur.

agree [ə'griː] *vt* (*price*) convenir de ♦ *vi*: **to ~ (with)** (*person*) être d'accord (avec); (*statements etc*) concorder (avec); (*LING*) s'accorder (avec); **to ~ to do** accepter de *or* consentir à faire; **to ~ to sth** consentir à qch; **to ~ that** (*admit*) convenir *or* reconnaître que; **it was ~d that ...** il a été convenu que ...; **they ~ on this** ils sont d'accord sur ce point; **they ~d on going/a price** ils se mirent d'accord pour y aller/sur un prix; **garlic doesn't ~ with me** je ne supporte pas l'ail.

agreeable [ə'griːəbl] *adj* (*pleasant*) agréable; (*willing*) consentant(e), d'accord; **are you ~ to this?** est-ce que vous êtes d'accord?

agreed [ə'griːd] *adj* (*time, place*) convenu(e); **to be ~** être d'accord.

agreement [ə'griːmənt] *n* accord *m*; **in ~** d'accord; **by mutual ~** d'un commun accord.

agricultural [ægrɪ'kʌltʃərəl] *adj* agricole.

agriculture ['ægrɪkʌltʃə*] *n* agriculture *f*.

aground [ə'graund] *adv*: **to run ~** s'échouer.

ahead [ə'hɛd] *adv* en avant; devant; **go right *or* straight ~** allez tout droit; **go ~!** (*fig*) allez-y!; **~ of** devant; (*fig*: *schedule etc*) en avance sur; **~ of time** en avance; **they were (right) ~ of us** ils nous précédaient (de peu), ils étaient (juste) devant nous.

AI *n abbr* = **Amnesty International**; (*COMPUT*) = **artificial intelligence**.

AIB *n abbr* (*BRIT*: = *Accident Investigation Bureau*) *commission d'enquête sur les accidents*.

AID *n abbr* (= *artificial insemination by donor*) IAD *f*; (*US*: = *Agency for International Development*) *agence pour le développement international*.

aid [eɪd] *n* aide *f* ♦ *vt* aider; **with the ~ of** avec l'aide de; **in ~ of** en faveur de; **to ~ and abet** (*LAW*) se faire le complice de.

aide [eɪd] *n* (*person*) assistant/e.

AIDS [eɪdz] *n abbr* (= *acquired immune (or immuno-)deficiency syndrome*) SIDA *m*.

AIH *n abbr* (= *artificial insemination by husband*) IAC *f*.

ailment ['eɪlmənt] *n* affection *f*.

aim [eɪm] *n* but *m* ♦ *vt*: **to ~ sth at** (*gun*,

camera) braquer or pointer qch sur, diriger qch contre; (missile) pointer qch vers or sur; (remark, blow) destiner or adresser qch à ♦ vi (also: to take ~) viser; to ~ at viser; (fig) viser (à); avoir pour but or ambition; to ~ to do avoir l'intention de faire.

aimless ['eɪmlɪs] adj sans but.

aimlessly ['eɪmlɪslɪ] adv sans but.

ain't [eɪnt] (col) = am not, aren't, isn't.

air [εə*] n air m ♦ vt aérer; (idea, grievance, views) mettre au tapis; (knowledge) faire étalage de ♦ cpd (currents, attack etc) aérien(ne); **by ~** par avion; **to be on the ~** (RADIO, TV: programme) être diffusé(e); (: station) émettre.

air bag n airbag m.

air base n base aérienne.

airbed ['εəbεd] n (BRIT) matelas m pneumatique.

airborne ['εəbɔːn] adj (plane) en vol; (troops) aeroporté(e); (particles) dans l'air; **as soon as the plane was ~** dès que l'avion eut décollé.

air cargo n fret aérien.

air-conditioned ['εəkən'dɪʃənd] adj climatisé(e), à air conditionné.

air conditioning [-kən'dɪʃnɪŋ] n climatisation f.

air-cooled ['εəkuːld] adj à refroidissement à air.

aircraft ['εəkrɑːft] n (pl inv) avion m.

aircraft carrier n porte-avions m inv.

air cushion n coussin m d'air.

airdrome ['εədrəum] n (US) aérodrome m.

airfield ['εəfiːld] n terrain m d'aviation.

Air Force n Armée f de l'air.

air freight n fret aérien.

airgun ['εəgʌn] n fusil m à air comprimé.

air hostess n (BRIT) hôtesse f de l'air.

airily ['εərɪlɪ] adv d'un air dégagé.

airing ['εərɪŋ] n: **to give an ~** to aérer; (fig: ideas, views etc) mettre sur le tapis.

air letter n (BRIT) aérogramme m.

airlift ['εəlɪft] n pont aérien.

airline ['εəlaɪn] n ligne aérienne, compagnie aérienne.

airliner ['εəlaɪnə*] n avion m de ligne.

airlock ['εəlɔk] n sas m.

airmail ['εəmeɪl] n: **by ~** par avion.

air mattress n matelas m pneumatique.

airplane ['εəpleɪn] n (US) avion m.

air pocket n trou m d'air.

airport ['εəpɔːt] n aéroport m.

air raid n attaque aérienne.

air rifle n carabine f à air comprimé.

airsick ['εəsɪk] adj: **to be ~** avoir le mal de l'air.

airspeed ['εəspiːd] n vitesse relative.

airstrip ['εəstrɪp] n terrain m d'atterrissage.

air terminal n aérogare f.

airtight ['εətaɪt] adj hermétique.

air time n (RADIO, TV) temps m d'antenne.

air traffic control n contrôle m de la navigation aérienne.

air traffic controller n aiguilleur m du ciel.

airway ['εəweɪ] n (AVIAT) voie aérienne; **~s** (ANAT) voies aériennes.

airy ['εərɪ] adj bien aéré(e); (manners) dégagé(e).

aisle [aɪl] n (of church) allée centrale; nef latérale; (in theatre) allée f; (on plane) couloir m.

ajar [ə'dʒɑː*] adj entrouvert(e).

AK abbr (US) = Alaska.

aka abbr (= also known as) alias.

akin [ə'kɪn] adj: **~ to** semblable à, du même ordre que.

AL abbr (US) = Alabama.

ALA n abbr = American Library Association.

Ala. abbr (US) = Alabama.

alacrity [ə'lækrɪtɪ] n: **with ~** avec empressement, promptement.

alarm [ə'lɑːm] n alarme f ♦ vt alarmer.

alarm clock n réveille-matin m inv, réveil m.

alarmed [ə'lɑːmd] adj (frightened) alarmé(e); (protected by an alarm) protégé(e) par un système d'alarme; **to become ~** prendre peur.

alarming [ə'lɑːmɪŋ] adj alarmant(e).

alarmingly [ə'lɑːmɪŋlɪ] adv d'une manière alarmante; **~ close** dangereusement proche; **~ quickly** à une vitesse inquiétante.

alarmist [ə'lɑːmɪst] n alarmiste m/f.

alas [ə'læs] excl hélas.

Alas. abbr (US) = Alaska.

Alaska [ə'læskə] n Alaska m.

Albania [æl'beɪnɪə] n Albanie f.

Albanian [æl'beɪnɪən] adj albanais(e) ♦ n Albanais/e; (LING) albanais m.

albatross ['ælbətrɔs] n albatros m.

albeit [ɔːl'biːɪt] conj bien que + sub, encore que + sub.

album ['ælbəm] n album m.

albumen ['ælbjumɪn] n albumine f; (of egg) albumen m.

alchemy ['ælkɪmɪ] n alchimie f.

alcohol ['ælkəhɔl] n alcool m.

alcohol-free ['ælkəhɔlfriː] adj sans alcool.

alcoholic [ælkə'hɔlɪk] adj, n alcoolique (m/f).

alcoholism ['ælkəhɔlɪzəm] n alcoolisme m.

alcove ['ælkəuv] n alcôve f.

Ald. abbr = alderman.

alderman ['ɔːldəmən] n conseiller municipal (en Angleterre).

ale [eɪl] n bière f.

alert [ə'lɜːt] adj alerte, vif(vive); (watchful) vigilant(e) ♦ n alerte f ♦ vt: **to ~ sb (to sth)** attirer l'attention de qn (sur qch); **to ~ sb to the dangers of sth** avertir qn des dangers de qch; **on the ~** sur le qui-vive; (MIL) en état d'alerte.

Aleutian Islands [ə'luːʃən-] npl îles Aléoutiennes.

A levels npl ≈ baccalauréat msg.

Alexandria [ælɪgˈzɑːndrɪə] *n* Alexandrie.
alfresco [ælˈfreskəʊ] *adj, adv* en plein air.
algebra [ˈældʒɪbrə] *n* algèbre *m*.
Algeria [ælˈdʒɪərɪə] *n* Algérie *f*.
Algerian [ælˈdʒɪərɪən] *adj* algérien(ne) ♦ *n* Algérien/ne.
Algiers [ælˈdʒɪəz] *n* Alger.
algorithm [ˈælgərɪðəm] *n* algorithme *m*.
alias [ˈeɪlɪəs] *adv* alias ♦ *n* faux nom, nom d'emprunt.
alibi [ˈælɪbaɪ] *n* alibi *m*.
alien [ˈeɪlɪən] *n* étranger/ère ♦ *adj:* ~ **(to)** étranger(ère) (à).
alienate [ˈeɪlɪəneɪt] *vt* aliéner; (*subj: person*) s'aliéner.
alienation [eɪlɪəˈneɪʃən] *n* aliénation *f*.
alight [əˈlaɪt] *adj, adv* en feu ♦ *vi* mettre pied à terre; (*passenger*) descendre; (*bird*) se poser.
align [əˈlaɪn] *vt* aligner.
alignment [əˈlaɪnmənt] *n* alignement *m*; **it's out of** ~ **(with)** ce n'est pas aligné (avec).
alike [əˈlaɪk] *adj* semblable, pareil(le) ♦ *adv* de même; **to look** ~ se ressembler.
alimony [ˈælɪmənɪ] *n* (*payment*) pension *f* alimentaire.
alive [əˈlaɪv] *adj* vivant(e); (*active*) plein(e) de vie; ~ **with** grouillant(e) de; ~ **to** sensible à.
alkali [ˈælkəlaɪ] *n* alcali *m*.

══════════════ *KEYWORD*

all [ɔːl] *adj* (*singular*) tout(e); (*plural*) tous(toutes); ~ **day** toute la journée; ~ **night** toute la nuit; ~ **men** tous les hommes; ~ **five** tous les cinq; ~ **the food** toute la nourriture; ~ **the books** tous les livres; ~ **the time** tout le temps; ~ **his life** toute sa vie
♦ *pron* **1** tout; **I ate it** ~, **I ate** ~ **of it** j'ai tout mangé; ~ **of us went** nous y sommes tous allés; ~ **of the boys went** tous les garçons y sont allés; **is that** ~? c'est tout?; (*in shop*) ce sera tout?
2 (*in phrases*): **above** ~ surtout, par-dessus tout; **after** ~ après tout; **at** ~: **not at** ~ (*in answer to question*) pas du tout; (*in answer to thanks*) je vous en prie!; **I'm not at** ~ **tired** je ne suis pas du tout fatigué(e); **anything at** ~ **will do** n'importe quoi fera l'affaire; ~ **in** ~ tout bien considéré, en fin de compte
♦ *adv*: ~ **alone** tout(e) seul(e); **it's not as hard as** ~ **that** ce n'est pas si difficile que ça; ~ **the more/the better** d'autant plus/mieux; ~ **but** presque, pratiquement; **to be** ~ **in** (*BRIT col*) être complètement à plat; ~ **out** *adv* à fond; **the score is 2** ~ le score est de 2 partout.

────────────────────

all-around [ɔːləˈraʊnd] *adj* (*US*) = **all-round**.
allay [əˈleɪ] *vt* (*fears*) apaiser, calmer.
all clear *n* (*also fig*) fin *f* d'alerte.
allegation [ælɪˈgeɪʃən] *n* allégation *f*.
allege [əˈledʒ] *vt* alléguer, prétendre; **he is** ~**d to have said** il aurait dit.

alleged [əˈledʒd] *adj* prétendu(e).
allegedly [əˈledʒɪdlɪ] *adv* à ce que l'on prétend, paraît-il.
allegiance [əˈliːdʒəns] *n* fidélité *f*, obéissance *f*.
allegory [ˈælɪgərɪ] *n* allégorie *f*.
all-embracing [ˈɔːlɪmˈbreɪsɪŋ] *adj* universel(le).
allergic [əˈlɜːdʒɪk] *adj:* ~ **to** allergique à.
allergy [ˈælədʒɪ] *n* allergie *f*.
alleviate [əˈliːvɪeɪt] *vt* soulager, adoucir.
alley [ˈælɪ] *n* ruelle *f*; (*in garden*) allée *f*.
alleyway [ˈælɪweɪ] *n* ruelle *f*.
alliance [əˈlaɪəns] *n* alliance *f*.
allied [ˈælaɪd] *adj* allié(e).
alligator [ˈælɪgeɪtə*] *n* alligator *m*.
all-important [ˈɔːlɪmˈpɔːtənt] *adj* capital(e), crucial(e).
all-in [ˈɔːlɪn] *adj, adv* (*BRIT: charge*) tout compris.
all-in wrestling *n* (*BRIT*) catch *m*.
alliteration [əlɪtəˈreɪʃən] *n* allitération *f*.
all-night [ˈɔːlˈnaɪt] *adj* ouvert(e) *or* qui dure toute la nuit.
allocate [ˈæləkeɪt] *vt* (*share out*) répartir, distribuer; (*duties*): **to** ~ **sth to** assigner *or* attribuer qch à; (*sum, time*): **to** ~ **sth to** allouer qch à; **to** ~ **sth for** affecter qch à.
allocation [æləʊˈkeɪʃən] *n* (*see vb*) répartition *f*; attribution *f*; allocation *f*; affectation *f*; (*money*) crédit(s) *m(pl)*, somme(s) allouée(s).
allot [əˈlɒt] *vt* (*share out*) répartir, distribuer; (*time*): **to** ~ **sth to** allouer qch à; (*duties*): **to** ~ **sth to** assigner qch à; **in the** ~**ted time** dans le temps imparti.
allotment [əˈlɒtmənt] *n* (*share*) part *f*; (*garden*) lopin *m* de terre (*loué à la municipalité*).
all-out [ˈɔːlaʊt] *adj* (*effort etc*) total(e).
allow [əˈlaʊ] *vt* (*practice, behaviour*) permettre, autoriser; (*sum to spend etc*) accorder, allouer; (*sum, time estimated*) compter, prévoir; (*concede*): **to** ~ **that** convenir que; **to** ~ **sb to do** permettre à qn de faire, autoriser qn à faire; **he is** ~**ed to ...** on lui permet de ...; **smoking is not** ~**ed** il est interdit de fumer; **we must** ~ **3 days for the journey** il faut compter 3 jours pour le voyage.
► **allow for** *vt fus* tenir compte de.
allowance [əˈlaʊəns] *n* (*money received*) allocation *f*; (: *from parent etc*) subside *m*; (: *for expenses*) indemnité *f*; (*TAX*) somme *f* déductible du revenu imposable, abattement *m*; **to make** ~**s for** tenir compte de.
alloy [ˈælɔɪ] *n* alliage *m*.
all right *adv* (*feel, work*) bien; (*as answer*) d'accord.
all-round [ˈɔːlˈraʊnd] *adj* compétent(e) dans tous les domaines; (*athlete etc*) complet(ète).
all-rounder [ɔːlˈraʊndə*] *n* (*BRIT*): **to be a good** ~ être doué(e) en tout.
allspice [ˈɔːlspaɪs] *n* poivre *m* de la Jamaïque.
all-time [ˈɔːlˈtaɪm] *adj* (*record*) sans précédent, absolu(e).
allude [əˈluːd] *vi:* **to** ~ **to** faire allusion à.

alluring [ə'ljuərɪŋ] *adj* séduisant(e), alléchant(e).

allusion [ə'luːʒən] *n* allusion *f*.

alluvium [ə'luːvɪəm] *n* alluvions *fpl*.

ally *n* ['ælaɪ] allié *m* ♦ *vt* [ə'laɪ]: **to ~ o.s. with** s'allier avec.

almighty [ɔːl'maɪtɪ] *adj* tout-puissant.

almond ['ɑːmənd] *n* amande *f*.

almost ['ɔːlməʊst] *adv* presque; **he ~ fell** il a failli tomber.

alms [ɑːmz] *n* aumône(s) *f(pl)*.

aloft [ə'lɔft] *adv* en haut, en l'air; (*NAUT*) dans la mâture.

alone [ə'ləʊn] *adj*, *adv* seul(e); **to leave sb ~** laisser qn tranquille; **to leave sth ~** ne pas toucher à qch; **let ~ ...** sans parler de ...; encore moins ....

along [ə'lɔŋ] *prep* le long de ♦ *adv*: **is he coming ~?** vient-il avec nous?; **he was hopping/limping ~** il venait *or* avançait en sautillant/boitant; **~ with** avec, en plus de; (*person*) en compagnie de.

alongside [ə'lɔŋ'saɪd] *prep* le long de; au côté de ♦ *adv* bord à bord; côte à côte; **we brought our boat ~** (*of a pier, shore etc*) nous avons accosté.

aloof [ə'luːf] *adj*, *adv* à distance, à l'écart; **to stand ~** se tenir à l'écart *or* à distance.

aloofness [ə'luːfnɪs] *n* réserve (hautaine), attitude distante.

aloud [ə'laʊd] *adv* à haute voix.

alphabet ['ælfəbɛt] *n* alphabet *m*.

alphabetical [ælfə'bɛtɪkl] *adj* alphabétique; **in ~ order** par ordre alphabétique.

alphanumeric [ælfənjuː'mɛrɪk] *adj* alphanumérique.

alpine ['ælpaɪn] *adj* alpin(e), alpestre; **~ hut** cabane *f* *or* refuge *m* de montagne; **~ pasture** pâturage *m* (de montagne); **~ skiing** ski alpin.

Alps [ælps] *npl*: **the ~** les Alpes *fpl*.

already [ɔːl'rɛdɪ] *adv* déjà.

alright ['ɔːl'raɪt] *adv* (*BRIT*) = **all right**.

Alsace [æl'sæs] *n* Alsace *f*.

Alsatian [æl'seɪʃən] *adj* alsacien(ne), d'Alsace ♦ *n* Alsacien/ne; (*BRIT: dog*) berger allemand.

also ['ɔːlsəʊ] *adv* aussi.

Alta. *abbr* (*Canada*) = **Alberta**.

altar ['ɔltə*] *n* autel *m*.

alter ['ɔltə*] *vt*, *vi* changer, modifier.

alteration [ɔltə'reɪʃən] *n* changement *m*, modification *f*; **~s** (*SEWING*) retouches *fpl*; (*ARCHIT*) modifications *fpl*; **timetable subject to ~** horaires sujets à modifications.

altercation [ɔltə'keɪʃən] *n* altercation *f*.

alternate *adj* [ɔl'təːnɪt] alterné(e), alternant(e), alternatif(ive) ♦ *vi* ['ɔltəːneɪt] alterner; **on ~ days** un jour sur deux, tous les deux jours.

alternately [ɔl'təːnɪtlɪ] *adv* alternativement, en alternant.

alternating ['ɔltəːneɪtɪŋ] *adj* (*current*) alternatif(ive).

alternative [ɔl'təːnətɪv] *adj* (*solutions*) interchangeable, possible; (*solution*) autre, de remplacement; (*energy*) doux(douce); (*society*) parallèle ♦ *n* (*choice*) alternative *f*; (*other possibility*) autre possibilité *f*.

alternatively [ɔl'təːnətɪvlɪ] *adv*: **~ one could** une autre *or* l'autre solution serait de.

alternative medicine *n* médecines *fpl* parallèles *or* douces.

alternator ['ɔltəːneɪtə*] *n* (*AUT*) alternateur *m*.

although [ɔːl'ðəʊ] *conj* bien que + *sub*.

altitude ['æltɪtjuːd] *n* altitude *f*.

alto ['æltəʊ] *n* (*female*) contralto *m*; (*male*) haute-contre *f*.

altogether [ɔːltə'gɛðə*] *adv* entièrement, tout à fait; (*on the whole*) tout compte fait; (*in all*) en tout; **how much is that ~?** ça fait combien en tout?

altruism ['æltruɪzəm] *n* altruisme *m*.

altruistic [æltru'ɪstɪk] *adj* altruiste.

aluminium [ælju'mɪnɪəm], (*US*) **aluminum** [ə'luːmɪnəm] *n* aluminium *m*.

alumna, *pl* **alumnae** [ə'lʌmnə, -niː] *n* (*US: SCOL*) ancienne élève; (: *UNIVERSITY*) ancienne étudiante.

alumnus, *pl* **alumni** [ə'lʌmnəs, -naɪ] *n* (*US: SCOL*) ancien élève; (:*UNIVERSITY*) ancien étudiant.

always ['ɔːlweɪz] *adv* toujours.

Alzheimer's disease ['æltshaɪməz-] *n* maladie *f* d'Alzheimer.

AM *abbr* = amplitude modulation.

am [æm] *vb see* **be**.

a.m. *adv abbr* (= *ante meridiem*) du matin.

AMA *n abbr* = American Medical Association.

amalgam [ə'mælgəm] *n* amalgame *m*.

amalgamate [ə'mælgəmeɪt] *vt*, *vi* fusionner.

amalgamation [əmælgə'meɪʃən] *n* fusion *f*; (*COMM*) fusionnement *m*.

amass [ə'mæs] *vt* amasser.

amateur ['æmətə*] *n* amateur *m* ♦ *adj* (*SPORT*) amateur *inv*; **~ dramatics** le théâtre amateur.

amateurish ['æmətərɪʃ] *adj* (*pej*) d'amateur, un peu amateur.

amaze [ə'meɪz] *vt* surprendre, étonner; **to be ~d (at)** être surpris *or* étonné (de).

amazement [ə'meɪzmənt] *n* surprise *f*, étonnement *m*.

amazing [ə'meɪzɪŋ] *adj* étonnant(e), incroyable; (*bargain, offer*) exceptionnel(le).

amazingly [ə'meɪzɪŋlɪ] *adv* incroyablement.

Amazon ['æməzən] *n* (*GEO, MYTHOLOGY*) Amazone *f* ♦ *cpd* amazonien(ne), de l'Amazone; **the ~ basin** le bassin de l'Amazone; **the ~ jungle** la forêt amazonienne.

Amazonian [æmə'zəʊnɪən] *adj* amazonien(ne).

ambassador [æm'bæsədə*] *n* ambassadeur *m*.

amber ['æmbə*] *n* ambre *m*; **at ~** (*BRIT AUT*) à l'orange.

ambidextrous [æmbɪ'dɛkstrəs] *adj* ambidextre.

ambience ['æmbɪəns] *n* ambiance *f*.

ambiguity [æmbɪ'gjuɪtɪ] *n* ambiguïté *f*.

ambiguous [æm'bɪgjuəs] *adj* ambigu(ë).

ambition [æm'bɪʃən] *n* ambition *f*.

ambitious [æm'bɪʃəs] *adj* ambitieux(euse).

ambivalent [æm'bɪvələnt] *adj* (*attitude*) ambivalent(e).

amble ['æmbl] *vi* (*also*: **to ~ along**) aller d'un pas tranquille.

ambulance ['æmbjuləns] *n* ambulance *f*.

ambush ['æmbuʃ] *n* embuscade *f* ♦ *vt* tendre une embuscade à.

ameba [ə'miːbə] *n* (*US*) = amoeba.

ameliorate [ə'miːlɪəreɪt] *vt* améliorer.

amen ['ɑːˈmɛn] *excl* amen.

amenable [ə'miːnəbl] *adj*: **~ to** (*advice etc*) disposé(e) à écouter *or* suivre; **~ to the law** responsable devant la loi.

amend [ə'mɛnd] *vt* (*law*) amender; (*text*) corriger; (*habits*) réformer ♦ *vi* s'amender, se corriger; **to make ~s** réparer ses torts, faire amende honorable.

amendment [ə'mɛndmənt] *n* (*to law*) amendement *m*; (*to text*) correction *f*.

amenities [ə'miːnɪtɪz] *npl* aménagements *mpl*, équipements *mpl*.

amenity [ə'miːnɪtɪ] *n* charme *m*, agrément *m*.

America [ə'mɛrɪkə] *n* Amérique *f*.

American [ə'mɛrɪkən] *adj* américain(e) ♦ *n* Américain/e.

americanize [ə'mɛrɪkənaɪz] *vt* américaniser.

amethyst ['æmɪθɪst] *n* améthyste *f*.

Amex ['æmɛks] *n abbr* = *American Stock Exchange*.

amiable ['eɪmɪəbl] *adj* aimable, affable.

amicable ['æmɪkəbl] *adj* amical(e).

amicably ['æmɪkəblɪ] *adv* amicalement.

amid(st) [ə'mɪd(st)] *prep* parmi, au milieu de.

amiss [ə'mɪs] *adj, adv*: **there's something ~** il y a quelque chose qui ne va pas *or* qui cloche; **to take sth ~** prendre qch mal *or* de travers.

ammo ['æməu] *n abbr* (*col*) = ammunition.

ammonia [ə'məunɪə] *n* (*gas*) ammoniac *m*; (*liquid*) ammoniaque *f*.

ammunition [æmju'nɪʃən] *n* munitions *fpl*; (*fig*) arguments *mpl*.

ammunition dump *n* dépôt *m* de munitions.

amnesia [æm'niːzɪə] *n* amnésie *f*.

amnesty ['æmnɪstɪ] *n* amnistie *f*; **to grant an ~** to accorder une amnistie à.

Amnesty International *n* Amnesty International.

amoeba, (*US*) **ameba** [ə'miːbə] *n* amibe *f*.

amok [ə'mɔk] *adv*: **to run ~** être pris(e) d'un accès de folie furieuse.

among(st) [ə'mʌŋ(st)] *prep* parmi, entre.

amoral [æ'mɔrəl] *adj* amoral(e).

amorous ['æmərəs] *adj* amoureux(euse).

amorphous [ə'mɔːfəs] *adj* amorphe.

amortization [əmɔːtaɪ'zeɪʃən] *n* (*COMM*) amor-

tissement *m*.

amount [ə'maunt] *n* (*sum of money*) somme *f*; (*total*) montant *m*; (*quantity*) quantité *f*, nombre *m* ♦ *vi*: **to ~ to** (*total*) s'élever à; (*be same as*) équivaloir à, revenir à; **this ~s to a refusal** cela équivaut à un refus; **the total ~** (*of money*) le montant total.

amp(ere) ['æmp(ɛə*)] *n* ampère *m*; **a 13 amp plug** une fiche de 13 A.

ampersand ['æmpəsænd] *n* signe &, "et" commercial.

amphetamine [æm'fɛtəmiːn] *n* amphétamine *f*.

amphibian [æm'fɪbɪən] *n* batracien *m*.

amphibious [æm'fɪbɪəs] *adj* amphibie.

amphitheatre, (*US*) **amphitheater** ['æmfɪθɪətə*] *n* amphithéâtre *m*.

ample ['æmpl] *adj* ample; spacieux(euse); (*enough*): **this is ~** c'est largement suffisant; **to have ~ time/room** avoir bien assez de temps/place, avoir largement le temps/la place.

amplifier ['æmplɪfaɪə*] *n* amplificateur *m*.

amplify ['æmplɪfaɪ] *vt* amplifier.

amply ['æmplɪ] *adv* amplement, largement.

ampoule, (*US*) **ampule** ['æmpuːl] *n* (*MED*) ampoule *f*.

amputate ['æmpjuteɪt] *vt* amputer.

amputee [æmpju'tiː] *n* amputé/e.

Amsterdam ['æmstədæm] *n* Amsterdam.

amt *abbr* = amount.

amuck [ə'mʌk] *adv* = amok.

amuse [ə'mjuːz] *vt* amuser; **to ~ o.s. with sth/by doing sth** se divertir avec qch/à faire qch; **to be ~d at** être amusé par; **he was not ~d** il n'a pas apprécié.

amusement [ə'mjuːzmənt] *n* amusement *m*.

amusement arcade *n* salle *f* de jeu.

amusement park *n* parc *m* d'attractions.

amusing [ə'mjuːzɪŋ] *adj* amusant(e), divertissant(e).

an [æn, ən, n] *indef art see* a.

ANA *n abbr* = *American Newspaper Association*; *American Nurses Association*.

anachronism [ə'nækrənɪzəm] *n* anachronisme *m*.

anaemia [ə'niːmɪə] *n* anémie *f*.

anaemic [ə'niːmɪk] *adj* anémique.

anaesthetic [ænɪs'θɛtɪk] *adj, n* anesthésique (*m*); **under the ~** sous anesthésie; **local/general ~** anesthésie locale/générale.

anaesthetist [æ'niːsθɪtɪst] *n* anesthésiste *m/f*.

anagram ['ænəgræm] *n* anagramme *m*.

anal ['eɪnl] *adj* anal(e).

analgesic [ænæl'dʒiːsɪk] *adj, n* analgésique (*m*).

analogous [ə'næləgəs] *adj*: **~ (to or with)** analogue (à).

analog(ue) ['ænəlɔg] *adj* (*watch, computer*) analogique.

analogy [ə'nælədʒɪ] *n* analogie *f*; **to draw an ~ between** établir une analogie entre.

analyse ['ænəlaɪz] *vt* (*BRIT*) analyser.

analysis, pl **analyses** [ə'næləsıs, -siːz] n analyse f; **in the last** ~ en dernière analyse.

analyst ['ænəlıst] n (political ~ etc) analyste m/ f; (US) psychanalyste m/f.

analytic(al) [ænə'lıtık(əl)] adj analytique.

analyze ['ænəlaız] vt (US) = **analyse.**

anarchic [æ'nɑːkık] adj anarchique.

anarchist ['ænəkıst] adj, n anarchiste (m/f).

anarchy ['ænəkı] n anarchie f.

anathema [ə'næθımə] n: **it is** ~ **to him** il a cela en abomination.

anatomical [ænə'tɔmıkəl] adj anatomique.

anatomy [ə'nætəmı] n anatomie f.

ANC n abbr (= African National Congress) ANC m.

ancestor ['ænsıstə*] n ancêtre m, aïeul m.

ancestral [æn'sɛstrəl] adj ancestral(e).

ancestry ['ænsıstrı] n ancêtres mpl; ascendance f.

anchor ['æŋkə*] n ancre f ♦ vi (also: to drop ~) jeter l'ancre, mouiller ♦ vt mettre à l'ancre.

anchorage ['æŋkərıdʒ] n mouillage m, ancrage m.

anchor man, anchor woman n (TV, RADIO) présentateur/trice.

anchovy ['æntʃəvı] n anchois m.

ancient ['eınʃənt] adj ancien(ne), antique; (fig) d'un âge vénérable, antique; ~ **monument** monument m historique.

ancillary [æn'sılərı] adj auxiliaire.

and [ænd] conj et; ~ **so on** et ainsi de suite; **try** ~ **come** tâchez de venir; **come** ~ **sit here** venez vous asseoir ici; **better** ~ **better** de mieux en mieux; **more** ~ **more** de plus en plus.

Andes ['ændiːz] npl: **the** ~ les Andes fpl.

anecdote ['ænıkdəut] n anecdote f.

anemia [ə'niːmıə] n = **anaemia.**

anemic [ə'niːmık] adj = **anaemic.**

anemone [ə'nɛmənı] n (BOT) anémone f; **sea** ~ anémone de mer.

anesthesiologist [ænısθiːzı'ɔlədʒıst] n (US) anesthésiste m/f.

anesthetic [ænıs'θɛtık] adj, n = **anaesthetic.**

anesthetist [æ'niːsθıtıst] n = **anaesthetist.**

anew [ə'njuː] adv à nouveau.

angel ['eındʒəl] n ange m.

angel dust n poussière f d'ange.

anger ['æŋgə*] n colère f ♦ vt mettre en colère, irriter.

angina [æn'dʒaınə] n angine f de poitrine.

angle ['æŋgl] n angle m ♦ vi: **to** ~ **for** (trout) pêcher; (compliments) chercher, quêter; **from their** ~ de leur point de vue.

angler ['æŋglə*] n pêcheur/euse à la ligne.

Anglican ['æŋglıkən] adj, n anglican(e).

anglicize ['æŋglısaız] vt angliciser.

angling ['æŋglıŋ] n pêche f à la ligne.

Anglo- ['æŋgləu] prefix anglo(-).

Anglo-French ['æŋgləu'frɛntʃ] adj anglo-français(e).

Anglo-Saxon ['æŋgləu'sæksən] adj, n anglo-saxon(ne).

Angola [æŋ'gəulə] n Angola m.

Angolan [æŋ'gəulən] adj angolais(e) ♦ n Angolais/e.

angrily ['æŋgrılı] adv avec colère.

angry ['æŋgrı] adj en colère, furieux(euse); **to be** ~ **with sb/at sth** être furieux contre qn/ de qch; **to get** ~ se fâcher, se mettre en colère; **to make sb** ~ mettre qn en colère.

anguish ['æŋgwıʃ] n angoisse f.

anguished ['æŋgwıʃt] adj (mentally) angoissé(e); (physically) plein(e) de souffrance.

angular ['æŋgjulə*] adj anguleux(euse).

animal ['ænıməl] n animal m ♦ adj animal(e).

animal rights npl droits mpl de l'animal.

animate vt ['ænımeıt] animer ♦ adj ['ænımıt] animé(e), vivant(e).

animated ['ænımeıtıd] adj animé(e).

animation [ænı'meıʃən] n (of person) entrain m; (of street, CINE) animation f.

animosity [ænı'mɔsıtı] n animosité f.

aniseed ['ænisiːd] n anis m.

Ankara ['æŋkərə] n Ankara f.

ankle ['æŋkl] n cheville f.

ankle socks npl socquettes fpl.

annex n ['ænɛks] (also: BRIT: **annexe**) annexe f ♦ vt [ə'nɛks] annexer.

annexation [ænɛks'eıʃən] n annexion f.

annihilate [ə'naıəleıt] vt annihiler, anéantir.

annihilation [ənaıə'leıʃən] n anéantissement m.

anniversary [ænı'vəːsərı] n anniversaire m.

anniversary dinner n dîner commémoratif or anniversaire.

annotate ['ænəuteıt] vt annoter.

announce [ə'nauns] vt annoncer; (birth, death) faire part de; **he** ~**d that he wasn't going** il a déclaré qu'il n'irait pas.

announcement [ə'naunsmənt] n annonce f; (for births etc: in newspaper) avis m de faire-part; (: letter, card) faire-part m; **I'd like to make an** ~ j'ai une communication à faire.

announcer [ə'naunsə*] n (RADIO, TV: between programmes) speaker/ine; (: in a programme) présentateur/trice.

annoy [ə'nɔı] vt agacer, ennuyer, contrarier; **to be** ~**ed (at sth/with sb)** être en colère or irrité (contre qch/qn); **don't get** ~**ed!** ne vous fâchez pas!

annoyance [ə'nɔıəns] n mécontentement m, contrariété f.

annoying [ə'nɔııŋ] adj ennuyeux(euse), agaçant(e), contrariant(e).

annual ['ænjuəl] adj annuel(le) ♦ n (BOT) plante annuelle; (book) album m.

annual general meeting (AGM) n (BRIT) assemblée générale annuelle (AGA).

annually ['ænjuəlı] adv annuellement.

annual report n rapport annuel.

annuity [ə'njuːıtı] n rente f; **life** ~ rente viagère.

annul [ə'nʌl] vt annuler; (law) abroger.

annulment [ə'nʌlmənt] *n* (*see vb*) annulation *f*; abrogation *f*.

annum ['ænəm] *n see* **per annum**.

Annunciation [ənʌnsɪ'eɪʃən] *n* Annonciation *f*.

anode ['ænəud] *n* anode *f*.

anoint [ə'nɔɪnt] *vt* oindre.

anomalous [ə'nɔmələs] *adj* anormal(e).

anomaly [ə'nɔməlɪ] *n* anomalie *f*.

anon. [ə'nɔn] *abbr* = **anonymous**.

anonymity [ænə'nɪmɪtɪ] *n* anonymat *m*.

anonymous [ə'nɔnɪməs] *adj* anonyme; **to remain** ~ garder l'anonymat.

anorak ['ænəræk] *n* anorak *m*.

anorexia [ænə'rɛksɪə] *n* (*also*: ~ **nervosa**) anorexie *f*.

anorexic [ænə'rɛksɪk] *adj, n* anorexique (*m/f*).

another [ə'nʌðə*] *adj*: ~ **book** (*one more*) un autre livre, encore un livre, un livre de plus; (*a different one*) un autre livre; ~ **drink?** encore un verre?; **in** ~ **5 years** dans 5 ans ♦ *pron* un(e) autre, encore un(e), un(e) de plus; *see also* **one**.

ANSI ['ænsɪ] *n abbr* (= *American National Standards Institution*) ANSI *m* (*Institut américain de normalisation*).

answer ['ɑːnsə*] *n* réponse *f*; (*to problem*) solution *f* ♦ *vi* répondre ♦ *vt* (*reply to*) répondre à; (*problem*) résoudre; (*prayer*) exaucer; **to** ~ **the phone** répondre (au téléphone); **in** ~ **to your letter** suite à *or* en réponse à votre lettre; **to** ~ **the bell** *or* **the door** aller *or* venir ouvrir (la porte).

▶**answer back** *vi* répondre, répliquer.

▶**answer for** *vt fus* répondre de, se porter garant de; (*crime, one's actions*) répondre de.

▶**answer to** *vt fus* (*description*) répondre *or* correspondre à.

answerable ['ɑːnsərəbl] *adj*: ~ (**to sb/for sth**) responsable (devant qn/de qch); **I am** ~ **to no-one** je n'ai de comptes à rendre à personne.

answering machine ['ɑːnsərɪŋ-] *n* répondeur *m*.

ant [ænt] *n* fourmi *f*.

ANTA *n abbr* = *American National Theater and Academy*.

antagonism [æn'tægənɪzəm] *n* antagonisme *m*.

antagonist [æn'tægənɪst] *n* antagoniste *m/f*, adversaire *m/f*.

antagonistic [æntægə'nɪstɪk] *adj* (*attitude, feelings*) hostile.

antagonize [æn'tægənaɪz] *vt* éveiller l'hostilité de, contrarier.

Antarctic [ænt'ɑːktɪk] *adj* antarctique, austral(e) ♦ *n*: **the** ~ l'Antarctique *m*.

Antarctica [ænt'ɑːktɪkə] *n* Antarctique *m*, Terres Australes.

Antarctic Circle *n* cercle *m* Antarctique.

Antarctic Ocean *n* océan *m* Antarctique *or* Austral.

ante ['æntɪ] *n*: **to up the** ~ faire monter les enjeux.

ante... ['æntɪ] *prefix* anté..., anti..., pré....

anteater ['æntiːtə*] *n* fourmilier *m*, tamanoir *m*.

antecedent [æntɪ'siːdənt] *n* antécédent *m*.

antechamber ['æntɪtʃeɪmbə*] *n* antichambre *f*.

antelope ['æntɪləup] *n* antilope *f*.

antenatal ['æntɪ'neɪtl] *adj* prénatal(e).

antenatal clinic *n* service *m* de consultation prénatale.

antenna, *pl* ~**e** [æn'tɛnə, -niː] *n* antenne *f*.

anthem ['ænθəm] *n* motet *m*; **national** ~ hymne national.

ant-hill ['ænthɪl] *n* fourmilière *f*.

anthology [æn'θɔlədʒɪ] *n* anthologie *f*.

anthropologist [ænθrə'pɔlədʒɪst] *n* anthropologue *m/f*.

anthropology [ænθrə'pɔlədʒɪ] *n* anthropologie *f*.

anti- [ænti] *prefix* anti-.

anti-aircraft ['æntɪ'ɛəkrɑːft] *adj* anti-aérien(ne).

anti-aircraft defence *n* défense *f* contre avions, DCA *f*.

antiballistic ['æntɪbə'lɪstɪk] *adj* antibalistique.

antibiotic ['æntɪbaɪ'ɔtɪk] *adj, n* antibiotique (*m*).

antibody ['æntɪbɔdɪ] *n* anticorps *m*.

anticipate [æn'tɪsɪpeɪt] *vt* s'attendre à, prévoir; (*wishes, request*) aller au devant de, devancer; **this is worse than I** ~**d** c'est pire que je ne pensais; **as** ~**d** comme prévu.

anticipation [æntɪsɪ'peɪʃən] *n* attente *f*; **thanking you in** ~ en vous remerciant d'avance, avec mes remerciements anticipés.

anticlimax ['æntɪ'klaɪmæks] *n* réalisation décevante d'un événement que l'on escomptait important, intéressant etc.

anticlockwise ['æntɪ'klɔkwaɪz] *adj* dans le sens inverse des aiguilles d'une montre.

antics ['æntɪks] *npl* singeries *fpl*.

anticyclone ['æntɪ'saɪkləun] *n* anticyclone *m*.

antidote ['æntɪdəut] *n* antidote *m*, contrepoison *m*.

antifreeze ['æntɪfriːz] *n* antigel *m*.

antihistamine [æntɪ'hɪstəmɪn] *n* antihistaminique *m*.

Antilles [æn'tɪliːz] *npl*: **the** ~ les Antilles *fpl*.

antipathy [æn'tɪpəθɪ] *n* antipathie *f*.

antiperspirant [æntɪ'pəːspɪrənt] *n* déodorant *m* anti-transpiration *f*.

Antipodean [æntɪpə'diːən] *adj* australien(ne) et néozélandais(e), d'Australie et de Nouvelle-Zélande.

Antipodes [æn'tɪpədiːz] *npl*: **the** ~ l'Australie *f* et la Nouvelle-Zélande.

antiquarian [æntɪ'kwɛərɪən] *adj*: ~ **bookshop** librairie *f* d'ouvrages anciens ♦ *n* expert *m* en objets *or* livres anciens; amateur *m* d'antiquités.

antiquated ['æntɪkweɪtɪd] *adj* vieilli(e), suranné(e), vieillot(te).

antique [æn'tiːk] *n* objet *m* d'art ancien, meuble ancien *or* d'époque, antiquité *f* ♦ *adj* ancien(ne); (*pre-mediaeval*) antique.

antique dealer *n* antiquaire *m/f*.

antique shop *n* magasin *m* d'antiquités.

antiquity [æn'tɪkwɪtɪ] *n* antiquité *f*.

anti-Semitic ['æntɪsɪ'mɪtɪk] *adj* antisémite.

anti-Semitism ['æntɪ'sɛmɪtɪzəm] *n* antisémitisme *m*.

antiseptic [æntɪ'sɛptɪk] *adj*, *n* antiseptique *(m)*.

antisocial ['æntɪ'səʊʃəl] *adj* peu liant(e), sauvage, insociable; (*against society*) anti-social(e).

antitank [æntɪ'tæŋk] *adj* antichar.

antithesis, *pl* **antitheses** [æn'tɪθɪsɪs, -siːz] *n* antithèse *f*.

antitrust [æntɪ'trʌst] *adj*: ~ **legislation** loi *f* anti-trust.

antlers ['æntləz] *npl* bois *mpl*, ramure *f*.

Antwerp ['æntwɔːp] *n* Anvers.

anus ['eɪnəs] *n* anus *m*.

anvil ['ænvɪl] *n* enclume *f*.

anxiety [æŋ'zaɪətɪ] *n* anxiété *f*; (*keenness*): ~ **to do** grand désir *or* impatience *f* de faire.

anxious ['æŋkʃəs] *adj* anxieux(euse), (très) inquiet(ète); (*keen*): ~ **to do/that** qui tient beaucoup à faire/à ce que; impatient(e) de faire/que; **I'm very** ~ **about you** je me fais beaucoup de souci pour toi.

anxiously ['æŋkʃəslɪ] *adv* anxieusement.

============================ *KEYWORD*

any ['ɛnɪ] *adj* **1** (*in questions etc: singular*) du, de l', de la; (*in questions etc: plural*) des; **have you** ~ **butter/children/ink?** avez-vous du beurre/des enfants/de l'encre?

2 (*with negative*) de, d'; **I haven't** ~ **money/books** je n'ai pas d'argent/de livres; **without** ~ **difficulty** sans la moindre difficulté

3 (*no matter which*) n'importe quel(le), quelconque; (*each and every*) tout(e), chaque; **choose** ~ **book you like** vous pouvez choisir n'importe quel livre

4 (*in phrases*): **in** ~ **case** de toute façon; ~ **day now** d'un jour à l'autre; **at** ~ **moment** à tout moment, d'un instant à l'autre; **at** ~ **rate** en tout cas

♦ *pron* **1** (*in questions etc*) en; **have you got** ~**?** est-ce que vous en avez?; **can** ~ **of you sing?** est-ce que parmi vous il y en a qui savent chanter?

2 (*with negative*) en; **I haven't** ~ **(of them)** je n'en ai pas, je n'en ai aucun

3 (*no matter which one(s)*) n'importe lequel (*or* laquelle); (*anybody*) n'importe qui; **take** ~ **of those books (you like)** vous pouvez prendre n'importe lequel de ces livres

♦ *adv* **1** (*in questions etc*): **do you want** ~ **more soup/sandwiches?** voulez-vous encore de la soupe/des sandwichs?; **are you feeling** ~ **better?** est-ce que vous vous sentez

mieux?

2 (*with negative*): **I can't hear him** ~ **more** je ne l'entends plus; **don't wait** ~ **longer** n'attendez pas plus longtemps.

anybody ['ɛnɪbɔdɪ] *pron* n'importe qui; (*in interrogative sentences*) quelqu'un; (*in negative sentences*): **I don't see** ~ je ne vois personne.

anyhow ['ɛnɪhaʊ] *adv* quoi qu'il en soit; (*haphazardly*) n'importe comment; **I shall go** ~ j'irai de toute façon.

anyone ['ɛnɪwʌn] = **anybody**.

anyplace ['ɛnɪpleɪs] *adv* (*US*) = **anywhere**.

anything ['ɛnɪθɪŋ] *pron* n'importe quoi; (*in interrogative sentences*) quelque chose; (*in negative sentences*): **I don't want** ~ je ne veux rien; ~ **else?** (*in shop*) et avec ça?; **it can cost** ~ **between £15 and £20** (*BRIT*) ça peut coûter dans les 15 à 20 livres.

anytime ['ɛnɪtaɪm] *adv* n'importe quand.

anyway ['ɛnɪweɪ] *adv* de toute façon.

anywhere ['ɛnɪwɛə*] *adv* n'importe où; (*in interrogative sentences*) quelque part; (*in negative sentences*): **I don't see him** ~ je ne le vois nulle part; ~ **in the world** n'importe où dans le monde.

Anzac ['ænzæk] *n abbr* (= *Australia-New Zealand Army Corps*) soldat du corps ANZAC.

Anzac Day est le 25 avril, jour férié en Australie et en Nouvelle-Zélande commémorant le débarquement des soldats du corps **ANZAC** à Gallipoli en 1915, pendant la Première Guerre mondiale. Ce fut la plus célèbre des campagnes du corps **ANZAC**.

---

apart [ə'pɑːt] *adv* (*to one side*) à part; de côté; à l'écart; (*separately*) séparément; **10 miles/a long way** ~ à 10 milles/très éloignés l'un de l'autre; **they are living** ~ ils sont séparés; ~ **from** *prep* à part, excepté.

apartheid [ə'pɑːteɪt] *n* apartheid *m*.

apartment [ə'pɑːtmənt] *n* (*US*) appartement *m*, logement *m*.

apartment building *n* (*US*) immeuble *m*; maison divisée en appartements.

apathetic [æpə'θɛtɪk] *adj* apathique, indifférent(e).

apathy ['æpəθɪ] *n* apathie *f*, indifférence *f*.

APB *n abbr* (*US*: = *all points bulletin*) expression de la police signifiant "découvrir et appréhender le suspect".

ape [eɪp] *n* (grand) singe ♦ *vt* singer.

Apennines ['æpənaɪnz] *npl*: **the** ~ les Apennins *mpl*.

apéritif [ə'pɛrɪtiːf] *n* apéritif *m*.

aperture ['æpətʃjʊə*] *n* orifice *m*, ouverture *f*; (*PHOT*) ouverture (du diaphragme).

APEX ['eɪpɛks] *n abbr* (*AVIAT*: = *advance purchase excursion*) APEX *m*.

apex ['eɪpɛks] *n* sommet *m*.

aphid ['eɪfɪd] *n* puceron *m*.

aphrodisiac [æfrəʊ'dızıæk] *adj, n* aphrodisiaque *(m)*.

API *n abbr* = *American Press Institute*.

apiece [ə'piːs] *adv (for each person)* chacun(e), par tête; *(for each item)* chacun(e), (la) pièce.

aplomb [ə'plɒm] *n* sang-froid *m*, assurance *f*.

APO *n abbr (US:* = *Army Post Office) service postal de l'armée*.

apocalypse [ə'pɒkəlıps] *n* apocalypse *f*.

apolitical [eıpə'lıtıkl] *adj* apolitique.

apologetic [əpɒlə'dʒetık] *adj (tone, letter)* d'excuse; **to be very ~ about** s'excuser vivement de.

apologetically [əpɒlə'dʒetıkəlı] *adv (say)* en s'excusant.

apologize [ə'pɒlədʒaız] *vi*: **to ~ (for sth to sb)** s'excuser (de qch auprès de qn), présenter des excuses (à qn pour qch).

apology [ə'pɒlədʒı] *n* excuses *fpl*; **to send one's apologies** envoyer une lettre *or* un mot d'excuse, s'excuser (de ne pas pouvoir venir); **please accept my apologies** vous voudrez bien m'excuser.

apoplectic [æpə'plektık] *adj (MED)* apoplectique; *(col)*: **~ with rage** fou(folle) de rage.

apoplexy ['æpəpleksı] *n* apoplexie *f*.

apostle [ə'pɒsl] *n* apôtre *m*.

apostrophe [ə'pɒstrəfı] *n* apostrophe *f*.

appal [ə'pɔːl] *vt* consterner, atterrer; horrifier.

Appalachian Mountains [æpə'leıʃən-] *npl*: **the ~** les (monts *mpl*) Appalaches *mpl*.

appalling [ə'pɔːlıŋ] *adj* épouvantable; *(stupidity)* consternant(e); **she's an ~ cook** c'est une très mauvaise cuisinière.

apparatus [æpə'reıtəs] *n* appareil *m*, dispositif *m*; *(in gymnasium)* agrès *mpl*.

apparel [ə'pærl] *n (US)* habillement *m*, confection *f*.

apparent [ə'pærənt] *adj* apparent(e); **it is ~ that** il est évident que.

apparently [ə'pærəntlı] *adv* apparemment.

apparition [æpə'rıʃən] *n* apparition *f*.

appeal [ə'piːl] *vi (LAW)* faire *or* interjeter appel ♦ *n (LAW)* appel *m*; *(request)* appel; prière *f*; *(charm)* attrait *m*, charme *m*; **to ~ for** demander (instamment); implorer; **to ~ to** *(subj: person)* faire appel à; *(subj: thing)* plaire à; **to ~ to sb for mercy** implorer la pitié de qn, prier *or* adjurer qn d'avoir pitié; **it doesn't ~ to me** cela ne m'attire pas; **right of ~** droit *m* de recours.

appealing [ə'piːlıŋ] *adj (nice)* attrayant(e); *(touching)* attendrissant(e).

appear [ə'pıə*] *vi* apparaître, se montrer; *(LAW)* comparaître; *(publication)* paraître, sortir, être publié(e); *(seem)* paraître, sembler; **it would ~ that** il semble que; **to ~ in Hamlet** jouer dans Hamlet; **to ~ on TV** passer à la télé.

appearance [ə'pıərəns] *n* apparition *f*; paru-

tion *f*; *(look, aspect)* apparence *f*, aspect *m*; **to put in** *or* **make an ~** faire acte de présence; *(THEAT)*: **by order of ~** par ordre d'entrée en scène; **to keep up ~s** sauver les apparences; **to all ~s** selon toute apparence.

appease [ə'piːz] *vt* apaiser, calmer.

appeasement [ə'piːzmənt] *n (POL)* apaisement *m*.

appellate court [ə'pelıt-] *n (US)* cour *f* d'appel.

append [ə'pend] *vt (COMPUT)* ajouter (à la fin d'un fichier).

appendage [ə'pendıdʒ] *n* appendice *m*.

appendicitis [əpendı'saıtıs] *n* appendicite *f*.

appendix, *pl* **appendices** [ə'pendıks, -siːz] *n* appendice *m*; **to have one's ~ out** se faire opérer de l'appendicite.

appetite ['æpıtaıt] *n* appétit *m*; **that walk has given me an ~** cette promenade m'a ouvert l'appétit.

appetizer ['æpıtaızə*] *n (food)* amuse-gueule *m*; *(drink)* apéritif *m*.

appetizing ['æpıtaızıŋ] *adj* appétissant(e).

applaud [ə'plɔːd] *vt, vi* applaudir.

applause [ə'plɔːz] *n* applaudissements *mpl*.

apple ['æpl] *n* pomme *f*; *(also:* **~ tree)** pommier *m*; **it's the ~ of my eye** j'y tiens comme à la prunelle de mes yeux.

apple turnover *n* chausson *m* aux pommes.

appliance [ə'plaıəns] *n* appareil *m*; **electrical ~s** l'électroménager *m*.

applicable [ə'plıkəbl] *adj* applicable; **the law is ~ from January** la loi entre en vigueur au mois de janvier; **to be ~ to** valoir pour.

applicant ['æplıkənt] *n*: **~ (for)** *(ADMIN: for benefit etc)* demandeur/euse (de); *(for post)* candidat/e (à).

application [æplı'keıʃən] *n* application *f*; *(for a job, a grant etc)* demande *f*; candidature *f*; **on ~** sur demande.

application form *n* formulaire *m* de demande.

application program *n (COMPUT)* programme *m* d'application.

applications package *n (COMPUT)* progiciel *m* d'application.

applied [ə'plaıd] *adj* appliqué(e); **~ arts** *npl* arts décoratifs.

apply [ə'plaı] *vt*: **to ~ (to)** *(paint, ointment)* appliquer (sur); *(theory, technique)* appliquer (à) ♦ *vi*: **to ~ to** *(ask)* s'adresser à; *(be suitable for, relevant to)* s'appliquer à, être valable pour; **to ~ (for)** *(permit, grant)* faire une demande (en vue d'obtenir); *(job)* poser sa candidature (pour), faire une demande d'emploi (concernant); **to ~ the brakes** actionner les freins, freiner; **to ~ o.s. to** s'appliquer à.

appoint [ə'pɔınt] *vt* nommer, engager; *(date, place)* fixer, désigner.

appointee [əpɔın'tiː] *n* personne nommée; candidat retenu.

appointment [ə'pɔɪntmənt] *n* (*to post*) nomination *f*; (*arrangement to meet*) rendez-vous *m*; **to make an ~ (with)** prendre rendez-vous (avec); **"~s (vacant)"** (*PRESS*) "offres d'emploi"; **by ~** sur rendez-vous.

apportion [ə'pɔːʃən] *vt* (*share out*) répartir, distribuer; **to ~ sth to sb** attribuer *or* assigner *or* allouer qch à qn.

appraisal [ə'preɪzl] *n* évaluation *f*.

appraise [ə'preɪz] *vt* (*value*) estimer; (*situation etc*) évaluer.

appreciable [ə'priːʃəbl] *adj* appréciable.

appreciably [ə'priːʃəblɪ] *adv* sensiblement, de façon appréciable.

appreciate [ə'priːʃɪeɪt] *vt* (*like*) apprécier, faire cas de; (*be grateful for*) être reconnaissant(e) de; (*assess*) évaluer; (*be aware of*) comprendre, se rendre compte de ♦ *vi* (*FINANCE*) prendre de la valeur; **I ~ your help** je vous remercie pour votre aide.

appreciation [əpriːʃɪ'eɪʃən] *n* appréciation *f*; (*gratitude*) reconnaissance *f*; (*FINANCE*) hausse *f*, valorisation *f*.

appreciative [ə'priːʃɪətɪv] *adj* (*person*) sensible; (*comment*) élogieux(euse).

apprehend [æprɪ'hɛnd] *vt* appréhender, arrêter; (*understand*) comprendre.

apprehension [æprɪ'hɛnʃən] *n* appréhension *f*, inquiétude *f*.

apprehensive [æprɪ'hɛnsɪv] *adj* inquiet(ète), appréhensif(ive).

apprentice [ə'prɛntɪs] *n* apprenti *m* ♦ *vt*: **to be ~d to** être en apprentissage chez.

apprenticeship [ə'prɛntɪsʃɪp] *n* apprentissage *m*; **to serve one's ~** faire son apprentissage.

appro. ['æprəu] *abbr* (*BRIT COMM: col*) = **approval**.

approach [ə'prəutʃ] *vi* approcher ♦ *vt* (*come near*) approcher de; (*ask, apply to*) s'adresser à; (*subject, passer-by*) aborder ♦ *n* approche *f*; accès *m*, abord *m*; démarche *f* (*auprès de qn*); démarche (*intellectuelle*); **to ~ sb about sth** aller *or* venir voir qn pour qch.

approachable [ə'prəutʃəbl] *adj* accessible.

approach road *n* voie *f* d'accès.

approbation [æprə'beɪʃən] *n* approbation *f*.

appropriate *vt* [ə'prəuprɪeɪt] (*take*) s'approprier; (*allot*): **to ~ sth for** affecter qch à ♦ *adj* [ə'prəuprɪət] qui convient, approprié(e); (*timely*) opportun(e); **~ for** *or* **to** approprié à; **it would not be ~ for me to comment** il ne me serait pas approprié de commenter.

appropriately [ə'prəuprɪətlɪ] *adv* pertinemment, avec à-propos.

appropriation [əprəuprɪ'eɪʃən] *n* dotation *f*, affectation *f*.

approval [ə'pruːvəl] *n* approbation *f*; **to meet with sb's ~** (*proposal etc*) recueillir l'assentiment de qn; **on ~** (*COMM*) à l'examen.

approve [ə'pruːv] *vt* approuver.

▶**approve of** *vt fus* approuver.

approved school [ə'pruːvd-] *n* (*BRIT*) centre *m* d'éducation surveillée.

approvingly [ə'pruːvɪŋlɪ] *adv* d'un air approbateur.

approx. *abbr* (= *approximately*) env.

approximate *adj* [ə'prɒksɪmɪt] approximatif(ive) ♦ *vt* [ə'prɒksɪmeɪt] se rapprocher de; être proche de.

approximation [ə'prɒksɪ'meɪʃən] *n* approximation *f*.

Apr. *abbr* = **April**.

apr *n abbr* (= *annual percentage rate*) taux (d'intérêt) annuel.

apricot ['eɪprɪkɒt] *n* abricot *m*.

April ['eɪprəl] *n* avril *m*; **~ fool!** poisson d'avril!; *for phrases see also* **July**.

April Fool's Day *n* le premier avril.

April Fool's Day *est le 1er avril, à l'occasion duquel on fait des farces de toutes sortes. Les victimes de ces farces sont les "April fools". Les médias britanniques se prennent aussi au jeu, diffusant de fausses nouvelles, comme la découverte d'îles de la taille de l'Irlande, ou faisant des reportages bidon, montrant par exemple la culture d'arbres à spaghettis en Italie.*

---

apron ['eɪprən] *n* tablier *m*; (*AVIAT*) aire *f* de stationnement.

apse [æps] *n* (*ARCHIT*) abside *f*.

APT *n abbr* (*BRIT*: = *advanced passenger train*) ≈ TGV *m*.

Apt. *abbr* (= *apartment*) appt.

apt [æpt] *adj* (*suitable*) approprié(e); (*able*): **~ (at)** doué(e) (pour); apte (à); (*likely*): **~ to do** susceptible de faire; ayant tendance à faire.

aptitude ['æptɪtjuːd] *n* aptitude *f*.

aptitude test *n* test *m* d'aptitude.

aptly ['æptlɪ] *adv* (fort) à propos.

aqualung ['ækwəlʌŋ] *n* scaphandre *m* autonome.

aquarium [ə'kwɛərɪəm] *n* aquarium *m*.

Aquarius [ə'kwɛərɪəs] *n* le Verseau; **to be ~** être du Verseau.

aquatic [ə'kwætɪk] *adj* aquatique; (*sport*) nautique.

aqueduct ['ækwɪdʌkt] *n* aqueduc *m*.

AR *abbr* (*US*) = **Arkansas**.

ARA *n abbr* (*BRIT*) = *Associate of the Royal Academy*.

Arab ['ærəb] *n* Arabe *m/f* ♦ *adj* arabe.

Arabia [ə'reɪbɪə] *n* Arabie *f*.

Arabian [ə'reɪbɪən] *adj* arabe.

Arabian Desert *n* désert *m* d'Arabie.

Arabian Sea *n* mer *f* d'Arabie.

Arabic ['ærəbɪk] *adj*, *n* arabe (*m*).

Arabic numerals *npl* chiffres *mpl* arabes.

arable ['ærəbl] *adj* arable.

ARAM *n abbr* (*BRIT*) = *Associate of the Royal Academy of Music*.

arbiter ['ɑːbɪtə*] *n* arbitre *m*.
arbitrary ['ɑːbɪtrərɪ] *adj* arbitraire.
arbitrate ['ɑːbɪtreɪt] *vi* arbitrer; trancher.
arbitration [ɑːbɪ'treɪʃən] *n* arbitrage *m*; **the dispute went to** ~ le litige a été soumis à arbitrage.
arbitrator ['ɑːbɪtreɪtə*] *n* arbitre *m*, médiateur/trice.
ARC *n abbr* = *American Red Cross.*
arc [ɑːk] *n* arc *m*.
arcade [ɑː'keɪd] *n* arcade *f*; (*passage with shops*) passage *m*, galerie *f*.
arch [ɑːtʃ] *n* arche *f*; (*of foot*) cambrure *f*, voûte *f* plantaire ♦ *vt* arquer, cambrer ♦ *adj* malicieux(euse) ♦ *prefix*: ~(-) achevé(e); par excellence; **pointed** ~ ogive *f*.
archaeological [ɑːkɪə'lɔdʒɪkl] *adj* archéologique.
archaeologist [ɑːkɪ'ɔlədʒɪst] *n* archéologue *m/f*.
archaeology [ɑːkɪ'ɔlədʒɪ] *n* archéologie *f*.
archaic [ɑː'keɪɪk] *adj* archaïque.
archangel ['ɑːkeɪndʒəl] *n* archange *m*.
archbishop [ɑːtʃ'bɪʃəp] *n* archevêque *m*.
archenemy ['ɑːtʃ'enɪmɪ] *n* ennemi *m* de toujours *or* par excellence.
archeology [ɑːkɪ'ɔlədʒɪ] *etc* (*US*) = **archaeology** *etc*.
archer ['ɑːtʃə*] *n* archer *m*.
archery ['ɑːtʃərɪ] *n* tir *m* à l'arc.
archetypal ['ɑːkɪtaɪpəl] *adj* archétype.
archetype ['ɑːkɪtaɪp] *n* prototype *m*, archétype *m*.
archipelago [ɑːkɪ'pɛlɪgəu] *n* archipel *m*.
architect ['ɑːkɪtɛkt] *n* architecte *m*.
architectural [ɑːkɪ'tɛktʃərəl] *adj* architectural(e).
architecture ['ɑːkɪtɛktʃə*] *n* architecture *f*.
archive ['ɑːkaɪv] *n* (*often pl*) archives *fpl*.
archive file *n* (*COMPUT*) fichier *m* d'archives.
archives ['ɑːkaɪvz] *npl* archives *fpl*.
archivist ['ɑːkɪvɪst] *n* archiviste *m/f*.
archway ['ɑːtʃweɪ] *n* voûte *f*, porche voûté *or* cintré.
ARCM *n abbr* (*BRIT*) = *Associate of the Royal College of Music.*
Arctic ['ɑːktɪk] *adj* arctique ♦ *n*: **the** ~ l'Arctique *m*.
Arctic Circle *n* cercle *m* Arctique.
Arctic Ocean *n* océan *m* Arctique.
ARD *n abbr* (*US MED*) = *acute respiratory disease.*
ardent ['ɑːdənt] *adj* fervent(e).
ardour, (*US*) **ardor** ['ɑːdə*] *n* ardeur *f*.
arduous ['ɑːdjuəs] *adj* ardu(e).
are [ɑː*] *vb see* **be**.
area ['ɛərɪə] *n* (*GEOM*) superficie *f*; (*zone*) région *f*; (: *smaller*) secteur *m*; **dining** ~ coin *m* salle à manger; **the London** ~ la région Londonienne.
area code *n* (*TEL*) indicatif *m* (téléphonique).
arena [ə'riːnə] *n* arène *f*.
aren't [ɑːnt] = **are not**.

Argentina [ɑːdʒən'tiːnə] *n* Argentine *f*.
Argentinian [ɑːdʒən'tɪnɪən] *adj* argentin(e) ♦ *n* Argentin/e.
arguable ['ɑːgjuəbl] *adj* discutable, contestable; **it is** ~ **whether** on peut se demander si.
arguably ['ɑːgjuəblɪ] *adv*: **it is** ~ ... on peut soutenir que c'est ....
argue ['ɑːgjuː] *vi* (*quarrel*) se disputer; (*reason*) argumenter ♦ *vt* (*debate: case, matter*) débattre; **to** ~ **about sth (with sb)** se disputer (avec qn) au sujet de qch; **to** ~ **that** objecter *or* alléguer que, donner comme argument que.
argument ['ɑːgjumənt] *n* (*reasons*) argument *m*; (*quarrel*) dispute *f*, discussion *f*; (*debate*) discussion, controverse *f*; ~ **for/against** argument pour/contre.
argumentative [ɑːgju'mɛntətɪv] *adj* ergoteur(euse), raisonneur(euse).
aria ['ɑːrɪə] *n* aria *f*.
ARIBA [ə'riːbə] *n abbr* (*BRIT*) = *Associate of the Royal Institute of British Architects.*
arid ['ærɪd] *adj* aride.
aridity [ə'rɪdɪtɪ] *n* aridité *f*.
Aries ['ɛərɪz] *n* le Bélier; **to be** ~ être du Bélier.
arise, *pt* **arose,** *pp* **arisen** [ə'raɪz, ə'rəuz, ə'rɪzn] *vi* survenir, se présenter; **to** ~ **from** résulter de; **should the need** ~ en cas de besoin.
aristocracy [ærɪs'tɔkrəsɪ] *n* aristocratie *f*.
aristocrat ['ærɪstəkræt] *n* aristocrate *m/f*.
aristocratic [ærɪstə'krætɪk] *adj* aristocratique.
arithmetic [ə'rɪθmətɪk] *n* arithmétique *f*.
arithmetical [ærɪθ'mɛtɪkl] *adj* arithmétique.
Ariz. *abbr* (*US*) = *Arizona.*
ark [ɑːk] *n*: **Noah's A**~ l'Arche *f* de Noé.
Ark. *abbr* (*US*) = *Arkansas.*
arm [ɑːm] *n* bras *m* ♦ *vt* armer; ~ **in** ~ bras dessus bras dessous.
armaments ['ɑːməmənts] *npl* (*weapons*) armement *m*.
armband ['ɑːmbænd] *n* brassard *m*.
armchair ['ɑːmtʃɛə*] *n* fauteuil *m*.
armed [ɑːmd] *adj* armé(e); **the** ~ **forces** les forces armées.
armed robbery *n* vol *m* à main armée.
Armenia [ɑː'miːnɪə] *n* Arménie *f*.
Armenian [ɑː'miːnɪən] *adj* arménien(ne) ♦ *n* Arménien/ne; (*LING*) arménien *m*.
armful ['ɑːmful] *n* brassée *f*.
armistice ['ɑːmɪstɪs] *n* armistice *m*.
armour, (*US*) **armor** ['ɑːmə*] *n* armure *f*; (*also:* ~-**plating**) blindage *m*; (*MIL: tanks*) blindés *mpl*.
armo(u)red car ['ɑːməd-] *n* véhicule blindé.
armo(u)ry ['ɑːmərɪ] *n* arsenal *m*.
armpit ['ɑːmpɪt] *n* aisselle *f*.
armrest ['ɑːmrɛst] *n* accoudoir *m*.
arms [ɑːmz] *npl* (*weapons*, *HERALDRY*) armes *fpl*.

arms control n contrôle m des armements.
arms race n course f aux armements.
army ['ɑ:mɪ] n armée f.
aroma [ə'rəumə] n arôme m.
aromatherapy [ərəumə'θerəpɪ] n aromathérapie f.
aromatic [ærə'mætɪk] adj aromatique.
arose [ə'rəuz] pt of **arise**.
around [ə'raund] adv (tout) autour; (nearby) dans les parages ♦ prep autour de; (fig: about) environ; vers; **is he ~?** est-il dans les parages or là?
arousal [ə'rauzəl] n (sexual) excitation sexuelle, éveil m.
arouse [ə'rauz] vt (sleeper) éveiller; (curiosity, passions) éveiller, susciter; exciter.
arpeggio [ɑ:'pedʒɪəu] n arpège m.
arrange [ə'reɪndʒ] vt arranger; (programme) arrêter, convenir de ♦ vi: **we have ~d for a car to pick you up** nous avons prévu qu'une voiture vienne vous prendre; **it was ~d that** ... il a été convenu que ..., il a été décidé que ...; **to ~ to do sth** prévoir de faire qch.
arrangement [ə'reɪndʒmənt] n arrangement m; (plans etc): **~s** dispositions fpl; **to come to an ~ (with sb)** se mettre d'accord (avec qn); **home deliveries by ~** livraison à domicile sur demande; **I'll make ~s for you to be met** je vous enverrai chercher.
arrant ['ærənt] adj: **he's talking ~ nonsense** il raconte vraiment n'importe quoi.
array [ə'reɪ] n (of objects) déploiement m, étalage m; (MATH, COMPUT) tableau m.
arrears [ə'rɪəz] npl arriéré m; **to be in ~ with one's rent** devoir un arriéré de loyer, être en retard pour le paiement de son loyer.
arrest [ə'rest] vt arrêter; (sb's attention) retenir, attirer ♦ n arrestation f; **under ~** en état d'arrestation.
arresting [ə'restɪŋ] adj (fig: beauty) saisissant(e); (: charm, candour) désarmant(e).
arrival [ə'raɪvl] n arrivée f; (COMM) arrivage m; (person) arrivant/e; **new ~** nouveau venu/nouvelle venue.
arrive [ə'raɪv] vi arriver.
►**arrive at** vt fus (fig) parvenir à.
arrogance ['ærəgəns] n arrogance f.
arrogant ['ærəgənt] adj arrogant(e).
arrow ['ærəu] n flèche f.
arse [ɑ:s] n (BRIT col!) cul m (!).
arsenal ['ɑ:sɪnl] n arsenal m.
arsenic ['ɑ:snɪk] n arsenic m.
arson ['ɑ:sn] n incendie criminel.
art [ɑ:t] n art m; (craft) métier m; **work of ~** œuvre f d'art.
artefact ['ɑ:tɪfækt] n objet fabriqué.
arterial [ɑ:'tɪərɪəl] adj (ANAT) artériel(le); (road etc) à grande circulation.
artery ['ɑ:tərɪ] n artère f.
artful ['ɑ:tful] adj rusé(e).
art gallery n musée m d'art; (small and private) galerie f de peinture.

arthritis [ɑ:'θraɪtɪs] n arthrite f.
artichoke ['ɑ:tɪtʃəuk] n artichaut m; **Jerusalem ~** topinambour m.
article ['ɑ:tɪkl] n article m; (BRIT LAW: training): **~s** npl ≈ stage m; **~s of clothing** vêtements mpl.
articles of association npl (COMM) statuts mpl d'une société.
articulate adj [ɑ:'tɪkjulɪt] (person) qui s'exprime clairement et aisément; (speech) bien articulé(e), prononcé(e) clairement ♦ vi [ɑ:'tɪkjuleɪt] articuler, parler distinctement.
articulated lorry [ɑ:'tɪkjuleɪtɪd-] n (BRIT) (camion m) semi-remorque m.
artifact ['ɑ:tɪfækt] n (US) objet fabriqué.
artifice ['ɑ:tɪfɪs] n ruse f.
artificial [ɑ:tɪ'fɪʃəl] adj artificiel(le).
artificial insemination [-ɪnsemɪ'neɪʃən] n insémination artificielle.
artificial intelligence (A.I.) n intelligence artificielle (IA).
artificial respiration n respiration artificielle.
artillery [ɑ:'tɪlərɪ] n artillerie f.
artisan ['ɑ:tɪzæn] n artisan/e.
artist ['ɑ:tɪst] n artiste m/f.
artistic [ɑ:'tɪstɪk] adj artistique.
artistry ['ɑ:tɪstrɪ] n art m, talent m.
artless ['ɑ:tlɪs] adj naïf(naïve), simple, ingénu(e).
arts [ɑ:ts] npl (SCOL) lettres fpl.
art school n ≈ école f des beaux-arts.
artwork ['ɑ:twɔ:k] n maquette f (prête pour la photogravure).
ARV n abbr (= American Revised Version) traduction américaine de la Bible.
AS n abbr (US SCOL: = Associate in/of Science) diplôme universitaire ♦ abbr (US) = American Samoa.

===================================== KEYWORD

as [æz] conj **1** (time: moment) comme, alors que; (: duration) tandis que; **he came in ~ I was leaving** il est arrivé comme je partais; **~ the years went by** à mesure que les années passaient; **~ from tomorrow** à partir de demain
2 (in comparisons): **~ big ~** aussi grand que; **twice ~ big ~** deux fois plus grand que; **big ~ it is** si grand que ce soit; **much ~ I like them, I ...** je les aime bien, mais je ...; **~ much or many ~** autant que; **~ much money/many books** autant d'argent/de livres que; **~ soon ~** dès que
3 (since, because) comme, puisque; **~ he had to be home by 10** ... comme il or puisqu'il devait être de retour avant 10 h ...
4 (referring to manner, way) comme; **do ~ you wish** faites comme vous voudrez
5 (concerning): **~ for or to that** quant à cela, pour ce qui est de cela

6: ~ **if** *or* **though** comme si; **he looked ~ if he was ill** il avait l'air d'être malade; *see also* **long; such; well**

♦ *prep* (*in the capacity of*) en tant que, en qualité de; **he works ~ a driver** il travaille comme chauffeur; ~ **chairman of the company, he ...** en tant que président de la société, il ...; **dressed up ~ a cowboy** déguisé en cowboy; **he gave me it ~ a present** il me l'a offert, il m'en a fait cadeau.

ASA *n abbr* (= *American Standards Association*) *association de normalisation*.

a.s.a.p. *abbr* = **as soon as possible**.

asbestos [æz'bɛstəs] *n* asbeste *m*, amiante *m*.

ascend [ə'sɛnd] *vt* gravir.

ascendancy [ə'sɛndənsɪ] *n* ascendant *m*.

ascendant [ə'sɛndənt] *n*: **to be in the ~** monter.

ascension [ə'sɛnʃən] *n*: **the A~** (*REL*) l'Ascension *f*.

Ascension Island *n* île *f* de l'Ascension.

ascent [ə'sɛnt] *n* ascension *f*.

ascertain [æsə'teɪn] *vt* s'assurer de, vérifier; établir.

ascetic [ə'sɛtɪk] *adj* ascétique.

asceticism [ə'sɛtɪsɪzəm] *n* ascétisme *m*.

ASCII [æskiː] *n abbr* (= *American Standard Code for Information Interchange*) ASCII.

ascribe [ə'skraɪb] *vt*: **to ~ sth to** attribuer qch à; (*blame*) imputer qch à.

ASCU *n abbr* (*US*) = *Association of State Colleges and Universities*.

ASE *n abbr* = *American Stock Exchange*.

ASH [æʃ] *n abbr* (*BRIT*: = *Action on Smoking and Health*) *ligue anti-tabac*.

ash [æʃ] *n* (*dust*) cendre *f*; (*also*: ~ **tree**) frêne *m*.

ashamed [ə'ʃeɪmd] *adj* honteux(euse), confus(e); **to be ~ of** avoir honte de; **to be ~ (of o.s.) for having done** avoir honte d'avoir fait.

ashen ['æʃən] *adj* (*pale*) cendreux(euse), blême.

ashore [ə'ʃɔː*] *adv* à terre; **to go ~** aller à terre, débarquer.

ashtray ['æʃtreɪ] *n* cendrier *m*.

Ash Wednesday *n* mercredi *m* des Cendres.

Asia ['eɪʃə] *n* Asie *f*.

Asia Minor *n* Asie Mineure.

Asian ['eɪʃən] *n* Asiatique *m/f* ♦ *adj* asiatique.

Asiatic [eɪsɪ'ætɪk] *adj* asiatique.

aside [ə'saɪd] *adv* de côté; à l'écart ♦ *n* aparté *m*; ~ **from** *prep* à part, excepté.

ask [ɑːsk] *vt* demander; (*invite*) inviter; **to ~ sb sth/to do sth** demander à qn qch/de faire qch; **to ~ sb the time** demander l'heure à qn; **to ~ sb about sth** questionner qn au sujet de qch; se renseigner auprès de qn au sujet de qch; **to ~ about the price** s'informer du prix, se renseigner au sujet du prix; **to ~ (sb) a question** poser une question (à qn); **to ~ sb out to dinner** inviter qn au restaurant.

▶**ask after** *vt fus* demander des nouvelles de.

▶**ask for** *vt fus* demander; **it's just ~ing for trouble** *or* **for it** ce serait chercher des ennuis.

askance [ə'skɑːns] *adv*: **to look ~ at sb** regarder qn de travers *or* d'un œil désapprobateur.

askew [ə'skjuː] *adv* de travers, de guinguois.

asking price ['ɑːskɪŋ-] *n* prix demandé.

asleep [ə'sliːp] *adj* endormi(e); **to be ~** dormir, être endormi; **to fall ~** s'endormir.

ASLEF [æzlɛf] *n abbr* (*BRIT*: = *Associated Society of Locomotive Engineers and Firemen*) *syndicat de cheminots*.

asp [æsp] *n* aspic *m*.

asparagus [əs'pærəgəs] *n* asperges *fpl*.

asparagus tips *npl* pointes *fpl* d'asperges.

ASPCA *n abbr* (= *American Society for the Prevention of Cruelty to Animals*) ≈ SPA *f*.

aspect ['æspɛkt] *n* aspect *m*; (*direction in which a building etc faces*) orientation *f*, exposition *f*.

aspersions [əs'pəːʃənz] *npl*: **to cast ~ on** dénigrer.

asphalt ['æsfælt] *n* asphalte *m*.

asphyxiate [æs'fɪksɪeɪt] *vt* asphyxier.

asphyxiation [æsfɪksɪ'eɪʃən] *n* asphyxie *f*.

aspirate *vt* ['æspəreɪt] aspirer ♦ *adj* ['æspərɪt] aspiré(e).

aspiration [æspə'reɪʃən] *n* aspiration *f*.

aspire [əs'paɪə*] *vi*: **to ~ to** aspirer à.

aspirin ['æsprɪn] *n* aspirine *f*.

aspiring [əs'paɪərɪŋ] *adj* (*artist, writer*) en herbe; (*manager*) potentiel(le).

ass [æs] *n* âne *m*; (*col*) imbécile *m/f*; (*US col!*) cul *m* (*!*).

assail [ə'seɪl] *vt* assaillir.

assailant [ə'seɪlənt] *n* agresseur *m*; assaillant *m*.

assassin [ə'sæsɪn] *n* assassin *m*.

assassinate [ə'sæsɪneɪt] *vt* assassiner.

assassination [əsæsɪ'neɪʃən] *n* assassinat *m*.

assault [ə'sɔːlt] *n* (*MIL*) assaut *m*; (*gen: attack*) agression *f*; (*LAW*): ~ **(and battery)** voies *fpl* de fait, coups *mpl* et blessures *fpl* ♦ *vt* attaquer; (*sexually*) violenter.

assemble [ə'sɛmbl] *vt* assembler ♦ *vi* s'assembler, se rassembler.

assembly [ə'sɛmblɪ] *n* (*meeting*) rassemblement *m*; (*construction*) assemblage *m*.

assembly language *n* (*COMPUT*) langage *m* d'assemblage.

assembly line *n* chaîne *f* de montage.

assent [ə'sɛnt] *n* assentiment *m*, consentement *m* ♦ *vi*: **to ~ (to sth)** donner son assentiment (à qch), consentir (à qch).

assert [ə'səːt] *vt* affirmer, déclarer; établir; **to ~ o.s.** s'imposer.

assertion [ə'səːʃən] *n* assertion *f*, affirmation *f*.

assertive [ə'səːtɪv] *adj* assuré(e); péremptoire.

assess [ə'sɛs] *vt* évaluer, estimer; (*tax, damages*) établir or fixer le montant de; (*property etc: for tax*) calculer la valeur imposable de.

assessment [ə'sɛsmənt] *n* évaluation *f*, estimation *f*; (*judgment*): ~ **(of)** jugement *m* or opinion *f* (sur).

assessor [ə'sɛsə*] *n* expert *m* (*en matière d'impôt et d'assurance*).

asset ['æsɛt] *n* avantage *m*, atout *m*; (*person*) atout; ~**s** *npl* (*COMM*) capital *m*; avoir(s) *m(pl)*; actif *m*.

asset-stripping ['æsɛt'strɪpɪŋ] *n* (*COMM*) récupération *f* (et démantèlement *m*) d'une entreprise en difficulté.

assiduous [ə'sɪdjuəs] *adj* assidu(e).

assign [ə'saɪn] *vt* (*date*) fixer, arrêter; (*task*): **to ~ sth to** assigner qch à; (*resources*): **to ~ sth to** affecter qch à; (*cause, meaning*): **to ~ sth to** attribuer qch à.

assignment [ə'saɪnmənt] *n* tâche *f*, mission *f*.

assimilate [ə'sɪmɪleɪt] *vt* assimiler.

assimilation [əsɪmɪ'leɪʃən] *n* assimilation *f*.

assist [ə'sɪst] *vt* aider, assister; (*injured person etc*) secourir.

assistance [ə'sɪstəns] *n* aide *f*, assistance *f*; secours *mpl*.

assistant [ə'sɪstənt] *n* assistant/e, adjoint/e; (*BRIT: also:* **shop** ~) vendeur/euse.

assistant manager *n* sous-directeur *m*.

assizes [ə'saɪzɪz] *npl* assises *fpl*.

associate *adj, n* [ə'səuʃɪɪt] associé(e) ♦ *vb* [ə'səuʃɪeɪt] *vt* associer ♦ *vi*: **to ~ with sb** fréquenter qn; ~ **director** directeur adjoint; ~**d company** société affiliée.

association [əsəusɪ'eɪʃən] *n* association *f*; **in ~ with** en collaboration avec.

association football *n* (*BRIT*) football *m*.

assorted [ə'sɔːtɪd] *adj* assorti(e); **in ~ sizes** en plusieurs tailles.

assortment [ə'sɔːtmənt] *n* assortiment *m*.

Asst. *abbr* = **assistant**.

assuage [ə'sweɪdʒ] *vt* (*grief, pain*) soulager; (*thirst, appetite*) assouvir.

assume [ə'sjuːm] *vt* supposer; (*responsibilities etc*) assumer; (*attitude, name*) prendre, adopter.

assumed name [ə'sjuːmd-] *n* nom *m* d'emprunt.

assumption [ə'sʌmpʃən] *n* supposition *f*, hypothèse *f*; **on the ~ that** dans l'hypothèse où; (*on condition that*) à condition que.

assurance [ə'ʃuərəns] *n* assurance *f*; **I can give you no ~s** je ne peux rien vous garantir.

assure [ə'ʃuə*] *vt* assurer.

assured [ə'ʃuəd] *adj* assuré(e).

AST *abbr* (*US: = Atlantic Standard Time*) heure d'hiver de New York.

asterisk ['æstərɪsk] *n* astérisque *m*.

astern [ə'stəːn] *adv* à l'arrière.

asteroid ['æstərɔɪd] *n* astéroïde *m*.

asthma ['æsmə] *n* asthme *m*.

asthmatic [æs'mætɪk] *adj, n* asthmatique *(m/f)*.

astigmatism [ə'stɪgmətɪzəm] *n* astigmatisme *m*.

astir [ə'stəː*] *adv* en émoi.

astonish [ə'stɔnɪʃ] *vt* étonner, stupéfier.

astonishing [ə'stɔnɪʃɪŋ] *adj* étonnant(e), stupéfiant(e); **I find it ~ that** ... je trouve incroyable que ....

astonishingly [ə'stɔnɪʃɪŋlɪ] *adv* incroyablement.

astonishment [ə'stɔnɪʃmənt] *n* (grand) étonnement, stupéfaction *f*.

astound [ə'staund] *vt* stupéfier, sidérer.

astray [ə'streɪ] *adv*: **to go ~** s'égarer; (*fig*) quitter le droit chemin; **to go ~ in one's calculations** faire fausse route dans ses calculs.

astride [ə'straɪd] *adv* à cheval ♦ *prep* à cheval sur.

astringent [əs'trɪndʒənt] *adj* astringent(e) ♦ *n* astringent *m*.

astrologer [əs'trɔlədʒə*] *n* astrologue *m*.

astrology [əs'trɔlədʒɪ] *n* astrologie *f*.

astronaut ['æstrənɔːt] *n* astronaute *m/f*.

astronomer [əs'trɔnəmə*] *n* astronome *m*.

astronomical [æstrə'nɔmɪkl] *adj* astronomique.

astronomy [əs'trɔnəmɪ] *n* astronomie *f*.

astrophysics ['æstrəu'fɪzɪks] *n* astrophysique *f*.

astute [əs'tjuːt] *adj* astucieux(euse), malin(igne).

asunder [ə'sʌndə*] *adv*: **to tear ~** déchirer.

ASV *n abbr* (= *American Standard Version*) traduction de la Bible.

asylum [ə'saɪləm] *n* asile *m*; **to seek political ~** demander l'asile politique.

asymmetric(al) [eɪsɪ'mɛtrɪk(l)] *adj* asymétrique.

at [æt] *prep* **1** (*referring to position, direction*) à; ~ **the top** au sommet; ~ **home/school** à la maison or chez soi/à l'école; ~ **the baker's** à la boulangerie, chez le boulanger; **to look ~ sth** regarder qch

2 (*referring to time*): ~ **4 o'clock** à 4 heures; ~ **Christmas** à Noël; ~ **night** la nuit; ~ **times** par moments, parfois

3 (*referring to rates, speed etc*) à; ~ **£1 a kilo** une livre le kilo; **two ~ a time** deux à la fois; ~ **50 km/h** à 50 km/h; ~ **full speed** à toute vitesse

4 (*referring to manner*): ~ **a stroke** d'un seul coup; ~ **peace** en paix

5 (*referring to activity*): **to be ~ work** être au travail, travailler; **to play ~ cowboys** jouer aux cowboys; **to be good ~ sth** être bon en qch

6 (*referring to cause*): **shocked/surprised/annoyed ~ sth** choqué par/étonné de/agacé

par qch; **I went ~ his suggestion** j'y suis
allé sur son conseil.

ate [eɪt] *pt of* **eat**.
atheism ['eɪθɪɪzəm] *n* athéisme *m*.
atheist ['eɪθɪɪst] *n* athée *m/f*.
Athenian [ə'θiːnɪən] *adj* athénien(ne) ♦ *n*
Athénien/ne.
Athens ['æθɪnz] *n* Athènes.
athlete ['æθliːt] *n* athlète *m/f*.
athletic [æθ'lɛtɪk] *adj* athlétique.
athletics [æθ'lɛtɪks] *n* athlétisme *m*.
Atlantic [ət'læntɪk] *adj* atlantique ♦ *n*: **the ~**
(Ocean) l'Atlantique *m*, l'océan *m* Atlantique.
atlas ['ætləs] *n* atlas *m*.
Atlas Mountains *npl*: **the ~** les monts *mpl* de
l'Atlas, l'Atlas *m*.
ATM *abbr* (= *Automated Telling Machine*)
guichet *m* automatique.
atmosphere ['ætməsfɪə*] *n* atmosphère *f*; (*air*)
air *m*.
atmospheric [ætməs'fɛrɪk] *adj* atmosphérique.
atmospherics [ætməs'fɛrɪks] *n* (*RADIO*) parasites *mpl*.
atoll ['ætɔl] *n* atoll *m*.
atom ['ætəm] *n* atome *m*.
atomic [ə'tɔmɪk] *adj* atomique.
atom(ic) bomb *n* bombe *f* atomique.
atomizer ['ætəmaɪzə*] *n* atomiseur *m*.
atone [ə'təun] *vi*: **to ~ for** expier, racheter.
atonement [ə'təunmənt] *n* expiation *f*.
A to Z *n* ® guide *m* A à Z; (*map*) plan *m* des
rues.
ATP *n abbr* (= *Association of Tennis Profes-*
sionals) ATP *f* (= *Association des tennismen*
professionnels).
atrocious [ə'trəuʃəs] *adj* (*very bad*) atroce,
exécrable.
atrocity [ə'trɔsɪtɪ] *n* atrocité *f*.
atrophy ['ætrəfɪ] *n* atrophie *f* ♦ *vt* atrophier
♦ *vi* s'atrophier.
attach [ə'tætʃ] *vt* (*gen*) attacher; (*document,*
letter) joindre; (*employee, troops*) affecter; **to**
be ~ed to sb/sth (*to like*) être attaché à qn/
qch; **the ~ed letter** la lettre ci-jointe.
attaché [ə'tæʃeɪ] *n* attaché *m*.
attaché case *n* mallette *f*, attaché-case *m*.
attachment [ə'tætʃmənt] *n* (*tool*) accessoire
m; (*love*): **~ (to)** affection *f* (pour), attachement *m* (à).
attack [ə'tæk] *vt* attaquer; (*task etc*) s'attaquer
à ♦ *n* attaque *f*; (*also*: **heart ~**) crise *f* cardiaque.
attacker [ə'tækə*] *n* attaquant *m*; agresseur *m*.
attain [ə'teɪn] *vt* (*also*: **to ~ to**) parvenir à, atteindre; acquérir.
attainments [ə'teɪnmənts] *npl* connaissances
fpl, résultats *mpl*.
attempt [ə'tɛmpt] *n* tentative *f* ♦ *vt* essayer,
tenter; **~ed theft** *etc* (*LAW*) tentative de vol

etc; **to make an ~ on sb's life** attenter à la
vie de qn; **he made no ~ to help** il n'a rien
fait pour m'aider (*or* l'aider *etc*).
attend [ə'tɛnd] *vt* (*course*) suivre; (*meeting,*
talk) assister à; (*school, church*) aller à, fréquenter; (*patient*) soigner, s'occuper de; **to**
~ (up)on servir; être au service de.
▶**attend to** *vt fus* (*needs, affairs etc*) s'occuper
de; (*customer*) s'occuper de, servir.
attendance [ə'tɛndəns] *n* (*being present*) présence *f*; (*people present*) assistance *f*.
attendant [ə'tɛndənt] *n* employé/e; gar-
dien/ne ♦ *adj* concomitant(e), qui accompagne *or* s'ensuit.
attention [ə'tɛnʃən] *n* attention *f*; **~s** attentions *fpl*, prévenances *fpl*; **~!** (*MIL*) garde-à-
vous!; **at ~** (*MIL*) au garde-à-vous; **for the ~**
of (*ADMIN*) à l'attention de; **it has come to**
my ~ that ... je constate que ....
attentive [ə'tɛntɪv] *adj* attentif(ive); (*kind*)
prévenant(e).
attentively [ə'tɛntɪvlɪ] *adv* attentivement,
avec attention.
attenuate [ə'tɛnjueɪt] *vt* atténuer ♦ *vi*
s'atténuer.
attest [ə'tɛst] *vi*: **to ~ to** témoigner de, attester (de).
attic ['ætɪk] *n* grenier *m*, combles *mpl*.
attire [ə'taɪə*] *n* habit *m*, atours *mpl*.
attitude ['ætɪtjuːd] *n* (*behaviour*) attitude *f*,
manière *f*; (*posture*) pose *f*, attitude; (*view*):
~ (to) attitude (envers).
attorney [ə'tɜːnɪ] *n* (*US: lawyer*) avocat *m*;
(*having proxy*) mandataire *m*; **power of ~**
procuration *f*.
Attorney General *n* (*BRIT*) ≈ procureur général; (*US*) ≈ garde *m* des Sceaux, ministre
m de la Justice.
attract [ə'trækt] *vt* attirer.
attraction [ə'trækʃən] *n* (*gen pl: pleasant*
things) attraction *f*, attrait *m*; (*PHYSICS*) attraction; (*fig: towards sth*) attirance *f*.
attractive [ə'træktɪv] *adj* séduisant(e), at-
trayant(e).
attribute *n* ['ætrɪbjuːt] attribut *m* ♦ *vt*
[ə'trɪbjuːt]: **to ~ sth to** attribuer qch à.
attrition [ə'trɪʃən] *n*: **war of ~** guerre *f*
d'usure.
Atty. Gen. *abbr* = **Attorney General**.
ATV *n abbr* (= *all terrain vehicle*) véhicule *m*
tout-terrain.
atypical [eɪ'tɪpɪkl] *adj* atypique.
aubergine ['əubəʒiːn] *n* aubergine *f*.
auburn ['ɔːbən] *adj* auburn *inv*, châtain roux
inv.
auction ['ɔːkʃən] *n* (*also*: **sale by ~**) vente *f*
aux enchères ♦ *vt* (*also*: **to sell by ~**) vendre
aux enchères; (*also*: **to put up for ~**) mettre
aux enchères.
auctioneer [ɔːkʃə'nɪə*] *n* commissaire-
priseur *m*.
auction room *n* salle *f* des ventes.

audacious [ɔːˈdeɪʃəs] *adj* impudent(e); audacieux(euse), intrépide.

audacity [ɔːˈdæsɪtɪ] *n* impudence *f*; audace *f*.

audible [ˈɔːdɪbl] *adj* audible.

audience [ˈɔːdɪəns] *n* (*people*) assistance *f*, auditoire *m*; auditeurs *mpl*; spectateurs *mpl*; (*interview*) audience *f*.

audiotypist [ˈɔːdɪəʊtaɪpɪst] *n* audiotypiste *m/f*.

audiovisual [ɔːdɪəʊˈvɪzjuəl] *adj* audiovisuel(le); ~ **aids** supports *or* moyens audiovisuels.

audit [ˈɔːdɪt] *n* vérification *f* des comptes, apurement *m* ♦ *vt* vérifier, apurer.

audition [ɔːˈdɪʃən] *n* audition *f* ♦ *vi* auditionner.

auditor [ˈɔːdɪtə*] *n* vérificateur *m* des comptes.

auditorium [ɔːdɪˈtɔːrɪəm] *n* auditorium *m*, salle *f* de concert *or* de spectacle.

Aug. *abbr* = **August**.

augment [ɔːgˈmɛnt] *vt*, *vi* augmenter.

augur [ˈɔːgə*] *vt* (*be a sign of*) présager, annoncer ♦ *vi*: **it ~s well** c'est bon signe *or* de bon augure, cela s'annonce bien.

August [ˈɔːgəst] *n* août *m*; *for phrases see also* **July**.

august [ɔːˈgʌst] *adj* majestueux(euse), imposant(e).

aunt [ɑːnt] *n* tante *f*.

auntie, aunty [ˈɑːntɪ] *n diminutive of* **aunt**.

au pair [ˈəʊˈpɛə*] *n* (*also*: ~ **girl**) jeune fille *f* au pair.

aura [ˈɔːrə] *n* atmosphère *f*.

auspices [ˈɔːspɪsɪz] *npl*: **under the ~ of** sous les auspices de.

auspicious [ɔːsˈpɪʃəs] *adj* de bon augure, propice.

austere [ɔsˈtɪə*] *adj* austère.

austerity [ɔsˈtɛrɪtɪ] *n* austérité *f*.

Australasia [ɔːstrəˈleɪzɪə] *n* Australasie *f*.

Australia [ɔsˈtreɪlɪə] *n* Australie *f*.

Australian [ɔsˈtreɪlɪən] *adj* australien(ne) ♦ *n* Australien/ne.

Austria [ˈɔstrɪə] *n* Autriche *f*.

Austrian [ˈɔstrɪən] *adj* autrichien(ne) ♦ *n* Autrichien/ne.

AUT *n abbr* (*BRIT*: = *Association of University Teachers*) syndicat universitaire.

authentic [ɔːˈθɛntɪk] *adj* authentique.

authenticate [ɔːˈθɛntɪkeɪt] *vt* établir l'authenticité de.

authenticity [ɔːθɛnˈtɪsɪtɪ] *n* authenticité *f*.

author [ˈɔːθə*] *n* auteur *m*.

authoritarian [ɔːθɔrɪˈtɛərɪən] *adj* autoritaire.

authoritative [ɔːˈθɔrɪtətɪv] *adj* (*account*) digne de foi; (*study, treatise*) qui fait autorité; (*manner*) autoritaire.

authority [ɔːˈθɔrɪtɪ] *n* autorité *f*; (*permission*) autorisation (formelle); **the authorities** les autorités, l'administration *f*; **to have ~ to do sth** être habilité à faire qch.

authorization [ɔːθəraɪˈzeɪʃən] *n* autorisation *f*.

authorize [ˈɔːθəraɪz] *vt* autoriser.

authorized capital [ˈɔːθəraɪzd-] *n* (*COMM*) capital social.

authorship [ˈɔːθəʃɪp] *n* paternité *f* (*littéraire etc*).

autistic [ɔːˈtɪstɪk] *adj* autistique.

auto [ˈɔːtəʊ] *n* (*US*) auto *f*, voiture *f*.

autobiography [ɔːtəbaɪˈɔgrəfɪ] *n* autobiographie *f*.

autocratic [ɔːtəˈkrætɪk] *adj* autocratique.

Autocue [ˈɔːtəʊkjuː] *n* ® (télé)prompteur *m*.

autograph [ˈɔːtəgrɑːf] *n* autographe *m* ♦ *vt* signer, dédicacer.

autoimmune [ɔːtəʊɪˈmjuːn] *adj* auto-immune.

automat [ˈɔːtəmæt] *n* (*vending machine*) distributeur *m* (automatique); (*US: place*) cafétéria *f* avec distributeurs automatiques.

automated [ˈɔːtəmeɪtɪd] *adj* automatisé(e).

automatic [ɔːtəˈmætɪk] *adj* automatique ♦ *n* (*gun*) automatique *m*; (*washing machine*) lave-linge *m* automatique; (*BRIT AUT*) voiture *f* à transmission automatique.

automatically [ɔːtəˈmætɪklɪ] *adv* automatiquement.

automatic data processing (ADP) *n* traitement *m* automatique des données.

automation [ɔːtəˈmeɪʃən] *n* automatisation *f*.

automaton, *pl* **automata** [ɔːˈtɔmətən, -tə] *n* automate *m*.

automobile [ˈɔːtəməbiːl] *n* (*US*) automobile *f*.

autonomous [ɔːˈtɔnəməs] *adj* autonome.

autonomy [ɔːˈtɔnəmɪ] *n* autonomie *f*.

autopsy [ˈɔːtɔpsɪ] *n* autopsie *f*.

autumn [ˈɔːtəm] *n* automne *m*.

auxiliary [ɔːgˈzɪlɪərɪ] *adj*, *n* auxiliaire (*m/f*).

AV *n abbr* (= *Authorized Version*) *traduction anglaise de la Bible* ♦ *abbr* = **audiovisual**.

Av. *abbr* (= *avenue*) Av.

avail [əˈveɪl] *vt*: **to ~ o.s. of** user de; profiter de ♦ *n*: **to no ~** sans résultat, en vain, en pure perte.

availability [əveɪləˈbɪlɪtɪ] *n* disponibilité *f*.

available [əˈveɪləbl] *adj* disponible; **every ~ means** tous les moyens possibles *or* à sa (*or* notre *etc*) disposition; **is the manager ~?** est-ce que le directeur peut (me) recevoir?; (*on phone*) pourrais-je parler au directeur?; **to make sth ~ to sb** mettre qch à la disposition de qn.

avalanche [ˈævəlɑːnʃ] *n* avalanche *f*.

avant-garde [ˈævɑ̃ˈɡɑːd] *adj* d'avant-garde.

avaricious [ævəˈrɪʃəs] *adj* âpre au gain.

avdp. *abbr* = *avoirdupois*.

Ave. *abbr* (= *avenue*) Av.

avenge [əˈvɛndʒ] *vt* venger.

avenue [ˈævənjuː] *n* avenue *f*.

average [ˈævərɪdʒ] *n* moyenne *f* ♦ *adj* moyen(ne) ♦ *vt* (*a certain figure*) atteindre *or* faire *etc* en moyenne; **on ~** en moyenne; **above/below (the) ~** au-dessus/en-dessous de la moyenne.

▶**average out** *vi*: **to ~ out at** représenter en

moyenne, donner une moyenne de.

averse [ə'vɜːs] *adj*: **to be ~ to sth/doing** éprouver une forte répugnance envers qch/à faire; **I wouldn't be ~ to a drink** un petit verre ne serait pas de refus, je ne dirais pas non à un petit verre.

aversion [ə'vɜːʃən] *n* aversion *f*, répugnance *f*.

avert [ə'vɜːt] *vt* prévenir, écarter; (*one's eyes*) détourner.

aviary ['eɪvɪərɪ] *n* volière *f*.

aviation [eɪvɪ'eɪʃən] *n* aviation *f*.

avid ['ævɪd] *adj* avide.

avidly ['ævɪdlɪ] *adv* avidement, avec avidité.

avocado [ævə'kɑːdəʊ] *n* (*also:* BRIT: ~ **pear**) avocat *m*.

avoid [ə'vɔɪd] *vt* éviter.

avoidable [ə'vɔɪdəbl] *adj* évitable.

avoidance [ə'vɔɪdəns] *n le fait d'éviter.*

avowed [ə'vaʊd] *adj* déclaré(e).

AVP *n abbr* (*US*) = assistant vice-president.

AWACS ['eɪwæks] *n abbr* (= *airborne warning and control system*) AWACS (*système aéroporté d'alerte et de contrôle*).

await [ə'weɪt] *vt* attendre; **~ing attention/ delivery** (*COMM*) en souffrance; **long ~ed** tant attendu(e).

awake [ə'weɪk] *adj* éveillé(e); (*fig*) en éveil ♦ *vb* (*pt* **awoke** [ə'wəʊk], *pp* **awoken** [ə'wəʊkən], **awaked**) *vt* éveiller ♦ *vi* s'éveiller; **~ to** conscient de; **he was still ~** il ne dormait pas encore.

awakening [ə'weɪknɪŋ] *n* réveil *m*.

award [ə'wɔːd] *n* récompense *f*, prix *m* ♦ *vt* (*prize*) décerner; (*LAW: damages*) accorder.

aware [ə'wɛə*] *adj*: **~ of** (*conscious*) conscient(e) de; (*informed*) au courant de; **to become ~ of** avoir conscience de, prendre conscience de; se rendre compte de; **politically/socially ~** sensibilisé(e) aux *or* ayant pris conscience des problèmes politiques/sociaux; **I am fully ~ that** je me rends parfaitement compte que.

awareness [ə'wɛənɪs] *n* conscience *f*, connaissance *f*; **to develop people's ~ (of)** sensibiliser le public (à).

awash [ə'wɒʃ] *adj* recouvert(e) (d'eau); **~ with** inondé(e) de.

away [ə'weɪ] *adj, adv* (au) loin; absent(e); **two kilometres ~** à (une distance de) deux kilomètres, à deux kilomètres de distance; **two hours ~ by car** à deux heures de voiture *or* de route; **the holiday was two weeks ~** il restait deux semaines jusqu'aux vacances; **~ from** loin de; **he's ~ for a week** il est parti (pour) une semaine; **he's ~ in Milan** il est (parti) à Milan; **to take ~** *vt* emporter; **to pedal/work/laugh** etc **~** *la particule indique la constance et l'énergie de l'action:* il pédalait etc tant qu'il pouvait; **to fade/wither** etc **~** *la particule renforce l'idée de la disparition,*

l'éloignement.

away game *n* (*SPORT*) match *m* à l'extérieur.

awe [ɔː] *n* respect mêlé de crainte, effroi mêlé d'admiration.

awe-inspiring ['ɔːɪnspaɪərɪŋ], **awesome** ['ɔːsəm] *adj* impressionnant(e).

awestruck ['ɔːstrʌk] *adj* frappé(e) d'effroi.

awful ['ɔːfəl] *adj* affreux(euse); **an ~ lot of** énormément de.

awfully ['ɔːfəlɪ] *adv* (*very*) terriblement, vraiment.

awhile [ə'waɪl] *adv* un moment, quelque temps.

awkward ['ɔːkwəd] *adj* (*clumsy*) gauche, maladroit(e); (*inconvenient*) malaisé(e), d'emploi malaisé, peu pratique; (*embarrassing*) gênant(e).

awkwardness ['ɔːkwədnɪs] *n* (*embarrassment*) gêne *f*.

awl [ɔːl] *n* alêne *f*.

awning ['ɔːnɪŋ] *n* (*of tent*) auvent *m*; (*of shop*) store *m*; (*of hotel etc*) marquise *f* (de toile).

awoke [ə'wəʊk] *pt of* **awake**.

awoken [ə'wəʊkən] *pp of* **awake**.

AWOL ['eɪwɒl] *abbr* (*MIL*) = **absent without leave.**

awry [ə'raɪ] *adv, adj* de travers; **to go ~** mal tourner.

axe, (*US*) **ax** [æks] *n* hache *f* ♦ *vt* (*employee*) renvoyer; (*project etc*) abandonner; (*jobs*) supprimer; **to have an ~ to grind** (*fig*) prêcher pour son saint.

axes ['æksiːz] *npl of* **axis.**

axiom ['æksɪəm] *n* axiome *m*.

axiomatic [æksɪəʊ'mætɪk] *adj* axiomatique.

axis, *pl* **axes** ['æksɪs, -siːz] *n* axe *m*.

axle ['æksl] *n* (*also:* ~**-tree**) essieu *m*.

ay(e) [aɪ] *excl* (*yes*) oui ♦ *n*: **the ~s** les oui.

AYH *n abbr* = *American Youth Hostels.*

AZ *abbr* (*US*) = *Arizona.*

azalea [ə'zeɪlɪə] *n* azalée *f*.

Azerbaijan [æzəbaɪ'dʒɑːn] *n* Azerbaïdjan *m*.

Azerbaijani, Azeri [æzəbaɪ'dʒɑːnɪ, ə'zɛərɪ] *adj* azerbaïdjanais(e) ♦ *n* Azerbaïdjanais/e.

Azores [ə'zɔːz] *npl*: **the ~** les Açores *fpl.*

AZT *n abbr* (= *azidothymidine*) AZT *f.*

Aztec ['æztɛk] *adj* aztèque ♦ *n* Aztèque *m/f.*

azure ['eɪʒə*] *adj* azuré(e).

B b

B, b [biː] n (letter) B, b m; (SCOL: mark) B; (MUS): **B** si m; **B for Benjamin**, (US) **B for Baker** B comme Berthe; **B road** n (BRIT AUT) route départementale.
b. abbr = **born**.
BA n abbr = **British Academy**; (SCOL) = **Bachelor of Arts**.
babble ['bæbl] vi babiller ♦ n babillage m.
baboon [bə'buːn] n babouin m.
baby ['beɪbɪ] n bébé m.
baby carriage n (US) voiture f d'enfant.
baby grand n (also: ~ **piano**) (piano m) demi-queue m.
babyhood ['beɪbɪhud] n petite enfance.
babyish ['beɪbɪɪʃ] adj enfantin(e), de bébé.
baby-minder ['beɪbɪmaɪndə*] n (BRIT) gardienne f (d'enfants).
baby-sit ['beɪbɪsɪt] vi garder les enfants.
baby-sitter ['beɪbɪsɪtə*] n baby-sitter m/f.
bachelor ['bætʃələ*] n célibataire m; **B~ of Arts/Science (BA/BSc)** ≈ licencié/e ès or en lettres/sciences; **B~ of Arts/Science degree (BA/BSc)** n ≈ licence f ès or en lettres/sciences.

Un **Bachelor's degree** est un diplôme accordé après trois ou quatre années d'université. Les Bachelor's degrees les plus courants sont le **BA** (Bachelor of Arts), le **BSc** (Bachelor of Science), le **BEd** (Bachelor of Education) et le **LLB** (Bachelor of Laws).

---

bachelorhood ['bætʃələhud] n célibat m.
bachelor party n (US) enterrement m de vie de garçon.
back [bæk] n (of person, horse) dos m; (of hand) dos, revers m; (of house) derrière m; (of car, train) arrière m; (of chair) dossier m; (of page) verso m; (SPORT) arrière m; **to have one's ~ to the wall** (fig) être au pied du mur; **to break the ~ of a job** (BRIT) faire le gros du travail; **~ to front** à l'envers ♦ vt (financially) soutenir (financièrement); (candidate: also: ~ **up**) soutenir, appuyer; (horse: at races) parier or miser sur; (car) (faire) reculer ♦ vi reculer; (car etc) faire marche arrière ♦ adj (in compounds) de derrière, à l'arrière; ~ **seats/wheels** (AUT) sièges mpl/roues fpl arrière; ~ **payments/rent** arriéré m de paiements/loyer; ~ **garden/room** jardin/pièce sur l'arrière; **to take a ~ seat** (fig) se contenter d'un second rôle, être relégué(e) au second plan ♦ adv (not forward) en arrière;

(returned): **he's ~** il est rentré, il est de retour; **when will you be ~?** quand seras-tu de retour?; **he ran ~** il est revenu en courant; (restitution): **throw the ball ~** renvoie la balle; **can I have it ~?** puis-je le ravoir?, peux-tu me le rendre?; (again): **he called ~** il a rappelé.
backbench ['bæk'bentʃ] n (BRIT) banc des députés sans portefeuille.
▶**back down** vi rabattre de ses prétentions.
▶**back on to** vt fus: **the house ~s on to the golf course** la maison donne derrière sur le terrain de golf.
▶**back out** vi (of promise) se dédire.
▶**back up** vt (COMPUT) faire une copie de sauvegarde de.
backache ['bækeɪk] n maux mpl de reins.

Le terme **back benches** désigne les bancs les plus éloignés de l'allée centrale de la Chambre des communes. Les députés qui occupent ces bancs sont les "backbenchers" et ils n'ont pas de portefeuille ministériel.

---

backbiting ['bækbaɪtɪŋ] n médisance(s) f(pl).
backbone ['bækbəun] n colonne vertébrale, épine dorsale; **he's the ~ of the organization** c'est sur lui que repose l'organisation.
backchat ['bæktʃæt] n (BRIT col) impertinences fpl.
back-cloth ['bækklɔθ] n (BRIT) toile f de fond.
backcomb ['bækkəum] vt (BRIT) crêper.
backdate [bæk'deɪt] vt (letter) antidater; ~**d pay rise** augmentation f avec effet rétroactif.
backdrop ['bækdrɔp] n = **backcloth**.
backer ['bækə*] n partisan m; (COMM) commanditaire m.
backfire [bæk'faɪə*] vi (AUT) pétarader; (plans) mal tourner.
backgammon ['bækgæmən] n trictrac m.
background ['bækgraund] n arrière-plan m; (of events) situation f, conjoncture f; (basic knowledge) éléments mpl de base; (experience) formation f ♦ cpd (noise, music) de fond; ~ **reading** lecture(s) générale(s) (sur un sujet); **family ~** milieu familial.
backhand ['bækhænd] n (TENNIS: also: ~ **stroke**) revers m.
backhanded ['bæk'hændɪd] adj (fig) déloyal(e); équivoque.
backhander ['bæk'hændə*] n (BRIT: bribe) pot-de-vin m.
backing ['bækɪŋ] n (fig) soutien m, appui m; (COMM) soutien (financier); (MUS) accompagnement m.
backlash ['bæklæʃ] n contre-coup m, répercussion f.
backlog ['bæklɔg] n: ~ **of work** travail m en retard.
back number n (of magazine etc) vieux numéro m.

backpack ['bækpæk] n sac m à dos.
backpacker ['bækpækə*] n randonneur/euse.
back pay n rappel m de salaire.
backpedal ['bækpɛdl] vi (fig) faire marche arrière.
backseat driver ['bæksi:t-] n passager qui donne des conseils au conducteur.
backside ['bæksaid] n (col) derrière m, postérieur m.
backslash ['bækslæʃ] n barre oblique inversée.
backslide ['bækslaid] vi retomber dans l'erreur.
backspace ['bækspeis] vi (in typing) appuyer sur la touche retour.
backstage [bæk'steidʒ] adv dans les coulisses.
back-street ['bækstri:t] adj (abortion) clandestin(e); ~ **abortionist** avorteur/euse (clandestin).
backstroke ['bækstrəuk] n dos crawlé.
backtrack ['bæktræk] vi (fig) = **backpedal**.
backup ['bækʌp] adj (train, plane) supplémentaire, de réserve; (COMPUT) de sauvegarde ♦ n (support) appui m, soutien m; (COMPUT: also: ~ **file**) sauvegarde f.
backward ['bækwəd] adj (movement) en arrière; (measure) rétrograde; (person, country) arriéré(e); attardé(e); (shy) hésitant(e); ~ **and forward movement** mouvement de va-et-vient.
backwards ['bækwədz] adv (move, go) en arrière; (read a list) à l'envers, à rebours; (fall) à la renverse; (walk) à reculons; (in time) en arrière, vers le passé; **to know sth** ~ or (US) ~ **and forwards** (col) connaître qch sur le bout des doigts.
backwater ['bækwɔ:tə*] n (fig) coin reculé; bled perdu.
back yard n arrière-cour f.
bacon ['beikən] n bacon m, lard m.
bacteria [bæk'tiəriə] npl bactéries fpl.
bacteriology [bæktiəri'ɔlədʒi] n bactériologie f.
bad [bæd] adj mauvais(e); (child) vilain(e); (meat, food) gâté(e), avarié(e); **his** ~ **leg** sa jambe malade; **to go** ~ (meat, food) se gâter; (milk) tourner; **to have a** ~ **time of it** traverser une mauvaise passe; **I feel** ~ **about it** (guilty) j'ai un peu mauvaise conscience; ~ **debt** créance douteuse; **in** ~ **faith** de mauvaise foi.
baddie, baddy ['bædi] n (col: CINE etc) méchant m.
bade [bæd] pt of **bid**.
badge [bædʒ] n insigne m; (of policeman) plaque f; (stick-on, sew-on) badge m.
badger ['bædʒə*] n blaireau m ♦ vt harceler.
badly ['bædli] adv (work, dress etc) mal; ~ **wounded** grièvement blessé; **he needs it** ~ il en a un absolument besoin; **things are going** ~ les choses vont mal; ~ **off** adj, adv dans la gêne.

bad-mannered ['bæd'mænəd] adj mal élevé(e).
badminton ['bædmintən] n badminton m.
bad-mouth ['bæd'mauθ] vt (US col) débiner.
bad-tempered ['bæd'tɛmpəd] adj (by nature) ayant mauvais caractère; (on one occasion) de mauvaise humeur.
baffle ['bæfl] vt (puzzle) déconcerter.
baffling ['bæflin] adj déroutant(e), déconcertant(e).
bag [bæg] n sac m; (of hunter) gibecière f, chasse f ♦ vt (col: take) empocher; s'approprier; (TECH) mettre en sacs; ~**s of** (col: lots of) des masses de; **to pack one's** ~**s** faire ses valises or bagages; ~**s under the eyes** poches fpl sous les yeux.
bagful ['bægful] n plein sac.
baggage ['bægidʒ] n bagages mpl.
baggage claim n (at airport) livraison f des bagages.
baggy ['bægi] adj avachi(e), qui fait des poches.
Baghdad [bæg'dæd] n Baghdâd, Bagdad.
bag lady n (col) clocharde f.
bagpipes ['bægpaips] npl cornemuse f.
bag-snatcher ['bægsnætʃə*] n (BRIT) voleur m à l'arraché.
bag-snatching ['bægsnætʃin] n (BRIT) vol m à l'arraché.
Bahamas [bə'hɑ:məz] npl: **the** ~ les Bahamas fpl.
Bahrain [bɑ:'rein] n Bahreïn m.
bail [beil] n caution f ♦ vt (prisoner: also: **grant** ~ **to**) mettre en liberté sous caution; (boat: also: ~ **out**) écoper; **to be released on** ~ être libéré(e) sous caution; see **bale**.
▶**bail out** vt (prisoner) payer la caution de.
bailiff ['beilif] n huissier m.
bait [beit] n appât m ♦ vt appâter; (fig) tourmenter.
bake [beik] vt (faire) cuire au four ♦ vi (bread etc) cuire (au four); (make cakes etc) faire de la pâtisserie.
baked beans [beikt-] npl haricots blancs à la sauce tomate.
baker ['beikə*] n boulanger m.
bakery ['beikəri] n boulangerie f; boulangerie industrielle.
baking ['beikin] n cuisson f.
baking powder n levure f (chimique).
baking tin n (for cake) moule m à gâteaux; (for meat) plat m pour le four.
baking tray n plaque f à gâteaux.
balaclava [bælə'klɑ:və] n (also: ~ **helmet**) passe-montagne m.
balance ['bæləns] n équilibre m; (COMM: sum) solde m; (scales) balance f ♦ vt mettre or faire tenir en équilibre; (pros and cons) peser; (budget) équilibrer; (account) balancer; (compensate) compenser, contrebalancer; ~ **of trade/payments** balance commerciale/des comptes or paiements; ~ **carried for-**

ward solde *m* à reporter; ~ **brought forward** solde reporté; **to** ~ **the books** arrêter les comptes, dresser le bilan.

balanced ['bælənst] *adj* (*personality, diet*) équilibré(e).

balance sheet *n* bilan *m*.

balcony ['bælkənɪ] *n* balcon *m*.

bald [bɔːld] *adj* chauve; (*tyre*) lisse.

baldness ['bɔːldnɪs] *n* calvitie *f*.

bale [beɪl] *n* balle *f*, ballot *m*.

►**bale out** *vi* (*of a plane*) sauter en parachute ♦ *vt* (*NAUT: water, boat*) écoper.

Balearic Islands [bælɪˈærɪk-] *npl*: **the** ~ les (îles *fpl*) Baléares *fpl*.

baleful ['beɪlful] *adj* funeste, maléfique.

balk [bɔːk] *vi*: **to** ~ **(at)** (*person*) regimber (contre); (*horse*) se dérober (devant).

Balkan ['bɔːlkən] *adj* balkanique ♦ *n*: **the** ~**s** les Balkans *mpl*.

ball [bɔːl] *n* boule *f*; (*football*) ballon *m*; (*for tennis, golf*) balle *f*; (*dance*) bal *m*; **to play** ~ **(with sb)** jouer au ballon (*or* à la balle) (avec qn); (*fig*) coopérer (avec qn); **to be on the** ~ (*fig: competent*) être à la hauteur; (: *alert*) être éveillé(e), être vif(vive); **to start the** ~ **rolling** (*fig*) commencer; **the** ~ **is in their court** (*fig*) la balle est dans leur camp.

ballad ['bæləd] *n* ballade *f*.

ballast ['bæləst] *n* lest *m*.

ball bearing *n* roulement *m* à billes.

ball cock *n* robinet *m* à flotteur.

ballerina [bæləˈriːnə] *n* ballerine *f*.

ballet ['bæleɪ] *n* ballet *m*; (*art*) danse *f* (classique).

ballet dancer *n* danseur/euse de ballet.

ballistic [bəˈlɪstɪk] *adj* balistique.

ballistics [bəˈlɪstɪks] *n* balistique *f*.

balloon [bəˈluːn] *n* ballon *m*; (*in comic strip*) bulle *f* ♦ *vi* gonfler.

balloonist [bəˈluːnɪst] *n* aéronaute *m/f*.

ballot ['bælət] *n* scrutin *m*.

ballot box *n* urne (électorale).

ballot paper *n* bulletin *m* de vote.

ballpark ['bɔːlpɑːk] *n* (*US*) stade *m* de baseball.

ballpark figure *n* (*col*) chiffre approximatif.

ball-point pen ['bɔːlpɔɪnt-] *n* stylo *m* à bille.

ballroom ['bɔːlrum] *n* salle *f* de bal.

balls [bɔːlz] *npl* (*col!*) couilles *fpl* (!).

balm [bɑːm] *n* baume *m*.

balmy ['bɑːmɪ] *adj* (*breeze, air*) doux(douce); (*BRIT col*) = **barmy**.

BALPA ['bælpə] *n abbr* (= *British Airline Pilots' Association*) syndicat des pilotes de ligne.

balsam ['bɔːlsəm] *n* baume *m*.

balsa (wood) ['bɔːlsə-] *n* balsa *m*.

Baltic [bɔːltɪk] *adj, n*: **the** ~ **(Sea)** la (mer) Baltique.

balustrade [bæləsˈtreɪd] *n* balustrade *f*.

bamboo [bæmˈbuː] *n* bambou *m*.

bamboozle [bæmˈbuːzl] *vt* (*col*) embobiner.

ban [bæn] *n* interdiction *f* ♦ *vt* interdire; **he was** ~**ned from driving** (*BRIT*) on lui a retiré le permis (de conduire).

banal [bəˈnɑːl] *adj* banal(e).

banana [bəˈnɑːnə] *n* banane *f*.

band [bænd] *n* bande *f*; (*at a dance*) orchestre *m*; (*MIL*) musique *f*, fanfare *f*.

►**band together** *vi* se liguer.

B & B *n abbr* = **bed and breakfast**.

bandage ['bændɪdʒ] *n* bandage *m*, pansement *m* ♦ *vt* (*wound, leg*) mettre un pansement *or* un bandage sur; (*person*) mettre un pansement *or* un bandage à.

Band-Aid ['bændeɪd] *n* ® (*US*) pansement adhésif.

bandit ['bændɪt] *n* bandit *m*.

bandstand ['bændstænd] *n* kiosque *m* (à musique).

bandwagon ['bændwægən] *n*: **to jump on the** ~ (*fig*) monter dans *or* prendre le train en marche.

bandy ['bændɪ] *vt* (*jokes, insults*) échanger.

►**bandy about** *vt* employer à tout bout de champ *or* à tort et à travers.

bandy-legged ['bændɪˈlɛgɪd] *adj* aux jambes arquées.

bane [beɪn] *n*: **it** (*or* **he etc**) **is the** ~ **of my life** c'est (*or* il est *etc*) le drame de ma vie.

bang [bæŋ] *n* détonation *f*; (*of door*) claquement *m*; (*blow*) coup (violent) ♦ *vt* frapper (violemment); (*door*) claquer ♦ *vi* détoner; claquer ♦ *adv*: **to be** ~ **on time** (*BRIT col*) être à l'heure pile; **to** ~ **at the door** cogner à la porte; **to** ~ **into sth** se cogner contre qch.

banger ['bæŋə*] *n* (*BRIT: car: also*: **old** ~) (vieux) tacot; (*BRIT col: sausage*) saucisse *f*; (*firework*) pétard *m*.

Bangkok [bæŋˈkɔk] *n* Bangkok.

Bangladesh [bæŋgləˈdɛʃ] *n* Bangladesh *m*.

bangle ['bæŋgl] *n* bracelet *m*.

bangs [bæŋz] *npl* (*US: fringe*) frange *f*.

banish ['bænɪʃ] *vt* bannir.

banister(s) ['bænɪstə(z)] *n(pl)* rampe *f* (d'escalier).

banjo, ~**es** *or* ~**s** ['bændʒəu] *n* banjo *m*.

bank [bæŋk] *n* banque *f*; (*of river, lake*) bord *m*, rive *f*; (*of earth*) talus *m*, remblai *m* ♦ *vi* (*AVIAT*) virer sur l'aile; (*COMM*): **they** ~ **with Pitt's** leur banque *or* banquier est Pitt's.

►**bank on** *vt fus* miser *or* tabler sur.

bank account *n* compte *m* en banque.

bank balance *n* solde *m* bancaire.

bank card *n* = **banker's card**.

bank charges *npl* (*BRIT*) frais *mpl* de banque.

bank draft *n* traite *f* bancaire.

banker ['bæŋkə*] *n* banquier *m*; ~**'s card** (*BRIT*) carte *f* d'identité bancaire; ~**'s order** (*BRIT*) ordre *m* de virement.

bank giro *n* paiement *m* par virement.

bank holiday *n* (*BRIT*) jour férié (*où les banques sont fermées*).

Un **bank holiday** *en Grande-Bretagne est un lundi férié et donc l'occasion d'un week-end prolongé. La circulation sur les routes et le trafic dans les gares et les aéroports augmentent considérablement à ces périodes. Les principaux bank holidays, à part Pâques et Noël, se situent au mois de mai et fin août.*

banking ['bæŋkɪŋ] n opérations fpl bancaires; profession f de banquier.
banking hours npl heures fpl d'ouverture des banques.
bank loan n prêt m bancaire.
bank manager n directeur m d'agence (bancaire).
banknote ['bæŋknəut] n billet m de banque.
bank rate n taux m de l'escompte.
bankrupt ['bæŋkrʌpt] n failli/e ♦ adj en faillite; **to go** ~ faire faillite.
bankruptcy ['bæŋkrʌptsɪ] n faillite f.
bank statement n relevé m de compte.
banner ['bænə*] n bannière f.
bannister(s) ['bænɪstə(z)] n(pl) = **banister(s)**.
banns [bænz] npl bans mpl (de mariage).
banquet ['bæŋkwɪt] n banquet m, festin m.
bantam-weight ['bæntəmweɪt] n poids m coq inv.
banter ['bæntə*] n badinage m.
BAOR n abbr (= British Army of the Rhine) forces britanniques en Allemagne.
baptism ['bæptɪzəm] n baptême m.
Baptist ['bæptɪst] n baptiste m/f.
baptize [bæp'taɪz] vt baptiser.
bar [ba:*] n barre f; (of window etc) barreau m; (of chocolate) tablette f, plaque f; (fig) obstacle m; mesure f d'exclusion; (pub) bar m; (counter: in pub) comptoir m, bar; (MUS) mesure f ♦ vt (road) barrer; (window) munir de barreaux; (person) exclure; (activity) interdire; ~ **of soap** savonnette f; **behind** ~s (prisoner) derrière les barreaux; **the B~** (LAW) le barreau; ~ **none** sans exception.
Barbados [ba:'beɪdɔs] n Barbade f.
barbaric [ba:'bærɪk] adj barbare.
barbarous ['ba:bərəs] adj barbare, cruel(le).
barbecue ['ba:bɪkju:] n barbecue m.
barbed wire ['ba:bd-] n fil m de fer barbelé.
barber ['ba:bə*] n coiffeur m (pour hommes).
barbiturate [ba:'bɪtjurɪt] n barbiturique m.
Barcelona [ba:sə'ləunə] n Barcelone.
bar chart n diagramme m en bâtons.
bar code n code m à barres.
bare [bɛə*] adj nu(e) ♦ vt mettre à nu, dénuder; (teeth) montrer; **the** ~ **essentials** le strict nécessaire.
bareback ['bɛəbæk] adv à cru, sans selle.
barefaced ['bɛəfeɪst] adj impudent(e), effronté(e).
barefoot ['bɛəfut] adj, adv nu-pieds, (les) pieds nus.
bareheaded [bɛə'hɛdɪd] adj, adv nu-tête, (la)

tête nue.
barely ['bɛəlɪ] adv à peine.
Barents Sea ['bærənts-] n: **the** ~ la mer de Barents.
bargain ['ba:gɪn] n (transaction) marché m; (good buy) affaire f, occasion f ♦ vi (haggle) marchander; (trade) négocier, traiter; **into the** ~ par-dessus le marché.
▶**bargain for** vi (col): **he got more than he** ~**ed for!** il en a eu pour son argent!
bargaining ['ba:gənɪŋ] n marchandage m; négociations fpl.
bargaining position n: **to be in a weak/strong** ~ être en mauvaise/bonne position pour négocier.
barge [ba:dʒ] n péniche f.
▶**barge in** vi (walk in) faire irruption; (interrupt talk) intervenir mal à propos.
▶**barge into** vt fus rentrer dans.
baritone ['bærɪtəun] n baryton m.
barium meal ['bɛərɪəm-] n (bouillie f de) sulfate m de baryum.
bark [ba:k] n (of tree) écorce f; (of dog) aboiement m ♦ vi aboyer.
barley ['ba:lɪ] n orge f.
barley sugar n sucre m d'orge.
barmaid ['ba:meɪd] n serveuse f (de bar), barmaid f.
barman ['ba:mən] n serveur m (de bar), barman m.
barmy ['ba:mɪ] adj (BRIT col) timbré(e), cinglé(e).
barn [ba:n] n grange f.
barnacle ['ba:nəkl] n anatife m, bernache f.
barn owl n chouette-effraie f, chat-huant m.
barometer [bə'rɔmɪtə*] n baromètre m.
baron ['bærən] n baron m; **the press/oil** ~**s** les magnats mpl or barons mpl de la presse/du pétrole.
baroness ['bærənɪs] n baronne f.
barrack ['bærək] vt (BRIT) chahuter.
barracking ['bærəkɪŋ] n (BRIT): **to give sb a** ~ chahuter qn.
barracks ['bærəks] npl caserne f.
barrage ['bæra:ʒ] n (MIL) tir m de barrage; (dam) barrage m; **a** ~ **of questions** un feu roulant de questions.
barrel ['bærəl] n tonneau m; (of gun) canon m.
barrel organ n orgue m de Barbarie.
barren ['bærən] adj stérile; (hills) aride.
barricade [bærɪ'keɪd] n barricade f ♦ vt barricader.
barrier ['bærɪə*] n barrière f; (BRIT: also: **crash** ~) rail m de sécurité.
barrier cream n (BRIT) crème protectrice.
barring ['ba:rɪŋ] prep sauf.
barrister ['bærɪstə*] n (BRIT) avocat (plaidant).

En Angleterre, un **barrister,** *que l'on appelle également "barrister-at-law", est un avocat qui représente ses clients devant la cour et plaide pour eux. Le client doit d'abord passer* *par l'intermédiaire d'un* **solicitor**. *On obtient le diplôme de barrister après avoir fait des études dans l'une des Inns of Court, les quatre écoles de droit londoniennes.*

barrow ['bærəu] *n* (*cart*) charrette *f* à bras.
barstool ['bɑːstuːl] *n* tabouret *m* de bar.
Bart. *abbr* (*BRIT*) = **baronet**.
bartender ['bɑːtɛndə*] *n* (*US*) serveur *m* (*de bar*), barman *m*.
barter ['bɑːtə*] *n* échange *m*, troc *m* ♦ *vt*: **to ~ sth for** échanger qch contre.
base [beɪs] *n* base *f* ♦ *vt* (*troops*): **to be ~d at** être basé(e) à; (*opinion, belief*): **to ~ sth on** baser *or* fonder qch sur ♦ *adj* vil(e), bas(se); **coffee-~d** à base de café; **a Paris-~d firm** une maison opérant de Paris *or* dont le siège est à Paris; **I'm ~d in London** je suis basé(e) à Londres.
baseball ['beɪsbɔːl] *n* base-ball *m*.
baseboard ['beɪsbɔːd] *n* (*US*) plinthe *f*.
base camp *n* camp *m* de base.
Basel ['bɑːl] *n* = **Basle**.
baseline ['beɪslaɪn] *n* (*TENNIS*) ligne *f* de fond.
basement ['beɪsmənt] *n* sous-sol *m*.
base rate *n* taux *m* de base.
bases ['beɪsiːz] *npl of* **basis**; ['beɪsɪz] *npl of* **base**.
bash [bæʃ] *vt* (*col*) frapper, cogner ♦ *n*: **I'll have a ~** (**at it**) (*BRIT col*) je vais essayer un coup; **~ed in** *adj* enfoncé(e), défoncé(e).
▶**bash up** *vt* (*col: car*) bousiller; (*: BRIT: person*) tabasser.
bashful ['bæʃful] *adj* timide; modeste.
bashing ['bæʃɪŋ] *n* (*col*) raclée *f*; **Paki-~≈** ratonnade *f*, **queer-~** chasse *f* aux pédés.
BASIC ['beɪsɪk] *n* (*COMPUT*) BASIC *m*.
basic ['beɪsɪk] *adj* (*precautions, rules*) élémentaire; (*principles, research*) fondamental(e); (*vocabulary, salary*) de base; réduit(e) au minimum, rudimentaire.
basically ['beɪsɪklɪ] *adv* (*really*) en fait; (*essentially*) fondamentalement.
basic rate *n* (*of tax*) première tranche d'imposition.
basil ['bæzl] *n* basilic *m*.
basin ['beɪsn] *n* (*vessel, also GEO*) cuvette *f*, bassin *m*; (*BRIT: for food*) bol *m*; (*: bigger*) saladier *m*; (*also: wash~*) lavabo *m*.
basis, *pl* **bases** ['beɪsɪs, -siːz] *n* base *f*; **on the ~ of what you've said** d'après *or* compte tenu de ce que vous dites.
bask [bɑːsk] *vi*: **to ~ in the sun** se chauffer au soleil.
basket ['bɑːskɪt] *n* corbeille *f*; (*with handle*) panier *m*.
basketball ['bɑːskɪtbɔːl] *n* basket-ball *m*.
basketball player *n* basketteur/euse.
Basle [bɑːl] *n* Bâle *f*.
basmati rice [bəz'mætɪ-] *n* riz *m* basmati.
Basque [bæsk] *adj* basque ♦ *n* Basque *m/f*.
bass [beɪs] *n* (*MUS*) basse *f*.
bass clef *n* clé *f* de fa.

bassoon [bə'suːn] *n* basson *m*.
bastard ['bɑːstəd] *n* enfant naturel(le), bâtard/e; (*col!*) salaud *m* (*!*).
baste [beɪst] *vt* (*CULIN*) arroser; (*SEWING*) bâtir, faufiler.
bastion ['bæstɪən] *n* bastion *m*.
bat [bæt] *n* chauve-souris *f*; (*for baseball etc*) batte *f*; (*BRIT: for table tennis*) raquette *f* ♦ *vt*: **he didn't ~ an eyelid** il n'a pas sourcillé *or* bronché; **off one's own ~** de sa propre initiative.
batch [bætʃ] *n* (*of bread*) fournée *f*; (*of papers*) liasse *f*; (*of applicants, letters*) paquet *m*; (*of work*) monceau *m*; (*of goods*) lot *m*.
batch processing *n* (*COMPUT*) traitement *m* par lot.
bated ['beɪtɪd] *adj*: **with ~ breath** en retenant son souffle.
bath [bɑːθ, *pl* bɑːðz] *n* bain *m*; (*bathtub*) baignoire *f* ♦ *vt* baigner, donner un bain à; **to have a ~** prendre un bain; *see also* **baths**.
Bath chair *n* (*BRIT*) fauteuil roulant.
bathe [beɪð] *vi* se baigner ♦ *vt* baigner; (*wound etc*) laver.
bather ['beɪðə*] *n* baigneur/euse.
bathing ['beɪðɪŋ] *n* baignade *f*.
bathing cap *n* bonnet *m* de bain.
bathing costume, (*US*) **bathing suit** *n* maillot *m* (de bain).
bathmat ['bɑːθmæt] *n* tapis *m* de bain.
bathrobe ['bɑːθrəub] *n* peignoir *m* de bain.
bathroom ['bɑːθrum] *n* salle *f* de bains.
baths [bɑːðz] *npl* établissement *m* de bains (-douches).
bath towel *n* serviette *f* de bain.
bathtub ['bɑːθtʌb] *n* baignoire *f*.
batman ['bætmən] *n* (*BRIT MIL*) ordonnance *f*.
baton ['bætən] *n* bâton *m*; (*MUS*) baguette *f*; (*club*) matraque *f*.
battalion [bə'tælɪən] *n* bataillon *m*.
batten ['bætn] *n* (*CARPENTRY*) latte *f*; (*NAUT: on sail*) latte de voile.
▶**batten down** *vt* (*NAUT*): **to ~ down the hatches** fermer les écoutilles.
batter ['bætə*] *vt* battre ♦ *n* pâte *f* à frire.
battered ['bætəd] *adj* (*hat, pan*) cabossé(e); **~ wife/child** épouse/enfant maltraité(e) *or* martyr(e).
battering ram ['bætərɪŋ-] *n* bélier *m* (*fig*).
battery ['bætərɪ] *n* batterie *f*; (*of torch*) pile *f*.
battery charger *n* chargeur *m*.
battery farming *n* élevage *m* en batterie.
battle ['bætl] *n* bataille *f*, combat *m* ♦ *vi* se battre, lutter; **that's half the ~** (*fig*) c'est déjà bien; **it's a** *or* **we're fighting a losing ~** (*fig*) c'est perdu d'avance, c'est peine perdue.
battle dress *n* tenue *f* de campagne *or* d'assaut.
battlefield ['bætlfiːld] *n* champ *m* de bataille.
battlements ['bætlmənts] *npl* remparts *mpl*.
battleship ['bætlʃɪp] *n* cuirassé *m*.

batty ['bætɪ] *adj (col: person)* toqué(e); (: *idea, behaviour)* loufoque.
bauble ['bɔːbl] *n* babiole *f*.
baud [bɔːd] *n (COMPUT)* baud *m*.
baud rate *n (COMPUT)* vitesse *f* de transmission.
baulk [bɔːlk] *vi* = **balk**.
bauxite ['bɔːksaɪt] *n* bauxite *f*.
Bavaria [bə'vɛərɪə] *n* Bavière *f*.
Bavarian [bə'vɛərɪən] *adj* bavarois(e) ♦ *n* Bavarois/e.
bawdy ['bɔːdɪ] *adj* paillard(e).
bawl [bɔːl] *vi* hurler, brailler.
bay [beɪ] *n (of sea)* baie *f*; (*BRIT: for parking)* place *f* de stationnement; (: *for loading)* aire *f* de chargement; (*horse)* bai/e *m/f*; **to hold sb at ~** tenir qn à distance *or* en échec.
bay leaf *n* laurier *m*.
bayonet ['beɪənɪt] *n* baïonnette *f*.
bay tree *n* laurier *m*.
bay window *n* baie vitrée.
bazaar [bə'zɑː*] *n* bazar *m*; vente *f* de charité.
bazooka [bə'zuːkə] *n* bazooka *m*.
BB *n abbr (BRIT: = Boys' Brigade)* mouvement de garçons.
BBB *n abbr (US: = Better Business Bureau)* organisme de défense du consommateur.
BBC *n abbr (= British Broadcasting Corporation) office de la radiodiffusion et télévision britannique.*

La **BBC** *est un organisme centralisé dont les membres, nommés par l'État, gèrent les chaînes de télévision publiques (BBC1, qui présente des émissions d'intérêt général, et BBC2, qui est plutôt orientée vers les émissions plus culturelles) et les stations de radio publiques (5 au niveau national, et 37 à l'échelle locale). Bien que non contrôlée par l'État, la BBC est responsable devant le* **Parliament** *quant au contenu des émissions qu'elle diffuse. Par ailleurs, la BBC offre un service mondial de diffusion d'émissions, en anglais et dans 35 autres langues, appelé BBC World Service. La BBC est financée par la redevance télévision et par l'exportation d'émissions.*

BC *adv abbr (= before Christ)* av. J.-C. ♦ *abbr (Canada) = British Columbia.*
BCG *n abbr (= Bacillus Calmette-Guérin)* BCG *m*.
BD *n abbr (= Bachelor of Divinity)* diplôme universitaire.
B/D *abbr = bank draft.*
BDS *n abbr (= Bachelor of Dental Surgery)* diplôme universitaire.

═══════════════════════ *KEYWORD*

be [biː] *(pt* **was, were,** *pp* **been)** *aux vb* **1** *(with present participle: forming continuous tenses)*: **what are you doing?** que faites-vous?; **they're coming tomorrow** ils viennent demain; **I've been waiting for you for 2 hours**
je t'attends depuis 2 heures
2 *(with pp: forming passives)* être; **to ~ killed** être tué(e); **he was nowhere to ~ seen** on ne le voyait nulle part
3 *(in tag questions)*: **it was fun, wasn't it?** c'était drôle, n'est-ce pas?; **she's back, is she?** elle est rentrée, n'est-ce pas *or* alors?
4 *(+to +infinitive)*: **the house is to ~ sold** la maison doit être vendue; **he's not to open it** il ne doit pas l'ouvrir; **am I to understand that ...?** dois-je comprendre que ...?; **he was to have come yesterday** il devait venir hier
5 *(possibility, supposition)*: **if I were you, I ...** à votre place, je ..., si j'étais vous, je ...
♦ *vb + complement* **1** *(gen)* être; **I'm English** je suis anglais(e); **I'm tired** je suis fatigué(e); **I'm hot/cold** j'ai chaud/froid; **he's a doctor** il est médecin; **2 and 2 are 4** 2 et 2 font 4
2 *(of health)* aller; **how are you?** comment allez-vous?; **he's fine now** il va bien maintenant; **he's very ill** il est très malade
3 *(of age)* avoir; **how old are you?** quel âge avez-vous?; **I'm sixteen (years old)** j'ai seize ans
4 *(cost)* coûter; **how much was the meal?** combien a coûté le repas?; **that'll ~ £5, please** ça fera 5 livres, s'il vous plaît
♦ *vi* **1** *(exist, occur etc)* être, exister; **the prettiest girl that ever was** la fille la plus jolie qui ait jamais existé; **~ that as it may** quoi qu'il en soit; **so ~ it** soit
2 *(referring to place)* être, se trouver; **I won't ~ here tomorrow** je ne serai pas là demain; **Edinburgh is in Scotland** Édimbourg est *or* se trouve en Écosse
3 *(referring to movement)* aller; **where have you been?** où êtes-vous allé(s)?
♦ *impers vb* **1** *(referring to time, distance)* être; **it's 5 o'clock** il est 5 heures; **it's the 28th of April** c'est le 28 avril; **it's 10 km to the village** le village est à 10 km
2 *(referring to the weather)* faire; **it's too hot/cold** il fait trop chaud/froid; **it's windy** il y a du vent
3 *(emphatic)*: **it's me/the postman** c'est moi/le facteur.

B/E *abbr = bill of exchange.*
beach [biːtʃ] *n* plage *f* ♦ *vt* échouer.
beachcomber ['biːtʃkəumə*] *n* ramasseur *m* d'épaves; (*fig)* glandeur *m*.
beachwear ['biːtʃwɛə*] *n* tenues *fpl* de plage.
beacon ['biːkən] *n (lighthouse)* fanal *m*; (*marker)* balise *f*; (*also:* **radio ~**) radiophare *m*.
bead [biːd] *n* perle *f*; (*of dew, sweat)* goutte *f*; **~s** (*necklace)* collier *m*.
beady ['biːdɪ] *adj*: **~ eyes** yeux *mpl* de fouine.
beagle ['biːgl] *n* beagle *m*.
beak [biːk] *n* bec *m*.
beaker ['biːkə*] *n* gobelet *m*.
beam [biːm] *n* poutre *f*; (*of light)* rayon *m*; (*RADIO)* faisceau *m* radio ♦ *vi* rayonner; **to**

drive on full *or* **main** *or* (*US*) **high** ~ rouler en pleins phares.
beaming ['biːmɪŋ] *adj* (*sun, smile*) radieux(euse).
bean [biːn] *n* haricot *m*; (*of coffee*) grain *m*.
beanpole ['biːnpəʊl] *n* (*col*) perche *f*.
bean sprouts *npl* pousses *fpl* (de soja).
bear [bɛə*] *n* ours *m*; (*STOCK EXCHANGE*) baissier *m* ♦ *vb* (*pt* **bore**, *pp* **borne** [bɔː*, bɔːn]) *vt* porter; (*endure*) supporter; (*traces, signs*) porter; (*COMM: interest*) rapporter ♦ *vi*: **to** ~ **right/left** obliquer à droite/gauche, se diriger vers la droite/gauche; **to** ~ **the responsibility of** assumer la responsabilité de; **to** ~ **comparison with** soutenir la comparaison avec; **I can't** ~ **him** je ne peux pas le supporter *or* souffrir; **to bring pressure to** ~ **on sb** faire pression sur qn.
▶**bear out** *vt* (*theory, suspicion*) confirmer.
▶**bear up** *vi* supporter, tenir le coup; **he bore up well** il a tenu le coup.
▶**bear with** *vt fus* (*sb's moods, temper*) supporter; ~ **with me a minute** un moment, s'il vous plaît.
bearable ['bɛərəbl] *adj* supportable.
beard [bɪəd] *n* barbe *f*.
bearded ['bɪədɪd] *adj* barbu(e).
bearer ['bɛərə*] *n* porteur *m*; (*of passport etc*) titulaire *m/f*.
bearing ['bɛərɪŋ] *n* maintien *m*, allure *f*; (*connection*) rapport *m*; (*TECH*): (**ball**) ~**s** *npl* roulement *m* (à billes); **to take a** ~ faire le point; **to find one's** ~**s** s'orienter.
beast [biːst] *n* bête *f*; (*col*): **he's a** ~ c'est une brute.
beastly ['biːstlɪ] *adj* infect(e).
beat [biːt] *n* battement *m*; (*MUS*) temps *m*, mesure *f*; (*of policeman*) ronde *f* ♦ *vt* (*pt* **beat**, *pp* **beaten**) battre; **off the** ~**en track** hors des chemins *or* sentiers battus; **to** ~ **about the bush** tourner autour du pot; **to** ~ **time** battre la mesure; **that** ~**s everything!** c'est le comble!
▶**beat down** *vt* (*door*) enfoncer; (*price*) faire baisser; (*seller*) faire descendre ♦ *vi* (*rain*) tambouriner; (*sun*) taper.
▶**beat off** *vt* repousser.
▶**beat up** *vt* (*eggs*) battre; (*col: person*) tabasser.
beater ['biːtə*] *n* (*for eggs, cream*) fouet *m*, batteur *m*.
beating ['biːtɪŋ] *n* raclée *f*.
beat-up ['biːt'ʌp] *adj* (*col*) déglingué(e).
beautician [bjuː'tɪʃən] *n* esthéticien/ne.
beautiful ['bjuːtɪfʊl] *adj* beau(belle).
beautifully ['bjuːtɪflɪ] *adv* admirablement.
beautify ['bjuːtɪfaɪ] *vt* embellir.
beauty ['bjuːtɪ] *n* beauté *f*; **the** ~ **of it is that ...** le plus beau, c'est que ....
beauty contest *n* concours *m* de beauté.
beauty queen *n* reine *f* de beauté.
beauty salon *n* institut *m* de beauté.

beauty sleep *n*: **I'm going to bed, I need my** ~ je vais me coucher, j'ai besoin de faire un gros dodo.
beauty spot *n* grain *m* de beauté; (*BRIT TOURISM*) site naturel (d'une grande beauté).
beaver ['biːvə*] *n* castor *m*.
becalmed [bɪ'kɑːmd] *adj* immobilisé(e) par le calme plat.
became [bɪ'keɪm] *pt of* **become**.
because [bɪ'kɔz] *conj* parce que; ~ **of** *prep* à cause de.
beck [bɛk] *n*: **to be at sb's** ~ **and call** être à l'entière disposition de qn.
beckon ['bɛkən] *vt* (*also*: ~ **to**) faire signe (de venir) à.
become [bɪ'kʌm] *vt* (*irreg: like* **come**) devenir; **to** ~ **fat/thin** grossir/maigrir; **to** ~ **angry** se mettre en colère; **it became known that** on apprit que; **what has** ~ **of him?** qu'est-il devenu?
becoming [bɪ'kʌmɪŋ] *adj* (*behaviour*) convenable, bienséant(e); (*clothes*) seyant(e).
BECTU ['bɛktu] *n abbr* (*BRIT*) = Broadcasting, Entertainment, Cinematographic and Theatre Union.
BEd *n abbr* (= Bachelor of Education) diplôme d'aptitude à l'enseignement.
bed [bɛd] *n* lit *m*; (*of flowers*) parterre *m*; (*of coal, clay*) couche *f*; (*of sea, lake*) fond *m*; **to go to** ~ aller se coucher.
▶**bed down** *vi* se coucher.
bed and breakfast (B & B) *n* (*terms*) chambre et petit déjeuner; (*place*) ≈ chambre *f* d'hôte.

Un bed and breakfast *est une petite pension dans une maison particulière ou une ferme où l'on peut louer une chambre avec petit déjeuner compris pour un prix modique par rapport à ce que l'on paierait dans un hôtel. Ces établissements sont communément appelés B & B, et sont signalés par une pancarte dans le jardin ou au-dessus de la porte.*

---

bedbug ['bɛdbʌg] *n* punaise *f*.
bedclothes ['bɛdkləʊðz] *npl* couvertures *fpl* et draps *mpl*.
bedcover ['bɛdkʌvə*] *n* couvre-lit *m*, dessus-de-lit *m*.
bedding ['bɛdɪŋ] *n* literie *f*.
bedevil [bɪ'dɛvl] *vt* (*harass*) harceler; **to be** ~**led by** être victime de.
bedfellow ['bɛdfɛləʊ] *n*: **they are strange** ~**s** (*fig*) ça fait un drôle de mélange.
bedlam ['bɛdləm] *n* chahut *m*, cirque *m*.
bedpan ['bɛdpæn] *n* bassin *m* (hygiénique).
bedpost ['bɛdpəʊst] *n* colonne *f* de lit.
bedraggled [bɪ'drægld] *adj* dépenaillé(e), les vêtements en désordre.
bedridden ['bɛdrɪdn] *adj* cloué(e) au lit.
bedrock ['bɛdrɔk] *n* (*fig*) principes essentiels *or* de base, essentiel *m*; (*GEO*) roche *f* en

place, socle *m*.

bedroom ['bɛdrum] *n* chambre *f* (à coucher).

Beds *abbr* (*BRIT*) = Bedfordshire.

bed settee *n* canapé-lit *m*.

bedside ['bɛdsaid] *n*: **at sb's** ~ au chevet de qn ♦ *cpd* (*book, lamp*) de chevet.

bedsit(ter) ['bɛdsɪt(ə*)] *n* (*BRIT*) chambre meublée, studio *m*.

bedspread ['bɛdsprɛd] *n* couvre-lit *m*, dessus-de-lit *m*.

bedtime ['bɛdtaim] *n*: **it's** ~ c'est l'heure de se coucher.

bee [bi:] *n* abeille *f*; **to have a** ~ **in one's bonnet (about sth)** être obnubilé(e) (par qch).

beech [bi:tʃ] *n* hêtre *m*.

beef [bi:f] *n* bœuf *m*.

▶**beef up** *vt* (*col: support*) renforcer; (: *essay*) étoffer.

beefburger ['bi:fbə:gə*] *n* hamburger *m*.

beefeater ['bi:fi:tə*] *n* hallebardier *m* (de la tour de Londres).

beehive ['bi:haiv] *n* ruche *f*.

bee-keeping ['bi:ki:pɪŋ] *n* apiculture *f*.

beeline ['bi:lain] *n*: **to make a** ~ **for** se diriger tout droit vers.

been [bi:n] *pp of* **be**.

beep [bi:p] *n* bip *m*.

beeper ['bi:pə*] *n* (*pager*) bip *m*.

beer [biə*] *n* bière *f*.

beer belly *n* (*col*) bedaine *f* (*de buveur de bière*).

beer can *n* canette *f* de bière.

beetle ['bi:tl] *n* scarabée *m*, coléoptère *m*.

beetroot ['bi:tru:t] *n* (*BRIT*) betterave *f*.

befall [bɪ'fɔ:l] *vi*(*vt*) (*irreg: like* **fall**) advenir (à).

befit [bɪ'fit] *vt* seoir à.

before [bɪ'fɔ:*] *prep* (*of time*) avant; (*of space*) devant ♦ *conj* avant que + *sub*; avant de ♦ *adv* avant; ~ **going** avant de partir; ~ **she goes** avant qu'elle (ne) parte; **the week** ~ la semaine précédente *or* d'avant; **I've seen it** ~ je l'ai déjà vu; **I've never seen it** ~ c'est la première fois que je le vois.

beforehand [bɪ'fɔ:hænd] *adv* au préalable, à l'avance.

befriend [bɪ'frɛnd] *vt* venir en aide à; traiter en ami.

befuddled [bɪ'fʌdld] *adj*: **to be** ~ avoir les idées brouillées.

beg [bɛg] *vi* mendier ♦ *vt* mendier; (*favour*) quémander, solliciter; (*entreat*) supplier; **I** ~ **your pardon** (*apologising*) excusez-moi; (: *not hearing*) pardon?; **that** ~**s the question of ...** cela soulève la question de ..., cela suppose réglée la question de ....

began [bɪ'gæn] *pt of* **begin**.

beggar ['bɛgə*] *n* (*also*: ~**man**, ~**woman**) mendiant/e.

begin, *pt* **began,** *pp* **begun** [bɪ'gɪn, -'gæn, -'gʌn] *vt, vi* commencer; **to** ~ **doing** *or* **to do sth** commencer à faire qch; ~**ning (from) Monday** à partir de lundi; **I can't** ~ **to thank**

you je ne saurais vous remercier; **to** ~ **with** d'abord, pour commencer.

beginner [bɪ'gɪnə*] *n* débutant/e.

beginning [bɪ'gɪnɪŋ] *n* commencement *m*, début *m*; **right from the** ~ dès le début.

begrudge [bɪ'grʌdʒ] *vt*: **to** ~ **sb sth** envier qch à qn; donner qch à contrecœur *or* à regret à qn.

beguile [bɪ'gail] *vt* (*enchant*) enjôler.

beguiling [bɪ'gailɪŋ] *adj* (*charming*) séduisant(e), enchanteur(eresse).

begun [bɪ'gʌn] *pp of* **begin**.

behalf [bɪ'hɑ:f] *n*: **on** ~ **of**, (*US*) **in** ~ **of** de la part de; au nom de; pour le compte de.

behave [bɪ'heiv] *vi* se conduire, se comporter; (*well: also:* ~ **o.s.**) se conduire bien *or* comme il faut.

behaviour, (*US*) **behavior** [bɪ'heivjə*] *n* comportement *m*, conduite *f*.

behead [bɪ'hɛd] *vt* décapiter.

beheld [bɪ'hɛld] *pt, pp of* **behold**.

behind [bɪ'haind] *prep* derrière; (*time*) en retard sur ♦ *adv* derrière; en retard ♦ *n* derrière *m*; ~ **the scenes** dans les coulisses; **to leave sth** ~ (*forget*) oublier de prendre qch; **to be** ~ (*schedule*) **with sth** être en retard dans qch.

behold [bɪ'həuld] *vt* (*irreg: like* **hold**) apercevoir, voir.

beige [beiʒ] *adj* beige.

being ['bi:ɪŋ] *n* être *m*; **to come into** ~ prendre naissance.

Beirut [bei'ru:t] *n* Beyrouth.

Belarus [bɛlə'rus] *n* Bélarus *f*.

Belarussian [bɛlə'rʌʃən] *adj* biélorusse ♦ *n* Biélorusse *m/f*; (*LING*) biélorusse *m*.

belated [bɪ'leitid] *adj* tardif(ive).

belch [bɛltʃ] *vi* avoir un renvoi, roter ♦ *vt* (*also:* ~ **out:** *smoke etc*) vomir, cracher.

beleaguered [bɪ'li:gid] *adj* (*city*) assiégé(e); (*army*) cerné(e); (*fig*) sollicité(e) de toutes parts.

Belfast ['bɛlfɑ:st] *n* Belfast.

belfry ['bɛlfri] *n* beffroi *m*.

Belgian ['bɛldʒən] *adj* belge, de Belgique ♦ *n* Belge *m/f*.

Belgium ['bɛldʒəm] *n* Belgique *f*.

Belgrade [bɛl'greid] *n* Belgrade.

belie [bɪ'lai] *vt* démentir; (*give false impression of*) occulter.

belief [bɪ'li:f] *n* (*opinion*) conviction *f*; (*trust, faith*) foi *f*; (*acceptance as true*) croyance *f*; **it's beyond** ~ c'est incroyable; **in the** ~ **that** dans l'idée que.

believable [bɪ'li:vəbl] *adj* croyable.

believe [bɪ'li:v] *vt, vi* croire, estimer; **to** ~ **in** (*God*) croire en; (*ghosts, method*) croire à; **I don't** ~ **in corporal punishment** je ne suis pas partisan des châtiments corporels; **he is** ~**d to be abroad** il serait à l'étranger.

believer [bɪ'li:və*] *n* (*in idea, activity*): ~ **in** partisan/e de; (*REL*) croyant/e.

belittle [bɪ'lɪtl] vt déprécier, rabaisser.
Belize [bɛ'liːz] n Bélize m.
bell [bɛl] n cloche f; (small) clochette f, grelot m; (on door) sonnette f; (electric) sonnerie f; **that rings a ~** (fig) cela me rappelle qch.
bell-bottoms ['bɛlbɔtəmz] npl pantalon m à pattes d'éléphant.
bellboy ['bɛlbɔɪ], (US) **bellhop** ['bɛlhɔp] n groom m, chasseur m.
belligerent [bɪ'lɪdʒərənt] adj (at war) belligérant(e); (fig) agressif(ive).
bellow ['bɛləu] vi mugir; beugler ♦ vt (orders) hurler.
bellows ['bɛləuz] npl soufflet m.
bell push n (BRIT) bouton m de sonnette.
belly ['bɛlɪ] n ventre m.
bellyache ['bɛlɪeɪk] (col) n colique f ♦ vi ronchonner.
bellybutton ['bɛlɪbʌtn] n nombril m.
bellyful ['bɛlɪful] n (col): **I've had a ~** j'en ai ras le bol.
belong [bɪ'lɔŋ] vi: **to ~ to** appartenir à; (club etc) faire partie de; **this book ~s here** ce livre va ici, la place de ce livre est ici.
belongings [bɪ'lɔŋɪŋz] npl affaires fpl, possessions fpl; **personal ~** effets personnels.
Belorussia [bɛlə'rʌʃə] n Biélorussie f.
Belorussian [bɛlə'rʌʃən] adj, n = **Belarussian**.
beloved [bɪ'lʌvɪd] adj (bien-)aimé(e), chéri(e) ♦ n bien-aimé/e.
below [bɪ'ləu] prep sous, au-dessous de ♦ adv en dessous; en contre-bas; **see ~** voir plus bas or plus loin or ci-dessous; **temperatures ~ normal** températures inférieures à la normale.
belt [bɛlt] n ceinture f; (TECH) courroie f ♦ vt (thrash) donner une raclée à ♦ vi (BRIT col) filer (à toutes jambes); **industrial ~** zone industrielle.
▶**belt out** vt (song) chanter à tue-tête or à pleins poumons.
▶**belt up** vi (BRIT col) la boucler.
beltway ['bɛltweɪ] n (US AUT) route f de ceinture; (: motorway) périphérique m.
bemoan [bɪ'məun] vt se lamenter sur.
bemused [bɪ'mjuːzd] adj médusé(e).
bench [bɛntʃ] n banc m; (in workshop) établi m; **the B~** (LAW) la magistrature, la Cour.
bench mark n repère m.
bend [bɛnd] vb (pt, pp **bent** [bɛnt]) vt courber; (leg, arm) plier ♦ vi se courber ♦ n (BRIT: in road) virage m, tournant m; (in pipe, river) coude m.
▶**bend down** vi se baisser.
▶**bend over** vi se pencher.
bends [bɛndz] npl (MED) maladie f des caissons.
beneath [bɪ'niːθ] prep sous, au-dessous de; (unworthy of) indigne de ♦ adv dessous, au-dessous, en bas.
benefactor ['bɛnɪfæktə*] n bienfaiteur m.
benefactress ['bɛnɪfæktrɪs] n bienfaitrice f.

beneficial [bɛnɪ'fɪʃəl] adj: **~ (to)** salutaire (pour), bénéfique (à).
beneficiary [bɛnɪ'fɪʃərɪ] n (LAW) bénéficiaire m/f.
benefit ['bɛnɪfɪt] n avantage m, profit m; (allowance of money) allocation f ♦ vt faire du bien à, profiter à ♦ vi: **he'll ~ from it** cela lui fera du bien, il y gagnera or s'en trouvera bien.
benefit performance n représentation f or gala m de bienfaisance.
Benelux ['bɛnɪlʌks] n Benelux m.
benevolent [bɪ'nɛvələnt] adj bienveillant(e).
BEng n abbr (= Bachelor of Engineering) diplôme universitaire.
benign [bɪ'naɪn] adj (person, smile) bienveillant(e), affable; (MED) bénin(igne).
bent [bɛnt] pt, pp of **bend** ♦ n inclination f, penchant m ♦ adj (wire, pipe) coudé(e); (col: dishonest) véreux(euse); **to be ~ on** être résolu(e) à.
bequeath [bɪ'kwiːð] vt léguer.
bequest [bɪ'kwɛst] n legs m.
bereaved [bɪ'riːvd] n: **the ~** la famille du disparu ♦ adj endeuillé(e).
bereavement [bɪ'riːvmənt] n deuil m.
beret ['bɛreɪ] n béret m.
Bering Sea ['beɪrɪŋ-] n: **the ~** la mer de Béring.
berk [bɜːk] n (BRIT col) andouille m/f.
Berks abbr (BRIT) = **Berkshire**.
Berlin [bɜː'lɪn] n Berlin; **East/West ~** Berlin Est/Ouest.
berm [bɜːm] n (US AUT) accotement m.
Bermuda [bɜː'mjuːdə] n Bermudes fpl.
Bermuda shorts npl bermuda m.
Bern [bɜːn] n Berne.
berry ['bɛrɪ] n baie f.
berserk [bə'sɜːk] adj: **to go ~** être pris(e) d'une rage incontrôlable; se déchaîner.
berth [bɜːθ] n (bed) couchette f; (for ship) poste m d'amarrage, mouillage m ♦ vi (in harbour) venir à quai; (at anchor) mouiller; **to give sb a wide ~** (fig) éviter qn.
beseech [bɪ'siːtʃ], pt, pp **besought** [bɪ'sɔːt] vt implorer, supplier.
beset [bɪ'sɛt], pt, pp **beset** vt assaillir ♦ adj: **~ with** semé(e) de.
besetting [bɪ'sɛtɪŋ] adj: **his ~ sin** son vice, son gros défaut.
beside [bɪ'saɪd] prep à côté de; (compared with) par rapport à; **that's ~ the point** ça n'a rien à voir; **to be ~ o.s.** (with anger) être hors de soi.
besides [bɪ'saɪdz] adv en outre, de plus ♦ prep en plus de; (except) excepté.
besiege [bɪ'siːdʒ] vt (town) assiéger; (fig) assaillir.
besotted [bɪ'sɔtɪd] adj (BRIT): **~ with** entiché(e) de.
besought [bɪ'sɔːt] pt, pp of **beseech**.
bespectacled [bɪ'spɛktɪkld] adj à lunettes.

bespoke [bɪ'spəuk] *adj* (*BRIT*: *garment*) fait(e) sur mesure; ~ **tailor** tailleur *m* à façon.

best [bɛst] *adj* meilleur(e) ♦ *adv* le mieux; **the** ~ **part of** (*quantity*) le plus clair de, la plus grande partie de; **at** ~ au mieux; **to make the** ~ **of sth** s'accommoder de qch (du mieux que l'on peut); **to do one's** ~ faire de son mieux; **to the** ~ **of my knowledge** pour autant que je sache; **to the** ~ **of my ability** du mieux que je pourrai; **he's not exactly patient at the** ~ **of times** il n'est jamais spécialement patient; **the** ~ **thing to do is** ... le mieux, c'est de ....

best man *n* garçon *m* d'honneur.

bestow [bɪ'stəu] *vt* accorder; (*title*) conférer.

bestseller ['bɛst'sɛlə*] *n* bestseller *m*, succès *m* de librairie.

bet [bɛt] *n* pari *m* ♦ *vt*, *vi* (*pt*, *pp* **bet** *or* **betted**) parier; **it's a safe** ~ (*fig*) il y a de fortes chances.

Bethlehem ['bɛθlɪhɛm] *n* Bethléem.

betray [bɪ'treɪ] *vt* trahir.

betrayal [bɪ'treɪəl] *n* trahison *f*.

better ['bɛtə*] *adj* meilleur(e) ♦ *adv* mieux ♦ *vt* améliorer ♦ *n*: **to get the** ~ **of** triompher de, l'emporter sur; **a change for the** ~ une amélioration; **I had** ~ **go** il faut que je m'en aille; **you had** ~ **do it** vous feriez mieux de le faire; **he thought** ~ **of it** il s'est ravisé; **to get** ~ aller mieux; s'améliorer; **that's** ~! c'est mieux!; ~ **off** *adj* plus à l'aise financièrement; (*fig*): **you'd be** ~ **off this way** vous vous trouveriez mieux ainsi, ce serait mieux *or* plus pratique ainsi.

betting ['bɛtɪŋ] *n* paris *mpl*.

betting shop *n* (*BRIT*) bureau *m* de paris.

between [bɪ'twiːn] *prep* entre ♦ *adv* au milieu, dans l'intervalle; **the road** ~ **here and London** la route d'ici à Londres; **we only had 5** ~ **us** nous n'en avions que 5 en tout.

bevel ['bɛvəl] *n* (*also*: ~ **edge**) biseau *m*.

beverage ['bɛvərɪdʒ] *n* boisson *f* (*gén sans alcool*).

bevy ['bɛvɪ] *n*: **a** ~ **of** un essaim *or* une volée de.

bewail [bɪ'weɪl] *vt* se lamenter sur.

beware [bɪ'wɛə*] *vt*, *vi*: **to** ~ (**of**) prendre garde (à).

bewildered [bɪ'wɪldəd] *adj* dérouté(e), ahuri(e).

bewildering [bɪ'wɪldrɪŋ] *adj* déroutant(e), ahurissant(e).

bewitching [bɪ'wɪtʃɪŋ] *adj* enchanteur(teresse).

beyond [bɪ'jɔnd] *prep* (*in space*) au-delà de; (*exceeding*) au-dessus de ♦ *adv* au-delà; ~ **doubt** hors de doute; ~ **repair** irréparable.

b/f *abbr* = brought forward.

BFPO *n abbr* (= British Forces Post Office) service postal de l'armée.

bhp *n abbr* (*AUT*: = brake horsepower) puissance *f* aux freins.

bi... [baɪ] *prefix* bi....

biannual [baɪ'ænjuəl] *adj* semestriel(le).

bias ['baɪəs] *n* (*prejudice*) préjugé *m*, parti pris; (*preference*) prévention *f*.

bias(s)ed ['baɪəst] *adj* partial(e), montrant un parti pris; **to be** ~ **against** avoir un préjugé contre.

biathlon [baɪ'æθlən] *n* biathlon *m*.

bib [bɪb] *n* bavoir *m*, bavette *f*.

Bible ['baɪbl] *n* Bible *f*.

Bible Belt *n* (*US*): **the** ~ *les États du Sud profondément protestants*.

bibliography [bɪblɪ'ɔgrəfɪ] *n* bibliographie *f*.

bicarbonate of soda [baɪ'kɑːbənɪt-] *n* bicarbonate *m* de soude.

bicentenary [baɪsɛn'tiːnərɪ] *n*, **bicentennial** [baɪsɛn'tɛnɪəl] *n* bicentenaire *m*.

biceps ['baɪsɛps] *n* biceps *m*.

bicker ['bɪkə*] *vi* se chamailler.

bicycle ['baɪsɪkl] *n* bicyclette *f*.

bicycle path *n*, **bicycle track** *n* piste *f* cyclable.

bicycle pump *n* pompe *f* à vélo.

bid [bɪd] *n* offre *f*; (*at auction*) enchère *f*; (*attempt*) tentative *f* ♦ *vb* (*pt* **bid** *or* **bade** [bæd], *pp* **bid** *or* **bidden** ['bɪdn]) *vi* faire une enchère *or* offre ♦ *vt* faire une enchère *or* offre de; **to** ~ **sb good day** souhaiter le bonjour à qn.

bidder ['bɪdə*] *n*: **the highest** ~ le plus offrant.

bidding ['bɪdɪŋ] *n* enchères *fpl*.

bide [baɪd] *vt*: **to** ~ **one's time** attendre son heure.

bidet ['biːdeɪ] *n* bidet *m*.

bidirectional ['baɪdɪ'rɛkʃənl] *adj* bidirectionnel(le).

biennial [baɪ'ɛnɪəl] *adj* biennal(e), bisannuel(le) ♦ *n* biennale *f*; (*plant*) plante bisannuelle.

bier [bɪə*] *n* bière *f* (*cercueil*).

bifocals [baɪ'fəuklz] *npl* lunettes *fpl* à double foyer.

big [bɪg] *adj* (*in height*: *person, building, tree*) grand(e); (*in bulk, amount*: *person, parcel, book*) gros(se); **to do things in a** ~ **way** faire les choses en grand.

bigamy ['bɪgəmɪ] *n* bigamie *f*.

big dipper [-'dɪpə*] *n* montagnes *fpl* russes.

big end *n* (*AUT*) tête *f* de bielle.

biggish ['bɪgɪʃ] *adj* (*see big*) assez grand(e); assez gros(se).

bigheaded ['bɪg'hɛdɪd] *adj* prétentieux(euse).

big-hearted ['bɪg'hɑːtɪd] *adj* au grand cœur.

bigot ['bɪgət] *n* fanatique *m/f*, sectaire *m/f*.

bigoted ['bɪgətɪd] *adj* fanatique, sectaire.

bigotry ['bɪgətrɪ] *n* fanatisme *m*, sectarisme *m*.

big toe *n* gros orteil.

big top *n* grand chapiteau.

big wheel *n* (*at fair*) grande roue.

bigwig ['bɪgwɪg] *n* (*col*) grosse légume, huile *f*.

bike [baɪk] n vélo m, bécane f.
bikini [bɪ'kiːnɪ] n bikini m.
bilateral [baɪ'lætərl] adj bilatéral(e).
bile [baɪl] n bile f.
bilingual [baɪ'lɪŋgwəl] adj bilingue.
bilious ['bɪlɪəs] adj bilieux(euse); (fig) maussade, irritable.
bill [bɪl] n note f, facture f; (POL) projet m de loi; (US: banknote) billet m (de banque); (in restaurant) addition f, note f; (notice) affiche f; (THEAT): **on the ~** à l'affiche; (of bird) bec m ♦ vt (item) facturer; (customer) remettre la facture à; **may I have the ~ please?** (est-ce que je peux avoir) l'addition, s'il vous plaît?; **"stick** or **post no ~s"** "défense d'afficher"; **to fit** or **fill the ~** (fig) faire l'affaire; **~ of exchange** lettre f de change; **~ of lading** connaissement m; **~ of sale** contrat m de vente.
billboard ['bɪlbɔːd] n panneau m d'affichage.
billet ['bɪlɪt] n cantonnement m (chez l'habitant) ♦ vt (troops) cantonner.
billfold ['bɪlfəʊld] n (US) portefeuille m.
billiards ['bɪljədz] n (jeu m de) billard m.
billion ['bɪljən] n (BRIT) billion m (million de millions); (US) milliard m.
billow ['bɪləʊ] n nuage m ♦ vi (smoke) s'élever en nuage; (sail) se gonfler.
billy goat ['bɪlɪgəʊt] n bouc m.
bimbo ['bɪmbəʊ] n (col) ravissante idiote f.
bin [bɪn] n boîte f; (BRIT: also: **dust~**, **litter~**) poubelle f; (for coal) coffre m.
binary ['baɪnərɪ] adj binaire.
bind, pt, pp **bound** [baɪnd, baʊnd] vt attacher; (book) relier; (oblige) obliger, contraindre.
▶**bind over** vt (LAW) mettre en liberté conditionnelle.
▶**bind up** vt (wound) panser; **to be bound up in** (work, research etc) être complètement absorbé par, être accroché par; **to be bound up with** (person) être accroché à.
binder ['baɪndə*] n (file) classeur m.
binding ['baɪndɪŋ] n (of book) reliure f ♦ adj (contract) qui constitue une obligation.
binge [bɪndʒ] n (col): **to go on a ~** faire la bringue.
bingo ['bɪŋgəʊ] n sorte de jeu de loto pratiqué dans des établissements publics.
bin liner n sac m poubelle.
binoculars [bɪ'nɔkjʊləz] npl jumelles fpl.
biochemistry [baɪə'kemɪstrɪ] n biochimie f.
biodegradable ['baɪəʊdɪ'greɪdəbl] adj biodégradable.
biodiversity ['baɪəʊdaɪ'vɔːsɪtɪ] n biodiversité f.
biofuel ['baɪəʊfjʊəl] n combustible m organique.
biographer [baɪ'ɔgrəfə*] n biographe m/f.
biographic(al) [baɪə'græfɪk(l)] adj biographique.
biography [baɪ'ɔgrəfɪ] n biographie f.
biological [baɪə'lɔdʒɪkl] adj biologique.

biological clock n horloge f physiologique.
biologist [baɪ'ɔlədʒɪst] n biologiste m/f.
biology [baɪ'ɔlədʒɪ] n biologie f.
biophysics ['baɪəʊ'fɪzɪks] n biophysique f.
biopic ['baɪəʊpɪk] n film m biographique.
biopsy ['baɪɒpsɪ] n biopsie f.
biosphere ['baɪəsfɪə*] n biosphère f.
biotechnology ['baɪəʊtɛk'nɒlədʒɪ] n biotechnologie f.
birch [bɔːtʃ] n bouleau m.
bird [bɔːd] n oiseau m; (BRIT col: girl) nana f.
bird of prey n oiseau m de proie.
bird's-eye view ['bɔːdzaɪ-] n vue f à vol d'oiseau; (fig) vue d'ensemble or générale.
bird watcher [-wɔtʃə*] n ornithologue m/f amateur.
Biro ['baɪərəʊ] n ® stylo m à bille.
birth [bɔːθ] n naissance f; **to give ~ to** donner naissance à, mettre au monde; (animal) mettre bas.
birth certificate n acte m de naissance.
birth control n limitation f des naissances; méthode(s) contraceptive(s).
birthday ['bɔːθdeɪ] n anniversaire m.
birthmark ['bɔːθmɑːk] n envie f, tache f de vin.
birthplace ['bɔːθpleɪs] n lieu m de naissance.
birth rate n (taux m de) natalité f.
Biscay ['bɪskeɪ] n: **the Bay of ~** le golfe de Gascogne.
biscuit ['bɪskɪt] n (BRIT) biscuit m; (US) petit pain au lait.
bisect [baɪ'sɛkt] vt couper or diviser en deux.
bisexual ['baɪ'sɛksjuəl] adj, n bisexuel(le).
bishop ['bɪʃəp] n évêque m; (CHESS) fou m.
bistro ['biːstrəʊ] n petit restaurant m, bistrot m.
bit [bɪt] pt of **bite** ♦ n morceau m; (of tool) mèche f; (of horse) mors m; (COMPUT) bit m, élément m binaire; **a ~ of** un peu de; **a ~ mad/dangerous** un peu fou/risqué; **~ by ~** petit à petit; **to come to ~s** (break) tomber en morceaux, se déglinguer; **bring all your ~s and pieces** apporte toutes tes affaires; **to do one's ~** y mettre du sien.
bitch [bɪtʃ] n (dog) chienne f; (col!) salope f (!), garce f.
bite [baɪt] vt, vi (pt **bit** [bɪt], pp **bitten** ['bɪtn]) mordre ♦ n morsure f; (insect ~) piqûre f; (mouthful) bouchée f; **let's have a ~ (to eat)** mangeons un morceau; **to ~ one's nails** se ronger les ongles.
biting ['baɪtɪŋ] adj mordant(e).
bit part n (THEAT) petit rôle m.
bitten ['bɪtn] pp of **bite**.
bitter ['bɪtə*] adj amer(ère); (criticism) cinglant(e); (icy: weather, wind) glacial(e) ♦ n (BRIT: beer) bière f (à forte teneur en houblon); **to the ~ end** jusqu'au bout.
bitterly ['bɪtəlɪ] adv (complain, weep) amèrement; (oppose, criticise) durement, âprement; (jealous, disappointed) horriblement; **it's ~ cold** il fait un froid de loup.

bitterness ['bɪtənɪs] *n* amertume *f*; goût amer.
bittersweet ['bɪtəswiːt] *adj* aigre-doux(douce).
bitty ['bɪtɪ] *adj* (*BRIT col*) décousu(e).
bitumen ['bɪtjumɪn] *n* bitume *m*.
bivouac ['bɪvuæk] *n* bivouac *m*.
bizarre [bɪ'zɑː*] *adj* bizarre.
bk *abbr* = bank, book.
BL *n abbr* (= *Bachelor of Law(s), Bachelor of Letters*) *diplôme universitaire*; (*US*: = *Bachelor of Literature*) *diplôme universitaire*.
bl *abbr* = bill of lading.
blab [blæb] *vi* jaser, trop parler ♦ *vt* (*also*: ~ out) laisser échapper, aller raconter.
black [blæk] *adj* noir(e) ♦ *n* (*colour*) noir *m*; (*person*): **B~** noir/e ♦ *vt* (*shoes*) cirer; (*BRIT INDUSTRY*) boycotter; **to give sb a ~ eye** pocher l'œil à qn, faire un œil au beurre noir à qn; **~ coffee** café noir; **there it is in ~ and white** (*fig*) c'est écrit noir sur blanc; **to be in the ~** (*in credit*) avoir un compte créditeur; **~ and blue** *adj* couvert(e) de bleus.
▶**black out** *vi* (*faint*) s'évanouir.
black belt *n* (*JUDO etc*) ceinture noire; **he's a ~** il est ceinture noire.
blackberry ['blækbərɪ] *n* mûre *f*.
blackbird ['blækbəːd] *n* merle *m*.
blackboard ['blækbɔːd] *n* tableau noir.
black box *n* (*AVIAT*) boîte noire.
Black Country *n* (*BRIT*): **the ~** le Pays Noir (*dans les Midlands*).
blackcurrant ['blæk'kʌrənt] *n* cassis *m*.
black economy *n* (*BRIT*) travail *m* (au) noir.
blacken ['blækn] *vt* noircir.
Black Forest *n*: **the ~** la Forêt Noire.
blackhead ['blækhed] *n* point noir.
black hole *n* (*ASTRONOMY*) trou noir.
black ice *n* verglas *m*.
blackjack ['blækdʒæk] *n* (*CARDS*) vingt-et-un *m*; (*US*: *truncheon*) matraque *f*.
blackleg ['blækleg] *n* (*BRIT*) briseur *m* de grève, jaune *m*.
blacklist ['blæklɪst] *n* liste noire ♦ *vt* mettre sur la liste noire.
blackmail ['blækmeɪl] *n* chantage *m* ♦ *vt* faire chanter, soumettre au chantage.
blackmailer ['blækmeɪlə*] *n* maître-chanteur *m*.
black market *n* marché noir.
blackout ['blækaut] *n* panne *f* d'électricité; (*in wartime*) black-out *m*; (*TV*) interruption *f* d'émission; (*fainting*) syncope *f*.
black pepper *n* poivre noir.
Black Sea *n*: **the ~** la mer Noire.
black sheep *n* brebis galeuse.
blacksmith ['blæksmɪθ] *n* forgeron *m*.
black spot *n* (*AUT*) point noir.
bladder ['blædə*] *n* vessie *f*.
blade [bleɪd] *n* lame *f*, (*of oar*) plat *m*; ~ **of grass** brin *m* d'herbe.
blame [bleɪm] *n* faute *f*, blâme *m* ♦ *vt*: **to ~ sb/sth for sth** attribuer à qn/qch la responsabi-lité de qch; reprocher qch à qn/qch; **who's to ~?** qui est le fautif *or* coupable *or* responsable?; **I'm not to ~** ce n'est pas ma faute.
blameless ['bleɪmlɪs] *adj* irréprochable.
blanch [blɑːntʃ] *vi* (*person, face*) blêmir ♦ *vt* (*CULIN*) blanchir.
bland [blænd] *adj* affable; (*taste*) doux(douce), fade.
blank [blæŋk] *adj* blanc(blanche); (*look*) sans expression, dénué(e) d'expression ♦ *n* espace *m* vide, blanc *m*; (*cartridge*) cartouche *f* à blanc; **we drew a ~** (*fig*) nous n'avons abouti à rien.
blank cheque, (*US*) **blank check** *n* chèque *m* en blanc; **to give sb a ~ to do ...** (*fig*) donner carte blanche à qn pour faire ....
blanket ['blæŋkɪt] *n* couverture *f* ♦ *adj* (*statement, agreement*) global(e), de portée générale; **to give ~ cover** (*subj: insurance policy*) couvrir tous les risques.
blare [blɛə*] *vi* (*brass band, horns, radio*) beugler.
blarney ['blɑːnɪ] *n* boniment *m*.
blasé ['blɑːzeɪ] *adj* blasé(e).
blasphemous ['blæsfɪməs] *adj* (*words*) blasphématoire; (*person*) blasphémateur(trice).
blasphemy ['blæsfɪmɪ] *n* blasphème *m*.
blast [blɑːst] *n* explosion *f*; (*shock wave*) souffle *m*; (*of air, steam*) bouffée *f* ♦ *vt* faire sauter *or* exploser ♦ *excl* (*BRIT col*) zut!; **(at) full ~** (*play music etc*) à plein volume.
▶**blast off** *vi* (*SPACE*) décoller.
blast-off ['blɑːstɔf] *n* (*SPACE*) lancement *m*.
blatant ['bleɪtənt] *adj* flagrant(e), criant(e).
blatantly ['bleɪtəntlɪ] *adv* (*lie*) ouvertement; **it's ~ obvious** c'est l'évidence même.
blaze [bleɪz] *n* (*fire*) incendie *m*; (*flames: of fire, sun etc*) embrasement *m*; (*: in hearth*) flamme *f*, flambée *f*; (*fig*) flamboiement *m* ♦ *vi* (*fire*) flamber; (*fig*) flamboyer, resplendir ♦ *vt*: **to ~ a trail** (*fig*) montrer la voie; **in a ~ of publicity** à grand renfort de publicité.
blazer ['bleɪzə*] *n* blazer *m*.
bleach [bliːtʃ] *n* (*also*: **household ~**) eau *f* de Javel ♦ *vt* (*linen*) blanchir.
bleached [bliːtʃt] *adj* (*hair*) oxygéné(e), décoloré(e).
bleachers ['bliːtʃəz] *npl* (*US SPORT*) gradins *mpl* (*en plein soleil*).
bleak [bliːk] *adj* morne, désolé(e); (*weather*) triste, maussade; (*smile*) lugubre; (*prospect, future*) morose.
bleary-eyed ['blɪərɪ'aɪd] *adj* aux yeux pleins de sommeil.
bleat [bliːt] *n* bêlement *m* ♦ *vi* bêler.
bleed, pt, pp bled [bliːd, bled] *vt* saigner; (*brakes, radiator*) purger ♦ *vi* saigner; **my nose is ~ing** je saigne du nez.
bleep [bliːp] *n* (*RADIO, TV*) top *m*; (*of pocket device*) bip *m* ♦ *vi* émettre des signaux ♦ *vt* (*doctor etc*) appeler (*au moyen d'un bip*).

bleeper ['bli:pə*] n (of doctor etc) bip m.
blemish ['blɛmɪʃ] n défaut m; (on reputation) tache f.
blend [blɛnd] n mélange m ♦ vt mélanger ♦ vi (colours etc) se mélanger, se fondre, s'allier.
blender ['blɛndə*] n (CULIN) mixeur m.
bless, pt, pp **blessed** or **blest** [blɛs, blɛst] vt bénir; **to be ~ed with** avoir le bonheur de jouir de or d'avoir.
blessed ['blɛsɪd] adj (REL: holy) béni(e); (happy) bienheureux(euse); **it rains every ~ day** il ne se passe pas de jour sans qu'il ne pleuve.
blessing ['blɛsɪŋ] n bénédiction f; bienfait m; **to count one's ~s** s'estimer heureux; **it was a ~ in disguise** c'est un bien pour un mal.
blew [blu:] pt of **blow**.
blight [blaɪt] n (of plants) rouille f ♦ vt (hopes etc) anéantir, briser.
blimey ['blaɪmɪ] excl (BRIT col) mince alors!
blind [blaɪnd] adj aveugle ♦ n (for window) store m ♦ vt aveugler; **to turn a ~ eye (on or to)** fermer les yeux (sur).
blind alley n impasse f.
blind corner n (BRIT) virage m sans visibilité.
blind date n rendez-vous galant (avec un(e) inconnu(e)).
blindfold ['blaɪndfəuld] n bandeau m ♦ adj, adv les yeux bandés ♦ vt bander les yeux à.
blindly ['blaɪndlɪ] adv aveuglément.
blindness ['blaɪndnɪs] n cécité f; (fig) aveuglement m.
blind spot n (AUT etc) angle m aveugle; (fig) angle mort.
blink [blɪŋk] vi cligner des yeux; (light) clignoter ♦ n: **the TV's on the ~** (col) la télé ne va pas tarder à nous lâcher.
blinkers ['blɪŋkəz] npl œillères fpl.
blinking ['blɪŋkɪŋ] adj (BRIT col): **this ~ ...** ce fichu or sacré ....
blip [blɪp] n (on radar etc) spot m; (on graph) petite aberration; (fig) petite anomalie (passagère).
bliss [blɪs] n félicité f, bonheur m sans mélange.
blissful ['blɪsful] adj (event, day) merveilleux(euse); (smile) de bonheur; **a ~ sigh** un soupir d'aise; **in ~ ignorance** dans une ignorance béate.
blissfully ['blɪsfulɪ] adv (smile) béatement; (happy) merveilleusement.
blister ['blɪstə*] n (on skin) ampoule f, cloque f; (on paintwork) boursouflure f ♦ vi (paint) se boursoufler, se cloquer.
blithely ['blaɪðlɪ] adv (unconcernedly) tranquillement; (joyfully) gaiement.
blithering ['blɪðərɪŋ] adj (col): **this ~ idiot** cet espèce d'idiot.
BLit(t) n abbr (= Bachelor of Literature) diplôme universitaire.
blitz [blɪts] n bombardement (aérien); **to have a ~ on sth** (fig) s'attaquer à qch.

blizzard ['blɪzəd] n blizzard m, tempête f de neige.
BLM n abbr (US: = Bureau of Land Management) ≈ les domaines.
bloated ['bləutɪd] adj (face) bouffi(e); (stomach) gonflé(e).
blob [blɔb] n (drop) goutte f; (stain, spot) tache f.
bloc [blɔk] n (POL) bloc m.
block [blɔk] n bloc m; (in pipes) obstruction f; (toy) cube m; (of buildings) pâté m (de maisons) ♦ vt bloquer; (COMPUT) grouper; **~ of flats** (BRIT) immeuble (locatif); **3 ~s from here** à trois rues d'ici; **mental ~** blocage m; **~ and tackle** (TECH) palan m.
▶**block up** vt boucher.
blockade [blɔ'keɪd] n blocus m ♦ vt faire le blocus de.
blockage ['blɔkɪdʒ] n obstruction f.
block booking n réservation f en bloc.
blockbuster ['blɔkbʌstə*] n (film, book) grand succès.
block capitals npl majuscules fpl d'imprimerie.
blockhead ['blɔkhɛd] n imbécile m/f.
block letters npl majuscules fpl.
block release n (BRIT) congé m de formation.
block vote n (BRIT) vote m de délégation.
bloke [bləuk] n (BRIT col) type m.
blonde [blɔnd] adj, n blond(e).
blood [blʌd] n sang m.
blood bank n banque f du sang.
blood count n numération f globulaire.
bloodcurdling ['blʌdkə:dlɪŋ] adj à vous glacer le sang.
blood donor n donneur/euse de sang.
blood group n groupe sanguin.
bloodhound ['blʌdhaund] n limier m.
bloodless ['blʌdlɪs] adj (victory) sans effusion de sang; (pale) anémié(e).
bloodletting ['blʌdlɛtɪŋ] n (MED) saignée f; (fig) effusion f de sang, représailles fpl.
blood poisoning n empoisonnement m du sang.
blood pressure n tension (artérielle); **to have high/low ~** faire de l'hypertension/l'hypotension.
bloodshed ['blʌdʃɛd] n effusion f de sang, carnage m.
bloodshot ['blʌdʃɔt] adj: **~ eyes** yeux injectés de sang.
bloodstained ['blʌdsteɪnd] adj taché(e) de sang.
bloodstream ['blʌdstri:m] n sang m, système sanguin.
blood test n analyse f de sang.
bloodthirsty ['blʌdθə:stɪ] adj sanguinaire.
blood transfusion n transfusion f de sang.
blood type n groupe sanguin.
blood vessel n vaisseau sanguin.
bloody ['blʌdɪ] adj sanglant(e); (BRIT col!): **this ~ ...** ce foutu ..., ce putain de ... (!); **~**

strong/good (*col!*) vachement *or* sacrément fort/bon.

bloody-minded ['blʌdɪ'maɪndɪd] *adj* (*BRIT col*) contrariant(e), obstiné(e).

bloom [blu:m] *n* fleur *f*; (*fig*) épanouissement *m* ♦ *vi* être en fleur; (*fig*) s'épanouir; être florissant(e).

blooming ['blu:mɪŋ] *adj* (*col*): **this** ~ ... ce fichu *or* sacré ....

blossom ['blɔsəm] *n* fleur(s) *f(pl)* ♦ *vi* être en fleurs; (*fig*) s'épanouir; **to** ~ **into** (*fig*) devenir.

blot [blɔt] *n* tache *f* ♦ *vt* tacher; (*ink*) sécher; **to be a** ~ **on the landscape** gâcher le paysage; **to** ~ **one's copy book** (*fig*) faire un impair.

▶**blot out** *vt* (*memories*) effacer; (*view*) cacher, masquer; (*nation, city*) annihiler.

blotchy ['blɔtʃɪ] *adj* (*complexion*) couvert(e) de marbrures.

blotter ['blɔtə*] *n*, **blotting paper** ['blɔtɪŋ-] *n* buvard *m*.

blotto ['blɔtəu] *adj* (*col*) bourré(e).

blouse [blauz] *n* (*feminine garment*) chemisier *m*, corsage *m*.

blow [bləu] *n* coup *m* ♦ *vb* (*pt* **blew**, *pp* **blown** [blu:, bləun]) *vi* souffler ♦ *vt* (*glass*) souffler; (*fuse*) faire sauter; **to** ~ **one's nose** se moucher; **to** ~ **a whistle** siffler; **to come to** ~**s** en venir aux coups.

▶**blow away** *vi* s'envoler ♦ *vt* chasser, faire s'envoler.

▶**blow down** *vt* faire tomber, renverser.

▶**blow off** *vi* s'envoler ♦ *vt* (*hat*) emporter; (*ship*): **to** ~ **off course** faire dévier.

▶**blow out** *vi* (*tyre*) éclater; (*fuse*) sauter.

▶**blow over** *vi* s'apaiser.

▶**blow up** *vi* exploser, sauter ♦ *vt* faire sauter; (*tyre*) gonfler; (*PHOT*) agrandir.

blow-dry ['bləudraɪ] *n* (*hairstyle*) brushing *m* ♦ *vt* faire un brushing à.

blowlamp ['bləulæmp] *n* (*BRIT*) chalumeau *m*.

blow-out ['bləuaut] *n* (*of tyre*) éclatement *m*; (*BRIT col: big meal*) gueuleton *m*.

blowtorch ['bləutɔ:tʃ] *n* chalumeau *m*.

blowzy ['blauzɪ] *adj* (*BRIT*) peu soigné(e).

BLS *n abbr* (*US*) = *Bureau of Labor Statistics*.

blubber ['blʌbə*] *n* blanc *m* de baleine ♦ *vi* (*pej*) pleurer comme un veau.

bludgeon ['blʌdʒən] *n* gourdin *m*, trique *f*.

blue [blu:] *adj* bleu(e); ~ **film/joke** film *m*/histoire *f* pornographique; **(only) once in a** ~ **moon** tous les trente-six du mois; **out of the** ~ (*fig*) à l'improviste, sans qu'on s'attende.

blue baby *n* enfant bleu(e).

bluebell ['blu:bɛl] *n* jacinthe *f* des bois.

blueberry ['blu:bərɪ] *n* myrtille *f*, airelle *f*.

bluebottle ['blu:bɔtl] *n* mouche *f* à viande.

blue cheese *n* (fromage) bleu *m*.

blue-chip ['blu:tʃɪp] *adj*: ~ **investment** investissement de premier ordre.

blue-collar worker ['blu:kɔlə*-] *n* ouvrier/ère, col bleu.

blue jeans *npl* blue-jeans *mpl*.

blueprint ['blu:prɪnt] *n* bleu *m*; (*fig*) projet *m*, plan directeur.

blues [blu:z] *npl*: **the** ~ (*MUS*) le blues; **to have the** ~ (*col: feeling*) avoir le cafard.

bluff [blʌf] *vi* bluffer ♦ *n* bluff *m*; (*cliff*) promontoire *m*, falaise *f* ♦ *adj* (*person*) bourru(e), brusque; **to call sb's** ~ mettre qn au défi d'exécuter ses menaces.

blunder ['blʌndə*] *n* gaffe *f*, bévue *f* ♦ *vi* faire une gaffe *or* une bévue; **to** ~ **into sb/sth** buter contre qn/qch.

blunt [blʌnt] *adj* émoussé(e), peu tranchant(e); (*pencil*) mal taillé(e); (*person*) brusque, ne mâchant pas ses mots ♦ *vt* émousser; ~ **instrument** (*LAW*) instrument contondant.

bluntly ['blʌntlɪ] *adv* carrément, sans prendre de gants.

bluntness ['blʌntnɪs] *n* (*of person*) brusquerie *f*, franchise brutale.

blur [blə:*] *n* tache *or* masse floue *or* confuse ♦ *vt* brouiller, rendre flou(e).

blurb [blə:b] *n* (*for book*) texte *m* de présentation; (*pej*) baratin *m*.

blurred [blə:d] *adj* flou(e).

blurt [blə:t]: **to** ~ **out** *vt* (*reveal*) lâcher; (*say*) balbutier, dire d'une voix entrecoupée.

blush [blʌʃ] *vi* rougir ♦ *n* rougeur *f*.

blusher ['blʌʃə*] *n* rouge *m* à joues.

bluster ['blʌstə*] *n* paroles *fpl* en l'air; (*boasting*) fanfaronnades *fpl*; (*threats*) menaces *fpl* en l'air ♦ *vi* parler en l'air; fanfaronner.

blustering ['blʌstərɪŋ] *adj* fanfaron(ne).

blustery ['blʌstərɪ] *adj* (*weather*) à bourrasques.

Blvd *abbr* (= *boulevard*) Bd.

BM *n abbr* = *British Museum*; (*SCOL*: = *Bachelor of Medicine*) diplôme universitaire.

BMA *n abbr* = *British Medical Association*.

BMJ *n abbr* = *British Medical Journal*.

BMus *n abbr* (= *Bachelor of Music*) diplôme universitaire.

BMX *n abbr* (= *bicycle motocross*) BMX *m*.

BO *n abbr* (*col*: = *body odour*) odeurs corporelles; (*US*) = **box office**.

boar [bɔ:*] *n* sanglier *m*.

board [bɔ:d] *n* planche *f*; (*on wall*) panneau *m*; (*for chess etc*) plateau *m*; (*committee*) conseil *m*, comité *m*; (*in firm*) conseil d'administration; (*NAUT, AVIAT*): **on** ~ à bord ♦ *vt* (*ship*) monter à bord de; (*train*) monter dans; **full** ~ (*BRIT*) pension complète; **half** ~ (*BRIT*) demi-pension *f*; ~ **and lodging** *n* chambre *f* avec pension; **with** ~ **and lodging** logé nourri; **above** ~ (*fig*) régulier(ère); **across the** ~ (*fig: ad*) systématiquement; (*: a*) de portée générale; **to go by the** ~ être abandonné(e); (*be unimportant*) compter pour rien, n'avoir aucune importance.

▶**board up** *vt* (*door*) condamner (*au moyen de planches, de tôle*).

boarder ['bɔːdə*] n pensionnaire m/f; (SCOL) interne m/f, pensionnaire.

board game n jeu m de société.

boarding card ['bɔːdɪŋ-] n (AVIAT, NAUT) carte f d'embarquement.

boarding house ['bɔːdɪŋ-] n pension f.

boarding party ['bɔːdɪŋ-] n section f d'abordage.

boarding pass ['bɔːdɪŋ-] n (BRIT) = **boarding card**.

boarding school ['bɔːdɪŋ-] n internat m, pensionnat m.

board meeting n réunion f du conseil d'administration.

board room n salle f du conseil d'administration.

boardwalk ['bɔːdwɔːk] n (US) cheminement m en planches.

boast [bəust] vi: to ~ (about or of) se vanter (de) ♦ vt s'enorgueillir de ♦ n vantardise f; sujet m d'orgueil or de fierté.

boastful ['bəustful] adj vantard(e).

boastfulness ['bəustfulnɪs] n vantardise f.

boat [bəut] n bateau m; (small) canot m; barque f; to go by ~ aller en bateau; to be in the same ~ (fig) être logé à la même enseigne.

boater ['bəutə*] n (hat) canotier m.

boating ['bəutɪŋ] n canotage m.

boat people npl boat people mpl.

boatswain ['bəusn] n maître m d'équipage.

bob [bɔb] vi (boat, cork on water. also: ~ up and down) danser, se balancer ♦ n (BRIT col) = **shilling**.

▶**bob up** vi surgir or apparaître brusquement.

bobbin ['bɔbɪn] n bobine f; (of sewing machine) navette f.

bobby ['bɔbɪ] n (BRIT col) ≈ agent m (de police).

bobby pin n (US) pince f à cheveux.

bobsleigh ['bɔbsleɪ] n bob m.

bode [bəud] vi: to ~ well/ill (for) être de bon/ mauvais augure (pour).

bodice ['bɔdɪs] n corsage m.

bodily ['bɔdɪlɪ] adj corporel(le); (pain, comfort) physique; (needs) matériel(le) ♦ adv (carry, lift) dans ses bras.

body ['bɔdɪ] n corps m; (of car) carrosserie f; (of plane) fuselage m; (also: ~ **stocking**) body m, justaucorps m; (fig: society) organe m, organisme m; (: quantity) ensemble m, masse f; (of wine) corps m; **ruling** ~ organe directeur; **in a** ~ en masse, ensemble; (speak) comme un seul et même homme.

body blow n (fig) coup dur, choc m.

body-building ['bɔdɪbɪldɪŋ] n body-building m, culturisme m.

bodyguard ['bɔdɪgɑːd] n garde m du corps.

body language n langage m du corps.

body repairs npl travaux mpl de carrosserie.

body search n fouille f (corporelle); **to carry out a** ~ **on sb** fouiller qn; **to submit to** or **undergo a** ~ se faire fouiller.

bodywork ['bɔdɪwɜːk] n carrosserie f.

boffin ['bɔfɪn] n (BRIT) savant m.

bog [bɔg] n tourbière f ♦ vt: **to get** ~**ged down** (in) (fig) s'enliser (dans).

boggle ['bɔgl] vi: **the mind** ~**s** c'est incroyable, on en reste sidéré.

bogie ['bəugɪ] n bogie m.

Bogotá [bəugə'tɑː] n Bogotá.

bogus ['bəugəs] adj bidon inv; fantôme.

Bohemia [bəu'hiːmɪə] n Bohême f.

Bohemian [bəu'hiːmɪən] adj bohémien(ne) ♦ n Bohémien/ne; (gipsy: also: **b**~) bohémien/ne.

boil [bɔɪl] vt (faire) bouillir ♦ vi bouillir ♦ n (MED) furoncle m; **to come to the** or (US) **a** ~ bouillir; **to bring to the** or (US) **a** ~ porter à ébullition; ~**ed egg** œuf m à la coque; ~**ed potatoes** pommes fpl à l'anglaise or à l'eau.

▶**boil down** vi (fig): **to** ~ **down to** se réduire or ramener à.

▶**boil over** vi déborder.

boiler ['bɔɪlə*] n chaudière f.

boiler suit n (BRIT) bleu m de travail, combinaison f.

boiling ['bɔɪlɪŋ] adj: **I'm** ~ **(hot)** (col) je crève de chaud.

boiling point n point m d'ébullition.

boil-in-the-bag [bɔɪlɪnðə'bæg] adj (rice etc) en sachet cuisson.

boisterous ['bɔɪstərəs] adj bruyant(e), tapageur(euse).

bold [bəuld] adj hardi(e), audacieux(euse); (pej) effronté(e); (outline, colour) franc(franche), tranché(e), marqué(e).

boldness ['bəuldnɪs] n hardiesse f, audace f; aplomb m, effronterie f.

bold type n (TYP) caractères mpl gras.

Bolivia [bə'lɪvɪə] n Bolivie f.

Bolivian [bə'lɪvɪən] adj bolivien(ne) ♦ n Bolivien/ne.

bollard ['bɔləd] n (NAUT) bitte f d'amarrage; (BRIT AUT) borne lumineuse or de signalisation.

bolshy ['bɔlʃɪ] adj râleur(euse); **to be in a** ~ **mood** être peu coopératif(ive).

bolster ['bəulstə*] n traversin m.

▶**bolster up** vt soutenir.

bolt [bəult] n verrou m; (with nut) boulon m ♦ adv: ~ **upright** droit(e) comme un piquet ♦ vt verrouiller; (food) engloutir ♦ vi se sauver, filer (comme une flèche); **a** ~ **from the blue** (fig) un coup de tonnerre dans un ciel bleu.

bomb [bɔm] n bombe f ♦ vt bombarder.

bombard [bɔm'bɑːd] vt bombarder.

bombardment [bɔm'bɑːdmənt] n bombardement m.

bombastic [bɔm'bæstɪk] adj grandiloquent(e), pompeux(euse).

bomb disposal n: ~ **unit** section f de déminage; ~ **expert** artificier m.

bomber ['bɔmə*] n caporal m d'artillerie; (AVIAT) bombardier m; (terrorist) poseur m de bombes.

bombing ['bɔmɪŋ] n bombardement m.

bomb scare n alerte f à la bombe.

bombshell ['bɔmʃɛl] n obus m; (fig) bombe f.

bomb site n zone f de bombardement.

bona fide ['bəʊnə'faɪdɪ] adj de bonne foi; (offer) sérieux(euse).

bonanza [bə'nænzə] n filon m.

bond [bɔnd] n lien m; (binding promise) engagement m, obligation f; (FINANCE) obligation; **in ~** (of goods) en entrepôt.

bondage ['bɔndɪdʒ] n esclavage m.

bonded warehouse ['bɔndɪd-] n entrepôt m sous douanes.

bone [bəʊn] n os m; (of fish) arête f ♦ vt désosser; ôter les arêtes de.

bone china n porcelaine f tendre.

bone-dry ['bəʊn'draɪ] adj absolument sec(sèche).

bone idle adj fainéant(e).

bone marrow n moelle osseuse.

boner ['bəʊnə*] n (US) gaffe f, bourde f.

bonfire ['bɔnfaɪə*] n feu m (de joie); (for rubbish) feu.

bonk [bɔŋk] (col!) vt s'envoyer (!), sauter (!) ♦ vi s'envoyer en l'air (!).

bonkers ['bɔŋkəz] adj (BRIT col) cinglé(e), dingue.

Bonn [bɔn] n Bonn.

bonnet ['bɔnɪt] n bonnet m; (BRIT: of car) capot m.

bonny [bɔnɪ] adj (Scottish) joli(e).

bonus ['bəʊnəs] n prime f, gratification f; (on wages) prime.

bony ['bəʊnɪ] adj (arm, face, MED: tissue) osseux(euse); (thin: person) squelettique; (meat) plein(e) d'os; (fish) plein d'arêtes.

boo [buː] excl hou!, peuh! ♦ vt huer ♦ n huée f.

boob [buːb] n (col: breast) nichon m; (: BRIT: mistake) gaffe f.

booby prize ['buːbɪ-] n timbale f (ironique).

booby trap ['buːbɪ-] n guet-apens m.

booby-trapped ['buːbɪtræpt] adj piégé(e).

book [buk] n livre m; (of stamps etc) carnet m; (COMM): **~s** comptes mpl, comptabilité f ♦ vt (ticket) prendre; (seat, room, table) réserver; (driver) dresser un procès-verbal à; (football player) prendre le nom de, donner un carton à; **to keep the ~s** tenir la comptabilité; **by the ~** à la lettre, selon les règles; **to throw the ~ at sb** passer un savon à qn.

▶**book in** vi (BRIT: at hotel) prendre sa chambre.

▶**book up** vt réserver; **all seats are ~ed up** tout est pris, c'est complet; **the hotel is ~ed up** l'hôtel est complet.

bookable ['bukəbl] adj: **seats are ~** on peut réserver ses places.

bookcase ['bukkeɪs] n bibliothèque f (meuble).

book ends npl serre-livres m inv.

booking ['bukɪŋ] n (BRIT) réservation f.

booking office n (BRIT) bureau m de location.

book-keeping ['buk'kiːpɪŋ] n comptabilité f.

booklet ['buklɪt] n brochure f.

bookmaker ['bukmeɪkə*] n bookmaker m.

bookseller ['bukselə*] n libraire m/f.

bookshelf ['bukʃelf] n (single) étagère f (à livres); **bookshelves** rayons mpl (de bibliothèque).

bookshop ['bukʃɔp] n librairie f.

bookstall ['bukstɔːl] n kiosque m à journaux.

book token n bon-cadeau m (pour un livre).

book value n valeur f comptable.

bookworm ['bukwəːm] n dévoreur/euse de livres.

boom [buːm] n (noise) grondement m; (busy period) boom m, vague f de prospérité ♦ vi gronder; prospérer.

boomerang ['buːməræŋ] n boomerang m.

boom town n ville f en plein essor.

boon [buːn] n bénédiction f, grand avantage.

boorish ['buərɪʃ] adj grossier(ère), rustre.

boost [buːst] n stimulant m, remontant m ♦ vt stimuler; **to give a ~ to sb's spirits** or **to sb** remonter le moral à qn.

booster ['buːstə*] n (TV) amplificateur m (de signal); (ELEC) survolteur m; (also: **~ rocket**) booster m; (MED: vaccine) rappel m.

booster seat n (AUT: for children) siège m rehausseur.

boot [buːt] n botte f; (for hiking) chaussure f (de marche); (for football etc) soulier m; (ankle ~) bottine f; (BRIT: of car) coffre m ♦ vt (COMPUT) lancer, mettre en route; **to ~** (in addition) par-dessus le marché, en plus; **to give sb the ~** (col) flanquer qn dehors, virer qn.

booth [buːð] n (at fair) baraque (foraine); (of cinema, telephone etc) cabine f; (also: **voting ~**) isoloir m.

bootleg ['buːtleg] adj de contrebande; **~ record** enregistrement m pirate.

booty ['buːtɪ] n butin m.

booze [buːz] (col) n boissons fpl alcooliques, alcool m ♦ vi boire, picoler.

boozer ['buːzə*] n (col: person): **he's a ~** il picole pas mal; (BRIT col: pub) pub m.

border ['bɔːdə*] n bordure f; bord m; (of a country) frontière f; **the B~** la frontière entre l'Écosse et l'Angleterre; **the B~s** la région frontière entre l'Écosse et l'Angleterre.

▶**border on** vt fus être voisin(e) de, toucher à.

borderline ['bɔːdəlaɪn] n (fig) ligne f de démarcation ♦ adj: **~ case** cas m limite.

bore [bɔː*] pt of **bear** ♦ vt (hole) percer; (person) ennuyer, raser ♦ n (person) raseur/euse; (of gun) calibre m; **he's ~d to tears** or **~d to death** or **~d stiff** il s'ennuie à mourir.

boredom ['bɔːdəm] n ennui m.

boring ['bɔːrɪŋ] adj ennuyeux(euse).

born [bɔːn] adj: **to be ~** naître; **I was ~ in 1960** je suis né en 1960; **~ blind** aveugle de nais-

sance; **a ~ comedian** un comédien-né.
born-again [bɔːnə'gɛn] *adj*: **~ Christian** ≈ évangeliste *m/f*.
borne [bɔːn] *pp of* **bear**.
Borneo ['bɔːnɪəu] *n* Bornéo *f*.
borough ['bʌrə] *n* municipalité *f*.
borrow ['bɔrəu] *vt*: **to ~ sth (from sb)** emprunter qch (à qn); **may I ~ your car?** est-ce que je peux vous emprunter votre voiture?
borrower ['bɔrəuə*] *n* emprunteur/euse.
borrowing ['bɔrəuɪŋ] *n* emprunt(s) *m(pl)*.
borstal ['bɔːstl] *n* (*BRIT*) ≈ maison *f* de correction.
Bosnia ['bɔznɪə] *n* Bosnie *f*.
Bosnia-Herzegovina ['bɔznɪəhəːtsəgəu'viːnə] *n* (*also*: **Bosnia-Hercegovina**) Bosnie-Herzégovine *f*.
Bosnian ['bɔznɪən] *adj* bosniaque, bosnien(ne) ♦ *n* Bosniaque *m/f*, Bosnien/ne.
bosom ['buzəm] *n* poitrine *f*; (*fig*) sein *m*.
bosom friend *n* ami/e intime.
boss [bɔs] *n* patron/ne ♦ *vt* (*also*: **~ about, ~ around**) mener à la baguette.
bossy ['bɔsɪ] *adj* autoritaire.
bosun ['bəusn] *n* maître *m* d'équipage.
botanical [bə'tænɪkl] *adj* botanique.
botanist ['bɔtənɪst] *n* botaniste *m/f*.
botany ['bɔtənɪ] *n* botanique *f*.
botch [bɔtʃ] *vt* (*also*: **~ up**) saboter, bâcler.
both [bəuθ] *adj* les deux, l'un(e) et l'autre ♦ *pron*: **~ (of them)** les deux, tous(toutes) (les) deux, l'un(e) et l'autre; **~ of us went, we ~ went** nous y sommes allés tous les deux ♦ *adv*: **they sell ~ the fabric and the finished curtains** ils vendent (et) le tissu et les rideaux (finis), ils vendent à la fois le tissu et les rideaux (finis).
bother ['bɔðə*] *vt* (*worry*) tracasser; (*needle, bait*) importuner, ennuyer; (*disturb*) déranger ♦ *vi* (*also*: **~ o.s.**) se tracasser, se faire du souci ♦ *n*: **it is a ~ to have to do** c'est vraiment ennuyeux d'avoir à faire ♦ *excl* zut!; **to ~ doing** prendre la peine de faire; **I'm sorry to ~ you** excusez-moi de vous déranger; **please don't ~** ne vous dérangez pas; **don't ~** ce n'est pas la peine; **it's no ~** aucun problème.
Botswana [bɔt'swɑːnə] *n* Botswana *m*.
bottle ['bɔtl] *n* bouteille *f*; (*baby's*) biberon *m*; (*of perfume, medicine*) flacon *m* ♦ *vt* mettre en bouteille(s); **~ of wine/milk** bouteille de vin/lait; **wine/milk ~** bouteille à vin/lait.
►**bottle up** *vt* refouler, contenir.
bottle bank *n* conteneur *m* (de bouteilles).
bottleneck ['bɔtlnɛk] *n* (*in traffic*) bouchon *m*; (*in production*) goulet *m* d'étranglement.
bottle-opener ['bɔtləupnə*] *n* ouvre-bouteille *m*.
bottom ['bɔtəm] *n* (*of container, sea etc*) fond *m*; (*buttocks*) derrière *m*; (*of page, list*) bas *m*; (*of chair*) siège *m*; (*of mountain, tree, hill*) pied *m* ♦ *adj* du fond; du bas; **to get to the ~ of sth**

(*fig*) découvrir le fin fond de qch.
bottomless ['bɔtəmlɪs] *adj* sans fond, insondable.
bottom line *n*: **the ~ is that ...** l'essentiel, c'est que ....
botulism ['bɔtjulɪzəm] *n* botulisme *m*.
bough [bau] *n* branche *f*, rameau *m*.
bought [bɔːt] *pt*, *pp of* **buy**.
boulder ['bəuldə*] *n* gros rocher (*gén lisse, arrondi*).
bounce [bauns] *vi* (*ball*) rebondir; (*cheque*) être refusé (*étant sans provision*); (*also*: **to ~ forward/out etc**) bondir, s'élancer ♦ *vt* faire rebondir ♦ *n* (*rebound*) rebond *m*; **he's got plenty of ~** (*fig*) il est plein d'entrain *or* d'allant.
bouncer ['baunsə*] *n* (*col*) videur *m*.
bouncy castle ['baunsɪ-] *n* ® château *m* gonflable.
bound [baund] *pt*, *pp of* **bind** ♦ *n* (*gen pl*) limite *f*; (*leap*) bond *m* ♦ *vt* (*leap*) bondir; (*limit*) borner ♦ *adj*: **to be ~ to do sth** (*obliged*) être obligé(e) *or* avoir obligation de faire qch; **he's ~ to fail** (*likely*) il est sûr d'échouer, son échec est inévitable *or* assuré; **~ for** à destination de; **out of ~s** dont l'accès est interdit.
boundary ['baundrɪ] *n* frontière *f*.
boundless ['baundlɪs] *adj* illimité(e), sans bornes.
bountiful ['bauntɪful] *adj* (*person*) généreux(euse); (*God*) bienfaiteur(trice); (*supply*) ample.
bounty ['bauntɪ] *n* (*generosity*) générosité *f*.
bouquet ['bukeɪ] *n* bouquet *m*.
bourbon ['buəbən] *n* (*US*: *also*: **~ whiskey**) bourbon *m*.
bourgeois ['buəʒwɑː] *adj*, *n* bourgeois(e).
bout [baut] *n* période *f*; (*of malaria etc*) accès *m*, crise *f*, attaque *f*; (*BOXING etc*) combat *m*, match *m*.
boutique [buː'tiːk] *n* boutique *f*.
bow[1] [bəu] *n* nœud *m*; (*weapon*) arc *m*; (*MUS*) archet *m*.
bow[2] [bau] *n* (*with body*) révérence *f*, inclination *f* (*du buste or corps*); (*NAUT*: *also*: **~s**) proue *f* ♦ *vi* faire une révérence, s'incliner; (*yield*): **to ~ to or before** s'incliner devant, se soumettre à; **to ~ to the inevitable** accepter l'inévitable *or* l'inéluctable.
bowels [bauəlz] *npl* intestins *mpl*; (*fig*) entrailles *fpl*.
bowl [bəul] *n* (*for eating*) bol *m*; (*for washing*) cuvette *f*; (*ball*) boule *f*; (*of pipe*) fourneau *m* ♦ *vi* (*CRICKET*) lancer (la balle).
►**bowl over** *vt* (*fig*) renverser.
bow-legged ['bəu'lɛgɪd] *adj* aux jambes arquées.
bowler ['bəulə*] *n* joueur *m* de boules; (*CRICKET*) lanceur *m* (de la balle); (*BRIT*: *also*: **~ hat**) (chapeau *m*) melon *m*.
bowling ['bəulɪŋ] *n* (*game*) jeu *m* de boules;

jeu de quilles.
bowling alley *n* bowling *m*.
bowling green *n* terrain *m* de boules (*gazonné et carré*).
bowls [bəulz] *n* (jeu *m* de) boules *fpl*.
bow tie [bəu-] *n* nœud *m* papillon.
box [bɒks] *n* boîte *f*; (*also:* **cardboard** ~) carton *m*; (*crate*) caisse *f*; (*THEAT*) loge *f*; (*BRIT AUT*) intersection *f* (*matérialisée par des marques au sol*) ♦ *vt* mettre en boîte; (*SPORT*) boxer avec ♦ *vi* boxer, faire de la boxe.
boxcar ['bɒkskɑː*] *n* (*US RAIL*) wagon *m* (de marchandises) couvert.
boxer ['bɒksə*] *n* (*person*) boxeur *m*; (*dog*) boxer *m*.
boxing ['bɒksɪŋ] *n* (*sport*) boxe *f*.
Boxing Day *n* (*BRIT*) le lendemain de Noël.

Boxing Day *est le lendemain de Noël, férié en Grande-Bretagne. Si Noël tombe un samedi, le jour férié est reculé jusqu'au lundi suivant. Ce nom vient d'une coutume du XIX*e *siècle qui consistait à donner des cadeaux de Noël (dans des boîtes) à ses employés etc le 26 décembre.*

---

boxing gloves *npl* gants *mpl* de boxe.
boxing ring *n* ring *m*.
box number *n* (*for advertisements*) numéro *m* d'annonce.
box office *n* bureau *m* de location.
box room *n* débarras *m*; chambrette *f*.
boy [bɔɪ] *n* garçon *m*.
boycott ['bɔɪkɒt] *n* boycottage *m* ♦ *vt* boycotter.
boyfriend ['bɔɪfrend] *n* (petit) ami.
boyish ['bɔɪɪʃ] *adj* d'enfant, de garçon; **to look** ~ (*man: appear youthful*) faire jeune.
Bp *abbr* = **bishop**.
BR *abbr* = **British Rail**.
Br. *abbr* (*REL*) = **brother**.
bra [brɑː] *n* soutien-gorge *m*.
brace [breɪs] *n* attache *f*, agrafe *f*; (*on teeth*) appareil *m* (dentaire); (*tool*) vilbrequin *m*; (*TYP: also:* ~ **bracket**) accolade *f* ♦ *vt* consolider, soutenir; **to** ~ **o.s.** (*fig*) se préparer mentalement.
bracelet ['breɪslɪt] *n* bracelet *m*.
braces ['breɪsɪz] *npl* (*BRIT*) bretelles *fpl*.
bracing ['breɪsɪŋ] *adj* tonifiant(e), tonique.
bracken ['brækən] *n* fougère *f*.
bracket ['brækɪt] *n* (*TECH*) tasseau *m*, support *m*; (*group*) classe *f*, tranche *f*; (*also:* **brace** ~) accolade *f*; (*also:* **round** ~) parenthèse *f*; (*also:* **square** ~) crochet *m* ♦ *vt* mettre entre parenthèses; (*fig: also:* ~ **together**) regrouper; **income** ~ tranche *f* des revenus; **in** ~**s** entre parenthèses (*or* crochets).
brackish ['brækɪʃ] *adj* (*water*) saumâtre.
brag [bræg] *vi* se vanter.
braid [breɪd] *n* (*trimming*) galon *m*; (*of hair*) tresse *f*, natte *f*.
Braille [breɪl] *n* braille *m*.

brain [breɪn] *n* cerveau *m*; ~**s** *npl* cervelle *f*; **he's got** ~**s** il est intelligent.
brainchild ['breɪntʃaɪld] *n* trouvaille (personnelle), invention *f*.
braindead ['breɪndɛd] *adj* (*MED*) dans un coma dépassé; (*col*) demeuré(e).
brainless ['breɪnlɪs] *adj* sans cervelle, stupide.
brainstorm ['breɪnstɔːm] *n* (*fig*) moment *m* d'égarement; (*US: brainwave*) idée *f* de génie.
brainwash ['breɪnwɒʃ] *vt* faire subir un lavage de cerveau à.
brainwave ['breɪnweɪv] *n* idée *f* de génie.
brainy ['breɪnɪ] *adj* intelligent(e), doué(e).
braise [breɪz] *vt* braiser.
brake [breɪk] *n* (*on vehicle*) frein *m* ♦ *vt, vi* freiner.
brake light *n* feu *m* de stop.
brake pedal *n* pédale *f* de frein.
bramble ['bræmbl] *n* ronces *fpl*; (*fruit*) mûre *f*.
bran [bræn] *n* son *m*.
branch [brɑːntʃ] *n* branche *f*; (*COMM*) succursale *f*; (*: bank*) agence *f*; (*of association*) section locale *f* ♦ *vi* bifurquer.
▶**branch out** *vi* diversifier ses activités; **to** ~ **out into** étendre ses activités à.
branch line *n* (*RAIL*) bifurcation *f*, embranchement *m*.
branch manager *n* directeur/trice de succursale (*or* d'agence).
brand [brænd] *n* marque (commerciale) ♦ *vt* (*cattle*) marquer (au fer rouge); (*fig: pej*): **to** ~ **sb a communist** *etc* traiter *or* qualifier qn de communiste *etc*.
brandish ['brændɪʃ] *vt* brandir.
brand name *n* nom *m* de marque.
brand-new ['brænd'njuː] *adj* tout(e) neuf(neuve), flambant neuf(neuve).
brandy ['brændɪ] *n* cognac *m*, fine *f*.
brash [bræʃ] *adj* effronté(e).
Brasilia [brə'zɪlɪə] *n* Brasilia.
brass [brɑːs] *n* cuivre *m* (jaune), laiton *m*; **the** ~ (*MUS*) les cuivres.
brass band *n* fanfare *f*.
brassiere ['bræsɪə*] *n* soutien-gorge *m*.
brass tacks *npl*: **to get down to** ~ en venir au fait.
brat [bræt] *n* (*pej*) mioche *m/f*, môme *m/f*.
bravado [brə'vɑːdəu] *n* bravade *f*.
brave [breɪv] *adj* courageux(euse), brave ♦ *n* guerrier indien ♦ *vt* braver, affronter.
bravery ['breɪvərɪ] *n* bravoure *f*, courage *m*.
bravo [brɑː'vəu] *excl* bravo!
brawl [brɔːl] *n* rixe *f*, bagarre *f* ♦ *vi* se bagarrer.
brawn [brɔːn] *n* muscle *m*; (*meat*) fromage *m* de tête.
brawny ['brɔːnɪ] *adj* musclé(e), costaud(e).
bray [breɪ] *n* braiement *m* ♦ *vi* braire.
brazen ['breɪzn] *adj* impudent(e), effronté(e) ♦ *vt*: **to** ~ **it out** payer d'effronterie, crâner.
brazier ['breɪzɪə*] *n* brasero *m*.
Brazil [brə'zɪl] *n* Brésil *m*.

Brazilian [brəˈzɪljən] *adj* brésilien(ne) ♦ *n* Brésilien/ne.

Brazil nut *n* noix *f* du Brésil.

breach [briːtʃ] *vt* ouvrir une brèche dans ♦ *n* (*gap*) brèche *f*; (*estrangement*) brouille *f*; (*breaking*): ~ **of contract** rupture *f* de contrat; ~ **of the peace** attentat *m* à l'ordre public; ~ **of trust** abus *m* de confiance.

bread [brɛd] *n* pain *m*; (*col: money*) fric *m*; ~ **and butter** *n* tartines (beurrées); (*fig*) subsistance *f*; **to earn one's daily** ~ gagner son pain; **to know which side one's** ~ **is buttered (on)** savoir où est son avantage *or* intérêt.

breadbin [ˈbrɛdbɪn] *n* (*BRIT*) boîte *f* or huche *f* à pain.

breadboard [ˈbrɛdbɔːd] *n* planche *f* à pain; (*COMPUT*) montage expérimental.

breadbox [ˈbrɛdbɔks] *n* (*US*) boîte *f* or huche *f* à pain.

breadcrumbs [ˈbrɛdkrʌmz] *npl* miettes *fpl* de pain; (*CULIN*) chapelure *f*, panure *f*.

breadline [ˈbrɛdlaɪn] *n*: **to be on the** ~ être sans le sou *or* dans l'indigence.

breadth [brɛtθ] *n* largeur *f*.

breadwinner [ˈbrɛdwɪnə*] *n* soutien *m* de famille.

break [breɪk] *vb* (*pt* **broke** [brəuk], *pp* **broken** [ˈbrəukən]) *vt* casser, briser; (*promise*) rompre; (*law*) violer ♦ *vi* (se) casser, se briser; (*weather*) tourner ♦ *n* (*gap*) brèche *f*; (*fracture*) cassure *f*; (*rest*) interruption *f*, arrêt *m*; (*: short*) pause *f*; (*: at school*) récréation *f*; (*chance*) chance *f*, occasion *f* favorable; **to** ~ **one's leg** *etc* se casser la jambe *etc*; **to** ~ **a record** battre un record; **to** ~ **the news to sb** annoncer la nouvelle à qn; **to** ~ **with sb** rompre avec qn; **to** ~ **even** *vi* rentrer dans ses frais; **to** ~ **free** *or* **loose** *vi* se dégager, s'échapper; **to take a** ~ (*few minutes*) faire une pause, s'arrêter cinq minutes; (*holiday*) prendre un peu de repos; **without a** ~ sans interruption, sans arrêt.

►**break down** *vt* (*door etc*) enfoncer; (*resistance*) venir à bout de; (*figures, data*) décomposer, analyser ♦ *vi* s'effondrer; (*MED*) faire une dépression (nerveuse); (*AUT*) tomber en panne.

►**break in** *vt* (*horse etc*) dresser ♦ *vi* (*burglar*) entrer par effraction.

►**break into** *vt fus* (*house*) s'introduire *or* pénétrer par effraction dans.

►**break off** *vi* (*speaker*) s'interrompre; (*branch*) se rompre ♦ *vt* (*talks, engagement*) rompre.

►**break open** *vt* (*door etc*) forcer, fracturer.

►**break out** *vi* éclater, se déclarer; **to** ~ **out in spots** se couvrir de boutons.

►**break through** *vi*: **the sun broke through** le soleil a fait son apparition ♦ *vt fus* (*defences, barrier*) franchir; (*crowd*) se frayer un passage à travers.

►**break up** *vi* (*partnership*) cesser, prendre fin; (*marriage*) se briser; (*friends*) se séparer ♦ *vt* fracasser, casser; (*fight etc*) interrompre, faire cesser; (*marriage*) désunir.

breakable [ˈbreɪkəbl] *adj* cassable, fragile ♦ *n*: ~**s** objets *mpl* fragiles.

breakage [ˈbreɪkɪdʒ] *n* casse *f*; **to pay for** ~**s** payer la casse.

breakaway [ˈbreɪkəweɪ] *adj* (*group etc*) dissident(e).

breakdown [ˈbreɪkdaun] *n* (*AUT*) panne *f*; (*in communications*) rupture *f*; (*MED: also*: **nervous** ~) dépression (nerveuse); (*of figures*) ventilation *f*, répartition *f*.

breakdown service *n* (*BRIT*) service *m* de dépannage.

breakdown van *n* (*BRIT*) dépanneuse *f*.

breaker [ˈbreɪkə*] *n* brisant *m*.

breakeven [ˈbreɪkˈiːvn] *cpd*: ~ **chart** graphique *m* de rentabilité; ~ **point** seuil *m* de rentabilité.

breakfast [ˈbrɛkfəst] *n* petit déjeuner *m*.

breakfast cereal *n* céréales *fpl*.

break-in [ˈbreɪkɪn] *n* cambriolage *m*.

breaking point [ˈbreɪkɪŋ-] *n* limites *fpl*.

breakthrough [ˈbreɪkθruː] *n* percée *f*.

break-up [ˈbreɪkʌp] *n* (*of partnership, marriage*) rupture *f*.

break-up value *n* (*COMM*) valeur *f* de liquidation.

breakwater [ˈbreɪkwɔːtə*] *n* brise-lames *m inv*, digue *f*.

breast [brɛst] *n* (*of woman*) sein *m*; (*chest*) poitrine *f*.

breast-feed [ˈbrɛstfiːd] *vt*, *vi* (*irreg: like* **feed**) allaiter.

breast pocket *n* poche *f* (de) poitrine.

breaststroke [ˈbrɛststrəuk] *n* brasse *f*.

breath [brɛθ] *n* haleine *f*, souffle *m*; **to go out for a** ~ **of air** sortir prendre l'air; **out of** ~ à bout de souffle, essoufflé(e).

breathalyse [ˈbrɛθəlaɪz] *vt* faire subir l'alcootest à.

Breathalyser [ˈbrɛθəlaɪzə*] *n* ® alcootest *m*.

breathe [briːð] *vt*, *vi* respirer; **I won't** ~ **a word about it** je n'en soufflerai pas mot, je n'en dirai rien à personne.

►**breathe in** *vi* inspirer ♦ *vt* aspirer.

►**breathe out** *vt*, *vi* expirer.

breather [ˈbriːðə*] *n* moment *m* de repos *or* de répit.

breathing [ˈbriːðɪŋ] *n* respiration *f*.

breathing space *n* (*fig*) (moment *m* de) répit *m*.

breathless [ˈbrɛθlɪs] *adj* essoufflé(e), haletant(e); oppressé(e); ~ **with excitement** le souffle coupé par l'émotion.

breath-taking [ˈbrɛθteɪkɪŋ] *adj* stupéfiant(e), à vous couper le souffle.

breath test *n* alcootest *m*.

-bred [brɛd] *suffix*: **well/ill**~ bien/mal élevé(e).

breed [briːd] (*pt*, *pp* **bred** [brɛd]) *vt* élever, faire l'élevage de; (*fig: hate, suspicion*) engendrer ♦ *vi* se reproduire ♦ *n* race *f*, variété *f*.

breeder ['bri:də*] *n* (*person*) éleveur *m*; (*PHYSICS: also:* ~ **reactor**) (réacteur *m*) surrégénérateur *m*.

breeding ['bri:dɪŋ] *n* reproduction *f*; élevage *m*; (*upbringing*) éducation *f*.

breeze [bri:z] *n* brise *f*.

breezeblock ['bri:zblɔk] *n* (*BRIT*) parpaing *m* (*de laitier*).

breezy ['bri:zɪ] *adj* frais(fraîche); aéré(e); désinvolte, jovial(e).

Breton ['brɛtən] *adj* breton(ne) ♦ *n* Breton/ne; (*LING*) breton *m*.

brevity ['brɛvɪtɪ] *n* brièveté *f*.

brew [bru:] *vt* (*tea*) faire infuser; (*beer*) brasser; (*plot*) tramer, préparer ♦ *vi* (*tea*) infuser; (*beer*) fermenter; (*fig*) se préparer, couver.

brewer ['bru:ə*] *n* brasseur *m*.

brewery ['bru:ərɪ] *n* brasserie *f* (*fabrique*).

briar ['braɪə*] *n* (*thorny bush*) ronces *fpl*; (*wild rose*) églantine *f*.

bribe [braɪb] *n* pot-de-vin *m* ♦ *vt* acheter; soudoyer; **to** ~ **sb to do sth** soudoyer qn pour qu'il fasse qch.

bribery ['braɪbərɪ] *n* corruption *f*.

bric-a-brac ['brɪkəbræk] *n* bric-à-brac *m*.

brick [brɪk] *n* brique *f*.

bricklayer ['brɪkleɪə*] *n* maçon *m*.

brickwork ['brɪkwə:k] *n* briquetage *m*, maçonnerie *f*.

brickworks ['brɪkwə:ks] *n* briqueterie *f*.

bridal ['braɪdl] *adj* nuptial(e); ~ **party** noce *f*.

bride [braɪd] *n* mariée *f*, épouse *f*.

bridegroom ['braɪdgru:m] *n* marié *m*, époux *m*.

bridesmaid ['braɪdzmeɪd] *n* demoiselle *f* d'honneur.

bridge [brɪdʒ] *n* pont *m*; (*NAUT*) passerelle *f* (*de commandement*); (*of nose*) arête *f*; (*CARDS, DENTISTRY*) bridge *m* ♦ *vt* (*river*) construire un pont sur; (*gap*) combler.

bridging loan ['brɪdʒɪŋ-] *n* (*BRIT*) prêt *m* relais.

bridle ['braɪdl] *n* bride *f* ♦ *vt* refréner, mettre la bride à; (*horse*) brider.

bridle path *n* piste *or* allée cavalière.

brief [bri:f] *adj* bref(brève) ♦ *n* (*LAW*) dossier *m*, cause *f* ♦ *vt* (*MIL etc*) donner des instructions à; **in** ~ ... (en) bref ...; **to** ~ **sb (about sth)** mettre qn au courant (de qch).

briefcase ['bri:fkeɪs] *n* serviette *f*, porte-documents *m inv*.

briefing ['bri:fɪŋ] *n* instructions *fpl*.

briefly ['bri:flɪ] *adv* brièvement; (*visit*) en coup de vent; **to glimpse** ~ entrevoir.

briefness ['bri:fnɪs] *n* brièveté *f*.

briefs [bri:fs] *npl* slip *m*.

Brig. *abbr* = **brigadier**.

brigade [brɪ'geɪd] *n* (*MIL*) brigade *f*.

brigadier [brɪgə'dɪə*] *n* brigadier général.

bright [braɪt] *adj* brillant(e); (*room, weather*) clair(e); (*person*) intelligent(e), doué(e); (*colour*) vif(vive); **to look on the** ~ **side** regarder le bon côté des choses.

brighten ['braɪtn] (*also:* ~ **up**) *vt* (*room*) éclaircir; égayer ♦ *vi* s'éclaircir; (*person*) retrouver un peu de sa gaieté.

brightly ['braɪtlɪ] *adv* brillamment.

brill [brɪl] *adj* (*BRIT col*) super *inv*.

brilliance ['brɪljəns] *n* éclat *m*; (*fig: of person*) brio *m*.

brilliant ['brɪljənt] *adj* brillant(e).

brim [brɪm] *n* bord *m*.

brimful ['brɪm'ful] *adj* plein(e) à ras bord; (*fig*) débordant(e).

brine [braɪn] *n* eau salée; (*CULIN*) saumure *f*.

bring, *pt, pp* **brought** [brɪŋ, brɔ:t] *vt* (*thing*) apporter; (*person*) amener; **to** ~ **sth to an end** mettre fin à qch; **I can't** ~ **myself to fire him** je ne peux me résoudre à le mettre à la porte.

▶**bring about** *vt* provoquer, entraîner.

▶**bring back** *vt* rapporter; (*person*) ramener.

▶**bring down** *vt* (*lower*) abaisser; (*shoot down*) abattre; (*government*) faire s'effondrer.

▶**bring forward** *vt* avancer; (*BOOK-KEEPING*) reporter.

▶**bring in** *vt* (*person*) faire entrer; (*object*) rentrer; (*POL: legislation*) introduire; (*LAW: verdict*) rendre; (*produce: income*) rapporter.

▶**bring off** *vt* (*task, plan*) réussir, mener à bien; (*deal*) mener à bien.

▶**bring out** *vt* (*meaning*) faire ressortir, mettre en relief; (*new product, book*) sortir.

▶**bring round, bring to** *vt* (*unconscious person*) ranimer.

▶**bring up** *vt* élever; (*question*) soulever; (*food: vomit*) vomir, rendre.

brink [brɪŋk] *n* bord *m*; **on the** ~ **of doing** sur le point de faire, à deux doigts de faire; **she was on the** ~ **of tears** elle était au bord des larmes.

brisk [brɪsk] *adj* vif(vive); (*abrupt*) brusque; (*trade etc*) actif(ive); **to go for a** ~ **walk** se promener d'un bon pas; **business is** ~ les affaires marchent (bien).

bristle ['brɪsl] *n* poil *m* ♦ *vi* se hérisser; **bristling with** hérissé(e) de.

bristly ['brɪslɪ] *adj* (*beard, hair*) hérissé(e); **your chin's all** ~ ton menton gratte.

Brit [brɪt] *n abbr* (*col: = British person*) Britannique *m/f*.

Britain ['brɪtən] *n* (*also:* **Great** ~) la Grande-Bretagne; **in** ~ en Grande-Bretagne.

British ['brɪtɪʃ] *adj* britannique; **the** ~ *npl* les Britanniques *mpl*; **the** ~ **Isles** les îles *fpl* Britanniques.

British Rail (BR) *n compagnie ferroviaire britannique*, ≈ SNCF *f*.

British Summer Time *n* heure *f* d'été britannique.

Briton ['brɪtən] *n* Britannique *m/f*.
Brittany ['brɪtənɪ] *n* Bretagne *f*.
brittle ['brɪtl] *adj* cassant(e), fragile.
Bro. *abbr* (*REL*) = **brother**.
broach [brəʊtʃ] *vt* (*subject*) aborder.
broad [brɔːd] *adj* large; (*distinction*) général(e); (*accent*) prononcé(e) ♦ *n* (*US col*) nana *f*; ~ **hint** allusion transparente; **in** ~ **daylight** en plein jour; **the** ~ **outlines** les grandes lignes.
broad bean *n* fève *f*.
broadcast ['brɔːdkɑːst] *n* émission *f* ♦ *vb* (*pt, pp* **broadcast**) *vt* radiodiffuser; téléviser ♦ *vi* émettre.
broadcaster ['brɔːdkɑːstə*] *n* personnalité *f* de la radio *or* de la télévision.
broadcasting ['brɔːdkɑːstɪŋ] *n* radiodiffusion *f*; télévision *f*.
broadcasting station *n* station *f* de radio (*or* de télévision).
broaden ['brɔːdn] *vt* élargir ♦ *vi* s'élargir.
broadly ['brɔːdlɪ] *adv* en gros, généralement.
broad-minded ['brɔːd'maɪndɪd] *adj* large d'esprit.
broadsheet ['brɔːdʃiːt] *n* (*BRIT*) journal *m* grand format.
broccoli ['brɔkəlɪ] *n* brocoli *m*.
brochure ['brəʊʃjuə*] *n* prospectus *m*, dépliant *m*.
brogue ['brəʊg] *n* (*accent*) accent régional; (*shoe*) (*sorte de*) chaussure basse de cuir épais.
broil [brɔɪl] *vt* rôtir.
broiler ['brɔɪlə*] *n* (*fowl*) poulet *m* (*à rôtir*).
broke [brəʊk] *pt of* **break** ♦ *adj* (*col*) fauché(e); **to go** ~ (*business*) faire faillite.
broken ['brəʊkn] *pp of* **break** ♦ *adj* (*stick, leg etc*) cassé(e); (*promise, vow*) rompu(e); **a** ~ **marriage** un couple dissocié; **a** ~ **home** un foyer désuni; **in** ~ **French/English** dans un français/anglais approximatif *or* hésitant.
broken-down ['brəʊkn'daʊn] *adj* (*car*) en panne; (*machine*) fichu(e); (*house*) en ruines.
broken-hearted ['brəʊkn'hɑːtɪd] *adj* (ayant) le cœur brisé.
broker ['brəʊkə*] *n* courtier *m*.
brokerage ['brəʊkrɪdʒ] *n* courtage *m*.
brolly ['brɔlɪ] *n* (*BRIT col*) pépin *m*, parapluie *m*.
bronchitis [brɔŋ'kaɪtɪs] *n* bronchite *f*.
bronze [brɔnz] *n* bronze *m*.
bronzed ['brɔnzd] *adj* bronzé(e), hâlé(e).
brooch [brəʊtʃ] *n* broche *f*.
brood [bruːd] *n* couvée *f* ♦ *vi* (*hen, storm*) couver; (*person*) méditer (sombrement), ruminer.
broody ['bruːdɪ] *adj* (*fig*) taciturne, mélancolique.
brook [brʊk] *n* ruisseau *m*.
broom [brum] *n* balai *m*.
broomstick ['brumstɪk] *n* manche *m* à balai.
Bros. *abbr* (*COMM*: = *brothers*) Frères.
broth [brɔθ] *n* bouillon *m* de viande et de légumes.
brothel ['brɔθl] *n* maison close, bordel *m*.
brother ['brʌðə*] *n* frère *m*.
brotherhood ['brʌðəhud] *n* fraternité *f*.
brother-in-law ['brʌðərɪn'lɔː*] *n* beau-frère *m*.
brotherly ['brʌðəlɪ] *adj* fraternel(le).
brought [brɔːt] *pt, pp of* **bring**.
brow [brau] *n* front *m*; (*rare: gen: eye*~) sourcil *m*; (*of hill*) sommet *m*.
browbeat ['braubiːt] *vt* intimider, brusquer.
brown [braun] *adj* brun(e), marron *inv*; (*hair*) châtain *inv*; (*rice, bread, flour*) complet(ète) ♦ *n* (*colour*) brun *m*, marron *m* ♦ *vt* brunir; (*CULIN*) faire dorer, faire roussir; **to go** ~ (*person*) bronzer; (*leaves*) jaunir.
brownie ['braunɪ] *n* jeannette *f*, éclaireuse (cadette).
brown paper *n* papier *m* d'emballage, papier kraft.
brown sugar *n* cassonade *f*.
browse [brauz] *vi* (*among books*) bouquiner, feuilleter les livres; (*animal*) paître; **to** ~ **through a book** feuilleter un livre.
browser ['brauzə*] *n* (*COMPUT*) navigateur *m*.
bruise [bruːz] *n* bleu *m*, ecchymose *f*, contusion *f* ♦ *vt* contusionner, meurtrir ♦ *vi* (*fruit*) se taler, se meurtrir; **to** ~ **one's arm** se faire un bleu au bras.
Brum [brʌm] *n* *abbr*, **Brummagem** ['brʌmədʒəm] *n* (*col*) = *Birmingham*.
Brummie ['brʌmɪ] *n* (*col*) habitant/e de Birmingham; natif/ive de Birmingham.
brunch [brʌntʃ] *n* brunch *m*.
brunette [bruː'nɛt] *n* (*femme*) brune.
brunt [brʌnt] *n*: **the** ~ **of** (*attack, criticism etc*) le plus gros de.
brush [brʌʃ] *n* brosse *f*; (*quarrel*) accrochage *m*, prise *f* de bec ♦ *vt* brosser; (*also:* ~ **past,** ~ **against**) effleurer, frôler; **to have a** ~ **with sb** s'accrocher avec qn; **to have a** ~ **with the police** avoir maille à partir avec la police.
▶**brush aside** *vt* écarter, balayer.
▶**brush up** *vt* (*knowledge*) rafraîchir, réviser.
brushed [brʌʃt] *adj* (*TECH: steel, chrome etc*) brossé(e); (*nylon, denim etc*) gratté(e).
brush-off ['brʌʃɔf] *n* (*col*): **to give sb the** ~ envoyer qn promener.
brushwood ['brʌʃwud] *n* broussailles *fpl*.
brusque [bruːsk] *adj* (*person, manner*) brusque, cassant(e); (*tone*) sec(sèche), cassant(e).
Brussels ['brʌslz] *n* Bruxelles.
Brussels sprout *n* chou *m* de Bruxelles.
brutal ['bruːtl] *adj* brutal(e).
brutality [bruː'tælɪtɪ] *n* brutalité *f*.
brutalize ['bruːtəlaɪz] *vt* (*harden*) rendre brutal(e); (*ill-treat*) brutaliser.
brute [bruːt] *n* brute *f* ♦ *adj*: **by** ~ **force** par la force.
brutish ['bruːtɪʃ] *adj* grossier(ère), brutal(e).
BS *n abbr* (*US*: = *Bachelor of Science*) diplôme universitaire.

bs *abbr* = **bill of sale**.
BSA *n abbr* = *Boy Scouts of America*.
BSc *n abbr* = **Bachelor of Science**.
BSE *n abbr* (= *bovine spongiform encephalopathy*) ESB *f*, BSE *f*.
BSI *n abbr* (= *British Standards Institution*) association de normalisation.
BST *abbr* (= *British Summer Time*) heure *f* d'été.
Bt. *abbr* (*BRIT*) = **baronet**.
btu *n abbr* (= *British thermal unit*) btu (= *1054,2 joules*).
bubble ['bʌbl] *n* bulle *f* ♦ *vi* bouillonner, faire des bulles; (*sparkle, fig*) pétiller.
bubble bath *n* bain moussant.
bubblejet printer ['bʌbldʒɛt-] *n* imprimante *f* à bulle d'encre.
bubbly ['bʌblɪ] *adj* (*drink*) pétillant(e); (*person*) plein(e) de vitalité ♦ *n* (*col*) champ *m*.
Bucharest [buːkə'rɛst] *n* Bucarest.
buck [bʌk] *n* mâle *m* (*d'un lapin, lièvre, daim etc*); (*US col*) dollar *m* ♦ *vi* ruer, lancer une ruade; **to pass the ~ (to sb)** se décharger de la responsabilité (sur qn).
▶**buck up** *vi* (*cheer up*) reprendre du poil de la bête, se remonter ♦ *vt*: **to ~ one's ideas up** se reprendre.
bucket ['bʌkɪt] *n* seau *m* ♦ *vi* (*BRIT col*): **the rain is ~ing (down)** il pleut à verse.

Buckingham Palace *est la résidence officielle londonienne du souverain britannique depuis 1762. Construit en 1703, il fut à l'origine le palais du duc de Buckingham. Il a été partiellement reconstruit au début du siècle.*

buckle ['bʌkl] *n* boucle *f* ♦ *vt* boucler, attacher; (*warp*) tordre, gauchir; (: *wheel*) voiler.
▶**buckle down** *vi* s'y mettre.
Bucks [bʌks] *abbr* (*BRIT*) = **Buckinghamshire**.
bud [bʌd] *n* bourgeon *m*; (*of flower*) bouton *m* ♦ *vi* bourgeonner; (*flower*) éclore.
Budapest [bjuːdə'pɛst] *n* Budapest.
Buddha ['budə] *n* Bouddha *m*.
Buddhism ['budɪzəm] *n* bouddhisme *m*.
Buddhist ['budɪst] *adj* bouddhiste ♦ *n* Bouddhiste *m/f*.
budding ['bʌdɪŋ] *adj* (*flower*) en bouton; (*poet etc*) en herbe; (*passion etc*) naissant(e).
buddy ['bʌdɪ] *n* (*US*) copain *m*.
budge [bʌdʒ] *vt* faire bouger ♦ *vi* bouger.
budgerigar ['bʌdʒərɪgaː*] *n* perruche *f*.
budget ['bʌdʒɪt] *n* budget *m* ♦ *vi*: **to ~ for sth** inscrire qch au budget; **I'm on a tight ~** je dois faire attention à mon budget.
budgie ['bʌdʒɪ] *n* budget *m* = **budgerigar**.
Buenos Aires ['bweɪnɔs'aɪrɪz] *n* Buenos Aires.
buff [bʌf] *adj* (couleur *f*) chamois *m* ♦ *n* (*enthusiast*) mordu/e.
buffalo, *pl* ~ or ~**es** ['bʌfələu] *n* buffle *m*; (*US*) bison *m*.
buffer ['bʌfə*] *n* tampon *m*; (*COMPUT*) mémoire *f* tampon.

buffering ['bʌfərɪŋ] *n* (*COMPUT*) mise *f* en mémoire tampon.
buffer state *n* état *m* tampon.
buffer zone *n* zone *f* tampon.
buffet *n* ['bufeɪ] (*food, BRIT*: *bar*) buffet *m* ♦ *vt* ['bʌfɪt] gifler, frapper; secouer, ébranler.
buffet car *n* (*BRIT RAIL*) voiture-bar *f*.
buffet lunch *n* lunch *m*.
buffoon [bə'fuːn] *n* buffon *m*, pitre *m*.
bug [bʌg] *n* (*insect*) punaise *f*; (: *gen*) insecte *m*, bestiole *f*; (*fig*: *germ*) virus *m*, microbe *m*; (*spy device*) dispositif *m* d'écoute (électronique), micro clandestin; (*COMPUT*: *of program*) erreur *f*; (: *of equipment*) défaut *m* ♦ *vt* (*room*) poser des micros dans; (*col*: *annoy*) embêter; **I've got the travel ~** (*fig*) j'ai le virus du voyage.
bugbear ['bʌgbɛə*] *n* cauchemar *m*, bête noire.
bugger ['bʌgə*] (*col!*) *n* salaud *m* (!); connard *m* (!) ♦ *vb*: ~ **off!** tire-toi! (!); ~ (**it**)! merde! (!).
bugle ['bjuːgl] *n* clairon *m*.
build [bɪld] *n* (*of person*) carrure *f*, charpente *f* ♦ *vt* (*pt, pp* **built** [bɪlt]) construire, bâtir.
▶**build on** *vt fus* (*fig*) tirer parti de, partir de.
▶**build up** *vt* accumuler, amasser; (*business*) développer; (*reputation*) bâtir; (*increase: production*) développer, accroître.
builder ['bɪldə*] *n* entrepreneur *m*.
building ['bɪldɪŋ] *n* construction *f*; (*structure*) bâtiment *m*, construction; (: *residential, offices*) immeuble *m*.
building contractor *n* entrepreneur *m* (en bâtiment).
building industry *n* (industrie *f* du) bâtiment *m*.
building site *n* chantier *m* (de construction).
building society *n* (*BRIT*) société *f* de crédit immobilier.

Une **building society** *est une mutuelle dont les épargnants et emprunteurs sont les propriétaires. Ces mutuelles offrent deux services principaux: on peut y avoir un compte d'épargne duquel on peut retirer son argent sur demande ou moyennant un court préavis; et on peut également y faire des emprunts à long terme, par exemple pour acheter une maison. Les building societies ont eu jusqu'en 1985 le quasi-monopole des comptes d'épargne et des prêts immobiliers, mais les banques ont maintenant une part importante de ce marché.*

building trade *n* = **building industry**.
build-up ['bɪldʌp] *n* (*of gas etc*) accumulation *f*; (*publicity*): **to give sb/sth a good ~** faire de la pub pour qn/qch.
built [bɪlt] *pt, pp of* **build**.
built-in ['bɪlt'ɪn] *adj* (*cupboard*) encastré(e); (*device*) incorporé(e); intégré(e).
built-up area ['bɪltʌp-] *n* agglomération (ur-

baine); zone urbanisée.

bulb [bʌlb] n (BOT) bulbe m, oignon m; (ELEC) ampoule f.

bulbous ['bʌlbəs] adj bulbeux(euse).

Bulgaria [bʌl'gɛərɪə] n Bulgarie f.

Bulgarian [bʌl'gɛərɪən] adj bulgare ♦ n Bulgare m/f; (LING) bulgare m.

bulge [bʌldʒ] n renflement m, gonflement m; (in birth rate, sales) brusque augmentation f ♦ vi faire saillie; présenter un renflement; **to be bulging with** être plein(e) à craquer de.

bulimia [bə'lɪmɪə] n boulimie f.

bulk [bʌlk] n masse f, volume m; **in ~** (COMM) en gros, en vrac; **the ~ of** la plus grande or grosse partie de.

bulk buying [-'baɪɪŋ] n achat m en gros.

bulk carrier n cargo m.

bulkhead ['bʌlkhɛd] n cloison f (étanche).

bulky ['bʌlkɪ] adj volumineux(euse), encombrant(e).

bull [bul] n taureau m; (STOCK EXCHANGE) haussier m; (REL) bulle f.

bulldog ['buldɔg] n bouledogue m.

bulldoze ['buldəuz] vt passer or raser au bulldozer; **I was ~d into doing it** (fig: col) on m'a forcé la main.

bulldozer ['buldəuzə*] n bulldozer m.

bullet ['bulɪt] n balle f (de fusil etc).

bulletin ['bulɪtɪn] n bulletin m, communiqué m.

bulletin board n (COMPUT) messagerie f (électronique).

bulletproof ['bulɪtpru:f] adj à l'épreuve des balles; **~ vest** gilet m pare-balles.

bullfight ['bulfaɪt] n corrida f, course f de taureaux.

bullfighter ['bulfaɪtə*] n torero m.

bullfighting ['bulfaɪtɪŋ] n tauromachie f.

bullion ['buljən] n or m or argent m en lingots.

bullock ['buljək] n bœuf m.

bullring ['bulrɪŋ] n arène f.

bull's-eye ['bulzaɪ] n centre m (de la cible).

bullshit ['bulʃɪt] (col!) n connerie(s) f(pl) (!) ♦ vt raconter des conneries à (!) ♦ vi déconner (!).

bully ['bulɪ] n brute f, tyran m ♦ vt tyranniser, rudoyer; (frighten) intimider.

bullying ['bulɪŋ] n brimades fpl.

bum [bʌm] n (col: backside) derrière m; (: tramp) vagabond/e, traîne-savates m/f inv; (: idler) glandeur m.

▶**bum around** vi (col) vagabonder.

bumblebee ['bʌmblbi:] n bourdon m.

bumf [bʌmf] n (col: forms etc) paperasses fpl.

bump [bʌmp] n (blow) coup m, choc m; (jolt) cahot m; (on road etc, on head) bosse f ♦ vt heurter, cogner; (car) emboutir.

▶**bump along** vi avancer en cahotant.

▶**bump into** vt fus rentrer dans; (col: meet) tomber sur.

bumper ['bʌmpə*] n pare-chocs m inv ♦ adj: ~ **crop/harvest** récolte/moisson exception-

nelle.

bumper cars npl (US) autos tamponneuses.

bumph [bʌmf] n = **bumf**.

bumptious ['bʌmpʃəs] adj suffisant(e), prétentieux(euse).

bumpy ['bʌmpɪ] adj cahoteux(euse); **it was a ~ flight/ride** on a été secoués dans l'avion/la voiture.

bun [bʌn] n petit pain au lait; (of hair) chignon m.

bunch [bʌntʃ] n (of flowers) bouquet m; (of keys) trousseau m; (of bananas) régime m; (of people) groupe m; ~ **of grapes** grappe f de raisin.

bundle ['bʌndl] n paquet m ♦ vt (also: ~ up) faire un paquet de; (put): **to ~ sth/sb into** fourrer or enfourner qch/qn dans.

▶**bundle off** vt (person) faire sortir (en toute hâte); expédier.

▶**bundle out** vt éjecter, sortir (sans ménagements).

bun fight n (BRIT col) réception f; (tea party) thé m.

bung [bʌŋ] n bonde f, bouchon m ♦ vt (BRIT: throw: also: ~ **into**) flanquer; (also: ~ **up**: pipe, hole) boucher; **my nose is ~ed up** j'ai le nez bouché.

bungalow ['bʌŋgələu] n bungalow m.

bungee jumping ['bʌndʒi:'dʒʌmpɪŋ] n saut m à l'élastique.

bungle ['bʌŋgl] vt bâcler, gâcher.

bunion ['bʌnjən] n oignon m (au pied).

bunk [bʌŋk] n couchette f; (BRIT col): **to do a ~** mettre les bouts or les voiles.

▶**bunk off** vi (BRIT col: SCOL) sécher (les cours); **I'll ~ off at 3 o'clock this afternoon** je vais mettre les bouts or les voiles à 3 heures cet après-midi.

bunk beds npl lits superposés.

bunker ['bʌŋkə*] n (coal store) soute f à charbon; (MIL, GOLF) bunker m.

bunny ['bʌnɪ] n (also: ~ **rabbit**) Jeannot m lapin.

bunny girl n (BRIT) hôtesse de cabaret.

bunny hill n (US SKI) piste f pour débutants.

bunting ['bʌntɪŋ] n pavoisement m, drapeaux mpl.

buoy [bɔɪ] n bouée f.

▶**buoy up** vt faire flotter; (fig) soutenir, épauler.

buoyancy ['bɔɪənsɪ] n (of ship) flottabilité f.

buoyant ['bɔɪənt] adj (ship) flottable; (carefree) gai(e), plein(e) d'entrain; (COMM: market) actif(ive); (: prices, currency) soutenu(e).

burden ['bə:dn] n fardeau m, charge f ♦ vt charger; (oppress) accabler, surcharger; **to be a ~ to sb** être un fardeau pour qn.

bureau, pl ~**x** ['bjuərəu, -z] n (BRIT: writing desk) bureau m, secrétaire m; (US: chest of drawers) commode f; (office) bureau, office m.

bureaucracy [bjuə'rɔkrəsɪ] n bureaucratie f.

bureaucrat ['bjuərəkræt] *n* bureaucrate *m/f*, rond-de-cuir *m*.
bureaucratic [bjuərə'krætık] *adj* bureaucratique.
burgeon ['bɜːdʒən] *vi* (*fig*) être en expansion rapide.
burger ['bɜːgə*] *n* hamburger *m*.
burglar ['bɜːglə*] *n* cambrioleur *m*.
burglar alarm *n* sonnerie *f* d'alarme.
burglarize ['bɜːgləraız] *vt* (*US*) cambrioler.
burglary ['bɜːglərı] *n* cambriolage *m*.
burgle ['bɜːgl] *vt* cambrioler.
Burgundy ['bɜːgəndı] *n* Bourgogne *f*.
burial ['berıəl] *n* enterrement *m*.
burial ground *n* cimetière *m*.
burlesque [bɜː'lesk] *n* caricature *f*, parodie *f*.
burly ['bɜːlı] *adj* de forte carrure, costaud(e).
Burma ['bɜːmə] *n* Birmanie *f*; *see also* **Myanmar**.
Burmese [bɜː'miːz] *adj* birman(e), de Birmanie ♦ *n* (*pl inv*) Birman/e; (*LING*) birman *m*.
burn [bɜːn] *vt*, *vi* (*pt*, *pp* **burned** *or* **burnt** [bɜːnt]) brûler ♦ *n* brûlure *f*; **the cigarette ~t a hole in her dress** la cigarette a fait un trou dans sa robe; **I've ~t myself!** je me suis brûlé(e)!
▶**burn down** *vt* incendier, détruire par le feu.
▶**burn out** *vt* (*subj: writer etc*): **to ~ o.s. out** s'user (à force de travailler).
burner ['bɜːnə*] *n* brûleur *m*.
burning ['bɜːnıŋ] *adj* (*building, forest*) en flammes; (*issue, question*) brûlant(e).
burnish ['bɜːnıʃ] *vt* polir.

Burns Night *est une fête qui a lieu le 25 janvier, à la mémoire du poète écossais Robert Burns (1759-1796), à l'occasion de laquelle les Écossais partout dans le monde organisent un souper, en général arrosé de whisky. Le plat principal est toujours le haggis, servi avec de la purée de pommes de terre et de la purée de rutabagas. On apporte le haggis au son des cornemuses et au cours du repas on lit des poèmes de Burns et on chante ses chansons.*

---

burnt [bɜːnt] *pt*, *pp of* **burn**.
burnt sugar *n* (*BRIT*) caramel *m*.
burp [bɜːp] (*col*) *n* rot *m* ♦ *vi* roter.
burrow ['bʌrəu] *n* terrier *m* ♦ *vt* creuser.
bursar ['bɜːsə*] *n* économe *m/f*; (*BRIT: student*) boursier/ère.
bursary ['bɜːsərı] *n* (*BRIT*) bourse *f* (d'études).
burst [bɜːst] *vb* (*pt*, *pp* **burst**) *vt* faire éclater ♦ *vi* éclater ♦ *n* explosion *f*; (*also*: ~ **pipe**) fuite *f* (*due à une rupture*); ~ **of energy** déploiement soudain d'énergie, activité soudaine; ~ **of laughter** éclat *m* de rire; **a ~ of applause** une salve d'applaudissement; **a ~ of speed** une pointe de vitesse; ~ **blood vessel** rupture *f* de vaisseau sanguin; **the river has ~ its banks** le cours d'eau est sorti de son lit; **to ~ into flames** s'enflammer

soudainement; **to ~ out laughing** éclater de rire; **to ~ into tears** fondre en larmes; **to ~ open** *vi* s'ouvrir violemment *or* soudainement; **to be ~ing with** être plein(e) (à craquer) de; regorger de.
▶**burst into** *vt fus* (*room etc*) faire irruption dans.
▶**burst out of** *vt fus* sortir précipitamment de.
bury ['berı] *vt* enterrer; **to ~ one's face in one's hands** se couvrir le visage de ses mains; **to ~ one's head in the sand** (*fig*) pratiquer la politique de l'autruche; **to ~ the hatchet** (*fig*) enterrer la hache de guerre.
bus, ~**es** [bʌs, 'bʌsız] *n* autobus *m*.
busboy ['bʌsbɔı] *n* (*US*) aide-serveur *m*.
bush [buʃ] *n* buisson *m*; (*scrub land*) brousse *f*.
bushed [buʃt] *adj* (*col*) crevé(e), claqué(e).
bushel ['buʃl] *n* boisseau *m*.
bushfire ['buʃfaıə*] *n* feu *m* de brousse.
bushy ['buʃı] *adj* broussailleux(euse), touffu(e).
busily ['bızılı] *adv*: **to be ~ doing sth** s'affairer à faire qch.
business ['bıznıs] *n* (*matter, firm*) affaire *f*; (*trading*) affaires *fpl*; (*job, duty*) travail *m*; **to be away on ~** être en déplacement d'affaires; **I'm here on ~** je suis là pour affaires; **he's in the insurance/transport ~** il est dans les assurances/les transports; **to do ~ with sb** traiter avec qn; **it's none of my ~** cela ne me regarde pas, ce ne sont pas mes affaires; **he means ~** il ne plaisante pas, il est sérieux.
business address *n* adresse professionnelle *or* au bureau.
business card *n* carte *f* de visite (professionnelle).
businesslike ['bıznıslaık] *adj* sérieux(euse); efficace.
businessman ['bıznısmən] *n* homme *m* d'affaires.
business trip *n* voyage *m* d'affaires.
businesswoman ['bıznıswumən] *n* femme *f* d'affaires.
busker ['bʌskə*] *n* (*BRIT*) artiste ambulant(e).
bus lane *n* (*BRIT*) voie réservée aux autobus.
bus shelter *n* abribus *m*.
bus station *n* gare routière.
bus stop *n* arrêt *m* d'autobus.
bust [bʌst] *n* buste *m* ♦ *adj* (*col: broken*) fichu(e), fini(e) ♦ *vt* (*col: POLICE: arrest*) pincer; **to go ~** faire faillite.
bustle ['bʌsl] *n* remue-ménage *m*, affairement *m* ♦ *vi* s'affairer, se démener.
bustling ['bʌslıŋ] *adj* (*person*) affairé(e); (*town*) très animé(e).
bust-up ['bʌstʌp] *n* (*BRIT col*) engueulade *f*.
busty ['bʌstı] *adj* (*col*) à la poitrine plantureuse.
busy ['bızı] *adj* occupé(e); (*shop, street*) très fréquenté(e); (*US: telephone, line*) occupé

♦ *vt*: **to ~ o.s.** s'occuper; **he's a ~ man** (*normally*) c'est un homme très pris; (*temporarily*) il est très pris.
busybody ['bɪzɪbɔdɪ] *n* mouche *f* du coche, âme *f* charitable.
busy signal *n* (*US*) tonalité *f* occupé.

═══════════════════════════ *KEYWORD*

but [bʌt] *conj* mais; **I'd love to come, ~ I'm busy** j'aimerais venir mais je suis occupé
♦ *prep* (*apart from, except*) sauf, excepté; **nothing ~** rien d'autre que; **we've had nothing ~ trouble** nous n'avons eu que des ennuis; **no-one ~ him can do it** lui seul peut le faire; **~ for you/your help** sans toi/ton aide; **anything ~ that** tout sauf *or* excepté ça, tout mais pas ça; **the last ~ one** (*BRIT*) l'avant-dernier(ère)
♦ *adv* (*just, only*) ne ... que; **she's ~ a child** elle n'est qu'une enfant; **had I ~ known** si seulement j'avais su; **all ~ finished** pratiquement terminé; **anything ~ finished** tout sauf fini, très loin d'être fini.

┕─────────────────────────────────┙

butane ['bjuːteɪn] *n* (*also*: **~ gas**) butane *m*.
butch [butʃ] *adj* (*col: man*) costaud, viril; (*: woman*) costaude, masculine.
butcher ['butʃə*] *n* boucher *m* ♦ *vt* massacrer; (*cattle etc for meat*) tuer; **~'s (shop)** boucherie *f*.
butler ['bʌtlə*] *n* maître *m* d'hôtel.
butt [bʌt] *n* (*cask*) gros tonneau; (*thick end*) (gros) bout; (*of gun*) crosse *f*; (*of cigarette*) mégot *m*; (*BRIT fig: target*) cible *f* ♦ *vt* donner un coup de tête à.
►**butt in** *vi* (*interrupt*) interrompre.
butter ['bʌtə*] *n* beurre *m* ♦ *vt* beurrer.
buttercup ['bʌtəkʌp] *n* bouton *m* d'or.
butter dish *n* beurrier *m*.
butterfingers ['bʌtəfɪŋgəz] *n* (*col*) maladroit/e.
butterfly ['bʌtəflaɪ] *n* papillon *m*; (*SWIMMING*: *also*: **~ stroke**) brasse *f* papillon.
buttocks ['bʌtəks] *npl* fesses *fpl*.
button ['bʌtn] *n* bouton *m* ♦ *vt* (*also*: **~ up**) boutonner ♦ *vi* se boutonner.
buttonhole ['bʌtnhəul] *n* boutonnière *f* ♦ *vt* accrocher, arrêter, retenir.
buttress ['bʌtrɪs] *n* contrefort *m*.
buxom ['bʌksəm] *adj* aux formes avantageuses *or* épanouies, bien galbé(e).
buy [baɪ] *vb* (*pt*, *pp* **bought** [bɔːt]) *vt* acheter; (*COMM: company*) (r)acheter ♦ *n*: **that was a good/bad ~** c'était un bon/mauvais achat; **to ~ sb sth/sth from sb** acheter qch à qn; **to ~ sb a drink** offrir un verre *or* à boire à qn.
►**buy back** *vt* racheter.
►**buy in** *vt* (*BRIT: goods*) acheter, faire venir.
►**buy into** *vt fus* (*BRIT COMM*) acheter des actions de.
►**buy off** *vt* (*bribe*) acheter.
►**buy out** *vt* (*partner*) désintéresser; (*busi-*

ness) racheter.
►**buy up** *vt* acheter en bloc, rafler.
buyer ['baɪə*] *n* acheteur/euse; **~'s market** marché *m* favorable aux acheteurs.
buy-out ['baɪaut] *n* (*COMM*) rachat *m* (*d'entreprise*).
buzz [bʌz] *n* bourdonnement *m*; (*col: phone call*) coup *m* de fil ♦ *vi* bourdonner ♦ *vt* (*call on intercom*) appeler; (*with buzzer*) sonner; (*AVIAT: plane, building*) raser; **my head is ~ing** j'ai la tête qui bourdonne.
►**buzz off** *vi* (*col*) s'en aller, ficher le camp.
buzzard ['bʌzəd] *n* buse *f*.
buzzer ['bʌzə*] *n* timbre *m* électrique.
buzz word *n* (*col*) mot *m* à la mode *or* dans le vent.

═══════════════════════════ *KEYWORD*

by [baɪ] *prep* **1** (*referring to cause, agent*) par, de; **killed ~ lightning** tué par la foudre; **surrounded ~ a fence** entouré d'une barrière; **a painting ~ Picasso** un tableau de Picasso
2 (*referring to method, manner, means*): **~ bus/car** en autobus/voiture; **~ train** par le *or* en train; **to pay ~ cheque** payer par chèque; **~ saving hard, he ...** à force d'économiser, il ...
3 (*via, through*) par; **we came ~ Dover** nous sommes venus par Douvres
4 (*close to, past*) à côté de; **the house ~ the school** la maison à côté de l'école; **a holiday ~ the sea** des vacances au bord de la mer; **she sat ~ his bed** elle était assise à son chevet; **she went ~ me** elle est passée à côté de moi; **I go ~ the post office every day** je passe devant la poste tous les jours
5 (*with time: not later than*) avant; (*: during*): **~ daylight** à la lumière du jour; **~ night** la nuit, de nuit; **~ 4 o'clock** avant 4 heures; **~ this time tomorrow** d'ici demain à la même heure; **~ the time I got here it was already too late** lorsque je suis arrivé il était déjà trop tard
6 (*amount*) à; **~ the kilo/metre** au kilo/au mètre; **paid ~ the hour** payé à l'heure; **to increase** *etc* **~ the hour** augmenter *etc* d'heure en heure
7 (*MATH, measure*): **to divide/multiply ~ 3** diviser/multiplier par 3; **a room 3 metres ~ 4** une pièce de 3 mètres sur 4; **it's broader ~ a metre** c'est plus large d'un mètre; **the bullet missed him ~ inches** la balle est passée à quelques centimètres de lui; **one ~ one** un à un; **little ~ little** petit à petit, peu à peu
8 (*according to*) d'après, selon; **it's 3 o'clock ~ my watch** il est 3 heures à ma montre; **it's all right ~ me** je n'ai rien contre
9: (**all**) **~ oneself** *etc* tout(e) seul(e)
10: **~ the way** au fait, à propos
♦ *adv* **1** *see* **go**; **pass** *etc*
2: **~ and ~** un peu plus tard, bientôt; **~ and large** dans l'ensemble.

bye(-bye) ['baɪ('baɪ)] *excl* au revoir!, salut!
by(e)-law ['baɪlɔ:] *n* arrêté municipal.
by-election ['baɪɪlɛkʃən] *n* (*BRIT*) élection (législative) partielle.
Byelorussia [bjɛləu'rʌʃə] *n* Biélorussie *f*.
Byelorussian [bjɛləu'rʌʃən] *adj*, *n* = **Belorussian**.
bygone ['baɪgɔn] *adj* passé(e) ♦ *n*: **let ~s be ~s** passons l'éponge, oublions le passé.
bypass ['baɪpɑ:s] *n* (route *f* de) contournement *m*; (*MED*) pontage *m* ♦ *vt* éviter.
by-product ['baɪprɔdʌkt] *n* sous-produit *m*, dérivé *m*; (*fig*) conséquence *f* secondaire, retombée *f*.
byre ['baɪə*] *n* (*BRIT*) étable *f* (à vaches).
bystander ['baɪstændə*] *n* spectateur/trice, badaud/e.
byte [baɪt] *n* (*COMPUT*) octet *m*.
byway ['baɪweɪ] *n* chemin détourné.
byword ['baɪwə:d] *n*: **to be a ~ for** être synonyme de (*fig*).
by-your-leave ['baɪjɔ:'li:v] *n*: **without so much as a ~** sans même demander la permission.

C c

C, c [si:] *n* (*letter*) C, c *m*; (*SCOL: mark*) C; (*MUS*): **C** do *m*; **C for Charlie** C comme Célestin.
C *abbr* (= *Celsius, centigrade*) C.
c *abbr* (= *century*) s.; (= *circa*) v.; (*US etc*) = **cent(s)**.
CA *n abbr* = **Central America**; (*BRIT*) = **chartered accountant** ♦ *abbr* (*US*) = **California**.
ca. *abbr* (= *circa*) v.
c/a *abbr* = **capital account, credit account, current account**.
CAA *n abbr* (*BRIT*: = *Civil Aviation Authority, US*: = *Civil Aeronautics Authority*) *direction de l'aviation civile*.
CAB *n abbr* (*BRIT*) = **Citizens' Advice Bureau**.
cab [kæb] *n* taxi *m*; (*of train, truck*) cabine *f*; (*horse-drawn*) fiacre *m*.
cabaret ['kæbəreɪ] *n* attractions *fpl*, spectacle *m* de cabaret.
cabbage ['kæbɪdʒ] *n* chou *m*.
cabbie, cabby ['kæbɪ] *n* (*col*), **cab driver** *n* taxi *m*, chauffeur *m* de taxi.
cabin ['kæbɪn] *n* cabane *f*, hutte *f*; (*on ship*) cabine *f*.
cabin cruiser *n* yacht *m* (à moteur).
cabinet ['kæbɪnɪt] *n* (*POL*) cabinet *m*; (*furniture*) petit meuble à tiroirs et rayons; (*also*: **display ~**) vitrine *f*, petite armoire vitrée.
cabinet-maker ['kæbɪnɪt'meɪkə*] *n* ébéniste

m.
cabinet minister *n* ministre *m* (*membre du cabinet*).
cable ['keɪbl] *n* câble *m* ♦ *vt* câbler, télégraphier.
cable-car ['keɪblkɑ:*] *n* téléphérique *m*.
cablegram ['keɪblgræm] *n* câblogramme *m*.
cable railway *n* (*BRIT*) funiculaire *m*.
cable television *n* télévision *f* par câble.
cache [kæʃ] *n* cachette *f*; **a ~ of food** *etc* un dépôt secret de provisions *etc*, une cachette contenant des provisions *etc*.
cackle ['kækl] *vi* caqueter.
cactus, *pl* **cacti** ['kæktəs, -taɪ] *n* cactus *m*.
CAD *n abbr* (= *computer-aided design*) CAO *f*.
caddie ['kædɪ] *n* caddie ® *m*.
cadet [kə'dɛt] *n* (*MIL*) élève *m* officier; **police ~** élève agent de police.
cadge [kædʒ] *vt* (*col*) se faire donner; **to ~ a meal (off sb)** se faire inviter à manger (par qn).
cadger ['kædʒə*] *n* pique-assiette *m/f inv*, tapeur/euse.
cadre ['kædrɪ] *n* cadre *m*.
Caesarean, (*US*) Cesarean [si:'zɛərɪən] *adj*: **~ (section)** césarienne *f*.
CAF *abbr* (*BRIT*: = *cost and freight*) C et F.
café ['kæfeɪ] *n* ≈ café(-restaurant) *m* (*sans alcool*).
cafeteria [kæfɪ'tɪərɪə] *n* cafeteria *f*.
caffein(e) ['kæfi:n] *n* caféine *f*.
cage [keɪdʒ] *n* cage *f* ♦ *vt* mettre en cage.
cagey ['keɪdʒɪ] *adj* (*col*) réticent(e); méfiant(e).
cagoule [kə'gu:l] *n* K-way *m* ®.
cahoots [kə'hu:ts] *n*: **to be in ~ (with)** être de mèche (avec).
CAI *n abbr* (= *computer-aided instruction*) EAO *m*.
Cairo ['kaɪərəu] *n* Le Caire.
cajole [kə'dʒəul] *vt* couvrir de flatteries *or* de gentillesses.
cake [keɪk] *n* gâteau *m*; **~ of soap** savonnette *f*; **it's a piece of ~** (*col*) c'est un jeu d'enfant; **he wants to have his ~ and eat it (too)** (*fig*) il veut tout avoir.
caked [keɪkt] *adj*: **~ with** raidi(e) par, couvert(e) d'une croûte de.
cake shop *n* pâtisserie *f*.
Cal. *abbr* (*US*) = **California**.
calamitous [kə'læmɪtəs] *adj* catastrophique, désastreux(euse).
calamity [kə'læmɪtɪ] *n* calamité *f*, désastre *m*.
calcium ['kælsɪəm] *n* calcium *m*.
calculate ['kælkjuleɪt] *vt* calculer; (*estimate: chances, effect*) évaluer.
▶**calculate on** *vt fus*: **to ~ on sth/on doing sth** compter sur qch/faire qch.
calculated ['kælkjuleɪtɪd] *adj* (*insult, action*) délibéré(e); **a ~ risk** un risque pris en toute connaissance de cause.

calculating ['kælkjuleɪtɪŋ] *adj* calculateur(trice).
calculation [kælkju'leɪʃən] *n* calcul *m*.
calculator ['kælkjuleɪtə*] *n* machine *f* à calculer, calculatrice *f*.
calculus ['kælkjuləs] *n* analyse *f* (mathématique), calcul infinitésimal; **integral/differential** ~ calcul intégral/différentiel.
calendar ['kæləndə*] *n* calendrier *m*.
calendar month *n* mois *m* (de calendrier).
calendar year *n* année civile.
calf, *pl* **calves** [kɑːf, kɑːvz] *n* (*of cow*) veau *m*; (*of other animals*) petit *m*; (*also*: ~**skin**) veau *m*, vachette *f*; (*ANAT*) mollet *m*.
caliber ['kælɪbə*] *n* (*US*) = **calibre**.
calibrate ['kælɪbreɪt] *vt* (*gun etc*) calibrer; (*scale of measuring instrument*) étalonner.
calibre, (*US*) **caliber** ['kælɪbə*] *n* calibre *m*.
calico ['kælɪkəʊ] *n* (*BRIT*) calicot *m*; (*US*) indienne *f*.
Calif. *abbr* (*US*) = *California*.
California [kælɪ'fɔːnɪə] *n* Californie *f*.
calipers ['kælɪpəz] *npl* (*US*) = **callipers**.
call [kɔːl] *vt* (*gen, also TEL*) appeler; (*announce: flight*) annoncer; (*meeting*) convoquer; (*strike*) lancer ♦ *vi* appeler; (*visit: also*: ~ **in,** ~ **round**): **to** ~ **(for)** passer (prendre) ♦ *n* (*shout*) appel *m*, cri *m*; (*summons: for flight etc, fig: lure*) appel; (*visit*) visite *f*; (*also*: **telephone** ~) coup *m* de téléphone; communication *f*; **to be on** ~ être de permanence; **she's** ~**ed Suzanne** elle s'appelle Suzanne; **who is** ~**ing?** (*TEL*) qui est à l'appareil?; **London** ~**ing** (*RADIO*) ici Londres; **please give me a** ~ **at 7** appelez-moi à 7 heures; **to make a** ~ téléphoner, passer un coup de fil; **to pay a** ~ **on sb** rendre visite à qn, passer voir qn; **there's not much** ~ **for these items** ces articles ne sont pas très demandés.
▶**call at** *vt fus* (*subj: ship*) faire escale à; (*: train*) s'arrêter à.
▶**call back** *vi* (*return*) repasser; (*TEL*) rappeler ♦ *vt* (*TEL*) rappeler.
▶**call for** *vt fus* demander.
▶**call in** *vt* (*doctor, expert, police*) appeler, faire venir.
▶**call off** *vt* annuler; **the strike was** ~**ed off** l'ordre de grève a été rapporté.
▶**call on** *vt fus* (*visit*) rendre visite à, passer voir; (*request*): **to** ~ **on sb to do** inviter qn à faire.
▶**call out** *vi* pousser un cri *or* des cris ♦ *vt* (*doctor, police, troops*) appeler.
▶**call up** *vt* (*MIL*) appeler, mobiliser.
Callanetics [kælə'netɪks] *n* ® stretching *m*.
callbox ['kɔːlbɒks] *n* (*BRIT*) cabine *f* téléphonique.
call centre *n* centre *m* d'appels.
caller ['kɔːlə*] *n* personne *f* qui appelle; visiteur *m*; **hold the line,** ~! (*TEL*) ne quittez pas, Monsieur (*or* Madame)!
call girl *n* call-girl *f*.

call-in ['kɔːlɪn] *n* (*US RADIO, TV*) programme *m* à ligne ouverte.
calling ['kɔːlɪŋ] *n* vocation *f*; (*trade, occupation*) état *m*.
calling card *n* (*US*) carte *f* de visite.
callipers, (*US*) **calipers** ['kælɪpəz] *npl* (*MATH*) compas *m*; (*MED*) appareil *m* orthopédique; gouttière *f*; étrier *m*.
callous ['kæləs] *adj* dur(e), insensible.
callousness ['kæləsnɪs] *n* dureté *f*, manque *m* de cœur, insensibilité *f*.
callow ['kæləʊ] *adj* sans expérience (de la vie).
calm [kɑːm] *adj* calme ♦ *n* calme *m* ♦ *vt* calmer, apaiser.
▶**calm down** *vi* se calmer, s'apaiser ♦ *vt* calmer, apaiser.
calmly ['kɑːmlɪ] *adv* calmement, avec calme.
calmness ['kɑːmnɪs] *n* calme *m*.
Calor gas ['kælə*-] *n* ® (*BRIT*) butane *m*, butagaz *m* ®.
calorie ['kælərɪ] *n* calorie *f*; **low** ~ **product** produit *m* pauvre en calories.
calve [kɑːv] *vi* vêler, mettre bas.
calves [kɑːvz] *npl of* **calf**.
CAM *n abbr* (= *computer-aided manufacturing*) FAO *f*.
camber ['kæmbə*] *n* (*of road*) bombement *m*.
Cambodia [kæm'bəʊdjə] *n* Cambodge *m*.
Cambodian [kæm'bəʊdɪən] *adj* cambodgien(ne) ♦ *n* Cambodgien/ne.
Cambs *abbr* (*BRIT*) = *Cambridgeshire*.
camcorder ['kæmkɔːdə*] *n* caméscope *m*.
came [keɪm] *pt of* **come**.
camel ['kæməl] *n* chameau *m*.
cameo ['kæmɪəʊ] *n* camée *m*.
camera ['kæmərə] *n* appareil *m* photo; (*CINE, TV*) caméra *f*; **35mm** ~ appareil 24 x 36 *or* petit format; **in** ~ à huis clos, en privé.
cameraman ['kæmərəmæn] *n* caméraman *m*.
Cameroon, Cameroun [kæmə'ruːn] *n* Cameroun *m*.
camouflage ['kæməflɑːʒ] *n* camouflage *m* ♦ *vt* camoufler.
camp [kæmp] *n* camp *m* ♦ *vi* camper; **to go** ~**ing** faire du camping.
campaign [kæm'peɪn] *n* (*MIL, POL etc*) campagne *f* ♦ *vi* (*also fig*) faire campagne; **to** ~ **for/against** militer pour/contre.
campaigner [kæm'peɪnə*] *n*: ~ **for** partisan/e de; ~ **against** opposant/e à.
campbed ['kæmp'bɛd] *n* (*BRIT*) lit *m* de camp.
camper ['kæmpə*] *n* campeur/euse.
camping ['kæmpɪŋ] *n* camping *m*.
camp(ing) site *n* (terrain *m* de) camping *m*.
campus ['kæmpəs] *n* campus *m*.
camshaft ['kæmʃɑːft] *n* arbre *m* à came.
can¹ [kæn] *aux vb see keyword* ♦ *n* (*of milk, oil, water*) bidon *m*; (*tin*) boîte *f* (de conserve) ♦ *vt* mettre en conserve; **a** ~ **of beer** une canette de bière; **he had to carry the** ~ (*BRIT col*) on lui a fait porter le chapeau.

===================== *KEYWORD*

can² [kæn] (*negative* **cannot**, **can't**; *conditional and pt* **could**) *aux vb* **1** (*be able to*) pouvoir; **you ~ do it if you try** vous pouvez le faire si vous essayez; **I ~'t hear you** je ne t'entends pas
2 (*know how to*) savoir; **I ~ swim/play tennis/drive** je sais nager/jouer au tennis/conduire; **~ you speak French?** parlez-vous français?
3 (*may*) pouvoir; **~ I use your phone?** puis-je me servir de votre téléphone?
4 (*expressing disbelief, puzzlement etc*): **it ~'t be true!** ce n'est pas possible!; **what CAN he want?** qu'est-ce qu'il peut bien vouloir?
5 (*expressing possibility, suggestion etc*): **he could be in the library** il est peut-être dans la bibliothèque; **she could have been delayed** il se peut qu'elle ait été retardée; **they could have forgotten** ils ont pu oublier.

Canada ['kænədə] *n* Canada *m*.
Canadian [kə'neɪdɪən] *adj* canadien(ne) ♦ *n* Canadien/ne.
canal [kə'næl] *n* canal *m*.
canary [kə'nɛərɪ] *n* canari *m*, serin *m*.
Canary Islands, Canaries [kə'nɛərɪz] *npl*: **the ~** les (îles *fpl*) Canaries *fpl*.
Canberra ['kænbərə] *n* Canberra.
cancel ['kænsəl] *vt* annuler; (*train*) supprimer; (*party, appointment*) décommander; (*cross out*) barrer, rayer; (*stamp*) oblitérer; (*cheque*) faire opposition à.
▶**cancel out** *vt* annuler; **they ~ each other out** ils s'annulent.
cancellation [kænsə'leɪʃən] *n* annulation *f*; suppression *f*; oblitération *f*; (*TOURISM*) réservation annulée, client *etc* qui s'est décommandé.
cancer ['kænsə*] *n* cancer *m*; **C~** (*sign*) le Cancer; **to be C~** être du Cancer.
cancerous ['kænsrəs] *adj* cancéreux(euse).
cancer patient *n* cancéreux/euse.
cancer research *n* recherche *f* contre le cancer.
C and F *abbr* (*BRIT*: = *cost and freight*) C et F.
candid ['kændɪd] *adj* (très) franc(franche), sincère.
candidacy ['kændɪdəsɪ] *n* candidature *f*.
candidate ['kændɪdeɪt] *n* candidat/e.
candidature ['kændɪdətʃə*] *n* (*BRIT*) = **candidacy**.
candied ['kændɪd] *adj* confit(e); **~ apple** (*US*) pomme caramélisée.
candle ['kændl] *n* bougie *f*; (*of tallow*) chandelle *f*; (*in church*) cierge *m*.
candlelight ['kændllaɪt] *n*: **by ~** à la lumière d'une bougie; (*dinner*) aux chandelles.
candlestick ['kændlstɪk] *n* (*also*: **candle holder**) bougeoir *m*; (*bigger, ornate*) chandelier *m*.
candour, (*US*) **candor** ['kændə*] *n* (grande)

franchise *or* sincérité.
C & W *n abbr* = **country and western (music)**.
candy ['kændɪ] *n* sucre candi; (*US*) bonbon *m*.
candy-floss ['kændɪflɔs] *n* (*BRIT*) barbe *f* à papa.
candy store *n* (*US*) confiserie *f*.
cane [keɪn] *n* canne *f*; (*for baskets, chairs etc*) rotin *m* ♦ *vt* (*BRIT SCOL*) administrer des coups de bâton à.
canine ['kænaɪn] *adj* canin(e).
canister ['kænɪstə*] *n* boîte *f* (*gén en métal*).
cannabis ['kænəbɪs] *n* (*drug*) cannabis *m*; (*also*: **~ plant**) chanvre indien.
canned ['kænd] *adj* (*food*) en boîte, en conserve; (*col: music*) enregistré(e); (*BRIT col: drunk*) bourré(e); (*US col: worker*) mis(e) à la porte.
cannibal ['kænɪbəl] *n* cannibale *m/f*, anthropophage *m/f*.
cannibalism ['kænɪbəlɪzəm] *n* cannibalisme *m*, anthropophagie *f*.
cannon, *pl* ~ *or* ~**s** ['kænən] *n* (*gun*) canon *m*.
cannonball ['kænənbɔːl] *n* boulet *m* de canon.
cannon fodder *n* chair *f* à canon.
cannot ['kænɔt] = **can not**.
canny ['kænɪ] *adj* madré(e), finaud(e).
canoe [kə'nuː] *n* pirogue *f*; (*SPORT*) canoë *m*.
canoeing [kə'nuːɪŋ] *n* (*sport*) canoë *m*.
canoeist [kə'nuːɪst] *n* canoéiste *m/f*.
canon ['kænən] *n* (*clergyman*) chanoine *m*; (*standard*) canon *m*.
canonize ['kænənaɪz] *vt* canoniser.
can opener [-'əʊpnə*] *n* ouvre-boîte *m*.
canopy ['kænəpɪ] *n* baldaquin *m*; dais *m*.
cant [kænt] *n* jargon *m* ♦ *vt, vi* pencher.
can't [kænt] = **can not**.
Cantab. *abbr* (*BRIT*: = *cantabrigiensis*) *of Cambridge*.
cantankerous [kæn'tæŋkərəs] *adj* querelleur(euse), acariâtre.
canteen [kæn'tiːn] *n* cantine *f*; (*BRIT*: *of cutlery*) ménagère *f*.
canter ['kæntə*] *n* petit galop ♦ *vi* aller au petit galop.
cantilever ['kæntɪliːvə*] *n* porte-à-faux *m inv*.
canvas ['kænvəs] *n* (*gen*) toile *f*; **under ~** (*camping*) sous la tente; (*NAUT*) toutes voiles dehors.
canvass ['kænvəs] *vt* (*POL: district*) faire la tournée électorale dans; (: *person*) solliciter le suffrage de; (*COMM: district*) prospecter; (*citizens, opinions*) sonder.
canvasser ['kænvəsə*] *n* (*POL*) agent électoral; (*COMM*) démarcheur *m*.
canvassing ['kænvəsɪŋ] *n* (*POL*) prospection électorale, démarche électoral; (*COMM*) démarchage, prospection.
canyon ['kænjən] *n* cañon *m*, gorge (profonde).
CAP *n abbr* (= *Common Agricultural Policy*) PAC *f*.
cap [kæp] *n* casquette *f*; (*for swimming*) bonnet

m de bain; (*of pen*) capuchon *m*; (*of bottle*) capsule *f*; (*BRIT: contraceptive: also:* Dutch ~) diaphragme *m*; (: *FOOTBALL*) sélection *f* pour l'équipe nationale ♦ *vt* capsuler; (*outdo*) surpasser; ~**ped with** coiffé(e) de; **and to** ~ **it all, he** ... (*BRIT*) pour couronner le tout, il ....

capability [keɪpə'bɪlɪtɪ] *n* aptitude *f*, capacité *f*.

capable ['keɪpəbl] *adj* capable; ~ **of** (*interpretation etc*) susceptible de.

capacious [kə'peɪʃəs] *adj* vaste.

capacity [kə'pæsɪtɪ] *n* (*of container*) capacité *f*, contenance *f*; (*ability*) aptitude *f*; **filled to** ~ plein(e); **in his** ~ **as** en sa qualité de; **this work is beyond my** ~ ce travail dépasse mes capacités; **in an advisory** ~ à titre consultatif; **to work at full** ~ travailler à plein rendement.

cape [keɪp] *n* (*garment*) cape *f*; (*GEO*) cap *m*.

Cape of Good Hope *n* cap *m* de Bonne Espérance.

caper ['keɪpə*] *n* (*CULIN: also:* ~**s**) câpre *f*.

Cape Town *n* Le Cap.

capita ['kæpɪtə] *see* **per capita**.

capital ['kæpɪtl] *n* (*also:* ~ **city**) capitale *f*; (*money*) capital *m*; (*also:* ~ **letter**) majuscule *f*.

capital account *n* balance *f* des capitaux; (*of country*) compte capital.

capital allowance *n* provision *f* pour amortissement.

capital assets *npl* immobilisations *fpl*.

capital expenditure *n* dépenses *fpl* d'équipement.

capital gains tax *n* impôt *m* sur les plus-values.

capital goods *n* biens *mpl* d'équipement.

capital-intensive ['kæpɪtlɪn'tɛnsɪv] *adj* à forte proportion de capitaux.

capitalism ['kæpɪtəlɪzəm] *n* capitalisme *m*.

capitalist ['kæpɪtəlɪst] *adj*, *n* capitaliste (*m/f*).

capitalize ['kæpɪtəlaɪz] *vt* (*provide with capital*) financer.

▶**capitalize on** *vt fus* (*fig*) profiter de.

capital punishment *n* peine capitale.

capital transfer tax *n* (*BRIT*) impôt *m* sur le transfert de propriété.

Capitol ['kæpɪtl] *n*: **the** ~ le Capitole.

> Le **Capitol** est le siège du **Congress**, à Washington. Il est situé sur Capitol Hill.

capitulate [kə'pɪtjuleɪt] *vi* capituler.

capitulation [kəpɪtju'leɪʃən] *n* capitulation *f*.

capricious [kə'prɪʃəs] *adj* capricieux(euse), fantasque.

Capricorn ['kæprɪkɔːn] *n* le Capricorne; **to be** ~ être du Capricorne.

caps [kæps] *abbr* = **capital letters**.

capsize [kæp'saɪz] *vt* faire chavirer ♦ *vi* chavirer.

capstan ['kæpstən] *n* cabestan *m*.

capsule ['kæpsjuːl] *n* capsule *f*.

Capt. *abbr* (= *captain*) Cne.

captain ['kæptɪn] *n* capitaine *m* ♦ *vt* commander, être le capitaine de.

caption ['kæpʃən] *n* légende *f*.

captivate ['kæptɪveɪt] *vt* captiver, fasciner.

captive ['kæptɪv] *adj*, *n* captif(ive).

captivity [kæp'tɪvɪtɪ] *n* captivité *f*.

captor ['kæptə*] *n* (*unlawful*) ravisseur *m*; (*lawful*): **his** ~**s** les gens (*or* ceux *etc*) qui l'ont arrêté.

capture ['kæptʃə*] *vt* capturer, prendre; (*attention*) capter ♦ *n* capture *f*.

car [kɑː*] *n* voiture *f*, auto *f*; (*US RAIL*) wagon *m*, voiture; **by** ~ en voiture.

Caracas [kə'rækəs] *n* Caracas.

carafe [kə'ræf] *n* carafe *f*.

carafe wine *n* (*in restaurant*) ≈ vin ouvert.

caramel ['kærəməl] *n* caramel *m*.

carat ['kærət] *n* carat *m*; **18** ~ **gold** or *m* à 18 carats.

caravan ['kærəvæn] *n* caravane *f*.

caravan site *n* (*BRIT*) camping *m* pour caravanes.

caraway ['kærəweɪ] *n*: ~ **seed** graine *f* de cumin, cumin *m*.

carbohydrates [kɑːbəʊ'haɪdreɪts] *npl* (*foods*) aliments *mpl* riches en hydrate de carbone.

carbolic acid [kɑː'bɒlɪk-] *n* phénol *m*.

car bomb *n* voiture piégée.

carbon ['kɑːbən] *n* carbone *m*.

carbonated ['kɑːbəneɪtɪd] *adj* (*drink*) gazeux(euse).

carbon copy *n* carbone *m*.

carbon dioxide *n* gas *m* carbonique, dioxyde *m* de carbone.

carbon paper *n* papier *m* carbone.

carbon ribbon *n* ruban *m* carbone.

car boot sale *n* marché aux puces où des particuliers vendent des objets entreposés dans le coffre de leur voiture.

carburettor, (*US*) **carburetor** [kɑːbju'rɛtə*] *n* carburateur *m*.

carcass ['kɑːkəs] *n* carcasse *f*.

carcinogenic [kɑːsɪnə'dʒɛnɪk] *adj* cancérigène.

card [kɑːd] *n* carte *f*; (*membership* ~) carte d'adhérent; **to play** ~**s** jouer aux cartes.

cardamom ['kɑːdəməm] *n* cardamome *f*.

cardboard ['kɑːdbɔːd] *n* carton *m*.

cardboard box *n* (boîte *f* en) carton *m*.

cardboard city *n* endroit de la ville où dorment les SDF dans des boîtes en carton.

card-carrying member ['kɑːdkærɪŋ-] *n* membre actif.

card game *n* jeu *m* de cartes.

cardiac ['kɑːdɪæk] *adj* cardiaque.

cardigan ['kɑːdɪgən] *n* cardigan *m*.

cardinal ['kɑːdɪnl] *adj* cardinal(e) ♦ *n* cardinal *m*.

card index *n* fichier *m* (alphabétique).

cardphone ['kɑːdfəʊn] *n* téléphone *m* à carte (magnétique).

cardsharp ['kɑ:dʃɑ:p] *n* tricheur/euse professionnel(le).

card vote *n* (*BRIT*) vote *m* de délégués.

CARE [kɛə*] *n abbr* (= *Cooperative for American Relief Everywhere*) *association charitable*.

care [kɛə*] *n* soin *m*, attention *f*; (*worry*) souci *m* ♦ *vi*: **to ~ about** se soucier de, s'intéresser à; **in sb's ~** à la garde de qn, confié à qn; **~ of (c/o)** (*on letter*) aux bons soins de; **"with ~"** "fragile"; **to take ~ (to do)** faire attention (à faire); **to take ~ of** *vt* s'occuper de, prendre soin de; (*details, arrangements*) s'occuper de; **the child has been taken into ~** l'enfant a été placé en institution; **would you ~ to/for ...?** voulez-vous ...?; **I wouldn't ~ to do it** je n'aimerais pas le faire; **I don't ~** ça m'est bien égal, peu m'importe; **I couldn't ~ less** cela m'est complètement égal, je m'en fiche complètement.

►**care for** *vt fus* s'occuper de; (*like*) aimer.

careen [kə'ri:n] *vi* (*ship*) donner de la bande ♦ *vt* caréner, mettre en carène.

career [kə'rɪə*] *n* carrière *f* ♦ *vi* (*also*: **~ along**) aller à toute allure.

career girl *n* jeune fille *f* (*or* femme *f*) qui veut faire carrière.

careers officer *n* conseiller/ère d'orientation (professionnelle).

carefree ['kɛəfri:] *adj* sans souci, insouciant(e).

careful ['kɛəful] *adj* soigneux(euse); (*cautious*) prudent(e); **(be) ~!** (*fais*) attention!; **to be ~ with one's money** regarder à la dépense.

carefully ['kɛəfəlɪ] *adv* avec soin, soigneusement; prudemment.

careless ['kɛəlɪs] *adj* négligent(e); (*heedless*) insouciant(e).

carelessly ['kɛəlɪslɪ] *adv* négligemment; avec insouciance.

carelessness ['kɛəlɪsnɪs] *n* manque *m* de soin, négligence *f*; insouciance *f*.

carer ['kɛərə*] *n* personne qui s'occupe d'un proche qui est malade.

caress [kə'rɛs] *n* caresse *f* ♦ *vt* caresser.

caretaker ['kɛəteɪkə*] *n* gardien/ne, concierge *m/f*.

caretaker government *n* (*BRIT*) gouvernement *m* intérimaire.

car-ferry ['kɑ:fɛrɪ] *n* (*on sea*) ferry(-boat) *m*; (*on river*) bac *m*.

cargo, *pl* **~es** ['kɑ:gəu] *n* cargaison *f*, chargement *m*.

cargo boat *n* cargo *m*.

cargo plane *n* avion-cargo *m*.

car hire *n* (*BRIT*) location *f* de voitures.

Caribbean [kærɪ'bi:ən] *adj* des Caraïbes; **the ~ (Sea)** la mer des Antilles *or* des Caraïbes.

caricature ['kærɪkətjuə*] *n* caricature *f*.

caring ['kɛərɪŋ] *adj* (*person*) bienveillant(e); (*society, organization*) humanitaire.

carnage ['kɑ:nɪdʒ] *n* carnage *m*.

carnal ['kɑ:nl] *adj* charnel(le).

carnation [kɑ:'neɪʃən] *n* œillet *m*.

carnival ['kɑ:nɪvl] *n* (*public celebration*) carnaval *m*; (*US*: *funfair*) fête foraine.

carnivorous [kɑ:'nɪvərəs] *adj* carnivore, carnassier(ière).

carol ['kærəl] *n*: **(Christmas) ~** chant *m* de Noël.

carouse [kə'rauz] *vi* faire la bringue.

carousel [kærə'sɛl] *n* (*US*) manège *m*.

carp [kɑ:p] *n* (*fish*) carpe *f*.

►**carp at** *vt fus* critiquer.

car park *n* parking *m*, parc *m* de stationnement.

carpenter ['kɑ:pɪntə*] *n* charpentier *m*.

carpentry ['kɑ:pɪntrɪ] *n* charpenterie *f*, métier *m* de charpentier; (*woodwork: at school etc*) menuiserie *f*.

carpet ['kɑ:pɪt] *n* tapis *m* ♦ *vt* recouvrir (d'un tapis); **fitted ~** (*BRIT*) moquette *f*.

carpet bombing *n* bombardement intensif.

carpet slippers *npl* pantoufles *fpl*.

carpet sweeper [-'swi:pə*] *n* balai *m* mécanique.

car phone *n* téléphone *m* de voiture.

car rental *n* (*US*) location *f* de voitures.

carriage ['kærɪdʒ] *n* voiture *f*; (*of goods*) transport *m*; (: *cost*) port *m*; (*of typewriter*) chariot *m*; (*bearing*) maintien *m*, port *m*; **~ forward** port dû; **~ free** franco de port; **~ paid** (en) port payé.

carriage return *n* retour *m* à la ligne.

carriageway ['kærɪdʒweɪ] *n* (*BRIT: part of road*) chaussée *f*.

carrier ['kærɪə*] *n* transporteur *m*, camionneur *m*; (*MED*) porteur/euse; (*NAUT*) porteavions *m inv*.

carrier bag *n* (*BRIT*) sac *m* en papier *or* en plastique.

carrier pigeon *n* pigeon voyageur.

carrion ['kærɪən] *n* charogne *f*.

carrot ['kærət] *n* carotte *f*.

carry ['kærɪ] *vt* (*subj: person*) porter; (: *vehicle*) transporter; (*a motion, bill*) voter, adopter; (*MATH: figure*) retenir; (*COMM: interest*) rapporter; (*involve: responsibilities etc*) comporter, impliquer ♦ *vi* (*sound*) porter; **to be carried away** (*fig*) s'emballer, s'enthousiasmer; **this loan carries 10% interest** ce prêt est à 10% (d'intérêt).

►**carry forward** *vt* (*gen, BOOK-KEEPING*) reporter.

►**carry on** *vi* (*continue*): **to ~ on with sth/ doing** continuer qch/à faire; (*col: make a fuss*) faire des histoires ♦ *vt* entretenir, poursuivre.

►**carry out** *vt* (*orders*) exécuter; (*investigation*) effectuer; (*idea, threat*) mettre à exécution.

carrycot ['kærɪkɔt] *n* (*BRIT*) porte-bébé *m*.

carry-on ['kærɪ'ɔn] *n* (*col: fuss*) histoires *fpl*; (: *annoying behaviour*) cirque *m*, cinéma *m*.

cart [kɑ:t] *n* charrette *f* ♦ *vt* transporter.

carte blanche ['kɑ:t'blɔnʃ] *n*: **to give sb ~**

donner carte blanche à qn.
cartel [kɑː'tɛl] n (COMM) cartel m.
cartilage ['kɑːtɪlɪdʒ] n cartilage m.
cartographer [kɑː'tɔgrəfə*] n cartographe m/f.
cartography [kɑː'tɔgrəfɪ] n cartographie f.
carton ['kɑːtən] n (box) carton m; (of yogurt) pot m (en carton); (of cigarettes) cartouche f.
cartoon [kɑː'tuːn] n (PRESS) dessin m (humoristique); (satirical) caricature f; (comic strip) bande dessinée; (CINE) dessin animé.
cartoonist [kɑː'tuːnɪst] n dessinateur/trice humoristique; caricaturiste m/f; auteur m de dessins animés; auteur de bandes dessinées.
cartridge ['kɑːtrɪdʒ] n (for gun, pen) cartouche f; (for camera) chargeur m; (music tape) cassette f; (of record player) cellule f.
cartwheel ['kɑːtwiːl] n roue f; **to turn a ~** faire la roue.
carve [kɑːv] vt (meat: also: **~ up**) découper; (wood, stone) tailler, sculpter.
carving ['kɑːvɪŋ] n (in wood etc) sculpture f.
carving knife n couteau m à découper.
car wash n station f de lavage (de voitures).
Casablanca [kæsə'blæŋkə] n Casablanca.
cascade [kæs'keɪd] n cascade f ♦ vi tomber en cascade.
case [keɪs] n cas m; (LAW) affaire f, procès m; (box) caisse f, boîte f, étui m; (BRIT: also: **suit~**) valise f; (TYP): **lower/upper ~** minuscule f/majuscule f; **to have a good ~** avoir de bons arguments; **there's a strong ~ for reform** il y aurait lieu d'engager une réforme; **in ~ of** en cas de; **in ~ he** au cas où il; **just in ~** à tout hasard.
case history n (MED) dossier médical, antécédents médicaux.
case study n étude f de cas.
cash [kæʃ] n argent m; (COMM) argent liquide, numéraire m; liquidités fpl; (: in payment) argent comptant, espèces fpl ♦ vt encaisser; **to pay (in) ~** payer (en argent) comptant or en espèces; **~ with order/on delivery** (COMM) payable or paiement à la commande/livraison; **to be short of ~** être à court d'argent.
►**cash in** vt (insurance policy etc) toucher.
►**cash in on** vt fus profiter de.
cash account n compte m caisse.
cash and carry n libre-service m de gros, cash and carry m inv.
cashbook ['kæʃbuk] n livre m de caisse.
cash box n caisse f.
cash card n carte de retrait or accréditive.
cash desk n (BRIT) caisse f.
cash discount n escompte m de caisse (pour paiement au comptant), remise f au comptant.
cash dispenser n distributeur m automatique de billets.
cashew [kæ'ʃuː] n (also: **~ nut**) noix f de cajou.

cash flow n cash-flow m, marge brute d'autofinancement.
cashier [kæ'ʃɪə*] n caissier/ère ♦ vt (MIL) destituer, casser.
cashmere ['kæʃmɪə*] n cachemire m.
cash payment n paiement comptant, versement m en espèces.
cash price n prix comptant.
cash register n caisse enregistreuse.
cash sale n vente f au comptant.
casing ['keɪsɪŋ] n revêtement (protecteur), enveloppe (protectrice).
casino [kə'siːnəu] n casino m.
cask [kɑːsk] n tonneau m.
casket ['kɑːskɪt] n coffret m; (US: coffin) cercueil m.
Caspian Sea ['kæspɪən-] n: **the ~** la mer Caspienne.
casserole ['kæsərəul] n cocotte f; (food) ragoût m (en cocotte).
cassette [kæ'sɛt] n cassette f, musicassette f.
cassette deck n platine f cassette.
cassette player n lecteur m de cassettes.
cassette recorder n magnétophone m à cassettes.
cast [kɑːst] vb (pt, pp **cast**) vt (throw) jeter; (shed) perdre; se dépouiller de; (metal) couler, fondre; (THEAT): **to ~ sb as Hamlet** attribuer à qn le rôle d'Hamlet ♦ n (THEAT) distribution f; (mould) moule m; (also: **plaster ~**) plâtre m; **to ~ one's vote** voter, exprimer son suffrage.
►**cast aside** vt (reject) rejeter.
►**cast off** vi (NAUT) larguer les amarres; (KNITTING) arrêter les mailles ♦ vt (KNITTING) arrêter.
►**cast on** (KNITTING) vt monter ♦ vi monter les mailles.
castanets [kæstə'nɛts] npl castagnettes fpl.
castaway ['kɑːstəweɪ] n naufragé/e.
caste [kɑːst] n caste f, classe sociale.
caster sugar ['kɑːstə-] n (BRIT) sucre m semoule.
casting vote ['kɑːstɪŋ-] n (BRIT) voix prépondérante (pour départager).
cast iron n fonte f ♦ adj: **cast-iron** (fig: will) de fer; (: alibi) en béton.
castle ['kɑːsl] n château-fort m; (manor) château m.
cast-offs ['kɑːstɔfs] npl vêtements mpl dont on ne veut plus.
castor ['kɑːstə*] n (wheel) roulette f.
castor oil n huile f de ricin.
castrate [kæs'treɪt] vt châtrer.
casual ['kæʒjul] adj (by chance) de hasard, fait(e) au hasard, fortuit(e); (irregular: work etc) temporaire; (unconcerned) désinvolte; **~ wear** vêtements mpl sport inv.
casual labour n main-d'œuvre f temporaire.
casually ['kæʒjulɪ] adv avec désinvolture, négligemment; (by chance) fortuitement.
casualty ['kæʒjultɪ] n accidenté/e, blessé/e;

(*dead*) victime *f*, mort/e; **heavy casualties** lourdes pertes.

casualty ward *n* (*BRIT*) service *m* des urgences.

cat [kæt] *n* chat *m*.

catacombs ['kætəkuːmz] *npl* catacombes *fpl*.

catalogue, (*US*) **catalog** ['kætəlɔg] *n* catalogue *m* ♦ *vt* cataloguer.

catalyst ['kætəlɪst] *n* catalyseur *m*.

catalytic converter [kætə'lɪtɪkkən'vɔːtə*] *n* pot *m* catalytique.

catapult ['kætəpʌlt] *n* lance-pierres *m inv*, fronde *m*; (*HISTORY*) catapulte *f*.

cataract ['kætərækt] *n* (*also MED*) cataracte *f*.

catarrh [kə'tɑː*] *n* rhume *m* chronique, catarrhe *f*.

catastrophe [kə'tæstrəfɪ] *n* catastrophe *f*.

catastrophic [kætə'strɔfɪk] *adj* catastrophique.

catcall ['kætkɔːl] *n* (*at meeting etc*) sifflet *m*.

catch [kætʃ] *vb* (*pt, pp* **caught** [kɔːt]) *vt* (*ball, train, thief, cold*) attraper; (*person: by surprise*) prendre, surprendre; (*understand*) saisir; (*get entangled*) accrocher ♦ *vi* (*fire*) prendre; (*get entangled*) s'accrocher ♦ *n* (*fish etc caught*) prise *f*; (*thief etc caught*) capture *f*; (*trick*) attrape *f*; (*TECH*) loquet *m*; cliquet *m*; **to ~ sb's attention** *or* **eye** attirer l'attention de qn; **to ~ fire** prendre feu; **to ~ sight of** apercevoir.

►**catch on** *vi* (*become popular*) prendre; (*understand*): **to ~ on (to sth)** saisir (qch).

►**catch out** *vt* (*BRIT fig: with trick question*) prendre en défaut.

►**catch up** *vi* se rattraper, combler son retard ♦ *vt* (*also*: ~ **up with**) rattraper.

catching ['kætʃɪŋ] *adj* (*MED*) contagieux(euse).

catchment area ['kætʃmənt-] *n* (*BRIT SCOL*) aire *f* de recrutement; (*GEO*) bassin *m* hydrographique.

catch phrase *n* slogan *m*; expression toute faite.

catch-22 ['kætʃtwentɪ'tuː] *n*: **it's a ~ situation** c'est (une situation) sans issue.

catchy ['kætʃɪ] *adj* (*tune*) facile à retenir.

catechism ['kætɪkɪzəm] *n* catéchisme *m*.

categoric(al) [kætɪ'gɔrɪk(l)] *adj* catégorique.

categorize ['kætɪgəraɪz] *vt* classer par catégories.

category ['kætɪgərɪ] *n* catégorie *f*.

cater ['keɪtə*] *vi* (*provide food*): **to ~ (for)** préparer des repas (pour), se charger de la restauration (pour).

►**cater for** *vt fus* (*BRIT: needs*) satisfaire, pourvoir à; (: *readers, consumers*) s'adresser à, pourvoir aux besoins de.

caterer ['keɪtərə*] *n* traiteur *m*; fournisseur *m*.

catering ['keɪtərɪŋ] *n* restauration *f*; approvisionnement *m*, ravitaillement *m*.

caterpillar ['kætəpɪlə*] *n* chenille *f* ♦ *cpd* (*vehicle*) à chenille; ~ **track** *n* chenille *f*.

cat flap *n* chatière *f*.

cathedral [kə'θiːdrəl] *n* cathédrale *f*.

cathode ['kæθəud] *n* cathode *f*.

cathode ray tube *n* tube *m* cathodique.

catholic ['kæθəlɪk] *adj* éclectique; universel(le); libéral(e); **C~** *adj, n* (*REL*) catholique (*m/f*).

cat's-eye ['kæts'aɪ] *n* (*BRIT AUT*) (clou *m* à) catadioptre *m*.

catsup ['kætsəp] *n* (*US*) ketchup *m*.

cattle ['kætl] *npl* bétail *m*, bestiaux *mpl*.

catty ['kætɪ] *adj* méchant(e).

catwalk ['kætwɔːk] *n* passerelle *f*; (*for models*) podium *m* (*de défilé de mode*).

Caucasian [kɔː'keɪzɪən] *adj, n* caucasien(ne).

Caucasus ['kɔːkəsəs] *n* Caucase *m*.

caucus ['kɔːkəs] *n* (*US POL*) comité électoral (pour désigner des candidats); (*BRIT POL: group*) comité local (*d'un parti politique*).

---

*Un **caucus** aux États-Unis est une réunion restreinte des principaux dirigeants d'un parti politique, précédant souvent une assemblée générale, dans le but de choisir des candidats ou de définir une ligne d'action. Par extension, ce terme désigne également l'état-major d'un parti politique.*

---

caught [kɔːt] *pt, pp of* **catch**.

cauliflower ['kɔlɪflauə*] *n* chou-fleur *m*.

cause [kɔːz] *n* cause *f* ♦ *vt* causer; **there is no ~ for concern** il n'y a pas lieu de s'inquiéter; **to ~ sth to be done** faire faire qch; **to ~ sb to do sth** faire faire qch à qn.

causeway ['kɔːzweɪ] *n* chaussée (surélevée).

caustic ['kɔːstɪk] *adj* caustique.

caution ['kɔːʃən] *n* prudence *f*; (*warning*) avertissement *m* ♦ *vt* avertir, donner un avertissement à.

cautious ['kɔːʃəs] *adj* prudent(e).

cautiously ['kɔːʃəslɪ] *adv* prudemment, avec prudence.

cautiousness ['kɔːʃəsnɪs] *n* prudence *f*.

cavalier [kævə'lɪə*] *adj* cavalier(ère), désinvolte ♦ *n* (*knight*) cavalier *m*.

cavalry ['kævəlrɪ] *n* cavalerie *f*.

cave [keɪv] *n* caverne *f*, grotte *f* ♦ *vi*: **to go caving** faire de la spéléo(logie).

►**cave in** *vi* (*roof etc*) s'effondrer.

caveman ['keɪvmæn] *n* homme *m* des cavernes.

cavern ['kævən] *n* caverne *f*.

caviar(e) ['kævɪɑː*] *n* caviar *m*.

cavity ['kævɪtɪ] *n* cavité *f*.

cavity wall insulation *n* isolation *f* des murs creux.

cavort [kə'vɔːt] *vi* cabrioler, faire des cabrioles.

cayenne [keɪ'ɛn] *n* (*also*: ~ **pepper**) poivre *m* de cayenne.

CB *n abbr* (= *Citizens' Band (Radio)*) CB *f*; (*BRIT*: = *Companion of (the Order of) the Bath*) titre honorifique.

CBC *n abbr* (= *Canadian Broadcasting Corporation*) *organisme de radiodiffusion.*

CBE *n abbr* (= *Companion of (the Order of) the British Empire*) *titre honorifique.*

CBI *n abbr* (= *Confederation of British Industry*) ≈ CNPF *m* (= *Conseil national du patronat français*).

CBS *n abbr* (*US*: = *Columbia Broadcasting System*) *chaîne de télévision.*

CC *abbr* (*BRIT*) = *county council.*

cc *abbr* (= *cubic centimetre*) cm³; (*on letter etc*) = **carbon copy.**

CCA *n abbr* (*US*: = *Circuit Court of Appeals*) cour d'appel itinérante.

CCTV *n abbr* = **closed-circuit television.**

CCU *n abbr* (*US*: = *coronary care unit*) unité *f* de soins cardiologiques.

CD *n abbr* (= *compact disc*) CD *m*; (*MIL*) = *Civil Defence (Corps)* (*BRIT*), *Civil Defense* (*US*) ♦ *abbr* (*BRIT*: = *Corps Diplomatique*) CD.

CDC *n abbr* (*US*) = *center for disease control.*

CD-I *n abbr* ® (= *Compact Disc Interactive*) CD-I *m*, disque compact interactif.

CD player *n* platine *f* laser.

Cdr. *abbr* (= *commander*) Cdt.

CD-ROM [siːdiːˈrɔm] *n abbr* (= *compact disc read-only memory*) CD-ROM *m inv.*

CDT *abbr* (*US*: = *Central Daylight Time*) heure d'été du centre.

CDW *n abbr* = **collision damage waiver.**

cease [siːs] *vt, vi* cesser.

ceasefire [ˈsiːsfaɪə*] *n* cessez-le-feu *m.*

ceaseless [ˈsiːslɪs] *adj* incessant(e), continuel(le).

CED *n abbr* (*US*) = *Committee for Economic Development.*

cedar [ˈsiːdə*] *n* cèdre *m.*

cede [siːd] *vt* céder.

cedilla [sɪˈdɪlə] *n* cédille *f.*

CEEB *n abbr* (*US*: = *College Entrance Examination Board*) *commission d'admission dans l'enseignement supérieur.*

ceilidh [ˈkeɪlɪ] *n* bal *m* folklorique écossais *or* irlandais.

ceiling [ˈsiːlɪŋ] *n* (*also fig*) plafond *m.*

celebrate [ˈsɛlɪbreɪt] *vt, vi* célébrer.

celebrated [ˈsɛlɪbreɪtɪd] *adj* célèbre.

celebration [sɛlɪˈbreɪʃən] *n* célébration *f.*

celebrity [sɪˈlɛbrɪtɪ] *n* célébrité *f.*

celeriac [səˈlɛrɪæk] *n* céleri(-rave) *m.*

celery [ˈsɛlərɪ] *n* céleri *m* (en branches).

celestial [sɪˈlɛstɪəl] *adj* céleste.

celibacy [ˈsɛlɪbəsɪ] *n* célibat *m.*

cell [sɛl] *n* (*gen*) cellule *f*; (*ELEC*) élément *m* (*de pile*).

cellar [ˈsɛlə*] *n* cave *f.*

'cellist [ˈtʃɛlɪst] *n* violoncelliste *m/f.*

'cello [ˈtʃɛləu] *n* violoncelle *m.*

cellophane [ˈsɛləfeɪn] *n* ® cellophane *f* ®.

cellphone [ˈsɛlfəun] *n* téléphone *m* cellulaire.

cellular [ˈsɛljulə*] *adj* cellulaire.

Celluloid [ˈsɛljulɔɪd] *n* ® celluloïd *m* ®.

cellulose [ˈsɛljuləus] *n* cellulose *f.*

Celsius [ˈsɛlsɪəs] *adj* Celsius *inv.*

Celt [kɛlt, sɛlt] *n* Celte *m/f.*

Celtic [ˈkɛltɪk, ˈsɛltɪk] *adj* celte, celtique ♦ *n* (*LING*) celtique *m.*

cement [səˈmɛnt] *n* ciment *m* ♦ *vt* cimenter.

cement mixer *n* bétonnière *f.*

cemetery [ˈsɛmɪtrɪ] *n* cimetière *m.*

cenotaph [ˈsɛnətɑːf] *n* cénotaphe *m.*

censor [ˈsɛnsə*] *n* censeur *m* ♦ *vt* censurer.

censorship [ˈsɛnsəʃɪp] *n* censure *f.*

censure [ˈsɛnʃə*] *vt* blâmer, critiquer.

census [ˈsɛnsəs] *n* recensement *m.*

cent [sɛnt] *n* (*US*: *coin*) cent *m* (= *1:100 du dollar*); *see also* **per.**

centenary [sɛnˈtiːnərɪ], **centennial** [sɛnˈtɛnɪəl] *n* centenaire *m.*

center [ˈsɛntə*] *n, vt* (*US*) = **centre.**

centigrade [ˈsɛntɪgreɪd] *adj* centigrade.

centilitre, (*US*) **centiliter** [ˈsɛntiliːtə*] *n* centilitre *m.*

centimetre, (*US*) **centimeter** [ˈsɛntimiːtə*] *n* centimètre *m.*

centipede [ˈsɛntipiːd] *n* mille-pattes *m inv.*

central [ˈsɛntrəl] *adj* central(e).

Central African Republic *n* République Centrafricaine.

Central America *n* Amérique centrale.

central heating *n* chauffage central.

centralize [ˈsɛntrəlaɪz] *vt* centraliser.

central processing unit (CPU) *n* (*COMPUT*) unité centrale (de traitement).

central reservation *n* (*BRIT AUT*) terre-plein central.

centre, (*US*) **center** [ˈsɛntə*] *n* centre *m* ♦ *vt* centrer; (*PHOT*) cadrer; (*concentrate*): **to ~ (on)** centrer (sur).

centrefold, (*US*) **centerfold** [ˈsɛntəfəuld] *n* (*PRESS*) pages centrales détachables (*avec photo de pin up*).

centre-forward [ˈsɛntəˈfɔːwəd] *n* (*SPORT*) avant-centre *m.*

centre-half [ˈsɛntəˈhɑːf] *n* (*SPORT*) demi-centre *m.*

centrepiece, (*US*) **centerpiece** [ˈsɛntəpiːs] *n* milieu *m* de table; (*fig*) pièce maîtresse.

centre spread *n* (*BRIT*) publicité *f* en double page.

centre-stage [sɛntəˈsteɪdʒ] *n*: **to take ~** occuper le centre de la scène.

centrifugal [sɛnˈtrɪfjugl] *adj* centrifuge.

century [ˈsɛntjurɪ] *n* siècle *m*; **in the twentieth ~** au vingtième siècle.

CEO *n abbr* (*US*) = **chief executive officer.**

ceramic [sɪˈræmɪk] *adj* céramique.

cereal [ˈsiːrɪəl] *n* céréale *f.*

cerebral [ˈsɛrɪbrəl] *adj* cérébral(e).

ceremonial [sɛrɪˈməunɪəl] *n* cérémonial *m*; (*rite*) rituel *m.*

ceremony [ˈsɛrɪmənɪ] *n* cérémonie *f*; **to stand on ~** faire des façons.

cert [səːt] *n* (*BRIT col*): **it's a dead ~** ça ne fait pas un pli.

certain ['sə:tən] *adj* certain(e); **to make ~ of** s'assurer de; **for ~** certainement, sûrement.

certainly ['sə:tənlɪ] *adv* certainement.

certainty ['sə:təntɪ] *n* certitude *f*.

certificate [sə'tɪfɪkɪt] *n* certificat *m*.

certified letter ['sə:tɪfaɪd-] *n* (*US*) lettre recommandée.

certified public accountant (CPA) ['sə:tɪfaɪd-] *n* (*US*) expert-comptable *m*.

certify ['sə:tɪfaɪ] *vt* certifier ♦ *vi*: **to ~ to** attester.

cervical ['sə:vɪkl] *adj*: **~ cancer** cancer *m* du col de l'utérus; **~ smear** frottis vaginal.

cervix ['sə:vɪks] *n* col *m* de l'utérus.

Cesarean [si:'zɛərɪən] *adj, n* (*US*) = **Caesarean**.

cessation [sə'seɪʃən] *n* cessation *f*, arrêt *m*.

cesspit ['sɛspɪt] *n* fosse *f* d'aisance.

CET *abbr* (= *Central European Time*) *heure d'Europe centrale*.

Ceylon [sɪ'lɔn] *n* Ceylan *m*.

cf. *abbr* (= *compare*) cf., voir.

c/f *abbr* (*COMM*) = *carried forward*.

CFC *n abbr* (= *chlorofluorocarbon*) CFC *m*.

CG *n abbr* (*US*) = **coastguard**.

cg *abbr* (= *centigram*) cg.

CH *n abbr* (*BRIT*: = *Companion of Honour*) titre honorifique.

ch *abbr* (*BRIT*: = *central heating*) c.c.

ch. *abbr* (= *chapter*) chap.

Chad [tʃæd] *n* Tchad *m*.

chafe [tʃeɪf] *vt* irriter, frotter contre ♦ *vi* (*fig*): **to ~ against** se rebiffer contre, regimber contre.

chaffinch ['tʃæfɪntʃ] *n* pinson *m*.

chagrin ['ʃægrɪn] *n* contrariété *f*, déception *f*.

chain [tʃeɪn] *n* (*gen*) chaîne *f* ♦ *vt* (*also*: **~ up**) enchaîner, attacher (avec une chaîne).

chain reaction *n* réaction *f* en chaîne.

chain-smoke ['tʃeɪnsməuk] *vi* fumer cigarette sur cigarette.

chain store *n* magasin *m* à succursales multiples.

chair [tʃɛə*] *n* chaise *f*; (*armchair*) fauteuil *m*; (*of university*) chaire *f* ♦ *vt* (*meeting*) présider; **the ~** (*US*: *electric ~*) la chaise électrique.

chairlift ['tʃɛəlɪft] *n* télésiège *m*.

chairman ['tʃɛəmən] *n* président *m*.

chairperson ['tʃɛəpə:sn] *n* président/e.

chairwoman ['tʃɛəwumən] *n* présidente *f*.

chalet ['ʃæleɪ] *n* chalet *m*.

chalice ['tʃælɪs] *n* calice *m*.

chalk [tʃɔ:k] *n* craie *f*.

▶**chalk up** *vt* écrire à la craie; (*fig: success etc*) remporter.

challenge ['tʃælɪndʒ] *n* défi *m* ♦ *vt* défier; (*statement, right*) mettre en question, contester; **to ~ sb to a fight/game** inviter qn à se battre/à jouer (*sous forme d'un défi*); **to ~ sb to do** mettre qn au défi de faire.

challenger ['tʃælɪndʒə*] *n* (*SPORT*) challenger *m*.

challenging ['tʃælɪndʒɪŋ] *adj* de défi, provocateur(trice).

chamber ['tʃeɪmbə*] *n* chambre *f*; **~ of commerce** chambre de commerce.

chambermaid ['tʃeɪmbəmeɪd] *n* femme *f* de chambre.

chamber music *n* musique *f* de chambre.

chamberpot ['tʃeɪmbəpɔt] *n* pot *m* de chambre.

chameleon [kə'mi:lɪən] *n* caméléon *m*.

chamois ['ʃæmwɑ:] *n* chamois *m*.

chamois leather ['ʃæmɪ-] *n* peau *f* de chamois.

champagne [ʃæm'peɪn] *n* champagne *m*.

champers ['ʃæmpəz] *n* (*col*) champ *m*.

champion ['tʃæmpɪən] *n* (*also of cause*) champion/ne ♦ *vt* défendre.

championship ['tʃæmpɪənʃɪp] *n* championnat *m*.

chance [tʃɑ:ns] *n* hasard *m*; (*opportunity*) occasion *f*, possibilité *f*; (*hope, likelihood*) chance *f* ♦ *vt* (*risk*): **to ~ it** risquer (le coup), essayer; (*happen*): **to ~ to do** faire par hasard ♦ *adj* fortuit(e), de hasard; **there is little ~ of his coming** il est peu probable *or* il y a peu de chances qu'il vienne; **to take a ~** prendre un risque; **it's the ~ of a lifetime** c'est une occasion unique; **by ~** par hasard.

▶**chance (up)on** *vt fus* (*person*) tomber sur, rencontrer par hasard; (*thing*) trouver par hasard.

chancel ['tʃɑ:nsəl] *n* chœur *m*.

chancellor ['tʃɑ:nsələ*] *n* chancelier *m*; **C~ of the Exchequer** (*BRIT*) chancelier de l'Échiquier.

chandelier [ʃændə'lɪə*] *n* lustre *m*.

change [tʃeɪndʒ] *vt* (*alter, replace, COMM: money*) changer; (*switch, substitute: gear, hands, trains, clothes, one's name etc*) changer de; (*transform*): **to ~ sb into** changer *or* transformer qn en ♦ *vi* (*gen*) changer; (*change clothes*) se changer; (*be transformed*): **to ~ into** se changer *or* transformer en ♦ *n* changement *m*; (*money*) monnaie *f*; **to ~ one's mind** changer d'avis; **she ~d into an old skirt** elle (s'est changée et) a enfilé une vieille jupe; **a ~ of clothes** des vêtements de rechange; **for a ~** pour changer; **small ~** petite monnaie; **to give sb ~ for** *or* **of £10** faire à qn la monnaie de 10 livres.

changeable ['tʃeɪndʒəbl] *adj* (*weather*) variable; (*person*) d'humeur changeante.

change machine *n* distributeur *m* de monnaie.

changeover ['tʃeɪndʒəuvə*] *n* (*to new system*) changement *m*, passage *m*.

changing ['tʃeɪndʒɪŋ] *adj* changeant(e).

changing room *n* (*BRIT: in shop*) salon *m* d'essayage; (: *SPORT*) vestiaire *m*.

channel ['tʃænl] *n* (*TV*) chaîne *f*; (*waveband, groove, fig: medium*) canal *m*; (*of river, sea*) chenal *m* ♦ *vt* canaliser; (*fig: interest, ener-*

gies): **to ~ into** diriger vers; **through the usual ~s** en suivant la filière habituelle; **green/red ~** (CUSTOMS) couloir m or sortie f "rien à déclarer"/"marchandises à déclarer"; **the (English) C~** la Manche.

Channel Islands npl: **the ~** les îles de la Manche, les îles anglo-normandes.

Channel Tunnel n: **the ~** le tunnel sous la Manche.

chant [tʃɑːnt] n chant m; mélopée f; psalmodie f ♦ vt chanter, scander; psalmodier.

chaos ['keɪɔs] n chaos m.

chaos theory n théorie f du chaos.

chaotic [keɪ'ɔtɪk] adj chaotique.

chap [tʃæp] n (BRIT col: man) type m; (term of address): **old ~** mon vieux ♦ vt (skin) gercer, crevasser.

chapel ['tʃæpl] n chapelle f.

chaperon ['ʃæpərəun] n chaperon m ♦ vt chaperonner.

chaplain ['tʃæplɪn] n aumônier m.

chapter ['tʃæptə*] n chapitre m.

char [tʃɑː*] vt (burn) carboniser ♦ vi (BRIT: cleaner) faire des ménages ♦ n (BRIT) = **charlady**.

character ['kærɪktə*] n caractère m; (in novel, film) personnage m; (eccentric) numéro m, phénomène m; **a person of good ~** une personne bien.

character code n (COMPUT) code m de caractère.

characteristic ['kærɪktə'rɪstɪk] adj, n caractéristique (f).

characterize ['kærɪktəraɪz] vt caractériser; **to ~ (as)** définir (comme).

charade [ʃə'rɑːd] n charade f.

charcoal ['tʃɑːkəul] n charbon m de bois.

charge [tʃɑːdʒ] n accusation f; (LAW) inculpation f; (cost) prix (demandé); (of gun, battery, MIL: attack) charge f ♦ vt (LAW): **to ~ sb (with)** inculper qn (de); (gun, battery, MIL: enemy) charger; (customer, sum) faire payer ♦ vi (gen with: up, along etc) foncer; **~s** npl: **bank/labour ~s** frais mpl de banque/main-d'œuvre; **to ~ in/out** entrer/sortir en trombe; **to ~ down/up** dévaler/grimper à toute allure; **is there a ~?** doit-on payer?; **there's no ~** c'est gratuit, on ne fait pas payer; **extra ~** supplément m; **to take ~ of** se charger de; **to be in ~ of** être responsable de, s'occuper de; **to have ~ of sb** avoir la charge de qn; **they ~d us £10 for the meal** ils nous ont fait payer le repas 10 livres, ils nous ont compté 10 livres pour le repas; **how much do you ~ for this repair?** combien demandez-vous pour cette réparation?; **to ~ an expense (up) to sb** mettre une dépense sur le compte de qn; **~ it to my account** facturez-le sur mon compte.

charge account n compte m client.

charge card n carte f de client (émise par un grand magasin).

chargehand ['tʃɑːdʒhænd] n (BRIT) chef m

d'équipe.

charger ['tʃɑːdʒə*] n (also: battery ~) chargeur m; (old: warhorse) cheval m de bataille.

charitable ['tʃærɪtəbl] adj charitable.

charity ['tʃærɪtɪ] n charité f; (organization) institution f charitable or de bienfaisance, œuvre f (de charité).

charlady ['tʃɑːleɪdɪ] n (BRIT) femme f de ménage.

charm [tʃɑːm] n charme m ♦ vt charmer, enchanter.

charm bracelet n bracelet m à breloques.

charming ['tʃɑːmɪŋ] adj charmant(e).

chart [tʃɑːt] n tableau m, diagramme m; graphique m; (map) carte marine; (weather ~) carte f du temps ♦ vt dresser or établir la carte de; (sales, progress) établir la courbe de; **to be in the ~s** (record, pop group) figurer au hit-parade.

charter ['tʃɑːtə*] vt (plane) affréter ♦ n (document) charte f; **on ~** (plane) affrété(e).

chartered accountant (CA) ['tʃɑːtəd-] n (BRIT) expert-comptable m.

charter flight n charter m.

charwoman ['tʃɑːwumən] n = **charlady**.

chase [tʃeɪs] vt poursuivre, pourchasser ♦ n poursuite f, chasse f.

▶**chase down** vt (US) = **chase up**.

▶**chase up** vt (BRIT: person) relancer; (: information) rechercher.

chasm ['kæzəm] n gouffre m, abîme m.

chassis ['ʃæsɪ] n châssis m.

chastened ['tʃeɪsnd] adj assagi(e), rappelé(e) à la raison.

chastening ['tʃeɪsnɪŋ] adj qui fait réfléchir.

chastise [tʃæs'taɪz] vt punir, châtier; corriger.

chastity ['tʃæstɪtɪ] n chasteté f.

chat [tʃæt] vi (also: **have a ~**) bavarder, causer ♦ n conversation f.

▶**chat up** vt (BRIT col: girl) baratiner.

chatline ['tʃætlaɪn] n numéro téléphonique qui permet de bavarder avec plusieurs personnes en même temps.

chat show n (BRIT) entretien télévisé.

chattel ['tʃætl] see **goods**.

chatter ['tʃætə*] vi (person) bavarder, papoter ♦ n bavardage m, papotage m; **my teeth are ~ing** je claque des dents.

chatterbox ['tʃætəbɔks] n moulin m à paroles, babillard/e.

chattering classes ['tʃætərɪŋ-] npl: **the ~** (col, pej) les intellos mpl.

chatty ['tʃætɪ] adj (style) familier(ière); (person) enclin(e) à bavarder or au papotage.

chauffeur ['ʃəufə*] n chauffeur m (de maître).

chauvinism ['ʃəuvɪnɪzəm] n (also: **male ~**) phallocratie f, machisme m; (nationalism) chauvinisme m.

chauvinist ['ʃəuvɪnɪst] n (also: **male ~**) phallocrate m, macho m; (nationalist) chauvin/e.

ChE abbr = **chemical engineer**.

cheap [tʃiːp] adj bon marché inv, pas cher(chère); (reduced: ticket) à prix réduit; (: fare) réduit(e); (joke) facile, d'un goût douteux; (poor quality) à bon marché, de qualité médiocre ♦ adv à bon marché, pour pas cher; ~**er** adj moins cher(chère).

cheapen [ˈtʃiːpn] vt rabaisser, déprécier.

cheaply [ˈtʃiːplɪ] adv à bon marché, à bon compte.

cheat [tʃiːt] vi tricher; (in exam) copier ♦ vt tromper, duper; (rob) escroquer ♦ n tricheur/euse; escroc m; (trick) duperie f, tromperie f; **to ~ on sb** (col: husband, wife etc) tromper qn.

cheating [ˈtʃiːtɪŋ] n tricherie f.

check [tʃɛk] vt vérifier; (passport, ticket) contrôler; (halt) enrayer; (restrain) maîtriser ♦ vi (official etc) se renseigner ♦ n vérification f; contrôle m; (curb) frein m; (bill) addition f; (pattern: gen pl) carreaux mpl; (US) = **cheque** ♦ adj (also: ~**ed**: pattern, cloth) à carreaux; **to ~ with sb** demander à qn; **to keep a ~ on sb/sth** surveiller qn/qch.

▶**check in** vi (in hotel) remplir sa fiche (d'hôtel); (at airport) se présenter à l'enregistrement ♦ vt (luggage) (faire) enregistrer.

▶**check off** vt cocher.

▶**check out** vi (in hotel) régler sa note ♦ vt (luggage) retirer; (investigate: story) vérifier; (person) prendre des renseignements sur.

▶**check up** vi: **to ~ up (on sth)** vérifier (qch); **to ~ up on sb** se renseigner sur le compte de qn.

checkered [ˈtʃɛkəd] adj (US) = **chequered**.

checkers [ˈtʃɛkəz] n (US) jeu m de dames.

check guarantee card n (US) carte f (d'identité) bancaire.

check-in [ˈtʃɛkɪn] n (also: ~ **desk**: at airport) enregistrement m.

checking account [ˈtʃɛkɪŋ-] n (US) compte courant.

checklist [ˈtʃɛklɪst] n liste f de contrôle.

checkmate [ˈtʃɛkmeɪt] n échec et mat m.

checkout [ˈtʃɛkaut] n (in supermarket) caisse f.

checkpoint [ˈtʃɛkpɔɪnt] n contrôle m.

checkup [ˈtʃɛkʌp] n (MED) examen médical, check-up m.

cheek [tʃiːk] n joue f; (impudence) toupet m, culot m.

cheekbone [ˈtʃiːkbəun] n pommette f.

cheeky [ˈtʃiːkɪ] adj effronté(e), culotté(e).

cheep [tʃiːp] n (of bird) piaulement m ♦ vi piauler.

cheer [tʃɪə*] vt acclamer, applaudir; (gladden) réjouir, réconforter ♦ vi applaudir ♦ n (gen pl) acclamations fpl, applaudissements mpl; bravos mpl, hourras mpl; ~**s!** (à votre) santé!

▶**cheer on** vt encourager (par des cris etc).

▶**cheer up** vi se dérider, reprendre courage ♦ vt remonter le moral à or de, dérider, égayer.

cheerful [ˈtʃɪəful] adj gai(e), joyeux(euse).

cheerfulness [ˈtʃɪəfulnɪs] n gaieté f, bonne humeur.

cheerio [tʃɪərɪˈəu] excl (BRIT) salut!, au revoir!

cheerleader [ˈtʃɪəliːdə*] n membre d'un groupe de majorettes qui chantent et dansent pour soutenir leur équipe pendant les matchs de football américain.

cheerless [ˈtʃɪəlɪs] adj sombre, triste.

cheese [tʃiːz] n fromage m.

cheeseboard [ˈtʃiːzbɔːd] n plateau m à fromages; (with cheese on it) plateau m de fromages.

cheeseburger [ˈtʃiːzbɔːgə*] n cheeseburger m.

cheesecake [ˈtʃiːzkeɪk] n tarte f au fromage.

cheetah [ˈtʃiːtə] n guépard m.

chef [ʃɛf] n chef (cuisinier).

chemical [ˈkɛmɪkl] adj chimique ♦ n produit m chimique.

chemist [ˈkɛmɪst] n (BRIT: pharmacist) pharmacien/ne; (scientist) chimiste m/f; ~**'s (shop)** n (BRIT) pharmacie f.

chemistry [ˈkɛmɪstrɪ] n chimie f.

chemotherapy [kiːməuˈθɛrəpɪ] n chimiothérapie f.

cheque, (US) **check** [tʃɛk] n chèque m; **to pay by ~** payer par chèque.

chequebook, (US) **checkbook** [ˈtʃɛkbuk] n chéquier m, carnet m de chèques.

cheque card n (BRIT) carte f (d'identité) bancaire.

chequered, (US) **checkered** [ˈtʃɛkəd] adj (fig) varié(e).

cherish [ˈtʃɛrɪʃ] vt chérir; (hope etc) entretenir.

cheroot [ʃəˈruːt] n cigare m de Manille.

cherry [ˈtʃɛrɪ] n cerise f.

Ches abbr (BRIT) = Cheshire.

chess [tʃɛs] n échecs mpl.

chessboard [ˈtʃɛsbɔːd] n échiquier m.

chessman [ˈtʃɛsmən] n pièce f (de jeu d'échecs).

chessplayer [ˈtʃɛspleɪə*] n joueur/euse d'échecs.

chest [tʃɛst] n poitrine f; (box) coffre m, caisse f; **to get sth off one's ~** (col) vider son sac; ~ **of drawers** n commode f.

chest measurement n tour m de poitrine.

chestnut [ˈtʃɛsnʌt] n châtaigne f; (also: ~ **tree**) châtaignier m; (colour) châtain m ♦ adj (hair) châtain inv; (horse) alezan.

chesty [ˈtʃɛstɪ] adj (cough) de poitrine.

chew [tʃuː] vt mâcher.

chewing gum [ˈtʃuːɪŋ-] n chewing-gum m.

chic [ʃiːk] adj chic inv, élégant(e).

chick [tʃɪk] n poussin m; (US col) pépée f.

chicken [ˈtʃɪkɪn] n poulet m; (col: coward) poule mouillée.

▶**chicken out** vi (col) se dégonfler.

chicken feed n (fig) broutilles fpl, bagatelle f.

chickenpox [ˈtʃɪkɪnpɔks] n varicelle f.

chickpea ['tʃɪkpiː] n pois m chiche.
chicory ['tʃɪkərɪ] n (for coffee) chicorée f; (salad) endive f.
chide [tʃaɪd] vt réprimander, gronder.
chief [tʃiːf] n chef m ♦ adj principal(e); **C~ of Staff** (MIL) chef d'État-major.
chief constable n (BRIT) ≈ préfet m de police.
chief executive, (US) **chief executive officer** n directeur général.
chiefly ['tʃiːflɪ] adv principalement, surtout.
chiffon ['ʃɪfɔn] n mousseline f de soie.
chilblain ['tʃɪlbleɪn] n engelure f.
child, pl **~ren** [tʃaɪld, 'tʃɪldrən] n enfant m/f.
child benefit n (BRIT) ≈ allocations familiales.
childbirth ['tʃaɪldbɜːθ] n accouchement m.
childhood ['tʃaɪldhud] n enfance f.
childish ['tʃaɪldɪʃ] adj puéril(e), enfantin(e).
childless ['tʃaɪldlɪs] adj sans enfants.
childlike ['tʃaɪldlaɪk] adj innocent(e), pur(e).
child minder n (BRIT) garde f d'enfants.
child prodigy n enfant m/f prodige.
children ['tʃɪldrən] npl of **child**.
children's home ['tʃɪldrənz-] n ≈ foyer m d'accueil (pour enfants).
Chile ['tʃɪlɪ] n Chili m.
Chilean ['tʃɪlɪən] adj chilien(ne) ♦ n Chilien/ne.
chill [tʃɪl] n froid m; (MED) refroidissement m, coup m de froid ♦ adj froid(e), glacial(e) ♦ vt faire frissonner; refroidir; (CULIN) mettre au frais, rafraîchir; **"serve ~ed"** "à servir frais".
► **chill out** vi (col: esp US) se relaxer.
chilli, (US) **chili** ['tʃɪlɪ] n piment m (rouge).
chilling ['tʃɪlɪŋ] adj (wind) frais(fraîche), froid(e); (look, smile) glacé(e); (thought) qui donne le frisson.
chilly ['tʃɪlɪ] adj froid(e), glacé(e); (sensitive to cold) frileux(euse); **to feel ~** avoir froid.
chime [tʃaɪm] n carillon m ♦ vi carillonner, sonner.
chimney ['tʃɪmnɪ] n cheminée f.
chimney sweep n ramoneur m.
chimpanzee [tʃɪmpæn'ziː] n chimpanzé m.
chin [tʃɪn] n menton m.
China ['tʃaɪnə] n Chine f.
china ['tʃaɪnə] n porcelaine f; (vaisselle f en) porcelaine.
Chinese [tʃaɪ'niːz] adj chinois(e) ♦ n (pl inv) Chinois/e; (LING) chinois m.
chink [tʃɪŋk] n (opening) fente f, fissure f; (noise) tintement m.
chinwag ['tʃɪnwæg] n (BRIT col): **to have a ~** tailler une bavette.
chip [tʃɪp] n (gen pl: CULIN) frite f; (: US: also: **potato ~**) chip m; (of wood) copeau m; (of glass, stone) éclat m; (also: **micro~**) puce f; (in gambling) fiche f ♦ vt (cup, plate) ébrécher; **when the ~s are down** (fig) au moment critique.
► **chip in** vi (col) mettre son grain de sel.

chipboard ['tʃɪpbɔːd] n aggloméré m, panneau m de particules.
chipmunk ['tʃɪpmʌŋk] n suisse m (animal).
chippings ['tʃɪpɪŋz] npl: **loose ~** gravillons mpl.
chip shop n (BRIT) friterie f.

Un **chip shop**, que l'on appelle également un "fish-and-chip shop", est un magasin où l'on vend des plats à emporter. Les chip shops sont d'ailleurs à l'origine des **takeaways**. On y achète en particulier du poisson frit et des frites, mais on y trouve également des plats traditionnels britanniques (steak pies, saucisses, etc). Tous les plats étaient à l'origine emballés dans du papier journal. Dans certains de ces magasins, on peut s'asseoir pour consommer sur place.

chiropodist [kɪ'rɔpədɪst] n (BRIT) pédicure m/f.
chiropody [kɪ'rɔpədɪ] n (BRIT) pédicurie f.
chirp [tʃəːp] n pépiement m, gazouillis m; (of crickets) stridulation f ♦ vi pépier, gazouiller; chanter, striduler.
chirpy ['tʃəːpɪ] adj (col) plein(e) d'entrain, tout guilleret(te).
chisel ['tʃɪzl] n ciseau m.
chit [tʃɪt] n mot m, note f.
chitchat ['tʃɪttʃæt] n bavardage m, papotage m.
chivalrous ['ʃɪvəlrəs] adj chevaleresque.
chivalry ['ʃɪvəlrɪ] n chevalerie f; esprit m chevaleresque.
chives [tʃaɪvz] npl ciboulette f, civette f.
chloride ['klɔːraɪd] n chlorure m.
chlorinate ['klɔrɪneɪt] vt chlorer.
chlorine ['klɔːriːn] n chlore m.
chock [tʃɔk] n cale f.
chock-a-block ['tʃɔkə'blɔk], **chock-full** [tʃɔk'ful] adj plein(e) à craquer.
chocolate ['tʃɔklɪt] n chocolat m.
choice [tʃɔɪs] n choix m ♦ adj de choix; **by** or **from ~** par choix; **a wide ~** un grand choix.
choir ['kwaɪə*] n chœur m, chorale f.
choirboy ['kwaɪəbɔɪ] n jeune choriste m, petit chanteur.
choke [tʃəuk] vi étouffer ♦ vt étrangler; étouffer; (block) boucher, obstruer ♦ n (AUT) starter m.
cholera ['kɔlərə] n choléra m.
cholesterol [kə'lestərɔl] n cholestérol m.
choose, pt **chose,** pp **chosen** [tʃuːz, tʃəuz, 'tʃəuzn] vt choisir ♦ vi: **to ~ between** choisir entre; **to ~ from** choisir parmi; **to ~ to do** décider de faire, juger bon de faire.
choosy ['tʃuːzɪ] adj: **(to be) ~** (faire le) difficile.
chop [tʃɔp] vt (wood) couper (à la hache); (CULIN: also: **~ up**) couper (fin), émincer, hacher (en morceaux) ♦ n coup m (de hache, du tranchant de la main); (CULIN) côtelette f; **to get the ~** (BRIT col: project) tomber à l'eau;

(: *person: be sacked*) se faire renvoyer.
▶**chop down** vt (*tree*) abattre.
chopper ['tʃɒpə*] n (*helicopter*) hélicoptère m, hélico m.
choppy ['tʃɒpɪ] adj (*sea*) un peu agité(e).
chops [tʃɒps] npl (*jaws*) mâchoires fpl; babines fpl.
chopsticks ['tʃɒpstɪks] npl baguettes fpl.
choral ['kɔːrəl] adj choral(e), chanté(e) en chœur.
chord [kɔːd] n (*MUS*) accord m.
chore [tʃɔː*] n travail m de routine; **household** ~s travaux mpl du ménage.
choreographer [kɒrɪ'ɒɡrəfə*] n chorégraphe m/f.
choreography [kɒrɪ'ɒɡrəfɪ] n chorégraphie f.
chorister ['kɒrɪstə*] n choriste m/f.
chortle ['tʃɔːtl] vi glousser.
chorus ['kɔːrəs] n chœur m; (*repeated part of song, also fig*) refrain m.
chose [tʃəuz] pt of **choose**.
chosen ['tʃəuzn] pp of **choose**.
chow [tʃau] n (*dog*) chow-chow m.
chowder ['tʃaudə*] n soupe f de poisson.
Christ [kraɪst] n Christ m.
christen ['krɪsn] vt baptiser.
christening ['krɪsnɪŋ] n baptême m.
Christian ['krɪstɪən] adj, n chrétien(ne).
Christianity [krɪstɪ'ænɪtɪ] n christianisme m.
Christian name n prénom m.
Christmas ['krɪsməs] n Noël m or f; **happy or merry** ~! joyeux Noël!
Christmas card n carte f de Noël.
Christmas Day n le jour de Noël.
Christmas Eve n la veille de Noël; la nuit de Noël.
Christmas Island n île f Christmas.
Christmas tree n arbre m de Noël.
chrome [krəum] n = **chromium**.
chromium ['krəumɪəm] n chrome m; (*also:* ~ **plating**) chromage m.
chromosome ['krəuməsəum] n chromosome m.
chronic ['krɒnɪk] adj chronique; (*fig: liar, smoker*) invétéré(e).
chronicle ['krɒnɪkl] n chronique f.
chronological [krɒnə'lɒdʒɪkl] adj chronologique.
chrysanthemum [krɪ'sænθəməm] n chrysanthème m.
chubby ['tʃʌbɪ] adj potelé(e), rondelet(te).
chuck [tʃʌk] vt lancer, jeter; **to** ~ (**up** or **in**) vt (*BRIT: job*) lâcher; (: *person*) plaquer.
▶**chuck out** vt flanquer dehors or à la porte.
chuckle ['tʃʌkl] vi glousser.
chuffed [tʃʌft] adj (*BRIT col*): **to be** ~ **about sth** être content(e) de qch.
chug [tʃʌɡ] vi faire teuf-teuf; souffler.
chum [tʃʌm] n copain/copine.
chump ['tʃʌmp] n (*col*) imbécile m/f, crétin/e.
chunk [tʃʌŋk] n gros morceau; (*of bread*) quignon m.

chunky ['tʃʌŋkɪ] adj (*furniture etc*) massif(ive); (*person*) trapu(e); (*knitwear*) en grosse laine.
Chunnel ['tʃʌnl] n = **Channel Tunnel**.
church [tʃəːtʃ] n église f; **the C~ of England** l'Église anglicane.
churchyard ['tʃəːtʃjɑːd] n cimetière m.
churlish ['tʃəːlɪʃ] adj grossier(ère); hargneux(euse).
churn [tʃəːn] n (*for butter*) baratte f; (*for transport: also:* **milk** ~) (grand) bidon à lait.
▶**churn out** vt débiter.
chute [ʃuːt] n glissoire f; (*also: rubbish* ~) vide-ordures m inv; (*BRIT: children's slide*) toboggan m.
chutney ['tʃʌtnɪ] n chutney m.
CIA n abbr (*US:* = *Central Intelligence Agency*) CIA f.
CID n abbr (*BRIT:* = *Criminal Investigation Department*) ≈ P.J. f (= *police judiciaire*).
cider ['saɪdə*] n cidre m.
CIF abbr (= *cost, insurance and freight*) CAF.
cigar [sɪ'ɡɑː*] n cigare m.
cigarette [sɪɡə'ret] n cigarette f.
cigarette case n étui m à cigarettes.
cigarette end n mégot m.
cigarette holder n fume-cigarettes m inv.
C-in-C abbr = **commander-in-chief**.
cinch [sɪntʃ] n (*col*): **it's a** ~ c'est du gâteau, c'est l'enfance de l'art.
cinder ['sɪndə*] n cendre f.
Cinderella [sɪndə'relə] n Cendrillon.
cine-camera ['sɪnɪ'kæmərə] n (*BRIT*) caméra f.
cine-film ['sɪnɪfɪlm] n (*BRIT*) film m.
cinema ['sɪnəmə] n cinéma m.
cine-projector ['sɪnɪprə'dʒektə*] n (*BRIT*) projecteur m de cinéma.
cinnamon ['sɪnəmən] n cannelle f.
cipher ['saɪfə*] n code secret; (*fig: faceless employee etc*) numéro m; **in** ~ codé(e).
circa ['səːkə] prep circa, environ.
circle ['səːkl] n cercle m; (*in cinema*) balcon m ♦ vi faire or décrire des cercles ♦ vt (*surround*) entourer, encercler; (*move round*) faire le tour de, tourner autour de.
circuit ['səːkɪt] n circuit m.
circuit board n plaquette f.
circuitous [səː'kjuɪtəs] adj indirect(e), qui fait un détour.
circular ['səːkjulə*] adj circulaire ♦ n circulaire f; (*as advertisement*) prospectus m.
circulate ['səːkjuleɪt] vi circuler ♦ vt faire circuler.
circulation [səːkju'leɪʃən] n circulation f; (*of newspaper*) tirage m.
circumcise ['səːkəmsaɪz] vt circoncire.
circumference [sə'kʌmfərəns] n circonférence f.
circumflex ['səːkəmfleks] n (*also:* ~ **accent**) accent m circonflexe.
circumscribe ['səːkəmskraɪb] vt circonscrire.
circumspect ['səːkəmspekt] adj circonspect(e).

circumstances ['sɔːkəmstənsɪz] *npl* circonstances *fpl*; (*financial condition*) moyens *mpl*, situation financière; **in the** ~ dans ces conditions; **under no** ~ en aucun cas, sous aucun prétexte.

circumstantial [sɔːkəm'stænʃl] *adj* (*report, statement*) circonstancié(e); ~ **evidence** preuve indirecte.

circumvent [sɔːkəm'vɛnt] *vt* (*rule etc*) tourner.

circus ['sɔːkəs] *n* cirque *m*; (*also:* **C~**: *in place names*) place *f*.

cirrhosis [sɪ'rəʊsɪs] *n* (*also:* ~ **of the liver**) cirrhose *f* (du foie).

CIS *n abbr* (= *Commonwealth of Independent States*) CEI *f*.

cissy ['sɪsɪ] *n* = **sissy**.

cistern ['sɪstən] *n* réservoir *m* (d'eau); (*in toilet*) réservoir de la chasse d'eau.

citation [saɪ'teɪʃən] *n* citation *f*; (*US*) P.-V. *m.*

cite [saɪt] *vt* citer.

citizen ['sɪtɪzn] *n* (*POL*) citoyen/ne; (*resident*): **the ~s of this town** les habitants de cette ville.

Citizens' Advice Bureau ['sɪtɪznz-] *n* (*BRIT*) ≈ Bureau *m* d'aide sociale.

citizenship ['sɪtɪznʃɪp] *n* citoyenneté *f.*

citric ['sɪtrɪk] *adj*: ~ **acid** acide *m* citrique.

citrus fruit ['sɪtrəs-] *n* agrume *m.*

city ['sɪtɪ] *n* ville *f*, cité *f*; **the C~** la Cité de Londres (*centre des affaires*).

city centre *n* centre-ville *m.*

City Hall *n* (*US*) ≈ hôtel *m* de ville.

City Technology College *n* (*BRIT*) établissement *m* d'enseignement technologique (*situé dans un quartier défavorisé*).

civic ['sɪvɪk] *adj* civique.

civic centre *n* (*BRIT*) centre administratif (municipal).

civil ['sɪvɪl] *adj* civil(e); (*polite*) poli(e), civil(e).

civil disobedience *n* désobéissance civile.

civil engineer *n* ingénieur civil.

civil engineering *n* génie civil, travaux publics.

civilian [sɪ'vɪlɪən] *adj, n* civil(e).

civilization [sɪvɪlaɪ'zeɪʃən] *n* civilisation *f.*

civilized ['sɪvɪlaɪzd] *adj* civilisé(e); (*fig*) où règnent les bonnes manières, empreint(e) d'une courtoisie de bon ton.

civil law *n* code civil; (*study*) droit civil.

civil liberties *npl* libertés *fpl* civiques.

civil rights *npl* droits *mpl* civiques.

civil servant *n* fonctionnaire *m/f.*

Civil Service *n* fonction publique, administration *f.*

civil war *n* guerre civile.

civvies ['sɪvɪz] *npl*: **in** ~ (*col*) en civil.

cl *abbr* (= *centilitre*) cl.

clad [klæd] *adj*: ~ **(in)** habillé(e) de, vêtu(e) de.

claim [kleɪm] *vt* (*rights etc*) revendiquer; (*compensation*) réclamer; **to** ~ **that/to be** prétendre que/être ♦ *vi* (*for insurance*) faire une déclaration de sinistre ♦ *n* revendication *f*;

prétention *f*; (*right*) droit *m*; (*for expenses*) note *f* de frais; (*insurance*) ~ demande *f* d'indemnisation, déclaration *f* de sinistre; **to put in a** ~ **for** (*pay rise etc*) demander.

claimant ['kleɪmənt] *n* (*ADMIN, LAW*) requérant/e.

claim form *n* (*gen*) formulaire *m* de demande.

clairvoyant [klɛə'vɔɪənt] *n* voyant/e, extralucide *m/f.*

clam [klæm] *n* palourde *f.*

►**clam up** *vi* (*col*) la boucler.

clamber ['klæmbə*] *vi* grimper, se hisser.

clammy ['klæmɪ] *adj* humide et froid(e) (au toucher), moite.

clamour, (*US*) **clamor** ['klæmə*] *n* (*noise*) clameurs *fpl*; (*protest*) protestations bruyantes ♦ *vi*: **to** ~ **for sth** réclamer qch à grands cris.

clamp [klæmp] *n* étau *m* à main; agrafe *f*, crampon *m* ♦ *vt* serrer; cramponner.

►**clamp down on** *vt fus* sévir contre, prendre des mesures draconiennes à l'égard de.

clampdown ['klæmpdaun] *n*: **there has been a** ~ **on ...** des mesures énergiques ont été prises contre ....

clan [klæn] *n* clan *m.*

clandestine [klæn'dɛstɪn] *adj* clandestin(e).

clang [klæŋ] *n* bruit *m or* fracas *m* métallique ♦ *vi* émettre un bruit *or* fracas métallique.

clanger ['klæŋə*] *n*: **to drop a** ~ (*BRIT col*) faire une boulette.

clansman ['klænzmən] *n* membre *m* d'un clan (écossais).

clap [klæp] *vi* applaudir ♦ *vt*: **to** ~ **(one's hands)** battre des mains ♦ *n* claquement *m*; tape *f*; **a** ~ **of thunder** un coup de tonnerre.

clapping ['klæpɪŋ] *n* applaudissements *mpl.*

claptrap ['klæptræp] *n* (*col*) baratin *m.*

claret ['klærət] *n* (vin *m* de) bordeaux *m* (rouge).

clarification [klærɪfɪ'keɪʃən] *n* (*fig*) clarification *f*, éclaircissement *m.*

clarify ['klærɪfaɪ] *vt* clarifier.

clarinet [klærɪ'nɛt] *n* clarinette *f.*

clarity ['klærɪtɪ] *n* clarté *f.*

clash [klæʃ] *n* (*sound*) choc *m*, fracas *m*; (*with police*) affrontement *m*; (*fig*) conflit *m* ♦ *vi* se heurter; être *or* entrer en conflit; (*dates, events*) tomber en même temps.

clasp [klɑːsp] *n* fermoir *m* ♦ *vt* serrer, étreindre.

class [klɑːs] *n* (*gen*) classe *f*; (*group, category*) catégorie *f* ♦ *vt* classer, classifier.

class-conscious [klɑːs'kɔnʃəs] *adj* conscient(e) de son appartenance sociale.

class consciousness *n* conscience *f* de classe.

classic ['klæsɪk] *adj* classique ♦ *n* (*author*) classique *m*; (*race etc*) classique *f.*

classical ['klæsɪkl] *adj* classique.

classics ['klæsɪks] *npl* (*SCOL*) lettres *fpl* classiques.

classification [klæsɪfɪ'keɪʃən] n classification f.

classified ['klæsɪfaɪd] adj (information) secret(ète); ~ **ads** petites annonces.

classify ['klæsɪfaɪ] vt classifier, classer.

classless society ['klɑːslɪs-] n société f sans classes.

classmate ['klɑːsmeɪt] n camarade m/f de classe.

classroom ['klɑːsrum] n (salle f de) classe f.

clatter ['klætə*] n cliquetis m ♦ vi cliqueter.

clause [klɔːz] n clause f; (LING) proposition f.

claustrophobia [klɔːstrə'fəubɪə] n claustrophobie f.

claustrophobic [klɔːstrə'fəubɪk] adj (person) claustrophobe; (place) claustrophobique.

claw [klɔː] n griffe f; (of bird of prey) serre f; (of lobster) pince f ♦ vt griffer; déchirer.

clay [kleɪ] n argile f.

clean [kliːn] adj propre; (clear, smooth) net(te) ♦ vt nettoyer ♦ adv: **he ~ forgot** il a complètement oublié; **to come ~** (col: admit guilt) se mettre à table; **to ~ one's teeth** (BRIT) se laver les dents; ~ **driving licence** or (US) **record** permis où n'est portée aucune indication de contravention.

▶**clean off** vt enlever.

▶**clean out** vt nettoyer (à fond).

▶**clean up** vt nettoyer, (fig) remettre de l'ordre dans ♦ vi (fig: make profit): **to ~ up on** faire son beurre avec.

clean-cut ['kliːn'kʌt] adj (man) soigné; (situation etc) bien délimité(e), net(te), clair(e).

cleaner ['kliːnə*] n (person) nettoyeur/euse, femme f de ménage; (also: **dry ~er**) teinturier/ière; (product) détachant m.

cleaning ['kliːnɪŋ] n nettoyage m.

cleaning lady n femme f de ménage.

cleanliness ['klɛnlɪnɪs] n propreté f.

cleanly ['kliːnlɪ] adv proprement; nettement.

cleanse [klɛnz] vt nettoyer; purifier.

cleanser ['klɛnzə*] n détergent m; (for face) démaquillant m.

clean-shaven ['kliːn'ʃeɪvn] adj rasé(e) de près.

cleansing department ['klɛnzɪŋ-] n (BRIT) service m de voirie.

clean sweep n: to make a ~ (SPORT) rafler tous les prix.

clean-up ['kliːnʌp] n nettoyage m.

clear [klɪə*] adj clair(e); (road, way) libre, dégagé(e); (profit, majority) net(te) ♦ vt dégager, déblayer, débarrasser; (room etc: of people) faire évacuer; (woodland) défricher; (cheque) compenser; (COMM: goods) liquider; (LAW: suspect) innocenter; (obstacle) franchir or sauter sans heurter ♦ vi (weather) s'éclaircir; (fog) se dissiper ♦ adv: ~ of à distance de, à l'écart de ♦ n: **to be in the ~** (out of debt) être dégagé(e) de toute dette; (out of suspicion) être lavé(e) de tout soup-

çon; (out of danger) être hors de danger; **to ~ the table** débarrasser la table, desservir; **to ~ one's throat** s'éclaircir la gorge; **to ~ a profit** faire un bénéfice net; **to make o.s. ~** se faire bien comprendre; **to make it ~ to sb that** ... bien faire comprendre à qn que ...; **I have a ~ day tomorrow** (BRIT) je n'ai rien de prévu demain; **to keep ~ of sb/sth** éviter qn/qch.

▶**clear off** vi (col: leave) dégager.

▶**clear up** vi s'éclaircir, se dissiper ♦ vt ranger, mettre en ordre; (mystery) éclaircir, résoudre.

clearance ['klɪərəns] n (removal) déblayage m; (free space) dégagement m; (permission) autorisation f.

clearance sale n (COMM) liquidation f.

clear-cut ['klɪə'kʌt] adj précis(e), nettement défini(e).

clearing ['klɪərɪŋ] n (in forest) clairière f; (BRIT BANKING) compensation f, clearing m.

clearing bank n (BRIT) banque f qui appartient à une chambre de compensation.

clearly ['klɪəlɪ] adv clairement; (obviously) de toute évidence.

clearway ['klɪəweɪ] n (BRIT) route f à stationnement interdit.

cleavage ['kliːvɪdʒ] n (of dress) décolleté m.

cleaver ['kliːvə*] n fendoir m, couperet m.

clef [klɛf] n (MUS) clé f.

cleft [klɛft] n (in rock) crevasse f, fissure f.

clemency ['klɛmənsɪ] n clémence f.

clement ['klɛmənt] adj (weather) clément(e).

clench [klɛntʃ] vt serrer.

clergy ['klɜːdʒɪ] n clergé m.

clergyman ['klɜːdʒɪmən] n ecclésiastique m.

clerical ['klɛrɪkl] adj de bureau, d'employé de bureau; (REL) clérical(e), du clergé.

clerk [klɑːk, (US) klɜːrk] n employé/e de bureau; (US: salesman/woman) vendeur/euse; **C~ of Court** (LAW) greffier m (du tribunal).

clever ['klɛvə*] adj (mentally) intelligent(e); (deft, crafty) habile, adroit(e); (device, arrangement) ingénieux(euse), astucieux(euse).

cleverly ['klɛvəlɪ] adv (skilfully) habilement; (craftily) astucieusement.

clew [kluː] n (US) = **clue**.

cliché ['kliːʃeɪ] n cliché m.

click [klɪk] vi faire un bruit sec or un déclic ♦ vt: **to ~ one's tongue** faire claquer sa langue; **to ~ one's heels** claquer les talons.

client ['klaɪənt] n client/e.

clientele [kliː̃ãːn'tɛl] n clientèle f.

cliff [klɪf] n falaise f.

cliffhanger ['klɪfhæŋə*] n (TV, fig) histoire pleine de suspense.

climactic [klaɪ'mæktɪk] adj à son point culminant, culminant(e).

climate ['klaɪmɪt] n climat m.

climax ['klaɪmæks] n apogée m, point culminant; (sexual) orgasme m.

climb [klaɪm] vi grimper, monter; (plane)

prendre de l'altitude ♦ vt gravir, escalader, monter sur ♦ n montée f, escalade f; to ~ over a wall passer par dessus un mur.
►**climb down** vi (re)descendre; (BRIT fig) rabattre de ses prétentions.
climbdown ['klaımdaun] n (BRIT) reculade f.
climber ['klaımə*] n (also: **rock ~**) grimpeur/euse, varappeur/euse.
climbing ['klaımıŋ] n (also: **rock ~**) escalade f, varappe f.
clinch [klıntʃ] vt (deal) conclure, sceller.
clincher ['klıntʃə*] n: **that was the ~** c'est ce qui a fait pencher la balance.
cling, pt, pp **clung** [klıŋ, klʌŋ] vi: **to ~ (to)** se cramponner (à), s'accrocher (à); (of clothes) coller (à).
clingfilm ['klıŋfılm] n film m alimentaire.
clinic ['klınık] n clinique f; centre médical; (session: MED) consultation(s) f(pl), séance(s) f(pl); (: SPORT) séance(s) de perfectionnement.
clinical ['klınıkl] adj clinique; (fig) froid(e).
clink [klıŋk] vi tinter, cliqueter.
clip [klıp] n (for hair) barrette f; (also: **paper ~**) trombone m; (BRIT: also: **bulldog ~**) pince f de bureau; (holding hose etc) collier m or bague f (métallique) de serrage ♦ vt (also: **~ together**: papers) attacher; (hair, nails) couper; (hedge) tailler.
clippers ['klıpəz] npl tondeuse f; (also: **nail ~**) coupe-ongles m inv.
clipping ['klıpıŋ] n (from newspaper) coupure f de journal.
clique [kliːk] n clique f, coterie f.
cloak [kləuk] n grande cape.
cloakroom ['kləukrum] n (for coats etc) vestiaire m; (BRIT: W.C.) toilettes fpl.
clock [klɔk] n (large) horloge f; (small) pendule f; **round the ~** (work etc) vingt-quatre heures sur vingt-quatre; **to sleep round the ~** or **the ~ round** faire le tour du cadran; **30,000 on the ~** (BRIT AUT) 30 000 milles au compteur; **to work against the ~** faire la course contre la montre.
►**clock in, clock on** vi (BRIT) pointer (en arrivant).
►**clock off, clock out** vi (BRIT) pointer (en partant).
►**clock up** vt (miles, hours etc) faire.
clockwise ['klɔkwaız] adv dans le sens des aiguilles d'une montre.
clockwork ['klɔkwəːk] n mouvement m (d'horlogerie); rouages mpl, mécanisme m ♦ adj (toy, train) mécanique.
clog [klɔg] n sabot m ♦ vt boucher, encrasser ♦ vi se boucher, s'encrasser.
cloister ['klɔıstə*] n cloître m.
clone [kləun] n clone m.
close adj, adv and derivatives [kləus] adj (near): **~ (to)** près (de), proche (de); (writing, texture) serré(e); (watch) étroit(e), strict(e); (examination) attentif(ive), minutieux(euse); (weather) lourd(e), étouffant(e); (room) mal aéré(e) ♦ adv près, à proximité; **~ to** prep près de; **~ by, ~ at hand** adj, adv tout(e) près; **how ~ is Edinburgh to Glasgow?** combien de kilomètres y-a-t-il entre Édimbourg et Glasgow?; **a ~ friend** un ami intime; **to have a ~ shave** (fig) l'échapper belle; **at ~ quarters** tout près, à côté ♦ vb and derivatives [kləuz] vt fermer; (bargain, deal) conclure ♦ vi (shop etc) fermer; (lid, door etc) se fermer; (end) se terminer, se conclure ♦ n (end) conclusion f; **to bring sth to a ~** mettre fin à qch.
►**close down** vt, vi fermer (définitivement).
►**close in** vi (hunters) approcher; (night, fog) tomber; **the days are closing in** les jours raccourcissent; **to ~ in on sb** cerner qn.
►**close off** vt (area) boucler.
closed [kləuzd] adj (shop etc) fermé(e); (road) fermé à la circulation.
closed-circuit ['kləuzd'səːkıt] adj: **~ television** télévision f en circuit fermé.
closed shop n organisation f qui n'admet que des travailleurs syndiqués.
close-knit ['kləus'nıt] adj (family, community) très uni(e).
closely ['kləuslı] adv (examine, watch) de près; **we are ~ related** nous sommes proches parents; **a ~ guarded secret** un secret bien gardé.
close season [kləus-] n (BRIT: HUNTING) fermeture f de la chasse/pêche; (: FOOTBALL) trêve f.
closet ['klɔzıt] n (cupboard) placard m, réduit m.
close-up ['kləusʌp] n gros plan.
closing ['kləuzıŋ] adj (stages, remarks) final(e); **~ price** (STOCK EXCHANGE) cours m de clôture; **~ time** heure f de fermeture.
closure ['kləuʒə*] n fermeture f.
clot [klɔt] n (gen: **blood ~**) caillot m; (col: person) ballot m ♦ vi (blood) former des caillots; (: external bleeding) se coaguler.
cloth [klɔθ] n (material) tissu m, étoffe f; (BRIT: also: **tea~**) torchon m; lavette f; (also: **table~**) nappe f.
clothe [kləuð] vt habiller, vêtir.
clothes [kləuðz] npl vêtements mpl, habits mpl; **to put one's ~ on** s'habiller; **to take one's ~ off** enlever ses vêtements.
clothes brush n brosse f à habits.
clothes line n corde f (à linge).
clothes peg, (US) **clothes pin** n pince f à linge.
clothing ['kləuðıŋ] n = **clothes**.
clotted cream ['klɔtıd-] n (BRIT) crème caillée.
cloud [klaud] n nuage m ♦ vt (liquid) troubler; **to ~ the issue** brouiller les cartes; **every ~ has a silver lining** (proverb) à quelque chose malheur est bon (proverbe).
►**cloud over** vi se couvrir; (fig) s'assombrir.

cloudburst ['klaudbə:st] n violente averse.
cloud-cuckoo-land ['klaud'kuku:'lænd] n (BRIT) monde m imaginaire.
cloudy ['klaudı] adj nuageux(euse), couvert(e); (liquid) trouble.
clout [klaut] n (blow) taloche f; (fig) pouvoir m ♦ vt flanquer une taloche à.
clove [kləuv] n clou m de girofle; ~ **of garlic** gousse f d'ail.
clover ['kləuvə*] n trèfle m.
cloverleaf ['kləuvəli:f] n feuille f de trèfle; (AUT) croisement m en trèfle.
clown [klaun] n clown m ♦ vi (also: ~ **about**, ~ **around**) faire le clown.
cloying ['kloiiŋ] adj (taste, smell) écœurant(e).
club [klʌb] n (society) club m; (weapon) massue f, matraque f; (also: golf ~) club ♦ vt matraquer ♦ vi: **to ~ together** s'associer; ~**s** npl (CARDS) trèfle m.
club car n (US RAIL) wagon-restaurant m.
club class n (AVIAT) classe f club.
clubhouse ['klʌbhaus] n pavillon m.
club soda n (US) eau f de seltz.
cluck [klʌk] vi glousser.
clue [klu:] n indice m; (in crosswords) définition f; **I haven't a** ~ je n'en ai pas la moindre idée.
clued up, (US) **clued in** [klu:d-] adj (col) (vachement) calé(e).
clump [klʌmp] n: ~ **of trees** bouquet m d'arbres.
clumsy ['klʌmzı] adj (person) gauche, maladroit(e); (object) malcommode, peu maniable.
clung [klʌŋ] pt, pp of **cling.**
cluster ['klʌstə*] n (petit) groupe ♦ vi se rassembler.
clutch [klʌtʃ] n (grip, grasp) étreinte f, prise f; (AUT) embrayage m ♦ vt agripper, serrer fort; **to ~ at** se cramponner à.
clutter ['klʌtə*] vt (also: ~ **up**) encombrer ♦ n désordre m, fouillis m.
CM abbr (US POST) = North Mariana Islands.
cm abbr (= centimetre) cm.
CNAA n abbr (BRIT: = Council for National Academic Awards) organisme non universitaire délivrant des diplômes.
CND n abbr = Campaign for Nuclear Disarmament.
CO n abbr (= commanding officer) Cdt; (BRIT) = Commonwealth Office ♦ abbr (US) = Colorado.
Co. abbr = **company, county.**
c/o abbr (= care of) c/o, aux bons soins de.
coach [kəutʃ] n (bus) autocar m; (horse-drawn) diligence f; (of train) voiture f, wagon m; (SPORT: trainer) entraîneur/euse; (school: tutor) répétiteur/trice ♦ vt entraîner; donner des leçons particulières à.
coach trip n excursion f en car.
coagulate [kəu'ægjuleit] vt coaguler ♦ vi se coaguler.
coal [kəul] n charbon m.

coal face n front m de taille.
coalfield ['kəulfi:ld] n bassin houiller.
coalition [kəuə'lıʃən] n coalition f.
coalman ['kəulmən] n charbonnier m, marchand m de charbon.
coal mine n mine f de charbon.
coal miner n mineur m.
coal mining n extraction f du charbon.
coarse [kɔ:s] adj grossier(ère), rude; (vulgar) vulgaire.
coast [kəust] n côte f ♦ vi (with cycle etc) descendre en roue libre.
coastal ['kəustl] adj côtier(ère).
coaster ['kəustə*] n (NAUT) caboteur m; (for glass) dessous m de verre.
coastguard ['kəustga:d] n garde-côte m.
coastline ['kəustlain] n côte f, littoral m.
coat [kəut] n manteau m; (of animal) pelage m, poil m; (of paint) couche f ♦ vt couvrir, enduire; ~ **of arms** n blason m, armoiries fpl.
coat hanger n cintre m.
coating ['kəutiŋ] n couche f, enduit m.
co-author ['kəu'ɔ:θə*] n co-auteur m.
coax [kəuks] vt persuader par des cajoleries.
cob [kɔb] n see **corn.**
cobbler ['kɔblə*] n cordonnier m.
cobbles, cobblestones ['kɔblz, 'kɔblstəunz] npl pavés (ronds).
COBOL ['kəubɔl] n COBOL m.
cobra ['kəubrə] n cobra m.
cobweb ['kɔbwɛb] n toile f d'araignée.
cocaine [kə'kein] n cocaïne f.
cock [kɔk] n (rooster) coq m; (male bird) mâle m ♦ vt (gun) armer; **to ~ one's ears** (fig) dresser l'oreille.
cock-a-hoop [kɔkə'hu:p] adj jubilant(e).
cockerel ['kɔkərl] n jeune coq m.
cock-eyed ['kɔkaid] adj (fig) de travers; qui louche; qui ne tient pas debout (fig).
cockle ['kɔkl] n coque f.
cockney ['kɔkni] n cockney m/f (habitant des quartiers populaires de l'East End de Londres), ≈ faubourien/ne.
cockpit ['kɔkpit] n (in aircraft) poste m de pilotage, cockpit m.
cockroach ['kɔkrəutʃ] n cafard m, cancrelat m.
cocktail ['kɔkteil] n cocktail m; **prawn** ~, (US) **shrimp** ~ cocktail de crevettes.
cocktail cabinet n (meuble-)bar m.
cocktail party n cocktail m.
cocktail shaker [-'ʃeikə*] n shaker m.
cocky ['kɔki] adj trop sûr(e) de soi.
cocoa ['kəukəu] n cacao m.
coconut ['kəukənʌt] n noix f de coco.
cocoon [kə'ku:n] n cocon m.
COD abbr = **cash on delivery, collect on delivery** (US).
cod [kɔd] n morue (fraîche), cabillaud m.
code [kəud] n code m; ~ **of behaviour** règles fpl de conduite; ~ **of practice** déontologie f.
codeine ['kəudi:n] n codéine f.

codger ['kɔdʒə*] n: **an old** ~ (BRIT col) un drôle de vieux bonhomme.
codicil ['kɔdɪsɪl] n codicille m.
codify ['kəudɪfaɪ] vt codifier.
cod-liver oil ['kɔdlɪvər-] n huile f de foie de morue.
co-driver ['kəu'draɪvə*] n (in race) copilote m; (of lorry) deuxième chauffeur m.
co-ed ['kəu'ɛd] adj abbr = **coeducational** ♦ n abbr (US: female student) étudiante d'une université mixte; (BRIT: school) école f mixte.
coeducational ['kəuɛdju'keɪʃənl] adj mixte.
coerce [kəu'ə:s] vt contraindre.
coercion [kəu'ə:ʃən] n contrainte f.
coexistence ['kəuɪg'zɪstəns] n coexistence f.
C. of C. n abbr = **chamber of commerce**.
C of E abbr = **Church of England**.
coffee ['kɔfɪ] n café m; **white** ~, (US) ~ **with cream** (café-)crème m.
coffee bar n (BRIT) café m.
coffee bean n grain m de café.
coffee break n pause-café f.
coffeecake ['kɔfɪkeɪk] n (US) ≈ petit pain aux raisins.
coffee cup n tasse f à café.
coffeepot ['kɔfɪpɔt] n cafetière f.
coffee table n (petite) table basse.
coffin ['kɔfɪn] n cercueil m.
C of I abbr = Church of Ireland.
C of S abbr = Church of Scotland.
cog [kɔg] n dent f (d'engrenage).
cogent ['kəudʒənt] adj puissant(e), convaincant(e).
cognac ['kɔnjæk] n cognac m.
cogwheel ['kɔgwi:l] n roue dentée.
cohabit [kəu'hæbɪt] vi (formal): **to** ~ **(with sb)** cohabiter (avec qn).
coherent [kəu'hɪərənt] adj cohérent(e).
cohesion [kəu'hi:ʒən] n cohésion f.
cohesive [kəu'hi:sɪv] adj (fig) cohésif(ive).
COI n abbr (BRIT: = Central Office of Information) service d'information gouvernemental.
coil [kɔɪl] n rouleau m, bobine f; (one loop) anneau m, spire f; (of smoke) volute f; (contraceptive) stérilet m ♦ vt enrouler.
coin [kɔɪn] n pièce f de monnaie ♦ vt (word) inventer.
coinage ['kɔɪnɪdʒ] n monnaie f, système m monétaire.
coin-box ['kɔɪnbɔks] n (BRIT) cabine f téléphonique.
coincide [kəuɪn'saɪd] vi coïncider.
coincidence [kəu'ɪnsɪdəns] n coïncidence f.
coin-operated ['kɔɪn'ɔpəreɪtɪd] adj (machine, launderette) automatique.
Coke [kəuk] n ® coca m.
coke [kəuk] n coke m.
Col. abbr (= colonel) Col; (US) = Colorado.
COLA n abbr (US: = cost-of-living adjustment) réajustement (des salaires, indemnités etc) en fonction du coût de la vie.
colander ['kɔləndə*] n passoire f (à légumes).

cold [kəuld] adj froid(e) ♦ n froid m; (MED) rhume m; **it's** ~ il fait froid; **to be** ~ avoir froid; **to catch** ~ prendre or attraper froid; **to catch a** ~ s'enrhumer, attraper un rhume; **in** ~ **blood** de sang-froid; **to have** ~ **feet** avoir froid aux pieds; (fig) avoir la frousse or la trouille; **to give sb the** ~ **shoulder** battre froid à qn.
cold-blooded ['kəuld'blʌdɪd] adj (ZOOL) à sang froid.
cold cream n crème f de soins.
coldly ['kəuldlɪ] adv froidement.
cold sore n bouton m de fièvre.
cold sweat n: **to be in a** ~ **(about sth)** avoir des sueurs froides (au sujet de qch).
cold turkey n (col) manque m; **to go** ~ être en manque.
Cold War n: **the** ~ la guerre froide.
coleslaw ['kəulslɔ:] n sorte de salade de chou cru.
colic ['kɔlɪk] n colique(s) f(pl).
colicky ['kɔlɪkɪ] adj qui souffre de coliques.
collaborate [kə'læbəreɪt] vi collaborer.
collaboration [kəlæbə'reɪʃən] n collaboration f.
collaborator [kə'læbəreɪtə*] n collaborateur/trice.
collage [kɔ'lɑ:ʒ] n (ART) collage m.
collagen ['kɔlədʒən] n collagène m.
collapse [kə'læps] vi s'effondrer, s'écrouler ♦ n effondrement m, écroulement m; (of government) chute f.
collapsible [kə'læpsəbl] adj pliant(e); télescopique.
collar ['kɔlə*] n (of coat, shirt) col m; (for dog) collier m; (TECH) collier, bague f ♦ vt (col: person) pincer.
collarbone ['kɔləbəun] n clavicule f.
collate [kɔ'leɪt] vt collationner.
collateral [kə'lætərl] n nantissement m.
collation [kə'leɪʃən] n collation f.
colleague ['kɔli:g] n collègue m/f.
collect [kə'lɛkt] vt rassembler; (pick up) ramasser; (as a hobby) collectionner; (BRIT: call for) (passer) prendre; (mail) faire la levée de, ramasser; (money owed) encaisser; (donations, subscriptions) recueillir ♦ vi (people) se rassembler; (dust, dirt) s'amasser; **to** ~ **one's thoughts** réfléchir, réunir ses idées; ~ **on delivery (COD)** (US COMM) payable or paiement à la livraison; **to call** ~ (US TEL) téléphoner en PCV.
collected [kə'lɛktɪd] adj: ~ **works** œuvres complètes.
collection [kə'lɛkʃən] n collection f; (of mail) levée f; (for money) collecte f, quête f.
collective [kə'lɛktɪv] adj collectif(ive) ♦ n collectif m.
collective bargaining n convention collective.
collector [kə'lɛktə*] n collectionneur m; (of taxes) percepteur m; (of rent, cash) encais-

seur _m_; ~'s **item** or **piece** pièce _f_ de collection.

college ['kɔlɪdʒ] _n_ collège _m_; (_of technology, agriculture etc_) institut _m_; **to go to** ~ faire des études supérieures; ~ **of education** ≈ école normale.

collide [kə'laɪd] _vi_: **to** ~ **(with)** entrer en collision (avec).

collie ['kɔlɪ] _n_ (_dog_) colley _m_.

colliery ['kɔlɪərɪ] _n_ (_BRIT_) mine _f_ de charbon, houillère _f_.

collision [kə'lɪʒən] _n_ collision _f_, heurt _m_; **to be on a** ~ **course** aller droit à la collision; (_fig_) aller vers l'affrontement.

collision damage waiver _n_ (_INSURANCE_) rachat _m_ de franchise.

colloquial [kə'ləukwɪəl] _adj_ familier(ère).

collusion [kə'luːʒən] _n_ collusion _f_; **in** ~ **with** en complicité avec.

Colo. _abbr_ (_US_) = _Colorado_.

cologne [kə'ləun] _n_ (_also:_ **eau de** ~) eau _f_ de cologne.

Colombia [kə'lɔmbɪə] _n_ Colombie _f_.

Colombian [kə'lɔmbɪən] _adj_ colombien(ne) ♦ _n_ Colombien/ne.

colon ['kəulən] _n_ (_sign_) deux-points _mpl_; (_MED_) côlon _m_.

colonel ['kɜːnl] _n_ colonel _m_.

colonial [kə'ləunɪəl] _adj_ colonial(e).

colonize ['kɔlənaɪz] _vt_ coloniser.

colony ['kɔlənɪ] _n_ colonie _f_.

color etc ['kʌlə*] (_US_) = **colour** etc.

Colorado beetle [kɔlə'rɑːdəu-] _n_ doryphore _m_.

colossal [kə'lɔsl] _adj_ colossal(e).

colour, (_US_) **color** ['kʌlə*] _n_ couleur _f_ ♦ _vt_ colorer; peindre; (_with crayons_) colorier; (_news_) fausser, exagérer ♦ _vi_ rougir ♦ _cpd_ (_film, photograph, television_) en couleur; ~**s** _npl_ (_of party, club_) couleurs _fpl_.

colo(u)r bar _n_ discrimination raciale (_dans un établissement etc_).

colo(u)r-blind ['kʌləblaɪnd] _adj_ daltonien(ne).

colo(u)red ['kʌləd] _adj_ coloré(e); (_photo_) en couleur.

colo(u)rful ['kʌləful] _adj_ coloré(e), vif(vive); (_personality_) pittoresque, haut(e) en couleurs.

colo(u)ring ['kʌlərɪŋ] _n_ colorant _m_; (_complexion_) teint _m_.

colo(u)r scheme _n_ combinaison _f_ de(s) couleur(s).

colour supplement _n_ (_BRIT PRESS_) supplément _m_ magazine.

colt [kəult] _n_ poulain _m_.

column ['kɔləm] _n_ colonne _f_; (_fashion/sports ~ etc_) rubrique _f_; **the editorial** ~ l'éditorial _m_.

columnist ['kɔləmnɪst] _n_ rédacteur/trice d'une rubrique.

coma ['kəumə] _n_ coma _m_.

comb [kəum] _n_ peigne _m_ ♦ _vt_ (_hair_) peigner; (_area_) ratisser, passer au peigne fin.

combat ['kɔmbæt] _n_ combat _m_ ♦ _vt_ combattre, lutter contre.

combination [kɔmbɪ'neɪʃən] _n_ (_gen_) combinaison _f_.

combination lock _n_ serrure _f_ à combinaison.

combine _vb_ [kəm'baɪn] _vt_ combiner; (_one quality with another_): **to** ~ **sth with sth** joindre qch à qch, allier qch à qch ♦ _vi_ s'associer; (_CHEM_) se combiner ♦ _n_ ['kɔmbaɪn] association _f_; (_ECON_) trust _m_; **a** ~**d effort** un effort conjugué.

combine (harvester) _n_ moissonneuse-batteuse(-lieuse) _f_.

combo ['kɔmbəu] _n_ (_JAZZ etc_) groupe _m_ de musiciens.

combustible [kəm'bʌstɪbl] _adj_ combustible.

combustion [kəm'bʌstʃən] _n_ combustion _f_.

come, _pt_ **came,** _pp_ **come** [kʌm, keɪm] _vi_ venir; (_col: sexually_) jouir; ~ **with me** suivez-moi; **we've just** ~ **from Paris** nous arrivons de Paris; ... **what might** ... ~ **of it** ... ce qui pourrait en résulter, ... ce qui pourrait advenir or se produire; **to** ~ **into sight** or **view** apparaître; **to** ~ **to** (_decision etc_) parvenir or arriver à; **to** ~ **undone/loose** se défaire/desserrer; **coming!** j'arrive!; **if it** ~**s to it** s'il le faut, dans le pire des cas.

▶**come about** _vi_ se produire, arriver.

▶**come across** _vt fus_ rencontrer par hasard, tomber sur ♦ _vi_: **to** ~ **across well/badly** faire une bonne/mauvaise impression.

▶**come along** _vi_ (_pupil, work_) faire des progrès, avancer; ~ **along!** viens!; allons!, allez!; **if you** ~ **along on Thursday** ... si vous venez jeudi ...

▶**come apart** _vi_ s'en aller en morceaux; se détacher.

▶**come away** _vi_ partir, s'en aller; (_become detached_) se détacher.

▶**come back** _vi_ revenir; (_reply_): **can I** ~ **back to you on that one?** est-ce qu'on peut revenir là-dessus plus tard?

▶**come by** _vt fus_ (_acquire_) obtenir, se procurer.

▶**come down** _vi_ descendre; (_prices_) baisser; (_buildings_) s'écrouler; (: _be demolished_) être démoli(e).

▶**come forward** _vi_ s'avancer; (_make o.s. known_) se présenter, s'annoncer.

▶**come from** _vt fus_ venir de; (_place_) venir de, être originaire de.

▶**come in** _vi_ entrer.

▶**come in for** _vt fus_ (_criticism etc_) être l'objet de.

▶**come into** _vt fus_ (_money_) hériter de.

▶**come off** _vi_ (_button_) se détacher; (_stain_) s'enlever; (_attempt_) réussir.

▶**come on** _vi_ (_lights, electricity_) s'allumer; (_central heating_) se mettre en marche; (_pupil, work, project_) faire des progrès, avancer; ~ **on!** viens!; allons!, allez!

▶**come out** _vi_ sortir; (_book_) paraître; (_strike_)

cesser le travail, se mettre en grève.

►**come over** *vt fus*: **I don't know what's ~ over him!** je ne sais pas ce qui lui a pris!

►**come round** *vi* (*after faint, operation*) revenir à soi, reprendre connaissance.

►**come through** *vi* (*survive*) s'en sortir; (*telephone call*): **the call came through** l'appel est bien parvenu.

►**come to** *vi* revenir à soi ♦ *vt* (*add up to: amount*): **how much does it ~ to?** ça fait combien?

►**come under** *vt fus* (*heading*) se trouver sous; (*influence*) subir.

►**come up** *vi* monter.

►**come up against** *vt fus* (*resistance, difficulties*) rencontrer.

►**come up to** *vt fus* arriver à; **the film didn't ~ up to our expectations** le film nous a déçu.

►**come up with** *vt fus*: **he came up with an idea** il a eu une idée, il a proposé quelque chose.

►**come upon** *vt fus* tomber sur.

comeback ['kʌmbæk] *n* (*reaction*) réaction *f*; (*response*) réponse *f*; (*THEAT etc*) rentrée *f*.

Comecon ['kɔmɪkɔn] *n abbr* (= *Council for Mutual Economic Aid*) COMECON *m*.

comedian [kə'miːdɪən] *n* (*in music hall etc*) comique *m*; (*THEAT*) comédien *m*.

comedienne [kəmiːdɪ'ɛn] *n* comique *f*.

comedown ['kʌmdaun] *n* déchéance *f*.

comedy ['kɔmɪdɪ] *n* comédie *f*.

comet ['kɔmɪt] *n* comète *f*.

comeuppance [kʌm'ʌpəns] *n*: **to get one's ~** recevoir ce qu'on mérite.

comfort ['kʌmfət] *n* confort *m*, bien-être *m*; (*solace*) consolation *f*, réconfort *m* ♦ *vt* consoler, réconforter.

comfortable ['kʌmfətəbl] *adj* confortable; **I don't feel very ~ about it** cela m'inquiète un peu.

comfortably ['kʌmfətəblɪ] *adv* (*sit*) confortablement; (*live*) à l'aise.

comforter ['kʌmfətə*] *n* (*US*) édredon *m*.

comforts ['kʌmfəts] *npl* aises *fpl*.

comfort station *n* (*US*) toilettes *fpl*.

comic ['kɔmɪk] *adj* comique ♦ *n* comique *m*; (*magazine*) illustré *m*.

comical ['kɔmɪkl] *adj* amusant(e).

comic strip *n* bande dessinée.

coming ['kʌmɪŋ] *n* arrivée *f* ♦ *adj* (*next*) prochain(e); (*future*) à venir; **in the ~ weeks** dans les prochaines semaines.

coming(s) and going(s) *n(pl)* va-et-vient *m inv*.

Comintern ['kɔmɪntəːn] *n* Comintern *m*.

comma ['kɔmə] *n* virgule *f*.

command [kə'mɑːnd] *n* ordre *m*, commandement *m*; (*MIL: authority*) commandement; (*mastery*) maîtrise *f*; (*COMPUT*) commande *f* ♦ *vt* (*troops*) commander; (*be able to get*) (pouvoir) disposer de, avoir à sa disposi-

tion; (*deserve*) avoir droit à; **to ~ sb to do** donner l'ordre *or* commander à qn de faire; **to have/take ~ of** avoir/prendre le commandement de; **to have at one's ~** (*money, resources etc*) disposer de.

command economy *n* économie planifiée.

commandeer [kɔmən'dɪə*] *vt* réquisitionner (par la force).

commander [kə'mɑːndə*] *n* chef *m*; (*MIL*) commandant *m*.

commander-in-chief [kə'mɑːndərɪn'tʃiːf] *n* (*MIL*) commandant *m* en chef.

commanding [kə'mɑːndɪŋ] *adj* (*appearance*) imposant(e); (*voice, tone*) autoritaire; (*lead, position*) dominant(e).

commanding officer *n* commandant *m*.

commandment [kə'mɑːndmənt] *n* (*REL*) commandement *m*.

command module *n* (*SPACE*) module *m* de commande.

commando [kə'mɑːndəu] *n* commando *m*; membre *m* d'un commando.

commemorate [kə'mɛməreɪt] *vt* commémorer.

commemoration [kəmɛmə'reɪʃən] *n* commémoration *f*.

commemorative [kə'mɛmərətɪv] *adj* commémoratif(ive).

commence [kə'mɛns] *vt*, *vi* commencer.

commend [kə'mɛnd] *vt* louer; recommander.

commendable [kə'mɛndəbl] *adj* louable.

commendation [kɔmɛn'deɪʃən] *n* éloge *m*; recommandation *f*.

commensurate [kə'mɛnʃərɪt] *adj*: **~ with/to** en rapport avec/selon.

comment ['kɔmɛnt] *n* commentaire *m* ♦ *vi* faire des remarques *or* commentaires; **to ~ on** faire des remarques sur; **to ~ that** faire remarquer que; **"no ~"** "je n'ai rien à déclarer".

commentary ['kɔməntərɪ] *n* commentaire *m*; (*SPORT*) reportage *m* (en direct).

commentator ['kɔmənteɪtə*] *n* commentateur *m*; (*SPORT*) reporter *m*.

commerce ['kɔməːs] *n* commerce *m*.

commercial [kə'məːʃəl] *adj* commercial(e) ♦ *n* (*RADIO, TV*) annonce *f* publicitaire, spot *m* (publicitaire).

commercial bank *n* banque *f* d'affaires.

commercial break *n* (*RADIO, TV*) spot *m* (publicitaire).

commercial college *n* école *f* de commerce.

commercialism [kə'məːʃəlɪzəm] *n* mercantilisme *m*.

commercial television *n* publicité *f* à la télévision; chaînes privées (financées par la publicité).

commercial traveller *n* voyageur *m* de commerce.

commercial vehicle *n* véhicule *m* utilitaire.

commiserate [kə'mɪzəreɪt] *vi*: **to ~ with sb** témoigner de la sympathie pour qn.

commission [kə'mɪʃən] n (*committee; fee: also for salesman*) commission f; (*order for work of art etc*) commande f ♦ vt (*MIL*) nommer (à un commandement); (*work of art*) commander, charger un artiste de l'exécution de; **out of** ~ (*NAUT*) hors de service; (*machine*) hors service; **I get 10%** ~ je reçois une commission de 10%; ~ **of inquiry** (*BRIT*) commission d'enquête.

commissionaire [kəmɪʃə'nɛə*] n (*BRIT: at shop, cinema etc*) portier m (en uniforme).

commissioner [kə'mɪʃənə*] n membre m d'une commission; (*POLICE*) préfet m (de police).

commit [kə'mɪt] vt (*act*) commettre; (*to sb's care*) confier (à); **to** ~ **o.s. (to do)** s'engager (à faire); **to** ~ **suicide** se suicider; **to** ~ **to writing** coucher par écrit; **to** ~ **sb for trial** traduire qn en justice.

commitment [kə'mɪtmənt] n engagement m; (*obligation*) responsabilité(s) f(pl).

committed [kə'mɪtɪd] adj (*writer, politician etc*) engagé(e).

committee [kə'mɪtɪ] n comité m; commission f; **to be on a** ~ siéger dans un comité (*or* une commission).

committee meeting n réunion f de comité *or* commission.

commodity [kə'mɒdɪtɪ] n produit m, marchandise f, article m; (*food*) denrée f.

commodity exchange n bourse f de marchandises.

common ['kɒmən] adj (*gen, also pej*) commun(e); (*usual*) courant(e) ♦ n terrain communal; **in** ~ en commun; **in** ~ **use** d'un usage courant; **it's** ~ **knowledge that** il est bien connu *or* notoire que; **to the** ~ **good** pour le bien de tous, dans l'intérêt général.

common cold n: **the** ~ le rhume.

common denominator n dénominateur commun.

commoner ['kɒmənə*] n roturier/ière.

common ground n (*fig*) terrain m d'entente.

common land n terrain communal.

common law n droit coutumier.

common-law ['kɒmənlɔː] adj: ~ **wife** épouse f de facto.

commonly ['kɒmənlɪ] adv communément, généralement; couramment.

Common Market n Marché commun.

commonplace ['kɒmənpleɪs] adj banal(e), ordinaire.

commonroom ['kɒmənrum] n salle commune; (*SCOL*) salle des professeurs.

Commons ['kɒmənz] npl (*BRIT POL*): **the (House of)** ~ la chambre des Communes.

common sense n bon sens.

Commonwealth ['kɒmənwɛlθ] n: **the** ~ le Commonwealth.

> Le **Commonwealth** regroupe 50 États indépendants et plusieurs territoires qui reconnaissent tous le souverain britannique comme chef de cette association.

commotion [kə'məuʃən] n désordre m, tumulte m.

communal ['kɒmjuːnl] adj (*life*) communautaire; (*for common use*) commun(e).

commune n ['kɒmjuːn] (*group*) communauté f ♦ vi [kə'mjuːn]: **to** ~ **with** converser intimement avec; communier avec.

communicate [kə'mjuːnɪkeɪt] vt communiquer, transmettre ♦ vi: **to** ~ **(with)** communiquer (avec).

communication [kəmjuːnɪ'keɪʃən] n communication f.

communication cord n (*BRIT*) sonnette f d'alarme.

communications network n réseau m de communications.

communications satellite n satellite m de télécommunications.

communicative [kə'mjuːnɪkətɪv] adj communicatif(ive).

communion [kə'mjuːnɪən] n (*also*: **Holy C**~) communion f.

communiqué [kə'mjuːnɪkeɪ] n communiqué m.

communism ['kɒmjunɪzəm] n communisme m.

communist ['kɒmjunɪst] adj, n communiste (m/f).

community [kə'mjuːnɪtɪ] n communauté f.

community centre n foyer socio-éducatif, centre m de loisirs.

community chest n (*US*) fonds commun.

community health centre n centre médico-social.

community service n ≈ travail m d'intérêt général, TIG m.

community spirit n solidarité f.

commutation ticket [kɒmjuː'teɪʃən-] n (*US*) carte f d'abonnement.

commute [kə'mjuːt] vi faire le trajet journalier (de son domicile à un lieu de travail assez éloigné) ♦ vt (*LAW*) commuer; (*MATH: terms etc*) opérer la commutation de.

commuter [kə'mjuːtə*] n banlieusard/e (qui ... see vi).

compact adj [kəm'pækt] compact(e) ♦ n ['kɒmpækt] contrat m, entente f; (*also*: **powder** ~) poudrier m.

compact disc n disque compact.

compact disc player n lecteur m de disques compacts.

companion [kəm'pænjən] n compagnon/compagne.

companionship [kəm'pænjənʃɪp] n camaraderie f.

companionway [kəm'pænjənweɪ] n (*NAUT*)

escalier *m* des cabines.

company ['kʌmpənɪ] *n* (*also COMM, MIL, THEAT*) compagnie *f*; **he's good** ~ il est d'une compagnie agréable; **we have** ~ nous avons de la visite; **to keep sb** ~ tenir compagnie à qn; **to part** ~ **with** se séparer de; **Smith and C**~ Smith et Compagnie.

company car *n* voiture *f* de fonction.

company director *n* administrateur/trice.

company secretary *n* (*BRIT COMM*) secrétaire général *m* (*d'une société*).

comparable ['kɔmpərəbl] *adj* comparable.

comparative [kəm'pærətɪv] *adj* comparatif(ive); (*relative*) relatif(ive).

comparatively [kəm'pærətɪvlɪ] *adv* (*relatively*) relativement.

compare [kəm'pɛə*] *vt*: **to** ~ **sth/sb with/to** comparer qch/qn avec *or* et/à ♦ *vi*: **to** ~ **(with)** se comparer (à); être comparable (à); **how do the prices** ~? comment sont les prix?, est-ce que les prix sont comparables?; ~**d with** *or* **to** par rapport à.

comparison [kəm'pærɪsn] *n* comparaison *f*; **in** ~ **(with)** en comparaison (de).

compartment [kəm'pɑːtmənt] *n* (*also RAIL*) compartiment *m*.

compass ['kʌmpəs] *n* boussole *f*; **within the** ~ **of** dans les limites de.

compasses ['kʌmpəsɪz] *npl* compas *m*.

compassion [kəm'pæʃən] *n* compassion *f*, humanité *f*.

compassionate [kəm'pæʃənɪt] *adj* accessible à la compassion, au cœur charitable et bienveillant; **on** ~ **grounds** pour raisons personnelles *or* de famille.

compassionate leave *n* congé exceptionnel (*pour raisons de famille*).

compatibility [kəmpætɪ'bɪlɪtɪ] *n* compatibilité *f*.

compatible [kəm'pætɪbl] *adj* compatible.

compel [kəm'pɛl] *vt* contraindre, obliger.

compelling [kəm'pɛlɪŋ] *adj* (*fig: argument*) irrésistible.

compendium [kəm'pɛndɪəm] *n* (*summary*) abrégé *m*.

compensate ['kɔmpənseɪt] *vt* indemniser, dédommager ♦ *vi*: **to** ~ **for** compenser.

compensation [kɔmpən'seɪʃən] *n* compensation *f*; (*money*) dédommagement *m*, indemnité *f*.

compere ['kɔmpɛə*] *n* présentateur/trice, animateur/trice.

compete [kəm'piːt] *vi* (*take part*) concourir; (*vie*): **to** ~ **(with)** rivaliser (avec), faire concurrence (à).

competence ['kɔmpɪtəns] *n* compétence *f*, aptitude *f*.

competent ['kɔmpɪtənt] *adj* compétent(e), capable.

competing [kəm'piːtɪŋ] *adj* (*ideas, theories*) opposé(e); (*companies*) concurrent(e).

competition [kɔmpɪ'tɪʃən] *n* compétition *f*,

concours *m*; (*ECON*) concurrence *f*; **in** ~ **with** en concurrence avec.

competitive [kəm'pɛtɪtɪv] *adj* (*ECON*) concurrentiel(le); (*sports*) de compétition.

competitive examination *n* concours *m*.

competitor [kəm'pɛtɪtə*] *n* concurrent/e.

compile [kəm'paɪl] *vt* compiler.

complacency [kəm'pleɪsnsɪ] *n* contentement *m* de soi, autosatisfaction *f*.

complacent [kəm'pleɪsnt] *adj* (trop) content(e) de soi.

complain [kəm'pleɪn] *vi*: **to** ~ **(about)** se plaindre (de); (*in shop etc*) réclamer (au sujet de).

▶**complain of** *vt fus* (*MED*) se plaindre de.

complaint [kəm'pleɪnt] *n* plainte *f*; (*in shop etc*) réclamation *f*; (*MED*) affection *f*.

complement ['kɔmplɪmənt] *n* complément *m*; (*esp of ship's crew etc*) effectif complet ♦ *vt* compléter.

complementary [kɔmplɪ'mɛntərɪ] *adj* complémentaire.

complete [kəm'pliːt] *adj* complet(ète) ♦ *vt* achever, parachever; (*a form*) remplir.

completely [kəm'pliːtlɪ] *adv* complètement.

completion [kəm'pliːʃən] *n* achèvement *m*; **to be nearing** ~ être presque terminé; **on** ~ **of contract** dès signature du contrat.

complex ['kɔmplɛks] *adj* complexe ♦ *n* (*PSYCH, buildings etc*) complexe *m*.

complexion [kəm'plɛkʃən] *n* (*of face*) teint *m*; (*of event etc*) aspect *m*, caractère *m*.

complexity [kəm'plɛksɪtɪ] *n* complexité *f*.

compliance [kəm'plaɪəns] *n* (*submission*) docilité *f*; (*agreement*): ~ **with** le fait de se conformer à; **in** ~ **with** en conformité avec, conformément à.

compliant [kəm'plaɪənt] *adj* docile, très accommodant(e).

complicate ['kɔmplɪkeɪt] *vt* compliquer.

complicated ['kɔmplɪkeɪtɪd] *adj* compliqué(e).

complication [kɔmplɪ'keɪʃən] *n* complication *f*.

complicity [kəm'plɪsɪtɪ] *n* complicité *f*.

compliment *n* ['kɔmplɪmənt] compliment *m* ♦ *vt* ['kɔmplɪment] complimenter; ~**s** *npl* compliments *mpl*, hommages *mpl*; vœux *mpl*; **to pay sb a** ~ faire *or* adresser un compliment à qn; **to** ~ **sb (on sth/on doing sth)** féliciter qn (pour qch/de faire qch).

complimentary [kɔmplɪ'mɛntərɪ] *adj* flatteur(euse); (*free*) à titre gracieux.

complimentary ticket *n* billet *m* de faveur.

compliments slip *n* fiche *f* de transmission.

comply [kəm'plaɪ] *vi*: **to** ~ **with** se soumettre à, se conformer à.

component [kəm'pəunənt] *adj* composant(e), constituant(e) ♦ *n* composant *m*, élément *m*.

compose [kəm'pəuz] *vt* composer; **to** ~ **o.s.** se calmer, se maîtriser; prendre une contenance.

composed [kəm'pəuzd] *adj* calme, posé(e).

composer [kəm'pəuzə*] n (*MUS*) compositeur m.

composite ['kɔmpəzɪt] adj composite; (*BOT, MATH*) composé(e).

composition [kɔmpə'zɪʃən] n composition f.

compost ['kɔmpɔst] n compost m.

composure [kəm'pəuʒə*] n calme m, maîtrise f de soi.

compound ['kɔmpaund] n (*CHEM, LING*) composé m; (*enclosure*) enclos m, enceinte f ♦ adj composé(e) ♦ vt [kəm'paund] (*fig: problem etc*) aggraver.

compound fracture n fracture compliquée.

compound interest n intérêt composé.

comprehend [kɔmprɪ'hend] vt comprendre.

comprehension [kɔmprɪ'henʃən] n compréhension f.

comprehensive [kɔmprɪ'hensɪv] adj (très) complet(ète).

comprehensive insurance policy n assurance f tous risques.

comprehensive (school) n (*BRIT*) école secondaire non sélective avec libre circulation d'une section à l'autre, ≈ CES m.

compress vt [kəm'pres] comprimer ♦ n ['kɔmpres] (*MED*) compresse f.

compression [kəm'preʃən] n compression f.

comprise [kəm'praɪz] vt (*also: be ~d of*) comprendre.

compromise ['kɔmprəmaɪz] n compromis m ♦ vt compromettre ♦ vi transiger, accepter un compromis ♦ cpd (*decision, solution*) de compromis.

compulsion [kəm'pʌlʃən] n contrainte f, force f; **under** ~ sous la contrainte.

compulsive [kəm'pʌlsɪv] adj (*PSYCH*) compulsif(ive); **he's a** ~ **smoker** c'est un fumeur invétéré.

compulsory [kəm'pʌlsərɪ] adj obligatoire.

compulsory purchase n expropriation f.

compunction [kəm'pʌŋkʃən] n scrupule m; **to have no** ~ **about doing sth** n'avoir aucun scrupule à faire qch.

computer [kəm'pju:tə*] n ordinateur m; (*mechanical*) calculatrice f.

computer game n jeu m vidéo.

computerize [kəm'pju:təraɪz] vt traiter or automatiser par ordinateur.

computer language n langage m machine or informatique.

computer literate adj initié(e) à l'informatique.

computer peripheral n périphérique m.

computer program n programme m informatique.

computer programmer n programmeur/euse.

computer programming n programmation f.

computer science n informatique f.

computer scientist n informaticien/ne.

computing [kəm'pju:tɪŋ] n informatique f.

comrade ['kɔmrɪd] n camarade m/f.

comradeship ['kɔmrɪdʃɪp] n camaraderie f.

comsat ['kɔmsæt] n abbr = **communications satellite**.

con [kɔn] vt duper; escroquer ♦ n escroquerie f; **to** ~ **sb into doing sth** tromper qn pour lui faire faire qch.

concave ['kɔn'keɪv] adj concave.

conceal [kən'si:l] vt cacher, dissimuler.

concede [kən'si:d] vt concéder ♦ vi céder.

conceit [kən'si:t] n vanité f, suffisance f, prétention f.

conceited [kən'si:tɪd] adj vaniteux(euse), suffisant(e).

conceivable [kən'si:vəbl] adj concevable, imaginable; **it is** ~ **that** il est concevable que.

conceivably [kən'si:vəblɪ] adv: **he may** ~ **be right** il n'est pas impossible qu'il ait raison.

conceive [kən'si:v] vt concevoir ♦ vi: **to** ~ **of sth/of doing sth** imaginer qch/de faire qch.

concentrate ['kɔnsəntreɪt] vi se concentrer ♦ vt concentrer.

concentration [kɔnsən'treɪʃən] n concentration f.

concentration camp n camp m de concentration.

concentric [kɔn'sentrɪk] adj concentrique.

concept ['kɔnsept] n concept m.

conception [kən'sepʃən] n conception f; (*idea*) idée f.

concern [kən'sə:n] n affaire f; (*COMM*) entreprise f, firme f; (*anxiety*) inquiétude f, souci m ♦ vt concerner; **to be** ~**ed (about)** s'inquiéter (de), être inquiet(ète) (au sujet de); **"to whom it may** ~**"** "à qui de droit"; **as far as I am** ~**ed** en ce qui me concerne; **to be** ~**ed with** (*person: involved with*) s'occuper de; **the department** ~**ed** (*under discussion*) le service en question; (*involved*) le service concerné.

concerning [kən'sə:nɪŋ] prep en ce qui concerne, à propos de.

concert ['kɔnsət] n concert m; **in** ~ à l'unisson, en chœur; ensemble.

concerted [kən'sə:tɪd] adj concerté(e).

concert hall n salle f de concert.

concertina [kɔnsə'ti:nə] n concertina m ♦ vi se télescoper, se caramboler.

concerto [kən'tʃə:təu] n concerto m.

concession [kən'seʃən] n concession f.

concessionaire [kənseʃə'neə*] n concessionnaire m/f.

concessionary [kən'seʃənrɪ] adj (*ticket, fare*) à tarif réduit.

conciliation [kənsɪlɪ'eɪʃən] n conciliation f, apaisement m.

conciliatory [kən'sɪlɪətrɪ] adj conciliateur(trice); conciliant(e).

concise [kən'saɪs] adj concis(e).

conclave ['kɔnkleɪv] n assemblée secrète; (*REL*) conclave m.

conclude [kən'klu:d] vt conclure ♦ vi (*speaker*)

conclure; (*events*): **to ~ (with)** se terminer (par).

concluding [kən'klu:dɪŋ] *adj* (*remarks etc*) final(e).

conclusion [kən'klu:ʒən] *n* conclusion *f*; **to come to the ~ that** (en) conclure que.

conclusive [kən'klu:sɪv] *adj* concluant(e), définitif(ive).

concoct [kən'kɔkt] *vt* confectionner, composer.

concoction [kən'kɔkʃən] *n* (*food, drink*) mélange *m*.

concord ['kɔŋkɔ:d] *n* (*harmony*) harmonie *f*; (*treaty*) accord *m*.

concourse ['kɔŋkɔ:s] *n* (*hall*) hall *m*, salle *f* des pas perdus; (*crowd*) affluence *f*, multitude *f*.

concrete ['kɔŋkri:t] *n* béton *m* ♦ *adj* concret(ète); (*CONSTR*) en béton.

concrete mixer *n* bétonnière *f*.

concur [kən'kə:*] *vi* être d'accord.

concurrently [kən'kʌrntlɪ] *adv* simultanément.

concussion [kən'kʌʃən] *n* (*MED*) commotion (cérébrale).

condemn [kən'dɛm] *vt* condamner.

condemnation [kɔndɛm'neɪʃən] *n* condamnation *f*.

condensation [kɔndɛn'seɪʃən] *n* condensation *f*.

condense [kən'dɛns] *vi* se condenser ♦ *vt* condenser.

condensed milk [kən'dɛnst-] *n* lait concentré (sucré).

condescend [kɔndɪ'sɛnd] *vi* condescendre, s'abaisser; **to ~ to do sth** daigner faire qch.

condescending [kɔndɪ'sɛndɪŋ] *adj* condescendant(e).

condition [kən'dɪʃən] *n* condition *f*; (*disease*) maladie *f* ♦ *vt* déterminer, conditionner; **in good/poor ~** en bon/mauvais état; **a heart ~** une maladie cardiaque; **weather ~s** conditions *fpl* météorologiques; **on ~ that** à condition que + *sub*, à condition de.

conditional [kən'dɪʃənl] *adj* conditionnel(le); **to be ~ upon** dépendre de.

conditioner [kən'dɪʃənə*] *n* (*for hair*) baume démêlant.

condo ['kɔndəu] *n abbr* (*US col*) = **condominium**.

condolences [kən'dəulənsɪz] *npl* condoléances *fpl*.

condom ['kɔndəm] *n* préservatif *m*.

condominium [kɔndə'mɪnɪəm] *n* (*US: building*) immeuble *m* (en copropriété); (*: rooms*) appartement *m* (dans un immeuble en copropriété).

condone [kən'dəun] *vt* fermer les yeux sur, approuver (tacitement).

conducive [kən'dju:sɪv] *adj*: **~ to** favorable à, qui contribue à.

conduct *n* ['kɔndʌkt] conduite *f* ♦ *vt* [kən'dʌkt] conduire; (*manage*) mener, diriger; (*MUS*) diriger; **to ~ o.s.** se conduire, se comporter.

conducted tour [kən'dʌktɪd-] *n* voyage organisé; (*of building*) visite guidée.

conductor [kən'dʌktə*] *n* (*of orchestra*) chef *m* d'orchestre; (*on bus*) receveur *m*; (*US: on train*) chef *m* de train; (*ELEC*) conducteur *m*.

conductress [kən'dʌktrɪs] *n* (*on bus*) receveuse *f*.

conduit ['kɔndɪt] *n* conduit *m*, tuyau *m*; tube *m*.

cone [kəun] *n* cône *m*; (*for ice-cream*) cornet *m*; (*BOT*) pomme *f* de pin, cône.

confectioner [kən'fɛkʃənə*] *n* (*of cakes*) pâtissier/ière; (*of sweets*) confiseur/euse; **~'s (shop)** confiserie(-pâtisserie) *f*.

confectionery [kən'fɛkʃənrɪ] *n* (*cakes*) pâtisserie *f*; (*sweets*) confiserie *f*.

confederate [kən'fɛdrɪt] *adj* confédéré(e) ♦ *n* (*pej*) acolyte *m*; (*US HISTORY*) confédéré/e.

confederation [kənfɛdə'reɪʃən] *n* confédération *f*.

confer [kən'fə:*] *vt*: **to ~ sth on** conférer qch à ♦ *vi* conférer, s'entretenir; **to ~ (with sb about sth)** s'entretenir (de qch avec qn).

conference ['kɔnfərns] *n* conférence *f*; **to be in ~** être en réunion *or* en conférence.

conference room *n* salle *f* de conférence.

confess [kən'fɛs] *vt* confesser, avouer ♦ *vi* se confesser.

confession [kən'fɛʃən] *n* confession *f*.

confessional [kən'fɛʃənl] *n* confessional *m*.

confessor [kən'fɛsə*] *n* confesseur *m*.

confetti [kən'fɛtɪ] *n* confettis *mpl*.

confide [kən'faɪd] *vi*: **to ~ in** s'ouvrir à, se confier à.

confidence ['kɔnfɪdns] *n* confiance *f*; (*also*: **self-~**) assurance *f*, confiance en soi; (*secret*) confidence *f*; **to have (every) ~ that** être certain que; **motion of no ~** motion *f* de censure; **to tell sb sth in strict ~** dire qch à qn en toute confidence.

confidence trick *n* escroquerie *f*.

confident ['kɔnfɪdənt] *adj* sûr(e), assuré(e).

confidential [kɔnfɪ'dɛnʃəl] *adj* confidentiel(le); (*secretary*) particulier(ère).

confidentiality ['kɔnfɪdɛnʃɪ'ælɪtɪ] *n* confidentialité *f*.

configuration [kən'fɪgju'reɪʃən] *n* (*also COMPUT*) configuration *f*.

confine [kən'faɪn] *vt* limiter, borner; (*shut up*) confiner, enfermer; **to ~ o.s. to doing sth/to sth** se contenter de faire qch/se limiter à qch.

confined [kən'faɪnd] *adj* (*space*) restreint(e), réduit(e).

confinement [kən'faɪnmənt] *n* emprisonnement *m*, détention *f*; (*MIL*) consigne *f* (au quartier); (*MED*) accouchement *m*.

confines ['kɔnfaɪnz] *npl* confins *mpl*, bornes *fpl*.

confirm [kən'fə:m] *vt* (*report, REL*) confirmer; (*appointment*) ratifier.

confirmation [kɔnfə'meɪʃən] *n* confirmation *f*; ratification *f*.

confirmed [kən'fə:md] *adj* invétéré(e), incorrigible.

confiscate ['kɔnfɪskeɪt] *vt* confisquer.

confiscation [kɔnfɪs'keɪʃən] *n* confiscation *f*.

conflagration [kɔnflə'greɪʃən] *n* incendie *m*; (*fig*) conflagration *f*.

conflict *n* ['kɔnflɪkt] conflit *m*, lutte *f* ♦ *vi* [kən'flɪkt] être *or* entrer en conflit; (*opinions*) s'opposer, se heurter.

conflicting [kən'flɪktɪŋ] *adj* contradictoire.

conform [kən'fɔ:m] *vi*: **to ~ (to)** se conformer (à).

conformist [kən'fɔ:mɪst] *n* conformiste *m/f*.

confound [kən'faund] *vt* confondre; (*amaze*) rendre perplexe.

confounded [kən'faundɪd] *adj* maudit(e), sacré(e).

confront [kən'frʌnt] *vt* confronter, mettre en présence; (*enemy, danger*) affronter, faire face à.

confrontation [kɔnfrən'teɪʃən] *n* confrontation *f*.

confrontational [kɔnfrən'teɪʃənl] *adj* conflictuel(le).

confuse [kən'fju:z] *vt* embrouiller; (*one thing with another*) confondre.

confused [kən'fju:zd] *adj* (*person*) dérouté(e), désorienté(e); (*situation*) embrouillé(e).

confusing [kən'fju:zɪŋ] *adj* peu clair(e), déroutant(e).

confusion [kən'fju:ʒən] *n* confusion *f*.

congeal [kən'dʒi:l] *vi* (*oil*) se figer; (*blood*) se coaguler.

congenial [kən'dʒi:nɪəl] *adj* sympathique, agréable.

congenital [kən'dʒenɪtl] *adj* congénital(e).

conger eel ['kɔngər-] *n* congre *m*.

congested [kən'dʒestɪd] *adj* (*MED*) congestionné(e); (*fig*) surpeuplé(e); congestionné; bloqué(e); (*telephone lines*) encombré(e).

congestion [kən'dʒestʃən] *n* congestion *f*; (*fig*) encombrement *m*.

conglomerate [kən'glɔmərɪt] *n* (*COMM*) conglomérat *m*.

conglomeration [kənglɔmə'reɪʃən] *n* groupement *m*; agglomération *f*.

Congo ['kɔŋgəu] *n* (*state*) (république *f* du) Congo.

congratulate [kən'grætjuleɪt] *vt*: **to ~ sb (on)** féliciter qn (de).

congratulations [kəngrætju'leɪʃənz] *npl*: **~ (on)** félicitations *fpl* (pour) ♦ *excl*: **~!** (toutes mes) félicitations!

congregate ['kɔngrɪgeɪt] *vi* se rassembler, réunir.

congregation [kɔngrɪ'geɪʃən] *n* assemblée *f* (des fidèles).

congress ['kɔngrɛs] *n* congrès *m*.

Le **Congress** est le parlement des États-Unis. Il comprend la **House of Representatives** et le **Senate**. Représentants et sénateurs sont élus au suffrage universel direct. Le Congrès se réunit au **Capitol**, à Washington.

congressman ['kɔngrɛsmən], **congresswoman** ['kɔngrɛswumən] *n* (*US*) membre *m* du Congrès.

conical ['kɔnɪkl] *adj* (de forme) conique.

conifer ['kɔnɪfə*] *n* conifère *m*.

coniferous [kə'nɪfərəs] *adj* (*forest*) de conifères.

conjecture [kən'dʒɛktʃə*] *n* conjecture *f* ♦ *vt*, *vi* conjecturer.

conjugal ['kɔndʒugl] *adj* conjugal(e).

conjugate ['kɔndʒugeɪt] *vt* conjuguer.

conjugation [kɔndʒə'geɪʃən] *n* conjugaison *f*.

conjunction [kən'dʒʌŋkʃən] *n* conjonction *f*; **in ~ with** (conjointement) avec.

conjunctivitis [kəndʒʌŋktɪ'vaɪtɪs] *n* conjonctivite *f*.

conjure ['kʌndʒə*] *vt* faire apparaître (par la prestidigitation); [kən'dʒuə*] conjurer, supplier ♦ *vi* faire des tours de passe-passe.

▸**conjure up** *vt* (*ghost, spirit*) faire apparaître; (*memories*) évoquer.

conjurer ['kʌndʒərə*] *n* prestidigitateur *m*, illusionniste *m/f*.

conjuring trick ['kʌndʒərɪŋ-] *n* tour *m* de prestidigitation.

conker ['kɔŋkə*] *n* (*BRIT*) marron *m* (d'Inde).

conk out [kɔŋk-] *vi* (*col*) tomber *or* rester en panne.

conman ['kɔnmæn] *n* escroc *m*.

Conn. *abbr* (*US*) = Connecticut.

connect [kə'nɛkt] *vt* joindre, relier; (*ELEC*) connecter; (*fig*) établir un rapport entre, faire un rapprochement entre ♦ *vi* (*train*): **to ~ with** assurer la correspondance avec; **to be ~ed with** avoir un rapport avec; (*have dealings with*) avoir des rapports avec, être en relation avec; **I am trying to ~ you** (*TEL*) j'essaie d'obtenir votre communication.

connection [kə'nɛkʃən] *n* relation *f*, lien *m*; (*ELEC*) connexion *f*, (*TEL*) communication *f*; (*train etc*) correspondance *f*; **in ~ with** à propos de; **what is the ~ between them?** quel est le lien entre eux?; **business ~s** relations d'affaires; **to miss/get one's ~** (*train etc*) rater/avoir sa correspondance.

connexion [kə'nɛkʃən] *n* (*BRIT*) = **connection**.

conning tower ['kɔnɪŋ-] *n* kiosque *m* (de sous-marin).

connive [kə'naɪv] *vi*: **to ~ at** se faire le complice de.

connoisseur [kɔnɪ'sə:*] *n* connaisseur *m*.

connotation [kɔnə'teɪʃən] *n* connotation *f*, implication *f*.

connubial [kə'nju:bɪəl] *adj* conjugal(e).

conquer ['kɔŋkə*] *vt* conquérir; (*feelings*) vaincre, surmonter.

conqueror ['kɔŋkərə*] *n* conquérant *m*, vainqueur *m*.

conquest ['kɔŋkwɛst] *n* conquête *f*.

cons [kɔnz] *npl see* **pro, convenience.**

conscience ['kɔnʃəns] *n* conscience *f*; **in all ~** en conscience.

conscientious [kɔnʃɪ'ɛnʃəs] *adj* consciencieux(euse); *(scruple, objection)* de conscience.

conscientious objector *n* objecteur *m* de conscience.

conscious ['kɔnʃəs] *adj* conscient(e); *(deliberate: insult, error)* délibéré(e); **to become ~ of sth/that** prendre conscience de qch/que.

consciousness ['kɔnʃəsnɪs] *n* conscience *f*; *(MED)* connaissance *f*; **to lose/regain ~** perdre/reprendre connaissance.

conscript ['kɔnskrɪpt] *n* conscrit *m*.

conscription [kən'skrɪpʃən] *n* conscription *f*.

consecrate ['kɔnsɪkreɪt] *vt* consacrer.

consecutive [kən'sɛkjutɪv] *adj* consécutif(ive); **on three ~ occasions** trois fois de suite.

consensus [kən'sɛnsəs] *n* consensus *m*; **the ~ (of opinion)** le consensus (d'opinion).

consent [kən'sɛnt] *n* consentement *m* ♦ *vi*: **to ~ (to)** consentir (à); **age of ~** âge nubile (légal); **by common ~** d'un commun accord.

consenting adults [kən'sɛntɪŋ-] *npl* personnes consentantes.

consequence ['kɔnsɪkwəns] *n* suites *fpl*, conséquence *f*; importance *f*; **in ~** en conséquence, par conséquent.

consequently ['kɔnsɪkwəntlɪ] *adv* par conséquent, donc.

conservation [kɔnsə'veɪʃən] *n* préservation *f*, protection *f*; *(also:* **nature ~)** défense *f* de l'environnement; **energy ~** économies *fpl* d'énergie.

conservationist [kɔnsə'veɪʃnɪst] *n* protecteur/trice de la nature.

conservative [kən'sɜːvətɪv] *adj* conservateur(trice); *(cautious)* prudent(e); **C~** *adj*, *n* *(BRIT POL)* conservateur(trice); **the C~ Party** le parti conservateur.

conservatory [kən'sɜːvətrɪ] *n* *(greenhouse)* serre *f*.

conserve [kən'sɜːv] *vt* conserver, préserver; *(supplies, energy)* économiser ♦ *n* confiture *f*, conserve *f* (de fruits).

consider [kən'sɪdə*] *vt* considérer, réfléchir à; *(take into account)* penser à, prendre en considération; *(regard, judge)* considérer, estimer; **to ~ doing sth** envisager de faire qch; **~ yourself lucky** estimez-vous heureux; **all things ~ed** (toute) réflexion faite.

considerable [kən'sɪdərəbl] *adj* considérable.

considerably [kən'sɪdərəblɪ] *adv* nettement.

considerate [kən'sɪdərɪt] *adj* prévenant(e), plein(e) d'égards.

consideration [kənsɪdə'reɪʃən] *n* considération *f*; *(reward)* rétribution *f*, rémunération *f*; **out of ~ for** par égard pour; **under ~** à l'étude; **my first ~ is my family** ma famille passe avant tout le reste.

considered [kən'sɪdəd] *adj*: **it is my ~ opinion that ...** après avoir mûrement réfléchi, je pense que ....

considering [kən'sɪdərɪŋ] *prep*: **~ (that)** étant donné (que).

consign [kən'saɪn] *vt* expédier, livrer.

consignee [kɔnsaɪ'niː] *n* destinataire *m/f*.

consignment [kən'saɪnmənt] *n* arrivage *m*, envoi *m*.

consignment note *n* *(COMM)* bordereau *m* d'expédition.

consignor [kən'saɪnə*] *n* expéditeur/trice.

consist [kən'sɪst] *vi*: **to ~ of** consister en, se composer de.

consistency [kən'sɪstənsɪ] *n* consistance *f*; *(fig)* cohérence *f*.

consistent [kən'sɪstənt] *adj* logique, cohérent(e); **~ with** compatible avec, en accord avec.

consolation [kɔnsə'leɪʃən] *n* consolation *f*.

console *vt* [kən'səul] consoler ♦ *n* ['kɔnsəul] console *f*.

consolidate [kən'sɔlɪdeɪt] *vt* consolider.

consols ['kɔnsɔlz] *npl* *(BRIT STOCK EXCHANGE)* rente *f* d'État.

consommé [kən'sɔmeɪ] *n* consommé *m*.

consonant ['kɔnsənənt] *n* consonne *f*.

consort *n* ['kɔnsɔːt] époux/épouse; **prince ~** prince *m* consort ♦ *vi* [kən'sɔːt] *(often pej)*: **to ~ with sb** frayer avec qn.

consortium [kən'sɔːtɪəm] *n* consortium *m*, comptoir *m*.

conspicuous [kən'spɪkjuəs] *adj* voyant(e), qui attire la vue *or* l'attention; **to make o.s. ~** se faire remarquer.

conspiracy [kən'spɪrəsɪ] *n* conspiration *f*, complot *m*.

conspiratorial [kən'spɪrə'tɔːrɪəl] *adj* *(behaviour)* de conspirateur; *(glance)* conspirateur(trice).

conspire [kən'spaɪə*] *vi* conspirer, comploter.

constable ['kʌnstəbl] *n* *(BRIT)* ≈ agent *m* de police, gendarme *m*.

constabulary [kən'stæbjulərɪ] *n* ≈ police *f*, gendarmerie *f*.

constant ['kɔnstənt] *adj* constant(e); incessant(e).

constantly ['kɔnstəntlɪ] *adv* constamment, sans cesse.

constellation [kɔnstə'leɪʃən] *n* constellation *f*.

consternation [kɔnstə'neɪʃən] *n* consternation *f*.

constipated ['kɔnstɪpeɪtɪd] *adj* constipé(e).

constipation [kɔnstɪ'peɪʃən] *n* constipation *f*.

constituency [kən'stɪtjuənsɪ] *n* circonscription électorale; *(people)* électorat *m*.

Une **constituency** *est à la fois une région qui élit un député au parlement et l'ensemble des électeurs dans cette région. En Grande-Bretagne, les députés font régulièrement des "permanences" dans leur circonscription élec-*

*torale lors desquelles les électeurs peuvent ve-
nir les voir pour parler de leurs problèmes de
logement etc.*

constituency party *n* section locale (d'un parti).

constituent [kən'stɪtjuənt] *n* électeur/trice; *(part)* élément constitutif, composant *m*.

constitute ['kɔnstɪtjuːt] *vt* constituer.

constitution [kɔnstɪ'tjuːʃən] *n* constitution *f*.

constitutional [kɔnstɪ'tjuːʃənl] *adj* constitutionnel(le).

constitutional monarchy *n* monarchie constitutionnelle.

constrain [kən'streɪn] *vt* contraindre, forcer.

constrained [kən'streɪnd] *adj* contraint(e), gêné(e).

constraint [kən'streɪnt] *n* contrainte *f*; *(embarrassment)* gêne *f*.

constrict [kən'strɪkt] *vt* rétrécir, resserrer; gêner, limiter.

construct [kən'strʌkt] *vt* construire.

construction [kən'strʌkʃən] *n* construction *f*; *(fig: interpretation)* interprétation *f*; **under ~** *(building etc)* en construction.

construction industry *n* (industrie *f* du) bâtiment.

constructive [kən'strʌktɪv] *adj* constructif(ive).

construe [kən'struː] *vt* analyser, expliquer.

consul ['kɔnsl] *n* consul *m*.

consulate ['kɔnsjulɪt] *n* consulat *m*.

consult [kən'sʌlt] *vt* consulter; **to ~ sb (about sth)** consulter qn (à propos de qch).

consultancy [kən'sʌltənsɪ] *n* service *m* de conseils.

consultancy fee *n* honoraires *mpl* d'expert.

consultant [kən'sʌltənt] *n (MED)* médecin consultant; *(other specialist)* consultant *m*, (expert-)conseil *m* ♦ *cpd*: **~ engineer** *n* ingénieur-conseil *m*; **~ paediatrician** *n* pédiatre *m*; **legal/management ~** conseiller *m* juridique/en gestion.

consultation [kɔnsəl'teɪʃən] *n* consultation *f*; **in ~ with** en consultation avec.

consultative [kən'sʌltətɪv] *adj* consultatif(ive).

consulting room [kən'sʌltɪŋ-] *n (BRIT)* cabinet *m* de consultation.

consume [kən'sjuːm] *vt* consommer.

consumer [kən'sjuːmə*] *n* consommateur/trice; *(of electricity, gas etc)* usager *m*.

consumer credit *n* crédit *m* aux consommateurs.

consumer durables *npl* biens *mpl* de consommation durables.

consumer goods *npl* biens *mpl* de consommation.

consumerism [kən'sjuːmərɪzəm] *n (consumer protection)* défense *f* du consommateur; *(ECON)* consumérisme *m*.

consumer society *n* société *f* de consomma-

tion.

consumer watchdog *n* organisme *m* pour la défense des consommateurs.

consummate ['kɔnsʌmeɪt] *vt* consommer.

consumption [kən'sʌmpʃən] *n* consommation *f*; *(MED)* consomption *f* (pulmonaire); **not fit for human ~** non comestible.

cont. *abbr* = **continued**.

contact ['kɔntækt] *n* contact *m*; *(person)* connaissance *f*, relation *f* ♦ *vt* se mettre en contact *or* en rapport avec; **to be in ~ with sb/ sth** être en contact avec qn/qch; **business ~s** relations *fpl* d'affaires, contacts *mpl*.

contact lenses *npl* verres *mpl* de contact.

contagious [kən'teɪdʒəs] *adj* contagieux(euse).

contain [kən'teɪn] *vt* contenir; **to ~ o.s.** se contenir, se maîtriser.

container [kən'teɪnə*] *n* récipient *m*; *(for shipping etc)* conteneur *m*.

containerize [kən'teɪnəraɪz] *vt* conteneuriser.

container ship *n* porte-conteneurs *m inv*.

contaminate [kən'tæmɪneɪt] *vt* contaminer.

contamination [kəntæmɪ'neɪʃən] *n* contamination *f*.

cont'd *abbr* = **continued**.

contemplate ['kɔntəmpleɪt] *vt* contempler; *(consider)* envisager.

contemplation [kɔntəm'pleɪʃən] *n* contemplation *f*.

contemporary [kən'tɛmpərərɪ] *adj* contemporain(e); *(design, wallpaper)* moderne ♦ *n* contemporain/e.

contempt [kən'tɛmpt] *n* mépris *m*, dédain *m*; **~ of court** *(LAW)* outrage *m* à l'autorité de la justice.

contemptible [kən'tɛmptəbl] *adj* méprisable, vil(e).

contemptuous [kən'tɛmptjuəs] *adj* dédaigneux(euse), méprisant(e).

contend [kən'tɛnd] *vt*: **to ~ that** soutenir *or* prétendre que ♦ *vi*: **to ~ with** *(compete)* lutter avec; **to have to ~ with** *(be faced with)* avoir affaire à, être aux prises avec.

contender [kən'tɛndə*] *n* prétendant/e; candidat/e.

content [kən'tɛnt] *adj* content(e), satisfait(e) ♦ *vt* contenter, satisfaire ♦ *n* ['kɔntɛnt] contenu *m*; teneur *f*; **~s** *npl* contenu *m*; **(table of) ~s** table *f* des matières; **to be ~ with** se contenter de; **to ~ o.s. with sth/with doing sth** se contenter de qch/de faire qch.

contented [kən'tɛntɪd] *adj* content(e), satisfait(e).

contentedly [kən'tɛntɪdlɪ] *adv* avec un sentiment de (profonde) satisfaction.

contention [kən'tɛnʃən] *n* dispute *f*, contestation *f*; *(argument)* assertion *f*, affirmation *f*; **bone of ~** sujet *m* de discorde.

contentious [kən'tɛnʃəs] *adj* querelleur(euse); litigieux(euse).

contentment [kən'tɛntmənt] *n* contentement

m, satisfaction *f*.

contest *n* ['kɔntɛst] combat *m*, lutte *f*; (*competition*) concours *m* ♦ *vt* [kən'tɛst] contester, discuter; (*compete for*) disputer; (*LAW*) attaquer.

contestant [kən'tɛstənt] *n* concurrent/e; (*in fight*) adversaire *m/f*.

context ['kɔntɛkst] *n* contexte *m*; **in/out of** ~ dans le/hors contexte.

continent ['kɔntɪnənt] *n* continent *m*; **the C~** (*BRIT*) l'Europe continentale; **on the C~** en Europe (continentale).

continental [kɔntɪ'nɛntl] *adj* continental(e) ♦ *n* (*BRIT*) Européen/ne (continental(e)).

continental breakfast *n* café (*or* thé) complet.

continental quilt *n* (*BRIT*) couette *f*.

contingency [kən'tɪndʒənsɪ] *n* éventualité *f*, événement imprévu.

contingency plan *n* plan *m* d'urgence.

contingent [kən'tɪndʒənt] *adj* contingent(e) ♦ *n* contingent *m*; **to be** ~ **upon** dépendre de.

continual [kən'tɪnjuəl] *adj* continuel(le).

continually [kən'tɪnjuəlɪ] *adv* continuellement, sans cesse.

continuation [kəntɪnju'eɪʃən] *n* continuation *f*; (*after interruption*) reprise *f*; (*of story*) suite *f*.

continue [kən'tɪnju:] *vi* continuer ♦ *vt* continuer; (*start again*) reprendre; **to be** ~d (*story*) à suivre; ~d **on page 10** suite page 10.

continuing education [kən'tɪnjuɪŋ-] *n* formation permanente *or* continue.

continuity [kɔntɪ'nju:ɪtɪ] *n* continuité *f*; (*CINE*) script *m*.

continuity girl *n* (*CINE*) script-girl *f*.

continuous [kən'tɪnjuəs] *adj* continu(e), permanent(e); ~ **performance** (*CINE*) séance permanente; ~ **stationery** (*COMPUT*) papier *m* en continu.

continuously [kən'tɪnjuəslɪ] *adv* (*repeatedly*) continuellement; (*uninterruptedly*) sans interruption.

contort [kən'tɔ:t] *vt* tordre, crisper.

contortion [kən'tɔ:ʃən] *n* crispation *f*, torsion *f*; (*of acrobat*) contorsion *f*.

contortionist [kən'tɔ:ʃənɪst] *n* contorsionniste *m/f*.

contour ['kɔntuə*] *n* contour *m*, profil *m*; (*also*: ~ **line**) courbe *f* de niveau.

contraband ['kɔntrəbænd] *n* contrebande *f* ♦ *adj* de contrebande.

contraception [kɔntrə'sɛpʃən] *n* contraception *f*.

contraceptive [kɔntrə'sɛptɪv] *adj* contraceptif(ive), anticonceptionnel(le) ♦ *n* contraceptif *m*.

contract *n* ['kɔntrækt] contrat *m* ♦ *cpd* ['kɔntrækt] (*price, date*) contractuel(le); (*work*) à forfait ♦ *vb* [kən'trækt] *vi* (*become smaller*) se contracter, se resserrer; (*COMM*): **to** ~ **to do sth** s'engager (par contrat) à faire qch ♦ *vt* contracter; ~ **of employment/service** contrat de travail/de service.

▶**contract in** *vi* s'engager (par contrat); (*BRIT ADMIN*) s'affilier au régime de retraite complémentaire.

▶**contract out** *vi* se dégager; (*BRIT ADMIN*) opter pour la non-affiliation au régime de retraite complémentaire.

contraction [kən'trækʃən] *n* contraction *f*; (*LING*) forme contractée.

contractor [kən'træktə*] *n* entrepreneur *m*.

contractual [kən'træktʃuəl] *adj* contractuel(le).

contradict [kɔntrə'dɪkt] *vt* contredire; (*be contrary to*) démentir, être en contradiction avec.

contradiction [kɔntrə'dɪkʃən] *n* contradiction *f*; **to be in** ~ **with** contredire, être en contradiction avec.

contradictory [kɔntrə'dɪktərɪ] *adj* contradictoire.

contralto [kən'træltəu] *n* contralto *m*.

contraption [kən'træpʃən] *n* (*pej*) machin *m*, truc *m*.

contrary¹ ['kɔntrərɪ] *adj* contraire, opposé(e) ♦ *n* contraire *m*; **on the** ~ au contraire; **unless you hear to the** ~ sauf avis contraire; ~ **to what we thought** contrairement à ce que nous pensions.

contrary² [kən'trɛərɪ] *adj* (*perverse*) contrariant(e), entêté(e).

contrast *n* ['kɔntrɑ:st] contraste *m* ♦ *vt* [kən'trɑ:st] mettre en contraste, contraster; **in** ~ **to** *or* **with** contrairement à, par opposition à.

contrasting [kən'trɑ:stɪŋ] *adj* opposé(e), contrasté(e).

contravene [kɔntrə'vi:n] *vt* enfreindre, violer, contrevenir à.

contravention [kɔntrə'vɛnʃən] *n*: ~ (**of**) infraction *f* (à).

contribute [kən'trɪbju:t] *vi* contribuer ♦ *vt*: **to** ~ **£10/an article to** donner 10 livres/un article à; **to** ~ **to** (*gen*) contribuer à; (*newspaper*) collaborer à; (*discussion*) prendre part à.

contribution [kɔntrɪ'bju:ʃən] *n* contribution *f*.

contributor [kən'trɪbjutə*] *n* (*to newspaper*) collaborateur/trice.

contributory [kən'trɪbjutərɪ] *adj* (*cause*) annexe; **it was a** ~ **factor in** ... ce facteur a contribué à ....

contributory pension scheme *n* (*BRIT*) régime *m* de retraite salariale.

contrite ['kɔntraɪt] *adj* contrit(e).

contrivance [kən'traɪvəns] *n* (*scheme*) machination *f*, combinaison *f*; (*device*) appareil *m*, dispositif *m*.

contrive [kən'traɪv] *vt* combiner, inventer ♦ *vi*: **to** ~ **to do** s'arranger pour faire, trouver le moyen de faire.

control [kən'trəul] *vt* maîtriser; (*check*) contrôler ♦ *n* maîtrise *f*; **~s** *npl* commandes *fpl*; **to take ~ of** se rendre maître de; (*COMM*) acquérir une participation majoritaire dans; **to be in ~ of** être maître de, maîtriser; (*in charge of*) être responsable de; **to ~ o.s.** se contrôler; **everything is under ~** j'ai (*or* il a *etc*) la situation en main; **the car went out of ~** j'ai (*or* il a *etc*) perdu le contrôle du véhicule; **beyond our ~** indépendant(e) de notre volonté.

control key *n* (*COMPUT*) touche *f* de commande.

controller [kən'trəulə*] *n* contrôleur *m*.

controlling interest [kən'trəulɪŋ-] *n* (*COMM*) participation *f* majoritaire.

control panel *n* (*on aircraft, ship, TV etc*) tableau *m* de commandes.

control point *n* (*poste m* de) contrôle *m*.

control room *n* (*NAUT, MIL*) salle *f* des commandes; (*RADIO, TV*) régie *f*.

control tower *n* (*AVIAT*) tour *f* de contrôle.

control unit *n* (*COMPUT*) unité *f* de contrôle.

controversial [kɔntrə'və:ʃl] *adj* discutable, controversé(e).

controversy ['kɔntrəvə:sɪ] *n* controverse *f*, polémique *f*.

conurbation [kɔnə'beɪʃən] *n* conurbation *f*.

convalesce [kɔnvə'lɛs] *vi* relever de maladie, se remettre (d'une maladie).

convalescence [kɔnvə'lɛsns] *n* convalescence *f*.

convalescent [kɔnvə'lɛsnt] *adj, n* convalescent(e).

convector [kən'vɛktə*] *n* radiateur *m* à convection, appareil *m* de chauffage par convection.

convene [kən'vi:n] *vt* convoquer, assembler ♦ *vi* se réunir, s'assembler.

convener [kən'vi:nə*] *n* organisateur *m*.

convenience [kən'vi:nɪəns] *n* commodité *f*; **at your ~** quand *or* comme cela vous convient; **at your earliest ~** (*COMM*) dans les meilleurs délais, le plus tôt possible; **all modern ~s,** (*BRIT*) **all mod cons** avec tout le confort moderne, tout confort.

convenience foods *npl* plats cuisinés.

convenient [kən'vi:nɪənt] *adj* commode; **if it is ~ to you** si cela vous convient, si cela ne vous dérange pas.

conveniently [kən'vi:nɪəntlɪ] *adv* (*happen*) à pic; (*situated*) commodément.

convent ['kɔnvənt] *n* couvent *m*.

convention [kən'vɛnʃən] *n* convention *f*.

conventional [kən'vɛnʃənl] *adj* conventionnel(le).

convent school *n* couvent *m*.

converge [kən'və:dʒ] *vi* converger.

conversant [kən'və:snt] *adj*: **to be ~ with** s'y connaître en; être au courant de.

conversation [kɔnvə'seɪʃən] *n* conversation *f*.

conversational [kɔnvə'seɪʃənl] *adj* de la conversation; (*COMPUT*) conversationnel(le).

conversationalist [kɔnvə'seɪʃnəlɪst] *n* brillant(e) causeur/euse.

converse *n* ['kɔnvə:s] contraire *m*, inverse *m* ♦ *vi* [kən'və:s]: **to ~ (with sb about sth)** s'entretenir (avec qn de qch).

conversely [kɔn'və:slɪ] *adv* inversement, réciproquement.

conversion [kən'və:ʃən] *n* conversion *f*; (*BRIT: of house*) transformation *f*, aménagement *m*.

conversion table *n* table *f* de conversion.

convert *vt* [kən'və:t] (*REL, COMM*) convertir; (*alter*) transformer, aménager; (*RUGBY*) transformer ♦ *n* ['kɔnvə:t] converti/e.

convertible [kən'və:təbl] *adj* convertible ♦ *n* (*voiture f*) décapotable *f*.

convex ['kɔn'vɛks] *adj* convexe.

convey [kən'veɪ] *vt* transporter; (*thanks*) transmettre; (*idea*) communiquer.

conveyance [kən'veɪəns] *n* (*of goods*) transport *m* de marchandises; (*vehicle*) moyen *m* de transport.

conveyancing [kən'veɪənsɪŋ] *n* (*LAW*) rédaction *f* des actes de cession de propriété.

conveyor belt [kən'veɪə*-] *n* convoyeur *m*, tapis roulant.

convict *vt* [kən'vɪkt] déclarer (*or* reconnaître) coupable ♦ *n* ['kɔnvɪkt] forçat *m*, convict *m*.

conviction [kən'vɪkʃən] *n* condamnation *f*; (*belief*) conviction *f*.

convince [kən'vɪns] *vt* convaincre, persuader; **to ~ sb (of sth/that)** persuader qn (de qch/que).

convincing [kən'vɪnsɪŋ] *adj* persuasif(ive), convaincant(e).

convincingly [kən'vɪnsɪŋlɪ] *adv* de façon convaincante.

convivial [kən'vɪvɪəl] *adj* joyeux(euse), plein(e) d'entrain.

convoluted ['kɔnvəlu:tɪd] *adj* (*shape*) tarabiscoté(e); (*argument*) compliqué(e).

convoy ['kɔnvɔɪ] *n* convoi *m*.

convulse [kən'vʌls] *vt* ébranler; **to be ~d with laughter** se tordre de rire.

convulsion [kən'vʌlʃən] *n* convulsion *f*.

coo [ku:] *vi* roucouler.

cook [kuk] *vt* (faire) cuire ♦ *vi* cuire; (*person*) faire la cuisine ♦ *n* cuisinier/ière.

▶**cook up** *vt* (*col: excuse, story*) inventer.

cookbook ['kukbuk] *n* livre *m* de cuisine.

cooker ['kukə*] *n* cuisinière *f*.

cookery ['kukərɪ] *n* cuisine *f*.

cookery book *n* (*BRIT*) = **cookbook**.

cookie ['kukɪ] *n* (*US*) biscuit *m*, petit gâteau sec.

cooking ['kukɪŋ] *n* cuisine *f* ♦ *cpd* (*apples, chocolate*) à cuire; (*utensils, salt*) de cuisine.

cookout ['kukaut] *n* (*US*) barbecue *m*.

cool [ku:l] *adj* frais(fraîche); (*not afraid*) calme; (*unfriendly*) froid(e); (*impertinent*) effronté(e) ♦ *vt, vi* rafraîchir, refroidir; **it's ~** (*weather*) il fait frais; **to keep sth ~** *or* **in a ~**

place garder *or* conserver qch au frais.
►**cool down** *vi* refroidir; (*fig: person, situation*) se calmer.
coolant ['ku:lənt] *n* liquide *m* de refroidissement.
cool box, (*US*) **cooler** ['ku:lə*] *n* boîte *f* isotherme.
cooling ['ku:lɪŋ] *adj* (*breeze*) rafraîchissant(e).
cooling tower *n* refroidisseur *m*.
coolly ['ku:lɪ] *adv* (*calmly*) calmement; (*audaciously*) sans se gêner; (*unenthusiastically*) froidement.
coolness ['ku:lnɪs] *n* fraîcheur *f*; sang-froid *m*, calme *m*; froideur *f*.
coop [ku:p] *n* poulailler *m* ♦ *vt*: **to ~ up** (*fig*) cloîtrer, enfermer.
co-op ['kəuɔp] *n abbr* (= *cooperative (society)*) coop *f*.
cooperate [kəu'ɔpəreɪt] *vi* coopérer, collaborer.
cooperation [kəuɔpə'reɪʃən] *n* coopération *f*, collaboration *f*.
cooperative [kəu'ɔpərətɪv] *adj* coopératif(ive) ♦ *n* coopérative *f*.
coopt [kəu'ɔpt] *vt*: **to ~ sb onto a committee** coopter qn pour faire partie d'un comité.
coordinate *vt* [kəu'ɔ:dɪneɪt] coordonner ♦ *n* [kəu'ɔdɪnət] (*MATH*) coordonnée *f*; **~s** *npl* (*clothes*) ensemble *m*, coordonnés *mpl*.
coordination [kəuɔ:dɪ'neɪʃən] *n* coordination *f*.
coot [ku:t] *n* foulque *f*.
co-ownership ['kəu'əunəʃɪp] *n* copropriété *f*.
cop [kɔp] *n* (*col*) flic *m*.
cope [kəup] *vi* s'en sortir, tenir le coup; **to ~ with** faire face à; (*take care of*) s'occuper de.
Copenhagen ['kəupn'heɪgən] *n* Copenhague.
copier ['kɔpɪə*] *n* (*also*: **photo~**) copieur *m*.
co-pilot ['kəu'paɪlət] *n* copilote *m*.
copious ['kəupɪəs] *adj* copieux(euse), abondant(e).
copper ['kɔpə*] *n* cuivre *m*; (*col: policeman*) flic *m*; **~s** *npl* petite monnaie.
coppice ['kɔpɪs], **copse** [kɔps] *n* taillis *m*.
copulate ['kɔpjuleɪt] *vi* copuler.
copy ['kɔpɪ] *n* copie *f*; (*book etc*) exemplaire *m*; (*material: for printing*) copie ♦ *vt* copier; (*imitate*) imiter; **rough ~** (*gen*) premier jet; (*SCOL*) brouillon *m*; **fair ~** version définitive; propre *m*; **to make good ~** (*PRESS*) faire un bon sujet d'article.
►**copy out** *vt* copier.
copycat ['kɔpɪkæt] *n* (*pej*) copieur/euse.
copyright ['kɔpɪraɪt] *n* droit d'auteur, copyright *m*; **~ reserved** tous droits (de reproduction) réservés.
copy typist *n* dactylo *m/f*.
copywriter ['kɔpɪraɪtə*] *n* rédacteur/trice publicitaire.
coral ['kɔrəl] *n* corail *m*.
coral reef *n* récif *m* de corail.
Coral Sea *n*: **the ~** la mer de Corail.

cord [kɔ:d] *n* corde *f*; (*fabric*) velours côtelé; whipcord *m*; corde *f*; (*ELEC*) cordon *m* (d'alimentation), fil *m* (électrique); **~s** *npl* (*trousers*) pantalon *m* de velours côtelé.
cordial ['kɔ:dɪəl] *adj* cordial(e), chaleureux(euse) ♦ *n* sirop *m*; cordial *m*.
cordless ['kɔ:dlɪs] *adj* sans fil.
cordon ['kɔ:dn] *n* cordon *m*.
►**cordon off** *vt* (*area*) interdire l'accès à; (*crowd*) tenir à l'écart.
corduroy ['kɔ:dərɔɪ] *n* velours côtelé.
CORE [kɔ:*] *n abbr* (*US*) = Congress of Racial Equality.
core [kɔ:*] *n* (*of fruit*) trognon *m*, cœur *m*; (*TECH: also of earth*) noyau *m*; (*of nuclear reactor, fig: of problem etc*) cœur ♦ *vt* enlever le trognon *or* le cœur de; **rotten to the ~** complètement pourri.
Corfu [kɔ:'fu:] *n* Corfou.
coriander [kɔrɪ'ændə*] *n* coriandre *f*.
cork [kɔ:k] *n* liège *m*; (*of bottle*) bouchon *m*.
corkage ['kɔ:kɪdʒ] *n* droit payé par le client qui apporte sa propre bouteille de vin.
corked [kɔ:kt], (*US*) **corky** ['kɔ:kɪ] *adj* (*wine*) qui sent le bouchon.
corkscrew ['kɔ:kskru:] *n* tire-bouchon *m*.
cormorant ['kɔ:mərnt] *n* cormoran *m*.
Corn *abbr* (*BRIT*) = Cornwall.
corn [kɔ:n] *n* (*BRIT: wheat*) blé *m*; (*US: maize*) maïs *m*; (*on foot*) cor *m*; **~ on the cob** (*CULIN*) épi *m* de maïs au naturel.
cornea ['kɔ:nɪə] *n* cornée *f*.
corned beef ['kɔ:nd-] *n* corned-beef *m*.
corner ['kɔ:nə*] *n* coin *m*; (*AUT*) tournant *m*, virage *m*; (*FOOTBALL: also*: **~ kick**) corner *m* ♦ *vt* acculer, mettre au pied du mur; coincer; (*COMM: market*) accaparer ♦ *vi* prendre un virage; **to cut ~s** (*fig*) prendre des raccourcis.
corner flag *n* (*FOOTBALL*) piquet *m* de coin.
corner kick *n* (*FOOTBALL*) corner *m*.
cornerstone ['kɔ:nəstəun] *n* pierre *f* angulaire.
cornet ['kɔ:nɪt] *n* (*MUS*) cornet *m* à pistons; (*BRIT: of ice-cream*) cornet (de glace).
cornflakes ['kɔ:nfleɪks] *npl* cornflakes *mpl*.
cornflour ['kɔ:nflauə*] *n* (*BRIT*) farine *f* de maïs, maïzena *f* ®.
cornice ['kɔ:nɪs] *n* corniche *f*.
Cornish ['kɔ:nɪʃ] *adj* de Cornouailles, cornouaillais(e).
corn oil *n* huile *f* de maïs.
cornstarch ['kɔ:nstɑ:tʃ] *n* (*US*) farine *f* de maïs, maïzena *f* ®.
cornucopia [kɔ:nju'kəupɪə] *n* corne *f* d'abondance.
Cornwall ['kɔ:nwɔl] *n* Cornouailles *f*.
corny ['kɔ:nɪ] *adj* (*col*) rebattu(e), galvaudé(e).
corollary [kə'rɔlərɪ] *n* corollaire *m*.
coronary ['kɔrənərɪ] *n*: **~ (thrombosis)** infarctus *m* (du myocarde), thrombose *f* coronaire.

coronation [kɔrə'neɪʃən] n couronnement m.
coroner ['kɔrənə*] n coroner m.
coronet ['kɔrənɪt] n couronne f.
Corp. abbr = **corporation**.
corporal ['kɔːpərl] n caporal m, brigadier m
♦ adj: ~ **punishment** châtiment corporel.
corporate ['kɔːpərɪt] adj en commun; (COMM)
constitué(e) (en corporation).
corporate hospitality n arrangement selon
lequel une entreprise offre des places de
théâtre, concert etc à ses clients.
corporate identity, corporate image n (of
organization) image f de l'entreprise.
corporation [kɔːpə'reɪʃən] n (of town) municipalité f, conseil municipal; (COMM) société f.
corporation tax n ≈ impôt m sur les bénéfices.
corps [kɔː*], pl **corps** [kɔːz] n corps m; the
press ~ la presse.
corpse [kɔːps] n cadavre m.
corpuscle ['kɔːpʌsl] n corpuscule m.
corral [kə'rɑːl] n corral m.
correct [kə'rɛkt] adj (accurate) correct(e),
exact(e); (proper) correct, convenable ♦ vt
corriger; **you are** ~ vous avez raison.
correction [kə'rɛkʃən] n correction f.
correlate ['kɔrɪleɪt] vt mettre en corrélation
♦ vi: **to** ~ **with** correspondre à.
correlation [kɔrɪ'leɪʃən] n corrélation f.
correspond [kɔrɪs'pɔnd] vi correspondre.
correspondence [kɔrɪs'pɔndəns] n correspondance f.
correspondence course n cours m par correspondance.
correspondent [kɔrɪs'pɔndənt] n corres-
pondant/e.
corridor ['kɔrɪdɔː*] n couloir m, corridor m.
corroborate [kə'rɔbəreɪt] vt corroborer, confirmer.
corrode [kə'rəud] vt corroder, ronger ♦ vi se
corroder.
corrosion [kə'rəuʒən] n corrosion f.
corrosive [kə'rəuzɪv] adj corrosif(ive).
corrugated ['kɔrəgeɪtɪd] adj plissé(e); ondu-
lé(e).
corrugated iron n tôle ondulée.
corrupt [kə'rʌpt] adj corrompu(e) ♦ vt corrompre; (data) altérer; ~ **practices** (dishonesty, bribery) malversation f.
corruption [kə'rʌpʃən] n corruption f; alté-
ration f (de données).
corset ['kɔːsɪt] n corset m.
Corsica ['kɔːsɪkə] n Corse f.
Corsican ['kɔːsɪkən] adj corse ♦ n Corse m/f.
cortège [kɔː'teɪʒ] n cortège m (gén funèbre).
cortisone ['kɔːtɪzəun] n cortisone f.
coruscating ['kɔrəskeɪtɪŋ] adj scintillant(e).
c.o.s. abbr (= cash on shipment) paiement m à
l'expédition.
cosh [kɔʃ] n (BRIT) matraque f.
cosignatory ['kəu'sɪgnətərɪ] n cosignataire m/
f.

cosiness ['kəuzɪnɪs] n atmosphère douillette,
confort m.
cos lettuce ['kɔs-] n (laitue f) romaine f.
cosmetic [kɔz'mɛtɪk] n produit m de beauté,
cosmétique m ♦ adj (preparation) cosmétique;
(surgery) esthétique; (fig: reforms) symbolique, superficiel(le).
cosmic ['kɔzmɪk] adj cosmique.
cosmonaut ['kɔzmənɔːt] n cosmonaute m/f.
cosmopolitan [kɔzmə'pɔlɪtn] adj cosmopolite.
cosmos ['kɔzmɔs] n cosmos m.
cosset ['kɔsɪt] vt choyer, dorloter.
cost [kɔst] n coût m ♦ vb (pt, pp **cost**) vi coûter
♦ vt établir or calculer le prix de revient de;
~**s** npl (LAW) dépens mpl; **how much does it**
~? combien ça coûte?; **it** ~**s £5/too much**
cela coûte 5 livres/trop cher; **what will it** ~
to have it repaired? combien cela coûtera de
le faire réparer?; **it** ~ **him his life/job** ça lui
a coûté la vie/son emploi; **the** ~ **of living** le
coût de la vie; **at all** ~**s** coûte que coûte, à
tout prix.
cost accountant n analyste m/f de coûts.
co-star ['kəustɑː*] n partenaire m/f.
Costa Rica ['kɔstə'riːkə] n Costa Rica m.
cost centre n centre m de coût.
cost control n contrôle m des coûts.
cost-effective ['kɔstɪ'fɛktɪv] adj rentable.
cost-effectiveness ['kɔstɪ'fɛktɪvnɪs] n rentabilité f.
costing ['kɔstɪŋ] n calcul m du prix de revient.
costly ['kɔstlɪ] adj coûteux(euse).
cost-of-living ['kɔstəv'lɪvɪŋ] adj: ~ **allowance**
indemnité f de vie chère; ~ **index** indice m
du coût de la vie.
cost price n (BRIT) prix coûtant or de revient.
costume ['kɔstjuːm] n costume m; (lady's suit)
tailleur m; (BRIT: also: **swimming** ~) maillot
m (de bain).
costume jewellery n bijoux mpl de fantaisie.
cosy, (US) **cozy** ['kəuzɪ] adj (bed) douillet(te);
(scarf, gloves) bien chaud(e); (atmosphere)
chaleureux(euse); (room) mignon(ne).
cot [kɔt] n (BRIT: child's) lit m d'enfant, petit
lit; (US: campbed) lit de camp.
cot death n mort subite du nourrisson.
Cotswolds ['kɔtswəuldz] npl: **the** ~ région de
collines du Gloucestershire.
cottage ['kɔtɪdʒ] n petite maison (à la campagne), cottage m.
cottage cheese n fromage blanc (maigre).
cottage industry n industrie familiale or artisanale.
cottage pie n ≈ hachis m Parmentier.
cotton ['kɔtn] n coton m; ~ **dress** etc robe etc
en or de coton.
▶**cotton on** vi (col): **to** ~ **on (to sth)** piger
(qch).
cotton wool n (BRIT) ouate f, coton m hydrophile.
couch [kautʃ] n canapé m; divan m; (doctor's)

table f d'examen; (*psychiatrist's*) divan ♦ vt formuler, exprimer.

couchette [kuːˈʃɛt] n couchette f.

couch potato n (*col*) mollasson/ne (*qui passe son temps devant la télé*).

cough [kɔf] vi tousser ♦ n toux f.

cough drop n pastille f pour or contre la toux.

cough mixture, cough syrup n sirop m pour la toux.

could [kud] pt of **can**.

couldn't ['kudnt] = **could not**.

council ['kaunsl] n conseil m; **city** or **town** ~ conseil municipal; **C~ of Europe** Conseil de l'Europe.

council estate n (*BRIT*) (quartier m or zone f de) logements loués à/par la municipalité.

council house n (*BRIT*) maison f (à loyer modéré) louée par la municipalité.

councillor ['kaunslə*] n conseiller/ère.

council tax n (*BRIT*) impôts locaux.

counsel ['kaunsl] n consultation f, délibération f; (*person*) avocat/e ♦ vt: **to ~ sth/sb to do sth** conseiller qch/à qn de faire qch; ~ **for the defence/the prosecution** (avocat de la) défense/avocat du ministère public.

counsellor, (*US*) **counselor** ['kaunslə*] n conseiller/ère; (*US LAW*) avocat m.

count [kaunt] vt, vi compter m; (*nobleman*) comte m; **to ~ (up) to 10** compter jusqu'à 10; **to keep ~ of sth** tenir le compte de qch; **not ~ing the children** sans compter les enfants; **10 ~ing him** 10 avec lui, 10 en le comptant; **to ~ the cost of** établir le coût de; **it ~s for very little** cela n'a pas beaucoup d'importance; ~ **yourself lucky** estimez-vous heureux.

▶**count on** vt fus compter sur; **to ~ on doing sth** compter faire qch.

▶**count up** vt compter, additionner.

countdown ['kauntdaun] n compte m à rebours.

countenance ['kauntɪnəns] n expression f ♦ vt approuver.

counter ['kauntə*] n comptoir m; (*in post office, bank*) guichet m; (*in game*) jeton m ♦ vt aller à l'encontre de, opposer; (*blow*) parer ♦ adv: ~ **to** à l'encontre de; contrairement à; **to buy under the** ~ (*fig*) acheter sous le manteau or en sous-main; **to ~ sth with sth/by doing sth** contrer or riposter à qch par qch/en faisant qch.

counteract ['kauntər'ækt] vt neutraliser, contrebalancer.

counterattack ['kauntərə'tæk] n contre-attaque f ♦ vi contre-attaquer.

counterbalance ['kauntə'bæləns] vt contrebalancer, faire contrepoids à.

counter-clockwise ['kauntə'klɔkwaɪz] adv en sens inverse des aiguilles d'une montre.

counter-espionage ['kauntər'ɛspɪənɑːʒ] n contre-espionnage m.

counterfeit ['kauntəfɪt] n faux m, contrefaçon f ♦ vt contrefaire ♦ adj faux(fausse).

counterfoil ['kauntəfɔɪl] n talon m, souche f.

counterintelligence ['kauntərɪn'tɛlɪdʒəns] n contre-espionnage m.

countermand ['kauntəmɑːnd] vt annuler.

countermeasure ['kauntəmɛʒə*] n contre-mesure f.

counteroffensive ['kauntərə'fɛnsɪv] n contre-offensive f.

counterpane ['kauntəpeɪn] n dessus-de-lit m.

counterpart ['kauntəpɑːt] n (*of document etc*) double m; (*of person*) homologue m/f.

counterproductive ['kauntəprə'dʌktɪv] adj contre-productif(ive).

counterproposal ['kauntəprə'pəuzl] n contre-proposition f.

countersign ['kauntəsaɪn] vt contresigner.

countersink ['kauntəsɪŋk] vt (*hole*) fraiser.

countess ['kauntɪs] n comtesse f.

countless ['kauntlɪs] adj innombrable.

countrified ['kʌntrɪfaɪd] adj rustique, à l'air campagnard.

country ['kʌntrɪ] n pays m; (*native land*) patrie f; (*as opposed to town*) campagne f; (*region*) région f, pays; **in the** ~ à la campagne; **mountainous** ~ pays de montagne, région montagneuse.

country and western (music) n musique f country.

country dancing n (*BRIT*) danse f folklorique.

country house n manoir m, (petit) château.

countryman ['kʌntrɪmən] n (*national*) compatriote m; (*rural*) habitant m de la campagne, campagnard m.

countryside ['kʌntrɪsaɪd] n campagne f.

countrywide ['kʌntrɪ'waɪd] adj s'étendant à l'ensemble du pays; (*problem*) à l'échelle nationale ♦ adv à travers or dans tout le pays.

county ['kauntɪ] n comté m.

county council n (*BRIT*) ≈ conseil régional.

county town n (*BRIT*) chef-lieu m.

coup, ~**s** [kuː, -z] n beau coup; (*also*: ~ **d'état**) coup d'État.

coupé [kuːˈpeɪ] n (*AUT*) coupé m.

couple ['kʌpl] n couple m ♦ vt (*carriages*) atteler; (*TECH*) coupler; (*ideas, names*) associer; **a ~ of** deux; (*a few*) deux ou trois.

couplet ['kʌplɪt] n distique m.

coupling ['kʌplɪŋ] n (*RAIL*) attelage m.

coupon ['kuːpɔn] n (*voucher*) bon-prime m, bon-réclame m; (*detachable form*) coupon m détachable, coupon-réponse m; (*FINANCE*) coupon.

courage ['kʌrɪdʒ] n courage m.

courageous [kə'reɪdʒəs] adj courageux(euse).

courgette [kuə'ʒɛt] n (*BRIT*) courgette f.

courier ['kurɪə*] n messager m, courrier m; (*for tourists*) accompagnateur/trice.

course [kɔːs] n cours m; (*of ship*) route f; (*for golf*) terrain m; (*part of meal*) plat m; **first** ~ entrée f; **of** ~ adv bien sûr; **(no) of** ~ **not!**

bien sûr que non!, évidemment que non!; **in the ~ of the next few days** au cours des prochains jours; **in due ~** en temps utile *or* voulu; **~ (of action)** parti *m*, ligne *f* de conduite; **the best ~ would be to ...** le mieux serait de ...; **we have no other ~ but to ...** nous n'avons pas d'autre solution que de ...; **~ of lectures** série *f* de conférences; **~ of treatment** (*MED*) traitement *m*.

court [kɔːt] *n* cour *f*; (*LAW*) cour, tribunal *m*; (*TENNIS*) court *m* ♦ *vt* (*woman*) courtiser, faire la cour à; (*fig: favour, popularity*) rechercher; (*: death, disaster*) courir après, flirter avec; **out of ~** (*LAW: settle*) à l'amiable; **to take to ~** actionner *or* poursuivre en justice; **~ of appeal** cour d'appel.

courteous [ˈkəːtɪəs] *adj* courtois(e), poli(e).

courtesan [kɔːtɪˈzæn] *n* courtisane *f*.

courtesy [ˈkəːtəsɪ] *n* courtoisie *f*, politesse *f*; **by ~ of** avec l'aimable autorisation de.

courtesy light *n* (*AUT*) plafonnier *m*.

court-house [ˈkɔːthaus] *n* (*US*) palais *m* de justice.

courtier [ˈkɔːtɪə*] *n* courtisan *m*, dame *f* de cour.

court martial, *pl* **courts martial** *n* cour martiale, conseil *m* de guerre.

courtroom [ˈkɔːtrum] *n* salle *f* de tribunal.

court shoe *n* escarpin *m*.

courtyard [ˈkɔːtjɑːd] *n* cour *f*.

cousin [ˈkʌzn] *n* cousin/e.

cove [kəuv] *n* petite baie, anse *f*.

covenant [ˈkʌvənənt] *n* contrat *m*, engagement *m* ♦ *vt*: **to ~ £200 per year to a charity** s'engager à verser 200 livres par an à une œuvre de bienfaisance.

Coventry [ˈkɔvəntrɪ] *n*: **to send sb to ~** (*fig*) mettre qn en quarantaine.

cover [ˈkʌvə*] *vt* couvrir; (*PRESS: report on*) faire un reportage sur ♦ *n* (*for bed, of book, COMM*) couverture *f*; (*of pan*) couvercle *m*; (*over furniture*) housse *f*; (*shelter*) abri *m*; **to take ~** se mettre à l'abri; **under ~** à l'abri; **under ~ of darkness** à la faveur de la nuit; **under separate ~** (*COMM*) sous pli séparé; **£10 will ~ everything** 10 livres suffiront (pour tout payer).

▶**cover up** *vt* (*person, object*): **to ~ up (with)** couvrir (de); (*fig: truth, facts*) occulter; **to ~ up for sb** (*fig*) couvrir qn.

coverage [ˈkʌvərɪdʒ] *n* (*in media*) reportage *m*; (*INSURANCE*) couverture *f*.

cover charge *n* couvert *m* (*supplément à payer*).

covering [ˈkʌvərɪŋ] *n* couverture *f*, enveloppe *f*.

covering letter, (*US*) **cover letter** *n* lettre explicative.

cover note *n* (*INSURANCE*) police *f* provisoire.

cover price *n* prix *m* de l'exemplaire.

covert [ˈkʌvət] *adj* (*threat*) voilé(e), caché(e); (*attack*) indirect(e); (*glance*) furtif(ive).

cover-up [ˈkʌvərʌp] *n* tentative *f* pour étouffer une affaire.

covet [ˈkʌvɪt] *vt* convoiter.

cow [kau] *n* vache *f* ♦ *cpd* femelle ♦ *vt* effrayer, intimider.

coward [ˈkauəd] *n* lâche *m/f*.

cowardice [ˈkauədɪs] *n* lâcheté *f*.

cowardly [ˈkauədlɪ] *adj* lâche.

cowboy [ˈkaubɔɪ] *n* cow-boy *m*.

cower [ˈkauə*] *vi* se recroqueviller; trembler.

cowshed [ˈkauʃed] *n* étable *f*.

cowslip [ˈkauslɪp] *n* (*BOT*) (fleur *f* de) coucou *m*.

coxswain [ˈkɔksn] *n* (*abbr*: **cox**) barreur *m*; (*of ship*) patron *m*.

coy [kɔɪ] *adj* faussement effarouché(e) *or* timide.

coyote [kɔɪˈəutɪ] *n* coyote *m*.

cozy [ˈkəuzɪ] *adj* (*US*) = **cosy**.

CP *n abbr* (= *Communist Party*) PC *m*.

cp. *abbr* (= *compare*) cf.

c/p *abbr* (*BRIT*) = **carriage paid**.

CPA *n abbr* (*US*) = **certified public accountant**.

CPI *n abbr* (= *Consumer Price Index*) IPC *m*.

Cpl. *abbr* (= *corporal*) C/C.

CP/M *n abbr* (= *Central Program for Microprocessors*) CP/M *m*.

c.p.s. *abbr* (= *characters per second*) caractères/seconde.

CPSA *n abbr* (*BRIT*: = *Civil and Public Services Association*) *syndicat de la fonction publique*.

CPU *n abbr* = **central processing unit**.

cr. *abbr* = **credit; creditor**.

crab [kræb] *n* crabe *m*.

crab apple *n* pomme *f* sauvage.

crack [kræk] *n* fente *f*, fissure *f*; (*in bone, dish, glass*) fêlure *f*; (*in wall*) lézarde *f*; (*noise*) craquement *m*, coup (sec); (*joke*) plaisanterie *f*; (*col: attempt*): **to have a ~ (at sth)** essayer (qch); (*DRUGS*) crack *m* ♦ *vt* fendre, fissurer; fêler; lézarder; (*whip*) faire claquer; (*nut*) casser; (*solve*) résoudre, trouver la clef de; déchiffrer ♦ *cpd* (*athlete*) de première classe, d'élite; **to ~ jokes** (*col*) raconter des blagues; **to get ~ing** (*col*) s'y mettre, se magner.

▶**crack down on** *vt fus* (*crime*) sévir contre, réprimer; (*spending*) mettre un frein à.

▶**crack up** *vi* être au bout de son rouleau, flancher.

crackdown [ˈkrækdaun] *n*: **~ (on)** (*on crime*) répression *f* (de); (*on spending*) restrictions *fpl* (de).

cracked [krækt] *adj* (*col*) toqué(e), timbré(e).

cracker [ˈkrækə*] *n* pétard *m*; (*biscuit*) biscuit (salé), craquelin *m*; **a ~ of a ...** (*BRIT col*) un(e) ... formidable; **he's ~s** (*BRIT col*) il est cinglé.

crackle [ˈkrækl] *vi* crépiter, grésiller.

crackling [ˈkræklɪŋ] *n* crépitement *m*, grésillement *m*; (*on radio, telephone*) grésillement, friture *f*; (*of pork*) couenne *f*.

crackpot ['krækpɔt] n (col) tordu/e.
cradle ['kreɪdl] n berceau m ♦ vt (child) bercer; (object) tenir dans ses bras.
craft [krɑːft] n métier (artisanal); (cunning) ruse f, astuce f; (boat) embarcation f, barque f.
craftsman ['krɑːftsmən] n artisan m, ouvrier (qualifié).
craftsmanship ['krɑːftsmənʃɪp] n métier m, habileté f.
crafty ['krɑːftɪ] adj rusé(e), malin(igne), astucieux(euse).
crag [kræg] n rocher escarpé.
craggy ['krægɪ] adj escarpé(e), rocheux(euse).
cram [kræm] vt (fill): **to ~ sth with** bourrer qch de; (put): **to ~ sth into** fourrer qch dans.
cramming ['kræmɪŋ] n (for exams) bachotage m.
cramp [kræmp] n crampe f ♦ vt gêner, entraver.
cramped [kræmpt] adj à l'étroit, très serré(e).
crampon ['kræmpən] n crampon m.
cranberry ['krænbərɪ] n canneberge f.
crane [kreɪn] n grue f ♦ vt, vi: **to ~ forward, to ~ one's neck** allonger le cou.
cranium, pl **crania** ['kreɪnɪəm, 'kreɪnɪə] n boîte crânienne.
crank [kræŋk] n manivelle f; (person) excentrique m/f.
crankshaft ['kræŋkʃɑːft] n vilebrequin m.
cranky ['kræŋkɪ] adj excentrique, loufoque; (bad-tempered) grincheux(euse), revêche.
cranny ['krænɪ] n see **nook**.
crap [kræp] n (col!) conneries fpl (!); **to have a ~** chier (!).
crappy ['kræpɪ] adj (col) merdique (!).
crash [kræʃ] n fracas m; (of car, plane) collision f; (of business) faillite f; (STOCK EXCHANGE) krach m ♦ vt (plane) écraser ♦ vi (plane) s'écraser; (two cars) se percuter, s'emboutir; (fig) s'effondrer; **to ~ into** se jeter or se fracasser contre; **he ~ed the car into a wall** il s'est écrasé contre un mur avec sa voiture.
crash barrier n (BRIT AUT) rail m de securité.
crash course n cours intensif.
crash helmet n casque (protecteur).
crash landing n atterrissage forcé or catastrophe.
crass [kræs] adj grossier(ière), crasse.
crate [kreɪt] n cageot m.
crater ['kreɪtə*] n cratère m.
cravat [krə'væt] n foulard (noué autour du cou).
crave [kreɪv] vt, vi: **to ~ for** désirer violemment, avoir un besoin physiologique de, avoir une envie irrésistible de.
craving ['kreɪvɪŋ] n: **~ (for)** (for food, cigarettes etc) envie f irrésistible (de).
crawl [krɔːl] vi ramper; (vehicle) avancer au pas ♦ n (SWIMMING) crawl m; **to ~ on one's hands and knees** aller à quatre pattes; **to ~**

to sb (col) faire de la lèche à qn.
crawler lane ['krɔːlə-] n (BRIT AUT) file f or voie f pour véhicules lents.
crayfish ['kreɪfɪʃ] n (pl inv) (freshwater) écrevisse f; (saltwater) langoustine f.
crayon ['kreɪən] n crayon m (de couleur).
craze [kreɪz] n engouement m.
crazed [kreɪzd] adj (look, person) affolé(e); (pottery, glaze) craquelé(e).
crazy ['kreɪzɪ] adj fou(folle); **to go ~** devenir fou; **to be ~ about sb** (col) aimer qn à la folie; **he's ~ about skiing** (col) c'est un fana(tique) de ski.
crazy paving n (BRIT) dallage irrégulier (en pierres plates).
creak [kriːk] vi (hinge) grincer; (floor, shoes) craquer.
cream [kriːm] n crème f ♦ adj (colour) crème inv; **whipped ~** crème fouettée.
▶**cream off** vt (fig) prélever.
cream cake n (petit) gâteau à la crème.
cream cheese n fromage m à la crème, fromage blanc.
creamery ['kriːmərɪ] n (shop) crémerie f; (factory) laiterie f.
creamy ['kriːmɪ] adj crémeux(euse).
crease [kriːs] n pli m ♦ vt froisser, chiffonner ♦ vi se froisser, se chiffonner.
crease-resistant ['kriːsrɪzɪstənt] adj infroissable.
create [kriː'eɪt] vt créer; (impression, fuss) faire.
creation [kriː'eɪʃən] n création f.
creative [kriː'eɪtɪv] adj créateur(trice).
creativity [kriːeɪ'tɪvɪtɪ] n créativité f.
creator [kriː'eɪtə*] n créateur/trice.
creature ['kriːtʃə*] n créature f.
creature comforts npl petit confort.
crèche [krɛʃ] n garderie f, crèche f.
credence ['kriːdns] n croyance f, foi f.
credentials [krɪ'denʃlz] npl (papers) références fpl; (letters of reference) pièces justificatives.
credibility [kredɪ'bɪlɪtɪ] n crédibilité f.
credible ['kredɪbl] adj digne de foi, crédible.
credit ['kredɪt] n crédit m; (SCOL) unité f de valeur ♦ vt (COMM) créditer; (believe: also: **give ~ to**) ajouter foi à, croire; **to ~ sb with** (fig) prêter or attribuer à qn; **to ~ £5 to sb** créditer (le compte de) qn de 5 livres; **to be in ~** (person, bank account) être créditeur(trice); **on ~** à crédit; **to one's ~** à son honneur; **to take the ~ for** s'attribuer le mérite de; **it does him ~** cela lui fait honneur.
creditable ['kredɪtəbl] adj honorable, estimable.
credit account n compte m client.
credit agency n (BRIT) agence f de renseignements commerciaux.
credit balance n solde créditeur.
credit bureau n (US) agence f de renseigne-

ments commerciaux.

credit card *n* carte *f* de crédit.

credit control *n* suivi *m* des factures.

credit facilities *npl* facilités *fpl* de paiement.

credit limit *n* limite *f* de crédit.

credit note *n* (*BRIT*) avoir *m*.

creditor ['krɛdɪtə*] *n* créancier/ière.

credits ['krɛdɪts] *npl* (*CINE*) générique *m*.

credit transfer *n* virement *m*.

creditworthy ['krɛdɪtwə:ðɪ] *adj* solvable.

credulity [krɪ'dju:lɪtɪ] *n* crédulité *f*.

creed [kri:d] *n* croyance *f*; credo *m*, principes *mpl*.

creek [kri:k] *n* crique *f*, anse *f*; (*US*) ruisseau *m*, petit cours d'eau.

creel ['kri:l] *n* panier *m* de pêche; (*also:* **lobster** ~) panier à homards.

creep, *pt, pp* **crept** [kri:p, krɛpt] *vi* ramper; (*fig*) se faufiler, se glisser; (*plant*) grimper ♦ *n* (*col*) saligaud *m*; **he's a** ~ c'est un type puant; **it gives me the** ~**s** cela me fait froid dans le dos; **to** ~ **up on sb** s'approcher furtivement de qn.

creeper ['kri:pə*] *n* plante grimpante.

creepers ['kri:pəz] *npl* (*US: for baby*) barboteuse *f*.

creepy ['kri:pɪ] *adj* (*frightening*) qui fait frissonner, qui donne la chair de poule.

creepy-crawly ['kri:pɪ'krɔ:lɪ] *n* (*col*) bestiole *f*.

cremate [krɪ'meɪt] *vt* incinérer.

cremation [krɪ'meɪʃən] *n* incinération *f*.

crematorium, *pl* **crematoria** [krɛmə'tɔ:rɪəm, -'tɔ:rɪə] *n* four *m* crématoire.

creosote ['krɪəsəut] *n* créosote *f*.

crepe [kreɪp] *n* crêpe *m*.

crepe bandage *n* (*BRIT*) bande *f* Velpeau ®.

crepe paper *n* papier *m* crépon.

crepe sole *n* semelle *f* de crêpe.

crept [krɛpt] *pt, pp of* **creep**.

crescendo [krɪ'ʃɛndəu] *n* crescendo *m*.

crescent ['krɛsnt] *n* croissant *m*; (*street*) rue *f* (*en arc de cercle*).

cress [krɛs] *n* cresson *m*.

crest [krɛst] *n* crête *f*; (*of helmet*) cimier *m*; (*of coat of arms*) timbre *m*.

crestfallen ['krɛstfɔ:lən] *adj* déconfit(e), découragé(e).

Crete ['kri:t] *n* Crète *f*.

crevasse [krɪ'væs] *n* crevasse *f*.

crevice ['krɛvɪs] *n* fissure *f*, lézarde *f*, fente *f*.

crew [kru:] *n* équipage *m*; (*CINE*) équipe *f* (de tournage); (*gang*) bande *f*.

crew-cut ['kru:kʌt] *n*: **to have a** ~ avoir les cheveux en brosse.

crew-neck ['kru:nɛk] *n* col ras.

crib [krɪb] *n* lit *m* d'enfant ♦ *vt* (*col*) copier.

cribbage ['krɪbɪdʒ] *n* sorte de jeu de cartes.

crick [krɪk] *n* crampe *f*, ~ **in the neck** torticolis *m*.

cricket ['krɪkɪt] *n* (*insect*) grillon *m*, cri-cri *m inv*; (*game*) cricket *m*.

cricketer ['krɪkɪtə*] *n* joueur *m* de cricket.

crime [kraɪm] *n* crime *m*; **minor** ~ délit *m or* infraction *f* mineur(e).

crime wave *n* poussée *f* de la criminalité.

criminal ['krɪmɪnl] *adj, n* criminel(le).

crimp [krɪmp] *vt* friser, frisotter.

crimson ['krɪmzn] *adj* cramoisi(e).

cringe [krɪndʒ] *vi* avoir un mouvement de recul; (*fig*) s'humilier, ramper.

crinkle ['krɪŋkl] *vt* froisser, chiffonner.

cripple ['krɪpl] *n* boiteux/euse, infirme *m/f* ♦ *vt* estropier, paralyser; (*ship, plane*) immobiliser; (*production, exports*) paralyser; ~**d with rheumatism** perclus(e) de rhumatismes.

crippling ['krɪplɪŋ] *adj* (*disease*) handicapant(e); (*taxation, debts*) écrasant(e).

crisis, *pl* **crises** ['kraɪsɪs, -si:z] *n* crise *f*.

crisp [krɪsp] *adj* croquant(e); (*fig*) vif(vive); brusque.

crisps [krɪsps] *npl* (*BRIT*) (pommes) chips *fpl*.

crisscross ['krɪskrɔs] *adj* entrecroisé(e), en croisillons ♦ *vt* sillonner; ~ **pattern** croisillons *mpl*.

criterion, *pl* **criteria** [kraɪ'tɪərɪən, -'tɪərɪə] *n* critère *m*.

critic ['krɪtɪk] *n* critique *m/f*.

critical ['krɪtɪkl] *adj* critique; **to be** ~ **of sb/sth** critiquer qn/qch.

critically ['krɪtɪklɪ] *adv* (*examine*) d'un œil critique; (*speak*) sévèrement; ~ **ill** gravement malade.

criticism ['krɪtɪsɪzəm] *n* critique *f*.

criticize ['krɪtɪsaɪz] *vt* critiquer.

croak [krəuk] *vi* (*frog*) coasser; (*raven*) croasser.

Croat ['krəuæt] *adj, n* = **Croatian**.

Croatia [krəu'eɪʃə] *n* Croatie *f*.

Croatian [krəu'eɪʃən] *adj* croate ♦ *n* Croate *m/f*; (*LING*) croate *m*.

crochet ['krəuʃeɪ] *n* travail *m* au crochet.

crock [krɔk] *n* cruche *f*; (*col: also:* **old** ~) épave *f*.

crockery ['krɔkərɪ] *n* vaisselle *f*.

crocodile ['krɔkədaɪl] *n* crocodile *m*.

crocus ['krəukəs] *n* crocus *m*.

croft [krɔft] *n* (*BRIT*) petite ferme.

crofter ['krɔftə*] *n* (*BRIT*) fermier *m*.

crone [krəun] *n* vieille bique, (vieille) sorcière.

crony ['krəunɪ] *n* copain/copine.

crook [kruk] *n* escroc *m*; (*of shepherd*) houlette *f*.

crooked ['krukɪd] *adj* courbé(e), tordu(e); (*action*) malhonnête.

crop [krɔp] *n* (*produce*) culture *f*; (*amount produced*) récolte *f*; (*riding* ~) cravache *f*; (*of bird*) jabot *m* ♦ *vt* (*hair*) tondre; (*subj: animals: grass*) brouter.

►**crop up** *vi* surgir, se présenter, survenir.

cropper ['krɔpə*] *n*: **to come a** ~ (*col*) faire la culbute, s'étaler.

crop spraying [-spreɪɪŋ] *n* pulvérisation *f* des cultures.

croquet ['krəukeɪ] *n* croquet *m*.

croquette [krə'kɛt] n croquette f.

cross [krɔs] n croix f; (BIOL) croisement m ♦ vt (street etc) traverser; (arms, legs, BIOL) croiser; (cheque) barrer; (thwart: person, plan) contrarier ♦ vi: **the boat ~es from ... to ...** le bateau fait la traversée de ... à ... ♦ adj en colère, fâché(e); **to ~ o.s.** se signer, faire le signe de (la) croix; **we have a ~ed line** (BRIT: on telephone) il y a des interférences; **they've got their lines ~ed** (fig) il y a un malentendu entre eux; **to be/get ~ with sb (about sth)** être en colère/se fâcher contre qn (à propos de qch).

▶**cross out** vt barrer, biffer.

▶**cross over** vi traverser.

crossbar ['krɔsbɑː*] n barre transversale.

crossbow ['krɔsbəu] n arbalète f.

crossbreed ['krɔsbriːd] n hybride m, métis/se.

cross-Channel ferry ['krɔs'tʃænl-] n ferry m qui fait la traversée de la Manche.

cross-check ['krɔstʃɛk] n recoupement m ♦ vi vérifier par recoupement.

cross-country (race) ['krɔs'kʌntrɪ-] n cross(-country) m.

cross-dressing [krɔs'drɛsɪŋ] n travestisme m.

cross-examination ['krɔsɪgzæmɪ'neɪʃən] n (LAW) examen m contradictoire (d'un témoin).

cross-examine ['krɔsɪg'zæmɪn] vt (LAW) faire subir un examen contradictoire à.

cross-eyed ['krɔsaɪd] adj qui louche.

crossfire ['krɔsfaɪə*] n feux croisés.

crossing ['krɔsɪŋ] n croisement m, carrefour m; (sea passage) traversée f; (also: pedestrian ~) passage clouté.

crossing point n poste frontalier.

cross-purposes ['krɔs'pəːpəsɪz] npl: **to be at ~ with sb** comprendre qn de travers; **we're (talking) at ~** on ne parle pas de la même chose.

cross-question ['krɔs'kwɛstʃən] vt faire subir un interrogatoire à.

cross-reference ['krɔs'rɛfrəns] n renvoi m, référence f.

crossroads ['krɔsrəudz] n carrefour m.

cross section n (BIOL) coupe transversale; (in population) échantillon m.

crosswalk ['krɔswɔːk] n (US) passage clouté.

crosswind ['krɔswɪnd] n vent m de travers.

crosswise ['krɔswaɪz] adv en travers.

crossword ['krɔswɔːd] n mots mpl croisés.

crotch [krɔtʃ] n (of garment) entre-jambes m inv.

crotchet ['krɔtʃɪt] n (MUS) noire f.

crotchety ['krɔtʃɪtɪ] adj (person) grognon(ne), grincheux(euse).

crouch [krautʃ] vi s'accroupir; se tapir; se ramasser.

croup [kruːp] n (MED) croup m.

crouton ['kruːtɔn] n croûton m.

crow [krəu] n (bird) corneille f; (of cock) chant m du coq, cocorico m ♦ vi (cock) chanter; (fig)

pavoiser, chanter victoire.

crowbar ['krəubɑː*] n levier m.

crowd [kraud] n foule f ♦ vt bourrer, remplir ♦ vi affluer, s'attrouper, s'entasser; **~s of people** une foule de gens.

crowded ['kraudɪd] adj bondé(e), plein(e); **~ with** plein de.

crowd scene n (CINE, THEAT) scène f de foule.

crown [kraun] n couronne f; (of head) sommet m de la tête, calotte crânienne; (of hat) fond m; (of hill) sommet m ♦ vt (also tooth) couronner.

crown court n (BRIT) ≈ Cour f d'assises.

En Angleterre et au Pays de Galles, une **crown court** est une cour de justice où sont jugées les affaires très graves, telles que le meurtre, l'homicide, le viol et le vol, en présence d'un jury. Tous les crimes et délits, quel que soit leur degré de gravité, doivent d'abord passer devant une **magistrates' court**. Il existe environ 90 crown courts.

crowning ['kraunɪŋ] adj (achievement, glory) suprême.

crown jewels npl joyaux mpl de la Couronne.

crown prince n prince héritier.

crow's-feet ['krəuzfiːt] npl pattes fpl d'oie (fig).

crow's-nest ['krəuznɛst] n (on sailing-ship) nid m de pie.

crucial ['kruːʃl] adj crucial(e), décisif(ive); **~ to** essentiel(le) à.

crucifix ['kruːsɪfɪks] n crucifix m.

crucifixion [kruːsɪ'fɪkʃən] n crucifiement m, crucifixion f.

crucify ['kruːsɪfaɪ] vt crucifier, mettre en croix; (fig) crucifier.

crude [kruːd] adj (materials) brut(e); non raffiné(e); (basic) rudimentaire, sommaire; (vulgar) cru(e), grossier(ière).

crude (oil) n (pétrole) brut m.

cruel ['kruəl] adj cruel(le).

cruelty ['kruəltɪ] n cruauté f.

cruet ['kruːɪt] n huilier m; vinaigrier m.

cruise [kruːz] n croisière f ♦ vi (ship) croiser; (car) rouler; (aircraft) voler; (taxi) être en maraude.

cruise missile n missile m de croisière.

cruiser ['kruːzə*] n croiseur m.

cruising speed ['kruːzɪŋ-] n vitesse f de croisière.

crumb [krʌm] n miette f.

crumble ['krʌmbl] vt émietter ♦ vi s'émietter; (plaster etc) s'effriter; (land, earth) s'ébouler; (building) s'écrouler, crouler; (fig) s'effondrer.

crumbly ['krʌmblɪ] adj friable.

crummy ['krʌmɪ] adj (col) minable; (: unwell) mal fichu(e), patraque.

crumpet ['krʌmpɪt] n petite crêpe (épaisse).

crumple ['krʌmpl] vt froisser, friper.

crunch [krʌntʃ] *vt* croquer; (*underfoot*) faire craquer, écraser; faire crisser ♦ *n* (*fig*) instant *m or* moment *m* critique, moment de vérité.

crunchy ['krʌntʃɪ] *adj* croquant(e), croustillant(e).

crusade [kruːˈseɪd] *n* croisade *f* ♦ *vi* (*fig*): **to ~ for/against** partir en croisade pour/contre.

crusader [kruːˈseɪdə*] *n* croisé *m*; (*fig*): **~ (for)** champion *m* (de).

crush [krʌʃ] *n* foule *f*, cohue *f*; (*love*): **to have a ~ on sb** avoir le béguin pour qn; (*drink*): **lemon ~** citron pressé ♦ *vt* écraser; (*crumple*) froisser; (*grind, break up: garlic, ice*) piler; (*: grapes*) presser.

crush barrier *n* (*BRIT*) barrière *f* de sécurité.

crushing ['krʌʃɪŋ] *adj* écrasant(e).

crust [krʌst] *n* croûte *f*.

crustacean [krʌsˈteɪʃən] *n* crustacé *m*.

crusty ['krʌstɪ] *adj* (*bread*) croustillant(e); (*col: person*) revêche, bourru(e); (*: remark*) irrité(e).

crutch [krʌtʃ] *n* béquille *f*; (*TECH*) support *m*; (*also*: **crotch**) entrejambe *m*.

crux [krʌks] *n* point crucial.

cry [kraɪ] *vi* pleurer; (*shout: also*: **~ out**) crier ♦ *n* cri *m*; **what are you ~ing about?** pourquoi pleures-tu?; **to ~ for help** appeler à l'aide; **she had a good ~** elle a pleuré un bon coup; **it's a far ~ from ...** (*fig*) on est loin de ....
▶**cry off** *vi* se dédire; se décommander.

crying ['kraɪɪŋ] *adj* (*fig*) criant(e), flagrant(e).

crypt [krɪpt] *n* crypte *f*.

cryptic ['krɪptɪk] *adj* énigmatique.

crystal ['krɪstl] *n* cristal *m*.

crystal-clear ['krɪstl'klɪə*] *adj* clair(e) comme de l'eau de roche.

crystallize ['krɪstəlaɪz] *vt* cristalliser ♦ *vi* (se) cristalliser; **~d fruits** (*BRIT*) fruits confits.

CSA *n abbr* = *Confederate States of America*; (*BRIT*: = *Child Support Agency*) organisme pour la protection des enfants de parents séparés, qui contrôle le versement des pensions alimentaires.

CSC *n abbr* (= *Civil Service Commission*) commission de recrutement des fonctionnaires.

CSE *n abbr* (*BRIT*: = *Certificate of Secondary Education*) ≈ BEPC *m*

CS gas *n* (*BRIT*) gaz *m* C.S.

CST *abbr* (*US*: = *Central Standard Time*) fuseau horaire.

CT *abbr* (*US*) = *Connecticut*.

ct *abbr* = *carat*.

CTC *n abbr* (*BRIT*) = *city technology college*.

CT scanner *n abbr* (*MED*: = *computerized tomography scanner*) scanner *m*, tomodensitomètre *m*.

cu. *abbr* = **cubic**.

cub [kʌb] *n* petit *m* (*d'un animal*); (*also*: **~ scout**) louveteau *m*.

Cuba ['kjuːbə] *n* Cuba *m*.

Cuban ['kjuːbən] *adj* cubain(e) ♦ *n* Cubain/e.

cubbyhole ['kʌbɪhəʊl] *n* cagibi *m*.

cube [kjuːb] *n* cube *m* ♦ *vt* (*MATH*) élever au cube.

cube root *n* racine *f* cubique.

cubic ['kjuːbɪk] *adj* cubique; **~ metre** *etc* mètre *m etc* cube; **~ capacity** (*AUT*) cylindrée *f*.

cubicle ['kjuːbɪkl] *n* box *m*, cabine *f*.

cuckoo ['kuku:] *n* coucou *m*.

cuckoo clock *n* (pendule *f* à) coucou *m*.

cucumber ['kjuːkʌmbə*] *n* concombre *m*.

cud [kʌd] *n*: **to chew the ~** ruminer.

cuddle ['kʌdl] *vt* câliner, caresser ♦ *vi* se blottir l'un contre l'autre.

cuddly ['kʌdlɪ] *adj* câlin(e).

cudgel ['kʌdʒl] *n* gourdin *m* ♦ *vt*: **to ~ one's brains** se creuser la tête.

cue [kjuː] *n* queue *f* de billard; (*THEAT etc*) signal *m*.

cuff [kʌf] *n* (*of shirt, coat etc*) poignet *m*, manchette *f*; (*US: on trousers*) revers *m*; (*blow*) gifle *f* ♦ *vt* gifler; **off the ~** *adv* de chic, à l'improviste.

cufflink ['kʌflɪŋk] *n* bouton *m* de manchette.

cu. in. *abbr* = *cubic inches*.

cuisine [kwɪˈziːn] *n* cuisine *f*, art *m* culinaire.

cul-de-sac ['kʌldəsæk] *n* cul-de-sac *m*, impasse *f*.

culinary ['kʌlɪnərɪ] *adj* culinaire.

cull [kʌl] *vt* sélectionner; (*kill selectively*) pratiquer l'abattage sélectif de.

culminate ['kʌlmɪneɪt] *vi*: **to ~ in** finir *or* se terminer par; (*lead to*) mener à.

culmination [kʌlmɪˈneɪʃən] *n* point culminant.

culottes [kjuːˈlɒts] *npl* jupe-culotte *f*.

culpable ['kʌlpəbl] *adj* coupable.

culprit ['kʌlprɪt] *n* coupable *m/f*.

cult [kʌlt] *n* culte *m*.

cult figure *n* idole *f*.

cultivate ['kʌltɪveɪt] *vt* (*also fig*) cultiver.

cultivation [kʌltɪˈveɪʃən] *n* culture *f*.

cultural ['kʌltʃərəl] *adj* culturel(le).

culture ['kʌltʃə*] *n* (*also fig*) culture *f*.

cultured ['kʌltʃəd] *adj* cultivé(e) (*fig*).

cumbersome ['kʌmbəsəm] *adj* encombrant(e), embarrassant(e).

cumin ['kʌmɪn] *n* (*spice*) cumin *m*.

cumulative ['kjuːmjʊlətɪv] *adj* cumulatif(ive).

cunning ['kʌnɪŋ] *n* ruse *f*, astuce *f* ♦ *adj* rusé(e), malin(igne); (*clever: device, idea*) astucieux(euse).

cunt [kʌnt] *n* (*col!*) chatte *f* (*!*); (*insult*) salaud *m* (*!*), salope *f* (*!*).

cup [kʌp] *n* tasse *f*; (*prize, event*) coupe *f*; (*of bra*) bonnet *m*; **a ~ of tea** une tasse de thé.

cupboard ['kʌbəd] *n* placard *m*.

cup final *n* (*BRIT FOOTBALL*) finale *f* de la coupe.

Cupid ['kjuːpɪd] *n* Cupidon *m*; (*figurine*) amour *m*.

cupidity [kjuːˈpɪdɪtɪ] *n* cupidité *f*.

cupola ['kjuːpələ] *n* coupole *f*.

cuppa ['kʌpə] n (BRIT col) tasse f de thé.
cup-tie ['kʌptaɪ] n (BRIT FOOTBALL) match m de coupe.
curable ['kjuərəbl] adj guérissable, curable.
curate ['kjuərɪt] n vicaire m.
curator [kjuə'reɪtə*] n conservateur m (d'un musée etc).
curb [kə:b] vt refréner, mettre un frein à; (expenditure) limiter, juguler ♦ n frein m (fig); (US) = **kerb**.
curd cheese n ≈ fromage blanc.
curdle ['kə:dl] vi (se) cailler.
curds [kə:dz] npl lait caillé.
cure [kjuə*] vt guérir; (CULIN) saler; fumer; sécher ♦ n remède m; **to be ~d of sth** être guéri de qch.
cure-all ['kjuərɔ:l] n (also fig) panacée f.
curfew ['kə:fju:] n couvre-feu m.
curio ['kjuərɪəu] n bibelot m, curiosité f.
curiosity [kjuərɪ'ɔsɪtɪ] n curiosité f.
curious ['kjuərɪəs] adj curieux(euse); **I'm ~ about him** il m'intrigue.
curiously ['kjuərɪəslɪ] adv curieusement; (inquisitively) avec curiosité; **~ enough, ...** bizarrement ....
curl [kə:l] n boucle f (de cheveux); (of smoke etc) volute f ♦ vt, vi boucler; (tightly) friser.
▶**curl up** vi s'enrouler; se pelotonner.
curler ['kə:lə*] n bigoudi m, rouleau m; (SPORT) joueur/euse de curling.
curlew ['kə:lu:] n courlis m.
curling ['kə:lɪŋ] n (sport) curling m.
curling tongs, (US) **curling irons** npl fer m à friser.
curly ['kə:lɪ] adj bouclé(e); (tightly curled) frisé(e).
currant ['kʌrnt] n raisin m de Corinthe, raisin sec.
currency ['kʌrnsɪ] n monnaie f; **foreign ~** devises étrangères, monnaie étrangère; **to gain ~** (fig) s'accréditer.
current ['kʌrnt] n courant m ♦ adj courant(e); (tendency, price, event) actuel(le); **direct/alternating ~** (ELEC) courant continu/alternatif; **the ~ issue of a magazine** le dernier numéro d'un magazine; **in ~ use** d'usage courant.
current account n (BRIT) compte courant.
current affairs npl (questions fpl d')actualité f.
current assets npl (COMM) actif m disponible.
current liabilities npl (COMM) passif m exigible.
currently ['kʌrntlɪ] adv actuellement.
curriculum, pl **~s** or **curricula** [kə'rɪkjuləm, -lə] n programme m d'études.
curriculum vitae (CV) [-'vi:taɪ] n curriculum vitae (CV) m.
curry ['kʌrɪ] n curry m ♦ vt: **to ~ favour with** chercher à gagner la faveur or à s'attirer les bonnes grâces de; **chicken ~** curry de poulet, poulet m au curry.

curry powder n poudre f de curry.
curse [kə:s] vi jurer, blasphémer ♦ vt maudire ♦ n malédiction f; fléau m; (swearword) juron m.
cursor ['kə:sə*] n (COMPUT) curseur m.
cursory ['kə:sərɪ] adj superficiel(le), hâtif(ive).
curt [kə:t] adj brusque, sec(sèche).
curtail [kə:'teɪl] vt (visit etc) écourter; (expenses etc) réduire.
curtain ['kə:tn] n rideau m; **to draw the ~s** (together) fermer or tirer les rideaux; (apart) ouvrir les rideaux.
curtain call n (THEAT) rappel m.
curts(e)y ['kə:tsɪ] n révérence f ♦ vi faire une révérence.
curvature ['kə:vətʃə*] n courbure f.
curve [kə:v] n courbe f; (in the road) tournant m, virage m ♦ vt courber ♦ vi se courber; (road) faire une courbe.
curved [kə:vd] adj courbe.
cushion ['kuʃn] n coussin m ♦ vt (seat) rembourrer; (shock) amortir.
cushy ['kuʃɪ] adj (col): **a ~ job** un boulot de tout repos; **to have a ~ time** se la couler douce.
custard ['kʌstəd] n (for pouring) crème anglaise.
custard powder n (BRIT) ≈ crème pâtissière instantanée.
custodial sentence [kʌs'təudɪəl-] n peine f de prison.
custodian [kʌs'təudɪən] n gardien/ne; (of collection etc) conservateur/trice.
custody ['kʌstədɪ] n (of child) garde f; (for offenders) détention préventive; **to take sb into ~** placer qn en détention préventive; **in the ~ of** sous la garde de.
custom ['kʌstəm] n coutume f, usage m; (LAW) droit coutumier, coutume; (COMM) clientèle f.
customary ['kʌstəmərɪ] adj habituel(le); **it is ~ to do it** l'usage veut qu'on le fasse.
custom-built ['kʌstəm'bɪlt] adj see **custom-made**.
customer ['kʌstəmə*] n client/e; **he's an awkward ~** (col) ce n'est pas quelqu'un de facile.
customer profile n profil m du client.
customized ['kʌstəmaɪzd] adj personnalisé(e).
custom-made ['kʌstəm'meɪd] adj (clothes) fait(e) sur mesure; (other goods: also: **custom-built**) hors série, fait(e) sur commande.
customs ['kʌstəmz] npl douane f; **to go through (the) ~** passer la douane.
Customs and Excise n (BRIT) administration f des douanes.
customs officer n douanier m.
cut [kʌt] vb (pt, pp **cut**) vt couper; (meat) découper; (shape, make) tailler; couper; creuser; graver; (reduce) réduire; (col: lecture, ap-

pointment) manquer ♦ vi couper; (intersect) se couper ♦ n (gen) coupure f; (of clothes) coupe f; (of jewel) taille f; (in salary etc) réduction f; (of meat) morceau m; **cold ~s** npl (US) viandes froides; **to ~ teeth** (baby) faire ses dents; **to ~ a tooth** percer une dent; **to ~ one's finger** se couper le doigt; **to get one's hair ~** se faire couper les cheveux; **to ~ sth short** couper court à qch; **to ~ sb dead** ignorer (complètement) qn.

►**cut back** vt (plants) tailler; (production, expenditure) réduire.

►**cut down** vt (tree) abattre; (reduce) réduire; **to ~ sb down to size** (fig) remettre qn à sa place.

►**cut down on** vt fus réduire.

►**cut in** vi (interrupt: conversation): **to ~ in (on)** couper la parole (à); (AUT) faire une queue de poisson.

►**cut off** vt couper; (fig) isoler; **we've been ~ off** (TEL) nous avons été coupés.

►**cut out** vt (picture etc) découper; (remove) ôter; supprimer.

►**cut up** vt découper.

cut-and-dried ['kʌtən'draɪd] adj (also: **cut-and-dry**) tout(e) fait(e), tout(e) décidé(e).

cutaway ['kʌtəweɪ] adj, n: **~ (drawing)** écorché m.

cutback ['kʌtbæk] n réduction f.

cute [kjuːt] adj mignon(ne), adorable; (clever) rusé(e), astucieux(euse).

cut glass n cristal taillé.

cuticle ['kjuːtɪkl] n (on nail): **~ remover** repousse-peaux m inv.

cutlery ['kʌtlərɪ] n couverts mpl; (trade) coutellerie f.

cutlet ['kʌtlɪt] n côtelette f.

cutoff ['kʌtɔf] n (also: **~ point**) seuil-limite m.

cutoff switch n interrupteur m.

cutout ['kʌtaut] n coupe-circuit m inv; (paper figure) découpage m.

cut-price ['kʌt'praɪs], (US) **cut-rate** ['kʌt'reɪt] adj au rabais, à prix réduit.

cutthroat ['kʌtθrəut] n assassin m ♦ adj: **~ competition** concurrence f sauvage.

cutting ['kʌtɪŋ] adj tranchant(e), coupant(e); (fig) cinglant(e), mordant(e) ♦ n (BRIT: from newspaper) coupure f (de journal); (: RAIL) tranchée f; (CINE) montage m.

cutting edge n (of knife) tranchant m; **on** or **at the ~ of** à la pointe de.

cuttlefish ['kʌtlfɪʃ] n seiche f.

cut-up ['kʌtʌp] adj affecté(e), démoralisé(e).

CV n abbr = **curriculum vitae**.

cwt. abbr = **hundredweight**.

cyanide ['saɪənaɪd] n cyanure m.

cybercafé ['saɪbə,kæfeɪ] n cybercafé m.

cybernetics [saɪbə'nɛtɪks] n cybernétique f.

cyclamen ['sɪkləmən] n cyclamen m.

cycle ['saɪkl] n cycle m ♦ vi faire de la bicyclette.

cycle race n course f cycliste.

cycle rack n râtelier m à bicyclette.

cycling ['saɪklɪŋ] n cyclisme m; **to go on a ~ holiday** (BRIT) faire du cyclotourisme.

cyclist ['saɪklɪst] n cycliste m/f.

cyclone ['saɪkləun] n cyclone m.

cygnet ['sɪgnɪt] n jeune cygne m.

cylinder ['sɪlɪndə*] n cylindre m.

cylinder block n bloc-cylindres m.

cylinder capacity n cylindrée f.

cylinder head n culasse f.

cylinder-head gasket ['sɪlɪndəhɛd-] n joint m de culasse.

cymbals ['sɪmblz] npl cymbales fpl.

cynic ['sɪnɪk] n cynique m/f.

cynical ['sɪnɪkl] adj cynique.

cynicism ['sɪnɪsɪzəm] n cynisme m.

CYO n abbr (US: = Catholic Youth Organization) ≈ JC f.

cypress ['saɪprɪs] n cyprès m.

Cypriot ['sɪprɪət] adj cypriote, chypriote ♦ n Cypriote m/f, Chypriote m/f.

Cyprus ['saɪprəs] n Chypre f.

cyst [sɪst] n kyste m.

cystitis [sɪs'taɪtɪs] n cystite f.

CZ n abbr (US: = Central Zone) zone f du canal de Panama.

czar [zɑː*] n tsar m.

Czech [tʃɛk] adj tchèque ♦ n Tchèque m/f; (LING) tchèque m; **the ~ Republic** la République tchèque.

Czechoslovak [tʃɛkə'sləuvæk] adj, n = **Czechoslovakian**.

Czechoslovakia [tʃɛkəslə'vækɪə] n Tchécoslovaquie f.

Czechoslovakian [tʃɛkəslə'vækɪən] adj tchécoslovaque ♦ n Tchécoslovaque m/f.

D d

D, d [diː] n (letter) D, d m; (MUS): **D** ré m; **D for David**, (US) **D for Dog** D comme Désirée.

D abbr (US POL) = **democrat(ic)**.

d abbr (BRIT: old) = **penny**.

d. abbr = **died**.

DA n abbr (US) = **district attorney**.

dab [dæb] vt (eyes, wound) tamponner; (paint, cream) appliquer (par petites touches or rapidement); **a ~ of paint** un petit coup de peinture.

dabble ['dæbl] vi: **to ~ in** faire or se mêler or s'occuper un peu de.

Dacca ['dækə] n Dacca.

dachshund ['dækshund] n teckel m.

dad, daddy [dæd, 'dædɪ] n papa m.

daddy-long-legs [dædɪ'lɔŋlɛgz] n tipule f;

daffodil – darkly

faucheux *m*.
daffodil ['dæfədıl] *n* jonquille *f*.
daft [dɑːft] *adj* (*col*) idiot(e), stupide; **to be ~ about** être toqué(e) *or* mordu(e) de.
dagger ['dægə*] *n* poignard *m*; **to be at ~s drawn with sb** être à couteaux tirés avec qn; **to look ~s at sb** foudroyer qn du regard.
dahlia ['deıljə] *n* dahlia *m*.
daily ['deılı] *adj* quotidien(ne), journalier(ière) ♦ *n* quotidien *m*; (*BRIT: servant*) femme *f* de ménage (*à la journée*) ♦ *adv* tous les jours; **twice ~** deux fois par jour.
dainty ['deıntı] *adj* délicat(e), mignon(ne).
dairy ['dɛərı] *n* (*shop*) crémerie *f*, laiterie *f*; (*on farm*) laiterie ♦ *adj* laitier(ière).
dairy cow *n* vache laitière.
dairy farm *n* exploitation *f* pratiquant l'élevage laitier.
dairy produce *n* produits laitiers.
dais ['deıs] *n* estrade *f*.
daisy ['deızı] *n* pâquerette *f*.
daisy wheel *n* (*on printer*) marguerite *f*.
daisy-wheel printer ['deızıwiːl-] *n* imprimante *f* à marguerite.
Dakar ['dækə] *n* Dakar.
dale [deıl] *n* vallon *m*.
dally ['dælı] *vi* musarder, flâner.
dalmatian [dæl'meıʃən] *n* (*dog*) dalmatien/ne.
dam [dæm] *n* barrage *m*; (*reservoir*) réservoir *m*, lac *m* de retenue ♦ *vt* endiguer.
damage ['dæmıdʒ] *n* dégâts *mpl*, dommages *mpl*; (*fig*) tort *m* ♦ *vt* endommager, abîmer; (*fig*) faire du tort à; **~ to property** dégâts matériels.
damages ['dæmıdʒız] *npl* (*LAW*) dommages-intérêts *mpl*; **to pay £5000 in ~** payer 5000 livres de dommages-intérêts.
damaging ['dæmıdʒıŋ] *adj*: **~ (to)** préjudiciable (à), nuisible (à).
Damascus [də'mɑːskəs] *n* Damas.
dame [deım] *n* (*title*) titre porté par une femme décorée de l'ordre de l'Empire Britannique ou d'un ordre de chevalerie; titre porté par la femme ou la veuve d'un chevalier ou baronnet; (*US col*) nana *f*; (*THEAT*) vieille dame (*rôle comique joué par un homme*).
damn [dæm] *vt* condamner; (*curse*) maudire ♦ *n* (*col*): **I don't give a ~** je m'en fous ♦ *adj* (*col*): **this ~ ...** ce sacré *or* foutu ...; **~ (it)!** zut!
damnable ['dæmnəbl] *adj* (*col: behaviour*) odieux(euse), détestable; (*: weather*) épouvantable, abominable.
damnation [dæm'neıʃən] *n* (*REL*) damnation *f* ♦ *excl* (*col*) malédiction!, merde!
damning ['dæmıŋ] *adj* (*evidence*) accablant(e).
damp [dæmp] *adj* humide ♦ *n* humidité *f* ♦ *vt* (*also*: **~en**: *cloth, rag*) humecter; (*: enthusiasm etc*) refroidir.
dampcourse ['dæmpkɔːs] *n* couche isolante

(contre l'humidité).
damper ['dæmpə*] *n* (*MUS*) étouffoir *m*; (*of fire*) registre *m*; **to put a ~ on** (*fig: atmosphere, enthusiasm*) refroidir.
dampness ['dæmpnıs] *n* humidité *f*.
damson ['dæmzən] *n* prune *f* de Damas.
dance [dɑːns] *n* danse *f*; (*ball*) bal *m* ♦ *vi* danser; **to ~ about** sautiller, gambader.
dance hall *n* salle *f* de bal, dancing *m*.
dancer ['dɑːnsə*] *n* danseur/euse.
dancing ['dɑːnsıŋ] *n* danse *f*.
D and C *n abbr* (*MED*: = *dilation and curettage*) curetage *m*.
dandelion ['dændılaıən] *n* pissenlit *m*.
dandruff ['dændrəf] *n* pellicules *fpl*.
dandy ['dændı] *n* dandy *m*, élégant *m* ♦ *adj* (*US col*) fantastique, super.
Dane [deın] *n* Danois/e.
danger ['deındʒə*] *n* danger *m*; **there is a ~ of fire** il y a (un) risque d'incendie; **in ~** en danger; **he was in ~ of falling** il risquait de tomber; **out of ~** hors de danger.
danger list *n* (*MED*): **on the ~** dans un état critique.
danger money *n* (*BRIT*) prime *f* de risque.
dangerous ['deındʒrəs] *adj* dangereux(euse).
dangerously ['deındʒrəslı] *adv* dangereusement; **~ ill** très gravement malade, en danger de mort.
danger zone *n* zone dangereuse.
dangle ['dæŋgl] *vt* balancer; (*fig*) faire miroiter ♦ *vi* pendre, se balancer.
Danish ['deınıʃ] *adj* danois(e) ♦ *n* (*LING*) danois *m*.
Danish pastry *n* feuilleté *m* (*recouvert d'un glaçage et fourré aux fruits etc*).
dank [dæŋk] *adj* froid(e) et humide.
Danube ['dænjuːb] *n*: **the ~** le Danube.
dapper ['dæpə*] *adj* pimpant(e).
Dardanelles [dɑːdə'nɛlz] *npl* Dardanelles *fpl*.
dare [dɛə*] *vt*: **to ~ sb to do** défier qn *or* mettre qn au défi de faire ♦ *vi*: **to ~ (to) do sth** oser faire qch; **I ~n't tell him** (*BRIT*) je n'ose pas le lui dire; **I ~ say he'll turn up** il est probable qu'il viendra.
daredevil ['dɛədɛvl] *n* casse-cou *m inv*.
Dar-es-Salaam ['dɑːrɛssə'lɑːm] *n* Dar-es-Salaam, Dar-es-Salaam.
daring ['dɛərıŋ] *adj* hardi(e), audacieux(euse) ♦ *n* audace *f*, hardiesse *f*.
dark [dɑːk] *adj* (*night, room*) obscur(e), sombre; (*colour, complexion*) foncé(e), sombre; (*fig*) sombre ♦ *n*: **in the ~** dans le noir; **in the ~ about** (*fig*) ignorant tout de; **after ~** après la tombée de la nuit; **it is/is getting ~** il fait nuit/commence à faire nuit.
darken ['dɑːkn] *vt* obscurcir, assombrir ♦ *vi* s'obscurcir, s'assombrir.
dark glasses *npl* lunettes noires.
dark horse *n* (*fig*): **he's a ~** on ne sait pas grand-chose de lui.
darkly ['dɑːklı] *adv* (*gloomily*) mélancolique-

ment; (*in a sinister way*) lugubrement.
darkness ['dɑːknɪs] *n* obscurité *f*.
darkroom ['dɑːkrum] *n* chambre noire.
darling ['dɑːlɪŋ] *adj, n* chéri(e).
darn [dɑːn] *vt* repriser.
dart [dɑːt] *n* fléchette *f* ♦ *vi:* **to ~ towards** (*also:* **make a ~ towards**) se précipiter *or* s'élancer vers; **to ~ away/along** partir/ passer comme une flèche.
dartboard ['dɑːtbɔːd] *n* cible *f* (de jeu de fléchettes).
darts [dɑːts] *n* jeu *m* de fléchettes.
dash [dæʃ] *n* (*sign*) tiret *m*; (*small quantity*) goutte *f*, larme *f* ♦ *vt* (*missile*) jeter *or* lancer violemment; (*hopes*) anéantir ♦ *vi:* **to ~ towards** (*also:* **make a ~ towards**) se précipiter *or* se ruer vers; **a ~ of soda** un peu d'eau gazeuse.
▶**dash away** *vi* partir à toute allure.
dashboard ['dæʃbɔːd] *n* (*AUT*) tableau *m* de bord.
dashing ['dæʃɪŋ] *adj* fringant(e).
dastardly ['dæstədlɪ] *adj* lâche.
DAT *n abbr* (= *digital audio tape*) cassette *f* audio digitale.
data ['deɪtə] *npl* données *fpl*.
database ['deɪtəbeɪs] *n* base *f* de données.
data capture *n* saisie *f* de données.
data processing *n* traitement *m* (électronique) de l'information.
data transmission *n* transmission *f* de données.
date [deɪt] *n* date *f*; (*appointment*) rendez-vous *m*; (*fruit*) datte *f* ♦ *vt* dater; (*col: girl etc*) sortir avec; **what's the ~ today?** quelle date sommes-nous aujourd'hui?; **~ of birth** date de naissance; **closing ~** date de clôture; **to ~** *adv* à ce jour; **out of ~** périmé(e); **up to ~** à la page; mis(e) à jour; moderne; **to bring up to ~** (*correspondence, information*) mettre à jour; (*method*) moderniser; (*person*) mettre au courant; **letter ~d 5th July** *or* (*US*) **July 5th** lettre (datée) du 5 juillet.
dated ['deɪtɪd] *adj* démodé(e).
dateline ['deɪtlaɪn] *n* ligne *f* de changement de date.
date rape *n* viol *m* (*à l'issue d'un rendez-vous galant*).
date stamp *n* timbre-dateur *m*.
daub [dɔːb] *vt* barbouiller.
daughter ['dɔːtə*] *n* fille *f*.
daughter-in-law ['dɔːtərɪnlɔː] *n* belle-fille *f*, bru *f*.
daunt [dɔːnt] *vt* intimider, décourager.
daunting ['dɔːntɪŋ] *adj* décourageant(e), intimidant(e).
dauntless ['dɔːntlɪs] *adj* intrépide.
dawdle ['dɔːdl] *vi* traîner, lambiner; **to ~ over one's work** traînasser *or* lambiner sur son travail.
dawn [dɔːn] *n* aube *f*, aurore *f* ♦ *vi* (*day*) se lever, poindre; (*fig*) naître, se faire jour; **at ~**

à l'aube; **from ~ to dusk** du matin au soir; **it ~ed on him that ...** il lui vint à l'esprit que ....
dawn chorus *n* (*BRIT*) chant *m* des oiseaux à l'aube.
day [deɪ] *n* jour *m*; (*as duration*) journée *f*, (*period of time, age*) époque *f*, temps *m*; **the ~ before** la veille, le jour précédent; **the ~ after, the following ~** le lendemain, le jour suivant; **the ~ before yesterday** avant-hier; **the ~ after tomorrow** après-demain; **(on) the ~ that ...** le jour où ...; **~ by ~** jour après jour; **by ~** de jour; **paid by the ~** payé(e) à la journée; **these ~s, in the present ~** de nos jours, à l'heure actuelle.
daybook ['deɪbuk] *n* (*BRIT*) main courante, brouillard *m*, journal *m*.
day boy *n* (*SCOL*) externe *m*.
daybreak ['deɪbreɪk] *n* point *m* du jour.
daycare centre ['deɪkɛə-] *n* garderie *f*.
daydream ['deɪdriːm] *n* rêverie *f* ♦ *vi* rêver (tout éveillé).
day girl *n* (*SCOL*) externe *f*.
daylight ['deɪlaɪt] *n* (lumière *f* du) jour *m*.
daylight robbery *n:* **it's ~** (*fig, col*) c'est du vol caractérisé *or* manifeste.
daylight saving time *n* (*US*) heure *f* d'été.
day release *n:* **to be on ~** avoir une journée de congé pour formation professionnelle.
day return (ticket) *n* (*BRIT*) billet *m* d'aller-retour (valable pour la journée).
day shift *n* équipe *f* de jour.
daytime ['deɪtaɪm] *n* jour *m*, journée *f*.
day-to-day ['deɪtə'deɪ] *adj* (*routine, expenses*) journalier(ière); **on a ~ basis** au jour le jour.
day trip *n* excursion *f* (d'une journée).
day tripper *n* excursionniste *m/f*.
daze [deɪz] *vt* (*subj: drug*) hébéter; (*: blow*) étourdir ♦ *n:* **in a ~** hébété(e); étourdi(e).
dazzle ['dæzl] *vt* éblouir, aveugler.
dazzling ['dæzlɪŋ] *adj* (*light*) aveuglant(e), éblouissant(e); (*fig*) éblouissant(e).
DC *abbr* (*ELEC*) = *direct current*; (*US*) = *District of Columbia*.
DCC *n abbr* ® (= *digital compact cassette*) DCC ®.
DD *n abbr* (= *Doctor of Divinity*) titre universitaire.
dd. *abbr* (*COMM*) = *delivered*.
D/D *abbr* = *direct debit*.
D-day ['diːdeɪ] *n* le jour J.
DDS *n abbr* (*US:* = *Doctor of Dental Science, Doctor of Dental Surgery*) titres universitaires.
DDT *n abbr* (= *dichlorodiphenyl trichloroethane*) DDT *m*.
DE *abbr* (*US*) = *Delaware*.
DEA *n abbr* (*US:* = *Drug Enforcement Administration*) ≈ brigade *f* des stupéfiants.
deacon ['diːkən] *n* diacre *m*.
dead [dɛd] *adj* mort(e); (*numb*) engourdi(e), insensible ♦ *adv* absolument, complètement;

the ~ *npl* les morts; **he was shot** ~ il a été tué d'un coup de revolver; ~ **on time** à l'heure pile; ~ **tired** éreinté(e), complètement fourbu(e); **to stop** ~ s'arrêter pile *or* net; **the line has gone** ~ (*TEL*) on n'entend plus rien.

dead beat *adj* (*col*) claqué(e), crevé(e).

deaden [dɛdn] *vt* (*blow, sound*) amortir; (*make numb*) endormir, rendre insensible.

dead end *n* impasse *f*.

dead-end ['dɛdɛnd] *adj*: **a** ~ **job** un emploi *or* poste sans avenir.

dead heat *n* (*SPORT*): **to finish in a** ~ terminer ex aequo.

dead-letter office [dɛd'lɛtər-] *n* ≈ centre *m* de recherche du courrier.

deadline ['dɛdlaɪn] *n* date *f or* heure *f* limite; **to work to a** ~ avoir des délais stricts à respecter.

deadlock ['dɛdlɔk] *n* impasse *f* (*fig*).

dead loss *n* (*col*): **to be a** ~ (*person*) n'être bon(bonne) à rien; (*thing*) ne rien valoir.

deadly ['dɛdlɪ] *adj* mortel(le); (*weapon*) meurtrier(ière); ~ **dull** ennuyeux(euse) à mourir, mortellement ennuyeux.

deadpan ['dɛdpæn] *adj* impassible; (*humour*) pince-sans-rire *inv*.

Dead Sea *n*: **the** ~ la mer Morte.

dead season *n* (*TOURISM*) morte saison.

deaf [dɛf] *adj* sourd(e); **to turn a** ~ **ear to sth** faire la sourde oreille à qch.

deaf-aid ['dɛfeɪd] *n* (*BRIT*) appareil auditif.

deaf-and-dumb ['dɛfən'dʌm] *adj* sourd(e)-muet(te); ~ **alphabet** alphabet *m* des sourds-muets.

deafen ['dɛfn] *vt* rendre sourd(e); (*fig*) assourdir.

deafening ['dɛfnɪŋ] *adj* assourdissant(e).

deaf-mute ['dɛfmjuːt] *n* sourd/e-muet/te.

deafness ['dɛfnɪs] *n* surdité *f*.

deal [diːl] *n* affaire *f*, marché *m* ♦ *vt* (*pt, pp* **dealt** [dɛlt]) (*blow*) porter; (*cards*) donner, distribuer; **to strike a** ~ **with sb** faire *or* conclure un marché avec qn; **it's a** ~! (*col*) marché conclu!, tope-là!, topez-là!; **he got a bad** ~ **from them** ils ont mal agi envers lui; **he got a fair** ~ **from them** ils ont agi loyalement envers lui; **a good** ~ (*a lot*) beaucoup; **a good** ~ **of, a great** ~ **of** beaucoup de, énormément de.

►**deal in** *vt fus* (*COMM*) faire le commerce de, être dans le commerce de.

►**deal with** *vt fus* (*COMM*) traiter avec; (*handle*) s'occuper *or* se charger de; (*be about: book etc*) traiter de.

dealer ['diːlə*] *n* marchand *m*.

dealership ['diːləʃɪp] *n* concession *f*.

dealings ['diːlɪŋz] *npl* (*in goods, shares*) opérations *fpl*, transactions *fpl*; (*relations*) relations *fpl*, rapports *mpl*.

dealt [dɛlt] *pt, pp of* **deal**.

dean [diːn] *n* (*REL, BRIT SCOL*) doyen *m*; (*US SCOL*) conseiller/ère (principal(e)) d'éducation.

dear [dɪə*] *adj* cher(chère); (*expensive*) cher, coûteux(euse) ♦ *n*: **my** ~ mon cher/ma chère; ~ **me!** mon Dieu!; **D~ Sir/Madam** (*in letter*) Monsieur/Madame; **D~ Mr/Mrs X** Cher Monsieur/Chère Madame X.

dearly ['dɪəlɪ] *adv* (*love*) tendrement; (*pay*) cher.

dearth [dɔːθ] *n* disette *f*, pénurie *f*.

death [dɛθ] *n* mort *f*; (*ADMIN*) décès *m*.

deathbed ['dɛθbɛd] *n* lit *m* de mort.

death certificate *n* acte *m* de décès.

death duties *npl* (*BRIT*) droits *mpl* de succession.

deathly ['dɛθlɪ] *adj* de mort ♦ *adv* comme la mort.

death penalty *n* peine *f* de mort.

death rate *n* taux *m* de mortalité.

death row [-'rəu] *n* (*US*) quartier *m* des condamnés à mort; **to be on** ~ être condamné à la peine de mort.

death sentence *n* condamnation *f* à mort.

death squad *n* escadron *m* de la mort.

deathtrap ['dɛθtræp] *n* endroit (*or* véhicule *etc*) dangereux.

deb [dɛb] *n abbr* (*col*) = **debutante**.

debar [dɪ'bɑː*] *vt*: **to** ~ **sb from a club** *etc* exclure qn d'un club *etc*; **to** ~ **sb from doing** interdire à qn de faire.

debase [dɪ'beɪs] *vt* (*currency*) déprécier, dévaloriser; (*person*) abaisser, avilir.

debatable [dɪ'beɪtəbl] *adj* discutable, contestable; **it is** ~ **whether** ... il est douteux que ....

debate [dɪ'beɪt] *n* discussion *f*, débat *m* ♦ *vt* discuter, débattre ♦ *vi* (*consider*): **to** ~ **whether** se demander si.

debauchery [dɪ'bɔːtʃərɪ] *n* débauche *f*.

debenture [dɪ'bɛntʃə*] *n* (*COMM*) obligation *f*.

debilitate [dɪ'bɪlɪteɪt] *vt* débiliter.

debit ['dɛbɪt] *n* débit *m* ♦ *vt*: **to** ~ **a sum to sb** *or* **to sb's account** porter une somme au débit de qn, débiter qn d'une somme.

debit balance *n* solde débiteur.

debit note *n* note *f* de débit.

debrief [diː'briːf] *vt* demander un compte rendu de fin de mission à.

debriefing [diː'briːfɪŋ] *n* compte rendu *m*.

debris ['dɛbriː] *n* débris *mpl*, décombres *mpl*.

debt [dɛt] *n* dette *f*; **to be in** ~ avoir des dettes, être endetté(e); **bad** ~ créance *f* irrécouvrable.

debt collector *n* agent *m* de recouvrements.

debtor ['dɛtə*] *n* débiteur/trice.

debug [diː'bʌg] *vt* (*COMPUT*) déverminer.

debunk [diː'bʌŋk] *vt* (*theory, claim*) montrer le ridicule de.

debut ['deɪbjuː] *n* début(s) *m(pl)*.

debutante ['dɛbjutænt] *n* débutante *f*.

Dec. *abbr* (= *December*) déc.

decade ['dɛkeɪd] *n* décennie *f*, décade *f*.

decadence ['dɛkədəns] *n* décadence *f*.

decadent ['dɛkədənt] adj décadent(e).

de-caff ['diːkæf] n (col) déca m.

decaffeinated [diːˈkæfɪneɪtɪd] adj décaféiné(e).

decamp [dɪˈkæmp] vi (col) décamper, filer.

decant [dɪˈkænt] vt (wine) décanter.

decanter [dɪˈkæntə*] n carafe f.

decarbonize [diːˈkɑːbənaɪz] vt (AUT) décalaminer.

decathlon [dɪˈkæθlən] n décathlon m.

decay [dɪˈkeɪ] n décomposition f, pourrissement m; (fig) déclin m, délabrement m; (also: **tooth** ~) carie f (dentaire) ♦ vi (rot) se décomposer, pourrir; (fig) se délabrer; décliner; se détériorer.

decease [dɪˈsiːs] n décès m.

deceased [dɪˈsiːst] n: **the** ~ le/la défunt/e.

deceit [dɪˈsiːt] n tromperie f, supercherie f.

deceitful [dɪˈsiːtful] adj trompeur(euse).

deceive [dɪˈsiːv] vt tromper; **to** ~ **o.s.** s'abuser.

decelerate [diːˈsɛləreɪt] vt, vi ralentir.

December [dɪˈsɛmbə*] n décembre m; for phrases see also **July**.

decency ['diːsənsɪ] n décence f.

decent ['diːsənt] adj décent(e), convenable; **they were very** ~ **about it** ils se sont montrés très chics.

decently ['diːsəntlɪ] adv (respectably) décemment, convenablement; (kindly) décemment.

decentralization [diːsɛntrəlaɪˈzeɪʃən] n décentralisation f.

decentralize [diːˈsɛntrəlaɪz] vt décentraliser.

deception [dɪˈsɛpʃən] n tromperie f.

deceptive [dɪˈsɛptɪv] adj trompeur(euse).

decibel ['dɛsɪbɛl] n décibel m.

decide [dɪˈsaɪd] vt (person) décider; (question, argument) trancher, régler ♦ vi se décider, décider; **to** ~ **to do/that** décider de faire/que; **to** ~ **on** décider, se décider pour; **to** ~ **on doing** décider de faire; **to** ~ **against doing** décider de ne pas faire.

decided [dɪˈsaɪdɪd] adj (resolute) résolu(e), décidé(e); (clear, definite) net(te), marqué(e).

decidedly [dɪˈsaɪdɪdlɪ] adv résolument; incontestablement, nettement.

deciding [dɪˈsaɪdɪŋ] adj décisif(ive).

deciduous [dɪˈsɪdjuəs] adj à feuilles caduques.

decimal ['dɛsɪməl] adj décimal(e) ♦ n décimale f; **to three** ~ **places** (jusqu')à la troisième décimale.

decimalize ['dɛsɪməlaɪz] vt (BRIT) décimaliser.

decimal point n ≈ virgule f.

decimate ['dɛsɪmeɪt] vt décimer.

decipher [dɪˈsaɪfə*] vt déchiffrer.

decision [dɪˈsɪʒən] n décision f; **to make a** ~ prendre une décision.

decisive [dɪˈsaɪsɪv] adj décisif(ive); (influence) décisif, déterminant(e); (manner, person) décidé(e), catégorique; (reply) ferme, catégorique.

deck [dɛk] n (NAUT) pont m; (of bus): **top** ~ impériale f; (of cards) jeu m; **to go up on** ~ monter sur le pont; **below** ~ dans l'entrepont; **record/cassette** ~ platine-disques/-cassettes f.

deckchair ['dɛktʃɛə*] n chaise longue.

deck hand n matelot m.

declaration [dɛkləˈreɪʃən] n déclaration f.

declare [dɪˈklɛə*] vt déclarer.

declassify [diːˈklæsɪfaɪ] vt rendre accessible au public or à tous.

decline [dɪˈklaɪn] n (decay) déclin m; (lessening) baisse f ♦ vt refuser, décliner ♦ vi décliner; être en baisse, baisser; ~ **in living standards** baisse du niveau de vie; **to** ~ **to do sth** refuser (poliment) de faire qch.

declutch ['diːˈklʌtʃ] vi (BRIT) débrayer.

decode ['diːˈkəud] vt décoder.

decoder [diːˈkəudə*] n (COMPUT, TV) décodeur m.

decompose [diːkəmˈpəuz] vi se décomposer.

decomposition [diːkɔmpəˈzɪʃən] n décomposition f.

decompression [diːkəmˈprɛʃən] n décompression f.

decompression chamber n caisson m de décompression.

decongestant [diːkənˈdʒɛstənt] n décongestif m.

decontaminate [diːkənˈtæmɪneɪt] vt décontaminer.

decontrol [diːkənˈtrəul] vt (prices etc) libérer.

décor ['deɪkɔː*] n décor m.

decorate ['dɛkəreɪt] vt (adorn, give a medal to) décorer; (paint and paper) peindre et tapisser.

decoration [dɛkəˈreɪʃən] n (medal etc, adornment) décoration f.

decorative ['dɛkərətɪv] adj décoratif(ive).

decorator ['dɛkəreɪtə*] n peintre m en bâtiment.

decorum [dɪˈkɔːrəm] n décorum m, bienséance f.

decoy ['diːkɔɪ] n piège m; **they used him as a** ~ **for the enemy** ils se sont servis de lui pour attirer l'ennemi.

decrease n ['diːkriːs] diminution f ♦ vt, vi [diːˈkriːs] diminuer; **to be on the** ~ diminuer, être en diminution.

decreasing [diːˈkriːsɪŋ] adj en voie de diminution.

decree [dɪˈkriː] n (POL, REL) décret m; (LAW) arrêt m, jugement m ♦ vt: **to** ~ **(that)** décréter (que), ordonner (que); ~ **absolute** jugement définitif (de divorce); ~ **nisi** jugement provisoire de divorce.

decrepit [dɪˈkrɛpɪt] adj (person) décrépit(e); (building) délabré(e).

decry [dɪˈkraɪ] vt condamner ouvertement, déplorer; (disparage) dénigrer, décrier.

dedicate ['dɛdɪkeɪt] vt consacrer; (book etc) dédier.

dedicated ['dɛdɪkeɪtɪd] adj (person) dévoué(e);

(*COMPUT*) spécialisé(e), dédié(e); ~ **word processor** station *f* de traitement de texte.

dedication [dɛdɪ'keɪʃən] *n* (*devotion*) dévouement *m*; (*in book*) dédicace *f*.

deduce [dɪ'djuːs] *vt* déduire, conclure.

deduct [dɪ'dʌkt] *vt*: **to ~ sth (from)** déduire qch (de), retrancher qch (de); (*from wage etc*) prélever qch (sur), retenir qch (sur).

deduction [dɪ'dʌkʃən] *n* (*deducting*) déduction *f*; (*from wage etc*) prélèvement *m*, retenue *f*; (*deducing*) déduction, conclusion, déduction *f*.

deed [diːd] *n* action *f*, acte *m*; (*LAW*) acte notarié, contrat *m*; ~ **of covenant** (acte *m* de) donation *f*.

deem [diːm] *vt* (*formal*) juger, estimer; **to ~ it wise to do** juger bon de faire.

deep [diːp] *adj* (*water, sigh, sorrow, thoughts*) profond(e); (*voice*) grave ♦ *adv*: ~ **in snow** recouvert(e) d'une épaisse couche de neige; **spectators stood 20 ~** il y avait 20 rangs de spectateurs; **knee-~ in water** dans l'eau jusqu'aux genoux; **4 metres ~** de 4 mètres de profondeur; **he took a ~ breath** il inspira profondément, il prit son souffle.

deepen [diːpn] *vt* (*hole*) approfondir ♦ *vi* s'approfondir; (*darkness*) s'épaissir.

deep-freeze ['diːp'friːz] *n* congélateur *m* ♦ *vt* surgeler.

deep-fry ['diːp'fraɪ] *vt* faire frire (dans une friteuse).

deeply ['diːplɪ] *adv* profondément; (*dig*) en profondeur; (*regret, interest*) vivement.

deep-rooted ['diːp'ruːtɪd] *adj* (*prejudice*) profondément enraciné(e); (*affection*) profond(e); (*habit*) invétéré(e).

deep-sea ['diːp'siː] *adj*: ~ **diver** plongeur sous-marin; ~ **diving** plongée sous-marine; ~ **fishing** pêche hauturière.

deep-seated ['diːp'siːtɪd] *adj* (*beliefs*) profondément enraciné(e).

deep-set ['diːpsɛt] *adj* (*eyes*) enfoncé(e).

deer [dɪə*] *n* (*pl inv*): **the** ~ les cervidés *mpl* (*ZOOL*); (**red**) ~ cerf *m*; (**fallow**) ~ daim *m*; (**roe**) ~ chevreuil *m*.

deerskin ['dɪəskɪn] *n* peau *f* de daim.

deerstalker ['dɪəstɔːkə*] *n* (*person*) chasseur *m* de cerf; (*hat*) casquette *f* à la Sherlock Holmes.

deface [dɪ'feɪs] *vt* dégrader; barbouiller; rendre illisible.

defamation [dɛfə'meɪʃən] *n* diffamation *f*.

defamatory [dɪ'fæmətrɪ] *adj* diffamatoire, diffamant(e).

default [dɪ'fɔːlt] *vi* (*LAW*) faire défaut; (*gen*) manquer à ses engagements ♦ *n* (*COMPUT*: *also*: ~ **value**) valeur *f* par défaut; **by** ~ (*LAW*) par défaut, par contumace; (*SPORT*) par forfait; **to ~ on a debt** ne pas s'acquitter d'une dette.

defaulter [dɪ'fɔːltə*] *n* (*on debt*) débiteur défaillant.

default option *n* (*COMPUT*) option *f* par défaut.

faut.

defeat [dɪ'fiːt] *n* défaite *f* ♦ *vt* (*team, opponents*) battre; (*fig: plans, efforts*) faire échouer.

defeatism [dɪ'fiːtɪzəm] *n* défaitisme *m*.

defeatist [dɪ'fiːtɪst] *adj, n* défaitiste (*m/f*).

defecate ['dɛfəkeɪt] *vi* déféquer.

defect *n* ['diːfɛkt] défaut *m* ♦ *vi* [dɪ'fɛkt]: **to ~ to the enemy/the West** passer à l'ennemi/ l'Ouest; **physical ~** malformation *f*, vice *m* de conformation; **mental ~** anomalie *or* déficience mentale.

defective [dɪ'fɛktɪv] *adj* défectueux(euse).

defector [dɪ'fɛktə*] *n* transfuge *m/f*.

defence, (*US*) **defense** [dɪ'fɛns] *n* défense *f*; **in ~ of** défendre; **witness for the ~** témoin *m* à décharge; **the Ministry of D~**, (*US*) **the Department of Defense** le ministère de la Défense nationale.

defenceless [dɪ'fɛnslɪs] *adj* sans défense.

defend [dɪ'fɛnd] *vt* défendre; (*decision, action, opinion*) justifier, défendre.

defendant [dɪ'fɛndənt] *n* défendeur/deresse; (*in criminal case*) accusé/e, prévenu/e.

defender [dɪ'fɛndə*] *n* défenseur *m*.

defending champion [dɪ'fɛndɪŋ-] *n* (*SPORT*) champion/ne en titre.

defending counsel [dɪ'fɛndɪŋ-] *n* (*LAW*) avocat *m* de la défense.

defense [dɪ'fɛns] *n* (*US*) = **defence**.

defensive [dɪ'fɛnsɪv] *adj* défensif(ive) ♦ *n* défensive *f*; **on the ~** sur la défensive.

defer [dɪ'fɜː*] *vt* (*postpone*) différer, ajourner ♦ *vi* (*submit*): **to ~ to sb/sth** déférer à qn/ qch, s'en remettre à qn/qch.

deference ['dɛfərəns] *n* déférence *f*, égards *mpl*; **out of** *or* **in ~ to** par déférence *or* égards pour.

defiance [dɪ'faɪəns] *n* défi *m*; **in ~ of** au mépris de.

defiant [dɪ'faɪənt] *adj* provocant(e), de défi.

defiantly [dɪ'faɪəntlɪ] *adv* d'un air (*or* d'un ton) de défi.

deficiency [dɪ'fɪʃənsɪ] *n* insuffisance *f*, déficience *f*; carence *f*; (*COMM*) déficit *m*, découvert *m*.

deficiency disease *n* maladie *f* de carence.

deficient [dɪ'fɪʃənt] *adj* insuffisant(e); défectueux(euse); déficient(e); **to be ~ in** manquer de.

deficit ['dɛfɪsɪt] *n* déficit *m*.

defile [dɪ'faɪl] *vt* souiller ♦ *vi* défiler ♦ *n* ['diːfaɪl] défilé *m*.

define [dɪ'faɪn] *vt* définir.

definite ['dɛfɪnɪt] *adj* (*fixed*) défini(e), (bien) déterminé(e); (*clear, obvious*) net(te), manifeste; (*LING*) défini(e); **he was ~ about it** il a été catégorique; il était sûr de son fait.

definitely ['dɛfɪnɪtlɪ] *adv* sans aucun doute.

definition [dɛfɪ'nɪʃən] *n* définition *f*.

definitive [dɪ'fɪnɪtɪv] *adj* définitif(ive).

deflate [diː'fleɪt] *vt* dégonfler; (*pompous person*) rabattre le caquet à; (*ECON*) provoquer la déflation de; (: _prices_) faire tomber _or_ baisser.

deflation [di:'fleɪʃən] _n_ (_ECON_) déflation _f_.

deflationary [di:'fleɪʃənrɪ] _adj_ (_ECON_) déflationniste.

deflect [dɪ'flɛkt] _vt_ détourner, faire dévier.

defog ['di:'fɔg] _vt_ (_US AUT_) désembuer.

defogger ['di:'fɔgə*] _n_ (_US AUT_) dispositif _m_ anti-buée _inv_.

deform [dɪ'fɔ:m] _vt_ déformer.

deformed [dɪ'fɔ:md] _adj_ difforme.

deformity [dɪ'fɔ:mɪtɪ] _n_ difformité _f_.

defraud [dɪ'frɔ:d] _vt_ frauder; **to ~ sb of sth** soutirer qch malhonnêtement à qn; escroquer qch à qn; frustrer qn de qch.

defray [dɪ'freɪ] _vt_: **to ~ sb's expenses** défrayer qn (de ses frais), rembourser _or_ payer à qn ses frais.

defrost [di:'frɔst] _vt_ (_fridge_) dégivrer; (_frozen food_) décongeler.

deft [dɛft] _adj_ adroit(e), preste.

defunct [dɪ'fʌŋkt] _adj_ défunt(e).

defuse [di:'fju:z] _vt_ désamorcer.

defy [dɪ'faɪ] _vt_ défier; (_efforts etc_) résister à.

degenerate _vi_ [dɪ'dʒɛnəreɪt] dégénérer ♦ _adj_ [dɪ'dʒɛnərɪt] dégénéré(e).

degradation [dɛgrə'deɪʃən] _n_ dégradation _f_.

degrade [dɪ'greɪd] _vt_ dégrader.

degrading [dɪ'greɪdɪŋ] _adj_ dégradant(e).

degree [dɪ'gri:] _n_ degré _m_; (_SCOL_) diplôme _m_ (universitaire); **10 ~s below (zero)** 10 degrés au-dessous de zéro; **a (first) ~ in maths** (_BRIT_) une licence en maths; **a considerable ~ of risk** un considérable facteur _or_ élément de risque; **by ~s** (_gradually_) par degrés; **to some ~, to a certain ~** jusqu'à un certain point, dans une certaine mesure.

dehydrated [di:haɪ'dreɪtɪd] _adj_ déshydraté(e); (_milk, eggs_) en poudre.

dehydration [di:haɪ'dreɪʃən] _n_ déshydratation _f_.

de-ice ['di:'aɪs] _vt_ (_windscreen_) dégivrer.

de-icer ['di:'aɪsə*] _n_ dégivreur _m_.

deign [deɪn] _vi_: **to ~ to do** daigner faire.

deity ['di:ɪtɪ] _n_ divinité _f_; dieu _m_, déesse _f_.

déjà vu [deɪʒɑ:'vu:] _n_: **I had a sense of ~** j'ai eu une impression de déjà-vu.

dejected [dɪ'dʒɛktɪd] _adj_ abattu(e), déprimé(e).

dejection [dɪ'dʒɛkʃən] _n_ abattement _m_, découragement _m_.

Del. _abbr_ (_US_) = _Delaware_.

del. _abbr_ = **delete**.

delay [dɪ'leɪ] _vt_ (_journey, operation_) retarder, différer; (_travellers, trains_) retarder; (_payment_) différer ♦ _vi_ s'attarder ♦ _n_ délai _m_, retard _m_; **without ~** sans délai, sans tarder.

delayed-action [dɪ'leɪd'ækʃən] _adj_ à retardement.

delectable [dɪ'lɛktəbl] _adj_ délicieux(euse).

delegate _n_ ['dɛlɪgɪt] délégué/e ♦ _vt_ [dɛlɪgeɪt] déléguer; **to ~ sth to sb/sb to do sth** déléguer qch à qn/qn pour faire qch.

delegation [dɛlɪ'geɪʃən] _n_ délégation _f_.

delete [dɪ'li:t] _vt_ rayer, supprimer; (_COMPUT_) effacer.

Delhi ['dɛlɪ] _n_ Delhi.

deli ['dɛlɪ] _n_ épicerie fine.

deliberate _adj_ [dɪ'lɪbərɪt] (_intentional_) délibéré(e); (_slow_) mesuré(e) ♦ _vi_ [dɪ'lɪbəreɪt] délibérer, réfléchir.

deliberately [dɪ'lɪbərɪtlɪ] _adv_ (_on purpose_) exprès, délibérément.

deliberation [dɪlɪbə'reɪʃən] _n_ délibération _f_, réflexion _f_; (_gen pl: discussion_) délibérations, débats _mpl_.

delicacy ['dɛlɪkəsɪ] _n_ délicatesse _f_; (_choice food_) mets fin _or_ délicat, friandise _f_.

delicate ['dɛlɪkɪt] _adj_ délicat(e).

delicately ['dɛlɪkɪtlɪ] _adv_ délicatement; (_act, express_) avec délicatesse, avec tact.

delicatessen [dɛlɪkə'tɛsn] _n_ épicerie fine.

delicious [dɪ'lɪʃəs] _adj_ délicieux(euse), exquis(e).

delight [dɪ'laɪt] _n_ (grande) joie, grand plaisir ♦ _vt_ enchanter; **a ~ to the eyes** un régal _or_ plaisir pour les yeux; **to take ~ in** prendre grand plaisir à; **to be the ~ of** faire les délices _or_ la joie de.

delighted [dɪ'laɪtɪd] _adj_: **~ (at _or_ with sth)** ravi(e) (de qch); **to be ~ to do sth/that** être enchanté(e) _or_ ravi(e) de faire qch/que; **I'd be ~** j'en serais enchanté _or_ ravi.

delightful [dɪ'laɪtfʊl] _adj_ (_person, child_) absolument charmant(e), adorable; (_evening, view_) merveilleux(euse); (_meal_) délicieux(euse).

delimit [di:'lɪmɪt] _vt_ délimiter.

delineate [dɪ'lɪnɪeɪt] _vt_ tracer, esquisser; (_fig_) dépeindre, décrire.

delinquency [dɪ'lɪŋkwənsɪ] _n_ délinquance _f_.

delinquent [dɪ'lɪŋkwənt] _adj, n_ délinquant(e).

delirious [dɪ'lɪrɪəs] _adj_ (_MED, fig_) délirant(e); **to be ~** délirer.

delirium [dɪ'lɪrɪəm] _n_ délire _m_.

deliver [dɪ'lɪvə*] _vt_ (_mail_) distribuer; (_goods_) livrer; (_message_) remettre; (_speech_) prononcer; (_warning, ultimatum_) lancer; (_free_) délivrer; (_MED_) accoucher; **to ~ the goods** (_fig_) tenir ses promesses.

deliverance [dɪ'lɪvrəns] _n_ délivrance _f_, libération _f_.

delivery [dɪ'lɪvərɪ] _n_ (_of mail_) distribution _f_; (_of goods_) livraison _f_; (_of speaker_) élocution _f_; (_MED_) accouchement _m_; **to take ~ of** prendre livraison de.

delivery note _n_ bon _m_ de livraison.

delivery van, (_US_) **delivery truck** _n_ fourgonnette _f or_ camionnette _f_ de livraison.

delouse [di:'laʊs] _vt_ épouiller, débarrasser de sa (_or_ leur _etc_) vermine.

delta ['dɛltə] _n_ delta _m_.

delude [dɪ'lu:d] _vt_ tromper, leurrer; **to ~ o.s.** se leurrer, se faire des illusions.

deluge ['dɛlju:dʒ] _n_ déluge _m_ ♦ _vt_ (_fig_): **to ~**

(with) inonder (de).

delusion [dɪ'luːʒən] n illusion f; **to have ~s of grandeur** être un peu mégalomane.

de luxe [də'lʌks] adj de luxe.

delve [dɛlv] vi: **to ~ into** fouiller dans.

Dem. abbr (US POL) = **democrat(ic)**.

demagogue ['dɛməgɔg] n démagogue m/f.

demand [dɪ'maːnd] vt réclamer, exiger; (need) exiger, requérir ♦ n exigence f; (claim) revendication f; (ECON) demande f; **to ~ sth (from or of sb)** exiger qch (de qn), réclamer qch (à qn); **in ~** demandé(e), recherché(e); **on ~** sur demande.

demanding [dɪ'maːndɪŋ] adj (person) exigeant(e); (work) astreignant(e).

demarcation [diːmaː'keɪʃən] n démarcation f.

demarcation dispute n (INDUSTRY) conflit m d'attributions.

demean [dɪ'miːn] vt: **to ~ o.s.** s'abaisser.

demeanour, (US) **demeanor** [dɪ'miːnə*] n comportement m; maintien m.

demented [dɪ'mɛntɪd] adj dément(e), fou(folle).

demilitarized zone [diː'mɪlɪtəraɪzd-] n zone démilitarisée.

demise [dɪ'maɪz] n décès m.

demist [diː'mɪst] vt (BRIT AUT) désembuer.

demister [diː'mɪstə*] n (BRIT AUT) dispositif m anti-buée inv.

demo ['dɛməʊ] n abbr (col: = **demonstration**) manif f.

demobilize [diː'məʊbɪlaɪz] vt démobiliser.

democracy [dɪ'mɔkrəsɪ] n démocratie f.

democrat ['dɛməkræt] n démocrate m/f.

democratic [dɛmə'krætɪk] adj démocratique; **the D~ Party** (US) le parti démocrate.

demography [dɪ'mɔgrəfɪ] n démographie f.

demolish [dɪ'mɔlɪʃ] vt démolir.

demolition [dɛmə'lɪʃən] n démolition f.

demon ['diːmən] n démon m ♦ cpd: **a ~ squash player** un crack en squash; **a ~ driver** un fou du volant.

demonstrate ['dɛmənstreɪt] vt démontrer, prouver ♦ vi: **to ~ (for/against)** manifester (en faveur de/contre).

demonstration [dɛmən'streɪʃən] n démonstration f; (POL etc) manifestation f; **to hold a ~** (POL etc) organiser une manifestation, manifester.

demonstrative [dɪ'mɔnstrətɪv] adj démonstratif(ive).

demonstrator ['dɛmənstreɪtə*] n (POL etc) manifestant/e; (COMM: sales person) vendeur/euse; (: car, computer etc) modèle m de démonstration.

demoralize [dɪ'mɔrəlaɪz] vt démoraliser.

demote [dɪ'məʊt] vt rétrograder.

demotion [dɪ'məʊʃən] n rétrogradation f.

demur [dɪ'mə:*] vi: **to ~ (at sth)** hésiter (devant qch); (object) élever des objections (contre qch) ♦ n: **without ~** sans hésiter; sans faire de difficultés.

demure [dɪ'mjuə*] adj sage, réservé(e); d'une modestie affectée.

demurrage [dɪ'mʌrɪdʒ] n droits mpl de magasinage; surestarie f.

den [dɛn] n tanière f, antre m.

denationalization [diːnæʃnəlaɪ'zeɪʃən] n dénationalisation f.

denationalize [diː'næʃnəlaɪz] vt dénationaliser.

denial [dɪ'naɪəl] n (of accusation) démenti m; (of rights, guilt, truth) dénégation f.

denier ['dɛnɪə*] n denier m; **15 ~ stockings** bas de 15 deniers.

denigrate ['dɛnɪgreɪt] vt dénigrer.

denim ['dɛnɪm] n coton émerisé.

denim jacket n veste f en jean.

denims ['dɛnɪmz] npl (blue-)jeans mpl.

denizen ['dɛnɪzn] n (inhabitant) habitant/e; (foreigner) étranger/ère.

Denmark ['dɛnmaːk] n Danemark m.

denomination [dɪnɔmɪ'neɪʃən] n (money) valeur f; (REL) confession f; culte m.

denominator [dɪ'nɔmɪneɪtə*] n dénominateur m.

denote [dɪ'nəʊt] vt dénoter.

denounce [dɪ'naʊns] vt dénoncer.

dense [dɛns] adj dense; (col: stupid) obtus(e), dur(e) or lent(e) à la comprenette.

densely ['dɛnslɪ] adv: **~ wooded** couvert(e) d'épaisses forêts; **~ populated** à forte densité (de population), très peuplé(e).

density ['dɛnsɪtɪ] n densité f; **single/double ~ disk** (COMPUT) disquette f (à) simple/double densité.

dent [dɛnt] n bosse f ♦ vt (also: **make a ~ in**) cabosser; **to make a ~ in** (fig) entamer.

dental ['dɛntl] adj dentaire.

dental floss [-flɔs] n fil m dentaire.

dental surgeon n (chirurgien/ne) dentiste.

dentifrice ['dɛntɪfrɪs] n dentifrice m.

dentist ['dɛntɪst] n dentiste m/f; **~'s surgery** (BRIT) cabinet m de dentiste.

dentistry ['dɛntɪstrɪ] n art m dentaire.

denture(s) ['dɛntʃə(z)] n(pl) dentier m.

denunciation [dɪnʌnsɪ'eɪʃən] n dénonciation f.

deny [dɪ'naɪ] vt nier; (refuse) refuser; (disown) renier; **he denies having said it** il nie l'avoir dit.

deodorant [diː'əʊdərənt] n désodorisant m, déodorant m.

depart [dɪ'paːt] vi partir; **to ~ from** (leave) quitter, partir de; (fig: differ from) s'écarter de.

departed [dɪ'paːtɪd] adj (dead) défunt(e); **the (dear) ~** le défunt/la défunte/les défunts.

department [dɪ'paːtmənt] n (COMM) rayon m; (SCOL) section f; (POL) ministère m, département m; **that's not my ~** (fig) ce n'est pas mon domaine or ma compétence, ce n'est pas mon rayon; **D~ of State** (US) Département m d'État.

departmental [diːpaːt'mɛntl] adj d'une or de

la section; d'un *or* du ministère, d'un *or* du département; ~ **manager** chef *m* de service; (*in shop*) chef de rayon.

department store *n* grand magasin.

departure [dɪˈpɑːtʃə*] *n* départ *m*; (*fig*): ~ **from** écart *m* par rapport à; **a new** ~ une nouvelle voie.

departure lounge *n* salle *f* de départ.

depend [dɪˈpend] *vi*: **to** ~ **(up)on** dépendre de; (*rely on*) compter sur; (*financially*) dépendre (financièrement) de, être à la charge de; **it** ~**s** cela dépend; ~**ing on the result** ... selon le résultat ....

dependable [dɪˈpendəbl] *adj* sûr(e), digne de confiance.

dependant [dɪˈpendənt] *n* personne *f* à charge.

dependence [dɪˈpendəns] *n* dépendance *f*.

dependent [dɪˈpendənt] *adj*: **to be** ~ **(on)** dépendre (de) ♦ *n* = **dependant**.

depict [dɪˈpɪkt] *vt* (*in picture*) représenter; (*in words*) (dé)peindre, décrire.

depilatory [dɪˈpɪlətrɪ] *n* (*also*: ~ **cream**) dépilatoire *m*, crème *f* à épiler.

depleted [dɪˈpliːtɪd] *adj* (considérablement) réduit(e) *or* diminué(e).

deplorable [dɪˈplɔːrəbl] *adj* déplorable, lamentable.

deplore [dɪˈplɔː*] *vt* déplorer.

deploy [dɪˈplɔɪ] *vt* déployer.

depopulate [diːˈpɒpjuleɪt] *vt* dépeupler.

depopulation [ˈdiːpɒpjuˈleɪʃən] *n* dépopulation *f*, dépeuplement *m*.

deport [dɪˈpɔːt] *vt* déporter, expulser.

deportation [diːpɔːˈteɪʃən] *n* déportation *f*, expulsion *f*.

deportation order *n* arrêté *m* d'expulsion.

deportee [diːpɔːˈtiː] *n* déporté/e.

deportment [dɪˈpɔːtmənt] *n* maintien *m*, tenue *f*.

depose [dɪˈpəuz] *vt* déposer.

deposit [dɪˈpɒzɪt] *n* (*CHEM, COMM, GEO*) dépôt *m*; (*of ore, oil*) gisement *m*; (*part payment*) arrhes *fpl*, acompte *m*; (*on bottle etc*) consigne *f*; (*for hired goods etc*) cautionnement *m*, garantie *f* ♦ *vt* déposer; (*valuables*) mettre *or* laisser en dépôt; **to put down a** ~ **of £50** verser 50 livres d'arrhes *or* d'acompte; laisser 50 livres en garantie.

deposit account *n* compte *m* de dépôt.

depositor [dɪˈpɒzɪtə*] *n* déposant/e.

depository [dɪˈpɒzɪtərɪ] *n* (*person*) dépositaire *m/f*; (*place*) dépôt *m*.

depot [ˈdepəu] *n* dépôt *m*.

depraved [dɪˈpreɪvd] *adj* dépravé(e), perverti(e).

depravity [dɪˈprævɪtɪ] *n* dépravation *f*.

deprecate [ˈdeprɪkeɪt] *vt* désapprouver.

deprecating [ˈdeprɪkeɪtɪŋ] *adj* (*disapproving*) désapprobateur(trice); (*apologetic*): **a** ~ **smile** un sourire d'excuse.

depreciate [dɪˈpriːʃɪeɪt] *vt* déprécier ♦ *vi* se déprécier, se dévaloriser.

depreciation [dɪpriːʃɪˈeɪʃən] *n* dépréciation *f*.

depress [dɪˈpres] *vt* déprimer; (*press down*) appuyer sur, abaisser.

depressant [dɪˈpresnt] *n* (*MED*) dépresseur *m*.

depressed [dɪˈprest] *adj* (*person*) déprimé(e), abattu(e); (*area*) en déclin, touché(e) par le sous-emploi; (*COMM: market, trade*) maussade; **to get** ~ se démoraliser, se laisser abattre.

depressing [dɪˈpresɪŋ] *adj* déprimant(e).

depression [dɪˈpreʃən] *n* (*also ECON*) dépression *f*.

deprivation [deprɪˈveɪʃən] *n* privation *f*; (*loss*) perte *f*.

deprive [dɪˈpraɪv] *vt*: **to** ~ **sb of** priver qn de; enlever à qn.

deprived [dɪˈpraɪvd] *adj* déshérité(e).

dept. *abbr* (= *department*) dép., dépt.

depth [depθ] *n* profondeur *f*; **in the** ~**s of** au fond de; au cœur de; au plus profond de; **at a** ~ **of 3 metres** à 3 mètres de profondeur; **to be out of one's** ~ (*BRIT: swimmer*) ne plus avoir pied; (*fig*) être dépassé(e), nager; **to study sth in** ~ étudier qch en profondeur.

depth charge *n* grenade sous-marine.

deputation [depjuˈteɪʃən] *n* députation *f*, délégation *f*.

deputize [ˈdepjutaɪz] *vi*: **to** ~ **for** assurer l'intérim de.

deputy [ˈdepjutɪ] *n* (*replacement*) suppléant/e, intérimaire *m/f*; (*second in command*) adjoint/e ♦ *adj*: ~ **chairman** vice-président *m*; ~ **head** (*SCOL*) directeur/trice adjoint(e), sous-directeur/trice; ~ **leader** (*BRIT POL*) vice-président/e, secrétaire adjoint(e).

derail [dɪˈreɪl] *vt* faire dérailler; **to be** ~**ed** dérailler.

derailment [dɪˈreɪlmənt] *n* déraillement *m*.

deranged [dɪˈreɪndʒd] *adj*: **to be (mentally)** ~ avoir le cerveau dérangé.

derby [ˈdəːrbɪ] *n* (*US*) (chapeau *m*) melon *m*.

Derbys *abbr* (*BRIT*) = *Derbyshire*.

deregulate [diːˈregjuleɪt] *vt* libérer, dérégler.

deregulation [dɪregjuˈleɪʃən] *n* libération *f*, dérèglement *m*.

derelict [ˈderɪlɪkt] *adj* abandonné(e), à l'abandon.

deride [dɪˈraɪd] *vt* railler.

derision [dɪˈrɪʒən] *n* dérision *f*.

derisive [dɪˈraɪsɪv] *adj* moqueur(euse), railleur(euse).

derisory [dɪˈraɪsərɪ] *adj* (*sum*) dérisoire; (*smile, person*) moqueur(euse), railleur(euse).

derivation [derɪˈveɪʃən] *n* dérivation *f*.

derivative [dɪˈrɪvətɪv] *n* dérivé *m* ♦ *adj* dérivé(e).

derive [dɪˈraɪv] *vt*: **to** ~ **sth from** tirer qch de; trouver qch dans ♦ *vi*: **to** ~ **from** provenir de, dériver de.

dermatitis [dəːməˈtaɪtɪs] *n* dermatite *f*.

dermatology [dəːməˈtɔlədʒɪ] *n* dermatologie

f.

derogatory [dɪˈrɔgətərɪ] *adj* désobligeant(e); péjoratif(ive).

derrick [ˈdɛrɪk] *n* mât *m* de charge; derrick *m*.

derv [dɜːv] *n* (*BRIT*) gas-oil *m*, diesel *m*.

DES *n abbr* (*BRIT*: = Department of Education and Science*) ministère de l'éducation nationale et des sciences.

desalination [diːsælɪˈneɪʃən] *n* dessalement *m*, dessalage *m*.

descend [dɪˈsɛnd] *vt, vi* descendre; **to ~ from** descendre de, être issu(e) de; **in ~ing order of importance** par ordre d'importance décroissante.

▶**descend on** *vt fus* (*subj: enemy, angry person*) tomber *or* sauter sur; (*: misfortune*) s'abattre sur; (*: gloom, silence*) envahir; **visitors ~ed (up)on us** des gens sont arrivés chez nous à l'improviste.

descendant [dɪˈsɛndənt] *n* descendant/e.

descent [dɪˈsɛnt] *n* descente *f*; (*origin*) origine *f*.

describe [dɪsˈkraɪb] *vt* décrire.

description [dɪsˈkrɪpʃən] *n* description *f*; (*sort*) sorte *f*, espèce *f*; **of every ~** de toutes sortes.

descriptive [dɪsˈkrɪptɪv] *adj* descriptif(ive).

desecrate [ˈdɛsɪkreɪt] *vt* profaner.

desert *n* [ˈdɛzət] désert *m* ♦ *vb* [dɪˈzɜːt] *vt* déserter, abandonner ♦ *vi* (*MIL*) déserter.

deserter [dɪˈzɜːtə*] *n* déserteur *m*.

desertion [dɪˈzɜːʃən] *n* désertion *f*.

desert island *n* île déserte.

deserts [dɪˈzɜːts] *npl*: **to get one's just ~** n'avoir que ce qu'on mérite.

deserve [dɪˈzɜːv] *vt* mériter.

deservedly [dɪˈzɜːvɪdlɪ] *adv* à juste titre, à bon droit.

deserving [dɪˈzɜːvɪŋ] *adj* (*person*) méritant(e); (*action, cause*) méritoire.

desiccated [ˈdɛsɪkeɪtɪd] *adj* séché(e).

design [dɪˈzaɪn] *n* (*sketch*) plan *m*, dessin *m*; (*layout, shape*) conception *f*, ligne *f*; (*pattern*) dessin, motif(s) *m(pl)*; (*of dress, car*) modèle *m*; (*art*) design *m*, stylisme *m*; (*intention*) dessein *m* ♦ *vt* dessiner; (*plan*) concevoir; **to have ~s on** avoir des visées sur; **well-~ed** *adj* bien conçu(e); **industrial ~** esthétique industrielle.

designate *vt* [ˈdɛzɪgneɪt] désigner ♦ *adj* [ˈdɛzɪgnɪt] désigné(e).

designation [dɛzɪgˈneɪʃən] *n* désignation *f*.

designer [dɪˈzaɪnə*] *n* (*ARCHIT, ART*) dessinateur/trice; (*INDUSTRY*) concepteur *m*, designer *m*; (*FASHION*) modéliste *m/f*.

desirability [dɪzaɪərəˈbɪlɪtɪ] *n* avantage *m*; attrait *m*.

desirable [dɪˈzaɪərəbl] *adj* désirable; **it is ~ that** il est souhaitable que.

desire [dɪˈzaɪə*] *n* désir *m* ♦ *vt* désirer, vouloir; **to ~ to do sth/that** désirer faire qch/que.

desirous [dɪˈzaɪərəs] *adj*: **~ of** désireux(euse) de.

desk [dɛsk] *n* (*in office*) bureau *m*; (*for pupil*) pupitre *m*; (*BRIT: in shop, restaurant*) caisse *f*; (*in hotel, at airport*) réception *f*.

desktop computer [ˈdɛsktɔp-] *n* ordinateur *m* de bureau *or* de table.

desktop publishing [ˈdɛsktɔp-] *n* publication assistée par ordinateur, PAO *f*.

desolate [ˈdɛsəlɪt] *adj* désolé(e).

desolation [dɛsəˈleɪʃən] *n* désolation *f*.

despair [dɪsˈpɛə*] *n* désespoir *m* ♦ *vi*: **to ~ of** désespérer de; **to be in ~** être au désespoir.

despatch [dɪsˈpætʃ] *n, vt* = **dispatch**.

desperate [ˈdɛspərɪt] *adj* désespéré(e); (*fugitive*) prêt(e) à tout; (*measures*) désespéré, extrême; **we are getting ~** nous commençons à désespérer.

desperately [ˈdɛspərɪtlɪ] *adv* désespérément; (*very*) terriblement, extrêmement; **~ ill** très gravement malade.

desperation [dɛspəˈreɪʃən] *n* désespoir *m*; **in ~** en désespoir de cause.

despicable [dɪsˈpɪkəbl] *adj* méprisable.

despise [dɪsˈpaɪz] *vt* mépriser, dédaigner.

despite [dɪsˈpaɪt] *prep* malgré, en dépit de.

despondent [dɪsˈpɔndənt] *adj* découragé(e), abattu(e).

despot [ˈdɛspɔt] *n* despote *m/f*.

dessert [dɪˈzɜːt] *n* dessert *m*.

dessertspoon [dɪˈzɜːtspuːn] *n* cuiller *f* à dessert.

destabilize [diːˈsteɪbɪlaɪz] *vt* déstabiliser.

destination [dɛstɪˈneɪʃən] *n* destination *f*.

destine [ˈdɛstɪn] *vt* destiner.

destined [ˈdɛstɪnd] *adj*: **to be ~ to do sth** être destiné(e) à faire qch; **~ for London** à destination de Londres.

destiny [ˈdɛstɪnɪ] *n* destinée *f*, destin *m*.

destitute [ˈdɛstɪtjuːt] *adj* indigent(e), dans le dénuement; **~ of** dépourvu(e) *or* dénué(e) de.

destroy [dɪsˈtrɔɪ] *vt* détruire.

destroyer [dɪsˈtrɔɪə*] *n* (*NAUT*) contre-torpilleur *m*.

destruction [dɪsˈtrʌkʃən] *n* destruction *f*.

destructive [dɪsˈtrʌktɪv] *adj* destructeur(trice).

desultory [ˈdɛsəltərɪ] *adj* (*reading, conversation*) décousu(e); (*contact*) irrégulier(ière).

detach [dɪˈtætʃ] *vt* détacher.

detachable [dɪˈtætʃəbl] *adj* amovible, détachable.

detached [dɪˈtætʃt] *adj* (*attitude*) détaché(e).

detached house *n* pavillon *m*, maison(nette) (individuelle).

detachment [dɪˈtætʃmənt] *n* (*MIL*) détachement *m*; (*fig*) détachement, indifférence *f*.

detail [ˈdiːteɪl] *n* détail *m*; (*MIL*) détachement *m* ♦ *vt* raconter en détail, énumérer; (*MIL*): **to ~ sb (for)** affecter qn (à), détacher qn (pour); **in ~** en détail; **to go into ~(s)** entrer dans les détails.

detailed [ˈdiːteɪld] *adj* détaillé(e).

detain [dɪ'teɪn] vt retenir; (*in captivity*) détenir; (*in hospital*) hospitaliser.

detainee [diːteɪ'niː] n détenu/e.

detect [dɪ'tɛkt] vt déceler, percevoir; (*MED, POLICE*) dépister; (*MIL, RADAR, TECH*) détecter.

detection [dɪ'tɛkʃən] n découverte f; (*MED, POLICE*) dépistage m; (*MIL, RADAR, TECH*) détection f; **to escape** ~ échapper aux recherches, éviter d'être découvert(e); (*mistake*) passer inaperçu(e); **crime** ~ le dépistage des criminels.

detective [dɪ'tɛktɪv] n agent m de la sûreté, policier m; **private** ~ détective privé.

detective story n roman policier.

detector [dɪ'tɛktə*] n détecteur m.

détente [deɪ'tɑːnt] n détente f.

detention [dɪ'tɛnʃən] n détention f; (*SCOL*) retenue f, consigne f.

deter [dɪ'tɜː*] vt dissuader.

detergent [dɪ'tə:dʒənt] n détersif m, détergent m.

deteriorate [dɪ'tɪərɪəreɪt] vi se détériorer, se dégrader.

deterioration [dɪtɪərɪə'reɪʃən] n détérioration f.

determination [dɪtə:mɪ'neɪʃən] n détermination f.

determine [dɪ'tə:mɪn] vt déterminer; **to** ~ **to do** résoudre de faire, se déterminer à faire.

determined [dɪ'tə:mɪnd] adj (*person*) déterminé(e), décidé(e); (*quantity*) déterminé, établi(e); (*effort*) très gros(se).

deterrence [dɪ'tɜːns] n dissuasion f.

deterrent [dɪ'tɛrənt] n effet m de dissuasion; force f de dissuasion; **to act as a** ~ avoir un effet dissuasif.

detest [dɪ'tɛst] vt détester, avoir horreur de.

detestable [dɪ'tɛstəbl] adj détestable, odieux(euse).

detonate ['dɛtəneɪt] vi exploser ♦ vt faire exploser *or* détoner.

detonator ['dɛtəneɪtə*] n détonateur m.

detour ['diːtuə*] n détour m; (*US AUT: diversion*) déviation f.

detract [dɪ'trækt] vt: **to** ~ **from** (*quality, pleasure*) diminuer; (*reputation*) porter atteinte à.

detractor [dɪ'træktə*] n détracteur/trice.

detriment ['dɛtrɪmənt] n: **to the** ~ **of** au détriment de, au préjudice de; **without** ~ **to** sans porter atteinte *or* préjudice à, sans conséquences fâcheuses pour.

detrimental [dɛtrɪ'mɛntl] adj: ~ **to** préjudiciable *or* nuisible à.

deuce [djuːs] n (*TENNIS*) égalité f.

devaluation [dɪvælju'eɪʃən] n dévaluation f.

devalue ['diː'væljuː] vt dévaluer.

devastate ['dɛvəsteɪt] vt dévaster; **he was ~d by the news** cette nouvelle lui a porté un coup terrible.

devastating ['dɛvəsteɪtɪŋ] adj dévasta-

teur(trice).

devastation [dɛvəs'teɪʃən] n dévastation f.

develop [dɪ'vɛləp] vt (*gen*) développer; (*habit*) contracter; (*resources*) mettre en valeur, exploiter; (*land*) aménager ♦ vi se développer; (*situation, disease: evolve*) évoluer; (*facts, symptoms: appear*) se manifester, se produire; **to** ~ **a taste for sth** prendre goût à qch; **to** ~ **into** devenir.

developer [dɪ'vɛləpə*] n (*PHOT*) révélateur m; (*of land*) promoteur m; (*also*: **property** ~) promoteur immobilier.

developing country [dɪ'vɛləpɪŋ-] n pays m en voie de développement.

development [dɪ'vɛləpmənt] n développement m; (*of affair, case*) rebondissement m, fait(s) nouveau(x).

development area n zone f à urbaniser.

deviate ['diːvɪeɪt] vi: **to** ~ (**from**) dévier (de).

deviation [diːvɪ'eɪʃən] n déviation f.

device [dɪ'vaɪs] n (*scheme*) moyen m, expédient m; (*apparatus*) engin m, dispositif m; **explosive** ~ engin explosif.

devil ['dɛvl] n diable m; démon m.

devilish ['dɛvlɪʃ] adj diabolique.

devil-may-care ['dɛvlmeɪ'kɛə*] adj je-m'en-foutiste.

devil's advocate n: **to play** ~ se faire avocat du diable.

devious ['diːvɪəs] adj (*means*) détourné(e); (*person*) sournois(e), dissimulé(e).

devise [dɪ'vaɪz] vt imaginer, concevoir.

devoid [dɪ'vɔɪd] adj: ~ **of** dépourvu(e) de, dénué(e) de.

devolution [diːvə'luːʃən] n (*POL*) décentralisation f.

devolve [dɪ'vɒlv] vi: **to** ~ (**up**)**on** retomber sur.

devote [dɪ'vəʊt] vt: **to** ~ **sth to** consacrer qch à.

devoted [dɪ'vəʊtɪd] adj dévoué(e); **to be** ~ **to** être dévoué(e) *or* très attaché(e) à; (*subj: book etc*) être consacré(e) à.

devotee [dɛvəʊ'tiː] n (*REL*) adepte m/f; (*MUS, SPORT*) fervent/e.

devotion [dɪ'vəʊʃən] n dévouement m, attachement m; (*REL*) dévotion f, piété f.

devour [dɪ'vaʊə*] vt dévorer.

devout [dɪ'vaʊt] adj pieux(euse), dévot(e).

dew [djuː] n rosée f.

dexterity [dɛks'tɛrɪtɪ] n dextérité f, adresse f.

dext(e)rous ['dɛkstrəs] adj adroit(e).

dg abbr (= *decigram*) dg.

diabetes [daɪə'biːtiːz] n diabète m.

diabetic [daɪə'bɛtɪk] n diabétique m/f ♦ adj (*person*) diabétique; (*chocolate, jam*) pour diabétiques.

diabolical [daɪə'bɒlɪkl] adj diabolique; (*col: dreadful*) infernal(e), atroce.

diaeresis [daɪ'ɛrɪsɪs] n tréma m.

diagnose [daɪəg'nəʊz] vt diagnostiquer.

diagnosis, pl **diagnoses** [daɪəg'nəʊsɪs, -siːz] n

diagnostic *m*.

diagonal [daɪˈægənl] *adj* diagonal(e) ♦ *n* diagonale *f*.

diagram ['daɪəgræm] *n* diagramme *m*, schéma *m*.

dial ['daɪəl] *n* cadran *m* ♦ *vt* (*number*) faire, composer; **to ~ a wrong number** faire un faux numéro; **can I ~ London direct?** puis-je *or* est-ce-que je peux avoir Londres par l'automatique?

dial. *abbr* = **dialect.**

dialect ['daɪəlɛkt] *n* dialecte *m*.

dialling code ['daɪəlɪŋ-] *n* indicatif *m* (téléphonique).

dialling tone ['daɪəlɪŋ-], (*US*) **dial tone** *n* tonalité *f*.

dialogue ['daɪəlɔg] *n* dialogue *m*.

dialysis [daɪˈælɪsɪs] *n* dialyse *f*.

diameter [daɪˈæmɪtə*] *n* diamètre *m*.

diametrically [daɪəˈmɛtrɪklɪ] *adv*: **~ opposed (to)** diamétralement opposé(e) (à).

diamond ['daɪəmənd] *n* diamant *m*; (*shape*) losange *m*; **~s** *npl* (*CARDS*) carreau *m*.

diamond ring *n* bague *f* de diamant(s).

diaper ['daɪəpə*] *n* (*US*) couche *f*.

diaphragm ['daɪəfræm] *n* diaphragme *m*.

diarrhoea, (*US*) **diarrhea** [daɪəˈriːə] *n* diarrhée *f*.

diary ['daɪərɪ] *n* (*daily account*) journal *m*; (*book*) agenda *m*; **to keep a ~** tenir un journal.

diatribe ['daɪətraɪb] *n* diatribe *f*.

dice [daɪs] *n* (*pl inv*) dé *m* ♦ *vt* (*CULIN*) couper en dés *or* en cubes.

dicey ['daɪsɪ] *adj* (*col*): **it's a bit ~** c'est un peu risqué.

dichotomy [daɪˈkɔtəmɪ] *n* dichotomie *f*.

dickhead ['dɪkhɛd] *n* (*BRIT col!*) tête *f* de nœud (*!*).

Dictaphone ['dɪktəfəun] *n* ® Dictaphone *m* ®.

dictate *vt* [dɪkˈteɪt] dicter ♦ *vi*: **to ~ to** (*person*) imposer sa volonté à, régenter; **I won't be ~d to** je n'ai d'ordres à recevoir de personne ♦ *n* ['dɪkteɪt] injonction *f*.

dictation [dɪkˈteɪʃən] *n* dictée *f*; **at ~ speed** à une vitesse de dictée.

dictator [dɪkˈteɪtə*] *n* dictateur *m*.

dictatorship [dɪkˈteɪtəʃɪp] *n* dictature *f*.

diction ['dɪkʃən] *n* diction *f*, élocution *f*.

dictionary ['dɪkʃənrɪ] *n* dictionnaire *m*.

did [dɪd] *pt of* **do.**

didactic [daɪˈdæktɪk] *adj* didactique.

didn't ['dɪdnt] = **did not.**

die [daɪ] *n* (*pl*: **dice**) dé *m*; (*pl*: **dies**) coin *m*; matrice *f*; étampe *f* ♦ *vi*: **to ~** (*of or from*) mourir (de); **to be dying** être mourant(e); **to be dying for sth** avoir une envie folle de qch; **to be dying to do sth** mourir d'envie de faire qch.

▶**die away** *vi* s'éteindre.

▶**die down** *vi* se calmer, s'apaiser.

▶**die out** *vi* disparaître, s'éteindre.

diehard ['daɪhɑːd] *n* réactionnaire *m/f*, jusqu'au-boutiste *m/f*.

diesel ['diːzl] *n* diesel *m*.

diesel engine *n* moteur *m* diesel.

diesel fuel, diesel oil *n* carburant *m* diesel.

diet ['daɪət] *n* alimentation *f*; (*restricted food*) régime *m* ♦ *vi* (*also*: **be on a ~**) suivre un régime; **to live on a ~ of** se nourrir de.

dietician [daɪəˈtɪʃən] *n* diététicien/ne.

differ ['dɪfə*] *vi*: **to ~ from sth** être différent(e) de; différer de; **to ~ from sb over sth** ne pas être d'accord avec qn au sujet de qch.

difference ['dɪfrəns] *n* différence *f*; (*quarrel*) différend *m*, désaccord *m*; **it makes no ~ to me** cela m'est égal, cela m'est indifférent; **to settle one's ~s** résoudre la situation.

different ['dɪfrənt] *adj* différent(e).

differential [dɪfəˈrɛnʃəl] *n* (*AUT, wages*) différentiel *m*.

differentiate [dɪfəˈrɛnʃɪeɪt] *vt* différencier ♦ *vi* se différencier; **to ~ between** faire une différence entre.

differently ['dɪfrəntlɪ] *adv* différemment.

difficult ['dɪfɪkəlt] *adj* difficile; **~ to understand** difficile à comprendre.

difficulty ['dɪfɪkəltɪ] *n* difficulté *f*; **to have difficulties with** avoir des ennuis *or* problèmes avec; **to be in ~** avoir des difficultés, avoir des problèmes.

diffidence ['dɪfɪdəns] *n* manque *m* de confiance en soi, manque d'assurance.

diffident ['dɪfɪdənt] *adj* qui manque de confiance *or* d'assurance, peu sûr(e) de soi.

diffuse *adj* [dɪˈfjuːs] diffus(e) ♦ *vt* [dɪˈfjuːz] diffuser, répandre.

dig [dɪg] *vt* (*pt, pp* **dug** [dʌg]) (*hole*) creuser; (*garden*) bêcher ♦ *n* (*prod*) coup *m* de coude; (*fig*) coup de griffe *or* de patte; (*ARCHAEOLOGY*) fouille *f*; **to ~ into** (*snow, soil*) creuser; **to ~ into one's pockets for sth** fouiller dans ses poches pour chercher *or* prendre qch; **to ~ one's nails into** enfoncer ses ongles dans.

▶**dig in** *vi* (*also*: **~ o.s. in:** *MIL*) se retrancher; (*: fig*) tenir bon, se braquer; (*col: eat*) attaquer (un repas *or* un plat *etc*) ♦ *vt* (*compost*) bien mélanger à la bêche; (*knife, claw*) enfoncer; **to ~ in one's heels** (*fig*) se braquer, se buter.

▶**dig out** *vt* (*survivors, car from snow*) sortir *or* dégager (à coups de pelles *or* pioches).

▶**dig up** *vt* déterrer.

digest *vt* [daɪˈdʒɛst] digérer ♦ *n* ['daɪdʒɛst] sommaire *m*, résumé *m*.

digestible [dɪˈdʒɛstəbl] *adj* digestible.

digestion [dɪˈdʒɛstʃən] *n* digestion *f*.

digestive [dɪˈdʒɛstɪv] *adj* digestif(ive).

digit ['dɪdʒɪt] *n* chiffre *m* (*de 0 à 9*); (*finger*) doigt *m*.

digital ['dɪdʒɪtl] *adj* digital(e); (*watch*) à affichage numérique *or* digital.

digital compact cassette n cassette f numérique.

digital TV n télévision f numérique.

dignified ['dɪgnɪfaɪd] adj digne.

dignitary ['dɪgnɪtərɪ] n dignitaire m.

dignity ['dɪgnɪtɪ] n dignité f.

digress [daɪ'grɛs] vi: **to ~ from** s'écarter de, s'éloigner de.

digression [daɪ'grɛʃən] n digression f.

digs [dɪgz] npl (BRIT col) chambre meublée.

dilapidated [dɪ'læpɪdeɪtɪd] adj délabré(e).

dilate [daɪ'leɪt] vt dilater ♦ vi se dilater.

dilatory ['dɪlətərɪ] adj dilatoire.

dilemma [daɪ'lɛmə] n dilemme m; **to be in a ~** être pris dans un dilemme.

diligent ['dɪlɪdʒənt] adj appliqué(e), assidu(e).

dill [dɪl] n aneth m.

dilly-dally ['dɪlɪ'dælɪ] vi hésiter, tergiverser; traînasser, lambiner.

dilute [daɪ'luːt] vt diluer ♦ adj dilué(e).

dim [dɪm] adj (light, eyesight) faible; (memory, outline) vague, indécis(e); (stupid) borné(e), obtus(e) ♦ vt (light) réduire, baisser; (US AUT) mettre en code, baisser; **to take a ~ view of sth** voir qch d'un mauvais œil.

dime [daɪm] n (US) = 10 cents.

dimension [daɪ'mɛnʃən] n dimension f.

-dimensional [dɪ'mɛnʃənl] adj suffix: **two~** à deux dimensions.

diminish [dɪ'mɪnɪʃ] vt, vi diminuer.

diminished [dɪ'mɪnɪʃt] adj: **~ responsibility** (LAW) responsabilité atténuée.

diminutive [dɪ'mɪnjutɪv] adj minuscule, tout(e) petit(e) ♦ n (LING) diminutif m.

dimly ['dɪmlɪ] adv faiblement; vaguement.

dimmer ['dɪmə*] n (also: **~ switch**) variateur m; **~s** npl (US AUT: dipped headlights) phares mpl code inv; (: parking lights) feux mpl de position.

dimple ['dɪmpl] n fossette f.

dim-witted ['dɪm'wɪtɪd] adj (col) stupide, borné(e).

din [dɪn] n vacarme m ♦ vt: **to ~ sth into sb** (col) enfoncer qch dans la tête or la caboche de qn.

dine [daɪn] vi dîner.

diner ['daɪnə*] n (person) dîneur/euse; (RAIL) = **dining car**; (US: eating place) petit restaurant.

dinghy ['dɪŋgɪ] n youyou m; (inflatable) canot m pneumatique; (also: **sailing ~**) voilier m, dériveur m.

dingy ['dɪndʒɪ] adj miteux(euse), minable.

dining car ['daɪnɪŋ-] n voiture-restaurant f, wagon-restaurant m.

dining room ['daɪnɪŋ-] n salle f à manger.

dinner ['dɪnə*] n dîner m; (public) banquet m; **~'s ready!** à table!

dinner jacket n smoking m.

dinner party n dîner m.

dinner time n heure f du dîner.

dinosaur ['daɪnəsɔː*] n dinosaure m.

dint [dɪnt] n: **by ~ of (doing) sth** à force de

(faire) qch.

diocese ['daɪəsɪs] n diocèse m.

dioxide [daɪ'ɔksaɪd] n dioxyde m.

Dip. abbr (BRIT) = **diploma**.

dip [dɪp] n déclivité f; (in sea) baignade f, bain m ♦ vt tremper, plonger; (BRIT AUT: lights) mettre en code, baisser ♦ vi plonger.

diphtheria [dɪf'θɪərɪə] n diphtérie f.

diphthong ['dɪfθɔŋ] n diphtongue f.

diploma [dɪ'pləumə] n diplôme m.

diplomacy [dɪ'pləuməsɪ] n diplomatie f.

diplomat ['dɪpləmæt] n diplomate m.

diplomatic [dɪplə'mætɪk] adj diplomatique; **to break off ~ relations (with)** rompre les relations diplomatiques (avec).

diplomatic corps n corps m diplomatique.

diplomatic immunity n immunité f diplomatique.

dipstick ['dɪpstɪk] n (AUT) jauge f de niveau d'huile.

dipswitch ['dɪpswɪtʃ] n (BRIT AUT) commutateur m de code.

dire [daɪə*] adj extrême, affreux(euse).

direct [daɪ'rɛkt] adj direct(e); (manner, person) direct, franc(franche) ♦ vt diriger, orienter; **can you ~ me to ...?** pouvez-vous m'indiquer le chemin de ...?; **to ~ sb to do sth** ordonner à qn de faire qch.

direct cost n (COMM) coût m variable.

direct current n (ELEC) courant continu.

direct debit n (BANKING) prélèvement m automatique.

direct dialling n (TEL) automatique m.

direct hit n (MIL) coup m au but, touché m.

direction [dɪ'rɛkʃən] n direction f; (THEAT) mise f en scène; (CINE, TV) réalisation f; **~s** npl (instructions: to a place) indications fpl; **~s for use** mode m d'emploi; **to ask for ~s** demander sa route or son chemin; **sense of ~** sens m de l'orientation; **in the ~ of** dans la direction de, vers.

directive [dɪ'rɛktɪv] n directive f; **a government ~** une directive du gouvernement.

direct labour n main-d'œuvre directe; employés municipaux.

directly [dɪ'rɛktlɪ] adv (in straight line) directement, tout droit; (at once) tout de suite, immédiatement.

direct mail n vente f par publicité directe.

direct mailshot n (BRIT) publicité postale.

directness [daɪ'rɛktnɪs] n (of person, speech) franchise f.

director [dɪ'rɛktə*] n directeur m; (board member) administrateur m; (THEAT) metteur m en scène; (CINE, TV) réalisateur/trice; **D~ of Public Prosecutions** (BRIT) ≈ procureur général.

directory [dɪ'rɛktərɪ] n annuaire m; (also: **street ~**) indicateur m de rues; (also: **trade ~**) annuaire du commerce; (COMPUT) répertoire m.

directory enquiries, (US) **directory assis-**

tance n (*TEL: service*) renseignements *mpl*.

dirt [dɔːt] n saleté *f*; (*mud*) boue *f*; **to treat sb like ~** traiter qn comme un chien.

dirt-cheap ['dɔːt'tʃiːp] *adj* (ne) coûtant presque rien.

dirt road n chemin non macadamisé *or* non revêtu.

dirty ['dɔːtɪ] *adj* sale ♦ *vt* salir; **~ story** histoire cochonne; **~ trick** coup tordu.

disability [dɪsə'bɪlɪtɪ] n invalidité *f*, infirmité *f*.

disability allowance n allocation *f* d'invalidité *or* d'infirmité.

disable [dɪs'eɪbl] *vt* (*subj: illness, accident*) rendre *or* laisser infirme; (*tank, gun*) mettre hors d'action.

disabled [dɪs'eɪbld] *adj* infirme, invalide; (*maimed*) mutilé(e); (*through illness, old age*) impotent(e).

disadvantage [dɪsəd'vɑːntɪdʒ] n désavantage *m*, inconvénient *m*.

disadvantaged [dɪsəd'vɑːntɪdʒd] *adj* (*person*) désavantagé(e).

disadvantageous [dɪsædvɑːn'teɪdʒəs] *adj* désavantageux(euse).

disaffected [dɪsə'fɛktɪd] *adj*: **~ (to or towards)** mécontent(e) (de).

disaffection [dɪsə'fɛkʃən] n désaffection *f*, mécontentement *m*.

disagree [dɪsə'griː] *vi* (*differ*) ne pas concorder; (*be against, think otherwise*): **to ~ (with)** ne pas être d'accord (avec); **garlic ~s with me** l'ail ne me convient pas, je ne supporte pas l'ail.

disagreeable [dɪsə'griːəbl] *adj* désagréable.

disagreement [dɪsə'griːmənt] n désaccord *m*, différend *m*.

disallow ['dɪsə'lau] *vt* rejeter, désavouer; (*BRIT FOOTBALL: goal*) refuser.

disappear [dɪsə'pɪə*] *vi* disparaître.

disappearance [dɪsə'pɪərəns] n disparition *f*.

disappoint [dɪsə'pɔɪnt] *vt* décevoir.

disappointed [dɪsə'pɔɪntɪd] *adj* déçu(e).

disappointing [dɪsə'pɔɪntɪŋ] *adj* décevant(e).

disappointment [dɪsə'pɔɪntmənt] n déception *f*.

disapproval [dɪsə'pruːvəl] n désapprobation *f*.

disapprove [dɪsə'pruːv] *vi*: **to ~ of** désapprouver.

disapproving [dɪsə'pruːvɪŋ] *adj* désapprobateur(trice), de désapprobation.

disarm [dɪs'ɑːm] *vt* désarmer.

disarmament [dɪs'ɑːməmənt] n désarmement *m*.

disarming [dɪs'ɑːmɪŋ] *adj* (*smile*) désarmant(e).

disarray [dɪsə'reɪ] n désordre *m*, confusion *f*; **in ~** (*troops*) en déroute; (*thoughts*) embrouillé(e); (*clothes*) en désordre; **to throw into ~** semer la confusion *or* le désordre dans (*or* parmi).

disaster [dɪ'zɑːstə*] n catastrophe *f*, désastre *m*.

disastrous [dɪ'zɑːstrəs] *adj* désastreux(euse).

disband [dɪs'bænd] *vt* démobiliser; disperser ♦ *vi* se séparer; se disperser.

disbelief ['dɪsbə'liːf] n incrédulité *f*; **in ~** avec incrédulité.

disbelieve ['dɪsbə'liːv] *vt* (*person*) ne pas croire; (*story*) mettre en doute; **I don't ~ you** je veux bien vous croire.

disc [dɪsk] n disque *m*.

disc. *abbr* (*COMM*) = **discount**.

discard [dɪs'kɑːd] *vt* (*old things*) se défaire de, mettre au rencart *or* au rebut; (*fig*) écarter, renoncer à.

disc brake n frein *m* à disque.

discern [dɪ'sɔːn] *vt* discerner, distinguer.

discernible [dɪ'sɔːnəbl] *adj* discernable, perceptible; (*object*) visible.

discerning [dɪ'sɔːnɪŋ] *adj* judicieux(euse), perspicace.

discharge *vt* [dɪs'tʃɑːdʒ] (*duties*) s'acquitter de; (*settle: debt*) s'acquitter de, régler; (*waste etc*) déverser; décharger; (*ELEC, MED*) émettre; (*patient*) renvoyer (chez lui); (*employee, soldier*) congédier, licencier; (*defendant*) relaxer, élargir ♦ n [dɪst'fɑːdʒ] (*ELEC, MED etc*) émission *f*; (*also: vaginal ~*) pertes blanches; (*dismissal*) renvoi *m*; licenciement *m*; élargissement *m*; **to ~ one's gun** faire feu; **~d bankrupt** failli/e réhabilité(e).

disciple [dɪ'saɪpl] n disciple *m*.

disciplinary ['dɪsɪplɪnərɪ] *adj* disciplinaire; **to take ~ action against sb** prendre des mesures disciplinaires à l'encontre de qn.

discipline ['dɪsɪplɪn] n discipline *f* ♦ *vt* discipliner; (*punish*) punir; **to ~ o.s. to do sth** s'imposer *or* s'astreindre à une discipline pour faire qch.

disc jockey (DJ) n disque-jockey *m* (DJ).

disclaim [dɪs'kleɪm] *vt* désavouer, dénier.

disclaimer [dɪs'kleɪmə*] n démenti *m*, dénégation *f*; **to issue a ~** publier un démenti.

disclose [dɪs'kləuz] *vt* révéler, divulguer.

disclosure [dɪs'kləuʒə*] n révélation *f*, divulgation *f*.

disco [dɪskəu] n *abbr* = **discothèque**.

discolour, (US) discolor [dɪs'kʌlə*] *vt* décolorer; (*sth white*) jaunir ♦ *vi* se décolorer; jaunir.

discolo(u)ration [dɪskʌlə'reɪʃən] n décoloration *f*; jaunissement *m*.

discolo(u)red [dɪs'kʌləd] *adj* décoloré(e); jauni(e).

discomfort [dɪs'kʌmfət] n malaise *m*, gêne *f*; (*lack of comfort*) manque *m* de confort.

disconcert [dɪskən'sɔːt] *vt* déconcerter, décontenancer.

disconnect [dɪskə'nɛkt] *vt* détacher; (*ELEC, RADIO*) débrancher; (*gas, water*) couper.

disconnected [dɪskə'nɛktɪd] *adj* (*speech, thoughts*) décousu(e), peu cohérent(e).

disconsolate [dɪs'kɒnsəlɪt] *adj* inconsolable.

discontent [dɪskən'tɛnt] n mécontentement

m.

discontented [dɪskən'tɛntɪd] *adj* mécontent(e).

discontinue [dɪskən'tɪnjuː] *vt* cesser, interrompre; **"~d"** (COMM) "fin de série".

discord ['dɪskɔːd] *n* discorde *f*, dissension *f*; (MUS) dissonance *f*.

discordant [dɪs'kɔːdənt] *adj* discordant(e), dissonant(e).

discotheque ['dɪskəutɛk] *n* discothèque *f*.

discount *n* ['dɪskaunt] remise *f*, rabais *m* ♦ *vt* [dɪs'kaunt] (report etc) ne pas tenir compte de; **to give sb a ~ on sth** faire une remise *or* un rabais à qn sur qch; **~ for cash** escompte *f* au comptant; **at a ~** avec une remise *or* réduction, au rabais.

discount house *n* (FINANCE) banque *f* d'escompte; (COMM: also: **discount store**) magasin *m* de discount.

discount rate *n* taux *m* de remise.

discourage [dɪs'kʌrɪdʒ] *vt* décourager; (dissuade, deter) dissuader, décourager.

discouragement [dɪs'kʌrɪdʒmənt] *n* (depression) découragement *m*; **to act as a ~ to sb** dissuader qn.

discouraging [dɪs'kʌrɪdʒɪŋ] *adj* décourageant(e).

discourteous [dɪs'kəːtɪəs] *adj* incivil(e), discourtois(e).

discover [dɪs'kʌvə*] *vt* découvrir.

discovery [dɪs'kʌvərɪ] *n* découverte *f*.

discredit [dɪs'krɛdɪt] *vt* mettre en doute; discréditer ♦ *n* discrédit *m*.

discreet [dɪ'skriːt] *adj* discret(ète).

discreetly [dɪ'skriːtlɪ] *adv* discrètement.

discrepancy [dɪ'skrɛpənsɪ] *n* divergence *f*, contradiction *f*.

discretion [dɪ'skrɛʃən] *n* discrétion *f*; **use your own ~** à vous de juger.

discretionary [dɪ'skrɛʃənrɪ] *adj* (powers) discrétionnaire.

discriminate [dɪ'skrɪmɪneɪt] *vi*: **to ~ between** établir une distinction entre, faire la différence entre; **to ~ against** pratiquer une discrimination contre.

discriminating [dɪ'skrɪmɪneɪtɪŋ] *adj* qui a du discernement.

discrimination [dɪskrɪmɪ'neɪʃən] *n* discrimination *f*; (judgment) discernement *m*; **racial/ sexual ~** discrimination raciale/sexuelle.

discus ['dɪskəs] *n* disque *m*.

discuss [dɪ'skʌs] *vt* discuter de; (debate) discuter.

discussion [dɪ'skʌʃən] *n* discussion *f*; **under ~** en discussion.

disdain [dɪs'deɪn] *n* dédain *m*.

disease [dɪ'ziːz] *n* maladie *f*.

diseased [dɪ'ziːzd] *adj* malade.

disembark [dɪsɪm'baːk] *vt, vi* débarquer.

disembarkation [dɪsɛmbaː'keɪʃən] *n* débarquement *m*.

disembodied ['dɪsɪm'bɔdɪd] *adj* désincar-

né(e).

disembowel ['dɪsɪm'bauəl] *vt* éviscérer, étriper.

disenchanted ['dɪsɪn'tʃaːntɪd] *adj*: **~ (with)** désenchanté(e) (de), désabusé(e) (de).

disenfranchise ['dɪsɪn'fræntʃaɪz] *vt* priver du droit de vote; (COMM) retirer la franchise à.

disengage [dɪsɪn'geɪdʒ] *vt* dégager; (TECH) déclencher; **to ~ the clutch** (AUT) débrayer.

disentangle [dɪsɪn'tæŋgl] *vt* démêler.

disfavour, (US) **disfavor** [dɪs'feɪvə*] *n* défaveur *f*; disgrâce *f*.

disfigure [dɪs'fɪgə*] *vt* défigurer.

disgorge [dɪs'gɔːdʒ] *vt* déverser.

disgrace [dɪs'greɪs] *n* honte *f*; (disfavour) disgrâce *f* ♦ *vt* déshonorer, couvrir de honte.

disgraceful [dɪs'greɪsful] *adj* scandaleux(euse), honteux(euse).

disgruntled [dɪs'grʌntld] *adj* mécontent(e).

disguise [dɪs'gaɪz] *n* déguisement *m* ♦ *vt* déguiser; (voice) déguiser, contrefaire; (feelings etc) masquer, dissimuler; **in ~** déguisé(e); **to ~ o.s. as** se déguiser en; **there's no disguising the fact that ...** on ne peut pas se dissimuler que ....

disgust [dɪs'gʌst] *n* dégoût *m*, aversion *f* ♦ *vt* dégoûter, écœurer.

disgusting [dɪs'gʌstɪŋ] *adj* dégoûtant(e), révoltant(e).

dish [dɪʃ] *n* plat *m*; **to do** *or* **wash the ~es** faire la vaisselle.

▶**dish out** *vt* distribuer.

▶**dish up** *vt* servir; (facts, statistics) sortir, débiter.

dishcloth ['dɪʃklɔθ] *n* (for drying) torchon *m*; (for washing) lavette *f*.

dishearten [dɪs'haːtn] *vt* décourager.

dishevelled, (US) **disheveled** [dɪ'ʃɛvəld] *adj* ébouriffé(e); décoiffé(e); débraillé(e).

dishonest [dɪs'ɔnɪst] *adj* malhonnête.

dishonesty [dɪs'ɔnɪstɪ] *n* malhonnêteté *f*.

dishonour, (US) **dishonor** [dɪs'ɔnə*] *n* déshonneur *m*.

dishono(u)rable [dɪs'ɔnərəbl] *adj* déshonorant(e).

dish soap *n* (US) produit *m* pour la vaisselle.

dishtowel ['dɪʃtauəl] *n* torchon *m* (à vaisselle).

dishwasher ['dɪʃwɔʃə*] *n* lave-vaisselle *m*; (person) plongeur/euse.

dishy ['dɪʃɪ] *adj* (BRIT col) séduisant(e), sexy *inv*.

disillusion [dɪsɪ'luːʒən] *vt* désabuser, désenchanter ♦ *n* désenchantement *m*; **to become ~ed (with)** perdre ses illusions (en ce qui concerne).

disillusionment [dɪsɪ'luːʒənmənt] *n* désillusionnement *m*, désillusion *f*.

disincentive [dɪsɪn'sɛntɪv] *n*: **it's a ~** c'est démotivant; **to be a ~ to sb** démotiver qn.

disinclined ['dɪsɪn'klaɪnd] *adj*: **to be ~ to do sth** être peu disposé(e) *or* peu enclin(e) à faire qch.

disinfect [dɪsɪn'fɛkt] vt désinfecter.

disinfectant [dɪsɪn'fɛktənt] n désinfectant m.

disinflation [dɪsɪn'fleɪʃən] n désinflation f.

disinformation [dɪsɪnfə'meɪʃən] n désinformation f.

disinherit [dɪsɪn'hɛrɪt] vt déshériter.

disintegrate [dɪs'ɪntɪgreɪt] vi se désintégrer.

disinterested [dɪs'ɪntrəstɪd] adj désintéressé(e).

disjointed [dɪs'dʒɔɪntɪd] adj décousu(e), incohérent(e).

disk [dɪsk] n (COMPUT) disquette f; **single-/double-sided** ~ disquette une face/double face.

disk drive n lecteur m de disquette.

diskette [dɪs'kɛt] n (COMPUT) disquette f.

disk operating system (DOS) n système m d'exploitation à disques (DOS).

dislike [dɪs'laɪk] n aversion f, antipathie f ♦ vt ne pas aimer; **to take a** ~ **to sb/sth** prendre qn/qch en grippe; **I** ~ **the idea** l'idée me déplaît.

dislocate ['dɪsləkeɪt] vt disloquer, déboîter; (services etc) désorganiser; **he has** ~**d his shoulder** il s'est disloqué l'épaule.

dislodge [dɪs'lɔdʒ] vt déplacer, faire bouger; (enemy) déloger.

disloyal [dɪs'lɔɪəl] adj déloyal(e).

dismal ['dɪzml] adj lugubre, maussade.

dismantle [dɪs'mæntl] vt démonter; (fort, warship) démanteler.

dismast [dɪs'mɑːst] vt démâter.

dismay [dɪs'meɪ] n consternation f ♦ vt consterner; **much to my** ~ à ma grande consternation, à ma grande inquiétude.

dismiss [dɪs'mɪs] vt congédier, renvoyer; (idea) écarter; (LAW) rejeter ♦ vi (MIL) rompre les rangs.

dismissal [dɪs'mɪsl] n renvoi m.

dismount [dɪs'maunt] vi mettre pied à terre.

disobedience [dɪsə'biːdɪəns] n désobéissance f.

disobedient [dɪsə'biːdɪənt] adj désobéissant(e), indiscipliné(e).

disobey [dɪsə'beɪ] vt désobéir à; (rule) transgresser, enfreindre.

disorder [dɪs'ɔːdə*] n désordre m; (rioting) désordres mpl; (MED) troubles mpl.

disorderly [dɪs'ɔːdəlɪ] adj (room) en désordre; (behaviour, retreat, crowd) désordonné(e).

disorderly conduct n (LAW) conduite f contraire aux bonnes mœurs.

disorganized [dɪs'ɔːgənaɪzd] adj désorganisé(e).

disorientated [dɪs'ɔːrɪɛnteɪtɪd] adj désorienté(e).

disown [dɪs'əun] vt renier.

disparaging [dɪs'pærɪdʒɪŋ] adj désobligeant(e); **to be** ~ **about sb/sth** faire des remarques désobligeantes sur qn/qch.

disparate ['dɪspərɪt] adj disparate.

disparity [dɪs'pærɪtɪ] n disparité f.

dispassionate [dɪs'pæʃənət] adj calme, froid(e); impartial(e), objectif(ive).

dispatch [dɪs'pætʃ] vt expédier, envoyer; (deal with: business) régler, en finir avec ♦ n envoi m, expédition f; (MIL, PRESS) dépêche f.

dispatch department n service m des expéditions.

dispatch rider n (MIL) estafette f.

dispel [dɪs'pɛl] vt dissiper, chasser.

dispensary [dɪs'pɛnsərɪ] n pharmacie f; (in chemist's) officine f.

dispense [dɪs'pɛns] vt distribuer, administrer; (medicine) préparer (et vendre); **to** ~ **sb from** dispenser qn de.

▶**dispense with** vt fus se passer de; (make unnecessary) rendre superflu(e).

dispenser [dɪs'pɛnsə*] n (device) distributeur m.

dispensing chemist [dɪs'pɛnsɪŋ-] n (BRIT) pharmacie f.

dispersal [dɪs'pɔːsl] n dispersion f; (ADMIN) déconcentration f.

disperse [dɪs'pɔːs] vt disperser; (knowledge) disséminer ♦ vi se disperser.

dispirited [dɪs'pɪrɪtɪd] adj découragé(e), déprimé(e).

displace [dɪs'pleɪs] vt déplacer.

displaced person [dɪs'pleɪst-] n (POL) personne déplacée.

displacement [dɪs'pleɪsmənt] n déplacement m.

display [dɪs'pleɪ] n (of goods) étalage m; affichage m; (computer ~: information) visualisation f; (: device) visuel m; (of feeling) manifestation f; (pej) ostentation f; (show, spectacle) spectacle m; (military ~) parade f militaire ♦ vt montrer; (goods) mettre à l'étalage, exposer; (results, departure times) afficher; (pej) faire étalage de; **on** ~ (exhibits) exposé(e), exhibé(e); (goods) à l'étalage.

display advertising n publicité rédactionnelle.

displease [dɪs'pliːz] vt mécontenter, contrarier; ~**d with** mécontent(e) de.

displeasure [dɪs'plɛʒə*] n mécontentement m.

disposable [dɪs'pəuzəbl] adj (pack etc) jetable; (income) disponible; ~ **nappy** (BRIT) couche f à jeter, couche-culotte f.

disposal [dɪs'pəuzl] n (availability, arrangement) disposition f; (of property etc: by selling) vente f; (: by giving away) cession f; (of rubbish) évacuation f, destruction f; **at one's** ~ à sa disposition; **to put sth at sb's** ~ mettre qch à la disposition de qn.

dispose [dɪs'pəuz] vt disposer.

▶**dispose of** vt fus (time, money) disposer de; (unwanted goods) se débarrasser de, se défaire de; (COMM: stock) écouler, vendre; (problem) expédier.

disposed [dɪs'pəuzd] adj: ~ **to do** disposé(e) à faire.

disposition [dɪspə'zɪʃən] *n* disposition *f*; (*temperament*) naturel *m*.

dispossess ['dɪspə'zɛs] *vt*: **to ~ sb (of)** déposséder qn (de).

disproportion [dɪsprə'pɔːʃən] *n* disproportion *f*.

disproportionate [dɪsprə'pɔːʃənət] *adj* disproportionné(e).

disprove [dɪs'pruːv] *vt* réfuter.

dispute [dɪs'pjuːt] *n* discussion *f*; (*also*: **industrial ~**) conflit *m* ♦ *vt* contester; (*matter*) discuter; (*victory*) disputer; **to be in** *or* **under ~** (*matter*) être en discussion; (*territory*) être contesté(e).

disqualification [dɪskwɔlɪfɪ'keɪʃən] *n* disqualification *f*; **~ (from driving)** (*BRIT*) retrait *m* du permis (de conduire).

disqualify [dɪs'kwɔlɪfaɪ] *vt* (*SPORT*) disqualifier; **to ~ sb for sth/from doing** (*status, situation*) rendre qn inapte à qch/à faire; (*authority*) signifier à qn l'interdiction de faire; **to ~ sb (from driving)** (*BRIT*) retirer à qn son permis (de conduire).

disquiet [dɪs'kwaɪət] *n* inquiétude *f*, trouble *m*.

disquieting [dɪs'kwaɪətɪŋ] *adj* inquiétant(e), alarmant(e).

disregard [dɪsrɪ'gɑːd] *vt* ne pas tenir compte de ♦ *n* (*indifference*): **~ (for)** (*feelings*) indifférence *f* (pour), insensibilité *f* (à); (*danger, money*) mépris *m* (pour).

disrepair ['dɪsrɪ'pɛə*] *n* mauvais état; **to fall into ~** (*building*) tomber en ruine; (*street*) se dégrader.

disreputable [dɪs'rɛpjutəbl] *adj* (*person*) de mauvaise réputation, peu recommandable; (*behaviour*) déshonorant(e); (*area*) mal famé(e), louche.

disrepute ['dɪsrɪ'pjuːt] *n* déshonneur *m*, discrédit *m*; **to bring into ~** faire tomber dans le discrédit.

disrespectful [dɪsrɪ'spɛktful] *adj* irrespectueux(euse).

disrupt [dɪs'rʌpt] *vt* (*plans, meeting, lesson*) perturber, déranger.

disruption [dɪs'rʌpʃən] *n* perturbation *f*, dérangement *m*.

disruptive [dɪs'rʌptɪv] *adj* perturbateur (trice).

dissatisfaction [dɪssætɪs'fækʃən] *n* mécontentement *m*, insatisfaction *f*.

dissatisfied [dɪs'sætɪsfaɪd] *adj*: **~ (with)** mécontent(e) *or* insatisfait(e) (de).

dissect [dɪ'sɛkt] *vt* disséquer; (*fig*) disséquer, éplucher.

disseminate [dɪ'sɛmɪneɪt] *vt* disséminer.

dissent [dɪ'sɛnt] *n* dissentiment *m*, différence *f* d'opinion.

dissenter [dɪ'sɛntə*] *n* (*REL, POL etc*) dissident/e.

dissertation [dɪsə'teɪʃən] *n* (*SCOL*) mémoire *m*.

disservice [dɪs'səːvɪs] *n*: **to do sb a ~** rendre

un mauvais service à qn; desservir qn.

dissident ['dɪsɪdnt] *adj, n* dissident(e).

dissimilar [dɪ'sɪmɪlə*] *adj*: **~ (to)** dissemblable (à), différent(e) (de).

dissipate ['dɪsɪpeɪt] *vt* dissiper; (*energy, efforts*) disperser.

dissipated ['dɪsɪpeɪtɪd] *adj* dissolu(e); débauché(e).

dissociate [dɪ'səʊʃɪeɪt] *vt* dissocier; **to ~ o.s. from** se désolidariser de.

dissolute ['dɪsəluːt] *adj* débauché(e), dissolu(e).

dissolution [dɪsə'luːʃən] *n* dissolution *f*.

dissolve [dɪ'zɔlv] *vt* dissoudre ♦ *vi* se dissoudre, fondre; (*fig*) disparaître.

dissuade [dɪ'sweɪd] *vt*: **to ~ sb (from)** dissuader qn (de).

distaff ['dɪstɑːf] *n*: **~ side** côté maternel.

distance ['dɪstns] *n* distance *f*; **what's the ~ to London?** à quelle distance se trouve Londres?; **it's within walking ~** on peut y aller à pied; **in the ~** au loin.

distant ['dɪstnt] *adj* lointain(e), éloigné(e); (*manner*) distant(e), froid(e).

distaste [dɪs'teɪst] *n* dégoût *m*.

distasteful [dɪs'teɪstful] *adj* déplaisant(e), désagréable.

Dist. Atty. *abbr* (*US*) = **district attorney**.

distemper [dɪs'tɛmpə*] *n* (*paint*) détrempe *f*, badigeon *m*; (*of dogs*) maladie *f* de Carré.

distended [dɪs'tɛndɪd] *adj* (*stomach*) dilaté(e).

distil, (*US*) **distill** [dɪs'tɪl] *vt* distiller.

distillery [dɪs'tɪlərɪ] *n* distillerie *f*.

distinct [dɪs'tɪŋkt] *adj* distinct(e); (*preference, progress*) marqué(e); **as ~ from** par opposition à, en contraste avec.

distinction [dɪs'tɪŋkʃən] *n* distinction *f*; (*in exam*) mention *f* très bien; **to draw a ~ between** faire une distinction entre; **a writer of ~** un écrivain réputé.

distinctive [dɪs'tɪŋktɪv] *adj* distinctif(ive).

distinctly [dɪs'tɪŋktlɪ] *adv* distinctement; (*specify*) expressément.

distinguish [dɪs'tɪŋgwɪʃ] *vt* distinguer ♦ *vi*: **to ~ between** (*concepts*) distinguer entre, faire une distinction entre; **to ~ o.s.** se distinguer.

distinguished [dɪs'tɪŋgwɪʃt] *adj* (*eminent, refined*) distingué(e); (*career*) remarquable, brillant(e).

distinguishing [dɪs'tɪŋgwɪʃɪŋ] *adj* (*feature*) distinctif(ive), caractéristique.

distort [dɪs'tɔːt] *vt* déformer.

distortion [dɪs'tɔːʃən] *n* déformation *f*.

distract [dɪs'trækt] *vt* distraire, déranger.

distracted [dɪs'træktɪd] *adj* (*look etc*) éperdu(e), égaré(e).

distraction [dɪs'trækʃən] *n* distraction *f*, dérangement *m*; **to drive sb to ~** rendre qn fou(folle).

distraught [dɪs'trɔːt] *adj* éperdu(e).

distress [dɪs'trɛs] *n* détresse *f*; (*pain*) douleur *f*

◆ *vt* affliger; **in ~** (*ship*) en perdition; (*plane*) en détresse; **~ed area** (*BRIT*) zone sinistrée.
distressing [dɪs'trɛsɪŋ] *adj* douloureux(euse), pénible, affligeant(e).
distress signal *n* signal *m* de détresse.
distribute [dɪs'trɪbjuːt] *vt* distribuer.
distribution [dɪstrɪ'bjuːʃən] *n* distribution *f*.
distribution cost *n* coût *m* de distribution.
distributor [dɪs'trɪbjutə*] *n* (*gen, TECH*) distributeur *m*; (*COMM*) concessionnaire *m/f*.
district ['dɪstrɪkt] *n* (*of country*) région *f*; (*of town*) quartier *m*; (*ADMIN*) district *m*.
district attorney *n* (*US*) ≈ procureur *m* de la République.
district council *n* (*BRIT*) ≈ conseil municipal.

En Grande-Bretagne, un **district council** *est une administration locale qui gère un* **district**. *Les conseillers ("***councillors***") sont élus au niveau local, en général tous les 4 ans. Le district council est financé par des impôts locaux et par des subventions du gouvernement.*

---

district nurse *n* (*BRIT*) infirmière visiteuse.
distrust [dɪs'trʌst] *n* méfiance *f*, doute *m* ◆ *vt* se méfier de.
distrustful [dɪs'trʌstful] *adj* méfiant(e).
disturb [dɪs'təːb] *vt* troubler; (*inconvenience*) déranger; **sorry to ~ you** excusez-moi de vous déranger.
disturbance [dɪs'təːbəns] *n* dérangement *m*; (*political etc*) troubles *mpl*; (*by drunks etc*) tapage *m*; **to cause a ~** troubler l'ordre public; **~ of the peace** (*LAW*) tapage injurieux ou nocturne.
disturbed [dɪs'təːbd] *adj* agité(e), troublé(e); **to be mentally/emotionally ~** avoir des problèmes psychologiques/affectifs.
disturbing [dɪs'təːbɪŋ] *adj* troublant(e), inquiétant(e).
disuse [dɪs'juːs] *n*: **to fall into ~** tomber en désuétude.
disused [dɪs'juːzd] *adj* désaffecté(e).
ditch [dɪtʃ] *n* fossé *m* ◆ *vt* (*col*) abandonner.
dither ['dɪðə*] *vi* hésiter.
ditto ['dɪtəu] *adv* idem.
divan [dɪ'væn] *n* divan *m*.
divan bed *n* divan-lit *m*.
dive [daɪv] *n* plongeon *m*; (*of submarine*) plongée *f*; (*AVIAT*) piqué *m*; (*pej: café, bar etc*) bouge *m* ◆ *vi* plonger.
diver ['daɪvə*] *n* plongeur *m*.
diverge [daɪ'vəːdʒ] *vi* diverger.
divergent [daɪ'vəːdʒənt] *adj* divergent(e).
diverse [daɪ'vəːs] *adj* divers(e).
diversification [daɪvəːsɪfɪ'keɪʃən] *n* diversification *f*.
diversify [daɪ'vəːsɪfaɪ] *vt* diversifier.
diversion [daɪ'vəːʃən] *n* (*BRIT AUT*) déviation *f*; (*distraction, MIL*) diversion *f*.
diversionary tactics [daɪ'vəːʃənrɪ-] *npl* tactique *fsg* de diversion.

diversity [daɪ'vəːsɪtɪ] *n* diversité *f*, variété *f*.
divert [daɪ'vəːt] *vt* (*BRIT: traffic*) dévier; (*plane*) dérouter; (*train, river*) détourner; (*amuse*) divertir.
divest [daɪ'vɛst] *vt*: **to ~ sb of** dépouiller qn de.
divide [dɪ'vaɪd] *vt* diviser; (*separate*) séparer ◆ *vi* se diviser; **to ~ (between** *or* **among)** répartir *or* diviser (entre); **40 ~d by 5** 40 divisé par 5.
▶**divide out** *vt*: **to ~ out (between** *or* **among)** distribuer *or* répartir (entre).
divided [dɪ'vaɪdɪd] *adj* (*fig: country, couple*) désuni(e); (*opinions*) partagé(e).
divided skirt *n* jupe-culotte *f*.
dividend ['dɪvɪdɛnd] *n* dividende *m*.
dividend cover *n* rapport *m* dividendes-résultat.
dividers [dɪ'vaɪdəz] *npl* compas *m* à pointes sèches; (*between pages*) feuillets *mpl* intercalaires.
divine [dɪ'vaɪn] *adj* divin(e) ◆ *vt* (*future*) prédire; (*truth*) deviner, entrevoir; (*water, metal*) détecter la présence de (*par l'intermédiaire de la radiesthésie*).
diving ['daɪvɪŋ] *n* plongée (sous-marine).
diving board *n* plongeoir *m*.
diving suit *n* scaphandre *m*.
divinity [dɪ'vɪnɪtɪ] *n* divinité *f*; (*as study*) théologie *f*.
division [dɪ'vɪʒən] *n* (*also BRIT FOOTBALL*) division *f*; (*separation*) séparation *f*; (*BRIT POL*) vote *m*; **~ of labour** division du travail.
divisive [dɪ'vaɪsɪv] *adj* qui entraîne la division, qui crée des dissensions.
divorce [dɪ'vɔːs] *n* divorce *m* ◆ *vt* divorcer d'avec.
divorced [dɪ'vɔːst] *adj* divorcé(e).
divorcee [dɪvɔː'siː] *n* divorcé/e.
divot ['dɪvət] *n* (*GOLF*) motte *f* de gazon.
divulge [daɪ'vʌldʒ] *vt* divulguer, révéler.
DIY *adj, n abbr* (*BRIT*) = **do-it-yourself**.
dizziness ['dɪzɪnɪs] *n* vertige *m*, étourdissement *m*.
dizzy ['dɪzɪ] *adj* (*height*) vertigineux(euse); **to make sb ~** donner le vertige à qn; **I feel ~** la tête me tourne, j'ai la tête qui tourne.
DJ *n abbr* = **disc jockey**.
d.j. *n abbr* = **dinner jacket**.
Djakarta [dʒə'kɑːtə] *n* Djakarta.
DJIA *n abbr* (*US STOCK EXCHANGE*) = *Dow-Jones Industrial Average*.
dl *abbr* (= *decilitre*) dl.
DLit(t) *n abbr* (= *Doctor of Literature, Doctor of Letters*) titre universitaire.
DLO *n abbr* = **dead-letter office**.
dm *abbr* (= *decimetre*) dm.
DMus *n abbr* (= *Doctor of Music*) titre universitaire.
DMZ *n abbr* = **demilitarized zone**.
DNA *n abbr* (= *deoxyribonucleic acid*) ADN *m*.
do *abbr* (= *ditto*) d°.

=== *KEYWORD*

do [du:] (*pt* **did**, *pp* **done**) *n* (*inf*: *party etc*) soirée *f*, fête *f*; (: *formal gathering*) réception *f*

♦ *vb* **1** (*in negative constructions*) *non traduit*; **I don't understand** je ne comprends pas

2 (*to form questions*) *non traduit*; **didn't you know?** vous ne le saviez pas?; **why didn't you come?** pourquoi n'êtes-vous pas venu?

3 (*for emphasis, in polite expressions*): **she does seem rather late** je trouve qu'elle est bien en retard; ~ **sit down/help yourself** asseyez-vous/servez-vous je vous en prie; **I DO wish I could go** j'aimerais tant y aller; **but I DO like it!** mais si, je l'aime!

4 (*used to avoid repeating vb*): **she swims better than I** ~ elle nage mieux que moi; ~ **you agree?** — **yes, I** ~/**no, I don't** vous êtes d'accord? — oui/non; **she lives in Glasgow** — **so** ~ **I** elle habite Glasgow — moi aussi; **who broke it?** — **I did** qui l'a cassé? — c'est moi

5 (*in question tags*): **he laughed, didn't he?** il a ri, n'est-ce pas?; **I don't know him,** ~ **I?** je ne crois pas le connaître

♦ *vt* (*gen: carry out, perform etc*) faire; (*visit: city, museum*) faire, visiter; **what are you** ~**ing tonight?** qu'est-ce que vous faites ce soir?; **what did he** ~ **with the cat?** qu'a t'il fait du chat?; **to** ~ **the cooking/washing-up** faire le cuisine/la vaisselle; **to** ~ **one's teeth/hair/nails** se brosser les dents/se coiffer/se faire les ongles; **the car was** ~**ing 100** la voiture faisait du 100 (à l'heure)

♦ *vi* **1** (*act, behave*) faire; ~ **as I** ~ faites comme moi

2 (*get on, fare*) marcher; **the firm is** ~**ing well** l'entreprise marche bien; **how** ~ **you** ~? comment allez-vous?; (*on being introduced*) enchanté(e)!

3 (*suit*) aller; **will it** ~? est-ce que ça ira?

4 (*be sufficient*) suffire, aller; **will £10** ~? est-ce que 10 livres suffiront?; **that'll** ~ ça suffit, ça ira; **that'll** ~! (*in annoyance*) ça va *or* suffit comme ça!; **to make** ~ **(with)** se contenter (de)

▶**do away with** *vt fus* abolir; (*kill*) supprimer

▶**do for** *vt fus* (*BRIT col: clean for*) faire le ménage chez

▶**do up** *vt* (*laces, dress*) attacher; (*buttons*) boutonner; (*zip*) fermer; (*renovate: room*) refaire; (: *house*) remettre à neuf; **to** ~ **o.s. up** se faire beau(belle)

▶**do with** *vt fus* (*need*): **I could** ~ **with a drink/some help** quelque chose à boire/un peu d'aide ne serait pas de refus; **it could** ~ **with a wash** ça ne lui ferait pas de mal d'être lavé; (*be connected*): **that has nothing to** ~ **with you** cela ne vous concerne pas; **I won't have anything to** ~ **with it** je ne veux pas m'en mêler; **what has that got to** ~ **with it?** quel est le rapport?, qu'est-ce que cela

vient faire là-dedans?

▶**do without** *vi* s'en passer ♦ *vt fus* se passer de.

===

DOA *abbr* (= *dead on arrival*) décédé(e) à l'admission.

d.o.b. *abbr* = **date of birth**.

doc [dɔk] *n* (*col*) toubib *m*.

docile ['dəusaɪl] *adj* docile.

dock [dɔk] *n* dock *m*; (*wharf*) quai *m*; (*LAW*) banc *m* des accusés ♦ *vi* se mettre à quai ♦ *vt*: **they** ~**ed a third of his wages** ils lui ont retenu *or* décompté un tiers de son salaire.

dock dues *npl* droits *mpl* de bassin.

docker ['dɔkə*] *n* docker *m*.

docket ['dɔkɪt] *n* bordereau *m*; (*on parcel etc*) étiquette *f or* fiche *f* (*décrivant le contenu d'un paquet etc*).

dockyard ['dɔkjɑːd] *n* chantier *m* de construction navale.

doctor ['dɔktə*] *n* médecin *m*, docteur *m*; (*PhD etc*) docteur ♦ *vt* (*cat*) couper; (*interfere with: food*) altérer; (: *drink*) frelater; (: *text, document*) arranger; ~**'s office** (*US*) cabinet *m* de consultation; **D~ of Philosophy (PhD)** doctorat *m*; titulaire *m/f* d'un doctorat.

doctorate ['dɔktərɪt] *n* doctorat *m*.

Le **doctorate** *est le diplôme universitaire le plus prestigieux. Il est le résultat d'au minimum trois années de recherches et est accordé après soutenance d'une thèse devant un jury. Le doctorat le plus courant est le PhD (Doctor of Philosophy), accordé en lettres, en sciences et en ingénierie, bien qu'il existe également d'autres doctorats spécialisés (en musique, en droit, etc); voir* **Bachelor's degree, Master's degree**

---

doctrine ['dɔktrɪn] *n* doctrine *f*.

docudrama ['dɔkjudrɑːmə] *n* (*TV*) docudrame *m*.

document *n* ['dɔkjumənt] document *m* ♦ *vt* ['dɔkjument] documenter.

documentary [dɔkju'mɛntərɪ] *adj, n* documentaire (*m*).

documentation [dɔkjumən'teɪʃən] *n* documentation *f*.

DOD *n abbr* (*US*) = **Department of Defense**.

doddering ['dɔdərɪŋ] *adj* (*senile*) gâteux(euse).

doddery ['dɔdərɪ] *adj* branlant(e).

doddle ['dɔdl] *n*: **it's a** ~ (*col*) c'est simple comme bonjour, c'est du gâteau.

Dodecanese (Islands) [dəudɪkə'niːz-] *n(pl)* Dodécanèse *m*.

dodge [dɔdʒ] *n* truc *m*; combine *f* ♦ *vt* esquiver, éviter ♦ *vi* faire un saut de côté; (*SPORT*) faire une esquive; **to** ~ **out of the way** s'esquiver; **to** ~ **through the traffic** se faufiler *or* faire de savantes manœuvres entre les voitures.

dodgems ['dɔdʒəmz] *npl* (*BRIT*) autos tampon-

neuses.
dodgy ['dɔdʒɪ] *adj* (*col: uncertain*) douteux(euse); (: *shady*) louche.
DOE *n abbr* (*BRIT*) = Department of the Environment; (*US*) = Department of Energy.
doe [dəu] *n* (*deer*) biche *f*; (*rabbit*) lapine *f*.
does [dʌz] *see* **do**.
doesn't ['dʌznt] = **does not**.
dog [dɔg] *n* chien/ne ♦ *vt* (*follow closely*) suivre de près, ne pas lâcher d'une semelle; (*fig: memory etc*) poursuivre, harceler; **to go to the ~s** (*nation etc*) aller à vau-l'eau.
dog biscuits *npl* biscuits *mpl* pour chien.
dog collar *n* collier *m* de chien; (*fig*) faux-col *m* d'ecclésiastique.
dog-eared ['dɔgɪəd] *adj* corné(e).
dog food *n* nourriture *f* pour les chiens *or* le chien.
dogged ['dɔgɪd] *adj* obstiné(e), opiniâtre.
doggy ['dɔgɪ] *n* (*col*) toutou *m*.
doggy bag *n petit sac pour emporter les restes.*
dogma ['dɔgmə] *n* dogme *m*.
dogmatic [dɔg'mætɪk] *adj* dogmatique.
do-gooder [du:'gudə*] *n* (*pej*) faiseur/euse de bonnes œuvres.
dogsbody ['dɔgzbɔdɪ] *n* (*BRIT*) bonne *f* à tout faire, tâcheron *m*.
doily ['dɔɪlɪ] *n* dessus *m* d'assiette.
doing ['duɪŋ] *n*: **this is your ~** c'est votre travail, c'est vous qui avez fait ça.
doings ['duɪŋz] *npl* activités *fpl*.
do-it-yourself ['du:ɪtjɔ:'sɛlf] *n* bricolage *m*.
doldrums ['dɔldrəmz] *npl*: **to be in the ~** avoir le cafard; être dans le marasme.
dole [dəul] *n* (*BRIT: payment*) allocation *f* de chômage; **on the ~** au chômage.
▶**dole out** *vt* donner au compte-goutte.
doleful ['dəulful] *adj* triste, lugubre.
doll [dɔl] *n* poupée *f*.
▶**doll up** *vt*: **to ~ o.s. up** se faire beau(belle).
dollar ['dɔlə*] *n* dollar *m*.
dollop ['dɔləp] *n* (*of butter, cheese*) bon morceau; (*of cream*) bonne cuillerée.
dolly ['dɔlɪ] *n* poupée *f*.
dolphin ['dɔlfɪn] *n* dauphin *m*.
domain [də'meɪn] *n* (*also fig*) domaine *m*.
dome [dəum] *n* dôme *m*.
domestic [də'mɛstɪk] *adj* (*duty, happiness*) familial(e); (*policy, affairs, flights*) intérieur(e); (*news*) national(e); (*animal*) domestique.
domesticated [də'mɛstɪkeɪtɪd] *adj* domestiqué(e); (*pej*) d'intérieur; **he's very ~** il participe volontiers aux tâches ménagères; question ménage, il est très organisé.
domesticity [dəumɛs'tɪsɪtɪ] *n* vie *f* de famille.
domestic servant *n* domestique *m/f*.
domicile ['dɔmɪsaɪl] *n* domicile *m*.
dominant ['dɔmɪnənt] *adj* dominant(e).
dominate ['dɔmɪneɪt] *vt* dominer.
domination [dɔmɪ'neɪʃən] *n* domination *f*.
domineering [dɔmɪ'nɪərɪŋ] *adj* domina-

teur(trice), autoritaire.
Dominican Republic [də'mɪnɪkən-] *n* République Dominicaine.
dominion [də'mɪnɪən] *n* domination *f*; territoire *m*; dominion *m*.
domino, **~es** ['dɔmɪnəu] *n* domino *m*; **~es** *n* (*game*) dominos *mpl*.
don [dɔn] *n* (*BRIT*) professeur *m* d'université ♦ *vt* revêtir.
donate [də'neɪt] *vt* faire don de, donner.
donation [də'neɪʃən] *n* donation *f*, don *m*.
done [dʌn] *pp of* **do**.
donkey ['dɔŋkɪ] *n* âne *m*.
donkey-work ['dɔŋkɪwə:k] *n* (*BRIT col*) le gros du travail, le plus dur (du travail).
donor ['dəunə*] *n* (*of blood etc*) donneur/euse; (*to charity*) donateur/trice.
donor card *n* carte *f* de don d'organes.
don't [dəunt] = **do not**.
doodle ['du:dl] *n* griffonnage *m*, gribouillage *m* ♦ *vi* griffonner, gribouiller.
doom [du:m] *n* (*fate*) destin *m*; (*ruin*) ruine *f* ♦ *vt*: **to be ~ed (to failure)** être voué(e) à l'échec.
doomsday ['du:mzdeɪ] *n* le Jugement dernier.
door [dɔ:*] *n* porte *f*; (*of vehicle*) portière *f*, porte; **to go from ~ to ~** aller de porte en porte.
doorbell ['dɔ:bɛl] *n* sonnette *f*.
door handle *n* poignée *f* de porte.
doorman ['dɔ:mən] *n* (*in hotel*) portier *m*; (*in block of flats*) concierge *m*.
doormat ['dɔ:mæt] *n* paillasson *m*.
doorpost ['dɔ:pəust] *n* montant *m* de porte.
doorstep ['dɔ:stɛp] *n* pas *m* de (la) porte, seuil *m*.
door-to-door ['dɔ:tə'dɔ:*] *adj*: **~ selling** vente *f* à domicile.
doorway ['dɔ:weɪ] *n* (*embrasure f de*) porte *f*.
dope [dəup] *n* (*col*) drogue *f*; (: *information*) tuyaux *mpl*, rancards *mpl* ♦ *vt* (*horse etc*) doper.
dopey ['dəupɪ] *adj* (*col*) à moitié endormi(e).
dormant ['dɔ:mənt] *adj* assoupi(e), en veilleuse; (*rule, law*) inappliqué(e).
dormer ['dɔ:mə*] *n* (*also*: **~ window**) lucarne *f*.
dormice ['dɔ:maɪs] *npl of* **dormouse**.
dormitory ['dɔ:mɪtrɪ] *n* dortoir *m*; (*US: hall of residence*) foyer *m* d'étudiants.
dormouse, *pl* **dormice** ['dɔ:maus, -maɪs] *n* loir *m*.
Dors *abbr* (*BRIT*) = Dorset.
DOS [dɔs] *n abbr* = **disk operating system**.
dosage ['dəusɪdʒ] *n* dose *f*; dosage *m*; (*on label*) posologie *f*.
dose [dəus] *n* dose *f*; (*BRIT: bout*) attaque *f* ♦ *vt*: **to ~ o.s.** se bourrer de médicaments; **a ~ of flu** une belle *or* bonne grippe.
dosser ['dɔsə*] *n* (*BRIT col*) clochard/e.
doss house ['dɔs-] *n* (*BRIT*) asile *m* de nuit.

dossier ['dɔsɪeɪ] *n* dossier *m*.

DOT *n abbr* (*US*) = Department of Transportation.

dot [dɔt] *n* point *m* ♦ *vt*: ~**ted with** parsemé(e) de; **on the ~** à l'heure tapante.

dot command *n* (*COMPUT*) commande précédée d'un point.

dote [dəut]: **to ~ on** *vt fus* être fou(folle) de.

dot-matrix printer [dɔt'meɪtrɪks-] *n* imprimante matricielle.

dotted line [dɔtɪd-] *n* ligne pointillée; (*AUT*) ligne discontinue; **to sign on the ~** signer à l'endroit indiqué *or* sur la ligne pointillée; (*fig*) donner son consentement.

dotty [dɔtɪ] *adj* (*col*) loufoque, farfelu(e).

double ['dʌbl] *adj* double ♦ *adv* (*fold*) en deux; (*twice*): **to cost ~** (**sth**) coûter le double (de qch) *or* deux fois plus (que qch) ♦ *n* double *m*; (*CINE*) doublure *f* ♦ *vt* doubler; (*fold*) plier en deux ♦ *vi* doubler; (*have two uses*): **to ~ as** servir aussi de; **~ five two six (5526)** (*BRIT TEL*) cinquante-cinq - vingt-six; **it's spelt with a ~ "l"** ça s'écrit avec deux "l"; **on the ~**, (*BRIT*) **at the ~** au pas de course.

▶**double back** *vi* (*person*) revenir sur ses pas.

▶**double up** *vi* (*bend over*) se courber, se plier; (*share room*) partager la chambre.

double bass *n* contrebasse *f*.

double bed *n* grand lit.

double-breasted ['dʌbl'brɛstɪd] *adj* croisé(e).

double-check ['dʌbl'tʃɛk] *vt, vi* revérifier.

double-clutch ['dʌbl'klʌtʃ] *vi* (*US*) faire un double débrayage.

double cream *n* (*BRIT*) crème fraîche épaisse.

doublecross ['dʌbl'krɔs] *vt* doubler, trahir.

doubledecker ['dʌbl'dɛkə*] *n* autobus *m* à impériale.

double declutch *vi* (*BRIT*) faire un double débrayage.

double exposure *n* (*PHOT*) surimpression *f*.

double glazing *n* (*BRIT*) double vitrage *m*.

double-page ['dʌblpeɪdʒ] *adj*: **~ spread** publicité *f* en double page.

double parking *n* stationnement *m* en double file.

double room *n* chambre *f* pour deux.

doubles ['dʌblz] *n* (*TENNIS*) double *m*.

double whammy [-'wæmɪ] *n* (*col*) double contretemps *m*.

doubly ['dʌblɪ] *adv* doublement, deux fois plus.

doubt [daut] *n* doute *m* ♦ *vt* douter de; **without (a) ~** sans aucun doute; **beyond ~** *adv* indubitablement ♦ *adj* indubitable; **to ~ that** douter que; **I ~ it very much** j'en doute fort.

doubtful ['dautful] *adj* douteux(euse); (*person*) incertain(e); **to be ~ about sth** avoir des doutes sur qch, ne pas être convaincu de qch; **I'm a bit ~** je n'en suis pas certain *or* sûr.

doubtless ['dautlɪs] *adv* sans doute, sûrement.

dough [dəu] *n* pâte *f*; (*col*: *money*) fric *m*, pognon *m*.

doughnut ['dəunʌt] *n* beignet *m*.

dour [duə*] *adj* austère.

douse [dauz] *vt* (*with water*) tremper, inonder; (*flames*) éteindre.

dove [dʌv] *n* colombe *f*.

Dover ['dəuvə*] *n* Douvres.

dovetail ['dʌvteɪl] *n*: **~ joint** assemblage *m* à queue d'aronde ♦ *vi* (*fig*) concorder.

dowager ['dauədʒə*] *n* douairière *f*.

dowdy ['daudɪ] *adj* démodé(e); mal fagoté(e).

Dow-Jones average ['dau'dʒəunz-] *n* (*US*) indice *m* Dow-Jones.

down [daun] *n* (*fluff*) duvet *m*; (*hill*) colline (dénudée) ♦ *adv* en bas ♦ *prep* en bas de ♦ *vt* (*enemy*) abattre; (*col*: *drink*) siffler; **~ there** là-bas (en bas), là au fond; **~ here** ici en bas; **the price of meat is ~** le prix de la viande a baissé; **I've got it ~ in my diary** c'est inscrit dans mon agenda; **to pay £2 ~** verser 2 livres d'arrhes *or* en acompte; **England is two goals ~** l'Angleterre a deux buts de retard; **to ~ tools** (*BRIT*) cesser le travail; **~ with X!** à bas X!

down-and-out ['daunəndaut] *n* (*tramp*) clochard/e.

down-at-heel ['daunət'hi:l] *adj* (*fig*) miteux(euse).

downbeat ['daunbi:t] *n* (*MUS*) temps frappé ♦ *adj* sombre, négatif(ive).

downcast ['daunka:st] *adj* démoralisé(e).

downer ['daunə*] *n* (*col*: *drug*) tranquillisant *m*; **to be on a ~** (*depressed*) flipper.

downfall ['daunfɔ:l] *n* chute *f*; ruine *f*.

downgrade ['daungreɪd] *vt* déclasser.

downhearted ['daun'ha:tɪd] *adj* découragé(e).

downhill ['daun'hɪl] *adv* (*face, look*) en aval, vers l'aval; (*roll, go*) vers le bas, en bas ♦ *n* (*SKI*: *also*: **~ race**) descente *f*; **to go ~** descendre; (*business*) péricliter, aller à vau-l'eau.

Downing Street ['daunɪŋ-] *n* (*BRIT*): **10 ~** résidence du Premier ministre.

Downing Street *est une rue de Westminster (à Londres) où se trouvent la résidence officielle du Premier ministre (numéro 10) et celle du ministre des Finances (numéro 11). Le nom "Downing Street" est souvent utilisé pour désigner le gouvernement britannique.*

download ['daunləud] *vt* télécharger.

down-market ['daun'ma:kɪt] *adj* (*product*) bas de gamme *inv*.

down payment *n* acompte *m*.

downplay ['daunpleɪ] *vt* (*US*) minimiser (l'importance de).

downpour ['daunpɔ:*] *n* pluie torrentielle, déluge *m*.

downright ['daunraɪt] *adj* franc(franche); (*refusal*) catégorique.

Downs [daunz] *npl* (*BRIT*): **the ~** *collines crayeuses du sud-est de l'Angleterre.*

downsize [daun'saız] *vt* réduire l'effectif de.

Down's syndrome [daunz-] *n* mongolisme *m*, trisomie *f*; **a ~ baby** un bébé mongolien *or* trisomique.

downstairs ['daun'steəz] *adv* (*on or to ground floor*) au rez-de-chaussée; (*on or to floor below*) à l'étage inférieur; **to come ~, to go ~** descendre (l'escalier).

downstream ['daunstri:m] *adv* en aval.

downtime ['dauntaım] *n* (*of machine etc*) temps mort; (*of person*) temps d'arrêt.

down-to-earth ['dauntu'ə:θ] *adj* terre à terre *inv*.

downtown ['daun'taun] *adv* en ville ♦ *adj* (*US*): **~ Chicago** le centre commerçant de Chicago.

downtrodden ['dauntrɔdn] *adj* opprimé(e).

down under *adv* en Australie (*or* Nouvelle Zélande).

downward ['daunwəd] *adj* vers le bas; **a ~ trend** une tendance à la baisse, une diminution progressive.

downward(s) ['daunwəd(z)] *adv* vers le bas.

dowry ['dauri] *n* dot *f*.

doz. *abbr* (= *dozen*) douz.

doze [dəuz] *vi* sommeiller.

▶**doze off** *vi* s'assoupir.

dozen ['dʌzn] *n* douzaine *f*; **a ~ books** une douzaine de livres; **80p a ~** 80p la douzaine; **~s of times** des centaines de fois.

DPh, DPhil *n abbr* (= *Doctor of Philosophy*) titre universitaire.

DPP *n abbr* (*BRIT*) = **Director of Public Prosecutions.**

DPT *n abbr* (*MED*: = *diphtheria, pertussis, tetanus*) DCT *m*.

DPW *n abbr* (*US*) = *Department of Public Works.*

Dr *abbr* (= *doctor*) Dr.

Dr. *abbr* (= *doctor*) Dr; (*in street names*) = **drive.**

dr *abbr* (*COMM*) = **debtor.**

drab [dræb] *adj* terne, morne.

draft [dra:ft] *n* brouillon *m*; (*of contract, document*) version *f* préliminaire; (*COMM*) traite *f*; (*US MIL*) contingent *m*; (*: call-up*) conscription *f* ♦ *vt* faire le brouillon de; (*document, report*) rédiger une version préliminaire de; *see also* **draught.**

drag [dræg] *vt* traîner; (*river*) draguer ♦ *vi* traîner ♦ *n* (*AVIAT, NAUT*) résistance *f*; (*col: person*) raseur/euse; (*: task etc*) corvée *f*; (*women's clothing*): **in ~** (en) travesti.

▶**drag away** *vt*: **to ~ away (from)** arracher *or* emmener de force (de).

▶**drag on** *vi* s'éterniser.

dragnet ['drægnɛt] *n* drège *f*, (*fig*) piège *m*, filets *mpl*.

dragon ['drægn] *n* dragon *m*.

dragonfly ['drægənflaı] *n* libellule *f*.

dragoon [drə'gu:n] *n* (*cavalryman*) dragon *m* ♦ *vt*: **to ~ sb into doing sth** (*BRIT*) forcer qn à faire qch.

drain [dreın] *n* égout *m*; (*on resources*) saignée *f* ♦ *vt* (*land, marshes*) drainer, assécher; (*vegetables*) égoutter; (*reservoir etc*) vider ♦ *vi* (*water*) s'écouler; **to feel ~ed (of energy** *or* **emotion)** être miné(e).

drainage ['dreınıdʒ] *n* système *m* d'égouts.

draining board ['dreınıŋ-], (*US*) **drainboard** ['dreınbɔ:d] *n* égouttoir *m*.

drainpipe ['dreınpaıp] *n* tuyau *m* d'écoulement.

drake [dreık] *n* canard *m* (mâle).

dram [dræm] *n* petit verre.

drama ['dra:mə] *n* (*art*) théâtre *m*, art *m* dramatique; (*play*) pièce *f*; (*event*) drame *m*.

dramatic [drə'mætık] *adj* (*THEAT*) dramatique; (*impressive*) spectaculaire.

dramatically [drə'mætıklı] *adv* de façon spectaculaire.

dramatist ['dræmətıst] *n* auteur *m* dramatique.

dramatize ['dræmətaız] *vt* (*events etc*) dramatiser; (*adapt*) adapter pour la télévision (*or* pour l'écran).

drank [dræŋk] *pt of* **drink.**

drape [dreıp] *vt* draper.

draper ['dreıpə*] *n* (*BRIT*) marchand/e de nouveautés.

drapes [dreıps] *npl* (*US*) rideaux *mpl*.

drastic ['dræstık] *adj* (*measures*) d'urgence, énergique; (*change*) radical(e).

drastically ['dræstıklı] *adv* radicalement.

draught, (*US*) **draft** [dra:ft] *n* courant *m* d'air; (*of chimney*) tirage *m*; (*NAUT*) tirant *m* d'eau; **on ~** (*beer*) à la pression.

draught beer *n* bière *f* (à la) pression.

draughtboard ['dra:ftbɔ:d] *n* (*BRIT*) damier *m*.

draughts [dra:fts] *n* (*BRIT*) (jeu *m* de) dames *fpl*.

draughtsman, (*US*) **draftsman** ['dra:ftsmən] *n* dessinateur/trice (industriel(le)).

draughtsmanship, (*US*) **draftsmanship** ['dra:ftsmənʃıp] *n* (*technique*) dessin industriel; (*art*) graphisme *m*.

draw [drɔ:] *vb* (*pt* **drew,** *pp* **drawn** [dru:, drɔ:n]) *vt* tirer; (*attract*) attirer; (*picture*) dessiner; (*line, circle*) tracer; (*money*) retirer; (*comparison, distinction*): **to ~ (between)** faire (entre) ♦ *vi* (*SPORT*) faire match nul ♦ *n* match nul; (*lottery*) loterie *f*; (*: picking of ticket*) tirage *m* au sort; **to ~ to a close** toucher à *or* tirer à sa fin; **to ~ near** *vi* s'approcher; approcher.

▶**draw back** *vi* (*move back*): **to ~ back (from)** reculer (de).

▶**draw in** *vi* (*BRIT: car*) s'arrêter le long du trottoir; (*: train*) entrer en gare *or* dans la station.

▶**draw on** *vt* (*resources*) faire appel à; (*imagination, person*) avoir recours à, faire appel à.

▶**draw out** *vi* (*lengthen*) s'allonger ♦ *vt* (*money*) retirer.

▶**draw up** *vi* (*stop*) s'arrêter ♦ *vt* (*document*) établir, dresser; (*plans*) formuler, dessiner.

drawback ['drɔːbæk] *n* inconvénient *m*, désavantage *m*.

drawbridge ['drɔːbrɪdʒ] *n* pont-levis *m*.

drawee [drɔː'iː] *n* tiré *m*.

drawer [drɔː*] *n* tiroir *m*; ['drɔːə*] (*of cheque*) tireur *m*.

drawing ['drɔːɪŋ] *n* dessin *m*.

drawing board *n* planche *f* à dessin.

drawing pin *n* (*BRIT*) punaise *f*.

drawing room *n* salon *m*.

drawl [drɔːl] *n* accent traînant.

drawn [drɔːn] *pp of* **draw** ♦ *adj* (*haggard*) tiré(e), crispé(e).

drawstring ['drɔːstrɪŋ] *n* cordon *m*.

dread [drɛd] *n* épouvante *f*, effroi *m* ♦ *vt* redouter, appréhender.

dreadful ['drɛdful] *adj* épouvantable, affreux(euse).

dream [driːm] *n* rêve *m* ♦ *vt, vi* (*pt, pp* **dreamed** *or* **dreamt** [drɛmt]) rêver; **to have a ~ about sb/sth** rêver à qn/qch; **sweet ~s!** faites de beaux rêves!

▶**dream up** *vt* inventer.

dreamer ['driːmə*] *n* rêveur/euse.

dream world *n* monde *m* imaginaire.

dreamy ['driːmɪ] *adj* (*absent-minded*) rêveur(euse).

dreary ['drɪərɪ] *adj* triste; monotone.

dredge [drɛdʒ] *vt* draguer.

▶**dredge up** *vt* draguer; (*fig: unpleasant facts*) (faire) ressortir.

dredger ['drɛdʒə*] *n* (*ship*) dragueur *m*; (*machine*) drague *f*; (*BRIT: also:* **sugar ~**) saupoudreuse *f*.

dregs [drɛgz] *npl* lie *f*.

drench [drɛntʃ] *vt* tremper; **~ed to the skin** trempé(e) jusqu'aux os.

dress [drɛs] *n* robe *f*; (*clothing*) habillement *m*, tenue *f* ♦ *vt* habiller; (*wound*) panser; (*food*) préparer ♦ *vi*: **she ~es very well** elle s'habille très bien; **to ~ o.s., to get ~ed** s'habiller; **to ~ a shop window** faire l'étalage *or* la vitrine.

▶**dress up** *vi* s'habiller; (*in fancy dress*) se déguiser.

dress circle *n* premier balcon.

dress designer *n* modéliste *m/f*, dessinateur/trice de mode.

dresser ['drɛsə*] *n* (*THEAT*) habilleur/euse; (*also:* **window ~**) étalagiste *m/f*; (*furniture*) vaisselier *m*.

dressing ['drɛsɪŋ] *n* (*MED*) pansement *m*; (*CULIN*) sauce *f*, assaisonnement *m*.

dressing gown *n* (*BRIT*) robe *f* de chambre.

dressing room *n* (*THEAT*) loge *f*; (*SPORT*) vestiaire *m*.

dressing table *n* coiffeuse *f*.

dressmaker ['drɛsmeɪkə*] *n* couturière *f*.

dressmaking ['drɛsmeɪkɪŋ] *n* couture *f*; travaux *mpl* de couture.

dress rehearsal *n* (répétition *f*) générale *f*.

dress shirt *n* chemise *f* à plastron.

dressy ['drɛsɪ] *adj* (*col: clothes*) (qui fait) habillé(e).

drew [druː] *pt of* **draw**.

dribble ['drɪbl] *vi* tomber goutte à goutte; (*baby*) baver ♦ *vt* (*ball*) dribbler.

dried [draɪd] *adj* (*fruit, beans*) sec(sèche); (*eggs, milk*) en poudre.

drier ['draɪə*] *n* = **dryer**.

drift [drɪft] *n* (*of current etc*) force *f*; direction *f*; (*of sand etc*) amoncellement *m*; (*of snow*) rafale *f*, coulée *f*; (*: on ground*) congère *f*; (*general meaning*) sens général ♦ *vi* (*boat*) aller à la dérive, dériver; (*sand, snow*) s'amonceler, s'entasser; **to let things ~** laisser les choses aller à la dérive; **to ~ apart** (*friends, lovers*) s'éloigner l'un de l'autre; **I get** *or* **catch your ~** je vois en gros ce que vous voulez dire.

drifter ['drɪftə*] *n* personne *f* sans but dans la vie.

driftwood ['drɪftwud] *n* bois flotté.

drill [drɪl] *n* perceuse *f*; (*bit*) foret *m*; (*of dentist*) roulette *f*, fraise *f*; (*MIL*) exercice *m* ♦ *vt* percer; (*soldiers*) faire faire l'exercice à; (*pupils: in grammar*) faire faire des exercices à ♦ *vi* (*for oil*) faire un *or* des forage(s).

drilling ['drɪlɪŋ] *n* (*for oil*) forage *m*.

drilling rig *n* (*on land*) tour *f* (de forage), derrick *m*; (*at sea*) plate-forme *f* de forage.

drily ['draɪlɪ] *adv* = **dryly**.

drink [drɪŋk] *n* boisson *f* ♦ *vt, vi* (*pt* **drank**, *pp* **drunk** [dræŋk, drʌŋk]) boire; **to have a ~** boire quelque chose, boire un verre; **a ~ of water** un verre d'eau; **would you like something to ~?** aimeriez-vous boire quelque chose?; **we had ~s before lunch** on a pris l'apéritif.

▶**drink in** *vt* (*fresh air*) inspirer profondément; (*story*) avaler, ne pas perdre une miette de; (*sight*) se remplir la vue de.

drinkable ['drɪŋkəbl] *adj* (*not dangerous*) potable; (*palatable*) buvable.

drink-driving ['drɪŋk'draɪvɪŋ] *n* conduite *f* en état d'ivresse.

drinker ['drɪŋkə*] *n* buveur/euse.

drinking ['drɪŋkɪŋ] *n* (*drunkenness*) boisson *f*, alcoolisme *m*.

drinking fountain *n* (*in park etc*) fontaine publique; (*in building*) jet *m* d'eau potable.

drinking water *n* eau *f* potable.

drip [drɪp] *n* goutte *f*; (*sound: of water etc*) bruit *m* de l'eau qui tombe goutte à goutte; (*MED*) goutte-à-goutte *m inv*, perfusion *f*; (*col: person*) lavette *f*, nouille *f* ♦ *vi* tomber goutte à goutte; (*washing*) s'égoutter; (*wall*) suinter.

drip-dry ['drɪp'draɪ] *adj* (*shirt*) sans repassage.

drip-feed ['drɪpfiːd] *vt* alimenter au goutte-à-goutte *or* par perfusion.

dripping ['drɪpɪŋ] *n* graisse *f* de rôti ♦ *adj*: **~ wet** trempé(e).

drive [draɪv] *n* promenade *f or* trajet *m* en voiture; (also: ~**way**) allée f; (energy) dynamisme m, énergie f; (PSYCH) besoin m; pulsion f; (push) effort (concerté); campagne f; (SPORT) drive m; (TECH) entraînement m; traction f; transmission f; (COMPUT: also: **disk** ~) lecteur m de disquette ♦ vb (pt **drove**, pp **driven** [drəuv, 'drɪvn]) vt conduire; (nail) enfoncer; (push) chasser, pousser; (TECH: motor) actionner; entraîner ♦ vi (be at the wheel) conduire; (travel by car) aller en voiture; **to go for a** ~ aller faire une promenade en voiture; **it's 3 hours'** ~ **from London** Londres est à 3 heures de route; **left-/right-hand** ~ (AUT) conduite f à gauche/droite; **front-/rear-wheel** ~ (AUT) traction f avant/arrière; **to** ~ **sb to (do) sth** pousser or conduire qn à (faire) qch; **to** ~ **sb mad** rendre qn fou(folle).

▶**drive at** vt fus (fig: intend, mean) vouloir dire, en venir à.

▶**drive on** vi poursuivre sa route, continuer; (after stopping) reprendre sa route, repartir ♦ vt (incite, encourage) inciter.

drive-by ['draɪvbaɪ] n (also: ~ **shooting**) (tentative d')assassinat par coups de feu tirés d'une voiture.

drive-in ['draɪvɪn] adj, n (esp US) drive-in (m).

drive-in window n (US) guichet-auto m.

drivel ['drɪvl] n (col) idioties fpl, imbécillités fpl.

driven ['drɪvn] pp of **drive**.

driver ['draɪvə*] n conducteur/trice; (of taxi, bus) chauffeur m.

driver's license n (US) permis m de conduire.

driveway ['draɪvweɪ] n allée f.

driving ['draɪvɪŋ] adj: ~ **rain** n pluie battante ♦ n conduite f.

driving force n locomotive f, élément m dynamique.

driving instructor n moniteur m d'auto-école.

driving lesson n leçon f de conduite.

driving licence n (BRIT) permis m de conduire.

driving school n auto-école f.

driving test n examen m du permis de conduire.

drizzle ['drɪzl] n bruine f, crachin m ♦ vi bruiner.

droll [drəul] adj drôle.

dromedary ['drɒmədərɪ] n dromadaire m.

drone [drəun] vi (bee) bourdonner; (engine etc) ronronner; (also: ~ **on**) parler d'une voix monocorde ♦ n bourdonnement m; ronronnement m; (male bee) faux-bourdon m.

drool [druːl] vi baver; **to** ~ **over sb/sth** (fig) baver d'admiration or être en extase devant qn/qch.

droop [druːp] vi s'affaisser; tomber.

drop [drɒp] n goutte f; (fall: also in price) baisse f; (: in salary) réduction f; (also: **parachute** ~) saut m; (of cliff) dénivellation f; à-pic m ♦ vt

laisser tomber; (voice, eyes, price) baisser; (set down from car) déposer ♦ vi (wind, temperature, price, voice) tomber; (numbers, attendance) diminuer; ~**s** npl (MED) gouttes; **cough** ~**s** pastilles fpl pour la toux; **a** ~ **of 10%** une baisse (or réduction) de 10%; **to** ~ **anchor** jeter l'ancre; **to** ~ **sb a line** mettre un mot à qn.

▶**drop in** vi (col: visit): **to** ~ **in (on)** faire un saut (chez), passer (chez).

▶**drop off** vi (sleep) s'assoupir ♦ vt: **to** ~ **sb off** déposer qn.

▶**drop out** vi (withdraw) se retirer; (student etc) abandonner, décrocher.

droplet ['drɒplɪt] n gouttelette f.

dropout ['drɒpaut] n (from society) marginal/e; (from university) drop-out m/f, dropé/e.

dropper ['drɒpə*] n (MED etc) compte-gouttes m inv.

droppings ['drɒpɪŋz] npl crottes fpl.

dross [drɒs] n déchets mpl; rebut m.

drought [draut] n sécheresse f.

drove [drəuv] pt of **drive** ♦ n: ~**s of people** une foule de gens.

drown [draun] vt noyer; (also: ~ **out**: sound) couvrir, étouffer ♦ vi se noyer.

drowse [drauz] vi somnoler.

drowsy ['drauzɪ] adj somnolent(e).

drudge [drʌdʒ] n bête f de somme (fig).

drudgery ['drʌdʒərɪ] n corvée f.

drug [drʌg] n médicament m; (narcotic) drogue f ♦ vt droguer; **he's on** ~**s** il se drogue; (MED) il est sous médication.

drug addict n toxicomane m/f.

druggist ['drʌgɪst] n (US) pharmacien/ne-droguiste.

drug peddler n revendeur/euse de drogue.

drugstore ['drʌgstɔː*] n (US) pharmacie-droguerie f, drugstore m.

drum [drʌm] n tambour m; (for oil, petrol) bidon m ♦ vt: **to** ~ **one's fingers on the table** pianoter or tambouriner sur la table; ~**s** npl (MUS) batterie f.

▶**drum up** vt (enthusiasm, support) susciter, rallier.

drummer ['drʌmə*] n (joueur m de) tambour m.

drum roll n roulement m de tambour.

drumstick ['drʌmstɪk] n (MUS) baguette f de tambour; (of chicken) pilon m.

drunk [drʌŋk] pp of **drink** ♦ adj ivre, soûl(e) ♦ n soûlard/e; homme/femme soûl(e); **to get** ~ s'enivrer, se soûler.

drunkard ['drʌŋkəd] n ivrogne m/f.

drunken ['drʌŋkən] adj ivre, soûl(e); (habitual) ivrogne, d'ivrogne; ~ **driving** conduite f en état d'ivresse.

drunkenness ['drʌŋkənnɪs] n ivresse f, ivrognerie f.

dry [draɪ] adj sec(sèche); (day) sans pluie; (humour) pince-sans-rire; (uninteresting) aride, rébarbatif(ive) ♦ vt sécher; (clothes) faire sécher ♦ *vi* sécher; **on ~ land** sur la terre ferme; **to ~ one's hands/hair/eyes** se sécher les mains/les cheveux/les yeux.

►**dry up** *vi* (*also fig: source of supply, imagination*) se tarir; (*: speaker*) sécher, rester sec.

dry-clean ['draɪ'kliːn] *vt* nettoyer à sec.

dry-cleaner ['draɪ'kliːnə*] *n* teinturier *m*.

dry-cleaner's ['draɪ'kliːnəz] *n* teinturerie *f*.

dry-cleaning ['draɪ'kliːnɪŋ] *n* nettoyage *m* à sec.

dry dock *n* (*NAUT*) cale sèche, bassin *m* de radoub.

dryer ['draɪə*] *n* séchoir *m*; (*spin-~*) essoreuse *f*.

dry goods *npl* (*COMM*) textiles *mpl*, mercerie *f*.

dry goods store *n* (*US*) magasin *m* de nouveautés.

dry ice *n* neige *f* carbonique.

dryly ['draɪlɪ] *adv* sèchement, d'un ton sec.

dryness ['draɪnɪs] *n* sécheresse *f*.

dry rot *n* pourriture sèche (*du bois*).

dry run *n* (*fig*) essai *m*.

dry ski slope *n* piste (de ski) artificielle.

DSc *n abbr* (= *Doctor of Science*) titre universitaire.

DSS *n abbr* (*BRIT*) = *Department of Social Security*.

DST *abbr* (*US: = Daylight Saving Time*) heure d'été.

DT *n abbr* (*COMPUT*) = **data transmission**.

DTI *n abbr* (*BRIT*) = *Department of Trade and Industry*.

DTP *n abbr* = **desktop publishing**.

DT's [diː'tiːz] *n abbr* (*col: = delirium tremens*) delirium tremens *m*.

dual ['djuəl] *adj* double.

dual carriageway *n* (*BRIT*) route *f* à quatre voies.

dual-control ['djuəlkən'trəul] *adj* à doubles commandes.

dual nationality *n* double nationalité *f*.

dual-purpose ['djuəl'pəːpəs] *adj* à double emploi.

dubbed [dʌbd] *adj* (*CINE*) doublé(e); (*nicknamed*) surnommé(e).

dubious ['djuːbɪəs] *adj* hésitant(e), incertain(e); (*reputation, company*) douteux(euse); **I'm very ~ about it** j'ai des doutes sur la question, je n'en suis pas sûr du tout.

Dublin ['dʌblɪn] *n* Dublin.

Dubliner ['dʌblɪnə*] *n* habitant/e de Dublin; originaire *m/f* de Dublin.

duchess ['dʌtʃɪs] *n* duchesse *f*.

duck [dʌk] *n* canard *m* ♦ *vi* se baisser vivement, baisser subitement la tête ♦ *vt* plonger dans l'eau.

duckling ['dʌklɪŋ] *n* caneton *m*.

duct [dʌkt] *n* conduite *f*, canalisation *f*; (*ANAT*) conduit *m*.

dud [dʌd] *n* (*shell*) obus non éclaté; (*object, tool*): **it's a ~** c'est de la camelote, ça ne marche pas ♦ *adj* (*BRIT: cheque*) sans provi-

sion; (*: note, coin*) faux(fausse).

due [djuː] *adj* dû(due); (*expected*) attendu(e); (*fitting*) qui convient ♦ *n* dû *m* ♦ *adv*: **~ north** droit vers le nord; **~s** *npl* (*for club, union*) cotisation *f*; (*in harbour*) droits *mpl* (de port); **in ~ course** en temps utile *or* voulu; (*in the end*) finalement; **~ to** dû à; causé par; **the rent is ~ on the 30th** il faut payer le loyer le 30; **the train is ~ at 8** le train est attendu à 8 h; **she is ~ back tomorrow** elle doit rentrer demain; **I am ~ 6 days' leave** j'ai droit à 6 jours de congé.

due date *n* date *f* d'échéance.

duel ['djuəl] *n* duel *m*.

duet [djuː'ɛt] *n* duo *m*.

duff [dʌf] *adj* (*BRIT col*) nullard(e), nul(le).

duffelbag, duffle bag ['dʌflbæg] *n* sac marin.

duffelcoat, duffle coat ['dʌflkəut] *n* duffel-coat *m*.

duffer ['dʌfə*] *n* (*col*) nullard/e.

dug [dʌg] *pt, pp of* **dig**.

dugout ['dʌgaut] *n* (*SPORT*) banc *m* de touche.

duke [djuːk] *n* duc *m*.

dull [dʌl] *adj* (*boring*) ennuyeux(euse); (*slow*) borné(e); (*lacklustre*) morne, terne; (*sound, pain*) sourd(e); (*weather, day*) gris(e), maussade; (*blade*) émoussé(e) ♦ *vt* (*pain, grief*) atténuer; (*mind, senses*) engourdir.

duly ['djuːlɪ] *adv* (*on time*) en temps voulu; (*as expected*) comme il se doit.

dumb [dʌm] *adj* muet(te); (*stupid*) bête; **to be struck ~** (*fig*) rester abasourdi(e), être sidéré(e).

dumbbell ['dʌmbɛl] *n* (*SPORT*) haltère *m*.

dumbfounded [dʌm'faundɪd] *adj* sidéré(e).

dummy ['dʌmɪ] *n* (*tailor's model*) mannequin *m*; (*SPORT*) feinte *f*; (*BRIT: for baby*) tétine *f* ♦ *adj* faux(fausse), factice.

dummy run *n* essai *m*.

dump [dʌmp] *n* tas *m* d'ordures; (*place*) décharge (publique); (*MIL*) dépôt *m*; (*COMPUT*) listage *m* (de la mémoire) ♦ *vt* (*put down*) déposer; déverser; (*get rid of*) se débarrasser de; (*COMPUT*) lister; (*COMM: goods*) vendre à perte (*sur le marché extérieur*); **to be (down) in the ~s** (*col*) avoir le cafard, broyer du noir.

dumping ['dʌmpɪŋ] *n* (*ECON*) dumping *m*; (*of rubbish*): **"no ~"** "décharge interdite".

dumpling ['dʌmplɪŋ] *n* boulette *f* (de pâte).

dumpy ['dʌmpɪ] *adj* courtaud(e), boulot(te).

dunce [dʌns] *n* âne *m*, cancre *m*.

dune [djuːn] *n* dune *f*.

dung [dʌŋ] *n* fumier *m*.

dungarees [dʌŋgə'riːz] *npl* bleu(s) *m(pl)*; (*for child, woman*) salopette *f*.

dungeon ['dʌndʒən] *n* cachot *m*.

dunk [dʌŋk] *vt* tremper.

Dunkirk [dʌn'kəːk] *n* Dunkerque *f*.

duo ['djuːəu] *n* (*gen, MUS*) duo *m*.

duodenal [djuːəu'diːnl] *adj* duodénal(e); **~ ulcer** ulcère *m* du duodénum.

dupe [dju:p] *n* dupe *f* ♦ *vt* duper, tromper.
duplex ['dju:plɛks] *n* (*US: also:* ~ **apartment**) duplex *m*.
duplicate *n* ['dju:plɪkət] double *m*, copie exacte; (*copy of letter etc*) duplicata *m* ♦ *adj* (*copy*) en double ♦ *vt* ['dju:plɪkeɪt] faire un double de; (*on machine*) polycopier; **in** ~ en deux exemplaires, en double; ~ **key** double *m* de la (*or* d'une) clé.
duplicating machine ['dju:plɪkeɪtɪŋ-], **duplicator** ['dju:plɪkeɪtə*] *n* duplicateur *m*.
duplicity [dju:'plɪsɪtɪ] *n* duplicité *f*, fausseté *f*.
Dur *abbr* (*BRIT*) = Durham.
durability [djuərə'bɪlɪtɪ] *n* solidité *f*; durabilité *f*.
durable ['djuərəbl] *adj* durable; (*clothes, metal*) résistant(e), solide.
duration [djuə'reɪʃən] *n* durée *f*.
duress [djuə'rɛs] *n*: **under** ~ sous la contrainte.
Durex ['djuərɛks] *n* ® (*BRIT*) préservatif (masculin).
during ['djuərɪŋ] *prep* pendant, au cours de.
dusk [dʌsk] *n* crépuscule *m*.
dusky ['dʌskɪ] *adj* sombre.
dust [dʌst] *n* poussière *f* ♦ *vt* (*furniture*) essuyer, épousseter; (*cake etc*) **to** ~ **with** saupoudrer de.
▶**dust off** *vt* (*also fig*) dépoussiérer.
dustbin ['dʌstbɪn] *n* (*BRIT*) poubelle *f*.
duster ['dʌstə*] *n* chiffon *m*.
dust jacket *n* jacquette *f*.
dustman ['dʌstmən] *n* (*BRIT*) boueux *m*, éboueur *m*.
dustpan ['dʌstpæn] *n* pelle *f* à poussière.
dusty ['dʌstɪ] *adj* poussiéreux(euse).
Dutch [dʌtʃ] *adj* hollandais(e), néerlandais(e) ♦ *n* (*LING*) hollandais *m*, néerlandais *m* ♦ *adv*: **to go** ~ *or* **d**~ partager les frais; **the** ~ *npl* les Hollandais, les Néerlandais.
Dutch auction *n* enchères *fpl* à la baisse.
Dutchman ['dʌtʃmən], **Dutchwoman** ['dʌtʃwumən] *n* Hollandais/e.
dutiable ['dju:tɪəbl] *adj* taxable; soumis(e) à des droits de douane.
dutiful ['dju:tɪful] *adj* (*child*) respectueux(euse); (*husband, wife*) plein(e) d'égards, prévenant(e); (*employee*) consciencieux(euse).
duty ['dju:tɪ] *n* devoir *m*; (*tax*) droit *m*, taxe *f*; **duties** *npl* fonctions *fpl*; **to make it one's** ~ **to do sth** se faire un devoir de faire qch; **to pay** ~ **on sth** payer un droit *or* une taxe sur qch; **on** ~ de service; (*at night etc*) de garde; **off** ~ libre, pas de service or de garde.
duty-free ['dju:tɪ'fri:] *adj* exempté(e) de douane, hors-taxe; ~ **shop** boutique *f* hors-taxe.
duty officer *n* (*MIL etc*) officier *m* de permanence.
duvet ['du:veɪ] *n* (*BRIT*) couette *f*.
DV *abbr* (= *Deo volente*) si Dieu le veut.

DVLA *n abbr* (*BRIT*: = *Driver and Vehicle Licensing Agency*) service qui délivre les cartes grises et les permis de conduire.
DVM *n abbr* (*US*: = *Doctor of Veterinary Medicine*) titre universitaire.
dwarf [dwɔ:f] *n* nain/e ♦ *vt* écraser.
dwell [dwɛl], *pt, pp* **dwelt** [dwɛl, dwɛlt] *vi* demeurer.
▶**dwell on** *vt fus* s'étendre sur.
dweller ['dwɛlə*] *n* habitant/e.
dwelling ['dwɛlɪŋ] *n* habitation *f*, demeure *f*.
dwindle ['dwɪndl] *vi* diminuer, décroître.
dwindling ['dwɪndlɪŋ] *adj* décroissant(e), en diminution.
dye [daɪ] *n* teinture *f* ♦ *vt* teindre; **hair** ~ teinture pour les cheveux.
dyestuffs ['daɪstʌfs] *npl* colorants *mpl*.
dying ['daɪɪŋ] *adj* mourant(e), agonisant(e).
dyke [daɪk] *n* (*embankment*) digue *f*.
dynamic [daɪ'næmɪk] *adj* dynamique.
dynamics [daɪ'næmɪks] *n or npl* dynamique *f*.
dynamite ['daɪnəmaɪt] *n* dynamite *f* ♦ *vt* dynamiter, faire sauter à la dynamite.
dynamo ['daɪnəməu] *n* dynamo *f*.
dynasty ['dɪnəstɪ] *n* dynastie *f*.
dysentery ['dɪsntrɪ] *n* dysenterie *f*.
dyslexia [dɪs'lɛksɪə] *n* dyslexie *f*.
dyslexic [dɪs'lɛksɪk] *adj, n* dyslexique *m/f*.
dyspepsia [dɪs'pɛpsɪə] *n* dyspepsie *f*.
dystrophy ['dɪstrəfɪ] *n* dystrophie *f*; **muscular** ~ dystrophie musculaire.

E e

E, e [i:] *n* (*letter*) E, e *m*; (*MUS*): **E** mi *m*; **E for Edward**, (*US*) **E for Easy** E comme Eugène.
E *abbr* (= *east*) E ♦ *n abbr* (*DRUGS*) = ecstasy.
E111 ['i:wʌnɪ'lɛvn] *n abbr* (*also:* **form** ~) formulaire *m* E111.
ea. *abbr* = **each**.
E.A. *n abbr* (*US*: = *educational age*) niveau scolaire.
each [i:tʃ] *adj* chaque ♦ *pron* chacun(e); ~ **one** chacun(e); ~ **other** se (*or* nous *etc*); **they hate** ~ **other** ils se détestent (mutuellement); **you are jealous of** ~ **other** vous êtes jaloux l'un de l'autre; ~ **day** chaque jour, tous les jours; **they have 2 books** ~ ils ont 2 livres chacun; **they cost £5** ~ ils coûtent 5 livres (la) pièce; ~ **of us** chacun(e) de nous.
eager ['i:gə*] *adj* impatient(e); avide; ardent(e), passionné(e); (*keen: pupil*) plein(e) d'enthousiasme, qui se passionne pour les études; **to be** ~ **to do sth** être impatient de faire qch, brûler de faire qch; désirer vivement faire qch; **to be** ~ **for** désirer vive-

ment, être avide de.

eagle ['iːgl] *n* aigle *m*.

E and OE *abbr* = **errors and omissions excepted**.

ear [ɪə*] *n* oreille *f*; (*of corn*) épi *m*; **up to one's ~s in debt** endetté(e) jusqu'au cou.

earache ['ɪəreɪk] *n* douleurs *fpl* aux oreilles.

eardrum ['ɪədrʌm] *n* tympan *m*.

earful ['ɪəful] *n* (*col*): **to give sb an ~** passer un savon à qn.

earl [əːl] *n* comte *m*.

earlier ['əːlɪə*] *adj* (*date etc*) plus rapproché(e); (*edition etc*) plus ancien(ne), antérieur(e) ♦ *adv* plus tôt.

early ['əːlɪ] *adv* tôt, de bonne heure; (*ahead of time*) en avance ♦ *adj* précoce; qui se manifeste (*or* se fait) tôt *or* de bonne heure; (*Christians, settlers*) premier(ière); **have an ~ night/start** couchez-vous/partez tôt *or* de bonne heure; **take the ~ train** prenez le premier train; **in the ~** *or* **~ in the spring/19th century** au début *or* commencement du printemps/19ème siècle; **you're ~!** tu es en avance!; **~ in the morning** tôt le matin; **she's in her ~ forties** elle a un peu plus de quarante ans *or* de la quarantaine; **at your earliest convenience** (*COMM*) dans les meilleurs délais.

early retirement *n* retraite anticipée.

early warning system *n* système *m* de première alerte.

earmark ['ɪəmɑːk] *vt*: **to ~ sth for** réserver *or* destiner qch à.

earn [əːn] *vt* gagner; (*COMM: yield*) rapporter; **to ~ one's living** gagner sa vie; **this ~ed him much praise, he ~ed much praise for this** ceci lui a valu de nombreux éloges; **he's ~ed his rest/reward** il mérite *or* a bien mérité *or* a bien gagné son repos/sa récompense.

earned income [əːnd-] *n* revenu *m* du travail.

earnest ['əːnɪst] *adj* sérieux(euse) ♦ *n* (*also:* **~ money**) acompte *m*, arrhes *fpl*; **in ~** *adv* sérieusement, pour de bon.

earnings ['əːnɪŋz] *npl* salaire *m*; gains *mpl*; (*of company etc*) profits *mpl*, bénéfices *mpl*.

ear, nose and throat specialist *n* oto-rhino-laryngologiste *m/f*.

earphones ['ɪəfəunz] *npl* écouteurs *mpl*.

earplugs ['ɪəplʌgz] *npl* boules *fpl* Quiès ®; (*to keep out water*) protège-tympans *mpl*.

earring ['ɪərɪŋ] *n* boucle *f* d'oreille.

earshot ['ɪəʃɔt] *n*: **out of/within ~** hors de portée/à portée de voix.

earth [əːθ] *n* (*gen, also BRIT ELEC*) terre *f*; (*of fox etc*) terrier *m* ♦ *vt* (*BRIT ELEC*) relier à la terre.

earthenware ['əːθnwɛə*] *n* poterie *f*; faïence *f* ♦ *adj* de *or* en faïence.

earthly ['əːθlɪ] *adj* terrestre; **~ paradise** paradis *m* terrestre; **there is no ~ reason to think** ... il n'y a absolument aucune raison *or* pas

la moindre raison de penser ....

earthquake ['əːθkweɪk] *n* tremblement *m* de terre, séisme *m*.

earth-shattering ['əːθʃætərɪŋ] *adj* stupéfiant(e).

earth tremor *n* secousse *f* sismique.

earthworks ['əːθwəːks] *npl* travaux *mpl* de terrassement.

earthworm ['əːθwəːm] *n* ver *m* de terre.

earthy ['əːθɪ] *adj* (*fig*) terre à terre *inv*; truculent(e).

earwax ['ɪəwæks] *n* cérumen *m*.

earwig ['ɪəwɪg] *n* perce-oreille *m*.

ease [iːz] *n* facilité *f*, aisance *f* ♦ *vt* (*soothe*) calmer; (*loosen*) relâcher, détendre; (*help pass*): **to ~ sth in/out** faire pénétrer/sortir qch délicatement *or* avec douceur; faciliter la pénétration/la sortie de qch ♦ *vi* (*situation*) se détendre; **with ~** sans difficulté, aisément; **life of ~** vie oisive; **at ~** à l'aise; (*MIL*) au repos.

▶**ease off, ease up** *vi* diminuer; (*slow down*) ralentir; (*relax*) se détendre.

easel ['iːzl] *n* chevalet *m*.

easily ['iːzɪlɪ] *adv* facilement.

easiness ['iːsɪnɪs] *n* facilité *f*; (*of manner*) aisance *f*; nonchalance *f*.

east [iːst] *n* est *m* ♦ *adj* d'est ♦ *adv* à l'est, vers l'est; **the E~** l'Orient *m*; (*POL*) les pays *mpl* de l'Est.

Easter ['iːstə*] *n* Pâques *fpl* ♦ *adj* (*holidays*) de Pâques, pascal(e).

Easter egg *n* œuf *m* de Pâques.

Easter Island *n* île *f* de Pâques.

easterly ['iːstəlɪ] *adj* d'est.

Easter Monday *n* le lundi de Pâques.

eastern ['iːstən] *adj* de l'est, oriental(e); **E~ Europe** l'Europe de l'Est; **the E~ bloc** (*POL*) les pays *mpl* de l'est.

Easter Sunday *n* le dimanche de Pâques.

East Germany *n* (*formerly*) Allemagne *f* de l'Est.

eastward(s) ['iːstwəd(z)] *adv* vers l'est, à l'est.

easy ['iːzɪ] *adj* facile; (*manner*) aisé(e) ♦ *adv*: **to take it** *or* **things ~** ne pas se fatiguer; (*not worry*) ne pas (trop) s'en faire; **payment on ~ terms** (*COMM*) facilités *fpl* de paiement; **that's easier said than done** c'est plus facile à dire qu'à faire, c'est vite dit; **I'm ~** (*col*) ça m'est égal.

easy chair *n* fauteuil *m*.

easy-going ['iːzɪ'gəuɪŋ] *adj* accommodant(e), facile à vivre.

easy touch *n* (*col*): **he's an ~** c'est une bonne poire.

eat, *pt* **ate**, *pp* **eaten** [iːt, eɪt, 'iːtn] *vt*, *vi* manger.

▶**eat away** *vt* (*subj: sea*) saper, éroder; (*: acid*) ronger, corroder.

▶**eat away at, eat into** *vt fus* ronger, attaquer.

►**eat out** vi manger au restaurant.
►**eat up** vt (food) finir (de manger); **it ~s up electricity** ça bouffe du courant, ça consomme beaucoup d'électricité.
eatable ['iːtəbl] adj mangeable; (safe to eat) comestible.
eau de Cologne ['əʊdəkə'ləʊn] n eau f de Cologne.
eaves [iːvz] npl avant-toit m.
eavesdrop ['iːvzdrɒp] vi: **to ~ (on)** écouter de façon indiscrète.
ebb [ɛb] n reflux m ♦ vi refluer; (fig: also: ~ **away**) décliner; **the ~ and flow** le flux et le reflux; **to be at a low ~** (fig) être bien bas(se), ne pas aller bien fort.
ebb tide n marée descendante, reflux m.
ebony ['ɛbənɪ] n ébène f.
ebullient [ɪ'bʌlɪənt] adj exubérant(e).
EC n abbr (= European Community) CE f (= Communauté européenne).
ECB n abbr (= European Central Bank) BCE f.
eccentric [ɪk'sɛntrɪk] adj, n excentrique (m/f).
ecclesiastic(al) [ɪkliːzɪ'æstɪk(l)] adj ecclésiastique.
ECG n abbr = electrocardiogram.
ECGD n abbr (= Export Credits Guarantee Department) service de garantie financière à l'exportation.
echo, **~es** ['ɛkəʊ] n écho m ♦ vt répéter; faire chorus avec ♦ vi résonner; faire écho.
éclair ['eɪklɛə*] n éclair m (CULIN).
eclipse [ɪ'klɪps] n éclipse f ♦ vt éclipser.
ECM n abbr (US) = European Common Market.
eco- ['iːkəʊ] prefix éco-.
eco-friendly [iːkəʊ'frɛndlɪ] adj non nuisible à or qui ne nuit pas à l'environnement.
ecological [iːkə'lɒdʒɪkəl] adj écologique.
ecologist [ɪ'kɒlədʒɪst] n écologiste m/f.
ecology [ɪ'kɒlədʒɪ] n écologie f.
economic [iːkə'nɒmɪk] adj économique; (profitable) rentable.
economical [iːkə'nɒmɪkl] adj économique; (person) économe.
economically [iːkə'nɒmɪklɪ] adv économiquement.
economics [iːkə'nɒmɪks] n économie f politique ♦ npl côté m or aspect m économique.
economist [ɪ'kɒnəmɪst] n économiste m/f.
economize [ɪ'kɒnəmaɪz] vi économiser, faire des économies.
economy [ɪ'kɒnəmɪ] n économie f; **economies of scale** économies d'échelle.
economy class n (AVIAT etc) classe f touriste.
economy size n taille f économique.
ecosystem ['iːkəʊsɪstəm] n écosystème m.
eco-tourism [iːkəʊ'tʊərɪzəm] n écotourisme m.
ECSC n abbr (= European Coal & Steel Community) CECA f (= Communauté européenne du charbon et de l'acier).
ecstasy ['ɛkstəsɪ] n extase f; (DRUGS) ecstasy m; **to go into ecstasies over** s'extasier sur.
ecstatic [ɛks'tætɪk] adj extatique, en extase.

ECT n abbr = electroconvulsive therapy.
ECU, ecu ['eɪkjuː] n abbr (= European Currency Unit) ECU m, écu m.
Ecuador ['ɛkwədɔː*] n Équateur m.
ecumenical [iːkjuː'mɛnɪkl] adj œcuménique.
eczema ['ɛksɪmə] n eczéma m.
eddy ['ɛdɪ] n tourbillon m.
edge [ɛdʒ] n bord m; (of knife etc) tranchant m, fil m ♦ vt border ♦ vi: **to ~ forward** avancer petit à petit; **to ~ away from** s'éloigner furtivement de; **on ~** (fig) = edgy; **to have the ~ on** (fig) l'emporter (de justesse) sur, être légèrement meilleur que.
edgeways ['ɛdʒweɪz] adv latéralement; **he couldn't get a word in ~** il ne pouvait pas placer un mot.
edging ['ɛdʒɪŋ] n bordure f.
edgy ['ɛdʒɪ] adj crispé(e), tendu(e).
edible ['ɛdɪbl] adj comestible; (meal) mangeable.
edict ['iːdɪkt] n décret m.
edifice ['ɛdɪfɪs] n édifice m.
edifying ['ɛdɪfaɪɪŋ] adj édifiant(e).
Edinburgh ['ɛdɪnbərə] n Édimbourg.
edit ['ɛdɪt] vt éditer; (magazine) diriger; (newspaper) être le rédacteur or la rédactrice en chef de.
edition [ɪ'dɪʃən] n édition f.
editor ['ɛdɪtə*] n (in newspaper) rédacteur/trice; rédacteur/trice en chef; (of sb's work) éditeur/trice; (also: film ~) monteur/euse.
editorial [ɛdɪ'tɔːrɪəl] adj de la rédaction, éditorial(e) ♦ n éditorial m; **the ~ staff** la rédaction.
EDP n abbr = electronic data processing.
EDT abbr (US: = Eastern Daylight Time) heure d'été de New York.
educate ['ɛdjukeɪt] vt instruire; éduquer; **~d at ...** qui a fait ses études à ....
educated guess ['ɛdjukeɪtɪd-] n supposition éclairée.
education [ɛdju'keɪʃən] n éducation f; (schooling) enseignement m, instruction f; (at university: subject etc) pédagogie f; **primary or** (US) **elementary/secondary ~** instruction f primaire/secondaire.
educational [ɛdju'keɪʃənl] adj pédagogique; scolaire; (useful) instructif(ive); (games, toys) éducatif(ive); **~ technology** technologie f de l'enseignement.
Edwardian [ɛd'wɔːdɪən] adj de l'époque du roi Édouard VII, des années 1900.
EE abbr = electrical engineer.
EEC n abbr (= European Economic Community) C.E.E. f (= Communauté économique européenne).
EEG n abbr = electroencephalogram.
eel [iːl] n anguille f.
EENT n abbr (US MED) = eye, ear, nose and throat.
EEOC n abbr (US) = Equal Employment Opportunity Commission.

eerie ['ɪərɪ] *adj* inquiétant(e), spectral(e), surnaturel(le).

EET *abbr* (= *Eastern European Time*) HEO (= *heure d'Europe orientale*).

effect [ɪ'fɛkt] *n* effet *m* ♦ *vt* effectuer; **to take ~** (*LAW*) entrer en vigueur, prendre effet; (*drug*) agir, faire son effet; **to put into ~** (*plan*) mettre en application *or* à exécution; **to have an ~ on sb/sth** avoir *or* produire un effet sur qn/qch; **in ~** en fait; **his letter is to the ~ that** ... sa lettre nous apprend que ....

effective [ɪ'fɛktɪv] *adj* efficace; (*striking: display, outfit*) frappant(e), qui produit *or* fait de l'effet; **to become ~** (*LAW*) entrer en vigueur, prendre effet; **~ date** date *f* d'effet *or* d'entrée en vigueur.

effectively [ɪ'fɛktɪvlɪ] *adv* efficacement; (*strikingly*) d'une manière frappante, avec beaucoup d'effet; (*in reality*) effectivement, en fait.

effectiveness [ɪ'fɛktɪvnɪs] *n* efficacité *f*.

effects [ɪ'fɛkts] *npl* (*THEAT*) effets *mpl*; (*property*) effets, affaires *fpl*.

effeminate [ɪ'fɛmɪnɪt] *adj* efféminé(e).

effervescent [ɛfə'vɛsnt] *adj* effervescent(e).

efficacy ['ɛfɪkəsɪ] *n* efficacité *f*.

efficiency [ɪ'fɪʃənsɪ] *n* efficacité *f*; rendement *m*.

efficiency apartment *n* (*US*) studio *m* avec coin cuisine.

efficient [ɪ'fɪʃənt] *adj* efficace; (*machine, car*) d'un bon rendement.

efficiently [ɪ'fɪʃəntlɪ] *adv* efficacement.

effigy ['ɛfɪdʒɪ] *n* effigie *f*.

effluent ['ɛfluənt] *n* effluent *m*.

effort ['ɛfət] *n* effort *m*; **to make an ~ to do sth** faire *or* fournir un effort pour faire qch.

effortless ['ɛfətlɪs] *adj* sans effort, aisé(e).

effrontery [ɪ'frʌntərɪ] *n* effronterie *f*.

effusive [ɪ'fjuːsɪv] *adj* (*person*) expansif(ive); (*welcome*) chaleureux(euse).

EFL *n abbr* (*SCOL*) = *English as a Foreign Language*.

EFTA ['ɛftə] *n abbr* (= *European Free Trade Association*) AELE *f* (= *Association européenne de libre-échange*).

e.g. *adv abbr* (= *exempli gratia*) par exemple, p. ex.

egalitarian [ɪgælɪ'tɛərɪən] *adj* égalitaire.

egg [ɛg] *n* œuf *m*.

▶**egg on** *vt* pousser.

eggcup ['ɛgkʌp] *n* coquetier *m*.

eggplant ['ɛgplɑːnt] *n* aubergine *f*.

eggshell ['ɛgʃɛl] *n* coquille *f* d'œuf ♦ *adj* (*colour*) blanc cassé *inv*.

egg-timer ['ɛgtaɪmə*] *n* sablier *m*.

egg white *n* blanc *m* d'œuf.

egg yolk *n* jaune *m* d'œuf.

ego ['iːgəu] *n* moi *m*.

egoism ['ɛgəuɪzəm] *n* égoïsme *m*.

egoist ['ɛgəuɪst] *n* égoïste *m/f*.

egotism ['ɛgəutɪzəm] *n* égotisme *m*.

egotist ['ɛgəutɪst] *n* égocentrique *m/f*.

ego trip *n*: **to be on an ~** être en plein délire d'autosatisfaction.

Egypt ['iːdʒɪpt] *n* Égypte *f*.

Egyptian [ɪ'dʒɪpʃən] *adj* égyptien(ne) ♦ *n* Egyptien/ne.

eiderdown ['aɪdədaun] *n* édredon *m*.

eight [eɪt] *num* huit.

eighteen [eɪ'tiːn] *num* dix-huit.

eighth [eɪtθ] *num* huitième.

eighty ['eɪtɪ] *num* quatre-vingt(s).

Eire ['ɛərə] *n* République *f* d'Irlande.

EIS *n abbr* (= *Educational Institute of Scotland*) syndicat enseignant.

either ['aɪðə*] *adj* l'un ou l'autre; (*both, each*) chaque; **on ~ side** de chaque côté ♦ *pron*: **~ (of them)** l'un ou l'autre; **I don't like ~** je n'aime ni l'un ni l'autre ♦ *adv* non plus; **no, I don't ~** moi non plus ♦ *conj*: **~ good or bad** ou bon ou mauvais, soit bon soit mauvais; **I haven't seen ~ one or the other** je n'ai vu ni l'un ni l'autre.

ejaculation [ɪdʒækju'leɪʃən] *n* (*PHYSIOL*) éjaculation *f*.

eject [ɪ'dʒɛkt] *vt* expulser; éjecter ♦ *vi* (*pilot*) s'éjecter.

ejector seat [ɪ'dʒɛktə-] *n* siège *m* éjectable.

eke [iːk]: **to ~ out** *vt* faire durer; augmenter.

EKG *n abbr* (*US*) = *electrocardiogram*.

el [ɛl] *n abbr* (*US col*) = *elevated railroad*.

elaborate *adj* [ɪ'læbərɪt] compliqué(e), recherché(e), minutieux(euse) ♦ *vb* [ɪ'læbəreɪt] *vt* élaborer ♦ *vi* entrer dans les détails.

elapse [ɪ'læps] *vi* s'écouler, passer.

elastic [ɪ'læstɪk] *adj*, *n* élastique (*m*).

elastic band *n* (*BRIT*) élastique *m*.

elasticity [ɪlæs'tɪsɪtɪ] *n* élasticité *f*.

elated [ɪ'leɪtɪd] *adj* transporté(e) de joie.

elation [ɪ'leɪʃən] *n* (grande) joie, allégresse *f*.

elbow ['ɛlbəu] *n* coude *m* ♦ *vt*: **to ~ one's way through the crowd** se frayer un passage à travers la foule (en jouant des coudes).

elbow grease *n*: **to use a bit of ~** mettre de l'huile de coude.

elder ['ɛldə*] *adj* aîné(e) ♦ *n* (*tree*) sureau *m*; **one's ~s** ses aînés.

elderly ['ɛldəlɪ] *adj* âgé(e) ♦ *npl*: **the ~** les personnes âgées.

elder statesman *n* vétéran *m* de la politique.

eldest ['ɛldɪst] *adj*, *n*: **the ~ (child)** l'aîné(e) (des enfants).

elect [ɪ'lɛkt] *vt* élire; (*choose*): **to ~ to do** choisir de faire ♦ *adj*: **the president ~** le président désigné.

election [ɪ'lɛkʃən] *n* élection *f*; **to hold an ~** procéder à une élection.

election campaign *n* campagne électorale.

electioneering [ɪlɛkʃə'nɪərɪŋ] *n* propagande électorale, manœuvres électorales.

elector [ɪ'lɛktə*] *n* électeur/trice.

electoral [ɪ'lɛktərəl] *adj* électoral(e).

electoral college n collège électoral.
electoral roll n (BRIT) liste électorale.
electorate [ɪ'lɛktərɪt] n électorat m.
electric [ɪ'lɛktrɪk] adj électrique.
electrical [ɪ'lɛktrɪkl] adj électrique.
electrical engineer n ingénieur électricien.
electrical failure n panne d'électricité or de courant.
electric blanket n couverture chauffante.
electric chair n chaise f électrique.
electric cooker n cuisinière f électrique.
electric current n courant m électrique.
electric fire n (BRIT) radiateur m électrique.
electrician [ɪlɛk'trɪʃən] n électricien m.
electricity [ɪlɛk'trɪsɪtɪ] n électricité f; **to switch on/off the ~** rétablir/couper le courant.
electricity board n (BRIT) ≈ agence régionale de l'E.D.F.
electric light n lumière f électrique.
electric shock n choc m or décharge f électrique.
electrify [ɪ'lɛktrɪfaɪ] vt (RAIL) électrifier; (audience) électriser.
electro... [ɪ'lɛktrəʊ] prefix électro....
electrocardiogram (ECG) [ɪ'lɛktrə'kɑːdɪəgræm] n électrocardiogramme m (ECG).
electro-convulsive therapy [ɪ'lɛktrə kən'vʌlsɪv-] n électrochocs mpl.
electrocute [ɪ'lɛktrəkjuːt] vt électrocuter.
electrode [ɪ'lɛktrəʊd] n électrode f.
electroencephalogram (EEG) [ɪ'lɛktrəʊ ɛn'sɛfələgræm] n électroencéphalogramme m (EEG).
electrolysis [ɪlɛk'trɒlɪsɪs] n électrolyse f.
electromagnetic [ɪ'lɛktrəmæg'nɛtɪk] adj électromagnétique.
electron [ɪ'lɛktrɒn] n électron m.
electronic [ɪlɛk'trɒnɪk] adj électronique.
electronic data processing (EDP) n traitement m électronique des données.
electronic mail n courrier m électronique.
electronics [ɪlɛk'trɒnɪks] n électronique f.
electronics engineer n électronicien/ne.
electron microscope n microscope m électronique.
electroplated [ɪ'lɛktrə'pleɪtɪd] adj plaqué(e) or doré(e) or argenté(e) par galvanoplastie.
electrotherapy [ɪ'lɛktrə'θɛrəpɪ] n électrothérapie f.
elegance ['ɛlɪgəns] n élégance f.
elegant ['ɛlɪgənt] adj élégant(e).
element ['ɛlɪmənt] n (gen) élément m; (of heater, kettle etc) résistance f.
elementary [ɛlɪ'mɛntərɪ] adj élémentaire; (school, education) primaire.

*Aux États-Unis et au Canada, une **elementary school** (également appelée "grade school" ou "grammar school" aux États-Unis) est une école publique où les enfants passent les six à huit premières années de leur scolarité.*

elephant ['ɛlɪfənt] n éléphant m.
elevate ['ɛlɪveɪt] vt élever.
elevated railroad ['ɛlɪveɪtɪd-] n (US) métro aérien.
elevation [ɛlɪ'veɪʃən] n élévation f; (height) altitude f.
elevator ['ɛlɪveɪtə*] n élévateur m, monte-charge m inv; (US: lift) ascenseur m.
eleven [ɪ'lɛvn] num onze.
elevenses [ɪ'lɛvnzɪz] npl (BRIT) ≈ pause-café f.
eleventh [ɪ'lɛvnθ] adj onzième; **at the ~ hour** (fig) à la dernière minute.
elf, pl **elves** [ɛlf, ɛlvz] n lutin m.
elicit [ɪ'lɪsɪt] vt: **to ~ (from)** obtenir (de); tirer (de).
eligible ['ɛlɪdʒəbl] adj éligible; (for membership) admissible; **~ for a pension** ayant droit à la retraite.
eliminate [ɪ'lɪmɪneɪt] vt éliminer.
elimination [ɪlɪmɪ'neɪʃən] n élimination f; **by process of ~** par élimination.
élite [eɪ'liːt] n élite f.
élitist [eɪ'liːtɪst] adj (pej) élitiste.
elixir [ɪ'lɪksə*] n élixir m.
Elizabethan [ɪlɪzə'biːθən] adj élisabéthain(e).
ellipse [ɪ'lɪps] n ellipse f.
elliptical [ɪ'lɪptɪkl] adj elliptique.
elm [ɛlm] n orme m.
elocution [ɛlə'kjuːʃən] n élocution f.
elongated ['iːlɒŋgeɪtɪd] adj étiré(e), allongé(e).
elope [ɪ'ləʊp] vi (lovers) s'enfuir (ensemble).
elopement [ɪ'ləʊpmənt] n fugue amoureuse.
eloquence ['ɛləkwəns] n éloquence f.
eloquent ['ɛləkwənt] adj éloquent(e).
else [ɛls] adv d'autre; **something ~** quelque chose d'autre, autre chose; **somewhere ~** ailleurs, autre part; **everywhere ~** partout ailleurs; **everyone ~** tous les autres; **nothing ~** rien d'autre; **is there anything ~ I can do?** est-ce que je peux faire quelque chose d'autre?; **where ~?** à quel autre endroit?; **little ~** pas grand-chose d'autre.
elsewhere [ɛls'wɛə*] adv ailleurs, autre part.
ELT n abbr (SCOL) = English Language Teaching.
elucidate [ɪ'luːsɪdeɪt] vt élucider.
elude [ɪ'luːd] vt échapper à; (question) éluder.
elusive [ɪ'luːsɪv] adj insaisissable; (answer) évasif(ive).
elves [ɛlvz] npl of **elf**.
emaciated [ɪ'meɪsɪeɪtɪd] adj émacié(e), décharné(e).
E-mail, e-mail ['iːmeɪl] n abbr (= electronic mail) courrier m électronique ♦ vt: **to ~ sb** envoyer un message électronique à qn.
emanate ['ɛməneɪt] vi: **to ~ from** émaner de.
emancipate [ɪ'mænsɪpeɪt] vt émanciper.
emancipation [ɪmænsɪ'peɪʃən] n émancipation f.

emasculate [ɪ'mæskjuleɪt] *vt* émasculer.

embalm [ɪm'bɑːm] *vt* embaumer.

embankment [ɪm'bæŋkmənt] *n* (*of road, railway*) remblai *m*, talus *m*; (*riverside*) berge *f*, quai *m*; (*dyke*) digue *f*.

embargo, ~es [ɪm'bɑːgəu] *n* (*COMM, NAUT*) embargo *m* ♦ *vt* frapper d'embargo, mettre l'embargo sur; **to put an ~ on sth** mettre l'embargo sur qch.

embark [ɪm'bɑːk] *vi*: **to ~ (on)** (s')embarquer (à bord de *or* sur) ♦ *vt* embarquer; **to ~ on** (*journey etc*) commencer, entreprendre; (*fig*) se lancer *or* s'embarquer dans.

embarkation [ɛmbɑː'keɪʃən] *n* embarquement *m*.

embarkation card *n* carte *f* d'embarquement.

embarrass [ɪm'bærəs] *vt* embarrasser, gêner; **to be ~ed** être gêné(e).

embarrassing [ɪm'bærəsɪŋ] *adj* gênant(e), embarrassant(e).

embarrassment [ɪm'bærəsmənt] *n* embarras *m*, gêne *f*.

embassy ['ɛmbəsɪ] *n* ambassade *f*; **the French E~** l'ambassade de France.

embed [ɪm'bɛd] *vt* enfoncer; sceller.

embellish [ɪm'bɛlɪʃ] *vt* embellir; enjoliver.

embers ['ɛmbəz] *npl* braise *f*.

embezzle [ɪm'bɛzl] *vt* détourner.

embezzlement [ɪm'bɛzlmənt] *n* détournement *m* (de fonds).

embezzler [ɪm'bɛzlə*] *n* escroc *m*.

embitter [ɪm'bɪtə*] *vt* aigrir; envenimer.

emblem ['ɛmbləm] *n* emblème *m*.

embodiment [ɪm'bɔdɪmənt] *n* personification *f*, incarnation *f*.

embody [ɪm'bɔdɪ] *vt* (*features*) réunir, comprendre; (*ideas*) formuler, exprimer.

embolden [ɪm'bəuldn] *vt* enhardir.

embolism ['ɛmbəlɪzəm] *n* embolie *f*.

embossed [ɪm'bɔst] *adj* repoussé(e); gaufré(e); **~ with** où figure(nt) en relief.

embrace [ɪm'breɪs] *vt* embrasser, étreindre; (*include*) embrasser, couvrir, comprendre ♦ *vi* s'embrasser, s'étreindre ♦ *n* étreinte *f*.

embroider [ɪm'brɔɪdə*] *vt* broder; (*fig: story*) enjoliver.

embroidery [ɪm'brɔɪdərɪ] *n* broderie *f*.

embroil [ɪm'brɔɪl] *vt*: **to become ~ed (in sth)** se retrouver mêlé(e) (à qch), se laisser entraîner (dans qch).

embryo ['ɛmbrɪəu] *n* (*also fig*) embryon *m*.

emend [ɪ'mɛnd] *vt* (*text*) corriger.

emerald ['ɛmərəld] *n* émeraude *f*.

emerge [ɪ'mɜːdʒ] *vi* apparaître, surgir; **it ~s that** (*BRIT*) il ressort que.

emergence [ɪ'mɜːdʒəns] *n* apparition *f*, (*of nation*) naissance *f*.

emergency [ɪ'mɜːdʒənsɪ] *n* urgence *f*; **in an ~** en cas d'urgence; **state of ~** état *m* d'urgence.

emergency exit *n* sortie *f* de secours.

emergency landing *n* atterrissage forcé.

emergency lane *n* (*US AUT*) accotement stabilisé.

emergency road service *n* (*US*) service *m* de dépannage.

emergency service *n* service *m* d'urgence.

emergency stop *n* (*BRIT AUT*) arrêt *m* d'urgence.

emergent [ɪ'mɜːdʒənt] *adj*: **~ nation** pays *m* en voie de développement.

emery board ['ɛmərɪ-] *n* lime *f* à ongles (*en carton émerisé*).

emery paper ['ɛmərɪ-] *n* papier *m* (d')émeri.

emetic [ɪ'mɛtɪk] *n* vomitif *m*, émétique *m*.

emigrant ['ɛmɪgrənt] *n* émigrant/e.

emigrate ['ɛmɪgreɪt] *vi* émigrer.

emigration [ɛmɪ'greɪʃən] *n* émigration *f*.

émigré ['ɛmɪgreɪ] *n* émigré/e.

eminence ['ɛmɪnəns] *n* éminence *f*.

eminent ['ɛmɪnənt] *adj* éminent(e).

eminently ['ɛmɪnəntlɪ] *adv* éminemment, admirablement.

emission [ɪ'mɪʃən] *n* émission *f*.

emit [ɪ'mɪt] *vt* émettre.

emolument [ɪ'mɔljumənt] *n* (*often pl: formal*) émoluments *mpl*; (*fee*) honoraires *mpl*; (*salary*) traitement *m*.

emotion [ɪ'məuʃən] *n* sentiment *m*; (*as opposed to reason*) émotion *f*, sentiments.

emotional [ɪ'məuʃənl] *adj* (*person*) émotif(ive), très sensible; (*scene*) émouvant(e); (*tone, speech*) qui fait appel aux sentiments.

emotionally [ɪ'məuʃnəlɪ] *adv* (*behave*) émotivement; (*be involved*) affectivement; (*speak*) avec émotion; **~ disturbed** qui souffre de troubles de l'affectivité.

emotive [ɪ'məutɪv] *adj* émotif(ive); **~ power** capacité *f* d'émouvoir *or* de toucher.

empathy ['ɛmpəθɪ] *n* communion *f* d'idées *or* de sentiments; empathie *f*; **to feel ~ with sb** se mettre à la place de qn.

emperor ['ɛmpərə*] *n* empereur *m*.

emphasis, pl -ases ['ɛmfəsɪs, -siːz] *n* accent *m*; force *f*, insistance *f*; **to lay** *or* **place ~ on sth** (*fig*) mettre l'accent sur, insister sur; **the ~ is on reading** la lecture tient une place primordiale, on accorde une importance particulière à la lecture.

emphasize ['ɛmfəsaɪz] *vt* (*syllable, word, point*) appuyer *or* insister sur; (*feature*) souligner, accentuer.

emphatic [ɛm'fætɪk] *adj* (*strong*) énergique, vigoureux(euse); (*unambiguous, clear*) catégorique.

emphatically [ɛm'fætɪklɪ] *adv* avec vigueur *or* énergie; catégoriquement.

empire ['ɛmpaɪə*] *n* empire *m*.

empirical [ɛm'pɪrɪkl] *adj* empirique.

employ [ɪm'plɔɪ] *vt* employer; **he's ~ed in a bank** il est employé de banque, il travaille dans une banque.

employee [ɪmplɔɪ'iː] *n* employé/e.

employer [ɪmˈplɔɪə*] n employeur/euse.
employment [ɪmˈplɔɪmənt] n emploi m; **to find** ~ trouver un emploi or du travail; **without** ~ au chômage, sans emploi; **place of** ~ lieu m de travail.
employment agency n agence f or bureau m de placement.
employment exchange n (BRIT) agence f pour l'emploi.
empower [ɪmˈpauə*] vt: **to** ~ **sb to do** autoriser or habiliter qn à faire.
empress [ˈɛmprɪs] n impératrice f.
emptiness [ˈɛmptɪnɪs] n vide m.
empty [ˈɛmptɪ] adj vide; (street, area) désert(e); (threat, promise) en l'air, vain(e) ♦ n (bottle) bouteille f vide ♦ vt vider ♦ vi se vider; (liquid) s'écouler; **on an** ~ **stomach** à jeun; **to** ~ **into** (river) se jeter dans, se déverser dans.
empty-handed [ˈɛmptɪˈhændɪd] adj les mains vides.
empty-headed [ˈɛmptɪˈhɛdɪd] adj écervelé(e), qui n'a rien dans la tête.
EMS n abbr (= European Monetary System) SME m.
EMT n abbr = emergency medical technician.
EMU n abbr (= European Monetary Union) UME f; (= economic and monetary union) UEM f.
emulate [ˈɛmjuleɪt] vt rivaliser avec, imiter.
emulsion [ɪˈmʌlʃən] n émulsion f; (also: ~ **paint**) peinture mate.
enable [ɪˈneɪbl] vt: **to** ~ **sb to do** permettre à qn de faire, donner à qn la possibilité de faire.
enact [ɪˈnækt] vt (LAW) promulguer; (play, scene) jouer, représenter.
enamel [ɪˈnæməl] n émail m.
enamel paint n peinture émaillée.
enamoured [ɪˈnæməd] adj: ~ **of** amoureux(euse) de; (idea) enchanté(e) par.
encampment [ɪnˈkæmpmənt] n campement m.
encased [ɪnˈkeɪst] adj: ~ **in** enfermé(e) dans, recouvert(e) de.
enchant [ɪnˈtʃɑːnt] vt enchanter.
enchanting [ɪnˈtʃɑːntɪŋ] adj ravissant(e), enchanteur(eresse).
encircle [ɪnˈsəːkl] vt entourer, encercler.
enc(l). abbr (on letters etc: = enclosed, enclosure) PJ.
enclose [ɪnˈkləuz] vt (land) clôturer; (letter etc): **to** ~ **(with)** joindre (à); **please find** ~**d** veuillez trouver ci-joint.
enclosure [ɪnˈkləuʒə*] n enceinte f; (in letter etc) annexe f.
encoder [ɪnˈkəudə*] n (COMPUT) encodeur m.
encompass [ɪnˈkʌmpəs] vt encercler, entourer; (include) contenir, inclure.
encore [ɔŋˈkɔː*] excl, n bis (m).
encounter [ɪnˈkauntə*] n rencontre f ♦ vt rencontrer.
encourage [ɪnˈkʌrɪdʒ] vt encourager; (industry, growth) favoriser; **to** ~ **sb to do sth** encourager qn à faire qch.

encouragement [ɪnˈkʌrɪdʒmənt] n encouragement m.
encouraging [ɪnˈkʌrɪdʒɪŋ] adj encourageant(e).
encroach [ɪnˈkrəutʃ] vi: **to** ~ **(up)on** empiéter sur.
encrust [ɪnˈkrʌst] vt encroûter; (with jewels etc) incruster.
encrusted [ɪnˈkrʌstɪd] adj: ~ **(with)** incrusté(e) (de).
encumber [ɪnˈkʌmbə*] vt: **to be** ~ed with (luggage) être encombré(e) de; (debts) être grevé(e) de.
encyclop(a)edia [ɛnsaɪkləuˈpiːdɪə] n encyclopédie f.
end [ɛnd] n (gen, also: aim) fin f; (of table, street, line, rope etc) bout m, extrémité f; (of pointed object) pointe f; (of town) bout m ♦ vt terminer; (also: **bring to an** ~, **put an** ~ **to**) mettre fin à ♦ vi se terminer, finir; **from** ~ **to** ~ d'un bout à l'autre; **to come to an** ~ prendre fin; **to be at an** ~ être fini(e), être terminé(e); **in the** ~ finalement; **on** ~ (object) debout, dressé(e); **to stand on** ~ (hair) se dresser sur la tête; **for 5 hours on** ~ durant 5 heures d'affilée or de suite; **for hours on** ~ pendant des heures (et des heures); **at the** ~ **of the day** (BRIT fig) en fin de compte; **to this** ~, **with this** ~ **in view** à cette fin, dans ce but.
▶**end up** vi: **to** ~ **up in** finir or se terminer par; (place) finir or aboutir à.
endanger [ɪnˈdeɪndʒə*] vt mettre en danger; **an** ~**ed species** une espèce en voie de disparition.
endear [ɪnˈdɪə*] vt: **to** ~ **o.s. to sb** se faire aimer de qn.
endearing [ɪnˈdɪərɪŋ] adj attachant(e).
endearment [ɪnˈdɪəmənt] n: **to whisper** ~**s** murmurer des mots or choses tendres; **term of** ~ terme m d'affection.
endeavour, (US) **endeavor** [ɪnˈdɛvə*] n tentative f, effort m ♦ vi: **to** ~ **to do** tenter or s'efforcer de faire.
endemic [ɛnˈdɛmɪk] adj endémique.
ending [ˈɛndɪŋ] n dénouement m, conclusion f; (LING) terminaison f.
endive [ˈɛndaɪv] n (curly) chicorée f; (smooth, flat) endive f.
endless [ˈɛndlɪs] adj sans fin, interminable; (patience, resources) inépuisable, sans limites; (possibilities) illimité(e).
endorse [ɪnˈdɔːs] vt (cheque) endosser; (approve) appuyer, approuver, sanctionner.
endorsee [ɪndɔːˈsiː] n bénéficiaire m/f, endossataire m/f.
endorsement [ɪnˈdɔːsmənt] n (approval) caution f, aval m; (signature) endossement m; (BRIT: on driving licence) contravention f (portée au permis de conduire).
endorser [ɪnˈdɔːsə*] n avaliste m, endosseur m.

endow [ɪn'dau] *vt* (*provide with money*) faire une donation à, doter; (*equip*): **to ~ with** gratifier de, doter de.

endowment [ɪn'daumənt] *n* dotation *f*.

endowment mortgage *n* hypothèque liée à une assurance-vie.

endowment policy *n* assurance *f* à capital différé.

end product *n* (*INDUSTRY*) produit fini; (*fig*) résultat *m*, aboutissement *m*.

end result *n* résultat final.

endurable [ɪn'djuərəbl] *adj* supportable.

endurance [ɪn'djuərəns] *n* endurance *f*, résistance *f*; patience *f*.

endurance test *n* test *m* d'endurance.

endure [ɪn'djuə*] *vt* supporter, endurer ♦ *vi* durer.

end user *n* (*COMPUT*) utilisateur final.

enema ['ɛnɪmə] *n* (*MED*) lavement *m*.

enemy ['ɛnəmɪ] *adj, n* ennemi(e); **to make an ~ of sb** se faire un(e) ennemi(e) de qn, se mettre qn à dos.

energetic [ɛnə'dʒɛtɪk] *adj* énergique; (*activity*) très actif(ive), qui fait se dépenser (physiquement).

energy ['ɛnədʒɪ] *n* énergie *f*; **Department of E~** ministère *m* de l'Énergie.

energy crisis *n* crise *f* de l'énergie.

energy-saving ['ɛnədʒɪ'seɪvɪŋ] *adj* (*policy*) d'économie d'énergie; (*device*) qui permet de réaliser des économies d'énergie.

enervating ['ɛnəveɪtɪŋ] *adj* débilitant(e), affaiblissant(e).

enforce [ɪn'fɔːs] *vt* (*LAW*) appliquer, faire respecter.

enforced [ɪn'fɔːst] *adj* forcé(e).

enfranchise [ɪn'fræntʃaɪz] *vt* accorder le droit de vote à; (*set free*) affranchir.

engage [ɪn'geɪdʒ] *vt* engager; (*MIL*) engager le combat avec; (*lawyer*) prendre ♦ *vi* (*TECH*) s'enclencher, s'engrener; **to ~ in** se lancer dans; **to ~ sb in conversation** engager la conversation avec qn.

engaged [ɪn'geɪdʒd] *adj* (*BRIT: busy, in use*) occupé(e); (*betrothed*) fiancé(e); **to get ~** se fiancer; **he is ~ in research/a survey** il fait de la recherche/une enquête.

engaged tone *n* (*BRIT TEL*) tonalité *f* occupé *inv*.

engagement [ɪn'geɪdʒmənt] *n* obligation *f*, engagement *m*; (*appointment*) rendez-vous *m inv*; (*to marry*) fiançailles *fpl*; (*MIL*) combat *m*; **I have a previous ~** j'ai déjà un rendez-vous, je suis déjà prise(e).

engagement ring *n* bague *f* de fiançailles.

engaging [ɪn'geɪdʒɪŋ] *adj* engageant(e), attirant(e).

engender [ɪn'dʒɛndə*] *vt* produire, causer.

engine ['ɛndʒɪn] *n* (*AUT*) moteur *m*; (*RAIL*) locomotive *f*.

engine driver *n* (*BRIT: of train*) mécanicien *m*.

engineer [ɛndʒɪ'nɪə*] *n* ingénieur *m*; (*BRIT: for domestic appliances*) réparateur *m*; (*US RAIL*) mécanicien *m*; **civil/mechanical ~** ingénieur des Travaux Publics *or* des Ponts et Chaussées/mécanicien.

engineering [ɛndʒɪ'nɪərɪŋ] *n* engineering *m*, ingénierie *f*; (*of bridges, ships*) génie *m*; (*of machine*) mécanique *f* ♦ *cpd*: **~ works** *or* **factory** atelier *m* de construction mécanique.

engine failure *n* panne *f*.

engine trouble *n* ennuis *mpl* mécaniques.

England ['ɪŋglənd] *n* Angleterre *f*.

English ['ɪŋglɪʃ] *adj* anglais(e) ♦ *n* (*LING*) anglais *m*; **the ~** *npl* les Anglais; **an ~ speaker** un anglophone.

English Channel *n*: **the ~** la Manche.

Englishman ['ɪŋglɪʃmən], **Englishwoman** ['ɪŋglɪʃwumən] *n* Anglais/e.

English-speaking ['ɪŋglɪʃ'spiːkɪŋ] *adj* qui parle anglais; anglophone.

engrave [ɪn'greɪv] *vt* graver.

engraving [ɪn'greɪvɪŋ] *n* gravure *f*.

engrossed [ɪn'grəust] *adj*: **~ in** absorbé(e) par, plongé(e) dans.

engulf [ɪn'gʌlf] *vt* engloutir.

enhance [ɪn'hɑːns] *vt* rehausser, mettre en valeur; (*position*) améliorer; (*reputation*) accroître.

enigma [ɪ'nɪgmə] *n* énigme *f*.

enigmatic [ɛnɪg'mætɪk] *adj* énigmatique.

enjoy [ɪn'dʒɔɪ] *vt* aimer, prendre plaisir à; (*have benefit of: health, fortune*) jouir de; (: *success*) connaître; **to ~ o.s.** s'amuser.

enjoyable [ɪn'dʒɔɪəbl] *adj* agréable.

enjoyment [ɪn'dʒɔɪmənt] *n* plaisir *m*.

enlarge [ɪn'lɑːdʒ] *vt* accroître; (*PHOT*) agrandir ♦ *vi*: **to ~ on** (*subject*) s'étendre sur.

enlarged [ɪn'lɑːdʒd] *adj* (*edition*) augmenté(e); (*MED: organ, gland*) anormalement gros(se), hypertrophié(e).

enlargement [ɪn'lɑːdʒmənt] *n* (*PHOT*) agrandissement *m*.

enlighten [ɪn'laɪtn] *vt* éclairer.

enlightened [ɪn'laɪtnd] *adj* éclairé(e).

enlightening [ɪn'laɪtnɪŋ] *adj* instructif(ive), révélateur(trice).

enlightenment [ɪn'laɪtnmənt] *n* édification *f*; éclaircissements *mpl*; (*HISTORY*): **the E~** ≈ le Siècle des lumières.

enlist [ɪn'lɪst] *vt* recruter; (*support*) s'assurer ♦ *vi* s'engager; **~ed man** (*US MIL*) simple soldat *m*.

enliven [ɪn'laɪvn] *vt* animer, égayer.

enmity ['ɛnmɪtɪ] *n* inimitié *f*.

ennoble [ɪ'nəubl] *vt* (*with title*) anoblir.

enormity [ɪ'nɔːmɪtɪ] *n* énormité *f*.

enormous [ɪ'nɔːməs] *adj* énorme.

enormously [ɪ'nɔːməslɪ] *adv* (*increase*) dans des proportions énormes; (*rich*) extrêmement.

enough [ɪ'nʌf] *adj, n*: **~ time/books** assez *or* suffisamment de temps/livres ♦ *adv*: **big ~** assez *or* suffisamment grand; **have you got**

~? (en) avez-vous assez?; **will 5 be** ~? est-ce que 5 suffiront?, est-ce qu'il y en aura assez avec 5?; **that's** ~! ça suffit!, assez!; **that's** ~, **thanks** cela suffit or c'est assez, merci; **I've had** ~! je n'en peux plus!; **he has not worked** ~ il n'a pas assez or suffisamment travaillé, il n'a pas travaillé assez or suffisamment; ~! assez!, ça suffit!; **it's hot** ~ **(as it is)**! il fait assez chaud comme ça!; **he was kind** ~ **to lend me the money** il a eu la gentillesse de me prêter l'argent; ... **which, funnily** ~ ... qui, chose curieuse.

enquire [ɪn'kwaɪə*] vt, vi = **inquire**.

enrage [ɪn'reɪdʒ] vt mettre en fureur or en rage, rendre furieux(euse).

enrich [ɪn'rɪtʃ] vt enrichir.

enrol, (US) **enroll** [ɪn'rəul] vt inscrire ♦ vi s'inscrire.

enrol(l)ment [ɪn'rəulmənt] n inscription f.

en route [ɔn'ru:t] adv en route, en chemin; ~ **for** or **to** en route vers, à destination de.

ensconced [ɪn'skɔnst] adj: ~ **in** bien calé(e) dans.

enshrine [ɪn'ʃraɪn] vt (fig) préserver.

ensign n (NAUT) ['ɛnsən] enseigne f, pavillon m; (MIL) ['ɛnsaɪn] porte-étendard m.

enslave [ɪn'sleɪv] vt asservir.

ensue [ɪn'sju:] vi s'ensuivre, résulter.

ensure [ɪn'ʃuə*] vt assurer, garantir; **to** ~ **that** s'assurer que.

ENT n abbr (= Ear, Nose and Throat) ORL f.

entail [ɪn'teɪl] vt entraîner, nécessiter.

entangle [ɪn'tæŋgl] vt emmêler, embrouiller; **to become** ~**d in sth** (fig) se laisser entraîner or empêtrer dans qch.

enter ['ɛntə*] vt (room) entrer dans, pénétrer dans; (club, army) entrer à; (profession) embrasser; (competition) s'inscrire à or pour; (sb for a competition) (faire) inscrire; (write down) inscrire, noter; (COMPUT) entrer, introduire ♦ vi entrer.

►**enter for** vt fus s'inscrire à, se présenter pour or à.

►**enter into** vt fus (explanation) se lancer dans; (negotiations) entamer; (debate) prendre part à; (agreement) conclure.

►**enter up** vt inscrire.

►**enter (up)on** vt fus commencer.

enteritis [ɛntə'raɪtɪs] n entérite f.

enterprise ['ɛntəpraɪz] n (company, undertaking) entreprise f; (initiative) (esprit m d')initiative f.

enterprising ['ɛntəpraɪzɪŋ] adj entreprenant(e), dynamique.

entertain [ɛntə'teɪn] vt amuser, distraire; (invite) recevoir (à dîner); (idea, plan) envisager.

entertainer [ɛntə'teɪnə*] n artiste m/f de variétés.

entertaining [ɛntə'teɪnɪŋ] adj amusant(e), distrayant(e) ♦ n: **to do a lot of** ~ beaucoup recevoir.

entertainment [ɛntə'teɪnmənt] n (amusement) distraction f, divertissement m, amusement m; (show) spectacle m.

entertainment allowance n frais mpl de représentation.

enthral [ɪn'θrɔ:l] vt captiver, passionner.

enthralling [ɪn'θrɔ:lɪŋ] adj captivant(e); enchanteur(eresse).

enthuse [ɪn'θu:z] vi: **to** ~ **about** or **over** parler avec enthousiasme de.

enthusiasm [ɪn'θu:zɪæzəm] n enthousiasme m.

enthusiast [ɪn'θu:zɪæst] n enthousiaste m/f; **a jazz** etc ~ un fervent or passionné du jazz etc.

enthusiastic [ɪnθu:zɪ'æstɪk] adj enthousiaste; **to be** ~ **about** être enthousiasmé(e) par.

entice [ɪn'taɪs] vt attirer, séduire.

enticing [ɪn'taɪsɪŋ] adj (person, offer) séduisant(e); (food) alléchant(e).

entire [ɪn'taɪə*] adj (tout) entier(ère).

entirely [ɪn'taɪəlɪ] adv entièrement, complètement.

entirety [ɪn'taɪərətɪ] n: **in its** ~ dans sa totalité.

entitle [ɪn'taɪtl] vt (allow): **to** ~ **sb to do** donner (le) droit à qn de faire; **to** ~ **sb to sth** donner droit à qch à qn.

entitled [ɪn'taɪtld] adj (book) intitulé(e); **to be** ~ **to sth/to do sth** avoir droit à qch/le droit de faire qch.

entity ['ɛntɪtɪ] n entité f.

entrails ['ɛntreɪlz] npl entrailles fpl.

entrance n ['ɛntrns] entrée f ♦ vt [ɪn'trɑ:ns] enchanter, ravir; **to gain** ~ **to** (university etc) être admis à.

entrance examination n examen m d'entrée or d'admission.

entrance fee n droit m d'inscription; (to museum etc) prix m d'entrée.

entrance ramp n (US AUT) bretelle f d'accès.

entrancing [ɪn'trɑ:nsɪŋ] adj enchanteur(teresse), ravissant(e).

entrant ['ɛntrnt] n (in race etc) participant/e, concurrent/e; (BRIT: in exam) candidat/e.

entreat [ɛn'tri:t] vt supplier.

entreaty [ɛn'tri:tɪ] n supplication f, prière f.

entrée ['ɔntreɪ] n (CULIN) entrée f.

entrenched [ɛn'trɛntʃt] adj retranché(e).

entrepreneur ['ɔntrəprə'nə:*] n entrepreneur m.

entrepreneurial ['ɔntrəprə'nə:rɪəl] adj animé(e) d'un esprit d'entreprise.

entrust [ɪn'trʌst] vt: **to** ~ **sth to** confier qch à.

entry ['ɛntrɪ] n entrée f; (in register, diary) inscription f; (in ledger) écriture f; **"no** ~**"** "défense d'entrer", "entrée interdite"; (AUT) "sens interdit"; **single/double** ~ **bookkeeping** comptabilité f en partie simple/double.

entry form n feuille f d'inscription.

entry phone n (BRIT) interphone m (à l'entrée d'un immeuble).

entwine [ɪn'twaɪn] *vt* entrelacer.
E-number ['iːnʌmbə*] *n* additif *m* (alimentaire).
enumerate [ɪ'njuːməreɪt] *vt* énumérer.
enunciate [ɪ'nʌnsɪeɪt] *vt* énoncer; prononcer.
envelop [ɪn'vɛləp] *vt* envelopper.
envelope ['ɛnvələup] *n* enveloppe *f*.
enviable ['ɛnvɪəbl] *adj* enviable.
envious ['ɛnvɪəs] *adj* envieux(euse).
environment [ɪn'vaɪərnmənt] *n* milieu *m*; environnement *m*; **Department of the E~** (*BRIT*) ministère de l'équipement et de l'aménagement du territoire.
environmental [ɪnvaɪərn'mɛntl] *adj* écologique, relatif(ive) à l'environnement; ~ **studies** (*in school etc*) écologie *f*.
environmentalist [ɪnvaɪərn'mɛntlɪst] *n* écologiste *m/f*.
environmentally [ɪnvaɪərn'mɛntlɪ] *adv*: ~ **sound/friendly** qui ne nuit pas à l'environnement.
Environmental Protection Agency (EPA) *n* (*US*) ≈ ministère *m* de l'Environnement.
envisage [ɪn'vɪzɪdʒ] *vt* envisager; prévoir.
envision [ɪn'vɪʒən] *vt* envisager, concevoir.
envoy ['ɛnvɔɪ] *n* envoyé/e.
envy ['ɛnvɪ] *n* envie *f* ♦ *vt* envier; **to ~ sb sth** envier qch à qn.
enzyme ['ɛnzaɪm] *n* enzyme *m*.
EPA *n abbr* (*US*) = **Environmental Protection Agency**.
ephemeral [ɪ'fɛmərl] *adj* éphémère.
epic ['ɛpɪk] *n* épopée *f* ♦ *adj* épique.
epicentre, (*US*) **epicenter** ['ɛpɪsɛntə*] *n* épicentre *m*.
epidemic [ɛpɪ'dɛmɪk] *n* épidémie *f*.
epilepsy ['ɛpɪlɛpsɪ] *n* épilepsie *f*.
epileptic [ɛpɪ'lɛptɪk] *adj*, *n* épileptique (*m/f*).
epilogue ['ɛpɪlɔg] *n* épilogue *m*.
episcopal [ɪ'pɪskəpl] *adj* épiscopal(e).
episode ['ɛpɪsəud] *n* épisode *m*.
epistle [ɪ'pɪsl] *n* épître *f*.
epitaph ['ɛpɪtɑːf] *n* épitaphe *f*.
epithet ['ɛpɪθɛt] *n* épithète *f*.
epitome [ɪ'pɪtəmɪ] *n* (*fig*) quintessence *f*, type *m*.
epitomize [ɪ'pɪtəmaɪz] *vt* (*fig*) illustrer, incarner.
epoch ['iːpɔk] *n* époque *f*, ère *f*.
epoch-making ['iːpɔkmeɪkɪŋ] *adj* qui fait époque.
eponymous [ɪ'pɔnɪməs] *adj* de ce *or* du même nom, éponyme.
equable ['ɛkwəbl] *adj* égal(e); de tempérament égal.
equal ['iːkwl] *adj* égal(e) ♦ *n* égal/e ♦ *vt* égaler; **~ to** (*task*) à la hauteur de; **~ to doing** de taille à *or* capable de faire.
equality [iː'kwɔlɪtɪ] *n* égalité *f*.
equalize ['iːkwəlaɪz] *vt*, *vi* égaliser.
equalizer ['iːkwəlaɪzə*] *n* but égalisateur.
equally ['iːkwəlɪ] *adv* également; (*just as*) tout

aussi; **they are ~ clever** ils sont tout aussi intelligents.
Equal Opportunities Commission, (*US*) **Equal Employment Opportunity Commission** *n* commission pour la non discrimination dans l'emploi.
equal(s) sign *n* signe *m* d'égalité.
equanimity [ɛkwə'nɪmɪtɪ] *n* égalité *f* d'humeur.
equate [ɪ'kweɪt] *vt*: **to ~ sth with** comparer qch à; assimiler qch à; **to ~ sth to** mettre qch en équation avec; égaler qch à.
equation [ɪ'kweɪʃən] *n* (*MATH*) équation *f*.
equator [ɪ'kweɪtə*] *n* équateur *m*.
equatorial [ɛkwə'tɔːrɪəl] *adj* équatorial(e).
Equatorial Guinea *n* Guinée équatoriale.
equestrian [ɪ'kwɛstrɪən] *adj* équestre ♦ *n* écuyer/ère, cavalier/ère.
equilibrium [iːkwɪ'lɪbrɪəm] *n* équilibre *m*.
equinox ['iːkwɪnɔks] *n* équinoxe *m*.
equip [ɪ'kwɪp] *vt* équiper; **to ~ sb/sth with** équiper *or* munir qn/qch de; **he is well ~ped for the job** il a les compétences *or* les qualités requises pour ce travail.
equipment [ɪ'kwɪpmənt] *n* équipement *m*; (*electrical etc*) appareillage *m*, installation *f*.
equitable ['ɛkwɪtəbl] *adj* équitable.
equities ['ɛkwɪtɪz] *npl* (*BRIT COMM*) actions cotées en Bourse.
equity ['ɛkwɪtɪ] *n* équité *f*.
equity capital *n* capitaux *mpl* propres.
equivalent [ɪ'kwɪvəlnt] *adj* équivalent(e) ♦ *n* équivalent *m*; **to be ~ to** équivaloir à, être équivalent(e) à.
equivocal [ɪ'kwɪvəkl] *adj* équivoque; (*open to suspicion*) douteux(euse).
equivocate [ɪ'kwɪvəkeɪt] *vi* user de faux-fuyants; éviter de répondre.
equivocation [ɪkwɪvə'keɪʃən] *n* équivoque *f*.
ER *abbr* (*BRIT*: = *Elizabeth Regina*) la reine Élisabeth.
ERA *n abbr* (*US POL*: = *Equal Rights Amendment*) amendement sur l'égalité des droits des femmes.
era ['ɪərə] *n* ère *f*, époque *f*.
eradicate [ɪ'rædɪkeɪt] *vt* éliminer.
erase [ɪ'reɪz] *vt* effacer.
eraser [ɪ'reɪzə*] *n* gomme *f*.
erect [ɪ'rɛkt] *adj* droit(e) ♦ *vt* construire; (*monument*) ériger, élever; (*tent etc*) dresser.
erection [ɪ'rɛkʃən] *n* (*PHYSIOL*) érection *f*; (*of building*) construction *f*; (*of machinery etc*) installation *f*.
ergonomics [əːgə'nɔmɪks] *n* ergonomie *f*.
ERISA *n abbr* (*US*: = *Employee Retirement Income Security Act*) loi sur les pensions de retraite.
Eritrea [ɛrɪ'treɪə] *n* Érythrée *f*.
ERM *n abbr* (= *Exchange Rate Mechanism*) MTC *m*.
ermine ['əːmɪn] *n* hermine *f*.
ERNIE ['əːnɪ] *n abbr* (*BRIT*: = *Electronic Random*

*Number Indicator Equipment) ordinateur ser-
vant au tirage des bons à lots gagnants.*
erode [ɪ'rəud] *vt* éroder; *(metal)* ronger.
erogenous zone [ɪ'rɔdʒənəs-] *n* zone *f* érogène.
erosion [ɪ'rəuʒən] *n* érosion *f.*
erotic [ɪ'rɔtɪk] *adj* érotique.
eroticism [ɪ'rɔtɪsɪzəm] *n* érotisme *m.*
err [əː*] *vi* se tromper; *(REL)* pécher.
errand ['ɛrnd] *n* course *f*, commission *f*; **to run
~s** faire des courses; **~ of mercy** mission *f*
de charité, acte *m* charitable.
errand boy *n* garçon *m* de courses.
erratic [ɪ'rætɪk] *adj* irrégulier(ière); incons-
tant(e).
erroneous [ɪ'rəunɪəs] *adj* erroné(e).
error ['ɛrə*] *n* erreur *f*; **typing/spelling ~** faute
f de frappe/d'orthographe; **in ~** par erreur,
par méprise; **~s and omissions excepted**
sauf erreur ou omission.
error message *n* *(COMPUT)* message *m*
d'erreur.
erstwhile ['əːstwaɪl] *adj* précédent(e),
d'autrefois.
erudite ['ɛrjudaɪt] *adj* savant(e).
erupt [ɪ'rʌpt] *vi* entrer en éruption; *(fig)* éclater, exploser.
eruption [ɪ'rʌpʃən] *n* éruption *f*, *(of anger, violence)* explosion *f.*
ESA *n abbr* (= *European Space Agency*) ASE *f*
(= *Agence spatiale européenne*).
escalate ['ɛskəleɪt] *vi* s'intensifier; *(costs)*
monter en flèche.
escalation [ɛskə'leɪʃən] *n* escalade *f.*
escalation clause *n* clause *f* d'indexation.
escalator ['ɛskəleɪtə*] *n* escalier roulant.
escapade [ɛskə'peɪd] *n* fredaine *f*; équipée *f.*
escape [ɪ'skeɪp] *n* évasion *f*, fuite *f*; *(of gas etc)*
fuite; (: *TECH)* échappement *m* ♦ *vi*
s'échapper, fuir; *(from jail)* s'évader; *(fig)*
s'en tirer, en réchapper; *(leak)* fuir;
s'échapper ♦ *vt* échapper à; **to ~ from** *(person)* échapper à; *(place)* s'échapper de; *(fig)*
fuir; **to ~ to** *(another place)* fuir à, s'enfuir à;
to ~ to safety se réfugier dans or gagner un
endroit sûr; **to ~ notice** passer inaperçu(e).
escape artist *n* virtuose *m/f* de l'évasion.
escape clause *n* clause *f* dérogatoire.
escapee [ɪskeɪ'piː] *n* évadé/e.
escape key *n* *(COMPUT)* touche *f*
d'échappement.
escape route *n* *(from fire)* issue *f* de secours;
(of prisoners etc) voie empruntée pour
s'échapper.
escapism [ɪ'skeɪpɪzəm] *n* évasion *f* *(fig).*
escapist [ɪ'skeɪpɪst] *adj* *(literature)* d'évasion
♦ *n* personne *f* qui se réfugie hors de la réalité.
escapologist [ɛskə'pɔlədʒɪst] *n* *(BRIT)* = **escape
artist.**
escarpment [ɪs'kɑːpmənt] *n* escarpement *m.*
eschew [ɪs'tʃuː] *vt* éviter.

escort *vt* [ɪ'skɔːt] escorter ♦ *n* ['ɛskɔːt] escorte
f; *(to dance etc)*: **her ~** son compagnon or cavalier; **his ~** sa compagne.
escort agency *n* bureau *m* d'hôtesses.
Eskimo ['ɛskɪməu] *adj* esquimau(de), eskimo
♦ *n* Esquimau/de; *(LING)* esquimau *m.*
ESL *n abbr* *(SCOL)* = *English as a Second Language.*
esophagus [iː'sɔfəgəs] *n* *(US)* = **oesophagus.**
esoteric [ɛsə'tɛrɪk] *adj* ésotérique.
ESP *n abbr* = **extrasensory perception**; *(SCOL)* =
English for Special Purposes.
esp. *abbr* = **especially.**
especially [ɪ'spɛʃlɪ] *adv* *(specifically)* spécialement, exprès; *(more than usually)* particulièrement; *(above all)* particulièrement, surtout.
espionage ['ɛspɪɒnɑːʒ] *n* espionnage *m.*
esplanade [ɛsplə'neɪd] *n* esplanade *f.*
espouse [ɪ'spauz] *vt* épouser, embrasser.
Esquire [ɪ'skwaɪə*] *n* *(BRIT: abbr Esq.)*: J.
Brown, **~** Monsieur J. Brown.
essay ['ɛseɪ] *n* *(SCOL)* dissertation *f*; *(LITERA-
TURE)* essai *m*; *(attempt)* tentative *f.*
essence ['ɛsns] *n* essence *f*; **in ~** en substance; **speed is of the ~** l'essentiel, c'est la
rapidité.
essential [ɪ'sɛnʃl] *adj* essentiel(le); *(basic)* fon-
damental(e) ♦ *n* élément essentiel; **it is ~
that** il est essentiel or primordial que.
essentially [ɪ'sɛnʃlɪ] *adv* essentiellement.
EST *abbr* *(US: = Eastern Standard Time)* heure
d'hiver de New York.
est. *abbr* = *established, estimate(d).*
establish [ɪ'stæblɪʃ] *vt* établir; *(business)* fonder, créer; *(one's power etc)* asseoir, affermir.
establishment [ɪ'stæblɪʃmənt] *n* établissement *m*; création *f*; *(institution)* établissement; **the E~** les pouvoirs établis; l'ordre
établi.
estate [ɪ'steɪt] *n* *(land)* domaine *m*, propriété *f*;
(LAW) biens *mpl*, succession *f*; *(BRIT: also:
housing ~)* lotissement *m.*
estate agency *n* *(BRIT)* agence immobilière.
estate agent *n* *(BRIT)* agent immobilier.
estate car *n* *(BRIT)* break *m.*
esteem [ɪ'stiːm] *n* estime *f* ♦ *vt* estimer; apprécier; **to hold sb in high ~** tenir qn en
haute estime.
esthetic [ɪs'θɛtɪk] *adj* *(US)* = **aesthetic.**
estimate *n* ['ɛstɪmət] estimation *f*; *(COMM)* devis *m* ♦ *vb* ['ɛstɪmeɪt] *vt* estimer ♦ *vi* *(BRIT
COMM)*: **to ~ for** estimer, faire une estimation de; *(bid for)* faire un devis pour; **to give
sb an ~ of** faire or donner un devis à qn
pour; **at a rough ~** approximativement.
estimation [ɛstɪ'meɪʃən] *n* opinion *f*; estime *f*;
in my ~ à mon avis, selon moi.
Estonia [ɛ'stəunɪə] *n* Estonie *f.*
Estonian [ɛ'stəunɪən] *adj* estonien(ne) ♦ *n*
Estonien/ne; *(LING)* estonien *m.*

estranged [ɪs'treɪndʒd] *adj* (*couple*) séparé(e); (*husband, wife*) dont on s'est séparé(e).
estrangement [ɪs'treɪndʒmənt] *n* (*from wife, family*) séparation *f*.
estrogen ['iːstrəudʒən] *n* (*US*) = **oestrogen**.
estuary ['ɛstjuərɪ] *n* estuaire *m*.
ET *abbr* (*US*: = *Eastern Time*) *heure de New York.*
ETA *n abbr* (= *estimated time of arrival*) HPA *f* (= *heure probable d'arrivée*).
et al. *abbr* (= *et alii: and others*) et coll.
etc. *abbr* (= *et cetera*) etc.
etch [ɛtʃ] *vt* graver à l'eau forte.
etching ['ɛtʃɪŋ] *n* eau-forte *f*.
ETD *n abbr* (= *estimated time of departure*) HPD *f* (= *heure probable de départ*).
eternal [ɪ'təːnl] *adj* éternel(le).
eternity [ɪ'təːnɪtɪ] *n* éternité *f*.
ether ['iːθə*] *n* éther *m*.
ethereal [ɪ'θɪərɪəl] *adj* éthéré(e).
ethical ['ɛθɪkl] *adj* moral(e).
ethics ['ɛθɪks] *n* éthique *f* ♦ *npl* moralité *f*.
Ethiopia [iːθɪ'əupɪə] *n* Éthiopie *f*.
Ethiopian [iːθɪ'əupɪən] *adj* éthiopien(ne) ♦ *n* Éthiopien/ne.
ethnic ['ɛθnɪk] *adj* ethnique; (*clothes, food*) folklorique, exotique; *propre aux minorités ethniques non-occidentales.*
ethnic cleansing [-'klɛnzɪŋ] *n* purification *f* ethnique.
ethnology [ɛθ'nɔlədʒɪ] *n* ethnologie *f*.
ethos ['iːθɔs] *n* (système *m* de) valeurs *fpl*.
etiquette ['ɛtɪkɛt] *n* convenances *fpl*, étiquette *f*.
ETV *n abbr* (*US*: = *Educational Television*) *télévision scolaire.*
etymology [ɛtɪ'mɔlədʒɪ] *n* étymologie *f*.
EU *n abbr* (= *European Union*) UE *f*.
eucalyptus [juːkə'lɪptəs] *n* eucalyptus *m*.
eulogy ['juːlədʒɪ] *n* éloge *m*.
euphemism ['juːfəmɪzəm] *n* euphémisme *m*.
euphemistic [juːfə'mɪstɪk] *adj* euphémique.
euphoria [juː'fɔːrɪə] *n* euphorie *f*.
Eurasia [juə'reɪʃə] *n* Eurasie *f*.
Eurasian [juə'reɪʃən] *adj* eurasien(ne); (*continent*) eurasiatique ♦ *n* Eurasien/ne.
Euratom [juə'rætəm] *n abbr* (= *European Atomic Energy Community*) EURATOM *f*.
euro ['juərəu] *n* (*currency*) euro *m*.
Euro- ['juərəu] *prefix* euro-.
Eurocheque ['juərəutʃɛk] *n* eurochèque *m*.
Eurocrat ['juərəukræt] *n* eurocrate *m/f*.
Eurodollar ['juərəudɔlə*] *n* eurodollar *m*.
Euroland ['juərəu,lænd] *n* Euroland *m*.
Europe ['juərəp] *n* Europe *f*.
European [juərə'piːən] *adj* européen(ne) ♦ *n* Européen/ne.
European Court of Justice *n* Cour *f* de Justice de la CEE.
Euro-sceptic ['juərəuskɛptɪk] *n* eurosceptique *m/f*.
euthanasia [juːθə'neɪzɪə] *n* euthanasie *f*.

evacuate [ɪ'vækjueɪt] *vt* évacuer.
evacuation [ɪvækju'eɪʃən] *n* évacuation *f*.
evacuee [ɪvækju'iː] *n* évacué/e.
evade [ɪ'veɪd] *vt* échapper à; (*question etc*) éluder; (*duties*) se dérober à.
evaluate [ɪ'væljueɪt] *vt* évaluer.
evangelist [ɪ'vændʒəlɪst] *n* évangéliste *m*.
evangelize [ɪ'vændʒəlaɪz] *vt* évangéliser, prêcher l'Évangile à.
evaporate [ɪ'væpəreɪt] *vi* s'évaporer ♦ *vt* faire évaporer.
evaporated milk [ɪ'væpəreɪtɪd-] *n* lait condensé (non sucré).
evaporation [ɪvæpə'reɪʃən] *n* évaporation *f*.
evasion [ɪ'veɪʒən] *n* dérobade *f*; (*excuse*) faux-fuyant *m*.
evasive [ɪ'veɪsɪv] *adj* évasif(ive).
eve [iːv] *n*: **on the ~ of** à la veille de.
even ['iːvn] *adj* régulier(ière), égal(e); (*number*) pair(e) ♦ *adv* même; **~ if** même si + *indicative*; **~ though** quand (bien) même + *conditional*, alors même que + *conditional*; **~ more** encore plus; **~ faster** encore plus vite; **~ so** quand même; **not ~** pas même; **to break ~** s'y retrouver, équilibrer ses comptes; **to get ~ with sb** prendre sa revanche sur qn.
▶**even out** *vi* s'égaliser.
even-handed [iːvn'hændɪd] *adj* équitable.
evening ['iːvnɪŋ] *n* soir *m*; (*as duration, event*) soirée *f*; **in the ~** le soir; **this ~** ce soir; **tomorrow/yesterday ~** demain/hier soir.
evening class *n* cours *m* du soir.
evening dress *n* (*man's*) habit *m* de soirée, smoking *m*; (*woman's*) robe *f* de soirée.
evenly ['iːvnlɪ] *adv* uniformément, également; (*space*) régulièrement.
evensong ['iːvnsɔŋ] *n* office *m* du soir.
event [ɪ'vɛnt] *n* événement *m*; (*SPORT*) épreuve *f*; **in the course of ~s** par la suite; **in the ~ of** en cas de; **in the ~** en réalité, en fait; **at all ~s** (*BRIT*), **in any ~** en tout cas, en toute manière.
eventful [ɪ'vɛntful] *adj* mouvementé(e).
eventing [ɪ'vɛntɪŋ] *n* (*HORSE-RIDING*) concours complet (*équitation*).
eventual [ɪ'vɛntʃuəl] *adj* final(e).
eventuality [ɪvɛntʃu'ælɪtɪ] *n* possibilité *f*, éventualité *f*.
eventually [ɪ'vɛntʃuəlɪ] *adv* finalement.
ever ['ɛvə*] *adv* jamais; (*at all times*) toujours; **the best ~** le meilleur qu'on ait jamais vu; **did you ~ meet him?** est-ce qu'il vous est arrivé de le rencontrer?; **have you ~ been there?** y êtes-vous déjà allé?; **for ~** pour toujours; **hardly ~** ne ... presque jamais; **~ since** *adv* depuis ♦ *conj* depuis que; **~ so pretty** si joli; **thank you ~ so much** merci mille fois;
Everest ['ɛvərɪst] *n* (*also*: **Mount ~**) le mont Everest, l'Everest *m*.
evergreen ['ɛvəgriːn] *n* arbre *m* à feuilles persistantes.

everlasting [ɛvə'lɑːstɪŋ] adj éternel(le).
every ['ɛvrɪ] adj chaque; ~ **day** tous les jours, chaque jour; ~ **other/third day** tous les deux/trois jours; ~ **other car** une voiture sur deux; ~ **now and then** de temps en temps; **I have** ~ **confidence in him** j'ai entièrement or pleinement confiance en lui.
everybody ['ɛvrɪbɔdɪ] pron tout le monde, tous pl; ~ **knows about it** tout le monde le sait; ~ **else** tous les autres.
everyday ['ɛvrɪdeɪ] adj (expression) courant(e), d'usage courant; (use) courant; (occurrence, experience) de tous les jours, ordinaire.
everyone ['ɛvrɪwʌn] = **everybody**.
everything ['ɛvrɪθɪŋ] pron tout; ~ **is ready** tout est prêt; **he did** ~ **possible** il a fait tout son possible.
everywhere ['ɛvrɪwɛə*] adv partout; ~ **you go you meet** ... où qu'on aille, on rencontre ....
evict [ɪ'vɪkt] vt expulser.
eviction [ɪ'vɪkʃən] n expulsion f.
eviction notice n préavis m d'expulsion.
evidence ['ɛvɪdns] n (proof) preuve(s) f(pl); (of witness) témoignage m; (sign): **to show** ~ **of** donner des signes de; **to give** ~ témoigner, déposer; **in** ~ (obvious) en évidence; en vue.
evident ['ɛvɪdnt] adj évident(e).
evidently ['ɛvɪdntlɪ] adv de toute évidence.
evil ['iːvl] adj mauvais(e) ♦ n mal m.
evince [ɪ'vɪns] vt manifester.
evocative [ɪ'vɔkətɪv] adj évocateur(trice).
evoke [ɪ'vəuk] vt évoquer; (admiration) susciter.
evolution [iːvə'luːʃən] n évolution f.
evolve [ɪ'vɔlv] vt élaborer ♦ vi évoluer, se transformer.
ewe [juː] n brebis f.
ewer ['juːə*] n broc m.
ex- [ɛks] prefix (former: husband, president etc) ex-; (out of): **the price** ~ **works** le prix départ usine.
exacerbate [ɛks'æsəbeɪt] vt (pain) exacerber, accentuer; (fig) aggraver.
exact [ɪg'zækt] adj exact(e) ♦ vt: **to** ~ **sth (from)** extorquer qch (à); exiger qch (de).
exacting [ɪg'zæktɪŋ] adj exigeant(e); (work) fatigant(e).
exactitude [ɪg'zæktɪtjuːd] n exactitude f, précision f.
exactly [ɪg'zæktlɪ] adv exactement; ~! parfaitement!, précisément!
exaggerate [ɪg'zædʒəreɪt] vt, vi exagérer.
exaggeration [ɪgzædʒə'reɪʃən] n exagération f.
exalted [ɪg'zɔːltɪd] adj (rank) élevé(e); (person) haut placé(e); (elated) exalté(e).
exam [ɪg'zæm] n abbr (SCOL) = **examination**.
examination [ɪgzæmɪ'neɪʃən] n (SCOL, MED) examen m; **to take** or (BRIT) **sit an** ~ passer un examen; **the matter is under** ~ la question est à l'examen.

examine [ɪg'zæmɪn] vt (gen) examiner; (SCOL, LAW: person) interroger; (inspect: machine, premises) inspecter; (passport) contrôler; (luggage) fouiller.
examiner [ɪg'zæmɪnə*] n examinateur/trice.
example [ɪg'zɑːmpl] n exemple m; **for** ~ par exemple; **to set a good/bad** ~ donner le bon/mauvais exemple.
exasperate [ɪg'zɑːspəreɪt] vt exaspérer, agacer.
exasperation [ɪgzɑːspə'reɪʃən] n exaspération f, irritation f.
excavate ['ɛkskəveɪt] vt excaver; (object) mettre au jour.
excavation [ɛkskə'veɪʃən] n excavation f.
excavator ['ɛkskəveɪtə*] n excavateur m, excavatrice f.
exceed [ɪk'siːd] vt dépasser; (one's powers) outrepasser.
exceedingly [ɪk'siːdɪŋlɪ] adv excessivement.
excel [ɪk'sɛl] vi exceller ♦ vt surpasser; **to** ~ **o.s.** (BRIT) se surpasser.
excellence ['ɛksələns] n excellence f.
Excellency ['ɛksələnsɪ] n: **His** ~ son Excellence f.
excellent ['ɛksələnt] adj excellent(e).
except [ɪk'sɛpt] prep (also: ~ **for**, ~**ing**) sauf, excepté, à l'exception de ♦ vt excepter; ~ **if/when** sauf si/quand; ~ **that** excepté que, si ce n'est que.
exception [ɪk'sɛpʃən] n exception f; **to take** ~ **to** s'offusquer de; **with the** ~ **of** à l'exception de.
exceptional [ɪk'sɛpʃənl] adj exceptionnel(le).
excerpt ['ɛksəːpt] n extrait m.
excess [ɪk'sɛs] n excès m; **in** ~ **of** plus de.
excess baggage n excédent m de bagages.
excess fare n supplément m.
excessive [ɪk'sɛsɪv] adj excessif(ive).
excess supply n suroffre f, offre f excédentaire.
exchange [ɪks'tʃeɪndʒ] n échange m; (also: **telephone** ~) central m ♦ vt: **to** ~ **(for)** échanger (contre); **in** ~ **for** en échange de; **foreign** ~ (COMM) change m.
exchange control n contrôle m des changes.
exchange market n marché m des changes.
exchange rate n taux m de change.
exchequer [ɪks'tʃɛkə*] n (BRIT) Échiquier m, ≈ ministère m des Finances.
excisable [ɪk'saɪzəbl] adj taxable.
excise n ['ɛksaɪz] taxe f ♦ vt [ɛk'saɪz] exciser.
excise duties npl impôts indirects.
excitable [ɪk'saɪtəbl] adj excitable, nerveux(euse).
excite [ɪk'saɪt] vt exciter; **to get** ~**d** s'exciter.
excitement [ɪk'saɪtmənt] n excitation f.
exciting [ɪk'saɪtɪŋ] adj passionnant(e).
excl. abbr = **excluding**, **exclusive (of)**.
exclaim [ɪk'skleɪm] vi s'exclamer.
exclamation [ɛksklə'meɪʃən] n exclamation f.
exclamation mark n point m d'exclamation.

exclude [ɪk'skluːd] *vt* exclure.

excluding [ɪk'skluːdɪŋ] *prep:* ~ **VAT** la TVA non comprise.

exclusion [ɪk'skluːʒən] *n* exclusion *f*; **to the ~ of** à l'exclusion de.

exclusion clause *n* clause *f* d'exclusion.

exclusion zone *n* zone interdite.

exclusive [ɪk'skluːsɪv] *adj* exclusif(ive); (*club, district*) sélect(e); (*item of news*) en exclusivité ♦ *adv* (*COMM*) exclusivement, non inclus; ~ **of VAT** TVA non comprise; ~ **of postage** (les) frais de poste non compris; **from 1st to 15th March** ~ du 1er au 15 mars exclusivement *or* exclu; ~ **rights** (*COMM*) exclusivité *f*.

exclusively [ɪk'skluːsɪvlɪ] *adv* exclusivement.

excommunicate [ɛkskə'mjuːnɪkeɪt] *vt* excommunier.

excrement ['ɛkskrəmənt] *n* excrément *m*.

excruciating [ɪk'skruːʃɪeɪtɪŋ] *adj* atroce, déchirant(e).

excursion [ɪk'skəːʃən] *n* excursion *f*.

excursion ticket *n* billet *m* tarif excursion.

excusable [ɪk'skjuːzəbl] *adj* excusable.

excuse *n* [ɪk'skjuːs] excuse *f* ♦ *vt* [ɪk'skjuːz] excuser; (*justify*) excuser, justifier; **to ~ sb from** (*activity*) dispenser qn de; ~ **me!** excusez-moi!, pardon!; **now if you will ~ me, ...** maintenant, si vous (le) permettez ...; **to make ~s for sb** trouver des excuses à qn; **to ~ o.s. for sth/for doing sth** s'excuser de/d'avoir fait qch.

ex-directory ['ɛksdɪ'rɛktərɪ] *adj* (*BRIT*): ~ **(phone) number** numéro *m* (de téléphone) sur la liste rouge.

execute ['ɛksɪkjuːt] *vt* exécuter.

execution [ɛksɪ'kjuːʃən] *n* exécution *f*.

executioner [ɛksɪ'kjuːʃnə*] *n* bourreau *m*.

executive [ɪg'zɛkjutɪv] *n* (*COMM*) cadre *m*; (*POL*) exécutif *m* ♦ *adj* exécutif(ive); (*position, job*) de cadre; (*secretary*) de direction; (*offices*) de la direction; (*car, plane*) de fonction.

executive director *n* administrateur/trice.

executor [ɪg'zɛkjutə*] *n* exécuteur/trice testamentaire.

exemplary [ɪg'zɛmplərɪ] *adj* exemplaire.

exemplify [ɪg'zɛmplɪfaɪ] *vt* illustrer.

exempt [ɪg'zɛmpt] *adj:* ~ **from** exempté(e) *or* dispensé(e) de ♦ *vt:* **to ~ sb from** exempter *or* dispenser qn de.

exemption [ɪg'zɛmpʃən] *n* exemption *f*, dispense *f*.

exercise ['ɛksəsaɪz] *n* exercice *m* ♦ *vt* exercer; (*patience etc*) faire preuve de; (*dog*) promener ♦ *vi* (*also:* **to take ~**) prendre de l'exercice.

exercise bike *n* vélo *m* d'appartement.

exercise book *n* cahier *m*.

exert [ɪg'zəːt] *vt* exercer, employer; (*strength, force*) employer; **to ~ o.s.** se dépenser.

exertion [ɪg'zəːʃən] *n* effort *m*.

ex gratia ['ɛks'ɡreɪʃə] *adj:* ~ **payment** gratification *f*.

exhale [ɛks'heɪl] *vt* expirer; exhaler ♦ *vi* expirer.

exhaust [ɪg'zɔːst] *n* (*also:* ~ **fumes**) gaz *mpl* d'échappement; (*also:* ~ **pipe**) tuyau *m* d'échappement ♦ *vt* épuiser; **to ~ o.s.** s'épuiser.

exhausted [ɪg'zɔːstɪd] *adj* épuisé(e).

exhausting [ɪg'zɔːstɪŋ] *adj* épuisant(e).

exhaustion [ɪg'zɔːstʃən] *n* épuisement *m*; **nervous ~** fatigue nerveuse.

exhaustive [ɪg'zɔːstɪv] *adj* très complet(ète).

exhibit [ɪg'zɪbɪt] *n* (*ART*) pièce *f or* objet *m* exposé(e); (*LAW*) pièce à conviction ♦ *vt* exposer; (*courage, skill*) faire preuve de.

exhibition [ɛksɪ'bɪʃən] *n* exposition *f*; ~ **of temper** manifestation *f* de colère.

exhibitionist [ɛksɪ'bɪʃənɪst] *n* exhibitionniste *m/f*.

exhibitor [ɪg'zɪbɪtə*] *n* exposant/e.

exhilarating [ɪg'zɪləreɪtɪŋ] *adj* grisant(e); stimulant(e).

exhilaration [ɪgzɪlə'reɪʃən] *n* euphorie *f*, ivresse *f*.

exhort [ɪg'zɔːt] *vt* exhorter.

exile ['ɛksaɪl] *n* exil *m*; (*person*) exilé/e ♦ *vt* exiler; **in ~** en exil.

exist [ɪg'zɪst] *vi* exister.

existence [ɪg'zɪstəns] *n* existence *f*; **to be in ~** exister.

existentialism [ɛgzɪs'tɛnʃlɪzəm] *n* existentialisme *m*.

existing [ɪg'zɪstɪŋ] *adj* (*laws*) existant(e); (*system, regime*) actuel(le).

exit ['ɛksɪt] *n* sortie *f* ♦ *vi* (*COMPUT, THEAT*) sortir.

exit poll *n* sondage *m* (*fait à la sortie de l'isoloir*).

exit ramp *n* (*US AUT*) bretelle *f* d'accès.

exit visa *n* visa *m* de sortie.

exodus ['ɛksədəs] *n* exode *m*.

ex officio ['ɛksə'fɪʃɪəu] *adj, adv* d'office, de droit.

exonerate [ɪg'zɔnəreɪt] *vt:* **to ~ from** disculper de.

exorbitant [ɪg'zɔːbɪtnt] *adj* (*price*) exorbitant(e), excessif(ive); (*demands*) exorbitant, démesuré(e).

exorcize ['ɛksɔːsaɪz] *vt* exorciser.

exotic [ɪg'zɔtɪk] *adj* exotique.

expand [ɪk'spænd] *vt* (*area*) agrandir; (*quantity*) accroître; (*influence etc*) étendre ♦ *vi* (*population, production*) s'accroître; (*trade, influence etc*) se développer, s'étendre; (*gas, metal*) se dilater; **to ~ on** (*notes, story etc*) développer.

expanse [ɪk'spæns] *n* étendue *f*.

expansion [ɪk'spænʃən] *n* (*see expand*) développement *m*; accroissement *m*; extension *f*; dilatation *f*.

expansionism [ɪk'spænʃənɪzəm] *n* expansionnisme m.

expansionist [ɪk'spænʃənɪst] adj expansionniste.

expatriate n [ɛks'pætrɪət] expatrié/e ♦ vt [ɛks'pætrɪeɪt] expatrier, exiler.

expect [ɪk'spɛkt] vt (anticipate) s'attendre à, s'attendre à ce que + sub; (count on) compter sur, escompter; (hope for) espérer; (require) demander, exiger; (suppose) supposer; (await, also baby) attendre ♦ vi: **to be ~ing** être enceinte; **to ~ sb to do** (anticipate) s'attendre à ce que qn fasse; (demand) attendre de qn qu'il fasse; **to ~ to do sth** penser or compter faire qch, s'attendre à faire qch; **as ~ed** comme prévu; **I ~ so** je crois que oui, je crois bien.

expectancy [ɪks'pɛktənsɪ] n attente f; **life ~** espérance f de vie.

expectant [ɪk'spɛktənt] adj qui attend (quelque chose); **~ mother** future maman.

expectantly [ɪk'spɛktəntlɪ] adv (look, listen) avec l'air d'attendre quelque chose.

expectation [ɛkspɛk'teɪʃən] n attente f, prévisions fpl; espérance(s) f(pl); **in ~ of** dans l'attente de, en prévision de; **against** or **contrary to all ~(s)** contre toute attente, contrairement à ce qu'on attendait; **to come** or **live up to sb's ~s** répondre à l'attente or aux espérances de qn.

expedience, expediency [ɪk'spiːdɪəns, ɪk'spiːdɪənsɪ] n opportunité f, convenance f (du moment); **for the sake of ~** parce que c'est (or c'était) plus simple or plus commode.

expedient [ɪk'spiːdɪənt] adj indiqué(e), opportun(e); commode ♦ n expédient m.

expedite ['ɛkspədaɪt] vt hâter; expédier.

expedition [ɛkspə'dɪʃən] n expédition f.

expeditionary force [ɛkspə'dɪʃənrɪ-] n corps m expéditionnaire.

expeditious [ɛkspə'dɪʃəs] adj expéditif(ive), prompt(e).

expel [ɪk'spɛl] vt chasser, expulser; (SCOL) renvoyer, exclure.

expend [ɪk'spɛnd] vt consacrer; (use up) dépenser.

expendable [ɪk'spɛndəbl] adj remplaçable.

expenditure [ɪk'spɛndɪtʃə*] n dépense f; dépenses fpl.

expense [ɪk'spɛns] n (cost) coût m; (spending) dépense f, frais mpl; **~s** npl frais mpl; dépenses; **to go to the ~ of** faire la dépense de; **at great/little ~** à grands/peu de frais; **at the ~ of** aux frais de; (fig) aux dépens de.

expense account n (note f de) frais mpl.

expensive [ɪk'spɛnsɪv] adj cher(chère), coûteux(euse); **to be ~** coûter cher; **~ tastes** goûts mpl de luxe.

experience [ɪk'spɪərɪəns] n expérience f ♦ vt connaître; éprouver; **to know by ~** savoir par expérience.

experienced [ɪk'spɪərɪənst] adj expérimen-

té(e).

experiment [ɪk'spɛrɪmənt] n expérience f ♦ vi faire une expérience; **to ~ with** expérimenter; **to perform** or **carry out an ~** faire une expérience; **as an ~** à titre d'expérience.

experimental [ɪkspɛrɪ'mɛntl] adj expérimental(e).

expert ['ɛkspəːt] adj expert(e) ♦ n expert m; **~ in** or **at doing sth** spécialiste de qch; **an ~ on sth** un spécialiste de qch; **~ witness** (LAW) expert m.

expertise [ɛkspəː'tiːz] n (grande) compétence.

expire [ɪk'spaɪə*] vi expirer.

expiry [ɪk'spaɪərɪ] n expiration f.

explain [ɪk'spleɪn] vt expliquer.

▶**explain away** vt justifier, excuser.

explanation [ɛksplə'neɪʃən] n explication f; **to find an ~ for sth** trouver une explication à qch.

explanatory [ɪk'splænətrɪ] adj explicatif(ive).

expletive [ɪk'spliːtɪv] n juron m.

explicit [ɪk'splɪsɪt] adj explicite; (definite) formel(le).

explode [ɪk'spləud] vi exploser ♦ vt faire exploser; (fig: theory) démolir; **to ~ a myth** détruire un mythe.

exploit n ['ɛksplɔɪt] exploit m ♦ vt [ɪk'splɔɪt] exploiter.

exploitation [ɛksplɔɪ'teɪʃən] n exploitation f.

exploration [ɛksplə'reɪʃən] n exploration f.

exploratory [ɪk'splɔrətrɪ] adj (fig: talks) préliminaire; **~ operation** (MED) intervention f (à visée) exploratrice.

explore [ɪk'splɔː*] vt explorer; (possibilities) étudier, examiner.

explorer [ɪk'splɔːrə*] n explorateur/trice.

explosion [ɪk'spləuʒən] n explosion f.

explosive [ɪk'spləusɪv] adj explosif(ive) ♦ n explosif m.

exponent [ɪk'spəunənt] n (of school of thought etc) interprète m, représentant m; (MATH) exposant m.

export vt [ɛk'spɔːt] exporter ♦ n ['ɛkspɔːt] exportation f ♦ cpd d'exportation.

exportation [ɛkspɔː'teɪʃən] n exportation f.

exporter [ɛk'spɔːtə*] n exportateur m.

export licence n licence f d'exportation.

expose [ɪk'spəuz] vt exposer; (unmask) démasquer, dévoiler; **to ~ o.s.** (LAW) commettre un outrage à la pudeur.

exposed [ɪk'spəuzd] adj (land, house) exposé(e); (ELEC: wire) à nu; (pipe, beam) apparent(e).

exposition [ɛkspə'zɪʃən] n exposition f.

exposure [ɪk'spəuʒə*] n exposition f; (PHOT) (temps m de) pose f; (: shot) pose; **suffering from ~** (MED) souffrant des effets du froid et de l'épuisement; **to die of ~** (MED) mourir de froid.

exposure meter n posemètre m.

expound [ɪk'spaund] vt exposer, expliquer.

express [ɪk'sprɛs] *adj* (*definite*) formel(le), exprès(esse); (*BRIT: letter etc*) exprès *inv* ♦ *n* (*train*) rapide *m* ♦ *adv* (*send*) exprès ♦ *vt* exprimer; **to ~ o.s.** s'exprimer.
expression [ɪk'sprɛʃən] *n* expression *f*.
expressionism [ɪk'sprɛʃənɪzəm] *n* expressionnisme *m*.
expressive [ɪk'sprɛsɪv] *adj* expressif(ive).
expressly [ɪk'sprɛslɪ] *adv* expressément, formellement.
expressway [ɪk'sprɛsweɪ] *n* (*US*) voie *f* express (à plusieurs files).
expropriate [ɛks'prəʊprɪeɪt] *vt* exproprier.
expulsion [ɪk'spʌlʃən] *n* expulsion *f*; renvoi *m*.
exquisite [ɛk'skwɪzɪt] *adj* exquis(e).
ex-serviceman ['ɛks'sə:vɪsmən] *n* ancien combattant.
ext. *abbr* (*TEL*) = **extension.**
extemporize [ɪk'stɛmpəraɪz] *vi* improviser.
extend [ɪk'stɛnd] *vt* (*visit, street*) prolonger; (*deadline*) reporter, remettre; (*building*) agrandir; (*offer*) présenter, offrir; (*COMM: credit*) accorder ♦ *vi* (*land*) s'étendre.
extension [ɪk'stɛnʃən] *n* (*see extend*) prolongation *f*; agrandissement *m*; (*building*) annexe *f*; (*to wire, table*) rallonge *f*; (*telephone: in offices*) poste *m*; (*: in private house*) téléphone *m* supplémentaire; **~ 3718** (*TEL*) poste 3718.
extension cable *n* (*ELEC*) rallonge *f*.
extensive [ɪk'stɛnsɪv] *adj* étendu(e), vaste; (*damage, alterations*) considérable; (*inquiries*) approfondi(e); (*use*) largement répandu(e).
extensively [ɪk'stɛnsɪvlɪ] *adv* (*altered, damaged etc*) considérablement; **he's travelled ~** il a beaucoup voyagé.
extent [ɪk'stɛnt] *n* étendue *f*; (*degree: of damage, loss*) importance *f*; **to some ~** dans une certaine mesure; **to a certain ~** dans une certaine mesure, jusqu'à un certain point; **to a large ~** en grande partie; **to what ~?** dans quelle mesure?, jusqu'à quel point?; **to such an ~ that ...** à tel point que ....
extenuating [ɪk'stɛnjueɪtɪŋ] *adj*: **~ circumstances** circonstances atténuantes.
exterior [ɛk'stɪərɪə*] *adj* extérieur(e), du dehors ♦ *n* extérieur *m*; dehors *m*.
exterminate [ɪk'stə:mɪneɪt] *vt* exterminer.
extermination [ɪkstə:mɪ'neɪʃən] *n* extermination *f*.
external [ɛk'stə:nl] *adj* externe ♦ *n*: **the ~s** les apparences *fpl*; **for ~ use only** (*MED*) à usage externe.
externally [ɛk'stə:nəlɪ] *adv* extérieurement.
extinct [ɪk'stɪŋkt] *adj* éteint(e).
extinction [ɪk'stɪŋkʃən] *n* extinction *f*.
extinguish [ɪk'stɪŋgwɪʃ] *vt* éteindre.
extinguisher [ɪk'stɪŋgwɪʃə*] *n* extincteur *m*.
extol, (*US*) **extoll** [ɪk'stəʊl] *vt* (*merits*) chanter, prôner; (*person*) chanter les louanges de.
extort [ɪk'stɔ:t] *vt*: **to ~ sth (from)** extorquer qch (à).

extortion [ɪk'stɔ:ʃən] *n* extorsion *f*.
extortionate [ɪk'stɔ:ʃnɪt] *adj* exorbitant(e).
extra ['ɛkstrə] *adj* supplémentaire, de plus ♦ *adv* (*in addition*) en plus ♦ *n* supplément *m*; (*THEAT*) figurant/e; **wine will cost ~** le vin sera en supplément; **~ large sizes** très grandes tailles.
extra... ['ɛkstrə] *prefix* extra....
extract *vt* [ɪk'strækt] extraire; (*tooth*) arracher; (*money, promise*) soutirer ♦ *n* ['ɛkstrækt] extrait *m*.
extraction [ɪk'strækʃən] *n* (*also descent*) extraction *f*.
extractor fan [ɪk'stræktə-] *n* exhausteur *m*, ventilateur *m* extracteur.
extracurricular ['ɛkstrəkə'rɪkjulə*] *adj* (*SCOL*) parascolaire.
extradite ['ɛkstrədaɪt] *vt* extrader.
extradition [ɛkstrə'dɪʃən] *n* extradition *f*.
extramarital ['ɛkstrə'mærɪtl] *adj* extraconjugal(e).
extramural ['ɛkstrə'mjuərl] *adj* hors-faculté *inv*.
extraneous [ɛk'streɪnɪəs] *adj*: **~ to** étranger(ère) à.
extraordinary [ɪk'strɔ:dnrɪ] *adj* extraordinaire; **the ~ thing is that ...** le plus étrange *or* étonnant c'est que ....
extraordinary general meeting *n* assemblée générale extraordinaire.
extrapolation [ɛkstræpə'leɪʃən] *n* extrapolation *f*.
extrasensory perception (ESP) ['ɛkstrə'sɛnsərɪ-] *n* perception extrasensorielle.
extra time *n* (*FOOTBALL*) prolongations *fpl*.
extravagance [ɪk'strævəgəns] *n* (*excessive spending*) prodigalités *fpl*; (*thing bought*) folie *f*, dépense excessive *or* exagérée.
extravagant [ɪk'strævəgənt] *adj* extravagant(e); (*in spending: person*) prodigue, dépensier(ière); (*: tastes*) dispendieux(euse).
extreme [ɪk'stri:m] *adj*, *n* extrême (*m*); **the ~ left/right** (*POL*) l'extrême gauche *f*/droite *f*; **~s of temperature** différences *fpl* extrêmes de température.
extremely [ɪk'stri:mlɪ] *adv* extrêmement.
extremist [ɪk'stri:mɪst] *adj*, *n* extrémiste (*m/f*).
extremity [ɪk'strɛmɪtɪ] *n* extrémité *f*.
extricate [ɪk'strɪkeɪt] *vt*: **to ~ sth (from)** dégager qch (de).
extrovert ['ɛkstrəvə:t] *n* extraverti/e.
exuberance [ɪg'zju:bərns] *n* exubérance *f*.
exuberant [ɪg'zju:bərnt] *adj* exubérant(e).
exude [ɪg'zju:d] *vt* exsuder; (*fig*) respirer; **the charm etc he ~s** le charme *etc* qui émane de lui.
exult [ɪg'zʌlt] *vi* exulter, jubiler.
exultant [ɪg'zʌltənt] *adj* (*shout, expression*) de triomphe; **to be ~** jubiler, triompher.
exultation [ɛgzʌl'teɪʃən] *n* exultation *f*, jubilation *f*.

eye [aɪ] n œil m (pl yeux); (of needle) trou m, chas m ♦ vt examiner; **as far as the ~ can see** à perte de vue; **to keep an ~ on** surveiller; **to have an ~ for sth** avoir l'œil pour qch; **in the public ~** en vue; **with an ~ to doing sth** (BRIT) en vue de faire qch; **there's more to this than meets the ~** ce n'est pas aussi simple que cela paraît.

eyeball ['aɪbɔːl] n globe m oculaire.

eyebath ['aɪbɑːθ] n (BRIT) œillère f (pour bains d'œil).

eyebrow ['aɪbrau] n sourcil m.

eyebrow pencil n crayon m à sourcils.

eye-catching ['aɪkætʃɪŋ] adj voyant(e), accrocheur(euse).

eye cup n (US) = eyebath.

eyedrops ['aɪdrɔps] npl gouttes fpl pour les yeux.

eyeful ['aɪful] n: **to get an ~ (of sth)** se rincer l'œil (en voyant qch).

eyeglass ['aɪglɑːs] n monocle m.

eyelash ['aɪlæʃ] n cil m.

eyelet ['aɪlɪt] n œillet m.

eye-level ['aɪlɛvl] adj en hauteur.

eyelid ['aɪlɪd] n paupière f.

eyeliner ['aɪlaɪnə*] n eye-liner m.

eye-opener ['aɪəupnə*] n révélation f.

eyeshadow ['aɪʃædəu] n ombre f à paupières.

eyesight ['aɪsaɪt] n vue f.

eyesore ['aɪsɔː*] n horreur f, chose f qui dépare or enlaidit.

eyestrain ['aɪstreɪn] adj: **to get ~** se fatiguer la vue or les yeux.

eyetooth, pl **-teeth** ['aɪtuːθ, -tiːθ] n canine supérieure; **to give one's eyeteeth for sth/to do sth** (fig) donner n'importe quoi pour qch/pour faire qch.

eyewash ['aɪwɔʃ] n bain m d'œil; (fig) frime f.

eye witness n témoin m oculaire.

eyrie ['ɪərɪ] n aire f.

F f

F, f [ɛf] n (letter) F, f m; (MUS): **F** fa m; **F for Frederick,** (US) **F for Fox** F comme François.

F abbr (= Fahrenheit) F.

FA n abbr (BRIT: = Football Association) fédération de football.

FAA n abbr (US) = Federal Aviation Administration.

fable ['feɪbl] n fable f.

fabric ['fæbrɪk] n tissu m ♦ cpd: **~ ribbon** n (for typewriter) ruban m (en) tissu.

fabricate ['fæbrɪkeɪt] vt fabriquer, inventer.

fabrication [fæbrɪ'keɪʃən] n fabrication f, invention f.

fabulous ['fæbjuləs] adj fabuleux(euse); (col: super) formidable, sensationnel(le).

façade [fə'sɑːd] n façade f.

face [feɪs] n visage m, figure f; expression f; grimace f; (of clock) cadran m; (of building) façade f; (side, surface) face f ♦ vt faire face à; (facts etc) accepter; **~ down** (person) à plat ventre; (card) face en dessous; **to lose/save ~** perdre/sauver la face; **to pull a ~** faire une grimace; **in the ~ of** (difficulties etc) face à, devant; **on the ~ of it** à première vue.

▶**face up to** vt fus faire face à, affronter.

face cloth n (BRIT) gant m de toilette.

face cream n crème f pour le visage.

face lift n lifting m; (of façade etc) ravalement m, retapage m.

face powder n poudre f (pour le visage).

face-saving ['feɪsseɪvɪŋ] adj qui sauve la face.

facet ['fæsɪt] n facette f.

facetious [fə'siːʃəs] adj facétieux(euse).

face-to-face ['feɪstə'feɪs] adv face à face.

face value ['feɪs'væljuː] n (of coin) valeur nominale; **to take sth at ~** (fig) prendre qch pour argent comptant.

facia ['feɪʃə] n = fascia.

facial ['feɪʃl] adj facial(e) ♦ n soin complet du visage.

facile ['fæsaɪl] adj facile.

facilitate [fə'sɪlɪteɪt] vt faciliter.

facility [fə'sɪlɪtɪ] n facilité f; **facilities** npl installations fpl, équipement m; **credit facilities** facilités de paiement.

facing ['feɪsɪŋ] prep face à, en face de ♦ n (of wall etc) revêtement m; (SEWING) revers m.

facsimile [fæk'sɪmɪlɪ] n (exact replica) facsimilé m; (also: **~ machine**) télécopieur m; (transmitted document) télécopie f.

fact [fækt] n fait m; **in ~** en fait; **to know for a ~ that ...** savoir pertinemment que ....

fact-finding ['fæktfaɪndɪŋ] adj: **a ~ tour** or **mission** une mission d'enquête.

faction ['fækʃən] n faction f.

factional ['fækʃənl] adj de factions.

factor ['fæktə*] n facteur m; (COMM) factor m, société f d'affacturage; (: agent) dépositaire m/f ♦ vi faire du factoring; **safety ~** facteur de sécurité.

factory ['fæktərɪ] n usine f, fabrique f.

factory farming n (BRIT) élevage industriel.

factory floor n: **the ~** (workers) les ouvriers mpl; (workshop) l'usine f; **on the ~** dans les ateliers.

factory ship n navire-usine m.

factual ['fæktjuəl] adj basé(e) sur les faits.

faculty ['fækəltɪ] n faculté f; (US: teaching staff) corps enseignant.

fad [fæd] n (col) manie f; engouement m.

fade [feɪd] vi se décolorer, passer; (light, sound, hope) s'affaiblir, disparaître; (flower) se faner.

▶**fade in** vt (picture) ouvrir en fondu; (sound) monter progressivement.

▶**fade out** vt (picture) fermer en fondu; (sound) baisser progressivement.

faeces, (US) **feces** ['fiːsiːz] npl fèces fpl.

fag [fæg] n (BRIT col: cigarette) sèche f; (: chore): **what a ~!** quelle corvée!; (US col: homosexual) pédé m.

fag end n (BRIT col) mégot m.

fagged out [fægd-] adj (BRIT col) crevé(e).

fail [feɪl] vt (exam) échouer à; (candidate) recaler; (subj: courage, memory) faire défaut à ♦ vi échouer; (supplies) manquer; (eyesight, health, light: also: **be ~ing**) baisser, s'affaiblir; (brakes) lâcher; **to ~ to do sth** (neglect) négliger de or ne pas faire qch; (be unable) ne pas arriver or parvenir à faire qch; **without ~** à coup sûr; sans faute.

failing ['feɪlɪŋ] n défaut m ♦ prep faute de; ~ **that** à défaut, sinon.

failsafe ['feɪlseɪf] adj (device etc) à sûreté intégrée.

failure ['feɪljə*] n échec m; (person) raté/e; (mechanical etc) défaillance f; **his ~ to turn up** le fait de n'être pas venu or qu'il ne soit pas venu.

faint [feɪnt] adj faible; (recollection) vague; (mark) à peine visible; (smell, breeze, trace) léger(ère) ♦ n évanouissement m ♦ vi s'évanouir; **to feel ~** défaillir.

faintest ['feɪntɪst] adj: **I haven't the ~ idea** je n'en ai pas la moindre idée.

faint-hearted ['feɪnt'hɑːtɪd] adj pusillanime.

faintly ['feɪntlɪ] adv faiblement; vaguement.

faintness ['feɪntnɪs] n faiblesse f.

fair [fɛə*] adj équitable, juste; (reasonable) correct(e), honnête; (hair) blond(e); (skin, complexion) pâle, blanc(blanche); (weather) beau(belle); (good enough) assez bon(ne) ♦ adv: **to play ~** jouer franc jeu ♦ n foire f; (BRIT: funfair) fête (foraine); (also: **trade ~**) foire(-exposition) commerciale; **it's not ~!** ce n'est pas juste!; **a ~ amount of** une quantité considérable de.

fair copy n copie f au propre; corrigé m.

fair game n: **to be ~ (for)** être une cible légitime (pour).

fairground ['fɛəgraund] n champ m de foire.

fair-haired [fɛə'hɛəd] adj (person) aux cheveux clairs, blond(e).

fairly ['fɛəlɪ] adv équitablement; (quite) assez; **I'm ~ sure** j'en suis quasiment or presque sûr.

fairness ['fɛənɪs] n (of trial etc) justice f, équité f; (of person) sens m de la justice; **in all ~** en toute justice.

fair play n fair play m.

fairy ['fɛərɪ] n fée f.

fairy godmother n bonne fée.

fairy lights npl (BRIT) guirlande f électrique.

fairy tale n conte m de fées.

faith [feɪθ] n foi f; (trust) confiance f; (sect) culte m, religion f; **to have ~ in sb/sth** avoir confiance en qn/qch.

faithful ['feɪθful] adj fidèle.

faithfully ['feɪθfəlɪ] adv fidèlement; **yours ~** (BRIT: in letters) veuillez agréer l'expression de mes salutations les plus distinguées.

faith healer [-hiːlə*] n guérisseur/euse.

fake [feɪk] n (painting etc) faux m; (photo) trucage m; (person) imposteur m ♦ adj faux(fausse) ♦ vt (emotions) simuler; (photo) truquer; (story) fabriquer; **his illness is a ~** sa maladie est une comédie or de la simulation.

falcon ['fɔːlkən] n faucon m.

Falkland Islands ['fɔːlklənd-] npl: **the ~** les Malouines fpl, les îles fpl Falkland.

fall [fɔːl] n chute f; (decrease) baisse f; (US: autumn) automne m ♦ vi (pt **fell** [fɛl], pp **fallen** ['fɔːlən]) tomber; **~s** npl (waterfall) chute f d'eau, cascade f; **to ~ flat** vi (on one's face) tomber de tout son long, s'étaler; (joke) tomber à plat; (plan) échouer; **to ~ short of** (sb's expectations) ne pas répondre à; **a ~ of snow** (BRIT) une chute de neige.

▶**fall apart** vi tomber en morceaux; (col: emotionally) craquer.

▶**fall back** vi reculer, se retirer.

▶**fall back on** vt fus se rabattre sur; **to have something to ~ back on** (money etc) avoir quelque chose en réserve; (job etc) avoir une solution de rechange.

▶**fall behind** vi prendre du retard.

▶**fall down** vi (person) tomber; (building, hopes) s'effondrer, s'écrouler.

▶**fall for** vt fus (trick) se laisser prendre à; (person) tomber amoureux(euse) de.

▶**fall in** vi s'effondrer; (MIL) se mettre en rangs.

▶**fall in with** vt fus (sb's plans etc) accepter.

▶**fall off** vi tomber; (diminish) baisser, diminuer.

▶**fall out** vi (friends etc) se brouiller.

▶**fall over** vi tomber (par terre).

▶**fall through** vi (plan, project) tomber à l'eau.

fallacy ['fæləsɪ] n erreur f, illusion f.

fallback ['fɔːlbæk] adj: **~ position** position f de repli.

fallen ['fɔːlən] pp of **fall**.

fallible ['fæləbl] adj faillible.

fallopian tube [fə'ləupɪən-] n (ANAT) trompe f de Fallope.

fallout ['fɔːlaut] n retombées (radioactives).

fallout shelter n abri m anti-atomique.

fallow ['fæləu] adj en jachère; en friche.

false [fɔːls] adj faux(fausse); **under ~ pretences** sous un faux prétexte.

false alarm n fausse alerte.

falsehood ['fɔːlshud] n mensonge m.

falsely ['fɔːlslɪ] adv (accuse) à tort.

false teeth npl (BRIT) fausses dents.

falsify ['fɔːlsɪfaɪ] vt falsifier; (accounts) maquiller.

falter ['fɔːltə*] vi chanceler, vaciller.
fame [feɪm] n renommée f, renom m.
familiar [fə'mɪlɪə*] adj familier(ière); **to be ~ with sth** connaître qch; **to make o.s. ~ with sth** se familiariser avec qch; **to be on ~ terms with sb** bien connaître qn.
familiarity [fəmɪlɪ'ærɪtɪ] n familiarité f.
familiarize [fə'mɪlɪəraɪz] vt familiariser.
family ['fæmɪlɪ] n famille f.
family allowance n (BRIT) allocations familiales.
family business n entreprise familiale.
family credit n (BRIT) complément familial.
family doctor n médecin m de famille.
family life n vie f de famille.
family man n père m de famille.
family planning clinic n centre m de planning familial.
family tree n arbre m généalogique.
famine ['fæmɪn] n famine f.
famished ['fæmɪʃt] adj affamé(e); **I'm ~!** (col) je meurs de faim!
famous ['feɪməs] adj célèbre.
famously ['feɪməslɪ] adv (get on) fameusement, à merveille.
fan [fæn] n (folding) éventail m; (ELEC) ventilateur m; (person) fan m, admirateur/trice; (: SPORT) supporter m/f ♦ vt éventer; (fire, quarrel) attiser.
▶**fan out** vi se déployer (en éventail).
fanatic [fə'nætɪk] n fanatique m/f.
fanatical [fə'nætɪkl] adj fanatique.
fan belt n courroie f de ventilateur.
fancied ['fænsɪd] adj imaginaire.
fanciful ['fænsɪful] adj fantaisiste.
fan club n fan-club m.
fancy ['fænsɪ] n fantaisie f, envie f; imagination f ♦ cpd (de) fantaisie inv ♦ vt (feel like, want) avoir envie de; (imagine) imaginer; **to take a ~ to** se prendre d'affection pour; s'enticher de; **it took** or **caught my ~** ça m'a plu; **when the ~ takes him** quand ça lui prend; **to ~ that** ... se figurer or s'imaginer que ...; **he fancies her** elle lui plaît.
fancy dress n déguisement m, travesti m.
fancy-dress ball [fænsɪ'drɛs-] n bal masqué or costumé.
fancy goods npl articles mpl (de) fantaisie.
fanfare ['fænfɛə*] n fanfare f (musique).
fanfold paper ['fænfəuld-] n papier m à pliage accordéon.
fang [fæŋ] n croc m; (of snake) crochet m.
fan heater n (BRIT) radiateur soufflant.
fanlight ['fænlaɪt] n imposte f.
fanny ['fænɪ] n (BRIT col!) chatte f (!); (US col) cul m (!).
fantasize ['fæntəsaɪz] vi fantasmer.
fantastic [fæn'tæstɪk] adj fantastique.
fantasy ['fæntəsɪ] n imagination f, fantaisie f; fantasme m.
fanzine ['fænziːn] n fanzine m.
FAO n abbr (= Food and Agriculture Organization)

FAO f.
FAQ abbr (= free alongside quay) FLQ.
far [fɑː*] adj: **the ~ side/end** l'autre côté/bout; **the ~ left/right** (POL) l'extrême gauche f/ droite f ♦ adv loin; **is it ~ to London?** est-ce qu'on est loin de Londres?; **it's not ~ (from here)** ce n'est pas loin (d'ici); **~ away, ~ off** au loin, dans le lointain; **~ better** beaucoup mieux; **~ from** loin de; **by ~** de loin, de beaucoup; **as ~ back as the 13th century** dès le 13e siècle; **go as ~ as the farm** allez jusqu'à la ferme; **as ~ as I know** pour autant que je sache; **as ~ as possible** dans la mesure du possible; **how ~ have you got with your work?** où en êtes-vous dans votre travail?
faraway ['fɑːrəweɪ] adj lointain(e); (look) absent(e).
farce [fɑːs] n farce f.
farcical ['fɑːsɪkl] adj grotesque.
fare [fɛə*] n (on trains, buses) prix m du billet; (in taxi) prix de la course; (passenger in taxi) client m; (food) table f, chère f ♦ vi se débrouiller.
Far East n: **the ~** l'Extrême-Orient m.
farewell [fɛə'wɛl] excl, n adieu (m) ♦ cpd (party etc) d'adieux.
far-fetched ['fɑː'fɛtʃt] adj exagéré(e), poussé(e).
farm [fɑːm] n ferme f ♦ vt cultiver.
▶**farm out** vt (work etc) distribuer.
farmer ['fɑːmə*] n fermier/ière; cultivateur/trice.
farmhand ['fɑːmhænd] n ouvrier/ière agricole.
farmhouse ['fɑːmhaus] n (maison f de) ferme f.
farming ['fɑːmɪŋ] n agriculture f; **intensive ~** culture intensive; **sheep ~** élevage m du mouton.
farm labourer n = **farmhand**.
farmland ['fɑːmlænd] n terres cultivées or arables.
farm produce n produits mpl agricoles.
farm worker n = **farmhand**.
farmyard ['fɑːmjɑːd] n cour f de ferme.
Faroe Islands ['fɛərəu-] npl, **Faroes** ['fɛərəuz] npl: **the ~** les îles fpl Féroé or Faeroe.
far-reaching ['fɑː'riːtʃɪŋ] adj d'une grande portée.
far-sighted ['fɑː'saɪtɪd] adj presbyte; (fig) prévoyant(e), qui voit loin.
fart [fɑːt] (col!) n pet m ♦ vi péter.
farther ['fɑːðə*] adv plus loin ♦ adj plus eloigné(e), plus lointain(e).
farthest ['fɑːðɪst] superlative of **far**.
FAS abbr (BRIT: = free alongside ship) FLB.
fascia ['feɪʃə] n (AUT) (garniture f du) tableau m de bord.
fascinate ['fæsɪneɪt] vt fasciner, captiver.
fascinating ['fæsɪneɪtɪŋ] adj fascinant(e).
fascination [fæsɪ'neɪʃən] n fascination f.

fascism ['fæʃɪzəm] n fascisme m.
fascist ['fæʃɪst] adj, n fasciste (m/f).
fashion ['fæʃən] n mode f; (manner) façon f, manière f ♦ vt façonner; **in** ~ à la mode; **out of** ~ démodé(e); **in the Greek** ~ à la grecque; **after a** ~ (finish, manage etc) tant bien que mal.
fashionable ['fæʃnəbl] adj à la mode.
fashion designer n (grand(e)) couturier/ière.
fashion show n défilé m de mannequins or de mode.
fast [fɑːst] adj rapide; (clock): **to be** ~ avancer; (dye, colour) grand or bon teint inv ♦ adv vite, rapidement; (stuck, held) solidement ♦ n jeûne m ♦ vi jeûner; **my watch is 5 minutes** ~ ma montre avance de 5 minutes; ~ **asleep** profondément endormi; **as** ~ **as I can** aussi vite que je peux; **to make a boat** ~ (BRIT) amarrer un bateau.
fasten ['fɑːsn] vt attacher, fixer; (coat) attacher, fermer ♦ vi se fermer, s'attacher.
▶**fasten (up)on** vt fus (idea) se cramponner à.
fastener ['fɑːsnə*], **fastening** ['fɑːsnɪŋ] n fermeture f, attache f; (BRIT: zip ~) fermeture éclair inv ® or à glissière f.
fast food n fast food m, restauration f rapide.
fastidious [fæs'tɪdɪəs] adj exigeant(e), difficile.
fast lane n (AUT: in Britain) voie f de droite.
fat [fæt] adj gros(se) ♦ n graisse f; (on meat) gras m; **to live off the** ~ **of the land** vivre grassement.
fatal ['feɪtl] adj fatal(e); (leading to death) mortel(le).
fatalism ['feɪtlɪzəm] n fatalisme m.
fatality [fə'tælɪtɪ] n (road death etc) victime f, décès m.
fatally ['feɪtəlɪ] adv fatalement; mortellement.
fate [feɪt] n destin m; (of person) sort m; **to meet one's** ~ trouver la mort.
fated ['feɪtɪd] adj (person) condamné(e); (project) voué(e) à l'échec.
fateful ['feɪtful] adj fatidique.
fat-free ['fæt'friː] adj sans matières grasses.
father ['fɑːðə*] n père m.
Father Christmas n le Père Noël.
fatherhood ['fɑːðəhud] n paternité f.
father-in-law ['fɑːðərənlɔː] n beau-père m.
fatherland ['fɑːðəlænd] n (mère f) patrie f.
fatherly ['fɑːðəlɪ] adj paternel(le).
fathom ['fæðəm] n brasse f (= 1828 mm) ♦ vt (mystery) sonder, pénétrer.
fatigue [fə'tiːg] n fatigue f; (MIL) corvée f; **metal** ~ fatigue du métal.
fatness ['fætnɪs] n corpulence f, grosseur f.
fatten ['fætn] vt, vi engraisser; **chocolate is** ~**ing** le chocolat fait grossir.
fatty ['fætɪ] adj (food) gras(se) ♦ n (col) gros/grosse.
fatuous ['fætjuəs] adj stupide.
faucet ['fɔːsɪt] n (US) robinet m.

fault [fɔːlt] n faute f; (defect) défaut m; (GEO) faille f ♦ vt trouver des défauts à, prendre en défaut; **it's my** ~ c'est de ma faute; **to find** ~ **with** trouver à redire or à critiquer à; **at** ~ fautif(ive), coupable; **to a** ~ à l'excès.
faultless ['fɔːltlɪs] adj impeccable; irréprochable.
faulty ['fɔːltɪ] adj défectueux(euse).
fauna ['fɔːnə] n faune f.
faux pas ['fəu'pɑː] n impair m, bévue f, gaffe f.
favour, (US) favor ['feɪvə*] n faveur f; (help) service m ♦ vt (proposition) être en faveur de; (pupil etc) favoriser; (team, horse) donner gagnant; **to do sb a** ~ rendre un service à qn; **in** ~ **of** en faveur de; **to be in** ~ **of sth/of doing sth** être partisan de qch/de faire qch; **to find** ~ **with sb** trouver grâce aux yeux de qn.
favo(u)rable ['feɪvrəbl] adj favorable; (price) avantageux(euse).
favo(u)rably ['feɪvrəblɪ] adv favorablement.
favo(u)rite ['feɪvrɪt] adj, n favori(te).
favo(u)ritism ['feɪvrɪtɪzəm] n favoritisme m.
fawn [fɔːn] n faon m ♦ adj (also: ~-coloured) fauve ♦ vi: **to** ~ **(up)on** flatter servilement.
fax [fæks] n (document) télécopie f; (machine) télécopieur m ♦ vt envoyer par télécopie.
FBI n abbr (US: = Federal Bureau of Investigation) FBI m.
FCC n abbr (US) = Federal Communications Commission.
FCO n abbr (BRIT: = Foreign and Commonwealth Office) ministère des Affaires étrangères et du Commonwealth.
FD n abbr (US) = **fire department**.
FDA n abbr (US: = Food and Drug Administration) office de contrôle des produits pharmaceutiques et alimentaires.
FE n abbr = **further education**.
fear [fɪə*] n crainte f, peur f ♦ vt craindre ♦ vi: **to** ~ **for** craindre pour; **to** ~ **that** craindre que; ~ **of heights** vertige m; **for** ~ **of** de peur que + sub or de + infinitive.
fearful ['fɪəful] adj craintif(ive); (sight, noise) affreux(euse), épouvantable; **to be** ~ **of** avoir peur de, craindre.
fearfully ['fɪəfəlɪ] adv (timidly) craintivement; (col: very) affreusement.
fearless ['fɪəlɪs] adj intrépide, sans peur.
fearsome ['fɪəsəm] adj (opponent) redoutable; (sight) épouvantable.
feasibility [fiːzə'bɪlɪtɪ] n (of plan) possibilité f de réalisation, faisabilité f.
feasibility study n étude f de faisabilité.
feasible ['fiːzəbl] adj faisable, réalisable.
feast [fiːst] n festin m, banquet m; (REL: also: ~ **day**) fête f ♦ vi festoyer; **to** ~ **on** se régaler de.
feat [fiːt] n exploit m, prouesse f.
feather ['fɛðə*] n plume f ♦ vt: **to** ~ **one's nest**

(*fig*) faire sa pelote ♦ *cpd* (*bed etc*) de plumes.

feather-weight ['fɛðəweit] *n* poids *m* plume *inv*.

feature ['fiːtʃə*] *n* caractéristique *f*; (*article*) chronique *f*, rubrique *f* ♦ *vt* (*subj: film*) avoir pour vedette(s) ♦ *vi* figurer (en bonne place); ~s *npl* (*of face*) traits *mpl*; **a (special)** ~ **on sth/sb** un reportage sur qch/qn; **it** ~**d prominently in** ... cela a figuré en bonne place sur *or* dans ....

feature film *n* long métrage.

featureless ['fiːtʃəlis] *adj* anonyme, sans traits distinctifs.

Feb. *abbr* (= *February*) fév.

February ['fɛbruərɪ] *n* février *m*; *for phrases see also* **July**.

feces ['fiːsiːz] *npl* (*US*) = **faeces**.

feckless ['fɛklɪs] *adj* inepte.

Fed *abbr* (*US*) = **federal; federation**.

fed [fɛd] *pt, pp of* **feed**; **to be** ~ **up** en avoir marre *or* plein le dos.

Fed. [fɛd] *n abbr* (*US col*) = **Federal Reserve Board**.

federal ['fɛdərəl] *adj* fédéral(e).

Federal Reserve Board *n* (*US*) organe de contrôle de la banque centrale américaine.

Federal Trade Commission (FTC) *n* (*US*) organisme de protection contre les pratiques commerciales abusives.

federation [fɛdə'reɪʃən] *n* fédération *f*.

fee [fiː] *n* rémunération *f*; (*of doctor, lawyer*) honoraires *mpl*; (*of school, college etc*) frais *mpl* de scolarité; (*for examination*) droits *mpl*; **entrance/membership** ~ droit d'entrée/d'inscription; **for a small** ~ pour une somme modique.

feeble ['fiːbl] *adj* faible.

feeble-minded ['fiːbl'maɪndɪd] *adj* faible d'esprit.

feed [fiːd] *n* (*of baby*) tétée *f*; (*of animal*) fourrage *m*; pâture *f*; (*on printer*) mécanisme *m* d'alimentation ♦ *vt* (*pt, pp* **fed** [fɛd]) nourrir; (*horse etc*) donner à manger à; (*machine*) alimenter; (*data etc*): **to** ~ **sth into** fournir qch à, introduire qch dans.

▶**feed back** *vt* (*results*) donner en retour.

▶**feed on** *vt fus* se nourrir de.

feedback ['fiːdbæk] *n* feed-back *m*; (*from person*) réactions *fpl*.

feeder ['fiːdə*] *n* (*bib*) bavette *f*.

feeding bottle ['fiːdɪŋ-] *n* (*BRIT*) biberon *m*.

feel [fiːl] *n* sensation *f* ♦ *vt* (*pt, pp* **felt** [fɛlt]) (*touch*) toucher; tâter, palper; (*cold, pain*) sentir; (*grief, anger*) ressentir, éprouver; (*think, believe*): **to** ~ (**that**) trouver que; **I** ~ **that you ought to do it** il me semble que vous devriez le faire; **to** ~ **hungry/cold** avoir faim/froid; **to** ~ **lonely/better** se sentir seul/mieux; **I don't** ~ **well** je ne me sens pas bien; **to** ~ **sorry for** avoir pitié de; **it** ~**s soft** c'est doux au toucher; **it** ~**s colder here**

je trouve qu'il fait plus froid ici; **it** ~**s like velvet** on dirait du velours, ça ressemble au velours; **to** ~ **like** (*want*) avoir envie de; **to** ~ **about** *or* **around** fouiller, tâtonner; **to get the** ~ **of sth** (*fig*) s'habituer à qch.

feeler ['fiːlə*] *n* (*of insect*) antenne *f*; (*fig*): **to put out a** ~ *or* ~**s** tâter le terrain.

feeling ['fiːlɪŋ] *n* sensation *f*, sentiment *m*; (*impression*) sentiment *m*; **to hurt sb's** ~**s** froisser qn; ~**s ran high about it** cela a déchaîné les passions; **what are your** ~**s about the matter?** quel est votre sentiment sur cette question?; **my** ~ **is that** ... j'estime que ...; **I have a** ~ **that** ... j'ai l'impression que ....

fee-paying school ['fiːpeɪɪŋ-] *n* établissement (d'enseignement) privé.

feet [fiːt] *npl of* **foot**.

feign [feɪn] *vt* feindre, simuler.

felicitous [fɪ'lɪsɪtəs] *adj* heureux(euse).

fell [fɛl] *pt of* **fall** ♦ *vt* (*tree*) abattre ♦ *n* (*BRIT: mountain*) montagne *f*; (: *moorland*): **the** ~**s** la lande ♦ *adj*: **with one** ~ **blow** d'un seul coup.

fellow ['fɛləu] *n* type *m*; (*comrade*) compagnon *m*; (*of learned society*) membre *m*; (*of university*) universitaire *m/f* (*membre du conseil*) ♦ *cpd*: **their** ~ **prisoners/students** leurs camarades prisonniers/étudiants; **his** ~ **workers** ses collègues *mpl* (de travail).

fellow citizen *n* concitoyen/ne.

fellow countryman *n* compatriote *m*.

fellow feeling *n* sympathie *f*.

fellow men *npl* semblables *mpl*.

fellowship ['fɛləuʃɪp] *n* (*society*) association *f*; (*comradeship*) amitié *f*, camaraderie *f*; (*SCOL*) sorte de bourse universitaire.

fellow traveller *n* compagnon/compagne de route; (*POL*) communiste *m/e*.

fell-walking ['fɛlwɔːkɪŋ] *n* (*BRIT*) randonnée *f* en montagne.

felon ['fɛlən] *n* (*LAW*) criminel/le.

felony ['fɛlənɪ] *n* (*LAW*) crime *m*, forfait *m*.

felt [fɛlt] *pt, pp of* **feel** ♦ *n* feutre *m*.

felt-tip pen ['fɛlttɪp-] *n* stylo-feutre *m*.

female ['fiːmeɪl] *n* (*ZOOL*) femelle *f*; (*pej: woman*) bonne femme ♦ *adj* (*BIOL, ELEC*) femelle; (*sex, character*) féminin(e); (*vote etc*) des femmes; (*child etc*) du sexe féminin; **male and** ~ **students** étudiants et étudiantes.

female impersonator *n* (*THEAT*) travesti *m*.

feminine ['fɛmɪnɪn] *adj* féminin(e) ♦ *n* féminin *m*.

femininity [fɛmɪ'nɪnɪtɪ] *n* féminité *f*.

feminism ['fɛmɪnɪzəm] *n* féminisme *m*.

feminist ['fɛmɪnɪst] *n* féministe *m/f*.

fen [fɛn] *n* (*BRIT*): **the F**~**s** les plaines *fpl* du Norfolk (*anciennement marécageuses*).

fence [fɛns] *n* barrière *f*; (*SPORT*) obstacle *m*; (*col: person*) receleur/euse ♦ *vt* (*also*: ~ **in**) clôturer ♦ *vi* faire de l'escrime; **to sit on the** ~ (*fig*) ne pas se mouiller.

fencing ['fɛnsɪŋ] *n* (*sport*) escrime *m*.

fend [fɛnd] *vi*: **to ~ for o.s.** se débrouiller (tout seul).
▶**fend off** *vt* (attack etc) parer.
fender ['fɛndə*] *n* (of fireplace) garde-feu *m inv*; (on boat) défense *f*; (*US*: of car) aile *f*.
fennel ['fɛnl] *n* fenouil *m*.
ferment *vi* [fə'mɛnt] fermenter ♦ *n* ['fə:mɛnt] agitation *f*, effervescence *f*.
fermentation [fə:mɛn'teɪʃən] *n* fermentation *f*.
fern [fə:n] *n* fougère *f*.
ferocious [fə'rəuʃəs] *adj* féroce.
ferocity [fə'rɔsɪtɪ] *n* férocité *f*.
ferret ['fɛrɪt] *n* furet *m*.
▶**ferret about, ferret around** *vi* fureter.
▶**ferret out** *vt* dénicher.
ferry ['fɛrɪ] *n* (small) bac *m*; (large: also: ~boat) ferry(-boat *m*) *m* ♦ *vt* transporter; **to ~ sth/sb across** *or* **over** faire traverser qch/qn.
ferryman ['fɛrɪmən] *n* passeur *m*.
fertile ['fə:taɪl] *adj* fertile; (BIOL) fécond(e); **~ period** période *f* de fécondité.
fertility [fə'tɪlɪtɪ] *n* fertilité *f*; fécondité *f*.
fertility drug *n* médicament *m* contre la stérilité.
fertilize ['fə:tɪlaɪz] *vt* fertiliser; féconder.
fertilizer ['fə:tɪlaɪzə*] *n* engrais *m*.
fervent ['fə:vənt] *adj* fervent(e), ardent(e).
fervour, (*US*) **fervor** ['fə:və*] *n* ferveur *f*.
fester ['fɛstə*] *vi* suppurer.
festival ['fɛstɪvəl] *n* (REL) fête *f*; (ART, MUS) festival *m*.
festive ['fɛstɪv] *adj* de fête; **the ~ season** (BRIT: Christmas) la période des fêtes.
festivities [fɛs'tɪvɪtɪz] *npl* réjouissances *fpl*.
festoon [fɛs'tu:n] *vt*: **to ~ with** orner de.
fetch [fɛtʃ] *vt* aller chercher; (BRIT: sell for) se vendre; **how much did it ~?** ça a atteint quel prix?
▶**fetch up** *vi* (BRIT) se retrouver.
fetching ['fɛtʃɪŋ] *adj* charmant(e).
fête [feɪt] *n* fête *f*, kermesse *f*.
fetid ['fɛtɪd] *adj* fétide.
fetish ['fɛtɪʃ] *n* fétiche *m*.
fetter ['fɛtə*] *vt* entraver.
fetters ['fɛtəz] *npl* chaînes *fpl*.
fettle ['fɛtl] *n* (BRIT): **in fine ~** en bonne forme.
fetus ['fi:təs] *n* (*US*) = **foetus**.
feud [fju:d] *n* dispute *f*, dissension *f* ♦ *vi* se disputer, se quereller; **a family ~** une querelle de famille.
feudal ['fju:dl] *adj* féodal(e).
feudalism ['fju:dlɪzəm] *n* féodalité *f*.
fever ['fi:və*] *n* fièvre *f*; **he has a ~** il a de la fièvre.
feverish ['fi:vərɪʃ] *adj* fiévreux(euse), fébrile.
few [fju:] *adj* peu de ♦ *pron*: **~ succeed** il y en a peu qui réussissent, (bien) peu réussissent; **they were ~** ils étaient peu (nombreux), il y en avait peu; **a ~ ...** quelques ...; **I know a ~** j'en connais quelques-uns; **quite a ~ ...** un certain nombre de ..., pas mal de ...; **in the**

next ~ days dans les jours qui viennent; **in the past ~ days** ces derniers jours; **every ~ days/months** tous les deux ou trois jours/mois; **a ~ more ...** encore quelques ..., quelques ... de plus.
fewer ['fju:ə*] *adj* moins de ♦ *pron* moins; **they are ~ now** il y en a moins maintenant, ils sont moins (nombreux) maintenant.
fewest ['fju:ɪst] *adj* le moins nombreux.
FFA *n abbr* = *Future Farmers of America*.
FH *abbr* (BRIT) = **fire hydrant**.
FHA *n abbr* (*US*: = *Federal Housing Administration*) office fédéral du logement.
fiancé [fɪ'ɑ:ŋseɪ] *n* fiancé *m*.
fiancée [fɪ'ɑ:ŋseɪ] *n* fiancée *f*.
fiasco [fɪ'æskəu] *n* fiasco *m*.
fib [fɪb] *n* bobard *m*.
fibre, (*US*) **fiber** ['faɪbə*] *n* fibre *f*.
fibreboard, (*US*) **fiberboard** ['faɪbəbɔ:d] *n* panneau *m* de fibres.
fibre-glass, (*US*) **fiber-glass** ['faɪbəglɑ:s] *n* fibre de verre.
fibrositis [faɪbrə'saɪtɪs] *n* aponévrosite *f*.
FICA *n abbr* (*US*) = *Federal Insurance Contributions Act*.
fickle ['fɪkl] *adj* inconstant(e), volage, capricieux(euse).
fiction ['fɪkʃən] *n* romans *mpl*, littérature *f* romanesque; (invention) fiction *f*.
fictional ['fɪkʃnl] *adj* fictif(ive).
fictionalize ['fɪkʃnəlaɪz] *vt* romancer.
fictitious [fɪk'tɪʃəs] *adj* fictif(ive), imaginaire.
fiddle ['fɪdl] *n* (MUS) violon *m*; (cheating) combine *f*; escroquerie *f* ♦ *vt* (BRIT: accounts) falsifier, maquiller; **tax ~** fraude fiscale, combine *f* pour échapper au fisc; **to work a ~** traficoter.
▶**fiddle with** *vt fus* tripoter.
fiddler ['fɪdlə*] *n* violoniste *m/f*.
fiddly ['fɪdlɪ] *adj* (task) minutieux(euse).
fidelity [fɪ'dɛlɪtɪ] *n* fidélité *f*.
fidget ['fɪdʒɪt] *vi* se trémousser, remuer.
fidgety ['fɪdʒɪtɪ] *adj* agité(e), qui a la bougeotte.
fiduciary [fɪ'dju:ʃɪərɪ] *n* agent *m* fiduciaire.
field [fi:ld] *n* champ *m*; (fig) domaine *m*, champ; (SPORT: ground) terrain *m*; (COMPUT) champ, zone *f*; **to lead the ~** (SPORT, COMM) dominer; **the children had a ~ day** (fig) c'était un grand jour pour les enfants.
field glasses *npl* jumelles *fpl*.
field hospital *n* antenne chirurgicale.
field marshal *n* maréchal *m*.
fieldwork ['fi:ldwə:k] *n* travaux *mpl* pratiques (*or* recherches *fpl*) sur le terrain.
fiend [fi:nd] *n* démon *m*.
fiendish ['fi:ndɪʃ] *adj* diabolique.
fierce [fɪəs] *adj* (look) féroce, sauvage; (wind, attack) (très) violent(e); (fighting, enemy) acharné(e).
fiery ['faɪərɪ] *adj* ardent(e), brûlant(e); fougueux(euse).

FIFA ['fi:fə] *n abbr* (= *Fédération internationale de Football Association*) FIFA *f*.
fifteen [fɪf'ti:n] *num* quinze.
fifth [fɪfθ] *num* cinquième.
fiftieth ['fɪftɪɪθ] *num* cinquantième.
fifty ['fɪftɪ] *num* cinquante.
fifty-fifty ['fɪftɪ'fɪftɪ] *adv*: **to share ~ with sb** partager moitié-moitié avec qn ♦ *adj*: **to have a ~ chance (of success)** avoir une chance sur deux (de réussir).
fig [fɪg] *n* figue *f*.
fight [faɪt] *n* bagarre *f*; (*MIL*) combat *m*; (*against cancer etc*) lutte *f* ♦ *vb* (*pt, pp* **fought** [fɔ:t]) *vt* se battre contre; (*cancer, alcoholism*) combattre, lutter contre; (*LAW: case*) défendre ♦ *vi* se battre; (*fig*): **to ~ (for/against)** lutter (pour/contre).
fighter ['faɪtə*] *n* lutteur *m* (*fig*); (*plane*) chasseur *m*.
fighter pilot *n* pilote *m* de chasse.
fighting ['faɪtɪŋ] *n* combats *mpl*; (*brawls*) bagarres *fpl*.
figment ['fɪgmənt] *n*: **a ~ of the imagination** une invention.
figurative ['fɪgjurətɪv] *adj* figuré(e).
figure ['fɪgə*] *n* (*DRAWING, GEOM*) figure *f*; (*number, cipher*) chiffre *m*; (*body, outline*) silhouette *f*, ligne *f*, formes *fpl*; (*person*) personnage *m* ♦ *vt* (*US*) supposer ♦ *vi* (*appear*) figurer; (*US: make sense*) s'expliquer; **public ~** personnalité *f*; **~ of speech** figure *f* de rhétorique.
▶**figure on** *vt fus* (*US*): **to ~ on doing** compter faire.
▶**figure out** *vt* arriver à comprendre; calculer.
figurehead ['fɪgəhɛd] *n* (*NAUT*) figure *f* de proue; (*pej*) prête-nom *m*.
figure skating *n* figures imposées (*en patinage*); patinage *m* artistique.
Fiji (Islands) ['fi:dʒi:-] *n(pl)* (îles *fpl*) Fi(d)ji *fpl*.
filament ['fɪləmənt] *n* filament *m*.
filch [fɪltʃ] *vt* (*col: steal*) voler, chiper.
file [faɪl] *n* (*tool*) lime *f*; (*dossier*) dossier *m*; (*folder*) dossier, chemise *f*; (: *binder*) classeur *m*; (*COMPUT*) fichier *m*; (*row*) file *f* ♦ *vt* (*nails, wood*) limer; (*papers*) classer; (*LAW: claim*) faire enregistrer; déposer ♦ *vi*: **to ~ in/out** entrer/sortir l'un derrière l'autre; **to ~ past** défiler devant; **to ~ a suit against sb** (*LAW*) intenter un procès à qn.
file name *n* (*COMPUT*) nom *m* de fichier.
filibuster ['fɪlɪbʌstə*] (*esp US POL*) *n* (*also:* **~er**) obstructionniste *m/f* ♦ *vi* faire de l'obstructionnisme.
filing ['faɪlɪŋ] *n* (*travaux mpl* de) classement *m*; **~s** *npl* limaille *f*.
filing cabinet *n* classeur *m* (*meuble*).
filing clerk *n* documentaliste *m/f*.
Filipino [fɪlɪ'pi:nəu] *n* (*person*) Philippin/e; (*LING*) tagalog *m*.
fill [fɪl] *vt* remplir; (*vacancy*) pourvoir à ♦ *n*: **to**

eat one's ~ manger à sa faim.
▶**fill in** *vt* (*hole*) boucher; (*form*) remplir; (*details, report*) compléter.
▶**fill out** *vt* (*form, receipt*) remplir.
▶**fill up** *vt* remplir ♦ *vi* (*AUT*) faire le plein; **~ it up, please** (*AUT*) le plein, s'il vous plaît.
fillet ['fɪlɪt] *n* filet *m* ♦ *vt* préparer en filets.
fillet steak *n* filet *m* de bœuf, tournedos *m*.
filling ['fɪlɪŋ] *n* (*CULIN*) garniture *f*, farce *f*; (*for tooth*) plombage *m*.
filling station *n* station *f* d'essence.
fillip ['fɪlɪp] *n* coup *m* de fouet (*fig*).
filly ['fɪlɪ] *n* pouliche *f*.
film [fɪlm] *n* film *m*; (*PHOT*) pellicule *f*, film ♦ *vt* (*scene*) filmer.
film star *n* vedette *f* de cinéma.
filmstrip ['fɪlmstrɪp] *n* (film *m* pour) projection *f* fixe.
film studio *n* studio *m* (de cinéma).
Filofax ['faɪləufæks] *n* ® Filofax *m* ®.
filter ['fɪltə*] *n* filtre *m* ♦ *vt* filtrer.
filter coffee *n* café *m* filtre.
filter lane *n* (*BRIT AUT: at traffic lights*) voie *f* de dégagement; (: *on motorway*) voie de sortie.
filter tip *n* bout *m* filtre.
filth [fɪlθ] *n* saleté *f*.
filthy ['fɪlθɪ] *adj* sale, dégoûtant(e); (*language*) ordurier(ière), grossier(ière).
fin [fɪn] *n* (*of fish*) nageoire *f*.
final ['faɪnl] *adj* final(e), dernier(ière); (*decision, answer*) définitif(ive) ♦ *n* (*SPORT*) finale *f*; **~s** *npl* (*SCOL*) examens *mpl* de dernière année; **~ demand** (*on invoice etc*) dernier rappel.
finale [fɪ'nɑ:lɪ] *n* finale *m*.
finalist ['faɪnəlɪst] *n* (*SPORT*) finaliste *m/f*.
finalize ['faɪnəlaɪz] *vt* mettre au point.
finally ['faɪnəlɪ] *adv* (*lastly*) en dernier lieu; (*eventually*) enfin, finalement; (*irrevocably*) définitivement.
finance [faɪ'næns] *n* finance *f* ♦ *vt* financer; **~s** *npl* finances *fpl*.
financial [faɪ'nænʃəl] *adj* financier(ière); **~ statement** bilan *m*, exercice financier.
financially [faɪ'nænʃəlɪ] *adv* financièrement.
financial year *n* année *f* budgétaire.
financier [faɪ'nænsɪə*] *n* financier *m*.
find [faɪnd] *vt* (*pt, pp* **found** [faund]) trouver; (*lost object*) retrouver ♦ *n* trouvaille *f*, découverte *f*; **to ~ sb guilty** (*LAW*) déclarer qn coupable; **to ~ (some) difficulty in doing sth** avoir du mal à faire qch.
▶**find out** *vt* se renseigner sur; (*truth, secret*) découvrir; (*person*) démasquer ♦ *vi*: **to ~ out about** se renseigner sur; (*by chance*) apprendre.
findings ['faɪndɪŋz] *npl* (*LAW*) conclusions *fpl*, verdict *m*; (*of report*) constatations *fpl*.
fine [faɪn] *adj* beau(belle); excellent(e); (*subtle, not coarse*) fin(e) ♦ *adv* (*well*) très bien; (*small*) fin, finement ♦ *n* (*LAW*) amende *f*; contravention *f* ♦ *vt* (*LAW*) condamner à une

amende; donner une contravention à; **he's ~** il va bien; **the weather is ~** il fait beau; **you're doing ~** c'est bien, vous vous débrouillez bien; **to cut it ~** calculer un peu juste.

fine arts *npl* beaux-arts *mpl*.

fine print *n*: **the ~** ce qui est imprimé en tout petit.

finery ['faɪnərɪ] *n* parure *f*.

finesse [fɪ'nɛs] *n* finesse *f*, élégance *f*.

fine-tooth comb ['faɪntu:θ-] *n*: **to go through sth with a ~** (*fig*) passer qch au peigne fin *or* au crible.

finger ['fɪŋgə*] *n* doigt *m* ♦ *vt* palper, toucher.

fingernail ['fɪŋgəneɪl] *n* ongle *m* (de la main).

fingerprint ['fɪŋgəprɪnt] *n* empreinte digitale ♦ *vt* (*person*) prendre les empreintes digitales de.

fingerstall ['fɪŋgəstɔ:l] *n* doigtier *m*.

fingertip ['fɪŋgətɪp] *n* bout *m* du doigt; (*fig*): **to have sth at one's ~s** avoir qch à sa disposition; (*knowledge*) savoir qch sur le bout du doigt.

finicky ['fɪnɪkɪ] *adj* tatillon(ne), méticuleux(euse); minutieux(euse).

finish ['fɪnɪʃ] *n* fin *f*; (*SPORT*) arrivée *f*; (*polish etc*) finition *f* ♦ *vt* finir, terminer ♦ *vi* finir, se terminer; (*session*) s'achever; **to ~ doing sth** finir de faire qch; **to ~ third** arriver *or* terminer troisième.

▶**finish off** *vt* finir, terminer; (*kill*) achever.

▶**finish up** *vi*, *vt* finir.

finished product ['fɪnɪʃt-] *n* produit fini.

finishing line ['fɪnɪʃɪŋ-] *n* ligne *f* d'arrivée.

finishing school ['fɪnɪʃɪŋ-] *n* institution privée (*pour jeunes filles*).

finite ['faɪnaɪt] *adj* fini(e); (*verb*) conjugué(e).

Finland ['fɪnlənd] *n* Finlande *f*.

Finn [fɪn] *n* Finnois/e; Finlandais/e.

Finnish ['fɪnɪʃ] *adj* finnois(e); finlandais(e) ♦ *n* (*LING*) finnois *m*.

fiord [fjɔ:d] *n* fjord *m*.

fir [fə:*] *n* sapin *m*.

fire ['faɪə*] *n* feu *m*; incendie *m* ♦ *vt* (*discharge*): **to ~ a gun** tirer un coup de feu; (*fig*) enflammer, animer; (*dismiss*) mettre à la porte, renvoyer ♦ *vi* tirer, faire feu ♦ *cpd*: **~ hazard**, **~ risk: that's a ~ hazard** *or* **risk** cela présente un risque d'incendie; **on ~** en feu; **to set ~ to sth, set sth on ~** mettre le feu à qch; **insured against ~** assuré contre l'incendie.

fire alarm *n* avertisseur *m* d'incendie.

firearm ['faɪərɑ:m] *n* arme *f* à feu.

fire brigade *n* (*BRIT*) (régiment *m* de sapeurs-)pompiers *mpl*.

fire chief *n* (*US*) = **fire master**.

fire department *n* (*US*) = **fire brigade**.

fire door *n* porte *f* coupe-feu.

fire engine *n* pompe *f* à incendie.

fire escape *n* escalier *m* de secours.

fire extinguisher *n* extincteur *m*.

fireguard ['faɪəgɑ:d] *n* (*BRIT*) garde-feu *m inv*.

fire insurance *n* assurance *f* incendie.

fireman ['faɪəmən] *n* pompier *m*.

fire master *n* (*BRIT*) capitaine *m* des pompiers.

fireplace ['faɪəpleɪs] *n* cheminée *f*.

fireproof ['faɪəpru:f] *adj* ignifuge.

fire regulations *npl* consignes *fpl* en cas d'incendie.

fire screen *n* (*decorative*) écran *m* de cheminée; (*for protection*) garde-feu *m inv*.

fireside ['faɪəsaɪd] *n* foyer *m*, coin *m* du feu.

fire station *n* caserne *f* de pompiers.

firewood ['faɪəwud] *n* bois *m* de chauffage.

firework ['faɪəwə:k] *n* feu *m* d'artifice; **~s** *npl* (*display*) feu(x) d'artifice.

firing ['faɪərɪŋ] *n* (*MIL*) feu *m*, tir *m*.

firing squad *n* peloton *m* d'exécution.

firm [fə:m] *adj* ferme ♦ *n* compagnie *f*, firme *f*.

firmly ['fə:mlɪ] *adv* fermement.

firmness ['fə:mnɪs] *n* fermeté *f*.

first [fə:st] *adj* premier(ière) ♦ *adv* (*before others*) le premier, la première; (*before other things*) en premier, d'abord; (*when listing reasons etc*) en premier lieu, premièrement ♦ *n* (*person: in race*) premier/ière; (*BRIT SCOL*) mention *f* très bien; (*AUT*) première *f*; **the ~ of January** le premier janvier; **at ~** au commencement, au début; **~ of all** tout d'abord, pour commencer; **in the ~ instance** en premier lieu; **I'll do it ~ thing tomorrow** je le ferai tout de suite demain matin.

first aid *n* premiers secours *or* soins.

first-aid kit [fə:st'eɪd-] *n* trousse *f* à pharmacie.

first-class ['fə:st'klɑ:s] *adj* de première classe.

first-class mail *n* courrier *m* rapide.

first-hand ['fə:st'hænd] *adj* de première main.

first lady *n* (*US*) femme *f* du président.

firstly ['fə:stlɪ] *adv* premièrement, en premier lieu.

first name *n* prénom *m*.

first night *n* (*THEAT*) première *f*.

first-rate ['fə:st'reɪt] *adj* excellent(e).

first-time buyer ['fə:sttaɪm-] *n* personne *achetant une maison ou un appartement pour la première fois.*

fir tree *n* sapin *m*.

FIS *n abbr* (*BRIT*: = *Family Income Supplement*) *complément familial.*

fiscal ['fɪskl] *adj* fiscal(e); **~ year** exercice financier.

fish [fɪʃ] *n* (*pl inv*) poisson *m*; poissons *mpl* ♦ *vt*, *vi* pêcher; **to ~ a river** pêcher dans une rivière; **to go ~ing** aller à la pêche.

fisherman ['fɪʃəmən] *n* pêcheur *m*.

fishery ['fɪʃərɪ] *n* pêcherie *f*.

fish factory *n* (*BRIT*) conserverie *f* de poissons.

fish farm *n* établissement *m* piscicole.

fish fingers *npl* (*BRIT*) bâtonnets de poisson (congelés).

fish hook *n* hameçon *m*.

fishing boat ['fɪʃɪŋ-] n barque f de pêche.
fishing industry ['fɪʃɪŋ-] n industrie f de la pêche.
fishing line ['fɪʃɪŋ-] n ligne f (de pêche).
fishing rod ['fɪʃɪŋ-] n canne f à pêche.
fishing tackle ['fɪʃɪŋ-] n attirail m de pêche.
fish market n marché m au poisson.
fishmonger ['fɪʃmʌŋgə*] n marchand m de poisson; ~'**s (shop)** poissonnerie f.
fish slice n (BRIT) pelle f à poisson.
fish sticks npl (US) = **fish fingers**.
fishy ['fɪʃɪ] adj (fig) suspect(e), louche.
fission ['fɪʃən] n fission f; **atomic** or **nuclear** ~ fission nucléaire.
fissure ['fɪʃə*] n fissure f.
fist [fɪst] n poing m.
fistfight ['fɪstfaɪt] n pugilat m, bagarre f (à coups de poing).
fit [fɪt] adj (MED, SPORT) en (bonne) forme; (proper) convenable; approprié(e) ♦ vt (subj: clothes) aller à; (adjust) ajuster; (put in, attach) installer, poser; adapter; (equip) équiper, garnir, munir ♦ vi (clothes) aller; (parts) s'adapter; (in space, gap) entrer, s'adapter ♦ n (MED) accès m, crise f; (of coughing) quinte f; ~ **to** en état de; ~ **for** digne de; apte à; **to keep** ~ se maintenir en forme; **this dress is a tight/good** ~ cette robe est un peu juste/(me) va très bien; **a** ~ **of anger** un accès de colère; **to have a** ~ (MED) faire or avoir une crise; (col) piquer une crise; **by** ~**s and starts** par à-coups.
▶**fit in** vi s'accorder; (person) s'adapter.
▶**fit out** vt (BRIT: also: **fit up**) équiper.
fitful ['fɪtful] adj intermittent(e).
fitment ['fɪtmənt] n meuble encastré, élément m.
fitness ['fɪtnɪs] n (MED) forme f physique; (of remark) à-propos m, justesse f.
fitted kitchen ['fɪtɪd-] n (BRIT) cuisine équipée.
fitter ['fɪtə*] n monteur m; (DRESSMAKING) essayeur/euse.
fitting ['fɪtɪŋ] adj approprié(e) ♦ n (of dress) essayage m; (of piece of equipment) pose f, installation f.
fitting room n (in shop) cabine f d'essayage.
fittings ['fɪtɪŋz] npl installations fpl.
five [faɪv] num cinq.
five-day week ['faɪvdeɪ-] n semaine f de cinq jours.
fiver ['faɪvə*] n (col: BRIT) billet m de cinq livres; (: US) billet de cinq dollars.
fix [fɪks] vt fixer; (sort out) arranger; (mend) réparer; (make ready: meal, drink) préparer; (col: game etc) truquer ♦ n: **to be in a** ~ être dans le pétrin.
▶**fix up** vt (meeting) arranger; **to** ~ **sb up with sth** faire avoir qch à qn.
fixation [fɪk'seɪʃən] n (PSYCH) fixation f; (fig) obsession f.
fixed [fɪkst] adj (prices etc) fixe; **there's a** ~

charge il y a un prix forfaitaire; **how are you** ~ **for money?** (col) question fric, ça va?
fixed assets npl immobilisations fpl.
fixture ['fɪkstʃə*] n installation f (fixe); (SPORT) rencontre f (au programme).
fizz [fɪz] vi pétiller.
fizzle ['fɪzl] vi pétiller.
▶**fizzle out** vi rater.
fizzy ['fɪzɪ] adj pétillant(e); gazeux(euse).
fjord [fjɔːd] n = **fiord**.
FL, Fla. abbr (US) = Florida.
flabbergasted ['flæbəgɑːstɪd] adj sidéré(e), ahuri(e).
flabby ['flæbɪ] adj mou(molle).
flag [flæg] n drapeau m; (also: ~**stone**) dalle f ♦ vi faiblir; fléchir; ~ **of convenience** pavillon m de complaisance.
▶**flag down** vt héler, faire signe (de s'arrêter) à.
flagon ['flægən] n bonbonne f.
flagpole ['flægpəul] n mât m.
flagrant ['fleɪgrənt] adj flagrant(e).
flag stop n (US: for bus) arrêt facultatif.
flair [fleə*] n flair m.
flak [flæk] n (MIL) tir antiaérien; (col: criticism) critiques fpl.
flake [fleɪk] n (of rust, paint) écaille f; (of snow, soap powder) flocon m ♦ vi (also: ~ **off**) s'écailler.
flaky ['fleɪkɪ] adj (paintwork) écaillé(e); (skin) desquamé(e); (pastry) feuilleté(e).
flamboyant [flæm'bɔɪənt] adj flamboyant(e), éclatant(e); (person) haut(e) en couleur.
flame [fleɪm] n flamme f.
flamingo [flə'mɪŋgəu] n flamant m (rose).
flammable ['flæməbl] adj inflammable.
flan [flæn] n (BRIT) tarte f.
Flanders ['flɑːndəz] n Flandre(s) f(pl).
flange [flændʒ] n boudin m; collerette f.
flank [flæŋk] n flanc m ♦ vt flanquer.
flannel ['flænl] n (BRIT: also: **face** ~) gant m de toilette; (fabric) flanelle f; (BRIT col) baratin m; ~**s** npl pantalon m de flanelle.
flap [flæp] n (of pocket, envelope) rabat m ♦ vt (wings) battre (de) ♦ vi (sail, flag) claquer; (col: also: **be in a** ~) paniquer.
flapjack ['flæpdʒæk] n (US: pancake) ≈ crêpe f; (BRIT: biscuit) galette f.
flare [fleə*] n fusée éclairante; (in skirt etc) évasement m.
▶**flare up** vi s'embraser; (fig: person) se mettre en colère, s'emporter; (: revolt) éclater.
flared ['fleəd] adj (trousers) à jambes évasées; (skirt) évasé(e).
flash [flæʃ] n éclair m; (also: **news** ~) flash m (d'information); (PHOT) flash ♦ vt (switch on) allumer (brièvement); (direct): **to** ~ **sth at** braquer qch sur; (flaunt) étaler, exhiber; (send: message) câbler ♦ vi briller; jeter des éclairs; (light on ambulance etc) clignoter; **in a** ~ en un clin d'œil; **to** ~ **one's headlights**

faire un appel de phares; **he ~ed by** *or* **past** il passa (devant nous) comme un éclair.

flashback ['flæʃbæk] *n* flashback *m*, retour *m* en arrière.

flashbulb ['flæʃbʌlb] *n* ampoule *f* de flash.

flash card *n* (SCOL) carte *f* (support visuel).

flashcube ['flæʃkjuːb] *n* cube-flash *m*.

flasher ['flæʃə*] *n* (AUT) clignotant *m*.

flashlight ['flæʃlaɪt] *n* lampe *f* de poche.

flashpoint ['flæʃpɔɪnt] *n* point *m* d'ignition; (*fig*): **to be at ~** être sur le point d'exploser.

flashy ['flæʃɪ] *adj* (*pej*) tape-à-l'œil *inv*, tapageur(euse).

flask [flɑːsk] *n* flacon *m*, bouteille *f*; (CHEM) ballon *m*; (*also*: **vacuum ~**) bouteille *f* thermos ®.

flat [flæt] *adj* plat(e); (*tyre*) dégonflé(e), à plat; (*denial*) catégorique; (MUS) bémolisé(e); (*: voice*) faux(fausse) ♦ *n* (BRIT: *rooms*) appartement *m*; (AUT) crevaison *f*, pneu crevé; (MUS) bémol *m*; **~ out** (*work*) sans relâche; (*race*) à fond; **~ rate of pay** (COMM) (salaire *m*) fixe.

flat-footed ['flæt'futɪd] *adj*: **to be ~** avoir les pieds plats.

flatly ['flætlɪ] *adv* catégoriquement.

flatmate ['flætmeɪt] *n* (BRIT): **he's my ~** il partage l'appartement avec moi.

flatness ['flætnɪs] *n* (*of land*) absence *f* de relief, aspect plat.

flat-screen ['flætskriːn] *adj* à écran plat.

flatten ['flætn] *vt* (*also*: **~ out**) aplatir; (*house, city*) raser.

flatter ['flætə*] *vt* flatter.

flatterer ['flætərə*] *n* flatteur *m*.

flattering ['flætərɪŋ] *adj* flatteur(euse); (*clothes etc*) seyant(e).

flattery ['flætərɪ] *n* flatterie *f*.

flatulence ['flætjuləns] *n* flatulence *f*.

flaunt [flɔːnt] *vt* faire étalage de.

flavour, (*US*) **flavor** ['fleɪvə*] *n* goût *m*, saveur *f*; (*of ice cream etc*) parfum *m* ♦ *vt* parfumer, aromatiser; **vanilla-~ed** à l'arôme de vanille, vanillé(e); **to give** *or* **add ~ to** donner du goût à, relever.

flavo(u)ring ['fleɪvərɪŋ] *n* arôme *m* (synthétique).

flaw [flɔː] *n* défaut *m*.

flawless ['flɔːlɪs] *adj* sans défaut.

flax [flæks] *n* lin *m*.

flaxen ['flæksən] *adj* blond(e).

flea [fliː] *n* puce *f*.

flea market *n* marché *m* aux puces.

fleck [flɛk] *n* (*of dust*) particule *f*; (*of mud, paint, colour*) tacheture *f*, moucheture *f* ♦ *vt* tacher, éclabousser; **brown ~ed with white** brun moucheté de blanc.

fledg(e)ling ['flɛdʒlɪŋ] *n* oisillon *m*.

flee, *pt, pp* **fled** [fliː, flɛd] *vt* fuir, s'enfuir de ♦ *vi* fuir, s'enfuir.

fleece [fliːs] *n* toison *f* ♦ *vt* (*col*) voler, filouter.

fleecy ['fliːsɪ] *adj* (*blanket*) moelleux(euse); (*cloud*) floconneux(euse).

fleet [fliːt] *n* flotte *f*; (*of lorries, cars etc*) parc *m*; convoi *m*.

fleeting ['fliːtɪŋ] *adj* fugace, fugitif(ive); (*visit*) très bref(brève).

Flemish ['flɛmɪʃ] *adj* flamand(e) ♦ *n* (LING) flamand *m*; **the ~** *npl* les Flamands.

flesh [flɛʃ] *n* chair *f*.

flesh wound [-wuːnd] *n* blessure superficielle.

flew [fluː] *pt of* **fly**.

flex [flɛks] *n* fil *m* *or* câble *m* électrique (souple) ♦ *vt* fléchir; (*muscles*) tendre.

flexibility [flɛksɪ'bɪlɪtɪ] *n* flexibilité *f*.

flexible ['flɛksəbl] *adj* flexible; (*person, schedule*) souple.

flexitime ['flɛksɪtaɪm] *n* horaire *m* variable *or* à la carte.

flick [flɪk] *n* petite tape; chiquenaude *f*; sursaut *m*.

▶**flick through** *vt fus* feuilleter.

flicker ['flɪkə*] *vi* vaciller ♦ *n* vacillement *m*; **a ~ of light** une brève lueur.

flick knife *n* (BRIT) couteau *m* à cran d'arrêt.

flicks [flɪks] *npl* (*col*) ciné *m*.

flier ['flaɪə*] *n* aviateur *m*.

flight [flaɪt] *n* vol *m*; (*escape*) fuite *f*; (*also*: **~ of steps**) escalier *m*; **to take ~** prendre la fuite; **to put to ~** mettre en fuite.

flight attendant *n* (US) steward *m*, hôtesse *f* de l'air.

flight crew *n* équipage *m*.

flight deck *n* (AVIAT) poste *m* de pilotage; (NAUT) pont *m* d'envol.

flight path *n* trajectoire *f* (de vol).

flight recorder *n* enregistreur *m* de vol.

flimsy ['flɪmzɪ] *adj* (*partition, fabric*) peu solide, mince; (*excuse*) pauvre, mince.

flinch [flɪntʃ] *vi* tressaillir; **to ~ from** se dérober à, reculer devant.

fling [flɪŋ] *vt* (*pt, pp* **flung** [flʌŋ]) jeter, lancer ♦ *n* (*love affair*) brève liaison, passade *f*.

flint [flɪnt] *n* silex *m*; (*in lighter*) pierre *f* (à briquet).

flip [flɪp] *n* chiquenaude *f* ♦ *vt* donner une chiquenaude à; (*US: pancake*) faire sauter ♦ *vi*: **to ~ for sth** (*US*) jouer qch à pile ou face.

▶**flip through** *vt fus* feuilleter.

flippant ['flɪpənt] *adj* désinvolte, irrévérencieux(euse).

flipper ['flɪpə*] *n* (*of animal*) nageoire *f*; (*for swimmer*) palme *f*.

flip side *n* (*of record*) deuxième face *f*.

flirt [flɜːt] *vi* flirter ♦ *n* flirteuse *f*.

flirtation [flɜː'teɪʃən] *n* flirt *m*.

flit [flɪt] *vi* voleter.

float [fləʊt] *n* flotteur *m*; (*in procession*) char *m*; (*sum of money*) réserve *f* ♦ *vi* flotter; (*bather*) flotter, faire la planche ♦ *vt* faire flotter; (*loan, business, idea*) lancer.

floating ['fləʊtɪŋ] *adj* flottant(e); **~ vote** voix flottante; **~ voter** électeur indécis.

flock [flɔk] n troupeau m; (of birds) vol m; (of people) foule f.

floe [fləu] n (also: **ice** ~) iceberg m.

flog [flɔg] vt fouetter.

flood [flʌd] n inondation f; (of words, tears etc) flot m, torrent m ♦ vt inonder; (AUT: carburettor) noyer; **to** ~ **the market** (COMM) inonder le marché; **in** ~ en crue.

flooding ['flʌdɪŋ] n inondation f.

floodlight ['flʌdlaɪt] n projecteur m ♦ vt éclairer aux projecteurs, illuminer.

floodlit ['flʌdlɪt] pt, pp of **floodlight** ♦ adj illuminé(e).

flood tide n marée montante.

floodwater ['flʌdwɔːtə*] n eau f de la crue.

floor [flɔː*] n sol m; (storey) étage m; (of sea, valley) fond m; (fig: at meeting): **the** ~ l'assemblée f, les membres mpl de l'assemblée ♦ vt terrasser; (baffle) désorienter; **on the** ~ par terre; **ground** ~, (US) **first** ~ rez-de-chaussée m; **first** ~, (US) **second** ~ premier étage; **top** ~ dernier étage; **to have the** ~ (speaker) avoir la parole.

floorboard ['flɔːbɔːd] n planche f (du plancher).

flooring ['flɔːrɪŋ] n sol m; (wooden) plancher m; (material to make floor) matériau(x) m(pl) pour planchers; (covering) revêtement m de sol.

floor lamp n (US) lampadaire m.

floor show n spectacle m de variétés.

floorwalker ['flɔːwɔːkə*] n (esp US) surveillant m (de grand magasin).

flop [flɔp] n fiasco m ♦ vi (fail) faire fiasco.

floppy ['flɔpɪ] adj lâche, flottant(e); ~ **hat** chapeau m à bords flottants.

floppy disk n disquette f, disque m souple.

flora ['flɔːrə] n flore f.

floral ['flɔːrl] adj floral(e).

Florence ['flɔrəns] n Florence.

florid ['flɔrɪd] adj (complexion) fleuri(e); (style) plein(e) de fioritures.

florist ['flɔrɪst] n fleuriste m/f; ~'**s (shop)** magasin m or boutique f de fleuriste.

flotation [fləu'teɪʃən] n (of shares) émission f; (of company) lancement m (en Bourse).

flounce [flauns] n volant m.

►**flounce out** vi sortir dans un mouvement d'humeur.

flounder ['flaundə*] n (ZOOL) flet m ♦ vi patauger.

flour ['flauə*] n farine f.

flourish ['flʌrɪʃ] vi prospérer ♦ vt brandir ♦ n fioriture f; (of trumpets) fanfare f.

flourishing ['flʌrɪʃɪŋ] adj prospère, florissant(e).

flout [flaut] vt se moquer de, faire fi de.

flow [fləu] n (of water, traffic etc) écoulement m; (tide, influx) flux m; (of orders, letters etc) flot m; (of blood, ELEC) circulation f; (of river) courant m ♦ vi couler; (traffic) s'écouler; (robes, hair) flotter.

flow chart, flow diagram n organigramme

m.

flower ['flauə*] n fleur f ♦ vi fleurir; **in** ~ en fleur.

flower bed n plate-bande f.

flowerpot ['flauəpɔt] n pot m (à fleurs).

flowery ['flauərɪ] adj fleuri(e).

flown [fləun] pp of **fly**.

flu [fluː] n grippe f.

fluctuate ['flʌktjueɪt] vi varier, fluctuer.

fluctuation [flʌktju'eɪʃən] n fluctuation f, variation f.

flue [fluː] n conduit m.

fluency ['fluːənsɪ] n facilité f, aisance f.

fluent ['fluːənt] adj (speech, style) coulant(e), aisé(e); **he's a** ~ **speaker/reader** il s'exprime/lit avec aisance or facilité; **he speaks** ~ **French, he's** ~ **in French** il parle le français couramment.

fluently ['fluːəntlɪ] adv couramment; avec aisance or facilité.

fluff [flʌf] n duvet m; peluche f.

fluffy ['flʌfɪ] adj duveteux(euse); pelucheux(euse); ~ **toy** jouet m en peluche.

fluid ['fluːɪd] n fluide m; (in diet) liquide m ♦ adj fluide.

fluid ounce n (BRIT) = 0.028 l; 0.05 pints.

fluke [fluːk] n (col) coup m de veine.

flummox ['flʌməks] vt dérouter, déconcerter.

flung [flʌŋ] pt, pp of **fling**.

flunky ['flʌŋkɪ] n larbin m.

fluorescent [fluə'rɛsnt] adj fluorescent(e).

fluoride ['fluəraɪd] n fluor m.

fluorine ['fluəriːn] n fluor m.

flurry ['flʌrɪ] n (of snow) rafale f, bourrasque f; ~ **of activity/excitement** affairement m/ excitation f soudain(e).

flush [flʌʃ] n rougeur f; (fig) éclat m; afflux m ♦ vt nettoyer à grande eau; (also: ~ **out**) débusquer ♦ vi rougir ♦ adj (col) en fonds; (level): ~ **with** au ras de, de niveau avec; **to** ~ **the toilet** tirer la chasse (d'eau); **hot** ~**es** (MED) bouffées fpl de chaleur.

flushed ['flʌʃt] adj (tout(e)) rouge.

fluster ['flʌstə*] n agitation f, trouble m.

flustered ['flʌstəd] adj énervé(e).

flute [fluːt] n flûte f.

fluted ['fluːtɪd] adj cannelé(e).

flutter ['flʌtə*] n agitation f; (of wings) battement m ♦ vi battre des ailes, voleter; (person) aller et venir dans une grande agitation.

flux [flʌks] n: **in a state of** ~ fluctuant sans cesse.

fly [flaɪ] n (insect) mouche f; (on trousers: also: **flies**) braguette f ♦ vb (pt **flew**, pp **flown** [fluː, fləun]) vt (plane) piloter; (passengers, cargo) transporter (par avion); (distances) parcourir ♦ vi voler; (passengers) aller en avion; (escape) s'enfuir, fuir; (flag) se déployer; **to** ~ **open** s'ouvrir brusquement; **to** ~ **off the handle** s'énerver, s'emporter.

►**fly away** vi s'envoler.

►**fly in** *vi* (*plane*) atterrir; (*person*): **he flew in yesterday** il est arrivé hier (par avion).

►**fly off** *vi* s'envoler.

►**fly out** *vi* (*see fly in*) s'envoler; partir (par avion).

fly-fishing ['flaɪfɪʃɪŋ] *n* pêche *f* à la mouche.

flying ['flaɪɪŋ] *n* (*activity*) aviation *f* ♦ *adj*: ~ **visit** visite *f* éclair *inv*; **with ~ colours** haut la main; **he doesn't like ~** il n'aime pas voyager en avion.

flying buttress *n* arc-boutant *m*.

flying picket *n* piquet *m* de grève volant.

flying saucer *n* soucoupe volante.

flying squad *n* (*POLICE*) brigade volante.

flying start *n*: **to get off to a ~** faire un excellent départ.

flyleaf ['flaɪliːf] *n* page *f* de garde.

flyover ['flaɪəuvə*] *n* (*BRIT: overpass*) saut-de-mouton *m*, pont autoroutier.

flypast ['flaɪpɑːst] *n* défilé aérien.

flysheet ['flaɪʃiːt] *n* (*for tent*) double toit *m*.

flyweight ['flaɪweɪt] *n* (*SPORT*) poids *m* mouche.

flywheel ['flaɪwiːl] *n* volant *m* (de commande).

FM *abbr* (*BRIT MIL*) = **field marshal**; (*RADIO*) = **frequency modulation**.

FMB *n abbr* (*US*) = *Federal Maritime Board*.

FMCS *n abbr* (*US*: = *Federal Mediation and Conciliation Services*) *organisme de conciliation en cas de conflits du travail*.

FO *n abbr* (*BRIT*) = **Foreign Office**.

foal [fəul] *n* poulain *m*.

foam [fəum] *n* écume *f*; (*on beer*) mousse *f*; (*also*: **plastic ~**) mousse cellulaire *or* de plastique ♦ *vi* écumer; (*soapy water*) mousser.

foam rubber *n* caoutchouc *m* mousse.

FOB *abbr* (= *free on board*) fob.

fob [fɔb] *n* (*also*: **watch ~**) chaîne *f*, ruban *m* ♦ *vt*: **to ~ sb off with** refiler à qn; se débarrasser de qn avec.

foc *abbr* (*BRIT*) = **free of charge**.

focal ['fəukl] *adj* (*also fig*) focal(e).

focal point *n* foyer *m*; (*fig*) centre *m* de l'attention, point focal.

focus ['fəukəs] *n* (*pl*: ~**es**) foyer *m*; (*of interest*) centre *m* ♦ *vt* (*field glasses etc*) mettre au point; (*light rays*) faire converger ♦ *vi*: **to ~ (on)** (*with camera*) régler la mise au point (sur); (*person*) fixer son regard (sur); **in ~** au point; **out of ~** pas au point.

fodder ['fɔdə*] *n* fourrage *m*.

FOE *n abbr* (= *Friends of the Earth*) AT *mpl* (= *Amis de la Terre*); (*US*: = *Fraternal Order of Eagles*) *organisation charitable*.

foe [fəu] *n* ennemi *m*.

foetus, (*US*) **fetus** ['fiːtəs] *n* fœtus *m*.

fog [fɔg] *n* brouillard *m*.

fogbound ['fɔgbaund] *adj* bloqué(e) par le brouillard.

foggy ['fɔgɪ] *adj*: **it's ~** il y a du brouillard.

fog lamp, (*US*) **fog light** *n* (*AUT*) phare *m* anti-brouillard.

foible ['fɔɪbl] *n* faiblesse *f*.

foil [fɔɪl] *vt* déjouer, contrecarrer ♦ *n* feuille *f* de métal; (*kitchen* ~) papier *m* alu(minium); (*FENCING*) fleuret *m*; **to act as a ~ to** (*fig*) servir de repoussoir *or* de faire-valoir à.

foist [fɔɪst] *vt*: **to ~ sth on sb** imposer qch à qn.

fold [fəuld] *n* (*bend, crease*) pli *m*; (*AGR*) parc *m* à moutons; (*fig*) bercail *m* ♦ *vt* plier; **to ~ one's arms** croiser les bras.

►**fold up** *vi* (*map etc*) se plier, se replier; (*business*) fermer boutique ♦ *vt* (*map etc*) plier, replier.

folder ['fəuldə*] *n* (*for papers*) chemise *f*; (*: binder*) classeur *m*; (*brochure*) dépliant *m*.

folding ['fəuldɪŋ] *adj* (*chair, bed*) pliant(e).

foliage ['fəulɪɪdʒ] *n* feuillage *m*.

folk [fəuk] *npl* gens *mpl* ♦ *cpd* folklorique; ~**s** *npl* famille *f*, parents *mpl*.

folklore ['fəuklɔː*] *n* folklore *m*.

folksong ['fəuksɔŋ] *n* chanson *f* folklorique; (*contemporary*) chanson folk *inv*.

follow ['fɔləu] *vt* suivre ♦ *vi* suivre; (*result*) s'ensuivre; **to ~ sb's advice** suivre les conseils de qn; **I don't quite ~ you** je ne vous suis plus; **to ~ in sb's footsteps** emboîter le pas à qn; (*fig*) suivre les traces de qn; **it ~s that ...** de ce fait, il s'ensuit que ...; **he ~ed suit** il fit de même.

►**follow out** *vt* (*idea, plan*) poursuivre, mener à terme.

►**follow through** *vt* = **follow out**.

►**follow up** *vt* (*victory*) tirer parti de; (*letter, offer*) donner suite à; (*case*) suivre.

follower ['fɔləuə*] *n* disciple *m/f*, partisan/e.

following ['fɔləuɪŋ] *adj* suivant(e) ♦ *n* partisans *mpl*, disciples *mpl*.

follow-up ['fɔləuʌp] *n* suite *f*; suivi *m*.

folly ['fɔlɪ] *n* inconscience *f*; sottise *f*; (*building*) folie *f*.

fond [fɔnd] *adj* (*memory, look*) tendre, affectueux(euse); **to be ~ of** aimer beaucoup.

fondle ['fɔndl] *vt* caresser.

fondly ['fɔndlɪ] *adv* (*lovingly*) tendrement; (*naïvely*) naïvement.

fondness ['fɔndnɪs] *n* (*for things*) attachement *m*; (*for people*) sentiments affectueux; **a special ~ for** une prédilection pour.

font [fɔnt] *n* (*REL*) fonts baptismaux; (*TYP*) police *f* de caractères.

food [fuːd] *n* nourriture *f*.

food chain *n* chaîne *f* alimentaire.

food mixer *n* mixeur *m*.

food poisoning *n* intoxication *f* alimentaire.

food processor *n* robot *m* de cuisine.

food stamp *n* (*US*) bon *m* de nourriture (*pour indigents*).

foodstuffs ['fuːdstʌfs] *npl* denrées *fpl* alimentaires.

fool [fuːl] *n* idiot/e; (*HISTORY: of king*) bouffon *m*, fou *m*; (*CULIN*) purée *f* de fruits à la crème

foolhardy – forage

♦ *vt* berner, duper ♦ *vi* (*also:* ~ **around**) faire l'idiot *or* l'imbécile; **to make a ~ of sb** (*ridicule*) ridiculiser qn; (*trick*) avoir *or* duper qn; **to make a ~ of o.s.** se couvrir de ridicule; **you can't ~ me** vous (ne) me la ferez pas, on (ne) me la fait pas.

▶**fool about, fool around** *vi* (*pej: waste time*) traînailler, glandouiller; (*: behave foolishly*) faire l'imbécile.

foolhardy ['fuːlhɑːdɪ] *adj* téméraire, imprudent(e).

foolish ['fuːlɪʃ] *adj* idiot(e), stupide; (*rash*) imprudent(e).

foolishly ['fuːlɪʃlɪ] *adv* stupidement.

foolishness ['fuːlɪʃnɪs] *n* idiotie *f*, stupidité *f*.

foolproof ['fuːlpruːf] *adj* (*plan etc*) infaillible.

foolscap ['fuːlskæp] *n* ≈ papier *m* ministre.

foot [fut] *n* (*pl:* **feet** [fiːt]) pied *m*; (*measure*) pied (*= 304 mm; 12 inches*); (*of animal*) patte *f* ♦ *vt* (*bill*) casquer, payer; **on** ~ à pied; **to find one's feet** (*fig*) s'acclimater; **to put one's** ~ **down** (*AUT*) appuyer sur le champignon; (*say no*) s'imposer.

footage ['futɪdʒ] *n* (*CINE: length*) ≈ métrage *m*; (*: material*) séquences *fpl*.

foot and mouth (disease) *n* fièvre aphteuse.

football ['futbɔːl] *n* ballon *m* (de football); (*sport: BRIT*) football *m* foot *m*; (*: US*) football américain.

footballer ['futbɔːlə*] *n* (*BRIT*) = **football player**.

football game *n* match *m* de football.

football ground *n* terrain *m* de football.

football match *n* (*BRIT*) match *m* de foot(ball).

football player *n* footballeur *m*, joueur *m* de football.

Les **football pools** *- ou plus familièrement les* "**pools**" *- sont une sorte de loto sportif britannique où l'on parie sur les matches de football qui se jouent tous les samedis. L'expression consacrée en anglais est "to do the pools". Les parieurs envoient à l'avance les fiches qu'ils ont complétées à l'organisme qui gère les paris et ils attendent les résultats, qui sont annoncés à 17 h le samedi. Les sommes gagnées se comptent parfois en milliers (ou même en millions) de livres sterling.*

---

footbrake ['futbreɪk] *n* frein *m* à pied.

footbridge ['futbrɪdʒ] *n* passerelle *f*.

foothills ['futhɪlz] *npl* contreforts *mpl*.

foothold ['futhəuld] *n* prise *f* (de pied).

footing ['futɪŋ] *n* (*fig*) position *f*; **to lose one's** ~ perdre pied; **on an equal** ~ sur pied d'égalité.

footlights ['futlaɪts] *npl* rampe *f*.

footman ['futmən] *n* laquais *m*.

footnote ['futnəut] *n* note *f* (en bas de page).

footpath ['futpɑːθ] *n* sentier *m*; (*in street*) trot-

toir *m*.

footprint ['futprɪnt] *n* trace *f* (de pied).

footrest ['futrɛst] *n* marchepied *m*.

footsie ['futsɪ] *n* (*col*): **to play** ~ **with sb** faire du pied à qn.

footsore ['futsɔː*] *adj*: **to be** ~ avoir mal aux pieds.

footstep ['futstɛp] *n* pas *m*.

footwear ['futwɛə*] *n* chaussure(s) *f(pl)* (*terme générique en anglais*).

FOR *abbr* (= *free on rail*) franco wagon.

═══════════════════ *KEYWORD*

for [fɔː*] *prep* **1** (*indicating destination, intention, purpose*) pour; **the train** ~ **London** le train pour *or* (à destination) de Londres; **he went** ~ **the paper** il est allé chercher le journal; **it's time** ~ **lunch** c'est l'heure du déjeuner; **what's it** ~? ça sert à quoi?; **what** ~? (*why*) pourquoi?; (*to what end*) pour quoi faire?, à quoi bon?; ~ **sale** à vendre

2 (*on behalf of, representing*) pour; **the MP** ~ **Hove** le député de Hove; **to work** ~ **sb/sth** travailler pour qn/qch; **G** ~ **George** G comme Georges

3 (*because of*) pour; ~ **this reason** pour cette raison; ~ **fear of being criticized** de peur d'être critiqué

4 (*with regard to*) pour; **it's cold** ~ **July** il fait froid pour juillet; **a gift** ~ **languages** un don pour les langues

5 (*in exchange for*): **I sold it** ~ **£5** je l'ai vendu 5 livres; **to pay 50 pence** ~ **a ticket** payer un billet 50 pence

6 (*in favour of*) pour; **are you** ~ **or against us?** êtes-vous pour ou contre nous?

7 (*referring to distance*) pendant, sur; **there are roadworks** ~ **5 km** il y a des travaux sur 5 km; **we walked** ~ **miles** nous avons marché pendant des kilomètres

8 (*referring to time*) pendant; depuis; pour; **he was away** ~ **2 years** il a été absent pendant 2 ans; **she will be away** ~ **a month** elle sera absente (pendant) un mois; **I have known her** ~ **years** je la connais depuis des années; **can you do it** ~ **tomorrow?** est-ce que tu peux le faire pour demain?

9 (*with infinitive clauses*): **it is not** ~ **me to decide** ce n'est pas à moi de décider; **it would be best** ~ **you to leave** le mieux serait que vous partiez; **there is still time** ~ **you to do it** vous avez encore le temps de le faire; ~ **this to be possible** ... pour que cela soit possible ...

10 (*in spite of*): ~ **all that** malgré cela, néanmoins; ~ **all his work/efforts** malgré tout son travail/tous ses efforts; ~ **all his complaints, he's very fond of her** il a beau se plaindre, il l'aime beaucoup

♦ *conj* (*since, as: rather formal*) car.

---

forage ['fɔrɪdʒ] *n* fourrage *m* ♦ *vi* fourrager,

fouiller.

forage cap n calot m.

foray ['fɔreɪ] n incursion f.

forbad(e) [fə'bæd] pt of **forbid**.

forbearing [fɔ:'bɛərɪŋ] adj patient(e), tolérant(e).

forbid, pt **forbad(e)**, pp **forbidden** [fə'bɪd, -'bæd, -'bɪdn] vt défendre, interdire; **to ~ sb to do** défendre or interdire à qn de faire.

forbidden [fə'bɪdn] adj défendu(e).

forbidding [fə'bɪdɪŋ] adj d'aspect or d'allure sévère or sombre.

force [fɔ:s] n force f ♦ vt forcer; **the F~s** npl (BRIT) l'armée f; **to ~ sb to do sth** forcer qn à faire qch; **in ~** en force; **to come into ~** entrer en vigueur; **a ~ 5 wind** un vent de force 5; **the sales ~** (COMM) la force de vente; **to join ~s** unir ses forces.

▶**force back** vt (crowd, enemy) repousser; (tears) refouler.

▶**force down** vt (food) se forcer à manger.

forced [fɔ:st] adj forcé(e).

force-feed ['fɔ:sfi:d] vt nourrir de force.

forceful ['fɔ:sful] adj énergique, volontaire.

forcemeat ['fɔ:smi:t] n (BRIT CULIN) farce f.

forceps ['fɔ:sɛps] npl forceps m.

forcibly ['fɔ:səblɪ] adv par la force, de force; (vigorously) énergiquement.

ford [fɔ:d] n gué m ♦ vt passer à gué.

fore [fɔ:*] n: **to the ~** en évidence.

forearm ['fɔ:rɑ:m] n avant-bras m inv.

forebear ['fɔ:bɛə*] n ancêtre m.

foreboding [fɔ:'bəudɪŋ] n pressentiment m (néfaste).

forecast ['fɔ:kɑ:st] n prévision f; (also: **weather ~**) prévisions météorologiques, météo f ♦ vt (irreg: like **cast**) prévoir.

foreclose [fɔ:'kləuz] vt (LAW: also: ~ **on**) saisir.

foreclosure [fɔ:'kləuʒə*] n saisie f du bien hypothéqué.

forecourt ['fɔ:kɔ:t] n (of garage) devant m.

forefathers ['fɔ:fɑ:ðəz] npl ancêtres mpl.

forefinger ['fɔ:fɪŋgə*] n index m.

forefront ['fɔ:frʌnt] n: **in the ~ of** au premier rang or plan de.

forego, pt **forewent**, pp **foregone** [fɔ:'gəu, -'wɛnt, -'gɔn] vt renoncer à.

foregoing ['fɔ:gəuɪŋ] adj susmentionné(e) ♦ n: **the ~** ce qui précède.

foregone ['fɔ:gɔn] adj: **it's a ~ conclusion** c'est à prévoir, c'est couru d'avance.

foreground ['fɔ:graund] n premier plan m ♦ cpd (COMPUT) prioritaire.

forehand ['fɔ:hænd] n (TENNIS) coup droit.

forehead ['fɔrɪd] n front m.

foreign ['fɔrɪn] adj étranger(ère); (trade) extérieur(e).

foreign body n corps étranger.

foreign currency n devises étrangères.

foreigner ['fɔrɪnə*] n étranger/ère.

foreign exchange n (system) change m; (money) devises fpl.

foreign exchange market n marché m des devises.

foreign exchange rate n cours m des devises.

foreign investment n investissement m à l'étranger.

Foreign Office n (BRIT) ministère m des Affaires étrangères.

foreign secretary n (BRIT) ministre m des Affaires étrangères.

foreleg ['fɔ:lɛg] n patte f de devant; jambe antérieure.

foreman ['fɔ:mən] n contremaître m; (LAW: of jury) président m (du jury).

foremost ['fɔ:məust] adj le(la) plus en vue; premier(ière) ♦ adv: **first and ~** avant tout, tout d'abord.

forename ['fɔ:neɪm] n prénom m.

forensic [fə'rɛnsɪk] adj: ~ **medicine** médecine légale; ~ **expert** expert m de la police, expert légiste.

foreplay ['fɔ:pleɪ] n stimulation f érotique, prélude m.

forerunner ['fɔ:rʌnə*] n précurseur m.

foresee, pt **foresaw**, pp **foreseen** [fɔ:'si:, -'sɔ:, -'si:n] vt prévoir.

foreseeable [fɔ:'si:əbl] adj prévisible.

foreshadow [fɔ:'ʃædəu] vt présager, annoncer, laisser prévoir.

foreshorten [fɔ:'ʃɔ:tn] vt (figure, scene) réduire, faire en raccourci.

foresight ['fɔ:saɪt] n prévoyance f.

foreskin ['fɔ:skɪn] n (ANAT) prépuce m.

forest ['fɔrɪst] n forêt f.

forestall [fɔ:'stɔ:l] vt devancer.

forestry ['fɔrɪstrɪ] n sylviculture f.

foretaste ['fɔ:teɪst] n avant-goût m.

foretell, pt, pp **foretold** [fɔ:'tɛl, -'təuld] vt prédire.

forethought ['fɔ:θɔ:t] n prévoyance f.

forever [fə'rɛvə*] adv pour toujours; (fig) continuellement.

forewarn [fɔ:'wɔ:n] vt avertir.

forewent [fɔ:'wɛnt] pt of **forego**.

foreword ['fɔ:wəd] n avant-propos m inv.

forfeit ['fɔ:fɪt] n prix m, rançon f ♦ vt perdre; (one's life, health) payer de.

forgave [fə'geɪv] pt of **forgive**.

forge [fɔ:dʒ] n forge f ♦ vt (signature) contrefaire; (wrought iron) forger; **to ~ documents/a will** fabriquer de faux papiers/un faux testament; **to ~ money** (BRIT) fabriquer de la fausse monnaie.

▶**forge ahead** vi pousser de l'avant, prendre de l'avance.

forger ['fɔ:dʒə*] n faussaire m.

forgery ['fɔ:dʒərɪ] n faux m, contrefaçon f.

forget, pt **forgot**, pp **forgotten** [fə'gɛt, -'gɔt, -'gɔtn] vt, vi oublier.

forgetful [fə'gɛtful] adj distrait(e), étourdi(e); ~ **of** oublieux(euse) de.

forgetfulness [fə'gɛtfulnɪs] n tendance f aux

oublis; (*oblivion*) oubli *m*.

forget-me-not [fə'gɛtmɪnɔt] *n* myosotis *m*.

forgive, *pt* **forgave**, *pp* **forgiven** [fə'gɪv, -'geɪv, -'gɪvn] *vt* pardonner; **to ~ sb for sth/ for doing sth** pardonner qch à qn/à qn de faire qch.

forgiveness [fə'gɪvnɪs] *n* pardon *m*.

forgiving [fə'gɪvɪŋ] *adj* indulgent(e).

forgo, *pt* **forwent**, *pp* **forgone** [fɔ:'gəu, -'wɛnt, -'gɔn] *vt* = **forego**.

forgot [fə'gɔt] *pt of* **forget**.

forgotten [fə'gɔtn] *pp of* **forget**.

fork [fɔːk] *n* (*for eating*) fourchette *f*; (*for gardening*) fourche *f*; (*of roads*) bifurcation *f*, (*of railways*) embranchement *m* ♦ *vi* (*road*) bifurquer.

▶**fork out** (*col: pay*) *vt* allonger, se fendre de ♦ *vi* casquer.

forked [fɔːkt] *adj* (*lightning*) en zigzags, ramifié(e).

fork-lift truck ['fɔːklɪft-] *n* chariot élévateur.

forlorn [fə'lɔːn] *adj* abandonné(e), délaissé(e); (*hope, attempt*) désespéré(e).

form [fɔːm] *n* forme *f*; (*SCOL*) classe *f*; (*questionnaire*) formulaire *m* ♦ *vt* former; **in the ~ of** sous forme de; **to ~ part of sth** faire partie de qch; **to be in good ~** (*SPORT, fig*) être en forme; **in top ~** en pleine forme.

formal ['fɔːməl] *adj* (*offer, receipt*) en bonne et due forme; (*person*) cérémonieux(euse), à cheval sur les convenances; (*occasion, dinner*) officiel(le); (*ART, PHILOSOPHY*) formel(le); **~ dress** tenue *f* de cérémonie; (*evening dress*) tenue de soirée.

formality [fɔː'mælɪtɪ] *n* formalité *f*; cérémonie(s) *f(pl)*.

formalize ['fɔːməlaɪz] *vt* officialiser.

formally ['fɔːməlɪ] *adv* officiellement; formellement; cérémonieusement.

format ['fɔːmæt] *n* format *m* ♦ *vt* (*COMPUT*) formater.

formation [fɔː'meɪʃən] *n* formation *f*.

formative ['fɔːmətɪv] *adj*: **~ years** années *fpl* d'apprentissage (*fig*) *or* de formation (*d'un enfant, d'un adolescent*).

former ['fɔːmə*] *adj* ancien(ne) (*before n*), précédent(e); **the ~ ... the latter** le premier ... le second, celui-là ... celui-ci; **the ~ president** l'ex-président; **the ~ Yugoslavia/Soviet Union** l'ex Yougoslavie/Union Soviétique.

formerly ['fɔːməlɪ] *adv* autrefois.

form feed *n* (*on printer*) alimentation *f* en feuilles.

formidable ['fɔːmɪdəbl] *adj* redoutable.

formula ['fɔːmjulə] *n* formule *f*; **F~ One** (*AUT*) Formule un.

formulate ['fɔːmjuleɪt] *vt* formuler.

fornicate ['fɔːnɪkeɪt] *vi* forniquer.

forsake, *pt* **forsook**, *pp* **forsaken** [fə'seɪk, -'suk, -'seɪkən] *vt* abandonner.

fort [fɔːt] *n* fort *m*; **to hold the ~** (*fig*) assurer la permanence.

forte ['fɔːtɪ] *n* (*point*) fort *m*.

forth [fɔːθ] *adv* en avant; **to go back and ~** aller et venir; **and so ~** et ainsi de suite.

forthcoming [fɔːθ'kʌmɪŋ] *adj* qui va paraître *or* avoir lieu prochainement; (*character*) ouvert(e), communicatif(ive).

forthright ['fɔːθraɪt] *adj* franc(franche), direct(e).

forthwith ['fɔːθ'wɪθ] *adv* sur le champ.

fortieth ['fɔːtɪɪθ] *num* quarantième.

fortification [fɔːtɪfɪ'keɪʃən] *n* fortification *f*.

fortified wine ['fɔːtɪfaɪd-] *n* vin liquoreux *or* de liqueur.

fortify ['fɔːtɪfaɪ] *vt* fortifier.

fortitude ['fɔːtɪtjuːd] *n* courage *m*, force *f* d'âme.

fortnight ['fɔːtnaɪt] *n* (*BRIT*) quinzaine *f*, quinze jours *mpl*; **it's a ~ since** ... il y a quinze jours que ....

fortnightly ['fɔːtnaɪtlɪ] *adj* bimensuel(le) ♦ *adv* tous les quinze jours.

FORTRAN ['fɔːtræn] *n* FORTRAN *m*.

fortress ['fɔːtrɪs] *n* forteresse *f*.

fortuitous [fɔː'tjuːɪtəs] *adj* fortuit(e).

fortunate ['fɔːtʃənɪt] *adj*: **to be ~** avoir de la chance; **it is ~ that** c'est une chance que, il est heureux que.

fortunately ['fɔːtʃənɪtlɪ] *adv* heureusement, par bonheur.

fortune ['fɔːtʃən] *n* chance *f*; (*wealth*) fortune *f*; **to make a ~** faire fortune.

fortuneteller ['fɔːtʃəntɛlə*] *n* diseuse *f* de bonne aventure.

forty ['fɔːtɪ] *num* quarante.

forum ['fɔːrəm] *n* forum *m*, tribune *f*.

forward ['fɔːwəd] *adj* (*movement, position*) en avant, vers l'avant; (*not shy*) effronté(e); (*COMM: delivery, sales, exchange*) à terme ♦ *adv* en avant ♦ *n* (*SPORT*) avant *m* ♦ *vt* (*letter*) faire suivre; (*parcel, goods*) expédier; (*fig*) promouvoir, contribuer au développement *or* à l'avancement de; **to move ~** avancer; **"please ~"** "prière de faire suivre"; **~ planning** planification *f* à long terme.

forwards ['fɔːwədz] *adv* en avant.

forwent [fɔː'wɛnt] *pt of* **forgo**.

fossil ['fɔsl] *adj, n* fossile (*m*); **~ fuel** combustible *m* fossile.

foster ['fɔstə*] *vt* encourager, favoriser.

foster brother *n* frère adoptif; frère de lait.

foster child *n* enfant adopté.

foster mother *n* mère adoptive; mère nourricière.

fought [fɔːt] *pt, pp of* **fight**.

foul [faul] *adj* (*weather, smell, food*) infect(e); (*language*) ordurier(ière); (*deed*) infâme ♦ *n* (*FOOTBALL*) faute *f* ♦ *vt* salir, encrasser; (*football player*) commettre une faute sur; (*entangle: anchor, propeller*) emmêler.

foul play *n* (*SPORT*) jeu déloyal; **~ is not suspected** la mort (*or* l'incendie *etc*) n'a pas de causes suspectes, on écarte l'hypothèse d'un meurtre (*or* d'un acte criminel).

found [faund] *pt, pp of* **find** ♦ *vt* (*establish*) fonder.

foundation [faun'deɪʃən] *n* (*act*) fondation *f*; (*base*) fondement *m*; (*also*: ~ **cream**) fond *m* de teint; ~**s** *npl* (*of building*) fondations *fpl*; **to lay the ~s** (*fig*) poser les fondements.

foundation stone *n* première pierre.

founder ['faundə*] *n* fondateur *m* ♦ *vi* couler, sombrer.

founding ['faundɪŋ] *adj*: ~ **fathers** (*esp US*) pères *mpl* fondateurs; ~ **member** membre *m* fondateur.

foundry ['faundrɪ] *n* fonderie *f*.

fount [faunt] *n* source *f*; (*TYP*) fonte *f*.

fountain ['fauntɪn] *n* fontaine *f*.

fountain pen *n* stylo *m* (à encre).

four [fɔ:*] *num* quatre; **on all ~s** à quatre pattes.

four-letter word ['fɔ:lɛtə-] *n* obscénité *f*, gros mot.

four-poster ['fɔ:'pəustə*] *n* (*also*: ~ **bed**) lit *m* à baldaquin.

foursome ['fɔ:səm] *n* partie *f* à quatre; sortie *f* à quatre.

fourteen ['fɔ:'ti:n] *num* quatorze.

fourth ['fɔ:θ] *num* quatrième ♦ *n* (*AUT: also*: ~ **gear**) quatrième *f*.

four-wheel drive ['fɔ:wi:l-] *n* (*AUT*): **with ~** à quatre roues motrices.

fowl [faul] *n* volaille *f*.

fox [fɔks] *n* renard *m* ♦ *vt* mystifier.

fox fur *n* renard *m*.

foxglove ['fɔksglʌv] *n* (*BOT*) digitale *f*.

fox-hunting ['fɔkshʌntɪŋ] *n* chasse *f* au renard.

foyer ['fɔɪeɪ] *n* vestibule *m*; (*THEAT*) foyer *m*.

FP *n abbr* (*BRIT*) = *former pupil*; (*US*) = *fireplug*.

FPA *n abbr* (*BRIT*) = *Family Planning Association*.

Fr. *abbr* (= *father; REL*) P; (= *friar*) F.

fr. *abbr* (= *franc*) F.

fracas ['fræka:] *n* bagarre *f*.

fraction ['frækʃən] *n* fraction *f*.

fractionally ['frækʃnəlɪ] *adv*: ~ **smaller** *etc* un poil plus petit *etc*.

fractious ['frækʃəs] *adj* grincheux(euse).

fracture ['fræktʃə*] *n* fracture *f* ♦ *vt* fracturer.

fragile ['frædʒaɪl] *adj* fragile.

fragment ['frægmənt] *n* fragment *m*.

fragmentary ['frægməntərɪ] *adj* fragmentaire.

fragrance ['freɪɡrəns] *n* parfum *m*.

fragrant ['freɪɡrənt] *adj* parfumé(e), odorant(e).

frail [freɪl] *adj* fragile, délicat(e).

frame [freɪm] *n* (*of building*) charpente *f*; (*of human, animal*) charpente, ossature *f*; (*of picture*) cadre *m*; (*of door, window*) encadrement *m*, chambranle *m*; (*of spectacles: also*: ~**s**) monture *f* ♦ *vt* encadrer; (*theory, plan*) construire, élaborer; **to ~ sb** (*col*) monter un coup contre qn; ~ **of mind** disposition *f* d'esprit.

framework ['freɪmwə:k] *n* structure *f*.

France [fra:ns] *n* la France; **in ~** en France.

franchise ['fræntʃaɪz] *n* (*POL*) droit *m* de vote; (*COMM*) franchise *f*.

franchisee [fræntʃaɪ'zi:] *n* franchisé *m*.

franchiser ['fræntʃaɪzə*] *n* franchiseur *m*.

frank [fræŋk] *adj* franc(franche) ♦ *vt* (*letter*) affranchir.

Frankfurt ['fræŋkfə:t] *n* Francfort.

franking machine ['fræŋkɪŋ-] *n* machine *f* à affranchir.

frankly ['fræŋklɪ] *adv* franchement.

frankness ['fræŋknɪs] *n* franchise *f*.

frantic ['fræntɪk] *adj* frénétique; (*desperate: need, desire*) effréné(e); (*person*) hors de soi.

frantically ['fræntɪklɪ] *adv* frénétiquement.

fraternal [frə'tə:nl] *adj* fraternel(le).

fraternity [frə'tə:nɪtɪ] *n* (*club*) communauté *f*, confrérie *f*; (*spirit*) fraternité *f*.

fraternize ['frætənaɪz] *vi* fraterniser.

fraud [frɔ:d] *n* supercherie *f*, fraude *f*, tromperie *f*; (*person*) imposteur *m*.

fraudulent ['frɔ:djulənt] *adj* frauduleux(euse).

fraught [frɔ:t] *adj* (*tense: person*) très tendu(e); (: *situation*) pénible; ~ **with** (*difficulties etc*) chargé(e) de, plein(e) de.

fray [freɪ] *n* bagarre *f*; (*MIL*) combat *m* ♦ *vt* effilocher ♦ *vi* s'effilocher; **tempers were ~ed** les gens commençaient à s'énerver; **her nerves were ~ed** elle était à bout de nerfs.

FRB *n abbr* (*US*) = *Federal Reserve Board*.

FRCM *n abbr* (*BRIT*) = *Fellow of the Royal College of Music*.

FRCO *n abbr* (*BRIT*) = *Fellow of the Royal College of Organists*.

FRCP *n abbr* (*BRIT*) = *Fellow of the Royal College of Physicians*.

FRCS *n abbr* (*BRIT*) = *Fellow of the Royal College of Surgeons*.

freak [fri:k] *n* (*also cpd*) phénomène *m*, créature ou événement exceptionnel par sa rareté, son caractère d'anomalie; (*pej: fanatic*): **health ~** fana *m/f* or obsédé/e de l'alimentation saine (*or* de la forme physique).

▶**freak out** *vi* (*col: drop out*) se marginaliser; (: *on drugs*) se défoncer.

freakish ['fri:kɪʃ] *adj* insolite; anormal(e).

freckle ['frɛkl] *n* tache *f* de rousseur.

free [fri:] *adj* libre; (*gratis*) gratuit(e); (*liberal*) généreux(euse), large ♦ *vt* (*prisoner etc*) libérer; (*jammed object or person*) dégager; **to give sb a ~ hand** donner carte blanche à qn; ~ **and easy** sans façon, décontracté(e); **admission ~** entrée libre; ~ (**of charge**) *adv* gratuitement.

freebie ['fri:bɪ] *n* (*col*): **it's a ~** c'est gratuit.

freedom ['fri:dəm] *n* liberté *f*.

freedom fighter *n* combattant *m* de la liberté.

free enterprise *n* libre entreprise *f*.

Freefone ['fri:fəun] *n* ® numéro vert.

free-for-all ['fri:fərɔ:l] n mêlée générale.
free gift n prime f.
freehold ['fri:həuld] n propriété foncière libre.
free kick n (SPORT) coup franc.
freelance ['fri:lɑ:ns] adj (journalist etc) indépendant(e); (work) à la pige, à la tâche.
freeloader ['fri:ləudə*] n (pej) parasite m.
freely ['fri:lı] adv librement; (liberally) libéralement.
free-market economy [fri:'mɑ:kıt-] n économie f de marché.
freemason ['fri:meısn] n franc-maçon m.
freemasonry ['fri:meısnrı] n franc-maçonnerie f.
freepost ['fri:pəust] n franchise postale.
free-range ['fri:'reındʒ] adj (eggs) de ferme.
free sample n échantillon gratuit.
free speech n liberté f d'expression.
free trade n libre-échange m.
freeway ['fri:weı] n (US) autoroute f.
freewheel [fri:'wi:l] vi descendre en roue libre.
freewheeling [fri:'wi:lıŋ] adj indépendant(e), libre.
free will n libre arbitre m; **of one's own** ~ de son plein gré.
freeze [fri:z] vb (pt **froze**, pp **frozen** [frəuz, 'frəuzn]) vi geler ♦ vt geler; (food) congeler; (prices, salaries) bloquer, geler ♦ n gel m; blocage m.
▶**freeze over** vi (river) geler; (windscreen) se couvrir de givre or de glace.
▶**freeze up** vi geler.
freeze-dried ['fri:zdraıd] adj lyophilisé(e).
freezer ['fri:zə*] n congélateur m.
freezing ['fri:zıŋ] adj: ~ (**cold**) (room etc) glacial(e); (person, hands) gelé(e), glacé(e) ♦ n: **3 degrees below** ~ 3 degrés au-dessous de zéro.
freezing point n point m de congélation.
freight [freıt] n (goods) fret m, cargaison f; (money charged) fret, prix m du transport; ~ **forward** port dû; ~ **inward** port payé par le destinataire.
freighter ['freıtə*] n (NAUT) cargo m.
freight forwarder [-fɔ:wədə*] n transitaire m.
freight train n (US) train m de marchandises.
French [frentʃ] adj français(e) ♦ n (LING) français m; **the** ~ npl les Français.
French bean n (BRIT) haricot vert.
French bread n pain m (français).
French Canadian adj canadien(ne) français(e) ♦ n Canadien/ne français(e).
French dressing n (CULIN) vinaigrette f.
French fried potatoes, (US) **French fries** npl (pommes de terre fpl) frites fpl.
French Guiana [-gaı'ænə] n Guyane française.
French loaf n ≈ pain m, ≈ parisien m.
Frenchman ['frentʃmən] n Français m.
French Riviera n: **the** ~ la Côte d'Azur.

French stick n ≈ baguette f.
French window n porte-fenêtre f.
Frenchwoman ['frentʃwumən] n Française f.
frenetic [frə'netık] adj frénétique.
frenzy ['frenzı] n frénésie f.
frequency ['fri:kwənsı] n fréquence f.
frequency modulation (FM) n modulation f de fréquence (FM, MF).
frequent adj ['fri:kwənt] fréquent(e) ♦ vt [frı'kwent] fréquenter.
frequently ['fri:kwəntlı] adv fréquemment.
fresco ['freskəu] n fresque f.
fresh [freʃ] adj frais(fraîche); (new) nouveau(nouvelle); (cheeky) familier(ière), culotté(e); **to make a** ~ **start** prendre un nouveau départ.
freshen ['freʃən] vi (wind, air) fraîchir.
▶**freshen up** vi faire un brin de toilette.
freshener ['freʃnə*] n: **skin** ~ astringent m; **air** ~ désodorisant m.
fresher ['freʃə*] n (BRIT SCOL: col) = freshman.
freshly ['freʃlı] adv nouvellement, récemment.
freshman ['freʃmən] n (SCOL) bizuth m, étudiant/e de première année.
freshness ['freʃnıs] n fraîcheur f.
freshwater ['freʃwɔ:tə*] adj (fish) d'eau douce.
fret [fret] vi s'agiter, se tracasser.
fretful ['fretful] adj (child) grincheux(euse).
Freudian ['frɔıdıən] adj freudien(ne); ~ **slip** lapsus m.
FRG n abbr (= Federal Republic of Germany) RFA f.
Fri. abbr (= Friday) ve.
friar ['fraıə*] n moine m, frère m.
friction ['frıkʃən] n friction f, frottement m.
friction feed n (on printer) entraînement m par friction.
Friday ['fraıdı] n vendredi m; for phrases see also **Tuesday**.
fridge [frıdʒ] n (BRIT) frigo m, frigidaire m ®.
fridge-freezer ['frıdʒ'fri:zə*] n réfrigérateur-congélateur m.
fried [fraıd] pt, pp of **fry** ♦ adj frit(e); ~ **egg** œuf m sur le plat.
friend [frend] n ami/e; **to make** ~**s with** se lier (d'amitié) avec.
friendliness ['frendlınıs] n attitude amicale.
friendly ['frendlı] adj amical(e); (kind) sympathique, gentil(le); (POL: country, government) ami(e) ♦ n (also: ~ **match**) match amical; **to be** ~ **with** être ami(e) avec; **to be** ~ **to** être bien disposé(e) à l'égard de.
friendly fire n: **they were killed by** ~ ils sont morts sous les tirs de leur propre camp.
friendly society n société f mutualiste.
friendship ['frendʃıp] n amitié f.
frieze [fri:z] n frise f, bordure f.
frigate ['frıgıt] n (NAUT: modern) frégate f.
fright [fraıt] n peur f, effroi m; **to take** ~ prendre peur, s'effrayer; **she looks a** ~ elle a l'air d'un épouvantail.

frighten ['fraitn] vt effrayer, faire peur à.
▶**frighten away, frighten off** vt (birds, children etc) faire fuir, effaroucher.
frightened ['fraitnd] adj: **to be ~ (of)** avoir peur (de).
frightening ['fraitnɪŋ] adj effrayant(e).
frightful ['fraitful] adj affreux(euse).
frightfully ['fraitfəlɪ] adv affreusement.
frigid ['frɪdʒɪd] adj (woman) frigide.
frigidity [frɪ'dʒɪdɪtɪ] n frigidité f.
frill [frɪl] n (of dress) volant m; (of shirt) jabot m; **without ~s** (fig) sans manières.
frilly ['frɪlɪ] adj à fanfreluches.
fringe [frɪndʒ] n frange f; (edge: of forest etc) bordure f; (fig): **on the ~** en marge.
fringe benefits npl avantages sociaux or en nature.
fringe theatre n théâtre m d'avant-garde.
Frisbee ['frɪzbɪ] n ® Frisbee m ®.
frisk [frɪsk] vt fouiller.
frisky ['frɪskɪ] adj vif(vive), sémillant(e).
fritter ['frɪtə*] n beignet m.
▶**fritter away** vt gaspiller.
frivolity [frɪ'vɔlɪtɪ] n frivolité f.
frivolous ['frɪvələs] adj frivole.
frizzy ['frɪzɪ] adj crépu(e).
fro [frəu] see **to**.
frock [frɔk] n robe f.
frog [frɔg] n grenouille f; **to have a ~ in one's throat** avoir un chat dans la gorge.
frogman ['frɔgmən] n homme-grenouille m.
frogmarch ['frɔgmɑːtʃ] vt (BRIT): **to ~ sb in/out** faire entrer/sortir qn de force.
frolic ['frɔlɪk] n ébats mpl ♦ vi folâtrer, batifoler.

═══════════════════ KEYWORD

from [frɔm] prep **1** (indicating starting place, origin etc) de; **where do you come ~?, where are you ~?** d'où venez-vous?; **where has he come ~?** d'où arrive-t-il?; ~ **London to Paris** de Londres à Paris; **a letter/telephone call ~ my sister** une lettre/un appel de ma sœur; **to drink ~ the bottle** boire à (même) la bouteille
2 (indicating time) (à partir) de; ~ **one o'clock to** or **until** or **till two** d'une heure à deux heures; ~ **January (on)** à partir de janvier
3 (indicating distance) de; **the hotel is one kilometre ~ the beach** l'hôtel est à un kilomètre de la plage
4 (indicating price, number etc) de; **the interest rate was increased ~ 9% to 10%** le taux d'intérêt est passé de 9 à 10%
5 (indicating difference) de; **he can't tell red ~ green** il ne peut pas distinguer le rouge du vert
6 (because of, on the basis of): ~ **what he says** d'après ce qu'il dit; **weak ~ hunger** affaibli par la faim.

frond [frɔnd] n fronde f.
front [frʌnt] n (of house, dress) devant m; (of coach, train) avant m; (of book) couverture f; (promenade: also: **sea ~**) bord m de mer; (MIL, POL, METEOROLOGY) front m; (fig: appearances) contenance f, façade f ♦ adj de devant; premier(ière) ♦ vi: **to ~ onto sth** donner sur qch; **in ~ (of)** devant.
frontage ['frʌntɪdʒ] n façade f; (of shop) devanture f.
frontal ['frʌntl] adj frontal(e).

┌───┐
Le **front bench** est le banc du gouvernement, placé à la droite du **Speaker**, ou celui du cabinet fantôme, placé à sa gauche. Ils se font face dans l'enceinte de la Chambre des communes. Par extension, **front bench** désigne les dirigeants des groupes parlementaires de la majorité et de l'opposition, qui sont appelés "frontbenchers" par opposition aux autres députés qui sont appelés "backbenchers".
└───┘

front desk n (US: in hotel, at doctor's) réception f.
front door n porte f d'entrée; (of car) portière f avant.
frontier ['frʌntɪə*] n frontière f.
frontispiece ['frʌntɪspiːs] n frontispice m.
front page n première page.
front room n (BRIT) pièce f de devant, salon m.
front runner n (fig) favori/te.
front-wheel drive ['frʌntwiːl-] n traction f avant.
frost [frɔst] n gel m, gelée f; (also: **hoar~**) givre m.
frostbite ['frɔstbaɪt] n gelures fpl.
frosted ['frɔstɪd] adj (glass) dépoli(e); (esp US: cake) glacé(e).
frosting ['frɔstɪŋ] n (esp US: on cake) glaçage m.
frosty ['frɔstɪ] adj (window) couvert(e) de givre; (welcome) glacial(e).
froth [frɔθ] n mousse f; écume f.
frown [fraun] n froncement m de sourcils ♦ vi froncer les sourcils.
▶**frown on** vt (fig) désapprouver.
froze [frəuz] pt of **freeze**.
frozen ['frəuzn] pp of **freeze** ♦ adj (food) congelé(e); (COMM: assets) gelé(e).
FRS n abbr (BRIT: = Fellow of the Royal Society) membre de l'Académie des sciences; (US: = Federal Reserve System) banque centrale américaine.
frugal ['fruːgl] adj frugal(e).
fruit [fruːt] n (pl inv) fruit m.
fruiterer ['fruːtərə*] n fruitier m, marchand/e de fruits; ~'**s (shop)** fruiterie f.
fruit fly n mouche f du vinaigre, drosophile f.
fruitful ['fruːtful] adj fructueux(euse); (plant, soil) fécond(e).
fruition [fruː'ɪʃən] n: **to come to ~** se réaliser.

fruit juice n jus m de fruit.
fruitless ['fruːtlɪs] adj (fig) vain(e), infructueux(euse).
fruit machine n (BRIT) machine f à sous.
fruit salad n salade f de fruits.
frump [frʌmp] n mocheté f.
frustrate [frʌs'treɪt] vt frustrer; (plot, plans) faire échouer.
frustrated [frʌs'treɪtɪd] adj frustré(e).
frustrating [frʌs'treɪtɪŋ] adj (job) frustrant(e); (day) démoralisant(e).
frustration [frʌs'treɪʃən] n frustration f.
fry, pt, pp **fried** [fraɪ, -d] vt (faire) frire; **the small ~** le menu fretin.
frying pan ['fraɪŋ-] n poêle f (à frire).
FT n abbr (BRIT: = Financial Times) journal financier.
ft. abbr = **foot, feet**.
FTC n abbr (US) = **Federal Trade Commission**.
FTSE 100 (Share) Index n abbr (= Financial Times Stock Exchange 100 (Share) Index) indice m Footsie des cent grandes valeurs.
fuchsia ['fjuːʃə] n fuchsia m.
fuck [fʌk] vt, vi (col!) baiser (!); ~ **off!** fous le camp! (!).
fuddled ['fʌdld] adj (muddled) embrouillé(e), confus(e).
fuddy-duddy ['fʌdɪdʌdɪ] adj (pej) vieux jeu inv, ringard(e).
fudge [fʌdʒ] n (CULIN) sorte de confiserie à base de sucre, de beurre et de lait ♦ vt (issue, problem) esquiver.
fuel [fjuəl] n (for heating) combustible m; (for propelling) carburant m.
fuel oil n mazout m.
fuel pump n (AUT) pompe f d'alimentation.
fuel tank n cuve f à mazout, citerne f; (in vehicle) réservoir m de or à carburant.
fug [fʌg] n (BRIT) puanteur f, odeur f de renfermé.
fugitive ['fjuːdʒɪtɪv] n fugitif/ive.
fulfil, (US) **fulfill** [ful'fɪl] vt (function) remplir; (order) exécuter; (wish, desire) satisfaire, réaliser.
fulfilled [ful'fɪld] adj (person) comblé(e), épanoui(e).
fulfil(l)ment [ful'fɪlmənt] n (of wishes) réalisation f.
full [ful] adj plein(e); (details, information) complet(ète); (price) fort(e), normal(e); (skirt) ample, large ♦ adv: **to know ~ well that** savoir fort bien que; ~ **(up)** (hotel etc) complet(ète); **I'm ~ (up)** j'ai bien mangé; ~ **employment/fare** plein emploi/tarif; **a two hours** deux bonnes heures; **at ~ speed** à toute vitesse; **in ~** (reproduce, quote, pay) intégralement; (write name etc) en toutes lettres.
fullback ['fulbæk] n (RUGBY, FOOTBALL) arrière m.
full-blooded ['ful'blʌdɪd] adj (vigorous) vigoureux(euse).

full-cream ['ful'kriːm] adj: ~ **milk** (BRIT) lait entier.
full-grown ['ful'grəun] adj arrivé(e) à maturité, adulte.
full-length ['ful'leŋθ] adj (portrait) en pied; ~ **film** long métrage.
full moon n pleine lune.
full-scale ['fulskeɪl] adj (model) grandeur nature inv; (search, retreat) complet(ète), total(e).
full-sized ['ful'saɪzd] adj (portrait etc) grandeur nature inv.
full stop n point m.
full-time ['ful'taɪm] adj (work) à plein temps ♦ n (SPORT) fin f du match.
fully ['fulɪ] adv entièrement, complètement; (at least): ~ **as big** au moins aussi grand.
fully-fledged ['fulɪ'fledʒd] adj (teacher, barrister) diplômé(e); (citizen, member) à part entière.
fulsome ['fulsəm] adj (pej: praise) excessif(ive); (: manner) exagéré(e).
fumble ['fʌmbl] vi fouiller, tâtonner ♦ vt (ball) mal réceptionner, cafouiller.
▶**fumble with** vt fus tripoter.
fume [fjuːm] vi rager; ~**s** npl vapeurs fpl, émanations fpl, gaz mpl.
fumigate ['fjuːmɪgeɪt] vt désinfecter (par fumigation).
fun [fʌn] n amusement m, divertissement m; **to have ~** s'amuser; **for ~** pour rire; **it's not much ~** ce n'est pas très drôle or amusant; **to make ~ of** se moquer de.
function ['fʌŋkʃən] n fonction f; (reception, dinner) cérémonie f, soirée officielle ♦ vi fonctionner; **to ~ as** faire office de.
functional ['fʌŋkʃənl] adj fonctionnel(le).
function key n (COMPUT) touche f de fonction.
fund [fʌnd] n caisse f, fonds m; (source, store) source f, mine f; ~**s** npl fonds mpl.
fundamental [fʌndə'mentl] adj fondamental(e); ~**s** npl principes mpl de base.
fundamentalism [fʌndə'mentəlɪzəm] n intégrisme m.
fundamentalist [fʌndə'mentəlɪst] intégriste m/f.
fundamentally [fʌndə'mentəlɪ] adv fondamentalement.
funding ['fʌndɪŋ] n financement m.
fund-raising ['fʌndreɪzɪŋ] n collecte f de fonds.
funeral ['fjuːnərəl] n enterrement m, obsèques fpl (more formal occasion).
funeral director n entrepreneur m des pompes funèbres.
funeral parlour n dépôt m mortuaire.
funeral service n service m funèbre.
funereal [fjuː'nɪərɪəl] adj lugubre, funèbre.
fun fair n (BRIT) fête (foraine).
fungus, pl **fungi** ['fʌŋgəs, -gaɪ] n champignon m; (mould) moisissure f.

funicular [fju:'nɪkjulə*] *n* (*also*: ~ **railway**) funiculaire *m*.

funky ['fʌŋkɪ] *adj* (*music*) funky *inv*; (*col*: *excellent*) super *inv*.

funnel ['fʌnl] *n* entonnoir *m*; (*of ship*) cheminée *f*.

funnily ['fʌnɪlɪ] *adv* (*see funny*) drôlement; curieusement.

funny ['fʌnɪ] *adj* amusant(e), drôle; (*strange*) curieux(euse), bizarre.

funny bone *n* endroit sensible du coude.

fun run *n* course *f* de fond (*pour amateurs*).

fur [fə:*] *n* fourrure *f*; (*BRIT*: *in kettle etc*) (dépôt *m* de) tartre *m*.

fur coat *n* manteau *m* de fourrure.

furious ['fjuərɪəs] *adj* furieux(euse); (*effort*) acharné(e); **to be** ~ **with sb** être dans une fureur noire contre qn.

furiously ['fjuərɪəslɪ] *adv* furieusement; avec acharnement.

furl [fə:l] *vt* rouler; (*NAUT*) ferler.

furlong ['fə:lɒŋ] *n* = 201.17 *m* (*terme d'hippisme*).

furlough ['fə:ləu] *n* permission *f*, congé *m*.

furnace ['fə:nɪs] *n* fourneau *m*.

furnish ['fə:nɪʃ] *vt* meubler; (*supply*) fournir; ~**ed flat** *or* (*US*) **apartment** meublé *m*.

furnishings ['fə:nɪʃɪŋz] *npl* mobilier *m*, articles *mpl* d'ameublement.

furniture ['fə:nɪtʃə*] *n* meubles *mpl*, mobilier *m*; **piece of** ~ meuble *m*.

furniture polish *n* encaustique *f*.

furore [fjuə'rɔ:rɪ] *n* (*protests*) protestations *fpl*.

furrier ['fʌrɪə*] *n* fourreur *m*.

furrow ['fʌrəu] *n* sillon *m*.

furry ['fə:rɪ] *adj* (*animal*) à fourrure; (*toy*) en peluche.

further ['fə:ðə*] *adj* supplémentaire, autre; nouveau(nouvelle) ♦ *adv* plus loin; (*more*) davantage; (*moreover*) de plus ♦ *vt* faire avancer *or* progresser, promouvoir; **how much** ~ **is it?** quelle distance *or* combien reste-t-il à parcourir?; **until** ~ **notice** jusqu'à nouvel ordre *or* avis; ~ **to your letter of ...** (*COMM*) suite à votre lettre du ....

further education *n* enseignement *m* postscolaire (*recyclage, formation professionnelle*).

furthermore [fə:ðə'mɔ:*] *adv* de plus, en outre.

furthermost ['fə:ðəməust] *adj* le(la) plus éloigné(e).

furthest ['fə:ðɪst] *superlative of* **far**.

furtive ['fə:tɪv] *adj* furtif(ive).

furtively ['fə:tɪvlɪ] *adv* furtivement.

fury ['fjuərɪ] *n* fureur *f*.

fuse, (*US*) **fuze** [fju:z] *n* fusible *m*; (*for bomb etc*) amorce *f*, détonateur *m* ♦ *vt*, *vi* (*metal*) fondre; (*fig*) fusionner; (*ELEC*): **to** ~ **the lights** faire sauter les fusibles *or* les plombs; **a** ~ **has blown** un fusible a sauté.

fuse box *n* boîte *f* à fusibles.

fuselage ['fju:zəla:ʒ] *n* fuselage *m*.

fuse wire *n* fusible *m*.

fusillade [fju:zɪ'leɪd] *n* fusillade *f*; (*fig*) feu roulant.

fusion ['fju:ʒən] *n* fusion *f*.

fuss [fʌs] *n* (*anxiety, excitement*) chichis *mpl*, façons *fpl*; (*commotion*) tapage *m*; (*complaining, trouble*) histoire(s) *f(pl)* ♦ *vi* faire des histoires ♦ *vt* (*person*) embêter; **to make a** ~ faire des façons (*or* des histoires); **to make a** ~ **of sb** dorloter qn.

►**fuss over** *vt fus* (*person*) dorloter.

fusspot ['fʌspɒt] *n* (*col*): **don't be such a** ~! ne fais pas tant d'histoires!

fussy ['fʌsɪ] *adj* (*person*) tatillon(ne), difficile; chichiteux(euse); (*dress, style*) tarabiscoté(e); **I'm not** ~ (*col*) ça m'est égal.

fusty ['fʌstɪ] *adj* (*old-fashioned*) vieillot(te); (*smell*) de renfermé *or* moisi.

futile ['fju:taɪl] *adj* futile.

futility [fju:'tɪlɪtɪ] *n* futilité *f*.

futon ['fu:tɒn] *n* futon *m*.

future ['fju:tʃə*] *adj* futur(e) ♦ *n* avenir *m*; (*LING*) futur *m*; **in (the)** ~ à l'avenir; **in the near/immediate** ~ dans un avenir proche/immédiat.

futures ['fju:tʃəz] *npl* (*COMM*) opérations *fpl* à terme.

futuristic [fju:tʃə'rɪstɪk] *adj* futuriste.

fuze [fju:z] *n*, *vt*, *vi* (*US*) = **fuse**.

fuzzy ['fʌzɪ] *adj* (*PHOT*) flou(e); (*hair*) crépu(e).

fwd. *abbr* = **forward**.

fwy *abbr* (*US*) = **freeway**.

FY *abbr* = **fiscal year**.

FYI *abbr* = **for your information**.

G g

G, g [dʒi:] *n* (*letter*) G, g *m*; (*MUS*): **G** sol *m*; **G for George** G comme Gaston.

G *n abbr* (*BRIT SCOL*: = *good*) b (= *bien*); (*US CINE*: = *general (audience)*) ≈ tous publics; **G7** (*POL*) G7 *m*.

g *abbr* (= *gram, gravity*) g.

GA *abbr* (*US*) = **Georgia**.

gab [gæb] *n* (*col*): **to have the gift of the** ~ avoir la langue bien pendue.

gabble ['gæbl] *vi* bredouiller; jacasser.

gaberdine [gæbə'di:n] *n* gabardine *f*.

gable ['geɪbl] *n* pignon *m*.

Gabon [gə'bɒn] *n* Gabon *m*.

gad about ['gædə'baut] *vi* (*col*) se balader.

gadget ['gædʒɪt] *n* gadget *m*.

Gaelic ['geɪlɪk] *adj, n* gaélique (*m*).

gaffe [gæf] *n* gaffe *f*.

gaffer ['gæfə*] *n* (*BRIT*: *foreman*) contremaître *m*; (*BRIT col*: *boss*) patron *m*.

gag [gæg] n bâillon m; (joke) gag m ♦ vt (prisoner etc) bâillonner ♦ vi (choke) étouffer.

gaga ['gɑːgɑː] adj: **to go** ~ devenir gaga or gâteux(euse).

gaiety ['geɪtɪ] n gaieté f.

gaily ['geɪlɪ] adv gaiement.

gain [geɪn] n gain m, profit m ♦ vt gagner ♦ vi (watch) avancer; **to** ~ **in/by** gagner en/à; **to** ~ **3lbs (in weight)** prendre 3 livres; **to** ~ **ground** gagner du terrain.

▶**gain (up)on** vt fus rattraper.

gainful ['geɪnful] adj profitable, lucratif(ive).

gainfully ['geɪnfəlɪ] adv: **to be** ~ **employed** avoir un emploi rémunéré.

gainsay [geɪn'seɪ] vt (irreg: like **say**) contredire; nier.

gait [geɪt] n démarche f.

gal. abbr = **gallon**.

gala ['gɑːlə] n gala m; **swimming** ~ grand concours de natation.

Galápagos (Islands) [gə'læpəgəs-] npl: **the** ~ les (îles fpl) Galapagos fpl.

galaxy ['gæləksɪ] n galaxie f.

gale [geɪl] n coup m de vent; ~ **force 10** vent m de force 10.

gall [gɔːl] n (ANAT) bile f; (fig) effronterie f ♦ vt ulcérer, irriter.

gall. abbr = **gallon**.

gallant ['gælənt] adj vaillant(e), brave; (towards ladies) empressé(e), galant(e).

gallantry ['gæləntrɪ] n bravoure f, vaillance f; empressement m, galanterie f.

gall-bladder ['gɔːlblædə*] n vésicule f biliaire.

galleon ['gælɪən] n galion m.

gallery ['gælərɪ] n galerie f; (for spectators) tribune f; (: in theatre) dernier balcon; (also: **art** ~) musée m; (: private) galerie.

galley ['gælɪ] n (ship's kitchen) cambuse f; (ship) galère f; (also: ~ **proof**) placard m, galée f.

Gallic ['gælɪk] adj (of Gaul) gaulois(e); (French) français(e).

galling ['gɔːlɪŋ] adj irritant(e).

gallon ['gælən] n gallon m (= 8 pints; BRIT = 4.543 l; US = 3.785 l).

gallop ['gæləp] n galop m ♦ vi galoper; ~**ing inflation** inflation galopante.

gallows ['gæləuz] n potence f.

gallstone ['gɔːlstəun] n calcul m (biliaire).

Gallup Poll ['gæləp-] n sondage m Gallup.

galore [gə'lɔː*] adv en abondance, à gogo.

galvanize ['gælvənaɪz] vt galvaniser; (fig): **to** ~ **sb into action** galvaniser qn.

Gambia ['gæmbɪə] n Gambie f.

gambit ['gæmbɪt] n (fig): **(opening)** ~ manœuvre f stratégique.

gamble ['gæmbl] n pari m, risque calculé ♦ vt, vi jouer; **to** ~ **on the Stock Exchange** jouer en or à la Bourse; **to** ~ **on** (fig) miser sur.

gambler ['gæmblə*] n joueur m.

gambling ['gæmblɪŋ] n jeu m.

gambol ['gæmbl] vi gambader.

game [geɪm] n jeu m; (event) match m; (HUNTING) gibier m ♦ adj brave; (ready): **to be** ~ **(for sth/to do)** être prêt(e) (à qch/à faire), se sentir de taille (à faire); **a** ~ **of football/tennis** une partie de football/tennis; ~**s** (SCOL) sport m; **big** ~ gros gibier.

game bird n gibier m à plume.

gamekeeper ['geɪmkiːpə*] n garde-chasse m.

gamely ['geɪmlɪ] adv vaillamment.

game reserve n réserve animalière.

games console ['geɪmz-] n console f de jeux vidéo.

gameshow ['geɪmʃəu] n jeu télévisé.

gamesmanship ['geɪmzmənʃɪp] n roublardise f.

gaming ['geɪmɪŋ] n jeu m, jeux mpl d'argent.

gammon ['gæmən] n (bacon) quartier m de lard fumé; (ham) jambon fumé.

gamut ['gæmət] n gamme f.

gang [gæŋ] n bande f, groupe m.

▶**gang up** vi: **to** ~ **up on sb** se liguer contre qn.

Ganges ['gændʒiːz] n: **the** ~ le Gange.

gangland ['gæŋlænd] adj: ~ **killer** tueur professionnel du milieu; ~ **boss** chef m de gang.

gangling ['gæŋglɪŋ], **gangly** ['gæŋglɪ] adj dégingandé(e).

gangplank ['gæŋplæŋk] n passerelle f.

gangrene ['gæŋgriːn] n gangrène f.

gangster ['gæŋstə*] n gangster m, bandit m.

gangway ['gæŋweɪ] n passerelle f; (BRIT: of bus) couloir central.

gantry ['gæntrɪ] n portique m; (for rocket) tour f de lancement.

GAO n abbr (US: = General Accounting Office) ≈ Cour f des comptes.

gaol [dʒeɪl] n, vt (BRIT) = **jail**.

gap [gæp] n trou m; (in time) intervalle m; (fig) lacune f; vide m.

gape [geɪp] vi être or rester bouche bée.

gaping ['geɪpɪŋ] adj (hole) béant(e).

garage ['gærɑːʒ] n garage m.

garb [gɑːb] n tenue f, costume m.

garbage ['gɑːbɪdʒ] n ordures fpl, détritus mpl; (fig: col) conneries fpl.

garbage can n (US) poubelle f, boîte f à ordures.

garbage collector n (US) éboueur m.

garbage disposal (unit) n (US) broyeur m d'ordures.

garbage truck n (US) camion m (du ramassage) des ordures, benne f à ordures.

garbled ['gɑːbld] adj déformé(e); faussé(e).

garden ['gɑːdn] n jardin m ♦ vi jardiner; ~**s** npl (public) jardin public; (private) parc m.

garden centre n garden-centre m, pépinière f.

garden city n (BRIT) cité-jardin f.

gardener ['gɑːdnə*] n jardinier m.

gardening ['gɑːdnɪŋ] n jardinage m.

gargle ['gɑːgl] vi se gargariser ♦ n gargarisme

m.

gargoyle ['gɑːgɔɪl] *n* gargouille *f*.

garish ['gɛərɪʃ] *adj* criard(e), voyant(e).

garland ['gɑːlənd] *n* guirlande *f*; couronne *f*.

garlic ['gɑːlɪk] *n* ail *m*.

garment ['gɑːmənt] *n* vêtement *m*.

garner ['gɑːnə*] *vt* engranger, amasser.

garnish ['gɑːnɪʃ] *vt* garnir.

garret ['gærɪt] *n* mansarde *f*.

garrison ['gærɪsn] *n* garnison *f* ♦ *vt* mettre en garnison, stationner.

garrulous ['gærjuləs] *adj* volubile, loquace.

garter ['gɑːtə*] *n* jarretière *f*; (*US: suspender*) jarretelle *f*.

garter belt *n* (*US*) porte-jarretelles *m inv*.

gas [gæs] *n* gaz *m*; (*used as anaesthetic*): **to be given** ~ se faire endormir; (*US: gasoline*) essence *f* ♦ *vt* asphyxier; (*MIL*) gazer.

Gascony ['gæskənɪ] *n* Gascogne *f*.

gas cooker *n* (*BRIT*) cuisinière *f* à gaz.

gas cylinder *n* bouteille *f* de gaz.

gaseous ['gæsɪəs] *adj* gazeux(euse).

gas fire *n* (*BRIT*) radiateur *m* à gaz.

gas-fired ['gæsfaɪəd] *adj* au gaz.

gash [gæʃ] *n* entaille *f*; (*on face*) balafre *f* ♦ *vt* taillader; balafrer.

gasket ['gæskɪt] *n* (*AUT*) joint *m* de culasse.

gas mask *n* masque *m* à gaz.

gas meter *n* compteur *m* à gaz.

gasoline ['gæsəliːn] *n* (*US*) essence *f*.

gasp [gɑːsp] *vi* haleter; (*fig*) avoir le souffle coupé.

▶**gasp out** *vt* (*say*) dire dans un souffle *or* d'une voix entrecoupée.

gas ring *n* brûleur *m*.

gas station *n* (*US*) station-service *f*.

gas stove *n* réchaud *m* à gaz; (*cooker*) cuisinière *f* à gaz.

gassy ['gæsɪ] *adj* gazeux(euse).

gas tank *n* (*US AUT*) réservoir *m* d'essence.

gas tap *n* bouton *m* (*de cuisinière à gaz*); (*on pipe*) robinet *m* à gaz.

gastric ['gæstrɪk] *adj* gastrique.

gastric ulcer *n* ulcère *m* de l'estomac.

gastroenteritis ['gæstrəuentə'raɪtɪs] *n* gastroentérite *f*.

gastronomy [gæs'trɔnəmɪ] *n* gastronomie *f*.

gasworks ['gæswəːks] *n*, *npl* usine *f* à gaz.

gate [geɪt] *n* (*of garden*) portail *m*; (*of farm, at level crossing*) barrière *f*; (*of building, town, at airport*) porte *f*; (*of lock*) vanne *f*.

gâteau, *pl* ~**x** ['gætəu, -z] *n* gros gâteau à la crème.

gatecrash ['geɪtkræʃ] *vt* s'introduire sans invitation dans.

gatecrasher ['geɪtkræʃə*] *n* intrus/e.

gatehouse ['geɪthaus] *n* loge *f*.

gateway ['geɪtweɪ] *n* porte *f*.

gather ['gæðə*] *vt* (*flowers, fruit*) cueillir; (*pick up*) ramasser; (*assemble*) rassembler, réunir; (*understand*) comprendre ♦ *vi* (*assemble*) se rassembler; (*dust*)

s'amasser; (*clouds*) s'amonceler; **to** ~ (**from/that**) conclure *or* déduire (de/que); **as far as I can** ~ d'après ce que je comprends; **to** ~ **speed** prendre de la vitesse.

gathering ['gæðərɪŋ] *n* rassemblement *m*.

GATT [gæt] *n abbr* (= *General Agreement on Tariffs and Trade*) GATT *m*.

gauche [gəuʃ] *adj* gauche, maladroit(e).

gaudy ['gɔːdɪ] *adj* voyant(e).

gauge [geɪdʒ] *n* (*standard measure*) calibre *m*; (*RAIL*) écartement *m*; (*instrument*) jauge *f* ♦ *vt* jauger; (*fig: sb's capabilities, character*) juger de; **to** ~ **the right moment** calculer le moment propice; **petrol** ~, (*US*) **gas** ~ jauge d'essence.

Gaul [gɔːl] *n* (*country*) Gaule *f*; (*person*) Gaulois/e.

gaunt [gɔːnt] *adj* décharné(e); (*grim, desolate*) désolé(e).

gauntlet ['gɔːntlɪt] *n* (*fig*): **to throw down the** ~ jeter le gant; **to run the** ~ **through an angry crowd** se frayer un passage à travers une foule hostile *or* entre deux haies de manifestants *etc* hostiles.

gauze [gɔːz] *n* gaze *f*.

gave [geɪv] *pt of* **give**.

gavel ['gævl] *n* marteau *m*.

gawky ['gɔːkɪ] *adj* dégingandé(e), godiche.

gawp [gɔːp] *vi*: **to** ~ **at** regarder bouche bée.

gay [geɪ] *adj* (*homosexual*) homosexuel(le); (*slightly old-fashioned: cheerful*) gai(e), réjoui(e); (*colour*) gai, vif(vive).

gaze [geɪz] *n* regard *m* fixe ♦ *vi*: **to** ~ **at** *vt* fixer du regard.

gazelle [gə'zɛl] *n* gazelle *f*.

gazette [gə'zɛt] *n* (*newspaper*) gazette *f*; (*official publication*) journal officiel.

gazetteer [gæzə'tɪə*] *n* dictionnaire *m* géographique.

gazump [gə'zʌmp] *vi* (*BRIT*) *revenir sur une promesse de vente pour accepter un prix plus élevé*.

gazumping [gə'zʌmpɪŋ] *n le fait de revenir sur une promesse de vente pour accepter un prix plus élevé*.

GB *abbr* = *Great Britain*.

GBH *n abbr* (*BRIT LAW: col*) = **grievous bodily harm**.

GC *n abbr* (*BRIT*: = *George Cross*) *distinction honorifique*.

GCE *n abbr* (*BRIT*) = *General Certificate of Education*.

GCHQ *n abbr* (*BRIT*: = *Government Communications Headquarters*) *centre d'interception des télécommunications étrangères*.

GCSE *n abbr* (*BRIT*: = *General Certificate of Secondary Education*) *examen passé à l'âge de 16 ans sanctionnant les connaissances de l'élève*; **she's got eight** ~**s** elle a réussi dans huit matières aux épreuves du GCSE.

Gdns. *abbr* = *gardens*.

GDP *n abbr* = **gross domestic product**.

GDR *n abbr* (*old*: = German Democratic Republic) RDA *f*.

gear [gɪə*] *n* matériel *m*, équipement *m*; (*TECH*) engrenage *m*; (*AUT*) vitesse *f* ♦ *vt* (*fig*: *adapt*) adapter; **top** *or* (*US*) **high/low/bottom** ~ quatrième (*or* cinquième)/deuxième/ première vitesse; **in** ~ en prise; **out of** ~ au point mort; **our service is** ~**ed to meet the needs of the disabled** notre service répond de façon spécifique aux besoins des handicapés.

▶**gear up** *vi*: **to** ~ **up (to do)** se préparer (à faire).

gear box *n* boîte *f* de vitesse.

gear lever, (*US*) **gear shift** *n* levier *m* de vitesse.

GED *n abbr* (*US SCOL*) = general educational development.

geese [giːs] *npl of* goose.

geezer ['giːzə*] *n* (*BRIT col*) mec *m*.

Geiger counter ['gaɪgə-] *n* compteur *m* Geiger.

gel [dʒɛl] *n* gelée *f*, (*CHEMISTRY*) colloïde *m*.

gelatin(e) ['dʒɛlətiːn] *n* gélatine *f*.

gelignite ['dʒɛlɪgnaɪt] *n* plastic *m*.

gem [dʒɛm] *n* pierre précieuse.

Gemini ['dʒɛmɪnaɪ] *n* les Gémeaux *mpl*; **to be** ~ être des Gémeaux.

gen [dʒɛn] *n* (*BRIT col*): **to give sb the** ~ **on sth** mettre qn au courant de qch.

Gen. *abbr* (*MIL*: = general) Gal.

gen. *abbr* (= general, generally) gén.

gender ['dʒɛndə*] *n* genre *m*.

gene [dʒiːn] *n* (*BIOL*) gène *m*.

genealogy [dʒiːnɪˈælədʒɪ] *n* généalogie *f*.

general ['dʒɛnərl] *n* général *m* ♦ *adj* général(e); **in** ~ en général; **the** ~ **public** le grand public; ~ **audit** (*COMM*) vérification annuelle.

general anaesthetic *n* anesthésie générale.

general election *n* élection(s) législative(s).

generalization ['dʒɛnrəlaɪˈzeɪʃən] *n* généralisation *f*.

generalize ['dʒɛnrəlaɪz] *vi* généraliser.

generally ['dʒɛnrəlɪ] *adv* généralement.

general manager *n* directeur général.

general practitioner (GP) *n* généraliste *m/f*; **who's your GP?** qui est votre médecin traitant?

general strike *n* grève générale.

generate ['dʒɛnəreɪt] *vt* engendrer; (*electricity*) produire.

generation [dʒɛnəˈreɪʃən] *n* génération *f*; (*of electricity etc*) production *f*.

generator ['dʒɛnəreɪtə*] *n* générateur *m*.

generic [dʒɪˈnɛrɪk] *adj* générique.

generosity [dʒɛnəˈrɔsɪtɪ] *n* générosité *f*.

generous ['dʒɛnərəs] *adj* généreux(euse); (*copious*) copieux(euse).

genesis ['dʒɛnɪsɪs] *n* genèse *f*.

genetic [dʒɪˈnɛtɪk] *adj* génétique.

genetic engineering *n* génie *m* génétique.

genetic fingerprinting [-ˈfɪŋgəprɪntɪŋ] *n* système *m* d'empreinte génétique.

genetics [dʒɪˈnɛtɪks] *n* génétique *f*.

Geneva [dʒɪˈniːvə] *n* Genève; **Lake** ~ le lac Léman.

genial ['dʒiːnɪəl] *adj* cordial(e), chaleureux(euse); (*climate*) clément(e).

genitals ['dʒɛnɪtlz] *npl* organes génitaux.

genitive ['dʒɛnɪtɪv] *n* génitif *m*.

genius ['dʒiːnɪəs] *n* génie *m*.

Genoa ['dʒɛnəʊə] *n* Gênes.

genocide ['dʒɛnəʊsaɪd] *n* génocide *m*.

gent [dʒɛnt] *n abbr* (*BRIT col*) = **gentleman**.

genteel [dʒɛnˈtiːl] *adj* de bon ton, distingué(e).

gentle ['dʒɛntl] *adj* doux(douce).

gentleman ['dʒɛntlmən] *n* monsieur *m*; (*well-bred man*) gentleman *m*; ~**'s agreement** gentleman's agreement *m*.

gentlemanly ['dʒɛntlmənlɪ] *adj* bien élevé(e).

gentleness ['dʒɛntlnɪs] *n* douceur *f*.

gently ['dʒɛntlɪ] *adv* doucement.

gentry ['dʒɛntrɪ] *n* petite noblesse.

gents [dʒɛnts] *n* W.-C. *mpl* (pour hommes).

genuine ['dʒɛnjuɪn] *adj* véritable, authentique; (*person, emotion*) sincère.

genuinely ['dʒɛnjuɪnlɪ] *adv* sincèrement, vraiment.

geographer [dʒɪˈɔgrəfə*] *n* géographe *m/f*.

geographic(al) [dʒɪəˈgræfɪk(l)] *adj* géographique.

geography [dʒɪˈɔgrəfɪ] *n* géographie *f*.

geological [dʒɪəˈlɔdʒɪkl] *adj* géologique.

geologist [dʒɪˈɔlədʒɪst] *n* géologue *m/f*.

geology [dʒɪˈɔlədʒɪ] *n* géologie *f*.

geometric(al) [dʒɪəˈmɛtrɪk(l)] *adj* géométrique.

geometry [dʒɪˈɔmɪtrɪ] *n* géométrie *f*.

Geordie ['dʒɔːdɪ] *n* (*col*) habitant/e de Tyneside; originaire *m/f* de Tyneside.

Georgia ['dʒɔːdʒə] *n* Géorgie *f*.

Georgian ['dʒɔːdʒən] *adj* (*GEO*) géorgien(ne) ♦ *n* Géorgien/ne; (*LING*) géorgien *m*.

geranium [dʒɪˈreɪnɪəm] *n* géranium *m*.

geriatric [dʒɛrɪˈætrɪk] *adj* gériatrique.

germ [dʒəːm] *n* (*MED*) microbe *m*; (*BIO, fig*) germe *m*.

German ['dʒəːmən] *adj* allemand(e) ♦ *n* Allemand/e; (*LING*) allemand *m*.

germane [dʒəːˈmeɪn] *adj* (*formal*): ~ **(to)** se rapportant (à).

German measles *n* rubéole *f*.

Germany ['dʒəːmənɪ] *n* Allemagne *f*.

germination [dʒəːmɪˈneɪʃən] *n* germination *f*.

germ warfare *n* guerre *f* bactériologique.

gerrymandering ['dʒɛrɪmændərɪŋ] *n* tripotage *m* du découpage électoral.

gestation [dʒɛsˈteɪʃən] *n* gestation *f*.

gesticulate [dʒɛsˈtɪkjuleɪt] *vi* gesticuler.

gesture ['dʒɛstjə*] *n* geste *m*; **as a** ~ **of friendship** en témoignage d'amitié.

=============================== KEYWORD

get [gɛt] (*pt, pp* **got,** *pp* **gotten** (*US*)) *vi* **1** (*become, be*) devenir; **to ~ old/tired** devenir vieux/fatigué, vieillir/se fatiguer; **to ~ drunk** s'enivrer; **to ~ ready/washed/shaved** *etc* se préparer/laver/raser *etc*; **to ~ killed** se faire tuer; **when do I ~ paid?** quand est-ce que je serai payé?; **it's ~ting late** il se fait tard

2 (*go*): **to ~ to/from** aller à/de; **to ~ home** rentrer chez soi; **how did you ~ here?** comment es-tu arrivé ici?; **he got across the bridge/under the fence** il a traversé le pont/ est passé au-dessous de la barrière

3 (*begin*) commencer *or* se mettre à; **I'm ~ting to like him** je commence à l'apprécier; **let's ~ going** *or* **started** allons-y

4 (*modal aux vb*): **you've got to do it** il faut que vous le fassiez; **I've got to tell the police** je dois le dire à la police

♦ *vt* **1**: **to ~ sth done** (*do*) faire qch; (*have done*) faire faire qch; **to ~ sth/sb ready** préparer qch/qn; **to ~ one's hair cut** se faire couper les cheveux; **to ~ sb to do sth** faire faire qch à qn; **to ~ sb drunk** enivrer qn

2 (*obtain: money, permission, results*) obtenir, avoir; (*find: job, flat*) trouver; (*fetch: person, doctor, object*) aller chercher; **to ~ sth for sb** procurer qch à qn; **~ me Mr Jones, please** (*on phone*) passez-moi Mr Jones, s'il vous plaît; **can I ~ you a drink?** est-ce que je peux vous servir à boire?

3 (*receive: present, letter*) recevoir, avoir; (*acquire: reputation*) avoir; (*: prize*) obtenir; **what did you ~ for your birthday?** qu'est-ce que tu as eu pour ton anniversaire?

4 (*catch*) prendre, saisir, attraper; (*hit: target etc*) atteindre; **to ~ sb by the arm/throat** prendre *or* saisir *or* attraper qn par le bras/à la gorge; **~ him!** arrête-le!; **he really ~s me!** il me porte sur les nerfs!

5 (*take, move*) faire parvenir; **do you think we'll ~ it through the door?** on arrivera à le faire passer par la porte?; **I'll ~ you there somehow** je me débrouillerai pour t'y emmener

6 (*catch, take: plane, bus etc*) prendre

7 (*understand*) comprendre, saisir; (*hear*) entendre; **I've got it!** j'ai compris!; **I didn't ~ your name** je n'ai pas entendu votre nom

8 (*have, possess*): **to have got** avoir; **how many have you got?** vous en avez combien?

▶**get about** *vi* se déplacer; (*news*) se répandre

▶**get across** *vt*: **to ~ across (to)** (*message, meaning*) faire passer à ♦ *vi*: **to ~ across to** (*subj: speaker*) se faire comprendre (par)

▶**get along** *vi* (*agree*) s'entendre; (*depart*) s'en aller; (*manage*) = **get by**

▶**get at** *vt fus* (*attack*) s'en prendre à; (*reach*) attraper, atteindre; **what are you ~ting at?**

à quoi voulez-vous en venir?

▶**get away** *vi* partir, s'en aller; (*escape*) s'échapper

▶**get away with** *vt fus* en être quitte pour; se faire passer *or* pardonner

▶**get back** *vi* (*return*) rentrer ♦ *vt* récupérer, recouvrer; **to ~ back to** (*start again*) retourner *or* revenir à; (*contact again*) recontacter

▶**get back at** *vt fus* (*col*): **to ~ back at sb** rendre la monnaie de sa pièce à qn

▶**get by** *vi* (*pass*) passer; (*manage*) se débrouiller; **I can ~ by in Dutch** je me débrouille en hollandais

▶**get down** *vi, vt fus* descendre ♦ *vt* descendre; (*depress*) déprimer

▶**get down to** *vt fus* (*work*) se mettre à (faire); **to ~ down to business** passer aux choses sérieuses

▶**get in** *vi* entrer; (*arrive home*) rentrer; (*train*) arriver ♦ *vt* (*bring in: harvest*) rentrer; (*: coal*) faire rentrer; (*: supplies*) faire des provisions de

▶**get into** *vt fus* entrer dans; (*car, train etc*) monter dans; (*clothes*) mettre, enfiler, endosser; **to ~ into bed/a rage** se mettre au lit/en colère

▶**get off** *vi* (*from train etc*) descendre; (*depart: person, car*) s'en aller; (*escape*) s'en tirer ♦ *vt* (*remove: clothes, stain*) enlever; (*send off*) expédier; (*have as leave: day, time*) **we got 2 days off** nous avons eu 2 jours de congé ♦ *vt fus* (*train, bus*) descendre de; **to ~ off to a good start** (*fig*) prendre un bon départ

▶**get on** *vi* (*at exam etc*) se débrouiller; (*agree*): **to ~ on (with)** s'entendre (avec); **how are you ~ting on?** comment ça va? ♦ *vt fus* monter dans; (*horse*) monter sur

▶**get on to** *vt fus* (*BRIT: deal with: problem*) s'occuper de; (*contact: person*) contacter

▶**get out** *vi* sortir; (*of vehicle*) descendre; (*news etc*) s'ébruiter ♦ *vt* sortir

▶**get out of** *vt fus* sortir de; (*duty etc*) échapper à, se soustraire à

▶**get over** *vt fus* (*illness*) se remettre de ♦ *vt* (*communicate: idea etc*) communiquer; (*finish*): **let's ~ it over (with)** finissons-en

▶**get round** *vi*: **to ~ round to doing sth** se mettre (finalement) à faire qch ♦ *vt fus* contourner; (*fig: person*) entortiller

▶**get through** *vi* (*TEL*) avoir la communication; **to ~ through to sb** atteindre qn ♦ *vt fus* (*finish: work, book*) finir, terminer

▶**get together** *vi* se réunir ♦ *vt* rassembler

▶**get up** *vi* (*rise*) se lever ♦ *vt fus* monter

▶**get up to** *vt fus* (*reach*) arriver à; (*prank etc*) faire.

getaway ['gɛtəweɪ] *n* fuite *f*.

getaway car *n* voiture prévue pour prendre la fuite.

get-together ['gɛttəgɛðə*] *n* petite réunion, petite fête.

get-up ['gɛtʌp] n (col: outfit) accoutrement m.
get-well card [gɛt'wɛl-] n carte f de vœux de bon rétablissement.
geyser ['giːzə*] n chauffe-eau m inv; (GEO) geyser m.
Ghana ['gɑːnə] n Ghana m.
Ghanaian [gɑː'neɪən] adj ghanéen(ne) ♦ n Ghanéen/ne.
ghastly ['gɑːstlɪ] adj atroce, horrible; (pale) livide, blême.
gherkin ['gɜːkɪn] n cornichon m.
ghetto ['gɛtəʊ] n ghetto m.
ghetto blaster [-blɑːstə*] n (col) gros radiocassette.
ghost [gəʊst] n fantôme m, revenant m ♦ vt (sb else's book) écrire.
ghostly ['gəʊstlɪ] adj fantomatique.
ghostwriter ['gəʊstraɪtə*] n nègre m (fig).
ghoul [guːl] n (ghost) vampire m.
ghoulish ['guːlɪʃ] adj (tastes etc) morbide.
GHQ n abbr (MIL: = general headquarters) GQG m.
GI n abbr (US col: = government issue) soldat de l'armée américaine, GI m.
giant ['dʒaɪənt] n géant/e ♦ adj géant(e), énorme; ~ (size) packet paquet géant.
giant killer n (SPORT) équipe inconnue qui remporte un match contre une équipe renommée.
gibber ['dʒɪbə*] vi émettre des sons inintelligibles.
gibberish ['dʒɪbərɪʃ] n charabia m.
gibe [dʒaɪb] n sarcasme m ♦ vi: to ~ at railler.
giblets ['dʒɪblɪts] npl abats mpl.
Gibraltar [dʒɪ'brɔːltə*] n Gibraltar m.
giddiness ['gɪdɪnɪs] n vertige m.
giddy ['gɪdɪ] adj (dizzy): to be (or feel) ~ avoir le vertige; (height) vertigineux(euse); (thoughtless) sot(te), étourdi(e).
gift [gɪft] n cadeau m, présent m; (donation) don m; (COMM: also: free ~) cadeau(-réclame) m; (talent): to have a ~ for sth avoir des dons pour or le don de qch.
gifted ['gɪftɪd] adj doué(e).
gift token, gift voucher n bon m d'achat.
gig [gɪg] n (col: of musician) gig f.
gigabyte ['dʒɪgəbaɪt] n gigaoctet m.
gigantic [dʒaɪ'gæntɪk] adj gigantesque.
giggle ['gɪgl] vi pouffer, ricaner sottement ♦ n petit rire sot, ricanement m.
GIGO ['gaɪgəʊ] abbr (COMPUT: col: = garbage in, garbage out) qualité d'entrée = qualité de sortie.
gild [gɪld] vt dorer.
gill [dʒɪl] n (measure) = 0.25 pints (BRIT = 0.148 l; US = 0.118 l).
gills [gɪlz] npl (of fish) ouïes fpl, branchies fpl.
gilt [gɪlt] n dorure f ♦ adj doré(e).
gilt-edged ['gɪltɛdʒd] adj (stocks, securities) de premier ordre.
gimlet ['gɪmlɪt] n vrille f.
gimmick ['gɪmɪk] n truc m; sales ~ offre promotionnelle.

gin [dʒɪn] n gin m.
ginger ['dʒɪndʒə*] n gingembre m.
▶**ginger up** vt secouer; animer.
ginger ale, ginger beer n boisson gazeuse au gingembre.
gingerbread ['dʒɪndʒəbrɛd] n pain m d'épices.
ginger group n (BRIT) groupe m de pression.
ginger-haired ['dʒɪndʒə'hɛəd] adj roux (rousse).
gingerly ['dʒɪndʒəlɪ] adv avec précaution.
gingham ['gɪŋəm] n vichy m.
ginseng ['dʒɪnsɛŋ] n ginseng m.
gipsy ['dʒɪpsɪ] n gitan/e, bohémien/ne ♦ cpd: ~ caravan n roulotte f.
giraffe [dʒɪ'rɑːf] n girafe f.
girder ['gɜːdə*] n poutrelle f.
girdle ['gɜːdl] n (corset) gaine f ♦ vt ceindre.
girl [gɜːl] n fille f, fillette f; (young unmarried woman) jeune fille; (daughter) fille; an English ~ une jeune Anglaise; a little English ~ une petite Anglaise.
girlfriend ['gɜːlfrɛnd] n (of girl) amie f; (of boy) petite amie.
girlish ['gɜːlɪʃ] adj de jeune fille.
Girl Scout n (US) guide f.
Giro ['dʒaɪrəʊ] n: the National ~ (BRIT) ≈ les comptes chèques postaux.
giro ['dʒaɪrəʊ] n (bank ~) virement m bancaire; (post office ~) mandat m.
girth [gɜːθ] n circonférence f; (of horse) sangle f.
gist [dʒɪst] n essentiel m.
give [gɪv] n (of fabric) élasticité f ♦ vb (pt gave, pp given [geɪv, 'gɪvn]) vt donner ♦ vi (break) céder; (stretch: fabric) se prêter; to ~ sb sth, ~ sth to sb donner qch à qn; to ~ a cry/sigh pousser un cri/un soupir; how much did you ~ for it? combien (l')avez-vous payé?; 12 o'clock, ~ or take a few minutes midi, à quelques minutes près; to ~ way vi céder; (BRIT AUT) donner la priorité.
▶**give away** vt donner; (give free) faire cadeau de; (betray) donner, trahir; (disclose) révéler; (bride) conduire à l'autel.
▶**give back** vt rendre.
▶**give in** vi céder ♦ vt donner.
▶**give off** vt dégager.
▶**give out** vt (food etc) distribuer; (news) annoncer ♦ vi (be exhausted: supplies) s'épuiser; (fail) lâcher.
▶**give up** vi renoncer ♦ vt renoncer à; to ~ up smoking arrêter de fumer; to ~ o.s. up se rendre.
give-and-take ['gɪvənd'teɪk] n concessions mutuelles.
giveaway ['gɪvəweɪ] n (col): her expression was a ~ son expression la trahissait; the exam was a ~! cet examen, c'était du gâteau! ♦ cpd: ~ prices prix sacrifiés.
given ['gɪvn] pp of **give** ♦ adj (fixed: time, amount) donné(e), déterminé(e) ♦ conj: ~ the

circumstances ... étant donné les circonstances ..., vu les circonstances ...; ~ **that** ... étant donné que ....

glacial ['gleɪsɪəl] adj (GEO) glaciaire; (wind, weather) glacial(e).

glacier ['glæsɪə*] n glacier m.

glad [glæd] adj content(e); **to be ~ about sth/ that** être heureux(euse) or bien content de qch/que; **I was ~ of his help** j'étais bien content de (pouvoir compter sur) son aide or qu'il m'aide.

gladden ['glædn] vt réjouir.

glade [gleɪd] n clairière f.

gladioli [glædɪ'əʊlaɪ] npl glaïeuls mpl.

gladly ['glædlɪ] adv volontiers.

glamorous ['glæmərəs] adj séduisant(e).

glamour ['glæmə*] n éclat m, prestige m.

glance [glɑːns] n coup m d'œil ♦ vi: **to ~ at** jeter un coup d'œil à.

▶**glance off** vt fus (bullet) ricocher sur.

glancing ['glɑːnsɪŋ] adj (blow) oblique.

gland [glænd] n glande f.

glandular ['glændjʊlə*] adj: **~ fever** (BRIT) mononucléose infectieuse.

glare [glɛə*] n lumière f éblouissante ♦ vi briller d'un éclat aveuglant; **to ~ at** lancer un or des regard(s) furieux à.

glaring ['glɛərɪŋ] adj (mistake) criant(e), qui saute aux yeux.

glasnost ['glæznɒst] n glasnost f.

glass [glɑːs] n verre m; (also: **looking ~**) miroir m.

glass-blowing ['glɑːsbləʊɪŋ] n soufflage m (du verre).

glass ceiling n (fig) plafond dans l'échelle hiérarchique au-dessus duquel les femmes ou les membres d'une minorité ethnique ne semblent pouvoir s'élever.

glasses ['glɑːsəz] npl lunettes fpl.

glass fibre n fibre f de verre.

glasshouse ['glɑːshaʊs] n serre f.

glassware ['glɑːswɛə*] n verrerie f.

glassy ['glɑːsɪ] adj (eyes) vitreux(euse).

Glaswegian [glæs'wiːdʒən] adj de Glasgow ♦ n habitant/e de Glasgow; natif/ive de Glasgow.

glaze [gleɪz] vt (door) vitrer; (pottery) vernir; (CULIN) glacer ♦ n vernis m; (CULIN) glaçage m.

glazed [gleɪzd] adj (eye) vitreux(euse); (pottery) verni(e); (tiles) vitrifié(e).

glazier ['gleɪzɪə*] n vitrier m.

gleam [gliːm] n lueur f ♦ vi luire, briller; **a ~ of hope** une lueur d'espoir.

gleaming ['gliːmɪŋ] adj luisant(e).

glean [gliːn] vt (information) recueillir.

glee [gliː] n joie f.

gleeful ['gliːful] adj joyeux(euse).

glen [glɛn] n vallée f.

glib [glɪb] adj qui a du bagou; facile.

glide [glaɪd] vi glisser; (AVIAT, bird) planer ♦ n glissement m; vol plané.

glider ['glaɪdə*] n (AVIAT) planeur m.

gliding ['glaɪdɪŋ] n (AVIAT) vol m à voile.

glimmer ['glɪmə*] vi luire ♦ n lueur f.

glimpse [glɪmps] n vision passagère, aperçu m ♦ vt entrevoir, apercevoir; **to catch a ~ of** entrevoir.

glint [glɪnt] n éclair m ♦ vi étinceler.

glisten ['glɪsn] vi briller, luire.

glitter ['glɪtə*] vi scintiller, briller ♦ n scintillement m.

glitz [glɪts] n (col) clinquant m.

gloat [gləʊt] vi: **to ~ (over)** jubiler (à propos de).

global ['gləʊbl] adj (world-wide) mondial(e); (overall) global(e).

global warming [-'wɔːmɪŋ] n réchauffement m de la planète.

globe [gləʊb] n globe m.

globe-trotter ['gləʊbtrɒtə*] n globe-trotter m.

globule ['glɒbjuːl] n (ANAT) globule m; (of water etc) gouttelette f.

gloom [gluːm] n obscurité f; (sadness) tristesse f, mélancolie f.

gloomy ['gluːmɪ] adj sombre, triste, mélancolique; **to feel ~** avoir or se faire des idées noires.

glorification [glɔːrɪfɪ'keɪʃən] n glorification f.

glorify ['glɔːrɪfaɪ] vt glorifier.

glorious ['glɔːrɪəs] adj glorieux(euse); (beautiful) splendide.

glory ['glɔːrɪ] n gloire f; splendeur f ♦ vi: **to ~ in** se glorifier de.

glory hole n (col) capharnaüm m.

Glos abbr (BRIT) = Gloucestershire.

gloss [glɒs] n (shine) brillant m, vernis m; (also: **~ paint**) peinture brillante or laquée.

▶**gloss over** vt fus glisser sur.

glossary ['glɒsərɪ] n glossaire m, lexique m.

glossy ['glɒsɪ] adj brillant(e), luisant(e) ♦ n (also: **~ magazine**) revue f de luxe.

glove [glʌv] n gant m.

glove compartment n (AUT) boîte f à gants, vide-poches m inv.

glow [gləʊ] vi rougeoyer; (face) rayonner ♦ vi rougeoiement m.

glower ['glaʊə*] vi lancer des regards mauvais.

glowing ['gləʊɪŋ] adj (fire) rougeoyant(e); (complexion) éclatant(e); (report, description etc) dithyrambique.

glow-worm ['gləʊwɔːm] n ver luisant.

glucose ['gluːkəʊs] n glucose m.

glue [gluː] n colle f ♦ vt coller.

glue-sniffing ['gluːsnɪfɪŋ] n inhalation f de colle.

glum [glʌm] adj maussade, morose.

glut [glʌt] n surabondance f ♦ vt rassasier; (market) encombrer.

glutinous ['gluːtɪnəs] adj visqueux(euse).

glutton ['glʌtn] n glouton/ne; **a ~ for work** un bourreau de travail.

gluttonous ['glʌtənəs] adj glouton(ne).

gluttony ['glʌtənɪ] n gloutonnerie f; (sin) gourmandise f.

glycerin(e) ['glɪsəriːn] n glycérine f.

GM abbr (= genetically modified) génétiquement modifié(e).

gm abbr (= gram) g.

GMAT n abbr (US: = Graduate Management Admissions Test) examen d'admission dans le 2e cycle de l'enseignement supérieur.

GMT abbr (= Greenwich Mean Time) GMT.

gnarled [nɑːld] adj noueux(euse).

gnash [næʃ] vt: **to ~ one's teeth** grincer des dents.

gnat [næt] n moucheron m.

gnaw [nɔː] vt ronger.

gnome [nəum] n gnome m, lutin m.

GNP n abbr = **gross national product**.

go [gəu] vb (pt **went**, pp **gone** [wɛnt, gɔn]) vi aller; (depart) partir, s'en aller; (work) marcher; (be sold): **to ~ for £10** se vendre 10 livres; (fit, suit): **to ~ with** aller avec; (become): **to ~ pale/mouldy** pâlir/moisir; (break etc) céder ♦ n (pl: ~es): **to have a ~ (at)** essayer (de faire); **to be on the ~** être en mouvement; **whose ~ is it?** à qui est-ce de jouer?; **to ~ by car/on foot** aller en voiture/à pied; **he's ~ing to do** il va faire, il est sur le point de faire; **to ~ for a walk** aller se promener; **to ~ dancing/shopping** aller danser/faire les courses; **to ~ looking for sb/sth** aller or partir à la recherche de qn/qch; **to ~ to sleep** s'endormir; **to ~ and see sb**, **to ~ to see sb** aller voir qn; **how is it ~ing?** comment ça marche?; **how did it ~?** comment est-ce que ça s'est passé?; **to ~ round the back/by the shop** passer par derrière/devant le magasin; **my voice has gone** j'ai une extinction de voix; **the cake is all gone** il n'y a plus de gâteau; **I'll take whatever is ~ing** (BRIT) je prendrai ce qu'il y a (or ce que vous avez); **... to ~** (US: food) ... à emporter.

▶**go about** vi (also: ~ **around**) aller çà et là; (: rumour) se répandre ♦ vt fus: **how do I ~ about this?** comment dois-je m'y prendre (pour faire ceci)?; **to ~ about one's business** s'occuper de ses affaires.

▶**go after** vt fus (pursue) poursuivre, courir après; (job, record etc) essayer d'obtenir.

▶**go against** vt fus (be unfavourable to) être défavorable à; (be contrary to) être contraire à.

▶**go ahead** vi (make progress) avancer; (get going) y aller.

▶**go along** vi aller, avancer ♦ vt fus longer, parcourir; **as you ~ along** (with your work) au fur et à mesure (de votre travail); **to ~ along with** (accompany) accompagner; (agree with: idea) être d'accord sur; (: person) suivre.

▶**go away** vi partir, s'en aller.

▶**go back** vi rentrer; revenir; (go again) retourner.

▶**go back on** vt fus (promise) revenir sur.

▶**go by** vi (years, time) passer, s'écouler ♦ vt fus s'en tenir à; (believe) en croire.

▶**go down** vi descendre; (ship) couler; (sun) se coucher ♦ vt fus descendre; **that should ~ down well with him** (fig) ça devrait lui plaire.

▶**go for** vt fus (fetch) aller chercher; (like) aimer; (attack) s'en prendre à; attaquer.

▶**go in** vi entrer.

▶**go in for** vt fus (competition) se présenter à; (like) aimer.

▶**go into** vt fus entrer dans; (investigate) étudier, examiner; (embark on) se lancer dans.

▶**go off** vi partir, s'en aller; (food) se gâter; (bomb) sauter; (lights etc) s'éteindre; (event) se dérouler ♦ vt fus ne plus aimer, ne plus avoir envie de; **the gun went off** le coup est parti; **to ~ off to sleep** s'endormir; **the party went off well** la fête s'est bien passée or était très réussie.

▶**go on** vi continuer; (happen) se passer; (lights) s'allumer ♦ vt fus (be guided by: evidence etc) se fonder sur; **to ~ on doing** continuer à faire; **what's ~ing on here?** qu'est-ce qui se passe ici?

▶**go on at** vt fus (nag) tomber sur le dos de.

▶**go on with** vt fus poursuivre, continuer.

▶**go out** vi sortir; (fire, light) s'éteindre; (tide) descendre; **to ~ out with sb** sortir avec qn.

▶**go over** vi (ship) chavirer ♦ vt fus (check) revoir, vérifier; **to ~ over sth in one's mind** repasser qch dans son esprit.

▶**go round** vi (circulate: news, rumour) circuler; (revolve) tourner; (visit): **to ~ round to sb's** passer chez qn; aller chez qn; (make a detour): **to ~ round (by)** faire un détour (par); (suffice) suffire (pour tout le monde).

▶**go through** vt fus (town etc) traverser; (search through) fouiller; (examine: list, book) lire or regarder en détail, éplucher; (perform: lesson) réciter; (: formalities) remplir; (: programme) exécuter.

▶**go through with** vt fus (plan, crime) aller jusqu'au bout de.

▶**go under** vi (sink: also fig) couler; (: person) succomber.

▶**go up** vi monter; (price) augmenter ♦ vt fus gravir; **to ~ up in flames** flamber, s'enflammer brusquement.

▶**go without** vt fus se passer de.

goad [gəud] vt aiguillonner.

go-ahead ['gəuəhɛd] adj dynamique, entreprenant(e) ♦ n feu vert.

goal [gəul] n but m.

goal difference n différence f de buts.

goalie ['gəulɪ] n (col) goal m.

goalkeeper ['gəulkiːpə*] n gardien m de but.

goal post n poteau m de but.

goat [gəut] n chèvre f.

gobble ['gɔbl] vt (also: ~ **down**, ~ **up**) engloutir.

go-between ['gəubɪtwi:n] n médiateur m.
Gobi Desert ['gəubɪ-] n désert m de Gobi.
goblet ['gɔblɪt] n goblet m.
goblin ['gɔblɪn] n lutin m.
go-cart ['gəukɑ:t] n kart m ♦ cpd: ~ **racing** n karting m.
god [gɔd] n dieu m; **G**~ Dieu.
god-awful [gɔd'ɔ:fəl] adj (col) franchement atroce.
godchild ['gɔdtʃaɪld] n filleul/e.
goddamn(ed) ['gɔddæm(d)] excl (esp US col): **goddamn (it)**! nom de Dieu! ♦ adj satané(e), sacré(e) ♦ adv sacrément.
goddaughter ['gɔddɔ:tə*] n filleule f.
goddess ['gɔdɪs] n déesse f.
godfather ['gɔdfɑ:ðə*] n parrain m.
god-fearing ['gɔdfɪərɪŋ] adj croyant(e).
god-forsaken ['gɔdfəseɪkən] adj maudit(e).
godmother ['gɔdmʌðə*] n marraine f.
godparents ['gɔdpɛərənts] npl: **the** ~ le parrain et la marraine.
godsend ['gɔdsɛnd] n aubaine f.
godson ['gɔdsʌn] n filleul m.
goes [gəuz] vb see **go**.
gofer ['gəufə*] n coursier/ière.
go-getter ['gəugɛtə*] n arriviste m/f.
goggle ['gɔgl] vi: **to** ~ **at** regarder avec des yeux ronds.
goggles ['gɔglz] npl lunettes (protectrices) (de motocycliste etc).
going ['gəuɪŋ] n (conditions) état m du terrain ♦ adj: **the** ~ **rate** le tarif (en vigueur); **a** ~ **concern** une affaire prospère; **it was slow** ~ les progrès étaient lents, ça n'avançait pas vite.
going-over [gəuɪŋ'əuvə*] n vérification f, révision f; (col: beating) passage m à tabac.
goings-on ['gəuɪŋz'ɔn] npl (col) manigances fpl.
go-kart ['gəukɑ:t] n = **go-cart**.
gold [gəuld] n or m ♦ adj en or; (reserves) d'or.
golden ['gəuldən] adj (made of gold) en or; (gold in colour) doré(e).
golden age n âge m d'or.
golden handshake n (BRIT) prime f de départ.
golden rule n règle f d'or.
goldfish ['gəuldfɪʃ] n poisson m rouge.
gold leaf n or m en feuille.
gold medal n (SPORT) médaille f d'or.
goldmine ['gəuldmaɪn] n mine f d'or.
gold-plated ['gəuld'pleɪtɪd] adj plaqué(e) or inv.
goldsmith ['gəuldsmɪθ] n orfèvre m.
gold standard n étalon-or m.
golf [gɔlf] n golf m.
golf ball n balle f de golf; (on typewriter) boule f.
golf club n club m de golf; (stick) club m, crosse f de golf.
golf course n terrain m de golf.
golfer ['gɔlfə*] n joueur/euse de golf.

golfing ['gɔlfɪŋ] n golf m.
gondola ['gɔndələ] n gondole f.
gondolier [gɔndə'lɪə*] n gondolier m.
gone [gɔn] pp of **go** ♦ adj parti(e).
goner ['gɔnə*] n (col): **to be a** ~ être fichu(e) or foutu(e).
gong [gɔŋ] n gong m.
good [gud] adj bon(ne); (kind) gentil(le); (child) sage ♦ n bien m; ~! bon!, très bien!; **to be** ~ **at** être bon en; **it's** ~ **for you** c'est bon pour vous; **it's a** ~ **thing you were there** heureusement que vous étiez là; **she is** ~ **with children/her hands** elle sait bien s'occuper des enfants/sait se servir de ses mains; **to feel** ~ se sentir bien; **it's** ~ **to see you** ça me fait plaisir de vous voir, je suis content de vous voir; **he's up to no** ~ il prépare quelque mauvais coup; **it's no** ~ **complaining** cela ne sert à rien de se plaindre; **for the common** ~ dans l'intérêt commun; **for** ~ (for ever) pour de bon, une fois pour toutes; **would you be** ~ **enough to ...?** auriez-vous la bonté or l'amabilité de ...?; **that's very** ~ **of you** c'est très gentil de votre part; **is this any** ~? (will it do?) est-ce que ceci fera l'affaire?, est-ce que cela peut vous rendre service?; (what's it like?) qu'est-ce que ça vaut?; **a** ~ **deal (of)** beaucoup (de); **a** ~ **many** beaucoup (de); ~ **morning/afternoon**! bonjour!; ~ **evening**! bonsoir!; ~ **night**! bonsoir!; (on going to bed) bonne nuit!
goodbye [gud'baɪ] excl au revoir!; **to say** ~ **to** dire au revoir à.
good faith n bonne foi.
good-for-nothing ['gudfənʌθɪŋ] adj bon(ne) or propre à rien.
Good Friday n Vendredi saint.
good-humoured ['gud'hju:məd] adj (person) jovial(e); (remark, joke) sans malice.
good-looking ['gud'lukɪŋ] adj bien inv.
good-natured ['gud'neɪtʃəd] adj (person) qui a un bon naturel; (discussion) enjoué(e).
goodness ['gudnɪs] n (of person) bonté f; **for** ~ **sake**! je vous en prie!; ~ **gracious**! mon Dieu!
goods [gudz] npl marchandise f, articles mpl; (COMM etc) marchandises; ~ **and chattels** biens mpl et effets mpl.
goods train n (BRIT) train m de marchandises.
goodwill [gud'wɪl] n bonne volonté; (COMM) réputation f (auprès de la clientèle).
goody-goody ['gudɪgudɪ] n (pej) petit saint, sainte nitouche.
gooey ['gu:ɪ] adj (BRIT col) gluant(e).
goose, pl **geese** [gu:s, gi:s] n oie f.
gooseberry ['guzbərɪ] n groseille f à maquereau; **to play** ~ (BRIT) tenir la chandelle.
gooseflesh ['gu:sfleʃ] n, **goosepimples** ['gu:spɪmplz] npl chair f de poule.
goose step n (MIL) pas m de l'oie.
GOP n abbr (US POL: col: = Grand Old Party) parti

républicain.

gopher ['gəufə*] *n* = **gofer.**

gore [gɔ:*] *vt* encorner ♦ *n* sang *m*.

gorge [gɔ:dʒ] *n* gorge *f* ♦ *vt*: **to ~ o.s. (on)** se gorger (de).

gorgeous ['gɔ:dʒəs] *adj* splendide, superbe.

gorilla [gə'rilə] *n* gorille *m*.

gormless ['gɔ:mlis] *adj* (*BRIT col*) lourdaud(e).

gorse [gɔ:s] *n* ajoncs *mpl*.

gory ['gɔ:rɪ] *adj* sanglant(e).

go-slow ['gəu'sləu] *n* (*BRIT*) grève perlée.

gospel ['gɔspl] *n* évangile *m*.

gossamer ['gɔsəmə*] *n* (*cobweb*) fils *mpl* de la vierge; (*light fabric*) étoffe très légère.

gossip ['gɔsip] *n* bavardages *mpl*; (*malicious*) commérage *m*, cancans *mpl*; (*person*) commère *f* ♦ *vi* bavarder; cancaner, faire des commérages; **a piece of ~** un ragot, un racontar.

gossip column *n* (*PRESS*) échos *mpl*.

got [gɔt] *pt, pp of* **get.**

Gothic ['gɔθɪk] *adj* gothique.

gotten ['gɔtn] (*US*) *pp of* **get.**

gouge [gaudʒ] *vt* (*also: ~ out: hole etc*) évider; (*: initials*) tailler; **to ~ sb's eyes out** crever les yeux à qn.

gourd [guəd] *n* calebasse *f*, gourde *f*.

gourmet ['guəmeɪ] *n* gourmet *m*, gastronome *m/f*.

gout [gaut] *n* goutte *f*.

govern ['gʌvən] *vt* (*gen, LING*) gouverner.

governess ['gʌvənis] *n* gouvernante *f*.

governing ['gʌvəniŋ] *adj* (*POL*) au pouvoir, au gouvernement; **~ body** conseil *m* d'administration.

government ['gʌvnmənt] *n* gouvernement *m*; (*BRIT: ministers*) ministère *m* ♦ *cpd* de l'État; **local ~** administration locale.

governmental [gʌvn'mentl] *adj* gouvernemental(e).

government housing *n* (*US*) logements sociaux.

government stock *n* titres *mpl* d'État.

governor ['gʌvənə*] *n* (*of colony, state, bank*) gouverneur *m*; (*of school, hospital etc*) administrateur/trice; (*BRIT: of prison*) directeur/trice.

Govt *abbr* (= *government*) gvt.

gown [gaun] *n* robe *f*; (*of teacher, BRIT: of judge*) toge *f*.

GP *n abbr* (*MED*) = **general practitioner.**

GPMU *n abbr* (*BRIT*) = *Graphical, Paper and Media Union.*

GPO *n abbr* (*BRIT: old*) = *General Post Office*; (*US*) = *Government Printing Office.*

gr. *abbr* (*COMM*) = **gross.**

grab [græb] *vt* saisir, empoigner; (*property, power*) se saisir de ♦ *vi*: **to ~ at** essayer de saisir.

grace [greis] *n* grâce *f* ♦ *vt* honorer; **5 days' ~** répit *m* de 5 jours; **to say ~** dire le bénédicité; (*after meal*) dire les grâces; **with a good/bad ~** de bonne/mauvaise grâce; **his sense of humour is his saving ~** il se rachète par son sens de l'humour.

graceful ['greisful] *adj* gracieux(euse), élégant(e).

gracious ['greiʃəs] *adj* (*kind*) charmant(e), bienveillant(e); (*elegant*) plein(e) d'élégance, d'une grande élégance; (*formal: pardon etc*) miséricordieux(euse) ♦ *excl*: **(good) ~!** mon Dieu!

gradation [grə'deiʃən] *n* gradation *f*.

grade [greid] *n* (*COMM*) qualité *f*; calibre *m*; catégorie *f*; (*in hierarchy*) grade *m*, échelon *m*; (*US: SCOL*) note *f*, classe *f*; (*: gradient*) pente *f* ♦ *vt* classer; calibrer; graduer; **to make the ~** (*fig*) réussir.

grade crossing *n* (*US*) passage *m* à niveau.

grade school *n* (*US*) école *f* primaire.

gradient ['greidiənt] *n* inclinaison *f*, pente *f*; (*GEOM*) gradient *m*.

gradual ['grædjuəl] *adj* graduel(le), progressif(ive).

gradually ['grædjuəli] *adv* peu à peu, graduellement.

graduate *n* ['grædjuit] diplômé/e d'université; (*US*) diplômé/e de fin d'études ♦ *vi* ['grædjueit] obtenir un diplôme d'université (*or* de fin d'études).

graduated pension ['grædjueitid-] *n* retraite calculée en fonction des derniers salaires.

graduation [grædju'eiʃən] *n* cérémonie *f* de remise des diplômes.

graffiti [grə'fi:ti] *npl* graffiti *mpl*.

graft [grɑ:ft] *n* (*AGR, MED*) greffe *f*; (*bribery*) corruption *f* ♦ *vt* greffer; **hard ~** (*col*) boulot acharné.

grain [grein] *n* grain *m*; (*no pl: cereals*) céréales *fpl*; (*US: corn*) blé *m*; **it goes against the ~** cela va à l'encontre de sa (*or* ma *etc*) nature.

gram [græm] *n* gramme *m*.

grammar ['græmə*] *n* grammaire *f*.

grammar school *n* (*BRIT*) ≈ lycée *m*.

grammatical [grə'mætikl] *adj* grammatical(e).

gramme [græm] *n* = **gram.**

gramophone ['græməfəun] *n* (*BRIT*) gramophone *m*.

granary ['grænəri] *n* grenier *m*.

grand [grænd] *adj* splendide, imposant(e); (*terrific*) magnifique, formidable; (*also humorous: gesture etc*) noble ♦ *n* (*col: thousand*) mille livres *fpl* (*or* dollars *mpl*).

grandchildren ['græntʃildrən] *npl* petits-enfants *mpl*.

granddad ['grændæd] *n* grand-papa *m*.

granddaughter ['grændɔ:tə*] *n* petite-fille *f*.

grandeur ['grændjə*] *n* magnificence *f*, splendeur *f*; (*of position etc*) éminence *f*.

grandfather ['grændfɑ:ðə*] *n* grand-père *m*.

grandiose ['grændiəus] *adj* grandiose; (*pej*) pompeux(euse).

grand jury *n* (*US*) jury *m* d'accusation (*formé*

de 12 à 23 jurés).

grandma ['grænmɑː] *n* grand-maman *f*.

grandmother ['grænmʌðə*] *n* grand-mère *f*.

grandpa ['grænpɑː] *n* = **granddad**.

grandparent ['grændpɛərənt] *n* grand-père/grand-mère.

grand piano *n* piano *m* à queue.

Grand Prix ['grɑː'priː] *n* (AUT) grand prix automobile.

grandson ['grænsʌn] *n* petit-fils *m*.

grandstand ['grændstænd] *n* (SPORT) tribune *f*.

grand total *n* total général.

granite ['grænɪt] *n* granit *m*.

granny ['grænɪ] *n* grand-maman *f*.

grant [grɑːnt] *vt* accorder; (*a request*) accéder à; (*admit*) concéder ♦ *n* (SCOL) bourse *f*; (ADMIN) subside *m*, subvention *f*; **to take sth for ~ed** considérer qch comme acquis; **to ~ that** admettre que.

granulated ['grænjuleɪtɪd] *adj*: **~ sugar** sucre *m* en poudre.

granule ['grænjuːl] *n* granule *m*.

grape [greɪp] *n* raisin *m*; **a bunch of ~s** une grappe de raisin.

grapefruit ['greɪpfruːt] *n* pamplemousse *m*.

grapevine ['greɪpvaɪn] *n* vigne *f*; **I heard it on the ~** (*fig*) je l'ai appris par le téléphone arabe.

graph [grɑːf] *n* graphique *m*, courbe *f*.

graphic ['græfɪk] *adj* graphique; (*vivid*) vivant(e).

graphic designer *n* graphiste *m/f*.

graphic equalizer *n* égaliseur *m* graphique.

graphics ['græfɪks] *n* (*art*) arts *mpl* graphiques; (*process*) graphisme *m*; (*pl: drawings*) illustrations *fpl*.

graphite ['græfaɪt] *n* graphite *m*.

graph paper *n* papier millimétré.

grapple ['græpl] *vi*: **to ~ with** être aux prises avec.

grappling iron ['græplɪŋ-] *n* (NAUT) grappin *m*.

grasp [grɑːsp] *vt* saisir, empoigner; (*understand*) saisir, comprendre ♦ *n* (*grip*) prise *f*; (*fig*) compréhension *f*, connaissance *f*; **to have sth within one's ~** avoir qch à sa portée; **to have a good ~ of sth** (*fig*) bien comprendre qch.

▶**grasp at** *vt fus* (*rope etc*) essayer de saisir; (*fig: opportunity*) sauter sur.

grasping ['grɑːspɪŋ] *adj* avide.

grass [grɑːs] *n* herbe *f*; (BRIT col: informer) mouchard/e; (: *ex-terrorist*) balanceur/euse.

grasshopper ['grɑːshɔpə*] *n* sauterelle *f*.

grassland ['grɑːslænd] *n* prairie *f*.

grass roots *npl* (*fig*) base *f*.

grass snake *n* couleuvre *f*.

grassy ['grɑːsɪ] *adj* herbeux(euse).

grate [greɪt] *n* grille *f* de cheminée ♦ *vi* grincer ♦ *vt* (CULIN) râper.

grateful ['greɪtful] *adj* reconnaissant(e).

gratefully ['greɪtfəlɪ] *adv* avec reconnaissance.

grater ['greɪtə*] *n* râpe *f*.

gratification [grætɪfɪ'keɪʃən] *n* satisfaction *f*.

gratify ['grætɪfaɪ] *vt* faire plaisir à; (*whim*) satisfaire.

gratifying ['grætɪfaɪɪŋ] *adj* agréable; satisfaisant(e).

grating ['greɪtɪŋ] *n* (*iron bars*) grille *f* ♦ *adj* (*noise*) grinçant(e).

gratitude ['grætɪtjuːd] *n* gratitude *f*.

gratuitous [grə'tjuːɪtəs] *adj* gratuit(e).

gratuity [grə'tjuːɪtɪ] *n* pourboire *m*.

grave [greɪv] *n* tombe *f* ♦ *adj* grave, sérieux(euse).

gravedigger ['greɪvdɪgə*] *n* fossoyeur *m*.

gravel ['grævl] *n* gravier *m*.

gravely ['greɪvlɪ] *adv* gravement, sérieusement; **~ ill** gravement malade.

gravestone ['greɪvstəun] *n* pierre tombale.

graveyard ['greɪvjɑːd] *n* cimetière *m*.

gravitate ['grævɪteɪt] *vi* graviter.

gravity ['grævɪtɪ] *n* (PHYSICS) gravité *f*; pesanteur *f*; (*seriousness*) gravité, sérieux *m*.

gravy ['greɪvɪ] *n* jus *m* (de viande); sauce *f* (au jus de viande).

gravy boat *n* saucière *f*.

gravy train *n* (*col*): **to ride the ~** avoir une bonne planque.

gray [greɪ] *adj* (US) = **grey**.

graze [greɪz] *vi* paître, brouter ♦ *vt* (*touch lightly*) frôler, effleurer; (*scrape*) écorcher ♦ *n* écorchure *f*.

grazing ['greɪzɪŋ] *n* (*pasture*) pâturage *m*.

grease [griːs] *n* (*fat*) graisse *f*; (*lubricant*) lubrifiant *m* ♦ *vt* graisser; lubrifier; **to ~ the skids** (US: *fig*) huiler les rouages.

grease gun *n* graisseur *m*.

greasepaint ['griːspeɪnt] *n* produits *mpl* de maquillage.

greaseproof paper ['griːspruːf-] *n* (BRIT) papier sulfurisé.

greasy ['griːsɪ] *adj* gras(se), graisseux(euse); (*hands, clothes*) graisseux; (BRIT: *road, surface*) glissant(e).

great [greɪt] *adj* grand(e); (*heat, pain etc*) très fort(e), intense; (*col*) formidable; **they're ~ friends** ils sont très amis, ce sont de grands amis; **we had a ~ time** nous nous sommes bien amusés; **it was ~!** c'était fantastique *or* super!; **the ~ thing is that ...** ce qu'il y a de vraiment bien c'est que ....

Great Barrier Reef *n*: **the ~** la Grande Barrière.

Great Britain *n* Grande-Bretagne *f*.

great-grandchild *pl* **-children** [greɪt'græntʃaɪld, -tʃɪldrən] *n* arrière-petit(e)-enfant.

great-grandfather [greɪt'grænfɑːðə*] *n* arrière-grand-père *m*.

great-grandmother [greɪt'grænmʌðə*] *n* arrière-grand-mère *f*.

Great Lakes *npl*: **the ~** les Grands Lacs.

greatly ['greɪtlɪ] *adv* très, grandement; (*with verbs*) beaucoup.

greatness ['greɪtnɪs] *n* grandeur *f*.

Grecian ['griːʃən] *adj* grec(grecque).

Greece [griːs] *n* Grèce *f*.

greed [griːd] *n* (*also*: ~**iness**) avidité *f*; (*for food*) gourmandise *f*.

greedily ['griːdɪlɪ] *adv* avidement; avec gourmandise.

greedy ['griːdɪ] *adj* avide; gourmand(e).

Greek [griːk] *adj* grec(grecque) ♦ *n* Grec/Grecque; (*LING*) grec *m*; **ancient/modern** ~ grec classique/moderne.

green [griːn] *adj* vert(e); (*inexperienced*) (bien) jeune, naïf(ïve); (*ecological: product etc*) écologique ♦ *n* (*colour, of golf course*) vert *m*; (*stretch of grass*) pelouse *f*; (*also*: **village** ~) ≈ place *f* du village; ~**s** *npl* légumes verts; **to have** ~ **fingers** *or* (*US*) **a** ~ **thumb** (*fig*) avoir le pouce vert; **G**~ (*POL*) écologiste (*m/f*); **the G**~ **Party** le parti écologiste.

green belt *n* (*round town*) ceinture verte.

green card *n* (*AUT*) carte verte.

greenery ['griːnərɪ] *n* verdure *f*.

greenfly ['griːnflaɪ] *n* (*BRIT*) puceron *m*.

greengage ['griːngeɪdʒ] *n* reine-claude *f*.

greengrocer ['griːngrəʊsə*] *n* (*BRIT*) marchand *m* de fruits et légumes.

greenhouse ['griːnhaʊs] *n* serre *f*.

greenhouse effect *n*: **the** ~ l'effet *m* de serre.

greenhouse gas *n* gaz *m* contribuant à l'effet de serre.

greenish ['griːnɪʃ] *adj* verdâtre.

Greenland ['griːnlənd] *n* Groenland *m*.

Greenlander ['griːnləndə*] *n* Groenlandais/e.

green light *n*: **to give sb/sth the** ~ donner le feu vert à qn/qch.

green pepper *n* poivron (vert).

green pound *n* (*ECON*) livre verte.

greet [griːt] *vt* accueillir.

greeting ['griːtɪŋ] *n* salutation *f*; **Christmas/birthday** ~**s** souhaits *mpl* de Noël/de bon anniversaire.

greeting(s) card *n* carte *f* de vœux.

gregarious [grə'gɛərɪəs] *adj* grégaire; sociable.

grenade [grə'neɪd] *n* (*also*: **hand** ~) grenade *f*.

grew [gruː] *pt of* **grow**.

grey [greɪ] *adj* gris(e); (*dismal*) sombre; **to go** ~ (commencer à) grisonner.

grey-haired [greɪ'hɛəd] *adj* aux cheveux gris.

greyhound ['greɪhaʊnd] *n* lévrier *m*.

grid [grɪd] *n* grille *f*; (*ELEC*) réseau *m*; (*US AUT*) intersection *f* (*matérialisée par des marques au sol*).

griddle [grɪdl] *n* (*on cooker*) plaque chauffante.

gridiron ['grɪdaɪən] *n* gril *m*.

gridlock ['grɪdlɒk] *n* (*traffic jam*) embouteillage *m*.

grief [griːf] *n* chagrin *m*, douleur *f*; **to come to**

~ (*plan*) échouer; (*person*) avoir un malheur.

grievance ['griːvəns] *n* doléance *f*, grief *m*; (*cause for complaint*) grief.

grieve [griːv] *vi* avoir du chagrin; se désoler ♦ *vt* faire de la peine à, affliger; **to** ~ **at** se désoler de; pleurer.

grievous ['griːvəs] *adj* grave; cruel(le); ~ **bodily harm** (*LAW*) coups *mpl* et blessures *fpl*.

grill [grɪl] *n* (*on cooker*) gril *m* ♦ *vt* (*BRIT*) griller; (*question*) interroger longuement, cuisiner.

grille [grɪl] *n* grillage *m*; (*AUT*) calandre *f*.

grill(room) ['grɪl(rʊm)] *n* rôtisserie *f*.

grim [grɪm] *adj* sinistre, lugubre.

grimace [grɪ'meɪs] *n* grimace *f* ♦ *vi* grimacer, faire une grimace.

grime [graɪm] *n* crasse *f*.

grimy ['graɪmɪ] *adj* crasseux(euse).

grin [grɪn] *n* large sourire *m* ♦ *vi* sourire; **to** ~ (**at**) faire un grand sourire (à).

grind [graɪnd] *vb* (*pt, pp* **ground** [graʊnd]) *vt* écraser; (*coffee, pepper etc*) moudre; (*US: meat*) hacher; (*make sharp*) aiguiser; (*polish: gem, lens*) polir ♦ *vi* (*car gears*) grincer ♦ *n* (*work*) corvée *f*; **to** ~ **one's teeth** grincer des dents; **to** ~ **to a halt** (*vehicle*) s'arrêter dans un grincement de freins; (*fig*) s'arrêter, s'immobiliser; **the daily** ~ (*col*) le train-train quotidien.

grinder ['graɪndə*] *n* (*machine: for coffee*) moulin *m* (à café); (: *for waste disposal etc*) broyeur *m*.

grindstone ['graɪndstəʊn] *n*: **to keep one's nose to the** ~ travailler sans relâche.

grip [grɪp] *n* (*control, grasp*) étreinte *f*; (*hold*) prise *f*; (*handle*) poignée *f*; (*holdall*) sac *m* de voyage ♦ *vt* saisir, empoigner; étreindre; **to come to** ~**s with** se colleter avec, en venir aux prises avec; **to** ~ **the road** (*AUT*) adhérer à la route; **to lose one's** ~ lâcher prise; (*fig*) perdre les pédales, être dépassé(e).

gripe [graɪp] *n* (*MED*) coliques *fpl*; (*col: complaint*) ronchonnement *m*, rouspétance *f* ♦ *vi* (*col*) râler.

gripping ['grɪpɪŋ] *adj* prenant(e), palpitant(e).

grisly ['grɪzlɪ] *adj* sinistre, macabre.

grist [grɪst] *n* (*fig*): **it's (all)** ~ **to his mill** ça l'arrange, ça apporte de l'eau à son moulin.

gristle ['grɪsl] *n* cartilage *m* (*de poulet etc*).

grit [grɪt] *n* gravillon *m*; (*courage*) cran *m* ♦ *vt* (*road*) sabler; **to** ~ **one's teeth** serrer les dents; **to have a piece of** ~ **in one's eye** avoir une poussière *or* saleté dans l'œil.

grits [grɪts] *npl* (*US*) gruau *m* de maïs.

grizzle ['grɪzl] *vi* (*BRIT*) pleurnicher.

grizzly ['grɪzlɪ] *n* (*also*: ~ **bear**) grizzli *m*, ours gris.

groan [grəʊn] *n* gémissement *m*; grognement *m* ♦ *vi* gémir; grogner.

grocer ['grəʊsə*] *n* épicier *m*; **at the** ~'**s** à l'épicerie, chez l'épicier.

groceries ['grəʊsərɪz] *npl* provisions *fpl*.

grocery ['grəʊsərɪ] *n* (*shop*) épicerie *f*.

grog [grɔg] *n* grog *m*.
groggy ['grɔgɪ] *adj* groggy *inv*.
groin [grɔɪn] *n* aine *f*.
groom [gruːm] *n* palefrenier *m*; (*also:* **bride~**) marié *m* ♦ *vt* (*horse*) panser; (*fig*): **to ~ sb for** former qn pour.
groove [gruːv] *n* sillon *m*, rainure *f*.
grope [grəup] *vi* tâtonner; **to ~ for** *vt fus* chercher à tâtons.
gross [grəus] *adj* grossier(ière); (*COMM*) brut(e) ♦ *n* (*pl inv*) (*twelve dozen*) grosse *f* ♦ *vt* (*COMM*): **to ~ £500,000** gagner 500 000 livres avant impôt.
gross domestic product (GDP) *n* produit brut intérieur (PIB).
grossly ['grəuslɪ] *adv* (*greatly*) très, grandement.
gross national product (GNP) *n* produit national brut (PNB).
grotesque [grə'tɛsk] *adj* grotesque.
grotto ['grɔtəu] *n* grotte *f*.
grotty ['grɔtɪ] *adj* (*BRIT col*) minable.
grouch [grautʃ] (*col*) *vi* rouspéter ♦ *n* (*person*) rouspéteur/euse.
ground [graund] *pt, pp of* **grind** ♦ *n* sol *m*, terre *f*; (*land*) terrain *m*, terres *fpl*; (*SPORT*) terrain; (*reason: gen pl*) raison *f*, (*US: also:* **~ wire**) terre *f* ♦ *vt* (*plane*) empêcher de décoller, retenir au sol; (*US ELEC*) équiper d'une prise de terre, mettre à la terre ♦ *vi* (*ship*) s'échouer ♦ *adj* (*coffee etc*) moulu(e); (*US: meat*) haché(e); **~s** *npl* (*gardens etc*) parc *m*, domaine *m*; (*of coffee*) marc *m*; **on the ~, to the ~** par terre; **below ~** sous terre; **to gain/lose ~** gagner/perdre du terrain; **common ~** terrain d'entente; **he covered a lot of ~ in his lecture** sa conférence a traité un grand nombre de questions *or* la question en profondeur.
ground cloth *n* (*US*) = **groundsheet**.
ground control *n* (*AVIAT, SPACE*) centre *m* de contrôle (au sol).
ground floor *n* (*BRIT*) rez-de-chaussée *m*.
grounding ['graundɪŋ] *n* (*in education*) connaissances *fpl* de base.
groundless ['graundlɪs] *adj* sans fondement.
groundnut ['graundnʌt] *n* arachide *f*.
ground rent *n* (*BRIT*) fermage *m*.
ground rules *npl*: **the ~** les principes *mpl* de base.
groundsheet ['graundʃiːt] *n* (*BRIT*) tapis *m* de sol.
groundsman ['graundzmən], (*US*) **groundskeeper** ['graundzkiːpə*] *n* (*SPORT*) gardien *m* de stade.
ground staff *n* équipage *m* au sol.
groundswell ['graundswɛl] *n* lame *f or* vague *f* de fond.
ground-to-air ['grauntu'ɛə*] *adj* (*MIL*) sol-air *inv*.
ground-to-ground ['grauntə'graund] *adj* (*MIL*) sol-sol *inv*.

groundwork ['graundwəːk] *n* préparation *f*.
group [gruːp] *n* groupe *m* ♦ *vt* (*also:* **~ together**) grouper ♦ *vi* (*also:* **~ together**) se grouper.
groupie ['gruːpɪ] *n* groupie *f*.
group therapy *n* thérapie *f* de groupe.
grouse [graus] *n* (*pl inv*) (*bird*) grouse *f* (*sorte de coq de bruyère*) ♦ *vi* (*complain*) rouspéter, râler.
grove [grəuv] *n* bosquet *m*.
grovel ['grɔvl] *vi* (*fig*): **to ~ (before)** ramper (devant).
grow, *pt* **grew**, *pp* **grown** [grəu, gruː, grəun] *vi* (*plant*) pousser, croître; (*person*) grandir; (*increase*) augmenter, se développer; (*become*): **to ~ rich/weak** s'enrichir/s'affaiblir ♦ *vt* cultiver, faire pousser.
▸**grow apart** *vi* (*fig*) se détacher (l'un de l'autre).
▸**grow away from** *vt fus* (*fig*) s'éloigner de.
▸**grow on** *vt fus*: **that painting is ~ing on me** je finirai par aimer ce tableau.
▸**grow out of** *vt fus* (*clothes*) devenir trop grand pour; (*habit*) perdre (avec le temps); **he'll ~ out of it** ça lui passera.
▸**grow up** *vi* grandir.
grower ['grəuə*] *n* producteur *m*; (*AGR*) cultivateur/trice.
growing ['grəuɪŋ] *adj* (*fear, amount*) croissant(e), grandissant(e); **~ pains** (*MED*) fièvre *f* de croissance; (*fig*) difficultés *fpl* de croissance.
growing pains *npl* (*fig*) difficultés *fpl* de croissance.
growl [graul] *vi* grogner.
grown [grəun] *pp of* **grow** ♦ *adj* adulte.
grown-up [grəun'ʌp] *n* adulte *m/f*, grande personne.
growth [grəuθ] *n* croissance *f*, développement *m*; (*what has grown*) pousse *f*, poussée *f*; (*MED*) grosseur *f*, tumeur *f*.
growth rate *n* taux *m* de croissance.
GRSM *n abbr* (*BRIT*) = *Graduate of the Royal Schools of Music*.
grub [grʌb] *n* larve *f*; (*col: food*) bouffe *f*.
grubby ['grʌbɪ] *adj* crasseux(euse).
grudge [grʌdʒ] *n* rancune *f* ♦ *vt*: **to ~ sb sth** donner qch à qn à contre-cœur; reprocher qch à qn; **to bear sb a ~ (for)** garder rancune *or* en vouloir à qn (de); **he ~s spending** il rechigne à dépenser.
grudgingly ['grʌdʒɪŋlɪ] *adv* à contre-cœur, de mauvaise grâce.
gruelling ['gruəlɪŋ] *adj* exténuant(e).
gruesome ['gruːsəm] *adj* horrible.
gruff [grʌf] *adj* bourru(e).
grumble ['grʌmbl] *vi* rouspéter, ronchonner.
grumpy ['grʌmpɪ] *adj* grincheux(euse).
grunge [grʌndʒ] *n* (*MUS, style*) grunge *m*.
grunt [grʌnt] *vi* grogner ♦ *n* grognement *m*.
G-string ['dʒiːstrɪŋ] *n* (*garment*) cache-sexe *m inv*.

GSUSA n abbr = Girl Scouts of the United States of America.

GU abbr (US) = Guam.

guarantee [gærən'tiː] n garantie f ♦ vt garantir; **he can't ~ (that) he'll come** il n'est pas absolument certain de pouvoir venir.

guarantor [gærən'tɔː*] n garant/e.

guard [gɑːd] n garde f, surveillance f; (squad, BOXING, FENCING) garde f; (one man) garde m; (BRIT RAIL) chef m de train; (safety device: on machine) dispositif m de sûreté; (also: **fire~**) garde-feu m inv ♦ vt garder, surveiller; (protect): **to ~ (against** or **from)** protéger (contre); **to be on one's ~** (fig) être sur ses gardes.

▶**guard against** vi: **to ~ against doing sth** se garder de faire qch.

guard dog n chien m de garde.

guarded ['gɑːdɪd] adj (fig) prudent(e).

guardian ['gɑːdɪən] n gardien/ne; (of minor) tuteur/trice.

guard's van n [gɑːdz-] n (BRIT RAIL) fourgon m.

Guatemala [gwɑːtɪ'mɑːlə] n Guatémala m.

Guernsey ['gəːnzɪ] n Guernesey m or f.

guerrilla [gə'rɪlə] n guérillero m.

guerrilla warfare n guérilla f.

guess [gɛs] vi deviner ♦ vt deviner; (US) croire, penser ♦ n supposition f, hypothèse f; **to take** or **have a ~** essayer de deviner; **to keep sb ~ing** laisser qn dans le doute or l'incertitude, tenir qn en haleine.

guesstimate ['gɛstɪmɪt] n (col) estimation f.

guesswork ['gɛswəːk] n hypothèse f; **I got the answer by ~** j'ai deviné la réponse.

guest [gɛst] n invité/e; (in hotel) client/e; **be my ~** faites comme chez vous.

guest-house ['gɛsthaus] n pension f.

guest room n chambre f d'amis.

guff [gʌf] n (col) bêtises fpl.

guffaw [gʌ'fɔː] n gros rire ♦ vi pouffer de rire.

guidance ['gaɪdəns] n conseils mpl; **under the ~ of** conseillé(e) or encadré(e) par, sous la conduite de; **vocational ~** orientation professionnelle; **marriage ~** conseils conjugaux.

guide [gaɪd] n (person, book etc) guide m; (also: **girl ~**) guide f ♦ vt guider; **to be ~d by sb/sth** se laisser guider par qn/qch.

guidebook ['gaɪdbuk] n guide m.

guided missile ['gaɪdɪd-] n missile téléguidé.

guide dog n chien m d'aveugle.

guide lines npl (fig) instructions générales, conseils mpl.

guild [gɪld] n corporation f; cercle m, association f.

guildhall ['gɪldhɔːl] n (BRIT) hôtel m de ville.

guile [gaɪl] n astuce f.

guileless ['gaɪlɪs] adj candide.

guillotine ['gɪlətiːn] n guillotine f; (for paper) massicot m.

guilt [gɪlt] n culpabilité f.

guilty ['gɪltɪ] adj coupable; **to plead ~/not ~** plaider coupable/non coupable; **to feel ~ about doing sth** avoir mauvaise conscience à faire qch.

Guinea ['gɪnɪ] n: **Republic of ~** (République f de) Guinée f.

guinea ['gɪnɪ] n (BRIT) guinée f (= 21 shillings: cette monnaie de compte ne s'emploie plus).

guinea pig n cobaye m.

guise [gaɪz] n aspect m, apparence f.

guitar [gɪ'tɑː*] n guitare f.

guitarist [gɪ'tɑːrɪst] n guitariste m/f.

gulch [gʌltʃ] n (US) ravin m.

gulf [gʌlf] n golfe m; (abyss) gouffre m; **the (Persian) G~** le golfe Persique.

Gulf States npl: **the ~** (in Middle East) les pays mpl du Golfe.

Gulf Stream n: **the ~** le Gulf Stream.

gull [gʌl] n mouette f.

gullet ['gʌlɪt] n gosier m.

gullibility [gʌlɪ'bɪlɪtɪ] n crédulité f.

gullible ['gʌlɪbl] adj crédule.

gully ['gʌlɪ] n ravin m; ravine f; couloir m.

gulp [gʌlp] vi avaler sa salive; (from emotion) avoir la gorge serrée, s'étrangler ♦ vt (also: **~ down**) avaler ♦ n (of drink) gorgée f; **at one ~** d'un seul coup.

gum [gʌm] n (ANAT) gencive f; (glue) colle f; (sweet) boule f de gomme; (also: **chewing-~**) chewing-gum m ♦ vt coller.

▶**gum up** vt: **to ~ up the works** (col) bousiller tout.

gumboil ['gʌmbɔɪl] n abcès m dentaire.

gumboots ['gʌmbuːts] npl (BRIT) bottes fpl en caoutchouc.

gumption ['gʌmpʃən] n bon sens, jugeote f.

gun [gʌn] n (small) revolver m, pistolet m; (rifle) fusil m, carabine f; (cannon) canon m ♦ vt (also: **~ down**) abattre; **to stick to one's ~s** (fig) ne pas en démordre.

gunboat ['gʌnbəut] n canonnière f.

gun dog n chien m de chasse.

gunfire ['gʌnfaɪə*] n fusillade f.

gunk [gʌŋk] n (col) saleté f.

gunman ['gʌnmən] n bandit armé.

gunner ['gʌnə*] n artilleur m.

gunpoint ['gʌnpɔɪnt] n: **at ~** sous la menace du pistolet (or fusil).

gunpowder ['gʌnpaudə*] n poudre f à canon.

gunrunner ['gʌnrʌnə*] n trafiquant m d'armes.

gunrunning ['gʌnrʌnɪŋ] n trafic m d'armes.

gunshot ['gʌnʃɔt] n coup m de feu; **within ~** à portée de fusil.

gunsmith ['gʌnsmɪθ] n armurier m.

gurgle ['gəːgl] n gargouillis m ♦ vi gargouiller.

guru ['guruː] n gourou m.

gush [gʌʃ] n jaillissement m, jet m ♦ vi jaillir; (fig) se répandre en effusions.

gushing ['gʌʃɪŋ] adj (person) trop exubérant(e) or expansif(ive); (compliments) exagéré(e).

gusset ['gʌsɪt] *n* gousset *m*, soufflet *m*; (*in tights, pants*) entre-jambes *m*.
gust [gʌst] *n* (*of wind*) rafale *f*; (*of smoke*) bouffée *f*.
gusto ['gʌstəu] *n* enthousiasme *m*.
gusty ['gʌstɪ] *adj* venteux(euse); ~ **winds** des rafales de vent.
gut [gʌt] *n* intestin *m*, boyau *m*; (*MUS etc*) boyau ♦ *vt* (*poultry, fish*) vider; (*building*) ne laisser que les murs de; ~**s** *npl* boyaux *mpl*; (*col: courage*) cran *m*; **to hate sb's** ~**s** ne pas pouvoir voir qn en peinture *or* sentir qn.
gut reaction *n* réaction instinctive.
gutsy ['gʌtsɪ] *adj* (*person*) qui a du cran; (*style*) qui a du punch.
gutted ['gʌtɪd] *adj*: **I was ~** (*col: disappointed*) j'étais carrément dégoûté.
gutter ['gʌtə*] *n* (*of roof*) gouttière *f*; (*in street*) caniveau *m*; (*fig*) ruisseau *m*.
gutter press *n*: **the ~** la presse de bas étage *or* à scandale.
guttural ['gʌtərl] *adj* guttural(e).
guy [gaɪ] *n* (*also*: ~**rope**) corde *f*; (*col: man*) type *m*; (*figure*) effigie de Guy Fawkes.
Guyana [gaɪ'ænə] *n* Guyane *f*.

Guy Fawkes' Night, *que l'on appelle également "bonfire night", commémore l'échec du complot (le "Gunpowder Plot") contre James Ist et son parlement le 5 novembre 1605. L'un des conspirateurs, Guy Fawkes, avait été surpris dans les caves du parlement alors qu'il s'apprêtait à y mettre le feu. Chaque année pour le 5 novembre, les enfants préparent à l'avance une effigie de Guy Fawkes et ils demandent aux passants "un penny pour le guy" avec lequel ils pourront s'acheter des fusées de feu d'artifice. Beaucoup de gens font encore un feu dans leur jardin sur lequel ils brûlent le "guy".*

guzzle ['gʌzl] *vi* s'empiffrer ♦ *vt* avaler gloutonnement.
gym [dʒɪm] *n* (*also*: **gymnasium**) gymnase *m*; (*also*: **gymnastics**) gym *f*.
gymkhana [dʒɪm'kɑːnə] *n* gymkhana *m*.
gymnasium [dʒɪm'neɪzɪəm] *n* gymnase *m*.
gymnast ['dʒɪmnæst] *n* gymnaste *m/f*.
gymnastics [dʒɪm'næstɪks] *n*, *npl* gymnastique *f*.
gym shoes *npl* chaussures *fpl* de gym(nastique).
gym slip *n* (*BRIT*) tunique *f* (d'écolière).
gynaecologist, (*US*) **gynecologist** [gaɪnɪ'kɔlədʒɪst] *n* gynécologue *m/f*.
gynaecology, (*US*) **gynecology** [gaɪnə'kɔlədʒɪ] *n* gynécologie *f*.
gypsy ['dʒɪpsɪ] *n* = **gipsy**.
gyrate [dʒaɪ'reɪt] *vi* tournoyer.
gyroscope ['dʒaɪərəskəup] *n* gyroscope *m*.

H h

H, h [eɪtʃ] *n* (*letter*) H, h *m*; **H for Harry**, (*US*) **H for How** H comme Henri.
habeas corpus ['heɪbɪəs'kɔːpəs] *n* (*LAW*) habeas corpus *m*.
haberdashery [hæbə'dæʃərɪ] *n* (*BRIT*) mercerie *f*.
habit ['hæbɪt] *n* habitude *f*; (*costume*) habit *m*, tenue *f*; **to get out of/into the ~ of doing sth** perdre/prendre l'habitude de faire qch.
habitable ['hæbɪtəbl] *adj* habitable.
habitat ['hæbɪtæt] *n* habitat *m*.
habitation [hæbɪ'teɪʃən] *n* habitation *f*.
habitual [hə'bɪtjuəl] *adj* habituel(le); (*drinker, liar*) invétéré(e).
habitually [hə'bɪtjuəlɪ] *adv* habituellement, d'habitude.
hack [hæk] *vt* hacher, tailler ♦ *n* (*cut*) entaille *f*; (*blow*) coup *m*; (*pej: writer*) nègre *m*; (*old horse*) canasson *m*.
hackles ['hæklz] *npl*: **to make sb's ~ rise** (*fig*) mettre qn hors de soi.
hackney cab ['hæknɪ-] *n* fiacre *m*.
hackneyed ['hæknɪd] *adj* usé(e), rebattu(e).
hacksaw ['hæksɔ:] *n* scie *f* à métaux.
had [hæd] *pt, pp of* **have**.
haddock, *pl* ~ *or* ~**s** ['hædək] *n* églefin *m*; **smoked ~** haddock *m*.
hadn't ['hædnt] = **had not**.
haematology, (*US*) **hematology** ['hi:mə'tɔlədʒɪ] *n* hématologie *f*.
haemoglobin, (*US*) **hemoglobin** ['hi:mə'gləubɪn] *n* hémoglobine *f*.
haemophilia, (*US*) **hemophilia** ['hi:mə'fɪlɪə] *n* hémophilie *f*.
haemorrhage, (*US*) **hemorrhage** ['hemərɪdʒ] *n* hémorragie *f*.
haemorrhoids, (*US*) **hemorrhoids** ['hemərɔɪdz] *npl* hémorroïdes *fpl*.
hag [hæg] *n* (*ugly*) vieille sorcière; (*nasty*) chameau *m*, harpie *f*; (*witch*) sorcière.
haggard ['hægəd] *adj* hagard(e), égaré(e).
haggis ['hægɪs] *n* haggis *m*.
haggle ['hægl] *vi* marchander; **to ~ over** chicaner sur.
haggling ['hæglɪŋ] *n* marchandage *m*.
Hague [heɪg] *n*: **The ~** La Haye.
hail [heɪl] *n* grêle *f* ♦ *vt* (*call*) héler; (*greet*) acclamer ♦ *vi* grêler; (*originate*): **he ~s from Scotland** il est originaire d'Écosse.
hailstone ['heɪlstəun] *n* grêlon *m*.
hailstorm ['heɪlstɔːm] *n* averse *f* de grêle.
hair [hɛə*] *n* cheveux *mpl*; (*on body*) poils *mpl*,

pilosité *f*; (*single hair: on head*) cheveu *m*; (: *on body*) poil *m*; **to do one's** ~ se coiffer.
hairbrush ['hεəbrʌʃ] *n* brosse *f* à cheveux.
haircut ['hεəkʌt] *n* coupe *f* (de cheveux).
hairdo ['hεədu:] *n* coiffure *f*.
hairdresser ['hεədrεsə*] *n* coiffeur/euse.
hair-dryer ['hεədraɪə*] *n* sèche-cheveux *m*.
-haired [hεəd] *suffix*: **fair/long**~ aux cheveux blonds/longs.
hair gel *n* gel *m* pour cheveux.
hairgrip ['hεəgrɪp] *n* pince *f* à cheveux.
hairline ['hεəlaɪn] *n* naissance *f* des cheveux.
hairline fracture *n* fêlure *f*.
hairnet ['hεənεt] *n* résille *f*.
hair oil *n* huile *f* capillaire.
hairpiece ['hεəpi:s] *n* postiche *m*.
hairpin ['hεəpɪn] *n* épingle *f* à cheveux.
hairpin bend, (*US*) **hairpin curve** *n* virage *m* en épingle à cheveux.
hairraising ['hεəreɪzɪŋ] *adj* à (vous) faire dresser les cheveux sur la tête.
hair remover *n* dépilateur *m*.
hair spray *n* laque *f* (pour les cheveux).
hairstyle ['hεəstaɪl] *n* coiffure *f*.
hairy ['hεərɪ] *adj* poilu(e); chevelu(e); (*fig*) effrayant(e).
Haiti ['heɪtɪ] *n* Haïti *m*.
hake [heɪk] *n* colin *m*, merlu *m*.
halcyon ['hælsɪən] *adj* merveilleux(euse).
hale [heɪl] *adj*: ~ **and hearty** robuste, en pleine santé.
half [hɑ:f] *n* (*pl* **halves** [hɑ:vz]) moitié *f*; (*SPORT: of match*) mi-temps *f*; (: *of ground*) moitié (du terrain) ♦ *adj* demi(e) ♦ *adv* (à) moitié, à demi; ~**-an-hour** une demi-heure; ~ **a dozen** une demi-douzaine; ~ **a pound** une demi-livre, ≈ 250 g; **two and a** ~ deux et demi; **a week and a** ~ une semaine et demie; ~ (**of it**) la moitié; ~ (**of**) la moitié de; ~ **the amount of the** **money** la moitié de; **to cut sth in** ~ couper qch en deux; ~ **past three** trois heures et demie; ~ **empty/closed** à moitié vide/fermé; **to go halves (with sb)** se mettre de moitié avec qn.
half-back ['hɑ:fbæk] *n* (*SPORT*) demi *m*.
half-baked ['hɑ:f'beɪkt] *adj* (*col*: *idea, scheme*) qui ne tient pas debout.
half-breed ['hɑ:fbri:d] *n* = **halfcaste**.
half-brother ['hɑ:fbrʌðə*] *n* demi-frère *m*.
half-caste ['hɑ:fkɑ:st] *n* métis/se.
half-hearted ['hɑ:f'hɑ:tɪd] *adj* tiède, sans enthousiasme.
half-hour [hɑ:f'auə*] *n* demi-heure *f*.
half-mast ['hɑ:f'mɑ:st] *n*: **at** ~ (*flag*) en berne, à mi-mât.
halfpenny ['heɪpnɪ] *n* demi-penny *m*.
half-price ['hɑ:f'praɪs] *adj* à moitié prix ♦ *adv* (*also*: **at** ~) à moitié prix.
half term *n* (*BRIT SCOL*) congé *m* de demi-trimestre.
half-time [hɑ:f'taɪm] *n* mi-temps *f*.
halfway ['hɑ:f'weɪ] *adv* à mi-chemin; **to meet**

sb ~ (*fig*) parvenir à un compromis avec qn.
halfway house *n* (*hostel*) centre *m* de réadaptation (*pour anciens prisonniers, malades mentaux etc*); (*fig*): **a** ~ (**between**) une étape intermédiaire (entre).
half-wit ['hɑ:fwɪt] *n* (*col*) idiot/e, imbécile *m/f*.
half-yearly [hɑ:f'jɪəlɪ] *adv* deux fois par an ♦ *adj* semestriel(le).
halibut ['hælɪbət] *n* (*pl inv*) flétan *m*.
halitosis [hælɪ'təusɪs] *n* mauvaise haleine.
hall [hɔ:l] *n* salle *f*; (*entrance way*) hall *m*, entrée *f*; (*corridor*) couloir *m*; (*mansion*) château *m*, manoir *m*; ~ **of residence** *n* (*BRIT*) pavillon *m* or résidence *f* universitaire.
hallmark ['hɔ:lmɑ:k] *n* poinçon *m*; (*fig*) marque *f*.
hallo [hə'ləu] *excl* = **hello**.
Hallowe'en ['hæləu'i:n] *n* veille *f* de la Toussaint.

Selon la tradition, **Hallowe'en** *est la nuit des fantômes et des sorcières. En Écosse et aux États-Unis surtout (beaucoup moins en Angleterre) les enfants, pour fêter Hallowe'en, se déguisent ce soir-là et ils vont ainsi de porte en porte en demandant de petits cadeaux (du chocolat, une pomme etc).*

---

hallucination [həlu:sɪ'neɪʃən] *n* hallucination *f*.
hallucinogenic [həlu:sɪnəu'dʒεnɪk] *adj* hallucinogène.
hallway ['hɔ:lweɪ] *n* vestibule *m*; couloir *m*.
halo ['heɪləu] *n* (*of saint etc*) auréole *f*; (*of sun*) halo *m*.
halt [hɔ:lt] *n* halte *f*, arrêt *m* ♦ *vt* faire arrêter ♦ *vi* faire halte, s'arrêter; **to call a** ~ **to sth** (*fig*) mettre fin à qch.
halter ['hɔ:ltə*] *n* (*for horse*) licou *m*.
halterneck ['hɔ:ltənεk] *adj* (*dress*) (avec) dos nu *inv*.
halve [hɑ:v] *vt* (*apple etc*) partager *or* diviser en deux; (*reduce by half*) réduire de moitié.
halves [hɑ:vz] *npl of* **half**.
ham [hæm] *n* jambon *m*; (*col: also*: **radio** ~) radio-amateur *m*; (: *also*: ~ **actor**) cabotin/e.
Hamburg ['hæmbə:g] *n* Hambourg.
hamburger ['hæmbə:gə*] *n* hamburger *m*.
ham-fisted ['hæm'fɪstɪd], (*US*) **ham-handed** ['hæm'hændɪd] *adj* maladroit(e).
hamlet ['hæmlɪt] *n* hameau *m*.
hammer ['hæmə*] *n* marteau *m* ♦ *vt* (*fig*) éreinter, démolir ♦ *vi* (*at door*) frapper à coups redoublés; **to** ~ **a point home to sb** faire rentrer qch dans la tête de qn.
▶**hammer out** *vt* (*metal*) étendre au marteau; (*fig: solution*) élaborer.
hammock ['hæmək] *n* hamac *m*.
hamper ['hæmpə*] *vt* gêner ♦ *n* panier *m* (d'osier).
hamster ['hæmstə*] *n* hamster *m*.
hamstring ['hæmstrɪŋ] *n* (*ANAT*) tendon *m* du

jarret.

hand [hænd] *n* main *f*; (*of clock*) aiguille *f*; (*handwriting*) écriture *f*; (*at cards*) jeu *m*; (*measurement: of horse*) paume *f*; (*worker*) ouvrier/ière ♦ *vt* passer, donner; **to give sb a ~** donner un coup de main à qn; **at ~** à portée de la main; **in ~** en main; (*work*) en cours; **we have the situation in ~** nous avons la situation bien en main; **to be on ~** (*person*) être disponible; (*emergency services*) se tenir prêt(e) (à intervenir); **to ~** (*information etc*) sous la main, à portée de la main; **to force sb's ~** forcer la main à qn; **to have a free ~** avoir carte blanche; **to have sth in one's ~** tenir qch à la main; **on the one ~ ...**, **on the other ~** d'une part ..., d'autre part.

►**hand down** *vt* passer; (*tradition, heirloom*) transmettre; (*US: sentence, verdict*) prononcer.

►**hand in** *vt* remettre.

►**hand out** *vt* distribuer.

►**hand over** *vt* remettre; (*powers etc*) transmettre.

►**hand round** *vt* (*BRIT: information*) faire circuler; (*: chocolates etc*) faire passer.

handbag ['hændbæg] *n* sac *m* à main.

hand baggage *n* bagages *mpl* à main; **one item of ~** un bagage à main.

handball ['hændbɔːl] *n* handball *m*.

handbasin ['hændbeɪsn] *n* lavabo *m*.

handbook ['hændbuk] *n* manuel *m*.

handbrake ['hændbreɪk] *n* frein *m* à main.

h & c *abbr* (*BRIT*) = hot and cold (water).

hand cream *n* crème *f* pour les mains.

handcuffs ['hændkʌfs] *npl* menottes *fpl*.

handful ['hændful] *n* poignée *f*.

hand-held ['hænd'held] *adj* à main.

handicap ['hændɪkæp] *n* handicap *m* ♦ *vt* handicaper; **mentally/physically ~ped** handicapé(e) mentalement/physiquement.

handicraft ['hændɪkrɑːft] *n* travail *m* d'artisanat, technique artisanale.

handiwork ['hændɪwɜːk] *n* ouvrage *m*; **this looks like his ~** (*pej*) ça a tout l'air d'être son œuvre.

handkerchief ['hæŋkətʃɪf] *n* mouchoir *m*.

handle ['hændl] *n* (*of door etc*) poignée *f*; (*of cup etc*) anse *f*; (*of knife etc*) manche *m*; (*of saucepan*) queue *f*; (*for winding*) manivelle *f* ♦ *vt* toucher, manier; (*deal with*) s'occuper de; (*treat: people*) prendre; **"~ with care"** "fragile".

handlebar(s) ['hændlbɑː(z)] *n(pl)* guidon *m*.

handling ['hændlɪŋ] *n* (*AUT*) maniement *m*; (*treatment*): **his ~ of the matter** la façon dont il a traité l'affaire.

handling charges *npl* frais *mpl* de manutention; (*BANKING*) agios *mpl*.

hand-luggage ['hændlʌgɪdʒ] *n* bagages *mpl* à main.

handmade ['hænd'meɪd] *adj* fait(e) à la main.

handout ['hændaut] *n* documentation *f*, prospectus *m*; (*press ~*) communiqué *m* de presse.

hand-picked ['hænd'pɪkt] *adj* (*produce*) cueilli(e) à la main; (*staff etc*) trié(e) sur le volet.

handrail ['hændreɪl] *n* (*on staircase etc*) rampe *f*, main courante.

handset ['hændset] *n* (*TEL*) combiné *m*.

handshake ['hændʃeɪk] *n* poignée *f* de main; (*COMPUT*) établissement *m* de la liaison.

handsome ['hænsəm] *adj* beau(belle); (*gift*) généreux(euse); (*profit*) considérable.

hands-on [hændz'ɔn] *adj* (*training, experience*) sur le tas; **she has a very ~ approach** sa politique est de mettre la main à la pâte.

handstand ['hændstænd] *n*: **to do a ~** faire l'arbre droit.

hand-to-mouth ['hændtə'mauθ] *adj* (*existence*) au jour le jour.

handwriting ['hændraɪtɪŋ] *n* écriture *f*.

handwritten ['hændrɪtn] *adj* manuscrit(e), écrit(e) à la main.

handy ['hændɪ] *adj* (*person*) adroit(e); (*close at hand*) sous la main; (*convenient*) pratique; **to come in ~** être (*or* s'avérer) utile.

handyman ['hændɪmæn] *n* bricoleur *m*; (*servant*) homme *m* à tout faire.

hang, *pt, pp* **hung** [hæŋ, hʌŋ] *vt* accrocher; (*criminal: pt, pp* **hanged**) pendre ♦ *vi* pendre; (*hair, drapery*) tomber ♦ *n*: **to get the ~ of (doing) sth** (*col*) attraper le coup pour faire qch.

►**hang about** *vi* flâner, traîner.

►**hang back** *vi* (*hesitate*): **to ~ back (from doing)** être réticent(e) (pour faire).

►**hang on** *vi* (*wait*) attendre ♦ *vt fus* (*depend on*) dépendre de; **to ~ on to** (*keep hold of*) ne pas lâcher; (*keep*) garder.

►**hang out** *vt* (*washing*) étendre (dehors) ♦ *vi* pendre; (*col: live*) habiter, percher.

►**hang together** *vi* (*argument etc*) se tenir, être cohérent(e).

►**hang up** *vi* (*TEL*) raccrocher ♦ *vt* accrocher, suspendre; **to ~ up on sb** (*TEL*) raccrocher au nez de qn.

hangar ['hæŋə*] *n* hangar *m*.

hangdog ['hæŋdɔg] *adj* (*look, expression*) de chien battu.

hanger ['hæŋə*] *n* cintre *m*, portemanteau *m*.

hanger-on [hæŋər'ɔn] *n* parasite *m*.

hang-glider ['hæŋglaɪdə*] *n* deltaplane *m*.

hang-gliding ['hæŋglaɪdɪŋ] *n* vol *m* libre *or* sur aile delta.

hanging ['hæŋɪŋ] *n* (*execution*) pendaison *f*.

hangman ['hæŋmən] *n* bourreau *m*.

hangover ['hæŋəuvə*] *n* (*after drinking*) gueule *f* de bois.

hang-up ['hæŋʌp] *n* complexe *m*.

hank [hæŋk] *n* écheveau *m*.

hanker ['hæŋkə*] *vi*: **to ~ after** avoir envie de.

hankering ['hæŋkərɪŋ] *n*: **to have a ~ for/to do sth** avoir une grande envie de/de faire qch.

hankie, hanky ['hæŋkɪ] *n abbr* = **handkerchief**.
Hants *abbr* (*BRIT*) = **Hampshire**.
haphazard [hæp'hæzəd] *adj* fait(e) au hasard, fait(e) au petit bonheur.
hapless ['hæplɪs] *adj* malheureux(euse).
happen ['hæpən] *vi* arriver, se passer, se produire; **what's** ~**ing?** que se passe-t-il?; **she** ~**ed to be free** il s'est trouvé (*or* se trouvait) qu'elle était libre; **if anything** ~**ed to him** s'il lui arrivait quoi que ce soit; **as it** ~**s** justement.
▶**happen (up)on** *vt fus* tomber sur.
happening ['hæpnɪŋ] *n* événement *m*.
happily ['hæpɪlɪ] *adv* heureusement.
happiness ['hæpɪnɪs] *n* bonheur *m*.
happy ['hæpɪ] *adj* heureux(euse); ~ **with** (*arrangements etc*) satisfait(e) de; **yes, I'd be** ~ **to** oui, avec plaisir *or* (bien) volontiers; ~ **birthday!** bon anniversaire!; ~ **Christmas/New Year!** joyeux Noël/bonne année!
happy-go-lucky ['hæpɪgəʊ'lʌkɪ] *adj* insouciant(e).
happy hour *n* l'heure *f* de l'apéritif, *heure pendant laquelle les consommations sont à prix réduit.*
harangue [hə'ræŋ] *vt* haranguer.
harass ['hærəs] *vt* accabler, tourmenter.
harassed ['hærəst] *adj* tracassé(e).
harassment ['hærəsmənt] *n* tracasseries *fpl*.
harbour, (*US*) **harbor** ['hɑːbə*] *n* port *m* ♦ *vt* héberger, abriter; (*hopes, suspicions*) entretenir; **to** ~ **a grudge against sb** en vouloir à qn.
harbo(u)r dues *npl* droits *mpl* de port.
harbo(u)r master *n* capitaine *m* du port.
hard [hɑːd] *adj* dur(e) ♦ *adv* (*work*) dur; (*think, try*) sérieusement; **to look** ~ **at** regarder fixement; regarder de près; **to drink** ~ boire sec; ~ **luck!** pas de veine!; **no** ~ **feelings!** sans rancune!; **to be** ~ **of hearing** être dur(e) d'oreille; **to be** ~ **done by** être traité(e) injustement; **to be** ~ **on sb** être dur(e) avec qn; **I find it** ~ **to believe that** ... je n'arrive pas à croire que ....
hard-and-fast ['hɑːdən'fɑːst] *adj* strict(e), absolu(e).
hardback ['hɑːdbæk] *n* livre relié.
hardboard ['hɑːdbɔːd] *n* Isorel *m* ®.
hard-boiled egg ['hɑːd'bɔɪld-] *n* œuf dur.
hard cash *n* espèces *fpl*.
hard copy *n* (*COMPUT*) sortie *f* or copie *f* papier.
hard-core ['hɑːd'kɔː*] *adj* (*pornography*) (dit(e)) dur(e); (*supporters*) inconditionnel(le).
hard court *n* (*TENNIS*) court *m* en dur.
hard disk *n* (*COMPUT*) disque dur.
harden ['hɑːdn] *vt* durcir; (*steel*) tremper; (*fig*) endurcir ♦ *vi* (*substance*) durcir.
hardened ['hɑːdnd] *adj* (*criminal*) endurci(e); **to be** ~ **to sth** s'être endurci(e) à qch, être (devenu(e)) insensible à qch.

hardening ['hɑːdnɪŋ] *n* durcissement *m*.
hard-headed ['hɑːd'hɛdɪd] *adj* réaliste; décidé(e).
hard-hearted ['hɑːd'hɑːtɪd] *adj* dur(e), impitoyable.
hard-hitting ['hɑːd'hɪtɪŋ] *adj* (*speech, article*) sans complaisance.
hard labour *n* travaux forcés.
hardliner [hɑːd'laɪnə*] *n* intransigeant/e, dur/e.
hard-luck story [hɑːd'lʌk-] *n* histoire larmoyante.
hardly ['hɑːdlɪ] *adv* (*scarcely*) à peine; (*harshly*) durement; **it's** ~ **the case** ce n'est guère le cas; ~ **anywhere/ever** presque nulle part/jamais; **I can** ~ **believe it** j'ai du mal à le croire.
hardness ['hɑːdnɪs] *n* dureté *f*.
hard-nosed ['hɑːd'nəʊzd] *adj* impitoyable, dur(e).
hard-pressed ['hɑːd'prɛst] *adj* sous pression.
hard sell *n* vente agressive.
hardship ['hɑːdʃɪp] *n* épreuves *fpl*; privations *fpl*.
hard shoulder *n* (*BRIT AUT*) accotement stabilisé.
hard-up [hɑːd'ʌp] *adj* (*col*) fauché(e).
hardware ['hɑːdwɛə*] *n* quincaillerie *f*; (*COMPUT*) matériel *m*.
hardware shop *n* quincaillerie *f*.
hard-wearing [hɑːd'wɛərɪŋ] *adj* solide.
hard-won ['hɑːd'wʌn] *adj* (si) durement gagné(e).
hard-working [hɑːd'wəːkɪŋ] *adj* travailleur(euse), consciencieux(euse).
hardy ['hɑːdɪ] *adj* robuste; (*plant*) résistant(e) au gel.
hare [hɛə*] *n* lièvre *m*.
hare-brained ['hɛəbreɪnd] *adj* farfelu(e); écervelé(e).
harelip ['hɛəlɪp] *n* (*MED*) bec-de-lièvre *m*.
harem [hɑː'riːm] *n* harem *m*.
hark back [hɑːk-] *vi*: **to** ~ **to** (en) revenir toujours à.
harm [hɑːm] *n* mal *m*; (*wrong*) tort *m* ♦ *vt* (*person*) faire du mal *or* du tort à; (*thing*) endommager; **to mean no** ~ ne pas avoir de mauvaises intentions; **there's no** ~ **in trying** on peut toujours essayer; **out of** ~**'s way** à l'abri du danger, en lieu sûr.
harmful ['hɑːmful] *adj* nuisible.
harmless ['hɑːmlɪs] *adj* inoffensif(ive); sans méchanceté.
harmonic [hɑː'mɔnɪk] *adj* harmonique.
harmonica [hɑː'mɔnɪkə] *n* harmonica *m*.
harmonics [hɑː'mɔnɪks] *npl* harmoniques *mpl or fpl*.
harmonious [hɑː'məʊnɪəs] *adj* harmonieux(euse).
harmonium [hɑː'məʊnɪəm] *n* harmonium *m*.
harmonize ['hɑːmənaɪz] *vt* harmoniser ♦ *vi* s'harmoniser.

harmony ['hɑːmənɪ] n harmonie f.
harness ['hɑːnɪs] n harnais m ♦ vt (horse) harnacher; (resources) exploiter.
harp [hɑːp] n harpe f ♦ vi: **to ~ on about** parler tout le temps de.
harpist ['hɑːpɪst] n harpiste m/f.
harpoon [hɑːˈpuːn] n harpon m.
harpsichord ['hɑːpsɪkɔːd] n clavecin m.
harrow ['hærəʊ] n (AGR) herse f.
harrowing ['hærəʊɪŋ] adj déchirant(e).
harry ['hærɪ] vt (MIL, fig) harceler.
harsh [hɑːʃ] adj (hard) dur(e), sévère; (rough: surface) rugueux(euse); (: sound) discordant(e); (: taste) âpre.
harshly ['hɑːʃlɪ] adv durement, sévèrement.
harshness ['hɑːʃnɪs] n dureté f, sévérité f.
harvest ['hɑːvɪst] n (of corn) moisson f; (of fruit) récolte f; (of grapes) vendange f ♦ vi, vt moissonner; récolter; vendanger.
harvester ['hɑːvɪstə*] n (machine) moissonneuse f; (also: **combine** ~) moissonneuse-batteuse(-lieuse f) f; (person) moissonneur/euse.
has [hæz] vb see **have**.
has-been ['hæzbiːn] n (col: person): **he/she's a ~** il/elle a fait son temps or est fini(e).
hash [hæʃ] n (CULIN) hachis m; (fig: mess) gâchis m ♦ n abbr (col) = **hashish**.
hashish ['hæʃɪʃ] n haschisch m.
hasn't ['hæznt] = **has not**.
hassle ['hæsl] n (col: fuss) histoire(s) f(pl).
haste [heɪst] n hâte f, précipitation f; **in ~** à la hâte, précipitemment.
hasten ['heɪsn] vt hâter, accélérer ♦ vi se hâter, s'empresser; **I ~ to add that** ... je m'empresse d'ajouter que ....
hastily ['heɪstɪlɪ] adv à la hâte, précipitamment.
hasty ['heɪstɪ] adj hâtif(ive), précipité(e).
hat [hæt] n chapeau m.
hatbox ['hætbɒks] n carton m à chapeau.
hatch [hætʃ] n (NAUT: also: ~**way**) écoutille f; (BRIT: also: **service** ~) passe-plats m inv ♦ vi éclore ♦ vt faire éclore; (fig: scheme) tramer, ourdir.
hatchback ['hætʃbæk] n (AUT) modèle m avec hayon arrière.
hatchet ['hætʃɪt] n hachette f.
hatchet job n (col) démolissage m.
hatchet man n (col) homme m de main.
hate [heɪt] vt haïr, détester ♦ n haine f; **to ~ to do** or **doing** détester faire; **I ~ to trouble you, but** ... désolé de vous déranger, mais ....
hateful ['heɪtful] adj odieux(euse), détestable.
hatred ['heɪtrɪd] n haine f.
hat trick n (BRIT SPORT, also fig): **to get a ~** réussir trois coups (or gagner trois matchs etc) consécutifs.
haughty ['hɔːtɪ] adj hautain(e), arrogant(e).
haul [hɔːl] vt traîner, tirer; (by lorry) camionner; (NAUT) haler ♦ n (of fish) prise f; (of stolen goods etc) butin m.
haulage ['hɔːlɪdʒ] n transport routier.
haulage contractor n (BRIT: firm) entreprise f de transport (routier); (: person) transporteur routier.
haulier ['hɔːlɪə*], (US) **hauler** ['hɔːlə*] n transporteur (routier), camionneur m.
haunch [hɔːntʃ] n hanche f; ~ **of venison** cuissot m de chevreuil.
haunt [hɔːnt] vt (subj: ghost, fear) hanter; (: person) fréquenter ♦ n repaire m.
haunted ['hɔːntɪd] adj (castle etc) hanté(e); (look) égaré(e), hagard(e).
haunting ['hɔːntɪŋ] adj (sight, music) obsédant(e).
Havana [həˈvænə] n La Havane.

═══════════════════════════════ KEYWORD

have [hæv] (pt, pp **had**) aux vb **1** (gen) avoir; être; **to ~ arrived/gone** être arrivé(e)/allé(e); **to ~ eaten/slept** avoir mangé/dormi; **he has been promoted** il a eu une promotion
2 (in tag questions): **you've done it, ~n't you?** vous l'avez fait, n'est-ce pas?
3 (in short answers and questions): **no I ~n't!/yes we ~!** mais non!/mais si!; **so I ~!** ah oui!, oui c'est vrai!; **I've been there before, ~ you?** j'y suis déjà allé, et vous?
♦ modal aux vb (be obliged): **to ~ (got) to do sth** devoir faire qch; être obligé(e) de faire qch; **she has (got) to do it** elle doit le faire, il faut qu'elle le fasse; **you ~n't to tell her** vous n'êtes pas obligé de le lui dire; (must not) ne le lui dites surtout pas
♦ vt **1** (possess, obtain) avoir; **he has (got) blue eyes/dark hair** il a les yeux bleus/les cheveux bruns; **may I ~ your address?** puis-je avoir votre adresse?
2 (+noun: take, hold etc): **to ~ breakfast/a bath/a shower** prendre le petit déjeuner/un bain/une douche; **to ~ dinner/lunch** dîner/déjeuner; **to ~ a swim** nager; **to ~ a meeting** se réunir; **to ~ a party** organiser une fête; **let me ~ a try** laissez-moi essayer
3: **to ~ sth done** faire faire qch; **to ~ one's hair cut** se faire couper les cheveux; **to ~ sb do sth** faire faire qch à qn
4 (experience, suffer) avoir; **to ~ a cold/flu** avoir un rhume/la grippe; **to ~ an operation** se faire opérer; **I won't ~ it** cela ne se passera pas ainsi
5 (inf: dupe) avoir; **he's been had** il s'est fait avoir or rouler
▶**have out** vt: **to ~ it out with sb** (settle a problem etc) s'expliquer (franchement) avec qn.

haven ['heɪvn] n port m; (fig) havre m.
haversack ['hævəsæk] n sac m à dos.
haves [hævz] npl (col): **the ~ and have-nots** les riches et les pauvres.
havoc ['hævək] n ravages mpl, dégâts mpl;

to play ~ with (*fig*) désorganiser complètement; détraquer.
Hawaii [həˈwaɪiː] *n* (îles *fpl*) Hawaii *m*.
Hawaiian [həˈwaɪjən] *adj* hawaïen(ne) ♦ *n* Hawaïen/ne; (*LING*) hawaïen *m*.
hawk [hɔːk] *n* faucon *m* ♦ *vt* (*goods for sale*) colporter.
hawker [ˈhɔːkə*] *n* colporteur *m*.
hawkish [ˈhɔːkɪʃ] *adj* belliciste.
hawthorn [ˈhɔːθɔːn] *n* aubépine *f*.
hay [heɪ] *n* foin *m*.
hay fever *n* rhume *m* des foins.
haystack [ˈheɪstæk] *n* meule *f* de foin.
haywire [ˈheɪwaɪə*] *adj* (*col*): **to go ~** perdre la tête; mal tourner.
hazard [ˈhæzəd] *n* (*chance*) hasard *m*, chance *f*; (*risk*) danger *m*, risque *m* ♦ *vt* risquer, hasarder; **to be a health/fire ~** présenter un risque d'incendie/pour la santé; **to ~ a guess** émettre *or* hasarder une hypothèse.
hazardous [ˈhæzədəs] *adj* hasardeux(euse), risqué(e).
hazard pay *n* (*US*) prime *f* de risque.
hazard warning lights *npl* (*AUT*) feux *mpl* de détresse.
haze [heɪz] *n* brume *f*.
hazel [heɪzl] *n* (*tree*) noisetier *m* ♦ *adj* (*eyes*) noisette *inv*.
hazelnut [ˈheɪzlnʌt] *n* noisette *f*.
hazy [ˈheɪzɪ] *adj* brumeux(euse); (*idea*) vague; (*photograph*) flou(e).
H-bomb [ˈeɪtʃbɔm] *n* bombe *f* H.
HE *abbr* = *high explosive*; (*REL, DIPLOMACY*) = *His (or Her) Excellency*.
he [hiː] *pron* il; **it is ~ who** ... c'est lui qui ...; **here ~** is le voici; **~-bear** *etc* ours *etc* mâle.
head [hɛd] *n* tête *f*; (*leader*) chef *m* ♦ *vt* (*list*) être en tête de; (*group*) être à la tête de; **~s** (*on coin*) (le côté) face; **~s or tails** pile ou face; **~ over heels in love** follement *or* éperdument amoureux(euse); **to ~ the ball** faire une tête; **10 francs a** *or* **per ~** 10 F par personne; **to sit at the ~ of the table** présider la tablée; **to have a ~ for business** avoir des dispositions pour les affaires; **to have no ~ for heights** être sujet(te) au vertige; **to come to a ~** (*fig: situation etc*) devenir critique.
►**head for** *vt fus* se diriger vers.
►**head off** *vt* (*threat, danger*) détourner.
headache [ˈhɛdeɪk] *n* mal *m* de tête; **to have a ~** avoir mal à la tête.
headband [ˈhɛdbænd] *n* bandeau *m*.
headboard [ˈhɛdbɔːd] *n* dosseret *m*.
head cold *n* rhume *m* de cerveau.
headdress [ˈhɛddrɛs] *n* coiffure *f*.
headed notepaper [ˈhɛdɪd-] *n* papier *m* à lettres à en-tête.
header [ˈhɛdə*] *n* (*BRIT col: FOOTBALL*) (coup *m* de) tête *f*; (: *fall*) chute *f* (*or* plongeon *m*) la tête la première.
head-first [ˈhɛdˈfɜːst] *adv* (*lit*) la tête la pre-

mière.
headhunt [ˈhɛdhʌnt] *vt*: **she was ~ed** elle a été recrutée par un chasseur de têtes.
headhunter [ˈhɛdhʌntə*] *n* chasseur *m* de têtes.
heading [ˈhɛdɪŋ] *n* titre *m*; (*subject title*) rubrique *f*.
headlamp [ˈhɛdlæmp] *n* = **headlight**.
headland [ˈhɛdlənd] *n* promontoire *m*, cap *m*.
headlight [ˈhɛdlaɪt] *n* phare *m*.
headline [ˈhɛdlaɪn] *n* titre *m*.
headlong [ˈhɛdlɔŋ] *adv* (*fall*) la tête la première; (*rush*) tête baissée.
headmaster [hɛdˈmɑːstə*] *n* directeur *m*, proviseur *m*.
headmistress [hɛdˈmɪstrɪs] *n* directrice *f*.
head office *n* siège *m*, direction *f* (générale).
head-on [hɛdˈɔn] *adj* (*collision*) de plein fouet.
headphones [ˈhɛdfəunz] *npl* casque *m* (à écouteurs).
headquarters (HQ) [ˈhɛdkwɔːtəz] *npl* (*of business*) siège *m*, direction *f* (générale); (*MIL*) quartier général.
head-rest [ˈhɛdrɛst] *n* appui-tête *m*.
headroom [ˈhɛdrum] *n* (*in car*) hauteur *f* de plafond; (*under bridge*) hauteur limite; dégagement *m*.
headscarf [ˈhɛdskɑːf] *n* foulard *m*.
headset [ˈhɛdsɛt] *n* = **headphones**.
headstone [ˈhɛdstəun] *n* (*on grave*) pierre tombale.
headstrong [ˈhɛdstrɔŋ] *adj* têtu(e), entêté(e).
head waiter *n* maître *m* d'hôtel.
headway [ˈhɛdweɪ] *n*: **to make ~** avancer, faire des progrès.
headwind [ˈhɛdwɪnd] *n* vent *m* contraire.
heady [ˈhɛdɪ] *adj* capiteux(euse); enivrant(e).
heal [hiːl] *vt, vi* guérir.
health [hɛlθ] *n* santé *f*; **Department of H~** (*US*) ≈ ministère *m* de la Santé; **Department of H~ (DH)** (*BRIT*) ≈ ministère de la Santé.
health care *n* services médicaux.
health centre *n* (*BRIT*) centre *m* de santé.
health food(s) *n(pl)* aliment(s) naturel(s).
health food shop *n* magasin *m* diététique.
health hazard *n* risque *m* pour la santé.
Health Service *n*: **the ~** (*BRIT*) ≈ la Sécurité Sociale.
healthy [ˈhɛlθɪ] *adj* (*person*) en bonne santé; (*climate, food, attitude etc*) sain(e).
heap [hiːp] *n* tas *m*, monceau *m* ♦ *vt* entasser, amonceler; **~s (of)** (*col: lots*) des tas (de); **to ~ favours/praise/gifts** *etc* **on sb** combler qn de faveurs/d'éloges/de cadeaux *etc*.
hear, *pt*, *pp* **heard** [hɪə*, hɜːd] *vt* entendre; (*news*) apprendre; (*lecture*) assister à, écouter ♦ *vi* entendre; **to ~ about** entendre parler de; (*have news of*) avoir des nouvelles de; **did you ~ about the move?** tu es au courant du déménagement?; **to ~ from sb** recevoir des nouvelles de qn; **I've never heard of that book** je n'ai jamais entendu

parler de ce livre.
▶**hear out** *vt* écouter jusqu'au bout.
hearing ['hɪərɪŋ] *n* (*sense*) ouïe *f*; (*of witnesses*) audition *f*; (*of a case*) audience *f*; (*of committee*) séance *f*; **to give sb a** ~ (*BRIT*) écouter ce que qn a à dire.
hearing aid *n* appareil *m* acoustique.
hearsay ['hɪəseɪ] *n* on-dit *mpl*, rumeurs *fpl*; **by** ~ *adv* par ouï-dire.
hearse [hɜːs] *n* corbillard *m*.
heart [hɑːt] *n* cœur *m*; ~**s** *npl* (*CARDS*) cœur; **at** ~ au fond; **by** ~ (*learn, know*) par cœur; **to have a weak** ~ avoir le cœur malade, avoir des problèmes de cœur; **to lose** ~ perdre courage, se décourager; **to take** ~ prendre courage; **to set one's** ~ **on sth/on doing sth** vouloir absolument qch/faire qch; **the** ~ **of the matter** le fond du problème.
heartache ['hɑːteɪk] *n* chagrin *m*, douleur *f*.
heart attack *n* crise *f* cardiaque.
heartbeat ['hɑːtbiːt] *n* battement *m* de cœur.
heartbreak ['hɑːtbreɪk] *n* immense chagrin *m*.
heartbreaking ['hɑːtbreɪkɪŋ] *adj* navrant(e), déchirant(e).
heartbroken ['hɑːtbrəukən] *adj*: **to be** ~ avoir beaucoup de chagrin.
heartburn ['hɑːtbɜːn] *n* brûlures *fpl* d'estomac.
-hearted ['hɑːtɪd] *suffix*: **kind**~ généreux(euse), qui a bon cœur.
heartening ['hɑːtnɪŋ] *adj* encourageant(e), réconfortant(e).
heart failure *n* (*MED*) arrêt *m* du cœur.
heartfelt ['hɑːtfelt] *adj* sincère.
hearth [hɑːθ] *n* foyer *m*, cheminée *f*.
heartily ['hɑːtɪlɪ] *adv* chaleureusement; (*laugh*) de bon cœur; (*eat*) de bon appétit; **to agree** ~ être entièrement d'accord; **to be** ~ **sick of** (*BRIT*) en avoir ras le bol de.
heartland ['hɑːtlænd] *n* centre *m*, cœur *m*; **France's** ~**s** la France profonde.
heartless ['hɑːtlɪs] *adj* sans cœur, insensible; cruel(le).
heartstrings ['hɑːtstrɪŋz] *npl*: **to tug (at) sb's** ~ toucher *or* faire vibrer les cordes sensibles de qn.
heartthrob ['hɑːtθrɔb] *n* idole *f*.
heart-to-heart ['hɑːt'tə'hɑːt] *adj, adv* à cœur ouvert.
heart transplant *n* greffe *f* du cœur.
heartwarming ['hɑːtwɔːmɪŋ] *adj* réconfortant(e).
hearty ['hɑːtɪ] *adj* chaleureux(euse); robuste; vigoureux(euse).
heat [hiːt] *n* chaleur *f*; (*fig*) ardeur *f*, feu *m*; (*SPORT*: *also*: **qualifying** ~) éliminatoire *f*; (*ZOOL*): **in** *or* (*BRIT*) **on** ~ en chaleur ♦ *vt* chauffer.
▶**heat up** *vi* (*liquids*) chauffer; (*room*) se réchauffer ♦ *vt* réchauffer.
heated ['hiːtɪd] *adj* chauffé(e); (*fig*) passionné(e); échauffé(e), excité(e).

heater ['hiːtə*] *n* appareil *m* de chauffage; radiateur *m*.
heath [hiːθ] *n* (*BRIT*) lande *f*.
heathen ['hiːðn] *adj, n* païen(ne).
heather ['hɛðə*] *n* bruyère *f*.
heating ['hiːtɪŋ] *n* chauffage *m*.
heat-resistant ['hiːtrɪzɪstənt] *adj* résistant(e) à la chaleur.
heat-seeking ['hiːtsiːkɪŋ] *adj* guidé(e) par infrarouge.
heatstroke ['hiːtstrəuk] *n* coup *m* de chaleur.
heatwave ['hiːtweɪv] *n* vague *f* de chaleur.
heave [hiːv] *vt* soulever (avec effort) ♦ *vi* se soulever; (*retch*) avoir des haut-le-cœur ♦ *n* (*push*) poussée *f*; **to** ~ **a sigh** pousser un gros soupir.
heaven ['hɛvn] *n* ciel *m*, paradis *m*; ~ **forbid!** surtout pas!; **thank** ~! Dieu merci!; **for** ~**'s sake!** (*pleading*) je vous en prie!; (*protesting*) mince alors!
heavenly ['hɛvnlɪ] *adj* céleste, divin(e).
heavily ['hɛvɪlɪ] *adv* lourdement; (*drink, smoke*) beaucoup; (*sleep, sigh*) profondément.
heavy ['hɛvɪ] *adj* lourd(e); (*work, rain, user, eater*) gros(se); (*drinker, smoker*) grand(e); **it's** ~ **going** ça ne va pas tout seul, c'est pénible.
heavy cream *n* (*US*) crème fraîche épaisse.
heavy-duty ['hɛvɪ'djuːtɪ] *adj* à usage intensif.
heavy goods vehicle (HGV) *n* (*BRIT*) poids lourd *m* (P.L.).
heavy-handed ['hɛvɪ'hændɪd] *adj* (*fig*) maladroit(e), qui manque de tact.
heavy metal *n* (*MUS*) heavy metal *m*.
heavy-set ['hɛvɪ'sɛt] *adj* (*esp US*) costaud(e).
heavyweight ['hɛvɪweɪt] *n* (*SPORT*) poids lourd.
Hebrew ['hiːbruː] *adj* hébraïque ♦ *n* (*LING*) hébreu *m*.
Hebrides ['hɛbrɪdiːz] *n*: **the** ~ les Hébrides *fpl*.
heck [hɛk] *n* (*col*): **why the** ~ ...? pourquoi diable ...?; **a** ~ **of a lot** une sacrée quantité; **he has done a** ~ **of a lot for us** il a vraiment beaucoup fait pour nous.
heckle ['hɛkl] *vt* interpeller (*un orateur*).
heckler ['hɛklə*] *n* interrupteur *m*; élément perturbateur.
hectare ['hɛktɑː*] *n* (*BRIT*) hectare *m*.
hectic ['hɛktɪk] *adj* agité(e), trépidant(e); (*busy*) trépidant.
hector ['hɛktə*] *vt* rudoyer, houspiller.
he'd [hiːd] = **he would, he had**.
hedge [hɛdʒ] *n* haie *f* ♦ *vi* se défiler ♦ *vt*: **to** ~ **one's bets** (*fig*) se couvrir; **as a** ~ **against inflation** pour se prémunir contre l'inflation.
▶**hedge in** *vt* entourer d'une haie.
hedgehog ['hɛdʒhɔg] *n* hérisson *m*.
hedgerow ['hɛdʒrəu] *n* haie(s) *f(pl)*.
hedonism ['hiːdənɪzəm] *n* hédonisme *m*.
heed [hiːd] *vt* (*also*: **take** ~ **of**) tenir compte de, prendre garde à.
heedless ['hiːdlɪs] *adj* insouciant(e).

heel [hi:l] n talon m ♦ vt (shoe) retalonner; **to bring to ~** (dog) faire venir à ses pieds; (fig: person) rappeler à l'ordre; **to take to one's ~s** prendre ses jambes à son cou.

hefty ['hɛftɪ] adj (person) costaud(e); (parcel) lourd(e); (piece, price) gros(se).

heifer ['hɛfə*] n génisse f.

height [haɪt] n (of person) taille f, grandeur f; (of object) hauteur f; (of plane, mountain) altitude f; (high ground) hauteur, éminence f; (fig: of glory) sommet m; (: of stupidity) comble m; **what ~ are you?** combien mesurez-vous?, quelle est votre taille?; **of average ~** de taille moyenne; **to be afraid of ~s** être sujet(te) au vertige; **it's the ~ of fashion** c'est le dernier cri.

heighten ['haɪtn] vt hausser, surélever; (fig) augmenter.

heinous ['heɪnəs] adj odieux(euse), atroce.

heir [ɛə*] n héritier m.

heir apparent n héritier présomptif.

heiress ['ɛərɛs] n héritière f.

heirloom ['ɛəlu:m] n meuble m (or bijou m or tableau m) de famille.

heist [haɪst] n (US col: hold-up) casse m.

held [hɛld] pt, pp of **hold**.

helicopter ['hɛlɪkɔptə*] n hélicoptère m.

heliport ['hɛlɪpɔ:t] n (AVIAT) héliport m.

helium ['hi:lɪəm] n hélium m.

hell [hɛl] n enfer m; **a ~ of a ...** (col) un(e) sacré(e) ...; **oh ~!** (col) merde!

he'll [hi:l] = he will, he shall.

hell-bent [hɛl'bɛnt] adj (col): **to be ~ on doing sth** vouloir à tout prix faire qch.

hellish ['hɛlɪʃ] adj infernal(e).

hello [hə'ləu] excl bonjour!; salut! (to sb one addresses as "tu"); (surprise) tiens!

helm [hɛlm] n (NAUT) barre f.

helmet ['hɛlmɪt] n casque m.

helmsman ['hɛlmzmən] n timonier m.

help [hɛlp] n aide f; (charwoman) femme f de ménage; (assistant etc) employé/e ♦ vt aider; **~!** au secours!; **~ yourself (to bread)** servez-vous (de pain); **can I ~ you?** (in shop) vous désirez?; **with the ~ of** (person) avec l'aide de; (tool etc) à l'aide de; **to be of ~ to sb** être utile à qn; **to ~ sb (to) do sth** aider qn à faire qch; **I can't ~ saying** je ne peux pas m'empêcher de dire; **he can't ~ it** il ne peut pas s'en empêcher.

helper ['hɛlpə*] n aide m/f, assistant/e.

helpful ['hɛlpful] adj serviable, obligeant(e); (useful) utile.

helping ['hɛlpɪŋ] n portion f.

helping hand n coup m de main; **to give sb a ~** prêter main-forte à qn.

helpless ['hɛlplɪs] adj impuissant(e); (baby) sans défense.

helplessly ['hɛlplɪslɪ] adv (watch) sans pouvoir rien faire.

helpline ['hɛlplaɪn] n numéro téléphonique que l'on peut appeler pour obtenir une assistance sociale, médicale, judiciaire etc ou des renseignements sur un produit commercial.

Helsinki ['hɛlsɪŋkɪ] n Helsinki.

helter-skelter ['hɛltə'skɛltə*] n (BRIT: at amusement park) toboggan m.

hem [hɛm] n ourlet m ♦ vt ourler.

▶**hem in** vt cerner; **to feel ~med in** (fig) avoir l'impression d'étouffer, se sentir oppressé(e) or écrasé(e).

he-man ['hi:mæn] n (col) macho m.

hematology ['hi:mə'tɔlədʒɪ] n (US) = **haematology**.

hemisphere ['hɛmɪsfɪə*] n hémisphère m.

hemlock ['hɛmlɔk] n cigüe f.

hemoglobin ['hi:mə'gləubɪn] n (US) = **haemoglobin**.

hemophilia ['hi:mə'fɪlɪə] n (US) = **haemophilia**.

hemorrhage ['hɛmərɪdʒ] n (US) = **haemorrhage**.

hemorrhoids ['hɛmərɔɪdz] npl (US) = **haemorrhoids**.

hemp [hɛmp] n chanvre m.

hen [hɛn] n poule f; (female bird) femelle f.

hence [hɛns] adv (therefore) d'où, de là; **2 years ~** d'ici 2 ans.

henceforth [hɛns'fɔ:θ] adv dorénavant.

henchman ['hɛntʃmən] n (pej) acolyte m, séide m.

henna ['hɛnə] n henné m.

hen party n (col) réunion f or fête f entre femmes.

henpecked ['hɛnpɛkt] adj dominé par sa femme.

hepatitis [hɛpə'taɪtɪs] n hépatite f.

her [hə:*] pron (direct) la, l' + vowel or h mute; (indirect) lui; (stressed, after prep) elle; see note at **she** ♦ adj son(sa), ses pl; **I see ~** je la vois; **give ~ a book** donne-lui un livre; **after ~** après elle.

herald ['hɛrəld] n héraut m ♦ vt annoncer.

heraldic [hɛ'rældɪk] adj héraldique.

heraldry ['hɛrəldrɪ] n héraldique f; (coat of arms) blason m.

herb [hə:b] n herbe f; **~s** npl (CULIN) fines herbes.

herbaceous [hə:'beɪʃəs] adj herbacé(e).

herbal ['hə:bl] adj à base de plantes; **~ tea** tisane f.

herbicide ['hə:bɪsaɪd] n herbicide m.

herd [hə:d] n troupeau m; (of wild animals, swine) troupeau, troupe f ♦ vt (drive: animals, people) mener, conduire; (gather) rassembler; **~ed together** parqués (comme du bétail).

here [hɪə*] adv ici ♦ excl tiens!, tenez!; **~!** présent!; **~ is, ~ are** voici; **~'s my sister** voici ma sœur; **~ he/she is** le/la voici; **~ she comes** la voici qui vient; **come ~!** viens ici!; **~ and there** ici et là.

hereabouts ['hɪərə'bauts] adv par ici, dans les parages.

hereafter [hɪər'ɑːftə*] _adv_ après, plus tard; ci-après ♦ _n_: **the** ~ l'au-delà _m_.
hereby [hɪə'baɪ] _adv_ (_in letter_) par la présente.
hereditary [hɪ'redɪtrɪ] _adj_ héréditaire.
heredity [hɪ'redɪtɪ] _n_ hérédité _f_.
heresy ['herəsɪ] _n_ hérésie _f_.
heretic ['herətɪk] _n_ hérétique _m/f_.
heretical [hɪ'retɪkl] _adj_ hérétique.
herewith [hɪə'wɪð] _adv_ avec ceci, ci-joint.
heritage ['herɪtɪdʒ] _n_ héritage _m_, patrimoine _m_; **our national** ~ notre patrimoine national.
hermetically [hə:'metɪklɪ] _adv_ hermétiquement; ~ **sealed** hermétiquement fermé _or_ clos.
hermit ['hə:mɪt] _n_ ermite _m_.
hernia ['hə:nɪə] _n_ hernie _f_.
hero, _pl_ ~**es** ['hɪərəʊ] _n_ héros _m_.
heroic [hɪ'rəʊɪk] _adj_ héroïque.
heroin ['herəʊɪn] _n_ héroïne _f_.
heroin addict _n_ héroïnomane _m/f_.
heroine ['herəʊɪn] _n_ héroïne _f_ (_femme_).
heroism ['herəʊɪzəm] _n_ héroïsme _m_.
heron ['herən] _n_ héron _m_.
hero worship _n_ culte _m_ (du héros).
herring ['herɪŋ] _n_ hareng _m_.
hers [hə:z] _pron_ le(la) sien(ne), les siens(siennes); **a friend of** ~ un(e) ami(e) à elle, un(e) de ses ami(e)s; **this is** ~ c'est à elle, c'est le sien.
herself [hə:'self] _pron_ (_reflexive_) se; (_emphatic_) elle-même; (_after prep_) elle.
Herts [hɑːts] _abbr_ (_BRIT_) = **Hertfordshire**.
he's [hiːz] = **he is, he has**.
hesitant ['hezɪtənt] _adj_ hésitant(e), indécis(e); **to be** ~ **about doing sth** hésiter à faire qch.
hesitate ['hezɪteɪt] _vi_: **to** ~ (**about/to do**) hésiter (sur/à faire).
hesitation [hezɪ'teɪʃən] _n_ hésitation _f_; **I have no** ~ **in saying (that)** ... je n'hésiterai pas à dire (que) ....
hessian ['hesɪən] _n_ (toile _f_ de) jute _m_.
heterogeneous ['hetərə'dʒiːnɪəs] _adj_ hétérogène.
heterosexual ['hetərəʊ'seksjuəl] _adj_, _n_ hétérosexuel(le).
het up [het'ʌp] _adj_ (_col_) agité(e), excité(e).
HEW _n abbr_ (_US_: = _Department of Health, Education and Welfare_) ministère de la santé publique, de l'enseignement et du bien-être.
hew [hjuː] _vt_ tailler (_à la hache_).
hex [heks] (_US_) _n_ sort _m_ ♦ _vt_ jeter un sort sur.
hexagon ['heksəgən] _n_ hexagone _m_.
hexagonal [hek'sægənl] _adj_ hexagonal(e).
hey [heɪ] _excl_ hé!
heyday ['heɪdeɪ] _n_: **the** ~ **of** l'âge _m_ d'or de, les beaux jours de.
HF _n abbr_ (= _high frequency_) HF _f_.
HGV _n abbr_ = **heavy goods vehicle**.
HI _abbr_ (_US_) = **Hawaii**.
hi [haɪ] _excl_ salut!
hiatus [haɪ'eɪtəs] _n_ trou _m_, lacune _f_; (_LING_) hiatus _m_.

hibernate ['haɪbəneɪt] _vi_ hiberner.
hibernation [haɪbə'neɪʃən] _n_ hibernation _f_.
hiccough, hiccup ['hɪkʌp] _vi_ hoqueter ♦ _n_ hoquet _m_; **to have (the)** ~**s** avoir le hoquet.
hick [hɪk] _n_ (_US col_) plouc _m_, péquenaud/e.
hid [hɪd] _pt of_ **hide**.
hidden ['hɪdn] _pp of_ **hide** ♦ _adj_: **there are no** ~ **extras** absolument tout est compris dans le prix; ~ **agenda** intentions non déclarées.
hide [haɪd] _n_ (_skin_) peau _f_ ♦ _vb_ (_pt_ **hid**, _pp_ **hidden** [hɪd, 'hɪdn]) _vt_: **to** ~ **sth (from sb)** cacher qch (à qn); (_feelings, truth_) dissimuler qch (à qn) ♦ _vi_: **to** ~ (**from sb**) se cacher de qn.
hide-and-seek ['haɪdən'siːk] _n_ cache-cache _m_.
hideaway ['haɪdəweɪ] _n_ cachette _f_.
hideous ['hɪdɪəs] _adj_ hideux(euse); atroce.
hide-out ['haɪdaut] _n_ cachette _f_.
hiding ['haɪdɪŋ] _n_ (_beating_) correction _f_, volée _f_ de coups; **to be in** ~ (_concealed_) se tenir caché(e).
hiding place _n_ cachette _f_.
hierarchy ['haɪərɑːkɪ] _n_ hiérarchie _f_.
hieroglyphic [haɪərə'glɪfɪk] _adj_ hiéroglyphique; ~**s** _npl_ hiéroglyphes _mpl_.
hi-fi ['haɪfaɪ] _adj_, _n abbr_ (= _high fidelity_) hi-fi (_f_) _inv_.
higgledy-piggledy ['hɪgldɪ'pɪgldɪ] _adv_ pêlemêle, dans le plus grand désordre.
high [haɪ] _adj_ haut(e); (_speed, respect, number_) grand(e); (_price_) élevé(e); (_wind_) fort(e), violent(e); (_voice_) aigu(aiguë); (_col: person: on drugs_) défoncé(e), fait(e); (_: on drink_) soûl(e), bourré(e); (_BRIT CULIN: meat, game_) faisandé(e); (_: spoilt_) avarié(e) ♦ _adv_ haut, en haut ♦ _n_: **exports have reached a new** ~ les exportations ont atteint un nouveau record; **20 m** ~ haut(e) de 20 m; **to pay a** ~ **price for sth** payer cher pour qch.
highball ['haɪbɔːl] _n_ (_US_) whisky _m_ à l'eau avec des glaçons.
highboy ['haɪbɔɪ] _n_ (_US_) grande commode.
highbrow ['haɪbrau] _adj_, _n_ intellectuel(le).
highchair ['haɪtʃeə*] _n_ chaise haute (_pour enfant_).
high-class ['haɪ'klɑːs] _adj_ (_neighbourhood, hotel_) chic _inv_, de grand standing; (_performance etc_) de haut niveau.
High Court _n_ (_LAW_) cour _f_ suprême.

_La_ **High Court** _en Grande-Bretagne est la plus haute cour de justice à laquelle les affaires les plus graves telles que le meurtre et le viol sont soumises et où elles sont jugées devant un jury._

higher ['haɪə*] _adj_ (_form of life, study etc_) supérieur(e) ♦ _adv_ plus haut.
higher education _n_ études supérieures.
highfalutin [haɪfə'luːtɪn] _adj_ (_col_) affecté(e).
high finance _n_ la haute finance.
high-flier, high-flyer [haɪ'flaɪə*] _n_ (_fig: ambitious_) ambitieux/euse; (_: gifted_) personne particulièrement douée et promise à un

avenir brillant.

high-flying [haɪˈflaɪɪŋ] *adj* (*fig*) ambitieux(euse), de haut niveau.

high-handed [haɪˈhændɪd] *adj* très autoritaire; très cavalier(ière).

high-heeled [haɪˈhiːld] *adj* à hauts talons.

highjack [ˈhaɪdʒæk] *n*, *vt* = **hijack**.

high jump *n* (*SPORT*) saut *m* en hauteur.

highlands [ˈhaɪləndz] *npl* région montagneuse; **the H~** (*in Scotland*) les Highlands *mpl*.

high-level [ˈhaɪlɛvl] *adj* (*talks etc*) à un haut niveau; **~ language** (*COMPUT*) langage évolué.

highlight [ˈhaɪlaɪt] *n* (*fig: of event*) point culminant ♦ *vt* faire ressortir, souligner; **~s** *npl* (*hairstyle*) reflets *mpl*.

highlighter [ˈhaɪlaɪtə*] *n* (*pen*) surligneur (lumineux).

highly [ˈhaɪlɪ] *adv* très, fort, hautement; **~ paid** très bien payé(e); **to speak ~ of** dire beaucoup de bien de.

highly-strung [ˈhaɪlɪˈstrʌŋ] *adj* nerveux(euse), toujours tendu(e).

High Mass *n* grand-messe *f*.

highness [ˈhaɪnɪs] *n* hauteur *f*; **Her H~** son Altesse *f*.

high-pitched [haɪˈpɪtʃt] *adj* aigu(ë).

high point *n*: **the ~ (of)** le clou (de), le point culminant (de).

high-powered [ˈhaɪˈpauəd] *adj* (*engine*) performant(e); (*fig: person*) dynamique; (: *job, businessman*) très important(e).

high-pressure [ˈhaɪprɛʃə*] *adj* à haute pression.

high-rise block [ˈhaɪraɪz-] *n* tour *f* (d'habitation).

high school *n* lycée *m*; (*US*) établissement *m* d'enseignement supérieur.

---

*Une **high school** est un établissement d'enseignement secondaire. Aux États-Unis, il y a la Junior High School, qui correspond au collège, et la Senior High School, qui correspond au lycée. En Grande-Bretagne, c'est un nom que l'on donne parfois aux écoles secondaires; voir **elementary school***

---

high season *n* (*BRIT*) haute saison *f*.

high spirits *npl* pétulance *f*; **to be in ~** être plein(e) d'entrain.

high street *n* (*BRIT*) grand-rue *f*.

highway [ˈhaɪweɪ] *n* grand'route *f*, route nationale; **the information ~** l'autoroute *f* de l'information.

Highway Code *n* (*BRIT*) code *m* de la route.

highwayman [ˈhaɪweɪmən] *n* voleur *m* de grand chemin.

hijack [ˈhaɪdʒæk] *vt* détourner (*par la force*) ♦ *n* (*also*: **~ing**) détournement *m* (d'avion).

hijacker [ˈhaɪdʒækə*] *n* auteur *m* d'un détournement d'avion, pirate *m* de l'air.

hike [haɪk] *vi* aller à pied ♦ *n* excursion *f* à

pied, randonnée *f*; (*col: in prices etc*) augmentation *f* ♦ *vt* (*col*) augmenter.

hiker [ˈhaɪkə*] *n* promeneur/euse, excursionniste *m/f*.

hiking [ˈhaɪkɪŋ] *n* excursions *fpl* à pied, randonnée *f*.

hilarious [hɪˈlɛərɪəs] *adj* (*behaviour, event*) désopilant(e).

hilarity [hɪˈlærɪtɪ] *n* hilarité *f*.

hill [hɪl] *n* colline *f*; (*fairly high*) montagne *f*; (*on road*) côte *f*.

hillbilly [ˈhɪlbɪlɪ] *n* (*US*) montagnard/e du sud des USA; (*pej*) péquenaud *m*.

hillock [ˈhɪlək] *n* petite colline, butte *f*.

hillside [ˈhɪlsaɪd] *n* (flanc *m* de) coteau *m*.

hill start *n* (*AUT*) démarrage *m* en côte.

hilly [ˈhɪlɪ] *adj* vallonné(e); montagneux(euse); (*road*) à fortes côtes.

hilt [hɪlt] *n* (*of sword*) garde *f*; **to the ~** (*fig: support*) à fond.

him [hɪm] *pron* (*direct*) le, l' + *vowel or h mute*; (*stressed, indirect, after prep*) lui; **I see ~** je le vois; **give ~ a book** donne-lui un livre; **after ~** après lui.

Himalayas [hɪməˈleɪəz] *npl*: **the ~** l'Himalaya *m*.

himself [hɪmˈsɛlf] *pron* (*reflexive*) se; (*emphatic*) lui-même; (*after prep*) lui.

hind [haɪnd] *adj* de derrière ♦ *n* biche *f*.

hinder [ˈhɪndə*] *vt* gêner; (*delay*) retarder; (*prevent*): **to ~ sb from doing** empêcher qn de faire.

hindquarters [ˈhaɪndˈkwɔːtəz] *npl* (*ZOOL*) arrière-train *m*.

hindrance [ˈhɪndrəns] *n* gêne *f*, obstacle *m*.

hindsight [ˈhaɪndsaɪt] *n* bon sens après coup; **with the benefit of ~** avec du recul, rétrospectivement.

Hindu [ˈhɪnduː] *n* Hindou/e.

hinge [hɪndʒ] *n* charnière *f* ♦ *vi* (*fig*): **to ~ on** dépendre de.

hint [hɪnt] *n* allusion *f*; (*advice*) conseil *m* ♦ *vt*: **to ~ that** insinuer que ♦ *vi*: **to ~ at** faire une allusion à; **to drop a ~** faire une allusion *or* insinuation; **give me a ~** (*clue*) mettez-moi sur la voie, donnez-moi une indication.

hip [hɪp] *n* hanche *f*; (*BOT*) fruit *m* de l'églantier *or* du rosier.

hip flask *n* flacon *m* (pour la poche).

hip hop *n* hip hop *m*.

hippie, hippy [ˈhɪpɪ] *n* hippie *m/f*.

hip pocket *n* poche-revolver *f*.

hippopotamus, *pl* **~es** *or* **hippopotami** [hɪpəˈpɔtəməs, -ˈpɔtəmaɪ] *n* hippopotame *m*.

hippy [ˈhɪpɪ] *n* = **hippie**.

hire [ˈhaɪə*] *vt* (*BRIT: car, equipment*) louer; (*worker*) embaucher, engager ♦ *n* location *f*; **for ~** à louer; (*taxi*) libre; **on ~** en location.

▶**hire out** *vt* louer.

hire(d) car [ˈhaɪə(d)-] *n* (*BRIT*) voiture louée.

hire purchase (H.P.) *n* (*BRIT*) achat *m* (*or* vente *f*) à tempérament *or* crédit; **to buy sth**

on ~ acheter qch en location-vente.

his [hɪz] *pron* le(la) sien(ne), les siens(siennes) ♦ *adj* son(sa), ses *pl*; **this is** ~ c'est à lui, c'est le sien.

hiss [hɪs] *vi* siffler ♦ *n* sifflement *m*.

histogram ['hɪstəgræm] *n* histogramme *m*.

historian [hɪ'stɔːrɪən] *n* historien/ne.

historic(al) [hɪ'stɔrɪk(l)] *adj* historique.

history ['hɪstərɪ] *n* histoire *f*; **medical** ~ (*of patient*) passé médical.

histrionics [hɪstrɪ'ɔnɪks] *n* gestes *mpl* dramatiques, cinéma *m* (*fig*).

hit [hɪt] *vt* (*pt, pp* hit) frapper; (*knock against*) cogner; (*reach: target*) atteindre, toucher; (*collide with: car*) entrer en collision avec, heurter; (*fig: affect*) toucher; (*find*) tomber sur ♦ *n* coup *m*; (*success*) coup réussi; succès *m*; (*song*) chanson *f* à succès, tube *m*; **to** ~ **it off with sb** bien s'entendre avec qn; **to** ~ **the headlines** être à la une des journaux; **to** ~ **the road** (*col*) se mettre en route.

►**hit back** *vi*: **to** ~ **back at sb** prendre sa revanche sur qn.

►**hit out at** *vt fus* envoyer un coup à; (*fig*) attaquer.

►**hit (up)on** *vt fus* (*answer*) trouver (par hasard); (*solution*) tomber sur (par hasard).

hit-and-miss ['hɪtænd'mɪs] *adj* au petit bonheur (la chance).

hit-and-run driver ['hɪtænd'rʌn-] *n* chauffard *m*.

hitch [hɪtʃ] *vt* (*fasten*) accrocher, attacher; (*also:* ~ **up**) remonter d'une saccade ♦ *n* (*knot*) nœud *m*; (*difficulty*) anicroche *f*, contretemps *m*; **to** ~ **a lift** faire du stop; **technical** ~ incident *m* technique.

►**hitch up** *vt* (*horse, cart*) atteler; *see also* **hitch**.

hitch-hike ['hɪtʃhaɪk] *vi* faire de l'auto-stop.

hitch-hiker ['hɪtʃhaɪkə*] *n* auto-stoppeur/euse.

hi-tech ['haɪ'tɛk] *adj* de pointe ♦ *n* high-tech *m*.

hitherto [hɪðə'tuː] *adv* jusqu'ici, jusqu'à présent.

hit list *n* liste noire.

hitman ['hɪtmæn] *n* (*col*) tueur *m* à gages.

hit-or-miss ['hɪtə'mɪs] *adj* au petit bonheur (la chance); **it's** ~ **whether** ... il est loin d'être certain que ... + *sub*.

hit parade *n* hit parade *m*.

HIV *n abbr* (= *human immunodeficiency virus*) HIV *m*, VIH *m*; ~-**negative/-positive** séronégatif(ive)/séropositif(ive).

hive [haɪv] *n* ruche *f*; **the shop was a** ~ **of activity** (*fig*) le magasin était une véritable ruche.

►**hive off** *vt* (*col*) mettre à part, séparer.

hl *abbr* (= *hectolitre*) hl.

HM *abbr* (= *His (or Her) Majesty*) SM.

HMG *abbr* (*BRIT*) = *His (or Her) Majesty's Government*.

HMI *n abbr* (*BRIT SCOL*) = *His (or Her) Majesty's Inspector*.

HMO *n abbr* (*US*: = *health maintenance organization*) organisme médical assurant un forfait entretien de santé.

HMS *abbr* (*BRIT*) = *His (or Her) Majesty's Ship*.

HMSO *n abbr* (*BRIT*: = *His (or Her) Majesty's Stationery Office*) ≈ Imprimerie nationale.

HNC *n abbr* (*BRIT*: = *Higher National Certificate*) ≈ DUT *m*.

HND *n abbr* (*BRIT*: = *Higher National Diploma*) ≈ licence *f* de sciences et techniques.

hoard [hɔːd] *n* (*of food*) provisions *fpl*, réserves *fpl*; (*of money*) trésor *m* ♦ *vt* amasser.

hoarding ['hɔːdɪŋ] *n* (*BRIT*) panneau *m* d'affichage *or* publicitaire.

hoarfrost ['hɔːfrɔst] *n* givre *m*.

hoarse [hɔːs] *adj* enroué(e).

hoax [həʊks] *n* canular *m*.

hob [hɔb] *n* plaque chauffante.

hobble ['hɔbl] *vi* boitiller.

hobby ['hɔbɪ] *n* passe-temps favori.

hobby-horse ['hɔbɪhɔːs] *n* cheval *m* à bascule; (*fig*) dada *m*.

hobnail(ed) boot ['hɔbneɪl(d)-] *n* chaussure (à semelle) cloutée.

hobnob ['hɔbnɔb] *vi*: **to** ~ **with** frayer avec, fréquenter.

hobo ['həʊbəʊ] *n* (*US*) vagabond *m*.

hock [hɔk] *n* (*BRIT: wine*) vin *m* du Rhin; (*of animal, CULIN*) jarret *m*; (*col*): **to be in** ~ (*person*) avoir des dettes; (*object*) être en gage *or* au clou.

hockey ['hɔkɪ] *n* hockey *m*.

hocus-pocus ['həʊkəs'pəʊkəs] *n* (*trickery*) supercherie *f*; (*words: of magician*) formules *fpl* magiques; (: *jargon*) galimatias *m*.

hod [hɔd] *n* oiseau *m*, hotte *f*.

hodgepodge ['hɔdʒpɔdʒ] *n* = **hotchpotch**.

hoe [həʊ] *n* houe *f*, binette *f* ♦ *vt* (*ground*) biner; (*plants etc*) sarcler.

hog [hɔg] *n* porc (châtré) ♦ *vt* (*fig*) accaparer; **to go the whole** ~ aller jusqu'au bout.

Hogmanay [hɔgmə'neɪ] *n* (*Scottish*) réveillon *m* du jour de l'An, Saint-Sylvestre *f*.

hogwash ['hɔgwɔʃ] *n* (*col*) foutaises *fpl*.

hoist [hɔɪst] *n* palan *m* ♦ *vt* hisser.

hoity-toity [hɔɪtɪ'tɔɪtɪ] *adj* (*col*) prétentieux(euse), qui se donne de grands airs.

hold [həʊld] *vb* (*pt, pp* held) *vt* tenir; (*contain*) contenir; (*keep back*) retenir; (*believe*) maintenir; considérer; (*possess*) avoir; détenir ♦ *vi* (*withstand pressure*) tenir (bon); (*be valid*) valoir ♦ *n* prise *f*; (*fig*) influence *f*; (*NAUT*) cale *f*; **to catch** *or* **get (a)** ~ **of** saisir; **to get** ~ **of** (*fig*) trouver; **to get** ~ **of o.s.** se contrôler; ~ **the line!** (*TEL*) ne quittez pas!; **to** ~ **one's own** (*fig*) (bien) se défendre; **to** ~ **office** (*POL*) avoir un portefeuille; **to** ~ **firm** *or* **fast** tenir bon; **he** ~**s the view that** ... il pense *or* estime que ..., d'après lui ...; **to** ~ **sb responsible for sth** tenir qn pour responsable de qch.

►**hold back** *vt* retenir; (*secret*) cacher; **to** ~

sb **back from doing sth** empêcher qn de faire qch.

►**hold down** vt (person) maintenir à terre; (job) occuper.

►**hold forth** vi pérorer.

►**hold off** vt tenir à distance ♦ vi (rain): **if the rain ~s off** s'il ne pleut pas, s'il ne se met pas à pleuvoir.

►**hold on** vi tenir bon; (wait) attendre; **~ on!** (TEL) ne quittez pas!

►**hold on to** vt fus se cramponner à; (keep) conserver, garder.

►**hold out** vt offrir ♦ vi (resist): **to ~ out (against)** résister (devant), tenir bon (devant).

►**hold over** vt (meeting etc) ajourner, reporter.

►**hold up** vt (raise) lever; (support) soutenir; (delay) retarder; (: traffic) ralentir; (rob) braquer.

holdall ['həuldɔːl] n (BRIT) fourre-tout m inv.

holder ['həuldə*] n (of ticket, record) détenteur/trice; (of office, title, passport etc) titulaire m/f.

holding ['həuldɪŋ] n (share) intérêts mpl; (farm) ferme f.

holding company n holding m.

holdup ['həuldʌp] n (robbery) hold-up m; (delay) retard m; (BRIT: in traffic) embouteillage m.

hole [həul] n trou m ♦ vt trouer, faire un trou dans; **~ in the heart** (MED) communication f interventriculaire; **to pick ~s (in)** (fig) chercher des poux (dans).

►**hole up** vi se terrer.

holiday ['hɔlədɪ] n (BRIT: vacation) vacances fpl; (day off) jour m de congé; (public) jour férié; **to be on ~** être en congé; **tomorrow is a ~** demain c'est fête, un jour de congé demain.

holiday camp n (BRIT: for children) colonie f de vacances; (: also: **holiday centre**) camp m de vacances.

holidaymaker ['hɔlədɪmeɪkə*] n (BRIT) vacancier/ière.

holiday pay n paie f des vacances.

holiday resort n centre m de villégiature or de vacances.

holiday season n période f des vacances.

holiness ['həulɪnɪs] n sainteté f.

holistic [həu'lɪstɪk] adj holiste, holistique.

Holland ['hɔlənd] n Hollande f.

holler ['hɔlə*] vi (col) brailler.

hollow ['hɔləu] adj creux(euse); (fig) faux(fausse) ♦ n creux m; (in land) dépression f (de terrain), cuvette f ♦ vt: **to ~ out** creuser, évider.

holly ['hɔlɪ] n houx m.

hollyhock ['hɔlɪhɔk] n rose trémière.

holocaust ['hɔləkɔːst] n holocauste m.

hologram ['hɔləgræm] n hologramme m.

hols [hɔlz] npl (col) vacances fpl.

holster ['həulstə*] n étui m de revolver.

holy ['həulɪ] adj saint(e); (bread, water) bé-

nit(e); (ground) sacré(e).

Holy Communion n la (sainte) communion.

Holy Ghost, Holy Spirit n Saint-Esprit m.

Holy Land n: **the ~** la Terre Sainte.

holy orders npl ordres (majeurs).

homage ['hɔmɪdʒ] n hommage m; **to pay ~ to** rendre hommage à.

home [həum] n foyer m, maison f; (country) pays natal, patrie f; (institution) maison ♦ adj de famille; (ECON, POL) national(e), intérieur(e); (SPORT: team) qui reçoit; (: match, win) sur leur (or notre) terrain ♦ adv chez soi, à la maison; au pays natal; (right in: nail etc) à fond; **at ~** chez soi, à la maison; **to go** (or **come**) **~** rentrer (chez soi), rentrer à la maison (or au pays); **make yourself at ~** faites comme chez vous; **near my ~** près de chez moi.

►**home in on** vt fus (missiles) se diriger automatiquement vers or sur.

home address n domicile permanent.

home-brew [həum'bruː] n vin m (or bière f) maison.

homecoming ['həumkʌmɪŋ] n retour m (au bercail).

home computer n ordinateur m domestique.

Home Counties npl les comtés autour de Londres.

home economics n économie f domestique.

home ground n: **to be on ~** être sur son terrain.

home-grown ['həumgrəun] adj (not foreign) du pays; (from garden) du jardin.

home help n (BRIT) aide-ménagère f.

homeland ['həumlænd] n patrie f.

homeless ['həumlɪs] adj sans foyer, sans abri; **the ~** npl les sans-abri mpl.

home loan n prêt m sur hypothèque.

homely ['həumlɪ] adj simple, sans prétention; accueillant(e).

home-made [həum'meɪd] adj fait(e) à la maison.

Home Office n (BRIT) ministère m de l'Intérieur.

homeopathy etc [həumɪ'ɔpəθɪ] (US) = **homoeopathy** etc.

homeowner ['həuməunə*] n propriétaire occupant.

home page n (COMPUT) page f d'accueil.

home rule n autonomie f.

Home Secretary n (BRIT) ministre m de l'Intérieur.

homesick ['həumsɪk] adj: **to be ~** avoir le mal du pays; (missing one's family) s'ennuyer de sa famille.

homestead ['həumstɛd] n propriété f; (farm) ferme f.

home town n ville natale.

home truth n: **to tell sb a few ~s** dire ses quatre vérités à qn.

homeward ['həumwəd] adj (journey) du retour ♦ adv = **homewards**.

homewards ['həumwədz] *adv* vers la maison.
homework ['həumwə:k] *n* devoirs *mpl*.
homicidal [həmɪ'saɪdl] *adj* homicide.
homicide ['həmɪsaɪd] *n* (*US*) homicide *m*.
homily ['hɒmɪlɪ] *n* homélie *f*.
homing ['həumɪŋ] *adj* (*device, missile*) à tête chercheuse; ~ **pigeon** pigeon voyageur.
homoeopath, (*US*) **homeopath** ['həumɪəupæθ] *n* homéopathe *m/f*.
homoeopathy, (*US*) **homeopathy** [həumɪ'ɒpəθɪ] *n* homéopathie *f*.
homogeneous [hɒməu'dʒi:nɪəs] *adj* homogène.
homogenize [hɒ'mɒdʒənaɪz] *vt* homogénéiser.
homosexual [hɒməu'sɛksjuəl] *adj, n* homosexuel(le).
Hon. *abbr* (= *honourable, honorary*) *dans un titre.*
Honduras [hɒn'djuərəs] *n* Honduras *m*.
hone [həun] *n* pierre *f* à aiguiser ♦ *vt* affûter, aiguiser.
honest ['ɒnɪst] *adj* honnête; (*sincere*) franc(franche); **to be quite ~ with you** ... à dire vrai ....
honestly ['ɒnɪstlɪ] *adv* honnêtement; franchement.
honesty ['ɒnɪstɪ] *n* honnêteté *f*.
honey ['hʌnɪ] *n* miel *m*; (*US col: darling*) chéri/e.
honeycomb ['hʌnɪkəum] *n* rayon *m* de miel; (*pattern*) nid *m* d'abeilles, motif alvéolé ♦ *vt* (*fig*): **to ~ with** cribler de.
honeymoon ['hʌnɪmu:n] *n* lune *f* de miel, voyage *m* de noces.
honeysuckle ['hʌnɪsʌkl] *n* chèvrefeuille *m*.
Hong Kong ['hɒŋ'kɒŋ] *n* Hong Kong.
honk [hɒŋk] *n* (*AUT*) coup *m* de klaxon ♦ *vi* klaxonner.
Honolulu [hɒnə'lu:lu:] *n* Honolulu *m*.
honorary ['ɒnərərɪ] *adj* honoraire; (*duty, title*) honorifique.
honour, (*US*) **honor** ['ɒnə*] *vt* honorer ♦ *n* honneur *m*; **in ~ of** en l'honneur de.
hono(u)rable ['ɒnərəbl] *adj* honorable.
hono(u)r-bound ['ɒnə'baund] *adj*: **to be ~ to do** se devoir de faire.
hono(u)rs degree ['ɒnəz-] *n* (*SCOL*) ≈ licence *f*.

Un **honours degree** *est un diplôme universitaire que l'on reçoit après trois années d'études en Angleterre et quatre années en Écosse. Les mentions qui l'accompagnent sont, par ordre décroissant: "first class" (très bien/bien), "upper second class" (assez bien), "lower second class" (passable), et "third class" (diplôme sans mention). Le titulaire d'un honours degree a un titre qu'il peut mettre à la suite de son nom, par exemple: Peter Jones BA Hons; voir* **ordinary degree**

---

honours list *n* (*BRIT*): **the ~** la liste des personnes auxquelles une distinction honorifique est conférée par le souverain.

---

*L'*honours list *est la liste des citoyens du Royaume-Uni et du Commonwealth auxquels le souverain confère un titre ou une décoration. Cette liste est préparée par le Premier ministre et paraît deux fois par an, au Nouvel An et lors de l'anniversaire officiel du règne du souverain. Des personnes qui se sont distinguées dans le monde des affaires, des sports et des médias, ainsi que dans les forces armées, mais également des citoyens "ordinaires" qui se consacrent à des œuvres de charité sont ainsi récompensées.*

Hons. *abbr* (*SCOL*) = **hono(u)rs degree**.
hood [hud] *n* capuchon *m*; (*BRIT AUT*) capote *f*; (*US AUT*) capot *m*; (*col*) truand *m*.
hoodlum ['hu:dləm] *n* truand *m*.
hoodwink ['hudwɪŋk] *vt* tromper.
hoof, *pl* ~**s** *or* **hooves** [hu:f, hu:vz] *n* sabot *m*.
hook [huk] *n* crochet *m*; (*on dress*) agrafe *f*; (*for fishing*) hameçon *m* ♦ *vt* accrocher; (*dress*) agrafer; ~ **and eye** agrafe; **by ~ or by crook** de gré ou de force, coûte que coûte; **to be ~ed (on)** (*col*) être accroché(e) (par); (*person*) être dingue (de).
►**hook up** *vt* (*RADIO, TV etc*) faire un duplex entre.
hooligan ['hu:lɪgən] *n* voyou *m*.
hoop [hu:p] *n* cerceau *m*; (*of barrel*) cercle *m*.
hoot [hu:t] *vi* (*AUT*) klaxonner; (*siren*) mugir; (*owl*) hululer ♦ *vt* (*jeer at*) huer ♦ *n* huée *f*; coup *m* de klaxon; mugissement *m*; hululement *m*; **to ~ with laughter** rire aux éclats.
hooter ['hu:tə*] *n* (*BRIT AUT*) klaxon *m*; (*NAUT, factory*) sirène *f*.
hoover ['hu:və*] *n* ® (*BRIT*) aspirateur *m* ♦ *vt* (*room*) passer l'aspirateur dans; (*carpet*) passer l'aspirateur sur.
hooves [hu:vz] *npl of* **hoof**.
hop [hɒp] *vi* sauter; (*on one foot*) sauter à cloche-pied ♦ *n* saut *m*.
hope [həup] *vt, vi* espérer ♦ *n* espoir *m*; **I ~ so** je l'espère; **I ~ not** j'espère que non.
hopeful ['həupful] *adj* (*person*) plein(e) d'espoir; (*situation*) prometteur(euse), encourageant(e); **I'm ~ that she'll manage to come** j'ai bon espoir qu'elle pourra venir.
hopefully ['həupfulɪ] *adv* avec espoir, avec optimisme; ~, **they'll come back** espérons bien qu'ils reviendront.
hopeless ['həuplɪs] *adj* désespéré(e), sans espoir; (*useless*) nul(le).
hopelessly ['həuplɪslɪ] *adv* (*live etc*) sans espoir; ~ **confused** *etc* complètement désorienté *etc*.
hopper ['hɒpə*] *n* (*chute*) trémie *f*.
hops [hɒps] *npl* houblon *m*.
horde [hɔ:d] *n* horde *f*.
horizon [hə'raɪzn] *n* horizon *m*.

horizontal [hɔrɪ'zɔntl] *adj* horizontal(e).
hormone ['hɔːməʊn] *n* hormone *f*.
hormone replacement therapy *n* hormonothérapie substitutive, traitement hormono-supplétif.
horn [hɔːn] *n* corne *f*; (*MUS*) cor *m*; (*AUT*) klaxon *m*.
horned [hɔːnd] *adj* (*animal*) à cornes.
hornet ['hɔːnɪt] *n* frelon *m*.
horny ['hɔːnɪ] *adj* corné(e); (*hands*) calleux(euse); (*col: aroused*) excité(e).
horoscope ['hɔrəskəʊp] *n* horoscope *m*.
horrendous [hə'rendəs] *adj* horrible, affreux(euse).
horrible ['hɔrɪbl] *adj* horrible, affreux(euse).
horrid ['hɔrɪd] *adj* méchant(e), désagréable.
horrific [hɔ'rɪfɪk] *adj* horrible.
horrify ['hɔrɪfaɪ] *vt* horrifier.
horrifying ['hɔrɪfaɪɪŋ] *adj* horrifiant(e).
horror ['hɔrə*] *n* horreur *f*.
horror film *n* film *m* d'épouvante.
horror-struck ['hɔrəstrʌk], **horror-stricken** ['hɔrəstrɪkn] *adj* horrifié(e).
hors d'œuvre [ɔː'dəːvrə] *n* hors d'œuvre *m*.
horse [hɔːs] *n* cheval *m*.
horseback ['hɔːsbæk]: **on ~** *adj, adv* à cheval.
horsebox ['hɔːsbɔks] *n* van *m*.
horse chestnut *n* marron *m* (d'Inde).
horse-drawn ['hɔːsdrɔːn] *adj* tiré(e) par des chevaux.
horsefly ['hɔːsflaɪ] *n* taon *m*.
horseman ['hɔːsmən] *n* cavalier *m*.
horsemanship ['hɔːsmənʃɪp] *n* talents *mpl* de cavalier.
horseplay ['hɔːspleɪ] *n* chahut *m* (*blagues etc*).
horsepower (hp) ['hɔːspaʊə*] *n* puissance *f* (en chevaux); cheval-vapeur *m* (CV).
horse-racing ['hɔːsreɪsɪŋ] *n* courses *fpl* de chevaux.
horseradish ['hɔːsrædɪʃ] *n* raifort *m*.
horseshoe ['hɔːsʃuː] *n* fer *m* à cheval.
horse show *n* concours *m* hippique.
horse-trading ['hɔːstreɪdɪŋ] *n* maquignonage *m*.
horse trials *npl* = **horse show**.
horsewhip ['hɔːswɪp] *vt* cravacher.
horsewoman ['hɔːswʊmən] *n* cavalière *f*.
horsey ['hɔːsɪ] *adj* féru(e) d'équitation *or* de cheval; (*appearance*) chevalin(e).
horticulture ['hɔːtɪkʌltʃə*] *n* horticulture *f*.
hose [həʊz] *n* tuyau *m*; (*also*: **garden ~**) tuyau d'arrosage.
▶**hose down** *vt* laver au jet.
hosepipe ['həʊzpaɪp] *n* tuyau *m*; (*in garden*) tuyau d'arrosage; (*for fire*) tuyau d'incendie.
hosiery ['həʊzɪərɪ] *n* (*in shop*) (rayon *m* des) bas *mpl*.
hospice ['hɔspɪs] *n* hospice *m*.
hospitable ['hɔspɪtəbl] *adj* hospitalier(ière).
hospital ['hɔspɪtl] *n* hôpital *m*; **in ~**, (*US*) **in the ~** à l'hôpital.
hospitality [hɔspɪ'tælɪtɪ] *n* hospitalité *f*.

hospitalize ['hɔspɪtəlaɪz] *vt* hospitaliser.
host [həʊst] *n* hôte *m*; (*in hotel etc*) patron *m*; (*TV, RADIO*) présentateur/trice, animateur/trice; (*large number*): **a ~ of** une foule de; (*REL*) hostie *f* ♦ *vt* (*TV programme*) présenter, animer.
hostage ['hɔstɪdʒ] *n* otage *m*.
host country *n* pays *m* d'accueil, pays-hôte *m*.
hostel ['hɔstl] *n* foyer *m*; (*also*: **youth ~**) auberge *f* de jeunesse.
hostelling ['hɔstlɪŋ] *n*: **to go (youth) ~** faire une virée *or* randonnée en séjournant dans des auberges de jeunesse.
hostess ['həʊstɪs] *n* hôtesse *f*; (*AVIAT*) hôtesse de l'air; (*in nightclub*) entraîneuse *f*.
hostile ['hɔstaɪl] *adj* hostile.
hostility [hɔ'stɪlɪtɪ] *n* hostilité *f*.
hot [hɔt] *adj* chaud(e); (*as opposed to only warm*) très chaud; (*spicy*) fort(e); (*fig*) acharné(e); brûlant(e); violent(e), passionné(e); **to be ~** (*person*) avoir chaud; (*thing*) être (très) chaud; (*weather*) faire chaud.
▶**hot up** (*BRIT col*) *vi* (*situation*) devenir tendu(e); (*party*) s'animer ♦ *vt* (*pace*) accélérer, forcer; (*engine*) gonfler.
hot-air balloon [hɔt'ɛə-] *n* montgolfière *f*, ballon *m*.
hotbed ['hɔtbed] *n* (*fig*) foyer *m*, pépinière *f*.
hotchpotch ['hɔtʃpɔtʃ] *n* (*BRIT*) mélange *m* hétéroclite.
hot dog *n* hot-dog *m*.
hotel [həʊ'tel] *n* hôtel *m*.
hotelier [həʊ'telɪə*] *n* hôtelier/ière.
hotel industry *n* industrie hôtelière.
hotel room *n* chambre *f* d'hôtel.
hot flush *n* (*BRIT*) bouffée *f* de chaleur.
hotfoot ['hɔtfʊt] *adv* à toute vitesse.
hothead ['hɔthed] *n* (*fig*) tête brûlée.
hotheaded [hɔt'hedɪd] *adj* impétueux(euse).
hothouse ['hɔthaʊs] *n* serre chaude.
hot line *n* (*POL*) téléphone *m* rouge, ligne directe.
hotly ['hɔtlɪ] *adv* passionnément, violemment.
hotplate ['hɔtpleɪt] *n* (*on cooker*) plaque chauffante.
hotpot ['hɔtpɔt] *n* (*BRIT CULIN*) ragoût *m*.
hot potato *n* (*BRIT col*) sujet brûlant; **to drop sb/sth like a ~** laisser tomber qn/qch brusquement.
hot seat *n* (*fig*) poste chaud.
hot spot *n* point chaud.
hot spring *n* source thermale.
hot-tempered ['hɔt'tempəd] *adj* emporté(e).
hot-water bottle [hɔt'wɔːtə-] *n* bouillotte *f*.
hot-wire ['hɔtwaɪə*] *vt* (*col: car*) démarrer en faisant se toucher les fils de contact.
hound [haʊnd] *vt* poursuivre avec acharnement ♦ *n* chien courant; the **~s** la meute.
hour ['aʊə*] *n* heure *f*; **at 30 miles an ~ ≈** à 50 km à l'heure; **lunch ~** heure du déjeuner; **to pay sb by the ~** payer qn à l'heure.

hourly ['auəlɪ] *adj* toutes les heures; (*rate*) horaire; ~ **paid** *adj* payé(e) à l'heure.

house *n* [haus] (*pl*: ~**s** ['hauzɪz]) maison *f*; (*POL*) chambre *f*; (*THEAT*) salle *f*; auditoire *m* ♦ *vt* [hauz] (*person*) loger, héberger; **at** (*or* **to**) **my** ~ chez moi; **the H~ of Commons/of Lords** (*BRIT*) la Chambre des communes/des lords; **the H~ (of Representatives)** (*US*) la Chambre des représentants; **on the** ~ (*fig*) aux frais de la maison.

Le parlement en Grande-Bretagne est constitué de deux assemblées:

-La **House of Lords**, *présidée par le Lord Chancellor et composée de membres du haut clergé et de lords séculiers dont le titre est, soit héréditaire, soit attribué par le souverain (dans ce dernier cas, il peut être héréditaire ou à vie); elle peut amender certains projets de loi votés par la Chambre des communes, mais elle n'est pas habilitée à débattre des projets de lois de finances. La Chambre des lords fait également office de la juridiction suprême en Angleterre et au Pays de Galles.*

-La **House of Commons**, *présidée par le* **Speaker** *et composée de plus de 600 députés (les* **MP***) élus au suffrage universel direct. Ceux-ci reçoivent tous un salaire. La Chambre des communes siège environ 175 jours par an.*

Aux États-Unis, le parlement, appelé le **Congress**, *est constitué du* **Senate** *et de la* **House of Représentatives**. *Cette dernière comprend actuellement 435 membres, le nombre de représentants par État étant proportionnel à la densité de population de cet État. Ils sont élus pour deux ans au suffrage universel direct et siègent au* **Capitol**, *à Washington D.C.*

---

house arrest *n* assignation *f* à domicile.

houseboat ['hausbəut] *n* bateau (aménagé en habitation).

housebound ['hausbaund] *adj* confiné(e) chez soi.

housebreaking ['hausbreɪkɪŋ] *n* cambriolage *m* (avec effraction).

house-broken ['hausbrəukn] *adj* (*US*) = **house-trained**.

housecoat ['hauskəut] *n* peignoir *m*.

household ['haushəuld] *n* ménage *m*; (*people*) famille *f*, maisonnée *f*; ~ **name** nom connu de tout le monde.

householder ['haushəuldə*] *n* propriétaire *m/f*; (*head of house*) chef *m* de ménage *or* de famille.

househunting ['haushʌntɪŋ] *n*: **to go** ~ se mettre en quête d'une maison (*or* d'un appartement).

housekeeper ['hauskiːpə*] *n* gouvernante *f*.

housekeeping ['hauskiːpɪŋ] *n* (*work*) ménage *m*; (*also*: ~ **money**) argent *m* du ménage; (*COMPUT*) gestion *f* (des disques).

houseman ['hausmən] *n* (*BRIT MED*) ≈ interne *m*.

house-owner ['hausəunə*] *n* propriétaire *m/f* (*de maison ou d'appartement*).

house-proud ['hauspraud] *adj* qui tient à avoir une maison impeccable.

house-to-house ['haustə'haus] *adj* (*enquiries etc*) chez tous les habitants (*du quartier etc*).

house-train ['haustreɪn] *vt* (*pet*) apprendre à être propre à.

house-trained ['haustreɪnd] *adj* (*BRIT: animal*) propre.

house-warming ['hauswɔːmɪŋ] *n* (*also*: ~ **party**) pendaison *f* de crémaillère.

housewife ['hauswaɪf] *n* ménagère *f*; femme *f* du foyer.

housework ['hauswɔːk] *n* (travaux *mpl* du) ménage *m*.

housing ['hauzɪŋ] *n* logement *m* ♦ *cpd* (*problem, shortage*) de *or* du logement.

housing association *n* fondation *f* charitable fournissant des logements.

housing benefit *n* (*BRIT*) ≈ allocations *fpl* logement.

housing conditions *npl* conditions *fpl* de logement.

housing development, (*BRIT*) **housing estate** *n* cité *f*, lotissement *m*.

hovel ['hɔvl] *n* taudis *m*.

hover ['hɔvə*] *vi* planer; **to** ~ **round sb** rôder *or* tourner autour de qn.

hovercraft ['hɔvəkrɑːft] *n* aéroglisseur *m*.

hoverport ['hɔvəpɔːt] *n* hoverport *m*.

how [hau] *adv* comment; ~ **are you?** comment allez-vous?; ~ **do you do?** bonjour; (*on being introduced*) enchanté(e); ~ **far is it to ...?** combien y a-t-il jusqu'à ...?; ~ **long have you been here?** depuis combien de temps êtes-vous là?; ~ **lovely!** que *or* comme c'est joli!; ~ **many/much?** combien?; ~ **many people/much milk** combien de gens/lait; ~ **old are you?** quel âge avez-vous?; ~**'s life?** (*col*) comment ça va?; ~ **about a drink?** si on buvait quelque chose?; ~ **is it that ...?** comment se fait-il que ... + *sub*?

however [hau'εvə*] *conj* pourtant, cependant ♦ *adv* de quelque façon *or* manière que + *sub*; (+ *adjective*) quelque *or* si ... que + *sub*; (*in questions*) comment.

howitzer ['hauɪtsə*] *n* (*MIL*) obusier *m*.

howl [haul] *n* hurlement *m* ♦ *vi* hurler.

howler ['haulə*] *n* gaffe *f*, bourde *f*.

howling ['haulɪŋ] *adj*: **a** ~ **wind** *or* **gale** un vent à décorner les bœufs.

HP *n abbr* (*BRIT*) = **hire purchase**.

hp *abbr* (*AUT*) = **horsepower**.

HQ *n abbr* (= *headquarters*) QG *m*.

HR *n abbr* (*US*) = **House of Representatives**.

HRH *abbr* (= *His (or Her) Royal Highness*) SAR.

hr(s) *abbr* (= *hour(s)*) h.

HRT *n abbr* = **hormone replacement therapy**.

HS *abbr* (*US*) = **high school**.
HST *abbr* (*US*: = *Hawaiian Standard Time*) *heure de Hawaii*.
hub [hʌb] *n* (*of wheel*) moyeu *m*; (*fig*) centre *m*, foyer *m*.
hubbub ['hʌbʌb] *n* brouhaha *m*.
hub cap *n* (*AUT*) enjoliveur *m*.
HUD *n abbr* (*US*: = *Department of Housing and Urban Development*) *ministère de l'urbanisme et du logement.*
huddle ['hʌdl] *vi*: **to ~ together** se blottir les uns contre les autres.
hue [hjuː] *n* teinte *f*, nuance *f*; **~ and cry** *n* tollé (général), clameur *f*.
huff [hʌf] *n*: **in a ~** fâché(e); **to take the ~** prendre la mouche.
huffy ['hʌfɪ] *adj* (*col*) froissé(e).
hug [hʌg] *vt* serrer dans ses bras; (*shore, kerb*) serrer ♦ *n* étreinte *f*; **to give sb a ~** serrer qn dans ses bras.
huge [hjuːdʒ] *adj* énorme, immense.
hulk [hʌlk] *n* (*ship*) vieux rafiot; (*car, building*) carcasse *f*; (*person*) mastodonte *m*, malabar *m*.
hulking ['hʌlkɪŋ] *adj* balourd(e).
hull [hʌl] *n* (*of ship, nuts*) coque *f*; (*of peas*) cosse *f*.
hullabaloo ['hʌləbə'luː] *n* (*col*: *noise*) tapage *m*, raffut *m*.
hullo [hə'ləu] *excl* = **hello**.
hum [hʌm] *vt* (*tune*) fredonner ♦ *vi* fredonner; (*insect*) bourdonner; (*plane, tool*) vrombir ♦ *n* fredonnement *m*; bourdonnement *m*; vrombissement *m*.
human ['hjuːmən] *adj* humain(e) ♦ *n* (*also*: **~ being**) être humain.
humane [hjuː'meɪn] *adj* humain(e), humanitaire.
humanism ['hjuːmənɪzəm] *n* humanisme *m*.
humanitarian [hjuːmænɪ'tɛərɪən] *adj* humanitaire.
humanity [hjuː'mænɪtɪ] *n* humanité *f*.
humanly ['hjuːmənlɪ] *adv* humainement.
humanoid ['hjuːmənɔɪd] *adj*, *n* humanoïde (*m/f*).
human rights *npl* droits *mpl* de l'homme.
humble ['hʌmbl] *adj* humble, modeste ♦ *vt* humilier.
humbly ['hʌmblɪ] *adv* humblement, modestement.
humbug ['hʌmbʌg] *n* fumisterie *f*; (*BRIT*: *sweet*) bonbon *m* à la menthe.
humdrum ['hʌmdrʌm] *adj* monotone, routinier(ière).
humid ['hjuːmɪd] *adj* humide.
humidifier [hjuː'mɪdɪfaɪə*] *n* humidificateur *m*.
humidity [hjuː'mɪdɪtɪ] *n* humidité *f*.
humiliate [hjuː'mɪlɪeɪt] *vt* humilier.
humiliation [hjuːmɪlɪ'eɪʃən] *n* humiliation *f*.
humility [hjuː'mɪlɪtɪ] *n* humilité *f*.
humorist ['hjuːmərɪst] *n* humoriste *m/f*.

humorous ['hjuːmərəs] *adj* humoristique; (*person*) plein(e) d'humour.
humour, (*US*) **humor** ['hjuːmə*] *n* humour *m*; (*mood*) humeur *f* ♦ *vt* (*person*) faire plaisir à; **sense of ~** sens *m* de l'humour; **to be in a good/bad ~** être de bonne/mauvaise humeur.
humo(u)rless ['hjuːməlɪs] *adj* dépourvu(e) d'humour.
hump [hʌmp] *n* bosse *f*.
humpback ['hʌmpbæk] *n* bossu/e; (*BRIT*: *also*: **~ bridge**) dos-d'âne *m*.
humus ['hjuːməs] *n* humus *m*.
hunch [hʌntʃ] *n* bosse *f*; (*premonition*) intuition *f*; **I have a ~ that** j'ai (comme une vague) idée que.
hunchback ['hʌntʃbæk] *n* bossu/e.
hunched [hʌntʃt] *adj* arrondi(e), voûté(e).
hundred ['hʌndrəd] *num* cent; **about a ~ people** une centaine de personnes; **~s of people** des centaines de gens; **I'm a ~ per cent sure** j'en suis absolument certain.
hundredweight ['hʌndrɪdweɪt] *n* (*BRIT*) = *50.8 kg; 112 lb*; (*US*) = *45.3 kg; 100 lb*.
hung [hʌŋ] *pt*, *pp of* **hang**.
Hungarian [hʌŋ'gɛərɪən] *adj* hongrois(e) ♦ *n* Hongrois/e; (*LING*) hongrois *m*.
Hungary ['hʌŋgərɪ] *n* Hongrie *f*.
hunger ['hʌŋgə*] *n* faim *f* ♦ *vi*: **to ~ for** avoir faim de, désirer ardemment.
hunger strike *n* grève *f* de la faim.
hungover [hʌŋ'əuvə*] *adj* (*col*): **to be ~** avoir la gueule de bois.
hungrily ['hʌŋgrəlɪ] *adv* voracement; (*fig*) avidement.
hungry ['hʌŋgrɪ] *adj* affamé(e); **to be ~** avoir faim; **~ for** (*fig*) avide de.
hung up *adj* (*col*) complexé(e), bourré(e) de complexes.
hunk [hʌŋk] *n* gros morceau; (*col*: *man*) beau mec.
hunt [hʌnt] *vt* (*seek*) chercher; (*SPORT*) chasser ♦ *vi* chasser ♦ *n* chasse *f*.
▶**hunt down** *vt* pourchasser.
hunter ['hʌntə*] *n* chasseur *m*; (*BRIT*: *horse*) cheval *m* de chasse.
hunting ['hʌntɪŋ] *n* chasse *f*.
hurdle ['hɜːdl] *n* (*for fences*) claie *f*; (*SPORT*) haie *f*; (*fig*) obstacle *m*.
hurl [hɜːl] *vt* lancer (avec violence).
hurling ['hɜːlɪŋ] *n* (*SPORT*) genre de hockey joué en Irlande.
hurly-burly ['hɜːlɪ'bɜːlɪ] *n* tohu-bohu *m inv*; brouhaha *m*.
hurrah, hurray [hu'rɑː, hu'reɪ] *n* hourra *m*.
hurricane ['hʌrɪkən] *n* ouragan *m*.
hurried ['hʌrɪd] *adj* pressé(e), précipité(e); (*work*) fait(e) à la hâte.
hurriedly ['hʌrɪdlɪ] *adv* précipitamment, à la hâte.
hurry ['hʌrɪ] *n* hâte *f*, précipitation *f* ♦ *vi* se presser, se dépêcher ♦ *vt* (*person*) faire

presser, faire se dépêcher; (*work*) presser; **to be in a** ~ être pressé(e); **to do sth in a** ~ faire qch en vitesse; **to** ~ **in/out** entrer/sortir précipitamment; **to** ~ **home** se dépêcher de rentrer.

▶**hurry along** *vi* marcher d'un pas pressé.

▶**hurry away**, **hurry off** *vi* partir précipitamment.

▶**hurry up** *vi* se dépêcher.

hurt [hɜːt] *vb* (*pt, pp* **hurt**) *vt* (*cause pain to*) faire mal à; (*injure, fig*) blesser; (*damage: business, interests etc*) nuire à, faire du tort à ♦ *vi* faire mal ♦ *adj* blessé(e); **I** ~ **my arm** je me suis fait mal au bras; **where does it** ~? où avez-vous mal?, où est-ce que ça vous fait mal?

hurtful ['hɜːtful] *adj* (*remark*) blessant(e).

hurtle ['hɜːtl] *vt* lancer (de toutes ses forces) ♦ *vi*: **to** ~ **past** passer en trombe; **to** ~ **down** dégringoler.

husband ['hʌzbənd] *n* mari *m*.

hush [hʌʃ] *n* calme *m*, silence *m* ♦ *vt* faire taire; ~! chut!

▶**hush up** *vt* (*fact*) étouffer.

hush-hush [hʌʃ'hʌʃ] *adj* (*col*) ultra-secret(ète).

husk [hʌsk] *n* (*of wheat*) balle *f*; (*of rice, maize*) enveloppe *f*; (*of peas*) cosse *f*.

husky ['hʌskɪ] *adj* rauque; (*burly*) costaud(e) ♦ *n* chien *m* esquimau *or* de traîneau.

hustings ['hʌstɪŋz] *npl* (*BRIT POL*) plate-forme électorale.

hustle ['hʌsl] *vt* pousser, bousculer ♦ *n* bousculade *f*; ~ **and bustle** *n* tourbillon *m* (d'activité).

hut [hʌt] *n* hutte *f*; (*shed*) cabane *f*.

hutch [hʌtʃ] *n* clapier *m*.

hyacinth ['haɪəsɪnθ] *n* jacinthe *f*.

hybrid ['haɪbrɪd] *adj, n* hybride (*m*).

hydrant ['haɪdrənt] *n* prise *f* d'eau; (*also:* **fire** ~) bouche *f* d'incendie.

hydraulic [haɪ'drɔːlɪk] *adj* hydraulique.

hydraulics [haɪ'drɔːlɪks] *n* hydraulique *f*.

hydrochloric ['haɪdrəu'klɔrɪk] *adj*: ~ **acid** acide *m* chlorhydrique.

hydroelectric ['haɪdrəuɪ'lɛktrɪk] *adj* hydro-électrique.

hydrofoil ['haɪdrəfɔɪl] *n* hydrofoil *m*.

hydrogen ['haɪdrədʒən] *n* hydrogène *m*.

hydrogen bomb *n* bombe *f* à hydrogène.

hydrophobia ['haɪdrə'fəubɪə] *n* hydrophobie *f*.

hydroplane ['haɪdrəpleɪn] *n* (*seaplane*) hydra-vion *m*; (*jetfoil*) hydroglisseur *m*.

hyena [haɪ'iːnə] *n* hyène *f*.

hygiene ['haɪdʒiːn] *n* hygiène *f*.

hygienic [haɪ'dʒiːnɪk] *adj* hygiénique.

hymn [hɪm] *n* hymne *m*; cantique *m*.

hype [haɪp] *n* (*col*) matraquage *m* publicitaire *or* médiatique.

hyperactive ['haɪpər'æktɪv] *adj* hyperactif(ive).

hypermarket ['haɪpəmɑːkɪt] *n* (*BRIT*) hypermarché *m*.

hypertension ['haɪpə'tɛnʃən] *n* (*MED*) hypertension *f*.

hypertext ['haɪpə‚tɛkst] *n* (*COMPUT*) hypertexte *m*.

hyphen ['haɪfn] *n* trait *m* d'union.

hypnosis [hɪp'nəusɪs] *n* hypnose *f*.

hypnotic [hɪp'nɔtɪk] *adj* hypnotique.

hypnotism ['hɪpnɒtɪzəm] *n* hypnotisme *m*.

hypnotist ['hɪpnɒtɪst] *n* hypnotiseur/euse.

hypnotize ['hɪpnətaɪz] *vt* hypnotiser.

hypoallergenic ['haɪpəuælə'dʒɛnɪk] *adj* hypoallergique.

hypochondriac [haɪpə'kɔndrɪæk] *n* hypocondriaque *m/f*.

hypocrisy [hɪ'pɔkrɪsɪ] *n* hypocrisie *f*.

hypocrite ['hɪpəkrɪt] *n* hypocrite *m/f*.

hypocritical [hɪpə'krɪtɪkl] *adj* hypocrite.

hypodermic [haɪpə'dəːmɪk] *adj* hypodermique ♦ *n* (*syringe*) seringue *f* hypodermique.

hypotenuse [haɪ'pɔtɪnjuːz] *n* hypoténuse *f*.

hypothermia [haɪpə'θəːmɪə] *n* hypothermie *f*.

hypothesis, *pl* **hypotheses** [haɪ'pɔθɪsɪs, -siːz] *n* hypothèse *f*.

hypothetic(al) [haɪpəu'θɛtɪk(l)] *adj* hypothétique.

hysterectomy [hɪstə'rɛktəmɪ] *n* hystérectomie *f*.

hysteria [hɪ'stɪərɪə] *n* hystérie *f*.

hysterical [hɪ'stɛrɪkl] *adj* hystérique; **to become** ~ avoir une crise de nerfs.

hysterics [hɪ'stɛrɪks] *npl* (violente) crise de nerfs; (*laughter*) crise de rire; **to have** ~ avoir une crise de nerfs; attraper un fou rire.

Hz *abbr* (= *hertz*) Hz.

I i

I, i [aɪ] *n* (*letter*) I, i *m*; **I for Isaac**, (*US*) **I for Item** I comme Irma.

I [aɪ] *pron* je; (*before vowel*) j'; (*stressed*) moi ♦ *abbr* (= *island, isle*) I.

IA, Ia. *abbr* (*US*) = *Iowa*.

IAEA *n abbr* = **International Atomic Energy Agency**.

IBA *n abbr* (*BRIT*: = *Independent Broadcasting Authority*) ≈ CNCL *f* (= *Commission nationale de la communication audio-visuelle*).

Iberian [aɪ'bɪərɪən] *adj* ibérique, ibérien(ne).

Iberian Peninsula *n*: **the** ~ la péninsule Ibérique.

i/c *abbr* (*BRIT*) = **in charge**.

ICBM *n abbr* (= *intercontinental ballistic missile*) ICBM *m*, engin *m* balistique à portée intercontinentale.

ICC *n abbr* (= *International Chamber of Commerce*) CCI *f*; (*US*) = *Interstate Commerce Commission.*

ice [aɪs] *n* glace *f*; (*on road*) verglas *m* ♦ *vt* (*cake*) glacer; (*drink*) faire rafraîchir ♦ *vi* (*also:* ~ **over**) geler; (*also:* ~ **up**) se givrer; **to put sth on** ~ (*fig*) mettre qch en attente.

Ice Age *n* ère *f* glaciaire.

ice axe *n* piolet *m*.

iceberg ['aɪsbəːg] *n* iceberg *m*; **the tip of the** ~ (*also fig*) la partie émergée de l'iceberg.

icebox ['aɪsbɔks] *n* (*US*) réfrigérateur *m*; (*BRIT*) compartiment *m* à glace; (*insulated box*) glacière *f*.

icebreaker ['aɪsbreɪkə*] *n* brise-glace *m*.

ice bucket *n* seau *m* à glace.

ice-cap ['aɪskæp] *n* calotte *f* glaciaire.

ice-cold [aɪs'kəuld] *adj* glacé(e).

ice cream *n* glace *f*.

ice cube *n* glaçon *m*.

iced [aɪst] *adj* (*drink*) frappé(e); (*coffee, tea, also cake*) glacé(e).

ice hockey *n* hockey *m* sur glace.

Iceland ['aɪslənd] *n* Islande *f*.

Icelander ['aɪsləndə*] *n* Islandais/e.

Icelandic [aɪs'lændɪk] *adj* islandais(e) ♦ *n* (*LING*) islandais *m*.

ice lolly [-'lɔlɪ] *n* (*BRIT*) esquimau *m*.

ice pick *n* pic *m* à glace.

ice rink *n* patinoire *f*.

ice-skate ['aɪsskeɪt] *n* patin *m* à glace ♦ *vi* faire du patin à glace.

ice-skating ['aɪsskeɪtɪŋ] *n* patinage *m* (sur glace).

icicle ['aɪsɪkl] *n* glaçon *m* (*naturel*).

icing ['aɪsɪŋ] *n* (*AVIAT etc*) givrage *m*; (*CULIN*) glaçage *m*.

icing sugar *n* (*BRIT*) sucre *m* glace.

ICJ *n abbr* = *International Court of Justice.*

icon ['aɪkɔn] *n* icône *f*.

ICR *n abbr* (*US*) = *Institute for Cancer Research.*

ICRC *n abbr* (= *International Committee of the Red Cross*) CICR *m*.

ICU *n abbr* = **intensive care unit.**

icy ['aɪsɪ] *adj* glacé(e); (*road*) verglacé(e); (*weather, temperature*) glacial(e).

ID *abbr* (*US*) = *Idaho.*

I'd [aɪd] = **I would, I had.**

Ida. *abbr* (*US*) = *Idaho.*

ID card *n* = **identity card.**

IDD *n abbr* (*BRIT TEL*: = *international direct dialling*) *automatique international.*

idea [aɪ'dɪə] *n* idée *f*; **good** ~! bonne idée!; **to have an** ~ **that** ... avoir idée que ...; **I haven't the least** ~ je n'ai pas la moindre idée.

ideal [aɪ'dɪəl] *n* idéal *m* ♦ *adj* idéal(e).

idealist [aɪ'dɪəlɪst] *n* idéaliste *m/f*.

ideally [aɪ'dɪəlɪ] *adv* idéalement, dans l'idéal; ~ **the book should have** ... l'idéal serait que le livre ait ....

identical [aɪ'dentɪkl] *adj* identique.

identification [aɪdentɪfɪ'keɪʃən] *n* identification *f*; **means of** ~ pièce *f* d'identité.

identify [aɪ'dentɪfaɪ] *vt* identifier ♦ *vi*: **to** ~ **with** s'identifier à.

Identikit [aɪ'dentɪkɪt] *n* ®: ~ **(picture)** portrait-robot *m*.

identity [aɪ'dentɪtɪ] *n* identité *f*.

identity card *n* carte *f* d'identité.

identity parade *n* (*BRIT*) parade *f* d'identification.

ideological [aɪdɪə'lɔdʒɪkl] *adj* idéologique.

ideology [aɪdɪ'ɔlədʒɪ] *n* idéologie *f*.

idiocy ['ɪdɪəsɪ] *n* idiotie *f*, stupidité *f*.

idiom ['ɪdɪəm] *n* langue *f*, idiome *m*; (*phrase*) expression *f* idiomatique.

idiomatic [ɪdɪə'mætɪk] *adj* idiomatique.

idiosyncrasy [ɪdɪəu'sɪŋkrəsɪ] *n* particularité *f*, caractéristique *f*.

idiot ['ɪdɪət] *n* idiot/e, imbécile *m/f*.

idiotic [ɪdɪ'ɔtɪk] *adj* idiot(e), bête, stupide.

idle ['aɪdl] *adj* sans occupation, désœuvré(e); (*lazy*) oisif(ive), paresseux(euse); (*unemployed*) au chômage; (*machinery*) au repos; (*question, pleasures*) vain(e), futile ♦ *vi* (*engine*) tourner au ralenti; **to lie** ~ être arrêté, ne pas fonctionner.

▸**idle away** *vt*: **to** ~ **away one's time** passer son temps à ne rien faire.

idleness ['aɪdlnɪs] *n* désœuvrement *m*; oisiveté *f*.

idler ['aɪdlə*] *n* désœuvré/e; oisif/ive.

idle time *n* (*COMM*) temps mort.

idol ['aɪdl] *n* idole *f*.

idolize ['aɪdəlaɪz] *vt* idolâtrer, adorer.

idyllic [ɪ'dɪlɪk] *adj* idyllique.

i.e. *abbr* (= *id est: that is*) c. à d., c'est-à-dire.

if [ɪf] *conj si* ♦ *n*: **there are a lot of** ~**s and buts** il y a beaucoup de si *mpl* et de mais *mpl*; **I'd be pleased** ~ **you could do it** je serais très heureux si vous pouviez le faire; ~ **necessary** si nécessaire, le cas échéant; ~ **only we were here** si seulement il était là; ~ **only to show him my gratitude** ne serait-ce que pour lui témoigner ma gratitude.

iffy ['ɪfɪ] *adj* (*col*) douteux(euse).

igloo ['ɪglu:] *n* igloo *m*.

ignite [ɪg'naɪt] *vt* mettre le feu à, enflammer ♦ *vi* s'enflammer.

ignition [ɪg'nɪʃən] *n* (*AUT*) allumage *m*; **to switch on/off the** ~ mettre/couper le contact.

ignition key *n* (*AUT*) clé *f* de contact.

ignoble [ɪg'nəubl] *adj* ignoble, indigne.

ignominious [ɪgnə'mɪnɪəs] *adj* honteux(euse), ignominieux(euse).

ignoramus [ɪgnə'reɪməs] *n* personne *f* ignare.

ignorance ['ɪgnərəns] *n* ignorance *f*; **to keep sb in** ~ **of sth** tenir qn dans l'ignorance de qch.

ignorant ['ɪgnərənt] *adj* ignorant(e); **to be** ~ **of** (*subject*) ne rien connaître en; (*events*) ne pas être au courant de.

ignore [ɪg'nɔː*] *vt* ne tenir aucun compte de, ne pas relever; (*person*) faire semblant de ne pas reconnaître, ignorer; (*fact*) méconnaître.

ikon ['aɪkɔn] *n* = **icon.**

IL *abbr* (*US*) = *Illinois.*

ILA *n abbr* (*US*: = *International Longshoremen's Association*) *syndicat international des dockers.*

ill [ɪl] *adj* (*sick*) malade; (*bad*) mauvais(e) ♦ *n* mal *m* ♦ *adv*: **to speak/think** ~ **of sb** dire/penser du mal de qn; **to take** *or* **be taken** ~ tomber malade.

Ill. *abbr* (*US*) = *Illinois.*

I'll [aɪl] = **I will, I shall.**

ill-advised [ɪləd'vaɪzd] *adj* (*decision*) peu judicieux(euse); (*person*) malavisé(e).

ill-at-ease [ɪlət'iːz] *adj* mal à l'aise.

ill-considered [ɪlkən'sɪdəd] *adj* (*plan*) inconsidéré(e), irréfléchi(e).

ill-disposed [ɪldɪs'pəuzd] *adj*: **to be** ~ **towards sb/sth** être mal disposé(e) envers qn/qch.

illegal [ɪ'liːgl] *adj* illégal(e).

illegally [ɪ'liːgəlɪ] *adv* illégalement.

illegible [ɪ'lɛdʒɪbl] *adj* illisible.

illegitimate [ɪlɪ'dʒɪtɪmət] *adj* illégitime.

ill-fated [ɪl'feɪtɪd] *adj* malheureux(euse); (*day*) néfaste.

ill-favoured, (*US*) **ill-favored** [ɪl'feɪvəd] *adj* déplaisant(e).

ill feeling *n* ressentiment *m*, rancune *f*.

ill-gotten ['ɪlgɔtn] *adj* (*gains etc*) mal acquis(e).

ill health *n* mauvaise santé.

illicit [ɪ'lɪsɪt] *adj* illicite.

ill-informed [ɪlɪn'fɔːmd] *adj* (*judgment*) erroné(e); (*person*) mal renseigné(e).

illiterate [ɪ'lɪtərət] *adj* illettré(e); (*letter*) plein(e) de fautes.

ill-mannered [ɪl'mænəd] *adj* impoli(e), grossier(ière).

illness ['ɪlnɪs] *n* maladie *f*.

illogical [ɪ'lɔdʒɪkl] *adj* illogique.

ill-suited [ɪl'suːtɪd] *adj* (*couple*) mal assorti(e); **he is** ~ **to the job** il n'est pas vraiment fait pour ce travail.

ill-timed [ɪl'taɪmd] *adj* inopportun(e).

ill-treat [ɪl'triːt] *vt* maltraiter.

ill-treatment [ɪl'triːtmənt] *n* mauvais traitement.

illuminate [ɪ'luːmɪneɪt] *vt* (*room, street*) éclairer; (*building*) illuminer; ~**d sign** enseigne lumineuse.

illuminating [ɪ'luːmɪneɪtɪŋ] *adj* éclairant(e).

illumination [ɪluːmɪ'neɪʃən] *n* éclairage *m*; illumination *f*.

illusion [ɪ'luːʒən] *n* illusion *f*; **to be under the** ~ **that** avoir l'illusion que.

illusive, illusory [ɪ'luːsɪv, ɪ'luːsərɪ] *adj* illusoire.

illustrate ['ɪləstreɪt] *vt* illustrer.

illustration [ɪlə'streɪʃən] *n* illustration *f*.

illustrator ['ɪləstreɪtə*] *n* illustrateur/trice.

illustrious [ɪ'lʌstrɪəs] *adj* illustre.

ill will *n* malveillance *f*.

ILO *n abbr* (= *International Labour Organization*) OIT *f*.

ILWU *n abbr* (*US*: = *International Longshoremen's and Warehousemen's Union*) *syndicat international des dockers et des magaziniers.*

I'm [aɪm] = **I am.**

image ['ɪmɪdʒ] *n* image *f*; (*public face*) image de marque.

imagery ['ɪmɪdʒərɪ] *n* images *fpl*.

imaginable [ɪ'mædʒɪnəbl] *adj* imaginable.

imaginary [ɪ'mædʒɪnərɪ] *adj* imaginaire.

imagination [ɪmædʒɪ'neɪʃən] *n* imagination *f*.

imaginative [ɪ'mædʒɪnətɪv] *adj* imaginatif(ive), plein(e) d'imagination.

imagine [ɪ'mædʒɪn] *vt* s'imaginer; (*suppose*) imaginer, supposer.

imbalance [ɪm'bæləns] *n* déséquilibre *m*.

imbecile ['ɪmbəsiːl] *n* imbécile *m/f*.

imbue [ɪm'bjuː] *vt*: **to** ~ **sth with** imprégner qch de.

IMF *n abbr* = **International Monetary Fund.**

imitate ['ɪmɪteɪt] *vt* imiter.

imitation [ɪmɪ'teɪʃən] *n* imitation *f*.

imitator ['ɪmɪteɪtə*] *n* imitateur/trice.

immaculate [ɪ'mækjulət] *adj* impeccable; (*REL*) immaculé(e).

immaterial [ɪmə'tɪərɪəl] *adj* sans importance, insignifiant(e).

immature [ɪmə'tjuə*] *adj* (*fruit*) qui n'est pas mûr(e); (*person*) qui manque de maturité.

immaturity [ɪmə'tjuərɪtɪ] *n* immaturité *f*.

immeasurable [ɪ'mɛʒrəbl] *adj* incommensurable.

immediacy [ɪ'miːdɪəsɪ] *n* (*of events etc*) caractère *or* rapport immédiat; (*of needs*) urgence *f*.

immediate [ɪ'miːdɪət] *adj* immédiat(e).

immediately [ɪ'miːdɪətlɪ] *adv* (*at once*) immédiatement; ~ **next to** juste à côté de.

immense [ɪ'mɛns] *adj* immense; énorme.

immensity [ɪ'mɛnsɪtɪ] *n* immensité *f*.

immerse [ɪ'məːs] *vt* immerger, plonger; **to** ~ **sth in** plonger qch dans.

immersion heater [ɪ'məːʃən-] *n* (*BRIT*) chauffe-eau *m* électrique.

immigrant ['ɪmɪgrənt] *n* immigrant/e; (*already established*) immigré/e.

immigration [ɪmɪ'greɪʃən] *n* immigration *f*.

immigration authorities *npl* service *m* de l'immigration.

immigration laws *npl* lois *fpl* sur l'immigration.

imminent ['ɪmɪnənt] *adj* imminent(e).

immobile [ɪ'məubaɪl] *adj* immobile.

immobilize [ɪ'məubɪlaɪz] *vt* immobiliser.

immoderate [ɪ'mɔdərət] *adj* immodéré(e), démesuré(e).

immodest [ɪ'mɔdɪst] *adj* (*indecent*) indécent(e); (*boasting*) pas modeste, présomptueux(euse).

immoral [ı'mɔrl] adj immoral(e).

immorality [ımɔ'rælıtı] n immoralité f.

immortal [ı'mɔ:tl] adj, n immortel(le).

immortalize [ı'mɔ:tlaız] vt immortaliser.

immovable [ı'mu:vəbl] adj (object) fixe; immobilier(ière); (person) inflexible; (opinion) immuable.

immune [ı'mju:n] adj: ~ (to) immunisé(e) (contre).

immune system n système m immunitaire.

immunity [ı'mju:nıtı] n immunité f; **diplomatic** ~ immunité diplomatique.

immunization [ımjunaı'zeıʃən] n immunisation f.

immunize ['ımjunaız] vt immuniser.

imp [ımp] n (small devil) lutin m; (child) petit diable.

impact ['ımpækt] n choc m, impact m; (fig) impact.

impair [ım'pɛə*] vt détériorer, diminuer.

impaired [ım'pɛəd] adj (make known) (organ, vision) abimé(e), détérioré(e); **his memory/circulation is** ~ il a des problèmes de mémoire/circulation; **visually** ~ malvoyant(e); **hearing** ~ malentendant(e); **mentally/physically** ~ intellectuellement/physiquement diminué(e).

impale [ım'peıl] vt empaler.

impart [ım'pɑ:t] vt (make known) communiquer, transmettre; (bestow) confier, donner.

impartial [ım'pɑ:ʃl] adj impartial(e).

impartiality [ımpɑ:ʃı'ælıtı] n impartialité f.

impassable [ım'pɑ:səbl] adj infranchissable; (road) impraticable.

impasse [æm'pɑ:s] n (fig) impasse f.

impassioned [ım'pæʃənd] adj passionné(e).

impassive [ım'pæsıv] adj impassible.

impatience [ım'peıʃəns] n impatience f.

impatient [ım'peıʃənt] adj impatient(e); **to get** or **grow** ~ s'impatienter.

impeach [ım'pi:tʃ] vt accuser, attaquer; (public official) mettre en accusation.

impeachment [ım'pi:tʃmənt] n (LAW) (mise f en) accusation f.

impeccable [ım'pɛkəbl] adj impeccable, parfait(e).

impecunious [ımpı'kju:nıəs] adj sans ressources.

impede [ım'pi:d] vt gêner.

impediment [ım'pɛdımənt] n obstacle m; (also: **speech** ~) défaut m d'élocution.

impel [ım'pɛl] vt (force): **to** ~ **sb (to do sth)** forcer qn (à faire qch).

impending [ım'pɛndıŋ] adj imminent(e).

impenetrable [ım'pɛnıtrəbl] adj impénétrable.

imperative [ım'pɛrətıv] adj nécessaire; urgent(e), pressant(e); (tone) impérieux(euse) ♦ n (LING) impératif m.

imperceptible [ımpə'sɛptıbl] adj imperceptible.

imperfect [ım'pə:fıkt] adj imparfait(e); (goods

etc) défectueux(euse) ♦ n (LING: also: ~ **tense**) imparfait m.

imperfection [ımpə:'fɛkʃən] n imperfection f; défectuosité f.

imperial [ım'pıərıəl] adj impérial(e); (BRIT: measure) légal(e).

imperialism [ım'pıərıəlızəm] n impérialisme m.

imperil [ım'pɛrıl] vt mettre en péril.

imperious [ım'pıərıəs] adj impérieux(euse).

impersonal [ım'pə:sənl] adj impersonnel(le).

impersonate [ım'pə:səneıt] vt se faire passer pour; (THEAT) imiter.

impersonation [ımpə:sə'neıʃən] n (LAW) usurpation f d'identité; (THEAT) imitation f.

impersonator [ım'pə:səneıtə*] n imposteur m; (THEAT) imitateur/trice.

impertinence [ım'pə:tınəns] n impertinence f, insolence f.

impertinent [ım'pə:tınənt] adj impertinent(e), insolent(e).

imperturbable [ımpə'tə:bəbl] adj imperturbable.

impervious [ım'pə:vıəs] adj imperméable; (fig): ~ **to** insensible à; inaccessible à.

impetuous [ım'pɛtjuəs] adj impétueux(euse), fougueux(euse).

impetus ['ımpətəs] n impulsion f; (of runner) élan m.

impinge [ım'pındʒ]: **to** ~ **on** vt fus (person) affecter, toucher; (rights) empiéter sur.

impish ['ımpıʃ] adj espiègle.

implacable [ım'plækəbl] adj implacable.

implant [ım'plɑ:nt] vt (MED) implanter; (fig) inculquer.

implausible [ım'plɔ:zıbl] adj peu plausible.

implement n ['ımplımənt] outil m, instrument m; (for cooking) ustensile m ♦ vt ['ımplımənt] exécuter, mettre à effet.

implicate ['ımplıkeıt] vt impliquer, compromettre.

implication [ımplı'keıʃən] n implication f; **by** ~ indirectement.

implicit [ım'plısıt] adj implicite; (complete) absolu(e), sans réserve.

implicitly [ım'plısıtlı] adv implicitement; absolument, sans réserve.

implore [ım'plɔ:*] vt implorer, supplier.

imply [ım'plaı] vt (hint) suggérer, laisser entendre; (mean) indiquer, supposer.

impolite [ımpə'laıt] adj impoli(e).

imponderable [ım'pɔndərəbl] adj impondérable.

import vt [ım'pɔ:t] importer ♦ n ['ımpɔ:t] (COMM) importation f; (meaning) portée f, signification f ♦ cpd (duty, licence etc) d'importation.

importance [ım'pɔ:tns] n importance f; **to be of great/little** ~ avoir beaucoup/peu d'importance.

important [ım'pɔ:tnt] adj important(e); **it is** ~ **that** il importe que, il est important que; **it's**

not ~ c'est sans importance, ce n'est pas important.

importantly [ɪmˈpɔːtntlɪ] adv (with an air of importance) d'un air important; (essentially): **but, more** ~ ... mais, (ce qui est) plus important encore ....

importation [ɪmpɔːˈteɪʃən] n importation f.

imported [ɪmˈpɔːtɪd] adj importé(e), d'importation.

importer [ɪmˈpɔːtə*] n importateur/trice.

impose [ɪmˈpəuz] vt imposer ♦ vi: **to ~ on sb** abuser de la gentillesse de qn.

imposing [ɪmˈpəuzɪŋ] adj imposant(e), impressionnant(e).

imposition [ɪmpəˈzɪʃən] n (of tax etc) imposition f; **to be an ~ on** (person) abuser de la gentillesse or la bonté de.

impossibility [ɪmpɔsəˈbɪlɪtɪ] n impossibilité f.

impossible [ɪmˈpɔsɪbl] adj impossible; **it is ~ for me to leave** il m'est impossible de partir.

impostor [ɪmˈpɔstə*] n imposteur m.

impotence [ˈɪmpətns] n impuissance f.

impotent [ˈɪmpətnt] adj impuissant(e).

impound [ɪmˈpaund] vt confisquer, saisir.

impoverished [ɪmˈpɔvərɪʃt] adj pauvre, appauvri(e).

impracticable [ɪmˈpræktɪkəbl] adj impraticable.

impractical [ɪmˈpræktɪkl] adj pas pratique, (person) qui manque d'esprit pratique.

imprecise [ɪmprɪˈsaɪs] adj imprécis(e).

impregnable [ɪmˈprɛgnəbl] adj (fortress) imprenable; (fig) inattaquable; irréfutable.

impregnate [ˈɪmprɛgneɪt] vt imprégner; (fertilize) féconder.

impresario [ɪmprɪˈsɑːrɪəu] n impresario m.

impress [ɪmˈprɛs] vt impressionner, faire impression sur; (mark) imprimer, marquer; **to ~ sth on sb** faire bien comprendre qch à qn.

impression [ɪmˈprɛʃən] n impression f; (of stamp, seal) empreinte f; **to make a good/bad ~ on sb** faire bonne/mauvaise impression sur qn; **to be under the ~ that** avoir l'impression que.

impressionable [ɪmˈprɛʃnəbl] adj impressionnable, sensible.

impressionist [ɪmˈprɛʃənɪst] n impressionniste m/f.

impressive [ɪmˈprɛsɪv] adj impressionnant(e).

imprint [ˈɪmprɪnt] n empreinte f; (PUBLISHING) notice f; (: label) nom m (de collection or d'éditeur).

imprinted [ɪmˈprɪntɪd] adj: ~ **on** imprimé(e) sur; (fig) imprimé(e) or gravé(e) dans.

imprison [ɪmˈprɪzn] vt emprisonner, mettre en prison.

imprisonment [ɪmˈprɪznmənt] n emprisonnement m.

improbable [ɪmˈprɔbəbl] adj improbable; (excuse) peu plausible.

impromptu [ɪmˈprɔmptjuː] adj impromptu(e) ♦ adv impromptu.

improper [ɪmˈprɔpə*] adj (wrong) incorrect(e); (unsuitable) déplacé(e), de mauvais goût; indécent(e).

impropriety [ɪmprəˈpraɪətɪ] n inconvenance f; (of expression) impropriété f.

improve [ɪmˈpruːv] vt améliorer ♦ vi s'améliorer; (pupil etc) faire des progrès.

▶**improve (up)on** vt fus (offer) enchérir sur.

improvement [ɪmˈpruːvmənt] n amélioration f; (of pupil etc) progrès m; **to make ~s to** apporter des améliorations à.

improvisation [ɪmprəvaɪˈzeɪʃən] n improvisation f.

improvise [ˈɪmprəvaɪz] vt, vi improviser.

imprudence [ɪmˈpruːdns] n imprudence f.

imprudent [ɪmˈpruːdnt] adj imprudent(e).

impudent [ˈɪmpjudnt] adj impudent(e).

impugn [ɪmˈpjuːn] vt contester, attaquer.

impulse [ˈɪmpʌls] n impulsion f; **on ~** impulsivement, sur un coup de tête.

impulse buy n achat m d'impulsion.

impulsive [ɪmˈpʌlsɪv] adj impulsif(ive).

impunity [ɪmˈpjuːnɪtɪ] n: **with ~** impunément.

impure [ɪmˈpjuə*] adj impur(e).

impurity [ɪmˈpjuərɪtɪ] n impureté f.

IN abbr (US) = Indiana.

══════════════════════ KEYWORD

in [ɪn] prep **1** (indicating place, position) dans; ~ **the house/the fridge** dans la maison/le frigo; ~ **the garden** dans le or au jardin; ~ **town** en ville; ~ **the country** à la campagne; ~ **school** à l'école; ~ **here/there** ici/là

2 (with place names: of town, region, country): ~ **London** à Londres; ~ **England** en Angleterre; ~ **Japan** au Japon; ~ **the United States** aux États-Unis

3 (indicating time: during): ~ **spring** au printemps; ~ **summer** en été; ~ **May/1992** en mai/1992; ~ **the afternoon** (dans) l'après-midi; **at 4 o'clock** ~ **the afternoon** à 4 heures de l'après-midi

4 (indicating time: in the space of) en; (: future) dans; **I did it** ~ **3 hours/days** je l'ai fait en 3 heures/jours; **I'll see you** ~ **2 weeks** or ~ **2 weeks' time** je te verrai dans 2 semaines; **once** ~ **a hundred years** une fois tous les cent ans

5 (indicating manner etc) à; ~ **a loud/soft voice** à voix haute/basse; ~ **pencil** au crayon; ~ **writing** par écrit; ~ **French** en français; **to pay** ~ **dollars** payer en dollars; **the boy** ~ **the blue shirt** le garçon à or avec la chemise bleue

6 (indicating circumstances): ~ **the sun** au soleil; ~ **the shade** à l'ombre; ~ **the rain** sous la pluie

7 (indicating mood, state): ~ **tears** en larmes; ~ **anger** sous le coup de la colère; ~ **despair** au désespoir; ~ **good condition** en bon état;

to live ~ **luxury** vivre dans le luxe
8 (*with ratios, numbers*): **1 ~ 10 (households),
1 (household)** ~ 10 1 (ménage) sur 10; **20
pence ~ the pound** 20 pence par livre sterling; **they lined up ~ twos** ils se mirent en
rangs (deux) par deux; ~ **hundreds** par centaines
9 (*referring to people, works*) chez; **the disease is common ~ children** c'est une maladie courante chez les enfants; ~ **(the
works of) Dickens** chez Dickens, dans
(l'œuvre de) Dickens
10 (*indicating profession etc*) dans; **to be ~
teaching** être dans l'enseignement
11 (*after superlative*) de; **the best pupil ~ the
class** le meilleur élève de la classe
12 (*with present participle*): ~ **saying this** en
disant ceci
♦ *adv*: **to be ~** (*person: at home, work*) être là;
(*train, ship, plane*) être arrivé(e); (*in fashion*)
être à la mode; **to ask sb ~** inviter qn à entrer; **to run/limp** *etc* ~ entrer en courant/
boitant *etc*; **their party is ~** leur parti est au
pouvoir
♦ *n*: **the ~s and outs (of)** (*of proposal, situation
etc*) les tenants et aboutissants (de).

in. *abbr* = **inch(es)**.
inability [ɪnə'bɪlɪtɪ] *n* incapacité *f*; ~ **to pay** incapacité de payer.
inaccessible [ɪnək'sɛsɪbl] *adj* inaccessible.
inaccuracy [ɪn'ækjurəsɪ] *n* inexactitude *f*;
manque *m* de précision.
inaccurate [ɪn'ækjurət] *adj* inexact(e); (*person*) qui manque de précision.
inaction [ɪn'ækʃən] *n* inaction *f*, inactivité *f*.
inactivity [ɪnæk'tɪvɪtɪ] *n* inactivité *f*.
inadequacy [ɪn'ædɪkwəsɪ] *n* insuffisance *f*.
inadequate [ɪn'ædɪkwət] *adj* insuffisant(e),
inadéquat(e).
inadmissible [ɪnəd'mɪsəbl] *adj* (*behaviour*)
inadmissible; (*LAW: evidence*) irrecevable.
inadvertent [ɪnəd'vɜːtnt] *adj* (*mistake*) commis(e) par inadvertance.
inadvertently [ɪnəd'vɜːtntlɪ] *adv* par mégarde.
inadvisable [ɪnəd'vaɪzəbl] *adj* à déconseiller;
it is ~ to il est déconseillé de.
inane [ɪ'neɪn] *adj* inepte, stupide.
inanimate [ɪn'ænɪmət] *adj* inanimé(e).
inapplicable [ɪn'æplɪkəbl] *adj* inapplicable.
inappropriate [ɪnə'prəuprɪət] *adj* inopportun(e), mal à propos; (*word, expression*) impropre.
inapt [ɪn'æpt] *adj* inapte; peu approprié(e).
inaptitude [ɪn'æptɪtjuːd] *n* inaptitude *f*.
inarticulate [ɪnɑː'tɪkjulət] *adj* (*person*) qui
s'exprime mal; (*speech*) indistinct(e).
inasmuch [ɪnəz'mʌtʃ] *adv*: ~ **as** vu que, en ce
sens que.
inattention [ɪnə'tɛnʃən] *n* manque *m*
d'attention.
inattentive [ɪnə'tɛntɪv] *adj* inattentif(ive), distrait(e); négligent(e).
inaudible [ɪn'ɔːdɪbl] *adj* inaudible.
inaugural [ɪ'nɔːgjurəl] *adj* inaugural(e).
inaugurate [ɪ'nɔːgjureɪt] *vt* inaugurer; (*president, official*) investir de ses fonctions.
inauguration [ɪnɔːgju'reɪʃən] *n* inauguration *f*;
investiture *f*.
inauspicious [ɪnɔːs'pɪʃəs] *adj* peu propice.
in-between [ɪnbɪ'twiːn] *adj* entre les deux.
inborn [ɪn'bɔːn] *adj* (*feeling*) inné(e); (*defect*)
congénital(e).
inbred [ɪn'brɛd] *adj* inné(e), naturel(le);
(*family*) consanguin(e).
inbreeding [ɪn'briːdɪŋ] *n* croisement *m*
d'animaux de même souche; unions consanguines.
Inc. *abbr* = **incorporated**.
Inca ['ɪŋkə] *adj* (*also:* ~**n**) inca *inv* ♦ *n* Inca *m/f*.
incalculable [ɪn'kælkjuləbl] *adj* incalculable.
incapability [ɪnkeɪpə'bɪlɪtɪ] *n* incapacité *f*.
incapable [ɪn'keɪpəbl] *adj*: ~ **(of)** incapable
(de).
incapacitate [ɪnkə'pæsɪteɪt] *vt*: **to ~ sb from
doing** rendre qn incapable de faire.
incapacitated [ɪnkə'pæsɪteɪtɪd] *adj* (*LAW*) frappé(e) d'incapacité.
incapacity [ɪnkə'pæsɪtɪ] *n* incapacité *f*.
incarcerate [ɪn'kɑːsəreɪt] *vt* incarcérer.
incarnate *adj* [ɪn'kɑːnɪt] incarné(e) ♦ *vt*
['ɪnkɑːneɪt] incarner.
incarnation [ɪnkɑː'neɪʃən] *n* incarnation *f*.
incendiary [ɪn'sɛndɪərɪ] *adj* incendiaire ♦ *n*
(*bomb*) bombe *f* incendiaire.
incense *n* ['ɪnsɛns] encens *m* ♦ *vt* [ɪn'sɛns] (*anger*) mettre en colère.
incense burner *n* encensoir *m*.
incentive [ɪn'sɛntɪv] *n* encouragement *m*, raison *f* de se donner de la peine.
incentive scheme *n* système *m* de primes
d'encouragement.
inception [ɪn'sɛpʃən] *n* commencement *m*, début *m*.
incessant [ɪn'sɛsnt] *adj* incessant(e).
incessantly [ɪn'sɛsntlɪ] *adv* sans cesse, constamment.
incest ['ɪnsɛst] *n* inceste *m*.
inch [ɪntʃ] *n* pouce *m* (= 25 mm; 12 in a foot);
within an ~ of à deux doigts de; **he wouldn't
give an ~** (*fig*) il n'a pas voulu céder d'un
pouce *or* faire la plus petite concession.
►**inch forward** *vi* avancer petit à petit.
inch tape *n* (*BRIT*) centimètre *m* (de couturière).
incidence ['ɪnsɪdns] *n* (*of crime, disease*) fréquence *f*.
incident ['ɪnsɪdnt] *n* incident *m*; (*in book*) péripétie *f*.
incidental [ɪnsɪ'dɛntl] *adj* accessoire; (*unplanned*) accidentel(le); ~ **to** qui accompagne; ~ **expenses** faux frais *mpl*.
incidentally [ɪnsɪ'dɛntəlɪ] *adv* (*by the way*) à
propos.

incidental music *n* musique *f* de fond.
incident room *n* (*POLICE*) salle *f* d'opérations.
incinerate [ɪnˈsɪnəreɪt] *vt* incinérer.
incinerator [ɪnˈsɪnəreɪtə*] *n* incinérateur *m*.
incipient [ɪnˈsɪpɪənt] *adj* naissant(e).
incision [ɪnˈsɪʒən] *n* incision *f*.
incisive [ɪnˈsaɪsɪv] *adj* incisif(ive); mordant(e).
incisor [ɪnˈsaɪzə*] *n* incisive *f*.
incite [ɪnˈsaɪt] *vt* inciter, pousser.
incl. *abbr* = **including, inclusive (of)**.
inclement [ɪnˈklemənt] *adj* inclément(e), rigoureux(euse).
inclination [ɪnklɪˈneɪʃən] *n* inclination *f*.
incline *n* [ˈɪnklaɪn] pente *f*, plan incliné ♦ *vb* [ɪnˈklaɪn] *vt* incliner ♦ *vi*: **to ~ to** avoir tendance à; **to be ~d to do** être enclin(e) à faire; (*have a tendency to do*) avoir tendance à faire; **to be well ~d towards sb** être bien disposé(e) à l'égard de qn.
include [ɪnˈkluːd] *vt* inclure, comprendre; **the tip is/is not ~d** le service est compris/n'est pas compris.
including [ɪnˈkluːdɪŋ] *prep* y compris; **~ tip** service compris.
inclusion [ɪnˈkluːʒən] *n* inclusion *f*.
inclusive [ɪnˈkluːsɪv] *adj* inclus(e), compris(e); **£50 ~ of all surcharges** 50 livres tous frais compris.
inclusive terms *npl* (*BRIT*) prix tout compris.
incognito [ɪnkɒgˈniːtəu] *adv* incognito.
incoherent [ɪnkəuˈhɪərənt] *adj* incohérent(e).
income [ˈɪnkʌm] *n* revenu *m*; **gross/net ~** revenu brut/net; **~ and expenditure account** compte *m* de recettes et de dépenses.
income support *n* (*BRIT*) ≈ revenu *m* minimum d'insertion, RMI *m*.
income tax *n* impôt *m* sur le revenu.
income tax inspector *n* inspecteur *m* des contributions directes.
income tax return *n* déclaration *f* des revenus.
incoming [ˈɪnkʌmɪŋ] *adj* (*passengers, mail*) à l'arrivée; (*government, tenant*) nouveau(nouvelle); **~ tide** marée montante.
incommunicado [ˈɪnkəmjuːnɪˈkɑːdəu] *adj*: **to hold sb ~** tenir qn au secret.
incomparable [ɪnˈkɒmpərəbl] *adj* incomparable.
incompatible [ɪnkəmˈpætɪbl] *adj* incompatible.
incompetence [ɪnˈkɒmpɪtns] *n* incompétence *f*, incapacité *f*.
incompetent [ɪnˈkɒmpɪtnt] *adj* incompétent(e), incapable.
incomplete [ɪnkəmˈpliːt] *adj* incomplet(ète).
incomprehensible [ɪnkɒmprɪˈhensɪbl] *adj* incompréhensible.
inconceivable [ɪnkənˈsiːvəbl] *adj* inconcevable.
inconclusive [ɪnkənˈkluːsɪv] *adj* peu concluant(e); (*argument*) peu convaincant(e).
incongruous [ɪnˈkɒŋgruəs] *adj* peu appro-

prié(e); (*remark, act*) incongru(e), déplacé(e).
inconsequential [ɪnkɒnsɪˈkwenʃl] *adj* sans importance.
inconsiderable [ɪnkənˈsɪdərəbl] *adj*: **not ~** non négligeable.
inconsiderate [ɪnkənˈsɪdərət] *adj* (*action*) inconsidéré(e); (*person*) qui manque d'égards.
inconsistency [ɪnkənˈsɪstənsɪ] *n* (*of actions etc*) inconséquence *f*; (*of work*) irrégularité *f*; (*of statement etc*) incohérence *f*.
inconsistent [ɪnkənˈsɪstnt] *adj* inconséquent(e); irregulier(ière); peu cohérent(e); **~ with** en contradiction avec.
inconsolable [ɪnkənˈsəuləbl] *adj* inconsolable.
inconspicuous [ɪnkənˈspɪkjuəs] *adj* qui passe inaperçu(e); (*colour, dress*) discret(ète); **to make o.s. ~** ne pas se faire remarquer.
inconstant [ɪnˈkɒnstnt] *adj* inconstant(e); variable.
incontinence [ɪnˈkɒntɪnəns] *n* incontinence *f*.
incontinent [ɪnˈkɒntɪnənt] *adj* incontinent(e).
incontrovertible [ɪnkɒntrəˈvəːtəbl] *adj* irréfutable.
inconvenience [ɪnkənˈviːnjəns] *n* inconvénient *m*; (*trouble*) dérangement *m* ♦ *vt* déranger; **don't ~ yourself** ne vous dérangez pas.
inconvenient [ɪnkənˈviːnjənt] *adj* malcommode; (*time, place*) mal choisi(e), qui ne convient pas; **that time is very ~ for me** c'est un moment qui ne me convient pas du tout.
incorporate [ɪnˈkɔːpəreɪt] *vt* incorporer; (*contain*) contenir ♦ *vi* fusionner; (*two firms*) se constituer en société.
incorporated [ɪnˈkɔːpəreɪtɪd] *adj*: **~ company** (*US: abbr* **Inc.**) ≈ société *f* anonyme (S.A.).
incorrect [ɪnkəˈrekt] *adj* incorrect(e); (*opinion, statement*) inexact(e).
incorrigible [ɪnˈkɒrɪdʒɪbl] *adj* incorrigible.
incorruptible [ɪnkəˈrʌptɪbl] *adj* incorruptible.
increase *n* [ˈɪnkriːs] augmentation *f* ♦ *vi, vt* [ɪnˈkriːs] augmenter; **an ~ of 5%** une augmentation de 5%; **to be on the ~** être en augmentation.
increasing [ɪnˈkriːsɪŋ] *adj* croissant(e).
increasingly [ɪnˈkriːsɪŋlɪ] *adv* de plus en plus.
incredible [ɪnˈkredɪbl] *adj* incroyable.
incredulous [ɪnˈkredjuləs] *adj* incrédule.
increment [ˈɪnkrɪmənt] *n* augmentation *f*.
incriminate [ɪnˈkrɪmɪneɪt] *vt* incriminer, compromettre.
incriminating [ɪnˈkrɪmɪneɪtɪŋ] *adj* compromettant(e).
incrust [ɪnˈkrʌst] *vt* = **encrust**.
incubate [ˈɪnkjubeɪt] *vt* (*egg*) couver, incuber ♦ *vi* (*eggs*) couver; (*disease*) couver.
incubation [ɪnkjuˈbeɪʃən] *n* incubation *f*.
incubation period *n* période *f* d'incubation.
incubator [ˈɪnkjubeɪtə*] *n* incubateur *m*; (*for babies*) couveuse *f*.
inculcate [ˈɪnkʌlkeɪt] *vt*: **to ~ sth in sb** inculquer qch à qn.

incumbent [ɪn'kʌmbənt] *adj*: **it is ~ on him to** ... il lui incombe *or* appartient de ... ♦ *n* titulaire *m/f*.

incur [ɪn'kəː*] *vt* (*expenses*) encourir; (*anger, risk*) s'exposer à; (*debt*) contracter; (*loss*) subir.

incurable [ɪn'kjuərəbl] *adj* incurable.

incursion [ɪn'kəːʃən] *n* incursion *f*.

Ind. *abbr* (*US*) = Indiana.

indebted [ɪn'dɛtɪd] *adj*: **to be ~ to sb (for)** être redevable à qn (de).

indecency [ɪn'diːsnsɪ] *n* indécence *f*.

indecent [ɪn'diːsnt] *adj* indécent(e), inconvenant(e).

indecent assault *n* (*BRIT*) attentat *m* à la pudeur.

indecent exposure *n* outrage *m* public à la pudeur.

indecipherable [ɪndɪ'saɪfərəbl] *adj* indéchiffrable.

indecision [ɪndɪ'sɪʒən] *n* indécision *f*.

indecisive [ɪndɪ'saɪsɪv] *adj* indécis(e); (*discussion*) peu concluant(e).

indeed [ɪn'diːd] *adv* en effet, effectivement; (*furthermore*) d'ailleurs; **yes ~!** certainement!

indefatigable [ɪndɪ'fætɪgəbl] *adj* infatigable.

indefensible [ɪndɪ'fɛnsɪbl] *adj* (*conduct*) indéfendable.

indefinable [ɪndɪ'faɪnəbl] *adj* indéfinissable.

indefinite [ɪn'dɛfɪnɪt] *adj* indéfini(e); (*answer*) vague; (*period, number*) indéterminé(e).

indefinitely [ɪn'dɛfɪnɪtlɪ] *adv* (*wait*) indéfiniment; (*speak*) vaguement, avec imprécision.

indelible [ɪn'dɛlɪbl] *adj* indélébile.

indelicate [ɪn'dɛlɪkɪt] *adj* (*tactless*) indélicat(e), grossier(ière); (*not polite*) inconvenant(e), malséant(e).

indemnify [ɪn'dɛmnɪfaɪ] *vt* indemniser, dédommager.

indemnity [ɪn'dɛmnɪtɪ] *n* (*insurance*) assurance *f*, garantie *f*; (*compensation*) indemnité *f*.

indent [ɪn'dɛnt] *vt* (*text*) commencer en retrait.

indentation [ɪndɛn'teɪʃən] *n* découpure *f*; (*TYP*) alinéa *m*; (*on metal*) bosse *f*.

indenture [ɪn'dɛntʃə*] *n* contrat *m* d'emploi-formation.

independence [ɪndɪ'pɛndns] *n* indépendance *f*.

L'**Independence Day** *est la fête nationale aux États-Unis, le 4 juillet. Il commémore l'adoption de la déclaration d'Indépendance, en 1776, écrite par Thomas Jefferson et proclamant la séparation des 13 colonies américaines de la Grande-Bretagne.*

independent [ɪndɪ'pɛndnt] *adj* indépendant(e); **to become ~** s'affranchir.

independently [ɪndɪ'pɛndntlɪ] *adv* de façon in-

dépendante; **~ of** indépendamment de.

in-depth ['ɪndɛpθ] *adj* approfondi(e).

indescribable [ɪndɪ'skraɪbəbl] *adj* indescriptible.

indeterminate [ɪndɪ'təːmɪnɪt] *adj* indéterminé(e).

index ['ɪndɛks] *n* (*pl*: ~**es**: *in book*) index *m*; (: *in library etc*) catalogue *m*; (*pl*: **indices** ['ɪndɪsiːz]) (*ratio, sign*) indice *m*.

index card *n* fiche *f*.

index finger *n* index *m*.

index-linked ['ɪndɛks'lɪŋkt], (*US*) **indexed** ['ɪndɛkst] *adj* indexé(e) (sur le coût de la vie *etc*).

India ['ɪndɪə] *n* Inde *f*.

Indian ['ɪndɪən] *adj* indien(ne) ♦ *n* Indien/ne.

Indian ink *n* encre *f* de Chine.

Indian Ocean *n*: **the ~** l'océan Indien.

Indian summer *n* (*fig*) été indien, beaux jours en automne.

India paper *n* papier *m* bible.

India rubber *n* gomme *f*.

indicate ['ɪndɪkeɪt] *vt* indiquer ♦ *vi* (*BRIT AUT*): **to ~ left/right** mettre son clignotant à gauche/à droite.

indication [ɪndɪ'keɪʃən] *n* indication *f*, signe *m*.

indicative [ɪn'dɪkətɪv] *adj* indicatif(ive) ♦ *n* (*LING*) indicatif *m*; **to be ~ of sth** être symptomatique de qch.

indicator ['ɪndɪkeɪtə*] *n* (*sign*) indicateur *m*; (*AUT*) clignotant *m*.

indices ['ɪndɪsiːz] *npl of* **index**.

indict [ɪn'daɪt] *vt* accuser.

indictable [ɪn'daɪtəbl] *adj* (*person*) passible de poursuites; **~ offence** délit *m* tombant sous le coup de la loi.

indictment [ɪn'daɪtmənt] *n* accusation *f*.

indifference [ɪn'dɪfrəns] *n* indifférence *f*.

indifferent [ɪn'dɪfrənt] *adj* indifférent(e); (*poor*) médiocre, quelconque.

indigenous [ɪn'dɪdʒɪnəs] *adj* indigène.

indigestible [ɪndɪ'dʒɛstɪbl] *adj* indigeste.

indigestion [ɪndɪ'dʒɛstʃən] *n* indigestion *f*, mauvaise digestion.

indignant [ɪn'dɪgnənt] *adj*: **~ (at sth/with sb)** indigné(e) (de qch/contre qn).

indignation [ɪndɪg'neɪʃən] *n* indignation *f*.

indignity [ɪn'dɪgnɪtɪ] *n* indignité *f*, affront *m*.

indigo ['ɪndɪgəu] *adj* indigo *inv* ♦ *n* indigo *m*.

indirect [ɪndɪ'rɛkt] *adj* indirect(e).

indirectly [ɪndɪ'rɛktlɪ] *adv* indirectement.

indiscreet [ɪndɪ'skriːt] *adj* indiscret(ète); (*rash*) imprudent(e).

indiscretion [ɪndɪ'skrɛʃən] *n* (*see indiscreet*) indiscrétion *f*; imprudence *f*.

indiscriminate [ɪndɪ'skrɪmɪnət] *adj* (*person*) qui manque de discernement; (*admiration*) aveugle; (*killings*) commis(e) au hasard.

indispensable [ɪndɪ'spɛnsəbl] *adj* indispensable.

indisposed [ɪndɪ'spəuzd] *adj* (*unwell*) indisposé(e), souffrant(e).

indisposition [ɪndɪspə'zɪʃən] n (*illness*) indisposition f, malaise m.

indisputable [ɪndɪ'spju:təbl] adj incontestable, indiscutable.

indistinct [ɪndɪ'stɪŋkt] adj indistinct(e); (*memory, noise*) vague.

indistinguishable [ɪndɪ'stɪŋgwɪʃəbl] adj impossible à distinguer.

individual [ɪndɪ'vɪdjuəl] n individu m ♦ adj individuel(le); (*characteristic*) particulier(ière), original(e).

individualist [ɪndɪ'vɪdjuəlɪst] n individualiste m/f.

individuality [ɪndɪvɪdju'ælɪtɪ] n individualité f.

individually [ɪndɪ'vɪdjuəlɪ] adv individuellement.

indivisible [ɪndɪ'vɪzɪbl] adj indivisible; (*MATH*) insécable.

Indo-China ['ɪndəu'tʃaɪnə] n Indochine f.

indoctrinate [ɪn'dɔktrɪneɪt] vt endoctriner.

indoctrination [ɪndɔktrɪ'neɪʃən] n endoctrinement m.

indolent ['ɪndələnt] adj indolent(e), nonchalant(e).

Indonesia [ɪndə'ni:zɪə] n Indonésie f.

Indonesian [ɪndə'ni:zɪən] adj indonésien(ne) ♦ n Indonésien/ne; (*LING*) indonésien m.

indoor ['ɪndɔ:*] adj d'intérieur; (*plant*) d'appartement; (*swimming pool*) couvert(e); (*sport, games*) pratiqué(e) en salle.

indoors [ɪn'dɔ:z] adv à l'intérieur; (*at home*) à la maison.

indubitable [ɪn'dju:bɪtəbl] adj indubitable, incontestable.

induce [ɪn'dju:s] vt persuader; (*bring about*) provoquer; **to ~ sb to do sth** inciter *or* pousser qn à faire qch.

inducement [ɪn'dju:smənt] n incitation f; (*incentive*) but m; (*pej: bribe*) pot-de-vin m.

induct [ɪn'dʌkt] vt établir dans ses fonctions; (*fig*) initier.

induction [ɪn'dʌkʃən] n (*MED: of birth*) accouchement provoqué.

induction course n (*BRIT*) stage m de mise au courant.

indulge [ɪn'dʌldʒ] vt (*whim*) céder à, satisfaire; (*child*) gâter ♦ vi: **to ~ in sth** s'offrir qch, se permettre qch; se livrer à qch.

indulgence [ɪn'dʌldʒəns] n fantaisie f (que l'on s'offre); (*leniency*) indulgence f.

indulgent [ɪn'dʌldʒənt] adj indulgent(e).

industrial [ɪn'dʌstrɪəl] adj industriel(le); (*injury*) du travail; (*dispute*) ouvrier(ière).

industrial action n action revendicative.

industrial estate n (*BRIT*) zone industrielle.

industrialist [ɪn'dʌstrɪəlɪst] n industriel m.

industrialize [ɪn'dʌstrɪəlaɪz] vt industrialiser.

industrial park n (*US*) zone industrielle.

industrial relations npl relations fpl dans l'entreprise.

industrial tribunal n (*BRIT*) ≈ conseil m de prud'hommes.

industrial unrest n (*BRIT*) agitation sociale, conflits sociaux.

industrious [ɪn'dʌstrɪəs] adj travailleur(euse).

industry ['ɪndəstrɪ] n industrie f; (*diligence*) zèle m, application f.

inebriated [ɪ'ni:brɪeɪtɪd] adj ivre.

inedible [ɪn'ɛdɪbl] adj immangeable; (*plant etc*) non comestible.

ineffective [ɪnɪ'fɛktɪv], **ineffectual** [ɪnɪ'fɛktʃuəl] adj inefficace; incompétent(e).

inefficiency [ɪnɪ'fɪʃənsɪ] n inefficacité f.

inefficient [ɪnɪ'fɪʃənt] adj inefficace.

inelegant [ɪn'ɛlɪgənt] adj peu élégant(e), inélégant(e).

ineligible [ɪn'ɛlɪdʒɪbl] adj (*candidate*) inéligible; **to be ~ for sth** ne pas avoir droit à qch.

inept [ɪ'nɛpt] adj inepte.

ineptitude [ɪ'nɛptɪtju:d] n ineptie f.

inequality [ɪnɪ'kwɔlɪtɪ] n inégalité f.

inequitable [ɪn'ɛkwɪtəbl] adj inéquitable, inique.

ineradicable [ɪnɪ'rædɪkəbl] adj indéracinable, tenace.

inert [ɪ'nə:t] adj inerte.

inertia [ɪ'nə:ʃə] n inertie f.

inertia-reel seat belt [ɪ'nə:ʃə'ri:l-] n ceinture f de sécurité à enrouleur.

inescapable [ɪnɪ'skeɪpəbl] adj inéluctable, inévitable.

inessential [ɪnɪ'sɛnʃl] adj superflu(e).

inestimable [ɪn'ɛstɪməbl] adj inestimable, incalculable.

inevitable [ɪn'ɛvɪtəbl] adj inévitable.

inevitably [ɪn'ɛvɪtəblɪ] adv inévitablement, fatalement.

inexact [ɪnɪg'zækt] adj inexact(e).

inexcusable [ɪnɪks'kju:zəbl] adj inexcusable.

inexhaustible [ɪnɪg'zɔ:stɪbl] adj inépuisable.

inexorable [ɪn'ɛksərəbl] adj inexorable.

inexpensive [ɪnɪk'spɛnsɪv] adj bon marché inv.

inexperience [ɪnɪk'spɪərɪəns] n inexpérience f, manque m d'expérience.

inexperienced [ɪnɪk'spɪərɪənst] adj inexpérimenté(e); **to be ~ in sth** manquer d'expérience dans qch.

inexplicable [ɪnɪk'splɪkəbl] adj inexplicable.

inexpressible [ɪnɪk'sprɛsɪbl] adj inexprimable, indicible.

inextricable [ɪnɪk'strɪkəbl] adj inextricable.

infallibility [ɪnfælə'bɪlɪtɪ] n infaillibilité f.

infallible [ɪn'fælɪbl] adj infaillible.

infamous ['ɪnfəməs] adj infâme, abominable.

infamy ['ɪnfəmɪ] n infamie f.

infancy ['ɪnfənsɪ] n petite enfance, bas âge; (*fig*) enfance, débuts mpl.

infant ['ɪnfənt] n (*baby*) nourrisson m; (*young child*) petit(e) enfant.

infantile ['ɪnfəntaɪl] adj infantile.

infant mortality n mortalité f infantile.

infantry ['ɪnfəntrɪ] n infanterie f.

infantryman ['ɪnfəntrɪmən] n fantassin m.

infant school n (BRIT) classes fpl préparatoires (entre 5 et 7 ans).

infatuated [ɪn'fætjueɪtɪd] adj: ~ **with** entiché(e) de; **to become ~ (with sb)** s'enticher (de qn).

infatuation [ɪnfætjuˈeɪʃən] n toquade f; engouement m.

infect [ɪn'fɛkt] vt infecter, contaminer; (fig: pej) corrompre; **~ed with** (illness) atteint(e) de; **to become ~ed** (wound) s'infecter.

infection [ɪn'fɛkʃən] n infection f; contagion f.

infectious [ɪn'fɛkʃəs] adj infectieux(euse); (also fig) contagieux(euse).

infer [ɪn'fə:*] vt: **to ~ (from)** conclure (de), déduire (de).

inference ['ɪnfərəns] n conclusion f, déduction f.

inferior [ɪn'fɪərɪə*] adj inférieur(e); (goods) de qualité inférieure ♦ n inférieur/e; (in rank) subalterne m/f; **to feel ~** avoir un sentiment d'infériorité.

inferiority [ɪnfɪərɪˈɔrətɪ] n infériorité f.

inferiority complex n complexe m d'infériorité.

infernal [ɪn'fə:nl] adj infernal(e).

inferno [ɪn'fə:nəu] n enfer m; brasier m.

infertile [ɪn'fə:taɪl] adj stérile.

infertility [ɪnfə:'tɪlɪtɪ] n infertilité f, stérilité f.

infested [ɪn'fɛstɪd] adj: ~ **(with)** infesté(e) (de).

infidelity [ɪnfɪ'dɛlɪtɪ] n infidélité f.

in-fighting ['ɪnfaɪtɪŋ] n querelles fpl internes.

infiltrate ['ɪnfɪltreɪt] vt (troops etc) faire s'infiltrer; (enemy line etc) s'infiltrer dans ♦ vi s'infiltrer.

infinite ['ɪnfɪnɪt] adj infini(e); (time, money) illimité(e).

infinitely ['ɪnfɪnɪtlɪ] adv infiniment.

infinitesimal [ɪnfɪnɪ'tɛsɪməl] adj infinitésimal(e).

infinitive [ɪn'fɪnɪtɪv] n infinitif m.

infinity [ɪn'fɪnɪtɪ] n infinité f; (also MATH) infini m.

infirm [ɪn'fə:m] adj infirme.

infirmary [ɪn'fə:mərɪ] n hôpital m; (in school, factory) infirmerie f.

infirmity [ɪn'fə:mɪtɪ] n infirmité f.

inflamed [ɪn'fleɪmd] adj enflammé(e).

inflammable [ɪn'flæməbl] adj (BRIT) inflammable.

inflammation [ɪnflə'meɪʃən] n inflammation f.

inflammatory [ɪn'flæmətərɪ] adj (speech) incendiaire.

inflatable [ɪn'fleɪtəbl] adj gonflable.

inflate [ɪn'fleɪt] vt (tyre, balloon) gonfler; (fig) grossir; gonfler; faire monter.

inflated [ɪn'fleɪtɪd] adj (style) enflé(e); (value) exagéré(e).

inflation [ɪn'fleɪʃən] n (ECON) inflation f.

inflationary [ɪn'fleɪʃənərɪ] adj inflationniste.

inflection [ɪn'flɛkʃən] n inflexion f; (ending) désinence f.

inflexible [ɪn'flɛksɪbl] adj inflexible, rigide.

inflict [ɪn'flɪkt] vt: **to ~ on** infliger à.

infliction [ɪn'flɪkʃən] n infliction f; affliction f.

in-flight ['ɪnflaɪt] adj (refuelling) en vol; (service etc) à bord.

inflow ['ɪnfləu] n afflux m.

influence ['ɪnfluəns] n influence f ♦ vt influencer; **under the ~ of** sous l'effet de; **under the ~ of drink** en état d'ébriété.

influential [ɪnflu'ɛnʃl] adj influent(e).

influenza [ɪnflu'ɛnzə] n grippe f.

influx ['ɪnflʌks] n afflux m.

inform [ɪn'fɔ:m] vt: **to ~ sb (of)** informer or avertir qn (de) ♦ vi: **to ~ on sb** dénoncer qn, informer contre qn; **to ~ sb about** renseigner qn sur, mettre qn au courant de.

informal [ɪn'fɔ:ml] adj (person, manner) simple, sans cérémonie; (announcement, visit) non officiel(le); "**dress ~**" "tenue de ville".

informality [ɪnfɔ:'mælɪtɪ] n simplicité f, absence f de cérémonie; caractère non officiel.

informal language n langage m de la conversation.

informally [ɪn'fɔ:məlɪ] adv sans cérémonie, en toute simplicité; non officiellement.

informant [ɪn'fɔ:mənt] n informateur/trice.

information [ɪnfə'meɪʃən] n information(s) f(pl); renseignements mpl; (knowledge) connaissances fpl; **to get ~ on** se renseigner sur; **a piece of ~** un renseignement; **for your ~** à titre d'information.

information bureau n bureau m de renseignements.

information processing n traitement m de l'information.

information retrieval n recherche f (informatique) de renseignements.

information superhighway n autoroute f de l'information.

information technology (IT) n informatique f.

informative [ɪn'fɔ:mətɪv] adj instructif(ive).

informed [ɪn'fɔ:md] adj (bien) informé(e); **an ~ guess** une hypothèse fondée sur la connaissance des faits.

informer [ɪn'fɔ:mə*] n dénonciateur/trice; (also: **police ~**) indicateur/trice.

infra dig ['ɪnfrə'dɪg] adj abbr (col: = infra dignitatem) au-dessous de ma (or sa etc) dignité.

infra-red [ɪnfrə'rɛd] adj infrarouge.

infrastructure ['ɪnfrəstrʌktʃə*] n infrastructure f.

infrequent [ɪn'fri:kwənt] adj peu fréquent(e), rare.

infringe [ɪn'frɪndʒ] vt enfreindre ♦ vi: **to ~ on** empiéter sur.

infringement [ɪn'frɪndʒmənt] n: ~ **(of)** infraction f (à).

infuriate [ɪn'fjuərɪeɪt] vt mettre en fureur.

infuriating [ɪn'fjuərɪeɪtɪŋ] adj exaspérant(e).

infuse [ɪn'fju:z] vt: **to ~ sb with sth** (fig) insuffler qch à qn.

infusion [ɪnˈfjuːʒən] *n* (*tea etc*) infusion *f*.
ingenious [ɪnˈdʒiːnjəs] *adj* ingénieux(euse).
ingenuity [ɪndʒɪˈnjuːɪtɪ] *n* ingéniosité *f*.
ingenuous [ɪnˈdʒɛnjuəs] *adj* franc(franche), ouvert(e).
ingot [ˈɪŋgət] *n* lingot *m*.
ingrained [ɪnˈgreɪnd] *adj* enraciné(e).
ingratiate [ɪnˈgreɪʃɪeɪt] *vt*: **to ~ o.s. with** s'insinuer dans les bonnes grâces de, se faire bien voir de.
ingratiating [ɪnˈgreɪʃɪeɪtɪŋ] *adj* (*smile, speech*) insinuant(e); (*person*) patelin(e).
ingratitude [ɪnˈgrætɪtjuːd] *n* ingratitude *f*.
ingredient [ɪnˈgriːdɪənt] *n* ingrédient *m*; élément *m*.
ingrowing [ˈɪngrəuɪŋ], **ingrown** [ˈɪngrəun] *adj*: **~ toenail** ongle incarné.
inhabit [ɪnˈhæbɪt] *vt* habiter.
inhabitable [ɪnˈhæbɪtəbl] *adj* habitable.
inhabitant [ɪnˈhæbɪtnt] *n* habitant/e.
inhale [ɪnˈheɪl] *vt* inhaler; (*perfume*) respirer ♦ *vi* (*in smoking*) avaler la fumée.
inhaler [ɪnˈheɪlə*] *n* inhalateur *m*.
inherent [ɪnˈhɪərənt] *adj*: **~ (in or to)** inhérent(e) (à).
inherently [ɪnˈhɪərəntlɪ] *adv* (*easy, difficult*) en soi; (*lazy*) fondamentalement.
inherit [ɪnˈhɛrɪt] *vt* hériter (de).
inheritance [ɪnˈhɛrɪtəns] *n* héritage *m*; **law of ~** droit *m* de la succession.
inhibit [ɪnˈhɪbɪt] *vt* (*PSYCH*) inhiber; **to ~ sb from doing** empêcher *or* retenir qn de faire.
inhibited [ɪnˈhɪbɪtɪd] *adj* (*person*) inhibé(e).
inhibiting [ɪnˈhɪbɪtɪŋ] *adj* gênant(e).
inhibition [ɪnhɪˈbɪʃən] *n* inhibition *f*.
inhospitable [ɪnhɔsˈpɪtəbl] *adj* inhospitalier(ière).
in-house [ˈɪnˈhaus] *adj* (*system*) interne; (*training*) effectué(e) sur place *or* dans le cadre de la compagnie ♦ *adv* (*train, produce*) sur place.
inhuman [ɪnˈhjuːmən] *adj* inhumain(e).
inhumane [ɪnhjuːˈmeɪn] *adj* inhumain(e).
inimitable [ɪˈnɪmɪtəbl] *adj* inimitable.
iniquity [ɪˈnɪkwɪtɪ] *n* iniquité *f*.
initial [ɪˈnɪʃl] *adj* initial(e) ♦ *n* initiale *f* ♦ *vt* parafer; **~s** *npl* initiales *fpl*; (*as signature*) parafe *m*.
initialize [ɪˈnɪʃəlaɪz] *vt* (*COMPUT*) initialiser.
initially [ɪˈnɪʃəlɪ] *adv* initialement, au début.
initiate [ɪˈnɪʃɪeɪt] *vt* (*start*) entreprendre; amorcer; lancer; (*person*) initier; **to ~ sb into a secret** initier qn à un secret; **to ~ proceedings against sb** (*LAW*) intenter une action à qn, engager des poursuites contre qn.
initiation [ɪnɪʃɪˈeɪʃən] *n* (*into secret etc*) initiation *f*.
initiative [ɪˈnɪʃətɪv] *n* initiative *f*; **to take the ~** prendre l'initiative.
inject [ɪnˈdʒɛkt] *vt* (*liquid, fig: money*) injecter; (*person*) faire une piqûre à.
injection [ɪnˈdʒɛkʃən] *n* injection *f*, piqûre *f*; **to**

have an ~ se faire faire une piqûre.
injudicious [ɪndʒuːˈdɪʃəs] *adj* peu judicieux(euse).
injunction [ɪnˈdʒʌŋkʃən] *n* (*LAW*) injonction *f*, ordre *m*.
injure [ˈɪndʒə*] *vt* blesser; (*wrong*) faire du tort à; (*damage: reputation etc*) compromettre; (*feelings*) heurter; **to ~ o.s.** se blesser.
injured [ˈɪndʒəd] *adj* (*person, leg etc*) blessé(e); (*tone, feelings*) offensé(e); **~ party** (*LAW*) partie lésée.
injurious [ɪnˈdʒuərɪəs] *adj*: **~ (to)** préjudiciable (à).
injury [ˈɪndʒərɪ] *n* blessure *f*; (*wrong*) tort *m*; **to escape without ~** s'en sortir sain et sauf.
injury time *n* (*SPORT*) arrêts *mpl* de jeu.
injustice [ɪnˈdʒʌstɪs] *n* injustice *f*; **you do me an ~** vous êtes injuste envers moi.
ink [ɪŋk] *n* encre *f*.
ink-jet printer [ˈɪŋkdʒɛt-] *n* imprimante *f* à jet d'encre.
inkling [ˈɪŋklɪŋ] *n* soupçon *m*, vague idée *f*.
inkpad [ˈɪŋkpæd] *n* tampon *m* encreur.
inky [ˈɪŋkɪ] *adj* taché(e) d'encre.
inlaid [ˈɪnleɪd] *adj* incrusté(e); (*table etc*) marqueté(e).
inland *adj* [ˈɪnlənd] intérieur(e) ♦ *adv* [ɪnˈlænd] à l'intérieur, dans les terres; **~ waterways** canaux *mpl* et rivières *fpl*.
Inland Revenue *n* (*BRIT*) fisc *m*.
in-laws [ˈɪnlɔːz] *npl* beaux-parents *mpl*; belle famille.
inlet [ˈɪnlɛt] *n* (*GEO*) crique *f*.
inlet pipe *n* (*TECH*) tuyau *m* d'arrivée.
inmate [ˈɪnmeɪt] *n* (*in prison*) détenu/e; (*in asylum*) interné/e.
inmost [ˈɪnməust] *adj* le(la) plus profond(e).
inn [ɪn] *n* auberge *f*.
innards [ˈɪnədz] *npl* (*col*) entrailles *fpl*.
innate [ɪˈneɪt] *adj* inné(e).
inner [ˈɪnə*] *adj* intérieur(e).
inner city *n* (vieux quartiers du) centre urbain (*souffrant souvent de délabrement, d'embouteillages etc*).
innermost [ˈɪnəməust] *adj* le(la) plus profond(e).
inner tube *n* (*of tyre*) chambre *f* à air.
innings [ˈɪnɪŋz] *n* (*CRICKET*) tour *m* de batte; (*BRIT fig*): **he has had a good ~** il (en) a bien profité.
innocence [ˈɪnəsns] *n* innocence *f*.
innocent [ˈɪnəsnt] *adj* innocent(e).
innocuous [ɪˈnɔkjuəs] *adj* inoffensif(ive).
innovation [ɪnəuˈveɪʃən] *n* innovation *f*.
innuendo, **~es** [ɪnjuˈɛndəu] *n* insinuation *f*, allusion (malveillante).
innumerable [ɪˈnjuːmrəbl] *adj* innombrable.
inoculate [ɪˈnɔkjuleɪt] *vt*: **to ~ sb with sth** inoculer qch à qn; **to ~ sb against sth** vacciner qn contre qch.
inoculation [ɪnɔkjuˈleɪʃən] *n* inoculation *f*.
inoffensive [ɪnəˈfɛnsɪv] *adj* inoffensif(ive).

inopportune [ɪn'ɔpətjuːn] *adj* inopportun(e).
inordinate [ɪ'nɔːdɪnət] *adj* démesuré(e).
inordinately [ɪ'nɔːdɪnətlɪ] *adv* démesurément.
inorganic [ɪnɔː'gænɪk] *adj* inorganique.
in-patient ['ɪnpeɪʃənt] *n* malade hospitalisé(e).
input ['ɪnput] *n* (*ELEC*) énergie *f*, puissance *f*; (*of machine*) consommation *f*; (*of computer*) information fournie ♦ *vt* (*COMPUT*) introduire, entrer.
inquest ['ɪnkwɛst] *n* enquête (criminelle).
inquire [ɪn'kwaɪə*] *vi* demander ♦ *vt* demander, s'informer de; **to ~ about** s'informer de, se renseigner sur; **to ~ when/where/ whether** demander quand/où/si.
▶**inquire after** *vt fus* demander des nouvelles de.
▶**inquire into** *vt fus* faire une enquête sur.
inquiring [ɪn'kwaɪərɪŋ] *adj* (*mind*) curieux(euse), investigateur(trice).
inquiry [ɪn'kwaɪərɪ] *n* demande *f* de renseignements; (*LAW*) enquête *f*, investigation *f*; **to hold an ~ into sth** enquêter sur qch.
inquiry desk *n* (*BRIT*) guichet *m* de renseignements.
inquiry office *n* (*BRIT*) bureau *m* de renseignements.
inquisition [ɪnkwɪ'zɪʃən] *n* enquête *f*, investigation *f*; (*REL*): **the I~** l'Inquisition *f*.
inquisitive [ɪn'kwɪzɪtɪv] *adj* curieux(euse).
inroads ['ɪnrəudz] *npl*: **to make ~ into** (*savings, supplies*) entamer.
ins *abbr* = **inches**.
insane [ɪn'seɪn] *adj* fou(folle); (*MED*) aliéné(e).
insanitary [ɪn'sænɪtərɪ] *adj* insalubre.
insanity [ɪn'sænɪtɪ] *n* folie *f*; (*MED*) aliénation (mentale).
insatiable [ɪn'seɪʃəbl] *adj* insatiable.
inscribe [ɪn'skraɪb] *vt* inscrire; (*book etc*): **to ~ (to sb)** dédicacer (à qn).
inscription [ɪn'skrɪpʃən] *n* inscription *f*; (*in book*) dédicace *f*.
inscrutable [ɪn'skruːtəbl] *adj* impénétrable.
inseam ['ɪnsiːm] *n* (*US*): **~ measurement** hauteur *f* d'entre-jambe.
insect ['ɪnsɛkt] *n* insecte *m*.
insect bite *n* piqûre *f* d'insecte.
insecticide [ɪn'sɛktɪsaɪd] *n* insecticide *m*.
insect repellent *n* crème *f* anti-insectes.
insecure [ɪnsɪ'kjuə*] *adj* peu solide; peu sûr(e); (*person*) anxieux(euse).
insecurity [ɪnsɪ'kjuərɪtɪ] *n* insécurité *f*.
insensible [ɪn'sɛnsɪbl] *adj* insensible; (*unconscious*) sans connaissance.
insensitive [ɪn'sɛnsɪtɪv] *adj* insensible.
insensitivity [ɪnsɛnsɪ'tɪvɪtɪ] *n* insensibilité *f*.
inseparable [ɪn'sɛprəbl] *adj* inséparable.
insert *vt* [ɪn'səːt] insérer ♦ *n* ['ɪnsəːt] insertion *f*.
insertion [ɪn'səːʃən] *n* insertion *f*.
in-service ['ɪn'səːvɪs] *adj* (*training*) continu(e); (*course*) d'initiation; de perfectionnement;

de recyclage.
inshore [ɪn'ʃɔː*] *adj* côtier(ière) ♦ *adv* près de la côte; vers la côte.
inside ['ɪn'saɪd] *n* intérieur *m*; (*of road*: *BRIT*) côté *m* gauche (*de la route*); (: *US, Europe etc*) côté droit (*de la route*) ♦ *adj* intérieur(e) ♦ *adv* à l'intérieur, dedans ♦ *prep* à l'intérieur de; (*of time*): **~ 10 minutes** en moins de 10 minutes; **~s** *npl* (*col*) intestins *mpl*; **~ out** *adv* à l'envers; **to turn sth ~ out** retourner qch; **to know sth ~ out** connaître qch à fond *or* comme sa poche; **~ information** renseignements *mpl* à la source; **~ story** histoire racontée par un témoin.
inside forward *n* (*SPORT*) intérieur *m*.
inside lane *n* (*AUT*: *in Britain*) voie *f* de gauche; (: *in US, Europe*) voie *f* de droite.
inside leg measurement *n* (*BRIT*) hauteur *f* d'entre-jambe.
insider [ɪn'saɪdə*] *n* initié/e.
insider dealing, insider trading *n* (*STOCK EXCHANGE*) délit *m* d'initiés.
insidious [ɪn'sɪdɪəs] *adj* insidieux(euse).
insight ['ɪnsaɪt] *n* perspicacité *f*; (*glimpse, idea*) aperçu *m*; **to gain (an) ~ into** parvenir à comprendre.
insignia [ɪn'sɪɡnɪə] *npl* insignes *mpl*.
insignificant [ɪnsɪɡ'nɪfɪknt] *adj* insignifiant(e).
insincere [ɪnsɪn'sɪə*] *adj* hypocrite.
insincerity [ɪnsɪn'sɛrɪtɪ] *n* manque *m* de sincérité, hypocrisie *f*.
insinuate [ɪn'sɪnjueɪt] *vt* insinuer.
insinuation [ɪnsɪnju'eɪʃən] *n* insinuation *f*.
insipid [ɪn'sɪpɪd] *adj* insipide, fade.
insist [ɪn'sɪst] *vi* insister; **to ~ on doing** insister pour faire; **to ~ that** insister pour que; (*claim*) maintenir *or* soutenir que.
insistence [ɪn'sɪstəns] *n* insistance *f*.
insistent [ɪn'sɪstənt] *adj* insistant(e), pressant(e).
insofar [ɪnsəu'fɑː*]: **~ as** *conj* dans la mesure où.
insole ['ɪnsəul] *n* semelle intérieure; (*fixed part of shoe*) première *f*.
insolence ['ɪnsələns] *n* insolence *f*.
insolent ['ɪnsələnt] *adj* insolent(e).
insoluble [ɪn'sɔljubl] *adj* insoluble.
insolvency [ɪn'sɔlvənsɪ] *n* insolvabilité *f*; faillite *f*.
insolvent [ɪn'sɔlvənt] *adj* insolvable; (*bankrupt*) en faillite.
insomnia [ɪn'sɔmnɪə] *n* insomnie *f*.
insomniac [ɪn'sɔmnɪæk] *n* insomniaque *m/f*.
inspect [ɪn'spɛkt] *vt* inspecter; (*BRIT*: *ticket*) contrôler.
inspection [ɪn'spɛkʃən] *n* inspection *f*; contrôle *m*.
inspector [ɪn'spɛktə*] *n* inspecteur/trice; contrôleur/euse.
inspiration [ɪnspə'reɪʃən] *n* inspiration *f*.
inspire [ɪn'spaɪə*] *vt* inspirer.
inspired [ɪn'spaɪəd] *adj* (*writer, book etc*) inspi-

ré(e); **in an ~ moment** dans un moment d'inspiration.

inspiring [ɪn'spaɪərɪŋ] *adj* inspirant(e).

inst. *abbr* (*BRIT COMM*: = *instant*): **of the 16th ~** du 16 courant.

instability [ɪnstə'bɪlɪtɪ] *n* instabilité *f*.

install [ɪn'stɔːl] *vt* installer.

installation [ɪnstə'leɪʃən] *n* installation *f*.

installment plan *n* (*US*) achat *m* (*or* vente *f*) à tempérament *or* crédit.

instalment, (*US*) **installment** [ɪn'stɔːlmənt] *n* acompte *m*, versement partiel; (*of TV serial etc*) épisode *m*; **in ~s** (*pay*) à tempérament; (*receive*) en plusieurs fois.

instance ['ɪnstəns] *n* exemple *m*; **for ~** par exemple; **in many ~s** dans bien des cas; **in that ~** dans ce cas; **in the first ~** tout d'abord, en premier lieu.

instant ['ɪnstənt] *n* instant *m* ♦ *adj* immédiat(e); urgent(e); (*coffee, food*) instanané(e), en poudre; **the 10th ~** le 10 courant.

instantaneous [ɪnstən'teɪnɪəs] *adj* instantané(e).

instantly ['ɪnstəntlɪ] *adv* immédiatement, tout de suite.

instant replay *n* (*US TV*) retour *m* sur une séquence.

instead [ɪn'stɛd] *adv* au lieu de cela; **~ of** au lieu de; **~ of sb** à la place de qn.

instep ['ɪnstɛp] *n* cou-de-pied *m*; (*of shoe*) cambrure *f*.

instigate ['ɪnstɪgeɪt] *vt* (*rebellion, strike, crime*) inciter à; (*new ideas etc*) susciter.

instigation [ɪnstɪ'geɪʃən] *n* instigation *f*; **at sb's ~** à l'instigation de qn.

instil [ɪn'stɪl] *vt*: **to ~ (into)** inculquer (à); (*courage*) insuffler (à).

instinct ['ɪnstɪŋkt] *n* instinct *m*.

instinctive [ɪn'stɪŋktɪv] *adj* instinctif(ive).

instinctively [ɪn'stɪŋktɪvlɪ] *adv* instinctivement.

institute ['ɪnstɪtjuːt] *n* institut *m* ♦ *vt* instituer, établir; (*inquiry*) ouvrir; (*proceedings*) entamer.

institution [ɪnstɪ'tjuːʃən] *n* institution *f*; (*school*) établissement *m* (scolaire); (*for care*) établissement (psychiatrique *etc*).

institutional [ɪnstɪ'tjuːʃənl] *adj* institutionnel(le); **~ care** soins fournis par un établissement médico-social.

instruct [ɪn'strʌkt] *vt* instruire, former; **to ~ sb in sth** enseigner qch à qn; **to ~ sb to do** charger qn *or* ordonner à qn de faire.

instruction [ɪn'strʌkʃən] *n* instruction *f*; **~s** *npl* directives *fpl*; **~s for use** mode *m* d'emploi.

instruction book *n* manuel *m* d'instructions.

instructive [ɪn'strʌktɪv] *adj* instructif(ive).

instructor [ɪn'strʌktə*] *n* professeur *m*; (*for skiing, driving*) moniteur *m*.

instrument ['ɪnstrumənt] *n* instrument *m*.

instrumental [ɪnstru'mɛntl] *adj* (*MUS*) instrumental(e); **to be ~ in sth/in doing sth** contribuer à qch/à faire qch.

instrumentalist [ɪnstru'mɛntəlɪst] *n* instrumentiste *m/f*.

instrument panel *n* tableau *m* de bord.

insubordinate [ɪnsə'bɔːdənɪt] *adj* insubordonné(e).

insubordination [ɪnsəbɔːdə'neɪʃən] *n* insubordination *f*.

insufferable [ɪn'sʌfrəbl] *adj* insupportable.

insufficient [ɪnsə'fɪʃənt] *adj* insuffisant(e).

insufficiently [ɪnsə'fɪʃəntlɪ] *adv* insuffisamment.

insular ['ɪnsjulə*] *adj* insulaire; (*outlook*) étroit(e); (*person*) aux vues étroites.

insulate ['ɪnsjuleɪt] *vt* isoler; (*against sound*) insonoriser.

insulating tape ['ɪnsjuleɪtɪŋ-] *n* ruban isolant.

insulation [ɪnsju'leɪʃən] *n* isolation *f*; insonorisation *f*.

insulin ['ɪnsjulɪn] *n* insuline *f*.

insult *n* ['ɪnsʌlt] insulte *f*, affront *m* ♦ *vt* [ɪn'sʌlt] insulter, faire un affront à.

insulting [ɪn'sʌltɪŋ] *adj* insultant(e), injurieux(euse).

insuperable [ɪn'sjuːprəbl] *adj* insurmontable.

insurance [ɪn'ʃuərəns] *n* assurance *f*; **fire/life ~** assurance-incendie/-vie; **to take out ~ (against)** s'assurer (contre).

insurance agent *n* agent *m* d'assurances.

insurance broker *n* courtier *m* en assurances.

insurance policy *n* police *f* d'assurance.

insurance premium *n* prime *f* d'assurance.

insure [ɪn'ʃuə*] *vt* assurer; **to ~ sb/sb's life** assurer qn/la vie de qn; **to be ~d for £5000** être assuré(e) pour 5 000 livres.

insured [ɪn'ʃuəd] *n*: **the ~** l'assuré/e.

insurer [ɪn'ʃuərə*] *n* assureur *m*.

insurgent [ɪn'sɔːdʒənt] *adj, n* insurgé(e).

insurmountable [ɪnsə'mauntəbl] *adj* insurmontable.

insurrection [ɪnsə'rɛkʃən] *n* insurrection *f*.

intact [ɪn'tækt] *adj* intact(e).

intake ['ɪnteɪk] *n* (*TECH*) admission *f*; adduction *f*; (*of food*) consommation *f*; (*BRIT SCOL*): **an ~ of 200 a year** 200 admissions par an.

intangible [ɪn'tændʒɪbl] *adj* intangible; (*assets*) immatériel(le).

integral ['ɪntɪgrəl] *adj* intégral(e); (*part*) intégrant(e).

integrate ['ɪntɪgreɪt] *vt* intégrer ♦ *vi* s'intégrer.

integrated circuit ['ɪntɪgreɪtɪd-] *n* (*COMPUT*) circuit intégré.

integration [ɪntɪ'greɪʃən] *n* intégration *f*; **racial ~** intégration raciale.

integrity [ɪn'tɛgrɪtɪ] *n* intégrité *f*.

intellect ['ɪntəlɛkt] *n* intelligence *f*.

intellectual [ɪntə'lɛktjuəl] *adj, n* intellectuel(le).

intelligence [ɪn'tɛlɪdʒəns] *n* intelligence *f*; (*MIL etc*) informations *fpl*, renseignements *mpl*.

intelligence quotient (IQ) n quotient intellectuel (QI).

Intelligence Service n services mpl de renseignements.

intelligence test n test m d'intelligence.

intelligent [ɪn'tɛlɪdʒənt] adj intelligent(e).

intelligently [ɪn'tɛlɪdʒəntlɪ] adv intelligemment.

intelligible [ɪn'tɛlɪdʒɪbl] adj intelligible.

intemperate [ɪn'tɛmpərət] adj immodéré(e); (drinking too much) adonné(e) à la boisson.

intend [ɪn'tɛnd] vt (gift etc): **to ~ sth for** destiner qch à; **to ~ to do** avoir l'intention de faire.

intended [ɪn'tɛndɪd] adj (insult) intentionnel(le); (journey) projeté(e); (effect) voulu(e).

intense [ɪn'tɛns] adj intense; (person) véhément(e).

intensely [ɪn'tɛnslɪ] adv intensément; (moving) profondément.

intensify [ɪn'tɛnsɪfaɪ] vt intensifier.

intensity [ɪn'tɛnsɪtɪ] n intensité f.

intensive [ɪn'tɛnsɪv] adj intensif(ive).

intensive care n: **to be in ~** être en réanimation; **~ unit** n service m de réanimation.

intent [ɪn'tɛnt] n intention f ♦ adj attentif(ive), absorbé(e); **to all ~s and purposes** en fait, pratiquement; **to be ~ on doing sth** être (bien) décidé à faire qch.

intention [ɪn'tɛnʃən] n intention f.

intentional [ɪn'tɛnʃənl] adj intentionnel(le), délibéré(e).

intently [ɪn'tɛntlɪ] adv attentivement.

inter [ɪn'tə:*] vt enterrer.

interact [ɪntər'ækt] vi avoir une action réciproque.

interaction [ɪntər'ækʃən] n interaction f.

interactive [ɪntər'æktɪv] adj (group) interactif(ive); (COMPUT) interactif, conversationnel(le).

intercede [ɪntə'si:d] vi: **to ~ with sb/on behalf of sb** intercéder auprès de qn/en faveur de qn.

intercept [ɪntə'sɛpt] vt intercepter; (person) arrêter au passage.

interception [ɪntə'sɛpʃən] n interception f.

interchange n ['ɪntətʃeɪndʒ] (exchange) échange m; (on motorway) échangeur m ♦ vt [ɪntə'tʃeɪndʒ] échanger; mettre à la place l'un(e) de l'autre.

interchangeable [ɪntə'tʃeɪndʒəbl] adj interchangeable.

intercity [ɪntə'sɪtɪ] adj: **~ (train)** train m rapide.

intercom ['ɪntəkɔm] n interphone m.

interconnect [ɪntəkə'nɛkt] vi (rooms) communiquer.

intercontinental ['ɪntəkɔntɪ'nɛntl] adj intercontinental(e).

intercourse ['ɪntəkɔ:s] n rapports mpl; **sexual ~** rapports sexuels.

interdependent [ɪntədɪ'pɛndənt] adj interdépendant(e).

interest ['ɪntrɪst] n intérêt m; (COMM: stake, share) participation f, intérêts mpl ♦ vt intéresser; **compound/simple ~** intérêt composé/simple; **British ~s in the Middle East** les intérêts britanniques au Moyen-Orient; **his main ~ is ...** ce qui l'intéresse le plus est ....

interested ['ɪntrɪstɪd] adj intéressé(e); **to be ~ in** s'intéresser à.

interest-free ['ɪntrɪst'fri:] adj sans intérêt.

interesting ['ɪntrɪstɪŋ] adj intéressant(e).

interest rate n taux m d'intérêt.

interface ['ɪntəfeɪs] n (COMPUT) interface f.

interfere [ɪntə'fɪə*] vi: **to ~ in** (quarrel, other people's business) se mêler à; **to ~ with** (object) tripoter, toucher à; (plans) contrecarrer; (duty) être en conflit avec; **don't ~** mêlez-vous de vos affaires.

interference [ɪntə'fɪərəns] n (gen) intrusion f; (PHYSICS) interférence f; (RADIO, TV) parasites mpl.

interfering [ɪntə'fɪərɪŋ] adj importun(e).

interim ['ɪntərɪm] adj provisoire; (post) intérimaire ♦ n: **in the ~** dans l'intérim.

interior [ɪn'tɪərɪə*] n intérieur m ♦ adj intérieur(e).

interior decorator, interior designer n décorateur/trice d'intérieur.

interjection [ɪntə'dʒɛkʃən] n interjection f.

interlock [ɪntə'lɔk] vi s'enclencher ♦ vt enclencher.

interloper ['ɪntələupə*] n intrus/e.

interlude ['ɪntəlu:d] n intervalle m; (THEAT) intermède m.

intermarry [ɪntə'mærɪ] vi former des alliances entre familles (or tribus); former des unions consanguines.

intermediary [ɪntə'mi:dɪərɪ] n intermédiaire m/f.

intermediate [ɪntə'mi:dɪət] adj intermédiaire; (SCOL: course, level) moyen(ne).

interment [ɪn'tə:mənt] n inhumation f, enterrement m.

interminable [ɪn'tə:mɪnəbl] adj sans fin, interminable.

intermission [ɪntə'mɪʃən] n pause f; (THEAT, CINE) entracte m.

intermittent [ɪntə'mɪtnt] adj intermittent(e).

intermittently [ɪntə'mɪtntlɪ] adv par intermittence, par intervalles.

intern vt [ɪn'tə:n] interner ♦ n ['ɪntə:n] (US) interne m/f.

internal [ɪn'tə:nl] adj interne; (dispute, reform etc) intérieur(e); **~ injuries** lésions fpl internes.

internally [ɪn'tə:nəlɪ] adv intérieurement; **"not to be taken ~"** "pour usage externe".

Internal Revenue (Service) (IRS) n (US) fisc m.

international [ɪntə'næʃənl] adj international(e) ♦ n (BRIT SPORT) international m.

International Atomic Energy Agency (IAEA) n Agence Internationale de l'Énergie Atomique (AIEA).

International Court of Justice (ICJ) n Cour internationale de justice (CIJ).

international date line n ligne f de changement de date.

internationally [ɪntəˈnæʃnəlɪ] adv dans le monde entier.

International Monetary Fund (IMF) n Fonds monétaire international (FMI).

international relations npl relations internationales.

internecine [ɪntəˈniːsaɪn] adj mutuellement destructeur(trice).

internee [ɪntəˈniː] n interné/e.

Internet [ˈɪntəˌnɛt] n: **the ~** l'Internet m.

internment [ɪnˈtəːnmənt] n internement m.

interplay [ˈɪntəpleɪ] n effet m réciproque, jeu m.

Interpol [ˈɪntəpɔl] n Interpol m.

interpret [ɪnˈtəːprɪt] vt interpréter ♦ vi servir d'interprète.

interpretation [ɪntəprɪˈteɪʃən] n interprétation f.

interpreter [ɪnˈtəːprɪtə*] n interprète m/f.

interpreting [ɪnˈtəːprɪtɪŋ] n (profession) interprétariat m.

interrelated [ɪntərɪˈleɪtɪd] adj en corrélation, en rapport étroit.

interrogate [ɪnˈtɛrəugeɪt] vt interroger; (suspect etc) soumettre à un interrogatoire.

interrogation [ɪntɛrəuˈgeɪʃən] n interrogation f; interrogatoire m.

interrogative [ɪntəˈrɔgətɪv] adj interrogateur(trice) ♦ n (LING) interrogatif m.

interrogator [ɪnˈtɛrəgeɪtə*] n interrogateur/trice.

interrupt [ɪntəˈrʌpt] vt interrompre.

interruption [ɪntəˈrʌpʃən] n interruption f.

intersect [ɪntəˈsɛkt] vt couper, croiser; (MATH) intersecter ♦ vi se croiser, se couper; s'intersecter.

intersection [ɪntəˈsɛkʃən] n intersection f; (of roads) croisement m.

intersperse [ɪntəˈspəːs] vt: **to ~ with** parsemer de.

intertwine [ɪntəˈtwaɪn] vt entrelacer ♦ vi s'entrelacer.

interval [ˈɪntəvl] n intervalle m; (BRIT: THEAT) entracte m; (: SPORT) mi-temps f; **bright ~s** (in weather) éclaircies fpl; **at ~s** par intervalles.

intervene [ɪntəˈviːn] vi (time) s'écouler (entre-temps); (event) survenir; (person) intervenir.

intervention [ɪntəˈvɛnʃən] n intervention f.

interview [ˈɪntəvjuː] n (RADIO, TV etc) interview f; (for job) entrevue f ♦ vt interviewer; avoir une entrevue avec.

interviewee [ɪntəvjuːˈiː] n (for job) candidat m (qui passe un entretien); (TV etc) invité/e, per-

sonne interviewée.

interviewer [ˈɪntəvjuə*] n interviewer m.

intestate [ɪnˈtɛsteɪt] adj intestat f inv.

intestinal [ɪnˈtɛstɪnl] adj intestinal(e).

intestine [ɪnˈtɛstɪn] n intestin m; **large ~** gros intestin; **small ~** intestin grêle.

intimacy [ˈɪntɪməsɪ] n intimité f.

intimate adj [ˈɪntɪmət] intime; (knowledge) approfondi(e) ♦ vt [ˈɪntɪmeɪt] suggérer, laisser entendre; (announce) faire savoir.

intimately [ˈɪntɪmətlɪ] adv intimement.

intimation [ɪntɪˈmeɪʃən] n annonce f.

intimidate [ɪnˈtɪmɪdeɪt] vt intimider.

intimidation [ɪntɪmɪˈdeɪʃən] n intimidation f.

into [ˈɪntu] prep dans; **~ pieces/French** en morceaux/français; **to change pounds ~ dollars** changer des livres en dollars.

intolerable [ɪnˈtɔlərəbl] adj intolérable.

intolerance [ɪnˈtɔlərns] n intolérance f.

intolerant [ɪnˈtɔlərnt] adj: **~ (of)** intolérant(e) (de); (MED) intolérant (à).

intonation [ɪntəuˈneɪʃən] n intonation f.

intoxicate [ɪnˈtɔksɪkeɪt] vt enivrer.

intoxicated [ɪnˈtɔksɪkeɪtɪd] adj ivre.

intoxication [ɪntɔksɪˈkeɪʃən] n ivresse f.

intractable [ɪnˈtræktəbl] adj (child, temper) indocile, insoumis(e); (problem) insoluble; (illness) incurable.

intranet [ˈɪntrənɛt] n intranet m.

intransigent [ɪnˈtrænsɪdʒənt] adj intransigeant(e).

intransitive [ɪnˈtrænsɪtɪv] adj intransitif(ive).

intra-uterine device (IUD) [ˈɪntrəˈjuːtəraɪn-] n dispositif intra-utérin (DIU), stérilet m.

intravenous [ɪntrəˈviːnəs] adj intraveineux(euse).

in-tray [ˈɪntreɪ] n courrier m "arrivée".

intrepid [ɪnˈtrɛpɪd] adj intrépide.

intricacy [ˈɪntrɪkəsɪ] n complexité f.

intricate [ˈɪntrɪkət] adj complexe, compliqué(e).

intrigue [ɪnˈtriːg] n intrigue f ♦ vt intriguer ♦ vi intriguer, comploter.

intriguing [ɪnˈtriːgɪŋ] adj fascinant(e).

intrinsic [ɪnˈtrɪnsɪk] adj intrinsèque.

introduce [ɪntrəˈdjuːs] vt introduire; **to ~ sb (to sb)** présenter qn (à qn); **to ~ sb to** (pastime, technique) initier qn à; **may I ~ ...?** je vous présente ....

introduction [ɪntrəˈdʌkʃən] n introduction f; (of person) présentation f; **a letter of ~** une lettre de recommendation.

introductory [ɪntrəˈdʌktərɪ] adj préliminaire, introductif(ive); **~ remarks** remarques fpl liminaires; **an ~ offer** une offre de lancement.

introspective [ɪntrəuˈspɛktɪv] adj introspectif(ive).

introvert [ˈɪntrəuvəːt] adj, n introverti(e).

intrude [ɪnˈtruːd] vi (person) être importun(e); **to ~ on** or **into** (conversation etc) s'immiscer dans; **am I intruding?** est-ce que je vous dé-

range?
intruder [ın'tru:də*] *n* intrus/e.
intrusion [ın'tru:ʒən] *n* intrusion *f*.
intrusive [ın'tru:sıv] *adj* importun(e), gênant(e).
intuition [ıntju:'ıʃən] *n* intuition *f*.
intuitive [ın'tju:ıtıv] *adj* intuitif(ive).
inundate ['ınʌndeıt] *vt:* **to ~ with** inonder de.
inure [ın'juə*] *vt:* **to ~ (to)** habituer (à).
invade [ın'veıd] *vt* envahir.
invader [ın'veıdə*] *n* envahisseur *m*.
invalid *n* ['ınvəlıd] malade *m/f*; (*with disability*) invalide *m/f* ♦ *adj* [ın'vælıd] (*not valid*) invalide, non valide.
invalidate [ın'vælıdeıt] *vt* invalider, annuler.
invalid chair ['ınvəlıd-] *n* (*BRIT*) fauteuil *m* d'infirme.
invaluable [ın'væljuəbl] *adj* inestimable, inappréciable.
invariable [ın'vɛərıəbl] *adj* invariable; (*fig*) immanquable.
invariably [ın'vɛərıəblı] *adv* invariablement; **she is ~ late** elle est toujours en retard.
invasion [ın'veıʒən] *n* invasion *f*.
invective [ın'vektıv] *n* invective *f*.
inveigle [ın'vi:gl] *vt:* **to ~ sb into (doing) sth** amener qn à (faire) qch (par la ruse *or* la flatterie).
invent [ın'vent] *vt* inventer.
invention [ın'venʃən] *n* invention *f*.
inventive [ın'ventıv] *adj* inventif(ive).
inventiveness [ın'ventıvnıs] *n* esprit inventif *or* d'invention.
inventor [ın'ventə*] *n* inventeur/trice.
inventory ['ınvəntrı] *n* inventaire *m*.
inventory control *n* (*COMM*) contrôle *m* des stocks.
inverse [ın'və:s] *adj* inverse ♦ *n* inverse *m*, contraire *m*; **in ~ proportion (to)** inversement proportionel(le) (à).
inversely [ın'və:slı] *adv* inversement.
invert [ın'və:t] *vt* intervertir; (*cup, object*) retourner.
invertebrate [ın'və:tıbrət] *n* invertébré *m*.
inverted commas [ın'və:tıd-] *npl* (*BRIT*) guillemets *mpl*.
invest [ın'vest] *vt* investir; (*endow*): **to ~ sb with sth** conférer qch à qn ♦ *vi* faire un investissement, investir; **to ~ in** placer de l'argent *or* investir dans; (*acquire*) s'offrir, faire l'acquisition de.
investigate [ın'vestıgeıt] *vt* étudier, examiner; (*crime*) faire une enquête sur.
investigation [ınvestı'geıʃən] *n* examen *m*; (*of crime*) enquête *f*, investigation *f*.
investigative [ın'vestıgeıtıv] *adj:* **~ journalism** enquête-reportage *f*, journalisme *m* d'enquête.
investigator [ın'vestıgeıtə*] *n* investigateur/ trice; **private ~** détective privé.
investiture [ın'vestıtʃə*] *n* investiture *f*.
investment [ın'vestmənt] *n* investissement *m*,

placement *m*.
investment income *n* revenu *m* de placement.
investment trust *n* société *f* d'investissements.
investor [ın'vestə*] *n* épargnant/e; (*shareholder*) actionnaire *m/f*.
inveterate [ın'vetərət] *adj* invétéré(e).
invidious [ın'vıdıəs] *adj* injuste; (*task*) déplaisant(e).
invigilate [ın'vıdʒıleıt] (*BRIT*) *vt* surveiller ♦ *vi* être de surveillance.
invigilator [ın'vıdʒıleıtə*] *n* (*BRIT*) surveillant *m* (d'examen).
invigorating [ın'vıgəreıtıŋ] *adj* vivifiant(e); stimulant(e).
invincible [ın'vınsıbl] *adj* invincible.
inviolate [ın'vaıələt] *adj* inviolé(e).
invisible [ın'vızıbl] *adj* invisible.
invisible assets *npl* (*BRIT*) actif incorporel.
invisible ink *n* encre *f* sympathique.
invisible mending *n* stoppage *m*.
invitation [ınvı'teıʃən] *n* invitation *f*; **by ~ only** sur invitation; **at sb's ~** à la demande de qn.
invite [ın'vaıt] *vt* inviter; (*opinions etc*) demander; (*trouble*) chercher; **to ~ sb (to do)** inviter qn (à faire); **to ~ sb to dinner** inviter qn à dîner.
▶**invite out** *vt* inviter (à sortir).
▶**invite over** *vt* inviter (chez soi).
inviting [ın'vaıtıŋ] *adj* engageant(e), attrayant(e); (*gesture*) encourageant(e).
invoice ['ınvoıs] *n* facture *f* ♦ *vt* facturer; **to ~ sb for goods** facturer des marchandises à qn.
invoke [ın'vəuk] *vt* invoquer.
involuntary [ın'vɔləntrı] *adj* involontaire.
involve [ın'vɔlv] *vt* (*entail*) impliquer; (*concern*) concerner; (*require*) nécessiter; **to ~ sb in** (*theft etc*) impliquer qn dans; (*activity, meeting*) faire participer qn à.
involved [ın'vɔlvd] *adj* complexe; **to feel ~** se sentir concerné(e); **to become ~** (*in love etc*) s'engager.
involvement [ın'vɔlvmənt] *n* (*personal role*) participation *f*; (*of resources, funds*) mise *f* en jeu.
invulnerable [ın'vʌlnərəbl] *adj* invulnérable.
inward ['ınwəd] *adj* (*movement*) vers l'intérieur; (*thought, feeling*) profond(e), intime ♦ *adv* = **inwards**.
inwardly ['ınwədlı] *adv* (*feel, think etc*) secrètement, en son for intérieur.
inwards ['ınwədz] *adv* vers l'intérieur.
I/O *abbr* (*COMPUT*: = *input/output*) E/S.
IOC *n abbr* (= *International Olympic Committee*) CIO *m* (= *Comité international olympique*).
iodine ['aıəudi:n] *n* iode *m*.
ion ['aıən] *n* ion *m*.
Ionian Sea [aı'əunıən-] *n:* **the ~** la mer Ionienne.

ioniser ['aɪənaɪzə*] n ioniseur m.

iota [aɪ'əʊtə] n (fig) brin m, grain m.

IOU n abbr (= I owe you) reconnaissance f de dette.

IOW abbr (BRIT) = Isle of Wight.

IPA n abbr (= International Phonetic Alphabet) A.P.I. m.

IQ n abbr = **intelligence quotient**.

IRA n abbr (= Irish Republican Army) IRA f; (US) = individual retirement account.

Iran [ɪ'rɑːn] n Iran m.

Iranian [ɪ'reɪnɪən] adj iranien(ne) ♦ n Iranien/ne; (LING) iranien m.

Iraq [ɪ'rɑːk] n Irak m.

Iraqi [ɪ'rɑːkɪ] adj irakien(ne) ♦ n Irakien/ne.

irascible [ɪ'ræsɪbl] adj irascible.

irate [aɪ'reɪt] adj courroucé(e).

Ireland ['aɪələnd] n Irlande f; **Republic of ~** République f d'Irlande.

iris, ~es ['aɪrɪs, -ɪz] n iris m.

Irish ['aɪrɪʃ] adj irlandais(e) ♦ n (LING) irlandais m; **the ~** npl les Irlandais.

Irishman ['aɪrɪʃmən] n Irlandais m.

Irish Sea n: **the ~** la mer d'Irlande.

Irishwoman ['aɪrɪʃwumən] n Irlandaise f.

irk [əːk] vt ennuyer.

irksome ['əːksəm] adj ennuyeux(euse).

IRN n abbr (= Independent Radio News) agence de presse radiophonique.

iron ['aɪən] n fer m; (for clothes) fer m à repasser ♦ adj de or en fer ♦ vt (clothes) repasser; **~s** npl (chains) fers mpl, chaînes fpl.

▶**iron out** vt (crease) faire disparaître au fer; (fig) aplanir; faire disparaître.

Iron Curtain n: **the ~** le rideau de fer.

iron foundry n fonderie f de fonte.

ironic(al) [aɪ'rɒnɪk(l)] adj ironique.

ironically [aɪ'rɒnɪklɪ] adv ironiquement.

ironing ['aɪənɪŋ] n repassage m.

ironing board n planche f à repasser.

ironmonger ['aɪənmʌŋgə*] n (BRIT) quincaillier m; **~'s (shop)** quincaillerie f.

iron ore n minerai m de fer.

ironworks ['aɪənwəːks] n usine f sidérurgique.

irony ['aɪrənɪ] n ironie f.

irrational [ɪ'ræʃənl] adj irrationnel(le); déraisonnable; qui manque de logique.

irreconcilable [ɪrekən'saɪləbl] adj irréconciliable; (opinion): **~ with** inconciliable avec.

irredeemable [ɪrɪ'diːməbl] adj (COMM) non remboursable.

irrefutable [ɪrɪ'fjuːtəbl] adj irréfutable.

irregular [ɪ'regjulə*] adj irrégulier(ière).

irregularity [ɪregju'lærɪtɪ] n irrégularité f.

irrelevance [ɪ'reləvəns] n manque m de rapport or d'à-propos.

irrelevant [ɪ'reləvənt] adj sans rapport, hors de propos.

irreligious [ɪrɪ'lɪdʒəs] adj irréligieux(euse).

irreparable [ɪ'reprəbl] adj irréparable.

irreplaceable [ɪrɪ'pleɪsəbl] adj irremplaçable.

irrepressible [ɪrɪ'presəbl] adj irrépressible.

irreproachable [ɪrɪ'prəutʃəbl] adj irréprochable.

irresistible [ɪrɪ'zɪstɪbl] adj irrésistible.

irresolute [ɪ'rezəluːt] adj irrésolu(e), indécis(e).

irrespective [ɪrɪ'spektɪv]: **~ of** prep sans tenir compte de.

irresponsible [ɪrɪ'spɒnsɪbl] adj (act) irréfléchi(e); (person) qui n'a pas le sens des responsabilités.

irretrievable [ɪrɪ'triːvəbl] adj irréparable, irrémédiable; (object) introuvable.

irreverent [ɪ'revərnt] adj irrévérencieux(euse).

irrevocable [ɪ'revəkəbl] adj irrévocable.

irrigate ['ɪrɪgeɪt] vt irriguer.

irrigation [ɪrɪ'geɪʃən] n irrigation f.

irritable ['ɪrɪtəbl] adj irritable.

irritate ['ɪrɪteɪt] vt irriter.

irritation [ɪrɪ'teɪʃən] n irritation f.

IRS n abbr (US) = **Internal Revenue Service**.

is [ɪz] vb see **be**.

ISBN n abbr (= International Standard Book Number) ISBN m.

ISDN n abbr (= Integrated Services Digital Network) RNIS m.

Islam ['ɪzlɑːm] n Islam m.

island ['aɪlənd] n île f; (also: **traffic ~**) refuge m (pour piétons).

islander ['aɪləndə*] n habitant/e d'une île, insulaire m/f.

isle [aɪl] n île f.

isn't ['ɪznt] = **is not**.

isolate ['aɪsəleɪt] vt isoler.

isolated ['aɪsəleɪtɪd] adj isolé(e).

isolation [aɪsə'leɪʃən] n isolement m.

isolationism [aɪsə'leɪʃənɪzəm] n isolationnisme m.

isotope ['aɪsəutəup] n isotope m.

Israel ['ɪzreɪl] n Israël m.

Israeli [ɪz'reɪlɪ] adj israélien(ne) ♦ n Israélien/ne.

issue ['ɪʃuː] n question f, problème m; (outcome) résultat m, issue f; (of banknotes etc) émission f; (of newspaper etc) numéro m; (offspring) descendance f ♦ vt (rations, equipment) distribuer; (orders) donner; (book) faire paraître, publier; (banknotes, cheques, stamps) émettre, mettre en circulation ♦ vi: **to ~ from** provenir de; **at ~** en jeu, en cause; **to avoid the ~** éluder le problème; **to take ~ with sb (over sth)** exprimer son désaccord avec qn (sur qch); **to make an ~ of sth** faire de qch un problème; **to confuse or obscure the ~** embrouiller la question.

Istanbul [ɪstæn'buːl] n Istamboul, Istanbul.

isthmus ['ɪsməs] n isthme m.

IT n abbr = **information technology**.

===================== KEYWORD

it [ɪt] *pron* **1** (*specific: subject*) il(elle); (: *direct object*) le(la, l'); (: *indirect object*) lui; ~'**s on the table** c'est *or* il (*or* elle) est sur la table; **about/from/of** ~ en; **I spoke to him about** ~ je lui en ai parlé; **what did you learn from** ~? qu'est-ce que vous en avez retiré?; **I'm proud of** ~ j'en suis fier; **I've come from** ~ j'en viens; **in/to** ~ y; **put the book in** ~ mettez-y le livre; **it's on** ~ c'est dessus; **he agreed to** ~ il y a consenti; **did you go to** ~? (*party, concert etc*) est-ce que vous y êtes allé(s)?; **above** ~, **over** ~ (au-)dessus; **below** ~, **under** ~ (en-)dessous; **in front of/behind** ~ devant/derrière

2 (*impersonal*) il; ce, cela, ça; ~'**s raining** il pleut; ~'**s Friday tomorrow** demain c'est vendredi *or* nous sommes vendredi; ~'**s 6 o'clock** il est 6 heures; ~'**s 2 hours by train** c'est à 2 heures de train; **who is** ~? — ~'**s me** qui est-ce? — c'est moi.

ITA *n abbr* (*BRIT*: = *initial teaching alphabet*) alphabet en partie phonétique utilisé pour l'enseignement de la lecture.
Italian [ɪˈtæljən] *adj* italien(ne) ♦ *n* Italien/ne; (*LING*) italien *m*.
italic [ɪˈtælɪk] *adj* italique; ~**s** *npl* italique *m*.
Italy [ˈɪtəlɪ] *n* Italie *f*.
itch [ɪtʃ] *n* démangeaison *f* ♦ *vi* (*person*) éprouver des démangeaisons; (*part of body*) démanger; **I'm** ~**ing to do** l'envie me démange de faire.
itching [ˈɪtʃɪŋ] *n* démangeaison *f*.
itchy [ˈɪtʃɪ] *adj* qui démange; **my back is** ~ j'ai le dos qui me démange.
it'd [ˈɪtd] = **it would, it had**.
item [ˈaɪtəm] *n* (*gen*) article *m*; (*on agenda*) question *f*, point *m*; (*in programme*) numéro *m*; (*also:* **news** ~) nouvelle *f*; ~**s of clothing** articles vestimentaires.
itemize [ˈaɪtəmaɪz] *vt* détailler, spécifier.
itemized bill [ˈaɪtəmaɪzd-] *n* facture détaillée.
itinerant [ɪˈtɪnərənt] *adj* itinérant(e); (*musician*) ambulant(e).
itinerary [aɪˈtɪnərərɪ] *n* itinéraire *m*.
it'll [ˈɪtl] = **it will, it shall**.
ITN *n abbr* (*BRIT*: = *Independent Television News*) chaîne de télévision commerciale.
its [ɪts] *adj* son(sa), ses *pl* ♦ *pron* le(la) sien(ne), les siens(siennes).
it's [ɪts] = **it is, it has**.
itself [ɪtˈsɛlf] *pron* (*emphatic*) lui-même(elle-même); (*reflexive*) se.
ITV *n abbr* (*BRIT*: = *Independent Television*) chaîne de télévision commerciale.

ITV est une chaîne de télévision britannique financée par la publicité. Les actualités, documentaires, débats, etc, constituent environ un tiers des émissions de ITV, le reste étant partagé entre les sports, les films, les feuilletons, les jeux, les séries, etc. Des compagnies indépendantes fournissent des émissions au niveau régional.

IUD *n abbr* = **intra-uterine device**.
I've [aɪv] = **I have**.
ivory [ˈaɪvərɪ] *n* ivoire *m*.
Ivory Coast *n* Côte *f* d'Ivoire.
ivory tower *n* (*fig*) tour *f* d'ivoire.
ivy [ˈaɪvɪ] *n* lierre *m*.

L'**Ivy League** regroupe les huit universités les plus prestigieuses du nord-est des États-Unis, ainsi surnommées à cause de leurs murs recouverts de lierre. Elles organisent des compétitions sportives entre elles. Ces universités sont: Brown, Columbia, Cornell, Dartmouth College, Harvard, Princeton, l'université de Pennsylvanie et Yale.

===================== **J j**

J, j [dʒeɪ] *n* (*letter*) J, j *m*; **J for Jack**, (*US*) **J for Jig** J comme Joseph.
JA *n abbr* = **judge advocate**.
J/A *abbr* = **joint account**.
jab [dʒæb] *vt*: **to** ~ **sth into** enfoncer *or* planter qch dans ♦ *n* coup *m*; (*MED*: *col*) piqûre *f*.
jabber [ˈdʒæbə*] *vt, vi* bredouiller, baragouiner.
jack [dʒæk] *n* (*AUT*) cric *m*; (*BOWLS*) cochonnet *m*; (*CARDS*) valet *m*.
▶**jack in** *vt* (*col*) laisser tomber.
▶**jack up** *vt* soulever (au cric).
jackal [ˈdʒækl] *n* chacal *m*.
jackass [ˈdʒækæs] *n* (*also fig*) âne *m*.
jackdaw [ˈdʒækdɔː] *n* choucas *m*.
jacket [ˈdʒækɪt] *n* veste *f*, veston *m*; (*of boiler etc*) enveloppe *f*; (*of book*) couverture *f*, jaquette *f*.
jacket potato *n* pomme *f* de terre en robe des champs.
jack-in-the-box [ˈdʒækɪnðəbɔks] *n* diable *m* à ressort.
jack-knife [ˈdʒæknaɪf] *n* couteau *m* de poche ♦ *vi*: **the lorry** ~**d** la remorque (du camion) s'est mise en travers.
jack-of-all-trades [ˈdʒækəvˈɔːltreɪdz] *n* bricoleur *m*.
jack plug *n* (*BRIT*) jack *m*.
jackpot [ˈdʒækpɔt] *n* gros lot.
Jacuzzi [dʒəˈkuːzɪ] *n* ® jacuzzi *m* ®.
jade [dʒeɪd] *n* (*stone*) jade *m*.

jaded ['dʒeɪdɪd] *adj* éreinté(e), fatigué(e).
JAG *n abbr* = **Judge Advocate General**.
jagged ['dʒægɪd] *adj* dentelé(e).
jaguar ['dʒægjuə*] *n* jaguar *m*.
jail [dʒeɪl] *n* prison *f* ♦ *vt* emprisonner, mettre en prison.
jailbird ['dʒeɪlbəːd] *n* récidiviste *m/f*.
jailbreak ['dʒeɪlbreɪk] *n* évasion *f*.
jailer ['dʒeɪlə*] *n* geôlier/ière.
jalopy [dʒə'lɔpɪ] *n* (*col*) vieux clou.
jam [dʒæm] *n* confiture *f*; (*of shoppers etc*) cohue *f*; (*also:* **traffic** ~) embouteillage *m* ♦ *vt* (*passage etc*) encombrer, obstruer; (*mechanism, drawer etc*) bloquer, coincer; (*RADIO*) brouiller ♦ *vi* (*mechanism, sliding part*) se coincer, se bloquer; (*gun*) s'enrayer; **to get sb out of a** ~ (*col*) sortir qn du pétrin; **to** ~ **sth into** entasser *or* comprimer qch dans; enfoncer qch dans; **the telephone lines are** ~**med** les lignes (téléphoniques) sont encombrées.
Jamaica [dʒə'meɪkə] *n* Jamaïque *f*.
Jamaican [dʒə'meɪkən] *adj* jamaïquain(e) ♦ *n* Jamaïquain/e.
jamb ['dʒæm] *n* jambage *m*.
jam-packed [dʒæm'pækt] *adj:* ~ **(with)** bourré(e) (de).
jam session *n* jam session *f*.
Jan. *abbr* (= *January*) janv.
jangle ['dʒæŋgl] *vi* cliqueter.
janitor ['dʒænɪtə*] *n* (*caretaker*) huissier *m*; concierge *m*.
January ['dʒænjuərɪ] *n* janvier *m*; *for phrases see also* **July.**
Japan [dʒə'pæn] *n* Japon *m*.
Japanese [dʒæpə'niːz] *adj* japonais(e) ♦ *n* (*pl inv*) Japonais/e; (*LING*) japonais *m*.
jar [dʒɑː*] *n* (*container*) pot *m*, bocal *m* ♦ *vi* (*sound*) produire un son grinçant *or* discordant; (*colours etc*) détonner, jurer ♦ *vt* (*shake*) ébranler, secouer.
jargon ['dʒɑːgən] *n* jargon *m*.
jarring ['dʒɑːrɪŋ] *adj* (*sound, colour*) discordant(e).
Jas. *abbr* = *James*.
jasmin(e) ['dʒæzmɪn] *n* jasmin *m*.
jaundice ['dʒɔːndɪs] *n* jaunisse *f*.
jaundiced ['dʒɔːndɪst] *adj* (*fig*) envieux(euse), désapprobateur(trice).
jaunt [dʒɔːnt] *n* balade *f*.
jaunty ['dʒɔːntɪ] *adj* enjoué(e); désinvolte.
Java ['dʒɑːvə] *n* Java *f*.
javelin ['dʒævlɪn] *n* javelot *m*.
jaw [dʒɔː] *n* mâchoire *f*.
jawbone ['dʒɔːbəun] *n* maxillaire *m*.
jay [dʒeɪ] *n* geai *m*.
jaywalker ['dʒeɪwɔːkə*] *n* piéton indiscipliné.
jazz [dʒæz] *n* jazz *m*.
► **jazz up** *vt* animer, égayer.
jazz band *n* orchestre *m or* groupe *m* de jazz.
jazzy ['dʒæzɪ] *adj* bariolé(e), tapageur(euse); (*beat*) de jazz.

JCB *n* ® excavatrice *f*.
JCS *n abbr* (*US*) = Joint Chiefs of Staff.
JD *n abbr* (*US*: = *Doctor of Laws*) *titre universitaire*; (: = *Justice Department*) *ministère de la Justice*.
jealous ['dʒeləs] *adj* jaloux(ouse).
jealously ['dʒeləslɪ] *adv* jalousement.
jealousy ['dʒeləsɪ] *n* jalousie *f*.
jeans [dʒiːnz] *npl* (blue-)jean *m*.
Jeep [dʒiːp] *n* ® jeep *f*.
jeer [dʒɪə*] *vi:* **to** ~ **(at)** huer; se moquer cruellement (de), railler.
jeering ['dʒɪərɪŋ] *adj* railleur(euse), moqueur(euse) ♦ *n* huées *fpl*.
jeers ['dʒɪəz] *npl* huées *fpl*; sarcasmes *mpl*.
jelly ['dʒelɪ] *n* gelée *f*.
jellyfish ['dʒelɪfɪʃ] *n* méduse *f*.
jeopardize ['dʒepədaɪz] *vt* mettre en danger *or* péril.
jeopardy ['dʒepədɪ] *n:* **in** ~ en danger *or* péril.
jerk [dʒəːk] *n* secousse *f*; saccade *f*; sursaut *m*, spasme *m*; (*col*) pauvre type *m* ♦ *vt* donner une secousse à ♦ *vi* (*vehicles*) cahoter.
jerkin ['dʒəːkɪn] *n* blouson *m*.
jerky ['dʒəːkɪ] *adj* saccadé(e); cahotant(e).
jerry-built ['dʒerɪbɪlt] *adj* de mauvaise qualité.
jerry can ['dʒerɪ-] *n* bidon *m*.
Jersey ['dʒəːzɪ] *n* Jersey *f*.
jersey ['dʒəːzɪ] *n* tricot *m*; (*fabric*) jersey *m*.
Jerusalem [dʒə'ruːsləm] *n* Jérusalem *m*.
jest [dʒest] *n* plaisanterie *f*; **in** ~ en plaisantant.
jester ['dʒestə*] *n* (*HIST*) plaisantin *m*.
Jesus ['dʒiːzəs] *n* Jésus; ~ **Christ** Jésus-Christ.
jet [dʒet] *n* (*of gas, liquid*) jet *m*; (*AUT*) gicleur *m*; (*AVIAT*) avion *m* à réaction, jet *m*.
jet-black ['dʒet'blæk] *adj* (d'un noir) de jais.
jet engine *n* moteur *m* à réaction.
jet lag *n* décalage *m* horaire.
jetsam ['dʒetsəm] *n* objets jetés à la mer (et rejetés sur la côte).
jet-setter ['dʒetsetə*] *n* membre *m* du *or* de la jet set.
jettison ['dʒetɪsn] *vt* jeter par-dessus bord.
jetty ['dʒetɪ] *n* jetée *f*, digue *f*.
Jew [dʒuː] *n* Juif *m*.
jewel ['dʒuːəl] *n* bijou *m*, joyau *m*.
jeweller ['dʒuːələ*] *n* bijoutier/ière, joaillier *m*; ~**'s (shop)** *n* bijouterie *f*, joaillerie *f*.
jewellery ['dʒuːəlrɪ] *n* bijoux *mpl*.
Jewess ['dʒuːɪs] *n* Juive *f*.
Jewish ['dʒuːɪʃ] *adj* juif(juive).
JFK *n abbr* (*US*) = John Fitzgerald Kennedy International Airport.
jib [dʒɪb] *n* (*NAUT*) foc *m*; (*of crane*) flèche *f* ♦ *vi* (*horse*) regimber; **to** ~ **at doing sth** rechigner à faire qch.
jibe [dʒaɪb] *n* sarcasme *m*.
jiffy ['dʒɪfɪ] *n* (*col*): **in a** ~ en un clin d'œil.
jig [dʒɪg] *n* (*dance, tune*) gigue *m*.
jigsaw ['dʒɪgsɔː] *n* (*also:* ~ **puzzle**) puzzle *m*;

(*tool*) scie sauteuse.

jilt [dʒɪlt] *vt* laisser tomber, plaquer.

jingle ['dʒɪŋgl] *n* (*advertising* ~) couplet *m* publicitaire ♦ *vi* cliqueter, tinter.

jingoism ['dʒɪŋgəʊɪzəm] *n* chauvinisme *m*.

jinx [dʒɪŋks] *n* (*col*) (mauvais) sort.

jitters ['dʒɪtəz] *npl* (*col*): **to get the** ~ avoir la trouille *or* la frousse.

jittery ['dʒɪtərɪ] *adj* (*col*) nerveux(euse); **to be** ~ avoir les nerfs en pelote.

jiujitsu [dʒuː'dʒɪtsuː] *n* jiu-jitsu *m*.

job [dʒɔb] *n* travail *m*; (*employment*) emploi *m*, poste *m*, place *f*; **a part-time/full-time** ~ un emploi à temps partiel/à plein temps; **he's only doing his** ~ il fait son boulot; **it's a good** ~ **that** ... c'est heureux *or* c'est une chance que ...; **just the** ~! (c'est) juste *or* exactement ce qu'il faut!

jobber ['dʒɔbə*] *n* (*BRIT STOCK EXCHANGE*) négociant *m* en titres.

jobbing ['dʒɔbɪŋ] *adj* (*BRIT: workman*) à la tâche, à la journée.

Jobcentre ['dʒɔbsɛntə*] *n* agence *f* pour l'emploi.

job creation scheme *n* plan *m* pour la création d'emplois.

job description *n* description *f* du poste.

jobless ['dʒɔblɪs] *adj* sans travail, au chômage ♦ *npl*: **the** ~ les sans-emploi *m inv*, les chômeurs *mpl*.

job lot *n* lot *m* (d'articles divers).

job satisfaction *n* satisfaction professionnelle.

job security *n* sécurité *f* de l'emploi.

job specification *n* caractéristiques *fpl* du poste.

Jock [dʒɔk] *n* (*col: Scotsman*) Écossais *m*.

jockey ['dʒɔkɪ] *n* jockey *m* ♦ *vi*: **to** ~ **for position** manœuvrer pour être bien placé.

jockey box *n* (*US AUT*) boîte *f* à gants, videpoches *m inv*.

jockstrap ['dʒɔkstræp] *n* slip *m* de sport.

jocular ['dʒɔkjulə*] *adj* jovial(e), enjoué(e); facétieux(euse).

jog [dʒɔg] *vt* secouer ♦ *vi* (*SPORT*) faire du jogging; **to** ~ **along** cahoter; trotter; **to** ~ **sb's memory** rafraîchir la mémoire de qn.

jogger ['dʒɔgə*] *n* jogger *m/f*.

jogging ['dʒɔgɪŋ] *n* jogging *m*.

john [dʒɔn] *n* (*US col*): **the** ~ (*toilet*) les cabinets *mpl*.

join [dʒɔɪn] *vt* unir, assembler; (*become member of*) s'inscrire à; (*meet*) rejoindre, retrouver; se joindre à ♦ *vi* (*roads, rivers*) se rejoindre, se rencontrer ♦ *n* raccord *m*; **will you** ~ **us for dinner?** vous dînerez bien avec nous?; **I'll** ~ **you later** je vous rejoindrai plus tard; **to** ~ **forces (with)** s'associer (à).

▶**join in** *vi* se mettre de la partie ♦ *vt* se mêler à.

▶**join up** *vi* s'engager.

joiner ['dʒɔɪnə*] *n* menuisier *m*.

joinery ['dʒɔɪnərɪ] *n* menuiserie *f*.

joint [dʒɔɪnt] *n* (*TECH*) jointure *f*; joint *m*; (*ANAT*) articulation *f*, jointure; (*BRIT: CULIN*) rôti *m*; (*col: place*) boîte *f* ♦ *adj* commun(e); (*committee*) mixte, paritaire; ~ **responsibility** coresponsabilité *f*.

joint account (J/A) *n* compte joint.

jointly ['dʒɔɪntlɪ] *adv* ensemble, en commun.

joint ownership *n* copropriété *f*.

joint-stock company ['dʒɔɪntstɔk-] *n* société *f* par actions.

joint venture *n* entreprise commune.

joist [dʒɔɪst] *n* solive *f*.

joke [dʒəʊk] *n* plaisanterie *f*; (*also*: **practical** ~) farce *f* ♦ *vi* plaisanter; **to play a** ~ **on** jouer un tour à, faire une farce à.

joker ['dʒəʊkə*] *n* plaisantin *m*, blagueur/euse; (*CARDS*) joker *m*.

joking ['dʒəʊkɪŋ] *n* plaisanterie *f*.

jollity ['dʒɔlɪtɪ] *n* réjouissances *fpl*, gaieté *f*.

jolly ['dʒɔlɪ] *adj* gai(e), enjoué(e) ♦ *adv* (*BRIT col*) rudement, drôlement ♦ *vt* (*BRIT*): **to** ~ **sb along** amadouer qn, convaincre *or* entraîner qn à force d'encouragements; ~ **good!** (*BRIT*) formidable!

jolt [dʒəʊlt] *n* cahot *m*, secousse *f* ♦ *vt* cahoter, secouer.

Jordan [dʒɔːdən] *n* (*country*) Jordanie *f*; (*river*) Jourdain *m*.

Jordanian [dʒɔː'deɪnɪən] *adj* jordanien(ne) ♦ *n* Jordanien/ne.

joss stick ['dʒɔsstɪk] *n* bâton *m* d'encens.

jostle ['dʒɔsl] *vt* bousculer, pousser ♦ *vi* jouer des coudes.

jot [dʒɔt] *n*: **not one** ~ pas un brin.

▶**jot down** *vt* inscrire rapidement, noter.

jotter ['dʒɔtə*] *n* (*BRIT*) cahier *m* (de brouillon); bloc-notes *m*.

journal ['dʒəːnl] *n* journal *m*.

journalese [dʒəːnə'liːz] *n* (*pej*) style *m* journalistique.

journalism ['dʒəːnəlɪzəm] *n* journalisme *m*.

journalist ['dʒəːnəlɪst] *n* journaliste *m/f*.

journey ['dʒəːnɪ] *n* voyage *m*; (*distance covered*) trajet *m*; **a 5-hour** ~ un voyage de 5 heures ♦ *vi* voyager.

jovial ['dʒəʊvɪəl] *adj* jovial(e).

jowl [dʒaul] *n* mâchoire *f* (*inférieure*); bajoue *f*.

joy [dʒɔɪ] *n* joie *f*.

joyful ['dʒɔɪful], **joyous** ['dʒɔɪəs] *adj* joyeux(euse).

joyride ['dʒɔɪraɪd] *vi*: **to go joyriding** faire une virée dans une voiture volée.

joyrider ['dʒɔɪraɪdə*] *n* voleur/euse de voiture (*qui fait une virée dans le véhicule volé*).

joystick ['dʒɔɪstɪk] *n* (*AVIAT*) manche *m* à balai; (*COMPUT*) manche à balai, manette *f* (de jeu).

JP *n abbr* = **Justice of the Peace**.

Jr. *abbr* = **junior**.

JTPA *n abbr* (*US*: = *Job Training Partnership Act*) *programme gouvernemental de formation*.

jubilant ['dʒuːbɪlnt] *adj* triomphant(e); réjoui(e).

jubilation [dʒuːbɪ'leɪʃən] *n* jubilation *f*.

jubilee ['dʒuːbɪliː] *n* jubilé *m*; **silver** ~ (jubilé du) vingt-cinquième anniversaire.

judge [dʒʌdʒ] *n* juge *m* ♦ *vt* juger; (*estimate: weight, size etc*) apprécier; (*consider*) estimer ♦ *vi*: **judging** *or* **to** ~ **by his expression** d'après son expression; **as far as I can** ~ autant que je puisse en juger; **I** ~**d it necessary to inform him** j'ai jugé nécessaire de l'informer.

judge advocate (JA) *n* (*MIL*) magistrat *m* militaire.

judg(e)ment ['dʒʌdʒmənt] *n* jugement *m*; (*punishment*) châtiment *m*; **in my** ~ à mon avis; **to pass** ~ **on** (*LAW*) prononcer un jugement (sur).

judicial [dʒuː'dɪʃl] *adj* judiciaire; (*fair*) impartial(e).

judiciary [dʒuː'dɪʃɪərɪ] *n* (pouvoir *m*) judiciaire *m*.

judicious [dʒuː'dɪʃəs] *adj* judicieux(euse).

judo ['dʒuːdəu] *n* judo *m*.

jug [dʒʌg] *n* pot *m*, cruche *f*.

jugged hare ['dʒʌgd-] *n* (*BRIT*) civet *m* de lièvre.

juggernaut ['dʒʌgənɔːt] *n* (*BRIT: huge truck*) mastodonte *m*.

juggle ['dʒʌgl] *vi* jongler.

juggler ['dʒʌglə*] *n* jongleur *m*.

Jugoslav ['juːgəu'slɑːv] *adj*, *n* = **Yugoslav**.

jugular ['dʒʌgjulə*] *adj*: ~ **(vein)** veine *f* jugulaire.

juice [dʒuːs] *n* jus *m*; (*col: petrol*): **we've run out of** ~ c'est la panne sèche.

juicy ['dʒuːsɪ] *adj* juteux(euse).

jukebox ['dʒuːkbɔks] *n* juke-box *m*.

Jul. *abbr* (= *July*) juil.

July [dʒuː'laɪ] *n* juillet *m*; **the first of** ~ le premier juillet; **(on) the eleventh of** ~ le onze juillet; **in the month of** ~ au mois de juillet; **at the beginning/end of** ~ au début/à la fin (du mois) de juillet, début/fin juillet; **in the middle of** ~ au milieu (du mois) de juillet, à la mi-juillet; **during** ~ pendant le mois de juillet; **in** ~ **of next year** en juillet de l'année prochaine; **each** *or* **every** ~ tous les ans *or* chaque année en juillet; ~ **was wet this year** il a beaucoup plu cette année en juillet.

jumble ['dʒʌmbl] *n* fouillis *m* ♦ *vt* (*also:* ~ **up**, ~ **together**) mélanger, brouiller.

jumble sale *n* (*BRIT*) vente *f* de charité.

---

*Les **jumble sales** ont lieu dans les églises, salles des fêtes ou halls d'écoles, et l'on y vend des articles de toutes sortes, en général bon marché et surtout d'occasion, pour collecter des fonds pour une œuvre de charité, une école (par exemple, pour acheter un ordinateur), ou encore une église (pour réparer un toit etc).*

---

jumbo ['dʒʌmbəu] *adj*: ~ **jet** (avion) gros porteur (à réaction); ~ **size** format maxi *or* extra-grand.

jump [dʒʌmp] *vi* sauter, bondir; (*start*) sursauter; (*increase*) monter en flèche ♦ *vt* sauter, franchir ♦ *n* saut *m*, bond *m*; sursaut *m*; (*fence*) obstacle *m*; **to** ~ **the queue** (*BRIT*) passer avant son tour.

▶**jump about** *vi* sautiller.

▶**jump at** *vt fus* (*fig*) sauter sur; **he** ~**ed at the offer** il s'est empressé d'accepter la proposition.

▶**jump down** *vi* sauter (pour descendre).

▶**jump up** *vi* se lever (d'un bond).

jumped-up ['dʒʌmptʌp] *adj* (*BRIT pej*) parvenu(e).

jumper ['dʒʌmpə*] *n* (*BRIT: pullover*) pull-over *m*; (*US: pinafore dress*) robe-chasuble *f*; (*SPORT*) sauteur/euse.

jump leads, (*US*) **jumper cables** *npl* câbles *mpl* de démarrage.

jump-start ['dʒʌmpstɑːt] *vt* (*car: push*) démarrer en poussant; (*: with jump leads*) démarrer avec des câbles (de démarrage); (*fig: project, situation*) faire redémarrer promptement.

jumpy ['dʒʌmpɪ] *adj* nerveux(euse), agité(e).

Jun. *abbr* = **June; junior**.

Junr *abbr* = **junior**.

junction ['dʒʌŋkʃən] *n* (*BRIT: of roads*) carrefour *m*; (*of rails*) embranchement *m*.

juncture ['dʒʌŋktʃə*] *n*: **at this** ~ à ce moment-là, sur ces entrefaites.

June [dʒuːn] *n* juin *m*; *for phrases see also* **July**.

jungle ['dʒʌŋgl] *n* jungle *f*.

junior ['dʒuːnɪə*] *adj*, *n*: **he's** ~ **to me (by 2 years), he's my** ~ **(by 2 years)** il est mon cadet (de 2 ans), il est plus jeune que moi (de 2 ans); **he's** ~ **to me** (*seniority*) il est en dessous de moi (dans la hiérarchie), j'ai plus d'ancienneté que lui.

junior executive *n* cadre moyen.

junior high school *n* (*US*) ≈ collège *m* d'enseignement secondaire.

junior minister *n* (*BRIT*) ministre *m* sous tutelle.

junior partner *n* associé(-adjoint) *m*.

junior school *n* (*BRIT*) école *f* primaire, cours moyen.

junior sizes *npl* (*COMM*) tailles *fpl* fillettes/garçonnets.

juniper ['dʒuːnɪpə*] *n*: ~ **berry** baie *f* de genièvre.

junk [dʒʌŋk] *n* (*rubbish*) bric-à-brac *m inv*; (*ship*) jonque *f* ♦ *vt* (*col*) abandonner, mettre au rancart.

junk bond *n* (*COMM*) obligation hautement spéculative utilisée dans les OPA agressives.

junk dealer *n* brocanteur/euse.

junket ['dʒʌŋkɪt] *n* (*CULIN*) lait caillé; (*BRIT col*): **to go on a** ~, **go** ~**ing** voyager aux frais de la princesse.

junk food n snacks vite prêts (*sans valeur nutritive*).

junkie ['dʒʌŋkɪ] n (*col*) junkie m, drogué/e.

junk mail n prospectus *mpl*.

junk room n (*US*) débarras m.

junk shop n (boutique f de) brocanteur m.

junta ['dʒʌntə] n junte f.

Jupiter ['dʒuːpɪtə*] n (*planet*) Jupiter f.

jurisdiction [dʒuərɪs'dɪkʃən] n juridiction f; **it falls** or **comes within/outside our ~** cela est/n'est pas de notre compétence or ressort.

jurisprudence [dʒuərɪs'pruːdəns] n jurisprudence f.

juror ['dʒuərə*] n juré m.

jury ['dʒuərɪ] n jury m.

jury box n banc m des jurés.

juryman ['dʒuərɪmən] n = **juror**.

just [dʒʌst] adj juste ♦ adv: **he's ~ done it/left** il vient de le faire/partir; **~ as I expected** exactement or précisément comme je m'y attendais; **~ right/two o'clock** exactement or juste ce qu'il faut/deux heures; **we were ~ going** nous partions; **I was ~ about to phone** j'allais téléphoner; **~ as he was leaving** au moment or à l'instant précis où il partait; **~ before/enough/here** juste avant/assez/là; **it's ~ me/a mistake** ce n'est que moi/(rien) qu'une erreur; **~ missed/caught** manqué/attrapé de justesse; **~ listen to this!** écoutez un peu ça!; **~ ask someone the way** vous n'avez qu'à demander votre chemin à quelqu'un; **it's ~ as good** c'est (vraiment) aussi bon; **it's ~ as well that you ...** heureusement que vous ...; **not ~ now** pas tout de suite; **~ a minute!**, **~ one moment!** un instant (s'il vous plaît)!

justice ['dʒʌstɪs] n justice f; **Lord Chief J~** (*BRIT*) premier président de la cour d'appel; **this photo doesn't do you ~** cette photo ne vous avantage pas.

Justice of the Peace (JP) n juge m de paix.

justifiable [dʒʌstɪ'faɪəbl] adj justifiable.

justifiably [dʒʌstɪ'faɪəblɪ] adv légitimement, à juste titre.

justification [dʒʌstɪfɪ'keɪʃən] n justification f.

justify ['dʒʌstɪfaɪ] vt justifier; **to be justified in doing sth** être en droit de faire qch.

justly ['dʒʌstlɪ] adv avec raison, justement.

justness ['dʒʌstnɪs] n justesse f.

jut [dʒʌt] vi (*also*: ~ **out**) dépasser, faire saillie.

jute [dʒuːt] n jute m.

juvenile ['dʒuːvənaɪl] adj juvénile; (*court, books*) pour enfants ♦ n adolescent/e.

juvenile delinquency n délinquance f juvénile.

juxtapose ['dʒʌkstəpəuz] vt juxtaposer.

juxtaposition ['dʒʌkstəpə'zɪʃən] n juxtaposition f.

K k

K, k [keɪ] n (*letter*) K, k m; **K for King** K comme Kléber.

K abbr (= *kilobyte*) Ko; (*BRIT*: = *Knight*) titre honorifique ♦ n abbr (= *one thousand*) K.

kaftan ['kæftæn] n cafetan m.

Kalahari Desert [kælə'hɑːrɪ-] n désert m de Kalahari.

kale [keɪl] n chou frisé.

kaleidoscope [kə'laɪdəskəup] n kaléidoscope m.

kamikaze [kæmɪ'kɑːzɪ] adj kamikaze.

Kampala [kæm'pɑːlə] n Kampala.

Kampuchea [kæmpu'tʃɪə] n Kampuchéa m.

kangaroo [kæŋgə'ruː] n kangourou m.

Kans. abbr (*US*) = **Kansas**.

kaput [kə'put] adj (*col*) kapout, capout.

karaoke [kɑːrə'əukɪ] n karaoke m.

karate [kə'rɑːtɪ] n karaté m.

Kashmir [kæʃ'mɪə*] n Cachemire m.

Kazakhstan [kɑːzɑːk'stæn] n Kazakhstan m.

KC n abbr (*BRIT LAW*: = *King's Counsel*) titre donné à certains avocats; *see also* **QC**.

kd abbr (*US*: = *knocked down*) en pièces détachées.

kebab [kə'bæb] n kebab m.

keel [kiːl] n quille f; **on an even ~** (*fig*) à flot.

▶**keel over** vi (*NAUT*) chavirer, dessaler; (*person*) tomber dans les pommes.

keen [kiːn] adj (*interest, desire, competition*) vif(vive); (*eye, intelligence*) pénétrant(e); (*edge*) effilé(e); (*eager*) plein(e) d'enthousiasme; **to be ~ to do** or **on doing sth** désirer vivement faire qch, tenir beaucoup à faire qch; **to be ~ on sth/sb** aimer beaucoup qch/qn; **I'm not ~ on going** je ne suis pas chaud pour aller, je n'ai pas très envie d'y aller.

keenly ['kiːnlɪ] adv (*enthusiastically*) avec enthousiasme; (*feel*) vivement, profondément; (*look*) intensément.

keenness ['kiːnnɪs] n (*eagerness*) enthousiasme m; **~ to do** vif désir de faire.

keep [kiːp] vb (*pt, pp* **kept** [kept]) vt (*retain, preserve*) garder; (*hold back*) retenir; (*a shop, the books, a diary*) tenir; (*feed: one's family etc*) entretenir, assurer la subsistance de; (*a promise*) tenir; (*chickens, bees, pigs etc*) élever ♦ vi (*food*) se conserver; (*remain: in a certain state or place*) rester ♦ n (*of castle*) donjon m; (*food etc*): **enough for his ~** assez pour (assurer) sa subsistance; **to ~ doing sth** continuer à faire qch; faire qch continuellement; **to ~ sb from doing/sth from happening** empêcher qn de faire *or* que qn (ne) fasse/que qch (n')arrive; **to ~ sb happy/a place tidy** faire que qn soit content/qu'un endroit reste propre; **to ~ sb waiting** faire attendre qn; **to ~ an appointment** ne pas manquer un rendez-vous; **to ~ a record of sth** prendre note de qch; **to ~ sth to o.s.** garder qch pour soi, tenir qch secret; **to ~ sth (back) from sb** cacher qch à qn; **to ~ time** (*clock*) être à l'heure, ne pas retarder.

▶**keep away** *vt*: **to ~ sth/sb away from sb** tenir qch/qn éloigné de qn ♦ *vi*: **to ~ away (from)** ne pas s'approcher (de).

▶**keep back** *vt* (*crowds, tears, money*) retenir ♦ *vi* rester en arrière.

▶**keep down** *vt* (*control: prices, spending*) empêcher d'augmenter, limiter; (*retain: food*) garder ♦ *vi* (*person*) rester assis(e); rester par terre.

▶**keep in** *vt* (*invalid, child*) garder à la maison; (*SCOL*) consigner ♦ *vi* (*col*): **to ~ in with sb** rester en bons termes avec qn.

▶**keep off** *vi* ne pas s'approcher; "*~* **off the grass**" "pelouse interdite".

▶**keep on** *vi* continuer; **to ~ on doing** continuer à faire.

▶**keep out** *vt* empêcher d'entrer ♦ *vi* rester en dehors; "*~* **out**" "défense d'entrer".

▶**keep up** *vi* se maintenir; (*fig: in comprehension*) suivre ♦ *vt* continuer, maintenir; **to ~ up with** se maintenir au niveau de; **to ~ up with sb** (*in race etc*) aller aussi vite que qn, être du même niveau que qn.

keeper ['kiːpə*] *n* gardien/ne.

keep-fit [kiːp'fɪt] *n* gymnastique *f* de maintien.

keeping ['kiːpɪŋ] *n* (*care*) garde *f*; **in ~ with** à l'avenant de; en accord avec.

keeps [kiːps] *n*: **for ~** (*col*) pour de bon, pour toujours.

keepsake ['kiːpseɪk] *n* souvenir *m*.

keg [kɛg] *n* barrique *f*, tonnelet *m*.

Ken. *abbr* (*US*) = **Kentucky.**

kennel ['kɛnl] *n* niche *f*; **~s** *npl* chenil *m*.

Kenya ['kɛnjə] *n* Kenya *m*.

Kenyan ['kɛnjən] *adj* kenyen(ne) ♦ *n* Kenyen/ne.

kept [kɛpt] *pt, pp of* **keep.**

kerb [kəːb] *n* (*BRIT*) bordure *f* du trottoir.

kerb crawler [-krɔːlə*] *n* personne qui accoste les prostitué(e)s en voiture.

kernel ['kəːnl] *n* amande *f*, (*fig*) noyau *m*.

kerosene ['kɛrəsiːn] *n* kérosène *m*.

ketchup ['kɛtʃəp] *n* ketchup *m*.

kettle ['kɛtl] *n* bouilloire *f*.

kettle drums *npl* timbales *fpl*.

key [kiː] *n* (*gen, MUS*) clé *f*; (*of piano, typewriter*) touche *f*; (*on map*) légende *f* ♦ *cpd* (-)clé.

▶**key in** *vt* (*text*) introduire au clavier.

keyboard ['kiːbɔːd] *n* clavier *m* ♦ *vt* (*text*) saisir.

keyboarder ['kiːbɔːdə*] *n* claviste *m/f*.

keyed up [kiːd'ʌp] *adj*: **to be (all) ~** être surexcité(e).

keyhole ['kiːhəul] *n* trou *m* de la serrure.

keyhole surgery *n* chirurgie très minutieuse où l'incision est minimale.

keynote ['kiːnəut] *n* (*MUS*) tonique *f*; (*fig*) note dominante.

keypad ['kiːpæd] *n* pavé *m* numérique.

key ring *n* porte-clés *m*.

keystroke ['kiːstrəuk] *n* frappe *f*.

kg *abbr* (= *kilogram*) K.

KGB *n abbr* KGB *m*.

khaki ['kɑːkɪ] *adj*, *n* kaki (*m*).

kibbutz [kɪ'buts] *n* kibboutz *m*.

kick [kɪk] *vt* donner un coup de pied à ♦ *vi* (*horse*) ruer ♦ *n* coup *m* de pied; (*of rifle*) recul *m*; (*col: thrill*): **he does it for ~s** il le fait parce que ça l'excite, il le fait pour le plaisir.

▶**kick around** *vi* (*col*) traîner.

▶**kick off** *vi* (*SPORT*) donner le coup d'envoi.

kick-off ['kɪkɔf] *n* (*SPORT*) coup *m* d'envoi.

kick-start ['kɪkstɑːt] *n* (*also*: **~er**) lanceur *m* au pied.

kid [kɪd] *n* (*col: child*) gamin/e, gosse *m/f*; (*animal, leather*) chevreau *m* ♦ *vi* (*col*) plaisanter, blaguer.

kid gloves *npl*: **to treat sb with ~** traiter qn avec ménagement.

kidnap ['kɪdnæp] *vt* enlever, kidnapper.

kidnapper ['kɪdnæpə*] *n* ravisseur/euse.

kidnapping ['kɪdnæpɪŋ] *n* enlèvement *m*.

kidney ['kɪdnɪ] *n* (*ANAT*) rein *m*; (*CULIN*) rognon *m*.

kidney bean *n* haricot *m* rouge.

kidney machine *n* (*MED*) rein artificiel.

Kilimanjaro [kɪlɪmən'dʒɑːrəu] *n*: **Mount ~** Kilimandjaro *m*.

kill [kɪl] *vt* tuer; (*fig*) faire échouer; détruire; supprimer ♦ *n* mise *f* à mort; **to ~ time** tuer le temps.

▶**kill off** *vt* exterminer; (*fig*) éliminer.

killer ['kɪlə*] *n* tueur/euse; meurtrier/ière.

killer instinct *n* combativité *f*; **to have the ~** avoir un tempérament de battant.

killing ['kɪlɪŋ] *n* meurtre *m*; tuerie *f*, massacre *m*; (*col*): **to make a ~** se remplir les poches, réussir un beau coup ♦ *adj* (*col*) tordant(e).

kill-joy ['kɪldʒɔɪ] *n* rabat-joie *m inv*.

kiln [kɪln] *n* four *m*.

kilo ['kiːləu] *n abbr* (= *kilogram*) kilo *m*.

kilobyte ['kiːləubaɪt] *n* kilo-octet *m*.

kilogram(me) ['kɪləugræm] *n* kilogramme *m*.

kilometre, (*US*) **kilometer** ['kɪləmiːtə*] *n* kilomètre *m*.

kilowatt ['kɪləuwɔt] *n* kilowatt *m*.

kilt [kɪlt] *n* kilt *m*.

kilter ['kɪltə*] *n*: **out of ~** déréglé(e), détraqué(e).

kimono [kɪ'məunəu] *n* kimono *m*.

kin [kɪn] *n see* **next-of-kin, kith.**

kind [kaɪnd] adj gentil(le), aimable ♦ n sorte f, espèce f, (species) genre m; **to be two of a ~** se ressembler; **would you be ~ enough to ...?, would you be so ~ as to ...?** auriez-vous la gentillesse or l'obligeance de ...?; **it's very ~ of you (to do)** c'est très aimable à vous (de faire); **in ~** (COMM) en nature; (fig): **to repay sb in ~** rendre la pareille à qn.

kindergarten ['kɪndəgɑːtn] n jardin m d'enfants.

kind-hearted [kaɪnd'hɑːtɪd] adj bon(bonne).

kindle ['kɪndl] vt allumer, enflammer.

kindling ['kɪndlɪŋ] n petit bois.

kindly ['kaɪndlɪ] adj bienveillant(e), plein(e) de gentillesse ♦ adv avec bonté; **will you ~ ...** auriez-vous la bonté or l'obligeance de ...; **he didn't take it ~** il l'a mal pris.

kindness ['kaɪndnɪs] n bonté f, gentillesse f.

kindred ['kɪndrɪd] adj apparenté(e); **~ spirit** âme f sœur.

kinetic [kɪ'nɛtɪk] adj cinétique.

king [kɪŋ] n roi m.

kingdom ['kɪŋdəm] n royaume m.

kingfisher ['kɪŋfɪʃə*] n martin-pêcheur m.

kingpin ['kɪŋpɪn] n (TECH) pivot m; (fig) cheville ouvrière.

king-size(d) ['kɪŋsaɪz(d)] adj (cigarette) (format) extra-long(longue).

kink [kɪŋk] n (of rope) entortillement m; (in hair) ondulation f; (col: fig) aberration f.

kinky ['kɪŋkɪ] adj (fig) excentrique; (pej) aux goûts spéciaux.

kinship ['kɪnʃɪp] n parenté f.

kinsman ['kɪnzmən] n parent m.

kinswoman ['kɪnzwumən] n parente f.

kiosk ['kiːɔsk] n kiosque m; (BRIT: also: **telephone ~**) cabine f (téléphonique); (: also: **newspaper ~**) kiosque à journaux.

kipper ['kɪpə*] n hareng fumé et salé.

Kirghizia [kəː'gɪzɪə] n Kirghizistan m.

kiss [kɪs] n baiser m ♦ vt embrasser; **to ~ (each other)** s'embrasser; **to ~ sb goodbye** dire au revoir à qn en l'embrassant; **~ of life** n (BRIT) bouche à bouche m.

kissagram ['kɪsəgræm] n baiser envoyé à l'occasion d'une célébration par l'intermédiaire d'une personne employée à cet effet.

kit [kɪt] n équipement m, matériel m; (set of tools etc) trousse f; (for assembly) kit m; **tool ~** nécessaire m à outils.

▶**kit out** vt (BRIT) équiper.

kitbag ['kɪtbæg] n sac m de voyage or de marin.

kitchen ['kɪtʃɪn] n cuisine f.

kitchen garden n jardin m potager.

kitchen sink n évier m.

kitchen unit n (BRIT) élément m de cuisine.

kitchenware ['kɪtʃɪnwɛə*] n vaisselle f; ustensiles mpl de cuisine.

kite [kaɪt] n (toy) cerf-volant m; (ZOOL) milan m.

kith [kɪθ] n: **~ and kin** parents et amis mpl.

kitten ['kɪtn] n petit chat, chaton m.

kitty ['kɪtɪ] n (money) cagnotte f.

kiwi ['kiːwiː] n: **~ (fruit)** kiwi m.

KKK n abbr (US) = Ku Klux Klan.

Kleenex ['kliːnɛks] n ® Kleenex m ®.

kleptomaniac [klɛptəu'meɪnɪæk] n kleptomane m/f.

km abbr (= kilometre) km.

km/h abbr (= kilometres per hour) km/h.

knack [næk] n: **to have the ~ (of doing)** avoir le coup (pour faire); **there's a ~** il y a un coup à prendre or une combine.

knackered ['nækəd] adj (col) crevé(e), nase.

knapsack ['næpsæk] n musette f.

knave [neɪv] n (CARDS) valet m.

knead [niːd] vt pétrir.

knee [niː] n genou m.

kneecap ['niːkæp] n rotule f ♦ vt tirer un coup de feu dans la rotule de.

knee-deep ['niːdiːp] adj: **the water was ~** l'eau arrivait aux genoux.

kneel, pt, pp **knelt** [niːl, nɛlt] vi (also: **~ down**) s'agenouiller.

kneepad ['niːpæd] n genouillère f.

knell [nɛl] n glas m.

knelt [nɛlt] pt, pp of **kneel**.

knew [njuː] pt of **know**.

knickers ['nɪkəz] npl (BRIT) culotte f (de femme).

knick-knack ['nɪknæk] n colifichet m.

knife [naɪf] n (pl **knives**) couteau m ♦ vt poignarder, frapper d'un coup de couteau; **~, fork and spoon** couvert m.

knife-edge ['naɪfɛdʒ] n: **to be on a ~** être sur le fil du rasoir.

knight [naɪt] n chevalier m; (CHESS) cavalier m.

knighthood ['naɪthud] n chevalerie f; (title): **to get a ~** être fait chevalier.

knit [nɪt] vt tricoter; (fig): **to ~ together** unir ♦ vi (broken bones) se ressouder.

knitted ['nɪtɪd] adj en tricot.

knitting ['nɪtɪŋ] n tricot m.

knitting machine n machine f à tricoter.

knitting needle n aiguille f à tricoter.

knitting pattern n modèle m (pour tricot).

knitwear ['nɪtwɛə*] n tricots mpl, lainages mpl.

knives [naɪvz] npl of **knife**.

knob [nɔb] n bouton m; (BRIT): **a ~ of butter** une noix de beurre.

knobbly ['nɔblɪ], (US) **knobby** ['nɔbɪ] adj (wood, surface) noueux(euse); (knees) noueux.

knock [nɔk] vt frapper; (make: hole etc): **to ~ a hole in** faire un trou dans, trouer; (force: nail etc): **to ~ a nail into** enfoncer un clou dans; (fig: col) dénigrer ♦ vi (engine) cogner; (at door etc): **to ~ at/on** frapper à/sur ♦ n coup m; **he ~ed at the door** il frappa à la porte.

▶**knock down** vt renverser; (price) réduire.

▶**knock off** vi (col: finish) s'arrêter (de travailler) ♦ *vt* (*vase, object*) faire tomber; (*col: steal*) piquer; (*fig: from price etc*): **to ~ off £10** faire une remise de 10 livres.

►**knock out** *vt* assommer; (*BOXING*) mettre k.-o.

►**knock over** *vt* (*object*) faire tomber; (*pedestrian*) renverser.

knockdown ['nɔkdaun] *adj* (*price*) sacrifié(e).

knocker ['nɔkə*] *n* (*on door*) heurtoir *m*.

knocking ['nɔkɪŋ] *n* coups *mpl*.

knock-kneed [nɔk'niːd] *adj* aux genoux cagneux.

knockout ['nɔkaut] *n* (*BOXING*) knock-out *m*, K.-O. *m*.

knockout competition *n* (*BRIT*) compétition *f* avec épreuves éliminatoires.

knock-up ['nɔkʌp] *n* (*TENNIS*): **to have a ~** faire des balles.

knot [nɔt] *n* (*gen*) nœud *m* ♦ *vt* nouer; **to tie a ~** faire un nœud.

knotty ['nɔtɪ] *adj* (*fig*) épineux(euse).

know [nəu] *vt* (*pt* **knew**, *pp* **known** [njuː, nəun]) savoir; (*person, place*) connaître; **to ~ that** savoir que; **to ~ how to do** savoir faire; **to ~ about/of sth** être au courant de/connaître qch; **to get to ~ sth** (*fact*) apprendre qch; (*place*) apprendre à connaître qch; **I don't ~ him** je ne le connais pas; **to ~ right from wrong** savoir distinguer le bon du mauvais; **as far as I ~ ...** à ma connaissance ..., autant que je sache ....

know-all ['nəuɔːl] *n* (*BRIT pej*) je-sais-tout *m/f*.

know-how ['nəuhau] *n* savoir-faire *m*, technique *f*, compétence *f*.

knowing ['nəuɪŋ] *adj* (*look etc*) entendu(e).

knowingly ['nəuɪŋlɪ] *adv* sciemment; d'un air entendu.

know-it-all ['nəuɪtɔːl] *n* (*US*) = **know-all**.

knowledge ['nɔlɪdʒ] *n* connaissance *f*; (*learning*) connaissances, savoir *m*; **to have no ~ of** ignorer; **not to my ~** pas à ma connaissance; **without my ~** à mon insu; **to have a working ~ of French** se débrouiller en français; **it is common ~ that ...** chacun sait que ...; **it has come to my ~ that ...** j'ai appris que ....

knowledgeable ['nɔlɪdʒəbl] *adj* bien informé(e).

known [nəun] *pp of* **know** ♦ *adj* (*thief, facts*) notoire; (*expert*) célèbre.

knuckle ['nʌkl] *n* articulation *f* (des phalanges), jointure *f*.

►**knuckle down** *vi* (*col*) s'y mettre.

►**knuckle under** *vi* (*col*) céder.

knuckleduster ['nʌkldʌstə*] *n* coup-de-poing américain.

KO *abbr* (= *knock out*) *n* K.-O. *m* ♦ *vt* mettre K.-O.

koala [kəu'ɑːlə] *n* (*also*: ~ **bear**) koala *m*.

kook [kuːk] *n* (*US col*) loufoque *m/f*.

Koran [kɔ'rɑːn] *n* Coran *m*.

Korea [kə'rɪə] *n* Corée *f*; **North/South ~** Corée

du Nord/Sud.

Korean [kə'rɪən] *adj* coréen(ne) ♦ *n* Coréen/ne.

kosher ['kəuʃə*] *adj* kascher *inv*.

kowtow ['kau'tau] *vi*: **to ~ to sb** s'aplatir devant qn.

Kremlin ['krɛmlɪn] *n*: **the ~** le Kremlin.

KS *abbr* (*US*) = *Kansas*.

Kt *abbr* (*BRIT*: = *Knight*) *titre honorifique*.

Kuala Lumpur ['kwɑːlə'lumpuə*] *n* Kuala Lumpur.

kudos ['kjuːdɔs] *n* gloire *f*, lauriers *mpl*.

Kurd [kəːd] *n* Kurde *m/f*.

Kuwait [ku'weɪt] *n* Koweït *f*, Kuweit *f*.

Kuwaiti [ku'weɪtɪ] *adj* koweïtien(ne) ♦ *n* Koweïtien/ne.

kW *abbr* (= *kilowatt*) kW.

KY, Ky. *abbr* (*US*) = *Kentucky*.

L l

L, l [ɛl] *n* (*letter*) L, l *m*; **L for Lucy**, (*US*) **L for Love** L comme Louis.

L *abbr* (= *lake, large*) L; (= *left*) g; (*BRIT AUT*: = *learner*) *signale un conducteur débutant*.

l *abbr* (= *litre*) l.

LA *n abbr* (*US*) = *Los Angeles* ♦ *abbr* (*US*) = *Louisiana*.

La. *abbr* (*US*) = *Louisiana*.

lab [læb] *n abbr* (= *laboratory*) labo *m*.

Lab. *abbr* (*Canada*) = *Labrador*.

label ['leɪbl] *n* étiquette *f*, (*brand: of record*) marque *f* ♦ *vt* étiqueter; **to ~ sb a ...** qualifier qn de ....

labor *etc* ['leɪbə*] (*US*) = **labour** *etc*.

laboratory [lə'bɔrətərɪ] *n* laboratoire *m*.

Labor Day *n* (*US, Canada*) fête *f* du travail (*le premier lundi de septembre*).

laborious [lə'bɔːrɪəs] *adj* laborieux(euse).

labor union *n* (*US*) syndicat *m*.

Labour ['leɪbə*] *n* (*BRIT POL: also*: **the ~ Party**) le parti travailliste, les travaillistes *mpl*.

labour, (*US*) **labor** ['leɪbə*] *n* (*task*) travail *m*; (*workmen*) main-d'œuvre *f*, (*MED*) travail, accouchement *m* ♦ *vi*: **to ~ (at)** travailler dur (à), peiner (sur); **in ~** (*MED*) en travail.

labo(u)r camp *n* camp *m* de travaux forcés.

labo(u)r cost *n* coût *m* de la main-d'œuvre; coût de la façon.

labo(u)red ['leɪbəd] *adj* lourd(e), laborieux(euse); (*breathing*) difficile, pénible; (*style*) lourd, embarrassé(e).

labo(u)rer ['leɪbərə*] *n* manœuvre *m*; (*on farm*) ouvrier *m* agricole.

labo(u)r force *n* main-d'œuvre *f*.

labo(u)r-intensive [leɪbərɪn'tɛnsɪv] *adj* intensif(ive) en main-d'œuvre.

labo(u)r market n marché m du travail.

labo(u)r pains npl douleurs fpl de l'accouchement.

labo(u)r relations npl relations fpl dans l'entreprise.

labo(u)r-saving ['leɪbəseɪvɪŋ] adj qui simplifie le travail.

labo(u)r unrest n agitation sociale.

labyrinth ['læbɪrɪnθ] n labyrinthe m, dédale m.

lace [leɪs] n dentelle f; (of shoe etc) lacet m ♦ vt (shoe) lacer; (drink) arroser, corser.

lacemaking ['leɪsmeɪkɪŋ] n fabrication f de dentelle.

laceration [læsə'reɪʃən] n lacération f.

lace-up ['leɪsʌp] adj (shoes etc) à lacets.

lack [læk] n manque m ♦ vt manquer de; **through** or **for ~ of** faute de, par manque de; **to be ~ing** manquer, faire défaut; **to be ~ing in** manquer de.

lackadaisical [lækə'deɪzɪkl] adj nonchalant(e), indolent(e).

lackey ['lækɪ] n (also fig) laquais m.

lacklustre ['læklʌstə*] adj terne.

laconic [lə'kɒnɪk] adj laconique.

lacquer ['lækə*] n laque f.

lacy ['leɪsɪ] adj comme de la dentelle, qui ressemble à de la dentelle.

lad [læd] n garçon m, gars m; (BRIT: in stable etc) lad m.

ladder ['lædə*] n échelle f; (BRIT: in tights) maille filée ♦ vt, vi (BRIT: tights) filer.

laden ['leɪdn] adj: **~ (with)** chargé(e) (de); **fully ~** (truck, ship) en pleine charge.

ladle ['leɪdl] n louche f.

lady ['leɪdɪ] n dame f; **L~ Smith** lady Smith; **the ladies' (room)** les toilettes fpl des dames; **a ~ doctor** une doctoresse, une femme médecin.

ladybird ['leɪdɪbɜːd], (US) **ladybug** ['leɪdɪbʌg] n coccinelle f.

lady-in-waiting ['leɪdɪɪn'weɪtɪŋ] n dame f d'honneur.

ladykiller ['leɪdɪkɪlə*] n don Juan m.

ladylike ['leɪdɪlaɪk] adj distingué(e).

ladyship ['leɪdɪʃɪp] n: **your L~** Madame la comtesse (or la baronne etc).

lag [læg] n = **time ~** ♦ vi (also: **~ behind**) rester en arrière, traîner ♦ vt (pipes) calorifuger.

lager ['lɑːgə*] n bière blonde.

lager lout n (BRIT col) jeune voyou m (porté sur la boisson).

lagging ['lægɪŋ] n enveloppe isolante, calorifuge m.

lagoon [lə'guːn] n lagune f.

Lagos ['leɪgɒs] n Lagos.

laid [leɪd] pt, pp of **lay**.

laid-back [leɪd'bæk] adj (col) relaxe, décontracté(e).

lain [leɪn] pp of **lie**.

lair [lɛə*] n tanière f, gîte m.

laissez-faire [lɛseɪ'fɛə*] n libéralisme m.

laity ['leɪətɪ] n laïques mpl.

lake [leɪk] n lac m.

Lake District n: **the ~** (BRIT) la région des lacs.

lamb [læm] n agneau m.

lamb chop n côtelette f d'agneau.

lambskin ['læmskɪn] n (peau f d')agneau m.

lambswool ['læmzwʊl] n laine f d'agneau.

lame [leɪm] adj boiteux(euse); **~ duck** (fig) canard boiteux.

lamely ['leɪmlɪ] adv (fig) sans conviction.

lament [lə'mɛnt] n lamentation f ♦ vt pleurer, se lamenter sur.

lamentable ['læməntəbl] adj déplorable, lamentable.

laminated ['læmɪneɪtɪd] adj laminé(e); (windscreen) (en verre) feuilleté.

lamp [læmp] n lampe f.

lamplight ['læmplaɪt] n: **by ~** à la lumière de la (or d'une) lampe.

lampoon [læm'puːn] n pamphlet m.

lamppost ['læmppəʊst] n (BRIT) réverbère m.

lampshade ['læmpʃeɪd] n abat-jour m inv.

lance [lɑːns] n lance f ♦ vt (MED) inciser.

lance corporal n (BRIT) (soldat m de) première classe m.

lancet ['lɑːnsɪt] n (MED) bistouri m.

Lancs [læŋks] abbr (BRIT) = Lancashire.

land [lænd] n (as opposed to sea) terre f (ferme); (country) pays m; (soil) terre; terrain m; (estate) terre(s), domaine(s) m(pl) ♦ vi (from ship) débarquer; (AVIAT) atterrir; (fig: fall) (re)tomber ♦ vt (passengers, goods) débarquer; (obtain) décrocher; **to go/travel by ~** se déplacer par voie de terre; **to own ~** être propriétaire foncier; **to ~ on one's feet** (also fig) retomber sur ses pieds.

▶**land up** vi atterrir, (finir par) se retrouver.

landed gentry ['lændɪd-] n (BRIT) propriétaires terriens or fonciers.

landfill site ['lændfɪl-] n centre m d'enfouissement des déchets.

landing ['lændɪŋ] n (from ship) débarquement m; (AVIAT) atterrissage m; (of staircase) palier m.

landing card n carte f de débarquement.

landing craft n péniche f de débarquement.

landing gear n train m d'atterrissage.

landing stage n (BRIT) débarcadère m, embarcadère m.

landing strip n piste f d'atterrissage.

landlady ['lændleɪdɪ] n propriétaire f, logeuse f.

landlocked ['lændlɒkt] adj entouré(e) de terre(s), sans accès à la mer.

landlord ['lændlɔːd] n propriétaire m, logeur m; (of pub etc) patron m.

landlubber ['lændlʌbə*] n terrien/ne.

landmark ['lændmɑːk] n (point m de) repère m; **to be a ~** (fig) faire date or époque.

landowner ['lændəʊnə*] n propriétaire foncier or terrien.

landscape ['lænskeɪp] n paysage m.
landscape architect, landscape gardener n paysagiste m/f.
landscape painting n (ART) paysage m.
landslide ['lændslaɪd] n (GEO) glissement m (de terrain); (fig: POL) raz-de-marée (électoral).
lane [leɪn] n (in country) chemin m; (in town) ruelle f; (AUT) voie f; file f; (in race) couloir m; **shipping** ~ route f maritime or de navigation.
language ['læŋgwɪdʒ] n langue f; (way one speaks) langage m; **bad** ~ grossièretés fpl, langage grossier.
language laboratory n laboratoire m de langues.
languid ['læŋgwɪd] adj languissant(e); langoureux(euse).
languish ['læŋgwɪʃ] vi languir.
lank [læŋk] adj (hair) raide et terne.
lanky ['læŋkɪ] adj grand(e) et maigre, efflanqué(e).
lanolin(e) ['lænəlɪn] n lanoline f.
lantern ['læntn] n lanterne f.
Laos [laus] n Laos m.
lap [læp] n (of track) tour m (de piste); (of body): **in** or **on one's** ~ sur les genoux ♦ vt (also: ~ **up**) laper ♦ vi (waves) clapoter.
▶**lap up** vt (fig) boire comme du petit-lait, se gargariser de; (: lies etc) gober.
La Paz [læ'pæz] n La Paz.
lapdog ['læpdɒg] n chien m d'appartement.
lapel [lə'pɛl] n revers m.
Lapland ['læplænd] n Laponie f.
lapse [læps] n défaillance f, (in behaviour) écart m (de conduite) ♦ vi (LAW) cesser d'être en vigueur; se périmer; **to** ~ **into bad habits** prendre de mauvaises habitudes; ~ **of time** laps m de temps, intervalle m; **a** ~ **of memory** un trou de mémoire.
laptop ['læptɒp] n (also: ~ **computer**) ordinateur portatif.
larceny ['lɑːsənɪ] n vol m.
lard [lɑːd] n saindoux m.
larder ['lɑːdə*] n garde-manger m inv.
large [lɑːdʒ] adj grand(e); (person, animal) gros(grosse); **to make** ~**r** agrandir; **a** ~ **number of people** beaucoup de gens; **by and** ~ en général; **on a** ~ **scale** sur une grande échelle; **at** ~ (free) en liberté; (generally) en général; pour la plupart.
largely ['lɑːdʒlɪ] adv en grande partie.
large-scale ['lɑːdʒ'skeɪl] adj (map, drawing etc) à grande échelle; (fig) important(e).
lark [lɑːk] n (bird) alouette f; (joke) blague f, farce f.
▶**lark about** vi faire l'idiot, rigoler.
larva, pl larvae ['lɑːvə, -iː] n larve f.
laryngitis [lærɪn'dʒaɪtɪs] n laryngite f.
larynx ['lærɪŋks] n larynx m.
lasagne [lə'zænjə] n lasagne f.
lascivious [lə'sɪvɪəs] adj lascif(ive).

laser ['leɪzə*] n laser m.
laser beam n rayon m laser.
laser printer n imprimante f laser.
lash [læʃ] n coup m de fouet; (also: **eye**~) cil m ♦ vt fouetter; (tie) attacher.
▶**lash down** vt attacher; amarrer; arrimer ♦ vi (rain) tomber avec violence.
▶**lash out** vi: **to** ~ **out** (**at** or **against sb/sth**) attaquer violemment (qn/qch); **to** ~ **out** (**on sth**) (col: spend) se fendre (de qch).
lashing ['læʃɪŋ] n: ~**s of** (BRIT col: cream etc) des masses de.
lass [læs] n (jeune) fille f.
lasso [læ'suː] n lasso m ♦ vt prendre au lasso.
last [lɑːst] adj dernier(ière) ♦ adv en dernier ♦ vi durer; ~ **week** la semaine dernière; ~ **night** hier soir; la nuit dernière; **at** ~ enfin; ~ **but one** avant-dernier(ière); **the** ~ **time** la dernière fois; **it** ~**s** (**for**) **2 hours** ça dure 2 heures.
last-ditch ['lɑːst'dɪtʃ] adj ultime, désespéré(e).
lasting ['lɑːstɪŋ] adj durable.
lastly ['lɑːstlɪ] adv en dernier lieu, pour finir.
last-minute ['lɑːstmɪnɪt] adj de dernière minute.
latch [lætʃ] n loquet m.
▶**latch on to** vt (cling to: person) s'accrocher à; (: idea) trouver bon(ne).
latchkey ['lætʃkiː] n clé f (de la porte d'entrée).
late [leɪt] adj (not on time) en retard; (far on in day etc) dernier(ière); tardif(ive); (recent) récent(e), dernier; (former) ancien(ne); (dead) défunt(e) ♦ adv tard; (behind time, schedule) en retard; **to be** ~ avoir du retard; **to be 10 minutes** ~ avoir 10 minutes de retard; **to work** ~ travailler tard; ~ **in life** sur le tard, à un âge avancé; **of** ~ dernièrement; **in** ~ **May** vers la fin (du mois) de mai, fin mai; **the** ~ **Mr X** feu M. X.
latecomer ['leɪtkʌmə*] n retardataire m/f.
lately ['leɪtlɪ] adv récemment.
lateness ['leɪtnɪs] n (of person) retard m; (of event) heure tardive.
latent ['leɪtnt] adj latent(e); ~ **defect** vice caché.
later ['leɪtə*] adj (date etc) ultérieur(e); (version etc) plus récent(e) ♦ adv plus tard; ~ **on today** plus tard dans la journée.
lateral ['lætərl] adj latéral(e).
latest ['leɪtɪst] adj tout(e) dernier(ière); **the** ~ **news** les dernières nouvelles; **at the** ~ au plus tard.
latex ['leɪtɛks] n latex m.
lath, ~s [læθ, læðz] n latte f.
lathe [leɪð] n tour m.
lather ['lɑːðə*] n mousse f (de savon) ♦ vt savonner ♦ vi mousser.
Latin ['lætɪn] n latin m ♦ adj latin(e).
Latin America n Amérique latine.
Latin American adj latino-américain(e), d'Amérique latine ♦ n Latino-Américain/e.

latitude ['lætɪtjuːd] n (*also fig*) latitude f.
latrine [lə'triːn] n latrines fpl.
latter ['lætə*] adj deuxième, dernier(ière) ♦ n: **the ~** ce dernier, celui-ci.
latterly ['lætəlɪ] adv dernièrement, récemment.
lattice ['lætɪs] n treillis m; treillage m.
lattice window n fenêtre treillissée, fenêtre à croisillons.
Latvia ['lætvɪə] n Lettonie f.
Latvian ['lætvɪən] adj letton(ne) ♦ n Letton/ne; (*LING*) letton m.
laudable ['lɔːdəbl] adj louable.
laudatory ['lɔːdətrɪ] adj élogieux(euse).
laugh [lɑːf] n rire m ♦ vi rire.
►**laugh at** vt fus se moquer de; (*joke*) rire de.
►**laugh off** vt écarter or rejeter par une plaisanterie or par une boutade.
laughable ['lɑːfəbl] adj risible, ridicule.
laughing ['lɑːfɪŋ] adj rieur(euse); **this is no ~ matter** il n'y a pas de quoi rire, ça n'a rien d'amusant.
laughing gas n gaz hilarant.
laughing stock n: **the ~ of** la risée de.
laughter ['lɑːftə*] n rire m; (*people laughing*) rires mpl.
launch [lɔːntʃ] n lancement m; (*boat*) chaloupe f, (*also: motor ~*) vedette f ♦ vt (*ship, rocket, plan*) lancer.
►**launch out** vi: **to ~ out (into)** se lancer (dans).
launching ['lɔːntʃɪŋ] n lancement m.
launch(ing) pad n rampe f de lancement.
launder ['lɔːndə*] vt blanchir.
Launderette [lɔːn'drɛt], (*US*) **Laundromat** ['lɔːndrəmæt] n ® laverie f (automatique).
laundry ['lɔːndrɪ] n blanchisserie f; (*clothes*) linge m; **to do the ~** faire la lessive.
laureate ['lɔːrɪət] adj see **poet laureate**.
laurel ['lɔrl] n laurier m; **to rest on one's ~s** se reposer sur ses lauriers.
lava ['lɑːvə] n lave f.
lavatory ['lævətərɪ] n toilettes fpl.
lavatory paper n (*BRIT*) papier m hygiénique.
lavender ['lævəndə*] n lavande f.
lavish ['lævɪʃ] adj copieux(euse); somptueux(euse); (*giving freely*): **~ with** prodigue de ♦ vt: **to ~ sth on sb** prodiguer qch à qn.
lavishly ['lævɪʃlɪ] adv (*give, spend*) sans compter; (*furnished*) luxueusement.
law [lɔː] n loi f; (*science*) droit m; **against the ~** contraire à la loi; **to study ~** faire du droit; **to go to ~** (*BRIT*) avoir recours à la justice; **~ and order** n l'ordre public.
law-abiding ['lɔːəbaɪdɪŋ] adj respectueux(euse) des lois.
lawbreaker ['lɔːbreɪkə*] n personne f qui transgresse la loi.
law court n tribunal m, cour f de justice.
lawful ['lɔːful] adj légal(e); permis(e).
lawfully ['lɔːfəlɪ] adv légalement.
lawless ['lɔːlɪs] adj sans loi.

Law Lord n (*BRIT*) juge siégant à la Chambre des Lords.
lawmaker ['lɔːmeɪkə*] n législateur/trice.
lawn [lɔːn] n pelouse f.
lawnmower ['lɔːnməuə*] n tondeuse f à gazon.
lawn tennis n tennis m.
law school n faculté f de droit.
law student n étudiant/e en droit.
lawsuit ['lɔːsuːt] n procès m; **to bring a ~ against** engager des poursuites contre.
lawyer ['lɔːjə*] n (*consultant, with company*) juriste m; (*for sales, wills etc*) ≈ notaire m; (*partner, in court*) ≈ avocat m.
lax [læks] adj relâché(e).
laxative ['læksətɪv] n laxatif m.
laxity ['læksɪtɪ] n relâchement m.
lay [leɪ] pt of **lie** ♦ adj laïque; profane ♦ vt (*pt, pp* **laid** [leɪd]) poser, mettre; (*eggs*) pondre; (*trap*) tendre; (*plans*) élaborer; **to ~ the table** mettre la table; **to ~ the facts/one's proposals before sb** présenter les faits/ses propositions à qn; **to get laid** (*col!*) baiser (*!*); se faire baiser (*!*).
►**lay aside**, **lay by** vt mettre de côté.
►**lay down** vt poser; **to ~ down the law** (*fig*) faire la loi.
►**lay in** vt accumuler, s'approvisionner en.
►**lay into** vi (*col: attack*) tomber sur; (*: scold*) passer une engueulade à.
►**lay off** vt (*workers*) licencier.
►**lay on** vt (*water, gas*) mettre, installer; (*provide: meal etc*) fournir; (*paint*) étaler.
►**lay out** vt (*design*) dessiner, concevoir; (*display*) disposer; (*spend*) dépenser.
►**lay up** vt (*to store*) amasser; (*car*) remiser; (*ship*) désarmer; (*subj: illness*) forcer à s'aliter.
layabout ['leɪəbaut] n fainéant/e.
lay-by ['leɪbaɪ] n (*BRIT*) aire f de stationnement (sur le bas-côté).
lay days npl (*NAUT*) estarie f.
layer ['leɪə*] n couche f.
layette [leɪ'ɛt] n layette f.
layman ['leɪmən] n laïque m; profane m.
lay-off ['leɪɔf] n licenciement m.
layout ['leɪaut] n disposition f, plan m, agencement m; (*PRESS*) mise f en page.
laze [leɪz] vi paresser.
laziness ['leɪzɪnɪs] n paresse f.
lazy ['leɪzɪ] adj paresseux(euse).
LB abbr (*Canada*) = Labrador.
lb. abbr (= libra: pound) unité de poids.
lbw abbr (*CRICKET*: = leg before wicket) faute dans laquelle le joueur a la jambe devant le guichet.
LC n abbr (*US*) = Library of Congress.
lc abbr (*TYP*: = lower case) b.d.c.
L/C abbr = **letter of credit**.
LCD n abbr = **liquid crystal display**.
Ld abbr (*BRIT*: = lord) titre honorifique.
LDS n abbr (= Licentiate in Dental Surgery) di-

plôme universitaire; (= *Latter-day Saints*) Église de Jésus-Christ des Saints du dernier jour.

LEA *n abbr* (*BRIT*: = *local education authority*) services locaux de l'enseignement.

lead¹ [li:d] *n* (*front position*) tête *f*; (*distance, time ahead*) avance *f*; (*clue*) piste *f*; (*to battery*) raccord *m*; (*ELEC*) fil *m*; (*for dog*) laisse *f*; (*THEAT*) rôle principal ♦ *vb* (*pt, pp* **led** [lɛd]) *vt* mener, conduire; (*induce*) amener; (*be leader of*) être à la tête de; (*SPORT*) être en tête de; (*orchestra: BRIT*) être le premier violon de; (: *US*) diriger ♦ *vi* mener, être en tête; **to ~ to** mener à; (*result in*) conduire à; aboutir à; **to ~sb astray** détourner qn du droit chemin; **to be in the ~** (*SPORT: in race*) mener, être en tête; (: *match*) mener (à la marque); **to take the ~** (*SPORT*) passer en tête, prendre la tête; mener; (*fig*) prendre l'initiative; **to ~ sb to believe that ...** amener qn à croire que ...; **to ~ sb to do sth** amener qn à faire qch.

▶**lead away** *vt* emmener.
▶**lead back** *vt* ramener.
▶**lead off** *vi* (*in game etc*) commencer.
▶**lead on** *vt* (*tease*) faire marcher; **to ~ sb on to** (*induce*) amener qn à.
▶**lead up to** *vt* conduire à.

lead² [lɛd] *n* (*chemical*) plomb *m*; (*in pencil*) mine *f*.

leaded [ˈlɛdɪd] *adj* (*windows*) à petits carreaux.

leaden [ˈlɛdn] *adj* de *or* en plomb.

leader [ˈliːdə*] *n* (*of team*) chef *m*; (*of party etc*) dirigeant/e, leader *m*; (*in newspaper*) éditorial *m*; **they are ~s in their field** (*fig*) ils sont à la pointe du progrès dans leur domaine; **the L~ of the House** (*BRIT*) le chef de la majorité ministérielle.

leadership [ˈliːdəʃɪp] *n* direction *f*; **under the ~ of ...** sous la direction de ...; **qualities of ~** qualités *fpl* de chef *or* de meneur.

lead-free [ˈlɛdfriː] *adj* sans plomb.

leading [ˈliːdɪŋ] *adj* de premier plan; (*main*) principal(e); **a ~ question** une question tendancieuse; **~ role** rôle prépondérant *or* de premier plan.

leading lady *n* (*THEAT*) vedette (féminine).

leading light *n* (*person*) sommité *f*, personnalité *f* de premier plan.

leading man *n* (*THEAT*) vedette (masculine).

lead pencil [lɛd-] *n* crayon noir *or* à papier.

lead poisoning [lɛd-] *n* saturnisme *m*.

lead time [liːd-] *n* (*COMM*) délai *m* de livraison.

lead weight [lɛd-] *n* plomb *m*.

leaf, *pl* **leaves** [liːf, liːvz] *n* feuille *f*; (*of table*) rallonge *f*; **to turn over a new ~** (*fig*) changer de conduite *or* d'existence; **to take a ~ out of sb's book** (*fig*) prendre exemple sur qn.

▶**leaf through** *vt* (*book*) feuilleter.

leaflet [ˈliːflɪt] *n* prospectus *m*, brochure *f*;

(*POL, REL*) tract *m*.

leafy [ˈliːfɪ] *adj* feuillu(e).

league [liːg] *n* ligue *f*; (*FOOTBALL*) championnat *m*; (*measure*) lieue *f*; **to be in ~ with** avoir partie liée avec, être de mèche avec.

league table *n* classement *m*.

leak [liːk] *n* (*out, also fig*) fuite *f*; (*in*) infiltration *f* ♦ *vi* (*pipe, liquid etc*) fuir; (*shoes*) prendre l'eau ♦ *vt* (*liquid*) répandre; (*information*) divulguer.

▶**leak out** *vi* fuir; (*information*) être divulgué(e).

leakage [ˈliːkɪdʒ] *n* (*also fig*) fuite *f*.

leaky [ˈliːkɪ] *adj* (*pipe, bucket*) qui fuit, percé(e); (*roof*) qui coule; (*shoe*) qui prend l'eau; (*boat*) qui fait eau.

lean [liːn] *adj* maigre ♦ *n* (*of meat*) maigre *m* ♦ *vb* (*pt, pp* **leaned** *or* **leant** [lɛnt]) *vt*: **to ~ sth on** appuyer qch sur ♦ *vi* (*slope*) pencher; (*rest*): **to ~ against** s'appuyer contre; être appuyé(e) contre; **to ~ on** s'appuyer sur.

▶**lean back** *vi* se pencher en arrière.
▶**lean forward** *vi* se pencher en avant.
▶**lean out** *vi*: **to ~ out (of)** se pencher au dehors (de).
▶**lean over** *vi* se pencher.

leaning [ˈliːnɪŋ] *adj* penché(e) ♦ *n*: **~ (towards)** penchant *m* (pour); **the L~ Tower of Pisa** la tour penchée de Pise.

leant [lɛnt] *pt, pp of* **lean**.

lean-to [ˈliːntuː] *n* appentis *m*.

leap [liːp] *n* bond *m*, saut *m* ♦ *vi* (*pt, pp* **leaped** *or* **leapt** [lɛpt]) bondir, sauter; **to ~ at an offer** saisir une offre.

▶**leap up** *vi* (*person*) faire un bond; se lever d'un bond.

leapfrog [ˈliːpfrɔg] *n* jeu *m* de saute-mouton.

leapt [lɛpt] *pt, pp of* **leap**.

leap year *n* année *f* bissextile.

learn, *pt, pp* **learned** *or* **learnt** [ləːn, -t] *vt, vi* apprendre; **to ~ how to do sth** apprendre à faire qch; **we were sorry to ~ that ...** nous apprenons avec regret que ...; **to ~ about sth** (*SCOL*) étudier qch; (*hear*) apprendre qch.

learned [ˈləːnɪd] *adj* érudit(e), savant(e).

learner [ˈləːnə*] *n* débutant/e; (*BRIT: also: ~ driver*) (conducteur/trice) débutant(e).

learning [ˈləːnɪŋ] *n* savoir *m*.

lease [liːs] *n* bail *m* ♦ *vt* louer à bail; **on ~** en location.

▶**lease back** *vt* vendre en cession-bail.

leaseback [ˈliːsbæk] *n* cession-bail *f*.

leasehold [ˈliːshəuld] *n* (*contract*) bail *m* ♦ *adj* loué(e) à bail.

leash [liːʃ] *n* laisse *f*.

least [liːst] *adj*: **the ~ + noun** le(la) plus petit(e), le(la) moindre; (*smallest amount of*) le moins de; **the ~ + adjective** le(la) moins; **the ~ money** le moins d'argent; **the ~ expensive** le moins cher; **at ~** au moins; **not in the ~** pas le moins du monde.

leather ['lɛðə*] n cuir m ♦ cpd en or de cuir; ~ **goods** maroquinerie f.

leave [li:v] vb (pt, pp **left** [lɛft]) vt laisser; (go away from) quitter ♦ vi partir, s'en aller ♦ n (time off) congé m; (MIL, also: consent) permission f; **to be left** rester; **there's some milk left over** il reste du lait; **to ~ school** quitter l'école, terminer sa scolarité; ~ **it to me!** laissez-moi faire!, je m'en occupe!; **on** ~ en permission; **to take one's ~ of** prendre congé de; ~ **of absence** n congé exceptionnel; (MIL) permission spéciale.

►**leave behind** vt (also fig) laisser; (opponent in race) distancer; (forget) laisser, oublier.

►**leave off** vt (cover, lid, heating) ne pas (re)mettre; (light) ne pas (r)allumer, laisser éteint(e); (BRIT col: stop): **to ~ off (doing sth)** s'arrêter (de faire qch).

►**leave on** vt (coat etc) garder, ne pas enlever; (lid) laisser dessus; (light, fire, cooker) laisser allumé(e).

►**leave out** vt oublier, omettre.

leaves [li:vz] npl of **leaf**.

leavetaking ['li:vteɪkɪŋ] n adieux mpl.

Lebanese [lɛbə'ni:z] adj libanais(e) ♦ n (pl inv) Libanais/e.

Lebanon ['lɛbənən] n Liban m.

lecherous ['lɛtʃərəs] adj lubrique.

lectern ['lɛktɜ:n] n lutrin m, pupitre m.

lecture ['lɛktʃə*] n conférence f; (SCOL) cours (magistral) ♦ vi donner des cours; enseigner ♦ vt (reprove) sermonner, réprimander; **to ~ on** faire un cours (or son cours) sur; **to give a ~ (on)** faire une conférence (sur); faire un cours (sur).

lecture hall n amphithéâtre m.

lecturer ['lɛktʃərə*] n (speaker) conférencier/ière; (BRIT: at university) professeur m (d'université), ≈ maître assistant, maître de conférences; **assistant ~** (BRIT) ≈ assistant/e; **senior ~** (BRIT) ≈ chargé/e d'enseignement.

lecture theatre n = **lecture hall**.

LED n abbr (= light-emitting diode) LED f, diode électroluminescente.

led [lɛd] pt, pp of **lead¹**.

ledge [lɛdʒ] n (of window, on wall) rebord m; (of mountain) saillie f, corniche f.

ledger ['lɛdʒə*] n registre m, grand livre m.

lee [li:] n côté m sous le vent; **in the ~ of** à l'abri de.

leech [li:tʃ] n sangsue f.

leek [li:k] n poireau m.

leer [lɪə*] vi: **to ~ at sb** regarder qn d'un air mauvais or concupiscent, lorgner qn.

leeward ['li:wəd] adj, adv sous le vent ♦ n côté m sous le vent; **to ~** sous le vent.

leeway ['li:weɪ] n (fig): **to make up ~** rattraper son retard; **to have some ~** avoir une certaine liberté d'action.

left [lɛft] pt, pp of **leave** ♦ adj gauche ♦ adv à gauche ♦ n gauche f; **on the ~, to the ~** à gauche; **the L~** (POL) la gauche.

left-hand drive ['lɛfthænd-] n (BRIT) conduite f à gauche.

left-handed [lɛft'hændɪd] adj gaucher(ère); (scissors etc) pour gauchers.

left-hand side ['lɛfthænd-] n gauche f, côté m gauche.

leftie ['lɛftɪ] n (col) gaucho m/f, gauchiste m/f.

leftist ['lɛftɪst] adj (POL) gauchiste, de gauche.

left-luggage (office) [lɛft'lʌgɪdʒ(-)] n (BRIT) consigne f.

left-overs ['lɛftəʊvəz] npl restes mpl.

left wing n (MIL, SPORT) aile f gauche; (POL) gauche f ♦ adj: **left-wing** (POL) de gauche.

left-winger ['lɛft'wɪŋgə*] n (POL) membre m de la gauche; (SPORT) ailier m gauche.

lefty ['lɛftɪ] n (col) = **leftie**.

leg [lɛg] n jambe f; (of animal) patte f; (of furniture) pied m; (CULIN: of chicken) cuisse f; **1st/2nd ~** (SPORT) match m aller/retour; (of journey) 1ère/2ème étape; ~ **of lamb** (CULIN) gigot m d'agneau; **to stretch one's ~s** se dégourdir les jambes.

legacy ['lɛgəsɪ] n (also fig) héritage m, legs m.

legal ['li:gl] adj légal(e); **to take ~ action or proceedings against sb** poursuivre qn en justice.

legal adviser n conseiller/ère juridique.

legality [lɪ'gælɪtɪ] n légalité f.

legalize ['li:gəlaɪz] vt légaliser.

legally ['li:gəlɪ] adv légalement; ~ **binding** juridiquement contraignant(e).

legal tender n monnaie légale.

legation [lɪ'geɪʃən] n légation f.

legend ['lɛdʒənd] n légende f.

legendary ['lɛdʒəndərɪ] adj légendaire.

-legged ['lɛgɪd] suffix: **two~** à deux pattes (or jambes or pieds).

leggings ['lɛgɪŋz] npl jambières fpl, guêtres fpl.

leggy ['lɛgɪ] adj aux longues jambes.

legibility [lɛdʒɪ'bɪlɪtɪ] n lisibilité f.

legible ['lɛdʒəbl] adj lisible.

legibly ['lɛdʒəblɪ] adv lisiblement.

legion ['li:dʒən] n légion f.

legionnaire [li:dʒə'nɛə*] n légionnaire m; ~**'s disease** maladie f du légionnaire.

legislate ['lɛdʒɪsleɪt] vi légiférer.

legislation [lɛdʒɪs'leɪʃən] n législation f; **a piece of ~** un texte de loi.

legislative ['lɛdʒɪslətɪv] adj législatif(ive).

legislator ['lɛdʒɪsleɪtə*] n législateur/trice.

legislature ['lɛdʒɪslətʃə*] n corps législatif.

legitimacy [lɪ'dʒɪtɪməsɪ] n légitimité f.

legitimate [lɪ'dʒɪtɪmət] adj légitime.

legitimize [lɪ'dʒɪtɪmaɪz] vt légitimer.

legless ['lɛglɪs] adj (BRIT col) bourré(e).

leg-room ['lɛgru:m] n place f pour les jambes.

Leics abbr (BRIT) = Leicestershire.

leisure ['lɛʒə*] n (time) loisir m, temps m; (free time) temps libre, loisirs mpl; **at ~** (tout) à loisir; à tête reposée.

leisure centre n centre m de loisirs.

leisurely ['lɛʒəlɪ] adj tranquille; fait(e) sans se presser.

leisure suit n (BRIT) survêtement m (mode).

lemon ['lɛmən] n citron m.

lemonade [lɛmə'neɪd] n limonade f.

lemon cheese n, **lemon curd** n crème f de citron.

lemon juice n jus m de citron.

lemon squeezer [-skwiːzə*] n presse-citron m inv.

lemon tea n thé m au citron.

lend, pt, pp **lent** [lɛnd, lɛnt] vt: to ~ sth (to sb) prêter qch (à qn); to ~ a hand donner un coup de main.

lender ['lɛndə*] n prêteur/euse.

lending library ['lɛndɪŋ-] n bibliothèque f de prêt.

length [lɛŋθ] n longueur f; (section: of road, pipe etc) morceau m, bout m; ~ of time durée f; what ~ is it? quelle longueur fait-il?; it is 2 metres in ~ cela fait 2 mètres de long; to fall full ~ tomber de tout son long; at ~ (at last) enfin, à la fin; (lengthily) longuement; to go to any ~(s) to do sth faire n'importe quoi pour faire qch, ne reculer devant rien pour faire qch.

lengthen ['lɛŋθən] vt allonger, prolonger ♦ vi s'allonger.

lengthways ['lɛŋθweɪz] adv dans le sens de la longueur, en long.

lengthy ['lɛŋθɪ] adj (très) long(longue).

leniency ['liːnɪənsɪ] n indulgence f, clémence f.

lenient ['liːnɪənt] adj indulgent(e), clément(e).

leniently ['liːnɪəntlɪ] adv avec indulgence or clémence.

lens [lɛnz] n lentille f; (of spectacles) verre m; (of camera) objectif m.

Lent [lɛnt] n carême m.

lent [lɛnt] pt, pp of **lend**.

lentil ['lɛntl] n lentille f.

Leo ['liːəu] n le Lion; to be ~ être du Lion.

leopard ['lɛpəd] n léopard m.

leotard ['liːətaːd] n maillot m (de danseur etc).

leper ['lɛpə*] n lépreux/euse.

leper colony n léproserie f.

leprosy ['lɛprəsɪ] n lèpre f.

lesbian ['lɛzbɪən] n· lesbienne f ♦ adj lesbien(ne).

lesion ['liːʒən] n (MED) lésion f.

Lesotho [lɪ'suːtuː] n Lesotho m.

less [lɛs] adj moins de ♦ pron, adv moins; ~ than that/you moins que cela/vous; ~ than half moins de la moitié; ~ than one/a kilo/3 metres moins de un/d'un kilo/de 3 mètres; ~ and ~ de moins en moins; the ~ he works ... moins il travaille ....

lessee [lɛ'siː] n locataire m/f (à bail), preneur/euse du bail.

lessen ['lɛsn] vi diminuer, s'amoindrir, s'atténuer ♦ vt diminuer, réduire, atténuer.

lesser ['lɛsə*] adj moindre; to a ~ extent or degree à un degré moindre.

lesson ['lɛsn] n leçon f; a maths ~ une leçon or un cours de maths; to give ~s in donner des cours de; it taught him a ~ (fig) cela lui a servi de leçon.

lessor ['lɛsɔː*, lɛ'sɔː*] n bailleur/eresse.

lest [lɛst] conj de peur de + infinitive, de peur que + sub.

let, pt, pp **let** [lɛt] vt laisser; (BRIT: lease) louer: to ~ sb do sth laisser qn faire qch; to ~ sb know sth faire savoir qch à qn, prévenir qn de qch; he ~ me go il m'a laissé partir; ~ the water boil and ... faites bouillir l'eau et ...; ~'s go allons-y; ~ him come qu'il vienne; "to ~" (BRIT) "à louer".
► **let down** vt (lower) baisser; (dress) rallonger; (hair) défaire; (BRIT: tyre) dégonfler; (disappoint) décevoir.
► **let go** vi lâcher prise ♦ vt lâcher.
► **let in** vt laisser entrer; (visitor etc) faire entrer; what have you ~ yourself in for? à quoi t'es-tu engagé?
► **let off** vt (allow to leave) laisser partir; (not punish) ne pas punir; (subj: taxi driver, bus driver) déposer; (firework etc) faire partir; (smell etc) dégager; to ~ off steam (fig: col) se défouler, décharger sa rate or bile.
► **let on** vi (col): to ~ on that ... révéler que ..., dire que ....
► **let out** vt laisser sortir; (dress) élargir; (scream) laisser échapper; (rent out) louer.
► **let up** vi diminuer, s'arrêter.

let-down ['lɛtdaun] n (disappointment) déception f.

lethal ['liːθl] adj mortel(le), fatal(e).

lethargic [lɛ'θaːdʒɪk] adj léthargique.

lethargy ['lɛθədʒɪ] n léthargie f.

letter ['lɛtə*] n lettre f; ~s npl (LITERATURE) lettres; **small/capital** ~ minuscule f/ majuscule f; ~ **of credit** lettre f de crédit.

letter bomb n lettre piégée.

letterbox ['lɛtəbɔks] n (BRIT) boîte f aux or à lettres.

letterhead ['lɛtəhɛd] n en-tête m.

lettering ['lɛtərɪŋ] n lettres fpl; caractères mpl.

letter opener n coupe-papier m.

letterpress ['lɛtəprɛs] n (method) typographie f.

letter quality n qualité f "courrier".

letters patent npl brevet m d'invention.

lettuce ['lɛtɪs] n laitue f, salade f.

let-up ['lɛtʌp] n répit m, détente f.

leukaemia, (US) **leukemia** [luː'kiːmɪə] n leucémie f.

level ['lɛvl] adj plat(e), plan(e), uni(e); horizontal(e) ♦ n niveau m; (flat place) terrain plat; (also: spirit ~) niveau à bulle ♦ vt niveler, aplanir; (gun) pointer, braquer; (accusation): to ~ (against) lancer or porter (contre) ♦ vi (col): to ~ with sb être franc(franche) avec qn; "A" ~s npl (BRIT: formerly) ≈ baccalauréat m; **"O"** ~**s** npl (BRIT: formerly) examens passés à l'âge de 16 ans sanctionnant les connaissances de l'élève, ≈ brevet m des collèges; **a** ~ **spoonful** (CU-LIN) une cuillerée à raser; **to be** ~ **with** être au même niveau que; **to draw** ~ **with** (team) arriver à égalité de points avec, égaliser avec; arriver au même classement que; (runner, car) arriver à la hauteur de, rattraper; **on the** ~ à l'horizontale; (fig: honest) régulier(ière).

▶**level off, level out** vi (prices etc) se stabiliser ♦ vt (ground) aplanir, niveler.

level crossing n (BRIT) passage m à niveau.

level-headed [lɛvl'hɛdɪd] adj équilibré(e).

levelling, (US) **leveling** ['lɛvlɪŋ] adj (process, effect) de nivellement.

level playing field n: **to compete on a** ~ jouer sur un terrain d'égalité.

lever ['li:və*] n levier m ♦ vt: **to** ~ **up/out** soulever/extraire au moyen d'un levier.

leverage ['li:vərɪdʒ] n: (**on** or **with**) prise f (sur).

levity ['lɛvɪtɪ] n manque m de sérieux, légèreté f.

levy ['lɛvɪ] n taxe f, impôt m ♦ vt prélever, imposer; percevoir.

lewd [lu:d] adj obscène, lubrique.

lexicographer [lɛksɪ'kɔgrəfə*] n lexicographe m/f.

lexicography [lɛksɪ'kɔgrəfɪ] n lexicographie f.

LGV n abbr (= Large Goods Vehicle) poids lourd.

LI abbr (US) = Long Island.

liabilities [laɪə'bɪlətɪz] npl (COMM) obligations fpl, engagements mpl; (on balance sheet) passif m.

liability [laɪə'bɪlətɪ] n responsabilité f; (handicap) handicap m.

liable ['laɪəbl] adj (subject): ~ **to** sujet(te) à; passible de; (responsible): ~ (**for**) responsable (de); (likely): ~ **to do** susceptible de faire; **to be** ~ **to a fine** être passible d'une amende.

liaise [li:'eɪz] vi: **to** ~ **with** rester en liaison avec.

liaison [li:'eɪzɔn] n liaison f.

liar ['laɪə*] n menteur/euse.

libel ['laɪbl] n écrit m diffamatoire; diffamation f ♦ vt diffamer.

libellous ['laɪbləs] adj diffamatoire.

liberal ['lɪbərl] adj libéral(e); (generous): ~ **with** prodigue de, généreux(euse) avec ♦ n: **L~** (POL) libéral/e.

Liberal Democrat n démocrate m/f.

liberality [lɪbə'rælɪtɪ] n (generosity) générosité f, libéralité f.

liberalize ['lɪbərəlaɪz] vt libéraliser.

liberal-minded ['lɪbərl'maɪndɪd] adj libéral(e), tolérant(e).

liberate ['lɪbəreɪt] vt libérer.

liberation [lɪbə'reɪʃən] n libération f.

liberation theology n théologie f de libération.

Liberia [laɪ'bɪərɪə] n Libéria m, Liberia m.

Liberian [laɪ'bɪərɪən] adj libérien(ne) ♦ n Libérien/ne.

liberty ['lɪbətɪ] n liberté f; **at** ~ **to do** libre de faire; **to take the** ~ **of** prendre la liberté de, se permettre de.

libido [lɪ'bi:dəu] n libido f.

Libra ['li:brə] n la Balance; **to be** ~ être de la Balance.

librarian [laɪ'brɛərɪən] n bibliothécaire m/f.

library ['laɪbrərɪ] n bibliothèque f.

library book n livre m de bibliothèque.

libretto [lɪ'brɛtəu] n livret m.

Libya ['lɪbɪə] n Libye f.

Libyan ['lɪbɪən] adj libyen(ne), de Libye ♦ n Libyen/ne.

lice [laɪs] npl of louse.

licence, (US) **license** ['laɪsns] n autorisation f, permis m; (COMM) licence f; (RADIO, TV) redevance f; (also: **driving** ~, (US) **driver's** ~) permis m (de conduire); (excessive freedom) licence; **import** ~ licence d'importation; **produced under** ~ fabriqué(e) sous licence.

licence number n (BRIT AUT) numéro m d'immatriculation.

license ['laɪsns] n (US) = **licence** ♦ vt donner une licence à; (car) acheter la vignette de; délivrer la vignette de.

licensed ['laɪsnst] adj (for alcohol) patenté(e) pour la vente des spiritueux, qui a une patente de débit de boissons.

licensee [laɪsən'si:] n (BRIT: of pub) patron/ne, gérant/e.

license plate n (esp US AUT) plaque f minéralogique.

licentious [laɪ'sɛnʃəs] adj licencieux(euse).

lichen ['laɪkən] n lichen m.

lick [lɪk] vt lécher; (col: defeat) écraser, flanquer une piquette or raclée à ♦ n coup m de langue; **a** ~ **of paint** un petit coup de peinture.

licorice ['lɪkərɪs] n = **liquorice**.

lid [lɪd] n couvercle m; **to take the** ~ **off sth** (fig) exposer or étaler qch au grand jour.

lido ['laɪdəu] n piscine f en plein air; complexe m balnéaire.

lie [laɪ] n mensonge m ♦ vi mentir; (pt **lay**, pp **lain** [leɪ, leɪn]) (rest) être étendu(e) or allongé(e) or couché(e); (in grave) être enterré(e), reposer; (of object: be situated) se trouver, être; **to** ~ **low** (fig) se cacher, rester caché(e); **to tell** ~**s** mentir.

▶**lie about, lie around** vi (things) traîner; (person) traînasser, flemmarder.

▶**lie back** vi se renverser en arrière.

▶**lie down** vi se coucher, s'étendre.

▶**lie up** vi (hide) se cacher.

Liechtenstein ['lɪktənstaɪn] n Liechtenstein m.

lie detector n détecteur m de mensonges.

lie-down ['laɪdaun] n (BRIT): **to have a** ~

s'allonger, se reposer.

lie-in ['laɪɪn] n (BRIT): **to have a** ~ faire la grasse matinée.

lieu [luː]: **in** ~ **of** prep au lieu de, à la place de.

Lieut. abbr (= lieutenant) Lt.

lieutenant [lɛf'tɛnənt, (US) luː'tɛnənt] n lieutenant m.

lieutenant-colonel [lɛf'tɛnənt'kəːnl, (US) luː'tɛnənt'kəːnl] n lieutenant-colonel m.

life, pl **lives** [laɪf, laɪvz] n vie f ♦ cpd de vie; de la vie; à vie; **true to** ~ réaliste, fidèle à la réalité; **to paint from** ~ peindre d'après nature; **to be sent to prison for** ~ être condamné(e) (à la réclusion criminelle) à perpétuité; **country/city** ~ la vie à la campagne/à la ville.

life annuity n pension f, rente viagère.

life assurance n (BRIT) = **life insurance.**

lifebelt ['laɪfbɛlt] n (BRIT) bouée f de sauvetage.

lifeblood ['laɪfblʌd] n (fig) élément moteur.

lifeboat ['laɪfbəut] n canot m or chaloupe f de sauvetage.

lifebuoy ['laɪfbɔɪ] n bouée f de sauvetage.

life expectancy n espérance f de vie.

lifeguard ['laɪfgɑːd] n surveillant m de baignade.

life imprisonment n prison f à vie; (LAW) réclusion f à perpétuité.

life insurance n assurance-vie f.

life jacket n gilet m or ceinture f de sauvetage.

lifeless ['laɪflɪs] adj sans vie, inanimé(e); (dull) qui manque de vie or de vigueur.

lifelike ['laɪflaɪk] adj qui semble vrai(e) or vivant(e); ressemblant(e).

lifeline ['laɪflaɪn] n corde f de sauvetage.

lifelong ['laɪflɔŋ] adj de toute une vie, de toujours.

life preserver [-prɪ'zəːvə*] n (US) gilet m or ceinture f de sauvetage.

lifer ['laɪfə*] n (col) condamné/e à perpète.

life-raft ['laɪfrɑːft] n radeau m de sauvetage.

life-saver ['laɪfseɪvə*] n surveillant m de baignade.

life sentence n condamnation f à vie or à perpétuité.

life-sized ['laɪfsaɪzd] adj grandeur nature inv.

life span n (durée f de) vie f.

life style n style m de vie.

life support system n (MED) respirateur artificiel.

lifetime ['laɪftaɪm] n: **in his** ~ de son vivant; **the chance of a** ~ la chance de ma (or sa etc) vie, une occasion unique.

lift [lɪft] vt soulever, lever; (steal) prendre, voler ♦ vi (fog) se lever ♦ n (BRIT: elevator) ascenseur m; **to give sb a** ~ (BRIT) emmener or prendre qn en voiture.

▶**lift off** vi (rocket, helicopter) décoller.

▶**lift out** vt sortir; (troops, evacuees etc) évacuer par avion or hélicoptère.

▶**lift up** vt soulever.

lift-off ['lɪftɔf] n décollage m.

ligament ['lɪgəmənt] n ligament m.

light [laɪt] n lumière f; (daylight) lumière, jour m; (lamp) lampe f; (AUT: traffic ~, rear ~) feu m; (: headlamp) phare m; (for cigarette etc): **have you got a** ~? avez-vous du feu? ♦ vt (pt, pp **lighted** or **lit** [lɪt]) (candle, cigarette, fire) allumer; (room) éclairer ♦ adj (room, colour) clair(e); (not heavy, also fig) léger(ère) ♦ adv (travel) avec peu de bagages; **to turn the** ~ **on/off** allumer/éteindre; **to cast** or **shed** or **throw** ~ **on** éclaircir; **to come to** ~ être dévoilé(e) or découvert(e); **in the** ~ **of** à la lumière de; étant donné; **to make** ~ **of sth** (fig) prendre qch à la légère, faire peu de cas de qch.

▶**light up** vi s'allumer; (face) s'éclairer ♦ vt (illuminate) éclairer, illuminer.

light bulb n ampoule f.

lighten ['laɪtn] vi s'éclairer ♦ vt (give light to) éclairer; (make lighter) éclaircir; (make less heavy) alléger.

lighter ['laɪtə*] n (also: **cigarette** ~) briquet m; (: in car) allume-cigare m inv; (boat) péniche f.

light-fingered [laɪt'fɪŋgəd] adj chapardeur(euse).

light-headed [laɪt'hɛdɪd] adj étourdi(e), écervelé(e).

light-hearted [laɪt'hɑːtɪd] adj gai(e), joyeux(euse), enjoué(e).

lighthouse ['laɪthaus] n phare m.

lighting ['laɪtɪŋ] n (on road) éclairage m; (in theatre) éclairages.

lighting-up time [laɪtɪŋ'ʌp-] n (BRIT) heure officielle de la tombée du jour.

lightly ['laɪtlɪ] adv légèrement; **to get off** ~ s'en tirer à bon compte.

light meter n (PHOT) photomètre m, cellule f.

lightness ['laɪtnɪs] n clarté f; (in weight) légèreté f.

lightning ['laɪtnɪŋ] n éclair m, foudre f.

lightning conductor, (US) **lightning rod** n paratonnerre m.

lightning strike n (BRIT) grève f surprise.

light pen n crayon m optique.

lightship ['laɪtʃɪp] n bateau-phare m.

lightweight ['laɪtweɪt] adj (suit) léger(ère); (boxer) poids léger inv.

light year ['laɪtjɪə*] n année-lumière f.

like [laɪk] vt aimer (bien) ♦ prep comme ♦ adj semblable, pareil(le) ♦ n: **the** ~ un(e) pareil(le) or semblable; le(la) pareil(le); (pej) (d')autres du même genre or acabit; **his** ~**s and dislikes** ses goûts mpl or préférences fpl; **I would** ~, **I'd** ~ je voudrais, j'aimerais; **would you** ~ **a coffee?** voulez-vous du café?; **to be/look** ~ **sb/sth** ressembler à qn/qch; **what's he** ~? comment est-il?; **what's the weather** ~? quel temps fait-il?; **that's just** ~ **him** c'est bien de lui, ça lui ressemble; **something** ~ **that** quelque chose comme ça;

I feel ~ a drink je boirais bien quelque chose; **if you ~** si vous voulez; **there's nothing ~** ... il n'y a rien de tel que ....

likeable ['laɪkəbl] adj sympathique, agréable.

likelihood ['laɪklɪhud] n probabilité f; **in all ~** selon toute vraisemblance.

likely ['laɪklɪ] adj (result, outcome) probable; (excuse) plausible; **he's ~ to leave** il va sûrement partir, il risque fort de partir; **not ~!** (col) pas de danger!

like-minded ['laɪk'maɪndɪd] adj de même opinion.

liken ['laɪkən] vt: **to ~ sth to** comparer qch à.

likeness ['laɪknɪs] n ressemblance f.

likewise ['laɪkwaɪz] adv de même, pareillement.

liking ['laɪkɪŋ] n affection f, penchant m; goût m; **to take a ~ to sb** se prendre d'amitié pour qn; **to be to sb's ~** être au goût de qn, plaire à qn.

lilac ['laɪlək] n lilas m ♦ adj lilas inv.

Lilo ['laɪləu] n ® matelas m pneumatique.

lilt [lɪlt] n rythme m, cadence f.

lilting ['lɪltɪŋ] adj aux cadences mélodieuses; chantant(e).

lily ['lɪlɪ] n lis m; **~ of the valley** muguet m.

Lima ['liːmə] n Lima.

limb [lɪm] n membre m; **to be out on a ~** (fig) être isolé(e).

limber ['lɪmbə*] : **to ~ up** vi se dégourdir, se mettre en train.

limbo ['lɪmbəu] n: **to be in ~** (fig) être tombé(e) dans l'oubli.

lime [laɪm] n (tree) tilleul m; (fruit) citron vert, lime f; (GEO) chaux f.

lime juice n jus m de citron vert.

limelight ['laɪmlaɪt] n: **in the ~** (fig) en vedette, au premier plan.

limerick ['lɪmərɪk] n petit poème humoristique.

limestone ['laɪmstəun] n pierre f à chaux; (GEO) calcaire m.

limit ['lɪmɪt] n limite f ♦ vt limiter; **weight/ speed ~** limite de poids/de vitesse.

limitation [lɪmɪ'teɪʃən] n limitation f, restriction f.

limited ['lɪmɪtɪd] adj limité(e), restreint(e); **~ edition** édition f à tirage limité.

limited (liability) company (Ltd) n (BRIT) ≈ société f anonyme (SA).

limitless ['lɪmɪtlɪs] adj illimité(e).

limousine ['lɪməziːn] n limousine f.

limp [lɪmp] n: **to have a ~** boiter ♦ vi boiter ♦ adj mou(molle).

limpet ['lɪmpɪt] n patelle f; **like a ~** (fig) comme une ventouse.

limpid ['lɪmpɪd] adj limpide.

linchpin ['lɪntʃpɪn] n esse f; (fig) pivot m.

Lincs [lɪŋks] abbr (BRIT) = Lincolnshire.

line [laɪn] n (gen) ligne f; (rope) corde f; (wire) fil m; (of poem) vers m; (row, series) rangée f; file f, queue f; (COMM: series of goods) arti-cle(s) m(pl), ligne de produits ♦ vt (clothes): **to ~ (with)** doubler (de); (box): **to ~ (with)** garnir or tapisser (de); (subj: trees, crowd) border; **to cut in ~** (US) passer avant son tour; **in his ~ of business** dans sa partie, dans son rayon; **on the right ~s** sur la bonne voie; **a new ~ in cosmetics** une nouvelle ligne de produits de beauté; **hold the ~ please** (BRIT TEL) ne quittez pas; **to be in ~ for sth** (fig) être en lice pour qch; **in ~ with** en accord avec, en conformité avec; **to bring sth into ~ with sth** aligner qch sur qch; **to draw the ~ at (doing) sth** (fig) se refuser à (faire) qch; ne pas tolérer or admettre (qu'on fasse) qch; **to take the ~ that** ... être d'avis or de l'opinion que ....

▶**line up** vi s'aligner, se mettre en rang(s) ♦ vt aligner; (set up, have ready) prévoir; trouver; **to have sb/sth ~d up** avoir qn/qch en vue or de prévu(e).

linear ['lɪnɪə*] adj linéaire.

lined [laɪnd] adj (paper) réglé(e); (face) marqué(e), ridé(e); (clothes) doublé(e).

line feed n (COMPUT) interligne m.

lineman ['laɪnmən] n (US: RAIL) poseur m de rails; (: TEL) ouvrier m de ligne; (: FOOTBALL) avant m.

linen ['lɪnɪn] n linge m (de corps or de maison); (cloth) lin m.

line printer n imprimante f (ligne par ligne).

liner ['laɪnə*] n paquebot m de ligne.

linesman ['laɪnzmən] n (TENNIS) juge m de ligne; (FOOTBALL) juge de touche.

line-up ['laɪnʌp] n file f; (also: police ~) parade f d'identification; (SPORT) (composition f de l'équipe f.

linger ['lɪŋgə*] vi s'attarder; traîner; (smell, tradition) persister.

lingerie ['læɲʒəriː] n lingerie f.

lingering ['lɪŋgərɪŋ] adj persistant(e); qui subsiste; (death) lent(e).

lingo, ~es ['lɪŋgəu] n (pej) jargon m.

linguist ['lɪŋgwɪst] n linguiste m/f; personne douée pour les langues.

linguistic [lɪŋ'gwɪstɪk] adj linguistique.

linguistics [lɪŋ'gwɪstɪks] n linguistique f.

lining ['laɪnɪŋ] n doublure f; (TECH) revêtement m; (: of brakes) garniture f.

link [lɪŋk] n (of a chain) maillon m; (connection) lien m, rapport m ♦ vt relier, lier, unir; **rail ~** liaison f ferroviaire.

▶**link up** vt relier ♦ vi se rejoindre; s'associer.

links [lɪŋks] npl (terrain m de) golf m.

link-up ['lɪŋkʌp] n lien m, rapport m; (of roads) jonction f, raccordement m; (of spaceships) arrimage m; (RADIO, TV) liaison f; (: programme) duplex m.

linoleum [lɪ'nəuliəm] n linoléum m.

linseed oil ['lɪnsiːd-] n huile f de lin.

lint [lɪnt] n tissu ouaté (pour pansements).

lintel ['lɪntl] n linteau m.

lion ['laɪən] n lion m.

lion cub n lionceau m.
lioness ['laɪənɪs] n lionne f.
lip [lɪp] n lèvre f; (of cup etc) rebord m; (insolence) insolences fpl.
liposuction ['lɪpəʊsʌkʃən] n liposuccion f.
lipread ['lɪpriːd] vi lire sur les lèvres.
lip salve [-sælv] n pommade f pour les lèvres, pommade rosat.
lip service n: **to pay ~ to sth** ne reconnaître le mérite de qch que pour la forme or qu'en paroles.
lipstick ['lɪpstɪk] n rouge m à lèvres.
liquefy ['lɪkwɪfaɪ] vt liquéfier ♦ vi se liquéfier.
liqueur [lɪ'kjuə*] n liqueur f.
liquid ['lɪkwɪd] n liquide m ♦ adj liquide.
liquid assets npl liquidités fpl, disponibilités fpl.
liquidate ['lɪkwɪdeɪt] vt liquider.
liquidation [lɪkwɪ'deɪʃən] n liquidation f; **to go into ~** déposer son bilan.
liquidator ['lɪkwɪdeɪtə*] n liquidateur m.
liquid crystal display (LCD) n affichage m à cristaux liquides.
liquidize ['lɪkwɪdaɪz] vt (BRIT CULIN) passer au mixer.
liquidizer ['lɪkwɪdaɪzə*] n (BRIT CULIN) mixer m.
liquor ['lɪkə*] n spiritueux m, alcool m.
liquorice ['lɪkərɪs] n (BRIT) réglisse m.
Lisbon ['lɪzbən] n Lisbonne.
lisp [lɪsp] n zézaiement m.
lissom ['lɪsəm] adj souple, agile.
list [lɪst] n liste f; (of ship) inclinaison f ♦ vt (write down) inscrire; faire la liste de; (enumerate) énumérer; (COMPUT) lister ♦ vi (ship) gîter, donner de la bande; **shopping ~** liste des courses.
listed building ['lɪstɪd-] n (ARCHIT) monument classé.
listed company ['lɪstɪd-] n société cotée en Bourse.
listen ['lɪsn] vi écouter; **to ~ to** écouter.
listener ['lɪsnə*] n auditeur/trice.
listeria [lɪs'tɪərɪə] n listéria f.
listing ['lɪstɪŋ] n (COMPUT) listage m; (: hard copy) liste f, listing m.
listless ['lɪstlɪs] adj indolent(e), apathique.
listlessly ['lɪstlɪslɪ] adv avec indolence or apathie.
list price n prix m de catalogue.
lit [lɪt] pt, pp of **light**.
litany ['lɪtənɪ] n litanie f.
liter ['liːtə*] n (US) = **litre**.
literacy ['lɪtərəsɪ] n degré m d'alphabétisation, fait m de savoir lire et écrire.
literal ['lɪtərl] adj littéral(e).
literally ['lɪtrəlɪ] adv littéralement.
literary ['lɪtərərɪ] adj littéraire.
literate ['lɪtərət] adj qui sait lire et écrire, instruit(e).
literature ['lɪtrɪtʃə*] n littérature f; (brochures etc) copie f publicitaire, prospectus mpl.

lithe [laɪð] adj agile, souple.
lithography [lɪ'θɔgrəfɪ] n lithographie f.
Lithuania [lɪθju'eɪnɪə] n Lituanie f.
Lithuanian [lɪθju'eɪnɪən] adj lituanien(ne) ♦ n Lituanien/ne; (LING) lituanien m.
litigate ['lɪtɪgeɪt] vt mettre en litige ♦ vi plaider.
litigation [lɪtɪ'geɪʃən] n litige m; contentieux m.
litmus ['lɪtməs] n: **~ paper** papier m de tournesol.
litre, (US) **liter** ['liːtə*] n litre m.
litter ['lɪtə*] n (rubbish) détritus mpl, ordures fpl; (young animals) portée f ♦ vt éparpiller; laisser des détritus dans; **~ed with** jonché(e) de, couvert(e) de.
litter bin n (BRIT) boîte f à ordures, poubelle f.
litter lout, (US) **litterbug** ['lɪtəbʌg] n personne qui jette des détritus par terre.
little ['lɪtl] adj (small) petit(e); (not much): **it's ~** c'est peu ♦ adv peu; **~ milk** peu de lait; **a ~** un peu (de); **a ~ milk** un peu de lait; **for a ~ while** pendant un petit moment; **with ~ difficulty** sans trop de difficulté; **as ~ as possible** le moins possible; **~ by ~** petit à petit, peu à peu; **to make ~ of** faire peu de cas de.
little-known ['lɪtl'nəʊn] adj peu connu(e).
liturgy ['lɪtədʒɪ] n liturgie f.
live vi [lɪv] vivre; (reside) vivre, habiter ♦ adj [laɪv] (animal) vivant(e), en vie; (wire) sous tension; (broadcast) (transmis(e)) en direct; (issue) d'actualité, brûlant(e); (unexploded) non explosé(e); **to ~ in London** habiter (à) Londres; **to ~ together** vivre ensemble, cohabiter; **~ ammunition** munitions fpl de combat.
▶**live down** vt faire oublier (avec le temps).
▶**live in** vi être logé(e) et nourri(e); être interne.
▶**live off** vt (land, fish etc) vivre de; (pej: parents etc) vivre aux crochets de.
▶**live on** vt fus (food) vivre de ♦ vi survivre; **to ~ on £50 a week** vivre avec 50 livres par semaine.
▶**live out** vi (BRIT: students) être externe ♦ vt: **to ~ out one's days** or **life** passer sa vie.
▶**live up** vt: **to ~ it up** (col) faire la fête; mener la grande vie.
▶**live up to** vt fus se montrer à la hauteur de.
live-in ['lɪvɪn] adj (nanny) à demeure; **~ partner** concubin/e.
livelihood ['laɪvlɪhʊd] n moyens mpl d'existence.
liveliness ['laɪvlɪnəs] n vivacité f, entrain m.
lively ['laɪvlɪ] adj vif(vive), plein(e) d'entrain.
liven up ['laɪvn-] vt (room etc) égayer; (discussion, evening) animer.
liver ['lɪvə*] n foie m.
liverish ['lɪvərɪʃ] adj qui a mal au foie; (fig) grincheux(euse).
Liverpudlian [lɪvə'pʌdlɪən] adj de Liverpool

♦ *n* habitant/e de Liverpool; natif/ive de Liverpool.
livery ['lɪvərɪ] *n* livrée *f*.
lives [laɪvz] *npl of* life.
livestock ['laɪvstɔk] *n* cheptel *m*, bétail *m*.
live wire [laɪv-] *n* (*col, fig*): **to be a (real)** ~ péter le feu.
livid ['lɪvɪd] *adj* livide, blafard(e); (*furious*) furieux(euse), furibond(e).
living ['lɪvɪŋ] *adj* vivant(e), en vie ♦ *n*: **to earn** *or* **make a** ~ gagner sa vie; **cost of** ~ coût *m* de la vie; **within** ~ **memory** de mémoire d'homme.
living conditions *npl* conditions *fpl* de vie.
living expenses *npl* dépenses courantes.
living room *n* salle *f* de séjour.
living wage *n* salaire *m* permettant de vivre (décemment).
lizard ['lɪzəd] *n* lézard *m*.
llama ['lɑːmə] *n* lama *m*.
LLB *n abbr* (= *Bachelor of Laws*) *titre universitaire*.
LLD *n abbr* (= *Doctor of Laws*) *titre universitaire*.
LMT *abbr* (*US*: = *Local Mean Time*) *heure locale*.
load [ləud] *n* (*weight*) poids *m*; (*thing carried*) chargement *m*, charge *f*, (*ELEC, TECH*) charge ♦ *vt* (*lorry, ship*): **to** ~ **(with)** charger (de); (*gun, camera*): **to** ~ **(with)** charger (avec); (*COMPUT*) charger; **a** ~ **of**, ~**s of** (*fig*) un *or* des tas de, des masses de.
loaded ['ləudɪd] *adj* (*dice*) pipé(e); (*question*) insidieux(euse); (*col: rich*) bourré(e) de fric; (: *drunk*) bourré.
loading bay ['ləudɪŋ-] *n* aire *f* de chargement.
loaf, loaves [ləuf, ləuvz] *n* pain *m*, miche *f* ♦ *vi* (*also*: ~ **about**, ~ **around**) fainéanter, traîner.
loam [ləum] *n* terreau *m*.
loan [ləun] *n* prêt *m* ♦ *vt* prêter; **on** ~ prêté(e), en prêt; **public** ~ emprunt public.
loan account *n* compte *m* de prêt.
loan capital *n* capital-obligations *m*.
loan shark *n* (*col, pej*) usurier *m*.
loath [ləuθ] *adj*: **to be** ~ **to do** répugner à faire.
loathe [ləuð] *vt* détester, avoir en horreur.
loathing ['ləuðɪŋ] *n* dégoût *m*, répugnance *f*.
loathsome ['ləuðsəm] *adj* répugnant(e), détestable.
loaves [ləuvz] *npl of* loaf.
lob [lɔb] *vt* (*ball*) lober.
lobby ['lɔbɪ] *n* hall *m*, entrée *f*, (*POL*) groupe *m* de pression, lobby *m* ♦ *vt* faire pression sur.
lobbyist ['lɔbɪɪst] *n* membre *m/f* d'un groupe de pression.
lobe [ləub] *n* lobe *m*.
lobster ['lɔbstə*] *n* homard *m*.
lobster pot *n* casier *m* à homards.
local ['ləukl] *adj* local(e) ♦ *n* (*BRIT: pub*) pub *m* or café *m* du coin; **the** ~**s** *npl* les gens *mpl* du pays *or* du coin.

local anaesthetic *n* anesthésie locale.
local authority *n* collectivité locale, municipalité *f*.
local call *n* (*TEL*) communication urbaine.
local government *n* administration locale *or* municipale.
locality [ləu'kælɪtɪ] *n* région *f*, environs *mpl*; (*position*) lieu *m*.
localize ['ləukəlaɪz] *vt* localiser.
locally ['ləukəlɪ] *adv* localement; dans les environs *or* la région.
locate [ləu'keɪt] *vt* (*find*) trouver, repérer; (*situate*) situer.
location [ləu'keɪʃən] *n* emplacement *m*; **on** ~ (*CINE*) en extérieur.
loch [lɔx] *n* lac *m*, loch *m*.
lock [lɔk] *n* (*of door, box*) serrure *f*; (*of canal*) écluse *f*; (*of hair*) mèche *f*, boucle *f* ♦ *vt* (*with key*) fermer à clé; (*immobilize*) bloquer ♦ *vi* (*door etc*) fermer à clé; (*wheels*) se bloquer; ~ **stock and barrel** (*fig*) en bloc; **on full** ~ (*BRIT AUT*) le volant tourné à fond.
►**lock away** *vt* (*valuables*) mettre sous clé; (*criminal*) mettre sous les verrous, enfermer.
►**lock out** *vt* enfermer dehors; (*on purpose*) mettre à la porte; (: *workers*) lock-outer.
►**lock up** *vi* tout fermer (à clé).
locker ['lɔkə*] *n* casier *m*.
locket ['lɔkɪt] *n* médaillon *m*.
lockjaw ['lɔkdʒɔː] *n* tétanos *m*.
lockout ['lɔkaut] *n* (*INDUSTRY*) lock-out *m*, grève patronale.
locksmith ['lɔksmɪθ] *n* serrurier *m*.
lock-up ['lɔkʌp] *n* (*prison*) prison *f*, (*cell*) cellule *f* provisoire; (*also*: ~ **garage**) box *m*.
locomotive [ləukə'məutɪv] *n* locomotive *f*.
locum ['ləukəm] *n* (*MED*) suppléant/e (de médecin).
locust ['ləukəst] *n* locuste *f*, sauterelle *f*.
lodge [lɔdʒ] *n* pavillon *m* (de gardien); (*FREEMASONRY*) loge *f* ♦ *vi* (*person*): **to** ~ **with** être logé(e) chez, être en pension chez ♦ *vt* (*appeal etc*) présenter; déposer; **to** ~ **a complaint** porter plainte; **to** ~ **(itself) in/between** se loger dans/entre.
lodger ['lɔdʒə*] *n* locataire *m/f*; (*with room and meals*) pensionnaire *m/f*.
lodging ['lɔdʒɪŋ] *n* logement *m*; *see also* board.
lodging house *n* (*BRIT*) pension *f* de famille.
lodgings ['lɔdʒɪŋz] *npl* chambre *f*, meublé *m*.
loft [lɔft] *n* grenier *m*; (*US*) grenier aménagé (en appartement) (*gén dans ancien entrepôt ou fabrique*).
lofty ['lɔftɪ] *adj* élevé(e); (*haughty*) hautain(e); (*sentiments, aims*) noble.
log [lɔg] *n* (*of wood*) bûche *f*; (*book*) = logbook ♦ *n abbr* (= *logarithm*) log *m* ♦ *vt* enregistrer.
►**log in, log on** *vi* (*COMPUT*) ouvrir une session, entrer dans le système.
►**log off, log out** *vi* (*COMPUT*) clore une session, sortir du système.

logarithm ['lɔgərɪðm] n logarithme m.

logbook ['lɔgbuk] n (*NAUT*) livre m or journal m de bord; (*AVIAT*) carnet m de vol; (*of lorry driver*) carnet de route; (*of events, movement of goods etc*) registre m; (*of car*) ≈ carte grise.

log cabin n cabane f en rondins.

log fire n feu m de bois.

logger ['lɔgə*] n bûcheron m.

loggerheads ['lɔgəhɛdz] npl: **at ~ (with)** à couteaux tirés (avec).

logic ['lɔdʒɪk] n logique f.

logical ['lɔdʒɪkl] adj logique.

logically ['lɔdʒɪkəlɪ] adv logiquement.

logistics [lɔ'dʒɪstɪks] n logistique f.

logjam ['lɔgdʒæm] n: **to break the ~** créer une ouverture dans l'impasse.

logo ['lɔugəu] n logo m.

loin [lɔɪn] n (*CULIN*) filet m, longe f; **~s** npl reins mpl.

loin cloth n pagne m.

loiter ['lɔɪtə*] vi s'attarder; **to ~ (about)** traîner, musarder; (*pej*) rôder.

loll [lɔl] vi (*also: ~ about*) se prélasser, fainéanter.

lollipop ['lɔlɪpɔp] n sucette f.

> *Les **lollipop men/ladies** sont employés pour aider les enfants à traverser la rue au voisinage des écoles à l'heure où ils entrent en classe et à la sortie. On les repère facilement à cause de leur long ciré blanc et ils portent une pancarte ronde pour faire signe aux automobilistes de s'arrêter. On les appelle ainsi car la forme circulaire de cette pancarte rappelle une sucette.*

lollop ['lɔləp] vi (*BRIT*) avancer (*or* courir) maladroitement.

lolly ['lɔlɪ] n (*col: ice*) esquimau m; (: *lollipop*) sucette f; (: *money*) fric m.

Lombardy ['lɔmbədɪ] n Lombardie f.

London ['lʌndən] n Londres.

Londoner ['lʌndənə*] n Londonien/ne.

lone [ləun] adj solitaire.

loneliness ['ləunlɪnɪs] n solitude f, isolement m.

lonely ['ləunlɪ] adj seul(e); (*childhood etc*) solitaire; (*place*) solitaire, isolé(e); **to feel ~** se sentir seul.

lonely hearts adj: **~ ad** petite annonce (personnelle); **~ club** club m de rencontres (*pour personnes seules*).

lone parent n parent m unique.

loner ['ləunə*] n solitaire m/f.

lonesome ['ləunsəm] adj seul(e); solitaire.

long [lɔŋ] adj long(longue) ♦ adv longtemps ♦ n: **the ~ and the short of it is that ...** (*fig*) le fin mot de l'histoire c'est que ... ♦ vi: **to ~ for sth/to do** avoir très envie de qch/de faire; attendre qch avec impatience/impatience de faire; **he had ~ understood that ...** il avait compris depuis longtemps que ...; **how ~ is this river/course?** quelle est la longueur de ce fleuve/la durée de ce cours?; **6 metres ~** (long) de 6 mètres; **6 months ~** qui dure 6 mois, de 6 mois; **all night ~** toute la nuit; **he no ~er comes** il ne vient plus; **~ before** longtemps avant; **before ~** (+ *future*) avant peu, dans peu de temps; (+ *past*) peu de temps après; **~ ago** il y a longtemps; **don't be ~!** fais vite!, dépêche-toi!; **I shan't be ~** je n'en ai pas pour longtemps; **at ~ last** enfin; **in the ~ run** à la longue; finalement; **so** *or* **as ~ as** pourvu que.

long-distance [lɔŋ'dɪstəns] adj (*race*) de fond; (*call*) interurbain(e).

long-haired ['lɔŋ'hɛəd] adj (*person*) aux cheveux longs; (*animal*) aux longs poils.

longhand ['lɔŋhænd] n écriture normale *or* courante.

longing ['lɔŋɪŋ] n désir m, envie f, nostalgie f ♦ adj plein(e) d'envie *or* de nostalgie.

longingly ['lɔŋɪŋlɪ] adv avec désir *or* nostalgie.

longitude ['lɔŋgɪtjuːd] n longitude f.

long johns [-dʒɔnz] npl caleçons longs.

long jump n saut m en longueur.

long-lost ['lɔŋlɔst] adj perdu(e) depuis longtemps.

long-playing ['lɔŋpleɪɪŋ] adj: **~ record (LP)** (disque m) 33 tours m inv.

long-range ['lɔŋ'reɪndʒ] adj à longue portée; (*weather forecast*) à long terme.

longshoreman ['lɔŋʃɔːmən] n (*US*) docker m, débardeur m.

long-sighted ['lɔŋ'saɪtɪd] adj (*BRIT*) presbyte; (*fig*) prévoyant(e).

long-standing ['lɔŋ'stændɪŋ] adj de longue date.

long-suffering [lɔŋ'sʌfərɪŋ] adj empreint(e) d'une patience résignée; extrêmement patient(e).

long-term ['lɔŋtəːm] adj à long terme.

long wave n (*RADIO*) grandes ondes, ondes longues.

long-winded [lɔŋ'wɪndɪd] adj intarissable, interminable.

loo [luː] n (*BRIT col*) w.-c. mpl, petit coin.

loofah ['luːfə] n sorte d'éponge végétale.

look [luk] vi regarder; (*seem*) sembler, paraître, avoir l'air; (*building etc*): **to ~ south/on to the sea** donner au sud/sur la mer ♦ n regard m; (*appearance*) air m, allure f, aspect m; **~s** npl physique m, beauté f; **to ~ like** ressembler à; **it ~s like him** on dirait que c'est lui; **it ~s about 4 metres long** je dirais que ça fait 4 mètres de long, à vue de nez, ça fait 4 mètres de long; **it ~s all right to me** ça me paraît bien; **to have a ~ at sth** jeter un coup d'œil à qch; **to have a ~ for sth** chercher qch; **to ~ ahead** regarder devant soi; (*fig*) envisager l'avenir.

▶**look after** vt fus s'occuper de, prendre soin de; (*luggage etc: watch over*) garder, surveiller.

►**look around** vi regarder autour de soi.

►**look at** vt fus regarder.

►**look back** vi: **to ~ back at sth/sb** se retourner pour regarder qch/qn; **to look back on** (event, period) évoquer, repenser à.

►**look down on** vt fus (fig) regarder de haut, dédaigner.

►**look for** vt fus chercher.

►**look forward to** vt fus attendre avec impatience; **I'm not ~ing forward to it** cette perspective ne me réjouit guère; **~ing forward to hearing from you** (in letter) dans l'attente de vous lire.

►**look in** vi: **to ~ in on sb** passer voir qn.

►**look into** vt fus (matter, possibility) examiner, étudier.

►**look on** vi regarder (en spectateur).

►**look out** vi (beware): **to ~ out (for)** prendre garde (à), faire attention (à).

►**look out for** vt fus être à la recherche de; guetter.

►**look over** vt (essay) jeter un coup d'œil à; (town, building) visiter (rapidement); (person) jeter un coup d'œil à; examiner de la tête aux pieds.

►**look round** vi (turn) regarder derrière soi, se retourner; **to ~ round for sth** chercher qch.

►**look through** vt fus (papers, book) examiner; (: briefly) parcourir; (telescope) regarder à travers.

►**look to** vt fus veiller à; (rely on) compter sur.

►**look up** vi lever les yeux; (improve) s'améliorer ♦ vt (word) chercher; (friend) passer voir.

►**look up to** vt fus avoir du respect pour.

look-out ['lukaut] n poste m de guet; guetteur m; **to be on the ~ (for)** guetter.

look-up table ['lukʌp-] n (COMPUT) table f à consulter.

LOOM n abbr (US: = Loyal Order of Moose) association charitable.

loom [luːm] n métier m à tisser ♦ vi surgir; (fig) menacer, paraître imminent(e).

loony ['luːnɪ] adj, n (col) timbré(e), cinglé(e) (m/f).

loop [luːp] n boucle f; (contraceptive) stérilet m.

loophole ['luːphəul] n porte f de sortie (fig); échappatoire f.

loose [luːs] adj (knot, screw) desserré(e); (stone) branlant(e); (clothes) vague, ample, lâche; (animal) en liberté, échappé(e); (life) dissolu(e); (morals, discipline) relâché(e); (thinking) peu rigoureux(euse), vague; (translation) approximatif(ive) ♦ vt (free: animal) lâcher; (: prisoner) relâcher, libérer; (slacken) détendre, relâcher, desserrer; défaire; donner du mou à; donner du ballant à; (BRIT: arrow) tirer; **~ connection** (ELEC) mauvais contact; **to be at a ~ end** or (US) **at ~ ends** (fig) ne pas trop savoir quoi faire; **to tie up ~ ends** (fig) mettre au point or régler

les derniers détails.

loose change n petite monnaie.

loose-fitting ['luːsfɪtɪŋ] adj (clothes) ample.

loose-leaf ['luːsliːf] adj: **~ binder** or **folder** classeur m à feuilles or feuillets mobiles.

loose-limbed [luːs'lɪmd] adj agile, souple.

loosely ['luːslɪ] adv sans serrer; approximativement.

loosely-knit ['luːslɪ'nɪt] adj élastique.

loosen ['luːsn] vt desserrer, relâcher, défaire.

►**loosen up** vi (before game) s'échauffer; (col: relax) se détendre, se laisser aller.

loot [luːt] n butin m ♦ vt piller.

looter ['luːtə*] n pillard m, casseur m.

looting ['luːtɪŋ] n pillage m.

lop [lɔp] n: **to ~ off** vt couper, trancher.

lop-sided ['lɔp'saɪdɪd] adj de travers, asymétrique.

lord [lɔːd] n seigneur m; **L~ Smith** lord Smith; **the L~** (REL) le Seigneur; **the (House of) L~s** (BRIT) la Chambre des Lords.

lordly ['lɔːdlɪ] adj noble, majestueux(euse); (arrogant) hautain(e).

lordship ['lɔːdʃɪp] n (BRIT): **your L~** Monsieur le comte (or le baron or le Juge).

lore [lɔː*] n tradition(s) f(pl).

lorry ['lɔrɪ] n (BRIT) camion m.

lorry driver n (BRIT) camionneur m, routier m.

lose, pt, pp **lost** [luːz, lɔst] vt perdre; (opportunity) manquer, perdre; (pursuers) distancer, semer ♦ vi perdre; **to ~ (time)** (clock) retarder; **to ~ no time (in doing sth)** ne pas perdre de temps (à faire qch); **to get lost** vi (person) se perdre; **my watch has got lost** ma montre est perdue.

loser ['luːzə*] n perdant/e; **to be a good/bad ~** être beau/mauvais joueur.

loss [lɔs] n perte f; **to cut one's ~es** limiter les dégâts; **to make a ~** enregistrer une perte; **to sell sth at a ~** vendre qch à perte; **to be at a ~** être perplexe or embarrassé(e); **to be at a ~ to do** se trouver incapable de faire.

loss adjuster n (INSURANCE) responsable m/f de l'évaluation des dommages.

loss leader n (COMM) article sacrifié.

lost [lɔst] pt, pp of **lose** ♦ adj perdu(e); **~ in thought** perdu dans ses pensées; **~ and found property** n (US) objets trouvés; **~ and found** n (US) (bureau m des) objets trouvés.

lost property n (BRIT) objets trouvés; **~ office** or **department** (bureau m des) objets trouvés.

lot [lɔt] n (at auctions) lot m; (destiny) sort m, destinée f; **the ~** le tout; tous mpl, toutes fpl; **a ~** beaucoup; **a ~ of** beaucoup de; **~s of** des tas de; **to draw ~s (for sth)** tirer (qch) au sort.

lotion ['ləuʃən] n lotion f.

lottery ['lɔtərɪ] n loterie f.

loud [laud] adj bruyant(e), sonore, fort(e); (gaudy) voyant(e), tapageur(euse) ♦ adv (*speak etc*) fort; **out** ~ tout haut.

loudhailer [laud'heɪlə*] *n* (*BRIT*) porte-voix *m* inv.

loudly ['laudlɪ] *adv* fort, bruyamment.

loudspeaker [laud'spiːkə*] *n* haut-parleur *m*.

lounge [laundʒ] *n* salon *m*; (*of airport*) salle *f* ♦ *vi* se prélasser, paresser.

lounge bar *n* (salle *f* de) bar *m*.

lounge suit *n* (*BRIT*) complet *m*; (: *on invitation*) "tenue de ville".

louse, *pl* **lice** [laus, laɪs] *n* pou *m*.

▶**louse up** *vt* (*col*) gâcher.

lousy ['lauzɪ] *adj* (*fig*) infect(e), moche.

lout [laut] *n* rustre *m*, butor *m*.

louvre, (*US*) **louver** ['luːvə*] *adj* (*door, window*) à claire-voie.

lovable ['lʌvəbl] *adj* très sympathique; adorable.

love [lʌv] *n* amour *m* ♦ *vt* aimer; aimer beaucoup; **to** ~ **to do** aimer beaucoup *or* adorer faire; **I'd** ~ **to come** cela me ferait très plaisir (de venir); **"15** ~**"** (*TENNIS*) "15 à rien *or* zéro"; **to be/fall in** ~ **with** être/tomber amoureux(euse) de; **to make** ~ faire l'amour; ~ **at first sight** le coup de foudre; **to send one's** ~ **to sb** adresser ses amitiés à qn; ~ **from Anne**, ~, **Anne** affectueusement, Anne.

love affair *n* liaison (amoureuse).

love child *n* enfant *m/f* illégitime *or* naturel(le).

loved ones ['lʌvdwʌnz] *npl* proches *mpl* et amis chers.

love-hate relationship [lʌv'heɪt-] *n* rapport ambigu; **they have a** ~ ils s'aiment et se détestent à la fois.

love letter *n* lettre *f* d'amour.

love life *n* vie sentimentale.

lovely ['lʌvlɪ] *adj* (*pretty: girl, house, garden*) ravissant(e); (*friend, wife*) charmant(e); (*holiday, surprise*) très agréable, merveilleux(euse); **we had a** ~ **time** c'était vraiment très bien.

lover ['lʌvə*] *n* amant *m*; (*amateur*): **a** ~ **of** un(e) ami(e) de, un(e) amoureux(euse) de.

lovesick ['lʌvsɪk] *adj* qui se languit d'amour.

lovesong ['lʌvsɔŋ] *n* chanson *f* d'amour.

loving ['lʌvɪŋ] *adj* affectueux(euse), tendre, aimant(e).

low [ləu] *adj* bas(basse) ♦ *adv* bas ♦ *n* (*METEOROLOGY*) dépression *f* ♦ *vi* (*cow*) mugir; **to feel** ~ se sentir déprimé(e); **he's very** ~ (*ill*) il est bien bas *or* très affaibli; **to turn (down)** ~ *vt* baisser; **to reach a new** *or* **an all-time** ~ tomber au niveau le plus bas.

low-alcohol [ləu'ælkəhɔl] *adj* à faible teneur en alcool, peu alcoolisé(e).

lowbrow ['ləubrau] *adj* sans prétentions intellectuelles.

low-calorie ['ləu'kælərɪ] *adj* hypocalorique.

low-cut ['ləukʌt] *adj* (*dress*) décolleté(e).

low-down ['ləudaun] *n* (*col*): **he gave me the**

~ (**on it**) il m'a mis au courant ♦ *adj* (*mean*) méprisable.

lower ['ləuə*] *adj, adv comparative of* **low** ♦ *vt* baisser; (*resistance*) diminuer ♦ *vi* ['lauə*] (*person*): **to** ~ **at sb** jeter un regard mauvais *or* noir à qn; (*sky, clouds*) être menaçant.

low-fat ['ləu'fæt] *adj* maigre.

low-key ['ləu'kiː] *adj* modéré(e); discret(ète).

lowland ['ləulənd] *n* plaine *f*.

low-level ['ləulɛvl] *adj* bas(basse); (*flying*) à basse altitude.

low-loader ['ləuləudə*] *n* semi-remorque *f* à plate-forme surbaissée.

lowly ['ləulɪ] *adj* humble, modeste.

low-lying [ləu'laɪɪŋ] *adj* à faible altitude.

low-paid [ləu'peɪd] *adj* mal payé(e), aux salaires bas.

low-rise ['ləuraɪz] *adj* bas(se), de faible hauteur.

low-tech ['ləutɛk] *adj* sommaire.

loyal ['lɔɪəl] *adj* loyal(e), fidèle.

loyalist ['lɔɪəlɪst] *n* loyaliste *m/f*.

loyalty ['lɔɪəltɪ] *n* loyauté *f*, fidélité *f*.

loyalty card *n* carte *f* de fidélité.

lozenge ['lɔzɪndʒ] *n* (*MED*) pastille *f*; (*GEOM*) losange *m*.

LP *n abbr* = **long-playing record**.

L-plates ['ɛlpleɪts] *npl* (*BRIT*) plaques *fpl* (obligatoires) d'apprenti conducteur.

Les **L-plates** sont des carrés blancs portant un "L" rouge que l'on met à l'avant et à l'arrière de sa voiture pour montrer qu'on n'a pas encore son permis de conduire. Jusqu'à l'obtention du permis, l'apprenti conducteur a un permis provisoire et n'a le droit de conduire que si un conducteur qualifié est assis à côté de lui. Il est interdit aux apprentis conducteurs de circuler sur les autoroutes, même s'ils sont accompagnés.

LPN *n abbr* (*US*: = *Licensed Practical Nurse*) infirmier/ière diplômé(e).

LRAM *n abbr* (*BRIT*) = *Licentiate of the Royal Academy of Music*.

LSAT *n abbr* (*US*) = *Law School Admissions Test*.

LSD *n abbr* (= *lysergic acid diethylamide*) LSD *m*; (*BRIT*: = *pounds, shillings and pence*) système monétaire en usage en GB jusqu'en 1971.

LSE *n abbr* = *London School of Economics*.

LT *abbr* (*ELEC*: = *low tension*) BT.

Lt. *abbr* (= *lieutenant*) Lt.

Ltd *abbr* (*COMM*) = **limited**.

lubricant ['luːbrɪkənt] *n* lubrifiant *m*.

lubricate ['luːbrɪkeɪt] *vt* lubrifier, graisser.

lucid ['luːsɪd] *adj* lucide.

lucidity [luːˈsɪdɪtɪ] *n* lucidité *f*.

luck [lʌk] *n* chance *f*; **bad** ~ malchance *f*, malheur *m*; **to be in** ~ avoir de la chance; **to be out of** ~ ne pas avoir de chance; **good** ~! bonne chance!

luckily ['lʌkɪlɪ] *adv* heureusement, par bon-

heur.
luckless ['lʌklɪs] *adj* (*person*) malchanceux(euse); (*trip*) marqué(e) par la malchance.
lucky ['lʌkɪ] *adj* (*person*) qui a de la chance; (*coincidence*) heureux(euse); (*number etc*) qui porte bonheur.
lucrative ['lu:krətɪv] *adj* lucratif(ive), rentable, qui rapporte.
ludicrous ['lu:dɪkrəs] *adj* ridicule, absurde.
ludo ['lu:dəu] *n* jeu *m* des petits chevaux.
lug [lʌg] *vt* traîner, tirer.
luggage ['lʌgɪdʒ] *n* bagages *mpl*.
luggage lockers *npl* consigne *f* automatique.
luggage rack *n* (*in train*) porte-bagages *m inv*; (: *made of string*) filet *m* à bagages; (*on car*) galerie *f*.
luggage van, (*US*) **luggage car** *n* (*RAIL*) fourgon *m* (à bagages).
lugubrious [lu'gu:brɪəs] *adj* lugubre.
lukewarm ['lu:kwɔ:m] *adj* tiède.
lull [lʌl] *n* accalmie *f* ♦ *vt* (*child*) bercer; (*person, fear*) apaiser, calmer.
lullaby ['lʌləbaɪ] *n* berceuse *f*.
lumbago [lʌm'beɪgəu] *n* lumbago *m*.
lumber ['lʌmbə*] *n* bric-à-brac *m inv* ♦ *vt* (*BRIT col*): **to ~ sb with sth/sb** coller *or* refiler qch/qn à qn ♦ *vi* (*also*: ~ **about**, ~ **along**) marcher pesamment.
lumberjack ['lʌmbədʒæk] *n* bûcheron *m*.
lumber room *n* (*BRIT*) débarras *m*.
lumber yard *n* entrepôt *m* de bois.
luminous ['lu:mɪnəs] *adj* lumineux(euse).
lump [lʌmp] *n* morceau *m*; (*in sauce*) grumeau *m*; (*swelling*) grosseur *f* ♦ *vt* (*also*: ~ **together**) réunir, mettre en tas.
lump sum *n* somme globale *or* forfaitaire.
lumpy ['lʌmpɪ] *adj* (*sauce*) qui a des grumeaux.
lunacy ['lu:nəsɪ] *n* démence *f*, folie *f*.
lunar ['lu:nə*] *adj* lunaire.
lunatic ['lu:nətɪk] *n* fou/folle, dément/e ♦ *adj* fou(folle), dément(e).
lunatic asylum *n* asile *m* d'aliénés.
lunch [lʌntʃ] *n* déjeuner *m* ♦ *vi* déjeuner; **it is his ~ hour** c'est l'heure où il déjeune; **to invite sb to** *or* **for ~** inviter qn à déjeuner.
luncheon ['lʌntʃən] *n* déjeuner *m*.
luncheon meat *n* sorte de saucisson.
luncheon voucher *n* chèque-repas *m*, ticket-repas *m*.
lunchtime ['lʌntʃtaɪm] *n* l'heure *f* du déjeuner.
lung [lʌŋ] *n* poumon *m*.
lung cancer *n* cancer *m* du poumon.
lunge [lʌndʒ] *vi* (*also*: ~ **forward**) faire un mouvement brusque en avant; **to ~ at sb** envoyer *or* assener un coup à qn.
lupin ['lu:pɪn] *n* lupin *m*.
lurch [lə:tʃ] *vi* vaciller, tituber ♦ *n* écart *m* brusque, embardée *f*; **to leave sb in the ~** laisser qn se débrouiller *or* se dépêtrer

tout(e) seul(e).
lure [luə*] *n* appât *m*, leurre *m* ♦ *vt* attirer *or* persuader par la ruse.
lurid ['luərɪd] *adj* affreux(euse), atroce.
lurk [lə:k] *vi* se tapir, se cacher.
luscious ['lʌʃəs] *adj* succulent(e); appétissant(e).
lush [lʌʃ] *adj* luxuriant(e).
lust [lʌst] *n* luxure *f*; lubricité *f*; désir *m*; (*fig*): **~ for** soif *f* de.
▶**lust after** *vt fus* convoiter, désirer.
luster ['lʌstə*] *n* (*US*) = **lustre**.
lustful ['lʌstful] *adj* lascif(ive).
lustre, (*US*) **luster** ['lʌstə*] *n* lustre *m*, brillant *m*.
lusty ['lʌstɪ] *adj* vigoureux(euse), robuste.
lute [lu:t] *n* luth *m*.
Luxembourg ['lʌksəmbə:g] *n* Luxembourg *m*.
luxuriant [lʌg'zjuərɪənt] *adj* luxuriant(e).
luxurious [lʌg'zjuərɪəs] *adj* luxueux(euse).
luxury ['lʌkʃərɪ] *n* luxe *m* ♦ *cpd* de luxe.
LV *n abbr* (*BRIT*) = **luncheon voucher**.
LW *abbr* (*RADIO*: = *long wave*) GO.
Lycra ['laɪkrə] *n* ® Lycra *m* ®.
lying ['laɪɪŋ] *n* mensonge(s) *m(pl)* ♦ *adj* (*statement, story*) mensonger(ère), faux(fausse); (*person*) menteur(euse).
lynch [lɪntʃ] *vt* lyncher.
lynx [lɪŋks] *n* lynx *m inv*.
Lyons ['laɪənz] *n* Lyon *m*.
lyre ['laɪə*] *n* lyre *f*.
lyric ['lɪrɪk] *adj* lyrique; ~**s** *npl* (*of song*) paroles *fpl*.
lyrical ['lɪrɪkl] *adj* lyrique.
lyricism ['lɪrɪsɪzəm] *n* lyrisme *m*.

M m

M, m [ɛm] *n* (*letter*) M, m *m*; **M for Mary,** (*US*) **M for Mike** *m* comme Marcel.
M *n abbr* (*BRIT*: = *motorway*): **the M8** ≈ l'A8 ♦ *abbr* (= *medium*) M.
m *abbr* (= *metre*) m; (= *million*) M; (= *mile*) mi.
MA *n abbr* (*SCOL*) = **Master of Arts** ♦ *abbr* (*US*) = *military academy*; (*US*) = *Massachusetts*.
mac [mæk] *n* (*BRIT*) imper(méable *m*) *m*.
macabre [mə'ka:brə] *adj* macabre.
macaroni [mækə'rəunɪ] *n* macaronis *mpl*.
macaroon [mækə'ru:n] *n* macaron *m*.
mace [meɪs] *n* masse *f*; (*spice*) macis *m*.
Macedonia [mæsɪ'dəunɪə] *n* Macédoine *f*.
Macedonian [mæsɪ'dəunɪən] *adj* macédonien(ne) ♦ *n* Macédonien/ne; (*LING*) macédonien *m*.
machinations [mækɪ'neɪʃənz] *npl* machina-

tions *fpl*, intrigues *fpl*.

machine [mə'ʃiːn] *n* machine *f* ♦ *vt* (*dress etc*) coudre à la machine; (*TECH*) usiner.

machine code *n* (*COMPUT*) code *m* machine.

machine gun *n* mitrailleuse *f*.

machine language *n* (*COMPUT*) langage *m* machine.

machine-readable [mə'ʃiːnriːdəbl] *adj* (*COMPUT*) exploitable par une machine.

machinery [mə'ʃiːnərɪ] *n* machinerie *f*, machines *fpl*; (*fig*) mécanisme(s) *m(pl)*.

machine shop *n* atelier *m* d'usinage.

machine tool *n* machine-outil *f*.

machine washable *adj* (*garment*) lavable en machine.

machinist [mə'ʃiːnɪst] *n* machiniste *m/f*.

macho ['mætʃəu] *adj* macho *inv*.

mackerel ['mækrl] *n* (*pl inv*) maquereau *m*.

mackintosh ['mækɪntɔʃ] *n* (*BRIT*) imperméable *m*.

macro... ['mækrəu] *prefix* macro....

macro-economics ['mækrəuiːkə'nɔmɪks] *n* macro-économie *f*.

mad [mæd] *adj* fou(folle); (*foolish*) insensé(e); (*angry*) furieux(euse); **to go ~** devenir fou; **to be ~ (keen) about** *or* **on sth** (*col*) être follement passionné de qch, être fou de qch.

madam ['mædəm] *n* madame *f*; **yes ~** oui Madame; **M~ Chairman** Madame la Présidente.

madcap ['mædkæp] *adj* (*col*) écervelé(e).

mad cow disease *n* maladie *f* des vaches folles.

madden ['mædn] *vt* exaspérer.

maddening ['mædnɪŋ] *adj* exaspérant(e).

made [meɪd] *pt, pp of* **make**.

Madeira [mə'dɪərə] *n* (*GEO*) Madère *f*, (*wine*) madère *m*.

made-to-measure ['meɪdtə'mɛʒə*] *adj* (*BRIT*) fait(e) sur mesure.

madhouse ['mædhaus] *n* (*also fig*) maison *f* de fous.

madly ['mædlɪ] *adv* follement.

madman ['mædmən] *n* fou *m*, aliéné *m*.

madness ['mædnɪs] *n* folie *f*.

Madrid [mə'drɪd] *n* Madrid.

Mafia ['mæfɪə] *n* maf(f)ia *f*.

mag. [mæg] *n abbr* (*BRIT col*) = **magazine** (*PRESS*).

magazine [mægə'ziːn] *n* (*PRESS*) magazine *m*, revue *f*; (*MIL: store*) dépôt *m*, arsenal *m*; (*of firearm*) magasin *m*.

maggot ['mægət] *n* ver *m*, asticot *m*.

magic ['mædʒɪk] *n* magie *f* ♦ *adj* magique.

magical ['mædʒɪkl] *adj* magique.

magician [mə'dʒɪʃən] *n* magicien/ne.

magistrate ['mædʒɪstreɪt] *n* magistrat *m*; juge *m*; **~s' court** (*BRIT*) ≈ tribunal *m* d'instance.

magnanimous [mæg'nænɪməs] *adj* magnanime.

magnate ['mægneɪt] *n* magnat *m*.

magnesium [mæg'niːzɪəm] *n* magnésium *m*.

magnet ['mægnɪt] *n* aimant *m*.

magnetic [mæg'nɛtɪk] *adj* magnétique.

magnetic disk *n* (*COMPUT*) disque *m* magnétique.

magnetic tape *n* bande *f* magnétique.

magnetism ['mægnɪtɪzəm] *n* magnétisme *m*.

magnification [mægnɪfɪ'keɪʃən] *n* grossissement *m*.

magnificence [mæg'nɪfɪsns] *n* magnificence *f*.

magnificent [mæg'nɪfɪsnt] *adj* superbe, magnifique.

magnify ['mægnɪfaɪ] *vt* grossir; (*sound*) amplifier.

magnifying glass ['mægnɪfaɪɪŋ-] *n* loupe *f*.

magnitude ['mægnɪtjuːd] *n* ampleur *f*.

magnolia [mæg'nəulɪə] *n* magnolia *m*.

magpie ['mægpaɪ] *n* pie *f*.

mahogany [mə'hɔgənɪ] *n* acajou *m* ♦ *cpd* en (bois d')acajou.

maid [meɪd] *n* bonne *f*; **old ~** (*pej*) vieille fille.

maiden ['meɪdn] *n* jeune fille *f* ♦ *adj* (*aunt etc*) non mariée; (*speech, voyage*) inaugural(e).

maiden name *n* nom *m* de jeune fille.

mail [meɪl] *n* poste *f*; (*letters*) courrier *m* ♦ *vt* envoyer (par la poste); **by ~** par la poste.

mailbag ['meɪlbæg] *n* (*US*) sac postal; (*postman's*) sacoche *f*.

mailbox ['meɪlbɔks] *n* (*US: for letters etc*; *COMPUT*) boîte *f* aux lettres.

mailing list ['meɪlɪŋ-] *n* liste *f* d'adresses.

mailman ['meɪlmæn] *n* (*US*) facteur *m*.

mail-order ['meɪlɔːdə*] *n* vente *f* *or* achat *m* par correspondance ♦ *cpd*: **~ firm** *or* **house** maison *f* de vente par correspondance.

mailshot ['meɪlʃɔt] *n* (*BRIT*) mailing *m*.

mail train *n* train postal.

mail truck *n* (*US AUT*) = **mail van**.

mail van *n* (*BRIT: AUT*) voiture *f* *or* fourgonnette *f* des postes; (*: RAIL*) wagon-poste *m*.

maim [meɪm] *vt* mutiler.

main [meɪn] *adj* principal(e) ♦ *n* (*pipe*) conduite principale, canalisation *f*; **the ~s** (*ELEC*) le secteur; **the ~ thing** l'essentiel *m*; **in the ~** dans l'ensemble.

main course *n* (*CULIN*) plat *m* de résistance.

mainframe ['meɪnfreɪm] *n* (*also:* **~ computer**) (gros) ordinateur, unité centrale.

mainland ['meɪnlənd] *n* continent *m*.

mainline ['meɪnlaɪn] *adj* (*RAIL*) de grande ligne ♦ *vb* (*drugs slang*) *vt* se shooter à ♦ *vi* se shooter.

main line *n* (*RAIL*) grande ligne.

mainly ['meɪnlɪ] *adv* principalement, surtout.

main road *n* grand axe, route nationale.

mainstay ['meɪnsteɪ] *n* (*fig*) pilier *m*.

mainstream ['meɪnstriːm] *n* (*fig*) courant principal.

maintain [meɪn'teɪn] *vt* entretenir; (*continue*) maintenir, préserver; (*affirm*) soutenir; **to ~ that ...** soutenir que ....

maintenance ['meɪntənəns] *n* entretien *m*; (*LAW: alimony*) pension *f* alimentaire.

maintenance contract *n* contrat *m*

d'entretien.

maintenance order n (LAW) obligation f alimentaire.

maisonette [meɪzə'nɛt] n (BRIT) appartement m en duplex.

maize [meɪz] n maïs m.

Maj. abbr (MIL) = **major**.

majestic [mə'dʒɛstɪk] adj majestueux(euse).

majesty ['mædʒɪstɪ] n majesté f.

major ['meɪdʒə*] n (MIL) commandant m ♦ adj important(e), principal(e); (MUS) majeur(e) ♦ vi (US SCOL): **to ~ (in)** se spécialiser (en); **a ~ operation** (MED) une grosse opération.

Majorca [mə'jɔːkə] n Majorque f.

major general n (MIL) général m de division.

majority [mə'dʒɔrɪtɪ] n majorité f ♦ cpd (verdict, holding) majoritaire.

make [meɪk] vt (pt, pp **made** [meɪd]) faire; (manufacture) faire, fabriquer; (cause to be): **to ~ sb sad** etc rendre qn triste etc; (force): **to ~ sb do sth** obliger qn à faire qch, faire faire qch à qn; (equal): **2 and 2 ~ 4** 2 et 2 font 4 ♦ n fabrication f; (brand) marque f; **to ~ it** (in time etc) y arriver; (succeed) réussir; **what time do you ~ it?** quelle heure avez-vous?; **to ~ good** vi (succeed) faire son chemin, réussir ♦ vt (deficit) combler; (losses) compenser; **to ~ do with** se contenter de; se débrouiller avec.

▶**make for** vt fus (place) se diriger vers.

▶**make off** vi filer.

▶**make out** vt (write out) écrire; (understand) comprendre; (see) distinguer; (claim, imply) prétendre, vouloir faire croire; **to ~ out a case for sth** présenter des arguments solides en faveur de qch.

▶**make over** vt (assign): **to ~ over (to)** céder (à), transférer (au nom de).

▶**make up** vt (invent) inventer, imaginer; (parcel) faire ♦ vi se réconcilier; (with cosmetics) se maquiller, se farder; **to be made up of** se composer de.

▶**make up for** vt fus compenser; racheter.

make-believe ['meɪkbɪliːv] n: **a world of ~** un monde de chimères or d'illusions; **it's just ~** c'est de la fantaisie; c'est une illusion.

maker ['meɪkə*] n fabricant m.

makeshift ['meɪkʃɪft] adj provisoire, improvisé(e).

make-up ['meɪkʌp] n maquillage m.

make-up bag n trousse f de maquillage.

make-up remover n démaquillant m.

making ['meɪkɪŋ] n (fig): **in the ~** en formation or gestation; **he has the ~s of an actor** il a l'étoffe d'un acteur.

maladjusted [mælə'dʒʌstɪd] adj inadapté(e).

malaise [mæ'leɪz] n malaise m.

malaria [mə'lɛərɪə] n malaria f, paludisme m.

Malawi [mə'lɑːwɪ] n Malawi m.

Malay [mə'leɪ] adj malais(e) ♦ n (person) Malais/e; (language) malais m.

Malaya [mə'leɪə] n Malaisie f.

Malayan [mə'leɪən] adj, n = **Malay**.

Malaysia [mə'leɪzɪə] n Malaisie f.

Malaysian [mə'leɪzɪən] adj malaisien(ne) ♦ n Malaisien/ne.

Maldives ['mɔːldaɪvz] npl: **the ~** les Maldives fpl.

male [meɪl] n (BIOL, ELEC) mâle m ♦ adj (sex, attitude) masculin(e); mâle; (child etc) du sexe masculin; **~ and female students** étudiants et étudiantes.

male chauvinist n phallocrate m.

male nurse n infirmier m.

malevolence [mə'lɛvələns] n malveillance f.

malevolent [mə'lɛvələnt] adj malveillant(e).

malfunction [mæl'fʌŋkʃən] n fonctionnement défectueux.

malice ['mælɪs] n méchanceté f, malveillance f.

malicious [mə'lɪʃəs] adj méchant(e), malveillant(e); (LAW) avec intention criminelle.

malign [mə'laɪn] vt diffamer, calomnier.

malignant [mə'lɪgnənt] adj (MED) malin(igne).

malingerer [mə'lɪŋɡərə*] n simulateur/trice.

mall [mɔːl] n (also: **shopping ~**) centre commercial.

malleable ['mælɪəbl] adj malléable.

mallet ['mælɪt] n maillet m.

malnutrition [mælnjuː'trɪʃən] n malnutrition f.

malpractice [mæl'præktɪs] n faute professionnelle; négligence f.

malt [mɔːlt] n malt m ♦ cpd (whisky) pur malt.

Malta ['mɔːltə] n Malte f.

Maltese [mɔːl'tiːz] adj maltais(e) ♦ n (pl inv) Maltais/e; (LING) maltais m.

maltreat [mæl'triːt] vt maltraiter.

mammal ['mæml] n mammifère m.

mammoth ['mæməθ] n mammouth m ♦ adj géant(e), monstre.

man, pl **men** [mæn, mɛn] n homme m; (CHESS) pièce f; (DRAUGHTS) pion m ♦ vt garnir d'hommes; servir, assurer le fonctionnement de; être de service à; **an old ~** un vieillard; **~ and wife** mari et femme.

Man. abbr (Canada) = Manitoba.

manacles ['mænəklz] npl menottes fpl.

manage ['mænɪdʒ] vi se débrouiller; y arriver, réussir ♦ vt (business) gérer; (team, operation) diriger; (device, things to do, carry etc) arriver à se débrouiller avec, s'en tirer avec; **to ~ to do** se débrouiller pour faire; (succeed) réussir à faire.

manageable ['mænɪdʒəbl] adj maniable; (task etc) faisable.

management ['mænɪdʒmənt] n administration f, direction f; (persons: of business, firm) dirigeants mpl, cadres mpl; (: of hotel, shop, theatre) direction; **"under new ~"** "changement de gérant", "changement de propriétaire".

management accounting n comptabilité f de gestion.

management consultant n conseiller/ère

de direction.

manager ['mænɪdʒə*] n (of business) directeur m; (of institution etc) administrateur m; (of department, unit) responsable m/f, chef m; (of hotel etc) gérant m; (of artist) impresario m; **sales** ~ responsable or chef des ventes.

manageress [mænɪdʒə'rɛs] n directrice f; (of hotel etc) gérante f.

managerial [mænɪ'dʒɪərɪəl] adj directorial(e); ~ **staff** cadres mpl.

managing director (MD) ['mænɪdʒɪŋ-] n directeur général.

Mancunian [mæŋ'kjuːnɪən] adj de Manchester ♦ n habitant/e de Manchester; natif/ive de Manchester.

mandarin ['mændərɪn] n (also: ~ **orange**) mandarine f; (person) mandarin m.

mandate ['mændeɪt] n mandat m.

mandatory ['mændətərɪ] adj obligatoire; (powers etc) mandataire.

mandolin(e) ['mændəlɪn] n mandoline f.

mane [meɪn] n crinière f.

maneuver etc [mə'nuːvə*] (US) = manoeuvre etc.

manfully ['mænfəlɪ] adv vaillamment.

manganese [mæŋgə'niːz] n manganèse m.

mangetout ['mɔnʒ'tuː] n mange-tout m inv.

mangle ['mæŋgl] vt déchiqueter; mutiler ♦ n essoreuse f; calandre f.

mango, ~es ['mæŋgəʊ] n mangue f.

mangrove ['mæŋgrəʊv] n palétuvier m.

mangy ['meɪndʒɪ] adj galeux(euse).

manhandle ['mænhændl] vt (mistreat) maltraiter, malmener; (move by hand) manutentionner.

manhole ['mænhəʊl] n trou m d'homme.

manhood ['mænhʊd] n âge m d'homme; virilité f.

man-hour ['mænaʊə*] n heure-homme f, heure f de main-d'œuvre.

manhunt ['mænhʌnt] n chasse f à l'homme.

mania ['meɪnɪə] n manie f.

maniac ['meɪnɪæk] n maniaque m/f.

manic ['mænɪk] adj maniaque.

manic-depressive ['mænɪkdɪ'presɪv] adj, n (PSYCH) maniaco-dépressif(ive).

manicure ['mænɪkjuə*] n manucure f ♦ vt (person) faire les mains à.

manicure set n trousse f à ongles.

manifest ['mænɪfest] vt manifester ♦ adj manifeste, évident(e) ♦ n (AVIAT, NAUT) manifeste m.

manifestation [mænɪfes'teɪʃən] n manifestation f.

manifesto [mænɪ'festəu] n manifeste m (POL).

manifold ['mænɪfəʊld] adj multiple, varié(e) ♦ n (AUT etc): **exhaust** ~ collecteur m d'échappement.

Manila [mə'nɪlə] n Manille, Manila.

manila [mə'nɪlə] adj: ~ **paper** papier m bulle.

manipulate [mə'nɪpjuleɪt] vt manipuler.

manipulation [mənɪpjuˈleɪʃən] n manipulation f.

mankind [mæn'kaɪnd] n humanité f, genre humain.

manliness ['mænlɪnɪs] n virilité f.

manly ['mænlɪ] adj viril(e); courageux(euse).

man-made ['mæn'meɪd] adj artificiel(le).

manna ['mænə] n manne f.

mannequin ['mænɪkɪn] n mannequin m.

manner ['mænə*] n manière f, façon f; (good) ~**s** (bonnes) manières; **bad** ~**s** mauvaises manières; **all** ~ **of** toutes sortes de.

mannerism ['mænərɪzəm] n particularité f de langage (or de comportement), tic m.

mannerly ['mænəlɪ] adj poli(e), courtois(e).

manoeuvrable, (US) **maneuverable** [mə'nuːvrəbl] adj facile à manœuvrer.

manoeuvre, (US) **maneuver** [mə'nuːvə*] vt, vi manœuvrer ♦ n manœuvre f; **to** ~ **sb into doing sth** manipuler qn pour lui faire faire qch.

manor ['mænə*] n (also: ~ **house**) manoir m.

manpower ['mænpaʊə*] n main-d'œuvre f.

manservant, pl **menservants** ['mænsəːvənt, 'men-] n domestique m.

mansion ['mænʃən] n château m, manoir m.

manslaughter ['mænslɔːtə*] n homicide m involontaire.

mantelpiece ['mæntlpiːs] n cheminée f.

mantle ['mæntl] n cape f; (fig) manteau m.

man-to-man ['mæntə'mæn] adj, adv d'homme à homme.

manual ['mænjuəl] adj manuel(le) ♦ n manuel m.

manual worker n travailleur manuel.

manufacture [mænju'fæktʃə*] vt fabriquer ♦ n fabrication f.

manufactured goods [mænju'fæktʃəd-] npl produits manufacturés.

manufacturer [mænju'fæktʃərə*] n fabricant m.

manufacturing industries [mænju'fæktʃərɪŋ-] npl industries fpl de transformation.

manure [mə'njuə*] n fumier m; (artificial) engrais m.

manuscript ['mænjuskrɪpt] n manuscrit m.

many ['menɪ] adj beaucoup de, de nombreux(euses) ♦ pron beaucoup, un grand nombre; **how** ~? combien?; **a great** ~ un grand nombre (de); **too** ~ **difficulties** trop de difficultés; **twice as** ~ deux fois plus; ~ **a** ... bien des ..., plus d'un(e) ....

Maori ['maurɪ] n Maori/e ♦ adj maori(e).

map [mæp] n carte f ♦ vt dresser la carte de.

▶**map out** vt tracer; (fig: career, holiday) organiser, préparer (à l'avance); (: essay) faire le plan de.

maple ['meɪpl] n érable m.

Mar. abbr = **March**.

mar [maː*] vt gâcher, gâter.

marathon ['mærəθən] n marathon m ♦ adj: **a** ~ **session** une séance-marathon.

marathon runner *n* coureur/euse de marathon, marathonien/ne.

marauder [mə'rɔːdə*] *n* maraudeur/euse.

marble ['mɑːbl] *n* marbre *m*; (*toy*) bille *f*; ~**s** *n* (*game*) billes.

March [mɑːtʃ] *n* mars *m*; *for phrases see also* **July**.

march [mɑːtʃ] *vi* marcher au pas; (*demonstrators*) défiler ♦ *n* marche *f*; (*demonstration*) rallye *m*; **to ~ out of/into** *etc* sortir de/entrer dans *etc* (*de manière décidée ou impulsive*).

marcher ['mɑːtʃə*] *n* (*demonstrator*) manifestant/e, marcheur/euse.

marching ['mɑːtʃɪŋ] *n*: **to give sb his ~ orders** (*fig*) renvoyer qn; envoyer promener qn.

march-past ['mɑːtʃpɑːst] *n* défilé *m*.

mare [mɛə*] *n* jument *f*.

marg. [mɑːdʒ] *n abbr* (*col*) = **margarine**.

margarine [mɑːdʒə'riːn] *n* margarine *f*.

margin ['mɑːdʒɪn] *n* marge *f*.

marginal ['mɑːdʒɪnl] *adj* marginal(e); ~ **seat** (*POL*) siège disputé.

marginally ['mɑːdʒɪnəlɪ] *adv* très légèrement, sensiblement.

marigold ['mærɪɡəʊld] *n* souci *m*.

marijuana [mærɪ'wɑːnə] *n* marijuana *f*.

marina [mə'riːnə] *n* marina *f*.

marinade *n* [mærɪ'neɪd] marinade *f* ♦ *vt* ['mærɪneɪd] = **marinate**.

marinate ['mærɪneɪt] *vt* (faire) mariner.

marine [mə'riːn] *adj* marin(e) ♦ *n* fusilier marin; (*US*) marine *m*.

marine insurance *n* assurance *f* maritime.

marital ['mærɪtl] *adj* matrimonial(e); ~ **status** situation *f* de famille.

maritime ['mærɪtaɪm] *adj* maritime.

maritime law *n* droit *m* maritime.

marjoram ['mɑːdʒərəm] *n* marjolaine *f*.

mark [mɑːk] *n* marque *f*; (*of skid etc*) trace *f*; (*BRIT SCOL*) note *f*; (*SPORT*) cible *f*; (*currency*) mark *m*; (*BRIT TECH*): **M~ 2/3** 2ème/3ème série *f or* version *f* ♦ *vt* (*also SPORT: player*) marquer; (*stain*) tacher; (*BRIT SCOL*) noter; corriger; **punctuation ~s** signes *mpl* de ponctuation; **to ~ time** marquer le pas; **to be quick off the ~ (in doing)** (*fig*) ne pas perdre de temps (pour faire); **up to the ~** (*in efficiency*) à la hauteur.

▸**mark down** *vt* (*prices, goods*) démarquer, réduire le prix de.

▸**mark off** *vt* (*tick off*) cocher, pointer.

▸**mark out** *vt* désigner.

▸**mark up** *vt* (*price*) majorer.

marked [mɑːkt] *adj* marqué(e), net(te).

markedly ['mɑːkɪdlɪ] *adv* visiblement, manifestement.

marker ['mɑːkə*] *n* (*sign*) jalon *m*; (*bookmark*) signet *m*.

market ['mɑːkɪt] *n* marché *m* ♦ *vt* (*COMM*) commercialiser; **to be on the ~** être sur le marché; **on the open ~** en vente libre; **to play the ~** jouer à la *or* spéculer en Bourse.

marketable ['mɑːkɪtəbl] *adj* commercialisable.

market analysis *n* analyse *f* de marché.

market day *n* jour *m* de marché.

market demand *n* besoins *mpl* du marché.

market economy *n* économie *f* de marché.

market forces *npl* tendances *fpl* du marché.

market garden *n* (*BRIT*) jardin maraîcher.

marketing ['mɑːkɪtɪŋ] *n* marketing *m*.

marketplace ['mɑːkɪtpleɪs] *n* place *f* du marché; (*COMM*) marché *m*.

market price *n* prix marchand.

market research *n* étude *f* de marché.

market value *n* valeur marchande; valeur du marché.

marking ['mɑːkɪŋ] *n* (*on animal*) marque *f*, tache *f*; (*on road*) signalisation *f*.

marksman ['mɑːksmən] *n* tireur *m* d'élite.

marksmanship ['mɑːksmənʃɪp] *n* adresse *f* au tir.

mark-up ['mɑːkʌp] *n* (*COMM: margin*) marge *f* (bénéficiaire); (*: increase*) majoration *f*.

marmalade ['mɑːməleɪd] *n* confiture *f* d'oranges.

maroon [mə'ruːn] *vt* (*fig*): **to be ~ed (in *or* at)** être bloqué(e) (à) ♦ *adj* bordeaux *inv*.

marquee [mɑː'kiː] *n* chapiteau *m*.

marquess, marquis ['mɑːkwɪs] *n* marquis *m*.

Marrakech, Marrakesh [mærə'kɛʃ] *n* Marrakech.

marriage ['mærɪdʒ] *n* mariage *m*.

marriage bureau *n* agence matrimoniale.

marriage certificate *n* extrait *m* d'acte de mariage.

marriage guidance, (*US*) **marriage counseling** *n* conseils conjugaux.

marriage of convenience *n* mariage *m* de convenance.

married ['mærɪd] *adj* marié(e); (*life, love*) conjugal(e).

marrow ['mærəʊ] *n* moelle *f*; (*vegetable*) courge *f*.

marry ['mærɪ] *vt* épouser, se marier avec; (*subj: father, priest etc*) marier ♦ *vi* (*also: get married*) se marier.

Mars [mɑːz] *n* (*planet*) Mars *f*.

Marseilles [mɑː'seɪlz] *n* Marseille.

marsh [mɑːʃ] *n* marais *m*, marécage *m*.

marshal ['mɑːʃl] *n* maréchal *m*; (*US: fire, police*) ≈ capitaine *m*; (*for demonstration, meeting*) membre *m* du service d'ordre ♦ *vt* rassembler.

marshalling yard ['mɑːʃlɪŋ-] *n* (*RAIL*) gare *f* de triage.

marshmallow [mɑːʃ'mæləʊ] *n* (*BOT*) guimauve *f*; (*sweet*) pâte *f* de) guimauve.

marshy ['mɑːʃɪ] *adj* marécageux(euse).

marsupial [mɑː'suːpɪəl] *adj* marsupial(e) ♦ *n* marsupial *m*.

martial ['mɑːʃl] *adj* martial(e).

martial arts *npl* arts martiaux.

martial law *n* loi martiale.

Martian ['mɑːʃən] *n* Martien/ne.

martin ['mɑːtɪn] *n* (*also*: **house** ~) martinet *m*.
martyr ['mɑːtə*] *n* martyr/e ♦ *vt* martyriser.
martyrdom ['mɑːtədəm] *n* martyre *m*.
marvel ['mɑːvl] *n* merveille *f* ♦ *vi*: **to** ~ **(at)** s'émerveiller (de).
marvellous, (*US*) **marvelous** ['mɑːvləs] *adj* merveilleux(euse).
Marxism ['mɑːksɪzəm] *n* marxisme *m*.
Marxist ['mɑːksɪst] *adj, n* marxiste (*m/f*).
marzipan ['mɑːzɪpæn] *n* pâte *f* d'amandes.
mascara [mæs'kɑːrə] *n* mascara *m*.
mascot ['mæskət] *n* mascotte *f*.
masculine ['mæskjulɪn] *adj* masculin(e) ♦ *n* masculin *m*.
masculinity [mæskju'lɪnɪtɪ] *n* masculinité *f*.
MASH [mæʃ] *n abbr* (*US MIL*) = *mobile army surgical hospital*.
mash [mæʃ] *vt* (*CULIN*) faire une purée de.
mashed [mæʃt] *adj*: ~ **potatoes** purée *f* de pommes de terre.
mask [mɑːsk] *n* masque *m* ♦ *vt* masquer.
masochism ['mæsəukɪzəm] *n* masochisme *m*.
masochist ['mæsəukɪst] *n* masochiste *m/f*.
mason ['meɪsn] *n* (*also*: **stone**~) maçon *m*; (*also*: **free**~) franc-maçon *m*.
masonic [mə'sɔnɪk] *adj* maçonnique.
masonry ['meɪsnrɪ] *n* maçonnerie *f*.
masquerade [mæskə'reɪd] *n* bal masqué; (*fig*) mascarade *f* ♦ *vi*: **to** ~ **as** se faire passer pour.
mass [mæs] *n* multitude *f*, masse *f*; (*PHYSICS*) masse; (*REL*) messe *f* ♦ *vi* se masser; **the** ~**es** les masses; **to go to** ~ aller à la messe.
Mass. *abbr* (*US*) = *Massachusetts*.
massacre ['mæsəkə*] *n* massacre *m* ♦ *vt* massacrer.
massage ['mæsɑːʒ] *n* massage *m* ♦ *vt* masser.
masseur [mæ'səː*] *n* masseur *m*.
masseuse [mæ'səːz] *n* masseuse *f*.
massive ['mæsɪv] *adj* énorme, massif(ive).
mass market *n* marché *m* grand public.
mass media *npl* mass-media *mpl*.
mass meeting *n* rassemblement *m* de masse.
mass-produce ['mæsprə'djuːs] *vt* fabriquer en série.
mass production *n* fabrication *f* en série.
mast [mɑːst] *n* mât *m*; (*RADIO, TV*) pylône *m*.
mastectomy [mæs'tɛktəmɪ] *n* mastectomie *f*.
master ['mɑːstə*] *n* maître *m*; (*in secondary school*) professeur *m*; (*title for boys*): **M~ X** Monsieur X ♦ *vt* maîtriser; (*learn*) apprendre à fond; (*understand*) posséder parfaitement *or* à fond; ~ **of ceremonies (MC)** *n* maître des cérémonies; **M~ of Arts/Science (MA/MSc)** *n* ≈ titulaire *m/f* d'une maîtrise (en lettres/science); **M~ of Arts/Science degree (MA/MSc)** *n* ≈ maîtrise *f*; **M~'s degree** *n* ≈ maîtrise.

Le **Master's degree** *est un diplôme que l'on prépare en général après le* **Bachelor's degree,** *bien que certaines universités décernent un*

Master's au lieu d'un Bachelor's. Pour l'obtenir, il faut suivre des cours, soit rédiger un mémoire à partir d'une recherche personnelle, soit encore les deux. Les principaux masters sont le MA (Master of Arts), et le MSc (Master of Science), qui comprennent cours et mémoire, et le MLitt (Master of Letters) et le MPhil (Master of Philosophy), qui reposent uniquement sur le mémoire; voir **doctorate**

---

master disk *n* (*COMPUT*) disque original.
masterful ['mɑːstəful] *adj* autoritaire, impérieux(euse).
master key *n* passe-partout *m inv*.
masterly ['mɑːstəlɪ] *adj* magistral(e).
mastermind ['mɑːstəmaɪnd] *n* esprit supérieur ♦ *vt* diriger, être le cerveau de.
masterpiece ['mɑːstəpiːs] *n* chef-d'œuvre *m*.
master plan *n* stratégie *f* d'ensemble.
master stroke *n* coup *m* de maître.
mastery ['mɑːstərɪ] *n* maîtrise *f*; connaissance parfaite.
mastiff ['mæstɪf] *n* mastiff *m*.
masturbate ['mæstəbeɪt] *vi* se masturber.
masturbation [mæstə'beɪʃən] *n* masturbation *f*.
mat [mæt] *n* petit tapis; (*also*: **door**~) paillasson *m* ♦ *adj* = **matt.**
match [mætʃ] *n* allumette *f*; (*game*) match *m*, partie *f*; (*fig*) égal/e; mariage *m*; parti *m* ♦ *vt* assortir; (*go well with*) aller bien avec, s'assortir à; (*equal*) égaler, valoir ♦ *vi* être assorti(e); **to be a good** ~ être bien assorti(e).
▶**match up** *vt* assortir.
matchbox ['mætʃbɒks] *n* boîte *f* d'allumettes.
matching ['mætʃɪŋ] *adj* assorti(e).
matchless ['mætʃlɪs] *adj* sans égal.
mate [meɪt] *n* camarade *m/f* de travail; (*col*) copain/copine; (*animal*) partenaire *m/f*, mâle/femelle; (*in merchant navy*) second *m* ♦ *vi* s'accoupler ♦ *vt* accoupler.
material [mə'tɪərɪəl] *n* (*substance*) matière *f*, matériau *m*; (*cloth*) tissu *m*, étoffe *f* ♦ *adj* matériel(le); (*important*) essentiel(le); ~**s** *npl* matériaux *mpl*; **reading** ~ de quoi lire, de la lecture.
materialistic [mətɪərɪə'lɪstɪk] *adj* matérialiste.
materialize [mə'tɪərɪəlaɪz] *vi* se matérialiser, se réaliser.
materially [mə'tɪərɪəlɪ] *adv* matériellement; essentiellement.
maternal [mə'təːnl] *adj* maternel(le).
maternity [mə'təːnɪtɪ] *n* maternité *f* ♦ *cpd* de maternité, de grossesse.
maternity benefit *n* prestation *f* de maternité.
maternity hospital *n* maternité *f*.
matey ['meɪtɪ] *adj* (*BRIT col*) copain-copain *inv*.
math. [mæθ] *n abbr* (*US*: = *mathematics*) maths *fpl*.
mathematical [mæθə'mætɪkl] *adj* mathémati-

que.

mathematician [mæθəmə'tɪʃən] n mathématicien/ne.

mathematics [mæθə'mætɪks] n mathématiques fpl.

maths [mæθs] n abbr (BRIT: = mathematics) maths fpl.

matinée ['mætɪneɪ] n matinée f.

mating ['meɪtɪŋ] n accouplement m.

mating call n appel m du mâle.

mating season n saison f des amours.

matriarchal [meɪtrɪ'ɑːkl] adj matriarcal(e).

matrices ['meɪtrɪsiːz] npl of **matrix**.

matriculation [mətrɪkjuˈleɪʃən] n inscription f.

matrimonial [mætrɪˈməʊnɪəl] adj matrimonial(e), conjugal(e).

matrimony ['mætrɪmənɪ] n mariage m.

matrix, pl **matrices** ['meɪtrɪks, 'meɪtrɪsiːz] n matrice f.

matron ['meɪtrən] n (in hospital) infirmière-chef f; (in school) infirmière f.

matronly ['meɪtrənlɪ] adj de matrone; imposant(e).

matt [mæt] adj mat(e).

matted ['mætɪd] adj emmêlé(e).

matter ['mætə*] n question f; (PHYSICS) matière f, substance f; (content) contenu m, fond m; (MED: pus) pus m ♦ vi importer; it doesn't ~ cela n'a pas d'importance; (I don't mind) cela ne fait rien; what's the ~? qu'est-ce qu'il y a?, qu'est-ce qui ne va pas?; no ~ what quoiqu'il arrive; that's another ~ c'est une autre affaire; as a ~ of course tout naturellement; as a ~ of fact en fait; it's a ~ of habit c'est une question d'habitude; printed ~ imprimés mpl; reading ~ (BRIT) de quoi lire, de la lecture.

matter-of-fact ['mætərəv'fækt] adj terre à terre, neutre.

matting ['mætɪŋ] n natte f.

mattress ['mætrɪs] n matelas m.

mature [mə'tjʊə*] adj mûr(e); (cheese) fait(e) ♦ vi mûrir; se faire.

mature student n étudiant/e plus âgé(e) que la moyenne.

maturity [mə'tjʊərɪtɪ] n maturité f.

maudlin ['mɔːdlɪn] adj larmoyant(e).

maul [mɔːl] vt lacérer.

Mauritania [mɔːrɪ'teɪnɪə] n Mauritanie f.

Mauritius [mə'rɪʃəs] n l'île f Maurice.

mausoleum [mɔːsə'lɪəm] n mausolée m.

mauve [məʊv] adj mauve.

maverick ['mævrɪk] n (fig) franc-tireur m, non-conformiste m/f.

mawkish ['mɔːkɪʃ] adj mièvre; fade.

max. abbr = **maximum**.

maxim ['mæksɪm] n maxime f.

maxima ['mæksɪmə] npl of **maximum**.

maximize ['mæksɪmaɪz] vt (profits etc, chances) maximiser.

maximum ['mæksɪməm] adj maximum ♦ n (pl **maxima** ['mæksɪmə]) maximum m.

May [meɪ] n mai m; for phrases see also **July**.

may [meɪ] vi (conditional: **might**) (indicating possibility): **he** ~ **come** il se peut qu'il vienne; (be allowed to): ~ **I smoke?** puis-je fumer?; (wishes): ~ **God bless you!** (que) Dieu vous bénisse!; ~ **I sit here?** vous permettez que je m'assoie ici?; **he might be there** il pourrait bien y être, il se pourrait qu'il y soit; **I might as well go** je ferais aussi bien d'y aller, autant y aller; **you might like to try** vous pourriez (peut-être) essayer.

maybe ['meɪbiː] adv peut-être; ~ **he'll** ... peut-être qu'il ...; ~ **not** peut-être pas.

May Day n le Premier mai.

mayday ['meɪdeɪ] n S.O.S. m.

mayhem ['meɪhem] n grabuge m.

mayonnaise [meɪə'neɪz] n mayonnaise f.

mayor [mɛə*] n maire m.

mayoress ['mɛərɛs] n maire m; épouse f du maire.

maypole ['meɪpəʊl] n mât enrubanné (autour duquel on danse).

maze [meɪz] n labyrinthe m, dédale m.

MB abbr (COMPUT) = **megabyte**; (Canada) = Manitoba.

MBA n abbr (= Master of Business Administration) titre universitaire.

MBBS, MBChB n abbr (BRIT: = Bachelor of Medicine and Surgery) titre universitaire.

MBE n abbr (BRIT: = Member of the Order of the British Empire) titre honorifique.

MC n abbr = **master of ceremonies**.

MCAT n abbr (US) = Medical College Admissions Test.

MCP n abbr (BRIT col: = male chauvinist pig) phallocrate m.

MD n abbr (= Doctor of Medicine) titre universitaire; (COMM) = **managing director** ♦ abbr (US) = Maryland.

Md. abbr (US) = Maryland.

MDT abbr (US: = Mountain Daylight Time) heure d'été des Montagnes Rocheuses.

ME n abbr (US: = medical examiner) médecin légiste m/f; (MED: = myalgic encephalomyelitis) encéphalomyélite f myalgique ♦ abbr (US) = Maine.

me [miː] pron me, m' + vowel; (stressed, after prep) moi; **it's** ~ c'est moi; **it's for** ~ c'est pour moi.

meadow ['mɛdəʊ] n prairie f, pré m.

meagre, (US) **meager** ['miːgə*] adj maigre.

meal [miːl] n repas m; (flour) farine f; **to go out for a** ~ sortir manger.

meals on wheels npl (BRIT) repas livrés à domicile aux personnes âgées ou handicapées.

mealtime ['miːltaɪm] n heure f du repas.

mealy-mouthed ['miːlɪmaʊðd] adj mielleux(euse).

mean [miːn] adj (with money) avare, radin(e); (unkind) mesquin(e), méchant(e); (US col: animal) méchant, vicieux(euse); (: person) vache; (*average*) moyen(ne) ♦ *vt* (*pt, pp* **meant** [mɛnt]) (*signify*) signifier, vouloir dire; (*intend*): **to ~ to do** avoir l'intention de faire ♦ *n* moyenne *f*; **to be meant for** être destiné(e) à; **do you ~ it?** vous êtes sérieux?; **what do you ~?** que voulez-vous dire?

meander [mɪ'ændə*] *vi* faire des méandres; (*fig*) flâner.

meaning ['miːnɪŋ] *n* signification *f*, sens *m*.

meaningful ['miːnɪŋful] *adj* significatif(ive); (*relationship*) valable.

meaningless ['miːnɪŋlɪs] *adj* dénué(e) de sens.

meanness ['miːnnɪs] *n* avarice *f*; mesquinerie *f*.

means [miːnz] *npl* moyens *mpl*; **by ~ of** par l'intermédiaire de; au moyen de; **by all ~** je vous en prie.

means test *n* (*ADMIN*) contrôle *m* des conditions de ressources.

meant [mɛnt] *pt, pp of* **mean**.

meantime ['miːntaɪm] *adv*, **meanwhile** ['miːnwaɪl] *adv* (*also*: **in the ~**) pendant ce temps.

measles ['miːzlz] *n* rougeole *f*.

measly ['miːzlɪ] *adj* (*col*) minable.

measurable ['mɛʒərəbl] *adj* mesurable.

measure ['mɛʒə*] *vt, vi* mesurer ♦ *n* mesure *f*; (*ruler*) règle (graduée); **a litre ~** un litre; **some ~ of success** un certain succès; **to take ~s to do sth** prendre des mesures pour faire qch.

▶**measure up** *vi*: **to ~ up (to)** être à la hauteur (de).

measured ['mɛʒəd] *adj* mesuré(e).

measurement ['mɛʒəmənt] *n*: **chest/hip ~** tour *m* de poitrine/hanches; **~s** *npl* mesures *fpl*; **to take sb's ~s** prendre les mesures de qn.

meat [miːt] *n* viande *f*; **cold ~s** (*BRIT*) viandes froides; **crab ~** crabe *f*.

meatball ['miːtbɔːl] *n* boulette *f* de viande.

meat pie *n* pâté *m* en croûte.

meaty ['miːtɪ] *adj* (*flavour*) de viande; (*fig: argument, book*) étoffé(e), substantiel(le).

Mecca ['mɛkə] *n* La Mecque; (*fig*): **a ~ (for)** la Mecque (de).

mechanic [mɪ'kænɪk] *n* mécanicien *m*.

mechanical [mɪ'kænɪkl] *adj* mécanique.

mechanical engineering *n* (*science*) mécanique *f*; (*industry*) construction *f* mécanique.

mechanics [mə'kænɪks] *n* mécanique *f* ♦ *npl* mécanisme *m*.

mechanism ['mɛkənɪzəm] *n* mécanisme *m*.

mechanization [mɛkənaɪ'zeɪʃən] *n* mécanisation *f*.

MEd *n abbr* (= *Master of Education*) *titre universitaire*.

medal ['mɛdl] *n* médaille *f*.

medallion [mɪ'dælɪən] *n* médaillon *m*.

medallist, (*US*) **medalist** ['mɛdlɪst] *n* (*SPORT*) médaillé/e.

meddle ['mɛdl] *vi*: **to ~ in** se mêler de,

s'occuper de; **to ~ with** toucher à.

meddlesome ['mɛdlsəm], **meddling** ['mɛdlɪŋ] *adj* indiscret(ète), qui se mêle de ce qui ne le (*or* la) regarde pas; touche-à-tout *inv*.

media ['miːdɪə] *npl* media *mpl*.

media circus *n* (*event*) battage *m* médiatique; (*group of journalists*) cortège *m* médiatique.

mediaeval [mɛdɪ'iːvl] *adj* = **medieval**.

median ['miːdɪən] *n* (*US: also*: **~ strip**) bande médiane.

media research *n* étude *f* de l'audience.

mediate ['miːdɪeɪt] *vi* s'interposer; servir d'intermédiaire.

mediation [miːdɪ'eɪʃən] *n* médiation *f*.

mediator ['miːdɪeɪtə*] *n* médiateur/trice.

Medicaid ['mɛdɪkeɪd] *n* (*US*) *assistance médicale aux indigents*.

medical ['mɛdɪkl] *adj* médical(e) ♦ *n* (*also*: **~ examination**) visite médicale; examen médical.

medical certificate *n* certificat médical.

medical student *n* étudiant/e en médecine.

Medicare ['mɛdɪkɛə*] *n* (*US*) *régime d'assurance maladie*.

medicated ['mɛdɪkeɪtɪd] *adj* traitant(e), médicamenteux(euse).

medication [mɛdɪ'keɪʃən] *n* (*drugs etc*) médication *f*.

medicinal [mɛ'dɪsɪnl] *adj* médicinal(e).

medicine ['mɛdsɪn] *n* médecine *f*; (*drug*) médicament *m*.

medicine chest *n* pharmacie *f* (*murale ou portative*).

medicine man *n* sorcier *m*.

medieval [mɛdɪ'iːvl] *adj* médiéval(e).

mediocre [miːdɪ'əʊkə*] *adj* médiocre.

mediocrity [miːdɪ'ɔkrɪtɪ] *n* médiocrité *f*.

meditate ['mɛdɪteɪt] *vi*: **to ~ (on)** méditer (sur).

meditation [mɛdɪ'teɪʃən] *n* méditation *f*.

Mediterranean [mɛdɪtə'reɪnɪən] *adj* méditerranéen(ne); **the ~ (Sea)** la (mer) Méditerranée.

medium ['miːdɪəm] *adj* moyen(ne) ♦ *n* (*pl* **media**) (*means*) moyen *m*; (*pl* **mediums**) (*person*) médium *m*; **the happy ~** le juste milieu.

medium-dry ['miːdɪəm'draɪ] *adj* demi-sec.

medium-sized ['miːdɪəm'saɪzd] *adj* de taille moyenne.

medium wave *n* (*RADIO*) ondes moyennes, petites ondes.

medley ['mɛdlɪ] *n* mélange *m*.

meek [miːk] *adj* doux(douce), humble.

meet, *pt, pp* **met** [miːt, mɛt] *vt* rencontrer; (*by arrangement*) retrouver, rejoindre; (*for the first time*) faire la connaissance de; (*go and fetch*): **I'll ~ you at the station** j'irai te chercher à la gare; (*problem*) faire face à; (*requirements*) satisfaire à, répondre à; (*bill, expenses*) régler, honorer ♦ *vi* se rencontrer; se retrouver; (*in session*) se réunir; (*join: objects*) se joindre ♦ *n* (*BRIT: HUNTING*) rendez-

vous *m* de chasse; (*US SPORT*) rencontre *f*, meeting *m*; **pleased to ~ you!** enchanté!
▶ **meet up** *vi*: **to ~ up with sb** rencontrer qn.
▶ **meet with** *vt fus* rencontrer.
meeting ['miːtɪŋ] *n* rencontre *f*; (*session: of club etc*) réunion *f*; (*formal*) assemblée *f*; (*SPORT: rally*) rencontre, meeting *m*; (*interview*) entrevue *f*; **she's at a ~** (*COMM*) elle est en conférence; **to call a ~** convoquer une réunion.
meeting place *n* lieu *m* de (la) réunion; (*for appointment*) lieu de rendez-vous.
megabyte ['mɛgəbaɪt] *n* (*COMPUT*) méga-octet *m*.
megalomaniac [mɛgələ'meɪnɪæk] *n* mégalomane *m/f*.
megaphone ['mɛgəfəun] *n* porte-voix *m inv*.
megawatt ['mɛgəwɔt] *n* mégawatt *m*.
melancholy ['mɛlənkəlɪ] *n* mélancolie *f* ♦ *adj* mélancolique.
mellow ['mɛləu] *adj* velouté(e); doux(douce); (*colour*) riche et profond(e); (*fruit*) mûr(e) ♦ *vi* (*person*) s'adoucir.
melodious [mɪ'ləudɪəs] *adj* mélodieux(euse).
melodrama ['mɛləudrɑːmə] *n* mélodrame *m*.
melodramatic [mɛlədrə'mætɪk] *adj* mélodramatique.
melody ['mɛlədɪ] *n* mélodie *f*.
melon ['mɛlən] *n* melon *m*.
melt [mɛlt] *vi* fondre; (*become soft*) s'amollir; (*fig*) s'attendrir ♦ *vt* faire fondre.
▶ **melt away** *vi* fondre complètement.
▶ **melt down** *vt* fondre.
meltdown ['mɛltdaun] *n* fusion *f* (du cœur d'un réacteur nucléaire).
melting point ['mɛltɪŋ-] *n* point *m* de fusion.
melting pot ['mɛltɪŋ-] *n* (*fig*) creuset *m*; **to be in the ~** être encore en discussion.
member ['mɛmbə*] *n* membre *m*; (*of club, political party*) membre, adhérent/e ♦ *cpd*: **~ country/state** *n* pays *m*/état *m* membre; **M~ of Parliament (MP)** *n* (*BRIT*) député *m*; **M~ of the European Parliament (MEP)** *n* Eurodéputé *m*; **M~ of the House of Representatives (MHR)** *n* (*US*) membre de la Chambre des représentants.
membership ['mɛmbəʃɪp] *n* (*becoming a member*) adhésion *f*; admission *f*; (*being a member*) qualité *f* de membre, fait *m* d'être membre; (*the members*) membres *mpl*, adhérents *mpl*; (*number of members*) nombre *m* des membres *or* adhérents.
membership card *n* carte *f* de membre.
membrane ['mɛmbreɪn] *n* membrane *f*.
memento [mə'mɛntəu] *n* souvenir *m*.
memo ['mɛməu] *n* note *f* (de service).
memoir ['mɛmwɑː*] *n* mémoire *m*, étude *f*; **~s** *npl* mémoires.
memo pad *n* bloc-notes *m*.
memorable ['mɛmərəbl] *adj* mémorable.
memorandum, *pl* **memoranda** [mɛmə'rændəm, -də] *n* note *f* (de service); (*DIPLOMACY*)

mémorandum *m*.
memorial [mɪ'mɔːrɪəl] *n* mémorial *m* ♦ *adj* commémoratif(ive).

Memorial Day *est un jour férié aux États-Unis, le dernier lundi de mai dans la plupart des États, à la mémoire des soldats américains morts au combat.*

---

memorize ['mɛməraɪz] *vt* apprendre *or* retenir par cœur.
memory ['mɛmərɪ] *n* mémoire *f*; (*recollection*) souvenir *m*; **to have a good/bad ~** avoir une bonne/mauvaise mémoire; **loss of ~** perte *f* de mémoire; **in ~ of** à la mémoire de.
men [mɛn] *npl of* **man**.
menace ['mɛnɪs] *n* menace *f*; (*col: nuisance*) peste *f*, plaie *f* ♦ *vt* menacer; **a public ~** un danger public.
menacing ['mɛnɪsɪŋ] *adj* menaçant(e).
menagerie [mɪ'nædʒərɪ] *n* ménagerie *f*.
mend [mɛnd] *vt* réparer; (*darn*) raccommoder, repriser ♦ *n* reprise *f*; **on the ~** en voie de guérison.
mending ['mɛndɪŋ] *n* raccommodages *mpl*.
menial ['miːnɪəl] *adj* de domestique, inférieur(e); subalterne.
meningitis [mɛnɪn'dʒaɪtɪs] *n* méningite *f*.
menopause ['mɛnəupɔːz] *n* ménopause *f*.
menservants ['mɛnsəvənts] *npl of* **manservant**.
men's room *n*: **the ~** (*esp US*) les toilettes *fpl* pour hommes.
menstruate ['mɛnstrueɪt] *vi* avoir ses règles.
menstruation [mɛnstru'eɪʃən] *n* menstruation *f*.
menswear ['mɛnzwɛə*] *n* vêtements *mpl* d'hommes.
mental ['mɛntl] *adj* mental(e); **~ illness** maladie mentale.
mental hospital *n* hôpital *m* psychiatrique.
mentality [mɛn'tælɪtɪ] *n* mentalité *f*.
mentally ['mɛntlɪ] *adv*: **to be ~ handicapped** être handicapé/e mental(e).
menthol ['mɛnθɔl] *n* menthol *m*.
mention ['mɛnʃən] *n* mention *f* ♦ *vt* mentionner, faire mention de; **don't ~ it!** je vous en prie, il n'y a pas de quoi!; **I need hardly ~ that** ... est-il besoin de rappeler que ...?; **not to ~ ..., without ~ing ...** sans parler de ..., sans compter ...
mentor ['mɛntɔː*] *n* mentor *m*.
menu ['mɛnjuː] *n* (*in restaurant, COMPUT*) menu *m*; (*printed*) carte *f*.
menu-driven ['mɛnjuːdrɪvn] *adj* (*COMPUT*) piloté(e) par menu.
MEP *n abbr* = **Member of the European Parliament**.
mercantile ['məːkəntaɪl] *adj* marchand(e); (*law*) commercial(e).
mercenary ['məːsɪnərɪ] *adj* mercantile ♦ *n* mercenaire *m*.

merchandise ['mə:tʃəndaɪz] *n* marchandises *fpl* ♦ *vt* commercialiser.
merchandiser ['mə:tʃəndaɪzə*] *n* marchandiseur *m*.
merchant ['mə:tʃənt] *n* négociant *m*, marchand *m*; **timber/wine** ~ négociant en bois/vins, marchand de bois/vins.
merchant bank *n* (*BRIT*) banque *f* d'affaires.
merchantman ['mə:tʃəntmən] *n* navire marchand.
merchant navy, (*US*) **merchant marine** *n* marine marchande.
merciful ['mə:sɪful] *adj* miséricordieux(euse), clément(e).
mercifully ['mə:sɪflɪ] *adv* avec clémence; (*fortunately*) par bonheur, Dieu merci.
merciless ['mə:sɪlɪs] *adj* impitoyable, sans pitié.
mercurial [mə:'kjuərɪəl] *adj* changeant(e); (*lively*) vif(vive).
mercury ['mə:kjurɪ] *n* mercure *m*.
mercy ['mə:sɪ] *n* pitié *f*, merci *f*; (*REL*) miséricorde *f*; **to have** ~ **on sb** avoir pitié de qn; **at the** ~ **of** à la merci de.
mercy killing *n* euthanasie *f*.
mere [mɪə*] *adj* simple.
merely ['mɪəlɪ] *adv* simplement, purement.
merge [mə:dʒ] *vt* unir; (*COMPUT*) fusionner, interclasser ♦ *vi* se fondre; (*COMM*) fusionner.
merger ['mə:dʒə*] *n* (*COMM*) fusion *f*.
meridian [mə'rɪdɪən] *n* méridien *m*.
meringue [mə'ræŋ] *n* meringue *f*.
merit ['mɛrɪt] *n* mérite *m*, valeur *f* ♦ *vt* mériter.
meritocracy [mɛrɪ'tɔkrəsɪ] *n* méritocratie *f*.
mermaid ['mə:meɪd] *n* sirène *f*.
merrily ['mɛrɪlɪ] *adv* joyeusement, gaiement.
merriment ['mɛrɪmənt] *n* gaieté *f*.
merry ['mɛrɪ] *adj* gai(e); **M~ Christmas!** joyeux Noël!
merry-go-round ['mɛrɪgəuraund] *n* manège *m*.
mesh [mɛʃ] *n* maille *f*; filet *m* ♦ *vi* (*gears*) s'engrener; **wire** ~ grillage *m* (métallique), treillis *m* (métallique).
mesmerize ['mɛzməraɪz] *vt* hypnotiser; fasciner.
mess [mɛs] *n* désordre *m*, fouillis *m*, pagaille *f*; (*MIL*) mess *m*, cantine *f*; **to be (in) a** ~ être en désordre; **to be/get o.s. in a** ~ (*fig*) être/se mettre dans le pétrin.
►**mess about, mess around** *vi* (*col*) perdre son temps.
►**mess about** *or* **around with** *vt fus* (*col*) chambarder, tripoter.
►**mess up** *vt* salir; chambarder; gâcher.
message ['mɛsɪdʒ] *n* message *m*; **to get the** ~ (*fig: col*) saisir, piger.
message switching [-swɪtʃɪŋ] *n* (*COMPUT*) commutation *f* de messages.
messenger ['mɛsɪndʒə*] *n* messager *m*.
Messiah [mɪ'saɪə] *n* Messie *m*.
Messrs, Messrs. ['mɛsəz] *abbr* (*on letters:* = *messieurs*) MM.
messy ['mɛsɪ] *adj* sale; en désordre.
Met [mɛt] *n abbr* (*US*) = *Metropolitan Opera*.
met [mɛt] *pt, pp of* **meet** ♦ *adj abbr* (= *meteorological*) météo *inv*.
metabolism [mɛ'tæbəlɪzəm] *n* métabolisme *m*.
metal ['mɛtl] *n* métal *m* ♦ *vt* empierrer.
metallic [mɛ'tælɪk] *adj* métallique.
metallurgy [mɛ'tælədʒɪ] *n* métallurgie *f*.
metalwork ['mɛtlwə:k] *n* (*craft*) ferronnerie *f*.
metamorphosis, *pl* **-ses** [mɛtə'mɔ:fəsɪs, -si:z] *n* métamorphose *f*.
metaphor ['mɛtəfə*] *n* métaphore *f*.
metaphysics [mɛtə'fɪzɪks] *n* métaphysique *f*.
mete [mi:t]: **to** ~ **out** *vt fus* infliger.
meteor ['mi:tɪə*] *n* météore *m*.
meteoric [mi:tɪ'ɔrɪk] *adj* (*fig*) fulgurant(e).
meteorite ['mi:tɪəraɪt] *n* météorite *m or f*.
meteorological [mi:tɪərə'lɔdʒɪkl] *adj* météorologique.
meteorology [mi:tɪə'rɔlədʒɪ] *n* météorologie *f*.
meter ['mi:tə*] *n* (*instrument*) compteur *m*; (*also:* **parking** ~) parc(o)mètre *m*; (*US*) = **metre**.
methane ['mi:θeɪn] *n* méthane *m*.
method ['mɛθəd] *n* méthode *f*, ~ **of payment** mode *m or* modalité *f* de paiement.
methodical [mɪ'θɔdɪkl] *adj* méthodique.
Methodist ['mɛθədɪst] *adj, n* méthodiste (*m/f*).
methylated spirit ['mɛθɪleɪtɪd-] *n* (*BRIT: also:* **meths**) alcool *m* à brûler.
meticulous [mɛ'tɪkjuləs] *adj* méticuleux(euse).
metre, (*US*) **meter** ['mi:tə*] *n* mètre *m*.
metric ['mɛtrɪk] *adj* métrique; **to go** ~ adopter le système métrique.
metrical ['mɛtrɪkl] *adj* métrique.
metrication [mɛtrɪ'keɪʃən] *n* conversion *f* au système métrique.
metric system *n* système *m* métrique.
metric ton *n* tonne *f*.
metronome ['mɛtrənəum] *n* métronome *m*.
metropolis [mɪ'trɔpəlɪs] *n* métropole *f*.
metropolitan [mɛtrə'pɔlɪtən] *adj* métropolitain(e).
Metropolitan Police *n* (*BRIT*): **the** ~ la police londonienne.
mettle ['mɛtl] *n* courage *m*.
mew [mju:] *vi* (*cat*) miauler.
mews [mju:z] *n* (*BRIT*): ~ **cottage** maisonnette aménagée dans une ancienne écurie ou remise.
Mexican ['mɛksɪkən] *adj* mexicain(e) ♦ *n* Mexicain/e.
Mexico ['mɛksɪkəu] *n* Mexique *m*.
Mexico City *n* Mexico.
mezzanine ['mɛtsəni:n] *n* mezzanine *f*; (*of shops, offices*) entresol *m*.
MFA *n abbr* (*US:* = *Master of Fine Arts*) titre universitaire.
mfr *abbr* = **manufacture, manufacturer**.
mg *abbr* (= *milligram*) mg.

Mgr *abbr* (= *Monseigneur, Monsignor*) Mgr; (= *manager*) dir.

MHR *n abbr* (*US*) = **Member of the House of Representatives**.

MHz *abbr* (= *megahertz*) MHz.

MI *abbr* (*US*) = *Michigan*.

MI5 *n abbr* (*BRIT*: = *Military Intelligence 5*) ≈ DST *f*.

MI6 *n abbr* (*BRIT*: = *Military Intelligence 6*) ≈ DGSE *f*.

MIA *abbr* (= *missing in action*) disparu au combat.

miaow [miː'au] *vi* miauler.

mice [maɪs] *npl of* **mouse**.

Mich. *abbr* (*US*) = *Michigan*.

microbe ['maɪkrəub] *n* microbe *m*.

microbiology [maɪkrəbaɪ'ɔlədʒɪ] *n* microbiologie *f*.

microchip ['maɪkrəutʃɪp] *n* (*ELEC*) puce *f*.

micro(computer) ['maɪkrəu(kəm'pjuːtə*)] *n* micro(-ordinateur *m*) *m*.

microcosm ['maɪkrəukɔzəm] *n* microcosme *m*.

microeconomics ['maɪkrəuiːkə'nɔmɪks] *n* micro-économie *f*.

microfiche ['maɪkrəufiːʃ] *n* microfiche *f*.

microfilm ['maɪkrəufɪlm] *n* microfilm *m* ♦ *vt* microfilmer.

microlight ['maɪkrəulaɪt] *n* ULM *m*.

micrometer [maɪ'krɔmɪtə*] *n* palmer *m*, micromètre *m*.

microphone ['maɪkrəfəun] *n* microphone *m*.

microprocessor ['maɪkrəu'prəusɛsə*] *n* microprocesseur *m*.

microscope ['maɪkrəskəup] *n* microscope *m*; **under the** ~ au microscope.

microscopic [maɪkrə'skɔpɪk] *adj* microscopique.

microwave ['maɪkrəuweɪv] *n* (*also*: ~ **oven**) four *m* à micro-ondes.

mid [mɪd] *adj*: ~ **May** la mi-mai; ~ **afternoon** le milieu de l'après-midi; **in** ~ **air** en plein ciel; **he's in his** ~ **thirties** il a dans les trente-cinq ans.

midday [mɪd'deɪ] *n* midi *m*.

middle ['mɪdl] *n* milieu *m*; (*waist*) ceinture *f*, taille *f* ♦ *adj* du milieu; **in the** ~ **of the night** au milieu de la nuit; **I'm in the** ~ **of reading it** je suis (justement) en train de le lire.

middle age *n* tranche d'âge aux limites floues, entre la quarantaine et le début du troisième âge.

middle-aged [mɪdl'eɪdʒd] *adj* (*people: see middle age*) d'un certain âge, ni vieux ni jeune; (*pej: values, outlook*) conventionnel(le), rassis(e).

Middle Ages *npl*: **the** ~ le moyen âge.

middle class *n*: **the** ~(**es**) ≈ les classes moyennes ♦ *adj* (*also*: **middle-class**) ≈ (petit(e)-)bourgeois(e).

Middle East *n*: **the** ~ le Proche-Orient, le Moyen-Orient.

middleman ['mɪdlmæn] *n* intermédiaire *m*.

middle management *n* cadres moyens.

middle name *n* second prénom.

middle-of-the-road ['mɪdləvðə'rəud] *adj* (*policy*) modéré(e), du juste milieu; (*music etc*) plutôt classique, assez traditionnel(le).

middleweight ['mɪdlweɪt] *n* (*BOXING*) poids moyen.

middling ['mɪdlɪŋ] *adj* moyen(ne).

Middx *abbr* (*BRIT*) = *Middlesex*.

midge [mɪdʒ] *n* moucheron *m*.

midget ['mɪdʒɪt] *n* nain/e ♦ *adj* minuscule.

midi system ['mɪdɪ-] *n* chaîne *f* midi.

Midlands ['mɪdləndz] *npl* comtés du centre de l'Angleterre.

midnight ['mɪdnaɪt] *n* minuit *m*; **at** ~ à minuit.

midriff ['mɪdrɪf] *n* estomac *m*, taille *f*.

midst [mɪdst] *n*: **in the** ~ **of** au milieu de.

midsummer [mɪd'sʌmə*] *n* milieu *m* de l'été.

midway [mɪd'weɪ] *adj, adv*: ~ (**between**) à mi-chemin (entre).

midweek [mɪd'wiːk] *adj* du milieu de la semaine ♦ *adv* au milieu de la semaine, en pleine semaine.

midwife, midwives ['mɪdwaɪf, -vz] *n* sage-femme *f*.

midwifery ['mɪdwɪfərɪ] *n* obstétrique *f*.

midwinter [mɪd'wɪntə*] *n* milieu *m* de l'hiver.

miffed [mɪft] *adj* (*col*) fâché(e), vexé(e).

might [maɪt] *vb see* **may** ♦ *n* puissance *f*, force *f*.

mighty ['maɪtɪ] *adj* puissant(e) ♦ *adv* (*col*) rudement.

migraine ['miːɡreɪn] *n* migraine *f*.

migrant ['maɪɡrənt] *n* (*bird, animal*) migrateur *m*; (*person*) migrant/e; nomade *m/f* ♦ *adj* migrateur(trice); migrant(e); nomade; (*worker*) saisonnier(ière).

migrate [maɪ'ɡreɪt] *vi* émigrer.

migration [maɪ'ɡreɪʃən] *n* migration *f*.

mike [maɪk] *n abbr* (= *microphone*) micro *m*.

Milan [mɪ'læn] *n* Milan.

mild [maɪld] *adj* doux(douce); (*reproach*) léger(ère); (*illness*) bénin(igne) ♦ *n* bière légère.

mildew ['mɪldjuː] *n* mildiou *m*.

mildly ['maɪldlɪ] *adv* doucement; légèrement; **to put it** ~ (*col*) c'est le moins qu'on puisse dire.

mildness ['maɪldnɪs] *n* douceur *f*.

mile [maɪl] *n* mil(l)e *m* (= *1609 m*); **to do 30** ~**s per gallon** ≈ faire 9,4 litres au cent.

mileage ['maɪlɪdʒ] *n* distance *f* en milles, ≈ kilométrage *m*.

mileage allowance *n* ≈ indemnité *f* kilométrique.

mileometer [maɪ'lɔmɪtə*] *n* (*BRIT*) = **milometer**.

milestone ['maɪlstəun] *n* borne *f*; (*fig*) jalon *m*.

milieu ['miːljəː] *n* milieu *m*.

militant ['mɪlɪtnt] *adj, n* militant(e).

militarism ['mɪlɪtərɪzəm] *n* militarisme *m*.

militaristic [mɪlɪtə'rɪstɪk] *adj* militariste.
military ['mɪlɪtərɪ] *adj* militaire ♦ *n*: **the ~** l'armée *f*, les militaires *mpl*.
military service *n* service *m* (militaire *ou* national).
militate ['mɪlɪteɪt] *vi*: **to ~ against** militer contre.
militia [mɪ'lɪʃə] *n* milice *f*.
milk [mɪlk] *n* lait *m* ♦ *vt* (*cow*) traire; (*fig*) dépouiller, plumer.
milk chocolate *n* chocolat *m* au lait.
milk float *n* (*BRIT*) voiture *f or* camionnette *f* du *or* de laitier.
milking ['mɪlkɪŋ] *n* traite *f*.
milkman ['mɪlkmən] *n* laitier *m*.
milk shake *n* milk-shake *m*.
milk tooth *n* dent *f* de lait.
milk truck *n* (*US*) = **milk float**.
milky ['mɪlkɪ] *adj* lacté(e); (*colour*) laiteux(euse).
Milky Way *n* Voie lactée.
mill [mɪl] *n* moulin *m*; (*factory*) usine *f*, fabrique *f*; (*spinning ~*) filature *f*; (*flour ~*) minoterie *f* ♦ *vt* moudre, broyer ♦ *vi* (*also: ~ about*) grouiller.
millennium, *pl* **~s** *or* **millennia** [mɪ'lɛnɪəm, -'lɛnɪə] *n* millénaire *m*.
millennium bug *n* bogue *m or* bug *m* de l'an 2000.
miller ['mɪlə*] *n* meunier *m*.
millet ['mɪlɪt] *n* millet *m*.
milli... ['mɪlɪ] *prefix* milli....
milligram(me) ['mɪlɪgræm] *n* milligramme *m*.
millilitre, (*US*) **milliliter** ['mɪlɪliːtə*] *n* millilitre *m*.
millimetre, (*US*) **millimeter** ['mɪlɪmiːtə*] *n* millimètre *m*.
milliner ['mɪlɪnə*] *n* modiste *f*.
millinery ['mɪlɪnərɪ] *n* modes *fpl*.
million ['mɪljən] *n* million *m*.
millionaire [mɪljə'nɛə*] *n* millionnaire *m*.
millipede ['mɪlɪpiːd] *n* mille-pattes *m inv*.
millstone ['mɪlstəun] *n* meule *f*.
millwheel ['mɪlwiːl] *n* roue *f* de moulin.
milometer [maɪ'lɒmɪtə*] *n* (*BRIT*) ≈ compteur *m* kilométrique.
mime [maɪm] *n* mime *m* ♦ *vt, vi* mimer.
mimic ['mɪmɪk] *n* imitateur/trice ♦ *vt, vi* imiter, contrefaire.
mimicry ['mɪmɪkrɪ] *n* imitation *f*; (*ZOOL*) mimétisme *m*.
Min. *abbr* (*BRIT POL*) = **ministry**.
min. *abbr* (= *minute*) mn.; (= *minimum*) min.
minaret [mɪnə'rɛt] *n* minaret *m*.
mince [mɪns] *vt* hacher ♦ *vi* (*in walking*) marcher à petits pas maniérés ♦ *n* (*BRIT CULIN*) viande hachée, hachis *m*; **he does not ~** (**his**) **words** il ne mâche pas ses mots.
mincemeat ['mɪnsmiːt] *n* hachis de fruits secs utilisés en pâtisserie.
mince pie *n* sorte de tarte aux fruits secs.
mincer ['mɪnsə*] *n* hachoir *m*.

mincing ['mɪnsɪŋ] *adj* affecté(e).
mind [maɪnd] *n* esprit *m* ♦ *vt* (*attend to, look after*) s'occuper de; (*be careful*) faire attention à; (*object to*): **I don't ~ the noise** je ne crains pas le bruit, le bruit ne me dérange pas; **do you ~ if ...?** est-ce que cela vous gêne si ...?; **I don't ~** cela ne me dérange pas; **~ you, ... remarquez, ...;** **never ~** peu importe, ça ne fait rien; **it is on my ~** cela me préoccupe; **to change one's ~** changer d'avis; **to be in two ~s about sth** (*BRIT*) être indécis(e) *or* irrésolu(e) en ce qui concerne qch; **to my ~** à mon avis, selon moi; **to be out of one's ~** ne plus avoir toute sa raison; **to keep sth in ~** ne pas oublier qch; **to bear sth in ~** tenir compte de qch; **to have sb/sth in ~** avoir qn/qch en tête; **to have in ~ to do** avoir l'intention de faire; **it went right out of my ~** ça m'est complètement sorti de la tête; **to bring** *or* **call sth to ~** se rappeler qch; **to make up one's ~** se décider; **"~ the step"** "attention à la marche".
mind-boggling ['maɪndbɒglɪŋ] *adj* (*col*) époustouflant(e), ahurissant(e).
-minded ['maɪndɪd] *adj*: **fair~** impartial(e); **an industrially~ nation** une nation orientée vers l'industrie.
minder ['maɪndə*] *n* (*child ~*) gardienne *f*; (*bodyguard*) ange gardien (*fig*).
mindful ['maɪndful] *adj*: **~ of** attentif(ive) à, soucieux(euse) de.
mindless ['maɪndlɪs] *adj* irréfléchi(e); (*violence, crime*) insensé(e).
mine [maɪn] *pron* le(la) mien(ne), les miens(miennes); **this book is ~** ce livre est à moi ♦ *n* mine *f* ♦ *vt* (*coal*) extraire; (*ship, beach*) miner.
mine detector *n* détecteur *m* de mines.
minefield ['maɪnfiːld] *n* champ *m* de mines.
miner ['maɪnə*] *n* mineur *m*.
mineral ['mɪnərəl] *adj* minéral(e) ♦ *n* minéral *m*; **~s** *npl* (*BRIT: soft drinks*) boissons gazeuses (sucrées).
mineralogy [mɪnə'rælədʒɪ] *n* minéralogie *f*.
mineral water *n* eau minérale.
minesweeper ['maɪnswiːpə*] *n* dragueur *m* de mines.
mingle ['mɪŋgl] *vt* mêler, mélanger ♦ *vi*: **to ~ with** se mêler à.
mingy ['mɪndʒɪ] *adj* (*col*) radin(e).
miniature ['mɪnətʃə*] *adj* (en) miniature ♦ *n* miniature *f*.
minibus ['mɪnɪbʌs] *n* minibus *m*.
minicab ['mɪnɪkæb] *n* (*BRIT*) minitaxi *m*.
minim ['mɪnɪm] *n* (*MUS*) blanche *f*.
minima ['mɪnɪmə] *npl of* **minimum**.
minimal ['mɪnɪml] *adj* minimal(e).
minimalist ['mɪnɪməlɪst] *adj, n* minimaliste (*m/f*).
minimize ['mɪnɪmaɪz] *vt* minimiser.
minimum ['mɪnɪməm] *n* (*pl*: **minima** ['mɪnɪmə]) minimum *m* ♦ *adj* minimum; **to reduce to a ~**

réduire au minimum.
minimum lending rate (MLR) *n* (*ECON*) taux *m* de crédit minimum.
mining ['maɪnɪŋ] *n* exploitation minière ♦ *adj* minier(ière); de mineurs.
minion ['mɪnjən] *n* (*pej*) laquais *m*; favori/te.
mini-series ['mɪnɪsɪəri:z] *n* téléfilm *m* en plusieurs parties.
miniskirt ['mɪnɪskə:t] *n* mini-jupe *f.*
minister ['mɪnɪstə*] *n* (*BRIT POL*) ministre *m*; (*REL*) pasteur *m* ♦ *vi*: **to ~ to sb** donner ses soins à qn; **to ~ to sb's needs** pourvoir aux besoins de qn.
ministerial [mɪnɪs'tɪərɪəl] *adj* (*BRIT POL*) ministériel(le).
ministry ['mɪnɪstrɪ] *n* (*BRIT POL*) ministère *m*; (*REL*): **to go into the ~** devenir pasteur.
mink [mɪŋk] *n* vison *m*.
mink coat *n* manteau *m* de vison.
Minn. *abbr* (*US*) = Minnesota.
minnow ['mɪnəu] *n* vairon *m*.
minor ['maɪnə*] *adj* petit(e), de peu d'importance; (*MUS*) mineur(e) ♦ *n* (*LAW*) mineur/e.
Minorca [mɪ'nɔ:kə] *n* Minorque *f.*
minority [maɪ'nɔrɪtɪ] *n* minorité *f*; **to be in a ~** être en minorité.
minster ['mɪnstə*] *n* église abbatiale.
minstrel ['mɪnstrəl] *n* trouvère *m*, ménestrel *m.*
mint [mɪnt] *n* (*plant*) menthe *f*; (*sweet*) bonbon *m* à la menthe ♦ *vt* (*coins*) battre; **the (Royal) M~**, (*US*) **the (US) M~** ≈ l'hôtel *m* de la Monnaie; **in ~ condition** à l'état de neuf.
mint sauce *n* sauce *f* à la menthe.
minuet [mɪnju'ɛt] *n* menuet *m.*
minus ['maɪnəs] *n* (*also:* **~ sign**) signe *m* moins ♦ *prep* moins.
minuscule ['mɪnəskju:l] *adj* minuscule.
minute *adj* [maɪ'nju:t] minuscule; (*detailed*) minutieux(euse) ♦ *n* ['mɪnɪt] minute *f*; (*official record*) procès-verbal *m*, compte rendu; **~s** *npl* procès-verbal; **it is 5 ~s past 3** il est 3 heures 5; **wait a ~!** (attendez) un instant!; **at the last ~** à la dernière minute; **up to the ~** (*fashion*) dernier cri; (*news*) de dernière minute; (*machine, technology*) de pointe; **in ~ detail** par le menu.
minute book *n* registre *m* des procès-verbaux.
minute hand *n* aiguille *f* des minutes.
minutely [maɪ'nju:tlɪ] *adv* (*by a small amount*) de peu, de manière infime; (*in detail*) minutieusement, dans les moindres détails.
minutiae [mɪ'nju:ʃi:] *npl* menus détails.
miracle ['mɪrəkl] *n* miracle *m.*
miraculous [mɪ'rækjuləs] *adj* miraculeux(euse).
mirage ['mɪrɑ:ʒ] *n* mirage *m.*
mire ['maɪə*] *n* bourbe *f*, boue *f.*
mirror ['mɪrə*] *n* miroir *m*, glace *f* ♦ *vt* refléter.
mirror image *n* image inversée.

mirth [mə:θ] *n* gaieté *f.*
misadventure [mɪsəd'vɛntʃə*] *n* mésaventure *f*; **death by ~** (*BRIT*) décès accidentel.
misanthropist [mɪ'zænθrəpɪst] *n* misanthrope *m/f.*
misapply [mɪsə'plaɪ] *vt* mal employer.
misapprehension ['mɪsæprɪ'hɛnʃən] *n* malentendu *m*, méprise *f.*
misappropriate [mɪsə'prəuprɪeɪt] *vt* détourner.
misappropriation ['mɪsəprəuprɪ'eɪʃən] *n* escroquerie *f*, détournement *m.*
misbehave [mɪsbɪ'heɪv] *vi* mal se conduire.
misbehaviour, (*US*) **misbehavior** [mɪsbɪ'heɪvjə*] *n* mauvaise conduite.
misc. *abbr* = miscellaneous.
miscalculate [mɪs'kælkjuleɪt] *vt* mal calculer.
miscalculation ['mɪskælkju'leɪʃən] *n* erreur *f* de calcul.
miscarriage ['mɪskærɪdʒ] *n* (*MED*) fausse couche; **~ of justice** erreur *f* judiciaire.
miscarry [mɪs'kærɪ] *vi* (*MED*) faire une fausse couche; (*fail: plans*) échouer, mal tourner.
miscellaneous [mɪsɪ'leɪnɪəs] *adj* (*items, expenses*) divers(es); (*selection*) varié(e).
miscellany [mɪ'sɛlənɪ] *n* recueil *m.*
mischance [mɪs'tʃɑ:ns] *n* malchance *f*; **by (some) ~** par malheur.
mischief ['mɪstʃɪf] *n* (*naughtiness*) sottises *fpl*; (*harm*) mal *m*, dommage *m*; (*maliciousness*) méchanceté *f.*
mischievous ['mɪstʃɪvəs] *adj* (*naughty*) coquin(e), espiègle; (*harmful*) méchant(e).
misconception ['mɪskən'sɛpʃən] *n* idée fausse.
misconduct [mɪs'kɔndʌkt] *n* inconduite *f*; **professional ~** faute professionnelle.
misconstrue [mɪskən'stru:] *vt* mal interpréter.
miscount [mɪs'kaunt] *vt, vi* mal compter.
misdeed ['mɪs'di:d] *n* méfait *m.*
misdemeanour, (*US*) **misdemeanor** [mɪsdɪ'mi:nə*] *n* écart *m* de conduite; infraction *f.*
misdirect [mɪsdɪ'rɛkt] *vt* (*person*) mal renseigner; (*letter*) mal adresser.
miser ['maɪzə*] *n* avare *m/f.*
miserable ['mɪzərəbl] *adj* malheureux(euse); (*wretched*) misérable; **to feel ~** avoir le cafard.
miserably ['mɪzərəblɪ] *adv* (*smile, answer*) tristement; (*live, pay*) misérablement; (*fail*) lamentablement.
miserly ['maɪzəlɪ] *adj* avare.
misery ['mɪzərɪ] *n* (*unhappiness*) tristesse *f*; (*pain*) souffrances *fpl*; (*wretchedness*) misère *f.*
misfire [mɪs'faɪə*] *vi* rater; (*car engine*) avoir des ratés.
misfit ['mɪsfɪt] *n* (*person*) inadapté/e.
misfortune [mɪs'fɔ:tʃən] *n* malchance *f*, malheur *m.*

misgiving(s) [mɪsˈgɪvɪŋ(z)] *n(pl)* craintes *fpl*, soupçons *mpl*; **to have ~s about sth** avoir des doutes quant à qch.

misguided [mɪsˈgaɪdɪd] *adj* malavisé(e).

mishandle [mɪsˈhændl] *vt (treat roughly)* malmener; *(mismanage)* mal s'y prendre pour faire *or* résoudre *etc*.

mishap [ˈmɪshæp] *n* mésaventure *f*.

mishear [mɪsˈhɪə*] *vt, vi irreg* mal entendre.

mishmash [ˈmɪʃmæʃ] *n (col)* fatras *m*, mélimélo *m*.

misinform [mɪsɪnˈfɔːm] *vt* mal renseigner.

misinterpret [mɪsɪnˈtəːprɪt] *vt* mal interpréter.

misinterpretation [ˈmɪsɪntəːprɪˈteɪʃən] *n* interprétation erronée, contresens *m*.

misjudge [mɪsˈdʒʌdʒ] *vt* méjuger, se méprendre sur le compte de.

mislay [mɪsˈleɪ] *vt irreg* égarer.

mislead [mɪsˈliːd] *vt irreg* induire en erreur.

misleading [mɪsˈliːdɪŋ] *adj* trompeur(euse).

misled [mɪsˈlɛd] *pt, pp of* **mislead.**

mismanage [mɪsˈmænɪdʒ] *vt* mal gérer; mal s'y prendre pour faire *or* résoudre *etc*.

mismanagement [mɪsˈmænɪdʒmənt] *n* mauvaise gestion.

misnomer [mɪsˈnəʊmə*] *n* terme *or* qualificatif trompeur *or* peu approprié.

misogynist [mɪˈsɔdʒɪnɪst] *n* misogyne *m/f*.

misplace [mɪsˈpleɪs] *vt* égarer; **to be ~d** *(trust etc)* être mal placé(e).

misprint [ˈmɪsprɪnt] *n* faute *f* d'impression.

mispronounce [mɪsprəˈnaʊns] *vt* mal prononcer.

misquote [ˈmɪsˈkwəʊt] *vt* citer erronément *or* inexactement.

misread [mɪsˈriːd] *vt irreg* mal lire.

misrepresent [mɪsrɛprɪˈzɛnt] *vt* présenter sous un faux jour.

Miss [mɪs] *n* Mademoiselle; **Dear ~ Smith** Chère Mademoiselle Smith.

miss [mɪs] *vt (fail to get)* manquer, rater; *(appointment, class)* manquer; *(escape, avoid)* échapper à, éviter; *(notice loss of: money etc)* s'apercevoir de l'absence de; *(regret the absence of)*: **I ~ him/it** il/cela me manque ♦ *vi* manquer ♦ *n (shot)* coup manqué; **the bus just ~ed the wall** le bus a évité le mur de justesse; **you're ~ing the point** vous êtes à côté de la question.

▶**miss out** *vt (BRIT)* oublier.

▶**miss out on** *vt fus (fun, party)* rater, manquer; *(chance, bargain)* laisser passer.

Miss. *abbr (US)* = Mississippi.

missal [ˈmɪsl] *n* missel *m*.

misshapen [mɪsˈʃeɪpən] *adj* difforme.

missile [ˈmɪsaɪl] *n (AVIAT)* missile *m*; *(object thrown)* projectile *m*.

missile base *n* base *f* de missiles.

missile launcher [-lɔːntʃə*] *n* lance-missiles *m*.

missing [ˈmɪsɪŋ] *adj* manquant(e); *(after escape, disaster: person)* disparu(e); **to go ~** disparaître; **~ person** personne disparue, disparu/e.

mission [ˈmɪʃən] *n* mission *f*; **on a ~ to sb** en mission auprès de qn.

missionary [ˈmɪʃənrɪ] *n* missionnaire *m/f*.

missive [ˈmɪsɪv] *n* missive *f*.

misspell [ˈmɪsˈspɛl] *vt (irreg: like* **spell***)* mal orthographier.

misspent [ˈmɪsˈspɛnt] *adj*: **his ~ youth** sa folle jeunesse.

mist [mɪst] *n* brume *f* ♦ *vi (also: ~ over, ~ up)* devenir brumeux(euse); *(BRIT: windows)* s'embuer.

mistake [mɪsˈteɪk] *n* erreur *f*, faute *f* ♦ *vt (irreg: like* **take***) (meaning)* mal comprendre; *(intentions)* se méprendre sur; **to ~ for** prendre pour; **by ~** par erreur, par inadvertance; **to make a ~** *(in writing)* faire une faute; *(in calculating etc)* faire une erreur; **to make a ~ about sb/sth** se tromper sur le compte de qn/sur qch.

mistaken [mɪsˈteɪkən] *pp of* **mistake** ♦ *adj (idea etc)* erroné(e); **to be ~** faire erreur, se tromper.

mistaken identity *n* erreur *f* d'identité.

mistakenly [mɪsˈteɪkənlɪ] *adv* par erreur, par mégarde.

mister [ˈmɪstə*] *n (col)* Monsieur *m*; *see* **Mr.**

mistletoe [ˈmɪsltəʊ] *n* gui *m*.

mistook [mɪsˈtʊk] *pt of* **mistake.**

mistranslation [mɪstrænsˈleɪʃən] *n* erreur *f* de traduction, contresens *m*.

mistreat [mɪsˈtriːt] *vt* maltraiter.

mistress [ˈmɪstrɪs] *n* maîtresse *f*; *(BRIT: in primary school)* institutrice *f*; *see* **Mrs.**

mistrust [mɪsˈtrʌst] *vt* se méfier de ♦ *n*: **~ (of)** méfiance *f* (à l'égard de).

mistrustful [mɪsˈtrʌstfʊl] *adj*: **~ (of)** méfiant(e) (à l'égard de).

misty [ˈmɪstɪ] *adj* brumeux(euse).

misty-eyed [ˈmɪstɪˈaɪd] *adj* les yeux embués de larmes; *(fig)* sentimental(e).

misunderstand [mɪsʌndəˈstænd] *vt, vi irreg* mal comprendre.

misunderstanding [ˈmɪsʌndəˈstændɪŋ] *n* méprise *f*, malentendu *m*.

misunderstood [mɪsʌndəˈstʊd] *pt, pp of* **misunderstand.**

misuse *n* [mɪsˈjuːs] mauvais emploi; *(of power)* abus *m* ♦ *vt* [mɪsˈjuːz] mal employer; abuser de.

MIT *n abbr (US)* = Massachusetts Institute of Technology.

mite [maɪt] *n (small quantity)* grain *m*, miette *f*; *(BRIT: small child)* petit/e.

mitigate [ˈmɪtɪgeɪt] *vt* atténuer; **mitigating circumstances** circonstances atténuantes.

mitigation [mɪtɪˈgeɪʃən] *n* atténuation *f*.

mitre, *(US)* **miter** [ˈmaɪtə*] *n* mitre *f*; *(CARPENTRY)* onglet *m*.

mitt(en) [ˈmɪt(n)] *n* mitaine *f*, moufle *f*.

mix [mɪks] *vt* mélanger ♦ *vi* se mélanger ♦ *n* mélange *m*; dosage *m*; **to ~ sth with sth** mélanger qch à qch; **to ~ business with pleasure** unir l'utile à l'agréable; **cake ~** préparation *f* pour gâteau.
▸**mix in** *vt* incorporer, mélanger.
▸**mix up** *vt* mélanger; (*confuse*) confondre; **to be ~ed up in sth** être mêlé(e) à qch *or* impliqué(e) dans qch.
mixed [mɪkst] *adj* (*assorted*) assortis(ies); (*school etc*) mixte.
mixed-ability ['mɪkstə'bɪlɪtɪ] *adj* (*class etc*) sans groupes de niveaux.
mixed bag *n*: **it's a (bit of a) ~** il y a (un peu) de tout.
mixed blessing *n*: **it's a ~** cela a du bon et du mauvais.
mixed doubles *npl* (*SPORT*) double *m* mixte.
mixed economy *n* économie *f* mixte.
mixed grill *n* (*BRIT*) assortiment *m* de grillades.
mixed marriage *n* mariage *m* mixte.
mixed-up [mɪkst'ʌp] *adj* (*person*) désorienté(e) *or* (*fig*).
mixer ['mɪksə*] *n* (*for food*) batteur *m*, mixeur *m*; (*person*): **he is a good ~** il est très sociable.
mixer tap *n* (robinet *m*) mélangeur *m*.
mixture ['mɪkstʃə*] *n* assortiment *m*, mélange *m*; (*MED*) préparation *f*.
mix-up ['mɪksʌp] *n* confusion *f*.
MK *abbr* (*BRIT TECH*) = **mark**.
mk *abbr* = **mark** (*currency*).
mkt *abbr* = **market**.
MLitt *n abbr* (= *Master of Literature, Master of Letters*) titre *universitaire*.
MLR *n abbr* (*BRIT*) = **minimum lending rate**.
mm *abbr* (= *millimetre*) mm.
MN *abbr* (*BRIT*) = **Merchant Navy**; (*US*) = Minnesota.
MO *n abbr* (*MED*) = *medical officer*; (*US col*: = *modus operandi*) méthode *f* ♦ *abbr* (*US*) = Missouri.
Mo. *abbr* (*US*) = Missouri.
m.o. *abbr* = **money order**.
moan [məun] *n* gémissement *m* ♦ *vi* gémir; (*col: complain*): **to ~ (about)** se plaindre (de).
moaner ['məunə*] *n* (*col*) rouspéteur/euse, râleur/euse.
moaning ['məunɪŋ] *n* gémissements *mpl*.
moat [məut] *n* fossé *m*, douves *fpl*.
mob [mɔb] *n* foule *f*; (*disorderly*) cohue *f*; (*pej*): **the ~** la populace ♦ *vt* assaillir.
mobile ['məubaɪl] *adj* mobile ♦ *n* (*ART*) mobile *m*; **applicants must be ~** (*BRIT*) les candidats devront être prêts à accepter tout déplacement.
mobile home *n* caravane *f*.
mobile phone *n* téléphone portatif.
mobile shop *n* (*BRIT*) camion *m* magasin.
mobility [məu'bɪlɪtɪ] *n* mobilité *f*.
mobilize ['məubɪlaɪz] *vt*, *vi* mobiliser.

moccasin ['mɔkəsɪn] *n* mocassin *m*.
mock [mɔk] *vt* ridiculiser, se moquer de ♦ *adj* faux(fausse).
mockery ['mɔkərɪ] *n* moquerie *f*, raillerie *f*; **to make a ~ of** ridiculiser, tourner en dérision.
mocking ['mɔkɪŋ] *adj* moqueur(euse).
mockingbird ['mɔkɪŋbəːd] *n* moqueur *m*.
mock-up ['mɔkʌp] *n* maquette *f*.
MOD *n abbr* (*BRIT*) = **Ministry of Defence**; *see* **defence**.
mod cons ['mɔd'kɔnz] *npl abbr* (*BRIT*) = **modern conveniences**; *see* **convenience**.
mode [məud] *n* mode *m*; (*of transport*) moyen *m*.
model ['mɔdl] *n* modèle *m*; (*person: for fashion*) mannequin *m*; (*: for artist*) modèle *m* ♦ *vt* modeler ♦ *vi* travailler comme mannequin ♦ *adj* (*railway: toy*) modèle réduit *inv*; (*child, factory*) modèle; **to ~ clothes** présenter des vêtements; **to ~ sb/sth on** modeler qn/qch sur.
modeller, (*US*) **modeler** ['mɔdlə*] *n* modeleur *m*; (*model maker*) maquettiste *m/f*; fabricant *m* de modèles réduits.
modem ['məudem] *n* modem *m*.
moderate *adj*, *n* ['mɔdərət] *adj* modéré(e) ♦ *n* (*POL*) modéré/e ♦ *vb* ['mɔdəreɪt] *vi* se modérer, se calmer ♦ *vt* modérer.
moderately ['mɔdərətlɪ] *adv* (*act*) avec modération *or* mesure; (*expensive, difficult*) moyennement; (*pleased, happy*) raisonnablement, assez; **~ priced** à un prix raisonnable.
moderation [mɔdə'reɪʃən] *n* modération *f*, mesure *f*; **in ~** à dose raisonnable, pris(e) *or* pratiqué(e) modérément.
moderator ['mɔdəreɪtə*] *n* (*REL*): **M~** président *m* (*de l'Assemblée générale de l'Église presbytérienne*); (*POL*) modérateur *m*.
modern ['mɔdən] *adj* moderne; **~ languages** langues vivantes.
modernization [mɔdənaɪ'zeɪʃən] *n* modernisation *f*.
modernize ['mɔdənaɪz] *vt* moderniser.
modest ['mɔdɪst] *adj* modeste.
modesty ['mɔdɪstɪ] *n* modestie *f*.
modicum ['mɔdɪkəm] *n*: **a ~ of** un minimum de.
modification [mɔdɪfɪ'keɪʃən] *n* modification *f*; **to make ~s** faire *or* apporter des modifications.
modify ['mɔdɪfaɪ] *vt* modifier.
modish ['məudɪʃ] *adj* à la mode.
Mods [mɔdz] *n abbr* (*BRIT:* = (*Honour*) *Moderations*) *premier examen universitaire* (à Oxford).
modular ['mɔdjulə*] *adj* (*filing, unit*) modulaire.
modulate ['mɔdjuleɪt] *vt* moduler.
modulation [mɔdju'leɪʃən] *n* modulation *f*.
module ['mɔdjuːl] *n* module *m*.
mogul ['məugl] *n* (*fig*) nabab *m*; (*SKI*) bosse *f*.

MOH *n abbr* (*BRIT*) = Medical Officer of Health.
mohair ['məʊhɛə*] *n* mohair *m*.
Mohammed [mə'hæmɛd] *n* Mahomet *m*.
moist [mɔɪst] *adj* humide, moite.
moisten ['mɔɪsn] *vt* humecter, mouiller légèrement.
moisture ['mɔɪstʃə*] *n* humidité *f*; (*on glass*) buée *f*.
moisturize ['mɔɪstʃəraɪz] *vt* (*skin*) hydrater.
moisturizer ['mɔɪstʃəraɪzə*] *n* produit hydratant.
molar ['məʊlə*] *n* molaire *f*.
molasses [məʊ'læsɪz] *n* mélasse *f*.
mold [məʊld] *n*, *vt* (*US*) = mould.
Moldavia [mɔl'deɪvɪə], **Moldova** [mɔl'dəʊvə] *n* Moldavie *f*.
Moldavian [mɔl'deɪvɪən], **Moldovan** [mɔl'dəʊvən] *adj* moldave.
mole [məʊl] *n* (*animal*) taupe *f*; (*spot*) grain *m* de beauté.
molecule ['mɔlɪkjuːl] *n* molécule *f*.
molehill ['məʊlhɪl] *n* taupinière *f*.
molest [məʊ'lɛst] *vt* tracasser; molester.
mollusc ['mɔləsk] *n* mollusque *m*.
mollycoddle ['mɔlɪkɔdl] *vt* chouchouter, couver.
Molotov cocktail ['mɔlətɔf-] *n* cocktail *m* Molotov.
molt [məʊlt] *vi* (*US*) = moult.
molten ['məʊltən] *adj* fondu(e).
mom [mɔm] *n* (*US*) = mum.
moment ['məʊmənt] *n* moment *m*, instant *m*; (*importance*) importance *f*; **at the ~** en ce moment; **for the ~** pour l'instant; **in a ~** dans un instant; **"one ~ please"** (*TEL*) "ne quittez pas".
momentarily ['məʊməntrɪlɪ] *adv* momentanément; (*US: soon*) bientôt.
momentary ['məʊməntərɪ] *adj* momentané(e), passager(ère).
momentous [məʊ'mɛntəs] *adj* important(e), capital(e).
momentum [məʊ'mɛntəm] *n* élan *m*, vitesse acquise; **to gather ~** prendre de la vitesse.
mommy ['mɔmɪ] *n* (*US: mother*) maman *f*.
Mon. *abbr* (= *Monday*) l.
Monaco ['mɔnəkəʊ] *n* Monaco *f*.
monarch ['mɔnək] *n* monarque *m*.
monarchist ['mɔnəkɪst] *n* monarchiste *m/f*.
monarchy ['mɔnəkɪ] *n* monarchie *f*.
monastery ['mɔnəstərɪ] *n* monastère *m*.
monastic [mə'næstɪk] *adj* monastique.
Monday ['mʌndɪ] *n* lundi *m*; *for phrases see also* Tuesday.
monetarist ['mʌnɪtərɪst] *n* monétariste *m/f*.
monetary ['mʌnɪtərɪ] *adj* monétaire.
money ['mʌnɪ] *n* argent *m*; **to make ~** (*person*) gagner de l'argent; (*business*) rapporter; **I've got no ~ left** je n'ai plus d'argent, je n'ai plus un sou.
moneyed ['mʌnɪd] *adj* riche.
moneylender ['mʌnɪlɛndə*] *n* prêteur/euse.

moneymaker ['mʌnɪmeɪkə*] *n* (*BRIT col: business*) affaire lucrative.
moneymaking ['mʌnɪmeɪkɪŋ] *adj* lucratif(ive), qui rapporte (de l'argent).
money market *n* marché financier.
money order *n* mandat *m*.
money-spinner ['mʌnɪspɪnə*] *n* (*col*) mine *f* d'or (*fig*).
money supply *n* masse *f* monétaire.
Mongol ['mɔŋgəl] *n* Mongol/e; (*LING*) mongol *m*.
mongol ['mɔŋgəl] *adj*, *n* (*MED*) mongolien(ne).
Mongolia [mɔŋ'gəʊlɪə] *n* Mongolie *f*.
Mongolian [mɔŋ'gəʊlɪən] *adj* mongol(e) ♦ *n* Mongol/e; (*LING*) mongol *m*.
mongoose ['mɔŋguːs] *n* mangouste *f*.
mongrel ['mʌŋgrəl] *n* (*dog*) bâtard *m*.
monitor ['mɔnɪtə*] *n* (*BRIT SCOL*) chef *m* de classe; (*US SCOL*) surveillant *m* (d'examen); (*TV, COMPUT*) écran *m*, moniteur *m* ♦ *vt* contrôler; (*foreign station*) être à l'écoute de.
monk [mʌŋk] *n* moine *m*.
monkey ['mʌŋkɪ] *n* singe *m*.
monkey nut *n* (*BRIT*) cacahuète *f*.
monkey wrench *n* clé *f* à molette.
mono ['mɔnəʊ] *adj* mono *inv*.
mono... ['mɔnəʊ] *prefix* mono....
monochrome ['mɔnəkrəʊm] *adj* monochrome.
monocle ['mɔnəkl] *n* monocle *m*.
monogamous [mə'nɔgəməs] *adj* monogame.
monogamy [mə'nɔgəmɪ] *n* monogamie *f*.
monogram ['mɔnəgræm] *n* monogramme *m*.
monolith ['mɔnəlɪθ] *n* monolithe *m*.
monologue ['mɔnəlɔg] *n* monologue *m*.
monoplane ['mɔnəpleɪn] *n* monoplan *m*.
monopolize [mə'nɔpəlaɪz] *vt* monopoliser.
monopoly [mə'nɔpəlɪ] *n* monopole *m*; **Monopolies and Mergers Commission** (*BRIT*) *commission britannique d'enquête sur les monopoles*.
monorail ['mɔnəʊreɪl] *n* monorail *m*.
monosodium glutamate [mɔnə'səʊdɪəm 'gluːtəmeɪt] *n* glutamate *m* de sodium.
monosyllabic [mɔnəsɪ'læbɪk] *adj* monosyllabique; (*person*) laconique.
monosyllable ['mɔnəsɪləbl] *n* monosyllabe *m*.
monotone ['mɔnətəʊn] *n* ton *m* (*or* voix *f*) monocorde; **to speak in a ~** parler sur un ton monocorde.
monotonous [mə'nɔtənəs] *adj* monotone.
monotony [mə'nɔtənɪ] *n* monotonie *f*.
monoxide [mə'nɔksaɪd] *n*: **carbon ~** oxyde *m* de carbone.
monsoon [mɔn'suːn] *n* mousson *f*.
monster ['mɔnstə*] *n* monstre *m*.
monstrosity [mɔns'trɔsɪtɪ] *n* monstruosité *f*, atrocité *f*.
monstrous ['mɔnstrəs] *adj* (*huge*) gigantesque; (*atrocious*) monstrueux(euse), atroce.
Mont. *abbr* (*US*) = Montana.
montage [mɔn'tɑːʒ] *n* montage *m*.
Mont Blanc [mɔ̃blɑ̃] *n* Mont Blanc *m*.

month [mʌnθ] n mois m; **every** ~ tous les mois; **300 dollars a** ~ 300 dollars par mois.

monthly ['mʌnθlı] adj mensuel(le) ♦ adv mensuellement ♦ n (magazine) mensuel m, publication mensuelle; **twice** ~ deux fois par mois.

Montreal [mɔntrı'ɔːl] n Montréal.

monument ['mɔnjumənt] n monument m.

monumental [mɔnju'mɛntl] adj monumental(e).

monumental mason n marbrier m.

moo [muː] vi meugler, beugler.

mood [muːd] n humeur f, disposition f; **to be in a good/bad** ~ être de bonne/mauvaise humeur; **to be in the** ~ **for** être d'humeur à, avoir envie de.

moody ['muːdı] adj (variable) d'humeur changeante, lunatique; (sullen) morose, maussade.

moon [muːn] n lune f.

moonbeam ['muːnbiːm] n rayon m de lune.

moon landing n alunissage m.

moonlight ['muːnlaıt] n clair m de lune ♦ vi travailler au noir.

moonlighting ['muːnlaıtıŋ] n travail m au noir.

moonlit ['muːnlıt] adj éclairé(e) par la lune; **a** ~ **night** une nuit de lune.

moonshot ['muːnʃɔt] n (SPACE) tir m lunaire.

moonstruck ['muːnstrʌk] adj fou(folle), dérangé(e).

moony ['muːnı] adj: **to have** ~ **eyes** avoir l'air dans la lune or rêveur.

Moor [muə*] n Maure/Mauresque.

moor [muə*] n lande f ♦ vt (ship) amarrer ♦ vi mouiller.

moorings ['muərıŋz] npl (chains) amarres fpl; (place) mouillage m.

Moorish ['muərıʃ] adj maure(mauresque).

moorland ['muələnd] n lande f.

moose [muːs] n (pl inv) élan m.

moot [muːt] vt soulever ♦ adj: ~ **point** point m discutable.

mop [mɔp] n balai m à laver ♦ vt éponger, essuyer; ~ **of hair** tignasse f.

▶**mop up** vt éponger.

mope [məup] vi avoir le cafard, se morfondre.

▶**mope about**, **mope around** vi broyer du noir, se morfondre.

moped ['məupɛd] n cyclomoteur m.

moquette [mɔ'kɛt] n moquette f.

MOR adj abbr (MUS: = middle-of-the-road) tous publics.

moral ['mɔrl] adj moral(e) ♦ n morale f; ~**s** npl moralité f.

morale [mɔ'rɑːl] n moral m.

morality [mə'rælıtı] n moralité f.

moralize ['mɔrəlaız] vi: **to** ~ **(about)** moraliser (sur).

morally ['mɔrəlı] adv moralement.

moral victory n victoire morale.

morass [mə'ræs] n marais m, marécage m.

moratorium [mɔrə'tɔːrıəm] n moratoire m.

morbid ['mɔːbıd] adj morbide.

========================= KEYWORD

more [mɔː*] adj **1** (greater in number etc) plus (de), davantage; ~ **people/work (than)** plus de gens/de travail (que)
2 (additional) encore (de); **do you want (some)** ~ **tea?** voulez-vous encore du thé?; **I have no** or **I don't have any** ~ **money** je n'ai plus d'argent; **it'll take a few** ~ **weeks** ça prendra encore quelques semaines
♦ pron plus, davantage; ~ **than 10** plus de 10; **it cost** ~ **than we expected** cela a coûté plus que prévu; **I want** ~ j'en veux plus or davantage; **is there any** ~? est-ce qu'il en reste?; **there's no** ~ il n'y en a plus; **a little** ~ un peu plus; **many/much** ~ beaucoup plus, bien davantage
♦ adv: ~ **dangerous/easily (than)** plus dangereux/facilement (que); ~ **and** ~ **expensive** de plus en plus cher; ~ **or less** plus ou moins; ~ **than ever** plus que jamais; **once** ~ encore une fois, une fois de plus; **and what's** ~ ... et de plus ..., et qui plus est ...

moreover [mɔː'rəuvə*] adv de plus.

morgue [mɔːg] n morgue f.

MORI ['mɔːrı] n abbr (BRIT: = Market & Opinion Research Institute) institut de sondage.

moribund ['mɔrıbʌnd] adj moribond(e).

morning ['mɔːnıŋ] n matin m; (as duration) matinée f; **in the** ~ le matin; **7 o'clock in the** ~ 7 heures du matin; **this** ~ ce matin.

morning-after pill ['mɔːnıŋ'ɑːftə-] n pilule f du lendemain.

morning sickness n nausées matinales.

Moroccan [mə'rɔkən] adj marocain(e) ♦ n Marocain/e.

Morocco [mə'rɔkəu] n Maroc m.

moron ['mɔːrɔn] n idiot/e, minus m/f.

moronic [mə'rɔnık] adj idiot(e), imbécile.

morose [mə'rəus] adj morose, maussade.

morphine ['mɔːfiːn] n morphine f.

morris dancing ['mɔrıs-] n (BRIT) danses folkloriques anglaises.

Morse [mɔːs] n (also: ~ **code**) morse m.

morsel ['mɔːsl] n bouchée f.

mortal ['mɔːtl] adj, n mortel(le).

mortality [mɔː'tælıtı] n mortalité f.

mortality rate n (taux m de) mortalité f.

mortar ['mɔːtə*] n mortier m.

mortgage ['mɔːgıdʒ] n hypothèque f; (loan) prêt m (or crédit m) hypothécaire ♦ vt hypothéquer; **to take out a** ~ prendre une hypothèque, faire un emprunt.

mortgage company n (US) société f de crédit immobilier.

mortgagee [mɔːgə'dʒiː] n prêteur/euse (sur hypothèque).

mortgagor ['mɔːgədʒə*] n emprunteur/euse

(sur hypothèque).

mortician [mɔː'tɪʃən] _n_ (_US_) entrepreneur _m_ de pompes funèbres.

mortified ['mɔːtɪfaɪd] _adj_ mortifié(e).

mortise lock ['mɔːtɪs-] _n_ serrure encastrée.

mortuary ['mɔːtjuərɪ] _n_ morgue _f_.

mosaic [mɔu'zeɪɪk] _n_ mosaïque _f_.

Moscow ['mɔskəu] _n_ Moscou.

Moslem ['mɔzləm] _adj_, _n_ = **Muslim**.

mosque [mɔsk] _n_ mosquée _f_.

mosquito, ~es [mɔs'kiːtəu] _n_ moustique _m_.

mosquito net _n_ moustiquaire _f_.

moss [mɔs] _n_ mousse _f_.

mossy ['mɔsɪ] _adj_ moussu(e).

most [məust] _adj_ la plupart de; le plus de ♦ _pron_ la plupart ♦ _adv_ le plus; (_very_) très, extrêmement; **the ~** (_also: + adjective_) le plus; **~ fish** la plupart des poissons; **~ of** la plus grande partie de; **~ of them** la plupart d'entre eux; **I saw ~** j'en ai vu la plupart; c'est moi qui en ai vu le plus; **at the (very) ~** au plus; **to make the ~ of** profiter au maximum de.

mostly ['məustlɪ] _adv_ surtout, principalement.

MOT _n abbr_ (_BRIT_: = _Ministry of Transport_): **the ~ (test)** visite technique (annuelle) obligatoire _des véhicules à moteur_.

motel [məu'tɛl] _n_ motel _m_.

moth [mɔθ] _n_ papillon _m_ de nuit; mite _f_.

mothball ['mɔθbɔːl] _n_ boule _f_ de naphtaline.

moth-eaten ['mɔθiːtn] _adj_ mité(e).

mother ['mʌðə*] _n_ mère _f_ ♦ _vt_ (_care for_) dorloter.

mother board _n_ (_COMPUT_) carte-mère _f_.

motherhood ['mʌðəhud] _n_ maternité _f_.

mother-in-law ['mʌðərɪnlɔː] _n_ belle-mère _f_.

motherly ['mʌðəlɪ] _adj_ maternel(le).

mother-of-pearl ['mʌðərəv'pɜːl] _n_ nacre _f_.

mother's help _n_ aide _f_ or auxiliaire _f_ familiale.

mother-to-be ['mʌðətə'biː] _n_ future maman _f_.

mother tongue _n_ langue maternelle.

mothproof ['mɔθpruːf] _adj_ traité(e) à l'antimite.

motif [məu'tiːf] _n_ motif _m_.

motion ['məuʃən] _n_ mouvement _m_; (_gesture_) geste _m_; (_at meeting_) motion _f_; (_BRIT_: _also_: **bowel ~**) selles _fpl_ ♦ _vt_, _vi_: **to ~ (to) sb to do** faire signe à qn de faire; **to be in ~** (_vehicle_) être en marche; **to set in ~** mettre en marche; **to go through the ~s of doing sth** (_fig_) faire qch machinalement _or_ sans conviction.

motionless ['məuʃənlɪs] _adj_ immobile, sans mouvement.

motion picture _n_ film _m_.

motivate ['məutɪveɪt] _vt_ motiver.

motivated ['məutɪveɪtɪd] _adj_ motivé(e).

motivation [məutɪ'veɪʃən] _n_ motivation _f_.

motive ['məutɪv] _n_ motif _m_, mobile _m_ ♦ _adj_ moteur(trice); **from the best (of) ~s** avec les meilleures intentions (du monde).

motley ['mɔtlɪ] _adj_ hétéroclite; bigarré(e), bariolé(e).

motor ['məutə*] _n_ moteur _m_; (_BRIT col_: _vehicle_) auto _f_ ♦ _adj_ moteur(trice).

motorbike ['məutəbaɪk] _n_ moto _f_.

motorboat ['məutəbəut] _n_ bateau _m_ à moteur.

motorcade ['məutəkeɪd] _n_ cortège _m_ d'automobiles _or_ de voitures.

motorcar ['məutəkɑː] _n_ (_BRIT_) automobile _f_.

motorcoach ['məutəkəutʃ] _n_ (_BRIT_) car _m_.

motorcycle ['məutəsaɪkl] _n_ vélomoteur _m_.

motorcyclist ['məutəsaɪklɪst] _n_ motocycliste _m/f_.

motoring ['məutərɪŋ] (_BRIT_) _n_ tourisme _m_ automobile ♦ _adj_ (_accident_) de voiture, de la route; **~ holiday** vacances _fpl_ en voiture; **~ offence** infraction _f_ au code de la route.

motorist ['məutərɪst] _n_ automobiliste _m/f_.

motorize ['məutəraɪz] _vt_ motoriser.

motor oil _n_ huile _f_ de graissage.

motor racing _n_ (_BRIT_) course _f_ automobile.

motor scooter _n_ scooter _m_.

motor vehicle _n_ véhicule _m_ automobile.

motorway ['məutəweɪ] _n_ (_BRIT_) autoroute _f_.

mottled ['mɔtld] _adj_ tacheté(e), marbré(e).

motto, ~es ['mɔtəu] _n_ devise _f_.

mould, (_US_) mold [məuld] _n_ moule _m_; (_mildew_) moisissure _f_ ♦ _vt_ mouler, modeler; (_fig_) façonner.

mo(u)lder ['məuldə*] _vi_ (_decay_) moisir.

mo(u)lding ['məuldɪŋ] _n_ (_ARCHIT_) moulure _f_.

mo(u)ldy ['məuldɪ] _adj_ moisi(e).

moult, (_US_) molt [məult] _vi_ muer.

mound [maund] _n_ monticule _m_, tertre _m_.

mount [maunt] _n_ mont _m_, montagne _f_; (_horse_) monture _f_; (_for jewel etc_) monture _f_ ♦ _vt_ monter; (_exhibition_) organiser, monter; (_picture_) monter sur carton; (_stamp_) coller dans un album ♦ _vi_ (_also_: **~ up**) s'élever, monter.

mountain ['mauntɪn] _n_ montagne _f_ ♦ _cpd_ (_de la_) montagne; **to make a ~ out of a molehill** (_fig_) se faire une montagne d'un rien.

mountain bike _n_ VTT _m_, vélo _m_ tout terrain.

mountaineer [mauntɪ'nɪə*] _n_ alpiniste _m/f_.

mountaineering [mauntɪ'nɪərɪŋ] _n_ alpinisme _m_; **to go ~** faire de l'alpinisme.

mountainous ['mauntɪnəs] _adj_ montagneux(euse).

mountain range _n_ chaîne _f_ de montagnes.

mountain rescue team _n_ colonne _f_ de secours.

mountainside ['mauntɪnsaɪd] _n_ flanc _m_ or versant _m_ de la montagne.

mounted ['mauntɪd] _adj_ monté(e).

Mount Everest _n_ le mont Everest.

mourn [mɔːn] _vt_ pleurer ♦ _vi_: **to ~ (for)** se lamenter (sur).

mourner ['mɔːnə*] _n_ parent/e _or_ ami/e du défunt; personne _f_ en deuil _or_ venue rendre hommage au défunt.

mournful ['mɔːnful] _adj_ triste, lugubre.

mourning ['mɔːnɪŋ] _n_ deuil _m_ ♦ _cpd_ (_dress_) de

deuil; **in ~** en deuil.

mouse, pl **mice** [maus, mais] n (also COMPUT) souris f.

mousetrap ['maustræp] n souricière f.

moussaka [mu'sɑːkə] n moussaka f.

mousse [muːs] n mousse f.

moustache [məs'tɑːʃ] n moustache(s) f(pl).

mousy ['mausɪ] adj (person) effacé(e); (hair) d'un châtain terne.

mouth, ~**s** [mauθ, -ðz] n bouche f; (of dog, cat) gueule f; (of river) embouchure f; (of bottle) goulot m; (opening) orifice m.

mouthful ['mauθful] n bouchée f.

mouth organ n harmonica m.

mouthpiece ['mauθpiːs] n (of musical instrument) bec m, embouchure f; (spokesman) porte-parole m inv.

mouth-to-mouth ['mauθtə'mauθ] adj: ~ **resuscitation** bouche à bouche m.

mouthwash ['mauθwɒʃ] n eau f dentifrice.

mouth-watering ['mauθwɔːtərɪŋ] adj qui met l'eau à la bouche.

movable ['muːvəbl] adj mobile.

move [muːv] n (movement) mouvement m; (in game) coup m; (: turn to play) tour m; (change of house) déménagement m ♦ vt déplacer, bouger; (emotionally) émouvoir; (POL: resolution etc) proposer ♦ vi (gen) bouger, remuer; (traffic) circuler; (also: ~ **house**) déménager; **to ~ towards** se diriger vers; **to ~ sb to do sth** pousser or inciter qn à faire qch; **to get a ~ on** se dépêcher, se remuer.

▶**move about, move around** vi (fidget) remuer; (travel) voyager, se déplacer.

▶**move along** vi se pousser.

▶**move away** vi s'en aller, s'éloigner.

▶**move back** vi revenir, retourner.

▶**move forward** vi avancer ♦ vt avancer; (people) faire avancer.

▶**move in** vi (to a house) emménager.

▶**move off** vi s'éloigner, s'en aller.

▶**move on** vi se remettre en route ♦ vt (onlookers) faire circuler.

▶**move out** vi (of house) déménager.

▶**move over** vi se pousser, se déplacer.

▶**move up** vi avancer; (employee) avoir de l'avancement.

movement ['muːvmənt] n mouvement m; ~ **(of the bowels)** (MED) selles fpl.

mover ['muːvə*] n auteur m d'une proposition.

movie ['muːvɪ] n film m; **the ~s** le cinéma.

movie camera n caméra f.

moviegoer ['muːvɪgəuə*] n (US) cinéphile m/f.

moving ['muːvɪŋ] adj en mouvement; (touching) émouvant(e) ♦ n (US) déménagement m.

mow, pt **mowed,** pp **mowed** or **mown** [məu, -n] vt faucher; (lawn) tondre.

▶**mow down** vt faucher.

mower ['məuə*] n (also: **lawn**~) tondeuse f à gazon.

Mozambique [məuzəm'biːk] n Mozambique m.

MP n abbr (= Military Police) PM; (BRIT) = **Member of Parliament**; (Canada) = Mounted Police.

mpg n abbr = miles per gallon (30 mpg = 9,4 l. aux 100 km).

mph abbr = miles per hour (60 mph = 96 km/h).

MPhil n abbr (US: = Master of Philosophy) titre universitaire.

MPS n abbr (BRIT) = Member of the Pharmaceutical Society.

Mr, Mr. ['mɪstə*] n: ~ **X** Monsieur X, M. X.

MRC n abbr (BRIT: = Medical Research Council) conseil de la recherche médicale.

MRCP n abbr (BRIT) = Member of the Royal College of Physicians.

MRCS n abbr (BRIT) = Member of the Royal College of Surgeons.

MRCVS n abbr (BRIT) = Member of the Royal College of Veterinary Surgeons.

Mrs, Mrs. ['mɪsɪz] n: ~ **X** Madame X, Mme X.

MS n abbr (= manuscript) ms; (= multiple sclerosis) SEP f; (US: = Master of Science) titre universitaire ♦ abbr (US) = Mississippi.

Ms, Ms. [mɪz] n (= Miss or Mrs): ~ **X** Madame X, Mme X.

MSA n abbr (US: = Master of Science in Agriculture) titre universitaire.

MSc n abbr = **Master of Science**.

MSG n abbr = monosodium glutamate.

MST abbr (US: = Mountain Standard Time) heure d'hiver des Montagnes Rocheuses.

MSW n abbr (US: = Master of Social Work) titre universitaire.

MT n abbr (= machine translation) TM ♦ abbr (US) = Montana.

Mt abbr (GEO: = mount) Mt.

MTV n abbr = music television.

much [mʌtʃ] adj beaucoup de ♦ adv, n or pron beaucoup; ~ **milk** beaucoup de lait; **how ~ is it?** combien est-ce que ça coûte?; **it's not** ~ ce n'est pas beaucoup; **too** ~ trop (de); **so** ~ tant (de); **I like it very/so** ~ j'aime beaucoup/tellement ça; **thank you very** ~ merci beaucoup; ~ **to my amazement** ... à mon grand étonnement ....

muck [mʌk] n (mud) boue f; (dirt) ordures fpl.

▶**muck about** vi (col) faire l'imbécile; (: waste time) traînasser; (: tinker) bricoler; tripoter.

▶**muck in** vi (BRIT col) donner un coup de main.

▶**muck out** vt (stable) nettoyer.

▶**muck up** vt (col: ruin) gâcher, esquinter; (: dirty) salir.

muckraking ['mʌkreɪkɪŋ] n (fig: col) déterrement m d'ordures.

mucky ['mʌkɪ] adj (dirty) boueux(euse), sale.

mucus ['mjuːkəs] n mucus m.

mud [mʌd] n boue f.

muddle ['mʌdl] n pagaille f; désordre m, fouillis m ♦ vt (also: ~ **up**) brouiller, embrouiller; **to be in a** ~ (person) ne plus savoir ou l'on

en est; **to get in a** ~ (*while explaining etc*) s'embrouiller.
▶**muddle along** *vi* aller son chemin tant bien que mal.
▶**muddle through** *vi* se débrouiller.
muddle-headed ['mʌdl'hɛdɪd] *adj* (*person*) à l'esprit embrouillé *or* confus, dans le brouillard.
muddy ['mʌdɪ] *adj* boueux(euse).
mud flats *npl* plage *f* de vase.
mudguard ['mʌdgɑːd] *n* garde-boue *m inv.*
mudpack ['mʌdpæk] *n* masque *m* de beauté.
mud-slinging ['mʌdslɪŋɪŋ] *n* médisance *f*, dénigrement *m.*
muesli ['mjuːzlɪ] *n* muesli *m.*
muff [mʌf] *n* manchon *m* ♦ *vt* (*col: shot, catch etc*) rater, louper; **to** ~ **it** rater *or* louper son coup.
muffin ['mʌfɪn] *n petit pain rond et plat.*
muffle ['mʌfl] *vt* (*sound*) assourdir, étouffer; (*against cold*) emmitoufler.
muffled ['mʌfld] *adj* étouffé(e), voilé(e).
muffler ['mʌflə*] *n* (*scarf*) cache-nez *m inv*; (*US AUT*) silencieux *m.*
mufti ['mʌftɪ] *n*: **in** ~ en civil.
mug [mʌg] *n* (*cup*) tasse *f* (*sans soucoupe*); (: *for beer*) chope *f*; (*col: face*) bouille *f*; (: *fool*) poire *f* ♦ *vt* (*assault*) agresser; **it's a** ~**'s game** (*BRIT*) c'est bon pour les imbéciles.
▶**mug up** *vt* (*BRIT col: also:* ~ **up on**) bosser, bûcher.
mugger ['mʌgə*] *n* agresseur *m.*
mugging ['mʌgɪŋ] *n* agression *f.*
muggins ['mʌgɪnz] *n* (*col*) ma pomme.
muggy ['mʌgɪ] *adj* lourd(e), moite.
mug shot *n* (*col: POLICE*) photo *f* de criminel; (: *gen: photo*) photo d'identité.
mulatto, ~**es** [mjuː'lætəu] *n* mulâtre/esse.
mulberry ['mʌlbrɪ] *n* (*fruit*) mûre *f*, (*tree*) mûrier *m.*
mule [mjuːl] *n* mule *f.*
mull [mʌl] *n*: **to** ~ **over** *vt* réfléchir à, ruminer.
mulled [mʌld] *adj*: ~ **wine** vin chaud.
multi... ['mʌltɪ] *prefix* multi....
multi-access ['mʌltɪ'ækses] *adj* (*COMPUT*) à accès multiple.
multicoloured, (*US*) **multicolored** ['mʌltɪkʌləd] *adj* multicolore.
multifarious [mʌltɪ'fɛərɪəs] *adj* divers(es), varié(e).
multilateral [mʌltɪ'lætərl] *adj* (*POL*) multilatéral(e).
multi-level ['mʌltɪlɛvl] *adj* (*US*) = **multistorey.**
multimillionaire [mʌltɪmɪljə'nɛə*] *n* milliardaire *m/f.*
multinational [mʌltɪ'næʃənl] *n* multinationale *f* ♦ *adj* multinational(e).
multiple ['mʌltɪpl] *adj* multiple ♦ *n* multiple *m*; (*BRIT: also:* ~ **store**) magasin *m* à succursales (multiples).
multiple choice *adj* à choix multiple.
multiple crash *n* carambolage *m.*

multiple sclerosis *n* sclérose *f* en plaques.
multiplex ['mʌltɪplɛks] *n* (*also:* ~ **cinema**) (cinéma *m*) multisalles *m.*
multiplication [mʌltɪplɪ'keɪʃən] *n* multiplication *f.*
multiplication table *n* table *f* de multiplication.
multiplicity [mʌltɪ'plɪsɪtɪ] *n* multiplicité *f.*
multiply ['mʌltɪplaɪ] *vt* multiplier ♦ *vi* se multiplier.
multiracial [mʌltɪ'reɪʃl] *adj* multiracial(e).
multistorey ['mʌltɪ'stɔːrɪ] *adj* (*BRIT: building*) à étages; (: *car park*) à étages *or* niveaux multiples.
multitude ['mʌltɪtjuːd] *n* multitude *f.*
mum [mʌm] *n* (*BRIT*) maman *f* ♦ *adj*: **to keep** ~ ne pas souffler mot; ~**'s the word!** motus et bouche cousue!
mumble ['mʌmbl] *vt*, *vi* marmotter, marmonner.
mumbo jumbo ['mʌmbəu-] *n* (*col*) baragouin *m*, charabia *m.*
mummify ['mʌmɪfaɪ] *vt* momifier.
mummy ['mʌmɪ] *n* (*BRIT: mother*) maman *f*; (*embalmed*) momie *f.*
mumps [mʌmps] *n* oreillons *mpl.*
munch [mʌntʃ] *vt*, *vi* mâcher.
mundane [mʌn'deɪn] *adj* banal(e), terre à terre *inv.*
municipal [mjuː'nɪsɪpl] *adj* municipal(e).
municipality [mjuːnɪsɪ'pælɪtɪ] *n* municipalité *f.*
munitions [mjuː'nɪʃənz] *npl* munitions *fpl.*
mural ['mjuərl] *n* peinture murale.
murder ['məːdə*] *n* meurtre *m*, assassinat *m* ♦ *vt* assassiner; **to commit** ~ commettre un meurtre.
murderer ['məːdərə*] *n* meurtrier *m*, assassin *m.*
murderess ['məːdərɪs] *n* meurtrière *f.*
murderous ['məːdərəs] *adj* meurtrier(ière).
murk [məːk] *n* obscurité *f.*
murky ['məːkɪ] *adj* sombre, ténébreux(euse).
murmur ['məːmə*] *n* murmure *m* ♦ *vt*, *vi* murmurer; **heart** ~ (*MED*) souffle *m* au cœur.
MusB(ac) *n abbr* (= *Bachelor of Music*) titre universitaire.
muscle ['mʌsl] *n* muscle *m.*
▶**muscle in** *vi* s'imposer, s'immiscer.
muscular ['mʌskjulə*] *adj* musculaire; (*person, arm*) musclé(e).
muscular dystrophy *n* dystrophie *f* musculaire.
MusD(oc) *n abbr* (= *Doctor of Music*) titre universitaire.
muse [mjuːz] *vi* méditer, songer ♦ *n* muse *f.*
museum [mjuː'zɪəm] *n* musée *m.*
mush [mʌʃ] *n* bouillie *f*; (*pej*) sentimentalité *f* à l'eau de rose.
mushroom ['mʌʃrum] *n* champignon *m* ♦ *vi* (*fig*) pousser comme un (*or* des) champignon(s).

mushy ['mʌʃɪ] *adj* (*vegetables, fruit*) en bouillie; (*movie etc*) à l'eau de rose.

music ['mjuːzɪk] *n* musique *f.*

musical ['mjuːzɪkl] *adj* musical(e); (*person*) musicien(ne) ♦ *n* (*show*) comédie musicale.

music(al) box *n* boîte *f* à musique.

musical chairs *npl* chaises musicales; (*fig*) **to play ~** faire des permutations.

musical instrument *n* instrument *m* de musique.

music centre *n* chaîne compacte.

music hall *n* music-hall *m.*

musician [mjuː'zɪʃən] *n* musicien/ne.

music stand *n* pupitre *m* à musique.

musk [mʌsk] *n* musc *m.*

musket ['mʌskɪt] *n* mousquet *m.*

muskrat ['mʌskræt] *n* rat musqué.

musk rose *n* (*BOT*) rose *f* muscade.

Muslim ['mʌzlɪm] *adj, n* musulman(e).

muslin ['mʌzlɪn] *n* mousseline *f.*

musquash ['mʌskwɔʃ] *n* loutre *f*; (*fur*) rat *m* d'Amérique, ondatra *m.*

mussel ['mʌsl] *n* moule *f.*

must [mʌst] *aux vb* (*obligation*): **I ~ do it** je dois le faire, il faut que je le fasse; (*probability*): **he ~ be there by now** il doit y être maintenant, il y est probablement maintenant; **I ~ have made a mistake** j'ai dû me tromper ♦ *n* nécessité *f*, impératif *m*; **it's a ~** c'est indispensable.

mustache ['mʌstæʃ] *n* (*US*) = **moustache**.

mustard ['mʌstəd] *n* moutarde *f.*

mustard gas *n* ypérite *f*, gaz *m* moutarde.

muster ['mʌstə*] *vt* rassembler; (*also*: **~ up**: *strength, courage*) rassembler.

mustiness ['mʌstɪnɪs] *n* goût *m* de moisi; odeur *f* de moisi *or* de renfermé.

mustn't ['mʌsnt] = **must not**.

musty ['mʌstɪ] *adj* qui sent le moisi *or* le renfermé.

mutant ['mjuːtənt] *adj* mutant(e) ♦ *n* mutant *m.*

mutate [mjuː'teɪt] *vi* subir une mutation.

mutation [mjuː'teɪʃən] *n* mutation *f.*

mute [mjuːt] *adj, n* muet(te).

muted ['mjuːtɪd] *adj* (*noise*) sourd(e), assourdi(e); (*criticism*) voilé(e); (*MUS*) en sourdine; (*: trumpet*) bouché(e).

mutilate ['mjuːtɪleɪt] *vt* mutiler.

mutilation [mjuːtɪ'leɪʃən] *n* mutilation *f.*

mutinous ['mjuːtɪnəs] *adj* (*troops*) mutiné(e); (*attitude*) rebelle.

mutiny ['mjuːtɪnɪ] *n* mutinerie *f* ♦ *vi* se mutiner.

mutter ['mʌtə*] *vt, vi* marmonner, marmotter.

mutton ['mʌtn] *n* mouton *m.*

mutual ['mjuːtʃuəl] *adj* mutuel(le), réciproque.

mutually ['mjuːtʃuəlɪ] *adv* mutuellement, réciproquement.

Muzak ['mjuːzæk] *n* ® (*often pej*) musique *f* d'ambiance.

muzzle ['mʌzl] *n* museau *m*; (*protective device*) muselière *f*; (*of gun*) gueule *f* ♦ *vt* museler.

MVP *n abbr* (*US SPORT*) = **most valuable player**.

MW *abbr* (= *medium wave*) PO.

my [maɪ] *adj* mon(ma), mes *pl.*

Myanmar ['maɪænmɑː*] *n* Myanmar *m.*

myopic [maɪ'ɔpɪk] *adj* myope.

myriad ['mɪrɪəd] *n* myriade *f.*

myself [maɪ'sɛlf] *pron* (*reflexive*) me; (*emphatic*) moi-même; (*after prep*) moi.

mysterious [mɪs'tɪərɪəs] *adj* mystérieux(euse).

mystery ['mɪstərɪ] *n* mystère *m.*

mystery story *n* roman *m* à suspense.

mystic ['mɪstɪk] *n* mystique *m/f* ♦ *adj* (*mysterious*) ésotérique.

mystical ['mɪstɪkl] *adj* mystique.

mystify ['mɪstɪfaɪ] *vt* mystifier; (*puzzle*) ébahir.

mystique [mɪs'tiːk] *n* mystique *f.*

myth [mɪθ] *n* mythe *m.*

mythical ['mɪθɪkl] *adj* mythique.

mythological [mɪθə'lɔdʒɪkl] *adj* mythologique.

mythology [mɪ'θɔlədʒɪ] *n* mythologie *f.*

N n

N, n [ɛn] *n* (*letter*) N, n *m*; **N for Nellie**, (*US*) **N for Nan** N comme Nicolas.

N *abbr* (= *north*) N.

NA *n abbr* (*US*: = *Narcotics Anonymous*) association *d'aide aux drogués*; (*US*) = *National Academy*.

n/a *abbr* (= *not applicable*) n.a.; (*COMM etc*) = *no account*.

NAACP *n abbr* (*US*) = *National Association for the Advancement of Colored People*.

NAAFI ['næfɪ] *n abbr* (*BRIT*: = *Navy, Army & Air Force Institute*) *organisme responsable des magasins et cantines de l'armée*.

nab [næb] *vt* (*col*) pincer, attraper.

NACU *n abbr* (*US*) = *National Association of Colleges and Universities*.

nadir ['neɪdɪə*] *n* (*ASTRONOMY*) nadir *m*; (*fig*) fond *m*, point *m* extrême.

nag [næg] *vt* (*person*) être toujours après, reprendre sans arrêt ♦ *n* (*pej: horse*) canasson *m*; (*person*): **she's an awful ~** elle est constamment après lui (*or* eux *etc*), elle est terriblement casse-pieds.

nagging ['nægɪŋ] *adj* (*doubt, pain*) persistant(e) ♦ *n* remarques continuelles.

nail [neɪl] *n* (*human*) ongle *m*; (*metal*) clou *m* ♦ *vt* clouer; **to ~ sb down to a date/price** contraindre qn à accepter *or* donner une date/un prix; **to pay cash on the ~** (*BRIT*) payer rubis sur l'ongle.

nailbrush ['neɪlbrʌʃ] *n* brosse *f* à ongles.

nailfile ['neɪlfaɪl] *n* lime *f* à ongles.

nail polish *n* vernis *m* à ongles.

nail polish remover *n* dissolvant *m*.

nail scissors *npl* ciseaux *mpl* à ongles.

nail varnish *n* (*BRIT*) = **nail polish**.

Nairobi [naɪˈrəʊbɪ] *n* Nairobi.

naïve [naɪˈiːv] *adj* naïf(ïve).

naïveté [naɪˈiːvteɪ], **naivety** [naɪˈiːvɪtɪ] *n* naïveté *f*.

naked ['neɪkɪd] *adj* nu(e); **with the ~ eye** à l'œil nu.

nakedness ['neɪkɪdnɪs] *n* nudité *f*.

NAM *n abbr* (*US*) = *National Association of Manufacturers.*

name [neɪm] *n* nom *m*; (*reputation*) réputation *f* ♦ *vt* nommer; citer; (*price, date*) fixer, donner; **by ~** par son nom; **de nom; in the ~ of** au nom de; **what's your ~?** quel est votre nom?; **my ~ is Peter** je m'appelle Peter; **to take sb's ~ and address** relever l'identité de qn *or* les nom et adresse de qn; **to make a ~ for o.s.** se faire un nom; **to get (o.s.) a bad ~** se faire une mauvaise réputation; **to call sb ~s** traiter qn de tous les noms.

name dropping *n* mention (*pour se faire valoir*) *du nom de personnalités qu'on connaît (ou prétend connaître).*

nameless ['neɪmlɪs] *adj* sans nom; (*witness, contributor*) anonyme.

namely ['neɪmlɪ] *adv* à savoir.

nameplate ['neɪmpleɪt] *n* (*on door etc*) plaque *f*.

namesake ['neɪmseɪk] *n* homonyme *m*.

nan bread [nɑːn-] *n* nan *m*.

nanny ['nænɪ] *n* bonne *f* d'enfants.

nanny goat *n* chèvre *f*.

nap [næp] *n* (*sleep*) (petit) somme ♦ *vi*: **to be caught ~ping** être pris(e) à l'improviste *or* en défaut.

NAPA *n abbr* (*US*: = *National Association of Performing Artists*) *syndicat des gens du spectacle.*

napalm ['neɪpɑːm] *n* napalm *m*.

nape [neɪp] *n*: **~ of the neck** nuque *f*.

napkin ['næpkɪn] *n* serviette *f* (de table).

Naples ['neɪplz] *n* Naples.

Napoleonic [nəpəʊlɪˈɒnɪk] *adj* napoléonien(ne).

nappy ['næpɪ] *n* (*BRIT*) couche *f* (gen *pl*).

nappy liner *n* (*BRIT*) protège-couche *m*.

narcissistic [nɑːsɪˈsɪstɪk] *adj* narcissique.

narcissus, *pl* **narcissi** [nɑːˈsɪsəs, -saɪ] *n* narcisse *m*.

narcotic [nɑːˈkɒtɪk] *n* (*MED*) narcotique *m*; **~s** *npl* (*drugs*) stupéfiants *mpl*.

nark [nɑːk] *vt* (*BRIT col*) mettre en rogne.

narrate [nəˈreɪt] *vt* raconter, narrer.

narration [nəˈreɪʃən] *n* narration *f*.

narrative ['nærətɪv] *n* récit *m* ♦ *adj* narra-

tif(ive).

narrator [nəˈreɪtə*] *n* narrateur/trice.

narrow ['nærəʊ] *adj* étroit(e); (*fig*) restreint(e), limité(e) ♦ *vi* devenir plus étroit, se rétrécir; **to have a ~ escape** l'échapper belle; **to ~ sth down to** réduire qch à.

narrow gauge *adj* (*RAIL*) à voie étroite.

narrowly ['nærəʊlɪ] *adv*: **he ~ missed injury/ the tree** il a failli se blesser/rentrer dans l'arbre; **he only ~ missed the target** il a manqué la cible de peu *or* de justesse.

narrow-minded [nærəʊˈmaɪndɪd] *adj* à l'esprit étroit, borné(e).

NAS *n abbr* (*US*) = *National Academy of Sciences.*

NASA ['næsə] *n abbr* (*US*: = *National Aeronautics and Space Administration*) NASA *f*.

nasal ['neɪzl] *adj* nasal(e).

Nassau ['næsɔː] *n* (*in Bahamas*) Nassau.

nastily ['nɑːstɪlɪ] *adv* (*say, act*) méchamment.

nastiness ['nɑːstɪnɪs] *n* (*of person, remark*) méchanceté *f*.

nasturtium [nəsˈtəːʃəm] *n* capucine *f*.

nasty ['nɑːstɪ] *adj* (*person*) méchant(e); très désagréable; (*smell*) dégoûtant(e); (*wound, situation*) mauvais(e), vilain(e); (*weather*) affreux(euse); **to turn ~** (*situation*) mal tourner; (*weather*) se gâter; (*person*) devenir méchant; **it's a ~ business** c'est une sale affaire.

NAS/UWT *n abbr* (*BRIT*: = *National Association of Schoolmasters/Union of Women Teachers*) *syndicat enseignant.*

nation ['neɪʃən] *n* nation *f*.

national ['næʃənl] *adj* national(e) ♦ *n* (*abroad*) ressortissant/e; (*when home*) national/e.

national anthem *n* hymne national.

National Curriculum *n* (*BRIT*) *programme scolaire commun à toutes les écoles publiques en Angleterre et au Pays de Galles comprenant dix disciplines.*

national debt *n* dette publique.

national dress *n* costume national.

National Guard *n* (*US*) milice *f* (*de volontaires dans chaque État*).

National Health Service (NHS) *n* (*BRIT*) *service national de santé*, ≈ Sécurité Sociale.

National Insurance *n* (*BRIT*) ≈ Sécurité Sociale.

nationalism ['næʃnəlɪzəm] *n* nationalisme *m*.

nationalist ['næʃnəlɪst] *adj, n* nationaliste (*m/f*).

nationality [næʃəˈnælɪtɪ] *n* nationalité *f*.

nationalization [næʃnəlaɪˈzeɪʃən] *n* nationalisation *f*.

nationalize ['næʃnəlaɪz] *vt* nationaliser.

nationally ['næʃnəlɪ] *adv* du point de vue national; dans le pays entier.

national park *n* parc national.

national press *n* presse nationale.

National Security Council *n* (*US*) conseil national de sécurité.

national service *n* (*MIL*) service *m* militaire.

*Le **National Trust** est un organisme indépendant, à but non lucratif, dont la mission est de protéger et de mettre en valeur les monuments et les sites britanniques en raison de leur intérêt historique ou de leur beauté naturelle.*

nation-wide ['neɪʃənwaɪd] *adj* s'étendant à l'ensemble du pays; (*problem*) à l'échelle du pays entier ♦ *adv* à travers *or* dans tout le pays.

native ['neɪtɪv] *n* habitant/e du pays, autochtone *m/f*; (*in colonies*) indigène *m/f* ♦ *adj* du pays, indigène; (*country*) natal(e); (*language*) maternel(le); (*ability*) inné(e); **a ~ of Russia** une personne originaire de Russie; **a ~ speaker of French** une personne de langue maternelle française.

Native American *n* Indien/ne d'Amérique.

Nativity [nə'tɪvɪtɪ] *n* (*REL*): **the ~** la Nativité.

nativity play *n* mystère *m or* miracle *m* de la Nativité.

NATO ['neɪtəu] *n abbr* (= *North Atlantic Treaty Organization*) OTAN *f*.

natter ['nætə*] *vi* (*BRIT*) bavarder.

natural ['nætʃrəl] *adj* naturel(le); **to die of ~ causes** mourir d'une mort naturelle.

natural childbirth *n* accouchement *m* sans douleur.

natural gas *n* gaz naturel.

natural history *n* histoire naturelle.

naturalist ['nætʃrəlɪst] *n* naturaliste *m/f*.

naturalization ['nætʃrəlaɪ'zeɪʃən] *n* naturalisation *f*; acclimatation *f*.

naturalize ['nætʃrəlaɪz] *vt* naturaliser; (*plant*) acclimater; **to become ~d** (*person*) se faire naturaliser.

naturally ['nætʃrəlɪ] *adv* naturellement.

naturalness ['nætʃrəlnɪs] *n* naturel *m*.

natural resources *npl* ressources naturelles.

natural selection *n* sélection naturelle.

natural wastage *n* (*INDUSTRY*) départs naturels et volontaires.

nature ['neɪtʃə*] *n* nature *f*; **by ~** par tempérament, de nature; **documents of a confidential ~** documents à caractère confidentiel.

-natured ['neɪtʃəd] *suffix*: **ill~** qui a mauvais caractère.

nature reserve *n* (*BRIT*) réserve naturelle.

nature trail *n* sentier de découverte de la nature.

naturist ['neɪtʃərɪst] *n* naturiste *m/f*.

naught [nɔːt] *n* = **nought**.

naughtiness ['nɔːtɪnɪs] *n* (*of child*) désobéissance *f*; (*of story etc*) grivoiserie *f*.

naughty ['nɔːtɪ] *adj* (*child*) vilain(e), pas sage; (*story, film*) grivois(e).

nausea ['nɔːsɪə] *n* nausée *f*.

nauseate ['nɔːsɪeɪt] *vt* écœurer, donner la nausée à.

nauseating ['nɔːsɪeɪtɪŋ] *adj* écœurant(e), dégoûtant(e).

nauseous ['nɔːsɪəs] *adj* nauséabond(e), écœurant(e); (*feeling sick*): **to be ~** avoir des nausées.

nautical ['nɔːtɪkl] *adj* nautique.

nautical mile *n* mille marin (= *1853 m*).

naval ['neɪvl] *adj* naval(e).

naval officer *n* officier *m* de marine.

nave [neɪv] *n* nef *f*.

navel ['neɪvl] *n* nombril *m*.

navigable ['nævɪgəbl] *adj* navigable.

navigate ['nævɪgeɪt] *vt* diriger, piloter ♦ *vi* naviguer; (*AUT*) indiquer la route à suivre.

navigation [nævɪ'geɪʃən] *n* navigation *f*.

navigator ['nævɪgeɪtə*] *n* navigateur *m*.

navvy ['nævɪ] *n* (*BRIT*) terrassier *m*.

navy ['neɪvɪ] *n* marine *f*; **Department of the N~** (*US*) ministère *m* de la Marine.

navy(-blue) ['neɪvɪ('bluː)] *adj* bleu marine *inv*.

Nazareth ['næzərɪθ] *n* Nazareth.

Nazi ['nɑːtsɪ] *adj* nazi(e) ♦ *n* Nazi/e.

NB *abbr* (= *nota bene*) NB; (*Canada*) = *New Brunswick*.

NBA *n abbr* (*US*) = *National Basketball Association, National Boxing Association*.

NBC *n abbr* (*US*: = *National Broadcasting Company*) chaîne de télévision.

NBS *n abbr* (*US*: = *National Bureau of Standards*) office de normalisation.

NC *abbr* (*COMM etc*) = *no charge*; (*US*) = *North Carolina*.

NCC *n abbr* (*BRIT*: = *Nature Conservancy Council*) organisme de protection de la nature; (*US*) = *National Council of Churches*.

NCCL *n abbr* (*BRIT*: = *National Council for Civil Liberties*) association de défense des libertés publiques.

NCO *n abbr* = *non-commissioned officer*.

ND, N. Dak. *abbr* (*US*) = *North Dakota*.

NE *abbr* (*US*) = *Nebraska, New England*.

NEA *n abbr* (*US*) = *National Education Association*.

neap [niːp] *n* (*also:* **~tide**) mortes-eaux *fpl*.

Neapolitan [nɪə'pɔlɪtən] *adj* napolitain(e) ♦ *n* Napolitain/e.

near [nɪə*] *adj* proche ♦ *adv* près ♦ *prep* (*also:* **~ to**) près de ♦ *vt* approcher de; **~ here/there** près d'ici/non loin de là; **£25,000 or ~est offer** (*BRIT*) 25 000 livres à débattre; **in the ~ future** dans un proche avenir; **the building is ~ing completion** le bâtiment est presque terminé; **to come ~** *vi* s'approcher.

nearby [nɪə'baɪ] *adj* proche ♦ *adv* tout près, à proximité.

Near East *n*: **the ~** le Proche-Orient.

nearer ['nɪərə*] *adj* plus proche ♦ *adv* plus près.

nearly ['nɪəlɪ] *adv* presque; **I ~ fell** j'ai failli tomber; **it's not ~ big enough** ce n'est vraiment pas assez grand, c'est loin d'être assez grand.

near miss *n* collision évitée de justesse; (*when aiming*) coup manqué de peu *or* de justesse.

nearness ['nɪənɪs] n proximité f.

nearside ['nɪəsaɪd] (AUT) n (right-hand drive) côté m gauche; (left-hand drive) côté droit ♦ adj de gauche; de droite.

near-sighted [nɪə'saɪtɪd] adj myope.

neat [niːt] adj (person, work) soigné(e); (room etc) bien tenu(e) or rangé(e); (solution, plan) habile; (spirits) pur(e); **I drink it** ~ je le bois sec or sans eau.

neatly ['niːtlɪ] adv avec soin or ordre; habilement.

neatness ['niːtnɪs] n (tidiness) netteté f; (skilfulness) habileté f.

Nebr. abbr (US) = Nebraska.

nebulous ['nɛbjuləs] adj nébuleux(euse).

necessarily ['nɛsɪsrɪlɪ] adv nécessairement; **not** ~ pas nécessairement or forcément.

necessary ['nɛsɪsrɪ] adj nécessaire; **if** ~ si besoin est, le cas échéant.

necessitate [nɪ'sɛsɪteɪt] vt nécessiter.

necessity [nɪ'sɛsɪtɪ] n nécessité f; chose nécessaire or essentielle; **in case of** ~ en cas d'urgence.

neck [nɛk] n cou m; (of horse, garment) encolure f; (of bottle) goulot m ♦ vi (col) se peloter; ~ **and** ~ à égalité; **to stick one's** ~ **out** (col) se mouiller.

necklace ['nɛklɪs] n collier m.

neckline ['nɛklaɪn] n encolure f.

necktie ['nɛktaɪ] n (esp US) cravate f.

nectar ['nɛktə*] n nectar m.

nectarine ['nɛktərɪn] n brugnon m, nectarine f.

NEDC n abbr (BRIT: = National Economic Development Council) conseil national pour le développement économique.

Neddy ['nɛdɪ] n abbr (BRIT col) = NEDC.

née [neɪ] adj: ~ **Scott** née Scott.

need [niːd] n besoin m ♦ vt avoir besoin de; **to** ~ **to do** devoir faire; avoir besoin de faire; **you don't** ~ **to go** vous n'avez pas besoin or vous n'êtes pas obligé de partir; **a signature is** ~**ed** il faut une signature; **to be in** ~ **of** or **have** ~ **of** avoir besoin de; **£10 will meet my immediate** ~**s** 10 livres suffiront pour mes besoins immédiats; **in case of** ~ en cas de besoin, au besoin; **there's no** ~ **to do ...** il n'y a pas lieu de faire ..., il n'est pas nécessaire de faire ...; **there's no** ~ **for that** ce n'est pas la peine, cela n'est pas nécessaire.

needle ['niːdl] n aiguille f; (on record player) saphir m ♦ vt (col) asticoter, tourmenter.

needlecord ['niːdlkɔːd] n (BRIT) velours m milleraies.

needless ['niːdlɪs] adj inutile; ~ **to say, ...** inutile de dire que ....

needlessly ['niːdlɪslɪ] adv inutilement.

needlework ['niːdlwɜːk] n (activity) travaux mpl d'aiguille; (object) ouvrage m.

needn't ['niːdnt] = need not.

needy ['niːdɪ] adj nécessiteux(euse).

negation [nɪ'geɪʃən] n négation f.

negative ['nɛgətɪv] n (PHOT, ELEC) négatif m; (LING) terme m de négation ♦ adj négatif(ive); **to answer in the** ~ répondre par la négative.

negative equity n situation dans laquelle la valeur d'une maison est inférieure à celle de l'emprunt-logement contracté pour la payer.

neglect [nɪ'glɛkt] vt négliger ♦ n (of person, duty, garden) le fait de négliger; (state of) ~ abandon m; **to** ~ **to do sth** négliger or omettre de faire qch.

neglected [nɪ'glɛktɪd] adj négligé(e), à l'abandon.

neglectful [nɪ'glɛktful] adj (gen) négligent(e); **to be** ~ **of sb/sth** négliger qn/qch.

negligee ['nɛglɪʒeɪ] n déshabillé m.

negligence ['nɛglɪdʒəns] n négligence f.

negligent ['nɛglɪdʒənt] adj négligent(e).

negligently ['nɛglɪdʒəntlɪ] adv par négligence; (offhandedly) négligemment.

negligible ['nɛglɪdʒɪbl] adj négligeable.

negotiable [nɪ'gəuʃɪəbl] adj négociable; **not** ~ (cheque) non négociable.

negotiate [nɪ'gəuʃɪeɪt] vi négocier ♦ vt (COMM) négocier; (obstacle) franchir, négocier; (bend in road) négocier; **to** ~ **with sb for sth** négocier avec qn en vue d'obtenir qch.

negotiating table [nɪ'gəuʃɪeɪtɪŋ-] n table f des négociations.

negotiation [nɪgəuʃɪ'eɪʃən] n négociation f, pourparlers mpl; **to enter into** ~**s with sb** engager des négociations avec qn.

negotiator [nɪ'gəuʃɪeɪtə*] n négociateur/trice.

Negress ['niːgrɪs] n négresse f.

Negro ['niːgrəu] adj (gen) noir(e); (music, arts) nègre, noir ♦ n (pl: ~**es**) Noir/e.

neigh [neɪ] vi hennir.

neighbour, (US) **neighbor** ['neɪbə*] n voisin/e.

neighbo(u)rhood ['neɪbəhud] n quartier m; voisinage m.

neighbourhood watch n (BRIT: also: ~ **scheme**) système de surveillance, assuré par les habitants d'un même quartier.

neighbo(u)ring ['neɪbərɪŋ] adj voisin(e), avoisinant(e).

neighbo(u)rly ['neɪbəlɪ] adj obligeant(e); (relations) de bon voisinage.

neither ['naɪðə*] adj, pron aucun(e) (des deux), ni l'un(e) ni l'autre ♦ conj: **I didn't move and** ~ **did Claude** je n'ai pas bougé, (et) Claude non plus ♦ adv: ~ **good nor bad** ni bon ni mauvais; ..., ~ **did I refuse** ..., (et or mais) je n'ai pas non plus refusé.

neo... ['niːəu] prefix néo-.

neolithic [niːəu'lɪθɪk] adj néolithique.

neologism [nɪ'ɒlədʒɪzəm] n néologisme m.

neon ['niːɒn] n néon m.

neon light n lampe f au néon.

neon sign n enseigne (lumineuse) au néon.

Nepal [nɪ'pɔːl] n Népal m.

nephew ['nɛvjuː] n neveu m.
nepotism ['nɛpətɪzəm] n népotisme m.
nerd [nɜːd] n (col) pauvre mec m, ballot m.
nerve [nɜːv] n nerf m; (bravery) sang-froid m, courage m; (cheek) aplomb m, toupet m; **he gets on my ~s** il m'énerve; **to have a fit of ~s** avoir le trac; **to lose one's ~** (self-confidence) perdre son sang-froid.
nerve centre n (ANAT) centre nerveux; (fig) centre névralgique.
nerve gas n gaz m neuroplégique.
nerve-racking ['nɜːvrækɪŋ] adj angoissant(e).
nervous ['nɜːvəs] adj nerveux(euse); (apprehensive) inquiet(ète), plein(e) d'appréhension.
nervous breakdown n dépression nerveuse.
nervously ['nɜːvəslɪ] adv nerveusement.
nervousness ['nɜːvəsnɪs] n nervosité f; inquiétude f, appréhension f.
nervous wreck n: **to be a ~** être une boule de nerfs.
nervy ['nɜːvɪ] adj: **he's very ~** il a les nerfs à fleur de peau or à vif.
nest [nɛst] n nid m ♦ vi (se) nicher, faire son nid; **~ of tables** table f gigogne.
nest egg n (fig) bas m de laine, magot m.
nestle ['nɛsl] vi se blottir.
nestling ['nɛstlɪŋ] n oisillon m.
net [nɛt] n (also called) filet m; **the N~** (Internet) le Net ♦ adj net(te) ♦ vt (fish etc) prendre au filet; (money: subj: person) toucher; (: deal, sale) rapporter; **~ of tax** net d'impôt; **he earns £10,000 ~ per year** il gagne 10 000 livres net par an.
netball ['nɛtbɔːl] n netball m.
net curtains npl voilages mpl.
Netherlands ['nɛðələndz] npl: **the ~** les Pays-Bas mpl.
net profit n bénéfice net.
nett [nɛt] adj = **net**.
netting ['nɛtɪŋ] n (for fence etc) treillis m, grillage m; (fabric) voile m.
nettle ['nɛtl] n ortie f.
network ['nɛtwɜːk] n réseau m ♦ vt (RADIO, TV) diffuser sur l'ensemble du réseau; (computers) interconnecter.
neuralgia [njʊəˈrældʒə] n névralgie f.
neurological [njʊərəˈlɒdʒɪkl] adj neurologique.
neurosis, pl **neuroses** [njʊəˈrəʊsɪs, -siːz] n névrose f.
neurotic [njʊəˈrɒtɪk] adj, n névrosé(e).
neuter ['njuːtə*] adj, n neutre (m) ♦ vt (cat etc) châtrer, couper.
neutral ['njuːtrəl] adj neutre ♦ n (AUT) point mort.
neutrality [njuːˈtrælɪtɪ] n neutralité f.
neutralize ['njuːtrəlaɪz] vt neutraliser.
Nev. abbr (US) = Nevada.
never ['nɛvə*] adv (ne ...) jamais; **~ again** plus jamais; **~ in my life** jamais de ma vie; see also **mind**.

never-ending [nɛvərˈɛndɪŋ] adj interminable.
nevertheless [nɛvəðəˈlɛs] adv néanmoins, malgré tout.
new [njuː] adj nouveau(nouvelle); (brand new) neuf(neuve); **as good as ~** comme neuf.
New Age n New Age m.
newborn ['njuːbɔːn] adj nouveau-né(e).
newcomer ['njuːkʌmə*] n nouveau venu/nouvelle venue.
new-fangled ['njuːfæŋgld] adj (pej) ultramoderne (et farfelu(e)).
new-found ['njuːfaʊnd] adj de fraîche date; (friend) nouveau(nouvelle).
Newfoundland ['njuːfənlənd] n Terre-Neuve f.
New Guinea n Nouvelle-Guinée f.
newly ['njuːlɪ] adv nouvellement, récemment.
newly-weds ['njuːlɪwɛdz] npl jeunes mariés mpl.
new moon n nouvelle lune.
newness ['njuːnɪs] n nouveauté f; (of fabric, clothes etc) état neuf.
New Orleans [-ˈɔːliːənz] n la Nouvelle-Orléans.
news [njuːz] n nouvelle(s) f(pl); (RADIO, TV) informations fpl; **a piece of ~** une nouvelle; **good/bad ~** bonne/mauvaise nouvelle; **financial ~** (PRESS, RADIO, TV) page financière.
news agency n agence f de presse.
newsagent ['njuːzeɪdʒənt] n (BRIT) marchand m de journaux.
news bulletin n (RADIO, TV) bulletin m d'informations.
newscaster ['njuːzkɑːstə*] n (RADIO, TV) présentateur/trice.
newsdealer ['njuːzdiːlə*] n (US) = **newsagent**.
news flash n flash m d'information.
newsletter ['njuːzlɛtə*] n bulletin m.
newspaper ['njuːzpeɪpə*] n journal m; **daily ~** quotidien m; **weekly ~** hebdomadaire m.
newsprint ['njuːzprɪnt] n papier m (de) journal.
newsreader ['njuːzriːdə*] n = **newscaster**.
newsreel ['njuːzriːl] n actualités (filmées).
newsroom ['njuːzruːm] n (PRESS) salle f de rédaction; (RADIO, TV) studio m.
news stand n kiosque m à journaux.
newsworthy ['njuːzwɜːðɪ] adj: **to be ~** valoir la peine d'être publié.
newt [njuːt] n triton m.
new town n (BRIT) ville nouvelle.
New Year n Nouvel An; **Happy ~!** Bonne Année!; **to wish sb a happy ~** souhaiter la Bonne Année à qn.
New Year's Day n le jour de l'An.
New Year's Eve n la Saint-Sylvestre.
New York [-ˈjɔːk] n New York; (also: **~ State**) New York m.
New Zealand [-ˈziːlənd] n Nouvelle-Zélande f ♦ adj néo-zélandais(e).

New Zealander [-'zi:ləndə*] n Néo-Zélandais/e.

next [nɛkst] adj (seat, room) voisin(e), d'à côté; (meeting, bus stop) suivant(e); prochain(e) ♦ adv la fois suivante; la prochaine fois; (afterwards) ensuite; ~ **to** prep à côté de; ~ **to nothing** presque rien; ~ **time** adv la prochaine fois; **the** ~ **day** le lendemain, le jour suivant or d'après; ~ **week** la semaine prochaine; **the** ~ **week** la semaine suivante; ~ **year** l'année prochaine; **"turn to the** ~ **page"** "voir page suivante"; **who's** ~? c'est à qui?; **the week after** ~ dans deux semaines; **when do we meet** ~? quand nous revoyons-nous?

next door adv à côté.

next-of-kin ['nɛkstəv'kın] n parent m le plus proche.

NF n abbr (BRIT POL: = National Front) ≈ FN ♦ abbr (Canada) = Newfoundland.

NFL n abbr (US) = National Football League.

Nfld. abbr (Canada) = Newfoundland.

NG abbr (US) = **National Guard**.

NGO n abbr (US: = non-governmental organization) ONG f.

NH abbr (US) = New Hampshire.

NHL n abbr (US) = National Hockey League.

NHS n abbr (BRIT) = **National Health Service**.

NI abbr = **Northern Ireland**; (BRIT) = **National Insurance**.

Niagara Falls [naı'ægərə-] npl: **the** ~ les chutes fpl du Niagara.

nib [nıb] n (of pen) (bec m de) plume f.

nibble ['nıbl] vt grignoter.

Nicaragua [nıkə'rægjuə] n Nicaragua m.

Nicaraguan [nıkə'rægjuən] adj nicaraguayen(ne) ♦ n Nicaraguayen/ne.

nice [naıs] adj (holiday, trip, taste) agréable; (flat, picture) joli(e); (person) gentil(le); (distinction, point) subtil(e).

nice-looking ['naıslukıŋ] adj joli(e).

nicely ['naıslı] adv agréablement; joliment; gentiment; subtilement; **that will do** ~ ce sera parfait.

niceties ['naısıtız] npl subtilités fpl.

niche [ni:ʃ] n (ARCHIT) niche f.

nick [nık] n encoche f; (BRIT col): **in good** ~ en bon état ♦ vt (cut): **to** ~ **o.s.** se couper; (col: steal) faucher, piquer; (: BRIT: arrest) choper, pincer; **in the** ~ **of time** juste à temps.

nickel ['nıkl] n nickel m; (US) pièce f de 5 cents.

nickname ['nıkneım] n surnom m ♦ vt surnommer.

Nicosia [nıkə'si:ə] n Nicosie f.

nicotine ['nıkəti:n] n nicotine f.

nicotine patch n timbre m anti-tabac, patch m.

niece [ni:s] n nièce f.

nifty ['nıftı] adj (col: car, jacket) qui a du chic or de la classe; (: gadget, tool) astucieux(euse).

Niger ['naıdʒə*] n (country, river) Niger m.

Nigeria [naı'dʒıərıə] n Nigéria m or f.

Nigerian [naı'dʒıərıən] adj nigérien(ne) ♦ n Nigérien/ne.

niggardly ['nıgədlı] adj (person) parcimonieux(euse), pingre; (allowance, amount) misérable.

nigger ['nıgə*] n (col!: highly offensive) nègre/négresse.

niggle ['nıgl] vt tracasser ♦ vi (find fault) trouver toujours à redire; (fuss) n'être jamais content(e).

niggling ['nıglıŋ] adj tatillon(ne); (detail) insignifiant(e); (doubt, pain) persistant(e).

night [naıt] n nuit f; (evening) soir m; **at** ~ la nuit; **by** ~ de nuit; **in the** ~, **during the** ~ pendant la nuit; **the** ~ **before last** avant-hier soir.

night-bird ['naıtbə:d] n oiseau m nocturne; (fig) couche-tard m inv, noctambule m/f.

nightcap ['naıtkæp] n boisson prise avant le coucher.

night club n boîte f de nuit.

nightdress ['naıtdrɛs] n chemise f de nuit.

nightfall ['naıtfɔ:l] n tombée f de la nuit.

nightie ['naıtı] n chemise f de nuit.

nightingale ['naıtıŋgeıl] n rossignol m.

night life n vie f nocturne.

nightly ['naıtlı] adj de chaque nuit or soir; (by night) nocturne ♦ adv chaque nuit or soir; nuitamment.

nightmare ['naıtmɛə*] n cauchemar m.

night porter n gardien m de nuit, concierge m de service la nuit.

night safe n coffre m de nuit.

night school n cours mpl du soir.

nightshade ['naıtʃeıd] n: **deadly** ~ (BOT) belladone f.

nightshift ['naıtʃıft] n équipe f de nuit.

night-time ['naıttaım] n nuit f.

night watchman n veilleur m de nuit; poste m de nuit.

nihilism ['naıılızəm] n nihilisme m.

nil [nıl] n rien m; (BRIT SPORT) zéro m.

Nile [naıl] n: **the** ~ le Nil.

nimble ['nımbl] adj agile.

nine [naın] num neuf.

nineteen ['naın'ti:n] num dix-neuf.

ninety ['naıntı] num quatre-vingt-dix.

ninth [naınθ] num neuvième.

nip [nıp] vt pincer ♦ vi (BRIT col): **to** ~ **out/down/up** sortir/descendre/monter en vitesse ♦ n pincement m; (drink) petit verre; **to** ~ **into a shop** faire un saut dans un magasin.

nipple ['nıpl] n (ANAT) mamelon m, bout m du sein.

nippy ['nıpı] adj (BRIT: person) alerte, leste; (: car) nerveux(euse).

nit [nıt] n (in hair) lente f; (col: idiot) imbécile m/f, crétin(e).

nit-pick ['nıtpık] vi (col) être tatillon(ne).

nitrogen ['naıtrədʒən] n azote m.

nitroglycerin(e) ['naɪtrəʊ'glɪsəriːn] n nitrogly-cérine f.
nitty-gritty ['nɪtɪ'grɪtɪ] n (fam): **to get down to the** ~ en venir au fond du problème.
nitwit ['nɪtwɪt] n (col) nigaud/e.
NJ abbr (US) = New Jersey.
NLF n abbr (= National Liberation Front) FLN m.
NLQ abbr (= near letter quality) qualité f courrier.
NLRB n abbr (US: = National Labor Relations Board) organisme de protection des travailleurs.
NM, N. Mex. abbr (US) = New Mexico.

==================== KEYWORD

no [nəʊ] (pl ~es) adv (opposite of "yes") non; **are you coming?** — ~ **(I'm not)** est-ce que vous venez? — non; **would you like some more?** — ~ **thank you** vous en voulez encore? — non merci
♦ adj (not any) pas de, aucun(e) (used with "ne"); **I have** ~ **money/books** je n'ai pas d'argent/de livres; ~ **student would have done it** aucun étudiant ne l'aurait fait; **"**~ **smoking"** "défense de fumer"; **"**~ **dogs"** "les chiens ne sont pas admis"
♦ n non m; **I won't take** ~ **for an answer** il n'est pas question de refuser.

no. abbr (= number) n°.
nobble ['nɒbl] vt (BRIT col: bribe: person) soudoyer, acheter; (: person: to speak to) mettre le grappin sur; (RACING: horse, dog) droguer (pour l'empêcher de gagner).
Nobel prize [nəʊ'bɛl-] n prix m Nobel.
nobility [nəʊ'bɪlɪtɪ] n noblesse f.
noble ['nəʊbl] adj noble.
nobleman ['nəʊblmən] n noble m.
nobly ['nəʊblɪ] adv noblement.
nobody ['nəʊbədɪ] pron personne (with negative).
no-claims bonus ['nəʊkleɪmz-] n bonus m.
nocturnal [nɒk'tɜːnl] adj nocturne.
nod [nɒd] vi faire un signe de (la) tête (affirmatif ou amical); (sleep) somnoler ♦ vt: **to** ~ **one's head** faire un signe de (la) tête; (in agreement) faire signe que oui ♦ n signe m de (la) tête; **they** ~**ded their agreement** ils ont acquiescé d'un signe de la tête.
▶**nod off** vi s'assoupir.
no-fly zone [nəʊ'flaɪ-] n zone interdite (aux avions et hélicoptères).
noise [nɔɪz] n bruit m.
noiseless ['nɔɪzlɪs] adj silencieux(euse).
noisily ['nɔɪzɪlɪ] adv bruyamment.
noisy ['nɔɪzɪ] adj bruyant(e).
nomad ['nəʊmæd] n nomade m/f.
nomadic [nəʊ'mædɪk] adj nomade.
no man's land n no man's land m.
nominal ['nɒmɪnl] adj (rent, fee) symbolique; (value) nominal(e).
nominate ['nɒmɪneɪt] vt (propose) proposer;

(elect) nommer.
nomination [nɒmɪ'neɪʃən] n nomination f.
nominee [nɒmɪ'niː] n candidat agréé; personne nommée.
non- [nɒn] prefix non-.
nonalcoholic [nɒnælkə'hɒlɪk] adj non-alcoolisé(e).
nonbreakable [nɒn'breɪkəbl] adj incassable.
nonce word ['nɒns-] n mot créé pour l'occasion.
nonchalant ['nɒnʃələnt] adj nonchalant(e).
noncommissioned [nɒnkə'mɪʃənd] adj: ~ **officer** sous-officier m.
noncommittal [nɒnkə'mɪtl] adj évasif(ive).
nonconformist [nɒnkən'fɔːmɪst] n nonconformiste m/f ♦ adj non-conformiste, dissident(e).
noncontributory [nɒnkən'trɪbjutərɪ] adj: ~ **pension scheme** or (US) **plan** régime de retraite payée par l'employeur.
noncooperation ['nɒnkəʊɒpə'reɪʃən] n refus m de coopérer, non-coopération f.
nondescript ['nɒndɪskrɪpt] adj quelconque, indéfinissable.
none [nʌn] pron aucun/e; ~ **of you** aucun d'entre vous, personne parmi vous; **I have** ~ je n'en ai pas; **I have** ~ **left** je n'en ai plus; ~ **at all** (not one) aucun(e); **how much milk?** — ~ **at all** combien de lait? — pas du tout; **he's** ~ **the worse for it** il ne s'en porte pas plus mal.
nonentity [nɒ'nɛntɪtɪ] n personne insignifiante.
nonessential [nɒnɪ'sɛnʃl] adj accessoire, superflu(e) ♦ n: ~**s** le superflu.
nonetheless ['nʌnðə'lɛs] adv néanmoins.
nonevent [nɒnɪ'vɛnt] n événement manqué.
nonexecutive [nɒnɪg'zɛkjutɪv] adj: ~ **director** administrateur/trice, conseiller/ère de direction.
nonexistent [nɒnɪg'zɪstənt] adj inexistant(e).
nonfiction [nɒn'fɪkʃən] n littérature f non-romanesque.
nonflammable [nɒn'flæməbl] adj ininflammable.
nonintervention ['nɒnɪntə'vɛnʃən] n nonintervention f.
no-no ['nəʊnəʊ] n (col): **it's a** ~ il n'en est pas question.
non obst. abbr (= non obstante: notwithstanding) nonobstant.
no-nonsense [nəʊ'nɒnsəns] adj (manner, person) plein(e) de bon sens.
nonpayment [nɒn'peɪmənt] n non-paiement m.
nonplussed [nɒn'plʌst] adj perplexe.
non-profit-making [nɒn'prɒfɪtmeɪkɪŋ] adj à but non lucratif.
nonsense ['nɒnsəns] n absurdités fpl, idioties fpl; ~! ne dites pas d'idioties!; **it is** ~ **to say that** ... il est absurde de dire que ....
nonsensical [nɒn'sɛnsɪkl] adj absurde, qui n'a

pas de sens.

nonshrink [nɔn'ʃrɪŋk] *adj* (*BRIT*) irrétrécissable.

nonskid [nɔn'skɪd] *adj* antidérapant(e).

nonsmoker ['nɔn'sməukə*] *n* non-fumeur *m*.

nonstarter [nɔn'stɑːtə*] *n*: **it's a** ~ c'est voué à l'échec.

nonstick ['nɔn'stɪk] *adj* qui n'attache pas.

nonstop ['nɔn'stɔp] *adj* direct(e), sans arrêt (*or* escale) ♦ *adv* sans arrêt.

nontaxable [nɔn'tæksəbl] *adj*: ~ **income** revenu *m* non imposable.

non-U ['nɔnjuː] *adj abbr* (*BRIT col*: = *non-upper class*) qui ne se dit (*or* se fait) pas.

nonvolatile [nɔn'vɔlətaɪl] *adj*: ~ **memory** (*COMPUT*) mémoire rémanente *or* non volatile.

nonvoting [nɔn'vəutɪŋ] *adj*: ~ **shares** actions *fpl* sans droit de vote.

non-white ['nɔn'waɪt] *adj* de couleur ♦ *n* personne *f* de couleur.

no-win situation [nəu'wɪn-] *n* impasse *f*; **we're in a** ~ nous sommes dans l'impasse.

noodles ['nuːdlz] *npl* nouilles *fpl*.

nook [nuk] *n*: ~**s and crannies** recoins *mpl*.

noon [nuːn] *n* midi *m*.

no one ['nəuwʌn] *pron* = **nobody**.

noose [nuːs] *n* nœud coulant; (*hangman's*) corde *f*.

nor [nɔː*] *conj* = **neither** ♦ *adv see* **neither**.

Norf *abbr* (*BRIT*) = **Norfolk**.

norm [nɔːm] *n* norme *f*.

normal ['nɔːml] *adj* normal(e) ♦ *n*: **to return to** ~ redevenir normal(e).

normality [nɔː'mælɪtɪ] *n* normalité *f*.

normally ['nɔːməlɪ] *adv* normalement.

Normandy ['nɔːməndɪ] *n* Normandie *f*.

north [nɔːθ] *n* nord *m* ♦ *adj* du nord, nord *inv* ♦ *adv* au *or* vers le nord.

North Africa *n* Afrique *f* du Nord.

North African *adj* nord-africain(e), d'Afrique du Nord ♦ *n* Nord-Africain/e.

North America *n* Amérique *f* du Nord.

North American *n* Nord-Américain/e ♦ *adj* nord-américain(e), d'Amérique du Nord.

Northants [nɔː'θænts] *abbr* (*BRIT*) = **Northamptonshire**.

northbound ['nɔːθbaund] *adj* (*traffic*) en direction du nord; (*carriageway*) nord *inv*.

Northd *abbr* (*BRIT*) = **Northumberland**.

north-east [nɔːθ'iːst] *n* nord-est *m*.

northerly ['nɔːðəlɪ] *adj* (*wind, direction*) du nord.

northern ['nɔːðən] *adj* du nord, septentrional(e).

Northern Ireland *n* Irlande *f* du Nord.

North Pole *n*: **the** ~ le pôle Nord.

North Sea *n*: **the** ~ la mer du Nord.

North Sea oil *n* pétrole *m* de la mer du Nord.

northward(s) ['nɔːθwəd(z)] *adv* vers le nord.

north-west [nɔːθ'wɛst] *n* nord-ouest *m*.

Norway ['nɔːweɪ] *n* Norvège *f*.

Norwegian [nɔː'wiːdʒən] *adj* norvégien(ne) ♦ *n* Norvégien/ne; (*LING*) norvégien *m*.

nos. *abbr* (= *numbers*) n°.

nose [nəuz] *n* nez *m*; (*fig*) flair *m* ♦ *vi* (*also:* ~ **one's way**) avancer précautionneusement; **to pay through the** ~ (**for sth**) (*col*) payer un prix excessif (pour qch).

►**nose about, nose around** *vi* fouiner *or* fureter (partout).

nosebleed ['nəuzbliːd] *n* saignement *m* de nez.

nose-dive ['nəuzdaɪv] *n* (descente *f* en) piqué *m*.

nose drops *npl* gouttes *fpl* pour le nez.

nosey ['nəuzɪ] *adj* curieux(euse).

nostalgia [nɔs'tældʒɪə] *n* nostalgie *f*.

nostalgic [nɔs'tældʒɪk] *adj* nostalgique.

nostril ['nɔstrɪl] *n* narine *f*; (*of horse*) naseau *m*.

nosy ['nəuzɪ] *adj* = **nosey**.

not [nɔt] *adv* (ne ...) pas; **I hope** ~ j'espère que non; ~ **at all** pas du tout; (*after thanks*) de rien; **you must** ~ *or* **mustn't do this** tu ne dois pas faire ça; **he isn't** ... il n'est pas ....

notable ['nəutəbl] *adj* notable.

notably ['nəutəblɪ] *adv* en particulier.

notary ['nəutərɪ] *n* (*also:* ~ **public**) notaire *m*.

notation [nəu'teɪʃən] *n* notation *f*.

notch [nɔtʃ] *n* encoche *f*.

►**notch up** *vt* (*score*) marquer; (*victory*) remporter.

note [nəut] *n* note *f*; (*letter*) mot *m*; (*banknote*) billet *m* ♦ *vt* (*also:* ~ **down**) noter; (*notice*) constater; **just a quick** ~ **to let you know** ... juste un mot pour vous dire ...; **to take** ~**s** prendre des notes; **to compare** ~**s** (*fig*) échanger des (*or* leurs *etc*) impressions; **to take** ~ **of** prendre note de; **a person of** ~ une personne éminente.

notebook ['nəutbuk] *n* carnet *m*; (*for shorthand etc*) bloc-notes *m*.

note-case ['nəutkeɪs] *n* (*BRIT*) porte-feuille *m*.

noted ['nəutɪd] *adj* réputé(e).

notepad ['nəutpæd] *n* bloc-notes *m*.

notepaper ['nəutpeɪpə*] *n* papier *m* à lettres.

noteworthy ['nəutwɜːðɪ] *adj* remarquable.

nothing ['nʌθɪŋ] *n* rien *m*; **he does** ~ il ne fait rien; ~ **new** rien de nouveau; **for** ~ (*free*) pour rien, gratuitement; ~ **at all** rien du tout.

notice ['nəutɪs] *n* avis *m*; (*of leaving*) congé *m*; (*BRIT: review: of play etc*) critique *f*, compte rendu *m* ♦ *vt* remarquer, s'apercevoir de; **without** ~ sans préavis; **advance** ~ préavis *m*; **to give sb** ~ **of sth** notifier qn de qch; **at short** ~ dans un délai très court; **until further** ~ jusqu'à nouvel ordre; **to give** ~, **hand in one's** ~ (*subj: employee*) donner sa démission, démissionner; **to take** ~ **of** prêter attention à; **to bring sth to sb's** ~ porter qch à la connaissance de qn; **it has come to my** ~ **that** ... on m'a signalé que ...; **to escape** *or* **avoid** ~ (essayer de) passer inaperçu *or* ne pas se faire remarquer.

noticeable ['nəutɪsəbl] *adj* visible.
notice board *n* (*BRIT*) panneau *m* d'affichage.
notification [nəutɪfɪ'keɪʃən] *n* notification *f*.
notify ['nəutɪfaɪ] *vt*: **to ~ sth to sb** notifier qch à qn; **to ~ sb of sth** avertir qn de qch.
notion ['nəuʃən] *n* idée *f*; (*concept*) notion *f*.
notions ['nəuʃənz] *npl* (*US: haberdashery*) mercerie *f*.
notoriety [nəutə'raɪətɪ] *n* notoriété *f*.
notorious [nəu'tɔːrɪəs] *adj* notoire (*souvent en mal*).
notoriously [nəu'tɔːrɪəslɪ] *adj* notoirement.
Notts [nɔts] *abbr* (*BRIT*) = **Nottinghamshire**.
notwithstanding [nɔtwɪθ'stændɪŋ] *adv* néanmoins ♦ *prep* en dépit de.
nougat ['nuːgɑː] *n* nougat *m*.
nought [nɔːt] *n* zéro *m*.
noun [naun] *n* nom *m*.
nourish ['nʌrɪʃ] *vt* nourrir.
nourishing ['nʌrɪʃɪŋ] *adj* nourrissant(e).
nourishment ['nʌrɪʃmənt] *n* nourriture *f*.
Nov. *abbr* (= *November*) nov.
Nova Scotia ['nəuvə'skəuʃə] *n* Nouvelle-Écosse *f*.
novel ['nɔvl] *n* roman *m* ♦ *adj* nouveau(nouvelle), original(e).
novelist ['nɔvəlɪst] *n* romancier *m*.
novelty ['nɔvəltɪ] *n* nouveauté *f*.
November [nəu'vɛmbə*] *n* novembre *m*; *for phrases see also* **July**.
novice ['nɔvɪs] *n* novice *m/f*.
NOW [nau] *n abbr* (*US*) = *National Organization for Women*.
now [nau] *adv* maintenant ♦ *conj*: **~ (that)** maintenant (que); **right ~** tout de suite; **by ~** à l'heure qu'il est; **just ~: that's the fashion just ~** c'est la mode en ce moment *or* maintenant; **I saw her just ~** je viens de la voir, je l'ai vue à l'instant; **I'll read it just ~** je vais le lire à l'instant *or* dès maintenant; **~ and then, ~ and again** de temps en temps; **from ~ on** dorénavant; **in 3 days from ~** dans *or* d'ici trois jours; **between ~ and Monday** d'ici (à) lundi; **that's all for ~** c'est tout pour l'instant.
nowadays ['nauədeɪz] *adv* de nos jours.
nowhere ['nəuwɛə*] *adv* nulle part; **~ else** nulle part ailleurs.
noxious ['nɔkʃəs] *adj* toxique.
nozzle ['nɔzl] *n* (*of hose*) jet *m*, lance *f*.
NP *n abbr* = *notary public*.
NS *abbr* (*Canada*) = **Nova Scotia**.
NSC *n abbr* (*US*) = **National Security Council**.
NSF *n abbr* (*US*) = *National Science Foundation*.
NSPCC *n abbr* (*BRIT*) = *National Society for the Prevention of Cruelty to Children*.
NSW *abbr* (*Australia*) = *New South Wales*.
NT *n abbr* (= *New Testament*) NT *m* ♦ *abbr* (*Canada*) = *Northwest Territories*.
nth [ɛnθ] *adj*: **for the ~ time** (*col*) pour la énième fois.
nuance ['njuːɑ̃ːns] *n* nuance *f*.

nubile ['njuːbaɪl] *adj* nubile; (*attractive*) jeune et désirable.
nuclear ['njuːklɪə*] *adj* nucléaire.
nuclear disarmament *n* désarmement *m* nucléaire.
nuclear family *n* famille *f* nucléaire.
nuclear-free zone ['njuːklɪə'friː-] *n* zone *f* où le nucléaire est interdit.
nucleus, *pl* **nuclei** ['njuːklɪəs, 'njuːklɪaɪ] *n* noyau *m*.
NUCPS *n abbr* (*BRIT*: = *National Union of Civil and Public Servants*) *syndicat des fonctionnaires.*
nude [njuːd] *adj* nu(e) ♦ *n* (*ART*) nu *m*; **in the ~** (tout(e)) nu(e).
nudge [nʌdʒ] *vt* donner un (petit) coup de coude à.
nudist ['njuːdɪst] *n* nudiste *m/f*.
nudist colony *n* colonie *f* de nudistes.
nudity ['njuːdɪtɪ] *n* nudité *f*.
nugget ['nʌgɪt] *n* pépite *f*.
nuisance ['njuːsns] *n*: **it's a ~** c'est (très) ennuyeux *or* gênant; **he's a ~** il est assommant *or* casse-pieds; **what a ~!** quelle barbe!
NUJ *n abbr* (*BRIT*: = *National Union of Journalists*) *syndicat des journalistes.*
nuke [njuːk] *n* (*col*) bombe *f* atomique.
null [nʌl] *adj*: **~ and void** nul(le) et non avenu(e).
nullify ['nʌlɪfaɪ] *vt* invalider.
NUM *n abbr* (*BRIT*: = *National Union of Mineworkers*) *syndicat des mineurs.*
numb [nʌm] *adj* engourdi(e) ♦ *vt* engourdir; **~ with cold** engourdi(e) par le froid, transi(e) (de froid); **~ with fear** transi de peur, paralysé(e) par la peur.
number ['nʌmbə*] *n* nombre *m*; (*numeral*) chiffre *m*; (*of house, car, telephone, newspaper*) numéro *m* ♦ *vt* numéroter; (*include*) compter; **a ~ of** un certain nombre de; **to be ~ed among** compter parmi; **the staff ~s 20** le nombre d'employés s'élève à *or* est de 20; **wrong ~** (*TEL*) mauvais numéro.
numbered account ['nʌmbəd-] *n* (*in bank*) compte numéroté.
number plate *n* (*BRIT AUT*) plaque *f* minéralogique *or* d'immatriculation.
Number Ten *n* (*BRIT*: = *10 Downing Street*) résidence du Premier ministre.
numbness ['nʌmnɪs] *n* torpeur *f*; (*due to cold*) engourdissement *m*.
numbskull ['nʌmskʌl] *n* (*col*) gourde *f*.
numeral ['njuːmərəl] *n* chiffre *m*.
numerate ['njuːmərɪt] *adj* (*BRIT*): **to be ~** avoir des notions d'arithmétique.
numerical [njuː'mɛrɪkl] *adj* numérique.
numerous ['njuːmərəs] *adj* nombreux(euse).
nun [nʌn] *n* religieuse *f*, sœur *f*.
nunnery ['nʌnərɪ] *n* couvent *m*.
nuptial ['nʌpʃəl] *adj* nuptial(e).
nurse [nəːs] *n* infirmière *f*; (*also*: **~maid**)

bonne *f* d'enfants ♦ *vt* (*patient, cold*) soigner; (*baby: BRIT*) bercer (dans ses bras); (: *US*) allaiter, nourrir; (*hope*) nourrir *m*.

nursery ['nɜːsərɪ] *n* (*room*) nursery *f*; (*institution*) pouponnière *f*; (*for plants*) pépinière *f*.

nursery rhyme *n* comptine *f*, chansonnette *f* pour enfants.

nursery school *n* école maternelle.

nursery slope *n* (*BRIT SKI*) piste *f* pour débutants.

nursing ['nɜːsɪŋ] *n* (*profession*) profession *f* d'infirmière ♦ *adj* (*mother*) qui allaite.

nursing home *n* clinique *f*; maison *f* de convalescence.

nurture ['nɜːtʃə*] *vt* élever.

NUS *n abbr* (*BRIT*: = *National Union of Students*) *syndicat des étudiants*.

NUT *n abbr* (*BRIT*: = *National Union of Teachers*) *syndicat enseignant*.

nut [nʌt] *n* (*of metal*) écrou *m*; (*fruit*) noix *f*, noisette *f*, cacahuète *f* (*terme générique en anglais*) ♦ *adj* (*chocolate etc*) aux noisettes; **he's ~s** (*col*) il est dingue.

nutcase ['nʌtkeɪs] *n* (*col*) dingue *m/f*.

nutcrackers ['nʌtkrækəz] *npl* casse-noix *m inv*, casse-noisette(s) *m*.

nutmeg ['nʌtmeg] *n* (*noix f*) muscade *f*.

nutrient ['njuːtrɪənt] *adj* nutritif(ive) ♦ *n* substance nutritive.

nutrition [njuːˈtrɪʃən] *n* nutrition *f*, alimentation *f*.

nutritionist [njuːˈtrɪʃənɪst] *n* nutritionniste *m/f*.

nutritious [njuːˈtrɪʃəs] *adj* nutritif(ive), nourrissant(e).

nutshell ['nʌtʃel] *n* coquille *f* de noix; **in a ~** en un mot.

nutty ['nʌtɪ] *adj* (*flavour*) à la noisette; (*col: person*) cinglé(e), dingue.

nuzzle ['nʌzl] *vi*: **to ~ up to** fourrer son nez contre.

NV *abbr* (*US*) = *Nevada*.

NWT *abbr* (*Canada*) = *Northwest Territories*.

NY *abbr* (*US*) = *New York*.

NYC *abbr* (*US*) = *New York City*.

nylon ['naɪlɒn] *n* nylon *m* ♦ *adj* de *or* en nylon; **~s** *npl* bas *mpl* nylon.

nymph [nɪmf] *n* nymphe *f*.

nymphomaniac ['nɪmfəuˈmeɪnɪæk] *adj, n* nymphomane (*f*).

NYSE *n abbr* (*US*) = *New York Stock Exchange*.

NZ *abbr* = *New Zealand*.

O o

O, o [əu] *n* (*letter*) O, o *m*; (*US SCOL*: = *outstanding*) tb (= *très bien*); **O for Oliver**, (*US*) **O for Oboe** O comme Oscar.

oaf [əuf] *n* balourd *m*.

oak [əuk] *n* chêne *m* ♦ *cpd* de *or* en (bois de) chêne.

O&M *n abbr* = *organization and method*.

OAP *n abbr* (*BRIT*) = **old age pensioner**.

oar [ɔː*] *n* aviron *m*, rame *f*; **to put** *or* **shove one's ~ in** (*fig: col*) mettre son grain de sel.

oarsman ['ɔːzmən], **oarswoman** ['ɔːzwumən] *n* rameur/euse; (*NAUT, SPORT*) nageur/euse.

OAS *n abbr* (= *Organization of American States*) OEA *f* (= *Organisation des États américains*).

oasis, *pl* **oases** [əuˈeɪsɪs, əuˈeɪsiːz] *n* oasis *f*.

oath [əuθ] *n* serment *m*; (*swear word*) juron *m*; **to take the ~** prêter serment; **on** (*BRIT*) *or* **under ~** sous serment; assermenté(e).

oatmeal ['əutmiːl] *n* flocons *mpl* d'avoine.

oats [əuts] *n* avoine *f*.

OAU *n abbr* (= *Organization of African Unity*) OUA *f* (= *Organisation de l'unité africaine*).

obdurate ['ɒbdjurɪt] *adj* obstiné(e); impénitent(e); intraitable.

OBE *n abbr* (*BRIT*: = *Order of the British Empire*) *distinction honorifique*.

obedience [əˈbiːdɪəns] *n* obéissance *f*; **in ~ to** conformément à.

obedient [əˈbiːdɪənt] *adj* obéissant(e); **to be ~ to sb/sth** obéir à qn/qch.

obelisk ['ɒbɪlɪsk] *n* obélisque *m*.

obese [əuˈbiːs] *adj* obèse.

obesity [əuˈbiːsɪtɪ] *n* obésité *f*.

obey [əˈbeɪ] *vt* obéir à; (*instructions, regulations*) se conformer à ♦ *vi* obéir.

obituary [əˈbɪtjuərɪ] *n* nécrologie *f*.

object *n* ['ɒbdʒɪkt] objet *m*; (*purpose*) but *m*, objet; (*LING*) complément *m* d'objet ♦ *vi* [əbˈdʒekt]: **to ~ to** (*attitude*) désapprouver; (*proposal*) protester contre, élever une objection contre; **I ~!** je proteste!; **he ~ed that** ... il a fait valoir *or* a objecté que ...; **do you ~ to my smoking?** est-ce que cela vous gêne si je fume?; **what's the ~ of doing that?** quel est l'intérêt de faire cela?; **money is no ~** l'argent n'est pas un problème.

objection [əbˈdʒekʃən] *n* objection *f*; (*drawback*) inconvénient *m*; **if you have no ~** si vous n'y voyez pas d'inconvénient; **to make** *or* **raise an ~** élever une objection.

objectionable [əbˈdʒekʃənəbl] *adj* très désagréable; choquant(e).

objective [əb'dʒɛktɪv] n objectif m ♦ adj objectif(ive).

objectivity [ɔbdʒɪk'tɪvɪtɪ] n objectivité f.

object lesson n (fig) (bonne) illustration.

objector [əb'dʒɛktə*] n opposant/e.

obligation [ɔblɪ'geɪʃən] n obligation f, devoir m; (debt) dette f (de reconnaissance); "without ~" "sans engagement".

obligatory [ə'blɪgətərɪ] adj obligatoire.

oblige [ə'blaɪdʒ] vt (force): to ~ sb to do obliger or forcer qn à faire; (do a favour) rendre service à, obliger; to be ~d to sb for sth être obligé(e) à qn de qch; anything to ~! (col) (toujours prêt à rendre) service!

obliging [ə'blaɪdʒɪŋ] adj obligeant(e), serviable.

oblique [ə'bliːk] adj oblique; (allusion) indirect(e) ♦ n (BRIT TYP): ~ (stroke) barre f oblique.

obliterate [ə'blɪtəreɪt] vt effacer.

oblivion [ə'blɪvɪən] n oubli m.

oblivious [ə'blɪvɪəs] adj: ~ of oublieux(euse) de.

oblong [ɔblɔŋ] adj oblong(ue) ♦ n rectangle m.

obnoxious [əb'nɔkʃəs] adj odieux(euse); (smell) nauséabond(e).

o.b.o. abbr (US: = or best offer. in classified ads) ≈ à débattre.

oboe ['əubəu] n hautbois m.

obscene [əb'siːn] adj obscène.

obscenity [əb'sɛnɪtɪ] n obscénité f.

obscure [əb'skjuə*] adj obscur(e) ♦ vt obscurcir; (hide: sun) cacher.

obscurity [əb'skjuərɪtɪ] n obscurité f.

obsequious [əb'siːkwɪəs] adj obséquieux(euse).

observable [əb'zəːvəbl] adj observable; (appreciable) notable.

observance [əb'zəːvns] n observance f, observation f; **religious ~s** observances religieuses.

observant [əb'zəːvnt] adj observateur(trice).

observation [ɔbzə'veɪʃən] n observation f; (by police etc) surveillance f.

observation post n (MIL) poste m d'observation.

observatory [əb'zəːvətrɪ] n observatoire m.

observe [əb'zəːv] vt observer; (remark) faire observer or remarquer.

observer [əb'zəːvə*] n observateur/trice.

obsess [əb'sɛs] vt obséder; to be ~ed by or with sb/sth être obsédé(e) par qn/qch.

obsession [əb'sɛʃən] n obsession f.

obsessive [əb'sɛsɪv] adj obsédant(e).

obsolescence [ɔbsə'lɛsns] n vieillissement m; obsolescence f; **built-in** or **planned** ~ (COMM) désuétude calculée.

obsolescent [ɔbsə'lɛsnt] adj obsolescent(e), en voie d'être périmé(e).

obsolete ['ɔbsəliːt] adj dépassé(e), périmé(e).

obstacle ['ɔbstəkl] n obstacle m.

obstacle race n course f d'obstacles.

obstetrician [ɔbstə'trɪʃən] n obstétricien/ne.

obstetrics [ɔb'stɛtrɪks] n obstétrique f.

obstinacy ['ɔbstɪnəsɪ] n obstination f.

obstinate ['ɔbstɪnɪt] adj obstiné(e); (pain, cold) persistant(e).

obstreperous [əb'strɛpərəs] adj turbulent(e).

obstruct [əb'strʌkt] vt (block) boucher, obstruer; (halt) arrêter; (hinder) entraver.

obstruction [əb'strʌkʃən] n obstruction f; obstacle m.

obstructive [əb'strʌktɪv] adj obstructionniste.

obtain [əb'teɪn] vt obtenir ♦ vi avoir cours.

obtainable [əb'teɪnəbl] adj qu'on peut obtenir.

obtrusive [əb'truːsɪv] adj (person) importun(e); (smell) pénétrant(e); (building etc) trop en évidence.

obtuse [əb'tjuːs] adj obtus(e).

obverse ['ɔbvəːs] n (of medal, coin) côté m face; (fig) contrepartie f.

obviate ['ɔbvɪeɪt] vt parer à, obvier à.

obvious ['ɔbvɪəs] adj évident(e), manifeste.

obviously ['ɔbvɪəslɪ] adv manifestement; (of course): ~, he ... or he ~ ... il est bien évident qu'il ...; ~! bien sûr!; ~ not! évidemment pas!, bien sûr que non!

OCAS n abbr (= Organization of Central American States) ODEAC f (= Organisation des États d'Amérique centrale).

occasion [ə'keɪʒən] n occasion f; (event) événement m ♦ vt occasionner, causer; **on that** ~ à cette occasion; **to rise to the** ~ se montrer à la hauteur de la situation.

occasional [ə'keɪʒənl] adj pris(e) (or fait(e) etc) de temps en temps; occasionnel(le).

occasionally [ə'keɪʒənəlɪ] adv de temps en temps; **very** ~ (assez) rarement.

occasional table n table décorative.

occult [ɔ'kʌlt] adj occulte ♦ n: **the** ~ le surnaturel.

occupancy ['ɔkjupənsɪ] n occupation f.

occupant ['ɔkjupənt] n occupant m.

occupation [ɔkju'peɪʃən] n occupation f; (job) métier m, profession f; **unfit for** ~ (house) impropre à l'habitation.

occupational [ɔkju'peɪʃənl] adj (accident, disease) du travail; (hazard) du métier.

occupational guidance n (BRIT) orientation professionnelle.

occupational pension n retraite professionnelle.

occupational therapy n ergothérapie f.

occupier ['ɔkjupaɪə*] n occupant/e.

occupy ['ɔkjupaɪ] vt occuper; **to** ~ **o.s. with** or **by doing** s'occuper à faire; **to be occupied with sth** être occupé(e) avec qch.

occur [ə'kəː*] vi se produire; (difficulty, opportunity) se présenter; (phenomenon, error) se rencontrer; **to** ~ **to sb** venir à l'esprit de qn.

occurrence [ə'kʌrəns] n présence f, existence f; cas m, fait m.

ocean ['əuʃən] n océan m; ~**s of** (col) des masses de.

ocean bed *n* fond (sous-)marin.

ocean-going ['əuʃəngəuɪŋ] *adj* de haute mer.

Oceania [əuʃɪ'eɪnɪə] *n* Océanie *f*.

ocean liner *n* paquebot *m*.

ochre ['əukə*] *adj* ocre.

o'clock [ə'klɔk] *adv*: **it is 5 ~** il est 5 heures.

OCR *n abbr* = **optical character reader, optical character recognition.**

Oct. *abbr* (= *October*) oct.

octagonal [ɔk'tægənl] *adj* octogonal(e).

octane ['ɔkteɪn] *n* octane *m*; **high-~ petrol** *or* (*US*) **gas** essence *f* à indice d'octane élevé.

octave ['ɔktɪv] *n* octave *f*.

October [ɔk'təubə*] *n* octobre *m*; *for phrases see also* **July.**

octogenarian ['ɔktəudʒɪ'nɛərɪən] *n* octogénaire *m/f*.

octopus ['ɔktəpəs] *n* pieuvre *f*.

odd [ɔd] *adj* (*strange*) bizarre, curieux(euse); (*number*) impair(e); (*left over*) qui reste, en plus; (*not of a set*) dépareillé(e); **60-~** 60 et quelques; **at ~ times** de temps en temps; **the ~ one out** l'exception *f*.

oddball ['ɔdbɔːl] *n* (*col*) excentrique *m/f*.

oddity ['ɔdɪtɪ] *n* bizarrerie *f*; (*person*) excentrique *m/f*.

odd-job man [ɔd'dʒɔb-] *n* homme *m* à tout faire.

odd jobs *npl* petits travaux divers.

oddly ['ɔdlɪ] *adv* bizarrement, curieusement.

oddments ['ɔdmənts] *npl* (*BRIT COMM*) fins *fpl* de série.

odds [ɔdz] *npl* (*in betting*) cote *f*; **the ~ are against his coming** il y a peu de chances qu'il vienne; **it makes no ~** cela n'a pas d'importance; **to succeed against all the ~** réussir contre toute attente; **~ and ends** de petites choses; **at ~** en désaccord.

odds-on [ɔdz'ɔn] *adj*: **the ~ favourite** le grand favori; **it's ~ that he'll come** il y a toutes les chances *or* gros à parier qu'il vienne.

ode [əud] *n* ode *f*.

odious ['əudɪəs] *adj* odieux(euse), détestable.

odometer [ɔ'dɔmɪtə*] *n* odomètre *m*.

odour, (*US*) **odor** ['əudə*] *n* odeur *f*.

odo(u)rless ['əudəlɪs] *adj* inodore.

OECD *n abbr* (= *Organization for Economic Co-operation and Development*) OCDE *f* (= *Organisation de coopération et de développement économique*).

oesophagus, (*US*) **esophagus** [iː'sɔfəgəs] *n* œsophage *m*.

oestrogen, (*US*) **estrogen** ['iːstraudʒən] *n* œstrogène *m*.

=============== *KEYWORD*

of [ɔv, əv] *prep* **1** (*gen*) de; **a friend ~ ours** un de nos amis; **a boy ~ 10** un garçon de 10 ans; **that was kind ~ you** c'était gentil de votre part
2 (*expressing quantity, amount, dates etc*) de;

a kilo ~ flour un kilo de farine; **how much ~ this do you need?** combien vous en faut-il?; **there were 3 ~ them** (*people*) ils étaient 3; (*objects*) il y en avait 3; **3 ~ us went** 3 d'entre nous y sont allé(e)s; **the 5th ~ July** le 5 juillet; **a quarter ~ 4** (*US*) 4 heures moins le quart
3 (*from, out of*) en, de; **a statue ~ marble** une statue de *or* en marbre; **made ~ wood** (fait) en bois.

off [ɔf] *adj, adv* (*engine*) coupé(e); (*tap*) fermé(e); (*BRIT: food*) mauvais(e), avancé(e); (*: milk*) tourné(e); (*absent*) absent(e); (*cancelled*) annulé(e); (*removed*): **the lid was ~** le couvercle était retiré *or* n'était pas mis ♦ *prep* de; sur; **to be ~** (*to leave*) partir, s'en aller; **I must be ~** il faut que je file; **to be ~ sick** être absent pour cause de maladie; **a day ~** un jour de congé; **to have an ~ day** n'être pas en forme; **he had his coat ~** il avait enlevé son manteau; **the hook is ~** le crochet s'est détaché; le crochet n'est pas mis; **10% ~** (*COMM*) 10% de rabais; **5 km ~ (the road)** à 5 km (de la route); **~ the coast** au large de la côte; **a house ~ the main road** une maison à l'écart de la grand-route; **it's a long way ~** c'est loin (d'ici); **I'm ~ meat** je ne mange plus de viande; je n'aime plus la viande; **on the ~ chance** à tout hasard; **to be well/badly ~** être bien/mal loti; (*financially*) être aisé/dans la gêne; **~ and on, on and ~** de temps à autre; **I'm afraid the chicken is ~** (*BRIT: not available*) je regrette, il n'y a plus de poulet; **that's a bit ~** (*fig: col*) c'est un peu fort.

offal ['ɔfl] *n* (*CULIN*) abats *mpl*.

offbeat ['ɔfbiːt] *adj* excentrique.

off-centre [ɔf'sɛntə*] *adj* décentré(e), excentré(e).

off-colour ['ɔf'kʌlə*] *adj* (*BRIT: ill*) malade, mal fichu(e); **to feel ~** être mal fichu.

offence, (*US*) **offense** [ə'fɛns] *n* (*crime*) délit *m*, infraction *f*; **to give ~ to** blesser, offenser; **to take ~ at** se vexer de, s'offenser de; **to commit an ~** commettre une infraction.

offend [ə'fɛnd] *vt* (*person*) offenser, blesser ♦ *vi*: **to ~ against** (*law, rule*) contrevenir à, enfreindre.

offender [ə'fɛndə*] *n* délinquant/e; (*against regulations*) contrevenant/e.

offending [ə'fɛndɪŋ] *adj* incriminé(e).

offense [ə'fɛns] *n* (*US*) = **offence.**

offensive [ə'fɛnsɪv] *adj* offensant(e), choquant(e); (*smell etc*) très déplaisant(e); (*weapon*) offensif(ive) ♦ *n* (*MIL*) offensive *f*.

offer ['ɔfə*] *n* offre *f*, proposition *f* ♦ *vt* offrir, proposer; **to make an ~ for sth** faire une offre pour qch; **to give ~ to sth** offrir qch; **~ sb sth** offrir qch à qn; **to ~ to do sth** proposer de faire qch; **"on special ~"** (*COMM*) "en promotion".

offering [ˈɔfərɪŋ] n offrande f.
offhand [ɔfˈhænd] adj désinvolte ♦ adv spontanément; **I can't tell you** ~ je ne peux pas vous le dire comme ça.
office [ˈɔfɪs] n (place) bureau m; (position) charge f, fonction f; **doctor's** ~ (US) cabinet (médical); **to take** ~ entrer en fonctions; **through his good** ~s (fig) grâce à ses bons offices; **O~ of Fair Trading** (BRIT) organisme de protection contre les pratiques commerciales abusives.
office automation n bureautique f.
office bearer n (of club etc) membre m du bureau.
office block, (US) **office building** n immeuble m de bureaux.
office boy n garçon m de bureau.
office hours npl heures fpl de bureau; (US MED) heures de consultation.
office manager n responsable administratif(ive).
officer [ˈɔfɪsə*] n (MIL etc) officier m; (of organization) membre m du bureau directeur; (also: **police** ~) agent m (de police).
office work n travail m de bureau.
office worker n employé/e de bureau.
official [əˈfɪʃl] adj (authorized) officiel(le) ♦ n officiel m; (civil servant) fonctionnaire m/f; employé/e.
officialdom [əˈfɪʃldəm] n bureaucratie f.
officially [əˈfɪʃəlɪ] adv officiellement.
official receiver n administrateur m judiciaire, syndic m de faillite.
officiate [əˈfɪʃɪeɪt] vi (REL) officier; **to** ~ **as Mayor** exercer les fonctions de maire; **to** ~ **at a marriage** célébrer un mariage.
officious [əˈfɪʃəs] adj trop empressé(e).
offing [ˈɔfɪŋ] n: **in the** ~ (fig) en perspective.
off-key [ɔfˈkiː] adj faux(fausse) ♦ adv faux.
off-licence [ˈɔflaɪsns] n (BRIT: shop) débit m de vins et de spiritueux.

Un **off-licence** est un magasin où l'on vend de l'alcool (à emporter) aux heures où les pubs sont fermés. On peut également y acheter des boissons non alcoolisées, des cigarettes, des chips, des bonbons, des chocolats etc.

---

off-limits [ɔfˈlɪmɪts] adj (esp US) dont l'accès est interdit.
off line adj (COMPUT) (en mode) autonome; (: switched off) non connecté(e).
off-load [ˈɔfləud] vt: **to** ~ **sth (onto)** (goods) décharger qch (sur); (job) se décharger de qch (sur).
off-peak [ˈɔfpiːk] adj aux heures creuses.
off-putting [ˈɔfputɪŋ] adj (BRIT) rébarbatif(ive); rebutant(e), peu engageant(e).
off-season [ˈɔfsiːzn] adj, adv hors-saison (inv).
offset [ˈɔfsɛt] vt irreg (counteract) contrebalancer, compenser ♦ n (also: ~ **printing**) offset m.

offshoot [ˈɔfʃuːt] n (fig) ramification f, antenne f; (: of discussion etc) conséquence f.
offshore [ɔfˈʃɔː*] adj (breeze) de terre; (island) proche du littoral; (fishing) côtier(ière); ~ **oilfield** gisement m pétrolifère en mer.
offside [ˈɔfˈsaɪd] n (AUT: with right-hand drive) côté droit; (: with left-hand drive) côté gauche ♦ adj (AUT) de droite; de gauche; (SPORT) hors jeu.
offspring [ˈɔfsprɪŋ] n progéniture f.
offstage [ɔfˈsteɪdʒ] adv dans les coulisses.
off-the-cuff [ɔfðəˈkʌf] adv au pied levé; de chic.
off-the-job [ˈɔfðəˈdʒɔb] adj: ~ **training** formation professionnelle extérieure.
off-the-peg [ˈɔfðəˈpɛg], (US) **off-the-rack** [ˈɔfðəˈræk] adv en prêt-à-porter.
off-the-record [ˈɔfðəˈrɛkɔːd] adj (remark) confidentiel(le), sans caractère officiel ♦ adv officieusement.
off-white [ˈɔfwaɪt] adj blanc cassé inv.
Ofgas [ˈɔfgæs] n (BRIT: = Office of Gas Supply) organisme qui surveille les activités des compagnies de gaz.
Oftel [ˈɔftɛl] n (BRIT: = Office of Telecommunications) organisme qui supervise les télécommunications.
often [ˈɔfn] adv souvent; **how** ~ **do you go?** vous y allez tous les combien?; **how** ~ **have you been there?** vous y êtes allé combien de fois?; **as** ~ **as not** la plupart du temps.
Ofwat [ˈɔfwɔt] n (BRIT: = Office of Water Services) organisme qui surveille les activités des compagnies des eaux.
ogle [ˈəugl] vt lorgner.
ogre [ˈəugə*] n ogre m.
OH abbr (US) = Ohio.
oh [əu] excl ô!, oh!, ah!
OHMS abbr (BRIT) = On His (or Her) Majesty's Service.
oil [ɔɪl] n huile f; (petroleum) pétrole m; (for central heating) mazout m ♦ vt (machine) graisser.
oilcan [ˈɔɪlkæn] n burette f de graissage; (for storing) bidon m à huile.
oil change n vidange f.
oilfield [ˈɔɪlfiːld] n gisement m de pétrole.
oil filter n (AUT) filtre m à huile.
oil-fired [ˈɔɪlfaɪəd] adj au mazout.
oil gauge n jauge f de niveau d'huile.
oil industry n industrie pétrolière.
oil level n niveau m d'huile.
oil painting n peinture f à l'huile.
oil refinery n raffinerie f de pétrole.
oil rig n derrick m; (at sea) plate-forme pétrolière.
oilskins [ˈɔɪlskɪnz] npl ciré m.
oil slick n nappe f de mazout.
oil tanker n pétrolier m.
oil well n puits m de pétrole.
oily [ˈɔɪlɪ] adj huileux(euse); (food) gras(se).
ointment [ˈɔɪntmənt] n onguent m.

OK *abbr* (*US*) = *Oklahoma*.

O.K., okay ['əu'keɪ] (*col*) *excl* d'accord! ♦ *vt* approuver, donner son accord à ♦ *n*: **to give sth one's** ~ donner son accord à qch ♦ *adj* en règle; en bon état; sain et sauf; acceptable; **is it** ~?, **are you** ~? ça va?; **are you** ~ **for money?** ça va *or* ira question argent?; **it's** ~ **with** *or* **by me** ça me va, c'est d'accord en ce qui me concerne.

Okla. *abbr* (*US*) = *Oklahoma*.

old [əuld] *adj* vieux(vieille); (*person*) vieux, âgé(e); (*former*) ancien(ne), vieux; **how** ~ **are you?** quel âge avez-vous?; **he's 10 years** ~ il a 10 ans, il est âgé de 10 ans; ~**er brother/sister** frère/sœur aîné(e); **any thing will do** n'importe quoi fera l'affaire.

old age *n* vieillesse *f*.

old age pensioner (OAP) *n* (*BRIT*) retraité/e.

old-fashioned ['əuld'fæʃnd] *adj* démodé(e); (*person*) vieux jeu *inv*.

old maid *n* vieille fille.

old people's home *n* maison *f* de retraite.

old-style ['əuldstaɪl] *adj* à l'ancienne (mode).

old-time ['əuld'taɪm] *adj* du temps jadis, d'autrefois.

old-timer ['əuld'taɪmə*] *n* ancien *m*.

old wives' tale *n* conte *m* de bonne femme.

O-level ['əulevl] *n* (*in England and Wales: formerly*) examen passé à l'âge de 16 ans sanctionnant les connaissances de l'élève, ≈ brevet *m* des collèges.

olive ['ɔlɪv] *n* (*fruit*) olive *f*; (*tree*) olivier *m* ♦ *adj* (*also*: ~**-green**) (vert) olive *inv*.

olive oil *n* huile *f* d'olive.

Olympic [əu'lɪmpɪk] *adj* olympique; **the** ~ **Games, the** ~**s** les Jeux *mpl* olympiques.

OM *n abbr* (*BRIT*: = *Order of Merit*) titre honorifique.

Oman [əu'mɑːn] *n* Oman *m*.

OMB *n abbr* (*US*: = *Office of Management and Budget*) service conseillant le président en matière budgétaire.

omelet(te) ['ɔmlɪt] *n* omelette *f*; **ham/cheese** ~ omelette au jambon/fromage.

omen ['əumən] *n* présage *m*.

ominous ['ɔmɪnəs] *adj* menaçant(e), inquiétant(e); (*event*) de mauvais augure.

omission [əu'mɪʃən] *n* omission *f*.

omit [əu'mɪt] *vt* omettre; **to** ~ **to do sth** négliger de faire qch.

omnivorous [ɔm'nɪvrəs] *adj* omnivore.

ON *abbr* (*Canada*) = *Ontario*.

========================= *KEYWORD*

on [ɔn] *prep* **1** (*indicating position*) sur; ~ **the table** sur la table; ~ **the wall** sur le *or* au mur; ~ **the left** à gauche; **I haven't any money** ~ **me** je n'ai pas d'argent sur moi

2 (*indicating means, method, condition etc*): ~ **foot** à pied; ~ **the train/plane** (*be*) dans le train/l'avion; (*go*) en train/avion; ~ **the telephone/radio/television** au téléphone/à la

radio/à la télévision; **to be** ~ **drugs** se droguer; ~ **holiday,** (*US*) ~ **vacation** en vacances; ~ **the continent** sur le continent

3 (*referring to time*): ~ **Friday** vendredi; ~ **Fridays** le vendredi; ~ **June 20th** le 20 juin; **a week** ~ **Friday** vendredi en huit; ~ **arrival** à l'arrivée; ~ **seeing this** en voyant cela

4 (*about, concerning*) sur, de; **a book** ~ **Balzac/physics** un livre sur Balzac/de physique

5 (*at the expense of*): **this round is** ~ **me** c'est ma tournée

♦ *adv* **1** (*referring to dress, covering*): **to have one's coat** ~ avoir (mis) son manteau; **to put one's coat** ~ mettre son manteau; **what's she got** ~? qu'est-ce qu'elle porte?; **screw the lid** ~ **tightly** vissez bien le couvercle

2 (*further, continuously*): **to walk** *etc* ~ continuer à marcher *etc*; ~ **and off** de temps à autre; **from that day** ~ depuis ce jour

♦ *adj* **1** (*in operation: machine*) en marche; (: *radio, TV, light*) allumé(e); (: *tap, gas*) ouvert(e); (: *brakes*) mis(e); **is the meeting still** ~? (*not cancelled*) est-ce que la réunion a bien lieu?; (*in progress*) la réunion dure-t-elle encore?; **it was well** ~ **in the evening** c'était tard dans la soirée; **when is this film** ~? quand passe ce film?

2 (*col*): **that's not** ~! (*not acceptable*) cela ne se fait pas!; (*not possible*) pas question!

========================

ONC *n abbr* (*BRIT*: = *Ordinary National Certificate*) ≈ BT *m*.

once [wʌns] *adv* une fois; (*formerly*) autrefois ♦ *conj* une fois que; ~ **he had left/it was done** une fois qu'il fut parti/que ce fut terminé; **at** ~ tout de suite, immédiatement; (*simultaneously*) à la fois; **all at** ~ *adv* tout d'un coup; ~ **a week** une fois par semaine; ~ **more** encore une fois; **I knew him** ~ je l'ai connu autrefois; ~ **and for all** une fois pour toutes; ~ **upon a time there was ...** il y avait une fois ..., il était une fois ...

oncoming ['ɔnkʌmɪŋ] *adj* (*traffic*) venant en sens inverse.

OND *n abbr* (*BRIT*: = *Ordinary National Diploma*) ≈ BTS *m*.

========================= *KEYWORD*

one [wʌn] *num* un(e); ~ **hundred and fifty** cent cinquante; ~ **day** un jour

♦ *adj* **1** (*sole*) seul(e), unique; **the** ~ **book which** l'unique *or* le seul livre qui; **the** ~ **man who** le seul (homme) qui

2 (*same*) même; **they came in the** ~ **car** ils sont venus dans la même voiture

♦ *pron* **1**: **this** ~ celui-ci(celle-ci); **that** ~ celui-là(celle-là); **I've already got** ~/**a red** ~ j'en ai déjà un(e)/un(e) rouge; ~ **by** ~ un(e) à *or* par un(e); **which** ~ **do you want?** lequel voulez-vous?

2: ~ **another** l'un(e) l'autre; **to look at** ~ **another** se regarder
3 (*impersonal*) on; ~ **never knows** on ne sait jamais; **to cut** ~**'s finger** se couper le doigt
4 (*phrases*): **to be** ~ **up on sb** avoir l'avantage sur qn; **to be at** ~ **(with sb)** être d'accord (avec qn).

one-armed bandit ['wɑnɑːmd-] *n* machine *f* à sous.
one-day excursion ['wʌndeɪ-] *n* (*US*) billet *m* d'aller-retour (valable pour la journée).
One-hundred share index ['wʌnhʌndrəd-] *n* indice *m* Footsie des cent grandes valeurs.
one-man ['wʌn'mæn] *adj* (*business*) dirigé(e) *etc* par un seul homme.
one-man band *n* homme-orchestre *m*.
one-off [wʌn'ɔf] (*BRIT col*) *n* exemplaire *m* unique ♦ *adj* unique.
one-parent family ['wʌnpɛərənt-] *n* famille monoparentale.
one-piece ['wʌnpiːs] *adj*: ~ **bathing suit** maillot *m* une pièce.
onerous ['ɔnərəs] *adj* (*task, duty*) pénible; (*responsibility*) lourd(e).
oneself [wʌn'sɛlf] *pron* se; (*after prep, also emphatic*) soi-même; **by** ~ tout seul.
one-sided [wʌn'saɪdɪd] *adj* (*decision*) unilatéral(e); (*judgment, account*) partial(e); (*contest*) inégal(e).
one-time ['wʌntaɪm] *adj* d'autrefois.
one-to-one ['wʌntəwʌn] *adj* (*relationship*) univoque.
one-upmanship [wʌn'ʌpmənʃɪp] *n*: **the art of** ~ l'art de faire mieux que les autres.
one-way ['wʌnweɪ] *adj* (*street, traffic*) à sens unique.
ongoing ['ɔngəuɪŋ] *adj* en cours; suivi(e).
onion ['ʌnjən] *n* oignon *m*.
on line *adj* (*COMPUT*) en ligne; (: *switched on*) connecté(e).
onlooker ['ɔnlukə*] *n* spectateur/trice.
only ['əunlɪ] *adv* seulement ♦ *adj* seul(e), unique ♦ *conj* seulement, mais; **an** ~ **child** un enfant unique; **not** ~ non seulement; **I** ~ **took one** j'en ai seulement pris un, je n'en ai pris qu'un; **I saw her** ~ **yesterday** je l'ai vue hier encore; **I'd be** ~ **too pleased to help** je ne serais que trop content de vous aider; **I would come,** ~ **I'm very busy** je viendrais bien mais j'ai beaucoup à faire.
ono *abbr* (*BRIT*: = *or nearest offer: in classified ads*) ≈ à débattre.
onset ['ɔnsɛt] *n* début *m*; (*of winter, old age*) approche *f*.
onshore ['ɔnʃɔː*] *adj* (*wind*) du large.
onslaught ['ɔnslɔːt] *n* attaque *f*, assaut *m*.
Ont. *abbr* (*Canada*) = Ontario.
on-the-job ['ɔnðə'dʒɔb] *adj*: ~ **training** formation *f* sur place.
onto ['ɔntu] *prep* = on to.
onus ['əunəs] *n* responsabilité *f*; **the** ~ **is upon** him **to prove it** c'est à lui de le prouver.

onward(s) ['ɔnwəd(z)] *adv* (*move*) en avant.
onyx ['ɔnɪks] *n* onyx *m*.
oops [ups] *excl* houp!; ~-**a-daisy!** houp-là!
ooze [uːz] *vi* suinter.
opacity [əu'pæsɪtɪ] *n* opacité *f*.
opal ['əupl] *n* opale *f*.
opaque [əu'peɪk] *adj* opaque.
OPEC ['əupɛk] *n* *abbr* (= *Organization of Petroleum-Exporting Countries*) OPEP *f* (= Organisation des pays exportateurs de pétrole).
open ['əupn] *adj* ouvert(e); (*car*) découvert(e); (*road, view*) dégagé(e); (*meeting*) public(ique); (*admiration*) manifeste; (*question*) non résolu(e); (*enemy*) déclaré(e) ♦ *vt* ouvrir ♦ *vi* (*flower, eyes, door, debate*) s'ouvrir; (*shop, bank, museum*) ouvrir; (*book etc: commence*) commencer, débuter; **in the** ~ (**air**) en plein air; **the** ~ **sea** le large; ~ **ground** (*among trees*) clairière *f*; (*waste ground*) terrain *m* vague; **to have an** ~ **mind** (**on sth**) avoir l'esprit ouvert (sur qch).
►**open on to** *vt fus* (*subj: room, door*) donner sur.
►**open out** *vt* ouvrir ♦ *vi* s'ouvrir.
►**open up** *vt* ouvrir; (*blocked road*) dégager ♦ *vi* s'ouvrir.
open-air [əupn'ɛə*] *adj* en plein air.
open-and-shut ['əupnən'ʃʌt] *adj*: ~ **case** cas *m* limpide.
open day *n* journée *f* portes ouvertes.
open-ended [əupn'ɛndɪd] *adj* (*fig*) non limité(e).
opener ['əupnə*] *n* (*also*: **can** ~, **tin** ~) ouvre-boîtes *m*.
open-heart surgery [əupn'hɑːt-] *n* chirurgie *f* à cœur ouvert.
opening ['əupnɪŋ] *n* ouverture *f*; (*opportunity*) occasion *f*; débouché *m*; (*job*) poste vacant.
opening night *n* (*THEAT*) première *f*.
open learning centre *n* centre ouvert à tous où l'on dispense un enseignement général à temps partiel.
openly ['əupnlɪ] *adv* ouvertement.
open-minded [əupn'maɪndɪd] *adj* à l'esprit ouvert.
open-necked ['əupnnɛkt] *adj* à col ouvert.
openness ['əupnɪs] *n* (*frankness*) franchise *f*.
open-plan ['əupn'plæn] *adj* sans cloisons.
open prison *n* prison ouverte.
open sandwich *n* canapé *m*.
open shop *n* entreprise qui admet les travailleurs non syndiqués.
Open University *n* (*BRIT*) cours universitaires par correspondance.

*L'***Open University** *a été fondée en 1969. L'enseignement comprend des cours (certaines plages horaires sont réservées à cet effet à la télévision et à la radio), des devoirs qui sont envoyés par l'étudiant à son directeur ou sa directrice d'études, et un stage obligatoire en* *université d'été. Il faut préparer un certain nombre d'unités de valeur pendant une période de temps déterminée et obtenir la moyenne à un certain nombre d'entre elles pour recevoir le diplôme visé.*

opera ['ɔpərə] n opéra m.

opera glasses npl jumelles fpl de théâtre.

opera house n opéra m.

opera singer n chanteur/euse d'opéra.

operate ['ɔpəreɪt] vt (machine) faire marcher, faire fonctionner; (system) pratiquer ♦ vi fonctionner; (drug) faire effet; **to ~ on sb (for)** (MED) opérer qn (de).

operatic [ɔpə'rætɪk] adj d'opéra.

operating ['ɔpəreɪtɪŋ] adj (COMM: costs, profit) d'exploitation; (MED): **~ table/theatre** table f/salle f d'opération.

operating room n (US) salle f d'opération.

operating system n (COMPUT) système m d'exploitation.

operation [ɔpə'reɪʃən] n opération f; (of machine) fonctionnement m; **to have an ~ (for)** se faire opérer (de); **to be in ~** (machine) être en service; (system) être en vigueur.

operational [ɔpə'reɪʃənl] adj opérationnel(le); (ready for use or action) en état de marche; **when the service is fully ~** lorsque le service fonctionnera pleinement.

operative ['ɔpərətɪv] adj (measure) en vigueur ♦ n (in factory) ouvrier/ière; **the ~ word** le mot clef.

operator ['ɔpəreɪtə*] n (of machine) opérateur/trice; (TEL) téléphoniste m/f.

operetta [ɔpə'retə] n opérette f.

ophthalmologist [ɔfθæl'mɔlədʒɪst] n ophtalmologiste m/f, ophtalmologue m/f.

opinion [ə'pɪnjən] n opinion f, avis m; **in my ~** à mon avis; **to seek a second ~** demander un deuxième avis.

opinionated [ə'pɪnjəneɪtɪd] adj aux idées bien arrêtées.

opinion poll n sondage m d'opinion.

opium ['əʊpɪəm] n opium m.

opponent [ə'pəunənt] n adversaire m/f.

opportune ['ɔpətjuːn] adj opportun(e).

opportunist [ɔpə'tjuːnɪst] n opportuniste m/f.

opportunity [ɔpə'tjuːnɪtɪ] n occasion f; **to take the ~ to do** or **of doing** profiter de l'occasion pour faire.

oppose [ə'pəuz] vt s'opposer à; **~d to** adj opposé(e) à; **as ~d to** par opposition à.

opposing [ə'pəuzɪŋ] adj (side) opposé(e).

opposite ['ɔpəzɪt] adj opposé(e); (house etc) d'en face ♦ adv en face ♦ prep en face de ♦ n opposé m, contraire m; (of word) contraire m; **"see ~ page"** "voir ci-contre".

opposite number n (BRIT) homologue m/f.

opposite sex n: **the ~** l'autre sexe.

opposition [ɔpə'zɪʃən] n opposition f.

oppress [ə'pres] vt opprimer.

oppression [ə'preʃən] n oppression f.

oppressive [ə'presɪv] adj oppressif(ive).

opprobrium [ə'prəubrɪəm] n (formal) opprobre m.

opt [ɔpt] vi: **to ~ for** opter pour; **to ~ to do** choisir de faire.

►**opt out** vi (school, hospital) devenir autonome; (health service) devenir privé(e); **to ~ out of** choisir de quitter.

optical ['ɔptɪkl] adj optique; (instrument) d'optique.

optical character reader/recognition (OCR) n lecteur m/lecture f optique.

optical fibre n fibre f optique.

optician [ɔp'tɪʃən] n opticien/ne.

optics ['ɔptɪks] n optique f.

optimism ['ɔptɪmɪzəm] n optimisme m.

optimist ['ɔptɪmɪst] n optimiste m/f.

optimistic [ɔptɪ'mɪstɪk] adj optimiste.

optimum ['ɔptɪməm] adj optimum.

option ['ɔpʃən] n choix m, option f; (SCOL) matière f à option; (COMM) option; **to keep one's ~s open** (fig) ne pas s'engager; **I have no ~** je n'ai pas le choix.

optional ['ɔpʃənl] adj facultatif(ive); (COMM) en option; **~ extras** accessoires mpl en option, options fpl.

opulence ['ɔpjuləns] n opulence f; abondance f.

opulent ['ɔpjulənt] adj opulent(e); abondant(e).

OR abbr (US) = Oregon.

or [ɔː*] conj ou; (with negative): **he hasn't seen ~ heard anything** il n'a rien vu ni entendu; **~ else** sinon; ou bien, ou alors.

oracle ['ɔrəkl] n oracle m.

oral ['ɔːrəl] adj oral(e) ♦ n oral m.

orange ['ɔrɪndʒ] n (fruit) orange f ♦ adj orange inv.

orangeade [ɔrɪndʒ'eɪd] n orangeade f.

oration [ɔː'reɪʃən] n discours solennel.

orator ['ɔrətə*] n orateur/trice.

oratorio [ɔrə'tɔːrɪəu] n oratorio m.

orb [ɔːb] n orbe m.

orbit ['ɔːbɪt] n orbite f ♦ vt décrire une or des orbite(s) autour de; **to be in/go into ~ (round)** être/entrer en orbite (autour de).

orbital ['ɔːbɪtl] n (also: **~ motorway**) périphérique f.

orchard ['ɔːtʃəd] n verger m; **apple ~** verger de pommiers.

orchestra ['ɔːkɪstrə] n orchestre m; (US: seating) (fauteuils mpl d')orchestre.

orchestral [ɔː'kestrəl] adj orchestral(e); (concert) symphonique.

orchestrate ['ɔːkɪstreɪt] vt (MUS, fig) orchestrer.

orchid ['ɔːkɪd] n orchidée f.

ordain [ɔː'deɪn] vt (REL) ordonner; (decide) décréter.

ordeal [ɔː'diːl] n épreuve f.

order ['ɔːdə*] n ordre m; (COMM) commande f

♦ *vt* ordonner; (*COMM*) commander; **in ~** en ordre; (*of document*) en règle; **out of ~** hors service; (*telephone*) en dérangement; **a machine in working ~** une machine en état de marche; **in ~ of size** par ordre de grandeur; **in ~ to do/that** pour faire/que + *sub*; **to ~ sb to do** ordonner à qn de faire; **to place an ~ for sth with sb** commander qch auprès de qn, passer commande de qch à qn; **to be on ~** être en commande; **made to ~** fait sur commande; **to be under ~s to do sth** avoir ordre de faire qch; **a point of ~** un point de procédure; **to the ~ of** (*BANKING*) à l'ordre de.

order book *n* carnet *m* de commandes.

order form *n* bon *m* de commande.

orderly ['ɔːdəlɪ] *n* (*MIL*) ordonnance *f* ♦ *adj* (*room*) en ordre; (*mind*) méthodique; (*person*) qui a de l'ordre.

order number *n* numéro *m* de commande.

ordinal ['ɔːdɪnl] *adj* (*number*) ordinal(e).

ordinary ['ɔːdnrɪ] *adj* ordinaire, normal(e); (*pej*) ordinaire, quelconque; **out of the ~** exceptionnel(le).

ordinary degree *n* (*SCOL*) ≈ licence *f* libre.

Un **ordinary degree** *est un diplôme inférieur à l'*honours degree *que l'on obtient en général après trois années d'études universitaires. Il peut aussi être décerné en cas d'échec à l'*honours degree.

---

ordinary seaman (OS) *n* (*BRIT*) matelot *m*.

ordinary shares *npl* actions *fpl* ordinaires.

ordination [ɔːdɪ'neɪʃən] *n* ordination *f*.

ordnance ['ɔːdnəns] *n* (*MIL: unit*) service *m* du matériel.

Ordnance Survey map *n* (*BRIT*) ≈ carte *f* d'État-major.

ore [ɔː*] *n* minerai *m*.

Ore(g). *abbr* (*US*) = Oregon.

organ ['ɔːgən] *n* organe *m*; (*MUS*) orgue *m*, orgues *fpl*.

organic [ɔː'gænɪk] *adj* organique; (*crops etc*) biologique, naturel(le).

organism ['ɔːgənɪzəm] *n* organisme *m*.

organist ['ɔːgənɪst] *n* organiste *m/f*.

organization [ɔːgənaɪ'zeɪʃən] *n* organisation *f*.

organization chart *n* organigramme *m*.

organize ['ɔːgənaɪz] *vt* organiser; **to get ~d** s'organiser.

organized crime ['ɔːgənaɪzd-] *n* crime organisé, grand banditisme.

organized labour ['ɔːgənaɪzd-] *n* main-d'œuvre syndiquée.

organizer ['ɔːgənaɪzə*] *n* organisateur/trice.

orgasm ['ɔːgæzəm] *n* orgasme *m*.

orgy ['ɔːdʒɪ] *n* orgie *f*.

Orient ['ɔːrɪənt] *n*: **the ~** l'Orient *m*.

oriental [ɔːrɪ'ɛntl] *adj* oriental(e) ♦ *n* Oriental/e.

orientate ['ɔːrɪənteɪt] *vt* orienter.

orifice ['ɔrɪfɪs] *n* orifice *m*.

origin ['ɔrɪdʒɪn] *n* origine *f*; **country of ~** pays *m* d'origine.

original [ə'rɪdʒɪnl] *adj* original(e); (*earliest*) originel(le) ♦ *n* original *m*.

originality [ərɪdʒɪ'nælɪtɪ] *n* originalité *f*.

originally [ə'rɪdʒɪnəlɪ] *adv* (*at first*) à l'origine.

originate [ə'rɪdʒɪneɪt] *vi*: **to ~ from** être originaire de; (*suggestion*) provenir de; **to ~ in** prendre naissance dans; avoir son origine dans.

originator [ə'rɪdʒɪneɪtə*] *n* auteur *m*.

Orkneys ['ɔːknɪz] *npl*: **the ~** (*also*: **the Orkney Islands**) les Orcades *fpl*.

ornament ['ɔːnəmənt] *n* ornement *m*; (*trinket*) bibelot *m*.

ornamental [ɔːnə'mɛntl] *adj* décoratif(ive); (*garden*) d'agrément.

ornamentation [ɔːnəmɛn'teɪʃən] *n* ornementation *f*.

ornate [ɔː'neɪt] *adj* très orné(e).

ornithologist [ɔːnɪ'θɔlədʒɪst] *n* ornithologue *m/f*.

ornithology [ɔːnɪ'θɔlədʒɪ] *n* ornithologie *f*.

orphan ['ɔːfn] *n* orphelin/e ♦ *vt*: **to be ~ed** devenir orphelin.

orphanage ['ɔːfənɪdʒ] *n* orphelinat *m*.

orthodox ['ɔːθədɔks] *adj* orthodoxe.

orthopaedic, (*US*) **orthopedic** [ɔːθə'piːdɪk] *adj* orthopédique.

OS *abbr* (*BRIT*: = *Ordnance Survey*) ≈ IGN *m* (= *Institut géographique national*); (: *NAUT*) = **ordinary seaman**; (: *DRESS*) = **outsize**.

O/S *abbr* = **out of stock**.

Oscar ['ɔskə*] *n* oscar *m*.

oscillate ['ɔsɪleɪt] *vi* osciller.

OSHA *n abbr* (*US*: = *Occupational Safety and Health Administration*) office de l'hygiène et de la sécurité au travail.

Oslo ['ɔzləu] *n* Oslo.

ostensible [ɔs'tɛnsɪbl] *adj* prétendu(e); apparent(e).

ostensibly [ɔs'tɛnsɪblɪ] *adv* en apparence.

ostentation [ɔstɛn'teɪʃən] *n* ostentation *f*.

ostentatious [ɔstɛn'teɪʃəs] *adj* prétentieux(euse); ostentatoire.

osteopath ['ɔstɪəpæθ] *n* ostéopathe *m/f*.

ostracize ['ɔstrəsaɪz] *vt* frapper d'ostracisme.

ostrich ['ɔstrɪtʃ] *n* autruche *f*.

OT *n abbr* (= *Old Testament*) AT *m*.

OTB *n abbr* (*US*: = *off-track betting*) paris pris en dehors du champ de course.

O.T.E. *abbr* (= *on-target earnings*) primes *fpl* sur objectifs inclus.

other ['ʌðə*] *adj* autre ♦ *pron*: **the ~ (one)** l'autre; **~s** (= *people*) d'autres; **some ~ people have still to arrive** on attend encore quelques personnes; **the ~ day** l'autre jour; **~ than** autrement que; à part; **some actor or ~** un certain acteur, je ne sais quel acteur; **somebody or ~** quelqu'un; **the car was none ~ than John's** la voiture n'était autre que celle de John.

otherwise ['ʌðəwaɪz] *adv, conj* autrement; **an ~ good piece of work** par ailleurs, un beau travail.

OTT *abbr* (*col*) = **over the top**; *see* **top**.

otter ['ɔtə*] *n* loutre *f*.

OU *n abbr* (*BRIT*) = **Open University**.

ouch [autʃ] *excl* aïe!

ought, *pt* **ought** [ɔːt] *aux vb*: **I ~ to do it** je devrais le faire, il faudrait que je le fasse; **this ~ to have been corrected** cela aurait dû être corrigé; **he ~ to win** il devrait gagner; **you ~ to go and see it** vous devriez aller le voir.

ounce [auns] *n* once *f* (= 28.35g; 16 in a pound).

our ['auə*] *adj* notre, nos *pl*.

ours [auəz] *pron* le(la) nôtre, les nôtres.

ourselves [auə'sɛlvz] *pron pl* (*reflexive, after preposition*) nous; (*emphatic*) nous-mêmes; **we did it (all) by ~** nous avons fait ça tout seuls.

oust [aust] *vt* évincer.

out [aut] *adv* dehors; (*published, not at home etc*) sorti(e); (*light, fire*) éteint(e); (*on strike*) en grève ♦ *vt*: **to ~ sb** révéler l'homosexualité de qn; **~ here** ici; **~ there** là-bas; **he's ~** (*absent*) il est sorti; (*unconscious*) il est sans connaissance; **to be ~ in one's calculations** s'être trompé dans ses calculs; **to run/back** *etc* **~** sortir en courant/en reculant *etc*; **to be ~ and about** *or* (*US*) **around again** être de nouveau sur pied; **before the week was ~** avant la fin de la semaine; **the journey ~** l'aller *m*; **the boat was 10 km ~** le bateau était à 10 km du rivage; **~ loud** *adv* à haute voix; **~ of** *prep* (*outside*) en dehors de; (*because of: anger etc*) par; (*from among*): **~ of 10** sur 10; (*without*): **~ of petrol** sans essence, à court d'essence; **made ~ of wood** en *or* de bois; **~ of order** (*machine*) en panne; (*TEL: line*) en dérangement; **~ of stock** (*COMM: article*) épuisé(e); (*: shop*) en rupture de stock.

outage ['autɪdʒ] *n* (*esp US: power failure*) panne *f or* coupure *f* de courant.

out-and-out ['autǝndaut] *adj* véritable.

outback ['autbæk] *n* campagne isolée; (*in Australia*) intérieur *m*.

outbid [aut'bɪd] *irreg vt* surenchérir.

outboard ['autbɔːd] *n*: **~ (motor)** (moteur *m*) hors-bord *m*.

outbound ['autbaund] *adj*: **~ (from/for)** en partance (de/pour).

outbreak ['autbreɪk] *n* éruption *f*, explosion *f*; (*start*) déclenchement *m*.

outbuilding ['autbɪldɪŋ] *n* dépendance *f*.

outburst ['autbɜːst] *n* explosion *f*, accès *m*.

outcast ['autkɑːst] *n* exilé/e; (*socially*) paria *m*.

outclass [aut'klɑːs] *vt* surclasser.

outcome ['autkʌm] *n* issue *f*, résultat *m*.

outcrop ['autkrɔp] *n* affleurement *m*.

outcry ['autkraɪ] *n* tollé (général).

outdated [aut'deɪtɪd] *adj* démodé(e).

outdistance [aut'dɪstəns] *vt* distancer.

outdo [aut'duː] *vt irreg* surpasser.

outdoor [aut'dɔː*] *adj* de *or* en plein air.

outdoors [aut'dɔːz] *adv* dehors; au grand air.

outer ['autə*] *adj* extérieur(e); **~ suburbs** grande banlieue.

outer space *n* espace *m* cosmique.

outfit [autfɪt] *n* équipement *m*; (*clothes*) tenue *f*; (*col: COMM*) organisation *f*, boîte *f*.

outfitter ['autfɪtə*] *n* (*BRIT*): **"(gent's) ~'s"** "confection pour hommes".

outgoing ['autgəʊɪŋ] *adj* (*president, tenant*) sortant(e); (*character*) ouvert(e), extraverti(e).

outgoings ['autgəʊɪŋz] *npl* (*BRIT: expenses*) dépenses *fpl*.

outgrow [aut'grəʊ] *vt irreg* (*clothes*) devenir trop grand(e) pour.

outhouse ['authaus] *n* appentis *m*, remise *f*.

outing ['autɪŋ] *n* sortie *f*; excursion *f*.

outlandish [aut'lændɪʃ] *adj* étrange.

outlast [aut'lɑːst] *vt* survivre à.

outlaw ['autlɔː] *n* hors-la-loi *m inv* ♦ *vt* (*person*) mettre hors la loi; (*practice*) proscrire.

outlay ['autleɪ] *n* dépenses *fpl*; (*investment*) mise *f* de fonds.

outlet [autlɛt] *n* (*for liquid etc*) issue *f*, sortie *f*; (*for emotion*) exutoire *m*; (*for goods*) débouché *m*; (*also: retail ~*) point *m* de vente; (*US: ELEC*) prise *f* de courant.

outline ['autlaɪn] *n* (*shape*) contour *m*; (*summary*) esquisse *f*, grandes lignes.

outlive [aut'lɪv] *vt* survivre à.

outlook ['autluk] *n* perspective *f*.

outlying ['autlaɪɪŋ] *adj* écarté(e).

outmanoeuvre [autmə'nuːvə*] *vt* (*rival etc*) avoir au tournant.

outmoded [aut'məudɪd] *adj* démodé(e); dépassé(e).

outnumber [aut'nʌmbə*] *vt* surpasser en nombre.

out-of-court [autəv'kɔːt] *adj, adv* à l'aimable.

out-of-date [autəv'deɪt] *adj* (*passport, ticket*) périmé(e); (*theory, idea*) dépassé(e); (*custom*) désuet(ète); (*clothes*) démodé(e).

out-of-the-way ['autəvðə'weɪ] *adj* loin de tout; (*fig*) insolite.

outpatient ['autpeɪʃənt] *n* malade *m/f* en consultation externe.

outpost ['autpəust] *n* avant-poste *m*.

outpouring ['autpɔːrɪŋ] *n* (*fig*) épanchement(s) *m(pl)*.

output ['autput] *n* rendement *m*, production *f* ♦ *vt* (*COMPUT*) sortir.

outrage ['autreɪdʒ] *n* atrocité *f*, acte *m* de violence; scandale *m* ♦ *vt* outrager.

outrageous [aut'reɪdʒəs] *adj* atroce; scandaleux(euse).

outrider ['autraɪdə*] *n* (*on motorcycle*) motard *m*.

outright *adv* [aut'raɪt] complètement; catégoriquement; carrément; sur le coup ♦ *adj* ['autraɪt] complet(ète); catégorique.

outrun [aut'rʌn] *vt irreg* dépasser.

outset ['autsɛt] n début m.

outshine [aut'ʃaɪn] vt irreg (fig) éclipser.

outside [aut'saɪd] n extérieur m ♦ adj extérieur(e); (remote, unlikely): **an ~ chance** une (très) faible chance ♦ adv (au) dehors, à l'extérieur ♦ prep hors de, à l'extérieur de; **at the ~** (fig) au plus or maximum; **~ left/right** n (FOOTBALL) ailier gauche/droit.

outside broadcast n (RADIO, TV) reportage m.

outside lane n (AUT: in Britain) voie f de droite; (: in US, Europe) voie de gauche.

outside line n (TEL) ligne extérieure.

outsider [aut'saɪdə*] n (in race etc) outsider m; (stranger) étranger/ère.

outsize ['autsaɪz] adj énorme; (clothes) grande taille inv.

outskirts ['autskəːts] npl faubourgs mpl.

outsmart [aut'smaːt] vt se montrer plus malin(igne) or futé(e) que.

outspoken [aut'spəukən] adj très franc(franche).

outspread [aut'sprɛd] adj (wings) déployé(e).

outstanding [aut'stændɪŋ] adj remarquable, exceptionnel(le); (unfinished) en suspens; en souffrance; non réglé(e); **your account is still ~** vous n'avez pas encore tout remboursé.

outstay [aut'steɪ] vt: **to ~ one's welcome** abuser de l'hospitalité de son hôte.

outstretched [aut'strɛtʃt] adj (hand) tendu(e); (body) étendu(e).

outstrip [aut'strɪp] vt (also fig) dépasser.

out-tray ['auttreɪ] n courrier m "départ".

outvote [aut'vaut] vt: **to ~ sb (by)** mettre qn en minorité (par); **to ~ sth (by)** rejeter qch (par).

outward ['autwəd] adj (sign, appearances) extérieur(e); (journey) (d')aller.

outwardly ['autwədlɪ] adv extérieurement; en apparence.

outweigh [aut'weɪ] vt l'emporter sur.

outwit [aut'wɪt] vt se montrer plus malin que.

oval ['əuvl] adj, n ovale (m).

L'**Oval Office** est le bureau personnel du président des États-Unis à la Maison-Blanche, ainsi appelé du fait de sa forme ovale. Par extension, ce terme désigne la présidence elle-même.

ovarian [əu'vɛərɪən] adj ovarien(ne); (cancer) des ovaires.

ovary ['əuvərɪ] n ovaire m.

ovation [əu'veɪʃən] n ovation f.

oven ['ʌvn] n four m.

ovenproof ['ʌvnpruːf] adj allant au four.

oven-ready ['ʌvnrɛdɪ] adj prêt(e) à cuire.

ovenware ['ʌvnwɛə*] n plats mpl allant au four.

over ['əuvə*] adv (par-)dessus; (excessively) trop ♦ adj (or adv) (finished) fini(e), terminé(e); (too much) en plus ♦ prep sur; par-dessus;

(above) au-dessus de; (on the other side of) de l'autre côté de; (more than) plus de; (during) pendant; (about, concerning): **they fell out ~ money/her** ils se sont brouillés pour des questions d'argent/à cause d'elle; **~ here** ici; **~ there** là-bas; **all ~** (everywhere) partout; (finished) fini(e); **~ and ~ (again)** à plusieurs reprises; **~ and above** en plus de; **to ask sb ~** inviter qn (à passer); **to go ~ to sb's** passer chez qn; **now ~ to our Paris correspondent** nous passons l'antenne à notre correspondant à Paris; **the world ~** dans le monde entier; **she's not ~ intelligent** (BRIT) elle n'est pas particulièrement intelligente.

over... ['əuvə*] prefix: **~abundant** surabondant(e).

overact [əuvər'ækt] vi (THEAT) outrer son rôle.

overall adj, n ['əuvərɔːl] adj (length) total(e); (study) d'ensemble ♦ n (BRIT) blouse f ♦ adv [əuvər'ɔːl] dans l'ensemble, en général; **~s** npl bleus mpl (de travail).

overall majority n majorité absolue.

overanxious [əuvər'æŋkʃəs] adj trop anxieux(euse).

overawe [əuvər'ɔː] vt impressionner.

overbalance [əuvə'bæləns] vi basculer.

overbearing [əuvə'bɛərɪŋ] adj impérieux(euse), autoritaire.

overboard ['əuvəbɔːd] adv (NAUT) par-dessus bord; **to go ~ for sth** (fig) s'emballer (pour qch).

overbook [əuvə'buk] vi faire du surbooking.

overcapitalize [əuvə'kæpɪtəlaɪz] vt surcapitaliser.

overcast ['əuvəkɑːst] adj couvert(e).

overcharge [əuvə'tʃɑːdʒ] vt: **to ~ sb for sth** faire payer qch trop cher à qn.

overcoat ['əuvəkəut] n pardessus m.

overcome [əuvə'kʌm] vt irreg triompher de; surmonter ♦ adj (emotionally) bouleversé(e); **~ with grief** accablé(e) de douleur.

overconfident [əuvə'kɒnfɪdənt] adj trop sûr(e) de soi.

overcrowded [əuvə'kraudɪd] adj bondé(e).

overcrowding [əuvə'kraudɪŋ] n surpeuplement m; (in bus) encombrement m.

overdo [əuvə'duː] vt irreg exagérer; (overcook) trop cuire; **to ~ it, to ~ things** (work too hard) en faire trop, se surmener.

overdose ['əuvədəus] n dose excessive.

overdraft ['əuvədrɑːft] n découvert m.

overdrawn [əuvə'drɔːn] adj (account) à découvert.

overdrive ['əuvədraɪv] n (AUT) (vitesse f) surmultipliée f.

overdue [əuvə'djuː] adj en retard; (bill) impayé(e); (recognition) tardif(ive); **that change was long ~** ce changement n'avait que trop tardé.

overemphasis [əuvər'ɛmfəsɪs] n: **to put an ~ on** accorder trop d'importance à.

overestimate [əuvər'ɛstɪmeɪt] vt surestimer.

overexcited [əuvərɪk'saɪtɪd] *adj* surexcité(e).

overexertion [əuvərɪg'zɔ:ʃən] *n* surmenage *m* (physique).

overexpose [əuvərɪk'spəuz] *vt* (*PHOT*) surexposer.

overflow *vi* [əuvə'fləu] déborder ♦ *n* ['əuvəfləu] trop-plein *m*; (*also:* ~ **pipe**) tuyau *m* d'écoulement, trop-plein *m*.

overfly [əuvə'flaɪ] *vt irreg* survoler.

overgenerous [əuvə'dʒɛnərəs] *adj* (*person*) prodigue; (*offer*) excessif(ive).

overgrown [əuvə'grəun] *adj* (*garden*) envahi(e) par la végétation; **he's just an ~ schoolboy** (*fig*) c'est un écolier attardé.

overhang ['əuvə'hæŋ] *irreg vt* surplomber ♦ *vi* faire saillie.

overhaul *vt* [əuvə'hɔ:l] réviser ♦ *n* ['əuvəhɔ:l] révision *f*.

overhead *adv* [əuvə'hɛd] au-dessus ♦ *adj, n* ['əuvəhɛd] *adj* aérien(ne); (*lighting*) vertical(e) ♦ *n* (*US*) = **overheads**.

overheads ['əuvəhɛdz] *npl* (*BRIT*) frais généraux.

overhear [əuvə'hɪə*] *vt irreg* entendre (par hasard).

overheat [əuvə'hi:t] *vi* devenir surchauffé(e); (*engine*) chauffer.

overjoyed [əuvə'dʒɔɪd] *adj* ravi(e), enchanté(e).

overkill ['əuvəkɪl] *n* (*fig*): **it would be ~** ce serait de trop.

overland ['əuvəlænd] *adj, adv* par voie de terre.

overlap *vi* [əuvə'læp] se chevaucher ♦ *n* ['əuvəlæp] chevauchement *m*.

overleaf [əuvə'li:f] *adv* au verso.

overload [əuvə'ləud] *vt* surcharger.

overlook [əuvə'luk] *vt* (*have view of*) donner sur; (*miss*) oublier, négliger; (*forgive*) fermer les yeux sur.

overlord ['əuvəlɔ:d] *n* chef *m* suprême.

overmanning [əuvə'mænɪŋ] *n* sureffectif *m*, main-d'œuvre *f* pléthorique.

overnight *adv* [əuvə'naɪt] (*happen*) durant la nuit; (*fig*) soudain ♦ *adj* ['əuvənaɪt] d'une (*or* de) nuit; soudain(e); **he stayed there ~** il y a passé la nuit; **if you travel ~** ... si tu fais le voyage de nuit ...; **he'll be away ~** il ne rentrera pas ce soir.

overpass ['əuvəpɑ:s] *n* pont autoroutier; (*US*) passerelle *f*, pont *m*.

overpay [əuvə'peɪ] *vt*: **to ~ sb by £50** donner à qn 50 livres de trop.

overplay [əuvə'pleɪ] *vt* exagérer; **to ~ one's hand** trop présumer de sa situation.

overpower [əuvə'pauə*] *vt* vaincre; (*fig*) accabler.

overpowering [əuvə'pauərɪŋ] *adj* irrésistible; (*heat, stench*) suffocant(e).

overproduction ['əuvəprə'dʌkʃən] *n* surproduction *f*.

overrate [əuvə'reɪt] *vt* surestimer.

overreact [əuvəri:'ækt] *vi* réagir de façon excessive.

override [əuvə'raɪd] *vt* (*irreg: like* **ride**) (*order, objection*) passer outre à; (*decision*) annuler.

overriding [əuvə'raɪdɪŋ] *adj* prépondérant(e).

overrule [əuvə'ru:l] *vt* (*decision*) annuler; (*claim*) rejeter.

overrun [əuvə'rʌn] *irreg vt* (*MIL: country etc*) occuper; (*time limit etc*) dépasser ♦ *vi* dépasser le temps imparti; **the town is ~ with tourists** la ville est envahie de touristes.

overseas [əuvə'si:z] *adv* outre-mer; (*abroad*) à l'étranger ♦ *adj* (*trade*) extérieur(e); (*visitor*) étranger(ère).

oversee [əuvə'si:] *vt irreg* surveiller.

overseer ['əuvəsɪə*] *n* (*in factory*) contremaître *m*.

overshadow [əuvə'ʃædəu] *vt* (*fig*) éclipser.

overshoot [əuvə'ʃu:t] *vt irreg* dépasser.

oversight ['əuvəsaɪt] *n* omission *f*, oubli *m*; **due to an ~** par suite d'une inadvertance.

oversimplify [əuvə'sɪmplɪfaɪ] *vt* simplifier à l'excès.

oversleep [əuvə'sli:p] *vi irreg* se réveiller (trop) tard.

overspend [əuvə'spɛnd] *vi irreg* dépenser de trop; **we have overspent by 5,000 dollars** nous avons dépassé notre budget de 5 000 dollars, nous avons dépensé 5 000 dollars de trop.

overspill ['əuvəspɪl] *n* excédent *m* de population.

overstaffed [əuvə'stɑ:ft] *adj*: **to be ~** avoir trop de personnel, être en surnombre.

overstate [əuvə'steɪt] *vt* exagérer.

overstatement [əuvə'steɪtmənt] *n* exagération *f*.

overstay [əuvə'steɪ] *vt*: **to ~ one's welcome (at sb's)** abuser de l'hospitalité de qn.

overstep [əuvə'stɛp] *vt*: **to ~ the mark** dépasser la mesure.

overstock [əuvə'stɔk] *vt* stocker en surabondance.

overstretched [əuvə'strɛtʃt] *adj* (*person*) débordé(e); **my budget is ~** j'ai atteint les limites de mon budget.

overstrike *n* ['əuvəstraɪk] (*on printer*) superposition *f*, double frappe *f* ♦ *vt irreg* [əuvə'straɪk] surimprimer.

overt [əu'vɔ:t] *adj* non dissimulé(e).

overtake [əuvə'teɪk] *vt irreg* dépasser; (*AUT*) dépasser, doubler.

overtaking [əuvə'teɪkɪŋ] *n* (*AUT*) dépassement *m*.

overtax [əuvə'tæks] *vt* (*ECON*) surimposer; (*fig: strength, patience*) abuser de; **to ~ o.s.** se surmener.

overthrow [əuvə'θrəu] *vt irreg* (*government*) renverser.

overtime ['əuvətaɪm] *n* heures *fpl* supplémentaires; **to do** *or* **work ~** faire des heures supplémentaires.

overtime ban n refus m de faire des heures supplémentaires.
overtone ['əuvətəun] n (also: ~s) note f, sous-entendus mpl.
overture ['əuvətʃuə*] n (MUS, fig) ouverture f.
overturn [əuvə'tə:n] vt renverser ♦ vi se retourner.
overview ['əuvəvju:] n vue f d'ensemble.
overweight [əuvə'weit] adj (person) trop gros(se); (luggage) trop lourd(e).
overwhelm [əuvə'wɛlm] vt accabler; submerger; écraser.
overwhelming [əuvə'wɛlmiŋ] adj (victory, defeat) écrasant(e); (desire) irrésistible; one's ~ **impression is of heat** on a une impression dominante de chaleur.
overwhelmingly [əuvə'wɛlmiŋli] adv (vote) en masse; (win) d'une manière écrasante.
overwork [əuvə'wə:k] n surmenage m ♦ vt surmener ♦ vi se surmener.
overwrite [əuvə'rait] vt irreg (COMPUT) écraser.
overwrought [əuvə'rɔ:t] adj excédé(e).
ovulation [ɔvju'leiʃən] n ovulation f.
owe [əu] vt devoir; **to ~ sb sth, to ~ sth to sb** devoir qch à qn.
owing to ['əuiŋtu:] prep à cause de, en raison de.
owl [aul] n hibou m.
own [əun] vt posséder ♦ vi (BRIT): **to ~ to sth** reconnaître or avouer qch; **to ~ to having done sth** avouer avoir fait qch ♦ adj propre; **a room of my ~** une chambre à moi, ma propre chambre; **can I have it for my (very) ~?** puis-je l'avoir pour moi (tout) seul?; **to get one's ~ back** prendre sa revanche; **on one's ~** tout(e) seul(e); **to come into one's ~** trouver sa voie; trouver sa justification.
▶**own up** vi avouer.
own brand n (COMM) marque f de distributeur.
owner ['əunə*] n propriétaire m/f.
owner-occupier ['əunər'ɔkjupaiə*] n propriétaire occupant.
ownership ['əunəʃip] n possession f; **it's under new ~** (shop etc) il y a eu un changement de propriétaire.
own goal n: **he scored an ~** (SPORT) il a marqué un but contre son camp; (fig) cela s'est retourné contre lui.
ox, pl **oxen** [ɔks, 'ɔksn] n bœuf m.

Oxbridge, nom formé à partir des mots Ox(ford) et (Cam)bridge, s'utilise pour parler de ces deux universités comme formant un tout, dans la mesure où elles sont toutes deux les universités britanniques les plus prestigieuses et mondialement connues.

Oxfam ['ɔksfæm] n abbr (BRIT: = Oxford Committee for Famine Relief) association humanitaire.

oxide ['ɔksaid] n oxyde m.
Oxon. ['ɔksn] abbr (BRIT: = Oxoniensis) = **of Oxford**.
oxtail ['ɔksteil] n: ~ **soup** soupe f à la queue de bœuf.
oxyacetylene ['ɔksiə'sɛtili:n] adj oxyacétylénique; ~ **burner**, ~ **lamp** chalumeau m oxyacétylénique.
oxygen ['ɔksidʒən] n oxygène m.
oxygen mask n masque m à oxygène.
oxygen tent n tente f à oxygène.
oyster ['ɔistə*] n huître f.
oz. abbr = **ounce**.
ozone ['əuzəun] n ozone m.

P p

P, p [pi:] n (letter) P, p m; **P for Peter** P comme Pierre.
P abbr = **president, prince**.
p abbr (= page) p; (BRIT) = **penny, pence**.
PA n abbr = **personal assistant, public address system** ♦ abbr (US) = **Pennsylvania**.
pa [pɑ:] n (col) papa m.
Pa. abbr (US) = **Pennsylvania**.
p.a. abbr = **per annum**.
PAC n abbr (US) = political action committee.
pace [peis] n pas m; (speed) allure f; vitesse f ♦ vi: **to ~ up and down** faire les cent pas; **to keep ~ with** aller à la même vitesse que; (events) se tenir au courant de; **to set the ~** (running) donner l'allure; (fig) donner le ton; **to put sb through his ~s** (fig) mettre qn à l'épreuve.
pacemaker ['peismeikə*] n (MED) stimulateur m cardiaque.
pacific [pə'sifik] adj pacifique ♦ n: **the P~** (Ocean) le Pacifique, l'océan m Pacifique.
pacification [pæsifi'keiʃən] n pacification f.
pacifier ['pæsifaiə*] n (US: dummy) tétine f.
pacifist ['pæsifist] n pacifiste m/f.
pacify ['pæsifai] vt pacifier; (soothe) calmer.
pack [pæk] n paquet m; ballot m; (of hounds) meute f; (of thieves, wolves etc) bande f; (of cards) jeu m ♦ vt (goods) empaqueter, emballer; (in suitcase etc) emballer; (box) remplir; (cram) entasser; (press down) tasser; damer; (COMPUT) grouper, tasser ♦ vi: **to ~ (one's bags)** faire ses bagages; **to ~ into** (room, stadium) s'entasser dans; **to send sb ~ing** (col) envoyer promener qn.
▶**pack in** (BRIT col) vi (machine) tomber en panne ♦ vt (boyfriend) plaquer; ~ **it in!** laisse tomber!
▶**pack off** vt (person) envoyer (promener),

expédier.

▶**pack up** *vi* (*BRIT col: machine*) tomber en panne; (*: person*) se tirer ♦ *vt* (*belongings*) ranger; (*goods, presents*) empaqueter, emballer.

package ['pækɪdʒ] *n* paquet *m*; (*of goods*) emballage *m*, conditionnement *m*; (*also:* ~ **deal**) marché global; forfait *m*; (*COMPUT*) progiciel *m* ♦ *vt* (*goods*) conditionner.

package holiday *n* (*BRIT*) vacances organisées.

package tour *n* voyage organisé.

packaging ['pækɪdʒɪŋ] *n* conditionnement *m*.

packed [pækt] *adj* (*crowded*) bondé(e); ~ **lunch** (*BRIT*) repas froid.

packer ['pækə*] *n* (*person*) emballeur/euse; conditionneur/euse.

packet ['pækɪt] *n* paquet *m*.

packet switching [-swɪtʃɪŋ] *n* (*COMPUT*) commutation *f* de paquets.

pack ice ['pækaɪs] *n* banquise *f*.

packing ['pækɪŋ] *n* emballage *m*.

packing case *n* caisse *f* (d'emballage).

pact [pækt] *n* pacte *m*, traité *m*.

pad [pæd] *n* bloc(-notes *m*) *m*; (*for inking*) tampon *m* encreur; (*col: flat*) piaule *f* ♦ *vt* rembourrer ♦ *vi*: **to** ~ **in/about** *etc* entrer/aller et venir *etc* à pas feutrés.

padded cell ['pædɪd-] *n* cellule capitonnée.

padding ['pædɪŋ] *n* rembourrage *m*; (*fig*) délayage *m*.

paddle ['pædl] *n* (*oar*) pagaie *f* ♦ *vi* barboter, faire trempette ♦ *vt*: **to** ~ **a canoe** *etc* pagayer.

paddle steamer *n* bateau *m* à aubes.

paddling pool ['pædlɪŋ-] *n* petit bassin.

paddock ['pædək] *n* enclos *m*; paddock *m*.

paddy ['pædɪ] *n* (*also:* ~ **field**) rizière *f*.

padlock ['pædlɔk] *n* cadenas *m* ♦ *vt* cadenasser.

padre ['pɑːdrɪ] *n* aumônier *m*.

paediatrician, (*US*) **pediatrician** [piːdɪə-'trɪʃən] *n* pédiatre *m/f*.

paediatrics, (*US*) **pediatrics** [piːdɪˈætrɪks] *n* pédiatrie *f*.

paedophile, (*US*) **pedophile** ['piːdəufaɪl] *n* pédophile *m*.

pagan ['peɪgən] *adj, n* païen(ne).

page [peɪdʒ] *n* (*of book*) page *f*; (*also:* ~ **boy**) groom *m*, chasseur *m*; (*at wedding*) garçon *m* d'honneur ♦ *vt* (*in hotel etc*) (faire) appeler.

pageant ['pædʒənt] *n* spectacle *m* historique; grande cérémonie.

pageantry ['pædʒəntrɪ] *n* apparat *m*, pompe *f*.

page break *n* fin *f* or saut *m* de page.

pager ['peɪdʒə*] *n* système *m* de téléappel, bip *m*.

paginate ['pædʒɪneɪt] *vt* paginer.

pagination [pædʒɪˈneɪʃən] *n* pagination *f*.

pagoda [pəˈgəudə] *n* pagode *f*.

paid [peɪd] *pt, pp of* **pay** ♦ *adj* (*work, official*) rémunéré(e); **to put** ~ **to** (*BRIT*) mettre fin à,

mettre par terre.

paid-up ['peɪdʌp], (*US*) **paid-in** ['peɪdɪn] *adj* (*member*) à jour de sa cotisation; (*shares*) libéré(e); ~ **capital** capital versé.

pail [peɪl] *n* seau *m*.

pain [peɪn] *n* douleur *f*; **to be in** ~ souffrir, avoir mal; **to have a** ~ **in** avoir mal à *or* dans; **to take** ~**s to do** se donner du mal pour faire; **on** ~ **of death** sous peine de mort.

pained ['peɪnd] *adj* peiné(e), chagrin(e).

painful ['peɪnful] *adj* douloureux(euse); (*difficult*) difficile, pénible.

painfully ['peɪnfəlɪ] *adv* (*fig: very*) terriblement.

painkiller ['peɪnkɪlə*] *n* calmant *m*.

painless ['peɪnlɪs] *adj* indolore.

painstaking ['peɪnzteɪkɪŋ] *adj* (*person*) soigneux(euse); (*work*) soigné(e).

paint [peɪnt] *n* peinture *f* ♦ *vt* peindre; (*fig*) dépeindre; **to** ~ **the door blue** peindre la porte en bleu; **to** ~ **in oils** faire de la peinture à l'huile.

paintbox ['peɪntbɔks] *n* boîte *f* de couleurs.

paintbrush ['peɪntbrʌʃ] *n* pinceau *m*.

painter ['peɪntə*] *n* peintre *m*.

painting ['peɪntɪŋ] *n* peinture *f*; (*picture*) tableau *m*.

paint-stripper ['peɪntstrɪpə*] *n* décapant *m*.

paintwork ['peɪntwɔːk] *n* (*BRIT*) peintures *fpl*; (*: of car*) peinture *f*.

pair [pɛə*] *n* (*of shoes, gloves etc*) paire *f*; (*couple*) couple *m*; (*twosome*) duo *m*; ~ **of scissors** (paire de) ciseaux *mpl*; ~ **of trousers** pantalon *m*.

▶**pair off** *vi* se mettre par deux.

pajamas [pəˈdʒɑːməz] *npl* (*US*) pyjama(s) *m(pl)*.

Pakistan [pɑːkɪˈstɑːn] *n* Pakistan *m*.

Pakistani [pɑːkɪˈstɑːnɪ] *adj* pakistanais(e) ♦ *n* Pakistanais/e.

PAL [pæl] *n abbr* (*TV:* = *phase alternation line*) PAL *m*.

pal [pæl] *n* (*col*) copain/copine.

palace ['pæləs] *n* palais *m*.

palatable ['pælɪtəbl] *adj* bon(bonne), agréable au goût.

palate ['pælɪt] *n* palais *m* (*ANAT*).

palatial [pəˈleɪʃəl] *adj* grandiose, magnifique.

palaver [pəˈlɑːvə*] *n* palabres *fpl* or *mpl*; histoire(s) *f(pl)*.

pale [peɪl] *adj* pâle ♦ *vi* pâlir ♦ *n*: **to be beyond the** ~ être au ban de la société; **to grow** *or* **turn** ~ (*person*) pâlir; ~ **blue** *adj* bleu pâle *inv*; **to** ~ **into insignificance (beside)** perdre beaucoup d'importance (par rapport à).

paleness ['peɪlnɪs] *n* pâleur *f*.

Palestine ['pælɪstaɪn] *n* Palestine *f*.

Palestinian [pælɪsˈtɪnɪən] *adj* palestinien(ne) ♦ *n* Palestinien/ne.

palette ['pælɪt] *n* palette *f*.

paling ['peɪlɪŋ] *n* (*stake*) palis *m*; (*fence*) palissade *f*.

palisade [pælɪ'seɪd] n palissade f.
pall [pɔːl] n (of smoke) voile m ♦ vi: **to ~ (on)** devenir lassant (pour).
pallet ['pælɪt] n (for goods) palette f.
pallid ['pælɪd] adj blême.
pallor ['pælə*] n pâleur f.
pally ['pælɪ] adj (col) copain(copine).
palm [pɑːm] n (ANAT) paume f; (also: ~ **tree**) palmier m; (leaf, symbol) palme f ♦ vt: **to ~ sth off on sb** (col) refiler qch à qn.
palmist ['pɑːmɪst] n chiromancien/ne.
Palm Sunday n le dimanche des Rameaux.
palpable ['pælpəbl] adj évident(e), manifeste.
palpitation [pælpɪ'teɪʃən] n palpitation f.
paltry ['pɔːltrɪ] adj dérisoire; piètre.
pamper ['pæmpə*] vt gâter, dorloter.
pamphlet ['pæmflət] n brochure f; (political etc) tract m.
pan [pæn] n (also: **sauce~**) casserole f; (also: **frying ~**) poêle f; (of lavatory) cuvette f ♦ vi (CINE) faire un panoramique ♦ vt (col: book, film) éreinter; **to ~ for gold** laver du sable aurifère.
panacea [pænə'sɪə] n panacée f.
Panama ['pænəmɑː] n Panama m.
Panama canal n canal m de Panama.
pancake ['pænkeɪk] n crêpe f.
Pancake Day n (BRIT) mardi gras.
pancake roll n rouleau m de printemps.
pancreas ['pæŋkrɪəs] n pancréas m.
panda ['pændə] n panda m.
panda car n (BRIT) ≈ voiture f pie inv.
pandemonium [pændɪ'məʊnɪəm] n tohu-bohu m.
pander ['pændə*] vi: **to ~ to** flatter bassement; obéir servilement à.
p&h abbr (US: = postage and handling) frais mpl de port.
P&L abbr = profit and loss.
p&p abbr (BRIT: = postage and packing) frais mpl de port.
pane [peɪn] n carreau m (de fenêtre).
panel ['pænl] n (of wood, cloth etc) panneau m; (RADIO, TV) panel m, invités mpl; (of experts) table ronde, comité m.
panel game n (BRIT) jeu m (radiophonique/télévisé).
panelling, (US) **paneling** ['pænəlɪŋ] n boiseries fpl.
panellist, (US) **panelist** ['pænəlɪst] n invité/e (d'un panel), membre d'un panel.
pang [pæŋ] n: **~s of remorse** pincements mpl de remords; **~s of hunger/conscience** tiraillements mpl d'estomac/de la conscience.
panhandler ['pænhændlə*] n (US col) mendiant/e.
panic ['pænɪk] n panique f, affolement m ♦ vi s'affoler, paniquer.
panic buying [-baɪɪŋ] n achats mpl de précaution.
panicky ['pænɪkɪ] adj (person) qui panique or s'affole facilement.

panic-stricken ['pænɪkstrɪkən] adj affolé(e).
pannier ['pænɪə*] n (on animal) bât m; (on bicycle) sacoche f.
panorama [pænə'rɑːmə] n panorama m.
panoramic [pænə'ræmɪk] adj panoramique.
pansy ['pænzɪ] n (BOT) pensée f; (col) tapette f, pédé m.
pant [pænt] vi haleter.
pantechnicon [pæn'tɛknɪkən] n (BRIT) (grand) camion de déménagement.
panther ['pænθə*] n panthère f.
panties ['pæntɪz] npl slip m, culotte f.
pantihose ['pæntɪhəʊz] n (US) collant m.
panto ['pæntəʊ] n = **pantomime**.
pantomime ['pæntəmaɪm] n (BRIT) spectacle m de Noël.

---

*Une **pantomime** (à ne pas confondre avec le mot tel qu'on l'utilise en français), que l'on appelle également de façon familière "panto", est un genre de farce où le personnage principal est souvent un jeune garçon et où il y a toujours une **dame**, c'est-à-dire une vieille femme jouée par un homme, et un méchant. La plupart du temps, l'histoire est basée sur un conte de fées comme Cendrillon ou Le Chat botté, et le public est encouragé à participer en prévenant le héros d'un danger imminent. Ce genre de spectacle, qui s'adresse surtout aux enfants, vise également un public d'adultes au travers des nombreuses plaisanteries faisant allusion à des faits d'actualité.*

---

pantry ['pæntrɪ] n garde-manger m inv; (room) office m.
pants [pænts] n (BRIT: woman's) culotte f, slip m; (: man's) slip m, caleçon m; (US: trousers) pantalon m.
pantsuit ['pæntsuːt] n (US) tailleur-pantalon m.
papacy ['peɪpəsɪ] n papauté f.
papal ['peɪpəl] adj papal(e), pontifical(e).
paparazzi [pæpə'rætsiː] npl paparazzi mpl.
paper ['peɪpə*] n papier m; (also: **wall~**) papier peint; (also: **news~**) journal m; (study, article) article m; (exam) épreuve écrite ♦ adj en or de papier ♦ vt tapisser (de papier peint); **a piece of ~** (odd bit) un bout de papier; (sheet) une feuille de papier; **to put sth down on ~** mettre qch par écrit.
paper advance n (on printer) avance f (du) papier.
paperback ['peɪpəbæk] n livre m de poche; livre broché or non relié ♦ adj: ~ **edition** édition brochée.
paper bag n sac m en papier.
paperboy ['peɪpəbɔɪ] n (selling) vendeur m de journaux; (delivering) livreur m de journaux.
paper clip n trombone m.
paper handkerchief n mouchoir m en papier.
paper mill n papeterie f.
paper money n papier-monnaie m.

paper profit n profit m théorique.
papers ['peɪpəz] npl (also: **identity** ~) papiers mpl (d'identité).
paper shop n (BRIT) marchand m de journaux.
paperweight ['peɪpəweɪt] n presse-papiers m inv.
paperwork ['peɪpəwɔːk] n paperasserie f.
papier-mâché ['pæpɪeɪ'mæʃeɪ] n papier mâché.
paprika ['pæprɪkə] n paprika m.
Pap test, Pap smear ['pæp-] n (MED) frottis m.
par [pɑː*] n pair m; (GOLF) normale f du parcours; **on a** ~ **with** à égalité avec, au même niveau que; **at** ~ au pair; **above/below** ~ au-dessus/au-dessous du pair; **to feel below** or **under** or **not up to** ~ ne pas se sentir en forme.
parable ['pærəbl] n parabole f (REL).
parabola [pə'ræbələ] n parabole f (MATH).
parachute ['pærəʃuːt] n parachute m ♦ vi sauter en parachute.
parachute jump n saut m en parachute.
parachutist ['pærəʃuːtɪst] n parachutiste m/f.
parade [pə'reɪd] n défilé m; (inspection) revue f; (street) boulevard m ♦ vt (fig) faire étalage de ♦ vi défiler; **a fashion** ~ (BRIT) un défilé de mode.
parade ground n terrain m de manœuvre.
paradise ['pærədaɪs] n paradis m.
paradox ['pærədɔks] n paradoxe m.
paradoxical [pærə'dɔksɪkl] adj paradoxal(e).
paradoxically [pærə'dɔksɪklɪ] adv paradoxalement.
paraffin ['pærəfɪn] n (BRIT): ~ (**oil**) pétrole (lampant); **liquid** ~ huile f de paraffine.
paraffin heater n (BRIT) poêle m à mazout.
paraffin lamp n (BRIT) lampe f à pétrole.
paragon ['pærəgən] n parangon m.
paragraph ['pærəgrɑːf] n paragraphe m; **to begin a new** ~ aller à la ligne.
Paraguay ['pærəgwaɪ] n Paraguay m.
Paraguayan [pærə'gwaɪən] adj paraguayen(ne) ♦ n Paraguayen/ne.
parallel ['pærəlɛl] adj: ~ (**with** or **to**) parallèle (à); (fig) analogue (à) ♦ n (line) parallèle f; (fig, GEO) parallèle m.
paralysis, pl **paralyses** [pə'rælɪsɪs, -siːz] n paralysie f.
paralytic [pærə'lɪtɪk] adj paralytique; (BRIT col: drunk) ivre mort(e).
paralyze ['pærəlaɪz] vt paralyser.
paramedic [pærə'mɛdɪk] n auxiliaire m/f médical(e).
parameter [pə'ræmɪtə*] n paramètre m.
paramilitary [pærə'mɪlɪtərɪ] adj paramilitaire.
paramount ['pærəmaunt] adj: **of** ~ **importance** de la plus haute or grande importance.
paranoia [pærə'nɔɪə] n paranoïa f.
paranoid ['pærənɔɪd] adj (PSYCH) paranoïaque; (neurotic) paranoïde.

paranormal [pærə'nɔːml] adj paranormal(e).
paraphernalia [pærəfə'neɪlɪə] n attirail m, affaires fpl.
paraphrase ['pærəfreɪz] vt paraphraser.
paraplegic [pærə'pliːdʒɪk] n paraplégique m/f.
parapsychology [pærəsaɪ'kɔlədʒɪ] n parapsychologie f.
parasite ['pærəsaɪt] n parasite m.
parasol ['pærəsɔl] n ombrelle f; (at café etc) parasol m.
paratrooper ['pærətruːpə*] n parachutiste m (soldat).
parcel ['pɑːsl] n paquet m, colis m ♦ vt (also: ~ up) empaqueter.
▶**parcel out** vt répartir.
parcel bomb n (BRIT) colis piégé.
parcel post n service m de colis postaux.
parch [pɑːtʃ] vt dessécher.
parched [pɑːtʃt] adj (person) assoiffé(e).
parchment ['pɑːtʃmənt] n parchemin m.
pardon ['pɑːdn] n pardon m; grâce f ♦ vt pardonner à; (LAW) gracier; ~! pardon!; ~ **me!** excusez-moi!; **I beg your** ~! pardon!, je suis désolé!; (**I beg your**) ~?, (US) ~ **me?** pardon?
pare [pɛə*] vt (BRIT: nails) couper; (fruit etc) peler; (fig: costs etc) réduire.
parent ['pɛərənt] n père m or mère f; ~**s** npl parents mpl.
parentage ['pɛərəntɪdʒ] n naissance f; **of unknown** ~ de parents inconnus.
parental [pə'rɛntl] adj parental(e), des parents.
parent company n société f mère.
parenthesis, pl **parentheses** [pə'rɛnθɪsɪs, -siːz] n parenthèse f; **in parentheses** entre parenthèses.
parenthood ['pɛərənthud] n paternité f or maternité f.
parenting ['pɛərəntɪŋ] n le métier de parent, le travail d'un parent.
Paris ['pærɪs] n Paris.
parish ['pærɪʃ] n paroisse f; (civil) ≈ commune f ♦ adj paroissial(e).
parish council n (BRIT) ≈ conseil municipal.
parishioner [pə'rɪʃənə*] n paroissien/ne.
Parisian [pə'rɪzɪən] adj parisien(ne) ♦ n Parisien/ne.
parity ['pærɪtɪ] n parité f.
park [pɑːk] n parc m, jardin public ♦ vt garer ♦ vi se garer.
parka ['pɑːkə] n parka m.
parking ['pɑːkɪŋ] n stationnement m; "**no** ~" "stationnement interdit".
parking lights npl feux mpl de stationnement.
parking lot n (US) parking m, parc m de stationnement.
parking meter n parc(o)mètre m.
parking offence, (US) **parking violation** n infraction f au stationnement.
parking place n place f de stationnement.
parking ticket n P.-V. m.
Parkinson's ['pɑːkɪnsənz] n (also: ~ **disease**)

maladie *f* de Parkinson, parkinson *m*.
parkway ['pɑːkweɪ] *n* (*US*) route *f* express (*en site vert ou aménagé*).
parlance ['pɑːləns] *n*: **in common/modern** ~ dans le langage courant/actuel.
parliament ['pɑːləmənt] *n* parlement *m*.

Le **Parliament** *est l'assemblée législative britannique; elle est composée de deux chambres:* la **House of Commons** *et la* **House of Lords**. *Ses bureaux sont les "Houses of Parliament" au palais de Westminster à Londres. Chaque Parliament est en général élu pour cinq ans. Les débats du Parliament sont maintenant retransmis à la télévision.*

---

parliamentary [pɑːlə'mentərɪ] *adj* parlementaire.
parlour, (*US*) **parlor** ['pɑːlə*] *n* salon *m*.
parlous ['pɑːləs] *adj* (*formal*) précaire.
Parmesan [pɑːmɪ'zæn] *n* (*also*: ~ **cheese**) Parmesan *m*.
parochial [pə'rəukɪəl] *adj* paroissial(e); (*pej*) à l'esprit de clocher.
parody ['pærədɪ] *n* parodie *f*.
parole [pə'rəul] *n*: **on** ~ en liberté conditionnelle.
paroxysm ['pærəksɪzəm] *n* (*MED*, *of grief*) paroxysme *m*; (*of anger*) accès *m*.
parquet ['pɑːkeɪ] *n*: ~ **floor(ing)** parquet *m*.
parrot ['pærət] *n* perroquet *m*.
parrot fashion *adv* comme un perroquet.
parry ['pærɪ] *vt* esquiver, parer à.
parsimonious [pɑːsɪ'məunɪəs] *adj* parcimonieux(euse).
parsley ['pɑːslɪ] *n* persil *m*.
parsnip ['pɑːsnɪp] *n* panais *m*.
parson ['pɑːsn] *n* ecclésiastique *m*; (*Church of England*) pasteur *m*.
parsonage ['pɑːsnɪdʒ] *n* presbytère *m*.
part [pɑːt] *n* partie *f*; (*of machine*) pièce *f*; (*THEAT etc*) rôle *m*; (*MUS*) voix *f*, partie ♦ *adj* partiel(le) ♦ *adv* = **partly** ♦ *vt* séparer ♦ *vi* (*people*) se séparer; (*roads*) se diviser; **to take** ~ **in** participer à, prendre part à; **to take sb's** ~ prendre le parti de qn, prendre parti pour qn; **on his** ~ de sa part; **for my** ~ en ce qui me concerne; **for the most** ~ en grande partie; dans la plupart des cas; **for the better** ~ **of the day** pendant la plus grande partie de la journée; **to be** ~ **and parcel of** faire partie de; **to take sth in good/bad** ~ prendre qch du bon/mauvais côté; ~ **of speech** (*LING*) partie *f* du discours.
▶**part with** *vt fus* se séparer de; se défaire de.
partake [pɑː'teɪk] *vi irreg* (*formal*): **to** ~ **of sth** prendre part à qch, partager qch.
part exchange *n* (*BRIT*): **in** ~ en reprise.
partial ['pɑːʃl] *adj* partiel(le); (*unjust*) partial(e); **to be** ~ **to** aimer, avoir un faible pour.
partially ['pɑːʃəlɪ] *adv* en partie, partiellement;

partialement.
participant [pɑː'tɪsɪpənt] *n*: ~ **(in)** participant/e (à).
participate [pɑː'tɪsɪpeɪt] *vi*: **to** ~ **(in)** participer (à), prendre part (à).
participation [pɑːtɪsɪ'peɪʃən] *n* participation *f*.
participle ['pɑːtɪsɪpl] *n* participe *m*.
particle ['pɑːtɪkl] *n* particule *f*.
particular [pə'tɪkjulə*] *adj* (*specific*) particulier(ière); (*special*) particulier, spécial(e); (*fussy*) difficile, exigeant(e); méticuleux(euse); ~**s** *npl* détails *mpl*; (*information*) renseignements *mpl*; **in** ~ surtout, en particulier.
particularly [pə'tɪkjuləlɪ] *adv* particulièrement; (*in particular*) en particulier.
parting ['pɑːtɪŋ] *n* séparation *f*; (*BRIT*: *in hair*) raie *f* ♦ *adj* d'adieu; **his** ~ **shot was ...** il lança en partant ....
partisan [pɑːtɪ'zæn] *n* partisan/e ♦ *adj* partisan(e); de parti.
partition [pɑː'tɪʃən] *n* (*POL*) partition *f*, division *f*; (*wall*) cloison *f*.
partly ['pɑːtlɪ] *adv* en partie, partiellement.
partner ['pɑːtnə*] *n* (*COMM*) partenaire *m/f*; (*at dance*) cavalier/ière ♦ *vt* être l'associé *or* le partenaire *or* le cavalier de.
partnership ['pɑːtnəʃɪp] *n* association *f*; **to go into** ~ **(with), form a** ~ **(with)** s'associer (avec).
part payment *n* acompte *m*.
partridge ['pɑːtrɪdʒ] *n* perdrix *f*.
part-time ['pɑːt'taɪm] *adj*, *adv* à mi-temps, à temps partiel.
part-timer [pɑːt'taɪmə*] *n* (*also*: **part-time worker**) travailleur/euse à temps partiel.
party ['pɑːtɪ] *n* (*POL*) parti *m*; (*team*) équipe *f*, groupe *m*; (*LAW*) partie *f*; (*celebration*) réception *f*; soirée *f*, réunion *f*, fête *f*; **dinner** ~ dîner *m*; **to give** *or* **throw a** ~ donner une réception; **we're having a** ~ **next Saturday** nous organisons une soirée *or* réunion entre amis samedi prochain; **it's for our son's birthday** ~ c'est pour la fête (*or* le goûter) d'anniversaire de notre garçon; **to be a** ~ **to a crime** être impliqué(e) dans un crime.
party line *n* (*POL*) ligne *f* politique; (*TEL*) ligne partagée.
party piece *n* numéro habituel.
party political broadcast *n* émission réservée à un parti politique.
pass [pɑːs] *vt* (*time, object*) passer; (*place*) passer devant; (*car, friend*) croiser; (*exam*) être reçu(e) à, réussir; (*candidate*) admettre; (*overtake, surpass*) dépasser; (*approve*) approuver, accepter; (*law*) promulguer ♦ *vi* passer; (*SCOL*) être reçu(e) *or* admis(e), réussir ♦ *n* (*permit*) laissez-passer *m inv*; carte *f* d'accès *or* d'abonnement; (*in mountains*) col *m*; (*SPORT*) passe *f*; (*SCOL*: *also*: ~ **mark**): **to get a** ~ être reçu(e) (sans mention); **she**

could ~ **for 25** on lui donnerait 25 ans; **to** ~ **sth through a ring** *etc* (faire) passer qch dans un anneau *etc*; **could you** ~ **the vegetables round?** pourriez-vous faire passer les légumes?; **things have come to a pretty** ~ (*BRIT*) voilà où on en est!; **to make a** ~ **at sb** (*col*) faire des avances à qn.

▶**pass away** *vi* mourir.

▶**pass by** *vi* passer ♦ *vt* négliger.

▶**pass down** *vt* (*customs, inheritance*) transmettre.

▶**pass on** *vi* (*die*) s'éteindre, décéder ♦ *vt* (*hand on*): **to** ~ **on (to)** transmettre (à); (: *illness*) passer (à); (: *price rises*) répercuter (sur).

▶**pass out** *vi* s'évanouir; (*BRIT MIL*) sortir (*d'une école militaire*).

▶**pass over** *vt* (*ignore*) passer sous silence.

▶**pass up** *vt* (*opportunity*) laisser passer.

passable ['pɑːsəbl] *adj* (*road*) praticable; (*work*) acceptable.

passage ['pæsɪdʒ] *n* (*also*: ~**way**) couloir *m*; (*gen, in book*) passage *m*; (*by boat*) traversée *f*.

passenger ['pæsɪndʒə*] *n* passager/ère.

passer-by [pɑːsə'baɪ] *n* passant/e.

passing ['pɑːsɪŋ] *adj* (*fig*) passager(ère); **in** ~ en passant.

passing place *n* (*AUT*) aire *f* de croisement.

passion ['pæʃən] *n* passion *f*; **to have a** ~ **for sth** avoir la passion de qch.

passionate ['pæʃənɪt] *adj* passionné(e).

passion fruit *n* fruit *m* de la passion.

passion play *n* mystère *m* de la Passion.

passive ['pæsɪv] *adj* (*also* LING) passif(ive).

passive smoking *n* tabagisme passif.

passkey ['pɑːskiː] *n* passe *m*.

Passover ['pɑːsəuvə*] *n* Pâque juive.

passport ['pɑːspɔːt] *n* passeport *m*.

passport control *n* contrôle *m* des passeports.

password ['pɑːswəːd] *n* mot *m* de passe.

past [pɑːst] *prep* (*further than*) au delà de, plus loin que; *après*; (*later than*) après ♦ *adj* passé(e); (*president etc*) ancien(ne) ♦ *n* passé *m*; **quarter/half** ~ **four** quatre heures et quart/demie; **ten/twenty** ~ **four** quatre heures dix/vingt; **he's** ~ **forty** il a dépassé la quarantaine, il a plus de *or* passé quarante ans; **it's** ~ **midnight** il est plus de minuit, il est passé minuit; **for the** ~ **few/3 days** depuis quelques/3 jours; ces derniers/3 derniers jours; **to run** ~ passer en courant; **he ran** ~ **me** il m'a dépassé en courant; il a passé devant moi en courant; **in the** ~ (*gen*) dans le temps, autrefois; (*LING*) au passé; **I'm** ~ **caring** je ne m'en fais plus; **to be** ~ **it** (*BRIT col*: *person*) avoir passé l'âge.

pasta ['pæstə] *n* pâtes *fpl*.

paste [peɪst] *n* (*glue*) colle *f* (de pâte); (*jewellery*) strass *m*; (*CULIN*) pâté *m* (à tartiner); pâte *f* ♦ *vt* coller; **tomato** ~ concentré *m* de tomate, purée *f* de tomate.

pastel ['pæstl] *adj* pastel *inv*.

pasteurized ['pæstəraɪzd] *adj* pasteurisé(e).

pastille ['pæstl] *n* pastille *f*.

pastime ['pɑːstaɪm] *n* passe-temps *m inv*, distraction *f*.

past master *n* (*BRIT*): **to be a** ~ **at** être expert en.

pastor ['pɑːstə*] *n* pasteur *m*.

pastoral ['pɑːstərl] *adj* pastoral(e).

pastry ['peɪstrɪ] *n* pâte *f*; (*cake*) pâtisserie *f*.

pasture ['pɑːstʃə*] *n* pâturage *m*.

pasty *n* ['pæstɪ] petit pâté (en croûte) ♦ *adj* ['peɪstɪ] pâteux(euse); (*complexion*) terreux(euse).

pat [pæt] *vt* donner une petite tape à ♦ *n*: **a** ~ **of butter** une noisette de beurre; **to give sb/o.s. a** ~ **on the back** (*fig*) congratuler qn/se congratuler; **he knows it (off)** ~, (*US*) **he has it down** ~ il sait cela sur le bout des doigts.

patch [pætʃ] *n* (*of material*) pièce *f*; (*spot*) tache *f*; (*of land*) parcelle *f* ♦ *vt* (*clothes*) rapiécer; **a bad** ~ (*BRIT*) une période difficile.

▶**patch up** *vt* réparer.

patchwork ['pætʃwəːk] *n* patchwork *m*.

patchy ['pætʃɪ] *adj* inégal(e).

pate [peɪt] *n*: **a bald** ~ un crâne chauve *or* dégarni.

pâté ['pæteɪ] *n* pâté *m*, terrine *f*.

patent ['peɪtnt, (*US*) 'pætənt] *n* brevet *m* (d'invention) ♦ *vt* faire breveter ♦ *adj* patent(e), manifeste.

patent leather *n* cuir verni.

patently ['peɪtntlɪ] *adv* manifestement.

patent medicine *n* spécialité *f* pharmaceutique.

patent office *n* bureau *m* des brevets.

paternal [pə'təːnl] *adj* paternel(le).

paternity [pə'təːnɪtɪ] *n* paternité *f*.

paternity suit *n* (*LAW*) action *f* en recherche de paternité.

path [pɑːθ] *n* chemin *m*, sentier *m*; allée *f*; (*of planet*) course *f*; (*of missile*) trajectoire *f*.

pathetic [pə'θetɪk] *adj* (*pitiful*) pitoyable; (*very bad*) lamentable, minable; (*moving*) pathétique.

pathological [pæθə'lɔdʒɪkl] *adj* pathologique.

pathologist [pə'θɔlədʒɪst] *n* pathologiste *m/f*.

pathology [pə'θɔlədʒɪ] *n* pathologie *f*.

pathos ['peɪθɔs] *n* pathétique *m*.

pathway ['pɑːθweɪ] *n* chemin *m*, sentier *m*.

patience ['peɪʃns] *n* patience *f*; (*BRIT*: *CARDS*) réussite *f*; **to lose (one's)** ~ perdre patience.

patient ['peɪʃnt] *n* patient/e; (*in hospital*) malade *m/f* ♦ *adj* patient(e).

patiently ['peɪʃntlɪ] *adv* patiemment.

patio ['pætɪəu] *n* patio *m*.

patriot ['peɪtrɪət] *n* patriote *m/f*.

patriotic [pætrɪ'ɔtɪk] *adj* patriotique; (*person*) patriote.

patriotism ['pætrɪətɪzəm] *n* patriotisme *m*.

patrol [pə'trəul] *n* patrouille *f* ♦ *vt* patrouiller

dans; **to be on** ~ être de patrouille.
patrol boat n patrouilleur m.
patrol car n voiture f de police.
patrolman [pə'trəulmən] n (US) agent m de police.
patron ['peɪtrən] n (in shop) client/e; (of charity) patron/ne; ~ **of the arts** mécène m.
patronage ['pætrənɪdʒ] n patronage m, appui m.
patronize ['pætrənaɪz] vt être (un) client or un habitué de; (fig) traiter avec condescendance.
patronizing ['pætrənaɪzɪŋ] adj condescendant(e).
patron saint n saint(e) patron/ne.
patter ['pætə*] n crépitement m, tapotement m; (sales talk) boniment m ♦ vi crépiter, tapoter.
pattern ['pætən] n modèle m; (SEWING) patron m; (design) motif m; (sample) échantillon m; **behaviour** ~ mode m de comportement.
patterned ['pætənd] adj à motifs.
paucity ['pɔːsɪtɪ] n pénurie f, carence f.
paunch [pɔːntʃ] n gros ventre, bedaine f.
pauper ['pɔːpə*] n indigent/e; ~**'s grave** fosse commune.
pause [pɔːz] n pause f, arrêt m; (MUS) silence m ♦ vi faire une pause, s'arrêter; **to** ~ **for breath** reprendre son souffle; (fig) faire une pause.
pave [peɪv] vt paver, daller; **to** ~ **the way for** ouvrir la voie à.
pavement ['peɪvmənt] n (BRIT) trottoir m; (US) chaussée f.
pavilion [pə'vɪlɪən] n pavillon m; tente f; (SPORT) stand m.
paving ['peɪvɪŋ] n pavage m, dallage m.
paving stone n pavé m.
paw [pɔː] n patte f ♦ vt donner un coup de patte à; (subj: person: pej) tripoter.
pawn [pɔːn] n gage m; (CHESS, also fig) pion m ♦ vt mettre en gage.
pawnbroker ['pɔːnbrəukə*] n prêteur m sur gages.
pawnshop ['pɔːnʃɔp] n mont-de-piété m.
pay [peɪ] n salaire m; (of manual worker) paie f ♦ vb (pt, pp **paid** [peɪd]) vt payer; (be profitable to: also fig) rapporter à ♦ vi payer; (be profitable) être rentable; **how much did you** ~ **for it?** combien l'avez-vous payé?, vous l'avez payé combien?; **I paid £5 for that record** j'ai payé ce disque 5 livres; **to** ~ **one's way** payer sa part; (company) couvrir ses frais; **to** ~ **dividends** (fig) porter ses fruits, s'avérer rentable; **it won't** ~ **you to do so** vous ne gagnerez rien à faire cela; **to** ~ **attention (to)** prêter attention (à).
▶**pay back** vt rembourser.
▶**pay in** vt verser.
▶**pay off** vt (debts) régler, acquitter; (creditor, mortgage) rembourser; (workers) licencier ♦ vi (plan, patience) se révéler payant(e); **to**

~ **sth off in instalments** payer qch à tempérament.
▶**pay out** vt (money) payer, sortir de sa poche; (rope) laisser filer.
▶**pay up** vt (debts) régler; (amount) payer.
payable ['peɪəbl] adj payable; **to make a cheque** ~ **to sb** établir un chèque à l'ordre de qn.
pay award n augmentation f.
pay day n jour m de paie.
PAYE n abbr (BRIT: = pay as you earn) système de retenue des impôts à la source.
payee [peɪ'iː] n bénéficiaire m/f.
pay envelope n (US) (enveloppe f de) paie f.
paying ['peɪɪŋ] adj payant(e); ~ **guest** hôte payant.
payload ['peɪləud] n charge f utile.
payment ['peɪmənt] n paiement m; (of bill) règlement m; (of deposit, cheque) versement m; **advance** ~ (part sum) acompte m; (total sum) paiement anticipé; **deferred** ~, ~ **by instalments** paiement par versements échelonnés; **monthly** ~ mensualité f; **in** ~ **for, in** ~ **of** en règlement de; **on** ~ **of £5** pour 5 livres.
pay packet n (BRIT) paie f.
payphone ['peɪfəun] n cabine f téléphonique, téléphone public.
payroll ['peɪrəul] n registre m du personnel; **to be on a firm's** ~ être employé par une entreprise.
pay slip n (BRIT) bulletin m de paie, feuille f de paie.
pay station n (US) cabine f téléphonique.
PBS n abbr (US: = Public Broadcasting Service) groupement d'aide à la réalisation d'émissions pour la TV publique.
PC n abbr = **personal computer**; (BRIT) = **police constable** ♦ adj abbr = **politically correct** ♦ abbr (BRIT) = Privy Councillor.
pc abbr = **per cent, postcard**.
p/c abbr = **petty cash**.
PCB n abbr = **printed circuit board**.
PD n abbr (US) = **police department**.
pd abbr = **paid**.
PDSA n abbr (BRIT) = People's Dispensary for Sick Animals.
PDT abbr (US: = Pacific Daylight Time) heure d'été du Pacifique.
PE n abbr (= physical education) EPS f ♦ abbr (Canada) = Prince Edward Island.
pea [piː] n (petit) pois.
peace [piːs] n paix f; (calm) calme m, tranquillité f; **to be at** ~ **with sb/sth** être en paix avec qn/qch; **to keep the** ~ (subj: policeman) assurer le maintien de l'ordre; (: citizen) ne pas troubler l'ordre.
peaceable ['piːsəbl] adj paisible, pacifique.
peaceful ['piːsful] adj paisible, calme.
peacekeeper ['piːskiːpə*] n (force) force gardienne de la paix.
peacekeeping ['piːskiːpɪŋ] n maintien m de la

paix.

peacekeeping force n forces fpl qui assurent le maintien de la paix.

peace offering n gage m de réconciliation; (humorous) gage de paix.

peach [piːtʃ] n pêche f.

peacock [ˈpiːkɔk] n paon m.

peak [piːk] n (mountain) pic m, cime f; (fig: highest level) maximum m; (: of career, fame) apogée m.

peak-hour [ˈpiːkauə*] adj (traffic etc) de pointe.

peak hours npl heures fpl d'affluence.

peak period n période f de pointe.

peak rate n plein tarif.

peaky [ˈpiːkɪ] adj (BRIT col) fatigué(e).

peal [piːl] n (of bells) carillon m; ~s of laughter éclats mpl de rire.

peanut [ˈpiːnʌt] n arachide f, cacahuète f.

peanut butter n beurre m de cacahuète.

pear [pɛə*] n poire f.

pearl [pəːl] n perle f.

peasant [ˈpɛznt] n paysan/ne.

peat [piːt] n tourbe f.

pebble [ˈpɛbl] n galet m, caillou m.

peck [pɛk] vt (also: ~ at) donner un coup de bec à; (food) picorer ♦ n coup m de bec; (kiss) bécot m.

pecking order [ˈpɛkɪŋ-] n ordre m hiérarchique.

peckish [ˈpɛkɪʃ] adj (BRIT col): I feel ~ je mangerais bien quelque chose, j'ai la dent.

peculiar [pɪˈkjuːliə*] adj (odd) étrange, bizarre, curieux(euse); (particular) particulier(ière); ~ to particulier à.

peculiarity [pɪkjuːliˈærɪtɪ] n bizarrerie f; particularité f.

pecuniary [pɪˈkjuːniərɪ] adj pécuniaire.

pedal [ˈpɛdl] n pédale f ♦ vi pédaler.

pedal bin n (BRIT) poubelle f à pédale.

pedantic [pɪˈdæntɪk] adj pédant(e).

peddle [ˈpɛdl] vt colporter; (drugs) faire le trafic de.

peddler [ˈpɛdlə*] n colporteur m; camelot m.

pedestal [ˈpɛdəstl] n piédestal m.

pedestrian [pɪˈdɛstriən] n piéton m ♦ adj piétonnier(ière); (fig) prosaïque, terre à terre inv.

pedestrian crossing n (BRIT) passage clouté.

pedestrian precinct n (BRIT) zone piétonne.

pediatrics [piːdɪˈætrɪks] n (US) = **paediatrics**.

pedigree [ˈpɛdɪgriː] n ascendance f; (of animal) pedigree m ♦ cpd (animal) de race.

pedlar [ˈpɛdlə*] n = **peddler**.

pee [piː] vi (col) faire pipi, pisser.

peek [piːk] vi jeter un coup d'œil (furtif).

peel [piːl] n pelure f, épluchure f; (of orange, lemon) écorce f ♦ vt peler, éplucher ♦ vi (paint etc) s'écailler; (wallpaper) se décoller.

▶**peel back** vt décoller.

peeler [ˈpiːlə*] n (potato etc ~) éplucheur m.

peelings [ˈpiːlɪŋz] npl pelures fpl, épluchures fpl.

peep [piːp] n (BRIT: look) coup d'œil furtif; (sound) pépiement m ♦ vi (BRIT) jeter un coup d'œil (furtif).

▶**peep out** vi (BRIT) se montrer (furtivement).

peephole [ˈpiːphəul] n judas m.

peer [pɪə*] vi: to ~ at regarder attentivement, scruter ♦ n (noble) pair m; (equal) pair, égal/e.

peerage [ˈpɪərɪdʒ] n pairie f.

peerless [ˈpɪəlɪs] adj incomparable, sans égal.

peeved [piːvd] adj irrité(e), ennuyé(e).

peevish [ˈpiːvɪʃ] adj grincheux(euse), maussade.

peg [pɛg] n cheville f; (for coat etc) patère f; (BRIT: also: clothes ~) pince f à linge ♦ vt (clothes) accrocher; (BRIT: groundsheet) fixer (avec des piquets); (fig: prices, wages) contrôler, stabiliser.

pejorative [pɪˈdʒɔrətɪv] adj péjoratif(ive).

Pekin [piːˈkɪn] n, **Peking** [piːˈkɪŋ] n Pékin.

pekinese [piːkɪˈniːz] n pékinois m.

pelican [ˈpɛlɪkən] n pélican m.

pelican crossing n (BRIT AUT) feu m à commande manuelle.

pellet [ˈpɛlɪt] n boulette f; (of lead) plomb m.

pell-mell [ˈpɛlˈmɛl] adv pêle-mêle.

pelmet [ˈpɛlmɪt] n cantonnière f; lambrequin m.

pelt [pɛlt] vt: to ~ sb (with) bombarder qn (de) ♦ vi (rain) tomber à seaux ♦ n peau f.

pelvis [ˈpɛlvɪs] n bassin m.

pen [pɛn] n (for writing) stylo m; (for sheep) parc m; (US col: prison) taule f, to put ~ to paper prendre la plume.

penal [ˈpiːnl] adj pénal(e).

penalize [ˈpiːnəlaɪz] vt pénaliser; (fig) désavantager.

penal servitude [-ˈsəːvɪtjuːd] n travaux forcés.

penalty [ˈpɛnltɪ] n pénalité f; sanction f; (fine) amende f; (SPORT) pénalisation f; (FOOTBALL: also: ~ kick) penalty m.

penalty area n (BRIT SPORT) surface f de réparation.

penalty clause n clause pénale.

penalty kick n (FOOTBALL) penalty m.

penalty shoot-out [-ˈʃuːtaut] n (FOOTBALL) épreuve f des penalties.

penance [ˈpɛnəns] n pénitence f.

pence [pɛns] npl (BRIT) see **penny**.

penchant [ˈpɑːʃɑːŋ] n penchant m.

pencil [ˈpɛnsl] n crayon m ♦ vt: to ~ sth in noter qch provisoirement.

pencil case n trousse f (d'écolier).

pencil sharpener n taille-crayon(s) m inv.

pendant [ˈpɛndnt] n pendentif m.

pending [ˈpɛndɪŋ] prep en attendant ♦ adj en suspens.

pendulum [ˈpɛndjuləm] n pendule m; (of clock) balancier m.

penetrate [ˈpɛnɪtreɪt] vt pénétrer dans; péné-

trer.
penetrating ['pɛnɪtreɪtɪŋ] adj pénétrant(e).
penetration [pɛnɪ'treɪʃən] n pénétration f.
penfriend ['pɛnfrɛnd] n (BRIT) correspondant/e.
penguin ['pɛŋgwɪn] n pingouin m.
penicillin [pɛnɪ'sɪlɪn] n pénicilline f.
peninsula [pə'nɪnsjulə] n péninsule f.
penis ['piːnɪs] n pénis m, verge f.
penitence ['pɛnɪtns] n repentir m.
penitent ['pɛnɪtnt] adj repentant(e).
penitentiary [pɛnɪ'tɛnʃərɪ] n (US) prison f.
penknife ['pɛnnaɪf] n canif m.
Penn(a). abbr (US) = Pennsylvania.
pen name n nom m de plume, pseudonyme m.
pennant ['pɛnənt] n flamme f, banderole f.
penniless ['pɛnɪlɪs] adj sans le sou.
Pennines ['pɛnaɪnz] npl: **the ~** les Pennines fpl.
penny, pl **pennies** or **pence** (BRIT) ['pɛnɪ, 'pɛnɪz, pɛns] n penny m (pl pennies) (new: 100 in a pound; old: 12 in a shilling; on tend à employer "pennies" ou "two-pence piece" etc pour les pièces, "pence" pour la valeur).
penpal ['pɛnpæl] n correspondant/e.
penpusher ['pɛnpuʃə*] n (pej) gratte-papier m inv.
pension ['pɛnʃən] n retraite f; (MIL) pension f.
▶**pension off** vt mettre à la retraite.
pensionable ['pɛnʃnəbl] adj qui a droit à une retraite.
pensioner ['pɛnʃənə*] n (BRIT) retraité/e.
pension fund n caisse f de retraite.
pensive ['pɛnsɪv] adj pensif(ive).
pentagon ['pɛntəgən] n pentagone m; **the P~** (US POL) le Pentagone.

> Le **Pentagon** est le nom donné aux bureaux du ministère de la Défense américain, situés à Arlington en Virginie, à cause de la forme pentagonale du bâtiment dans lequel ils se trouvent. Par extension, ce terme est également utilisé en parlant du ministère lui-même.

Pentecost ['pɛntɪkɔst] n Pentecôte f.
penthouse ['pɛnthaus] n appartement m (de luxe) en attique.
pent-up ['pɛntʌp] adj (feelings) refoulé(e).
penultimate [pɪ'nʌltɪmət] adj pénultième, avant-dernier(ière).
penury ['pɛnjurɪ] n misère f.
people ['piːpl] npl gens mpl; personnes fpl; (citizens) peuple m ♦ n (nation, race) peuple m ♦ vt peupler; **several ~ came** plusieurs personnes sont venues; **I know ~ who ...** je connais des gens qui ...; **the room was full of ~** la salle était pleine de monde or de gens; **~ say that ...** on dit or les gens disent que ...; **old ~** les personnes âgées; **young ~** les jeunes; **a man of the ~** un homme du peuple.
PEP [pɛp] n (= personal equity plan) ≈ CEA m (= compte d'épargne en actions)
pep [pɛp] n (col) entrain m, dynamisme m.
▶**pep up** vt (col) remonter.
pepper ['pɛpə*] n poivre m; (vegetable) poivron m ♦ vt poivrer.
peppermint ['pɛpəmɪnt] n (plant) menthe poivrée; (sweet) pastille f de menthe.
pepperoni [pɛpə'rəunɪ] n saucisson sec de porc et de bœuf très poivré.
pepperpot ['pɛpəpɔt] n poivrière f.
peptalk ['pɛptɔːk] n (col) (petit) discours d'encouragement.
per [pə:*] prep par; **~ hour** (miles etc) à l'heure; (fee) (de) l'heure; **~ kilo** etc le kilo etc; **~ day/person** par jour/personne; **as ~ your instructions** conformément à vos instructions.
per annum adv par an.
per capita adj, adv par habitant, par personne.
perceive [pə'siːv] vt percevoir; (notice) remarquer, s'apercevoir de.
per cent adv pour cent; **a 20 ~ discount** une réduction de 20 pour cent.
percentage [pə'sɛntɪdʒ] n pourcentage m; **on a ~ basis** au pourcentage.
percentage point n: **ten ~s** dix pour cent.
perceptible [pə'sɛptɪbl] adj perceptible.
perception [pə'sɛpʃən] n perception f; (insight) sensibilité f.
perceptive [pə'sɛptɪv] adj (remark, person) perspicace.
perch [pə:tʃ] n (fish) perche f; (for bird) perchoir m ♦ vi (se) percher.
percolate ['pə:kəleɪt] vt, vi passer.
percolator ['pə:kəleɪtə*] n percolateur m; cafetière f électrique.
percussion [pə'kʌʃən] n percussion f.
peremptory [pə'rɛmptərɪ] adj péremptoire.
perennial [pə'rɛnɪəl] adj perpétuel(le); (BOT) vivace ♦ n plante f vivace.
perfect adj, n ['pə:fɪkt] adj parfait(e) ♦ n (also: **~ tense**) parfait m ♦ vt [pə'fɛkt] parfaire; mettre au point; **he's a ~ stranger to me** il m'est totalement inconnu.
perfection [pə'fɛkʃən] n perfection f.
perfectionist [pə'fɛkʃənɪst] n perfectionniste m/f.
perfectly ['pə:fɪktlɪ] adv parfaitement; **I'm ~ happy with the situation** cette situation me convient parfaitement; **you know ~ well** vous le savez très bien.
perforate ['pə:fəreɪt] vt perforer, percer.
perforated ulcer ['pə:fəreɪtɪd-] n (MED) ulcère perforé.
perforation [pə:fə'reɪʃən] n perforation f; (line of holes) pointillé m.
perform [pə'fɔ:m] vt (carry out) exécuter, remplir; (concert etc) jouer, donner ♦ vi jouer.
performance [pə'fɔ:məns] n représentation f, spectacle m; (of an artist) interprétation f; (of player etc) prestation f; (of car, engine) performance f; **the team put up a good ~**

l'équipe a bien joué.
performer [pə'fɔːmə*] n artiste m/f.
performing [pə'fɔːmɪŋ] adj (animal) savant(e).
performing arts npl: **the ~** les arts mpl du spectacle.
perfume ['pəːfjuːm] n parfum m ♦ vt parfumer.
perfunctory [pə'fʌŋktərɪ] adj négligent(e), pour la forme.
perhaps [pə'hæps] adv peut-être; **~ he'll ...** peut-être qu'il ...; **~ so/not** peut-être que oui/que non.
peril ['pɛrɪl] n péril m.
perilous ['pɛrɪləs] adj périlleux(euse).
perilously ['pɛrɪləslɪ] adv: **they came ~ close to being caught** ils ont été à deux doigts de se faire prendre.
perimeter [pə'rɪmɪtə*] n périmètre m.
perimeter wall n mur m d'enceinte.
period ['pɪərɪəd] n période f; (HISTORY) époque f; (SCOL) cours m; (full stop) point m; (MED) règles fpl ♦ adj (costume, furniture) d'époque; **for a ~ of three weeks** pour (une période de) trois semaines; **the holiday ~** (BRIT) la période des vacances.
periodic [pɪərɪ'ɔdɪk] adj périodique.
periodical [pɪərɪ'ɔdɪkl] adj périodique ♦ n périodique m.
periodically [pɪərɪ'ɔdɪklɪ] adv périodiquement.
period pains npl (BRIT) douleurs menstruelles.
peripatetic [pɛrɪpə'tɛtɪk] adj (salesman) ambulant; (BRIT: teacher) qui travaille dans plusieurs établissements.
peripheral [pə'rɪfərəl] adj périphérique ♦ n (COMPUT) périphérique m.
periphery [pə'rɪfərɪ] n périphérie f.
periscope ['pɛrɪskəup] n périscope m.
perish ['pɛrɪʃ] vi périr, mourir; (decay) se détériorer.
perishable ['pɛrɪʃəbl] adj périssable.
perishables ['pɛrɪʃəblz] npl denrées fpl périssables.
perishing ['pɛrɪʃɪŋ] adj (BRIT col: cold) glacial(e).
peritonitis [pɛrɪtə'naɪtɪs] n péritonite f.
perjure ['pəːdʒə*] vt: **to ~ o.s.** se parjurer.
perjury ['pəːdʒərɪ] n (LAW: in court) faux témoignage; (breach of oath) parjure m.
perk [pəːk] n (col) avantage m, à-côté m.
▶**perk up** vi (col: cheer up) se ragaillardir.
perky ['pəːkɪ] adj (cheerful) guilleret(te), gai(e).
perm [pəːm] n (for hair) permanente f ♦ vt: **to have one's hair ~ed** se faire faire une permanente.
permanence ['pəːmənəns] n permanence f.
permanent ['pəːmənənt] adj permanent(e); (job, position) permanent, fixe; (dye, ink) indélébile; **I'm not ~ here** je ne suis pas ici à titre définitif; **~ address** adresse habituelle.
permanently ['pəːmənəntlɪ] adv de façon per-

manente.
permeable ['pəːmɪəbl] adj perméable.
permeate ['pəːmɪeɪt] vi s'infiltrer ♦ vt s'infiltrer dans; pénétrer.
permissible [pə'mɪsɪbl] adj permis(e), acceptable.
permission [pə'mɪʃən] n permission f, autorisation f; **to give sb ~ to do sth** donner à qn la permission de faire qch.
permissive [pə'mɪsɪv] adj tolérant(e); **the ~ society** la société de tolérance.
permit n ['pəːmɪt] permis m; (entrance pass) autorisation f, laisser-passer m; (for goods) licence f ♦ vt [pə'mɪt] permettre; **to ~ sb to do** autoriser qn à faire, permettre à qn de faire; **weather ~ting** si le temps le permet.
permutation [pəːmju'teɪʃən] n permutation f.
pernicious [pəː'nɪʃəs] adj pernicieux(euse), nocif(ive).
pernickety [pə'nɪkɪtɪ] adj (col) pointilleux(euse), tatillon(ne); (task) minutieux(euse).
perpendicular [pəːpən'dɪkjulə*] adj, n perpendiculaire (f).
perpetrate ['pəːpɪtreɪt] vt perpétrer, commettre.
perpetual [pə'pɛtjuəl] adj perpétuel(le).
perpetuate [pə'pɛtjueɪt] vt perpétuer.
perpetuity [pəːpɪ'tjuːɪtɪ] n: **in ~** à perpétuité.
perplex [pə'plɛks] vt rendre perplexe; (complicate) embrouiller.
perplexing [pəː'plɛksɪŋ] adj embarrassant(e).
perquisites ['pəːkwɪzɪts] npl (also: **perks**) avantages mpl annexes.
persecute ['pəːsɪkjuːt] vt persécuter.
persecution [pəːsɪ'kjuːʃən] n persécution f.
perseverance [pəːsɪ'vɪərns] n persévérance f, ténacité f.
persevere [pəːsɪ'vɪə*] vi persévérer.
Persia ['pəːʃə] n Perse f.
Persian ['pəːʃən] adj persan(e) ♦ n (LING) persan m; **the (~) Gulf** le golfe Persique.
Persian cat n chat persan.
persist [pə'sɪst] vi: **to ~ (in doing)** persister (à faire), s'obstiner (à faire).
persistence [pə'sɪstəns] n persistance f, obstination f; opiniâtreté f.
persistent [pə'sɪstənt] adj persistant(e), tenace; (lateness, rain) persistant; **~ offender** (LAW) multirécidiviste m/f.
persnickety [pə'snɪkɪtɪ] adj (US col) = **pernickety**.
person ['pəːsn] n personne f; **in ~** en personne; **on or about one's ~** sur soi; **~ to ~ call** (TEL) appel m avec préavis.
personable ['pəːsnəbl] adj de belle prestance, au physique attrayant.
personal ['pəːsnl] adj personnel(le); **~ belongings, ~ effects** effets personnels; **~ hygiene** hygiène f intime; **a ~ interview** un entretien.
personal allowance n (TAX) part f du revenu non imposable.

personal assistant (PA) n secrétaire personnel(le).

personal call n (*TEL*) communication f avec préavis.

personal column n annonces personnelles.

personal computer (PC) n ordinateur individuel, PC m.

personal details npl (*on form etc*) coordonnées fpl.

personal identification number (PIN) n (*COMPUT, BANKING*) numéro m d'identification personnel.

personality [pɜːsəˈnælɪtɪ] n personnalité f.

personally [ˈpɜːsnəlɪ] adv personnellement.

personal organizer n agenda (personnel) (*style Filofax*); (*electronic*) agenda électronique.

personal property n biens personnels.

personal stereo n walkman m ®, baladeur m.

personify [pɜːˈsɒnɪfaɪ] vt personnifier.

personnel [pɜːsəˈnɛl] n personnel m.

personnel department n service m du personnel.

personnel manager n chef m du personnel.

perspective [pəˈspɛktɪv] n perspective f; **to get sth into ~** ramener qch à sa juste mesure.

perspex [ˈpɜːspɛks] n ® (*BRIT*) Plexiglas m ®.

perspicacity [pɜːspɪˈkæsɪtɪ] n perspicacité f.

perspiration [pɜːspɪˈreɪʃən] n transpiration f.

perspire [pəˈspaɪə*] vi transpirer.

persuade [pəˈsweɪd] vt: **to ~ sb to do sth** persuader qn de faire qch, amener or décider qn à faire qch; **to ~ sb of sth/that** persuader qn de qch/que.

persuasion [pəˈsweɪʒən] n persuasion f; (*creed*) conviction f.

persuasive [pəˈsweɪsɪv] adj persuasif(ive).

pert [pɜːt] adj coquin(e), mutin(e).

pertaining [pəˈteɪnɪŋ]: **~ to** prep relatif(ive) à.

pertinent [ˈpɜːtɪnənt] adj pertinent(e).

perturb [pəˈtɜːb] vt troubler, inquiéter.

perturbing [pəˈtɜːbɪŋ] adj troublant(e).

Peru [pəˈruː] n Pérou m.

perusal [pəˈruːzl] n lecture (attentive).

Peruvian [pəˈruːvjən] adj péruvien(ne) ♦ n Péruvien/ne.

pervade [pəˈveɪd] vt se répandre dans, envahir.

pervasive [pəˈveɪsɪv] adj (*smell*) pénétrant(e); (*influence*) insidieux(euse); (*gloom, ideas*) diffus(e).

perverse [pəˈvɜːs] adj pervers(e); (*stubborn*) entêté(e), contrariant(e).

perversion [pəˈvɜːʃən] n perversion f.

perversity [pəˈvɜːsɪtɪ] n perversité f.

pervert n [ˈpɜːvɜːt] perverti/e ♦ vt [pəˈvɜːt] pervertir.

pessimism [ˈpɛsɪmɪzəm] n pessimisme m.

pessimist [ˈpɛsɪmɪst] n pessimiste m/f.

pessimistic [pɛsɪˈmɪstɪk] adj pessimiste.

pest [pɛst] n animal m (*or* insecte m) nuisible; (*fig*) fléau m.

pest control n lutte f contre les nuisibles.

pester [ˈpɛstə*] vt importuner, harceler.

pesticide [ˈpɛstɪsaɪd] n pesticide m.

pestilence [ˈpɛstɪləns] n peste f.

pestle [ˈpɛsl] n pilon m.

pet [pɛt] n animal familier; (*favourite*) chouchou m ♦ vt choyer ♦ vi (*col*) se peloter; **~ lion** etc lion etc apprivoisé.

petal [ˈpɛtl] n pétale m.

peter [ˈpiːtə*]: **to ~ out** vi s'épuiser; s'affaiblir.

petite [pəˈtiːt] adj menu(e).

petition [pəˈtɪʃən] n pétition f ♦ vt adresser une pétition à ♦ vi: **to ~ for divorce** demander le divorce.

pet name n (*BRIT*) petit nom.

petrified [ˈpɛtrɪfaɪd] adj (*fig*) mort(e) de peur.

petrify [ˈpɛtrɪfaɪ] vt pétrifier.

petrochemical [pɛtrəˈkɛmɪkl] adj pétrochimique.

petrodollars [ˈpɛtrəudɒləz] npl pétrodollars mpl.

petrol [ˈpɛtrəl] n (*BRIT*) essence f.

petrol bomb n cocktail m Molotov.

petrol can n (*BRIT*) bidon m à essence.

petrol engine n (*BRIT*) moteur m à essence.

petroleum [pəˈtrəuliəm] n pétrole m.

petroleum jelly n vaseline f.

petrol pump n (*BRIT: in car, at garage*) pompe f à essence.

petrol station n (*BRIT*) station-service f.

petrol tank n (*BRIT*) réservoir m d'essence.

petticoat [ˈpɛtɪkəut] n jupon m.

pettifogging [ˈpɛtɪfɒgɪŋ] adj chicanier(ière).

pettiness [ˈpɛtɪnɪs] n mesquinerie f.

petty [ˈpɛtɪ] adj (*mean*) mesquin(e); (*unimportant*) insignifiant(e), sans importance.

petty cash n caisse f des dépenses courantes, petite caisse.

petty officer n second-maître m.

petulant [ˈpɛtjulənt] adj irritable.

pew [pjuː] n banc m (d'église).

pewter [ˈpjuːtə*] n étain m.

Pfc abbr (*US MIL*) = private first class.

PG n abbr (*CINE*: = parental guidance) avis des parents recommandé.

PGA n abbr = Professional Golfers Association.

PH n abbr (*US MIL*: = Purple Heart) décoration accordée aux blessés de guerre.

PHA n abbr (*US*: = Public Housing Administration) organisme d'aide à la construction.

phallic [ˈfælɪk] adj phallique.

phantom [ˈfæntəm] n fantôme m; (*vision*) fantasme m.

Pharaoh [ˈfɛərəu] n pharaon m.

pharmaceutical [fɑːməˈsjuːtɪkl] adj pharmaceutique ♦ n: **~s** produits mpl pharmaceutiques.

pharmacist [ˈfɑːməsɪst] n pharmacien/ne.

pharmacy [ˈfɑːməsɪ] n pharmacie f.

phase [feɪz] n phase f, période f ♦ vt: **to ~ sth in/out** introduire/supprimer qch progressivement.

PhD abbr (= Doctor of Philosophy) title ≈ Docteur m en Droit or Lettres etc ♦ n ≈ doctorat m; titulaire m d'un doctorat; see also **doctorate.**

pheasant ['feznt] n faisan m.

phenomenon, pl phenomena [fə'nɒmɪnən, -nə] n phénomène m.

phew [fju:] excl ouf!

phial ['faɪəl] n fiole f.

philanderer [fɪ'lændərə*] n don Juan m.

philanthropic [fɪlən'θrɒpɪk] adj philanthropique.

philanthropist [fɪ'lænθrəpɪst] n philanthrope m/f.

philatelist [fɪ'lætəlɪst] n philatéliste m/f.

philately [fɪ'lætəlɪ] n philatélie f.

Philippines ['fɪlɪpiːnz] npl (also: **Philippine Islands**): the ~ les Philippines fpl.

philosopher [fɪ'lɒsəfə*] n philosophe m.

philosophical [fɪlə'sɒfɪkl] adj philosophique.

philosophy [fɪ'lɒsəfɪ] n philosophie f.

phlegm [flɛm] n flegme m.

phlegmatic [flɛg'mætɪk] adj flegmatique.

phobia ['fəʊbjə] n phobie f.

phone [fəʊn] n téléphone m ♦ vt téléphoner à ♦ vi téléphoner; **to be on the ~** avoir le téléphone; (be calling) être au téléphone.
►**phone back** vt, vi rappeler.

phone book n annuaire m.

phone box, phone booth n cabine f téléphonique.

phone call n coup m de fil or de téléphone.

phonecard ['fəʊnkɑːd] n télécarte f.

phone-in ['fəʊnɪn] n (BRIT RADIO, TV) programme m à ligne ouverte.

phone tapping [-tæpɪŋ] n mise f sur écoutes téléphoniques.

phonetics [fə'nɛtɪks] n phonétique f.

phoney ['fəʊnɪ] adj faux(fausse), factice ♦ n (person) charlatan m; fumiste m/f.

phonograph ['fəʊnəgrɑːf] n (US) électrophone m.

phony ['fəʊnɪ] adj, n = **phoney.**

phosphate ['fɒsfeɪt] n phosphate m.

phosphorus ['fɒsfərəs] n phosphore m.

photo ['fəʊtəʊ] n photo f.

photo... ['fəʊtəʊ] prefix photo....

photocall ['fəʊtəʊkɔːl] n séance f de photos pour la presse.

photocopier ['fəʊtəʊkɒpɪə*] n copieur m.

photocopy ['fəʊtəʊkɒpɪ] n photocopie f ♦ vt photocopier.

photoelectric [fəʊtəʊɪ'lɛktrɪk] adj photoélectrique; ~ **cell** cellule f photoélectrique.

Photofit ['fəʊtəʊfɪt] n ® portrait-robot m.

photogenic [fəʊtəʊ'dʒɛnɪk] adj photogénique.

photograph ['fəʊtəgræf] n photographie f ♦ vt photographier; **to take a ~ of sb** prendre qn en photo.

photographer [fə'tɒgrəfə*] n photographe m/f.

photographic [fəʊtə'græfɪk] adj photographique.

photography [fə'tɒgrəfɪ] n photographie f.

photo opportunity n occasion, souvent arrangée, pour prendre des photos d'une personnalité.

Photostat ['fəʊtəʊstæt] n ® photocopie f, photostat m.

photosynthesis [fəʊtəʊ'sɪnθəsɪs] n photosynthèse f.

phrase [freɪz] n expression f; (LING) locution f ♦ vt exprimer; (letter) rédiger.

phrasebook ['freɪzbʊk] n recueil m d'expressions (pour touristes).

physical ['fɪzɪkl] adj physique; ~ **examination** examen médical; ~ **education** éducation physique; ~ **exercises** gymnastique f.

physically ['fɪzɪklɪ] adv physiquement.

physician [fɪ'zɪʃən] n médecin m.

physicist ['fɪzɪsɪst] n physicien/ne.

physics ['fɪzɪks] n physique f.

physiological [fɪzɪə'lɒdʒɪkl] adj physiologique.

physiology [fɪzɪ'ɒlədʒɪ] n physiologie f.

physiotherapist [fɪzɪəʊ'θɛrəpɪst] n kinésithérapeute m/f.

physiothera-py [fɪzɪəʊ'θɛrəpɪ] n kinésithérapie f.

physique [fɪ'ziːk] n (appearance) physique m; (health etc) constitution f.

pianist ['piːənɪst] n pianiste m/f.

piano [pɪ'ænəʊ] n piano m.

piano accordion n (BRIT) accordéon m à touches.

Picardy ['pɪkədɪ] n Picardie f.

piccolo ['pɪkələʊ] n piccolo m.

pick [pɪk] n (tool: also: ~-**axe**) pic m, pioche f ♦ vt choisir; (gather) cueillir; (scab, spot) gratter, écorcher; **take your ~** faites votre choix; **the ~ of** le(la) meilleur(e) de; **to ~ a bone** ronger un os; **to ~ one's nose** se mettre le doigt dans le nez; **to ~ one's teeth** se curer les dents; **to ~ sb's brains** faire appel aux lumières de qn; **to ~ pockets** pratiquer le vol à la tire; **to ~ a quarrel/fight with sb** chercher querelle à/la bagarre avec qn.
►**pick off** vt (kill) (viser soigneusement et) abattre.
►**pick on** vt fus (person) harceler.
►**pick out** vt choisir; (distinguish) distinguer.
►**pick up** vi (improve) remonter, s'améliorer ♦ vt ramasser; (telephone) décrocher; (collect) passer prendre; (AUT: give lift to) prendre; (learn) apprendre; (RADIO, TV, TEL) capter; **to ~ up speed** prendre de la vitesse; **to ~ o.s. up** se relever; **to ~ up where one left off** reprendre là où l'on s'est arrêté.

pickaxe, (US) **pickax** ['pɪkæks] n pioche f.

picket ['pɪkɪt] n (in strike) gréviste m/f participant à un piquet de grève; piquet m de grève ♦ vt mettre un piquet de grève devant.

picket line n piquet m de grève.

pickings ['pɪkɪŋz] npl: **there are rich ~ to be had in ...** il y a gros à gagner dans ....

pickle ['pɪkl] n (also: ~s: as condiment) pickles mpl; (fig): **in a ~** dans le pétrin ♦ vt conserver dans du vinaigre or dans de la saumure.

pick-me-up ['pɪkmiːʌp] n remontant m.

pickpocket ['pɪkpɔkɪt] n pickpocket m.

pickup ['pɪkʌp] n (BRIT: on record player) bras m pick-up; (small truck: also: ~ **truck**, ~ **van**) camionnette f.

picnic ['pɪknɪk] n pique-nique m ♦ vi piqueniquer.

picnicker ['pɪknɪkə*] n pique-niqueur/euse.

pictorial [pɪk'tɔːrɪəl] adj illustré(e).

picture ['pɪktʃə*] n (also TV) image f; (painting) peinture f, tableau m; (photograph) photo(graphie) f; (drawing) dessin m; (film) film m ♦ vt se représenter; (describe) dépeindre, représenter; **the ~s** (BRIT) le cinéma; **to take a ~ of sb/sth** prendre qn/qch en photo; **the overall ~** le tableau d'ensemble; **to put sb in the ~** mettre qn au courant.

picture book n livre m d'images.

picturesque [pɪktʃə'rɛsk] adj pittoresque.

picture window n baie vitrée, fenêtre f panoramique.

piddling ['pɪdlɪŋ] adj (col) insignifiant(e).

pidgin ['pɪdʒɪn] adj: ~ **English** pidgin m.

pie [paɪ] n tourte f; (of meat) pâté m en croûte.

piebald ['paɪbɔːld] adj pie inv.

piece [piːs] n morceau m; (of land) parcelle f; (item): **a ~ of furniture/advice** un meuble/conseil; (DRAUGHTS etc) pion m ♦ vt: **to ~ together** rassembler; **in ~s** (broken) en morceaux, en miettes; (not yet assembled) en pièces détachées; **to take to ~s** démonter; **in one ~** (object) intact(e); **to get back all in one ~** (person) rentrer sain et sauf; **a 10p ~** (BRIT) une pièce de 10p; **~ by ~** morceau par morceau; **a six-~ band** un orchestre de six musiciens; **to say one's ~** réciter son morceau.

piecemeal ['piːsmiːl] adv par bouts.

piece rate n taux m or tarif m à la pièce.

piecework ['piːswəːk] n travail m aux pièces or à la pièce.

pie chart n graphique m à secteurs, camembert m.

Piedmont ['piːdmɔnt] n Piémont m.

pier [pɪə*] n jetée f; (of bridge etc) pile f.

pierce [pɪəs] vt percer, transpercer; **to have one's ears ~d** se faire percer les oreilles.

piercing ['pɪəsɪŋ] adj (cry) perçant(e).

piety ['paɪətɪ] n piété f.

piffling ['pɪflɪŋ] adj insignifiant(e).

pig [pɪg] n cochon m, porc m.

pigeon ['pɪdʒən] n pigeon m.

pigeonhole ['pɪdʒənhəul] n casier m.

pigeon-toed ['pɪdʒəntəud] adj marchant les pieds en dedans.

piggy bank ['pɪgɪ-] n tirelire f.

pigheaded ['pɪg'hɛdɪd] adj entêté(e), têtu(e).

piglet ['pɪglɪt] n petit cochon, porcelet m.

pigment ['pɪgmənt] n pigment m.

pigmentation [pɪgmən'teɪʃən] n pigmentation f.

pigmy ['pɪgmɪ] n = **pygmy**.

pigskin ['pɪgskɪn] n (peau f de) porc m.

pigsty ['pɪgstaɪ] n porcherie f.

pigtail ['pɪgteɪl] n natte f, tresse f.

pike [paɪk] n (spear) pique f; (fish) brochet m.

pilchard ['pɪltʃəd] n pilchard m (sorte de sardine).

pile [paɪl] n (pillar, of books) pile f; (heap) tas m; (of carpet) épaisseur f ♦ vb (also: ~ **up**) vt empiler, entasser ♦ vi s'entasser; **in a ~** en tas.

▶**pile on** vt: **to ~ it on** (col) exagérer.

piles [paɪlz] npl hémorroïdes fpl.

pileup ['paɪlʌp] n (AUT) télescopage m, collision f en série.

pilfer ['pɪlfə*] vt chaparder ♦ vi commettre des larcins.

pilfering ['pɪlfərɪŋ] n chapardage m.

pilgrim ['pɪlgrɪm] n pèlerin m.

pilgrimage ['pɪlgrɪmɪdʒ] n pèlerinage m.

pill [pɪl] n pilule f; **the ~** la pilule; **to be on the ~** prendre la pilule.

pillage ['pɪlɪdʒ] vt piller.

pillar ['pɪlə*] n pilier m.

pillar box n (BRIT) boîte f aux lettres (publique).

pillion ['pɪljən] n (of motor cycle) siège m arrière; **to ride ~** être derrière; (on horse) être en croupe.

pillory ['pɪlərɪ] n pilori m ♦ vt mettre au pilori.

pillow ['pɪləu] n oreiller m.

pillowcase ['pɪləukeɪs], **pillowslip** ['pɪləuslɪp] n taie f d'oreiller.

pilot ['paɪlət] n pilote m ♦ cpd (scheme etc) pilote, expérimental(e) ♦ vt piloter.

pilot boat n bateau-pilote m.

pilot light n veilleuse f.

pimento [pɪ'mɛntəu] n piment m.

pimp [pɪmp] n souteneur m, maquereau m.

pimple ['pɪmpl] n bouton m.

pimply ['pɪmplɪ] adj boutonneux(euse).

PIN n abbr = **personal identification number**.

pin [pɪn] n épingle f; (TECH) cheville f; (BRIT: drawing ~) punaise f; (in grenade) goupille f; (BRIT ELEC: of plug) broche f ♦ vt épingler; **~s and needles** fourmis fpl; **to ~ sb against/to sth** clouer qn contre/à; **to ~ sth on sb** (fig) mettre qch sur le dos de qn.

▶**pin down** vt (fig): **to ~ sb down** obliger qn à répondre; **there's something strange here but I can't quite ~ it down** il y a quelque chose d'étrange ici, mais je n'arrive pas exactement à savoir quoi.

pinafore ['pɪnəfɔː*] n tablier m.

pinafore dress n robe-chasuble f.

pinball ['pɪnbɔːl] n flipper m.

pincers ['pɪnsəz] npl tenailles fpl.

pinch [pɪntʃ] n pincement m; (of salt etc) pincée f ♦ vt pincer; (col: steal) piquer, chiper ♦ vi (shoe) serrer; **at a ~** à la rigueur; **to feel the ~** (fig) se ressentir des restrictions (or de la récession etc).

pinched [pɪntʃt] adj (drawn) tiré(e); **~ with cold** transi(e) de froid; **~ for** (short of): **~ for money** à court d'argent; **~ for space** à l'étroit.

pincushion ['pɪnkuʃən] n pelote f à épingles.

pine [paɪn] n (also: **~ tree**) pin m ♦ vi: **to ~ for** aspirer à, désirer ardemment.

►**pine away** vi dépérir.

pineapple ['paɪnæpl] n ananas m.

pine cone n pomme f de pin.

pine needle n aiguille f de pin.

ping [pɪŋ] n (noise) tintement m.

Ping-Pong ['pɪŋpɔŋ] n ℞ ping-pong m ℞.

pink [pɪŋk] adj rose ♦ n (colour) rose m; (BOT) œillet m, mignardise f.

pinking shears ['pɪŋkɪŋ-] npl ciseaux mpl à denteler.

pin money n (BRIT) argent m de poche.

pinnacle ['pɪnəkl] n pinacle m.

pinpoint ['pɪnpɔɪnt] vt indiquer (avec précision).

pinstripe ['pɪnstraɪp] n rayure très fine.

pint [paɪnt] n pinte f (BRIT = 0.57 l; US = 0.47 l); (BRIT col) ≈ demi m, ≈ pot m.

pinup ['pɪnʌp] n pin-up f inv.

pioneer [paɪə'nɪə*] n explorateur/trice; (early settler) pionnier m; (fig) pionnier, précurseur m ♦ vt être un pionnier de.

pious ['paɪəs] adj pieux(euse).

pip [pɪp] n (seed) pépin m; (BRIT: time signal on radio) top m.

pipe [paɪp] n tuyau m, conduite f; (for smoking) pipe f; (MUS) pipeau m ♦ vt amener par tuyau; **~s** npl (also: **bag~s**) cornemuse f.

►**pipe down** vi (col) se taire.

pipe cleaner n cure-pipe m.

piped music [paɪpt-] n musique f de fond.

pipe dream n chimère f, utopie f.

pipeline ['paɪplaɪn] n (for gas) gazoduc m, pipeline m; (for oil) oléoduc m, pipeline; **it is in the ~** (fig) c'est en route, ça va se faire.

piper ['paɪpə*] n joueur/euse de pipeau (or de cornemuse).

pipe tobacco n tabac m pour la pipe.

piping ['paɪpɪŋ] adv: **~ hot** très chaud(e).

piquant ['pi:kənt] adj piquant(e).

pique [pi:k] n dépit m.

piracy ['paɪərəsɪ] n piraterie f.

pirate ['paɪərət] n pirate m ♦ vt (record, video, book) pirater.

pirate radio n (BRIT) radio f pirate.

pirouette [pɪru'et] n pirouette f ♦ vi faire une or des pirouette(s).

Pisces ['paɪsi:z] n les Poissons mpl; **to be ~** être des Poissons.

piss [pɪs] vi (col!) pisser (!); **~ off!** tire-toi! (!).

pissed [pɪst] adj (BRIT col: drunk) bourré(e).

pistol ['pɪstl] n pistolet m.

piston ['pɪstən] n piston m.

pit [pɪt] n trou m, fosse f; (also: **coal ~**) puits m de mine; (also: **orchestra ~**) fosse d'orchestre ♦ vt: **to ~ sb against sb** opposer qn à qn; **to ~ o.s. against** se mesurer à; **~s** npl (in motor racing) aire f de service.

pitapat ['pɪtə'pæt] adv (BRIT): **to go ~** (heart) battre la chamade; (rain) tambouriner.

pitch [pɪtʃ] n (throw) lancement m; (MUS) ton m; (of voice) hauteur f; (fig: degree) degré m; (also: **sales ~**) baratin m, boniment m; (BRIT SPORT) terrain m; (NAUT) tangage m; (tar) poix f ♦ vt (throw) lancer; (tent) dresser; (set: price, message) adapter, positionner ♦ vi (NAUT) tanguer; (fall): **to ~ into/off** tomber dans/de; **to be ~ed forward** être projeté(e) en avant; **at this ~** à ce rythme.

pitch-black ['pɪtʃ'blæk] adj noir(e) comme poix.

pitched battle [pɪtʃt-] n bataille rangée.

pitcher ['pɪtʃə*] n cruche f.

pitchfork ['pɪtʃfɔːk] n fourche f.

piteous ['pɪtɪəs] adj pitoyable.

pitfall ['pɪtfɔːl] n trappe f, piège m.

pith [pɪθ] n (of plant) moelle f; (of orange) intérieur m de l'écorce; (fig) essence f, vigueur f.

pithead ['pɪthed] n (BRIT) bouche f de puits.

pithy ['pɪθɪ] adj piquant(e); vigoureux(euse).

pitiable ['pɪtɪəbl] adj pitoyable.

pitiful ['pɪtɪful] adj (touching) pitoyable; (contemptible) lamentable.

pitifully ['pɪtɪfəlɪ] adv pitoyablement; lamentablement.

pitiless ['pɪtɪlɪs] adj impitoyable.

pittance ['pɪtns] n salaire m de misère.

pitted ['pɪtɪd] adj: **~ with** (chickenpox) grêlé(e) par; (rust) piqué(e) de.

pity ['pɪtɪ] n pitié f ♦ vt plaindre; **what a ~!** quel dommage!; **it is a ~ that you can't come** c'est dommage que vous ne puissiez venir; **to have** or **take ~ on sb** avoir pitié de qn.

pitying ['pɪtɪɪŋ] adj compatissant(e).

pivot ['pɪvət] n pivot m ♦ vi pivoter.

pixel ['pɪksl] n (COMPUT) pixel m.

pixie ['pɪksɪ] n lutin m.

pizza ['piːtsə] n pizza f.

placard ['plækaːd] n affiche f.

placate [plə'keɪt] vt apaiser, calmer.

placatory [plə'keɪtərɪ] adj d'apaisement, lénifiant(e).

place [pleɪs] n endroit m, lieu m; (proper position, rank, seat) place f; (house) maison f, logement m; (in street names): **Laurel ~** ≈ rue des Lauriers; (home): **at/to his ~** chez lui ♦ vt (position) placer, mettre; (identify) situer; reconnaître; **to take ~** avoir lieu; (occur) se produire; **from ~ to ~** d'un endroit à l'autre; **all over the ~** partout; **out of ~** (not suitable) déplacé(e), inopportun(e); **I feel out of ~ here** je ne me sens pas à ma place ici;

in the first ~ d'abord, en premier; to put sb in his ~ (fig) remettre qn à sa place; he's going ~s (fig: col) il fait son chemin; it is not my ~ to do it ce n'est pas à moi de le faire; to ~ an order with sb (for) (COMM) passer commande à qn (de); to be ~d (in race, exam) se placer; how are you ~d next week? comment ça se présente pour la semaine prochaine?

placebo [plə'si:bəu] n placebo m.

place mat n set m de table; (in linen etc) napperon m.

placement ['pleɪsmənt] n placement m; poste m.

place name n nom m de lieu.

placenta [plə'sɛntə] n placenta m.

placid ['plæsɪd] adj placide.

placidity [plə'sɪdɪtɪ] n placidité f.

plagiarism ['pleɪdʒərɪzəm] n plagiat m.

plagiarist ['pleɪdʒərɪst] n plagiaire m/f.

plagiarize ['pleɪdʒəraɪz] vt plagier.

plague [pleɪg] n fléau m; (MED) peste f ♦ vt (fig) tourmenter; to ~ sb with questions harceler qn de questions.

plaice [pleɪs] n (pl inv) carrelet m.

plaid [plæd] n tissu écossais.

plain [pleɪn] adj (clear) clair(e), évident(e); (simple) simple, ordinaire; (frank) franc(franche); (not handsome) quelconque, ordinaire; (cigarette) sans filtre; (without seasoning etc) nature inv; (in one colour) uni(e) ♦ adv franchement, carrément ♦ n plaine f; in ~ clothes (police) en civil; to make sth ~ to sb faire clairement comprendre qch à qn.

plain chocolate n chocolat m à croquer.

plainly ['pleɪnlɪ] adv clairement; (frankly) carrément, sans détours.

plainness ['pleɪnnɪs] n simplicité f.

plain speaking n propos mpl sans équivoque; she has a reputation for ~ elle est bien connue pour son franc parler or sa franchise.

plaintiff ['pleɪntɪf] n plaignant/e.

plaintive ['pleɪntɪv] adj plaintif(ive).

plait [plæt] n tresse f, natte f ♦ vt tresser, natter.

plan [plæn] n plan m; (scheme) projet m ♦ vt (think in advance) projeter; (prepare) organiser ♦ vi faire des projets; to ~ to do projeter de faire; how long do you ~ to stay? combien de temps comptez-vous rester?

plane [pleɪn] n (AVIAT) avion m; (tree) platane m; (tool) rabot m; (ART, MATH etc) plan m ♦ adj plan(e), plat(e) ♦ vt (with tool) raboter.

planet ['plænɪt] n planète f.

planetarium [plænɪ'tɛərɪəm] n planétarium m.

plank [plæŋk] n planche f; (POL) point m d'un programme.

plankton ['plæŋktən] n plancton m.

planned economy [plænd-] n économie planifiée.

planner ['plænə*] n planificateur/trice; (chart) planning m; town or (US) city ~ urbaniste

m/f.

planning ['plænɪŋ] n planification f; family ~ planning familial.

planning permission n (BRIT) permis m de construire.

plant [plɑːnt] n plante f; (machinery) matériel m; (factory) usine f ♦ vt planter; (bomb) déposer, poser.

plantation [plæn'teɪʃən] n plantation f.

plant pot n (BRIT) pot m de fleurs.

plaque [plæk] n plaque f.

plasma ['plæzmə] n plasma m.

plaster ['plɑːstə*] n plâtre m; (BRIT: also: sticking ~) pansement adhésif ♦ vt plâtrer; (cover): to ~ with couvrir de; in ~ (BRIT: leg etc) dans le plâtre; ~ of Paris plâtre à mouler.

plasterboard ['plɑːstəbɔːd] n Placoplâtre m ®.

plaster cast n (MED) plâtre m; (model, statue) moule m.

plastered ['plɑːstəd] adj (col) soûl(e).

plasterer ['plɑːstərə*] n plâtrier m.

plastic ['plæstɪk] n plastique m ♦ adj (made of plastic) en plastique; (flexible) plastique, malléable; (art) plastique.

plastic bag n sac m en plastique.

plastic bullet n balle f de plastique.

plastic explosive n plastic m.

plasticine ['plæstɪsiːn] n ® pâte f à modeler.

plastic surgery n chirurgie f esthétique.

plate [pleɪt] n (dish) assiette f; (sheet of metal, on door, PHOT) plaque f; (TYP) cliché m; (in book) gravure f; (AUT: number ~) plaque minéralogique; gold/silver ~ (dishes) vaisselle f d'or/d'argent.

plateau, ~s or ~x ['plætəu, -z] n plateau m.

plateful ['pleɪtful] n assiette f, assiettée f.

plate glass n verre m à vitre, vitre f.

platen ['plætən] n (on typewriter, printer) rouleau m.

plate rack n égouttoir m.

platform ['plætfɔːm] n (at meeting) tribune f; (BRIT: of bus) plate-forme f; (stage) estrade f; (RAIL) quai m; the train leaves from ~ 7 le train part de la voie 7.

platform ticket n (BRIT) billet m de quai.

platinum ['plætɪnəm] n platine m.

platitude ['plætɪtjuːd] n platitude f, lieu commun.

platoon [plə'tuːn] n peloton m.

platter ['plætə*] n plat m.

plaudits ['plɔːdɪts] npl applaudissements mpl.

plausible ['plɔːzɪbl] adj plausible; (person) convaincant(e).

play [pleɪ] n jeu m; (THEAT) pièce f (de théâtre) ♦ vt (game) jouer à; (team, opponent) jouer contre; (instrument) jouer de; (part, piece of music, note) jouer ♦ vi jouer; to bring or call into ~ faire entrer en jeu; ~ on words jeu de mots; to ~ a trick on sb jouer un tour à qn; they're ~ing at soldiers ils jouent aux soldats; to ~ for time (fig) chercher à gagner du temps; to ~ into sb's hands (fig)

faire le jeu de qn.
▶**play about, play around** vi (*person*) s'amuser.
▶**play along** vi (*fig*): **to ~ along with** (*person*) entrer dans le jeu de ♦ vt (*fig*): **to ~ sb along** faire marcher qn.
▶**play back** vt repasser, réécouter.
▶**play down** vt minimiser.
▶**play on** vt fus (*sb's feelings, credulity*) jouer sur; **to ~ on sb's nerves** porter sur les nerfs de qn.
▶**play up** vi (*cause trouble*) faire des siennes.
playact ['pleɪækt] vi jouer la comédie.
playboy ['pleɪbɔɪ] n playboy m.
played-out ['pleɪd'aut] adj épuisé(e).
player ['pleɪə*] n joueur/euse; (*THEAT*) acteur/trice; (*MUS*) musicien/ne.
playful ['pleɪful] adj enjoué(e).
playgoer ['pleɪɡəuə*] n amateur/trice de théâtre, habitué/e des théâtres.
playground ['pleɪɡraund] n cour f de récréation.
playgroup ['pleɪɡruːp] n garderie f.
playing card ['pleɪɪŋ-] n carte f à jouer.
playing field ['pleɪɪŋ-] n terrain m de sport.
playmaker ['pleɪmeɪkə*] n (*SPORT*) joueur qui crée des occasions de marquer des buts pour ses coéquipiers.
playmate ['pleɪmeɪt] n camarade m/f, copain/copine.
play-off ['pleɪɔf] n (*SPORT*) belle f.
playpen ['pleɪpen] n parc m (pour bébé).
playroom ['pleɪruːm] n salle f de jeux.
plaything ['pleɪθɪŋ] n jouet m.
playtime ['pleɪtaɪm] n (*SCOL*) récréation f.
playwright ['pleɪraɪt] n dramaturge m.
plc abbr (*BRIT*) = **public limited company**.
plea [pliː] n (*request*) appel m; (*excuse*) excuse f; (*LAW*) défense f.
plea bargaining n (*LAW*) négociations entre le procureur, l'avocat de la défense et parfois le juge, pour réduire la gravité des charges.
plead [pliːd] vt plaider; (*give as excuse*) invoquer ♦ vi (*LAW*) plaider; (*beg*): **to ~ with sb (for sth)** implorer qn (d'accorder qch); **to ~ for sth** implorer qch; **to ~ guilty/not guilty** plaider coupable/non coupable.
pleasant ['pleznt] adj agréable.
pleasantly ['plezntlɪ] adv agréablement.
pleasantry ['plezntrɪ] n (*joke*) plaisanterie f; **pleasantries** npl (*polite remarks*) civilités fpl.
please [pliːz] vt plaire à ♦ vi (*think fit*): **do as you ~** faites comme il vous plaira; **~!** s'il te (*or* vous) plaît; **my bill, ~** l'addition, s'il vous plaît; **~ don't cry!** je t'en prie, ne pleure pas!; **~ yourself!** (faites) comme vous voulez!
pleased [pliːzd] adj: **(with)** content(e) (de); **~ to meet you** enchanté (de faire votre connaissance); **we are ~ to inform you that ...** nous sommes heureux de vous annoncer

que ....
pleasing ['pliːzɪŋ] adj plaisant(e), qui fait plaisir.
pleasurable ['pleʒərəbl] adj très agréable.
pleasure ['pleʒə*] n plaisir m; **"it's a ~"** "je vous en prie"; **with ~** avec plaisir; **is this trip for business or ~?** est-ce un voyage d'affaires ou d'agrément?
pleasure cruise n croisière f.
pleat [pliːt] n pli m.
plebiscite ['plebɪsɪt] n plébiscite m.
plebs [plebz] npl (*pej*) bas peuple.
plectrum ['plektrəm] n plectre m.
pledge [pledʒ] n gage m; (*promise*) promesse f ♦ vt engager; promettre; **to ~ support for sb** s'engager à soutenir qn; **to ~ sb to secrecy** faire promettre à qn de garder le secret.
plenary ['pliːnərɪ] adj: **in ~ session** en séance plénière.
plentiful ['plentɪful] adj abondant(e), copieux(euse).
plenty ['plentɪ] n abondance f; **~ of** beaucoup de; (*sufficient*) (bien) assez de; **we've got ~ of time** nous avons largement le temps.
pleurisy ['pluərɪsɪ] n pleurésie f.
Plexiglas ['pleksɪɡlɑːs] n ® (*US*) Plexiglas m ®.
pliable ['plaɪəbl] adj flexible; (*person*) malléable.
pliers ['plaɪəz] npl pinces fpl.
plight [plaɪt] n situation f critique.
plimsolls ['plɪmsəlz] npl (*BRIT*) (chaussures fpl) tennis fpl.
plinth [plɪnθ] n socle m.
PLO n abbr (= *Palestine Liberation Organization*) OLP f.
plod [plɔd] vi avancer péniblement; (*fig*) peiner.
plodder ['plɔdə*] n bûcheur/euse.
plodding ['plɔdɪŋ] adj pesant(e).
plonk [plɔŋk] (*col*) n (*BRIT: wine*) pinard m, piquette f ♦ vt: **to ~ sth down** poser brusquement qch.
plot [plɔt] n complot m, conspiration f; (*of story, play*) intrigue f; (*of land*) lot m de terrain, lopin m ♦ vt (*mark out*) pointer; relever; (*conspire*) comploter ♦ vi comploter; **a vegetable ~** (*BRIT*) un carré de légumes.
plotter ['plɔtə*] n conspirateur/trice; (*COMPUT*) traceur m.
plough, (*US*) **plow** [plau] n charrue f ♦ vt (*earth*) labourer.
▶**plough back** vt (*COMM*) réinvestir.
▶**plough through** vt fus (*snow etc*) avancer péniblement dans.
ploughing, (*US*) **plowing** ['plauɪŋ] n labourage m.
ploughman, (*US*) **plowman** ['plaumən] n laboureur m; **~'s lunch** (*BRIT*) repas sommaire de pain et de fromage.
ploy [plɔɪ] n stratagème m.
pluck [plʌk] vt (*fruit*) cueillir; (*musical instru-*

ment) pincer; (*bird*) plumer ♦ *n* courage *m*, cran *m*; **to ~ one's eyebrows** s'épiler les sourcils; **to ~ up courage** prendre son courage à deux mains.

plucky ['plʌkɪ] *adj* courageux(euse).

plug [plʌg] *n* bouchon *m*, bonde *f*; (*ELEC*) prise *f* de courant; (*AUT: also*: **spark(ing) ~**) bougie *f* ♦ *vt* (*hole*) boucher; (*col: advertise*) faire du battage pour, matraquer; **to give sb/sth a ~** (*col*) faire de la pub pour qn/qch.
►**plug in** (*ELEC*) *vt* brancher ♦ *vi* se brancher.

plughole ['plʌghəul] *n* (*BRIT*) trou *m* (d'écoulement).

plum [plʌm] *n* (*fruit*) prune *f* ♦ *adj*: **~ job** (*col*) travail *m* en or.

plumage ['plu:mɪdʒ] *n* plumage *m*.

plumb [plʌm] *adj* vertical(e) ♦ *n* plomb *m* ♦ *adv* (*exactly*) en plein ♦ *vt* sonder.
►**plumb in** *vt* (*washing machine*) faire le raccordement de.

plumber ['plʌmə*] *n* plombier *m*.

plumbing ['plʌmɪŋ] *n* (*trade*) plomberie *f*; (*piping*) tuyauterie *f*.

plumbline ['plʌmlaɪn] *n* fil *m* à plomb.

plume [plu:m] *n* plume *f*, plumet *m*.

plummet ['plʌmɪt] *vi* plonger, dégringoler.

plump [plʌmp] *adj* rondelet(te), dodu(e), bien en chair ♦ *vt*: **to ~ sth (down) on** laisser tomber qch lourdement sur.
►**plump for** *vt fus* (*col: choose*) se décider pour.
►**plump up** *vt* (*cushion*) battre (pour lui redonner forme).

plunder ['plʌndə*] *n* pillage *m* ♦ *vt* piller.

plunge [plʌndʒ] *n* plongeon *m* ♦ *vt* plonger ♦ *vi* (*fall*) tomber, dégringoler; **to take the ~** se jeter à l'eau; **to ~ a room into darkness** plonger une pièce dans l'obscurité.

plunger ['plʌndʒə*] *n* piston *m*; (*for blocked sink*) (débouchoir *m* à) ventouse *f*.

plunging ['plʌndʒɪŋ] *adj* (*neckline*) plongeant(e).

pluperfect [plu:'pə:fɪkt] *n* plus-que-parfait *m*.

plural ['pluərl] *adj* pluriel(le) ♦ *n* pluriel *m*.

plus [plʌs] *n* (*also*: **~ sign**) signe *m* plus ♦ *prep* plus; **ten/twenty ~** plus de dix/vingt; **it's a ~** c'est un atout.

plus fours *npl* pantalon *m* (de) golf.

plush [plʌʃ] *adj* somptueux(euse) ♦ *n* peluche *f*.

plutonium [plu:'təunɪəm] *n* plutonium *m*.

ply [plaɪ] *n* (*of wool*) fil *m*; (*of wood*) feuille *f*, épaisseur *f* ♦ *vt* (*tool*) manier; (*a trade*) exercer ♦ *vi* (*ship*) faire la navette; **three ~ (wool)** *n* laine *f* trois fils; **to ~ sb with drink** donner continuellement à boire à qn.

plywood ['plaɪwud] *n* contreplaqué *m*.

PM *n abbr* (*BRIT*) = **prime minister**.

p.m. *adv abbr* (= *post meridiem*) de l'après-midi.

PMS *n abbr* (= *premenstrual syndrome*) syndrome prémenstruel.

PMT *n abbr* = **premenstrual tension**.

pneumatic [nju:'mætɪk] *adj* pneumatique; **~ drill** marteau-piqueur *m*.

pneumonia [nju:'məunɪə] *n* pneumonie *f*.

PO *n abbr* (= *Post Office*) PTT *fpl*; (*MIL*) = **petty officer**.

po *abbr* = **postal order**.

POA *n abbr* (*BRIT*) = *Prison Officers' Association*.

poach [pəutʃ] *vt* (*cook*) pocher; (*steal*) pêcher (*or* chasser) sans permis ♦ *vi* braconner.

poached [pəutʃt] *adj* (*egg*) poché(e).

poacher ['pəutʃə*] *n* braconnier *m*.

poaching ['pəutʃɪŋ] *n* braconnage *m*.

PO box *n abbr* = **post office box**.

pocket ['pɔkɪt] *n* poche *f* ♦ *vt* empocher; **to be (£5) out of ~** (*BRIT*) en être de sa poche (pour 5 livres).

pocketbook ['pɔkɪtbuk] *n* (*wallet*) portefeuille *m*; (*notebook*) carnet *m*; (*US: handbag*) sac *m* à main.

pocket knife *n* canif *m*.

pocket money *n* argent *m* de poche.

pockmarked ['pɔkmɑ:kt] *adj* (*face*) grêlé(e).

pod [pɔd] *n* cosse *f* ♦ *vt* écosser.

podgy ['pɔdʒɪ] *adj* rondelet(te).

podiatrist [pɔ'di:ətrɪst] *n* (*US*) pédicure *m/f*.

podiatry [pɔ'di:ətrɪ] *n* (*US*) pédicurie *f*.

podium ['pəudɪəm] *n* podium *m*.

POE *n abbr* = **port of embarkation**, **port of entry**.

poem ['pəuɪm] *n* poème *m*.

poet ['pəuɪt] *n* poète *m*.

poetic [pəu'etɪk] *adj* poétique.

poet laureate *n* poète lauréat.

> *En Grande-Bretagne, le* **poet laureate** *est un poète qui reçoit un traitement en tant que poète de la cour et qui est officier de la maison royale à vie. Le premier d'entre eux fut Ben Jonson, en 1616. Jadis, le poète lauréat écrivait des poèmes lors des grandes occasions, mais cette tradition n'est plus guère observée.*

poetry ['pəuɪtrɪ] *n* poésie *f*.

poignant ['pɔɪnjənt] *adj* poignant(e); (*sharp*) vif(vive).

point [pɔɪnt] *n* (*tip*) pointe *f*; (*in time*) moment *m*; (*in space*) endroit *m*; (*GEOM, SCOL, SPORT, on scale*) point *m*; (*subject, idea*) point, sujet *m*; (*also*: **decimal ~**): **2 ~ 3 (2.3)** 2 virgule 3 (2,3); (*BRIT ELEC: also*: **power ~**) prise *f* (de courant) ♦ *vt* (*show*) indiquer; (*wall, window*) jointoyer; (*gun etc*): **to ~ sth at** braquer *or* diriger qch sur ♦ *vi*: **to ~** montrer du doigt; **to ~ to** montrer du doigt; (*fig*) signaler; **~s** *npl* (*AUT*) vis platinées; (*RAIL*) aiguillage *m*; **good ~s** qualités *fpl*; **the train stops at Carlisle and all ~s south** le train dessert Carlisle et toutes les gares vers le sud; **to make a ~** faire une remarque; **to make a ~ of doing sth** ne pas manquer de faire qch; **to make one's ~** se faire comprendre; **to get the ~** comprendre, saisir; **to come to the ~** en venir au fait; **when it comes to the ~** le moment venu; **there's no ~ (in doing)** cela ne sert à rien (de faire); **to be on the ~ of doing sth** être sur le point de faire qch; **that's the whole ~!** précisément!; **to be beside the ~** être à côté de la question; **you've got a ~ there!** (c'est) juste!; **in ~ of fact** en fait, en réalité; **~ of departure** (*also fig*) point de départ; **~ of order** point de procédure; **~ of sale** (*COMM*) point de vente; **~ of view** point de vue.

►**point out** *vt* faire remarquer, souligner.

point-blank ['pɔɪnt'blæŋk] *adv* (*also:* **at ~ range**) à bout portant ♦ *adj* (*fig*) catégorique.

point duty *n* (*BRIT*): **to be on ~** diriger la circulation.

pointed ['pɔɪntɪd] *adj* (*shape*) pointu(e); (*remark*) plein(e) de sous-entendus.

pointedly ['pɔɪntɪdlɪ] *adv* d'une manière significative.

pointer ['pɔɪntə*] *n* (*stick*) baguette *f*; (*needle*) aiguille *f*; (*dog*) chien *m* d'arrêt; (*clue*) indication *f*; (*advice*) tuyau *m*.

pointless ['pɔɪntlɪs] *adj* inutile, vain(e).

poise [pɔɪz] *n* (*balance*) équilibre *m*; (*of head, body*) port *m*; (*calmness*) calme *m* ♦ *vt* placer en équilibre; **to be ~d for** (*fig*) être prêt à.

poison ['pɔɪzn] *n* poison *m* ♦ *vt* empoisonner.

poisoning ['pɔɪznɪŋ] *n* empoisonnement *m*.

poisonous ['pɔɪznəs] *adj* (*snake*) venimeux(euse); (*substance etc*) vénéneux(euse); (*fumes*) toxique; (*fig*) pernicieux(euse).

poke [pəuk] *vt* (*fire*) tisonner; (*jab with finger, stick etc*) piquer; pousser du doigt; (*put*): **to ~ sth into** fourrer *or* enfoncer qch dans ♦ *n* (*jab*) (petit) coup; (*to fire*) coup *m* de tisonnier; **to ~ one's head out of the window** passer la tête par la fenêtre; **to ~ fun at sb** se moquer de qn.

►**poke about** *vi* fureter.

poker ['pəukə*] *n* tisonnier *m*; (*CARDS*) poker *m*.

poker-faced ['pəukə'feɪst] *adj* au visage impassible.

poky ['pəukɪ] *adj* exigu(ë).

Poland ['pəulənd] *n* Pologne *f*.

polar ['pəulə*] *adj* polaire.

polar bear *n* ours blanc.

polarize ['pəuləraɪz] *vt* polariser.

Pole [pəul] *n* Polonais/e.

pole [pəul] *n* (*of wood*) mât *m*, perche *f*; (*ELEC*) poteau *m*; (*GEO*) pôle *m*.

poleaxe ['pəulæks] *vt* (*fig*) terrasser.

pole bean *n* (*US*) haricot *m* (à rames).

polecat ['pəulkæt] *n* putois *m*.

Pol. Econ. ['pɒlɪkɒn] *n abbr* = *political economy*.

polemic [pɒ'lɛmɪk] *n* polémique *f*.

pole star ['pəulstɑ:*] *n* étoile *f* polaire.

pole vault ['pəulvɔːlt] *n* saut *m* à la perche.

police [pə'liːs] *npl* police *f* ♦ *vt* maintenir l'ordre dans; **a large number of ~ were hurt** de nombreux policiers ont été blessés.

police car *n* voiture *f* de police.

police constable *n* (*BRIT*) agent *m* de police.

police department *n* (*US*) services *mpl* de police.

police force *n* police *f*, forces *fpl* de l'ordre.

policeman [pə'liːsmən] *n* agent *m* de police, policier *m*.

police officer *n* agent *m* de police.

police record *n* casier *m* judiciaire.

police state *n* état policier.

police station *n* commissariat *m* de police.

policewoman [pə'liːswumən] *n* femme-agent *f*.

policy ['pɒlɪsɪ] *n* politique *f*; (*also:* **insurance ~**) police *f* (d'assurance); (*of newspaper, company*) politique générale; **to take out a ~** (*INSURANCE*) souscrire une police d'assurance.

policy holder *n* assuré/e.

policy-making ['pɒlɪsɪmeɪkɪŋ] *n* élaboration *f* de nouvelles lignes d'action.

polio ['pəulɪəu] *n* polio *f*.

Polish ['pəulɪʃ] *adj* polonais(e) ♦ *n* (*LING*) polonais *m*.

polish ['pɒlɪʃ] *n* (*for shoes*) cirage *m*; (*for floor*) cire *f*, encaustique *f*; (*for nails*) vernis *m*; (*shine*) éclat *m*, poli *m*; (*fig: refinement*) raffinement *m* ♦ *vt* (*put polish on: shoes, wood*) cirer; (*make shiny*) astiquer, faire briller; (*fig: improve*) perfectionner.

►**polish off** *vt* (*work*) expédier; (*food*) liquider.

polished ['pɒlɪʃt] *adj* (*fig*) raffiné(e).

polite [pə'laɪt] *adj* poli(e); **it's not ~ to do that** ça ne se fait pas.

politely [pə'laɪtlɪ] *adv* poliment.

politeness [pə'laɪtnɪs] *n* politesse *f*.

politic ['pɒlɪtɪk] *adj* diplomatique.

political [pə'lɪtɪkl] *adj* politique.

political asylum *n* asile *m* politique.

politically [pə'lɪtɪklɪ] *adv* politiquement.

politically correct *adj* politiquement correct(e).

politician [pɒlɪ'tɪʃən] *n* homme/femme politique, politicien/ne.

politics ['pɒlɪtɪks] *n* politique *f*.

polka ['pɒlkə] *n* polka *f*.

polka dot *n* pois *m*.

poll [pəul] *n* scrutin *m*, vote *m*; (*also:* **opinion ~**) sondage *m* (d'opinion) ♦ *vt* obtenir; **to go to the ~s** (*voters*) aller aux urnes; (*government*) tenir des élections.

pollen ['pɒlən] *n* pollen *m*.

pollen count *n* taux *m* de pollen.

pollination [pɒlɪ'neɪʃən] *n* pollinisation *f*.

polling ['pəulɪŋ] *n* (*BRIT POL*) élections *fpl*; (*TEL*) invitation *f* à émettre.

polling booth *n* (*BRIT*) isoloir *m*.

polling day *n* (*BRIT*) jour *m* des élections.

polling station *n* (*BRIT*) bureau *m* de vote.

pollster ['pəulstə*] *n* sondeur *m*, enquêteur/euse.

poll tax *n* (*BRIT: formerly*) ≈ impôts locaux.

pollutant [pə'luːtənt] *n* polluant *m*.

pollute [pə'luːt] vt polluer.
pollution [pə'luːʃən] n pollution f.
polo ['pəuləu] n polo m.
poloneck ['pəuləunɛk] n col roulé ♦ adj à col roulé.
poly ['pɔlɪ] n abbr (BRIT) = **polytechnic**.
poly bag n (BRIT col) sac m en plastique.
polyester [pɔlɪ'ɛstə*] n polyester m.
polygamy [pə'lɪɡəmɪ] n polygamie f.
polygraph ['pɔlɪɡrɑːf] n détecteur m de mensonges.
Polynesia [pɔlɪ'niːzɪə] n Polynésie f.
Polynesian [pɔlɪ'niːzɪən] adj polynésien(ne) ♦ n Polynésien/ne.
polyp ['pɔlɪp] n (MED) polype m.
polystyrene [pɔlɪ'staɪriːn] n polystyrène m.
polytechnic [pɔlɪ'tɛknɪk] n (college) IUT m, Institut m universitaire de technologie.
polythene ['pɔlɪθiːn] n polyéthylène m.
polythene bag n sac m en plastique.
polyurethane [pɔlɪ'juərɪθeɪn] n polyuréthane m.
pomegranate ['pɔmɪɡrænɪt] n grenade f.
pommel ['pɔml] n pommeau m ♦ vt = **pummel**.
pomp [pɔmp] n pompe f, faste f, apparat m.
pompom ['pɔmpɔm] n pompon m.
pompous ['pɔmpəs] adj pompeux(euse).
pond [pɔnd] n étang m; (stagnant) mare f.
ponder ['pɔndə*] vi réfléchir ♦ vt considérer, peser.
ponderous ['pɔndərəs] adj pesant(e), lourd(e).
pong [pɔŋ] (BRIT col) n puanteur f ♦ vi schlinguer.
pontiff ['pɔntɪf] n pontife m.
pontificate [pɔn'tɪfɪkeɪt] vi (fig): **to ~ (about)** pontifier (sur).
pontoon [pɔn'tuːn] n ponton m; (BRIT: CARDS) vingt-et-un m.
pony ['pəunɪ] n poney m.
ponytail ['pəunɪteɪl] n queue f de cheval.
pony trekking [-trɛkɪŋ] n (BRIT) randonnée f équestre or à cheval.
poodle ['puːdl] n caniche m.
pooh-pooh ['puː'puː] vt dédaigner.
pool [puːl] n (of rain) flaque f; (pond) mare f; (artificial) bassin m; (also: **swimming ~**) piscine f; (sth shared) fonds commun; (money at cards) cagnotte f; (billiards) poule f; (COMM: consortium) pool m; (US: monopoly trust) trust m ♦ vt mettre en commun; **typing ~**, (US) **secretary ~** pool m dactylographique; **to do the (football) ~s** (BRIT) ≈ jouer au loto sportif; see also **football pools**.
poor [puə*] adj pauvre; (mediocre) médiocre, faible, mauvais(e) ♦ npl: **the ~** les pauvres mpl.
poorly ['puəlɪ] adv pauvrement; médiocrement ♦ adj souffrant(e), malade.
pop [pɔp] n (noise) bruit sec; (MUS) musique f pop; (col: drink) soda m; (US col: father) papa m ♦ vt (put) fourrer, mettre (rapidement) ♦ vi éclater; (cork) sauter; **she ~ped her head**

out of the window elle passa la tête par la fenêtre.
▶**pop in** vi entrer en passant.
▶**pop out** vi sortir.
▶**pop up** vi apparaître, surgir.
pop concert n concert m pop.
popcorn ['pɔpkɔːn] n pop-corn m.
pope [pəup] n pape m.
poplar ['pɔplə*] n peuplier m.
poplin ['pɔplɪn] n popeline f.
popper ['pɔpə*] n (BRIT) bouton-pression m.
poppy ['pɔpɪ] n coquelicot m; pavot m.
poppycock ['pɔpɪkɔk] n (col) balivernes fpl.
Popsicle ['pɔpsɪkl] n ® (US) esquimau m (glace).
populace ['pɔpjuləs] n peuple m.
popular ['pɔpjulə*] adj populaire; (fashionable) à la mode; **to be ~ (with)** (person) avoir du succès (auprès de); (decision) être bien accueilli(e) (par).
popularity [pɔpju'lærɪtɪ] n popularité f.
popularize ['pɔpjuləraɪz] vt populariser; (science) vulgariser.
populate ['pɔpjuleɪt] vt peupler.
population [pɔpju'leɪʃən] n population f.
population explosion n explosion f démographique.
populous ['pɔpjuləs] adj populeux(euse).
porcelain ['pɔːslɪn] n porcelaine f.
porch [pɔːtʃ] n porche m.
porcupine ['pɔːkjupaɪn] n porc-épic m.
pore [pɔː*] n pore m ♦ vi: **to ~ over** s'absorber dans, être plongé(e) dans.
pork [pɔːk] n porc m.
pork chop n côte f de porc.
porn [pɔːn] adj, n (col) porno (m).
pornographic [pɔːnə'ɡræfɪk] adj pornographique.
pornography [pɔː'nɔɡrəfɪ] n pornographie f.
porous ['pɔːrəs] adj poreux(euse).
porpoise ['pɔːpəs] n marsouin m.
porridge ['pɔrɪdʒ] n porridge m.
port [pɔːt] n (harbour) port m; (opening in ship) sabord m; (NAUT: left side) bâbord m; (wine) porto m; (COMPUT) port m, accès m ♦ cpd portuaire, du port; **to ~** (NAUT) à bâbord; **~ of call** (port d')escale f.
portable ['pɔːtəbl] adj portatif(ive).
portal ['pɔːtl] n portail m.
portcullis [pɔːt'kʌlɪs] n herse f.
portend [pɔː'tɛnd] vt présager, annoncer.
portent ['pɔːtɛnt] n présage m.
porter ['pɔːtə*] n (for luggage) porteur m; (doorkeeper) gardien/ne; portier m.
portfolio [pɔːt'fəulɪəu] n portefeuille m; (of artist) portfolio m.
porthole ['pɔːthəul] n hublot m.
portico ['pɔːtɪkəu] n portique m.
portion ['pɔːʃən] n portion f, part f.
portly ['pɔːtlɪ] adj corpulent(e).
portrait ['pɔːtreɪt] n portrait m.
portray [pɔː'treɪ] vt faire le portrait de; (in

writing) dépeindre, représenter.

portrayal [pɔ:'treɪəl] *n* portrait *m*, représentation *f*.

Portugal ['pɔ:tjugl] *n* Portugal *m*.

Portuguese [pɔ:tju'gi:z] *adj* portugais(e) ♦ *n* (*pl inv*) Portugais/e; (*LING*) portugais *m*.

Portuguese man-of-war [-mænəv'wɔ:*] *n* (*jellyfish*) galère *f*.

pose [pəuz] *n* pose *f*; (*pej*) affectation *f* ♦ *vi* poser; (*pretend*): **to ~ as** se poser en ♦ *vt* poser, créer; **to strike a ~** poser (pour la galerie).

poser ['pəuzə*] *n* question difficile *or* embarrassante; (*person*) = **poseur.**

poseur [pəu'zə:*] *n* (*pej*) poseur/euse.

posh [pɔʃ] *adj* (*col*) chic *inv*; **to talk ~** parler d'une manière affectée.

position [pə'zɪʃən] *n* position *f*; (*job*) situation *f* ♦ *vt* mettre en place *or* en position; **to be in a ~ to do sth** être en mesure de faire qch.

positive ['pɔzɪtɪv] *adj* positif(ive); (*certain*) sûr(e), certain(e); (*definite*) formel(le), catégorique; (*clear*) indéniable, réel(le).

posse ['pɔsɪ] *n* (*US*) détachement *m*.

possess [pə'zɛs] *vt* posséder; **like one ~ed** comme un fou; **whatever can have ~ed you?** qu'est-ce qui vous a pris?

possession [pə'zɛʃən] *n* possession *f*; **to take ~ of sth** prendre possession de qch.

possessive [pə'zɛsɪv] *adj* possessif(ive).

possessiveness [pə'zɛsɪvnɪs] *n* possessivité *f*.

possessor [pə'zɛsə*] *n* possesseur *m*.

possibility [pɔsɪ'bɪlɪtɪ] *n* possibilité *f*; éventualité *f*; **he's a ~ for the part** c'est un candidat possible pour le rôle.

possible ['pɔsɪbl] *adj* possible; (*solution*) envisageable, éventuel(le); **it is ~ to do it** il est possible de le faire; **as far as ~** dans la mesure du possible, autant que possible; **if ~** si possible; **as big as ~** aussi gros que possible.

possibly ['pɔsɪblɪ] *adv* (*perhaps*) peut-être; **if you ~ can** si cela vous est possible; **I cannot ~ come** il m'est impossible de venir.

post [pəust] *n* (*BRIT: mail*) poste *f*; (*: collection*) levée *f*; (*: letters, delivery*) courrier *m*; (*job, situation*) poste *m*; (*pole*) poteau *m*; (*trading ~*) comptoir (commercial) ♦ *vt* (*BRIT: send by post, MIL*) poster; (*BRIT: appoint*): **to ~ to** affecter à; (*notice*) afficher; **by ~** (*BRIT*) par la poste; **by return of ~** (*BRIT*) par retour du courrier; **to keep sb ~ed** tenir qn au courant.

post... [pəust] *prefix* post...; **~ 1990** *adj* d'après 1990 ♦ *adv* après 1990.

postage ['pəustɪdʒ] *n* affranchissement *m*; **~ paid** port payé; **~ prepaid** (*US*) franco (de port).

postage stamp *n* timbre-poste *m*.

postal ['pəustl] *adj* postal(e).

postal order *n* mandat(-poste *m*) *m*.

postbag ['pəustbæg] *n* (*BRIT*) sac postal; (*postman's*) sacoche *f*.

postbox ['pəustbɔks] *n* (*BRIT*) boîte *f* aux lettres (*publique*).

postcard ['pəustka:d] *n* carte postale.

postcode ['pəustkəud] *n* (*BRIT*) code postal.

postdate ['pəust'deɪt] *vt* (*cheque*) postdater.

poster ['pəustə*] *n* affiche *f*.

poste restante [pəust'rɛstã:nt] *n* (*BRIT*) poste restante.

posterior [pɔs'tɪərɪə*] *n* (*col*) postérieur *m*, derrière *m*.

posterity [pɔs'tɛrɪtɪ] *n* postérité *f*.

poster paint *n* gouache *f*.

post exchange (PX) *n* (*US MIL*) magasin *m* de l'armée.

post-free ['pəust'fri:] *adj* (*BRIT*) franco (de port).

postgraduate ['pəust'grædjuət] *n* ≈ étudiant/e de troisième cycle.

posthumous ['pɔstjuməs] *adj* posthume.

posthumously ['pɔstjuməslɪ] *adv* après la mort de l'auteur, à titre posthume.

posting ['pəustɪŋ] *n* (*BRIT*) affectation *f*.

postman ['pəustmən] *n* facteur *m*.

postmark ['pəustma:k] *n* cachet *m* (de la poste).

postmaster ['pəustma:stə*] *n* receveur *m* des postes.

Postmaster General *n* ≈ ministre *m* des Postes et Télécommunications.

postmistress ['pəustmɪstrɪs] *n* receveuse *f* des postes.

post-mortem [pəust'mɔ:təm] *n* autopsie *f*.

postnatal ['pəust'neɪtl] *adj* post-natal(e).

post office *n* (*building*) poste *f*; (*organization*) postes *fpl*.

post office box (PO box) *n* boîte postale (B.P.).

post-paid ['pəust'peɪd] *adj* (*BRIT*) port payé.

postpone [pəs'pəun] *vt* remettre (à plus tard), reculer.

postponement [pəs'pəunmənt] *n* ajournement *m*, renvoi *m*.

postscript ['pəustskrɪpt] *n* post-scriptum *m*.

postulate ['pɔstjuleɪt] *vt* postuler.

posture ['pɔstʃə*] *n* posture *f*, attitude *f* ♦ *vi* poser.

postwar [pəust'wɔ:*] *adj* d'après-guerre.

posy ['pəuzɪ] *n* petit bouquet.

pot [pɔt] *n* (*for cooking*) marmite *f*; casserole *f*; (*for plants, jam*) pot *m*; (*piece of pottery*) poterie *f*; (*col: marijuana*) herbe *f* ♦ *vt* (*plant*) mettre en pot; **to go to ~** aller à vau-l'eau; **~s of** (*BRIT col*) beaucoup de, plein de.

potash ['pɔtæʃ] *n* potasse *f*.

potassium [pə'tæsɪəm] *n* potassium *m*.

potato, ~es [pə'teɪtəu] *n* pomme *f* de terre.

potato crisps, (*US*) **potato chips** *npl* chips *mpl*.

potato flour *n* fécule *f*.

potato peeler *n* épluche-légumes *m*.

potbellied ['pɔtbɛlɪd] *adj* (*from overeating*) bedonnant(e); (*from malnutrition*) au ventre ballonné.

potency ['pəutnsɪ] *n* puissance *f*, force *f*; (*of drink*) degré *m* d'alcool.

potent ['pəutnt] *adj* puissant(e); (*drink*) fort(e), très alcoolisé(e).

potentate ['pəutnteɪt] *n* potentat *m*.

potential [pə'tɛnʃl] *adj* potentiel(le) ♦ *n* potentiel *m*; **to have** ~ être prometteur(euse); ouvrir des possibilités.

potentially [pə'tɛnʃəlɪ] *adv* potentiellement; **it's** ~ **dangerous** ça pourrait se révéler dangereux, il y a possibilité de danger.

pothole ['pɔthəul] *n* (*in road*) nid *m* de poule; (*BRIT: underground*) gouffre *m*, caverne *f*.

potholer ['pɔthəulə*] *n* (*BRIT*) spéléologue *m/f*.

potholing ['pɔthəulɪŋ] *n* (*BRIT*): **to go** ~ faire de la spéléologie.

potion ['pəuʃən] *n* potion *f*.

potluck [pɔt'lʌk] *n*: **to take** ~ tenter sa chance.

potpourri [pəu'puːriː] *n* pot-pourri *m*.

pot roast *n* rôti *m* à la cocotte.

potshot ['pɔtʃɔt] *n*: **to take** ~s **at** canarder.

potted ['pɔtɪd] *adj* (*food*) en conserve; (*plant*) en pot; (*fig: shortened*) abrégé(e).

potter ['pɔtə*] *n* potier *m* ♦ *vi* (*BRIT*): **to** ~ **around**, ~ **about** bricoler; ~**'s wheel** tour *m* de potier.

pottery ['pɔtərɪ] *n* poterie *f*; **a piece of** ~ une poterie.

potty ['pɔtɪ] *adj* (*BRIT col: mad*) dingue ♦ *n* (*child's*) pot *m*.

potty-training ['pɔtɪtreɪnɪŋ] *n* apprentissage *m* de la propreté.

pouch [pautʃ] *n* (*ZOOL*) poche *f*; (*for tobacco*) blague *f*.

pouf(fe) [puːf] *n* (*stool*) pouf *m*.

poultice ['pəultɪs] *n* cataplasme *m*.

poultry ['pəultrɪ] *n* volaille *f*.

poultry farm *n* élevage *m* de volaille.

poultry farmer *n* aviculteur *m*.

pounce [pauns] *vi*: **to** ~ **(on)** bondir (sur), fondre (sur) ♦ *n* bond *m*, attaque *f*.

pound [paund] *n* livre *f* (*weight = 453g, 16 ounces; money = 100 pence*); (*for dogs, cars*) fourrière *f* ♦ *vt* (*beat*) bourrer de coups, marteler; (*crush*) piler, pulvériser; (*with guns*) pilonner ♦ *vi* (*beat*) battre violemment, taper; **half a** ~ **(of)** une demi-livre (de); **a five-~ note** un billet de cinq livres.

pounding ['paundɪŋ] *n*: **to take a** ~ (*fig*) prendre une râclée.

pound sterling *n* livre *f* sterling.

pour [pɔː*] *vt* verser ♦ *vi* couler à flots; (*rain*) pleuvoir à verse; **to come** ~**ing in** (*water*) entrer à flots; (*letters*) arriver par milliers; (*cars, people*) affluer.

▶**pour away, pour off** *vt* vider.

▶**pour in** *vi* (*people*) affluer, se précipiter.

▶**pour out** *vi* (*people*) sortir en masse ♦ *vt* vider; déverser; (*serve: a drink*) verser.

pouring ['pɔːrɪŋ] *adj*: ~ **rain** pluie torrentielle.

pout [paut] *n* moue *f* ♦ *vi* faire la moue.

poverty ['pɔvətɪ] *n* pauvreté *f*, misère *f*.

poverty line *n* seuil *m* de pauvreté.

poverty-stricken ['pɔvətɪstrɪkn] *adj* pauvre, déshérité(e).

poverty trap *n* (*BRIT*) piège *m* de la pauvreté.

POW *n abbr* = **prisoner of war.**

powder ['paudə*] *n* poudre *f* ♦ *vt* poudrer; **to** ~ **one's nose** se poudrer; (*euphemism*) aller à la salle de bain; ~**ed milk** lait *m* en poudre.

powder compact *n* poudrier *m*.

powder keg *n* (*fig*) poudrière *f*.

powder puff *n* houppette *f*.

powder room *n* toilettes *fpl* (pour dames).

powdery ['paudərɪ] *adj* poudreux(euse).

power ['pauə*] *n* (*strength*) puissance *f*, force *f*; (*ability, POL: of party, leader*) pouvoir *m*; (*MATH*) puissance *f*; (*of speech, thought*) faculté *f*; (*ELEC*) courant *m* ♦ *vt* faire marcher, actionner; **to do all in one's** ~ **to help sb** faire tout ce qui est en son pouvoir pour aider qn; **the world** ~**s** les grandes puissances; **to be in** ~ être au pouvoir.

powerboat ['pauəbəut] *n* (*BRIT*) hors-bord *m*.

power cut *n* (*BRIT*) coupure *f* de courant.

powered ['pauəd] *adj*: ~ **by** actionné(e) par, fonctionnant à; **nuclear-~ submarine** sous-marin *m* (à propulsion) nucléaire.

power failure *n* panne *f* de courant.

powerful ['pauəful] *adj* puissant(e).

powerhouse ['pauəhaus] *n* (*fig: person*) fonceur *m*; **a** ~ **of ideas** une mine d'idées.

powerless ['pauəlɪs] *adj* impuissant(e).

power line *n* ligne *f* électrique.

power of attorney *n* procuration *f*.

power point *n* (*BRIT*) prise *f* de courant.

power station *n* centrale *f* électrique.

power steering *n* direction assistée.

powwow ['pauwau] *n* conciliabule *m*.

pox [pɔks] *n see* **chickenpox.**

pp *abbr* (= *per procurationem: by proxy*) p.p.

PPE *n abbr* (*BRIT SCOL*) = *philosophy, politics and economics*.

PPS *n abbr* (= *post postscriptum*) PPS; (*BRIT*: = *parliamentary private secretary*) *parlementaire chargé de mission auprès d'un ministre*.

PQ *abbr* (*Canada*: = *Province of Quebec*) PQ.

PR *n abbr* = **proportional representation, public relations** ♦ *abbr* (*US*) = *Puerto Rico.*

Pr. *abbr* (= *prince*) Pce.

practicability [præktɪkə'bɪlɪtɪ] *n* possibilité *f* de réalisation.

practicable ['præktɪkəbl] *adj* (*scheme*) réalisable.

practical ['præktɪkl] *adj* pratique.

practicality [præktɪ'kælɪtɪ] *n* (*of plan*) aspect *m* pratique; (*of person*) sens *m* pratique; **practicalities** *npl* détails *mpl* pratiques.

practical joke *n* farce *f*.

practically ['præktɪklɪ] *adv* (*almost*) pratiquement.

practice ['præktɪs] *n* pratique *f*; (*of profession*)

exercice m; (at football etc) entraînement m; (business) cabinet m; clientèle f ♦ vt, vi (US) = **practise; in** ~ (in reality) en pratique; **out of** ~ rouillé(e); **2 hours' piano** ~ 2 heures de travail or d'exercices au piano; **target** ~ exercices de tir; **it's common** ~ c'est courant, ça se fait couramment; **to put sth into** ~ mettre qch en pratique.

practice match n match m d'entraînement.

practise, (US) **practice** ['præktɪs] vt (work at: piano, one's backhand etc) s'exercer à, travailler; (train for: skiing, running etc) s'entraîner à; (a sport, religion, method) pratiquer; (profession) exercer ♦ vi s'exercer, travailler; (train) s'entraîner; **to** ~ **for a match** s'entraîner pour un match.

practised, (US) **practiced** ['præktɪst] adj (person) expérimenté(e); (performance) impeccable; (liar) invétéré(e); **with a** ~ **eye** d'un œil exercé.

practising, (US) **practicing** ['præktɪsɪŋ] adj (Christian etc) pratiquant(e); (lawyer) en exercice; (homosexual) déclaré.

practitioner [præk'tɪʃənə*] n praticien/ne.

pragmatic [præg'mætɪk] adj pragmatique.

Prague [prɑːg] n Prague.

prairie ['prɛərɪ] n savane f, (US): **the** ~**s** la Prairie.

praise [preɪz] n éloge(s) m(pl), louange(s) f(pl) ♦ vt louer, faire l'éloge de.

praiseworthy ['preɪzwɜːðɪ] adj digne de louanges.

pram [præm] n (BRIT) landau m, voiture f d'enfant.

prance [prɑːns] vi (horse) caracoler.

prank [præŋk] n farce f.

prat [præt] n (BRIT col) imbécile m, andouille f.

prattle ['prætl] vi jacasser.

prawn [prɔːn] n crevette f (rose).

pray [preɪ] vi prier.

prayer [prɛə*] n prière f.

prayer book n livre m de prières.

pre... ['priː] prefix pré...; ~**-1970** adj d'avant 1970 ♦ adv avant 1970.

preach [priːtʃ] vt, vi prêcher; **to** ~ **at sb** faire la morale à qn.

preacher ['priːtʃə*] n prédicateur m; (US: clergyman) pasteur m.

preamble [prɪ'æmbl] n préambule m.

prearranged [priːə'reɪndʒd] adj organisé(e) or fixé(e) à l'avance.

precarious [prɪ'kɛərɪəs] adj précaire.

precaution [prɪ'kɔːʃən] n précaution f.

precautionary [prɪ'kɔːʃənrɪ] adj (measure) de précaution.

precede [prɪ'siːd] vt, vi précéder.

precedence ['prɛsɪdəns] n préséance f.

precedent ['prɛsɪdənt] n précédent m; **to establish** or **set a** ~ créer un précédent.

preceding [prɪ'siːdɪŋ] adj qui précède (or précédait).

precept ['priːsɛpt] n précepte m.

precinct ['priːsɪŋkt] n (round cathedral) pourtour m, enceinte f; (US: district) circonscription f, arrondissement m; ~**s** npl (neighbourhood) alentours mpl, environs mpl; **pedestrian** ~ zone piétonne; **shopping** ~ (BRIT) centre commercial.

precious ['prɛʃəs] adj précieux(euse) ♦ adv (col): ~ **little** or **few** fort peu; **your** ~ **dog** (ironic) ton chien chéri, ton chéri chien.

precipice ['prɛsɪpɪs] n précipice m.

precipitate adj [prɪ'sɪpɪtɪt] (hasty) précipité(e) ♦ vt [prɪ'sɪpɪteɪt] précipiter.

precipitation [prɪsɪpɪ'teɪʃən] n précipitation f.

precipitous [prɪ'sɪpɪtəs] adj (steep) abrupt(e), à pic.

précis, pl **précis** ['preɪsiː, -z] n résumé m.

precise [prɪ'saɪs] adj précis(e).

precisely [prɪ'saɪslɪ] adv précisément.

precision [prɪ'sɪʒən] n précision f.

preclude [prɪ'kluːd] vt exclure, empêcher; **to** ~ **sb from doing** empêcher qn de faire.

precocious [prɪ'kəuʃəs] adj précoce.

preconceived [priːkən'siːvd] adj (idea) préconçu(e).

preconception [priːkən'sɛpʃən] n idée préconçue.

precondition [priːkən'dɪʃən] n condition f nécessaire.

precursor [priː'kɜːsə*] n précurseur m.

predate [priː'deɪt] vt (precede) antidater.

predator ['prɛdətə*] n prédateur m, rapace m.

predatory ['prɛdətərɪ] adj rapace.

predecessor ['priːdɪsɛsə*] n prédécesseur m.

predestination [priːdɛstɪ'neɪʃən] n prédestination f.

predetermine [priːdɪ'tɜːmɪn] vt déterminer à l'avance.

predicament [prɪ'dɪkəmənt] n situation f difficile.

predicate ['prɛdɪkɪt] n (LING) prédicat m.

predict [prɪ'dɪkt] vt prédire.

predictable [prɪ'dɪktəbl] adj prévisible.

predictably [prɪ'dɪktəblɪ] adv (behave, react) de façon prévisible; ~ **she didn't arrive** comme on pouvait s'y attendre, elle n'est pas venue.

prediction [prɪ'dɪkʃən] n prédiction f.

predispose [priːdɪs'pəuz] vt prédisposer.

predominance [prɪ'dɒmɪnəns] n prédominance f.

predominant [prɪ'dɒmɪnənt] adj prédominant(e).

predominantly [prɪ'dɒmɪnəntlɪ] adv en majeure partie; surtout.

predominate [prɪ'dɒmɪneɪt] vi prédominer.

pre-eminent [priː'ɛmɪnənt] adj prééminent(e).

pre-empt [priː'ɛmt] vt (BRIT) acquérir par droit de préemption; (fig) anticiper sur; **to** ~ **the issue** conclure avant même d'ouvrir les débats.

pre-emptive [prɪ'ɛmtɪv] adj: ~ **strike** attaque (or action) préventive.

preen [pri:n] *vt*: **to ~ itself** (*bird*) se lisser les plumes; **to ~ o.s.** s'admirer.

prefab ['pri:fæb] *n* bâtiment préfabriqué.

prefabricated [pri:'fæbrɪkeɪtɪd] *adj* préfabriqué(e).

preface ['prefəs] *n* préface *f*.

prefect ['pri:fɛkt] *n* (*BRIT*: *in school*) élève chargé de certaines fonctions de discipline; (*in France*) préfet *m*.

prefer [prɪ'fə:*] *vt* préférer; (*LAW*): **to ~ charges** procéder à une inculpation; **to ~ coffee to tea** préférer le café au thé.

preferable ['prefrəbl] *adj* préférable.

preferably ['prefrəblɪ] *adv* de préférence.

preference ['prefrəns] *n* préférence *f*; **in ~ to sth** plutôt que qch, de préférence à qch.

preference shares *npl* (*BRIT*) actions privilégiées.

preferential [prefə'renʃəl] *adj* préférentiel(le); **~ treatment** traitement *m* de faveur.

preferred stock [prɪ'fə:d-] *npl* (*US*) = **preference shares**.

prefix ['pri:fɪks] *n* préfixe *m*.

pregnancy ['pregnənsɪ] *n* grossesse *f*.

pregnancy test *n* test *m* de grossesse.

pregnant ['pregnənt] *adj* enceinte *adj f*; **3 months ~** enceinte de 3 mois.

prehistoric ['pri:hɪs'tɔrɪk] *adj* préhistorique.

prehistory [pri:'hɪstərɪ] *n* préhistoire *f*.

prejudge [pri:'dʒʌdʒ] *vt* préjuger de.

prejudice ['predʒudɪs] *n* préjugé *m*; (*harm*) tort *m*, préjudice *m* ♦ *vt* porter préjudice à; (*bias*): **to ~ sb in favour of/against** prévenir qn en faveur de/contre.

prejudiced ['predʒudɪst] *adj* (*person*) plein(e) de préjugés; (*view*) préconçu(e), partial(e); **to be ~ against sb/sth** avoir un parti-pris contre qn/qch.

prelate ['prelət] *n* prélat *m*.

preliminaries [prɪ'lɪmɪnərɪz] *npl* préliminaires *mpl*.

preliminary [prɪ'lɪmɪnərɪ] *adj* préliminaire.

prelude ['prelju:d] *n* prélude *m*.

premarital ['pri:'mærɪtl] *adj* avant le mariage.

premature ['premətʃuə*] *adj* prématuré(e); **to be ~ (in doing sth)** aller un peu (trop) vite (en faisant qch).

premeditated [pri:'medɪteɪtɪd] *adj* prémédité(e).

premeditation [pri:medɪ'teɪʃən] *n* préméditation *f*.

premenstrual [pri:'menstruəl] *adj* prémenstruel(le).

premenstrual tension *n* irritabilité *f* avant les règles.

premier ['premɪə*] *adj* premier(ière), principal(e) ♦ *n* (*POL*) premier ministre.

premiere ['premɪeə*] *n* première *f*.

premise ['premɪs] *n* prémisse *f*.

premises ['premɪsɪz] *npl* locaux *mpl*; **on the ~** sur les lieux; sur place; **business ~** locaux commerciaux.

premium ['pri:mɪəm] *n* prime *f*; **to be at a ~** (*fig: housing etc*) être très demandé(e), être rarissime; **to sell at a ~** (*shares*) vendre au-dessus du pair.

premium bond *n* (*BRIT*) bon *m* à lots.

> *Les* **premium bonds** *sont des bons du Trésor que le public peut acheter. Les intérêts ne sont pas versés, mais il y a chaque mois un tirage au sort par ordinateur. Les personnes dont le bon a été sélectionné gagnent une somme d'argent pouvant aller de quelques livres à plusieurs milliers de livres.*

premium deal *n* (*COMM*) offre spéciale.

premium gasoline *n* (*US*) super *m*.

premonition [premə'nɪʃən] *n* prémonition *f*.

preoccupation [pri:ɔkju'peɪʃən] *n* préoccupation *f*.

preoccupied [pri:'ɔkjupaɪd] *adj* préoccupé(e).

prep [prep] *adj abbr*: **~ school = preparatory school** ♦ *n abbr* (*SCOL*: = *preparation*) étude *f*.

prepackaged [pri:'pækɪdʒd] *adj* préempaqueté(e).

prepaid [pri:'peɪd] *adj* payé(e) d'avance.

preparation [prepə'reɪʃən] *n* préparation *f*; **~s** (*for trip, war*) préparatifs *mpl*; **in ~ for** en vue de.

preparatory [prɪ'pærətɔrɪ] *adj* préparatoire; **~ to sth/to doing sth** en prévision de qch/avant de faire qch.

preparatory school *n* école primaire privée; (*US*) lycée privé.

> *En Grande-Bretagne, une* **preparatory school** *- ou, plus familièrement, une* **prep school** *- est une école payante qui prépare les enfants de 7 à 13 ans aux* **public schools**.

prepare [prɪ'peə*] *vt* préparer ♦ *vi*: **to ~ for** se préparer à.

prepared [prɪ'peəd] *adj*: **~ for** préparé(e) à; **~ to** prêt(e) à.

preponderance [prɪ'pɔndərns] *n* prépondérance *f*.

preposition [prepə'zɪʃən] *n* préposition *f*.

prepossessing [pri:pə'zesɪŋ] *adj* avenant(e), engageant(e).

preposterous [prɪ'pɔstərəs] *adj* absurde.

prep school *n* = **preparatory school**.

prerecord ['pri:rɪ'kɔ:d] *vt*: **~ed broadcast** émission *f* en différé; **~ed cassette** cassette *f* enregistrée.

prerequisite [pri:'rekwɪzɪt] *n* condition *f* préalable.

prerogative [prɪ'rɔgətɪv] *n* prérogative *f*.

presbyterian [prezbɪ'tɪərɪən] *adj*, *n* presbytérien(ne).

presbytery ['prezbɪtərɪ] *n* presbytère *m*.

preschool ['pri:'sku:l] *adj* préscolaire; (*child*) d'âge préscolaire.

prescribe [prɪ'skraɪb] *vt* prescrire; **~d books**

(*BRIT SCOL*) œuvres *fpl* au programme.
prescription [prɪ'skrɪpʃən] *n* prescription *f*; (*MED*) ordonnance *f*; **to make up** or (*US*) **fill a** ~ faire une ordonnance; "**only available on** ~" "uniquement sur ordonnance".
prescription charges *npl* (*BRIT*) participation *f* fixe au coût de l'ordonnance.
prescriptive [prɪ'skrɪptɪv] *adj* normatif(ive).
presence ['prɛzns] *n* présence *f*; ~ **of mind** présence d'esprit.
present ['prɛznt] *adj* présent(e) ♦ *n* cadeau *m*; (*also:* ~ **tense**) présent *m* ♦ *vt* [prɪ'zɛnt] présenter; (*give*): **to** ~ **sb with sth** offrir qch à qn; **to be** ~ **at** assister à; **those** ~ les présents; **at** ~ en ce moment; **to give sb a** ~ offrir un cadeau à qn; **to** ~ **sb (to sb)** présenter qn (à qn).
presentable [prɪ'zɛntəbl] *adj* présentable.
presentation [prɛzn'teɪʃən] *n* présentation *f*; (*gift*) cadeau *m*, présent *m*; (*ceremony*) remise *f* du cadeau; **on** ~ **of** (*voucher etc*) sur présentation de.
present-day ['prɛzntdeɪ] *adj* contemporain(e), actuel(le).
presenter [prɪ'zɛntə*] *n* (*BRIT RADIO, TV*) présentateur/trice.
presently ['prɛzntlɪ] *adv* (*soon*) tout à l'heure, bientôt; (*at present*) en ce moment; (*US: now*) maintenant.
preservation [prɛzə'veɪʃən] *n* préservation *f*, conservation *f*.
preservative [prɪ'zə:vətɪv] *n* agent *m* de conservation.
preserve [prɪ'zə:v] *vt* (*keep safe*) préserver, protéger; (*maintain*) conserver, garder; (*food*) mettre en conserve ♦ *n* (*for game, fish*) réserve *f*; (*often pl: jam*) confiture *f*; (: *fruit*) fruits *mpl* en conserve.
preshrunk [pri:'ʃrʌŋk] *adj* irrétrécissable.
preside [prɪ'zaɪd] *vi* présider.
presidency ['prɛzɪdənsɪ] *n* présidence *f*.
president ['prɛzɪdənt] *n* président/e; (*US: of company*) président-directeur général, PDG *m*.
presidential [prɛzɪ'dɛnʃl] *adj* présidentiel(le).
press [prɛs] *n* (*tool, machine, newspapers*) presse *f*; (*for wine*) pressoir *m*; (*crowd*) cohue *f*, foule *f* ♦ *vt* (*push*) appuyer sur; (*squeeze*) presser, serrer; ⟨*clothes: iron*⟩ repasser; (*pursue*) talonner; (*insist*): **to** ~ **sth on sb** presser qn d'accepter qch; (*urge, entreat*): **to** ~ **sb to do** or **into doing sth** pousser qn à faire qch ♦ *vi* appuyer, peser; se presser; **we are** ~**ed for time** le temps nous manque; **to** ~ **for sth** faire pression pour obtenir qch; **to** ~ **sb for an answer** presser qn de répondre; **to** ~ **charges against sb** (*LAW*) engager des poursuites contre qn; **to go to** ~ (*newspaper*) aller à l'impression; **to be in the** ~ (*being printed*) être sous presse; (*in the newspapers*) être dans le journal.
►**press ahead** *vi* = **press on**.

►**press on** *vi* continuer.
press agency *n* agence *f* de presse.
press clipping *n* coupure *f* de presse.
press conference *n* conférence *f* de presse.
press cutting *n* = **press clipping**.
press-gang ['prɛsgæŋ] *vt* (*fig*): **to** ~ **sb into doing sth** faire pression sur qn pour qu'il fasse qch.
pressing ['prɛsɪŋ] *adj* urgent(e), pressant(e) ♦ *n* repassage *m*.
press officer *n* attaché/e de presse.
press release *n* communiqué *m* de presse.
press stud *n* (*BRIT*) bouton-pression *m*.
press-up ['prɛsʌp] *n* (*BRIT*) traction *f*.
pressure ['prɛʃə*] *n* pression *f*; (*stress*) tension *f* ♦ *vt* = **to put** ~ **on**; **to put** ~ **on sb (to do sth)** faire pression sur qn (pour qu'il fasse qch).
pressure cooker *n* cocotte-minute *f*.
pressure gauge *n* manomètre *m*.
pressure group *n* groupe *m* de pression.
pressurize ['prɛʃəraɪz] *vt* pressuriser; (*BRIT fig*): **to** ~ **sb (into doing sth)** faire pression sur qn (pour qu'il fasse qch).
pressurized ['prɛʃəraɪzd] *adj* pressurisé(e).
Prestel ['prɛstɛl] *n* ® ≈ Minitel *m* ®.
prestige [prɛs'ti:ʒ] *n* prestige *m*.
prestigious [prɛs'tɪdʒəs] *adj* prestigieux(euse).
presumably [prɪ'zju:məblɪ] *adv* vraisemblablement; ~ **he did it** c'est sans doute lui (qui a fait cela).
presume [prɪ'zju:m] *vt* présumer, supposer; **to** ~ **to do** (*dare*) se permettre de faire.
presumption [prɪ'zʌmpʃən] *n* supposition *f*, présomption *f*; (*boldness*) audace *f*.
presumptuous [prɪ'zʌmpʃəs] *adj* présomptueux(euse).
presuppose [pri:sə'pəuz] *vt* présupposer.
pre-tax [pri:'tæks] *adj* avant impôt(s).
pretence, (*US*) **pretense** [prɪ'tɛns] *n* (*claim*) prétention *f*; (*pretext*) prétexte *m*; **she is devoid of all** ~ elle n'est pas du tout prétentieuse; **to make a** ~ **of doing** faire semblant de faire; **on** or **under the** ~ **of doing sth** sous prétexte de faire qch.
pretend [prɪ'tɛnd] *vt* (*feign*) feindre, simuler ♦ *vi* (*feign*) faire semblant; (*claim*): **to** ~ **to sth** prétendre à qch; **to** ~ **to do** faire semblant de faire.
pretense [prɪ'tɛns] *n* (*US*) = **pretence**.
pretension [prɪ'tɛnʃən] *n* (*claim*) prétention *f*; **to have no** ~**s to being sth** n'avoir aucune prétention à qch/à être qch.
pretentious [prɪ'tɛnʃəs] *adj* prétentieux(euse).
preterite ['prɛtərɪt] *n* prétérit *m*.
pretext ['pri:tɛkst] *n* prétexte *m*; **on** or **under the** ~ **of doing sth** sous prétexte de faire qch.
pretty ['prɪtɪ] *adj* joli(e) ♦ *adv* assez.
prevail [prɪ'veɪl] *vi* (*win*) l'emporter, prévaloir; (*be usual*) avoir cours; (*persuade*): **to** ~ **(up)on sb to do** persuader qn de faire.
prevailing [prɪ'veɪlɪŋ] *adj* dominant(e).

prevalent ['prɛvələnt] adj répandu(e), courant(e); (fashion) en vogue.

prevarication [prɪværɪ'keɪʃən] n (usage m de) faux-fuyants mpl.

prevent [prɪ'vɛnt] vt: **to ~ (from doing)** empêcher (de faire).

preventable [prɪ'vɛntəbl] adj évitable.

preventative [prɪ'vɛntətɪv] adj préventif(ive).

prevention [prɪ'vɛnʃən] n prévention f.

preventive [prɪ'vɛntɪv] adj préventif(ive).

preview ['priːvjuː] n (of film) avant-première f; (fig) aperçu m.

previous ['priːvɪəs] adj (last) précédent(e); (earlier) antérieur(e); (question, experience) préalable; **I have a ~ engagement** je suis déjà pris(e); **~ to doing** avant de faire.

previously ['priːvɪəslɪ] adv précédemment, auparavant.

prewar [priː'wɔː*] adj d'avant-guerre.

prey [preɪ] n proie f ♦ vi: **to ~ on** s'attaquer à; **it was ~ing on his mind** ça le rongeait or minait.

price [praɪs] n prix m; (BETTING: odds) cote f ♦ vt (goods) fixer le prix de; tarifer; **what is the ~ of ...?** combien coûte ...?, quel est le prix de ...?; **to go up or rise in ~** augmenter; **to put a ~ on sth** chiffrer qch; **to be ~d out of the market** (article) être trop cher pour soutenir la concurrence; (producer, nation) ne pas pouvoir soutenir la concurrence; **what ~ his promises now?** (BRIT) que valent maintenant toutes ses promesses?; **he regained his freedom, but at a ~** il a retrouvé sa liberté, mais cela lui a coûté cher.

price control n contrôle m des prix.

price-cutting ['praɪskʌtɪŋ] n réductions fpl de prix.

priceless ['praɪslɪs] adj sans prix, inestimable; (col: amusing) impayable.

price list n tarif m.

price range n gamme f de prix; **it's within my ~** c'est dans mes prix.

price tag n étiquette f.

price war n guerre f des prix.

pricey ['praɪsɪ] adj (col) chérot inv.

prick [prɪk] n piqûre f; (col!) bitte f (!); connard m (!) ♦ vt piquer; **to ~ up one's ears** dresser or tendre l'oreille.

prickle ['prɪkl] n (of plant) épine f; (sensation) picotement m.

prickly ['prɪklɪ] adj piquant(e), épineux(euse); (fig: person) irritable.

prickly heat n fièvre f miliaire.

prickly pear n figue f de Barbarie.

pride [praɪd] n (feeling proud) fierté f; (: pej) orgueil m; (self-esteem) amour-propre m ♦ vt: **to ~ o.s. on** se flatter de; s'enorgueillir de; **to take (a) ~ in** être (très) fier(ère) de; **to take a ~ in doing** mettre sa fierté à faire; **to have ~ of place** (BRIT) avoir la place d'honneur.

priest [priːst] n prêtre m.

priestess ['priːstɪs] n prêtresse f.

priesthood ['priːsthud] n prêtrise f, sacerdoce m.

prig [prɪg] n poseur/euse, fat m.

prim [prɪm] adj collet monté inv, guindé(e).

primacy ['praɪməsɪ] n primauté f.

prima facie ['praɪmə'feɪʃɪ] adj: **to have a ~ case** (LAW) avoir une affaire qui paraît fondée.

primal ['praɪməl] adj (first in time) primitif(ive); (first in importance) primordial(e).

primarily ['praɪmərɪlɪ] adv principalement, essentiellement.

primary ['praɪmərɪ] adj primaire; (first in importance) premier(ière), primordial(e) ♦ n (US: election) (élection f) primaire f.

> Aux États-Unis, les **primaries** constituent un processus de sélection préliminaire des candidats qui seront choisis par les principaux partis lors de la campagne électorale pour l'élection présidentielle. Elles ont lieu dans 35 États, de février à juin, l'année de l'élection. Chaque État envoie en juillet - août des **delegates** aux conventions démocrate et républicaine chargées de désigner leur candidat à la présidence. Ces **delegates** sont généralement choisis en fonction du nombre de voix obtenu par les candidats lors des **primaries**.

primary colour n couleur fondamentale.

primary school n (BRIT) école f primaire.

> Les **primary schools** en Grande-Bretagne accueillent les enfants de 5 à 11 ans. Elles marquent le début du cycle scolaire obligatoire et elles comprennent deux sections: la section des petits ("infant school") et la section des grands ("junior school"); voir **secondary school**

primate n (REL) ['praɪmɪt] primat m; (ZOOL) ['praɪmeɪt] primate m.

prime [praɪm] adj primordial(e), fondamental(e); (excellent) excellent(e) ♦ vt (gun, pump) amorcer; (fig) mettre au courant; **in the ~ of life** dans la fleur de l'âge.

prime minister n Premier ministre m.

primer ['praɪmə*] n (book) premier livre, manuel m élémentaire; (paint) apprêt m; (of gun) amorce f.

prime time n (RADIO, TV) heure(s) f(pl) de grande écoute.

primeval [praɪ'miːvl] adj primitif(ive).

primitive ['prɪmɪtɪv] adj primitif(ive).

primrose ['prɪmrəuz] n primevère f.

primus (stove) ['praɪməs-] n ® (BRIT) réchaud m de camping.

prince [prɪns] n prince m.

princess [prɪn'sɛs] n princesse f.

principal ['prɪnsɪpl] adj principal(e) ♦ n (headmaster) directeur m, principal m; (in play) rôle principal; (money) principal m.

principality [prɪnsɪ'pælɪtɪ] n principauté f.
principally ['prɪnsɪplɪ] adv principalement.
principle ['prɪnsɪpl] n principe m; **in ~** en principe; **on ~** par principe.
print [prɪnt] n (mark) empreinte f; (letters) caractères mpl; (fabric) imprimé m; (ART) gravure f, estampe f; (PHOT) épreuve f ♦ vt imprimer; (publish) publier; (write in capitals) écrire en majuscules; **out of ~** épuisé(e).
▶**print out** vt (COMPUT) imprimer.
printed circuit board (PCB) ['prɪntɪd-] n carte f à circuit imprimé.
printed matter ['prɪntɪd-] n imprimés mpl.
printer ['prɪntə*] n imprimeur m; (machine) imprimante f.
printhead ['prɪnthɛd] n tête f d'impression.
printing ['prɪntɪŋ] n impression f.
printing press n presse f typographique.
print-out ['prɪntaʊt] n copie f papier, tirage m.
print wheel n marguerite f.
prior ['praɪə*] adj antérieur(e), précédent(e) ♦ n (REL) prieur m; **~ to doing** avant de faire; **without ~ notice** sans préavis; **to have a ~ claim to sth** avoir priorité pour qch.
priority [praɪ'ɔrɪtɪ] n priorité f; **to have or take ~ over sth/sb** avoir la priorité sur qch/qn.
priory ['praɪərɪ] n prieuré m.
prise [praɪz] vt: **to ~ open** forcer.
prism ['prɪzəm] n prisme m.
prison ['prɪzn] n prison f.
prison camp n camp m de prisonniers.
prisoner ['prɪznə*] n prisonnier/ière; **the ~ at the bar** l'accusé/e; **to take sb ~** faire qn prisonnier; **~ of war** prisonnier de guerre.
prissy ['prɪsɪ] adj bégueule.
pristine ['prɪstiːn] adj virginal(e).
privacy ['prɪvəsɪ] n intimité f, solitude f.
private ['praɪvɪt] adj (not public) privé(e); (personal) personnel(le); (house, car, lesson) particulier(ière) ♦ n soldat m de deuxième classe; **"~"** (on envelope) "personnelle"; **in ~** en privé; **in (his) ~ life** dans sa vie privée; **he is a very ~ person** il est très secret; **to be in ~ practice** être médecin (or dentiste etc) non conventionné; **~ hearing** (LAW) audience f à huis-clos.
private enterprise n entreprise privée.
private eye n détective privé.
private limited company n (BRIT) société f à participation restreinte (non cotée en Bourse).
privately ['praɪvɪtlɪ] adv en privé; (within oneself) intérieurement.
private parts npl parties (génitales).
private property n propriété privée.
private school n école privée.
privation [praɪ'veɪʃən] n privation f.
privatize ['praɪvɪtaɪz] vt privatiser.
privet ['prɪvɪt] n troène m.
privilege ['prɪvɪlɪdʒ] n privilège m.
privileged ['prɪvɪlɪdʒd] adj privilégié(e); **to be ~ to do sth** avoir le privilège de faire qch.

privy ['prɪvɪ] adj: **to be ~ to** être au courant de.
privy council n conseil privé.

Le **privy council** existe en Angleterre depuis l'avènement des Normands. À l'époque, ses membres étaient les conseillers privés du roi, mais en 1688 le cabinet les a supplantés. Les ministres du cabinet sont aujourd'hui automatiquement conseillers du roi, et ce titre est également accordé aux personnes qui ont occupé de hautes fonctions en politique, dans le clergé ou dans les milieux juridiques. Les pouvoirs de ces conseillers en tant que tels sont maintenant limités.

prize [praɪz] n prix m ♦ adj (example, idiot) parfait(e); (bull, novel) primé(e) ♦ vt priser, faire grand cas de.
prize-fighter ['praɪzfaɪtə*] n boxeur professionnel.
prize giving n distribution f des prix.
prize money n argent m du prix.
prizewinner ['praɪzwɪnə*] n gagnant/e.
prizewinning ['praɪzwɪnɪŋ] adj gagnant(e); (novel, essay etc) primé(e).
PRO n abbr = **public relations officer**.
pro [prəʊ] n (SPORT) professionnel/le; **the ~s and cons** le pour et le contre.
pro- [prəʊ] prefix (in favour of) pro-.
pro-active [prəʊ'æktɪv] adj dynamique.
probability [prɔbə'bɪlɪtɪ] n probabilité f; **in all ~** très probablement.
probable ['prɔbəbl] adj probable; **it is ~/hardly ~ that ...** il est probable/peu probable que ....
probably ['prɔbəblɪ] adv probablement.
probate ['prəʊbɪt] n (LAW) validation f, homologation f.
probation [prə'beɪʃən] n (in employment) (période f d')essai m; (LAW) liberté surveillée; (REL) noviciat m, probation f; **on ~** (employee) à l'essai; (LAW) en liberté surveillée.
probationary [prə'beɪʃənrɪ] adj (period) d'essai.
probe [prəʊb] n (MED, SPACE) sonde f; (enquiry) enquête f, investigation f ♦ vt sonder, explorer.
probity ['prəʊbɪtɪ] n probité f.
problem ['prɔbləm] n problème m; **to have ~s with the car** avoir des ennuis avec la voiture; **what's the ~?** qu'y a-t-il?, quel est le problème?; **I had no ~ in finding her** je n'ai pas eu de mal à la trouver; **no ~!** pas de problème!
problematic [prɔblə'mætɪk] adj problématique.
problem-solving ['prɔbləmsɒlvɪŋ] n résolution f de problèmes; **an approach to ~** une approche en matière de résolution de problèmes.
procedure [prə'siːdʒə*] n (ADMIN, LAW) procé-

dure *f*; (*method*) marche *f* à suivre, façon *f* de procéder.

proceed [prə'siːd] *vi* (*go forward*) avancer; (*go about it*) procéder; (*continue*): **to ~ (with)** continuer, poursuivre; **to ~ to** aller à; passer à; **to ~ to do se** mettre à faire; **I am not sure how to ~** je ne sais pas exactement comment m'y prendre; **to ~ against sb** (*LAW*) intenter des poursuites contre qn.

proceedings [prə'siːdɪŋz] *npl* mesures *fpl*; (*LAW*) poursuites *fpl*; (*meeting*) réunion *f*, séance *f*; (*records*) compte rendu; actes *mpl*.

proceeds ['prəusiːdz] *npl* produit *m*, recette *f*.

process ['prəusɛs] *n*; (*method*) procédé *m* ♦ *vt* traiter ♦ *vi* [prə'sɛs] (*BRIT formal: go in procession*) défiler; **in ~** en cours; **we are in the ~ of doing** nous sommes en train de faire.

processed cheese ['prəusɛst-] *n* ≈ fromage fondu.

processing ['prəusɛsɪŋ] *n* traitement *m*.

procession [prə'sɛʃən] *n* défilé *m*, cortège *m*; **funeral ~** cortège funèbre, convoi *m* mortuaire.

pro-choice [prəu'tʃɔɪs] *adj* en faveur de l'avortement.

proclaim [prə'kleɪm] *vt* déclarer, proclamer.

proclamation [prɔklə'meɪʃən] *n* proclamation *f*.

proclivity [prə'klɪvɪtɪ] *n* inclination *f*.

procrastination [prəukræstɪ'neɪʃən] *n* procrastination *f*.

procreation [prəukrɪ'eɪʃən] *n* procréation *f*.

Procurator Fiscal ['prɔkjureɪtə-] *n* (*Scottish*) ≈ procureur *m* (*de la République*).

procure [prə'kjuə*] *vt* (*for o.s.*) se procurer; (*for sb*) procurer.

procurement [prə'kjuəmənt] *n* achat *m*, approvisionnement *m*.

prod [prɔd] *vt* pousser ♦ *n* (*push, jab*) petit coup, poussée *f*.

prodigal ['prɔdɪgl] *adj* prodigue.

prodigious [prə'dɪdʒəs] *adj* prodigieux(euse).

prodigy ['prɔdɪdʒɪ] *n* prodige *m*.

produce *n* ['prɔdjuːs] (*AGR*) produits *mpl* ♦ *vt* [prə'djuːs] produire; (*to show*) présenter; (*cause*) provoquer, causer; (*THEAT*) monter, mettre en scène.

producer [prə'djuːsə*] *n* (*THEAT*) metteur *m* en scène; (*AGR, CINE*) producteur *m*.

product ['prɔdʌkt] *n* produit *m*.

production [prə'dʌkʃən] *n* production *f*; (*THEAT*) mise *f* en scène; **to put into ~** (*goods*) entreprendre la fabrication de.

production agreement *n* (*US*) accord *m* de productivité.

production line *n* chaîne *f* (de fabrication).

production manager *n* directeur/trice de la production.

productive [prə'dʌktɪv] *adj* productif(ive).

productivity [prɔdʌk'tɪvɪtɪ] *n* productivité *f*.

productivity agreement *n* (*BRIT*) accord *m*

de productivité.

productivity bonus *n* prime *f* de rendement.

Prof. [prɔf] *abbr* (= *professor*) Prof.

profane [prə'feɪn] *adj* sacrilège; (*lay*) profane.

profess [prə'fɛs] *vt* professer; **I do not ~ to be an expert** je ne prétends pas être spécialiste.

professed [prə'fɛst] *adj* (*self-declared*) déclaré(e).

profession [prə'fɛʃən] *n* profession *f*; **the ~s** les professions libérales.

professional [prə'fɛʃənl] *n* (*SPORT*) professionnel/le ♦ *adj* professionnel(le); (*work*) de professionnel; **he's a ~ man** il exerce une profession libérale; **to take ~ advice** consulter un spécialiste.

professionalism [prə'fɛʃnəlɪzəm] *n* professionnalisme *m*.

professionally [prə'fɛʃnəlɪ] *adv* professionnellement; (*SPORT: play*) en professionnel; **I only know him ~** je n'ai avec lui que des relations de travail.

professor [prə'fɛsə*] *n* professeur *m* (*titulaire d'une chaire*); (*US: teacher*) professeur *m*.

professorship [prə'fɛsəʃɪp] *n* chaire *f*.

proffer ['prɔfə*] *vt* (*hand*) tendre; (*remark*) faire; (*apologies*) présenter.

proficiency [prə'fɪʃənsɪ] *n* compétence *f*, aptitude *f*.

proficient [prə'fɪʃənt] *adj* compétent(e), capable.

profile ['prəufaɪl] *n* profil *m*; **to keep a high/low ~** (*fig*) rester *or* être très en évidence/discret(ète).

profit ['prɔfɪt] *n* (*from trading*) bénéfice *m*; (*advantage*) profit *m* ♦ *vi*: **to ~ (by *or* from)** profiter (de); **~ and loss account** compte *m* de profits et pertes; **to make a ~** faire un *or* des bénéfice(s); **to sell sth at a ~** vendre qch à profit.

profitability [prɔfɪtə'bɪlɪtɪ] *n* rentabilité *f*.

profitable ['prɔfɪtəbl] *adj* lucratif(ive), rentable; (*fig: beneficial*) avantageux(euse); (: *meeting*) fructueux(euse).

profit centre *n* centre *m* de profit.

profiteering [prɔfɪ'tɪərɪŋ] *n* (*pej*) mercantilisme *m*.

profit-making ['prɔfɪtmeɪkɪŋ] *adj* à but lucratif.

profit margin *n* marge *f* bénéficiaire.

profit-sharing ['prɔfɪtʃɛərɪŋ] *n* intéressement *m* aux bénéfices.

profits tax *n* (*BRIT*) impôt *m* sur les bénéfices.

profligate ['prɔflɪgɪt] *adj* (*behaviour, act*) dissolu(e); (*person*) débauché(e); (*extravagant*): **~ (with)** prodigue (de).

pro forma ['prəu'fɔːmə] *adj*: **~ invoice** facture *f* pro-forma.

profound [prə'faund] *adj* profond(e).

profuse [prə'fjuːs] *adj* abondant(e).

profusely [prə'fjuːslɪ] *adv* abondamment; (*thank etc*) avec effusion.

profusion [prə'fjuːʒən] *n* profusion *f*, abon-

dance *f*.
progeny ['prɔdʒɪnɪ] *n* progéniture *f*; descendants *mpl*.
programme, (*US, also:* BRIT COMPUT) **program** ['prəugræm] *n* programme *m*; (*RADIO, TV*) émission *f* ♦ *vt* programmer.
program(m)er ['prəugræmə*] *n* programmeur/euse.
program(m)ing ['prəugræmɪŋ] *n* programmation *f*.
program(m)ing language *n* langage *m* de programmation.
progress *n* ['prəugrɛs] progrès *m* ♦ *vi* [prə'grɛs] progresser, avancer; **in** ~ en cours; **to make** ~ progresser, faire des progrès, être en progrès; **as the match** ~ed au fur et à mesure que la partie avançait.
progression [prə'grɛʃən] *n* progression *f*.
progressive [prə'grɛsɪv] *adj* progressif(ive); (*person*) progressiste.
progressively [prə'grɛsɪvlɪ] *adv* progressivement.
progress report *n* (*MED*) bulletin *m* de santé; (*ADMIN*) rapport *m* d'activité; rapport sur l'état (d'avancement) des travaux.
prohibit [prə'hɪbɪt] *vt* interdire, défendre; **to** ~ **sb from doing sth** défendre *or* interdire à qn de faire qch; **"smoking** ~**ed"** "défense de fumer".
prohibition [prəuɪ'bɪʃən] *n* prohibition *f*.
prohibitive [prə'hɪbɪtɪv] *adj* (*price etc*) prohibitif(ive).
project *n* ['prɔdʒɛkt] (*plan*) projet *m*, plan *m*; (*venture*) opération *f*, entreprise *f*; (*gen SCOL: research*) étude *f*, dossier *m* ♦ *vb* [prə'dʒɛkt] *vt* projeter ♦ *vi* (*stick out*) faire saillie, s'avancer.
projectile [prə'dʒɛktaɪl] *n* projectile *m*.
projection [prə'dʒɛkʃən] *n* projection *f*; (*overhang*) saillie *f*.
projectionist [prə'dʒɛkʃənɪst] *n* (*CINE*) projectionniste *m/f*.
projection room *n* (*CINE*) cabine *f* de projection.
projector [prə'dʒɛktə*] *n* (*CINE etc*) projecteur *m*.
proletarian [prəulɪ'tɛərɪən] *adj* prolétarien(ne) ♦ *n* prolétaire *m/f*.
proletariat [prəulɪ'tɛərɪət] *n* prolétariat *m*.
pro-life [prəu'laɪf] *adj* contre l'avortement.
proliferate [prə'lɪfəreɪt] *vi* proliférer.
proliferation [prəlɪfə'reɪʃən] *n* prolifération *f*.
prolific [prə'lɪfɪk] *adj* prolifique.
prologue ['prəulɔg] *n* prologue *m*.
prolong [prə'lɔŋ] *vt* prolonger.
prom [prɔm] *n abbr* = **promenade, promenade concert**; (*US: ball*) bal *m* d'étudiants.
promenade [prɔmə'nɑːd] *n* (*by sea*) esplanade *f*, promenade *f*.
promenade concert *n* concert *m* (de musique classique).

En Grande-Bretagne, un **promenade concert** (*ou* **prom**) *est un concert de musique classique, ainsi appelé car, à l'origine, le public restait debout et se promenait au lieu de rester assis. De nos jours, une partie du public reste debout, mais il y a également des places assises (plus chères). Les Proms les plus connus sont les Proms londoniens. La dernière séance (the Last Night of the Proms) est un grand événement médiatique où se jouent des airs traditionnels et patriotiques.*
Aux États-Unis et au Canada, le **prom** *ou* **promenade** *est un bal organisé par le lycée.*

---

promenade deck *n* (*NAUT*) pont *m* promenade.
prominence ['prɔmɪnəns] *n* proéminence *f*; importance *f*.
prominent ['prɔmɪnənt] *adj* (*standing out*) proéminent(e); (*important*) important(e); **he is** ~ **in the field of** ... il est très connu dans le domaine de ....
prominently ['prɔmɪnəntlɪ] *adv* (*display, set*) bien en évidence; **he figured** ~ **in the case** il a joué un rôle important dans l'affaire.
promiscuity [prɔmɪs'kjuːɪtɪ] *n* (*sexual*) légèreté *f* de mœurs.
promiscuous [prə'mɪskjuəs] *adj* (*sexually*) de mœurs légères.
promise ['prɔmɪs] *n* promesse *f* ♦ *vt, vi* promettre; **to make sb a** ~ faire une promesse à qn; **to** ~ **(sb) to do sth** promettre (à qn) de faire qch; **a young man of** ~ un jeune homme plein d'avenir; **to** ~ **well** *vi* promettre.
promising ['prɔmɪsɪŋ] *adj* prometteur(euse).
promissory note ['prɔmɪsərɪ-] *n* billet *m* à ordre.
promontory ['prɔməntrɪ] *n* promontoire *m*.
promote [prə'məut] *vt* promouvoir; (*venture, event*) organiser, mettre sur pied; (*new product*) lancer; **the team was** ~**d to the second division** (BRIT FOOTBALL) l'équipe est montée en 2e division.
promoter [prə'məutə*] *n* (*of event*) organisateur/trice; (*of cause etc*) partisan/e, défenseur *m*.
promotion [prə'məuʃən] *n* promotion *f*.
prompt [prɔmpt] *adj* rapide ♦ *n* (COMPUT) message *m* (de guidage) ♦ *vt* inciter; (*cause*) entraîner, provoquer; (THEAT) souffler (son rôle *or* ses répliques) à; **they're very** ~ (*punctual*) ils sont ponctuels; **at 8 o'clock** ~ à 8 heures précises; **he was** ~ **to accept** il a tout de suite accepté; **to** ~ **sb to do** inciter *or* pousser qn à faire.
prompter ['prɔmptə*] *n* (THEAT) souffleur *m*.
promptly ['prɔmptlɪ] *adv* rapidement, sans délai; ponctuellement.
promptness ['prɔmptnɪs] *n* rapidité *f*; promptitude *f*; ponctualité *f*.

promulgate ['prɔmǝlgeɪt] vt promulguer.

prone [prǝun] adj (lying) couché(e) (face contre terre); (liable): ~ **to** enclin(e) à; **to be ~ to illness** être facilement malade; **to be ~ to an illness** être sujet à une maladie; **she is ~ to burst into tears if** ... elle a tendance à tomber en larmes si ....

prong [prɔŋ] n pointe f, (of fork) dent f.

pronoun ['prǝunaun] n pronom m.

pronounce [prǝ'nauns] vt prononcer ♦ vi: **to ~ (up)on** se prononcer sur; **they ~d him unfit to drive** ils l'ont déclaré inapte à la conduite.

pronounced [prǝ'naunst] adj (marked) prononcé(e).

pronouncement [prǝ'naunsmǝnt] n déclaration f.

pronunciation [prǝnʌnsɪ'eɪʃǝn] n prononciation f.

proof [pruːf] n preuve f, (test, of book, PHOT) épreuve f; (of alcohol) degré m ♦ adj: ~ **against** à l'épreuve de ♦ vt (BRIT: tent, anorak) imperméabiliser; **to be 70° ~** ≈ titrer 40 degrés.

proofreader ['pruːfriːdǝ*] n correcteur/trice (d'épreuves).

prop [prɔp] n support m, étai m ♦ vt (also: ~ **up**) étayer, soutenir; (lean): **to ~ sth against** appuyer qch contre or à.

Prop. abbr (COMM) = **proprietor**.

propaganda [prɔpǝ'gændǝ] n propagande f.

propagation [prɔpǝ'geɪʃǝn] n propagation f.

propel [prǝ'pɛl] vt propulser, faire avancer.

propeller [prǝ'pɛlǝ*] n hélice f.

propelling pencil [prǝ'pɛlɪŋ-] n (BRIT) porte-mine m inv.

propensity [prǝ'pɛnsɪtɪ] n propension f.

proper ['prɔpǝ*] adj (suited, right) approprié(e), bon(bonne); (seemly) correct(e), convenable; (authentic) vrai(e), véritable; (col: real) fini(e), vrai(e); **to go through the ~ channels** (ADMIN) passer par la voie officielle.

properly ['prɔpǝlɪ] adv correctement, convenablement; (really) bel et bien.

proper noun n nom m propre.

property ['prɔpǝtɪ] n (possessions) biens mpl; (house etc) propriété f; (land) terres fpl, domaine m; (CHEM etc: quality) propriété f; **it's their ~** cela leur appartient, c'est leur propriété.

property developer n (BRIT) promoteur immobilier.

property owner n propriétaire m.

property tax n impôt foncier.

prophecy ['prɔfɪsɪ] n prophétie f.

prophesy ['prɔfɪsaɪ] vt prédire ♦ vi prophétiser.

prophet ['prɔfɪt] n prophète m.

prophetic [prǝ'fɛtɪk] adj prophétique.

proportion [prǝ'pɔːʃǝn] n proportion f; (share) part f, partie f ♦ vt proportionner; **to be in/out of ~ to** or **with sth** être à la mesure de/hors de proportion avec qch; **to see sth in ~** (fig) ramener qch à de justes proportions.

proportional [prǝ'pɔːʃǝnl], **proportionate** [prǝ'pɔːʃǝnɪt] adj proportionnel(le).

proportional representation (PR) n (POL) représentation proportionnelle.

proposal [prǝ'pǝuzl] n proposition f, offre f; (plan) projet m; (of marriage) demande f en mariage.

propose [prǝ'pǝuz] vt proposer, suggérer; (have in mind): **to ~ sth/to do** or **doing sth** envisager qch/de faire qch ♦ vi faire sa demande en mariage; **to ~ to do** avoir l'intention de faire.

proposer [prǝ'pǝuzǝ*] n (BRIT: of motion etc) auteur m.

proposition [prɔpǝ'zɪʃǝn] n proposition f; **to make sb a ~** faire une proposition à qn.

propound [prǝ'paund] vt proposer, soumettre.

proprietary [prǝ'praɪǝtǝrɪ] adj de marque déposée; ~ **article** article m or produit m de marque; ~ **brand** marque déposée.

proprietor [prǝ'praɪǝtǝ*] n propriétaire m/f.

propriety [prǝ'praɪǝtɪ] n (seemliness) bienséance f, convenance f.

propulsion [prǝ'pʌlʃǝn] n propulsion f.

pro rata [prǝu'rɑːtǝ] adv au prorata.

prosaic [prǝu'zeɪɪk] adj prosaïque.

Pros. Atty. abbr (US) = **prosecuting attorney**.

proscribe [prǝ'skraɪb] vt proscrire.

prose [prǝuz] n prose f; (SCOL: translation) thème m.

prosecute ['prɔsɪkjuːt] vt poursuivre.

prosecuting attorney (Pros. Atty.) ['prɔsɪkjuːtɪŋ-] n (US) procureur m.

prosecution [prɔsɪ'kjuːʃǝn] n poursuites fpl judiciaires; (accusing side) accusation f.

prosecutor ['prɔsɪkjuːtǝ*] n procureur m; (also: **public ~**) ministère public.

prospect n ['prɔspɛkt] perspective f; (hope) espoir m, chances fpl ♦ vt, vi [prǝ'spɛkt] prospecter; **we are faced with the ~ of leaving** nous risquons de devoir partir; **there is every ~ of an early victory** tout laisse prévoir une victoire rapide.

prospecting [prǝ'spɛktɪŋ] n prospection f.

prospective [prǝ'spɛktɪv] adj (possible) éventuel(le); (future) futur(e).

prospector [prǝ'spɛktǝ*] n prospecteur m; **gold ~** chercheur m d'or.

prospects ['prɔspɛkts] npl (for work etc) possibilités fpl d'avenir, débouchés mpl.

prospectus [prǝ'spɛktǝs] n prospectus m.

prosper ['prɔspǝ*] vi prospérer.

prosperity [prɔ'spɛrɪtɪ] n prospérité f.

prosperous ['prɔspǝrǝs] adj prospère.

prostate ['prɔsteɪt] n (also: ~ **gland**) prostate f.

prostitute ['prɔstɪtjuːt] n prostituée f; **male ~** prostitué m.

prostitution [prɔstɪ'tjuːʃǝn] n prostitution f.

prostrate *adj* ['prɔstreɪt] prosterné(e); *(fig)* prostré(e) ◆ *vt* [prɔ'streɪt]: **to ~ o.s. (before sb)** se prosterner (devant qn).

protagonist [prə'tægənɪst] *n* protagoniste *m*.

protect [prə'tɛkt] *vt* protéger.

protection [prə'tɛkʃən] *n* protection *f*; **to be under sb's ~** être sous la protection de qn.

protectionism [prə'tɛkʃənɪzəm] *n* protectionnisme *m*.

protection racket *n* racket *m*.

protective [prə'tɛktɪv] *adj* protecteur(trice); **~ custody** *(LAW)* détention préventive.

protector [prə'tɛktə*] *n* protecteur/trice.

protégé ['prəutɛʒeɪ] *n* protégé *m*.

protégée ['prəutɛʒeɪ] *n* protégée *f*.

protein ['prəutiːn] *n* protéine *f*.

pro tem [prəu'tɛm] *adv abbr* (= *pro tempore: for the time being*) provisoirement.

protest *n* ['prəutɛst] protestation *f* ◆ *vb* [prə'tɛst] *vi*: **to ~ against/about** protester contre/à propos de ◆ *vt* protester de.

Protestant ['prɔtɪstənt] *adj*, *n* protestant(e).

protester, protestor [prə'tɛstə*] *n* (*in demonstration*) manifestant/e.

protest march *n* manifestation *f*.

protocol ['prəutəkɔl] *n* protocole *m*.

prototype ['prəutətaɪp] *n* prototype *m*.

protracted [prə'træktɪd] *adj* prolongé(e).

protractor [prə'træktə*] *n* (*GEOM*) rapporteur *m*.

protrude [prə'truːd] *vi* avancer, dépasser.

protuberance [prə'tjuːbərəns] *n* protubérance *f*.

proud [praud] *adj* fier(ère); (*pej*) orgueilleux(euse); **to be ~ to do sth** être fier de faire qch; **to do sb ~** (*col*) faire honneur à qn; **to do o.s. ~** (*col*) ne se priver de rien.

proudly ['praudlɪ] *adv* fièrement.

prove [pruːv] *vt* prouver, démontrer ◆ *vi*: **to ~ correct** *etc* s'avérer juste *etc*; **to ~ o.s.** montrer ce dont on est capable; **to ~ o.s./itself (to be) useful** *etc* se montrer *or* se révéler utile *etc*; **he was ~d right in the end** il s'est avéré qu'il avait raison.

proverb ['prɔvə:b] *n* proverbe *m*.

proverbial [prə'və:bɪəl] *adj* proverbial(e).

provide [prə'vaɪd] *vt* fournir; **to ~ sb with sth** fournir qch à qn; **to be ~d with** (*person*) disposer de; (*thing*) être équipé(e) *or* muni(e) de.

▶**provide for** *vt fus* (*person*) subvenir aux besoins de; (*emergency*) prévoir.

provided [prə'vaɪdɪd] *conj*: **~ (that)** à condition que + *sub*.

Providence ['prɔvɪdəns] *n* la Providence.

providing [prə'vaɪdɪŋ] *conj* à condition que + *sub*.

province ['prɔvɪns] *n* province *f*.

provincial [prə'vɪnʃəl] *adj* provincial(e).

provision [prə'vɪʒən] *n* (*supply*) provision *f*; (*supplying*) fourniture *f*; approvisionnement *m*; (*stipulation*) disposition *f*; **~s** *npl* (*food*)

provisions *fpl*; **to make ~ for** (*one's future*) assurer; (*one's family*) assurer l'avenir de; **there's no ~ for this in the contract** le contrat ne prévoit pas cela.

provisional [prə'vɪʒənl] *adj* provisoire ◆ *n*: **P~** (*Irish POL*) Provisional *m* (*membre de la tendance activiste de l'IRA*).

provisional licence *n* (*BRIT AUT*) permis *m* provisoire.

provisionally [prə'vɪʒnəlɪ] *adv* provisoirement.

proviso [prə'vaɪzəu] *n* condition *f*; **with the ~ that** à la condition (expresse) que.

Provo ['prɔvəu] *n abbr* (*col*) = **Provisional**.

provocation [prɔvə'keɪʃən] *n* provocation *f*.

provocative [prə'vɔkətɪv] *adj* provocateur(trice), provocant(e).

provoke [prə'vəuk] *vt* provoquer; **to ~ sb to sth/to do** *or* **into doing sth** pousser qn à qch/à faire qch.

provoking [prə'vəukɪŋ] *adj* énervant(e), exaspérant(e).

provost ['prɔvəst] *n* (*BRIT: of university*) principal *m*; (*Scottish*) maire *m*.

prow [prau] *n* proue *f*.

prowess ['prauɪs] *n* prouesse *f*.

prowl [praul] *vi* (*also*: **~ about, ~ around**) rôder ◆ *n*: **to be on the ~** rôder.

prowler ['praulə*] *n* rôdeur/euse.

proximity [prɔk'sɪmɪtɪ] *n* proximité *f*.

proxy ['prɔksɪ] *n* procuration *f*; **by ~** par procuration.

PRP *n abbr* (= *performance related pay*) salaire *m* au rendement.

prude [pruːd] *n* prude *f*.

prudence ['pruːdns] *n* prudence *f*.

prudent ['pruːdnt] *adj* prudent(e).

prudish ['pruːdɪʃ] *adj* prude, pudibond(e).

prune [pruːn] *n* pruneau *m* ◆ *vt* élaguer.

pry [praɪ] *vi*: **to ~ into** fourrer son nez dans.

PS *n abbr* (= *postscript*) PS *m*.

psalm [sɑːm] *n* psaume *m*.

PSAT *n abbr* (*US*) = *Preliminary Scholastic Aptitude Test*.

PSBR *n abbr* (*BRIT*: = *public sector borrowing requirement*) besoins *mpl* d'emprunts des pouvoirs publics.

pseud [sjuːd] *n* (*BRIT col: intellectually*) pseudo-intello *m*; (: *socially*) snob *m/f*.

pseudo- ['sjuːdəu] *prefix* pseudo-.

pseudonym ['sjuːdənɪm] *n* pseudonyme *m*.

PST *abbr* (*US*: = *Pacific Standard Time*) heure d'hiver du Pacifique.

PSV *n abbr* (*BRIT*) = **public service vehicle**.

psyche ['saɪkɪ] *n* psychisme *m*.

psychiatric [saɪkɪ'ætrɪk] *adj* psychiatrique.

psychiatrist [saɪ'kaɪətrɪst] *n* psychiatre *m/f*.

psychiatry [saɪ'kaɪətrɪ] *n* psychiatrie *f*.

psychic ['saɪkɪk] *adj* (*also*: **~al**) (méta)psychique; (*person*) doué(e) de télépathie *or* d'un sixième sens.

psycho ['saɪkəu] *n* (*col*) psychopathe *m/f*.

psychoanalyse – pudding

psychoanalyse [saɪkəu'ænəlaɪz] *vt* psychanalyser.
psychoanalysis, *pl* -ses [saɪkəuə'næləsɪs, -siːz] *n* psychanalyse *f*.
psychoanalyst [saɪkəu'ænəlɪst] *n* psychanalyste *m/f*.
psychological [saɪkə'lɔdʒɪkl] *adj* psychologique.
psychologist [saɪ'kɔlədʒɪst] *n* psychologue *m/f*.
psychology [saɪ'kɔlədʒɪ] *n* psychologie *f*.
psychopath ['saɪkəupæθ] *n* psychopathe *m/f*.
psychosis, *pl* psychoses [saɪ'kəusɪs, -siːz] *n* psychose *f*.
psychosomatic [saɪkəusə'mætɪk] *adj* psychosomatique.
psychotherapy [saɪkəu'θɛrəpɪ] *n* psychothérapie *f*.
psychotic [saɪ'kɔtɪk] *adj, n* psychotique (*m/f*).
PT *n abbr* (*BRIT*: = *physical training*) EPS *f*.
Pt. *abbr* (*in place names*: = *Point*) Pte.
pt *abbr* = pint, point.
PTA *n abbr* = Parent-Teacher Association.
Pte. *abbr* (*BRIT MIL*) = private.
PTO *abbr* (= *please turn over*) TSVP (= *tournez s'il vous plaît*).
PTV *n abbr* (*US*) = pay television, public television.
pub [pʌb] *n abbr* (= *public house*) pub *m*.

Un pub *comprend en général deux salles: l'une ("the lounge") est plutôt confortable, avec des fauteuils et des bancs capitonnés, tandis que l'autre ("the public bar") est simplement un bar où les consommations sont en général moins chères. Cette dernière est souvent aussi une salle de jeux, les jeux les plus courants étant les fléchettes, les dominos et le billard. Il y a parfois aussi une petite arrière-salle douillette appelée "the snug". Beaucoup de pubs servent maintenant des repas, surtout à l'heure du déjeuner, et c'est alors le seul moment où les enfants sont acceptés, à condition d'être accompagnés. Les pubs sont en général ouverts de 11 h à 23 h, mais cela peut varier selon leur licence; certains pubs ferment l'après-midi.*

pub crawl *n* (*BRIT col*): to go on a ~ faire la tournée des bars.
puberty ['pjuːbətɪ] *n* puberté *f*.
pubic ['pjuːbɪk] *adj* pubien(ne), du pubis.
public ['pʌblɪk] *adj* public(ique) ♦ *n* public *m*; in ~ en public; the general ~ le grand public; to be ~ knowledge être de notoriété publique; to go ~ (*COMM*) être coté(e) en Bourse.
public address system (PA) *n* (système *m* de) sonorisation *f*, sono *f* (*col*).
publican ['pʌblɪkən] *n* patron *m* or gérant *m* de pub.
publication [pʌblɪ'keɪʃən] *n* publication *f*.

public company *n* société *f* anonyme (*cotée en Bourse*).
public convenience *n* (*BRIT*) toilettes *fpl*.
public holiday *n* (*BRIT*) jour férié.
public house *n* (*BRIT*) pub *m*.
publicity [pʌb'lɪsɪtɪ] *n* publicité *f*.
publicize ['pʌblɪsaɪz] *vt* faire connaître, rendre public.
public limited company (plc) *n* ≈ société *f* anonyme (SA) (*cotée en Bourse*).
publicly ['pʌblɪklɪ] *adv* publiquement, en public.
public opinion *n* opinion publique.
public ownership *n*: to be taken into ~ être nationalisé(e), devenir propriété de l'État.
public prosecutor *n* ≈ procureur *m* (*de la République*); ~'s office parquet *m*.
public relations (PR) *n or npl* relations publiques (RP).
public relations officer *n* responsable *m/f* des relations publiques.
public school *n* (*BRIT*) école privée; (*US*) école publique.

Une public school *est un établissement d'enseignement secondaire privé. Bon nombre d'entre elles sont des pensionnats. Beaucoup ont également une école primaire qui leur est rattachée (une* prep *ou* preparatory school) *pour préparer les élèves au cycle secondaire. Ces écoles sont en général prestigieuses, et les frais de scolarité sont très élevés dans les plus connues (Westminster, Eton, Harrow). Beaucoup d'élèves vont ensuite à l'université, et un grand nombre entre à Oxford ou à Cambridge. Les grands industriels, les députés et les hauts fonctionnaires sortent souvent de ces écoles. En Écosse et aux États-Unis, le terme "public school" désigne tout simplement une école publique gratuite.*

public sector *n* secteur public.
public service vehicle (PSV) *n* (*BRIT*) véhicule affecté au transport de personnes.
public-spirited [pʌblɪk'spɪrɪtɪd] *adj* qui fait preuve de civisme.
public transport, (*US*) public transportation *n* transports *mpl* en commun.
public utility *n* service public.
public works *npl* travaux publics.
publish ['pʌblɪʃ] *vt* publier.
publisher ['pʌblɪʃə*] *n* éditeur *m*.
publishing ['pʌblɪʃɪŋ] *n* (*industry*) édition *f*; (*of a book*) publication *f*.
publishing company *n* maison *f* d'édition.
puce [pjuːs] *adj* puce.
puck [pʌk] *n* (*elf*) lutin *m*; (*ICE HOCKEY*) palet *m*.
pucker ['pʌkə*] *vt* plisser.
pudding ['pudɪŋ] *n* (*BRIT*: *sweet*) dessert *m*, entremets *m*; (*sausage*) boudin *m*; rice ~ ≈ riz *m* au lait; black ~, (*US*) blood ~ boudin (noir).

puddle – purchase

puddle ['pʌdl] n flaque f d'eau.
puerile ['pjuəraɪl] adj puéril(e).
Puerto Rico ['pwɔːˈtəuˈriːkəu] n Porto Rico f.
puff [pʌf] n bouffée f ♦ vt: **to ~ one's pipe** tirer sur sa pipe; (also: ~ **out**: sails, cheeks) gonfler ♦ vi sortir par bouffées; (pant) haleter; **to ~ out smoke** envoyer des bouffées de fumée.
puffed [pʌft] adj (col: out of breath) tout(e) essoufflé(e).
puffin ['pʌfɪn] n macareux m.
puff pastry, (US) **puff paste** n pâte feuilletée.
puffy ['pʌfɪ] adj bouffi(e), boursouflé(e).
pugnacious [pʌgˈneɪʃəs] adj pugnace, batailleur(euse).
pull [pul] n (of moon, magnet, the sea etc) attraction f; (fig) influence f ♦ vt tirer; (strain: muscle, tendon) se claquer ♦ vi tirer; **to give sth a ~** (tug) tirer sur qch; **to ~ a face** faire une grimace; **to ~ to pieces** mettre en morceaux; **to ~ one's punches** (also fig) ménager son adversaire; **to ~ one's weight** y mettre du sien; **to ~ o.s. together** se ressaisir; **to ~ sb's leg** (fig) faire marcher qn; **to ~ strings (for sb)** intervenir (en faveur de qn).
▶**pull about** vt (BRIT: handle roughly: object) maltraiter; (: person) malmener.
▶**pull apart** vt séparer; (break) mettre en pièces, démantibuler.
▶**pull down** vt baisser, abaisser; (house) démolir; (tree) abattre.
▶**pull in** vi (AUT) se ranger; (RAIL) entrer en gare.
▶**pull off** vt enlever, ôter; (deal etc) conclure.
▶**pull out** vi démarrer, partir; (withdraw) se retirer; (AUT: come out of line) déboîter ♦ vt sortir; arracher; (withdraw) retirer.
▶**pull over** vi (AUT) se ranger.
▶**pull round** vi (unconscious person) revenir à soi; (sick person) se rétablir.
▶**pull through** vi s'en sortir.
▶**pull up** vi (stop) s'arrêter ♦ vt remonter; (uproot) déraciner, arracher; (stop) arrêter.
pulley ['pulɪ] n poulie f.
pull-out ['pulaut] n (of forces etc) retrait m ♦ cpd (magazine, pages) détachable.
pullover ['puləuvə*] n pull-over m, tricot m.
pulp [pʌlp] n (of fruit) pulpe f; (for paper) pâte f à papier; (pej: also: ~ **magazines** etc) presse f à sensation or de bas étage; **to reduce sth to (a) ~** réduire qch en purée.
pulpit ['pulpɪt] n chaire f.
pulsate [pʌlˈseɪt] vi battre, palpiter; (music) vibrer.
pulse [pʌls] n (of blood) pouls m; (of heart) battement m; (of music, engine) vibrations fpl; **to feel or take sb's ~** prendre le pouls à qn.
pulses ['pʌlsəz] npl (CULIN) légumineuses fpl.
pulverize ['pʌlvəraɪz] vt pulvériser.
puma ['pjuːmə] n puma m.
pumice ['pʌmɪs] n (also: ~ **stone**) pierre f ponce.

pummel ['pʌml] vt rouer de coups.
pump [pʌmp] n pompe f; (shoe) escarpin m ♦ vt pomper; (fig: col) faire parler; **to ~ sb for information** essayer de soutirer des renseignements à qn.
▶**pump up** vt gonfler.
pumpkin ['pʌmpkɪn] n potiron m, citrouille f.
pun [pʌn] n jeu m de mots, calembour m.
punch [pʌntʃ] n (blow) coup m de poing; (fig: force) vivacité f, mordant m; (tool) poinçon m; (drink) punch m ♦ vt (make a hole) poinçonner, perforer; (hit): **to ~ sb/sth** donner un coup de poing à qn/sur qch; **to ~ a hole (in)** faire un trou (dans).
▶**punch in** vi (US) pointer (en arrivant).
▶**punch out** vi (US) pointer (en partant).
punch-drunk ['pʌntʃdrʌŋk] adj (BRIT) sonné(e).
punch(ed) card [pʌntʃ(t)-] n carte perforée.
punch line n (of joke) conclusion f.
punch-up ['pʌntʃʌp] n (BRIT col) bagarre f.
punctual ['pʌŋktjuəl] adj ponctuel(le).
punctuality [pʌŋktjuˈælɪtɪ] n ponctualité f.
punctually ['pʌŋktjuəlɪ] adv ponctuellement; **it will start ~ at 6** cela commencera à 6 heures précises.
punctuate ['pʌŋktjueɪt] vt ponctuer.
punctuation [pʌŋktjuˈeɪʃən] n ponctuation f.
punctuation mark n signe m de ponctuation.
puncture ['pʌŋktʃə*] n (BRIT) crevaison f ♦ vt crever; **I have a ~** (AUT) j'ai (un pneu) crevé.
pundit ['pʌndɪt] n individu m qui pontifie, pontife m.
pungent ['pʌndʒənt] adj piquant(e); (fig) mordant(e), caustique.
punish ['pʌnɪʃ] vt punir; **to ~ sb for sth/for doing sth** punir qn de qch/d'avoir fait qch.
punishable ['pʌnɪʃəbl] adj punissable.
punishing ['pʌnɪʃɪŋ] adj (fig: exhausting) épuisant(e) ♦ n punition f.
punishment ['pʌnɪʃmənt] n punition f, châtiment m; (fig: col): **to take a lot of ~** (boxer) encaisser; (car, person etc) être mis(e) à dure épreuve.
punk [pʌŋk] n (person: also: ~ **rocker**) punk m/f; (music: also: ~ **rock**) le punk; (US col: hoodlum) voyou m.
punt [pʌnt] n (boat) bachot m; (IRELAND) livre irlandaise ♦ vi (BRIT: bet) parier.
punter ['pʌntə*] n (BRIT: gambler) parieur/euse; (: col) Monsieur m tout le monde; type m.
puny ['pjuːnɪ] adj chétif(ive).
pup [pʌp] n chiot m.
pupil ['pjuːpl] n élève m/f; (of eye) pupille f.
puppet ['pʌpɪt] n marionnette f, pantin m.
puppet government n gouvernement m fantoche.
puppy ['pʌpɪ] n chiot m, petit chien.
purchase ['pɔːtʃɪs] n achat m; (grip) prise f ♦ vt

acheter; **to get a ~ on** trouver appui sur.
purchase order *n* ordre *m* d'achat.
purchase price *n* prix *m* d'achat.
purchaser ['pɜːtʃɪsə*] *n* acheteur/euse.
purchase tax *n* (*BRIT*) taxe *f* à l'achat.
purchasing power ['pɜːtʃɪsɪŋ-] *n* pouvoir *m* d'achat.
pure [pjuə*] *adj* pur(e); **a ~ wool jumper** un pull en pure laine; **~ and simple** pur(e) et simple.
purebred ['pjuəbred] *adj* de race.
purée ['pjuəreɪ] *n* purée *f.*
purely ['pjuəlɪ] *adv* purement.
purge [pɜːdʒ] *n* (*MED*) purge *f*; (*POL*) épuration *f*, purge ♦ *vt* purger; (*fig*) épurer, purger.
purification [pjuərɪfɪ'keɪʃən] *n* purification *f.*
purify ['pjuərɪfaɪ] *vt* purifier, épurer.
purist ['pjuərɪst] *n* puriste *m/f.*
puritan ['pjuərɪtən] *n* puritain/e.
puritanical [pjuərɪ'tænɪkl] *adj* puritain(e).
purity ['pjuərɪtɪ] *n* pureté *f.*
purl [pɜːl] *n* maille *f* à l'envers ♦ *vt* tricoter à l'envers.
purloin [pɜː'lɔɪn] *vt* dérober.
purple ['pɜːpl] *adj* violet(te); cramoisi(e).
purport [pɜː'pɔːt] *vi*: **to ~ to be/do** prétendre être/faire.
purpose ['pɜːpəs] *n* intention *f*, but *m*; **on ~** exprès; **for illustrative ~s** à titre d'illustration; **for teaching ~s** dans un but pédagogique; **for the ~s of this meeting** pour cette réunion; **to no ~** en pure perte.
purpose-built ['pɜːpəs'bɪlt] *adj* (*BRIT*) fait(e) sur mesure.
purposeful ['pɜːpəsful] *adj* déterminé(e), résolu(e).
purposely ['pɜːpəslɪ] *adv* exprès.
purr [pɜː*] *n* ronronnement *m* ♦ *vi* ronronner.
purse [pɜːs] *n* porte-monnaie *m inv*, bourse *f*; (*US: handbag*) sac *m* (à main) ♦ *vt* serrer, pincer.
purser ['pɜːsə*] *n* (*NAUT*) commissaire *m* du bord.
purse snatcher [-'snætʃə*] *n* (*US*) voleur *m* à l'arraché.
pursue [pə'sjuː] *vt* poursuivre; (*pleasures*) rechercher; (*inquiry, matter*) approfondir.
pursuer [pə'sjuːə*] *n* poursuivant/e.
pursuit [pə'sjuːt] *n* poursuite *f*; (*occupation*) occupation *f*, activité *f*; **scientific ~s** recherches *fpl* scientifiques; **in (the) ~ of sth** à la recherche de qch.
purveyor [pə'veɪə*] *n* fournisseur *m.*
pus [pʌs] *n* pus *m.*
push [puʃ] *n* poussée *f*; (*effort*) gros effort; (*drive*) énergie *f* ♦ *vt* pousser; (*button*) appuyer sur; (*thrust*): **to ~ sth (into)** enfoncer qch (dans); (*fig*) mettre en avant, faire de la publicité pour ♦ *vi* pousser; appuyer; **to ~ a door open/shut** pousser une porte (pour l'ouvrir/pour la fermer); **"~"** (*on door*) "pousser"; (*on bell*) "appuyer"; **to ~ for** (*bet-*

ter pay, conditions) réclamer; **to be ~ed for time/money** être à court de temps/d'argent; **she is ~ing fifty** (*col*) elle frise la cinquantaine; **at a ~** (*BRIT col*) à la limite, à la rigueur.
►**push aside** *vt* écarter.
►**push in** *vi* s'introduire de force.
►**push off** *vi* (*col*) filer, ficher le camp.
►**push on** *vi* (*continue*) continuer.
►**push over** *vt* renverser.
►**push through** *vt* (*measure*) faire voter.
►**push up** *vt* (*total, prices*) faire monter.
push-bike ['puʃbaɪk] *n* (*BRIT*) vélo *m.*
push-button ['puʃbʌtn] *n* bouton(-poussoir *m*) *m.*
pushchair ['puʃtʃeə*] *n* (*BRIT*) poussette *f.*
pusher ['puʃə*] *n* (*also:* **drug ~**) revendeur/euse (de drogue), ravitailleur/euse (en drogue).
pushover ['puʃəuvə*] *n* (*col*): **it's a ~** c'est un jeu d'enfant.
push-up ['puʃʌp] *n* (*US*) traction *f.*
pushy ['puʃɪ] *adj* (*pej*) arriviste.
puss, pussy(-cat) [pus, 'pusɪ(kæt)] *n* minet *m.*
put, *pt, pp* **put** [put] *vt* mettre; (*place*) poser, placer; (*say*) dire, exprimer; (*a question*) poser; (*estimate*) estimer; **to ~ sb in a good/bad mood** mettre qn de bonne/mauvaise humeur; **to ~ sb to bed** mettre qn au lit, coucher qn; **to ~ sb to a lot of trouble** déranger qn; **how shall I ~ it?** comment dirais-je?, comment dire?; **to ~ a lot of time into sth** passer beaucoup de temps à qch; **to ~ money on a horse** miser sur un cheval; **I ~ it to you that ...** (*BRIT*) je (vous) suggère que ..., je suis d'avis que ...; **to stay ~** ne pas bouger.
►**put about** *vi* (*NAUT*) virer de bord ♦ *vt* (*rumour*) faire courir.
►**put across** *vt* (*ideas etc*) communiquer; faire comprendre.
►**put aside** *vt* mettre de côté.
►**put away** *vt* (*store*) ranger.
►**put back** *vt* (*replace*) remettre, replacer; (*postpone*) remettre; (*delay, also: watch, clock*) retarder; **this will ~ us back ten years** cela nous ramènera dix ans en arrière.
►**put by** *vt* (*money*) mettre de côté, économiser.
►**put down** *vt* (*parcel etc*) poser, déposer; (*pay*) verser; (*in writing*) mettre par écrit, inscrire; (*suppress: revolt etc*) réprimer, écraser; (*attribute*) attribuer.
►**put forward** *vt* (*ideas*) avancer, proposer; (*date, watch, clock*) avancer.
►**put in** *vt* (*gas, electricity*) installer; (*application, complaint*) faire.
►**put in for** *vt fus* (*job*) poser sa candidature pour; (*promotion*) solliciter.
►**put off** *vt* (*light etc*) éteindre; (*postpone*) remettre à plus tard, ajourner; (*discourage*) dissuader.

►**put on** vt (clothes, lipstick etc) mettre; (light etc) allumer; (play etc) monter; (extra bus, train etc) mettre en service; (food, meal) servir; (weight) prendre; (assume: accent, manner) prendre; (: airs) se donner, prendre; (brake) mettre; (col: tease) faire marcher; (inform, indicate): **to ~ sb on to sb/sth** indiquer qn/qch à qn.

►**put out** vt mettre dehors; (one's hand) tendre; (news, rumour) faire courir, répandre; (light etc) éteindre; (person: inconvenience) déranger, gêner; (BRIT: dislocate) se démettre ♦ vi (NAUT): **to ~ out to sea** prendre le large; **to ~ out from Plymouth** quitter Plymouth.

►**put through** vt (caller) mettre en communication; (call) passer; **~ me through to Miss Blair** passez-moi Miss Blair.

►**put together** vt mettre ensemble; (assemble: furniture, toy etc) monter, assembler; (meal) préparer.

►**put up** vt (raise) lever, relever, remonter; (pin up) afficher; (hang) accrocher; (build) construire, ériger; (a tent) monter; (increase) augmenter; (accommodate) loger; (incite): **to ~ sb up to doing sth** pousser qn à faire qch; **to ~ sth up for sale** mettre qch en vente.

►**put upon** vt fus: **to be ~ upon** (imposed on) se laisser faire.

►**put up with** vt fus supporter.

putrid ['pjuːtrɪd] adj putride.

putt [pʌt] vt, vi putter ♦ n putt m.

putter ['pʌtə*] n (GOLF) putter m.

putting green ['pʌtɪŋ-] n green m.

putty ['pʌtɪ] n mastic m.

put-up ['putʌp] adj: **~ job** coup monté.

puzzle ['pʌzl] n énigme f, mystère m; (jigsaw) puzzle m; (also: crossword ~) problème m de mots croisés ♦ vt intriguer, rendre perplexe ♦ vi se creuser la tête; **to ~ over** chercher à comprendre; **to be ~d about sth** être perplexe au sujet de qch.

puzzling ['pʌzlɪŋ] adj déconcertant(e), inexplicable.

PVC n abbr (= polyvinyl chloride) PVC m.

Pvt. abbr (US MIL) = **private**.

pw abbr (= per week) p.sem.

PX n abbr (US MIL) = **post exchange**.

pygmy ['pɪgmɪ] n pygmée m/f.

pyjamas [pɪ'dʒɑːməz] npl (BRIT) pyjama m; **a pair of ~** un pyjama.

pylon ['paɪlən] n pylône m.

pyramid ['pɪrəmɪd] n pyramide f.

Pyrenean [pɪrə'niːən] adj pyrénéen(ne), des Pyrénées.

Pyrenees [pɪrə'niːz] npl: **the ~** les Pyrénées fpl.

Pyrex ['paɪrɛks] n ® Pyrex m ® ♦ cpd: **~ dish** plat m en Pyrex.

python ['paɪθən] n python m.

Q q

Q, q [kjuː] n (letter) Q, q m; **Q for Queen** Q comme Quintal.

Qatar [kæ'tɑː*] n Qatar m, Katar m.

En Angleterre, un **QC** ou **Queen's Counsel** (ou **KC** pour **King's Counsel**, sous le règne d'un roi) est un avocat qui reçoit un poste de haut fonctionnaire sur recommandation du Lord Chancellor. Il fait alors souvent suivre son nom des lettres QC, et lorsqu'il va au tribunal, il est toujours accompagné par un autre avocat (un "junior barrister").

QED abbr (= quod erat demonstrandum) CQFD.

QM n abbr = **quartermaster**.

q.t. n abbr (col: = quiet): **on the ~** discrètement.

qty abbr (= quantity) qté.

quack [kwæk] n (of duck) coin-coin m inv; (pej: doctor) charlatan m ♦ vi faire coin-coin.

quad [kwɔd] n abbr = **quadruple, quadruplet, quadrangle**.

quadrangle ['kwɔdræŋgl] n (MATH) quadrilatère m; (courtyard: abbr: **quad**) cour f.

quadruped ['kwɔdruped] n quadrupède m.

quadruple [kwɔ'druːpl] adj, n quadruple (m) ♦ vt, vi quadrupler.

quadruplet [kwɔ'druːplɪt] n un/une des quadruplé(e)s.

quagmire ['kwægmaɪə*] n bourbier m.

quail [kweɪl] n (ZOOL) caille f ♦ vi: **to ~ at** or **before** se décourager devant.

quaint [kweɪnt] adj bizarre; (old-fashioned) désuet(ète); au charme vieillot, pittoresque.

quake [kweɪk] vi trembler ♦ n abbr = **earthquake**.

Quaker ['kweɪkə*] n quaker/esse.

qualification [kwɔlɪfɪ'keɪʃən] n (degree etc) diplôme m; (ability) compétence f, qualification f; (limitation) réserve f, restriction f; **what are your ~s?** qu'avez-vous comme diplômes?; quelles sont vos qualifications?

qualified ['kwɔlɪfaɪd] adj diplômé(e); (able) compétent(e), qualifié(e); (limited) conditionnel(le); **it was a ~ success** ce fut un succès mitigé; **~ for/to do** qui a les diplômes requis pour/pour faire; qualifié pour/pour faire.

qualify ['kwɔlɪfaɪ] vt qualifier; (limit: statement) apporter des réserves à ♦ vi: **to ~ (as)** obtenir son diplôme (de); **to ~ (for)** remplir les conditions requises (pour); (SPORT) se qualifier (pour).

qualifying ['kwɔlɪfaɪɪŋ] *adj*: ~ **exam** examen *m* d'entrée; ~ **round** éliminatoires *fpl*.
qualitative ['kwɔlɪtətɪv] *adj* qualitatif(ive).
quality ['kwɔlɪtɪ] *n* qualité *f* ♦ *cpd* de qualité; **of good/poor** ~ de bonne/mauvaise qualité.
quality control *n* contrôle *m* de qualité.
quality of life *n* qualité *f* de la vie.
quality papers *npl* (*BRIT*): **the** ~ la presse d'information.

Les **quality (news)papers** (*ou* la **quality press**) englobent les journaux sérieux, quotidiens ou hebdomadaires, par opposition aux journaux populaires (**tabloid press**). Ces journaux visent un public qui souhaite des informations détaillées sur un éventail très vaste de sujets et qui est prêt à consacrer beaucoup de temps à leur lecture. Les **quality** newspapers sont en général de grand format.

qualm [kwɑːm] *n* doute *m*; scrupule *m*; **to have ~s about sth** avoir des doutes sur qch; éprouver des scrupules à propos de qch.
quandary ['kwɔndrɪ] *n*: **in a** ~ devant un dilemme, dans l'embarras.
quango ['kwæŋgəʊ] *n abbr* (*BRIT*: = *quasi-autonomous non-governmental organization*) commission nommée par le gouvernement.
quantifiable [kwɔntɪ'faɪəbl] *adj* quantifiable.
quantitative ['kwɔntɪtətɪv] *adj* quantitatif(ive).
quantity ['kwɔntɪtɪ] *n* quantité *f*; **in** ~ en grande quantité.
quantity surveyor *n* (*BRIT*) métreur vérificateur.
quantum leap ['kwɔntəm-] *n* (*fig*) bond *m* en avant.
quarantine ['kwɔrntiːn] *n* quarantaine *f*.
quark [kwɑːk] *n* quark *m*.
quarrel ['kwɔrl] *n* querelle *f*, dispute *f* ♦ *vi* se disputer, se quereller; **to have a** ~ **with sb** se quereller avec qn; **I've no** ~ **with him** je n'ai rien contre lui; **I can't** ~ **with that** je ne vois rien à redire à cela.
quarrelsome ['kwɔrəlsəm] *adj* querelleur(euse).
quarry ['kwɔrɪ] *n* (*for stone*) carrière *f*; (*animal*) proie *f*, gibier *m* ♦ *vt* (*marble etc*) extraire.
quart [kwɔːt] *n* ≈ litre *m*.
quarter ['kwɔːtə*] *n* quart *m*; (*of year*) trimestre *m*; (*district*) quartier *m*; (*US, Canada*: *25 cents*) (pièce *f* de) vingt-cinq cents *mpl* ♦ *vt* partager en quartiers *or* en quatre; (*MIL*) caserner, cantonner; ~s *npl* logement *m*; (*MIL*) quartiers *mpl*, cantonnement *m*; **a** ~ **of an hour** un quart d'heure; **it's a** ~ **to 3,** (*US*) **it's a** ~ **of 3** il est 3 heures moins le quart; **it's a** ~ **past 3,** (*US*) **it's a** ~ **after 3** il est 3 heures et quart; **from all** ~s de tous côtés; **at close** ~s tout près.
quarterback ['kwɔːtəbæk] *n* (*US FOOTBALL*) quarterback *m/f*.

quarter-deck ['kwɔːtədɛk] *n* (*NAUT*) plage *f* arrière.
quarter final *n* quart *m* de finale.
quarterly ['kwɔːtəlɪ] *adj* trimestriel(le) ♦ *adv* tous les trois mois ♦ *n* (*PRESS*) revue trimestrielle.
quartermaster ['kwɔːtəmɑːstə*] *n* (*MIL*) intendant *m* militaire de troisième classe; (*NAUT*) maître *m* de manœuvre.
quartet(te) [kwɔːˈtɛt] *n* quatuor *m*; (*jazz players*) quartette *m*.
quarto ['kwɔːtəʊ] *adj, n* in-quarto *(m) inv*.
quartz [kwɔːts] *n* quartz *m* ♦ *cpd* de *or* en quartz; (*watch, clock*) à quartz.
quash [kwɔʃ] *vt* (*verdict*) annuler, casser.
quasi- ['kweɪzaɪ] *prefix* quasi- + *noun*; quasi, presque + *adjective*.
quaver ['kweɪvə*] *n* (*BRIT MUS*) croche *f* ♦ *vi* trembler.
quay [kiː] *n* (*also*: ~**side**) quai *m*.
Que. *abbr* (*Canada*) = *Quebec*.
queasy ['kwiːzɪ] *adj* (*stomach*) délicat(e); **to feel** ~ avoir mal au cœur.
Quebec [kwɪˈbɛk] *n* Québec *m*.
queen [kwiːn] *n* (*gen*) reine *f*; (*CARDS etc*) dame *f*.
queen mother *n* reine mère *f*.

Le **Queen's speech** (*ou* **King's speech**) est le discours lu par le souverain à l'ouverture du **Parliament**, dans la **House of Lords**, en présence des lords et des députés. Il contient le programme de politique générale que propose le gouvernement pour la session, et il est préparé par le Premier ministre en consultation avec le cabinet.

queer [kwɪə*] *adj* étrange, curieux(euse); (*suspicious*) louche; (*BRIT*: *sick*): **I feel** ~ je ne me sens pas bien ♦ *n* (*col*) homosexuel *m*.
quell [kwɛl] *vt* réprimer, étouffer.
quench [kwɛntʃ] *vt* (*flames*) éteindre; **to** ~ **one's thirst** se désaltérer.
querulous ['kwɛrʊləs] *adj* (*person*) récriminateur(trice); (*voice*) plaintif(ive).
query ['kwɪərɪ] *n* question *f*; (*doubt*) doute *m*; (*question mark*) point *m* d'interrogation ♦ *vt* (*disagree with, dispute*) mettre en doute, questionner.
quest [kwɛst] *n* recherche *f*, quête *f*.
question ['kwɛstʃən] *n* question *f* ♦ *vt* (*person*) interroger; (*plan, idea*) mettre en question *or* en doute; **to ask sb a** ~, **to put a** ~ **to sb** poser une question à qn; **to bring** *or* **call sth into** ~ remettre qch en question; **the** ~ **is ...** la question est de savoir ...; **it's a** ~ **of doing** il s'agit de faire; **there's some** ~ **of doing** il est question de faire; **beyond** ~ sans aucun doute; **out of the** ~ hors de question.
questionable ['kwɛstʃənəbl] *adj* discutable.
questioner ['kwɛstʃənə*] *n* personne *f* qui pose une question (*or* qui a posé la question

etc).

questioning ['kwɛstʃənɪŋ] adj interrogateur(trice) ♦ n interrogatoire m.

question mark n point m d'interrogation.

questionnaire [kwɛstʃə'nɛə*] n questionnaire m.

queue [kjuː] (BRIT) n queue f, file f ♦ vi faire la queue; **to jump the** ~ passer avant son tour.

quibble ['kwɪbl] vi ergoter, chicaner.

quick [kwɪk] adj rapide; (reply) prompt(e), rapide; (mind) vif(vive) ♦ adv vite, rapidement ♦ n: **cut to the** ~ (fig) touché(e) au vif; **be** ~! dépêche-toi!; **to be** ~ **to act** agir tout de suite.

quicken ['kwɪkən] vt accélérer, presser; (rouse) stimuler ♦ vi s'accélérer, devenir plus rapide.

quick fix n solution f de fortune.

quicklime ['kwɪklaɪm] n chaux vive.

quickly ['kwɪklɪ] adv (fast) vite, rapidement; (immediately) tout de suite.

quickness ['kwɪknɪs] n rapidité f, promptitude f; (of mind) vivacité f.

quicksand ['kwɪksænd] n sables mouvants.

quickstep ['kwɪkstɛp] n fox-trot m.

quick-tempered [kwɪk'tɛmpəd] adj emporté(e).

quick-witted [kwɪk'wɪtɪd] adj à l'esprit vif.

quid [kwɪd] n (pl inv: BRIT col) livre f.

quid pro quo ['kwɪdprəu'kwəu] n contrepartie f.

quiet ['kwaɪət] adj tranquille, calme; (not noisy: engine) silencieux(euse); (reserved) réservé(e); (not busy: day, business) calme; (ceremony, colour) discret(ète) ♦ n tranquillité f, calme m ♦ vt, vi (US) = **quieten**; **keep** ~! tais-toi!; **on the** ~ en secret, discrètement; **I'll have a** ~ **word with him** je lui en parlerai discrètement.

quieten ['kwaɪətn] (also: ~ **down**) vi se calmer, s'apaiser ♦ vt calmer, apaiser.

quietly ['kwaɪətlɪ] adv tranquillement, calmement; discrètement.

quietness ['kwaɪətnɪs] n tranquillité f, calme m; silence m.

quill [kwɪl] n plume f (d'oie).

quilt [kwɪlt] n édredon m; (continental ~) couette f.

quin [kwɪn] n abbr = **quintuplet**.

quince [kwɪns] n coing m; (tree) cognassier m.

quinine [kwɪ'niːn] n quinine f.

quintet(te) [kwɪn'tɛt] n quintette m.

quintuplet [kwɪn'tjuːplɪt] n quintuplé/e.

quip [kwɪp] n remarque piquante or spirituelle, pointe f ♦ vt: ... **he** ~**ped** ... lança-t-il.

quire ['kwaɪə*] n ≈ main f (de papier).

quirk [kwəːk] n bizarrerie f; **by some** ~ **of fate** par un caprice du hasard.

quit, pt, pp **quit** or **quitted** [kwɪt] vt quitter ♦ vi (give up) abandonner, renoncer; (resign) démissionner; **to** ~ **doing** arrêter de faire; ~ **stalling!** (US col) arrête de te dérober!;

notice to ~ (BRIT) congé m (signifié au locataire).

quite [kwaɪt] adv (rather) assez, plutôt; (entirely) complètement, tout à fait; ~ **new** plutôt neuf; tout à fait neuf; **she's** ~ **pretty** elle est plutôt jolie; **I** ~ **understand** je comprends très bien; ~ **a few of them** un assez grand nombre d'entre eux; **that's not** ~ **right** ce n'est pas tout à fait juste; **not** ~ **as many as last time** pas tout à fait autant que la dernière fois; ~ **(so)!** exactement!

Quito ['kiːtəu] n Quito.

quits [kwɪts] adj: ~ **(with)** quitte (envers); **let's call it** ~ restons-en là.

quiver ['kwɪvə*] vi trembler, frémir ♦ n (for arrows) carquois m.

quiz [kwɪz] n (on TV) jeu-concours m (télévisé); (in magazine etc) test m de connaissances ♦ vt interroger.

quizzical ['kwɪzɪkl] adj narquois(e).

quoits [kwɔɪts] npl jeu m du palet.

quorum ['kwɔːrəm] n quorum m.

quota ['kwəutə] n quota m.

quotation [kwəu'teɪʃən] n citation f; (of shares etc) cote f, cours m; (estimate) devis m.

quotation marks npl guillemets mpl.

quote [kwəut] n citation f ♦ vt (sentence, author) citer; (price) donner, soumettre; (shares) coter ♦ vi: **to** ~ **from** citer; **to** ~ **for a job** établir un devis pour des travaux; ~**s** npl (col) = **quotation marks**; **in** ~**s** entre guillemets; ~ ... **unquote** (in dictation) ouvrez les guillemets ... fermez les guillemets.

quotient ['kwəuʃənt] n quotient m.

qv abbr (= quod vide: which see) voir.

qwerty keyboard ['kwəːtɪ-] n clavier m QWERTY.

R r

R, r [ɑː*] n (letter) R, r m; **R for Robert,** (US) **R for Roger** R comme Raoul.

R abbr (= right) dr; (= river) riv., fl.; (= Réaumur (scale)) R; (US CINE: = restricted) interdit aux moins de 17 ans; (US POL) = **republican**; (BRIT) = Rex, Regina.

RA abbr = **rear admiral** ♦ n abbr (BRIT) = **Royal Academy**, Royal Academician.

RAAF n abbr = Royal Australian Air Force.

Rabat [rə'bɑːt] n Rabat.

rabbi ['ræbaɪ] n rabbin m.

rabbit ['ræbɪt] n lapin m ♦ vi: **to** ~ **(on)** (BRIT) parler à n'en plus finir.

rabbit hole n terrier m (de lapin).

rabbit hutch n clapier m.

rabble ['ræbl] n (pej) populace f.
rabid ['ræbɪd] adj enragé(e).
rabies ['reɪbiːz] n rage f.
RAC n abbr (BRIT: = Royal Automobile Club) ≈ ACF m.
raccoon [rə'kuːn] n raton m laveur.
race [reɪs] n race f; (competition, rush) course f ♦ vt (person) faire la course avec; (horse) faire courir; (engine) emballer ♦ vi courir; (engine) s'emballer; **the human ~** la race humaine; **to ~ in/out** etc entrer/sortir etc à toute vitesse.
race car n (US) = **racing car**.
race car driver n (US) = **racing driver**.
racecourse ['reɪskɔːs] n champ m de courses.
racehorse ['reɪshɔːs] n cheval m de course.
race relations npl rapports mpl entre les races.
racetrack ['reɪstræk] n piste f.
racial ['reɪʃl] adj racial(e).
racialism ['reɪʃlɪzəm] n racisme m.
racialist ['reɪʃlɪst] adj, n raciste (m/f).
racing ['reɪsɪŋ] n courses fpl.
racing car n (BRIT) voiture f de course.
racing driver n (BRIT) pilote m de course.
racism ['reɪsɪzəm] n racisme m.
racist ['reɪsɪst] adj, n (pej) raciste (m/f).
rack [ræk] n (also: **luggage ~**) filet m à bagages; (also: **roof ~**) galerie f ♦ vt tourmenter; **magazine ~** porte-revues m inv; **shoe ~** étagère f à chaussures; **toast ~** porte-toast m; **to ~ one's brains** se creuser la cervelle; **to go to ~ and ruin** (building) tomber en ruine; (business) péricliter.
▶**rack up** vt accumuler.
racket ['rækɪt] n (for tennis) raquette f; (noise) tapage m, vacarme m; (swindle) escroquerie f; (organized crime) racket m.
racketeer [rækɪ'tɪə*] n (esp US) racketteur m.
racoon [rə'kuːn] n = **raccoon**.
racquet ['rækɪt] n raquette f.
racy ['reɪsɪ] adj plein(e) de verve; osé(e).
RADA [rɑːdə] n abbr (BRIT) = Royal Academy of Dramatic Art.
radar ['reɪdɑː*] n radar m ♦ cpd radar inv.
radar trap n contrôle m radar.
radial ['reɪdɪəl] adj (also: **~-ply**) à carcasse radiale.
radiance ['reɪdɪəns] n éclat m, rayonnement m.
radiant ['reɪdɪənt] adj rayonnant(e); (PHYSICS) radiant(e).
radiate ['reɪdɪeɪt] vt (heat) émettre, dégager ♦ vi (lines) rayonner.
radiation [reɪdɪ'eɪʃən] n rayonnement m; (radioactive) radiation f.
radiation sickness n mal m des rayons.
radiator ['reɪdɪeɪtə*] n radiateur m.
radiator cap n bouchon m de radiateur.
radiator grill n (AUT) calandre f.
radical ['rædɪkl] adj radical(e).
radii ['reɪdɪaɪ] npl of **radius**.
radio ['reɪdɪəu] n radio f ♦ vi: **to ~ to sb** en-

voyer un message radio à qn ♦ vt (information) transmettre par radio; (one's position) signaler par radio; (person) appeler par radio; **on the ~** à la radio.
radioactive ['reɪdɪəu'æktɪv] adj radioactif(ive).
radioactivity ['reɪdɪəuæk'tɪvɪtɪ] n radioactivité f.
radio announcer n annonceur m.
radio-controlled ['reɪdɪəukən'trəuld] adj radioguidé(e).
radiographer [reɪdɪ'ɔgrəfə*] n radiologue m/f (technicien).
radiography [reɪdɪ'ɔgrəfɪ] n radiographie f.
radiologist [reɪdɪ'ɔlədʒɪst] n radiologue m/f (médecin).
radiology [reɪdɪ'ɔlədʒɪ] n radiologie f.
radio station n station f de radio.
radio taxi n radio-taxi m.
radiotelephone ['reɪdɪəu'telɪfəun] n radiotéléphone m.
radiotherapist ['reɪdɪəu'θerəpɪst] n radiothérapeute m/f.
radiotherapy ['reɪdɪəu'θerəpɪ] n radiothérapie f.
radish ['rædɪʃ] n radis m.
radium ['reɪdɪəm] n radium m.
radius, pl **radii** ['reɪdɪəs, -ɪaɪ] n rayon m; (ANAT) radius m; **within a ~ of 50 miles** dans un rayon de 50 milles.
RAF n abbr (BRIT) = **Royal Air Force**.
raffia ['ræfɪə] n raphia m.
raffish ['ræfɪʃ] adj dissolu(e); canaille.
raffle ['ræfl] n tombola f ♦ vt mettre comme lot dans une tombola.
raft [rɑːft] n (craft; also: **life ~**) radeau m; (logs) train m de flottage.
rafter ['rɑːftə*] n chevron m.
rag [ræg] n chiffon m; (pej: newspaper) feuille f, torchon m; (for charity) attractions organisées par les étudiants au profit d'œuvres de charité ♦ vt (BRIT) chahuter, mettre en boîte; **~s** npl haillons mpl; **in ~s** (person) en haillons; (clothes) en lambeaux.
rag-and-bone man [rægən'bəunmæn] n chiffonnier m.
ragbag ['rægbæg] n (fig) ramassis m.

> **Rag Day** ou plus communément **Rag Week**, est un jour, ou une semaine, où les étudiants se déguisent et collectent de l'argent pour les œuvres de charité. Toutes sortes d'animations sont organisées à cette occasion (marches sponsorisées, spectacles de rue etc). Des magazines (les "rag mags") contenant des plaisanteries osées sont vendus dans les rues, également au profit des œuvres. Enfin, la plupart des universités organisent un bal (le "rag ball").

rag doll n poupée f de chiffon.
rage [reɪdʒ] n (fury) rage f, fureur f ♦ vi (per-

son) être fou(folle) de rage; (*storm*) faire rage, être déchaîné(e); **to fly into a** ~ se mettre en rage; **it's all the** ~ cela fait fureur.

ragged ['rægɪd] *adj* (*edge*) inégal(e), qui accroche; (*cuff*) effiloché(e); (*appearance*) déguenillé(e).

raging ['reɪdʒɪŋ] *adj* (*sea, storm*) en furie; (*fever, pain*) violent(e); ~ **toothache** rage *f* de dents; **in a** ~ **temper** dans une rage folle.

rag trade *n* (*col*): **the** ~ la confection.

raid [reɪd] *n* (*MIL*) raid *m*; (*criminal*) hold-up *m inv*; (*by police*) descente *f*, rafle *f* ♦ *vt* faire un raid sur *or* un hold-up dans *or* une descente dans.

raider ['reɪdə*] *n* malfaiteur *m*.

rail [reɪl] *n* (*on stair*) rampe *f*; (*on bridge, balcony*) balustrade *f*; (*of ship*) bastingage *m*; (*for train*) rail *m*; ~**s** *npl* rails *mpl*, voie ferrée; **by** ~ par chemin de fer, par le train.

railcard ['reɪlkɑːd] *n* (*BRIT*) carte *f* de chemin de fer; **young person's** ~ carte *f* jeune.

railing(s) ['reɪlɪŋ(z)] *n(pl)* grille *f*.

railway ['reɪlweɪ], (*US*) **railroad** ['reɪlrəud] *n* chemin *m* de fer.

railway engine *n* locomotive *f*.

railway line *n* ligne *f* de chemin de fer; (*track*) voie ferrée.

railwayman ['reɪlweɪmən] *n* cheminot *m*.

railway station *n* gare *f*.

rain [reɪn] *n* pluie *f* ♦ *vi* pleuvoir; **in the** ~ sous la pluie; **it's** ~**ing** il pleut; **it's** ~**ing cats and dogs** il pleut à torrents.

rainbow ['reɪnbəu] *n* arc-en-ciel *m*.

raincoat ['reɪnkəut] *n* imperméable *m*.

raindrop ['reɪndrɔp] *n* goutte *f* de pluie.

rainfall ['reɪnfɔːl] *n* chute *f* de pluie; (*measurement*) hauteur *f* des précipitations.

rainforest ['reɪnfɔrɪst] *n* forêt tropicale.

rainproof ['reɪnpruːf] *adj* imperméable.

rainstorm ['reɪnstɔːm] *n* pluie torrentielle.

rainwater ['reɪnwɔːtə*] *n* eau *f* de pluie.

rainy ['reɪnɪ] *adj* pluvieux(euse).

raise [reɪz] *n* augmentation *f* ♦ *vt* (*lift*) lever; hausser; (*end: siege, embargo*) lever; (*build*) ériger; (*increase*) augmenter; (*a protest, doubt*) provoquer, causer; (*a question*) soulever; (*cattle, family*) élever; (*crop*) faire pousser; (*army, funds*) rassembler; (*loan*) obtenir; **to** ~ **one's glass to sb/sth** porter un toast en l'honneur de qn/qch; **to** ~ **one's voice** élever la voix; **to** ~ **sb's hopes** donner de l'espoir à qn; **to** ~ **a laugh/a smile** faire rire/sourire.

raisin ['reɪzn] *n* raisin sec.

Raj [rɑːdʒ] *n*: **the** ~ l'empire *m* (*aux Indes*).

rajah ['rɑːdʒə] *n* radja(h) *m*.

rake [reɪk] *n* (*tool*) râteau *m*; (*person*) débauché *m* ♦ *vt* (*garden*) ratisser; (*fire*) tisonner; (*with machine gun*) balayer ♦ *vi*: **to** ~ **through** (*fig: search*) fouiller (dans).

rake-off ['reɪkɔf] *n* (*col*) pourcentage *m*.

rakish ['reɪkɪʃ] *adj* dissolu(e); cavalier(ière).

rally ['rælɪ] *n* (*POL etc*) meeting *m*, rassemblement *m*; (*AUT*) rallye *m*; (*TENNIS*) échange *m* ♦ *vt* rassembler, rallier ♦ *vi* se rallier; (*sick person*) aller mieux; (*Stock Exchange*) reprendre.

▶**rally round** *vi* venir en aide ♦ *vt fus* se rallier à; venir en aide à.

rallying point ['rælɪŋ-] *n* (*MIL*) point *m* de ralliement.

RAM [ræm] *n abbr* (*COMPUT*) = **random access memory**.

ram [ræm] *n* bélier *m* ♦ *vt* enfoncer; (*soil*) tasser; (*crash into*) emboutir; percuter; éperonner.

ramble ['ræmbl] *n* randonnée *f* ♦ *vi* (*pej: also* ~ **on**) discourir, pérorer.

rambler ['ræmblə*] *n* promeneur/euse, randonneur/euse; (*BOT*) rosier grimpant.

rambling ['ræmblɪŋ] *adj* (*speech*) décousu(e); (*house*) plein(e) de coins et de recoins; (*BOT*) grimpant(e).

RAMC *n abbr* (*BRIT*) = Royal Army Medical Corps.

ramification [ræmɪfɪ'keɪʃən] *n* ramification *f*.

ramp [ræmp] *n* (*incline*) rampe *f*; dénivellation *f*; (*in garage*) pont *m*.

rampage [ræm'peɪdʒ] *n*: **to be on the** ~ se déchaîner ♦ *vi*: **they went rampaging through the town** ils ont envahi les rues et ont tout saccagé sur leur passage.

rampant ['ræmpənt] *adj* (*disease etc*) qui sévit.

rampart ['ræmpɑːt] *n* rempart *m*.

ram raiding [-reɪdɪŋ] *n* pillage d'un magasin en enfonçant la vitrine avec une voiture volée.

ramshackle ['ræmʃækl] *adj* (*house*) délabré(e); (*car etc*) déglingué(e).

RAN *n abbr* = Royal Australian Navy.

ran [ræn] *pt of* **run**.

ranch [rɑːntʃ] *n* ranch *m*.

rancher ['rɑːntʃə*] *n* (*owner*) propriétaire *m* de ranch; (*ranch hand*) cowboy *m*.

rancid ['rænsɪd] *adj* rance.

rancour, (*US*) **rancor** ['ræŋkə*] *n* rancune *f*, rancœur *f*.

R&B *n abbr* = rhythm and blues.

R&D *n abbr* (= research and development) R-D *f*.

random ['rændəm] *adj* fait(e) *or* établi(e) au hasard; (*COMPUT, MATH*) aléatoire ♦ *n*: **at** ~ au hasard.

random access memory (RAM) *n* (*COMPUT*) mémoire vive, RAM *f*.

R&R *n abbr* (*US MIL*) = rest and recreation.

randy ['rændɪ] *adj* (*BRIT col*) excité(e); lubrique.

rang [ræŋ] *pt of* **ring**.

range [reɪndʒ] *n* (*of mountains*) chaîne *f*; (*of missile, voice*) portée *f*; (*of products*) choix *m*, gamme *f*; (*also*: **shooting** ~) champ *m* de tir; (*: indoor*) stand *m* de tir; (*also*: **kitchen** ~) fourneau *m* (de cuisine) ♦ *vt* (*place*) mettre en rang, placer; (*roam*) parcourir ♦ *vi*: **to** ~ **over** couvrir; **to** ~ **from ... to** aller de ... à;

price ~ éventail m des prix; **do you have anything else in this price** ~? avez-vous autre chose dans ces prix?; **within (firing)** ~ à portée (de tir); ~**d left/right** (text) justifié à gauche/à droite.

ranger ['reɪndʒə*] n garde m forestier.

Rangoon [ræŋ'guːn] n Rangoon.

rank [ræŋk] n rang m; (MIL) grade m; (BRIT: also: taxi ~) station f de taxis ♦ vi: **to** ~ **among** compter or se classer parmi ♦ vt: **I** ~ **him sixth** je le place sixième ♦ adj (smell) nauséabond(e); (hypocrisy, injustice etc) flagrant(e); **he's a** ~ **outsider** il n'est vraiment pas dans la course; **the** ~**s** (MIL) la troupe; **the** ~ **and file** (fig) la masse, la base; **to close** ~**s** (MIL, fig) serrer les rangs.

rankle ['ræŋkl] vi (insult) rester sur le cœur.

ransack ['rænsæk] vt fouiller (à fond); (plunder) piller.

ransom ['rænsəm] n rançon f; **to hold sb to** ~ (fig) exercer un chantage sur qn.

rant [rænt] vi fulminer.

ranting ['ræntɪŋ] n invectives fpl.

rap [ræp] n petit coup sec; tape f ♦ vt frapper sur or à; taper sur.

rape [reɪp] n viol m; (BOT) colza m ♦ vt violer.

rape(seed) oil ['reɪp(siːd)-] n huile f de colza.

rapid ['ræpɪd] adj rapide.

rapidity [rə'pɪdɪtɪ] n rapidité f.

rapidly ['ræpɪdlɪ] adv rapidement.

rapids ['ræpɪdz] npl (GEO) rapides mpl.

rapist ['reɪpɪst] n auteur m d'un viol.

rapport [ræ'pɔː*] n entente f.

rapt [ræpt] adj (attention) extrême; **to be** ~ **in contemplation** être perdu(e) dans la contemplation.

rapture ['ræptʃə*] n extase f, ravissement m; **to go into** ~**s over** s'extasier sur.

rapturous ['ræptʃərəs] adj extasié(e); frénétique.

rare [rɛə*] adj rare; (CULIN: steak) saignant(e).

rarebit ['rɛəbɪt] n see **Welsh rarebit**.

rarefied ['rɛərɪfaɪd] adj (air, atmosphere) raréfié(e).

rarely ['rɛəlɪ] adv rarement.

raring ['rɛərɪŋ] adj: **to be** ~ **to go** (col) être très impatient(e) de commencer.

rarity ['rɛərɪtɪ] n rareté f.

rascal ['rɑːskl] n vaurien m.

rash [ræʃ] adj imprudent(e), irréfléchi(e) ♦ n (MED) rougeur f, éruption f; **to come out in a** ~ avoir une éruption.

rasher ['ræʃə*] n fine tranche (de lard).

rasp [rɑːsp] n (tool) lime f ♦ vt (speak: also: ~ out) dire d'une voix grinçante.

raspberry ['rɑːzbərɪ] n framboise f.

raspberry bush n framboisier m.

rasping ['rɑːspɪŋ] adj: ~ **noise** grincement m.

Rastafarian [ræstə'fɛərɪən] adj, n rastafari (m/f).

rat [ræt] n rat m.

ratable ['reɪtəbl] adj = **rateable**.

ratchet ['rætʃɪt] n: ~ **wheel** roue f à rochet.

rate [reɪt] n (ratio) taux m, pourcentage m; (speed) vitesse f, rythme m; (price) tarif m ♦ vt classer; évaluer; **to** ~ **sb/sth as** considérer qn/qch comme; **to** ~ **sb/sth among** classer qn/qch parmi; **to** ~ **sb/sth highly** avoir une haute opinion de qn/qch; **at a** ~ **of 60 kph** à une vitesse de 60 km/h; ~ **of exchange** taux or cours m du change; ~ **of flow** débit m; ~ **of return** (taux de) rendement m; **pulse** ~ fréquence f des pulsations.

rateable value ['reɪtəbl-] n (BRIT) valeur locative imposable.

ratepayer ['reɪtpeɪə*] n (BRIT) contribuable m/f (payant les impôts locaux).

rates ['reɪts] npl (BRIT) impôts locaux.

rather ['rɑːðə*] adv (somewhat) assez, plutôt; (to some extent) un peu; **it's** ~ **expensive** c'est assez cher; (too much) c'est un peu cher; **there's** ~ **a lot** il y en a beaucoup; **I would** or **I'd** ~ **go** j'aimerais mieux or je préférerais partir; **I had** ~ **go** il vaudrait mieux que je parte; **I'd** ~ **not leave** j'aimerais mieux ne pas partir; **or** ~ (more accurately) ou plutôt; **I** ~ **think he won't come** je crois bien qu'il ne viendra pas.

ratification [rætɪfɪ'keɪʃən] n ratification f.

ratify ['rætɪfaɪ] vt ratifier.

rating ['reɪtɪŋ] n classement m; cote f; (NAUT: category) classe f; (: sailor: BRIT) matelot m; ~**s** npl (RADIO, TV) indice(s) m(pl) d'écoute.

ratio ['reɪʃɪəu] n proportion f; **in the** ~ **of 100 to 1** dans la proportion de 100 contre 1.

ration ['ræʃən] n (gen pl) ration(s) f(pl) ♦ vt rationner.

rational ['ræʃənl] adj raisonnable, sensé(e); (solution, reasoning) logique; (MED) lucide.

rationale [ræʃə'nɑːl] n raisonnement m; justification f.

rationalization [ræʃnəlaɪ'zeɪʃən] n rationalisation f.

rationalize ['ræʃnəlaɪz] vt rationaliser; (conduct) essayer d'expliquer or de motiver.

rationally ['ræʃnəlɪ] adv raisonnablement; logiquement.

rationing ['ræʃnɪŋ] n rationnement m.

ratpack ['rætpæk] n (BRIT col) journalistes mpl de la presse à sensation.

rat poison n mort-aux-rats f inv.

rat race n foire f d'empoigne.

rattan [ræ'tæn] n rotin m.

rattle ['rætl] n cliquetis m; (louder) bruit m de ferraille; (object: of baby) hochet m; (: of sports fan) crécelle f ♦ vi cliqueter; faire un bruit de ferraille or du bruit ♦ vt agiter (bruyamment); (col: disconcert) décontenancer; (: annoy) embêter.

rattlesnake ['rætlsneɪk] n serpent m à sonnettes.

ratty ['rætɪ] adj (col) en rogne.

raucous ['rɔːkəs] adj rauque.

raucously ['rɔːkəslɪ] adv d'une voix rauque.

raunchy ['rɔːntʃɪ] adj (col: voice, image, act)

sexy; (:*scenes, film*) lubrique.
ravage ['rævɪdʒ] *vt* ravager.
ravages ['rævɪdʒɪz] *npl* ravages *mpl*.
rave [reɪv] *vi* (*in anger*) s'emporter; (*with enthusiasm*) s'extasier; (*MED*) délirer ♦ *n*: a ~ (**party**) une rave, une soirée techno ♦ *adj* (*scene, culture, music*) rave, techno ♦ *cpd*: ~ **review** (*col*) critique *f* dithyrambique.
raven ['reɪvən] *n* grand corbeau.
ravenous ['rævənəs] *adj* affamé(e).
ravine [rə'viːn] *n* ravin *m*.
raving ['reɪvɪŋ] *adj*: ~ **lunatic** *n* fou furieux/folle furieuse.
ravings ['reɪvɪŋz] *npl* divagations *fpl*.
ravioli [rævɪ'əulɪ] *n* ravioli *mpl*.
ravish ['rævɪʃ] *vt* ravir.
ravishing ['rævɪʃɪŋ] *adj* enchanteur(eresse).
raw [rɔː] *adj* (*uncooked*) cru(e); (*not processed*) brut(e); (*sore*) à vif, irrité(e); (*inexperienced*) inexpérimenté(e); ~ **deal** (*col: bad bargain*) sale coup *m*; (: *unfair treatment*): **to get a ~ deal** être traité(e) injustement.
Rawalpindi [rɔːl'pɪndɪ] *n* Rawalpindi.
raw material *n* matière première.
ray [reɪ] *n* rayon *m*; ~ **of hope** lueur *f* d'espoir.
rayon ['reɪɔn] *n* rayonne *f*.
raze [reɪz] *vt* (*also*: ~ **to the ground**) raser.
razor ['reɪzə*] *n* rasoir *m*.
razor blade *n* lame *f* de rasoir.
razzle(-dazzle) ['ræzl('dæzl)] *n* (*BRIT col*): **to go on the ~** faire la bringue.
razzmatazz ['ræzmə'tæz] *n* (*col*) tralala *m*, tapage *m*.
RC *abbr* = **Roman Catholic**.
RCAF *n abbr* = Royal Canadian Air Force.
RCMP *n abbr* = Royal Canadian Mounted Police.
RCN *n abbr* = Royal Canadian Navy.
RD *abbr* (*US*) = rural delivery.
Rd *abbr* = road.
RDC *n abbr* (*BRIT*) = rural district council.
RE *n abbr* (*BRIT*) = religious education; (*BRIT MIL*) = Royal Engineers.
re [riː] *prep* concernant.
reach [riːtʃ] *n* portée *f*, atteinte *f*; (*of river etc*) étendue *f* ♦ *vt* atteindre, arriver à ♦ *vi* s'étendre; (*stretch out hand*): **to ~ up/down/out** *etc* (**for sth**) lever/baisser/allonger *etc* le bras (pour prendre qch); **to ~ sb by phone** joindre qn par téléphone; **out of/within ~** (*object*) hors de/à portée; **within easy ~ (of)** (*place*) à proximité (de), proche (de).
react [riː'ækt] *vi* réagir.
reaction [riː'ækʃən] *n* réaction *f*.
reactionary [riː'ækʃənrɪ] *adj, n* réactionnaire (*m/f*).
reactor [riː'æktə*] *n* réacteur *m*.
read, *pt, pp* **read** [riːd, rɛd] *vi* lire ♦ *vt* lire; (*understand*) comprendre, interpréter; (*study*) étudier; (*subj: instrument etc*) indiquer, marquer; **to take sth as read** (*fig*) considérer qch comme accepté; **do you ~ me?** (*TEL*) est-ce que vous me recevez?

►**read out** *vt* lire à haute voix.
►**read over** *vt* relire.
►**read through** *vt* (*quickly*) parcourir; (*thoroughly*) lire jusqu'au bout.
►**read up** *vt*, **read up on** *vt fus* étudier.
readable ['riːdəbl] *adj* facile *or* agréable à lire.
reader ['riːdə*] *n* lecteur/trice; (*book*) livre *m* de lecture; (*BRIT: at university*) maître *m* de conférences.
readership ['riːdəʃɪp] *n* (*of paper etc*) (nombre *m* de) lecteurs *mpl*.
readily ['rɛdɪlɪ] *adv* volontiers, avec empressement; (*easily*) facilement.
readiness ['rɛdɪnɪs] *n* empressement *m*; **in ~** (*prepared*) prêt(e).
reading ['riːdɪŋ] *n* lecture *f*; (*understanding*) interprétation *f*; (*on instrument*) indications *fpl*.
reading lamp *n* lampe *f* de bureau.
reading room *n* salle *f* de lecture.
readjust [riːə'dʒʌst] *vt* rajuster; (*instrument*) régler de nouveau ♦ *vi* (*person*): **to ~ (to)** se réadapter (à).
ready ['rɛdɪ] *adj* prêt(e); (*willing*) prêt, disposé(e); (*quick*) prompt(e); (*available*) disponible ♦ *n*: **at the ~** (*MIL*) prêt à faire feu; (*fig*) tout(e) prêt(e); ~ **for use** prêt à l'emploi; **to be ~ to do sth** être prêt à faire qch; **to get ~** *vi* se préparer ♦ *vt* préparer.
ready cash *n* (argent *m*) liquide *m*.
ready-made ['rɛdɪ'meɪd] *adj* tout(e) fait(e).
ready-mix ['rɛdɪmɪks] *n* (*for cakes etc*) préparation *f* en sachet.
ready reckoner [-'rɛknə*] *n* (*BRIT*) barème *m*.
ready-to-wear ['rɛdɪtə'wɛə*] *adj* (en) prêt-à-porter.
reagent [riː'eɪdʒənt] *n* réactif *m*.
real [rɪəl] *adj* réel(le); (*genuine*) véritable; (*proper*) vrai(e) ♦ *adv* (*US col: very*) vraiment; **in ~ life** dans la réalité.
real ale *n* bière traditionnelle.
real estate *n* biens fonciers *or* immobiliers.
realism ['rɪəlɪzəm] *n* réalisme *m*.
realist ['rɪəlɪst] *n* réaliste *m/f*.
realistic [rɪə'lɪstɪk] *adj* réaliste.
reality [riː'ælɪtɪ] *n* réalité *f*; **in ~** en réalité, en fait.
realization [rɪəlaɪ'zeɪʃən] *n* prise *f* de conscience; réalisation *f*.
realize ['rɪəlaɪz] *vt* (*understand*) se rendre compte de, prendre conscience de; (*a project, COMM: asset*) réaliser.
really ['rɪəlɪ] *adv* vraiment.
realm [rɛlm] *n* royaume *m*.
real-time ['rɪːltaɪm] *adj* (*COMPUT*) en temps réel
Realtor ['rɪəltɔː*] *n* ® (*US*) agent immobilier.
ream [riːm] *n* rame *f* (*de papier*); ~**s** *npl* (*fig: col*) des pages et des pages.
reap [riːp] *vt* moissonner; (*fig*) récolter.
reaper ['riːpə*] *n* (*machine*) moissonneuse *f*.
reappear [riːə'pɪə*] *vi* réapparaître, reparaître.

reappearance [ri:ə'piərəns] n réapparition f.
reapply [ri:ə'plai] vi: **to ~ for** (job) faire une nouvelle demande d'emploi concernant; reposer sa candidature à; (loan, grant) faire une nouvelle demande de.
reappraisal [ri:ə'preizl] n réévaluation f.
rear [riə*] adj de derrière, arrière inv; (AUT: wheel etc) arrière ♦ n arrière m, derrière m ♦ vt (cattle, family) élever ♦ vi (also: ~ **up**: animal) se cabrer.
rear admiral (RA) n vice-amiral m.
rear-engined ['riər'ɛndʒind] adj (AUT) avec moteur à l'arrière.
rearguard ['riəgɑ:d] n arrière-garde f.
rearm [ri:'ɑ:m] vt, vi réarmer.
rearmament [ri:'ɑ:məmənt] n réarmement m.
rearrange [ri:ə'reindʒ] vt réarranger.
rear-view ['riəvju:]: **~ mirror** n (AUT) rétroviseur m.
reason ['ri:zn] n raison f ♦ vi: **to ~ with sb** raisonner qn, faire entendre raison à qn; **the ~ for/why** la raison de/pour laquelle; **to have ~ to think** avoir lieu de penser; **it stands to ~ that** il va sans dire que; **she claims with good ~ that** ... elle affirme à juste titre que ...; **all the more ~ why** raison de plus pour + infinitive or pour que + sub.
reasonable ['ri:znəbl] adj raisonnable; (not bad) acceptable.
reasonably ['ri:znəbli] adv (to behave) raisonnablement; (fairly) assez; **one can ~ assume that** ... on est fondé à or il est permis de supposer que ....
reasoned ['ri:znd] adj (argument) raisonné(e).
reasoning ['ri:znin] n raisonnement m.
reassemble [ri:ə'sɛmbl] vt rassembler; (machine) remonter.
reassert [ri:ə'sə:t] vt réaffirmer.
reassurance [ri:ə'ʃuərəns] n assurance f, garantie f; (comfort) réconfort m.
reassure [ri:ə'ʃuə*] vt rassurer; **to ~ sb of** donner à qn l'assurance répétée de.
reassuring [ri:ə'ʃuərin] adj rassurant(e).
reawakening [ri:ə'weiknin] n réveil m.
rebate ['ri:beit] n (on product) rabais m; (on tax etc) dégrèvement m; (repayment) remboursement m.
rebel n ['rɛbl] rebelle m/f ♦ vi [ri'bɛl] se rebeller, se révolter.
rebellion [ri'bɛljən] n rébellion f, révolte f.
rebellious [ri'bɛljəs] adj rebelle.
rebirth [ri:'bə:θ] n renaissance f.
rebound vi [ri'baund] (ball) rebondir ♦ n ['ri:baund] rebond m.
rebuff [ri'bʌf] n rebuffade f ♦ vt repousser.
rebuild [ri:'bild] vt irreg reconstruire.
rebuke [ri'bju:k] n réprimande f, reproche m ♦ vt réprimander.
rebut [ri'bʌt] vt réfuter.
rebuttal [ri'bʌtl] n réfutation f.
recalcitrant [ri'kælsitrənt] adj récalcitrant(e).
recall [ri'kɔ:l] vt rappeler; (remember) se rap-

peler, se souvenir de ♦ n rappel m; **beyond ~** adj irrévocable.
recant [ri'kænt] vi se rétracter; (REL) abjurer.
recap ['ri:kæp] n récapitulation f ♦ vt, vi récapituler.
recapitulate [ri:kə'pitjuleit] vt, vi récapituler.
recapture [ri:'kæptʃə*] vt reprendre; (atmosphere) recréer.
recd. abbr = received.
recede [ri'si:d] vi s'éloigner; reculer; redescendre.
receding [ri'si:din] adj (forehead, chin) fuyant(e); **~ hairline** front dégarni.
receipt [ri'si:t] n (document) reçu m; (for parcel etc) accusé m de réception; (act of receiving) réception f; **~s** npl (COMM) recettes fpl; **to acknowledge ~ of** accuser réception de; **we are in ~ of** ... nous avons reçu ....
receivable [ri'si:vəbl] adj (COMM) recevable; (: owing) à recevoir.
receive [ri'si:v] vt recevoir; (guest) recevoir, accueillir; **"~d with thanks"** (COMM) "pour acquit".

> En Grande-Bretagne, la **received pronunciation** ou **RP** est une prononciation de la langue anglaise qui, récemment encore, était surtout associée à l'aristocratie et à la bourgeoisie, mais qui maintenant est en général considérée comme la prononciation correcte.

receiver [ri'si:və*] n (TEL) récepteur m, combiné m; (RADIO) récepteur m; (of stolen goods) receleur m; (COMM) administrateur m judiciaire.
receivership [ri'si:vəʃip] n: **to go into ~** être placé sous administration judiciaire.
recent ['ri:snt] adj récent(e); **in ~ years** au cours de ces dernières années.
recently ['ri:sntli] adv récemment; **as ~ as** pas plus tard que; **until ~** jusqu'à il y a peu de temps encore.
receptacle [ri'sɛptikl] n récipient m.
reception [ri'sɛpʃən] n réception f; (welcome) accueil m, réception.
reception centre n (BRIT) centre m d'accueil.
reception desk n réception f.
receptionist [ri'sɛpʃənist] n réceptionniste m/f.
receptive [ri'sɛptiv] adj réceptif(ive).
recess [ri'sɛs] n (in room) renfoncement m; (for bed) alcôve f; (secret place) recoin m; (POL etc: holiday) vacances fpl; (US: LAW: short break) suspension f d'audience; (SCOL: esp US) récréation f.
recession [ri'sɛʃən] n (ECON) récession f.
recharge [ri:'tʃɑ:dʒ] vt (battery) recharger.
rechargeable [ri:'tʃɑ:dʒəbl] adj rechargeable.
recipe ['rɛsipi] n recette f.
recipient [ri'sipiənt] n bénéficiaire m/f; (of letter) destinataire m/f.
reciprocal [ri'siprəkl] adj réciproque.

reciprocate [rɪ'sɪprəkeɪt] *vt* retourner, offrir en retour ♦ *vi* en faire autant.

recital [rɪ'saɪtl] *n* récital *m*.

recite [rɪ'saɪt] *vt* (*poem*) réciter; (*complaints etc*) énumérer.

reckless ['rɛkləs] *adj* (*driver etc*) imprudent(e); (*spender etc*) insouciant(e).

recklessly ['rɛkləslɪ] *adv* imprudemment; avec insouciance.

reckon ['rɛkən] *vt* (*count*) calculer, compter; (*consider*) considérer, estimer; (*think*): I ~ (that) ... je pense (que) ..., j'estime (que) ... ♦ *vi*: **he is somebody to be ~ed with** il ne faut pas le sous-estimer; **to ~ without sb/ sth** ne pas tenir compte de qn/qch.
▶**reckon on** *vt fus* compter sur, s'attendre à.

reckoning ['rɛknɪŋ] *n* compte *m*, calcul *m*; estimation *f*; **the day of ~** le jour du Jugement.

reclaim [rɪ'kleɪm] *vt* (*land*) amender; (*: from sea*) assécher; (*: from forest*) défricher; (*demand back*) réclamer (le remboursement *or* la restitution de).

reclamation [rɛklə'meɪʃən] *n* (*of land*) amendement *m*; assèchement *m*; défrichement *m*.

recline [rɪ'klaɪn] *vi* être allongé(e) *or* étendu(e).

reclining [rɪ'klaɪnɪŋ] *adj* (*seat*) à dossier réglable.

recluse [rɪ'kluːs] *n* reclus/e, ermite *m*.

recognition [rɛkəg'nɪʃən] *n* reconnaissance *f*; **in ~ of** en reconnaissance de; **to gain ~** être reconnu(e); **transformed beyond ~** méconnaissable.

recognizable ['rɛkəgnaɪzəbl] *adj*: ~ **(by)** reconnaissable (à).

recognize ['rɛkəgnaɪz] *vt*: **to ~ (by/as)** reconnaître (à/comme étant).

recoil [rɪ'kɔɪl] *vi* (*person*): **to ~ (from)** reculer (devant) ♦ *n* (*of gun*) recul *m*.

recollect [rɛkə'lɛkt] *vt* se rappeler, se souvenir de.

recollection [rɛkə'lɛkʃən] *n* souvenir *m*; **to the best of my ~** autant que je m'en souvienne.

recommend [rɛkə'mɛnd] *vt* recommander; **she has a lot to ~ her** elle a beaucoup de choses en sa faveur.

recommendation [rɛkəmɛn'deɪʃən] *n* recommandation *f*.

recommended retail price (RRP) [rɛkə'mɛndɪd-] *n* (*BRIT*) prix conseillé.

recompense ['rɛkəmpɛns] *vt* récompenser; (*compensate*) dédommager ♦ *n* récompense *f*; dédommagement *m*.

reconcilable ['rɛkənsaɪləbl] *adj* (*ideas*) conciliable.

reconcile ['rɛkənsaɪl] *vt* (*two people*) réconcilier; (*two facts*) concilier, accorder; **to ~ o.s. to** se résigner à.

reconciliation [rɛkənsɪlɪ'eɪʃən] *n* réconciliation *f*; conciliation *f*.

recondite [rɪ'kɔndaɪt] *adj* abstrus(e), obscur(e).

recondition [riːkən'dɪʃən] *vt* remettre à neuf; réviser entièrement.

reconnaissance [rɪ'kɔnɪsns] *n* (*MIL*) reconnaissance *f*.

reconnoitre, (*US*) **reconnoiter** [rɛkə'nɔɪtə*] (*MIL*) *vt* reconnaître ♦ *vi* faire une reconnaissance.

reconsider [riːkən'sɪdə*] *vt* reconsidérer.

reconstitute [riː'kɔnstɪtjuːt] *vt* reconstituer.

reconstruct [riːkən'strʌkt] *vt* (*building*) reconstruire; (*crime*) reconstituer.

reconstruction [riːkən'strʌkʃən] *n* reconstruction *f*; reconstitution *f*.

reconvene [riːkən'viːn] *vt* reconvoquer ♦ *vi* se réunir *or* s'assembler de nouveau.

record *n* ['rɛkɔːd] rapport *m*, récit *m*; (*of meeting etc*) procès-verbal *m*; (*register*) registre *m*; (*file*) dossier *m*; (*COMPUT*) article *m*; (*also*: **police ~**) casier *m* judiciaire; (*MUS: disc*) disque *m*; (*SPORT*) record *m* ♦ *vt* [rɪ'kɔːd] (*set down*) noter; (*relate*) rapporter; (*MUS: song etc*) enregistrer; **in ~ time** dans un temps record *inv*; **public ~s** archives *fpl*; **to keep a ~ of** noter; **to keep the ~ straight** (*fig*) mettre les choses au point; **he is on ~ as saying that** ... il a déclaré en public que ...; **Italy's excellent ~** les excellents résultats obtenus par l'Italie; **off the ~** *adj* officieux(euse) ♦ *adv* officieusement.

record card *n* (*in file*) fiche *f*.

recorded delivery letter [rɪ'kɔːdɪd-] *n* (*BRIT POST*) ≈ lettre recommandée.

recorder [rɪ'kɔːdə*] *n* (*LAW*) avocat nommé à la fonction de juge; (*MUS*) flûte *f* à bec.

record holder *n* (*SPORT*) détenteur/trice du record.

recording [rɪ'kɔːdɪŋ] *n* (*MUS*) enregistrement *m*.

recording studio *n* studio *m* d'enregistrement.

record library *n* discothèque *f*.

record player *n* électrophone *m*.

recount [rɪ'kaunt] *vt* raconter.

re-count *n* ['riːkaunt] (*POL: of votes*) nouveau décompte (des suffrages) ♦ *vt* [riː'kaunt] recompter.

recoup [rɪ'kuːp] *vt*: **to ~ one's losses** récupérer ce qu'on a perdu, se refaire.

recourse [rɪ'kɔːs] *n* recours *m*; expédient *m*; **to have ~ to** recourir à, avoir recours à.

recover [rɪ'kʌvə*] *vt* récupérer ♦ *vi* (*from illness*) se rétablir; (*from shock*) se remettre; (*country*) se redresser.

re-cover [riː'kʌvə*] *vt* (*chair etc*) recouvrir.

recovery [rɪ'kʌvərɪ] *n* récupération *f*; rétablissement *m*; redressement *m*.

recreate [riːkrɪ'eɪt] *vt* recréer.

recreation [rɛkrɪ'eɪʃən] *n* récréation *f*, détente *f*.

recreational [rɛkrɪ'eɪʃənl] *adj* pour la détente, récréatif(ive).

recreational drug *n* drogue que l'on prend pour le plaisir et non pour des raisons médicales ou par dépendance.

recreational vehicle (RV) *n* (*US*) camping-car *m*.

recrimination [rɪkrɪmɪ'neɪʃən] *n* récrimination *f*.

recruit [rɪ'kruːt] *n* recrue *f* ♦ *vt* recruter.

recruiting office [rɪ'kruːtɪŋ-] *n* bureau *m* de recrutement.

recruitment [rɪ'kruːtmənt] *n* recrutement *m*.

rectangle ['rɛktæŋgl] *n* rectangle *m*.

rectangular [rɛk'tæŋgjulə*] *adj* rectangulaire.

rectify ['rɛktɪfaɪ] *vt* (*error*) rectifier, corriger; (*omission*) réparer.

rector ['rɛktə*] *n* (*REL*) pasteur *m*; (*in Scottish universities*) personnalité élue par les étudiants pour les représenter.

rectory ['rɛktərɪ] *n* presbytère *m*.

rectum ['rɛktəm] *n* (*ANAT*) rectum *m*.

recuperate [rɪ'kjuːpəreɪt] *vi* (*from illness*) se rétablir.

recur [rɪ'kə:*] *vi* se reproduire; (*idea, opportunity*) se retrouver; (*symptoms*) réapparaître.

recurrence [rɪ'kə:rns] *n* répétition *f*; réapparition *f*.

recurrent [rɪ'kə:rnt] *adj* périodique, fréquent(e).

recurring [rɪ'kə:rɪŋ] *adj* (*MATH*) périodique.

recycle [riː'saɪkl] *vt, vi* recycler.

red [rɛd] *n* rouge *m*; (*POL: pej*) rouge *m/f* ♦ *adj* rouge; **in the ~** (*account*) à découvert; (*business*) en déficit.

red alert *n* alerte *f* rouge.

red-blooded [rɛd'blʌdɪd] *adj* (*col*) viril, vigoureux(euse).

Une **redbrick university**, ainsi nommée à cause du matériau de construction répandu à l'époque (la brique), est une université britannique provinciale construite assez récemment, en particulier fin XIXe-début XXe siècle. Il y en a notamment une à Manchester, une à Liverpool et une à Bristol. Ce terme est utilisé pour établir une distinction avec les universités les plus anciennes et traditionnelles.

red carpet treatment *n* réception *f* en grande pompe.

Red Cross *n* Croix-Rouge *f*.

redcurrant ['rɛdkʌrənt] *n* groseille *f* (rouge).

redden ['rɛdn] *vt, vi* rougir.

reddish ['rɛdɪʃ] *adj* rougeâtre; (*hair*) plutôt roux(rousse).

redecorate [riː'dɛkəreɪt] *vt* refaire à neuf, repeindre et retapisser.

redecoration [riːdɛkə'reɪʃən] *n* remise *f* à neuf.

redeem [rɪ'diːm] *vt* (*debt*) rembourser; (*sth in pawn*) dégager; (*fig, also REL*) racheter.

redeemable [rɪ'diːməbl] *adj* rachetable; remboursable, amortissable.

redeeming [rɪ'diːmɪŋ] *adj* (*feature*) qui sauve, qui rachète (le reste).

redefine [riːdɪ'faɪn] *vt* redéfinir.

redemption [rɪ'dɛmʃən] *n* (*REL*) rédemption *f*; **past** *or* **beyond ~** (*situation*) irrémédiable; (*place*) qui ne peut plus être sauvé(e); (*person*) irrécupérable.

redeploy [riːdɪ'plɔɪ] *vt* (*MIL*) redéployer; (*staff, resources*) reconvertir.

redeployment [riːdɪ'plɔɪmənt] *n* redéploiement *m*; reconversion *f*.

redevelop [riːdɪ'vɛləp] *vt* rénover.

redevelopment [riːdɪ'vɛləpmənt] *n* rénovation *f*, reconstruction *f*.

red-handed [rɛd'hændɪd] *adj*: **to be caught ~** être pris(e) en flagrant délit *or* la main dans le sac.

redhead ['rɛdhɛd] *n* roux/rousse.

red herring *n* (*fig*) diversion *f*, fausse piste.

red-hot [rɛd'hɔt] *adj* chauffé(e) au rouge, brûlant(e).

redirect [riːdaɪ'rɛkt] *vt* (*mail*) faire suivre.

redistribute [riːdɪ'strɪbjuːt] *vt* redistribuer.

red-letter day ['rɛdlɛtə-] *n* grand jour, jour mémorable.

red light *n*: **to go through a ~** (*AUT*) brûler un feu rouge.

red-light district ['rɛdlaɪt-] *n* quartier réservé.

red meat *n* viande *f* rouge.

redness ['rɛdnɪs] *n* rougeur *f*; (*of hair*) rousseur *f*.

redo [riː'duː] *vt irreg* refaire.

redolent ['rɛdələnt] *adj*: **~ of** qui sent; (*fig*) qui évoque.

redouble [riː'dʌbl] *vt*: **to ~ one's efforts** redoubler d'efforts.

redraft [riː'drɑːft] *vt* remanier.

redress [rɪ'drɛs] *n* réparation *f* ♦ *vt* redresser; **to ~ the balance** rétablir l'équilibre.

Red Sea *n*: **the ~** la mer Rouge.

redskin ['rɛdskɪn] *n* Peau-Rouge *m/f*.

red tape *n* (*fig*) paperasserie (administrative).

reduce [rɪ'djuːs] *vt* réduire; (*lower*) abaisser; **"~ speed now"** (*AUT*) "ralentir"; **to ~ sth by/to** réduire qch de/à; **to ~ sb to tears** faire pleurer qn.

reduced [rɪ'djuːst] *adj* réduit(e); **"greatly ~ prices"** "gros rabais"; **at a ~ price** (*goods*) au rabais; (*ticket etc*) à prix réduit.

reduction [rɪ'dʌkʃən] *n* réduction *f*; (*of price*) baisse *f*; (*discount*) rabais *m*; réduction.

redundancy [rɪ'dʌndənsɪ] *n* (*BRIT*) licenciement *m*, mise *f* au chômage; **compulsory ~** licenciement; **voluntary ~** départ *m* volontaire.

redundancy payment *n* (*BRIT*) indemnité *f* de licenciement.

redundant [rɪ'dʌndnt] *adj* (*BRIT: worker*) licencié(e), mis(e) au chômage; (*detail, object*) superflu(e); **to be made ~** (*worker*) être li-

cencié, être mis au chômage.
reed [riːd] *n* (*BOT*) roseau *m*; (*MUS*: *of clarinet etc*) anche *f*.
re-educate [riːˈedjukeɪt] *vt* rééduquer.
reedy [ˈriːdɪ] *adj* (*voice, instrument*) ténu(e).
reef [riːf] *n* (*at sea*) récif *m*, écueil *m*.
reek [riːk] *vi*: **to ~ (of)** puer, empester.
reel [riːl] *n* bobine *f*; (*TECH*) dévidoir *m*; (*FISHING*) moulinet *m*; (*CINE*) bande *f* ♦ *vt* (*TECH*) bobiner; (*also*: **~ up**) enrouler ♦ *vi* (*sway*) chanceler; **my head is ~ing** j'ai la tête qui tourne.
▶**reel off** *vt* (*say*) énumérer, débiter.
re-election [riːɪˈlɛkʃən] *n* réélection *f*.
re-enter [riːˈɛntə*] *vt* (*also SPACE*) rentrer dans.
re-entry [riːˈɛntrɪ] *n* (*also SPACE*) rentrée *f*.
re-export *vt* [ˈriːɪksˈpɔːt] réexporter ♦ *n* [riːˈɛkspɔːt] marchandise réexportée; (*act*) réexportation *f*.
ref [rɛf] *n abbr* (*col*: = *referee*) arbitre *m*.
ref. *abbr* (*COMM*: = *with reference to*) réf.
refectory [rɪˈfɛktərɪ] *n* réfectoire *m*.
refer [rɪˈfəː*] *vt*: **to ~ sth to** (*dispute, decision*) soumettre qch à; **to ~ sb to** (*inquirer: for information*) adresser *or* envoyer qn à; (*reader: to text*) renvoyer qn à; **he ~red me to the manager** il m'a dit de m'adresser au directeur.
▶**refer to** *vt fus* (*allude to*) parler de, faire allusion à; (*apply to*) s'appliquer à; (*consult*) se reporter à; **~ring to your letter** (*COMM*) en réponse à votre lettre.
referee [rɛfəˈriː] *n* arbitre *m*; (*TENNIS*) juge-arbitre *m*; (*BRIT*: *for job application*) répondant/e ♦ *vt* arbitrer.
reference [ˈrɛfrəns] *n* référence *f*, renvoi *m*; (*mention*) allusion *f*, mention *f*; (*for job application: letter*) références; lettre *f* de recommandation; (: *person*) répondant/e; **with ~ to** en ce qui concerne; (*COMM*: *in letter*) me référant à; **"please quote this ~"** (*COMM*) "prière de rappeler cette référence".
reference book *n* ouvrage *m* de référence.
reference library *n* bibliothèque *f* d'ouvrages à consulter.
reference number *n* (*COMM*) numéro *m* de référence.
referendum, *pl* **referenda** [rɛfəˈrɛndəm, -də] *n* référendum *m*.
referral [rɪˈfəːrəl] *n* soumission *f*; **she got a ~ to a specialist** elle a été adressée à un spécialiste.
refill *vt* [riːˈfɪl] remplir à nouveau; (*pen, lighter etc*) recharger ♦ *n* [ˈriːfɪl] (*for pen etc*) recharge *f*.
refine [rɪˈfaɪn] *vt* (*sugar, oil*) raffiner; (*taste*) affiner.
refined [rɪˈfaɪnd] *adj* (*person, taste*) raffiné(e).
refinement [rɪˈfaɪnmənt] *n* (*of person*) raffinement *m*.
refinery [rɪˈfaɪnərɪ] *n* raffinerie *f*.

refit (*NAUT*) *n* [ˈriːfɪt] remise *f* en état ♦ *vt* [riːˈfɪt] remettre en état.
reflate [riːˈfleɪt] *vt* (*economy*) relancer.
reflation [riːˈfleɪʃən] *n* relance *f*.
reflationary [riːˈfleɪʃənrɪ] *adj* de relance.
reflect [rɪˈflɛkt] *vt* (*light, image*) réfléchir, refléter; (*fig*) refléter ♦ *vi* (*think*) réfléchir, méditer.
▶**reflect on** *vt fus* (*discredit*) porter atteinte à, faire tort à.
reflection [rɪˈflɛkʃən] *n* réflexion *f*; (*image*) reflet *m*; (*criticism*): **~ on** critique *f* de; atteinte *f* à; **on ~** réflexion faite.
reflector [rɪˈflɛktə*] *n* (*also AUT*) réflecteur *m*.
reflex [ˈriːflɛks] *adj*, *n* réflexe (*m*).
reflexive [rɪˈflɛksɪv] *adj* (*LING*) réfléchi(e).
reform [rɪˈfɔːm] *n* réforme *f* ♦ *vt* réformer.
reformat [riːˈfɔːmæt] *vt* (*COMPUT*) reformater.
Reformation [rɛfəˈmeɪʃən] *n*: **the ~** la Réforme.
reformatory [rɪˈfɔːmətərɪ] *n* (*US*) centre *m* d'éducation surveillée.
reformed [rɪˈfɔːmd] *adj* amendé(e), assagi(e).
reformer [rɪˈfɔːmə*] *n* réformateur/trice.
refrain [rɪˈfreɪn] *vi*: **to ~ from doing** s'abstenir de faire ♦ *n* refrain *m*.
refresh [rɪˈfrɛʃ] *vt* rafraîchir; (*subj*: *food, sleep etc*) redonner des forces à.
refresher course [rɪˈfrɛʃə-] *n* (*BRIT*) cours *m* de recyclage.
refreshing [rɪˈfrɛʃɪŋ] *adj* rafraîchissant(e); (*sleep*) réparateur(trice); (*fact, idea etc*) qui réjouit par son originalité *or* sa rareté.
refreshment [rɪˈfrɛʃmənt] *n*: **for some ~** (*eating*) pour se restaurer *or* sustenter; **in need of ~** (*resting etc*) ayant besoin de refaire ses forces; **~(s)** rafraîchissement(s) *m(pl)*.
refrigeration [rɪfrɪdʒəˈreɪʃən] *n* réfrigération *f*.
refrigerator [rɪˈfrɪdʒəreɪtə*] *n* réfrigérateur *m*, frigidaire *m*.
refuel [riːˈfjuəl] *vt* ravitailler en carburant ♦ *vi* se ravitailler en carburant.
refuge [ˈrɛfjuːdʒ] *n* refuge *m*; **to take ~ in** se réfugier dans.
refugee [rɛfjuˈdʒiː] *n* réfugié/e.
refugee camp *n* camp *m* de réfugiés.
refund *n* [ˈriːfʌnd] remboursement *m* ♦ *vt* [rɪˈfʌnd] rembourser.
refurbish [riːˈfəːbɪʃ] *vt* remettre à neuf.
refurnish [riːˈfəːnɪʃ] *vt* remeubler.
refusal [rɪˈfjuːzəl] *n* refus *m*; **to have first ~ on sth** avoir droit de préemption sur qch.
refuse *n* [ˈrɛfjuːs] ordures *fpl*, détritus *mpl* ♦ *vt*, *vi* [rɪˈfjuːz] refuser; **to ~ to do sth** refuser de faire qch.
refuse collection *n* ramassage *m* d'ordures.
refuse disposal *n* élimination *f* des ordures.
refusenik [rɪˈfjuːznɪk] *n* refuznik *m/f*.
refute [rɪˈfjuːt] *vt* réfuter.
regain [rɪˈgeɪn] *vt* regagner; retrouver.
regal [ˈriːgl] *adj* royal(e).

regale [rɪ'geɪl] *vt*: **to ~ sb with sth** régaler qn de qch.

regalia [rɪ'geɪlɪə] *n* insignes *mpl* de la royauté.

regard [rɪ'gɑːd] *n* respect *m*, estime *f*, considération *f* ♦ *vt* considérer; **to give one's ~s to** faire ses amitiés à; **"with kindest ~s"** "bien amicalement"; **as ~s, with ~ to** en ce qui concerne.

regarding [rɪ'gɑːdɪŋ] *prep* en ce qui concerne.

regardless [rɪ'gɑːdlɪs] *adv* quand même; **~ of** sans se soucier de.

regatta [rɪ'gætə] *n* régate *f*.

regency ['riːdʒənsɪ] *n* régence *f*.

regenerate [rɪ'dʒenəreɪt] *vt* régénérer ♦ *vi* se régénérer.

regent ['riːdʒənt] *n* régent/e.

reggae ['regeɪ] *n* reggae *m*.

régime [reɪ'ʒiːm] *n* régime *m*.

regiment *n* ['redʒɪmənt] régiment *m* ♦ *vt* ['redʒɪment] imposer une discipline trop stricte à.

regimental [redʒɪ'mentl] *adj* d'un *or* du régiment.

regimentation [redʒɪmen'teɪʃən] *n* réglementation excessive.

region ['riːdʒən] *n* région *f*; **in the ~ of** (*fig*) aux alentours de.

regional ['riːdʒənl] *adj* régional(e).

En Écosse, le **regional council** *est une assemblée délibérante régionale dont les membres sont élus tous les quatre ans. Elle est responsable, entre autres, de l'urbanisme, des transports, de l'éducation, de la police et des pompiers; voir* **district council**

---

regional development *n* aménagement *m* du territoire.

register ['redʒɪstə*] *n* registre *m*; (*also:* **electoral ~**) liste électorale ♦ *vt* enregistrer, inscrire; (*birth*) déclarer; (*vehicle*) immatriculer; (*luggage*) enregistrer; (*letter*) envoyer en recommandé; (*subj: instrument*) marquer ♦ *vi* se faire inscrire; (*at hotel*) signer le registre; (*make impression*) être (bien) compris(e); **to ~ for a course** s'inscrire à un cours; **to ~ a protest** protester.

registered ['redʒɪstəd] *adj* (*design*) déposé(e); (*BRIT: letter*) recommandé(e); (*student, voter*) inscrit(e).

registered company *n* société immatriculée.

registered nurse *n* (*US*) infirmier/ière diplômé(e) d'État.

registered office *n* siège social.

registered trademark *n* marque déposée.

registrar ['redʒɪstrɑː*] *n* officier *m* de l'état civil; secrétaire (général).

registration [redʒɪs'treɪʃən] *n* (*act*) enregistrement *m*; inscription *f*; (*BRIT AUT: also:* **~ number**) numéro *m* d'immatriculation.

registry ['redʒɪstrɪ] *n* bureau *m* de l'enregistrement.

registry office *n* (*BRIT*) bureau *m* de l'état civil; **to get married in a ~** ≈ se marier à la mairie.

regret [rɪ'gret] *n* regret *m* ♦ *vt* regretter; **to ~ that** regretter que + *sub*; **we ~ to inform you that ...** nous sommes au regret de vous informer que ....

regretfully [rɪ'gretfəlɪ] *adv* à *or* avec regret.

regrettable [rɪ'gretəbl] *adj* regrettable, fâcheux(euse).

regrettably [rɪ'gretəblɪ] *adv* (*drunk, late*) fâcheusement; **~, he ...** malheureusement, il ....

regroup [riː'gruːp] *vt* regrouper ♦ *vi* se regrouper.

regt *abbr* = **regiment**.

regular ['regjulə*] *adj* régulier(ière); (*usual*) habituel(le), normal(e); (*listener, reader*) fidèle; (*soldier*) de métier; (*COMM: size*) ordinaire ♦ *n* (*client etc*) habitué/e.

regularity [regju'lærɪtɪ] *n* régularité *f*.

regularly ['regjuləlɪ] *adv* régulièrement.

regulate ['regjuleɪt] *vt* régler.

regulation [regju'leɪʃən] *n* (*rule*) règlement *m*; (*adjustment*) réglage *m* ♦ *cpd* réglementaire.

rehabilitate [riːə'bɪlɪteɪt] *vt* (*criminal*) réinsérer; (*drug addict*) désintoxiquer; (*invalid*) rééduquer.

rehabilitation ['riːəbɪlɪ'teɪʃən] *n* (*of offender*) réhabilitation *f*; (*of disabled*) rééducation *f*, réadaptation *f*.

rehash [riː'hæʃ] *vt* (*col*) remanier.

rehearsal [rɪ'həːsəl] *n* répétition *f*; **dress ~** (répétition) générale *f*.

rehearse [rɪ'həːs] *vt* répéter.

rehouse [riː'hauz] *vt* reloger.

reign [reɪn] *n* règne *m* ♦ *vi* régner.

reigning ['reɪnɪŋ] *adj* (*monarch*) régnant(e); (*champion*) actuel(le).

reimburse [riːɪm'bəːs] *vt* rembourser.

rein [reɪn] *n* (*for horse*) rêne *f*; **to give sb free ~** (*fig*) donner carte blanche à qn.

reincarnation [riːɪnkɑː'neɪʃən] *n* réincarnation *f*.

reindeer ['reɪndɪə*] *n* (*pl inv*) renne *m*.

reinforce [riːɪn'fɔːs] *vt* renforcer.

reinforced concrete [riːɪn'fɔst-] *n* béton armé.

reinforcement [riːɪn'fɔːsmənt] *n* (*action*) renforcement *m*; **~s** *npl* (*MIL*) renfort(s) *m(pl)*.

reinstate [riːɪn'steɪt] *vt* rétablir, réintégrer.

reinstatement [riːɪn'steɪtmənt] *n* réintégration *f*.

reissue [riː'ɪʃjuː] *vt* (*book*) rééditer; (*film*) ressortir.

reiterate [riː'ɪtəreɪt] *vt* réitérer, répéter.

reject *n* ['riːdʒekt] (*COMM*) article *m* de rebut ♦ *vt* [rɪ'dʒekt] refuser; (*COMM: goods*) mettre au rebut; (*idea*) rejeter.

rejection [rɪ'dʒekʃən] *n* rejet *m*, refus *m*.

rejoice [rɪ'dʒɔɪs] *vi*: **to ~ (at or over)** se réjouir (de).

rejoinder [rɪ'dʒɔɪndə*] *n* (*retort*) réplique *f*.

rejuvenate [rɪ'dʒuːvəneɪt] *vt* rajeunir.

rekindle [riː'kɪndl] *vt* rallumer; (*fig*) raviver.

relapse [rɪ'læps] *n* (*MED*) rechute *f*.

relate [rɪ'leɪt] *vt* (*tell*) raconter; (*connect*) établir un rapport entre ♦ *vi*: **to ~ to** (*connect*) se rapporter à; (*interact*) établir un rapport *or* une entente avec.

related [rɪ'leɪtɪd] *adj* apparenté(e).

relating [rɪ'leɪtɪŋ]: **~ to** *prep* concernant.

relation [rɪ'leɪʃən] *n* (*person*) parent/e; (*link*) rapport *m*, lien *m*; **diplomatic/international ~s** relations diplomatiques/internationales; **in ~ to** en ce qui concerne; par rapport à; **to bear no ~ to** être sans rapport avec.

relationship [rɪ'leɪʃənʃɪp] *n* rapport *m*, lien *m*; (*personal ties*) relations *fpl*, rapports; (*also*: **family ~**) lien de parenté; (*affair*) liaison *f*; **they have a good ~** ils s'entendent bien.

relative ['rɛlətɪv] *n* parent/e ♦ *adj* relatif(ive); (*respective*) respectif(ive); **all her ~s** toute sa famille.

relatively ['rɛlətɪvlɪ] *adv* relativement.

relax [rɪ'læks] *vi* se relâcher; (*person: unwind*) se détendre; (*calm down*) se calmer ♦ *vt* relâcher; (*mind, person*) détendre.

relaxation [riːlæk'seɪʃən] *n* relâchement *m*; détente *f*; (*entertainment*) distraction *f*.

relaxed [rɪ'lækst] *adj* relâché(e); détendu(e).

relaxing [rɪ'læksɪŋ] *adj* délassant(e).

relay ['riːleɪ] *n* (*SPORT*) course *f* de relais ♦ *vt* (*message*) retransmettre, relayer.

release [rɪ'liːs] *n* (*from prison, obligation*) libération *f*; (*of gas etc*) émission *f*; (*of film etc*) sortie *f*; (*record*) disque *m*; (*device*) déclencheur *m* ♦ *vt* (*prisoner*) libérer; (*book, film*) sortir; (*report, news*) rendre public, publier; (*gas etc*) émettre, dégager; (*free: from wreckage etc*) dégager; (*TECH: catch, spring etc*) déclencher; (*let go*) relâcher; lâcher; desserrer; **to ~ one's grip** *or* **hold** lâcher prise; **to ~ the clutch** (*AUT*) débrayer.

relegate ['rɛləgeɪt] *vt* reléguer; (*SPORT*): **to be ~d** descendre dans une division inférieure.

relent [rɪ'lɛnt] *vi* se laisser fléchir.

relentless [rɪ'lɛntlɪs] *adj* implacable.

relevance ['rɛləvəns] *n* pertinence *f*; **~ of sth to sth** rapport *m* entre qch et qch.

relevant ['rɛləvənt] *adj* approprié(e); (*fact*) significatif(ive); (*information*) utile, pertinent(e); **~ to** ayant rapport à, approprié à.

reliability [rɪlaɪə'bɪlɪtɪ] *n* sérieux *m*; fiabilité *f*.

reliable [rɪ'laɪəbl] *adj* (*person, firm*) sérieux(euse), fiable; (*method, machine*) fiable.

reliably [rɪ'laɪəblɪ] *adv*: **to be ~ informed** savoir de source sûre.

reliance [rɪ'laɪəns] *n*: **~ (on)** (*trust*) confiance *f* (en); (*dependence*) besoin *m* (de), dépendance *f* (de).

reliant [rɪ'laɪənt] *adj*: **to be ~ on sth/sb** dé-

pendre de qch/qn.

relic ['rɛlɪk] *n* (*REL*) relique *f*; (*of the past*) vestige *m*.

relief [rɪ'liːf] *n* (*from pain, anxiety*) soulagement *m*; (*help, supplies*) secours *m(pl)*; (*of guard*) relève *f*; (*ART, GEO*) relief *m*; **by way of light ~** pour faire diversion.

relief map *n* carte *f* en relief.

relief road *n* (*BRIT*) route *f* de délestage.

relieve [rɪ'liːv] *vt* (*pain, patient*) soulager; (*bring help*) secourir; (*take over from: gen*) relayer; (*: guard*) relever; **to ~ sb of sth** débarrasser qn de qch; **to ~ sb of his command** (*MIL*) relever qn de ses fonctions; **to ~ o.s.** (*euphemism*) se soulager, faire ses besoins.

relieved [rɪ'liːvd] *adj* soulagé(e); **to be ~ that ...** être soulagé que ...; **I'm ~ to hear it** je suis soulagé de l'entendre.

religion [rɪ'lɪdʒən] *n* religion *f*.

religious [rɪ'lɪdʒəs] *adj* religieux(euse); (*book*) de piété.

religious education *n* instruction religieuse.

relinquish [rɪ'lɪŋkwɪʃ] *vt* abandonner; (*plan, habit*) renoncer à.

relish ['rɛlɪʃ] *n* (*CULIN*) condiment *m*; (*enjoyment*) délectation *f* ♦ *vt* (*food etc*) savourer; **to ~ doing** se délecter à faire.

relive [riː'lɪv] *vt* revivre.

reload [riː'ləud] *vt* recharger.

relocate [riːləu'keɪt] *vt* (*business*) transférer ♦ *vi* se transférer, s'installer *or* s'établir ailleurs; **to ~ in** (déménager et) s'installer *or* s'établir à, se transférer à.

reluctance [rɪ'lʌktəns] *n* répugnance *f*.

reluctant [rɪ'lʌktənt] *adj* peu disposé(e), qui hésite; **to be ~ to do sth** hésiter à faire qch.

reluctantly [rɪ'lʌktəntlɪ] *adv* à contrecœur, sans enthousiasme.

rely [rɪ'laɪ]: **to ~ on** *vt fus* compter sur; (*be dependent*) dépendre de.

remain [rɪ'meɪn] *vi* rester; **to ~ silent** garder le silence; **I ~, yours faithfully** (*BRIT: in letters*) je vous prie d'agréer, Monsieur (*etc*), l'assurance de mes sentiments distingués.

remainder [rɪ'meɪndə*] *n* reste *m*; (*COMM*) fin *f* de série.

remaining [rɪ'meɪnɪŋ] *adj* qui reste.

remains [rɪ'meɪnz] *npl* restes *mpl*.

remand [rɪ'maːnd]: **on ~** en détention préventive ♦ *vt*: **to ~ in custody** écrouer; renvoyer en détention provisoire.

remand home *n* (*BRIT*) centre *m* d'éducation surveillée.

remark [rɪ'maːk] *n* remarque *f*, observation *f* ♦ *vt* (*faire*) remarquer, dire; (*notice*) remarquer; **to ~ on sth** faire une *or* des remarque(s) sur qch.

remarkable [rɪ'maːkəbl] *adj* remarquable.

remarry [riː'mærɪ] *vi* se remarier.

remedial [rɪ'miːdɪəl] *adj* (*tuition, classes*) de rattrapage.

remedy ['rɛmədɪ] *n*: **~ (for)** remède *m* (contre

or à) ♦ *vt* remédier à.

remember [rɪ'mɛmbə*] *vt* se rappeler, se souvenir de; **I ~ seeing it, I ~ having seen it** je me rappelle l'avoir vu *or* que je l'ai vu; **she ~ed to do it** elle a pensé à le faire; **~ me to your wife** rappelez-moi au bon souvenir de votre femme.

remembrance [rɪ'mɛmbrəns] *n* souvenir *m*; mémoire *f*.

Remembrance Sunday *ou* **Remembrance Day** *est le dimanche le plus proche du 11 novembre, jour où la Première Guerre mondiale a officiellement pris fin. Il rend hommage aux victimes des deux guerres mondiales. À cette occasion, on observe deux minutes de silence à 11 h, heure de la signature de l'armistice avec l'Allemagne en 1918; certains membres de la famille royale et du gouvernement déposent des gerbes de coquelicots au cénotaphe de Whitehall, et des couronnes sont placées sur les monuments aux morts dans toute la Grande-Bretagne; par ailleurs, les gens portent des coquelicots artificiels fabriqués et vendus par des membres de la légion britannique blessés au combat, au profit des blessés de guerre et de leur famille.*

---

remind [rɪ'maɪnd] *vt*: **to ~ sb of sth** rappeler qch à qn; **to ~ sb to do** faire penser à qn à faire, rappeler à qn qu'il doit faire; **that ~s me!** j'y pense!

reminder [rɪ'maɪndə*] *n* rappel *m*; (*note etc*) pense-bête *m*.

reminisce [rɛmɪ'nɪs] *vi*: **to ~ (about)** évoquer ses souvenirs (de).

reminiscences [rɛmɪ'nɪsnsɪz] *npl* réminiscences *fpl*, souvenirs *mpl*.

reminiscent [rɛmɪ'nɪsnt] *adj*: **~ of** qui rappelle, qui fait penser à.

remiss [rɪ'mɪs] *adj* négligent(e); **it was ~ of me** c'était une négligence de ma part.

remission [rɪ'mɪʃən] *n* rémission *f*; (*of debt, sentence*) remise *f*; (*of fee*) exemption *f*.

remit [rɪ'mɪt] *vt* (*send: money*) envoyer.

remittance [rɪ'mɪtns] *n* envoi *m*, paiement *m*.

remnant [ˈrɛmnənt] *n* reste *m*, restant *m*; **~s** *npl* (*COMM*) coupons *mpl*; fins *fpl* de série.

remonstrate [ˈrɛmənstreɪt] *vi*: **to ~ (with sb about sth)** se plaindre (à qn de qch).

remorse [rɪ'mɔːs] *n* remords *m*.

remorseful [rɪ'mɔːsful] *adj* plein(e) de remords.

remorseless [rɪ'mɔːslɪs] *adj* (*fig*) impitoyable.

remote [rɪ'məut] *adj* éloigné(e), lointain(e); (*person*) distant(e); **there is a ~ possibility that ...** il est tout juste possible que ....

remote control *n* télécommande *f*.

remote-controlled [rɪ'məutkən'trəuld] *adj* téléguidé(e).

remotely [rɪ'məutlɪ] *adv* au loin; (*slightly*) très vaguement.

remoteness [rɪ'məutnɪs] *n* éloignement *m*.

remould ['riːməuld] *n* (*BRIT: tyre*) pneu rechapé.

removable [rɪ'muːvəbl] *adj* (*detachable*) amovible.

removal [rɪ'muːvəl] *n* (*taking away*) enlèvement *m*; suppression *f*; (*BRIT: from house*) déménagement *m*; (*from office: dismissal*) renvoi *m*; (*MED*) ablation *f*.

removal man *n* (*BRIT*) déménageur *m*.

removal van *n* (*BRIT*) camion *m* de déménagement.

remove [rɪ'muːv] *vt* enlever, retirer; (*employee*) renvoyer; (*stain*) faire partir; (*doubt, abuse*) supprimer; **first cousin once ~d** cousin/e au deuxième degré.

remover [rɪ'muːvə*] *n* (*for paint*) décapant *m*; (*for varnish*) dissolvant *m*; **make-up ~** démaquillant *m*.

remunerate [rɪ'mjuːnəreɪt] *vt* rémunérer.

remuneration [rɪmjuːnə'reɪʃən] *n* rémunération *f*.

rename [riː'neɪm] *vt* rebaptiser.

rend, *pt, pp* **rent** [rɛnd, rɛnt] *vt* déchirer.

render ['rɛndə*] *vt* rendre; (*CULIN: fat*) clarifier.

rendering ['rɛndərɪŋ] *n* (*MUS etc*) interprétation *f*.

rendez-vous ['rɒndɪvuː] *n* rendez-vous *m inv* ♦ *vi* opérer une jonction, se rejoindre; (*spaceship*) effectuer un rendez-vous (dans l'espace); **to ~ with sb** rejoindre qn.

renegade ['rɛnɪgeɪd] *n* rénégat/e.

renew [rɪ'njuː] *vt* renouveler; (*negotiations*) reprendre; (*acquaintance*) renouer.

renewable [rɪ'njuːəbl] *adj* renouvelable; **~ energy, ~s** énergies renouvelables.

renewal [rɪ'njuːəl] *n* renouvellement *m*; reprise *f*.

renounce [rɪ'nauns] *vt* renoncer à; (*disown*) renier.

renovate ['rɛnəveɪt] *vt* rénover; (*work of art*) restaurer.

renovation [rɛnə'veɪʃən] *n* rénovation *f*; restauration *f*.

renown [rɪ'naun] *n* renommée *f*.

renowned [rɪ'naund] *adj* renommé(e).

rent [rɛnt] *pt, pp of* **rend** ♦ *n* loyer *m* ♦ *vt* louer; (*car, TV*) louer, prendre en location; (*also: ~ out: car, TV*) louer, donner en location.

rental ['rɛntl] *n* (*for television, car*) (prix *m* de) location *f*.

rent boy *n* (*BRIT col*) jeune prostitué.

renunciation [rɪnʌnsɪ'eɪʃən] *n* renonciation *f*; (*self-denial*) renoncement *m*.

reopen [riː'əupən] *vt* rouvrir.

reopening [riː'əupnɪŋ] *n* réouverture *f*.

reorder [riː'ɔːdə*] *vt* commander de nouveau; (*rearrange*) réorganiser.

reorganize [riː'ɔːgənaɪz] *vt* réorganiser.

rep [rɛp] *n abbr* (*COMM*) = **representative**; (*THEAT*) = **repertory**.

Rep. *abbr* (*US POL*) = **representative**, **republi-**

can.

repair [rɪ'pɛə*] *n* réparation *f* ♦ *vt* réparer; **in good/bad** ~ en bon/mauvais état; **under** ~ en réparation.

repair kit *n* trousse *f* de réparations.

repair man *n* réparateur *m*.

repair shop *n* (AUT etc) atelier *m* de réparations.

repartee [rɛpɑ:'ti:] *n* repartie *f*.

repast [rɪ'pɑ:st] *n* (formal) repas *m*.

repatriate [ri:'pætrɪeɪt] *vt* rapatrier.

repay [ri:'peɪ] *vt irreg* (money, creditor) rembourser; (sb's efforts) récompenser.

repayment [ri:'peɪmənt] *n* remboursement *m*; récompense *f*.

repeal [rɪ'pi:l] *n* (of law) abrogation *f*; (of sentence) annulation *f* ♦ *vt* abroger; annuler.

repeat [rɪ'pi:t] *n* (RADIO, TV) reprise *f* ♦ *vt* répéter; (pattern) reproduire; (promise, attack, also COMM: order) renouveler; (SCOL: a class) redoubler ♦ *vi* répéter.

repeatedly [rɪ'pi:tɪdlɪ] *adv* souvent, à plusieurs reprises.

repel [rɪ'pɛl] *vt* repousser.

repellent [rɪ'pɛlənt] *adj* repoussant(e) ♦ *n*: **insect** ~ insectifuge *m*; **moth** ~ produit *m* antimite(s).

repent [rɪ'pɛnt] *vi*: **to** ~ **(of)** se repentir (de).

repentance [rɪ'pɛntəns] *n* repentir *m*.

repercussion [ri:pə'kʌʃən] *n* (consequence) répercussion *f*.

repertoire ['rɛpətwɑ:*] *n* répertoire *m*.

repertory ['rɛpətərɪ] *n* (also: ~ **theatre**) théâtre *m* de répertoire.

repertory company *n* troupe théâtrale permanente.

repetition [rɛpɪ'tɪʃən] *n* répétition *f*.

repetitious [rɛpɪ'tɪʃəs] *adj* (speech) plein(e) de redites.

repetitive [rɪ'pɛtɪtɪv] *adj* (movement, work) répétitif(ive); (speech) plein(e) de redites.

replace [rɪ'pleɪs] *vt* (put back) remettre, replacer; (take the place of) remplacer; (TEL): *"*~ **the receiver"** "raccrochez".

replacement [rɪ'pleɪsmənt] *n* replacement *m*; remplacement *m*; (person) remplaçant/e.

replacement part *n* pièce *f* de rechange.

replay [ri:pleɪ] *n* (of match) match rejoué; (of tape, film) répétition *f*.

replenish [rɪ'plɛnɪʃ] *vt* (glass) remplir (de nouveau); (stock etc) réapprovisionner.

replete [rɪ'pli:t] *adj* rempli(e); (well-fed): ~ **(with)** rassasié(e) (de).

replica ['rɛplɪkə] *n* réplique *f*, copie exacte.

reply [rɪ'plaɪ] *n* réponse *f* ♦ *vi* répondre; **in** ~ **(to)** en réponse (à); **there's no** ~ (TEL) ça ne répond pas.

reply coupon *n* coupon-réponse *m*.

report [rɪ'pɔ:t] *n* rapport *m*; (PRESS etc) reportage *m*; (BRIT: also: **school** ~) bulletin *m* (scolaire); (of gun) détonation *f* ♦ *vt* rapporter, faire un compte rendu de; (PRESS etc) faire

un reportage sur; (bring to notice: occurrence) signaler; (: person) dénoncer ♦ *vi* (make a report): **to** ~ **(on)** faire un rapport (sur); (for newspaper) faire un reportage (sur); (present o.s.): **to** ~ **(to sb)** se présenter (chez qn); **it is** ~**ed that** on dit *or* annonce que; **it is** ~**ed from Berlin that** on nous apprend de Berlin que.

report card *n* (US, Scottish) bulletin *m* (scolaire).

reportedly [rɪ'pɔ:tɪdlɪ] *adv*: **she is** ~ **living in Spain** elle habiterait en Espagne; **he** ~ **ordered them to ...** il leur aurait ordonné de ....

reported speech *n* (LING) discours indirect.

reporter [rɪ'pɔ:tə*] *n* reporter *m*.

repose [rɪ'pəʊz] *n*: **in** ~ en *or* au repos.

repossess [ri:pə'zɛs] *vt* saisir.

repossession order [ri:pə'zɛʃən-] *n* ordre *m* de reprise de possession.

reprehensible [rɛprɪ'hɛnsɪbl] *adj* répréhensible.

represent [rɛprɪ'zɛnt] *vt* représenter; (explain): **to** ~ **to sb that** expliquer à qn que.

representation [rɛprɪzɛn'teɪʃən] *n* représentation *f*; ~**s** *npl* (protest) démarche *f*.

representative [rɛprɪ'zɛntətɪv] *n* représentant/e; (COMM) représentant/e (de commerce); (US POL) député *m* ♦ *adj*: ~ **(of)** représentatif(ive) (de), caractéristique (de).

repress [rɪ'prɛs] *vt* réprimer.

repression [rɪ'prɛʃən] *n* répression *f*.

repressive [rɪ'prɛsɪv] *adj* répressif(ive).

reprieve [rɪ'pri:v] *n* (LAW) grâce *f*; (fig) sursis *m*, délai *m* ♦ *vt* gracier; accorder un sursis *or* un délai à.

reprimand ['rɛprɪmɑ:nd] *n* réprimande *f* ♦ *vt* réprimander.

reprint *n* ['ri:prɪnt] réimpression *f* ♦ *vt* [ri:'prɪnt] réimprimer.

reprisal [rɪ'praɪzl] *n* représailles *fpl*; **to take** ~**s** user de représailles.

reproach [rɪ'prəʊtʃ] *n* reproche *m* ♦ *vt*: **to** ~ **sb with sth** reprocher qch à qn; **beyond** ~ irréprochable.

reproachful [rɪ'prəʊtʃful] *adj* de reproche.

reproduce [ri:prə'dju:s] *vt* reproduire ♦ *vi* se reproduire.

reproduction [ri:prə'dʌkʃən] *n* reproduction *f*.

reproductive [ri:prə'dʌktɪv] *adj* repro- ducteur(trice).

reproof [rɪ'pru:f] *n* reproche *m*.

reprove [rɪ'pru:v] *vt* (action) réprouver; (person): **to** ~ **(for)** blâmer (de).

reproving [rɪ'pru:vɪŋ] *adj* réprobateur(trice).

reptile ['rɛptaɪl] *n* reptile *m*.

Repub. *abbr* (US POL) = **republican**.

republic [rɪ'pʌblɪk] *n* république *f*.

republican [rɪ'pʌblɪkən] *adj*, *n* républicain(e).

repudiate [rɪ'pju:dɪeɪt] *vt* (ally, behaviour) désavouer; (accusation) rejeter; (wife) répu-

dier.
repugnant [rɪ'pʌɡnənt] *adj* répugnant(e).
repulse [rɪ'pʌls] *vt* repousser.
repulsion [rɪ'pʌlʃən] *n* répulsion *f*.
repulsive [rɪ'pʌlsɪv] *adj* repoussant(e), répulsif(ive).
reputable ['repjutəbl] *adj* de bonne réputation; (*occupation*) honorable.
reputation [repju'teɪʃən] *n* réputation *f*; **to have a ~ for** être réputé(e) pour; **he has a ~ for being awkward** il a la réputation de ne pas être commode.
repute [rɪ'pju:t] *n* (bonne) réputation.
reputed [rɪ'pju:tɪd] *adj* réputé(e); **he is ~ to be rich/intelligent** *etc* on dit qu'il est riche/intelligent *etc*.
reputedly [rɪ'pju:tɪdlɪ] *adv* d'après ce qu'on dit.
request [rɪ'kwest] *n* demande *f*; (*formal*) requête *f* ♦ *vt*: **to ~ (of or from sb)** demander (à qn); **at the ~ of** à la demande de.
request stop *n* (*BRIT: for bus*) arrêt facultatif.
requiem ['rekwɪəm] *n* requiem *m*.
require [rɪ'kwaɪə*] *vt* (*need: subj: person*) avoir besoin de; (*: thing, situation*) nécessiter, demander; (*demand*) exiger, requérir; (*order*): **to ~ sb to do sth/sth of sb** exiger que qn fasse qch/qch de qn; **if ~d** s'il le faut; **what qualifications are ~d?** quelles sont les qualifications requises?; **~d by law** requis par la loi.
required [rɪ'kwaɪəd] *adj* requis(e), voulu(e).
requirement [rɪ'kwaɪəmənt] *n* exigence *f*; besoin *m*; condition *f* (requise).
requisite ['rekwɪzɪt] *n* chose *f* nécessaire ♦ *adj* requis(e), nécessaire; **toilet ~s** accessoires *mpl* de toilette.
requisition [rekwɪ'zɪʃən] *n*: **~ (for)** demande *f* (de) ♦ *vt* (*MIL*) réquisitionner.
reroute [ri:'ru:t] *vt* (*train etc*) dérouter.
resale ['ri:'seɪl] *n* revente *f*.
resale price maintenance (RPM) *n* vente au détail à prix imposé.
rescind [rɪ'sɪnd] *vt* annuler; (*law*) abroger; (*judgment*) rescinder.
rescue ['reskju:] *n* sauvetage *m*; (*help*) secours *mpl* ♦ *vt* sauver; **to come to sb's ~** venir au secours de qn.
rescue party *n* équipe *f* de sauvetage.
rescuer ['reskjuə*] *n* sauveteur *m*.
research [rɪ'sə:tʃ] *n* recherche(s) *f(pl)* ♦ *vt* faire des recherches sur ♦ *vi*: **to ~ (into sth)** faire des recherches (sur qch); **a piece of ~** un travail de recherche; **~ and development (R & D)** recherche-développement (R-D).
researcher [rɪ'sə:tʃə*] *n* chercheur/euse.
research work *n* recherches *fpl*.
resell [ri:'sel] *vt irreg* revendre.
resemblance [rɪ'zembləns] *n* ressemblance *f*; **to bear a strong ~ to** ressembler beaucoup à.

resemble [rɪ'zembl] *vt* ressembler à.
resent [rɪ'zent] *vt* éprouver du ressentiment de, être contrarié(e) par.
resentful [rɪ'zentful] *adj* irrité(e), plein(e) de ressentiment.
resentment [rɪ'zentmənt] *n* ressentiment *m*.
reservation [rezə'veɪʃən] *n* (*booking*) réservation *f*; (*doubt; protected area*) réserve *f*; (*BRIT AUT: also*: **central ~**) bande médiane; **to make a ~ (in an hotel/a restaurant/on a plane)** réserver *or* retenir une chambre/une table/une place; **with ~s** (*doubts*) avec certaines réserves.
reservation desk *n* (*US: in hotel*) réception *f*.
reserve [rɪ'zə:v] *n* réserve *f*; (*SPORT*) remplaçant/e ♦ *vt* (*seats etc*) réserver, retenir; **~s** *npl* (*MIL*) réservistes *mpl*; **in ~** en réserve.
reserve currency *n* monnaie *f* de réserve.
reserved [rɪ'zə:vd] *adj* réservé(e).
reserve price *n* (*BRIT*) mise *f* à prix, prix *m* de départ.
reserve team *n* (*BRIT SPORT*) deuxième équipe *f*.
reservist [rɪ'zə:vɪst] *n* (*MIL*) réserviste *m*.
reservoir ['rezəvwɑ:*] *n* réservoir *m*.
reset [ri:'set] *vt irreg* remettre; (*clock, watch*) mettre à l'heure; (*COMPUT*) remettre à zéro.
reshape [ri:'ʃeɪp] *vt* (*policy*) réorganiser.
reshuffle [ri:'ʃʌfl] *n*: **Cabinet ~** (*POL*) remaniement ministériel.
reside [rɪ'zaɪd] *vi* résider.
residence ['rezɪdəns] *n* résidence *f*; **to take up ~** s'installer; **in ~** (*queen etc*) en résidence; (*doctor*) résidant(e).
residence permit *n* (*BRIT*) permis *m* de séjour.
resident ['rezɪdənt] *n* résident/e ♦ *adj* résidant(e).
residential [rezɪ'denʃəl] *adj* de résidence; (*area*) résidentiel(le).
residue ['rezɪdju:] *n* reste *m*; (*CHEM, PHYSICS*) résidu *m*.
resign [rɪ'zaɪn] *vt* (*one's post*) se démettre de ♦ *vi*: **to ~ (from)** démissionner (de); **to ~ o.s. to** (*endure*) se résigner à.
resignation [rezɪɡ'neɪʃən] *n* démission *f*; résignation *f*; **to tender one's ~** donner sa démission.
resigned [rɪ'zaɪnd] *adj* résigné(e).
resilience [rɪ'zɪlɪəns] *n* (*of material*) élasticité *f*; (*of person*) ressort *m*.
resilient [rɪ'zɪlɪənt] *adj* (*person*) qui réagit, qui a du ressort.
resin ['rezɪn] *n* résine *f*.
resist [rɪ'zɪst] *vt* résister à.
resistance [rɪ'zɪstəns] *n* résistance *f*.
resistant [rɪ'zɪstənt] *adj*: **~ (to)** résistant(e) (à).
resolute ['rezəlu:t] *adj* résolu(e).
resolution [rezə'lu:ʃən] *n* résolution *f*; **to make a ~** prendre une résolution.

resolve [rɪ'zɔlv] *n* résolution *f* ♦ *vt* (*decide*): **to ~ to do** résoudre *or* décider de faire; (*problem*) résoudre.

resolved [rɪ'zɔlvd] *adj* résolu(e).

resonance ['rɛzənəns] *n* résonance *f*.

resonant ['rɛzənənt] *adj* résonnant(e).

resort [rɪ'zɔ:t] *n* (*town*) station *f* (de vacances); (*recourse*) recours *m* ♦ *vi*: **to ~ to** avoir recours à; **seaside/winter sports ~** station balnéaire/de sports d'hiver; **in the last ~** en dernier ressort.

resound [rɪ'zaund] *vi*: **to ~ (with)** retentir (de).

resounding [rɪ'zaundɪŋ] *adj* retentissant(e).

resource [rɪ'sɔ:s] *n* ressource *f*; **~s** *npl* ressources; **natural ~s** ressources naturelles; **to leave sb to his** (*or* **her**) **own ~s** (*fig*) livrer qn à lui-même (*or* elle-même).

resourceful [rɪ'sɔ:sful] *adj* plein(e) de ressource, débrouillard(e).

resourcefulness [rɪ'sɔ:sfəlnıs] *n* ressource *f*.

respect [rɪs'pɛkt] *n* respect *m*; (*point, detail*): **in some ~s** à certains égards ♦ *vt* respecter; **~s** *npl* respects, hommages *mpl*; **to have** *or* **show ~ for sb/sth** respecter qn/qch; **out of ~ for** par respect pour; **with ~ to** en ce qui concerne; **in ~ of** sous le rapport de, quant à; **in this ~** sous ce rapport, à cet égard; **with due ~ I** ... malgré le respect que je vous dois, je ....

respectability [rɪspɛktə'bɪlɪtɪ] *n* respectabilité *f*.

respectable [rɪs'pɛktəbl] *adj* respectable; (*quite good: result etc*) honorable; (*player*) assez bon(bonne).

respectful [rɪs'pɛktful] *adj* respectueux(euse).

respective [rɪs'pɛktɪv] *adj* respectif(ive).

respectively [rɪs'pɛktɪvlɪ] *adv* respectivement.

respiration [rɛspɪ'reɪʃən] *n* respiration *f*.

respirator ['rɛspɪreɪtə*] *n* respirateur *m*.

respiratory ['rɛspərətərɪ] *adj* respiratoire.

respite ['rɛspaɪt] *n* répit *m*.

resplendent [rɪs'plɛndənt] *adj* resplendissant(e).

respond [rɪs'pɔnd] *vi* répondre; (*to treatment*) réagir.

respondent [rɪs'pɔndənt] *n* (*LAW*) défendeur/ deresse.

response [rɪs'pɔns] *n* réponse *f*; (*to treatment*) réaction *f*; **in ~ to** en réponse à.

responsibility [rɪspɔnsɪ'bɪlɪtɪ] *n* responsabilité *f*; **to take ~ for sth/sb** accepter la responsabilité de qch/d'être responsable de qn.

responsible [rɪs'pɔnsɪbl] *adj* (*liable*): **~ (for)** responsable (de); (*person*) digne de confiance; (*job*) qui comporte des responsabilités; **to be ~ to sb (for sth)** être responsable devant qn (de qch).

responsibly [rɪs'pɔnsɪblɪ] *adv* avec sérieux.

responsive [rɪs'pɔnsɪv] *adj* qui n'est pas réservé(e) *or* indifférent(e).

rest [rɛst] *n* repos *m*; (*stop*) arrêt *m*, pause *f*; (*MUS*) silence *m*; (*support*) support *m*, appui *m*; (*remainder*) reste *m*, restant *m* ♦ *vi* se reposer; (*be supported*): **to ~ on** appuyer *or* reposer sur; (*remain*) rester ♦ *vt* (*lean*): **to ~ sth on/against** appuyer qch sur/contre; **the ~ of them** les autres; **to set sb's mind at ~** tranquilliser qn; **it ~s with him to** c'est à lui de; **~ assured that ...** soyez assuré que ....

restart [ri:'stɑ:t] *vt* (*engine*) remettre en marche; (*work*) reprendre.

restaurant ['rɛstərɔŋ] *n* restaurant *m*.

restaurant car *n* (*BRIT*) wagon-restaurant *m*.

rest cure *n* cure *f* de repos.

restful ['rɛstful] *adj* reposant(e).

rest home *n* maison *f* de repos.

restitution [rɛstɪ'tju:ʃən] *n* (*act*) restitution *f*; (*reparation*) réparation *f*.

restive ['rɛstɪv] *adj* agité(e), impatient(e); (*horse*) rétif(ive).

restless ['rɛstlɪs] *adj* agité(e); **to get ~** s'impatienter.

restlessly ['rɛstlɪslɪ] *adv* avec agitation.

restock [ri:'stɔk] *vt* réapprovisionner.

restoration [rɛstə'reɪʃən] *n* restauration *f*; restitution *f*.

restorative [rɪ'stɔrətɪv] *adj* reconstituant(e) ♦ *n* reconstituant *m*.

restore [rɪ'stɔ:*] *vt* (*building*) restaurer; (*sth stolen*) restituer; (*peace, health*) rétablir.

restorer [rɪ'stɔ:rə*] *n* (*ART etc*) restaurateur/ trice (d'œuvres d'art).

restrain [rɪs'treɪn] *vt* (*feeling*) contenir; (*person*): **to ~ (from doing)** retenir (de faire).

restrained [rɪs'treɪnd] *adj* (*style*) sobre; (*manner*) mesuré(e).

restraint [rɪs'treɪnt] *n* (*restriction*) contrainte *f*; (*moderation*) retenue *f*; (*of style*) sobriété *f*; **wage ~** limitations salariales.

restrict [rɪs'trɪkt] *vt* restreindre, limiter.

restricted area [rɪs'trɪktɪd-] *n* (*AUT*) zone *f* à vitesse limitée.

restriction [rɪs'trɪkʃən] *n* restriction *f*, limitation *f*.

restrictive [rɪs'trɪktɪv] *adj* restrictif(ive).

restrictive practices *npl* (*INDUSTRY*) pratiques *fpl* entravant la libre concurrence.

rest room *n* (*US*) toilettes *fpl*.

restructure [ri:'strʌktʃə*] *vt* restructurer.

result [rɪ'zʌlt] *n* résultat *m* ♦ *vi*: **to ~ (from)** résulter (de); **to ~ in** aboutir à, se terminer par; **as a ~ it is too expensive** il en résulte que c'est trop cher; **as a ~ of** à la suite de.

resultant [rɪ'zʌltənt] *adj* résultant(e).

resume [rɪ'zju:m] *vt* (*work, journey*) reprendre; (*sum up*) résumer ♦ *vi* (*work etc*) reprendre.

résumé ['reɪzju:meɪ] *n* (*summary*) résumé *m*; (*US: curriculum vitae*) curriculum vitae *m inv*.

resumption [rɪ'zʌmpʃən] *n* reprise *f*.

resurgence [rɪ'sɜ:dʒəns] *n* réapparition *f*.

resurrection [rɛzə'rɛkʃən] *n* résurrection *f*.

resuscitate [rɪ'sʌsɪteɪt] vt (MED) réanimer.
resuscitation [rɪsʌsɪ'teɪʃən] n réanimation f.
retail ['riːteɪl] n (vente f au) détail m ♦ cpd de or au détail ♦ vt vendre au détail ♦ vi: **to ~ at 10 francs** se vendre au détail à 10 francs.
retailer ['riːteɪlə*] n détaillant/e.
retail outlet n point m de vente.
retail price n prix m de détail.
retail price index n ≈ indice m des prix.
retain [rɪ'teɪn] vt (keep) garder, conserver; (employ) engager.
retainer [rɪ'teɪnə*] n (servant) serviteur m; (fee) acompte m, provision f.
retaliate [rɪ'tælɪeɪt] vi: **to ~ (against)** se venger (de); **to ~ (on sb)** rendre la pareille (à qn).
retaliation [rɪtælɪ'eɪʃən] n représailles fpl, vengeance f; **in ~ for** par représailles pour.
retaliatory [rɪ'tælɪətərɪ] adj de représailles.
retarded [rɪ'tɑːdɪd] adj retardé(e).
retch [retʃ] vi avoir des haut-le-cœur.
retentive [rɪ'tentɪv] adj: **~ memory** excellente mémoire.
rethink ['riː'θɪŋk] vt repenser.
reticence ['retɪsns] n réticence f.
reticent ['retɪsnt] adj réticent(e).
retina ['retɪnə] n rétine f.
retinue ['retɪnjuː] n suite f, cortège m.
retire [rɪ'taɪə*] vi (give up work) prendre sa retraite; (withdraw) se retirer, partir; (go to bed) (aller) se coucher.
retired [rɪ'taɪəd] adj (person) retraité(e).
retirement [rɪ'taɪəmənt] n retraite f.
retirement age n âge m de la retraite.
retiring [rɪ'taɪərɪŋ] adj (person) réservé(e); (chairman etc) sortant(e).
retort [rɪ'tɔːt] n (reply) riposte f; (container) cornue f ♦ vi riposter.
retrace [riː'treɪs] vt reconstituer; **to ~ one's steps** revenir sur ses pas.
retract [rɪ'trækt] vt (statement, claws) rétracter; (undercarriage, aerial) rentrer, escamoter ♦ vi se rétracter; rentrer.
retractable [rɪ'træktəbl] adj escamotable.
retrain [riː'treɪn] vt recycler ♦ vi se recycler.
retraining [riː'treɪnɪŋ] n recyclage m.
retread vt [riː'tred] (AUT: tyre) rechaper ♦ n ['riːtred] pneu rechapé.
retreat [rɪ'triːt] n retraite f ♦ vi battre en retraite; (flood) reculer; **to beat a hasty ~** (fig) partir avec précipitation.
retrial [riː'traɪəl] n nouveau procès.
retribution [retrɪ'bjuːʃən] n châtiment m.
retrieval [rɪ'triːvəl] n récupération f; réparation f; recherche f et extraction f.
retrieve [rɪ'triːv] vt (sth lost) récupérer; (situation, honour) sauver; (error, loss) réparer; (COMPUT) rechercher.
retriever [rɪ'triːvə*] n chien m d'arrêt.
retroactive [retrəʊ'æktɪv] adj rétroactif(ive).
retrograde ['retrəgreɪd] adj rétrograde.
retrospect ['retrəspekt] n: **in ~** rétrospective-

ment, après coup.
retrospective [retrə'spektɪv] adj (law) rétroactif(ive) ♦ n (ART) rétrospective f.
return [rɪ'tɜːn] n (going or coming back) retour m; (of sth stolen etc) restitution f; (recompense) récompense f; (FINANCE: from land, shares) rapport m; (report) relevé m, rapport ♦ cpd (journey) de retour; (BRIT: ticket) aller et retour; (match) retour ♦ vi (person etc: come back) revenir; (: go back) retourner ♦ vt rendre; (bring back) rapporter; (send back) renvoyer; (put back) remettre; (POL: candidate) élire; **~s** npl (COMM) recettes fpl; bénéfices mpl; (: ~of goods) marchandises renvoyées; **many happy ~s (of the day)!** bon anniversaire!; **by ~ (of post)** par retour (du courrier); **in ~ (for)** en échange (de).
returnable [rɪ'tɜːnəbl] adj (bottle etc) consigné(e).
returner [rɪ'tɜːnə*] n femme qui reprend un travail après avoir élevé ses enfants.
returning officer [rɪ'tɜːnɪŋ-] n (BRIT POL) président m de bureau de vote.
return key n (COMPUT) touche f de retour.
reunion [riː'juːnɪən] n réunion f.
reunite [riːjuː'naɪt] vt réunir.
rev [rev] n abbr (= revolution: AUT) tour m ♦ vb (also: ~ up) vt emballer ♦ vi s'emballer.
Rev. abbr = **reverend**.
revaluation [riːvælju'eɪʃən] n réévaluation f.
revamp [riː'væmp] vt (house) retaper; (firm) réorganiser.
rev counter n (BRIT) compte-tours m inv.
Revd. abbr = **reverend**.
reveal [rɪ'viːl] vt (make known) révéler; (display) laisser voir.
revealing [rɪ'viːlɪŋ] adj révélateur(trice); (dress) au décolleté généreux or suggestif.
reveille [rɪ'vælɪ] n (MIL) réveil m.
revel ['revl] vi: **to ~ in sth/in doing** se délecter de qch/à faire.
revelation [revə'leɪʃən] n révélation f.
reveller ['revlə*] n fêtard m.
revelry ['revlrɪ] n festivités fpl.
revenge [rɪ'vendʒ] n vengeance f; (in game etc) revanche f ♦ vt venger; **to take ~** se venger.
revengeful [rɪ'vendʒful] adj vengeur(eresse); vindicatif(ive).
revenue ['revənjuː] n revenu m.
reverberate [rɪ'vɜːbəreɪt] vi (sound) retentir, se répercuter; (light) se réverbérer.
reverberation [rɪvɜːbə'reɪʃən] n répercussion f; réverbération f.
revere [rɪ'vɪə*] vt vénérer, révérer.
reverence ['revərəns] n vénération f, révérence f.
reverend ['revərənd] adj vénérable; **the R~ John Smith** (Anglican) le révérend John Smith; (Catholic) l'abbé John Smith; (Protestant) le pasteur John Smith.
reverent ['revərənt] adj respectueux(euse).
reverie ['revərɪ] n rêverie f.

reversal [rɪ'vɔːsl] n (of opinion) revirement m.

reverse [rɪ'vɔːs] n contraire m, opposé m; (back) dos m, envers m; (AUT: also: ~ **gear**) marche f arrière ♦ adj (order, direction) opposé(e), inverse ♦ vt (turn) renverser, retourner; (change) renverser, changer complètement; (LAW: judgment) réformer ♦ vi (BRIT AUT) faire marche arrière; **to go into** ~ faire marche arrière; **in** ~ **order** en ordre inverse.

reversed charge call [rɪ'vɔːst-] n (BRIT TEL) communication f en PCV.

reverse video n vidéo m inverse.

reversible [rɪ'vɔːsəbl] adj (garment) réversible; (procedure) révocable.

reversing lights [rɪ'vɔːsɪŋ-] npl (BRIT AUT) feux mpl de marche arrière or de recul.

reversion [rɪ'vɔːʃən] n retour m.

revert [rɪ'vɔːt] vi: **to** ~ **to** revenir à, retourner à.

review [rɪ'vjuː] n revue f; (of book, film) critique f ♦ vt passer en revue; faire la critique de; **to come under** ~ être révisé(e).

reviewer [rɪ'vjuːə*] n critique m.

revile [rɪ'vaɪl] vt injurier.

revise [rɪ'vaɪz] vt (manuscript) revoir, corriger; (opinion) réviser, modifier; (study: subject, notes) réviser; ~**d edition** édition revue et corrigée.

revision [rɪ'vɪʒən] n révision f; (revised version) version corrigée.

revitalize [riː'vaɪtəlaɪz] vt revitaliser.

revival [rɪ'vaɪvəl] n reprise f; rétablissement m; (of faith) renouveau m.

revive [rɪ'vaɪv] vt (person) ranimer; (custom) rétablir; (hope, courage) redonner; (play, fashion) reprendre ♦ vi (person) reprendre connaissance; (hope) renaître; (activity) reprendre.

revoke [rɪ'vəuk] vt révoquer; (promise, decision) revenir sur.

revolt [rɪ'vəult] n révolte f ♦ vi se révolter, se rebeller.

revolting [rɪ'vəultɪŋ] adj dégoûtant(e).

revolution [rɛvə'luːʃən] n révolution f; (of wheel etc) tour m, révolution f.

revolutionary [rɛvə'luːʃənrɪ] adj, n révolutionnaire (m/f).

revolutionize [rɛvə'luːʃənaɪz] vt révolutionner.

revolve [rɪ'vɔlv] vi tourner.

revolver [rɪ'vɔlvə*] n revolver m.

revolving [rɪ'vɔlvɪŋ] adj (chair) pivotant(e); (light) tournant(e).

revolving door n (porte f à) tambour m.

revue [rɪ'vjuː] n (THEAT) revue f.

revulsion [rɪ'vʌlʃən] n dégoût m, répugnance f.

reward [rɪ'wɔːd] n récompense f ♦ vt: **to** ~ **(for)** récompenser (de).

rewarding [rɪ'wɔːdɪŋ] adj (fig) qui (en) vaut la peine, gratifiant(e); **financially** ~ finan-cièrement intéressant(e).

rewind [riː'waɪnd] vt irreg (watch) remonter; (ribbon etc) réembobiner.

rewire [riː'waɪə*] vt (house) refaire l'installation électrique de.

reword [riː'wɔːd] vt formuler or exprimer différemment.

rewrite [riː'raɪt] vt irreg récrire.

Reykjavik ['reɪkjəviːk] n Reykjavik.

RFD abbr (US POST) = rural free delivery.

Rh abbr (= rhesus) Rh.

rhapsody ['ræpsədɪ] n (MUS) rhapsodie f; (fig) éloge délirant.

rhesus negative ['riːsəs-] adj (MED) de rhésus négatif.

rhesus positive ['riːsəs-] adj (MED) de rhésus positif.

rhetoric ['rɛtərɪk] n rhétorique f.

rhetorical [rɪ'tɔrɪkl] adj rhétorique.

rheumatic [ruː'mætɪk] adj rhumatismal(e).

rheumatism ['ruːmətɪzəm] n rhumatisme m.

rheumatoid arthritis ['ruːmətɔɪd-] n polyarthrite f chronique.

Rhine [raɪn] n: **the** ~ le Rhin.

rhinestone ['raɪnstəun] n faux diamant.

rhinoceros [raɪ'nɔsərəs] n rhinocéros m.

Rhodes [rəudz] n Rhodes f.

Rhodesia [rəu'diːʒə] n Rhodésie f.

Rhodesian [rəu'diːʒən] adj rhodésien(ne) ♦ n Rhodésien/ne.

rhododendron [rəudə'dɛndrn] n rhododendron m.

Rhône [rəun] n: **the** ~ le Rhône.

rhubarb ['ruːbɑːb] n rhubarbe f.

rhyme [raɪm] n rime f; (verse) vers mpl ♦ vi: **to** ~ **(with)** rimer (avec); **without** ~ **or reason** sans rime ni raison.

rhythm ['rɪðm] n rythme m.

rhythmic(al) ['rɪðmɪk(l)] adj rythmique.

rhythmically ['rɪðmɪklɪ] adv avec rythme.

rhythm method n méthode f des températures.

RI n abbr (BRIT) = religious instruction ♦ abbr (US) = Rhode Island.

rib [rɪb] n (ANAT) côte f ♦ vt (mock) taquiner.

ribald ['rɪbəld] adj paillard(e).

ribbed [rɪbd] adj (knitting) à côtes; (shell) strié(e).

ribbon ['rɪbən] n ruban m; **in** ~**s** (torn) en lambeaux.

rice [raɪs] n riz m.

ricefield ['raɪsfiːld] n rizière f.

rice pudding n riz m au lait.

rich [rɪtʃ] adj riche; (gift, clothes) somptueux(euse); **the** ~ npl les riches mpl; ~**es** npl richesses fpl; **to be** ~ **in sth** être riche en qch.

richly ['rɪtʃlɪ] adv richement; (deserved, earned) largement, grandement.

richness ['rɪtʃnɪs] n richesse f.

rickets ['rɪkɪts] n rachitisme m.

rickety ['rɪkɪtɪ] adj branlant(e).

rickshaw ['rɪkʃɔ:] n pousse(-pousse) m inv.

ricochet ['rɪkəʃeɪ] n ricochet m ♦ vi ricocher.

rid, pt, pp **rid** [rɪd] vt: **to ~ sb of** débarrasser qn de; **to get ~ of** se débarrasser de.

riddance ['rɪdns] n: **good ~!** bon débarras!

ridden ['rɪdn] pp of **ride**.

riddle ['rɪdl] n (puzzle) énigme f ♦ vt: **to be ~d with** être criblé(e) de.

ride [raɪd] n promenade f, tour m; (distance covered) trajet m ♦ vb (pt **rode**, pp **ridden** [rəud, 'rɪdn]) vi (as sport) monter (à cheval), faire du cheval; (go somewhere: on horse, bicycle) aller (à cheval or bicyclette etc); (journey: on bicycle, motor cycle, bus) rouler ♦ vt (a certain horse) monter; (distance) parcourir, faire; **we rode all day/all the way** nous sommes restés toute la journée en selle/ avons fait tout le chemin en selle or à cheval; **to ~ a horse/bicycle/camel** monter à cheval/à bicyclette/à dos de chameau; **can you ~ a bike?** est-ce que tu sais monter à bicyclette?; **to ~ at anchor** (NAUT) être à l'ancre; **horse/car ~** promenade or tour à cheval/en voiture; **to go for a ~** faire une promenade (en voiture or à bicyclette etc); **to take sb for a ~** (fig) faire marcher qn; rouler qn.

▶**ride out** vt: **to ~ out the storm** (fig) surmonter les difficultés.

rider ['raɪdə*] n cavalier/ière; (in race) jockey m; (on bicycle) cycliste m/f; (on motorcycle) motocycliste m/f; (in document) annexe f, clause additionnelle.

ridge [rɪdʒ] n (of hill) faîte m; (of roof, mountain) arête f; (on object) strie f.

ridicule ['rɪdɪkju:l] n ridicule m; dérision f ♦ vt ridiculiser, tourner en dérision; **to hold sb/ sth up to ~** tourner qn/qch en ridicule.

ridiculous [rɪ'dɪkjuləs] adj ridicule.

riding ['raɪdɪŋ] n équitation f.

riding school n manège m, école f d'équitation.

rife [raɪf] adj répandu(e); **~ with** abondant(e) en.

riffraff ['rɪfræf] n racaille f.

rifle ['raɪfl] n fusil m (à canon rayé) ♦ vt vider, dévaliser.

▶**rifle through** vt fus fouiller dans.

rifle range n champ m de tir; (indoor) stand m de tir.

rift [rɪft] n fente f, fissure f; (fig: disagreement) désaccord m.

rig [rɪg] n (also: **oil ~**: on land) derrick m; (: at sea) plate-forme pétrolière ♦ vt (election etc) truquer.

▶**rig out** vt (BRIT) habiller; (: pej) fringuer, attifer.

▶**rig up** vt arranger, faire avec des moyens de fortune.

rigging ['rɪgɪŋ] n (NAUT) gréement m.

right [raɪt] adj (true) juste, exact(e); (correctly chosen: answer, road etc) bon(bonne); (suitable) approprié(e), convenable; (just) juste, équitable; (morally good) bien inv; (not left) droit(e) ♦ n (title, claim) droit m; (not left) droite f ♦ adv (answer) correctement; (not on the left) à droite ♦ vt redresser ♦ excl bon!; **the ~ time** (precise) l'heure exacte; (not wrong) la bonne heure; **to be ~** (person) avoir raison; (answer) être juste or correct(e); **to get sth ~** ne pas se tromper sur qch; **let's get it ~ this time!** essayons de ne pas nous tromper cette fois-ci!; **you did the ~ thing** vous avez bien fait; **to put a mistake ~** (BRIT) rectifier une erreur; **~ now** en ce moment même; tout de suite; **~ before/after** juste avant/après; **~ against the wall** tout contre le mur; **~ ahead** tout droit; droit devant; **~ in the middle** en plein milieu; **~ away** immédiatement; **to go ~ to the end of sth** aller jusqu'au bout de qch; **by ~s** en toute justice; **on the ~** à droite; **~ and wrong** le bien et le mal; **to be in the ~** avoir raison; **film ~s** droits d'adaptation cinématographique; **~ of way** droit m de passage; (AUT) priorité f.

right angle n angle droit.

righteous ['raɪtʃəs] adj droit(e), vertueux(euse); (anger) justifié(e).

righteousness ['raɪtʃəsnɪs] n droiture f, vertu f.

rightful ['raɪtful] adj (heir) légitime.

rightfully ['raɪtfəlɪ] adv à juste titre, légitimement.

right-handed [raɪt'hændɪd] adj (person) droitier(ière).

right-hand man ['raɪthænd-] n bras droit (fig).

right-hand side ['raɪthænd-] n côté droit.

rightly ['raɪtlɪ] adv bien, correctement; (with reason) à juste titre; **if I remember ~** (BRIT) si je me souviens bien.

right-minded ['raɪt'maɪndɪd] adj sensé(e), sain(e) d'esprit.

rights issue n (STOCK EXCHANGE) émission préférentielle or de droit de souscription.

right wing n (MIL, SPORT) aile droite; (POL) droite f ♦ adj: **right-wing** (POL) de droite.

right-winger [raɪt'wɪŋə*] n (POL) membre m de la droite; (SPORT) ailier droit.

rigid ['rɪdʒɪd] adj rigide; (principle) strict(e).

rigidity [rɪ'dʒɪdɪtɪ] n rigidité f.

rigidly ['rɪdʒɪdlɪ] adv rigidement; (behave) inflexiblement.

rigmarole ['rɪgmərəul] n galimatias m, comédie f.

rigor ['rɪgə*] n (US) = **rigour**.

rigor mortis ['rɪgə'mɔ:tɪs] n rigidité f cadavérique.

rigorous ['rɪgərəs] adj rigoureux(euse).

rigorously ['rɪgərəslɪ] adv rigoureusement.

rigour, (US) **rigor** ['rɪgə*] n rigueur f.

rig-out ['rɪgaut] n (BRIT col) tenue f.

rile [raɪl] vt agacer.

rim [rɪm] *n* bord *m*; (*of spectacles*) monture *f*; (*of wheel*) jante *f*.

rimless ['rɪmlɪs] *adj* (*spectacles*) à monture invisible.

rind [raɪnd] *n* (*of bacon*) couenne *f*; (*of lemon etc*) écorce *f*.

ring [rɪŋ] *n* anneau *m*; (*on finger*) bague *f*; (*also*: **wedding ~**) alliance *f*; (*for napkin*) rond *m*; (*of people, objects*) cercle *m*; (*of spies*) réseau *m*; (*of smoke etc*) rond; (*arena*) piste *f*, arène *f*; (*for boxing*) ring *m*; (*sound of bell*) sonnerie *f*; (*telephone call*) coup *m* de téléphone ♦ *vb* (*pt* **rang**, *pp* **rung** [ræŋ, rʌŋ]) *vi* (*person, bell*) sonner; (*also*: **~ out**: *voice, words*) retentir; (*TEL*) téléphoner ♦ *vt* (*BRIT TEL*: *also*: **~ up**) téléphoner à; **to ~ the bell** sonner; **to give sb a ~** (*TEL*) passer un coup de téléphone *or* de fil à qn; **that has the ~ of truth about it** cela sonne vrai; **the name doesn't ~ a bell (with me)** ce nom ne me dit rien.

▶**ring back** *vt, vi* (*BRIT TEL*) rappeler.

▶**ring off** *vi* (*BRIT TEL*) raccrocher.

ring binder *n* classeur *m* à anneaux.

ring finger *n* annulaire *m*.

ringing ['rɪŋɪŋ] *n* (*of bell*) tintement *m*; (*louder, also of telephone*) sonnerie *f*; (*in ears*) bourdonnement *m*.

ringing tone *n* (*BRIT TEL*) sonnerie *f*.

ringleader ['rɪŋliːdə*] *n* (*of gang*) chef *m*, meneur *m*.

ringlets ['rɪŋlɪts] *npl* anglaises *fpl*.

ring road *n* (*BRIT*) route *f* de ceinture.

rink [rɪŋk] *n* (*also*: **ice ~**) patinoire *f*; (*for roller-skating*) skating *m*.

rinse [rɪns] *n* rinçage *m* ♦ *vt* rincer.

Rio (de Janeiro) ['riːəu(dədʒə'nɪərəu)] *n* Rio de Janeiro.

riot ['raɪət] *n* émeute *f*, bagarres *fpl* ♦ *vi* manifester avec violence; **a ~ of colours** une débauche *or* orgie de couleurs; **to run ~** se déchaîner.

rioter ['raɪətə*] *n* émeutier/ière, manifestant/e.

riot gear *n*: **in ~** casqué et portant un bouclier.

riotous ['raɪətəs] *adj* tapageur(euse); tordant(e).

riotously ['raɪətəslɪ] *adv*: **~ funny** tordant(e).

riot police *n* forces *fpl* de police intervenant en cas d'émeute; **hundreds of ~** des centaines de policiers casqués et armés.

RIP *abbr* (= *rest in peace*) RIP.

rip [rɪp] *n* déchirure *f* ♦ *vt* déchirer ♦ *vi* se déchirer.

▶**rip up** *vt* déchirer.

ripcord ['rɪpkɔːd] *n* poignée *f* d'ouverture.

ripe [raɪp] *adj* (*fruit*) mûr(e); (*cheese*) fait(e).

ripen ['raɪpn] *vt* mûrir ♦ *vi* mûrir; se faire.

ripeness ['raɪpnɪs] *n* maturité *f*.

rip-off ['rɪpɔf] *n* (*col*): **it's a ~!** c'est du vol manifeste!

riposte [rɪ'pɔst] *n* riposte *f*.

ripple ['rɪpl] *n* ride *f*, ondulation *f*; égrènement *m*, cascade *f* ♦ *vi* se rider, onduler ♦ *vt* rider, faire onduler.

rise [raɪz] *n* (*slope*) côte *f*, pente *f*; (*hill*) élévation *f*; (*increase: in wages*: *BRIT*) augmentation *f*; (: *in prices, temperature*) hausse *f*, augmentation; (*fig*) ascension *f* ♦ *vi* (*pt* **rose**, *pp* **risen** [rəuz, rɪzn]) s'élever, monter; (*prices*) augmenter, monter; (*waters, river*) monter; (*sun, wind, person: from chair, bed*) se lever; (*also*: **~ up**: *rebel*) se révolter; se rebeller; **~ to power** montée *f* au pouvoir; **to give ~ to** donner lieu à; **to ~ to the occasion** se montrer à la hauteur.

rising ['raɪzɪŋ] *adj* (*increasing: number, prices*) en hausse; (*tide*) montant(e); (*sun, moon*) levant(e) ♦ *n* (*uprising*) soulèvement *m*, insurrection *f*.

rising damp *n* humidité *f* (montant des fondations).

rising star *n* (*also fig*) étoile montante.

risk [rɪsk] *n* risque *m*, danger *m*; (*deliberate*) risque ♦ *vt* risquer; **to take** *or* **run the ~ of doing** courir le risque de faire; **at ~** en danger; **at one's own ~** à ses risques et périls; **it's a fire/health ~** cela présente un risque d'incendie/pour la santé; **I'll ~ it** je vais risquer le coup.

risk capital *n* capital-risques *m*.

risky ['rɪskɪ] *adj* risqué(e).

risqué ['riːskeɪ] *adj* (*joke*) risqué(e).

rissole ['rɪsəul] *n* croquette *f*.

rite [raɪt] *n* rite *m*; **the last ~s** les derniers sacrements.

ritual ['rɪtjuəl] *adj* rituel(le) ♦ *n* rituel *m*.

rival ['raɪvl] *n* rival/e; (*in business*) concurrent/e ♦ *adj* rival(e); qui fait concurrence ♦ *vt* être en concurrence avec; **to ~ sb/sth in** rivaliser avec qn/qch de.

rivalry ['raɪvlrɪ] *n* rivalité *f*; concurrence *f*.

river ['rɪvə*] *n* rivière *f*; (*major, also fig*) fleuve *m* ♦ *cpd* (*port, traffic*) fluvial(e); **up/down ~** en amont/aval.

riverbank ['rɪvəbæŋk] *n* rive *f*, berge *f*.

riverbed ['rɪvəbed] *n* lit *m* (de rivière *or* de fleuve).

riverside ['rɪvəsaɪd] *n* bord *m* de la rivière *or* du fleuve.

rivet ['rɪvɪt] *n* rivet *m* ♦ *vt* riveter; (*fig*) river, fixer.

riveting ['rɪvɪtɪŋ] *adj* (*fig*) fascinant(e).

Riviera [rɪvɪ'ɛərə] *n*: **the (French) ~** la Côte d'Azur; **the Italian ~** la Riviera (italienne).

Riyadh [rɪ'jɑːd] *n* Riyad.

RMT *n abbr* (= *Rail, Maritime and Transport*) syndicat des transports.

RN *n abbr* (*BRIT*) = **Royal Navy**; (*US*) = **registered nurse**.

RNA *n abbr* (= *ribonucleic acid*) ARN *m*.

RNLI *n abbr* (*BRIT*: = *Royal National Lifeboat Institution*) ≈ SNSM *f*.

RNZAF *n abbr* = *Royal New Zealand Air Force*.

RNZN n abbr = Royal New Zealand Navy.
road [rəud] n route f; (in town) rue f; (fig) chemin, voie f; **main** ~ grande route; **major** ~ route principale or à priorité; **minor** ~ voie secondaire; **it takes four hours by** ~ il y a quatre heures de route; **"~ up"** (BRIT) "attention travaux".
roadblock ['rəudblɔk] n barrage routier.
road haulage n transports routiers.
roadhog ['rəudhɔg] n chauffard m.
road map n carte routière.
road safety n sécurité routière.
roadside ['rəudsaɪd] n bord m de la route, bas-côté m ♦ cpd (situé(e) etc) au bord de la route; **by the** ~ au bord de la route.
roadsign ['rəudsaɪn] n panneau m de signalisation.
roadsweeper ['rəudswiːpə*] n (BRIT: person) balayeur/euse.
road user n usager m de la route.
roadway ['rəudweɪ] n chaussée f.
roadworks ['rəudwɔːks] npl travaux mpl (de réfection des routes).
roadworthy ['rəudwɔːðɪ] adj en bon état de marche.
roam [rəum] vi errer, vagabonder ♦ vt parcourir, errer par.
roar [rɔː*] n rugissement m; (of crowd) hurlements mpl; (of vehicle, thunder, storm) grondement m ♦ vi rugir; hurler; gronder; **to** ~ **with laughter** rire à gorge déployée.
roaring ['rɔːrɪŋ] adj: **a** ~ **fire** une belle flambée; **a** ~ **success** un succès fou; **to do a** ~ **trade** faire des affaires d'or.
roast [rəust] n rôti m ♦ vt (meat) (faire) rôtir.
roast beef n rôti m de bœuf, rosbif m.
roasting ['rəustɪŋ] n (col): **to give sb a** ~ sonner les cloches à qn.
rob [rɔb] vt (person) voler; (bank) dévaliser; **to** ~ **sb of sth** voler or dérober qch à qn; (fig: deprive) priver qn de qch.
robber ['rɔbə*] n bandit m, voleur m.
robbery ['rɔbərɪ] n vol m.
robe [rəub] n (for ceremony etc) robe f; (also: **bath**~) peignoir m ♦ vt revêtir (d'une robe).
robin ['rɔbɪn] n rouge-gorge m.
robot ['rəubɔt] n robot m.
robotics [rə'bɔtɪks] n robotique m.
robust [rəu'bʌst] adj robuste; (material, appetite) solide.
rock [rɔk] n (substance) roche f, roc m; (boulder) rocher m; roche; (BRIT: sweet) ≈ sucre m d'orge ♦ vt (swing gently: cradle) balancer; (: child) bercer; (shake) ébranler, secouer ♦ vi (se) balancer; être ébranlé(e) or secoué(e); **on the** ~**s** (drink) avec des glaçons; (ship) sur les écueils; (marriage etc) en train de craquer; **to** ~ **the boat** (fig) jouer les trouble-fête.
rock and roll n rock (and roll) m, rock'n'roll m.
rock bottom ['rɔk'bɔtəm] n (fig) niveau le

plus bas ♦ adj: **rock-bottom** (fig: prices) sacrifié(e); **to reach** or **touch rock bottom** (price, person) tomber au plus bas.
rock climber n varappeur/euse.
rock climbing n varappe f.
rockery ['rɔkərɪ] n (jardin m de) rocaille f.
rocket ['rɔkɪt] n fusée f; (MIL) fusée, roquette f ♦ vi (prices) monter en flèche.
rocket launcher [-lɔːnʃə*] n lance-roquettes m inv.
rock face n paroi rocheuse.
rock fall n chute f de pierres.
rocking chair ['rɔkɪŋ-] n fauteuil m à bascule.
rocking horse ['rɔkɪŋ-] n cheval m à bascule.
rocky ['rɔkɪ] adj (hill) rocheux(euse); (path) rocailleux(euse); (unsteady: table) branlant(e).
Rocky Mountains npl: **the** ~ les (montagnes fpl) Rocheuses fpl.
rod [rɔd] n (metallic) tringle f; (TECH) tige f; (wooden) baguette f; (also: **fishing** ~) canne f à pêche.
rode [rəud] pt of ride.
rodent ['rəudnt] n rongeur m.
rodeo ['rəudɪəu] n rodéo m.
roe [rəu] n (species: also: ~ **deer**) chevreuil m; (of fish: also: **hard** ~) œufs mpl de poisson; **soft** ~ laitance f.
roe deer n chevreuil m; chevreuil femelle.
rogue [rəug] n coquin/e.
roguish ['rəugɪʃ] adj coquin(e).
role [rəul] n rôle m.
role model n modèle m à émuler.
role play, role playing n jeu m de rôle.
roll [rəul] n rouleau m; (of banknotes) liasse f; (also: **bread** ~) petit pain; (register) liste f; (sound: of drums etc) roulement m; (movement: of ship) roulis m ♦ vt rouler; (also: ~ **up:** string) enrouler; (also: ~ **out:** pastry) étendre au rouleau ♦ vi rouler; (wheel) tourner; **cheese** ~ ≈ sandwich m au fromage (dans un petit pain).
▶**roll about, roll around** vi rouler çà et là; (person) se rouler par terre.
▶**roll by** vi (time) s'écouler, passer.
▶**roll in** vi (mail, cash) affluer.
▶**roll over** vi se retourner.
▶**roll up** vi (col: arrive) arriver, s'amener ♦ vt (carpet, cloth, map) rouler; (sleeves) retrousser; **to** ~ **o.s. up into a ball** se rouler en boule.
roll call n appel m.
rolled-gold ['rəuldgəuld] adj plaqué or inv.
roller ['rəulə*] n rouleau m; (wheel) roulette f.
roller blind n (BRIT) store m.
roller coaster n montagnes fpl russes.
roller skates npl patins mpl à roulettes.
rollicking ['rɔlɪkɪŋ] adj bruyant(e) et joyeux(euse); (play) bouffon(ne); **to have a** ~ **time** s'amuser follement.
rolling ['rəulɪŋ] adj (landscape) onduleux(euse).
rolling mill n laminoir m.

rolling pin n rouleau m à pâtisserie.

rolling stock n (RAIL) matériel roulant.

roll-on-roll-off ['rəʊlɒn'rəʊlɒf] adj (BRIT: ferry) transroulier(ière).

roly-poly ['rəʊlɪ'pəʊlɪ] n (BRIT CULIN) roulé m à la confiture.

ROM [rɒm] n abbr (COMPUT: = read-only memory) mémoire morte, ROM f.

Roman ['rəʊmən] adj romain(e) ♦ n Romain/e.

Roman Catholic adj, n catholique (m/f).

romance [rə'mæns] n histoire f (or film m or aventure f) romanesque; (charm) poésie f; (love affair) idylle f.

Romanesque [rəʊmə'nɛsk] adj roman(e).

Romania [rəʊ'meɪnɪə] n Roumanie f.

Romanian [rəʊ'meɪnɪən] adj roumain(e) ♦ n Roumain/e; (LING) roumain m.

Roman numeral n chiffre romain.

romantic [rə'mæntɪk] adj romantique; (play, attachment) sentimental(e).

romanticism [rə'mæntɪsɪzəm] n romantisme m.

Romany ['rɒmənɪ] adj de bohémien ♦ n bohémien/ne; (LING) romani m.

Rome [rəʊm] n Rome f.

romp [rɒmp] n jeux bruyants ♦ vi (also: ~ about) s'ébattre, jouer bruyamment; to ~ home (horse) arriver bon premier.

rompers ['rɒmpəz] npl barboteuse f.

rondo ['rɒndəʊ] n (MUS) rondeau m.

roof [ruːf] n toit m; (of tunnel, cave) plafond m ♦ vt couvrir (d'un toit); the ~ of the mouth la voûte du palais.

roof garden n toit-terrasse m.

roofing ['ruːfɪŋ] n toiture f.

roof rack n (AUT) galerie f.

rook [rʊk] n (bird) freux m; (CHESS) tour f ♦ vt (col: cheat) rouler, escroquer.

rookie ['rʊkɪ] n (col: esp MIL) bleu m.

room [ruːm] n (in house) pièce f; (also: bed~) chambre f (à coucher); (in school etc) salle f; (space) place f; ~s npl (lodging) meublé m; "~s to let", (US) "~s for rent" "chambres à louer"; is there ~ for this? est-ce qu'il y a de la place pour ceci?; to make ~ for sb faire de la place à qn; there is ~ for improvement on peut faire mieux.

rooming house ['ruːmɪŋ-] n (US) maison f de rapport.

roommate ['ruːmmeɪt] n camarade m/f de chambre.

room service n service m des chambres (dans un hôtel).

room temperature n température ambiante; **"serve at ~"** (wine) "servir chambré".

roomy ['ruːmɪ] adj spacieux(euse); (garment) ample.

roost [ruːst] n juchoir m ♦ vi se jucher.

rooster ['ruːstə*] n coq m.

root [ruːt] n (BOT, MATH) racine f; (fig: of problem) origine f, fond m ♦ vi (plant) s'enraciner; **to take ~** (plant, idea) prendre racine.

▶**root about** vi (fig) fouiller.

▶**root for** vt fus (col) applaudir.

▶**root out** vt extirper.

root beer n (US) sorte de limonade à base d'extraits végétaux.

rope [rəʊp] n corde f; (NAUT) cordage m ♦ vt (box) corder; (climbers) encorder; **to ~ sb in** (fig) embringuer qn; **to know the ~s** (fig) être au courant, connaître les ficelles.

rope ladder n échelle f de corde.

ropey ['rəʊpɪ] adj (col) pas fameux(euse) or brillant(e); **I feel a bit ~ today** c'est pas la forme aujourd'hui.

rosary ['rəʊzərɪ] n chapelet m.

rose [rəʊz] pt of rise ♦ n rose f; (also: ~bush) rosier m; (on watering can) pomme f ♦ adj rose.

rosé ['rəʊzeɪ] n rosé m.

rosebed ['rəʊzbɛd] n massif m de rosiers.

rosebud ['rəʊzbʌd] n bouton m de rose.

rosebush ['rəʊzbʊʃ] n rosier m.

rosemary ['rəʊzmərɪ] n romarin m.

rosette [rəʊ'zɛt] n rosette f; (larger) cocarde f.

ROSPA ['rɒspə] n abbr (BRIT) = Royal Society for the Prevention of Accidents.

roster ['rɒstə*] n: **duty ~** tableau m de service.

rostrum ['rɒstrəm] n tribune f (pour un orateur etc).

rosy ['rəʊzɪ] adj rose; **a ~ future** un bel avenir.

rot [rɒt] n (decay) pourriture f; (fig: pej) idioties fpl, balivernes fpl ♦ vt, vi pourrir; **to stop the ~** (BRIT fig) rétablir la situation; **dry ~** pourriture sèche (du bois); **wet ~** pourriture (du bois).

rota ['rəʊtə] n liste f, tableau m de service; **on a ~ basis** par roulement.

rotary ['rəʊtərɪ] adj rotatif(ive).

rotate [rəʊ'teɪt] vt (revolve) faire tourner; (change round: crops) alterner; (: jobs) faire à tour de rôle ♦ vi (revolve) tourner.

rotating [rəʊ'teɪtɪŋ] adj (movement) tournant(e).

rotation [rəʊ'teɪʃən] n rotation f; **in ~** à tour de rôle.

rote [rəʊt] n: **by ~** machinalement, par cœur.

rotor ['rəʊtə*] n rotor m.

rotten ['rɒtn] adj (decayed) pourri(e); (dishonest) corrompu(e); (col: bad) mauvais(e), moche; **to feel ~** (ill) être mal fichu(e).

rotting ['rɒtɪŋ] adj pourrissant(e).

rotund [rəʊ'tʌnd] adj rondelet(te); arrondi(e).

rouble, (US) **ruble** ['ruːbl] n rouble m.

rouge [ruːʒ] n rouge m (à joues).

rough [rʌf] adj (cloth, skin) rêche, rugueux(euse); (terrain) accidenté(e); (path) rocailleux(euse); (voice) rauque, rude; (person, manner: coarse) rude, fruste; (: violent) brutal(e); (district, weather) mauvais(e); (plan) ébauché(e); (guess) approximatif(ive) ♦ n (GOLF) rough m ♦ vt: **to ~ it** vivre à la dure; **the sea is ~ today** la mer est agitée aujourd'hui; **to have a ~ time (of it)** en voir de dures; **~ estimate** approximation f; **to play ~** jouer avec brutalité; **to sleep ~** (*BRIT*) coucher à la dure; **to feel ~** (*BRIT*) être mal fichu(e).

▶**rough out** *vt* (*draft*) ébaucher.

roughage ['rʌfɪdʒ] *n* fibres *fpl* diététiques.

rough-and-ready ['rʌfən'rɛdɪ] *adj* (*accommodation, method*) rudimentaire.

rough-and-tumble ['rʌfən'tʌmbl] *n* agitation *f*.

roughcast ['rʌfkɑːst] *n* crépi *m*.

rough copy, rough draft *n* brouillon *m*.

roughen ['rʌfn] *vt* (*a surface*) rendre rude *or* rugueux(euse).

rough justice *n* justice *f* sommaire.

roughly ['rʌflɪ] *adv* (*handle*) rudement, brutalement; (*make*) grossièrement; (*approximately*) à peu près, en gros; **~ speaking** en gros.

roughness ['rʌfnɪs] *n* (*of cloth, skin*) rugosité *f*; (*of person*) rudesse *f*; brutalité *f*.

roughshod ['rʌfʃɔd] *adv*: **to ride ~ over** ne tenir aucun compte de.

rough work *n* (*at school etc*) brouillon *m*.

roulette [ruː'lɛt] *n* roulette *f*.

Roumania *etc* [ruː'meɪnɪə] = **Romania** *etc*.

round [raund] *adj* rond(e) ♦ *n* rond *m*, cercle *m*; (*BRIT: of toast*) tranche *f*; (*duty: of policeman, milkman etc*) tournée *f*; (*: of doctor*) visites *fpl*; (*game: of cards, in competition*) partie *f*; (*BOXING*) round *m*; (*of talks*) série *f* ♦ *vt* (*corner*) tourner; (*bend*) prendre; (*cape*) doubler ♦ *prep* autour de ♦ *adv*: **right ~, all ~** tout autour; **the long way ~** (par) le chemin le plus long; **all the year ~** toute l'année; **in ~ figures** en chiffres ronds; **it's just ~ the corner** c'est juste après le coin; (*fig*) c'est tout près; **to ask sb ~** inviter qn (chez soi); **I'll be ~ at 6 o'clock** je serai là à 6 heures; **to go ~** faire le tour *or* un détour; **to go ~ to sb's (house)** aller chez qn; **to go ~ an obstacle** contourner un obstacle; **go ~ the back** passez par derrière; **to go ~ a house** visiter une maison, faire le tour d'une maison; **enough to go ~** assez pour tout le monde; **she arrived ~ (about) noon** (*BRIT*) elle est arrivée vers midi; **~ the clock** 24 heures sur 24; **to go the ~s** (*disease, story*) circuler; **the daily ~** (*fig*) la routine quotidienne; **~ of ammunition** cartouche *f*; **~ of applause** ban *m*, applaudissements *mpl*; **~ of drinks** tournée *f*; **~ of sandwiches** (*BRIT*) sandwich de pain de mie.

▶**round off** *vt* (*speech etc*) terminer.

▶**round up** *vt* rassembler; (*criminals*) effectuer une rafle de; (*prices*) arrondir (au chiffre supérieur).

roundabout ['raundəbaut] *n* (*BRIT AUT*) rond-point *m* (à sens giratoire); (*at fair*) manège *m* (de chevaux de bois) ♦ *adj* (*route, means*) dé-

tourné(e).

rounded ['raundɪd] *adj* arrondi(e); (*style*) harmonieux(euse).

rounders ['raundəz] *npl* (*game*) ≈ balle *f* au camp.

roundly ['raundlɪ] *adv* (*fig*) tout net, carrément.

round-robin ['raundrɔbɪn] *n* (*SPORT: also:* ~ **tournament**) tournoi où tous les joueurs se rencontrent.

round-shouldered ['raund'ʃəuldəd] *adj* au dos rond.

round trip *n* (voyage *m*) aller et retour *m*.

roundup ['raundʌp] *n* rassemblement *m*; (*of criminals*) rafle *f*; **a ~ of the latest news** un rappel des derniers événements.

rouse [rauz] *vt* (*wake up*) réveiller; (*stir up*) susciter; provoquer; éveiller.

rousing ['rauzɪŋ] *adj* (*welcome*) enthousiaste.

rout [raut] *n* (*MIL*) déroute *f* ♦ *vt* mettre en déroute.

route [ruːt] *n* itinéraire *m*; (*of bus*) parcours *m*; (*of trade, shipping*) route *f*; **"all ~s"** (*AUT*) "toutes directions"; **the best ~ to London** le meilleur itinéraire pour aller à Londres; **en ~ for** en route pour.

route map *n* (*BRIT: for journey*) croquis *m* d'itinéraire; (*for trains etc*) carte *f* du réseau.

routine [ruː'tiːn] *adj* (*work*) ordinaire, courant(e); (*procedure*) d'usage ♦ *n* routine *f*; (*THEAT*) numéro *m*; **daily ~** occupations journalières.

roving ['rəuvɪŋ] *adj* (*life*) vagabond(e).

roving reporter *n* reporter volant.

row[1] [rəu] *n* (*line*) rangée *f*; (*of people, seats, KNITTING*) rang *m*; (*behind one another: of cars, people*) file *f* ♦ *vi* (*in boat*) ramer; (*as sport*) faire de l'aviron ♦ *vt* (*boat*) faire aller à la rame *or* à l'aviron; **in a ~** (*fig*) d'affilée.

row[2] [rau] *n* (*noise*) vacarme *m*; (*dispute*) dispute *f*, querelle *f*; (*scolding*) réprimande *f*, savon *m* ♦ *vi* (*also:* **to have a ~**) se disputer, se quereller.

rowboat ['rəubəut] *n* (*US*) canot *m* (à rames).

rowdiness ['raudɪnɪs] *n* tapage *m*, chahut *m*; (*fighting*) bagarre *f*.

rowdy ['raudɪ] *adj* chahuteur(euse); bagarreur(euse) ♦ *n* voyou *m*.

rowdyism ['raudɪɪzəm] *n* tendances *fpl* à la violence; actes *mpl* de violence.

rowing ['rəuɪŋ] *n* canotage *m*; (*as sport*) aviron *m*.

rowing boat *n* (*BRIT*) canot *m* (à rames).

rowlock ['rɔlək] *n* (*BRIT*) dame *f* de nage, tolet *m*.

royal ['rɔɪəl] *adj* royal(e).

La **Royal Academy** *ou* **Royal Academy of Arts**, *fondée en 1768 par George III pour encourager la peinture, la sculpture et l'architecture, est située à Burlington House, sur Piccadilly. Une exposition des œuvres d'artistes contempo-*

rains a lieu tous les étés. L'Académie dispense également des cours en peinture, sculpture et architecture.

Royal Air Force (RAF) *n* (*BRIT*) *armée de l'air britannique.*

royal blue *adj* bleu roi *inv*.

royalist ['rɔɪəlɪst] *adj*, *n* royaliste (*m/f*).

Royal Navy (RN) *n* (*BRIT*) *marine de guerre britannique.*

royalty ['rɔɪəltɪ] *n* (*royal persons*) (membres *mpl* de la) famille royale; (*payment: to author*) droits *mpl* d'auteur; (*: to inventor*) royalties *fpl*.

RP *n abbr* (*BRIT*: = *received pronunciation*) prononciation *f* standard.

rpm *abbr* (= *revolutions per minute*) t/mn (= *tours/minute*).

RR *abbr* (*US*) = **railroad**.

RSA *n abbr* (*BRIT*) = *Royal Society of Arts, Royal Scottish Academy*.

RSI *n abbr* (*MED*: = *repetitive strain injury*) microtraumatisme permanent.

RSPB *n abbr* (*BRIT*: = *Royal Society for the Protection of Birds*) ≈ LPO *f*.

RSPCA *n abbr* (*BRIT*: = *Royal Society for the Prevention of Cruelty to Animals*) ≈ SPA *f*.

RSVP *abbr* (= *répondez s'il vous plaît*) RSVP.

RTA *n abbr* (= *road traffic accident*) accident *m* de la route.

Rt Hon. *abbr* (*BRIT*: = *Right Honourable*) titre donné aux députés de la Chambre des communes.

Rt Rev. *abbr* (= *Right Reverend*) très révérend.

rub [rʌb] *n* (*with cloth*) coup *m* de chiffon *or* de torchon; (*on person*) friction *f* ♦ *vt* frotter; frictionner; **to ~ sb up** *or* (*US*) **~ sb the wrong way** prendre qn à rebrousse-poil.

▶**rub down** *vt* (*body*) frictionner; (*horse*) bouchonner.

▶**rub in** *vt* (*ointment*) faire pénétrer.

▶**rub off** *vi* partir; **to ~ off on** déteindre sur.

▶**rub out** *vt* effacer ♦ *vi* s'effacer.

rubber ['rʌbə*] *n* caoutchouc *m*; (*BRIT*: *eraser*) gomme *f* (à effacer).

rubber band *n* élastique *m*.

rubber bullet *n* balle *f* en caoutchouc.

rubber plant *n* caoutchouc *m* (*plante verte*).

rubber ring *n* (*for swimming*) bouée *f* (de natation).

rubber stamp *n* tampon *m*.

rubber-stamp [rʌbə'stæmp] *vt* (*fig*) approuver sans discussion.

rubbery ['rʌbərɪ] *adj* caoutchouteux(euse).

rubbish ['rʌbɪʃ] *n* (*from household*) ordures *fpl*; (*fig: pej*) choses *fpl* sans valeur; camelote *f*; (*nonsense*) bêtises *fpl*, idioties *fpl* ♦ *vt* (*BRIT col*) dénigrer, rabaisser; **what you've just said is ~** tu viens de dire une bêtise.

rubbish bin *n* (*BRIT*) boîte *f* à ordures, poubelle *f*.

rubbish dump *n* (*in town*) décharge publi-

que, dépotoir *m*.

rubbishy ['rʌbɪʃɪ] *adj* (*BRIT col*) qui ne vaut rien, moche.

rubble ['rʌbl] *n* décombres *mpl*; (*smaller*) gravats *mpl*.

ruble ['ruːbl] *n* (*US*) = **rouble**.

ruby ['ruːbɪ] *n* rubis *m*.

RUC *n abbr* (*BRIT*) = *Royal Ulster Constabulary*.

rucksack ['rʌksæk] *n* sac *m* à dos.

ructions ['rʌkʃənz] *npl* grabuge *m*.

rudder ['rʌdə*] *n* gouvernail *m*.

ruddy ['rʌdɪ] *adj* (*face*) coloré(e); (*col: damned*) sacré(e), fichu(e).

rude [ruːd] *adj* (*impolite: person*) impoli(e); (*: word, manners*) grossier(ière); (*shocking*) indécent(e), inconvenant(e); **to be ~ to sb** être grossier envers qn.

rudely ['ruːdlɪ] *adv* impoliment; grossièrement.

rudeness ['ruːdnɪs] *n* impolitesse *f*; grossièreté *f*.

rudiment ['ruːdɪmənt] *n* rudiment *m*.

rudimentary [ruːdɪ'mɛntərɪ] *adj* rudimentaire.

rue [ruː] *vt* se repentir de, regretter amèrement.

rueful ['ruːful] *adj* triste.

ruff [rʌf] *n* fraise *f*, collerette *f*.

ruffian ['rʌfɪən] *n* brute *f*, voyou *m*.

ruffle ['rʌfl] *vt* (*hair*) ébouriffer; (*clothes*) chiffonner; (*water*) agiter; (*fig: person*) émouvoir, faire perdre son flegme à.

rug [rʌg] *n* petit tapis; (*BRIT*: *for knees*) couverture *f*.

rugby ['rʌgbɪ] *n* (*also*: ~ *football*) rugby *m*.

rugged ['rʌgɪd] *adj* (*landscape*) accidenté(e); (*features, kindness, character*) rude; (*determination*) farouche.

rugger ['rʌgə*] *n* (*BRIT col*) rugby *m*.

ruin ['ruːɪn] *n* ruine *f* ♦ *vt* ruiner; (*spoil: clothes*) abîmer; **~s** *npl* ruine(s); **in ~s** en ruine.

ruination [ruːɪ'neɪʃən] *n* ruine *f*.

ruinous ['ruːɪnəs] *adj* ruineux(euse).

rule [ruːl] *n* règle *f*; (*regulation*) règlement *m*; (*government*) autorité *f*, gouvernement *m*; (*dominion etc*): **under British ~** sous l'autorité britannique ♦ *vt* (*country*) gouverner; (*person*) dominer; (*decide*) décider ♦ *vi* commander; décider; (*LAW*): **to ~ against/in favour of/on** statuer contre/en faveur de/ sur; **to ~ that** (*umpire, judge etc*) décider que; **it's against the ~s** c'est contraire au règlement; **by ~ of thumb** à vue de nez; **as a ~ normalement**, en règle générale.

▶**rule out** *vt* exclure; **murder cannot be ~d out** l'hypothèse d'un meurtre ne peut être exclue.

ruled [ruːld] *adj* (*paper*) réglé(e).

ruler ['ruːlə*] *n* (*sovereign*) souverain/e; (*leader*) chef *m* (d'État); (*for measuring*) règle *f*.

ruling ['ruːlɪŋ] *adj* (*party*) au pouvoir; (*class*) dirigeant(e) ♦ *n* (*LAW*) décision *f*.

rum [rʌm] *n* rhum *m* ♦ *adj* (*BRIT col*) bizarre.

Rumania *etc* [ruːˈmeɪnɪə] = **Romania** *etc.*

rumble [ˈrʌmbl] *n* grondement *m*; gargouillement *m* ♦ *vi* gronder; (*stomach, pipe*) gargouiller.

rumbustious [rʌmˈbʌstʃəs], (*US*) **rumbunctious** [rʌmˈbʌŋkʃəs] *adj* (*person*) exubérant(e).

rummage [ˈrʌmɪdʒ] *vi* fouiller.

rumour, (*US*) **rumor** [ˈruːmə*] *n* rumeur *f*, bruit *m* (qui court) ♦ *vt*: **it is ~ed that** le bruit court que.

rump [rʌmp] *n* (*of animal*) croupe *f*; (*also:* ~ **steak**) romsteck *m*.

rumple [ˈrʌmpl] *vt* (*hair*) ébouriffer; (*clothes*) chiffonner, friper.

rumpus [ˈrʌmpəs] *n* (*col*) tapage *m*, chahut *m*; (*quarrel*) prise *f* de bec; **to kick up a ~** faire toute une histoire.

run [rʌn] *n* (*race etc*) course *f*; (*outing*) tour *m* *or* promenade *f* (en voiture); (*journey*) parcours *m*, trajet *m*; (*series*) suite *f*, série *f*; (*THEAT*) série de représentations; (*SKI*) piste *f*; (*in tights, stockings*) maille filée, échelle *f* ♦ *vb* (*pt* **ran**, *pp* **run** [ræn, rʌn]) *vt* (*business*) diriger; (*competition, course*) organiser; (*hotel, house*) tenir; (*COMPUT: program*) exécuter; (*force through: rope, pipe*): **to ~ sth through** faire passer qch à travers; (*to pass: hand, finger*): **to ~ sth over** promener *or* passer qch sur; (*water, bath*) faire couler ♦ *vi* courir; (*pass: road etc*) passer; (*work: machine, factory*) marcher; (*bus, train*) circuler; (*continue: play*) se jouer, être à l'affiche; (*: contract*) être valide *or* en vigueur; (*slide: drawer etc*) glisser; (*flow: river, bath*) couler; (*colours, washing*) déteindre; (*in election*) être candidat, se présenter; **to go for a ~** aller courir *or* faire un peu de course à pied; (*in car*) faire un tour *or* une promenade (en voiture); **to break into a ~** se mettre à courir; **a ~ of luck** une série de coups de chance; **to have the ~ of sb's house** avoir la maison de qn à sa disposition; **there was a ~ on** (*meat, tickets*) les gens se sont rués sur; **in the long ~** à longue échéance; à la longue; en fin de compte; **in the short ~** à brève échéance, à court terme; **on the ~** en fuite; **to make a ~ for it** s'enfuir; **I'll ~ you to the station** je vais vous emmener *or* conduire à la gare; **to ~ errands** faire des commissions; **the train ~s between Gatwick and Victoria** le train assure le service entre Gatwick et Victoria; **the bus ~s every 20 minutes** il y a un autobus toutes les 20 minutes; **it's very cheap to ~** (*car, machine*) c'est très économique; **to ~ on petrol** *or* (*US*) **gas/on diesel/off batteries** marcher à l'essence/au diesel/sur piles; **to ~ for president** être candidat à la présidence; **their losses ran into millions** leurs pertes se sont élevées à plusieurs millions; **to be ~ off one's feet** (*BRIT*) ne plus savoir où donner de la tête.

▶**run about** *vi* (*children*) courir çà et là.

▶**run across** *vt fus* (*find*) trouver par hasard.

▶**run away** *vi* s'enfuir.

▶**run down** *vi* (*clock*) s'arrêter (faute d'avoir été remonté) ♦ *vt* (*AUT*) renverser; (*BRIT: reduce: production*) réduire progressivement; (*: factory/shop*) réduire progressivement la production/l'activité de; (*criticize*) critiquer, dénigrer; **to be ~ down** être fatigué(e) *or* à plat.

▶**run in** *vt* (*BRIT: car*) roder.

▶**run into** *vt fus* (*meet: person*) rencontrer par hasard; (*: trouble*) se heurter à; (*collide with*) heurter; **to ~ into debt** contracter des dettes.

▶**run off** *vi* s'enfuir ♦ *vt* (*water*) laisser s'écouler.

▶**run out** *vi* (*person*) sortir en courant; (*liquid*) couler; (*lease*) expirer; (*money*) être épuisé(e).

▶**run out of** *vt fus* se trouver à court de; **I've ~ out of petrol** *or* (*US*) **gas** je suis en panne d'essence.

▶**run over** *vt* (*AUT*) écraser ♦ *vt fus* (*revise*) revoir, reprendre.

▶**run through** *vt fus* (*instructions*) reprendre, revoir.

▶**run up** *vt* (*debt*) laisser accumuler; **to ~ up against** (*difficulties*) se heurter à.

runaround [ˈrʌnəraund] *n* (*col*): **to give sb the ~** rester très évasif.

runaway [ˈrʌnəweɪ] *adj* (*horse*) emballé(e); (*truck*) fou(folle); (*inflation*) galopant(e).

rundown [ˈrʌndaun] *n* (*BRIT: of industry etc*) réduction progressive.

rung [rʌŋ] *pp of* **ring** ♦ *n* (*of ladder*) barreau *m*.

run-in [ˈrʌnɪn] *n* (*col*) accrochage *m*, prise *f* de bec.

runner [ˈrʌnə*] *n* (*in race: person*) coureur/euse; (*: horse*) partant *m*; (*on sledge*) patin *m*; (*for drawer etc*) coulisseau *m*; (*carpet: in hall etc*) chemin *m*.

runner bean *n* (*BRIT*) haricot *m* (à rames).

runner-up [rʌnərˈʌp] *n* second/e.

running [ˈrʌnɪŋ] *n* (*in race etc*) course *f*; (*of business*) direction *f*; (*of event*) organisation *f*; (*of machine etc*) marche *f*, fonctionnement *m* ♦ *adj* (*water*) courant(e); (*commentary*) suivi(e); **6 days** ~ 6 jours de suite; **to be in/out of the ~ for sth** être/ne pas être sur les rangs pour qch.

running costs *npl* (*of business*) frais *mpl* de gestion; (*of car*): **the ~ are high** elle revient cher.

running head *n* (*TYP, WORD PROCESSING*) titre courant.

running mate *n* (*US POL*) candidat à la vice-présidence.

runny [ˈrʌnɪ] *adj* qui coule.

run-off [ˈrʌnɔf] *n* (*in contest, election*) deuxième tour *m*; (*extra race etc*) épreuve *f* supplémentaire.

run-of-the-mill ['rʌnəvðə'mɪl] *adj* ordinaire, banal(e).

runt [rʌnt] *n* (*also pej*) avorton *m*.

run-through ['rʌnθru:] *n* répétition *f*, essai *m*.

run-up ['rʌnʌp] *n* (*BRIT*): ~ **to sth** période *f* précédant qch.

runway ['rʌnweɪ] *n* (*AVIAT*) piste *f* (d'envol *or* d'atterrissage).

rupee [ru:'pi:] *n* roupie *f*.

rupture ['rʌptʃə*] *n* (*MED*) hernie *f* ♦ *vt*: **to ~ o.s.** se donner une hernie.

rural ['ruərl] *adj* rural(e).

ruse [ru:z] *n* ruse *f*.

rush [rʌʃ] *n* course précipitée; (*of crowd*) ruée *f*, bousculade *f*; (*hurry*) hâte *f*, bousculade; (*current*) flot *m*; (*BOT*) jonc *m*; (*for chair*) paille *f* ♦ *vt* transporter *or* envoyer d'urgence; (*attack: town etc*) prendre d'assaut; (*BRIT col: overcharge*) estamper; faire payer ♦ *vi* se précipiter; **don't ~ me!** laissez-moi le temps de souffler!; **to ~ sth off** (*do quickly*) faire qch à la hâte; (*send*) envoyer d'urgence; **is there any ~ for this?** est-ce urgent?; **we've had a ~ of orders** nous avons reçu une avalanche de commandes; **I'm in a ~ (to do)** je suis vraiment pressé (de faire); **gold ~** ruée vers l'or.

▶**rush through** *vt fus* (*work*) exécuter à la hâte ♦ *vt* (*COMM: order*) exécuter d'urgence.

rush hour *n* heures *fpl* de pointe *or* d'affluence.

rush job *n* travail urgent.

rush matting *n* natte *f* de paille.

rusk [rʌsk] *n* biscotte *f*.

Russia ['rʌʃə] *n* Russie *f*.

Russian ['rʌʃən] *adj* russe ♦ *n* Russe *m/f*; (*LING*) russe *m*.

rust [rʌst] *n* rouille *f* ♦ *vi* rouiller.

rustic ['rʌstɪk] *adj* rustique ♦ *n* (*pej*) rustaud/e.

rustle ['rʌsl] *vi* bruire, produire un bruissement ♦ *vt* (*paper*) froisser; (*US: cattle*) voler.

rustproof ['rʌstpru:f] *adj* inoxydable.

rustproofing ['rʌstpru:fɪŋ] *n* traitement *m* antirouille.

rusty ['rʌstɪ] *adj* rouillé(e).

rut [rʌt] *n* ornière *f*, (*ZOOL*) rut *m*; **to be in a ~** (*fig*) suivre l'ornière, s'encroûter.

rutabaga [ru:tə'beɪgə] *n* (*US*) rutabaga *m*.

ruthless ['ru:θlɪs] *adj* sans pitié, impitoyable.

ruthlessness ['ru:θlɪsnɪs] *n* dureté *f*, cruauté *f*.

RV *abbr* (= *revised version*) *traduction anglaise de la Bible de 1885* ♦ *n abbr* (*US*) = **recreational vehicle**.

rye [raɪ] *n* seigle *m*.

rye bread *n* pain *m* de seigle.

S s

S, s [ɛs] *n* (*letter*) S, s *m*; (*US SCOL*: = *satisfactory*) ≈ assez bien; **S for Sugar** S comme Suzanne.

S *abbr* (= *south, small*) S; (= *saint*) St.

SA *n abbr* = **South Africa, South America**.

Sabbath ['sæbəθ] *n* (*Jewish*) sabbat *m*; (*Christian*) dimanche *m*.

sabbatical [sə'bætɪkl] *adj*: ~ **year** année *f* sabbatique.

sabotage ['sæbətɑːʒ] *n* sabotage *m* ♦ *vt* saboter.

saccharin(e) ['sækərɪn] *n* saccharine *f*.

sachet ['sæʃeɪ] *n* sachet *m*.

sack [sæk] *n* (*bag*) sac *m* ♦ *vt* (*dismiss*) renvoyer, mettre à la porte; (*plunder*) piller, mettre à sac; **to give sb the ~** renvoyer qn, mettre qn à la porte; **to get the ~** être renvoyé(e) *or* mis(e) à la porte.

sackful ['sækful] *n*: **a ~ of** un (plein) sac de.

sacking ['sækɪŋ] *n* toile *f* à sac; (*dismissal*) renvoi *m*.

sacrament ['sækrəmənt] *n* sacrement *m*.

sacred ['seɪkrɪd] *adj* sacré(e).

sacred cow *n* (*fig*) chose sacro-sainte.

sacrifice ['sækrɪfaɪs] *n* sacrifice *m* ♦ *vt* sacrifier; **to make ~s (for sb)** se sacrifier *or* faire des sacrifices (pour qn).

sacrilege ['sækrɪlɪdʒ] *n* sacrilège *m*.

sacrosanct ['sækrəusæŋkt] *adj* sacro-saint(e).

sad [sæd] *adj* (*unhappy*) triste; (*deplorable*) triste, fâcheux(euse).

sadden ['sædn] *vt* attrister, affliger.

saddle ['sædl] *n* selle *f* ♦ *vt* (*horse*) seller; **to be ~d with sth** (*col*) avoir qch sur les bras.

saddlebag ['sædlbæg] *n* sacoche *f*.

sadism ['seɪdɪzəm] *n* sadisme *m*.

sadist ['seɪdɪst] *n* sadique *m/f*.

sadistic [sə'dɪstɪk] *adj* sadique.

sadly ['sædlɪ] *adv* tristement; (*regrettably*) malheureusement.

sadness ['sædnɪs] *n* tristesse *f*.

sado-masochism [seɪdəu'mæsəkɪzəm] *n* sado-masochisme *m*.

sae *abbr* (*BRIT*: = *stamped addressed envelope*) enveloppe affranchie pour la réponse.

safari [sə'fɑːrɪ] *n* safari *m*.

safari park *n* réserve *f*.

safe [seɪf] *adj* (*out of danger*) hors de danger, en sécurité; (*not dangerous*) sans danger; (*cautious*) prudent(e); (*sure: bet etc*) assuré(e) ♦ *n* coffre-fort *m*; ~ **from** à l'abri de; ~ **and sound** sain(e) et sauf(sauve); (**just) to**

be on the ~ **side** pour plus de sûreté, par précaution; **to play** ~ ne prendre aucun risque; **it is** ~ **to say that ...** on peut dire sans crainte que ...; ~ **journey!** bon voyage!

safe bet *n*: **it was a** ~ ça ne comportait pas trop de risques; **it's a** ~ **that he'll be late** il y a toutes les chances pour qu'il soit en retard.

safe-breaker ['seifbreikə*] *n* (*BRIT*) perceur *m* de coffre-fort.

safe-conduct [seif'kɔndʌkt] *n* sauf-conduit *m*.

safe-cracker ['seifkrækə*] *n* = **safe-breaker**.

safe-deposit ['seifdipɔzit] *n* (*vault*) dépôt *m* de coffres-forts; (*box*) coffre-fort *m*.

safeguard ['seifgɑːd] *n* sauvegarde *f*, protection *f* ♦ *vt* sauvegarder, protéger.

safe haven *n* zone *f* de sécurité.

safekeeping ['seif'kiːpiŋ] *n* bonne garde.

safely ['seifli] *adv* sans danger, sans risque; (*without mishap*) sans accident; **I can** ~ **say ...** je peux dire à coup sûr ....

safe passage *n*: **to grant sb** ~ accorder un laissez-passer à qn.

safe sex *n* rapports sexuels protégés.

safety ['seifti] *n* sécurité *f*; ~ **first!** la sécurité d'abord!

safety belt *n* ceinture *f* de sécurité.

safety catch *n* cran *m* de sûreté *or* sécurité.

safety net *n* filet *m* de sécurité.

safety pin *n* épingle *f* de sûreté *or* de nourrice.

safety valve *n* soupape *f* de sûreté.

saffron ['sæfrən] *n* safran *m*.

sag [sæg] *vi* s'affaisser, fléchir; pendre.

saga ['sɑːgə] *n* saga *f*; (*fig*) épopée *f*.

sage [seidʒ] *n* (*herb*) sauge *f*; (*man*) sage *m*.

Sagittarius [sædʒɪ'tɛərɪəs] *n* le Sagittaire; **to be** ~ être du Sagittaire.

sago ['seigəu] *n* sagou *m*.

Sahara [sə'hɑːrə] *n*: **the** ~ (**Desert**) le (désert du) Sahara *m*.

Sahel [sæ'hel] *n* Sahel *m*.

said [sɛd] *pt, pp of* **say**.

Saigon [sai'gɔn] *n* Saigon.

sail [seil] *n* (*on boat*) voile *f*; (*trip*): **to go for a** ~ faire un tour en bateau ♦ *vt* (*boat*) manœuvrer, piloter ♦ *vi* (*travel: ship*) avancer, naviguer; (: *passenger*) aller *or* se rendre (en bateau); (*set off*) partir, prendre la mer; (*SPORT*) faire de la voile; **they** ~**ed into Le Havre** ils sont entrés dans le port du Havre.
▶**sail through** *vi, vt fus* (*fig*) réussir haut la main.

sailboat ['seilbəut] *n* (*US*) bateau *m* à voiles, voilier *m*.

sailing ['seiliŋ] *n* (*SPORT*) voile *f*; **to go** ~ faire de la voile.

sailing boat *n* bateau *m* à voiles, voilier *m*.

sailing ship *n* grand voilier.

sailor ['seilə*] *n* marin *m*, matelot *m*.

saint [seint] *n* saint/e.

saintly ['seintli] *adj* saint(e), plein(e) de bonté.

sake [seik] *n*: **for the** ~ **of** (*out of concern for*) pour, dans l'intérêt de; (*out of consideration for*) par égard pour; (*in order to achieve*) pour plus de, par souci de; **arguing for arguing's** ~ discuter pour (le plaisir de) discuter; **for the** ~ **of argument** à titre d'exemple; **for heaven's** ~! pour l'amour du ciel!

salad ['sæləd] *n* salade *f*; **tomato** ~ salade de tomates.

salad bowl *n* saladier *m*.

salad cream *n* (*BRIT*) (sorte *f* de) mayonnaise *f*.

salad dressing *n* vinaigrette *f*.

salad oil *n* huile *f* de table.

salami [sə'lɑːmɪ] *n* salami *m*.

salaried ['sælərɪd] *adj* (*staff*) salarié(e), qui touche un traitement.

salary ['sælərɪ] *n* salaire *m*, traitement *m*.

salary scale *n* échelle *f* des traitements.

sale [seil] *n* vente *f*; (*at reduced prices*) soldes *mpl*; **"for** ~**"** "à vendre"; **on** ~ en vente; **on** ~ **or return** vendu(e) avec faculté de retour; **closing-down** *or* (*US*) **liquidation** ~ liquidation *f* (*avant fermeture*); ~ **and lease back** *n* cession-bail *f*.

saleroom ['seilruːm] *n* salle *f* des ventes.

sales assistant *n* (*BRIT*) vendeur/euse.

sales clerk *n* (*US*) vendeur/euse.

sales conference *n* réunion *f* de vente.

sales drive *n* campagne commerciale, animation *f* des ventes.

sales force *n* (ensemble *m* du) service des ventes.

salesman ['seilzmən] *n* vendeur *m*; (*representative*) représentant *m* de commerce.

sales manager *n* directeur commercial.

salesmanship ['seilzmənʃɪp] *n* art *m* de la vente.

sales tax *n* (*US*) taxe *f* à l'achat.

saleswoman ['seilzwumən] *n* vendeuse *f*.

salient ['seilɪənt] *adj* saillant(e).

saline ['seilaɪn] *adj* salin(e).

saliva [sə'laɪvə] *n* salive *f*.

sallow ['sæləu] *adj* cireux(euse).

sally forth, **sally out** ['sælɪ-] *vi* partir plein(e) d'entrain.

salmon ['sæmən] *n* (*pl inv*) saumon *m*.

salmon trout *n* truite saumonée.

saloon [sə'luːn] *n* (*US*) bar *m*; (*BRIT AUT*) berline *f*; (*ship's lounge*) salon *m*.

SALT [sɔːlt] *n abbr* (= *Strategic Arms Limitation Talks/Treaty*) SALT *m*.

salt [sɔːlt] *n* sel *m* ♦ *vt* saler ♦ *cpd* de sel; (*CULIN*) salé(e); **an old** ~ un vieux loup de mer.
▶**salt away** *vt* mettre de côté.

salt cellar *n* salière *f*.

salt-free ['sɔːlt'friː] *adj* sans sel.

saltwater ['sɔːlt'wɔːtə*] *adj* (*fish etc*) (d'eau) de mer.

salty ['sɔːltɪ] *adj* salé(e).

salubrious [sə'luːbrɪəs] *adj* salubre.

salutary ['sæljutərɪ] *adj* salutaire.

salute [sə'luːt] *n* salut *m* ♦ *vt* saluer.
salvage ['sælvɪdʒ] *n* (*saving*) sauvetage *m*; (*things saved*) biens sauvés *or* récupérés ♦ *vt* sauver, récupérer.
salvage vessel *n* bateau *m* de sauvetage.
salvation [sæl'veɪʃən] *n* salut *m*.
Salvation Army *n* Armée *f* du Salut.
salver ['sælvə*] *n* plateau *m* de métal.
salvo ['sælvəu] *n* salve *f*.
Samaritan [sə'mærɪtən] *n*: **the ~s** (*organization*) ≈ S.O.S. Amitié.
same [seɪm] *adj* même ♦ *pron*: **the ~ le(la) même, les mêmes; the ~ book as** le même livre que; **on the ~ day** le même jour; **at the ~ time** en même temps; **all** *or* **just the ~** tout de même, quand même; **they're one and the ~** (*person/thing*) c'est une seule et même personne/chose; **to do the ~** faire de même, en faire autant; **to do the ~ as sb** faire comme qn; **and the ~ to you!** et à vous de même!; (*after insult*) toi-même!; **~ here!** moi aussi!; **the ~ again!** (*in bar etc*) la même chose!
sample ['sɑːmpl] *n* échantillon *m*; (*MED*) prélèvement *m* ♦ *vt* (*food, wine*) goûter; **to take a ~** prélever un échantillon; **free ~** échantillon gratuit.
sanatorium, *pl* **sanatoria** [sænə'tɔːrɪəm, -rɪə] *n* sanatorium *m*.
sanctify ['sæŋktɪfaɪ] *vt* sanctifier.
sanctimonious [sæŋktɪ'məunɪəs] *adj* moralisateur(trice).
sanction ['sæŋkʃən] *n* sanction *f* ♦ *vt* cautionner, sanctionner; **to impose economic ~s on** *or* **against** prendre des sanctions économiques contre.
sanctity ['sæŋktɪtɪ] *n* sainteté *f*, caractère sacré.
sanctuary ['sæŋktjuərɪ] *n* (*holy place*) sanctuaire *m*; (*refuge*) asile *m*; (*for wild life*) réserve *f*.
sand [sænd] *n* sable *m* ♦ *vt* sabler; (*also: ~ down: wood etc*) poncer.
sandal ['sændl] *n* sandale *f*.
sandbag ['sændbæg] *n* sac *m* de sable.
sandblast ['sændblɑːst] *vt* décaper à la sableuse.
sandbox ['sændbɔks] *n* (*US: for children*) tas *m* de sable.
sandcastle ['sændkɑːsl] *n* château *m* de sable.
sand dune *n* dune *f* de sable.
sander ['sændə*] *n* ponceuse *f*.
S&M *n abbr* (= *sadomasochism*) sadomasochisme *m*.
sandpaper ['sændpeɪpə*] *n* papier *m* de verre.
sandpit ['sændpɪt] *n* (*BRIT: for children*) tas *m* de sable.
sands [sændz] *npl* plage *f* (de sable).
sandstone ['sændstəun] *n* grès *m*.
sandstorm ['sændstɔːm] *n* tempête *f* de sable.
sandwich ['sændwɪtʃ] *n* sandwich *m* ♦ *vt* (*also: ~ in*) intercaler; **~ed between** pris en sand-

wich entre; **cheese/ham ~** sandwich au fromage/jambon.
sandwich board *n* panneau *m* publicitaire (porté par un homme-sandwich).
sandwich course *n* (*BRIT*) cours *m* de formation professionnelle.
sandy ['sændɪ] *adj* sablonneux(euse); couvert(e) de sable; (*colour*) sable *inv*, blond roux *inv*.
sane [seɪn] *adj* (*person*) sain(e) d'esprit; (*outlook*) sensé(e), sain(e).
sang [sæŋ] *pt of* **sing**.
sanguine ['sæŋgwɪn] *adj* optimiste.
sanitarium, *pl* **sanitaria** [sænɪ'tɛərɪəm, -rɪə] *n* (*US*) = **sanatorium**.
sanitary ['sænɪtərɪ] *adj* (*system, arrangements*) sanitaire; (*clean*) hygiénique.
sanitary towel, (*US*) **sanitary napkin** *n* serviette *f* hygiénique.
sanitation [sænɪ'teɪʃən] *n* (*in house*) installations *fpl* sanitaires; (*in town*) système *m* sanitaire.
sanitation department *n* (*US*) service *m* de voirie.
sanity ['sænɪtɪ] *n* santé mentale; (*common sense*) bon sens.
sank [sæŋk] *pt of* **sink**.
San Marino ['sænmə'riːnəu] *n* Saint-Marin *m*.
Santa Claus [sæntə'klɔːz] *n* le Père Noël.
Santiago [sæntɪ'ɑːgəu] *n* (*also: ~ de Chile*) Santiago (du Chili).
sap [sæp] *n* (*of plants*) sève *f* ♦ *vt* (*strength*) saper, miner.
sapling ['sæplɪŋ] *n* jeune arbre *m*.
sapphire ['sæfaɪə*] *n* saphir *m*.
sarcasm ['sɑːkæzm] *n* sarcasme *m*, raillerie *f*.
sarcastic [sɑː'kæstɪk] *adj* sarcastique.
sarcophagus, *pl* **sarcophagi** [sɑː'kɔfəgəs, -gaɪ] *n* sarcophage *m*.
sardine [sɑː'diːn] *n* sardine *f*.
Sardinia [sɑː'dɪnɪə] *n* Sardaigne *f*.
Sardinian [sɑː'dɪnɪən] *adj* sarde ♦ *n* Sarde *m/f*; (*LING*) sarde *m*.
sardonic [sɑː'dɔnɪk] *adj* sardonique.
sari ['sɑːrɪ] *n* sari *m*.
sartorial [sɑː'tɔːrɪəl] *adj* vestimentaire.
SAS *n abbr* (*BRIT MIL*: = *Special Air Service*) ≈ GIGN *m*.
SASE *n abbr* (*US*: = *self-addressed stamped envelope*) enveloppe affranchie pour la réponse.
sash [sæʃ] *n* écharpe *f*.
sash window *n* fenêtre *f* à guillotine.
Sask. *abbr* (*Canada*) = **Saskatchewan**.
SAT *n abbr* (*US*) = **Scholastic Aptitude Test**.
sat [sæt] *pt, pp of* **sit**.
Sat. *abbr* (= *Saturday*) sa.
Satan ['seɪtn] *n* Satan *m*.
satanic [sə'tænɪk] *adj* satanique, démoniaque.
satchel ['sætʃl] *n* cartable *m*.
sated ['seɪtɪd] *adj* repu(e); blasé(e).
satellite ['sætəlaɪt] *adj, n* satellite (*m*).
satellite television *n* télévision *f* par satel-

lite.
satiate ['seɪʃɪeɪt] vt rassasier.
satin ['sætɪn] n satin m ♦ adj en or de satin, satiné(e); **with a ~ finish** satiné(e).
satire ['sætaɪə*] n satire f.
satirical [sə'tɪrɪkl] adj satirique.
satirist ['sætɪrɪst] n (writer) auteur m satirique; (cartoonist) caricaturiste m/f.
satirize ['sætɪraɪz] vt faire la satire de, satiriser.
satisfaction [sætɪs'fækʃən] n satisfaction f.
satisfactory [sætɪs'fæktərɪ] adj satisfaisant(e).
satisfied ['sætɪsfaɪd] adj satisfait(e); **to be ~ with sth** être satisfait de qch.
satisfy ['sætɪsfaɪ] vt satisfaire, contenter; (convince) convaincre, persuader; **to ~ the requirements** remplir les conditions; **to ~ sb (that)** convaincre qn (que); **to ~ o.s. of sth** vérifier qch, s'assurer de qch.
satisfying ['sætɪsfaɪɪŋ] adj satisfaisant(e).
satsuma [sæt'suːmə] n satsuma f.
saturate ['sætʃəreɪt] vt: **to ~ (with)** saturer (de).
saturated fat ['sætʃəreɪtɪd-] n graisse saturée.
saturation [sætʃə'reɪʃən] n saturation f.
Saturday ['sætədɪ] n samedi m; for phrases see also **Tuesday**.
sauce [sɔːs] n sauce f.
saucepan ['sɔːspən] n casserole f.
saucer ['sɔːsə*] n soucoupe f.
saucy ['sɔːsɪ] adj impertinent(e).
Saudi Arabia ['saudɪ-] n Arabie f Saoudite or Séoudite.
Saudi (Arabian) ['saudɪ-] adj saoudien(ne) ♦ n Saoudien/ne.
sauna ['sɔːnə] n sauna m.
saunter ['sɔːntə*] vi: **to ~ to** aller en flânant or se balader jusqu'à.
sausage ['sɔsɪdʒ] n saucisse f; (salami etc) saucisson m.
sausage roll n friand m.
sauté ['səuteɪ] adj (CULIN: potatoes) sauté(e); (: onions) revenu(e) ♦ vt faire sauter; faire revenir.
savage ['sævɪdʒ] adj (cruel, fierce) brutal(e), féroce; (primitive) primitif(ive), sauvage ♦ n sauvage m/f ♦ vt attaquer férocement.
savagery ['sævɪdʒrɪ] n sauvagerie f, brutalité f, férocité f.
save [seɪv] vt (person, belongings) sauver; (money) mettre de côté, économiser; (time) (faire) gagner; (food) garder; (COMPUT) sauvegarder; (avoid: trouble) éviter ♦ vi (also: ~ up) mettre de l'argent de côté ♦ n (SPORT) arrêt m (du ballon) ♦ prep sauf, à l'exception de; **it will ~ me an hour** ça me fera gagner une heure; **to ~ face** sauver la face; **God ~ the Queen!** vive la Reine!
saving ['seɪvɪŋ] n économie f ♦ adj: **the ~ grace of** ce qui rachète; **~s** npl économies fpl; **to make ~s** faire des économies.

savings account n compte m d'épargne.
savings bank n caisse f d'épargne.
saviour, (US) **savior** ['seɪvjə*] n sauveur m.
savour, (US) **savor** ['seɪvə*] n saveur f, goût m ♦ vt savourer.
savo(u)ry ['seɪvərɪ] adj savoureux(euse); (dish: not sweet) salé(e).
savvy ['sævɪ] n (col) jugeote f.
saw [sɔː] pt of **see** ♦ n (tool) scie f ♦ vt (pt **sawed**, pp **sawed** or **sawn** [sɔːn]) scier; **to ~ sth up** débiter qch à la scie.
sawdust ['sɔːdʌst] n sciure f.
sawmill ['sɔːmɪl] n scierie f.
sawn-off ['sɔːnɔf], (US) **sawed-off** ['sɔːdɔf] adj: **~ shotgun** carabine f à canon scié.
saxophone ['sæksəfəun] n saxophone m.
say [seɪ] n: **to have one's ~** dire ce qu'on a à dire ♦ vt (pt, pp **said** [sed]) dire; **to have a ~** avoir voix au chapitre; **could you ~ that again?** pourriez-vous répéter ceci?; **to ~ yes/no** dire oui/non; **she said (that) I was to give you this** elle m'a chargé de vous remettre ceci; **my watch ~s 3 o'clock** ma montre indique 3 heures, il est 3 heures à ma montre; **shall we ~ Tuesday?** disons mardi?; **that doesn't ~ much for him** ce n'est pas vraiment à son honneur; **when all is said and done** en fin de compte, en définitive; **there is something** or **a lot to be said for it** cela a des avantages; **that is to ~** c'est-à-dire; **to ~ nothing of** sans compter; **~ that …** mettons or disons que …; **that goes without ~ing** cela va sans dire, cela va de soi.
saying ['seɪɪŋ] n dicton m, proverbe m.
SBA n abbr (US: = Small Business Administration) organisme d'aide aux PME.
SC n abbr (US) = **supreme court** ♦ abbr (US) = **South Carolina**.
s/c abbr = **self-contained**.
scab [skæb] n croûte f; (pej) jaune m.
scabby ['skæbɪ] adj croûteux(euse).
scaffold ['skæfəld] n échafaud m.
scaffolding ['skæfəldɪŋ] n échafaudage m.
scald [skɔːld] n brûlure f ♦ vt ébouillanter.
scalding ['skɔːldɪŋ] adj (also: ~ **hot**) brûlant(e), bouillant(e).
scale [skeɪl] n (of fish) écaille f; (MUS) gamme f; (of ruler, thermometer etc) graduation f, échelle (graduée); (of salaries, fees etc) barème m; (of map, also size, extent) échelle ♦ vt (mountain) escalader; (fish) écailler; **pay ~** échelle des salaires; **~ of charges** tarif m (des consultations or prestations etc); **on a large ~** sur une grande échelle, en grand; **to draw sth to ~** dessiner qch à l'échelle; **small-~ model** modèle réduit.
▶**scale down** vt réduire.
scaled-down [skeɪld'daun] adj à échelle réduite.
scale drawing n dessin m à l'échelle.
scale model n modèle m à l'échelle.

scales [skeɪlz] *npl* balance *f*; (*larger*) bascule *f*.

scallion ['skæljən] *n* oignon *m*; (*US: shaliot*) échalote *f*; (: *leek*) poireau *m*.

scallop ['skɔləp] *n* coquille *f* Saint-Jacques.

scalp [skælp] *n* cuir chevelu ♦ *vt* scalper.

scalpel ['skælpl] *n* scalpel *m*.

scalper ['skælpə*] *n* (*US col: of tickets*) revendeur *m* de billets.

scam [skæm] *n* (*col*) arnaque *f*.

scamp [skæmp] *vt* bâcler.

scamper ['skæmpə*] *vi*: **to ~ away, ~ off** détaler.

scampi ['skæmpɪ] *npl* langoustines (frites), scampi *mpl*.

scan [skæn] *vt* scruter, examiner; (*glance at quickly*) parcourir; (*poetry*) scander; (*TV, RADAR*) balayer ♦ *n* (*MED*) scanographie *f*.

scandal ['skændl] *n* scandale *m*; (*gossip*) ragots *mpl*.

scandalize ['skændəlaɪz] *vt* scandaliser, indigner.

scandalous ['skændələs] *adj* scandaleux(euse).

Scandinavia [skændɪ'neɪvɪə] *n* Scandinavie *f*.

Scandinavian [skændɪ'neɪvɪən] *adj* scandinave ♦ *n* Scandinave *m/f*.

scanner ['skænə*] *n* (*RADAR, MED*) scanner *m*, scanographe *m*.

scant [skænt] *adj* insuffisant(e).

scantily ['skæntɪlɪ] *adv*: **~ clad** *or* **dressed** vêtu(e) du strict minimum.

scanty ['skæntɪ] *adj* peu abondant(e), insuffisant(e), maigre.

scapegoat ['skeɪpgəut] *n* bouc *m* émissaire.

scar [skɑ:] *n* cicatrice *f* ♦ *vt* laisser une cicatrice *or* une marque à.

scarce [skɛəs] *adj* rare, peu abondant(e).

scarcely ['skɛəslɪ] *adv* à peine, presque pas; **~ anybody** pratiquement personne; **I can ~ believe it** j'ai du mal à le croire.

scarcity ['skɛəsɪtɪ] *n* rareté *f*, manque *m*.

scarcity value *n* valeur *f* de rareté.

scare [skɛə*] *n* peur *f*, panique *f* ♦ *vt* effrayer, faire peur à; **to ~ sb stiff** faire une peur bleue à qn; **bomb ~** alerte *f* à la bombe.

▶**scare away, scare off** *vt* faire fuir.

scarecrow ['skɛəkrəu] *n* épouvantail *m*.

scared ['skɛəd] *adj*: **to be ~** avoir peur.

scaremonger ['skɛəmʌŋgə*] *n* alarmiste *m/f*.

scarf, *pl* **scarves** [skɑ:f, skɑ:vz] *n* (*long*) écharpe *f*; (*square*) foulard *m*.

scarlet ['skɑ:lɪt] *adj* écarlate.

scarlet fever *n* scarlatine *f*.

scarper ['skɑ:pə*] *vi* (*BRIT col*) ficher le camp.

SCART socket ['skɑ:t-] *n* prise *f* péritel.

scarves [skɑ:vz] *npl of* **scarf**.

scary ['skɛərɪ] *adj* (*col*) qui fiche la frousse.

scathing ['skeɪðɪŋ] *adj* cinglant(e), acerbe; **to be ~ about sth** être très critique vis-à-vis de qch.

scatter ['skætə*] *vt* éparpiller, répandre; (*crowd*) disperser ♦ *vi* se disperser.

scatterbrained ['skætəbreɪnd] *adj* écervelé(e), étourdi(e).

scattered ['skætəd] *adj* épars(e), dispersé(e).

scatty ['skætɪ] *adj* (*BRIT col*) loufoque.

scavenge ['skævəndʒ] *vi* (*person*): **to ~ (for)** faire les poubelles (pour trouver); **to ~ for food** (*hyenas etc*) se nourrir de charognes.

scavenger ['skævəndʒə*] *n* éboueur *m*.

SCE *n abbr* = *Scottish Certificate of Education*.

scenario [sɪ'nɑ:rɪəu] *n* scénario *m*.

scene [si:n] *n* (*THEAT, fig etc*) scène *f*; (*of crime, accident*) lieu(x) *m(pl)*, endroit *m*; (*sight, view*) spectacle *m*, vue *f*; **behind the ~s** (*also fig*) dans les coulisses; **to make a ~** (*col: fuss*) faire une scène *or* toute une histoire; **to appear on the ~** (*also fig*) faire son apparition, arriver; **the political ~** la situation politique.

scenery ['si:nərɪ] *n* (*THEAT*) décor(s) *m(pl)*; (*landscape*) paysage *m*.

scenic ['si:nɪk] *adj* scénique; offrant de beaux paysages *or* panoramas.

scent [sɛnt] *n* parfum *m*, odeur *f*; (*fig: track*) piste *f*; (*sense of smell*) odorat *m* ♦ *vt* parfumer; (*smell, also fig*) flairer; **to put** *or* **throw sb off the ~** (*fig*) mettre *or* lancer qn sur une mauvaise piste.

sceptic, (*US*) **skeptic** ['skɛptɪk] *n* sceptique *m/f*.

sceptical, (*US*) **skeptical** ['skɛptɪkl] *adj* sceptique.

scepticism, (*US*) **skepticism** ['skɛptɪsɪzəm] *n* scepticisme *m*.

sceptre, (*US*) **scepter** ['sɛptə*] *n* sceptre *m*.

schedule ['ʃɛdju:l, (*US*) 'skɛdju:l] *n* programme *m*, plan *m*; (*of trains*) horaire *m*; (*of prices etc*) barème *m*, tarif *m* ♦ *vt* prévoir; **as ~d** comme prévu; **on ~** à l'heure (prévue); à la date prévue; **to be ahead of/behind ~** avoir de l'avance/du retard; **we are working to a very tight ~** notre programme de travail est très serré *or* intense; **everything went according to ~** tout s'est passé comme prévu.

scheduled ['ʃɛdju:ld, (*US*) 'skɛdju:ld] *adj* (*date, time*) prévu(e), indiqué(e); (*visit, event*) programmé(e), prévu; (*train, bus, stop, flight*) régulier(ière).

schematic [skɪ'mætɪk] *adj* schématique.

scheme [ski:m] *n* plan *m*, projet *m*; (*method*) procédé *m*; (*dishonest plan, plot*) complot *m*, combine *f*; (*arrangement*) arrangement *m*, classification *f*; (*pension ~ etc*) régime *m* ♦ *vt*, *vi* comploter, manigancer; **colour ~** combinaison *f* de(s) couleurs.

scheming ['ski:mɪŋ] *adj* rusé(e), intrigant(e) ♦ *n* manigances *fpl*, intrigues *fpl*.

schism ['skɪzəm] *n* schisme *m*.

schizophrenia [skɪtsə'fri:nɪə] *n* schizophrénie *f*.

schizophrenic [skɪtsə'frɛnɪk] *adj* schizophrène.

scholar ['skɔlə*] n érudit/e.
scholarly ['skɔləlɪ] adj érudit(e), savant(e).
scholarship ['skɔləʃɪp] n érudition f; (grant) bourse f (d'études).
school [sku:l] n (gen) école f; (in university) faculté f; (secondary school) collège m, lycée m; (of fish) banc m ♦ cpd scolaire ♦ vt (animal) dresser.
school age n âge m scolaire.
schoolbook ['sku:lbuk] n livre m scolaire or de classe.
schoolboy ['sku:lbɔɪ] n écolier m; collégien m, lycéen m.
schoolchild, pl **-children** ['sku:ltʃaɪld, -'tʃɪldrən] n écolier/ière, collégien/ne, lycéen/ne.
schooldays ['sku:ldeɪz] npl années fpl de scolarité.
schoolgirl ['sku:lgɜ:l] n écolière f; collégienne f, lycéenne f.
schooling ['sku:lɪŋ] n instruction f, études fpl.
school-leaver ['sku:lli:və*] n (BRIT) jeune qui vient de terminer ses études secondaires.
schoolmaster ['sku:lmɑ:stə*] n (primary) instituteur m; (secondary) professeur m.
schoolmistress ['sku:lmɪstrɪs] n (primary) institutrice f; (secondary) professeur m.
school report n (BRIT) bulletin m (scolaire).
schoolroom ['sku:lru:m] n (salle f de) classe f.
schoolteacher ['sku:lti:tʃə*] n (primary) instituteur/trice; (secondary) professeur m.
schoolyard ['sku:ljɑ:d] n (US) cour f de récréation.
schooner ['sku:nə*] n (ship) schooner m, goélette f; (glass) grand verre (à xérès).
sciatica [saɪ'ætɪkə] n sciatique f.
science ['saɪəns] n science f; the ~s les sciences; (SCOL) les matières fpl scientifiques.
science fiction n science-fiction f.
scientific [saɪən'tɪfɪk] adj scientifique.
scientist ['saɪəntɪst] n scientifique m/f.
sci-fi ['saɪfaɪ] n abbr (col: = science fiction) SF f.
Scilly Isles ['sɪlɪ'aɪlz] npl, **Scillies** ['sɪlɪz] npl: the ~ les Sorlingues fpl, les îles fpl Scilly.
scintillating ['sɪntɪleɪtɪŋ] adj scintillant(e), étincelant(e); (wit etc) brillant(e).
scissors ['sɪzəz] npl ciseaux mpl; a pair of ~ une paire de ciseaux.
sclerosis [sklɪ'rəusɪs] n sclérose f.
scoff [skɔf] vt (BRIT col: eat) avaler, bouffer ♦ vi: to ~ (at) (mock) se moquer (de).
scold [skəuld] vt gronder, attraper, réprimander.
scolding ['skəuldɪŋ] n réprimande f.
scone [skɔn] n sorte de petit pain rond au lait.
scoop [sku:p] n pelle f (à main); (for ice cream) boule f à glace; (PRESS) reportage exclusif or à sensation.
▶**scoop out** vt évider, creuser.
▶**scoop up** vt ramasser.
scooter ['sku:tə*] n (motor cycle) scooter m;

(toy) trottinette f.
scope [skəup] n (capacity: of plan, undertaking) portée f, envergure f; (: of person) compétence f, capacités fpl; (opportunity) possibilités fpl; **within the ~ of** dans les limites de; **there is plenty of ~ for improvement** (BRIT) cela pourrait être beaucoup mieux.
scorch [skɔ:tʃ] vt (clothes) brûler (légèrement), roussir; (earth, grass) dessécher, brûler.
scorched earth policy ['skɔ:tʃt-] n politique f de la terre brûlée.
scorcher ['skɔ:tʃə*] n (col: hot day) journée f torride.
scorching ['skɔ:tʃɪŋ] adj torride, brûlant(e).
score [skɔ:*] n score m, décompte m des points: (MUS) partition f; (twenty) vingt ♦ vt (goal, point) marquer; (success) remporter; (cut: leather, wood, card) entailler, inciser ♦ vi marquer des points; (FOOTBALL) marquer un but; (keep score) compter les points; **on that ~** sur ce chapitre, à cet égard; **to have an old ~ to settle with sb** (fig) avoir un (vieux) compte à régler avec qn; **~s of** (fig) des tas de; **to ~ well/6 out of 10** obtenir un bon résultat/6 sur 10.
▶**score out** vt rayer, barrer, biffer.
scoreboard ['skɔ:bɔ:d] n tableau m.
scorecard ['skɔ:kɑ:d] n (SPORT) carton m, feuille f de marque.
scoreline ['skɔ:laɪn] n (SPORT) score m.
scorer ['skɔ:rə*] n (FOOTBALL) auteur m du but; buteur m; (keeping score) marqueur m.
scorn [skɔ:n] n mépris m, dédain m ♦ vt mépriser, dédaigner.
scornful ['skɔ:nful] adj méprisant(e), dédaigneux(euse).
Scorpio ['skɔ:pɪəu] n le Scorpion; **to be ~** être du Scorpion.
scorpion ['skɔ:pɪən] n scorpion m.
Scot [skɔt] n Écossais/e.
Scotch [skɔtʃ] n whisky m, scotch m.
scotch [skɔtʃ] vt faire échouer; enrayer; étouffer.
Scotch tape n ® scotch m ®, ruban adhésif m.
scot-free ['skɔt'fri:] adj: **to get off ~** s'en tirer sans être puni(e) (or sans payer); s'en sortir indemne.
Scotland ['skɔtlənd] n Écosse f.
Scots [skɔts] adj écossais(e).
Scotsman ['skɔtsmən] n Écossais m.
Scotswoman ['skɔtswumən] n Écossaise f.
Scottish ['skɔtɪʃ] adj écossais(e); **the ~ National Party** le parti national écossais.
scoundrel ['skaundrl] n vaurien m.
scour ['skauə*] vt (clean) récurer; frotter; décaper; (search) battre, parcourir.
scourer ['skauərə*] n tampon abrasif or à récurer; (powder) poudre f à récurer.
scourge [skɜ:dʒ] n fléau m.
scouring pad ['skauərɪŋ-] n tampon abrasif or à récurer.

scout [skaut] n (MIL) éclaireur m; (also: **boy** ~) scout m.
▶**scout around** vi chercher.

scowl [skaul] vi se renfrogner, avoir l'air maussade; **to** ~ **at** regarder de travers.

scrabble ['skræbl] vi (claw): **to** ~ **(at)** gratter; **to** ~ **about** or **around for sth** chercher qch à tâtons ♦ n: **S**~ ® Scrabble m ®.

scraggy ['skrægɪ] adj décharné(e), efflanqué(e), famélique.

scram [skræm] vi (col) ficher le camp.

scramble ['skræmbl] n bousculade f, ruée f ♦ vi avancer tant bien que mal (à quatre pattes or en grimpant); **to** ~ **for** se bousculer or se disputer pour (avoir); **to go scrambling** (SPORT) faire du trial.

scrambled eggs ['skræmbld-] npl œufs brouillés.

scrap [skræp] n bout m, morceau m; (fight) bagarre f, (also: ~ **iron**) ferraille f ♦ vt jeter, mettre au rebut; (fig) abandonner, laisser tomber; ~**s** npl (waste) déchets mpl; **to sell sth for** ~ vendre qch à la casse or à la ferraille.

scrapbook ['skræpbuk] n album m.

scrap dealer n marchand m de ferraille.

scrape [skreɪp] vt, vi gratter, racler ♦ n: **to get into a** ~ s'attirer des ennuis.
▶**scrape through** vi (in exam etc) réussir de justesse.

scraper ['skreɪpə*] n grattoir m, racloir m.

scrap heap n tas m de ferraille; (fig): **on the** ~ au rancart or rebut.

scrap merchant n (BRIT) marchand m de ferraille.

scrap metal n ferraille f.

scrap paper n papier m brouillon.

scrappy ['skræpɪ] adj fragmentaire, décousu(e).

scrap yard n parc m à ferrailles; (for cars) cimetière m de voitures.

scratch [skrætʃ] n égratignure f, rayure f, éraflure f; (from claw) coup m de griffe ♦ adj: ~ **team** équipe de fortune or improvisée ♦ vt (record) rayer; (paint etc) érafler; (with claw, nail) griffer; (COMPUT) effacer ♦ vi (se) gratter; **to start from** ~ partir de zéro; **to be up to** ~ être à la hauteur.

scrawl [skrɔːl] n gribouillage m ♦ vi gribouiller.

scrawny ['skrɔːnɪ] adj décharné(e).

scream [skriːm] n cri perçant, hurlement m ♦ vi crier, hurler; **to be a** ~ (col) être impayable; **to** ~ **at sb to do sth** crier or hurler à qn de faire qch.

scree [skriː] n éboulis m.

screech [skriːtʃ] n cri strident, hurlement m; (of tyres, brakes) crissement m, grincement m ♦ vi hurler; crisser, grincer.

screen [skriːn] n écran m, paravent m; (CINE, TV) écran m; (fig) écran, rideau m ♦ vt masquer, cacher; (from the wind etc) abriter, protéger; (film) projeter; (candidates etc) filtrer; (for illness): **to** ~ **sb for sth** faire subir un test de dépistage de qch à qn.

screen editing [-'edɪtɪŋ] n (COMPUT) édition f or correction f sur écran.

screening ['skriːnɪŋ] n (of film) projection f; (MED) test m (or tests) de dépistage; (for security) filtrage m.

screen memory n (COMPUT) mémoire f écran.

screenplay ['skriːnpleɪ] n scénario m.

screen saver n (COMPUT) économiseur m d'écran.

screen test n bout m d'essai.

screw [skruː] n vis f; (propeller) hélice f ♦ vt visser; (col!: woman) baiser (!); **to** ~ **sth to the wall** visser qch au mur; **to have one's head** ~**ed on** (fig) avoir la tête sur les épaules.
▶**screw up** vt (paper, material) froisser; (col!: ruin) bousiller; **to** ~ **up one's face** faire la grimace.

screwdriver ['skruːdraɪvə*] n tournevis m.

screwed-up ['skruːd'ʌp] adj (col): **to be** ~ être paumé(e).

screwy ['skruːɪ] adj (col) dingue, cinglé(e).

scribble ['skrɪbl] n gribouillage m ♦ vt gribouiller, griffonner; **to** ~ **sth down** griffonner qch.

scribe [skraɪb] n scribe m.

script [skrɪpt] n (CINE etc) scénario m, texte m; (in exam) copie f; (writing) (écriture f) script m.

Scripture ['skrɪptʃə*] n Écriture sainte.

scriptwriter ['skrɪptraɪtə*] n scénariste m/f, dialoguiste m/f.

scroll [skrəul] n rouleau m ♦ vt (COMPUT) faire défiler (sur l'écran).

scrotum ['skrəutəm] n scrotum m.

scrounge [skraundʒ] (col) vt: **to** ~ **sth (off** or **from sb)** se faire payer qch (par qn), emprunter qch (à qn) ♦ vi: **to** ~ **on sb** vivre aux crochets de qn.

scrounger ['skraundʒə*] n parasite m.

scrub [skrʌb] n (clean) nettoyage m (à la brosse); (land) broussailles fpl ♦ vt (floor) nettoyer à la brosse; (pan) récurer; (washing) frotter; (reject) annuler.

scrubbing brush ['skrʌbɪŋ-] n brosse dure.

scruff [skrʌf] n: **by the** ~ **of the neck** par la peau du cou.

scruffy ['skrʌfɪ] adj débraillé(e).

scrum(mage) ['skrʌm(ɪdʒ)] n mêlée f.

scruple ['skruːpl] n scrupule m; **to have no** ~**s about doing sth** n'avoir aucun scrupule à faire qch.

scrupulous ['skruːpjuləs] adj scrupuleux(euse).

scrupulously ['skruːpjuləslɪ] adv scrupuleusement; **to be** ~ **honest** être d'une honnêteté scrupuleuse.

scrutinize ['skruːtɪnaɪz] vt scruter, examiner

minutieusement.

scrutiny ['skru:tɪnɪ] n examen minutieux; **under the ~ of sb** sous la surveillance de qn.

scuba ['sku:bə] n scaphandre m (autonome).

scuba diving n plongée sous-marine (autonome).

scuff [skʌf] vt érafler.

scuffle ['skʌfl] n échauffourée f, rixe f.

scull [skʌl] n aviron m.

scullery ['skʌlərɪ] n arrière-cuisine f.

sculptor ['skʌlptə*] n sculpteur m.

sculpture ['skʌlptʃə*] n sculpture f.

scum [skʌm] n écume f, mousse f; (pej: people) rebut m, lie f.

scupper ['skʌpə*] vt (BRIT) saborder.

scurrilous ['skʌrɪləs] adj haineux(euse), virulent(e); calomnieux(euse).

scurry ['skʌrɪ] vi filer à toute allure; **to ~ off** détaler, se sauver.

scurvy ['skə:vɪ] n scorbut m.

scuttle ['skʌtl] n (NAUT) écoutille f; (also: coal ~) seau m (à charbon) ♦ vt (ship) saborder ♦ vi (scamper): **to ~ away, ~ off** détaler.

scythe [saɪð] n faux f.

SD, S. Dak. abbr (US) = South Dakota.

SDI n abbr (= Strategic Defense Initiative) IDS f.

SDLP n abbr (BRIT POL) = Social Democratic and Labour Party

SDP n abbr (BRIT POL) = Social Democratic Party.

sea [si:] n mer f ♦ cpd marin(e), de (la) mer, maritime; **on the ~** (boat) en mer; (town) au bord de la mer; **by or beside the ~** (holiday) au bord de la mer; (village) près de la mer; **by ~** par mer, en bateau; **out to ~** au large; **(out) at ~** en mer; **heavy or rough ~(s)** grosse mer, mer agitée; **a ~ of faces** (fig) une multitude de visages; **to be all at ~** (fig) nager complètement.

sea bed n fond m de la mer.

sea bird n oiseau m de mer.

seaboard ['si:bɔ:d] n côte f.

sea breeze n brise f de mer.

seafarer ['si:fɛərə*] n marin m.

seafaring ['si:fɛərɪŋ] adj (life) de marin; **~ people** les gens mpl de mer.

seafood ['si:fu:d] n fruits mpl de mer.

sea front n bord m de mer.

seagoing ['si:gəʊɪŋ] adj (ship) de haute mer.

seagull ['si:gʌl] n mouette f.

seal [si:l] n (animal) phoque m; (stamp) sceau m, cachet m; (impression) cachet, estampille f ♦ vt sceller; (envelope) coller; (: with seal) cacheter; (decide: sb's fate) décider (de); (: bargain) conclure; **~ of approval** approbation f.

▶**seal off** vt (close) condamner; (forbid entry to) interdire l'accès de.

sea level n niveau m de la mer.

sealing wax ['si:lɪŋ-] n cire f à cacheter.

sea lion n lion m de mer.

sealskin ['si:lskɪn] n peau f de phoque.

seam [si:m] n couture f; (of coal) veine f, filon

m; **the hall was bursting at the ~s** la salle était pleine à craquer.

seaman ['si:mən] n marin m.

seamanship ['si:mənʃɪp] n qualités fpl de marin.

seamless ['si:mlɪs] adj sans couture(s).

seamy ['si:mɪ] adj louche, mal famé(e).

seance ['seɪɔns] n séance f de spiritisme.

seaplane ['si:pleɪn] n hydravion m.

seaport ['si:pɔ:t] n port m de mer.

search [sə:tʃ] n (for person, thing) recherche(s) f(pl); (of drawer, pockets) fouille f; (LAW: at sb's home) perquisition f ♦ vt fouiller; (examine) examiner minutieusement; scruter ♦ vi: **~ for** chercher; **in ~ of** à la recherche de; **"~ and replace"** (COMPUT) "rechercher et remplacer".

▶**search through** vt fus fouiller.

searcher ['sə:tʃə*] n chercheur/euse.

searching ['sə:tʃɪŋ] adj (look, question) pénétrant(e); (examination) minutieux(euse).

searchlight ['sə:tʃlaɪt] n projecteur m.

search party n expédition f de secours.

search warrant n mandat m de perquisition.

searing ['sɪərɪŋ] adj (heat) brûlant(e); (pain) aigu(ë).

seashore ['si:ʃɔ:*] n rivage m, plage f, bord m de (la) mer; **on the ~** sur le rivage.

seasick ['si:sɪk] adj: **to be ~** avoir le mal de mer.

seaside ['si:saɪd] n bord m de la mer.

seaside resort n station f balnéaire.

season ['si:zn] n saison f ♦ vt assaisonner, relever; **to be in/out of ~** être/ne pas être de saison; **the busy ~** (for shops) la période de pointe; (for hotels etc) la pleine saison; **the open ~** (HUNTING) la saison de la chasse.

seasonal ['si:znl] adj saisonnier(ière).

seasoned ['si:znd] adj (wood) séché(e); (fig: worker, actor, troops) expérimenté(e); **a ~ campaigner** un vieux militant, un vétéran.

seasoning ['si:znɪŋ] n assaisonnement m.

season ticket n carte f d'abonnement.

seat [si:t] n siège m; (in bus, train: place) place f; (PARLIAMENT) siège; (buttocks) postérieur m; (of trousers) fond m ♦ vt faire asseoir, placer; (have room for) avoir des places assises pour, pouvoir accueillir; **are there any ~s left?** est-ce qu'il reste des places?; **to take one's ~** prendre place; **to be ~ed** être assis; **please be ~ed** veuillez vous asseoir.

seat belt n ceinture f de sécurité.

seating capacity ['si:tɪŋ-] n nombre m de places assises.

SEATO ['si:təʊ] n abbr (= Southeast Asia Treaty Organization) OTASE f (= Organisation du traité de l'Asie du Sud-Est).

sea urchin n oursin m.

sea water n eau f de mer.

seaweed ['si:wi:d] n algues fpl.

seaworthy ['si:wə:ðɪ] adj en état de naviguer.

SEC n abbr (US: = Securities and Exchange Commission) ≈ COB *f* (= *Commission des opérations de Bourse*).

sec. *abbr* (= *second*) sec.

secateurs [sɛkə'tɜːz] *npl* sécateur *m*.

secede [sɪ'siːd] *vi* faire sécession.

secluded [sɪ'kluːdɪd] *adj* retiré(e), à l'écart.

seclusion [sɪ'kluːʒən] *n* solitude *f*.

second¹ ['sɛkənd] *num* deuxième, second(e) ◊ *adv* (*in race etc*) en seconde position ◊ *n* (*unit of time*) seconde *f*; (*in series, position*) deuxième *m/f*, second/e; (*BRIT SCOL*) ≈ licence *f* avec mention bien *or* assez bien; (*AUT: also:* ~ *gear*) seconde *f*; (*COMM: imperfect*) article *m* de second choix ◊ *vt* (*motion*) appuyer; **Charles the S**~ Charles II; **just a ~!** une seconde!, un instant!; (*stopping sb*) pas si vite!; ~ **floor** (*BRIT*) deuxième (étage) *m*; (*US*) premier (étage) *m*; **to ask for a ~ opinion** (*MED*) demander l'avis d'un autre médecin; **to have ~ thoughts (about doing sth)** changer d'avis (à propos de faire qch); **on ~ thoughts** *or* (*US*) **thought** à la réflexion.

second² [sɪ'kɔnd] *vt* (*employee*) détacher, mettre en détachement.

secondary ['sɛkəndərɪ] *adj* secondaire.

secondary school *n* collège *m*, lycée *m*.

Une **secondary school** *est un établissement d'enseignement pour les élèves de 11 à 18 ans, certains d'entre eux pouvant décider d'arrêter leurs études à 16 ans. La plupart de ces écoles sont des* **comprehensive schools** *sans examen d'entrée; mais certaines sont encore à recrutement sélectif; voir* **primary school**

---

second-best [sɛkənd'bɛst] *n* deuxième choix *m*; **as a ~** faute de mieux.

second-class ['sɛkənd'klɑːs] *adj* de deuxième classe ◊ *adv*: **to send sth ~** envoyer qch à tarif réduit; **to travel ~** voyager en seconde; ~ **citizen** citoyen/ne de deuxième classe.

second cousin *n* cousin/e issu(e) de germains.

seconder ['sɛkəndə*] *n* personne *f* qui appuie une motion.

second-guess ['sɛkənd'gɛs] *vt* (*predict*) (essayer d')anticiper; **they're still trying to ~ his motives** ils essaient toujours de comprendre ses raisons.

second hand *n* (*on clock*) trotteuse *f*.

secondhand ['sɛkənd'hænd] *adj* d'occasion ◊ *adv* (*buy*) d'occasion; **to hear sth ~** apprendre qch indirectement.

second-in-command ['sɛkəndɪnkə'mɑːnd] *n* (*MIL*) commandant *m* en second; (*ADMIN*) adjoint/e, sous-chef *m*.

secondly ['sɛkəndlɪ] *adv* deuxièmement; **firstly ... ~ ...** d'abord ... ensuite ... *or* de plus ...

secondment [sɪ'kɔndmənt] *n* (*BRIT*) détachement *m*.

second-rate ['sɛkənd'reɪt] *adj* de deuxième ordre, de qualité inférieure.

Second World War *n* Deuxième *or* Seconde Guerre mondiale.

secrecy ['siːkrəsɪ] *n* secret *m*; **in ~** en secret, dans le secret.

secret ['siːkrɪt] *adj* secret(ète) ◊ *n* secret *m*; **in ~** en secret, secrètement en cachette; **to keep sth ~ from sb** cacher qch à qn, ne pas révéler qch à qn; **keep it ~** n'en parle à personne; **to make no ~ of sth** ne pas cacher qch.

secret agent *n* agent secret.

secretarial [sɛkrɪ'tɛərɪəl] *adj* de secrétaire, de secrétariat.

secretariat [sɛkrɪ'tɛərɪət] *n* secrétariat *m*.

secretary ['sɛkrətrɪ] *n* secrétaire *m/f*; (*COMM*) secrétaire général; **S~ of State** (*US POL*) ≈ ministre *m* des Affaires étrangères; **S~ of State (for)** (*BRIT POL*) ministre *m* (de).

secretary-general ['sɛkrətrɪ'dʒɛnərl] *n* secrétaire général.

secrete [sɪ'kriːt] *vt* (*ANAT, BIOL, MED*) sécréter; (*hide*) cacher.

secretion [sɪ'kriːʃən] *n* sécrétion *f*.

secretive ['siːkrətɪv] *adj* réservé(e); (*pej*) cachottier(ière), dissimulé(e).

secretly ['siːkrɪtlɪ] *adv* en secret, secrètement, en cachette.

secret police *n* police secrète.

secret service *n* services secrets.

sect [sɛkt] *n* secte *f*.

sectarian [sɛk'tɛərɪən] *adj* sectaire.

section ['sɛkʃən] *n* coupe *f*, section *f*; (*department*) section; (*COMM*) rayon *m*; (*of document*) section, article *m*, paragraphe *m* ◊ *vt* sectionner; **the business etc ~** (*PRESS*) la page des affaires *etc*.

sectional ['sɛkʃənl] *adj* (*drawing*) en coupe.

sector ['sɛktə*] *n* secteur *m*.

secular ['sɛkjulə*] *adj* profane; laïque; séculier(ière).

secure [sɪ'kjuə*] *adj* (*free from anxiety*) sans inquiétude, sécurisé(e); (*firmly fixed*) solide, bien attaché(e) (*or* fermé(e) *etc*); (*in safe place*) en lieu sûr, en sûreté ◊ *vt* (*fix*) fixer, attacher; (*get*) obtenir, se procurer; (*COMM: loan*) garantir; **to make sth ~** bien fixer *or* attacher qch; **to ~ sth for sb** obtenir qch pour qn, procurer qch à qn.

secured creditor [sɪ'kjuəd-] *n* créancier/ière privilégié(e).

security [sɪ'kjuərɪtɪ] *n* sécurité *f*, mesures *fpl* de sécurité; (*for loan*) caution *f*, garantie *f*; **securities** *npl* (*STOCK EXCHANGE*) valeurs *fpl*, titres *mpl*; **to increase** *or* **tighten ~** renforcer les mesures de sécurité; ~ **of tenure** stabilité *f* d'un emploi, titularisation *f*.

Security Council *n*: **the ~** le Conseil de sécurité.

security forces *npl* forces *fpl* de sécurité.

security guard *n* garde chargé de la sécurité; (*transporting money*) convoyeur *m* de fonds.

security risk n menace f pour la sécurité de l'état (or d'une entreprise etc).

secy abbr (= secretary) secr.

sedan [sə'dæn] n (US AUT) berline f.

sedate [sɪ'deɪt] adj calme; posé(e) ♦ vt donner des sédatifs à.

sedation [sɪ'deɪʃən] n (MED) sédation f; **to be under** ~ être sous calmants.

sedative ['sɛdɪtɪv] n calmant m, sédatif m.

sedentary ['sɛdntrɪ] adj sédentaire.

sediment ['sɛdɪmənt] n sédiment m, dépôt m.

sedition [sɪ'dɪʃən] n sédition f.

seduce [sɪ'djuːs] vt séduire.

seduction [sɪ'dʌkʃən] n séduction f.

seductive [sɪ'dʌktɪv] adj séduisant(e), séducteur(trice).

see [siː] vb (pt saw, pp seen [sɔː, siːn]) vt (gen) voir; (accompany): **to** ~ **sb to the door** reconduire or raccompagner qn jusqu'à la porte ♦ vi voir ♦ n évêché m; **to** ~ **that** (ensure) veiller à ce que + sub, faire en sorte que + sub, s'assurer que; **there was nobody to be** ~**n** il n'y avait pas un chat; **let me** ~ (show me) fais(-moi) voir; (let me think) voyons (un peu); **to go and** ~ **sb** aller voir qn; ~ **for yourself** voyez vous-même; **I don't know what she** ~**s in him** je ne sais pas ce qu'elle lui trouve; **as far as I can** ~ pour autant que je puisse en juger; ~ **you!** au revoir!, à bientôt!; ~ **you soon/later/ tomorrow!** à bientôt/plus tard/demain!

▶**see about** vt fus (deal with) s'occuper de.

▶**see off** vt accompagner (à la gare or à l'aéroport etc).

▶**see through** vt mener à bonne fin ♦ vt fus voir clair dans.

▶**see to** vt fus s'occuper de, se charger de.

seed [siːd] n graine f; (fig) germe m; (TENNIS etc) tête f de série; **to go to** ~ monter en graine; (fig) se laisser aller.

seedless ['siːdlɪs] adj sans pépins.

seedling ['siːdlɪŋ] n jeune plant m, semis m.

seedy ['siːdɪ] adj (shabby) minable, miteux(euse).

seeing ['siːɪŋ] conj: ~ **(that)** vu que, étant donné que.

seek, pt, pp **sought** [siːk, sɔːt] vt chercher, rechercher; **to** ~ **advice/help from sb** demander conseil/de l'aide à qn.

▶**seek out** vt (person) chercher.

seem [siːm] vi sembler, paraître; **there** ~**s to be** ... il semble qu'il y a ..., on dirait qu'il y a ...; **it** ~**s (that)** ... il semble que ...; **what** ~**s to be the trouble?** qu'est-ce qui ne va pas?

seemingly ['siːmɪŋlɪ] adv apparemment.

seen [siːn] pp of **see**.

seep [siːp] vi suinter, filtrer.

seer [sɪə*] n prophète/prophétesse, voyant/e.

seersucker ['sɪəsʌkə*] n cloqué m, étoffe cloquée.

seesaw ['siːsɔː] n (jeu m de) bascule f.

seethe [siːð] vi être en effervescence; **to** ~ **with anger** bouillir de colère.

see-through ['siːθruː] adj transparent(e).

segment ['sɛgmənt] n segment m.

segregate ['sɛgrɪgeɪt] vt séparer, isoler.

segregation [sɛgrɪ'geɪʃən] n ségrégation f.

Seine [seɪn] n: **the** ~ la Seine.

seismic ['saɪzmɪk] adj sismique.

seize [siːz] vt (grasp) saisir, attraper; (take possession of) s'emparer de; (LAW) saisir.

▶**seize up** vi (TECH) se gripper.

▶**seize (up)on** vt fus saisir, sauter sur.

seizure ['siːʒə*] n (MED) crise f, attaque f; (LAW) saisie f.

seldom ['sɛldəm] adv rarement.

select [sɪ'lɛkt] adj choisi(e), d'élite; (hotel, restaurant, club) chic inv, sélect inv ♦ vt sélectionner, choisir; **a** ~ **few** quelques privilégiés.

selection [sɪ'lɛkʃən] n sélection f, choix m.

selection committee n comité m de sélection.

selective [sɪ'lɛktɪv] adj sélectif(ive); (school) à recrutement sélectif.

selector [sɪ'lɛktə*] n (person) sélectionneur/ euse; (TECH) sélecteur m.

self [sɛlf] n (pl **selves** [sɛlvz]): **the** ~ le moi inv ♦ prefix auto-.

self-addressed ['sɛlfə'drɛst] adj: ~ **envelope** enveloppe f à mon (or votre etc) nom.

self-adhesive [sɛlfəd'hiːzɪv] adj autocollant(e).

self-assertive [sɛlfə'sə:tɪv] adj autoritaire.

self-assurance [sɛlfə'ʃuərəns] n assurance f.

self-assured [sɛlfə'ʃuəd] adj sûr(e) de soi, plein(e) d'assurance.

self-catering [sɛlf'keɪtərɪŋ] adj (BRIT: flat) avec cuisine, où l'on peut faire sa cuisine; (: holiday) en appartement (or chalet etc) loué.

self-centred, (US) self-centered [sɛlf'sɛntəd] adj égocentrique.

self-cleaning [sɛlf'kliːnɪŋ] adj autonettoyant(e).

self-confessed [sɛlfkən'fɛst] adj (alcoholic etc) déclaré(e), qui ne s'en cache pas.

self-confidence [sɛlf'kɔnfɪdns] n confiance f en soi.

self-conscious [sɛlf'kɔnʃəs] adj timide, qui manque d'assurance.

self-contained [sɛlfkən'teɪnd] adj (BRIT: flat) avec entrée particulière, indépendant(e).

self-control [sɛlfkən'trəul] n maîtrise f de soi.

self-defeating [sɛlfdɪ'fiːtɪŋ] adj qui a un effet contraire à l'effet recherché.

self-defence, (US) self-defense [sɛlfdɪ'fɛns] n légitime défense f.

self-discipline [sɛlf'dɪsɪplɪn] n discipline personnelle.

self-employed [sɛlfɪm'plɔɪd] adj qui travaille à son compte.

self-esteem [sɛlfɪ'stiːm] n amour-propre m.

self-evident [sɛlf'ɛvɪdnt] adj évident(e), qui va de soi.

self-explanatory [sɛlfɪk'splænətrɪ] adj qui se

passe d'explication.

self-governing [sɛlf'gʌvənɪŋ] *adj* autonome.

self-help ['sɛlf'hɛlp] *n* initiative personnelle, efforts personnels.

self-importance [sɛlfɪm'pɔːtns] suffisance *f.*

self-indulgent [sɛlfɪn'dʌldʒənt] *adj* qui ne se refuse rien.

self-inflicted [sɛlfɪn'flɪktɪd] *adj* volontaire.

self-interest [sɛlf'ɪntrɪst] *n* intérêt personnel.

selfish ['sɛlfɪʃ] *adj* égoïste.

selfishness ['sɛlfɪʃnɪs] *n* égoïsme *m.*

selfless ['sɛlflɪs] *adj* désintéressé(e).

selflessly ['sɛlflɪslɪ] *adv* sans penser à soi.

self-made man ['sɛlfmeɪd-] *n* self-made man *m.*

self-pity [sɛlf'pɪtɪ] *n* apitoiement *m* sur soi-même.

self-portrait [sɛlf'pɔːtreɪt] *n* autoportrait *m.*

self-possessed [sɛlfpə'zɛst] *adj* assuré(e).

self-preservation ['sɛlfprɛzə'veɪʃən] *n* instinct *m* de conservation.

self-raising [sɛlf'reɪzɪŋ], (*US*) **self-rising** [sɛlf'raɪzɪŋ] *adj*: ~ **flour** farine *f* pour gâteaux (*avec levure incorporée*).

self-reliant [sɛlfrɪ'laɪənt] *adj* indépendant(e).

self-respect [sɛlfrɪs'pɛkt] *n* respect *m* de soi, amour-propre *m.*

self-respecting [sɛlfrɪs'pɛktɪŋ] *adj* qui se respecte.

self-righteous [sɛlf'raɪtʃəs] *adj* satisfait(e) de soi, pharisaïque.

self-rising [sɛlf'raɪzɪŋ] *adj* (*US*) = **self-raising**.

self-sacrifice [sɛlf'sækrɪfaɪs] *n* abnégation *f.*

self-same ['sɛlfseɪm] *adj* même.

self-satisfied [sɛlf'sætɪsfaɪd] *adj* content(e) de soi, suffisant(e).

self-sealing [sɛlf'siːlɪŋ] *adj* (*envelope*) autocollant(e).

self-service [sɛlf'səːvɪs] *adj, n* libre-service (*m*), self-service (*m*).

self-styled ['sɛlfstaɪld] *adj* soi-disant *inv.*

self-sufficient [sɛlfsə'fɪʃənt] *adj* indépendant(e).

self-supporting [sɛlfsə'pɔːtɪŋ] *adj* financièrement indépendant(e).

self-taught [sɛlf'tɔːt] *adj* autodidacte.

self-test ['sɛlftɛst] *n* (*COMPUT*) test *m* automatique.

sell, *pt, pp* **sold** [sɛl, səʊld] *vt* vendre ♦ *vi* se vendre; **to ~ at** *or* **for 10 F** se vendre 10 F; **to ~ sb an idea** (*fig*) faire accepter une idée à qn.

▶**sell off** *vt* liquider.

▶**sell out** *vi*: **to ~ out (to)** (*COMM*) vendre son fonds *or* son affaire (à) ♦ *vt* vendre tout son stock de; **the tickets are all sold out** il ne reste plus de billets.

▶**sell up** *vi* vendre son fonds *or* son affaire.

sell-by date ['sɛlbaɪ-] *n* date *f* limite de vente.

seller ['sɛlə*] *n* vendeur/euse, marchand/e; **~'s market** marché *m* à la hausse.

selling price ['sɛlɪŋ-] *n* prix *m* de vente.

Sellotape ['sɛləʊteɪp] *n* ® (*BRIT*) papier collant, scotch *m* ®.

sellout ['sɛlaʊt] *n* trahison *f*, capitulation *f*; (*of tickets*): **it was a** ~ tous les billets ont été vendus.

selves [sɛlvz] *npl of* **self**.

semantic [sɪ'mæntɪk] *adj* sémantique.

semantics [sɪ'mæntɪks] *n* sémantique *f.*

semaphore ['sɛməfɔː*] *n* signaux *mpl* à bras; (*RAIL*) sémaphore *m.*

semblance ['sɛmblns] *n* semblant *m.*

semen ['siːmən] *n* sperme *m.*

semester [sɪ'mɛstə*] *n* (*esp US*) semestre *m.*

semi... ['sɛmɪ] *prefix* semi-, demi-; à demi, à moitié ♦ *n*: **semi = semidetached (house)**.

semi-breve ['sɛmɪbriːv] *n* (*BRIT*) ronde *f.*

semicircle ['sɛmɪsəːkl] *n* demi-cercle *m.*

semicircular ['sɛmɪ'səːkjʊlə*] *adj* en demi-cercle, semi-circulaire.

semicolon [sɛmɪ'kəʊlən] *n* point-virgule *m.*

semiconductor [sɛmɪkən'dʌktə*] *n* semiconducteur *m.*

semiconscious [sɛmɪ'kɔnʃəs] *adj* à demi conscient(e).

semidetached (house) [sɛmɪdɪ'tætʃt-] *n* (*BRIT*) maison jumelée *or* jumelle.

semifinal [sɛmɪ'faɪnl] *n* demi-finale *f.*

seminar ['sɛmɪnɑː*] *n* séminaire *m.*

seminary ['sɛmɪnərɪ] *n* (*REL: for priests*) séminaire *m.*

semiprecious [sɛmɪ'prɛʃəs] *adj* semi-précieux(euse).

semiquaver ['sɛmɪkweɪvə*] *n* (*BRIT*) double croche *f.*

semiskilled [sɛmɪ'skɪld] *adj*: ~ **worker** ouvrier/ière spécialisé(e).

semi-skimmed ['sɛmɪ'skɪmd] *adj* demi-écrémé(e).

semitone ['sɛmɪtəʊn] *n* (*MUS*) demi-ton *m.*

semolina [sɛmə'liːnə] *n* semoule *f.*

SEN *n abbr* (*BRIT*) = *State Enrolled Nurse.*

Sen., sen. *abbr* = **senator, senior.**

senate ['sɛnɪt] *n* sénat *m.*

Le **Senate** est la chambre haute du **Congress**, le parlement des États-Unis. Il est composé de 100 sénateurs, 2 par État, élus au suffrage universel direct tous les 6 ans, un tiers d'entre eux étant renouvelé tous les 2 ans.

senator ['sɛnɪtə*] *n* sénateur *m.*

send, *pt, pp* **sent** [sɛnd, sɛnt] *vt* envoyer; **to ~ by post** *or* (*US*) **mail** envoyer *or* expédier par la poste; **to ~ sb for sth** envoyer qn chercher qch; **to ~ word that ...** faire dire que ...; **she ~s (you) her love** elle vous adresse ses amitiés; **to ~ sb to Coventry** (*BRIT*) mettre qn en quarantaine; **to ~ sb to sleep** endormir qn; **to ~ sb into fits of laughter** faire rire qn aux éclats; **to ~ sth flying** envoyer valser qch.

▶**send away** *vt* (*letter, goods*) envoyer, expédier.

▶**send away for** *vt fus* commander par correspondance, se faire envoyer.

▶**send back** *vt* renvoyer.

▶**send for** *vt fus* envoyer chercher; faire venir; (*by post*) se faire envoyer, commander par correspondance.

▶**send in** *vt* (*report, application, resignation*) remettre.

▶**send off** *vt* (*goods*) envoyer, expédier; (*BRIT SPORT: player*) expulser *or* renvoyer du terrain.

▶**send on** *vt* (*BRIT: letter*) faire suivre; (*luggage etc: in advance*) (faire) expédier à l'avance.

▶**send out** *vt* (*invitation*) envoyer (par la poste); (*emit: light, heat, signals*) émettre.

▶**send round** *vt* (*letter, document etc*) faire circuler.

▶**send up** *vt* (*person, price*) faire monter; (*BRIT: parody*) mettre en boîte, parodier.

sender ['sɛndə*] *n* expéditeur/trice.

send-off ['sɛndɔf] *n*: **a good ~** des adieux chaleureux.

Senegal [sɛnɪ'gɔːl] *n* Sénégal *m*.

Senegalese [sɛnɪgə'liːz] *adj* sénégalais(e) ♦ *n* (*pl inv*) Sénégalais/e.

senile ['siːnaɪl] *adj* sénile.

senility [sɪ'nɪlɪtɪ] *n* sénilité *f*.

senior ['siːnɪə*] *adj* (*older*) aîné(e), plus âgé(e); (*of higher rank*) supérieur(e) ♦ *n* aîné/e; (*in service*) personne *f* qui a plus d'ancienneté; **P. Jones ~** P. Jones père.

senior citizen *n* personne âgée.

senior high school *n* (*US*) ≈ lycée *m*.

seniority [siːnɪ'ɔrɪtɪ] *n* priorité *f* d'âge, ancienneté *f*; (*in rank*) supériorité *f* (hiérarchique).

sensation [sɛn'seɪʃən] *n* sensation *f*; **to create a ~** faire sensation.

sensational [sɛn'seɪʃənl] *adj* qui fait sensation; (*marvellous*) sensationnel(le).

sense [sɛns] *n* sens *m*; (*feeling*) sentiment *m*; (*meaning*) signification *f*; (*wisdom*) bon sens ♦ *vt* sentir, pressentir; **~s** *npl* raison *f*; **it makes ~** c'est logique; **~ of humour** sens de l'humour; **there is no ~ in (doing) that** cela n'a pas de sens; **to come to one's ~s** (*regain consciousness*) reprendre conscience; (*become reasonable*) revenir à la raison; **to take leave of one's ~s** perdre la tête.

senseless ['sɛnslɪs] *adj* insensé(e), stupide; (*unconscious*) sans connaissance.

sensibility [sɛnsɪ'bɪlɪtɪ] *n* sensibilité *f*; **sensibilities** *npl* susceptibilité *f*.

sensible ['sɛnsɪbl] *adj* sensé(e), raisonnable; (*shoes etc*) pratique.

sensitive ['sɛnsɪtɪv] *adj*: **~ (to)** sensible (à); **he is very ~ about it** c'est un point très sensible (chez lui).

sensitivity [sɛnsɪ'tɪvɪtɪ] *n* sensibilité *f*.

sensual ['sɛnsjuəl] *adj* sensuel(le).

sensuous ['sɛnsjuəs] *adj* voluptueux(euse),

sensuel(le).

sent [sɛnt] *pt, pp of* **send**.

sentence ['sɛntns] *n* (*LING*) phrase *f*; (*LAW: judgment*) condamnation *f*, sentence *f*; (*: punishment*) peine *f* ♦ *vt*: **to ~ sb to death/to 5 years** condamner qn à mort/à 5 ans; **to pass ~ on sb** prononcer une peine contre qn.

sentiment ['sɛntɪmənt] *n* sentiment *m*; (*opinion*) opinion *f*, avis *m*.

sentimental [sɛntɪ'mɛntl] *adj* sentimental(e).

sentimentality [sɛntɪmɛn'tælɪtɪ] *n* sentimentalité *f*, sensiblerie *f*.

sentry ['sɛntrɪ] *n* sentinelle *f*, factionnaire *m*.

sentry duty *n*: **to be on ~** être de faction.

Seoul [səul] *n* Séoul.

separable ['sɛprəbl] *adj* séparable.

separate *adj* ['sɛprɪt] séparé(e), indépendant(e), différent(e) ♦ *vb* ['sɛpəreɪt] *vt* séparer ♦ *vi* se séparer; **~ from** se distinct(e) de; **under ~ cover** (*COMM*) sous pli séparé; **to ~ into** diviser en.

separately ['sɛprɪtlɪ] *adv* séparément.

separates ['sɛprɪts] *npl* (*clothes*) coordonnés *mpl*.

separation [sɛpə'reɪʃən] *n* séparation *f*.

Sept. *abbr* (= *September*) sept.

September [sɛp'tɛmbə*] *n* septembre *m*; *for phrases see also* **July**.

septic ['sɛptɪk] *adj* septique; (*wound*) infecté(e); **to go ~** s'infecter.

septicaemia [sɛptɪ'siːmɪə] *n* septicémie *f*.

septic tank *n* fosse *f* septique.

sequel ['siːkwl] *n* conséquence *f*, séquelles *fpl*; (*of story*) suite *f*.

sequence ['siːkwəns] *n* ordre *m*, suite *f*; **in ~** par ordre, dans l'ordre, les uns après les autres; **~ of tenses** concordance *f* des temps.

sequential [sɪ'kwɛnʃəl] *adj*: **~ access** (*COMPUT*) accès séquentiel.

sequin ['siːkwɪn] *n* paillette *f*.

Serb [səːb] *adj, n* = **Serbian**.

Serbia ['səːbɪə] *n* Serbie *f*.

Serbian ['səːbɪən] *adj* serbe ♦ *n* Serbe *m/f*; (*LING*) serbe *m*.

Serbo-Croat ['səːbəu'krəuæt] *n* (*LING*) serbo-croate *m*.

serenade [sɛrə'neɪd] *n* sérénade *f* ♦ *vt* donner une sérénade à.

serene [sɪ'riːn] *adj* serein(e), calme, paisible.

serenity [sə'rɛnɪtɪ] *n* sérénité *f*, calme *m*.

sergeant ['saːdʒənt] *n* sergent *m*; (*POLICE*) brigadier *m*.

sergeant major *n* sergent-major *m*.

serial ['sɪərɪəl] *n* feuilleton *m* ♦ *adj* (*COMPUT: interface, printer*) série *inv*; (*: access*) séquentiel(le).

serialize ['sɪərɪəlaɪz] *vt* publier (*or* adapter) en feuilleton.

serial killer *n* meurtrier *m* tuant en série.

serial number *n* numéro *m* de série.

series ['sɪərɪz] *n* série *f*; (*PUBLISHING*) collection *f*.

serious ['sɪərɪəs] *adj* sérieux(euse); (*accident etc*) grave; **are you ~ (about it?)** parlez-vous sérieusement?

seriously ['sɪərɪəslɪ] *adv* sérieusement, gravement; **~ rich/difficult** (*col: extremely*) drôlement riche/difficile; **to take sth/sb ~** prendre qch/qn au sérieux.

seriousness ['sɪərɪəsnɪs] *n* sérieux *m*, gravité *f*.

sermon ['sɜːmən] *n* sermon *m*.

serrated [sɪ'reɪtɪd] *adj* en dents de scie.

serum ['sɪərəm] *n* sérum *m*.

servant ['sɜːvənt] *n* domestique *m/f*; (*fig*) serviteur/servante.

serve [sɜːv] *vt* (*employer etc*) servir, être au service de; (*purpose*) servir à; (*customer, food, meal*) servir; (*apprenticeship*) faire, accomplir; (*prison term*) faire; purger ♦ *vi* (*also TENNIS*) servir; (*be useful*): **to ~ as/for/to do** servir de/à/à faire ♦ *n* (*TENNIS*) service *m*; **are you being ~d?** est-ce qu'on s'occupe de vous?; **to ~ on a committee/jury** faire partie d'un comité/jury; **it ~s him right** c'est bien fait pour lui; **it ~s my purpose** cela fait mon affaire.

►**serve out, serve up** *vt* (*food*) servir.

service ['sɜːvɪs] *n* (*gen*) service *m*; (*AUT: maintenance*) révision *f*; (*REL*) office *m* ♦ *vt* (*car, washing machine*) réviser; **the S~s** *npl* les forces armées; **to be of ~ to sb, to do sb a ~** rendre service à qn; **to put one's car in for ~** donner sa voiture à réviser; **dinner ~** service de table.

serviceable ['sɜːvɪsəbl] *adj* pratique, commode.

service area *n* (*on motorway*) aire *f* de services.

service charge *n* (*BRIT*) service *m*.

service industries *npl* les industries *fpl* de service, les services *mpl*.

serviceman ['sɜːvɪsmən] *n* militaire *m*.

service station *n* station-service *f*.

serviette [sɜːvɪ'et] *n* (*BRIT*) serviette *f* (de table).

servile ['sɜːvaɪl] *adj* servile.

session ['seʃən] *n* (*sitting*) séance *f*; (*SCOL*) année *f* scolaire (*or* universitaire); **to be in ~** siéger, être en session *or* en séance.

session musician *n* musicien/ne de studio.

set [set] *n* série *f*, assortiment *m*; (*of tools etc*) jeu *m*; (*RADIO, TV*) poste *m*; (*TENNIS*) set *m*; (*group of people*) cercle *m*, milieu *m*; (*CINE*) plateau *m*; (*THEAT: stage*) scène *f*; (*: scenery*) décor *m*; (*MATH*) ensemble *m*; (*HAIRDRESSING*) mise *f* en plis ♦ *adj* (*fixed*) fixe, déterminé(e); (*ready*) prêt(e) ♦ *vb* (*pt, pp* **set**) *vt* (*place*) mettre, poser, placer; (*fix, establish*) fixer; (*: record*) établir; (*assign: task, homework*) donner; (*adjust*) régler; (*decide: rules etc*) fixer, choisir; (*TYP*) composer ♦ *vi* (*sun*) se coucher; (*jam, jelly, concrete*) prendre; **to be**

~ on doing être résolu(e) à faire; **to be all ~ to do** être (fin) prêt(e) pour faire; **to be (dead) ~ against** être (totalement) opposé à; **he's ~ in his ways** il n'est pas très souple, il tient à ses habitudes; **to ~ to music** mettre en musique; **to ~ on fire** mettre le feu à; **to ~ free** libérer; **to ~ sth going** déclencher qch; **to ~ the alarm clock for 7 o'clock** mettre le réveil à sonner à sept heures; **to ~ sail** partir, prendre la mer; **a ~ phrase** une expression toute faite, une locution; **a ~ of false teeth** un dentier; **a ~ of dining-room furniture** une salle à manger.

►**set about** *vt fus* (*task*) entreprendre, se mettre à; **to ~ about doing sth** se mettre à faire qch.

►**set aside** *vt* mettre de côté.

►**set back** *vt* (*in time*): **to ~ back (by)** retarder (de); (*place*): **a house ~ back from the road** une maison située en retrait de la route.

►**set in** *vi* (*infection, bad weather*) s'installer; (*complications*) survenir, surgir; **the rain has ~ in for the day** c'est parti pour qu'il pleuve toute la journée.

►**set off** *vi* se mettre en route, partir ♦ *vt* (*bomb*) faire exploser; (*cause to start*) déclencher; (*show up well*) mettre en valeur, faire valoir.

►**set out** *vi*: **to ~ out to do** entreprendre de faire; avoir pour but *or* intention de faire ♦ *vt* (*arrange*) disposer; (*state*) présenter, exposer; **to ~ out (from)** partir (de).

►**set up** *vt* (*organization*) fonder, constituer; (*monument*) ériger; **to ~ up shop** (*fig*) s'établir, s'installer.

setback ['setbæk] *n* (*hitch*) revers *m*, contretemps *m*; (*in health*) rechute *f*.

set menu *n* menu *m*.

set square *n* équerre *f*.

settee [se'tiː] *n* canapé *m*.

setting ['setɪŋ] *n* cadre *m*; (*of jewel*) monture *f*.

setting lotion *n* lotion *f* pour mise en plis.

settle ['setl] *vt* (*argument, matter, account*) régler; (*problem*) résoudre; (*MED: calm*) calmer; (*colonize: land*) coloniser ♦ *vi* (*bird, dust etc*) se poser; (*sediment*) se déposer; (*also: ~ down*) s'installer, se fixer; (*: become calmer*) se calmer; se ranger; **to ~ to sth** se mettre sérieusement à qch; **to ~ for sth** accepter qch, se contenter de qch; **to ~ on sth** opter *or* se décider pour qch; **that's ~d then** alors, c'est d'accord!; **to ~ one's stomach** calmer des maux d'estomac.

►**settle in** *vi* s'installer.

►**settle up** *vi*: **to ~ up with sb** régler (ce que l'on doit à) qn.

settlement ['setlmənt] *n* (*payment*) règlement *m*; (*agreement*) accord *m*; (*colony*) colonie *f*; (*village etc*) établissement *m*; hameau *m*; **in ~ of our account** (*COMM*) en règlement de notre compte.

settler ['setlə*] *n* colon *m*.

setup ['sɛtʌp] n (arrangement) manière f dont les choses sont organisées; (situation) situation f, allure f des choses.

seven ['sɛvn] num sept.

seventeen [sɛvn'tiːn] num dix-sept.

seventh ['sɛvnθ] num septième.

seventy ['sɛvntɪ] num soixante-dix.

sever ['sɛvə*] vt couper, trancher; (relations) rompre.

several ['sɛvərl] adj, pron plusieurs (m/fpl); ~ **of us** plusieurs d'entre nous; ~ **times** plusieurs fois.

severance ['sɛvərəns] n (of relations) rupture f.

severance pay n indemnité f de licenciement.

severe [sɪ'vɪə*] adj sévère, strict(e); (serious) grave, sérieux(euse); (hard) rigoureux(euse), dur(e); (plain) sévère, austère.

severely [sɪ'vɪəlɪ] adv sévèrement; (wounded, ill) gravement.

severity [sɪ'vɛrɪtɪ] n sévérité f; gravité f; rigueur f.

sew, pt sewed, pp sewn [səu, səud, səun] vt, vi coudre.

▶**sew up** vt (re)coudre; **it is all sewn up** (fig) c'est dans le sac or dans la poche.

sewage ['suːɪdʒ] n vidange(s) f(pl).

sewage works n champ m d'épandage.

sewer ['suːə*] n égout m.

sewing ['səuɪŋ] n couture f.

sewing machine n machine f à coudre.

sewn [səun] pp of **sew**.

sex [sɛks] n sexe m; **to have** ~ **with** avoir des rapports (sexuels) avec.

sex act n acte sexuel.

sex appeal n sex-appeal m.

sex education n éducation sexuelle.

sexism ['sɛksɪzəm] n sexisme m.

sexist ['sɛksɪst] adj sexiste.

sex life n vie sexuelle.

sex object n femme-objet f, objet sexuel.

sextet [sɛks'tɛt] n sextuor m.

sexual ['sɛksjuəl] adj sexuel(le); ~ **assault** attentat m à la pudeur; ~ **harassment** harcèlement sexuel; ~ **intercourse** rapports sexuels.

sexy ['sɛksɪ] adj sexy inv.

Seychelles [seɪ'ʃɛl(z)] npl: **the** ~ **les** Seychelles fpl.

SF n abbr (= science fiction) SF f.

SG n abbr (US) = **Surgeon General**.

Sgt abbr (= sergeant) Sgt.

shabbiness ['ʃæbɪnɪs] n aspect miteux; mesquinerie f.

shabby ['ʃæbɪ] adj miteux(euse); (behaviour) mesquin(e), méprisable.

shack [ʃæk] n cabane f, hutte f.

shackles ['ʃæklz] npl chaînes fpl, entraves fpl.

shade [ʃeɪd] n ombre f; (for lamp) abat-jour m inv; (of colour) nuance f, ton m; (US: window ~) store m; (small quantity): **a** ~ **of** un soupçon de ♦ vt abriter du soleil, ombrager; ~**s** npl (US: sunglasses) lunettes fpl de soleil; **in the** ~ à l'ombre; **a** ~ **smaller** un tout petit peu plus petit.

shadow ['ʃædəu] n ombre f ♦ vt (follow) filer; **without** or **beyond a** ~ **of doubt** sans l'ombre d'un doute.

shadow cabinet n (BRIT POL) cabinet parallèle formé par le parti qui n'est pas au pouvoir.

shadowy ['ʃædəuɪ] adj ombragé(e); (dim) vague, indistinct(e).

shady ['ʃeɪdɪ] adj ombragé(e); (fig: dishonest) louche, véreux(euse).

shaft [ʃɑːft] n (of arrow, spear) hampe f; (AUT, TECH) arbre m; (of mine) puits m; (of lift) cage f; (of light) rayon m, trait m; **ventilator** ~ conduit m d'aération or de ventilation.

shaggy ['ʃægɪ] adj hirsute; en broussaille.

shake [ʃeɪk] vb (pt **shook**, pp **shaken** [ʃuk, 'ʃeɪkn]) vt secouer; (bottle, cocktail) agiter; (house, confidence) ébranler ♦ vi trembler ♦ n secousse f; **to** ~ **one's head** (in refusal etc) dire or faire non de la tête; (in dismay) secouer la tête; **to** ~ **hands with sb** serrer la main à qn.

▶**shake off** vt secouer; (fig) se débarrasser de.

▶**shake up** vt secouer.

shake-up ['ʃeɪkʌp] n grand remaniement.

shakily ['ʃeɪkɪlɪ] adv (reply) d'une voix tremblante; (walk) d'un pas mal assuré; (write) d'une main tremblante.

shaky ['ʃeɪkɪ] adj (hand, voice) tremblant(e); (building) branlant(e), peu solide; (memory) chancelant(e); (knowledge) incertain(e).

shale [ʃeɪl] n schiste argileux.

shall [ʃæl] aux vb: **I** ~ **go** j'irai.

shallot [ʃə'lɔt] n (BRIT) échalote f.

shallow ['ʃæləu] adj peu profond(e); (fig) superficiel(le), qui manque de profondeur.

sham [ʃæm] n frime f; (jewellery, furniture) imitation f ♦ adj feint(e), simulé(e) ♦ vt feindre, simuler.

shambles ['ʃæmblz] n confusion f, pagaïe f, fouillis m; **the economy is (in) a complete** ~ l'économie est dans la confusion la plus totale.

shambolic [ʃæm'bɔlɪk] adj (col) bordélique.

shame [ʃeɪm] n honte f ♦ vt faire honte à; **it is a** ~ **(that/to do)** c'est dommage (que + sub/de faire); **what a** ~! quel dommage!; **to put sb/sth to** ~ (fig) faire honte à qn/qch.

shamefaced ['ʃeɪmfeɪst] adj honteux(euse), penaud(e).

shameful ['ʃeɪmful] adj honteux(euse), scandaleux(euse).

shameless ['ʃeɪmlɪs] adj éhonté(e), effronté(e); (immodest) impudique.

shampoo [ʃæm'puː] n shampooing m ♦ vt faire un shampooing à; ~ **and set** shampooing et mise f en plis.

shamrock ['ʃæmrɔk] n trèfle m (emblème national de l'Irlande).

shandy ['ʃændɪ] n bière panachée.

shan't [ʃɑːnt] = **shall not.**

shantytown ['ʃæntɪtaun] n bidonville m.

SHAPE [ʃeɪp] n abbr (= Supreme Headquarters Allied Powers, Europe) quartier général des forces alliées en Europe.

shape [ʃeɪp] n forme f ♦ vt façonner, modeler; (clay, stone) donner forme à; (statement) formuler; (sb's ideas, character) former; (sb's life) déterminer; (course of events) influer sur le cours de ♦ vi (also: ~ up: events) prendre tournure; (: person) faire des progrès, s'en sortir; **to take ~** prendre forme or tournure; **in the ~ of a heart** en forme de cœur; **I can't bear gardening in any ~ or form** je déteste le jardinage sous quelque forme que ce soit; **to get o.s. into ~** (re)trouver la forme.

-shaped [ʃeɪpt] suffix: **heart-~** en forme de cœur.

shapeless ['ʃeɪplɪs] adj informe, sans forme.

shapely ['ʃeɪplɪ] adj bien proportionné(e), beau(belle).

share [ʃɛə*] n (thing received, contribution) part f; (COMM) action f ♦ vt partager; (have in common) avoir en commun; **to ~ out (among or between)** partager (entre); **to ~ in** (joy, sorrow) prendre part à; (profits) participer à, avoir part à; (work) partager.

share capital n capital social.

share certificate n certificat m or titre m d'action.

shareholder ['ʃɛəhəuldə*] n actionnaire m/f.

share index n indice m de la Bourse.

shark [ʃɑːk] n requin m.

sharp [ʃɑːp] adj (razor, knife) tranchant(e), bien aiguisé(e); (point) aigu(ë); (nose, chin) pointu(e); (outline) net(te); (curve, bend) brusque; (cold, pain) vif(vive); (MUS) dièse; (voice) coupant(e); (person: quick-witted) vif(vive), éveillé(e); (: unscrupulous) malhonnête ♦ n (MUS) dièse m ♦ adv: **at 2 o'clock ~** à 2 heures pile or tapantes; **turn ~ left** tournez immédiatement à gauche; **to be ~ with sb** être brusque avec qn; **look ~!** dépêche-toi!

sharpen ['ʃɑːpn] vt aiguiser; (pencil) tailler; (fig) aviver.

sharpener ['ʃɑːpnə*] n (also: **pencil ~**) taille-crayon(s) m inv; (also: **knife ~**) aiguisoir m.

sharp-eyed [ʃɑːp'aɪd] adj à qui rien n'échappe.

sharpish ['ʃɑːpɪʃ] adv (BRIT col: quickly) en vitesse.

sharply ['ʃɑːplɪ] adv (abruptly) brusquement; (clearly) nettement; (harshly) sèchement, vertement.

sharp-tempered [ʃɑːp'tempəd] adj prompt(e) à se mettre en colère.

sharp-witted [ʃɑːp'wɪtɪd] adj à l'esprit vif, malin(igne).

shatter ['ʃætə*] vt fracasser, briser, faire voler en éclats; (fig: upset) bouleverser; (: ruin) briser, ruiner ♦ vi voler en éclats, se briser, se fracasser.

shattered ['ʃætəd] adj (overwhelmed, grief-stricken) bouleversé(e); (col: exhausted) éreinté(e).

shatterproof ['ʃætəpruːf] adj incassable.

shave [ʃeɪv] vt raser ♦ vi se raser ♦ n: **to have a ~** se raser.

shaven ['ʃeɪvn] adj (head) rasé(e).

shaver ['ʃeɪvə*] n (also: **electric ~**) rasoir m électrique.

shaving ['ʃeɪvɪŋ] n (action) rasage m; **~s** npl (of wood etc) copeaux mpl.

shaving brush n blaireau m.

shaving cream n crème f à raser.

shaving soap n savon m à barbe.

shawl [ʃɔːl] n châle m.

she [ʃiː] pron elle; **there ~ is** la voilà; **~-elephant** etc éléphant m etc femelle; NB: for ships, countries follow the gender of your translation.

sheaf, pl **sheaves** [ʃiːf, ʃiːvz] n gerbe f.

shear [ʃɪə*] vt (pt ~ed, pp ~ed or shorn [ʃɔːn]) (sheep) tondre.

▶**shear off** vt tondre; (branch) élaguer.

shears ['ʃɪəz] npl (for hedge) cisaille(s) f(pl).

sheath [ʃiːθ] n gaine f, fourreau m, étui m; (contraceptive) préservatif m.

sheathe [ʃiːð] vt gainer; (sword) rengainer.

sheath knife n couteau m à gaine.

sheaves [ʃiːvz] npl of **sheaf.**

shed [ʃed] n remise f, resserre f; (INDUSTRY, RAIL) hangar m ♦ vt (pt, pp shed) (leaves, fur etc) perdre; (tears) verser, répandre; **to ~ light on** (problem, mystery) faire la lumière sur.

she'd [ʃiːd] = **she had, she would.**

sheen [ʃiːn] n lustre m.

sheep [ʃiːp] n (pl inv) mouton m.

sheepdog ['ʃiːpdɔg] n chien m de berger.

sheep farmer n éleveur m de moutons.

sheepish ['ʃiːpɪʃ] adj penaud(e), timide.

sheepskin ['ʃiːpskɪn] n peau f de mouton.

sheepskin jacket n canadienne f.

sheer [ʃɪə*] adj (utter) pur(e), pur et simple; (steep) à pic, abrupt(e); (almost transparent) extrêmement fin(e) ♦ adv à pic, abruptement; **by ~ chance** par pur hasard.

sheet [ʃiːt] n (on bed) drap m; (of paper) feuille f; (of glass, metal) feuille, plaque f.

sheet feed n (on printer) alimentation f en papier (feuille à feuille).

sheet lightning n éclair m en nappe(s).

sheet metal n tôle f.

sheet music n partition(s) f(pl).

sheik(h) [ʃeɪk] n cheik m.

shelf, pl **shelves** [ʃelf, ʃelvz] n étagère f, rayon m; **set of shelves** rayonnage m.

shelf life n (COMM) durée f de conservation (avant la vente).

shell [ʃel] n (on beach) coquillage m; (of egg,

nut etc) coquille f; (explosive) obus m; (of building) carcasse f ♦ vt (crab, prawn etc) décortiquer; (peas) écosser; (MIL) bombarder (d'obus).

►**shell out** vi (col): **to ~ out (for)** casquer (pour).

she'll [ʃiːl] = **she will, she shall.**

shellfish ['ʃɛlfɪʃ] n (pl inv) (crab etc) crustacé m; (scallop etc) coquillage m; (pl: as food) crustacés; coquillages.

shellsuit ['ʃɛlsuːt] n survêtement m.

shelter ['ʃɛltə*] n abri m, refuge m ♦ vt abriter, protéger; (give lodging to) donner asile à ♦ vi s'abriter, se mettre à l'abri; **to take ~ (from)** s'abriter (de).

sheltered ['ʃɛltəd] adj (life) retiré(e), à l'abri des soucis; (spot) abrité(e).

shelve [ʃɛlv] vt (fig) mettre en suspens or en sommeil.

shelves ['ʃɛlvz] npl of **shelf.**

shelving ['ʃɛlvɪŋ] n (shelves) rayonnage(s) m(pl).

shepherd ['ʃɛpəd] n berger m ♦ vt (guide) guider, escorter.

shepherdess ['ʃɛpədɪs] n bergère f.

shepherd's pie ['ʃɛpədz-] n ≈ hachis m Parmentier.

sherbet ['ʃəːbət] n (BRIT: powder) poudre acidulée; (US: water ice) sorbet m.

sheriff ['ʃɛrɪf] n shérif m.

sherry ['ʃɛrɪ] n xérès m, sherry m.

she's [ʃiːz] = **she is, she has.**

Shetland ['ʃɛtlənd] n (also: **the ~s, the ~ Isles** or **Islands**) les îles fpl Shetland.

Shetland pony n poney m des îles Shetland.

shield [ʃiːld] n bouclier m ♦ vt: **to ~ (from)** protéger (de or contre).

shift [ʃɪft] n (change) changement m; (of workers) équipe f, poste m ♦ vt déplacer, changer de place; (remove) enlever ♦ vi changer de place, bouger; **the wind has ~ed to the south** le vent a tourné au sud; **a ~ in demand** (COMM) un déplacement de la demande.

shift key n (on typewriter) touche f de majuscule.

shiftless ['ʃɪftlɪs] adj fainéant(e).

shift work n travail m par roulement; **to do ~** travailler par roulement.

shifty ['ʃɪftɪ] adj sournois(e); (eyes) fuyant(e).

Shiite ['ʃiːaɪt] n Chiite m/f ♦ adj chiite.

shilling ['ʃɪlɪŋ] n (BRIT) shilling m (= 12 old pence; 20 in a pound).

shilly-shally ['ʃɪlɪʃælɪ] vi tergiverser, atermoyer.

shimmer ['ʃɪmə*] n miroitement m, chatoiement m ♦ vi miroiter, chatoyer.

shin [ʃɪn] n tibia m ♦ vi: **to ~ up/down a tree** grimper dans l'arbre/descendre d'un arbre.

shindig ['ʃɪndɪg] n (col) bamboula f.

shine [ʃaɪn] n éclat m, brillant m ♦ vb (pt, pp **shone** [ʃɔn]) vi briller ♦ vt faire briller or re-

luire; (torch): **to ~ on** braquer sur.

shingle ['ʃɪŋgl] n (on beach) galets mpl; (on roof) bardeau m.

shingles ['ʃɪŋglz] n (MED) zona m.

shining ['ʃaɪnɪŋ] adj brillant(e).

shiny ['ʃaɪnɪ] adj brillant(e).

ship [ʃɪp] n bateau m; (large) navire m ♦ vt transporter (par mer); (send) expédier (par mer); (load) charger, embarquer; **on board ~** à bord.

shipbuilder ['ʃɪpbɪldə*] n constructeur m de navires.

shipbuilding ['ʃɪpbɪldɪŋ] n construction navale.

ship canal n canal m maritime or de navigation.

ship chandler [-'tʃɑːndlə*] n fournisseur m maritime, shipchandler m.

shipment ['ʃɪpmənt] n cargaison f.

shipowner ['ʃɪpəunə*] n armateur m.

shipper ['ʃɪpə*] n affréteur m, expéditeur m.

shipping ['ʃɪpɪŋ] n (ships) navires mpl; (traffic) navigation f.

shipping agent n agent m maritime.

shipping company n compagnie f de navigation.

shipping lane n couloir m de navigation.

shipping line n = **shipping company.**

shipshape ['ʃɪpʃeɪp] adj en ordre impeccable.

shipwreck ['ʃɪprɛk] n épave f; (event) naufrage m ♦ vt: **to be ~ed** faire naufrage.

shipyard ['ʃɪpjɑːd] n chantier naval.

shire ['ʃaɪə*] n (BRIT) comté m.

shirk [ʃəːk] vt esquiver, se dérober à.

shirt [ʃəːt] n chemise f; **in ~ sleeves** en bras de chemise.

shirty ['ʃəːtɪ] adj (BRIT col) de mauvais poil.

shit [ʃɪt] excl (col!) merde (!).

shiver ['ʃɪvə*] n frisson m ♦ vi frissonner.

shoal [ʃəul] n (of fish) banc m.

shock [ʃɔk] n (impact) choc m, heurt m; (ELEC) secousse f, décharge f; (emotional) choc; (MED) commotion f, choc ♦ vt (scandalize) choquer, scandaliser; (upset) bouleverser; **suffering from ~** (MED) commotionné(e); **it gave us a ~** ça nous a fait un choc; **it came as a ~ to hear that ...** nous avons appris avec stupeur que ....

shock absorber [-əbzɔːbə*] n amortisseur m.

shocker ['ʃɔkə*] n (col): **the news was a real ~ to him** il a vraiment été choqué par cette nouvelle.

shocking ['ʃɔkɪŋ] adj choquant(e), scandaleux(euse); (weather, handwriting) épouvantable.

shockproof ['ʃɔkpruːf] adj anti-choc inv.

shock therapy, shock treatment n (MED) (traitement m par) électrochoc(s) m(pl).

shock wave n (also fig) onde f de choc.

shod [ʃɔd] pt, pp of **shoe; well-~** bien chaussé(e).

shoddy ['ʃɔdɪ] adj de mauvaise qualité, mal

fait(e).

shoe [ʃuː] n chaussure f, soulier m; (also: **horse~**) fer m à cheval; (also: **brake ~**) mâchoire f de frein ♦ vt (pt, pp **shod** [ʃɔd]) (horse) ferrer.

shoebrush [ˈʃuːbrʌʃ] n brosse f à chaussures.

shoehorn [ˈʃuːhɔːn] n chausse-pied m.

shoelace [ˈʃuːleɪs] n lacet m (de soulier).

shoemaker [ˈʃuːmeɪkə*] n cordonnier m, fabricant m de chaussures.

shoe polish n cirage m.

shoeshop [ˈʃuːʃɔp] n magasin m de chaussures.

shoestring [ˈʃuːstrɪŋ] n: **on a ~** (fig) avec un budget dérisoire; avec des moyens très restreints.

shoetree [ˈʃuːtriː] n embauchoir m.

shone [ʃɔn] pt, pp of **shine**.

shoo [ʃuː] excl (allez,) ouste! ♦ vt (also: ~ **away**, ~ **off**) chasser.

shook [ʃuk] pt of **shake**.

shoot [ʃuːt] n (on branch, seedling) pousse f; (shooting party) partie f de chasse ♦ vb (pt, pp **shot** [ʃɔt]) vt (game: BRIT) chasser; tirer; abattre; (person) blesser (or tuer) d'un coup de fusil (or de revolver); (execute) fusiller; (CINE) tourner ♦ vi (with gun, bow): **to ~ (at)** tirer (sur); (FOOTBALL) shooter, tirer; **to ~ past sb** passer en flèche devant qn; **to ~ in/out** entrer/sortir comme une flèche.

▶**shoot down** vt (plane) abattre.

▶**shoot up** vi (fig) monter en flèche.

shooting [ˈʃuːtɪŋ] n (shots) coups mpl de feu; (attack) fusillade f; (: murder) homicide m (à l'aide d'une arme à feu); (HUNTING) chasse f; (CINE) tournage m.

shooting range n stand m de tir.

shooting star n étoile filante.

shop [ʃɔp] n magasin m; (workshop) atelier m ♦ vi (also: **go ~ping**) faire ses courses or ses achats; **repair ~** atelier de réparations; **to talk ~** (fig) parler boutique.

▶**shop around** vi faire le tour des magasins (pour comparer les prix); (fig) se renseigner avant de choisir or décider.

shopaholic [ʃɔpəˈhɔlɪk] n (col) personne qui achète sans pouvoir s'arrêter.

shop assistant n (BRIT) vendeur/euse.

shop floor n (BRIT: fig) ouvriers mpl.

shopkeeper [ˈʃɔpkiːpə*] n marchand/e, commerçant/e.

shoplift [ˈʃɔplɪft] vi voler à l'étalage.

shoplifter [ˈʃɔplɪftə*] n voleur/euse à l'étalage.

shoplifting [ˈʃɔplɪftɪŋ] n vol m à l'étalage.

shopper [ˈʃɔpə*] n personne f qui fait ses courses, acheteur/euse.

shopping [ˈʃɔpɪŋ] n (goods) achats mpl, provisions fpl.

shopping bag n sac m (à provisions).

shopping centre n centre commercial.

shopping mall n centre commercial.

shop-soiled [ˈʃɔpsɔɪld] adj défraîchi(e), qui a fait la vitrine.

shop steward n (BRIT INDUSTRY) délégué/e syndical(e).

shop window n vitrine f.

shore [ʃɔː*] n (of sea, lake) rivage m, rive f ♦ vt: **to ~ (up)** étayer; **on ~** à terre.

shore leave n (NAUT) permission f à terre.

shorn [ʃɔːn] pp of **shear** ♦ adj: ~ **of** dépouillé(e) de.

short [ʃɔːt] adj (not long) court(e); (soon finished) court, bref(brève); (person, step) petit(e); (curt) brusque, sec(sèche); (insufficient) insuffisant(e) ♦ n (also: ~ **film**) court métrage; **to be ~ of sth** être à court de or manquer de qch; **to be in ~ supply** manquer, être difficile à trouver; **I'm 3 ~** il m'en manque 3; **in ~** bref; en bref; ~ **of doing** à moins de faire; **everything ~ of** tout sauf; **it is ~ for** c'est l'abréviation or le diminutif de; **a ~ time ago** il y a peu de temps; **in the ~ term** à court terme; **to cut ~** (speech, visit) abréger, écourter; (person) couper la parole à; **to fall ~ of** ne pas être à la hauteur de; **to stop ~** s'arrêter net; **to stop ~ of** ne pas aller jusqu'à.

shortage [ˈʃɔːtɪdʒ] n manque m, pénurie f.

shortbread [ˈʃɔːtbred] n ≈ sablé m.

short-change [ʃɔːtˈtʃeɪndʒ] vt: **to ~ sb** ne pas rendre assez à qn.

short-circuit [ʃɔːtˈsəːkɪt] n court-circuit m ♦ vt court-circuiter ♦ vi se mettre en court-circuit.

shortcoming [ˈʃɔːtkʌmɪŋ] n défaut m.

short(crust) pastry [ˈʃɔːt(krʌst)-] n (BRIT) pâte brisée.

shortcut [ˈʃɔːtkʌt] n raccourci m.

shorten [ˈʃɔːtn] vt raccourcir; (text, visit) abréger.

shortening [ˈʃɔːtnɪŋ] n (CULIN) matière grasse.

shortfall [ˈʃɔːtfɔːl] n déficit m.

shorthand [ˈʃɔːthænd] n (BRIT) sténo(graphie) f; **to take sth down in ~** prendre qch en sténo.

shorthand notebook n bloc m sténo.

shorthand typist n (BRIT) sténodactylo m/f.

short list n (BRIT: for job) liste f des candidats sélectionnés.

short-lived [ˈʃɔːtˈlɪvd] adj de courte durée.

shortly [ˈʃɔːtlɪ] adv bientôt, sous peu.

shortness [ˈʃɔːtnɪs] n brièveté f.

shorts [ʃɔːts] npl (also: **a pair of ~**) un short.

short-sighted [ˈʃɔːtˈsaɪtɪd] adj (BRIT) myope; (fig) qui manque de clairvoyance.

short-staffed [ˈʃɔːtˈstɑːft] adj à court de personnel.

short story n nouvelle f.

short-tempered [ˈʃɔːtˈtempəd] adj qui s'emporte facilement.

short-term [ˈʃɔːttəːm] adj (effect) à court terme.

short time *n*: **to work ~, to be on ~** (*IN-DUSTRY*) être en chômage partiel, travailler à horaire réduit.

short wave *n* (*RADIO*) ondes courtes.

shot [ʃɔt] *pt, pp of* **shoot** ♦ *n* coup *m* (de feu); (*shotgun pellets*) plombs *mpl*; (*person*) tireur *m*; (*try*) coup, essai *m*; (*injection*) piqûre *f*; (*PHOT*) photo *f*; **to fire a ~ at sb/sth** tirer sur qn/qch; **to have a ~ at (doing) sth** essayer de faire qch; **like a ~** comme une flèche; (*very readily*) sans hésiter; **to get ~ of sb/sth** (*col*) se débarrasser de qn/qch; **a big ~** (*col*) un gros bonnet.

shotgun [ʃɔtɡʌn] *n* fusil *m* de chasse.

should [ʃud] *aux vb*: **I ~ go now** je devrais partir maintenant; **he ~ be there now** il devrait être arrivé maintenant; **I ~ go if I were you** si j'étais vous j'irais; **I ~ like to** j'aimerais bien, volontiers; **~ he phone ...** si jamais il téléphone ....

shoulder [ʃəuldə*] *n* épaule *f*; (*BRIT: of road*): **hard ~** accotement *m* ♦ *vt* (*fig*) endosser, se charger de; **to look over one's ~** regarder derrière soi (en tournant la tête); **to rub ~s with sb** (*fig*) côtoyer qn; **to give sb the cold ~** (*fig*) battre froid à qn.

shoulder bag *n* sac *m* à bandoulière.

shoulder blade *n* omoplate *f*.

shoulder strap *n* bretelle *f*.

shouldn't [ʃudnt] = **should not**.

shout [ʃaut] *n* cri *m* ♦ *vt* crier ♦ *vi* crier, pousser des cris; **to give sb a ~** appeler qn.

▶**shout down** *vt* huer.

shouting [ʃautɪŋ] *n* cris *mpl*.

shouting match *n* (*col*) engueulade *f*, empoignade *f*.

shove [ʃʌv] *vt* pousser; (*col: put*): **to ~ sth in** fourrer *or* ficher qch dans ♦ *n* poussée *f*; **he ~d me out of the way** il m'a écarté en me poussant.

▶**shove off** *vi* (*NAUT*) pousser au large; (*fig: col*) ficher le camp.

shovel [ʃʌvl] *n* pelle *f* ♦ *vt* pelleter, enlever (*or* enfourner) à la pelle.

show [ʃəu] *n* (*of emotion*) manifestation *f*, démonstration *f*; (*semblance*) semblant *m*, apparence *f*; (*exhibition*) exposition *f*, salon *m*; (*THEAT*) spectacle *m*, représentation *f*; (*CINE*) séance *f* ♦ *vb* (*pt* **~ed**, *pp* **shown** [ʃəun]) *vt* montrer; (*courage etc*) faire preuve de, manifester; (*exhibit*) exposer ♦ *vi* se voir, être visible; **to ask for a ~ of hands** demander que l'on vote à main levée; **to be on ~** être exposé(e); **it's just for ~** c'est juste pour l'effet; **who's running the ~ here?** (*col*) qui est-ce qui commande ici?; **to ~ sb to his seat/to the door** accompagner qn jusqu'à sa place/la porte; **to ~ a profit/ loss** (*COMM*) indiquer un bénéfice/une perte; **it just goes to ~ that ...** ça prouve bien que ....

▶**show in** *vt* faire entrer.

▶**show off** *vi* (*pej*) crâner ♦ *vt* (*display*) faire valoir; (*pej*) faire étalage de.

▶**show out** *vt* reconduire à la porte.

▶**show up** *vi* (*stand out*) ressortir; (*col: turn up*) se montrer ♦ *vt* démontrer; (*unmask*) démasquer, dénoncer.

showbiz [ʃəubɪz] *n* (*col*) showbiz *m*.

show business *n* le monde du spectacle.

showcase [ʃəukeɪs] *n* vitrine *f*.

showdown [ʃəudaun] *n* épreuve *f* de force.

shower [ʃauə*] *n* (*also:* **~ bath**) douche *f*; (*rain*) averse *f*; (*of stones etc*) pluie *f*, grêle *f*; (*US: party*) réunion organisée pour la remise de cadeaux ♦ *vi* prendre une douche, se doucher ♦ *vt*: **to ~ sb with** (*gifts etc*) combler qn de; (*abuse etc*) accabler qn de; (*missiles*) bombarder qn de; **to have** *or* **take a ~** prendre une douche, se doucher.

shower cap *n* bonnet *m* de douche.

showerproof [ʃauəpruːf] *adj* imperméable.

showery [ʃauərɪ] *adj* (*weather*) pluvieux(euse).

showground [ʃəugraund] *n* champ *m* de foire.

showing [ʃəuɪŋ] *n* (*of film*) projection *f*.

show jumping [-dʒʌmpɪŋ] *n* concours *m* hippique.

showman [ʃəumən] *n* (*at fair, circus*) forain *m*; (*fig*) comédien *m*.

showmanship [ʃəumənʃɪp] *n* art *m* de la mise en scène.

shown [ʃəun] *pp of* **show**.

show-off [ʃəuɔf] *n* (*col: person*) crâneur/euse, m'as-tu-vu/e.

showpiece [ʃəupiːs] *n* (*of exhibition etc*) joyau *m*, clou *m*; **that hospital is a ~** cet hôpital est un modèle du genre.

showroom [ʃəurum] *n* magasin *m or* salle *f* d'exposition.

show trial *n* grand procès *m* médiatique (*qui fait un exemple*).

showy [ʃəuɪ] *adj* tapageur(euse).

shrank [ʃræŋk] *pt of* **shrink**.

shrapnel [ʃræpnl] *n* éclats *mpl* d'obus.

shred [ʃred] *n* (*gen pl*) lambeau *m*, petit morceau; (*fig: of truth, evidence*) parcelle *f* ♦ *vt* mettre en lambeaux, déchirer; (*documents*) détruire; (*CULIN*) râper; couper en lanières.

shredder [ʃredə*] *n* (*for vegetables*) râpeur *m*; (*for documents, papers*) déchiqueteuse *f*.

shrewd [ʃruːd] *adj* astucieux(euse), perspicace.

shrewdness [ʃruːdnɪs] *n* perspicacité *f*.

shriek [ʃriːk] *n* cri perçant *or* aigu, hurlement *m* ♦ *vt, vi* hurler, crier.

shrift [ʃrɪft] *n*: **to give sb short ~** expédier qn sans ménagements.

shrill [ʃrɪl] *adj* perçant(e), aigu(ë), strident(e).

shrimp [ʃrɪmp] *n* crevette grise.

shrine [ʃraɪn] *n* châsse *f*; (*place*) lieu *m* de pèlerinage.

shrink, *pt* **shrank**, *pp* **shrunk** [ʃrɪŋk, ʃræŋk, ʃrʌŋk] *vi* rétrécir; (*fig*) se réduire; se con-

tracter ♦ vt (wool) (faire) rétrécir ♦ n (col:
pej) psychanalyste m/f; **to ~ from (doing) sth**
reculer devant (la pensée de faire) qch.

shrinkage ['ʃrɪŋkɪdʒ] n (of clothes) rétrécissement m.

shrink-wrap ['ʃrɪŋkræp] vt emballer sous film
plastique.

shrivel ['ʃrɪvl] (also: ~ **up**) vt ratatiner, flétrir
♦ vi se ratatiner, se flétrir.

shroud [ʃraud] n linceul m ♦ vt: ~**ed in mystery**
enveloppé(e) de mystère.

Shrove Tuesday ['ʃrəuv-] n (le) Mardi gras.

shrub [ʃrʌb] n arbuste m.

shrubbery ['ʃrʌbərɪ] n massif m d'arbustes.

shrug [ʃrʌg] n haussement m d'épaules ♦ vt, vi:
to ~ (one's shoulders) hausser les épaules.

►**shrug off** vt faire fi de; (cold, illness) se débarrasser de.

shrunk [ʃrʌŋk] pp of **shrink**.

shrunken ['ʃrʌŋkn] adj ratatiné(e).

shudder ['ʃʌdə*] n frisson m, frémissement m
♦ vi frissonner, frémir.

shuffle ['ʃʌfl] vt (cards) battre; **to ~ (one's
feet)** traîner les pieds.

shun [ʃʌn] vt éviter, fuir.

shunt [ʃʌnt] vt (RAIL: direct) aiguiller; (: divert)
détourner ♦ vi: **to ~ (to and fro)** faire la navette.

shunting yard ['ʃʌntɪŋ-] n voies fpl de garage
or de triage.

shush [ʃuʃ] excl chut!

shut, pt, pp **shut** [ʃʌt] vt fermer ♦ vi (se) fermer.

►**shut down** vt fermer définitivement;
(machine) arrêter ♦ vi fermer définitivement.

►**shut off** vt couper, arrêter.

►**shut out** vt (person, cold) empêcher
d'entrer; (noise) éviter d'entendre; (block:
view) boucher; (: memory of sth) chasser de
son esprit.

►**shut up** vi (col: keep quiet) se taire ♦ vt
(close) fermer; (silence) faire taire.

shutdown ['ʃʌtdaun] n fermeture f.

shutter ['ʃʌtə*] n volet m; (PHOT) obturateur
m.

shuttle ['ʃʌtl] n navette f; (also: ~ **service**)
(service m de) navette f ♦ vi (vehicle, person)
faire la navette ♦ vt (passengers) transporter
par un système de navette.

shuttlecock ['ʃʌtlkɔk] n volant m (de badminton).

shuttle diplomacy n navettes fpl diplomatiques.

shy [ʃaɪ] adj timide; **to fight ~ of** se dérober
devant; **to be ~ of doing sth** hésiter à faire
qch, ne pas oser faire qch ♦ vi: **to ~ away
from doing sth** (fig) craindre de faire qch.

shyness ['ʃaɪnɪs] n timidité f.

Siam [saɪ'æm] n Siam m.

Siamese [saɪə'miːz] adj: ~ **cat** chat siamois
mpl; ~ **twins** (frères mpl) siamois mpl, (sœurs

fpl) siamoises fpl.

Siberia [saɪ'bɪərɪə] n Sibérie f.

siblings ['sɪblɪŋz] npl (formal) enfants mpl d'un
même couple.

Sicilian [sɪ'sɪlɪən] adj sicilien(ne) ♦ n Sicilien/
ne.

Sicily ['sɪsɪlɪ] n Sicile f.

sick [sɪk] adj (ill) malade; (vomiting): **to be ~**
vomir; (humour) noir(e), macabre; **to feel ~**
avoir envie de vomir, avoir mal au cœur; **to
fall ~** tomber malade; **to be (off) ~** être ab-
sent(e) pour cause de maladie; **a ~ person**
un(e) malade; **to be ~ of** (fig) en avoir assez
de.

sickbag ['sɪkbæg] n sac m vomitoire.

sick bay n infirmerie f.

sick building syndrome n maladie dûe à la
climatisation, l'éclairage artificiel etc des
bureaux.

sicken ['sɪkn] vt écœurer ♦ vi: **to be ~ing for**
sth (cold, flu etc) couver qch.

sickening ['sɪknɪŋ] adj (fig) écœurant(e), ré-
voltant(e), répugnant(e).

sickle ['sɪkl] n faucille f.

sick leave n congé m de maladie.

sickle-cell anaemia ['sɪklsɛl-] n anémie f à
hématies falciformes, drépanocytose f.

sickly ['sɪklɪ] adj maladif(ive), souffre-
teux(euse); (causing nausea) écœurant(e).

sickness ['sɪknɪs] n maladie f; (vomiting) vo-
missement(s) m(pl).

sickness benefit n (prestations fpl de
l')assurance-maladie f.

sick pay n indemnité f de maladie (versée par
l'employeur).

sickroom ['sɪkruːm] n infirmerie f.

side [saɪd] n côté m; (of animal) flanc m; (of lake,
road) bord m; (of mountain) versant m; (fig:
aspect) côté, aspect m; (team: SPORT) équipe f
♦ cpd (door, entrance) latéral(e) ♦ vi: **to ~ with**
sb prendre le parti de qn, se ranger du côté
de qn; **by the ~ of** au bord de; ~ **by** ~ côte à
côte; **the right/ wrong** ~ le bon/mauvais
côté, l'endroit/l'envers m; **they are on our** ~
ils sont avec nous; **from all** ~**s** de tous côtés;
to take ~**s (with)** prendre parti (pour); **a** ~
of beef ≈ un quartier de bœuf.

sideboard ['saɪdbɔːd] n buffet m.

sideboards ['saɪdbɔːdz] (BRIT), **sideburns**
['saɪdbɜːnz] npl (whiskers) pattes fpl.

sidecar ['saɪdkɑː*] n side-car m.

side dish n (plat m d')accompagnement m.

side drum n (MUS) tambour plat, caisse
claire.

side effect n (MED) effet m secondaire.

sidekick ['saɪdkɪk] n (col) sous-fifre m.

sidelight ['saɪdlaɪt] n (AUT) veilleuse f.

sideline ['saɪdlaɪn] n (SPORT) (ligne f de)
touche f; (fig) activité f secondaire.

sidelong ['saɪdlɔŋ] adj: **to give sb a** ~ **glance**
regarder qn du coin de l'œil.

side plate n petite assiette f.

side road n petite route, route transversale.
sidesaddle ['saɪdsædl] adv en amazone.
side show n attraction f.
sidestep ['saɪdstɛp] vt (question) éluder; (problem) éviter ♦ vi (BOXING etc) esquiver.
side street n rue transversale.
sidetrack ['saɪdtræk] vt (fig) faire dévier de son sujet.
sidewalk ['saɪdwɔːk] n (US) trottoir m.
sideways ['saɪdweɪz] adv de côté.
siding ['saɪdɪŋ] n (RAIL) voie f de garage.
sidle ['saɪdl] vi: **to ~ up (to)** s'approcher furtivement (de).
SIDS [sɪdz] n abbr (= sudden infant death syndrome) mort subite du nourrisson, mort f au berceau.
siege [siːdʒ] n siège m; **to lay ~ to** assiéger.
siege economy n économie f de (temps de) siège.
Sierra Leone [sɪˈɛrəlɪˈəun] n Sierra Leone f.
sieve [sɪv] n tamis m, passoire f ♦ vt tamiser, passer (au tamis).
sift [sɪft] vt passer au tamis or au crible; (fig) passer au crible ♦ vi (fig): **to ~ through** passer en revue.
sigh [saɪ] n soupir m ♦ vi soupirer, pousser un soupir.
sight [saɪt] n (faculty) vue f; (spectacle) spectacle m; (on gun) mire f ♦ vt apercevoir; **in ~** visible; (fig) en vue; **out of ~** hors de vue; **at ~** (COMM) à vue; **at first ~** à première vue, au premier abord; **I know her by ~** je la connais de vue; **to catch ~ of sb/sth** apercevoir qn/qch; **to lose ~ of sb/sth** perdre qn/qch de vue; **to set one's ~s on sth** jeter son dévolu sur qch.
sighted ['saɪtɪd] adj qui voit; **partially ~** qui a un certain degré de vision.
sightseeing ['saɪtsiːɪŋ] n tourisme m; **to go ~** faire du tourisme.
sightseer ['saɪtsiːə*] n touriste m/f.
sign [saɪn] n (gen) signe m; (with hand etc) signe, geste m; (notice) panneau m, écriteau m; (also: **road ~**) panneau m de signalisation ♦ vt signer; **as a ~ of** en signe de; **it's a good/bad ~** c'est bon/mauvais signe; **plus/minus ~** signe plus/moins; **there's no ~ of a change of mind** rien ne laisse présager un revirement; **he was showing ~s of improvement** il commençait visiblement à faire des progrès; **to ~ one's name** signer.
▶**sign away** vt (rights etc) renoncer officiellement à.
▶**sign in** vi signer le registre (en arrivant).
▶**sign off** vi (RADIO, TV) terminer l'émission.
▶**sign on** vi (MIL) s'engager; (as unemployed) s'inscrire au chômage; (enrol): **to ~ on for a course** s'inscrire pour un cours ♦ vt (MIL) engager; (employee) embaucher.
▶**sign out** vi signer le registre (en partant).
▶**sign over** vt: **to ~ sth over to sb** céder qch par écrit à qn.

▶**sign up** (MIL) vt engager ♦ vi s'engager.
signal ['sɪgnl] n signal m ♦ vi (AUT) mettre son clignotant ♦ vt (person) faire signe à; (message) communiquer par signaux; **to ~ a left/right turn** (AUT) indiquer or signaler que l'on tourne à gauche/droite; **to ~ to sb (to do sth)** faire signe à qn (de faire qch).
signal box n (RAIL) poste m d'aiguillage.
signalman ['sɪgnlmən] n (RAIL) aiguilleur m.
signatory ['sɪgnətərɪ] n signataire m/f.
signature ['sɪgnətʃə*] n signature f.
signature tune n indicatif musical.
signet ring ['sɪgnət-] n chevalière f.
significance [sɪgˈnɪfɪkəns] n signification f; importance f; **that is of no ~** ceci n'a pas d'importance.
significant [sɪgˈnɪfɪkənt] adj significatif(ive); (important) important(e), considérable.
significantly [sɪgˈnɪfɪkəntlɪ] adv (improve, increase) sensiblement; (smile) d'un air entendu, éloquemment; **~, ...** fait significatif, ...
signify ['sɪgnɪfaɪ] vt signifier.
sign language n langage m par signes.
signpost ['saɪnpəust] n poteau indicateur.
silage ['saɪlɪdʒ] n (fodder) fourrage vert; (method) ensilage m.
silence ['saɪlns] n silence m ♦ vt faire taire, réduire au silence.
silencer ['saɪlənsə*] n (on gun, BRIT AUT) silencieux m.
silent ['saɪlnt] adj silencieux(euse); (film) muet(te); **to keep** or **remain ~** garder le silence, ne rien dire.
silently ['saɪlntlɪ] adv silencieusement.
silent partner n (COMM) bailleur m de fonds, commanditaire m.
silhouette [sɪluːˈet] n silhouette f ♦ vt: **~d against** se profilant sur, se découpant contre.
silicon ['sɪlɪkən] n silicium m.
silicon chip n puce f électronique.
silicone ['sɪlɪkəun] n silicone f.
silk [sɪlk] n soie f ♦ cpd de or en soie.
silky ['sɪlkɪ] adj soyeux(euse).
sill [sɪl] n (also: **window~**) rebord m (de la fenêtre); (of door) seuil m; (AUT) bas m de marche.
silly ['sɪlɪ] adj stupide, sot(te), bête; **to do something ~** faire une bêtise.
silo ['saɪləu] n silo m.
silt [sɪlt] n vase f; limon m.
silver ['sɪlvə*] n argent m; (money) monnaie f (en pièces d'argent); (also: **~ware**) argenterie f ♦ cpd d'argent, en argent.
silver paper (BRIT), **silver foil** n papier m d'argent or d'étain.
silver-plated [sɪlvəˈpleɪtɪd] adj plaqué(e) argent.
silversmith ['sɪlvəsmɪθ] n orfèvre m/f.
silverware ['sɪlvəwɛə*] n argenterie f.
silver wedding (anniversary) n noces fpl d'argent.

silvery ['sɪlvrɪ] *adj* argenté(e).
similar ['sɪmɪlə*] *adj*: ~ **(to)** semblable (à).
similarity [sɪmɪ'lærɪtɪ] *n* ressemblance *f*, similarité *f*.
similarly ['sɪmɪləlɪ] *adv* de la même façon, de même.
simile ['sɪmɪlɪ] *n* comparaison *f*.
simmer ['sɪmə*] *vi* cuire à feu doux, mijoter.
▶**simmer down** *vi* (*fig: col*) se calmer.
simper ['sɪmpə*] *vi* minauder.
simpering ['sɪmprɪŋ] *adj* stupide.
simple ['sɪmpl] *adj* simple; **the** ~ **truth** la vérité pure et simple.
simple interest *n* (*MATH, COMM*) intérêts *mpl* simples.
simple-minded [sɪmpl'maɪndɪd] *adj* simplet(te), simple d'esprit.
simpleton ['sɪmpltən] *n* nigaud/e, niais/e.
simplicity [sɪm'plɪsɪtɪ] *n* simplicité *f*.
simplification [sɪmplɪfɪ'keɪʃən] *n* simplification *f*.
simplify ['sɪmplɪfaɪ] *vt* simplifier.
simply ['sɪmplɪ] *adv* simplement; (*without fuss*) avec simplicité.
simulate ['sɪmjuleɪt] *vt* simuler, feindre.
simulation [sɪmju'leɪʃən] *n* simulation *f*.
simultaneous [sɪməl'teɪnɪəs] *adj* simultané(e).
simultaneously [sɪməl'teɪnɪəslɪ] *adv* simultanément.
sin [sɪn] *n* péché *m* ♦ *vi* pécher.
Sinai ['saɪneɪaɪ] *n* Sinaï *m*.
since [sɪns] *adv*, *prep* depuis ♦ *conj* (*time*) depuis que; (*because*) puisque, étant donné que, comme; ~ **then** depuis c̀e moment-là; ~ **Monday** depuis lundi; **(ever)** ~ **I arrived** depuis mon arrivée, depuis que je suis arrivé.
sincere [sɪn'sɪə*] *adj* sincère.
sincerely [sɪn'sɪəlɪ] *adv* sincèrement; **Yours** ~ (*at end of letter*) veuillez agréer, Monsieur (*or* Madame), l'expression de mes sentiments distingués *or* les meilleurs.
sincerity [sɪn'sɛrɪtɪ] *n* sincérité *f*.
sine [saɪn] *n* (*MATH*) sinus *m*.
sinew ['sɪnjuː] *n* tendon *m*; ~**s** *npl* muscles *mpl*.
sinful ['sɪnful] *adj* coupable.
sing, *pt* **sang,** *pp* **sung** [sɪŋ, sæŋ, sʌŋ] *vt*, *vi* chanter.
Singapore [sɪŋgə'pɔː*] *n* Singapour *m*.
singe [sɪndʒ] *vt* brûler légèrement; (*clothes*) roussir.
singer ['sɪŋə*] *n* chanteur/euse.
Singhalese [sɪŋə'liːz] *adj* = **Sinhalese**.
singing ['sɪŋɪŋ] *n* (*of person, bird*) chant *m*; façon *f* de chanter; (*of kettle, bullet, in ears*) sifflement *m*.
single ['sɪŋgl] *adj* seul(e), unique; (*unmarried*) célibataire; (*not double*) simple ♦ *n* (*BRIT: also*: ~ **ticket**) aller *m* (simple); (*record*) 45 tours *m*; **not a** ~ **one was left** il n'en est pas resté un(e) seul(e); **every** ~ **day** chaque jour sans exception.
▶**single out** *vt* choisir; distinguer.

single bed *n* lit *m* à une place.
single-breasted ['sɪŋglbrɛstɪd] *adj* droit(e).
Single European Market *n*: **the** ~ le marché unique européen.
single file *n*: **in** ~ en file indienne.
single-handed [sɪŋgl'hændɪd] *adv* tout(e) seul(e), sans (aucune) aide.
single-minded [sɪŋgl'maɪndɪd] *adj* résolu(e), tenace.
single parent *n* parent unique (*or* célibataire).
single room *n* chambre *f* à un lit *or* pour une personne.
singles ['sɪŋglz] *npl* (*TENNIS*) simple *m*; (*US: single people*) célibataires *m/fpl*.
singles bar *n* (*esp US*) bar *m* de rencontres pour célibataires.
single-sex school [sɪŋgl'sɛks-] *n* école *f* non mixte.
singlet ['sɪŋglɪt] *n* tricot *m* de corps.
singly ['sɪŋglɪ] *adv* séparément.
singsong ['sɪŋsɔŋ] *adj* (*tone*) chantant(e) ♦ *n* (*songs*): **to have a** ~ chanter quelque chose (ensemble).
singular ['sɪŋgjulə*] *adj* singulier(ière); (*odd*) singulier, étrange; (*LING*) (au) singulier, du singulier ♦ *n* (*LING*) singulier *m*; **in the feminine** ~ au féminin singulier.
singularly ['sɪŋgjuləlɪ] *adv* singulièrement; étrangement.
Sinhalese [sɪnhə'liːz] *adj* cingalais(e).
sinister ['sɪnɪstə*] *adj* sinistre.
sink [sɪŋk] *n* évier *m* ♦ *vb* (*pt* **sank**, *pp* **sunk** [sæŋk, sʌŋk]) *vt* (*ship*) (faire) couler, faire sombrer; (*foundations*) creuser; (*piles etc*): **to** ~ **sth into** enfoncer qch dans ♦ *vi* couler, sombrer; (*ground etc*) s'affaisser; **he sank into a chair/the mud** il s'est enfoncé dans un fauteuil/la boue; **a** ~**ing feeling** un serrement de cœur.
▶**sink in** *vi* s'enfoncer, pénétrer; (*explanation*): **it took a long time to** ~ **in** il a fallu longtemps pour que ça rentre.
sinking ['sɪŋkɪŋ] *adj*: **that** ~ **feeling** un serrement de cœur.
sinking fund *n* fonds *mpl* d'amortissement.
sink unit *n* bloc-évier *m*.
sinner ['sɪnə*] *n* pécheur/eresse.
Sinn Féin [ʃɪn'feɪn] *n* Sinn Féin *m* (*parti politique irlandais qui soutient l'IRA*).
Sino- ['saɪnəu] *prefix* sino-.
sinuous ['sɪnjuəs] *adj* sinueux(euse).
sinus ['saɪnəs] *n* (*ANAT*) sinus *m inv*.
sip [sɪp] *n* petite gorgée ♦ *vt* boire à petites gorgées.
siphon ['saɪfən] *n* siphon *m* ♦ *vt* (*also*: ~ **off**) siphonner; (: *fig: funds*) transférer; (: *illegally*) détourner.
sir [sə*] *n* monsieur *m*; **S**~ **John Smith** sir John Smith; **yes** ~ oui Monsieur; **Dear S**~ (*in letter*) Monsieur.
siren ['saɪərn] *n* sirène *f*.

sirloin ['sə:lɔɪn] n aloyau m.
sirloin steak n bifteck m dans l'aloyau.
sirocco [sɪ'rɔkəʊ] n sirocco m.
sisal ['saɪsəl] n sisal m.
sissy ['sɪsɪ] n (col: coward) poule mouillée.
sister ['sɪstə*] n sœur f; (nun) religieuse f, (bonne) sœur, (BRIT: nurse) infirmière f en chef ♦ cpd: ~ **organization** organisation f sœur; ~ **ship** sister(-)ship m.
sister-in-law ['sɪstərɪnlɔ:] n belle-sœur f.
sit [sɪt] pt, pp **sat** [sɪt, sæt] vi s'asseoir; (assembly) être en séance, siéger; (for painter) poser; (dress etc) tomber ♦ vt (exam) passer, se présenter à; **to** ~ **on a committee** faire partie d'un comité; **to** ~ **tight** ne pas bouger.
▶**sit about, sit around** vi être assis(e) or rester à ne rien faire.
▶**sit back** vi (in seat) bien s'installer, se carrer.
▶**sit down** vi s'asseoir; **to be ~ting down** être assis(e).
▶**sit in** vi: **to** ~ **in on a discussion** assister à une discussion.
▶**sit up** vi s'asseoir; (not go to bed) rester debout, ne pas se coucher.
sitcom ['sɪtkɔm] n abbr (TV: = situation comedy) série f comique.
sit-down ['sɪtdaʊn] adj: **a** ~ **strike** une grève sur le tas; **a** ~ **meal** un repas assis.
site [saɪt] n emplacement m, site m; (also: **building** ~) chantier m ♦ vt placer.
sit-in ['sɪtɪn] n (demonstration) sit-in m inv, occupation f de locaux.
siting ['saɪtɪŋ] n (location) emplacement m.
sitter ['sɪtə*] n (for painter) modèle m; (also: **baby~**) baby-sitter m/f.
sitting ['sɪtɪŋ] n (of assembly etc) séance f; (in canteen) service m.
sitting member n (POL) parlementaire m/f en exercice.
sitting room n salon m.
sitting tenant n (BRIT) locataire occupant(e).
situate ['sɪtjʊeɪt] vt situer.
situated ['sɪtjʊeɪtɪd] adj situé(e).
situation [sɪtjʊ'eɪʃən] n situation f; **"~s vacant/wanted"** (BRIT) "offres/demandes d'emploi".
situation comedy n (THEAT) comédie f de situation.
six [sɪks] num six.
six-pack ['sɪkspæk] n (esp US) pack m de six canettes.
sixteen [sɪks'ti:n] num seize.
sixth ['sɪksθ] adj sixième; **the upper/lower** ~ (BRIT SCOL) la terminale/la première.
sixty ['sɪkstɪ] num soixante.
size [saɪz] n dimensions fpl; (of person) taille f; (of estate, area) étendue f; (of problem) ampleur f; (of company) importance f; (of clothing) taille f; (of shoes) pointure f; (glue) colle f; **I take** ~ **14** (of dress etc) ≈ je prends du 42 or la taille 42; **the small/large** ~ (of soap pow-der etc) le petit/grand modèle; **it's the** ~ **of ...** c'est de la taille (or grosseur) de ..., c'est grand (or gros) comme ...; **cut to** ~ découpé(e) aux dimensions voulues.
▶**size up** vt juger, jauger.
sizeable ['saɪzəbl] adj assez grand(e) or gros(se); assez important(e).
sizzle ['sɪzl] vi grésiller.
SK abbr (Canada) = Saskatchewan.
skate [skeɪt] n patin m; (fish: pl inv) raie f ♦ vi patiner.
▶**skate over, skate around** vt (problem, issue) éluder.
skateboard ['skeɪtbɔ:d] n skateboard m, planche f à roulettes.
skater ['skeɪtə*] n patineur/euse.
skating ['skeɪtɪŋ] n patinage m.
skating rink n patinoire f.
skeleton ['skelɪtn] n squelette m; (outline) schéma m.
skeleton key n passe-partout m.
skeleton staff n effectifs réduits.
skeptic etc ['skeptɪk] (US) = **sceptic** etc.
sketch [sketʃ] n (drawing) croquis m, esquisse f; (THEAT) sketch m, saynète f ♦ vt esquisser, faire un croquis or une esquisse de.
sketch book n carnet m à dessin.
sketch pad n bloc m à dessin.
sketchy ['sketʃɪ] adj incomplet(ète), fragmentaire.
skew [skju:] n (BRIT): **on the** ~ de travers, en biais.
skewer ['skju:ə*] n brochette f.
ski [ski:] n ski m ♦ vi skier, faire du ski.
ski boot n chaussure f de ski.
skid [skɪd] n dérapage m ♦ vi déraper; **to go into a** ~ déraper.
skid mark n trace f de dérapage.
skier ['ski:ə*] n skieur/euse.
skiing ['ski:ɪŋ] n ski m; **to go** ~ (aller) faire du ski.
ski instructor n moniteur/trice de ski.
ski jump n (ramp) tremplin m; (event) saut m à skis.
skilful, (US) **skillful** ['skɪlful] adj habile, adroit(e).
ski lift n remonte-pente m inv.
skill [skɪl] n (ability) habileté f, adresse f, talent m; (art, craft) technique(s) f(pl), compétences fpl.
skilled [skɪld] adj habile, adroit(e); (worker) qualifié(e).
skillet ['skɪlɪt] n poêlon m.
skillful etc ['skɪlful] (US) = **skilful** etc.
skil(l)fully ['skɪlfəlɪ] adv habilement, adroitement.
skim [skɪm] vt (milk) écrémer; (soup) écumer; (glide over) raser, effleurer ♦ vi: **to** ~ **through** (fig) parcourir.
skimmed milk [skɪmd-] n lait écrémé.
skimp [skɪmp] vt (work) bâcler, faire à la vavite; (cloth etc) lésiner sur.

skimpy ['skɪmpɪ] *adj* étriqué(e); maigre.
skin [skɪn] *n* peau *f* ♦ *vt* (*fruit etc*) éplucher; (*animal*) écorcher; **wet** *or* **soaked to the** ~ trempé(e) jusqu'aux os.
skin cancer *n* cancer *m* de la peau.
skin-deep ['skɪn'diːp] *adj* superficiel(le).
skin diver *n* plongeur/euse sous-marin(e).
skin diving *n* plongée sous-marine.
skinflint ['skɪnflɪnt] *n* grippe-sou *m*.
skin graft *n* greffe *f* de peau.
skinhead ['skɪnhɛd] *n* skinhead *m*.
skinny ['skɪnɪ] *adj* maigre, maigrichon(ne).
skin test *n* cuti(-réaction *f*) *f*.
skintight ['skɪntaɪt] *adj* (*dress etc*) collant(e), ajusté(e).
skip [skɪp] *n* petit bond *or* saut; (*container*) benne *f* ♦ *vi* gambader, sautiller; (*with rope*) sauter à la corde ♦ *vt* (*pass over*) sauter; **to** ~ **school** (*esp US*) faire l'école buissonnière.
ski pants *npl* pantalon *m* de ski.
ski pole *n* bâton *m* de ski.
skipper ['skɪpə*] *n* (*NAUT, SPORT*) capitaine *m* ♦ *vt* (*boat*) commander; (*team*) être le chef de.
skipping rope ['skɪpɪŋ-] *n* (*BRIT*) corde *f* à sauter.
ski resort *n* station *f* de sports d'hiver.
skirmish ['skəːmɪʃ] *n* escarmouche *f*, accrochage *m*.
skirt [skəːt] *n* jupe *f* ♦ *vt* longer, contourner.
skirting board ['skəːtɪŋ-] *n* (*BRIT*) plinthe *f*.
ski run *n* piste *f* de ski.
ski suit *n* combinaison *f* de ski.
skit [skɪt] *n* sketch *m* satirique.
ski tow *n* = **ski lift**.
skittle ['skɪtl] *n* quille *f*; ~**s** (*game*) (jeu *m* de) quilles *fpl*.
skive [skaɪv] *vi* (*BRIT col*) tirer au flanc.
skulk [skʌlk] *vi* rôder furtivement.
skull [skʌl] *n* crâne *m*.
skullcap ['skʌlkæp] *n* calotte *f*.
skunk [skʌŋk] *n* mouffette *f*; (*fur*) sconse *m*.
sky [skaɪ] *n* ciel *m*; **to praise sb to the skies** porter qn aux nues.
sky-blue [skaɪ'bluː] *adj* bleu ciel *inv*.
skydiving ['skaɪdaɪvɪŋ] *n* parachutisme *m* (*en chute libre*).
sky-high ['skaɪ'haɪ] *adv* très haut ♦ *adj* exorbitant(e); **prices are** ~ les prix sont exorbitants.
skylark ['skaɪlɑːk] *n* (*bird*) alouette *f* (*des champs*).
skylight ['skaɪlaɪt] *n* lucarne *f*.
skyline ['skaɪlaɪn] *n* (*horizon*) (ligne *f* d')horizon *m*; (*of city*) ligne des toits.
skyscraper ['skaɪskreɪpə*] *n* gratte-ciel *m inv*.
slab [slæb] *n* plaque *f*; dalle *f*; (*of wood*) bloc *m*; (*of meat, cheese*) tranche épaisse.
slack [slæk] *adj* (*loose*) lâche, desserré(e); (*slow*) stagnant(e); (*careless*) négligent(e), peu sérieux(euse) *or* consciencieux(euse); (*COMM: market*) peu actif(ive); (: *demand*)

faible; (*period*) creux(euse) ♦ *n* (*in rope etc*) mou *m*; **business is** ~ les affaires vont mal.
slacken ['slækn] (*also:* ~ **off**) *vi* ralentir, diminuer ♦ *vt* relâcher.
slacks [slæks] *npl* pantalon *m*.
slag [slæg] *n* scories *fpl*.
slag heap *n* crassier *m*.
slain [sleɪn] *pp of* **slay**.
slake [sleɪk] *vt* (*one's thirst*) étancher.
slalom ['slɑːləm] *n* slalom *m*.
slam [slæm] *vt* (*door*) (faire) claquer; (*throw*) jeter violemment, flanquer; (*criticize*) éreinter, démolir ♦ *vi* claquer.
slammer ['slæmə*] *n* (*col*): **the** ~ la taule.
slander ['slɑːndə*] *n* calomnie *f*; (*LAW*) diffamation *f* ♦ *vt* calomnier; diffamer.
slanderous ['slɑːndrəs] *adj* calomnieux(euse); diffamatoire.
slang [slæŋ] *n* argot *m*.
slanging match ['slæŋɪŋ-] *n* (*BRIT col*) engueulade *f*, empoignade *f*.
slant [slɑːnt] *n* inclinaison *f*; (*fig*) angle *m*, point *m* de vue.
slanted ['slɑːntɪd] *adj* tendancieux(euse).
slanting ['slɑːntɪŋ] *adj* en pente, incliné(e); couché(e).
slap [slæp] *n* claque *f*, gifle *f*; (*on the back*) tape *f* ♦ *vt* donner une claque *or* une gifle (*or* une tape) à ♦ *adv* (*directly*) tout droit, en plein.
slapdash ['slæpdæʃ] *adj* (*work*) fait(e) sans soin *or* à la va-vite; (*person*) insouciant(e), négligent(e).
slaphead ['slæphɛd] *n* (*BRIT col*) abruti/e, taré/e.
slapstick ['slæpstɪk] *n* (*comedy*) grosse farce (*style tarte à la crème*).
slap-up ['slæpʌp] *adj* (*BRIT*): **a** ~ **meal** un repas extra *or* fameux.
slash [slæʃ] *vt* entailler, taillader; (*fig: prices*) casser.
slat [slæt] *n* (*of wood*) latte *f*, lame *f*.
slate [sleɪt] *n* ardoise *f* ♦ *vt* (*fig: criticize*) éreinter, démolir.
slaughter ['slɔːtə*] *n* carnage *m*, massacre *m*; (*of animals*) abattage *m* ♦ *vt* (*animal*) abattre; (*people*) massacrer.
slaughterhouse ['slɔːtəhaus] *n* abattoir *m*.
Slav [slɑːv] *adj* slave.
slave [sleɪv] *n* esclave *m/f* ♦ *vi* (*also:* ~ **away**) trimer, travailler comme un forçat; **to** ~ (**away**) **at sth/at doing sth** se tuer à qch/à faire qch.
slave driver *n* (*col, pej*) négrier/ière.
slave labour *n* travail *m* d'esclave; **it's just** ~ (*fig*) c'est de l'esclavage.
slaver ['slævə*] *vi* (*dribble*) baver.
slavery ['sleɪvərɪ] *n* esclavage *m*.
Slavic ['slævɪk] *adj* slave.
slavish ['sleɪvɪʃ] *adj* servile.
slavishly ['sleɪvɪʃlɪ] *adv* (*copy*) servilement.
Slavonic [slə'vɔnɪk] *adj* slave.
slay, *pt* **slew,** *pp* **slain** [sleɪ, sluː, sleɪn] *vt* (*liter-*

ary) tuer.

sleazy ['sli:zɪ] *adj* miteux(euse), minable.

sledge [slɛdʒ] *n* luge *f*.

sledgehammer ['slɛdʒhæmə*] *n* marteau *m* de forgeron.

sleek [sli:k] *adj* (*hair, fur*) brillant(e), luisant(e); (*car, boat*) aux lignes pures *or* élégantes.

sleep [sli:p] *n* sommeil *m* ♦ *vi* (*pt, pp* **slept** [slɛpt]) dormir; (*spend night*) dormir, coucher ♦ *vt*: **we can ~ 4** on peut coucher *or* loger 4 personnes; **to go to ~** s'endormir; **to have a good night's ~** passer une bonne nuit; **to put to ~** (*patient*) endormir; (*animal: euphemism: kill*) piquer; **to ~ lightly** avoir le sommeil léger; **to ~ with sb** (*euphemism*) coucher avec qn.

▶**sleep in** *vi* (*lie late*) faire la grasse matinée; (*oversleep*) se réveiller trop tard.

sleeper ['sli:pə*] *n* (*person*) dormeur/euse; (*BRIT RAIL: on track*) traverse *f*; (*: train*) train *m* de voitures-lits; (*: carriage*) wagon-lits *m*, voiture-lits *f*; (*: berth*) couchette *f*.

sleepily ['sli:pɪlɪ] *adv* d'un air endormi.

sleeping ['sli:pɪŋ] *adj* qui dort, endormi(e).

sleeping bag *n* sac *m* de couchage.

sleeping car *n* wagon-lits *m*, voiture-lits *f*.

sleeping partner *n* (*BRIT COMM*) = **silent partner**.

sleeping pill *n* somnifère *m*.

sleeping sickness *n* maladie *f* du sommeil.

sleepless ['sli:plɪs] *adj*: **a ~ night** une nuit blanche.

sleeplessness ['sli:plɪsnɪs] *n* insomnie *f*.

sleepwalk ['sli:pwɔ:k] *vi* marcher en dormant.

sleepwalker ['sli:pwɔ:kə*] *n* somnambule *m/f*.

sleepy ['sli:pɪ] *adj* qui a envie de dormir; (*fig*) endormi(e); **to be** *or* **feel ~** avoir sommeil, avoir envie de dormir.

sleet [sli:t] *n* neige fondue.

sleeve [sli:v] *n* manche *f*; (*of record*) pochette *f*.

sleeveless ['sli:vlɪs] *adj* (*garment*) sans manches.

sleigh [sleɪ] *n* traîneau *m*.

sleight [slaɪt] *n*: **~ of hand** tour *m* de passe-passe.

slender ['slɛndə*] *adj* svelte, mince; (*fig*) faible, ténu(e).

slept [slɛpt] *pt, pp of* **sleep**.

sleuth [slu:θ] *n* (*col*) détective (privé).

slew [slu:] *vi* (*also:* **~ round**) virer, pivoter ♦ *pt of* **slay**.

slice [slaɪs] *n* tranche *f*; (*round*) rondelle *f* ♦ *vt* couper en tranches (*or* en rondelles); **~d bread** pain *m* en tranches.

slick [slɪk] *adj* brillant(e) en apparence; mielleux(euse) ♦ *n* (*also:* **oil ~**) nappe *f* de pétrole, marée noire.

slid [slɪd] *pt, pp of* **slide**.

slide [slaɪd] *n* (*in playground*) toboggan *m*; (*PHOT*) diapositive *f*; (*BRIT: also:* **hair ~**) bar-

rette *f*; (*microscope ~*) (lame *f*) porte-objet *m*; (*in prices*) chute *f*, baisse *f* ♦ *vb* (*pt, pp* **slid** [slɪd]) *vt* (faire) glisser ♦ *vi* glisser; **to let things ~** (*fig*) laisser les choses aller à la dérive.

slide projector *n* (*PHOT*) projecteur *m* de diapositives.

slide rule *n* règle *f* à calcul.

sliding ['slaɪdɪŋ] *adj* (*door*) coulissant(e); **~ roof** (*AUT*) toit ouvrant.

sliding scale *n* échelle *f* mobile.

slight [slaɪt] *adj* (*slim*) mince, menu(e); (*frail*) frêle; (*trivial*) faible, insignifiant(e); (*small*) petit(e), léger(ère) (*before n*) ♦ *n* offense *f*, affront *m* ♦ *vt* (*offend*) blesser, offenser; **the ~est** le (*or* la) moindre; **not in the ~est** pas le moins du monde, pas du tout.

slightly ['slaɪtlɪ] *adv* légèrement, un peu; **~ built** fluet(te).

slim [slɪm] *adj* mince ♦ *vi* maigrir, suivre un régime amaigrissant.

slime [slaɪm] *n* vase *f*; substance visqueuse.

slimming ['slɪmɪŋ] *n* amaigrissement *m* ♦ *adj* (*diet, pills*) amaigrissant(e), pour maigrir.

slimy ['slaɪmɪ] *adj* visqueux(euse), gluant(e); (*covered with mud*) vaseux(euse).

sling [slɪŋ] *n* (*MED*) écharpe *f* ♦ *vt* (*pt, pp* **slung** [slʌŋ]) lancer, jeter; **to have one's arm in a ~** avoir le bras en écharpe.

slink, *pt, pp* **slunk** [slɪŋk, slʌŋk] *vi*: **to ~ away** *or* **off** s'en aller furtivement.

slinky ['slɪŋkɪ] *adj* (*clothes*) moulant(e).

slip [slɪp] *n* faux pas; (*mistake*) erreur *f*, bévue *f*; (*underskirt*) combinaison *f*; (*of paper*) petite feuille, fiche *f* ♦ *vt* (*slide*) glisser ♦ *vi* (*slide*) glisser; (*move smoothly*): **to ~ into/out of** se glisser *or* se faufiler dans/hors de; (*decline*) baisser; **to let a chance ~ by** laisser passer une occasion; **to ~ sth on/off** enfiler/enlever qch; **it ~ped from her hand** cela lui a glissé des mains; **to give sb the ~** fausser compagnie à qn; **a ~ of the tongue** un lapsus.

▶**slip away** *vi* s'esquiver.

▶**slip in** *vt* glisser.

▶**slip out** *vi* sortir.

slip-on ['slɪpɔn] *adj* facile à enfiler; **~ shoes** mocassins *mpl*.

slipped disc [slɪpt-] *n* hernie discale.

slipper ['slɪpə*] *n* pantoufle *f*.

slippery ['slɪpərɪ] *adj* glissant(e); (*fig: person*) insaisissable.

slip road *n* (*BRIT: to motorway*) bretelle *f* d'accès.

slipshod ['slɪpʃɔd] *adj* négligé(e), peu soigné(e).

slip-up ['slɪpʌp] *n* bévue *f*.

slipway ['slɪpweɪ] *n* cale *f* (de construction *or* de lancement).

slit [slɪt] *n* fente *f*; (*cut*) incision *f*; (*tear*) déchirure *f* ♦ *vt* (*pt, pp* **slit**) fendre; couper; inciser; déchirer; **to ~ sb's throat** trancher la gorge à qn.

slither ['slɪðə*] vi glisser, déraper.

sliver ['slɪvə*] n (of glass, wood) éclat m; (of cheese, sausage) petit morceau.

slob [slɔb] n (col) rustaud/e.

slog [slɔg] n (BRIT) gros effort; tâche fastidieuse ♦ vi travailler très dur.

slogan ['sləugən] n slogan m.

slop [slɔp] vi (also: ~ over) se renverser; déborder ♦ vt répandre; renverser.

slope [sləup] n pente f; (side of mountain) versant m; (slant) inclinaison f ♦ vi: to ~ down être or descendre en pente; to ~ up monter.

sloping ['sləupɪŋ] adj en pente, incliné(e); (handwriting) penché(e).

sloppy ['slɔpɪ] adj (work) peu soigné(e), bâclé(e); (appearance) négligé(e), débraillé(e); (film etc) sentimental(e).

slosh [slɔʃ] vi (col): to ~ about or around (children) patauger; (liquid) clapoter.

sloshed [slɔʃt] adj (col: drunk) bourré(e).

slot [slɔt] n fente f; (in timetable, RADIO, TV) créneau m, plage f ♦ vt: to ~ into encastrer or insérer dans ♦ vi: to ~ into s'encastrer or s'insérer dans.

sloth [sləuθ] n (vice) paresse f; (ZOOL) paresseux m.

slot machine n (BRIT: vending machine) distributeur m (automatique), machine f à sous; (for gambling) appareil m or machine à sous.

slot meter n (BRIT) compteur m à pièces.

slouch [slautʃ] vi avoir le dos rond, être voûté(e).

▶**slouch about, slouch around** vi traîner à ne rien faire.

Slovak ['sləuvæk] adj slovaque ♦ n Slovaque m/f; (LING) slovaque m; **the ~ Republic** la République slovaque.

Slovakia [sləu'vækɪə] n Slovaquie f.

Slovakian [sləu'vækɪən] adj, n = **Slovak**.

Slovene [sləu'vi:n] adj slovène ♦ n Slovène m/f; (LING) slovène m.

Slovenia [sləu'vi:nɪə] n Slovénie f.

Slovenian [sləu'vi:nɪən] adj, n = **Slovene**.

slovenly ['slʌvənlɪ] adj sale, débraillé(e), négligé(e).

slow [sləu] adj lent(e); (watch): **to be ~** retarder ♦ adv lentement ♦ vt, vi (also: ~ down, ~ up) ralentir; " ~ " (road sign) "ralentir"; **at a ~ speed** à petite vitesse; **to be ~ to act/decide** être lent à agir/décider; **my watch is 20 minutes ~** ma montre retarde de 20 minutes; **business is ~** les affaires marchent au ralenti; **to go ~** (driver) rouler lentement; (in industrial dispute) faire la grève perlée.

slow-acting [sləu'æktɪŋ] adj qui agit lentement, à action lente.

slowcoach ['sləukəutʃ] n (BRIT col) lambin/e.

slowly ['sləulɪ] adv lentement.

slow motion n: **in ~** au ralenti.

slowness ['sləunɪs] n lenteur f.

slowpoke ['sləupəuk] n (US col) = **slowcoach**.

sludge [slʌdʒ] n boue f.

slug [slʌg] n limace f; (bullet) balle f.

sluggish ['slʌgɪʃ] adj mou(molle), lent(e); (business, sales) stagnant(e).

sluice [slu:s] n écluse f; (also: ~ gate) vanne f ♦ vt: **to ~ down** or **out** laver à grande eau.

slum [slʌm] n taudis m.

slumber ['slʌmbə*] n sommeil m.

slump [slʌmp] n baisse soudaine, effondrement m; crise f ♦ vi s'effondrer, s'affaisser.

slung [slʌŋ] pt, pp of **sling**.

slunk [slʌŋk] pt, pp of **slink**.

slur [slə:*] n bredouillement m; (smear): ~ (on) atteinte f (à); insinuation f (contre) ♦ vt mal articuler; **to be a ~ on** porter atteinte à.

slurp [slə:p] vt, vi boire à grand bruit.

slurred [slə:d] adj (pronunciation) inarticulé(e), indistinct(e).

slush [slʌʃ] n neige fondue.

slush fund n caisse noire, fonds secrets.

slushy ['slʌʃɪ] adj (snow) fondu(e); (street) couvert(e) de neige fondue; (BRIT: fig) à l'eau de rose.

slut [slʌt] n souillon f.

sly [slaɪ] adj rusé(e); sournois(e); **on the ~** en cachette.

smack [smæk] n (slap) tape f; (on face) gifle f ♦ vt donner une tape à; gifler; (child) donner la fessée à ♦ vi: **to ~ of** avoir des relents de, sentir ♦ adv (col): **it fell ~ in the middle** c'est tombé en plein milieu or en plein dedans; **to ~ one's lips** se lécher les babines.

smacker ['smækə*] n (col: kiss) bisou m or bise f sonore; (: BRIT: pound note) livre f; (: US: dollar bill) dollar m.

small [smɔ:l] adj petit(e); (letter) minuscule ♦ n: **the ~ of the back** le creux des reins; **to get** or **grow ~er** diminuer; **to make ~er** (amount, income) diminuer; (object, garment) rapetisser; **a ~ shopkeeper** un petit commerçant.

small ads npl (BRIT) petites annonces.

small arms npl armes individuelles.

small business n petit commerce, petite affaire.

small change n petite or menue monnaie.

smallholder ['smɔ:lhəuldə*] n (BRIT) petit cultivateur.

smallholding ['smɔ:lhəuldɪŋ] n (BRIT) petite ferme.

small hours npl: **in the ~** au petit matin.

smallish ['smɔ:lɪʃ] adj plutôt or assez petit(e).

small-minded [smɔ:l'maɪndɪd] adj mesquin(e).

smallpox ['smɔ:lpɔks] n variole f.

small print n (in contract etc) clause(s) imprimée(s) en petits caractères.

small-scale ['smɔ:lskeɪl] adj (map, model) à échelle réduite, à petite échelle; (business, farming) peu important(e), modeste.

small talk n menus propos.

small-time ['smɔ:ltaɪm] adj (farmer etc) petit(e); **a ~ thief** un voleur à la petite semaine.

small-town ['smɔːltaun] *adj* provincial(e).

smarmy ['smɑːmɪ] *adj* (*BRIT pej*) flagorneur(euse), lécheur(euse).

smart [smɑːt] *adj* élégant(e), chic *inv*; (*clever*) intelligent(e); (*pej*) futé(e); (*quick*) vif(vive), prompt(e) ♦ *vi* faire mal, brûler; **the ~ set** le beau monde; **to look ~** être élégant(e); **my eyes are ~ing** j'ai les yeux irrités *or* qui me piquent.

smartcard ['smɑːtkɑːd] *n* carte *f* à puce.

smarten up ['smɑːtn-] *vi* devenir plus élégant(e), se faire beau(belle) ♦ *vt* rendre plus élégant(e).

smash [smæʃ] *n* (*also*: ~-**up**) collision *f*, accident *m*; (*sound*) fracas *m* ♦ *vt* casser, briser, fracasser; (*opponent*) écraser; (*hopes*) ruiner, détruire; (*SPORT*: *record*) pulvériser ♦ *vi* se briser, se fracasser; s'écraser.

▶**smash up** *vt* (*car*) bousiller; (*room*) tout casser dans.

smash hit *n* (grand) succès.

smashing ['smæʃɪŋ] *adj* (*col*) formidable.

smattering ['smætərɪŋ] *n*: **a ~ of** quelques notions de.

smear [smɪə*] *n* tache *f*, salissure *f*; trace *f*; (*MED*) frottis *m*; (*insult*) calomnie *f* ♦ *vt* enduire; (*fig*) porter atteinte à; **his hands were ~ed with oil/ink** il avait les mains maculées de cambouis/d'encre.

smear campaign *n* campagne *f* de dénigrement.

smear test *n* (*BRIT MED*) frottis *m*.

smell [smɛl] *n* odeur *f*; (*sense*) odorat *m* ♦ *vb* (*pt, pp* **smelt** *or* **smelled** [smɛlt, smɛld]) *vt* sentir ♦ *vi* (*food etc*): **to ~ (of)** sentir; (*pej*) sentir mauvais; **it ~s good** ça sent bon.

smelly ['smɛlɪ] *adj* qui sent mauvais, malodorant(e).

smelt [smɛlt] *pt, pp of* **smell** ♦ *vt* (*ore*) fondre.

smile [smaɪl] *n* sourire *m* ♦ *vi* sourire.

smiling ['smaɪlɪŋ] *adj* souriant(e).

smirk [smɜːk] *n* petit sourire suffisant *or* affecté.

smith [smɪθ] *n* maréchal-ferrant *m*; forgeron *m*.

smithy ['smɪðɪ] *n* forge *f*.

smitten ['smɪtn] *adj*: ~ **with** pris(e) de; frappé(e) de.

smock [smɔk] *n* blouse *f*, sarrau *m*.

smog [smɔg] *n* brouillard mêlé de fumée.

smoke [sməuk] *n* fumée *f* ♦ *vt*, *vi* fumer; **to have a ~** fumer une cigarette; **do you ~?** est-ce que vous fumez?; **to go up in ~** (*house etc*) brûler; (*fig*) partir en fumée.

smoked ['sməukt] *adj* (*bacon, glass*) fumé(e).

smokeless fuel ['sməuklɪs-] *n* combustible non polluant.

smokeless zone ['sməuklɪs-] *n* (*BRIT*) zone *f* où l'usage du charbon est réglementé.

smoker ['sməukə*] *n* (*person*) fumeur/euse; (*RAIL*) wagon *m* fumeurs.

smoke screen *n* rideau *m* *or* écran *m* de fumée; (*fig*) paravent *m*.

smoke shop *n* (*US*) (bureau *m* de) tabac *m*.

smoking ['sməukɪŋ] *n*: "**no ~**" (*sign*) "défense de fumer"; **he's given up ~** il a arrêté de fumer.

smoking compartment, (*US*) **smoking car** *n* wagon *m* fumeurs.

smoking room *n* fumoir *m*.

smoky ['sməukɪ] *adj* enfumé(e).

smolder ['sməuldə*] *vi* (*US*) = **smoulder**.

smoochy ['smuːtʃɪ] *adj* (*col*) langoureux(euse).

smooth [smuːð] *adj* lisse; (*sauce*) onctueux(euse); (*flavour, whisky*) moelleux(euse); (*cigarette*) doux(douce); (*movement*) régulier(ière), sans à-coups *or* heurts; (*landing, takeoff*) en douceur; (*flight*) sans secousses; (*person*) doucereux(euse), mielleux(euse) ♦ *vt* lisser, défroisser; (*also*: ~ **out**: *creases, difficulties*) faire disparaître.

▶**smooth over** *vt*: **to ~ things over** (*fig*) arranger les choses.

smoothly ['smuːðlɪ] *adv* (*easily*) facilement, sans difficulté(s); **everything went ~** tout s'est bien passé.

smother ['smʌðə*] *vt* étouffer.

smoulder, (*US*) **smolder** ['sməuldə*] *vi* couver.

smudge [smʌdʒ] *n* tache *f*, bavure *f* ♦ *vt* salir, maculer.

smug [smʌg] *adj* suffisant(e), content(e) de soi.

smuggle ['smʌgl] *vt* passer en contrebande *or* en fraude; **to ~ in/out** (*goods etc*) faire entrer/sortir clandestinement *or* en fraude.

smuggler ['smʌglə*] *n* contrebandier/ière.

smuggling ['smʌglɪŋ] *n* contrebande *f*.

smut [smʌt] *n* (*grain of soot*) grain *m* de suie; (*mark*) tache *f* de suie; (*in conversation etc*) obscénités *fpl*.

smutty ['smʌtɪ] *adj* (*fig*) grossier(ière), obscène.

snack [snæk] *n* casse-croûte *m inv*; **to have a ~** prendre un en-cas, manger quelque chose (de léger).

snack bar *n* snack(-bar) *m*.

snag [snæg] *n* inconvénient *m*, difficulté *f*.

snail [sneɪl] *n* escargot *m*.

snake [sneɪk] *n* serpent *m*.

snap [snæp] *n* (*sound*) claquement *m*, bruit sec; (*photograph*) photo *f*, instantané *m*; (*game*) sorte de jeu de bataille ♦ *adj* subit(e); fait(e) sans réfléchir ♦ *vt* faire claquer; (*break*) casser net; (*photograph*) prendre un instantané de ♦ *vi* se casser net *or* avec un bruit sec; (*fig*: *person*) craquer; **to ~ at sb** (*subj*: *person*) parler d'un ton brusque à qn; (: *dog*) essayer de mordre qn; **to ~ open/ shut** s'ouvrir/se refermer brusquement; **to ~ one's fingers at** (*fig*) se moquer de; **a cold ~** (*of weather*) un refroidissement soudain de la température.

►**snap off** *vt* (*break*) casser net.

►**snap up** *vt* sauter sur, saisir.

snap fastener *n* bouton-pression *m*.

snappy ['snæpɪ] *adj* prompt(e); (*slogan*) qui a du punch; **make it ~!** (*col: hurry up*) grouille-toi!, magne-toi!

snapshot ['snæpʃɔt] *n* photo *f*, instantané *m*.

snare [snɛə*] *n* piège *m* ♦ *vt* attraper, prendre au piège.

snarl [snɑːl] *n* grondement *m or* grognement *m* féroce ♦ *vi* gronder ♦ *vt*: **to get ~ed up** (*wool, plans*) s'emmêler; (*traffic*) se bloquer.

snatch [snætʃ] *n* (*fig*) vol *m*; (*BRIT: small amount*): **~es** *des* fragments *mpl or* bribes *fpl de* ♦ *vt* saisir (*d'un geste vif*); (*steal*) voler ♦ *vi*: **don't ~!** doucement!; **to ~ a sandwich** manger *or* avaler un sandwich à la hâte; **to ~ some sleep** arriver à dormir un peu.

►**snatch up** *vt* saisir, s'emparer de.

snazzy ['snæzɪ] *adj* (*col: clothes*) classe *inv*, chouette.

sneak [sniːk] *vi*: **to ~ in/out** entrer/sortir furtivement *or* à la dérobée ♦ *vt*: **to ~ a look at sth** regarder furtivement qch.

sneakers ['sniːkəz] *npl* chaussures *fpl* de tennis *or* basket.

sneaking ['sniːkɪŋ] *adj*: **to have a ~ feeling** *or* **suspicion that ...** avoir la vague impression que ....

sneaky ['sniːkɪ] *adj* sournois(e).

sneer [snɪə*] *n* ricanement *m* ♦ *vi* ricaner, sourire d'un air sarcastique; **to ~ at sb/sth** se moquer de qn/qch avec mépris.

sneeze [sniːz] *n* éternuement *m* ♦ *vi* éternuer.

snide [snaɪd] *adj* sarcastique, narquois(e).

sniff [snɪf] *n* reniflement *m* ♦ *vi* renifler ♦ *vt* renifler, flairer; (*glue, drug*) sniffer, respirer.

►**sniff at** *vt fus*: **it's not to be ~ed at** il ne faut pas cracher dessus, ce n'est pas à dédaigner.

sniffer dog ['snɪfə-] *n* (*POLICE*) *chien dressé pour la recherche d'explosifs et de stupéfiants.*

snigger ['snɪgə*] *n* ricanement *m*; rire moqueur ♦ *vi* ricaner; pouffer de rire.

snip [snɪp] *n* petit bout; (*bargain*) (bonne) occasion *or* affaire ♦ *vt* couper.

sniper ['snaɪpə*] *n* (*marksman*) tireur embusqué.

snippet ['snɪpɪt] *n* bribes *fpl*.

snivelling ['snɪvlɪŋ] *adj* larmoyant(e), pleurnicheur(euse).

snob [snɔb] *n* snob *m/f*.

snobbery ['snɔbərɪ] *n* snobisme *m*.

snobbish ['snɔbɪʃ] *adj* snob *inv*.

snog [snɔg] *vi* (*col*) se bécoter.

snooker ['snuːkə*] *n* *sorte de jeu de billard.*

snoop [snuːp] *vi*: **to ~ on sb** espionner qn; **to ~ about somewhere** fourrer son nez quelque part.

snooper ['snuːpə*] *n* fureteur/euse.

snooty ['snuːtɪ] *adj* snob *inv*, prétentieux(euse).

snooze [snuːz] *n* petit somme ♦ *vi* faire un petit somme.

snore [snɔː*] *vi* ronfler ♦ *n* ronflement *m*.

snoring ['snɔːrɪŋ] *n* ronflement(s) *m(pl)*.

snorkel ['snɔːkl] *n* (*of swimmer*) tuba *m*.

snort [snɔːt] *n* grognement *m* ♦ *vi* grogner; (*horse*) renâcler ♦ *vt* (*col: drugs*) sniffer.

snotty ['snɔtɪ] *adj* morveux(euse).

snout [snaut] *n* museau *m*.

snow [snəu] *n* neige *f* ♦ *vi* neiger ♦ *vt*: **to be ~ed under with work** être débordé(e) de travail.

snowball ['snəubɔːl] *n* boule *f* de neige.

snowbound ['snəubaund] *adj* enneigé(e), bloqué(e) par la neige.

snow-capped ['snəukæpt] *adj* (*peak, mountain*) couvert(e) de neige.

snowdrift ['snəudrɪft] *n* congère *f*.

snowdrop ['snəudrɔp] *n* perce-neige *m*.

snowfall ['snəufɔːl] *n* chute *f* de neige.

snowflake ['snəufleɪk] *n* flocon *m* de neige.

snowman ['snəumæn] *n* bonhomme *m* de neige.

snowplough, (*US*) **snowplow** ['snəuplau] *n* chasse-neige *m inv*.

snowshoe ['snəuʃuː] *n* raquette *f* (*pour la neige*).

snowstorm ['snəustɔːm] *n* tempête *f* de neige.

snowy ['snəuɪ] *adj* neigeux(euse); (*covered with snow*) enneigé(e).

SNP *n abbr* (*BRIT POL*) = **Scottish National Party.**

snub [snʌb] *vt* repousser, snober ♦ *n* rebuffade *f*.

snub-nosed [snʌb'nəuzd] *adj* au nez retroussé.

snuff [snʌf] *n* tabac *m* à priser ♦ *vt* (*also: ~ out: candle*) moucher.

snuff movie *n* (*col*) *film pornographique qui se termine par le meurtre réel de l'un des acteurs.*

snug [snʌg] *adj* douillet(te), confortable; **it's a ~ fit** c'est bien juste(e).

snuggle ['snʌgl] *vi*: **to ~ down in bed/up to sb** se pelotonner dans son lit/contre qn.

SO *abbr* (*BANKING*) = **standing order.**

═══════════════════════════ *KEYWORD*

so [səu] *adv* **1** (*thus, likewise*) ainsi, de cette façon; **if ~** si oui; **~ do** *or* **have I** moi aussi; **it's 5 o'clock — ~ it is!** il est 5 heures — en effet! *or* c'est vrai!; **I hope/think ~** je l'espère/le crois; **~ far** jusqu'ici, jusqu'à maintenant; (*in past*) jusque-là; **quite ~!** exactement!, c'est bien ça!; **even ~** quand même, tout de même

2 (*in comparisons etc: to such a degree*) si, tellement; **~ big (that)** si *or* tellement grand (que); **she's not ~ clever as her brother** elle n'est pas aussi intelligente que son frère

3: **~ much** *adj, adv* tant (de); **I've got ~ much**

work j'ai tant de travail; **I love you ~ much** je vous aime tant; **~ many** tant (de)
4 (*phrases*): **10 or ~** à peu près or environ 10; **~ long!** (*inf*: *goodbye*) au revoir!, à un de ces jours!; **~ to speak** pour ainsi dire; **~ (what)?** (*col*) (bon) et alors?, et après?
♦ *conj* **1** (*expressing purpose*): **~ as to do** pour faire, afin de faire; **~ (that)** pour que or afin que +*sub*
2 (*expressing result*) donc, par conséquent; **~ that** si bien que, de (telle) sorte que; **~ that's the reason!** c'est donc (pour) ça!

soak [səuk] *vt* faire or laisser tremper ♦ *vi* tremper; **to be ~ed through** être trempé jusqu'aux os.
►**soak in** *vi* pénétrer, être absorbé(e).
►**soak up** *vt* absorber.
soaking ['səukɪŋ] *adj* (*also*: **~ wet**) trempé(e).
so and so *n* un tel/une telle.
soap [səup] *n* savon *m*.
soapbox ['səupbɒks] *n* tribune improvisée (*en plein air*).
soapflakes ['səupfleɪks] *npl* paillettes *fpl* de savon.
soap opera *n* feuilleton télévisé (*quotidienneté réaliste ou embellie*).
soap powder *n* lessive *f*, détergent *m*.
soapsuds ['səupsʌds] *npl* mousse *f* de savon.
soapy ['səupɪ] *adj* savonneux(euse).
soar [sɔː*] *vi* monter (en flèche), s'élancer; **~ing prices** prix qui grimpent.
sob [sɒb] *n* sanglot *m* ♦ *vi* sangloter.
s.o.b. *n abbr* (*US col!*: = *son of a bitch*) salaud *m* (*!*).
sober ['səubə*] *adj* qui n'est pas (or plus) ivre; (*sedate*) sérieux(euse), sensé(e); (*moderate*) mesuré(e); (*colour*, *style*) sobre, discret(ète).
►**sober up** *vt* dégriser ♦ *vi* se dégriser.
sobriety [sə'braɪətɪ] *n* (*not being drunk*) sobriété *f*, (*seriousness*, *sedateness*) sérieux *m*.
sob story *n* (*col*, *pej*) histoire larmoyante.
Soc. *abbr* (= *society*) Soc.
so-called ['səu'kɔːld] *adj* soi-disant *inv*.
soccer ['sɒkə*] *n* football *m*.
soccer pitch *n* terrain *m* de football.
soccer player *n* footballeur *m*.
sociable ['səuʃəbl] *adj* sociable.
social ['səuʃl] *adj* social(e) ♦ *n* (petite) fête.
social climber *n* arriviste *m/f*.
social club *n* amicale *f*, foyer *m*.
Social Democrat *n* social-démocrate *m/f*.
social insurance *n* (*US*) sécurité sociale.
socialism ['səuʃəlɪzəm] *n* socialisme *m*.
socialist ['səuʃəlɪst] *adj*, *n* socialiste (*m/f*).
socialite ['səuʃəlaɪt] *n* personnalité mondaine.
socialize ['səuʃəlaɪz] *vi* voir or rencontrer des gens, se faire des amis; **to ~ with** fréquenter; lier connaissance or parler avec.
social life *n* vie sociale; **how's your ~?** est-ce que tu sors beaucoup?
socially ['səuʃəlɪ] *adv* socialement, en société.

social science *n* sciences humaines.
social security *n* aide sociale.
social services *npl* services sociaux.
social welfare *n* sécurité sociale.
social work *n* assistance sociale.
social worker *n* assistant/e social(e).
society [sə'saɪətɪ] *n* société *f*; (*club*) société, association *f*; (*also*: **high ~**) (haute) société, grand monde ♦ *cpd* (*party*) mondain(e).
socio-economic ['səusɪəuiː:kə'nɒmɪk] *adj* socioéconomique.
sociological [səusɪə'lɒdʒɪkl] *adj* sociologique.
sociologist [səusɪ'ɔlədʒɪst] *n* sociologue *m/f*.
sociology [səusɪ'ɔlədʒɪ] *n* sociologie *f*.
sock [sɒk] *n* chaussette *f* ♦ *vt* (*col*: *hit*) flanquer un coup à; **to pull one's ~s up** (*fig*) se secouer (les puces).
socket ['sɒkɪt] *n* cavité *f*; (*ELEC*: *also*: **wall ~**) prise *f* de courant; (*: for light bulb*) douille *f*.
sod [sɒd] *n* (*of earth*) motte *f*; (*BRIT col!*) con *m* (*!*); salaud *m* (*!*).
►**sod off** *vi*: **~ off!** (*BRIT col!*) fous le camp!, va te faire foutre! (*!*).
soda ['səudə] *n* (*CHEM*) soude *f*; (*also*: **~ water**) eau *f* de Seltz; (*US*: *also*: **~ pop**) soda *m*.
sodden ['sɒdn] *adj* trempé(e); détrempé(e).
sodium ['səudɪəm] *n* sodium *m*.
sodium chloride *n* chlorure *m* de sodium.
sofa ['səufə] *n* sofa *m*, canapé *m*.
Sofia ['səufɪə] *n* Sofia.
soft [sɒft] *adj* (*not rough*) doux(douce); (*not hard*) doux; mou(molle); (*not loud*) doux, léger(ère); (*kind*) doux, gentil(le); (*weak*) indulgent(e); (*stupid*) stupide, débile.
soft-boiled ['sɒftbɔɪld] *adj* (*egg*) à la coque.
soft drink *n* boisson non alcoolisée.
soft drugs *npl* drogues douces.
soften ['sɒfn] *vt* (r)amollir; adoucir; atténuer ♦ *vi* se ramollir; s'adoucir; s'atténuer.
softener ['sɒfnə*] *n* (*water ~*) adoucisseur *m*; (*fabric ~*) produit assouplissant.
soft fruit *n* (*BRIT*) baies *fpl*.
soft furnishings *npl* tissus *mpl* d'ameublement.
soft-hearted [sɒft'hɑːtɪd] *adj* au cœur tendre.
softly ['sɒftlɪ] *adv* doucement; légèrement; gentiment.
softness ['sɒftnɪs] *n* douceur *f*.
soft option *n* solution *f* de facilité.
soft sell *n* promotion *f* de vente discrète.
soft target *n* cible *f* facile.
soft toy *n* jouet *m* en peluche.
software ['sɒftwɛə*] *n* logiciel *m*, software *m*.
software package *n* progiciel *m*.
soggy ['sɒgɪ] *adj* trempé(e); détrempé(e).
soil [sɔɪl] *n* (*earth*) sol *m*, terre *f* ♦ *vt* salir; (*fig*) souiller.
soiled [sɔɪld] *adj* sale; (*COMM*) défraîchi(e).
sojourn ['sɒdʒəːn] *n* (*formal*) séjour *m*.
solace ['sɒlɪs] *n* consolation *f*, réconfort *m*.
solar ['səulə*] *adj* solaire.
solarium, *pl* **solaria** [sə'lɛərɪəm, -rɪə] *n* sola-

rium *m*.

solar panel *n* panneau *m* solaire.

solar plexus [-'plɛksəs] *n* (*ANAT*) plexus *m* solaire.

solar power *n* énergie *f* solaire.

sold [səuld] *pt, pp of* **sell**.

solder ['səuldə*] *vt* souder (*au fil à souder*) ♦ *n* soudure *f*.

soldier ['səuldʒə*] *n* soldat *m*, militaire *m* ♦ *vi*: **to ~ on** persévérer, s'accrocher; **toy ~** petit soldat.

sold out *adj* (*COMM*) épuisé(e).

sole [səul] *n* (*of foot*) plante *f*; (*of shoe*) semelle *f*; (*fish: pl inv*) sole *f* ♦ *adj* seul(e), unique; **the ~ reason** la seule et unique raison.

solely ['səulli] *adv* seulement, uniquement; **I will hold you ~ responsible** je vous en tiendrai pour seul responsable.

solemn ['sɔləm] *adj* solennel(le); sérieux(euse), grave.

sole trader *n* (*COMM*) chef *m* d'entreprise individuelle.

solicit [sə'lɪsɪt] *vt* (*request*) solliciter ♦ *vi* (*prostitute*) racoler.

solicitor [sə'lɪsɪtə*] *n* (*BRIT: for wills etc*) ≈ notaire *m*; (*: in court*) ≈ avocat *m*.

solid ['sɔlɪd] *adj* (*not hollow*) plein(e), compact(e), massif(ive); (*strong, sound, reliable, not liquid*) solide; (*meal*) consistant(e), substantiel(le); (*vote*) unanime ♦ *n* solide *m*; **to be on ~ ground** être sur la terre ferme; (*fig*) être en terrain sûr; **we waited 2 ~ hours** nous avons attendu deux heures entières.

solidarity [sɔlɪ'dærɪtɪ] *n* solidarité *f*.

solid fuel *n* combustible *m* solide.

solidify [sə'lɪdɪfaɪ] *vi* se solidifier ♦ *vt* solidifier.

solidity [sə'lɪdɪtɪ] *n* solidité *f*.

solid-state ['sɔlɪdsteɪt] *adj* (*ELEC*) à circuits intégrés.

soliloquy [sə'lɪləkwɪ] *n* monologue *m*.

solitaire [sɔlɪ'tɛə*] *n* (*gem, BRIT: game*) solitaire *m*; (*US: card game*) réussite *f*.

solitary ['sɔlɪtərɪ] *adj* solitaire.

solitary confinement *n* (*LAW*) isolement *m* (cellulaire).

solitude ['sɔlɪtjuːd] *n* solitude *f*.

solo ['səuləu] *n* solo *m*.

soloist ['səuləuɪst] *n* soliste *m/f*.

Solomon Islands ['sɔləmən-] *npl*: **the ~** les (îles *fpl*) Salomon *fpl*.

solstice ['sɔlstɪs] *n* solstice *m*.

soluble ['sɔljubl] *adj* soluble.

solution [sə'luːʃən] *n* solution *f*.

solve [sɔlv] *vt* résoudre.

solvency ['sɔlvənsɪ] *n* (*COMM*) solvabilité *f*.

solvent ['sɔlvənt] *adj* (*COMM*) solvable ♦ *n* (*CHEM*) (dis)solvant *m*.

solvent abuse *n* usage *m* de solvants hallucinogènes.

Som. *abbr* (*BRIT*) = **Somerset**.

Somali [səu'mɑːlɪ] *adj* somali(e), somalien(ne)

♦ *n* Somali/e, Somalien/ne.

Somalia [səu'mɑːlɪə] *n* (République *f* de) Somalie *f*.

Somaliland [səu'mɑːlɪlænd] *n* Somaliland *m*.

sombre, (*US*) **somber** ['sɔmbə*] *adj* sombre, morne.

=============================== *KEYWORD*

some [sʌm] *adj* **1** (*a certain amount or number of*): ~ **tea/water/ice cream** du thé/de l'eau/de la glace; ~ **children/apples** des enfants/pommes

2 (*certain: in contrasts*): ~ **people say that ...** il y a des gens qui disent que ...; ~ **films were excellent, but others ...** certains films étaient excellents, mais la plupart ...

3 (*unspecified*): ~ **woman was asking for you** il y avait une dame qui vous demandait; **he was asking for ~ book (or other)** il demandait un livre quelconque; ~ **day** un de ces jours; ~ **day next week** un jour la semaine prochaine; **after ~ time** après un certain temps; **at ~ length** assez longuement; **in ~ form or other** sous une forme ou une autre, sous une forme quelconque

♦ *pron* **1** (*a certain number*) quelques-un(e)s, certain(e)s; **I've got ~** (*books etc*) j'en ai (quelques-uns); ~ **(of them) have been sold** certains ont été vendus

2 (*a certain amount*) un peu; **I've got ~** (*money, milk*) j'en ai (un peu); **would you like ~?** est-ce que vous en voulez?, en voulez-vous?

♦ *adv*: ~ **10 people** quelque 10 personnes, 10 personnes environ.

somebody ['sʌmbədɪ] *pron* quelqu'un; ~ **or other** quelqu'un, je ne sais qui.

someday ['sʌmdeɪ] *adv* un de ces jours, un jour ou l'autre.

somehow ['sʌmhau] *adv* d'une façon ou d'une autre; (*for some reason*) pour une raison ou une autre.

someone ['sʌmwʌn] *pron* = **somebody**.

someplace ['sʌmpleɪs] *adv* (*US*) = **somewhere**.

somersault ['sʌməsɔːlt] *n* culbute *f*, saut périlleux ♦ *vi* faire la culbute *or* un saut périlleux; (*car*) faire un tonneau.

something ['sʌmθɪŋ] *pron* quelque chose *m*; ~ **interesting** quelque chose d'intéressant; ~ **to do** quelque chose à faire; **he's ~ like me** il est un peu comme moi; **it's ~ of a problem** il y a là un problème.

sometime ['sʌmtaɪm] *adv* (*in future*) un de ces jours, un jour ou l'autre; (*in past*): ~ **last month** au cours du mois dernier.

sometimes ['sʌmtaɪmz] *adv* quelquefois, parfois.

somewhat ['sʌmwɔt] *adv* quelque peu, un peu.

somewhere ['sʌmwɛə*] *adv* quelque part; ~ **else** ailleurs, autre part.

son [sʌn] n fils m.
sonar ['səʊnɑːʳ] n sonar m.
sonata [sə'nɑːtə] n sonate f.
song [sɒŋ] n chanson f.
songbook ['sɒŋbʊk] n chansonnier m.
songwriter ['sɒŋraɪtəʳ] n auteur-compositeur m.
sonic ['sɒnɪk] adj (boom) supersonique.
son-in-law ['sʌnɪnlɔː] n gendre m, beau-fils m.
sonnet ['sɒnɪt] n sonnet m.
sonny ['sʌnɪ] n (col) fiston m.
soon [suːn] adv bientôt; (early) tôt; ~ afterwards peu après; quite ~ sous peu; how ~ can you do it? combien de temps vous fautil pour le faire, au plus pressé?; how ~ can you come back? quand or dans combien de temps pouvez-vous revenir, au plus tôt; see you ~! à bientôt!; see also as.
sooner ['suːnəʳ] adv (time) plus tôt; (preference): I would ~ do j'aimerais autant or je préférerais faire; ~ or later tôt ou tard; no ~ said than done sitôt dit, sitôt fait; the ~ the better le plus tôt sera le mieux; no ~ had we left than ... à peine étions-nous partis que ....
soot [sut] n suie f.
soothe [suːð] vt calmer, apaiser.
soothing ['suːðɪŋ] adj (ointment etc) lénitif(ive), lénifiant(e); (tone, words etc) apaisant(e); (drink, bath) relaxant(e).
SOP n abbr = standard operating procedure.
sop [sɒp] n: that's only a ~ c'est pour nous (or les etc) amadouer.
sophisticated [sə'fɪstɪkeɪtɪd] adj raffiné(e), sophistiqué(e); (system etc) très perfectionné(e), sophistiqué.
sophistication [səfɪstɪ'keɪʃən] n raffinement m; (niveau m de) perfectionnement m.
sophomore ['sɒfəmɔːʳ] n (US) étudiant/e de seconde année.
soporific [sɒpə'rɪfɪk] adj soporifique ♦ n somnifère m.
sopping ['sɒpɪŋ] adj (also: ~ wet) tout(e) trempé(e).
soppy ['sɒpɪ] adj (pej) sentimental(e).
soprano [sə'prɑːnəʊ] n (voice) soprano m; (singer) soprano m/f.
sorbet ['sɔːbeɪ] n sorbet m.
sorcerer ['sɔːsərəʳ] n sorcier m.
sordid ['sɔːdɪd] adj sordide.
sore [sɔːʳ] adj (painful) douloureux(euse), sensible; (offended) contrarié(e), vexé(e) ♦ n plaie f; to have a ~ throat avoir mal à la gorge; it's a ~ point (fig) c'est un point délicat.
sorely ['sɔːlɪ] adv (tempted) fortement.
sorrel ['sɔrəl] n oseille f.
sorrow ['sɔrəʊ] n peine f, chagrin m.
sorrowful ['sɔrəʊful] adj triste.
sorry ['sɔrɪ] adj désolé(e); (condition, excuse, tale) triste, déplorable; (sight) désolant(e); ~! pardon!, excusez-moi!; to feel ~ for sb

plaindre qn; I'm ~ to hear that ... je suis désolé(e) or navré(e) d'apprendre que ...; to be ~ about sth regretter qch.
sort [sɔːt] n genre m, espèce f, sorte f; (make: of coffee, car etc) marque f ♦ vt (also: ~ out: papers) trier; classer; ranger; (: letters etc) trier; (: problems) résoudre, régler; (COMPUT) trier; what ~ do you want? quelle sorte or quel genre voulez-vous?; what ~ of car? quelle marque de voiture?; I'll do nothing of the ~! je ne ferai rien de tel!; it's ~ of awkward (col) c'est plutôt gênant.
sortie ['sɔːtɪ] n sortie f.
sorting office ['sɔːtɪŋ-] n (POST) bureau m de tri.
SOS n abbr (= save our souls) SOS m.
so-so ['səʊsəʊ] adv comme ci comme ça.
soufflé ['suːfleɪ] n soufflé m.
sought [sɔːt] pt, pp of seek.
sought-after ['sɔːtɑːftəʳ] adj recherché(e).
soul [səʊl] n âme f; the poor ~ had nowhere to sleep le pauvre n'avait nulle part où dormir; I didn't see a ~ je n'ai vu (absolument) personne.
soul-destroying ['səʊldɪstrɔɪɪŋ] adj démoralisant(e).
soulful ['səʊlful] adj plein(e) de sentiment.
soulless ['səʊllɪs] adj sans cœur, inhumain(e).
soul mate n âme f sœur.
soul-searching ['səʊlsɜːtʃɪŋ] n: after much ~, I decided ... j'ai longuement réfléchi avant de décider ....
sound [saʊnd] adj (healthy) en bonne santé, sain(e); (safe, not damaged) solide, en bon état; (reliable, not superficial) sérieux(euse), solide; (sensible) sensé(e) ♦ adv: ~ asleep dormant d'un profond sommeil ♦ n (noise) son m; bruit m; (GEO) détroit m, bras m de mer ♦ vt (alarm) sonner; (also: ~ out: opinions) sonder ♦ vi sonner, retentir; (fig: seem) sembler (être); to be of ~ mind être sain(e) d'esprit; I don't like the ~ of it ça ne me dit rien qui vaille; to ~ one's horn (AUT) klaxonner, actionner son avertisseur; to ~ like ressembler à; it ~s as if ... il semblerait que ..., j'ai l'impression que ....
▶**sound off** vi (col): to ~ off (about) la ramener (sur).
sound barrier n mur m du son.
soundbite ['saʊndbaɪt] n phrase toute faite (pour être citée dans les médias).
sound effects npl bruitage m.
sound engineer n ingénieur m du son.
sounding ['saʊndɪŋ] n (NAUT etc) sondage m.
sounding board n (MUS) table f d'harmonie; (fig): to use sb as a ~ for one's ideas essayer ses idées sur qn.
soundly ['saʊndlɪ] adv (sleep) profondément; (beat) complètement, à plate couture.
soundproof ['saʊndpruːf] vt insonoriser ♦ adj insonorisé(e).
sound system n sono(risation) f.

soundtrack ['saundtræk] *n* (*of film*) bande *f* sonore.

sound wave *n* (*PHYSICS*) onde *f* sonore.

soup [su:p] *n* soupe *f*, potage *m*; **in the ~** (*fig*) dans le pétrin.

soup course *n* potage *m*.

soup kitchen *n* soupe *f* populaire.

soup plate *n* assiette creuse *or* à soupe.

soupspoon ['su:pspu:n] *n* cuiller *f* à soupe.

sour ['sauə*] *adj* aigre, acide; (*milk*) tourné(e), aigre; (*fig*) acerbe, aigre; revêche; **to go** *or* **turn ~** (*milk, wine*) tourner; (*fig: relationship, plans*) mal tourner; **it's ~ grapes** c'est du dépit.

source [sɔ:s] *n* source *f*; **I have it from a reliable ~ that** je sais de source sûre que.

south [sauθ] *n* sud *m* ♦ *adj* sud *inv*, du sud ♦ *adv* au sud, vers le sud; **(to the) ~ of** au sud de; **to travel ~** aller en direction du sud; **the S~ of France** le Sud de la France, le Midi.

South Africa *n* Afrique *f* du Sud.

South African *adj* sud-africain(e) ♦ *n* Sud-Africain/e.

South America *n* Amérique *f* du Sud.

South American *adj* sud-américain(e) ♦ *n* Sud-Américain/e.

southbound ['sauθbaund] *adj* en direction du sud; (*carriageway*) sud *inv*.

south-east [sauθ'i:st] *n* sud-est *m*.

South-East Asia *n* le Sud-Est asiatique.

southerly ['sʌðəlɪ] *adj* du sud; au sud.

southern ['sʌðən] *adj* (du) sud; méridional(e); **with a ~ aspect** orienté(e) *or* exposé(e) au sud; **the ~ hemisphere** l'hémisphère sud *or* austral.

South Pole *n* Pôle *m* Sud.

South Sea Islands *npl*: **the ~** l'Océanie *f*.

South Seas *npl*: **the ~** les mers *fpl* du Sud.

South Vietnam *n* Viêt-Nam *m* du Sud.

southward(s) ['sauθwəd(z)] *adv* vers le sud.

south-west [sauθ'wɛst] *n* sud-ouest *m*.

souvenir [su:və'nɪə*] *n* souvenir *m* (*objet*).

sovereign ['sɔvrɪn] *adj, n* souverain(e).

sovereignty ['sɔvrɪntɪ] *n* souveraineté *f*.

soviet ['səuvɪət] *adj* soviétique.

Soviet Union *n*: **the ~** l'Union *f* soviétique.

sow *n* [sau] truie *f* ♦ *vt* [səu] (*pt* **~ed**, *pp* **sown** [səun]) semer.

soya ['sɔɪə], (*US*) **soy** [sɔɪ] *n*: **~ bean** graine *f* de soja; **~ sauce** sauce *f* au soja.

sozzled ['sɔzld] *adj* (*BRIT col*) paf *inv*.

spa [spɑ:] *n* (*town*) station thermale; (*US: also*: **health ~**) établissement *m* de cure de rajeunissement.

space [speɪs] *n* (*gen*) espace *m*; (*room*) place *f*; espace; (*length of time*) laps *m* de temps ♦ *cpd* spatial(e) ♦ *vt* (*also*: **~ out**) espacer; **to clear a ~ for sth** faire de la place pour qch; **in a confined ~** dans un espace réduit *or* restreint; **in a short ~ of time** dans peu de temps; **(with)in the ~ of an hour** en l'espace d'une heure.

space bar *n* (*on typewriter*) barre *f* d'espacement.

spacecraft ['speɪskrɑ:ft] *n* engin spatial.

spaceman ['speɪsmæn] *n* astronaute *m*, cosmonaute *m*.

spaceship ['speɪsʃɪp] *n* engin *or* vaisseau spatial.

space shuttle *n* navette spatiale.

spacesuit ['speɪssu:t] *n* combinaison spatiale.

spacewoman ['speɪswumən] *n* astronaute *f*, cosmonaute *f*.

spacing ['speɪsɪŋ] *n* espacement *m*; **single/double ~** (*TYP etc*) interligne *m* simple/double.

spacious ['speɪʃəs] *adj* spacieux(euse), grand(e).

spade [speɪd] *n* (*tool*) bêche *f*, pelle *f*; (*child's*) pelle; **~s** *npl* (*CARDS*) pique *m*.

spadework ['speɪdwə:k] *n* (*fig*) gros *m* du travail.

spaghetti [spə'gɛtɪ] *n* spaghetti *mpl*.

Spain [speɪn] *n* Espagne *f*.

span [spæn] *n* (*of bird, plane*) envergure *f*; (*of arch*) portée *f*; (*in time*) espace *m* de temps, durée *f* ♦ *vt* enjamber, franchir; (*fig*) couvrir, embrasser.

Spaniard ['spænjəd] *n* Espagnol/e.

spaniel ['spænjəl] *n* épagneul *m*.

Spanish ['spænɪʃ] *adj* espagnol(e), d'Espagne ♦ *n* (*LING*) espagnol *m*; **the ~** *npl* les Espagnols; **~ omelette** omelette *f* à l'espagnole.

spank [spæŋk] *vt* donner une fessée à.

spanner ['spænə*] *n* (*BRIT*) clé *f* (de mécanicien).

spar [spɑ:*] *n* espar *m* ♦ *vi* (*BOXING*) s'entraîner.

spare [spɛə*] *adj* de réserve, de rechange; (*surplus*) de *or* en trop, de reste ♦ *n* (*part*) pièce *f* de rechange, pièce détachée ♦ *vt* (*do without*) se passer de; (*afford to give*) donner, accorder, passer; (*refrain from hurting*) épargner; (*refrain from using*) ménager; **to ~** (*surplus*) en surplus, de trop; **there are 2 going ~** (*BRIT*) il y en a 2 de disponible; **to ~ no expense** ne pas reculer devant la dépense; **can you ~ the time?** est-ce que vous avez le temps?; **there is no time to ~** il n'y a pas de temps à perdre; **I've a few minutes to ~** je dispose de quelques minutes.

spare part *n* pièce *f* de rechange, pièce détachée.

spare room *n* chambre *f* d'ami.

spare time *n* moments *mpl* de loisir.

spare tyre *n* (*AUT*) pneu *m* de rechange.

spare wheel *n* (*AUT*) roue *f* de secours.

sparing ['spɛərɪŋ] *adj*: **to be ~ with** ménager.

sparingly ['spɛərɪŋlɪ] *adv* avec modération.

spark [spɑ:k] *n* étincelle *f*; (*fig*) étincelle, lueur *f*.

spark(ing) plug ['spɑ:k(ɪŋ)-] *n* bougie *f*.

sparkle ['spɑ:kl] *n* scintillement *m*, étincellement *m*, éclat *m* ♦ *vi* étinceler, scintiller;

(*bubble*) pétiller.

sparkler ['spɑːklə*] n cierge m magique.

sparkling ['spɑːklɪŋ] adj étincelant(e), scintillant(e); (*wine*) mousseux(euse), pétillant(e).

sparring partner ['spɑːrɪŋ-] n sparringpartner m; (*fig*) vieil(le) ennemi/e.

sparrow ['spærəu] n moineau m.

sparse [spɑːs] adj clairsemé(e).

spartan ['spɑːtən] adj (*fig*) spartiate.

spasm ['spæzəm] n (MED) spasme m; (*fig*) accès m.

spasmodic [spæz'mɔdɪk] adj (*fig*) intermittent(e).

spastic ['spæstɪk] n handicapé/e moteur.

spat [spæt] pt, pp of **spit** ♦ n (US) prise f de bec.

spate [speɪt] n (*fig*): ~ **of** avalanche f or torrent m de; **in** ~ (*river*) en crue.

spatial ['speɪʃl] adj spatial(e).

spatter ['spætə*] n éclaboussure(s) f(pl) ♦ vt éclabousser ♦ vi gicler.

spatula ['spætjulə] n spatule f.

spawn [spɔːn] vt pondre; (*pej*) engendrer ♦ vi frayer ♦ n frai m.

SPCA n abbr (US: = Society for the Prevention of Cruelty to Animals) ≈ SPA f.

SPCC n abbr (US) = Society for the Prevention of Cruelty to Children.

speak, pt **spoke,** pp **spoken** [spiːk, spəuk, 'spəukn] vt (*language*) parler; (*truth*) dire ♦ vi parler; (*make a speech*) prendre la parole; **to ~ to sb/of or about sth** parler à qn/de qch; **~ing!** (*on telephone*) c'est moi-même!; **to ~ one's mind** dire ce que l'on pense; **it ~s for itself** c'est évident; ~ **up!** parle plus fort!; **he has no money to ~ of** il n'a pas d'argent.

▶**speak for** vt fus: **to ~ for sb** parler pour qn; **that picture is already spoken for** (*in shop*) ce tableau est déjà réservé.

speaker ['spiːkə*] n (*in public*) orateur m; (*also*: **loud~**) haut-parleur m; (POL): **the S~** le président de la Chambre des communes (BRIT) or des représentants (US); **are you a Welsh ~?** parlez-vous gallois?

speaking ['spiːkɪŋ] adj parlant(e); **French-~ people** les francophones; **to be on ~ terms** se parler.

spear [spɪə*] n lance f ♦ vt transpercer.

spearhead ['spɪəhɛd] n fer m de lance; (MIL) colonne f d'attaque ♦ vt (*attack etc*) mener.

spearmint ['spɪəmɪnt] n (BOT etc) menthe verte.

spec [spɛk] n (BRIT col): **on ~** à tout hasard; **to buy on ~** acheter avec l'espoir de faire une bonne affaire.

special ['spɛʃl] adj spécial(e) ♦ n (*train*) train spécial; **take ~ care** soyez particulièrement prudents; **nothing ~** rien de spécial; **today's ~** (*at restaurant*) le plat du jour.

special agent n agent secret.

special correspondent n envoyé spécial.

special delivery n (POST): **by ~** en exprès.

special effects npl (CINE) effets spéciaux.

specialist ['spɛʃəlɪst] n spécialiste m/f; **heart ~** cardiologue m/f.

speciality [spɛʃɪ'ælɪtɪ] n spécialité f.

specialize ['spɛʃəlaɪz] vi: **to ~ (in)** se spécialiser (dans).

specially ['spɛʃlɪ] adv spécialement, particulièrement.

special offer n (COMM) réclame f.

specialty ['spɛʃəltɪ] n (US) = **speciality.**

species ['spiːʃiːz] n (pl inv) espèce f.

specific [spə'sɪfɪk] adj (*not vague*) précis(e), explicite; (*particular*) particulier(ière); (BOT, CHEM etc) spécifique; **to be ~ to** être particulier à, être le or un caractère (or les caractères) spécifique(s) de.

specifically [spə'sɪfɪklɪ] adv explicitement, précisément; (*intend, ask, design*) expressément, spécialement; (*exclusively*) exclusivement, spécifiquement.

specification [spɛsɪfɪ'keɪʃən] n spécification f; stipulation f; **~s** npl (of car, building etc) spécification.

specify ['spɛsɪfaɪ] vt spécifier, préciser; **unless otherwise specified** sauf indication contraire.

specimen ['spɛsɪmən] n spécimen m, échantillon m; (MED) prélèvement m.

specimen copy n spécimen m.

specimen signature n spécimen m de signature.

speck [spɛk] n petite tache, petit point; (*particle*) grain m.

speckled ['spɛkld] adj tacheté(e), moucheté(e).

specs [spɛks] npl (col) lunettes fpl.

spectacle ['spɛktəkl] n spectacle m.

spectacle case n (BRIT) étui m à lunettes.

spectacles ['spɛktəklz] npl (BRIT) lunettes fpl.

spectacular [spɛk'tækjulə*] adj spectaculaire ♦ n (CINE etc) superproduction f.

spectator [spɛk'teɪtə*] n spectateur/trice.

spectator sport n: **football is a great ~** le football est un sport qui passionne les foules.

spectra ['spɛktrə] npl of **spectrum.**

spectre, (US) **specter** ['spɛktə*] n spectre m, fantôme m.

spectrum, pl **spectra** ['spɛktrəm, -rə] n spectre m; (*fig*) gamme f.

speculate ['spɛkjuleɪt] vi spéculer; (*try to guess*): **to ~ about** s'interroger sur.

speculation [spɛkju'leɪʃən] n spéculation f; conjectures fpl.

speculative ['spɛkjulətɪv] adj spéculatif(ive).

speculator ['spɛkjuleɪtə*] n spéculateur/trice.

speech [spiːtʃ] n (*faculty*) parole f; (*talk*) discours m, allocution f; (*manner of speaking*) façon f de parler, langage m; (*language*) langage m; (*enunciation*) élocution f.

speech day n (BRIT SCOL) distribution f des prix.

speech impediment n défaut m d'élocution.

speechless ['spi:tʃlɪs] *adj* muet(te).
speech therapy *n* orthophonie *f*.
speed [spi:d] *n* vitesse *f*; *(promptness)* rapidité *f* ♦ *vi* (*pt, pp* **sped** [sped]): **to ~ along/by** *etc* aller/passer *etc* à toute vitesse; (*AUT: exceed* ~ *limit*) faire un excès de vitesse; **at ~** (*BRIT*) rapidement; **at full** *or* **top ~** à toute vitesse *or* allure; **at a ~ of 70 km/h** à une vitesse de 70 km/h; **shorthand/typing ~s** nombre *m* de mots à la minute en sténographie/ dactylographie; **a five-~ gearbox** une boîte cinq vitesses.
▶**speed up**, *pt, pp* ~**ed up** *vi* aller plus vite, accélérer ♦ *vt* accélérer.
speedboat ['spi:dbəut] *n* vedette *f*, hors-bord *m inv*.
speedily ['spi:dɪlɪ] *adv* rapidement, promptement.
speeding ['spi:dɪŋ] *n* (*AUT*) excès *m* de vitesse.
speed limit *n* limitation *f* de vitesse, vitesse maximale permise.
speedometer [spɪ'dɔmɪtə*] *n* compteur *m* (de vitesse).
speed trap *n* (*AUT*) piège *m* de police pour contrôle de vitesse.
speedway *n* (*SPORT*) piste *f* de vitesse pour motos; (: *also*: ~ **racing**) épreuve(s) *f(pl)* de vitesse de motos.
speedy [spi:dɪ] *adj* rapide, prompt(e).
speleologist [spelɪ'ɔlədʒɪst] *n* spéléologue *m/f*.
spell [spel] *n* (*also*: **magic ~**) sortilège *m*, charme *m*; (*period of time*) (courte) période ♦ *vt* (*pt, pp* **spelt** *or* ~**ed** [spelt, speld]) (*in writing*) écrire, orthographier; (*aloud*) épeler; (*fig*) signifier; **to cast a ~ on sb** jeter un sort à qn; **he can't ~** il fait des fautes d'orthographe; **how do you ~ your name?** comment écrivez-vous votre nom?; **can you ~ it for me?** pouvez-vous me l'épeler?
spellbound ['spelbaund] *adj* envoûté(e), subjugué(e).
spelling ['spelɪŋ] *n* orthographe *f*.
spelt [spelt] *pt, pp of* **spell**.
spend, *pt, pp* **spent** [spend, spent] *vt* (*money*) dépenser; (*time, life*) passer; (*devote*): **to ~ time/money/effort on sth** consacrer du temps/de l'argent/de l'énergie à qch.
spending ['spendɪŋ] *n* dépenses *fpl*; **government ~** les dépenses publiques.
spending money *n* argent *m* de poche.
spending power *n* pouvoir *m* d'achat.
spendthrift ['spendθrɪft] *n* dépensier/ière.
spent [spent] *pt, pp of* **spend** ♦ *adj* (*patience*) épuisé(e), à bout; (*cartridge, bullets*) vide; ~ **matches** vieilles allumettes.
sperm [spə:m] *n* spermatozoïde *m*; (*semen*) sperme *m*.
sperm bank *n* banque *f* du sperme.
sperm whale *n* cachalot *m*.
spew [spju:] *vt* vomir.
sphere [sfɪə*] *n* sphère *f*; (*fig*) sphère, domaine *m*.

spherical ['sfɛrɪkl] *adj* sphérique.
sphinx [sfɪŋks] *n* sphinx *m*.
spice [spaɪs] *n* épice *f* ♦ *vt* épicer.
spick-and-span ['spɪkən'spæn] *adj* impeccable.
spicy ['spaɪsɪ] *adj* épicé(e), relevé(e); (*fig*) piquant(e).
spider ['spaɪdə*] *n* araignée *f*; ~'**s web** toile *f* d'araignée.
spiel [spi:l] *n* laïus *m inv*.
spike [spaɪk] *n* pointe *f*; (*ELEC*) pointe de tension; ~**s** *npl* (*SPORT*) chaussures *fpl* à pointes.
spike heel *n* (*US*) talon *m* aiguille.
spiky ['spaɪkɪ] *adj* (*bush, branch*) épineux(euse); (*animal*) plein(e) de piquants.
spill, *pt, pp* **spilt** *or* ~**ed** [spɪl, -t, -d] *vt* renverser; répandre ♦ *vi* se répandre; **to ~ the beans** (*col*) vendre la mèche; (: *confess*) lâcher le morceau.
▶**spill out** *vi* sortir à flots, se répandre.
▶**spill over** *vi* déborder.
spillage ['spɪlɪdʒ] *n* (*of oil*) déversement *m* (accidentel).
spin [spɪn] *n* (*revolution of wheel*) tour *m*; (*AVIAT*) (chute *f* en) vrille *f*; (*trip in car*) petit tour, balade *f* ♦ *vb* (*pt, pp* **spun** [spʌn]) *vt* (*wool etc*) filer; (*wheel*) faire tourner; (*BRIT: clothes*) essorer ♦ *vi* tourner, tournoyer; **to ~ a yarn** débiter une longue histoire; **to ~ a coin** (*BRIT*) jouer à pile ou face.
▶**spin out** *vt* faire durer.
spina bifida ['spaɪnə'bɪfɪdə] *n* spina-bifida *m inv*.
spinach ['spɪnɪtʃ] *n* épinard *m*; (*as food*) épinards.
spinal ['spaɪnl] *adj* vertébral(e), spinal(e).
spinal column *n* colonne vertébrale.
spinal cord *n* moelle épinière.
spindly ['spɪndlɪ] *adj* grêle, filiforme.
spin doctor *n* (*col*) personne employée pour présenter un parti politique sous un jour favorable.
spin-dry ['spɪn'draɪ] *vt* essorer.
spin-dryer [spɪn'draɪə*] *n* (*BRIT*) essoreuse *f*.
spine [spaɪn] *n* colonne vertébrale; (*thorn*) épine *f*, piquant *m*.
spine-chilling ['spaɪntʃɪlɪŋ] *adj* terrifiant(e).
spineless ['spaɪnlɪs] *adj* invertébré(e); (*fig*) mou(molle), sans caractère.
spinner ['spɪnə*] *n* (*of thread*) fileur/euse.
spinning ['spɪnɪŋ] *n* (*of thread*) filage *m*; (*by machine*) filature *f*.
spinning top *n* toupie *f*.
spinning wheel *n* rouet *m*.
spin-off ['spɪnɔf] *n* sous-produit *m*; avantage inattendu.
spinster ['spɪnstə*] *n* célibataire *f*; vieille fille.
spiral ['spaɪərl] *n* spirale *f* ♦ *vi* (*fig: prices etc*) monter en flèche; **the inflationary ~** la spirale inflationniste.
spiral staircase *n* escalier *m* en colimaçon.
spire ['spaɪə*] *n* flèche *f*, aiguille *f*.

spirit ['spɪrɪt] n (soul) esprit m, âme f; (ghost) esprit, revenant m; (mood) esprit, état m d'esprit; (courage) courage m, énergie f; ~s npl (drink) spiritueux mpl, alcool m; **in good ~s** de bonne humeur; **in low ~s** démoralisé(e); **community ~** solidarité f; **public ~** civisme m.

spirit duplicator n duplicateur m à alcool.

spirited ['spɪrɪtɪd] adj vif(vive), fougueux(euse), plein(e) d'allant.

spirit level n niveau m à bulle.

spiritual ['spɪrɪtjuəl] adj spirituel(le); religieux(euse) ♦ n (also: **Negro ~**) spiritual m.

spiritualism ['spɪrɪtjuəlɪzəm] n spiritisme m.

spit [spɪt] n (for roasting) broche f; (spittle) crachat m; (saliva) salive f ♦ vi (pt, pp **spat** [spæt]) cracher; (sound) crépiter.

spite [spaɪt] n rancune f, dépit m ♦ vt contrarier, vexer; **in ~ of** en dépit de, malgré.

spiteful ['spaɪtful] adj malveillant(e), rancunier(ière).

spitroast ['spɪt'rəust] vt faire rôtir à la broche.

spitting ['spɪtɪŋ] n: "~ **prohibited**" "défense de cracher" ♦ adj: **to be the ~ image of sb** être le portrait tout craché de qn.

spittle ['spɪtl] n salive f; bave f; crachat m.

spiv [spɪv] n (BRIT col) chevalier m d'industrie, aigrefin m.

splash [splæʃ] n éclaboussement m; (of colour) tache f ♦ excl (sound) plouf! ♦ vt éclabousser ♦ vi (also: **~ about**) barboter, patauger.

splashdown ['splæʃdaun] n amerrissage m.

splay [spleɪ] adj: **~footed** marchant les pieds en dehors.

spleen [spliːn] n (ANAT) rate f.

splendid ['splɛndɪd] adj splendide, superbe, magnifique.

splendour, (US) **splendor** ['splɛndə*] n splendeur f, magnificence f.

splice [splaɪs] vt épisser.

splint [splɪnt] n attelle f, éclisse f.

splinter ['splɪntə*] n (wood) écharde f; (metal) éclat m ♦ vi se fragmenter.

splinter group n groupe dissident.

split [splɪt] n fente f, déchirure f; (fig: POL) scission f ♦ vb (pt, pp **split**) vt fendre, déchirer; (party) diviser; (work, profits) partager, répartir ♦ vi (break) se fendre, se briser; (divide) se diviser; **let's ~ the difference** coupons la poire en deux; **to do the ~s** faire le grand écart.

▶**split up** vi (couple) se séparer, rompre; (meeting) se disperser.

split-level ['splɪtlɛvl] adj (house) à deux or plusieurs niveaux.

split peas npl pois cassés.

split personality n double personnalité f.

split second n fraction f de seconde.

splitting ['splɪtɪŋ] adj: **a ~ headache** un mal de tête atroce.

splutter ['splʌtə*] vi bafouiller; postillonner.

spoil, pt, pp **spoilt** or **~ed** [spɔɪl, -t, -d] vt (damage) abîmer; (mar) gâcher; (child) gâter; (ballot paper) rendre nul ♦ vi: **to be ~ing for a fight** chercher la bagarre.

spoils [spɔɪlz] npl butin m.

spoilsport ['spɔɪlspɔːt] n trouble-fête m/f inv, rabat-joie m inv.

spoilt [spɔɪlt] pt, pp of **spoil** ♦ adj (child) gâté(e); (ballot paper) nul(le).

spoke [spəuk] pt of **speak** ♦ n rayon m.

spoken ['spəukn] pp of **speak**.

spokesman ['spəuksmən], **spokeswoman** [-wumən] n porte-parole m inv.

spokesperson ['spəukspəːsn] n porte-parole m inv.

sponge [spʌndʒ] n éponge f; (CULIN: also: **~ cake**) ≈ biscuit m de Savoie ♦ vt éponger ♦ vi: **to ~ on** or (US) **off of** vivre aux crochets de.

sponge bag n (BRIT) trousse f de toilette.

sponge cake n ≈ biscuit m de Savoie.

sponger ['spʌndʒə*] n (pej) parasite m.

spongy ['spʌndʒɪ] adj spongieux(euse).

sponsor ['spɔnsə*] n sponsor m, personne f (or organisme m) qui assure le parrainage; (of new member) parrain m/marraine f ♦ vt (programme, competition etc) parrainer, patronner, sponsoriser; (POL: bill) présenter; (new member) parrainer; **I ~ed him at 3p a mile** (in fund-raising race) je me suis engagé à lui donner 3p par mile.

sponsorship ['spɔnsəʃɪp] n patronage m, parrainage m.

spontaneity [spɔntə'neɪtɪ] n spontanéité f.

spontaneous [spɔn'teɪnɪəs] adj spontané(e).

spoof [spuːf] n (parody) parodie f; (trick) canular m.

spooky ['spuːkɪ] adj qui donne la chair de poule.

spool [spuːl] n bobine f.

spoon [spuːn] n cuiller f.

spoon-feed ['spuːnfiːd] vt nourrir à la cuiller; (fig) mâcher le travail à.

spoonful ['spuːnful] n cuillerée f.

sporadic [spə'rædɪk] adj sporadique.

sport [spɔːt] n sport m; (amusement) divertissement m; (person) chic type/chic fille ♦ vt arborer; **indoor/outdoor ~s** sports en salle/de plein air; **to say sth in ~** dire qch pour rire.

sporting ['spɔːtɪŋ] adj sportif(ive); **to give sb a ~ chance** donner sa chance à qn.

sport jacket n (US) = **sports jacket**.

sports car n voiture f de sport.

sports ground n terrain m de sport.

sports jacket n veste f de sport.

sportsman ['spɔːtsmən] n sportif m.

sportsmanship ['spɔːtsmənʃɪp] n esprit sportif, sportivité f.

sports page n page f des sports.

sportswear ['spɔːtswɛə*] n vêtements mpl de sport.

sportswoman ['spɔːtswʊmən] *n* sportive *f*.
sporty ['spɔːtɪ] *adj* sportif(ive).
spot [spɔt] *n* tache *f*; (*dot: on pattern*) pois *m*; (*pimple*) bouton *m*; (*place*) endroit *m*, coin *m*; (*also:* ~ **advertisement**) message *m* publicitaire; (*small amount*): **a** ~ **of** un peu de ♦ *vt* (*notice*) apercevoir, repérer; **on the** ~ sur place, sur les lieux; (*immediately*) sur le champ; **to put sb on the** ~ (*fig*) mettre qn dans l'embarras; **to come out in** ~s se couvrir de boutons, avoir une éruption de boutons.
spot check *n* contrôle intermittent.
spotless ['spɔtlɪs] *adj* immaculé(e).
spotlight ['spɔtlaɪt] *n* projecteur *m*; (*AUT*) phare *m* auxiliaire.
spot-on [spɔt'ɔn] *adj* (*BRIT col*) en plein dans le mille.
spot price *n* prix *m* sur place.
spotted ['spɔtɪd] *adj* tacheté(e), moucheté(e); à pois; ~ **with** tacheté(e) de.
spotty ['spɔtɪ] *adj* (*face*) boutonneux(euse).
spouse [spauz] *n* époux/épouse.
spout [spaut] *n* (*of jug*) bec *m*; (*of liquid*) jet *m* ♦ *vi* jaillir.
sprain [spreɪn] *n* entorse *f*, foulure *f* ♦ *vt*: **to** ~ **one's ankle** se fouler *or* se tordre la cheville.
sprang [spræŋ] *pt of* **spring**.
sprawl [sprɔːl] *vi* s'étaler ♦ *n*: **urban** ~ expansion urbaine; **to send sb** ~**ing** envoyer qn rouler par terre.
spray [spreɪ] *n* jet *m* (*en fines gouttelettes*); (*container*) vaporisateur *m*, bombe *f*; (*of flowers*) petit bouquet ♦ *vt* vaporiser, pulvériser; (*crops*) traiter ♦ *cpd* (*deodorant etc*) en bombe *or* atomiseur.
spread [sprɛd] *n* (*distribution*) répartition *f*; (*CULIN*) pâte *f* à tartiner; (*PRESS, TYP: two pages*) double page *f* ♦ *vb* (*pt, pp* **spread**) *vt* (*paste, contents*) étendre, étaler; (*rumour, disease*) répandre, propager; (*repayments*) échelonner, étaler; (*wealth*) répartir ♦ *vi* s'étendre; se répandre; se propager; **middle-age** ~ embonpoint *m* (*pris avec l'âge*).
spread-eagled ['sprɛdiːɡld] *adj*: **to be** *or* **lie** ~ être étendu(e) bras et jambes écartés.
spreadsheet ['sprɛdʃiːt] *n* (*COMPUT*) tableur *m*.
spree [spriː] *n*: **to go on a** ~ faire la fête.
sprig [sprɪɡ] *n* rameau *m*.
sprightly ['spraɪtlɪ] *adj* alerte.
spring [sprɪŋ] *n* (*leap*) bond *m*, saut *m*; (*coiled metal*) ressort *m*; (*bounciness*) élasticité *f*; (*season*) printemps *m*; (*of water*) source *f* ♦ *vb* (*pt* **sprang**, *pp* **sprung** [spræŋ, sprʌŋ]) *vi* bondir, sauter ♦ *vt*: **to** ~ **a leak** (*pipe etc*) se mettre à fuir; **he sprang the news on me** il m'a annoncé la nouvelle de but en blanc; **in** ~, **in the** ~ au printemps; **to** ~ **from** provenir de; **to** ~ **into action** passer à l'action; **to**

walk with a ~ **in one's step** marcher d'un pas souple.
▶**spring up** *vi* (*problem*) se présenter, surgir.
springboard ['sprɪŋbɔːd] *n* tremplin *m*.
spring-clean [sprɪŋ'kliːn] *n* (*also:* ~**ing**) grand nettoyage de printemps.
spring onion *n* (*BRIT*) ciboule *f*, cive *f*.
spring roll *n* rouleau *m* de printemps.
springtime ['sprɪŋtaɪm] *n* printemps *m*.
springy ['sprɪŋɪ] *adj* élastique, souple.
sprinkle ['sprɪŋkl] *vt* (*pour*) répandre; verser; **to** ~ **water** *etc* **on**, ~ **with water** *etc* asperger d'eau *etc*; **to** ~ **sugar** *etc* **on**, ~ **with sugar** *etc* saupoudrer de sucre *etc*; ~**d with** (*fig*) parsemé(e) de.
sprinkler ['sprɪŋklə*] *n* (*for lawn etc*) arroseur *m*; (*to put out fire*) diffuseur *m* d'extincteur automatique d'incendie.
sprinkling ['sprɪŋklɪŋ] *n* (*of water*) quelques gouttes *fpl*; (*of salt*) pincée *f*; (*of sugar*) légère couche.
sprint [sprɪnt] *n* sprint *m* ♦ *vi* sprinter.
sprinter ['sprɪntə*] *n* sprinteur/euse.
sprite [spraɪt] *n* lutin *m*.
spritzer ['sprɪtsə*] *n* boisson à base de vin blanc et d'eau de Seltz.
sprocket ['sprɔkɪt] *n* (*on printer etc*) picot *m*.
sprout [spraut] *vi* germer, pousser.
sprouts [sprauts] *npl* (*also:* **Brussels** ~) choux *mpl* de Bruxelles.
spruce [spruːs] *n* épicéa *m* ♦ *adj* net(te), pimpant(e).
▶**spruce up** *vt* (*smarten up: room etc*) apprêter; **to** ~ **o.s. up** se faire beau(belle).
sprung [sprʌŋ] *pp of* **spring**.
spry [spraɪ] *adj* alerte, vif(vive).
SPUC *n abbr* = *Society for the Protection of Unborn Children*.
spud [spʌd] *n* (*col: potato*) patate *f*.
spun [spʌn] *pt, pp of* **spin**.
spur [spəː*] *n* éperon *m*; (*fig*) aiguillon *m* ♦ *vt* (*also:* ~ **on**) éperonner; aiguillonner; **on the** ~ **of the moment** sous l'impulsion du moment.
spurious ['spjuərɪəs] *adj* faux(fausse).
spurn [spəːn] *vt* repousser avec mépris.
spurt [spəːt] *n* jet *m*; (*of energy*) sursaut *m* ♦ *vi* jaillir, gicler; **to put in** *or* **on a** ~ (*runner*) piquer un sprint; (*fig: in work etc*) donner un coup de collier.
sputter ['spʌtə*] *vi* = **splutter**.
spy [spaɪ] *n* espion/ne ♦ *vi*: **to** ~ **on** espionner, épier ♦ *vt* (*see*) apercevoir ♦ *cpd* (*film, story*) d'espionnage.
spying ['spaɪɪŋ] *n* espionnage *m*.
Sq. *abbr* (*in address*) = **square**.
sq. *abbr* (*MATH etc*) = **square**.
squabble ['skwɔbl] *n* querelle *f*, chamaillerie *f* ♦ *vi* se chamailler.
squad [skwɔd] *n* (*MIL, POLICE*) escouade *f*, groupe *m*; (*FOOTBALL*) contingent *m*; **flying** ~ (*POLICE*) brigade volante.

squad car n (BRIT POLICE) voiture f de police.
squaddie ['skwɔdı] n (MIL col) troufion m, bidasse m.
squadron ['skwɔdrn] n (MIL) escadron m; (AVIAT, NAUT) escadrille f.
squalid ['skwɔlıd] adj sordide, ignoble.
squall [skwɔːl] n rafale f, bourrasque f.
squalor ['skwɔlə*] n conditions fpl sordides.
squander ['skwɔndə*] vt gaspiller, dilapider.
square [skwɛə*] n carré m; (in town) place f; (US: block of houses) îlot m, pâté m de maisons; (instrument) équerre f ♦ adj carré(e); (honest) honnête, régulier(ière); (col: ideas, tastes) vieux jeu inv, qui retarde ♦ vt (arrange) régler; arranger; (MATH) élever au carré; (reconcile) concilier ♦ vi (agree) cadrer, s'accorder; all ~ quitte; à égalité; a ~ meal un repas convenable; 2 metres ~ (de) 2 mètres sur 2; 1 ~ metre 1 mètre carré; we're back to ~ one (fig) on se retrouve à la case départ.
▶**square up** vi (BRIT: settle) régler; to ~ up with sb régler ses comptes avec qn.
square bracket n (TYP) crochet m.
squarely ['skwɛəlı] adv carrément; (honestly, fairly) honnêtement, équitablement.
square root n racine carrée.
squash [skwɔʃ] n (BRIT: drink): lemon/orange ~ citronnade/orangeade f; (SPORT) squash m; (vegetable) courge f ♦ vt écraser.
squat [skwɔt] adj petit(e) et épais(se), ramassé(e) ♦ vi s'accroupir; (on property) squatter, squattériser.
squatter ['skwɔtə*] n squatter m.
squawk [skwɔːk] vi pousser un or des gloussement(s).
squeak [skwiːk] n (of hinge, wheel etc) grincement m; (of shoes) craquement m; (of mouse etc) petit cri aigu ♦ vi grincer, crier.
squeaky ['skwiːkı] adj grinçant(e); to be ~ clean (fig) être au-dessus de tout soupçon.
squeal [skwiːl] vi pousser un or des cri(s) aigu(s) or perçant(s).
squeamish ['skwiːmıʃ] adj facilement dégoûté(e); facilement scandalisé(e).
squeeze [skwiːz] n pression f; (also: credit ~) encadrement m du crédit, restrictions fpl de crédit ♦ vt presser; (hand, arm) serrer ♦ vi: to ~ past/under sth se glisser avec (beaucoup de) difficulté devant/sous qch; a ~ of lemon quelques gouttes de citron.
▶**squeeze out** vt exprimer; (fig) soutirer.
squelch [skwɛltʃ] vi faire un bruit de succion; patauger.
squib [skwıb] n pétard m.
squid [skwıd] n calmar m.
squiggle ['skwıgl] n gribouillis m.
squint [skwınt] vi loucher ♦ n: he has a ~ il louche, il souffre de strabisme; to ~ at sth regarder qch du coin de l'œil; (quickly) jeter un coup d'œil à qch.
squire ['skwaıə*] n (BRIT) propriétaire terrien.

squirm [skwɔːm] vi se tortiller.
squirrel ['skwırəl] n écureuil m.
squirt [skwɔːt] n jet m ♦ vi jaillir, gicler.
Sr abbr = senior, sister (REL).
SRC n abbr (BRIT: = Students' Representative Council) ≈ CROUS m.
Sri Lanka [srı'læŋkə] n Sri Lanka m or f.
SRN n abbr (BRIT) = State Registered Nurse.
SRO abbr (US) = standing room only.
SS abbr (= steamship) S/S.
SSA n abbr (US: = Social Security Administration) organisme de sécurité sociale.
SST n abbr (US) = supersonic transport.
ST abbr (US: = Standard Time) heure officielle.
St abbr (= saint) St; (= street) R.
stab [stæb] n (with knife etc) coup m (de couteau etc); (col: try): to have a ~ at (doing) sth s'essayer à (faire) qch ♦ vt poignarder; to ~ sb to death tuer qn à coups de couteau.
stabbing ['stæbıŋ] n: there's been a ~ quelqu'un a été attaqué à coups de couteau ♦ adj (pain, ache) lancinant(e).
stability [stə'bılıtı] n stabilité f.
stabilization [steıbəlaı'zeıʃən] n stabilisation f.
stabilize ['steıbəlaız] vt stabiliser ♦ vi se stabiliser.
stabilizer ['steıbəlaızə*] n stabilisateur m.
stable ['steıbl] n écurie f ♦ adj stable; riding ~s centre m d'équitation.
staccato [stə'kɑːtəu] adv staccato ♦ adj (MUS) piqué(e); (noise, voice) saccadé(e).
stack [stæk] n tas m, pile f ♦ vt empiler, entasser; there's ~s of time (BRIT col) on a tout le temps.
stadium ['steıdıəm] n stade m.
staff [stɑːf] n (work force) personnel m; (BRIT SCOL: also: teaching ~) professeurs mpl, enseignants mpl, personnel enseignant; (servants) domestiques mpl; (MIL) état-major m; (stick) perche f, bâton m ♦ vt pourvoir en personnel.
staffroom ['stɑːfruːm] n salle f des professeurs.
Staffs abbr (BRIT) = Staffordshire.
stag [stæg] n cerf m; (BRIT STOCK EXCHANGE) loup m.
stage [steıdʒ] n scène f; (profession): the ~ le théâtre; (point) étape f, stade m; (platform) estrade f ♦ vt (play) monter, mettre en scène; (demonstration) organiser; (fig: recovery etc) effectuer; in ~s par étapes, par degrés; to go through a difficult ~ traverser une période difficile; in the early ~s au début; in the final ~s à la fin.
stagecoach ['steıdʒkəutʃ] n diligence f.
stage door n entrée f des artistes.
stage fright n trac m.
stagehand ['steıdʒhænd] n machiniste m.
stage-manage ['steıdʒmænıdʒ] vt (fig) orchestrer.
stage manager n régisseur m.

stagger ['stægə*] *vi* chanceler, tituber ♦ *vt* (*person*) stupéfier; bouleverser; (*hours, holidays*) étaler, échelonner.

staggering ['stægərɪŋ] *adj* (*amazing*) stupéfiant(e), renversant(e).

staging post ['steɪdʒɪŋ-] *n* relais *m*.

stagnant ['stægnənt] *adj* stagnant(e).

stagnate [stæg'neɪt] *vi* stagner, croupir.

stagnation [stæg'neɪʃən] *n* stagnation *f*.

stag night, stag party *n* enterrement *m* de vie de garçon.

staid [steɪd] *adj* posé(e), rassis(e).

stain [steɪn] *n* tache *f*; (*colouring*) colorant *m* ♦ *vt* tacher; (*wood*) teindre.

stained glass window [steɪnd-] *n* vitrail *m*.

stainless ['steɪnlɪs] *adj* (*steel*) inoxydable.

stain remover *n* détachant *m*.

stair [stɛə*] *n* (*step*) marche *f*; ~s *npl* escalier *m*; **on the** ~s dans l'escalier.

staircase ['stɛəkeɪs], **stairway** ['stɛəweɪ] *n* escalier *m*.

stairwell ['stɛəwɛl] *n* cage *f* d'escalier.

stake [steɪk] *n* pieu *m*, poteau *m*; (*BETTING*) enjeu *m* ♦ *vt* risquer, jouer; (*also*: ~ **out**: *area*) marquer, délimiter; **to be at** ~ être en jeu; **to have a** ~ **in sth** avoir des intérêts (en jeu) dans qch; **to** ~ **a claim (to sth)** revendiquer (qch).

stakeout ['steɪkaut] *n* surveillance *f*; **to be on a** ~ effectuer une surveillance.

stalactite ['stæləktaɪt] *n* stalactite *f*.

stalagmite ['stæləgmaɪt] *n* stalagmite *f*.

stale [steɪl] *adj* (*bread*) rassis(e); (*beer*) éventé(e); (*smell*) de renfermé.

stalemate ['steɪlmeɪt] *n* pat *m*; (*fig*) impasse *f*.

stalk [stɔːk] *n* tige *f* ♦ *vt* traquer ♦ *vi*: **to** ~ **in/out** entrer/sortir *etc* avec raideur.

stall [stɔːl] *n* (*BRIT: in street, market etc*) éventaire *m*, étal *m*; (*in stable*) stalle *f* ♦ *vt* (*AUT*) caler ♦ *vi* (*AUT*) caler; (*fig*) essayer de gagner du temps; ~s *npl* (*BRIT: in cinema, theatre*) orchestre *m*; **a newspaper/flower** ~ un kiosque à journaux/de fleuriste.

stallholder ['stɔːlhəuldə*] *n* (*BRIT*) marchand/e en plein air.

stallion ['stæljən] *n* étalon *m* (*cheval*).

stalwart ['stɔːlwət] *n* partisan *m* fidèle.

stamen ['steɪmɛn] *n* étamine *f*.

stamina ['stæmɪnə] *n* vigueur *f*, endurance *f*.

stammer ['stæmə*] *n* bégaiement *m* ♦ *vi* bégayer.

stamp [stæmp] *n* timbre *m*; (*mark, also fig*) empreinte *f*; (*on document*) cachet *m* ♦ *vi* (*also*: ~ **one's foot**) taper du pied ♦ *vt* tamponner, estamper; (*letter*) timbrer; ~**ed addressed envelope (s.a.e.)** enveloppe affranchie pour la réponse.

▶**stamp out** *vt* (*fire*) piétiner; (*crime*) éradiquer; (*opposition*) éliminer.

stamp album *n* album *m* de timbres(-poste).

stamp collecting [-kəlɛktɪŋ] *n* philatélie *f*.

stamp duty *n* (*BRIT*) droit *m* de timbre.

stampede [stæm'piːd] *n* ruée *f*; (*of cattle*) débandade *f*.

stamp machine *n* distributeur *m* de timbres-poste.

stance [stæns] *n* position *f*.

stand [stænd] *n* (*position*) position *f*; (*MIL*) résistance *f*; (*structure*) guéridon *m*; support *m*; (*COMM*) étalage *m*, stand *m*; (*SPORT*) tribune *f*; (*also*: **music** ~) pupitre *m* ♦ *vb* (*pt, pp* **stood** [stud]) *vi* être *or* se tenir (debout); (*rise*) se lever, se mettre debout; (*be placed*) se trouver ♦ *vt* (*place*) mettre, poser; (*tolerate, withstand*) supporter; **to make a** ~ prendre position; **to take a** ~ **on an issue** prendre position sur un problème; **to** ~ **for parliament** (*BRIT*) se présenter aux élections (*comme candidat à la députation*); **to** ~ **guard** *or* **watch** (*MIL*) monter la garde; **it** ~**s to reason** c'est logique; cela va de soi; **as things** ~ dans l'état actuel des choses; **to** ~ **sb a drink/meal** payer à boire/à manger à qn; **I can't** ~ **him** je ne peux pas le voir.

▶**stand aside** *vi* s'écarter.

▶**stand by** *vi* (*be ready*) se tenir prêt(e) ♦ *vt fus* (*opinion*) s'en tenir à.

▶**stand down** *vi* (*withdraw*) se retirer; (*LAW*) renoncer à ses droits.

▶**stand for** *vt fus* (*signify*) représenter, signifier; (*tolerate*) supporter, tolérer.

▶**stand in for** *vt fus* remplacer.

▶**stand out** *vi* (*be prominent*) ressortir.

▶**stand up** *vi* (*rise*) se lever, se mettre debout.

▶**stand up for** *vt fus* défendre.

▶**stand up to** *vt fus* tenir tête à, résister à.

stand-alone ['stændələun] *adj* (*COMPUT*) autonome.

standard ['stændəd] *n* (*reference*) norme *f*; (*level*) niveau *m*; (*flag*) étendard *m* ♦ *adj* (*size etc*) ordinaire, normal(e); (*model, feature*) standard *inv*; (*practice*) courant(e); (*text*) de base; ~**s** *npl* (*morals*) morale *f*, principes *mpl*; **to be** *or* **come up to** ~ être du niveau voulu *or* à la hauteur; **to apply a double** ~ avoir *or* appliquer deux poids deux mesures; ~ **of living** niveau de vie.

standardization [stændədaɪ'zeɪʃən] *n* standardisation *f*.

standardize ['stændədaɪz] *vt* standardiser.

standard lamp *n* (*BRIT*) lampadaire *m*.

standard time *n* heure légale.

stand-by ['stændbaɪ] *n* remplaçant/e ♦ *adj* (*provisions*) de réserve; **to be on** ~ se tenir prêt(e) (à intervenir); (*doctor*) être de garde.

stand-by generator *n* générateur *m* de secours.

stand-by passenger *n* passager/ère en stand-by *or* en attente.

stand-by ticket *n* billet *m* stand-by.

stand-in ['stændɪn] *n* remplaçant/e; (*CINE*) doublure *f*.

standing ['stændɪŋ] adj debout inv; (permanent: rule) immuable; (army) de métier; (grievance) constant(e), de longue date ♦ n réputation f, rang m, standing m; (duration): **of 6 months'** ~ qui dure depuis 6 mois; **of many years'** ~ qui dure or existe depuis longtemps; **he was given a** ~ **ovation** on s'est levé pour l'acclamer; **it's a** ~ **joke** c'est un vieux sujet de plaisanterie; **a man of some** ~ un homme estimé.

standing committee n commission permanente.

standing order n (BRIT: at bank) virement permanent; ~**s** npl (MIL) règlement m.

standing room n places fpl debout.

stand-off ['stændɔf] n (esp US: stalemate) impasse f.

stand-offish [stænd'ɔfɪʃ] adj distant(e), froid(e).

standpat ['stændpæt] adj (US) inflexible, rigide.

standpipe ['stændpaɪp] n colonne f d'alimentation.

standpoint ['stændpɔɪnt] n point m de vue.

standstill ['stændstɪl] n: **at a** ~ à l'arrêt; (fig) au point mort; **to come to a** ~ s'immobiliser, s'arrêter.

stank [stæŋk] pt of **stink**.

stanza ['stænzə] n strophe f; couplet m.

staple ['steɪpl] n (for papers) agrafe f; (chief product) produit m de base ♦ adj (food, crop, industry etc) de base, principal(e) ♦ vt agrafer.

stapler ['steɪplə*] n agrafeuse f.

star [stɑː*] n étoile f; (celebrity) vedette f ♦ vi: **to** ~ **(in)** être la vedette (de) ♦ vt (CINE) avoir pour vedette; **4-**~ **hotel** hôtel m 4 étoiles; **2-**~ **petrol** (BRIT) essence f ordinaire; **4-**~ **petrol** (BRIT) super m.

star attraction n grande attraction.

starboard ['stɑːbəd] n tribord m; **to** ~ à tribord.

starch [stɑːtʃ] n amidon m.

starched ['stɑːtʃt] adj (collar) amidonné(e), empesé(e).

starchy ['stɑːtʃɪ] adj riche en féculents; (person) guindé(e).

stardom ['stɑːdəm] n célébrité f.

stare [stɛə*] n regard m fixe ♦ vi: **to** ~ **at** regarder fixement.

starfish ['stɑːfɪʃ] n étoile f de mer.

stark [stɑːk] adj (bleak) désolé(e), morne; (simplicity, colour) austère; (reality, poverty) nu(e) ♦ adv: ~ **naked** complètement nu(e).

starkers ['stɑːkəz] adj: **to be** ~ (BRIT col) être à poil.

starlet ['stɑːlɪt] n (CINE) starlette f.

starlight ['stɑːlaɪt] n: **by** ~ à la lumière des étoiles.

starling ['stɑːlɪŋ] n étourneau m.

starlit ['stɑːlɪt] adj étoilé(e); illuminé(e) par les étoiles.

starry ['stɑːrɪ] adj étoilé(e).

starry-eyed [stɑːrɪ'aɪd] adj (innocent) ingénu(e).

Stars and Stripes npl: **the** ~ la bannière étoilée.

star sign n signe zodiacal or du zodiaque.

star-studded ['stɑːstʌdɪd] adj: **a** ~ **cast** une distribution prestigieuse.

start [stɑːt] n commencement m, début m; (of race) départ m; (sudden movement) sursaut m; (advantage) avance f ♦ vt commencer; (found: business, newspaper) lancer, créer ♦ vi partir, se mettre en route; (jump) sursauter; **at the** ~ au début; **for a** ~ d'abord, pour commencer; **to make an early** ~ partir or commencer de bonne heure; **to** ~ **doing** sth se mettre à faire qch; **to** ~ **(off) with ...** (firstly) d'abord ...; (at the beginning) au commencement ....

▶**start off** vi commencer; (leave) partir.

▶**start over** vi (US) recommencer.

▶**start up** vi commencer; (car) démarrer ♦ vt déclencher; (car) mettre en marche.

starter ['stɑːtə*] n (AUT) démarreur m; (SPORT: official) starter m; (: runner, horse) partant m; (BRIT CULIN) entrée f.

starting handle ['stɑːtɪŋ-] n (BRIT) manivelle f.

starting point ['stɑːtɪŋ-] n point m de départ.

starting price ['stɑːtɪŋ-] n prix initial.

startle ['stɑːtl] vt faire sursauter; donner un choc à.

startling ['stɑːtlɪŋ] adj surprenant(e), saisissant(e).

star turn n (BRIT) vedette f.

starvation [stɑː'veɪʃən] n faim f, famine f; **to die of** ~ mourir de faim or d'inanition.

starve [stɑːv] vi mourir de faim; être affamé(e) ♦ vt affamer; **I'm starving** je meurs de faim.

stash [stæʃ] vt (col): **to** ~ **sth away** planquer qch.

state [steɪt] n état m; (pomp): **in** ~ en grande pompe ♦ vt (declare) déclarer, affirmer; (specify) indiquer, spécifier; **to be in a** ~ être dans tous ses états; ~ **of emergency** état d'urgence; ~ **of mind** état d'esprit; **the** ~ **of the art** l'état actuel de la technologie (or des connaissances).

state control n contrôle m de l'État.

stated ['steɪtɪd] adj fixé(e), prescrit(e).

State Department n (US) Département m d'État, ≈ ministère m des Affaires étrangères.

state education n (BRIT) enseignement public.

stateless ['steɪtlɪs] adj apatride.

stately ['steɪtlɪ] adj majestueux(euse), imposant(e).

statement ['steɪtmənt] n déclaration f; (LAW) déposition f; (ECON) relevé m; **official** ~ communiqué officiel; ~ **of account, bank** ~ relevé de compte.

state-owned ['steɪtəund] *adj* étatisé(e).

States [steɪts] *npl:* **the** ~ les États-Unis *mpl.*

state school *n* école publique.

state secret *n* secret *m* d'État.

statesman ['steɪtsmən] *n* homme *m* d'État.

statesmanship ['steɪtsmənʃɪp] *n* qualités *fpl* d'homme d'État.

static ['stætɪk] *n* (*RADIO*) parasites *mpl;* (*also:* ~ **electricity**) électricité *f* statique ♦ *adj* statique.

station ['steɪʃən] *n* gare *f;* (*MIL, POLICE*) poste *m* (militaire *or* de police *etc*); (*rank*) condition *f*, rang *m* ♦ *vt* placer, poster; **action** ~**s** postes *mpl* de combat; **to be** ~**ed in** (*MIL*) être en garnison à.

stationary ['steɪʃnərɪ] *adj* à l'arrêt, immobile.

stationer ['steɪʃənə*] *n* papetier/ière; ~**'s (shop)** papeterie *f.*

stationery ['steɪʃnərɪ] *n* papier *m* à lettres, petit matériel de bureau.

station master *n* (*RAIL*) chef *m* de gare.

station wagon *n* (*US*) break *m.*

statistic [stə'tɪstɪk] *n* statistique *f.*

statistical [stə'tɪstɪkl] *adj* statistique.

statistics [stə'tɪstɪks] *n* (*science*) statistique *f.*

statue ['stætjuː] *n* statue *f.*

statuesque [stætju'esk] *adj* sculptural(e).

statuette [stætju'et] *n* statuette *f.*

stature ['stætʃə*] *n* stature *f;* (*fig*) envergure *f.*

status ['steɪtəs] *n* position *f*, situation *f;* (*prestige*) prestige *m;* (*ADMIN, official position*) statut *m.*

status quo [-'kwəu] *n:* **the** ~ le statu quo.

status symbol *n* marque *f* de standing, signe extérieur de richesse.

statute ['stætjuːt] *n* loi *f;* ~**s** *npl* (*of club etc*) statuts *mpl.*

statute book *n* ≈ code *m*, textes *mpl* de loi.

statutory ['stætjutrɪ] *adj* statutaire, prévu(e) par un article de loi; ~ **meeting** assemblée constitutive *or* statutaire.

staunch [stɔːntʃ] *adj* sûr(e), loyal(e) ♦ *vt* étancher.

stave [steɪv] *n* (*MUS*) portée *f* ♦ *vt:* **to** ~ **off** (*attack*) parer; (*threat*) conjurer.

stay [steɪ] *n* (*period of time*) séjour *m;* (*LAW*): ~ **of execution** sursis *m* à statuer ♦ *vi* rester; (*reside*) loger; (*spend some time*) séjourner; **to** ~ **put** ne pas bouger; **to** ~ **with friends** loger chez des amis; **to** ~ **the night** passer la nuit.

▶**stay behind** *vi* rester en arrière.

▶**stay in** *vi* (*at home*) rester à la maison.

▶**stay on** *vi* rester.

▶**stay out** *vi* (*of house*) ne pas rentrer; (*strikers*) rester en grève.

▶**stay up** *vi* (*at night*) ne pas se coucher.

staying power ['steɪɪŋ-] *n* endurance *f.*

STD *n abbr* (*BRIT:* = *subscriber trunk dialling*) l'automatique *m;* (= *sexually transmitted disease*) MST *f.*

stead [sted] *n* (*BRIT*): **in sb's** ~ à la place de qn; **to stand sb in good** ~ être très utile *or* servir beaucoup à qn.

steadfast ['stedfɑːst] *adj* ferme, résolu(e).

steadily ['stedɪlɪ] *adv* régulièrement; fermement; d'une voix *etc* ferme.

steady ['stedɪ] *adj* stable, solide, ferme; (*regular*) constant(e), régulier(ière); (*person*) calme, pondéré(e) ♦ *vt* assurer, stabiliser; (*voice*) assurer; **to** ~ **oneself** reprendre son aplomb.

steak [steɪk] *n* (*meat*) bifteck *m*, steak *m;* (*fish*) tranche *f.*

steakhouse ['steɪkhaus] *n* ≈ grill-room *m.*

steal, *pt* **stole,** *pp* **stolen** [stiːl, stəul, 'stəuln] *vt, vi* voler.

▶**steal away, steal off** *vi* s'esquiver.

stealth [stelθ] *n:* **by** ~ furtivement.

stealthy ['stelθɪ] *adj* furtif(ive).

steam [stiːm] *n* vapeur *f* ♦ *vt* passer à la vapeur; (*CULIN*) cuire à la vapeur ♦ *vi* fumer; (*ship*): **to** ~ **along** filer; **under one's own** ~ (*fig*) par ses propres moyens; **to run out of** ~ (*fig: person*) caler; être à bout; **to let off** ~ (*fig: col*) se défouler.

▶**steam up** *vi* (*window*) se couvrir de buée; **to get** ~**ed up about sth** (*fig: col*) s'exciter à propos de qch.

steam engine *n* locomotive *f* à vapeur.

steamer ['stiːmə*] *n* (bateau *m* à) vapeur *m;* (*CULIN*) ≈ couscoussier *m.*

steam iron *n* fer *m* à repasser à vapeur.

steamroller ['stiːmrəulə*] *n* rouleau compresseur.

steamy ['stiːmɪ] *adj* embué(e), humide.

steed [stiːd] *n* (*literary*) coursier *m.*

steel [stiːl] *n* acier *m* ♦ *cpd* d'acier.

steel band *n* steel band *m.*

steel industry *n* sidérurgie *f.*

steel mill *n* aciérie *f*, usine *f* sidérurgique.

steelworks ['stiːlwəːks] *n* aciérie *f.*

steely ['stiːlɪ] *adj* (*determination*) inflexible; (*eyes, gaze*) d'acier.

steep [stiːp] *adj* raide, escarpé(e); (*price*) très élevé(e), excessif(ive) ♦ *vt* (faire) tremper.

steeple ['stiːpl] *n* clocher *m.*

steeplechase ['stiːpltʃeɪs] *n* steeple(-chase) *m.*

steeplejack ['stiːpldʒæk] *n* réparateur *m* de clochers et de hautes cheminées.

steeply ['stiːplɪ] *adv* en pente raide.

steer [stɪə*] *n* bœuf *m* ♦ *vt* diriger, gouverner; (*lead*) guider ♦ *vi* tenir le gouvernail; **to** ~ **clear of sb/sth** (*fig*) éviter qn/qch.

steering ['stɪərɪŋ] *n* (*AUT*) conduite *f.*

steering column *n* (*AUT*) colonne *f* de direction.

steering committee *n* comité *m* d'organisation.

steering wheel *n* volant *m.*

stellar ['stelə*] *adj* stellaire.

stem [stem] *n* (*of plant*) tige *f;* (*of leaf, fruit*) queue *f*; (*of glass*) pied *m* ♦ *vt* contenir, endiguer, juguler.

▶**stem from** *vt fus* provenir de, découler de.

stench [stɛntʃ] *n* puanteur *f*.

stencil ['stɛnsl] *n* stencil *m*; pochoir *m* ♦ *vt* polycopier.

stenographer [stɛ'nɔgrəfə*] *n* (*US*) sténographe *m/f*.

stenography [stɛ'nɔgrəfɪ] *n* (*US*) sténo(graphie) *f*.

step [stɛp] *n* pas *m*; (*stair*) marche *f*; (*action*) mesure *f*, disposition *f* ♦ *vi*: **to ~ forward** faire un pas en avant, avancer; **~s** *npl* (*BRIT*) = **stepladder**; **~ by ~** pas à pas; (*fig*) petit à petit; **to be in ~ (with)** (*fig*) aller dans le sens (de); **to be out of ~ (with)** (*fig*) être déphasé(e) (par rapport à).

▶**step down** *vi* (*fig*) se retirer, se désister.

▶**step in** *vi* (*fig*) intervenir.

▶**step off** *vt fus* descendre de.

▶**step over** *vt fus* enjamber.

▶**step up** *vt* augmenter; intensifier.

step aerobics *npl* ® step *m* ®.

stepbrother ['stɛpbrʌðə*] *n* demi-frère *m*.

stepchild ['stɛptʃaɪld] *n* beau-fils/belle-fille.

stepdaughter ['stɛpdɔːtə*] *n* belle-fille *f*.

stepfather ['stɛpfɑːðə*] *n* beau-père *m*.

stepladder ['stɛplædə*] *n* (*BRIT*) escabeau *m*.

stepmother ['stɛpmʌðə*] *n* belle-mère *f*.

stepping stone ['stɛpɪŋ-] *n* pierre *f* de gué; (*fig*) tremplin *m*.

step Reebok [-'riːbɔk] *n* ® step *m* ®.

stepsister ['stɛpsɪstə*] *n* demi-sœur *f*.

stepson ['stɛpsʌn] *n* beau-fils *m*.

stereo ['stɛrɪəʊ] *n* (*system*) stéréo *f*; (*record player*) chaîne *f* stéréo ♦ *adj* (*also*: ~**phonic**) stéréophonique; **in ~** en stéréo.

stereotype ['stɪərɪətaɪp] *n* stéréotype *m* ♦ *vt* stéréotyper.

sterile ['stɛraɪl] *adj* stérile.

sterility [stɛ'rɪlɪtɪ] *n* stérilité *f*.

sterilization [stɛrɪlaɪ'zeɪʃən] *n* stérilisation *f*.

sterilize ['stɛrɪlaɪz] *vt* stériliser.

sterling ['stəːlɪŋ] *adj* sterling *inv*; (*silver*) de bon aloi, fin(e); (*fig*) à toute épreuve, excellent(e) ♦ *n* (*currency*) livre *f* sterling *inv*; **a pound ~** une livre sterling.

sterling area *n* zone *f* sterling *inv*.

stern [stəːn] *adj* sévère ♦ *n* (*NAUT*) arrière *m*, poupe *f*.

sternum ['stəːnəm] *n* sternum *m*.

steroid ['stɪərɔɪd] *n* stéroïde *m*.

stethoscope ['stɛθəskəʊp] *n* stéthoscope *m*.

stevedore ['stiːvədɔː*] *n* docker *m*, débardeur *m*.

stew [stjuː] *n* ragoût *m* ♦ *vt*, *vi* cuire à la casserole; **~ed tea** thé trop infusé; **~ed fruit** fruits cuits *or* en compote.

steward ['stjuːəd] *n* (*AVIAT, NAUT, RAIL*) steward *m*; (*in club etc*) intendant *m*; (*also*: **shop ~**) délégué syndical.

stewardess ['stjuːədɛs] *n* hôtesse *f*.

stewardship ['stjuːədʃɪp] *n* intendance *f*.

stewing steak ['stjuːɪŋ-], (*US*) **stew meat** *n* bœuf *m* à braiser.

St. Ex. *abbr* = **stock exchange**.

stg *abbr* = **sterling**.

stick [stɪk] *n* bâton *m*; (*of chalk etc*) morceau *m* ♦ *vb* (*pt, pp* **stuck** [stʌk]) *vt* (*glue*) coller; (*thrust*): **to ~ sth into** piquer *or* planter *or* enfoncer qch dans; (*col: put*) mettre, fourrer; (*: tolerate*) supporter ♦ *vi* (*adhere*) coller; (*remain*) rester; (*get jammed: door, lift*) se bloquer; **to get hold of the wrong end of the ~** (*BRIT fig*) comprendre de travers; **to ~ to** (*one's word, promise*) s'en tenir à; (*principles*) rester fidèle à.

▶**stick around** *vi* (*col*) rester (dans les parages).

▶**stick out** *vi* dépasser, sortir ♦ *vt*: **to ~ it out** (*col*) tenir le coup.

▶**stick up** *vi* dépasser, sortir.

▶**stick up for** *vt fus* défendre.

sticker ['stɪkə*] *n* auto-collant *m*.

sticking plaster ['stɪkɪŋ-] *n* sparadrap *m*, pansement adhésif.

sticking point ['stɪkɪŋ-] *n* (*fig*) point *m* de friction.

stickleback ['stɪklbæk] *n* épinoche *f*.

stickler ['stɪklə*] *n*: **to be a ~ for** être pointilleux(euse) sur.

stick shift *n* (*US AUT*) levier *m* de vitesses.

stick-up ['stɪkʌp] *n* (*col*) braquage *m*, hold-up *m*.

sticky ['stɪkɪ] *adj* poisseux(euse); (*label*) adhésif(ive).

stiff [stɪf] *adj* (*gen*) raide, rigide; (*door, brush*) dur(e); (*difficult*) difficile, ardu(e); (*cold*) froid(e), distant(e); (*strong, high*) fort(e), élevé(e); **to be** *or* **feel ~** (*person*) avoir des courbatures; **to have a ~ back** avoir mal au dos; **~ upper lip** (*BRIT: fig*) flegme *m* (*typiquement britannique*).

stiffen ['stɪfn] *vt* raidir, renforcer ♦ *vi* se raidir; se durcir.

stiffness ['stɪfnɪs] *n* raideur *f*.

stifle ['staɪfl] *vt* étouffer, réprimer.

stifling ['staɪflɪŋ] *adj* (*heat*) suffocant(e).

stigma *pl* (*BOT, MED, REL*) **~ta**, (*fig*) **~s** ['stɪgmə, stɪg'mɑːtə] *n* stigmate *m*.

stile [staɪl] *n* échalier *m*.

stiletto [stɪ'lɛtəʊ] *n* (*BRIT: also*: **~ heel**) talon *m* aiguille.

still [stɪl] *adj* (*motionless*) immobile; (*calm*) calme, tranquille; (*BRIT: orange drink etc*) non gazeux(euse) ♦ *adv* (*up to this time*) encore, toujours; (*even*) encore; (*nonetheless*) quand même, tout de même ♦ *n* (*CINE*) photo *f*; **to stand ~** rester immobile, ne pas bouger; **keep ~!** ne bouge pas!; **he ~ hasn't arrived** il n'est pas encore arrivé, il n'est toujours pas arrivé.

stillborn ['stɪlbɔːn] *adj* mort-né(e).

still life *n* nature morte.

stilt [stɪlt] *n* échasse *f*; (*pile*) pilotis *m*.
stilted ['stɪltɪd] *adj* guindé(e), emprunté(e).
stimulant ['stɪmjulənt] *n* stimulant *m*.
stimulate ['stɪmjuleɪt] *vt* stimuler.
stimulating ['stɪmjuleɪtɪŋ] *adj* stimulant(e).
stimulation [stɪmju'leɪʃən] *n* stimulation *f*.
stimulus, *pl* **stimuli** ['stɪmjuləs, 'stɪmjulaɪ] *n* stimulant *m*; (*BIOL, PSYCH*) stimulus *m*.
sting [stɪŋ] *n* piqûre *f*; (*organ*) dard *m*; (*col: confidence trick*) arnaque *m* ♦ *vt* (*pt, pp* **stung** [stʌŋ]) piquer ♦ *vi* piquer; **my eyes are** ~**ing** j'ai les yeux qui piquent.
stingy ['stɪndʒɪ] *adj* avare, pingre, chiche.
stink [stɪŋk] *n* puanteur *f* ♦ *vi* (*pt* **stank,** *pp* **stunk** [stæŋk, stʌŋk]) puer, empester.
stinker ['stɪŋkə*] *n* (*col: problem, exam*) vacherie *f*; (: *person*) dégueulasse *m/f*.
stinking ['stɪŋkɪŋ] *adj* (*fig: col*) infect(e); ~ **rich** bourré(e) de pognon.
stint [stɪnt] *n* part *f* de travail ♦ *vi*: **to** ~ **on** lésiner sur, être chiche de.
stipend ['staɪpɛnd] *n* (*of vicar etc*) traitement *m*.
stipendiary [staɪ'pɛndɪərɪ] *adj*: ~ **magistrate** juge *m* de tribunal d'instance.
stipulate ['stɪpjuleɪt] *vt* stipuler.
stipulation [stɪpju'leɪʃən] *n* stipulation *f*, condition *f*.
stir [stə:*] *n* agitation *f*, sensation *f* ♦ *vt* remuer ♦ *vi* remuer, bouger; **to give sth a** ~ remuer qch; **to cause a** ~ faire sensation.
▶**stir up** *vt* exciter.
stir-fry ['stə:'fraɪ] *vt* faire sauter ♦ *n*: **vegetable** ~ légumes sautés à la poêle.
stirring ['stə:rɪŋ] *adj* excitant(e); émouvant(e).
stirrup ['stɪrəp] *n* étrier *m*.
stitch [stɪtʃ] *n* (*SEWING*) point *m*; (*KNITTING*) maille *f*; (*MED*) point de suture; (*pain*) point de côté ♦ *vt* coudre, piquer; suturer.
stoat [stəut] *n* hermine *f* (*avec son pelage d'été*).
stock [stɔk] *n* réserve *f*, provision *f*; (*COMM*) stock *m*; (*AGR*) cheptel *m*, bétail *m*; (*CULIN*) bouillon *m*; (*FINANCE*) valeurs *fpl*, titres *mpl*; (*RAIL: also: rolling* ~) matériel roulant; (*descent, origin*) souche *f* ♦ *adj* (*fig: reply etc*) courant(e); classique ♦ *vt* (*have in stock*) avoir, vendre; **well-**~**ed** bien approvisionné(e) *or* fourni(e); **in** ~ en stock, en magasin; **out of** ~ épuisé(e); **to take** ~ (*fig*) faire le point; ~**s and shares** valeurs (mobilières), titres; **government** ~ fonds publics.
▶**stock up** *vi*: **to** ~ **up (with)** s'approvisionner (en).
stockade [stɔ'keɪd] *n* palissade *f*.
stockbroker ['stɔkbrəukə*] *n* agent *m* de change.
stock control *n* (*COMM*) gestion *f* des stocks.
stock cube *n* (*BRIT CULIN*) bouillon-cube *m*.
stock exchange *n* Bourse *f* (des valeurs).
stockholder ['stɔkhəuldə*] *n* actionnaire *m/f*.
Stockholm ['stɔkhəum] *n* Stockholm.

stocking ['stɔkɪŋ] *n* bas *m*.
stock-in-trade ['stɔkɪn'treɪd] *n* (*fig*): **it's his** ~ c'est sa spécialité.
stockist ['stɔkɪst] *n* (*BRIT*) stockiste *m*.
stock market *n* (*BRIT*) Bourse *f*, marché financier.
stock phrase *n* cliché *m*.
stockpile ['stɔkpaɪl] *n* stock *m*, réserve *f* ♦ *vt* stocker, accumuler.
stockroom ['stɔkru:m] *n* réserve *f*, magasin *m*.
stocktaking ['stɔkteɪkɪŋ] *n* (*BRIT COMM*) inventaire *m*.
stocky ['stɔkɪ] *adj* trapu(e), râblé(e).
stodgy ['stɔdʒɪ] *adj* bourratif(ive), lourd(e).
stoic ['stəuɪk] *n* stoïque *m/f*.
stoical ['stəuɪkl] *adj* stoïque.
stoke [stəuk] *vt* garnir, entretenir; chauffer.
stoker ['stəukə*] *n* (*RAIL, NAUT etc*) chauffeur *m*.
stole [stəul] *pt of* **steal** ♦ *n* étole *f*.
stolen ['stəuln] *pp of* **steal**.
stolid ['stɔlɪd] *adj* impassible, flegmatique.
stomach ['stʌmək] *n* estomac *m*; (*abdomen*) ventre *m* ♦ *vt* supporter, digérer.
stomach ache *n* mal *m* à l'estomac *or* au ventre.
stomach pump *n* pompe stomacale.
stomach ulcer *n* ulcère *m* à l'estomac.
stomp [stɔmp] *vi*: **to** ~ **in/out** entrer/sortir d'un pas bruyant.
stone [stəun] *n* pierre *f*; (*pebble*) caillou *m*, galet *m*; (*in fruit*) noyau *m*; (*MED*) calcul *m*; (*BRIT: weight*) = 6.348 kg; 14 pounds ♦ *cpd* de *or* en pierre ♦ *vt* dénoyauter; **within a** ~'s **throw of the station** à deux pas de la gare.
Stone Age *n*: **the** ~ l'âge *m* de pierre.
stone-cold ['stəun'kəuld] *adj* complètement froid(e).
stoned [stəund] *adj* (*col: drunk*) bourré(e); (: *on drugs*) défoncé(e).
stone-deaf ['stəun'dɛf] *adj* sourd(e) comme un pot.
stonemason ['stəunmeɪsn] *n* tailleur *m* de pierre(s).
stonewall [stəun'wɔ:l] *vi* faire de l'obstruction ♦ *vt* faire obstruction à.
stonework ['stəunwə:k] *n* maçonnerie *f*.
stony ['stəunɪ] *adj* pierreux(euse), rocailleux(euse).
stood [stud] *pt, pp of* **stand**.
stooge [stu:dʒ] *n* (*col*) larbin *m*.
stool [stu:l] *n* tabouret *m*.
stoop [stu:p] *vi* (*also:* **have a** ~) être voûté(e); (*bend*) se baisser, se courber; (*fig*): **to** ~ **to sth/doing sth** s'abaisser jusqu'à qch/jusqu'à faire qch.
stop [stɔp] *n* arrêt *m*; (*short stay*) halte *f*; (*in punctuation*) point *m* ♦ *vt* arrêter; (*break off*) interrompre; (*also:* **put a** ~ **to**) mettre fin à; (*prevent*) empêcher ♦ *vi* s'arrêter; (*rain, noise etc*) cesser, s'arrêter; **to** ~ **doing sth** cesser

or arrêter de faire qch; **to ~ sb (from) doing sth** empêcher qn de faire qch; **to ~ dead** *vi* s'arrêter net; **~ it!** arrête!

▶**stop by** *vi* s'arrêter (au passage).

▶**stop off** *vi* faire une courte halte.

▶**stop up** *vt* (*hole*) boucher.

stopcock ['stɔpkɔk] *n* robinet *m* d'arrêt.

stopgap ['stɔpgæp] *n* (*person*) bouche-trou *m*; (*also:* ~ **measure**) mesure *f* intérimaire.

stoplights ['stɔplaɪts] *npl* (*AUT*) signaux *mpl* de stop, feux *mpl* arrière.

stopover ['stɔpəuvə*] *n* halte *f*; (*AVIAT*) escale *f*.

stoppage ['stɔpɪdʒ] *n* arrêt *m*; (*of pay*) retenue *f*; (*strike*) arrêt de travail.

stopper ['stɔpə*] *n* bouchon *m*.

stop press *n* nouvelles *fpl* de dernière heure.

stopwatch ['stɔpwɔtʃ] *n* chronomètre *m*.

storage ['stɔːrɪdʒ] *n* emmagasinage *m*; (*of nuclear waste etc*) stockage *m*; (*in house*) rangement *m*; (*COMPUT*) mise *f* en mémoire *or* réserve.

storage heater *n* (*BRIT*) radiateur *m* électrique par accumulation.

store [stɔː*] *n* provision *f*, réserve *f*; (*depot*) entrepôt *m*; (*BRIT: large shop*) grand magasin; (*US: shop*) magasin *m* ♦ *vt* emmagasiner; (*nuclear waste etc*) stocker; (*in filing system*) classer, ranger; (*COMPUT*) mettre en mémoire; **~s** *npl* provisions; **who knows what is in ~ for us?** qui sait ce que l'avenir nous réserve *or* ce qui nous attend?; **to set great/little ~ by sth** faire grand cas/peu de cas de qch.

▶**store up** *vt* mettre en réserve, emmagasiner.

storehouse ['stɔːhaus] *n* entrepôt *m*.

storekeeper ['stɔːkiːpə*] *n* (*US*) commerçant/e.

storeroom ['stɔːruːm] *n* réserve *f*, magasin *m*.

storey, (*US*) **story** ['stɔːrɪ] *n* étage *m*.

stork [stɔːk] *n* cigogne *f*.

storm [stɔːm] *n* tempête *f*; (*also:* **electric ~**) orage *m* ♦ *vi* (*fig*) fulminer ♦ *vt* prendre d'assaut.

storm cloud *n* nuage *m* d'orage.

storm door *n* double-porte (extérieure).

stormy ['stɔːmɪ] *adj* orageux(euse).

story ['stɔːrɪ] *n* histoire *f*; récit *m*; (*PRESS: article*) article *m*; (*: subject*) affaire *f*; (*US*) = **storey**.

storybook ['stɔːrɪbuk] *n* livre *m* d'histoires *or* de contes.

storyteller ['stɔːrɪtɛlə*] *n* conteur/euse.

stout [staut] *adj* solide; (*brave*) intrépide; (*fat*) gros(se), corpulent(e) ♦ *n* bière brune.

stove [stəuv] *n* (*for cooking*) fourneau *m*; (*: small*) réchaud *m*; (*for heating*) poêle *m*; **gas/electric ~** (*cooker*) cuisinière *f* à gaz/électrique.

stow [stəu] *vt* ranger; cacher.

stowaway ['stəuəweɪ] *n* passager/ère clan-

destin(e).

straddle ['strædl] *vt* enjamber, être à cheval sur.

strafe [strɑːf] *vt* mitrailler.

straggle ['strægl] *vi* être (*or* marcher) en désordre; **~d along the coast** disséminé(e) tout au long de la côte.

straggler ['stræglə*] *n* traînard/e.

straggling ['stræglɪŋ], **straggly** ['stræglɪ] *adj* (*hair*) en désordre.

straight [streɪt] *adj* droit(e); (*frank*) honnête, franc(franche); (*plain, uncomplicated*) simple; (*THEAT: part, play*) sérieux(euse); (*col: heterosexual*) hétéro *inv* ♦ *adv* (tout) droit; (*drink*) sec, sans eau ♦ *n*: **the ~** (*SPORT*) la ligne droite; **to put** *or* **get ~** mettre en ordre, mettre de l'ordre dans; **let's get this ~** mettons les choses au point; **10 ~ wins** 10 victoires d'affilée; **to go ~ home** rentrer directement à la maison; **~ away, ~ off** (*at once*) tout de suite; **~ off, ~ out** sans hésiter.

straighten ['streɪtn] *vt* (*also:* ~ **out**) redresser; **to ~ things out** arranger les choses.

straight-faced [streɪt'feɪst] *adj* impassible ♦ *adv* en gardant son sérieux.

straightforward [streɪt'fɔːwəd] *adj* simple; (*frank*) honnête, direct(e).

strain [streɪn] *n* (*TECH*) tension *f*, pression *f*; (*physical*) effort *m*; (*mental*) tension (nerveuse); (*MED*) entorse *f*; (*streak, trace*) tendance *f*; élément *m*; (*breed*) variété *f*; (*of virus*) souche *f*; **~s** *npl* (*of music*) accents *mpl*, accords *mpl* ♦ *vt* tendre fortement; mettre à l'épreuve; (*filter*) passer, filtrer ♦ *vi* peiner, fournir un gros effort; **he's been under a lot of ~** il a traversé des moments très difficiles, il est très éprouvé nerveusement.

strained [streɪnd] *adj* (*laugh etc*) forcé(e), contraint(e); (*relations*) tendu(e).

strainer ['streɪnə*] *n* passoire *f*.

strait [streɪt] *n* (*GEO*) détroit *m*; **to be in dire ~s** (*fig*) être dans une situation désespérée.

straitjacket ['streɪtdʒækɪt] *n* camisole *f* de force.

strait-laced [streɪt'leɪst] *adj* collet monté *inv*.

strand [strænd] *n* (*of thread*) fil *m*, brin *m* ♦ *vt* (*boat*) échouer.

stranded ['strændɪd] *adj* en rade, en plan.

strange [streɪndʒ] *adj* (*not known*) inconnu(e); (*odd*) étrange, bizarre.

strangely ['streɪndʒlɪ] *adv* étrangement, bizarrement.

stranger ['streɪndʒə*] *n* (*unknown*) inconnu/e; (*from somewhere else*) étranger/ère; **I'm a ~ here** je ne suis pas d'ici.

strangle ['stræŋgl] *vt* étrangler.

stranglehold ['stræŋglhəuld] *n* (*fig*) emprise totale, mainmise *f*.

strangulation [stræŋgju'leɪʃən] *n* strangulation *f*.

strap [stræp] *n* lanière *f*, courroie *f*, sangle *f*;

(*of slip, dress*) bretelle *f* ♦ *vt* attacher (avec une courroie *etc*).

straphanging ['stræphæŋɪŋ] *n* (fait *m* de) voyager debout (dans le métro *etc*).

strapless ['stræplɪs] *adj* (*bra, dress*) sans bretelles.

strapped [stræpt] *adj*: **to be ~ for cash** (*col*) être à court d'argent.

strapping ['stræpɪŋ] *adj* bien découplé(e), costaud(e).

Strasbourg ['stræzbɔːg] *n* Strasbourg.

strata ['strɑːtə] *npl of* stratum.

stratagem ['strætɪdʒəm] *n* stratagème *m*.

strategic [strə'tiːdʒɪk] *adj* stratégique.

strategist ['strætɪdʒɪst] *n* stratège *m*.

strategy ['strætɪdʒɪ] *n* stratégie *f*.

stratosphere ['strætəsfɪə*] *n* stratosphère *f*.

stratum, *pl* **strata** ['strɑːtəm, 'strɑːtə] *n* strate *f*, couche *f*.

straw [strɔː] *n* paille *f*; **that's the last ~!** ça c'est le comble!

strawberry ['strɔːbərɪ] *n* fraise *f*; (*plant*) fraisier *m*.

stray [streɪ] *adj* (*animal*) perdu(e), errant(e) ♦ *vi* s'égarer; **~ bullet** balle perdue.

streak [striːk] *n* raie *f*, bande *f*, filet *m*; (*fig: of madness etc*): **a ~ of** une *or* des tendance(s) à ♦ *vt* zébrer, strier ♦ *vi*: **to ~ past** passer à toute allure; **to have ~s in one's hair** s'être fait faire des mèches; **a winning/losing ~** une bonne/mauvaise série *or* période.

streaker ['striːkə*] *n* personne qui traverse une foule en courant toute nue.

streaky ['striːkɪ] *adj* zébré(e), strié(e).

streaky bacon *n* (*BRIT*) ≈ lard *m* (maigre).

stream [striːm] *n* (*brook*) ruisseau *m*; (*current*) courant *m*, flot *m*; (*of people*) défilé ininterrompu, flot ♦ *vt* (*SCOL*) répartir par niveau ♦ *vi* ruisseler; **to ~ in/out** entrer/sortir à flots; **against the ~** à contre courant; **on ~** (*new power plant etc*) en service.

streamer ['striːmə*] *n* serpentin *m*, banderole *f*.

stream feed *n* (*on photocopier etc*) alimentation *f* en continu.

streamline ['striːmlaɪn] *vt* donner un profil aérodynamique à; (*fig*) rationaliser.

streamlined ['striːmlaɪnd] *adj* (*AVIAT*) fuselé(e), profilé(e); (*AUT*) aérodynamique; (*fig*) rationalisé(e).

street [striːt] *n* rue *f*; **the back ~s** les quartiers pauvres; **to be on the ~s** (*homeless*) être à la rue *or* sans abri; (*as prostitute*) faire le trottoir.

streetcar ['striːtkɑː*] *n* (*US*) tramway *m*.

street cred [-krɛd] *n* (*col*): **to have ~** être branché(e).

street lamp *n* réverbère *m*.

street lighting *n* éclairage public.

street map, street plan *n* plan *m* des rues.

street market *n* marché *m* à ciel ouvert.

streetwise ['striːtwaɪz] *adj* (*col*) futé(e), réa-

liste.

strength [strɛŋθ] *n* force *f*; (*of girder, knot etc*) solidité *f*; (*of chemical solution*) titre *m*; (*of wine*) degré *m* d'alcool; **on the ~ of** en vertu de; **at full ~** au grand complet; **below ~** à effectifs réduits.

strengthen ['strɛŋθn] *vt* renforcer; (*muscle*) fortifier.

strenuous ['strɛnjuəs] *adj* vigoureux(euse), énergique; (*tiring*) ardu(e), fatigant(e).

stress [strɛs] *n* (*force, pressure*) pression *f*; (*mental strain*) tension (nerveuse); (*accent*) accent *m*; (*emphasis*) insistance *f* ♦ *vt* insister sur, souligner; **to lay great ~ on sth** insister beaucoup sur qch; **to be under ~** être stressé(e).

stressful ['strɛsful] *adj* (*job*) stressant(e).

stretch [strɛtʃ] *n* (*of sand etc*) étendue *f*; (*of time*) période *f* ♦ *vi* s'étirer; (*extend*): **to ~ to** *or* **as far as** s'étendre jusqu'à; (*be enough: money, food*): **to ~ to** aller pour ♦ *vt* tendre, étirer; (*spread*) étendre; (*fig*) pousser (au maximum); **at a ~** sans discontinuer, sans interruption; **to ~ a muscle** se distendre un muscle; **to ~ one's legs** se dégourdir les jambes.

►**stretch out** *vi* s'étendre ♦ *vt* (*arm etc*) allonger, tendre; (*to spread*) étendre; **to ~ out for sth** allonger la main pour prendre qch.

stretcher ['strɛtʃə*] *n* brancard *m*, civière *f*.

stretcher-bearer ['strɛtʃəbɛərə*] *n* brancardier *m*.

stretch marks *npl* (*on skin*) vergetures *fpl*.

strewn [struːn] *adj*: **~ with** jonché(e) de.

stricken ['strɪkən] *adj* très éprouvé(e); dévasté(e); (*ship*) très endommagé(e); **~ with** frappé(e) *or* atteint(e) de.

strict [strɪkt] *adj* strict(e); **in ~ confidence** tout à fait confidentiellement.

strictly ['strɪktlɪ] *adv* strictement; **~ confidential** strictement confidentiel(le); **~ speaking** à strictement parler.

strictness ['strɪktnɪs] *n* sévérité *f*.

stride [straɪd] *n* grand pas, enjambée *f* ♦ *vi* (*pt* **strode**, *pp* **stridden** [strəud, 'strɪdn]) marcher à grands pas; **to take in one's ~** (*fig: changes etc*) accepter sans sourciller.

strident ['straɪdnt] *adj* strident(e).

strife [straɪf] *n* conflit *m*, dissensions *fpl*.

strike [straɪk] *n* grève *f*; (*of oil etc*) découverte *f*; (*attack*) raid *m* ♦ *vb* (*pt, pp* **struck** [strʌk]) *vt* frapper; (*oil etc*) trouver, découvrir; (*make: agreement, deal*) conclure ♦ *vi* faire grève; (*attack*) attaquer; (*clock*) sonner; **to go on** *or* **come out on ~** se mettre en grève, faire grève; **to ~ a match** frotter une allumette; **to ~ a balance** (*fig*) trouver un juste milieu.

►**strike back** *vi* (*MIL, fig*) contre-attaquer.

►**strike down** *vt* (*fig*) terrasser.

►**strike off** *vt* (*from list*) rayer; (*: doctor etc*) radier.

►**strike out** *vt* rayer.

►**strike up** vt (MUS) se mettre à jouer; **to ~ up a friendship with** se lier d'amitié avec.

strikebreaker ['straɪkbreɪkə*] n briseur m de grève.

striker ['straɪkə*] n gréviste m/f; (SPORT) buteur m.

striking ['straɪkɪŋ] adj frappant(e), saisissant(e).

strimmer ['strɪmə*] n ® (BRIT) coupe-bordures m.

string [strɪŋ] n ficelle f, fil m; (row: of beads) rang m; (: of onions, excuses) chapelet m; (: of people, cars) file f; (MUS) corde f; (COMPUT) châine f ♦ vt (pt, pp **strung** [strʌŋ]): **to ~ out** échelonner; **to ~ together** enchaîner; **the ~s** (MUS) les instruments mpl à cordes; **to get a job by pulling ~s** obtenir un emploi en faisant jouer le piston; **with no ~s attached** (fig) sans conditions.

string bean n haricot vert.

string(ed) instrument [strɪŋ(d)-] n (MUS) instrument m à cordes.

stringent ['strɪndʒənt] adj rigoureux(euse); (need) impérieux(euse).

string quartet n quatuor m à cordes.

strip [strɪp] n bande f; (SPORT): **wearing the Celtic ~** en tenue du Celtic ♦ vt déshabiller; (fig) dégarnir, dépouiller; (also: ~ **down**: machine) démonter ♦ vi se déshabiller.

strip cartoon n bande dessinée.

stripe [straɪp] n raie f, rayure f.

striped ['straɪpt] adj rayé(e), à rayures.

strip light n (BRIT) (tube m au) néon m.

stripper ['strɪpə*] n strip-teaseuse f.

strip-search ['strɪpsə:tʃ] n fouille corporelle (en faisant se déshabiller la personne) ♦ vt: **to ~ sb** fouiller qn (en le faisant se déshabiller).

striptease ['strɪpti:z] n strip-tease m.

strive, pt **strove**, pp **striven** [straɪv, strəʊv, 'strɪvn] vi: **to ~ to do** s'efforcer de faire.

strobe [strəʊb] n (also: ~ **light**) stroboscope m.

strode [strəʊd] pt of **stride**.

stroke [strəʊk] n coup m; (MED) attaque f; (caress) caresse f; (SWIMMING: style) (sorte f de) nage f; (of piston) course f ♦ vt caresser; **at a ~ d'un** (seul) coup; **on the ~ of 5** à 5 heures sonnantes; **a ~ of luck** un coup de chance; **a 2-~ engine** un moteur à 2 temps.

stroll [strəʊl] n petite promenade ♦ vi flâner, se promener nonchalamment; **to go for a ~** aller se promener or faire un tour.

stroller ['strəʊlə*] n (US) poussette f.

strong [strɒŋ] adj (gen) fort(e); (healthy) vigoureux(euse); (object, material) solide; (distaste, desire) vif(vive); (drugs, chemicals) puissant(e) ♦ adv: **to be going ~** (company) marcher bien; (person) être toujours solide; **they are 50 ~** ils sont au nombre de 50.

strong-arm ['strɒŋɑ:m] adj (tactics, methods) musclé(e).

strongbox ['strɒŋbɒks] n coffre-fort m.

stronghold ['strɒŋhəʊld] n bastion m.

strongly ['strɒŋlɪ] adv fortement, avec force; vigoureusement; solidement; **I feel ~ about it** c'est une question qui me tient particulièrement à cœur; (negatively) j'y suis profondément opposé(e).

strongman ['strɒŋmæn] n hercule m, colosse m; (fig) homme m à poigne.

strongroom ['strɒŋru:m] n chambre forte.

stroppy ['strɒpɪ] adj (BRIT col) contrariant(e), difficile.

strove [strəʊv] pt of **strive**.

struck [strʌk] pt, pp of **strike**.

structural ['strʌktʃrəl] adj structural(e); (CONSTR) de construction; affectant les parties portantes.

structurally ['strʌktʃrəlɪ] adv du point de vue de la construction.

structure ['strʌktʃə*] n structure f; (building) construction f.

struggle ['strʌgl] n lutte f ♦ vi lutter, se battre; **to have a ~ to do sth** avoir beaucoup de mal à faire qch.

strum [strʌm] vt (guitar) gratter de.

strung [strʌŋ] pt, pp of **string**.

strut [strʌt] n étai m, support m ♦ vi se pavaner.

strychnine ['strɪkni:n] n strychnine f.

stub [stʌb] n bout m; (of ticket etc) talon m ♦ vt: **to ~ one's toe (on sth)** se heurter le doigt de pied (contre qch).

►**stub out** vt écraser.

stubble ['stʌbl] n chaume m; (on chin) barbe f de plusieurs jours.

stubborn ['stʌbən] adj têtu(e), obstiné(e), opiniâtre.

stubby ['stʌbɪ] adj trapu(e); gros(se) et court(e).

stucco ['stʌkəʊ] n stuc m.

stuck [stʌk] pt, pp of **stick** ♦ adj (jammed) bloqué(e), coincé(e); **to get ~** se bloquer or coincer.

stuck-up [stʌk'ʌp] adj prétentieux(euse).

stud [stʌd] n clou m (à grosse tête); (collar ~) bouton m de col; (of horses) écurie f, haras m; (also: ~ **horse**) étalon m ♦ vt (fig): **~ded with** parsemé(e) or criblé(e) de.

student ['stju:dənt] n étudiant/e ♦ cpd estudiantin(e); universitaire; d'étudiant; **law/ medical ~** étudiant en droit/médecine.

student driver n (US) conducteur/trice débutant/e.

students' union n (BRIT: association) ≈ union f des étudiants; (: building) ≈ foyer m des étudiants.

studied ['stʌdɪd] adj étudié(e), calculé(e).

studio ['stju:dɪəʊ] n studio m, atelier m.

studio flat, (US) **studio apartment** n studio m.

studious ['stju:dɪəs] adj studieux(euse), appliqué(e); (studied) étudié(e).

studiously ['stju:dɪəslɪ] adv (carefully) soigneusement.

study ['stʌdɪ] *n* étude *f*; (*room*) bureau *m* ♦ *vt* étudier ♦ *vi* étudier, faire ses études; **to make a ~ of sth** étudier qch, faire une étude de qch; **to ~ for an exam** préparer un examen.

stuff [stʌf] *n* (*gen*) chose(s) *f(pl)*, truc *m*; (*belongings*) affaires *fpl*, trucs; (*substance*) substance *f* ♦ *vt* rembourrer; (*CULIN*) farcir; (*animal: for exhibition*) empailler; **my nose is ~ed up** j'ai le nez bouché; **get ~ed!** (*col!*) va te faire foutre! (*!*); **~ed toy** jouet *m* en peluche.

stuffing ['stʌfɪŋ] *n* bourre *f*, rembourrage *m*; (*CULIN*) farce *f*.

stuffy ['stʌfɪ] *adj* (*room*) mal ventilé(e) *or* aéré(e); (*ideas*) vieux jeu *inv*.

stumble ['stʌmbl] *vi* trébucher.
►**stumble across** *vt fus* (*fig*) tomber sur.

stumbling block ['stʌmblɪŋ-] *n* pierre *f* d'achoppement.

stump [stʌmp] *n* souche *f*; (*of limb*) moignon *m* ♦ *vt*: **to be ~ed** sécher, ne pas savoir que répondre.

stun [stʌn] *vt* (*subj: blow*) étourdir; (*: news*) abasourdir, stupéfier.

stung [stʌŋ] *pt, pp of* **sting**.

stunk [stʌŋk] *pp of* **stink**.

stunning ['stʌnɪŋ] *adj* étourdissant(e); (*fabulous*) stupéfiant(e), sensationnel(le).

stunt [stʌnt] *n* tour *m* de force; truc *m* publicitaire; (*AVIAT*) acrobatie *f* ♦ *vt* retarder, arrêter.

stunted ['stʌntɪd] *adj* rabougri(e).

stuntman ['stʌntmæn] *n* cascadeur *m*.

stupefaction [stjuːpɪ'fækʃən] *n* stupéfaction *f*, stupeur *f*.

stupefy ['stjuːpɪfaɪ] *vt* étourdir; abrutir; (*fig*) stupéfier.

stupendous [stjuː'pɛndəs] *adj* prodigieux(euse), fantastique.

stupid ['stjuːpɪd] *adj* stupide, bête.

stupidity [stjuː'pɪdɪtɪ] *n* stupidité *f*, bêtise *f*.

stupidly ['stjuːpɪdlɪ] *adv* stupidement, bêtement.

stupor ['stjuːpə*] *n* stupeur *f*.

sturdy ['stɜːdɪ] *adj* robuste, vigoureux(euse), solide.

sturgeon ['stɜːdʒən] *n* esturgeon *m*.

stutter ['stʌtə*] *n* bégaiement *m* ♦ *vi* bégayer.

sty [staɪ] *n* (*of pigs*) porcherie *f*.

stye [staɪ] *n* (*MED*) orgelet *m*.

style [staɪl] *n* style *m*; (*of dress etc*) genre *m*; (*distinction*) allure *f*, cachet *m*, style; **in the latest ~** à la dernière mode; **hair ~** coiffure *f*.

stylish ['staɪlɪʃ] *adj* élégant(e), chic *inv*.

stylist ['staɪlɪst] *n* (*hair ~*) coiffeur/euse; (*literary ~*) styliste *m/f*.

stylized ['staɪlaɪzd] *adj* stylisé(e).

stylus, *pl* **styli** *or* **styluses** ['staɪləs, -laɪ] *n* (*of record player*) pointe *f* de lecture.

Styrofoam ['staɪrəfəum] *n* ® (*US*) polystyrène expansé ♦ *adj* en polystyrène.

suave [swɑːv] *adj* doucereux(euse), onctueux(euse).

sub [sʌb] *n abbr* = **submarine**, **subscription**.

sub... [sʌb] *prefix* sub..., sous-.

subcommittee ['sʌbkəmɪtɪ] *n* sous-comité *m*.

subconscious [sʌb'kɒnʃəs] *adj* subconscient(e) ♦ *n* subconscient *m*.

subcontinent [sʌb'kɒntɪnənt] *n*: **the (Indian) ~** le sous-continent indien.

subcontract *n* ['sʌb'kɒntrækt] contrat *m* de sous-traitance ♦ *vt* [sʌbkən'trækt] soustraiter.

subcontractor ['sʌbkən'træktə*] *n* soustraitant *m*.

subdivide [sʌbdɪ'vaɪd] *vt* subdiviser.

subdivision ['sʌbdɪvɪʒən] *n* subdivision *f*.

subdue [səb'djuː] *vt* subjuguer, soumettre.

subdued [səb'djuːd] *adj* contenu(e), atténué(e); (*light*) tamisé(e); (*person*) qui a perdu de son entrain.

sub-editor ['sʌb'edɪtə*] *n* (*BRIT*) secrétaire *m/f* de (la) rédaction.

subject *n* ['sʌbdʒɪkt] sujet *m*; (*SCOL*) matière *f* ♦ *vt* [səb'dʒɛkt]: **to ~ to** soumettre à; exposer à; **to be ~ to** (*law*) être soumis(e) à; (*disease*) être sujet(te) à; **~ to confirmation in writing** sous réserve de confirmation écrite; **to change the ~** changer de conversation.

subjection [səb'dʒɛkʃən] *n* soumission *f*, sujétion *f*.

subjective [səb'dʒɛktɪv] *adj* subjectif(ive).

subject matter *n* sujet *m*; contenu *m*.

sub judice [sʌb'djuːdɪsɪ] *adj* (*LAW*) devant les tribunaux.

subjugate ['sʌbdʒugeɪt] *vt* subjuguer.

subjunctive [səb'dʒʌŋktɪv] *adj* subjonctif(ive) ♦ *n* subjonctif *m*.

sublet [sʌb'let] *vt* sous-louer.

sublime [sə'blaɪm] *adj* sublime.

subliminal [sʌb'lɪmɪnl] *adj* subliminal(e).

submachine gun ['sʌbmə'ʃiːn-] *n* mitraillette *f*.

submarine [sʌbmə'riːn] *n* sous-marin *m*.

submerge [səb'mɜːdʒ] *vt* submerger; immerger ♦ *vi* plonger.

submersion [səb'mɜːʃən] *n* submersion *f*; immersion *f*.

submission [səb'mɪʃən] *n* soumission *f*; (*to committee etc*) présentation *f*.

submissive [səb'mɪsɪv] *adj* soumis(e).

submit [səb'mɪt] *vt* soumettre ♦ *vi* se soumettre.

subnormal [sʌb'nɔːml] *adj* au-dessous de la normale; (*person*) arriéré(e).

subordinate [sə'bɔːdɪnət] *adj*, *n* subordonné(e).

subpoena [səb'piːnə] (*LAW*) *n* citation *f*, assignation *f* ♦ *vt* citer *or* assigner (à comparaître).

subroutine [sʌbruː'tiːn] *n* (*COMPUT*) sousprogramme *m*.

subscribe [səb'skraɪb] *vi* cotiser; **to ~ to** (*opin-*

ion, fund) souscrire à; (*newspaper*) s'abonner à; être abonné(e) à.
subscriber [səb'skraɪbə*] *n* (*to periodical, telephone*) abonné/e.
subscript ['sʌbskrɪpt] *n* (*TYP*) indice inférieur.
subscription [səb'skrɪpʃən] *n* (*to fund*) souscription *f*; (*to magazine etc*) abonnement *m*; (*membership dues*) cotisation *f*; **to take out a ~ to** s'abonner à.
subsequent ['sʌbsɪkwənt] *adj* ultérieur(e), suivant(e); **~ to** *prep* à la suite de.
subsequently ['sʌbsɪkwəntlɪ] *adv* par la suite.
subservient [səb'səːvɪənt] *adj* obséquieux(euse).
subside [səb'saɪd] *vi* s'affaisser; (*flood*) baisser; (*wind*) tomber.
subsidence [səb'saɪdns] *n* affaissement *m*.
subsidiarity [səbsɪdɪ'ærɪtɪ] *n* (*POL*) subsidiarité *f*.
subsidiary [səb'sɪdɪərɪ] *adj* subsidiaire; accessoire; (*BRIT SCOL: subject*) complémentaire ♦ *n* filiale *f*.
subsidize ['sʌbsɪdaɪz] *vt* subventionner.
subsidy ['sʌbsɪdɪ] *n* subvention *f*.
subsist [səb'sɪst] *vi*: **to ~ on sth** (arriver à) vivre avec *or* subsister avec qch.
subsistence [səb'sɪstəns] *n* existence *f*, subsistance *f*.
subsistence allowance *n* indemnité *f* de séjour.
subsistence level *n* niveau *m* de vie minimum.
substance ['sʌbstəns] *n* substance *f*; (*fig*) essentiel *m*; **a man of ~** un homme jouissant d'une certaine fortune; **to lack ~** être plutôt mince (*fig*).
substance abuse *n* abus *m* de substances toxiques.
substandard [sʌb'stændəd] *adj* (*goods*) de qualité inférieure, qui laisse à désirer; (*housing*) inférieur(e) aux normes requises.
substantial [səb'stænʃl] *adj* substantiel(le); (*fig*) important(e).
substantially [səb'stænʃəlɪ] *adv* considérablement; en grande partie.
substantiate [səb'stænʃɪeɪt] *vt* étayer, fournir des preuves à l'appui de.
substitute ['sʌbstɪtjuːt] *n* (*person*) remplaçant/e; (*thing*) succédané *m* ♦ *vt*: **to ~ sth/sb for** substituer qch/qn à, remplacer par qch/qn.
substitute teacher *n* (*US*) suppléant/e.
substitution [sʌbstɪ'tjuːʃən] *n* substitution *f*.
subterfuge ['sʌbtəfjuːdʒ] *n* subterfuge *m*.
subterranean [sʌbtə'reɪnɪən] *adj* souterrain(e).
subtitle ['sʌbtaɪtl] *n* (*CINE*) sous-titre *m*.
subtle ['sʌtl] *adj* subtil(e).
subtlety ['sʌtltɪ] *n* subtilité *f*.
subtly ['sʌtlɪ] *adv* subtilement.
subtotal [sʌb'təutl] *n* total partiel.
subtract [səb'trækt] *vt* soustraire, retrancher.

subtraction [səb'trækʃən] *n* soustraction *f*.
subtropical [sʌb'trɔpɪkl] *adj* subtropical(e).
suburb ['sʌbəːb] *n* faubourg *m*; **the ~s** la banlieue.
suburban [sə'bəːbən] *adj* de banlieue, suburbain(e).
suburbia [sə'bəːbɪə] *n* la banlieue.
subvention [səb'vɛnʃən] *n* (*subsidy*) subvention *f*.
subversion [səb'vəːʃən] *n* subversion *f*.
subversive [səb'vəːsɪv] *adj* subversif(ive).
subway ['sʌbweɪ] *n* (*US*) métro *m*; (*BRIT*) passage souterrain.
sub-zero [sʌb'zɪərəu] *adj* au-dessous de zéro.
succeed [sək'siːd] *vi* réussir ♦ *vt* succéder à; **to ~ in doing** réussir à faire.
succeeding [sək'siːdɪŋ] *adj* suivant(e), qui suit (*or* suivent *or* suivront *etc*).
success [sək'sɛs] *n* succès *m*; réussite *f*.
successful [sək'sɛsful] *adj* qui a du succès; (*candidate*) choisi(e), agréé(e); (*business*) prospère, qui réussit; (*attempt*) couronné(e) de succès; **to be ~ (in doing)** réussir (à faire).
successfully [sək'sɛsfəlɪ] *adv* avec succès.
succession [sək'sɛʃən] *n* succession *f*; **in ~** successivement; **3 years in ~** 3 ans de suite.
successive [sək'sɛsɪv] *adj* successif(ive); **on 3 ~ days** 3 jours de suite *or* consécutifs.
successor [sək'sɛsə*] *n* successeur *m*.
succinct [sək'sɪŋkt] *adj* succinct(e), bref(brève).
succulent ['sʌkjulənt] *adj* succulent(e) ♦ *n* (*BOT*): **~s** plantes grasses.
succumb [sə'kʌm] *vi* succomber.
such [sʌtʃ] *adj* tel(telle); (*of that kind*): **~ a book** un livre de ce genre *or* pareil, un tel livre ♦ *adv* si; **~ books** des livres de ce genre *or* pareils, de tels livres; (*so much*): **~ courage** un tel courage; **~ a long trip** un si long voyage; **~ good books** de si bons livres; **~ a long trip that** un voyage si *or* tellement long que; **~ a lot of** tellement *or* tant de; **making ~ a noise that** faisant un tel bruit que *or* tellement de bruit que; **~ a long time ago** il y a si *or* tellement longtemps; **~ as** (*like*) tel(telle) que, comme; **a noise ~ as** to so un bruit de nature à; **~ books as I have** les quelques livres que j'ai; **as ~** *adv* en tant que tel(telle), à proprement parler.
such-and-such ['sʌtʃənsʌtʃ] *adj* tel(telle) ou tel(telle).
suchlike ['sʌtʃlaɪk] *pron* (*col*): **and ~** et le reste.
suck [sʌk] *vt* sucer; (*breast, bottle*) téter; (*subj: pump, machine*) aspirer.
sucker ['sʌkə*] *n* (*BOT, ZOOL, TECH*) ventouse *f*; (*col*) naïf/ive, poire *f*.
suckle ['sʌkl] *vt* allaiter.
sucrose ['suːkrəuz] *n* saccharose *m*.
suction ['sʌkʃən] *n* succion *f*.

suction pump *n* pompe aspirante.
Sudan [su'dɑːn] *n* Soudan *m*.
Sudanese [suːdə'niːz] *adj* soudanais(e) ♦ *n* Soudanais/e.
sudden ['sʌdn] *adj* soudain(e), subit(e); **all of a ~** soudain, tout à coup.
sudden-death [sʌdn'dɛθ] *n*: **~ play-off** partie supplémentaire pour départager les adversaires.
suddenly ['sʌdnlɪ] *adv* brusquement, tout à coup, soudain.
suds [sʌdz] *npl* eau savonneuse.
sue [suː] *vt* poursuivre en justice, intenter un procès à ♦ *vi*: **to ~ (for)** intenter un procès (pour); **to ~ for divorce** engager une procédure de divorce; **to ~ sb for damages** poursuivre qn en dommages-intérêts.
suede [sweɪd] *n* daim *m*, cuir suédé ♦ *cpd* de daim.
suet ['suɪt] *n* graisse *f* de rognon *or* de bœuf.
Suez Canal ['suːɪz-] *n* canal *m* de Suez.
Suff. *abbr* (*BRIT*) = Suffolk.
suffer ['sʌfə*] *vt* souffrir, subir; (*bear*) tolérer, supporter, subir ♦ *vi* souffrir; **to ~ from** (*illness*) souffrir de, avoir; **to ~ from the effects of alcohol/a fall** se ressentir des effets de l'alcool/des conséquences d'une chute.
sufferance ['sʌfərns] *n*: **he was only there on ~** sa présence était seulement tolérée.
sufferer ['sʌfərə*] *n* malade *m/f*; victime *m/f*.
suffering ['sʌfərɪŋ] *n* souffrance(s) *f(pl)*.
suffice [sə'faɪs] *vi* suffire.
sufficient [sə'fɪʃənt] *adj* suffisant(e); **~ money** suffisamment d'argent.
sufficiently [sə'fɪʃəntlɪ] *adv* suffisamment, assez.
suffix ['sʌfɪks] *n* suffixe *m*.
suffocate ['sʌfəkeɪt] *vi* suffoquer; étouffer.
suffocation [sʌfə'keɪʃən] *n* suffocation *f*; (*MED*) asphyxie *f*.
suffrage ['sʌfrɪdʒ] *n* suffrage *m*; droit *m* de suffrage *or* de vote.
suffuse [sə'fjuːz] *vt* baigner, imprégner; **the room was ~d with light** la pièce baignait dans la lumière *or* était imprégnée de lumière.
sugar ['ʃugə*] *n* sucre *m* ♦ *vt* sucrer.
sugar beet *n* betterave sucrière.
sugar bowl *n* sucrier *m*.
sugar cane *n* canne *f* à sucre.
sugar-coated ['ʃugə'kəutɪd] *adj* dragéifié(e).
sugar lump *n* morceau *m* de sucre.
sugar refinery *n* raffinerie *f* de sucre.
sugary ['ʃugərɪ] *adj* sucré(e).
suggest [sə'dʒɛst] *vt* suggérer, proposer; (*indicate*) laisser supposer, suggérer; **what do you ~ I do?** que vous me suggérez de faire?
suggestion [sə'dʒɛstʃən] *n* suggestion *f*.
suggestive [sə'dʒɛstɪv] *adj* suggestif(ive).
suicidal [suɪ'saɪdl] *adj* suicidaire.
suicide ['suɪsaɪd] *n* suicide *m*; **to commit ~** se suicider.

suicide attempt, suicide bid *n* tentative *f* de suicide.
suit [suːt] *n* (*man's*) costume *m*, complet *m*; (*woman's*) tailleur *m*, ensemble *m*; (*CARDS*) couleur *f*; (*law~*) procès *m* ♦ *vt* aller à; convenir à; (*adapt*): **to ~ sth to** adapter *or* approprier qch à; **to be ~ed to sth** (*suitable for*) être adapté(e) *or* approprié(e) à qch; **well ~ed** (*couple*) faits l'un pour l'autre, très bien assortis; **to bring a ~ against sb** intenter un procès contre qn; **to follow ~** (*fig*) faire de même.
suitable ['suːtəbl] *adj* qui convient; approprié(e), adéquat(e); **would tomorrow be ~?** est-ce que demain vous convien- drait?; **we found somebody ~** nous avons trouvé la personne qu'il nous faut.
suitably ['suːtəblɪ] *adv* comme il se doit (*or* se devait *etc*), convenablement.
suitcase ['suːtkeɪs] *n* valise *f*.
suite [swiːt] *n* (*of rooms, also MUS*) suite *f*; (*furniture*): **bedroom/dining room ~** (ensemble *m* de) chambre *f* à coucher/salle *f* à manger; **a three-piece ~** un salon (canapé et deux fauteuils).
suitor ['suːtə*] *n* soupirant *m*, prétendant *m*.
sulfate ['sʌlfeɪt] *n* (*US*) = **sulphate**.
sulfur *etc* ['sʌlfə*] (*US*) = **sulphur** *etc*.
sulk [sʌlk] *vi* bouder.
sulky ['sʌlkɪ] *adj* boudeur(euse), maussade.
sullen ['sʌlən] *adj* renfrogné(e), maussade; morne.
sulphate, (*US*) sulfate ['sʌlfeɪt] *n* sulfate *m*; **copper ~** sulfate de cuivre.
sulphur, (*US*) sulfur ['sʌlfə*] *n* soufre *m*.
sulphur dioxide *n* anhydride sulfureux.
sulphuric, (*US*) sulfuric [sʌl'fjuərɪk] *adj*: **~ acid** acide *m* sulfurique.
sultan ['sʌltən] *n* sultan *m*.
sultana [sʌl'tɑːnə] *n* (*fruit*) raisin (sec) de Smyrne.
sultry ['sʌltrɪ] *adj* étouffant(e).
sum [sʌm] *n* somme *f*; (*SCOL etc*) calcul *m*.
▶**sum up** *vt* résumer; (*evaluate rapidly*) récapituler ♦ *vi* résumer.
Sumatra [su'mɑːtrə] *n* Sumatra.
summarize ['sʌməraɪz] *vt* résumer.
summary ['sʌmərɪ] *n* résumé *m* ♦ *adj* (*justice*) sommaire.
summer ['sʌmə*] *n* été *m* ♦ *cpd* d'été, estival(e); **in (the) ~** en été, pendant l'été.
summer camp *n* (*US*) colonie *f* de vacances.
summerhouse ['sʌməhaus] *n* (*in garden*) pavillon *m*.
summertime ['sʌmətaɪm] *n* (*season*) été *m*.
summer time *n* (*by clock*) heure *f* d'été.
summery ['sʌmərɪ] *adj* estival(e); d'été.
summing-up [sʌmɪŋ'ʌp] *n* résumé *m*, récapitulation *f*.
summit ['sʌmɪt] *n* sommet *m*; (*also*: **~ conference**) (conférence *f* au) sommet *m*.
summon ['sʌmən] *vt* appeler, convoquer; **to**

~ **a witness** citer *or* assigner un témoin.
▶**summon up** *vt* rassembler, faire appel à.
summons ['sʌmənz] *n* citation *f*, assignation *f*
♦ *vt* citer, assigner; **to serve a ~ on sb** remettre une assignation à qn.
sumo ['suːməu] *n:* ~ **wrestling** sumo *m*.
sump [sʌmp] *n* (*BRIT AUT*) carter *m*.
sumptuous ['sʌmptjuəs] *adj* somptueux(euse).
sun [sʌn] *n* soleil *m*; **in the ~** au soleil; **to catch the ~** prendre le soleil; **everything under the ~** absolument tout.
Sun. *abbr* (= *Sunday*) dim.
sunbathe ['sʌnbeɪð] *vi* prendre un bain de soleil.
sunbeam ['sʌnbiːm] *n* rayon *m* de soleil.
sunbed ['sʌnbɛd] *n* lit pliant; (*with sun lamp*) lit à ultra-violets.
sunburn ['sʌnbəːn] *n* coup *m* de soleil.
sunburnt ['sʌnbəːnt], **sunburned** ['sʌnbəːnd] *adj* bronzé(e), hâlé(e); (*painfully*) brûlé(e) par le soleil.
sun cream *n* crème *f* (anti-)solaire.
sundae ['sʌndeɪ] *n* sundae *m*, coupe glacée.
Sunday ['sʌndɪ] *n* dimanche *m; for phrases see also* **Tuesday.**
Sunday paper *n* journal *m* du dimanche.

Les **Sunday papers** *sont une véritable institution en Grande-Bretagne. Il y a des "quality" Sunday papers et des "popular" Sunday papers, et la plupart des quotidiens ont un journal du dimanche qui leur est associé, bien que leurs équipes de rédacteurs soient différentes. Les quality Sunday papers ont plusieurs suppléments et magazines; voir* **quality press** *et* **tabloid press**

Sunday school *n* ≈ catéchisme *m*.
sundial ['sʌndaɪəl] *n* cadran *m* solaire.
sundown ['sʌndaun] *n* coucher *m* du soleil.
sundries ['sʌndrɪz] *npl* articles divers.
sundry ['sʌndrɪ] *adj* divers(e), différent(e); **all and ~** tout le monde, n'importe qui.
sunflower ['sʌnflauə*] *n* tournesol *m*.
sung [sʌŋ] *pp of* **sing.**
sunglasses ['sʌnglɑːsɪz] *npl* lunettes *fpl* de soleil.
sunk [sʌŋk] *pp of* **sink.**
sunken ['sʌŋkn] *adj* (*rock, ship*) submergé(e); (*eyes, cheeks*) creux(euse); (*bath*) encastré(e).
sunlamp ['sʌnlæmp] *n* lampe *f* à rayons ultra-violets.
sunlight ['sʌnlaɪt] *n* (lumière *f* du) soleil *m*.
sunlit ['sʌnlɪt] *adj* ensoleillé(e).
sunny ['sʌnɪ] *adj* ensoleillé(e); (*fig*) épanoui(e), radieux(euse); **it is ~** il fait (du) soleil, il y a du soleil.
sunrise ['sʌnraɪz] *n* lever *m* du soleil.
sun roof *n* (*AUT*) toit ouvrant.
sunscreen ['sʌnskriːn] *n* crème *f* solaire.

sunset ['sʌnsɛt] *n* coucher *m* du soleil.
sunshade ['sʌnʃeɪd] *n* (*lady's*) ombrelle *f*; (*over table*) parasol *m*.
sunshine ['sʌnʃaɪn] *n* (lumière *f* du) soleil *m*.
sunspot ['sʌnspɔt] *n* tache *f* solaire.
sunstroke ['sʌnstrəuk] *n* insolation *f*, coup *m* de soleil.
suntan ['sʌntæn] *n* bronzage *m*.
suntanned ['sʌntænd] *adj* bronzé(e).
suntan oil *n* huile *f* solaire.
suntrap ['sʌntræp] *n* coin très ensoleillé.
super ['suːpə*] *adj* (*col*) formidable.
superannuation [suːpərænjuˈeɪʃən] *n* cotisations *fpl* pour la pension.
superb [suːˈpəːb] *adj* superbe, magnifique.
Super Bowl *n* (*US SPORT*) Super Bowl *m*.
supercilious [suːpəˈsɪlɪəs] *adj* hautain(e), dédaigneux(euse).
superconductor [suːpəkənˈdʌktə*] *n* supraconducteur *m*.
superficial [suːpəˈfɪʃəl] *adj* superficiel(le).
superficially [suːpəˈfɪʃəlɪ] *adv* superficiellement.
superfluous [suˈpəːfluəs] *adj* superflu(e).
superglue ['suːpəgluː] *n* colle forte.
superhighway ['suːpəhaɪweɪ] *n* (*US*) voie *f* express (à plusieurs files); **the information ~** la super-autoroute de l'information.
superhuman [suːpəˈhjuːmən] *adj* surhumain(e).
superimpose ['suːpərɪmˈpəuz] *vt* superposer.
superintend [suːpərɪnˈtɛnd] *vt* surveiller.
superintendent [suːpərɪnˈtɛndənt] *n* directeur/trice; (*POLICE*) ≈ commissaire *m*.
superior [suˈpɪərɪə*] *adj* supérieur(e); (*COMM: goods, quality*) de qualité supérieure; (*smug*) condescendant(e), méprisant(e) ♦ *n* supérieur/e; **Mother S~** (*REL*) Mère supérieure.
superiority [supɪərɪˈɔrɪtɪ] *n* supériorité *f*.
superlative [suˈpəːlətɪv] *adj* sans pareil(le), suprême ♦ *n* (*LING*) superlatif *m*.
superman ['suːpəmæn] *n* surhomme *m*.
supermarket ['suːpəmɑːkɪt] *n* supermarché *m*.
supermodel ['suːpəmɔdl] *n* top model *m*.
supernatural [suːpəˈnætʃərəl] *adj* surnaturel(le).
supernova [suːpəˈnəuvə] *n* supernova *f*.
superpower ['suːpəpauə*] *n* (*POL*) superpuissance *f*.
supersede [suːpəˈsiːd] *vt* remplacer, supplanter.
supersonic ['suːpəˈsɔnɪk] *adj* supersonique.
superstar ['suːpəstɑː*] *n* (*CINE etc*) superstar *f*; (*SPORT*) superchampion/ne ♦ *adj* (*status, lifestyle*) de superstar.
superstition [suːpəˈstɪʃən] *n* superstition *f*.
superstitious [suːpəˈstɪʃəs] *adj* superstitieux(euse).
superstore ['suːpəstɔː*] *n* (*BRIT*) hypermarché *m*, grand surface.

supertanker ['su:pətæŋkə*] *n* pétrolier géant, superpétrolier *m*.

supertax ['su:pətæks] *n* tranche supérieure de l'impôt.

supervise ['su:pəvaɪz] *vt* (*children etc*) surveiller; (*organization, work*) diriger.

supervision [su:pə'vɪʒən] *n* surveillance *f*; direction *f*; **under medical** ~ sous contrôle du médecin.

supervisor ['su:pəvaɪzə*] *n* surveillant/e; (*in shop*) chef *m* de rayon; (*SCOL*) directeur/trice de thèse.

supervisory ['su:pəvaɪzərɪ] *adj* de surveillance.

supine ['su:paɪn] *adj* couché(e) *or* étendu(e) sur le dos.

supper ['sʌpə*] *n* dîner *m*; (*late*) souper *m*; **to have** ~ dîner; souper.

supplant [sə'plɑ:nt] *vt* supplanter.

supple ['sʌpl] *adj* souple.

supplement *n* ['sʌplɪmənt] supplément *m* ♦ *vt* [sʌplɪ'ment] ajouter à, compléter.

supplementary [sʌplɪ'mentərɪ] *adj* supplémentaire.

supplementary benefit *n* (*BRIT*) allocation *f* supplémentaire d'aide sociale.

supplier [sə'plaɪə*] *n* fournisseur *m*.

supply [sə'plaɪ] *vt* (*goods*): **to** ~ **sth** (**to sb**) fournir qch (à qn); (*people, organization*): **to** ~ **sb** (**with sth**) approvisionner *or* ravitailler qn (en qch); fournir qn (en qch); fournir qch à qn; (*system, machine*): **to** ~ **sth** (**with sth**) alimenter qch (en qch); (*a need*) répondre à ♦ *n* provision *f*, réserve *f*; (*supplying*) approvisionnement *m*; (*TECH*) alimentation *f*; **supplies** *npl* (*food*) vivres *mpl*; (*MIL*) subsistances *fpl*; **office supplies** fournitures *fpl* de bureau; **to be in short** ~ être rare, manquer; **the electricity/water/gas** ~ l'alimentation en électricité/eau/gaz; ~ **and demand** l'offre *f* et la demande; **it comes supplied with an adaptor** il (*or* elle) est pourvu(e) d'un adaptateur.

supply teacher *n* (*BRIT*) suppléant/e.

support [sə'pɔ:t] *n* (*moral, financial etc*) soutien *m*, appui *m*; (*TECH*) support *m*, soutien ♦ *vt* soutenir, supporter; (*financially*) subvenir aux besoins de; (*uphold*) être pour, être partisan de, appuyer; (*SPORT: team*) être pour; **to** ~ **o.s.** (*financially*) gagner sa vie.

supporter [sə'pɔ:tə*] *n* (*POL etc*) partisan/e; (*SPORT*) supporter *m*.

supporting [sə'pɔ:tɪŋ] *adj* (*wall*) d'appui.

supporting actor/actress *n* second rôle *m/f*.

supporting role *n* second rôle *m*.

supportive [sə'pɔ:tɪv] *adj*: **my family were very** ~ ma famille m'a été d'un grand soutien.

suppose [sə'pəuz] *vt, vi* supposer; imaginer; **to be** ~**d to do/be** être censé(e) faire/être; **I don't** ~ **she'll come** je suppose qu'elle ne viendra pas, cela m'étonnerait qu'elle

vienne.

supposedly [sə'pəuzɪdlɪ] *adv* soi-disant.

supposing [sə'pəuzɪŋ] *conj* si, à supposer que + *sub*.

supposition [sʌpə'zɪʃən] *n* supposition *f*, hypothèse *f*.

suppository [sə'pozɪtrɪ] *n* suppositoire *m*.

suppress [sə'pres] *vt* (*revolt, feeling*) réprimer; (*publication*) supprimer; (*scandal*) étouffer.

suppression [sə'preʃən] *n* suppression *f*, répression *f*.

suppressor [sə'presə*] *n* (*ELEC etc*) dispositif *m* antiparasite.

supremacy [su'preməsɪ] *n* suprématie *f*.

supreme [su'pri:m] *adj* suprême.

Supreme Court *n* (*US*) Cour *f* suprême.

supremo [su'pri:məu] *n* grand chef.

Supt. *abbr* (*POLICE*) = **superintendent**.

surcharge ['sə:tʃɑ:dʒ] *n* surcharge *f*; (*extra tax*) surtaxe *f*.

sure [ʃuə*] *adj* (*gen*) sûr(e); (*definite, convinced*) sûr, certain(e) ♦ *adv* (*col: esp US*): **that's is pretty, that's** ~ **pretty** c'est drôlement joli(e); ~! (*of course*) bien sûr!; ~ **enough** effectivement; **I'm not** ~ **how/why/when** je ne sais pas très bien comment/pourquoi/quand; **to be** ~ **of o.s.** être sûr de soi; **to make** ~ **of** s'assurer de; vérifier.

sure-fire ['ʃuəfaɪə*] *adj* (*col*) certain(e), infaillible.

sure-footed [ʃuə'futɪd] *adj* au pied sûr.

surely ['ʃuəlɪ] *adv* sûrement; certainement; ~ **you don't mean that!** vous ne parlez pas sérieusement!

surety ['ʃuərətɪ] *n* caution *f*; **to go** *or* **stand** ~ **for sb** se porter caution pour qn.

surf [sə:f] *n* ressac *m*.

surface ['sə:fɪs] *n* surface *f* ♦ *vt* (*road*) poser le revêtement de ♦ *vi* remonter à la surface; faire surface; **on the** ~ (*fig*) au premier abord.

surface area *n* superficie *f*, aire *f*.

surface mail *n* courrier *m* par voie de terre (*or* maritime).

surface-to-surface ['sə:fɪstə'sə:fɪs] *adj* (*MIL*) sol-sol *inv*.

surfboard ['sə:fbɔ:d] *n* planche *f* de surf.

surfeit ['sə:fɪt] *n*: **a** ~ **of** un excès de; une indigestion de.

surfer ['sə:fə*] *n* surfiste *m/f*.

surfing ['sə:fɪŋ] *n* surf *m*.

surge [sə:dʒ] *n* vague *f*, montée *f*; (*ELEC*) pointe *f* de courant ♦ *vi* déferler; **to** ~ **forward** se précipiter (en avant).

surgeon ['sə:dʒən] *n* chirurgien *m*.

Surgeon General *n* (*US*) chef *m* du service fédéral de la santé publique.

surgery ['sə:dʒərɪ] *n* chirurgie *f*; (*BRIT: room*) cabinet *m* (de consultation); (: *session*) consultation *f*; (: *of MP etc*) permanence *f* (*où le député etc reçoit les électeurs etc*); **to undergo** ~ être opéré(e).

surgery hours npl (BRIT) heures fpl de consultation.

surgical ['sə:dʒɪkl] adj chirurgical(e).

surgical spirit n (BRIT) alcool m à 90°.

surly ['sə:lɪ] adj revêche, maussade.

surmise [sə:'maɪz] vt présumer, conjecturer.

surmount [sə:'maunt] vt surmonter.

surname ['sə:neɪm] n nom m de famille.

surpass [sə:'pɑ:s] vt surpasser, dépasser.

surplus ['sə:pləs] n surplus m, excédent m ♦ adj en surplus, de trop; **it is ~ to our requirements** cela dépasse nos besoins; ~ **stock** surplus m.

surprise [sə'praɪz] n (gen) surprise f; (astonishment) étonnement m ♦ vt surprendre; étonner; **to take by ~** (person) prendre au dépourvu; (MIL: town, fort) prendre par surprise.

surprising [sə'praɪzɪŋ] adj surprenant(e), étonnant(e).

surprisingly [sə'praɪzɪŋlɪ] adv (easy, helpful) étonnamment, étrangement; (somewhat) ~, **he agreed** curieusement, il a accepté.

surrealism [sə'rɪəlɪzəm] n surréalisme m.

surrealist [sə'rɪəlɪst] adj, n surréaliste (m/f).

surrender [sə'rendə*] n reddition f, capitulation f ♦ vi se rendre, capituler ♦ vt (claim, right) renoncer à.

surrender value n valeur f de rachat.

surreptitious [sʌrəp'tɪʃəs] adj subreptice, furtif(ive).

surrogate ['sʌrəgɪt] n (BRIT: substitute) substitut m ♦ adj de substitution, de remplacement; **a food ~** un succédané alimentaire; ~ **coffee** ersatz m or succédané m de café.

surrogate mother n mère porteuse or de substitution.

surround [sə'raund] vt entourer; (MIL etc) encercler.

surrounding [sə'raundɪŋ] adj environnant(e).

surroundings [sə'raundɪŋz] npl environs mpl, alentours mpl.

surtax ['sə:tæks] n surtaxe f.

surveillance [sə:'veɪləns] n surveillance f.

survey n ['sə:veɪ] enquête f, étude f; (in house buying etc) inspection f, (rapport m d')expertise f; (of land) levé m; (comprehensive view: of situation etc) vue f d'ensemble ♦ vt [sə:'veɪ] passer en revue; enquêter sur; inspecter; (building) expertiser; (land) faire le levé de.

surveying [sə'veɪɪŋ] n arpentage m.

surveyor [sə'veɪə*] n (of building) expert m; (of land) (arpenteur m) géomètre m.

survival [sə'vaɪvl] n survie f; (relic) vestige m ♦ cpd (course, kit) de survie.

survive [sə'vaɪv] vi survivre; (custom etc) subsister ♦ vt survivre à, réchapper de; (person) survivre à.

survivor [sə'vaɪvə*] n survivant/e.

susceptible [sə'septəbl] adj: ~ **(to)** sensible (à); (disease) prédisposé(e) (à).

suspect adj, n ['sʌspekt] suspect(e) ♦ vt [səs'pekt] soupçonner, suspecter.

suspected [səs'pektɪd] adj: **a ~ terrorist** une personne soupçonnée de terrorisme; **he had a ~ broken arm** il avait une supposée fracture du bras.

suspend [səs'pend] vt suspendre.

suspended animation [səs'pendɪd-] n: **in a state of ~** en hibernation.

suspended sentence [səs'pendɪd-] n condamnation f avec sursis.

suspender belt [səs'pendə-] n (BRIT) portejarretelles m inv.

suspenders [səs'pendəz] npl (BRIT) jarretelles fpl; (US) bretelles fpl.

suspense [səs'pens] n attente f; (in film etc) suspense m.

suspension [səs'penʃən] n (gen, AUT) suspension f; (of driving licence) retrait m provisoire.

suspension bridge n pont suspendu.

suspicion [səs'pɪʃən] n soupçon(s) m(pl); **to be under ~** être considéré(e) comme suspect(e), être suspecté(e); **arrested on ~ of murder** arrêté sur présomption de meurtre.

suspicious [səs'pɪʃəs] adj (suspecting) soupçonneux(euse), méfiant(e); (causing suspicion) suspect(e); **to be ~ of or about sb/sth** avoir des doutes à propos de qn/sur qch, trouver qn/qch suspect(e).

suss out ['sʌs'aut] vt (BRIT col: discover) supputer; (: understand) piger.

sustain [səs'teɪn] vt supporter; soutenir; corroborer; (suffer) subir; recevoir.

sustainable [səs'teɪnəbl] adj (rate, growth) qui peut être maintenu(e); (agriculture, development) durable.

sustained [səs'teɪnd] adj (effort) soutenu(e), prolongé(e).

sustenance ['sʌstɪnəns] n nourriture f; moyens mpl de subsistance.

suture ['su:tʃə*] n suture f.

SW abbr (= short wave) OC.

swab [swɔb] n (MED) tampon m; prélèvement m ♦ vt (NAUT: also: ~ **down**) nettoyer.

swagger ['swægə*] vi plastronner, parader.

swallow ['swɔləu] n (bird) hirondelle f; (of food etc) gorgée f ♦ vt avaler; (fig) gober.

▶**swallow up** vt engloutir.

swam [swæm] pt of **swim**.

swamp [swɔmp] n marais m, marécage m ♦ vt submerger.

swampy ['swɔmpɪ] adj marécageux(euse).

swan [swɔn] n cygne m.

swank [swæŋk] vi (col) faire de l'épate.

swan song n (fig) chant m du cygne.

swap [swɔp] n échange m, troc m ♦ vt: **to ~ (for)** échanger (contre), troquer (contre).

SWAPO ['swɑ:pəu] n abbr (= South-West Africa People's Organization) SWAPO f.

swarm [swɔ:m] n essaim m ♦ vi essaimer; fourmiller, grouiller.

swarthy ['swɔːðɪ] *adj* basané(e), bistré(e).
swashbuckling ['swɔʃbʌklɪŋ] *adj* (*film*) de cape et d'épée.
swastika ['swɒstɪkə] *n* croix gammée
SWAT *n abbr* (*US*: = *Special Weapons and Tactics*) ≈ CRS *f*.
swat [swɔt] *vt* écraser ♦ *n* (*BRIT: also:* **fly ~**) tapette *f*.
swathe [sweɪð] *vt:* **to ~ in** (*bandages, blankets*) emboîner de.
swatter ['swɔtə*] *n* (*also:* **fly ~**) tapette *f*.
sway [sweɪ] *vi* se balancer, osciller; tanguer ♦ *vt* (*influence*) influencer ♦ *n* (*rule, power*): **~ (over)** emprise *f* (sur); **to hold ~ over sb** avoir de l'emprise sur qn.
Swaziland ['swɑːzɪlænd] *n* Swaziland *m*.
swear, *pt* **swore**, *pp* **sworn** [swɛə*, swɔː*, swɔːn] *vi* jurer; **to ~ to sth** jurer de qch; **to ~ an oath** prêter serment.
▶**swear in** *vt* assermenter.
swearword ['swɛəwəːd] *n* gros mot, juron *m*.
sweat [swɛt] *n* sueur *f*, transpiration *f* ♦ *vi* suer; **in a ~** en sueur.
sweatband ['swɛtbænd] *n* (*SPORT*) bandeau *m*.
sweater ['swɛtə*] *n* tricot *m*, pull *m*.
sweatshirt ['swɛtʃəːt] *n* sweat-shirt *m*.
sweatshop ['swɛtʃɔp] *n* atelier *m* où les ouvriers sont exploités.
sweaty ['swɛtɪ] *adj* en sueur, moite *or* mouillé(e) de sueur.
Swede [swiːd] *n* Suédois/e.
swede [swiːd] *n* (*BRIT*) rutabaga *m*.
Sweden ['swiːdn] *n* Suède *f*.
Swedish ['swiːdɪʃ] *adj* suédois(e) ♦ *n* (*LING*) suédois *m*.
sweep [swiːp] *n* coup *m* de balai; (*curve*) grande courbe; (*range*) champ *m*; (*also:* **chimney ~**) ramoneur *m* ♦ *vb* (*pt, pp* **swept** [swɛpt]) *vt* balayer; (*fashion, craze*) se répandre dans ♦ *vi* avancer majestueusement *or* rapidement; s'élancer; s'étendre.
▶**sweep away** *vt* balayer; entraîner; emporter.
▶**sweep past** *vi* passer majestueusement *or* rapidement.
▶**sweep up** *vt, vi* balayer.
sweeper ['swiːpə*] *n* (*person*) balayeur *m*; (*machine*) balayeuse *f*; (*FOOTBALL*) libéro *m*.
sweeping ['swiːpɪŋ] *adj* (*gesture*) large; circulaire; (*changes, reforms*) radical(e); **a ~ statement** une généralisation hâtive.
sweepstake ['swiːpsteɪk] *n* sweepstake *m*.
sweet [swiːt] *n* (*BRIT*) dessert *m*; (*candy*) bonbon *m* ♦ *adj* doux(douce); (*not savoury*) sucré(e); (*fresh*) frais(fraîche), pur(e); (*kind*) gentil(le); (*cute*) mignon(ne) ♦ *adv:* **to smell ~** sentir bon; **to taste ~** avoir un goût sucré; **~ and sour** *adj* aigre-doux(douce).
sweetbread ['swiːtbrɛd] *n* ris *m* de veau.
sweetcorn ['swiːtkɔːn] *n* maïs doux.
sweeten ['swiːtn] *vt* sucrer; (*fig*) adoucir.
sweetener ['swiːtnə*] *n* (*CULIN*) édulcorant *m*.

sweetheart ['swiːthɑːt] *n* amoureux/euse.
sweetly ['swiːtlɪ] *adv* (*smile*) gentiment; (*sing, play*) mélodieusement.
sweetness ['swiːtnɪs] *n* douceur *f*; (*of taste*) goût sucré.
sweet pea *n* pois *m* de senteur.
sweet potato *n* patate douce.
sweetshop ['swiːtʃɔp] *n* (*BRIT*) confiserie *f*.
sweet tooth *n:* **to have a ~** aimer les sucreries.
swell [swɛl] *n* (*of sea*) houle *f* ♦ *adj* (*col: excellent*) chouette ♦ *vb* (*pt* **~ed**, *pp* **swollen** *or* **~ed** ['swəulən]) *vt* augmenter; grossir ♦ *vi* grossir, augmenter; (*sound*) s'enfler; (*MED*) enfler.
swelling ['swɛlɪŋ] *n* (*MED*) enflure *f*; grosseur *f*.
sweltering ['swɛltərɪŋ] *adj* étouffant(e), oppressant(e).
swept [swɛpt] *pt, pp of* **sweep**.
swerve [swəːv] *vi* faire une embardée *or* un écart; dévier.
swift [swɪft] *n* (*bird*) martinet *m* ♦ *adj* rapide, prompt(e).
swiftly ['swɪftlɪ] *adv* rapidement, vite.
swiftness ['swɪftnɪs] *n* rapidité *f*.
swig [swɪg] *n* (*col: drink*) lampée *f*.
swill [swɪl] *n* pâtée *f* ♦ *vt* (*also:* **~ out, ~ down**) laver à grande eau.
swim [swɪm] *n:* **to go for a ~** aller nager *or* se baigner ♦ *vb* (*pt* **swam**, *pp* **swum** [swæm, swʌm]) *vi* nager; (*SPORT*) faire de la natation; (*fig: head, room*) tourner ♦ *vt* traverser (à la nage); (*distance*) faire (à la nage); **to ~ a length** nager une longueur; **to go ~ming** aller nager.
swimmer ['swɪmə*] *n* nageur/euse.
swimming ['swɪmɪŋ] *n* nage *f*, natation *f*.
swimming baths *npl* (*BRIT*) piscine *f*.
swimming cap *n* bonnet *m* de bain.
swimming costume *n* (*BRIT*) maillot *m* (de bain).
swimmingly ['swɪmɪŋlɪ] *adv:* **to go ~** (*wonderfully*) se dérouler à merveille.
swimming pool *n* piscine *f*.
swimming trunks *npl* maillot *m* de bain.
swimsuit ['swɪmsuːt] *n* maillot *m* (de bain).
swindle ['swɪndl] *n* escroquerie *f* ♦ *vt* escroquer.
swindler ['swɪndlə*] *n* escroc *m*.
swine [swaɪn] *n* (*pl inv*) pourceau *m*, porc *m*; (*col!*) salaud *m* (*!*).
swing [swɪŋ] *n* balançoire *f*; (*movement*) balancement *m*, oscillations *fpl*; (*MUS*) swing *m*; rythme *m* ♦ *vb* (*pt, pp* **swung** [swʌŋ]) *vt* balancer, faire osciller; (*also:* **~ round**) tourner, faire virer ♦ *vi* se balancer, osciller; (*also:* **~ round**) virer, tourner; **a ~ to the left** (*POL*) un revirement en faveur de la gauche; **to be in full ~** battre son plein; **to get into the ~ of things** se mettre dans le bain; **the road ~s south** la route prend la direction sud.

swing bridge n pont tournant.
swing door n (BRIT) porte battante.
swingeing ['swɪndʒɪŋ] adj (BRIT) écrasant(e); considérable.
swinging ['swɪŋɪŋ] adj rythmé(e); entraînant(e); (fig) dans le vent; ~ **door** (US) porte battante.
swipe [swaɪp] n grand coup; gifle f ♦ vt (hit) frapper à toute volée; gifler; (col: steal) piquer; (credit card etc) faire passer (dans la machine).
swirl [swə:l] n tourbillon m ♦ vi tourbillonner, tournoyer.
swish [swɪʃ] adj (BRIT col: smart) rupin(e) ♦ vi (whip) siffler; (skirt, long grass) bruire.
Swiss [swɪs] adj suisse ♦ n (pl inv) Suisse/esse.
Swiss French adj suisse romand(e).
Swiss German adj suisse-allemand(e).
Swiss roll n gâteau roulé.
switch [swɪtʃ] n (for light, radio etc) bouton m; (change) changement m, revirement m ♦ vt (change) changer; (exchange) intervertir; (invert): **to ~ (round** or **over)** changer de place.
▶**switch off** vt éteindre; (engine) arrêter.
▶**switch on** vt allumer; (engine, machine) mettre en marche; (BRIT: water supply) ouvrir.
switchback ['swɪtʃbæk] n (BRIT) montagnes fpl russes.
switchblade ['swɪtʃbleɪd] n (also: ~ **knife**) couteau m à cran d'arrêt.
switchboard ['swɪtʃbɔ:d] n (TEL) standard m.
switchboard operator n (TEL) standardiste m/f.
Switzerland ['swɪtsələnd] n Suisse f.
swivel ['swɪvl] vi (also: ~ **round**) pivoter, tourner.
swollen ['swəulən] pp of swell ♦ adj (ankle etc) enflé(e).
swoon [swu:n] vi se pâmer.
swoop [swu:p] n (by police etc) rafle f, descente f; (of bird etc) descente f en piqué ♦ vi (also: ~ **down**) descendre en piqué, piquer.
swop [swɔp] n, vt = swap.
sword [sɔ:d] n épée f.
swordfish ['sɔ:dfɪʃ] n espadon m.
swore [swɔ:*] pt of swear.
sworn [swɔ:n] pp of swear.
swot [swɔt] vt, vi bûcher, potasser.
swum [swʌm] pp of swim.
swung [swʌŋ] pt, pp of swing.
sycamore ['sɪkəmɔ:*] n sycomore m.
sycophant ['sɪkəfænt] n flagorneur/euse.
sycophantic [sɪkə'fæntɪk] adj flagorneur(euse).
Sydney ['sɪdnɪ] n Sydney.
syllable ['sɪləbl] n syllabe f.
syllabus ['sɪləbəs] n programme m; **on the ~** au programme.
symbol ['sɪmbl] n symbole m.
symbolic(al) [sɪm'bɔlɪk(l)] adj symbolique.

symbolism ['sɪmbəlɪzəm] n symbolisme m.
symbolize ['sɪmbəlaɪz] vt symboliser.
symmetrical [sɪ'mɛtrɪkl] adj symétrique.
symmetry ['sɪmɪtrɪ] n symétrie f.
sympathetic [sɪmpə'θɛtɪk] adj (showing pity) compatissant(e); (understanding) bienveillant(e), compréhensif(ive); ~ **towards** bien disposé(e) envers.
sympathetically [sɪmpə'θɛtɪklɪ] adv avec compassion (or bienveillance).
sympathize ['sɪmpəθaɪz] vi: **to ~ with sb** (in grief) être de tout cœur avec qn, compatir à la douleur de qn; (in predicament) partager les sentiments de qn; **to ~ with** (sb's feelings) comprendre.
sympathizer ['sɪmpəθaɪzə*] n (POL) sympathisant/e.
sympathy ['sɪmpəθɪ] n compassion f; **in ~ with** en accord avec; (strike) en or par solidarité avec; **with our deepest ~** en vous priant d'accepter nos sincères condoléances.
symphonic [sɪm'fɔnɪk] adj symphonique.
symphony ['sɪmfənɪ] n symphonie f.
symphony orchestra n orchestre m symphonique.
symposium [sɪm'pəuzɪəm] n symposium m.
symptom ['sɪmptəm] n symptôme m; indice m.
symptomatic [sɪmptə'mætɪk] adj symptomatique.
synagogue ['sɪnəgɔg] n synagogue f.
sync [sɪŋk] n (col): **in/out of ~** bien/mal synchronisé(e); **they're in ~ with each other** (fig) le courant passe bien entre eux.
synchromesh [sɪŋkrəu'mɛʃ] n (AUT) synchronisation f.
synchronize ['sɪŋkrənaɪz] vt synchroniser ♦ vi: **to ~ with** se produire en même temps que.
synchronized swimming ['sɪŋkrənaɪzd-] n natation synchronisée.
syncopated ['sɪŋkəpeɪtɪd] adj syncopé(e).
syndicate ['sɪndɪkɪt] n syndicat m, coopérative f; (PRESS) agence f de presse.
syndrome ['sɪndrəum] n syndrome m.
synonym ['sɪnənɪm] n synonyme m.
synonymous [sɪ'nɔnɪməs] adj: ~ **(with)** synonyme (de).
synopsis, pl **synopses** [sɪ'nɔpsɪs, -si:z] n résumé m, synopsis m or f.
syntax ['sɪntæks] n syntaxe f.
synthesis, pl **syntheses** ['sɪnθəsɪs, -si:z] n synthèse f.
synthesizer ['sɪnθəsaɪzə*] n (MUS) synthétiseur m.
synthetic [sɪn'θɛtɪk] adj synthétique ♦ n matière f synthétique; ~**s** npl textiles artificiels.
syphilis ['sɪfɪlɪs] n syphilis f.
syphon ['saɪfən] n, vb = siphon.
Syria ['sɪrɪə] n Syrie f.
Syrian ['sɪrɪən] adj syrien(ne) ♦ n Syrien/ne.
syringe [sɪ'rɪndʒ] n seringue f.

syrup ['sırəp] _n_ sirop _m_; (_BRIT: also:_ **golden ~**) mélasse raffinée.
syrupy ['sırəpı] _adj_ sirupeux(euse).
system ['sıstəm] _n_ système _m_; (_order_) méthode _f_; (_ANAT_) organisme _m_.
systematic [sıstə'mætık] _adj_ systématique; méthodique.
system disk _n_ (_COMPUT_) disque _m_ système.
systems analyst _n_ analyste-programmeur _m/f_.

T t

T, t [tiː] _n_ (_letter_) T, t _m_; **T for Tommy** T comme Thérèse.
TA _n abbr_ (_BRIT_) = Territorial Army.
ta [tɑː] _excl_ (_BRIT col_) merci!
tab [tæb] _n abbr_ = **tabulator** ♦ _n_ (_loop on coat etc_) attache _f_; (_label_) étiquette _f_; **to keep ~s on** (_fig_) surveiller.
tabby ['tæbı] _n_ (_also:_ **~ cat**) chat/te tigré(e).
tabernacle ['tæbənækl] _n_ tabernacle _m_.
table ['teıbl] _n_ table _f_ ♦ _vt_ (_BRIT: motion etc_) présenter; **to lay** _or_ **set the ~** mettre le couvert _or_ la table; **to clear the ~** débarrasser la table; **league ~** (_BRIT FOOTBALL, RUGBY_) classement _m_ (du championnat); **~ of contents** table des matières.
tablecloth ['teıblklɔθ] _n_ nappe _f_.
table d'hôte [tɑːbl'dəut] _adj_ (_meal_) à prix fixe.
table football _n_ baby-foot _m_.
table lamp _n_ lampe décorative.
tablemat ['teıblmæt] _n_ (_for plate_) napperon _m_, set _m_; (_for hot dish_) dessous-de-plat _m inv_.
table salt _n_ sel fin _or_ de table.
tablespoon ['teıblspuːn] _n_ cuiller _f_ de service; (_also:_ **~ful:** _as measurement_) cuillerée _f_ à soupe.
tablet ['tæblıt] _n_ (_MED_) comprimé _m_; (: _for sucking_) pastille _f_; (_for writing_) bloc _m_; (_of stone_) plaque _f_; **~ of soap** (_BRIT_) savonnette _f_.
table tennis _n_ ping-pong _m_, tennis _m_ de table.
table wine _n_ vin _m_ de table.
tabloid ['tæblɔıd] _n_ (_newspaper_) tabloïde _m_; **the ~s** les journaux _mpl_ populaires.

> _Le terme_ **tabloid press** _désigne les journaux populaires de demi-format où l'on trouve beaucoup de photos et qui adoptent un style très concis. Ce type de journaux vise des lecteurs s'intéressant aux faits divers ayant un parfum de scandale; voir_ **quality press**

taboo [tə'buː] _adj, n_ tabou (_m_).

tabulate ['tæbjuleıt] _vt_ (_data, figures_) mettre sous forme de table(s).
tabulator ['tæbjuleıtə*] _n_ tabulateur _m_.
tachograph ['tækəgrɑːf] _n_ tachygraphe _m_.
tachometer [tæ'kɔmıtə*] _n_ tachymètre _m_.
tacit ['tæsıt] _adj_ tacite.
taciturn ['tæsıtəːn] _adj_ taciturne.
tack [tæk] _n_ (_nail_) petit clou; (_stitch_) point _m_ de bâti; (_NAUT_) bord _m_, bordée _f_ ♦ _vt_ clouer; bâtir ♦ _vi_ tirer un _or_ des bord(s); **to change ~** virer de bord; **on the wrong ~** (_fig_) sur la mauvaise voie; **to ~ sth on to (the end of) sth** (_of letter, book_) rajouter qch à la fin de qch.
tackle ['tækl] _n_ matériel _m_, équipement _m_; (_for lifting_) appareil _m_ de levage; (_FOOTBALL, RUGBY_) plaquage _m_ ♦ _vt_ (_difficulty_) s'attaquer à; (_FOOTBALL, RUGBY_) plaquer.
tacky ['tækı] _adj_ collant(e); pas sec(sèche); (_col: shabby_) moche.
tact [tækt] _n_ tact _m_.
tactful ['tæktful] _adj_ plein(e) de tact.
tactfully ['tæktfəlı] _adv_ avec tact.
tactical ['tæktıkl] _adj_ tactique; **~ error** erreur _f_ de tactique.
tactical voting _n_ vote _m_ tactique.
tactician [tæk'tıʃən] _n_ tacticien/ne.
tactics ['tæktıks] _n, npl_ tactique _f_.
tactless ['tæktlıs] _adj_ qui manque de tact.
tactlessly ['tæktlıslı] _adv_ sans tact.
tadpole ['tædpəul] _n_ têtard _m_.
Tadzhikistan [tædʒıkı'stɑːn] _n_ = **Tajikistan**.
taffy ['tæfı] _n_ (_US_) (bonbon _m_ au) caramel _m_.
tag [tæg] _n_ étiquette _f_; **price/name ~** étiquette (portant le prix/le nom).
▶**tag along** _vi_ suivre.
Tahiti [tɑː'hiːtı] _n_ Tahiti _m_.
tail [teıl] _n_ queue _f_; (_of shirt_) pan _m_ ♦ _vt_ (_follow_) suivre, filer; **to turn ~** se sauver à toutes jambes; _see also_ **head**.
▶**tail away, tail off** _vi_ (_in size, quality etc_) baisser peu à peu.
tailback ['teılbæk] _n_ (_BRIT_) bouchon _m_.
tail coat _n_ habit _m_.
tail end _n_ bout _m_, fin _f_.
tailgate ['teılgeıt] _n_ (_AUT_) hayon _m_ arrière.
tail light _n_ (_AUT_) feu _m_ arrière.
tailor ['teılə*] _n_ tailleur _m_ (_artisan_) ♦ _vt_: **to ~ sth (to)** adapter qch exactement (à); **~'s (shop)** (boutique _f_ de) tailleur _m_.
tailoring ['teılərıŋ] _n_ (_cut_) coupe _f_.
tailor-made ['teılə'meıd] _adj_ fait(e) sur mesure; (_fig_) conçu(e) spécialement.
tailwind ['teılwınd] _n_ vent _m_ arrière _inv_.
taint [teınt] _vt_ (_meat, food_) gâter; (_fig: reputation_) salir.
tainted ['teıntıd] _adj_ (_food_) gâté(e); (_water, air_) infecté(e); (_fig_) souillé(e).
Taiwan ['taı'wɑːn] _n_ Taiwan (_no article_).
Tajikistan [tædʒıkı'stɑːn] _n_ Tajikistan _m/f_.
take [teık] _vb_ (_pt_ **took**, _pp_ **taken** [tuk, 'teıkn]) _vt_ prendre; (_gain: prize_) remporter; (_require: ef-_

fort, courage) demander; (tolerate) accepter, supporter; (hold: passengers etc) contenir; (accompany) emmener, accompagner; (bring, carry) apporter, emporter; (exam) passer, se présenter à; (conduct: meeting) présider ♦ vi (dye, fire etc) prendre ♦ n (CINE) prise f de vues; **to ~ sth from** (drawer etc) prendre qch dans; (person) prendre qch à; **I ~ it that** je suppose que; **I took him for a doctor** je l'ai pris pour un docteur; **to ~ sb's hand** prendre qn par la main; **to ~ for a walk** (child, dog) emmener promener; **to be taken ill** tomber malade; **to ~ it upon o.s. to do sth** prendre sur soi de faire qch; **to ~ the first (street) on the left** prenez la première à gauche; **it won't ~ long** ça ne prendra pas longtemps; **I was quite taken with her/it** elle/cela m'a beaucoup plu.
▶**take after** vt fus ressembler à.
▶**take apart** vt démonter.
▶**take away** vt emporter; (remove) enlever; (subtract) soustraire ♦ vi: **to ~ away from** diminuer.
▶**take back** vt (return) rendre, rapporter; (one's words) retirer.
▶**take down** vt (building) démolir; (dismantle: scaffolding) démonter; (letter etc) prendre, écrire.
▶**take in** vt (deceive) tromper, rouler; (understand) comprendre, saisir; (include) couvrir, inclure; (lodger) prendre; (orphan, stray dog) recueillir; (dress, waistband) reprendre.
▶**take off** vi (AVIAT) décoller ♦ vt (remove) enlever; (imitate) imiter, pasticher.
▶**take on** vt (work) accepter, se charger de; (employee) prendre, embaucher; (opponent) accepter de se battre contre.
▶**take out** vt sortir; (remove) enlever; (licence) prendre, se procurer; **to ~ sth out of** enlever qch de; prendre qch dans; **don't ~ it out on me!** ne t'en prends pas à moi!
▶**take over** vt (business) reprendre ♦ vi: **to ~ over from sb** prendre la relève de qn.
▶**take to** vt fus (person) se prendre d'amitié pour; (activity) prendre goût à; **to ~ to doing sth** prendre l'habitude de faire qch.
▶**take up** vt (one's story, a dress) reprendre; (occupy: time, space) prendre, occuper; (engage in: hobby etc) se mettre à; (accept: offer, challenge) accepter; (absorb: liquids) absorber ♦ vi: **to ~ up with sb** se lier d'amitié avec qn.
takeaway ['teɪkəweɪ] (BRIT) adj (food) à emporter ♦ n (shop, restaurant) ≈ traiteur m (qui vend des plats à emporter).
take-home pay ['teɪkhəum-] n salaire net.
taken ['teɪkən] pp of **take**.
takeoff ['teɪkɔf] n (AVIAT) décollage m.
takeout ['teɪkaut] adj (US) = **takeaway**.
takeover ['teɪkəuvə*] n (COMM) rachat m.
takeover bid n offre publique d'achat, OPA f.
takings ['teɪkɪŋz] npl (COMM) recette f.

talc [tælk] n (also: ~**um powder**) talc m.
tale [teɪl] n (story) conte m, histoire f; (account) récit m; (pej) histoire f; **to tell ~s** (fig) rapporter.
talent ['tælnt] n talent m, don m.
talented ['tæləntɪd] adj doué(e), plein(e) de talent.
talent scout n découvreur m de vedettes (or joueurs etc).
talisman ['tælɪzmən] n talisman m.
talk [tɔːk] n propos mpl; (gossip) racontars mpl (pej); (conversation) discussion f; (interview) entretien m; (a speech) causerie f, exposé m ♦ vi (chatter) bavarder; ~**s** npl (POL etc) entretiens mpl; conférence f; **to give a ~** faire un exposé; **to ~ about** parler de; (converse) s'entretenir or parler de; ~**ing of films, have you seen ...?** à propos de films, avez-vous vu ...?; **to ~ sb out of/into doing** persuader qn de ne pas faire/de faire; **to ~ shop** parler métier or affaires.
▶**talk over** vt discuter (de).
talkative ['tɔːkətɪv] adj bavard(e).
talker ['tɔːkə*] n causeur/euse; (pej) bavard/e.
talking point ['tɔːkɪŋ-] n sujet m de conversation.
talking-to ['tɔːkɪŋtu] n: **to give sb a good ~** passer un savon à qn.
talk show n (TV, RADIO) causerie (télévisée or radiodiffusée).
tall [tɔːl] adj (person) grand(e); (building, tree) haut(e); **to be 6 feet ~** ≈ mesurer 1 mètre 80; **how ~ are you?** combien mesurez-vous?
tallboy ['tɔːlbɔɪ] n (BRIT) grande commode.
tallness ['tɔːlnɪs] n grande taille; hauteur f.
tall story n histoire f invraisemblable.
tally ['tælɪ] n compte m ♦ vi: **to ~ (with)** correspondre (à); **to keep a ~ of sth** tenir le compte de qch.
talon ['tælən] n griffe f; (of eagle) serre f.
tambourine [tæmbə'riːn] n tambourin m.
tame [teɪm] adj apprivoisé(e); (fig: story, style) insipide.
Tamil ['tæmɪl] adj tamoul(e) or tamil(e) ♦ n Tamoul/e or Tamil/e; (LING) tamoul m or tamil m.
tamper ['tæmpə*] vi: **to ~ with** toucher à (en cachette ou sans permission).
tampon ['tæmpən] n tampon m hygiénique or périodique.
tan [tæn] n (also: **sun~**) bronzage m ♦ vt, vi bronzer, brunir ♦ adj (colour) brun roux inv; **to get a ~** bronzer.
tandem ['tændəm] n tandem m.
tandoori [tæn'duərɪ] adj tandouri.
tang [tæŋ] n odeur (or saveur) piquante.
tangent ['tændʒənt] n (MATH) tangente f; **to go off at a ~** (fig) changer complètement de direction.
tangerine [tændʒə'riːn] n mandarine f.
tangible ['tændʒəbl] adj tangible; ~ **assets** biens réels.

Tangier [tæn'dʒɪə*] *n* Tanger.
tangle ['tæŋgl] *n* enchevêtrement *m* ♦ *vt* enchevêtrer; **to get in(to) a ~** s'emmêler.
tango ['tæŋgəu] *n* tango *m*.
tank [tæŋk] *n* réservoir *m*; (*for processing*) cuve *f*; (*for fish*) aquarium *m*; (*MIL*) char *m* d'assaut, tank *m*.
tankard ['tæŋkəd] *n* chope *f*.
tanker ['tæŋkə*] *n* (*ship*) pétrolier *m*, tanker *m*; (*truck*) camion-citerne *m*; (*RAIL*) wagon-citerne *m*.
tanned [tænd] *adj* bronzé(e).
tannin ['tænɪn] *n* tanin *m*.
tanning ['tænɪŋ] *n* (*of leather*) tannage *m*.
tannoy ['tænɔɪ] *n* ® (*BRIT*) haut-parleur *m*; **over the ~** par haut-parleur.
tantalizing ['tæntəlaɪzɪŋ] *adj* (*smell*) extrêmement appétissant(e); (*offer*) terriblement tentant(e).
tantamount ['tæntəmaunt] *adj*: **~ to** qui équivaut à.
tantrum ['tæntrəm] *n* accès *m* de colère; **to throw a ~** piquer une colère.
Tanzania [tænzə'nɪə] *n* Tanzanie *f*.
Tanzanian [tænzə'nɪən] *adj* tanzanien(ne) ♦ *n* Tanzanien/ne.
tap [tæp] *n* (*on sink etc*) robinet *m*; (*gentle blow*) petite tape ♦ *vt* frapper *or* taper légèrement; (*resources*) exploiter, utiliser; (*telephone*) mettre sur écoute; **on ~** (*beer*) en tonneau; (*fig: resources*) disponible.
tap-dancing ['tæpdɑːnsɪŋ] *n* claquettes *fpl*.
tape [teɪp] *n* ruban *m*; (*also:* **magnetic ~**) bande *f* (magnétique) ♦ *vt* (*record*) enregistrer (au magnétophone *or* sur bande); **on ~** (*song etc*) enregistré(e).
tape deck *n* platine *f* d'enregistrement.
tape measure *n* mètre *m* à ruban.
taper ['teɪpə*] *n* cierge *m* ♦ *vi* s'effiler.
tape-record ['teɪprɪkɔːd] *vt* enregistrer (au magnétophone *or* sur bande).
tape recorder *n* magnétophone *m*.
tape recording *n* enregistrement *m* (au magnétophone).
tapered ['teɪpəd], **tapering** ['teɪpərɪŋ] *adj* fuselé(e), effilé(e).
tapestry ['tæpɪstrɪ] *n* tapisserie *f*.
tape-worm ['teɪpwəːm] *n* ver *m* solitaire, ténia *m*.
tapioca [tæpɪ'əukə] *n* tapioca *m*.
tappet ['tæpɪt] *n* (*AUT*) poussoir *m* (de soupape).
tar [tɑː] *n* goudron *m*; **low-/middle-~** cigarettes *fpl* à faible/moyenne teneur en goudron.
tarantula [tə'ræntjulə] *n* tarentule *f*.
tardy ['tɑːdɪ] *adj* tardif(ive).
target ['tɑːgɪt] *n* cible *f*; (*fig: objective*) objectif *m*; **to be on ~** (*project*) progresser comme prévu.
target practice *n* exercices *mpl* de tir (à la cible).

tariff ['tærɪf] *n* (*COMM*) tarif *m*; (*taxes*) tarif douanier.
tariff barrier *n* barrière douanière.
tarmac ['tɑːmæk] *n* (*BRIT: on road*) macadam *m*; (*AVIAT*) aire *f* d'envol ♦ *vt* (*BRIT*) goudronner.
tarnish ['tɑːnɪʃ] *vt* ternir.
tarot ['tærəu] *n* tarot *m*.
tarpaulin [tɑː'pɔːlɪn] *n* bâche goudronnée.
tarragon ['tærəgən] *n* estragon *m*.
tart [tɑːt] *n* (*CULIN*) tarte *f*; (*BRIT col: pej: woman*) poule *f* ♦ *adj* (*flavour*) âpre, aigrelet(te).
▶**tart up** *vt* (*col*): **to ~ o.s. up** se faire beau(belle); (*: pej*) s'attifer.
tartan ['tɑːtn] *n* tartan *m* ♦ *adj* écossais(e).
tartar ['tɑːtə*] *n* (*on teeth*) tartre *m*.
tartar sauce *n* sauce *f* tartare.
task [tɑːsk] *n* tâche *f*; **to take to ~** prendre à partie.
task force *n* (*MIL, POLICE*) détachement spécial.
taskmaster ['tɑːskmɑːstə*] *n*: **he's a hard ~** il est très exigeant dans le travail.
Tasmania [tæz'meɪnɪə] *n* Tasmanie *f*.
tassel ['tæsl] *n* gland *m*; pompon *m*.
taste [teɪst] *n* goût *m*; (*fig: glimpse, idea*) idée *f*, aperçu *m* ♦ *vt* goûter ♦ *vi*: **to ~ of** (*fish etc*) avoir le *or* un goût de; **it ~s like fish** ça a un *or* le goût de poisson, on dirait du poisson; **what does it ~ like?** quel goût ça a?; **you can ~ the garlic (in it)** on sent bien l'ail; **can I have a ~ of this wine?** puis-je goûter un peu de ce vin?; **to have a ~ of sth** goûter (à) qch; **to have a ~ for sth** aimer qch, avoir un penchant pour qch; **to be in good/bad** *or* **poor ~** être de bon/mauvais goût.
taste bud *n* papille *f*.
tasteful ['teɪstful] *adj* de bon goût.
tastefully ['teɪstfəlɪ] *adv* avec goût.
tasteless ['teɪstlɪs] *adj* (*food*) qui n'a aucun goût; (*remark*) de mauvais goût.
tasty ['teɪstɪ] *adj* savoureux(euse), délicieux(euse).
tattered ['tætəd] *adj see* **tatters**.
tatters ['tætəz] *npl*: **in ~** (*also:* **tattered**) en lambeaux.
tattoo [tə'tuː] *n* tatouage *m*; (*spectacle*) parade *f* militaire ♦ *vt* tatouer.
tatty ['tætɪ] *adj* (*BRIT col*) défraîchi(e), en piteux état.
taught [tɔːt] *pt, pp of* **teach**.
taunt [tɔːnt] *n* raillerie *f* ♦ *vt* railler.
Taurus ['tɔːrəs] *n* le Taureau; **to be ~** être du Taureau.
taut [tɔːt] *adj* tendu(e).
tavern ['tævən] *n* taverne *f*.
tawdry ['tɔːdrɪ] *adj* (d'un mauvais goût) criard.
tawny ['tɔːnɪ] *adj* fauve (*couleur*).
tax [tæks] *n* (*on goods etc*) taxe *f*; (*on income*) impôts *mpl*, contributions *fpl* ♦ *vt* taxer; imposer; (*fig: strain: patience etc*) mettre à

l'épreuve; **before/after** ~ avant/après l'impôt; **free of** ~ exonéré(e) d'impôt.
taxable ['tæksəbl] *adj (income)* imposable.
tax allowance *n* part *f* du revenu non imposable, abattement *m* à la base.
taxation [tæk'seɪʃən] *n* taxation *f*; impôts *mpl*, contributions *fpl*; **system of** ~ système fiscal.
tax avoidance *n* évasion fiscale.
tax collector *n* percepteur *m*.
tax disc *n (BRIT AUT)* vignette *f* (automobile).
tax evasion *n* fraude fiscale.
tax exemption *n* exonération fiscale, exemption *f* d'impôts.
tax exile *n personne qui s'expatrie pour raisons fiscales.*
tax-free ['tæksfriː] *adj* exempt(e) d'impôts.
tax haven *n* paradis fiscal.
taxi ['tæksɪ] *n* taxi *m* ♦ *vi (AVIAT)* rouler (lentement) au sol.
taxidermist ['tæksɪdəːmɪst] *n* empailleur/euse *(d'animaux).*
taxi driver *n* chauffeur *m* de taxi.
tax inspector *n (BRIT)* percepteur *m*.
taxi rank *(BRIT)*, **taxi stand** *n* station *f* de taxis.
tax payer [-peɪə*] *n* contribuable *m/f*.
tax rebate *n* ristourne *f* d'impôt.
tax relief *n* dégrèvement *or* allègement fiscal, réduction *f* d'impôt.
tax return *n* déclaration *f* d'impôts *or* de revenus.
tax year *n* année fiscale.
TB *n abbr* = **tuberculosis.**
TD *n abbr (US)* = **Treasury Department**; *(: FOOTBALL)* = **touchdown.**
tea [tiː] *n* thé *m*; *(BRIT: snack: for children)* goûter *m*; **high** ~ *(BRIT) collation combinant goûter et dîner.*
tea bag *n* sachet *m* de thé.
tea break *n (BRIT)* pause-thé *f*.
teacake ['tiːkeɪk] *n (BRIT)* ≈ petit pain aux raisins.
teach, *pt, pp* **taught** [tiːtʃ, tɔːt] *vt:* **to** ~ **sb sth**, ~ **sth to sb** apprendre qch à qn; *(in school etc)* enseigner qch à qn ♦ *vi* enseigner; **it taught him a lesson** *(fig)* ça lui a servi de leçon.
teacher ['tiːtʃə*] *n (in secondary school)* professeur *m*; *(in primary school)* instituteur/trice; **French** ~ professeur *m* de français.
teacher training college *n (for primary schools)* ≈ école normale d'instituteurs; *(for secondary schools)* collège *m* de formation pédagogique *(pour l'enseignement secondaire).*
teaching ['tiːtʃɪŋ] *n* enseignement *m*.
teaching aids *npl* supports *mpl* pédagogiques.
teaching hospital *n (BRIT)* C.H.U. *m*, centre *m* hospitalo-universitaire.
teaching staff *n (BRIT)* enseignants *mpl*.
tea cosy *n* couvre-théière *m*.

teacup ['tiːkʌp] *n* tasse *f* à thé.
teak [tiːk] *n* teck *m* ♦ *adj* en *or* de teck.
tea leaves *npl* feuilles *fpl* de thé.
team [tiːm] *n* équipe *f*; *(of animals)* attelage *m*.
▶**team up** *vi:* **to** ~ **up (with)** faire équipe (avec).
team games *npl* jeux *mpl* d'équipe.
teamwork ['tiːmwəːk] *n* travail *m* d'équipe.
tea party *n* thé *m (réception)*.
teapot ['tiːpɔt] *n* théière *f*.
tear¹ *n* [tɛə*] déchirure *f* ♦ *vb (pt* **tore**, *pp* **torn** [tɔː*, tɔːn]) *vt* déchirer ♦ *vi* se déchirer; **to** ~ **to pieces** *or* **to bits** *or* **to shreds** mettre en pièces; *(fig)* démolir.
▶**tear along** *vi (rush)* aller à toute vitesse.
▶**tear apart** *vt (also fig)* déchirer.
▶**tear away** *vt:* **to** ~ **o.s. away (from sth)** *(fig)* s'arracher (de qch).
▶**tear out** *vt (sheet of paper, cheque)* arracher.
▶**tear up** *vt (sheet of paper etc)* déchirer, mettre en morceaux *or* pièces.
tear² ['tɪə*] *n* larme *f*; **in** ~**s** en larmes; **to burst into** ~**s** fondre en larmes.
tearaway ['tɛərəweɪ] *n (col)* casse-cou *m inv*.
teardrop ['tɪədrɔp] *n* larme *f*.
tearful ['tɪəful] *adj* larmoyant(e).
tear gas ['tɪə-] *n* gaz *m* lacrymogène.
tearoom ['tiːruːm] *n* salon *m* de thé.
tease [tiːz] *n* taquin/e ♦ *vt* taquiner; *(unkindly)* tourmenter.
tea set *n* service *m* à thé.
teashop ['tiːʃɔp] *n (BRIT)* pâtisserie-salon de thé *f*.
Teasmade ['tiːzmeɪd] *n* ® machine *f* à faire le thé.
teaspoon ['tiːspuːn] *n* petite cuiller; *(also:* ~**ful:** *as measurement)* ≈ cuillerée *f* à café.
tea strainer *n* passoire *f* (à thé).
teat [tiːt] *n* tétine *f*.
teatime ['tiːtaɪm] *n* l'heure *f* du thé.
tea towel *n (BRIT)* torchon *m* (à vaisselle).
tea urn *n* fontaine *f* à thé.
tech [tɛk] *n abbr (col)* = **technology, technical college.**
technical ['tɛknɪkl] *adj* technique.
technical college *n* C.E.T. *m*, collège *m* d'enseignement technique.
technicality [tɛknɪ'kælɪtɪ] *n* technicité *f*; *(detail)* détail *m* technique; **on a legal** ~ à cause de *(or* grâce à) l'application à la lettre d'une subtilité juridique; pour vice de forme.
technically ['tɛknɪklɪ] *adv* techniquement; *(strictly speaking)* en théorie, en principe.
technician [tɛk'nɪʃən] *n* technicien/ne.
technique [tɛk'niːk] *n* technique *f*.
techno ['tɛknəu] *n (MUS)* techno *f*.
technocrat ['tɛknəkræt] *n* technocrate *m/f*.
technological [tɛknə'lɔdʒɪkl] *adj* technologique.
technologist [tɛk'nɔlədʒɪst] *n* technologue *m/f*.
technology [tɛk'nɔlədʒɪ] *n* technologie *f*.
teddy (bear) ['tɛdɪ-] *n* ours *m* (en peluche).

tedious ['ti:dɪəs] *adj* fastidieux(euse).

tedium ['ti:dɪəm] *n* ennui *m*.

tee [ti:] *n* (*GOLF*) tee *m*.

teem [ti:m] *vi*: **to ~ (with)** grouiller (de); **it is ~ing (with rain)** il pleut à torrents.

teenage ['ti:neɪdʒ] *adj* (*fashions etc*) pour jeunes, pour adolescents.

teenager ['ti:neɪdʒə*] *n* jeune *m/f*, adolescent/e.

teens [ti:nz] *npl*: **to be in one's ~** être adolescent(e).

tee-shirt ['ti:ʃə:t] *n* = T-shirt.

teeter ['ti:tə*] *vi* chanceler, vaciller.

teeth [ti:θ] *npl of* tooth.

teethe [ti:ð] *vi* percer ses dents.

teething ring ['ti:ðɪŋ-] *n* anneau *m* (*pour bébé qui perce ses dents*).

teething troubles ['ti:ðɪŋ-] *npl* (*fig*) difficultés initiales.

teetotal ['ti:'təutl] *adj* (*person*) qui ne boit jamais d'alcool.

teetotaller, (*US*) **teetotaler** ['ti:'təutlə*] *n* personne *f* qui ne boit jamais d'alcool.

TEFL ['tefl] *n abbr* = *Teaching of English as a Foreign Language*.

Teflon ['teflɔn] *n* ® Téflon *m* ®.

Teheran [tɛə'rɑ:n] *n* Téhéran.

tel. *abbr* (= *telephone*) tél.

Tel Aviv ['tɛlə'vi:v] *n* Tel Aviv.

telecast ['tɛlɪkɑ:st] *vt* télédiffuser, téléviser.

telecommunications ['tɛlɪkəmju:nɪ'keɪʃənz] *n* télécommunications *fpl*.

teleconferencing ['tɛlɪkɒnfərənsɪŋ] *n* téléconférence *f*.

telegram ['tɛlɪgræm] *n* télégramme *m*.

telegraph ['tɛlɪgrɑ:f] *n* télégraphe *m*.

telegraphic [tɛlɪ'græfɪk] *adj* télégraphique.

telegraph pole *n* poteau *m* télégraphique.

telegraph wire *n* fil *m* télégraphique.

telepathic [tɛlɪ'pæθɪk] *adj* télépathique.

telepathy [tə'lɛpəθɪ] *n* télépathie *f*.

telephone ['tɛlɪfəun] *n* téléphone *m* ♦ *vt* (*person*) téléphoner à; (*message*) téléphoner; **to have a ~,** (*BRIT*) **to be on the ~** (*subscriber*) être abonné(e) au téléphone; **to be on the ~** (*be speaking*) être au téléphone.

telephone booth, (*BRIT*) **telephone box** *n* cabine *f* téléphonique.

telephone call *n* appel *m* téléphonique, communication *f* téléphonique.

telephone directory *n* annuaire *m* (du téléphone).

telephone number *n* numéro *m* de téléphone.

telephone operator *n* téléphoniste *m/f*, standardiste *m/f*.

telephone tapping [-tæpɪŋ] *n* mise *f* sur écoute.

telephonist [tə'lɛfənɪst] *n* (*BRIT*) téléphoniste *m/f*.

telephoto ['tɛlɪfəutəu] *adj*: **~ lens** téléobjectif *m*.

teleprinter ['tɛlɪprɪntə*] *n* téléscripteur *m*.

Teleprompter ['tɛlɪprɒmptə*] *n* ® (*US*) prompteur *m*.

telesales ['tɛlɪseɪlz] *npl* télévente *f*.

telescope ['tɛlɪskəup] *n* télescope *m* ♦ *vi* se télescoper ♦ *vt* télescoper.

telescopic [tɛlɪ'skɒpɪk] *adj* télescopique; (*umbrella*) à manche télescopique.

Teletext ['tɛlɪtɛkst] *n* ® télétexte *m*.

telethon ['tɛlɪθɒn] *n* téléthon *m*.

televise ['tɛlɪvaɪz] *vt* téléviser.

television ['tɛlɪvɪʒən] *n* télévision *f*.

television licence *n* (*BRIT*) redevance *f* (de l'audio-visuel).

television programme *n* émission *f* de télévision.

television set *n* poste *m* de télévision, téléviseur *m*.

teleworking ['tɛlɪwɜ:kɪŋ] *n* télétravail *m*.

telex ['tɛlɛks] *n* télex *m* ♦ *vt* (*message*) envoyer par télex; (*person*) envoyer un télex à ♦ *vi* envoyer un télex.

tell, *pt, pp* **told** [tɛl, təuld] *vt* dire; (*relate: story*) raconter; (*distinguish*): **to ~ sth from** distinguer qch de ♦ *vi* (*talk*): **to ~ (of)** parler (de); (*have effect*) se faire sentir, se voir; **to ~ sb to do** dire à qn de faire; **to ~ sb about sth** (*place, object etc*) parler de qch à qn; (*what happened etc*) raconter qch à qn; **to ~ the time** (*know how to*) savoir lire l'heure; **can you ~ me the time?** pourriez-vous me dire l'heure?; **(I) ~ you what ...** écoute, ...; **I can't ~ them apart** je n'arrive pas à les distinguer.

▶**tell off** *vt* réprimander, gronder.

▶**tell on** *vt fus* (*inform against*) dénoncer, rapporter contre.

teller ['tɛlə*] *n* (*in bank*) caissier/ière.

telling ['tɛlɪŋ] *adj* (*remark, detail*) révélateur(trice).

telltale ['tɛlteɪl] *n* rapporteur/euse ♦ *adj* (*sign*) éloquent(e), révélateur(trice).

telly ['tɛlɪ] *n abbr* (*BRIT col*: = television) télé *f*.

temerity [tə'mɛrɪtɪ] *n* témérité *f*.

temp [tɛmp] *abbr* (*BRIT col*: = temporary) *n* intérimaire *m/f* ♦ *vi* travailler comme intérimaire.

temper ['tɛmpə*] *n* (*nature*) caractère *m*; (*mood*) humeur *f*; (*fit of anger*) colère *f* ♦ *vt* (*moderate*) tempérer, adoucir; **to be in a ~** être en colère; **to lose one's ~** se mettre en colère; **to keep one's ~** rester calme.

temperament ['tɛmprəmənt] *n* (*nature*) tempérament *m*.

temperamental [tɛmprə'mɛntl] *adj* capricieux(euse).

temperance ['tɛmpərns] *n* modération *f*; (*in drinking*) tempérance *f*.

temperate ['tɛmprət] *adj* modéré(e); (*climate*) tempéré(e).

temperature ['tɛmprətʃə*] *n* température *f*; **to have** *or* **run a ~** avoir de la fièvre.

temperature chart *n* (*MED*) feuille *f* de température.

tempered ['tɛmpəd] *adj* (*steel*) trempé(e).

tempest ['tɛmpɪst] *n* tempête *f*.

tempestuous [tɛm'pɛstjuəs] *adj* (*fig*) orageux(euse); (*: person*) passionné(e).

tempi ['tɛmpiː] *npl of* **tempo**.

template ['tɛmplɪt] *n* patron *m*.

temple ['tɛmpl] *n* (*building*) temple *m*; (*ANAT*) tempe *f*.

templet ['tɛmplɪt] *n* = **template**.

tempo, ~s *or* **tempi** ['tɛmpəu, 'tɛmpiː] *n* tempo *m*; (*fig: of life etc*) rythme *m*.

temporal ['tɛmpərl] *adj* temporel(le).

temporarily ['tɛmpərərɪlɪ] *adv* temporairement; provisoirement.

temporary ['tɛmpərərɪ] *adj* temporaire, provisoire; (*job, worker*) temporaire; **~ secretary** (secrétaire *f*) intérimaire *f*; **a ~ teacher** un professeur remplaçant *or* suppléant.

temporize ['tɛmpəraɪz] *vi* atermoyer; transiger.

tempt [tɛmpt] *vt* tenter; **to ~ sb into doing** induire qn à faire; **to be ~ed to do sth** être tenté(e) de faire qch.

temptation [tɛmp'teɪʃən] *n* tentation *f*.

tempting ['tɛmptɪŋ] *adj* tentant(e).

ten [tɛn] *num* dix ♦ *n*: **~s of thousands** des dizaines *fpl* de milliers.

tenable ['tɛnəbl] *adj* défendable.

tenacious [tə'neɪʃəs] *adj* tenace.

tenacity [tə'næsɪtɪ] *n* ténacité *f*.

tenancy ['tɛnənsɪ] *n* location *f*; état *m* de locataire.

tenant ['tɛnənt] *n* locataire *m/f*.

tend [tɛnd] *vt* s'occuper de; (*sick etc*) soigner ♦ *vi*: **to ~ to do** avoir tendance à faire; (*colour*): **to ~ to** tirer sur.

tendency ['tɛndənsɪ] *n* tendance *f*.

tender ['tɛndə*] *adj* tendre; (*delicate*) délicat(e); (*sore*) sensible; (*affectionate*) tendre, doux(douce) ♦ *n* (*COMM: offer*) soumission *f*; (*money*): **legal ~** cours légal ♦ *vt* offrir; **to ~ one's resignation** donner *or* remettre sa démission; **to put in a ~ (for)** faire une soumission (pour); **to put work out to ~** (*BRIT*) mettre un contrat en adjudication.

tenderize ['tɛndəraɪz] *vt* (*CULIN*) attendrir.

tenderly ['tɛndəlɪ] *adv* tendrement.

tenderness ['tɛndənɪs] *n* tendresse *f*; (*of meat*) tendreté *f*.

tendon ['tɛndən] *n* tendon *m*.

tenement ['tɛnəmənt] *n* immeuble *m* (de rapport).

Tenerife [tɛnə'riːf] *n* Ténérife *f*.

tenet ['tɛnət] *n* principe *m*.

Tenn. *abbr* (*US*) = *Tennessee*.

tenner ['tɛnə*] *n* (*BRIT col*) billet *m* de dix livres.

tennis ['tɛnɪs] *n* tennis *m* ♦ *cpd* (*club, match, racket, player*) de tennis.

tennis ball *n* balle *f* de tennis.

tennis court *n* (court *m* de) tennis *m*.

tennis elbow *n* (*MED*) synovite *f* du coude.

tennis shoes *npl* (chaussures *fpl* de) tennis *mpl*.

tenor ['tɛnə*] *n* (*MUS*) ténor *m*; (*of speech etc*) sens général.

tenpin bowling ['tɛnpɪn-] *n* (*BRIT*) bowling *m* (*à 10 quilles*).

tense [tɛns] *adj* tendu(e); (*person*) tendu, crispé(e) ♦ *n* (*LING*) temps *m* ♦ *vt* (*tighten: muscles*) tendre.

tenseness ['tɛnsnɪs] *n* tension *f*.

tension ['tɛnʃən] *n* tension *f*.

tent [tɛnt] *n* tente *f*.

tentacle ['tɛntəkl] *n* tentacule *m*.

tentative ['tɛntətɪv] *adj* timide, hésitant(e); (*conclusion*) provisoire.

tenterhooks ['tɛntəhuks] *npl*: **on ~** sur des charbons ardents.

tenth [tɛnθ] *num* dixième.

tent peg *n* piquet *m* de tente.

tent pole *n* montant *m* de tente.

tenuous ['tɛnjuəs] *adj* ténu(e).

tenure ['tɛnjuə*] *n* (*of property*) bail *m*; (*of job*) période *f* de jouissance; statut *m* de titulaire.

tepid ['tɛpɪd] *adj* tiède.

Ter. *abbr* = **terrace**.

term [təːm] *n* (*limit*) terme *m*; (*word*) terme, mot *m*; (*SCOL*) trimestre *m*; (*LAW*) session *f* ♦ *vt* appeler; **~s** *npl* (*conditions*) conditions *fpl*; (*COMM*) tarif *m*; **~ of imprisonment** peine *f* de prison; **his ~ of office** la période où il était en fonction; **in the short/long ~** à court/long terme; **"easy ~s"** (*COMM*) "facilités de paiement"; **to come to ~s with** (*problem*) faire face à; **to be on good ~s with** bien s'entendre avec, être en bons termes avec.

terminal ['təːmɪnl] *adj* terminal(e); (*disease*) dans sa phase terminale ♦ *n* (*ELEC*) borne *f*; (*for oil, ore etc, also* COMPUT) terminal *m*; (*also*: **air ~**) aérogare *f*; (*BRIT: also*: **coach ~**) gare routière.

terminate ['təːmɪneɪt] *vt* mettre fin à ♦ *vi*: **to ~ in** finir en or par.

termination [təːmɪ'neɪʃən] *n* fin *f*; cessation *f*; (*of contract*) résiliation *f*; **~ of pregnancy** (*MED*) interruption *f* de grossesse.

termini ['təːmɪnaɪ] *npl of* **terminus**.

terminology [təːmɪ'nɔlədʒɪ] *n* terminologie *f*.

terminus, *pl* termini ['təːmɪnəs, 'təːmɪnaɪ] *n* terminus *m inv*.

termite ['təːmaɪt] *n* termite *m*.

term paper *n* (*US UNIVERSITY*) dissertation trimestrielle.

Terr. *abbr* = **terrace**.

terrace ['tɛrəs] *n* terrasse *f*; (*BRIT: row of houses*) rangée *f* de maisons (*attenantes les unes aux autres*); **the ~s** (*BRIT SPORT*) les gradins *mpl*.

terraced ['tɛrəst] *adj* (*garden*) en terrasses; (*in a row: house, cottage etc*) attenant(e) aux maisons voisines.

terracotta ['tɛrə'kɒtə] n terre cuite.

terrain [tɛ'reɪn] n terrain m (sol).

terrible ['tɛrɪbl] adj terrible, atroce; (weather, work) affreux(euse), épouvantable.

terribly ['tɛrɪblɪ] adv terriblement; (very badly) affreusement mal.

terrier ['tɛrɪə*] n terrier m (chien).

terrific [tə'rɪfɪk] adj fantastique, incroyable, terrible; (wonderful) formidable, sensationnel(le).

terrify ['tɛrɪfaɪ] vt terrifier.

territorial [tɛrɪ'tɔːrɪəl] adj territorial(e).

territorial waters npl eaux territoriales.

territory ['tɛrɪtərɪ] n territoire m.

terror ['tɛrə*] n terreur f.

terrorism ['tɛrərɪzəm] n terrorisme m.

terrorist ['tɛrərɪst] n terroriste m/f.

terrorize ['tɛrəraɪz] vt terroriser.

terse [tɜːs] adj (style) concis(e); (reply) laconique.

tertiary ['tɜːʃərɪ] adj tertiaire; ~ **education** (BRIT) enseignement m postscolaire.

Terylene ['tɛrɪliːn] n ® (BRIT) tergal m ®.

TESL ['tɛsl] n abbr = Teaching of English as a Second Language.

TESSA ['tɛsə] n abbr (BRIT: = Tax Exempt Special Savings Account) compte de dépôt aux intérêts exempts d'impôts si le capital reste bloqué.

test [tɛst] n (trial, check) essai m; (: of goods in factory) contrôle m; (of courage etc) épreuve f; (MED) examens mpl; (CHEM) analyses fpl; (exam: of intelligence etc) test m (d'aptitude); (: in school) interrogation f de contrôle; (also: driving ~) (examen du) permis m de conduire ♦ vt essayer; contrôler; mettre à l'épreuve; examiner; analyser; tester; faire subir une interrogation (de contrôle) à; **to put sth to the ~** mettre qch à l'épreuve.

testament ['tɛstəmənt] n testament m; **the Old/New T~** l'Ancien/le Nouveau Testament.

test ban n (also: nuclear ~) interdiction f des essais nucléaires.

test case n (LAW, fig) affaire-test f.

testes ['tɛstiːz] npl testicules mpl.

test flight n vol m d'essai.

testicle ['tɛstɪkl] n testicule m.

testify ['tɛstɪfaɪ] vi (LAW) témoigner, déposer; **to ~ to sth** (LAW) attester qch; (gen) témoigner de qch.

testimonial [tɛstɪ'məʊnɪəl] n (BRIT: reference) recommandation f; (gift) témoignage m d'estime.

testimony ['tɛstɪmənɪ] n (LAW) témoignage m, déposition f.

testing ['tɛstɪŋ] adj (situation, period) difficile.

test match n (CRICKET, RUGBY) match international.

testosterone [tɛs'tɒstərəʊn] n testostérone f.

test paper n (SCOL) interrogation écrite.

test pilot n pilote m d'essai.

test tube n éprouvette f.

test-tube baby ['tɛsttjuːb-] n bébé-éprouvette m.

testy ['tɛstɪ] adj irritable.

tetanus ['tɛtənəs] n tétanos m.

tetchy ['tɛtʃɪ] adj hargneux(euse).

tether ['tɛðə*] vt attacher ♦ n: **at the end of one's ~** à bout (de patience).

Tex. abbr (US) = Texas.

text [tɛkst] n texte m.

textbook ['tɛkstbuk] n manuel m.

textile ['tɛkstaɪl] n textile m.

textual ['tɛkstjuəl] adj textuel(le).

texture ['tɛkstʃə*] n texture f; (of skin, paper etc) grain m.

TGIF abbr (col) = thank God it's Friday.

TGWU n abbr (BRIT: = Transport and General Workers' Union) syndicat de transporteurs.

Thai [taɪ] adj thaïlandais(e) ♦ n Thaïlandais/e; (LING) thaï m.

Thailand ['taɪlænd] n Thaïlande f.

thalidomide [θə'lɪdəmaɪd] n ® thalidomide f ®.

Thames [tɛmz] n: **the ~** la Tamise.

than [ðæn, ðən] conj que; (with numerals): **more ~ 10/once** plus de 10/d'une fois; **I have more/less ~ you** j'en ai plus/moins que toi; **she has more apples ~ pears** elle a plus de pommes que de poires; **it is better to phone ~ to write** il vaut mieux téléphoner (plutôt) qu'écrire; **no sooner did he leave ~ the phone rang** il venait de partir quand le téléphone a sonné.

thank [θæŋk] vt remercier, dire merci à; ~ **you (very much)** merci (beaucoup); ~ **heavens, ~ God** Dieu merci.

thankful ['θæŋkful] adj: ~ **(for)** reconnaissant(e) (de); ~ **for/that** (relieved) soulagé(e) de/que.

thankfully ['θæŋkfəlɪ] adv avec reconnaissance; avec soulagement; ~ **there were few victims** il y eut fort heureusement peu de victimes.

thankless ['θæŋklɪs] adj ingrat(e).

thanks [θæŋks] npl remerciements mpl ♦ excl merci!; ~ **to** prep grâce à.

Thanksgiving (Day) ['θæŋksgɪvɪŋ-] n jour m d'action de grâce.

Thanksgiving Day est un jour de congé aux États-Unis, le quatrième jeudi du mois de novembre, commémorant la bonne récolte que les Pélerins venus de Grande-Bretagne ont eue en 1621; traditionnellement, c'était un jour où l'on remerciait Dieu et où l'on organisait un grand festin.
Une fête semblable, mais qui n'a aucun rapport avec les Pères Pélerins, a lieu au Canada le deuxième lundi d'octobre.

===================== KEYWORD

that [ðæt] adj (demonstrative: pl **those**) ce, cet +vowel or h mute, f cette; ~ **man/woman/book** cet homme/cette femme/ce livre; (not this) cet homme-là/cette femme-là/ce livre-là; ~ **one** celui-là(celle-là)

♦ pron **1** (demonstrative: pl **those**) ce; (not this one) cela, ça; (the one) celui(celle); **who's ~?** qui est-ce?; **what's ~?** qu'est-ce que c'est?; **is ~ you?** c'est toi?; **I prefer this to ~** je préfère ceci à cela or ça; **~'s what he said** c'est or voilà ce qu'il a dit; **all ~** tout cela, tout ça; **~ is (to say)** c'est-à-dire, à savoir; **at** or **with ~, she ...** là-dessus, elle ...; **do it like ~** fais-le comme ça

2 (relative: subject) qui; (: object) que; (: indirect) lequel(laquelle), lesquels(lesquelles) pl; **the book ~ I read** le livre que j'ai lu; **the books ~ are in the library** les livres qui sont dans la bibliothèque; **all ~ I have** tout ce que j'ai; **the box ~ I put it in** la boîte dans laquelle je l'ai mis; **the people ~ I spoke to** les gens auxquels or à qui j'ai parlé; **not ~ I know of** pas à ma connaissance

3 (relative: of time) où; **the day ~ he came** le jour où il est venu

♦ conj que; **he thought ~ I was ill** il pensait que j'étais malade

♦ adv (demonstrative): **I can't work ~ much** je ne peux pas travailler autant que cela; **I didn't know it was ~ bad** je ne savais pas que c'était si or aussi mauvais; **~ high** aussi haut; si haut; **it's about ~ high** c'est à peu près de cette hauteur.

thatched [θætʃt] adj (roof) de chaume; ~ **cottage** chaumière f.

Thatcherism ['θætʃərɪzəm] n thatchérisme m.

thaw [θɔː] n dégel m ♦ vi (ice) fondre; (food) dégeler ♦ vt (food) (faire) dégeler; **it's ~ing** (weather) il dégèle.

===================== KEYWORD

the [ðiː, ðə] def art **1** (gen) le, la f, l' +vowel or h mute, les pl; (NB: à +le(s) = au(x); de + le = du; de +les = des); ~ **boy/girl/ink** le garçon/la fille/l'encre; ~ **children** les enfants; ~ **history of ~ world** l'histoire du monde; **give it to ~ postman** donne-le au facteur; **to play ~ piano/flute** jouer du piano/de la flûte; ~ **rich and ~ poor** les riches et les pauvres

2 (in titles): **Elizabeth ~ First** Elisabeth première; **Peter ~ Great** Pierre le Grand

3 (in comparisons): **~ more he works, ~ more he earns** plus il travaille, plus il gagne de l'argent; **~ sooner ~ better** le plus tôt sera le mieux.

theatre, (US) **theater** ['θɪətə*] n théâtre m.

theatre-goer ['θɪətəgəuə*] n habitué/e du théâtre.

theatrical [θɪ'ætrɪkl] adj théâtral(e); ~ **compa-ny** troupe f de théâtre.

theft [θɛft] n vol m (larcin).

their [ðɛə*] adj leur, leurs pl.

theirs [ðɛəz] pron le(la) leur, les leurs; **it is ~** c'est à eux; **a friend of ~** un de leurs amis.

them [ðɛm, ðəm] pron (direct) les; (indirect) leur; (stressed, after prep) eux(elles); **I see ~** je les vois; **give ~ the book** donne-leur le livre; **give me a few of ~** donnez m'en quelques uns (or quelques unes).

theme [θiːm] n thème m.

theme park n parc m à thème.

theme song n chanson principale.

themselves [ðəm'sɛlvz] pl pron (reflexive) se; (emphatic) eux-mêmes(elles-mêmes); **be-tween ~** entre eux(elles).

then [ðɛn] adv (at that time) alors, à ce moment-là; (next) puis, ensuite; (and also) et puis ♦ conj (therefore) alors, dans ce cas ♦ adj: **the ~ president** le président d'alors or de l'époque; **by ~** (past) à ce moment-là; (future) d'ici là; **from ~ on** dès lors; **before ~** avant; **until ~** jusqu'à ce moment-là, jusque-là; **and ~ what?** et puis après?; **what do you want me to do ~?** (afterwards) que veux-tu que je fasse ensuite?; (in that case) bon alors, qu'est-ce que je fais?

theologian [θɪə'ləudʒən] n théologien/ne.

theological [θɪə'lɔdʒɪkl] adj théologique.

theology [θɪ'ɔlədʒɪ] n théologie f.

theorem ['θɪərəm] n théorème m.

theoretical [θɪə'rɛtɪkl] adj théorique.

theorize ['θɪəraɪz] vi élaborer une théorie; (pej) faire des théories.

theory ['θɪərɪ] n théorie f.

therapeutic(al) [θɛrə'pjuːtɪk(l)] adj thérapeu-tique.

therapist ['θɛrəpɪst] n thérapeute m/f.

therapy ['θɛrəpɪ] n thérapie f.

===================== KEYWORD

there [ðɛə*] adv **1**: ~ **is,** ~ **are** il y a; ~ **are 3 of them** (people, things) il y en a 3; ~ **has been an accident** il y a eu un accident

2 (referring to place) là, là-bas; **it's ~** c'est là(-bas); **in/on/up/down ~** là-dedans/là-dessus/là-haut/en bas; **he went ~ on Friday** il y est allé vendredi; **to go ~ and back** faire l'aller-retour; **I want that book ~** je veux ce livre-là; ~ **he is!** le voilà!

3: ~, ~ (esp to child) allons, allons!

thereabouts ['ðɛərə'bauts] adv (place) par là, près de là; (amount) environ, à peu près.

thereafter [ðɛər'ɑːftə*] adv par la suite.

thereby ['ðɛəbaɪ] adv ainsi.

therefore ['ðɛəfɔː*] adv donc, par conséquent.

there's ['ðɛəz] = **there is, there has.**

thereupon [ðɛərə'pɔn] adv (at that point) sur ce; (formal: on that subject) à ce sujet.

thermal ['θəːml] adj thermique; ~ **paper/**

printer papier *m*/imprimante *f* thermique.
thermodynamics ['θə:dəʊ'næmɪks] *n* thermodynamique *f*.
thermometer [θə'mɒmɪtə*] *n* thermomètre *m*.
thermonuclear ['θə:məʊ'nju:klɪə*] *adj* thermonucléaire.
Thermos ['θə:məs] *n* ® (*also*: ~ **flask**) thermos *m or f inv* ®.
thermostat ['θə:məʊstæt] *n* thermostat *m*.
thesaurus [θɪ'sɔ:rəs] *n* dictionnaire *m* synonymique.
these [ði:z] *pl pron* ceux-ci(celles-ci) ♦ *pl adj* ces; (*not those*): ~ **books** ces livres-ci.
thesis, *pl* **theses** ['θi:sɪs, 'θi:si:z] *n* thèse *f*.
they [ðeɪ] *pl pron* ils(elles); (*stressed*) eux(elles); ~ **say that ...** (*it is said that*) on dit que ....
they'd [ðeɪd] = **they had, they would**.
they'll [ðeɪl] = **they shall, they will**.
they're [ðɛə*] = **they are**.
they've [ðeɪv] = **they have**.
thick [θɪk] *adj* épais(se); (*crowd*) dense; (*stupid*) bête, borné(e) ♦ *n*: **in the ~ of** au beau milieu de, en plein cœur de; **it's 20 cm ~** ça a 20 cm d'épaisseur.
thicken ['θɪkn] *vi* s'épaissir ♦ *vt* (*sauce etc*) épaissir.
thicket ['θɪkɪt] *n* fourré *m*, hallier *m*.
thickly ['θɪklɪ] *adv* (*spread*) en couche épaisse; (*cut*) en tranches épaisses; ~ **populated** à forte densité de population.
thickness ['θɪknɪs] *n* épaisseur *f*.
thickset [θɪk'sɛt] *adj* trapu(e), costaud(e).
thickskinned [θɪk'skɪnd] *adj* (*fig*) peu sensible.
thief, *pl* **thieves** [θi:f, θi:vz] *n* voleur/euse.
thieving ['θi:vɪŋ] *n* vol *m* (*larcin*).
thigh [θaɪ] *n* cuisse *f*.
thighbone ['θaɪbəʊn] *n* fémur *m*.
thimble ['θɪmbl] *n* dé *m* (à coudre).
thin [θɪn] *adj* mince; (*person*) maigre; (*soup*) peu épais(se); (*hair, crowd*) clairsemé(e); (*fog*) léger(ère) ♦ *vt* (*hair*) éclaircir; (*also*: ~ **down**: *sauce, paint*) délayer ♦ *vi* (*fog*) s'éclaircir; (*also*: ~ **out**: *crowd*) se disperser; **his hair is ~ning** il se dégarnit.
thing [θɪŋ] *n* chose *f*; (*object*) objet *m*; (*contraption*) truc *m*; ~**s** *npl* (*belongings*) affaires *fpl*; **first ~ (in the morning)** à la première heure, tout de suite (le matin); **last ~ (at night)**, he ... juste avant de se coucher, il ...; **the ~ is ...** c'est que ...; **for one ~** d'abord; **the best ~ would be to** le mieux serait de; **how are ~s?** comment ça va?; **she's got a ~ about ...** elle déteste ...; **poor ~!** le (*or* la) pauvre!
think, *pt, pp* **thought** [θɪŋk, θɔ:t] *vi* penser, réfléchir ♦ *vt* penser, croire; (*imagine*) s'imaginer; **to ~ of** penser à; **what do you ~ of it?** qu'en pensez-vous?; **what did you ~ of them?** qu'avez-vous pensé d'eux?; **to ~ about sth/sb** penser à qch/qn; **I'll ~ about it** je vais y réfléchir; **to ~ of doing** avoir l'idée de faire; **I ~ so/not** je crois *or* pense que

oui/non; **to ~ well of** avoir une haute opinion de; **~ again!** attention, réfléchis bien!; **to ~ aloud** penser tout haut.
▶**think out** *vt* (*plan*) bien réfléchir à; (*solution*) trouver.
▶**think over** *vt* bien réfléchir à; **I'd like to ~ things over** (*offer, suggestion*) j'aimerais bien y réfléchir un peu.
▶**think through** *vt* étudier dans tous les détails.
▶**think up** *vt* inventer, trouver.
thinking ['θɪŋkɪŋ] *n*: **to my (way of) ~** selon moi.
think tank *n* groupe *m* de réflexion.
thinly ['θɪnlɪ] *adv* (*cut*) en tranches fines; (*spread*) en couche mince.
thinness ['θɪnnɪs] *n* minceur *f*; maigreur *f*.
third [θə:d] *num* troisième ♦ *n* troisième *m/f*; (*fraction*) tiers *m*; (*BRIT SCOL*: *degree*) ≈ licence *f* avec mention passable; **a ~ of** le tiers de.
third-degree burns ['θə:ddɪgri:-] *npl* brûlures *fpl* au troisième degré.
thirdly ['θə:dlɪ] *adv* troisièmement.
third party insurance *n* (*BRIT*) assurance *f* au tiers.
third-rate ['θə:d'reɪt] *adj* de qualité médiocre.
Third World *n*: **the ~** le Tiers-Monde.
thirst [θə:st] *n* soif *f*.
thirsty ['θə:stɪ] *adj* qui a soif, assoiffé(e); **to be ~** avoir soif.
thirteen [θə:'ti:n] *num* treize.
thirtieth ['θə:tɪɪθ] *num* trentième.
thirty ['θə:tɪ] *num* trente.

════════════════════ *KEYWORD*

this [ðɪs] *adj* (*demonstrative*: *pl* **these**) ce, cet +*vowel or h mute*, cette *f*; ~ **man/woman/book** cet homme/cette femme/ce livre; (*not that*) cet homme-ci/cette femme-ci/ce livre-ci; ~ **one** celui-ci(celle-ci); ~ **time** cette fois-ci; ~ **time last year** l'année dernière à la même époque; ~ **way** (*in this direction*) par ici; (*in this fashion*) de cette façon, ainsi
♦ *pron* (*demonstrative*: *pl* **these**) ce; (*not that one*) celui-ci(celle-ci), ceci; **who's ~?** qui est-ce?; **what's ~?** qu'est-ce que c'est?; **I prefer ~ to that** je préfère ceci à cela; **they were talking of ~ and that** ils parlaient de choses et d'autres; ~ **is what he said** voici ce qu'il a dit; ~ **is Mr Brown** (*in introductions*) je vous présente Mr Brown; (*in photo*) c'est Mr Brown; (*on telephone*) ici Mr Brown
♦ *adv* (*demonstrative*): **it was about ~ big** c'était à peu près de cette grandeur *or* grand comme ça; **I didn't know it was ~ bad** je ne savais pas que c'était si *or* aussi mauvais.

thistle ['θɪsl] *n* chardon *m*.
thong [θɒŋ] *n* lanière *f*.
thorn [θɔ:n] *n* épine *f*.

thorny ['θɔːnɪ] *adj* épineux(euse).

thorough ['θʌrə] *adj* (*search*) minutieux(euse); (*knowledge, research*) approfondi(e); (*work*) consciencieux(euse); (*cleaning*) à fond.

thoroughbred ['θʌrəbrɛd] *n* (*horse*) pur-sang *m inv*.

thoroughfare ['θʌrəfɛə*] *n* rue *f*; "no ~" (*BRIT*) "passage interdit".

thoroughgoing ['θʌrəgəʊɪŋ] *adj* (*analysis*) approfondi(e); (*reform*) profond(e).

thoroughly ['θʌrəlɪ] *adv* minutieusement; en profondeur; à fond; **he ~ agreed** il était tout à fait d'accord.

thoroughness ['θʌrənɪs] *n* soin (méticuleux).

those [ðəʊz] *pl pron* ceux-là(celles-là) ♦ *pl adj* ces; (*not these*): ~ **books** ces livres-là.

though [ðəʊ] *conj* bien que + *sub*, quoique + *sub* ♦ *adv* pourtant; **even ~** quand bien même + *conditional*; **it's not easy, ~** pourtant, ce n'est pas facile.

thought [θɔːt] *pt, pp of* **think** ♦ *n* pensée *f*; (*opinion*) avis *m*; (*intention*) intention *f*; **after much ~** après mûre réflexion; **I've just had a ~** je viens de penser à quelque chose; **to give sth some ~** réfléchir à qch.

thoughtful ['θɔːtful] *adj* pensif(ive); (*considerate*) prévenant(e).

thoughtfully ['θɔːtfəlɪ] *adv* pensivement; avec prévenance.

thoughtless ['θɔːtlɪs] *adj* étourdi(e); qui manque de considération.

thoughtlessly ['θɔːtlɪslɪ] *adv* inconsidérément.

thought-provoking ['θɔːtprəvəʊkɪŋ] *adj* stimulant(e).

thousand ['θaʊzənd] *num* mille; **one ~** mille; **~s of** des milliers de.

thousandth ['θaʊzəntθ] *num* millième.

thrash [θræʃ] *vt* rouer de coups; donner une correction à; (*defeat*) battre à plate(s) couture(s).

▶**thrash about** *vi* se débattre.

▶**thrash out** *vt* débattre de.

thrashing ['θræʃɪŋ] *n*: **to give sb a ~ = to thrash sb**.

thread [θrɛd] *n* fil *m*; (*of screw*) pas *m*, filetage *m* ♦ *vt* (*needle*) enfiler; **to ~ one's way between** se faufiler entre.

threadbare ['θrɛdbɛə*] *adj* râpé(e), élimé(e).

threat [θrɛt] *n* menace *f*; **to be under ~ of** être menacé(e) de.

threaten ['θrɛtn] *vi* (*storm*) menacer ♦ *vt*: **to ~ sb with sth/to do** menacer qn de qch/de faire.

threatening ['θrɛtnɪŋ] *adj* menaçant(e).

three [θriː] *num* trois.

three-dimensional [θriːdɪˈmɛnʃənl] *adj* à trois dimensions; (*film*) en relief.

threefold ['θriːfəʊld] *adv*: **to increase ~** tripler.

three-piece ['θriːpiːs]: ~ **suit** *n* complet *m* (avec gilet); ~ **suite** *n* salon *m* comprenant un canapé et deux fauteuils assortis.

three-ply [θriːˈplaɪ] *adj* (*wood*) à trois épaisseurs; (*wool*) trois fils *inv*.

three-quarters [θriːˈkwɔːtəz] *npl* trois-quarts *mpl*; ~ **full** aux trois-quarts plein.

three-wheeler [θriːˈwiːlə*] *n* (*car*) voiture *f* à trois roues.

thresh [θrɛʃ] *vt* (*AGR*) battre.

threshing machine ['θrɛʃɪŋ-] *n* batteuse *f*.

threshold ['θrɛʃhəʊld] *n* seuil *m*; **to be on the ~ of** (*fig*) être au seuil de.

threshold agreement *n* (*ECON*) accord *m* d'indexation des salaires.

threw [θruː] *pt of* **throw**.

thrift [θrɪft] *n* économie *f*.

thrifty ['θrɪftɪ] *adj* économe.

thrill [θrɪl] *n* frisson *m*, émotion *f* ♦ *vi* tressaillir, frissonner ♦ *vt* (*audience*) électriser; **to be ~ed** (*with gift etc*) être ravi(e).

thriller ['θrɪlə*] *n* film *m* (*or* roman *m* *or* pièce *f*) à suspense.

thrilling ['θrɪlɪŋ] *adj* (*book, play etc*) saisissant(e); (*news, discovery*) excitant(e).

thrive, *pt* **thrived**, **throve**, *pp* **thrived**, **thriven** [θraɪv, θrəʊv, 'θrɪvn] *vi* pousser *or* se développer bien; (*business*) prospérer; **he ~s on it** cela lui réussit.

thriving ['θraɪvɪŋ] *adj* vigoureux(euse); (*industry etc*) prospère.

throat [θrəʊt] *n* gorge *f*; **to have a sore ~** avoir mal à la gorge.

throb [θrɒb] *n* (*of heart*) pulsation *f*; (*of engine*) vibration *f*; (*of pain*) élancement *m* ♦ *vi* (*heart*) palpiter; (*engine*) vibrer; (*pain*) lanciner; (*wound*) causer des élancements; **my head is ~bing** j'ai des élancements dans la tête.

throes [θrəʊz] *npl*: **in the ~ of** au beau milieu de; en proie à; **in the ~ of death** à l'agonie.

thrombosis [θrɒmˈbəʊsɪs] *n* thrombose *f*.

throne [θrəʊn] *n* trône *m*.

throng ['θrɒŋ] *n* foule *f* ♦ *vt* se presser dans.

throttle ['θrɒtl] *n* (*AUT*) accélérateur *m* ♦ *vt* étrangler.

through [θruː] *prep* à travers; (*time*) pendant, durant; (*by means of*) par, par l'intermédiaire de; (*owing to*) à cause de ♦ *adj* (*ticket, train, passage*) direct(e) ♦ *adv* à travers; (*from*) **Monday ~ Friday** (*US*) de lundi à vendredi; **to let sb ~** laisser passer qn; **to put sb ~ to sb** (*TEL*) passer qn à qn; **to be ~** (*TEL*) avoir la communication; (*have finished*) avoir fini; "**no ~ traffic**" (*US*) "passage interdit"; "**no ~ way**" (*BRIT*) "impasse".

throughout [θruːˈaʊt] *prep* (*place*) partout dans; (*time*) durant tout(e) le(la) ♦ *adv* partout.

throughput ['θruːpʊt] *n* (*of goods, materials*) quantité de matières premières utilisée; (*COMPUT*) débit *m*.

throve [θrəʊv] *pt of* **thrive**.

throw [θrəʊ] *n* jet *m*; (*SPORT*) lancer *m* ♦ *vt* (*pt* **threw**, *pp* **thrown** [θruː, θrəʊn]) lancer, jeter;

(SPORT) lancer; (rider) désarçonner; (fig) décontenancer; (pottery) tourner; **to ~ a party** donner une réception.
▶**throw about, throw around** vt (litter etc) éparpiller.
▶**throw away** vt jeter.
▶**throw off** vt se débarrasser de.
▶**throw out** vt jeter dehors; (reject) rejeter.
▶**throw together** vt (clothes, meal etc) assembler à la hâte; (essay) bâcler.
▶**throw up** vi vomir.
throwaway ['θrəuəweɪ] adj à jeter.
throwback ['θrəubæk] n: **it's a ~ to** ça nous etc ramène à.
throw-in ['θrəuɪn] n (SPORT) remise f en jeu.
thru [θruː] prep, adj, adv (US) = **through**.
thrush [θrʌʃ] n (ZOOL) grive f; (MED: esp in children) muguet m; (: BRIT: in women) muguet vaginal.
thrust [θrʌst] n (TECH) poussée f ♦ vt (pt, pp **thrust**) pousser brusquement; (push in) enfoncer.
thrusting ['θrʌstɪŋ] adj dynamique; qui se met trop en avant.
thud [θʌd] n bruit sourd.
thug [θʌg] n voyou m.
thumb [θʌm] n (ANAT) pouce m ♦ vt (book) feuilleter; **to ~ a lift** faire de l'auto-stop, arrêter une voiture; **to give sb/sth the ~s up/ ~s down** donner/refuser de donner le feu vert à qn/qch.
thumb index n répertoire m (à onglets).
thumbnail ['θʌmneɪl] n ongle m du pouce.
thumbnail sketch n croquis m.
thumbtack ['θʌmtæk] n (US) punaise f (clou).
thump [θʌmp] n grand coup; (sound) bruit sourd ♦ vt cogner sur ♦ vi cogner, frapper.
thunder ['θʌndə*] n tonnerre m ♦ vi tonner; (train etc): **to ~ past** passer dans un grondement or un bruit de tonnerre.
thunderbolt ['θʌndəbəult] n foudre f.
thunderclap ['θʌndəklæp] n coup m de tonnerre.
thunderous ['θʌndrəs] adj étourdissant(e).
thunderstorm ['θʌndəstɔːm] n orage m.
thunderstruck ['θʌndəstrʌk] adj (fig) abasourdi(e).
thundery ['θʌndərɪ] adj orageux(euse).
Thur(s). abbr (= Thursday) jeu.
Thursday ['θəːzdɪ] n jeudi m; for phrases see also **Tuesday**.
thus [ðʌs] adv ainsi.
thwart [θwɔːt] vt contrecarrer.
thyme [taɪm] n thym m.
thyroid ['θaɪrɔɪd] n thyroïde f.
tiara [tɪˈɑːrə] n (woman's) diadème m.
Tibet [tɪˈbɛt] n Tibet m.
Tibetan [tɪˈbɛtən] adj tibétain(e) ♦ n Tibétain/ e; (LING) tibétain m.
tibia ['tɪbɪə] n tibia m.
tic [tɪk] n tic (nerveux).
tick [tɪk] n (sound: of clock) tic-tac m; (mark)

coche f; (ZOOL) tique f; (BRIT col): **in a ~** dans un instant; (BRIT col: credit): **to buy sth on ~** acheter qch à crédit ♦ vi faire tic-tac ♦ vt cocher; **to put a ~ against sth** cocher qch.
▶**tick off** vt cocher; (person) réprimander, attraper.
▶**tick over** vi (BRIT: engine) tourner au ralenti; (: fig) aller or marcher doucement.
ticker tape ['tɪkə-] n bande f de téléscripteur; (US: in celebrations) ≈ serpentin m.
ticket ['tɪkɪt] n billet m; (for bus, tube) ticket m; (in shop: on goods) étiquette f, (: from cash register) reçu m, ticket; (for library) carte f; (US POL) liste électorale (soutenue par un parti); **to get a (parking) ~** (AUT) attraper une contravention (pour stationnement illégal).
ticket agency n (THEAT) agence f de spectacles.
ticket collector n contrôleur/euse.
ticket holder n personne munie d'un billet.
ticket inspector n contrôleur/euse.
ticket office n guichet m, bureau m de vente des billets.
tickle ['tɪkl] n chatouillement m ♦ vt chatouiller; (fig) plaire à; faire rire.
ticklish ['tɪklɪʃ] adj (person) chatouilleux(euse); (which tickles: blanket) qui chatouille; (: cough) qui irrite.
tidal ['taɪdl] adj à marée.
tidal wave n raz-de-marée m inv.
tidbit ['tɪdbɪt] n (esp US) = **titbit**.
tiddlywinks ['tɪdlɪwɪŋks] n jeu m de puce.
tide [taɪd] n marée f; (fig: of events) cours m ♦ vt: **to ~ sb over** dépanner qn; **high/low ~** marée haute/basse.
tidily ['taɪdɪlɪ] adv avec soin, soigneusement.
tidiness ['taɪdɪnɪs] n bon ordre; goût m de l'ordre.
tidy ['taɪdɪ] adj (room) bien rangé(e); (dress, work) net(nette), soigné(e); (person) ordonné(e), qui a de l'ordre; (: in character) soigneux(euse); (mind) méthodique ♦ vt (also: ~ **up**) ranger; **to ~ o.s. up** s'arranger.
tie [taɪ] n (string etc) cordon m; (BRIT: also: **neck~**) cravate f; (fig: link) lien m; (SPORT: draw) égalité f de points; match nul; (: match) rencontre f; (US RAIL) traverse f ♦ vt (parcel) attacher; (ribbon) nouer ♦ vi (SPORT) faire match nul; finir à égalité de points; **"black/white ~"** "smoking/habit de rigueur"; **family ~s** liens de famille; **to ~ sth in a bow** faire un nœud à or avec qch; **to ~ a knot in sth** faire un nœud à qch.
▶**tie down** vt attacher; (fig): **to ~ sb down to** contraindre qn à accepter.
▶**tie in** vi: **to ~ in (with)** (correspond) correspondre (à).
▶**tie on** vt (BRIT: label etc) attacher (avec une ficelle).
▶**tie up** vt (parcel) ficeler; (dog, boat) attacher; (arrangements) conclure; **to be ~d up** (busy) être pris or occupé.

tie-break(er) ['taɪbreɪk(ə*)] n (TENNIS) tie-break m; (in quiz) question f subsidiaire.
tie-on ['taɪɔn] adj (BRIT: label) qui s'attache.
tie-pin ['taɪpɪn] n (BRIT) épingle f de cravate.
tier [tɪə*] n gradin m; (of cake) étage m.
Tierra del Fuego [tɪ'ɛrədɛl'fweɪgəu] n Terre f de Feu.
tie tack n (US) épingle f de cravate.
tiff [tɪf] n petite querelle.
tiger ['taɪgə*] n tigre m.
tight [taɪt] adj (rope) tendu(e), raide; (clothes) étroit(e), très juste; (budget, programme, bend) serré(e); (control) strict(e), sévère; (col: drunk) ivre, rond(e) ♦ adv (squeeze) très fort; (shut) à bloc, hermétiquement; **to be packed** ~ (suitcase) être bourré(e); (people) être serré(e); **everybody hold** ~! accrochez-vous bien!
tighten ['taɪtn] vt (rope) tendre; (screw) resserrer; (control) renforcer ♦ vi se tendre; se resserrer.
tight-fisted [taɪt'fɪstɪd] adj avare.
tight-lipped ['taɪt'lɪpt] adj: **to be** ~ **(about sth)** (silent) ne pas desserrer les lèvres or les dents (au sujet de qch); **she was** ~ **with anger** elle pinçait les lèvres de colère.
tightly ['taɪtlɪ] adv (grasp) bien, très fort.
tight-rope ['taɪtrəup] n corde f raide.
tight-rope walker n funambule m/f.
tights [taɪts] npl (BRIT) collant m.
tigress ['taɪgrɪs] n tigresse f.
tilde ['tɪldə] n tilde m.
tile [taɪl] n (on roof) tuile f; (on wall or floor) carreau m ♦ vt (floor, bathroom etc) carreler.
tiled [taɪld] adj en tuiles; carrelé(e).
till [tɪl] n caisse (enregistreuse) ♦ vt (land) cultiver ♦ prep, conj = until.
tiller ['tɪlə*] n (NAUT) barre f (du gouvernail).
tilt [tɪlt] vt pencher, incliner ♦ vi pencher, être incliné(e) ♦ n (slope) inclinaison f; **to wear one's hat at a** ~ porter son chapeau incliné sur le côté; **(at) full** ~ à toute vitesse.
timber ['tɪmbə*] n (material) bois m de construction; (trees) arbres mpl.
time [taɪm] n temps m; (epoch: often pl) époque f, temps; (by clock) heure f; (moment) moment m; (occasion, also MATH) fois f; (MUS) mesure f ♦ vt (race) chronométrer; (programme) minuter; (remark etc) choisir le moment de; **a long** ~ un long moment, longtemps; **for the** ~ **being** pour le moment; **from** ~ **to** ~ de temps en temps; ~ **after** ~, ~ **and again** bien des fois; **in** ~ (soon enough) à temps; (after some time) avec le temps, à la longue; (MUS) en mesure; **in a week's** ~ dans une semaine; **in no** ~ en un rien de temps; **on** ~ à l'heure; **to be 30 minutes behind/ahead of** ~ avoir 30 minutes de retard/d'avance; **by the** ~ **he arrived** quand il est arrivé, le temps qu'il arrive sub; **5** ~**s 5** 5 fois 5; **what** ~ **is it?** quelle heure est-il?; **what** ~ **do you make it?** quelle heure avez-

vous?; **to have a good** ~ bien s'amuser; **we (or they etc) had a hard** ~ ça a été difficile or pénible; ~**'s up!** c'est l'heure!; **I've no** ~ **for it** (fig) cela m'agace; **he'll do it in his own (good)** ~ (without being hurried) il le fera quand il en aura le temps; **he'll do it in** or (US) **on his own** ~ (out of working hours) il le fera à ses heures perdues; **to be behind the** ~**s** retarder (sur son temps).
time-and-motion study ['taɪmənd'məuʃən-] n étude f des cadences.
time bomb n bombe f à retardement.
time clock n horloge pointeuse.
time-consuming ['taɪmkənsju:mɪŋ] adj qui prend beaucoup de temps.
time difference n décalage m horaire.
time frame n délais mpl.
time-honoured, (US) **time-honored** ['taɪmɔnəd] adj consacré(e).
timekeeper ['taɪmki:pə*] n (SPORT) chronomètre m.
time lag n (BRIT) décalage m; (: in travel) décalage horaire.
timeless ['taɪmlɪs] adj éternel(le).
time limit n limite f de temps, délai m.
timely ['taɪmlɪ] adj opportun(e).
time off n temps m libre.
timer ['taɪmə*] n (in kitchen) compte-minutes m inv; (TECH) minuteur m.
time-saving ['taɪmseɪvɪŋ] adj qui fait gagner du temps.
time scale n délais mpl.
time-sharing ['taɪmʃɛərɪŋ] n (COMPUT) temps partagé.
time sheet n feuille f de présence.
time signal n signal m horaire.
time switch n (BRIT) minuteur m; (: for lighting) minuterie f.
timetable ['taɪmteɪbl] n (RAIL) (indicateur m) horaire m; (SCOL) emploi m du temps; (programme of events etc) programme m.
time zone n fuseau m horaire.
timid ['tɪmɪd] adj timide; (easily scared) peureux(euse).
timidity [tɪ'mɪdɪtɪ] n timidité f.
timing ['taɪmɪŋ] n minutage m; chronométrage m; **the** ~ **of his resignation** le moment choisi pour sa démission.
timing device n (on bomb) mécanisme m de retardement.
timpani ['tɪmpənɪ] npl timbales fpl.
tin [tɪn] n étain m; (also: ~ **plate**) fer-blanc m; (BRIT: can) boîte f (de conserve); (: for baking) moule m (à gâteau); **a** ~ **of paint** un pot de peinture.
tin foil n papier m d'étain.
tinge [tɪndʒ] n nuance f ♦ vt: ~**d with** teinté(e) de.
tingle ['tɪŋgl] n picotement m; frisson m ♦ vi picoter.
tinker ['tɪŋkə*] n rétameur ambulant; (gipsy) romanichel m.

▶**tinker with** vt fus bricoler, rafistoler.

tinkle ['tɪŋkl] vi tinter ♦ n (col): **to give sb a ~** passer un coup de fil à qn.

tin mine n mine f d'étain.

tinned [tɪnd] adj (BRIT: food) en boîte, en conserve.

tinnitus ['tɪnɪtəs] n (MED) acouphène m.

tinny ['tɪnɪ] adj métallique.

tin opener [-'əupnə*] n (BRIT) ouvre-boîte(s) m.

tinsel ['tɪnsl] n guirlandes fpl de Noël (argentées).

tint [tɪnt] n teinte f; (for hair) shampooing colorant ♦ vt (hair) faire un shampooing colorant à.

tinted ['tɪntɪd] adj (hair) teint(e); (spectacles, glass) teinté(e).

tiny ['taɪnɪ] adj minuscule.

tip [tɪp] n (end) bout m; (protective: on umbrella etc) embout m; (gratuity) pourboire m; (BRIT: for coal) terril m; (: for rubbish) décharge f; (advice) tuyau m ♦ vt (waiter) donner un pourboire à; (tilt) incliner; (overturn: also: ~ **over**) renverser; (empty: also: ~ **out**) déverser; (predict: winner etc) pronostiquer; **he ~ped out the contents of the box** il a vidé le contenu de la boîte.

▶**tip off** vt prévenir, avertir.

tip-off ['tɪpɔf] n (hint) tuyau m.

tipped ['tɪpt] adj (BRIT: cigarette) (à bout) filtre inv; **steel-~** à bout métallique, à embout de métal.

Tipp-Ex ['tɪpɛks] n ® (BRIT) Tipp-Ex m ®.

tipple ['tɪpl] (BRIT) vi picoler ♦ n: **to have a ~** boire un petit coup.

tipster ['tɪpstə*] n (RACING) pronostiqueur m.

tipsy ['tɪpsɪ] adj un peu ivre, éméché(e).

tiptoe ['tɪptəu] n: **on ~** sur la pointe des pieds.

tiptop ['tɪptɔp] adj: **in ~ condition** en excellent état.

tirade [taɪ'reɪd] n diatribe f.

tire ['taɪə*] n (US) = **tyre** ♦ vt fatiguer ♦ vi se fatiguer.

▶**tire out** vt épuiser.

tired ['taɪəd] adj fatigué(e); **to be/feel/look ~** être/se sentir/avoir l'air fatigué; **to be ~ of** en avoir assez de, être las(lasse) de.

tiredness ['taɪədnɪs] n fatigue f.

tireless ['taɪəlɪs] adj infatigable, inlassable.

tiresome ['taɪəsəm] adj ennuyeux(euse).

tiring ['taɪərɪŋ] adj fatigant(e).

tissue ['tɪʃu:] n tissu m; (paper handkerchief) mouchoir m en papier, kleenex m ®.

tissue paper n papier m de soie.

tit [tɪt] n (bird) mésange f; (col: breast) nichon m; **to give ~ for tat** rendre coup pour coup.

titanium [tɪ'teɪnɪəm] n titane m.

titbit ['tɪtbɪt] n (food) friandise f; (before meal) amuse-gueule m inv; (news) potin m.

titillate ['tɪtɪleɪt] vt titiller, exciter.

titivate ['tɪtɪveɪt] vt pomponner.

title ['taɪtl] n titre m; (LAW: right): **~ (to)** droit m (à).

title deed n (LAW) titre (constitutif) de propriété.

title page n page f de titre.

title role n rôle principal.

titter ['tɪtə*] vi rire (bêtement).

tittle-tattle ['tɪtltætl] n bavardages mpl.

titular ['tɪtjulə*] adj (in name only) nominal(e).

tizzy ['tɪzɪ] n: **to be in a ~** être dans tous ses états.

T-junction ['ti:'dʒʌŋkʃən] n croisement m en T.

TM n abbr = **trademark, transcendental meditation**.

TN abbr (US) = **Tennessee**.

TNT n abbr (= trinitrotoluene) TNT m.

═══════════════════════════════ KEYWORD

to [tu:, tə] prep **1** (direction) à; (towards) vers; envers; **to go ~ France/Portugal/London/school** aller en France/au Portugal/à Londres/à l'école; **to go ~ Claude's/the doctor's** aller chez Claude/le docteur; **the road ~ Edinburgh** la route d'Édimbourg

2 (as far as) (jusqu'à)à; **to count ~ 10** compter jusqu'à 10; **from 40 ~ 50 people** de 40 à 50 personnes

3 (with expressions of time): **a quarter ~ 5** 5 heures moins le quart; **it's twenty ~ 3** il est 3 heures moins vingt

4 (for, of) de; **the key ~ the front door** la clé de la porte d'entrée; **a letter ~ his wife** une lettre (adressée) à sa femme

5 (expressing indirect object) à; **to give sth ~ sb** donner qch à qn; **to talk ~ sb** parler à qn; **it belongs ~ him** cela lui appartient, c'est à lui

6 (in relation to) à; **3 goals ~ 2** 3 (buts) à 2; **30 miles ~ the gallon** ≈ 9,4 litres aux cent (km)

7 (purpose, result): **to come ~ sb's aid** venir au secours de qn, porter secours à qn; **to sentence sb ~ death** condamner qn à mort; **~ my surprise** à ma grande surprise

♦ with vb **1** (simple infinitive): **~ go/eat** aller/manger

2 (following another vb): **to want/try/start ~ do** vouloir/essayer de/commencer à faire

3 (with vb omitted): **I don't want ~** je ne veux pas

4 (purpose, result) pour; **I did it ~ help you** je l'ai fait pour vous aider

5 (equivalent to relative clause): **I have things ~ do** j'ai des choses à faire; **the main thing is ~ try** l'important est d'essayer

6 (after adjective etc): **ready ~ go** prêt(e) à partir; **too old/young ~ ...** trop vieux/jeune pour ...

♦ adv: **push/pull the door ~** tirez/poussez la porte; **to go ~ and fro** aller et venir.

toad [təud] n crapaud m.

toadstool ['təudstu:l] n champignon (vénéneux).

toady ['təudɪ] vi flatter bassement.

toast [təust] n (CULIN) pain grillé, toast m; (drink, speech) toast ♦ vt (CULIN) faire griller; (drink to) porter un toast à; **a piece** or **slice of ~** un toast.

toaster ['təustə*] n grille-pain m inv.

toastmaster ['təustmɑːstə*] n animateur m pour réceptions.

toast rack n porte-toast m inv.

tobacco [tə'bækəu] n tabac m; **pipe ~** tabac à pipe.

tobacconist [tə'bækənɪst] n marchand/e de tabac; **~'s (shop)** (bureau m de) tabac m.

Tobago [tə'beɪgəu] n see **Trinidad and Tobago**.

toboggan [tə'bɔgən] n toboggan m; (child's) luge f.

today [tə'deɪ] adv, n (also fig) aujourd'hui (m); **what day is it ~?** quel jour sommes-nous aujourd'hui?; **what date is it ~?** quelle est la date aujourd'hui?; **~ is the 4th of March** aujourd'hui nous sommes le 4 mars; **a week ago ~** il y a huit jours aujourd'hui.

toddler ['tɔdlə*] n enfant m/f qui commence à marcher, bambin m.

toddy ['tɔdɪ] n grog m.

to-do [tə'du:] n (fuss) histoire f, affaire f.

toe [təu] n doigt m de pied, orteil m; (of shoe) bout m ♦ vt: **to ~ the line** (fig) obéir, se conformer; **big ~** gros orteil; **little ~** petit orteil.

TOEFL n abbr = Test(ing) of English as a Foreign Language.

toehold ['təuhəuld] n prise f.

toenail ['təuneɪl] n ongle m de l'orteil.

toffee ['tɔfɪ] n caramel m.

toffee apple n (BRIT) pomme caramélisée.

tofu ['təufu:] n fromage m de soja.

toga ['təugə] n toge f.

together [tə'gɛðə*] adv ensemble; (at same time) en même temps; **~ with** prep avec.

togetherness [tə'gɛðənɪs] n camaraderie f, intimité f.

toggle switch ['tɔgl-] n (COMPUT) interrupteur m à bascule.

Togo ['təugəu] n Togo m.

togs [tɔgz] npl (col: clothes) fringues fpl.

toil [tɔɪl] n dur travail, labeur m ♦ vi travailler dur; peiner.

toilet ['tɔɪlət] n (BRIT: lavatory) toilettes fpl, cabinets mpl ♦ cpd (bag, soap etc) de toilette; **to go to the ~** aller aux toilettes.

toilet bag n (BRIT) nécessaire m de toilette.

toilet bowl n cuvette f des W.-C.

toilet paper n papier m hygiénique.

toiletries ['tɔɪlətrɪz] npl articles mpl de toilette.

toilet roll n rouleau m de papier hygiénique.

toilet water n eau f de toilette.

to-ing and fro-ing ['tu:ɪŋən'frəuɪŋ] n (BRIT) al-

lées et venues fpl.

token ['təukən] n (sign) marque f, témoignage m; (voucher) bon m, coupon m ♦ cpd (fee, strike) symbolique; **by the same ~** (fig) de même; **book/record ~** (BRIT) chèque-livre/disque m.

tokenism ['təukənɪzəm] n (POL): **it's just ~** c'est une politique de pure forme.

Tokyo ['təukjəu] n Tokyo.

told [təuld] pt, pp of **tell**.

tolerable ['tɔlərəbl] adj (bearable) tolérable; (fairly good) passable.

tolerably ['tɔlərəblɪ] adv: **~ good** tolérable.

tolerance ['tɔlərns] n (also TECH) tolérance f.

tolerant ['tɔlərnt] adj: **~ (of)** tolérant(e) (à l'égard de).

tolerate ['tɔləreɪt] vt supporter; (MED, TECH) tolérer.

toleration [tɔlə'reɪʃən] n tolérance f.

toll [təul] n (tax, charge) péage m ♦ vi (bell) sonner; **the accident ~ on the roads** le nombre des victimes de la route.

tollbridge ['təulbrɪdʒ] n pont m à péage.

toll call n (US TEL) appel m (à) longue distance.

toll-free ['təul'fri:] adj (US) gratuit(e) ♦ adv gratuitement.

tomato, ~es [tə'mɑːtəu] n tomate f.

tomb [tu:m] n tombe f.

tombola [tɔm'bəulə] n tombola f.

tomboy ['tɔmbɔɪ] n garçon manqué.

tombstone ['tu:mstəun] n pierre tombale.

tomcat ['tɔmkæt] n matou m.

tomorrow [tə'mɔrəu] adv, n (also fig) demain (m); **the day after ~** après-demain; **a week ~** demain en huit; **~ morning** demain matin.

ton [tʌn] n tonne f (Brit: = 1016 kg; US = 907 kg; metric = 1000 kg); (NAUT: also: **register ~**) tonneau m (= 2.83 cu.m); **~s of** (col) des tas de.

tonal ['təunl] adj tonal(e).

tone [təun] n ton m; (of radio, BRIT TEL) tonalité f ♦ vi s'harmoniser.

▶tone down vt (colour, criticism) adoucir; (sound) baisser.

▶tone up vt (muscles) tonifier.

tone-deaf [təun'dɛf] adj qui n'a pas d'oreille.

toner ['təunə*] n (for photocopier) encre f.

Tonga ['tɔŋə] n îles fpl Tonga.

tongs [tɔŋz] npl pinces fpl; (for coal) pincettes fpl; (for hair) fer m à friser.

tongue [tʌŋ] n langue f; **~ in cheek** adv ironiquement.

tongue-tied ['tʌŋtaɪd] adj (fig) muet(te).

tongue-twister ['tʌŋtwɪstə*] n phrase f très difficile à prononcer.

tonic ['tɔnɪk] n (MED) tonique m; (MUS) tonique f; (also: **~ water**) tonic m.

tonight [tə'naɪt] adv, n cette nuit; (this evening) ce soir; **(I'll) see you ~!** à ce soir!

tonnage ['tʌnɪdʒ] n (NAUT) tonnage m.

tonne [tʌn] n (BRIT: metric ton) tonne f.

tonsil ['tɔnsl] n amygdale f; **to have one's ~s**

out se faire opérer des amygdales.

tonsillitis [tɔnsɪ'laɪtɪs] n amygdalite f; **to have ~** avoir une angine or une amygdalite.

too [tuː] adv (excessively) trop; (also) aussi; **it's ~ sweet** c'est trop sucré; **I went ~** moi aussi, j'y suis allé; **~ much** adv trop ♦ adj trop de; **~ many** adj trop de; **~ bad!** tant pis!

took [tuk] pt of **take**.

tool [tuːl] n outil m; (fig) instrument m ♦ vt travailler, ouvrager.

tool box n boîte f à outils.

tool kit n trousse f à outils.

toot [tuːt] n coup m de sifflet (or de klaxon) ♦ vi siffler; (with car-horn) klaxonner.

tooth, pl **teeth** [tuːθ, tiːθ] n (ANAT, TECH) dent f; **to have a ~ out** or (US) **pulled** se faire arracher une dent; **to brush one's teeth** se laver les dents; **by the skin of one's teeth** (fig) de justesse.

toothache ['tuːθeɪk] n mal m de dents; **to have ~** avoir mal aux dents.

toothbrush ['tuːθbrʌʃ] n brosse f à dents.

toothpaste ['tuːθpeɪst] n (pâte f) dentifrice m.

toothpick ['tuːθpɪk] n cure-dent m.

tooth powder n poudre f dentifrice.

top [tɔp] n (of mountain, head) sommet m; (of page, ladder) haut m; (of list, queue) commencement m; (of box, cupboard, table) dessus m; (lid: of box, jar) couvercle m; (: of bottle) bouchon m; (toy) toupie f; (DRESS: blouse etc) haut; (of pyjamas) veste f ♦ adj du haut; (in rank) premier(ière); (best) meilleur(e) ♦ vt (exceed) dépasser; (be first in) être en tête de; **the ~ of the milk** (BRIT) la crème du lait; **at the ~ of the stairs/ page/street** en haut de l'escalier/de la page/de la rue; **on ~ of** sur; (in addition to) en plus de; **from ~ to toe** (BRIT) de la tête aux pieds; **at the ~ of the list** en tête de liste; **at the ~ of one's voice** à tue-tête; **at ~ speed** à toute vitesse; **over the ~** (col: behaviour etc) qui dépasse les limites.

▶**top up**, (US) **top off** vt remplir.

topaz ['təupæz] n topaze f.

top-class ['tɔp'klɑːs] adj de première classe; (SPORT) de haute compétition.

topcoat ['tɔpkəut] n pardessus m.

topflight ['tɔpflaɪt] adj excellent(e).

top floor n dernier étage.

top hat n haut-de-forme m.

top-heavy [tɔp'hɛvɪ] adj (object) trop lourd(e) du haut.

topic ['tɔpɪk] n sujet m, thème m.

topical ['tɔpɪkl] adj d'actualité.

topless ['tɔplɪs] adj (bather etc) aux seins nus; **~ swimsuit** monokini m.

top-level ['tɔplɛvl] adj (talks) à l'échelon le plus élevé.

topmost ['tɔpməust] adj le(la) plus haut(e).

top-notch ['tɔp'nɔtʃ] adj (col) de premier ordre.

topography [tə'pɔgrəfɪ] n topographie f.

topping ['tɔpɪŋ] n (CULIN) couche de crème, fromage etc qui recouvre un plat.

topple ['tɔpl] vt renverser, faire tomber ♦ vi basculer; tomber.

top-ranking ['tɔpræŋkɪŋ] adj très haut placé(e).

top-secret ['tɔp'siːkrɪt] adj ultra-secret(ète).

top-security ['tɔpsə'kjuərɪtɪ] adj (BRIT) de haute sécurité.

topsy-turvy ['tɔpsɪ'təːvɪ] adj, adv sens dessus-dessous.

top-up ['tɔpʌp] n: **would you like a ~?** je vous en remets or rajoute?

top-up loan n (BRIT) prêt m complémentaire.

torch [tɔːtʃ] n torche f; (BRIT: electric) lampe f de poche.

tore [tɔː*] pt of **tear**.

torment n ['tɔːmɛnt] tourment m ♦ vt [tɔː'mɛnt] tourmenter; (fig: annoy) agacer.

torn [tɔːn] pp of **tear** ♦ adj: **~ between** (fig) tiraillé(e) entre.

tornado, **~es** [tɔː'neɪdəu] n tornade f.

torpedo, **~es** [tɔː'piːdəu] n torpille f.

torpedo boat n torpilleur m.

torpor ['tɔːpə*] n torpeur f.

torrent ['tɔrnt] n torrent m.

torrential [tɔ'rɛnʃl] adj torrentiel(le).

torrid ['tɔrɪd] adj torride; (fig) ardent(e).

torso ['tɔːsəu] n torse m.

tortoise ['tɔːtəs] n tortue f.

tortoiseshell ['tɔːtəʃɛl] adj en écaille.

tortuous ['tɔːtjuəs] adj tortueux(euse).

torture ['tɔːtʃə*] n torture f ♦ vt torturer.

torturer ['tɔːtʃərə*] n tortionnaire m.

Tory ['tɔːrɪ] adj (BRIT POL) tory (pl tories), conservateur(trice) ♦ n tory m/f, conservateur/trice.

toss [tɔs] vt lancer, jeter; (BRIT: pancake) faire sauter; (head) rejeter en arrière ♦ vi: **to ~ up for sth** (BRIT) jouer qch à pile ou face ♦ n (movement: of head etc) mouvement soudain; (of coin) tirage m à pile ou face; **to ~ a coin** jouer à pile ou face; **to ~ and turn** (in bed) se tourner et se retourner; **to win/lose the ~** gagner/perdre à pile ou face; (SPORT) gagner/perdre le tirage au sort.

tot [tɔt] n (BRIT: drink) petit verre; (child) bambin m.

▶**tot up** vt (BRIT: figures) additionner.

total ['təutl] adj total(e) ♦ n total m ♦ vt (add up) faire le total de, totaliser; (amount to) s'élever à; **in ~** au total.

totalitarian [təutælɪ'tɛərɪən] adj totalitaire.

totality [təu'tælɪtɪ] n totalité f.

totally ['təutəlɪ] adv totalement.

tote bag [təut-] n fourre-tout m inv.

totem pole ['təutəm-] n mât m totémique.

totter ['tɔtə*] vi chanceler; (object, government) être chancelant(e).

touch [tʌtʃ] n contact m, toucher m; (sense, also skill: of pianist etc) toucher; (fig: note, also FOOTBALL) touche f ♦ vt (gen) toucher; (tamper with) toucher à; **the personal ~** la petite note personnelle; **to put the finishing ~es to sth** mettre la dernière main à qch; **a ~ of** *(fig)* un petit peu de; une touche de; **in ~ with** en contact *or* rapport avec; **to get in ~ with** prendre contact avec; **I'll be in ~** je resterai en contact; **to lose ~** *(friends)* se perdre de vue; **to be out of ~ with events** ne pas être au courant de ce qui se passe.

▶**touch on** *vt fus (topic)* effleurer, toucher.

▶**touch up** *vt (paint)* retoucher.

touch-and-go ['tʌtʃən'gəu] *adj* incertain(e); **it was ~ whether we did it** nous avons failli ne pas le faire.

touchdown ['tʌtʃdaun] *n* atterrissage *m*; *(on sea)* amerrissage *m*; *(US FOOTBALL)* essai *m*.

touched [tʌtʃt] *adj* touché(e); *(col)* cinglé(e).

touching ['tʌtʃɪŋ] *adj* touchant(e), attendrissant(e).

touchline ['tʌtʃlaɪn] *n (SPORT)* (ligne *f* de) touche *f*.

touch-sensitive ['tʌtʃsɛnsɪtɪv] *adj (keypad)* à effleurement; *(screen)* tactile.

touch-type ['tʌtʃtaɪp] *vi* taper au toucher.

touchy ['tʌtʃi] *adj (person)* susceptible.

tough [tʌf] *adj* dur(e); *(resistant)* résistant(e), solide; *(meat)* dur, coriace; *(journey)* pénible; *(task, problem, situation)* difficile; *(rough)* dur ♦ *n (gangster etc)* dur *m*; **~ luck!** pas de chance!; tant pis!

toughen ['tʌfn] *vt* rendre plus dur(e) *(or* plus résistant(e) *or* plus solide).

toughness ['tʌfnɪs] *n* dureté *f*; résistance *f*; solidité *f*.

toupee ['tu:peɪ] *n* postiche *m*.

tour ['tuə*] *n* voyage *m*; *(also:* **package ~)** voyage organisé; *(of town, museum)* tour *m*, visite *f*; *(by artist)* tournée *f* ♦ *vt* visiter; **to go on a ~ of** *(museum, region)* visiter; **to go on ~** partir en tournée.

touring ['tuərɪŋ] *n* voyages *mpl* touristiques, tourisme *m*.

tourism ['tuərɪzm] *n* tourisme *m*.

tourist ['tuərɪst] *n* touriste *m/f* ♦ *adv (travel)* en classe touriste ♦ *cpd* touristique; **the ~ trade** le tourisme.

tourist class *n (AVIAT)* classe *f* touriste.

tourist office *n* syndicat *m* d'initiative.

tournament ['tuənəmənt] *n* tournoi *m*.

tourniquet ['tuənɪkeɪ] *n (MED)* garrot *m*.

tour operator *n (BRIT)* organisateur *m* de voyages, tour-opérateur *m*.

tousled ['tauzld] *adj (hair)* ébouriffé(e).

tout [taut] *vi:* **to ~ for** essayer de raccrocher, racoler; **to ~ sth (around)** *(BRIT)* essayer de placer *or* (re)vendre qch ♦ *n (BRIT:* **ticket ~)** revendeur *m* de billets.

tow [təu] *n:* **to give sb a ~** *(AUT)* remorquer qn ♦ *vt* remorquer; **"on ~",** *(US)* **"in ~"** *(AUT)* "véhicule en remorque".

toward(s) [tə'wɔːd(z)] *prep* vers; *(of attitude)* envers, à l'égard de; *(of purpose)* pour; **~ noon/the end of the year** vers midi/la fin de

l'année; **to feel friendly ~ sb** être bien disposé envers qn.

towel ['tauəl] *n* serviette *f* (de toilette); *(also:* **tea ~)** torchon *m*; **to throw in the ~** *(fig)* jeter l'éponge.

towelling ['tauəlɪŋ] *n (fabric)* tissu-éponge *m*.

towel rail, *(US)* **towel rack** *n* porte-serviettes *m inv*.

tower ['tauə*] *n* tour *f* ♦ *vi (building, mountain)* se dresser (majestueusement); **to ~ above** *or* **over sb/sth** dominer qn/qch.

tower block *n (BRIT)* tour *f* (d'habitation).

towering ['tauərɪŋ] *adj* très haut(e), imposant(e).

towline ['təulaɪn] *n (câble m de)* remorque *f*.

town [taun] *n* ville *f*; **to go to ~** aller en ville; *(fig)* y mettre le paquet; **in the ~** dans la ville, en ville; **to be out of ~** *(person)* être en déplacement.

town centre *n* centre *m* de la ville, centre-ville *m*.

town clerk *n ≈* secrétaire *m/f* de mairie.

town council *n* conseil municipal.

town crier [-'kraɪə*] *n (BRIT)* crieur public.

town hall *n ≈* mairie *f*.

townie ['tauni] *n (BRIT col)* citadin/e.

town plan *n* plan *m* de ville.

town planner *n* urbaniste *m/f*.

town planning *n* urbanisme *m*.

township ['taunʃɪp] *n* banlieue noire *(établie sous le régime de l'apartheid)*.

townspeople ['taunzpi:pl] *npl* citadins *mpl*.

towpath ['təupɑ:θ] *n (chemin m de)* halage *m*.

towrope ['təurəup] *n (câble m de)* remorque *f*.

tow truck *n (US)* dépanneuse *f*.

toxic ['tɔksɪk] *adj* toxique.

toxin ['tɔksɪn] *n* toxine *f*.

toy [tɔɪ] *n* jouet *m*.

▶**toy with** *vt fus* jouer avec; *(idea)* caresser.

toyshop ['tɔɪʃɔp] *n* magasin *m* de jouets.

trace [treɪs] *n* trace *f* ♦ *vt (draw)* tracer, dessiner; *(follow)* suivre la trace de; *(locate)* retrouver; **without ~** *(disappear)* sans laisser de traces; **there was no ~ of it** il n'y en avait pas trace.

trace element *n* oligo-élément *m*.

trachea [trə'kɪə] *n (ANAT)* trachée *f*.

tracing paper ['treɪsɪŋ-] *n* papier-calque *m*.

track [træk] *n (mark)* trace *f*; *(path: gen)* chemin *m*, piste *f*; *(: of bullet etc)* trajectoire *f*; *(: of suspect, animal)* piste; *(RAIL)* voie ferrée, rails *mpl*; *(on tape, COMPUT, SPORT)* piste; *(on record)* plage *f* ♦ *vt* suivre la trace *or* la piste de; **to keep ~ of** suivre; **to be on the right ~** *(fig)* être sur la bonne voie.

▶**track down** *vt (prey)* trouver et capturer; *(sth lost)* finir par retrouver.

tracked [trækt] *adj (AUT)* à chenille.

tracker dog ['trækə-] *n (BRIT)* chien dressé pour suivre une piste.

track events *npl (SPORT)* épreuves *fpl* sur piste.

tracking station ['trækɪŋ-] n (SPACE) centre m d'observation de satellites.
track meet n (US) réunion sportive sur piste.
track record n: **to have a good ~** (fig) avoir fait ses preuves.
track suit n survêtement m.
tract [trækt] n (GEO) étendue f, zone f; (pamphlet) tract m; **respiratory ~** (ANAT) système m respiratoire.
traction ['trækʃən] n traction f.
tractor ['træktə*] n tracteur m.
trade [treɪd] n commerce m; (skill, job) métier m ♦ vi faire du commerce; **to ~ with/in** faire du commerce avec/le commerce de; **foreign ~** commerce extérieur; **Department of T~ and Industry (DTI)** (BRIT) ministère m du Commerce et de l'Industrie.
▶**trade in** vt (old car etc) faire reprendre.
trade barrier n barrière commerciale.
trade deficit n déficit extérieur.
Trade Descriptions Act n (BRIT) loi contre les appellations et la publicité mensongères.
trade discount n remise f au détaillant.
trade fair n foire(-exposition) commerciale.
trade-in ['treɪdɪn] n reprise f.
trade-in price n prix m à la reprise.
trademark ['treɪdmɑːk] n marque f de fabrique.
trade mission n mission commerciale.
trade name n marque déposée.
trade-off ['treɪdɔf] n (exchange) échange f; (balancing) équilibre m.
trader ['treɪdə*] n commerçant/e, négociant/e.
trade secret n secret m de fabrication.
tradesman ['treɪdzmən] n (shopkeeper) commerçant m; (skilled worker) ouvrier qualifié.
trade union n syndicat m.
trade unionist [-'juːnjənɪst] n syndicaliste m/f.
trade wind n alizé m.
trading ['treɪdɪŋ] n affaires fpl, commerce m.
trading estate n (BRIT) zone industrielle.
trading stamp n timbre-prime m.
tradition [trə'dɪʃən] n tradition f; **~s** npl coutumes fpl, traditions.
traditional [trə'dɪʃənl] adj traditionnel(le).
traffic ['træfɪk] n trafic m; (cars) circulation f ♦ vi: **to ~ in** (pej: liquor, drugs) faire le trafic de.
traffic calming [-'kɑːmɪŋ] n ralentissement m de la circulation.
traffic circle n (US) rond-point m.
traffic island n refuge m (pour piétons).
traffic jam n embouteillage m.
trafficker ['træfɪkə*] n trafiquant/e.
traffic lights npl feux mpl (de signalisation).
traffic offence n (BRIT) infraction f au code de la route.
traffic sign n panneau m de signalisation.
traffic violation n (US) = **traffic offence**.
traffic warden n contractuel/le.
tragedy ['trædʒədɪ] n tragédie f.

tragic ['trædʒɪk] adj tragique.
trail [treɪl] n (tracks) trace f, piste f; (path) chemin m, piste; (of smoke etc) traînée f ♦ vt traîner, tirer; (follow) suivre ♦ vi traîner; **to be on sb's ~** être sur la piste de qn.
▶**trail away, trail off** vi (sound, voice) s'évanouir; (interest) disparaître.
▶**trail behind** vi traîner, être à la traîne.
trailer ['treɪlə*] n (AUT) remorque f; (US) caravane f; (CINE) bande-annonce f.
trailer truck n (US) (camion m) semi-remorque m.
train [treɪn] n train m; (in underground) rame f; (of dress) traîne f; (BRIT: series): **~ of events** série f d'événements ♦ vt (apprentice, doctor etc) former; (sportsman) entraîner; (dog) dresser; (memory) exercer; (point: gun etc): **to ~ sth on** braquer qch sur ♦ vi recevoir sa formation; s'entraîner; **one's ~ of thought** le fil de sa pensée; **to go by ~** voyager par le train or en train; **to ~ sb to do sth** apprendre à qn à faire qch; (employee) former qn à faire qch.
train attendant n (US) employé/e des wagons-lits.
trained [treɪnd] adj qualifié(e), qui a reçu une formation; dressé(e).
trainee [treɪ'niː] n stagiaire m/f; (in trade) apprenti/e.
trainer ['treɪnə*] n (SPORT) entraîneur/euse; (of dogs etc) dresseur/euse; **~s** npl (shoes) chaussures fpl de sport.
training ['treɪnɪŋ] n formation f; entraînement m; dressage m; **in ~** (SPORT) à l'entraînement; (fit) en forme.
training college n école professionnelle; (for teachers) ≈ école normale.
training course n cours m de formation professionnelle.
traipse [treɪps] vi (se) traîner, déambuler.
trait [treɪt] n trait m (de caractère).
traitor ['treɪtə*] n traître m.
trajectory [trə'dʒɛktərɪ] n trajectoire f.
tram [træm] n (BRIT: also: **~car**) tram(way) m.
tramline ['træmlaɪn] n ligne f de tram(way).
tramp [træmp] n (person) vagabond/e, clochard/e; (col: pej: woman): **to be a ~** être coureuse ♦ vi marcher d'un pas lourd ♦ vt (walk through: town, streets) parcourir à pied.
trample ['træmpl] vt: **to ~ (underfoot)** piétiner; (fig) bafouer.
trampoline ['træmpəliːn] n trampolino m.
trance [trɑːns] n transe f; (MED) catalepsie f; **to go into a ~** entrer en transe.
tranquil ['træŋkwɪl] adj tranquille.
tranquillity [træŋ'kwɪlɪtɪ] n tranquillité f.
tranquillizer ['træŋkwɪlaɪzə*] n (MED) tranquillisant m.
transact [træn'zækt] vt (business) traiter.
transaction [træn'zækʃən] n transaction f; **~s** npl (minutes) actes mpl; **cash ~** transaction au comptant.

transatlantic ['trænzət'læntık] *adj* transatlantique.

transcend [træn'sɛnd] *vt* transcender; *(excel over)* surpasser.

transcendental [trænsɛn'dɛntl] *adj*: ~ **meditation** méditation transcendantale.

transcribe [træn'skraıb] *vt* transcrire.

transcript ['trænskrıpt] *n* transcription *f* *(texte)*.

transcription [træn'skrıpʃən] *n* transcription *f*.

transept ['trænsɛpt] *n* transept *m*.

transfer *n* ['trænsfə*] *(gen, also* SPORT*)* transfert *m*; *(*POL: *of power)* passation *f*; *(of money)* virement *m*; *(picture, design)* décalcomanie *f*; *(: stick-on)* autocollant *m* ♦ *vt* [træns'fə:*] transférer; passer; virer; décalquer; **to ~ the charges** *(*BRIT TEL*)* téléphoner en P.C.V.; **by bank** ~ par virement bancaire.

transferable [træns'fɔ:rəbl] *adj* transmissible, transférable; **"not ~"** "personnel".

transfix [træns'fıks] *vt* transpercer; *(fig)*: ~**ed with fear** paralysé(e) par la peur.

transform [træns'fɔ:m] *vt* transformer.

transformation [trænsfə'meıʃən] *n* transformation *f*.

transformer [træns'fɔ:mə*] *n* *(*ELEC*)* transformateur *m*.

transfusion [træns'fju:ʒən] *n* transfusion *f*.

transgress [træns'grɛs] *vt* transgresser.

transient ['trænzıənt] *adj* transitoire, éphémère.

transistor [træn'zıstə*] *n* *(*ELEC; *also:* ~ **radio**) transistor *m*.

transit ['trænzıt] *n*: **in** ~ en transit.

transit camp *n* camp *m* de transit.

transition [træn'zıʃən] *n* transition *f*.

transitional [træn'zıʃənl] *adj* transitoire.

transitive ['trænzıtıv] *adj* *(*LING*)* transitif(ive).

transit lounge *n* *(*AVIAT*)* salle *f* de transit.

transitory ['trænzıtərı] *adj* transitoire.

translate [trænz'leıt] *vt*: **to** ~ **(from/into)** traduire (du/en).

translation [trænz'leıʃən] *n* traduction *f*; *(*SCOL: *as opposed to prose)* version *f*.

translator [trænz'leıtə*] *n* traducteur/trice.

translucent [trænz'lu:snt] *adj* translucide.

transmission [trænz'mıʃən] *n* transmission *f*.

transmit [trænz'mıt] *vt* transmettre; *(*RADIO, TV*)* émettre.

transmitter [trænz'mıtə*] *n* émetteur *m*.

transparency [træns'pɛərnsı] *n* *(*BRIT PHOT*)* diapositive *f*.

transparent [træns'pærnt] *adj* transparent(e).

transpire [træns'paıə*] *vi* *(become known)*: **it finally ~d that ...** on a finalement appris que ...; *(happen)* arriver.

transplant *vt* [træns'plɑ:nt] transplanter; *(seedlings)* repiquer ♦ *n* ['trænsplɑ:nt] *(*MED*)* transplantation *f*; **to have a heart** ~ subir une greffe du cœur.

transport *n* ['trænspɔ:t] transport *m* ♦ *vt*

[træns'pɔ:t] transporter; **public** ~ **transports en commun; Department of T~** *(*BRIT*)* ministère *m* des Transports.

transportation [trænspɔ:'teıʃən] *n* (moyen *m* de) transport *m*; *(of prisoners)* transportation *f*; **Department of T~** *(*US*)* ministère *m* des Transports.

transport café *n* *(*BRIT*)* ≈ routier *m*.

transpose [træns'pəuz] *vt* transposer.

transsexual [trænz'sɛksjuəl] *adj*, *n* transsexuel(le).

transverse ['trænzvə:s] *adj* transversal(e).

transvestite [trænz'vɛstaıt] *n* travesti/e.

trap [træp] *n* *(snare, trick)* piège *m*; *(carriage)* cabriolet *m* ♦ *vt* prendre au piège; *(immobilize)* bloquer; *(jam)* coincer; **to set** *or* **lay a** ~ **(for sb)** tendre un piège (à qn); **to shut one's** ~ *(col)* la fermer.

trap door *n* trappe *f*.

trapeze [trə'pi:z] *n* trapèze *m*.

trapper ['træpə*] *n* trappeur *m*.

trappings ['træpıŋz] *npl* ornements *mpl*; attributs *mpl*.

trash [træʃ] *n* *(pej: goods)* camelote *f*; *(: nonsense)* sottises *fpl*; *(*US: *rubbish)* ordures *fpl*.

trash can *n* *(*US*)* boîte *f* à ordures.

trashy ['træʃı] *adj* *(col)* de camelote, qui ne vaut rien.

trauma ['trɔ:mə] *n* traumatisme *m*.

traumatic [trɔ:'mætık] *adj* traumatisant(e).

travel ['trævl] *n* voyage(s) *m(pl)* ♦ *vi* voyager; *(move)* aller, se déplacer ♦ *vt* *(distance)* parcourir; **this wine doesn't** ~ **well** ce vin voyage mal.

travel agency *n* agence *f* de voyages.

travel agent *n* agent *m* de voyages.

travel brochure *n* brochure *f* touristique.

traveller, *(*US*)* **traveler** ['trævlə*] *n* voyageur/euse; *(*COMM*)* représentant *m* de commerce.

traveller's cheque, *(*US*)* **traveler's check** *n* chèque *m* de voyage.

travelling, *(*US*)* **traveling** ['trævlıŋ] *n* voyage(s) *m(pl)* ♦ *adj* *(circus, exhibition)* ambulant(e) ♦ *cpd* *(bag, clock)* de voyage; *(expenses)* de déplacement.

travel(l)ing salesman *n* voyageur *m* de commerce.

travelogue ['trævəlɔg] *n* *(book, talk)* récit *m* de voyage; *(film)* documentaire *m* de voyage.

travel sickness *n* mal *m* de la route *(or* de mer *or* de l'air).

traverse ['trævəs] *vt* traverser.

travesty ['trævəstı] *n* parodie *f*.

trawler ['trɔ:lə*] *n* chalutier *m*.

tray [treı] *n* *(for carrying)* plateau *m*; *(on desk)* corbeille *f*.

treacherous ['trɛtʃərəs] *adj* traître(sse); **road conditions are** ~ l'état des routes est dangereux.

treachery ['trɛtʃərı] *n* traîtrise *f*.

treacle ['tri:kl] *n* mélasse *f*.

tread [trɛd] n pas m; (sound) bruit m de pas; (of tyre) chape f, bande f de roulement ♦ vi (pt trod, pp trodden [trɔd, 'trɔdn]) marcher.
▶**tread on** vt fus marcher sur.
treadle ['trɛdl] n pédale f (de machine).
treas. abbr = treasurer.
treason ['tri:zn] n trahison f.
treasure ['trɛʒə*] n trésor m ♦ vt (value) tenir beaucoup à; (store) conserver précieusement.
treasure hunt n chasse f au trésor.
treasurer ['trɛʒərə*] n trésorier/ière.
treasury ['trɛʒərɪ] n trésorerie f; **the T~**, (US) **the T~ Department** ≈ le ministère des Finances.
treasury bill n bon m du Trésor.
treat [tri:t] n petit cadeau, petite surprise ♦ vt traiter; **it was a ~** ça m'a (or nous a etc) vraiment fait plaisir; **to ~ sb to sth** offrir qch à qn; **to ~ sth as a joke** prendre qch à la plaisanterie.
treatise ['tri:tɪz] n traité m (ouvrage).
treatment ['tri:tmənt] n traitement m; **to have ~ for sth** (MED) suivre un traitement pour qch.
treaty ['tri:tɪ] n traité m.
treble ['trɛbl] adj triple ♦ n (MUS) soprano m ♦ vt, vi tripler.
treble clef n clé f de sol.
tree [tri:] n arbre m.
tree-lined ['tri:laɪnd] adj bordé(e) d'arbres.
treetop ['tri:tɔp] n cime f d'un arbre.
tree trunk n tronc m d'arbre.
trek [trɛk] n voyage m; randonnée f; (tiring walk) tirée f ♦ vi (as holiday) faire de la randonnée.
trellis ['trɛlɪs] n treillis m, treillage m.
tremble ['trɛmbl] vi trembler.
trembling ['trɛmblɪŋ] n tremblement m ♦ adj tremblant(e).
tremendous [trɪ'mɛndəs] adj énorme, formidable; (excellent) fantastique, formidable.
tremendously [trɪ'mɛndəslɪ] adv énormément, extrêmement + adjective; formidablement.
tremor ['trɛmə*] n tremblement m; (also: earth ~) secousse f sismique.
trench [trɛntʃ] n tranchée f.
trench coat n trench-coat m.
trench warfare n guerre f de tranchées.
trend [trɛnd] n (tendency) tendance f; (of events) cours m; (fashion) mode f; **~ towards/away from doing** tendance à faire/à ne pas faire; **to set the ~** donner le ton; **to set a ~** lancer une mode.
trendy ['trɛndɪ] adj (idea) dans le vent; (clothes) dernier cri inv.
trepidation [trɛpɪ'deɪʃən] n vive agitation.
trespass ['trɛspəs] vi: **to ~ on** s'introduire sans permission dans; (fig) empiéter sur; **"no ~ing"** "propriété privée", "défense d'entrer".

trespasser ['trɛspəsə*] n intrus/e; **"~s will be prosecuted"** "interdiction d'entrer sous peine de poursuites".
tress [trɛs] n boucle f de cheveux.
trestle ['trɛsl] n tréteau m.
trestle table n table f à tréteaux.
trial ['traɪəl] n (LAW) procès m, jugement m; (test: of machine etc) essai m; (hardship) épreuve f, (worry) souci m; **~s** npl (SPORT) épreuves éliminatoires; **horse ~s** concours m hippique; **~ by jury** jugement par jury; **to be sent for ~** être traduit(e) en justice; **to be on ~** passer en jugement; **by ~ and error** par tâtonnements.
trial balance n (COMM) balance f de vérification.
trial basis n: **on a ~** pour une période d'essai.
trial run n essai m.
triangle ['traɪæŋgl] n (MATH, MUS) triangle m.
triangular [traɪ'æŋgjulə*] adj triangulaire.
triathlon [traɪ'æθlən] n triathlon m.
tribal ['traɪbl] adj tribal(e).
tribe [traɪb] n tribu f.
tribesman ['traɪbzmən] n membre m de la tribu.
tribulation [trɪbju'leɪʃən] n tribulation f, malheur m.
tribunal [traɪ'bju:nl] n tribunal m.
tributary ['trɪbjutərɪ] n (river) affluent m.
tribute ['trɪbju:t] n tribut m, hommage m; **to pay ~ to** rendre hommage à.
trice [traɪs] n: **in a ~** en un clin d'œil.
trick [trɪk] n ruse f; (clever act) astuce f; (joke) tour m; (CARDS) levée f ♦ vt attraper, rouler; **to play a ~ on sb** jouer un tour à qn; **to ~ sb into doing sth** persuader qn par la ruse de faire qch; **to ~ sb out of sth** obtenir qch de qn par la ruse; **it's a ~ of the light** c'est une illusion d'optique causée par la lumière; **that should do the ~** (col) ça devrait faire l'affaire.
trickery ['trɪkərɪ] n ruse f.
trickle ['trɪkl] n (of water etc) filet m ♦ vi couler en un filet or goutte à goutte; **to ~ in/out** (people) entrer/sortir par petits groupes.
trick question n question-piège f.
trickster ['trɪkstə*] n arnaqueur/euse, filou m.
tricky ['trɪkɪ] adj difficile, délicat(e).
tricycle ['traɪsɪkl] n tricycle m.
trifle ['traɪfl] n bagatelle f; (CULIN) ≈ diplomate m ♦ adv: **a ~ long** un peu long ♦ vi: **to ~ with** traiter à la légère.
trifling ['traɪflɪŋ] adj insignifiant(e).
trigger ['trɪgə*] n (of gun) gâchette f.
▶**trigger off** vt déclencher.
trigonometry [trɪgə'nɔmətrɪ] n trigonométrie f.
trilby ['trɪlbɪ] n (BRIT: also: ~ hat) chapeau mou, feutre m.
trill [trɪl] n (of bird, MUS) trille m.
trilogy ['trɪlədʒɪ] n trilogie f.
trim [trɪm] adj net(te); (house, garden) bien

tenu(e); (*figure*) svelte ♦ *n* (*haircut etc*) légère coupe; (*embellishment*) finitions *fpl*; (*on car*) garnitures *fpl* ♦ *vt* couper légèrement; (*decorate*): **to ~ (with)** décorer (de); (*NAUT: a sail*) gréer; **to keep in (good) ~** maintenir en (bon) état.

trimmings ['trɪmɪŋz] *npl* décorations *fpl*; (*extras: gen CULIN*) garniture *f*.

Trinidad and Tobago ['trɪnɪdæd-] *n* Trinité et Tobago *f*.

Trinity ['trɪnɪtɪ] *n*: **the ~** la Trinité.

trinket ['trɪŋkɪt] *n* bibelot *m*; (*piece of jewellery*) colifichet *m*.

trio ['triːəʊ] *n* trio *m*.

trip [trɪp] *n* voyage *m*; (*excursion*) excursion *f*; (*stumble*) faux pas ♦ *vi* faire un faux pas, trébucher; (*go lightly*) marcher d'un pas léger; **on a ~** en voyage.

►**trip up** *vi* trébucher ♦ *vt* faire un croc-en-jambe à.

tripartite [traɪ'pɑːtaɪt] *adj* triparti(e).

tripe [traɪp] *n* (*CULIN*) tripes *fpl*; (*pej: rubbish*) idioties *fpl*.

triple ['trɪpl] *adj* triple ♦ *adv*: **~ the distance/the speed** trois fois la distance/la vitesse.

triple jump *n* triple saut *m*.

triplets ['trɪplɪts] *npl* triplés/ées.

triplicate ['trɪplɪkət] *n*: **in ~** en trois exemplaires.

tripod ['traɪpɔd] *n* trépied *m*.

Tripoli ['trɪpəlɪ] *n* Tripoli.

tripper ['trɪpə*] *n* (*BRIT*) touriste *m/f*; excursionniste *m/f*.

tripwire ['trɪpwaɪə*] *n* fil *m* de déclenchement.

trite [traɪt] *adj* banal(e).

triumph ['traɪʌmf] *n* triomphe *m* ♦ *vi*: **to ~ (over)** triompher (de).

triumphal [traɪ'ʌmfl] *adj* triomphal(e).

triumphant [traɪ'ʌmfənt] *adj* triomphant(e).

trivia ['trɪvɪə] *npl* futilités *fpl*.

trivial ['trɪvɪəl] *adj* insignifiant(e); (*commonplace*) banal(e).

triviality [trɪvɪ'ælɪtɪ] *n* caractère insignifiant; banalité *f*.

trivialize ['trɪvɪəlaɪz] *vt* rendre banal(e).

trod [trɔd] *pt of* **tread**.

trodden ['trɔdn] *pp of* **tread**.

trolley ['trɔlɪ] *n* chariot *m*.

trolley bus *n* trolleybus *m*.

trollop ['trɔləp] *n* prostituée *f*.

trombone [trɔm'bəʊn] *n* trombone *m*.

troop [truːp] *n* bande *f*, groupe *m* ♦ *vi*: **to ~ in/out** entrer/sortir en groupe; **~ing the colour** (*BRIT: ceremony*) le salut au drapeau.

troop carrier *n* (*plane*) avion *m* de transport de troupes; (*NAUT: also:* **troopship**) transport *m* (*navire*).

trooper ['truːpə*] *n* (*MIL*) soldat *m* de cavalerie; (*US: policeman*) ≈ gendarme *m*.

troops [truːps] *npl* (*MIL*) troupes *fpl*; (: *men*) hommes *mpl*, soldats *mpl*.

troopship ['truːpʃɪp] *n* transport *m* (*navire*).

trophy ['trəʊfɪ] *n* trophée *m*.

tropic ['trɔpɪk] *n* tropique *m*; **in the ~s** sous les tropiques; **T~ of Cancer/Capricorn** tropique du Cancer/Capricorne.

tropical ['trɔpɪkl] *adj* tropical(e).

trot [trɔt] *n* trot *m* ♦ *vi* trotter; **on the ~** (*BRIT: fig*) d'affilée.

►**trot out** *vt* (*excuse, reason*) débiter; (*names, facts*) réciter les uns après les autres.

trouble ['trʌbl] *n* difficulté(s) *f(pl)*, problème(s) *m(pl)*; (*worry*) ennuis *mpl*, soucis *mpl*; (*bother, effort*) peine *f*, (*POL*) conflit(s) *m(pl)*, troubles *mpl*; (*MED*): **stomach etc ~** troubles gastriques *etc* ♦ *vt* déranger, gêner; (*worry*) inquiéter ♦ *vi*: **to ~ to do** prendre la peine de faire; **~s** *npl* (*POL etc*) troubles; **to be in ~** avoir des ennuis; (*ship, climber etc*) être en difficulté; **to have ~ doing sth** avoir du mal à faire qch; **to go to the ~ of doing** se donner le mal de faire; **it's no ~!** je vous en prie!; **please don't ~ yourself** je vous en prie, ne vous dérangez pas!; **the ~ is ...** le problème, c'est que ...; **what's the ~?** qu'est-ce qui ne va pas?

troubled ['trʌbld] *adj* (*person*) inquiet(ète); (*epoch, life*) agité(e).

trouble-free ['trʌblfriː] *adj* sans problèmes *or* ennuis.

troublemaker ['trʌblmeɪkə*] *n* élément perturbateur, fauteur *m* de troubles.

troubleshooter ['trʌblʃuːtə*] *n* (*in conflict*) conciliateur *m*.

troublesome ['trʌblsəm] *adj* ennuyeux(euse), gênant(e).

trouble spot *n* point chaud (*fig*).

troubling ['trʌblɪŋ] *adj* (*times, thought*) inquiétant(e).

trough [trɔf] *n* (*also:* **drinking ~**) abreuvoir *m*; (*also:* **feeding ~**) auge *f*; (*channel*) chenal *m*; **~ of low pressure** (*METEOROLOGY*) dépression *f*.

trounce [traʊns] *vt* (*defeat*) battre à plates coutures.

troupe [truːp] *n* troupe *f*.

trouser press *n* presse-pantalon *m inv*.

trousers ['traʊzəz] *npl* pantalon *m*; **short ~** (*BRIT*) culottes courtes.

trouser suit *n* (*BRIT*) tailleur-pantalon *m*.

trousseau, *pl* **~x** *or* **~s** ['truːsəʊ, -z] *n* trousseau *m*.

trout [traʊt] *n* (*pl inv*) truite *f*.

trowel ['traʊəl] *n* truelle *f*.

truant ['truːənt] *n*: **to play ~** (*BRIT*) faire l'école buissonnière.

truce [truːs] *n* trêve *f*.

truck [trʌk] *n* camion *m*; (*RAIL*) wagon *m* à plate-forme; (*for luggage*) chariot *m* (à bagages).

truck driver *n* camionneur *m*.

trucker ['trʌkə*] *n* (*esp US*) camionneur *m*.

truck farm *n* (*US*) jardin maraîcher.

trucking ['trʌkɪŋ] *n* (*esp US*) transport routier.

trucking company n (*US*) entreprise f de transport (routier).

truck stop (*US*) routier m, restaurant m de routiers.

truculent ['trʌkjulənt] adj agressif(ive).

trudge [trʌdʒ] vi marcher lourdement, se traîner.

true [tru:] adj vrai(e); (*accurate*) exact(e); (*genuine*) vrai, véritable; (*faithful*) fidèle; (*wall*) d'aplomb; (*beam*) droit(e); (*wheel*) dans l'axe; **to come** ~ se réaliser; ~ **to life** réaliste.

truffle ['trʌfl] n truffe f.

truly ['tru:lɪ] adv vraiment, réellement; (*truthfully*) sans mentir; (*faithfully*) fidèlement; **yours** ~ (*in letter*) je vous prie d'agréer, Monsieur (*or* Madame *etc*), l'expression de mes sentiments respectueux.

trump [trʌmp] n atout m; **to turn up** ~s (*fig*) faire des miracles.

trump card n atout m; (*fig*) carte maîtresse f.

trumped-up [trʌmpt'ʌp] adj inventé(e) (de toutes pièces).

trumpet ['trʌmpɪt] n trompette f.

truncated [trʌŋ'keɪtɪd] adj tronqué(e).

truncheon ['trʌntʃən] n bâton m (d'agent de police); matraque f.

trundle ['trʌndl] vt, vi: **to** ~ **along** rouler bruyamment.

trunk [trʌŋk] n (*of tree, person*) tronc m; (*of elephant*) trompe f; (*case*) malle f; (*US AUT*) coffre m.

trunk call n (*BRIT TEL*) communication interurbaine.

trunk road n (*BRIT*) ≈ (route f) nationale f.

trunks [trʌŋks] npl (*also:* **swimming** ~) maillot m or slip m de bain.

truss [trʌs] n (*MED*) bandage m herniaire ♦ vt: **to** ~ **(up)** (*CULIN*) brider.

trust [trʌst] n confiance f; (*LAW*) fidéicommis m; (*COMM*) trust m ♦ vt (*rely on*) avoir confiance en; (*entrust*): **to** ~ **sth to sb** confier qch à qn; (*hope*): **to** ~ **(that)** espérer (que); **to take sth on** ~ accepter qch sans garanties (*or* sans preuves); **in** ~ (*LAW*) par fidéicommis.

trust company n société f fiduciaire.

trusted ['trʌstɪd] adj en qui l'on a confiance.

trustee [trʌs'ti:] n (*LAW*) fidéicommissaire m/f; (*of school etc*) administrateur/trice.

trustful ['trʌstful] adj confiant(e).

trust fund n fonds m en fidéicommis.

trusting ['trʌstɪŋ] adj confiant(e).

trustworthy ['trʌstwə:ðɪ] adj digne de confiance.

trusty ['trʌstɪ] adj fidèle.

truth, ~s [tru:θ, tru:ðz] n vérité f.

truthful ['tru:θful] adj (*person*) qui dit la vérité; (*description*) exact(e), vrai(e).

truthfully ['tru:θfəlɪ] adv sincèrement, sans mentir.

truthfulness ['tru:θfəlnɪs] n véracité f.

try [traɪ] n essai m, tentative f; (*RUGBY*) essai ♦ vt (*LAW*) juger; (*test: sth new*) essayer, tester; (*strain*) éprouver ♦ vi essayer; **to** ~ **to do** essayer de faire; (*seek*) chercher à faire; **to** ~ **one's (very) best** *or* **one's (very) hardest** faire de son mieux; **to give sth a** ~ essayer qch.

▶**try on** vt (*clothes*) essayer; **to** ~ **it on** (*fig*) tenter le coup, bluffer.

▶**try out** vt essayer, mettre à l'essai.

trying ['traɪɪŋ] adj pénible.

tsar [zɑ:*] n tsar m.

T-shirt ['ti:ʃə:t] n tee-shirt m.

T-square ['ti:skwɛə*] n équerre f en T.

TT adj abbr (*BRIT col*) = **teetotal** ♦ abbr (*US*) = *Trust Territory*.

tub [tʌb] n cuve f, baquet m; (*bath*) baignoire f.

tuba ['tju:bə] n tuba m.

tubby ['tʌbɪ] adj rondelet(te).

tube [tju:b] n tube m; (*BRIT: underground*) métro m; (*for tyre*) chambre f à air; (*col: television*): **the** ~ la télé.

tubeless ['tju:blɪs] adj (*tyre*) sans chambre à air.

tuber ['tju:bə*] n (*BOT*) tubercule m.

tuberculosis [tjubə:kju'ləusɪs] n tuberculose f.

tube station n (*BRIT*) station f de métro.

tubing ['tju:bɪŋ] n tubes mpl; **a piece of** ~ un tube.

tubular ['tju:bjulə*] adj tubulaire.

TUC n abbr (*BRIT*: = *Trades Union Congress*) confédération f des syndicats britanniques.

tuck [tʌk] n (*SEWING*) pli m, rempli m ♦ vt (*put*) mettre.

▶**tuck away** vt cacher, ranger.

▶**tuck in** vt rentrer; (*child*) border ♦ vi (*eat*) manger de bon appétit; attaquer le repas.

▶**tuck up** vt (*child*) border.

tuck shop n (*BRIT SCOL*) boutique f à provisions.

Tue(s). abbr (= *Tuesday*) ma.

Tuesday ['tju:zdɪ] n mardi m; **(the date) today is** ~ **23rd March** nous sommes aujourd'hui le mardi 23 mars; **on** ~ mardi; **on** ~s le mardi; **every** ~ tous les mardis, chaque mardi; **every other** ~ un mardi sur deux; **last/next** ~ mardi dernier/prochain; ~ **next** mardi qui vient; **the following** ~ le mardi suivant; **a week/fortnight on** ~, ~ **week/fortnight** mardi en huit/quinze; **the** ~ **before last** l'autre mardi; **the** ~ **after next** mardi en huit; ~ **morning/lunchtime/afternoon/evening** mardi matin/midi/après-midi/soir; ~ **night** mardi soir; (*overnight*) la nuit de mardi (à mercredi); ~**'s newspaper** le journal de mardi.

tuft [tʌft] n touffe f.

tug [tʌg] n (*ship*) remorqueur m ♦ vt tirer (sur).

tug-of-love [tʌgəv'lʌv] n lutte acharnée entre parents divorcés pour avoir la garde d'un enfant.

tug-of-war [tʌgəv'wɔ:*] n lutte f à la corde.
tuition [tju:'ɪʃən] n (BRIT: lessons) leçons fpl; (US: fees) frais mpl de scolarité.
tulip ['tju:lɪp] n tulipe f.
tumble ['tʌmbl] n (fall) chute f, culbute f ♦ vi tomber, dégringoler; (somersault) faire une or des culbute(s) ♦ vt renverser, faire tomber; **to ~ to sth** (col) réaliser qch.
tumbledown ['tʌmbldaun] adj délabré(e).
tumble dryer n (BRIT) séchoir m (à linge) à air chaud.
tumbler ['tʌmblə*] n verre (droit), gobelet m.
tummy ['tʌmɪ] n (col) ventre m.
tumour, (US) **tumor** ['tju:mə*] n tumeur f.
tumult ['tju:mʌlt] n tumulte m.
tumultuous [tju:'mʌltjuəs] adj tumultueux(euse).
tuna ['tju:nə] n (pl inv) (also: ~ **fish**) thon m.
tune [tju:n] n (melody) air m ♦ vt (MUS) accorder; (RADIO, TV, AUT) régler, mettre au point; **to be in/out of ~** (instrument) être accordé/désaccordé; (singer) chanter juste/faux; **to be in/out of ~ with** (fig) être en accord/désaccord avec; **she was robbed to the ~ of £10,000** (fig) on lui a volé la jolie somme de 10 000 livres.
▶**tune in** vi (RADIO, TV): **to ~ in (to)** se mettre à l'écoute (de).
▶**tune up** vi (musician) accorder son instrument.
tuneful ['tju:nful] adj mélodieux(euse).
tuner ['tju:nə*] n (radio set) radio-préamplificateur m; **piano ~** accordeur m de pianos.
tuner amplifier n radio-ampli m.
tungsten ['tʌŋstn] n tungstène m.
tunic ['tju:nɪk] n tunique f.
tuning ['tju:nɪŋ] n réglage m.
tuning fork n diapason m.
Tunis ['tju:nɪs] n Tunis.
Tunisia [tju:'nɪzɪə] n Tunisie f.
Tunisian [tju:'nɪzɪən] adj tunisien(ne) ♦ n Tunisien/ne.
tunnel ['tʌnl] n tunnel m; (in mine) galerie f ♦ vi creuser un tunnel (or une galerie).
tunnel vision n (MED) rétrécissement m du champ visuel; (fig) vision étroite des choses.
tunny ['tʌnɪ] n thon m.
turban ['tə:bən] n turban m.
turbid ['tə:bɪd] adj trouble(euse).
turbine ['tə:baɪn] n turbine f.
turbo ['tə:bəu] n turbo m.
turbojet [tə:bəu'dʒet] n turboréacteur m.
turboprop [tə:bəu'prɔp] n (engine) turbopropulseur m.
turbot ['tə:bət] n (pl inv) turbot m.
turbulence ['tə:bjuləns] n (AVIAT) turbulence f.
turbulent ['tə:bjulənt] adj turbulent(e); (sea) agité(e).
tureen [tə'ri:n] n soupière f.

turf [tə:f] n gazon m; (clod) motte f (de gazon) ♦ vt gazonner; **the T~** le turf, les courses fpl.
▶**turf out** vt (col) jeter; jeter dehors.
turf accountant n (BRIT) bookmaker m.
turgid ['tə:dʒɪd] adj (speech) pompeux(euse).
Turin [tjuə'rɪn] n Turin.
Turk [tə:k] n Turc/Turque.
Turkey ['tə:kɪ] n Turquie f.
turkey ['tə:kɪ] n dindon m, dinde f.
Turkish ['tə:kɪʃ] adj turc(turque) ♦ n (LING) turc m.
Turkish bath n bain turc.
Turkish delight n loukoum m.
turmeric ['tə:mərɪk] n curcuma m.
turmoil ['tə:mɔɪl] n trouble m, bouleversement m.
turn [tə:n] n tour m; (in road) tournant m; (tendency: of mind, events) tournure f; (performance) numéro m; (MED) crise f, attaque f ♦ vt tourner; (collar, steak) retourner; (milk) faire tourner; (change): **to ~ sth into** changer qch en; (shape: wood, metal) tourner ♦ vi tourner; (person: look back) se (re)tourner; (reverse direction) faire demi-tour; (change) changer; (become) devenir; **to ~ into** se changer en, se transformer en; **a good ~** un service; **a bad ~** un mauvais tour; **it gave me quite a ~** ça m'a fait un coup; **"no left ~"** (AUT) "défense de tourner à gauche"; **it's your ~** c'est (à) votre tour; **in ~** à son tour; à tour de rôle; **to take ~s** se relayer; **to take ~s at** faire à tour de rôle; **at the ~ of the year/ century** à la fin de l'année/du siècle; **to take a ~ for the worse** (situation, events) empirer; **his health or he has taken a ~ for the worse** son état s'est aggravé.
▶**turn about** vi faire demi-tour; faire un demi-tour.
▶**turn away** vi se détourner, tourner la tête ♦ vt (reject: person) renvoyer; (: business) refuser.
▶**turn back** vi revenir, faire demi-tour.
▶**turn down** vt (refuse) rejeter, refuser; (reduce) baisser; (fold) rabattre.
▶**turn in** vi (col: go to bed) aller se coucher ♦ vt (fold) rentrer.
▶**turn off** vi (from road) tourner ♦ vt (light, radio etc) éteindre; (engine) arrêter.
▶**turn on** vt (light, radio etc) allumer; (engine) mettre en marche.
▶**turn out** vt (light, gas) éteindre; (produce: goods, novel, good pupils) produire ♦ vi (appear, attend: troops, doctor etc) être présent(e); **to ~ out to be ...** s'avérer ..., se révéler ...
▶**turn over** vi (person) se retourner ♦ vt (object) retourner; (page) tourner.
▶**turn round** vi faire demi-tour; (rotate) tourner.
▶**turn up** vi (person) arriver, se pointer; (lost object) être retrouvé(e) ♦ vt (collar) remonter; (increase: sound, volume etc) mettre plus

fort.

turnabout ['tə:nəbaut], **turnaround** ['tə:nəraund] *n* volte-face *f inv*.

turncoat ['tə:nkəut] *n* rénégat/e.

turned-up ['tə:ndʌp] *adj* (*nose*) retroussé(e).

turning ['tə:nɪŋ] *n* (*in road*) tournant *m*; **the first** ~ **on the right** la première (rue *or* route) à droite.

turning circle *n* (*BRIT*) rayon *m* de braquage.

turning point *n* (*fig*) tournant *m*, moment décisif.

turning radius *n* (*US*) = turning circle.

turnip ['tə:nɪp] *n* navet *m*.

turnout ['tə:naut] *n* (nombre *m* de personnes dans l')assistance *f*.

turnover ['tə:nəuvə*] *n* (*COMM: amount of money*) chiffre *m* d'affaires; (: *of goods*) roulement *m*; (*CULIN*) sorte de chausson; **there is a rapid** ~ **in staff** le personnel change souvent.

turnpike ['tə:npaɪk] *n* (*US*) autoroute *f* à péage.

turnstile ['tə:nstaɪl] *n* tourniquet *m* (*d'entrée*).

turntable ['tə:nteɪbl] *n* (*on record player*) platine *f*.

turn-up ['tə:nʌp] *n* (*BRIT: on trousers*) revers *m*.

turpentine ['tə:pəntaɪn] *n* (*also:* **turps**) (essence *f* de) térébenthine *f*.

turquoise ['tə:kwɔɪz] *n* (*stone*) turquoise *f* ♦ *adj* turquoise *inv*.

turret ['tʌrɪt] *n* tourelle *f*.

turtle ['tə:tl] *n* tortue marine.

turtleneck (sweater) ['tə:tlnɛk-] *n* pullover *m* à col montant.

Tuscany ['tʌskənɪ] *n* Toscane *f*.

tusk [tʌsk] *n* défense *f* (*d'éléphant*).

tussle ['tʌsl] *n* bagarre *f*, mêlée *f*.

tutor ['tju:tə*] *n* (*BRIT SCOL*) directeur/trice d'études; (*private teacher*) précepteur/trice.

tutorial [tju:'tɔ:rɪəl] *n* (*SCOL*) (séance *f* de) travaux *mpl* pratiques.

tuxedo [tʌk'si:dəu] *n* (*US*) smoking *m*.

TV [ti:'vi:] *n abbr* (= television) télé *f*, TV *f*.

TV dinner *n* plateau-repas surgelé.

twaddle ['twɔdl] *n* balivernes *fpl*.

twang [twæŋ] *n* (*of instrument*) son vibrant; (*of voice*) ton nasillard ♦ *vi* vibrer ♦ *vt* (*guitar*) pincer les cordes de.

tweak [twi:k] *vt* (*nose*) tordre; (*ear, hair*) tirer.

tweed [twi:d] *n* tweed *m*.

tweezers ['twi:zəz] *npl* pince *f* à épiler.

twelfth [twɛlfθ] *num* douzième.

Twelfth Night *n* la fête des Rois.

twelve [twɛlv] *num* douze; **at** ~ **(o'clock)** à midi; (*midnight*) à minuit.

twentieth ['twɛntɪɪθ] *num* vingtième.

twenty ['twɛntɪ] *num* vingt.

twerp [twə:p] *n* (*col*) imbécile *m/f*.

twice [twaɪs] *adv* deux fois; ~ **as much** deux fois plus; ~ **a week** deux fois par semaine; **she is** ~ **your age** elle a deux fois ton âge.

twiddle ['twɪdl] *vt, vi*: **to** ~ **(with)** sth tripoter

qch; **to** ~ **one's thumbs** (*fig*) se tourner les pouces.

twig [twɪg] *n* brindille *f* ♦ *vt, vi* (*col*) piger.

twilight ['twaɪlaɪt] *n* crépuscule *m*; (*morning*) aube *f*; **in the** ~ dans la pénombre.

twill [twɪl] *n* sergé *m*.

twin [twɪn] *adj, n* jumeau(elle) ♦ *vt* jumeler.

twin(-bedded) room ['twɪn('bɛdɪd)-] *n* chambre *f* à deux lits.

twin beds *npl* lits *mpl* jumeaux.

twin-carburettor ['twɪnka:bju'rɛtə*] *adj* à double carburateur.

twine [twaɪn] *n* ficelle *f* ♦ *vi* (*plant*) s'enrouler.

twin-engined [twɪn'ɛndʒɪnd] *adj* bimoteur; ~ **aircraft** bimoteur *m*.

twinge [twɪndʒ] *n* (*of pain*) élancement *m*; (*of conscience*) remords *m*.

twinkle ['twɪŋkl] *n* scintillement *m*; pétillement *m* ♦ *vi* scintiller; (*eyes*) pétiller.

twin town *n* ville jumelée.

twirl [twə:l] *n* tournoiement *m* ♦ *vt* faire tournoyer ♦ *vi* tournoyer.

twist [twɪst] *n* torsion *f*, tour *m*; (*in wire, flex*) tortillon *m*; (*bend: in road*) tournant *m*; (*in story*) coup *m* de théâtre ♦ *vt* tordre; (*weave*) entortiller; (*roll around*) enrouler; (*fig*) déformer ♦ *vi* s'entortiller; s'enrouler; (*road*) serpenter; **to** ~ **one's ankle/wrist** (*MED*) se tordre la cheville/le poignet.

twisted ['twɪstɪd] *adj* (*wire, rope*) entortillé(e); (*ankle, wrist*) tordu(e), foulé(e); (*fig: logic, mind*) tordu.

twit [twɪt] *n* (*col*) crétin/e.

twitch [twɪtʃ] *n* saccade *f*; (*nervous*) tic *m* ♦ *vi* se convulser; avoir un tic.

two [tu:] *num* deux; ~ **by** ~, **in** ~**s** par deux; **to put** ~ **and** ~ **together** (*fig*) faire le rapport.

two-bit [tu:'bɪt] *adj* (*esp US col, pej*) de pacotille.

two-door [tu:'dɔ:*] *adj* (*AUT*) à deux portes.

two-faced [tu:'feɪst] *adj* (*pej: person*) faux(fausse).

twofold ['tu:fəuld] *adv*: **to increase** ~ doubler ♦ *adj* (*increase*) de cent pour cent; (*reply*) en deux parties.

two-piece ['tu:'pi:s] *n* (*also:* ~ **suit**) (costume *m*) deux-pièces *m inv*; (*also:* ~ **swimsuit**) (maillot *m* de bain) deux-pièces.

two-seater [tu:'si:tə*] *n* (*plane*) (avion *m*) biplace *m*; (*car*) voiture *f* à deux places.

twosome ['tu:səm] *n* (*people*) couple *m*.

two-stroke ['tu:strəuk] *n* (*also:* ~ **engine**) moteur *m* à deux temps ♦ *adj* à deux temps.

two-tone ['tu:'təun] *adj* (*in colour*) à deux tons.

two-way ['tu:weɪ] *adj* (*traffic*) dans les deux sens; ~ **radio** émetteur-récepteur *m*.

TX *abbr* (*US*) = Texas.

tycoon [taɪ'ku:n] *n*: **(business)** ~ gros homme d'affaires.

type [taɪp] *n* (*category*) genre *m*, espèce *f*; (*model*) modèle *m*; (*example*) type *m*; (*TYP*) type, caractère *m* ♦ *vt* (*letter etc*) taper (à la machine); **what ~ do you want?** quel genre voulez-vous?; **in bold/italic ~** en caractères gras/en italiques.

typecast ['taɪpkɑːst] *adj* condamné(e) à toujours jouer le même rôle.

typeface ['taɪpfeɪs] *n* police *f* (de caractères).

typescript ['taɪpskrɪpt] *n* texte dactylographié.

typeset ['taɪpsɛt] *vt* composer (*en imprimerie*).

typesetter ['taɪpsɛtə*] *n* compositeur *m*.

typewriter ['taɪpraɪtə*] *n* machine *f* à écrire.

typewritten ['taɪprɪtn] *adj* dactylographié(e).

typhoid ['taɪfɔɪd] *n* typhoïde *f*.

typhoon [taɪ'fuːn] *n* typhon *m*.

typhus ['taɪfəs] *n* typhus *m*.

typical ['tɪpɪkl] *adj* typique, caractéristique.

typify ['tɪpɪfaɪ] *vt* être caractéristique de.

typing ['taɪpɪŋ] *n* dactylo(graphie) *f*.

typing error *n* faute *f* de frappe.

typing pool *n* pool *m* de dactylos.

typist ['taɪpɪst] *n* dactylo *m/f*.

typo ['taɪpəu] *n abbr* (*col*: = *typographical error*) coquille *f*.

typography [taɪ'pɔgrəfɪ] *n* typographie *f*.

tyranny ['tɪrənɪ] *n* tyrannie *f*.

tyrant ['taɪərnt] *n* tyran *m*.

tyre, (*US*) **tire** ['taɪə*] *n* pneu *m*.

tyre pressure *n* pression *f* (de gonflage).

Tyrol [tɪ'rəul] *n* Tyrol *m*.

Tyrolean [tɪrə'liːən], **Tyrolese** [tɪrə'liːz] *adj* tyrolien(ne) ♦ *n* Tyrolien/ne.

Tyrrhenian Sea [tɪ'riːnɪən-] *n*: **the ~** la mer Tyrrhénienne.

tzar [zɑː*] *n* = **tsar**.

U u

U, u [juː] *n* (*letter*) U, u *m*; **U for Uncle** U comme Ursule.

U *n abbr* (*BRIT CINE*: = *universal*) ≈ tous publics.

UAW *n abbr* (*US*: = *United Automobile Workers*) syndicat des ouvriers de l'automobile.

UB40 *n abbr* (*BRIT*: = *unemployment benefit form 40*) numéro de référence d'un formulaire d'inscription au chômage: par extension, le bénéficiaire.

U-bend ['juːbɛnd] *n* (*BRIT AUT*) coude *m*, virage *m* en épingle à cheveux; (*in pipe*) coude.

ubiquitous [juː'bɪkwɪtəs] *adj* doué(e) d'ubiquité, omniprésent(e).

UCAS ['juːkæs] *n abbr* (*BRIT*) = *Universities and Colleges Admissions Service*.

UDA *n abbr* (*BRIT*) = *Ulster Defence Association*.

UDC *n abbr* (*BRIT*) = *Urban District Council*.

udder ['ʌdə*] *n* pis *m*, mamelle *f*.

UDI *n abbr* (*BRIT POL*) = *unilateral declaration of independence*.

UDR *n abbr* (*BRIT*) = *Ulster Defence Regiment*.

UEFA [juː'eɪfə] *n abbr* (= *Union of European Football Associations*) UEFA *f*.

UFO ['juːfəu] *n abbr* (= *unidentified flying object*) ovni *m* (= *objet volant non identifié*).

Uganda [juː'gændə] *n* Ouganda *m*.

Ugandan [juː'gændən] *adj* ougandais(e) ♦ *n* Ougandais/e.

UGC *n abbr* (*BRIT*: = *University Grants Committee*) commission d'attribution des dotations aux universités.

ugh [əːh] *excl* pouah!

ugliness ['ʌglɪnɪs] *n* laideur *f*.

ugly ['ʌglɪ] *adj* laid(e), vilain(e); (*fig*) répugnant(e).

UHF *abbr* (= *ultra-high frequency*) UHF.

UHT *adj abbr* (= *ultra-heat treated*): **~ milk** lait *m* UHT *or* longue conservation.

UK *n abbr* = *United Kingdom*.

Ukraine [juː'kreɪn] *n* Ukraine *f*.

Ukrainian [juː'kreɪnɪən] *adj* ukrainien(ne) ♦ *n* Ukrainien/ne; (*LING*) ukrainien *m*.

ulcer ['ʌlsə*] *n* ulcère *m*; **mouth ~** aphte *f*.

Ulster ['ʌlstə*] *n* Ulster *m*.

ulterior [ʌl'tɪərɪə*] *adj* ultérieur(e); **~ motive** arrière-pensée *f*.

ultimate ['ʌltɪmət] *adj* ultime, final(e); (*authority*) suprême ♦ *n*: **the ~ in luxury** le summum du luxe.

ultimately ['ʌltɪmətlɪ] *adv* (*in the end*) en fin de compte; (*at last*) finalement; (*eventually*) par la suite.

ultimatum, *pl* **~s** *or* **ultimata** [ʌltɪ'meɪtəm, -tə] *n* ultimatum *m*.

ultrasonic [ʌltrə'sɔnɪk] *adj* ultrasonique.

ultrasound ['ʌltrəsaund] *n* (*MED*) ultrason *m*.

ultraviolet ['ʌltrə'vaɪəlɪt] *adj* ultraviolet(te).

umbilical [ʌmbɪ'laɪkl] *adj*: **~ cord** cordon ombilical.

umbrage ['ʌmbrɪdʒ] *n*: **to take ~** prendre ombrage, se froisser.

umbrella [ʌm'brɛlə] *n* parapluie *m*; (*fig*): **under the ~ of** sous les auspices de; chapeauté(e) par.

umlaut ['umlaut] *n* tréma *m*.

umpire ['ʌmpaɪə*] *n* arbitre *m*; (*TENNIS*) juge *m* de chaise ♦ *vt* arbitrer.

umpteen [ʌmp'tiːn] *adj* je ne sais combien de; **for the ~th time** pour la nième fois.

UMW *n abbr* (= *United Mineworkers of America*) syndicat des mineurs.

UN *n abbr* = *United Nations*.

unabashed [ʌnə'bæʃt] *adj* nullement intimidé(e).

unabated [ʌnə'beɪtɪd] *adj* non diminué(e).

unable [ʌn'eɪbl] *adj*: **to be ~ to** ne (pas) pouvoir, être dans l'impossibilité de; (*not capable*) être incapable de.

unabridged [ʌnə'brɪdʒd] *adj* complet(ète), intégral(e).

unacceptable [ʌnək'sɛptəbl] *adj* (*behaviour*) inadmissible; (*price, proposal*) inacceptable.

unaccompanied [ʌnə'kʌmpənɪd] *adj* (*child, lady*) non accompagné(e); (*singing, song*) sans accompagnement.

unaccountably [ʌnə'kauntəblɪ] *adv* inexplicablement.

unaccounted [ʌnə'kauntɪd] *adj*: **two passengers are ~ for** on est sans nouvelles de deux passagers.

unaccustomed [ʌnə'kʌstəmd] *adj* inaccoutumé(e), inhabituel(le); **to be ~ to sth** ne pas avoir l'habitude de qch.

unacquainted [ʌnə'kweɪntɪd] *adj*: **to be ~ with** ne pas connaître.

unadulterated [ʌnə'dʌltəreɪtɪd] *adj* pur(e), naturel(le).

unaffected [ʌnə'fɛktɪd] *adj* (*person, behaviour*) naturel(le); (*emotionally*): **to be ~ by** ne pas être touché(e) par.

unafraid [ʌnə'freɪd] *adj*: **to be ~** ne pas avoir peur.

unaided [ʌn'eɪdɪd] *adj* sans aide, tout(e) seul(e).

unanimity [juːnə'nɪmɪtɪ] *n* unanimité *f*.

unanimous [juː'nænɪməs] *adj* unanime.

unanimously [juː'nænɪməslɪ] *adv* à l'unanimité.

unanswered [ʌn'ɑːnsəd] *adj* (*question, letter*) sans réponse.

unappetizing [ʌn'æpɪtaɪzɪŋ] *adj* peu appétissant(e).

unappreciative [ʌnə'priːʃɪətɪv] *adj* indifférent(e).

unarmed [ʌn'ɑːmd] *adj* (*person*) non armé(e); (*combat*) sans armes.

unashamed [ʌnə'ʃeɪmd] *adj* sans honte; impudent(e).

unassisted [ʌnə'sɪstɪd] *adj* non assisté(e) ♦ *adv* sans aide, tout(e) seul(e).

unassuming [ʌnə'sjuːmɪŋ] *adj* modeste, sans prétentions.

unattached [ʌnə'tætʃt] *adj* libre, sans attaches.

unattended [ʌnə'tɛndɪd] *adj* (*car, child, luggage*) sans surveillance.

unattractive [ʌnə'træktɪv] *adj* peu attrayant(e).

unauthorized [ʌn'ɔːθəraɪzd] *adj* non autorisé(e), sans autorisation.

unavailable [ʌnə'veɪləbl] *adj* (*article, room, book*) (qui n'est) pas disponible; (*person*) (qui n'est) pas libre.

unavoidable [ʌnə'vɔɪdəbl] *adj* inévitable.

unavoidably [ʌnə'vɔɪdəblɪ] *adv* inévitablement.

unaware [ʌnə'wɛə*] *adj*: **to be ~ of** ignorer, ne pas savoir, être inconscient(e) de.

unawares [ʌnə'wɛəz] *adv* à l'improviste, au dépourvu.

unbalanced [ʌn'bælənst] *adj* déséquilibré(e).

unbearable [ʌn'bɛərəbl] *adj* insupportable.

unbeatable [ʌn'biːtəbl] *adj* imbattable.

unbeaten [ʌn'biːtn] *adj* invaincu(e); (*record*) non battu(e).

unbecoming [ʌnbɪ'kʌmɪŋ] *adj* (*unseemly: language, behaviour*) malséant(e), inconvenant(e); (*unflattering: garment*) peu seyant(e).

unbeknown(st) [ʌnbɪ'nəun(st)] *adv*: **~ to** à l'insu de.

unbelief [ʌnbɪ'liːf] *n* incrédulité *f*.

unbelievable [ʌnbɪ'liːvəbl] *adj* incroyable.

unbelievingly [ʌnbɪ'liːvɪŋlɪ] *adv* avec incrédulité.

unbend [ʌn'bɛnd] *vb* (*irreg*) *vi* se détendre ♦ *vt* (*wire*) redresser, détordre.

unbending [ʌn'bɛndɪŋ] *adj* (*fig*) inflexible.

unbias(s)ed [ʌn'baɪəst] *adj* impartial(e).

unblemished [ʌn'blɛmɪʃt] *adj* impeccable.

unblock [ʌn'blɔk] *vt* (*pipe*) déboucher; (*road*) dégager.

unborn [ʌn'bɔːn] *adj* à naître.

unbounded [ʌn'baundɪd] *adj* sans bornes, illimité(e).

unbreakable [ʌn'breɪkəbl] *adj* incassable.

unbridled [ʌn'braɪdld] *adj* débridé(e), déchaîné(e).

unbroken [ʌn'brəukn] *adj* intact(e); (*line*) continu(e); (*record*) non battu(e).

unbuckle [ʌn'bʌkl] *vt* déboucler.

unburden [ʌn'bɔːdn] *vt*: **to ~ o.s.** s'épancher, se livrer.

unbutton [ʌn'bʌtn] *vt* déboutonner.

uncalled-for [ʌn'kɔːldfɔː*] *adj* déplacé(e), injustifié(e).

uncanny [ʌn'kænɪ] *adj* étrange, troublant(e).

unceasing [ʌn'siːsɪŋ] *adj* incessant(e), continu(e).

unceremonious [ʌnsɛrɪ'məunɪəs] *adj* (*abrupt, rude*) brusque.

uncertain [ʌn'sɔːtn] *adj* incertain(e); **we were ~ whether ...** nous ne savions pas vraiment si ...; **in no ~ terms** sans équivoque possible.

uncertainty [ʌn'sɔːtntɪ] *n* incertitude *f*, doutes *mpl*.

unchallenged [ʌn'tʃælɪndʒd] *adj* (*gen*) incontesté(e); (*information*) non contesté(e); **to go ~** ne pas être contesté.

unchanged [ʌn'tʃeɪndʒd] *adj* inchangé(e).

uncharitable [ʌn'tʃærɪtəbl] *adj* peu charitable.

uncharted [ʌn'tʃɑːtɪd] *adj* inexploré(e).

unchecked [ʌn'tʃɛkt] *adj* non réprimé(e).

uncivilized [ʌn'sɪvɪlaɪzd] *adj* non civilisé(e); (*fig*) barbare.

uncle ['ʌŋkl] *n* oncle *m*.

unclear [ʌn'klɪə*] *adj* (qui n'est) pas clair(e) or évident(e); **I'm still ~ about what I'm supposed to do** je ne sais pas encore exactement ce que je dois faire.

uncoil [ʌn'kɔɪl] *vt* dérouler ♦ *vi* se dérouler.

uncomfortable [ʌn'kʌmfətəbl] *adj* inconfortable; (*uneasy*) mal à l'aise, gêné(e); (*situation*) désagréable.

uncomfortably [ʌn'kʌmfətəblɪ] adv inconfortablement; d'un ton etc gêné or embarrassé; désagréablement.

uncommitted [ʌnkə'mɪtɪd] adj (attitude, country) non engagé(e).

uncommon [ʌn'kɔmən] adj rare, singulier(ière), peu commun(e).

uncommunicative [ʌnkə'mjuːnɪkətɪv] adj réservé(e).

uncomplicated [ʌn'kɔmplɪkeɪtɪd] adj simple, peu compliqué(e).

uncompromising [ʌn'kɔmprəmaɪzɪŋ] adj intransigeant(e), inflexible.

unconcerned [ʌnkən'səːnd] adj (unworried): **to be ~ (about)** ne pas s'inquiéter (de).

unconditional [ʌnkən'dɪʃənl] adj sans conditions.

uncongenial [ʌnkən'dʒiːnɪəl] adj peu agréable.

unconnected [ʌnkə'nɛktɪd] adj (unrelated): ~ **(with)** sans rapport (avec).

unconscious [ʌn'kɔnʃəs] adj sans connaissance, évanoui(e); (unaware) inconscient(e) ♦ n: **the ~** l'inconscient m; **to knock sb ~** assommer qn.

unconsciously [ʌn'kɔnʃəslɪ] adv inconsciemment.

unconstitutional [ʌnkɔnstɪ'tjuːʃənl] adj anticonstitutionnel(le).

uncontested [ʌnkən'tɛstɪd] adj (champion) incontesté(e); (POL: seat) non disputé(e).

uncontrollable [ʌnkən'trəuləbl] adj (child, dog) indiscipliné(e); (emotion) irrépressible.

uncontrolled [ʌnkən'trəuld] adj (laughter, price rises) incontrôlé(e).

unconventional [ʌnkən'vɛnʃənl] adj non conventionnel(le).

unconvinced [ʌnkən'vɪnst] adj: **to be ~** ne pas être convaincu(e).

unconvincing [ʌnkən'vɪnsɪŋ] adj peu convaincant(e).

uncork [ʌn'kɔːk] vt déboucher.

uncorroborated [ʌnkə'rɔbəreɪtɪd] adj non confirmé(e).

uncouth [ʌn'kuːθ] adj grossier(ière), fruste.

uncover [ʌn'kʌvə*] vt découvrir.

unctuous ['ʌŋktjuəs] adj onctueux(euse), mielleux(euse).

undamaged [ʌn'dæmɪdʒd] adj (goods) intact(e), en bon état; (fig: reputation) intact.

undaunted [ʌn'dɔːntɪd] adj non intimidé(e), inébranlable.

undecided [ʌndɪ'saɪdɪd] adj indécis(e), irrésolu(e).

undelivered [ʌndɪ'lɪvəd] adj non remis(e), non livré(e).

undeniable [ʌndɪ'naɪəbl] adj indéniable, incontestable.

under ['ʌndə*] prep sous; (less than) (de) moins de; au-dessous de; (according to) selon, en vertu de ♦ adv au-dessous; en dessous; **from ~ sth** de dessous or de sous qch; **~ there** là-dessous; **in ~ 2 hours** en moins de 2 heures; **~ anaesthetic** sous anesthésie; **~ discussion** en discussion; **~ the circumstances** étant donné les circonstances; **~ repair** en (cours de) réparation.

under... ['ʌndə*] prefix sous-.

under-age [ʌndər'eɪdʒ] adj qui n'a pas l'âge réglementaire.

underarm ['ʌndərɑːm] adv par en-dessous ♦ adj (throw) par en-dessous; (deodorant) pour les aisselles.

undercapitalized [ʌndə'kæpɪtəlaɪzd] adj souscapitalisé(e).

undercarriage ['ʌndəkærɪdʒ] n (BRIT AVIAT) train m d'atterrissage.

undercharge [ʌndə'tʃɑːdʒ] vt ne pas faire payer assez à.

underclass ['ʌndəklɑːs] n ≈ quart-monde m.

underclothes ['ʌndəkləuðz] npl sousvêtements mpl; (women's only) dessous mpl.

undercoat ['ʌndəkəut] n (paint) couche f de fond.

undercover [ʌndə'kʌvə*] adj secret(ète), clandestin(e).

undercurrent ['ʌndəkʌrnt] n courant sousjacent.

undercut [ʌndə'kʌt] vt irreg vendre moins cher que.

underdeveloped ['ʌndədɪ'vɛləpt] adj sousdéveloppé(e).

underdog ['ʌndədɔg] n opprimé m.

underdone [ʌndə'dʌn] adj (food) pas assez cuit(e).

underemployment [ʌndərɪm'plɔɪmənt] n sous-emploi m.

underestimate ['ʌndər'ɛstɪmeɪt] vt sousestimer, mésestimer.

underexposed ['ʌndərɪks'pəuzd] adj (PHOT) sous-exposé(e).

underfed [ʌndə'fɛd] adj sous-alimenté(e).

underfoot [ʌndə'fut] adv sous les pieds.

under-funded ['ʌndə'fʌndɪd] adj: **to be ~** (organization) ne pas être doté(e) de fonds suffisants.

undergo [ʌndə'gəu] vt irreg subir; (treatment) suivre; **the car is ~ing repairs** la voiture est en réparation.

undergraduate [ʌndə'grædjuɪt] n étudiant/e (qui prépare la licence) ♦ cpd: ~ **courses** cours mpl préparant à la licence.

underground ['ʌndəgraund] adj souterrain(e); (fig) clandestin(e) ♦ n (BRIT) métro m; (POL) clandestinité f.

undergrowth ['ʌndəgrəuθ] n broussailles fpl, sous-bois m.

underhand(ed) [ʌndə'hænd(ɪd)] adj (fig) sournois(e), en dessous.

underinsured [ʌndərɪn'ʃuəd] adj sousassuré(e).

underlie [ʌndə'laɪ] vt irreg être à la base de; **the underlying cause** la cause sous-jacente.

underline [ʌndə'laɪn] vt souligner.

underling [ˈʌndəlɪŋ] n (pej) sous-fifre m, subalterne m.

undermanning [ʌndəˈmænɪŋ] n pénurie f de main-d'œuvre.

undermentioned [ʌndəˈmɛnʃənd] adj mentionné(e) ci-dessous.

undermine [ʌndəˈmaɪn] vt saper, miner.

underneath [ʌndəˈniːθ] adv (en) dessous ♦ prep sous, au-dessous de.

undernourished [ʌndəˈnʌrɪʃt] adj sous-alimenté(e).

underpaid [ʌndəˈpeɪd] adj sous-payé(e).

underpants [ˈʌndəpænts] npl caleçon m, slip m.

underpass [ˈʌndəpɑːs] n (BRIT) passage souterrain; (: on motorway) passage inférieur.

underpin [ʌndəˈpɪn] vt (argument, case) étayer.

underplay [ʌndəˈpleɪ] vt (BRIT) minimiser.

underpopulated [ʌndəˈpɔpjuleɪtɪd] adj sous-peuplé(e).

underprice [ʌndəˈpraɪs] vt vendre à un prix trop bas.

underprivileged [ʌndəˈprɪvɪlɪdʒd] adj défavorisé(e), déshérité(e).

underrate [ʌndəˈreɪt] vt sous-estimer, mésestimer.

underscore [ʌndəˈskɔː*] vt souligner.

underseal [ʌndəˈsiːl] vt (BRIT) traiter contre la rouille.

undersecretary [ˈʌndəˈsɛkrətrɪ] n sous-secrétaire m.

undersell [ʌndəˈsɛl] vt (competitors) vendre moins cher que.

undershirt [ˈʌndəʃəːt] n (US) tricot m de corps.

undershorts [ˈʌndəʃɔːts] npl (US) caleçon m, slip m.

underside [ˈʌndəsaɪd] n dessous m.

undersigned [ˈʌndəˈsaɪnd] adj, n soussigné(e) (m/f).

underskirt [ˈʌndəskəːt] n (BRIT) jupon m.

understaffed [ʌndəˈstɑːft] adj qui manque de personnel.

understand [ʌndəˈstænd] vb (irreg: like stand) vt, vi comprendre; I ~ that ... je me suis laissé dire que ...; je crois comprendre que ...; to make o.s. understood se faire comprendre.

understandable [ʌndəˈstændəbl] adj compréhensible.

understanding [ʌndəˈstændɪŋ] adj compréhensif(ive) ♦ n compréhension f; (agreement) accord m; to come to an ~ with sb s'entendre avec qn; on the ~ that ... à condition que ....

understate [ʌndəˈsteɪt] vt minimiser.

understatement [ˈʌndəsteɪtmənt] n: that's an ~ c'est (bien) peu dire, le terme est faible.

understood [ʌndəˈstud] pt, pp of understand ♦ adj entendu(e); (implied) sous-entendu(e).

understudy [ˈʌndəstʌdɪ] n doublure f.

undertake [ʌndəˈteɪk] vt irreg (job, task) entre-

prendre; (duty) se charger de; to ~ to do sth s'engager à faire qch.

undertaker [ˈʌndəteɪkə*] n entrepreneur m des pompes funèbres, croque-mort m.

undertaking [ˈʌndəteɪkɪŋ] n entreprise f; (promise) promesse f.

undertone [ˈʌndətəʊn] n (low voice): in an ~ à mi-voix; (of criticism etc) nuance cachée.

undervalue [ʌndəˈvæljuː] vt sous-estimer.

underwater [ʌndəˈwɔːtə*] adv sous l'eau ♦ adj sous-marin(e).

underwear [ˈʌndəwɛə*] n sous-vêtements mpl; (women's only) dessous mpl.

underweight [ʌndəˈweɪt] adj d'un poids insuffisant; (person) (trop) maigre.

underworld [ˈʌndəwəːld] n (of crime) milieu m, pègre f.

underwrite [ʌndəˈraɪt] vt (FINANCE) garantir; (INSURANCE) souscrire.

underwriter [ˈʌndəraɪtə*] n (INSURANCE) souscripteur m.

undeserving [ʌndɪˈzəːvɪŋ] adj: to be ~ of ne pas mériter.

undesirable [ʌndɪˈzaɪərəbl] adj peu souhaitable; indésirable.

undeveloped [ʌndɪˈvɛləpt] adj (land, resources) non exploité(e).

undies [ˈʌndɪz] npl (col) dessous mpl, lingerie f.

undiluted [ˈʌndaɪˈluːtɪd] adj pur(e), non dilué(e).

undiplomatic [ˈʌndɪpləˈmætɪk] adj peu diplomatique, maladroit(e).

undischarged [ˈʌndɪsˈtʃɑːdʒd] adj: ~ bankrupt failli/e non réhabilité(e).

undisciplined [ʌnˈdɪsɪplɪnd] adj indiscipliné(e).

undisguised [ˈʌndɪsˈgaɪzd] adj (dislike, amusement etc) franc(franche).

undisputed [ˈʌndɪsˈpjuːtɪd] adj incontesté(e).

undistinguished [ˈʌndɪsˈtɪŋgwɪʃt] adj médiocre, quelconque.

undisturbed [ʌndɪsˈtəːbd] adj (sleep) tranquille, paisible; to leave ~ ne pas déranger.

undivided [ʌndɪˈvaɪdɪd] adj: can I have your ~ attention? puis-je avoir toute votre attention?

undo [ʌnˈduː] vt irreg défaire.

undoing [ʌnˈduːɪŋ] n ruine f, perte f.

undone [ʌnˈdʌn] pp of undo; to come ~ se défaire.

undoubted [ʌnˈdautɪd] adj indubitable, certain(e).

undoubtedly [ʌnˈdautɪdlɪ] adv sans aucun doute.

undress [ʌnˈdrɛs] vi se déshabiller ♦ vt déshabiller.

undrinkable [ʌnˈdrɪŋkəbl] adj (unpalatable) imbuvable; (poisonous) non potable.

undue [ʌnˈdjuː] adj indu(e), excessif(ive).

undulating [ˈʌndjuleɪtɪŋ] adj ondoyant(e), onduleux(euse).

unduly [ʌnˈdjuːlɪ] adv trop, excessivement.

undying [ʌn'daɪɪŋ] *adj* éternel(le).
unearned [ʌn'ə:nd] *adj* (*praise, respect*) immérité(e); ~ **income** rentes *fpl*.
unearth [ʌn'ə:θ] *vt* déterrer; (*fig*) dénicher.
unearthly [ʌn'ə:θlɪ] *adj* surnaturel(le); (*hour*) indu(e), impossible.
uneasy [ʌn'i:zɪ] *adj* mal à l'aise, gêné(e); (*worried*) inquiet(ète); **to feel** ~ **about doing sth** se sentir mal à l'aise à l'idée de faire qch.
uneconomic(al) ['ʌni:kə'nɔmɪk(l)] *adj* peu économique; peu rentable.
uneducated [ʌn'ɛdjukeɪtɪd] *adj* sans éducation.
unemployed [ʌnɪm'plɔɪd] *adj* sans travail, au chômage ♦ *n*: **the** ~ les chômeurs *mpl*.
unemployment [ʌnɪm'plɔɪmənt] *n* chômage *m*.
unemployment benefit, (*US*) **unemployment compensation** *n* allocation *f* de chômage.
unending [ʌn'ɛndɪŋ] *adj* interminable.
unenviable [ʌn'ɛnvɪəbl] *adj* peu enviable.
unequal [ʌn'i:kwəl] *adj* inégal(e).
unequalled, (*US*) **unequaled** [ʌn'i:kwəld] *adj* inégalé(e).
unequivocal [ʌnɪ'kwɪvəkl] *adj* (*answer*) sans équivoque; (*person*) catégorique.
unerring [ʌn'ə:rɪŋ] *adj* infaillible, sûr(e).
UNESCO [ju:'nɛskəu] *n abbr* (= *United Nations Educational, Scientific and Cultural Organization*) UNESCO *f*.
unethical [ʌn'ɛθɪkl] *adj* (*methods*) immoral(e); (*doctor's behaviour*) qui ne respecte pas l'éthique.
uneven [ʌn'i:vn] *adj* inégal(e); irrégulier(ière).
uneventful [ʌnɪ'vɛntful] *adj* tranquille, sans histoires.
unexceptional [ʌnɪk'sɛpʃənl] *adj* banal(e), quelconque.
unexciting [ʌnɪk'saɪtɪŋ] *adj* pas passionnant(e).
unexpected [ʌnɪk'spɛktɪd] *adj* inattendu(e), imprévu(e).
unexpectedly [ʌnɪk'spɛktɪdlɪ] *adv* contre toute attente; (*arrive*) à l'improviste.
unexplained [ʌnɪk'spleɪnd] *adj* inexpliqué(e).
unexploded [ʌnɪk'spləudɪd] *adj* non explosé(e) *or* éclaté(e).
unfailing [ʌn'feɪlɪŋ] *adj* inépuisable; infaillible.
unfair [ʌn'fɛə*] *adj*: ~ **(to)** injuste (envers); **it's** ~ **that** ... il n'est pas juste que ....
unfair dismissal *n* licenciement abusif.
unfairly [ʌn'fɛəlɪ] *adv* injustement.
unfaithful [ʌn'feɪθful] *adj* infidèle.
unfamiliar [ʌnfə'mɪlɪə*] *adj* étrange, inconnu(e); **to be** ~ **with sth** mal connaître qch.
unfashionable [ʌn'fæʃnəbl] *adj* (*clothes*) démodé(e); (*district*) déshérité(e), pas à la mode.
unfasten [ʌn'fɑ:sn] *vt* défaire; détacher.
unfathomable [ʌn'fæðəməbl] *adj* insondable.

unfavourable, (*US*) **unfavorable** [ʌn'feɪvrəbl] *adj* défavorable.
unfavo(u)rably [ʌn'feɪvrəblɪ] *adv*: **to look** ~ **upon** ne pas être favorable à.
unfeeling [ʌn'fi:lɪŋ] *adj* insensible, dur(e).
unfinished [ʌn'fɪnɪʃt] *adj* inachevé(e).
unfit [ʌn'fɪt] *adj* (*physically*) pas en forme; (*incompetent*): ~ **(for)** impropre (à); (*work, service*) inapte (à).
unflagging [ʌn'flægɪŋ] *adj* infatigable, inlassable.
unflappable [ʌn'flæpəbl] *adj* imperturbable.
unflattering [ʌn'flætərɪŋ] *adj* (*dress, hairstyle*) qui n'avantage pas; (*remark*) peu flatteur(euse).
unflinching [ʌn'flɪntʃɪŋ] *adj* stoïque.
unfold [ʌn'fəuld] *vt* déplier; (*fig*) révéler, exposer ♦ *vi* se dérouler.
unforeseeable [ʌnfɔ:'si:əbl] *adj* imprévisible.
unforeseen ['ʌnfɔ:'si:n] *adj* imprévu(e).
unforgettable [ʌnfə'gɛtəbl] *adj* inoubliable.
unforgivable [ʌnfə'gɪvəbl] *adj* impardonnable.
unformatted [ʌn'fɔ:mætɪd] *adj* (*disk, text*) non formaté(e).
unfortunate [ʌn'fɔ:tʃnət] *adj* malheureux(euse); (*event, remark*) malencontreux(euse).
unfortunately [ʌn'fɔ:tʃnətlɪ] *adv* malheureusement.
unfounded [ʌn'faundɪd] *adj* sans fondement.
unfriendly [ʌn'frɛndlɪ] *adj* froid(e), inamical(e).
unfulfilled [ʌnful'fɪld] *adj* (*ambition, prophecy*) non réalisé(e); (*desire*) insatisfait(e); (*promise*) non tenu(e); (*terms of contract*) non rempli(e); (*person*) qui n'a pas su se réaliser.
unfurl [ʌn'fə:l] *vt* déployer.
unfurnished [ʌn'fə:nɪʃt] *adj* non meublé(e).
ungainly [ʌn'geɪnlɪ] *adj* gauche, dégingandé(e).
ungodly [ʌn'gɔdlɪ] *adj* impie; **at an** ~ **hour** à une heure indue.
ungrateful [ʌn'greɪtful] *adj* qui manque de reconnaissance, ingrat(e).
unguarded [ʌn'gɑ:dɪd] *adj*: ~ **moment** moment *m* d'inattention.
unhappily [ʌn'hæpɪlɪ] *adv* tristement; (*unfortunately*) malheureusement.
unhappiness [ʌn'hæpɪnɪs] *n* tristesse *f*, peine *f*.
unhappy [ʌn'hæpɪ] *adj* triste, malheureux(euse); (*unfortunate: remark etc*) malheureux(euse); (*not pleased*): ~ **with** mécontent(e) de, peu satisfait(e) de.
unharmed [ʌn'hɑ:md] *adj* indemne, sain(e) et sauf(sauve).
UNHCR *n abbr* (= *United Nations High Commission for Refugees*) HCR *m*.
unhealthy [ʌn'hɛlθɪ] *adj* (*gen*) malsain(e); (*person*) maladif(ive).
unheard-of [ʌn'hə:dɔv] *adj* inouï(e), sans précédent.

unhelpful [ʌn'hɛlpful] *adj* (*person*) peu serviable; (*advice*) peu utile.
unhesitating [ʌn'hɛzɪteɪtɪŋ] *adj* (*loyalty*) spontané(e); (*reply, offer*) immédiat(e).
unholy [ʌn'həulɪ] *adj*: **an ~ alliance** une alliance contre nature; **he got home at an ~ hour** il est rentré à une heure impossible.
unhook [ʌn'huk] *vt* décrocher; dégrafer.
unhurt [ʌn'hɜːt] *adj* indemne, sain(e) et sauf(sauve).
unhygienic ['ʌnhaɪ'dʒiːnɪk] *adj* antihygiénique.
UNICEF ['juːnɪsɛf] *n abbr* (= *United Nations Children's Fund*) UNICEF *m*, FISE *m*.
unicorn ['juːnɪkɔːn] *n* licorne *f*.
unidentified [ʌnaɪ'dɛntɪfaɪd] *adj* non identifié(e).
uniform ['juːnɪfɔːm] *n* uniforme *m* ♦ *adj* uniforme.
uniformity [juːnɪ'fɔːmɪtɪ] *n* uniformité *f*.
unify ['juːnɪfaɪ] *vt* unifier.
unilateral [juːnɪ'lætərəl] *adj* unilatéral(e).
unimaginable [ʌnɪ'mædʒɪnəbl] *adj* inimaginable, inconcevable.
unimaginative [ʌnɪ'mædʒɪnətɪv] *adj* sans imagination.
unimpaired [ʌnɪm'pɛəd] *adj* intact(e).
unimportant [ʌnɪm'pɔːtənt] *adj* sans importance.
unimpressed [ʌnɪm'prɛst] *adj* pas impressionné(e).
uninhabited [ʌnɪn'hæbɪtɪd] *adj* inhabité(e).
uninhibited [ʌnɪn'hɪbɪtɪd] *adj* sans inhibitions; sans retenue.
uninjured [ʌn'ɪndʒəd] *adj* indemne.
uninspiring [ʌnɪn'spaɪərɪŋ] *adj* peu inspirant(e).
unintelligent [ʌnɪn'tɛlɪdʒənt] *adj* inintelligent(e).
unintentional [ʌnɪn'tɛnʃənəl] *adj* involontaire.
unintentionally [ʌnɪn'tɛnʃnəlɪ] *adv* sans le vouloir.
uninvited [ʌnɪn'vaɪtɪd] *adj* (*guest*) qui n'a pas été invité(e).
uninviting [ʌnɪn'vaɪtɪŋ] *adj* (*place*) peu attirant(e); (*food*) peu appétissant(e).
union ['juːnjən] *n* union *f*; (*also*: **trade ~**) syndicat *m* ♦ *cpd* du syndicat, syndical(e).
unionize ['juːnjənaɪz] *vt* syndiquer.
Union Jack *n* drapeau du *Royaume-Uni*.
Union of Soviet Socialist Republics (USSR) *n* (*formerly*) Union *f* des républiques socialistes soviétiques (URSS).
union shop *n entreprise où tous les travailleurs doivent être syndiqués.*
unique [juː'niːk] *adj* unique.
unisex ['juːnɪsɛks] *adj* unisexe.
UNISON ['juːnɪsn] *n* (*trade union*) grand *syndicat des services publics en Grande-Bretagne.*
unison ['juːnɪsn] *n*: **in ~** à l'unisson, en chœur.
unit ['juːnɪt] *n* unité *f*; (*section: of furniture etc*)

élément *m*, bloc *m*; (*team, squad*) groupe *m*, service *m*; **production ~** atelier *m* de fabrication; **sink ~** bloc-évier *m*.
unit cost *n* coût *m* unitaire.
unite [juː'naɪt] *vt* unir ♦ *vi* s'unir.
united [juː'naɪtɪd] *adj* uni(e); unifié(e); (*efforts*) conjugué(e).
United Arab Emirates *npl* Émirats Arabes Unis.
United Kingdom (UK) *n* Royaume-Uni *m* (R.U.).
United Nations (Organization) (UN, UNO) *n* (Organisation *f* des) Nations unies (ONU).
United States (of America) (US, USA) *n* États-Unis *mpl*.
unit price *n* prix *m* unitaire.
unit trust *n* (*BRIT COMM*) fonds commun de placement, FCP *m*.
unity ['juːnɪtɪ] *n* unité *f*.
Univ. *abbr* = **university**.
universal [juːnɪ'vɜːsl] *adj* universel(le).
universe ['juːnɪvɜːs] *n* univers *m*.
university [juːnɪ'vɜːsɪtɪ] *n* université *f* ♦ *cpd* (*student, professor*) d'université; (*education, year, degree*) universitaire.
unjust [ʌn'dʒʌst] *adj* injuste.
unjustifiable ['ʌndʒʌstɪ'faɪəbl] *adj* injustifiable.
unjustified [ʌn'dʒʌstɪfaɪd] *adj* injustifié(e); (*text*) non justifié(e).
unkempt [ʌn'kɛmpt] *adj* mal tenu(e), débraillé(e); mal peigné(e).
unkind [ʌn'kaɪnd] *adj* peu gentil(le), méchant(e).
unkindly [ʌn'kaɪndlɪ] *adv* (*treat, speak*) avec méchanceté.
unknown [ʌn'nəun] *adj* inconnu(e); **~ to me** sans que je le sache; **~ quantity** (*MATH, fig*) inconnue *f*.
unladen [ʌn'leɪdn] *adj* (*ship, weight*) à vide.
unlawful [ʌn'lɔːful] *adj* illégal(e).
unleaded [ʌn'lɛdɪd] *n* (*also*: **petrol**) essence *f* sans plomb.
unleash [ʌn'liːʃ] *vt* détacher; (*fig*) déchaîner, déclencher.
unleavened [ʌn'lɛvnd] *adj* sans levain.
unless [ʌn'lɛs] *conj*: ~ **he leaves** à moins qu'il (ne) parte; ~ **we leave** à moins de partir, à moins que nous (ne) partions; ~ **otherwise stated** sauf indication contraire; ~ **I am mistaken** si je ne me trompe.
unlicensed [ʌn'laɪsnst] *adj* (*BRIT*) non patenté(e) pour la vente des spiritueux.
unlike [ʌn'laɪk] *adj* dissemblable, différent(e) ♦ *prep* à la différence de, contrairement à.
unlikelihood [ʌn'laɪklɪhud] *adj* improbabilité *f*.
unlikely [ʌn'laɪklɪ] *adj* (*result, event*) improbable; (*explanation*) invraisemblable.
unlimited [ʌn'lɪmɪtɪd] *adj* illimité(e).
unlisted ['ʌn'lɪstɪd] *adj* (*US TEL*) sur la liste rouge; (*STOCK EXCHANGE*) non coté(e) en

Bourse.

unlit [ʌn'lɪt] *adj (room)* non éclairé(e).

unload [ʌn'ləud] *vt* décharger.

unlock [ʌn'lɔk] *vt* ouvrir.

unlucky [ʌn'lʌkɪ] *adj* malchanceux(euse); *(object, number)* qui porte malheur; **to be ~** *(person)* ne pas avoir de chance.

unmanageable [ʌn'mænɪdʒəbl] *adj (unwieldy: tool, vehicle)* peu maniable; (: *situation)* inextricable.

unmanned [ʌn'mænd] *adj* sans équipage.

unmannerly [ʌn'mænəlɪ] *adj* mal élevé(e), impoli(e).

unmarked [ʌn'mɑːkt] *adj (unstained)* sans marque; **~ police car** voiture de police banalisée.

unmarried [ʌn'mærɪd] *adj* célibataire.

unmask [ʌn'mɑːsk] *vt* démasquer.

unmatched [ʌn'mætʃt] *adj* sans égal(e).

unmentionable [ʌn'menʃnəbl] *adj (topic)* dont on ne parle pas; *(word)* qui ne se dit pas.

unmerciful [ʌn'məːsɪful] *adj* sans pitié.

unmistakable [ʌnmɪs'teɪkəbl] *adj* indubitable; qu'on ne peut pas ne pas reconnaître.

unmitigated [ʌn'mɪtɪgeɪtɪd] *adj* non mitigé(e), absolu(e), pur(e).

unnamed [ʌn'neɪmd] *adj (nameless)* sans nom; *(anonymous)* anonyme.

unnatural [ʌn'nætʃrəl] *adj* non naturel(le); contre nature.

unnecessary [ʌn'nesəsərɪ] *adj* inutile, superflu(e).

unnerve [ʌn'nəːv] *vt* faire perdre son sang-froid à.

unnoticed [ʌn'nəutɪst] *adj* inaperçu(e); **to go ~** passer inaperçu.

UNO ['juːnəu] *n abbr* = **United Nations Organization**.

unobservant [ʌnəb'zəːvnt] *adj* pas observateur(trice).

unobtainable [ʌnəb'teɪnəbl] *adj (TEL)* impossible à obtenir.

unobtrusive [ʌnəb'truːsɪv] *adj* discret(ète).

unoccupied [ʌn'ɔkjupaɪd] *adj (seat, table, also MIL)* libre; *(house)* inoccupé(e).

unofficial [ʌnə'fɪʃl] *adj* non officiel(le); *(strike)* ≈ non sanctionné(e) par la centrale.

unopposed [ʌnə'pəuzd] *adj* sans opposition.

unorthodox [ʌn'ɔːθədɔks] *adj* peu orthodoxe.

unpack [ʌn'pæk] *vi* défaire sa valise, déballer ses affaires.

unpaid [ʌn'peɪd] *adj (bill)* impayé(e); *(holiday)* non-payé(e), sans salaire; *(work)* non rétribué(e); *(worker)* bénévole.

unpalatable [ʌn'pælətəbl] *adj (truth)* désagréable (à entendre).

unparalleled [ʌn'pærəleld] *adj* incomparable, sans égal.

unpatriotic ['ʌnpætrɪ'ɔtɪk] *adj (person)* manquant de patriotisme; *(speech, attitude)* antipatriotique.

unplanned [ʌn'plænd] *adj (visit)* imprévu(e);

(baby) non prévu(e).

unpleasant [ʌn'pleznt] *adj* déplaisant(e), désagréable.

unplug [ʌn'plʌg] *vt* débrancher.

unpolluted [ʌnpə'luːtɪd] *adj* non pollué(e).

unpopular [ʌn'pɔpjulə*] *adj* impopulaire; **to make o.s. ~ (with)** se rendre impopulaire (auprès de).

unprecedented [ʌn'presɪdentɪd] *adj* sans précédent.

unpredictable [ʌnprɪ'dɪktəbl] *adj* imprévisible.

unprejudiced [ʌn'predʒudɪst] *adj (not biased)* impartial(e); *(having no prejudices)* qui n'a pas de préjugés.

unprepared [ʌnprɪ'peəd] *adj (person)* qui n'est pas suffisamment préparé(e); *(speech)* improvisé(e).

unprepossessing ['ʌnpriːpə'zesɪŋ] *adj* peu avenant(e).

unpretentious [ʌnprɪ'tenʃəs] *adj* sans prétention(s).

unprincipled [ʌn'prɪnsɪpld] *adj* sans principes.

unproductive [ʌnprə'dʌktɪv] *adj* improductif(ive); *(discussion)* stérile.

unprofessional [ʌnprə'feʃənl] *adj (conduct)* contraire à la déontologie.

unprofitable [ʌn'prɔfɪtəbl] *adj* non rentable.

UNPROFOR [ʌn'prəufɔː*] *n abbr (= United Nations Protection Force)* FORPRONU *f.*

unprotected ['ʌnprə'tektɪd] *adj (sex)* non protégé(e).

unprovoked [ʌnprə'vəukt] *adj (attack)* sans provocation.

unpunished [ʌn'pʌnɪʃt] *adj* impuni(e); **to go ~** rester impuni.

unqualified [ʌn'kwɔlɪfaɪd] *adj (teacher)* non diplômé(e), sans titres; *(success)* sans réserve, total(e).

unquestionably [ʌn'kwestʃənəblɪ] *adv* incontestablement.

unquestioning [ʌn'kwestʃənɪŋ] *adj (obedience, acceptance)* inconditionnel(le).

unravel [ʌn'rævl] *vt* démêler.

unreal [ʌn'rɪəl] *adj* irréel(le).

unrealistic ['ʌnrɪə'lɪstɪk] *adj (idea)* irréaliste; *(estimate)* peu réaliste.

unreasonable [ʌn'riːznəbl] *adj* qui n'est pas raisonnable; **to make ~ demands on sb** exiger trop de qn.

unrecognizable [ʌn'rekəgnaɪzəbl] *adj* pas reconnaissable.

unrecognized [ʌn'rekəgnaɪzd] *adj (talent, genius)* méconnu(e); *(POL: régime)* non reconnu(e).

unrecorded [ʌnrɪ'kɔːdɪd] *adj* non enregistré(e).

unrefined [ʌnrɪ'faɪnd] *adj (sugar, petroleum)* non raffiné(e).

unrehearsed [ʌnrɪ'həːst] *adj (THEAT etc)* qui n'a pas été répété(e); *(spontaneous)* spontané(e).

unrelated [ˌʌnrɪ'leɪtɪd] *adj* sans rapport; sans lien de parenté.

unrelenting [ˌʌnrɪ'lentɪŋ] *adj* implacable; acharné(e).

unreliable [ˌʌnrɪ'laɪəbl] *adj* sur qui (*or* quoi) on ne peut pas compter, peu fiable.

unrelieved [ˌʌnrɪ'liːvd] *adj* (*monotony*) constant(e), uniforme.

unremitting [ˌʌnrɪ'mɪtɪŋ] *adj* inlassable, infatigable, acharné(e).

unrepeatable [ˌʌnrɪ'piːtəbl] *adj* (*offer*) unique, exceptionnel(le).

unrepentant [ˌʌnrɪ'pentənt] *adj* impénitent(e).

unrepresentative [ˈʌnreprɪ'zentətɪv] *adj*: ~ (of) peu représentatif(ive) (de).

unreserved [ˌʌnrɪ'zɜːvd] *adj* (*seat*) non réservé(e); (*approval, admiration*) sans réserve.

unresponsive [ˌʌnrɪs'pɒnsɪv] *adj* insensible.

unrest [ʌn'rest] *n* agitation *f*, troubles *mpl*.

unrestricted [ˌʌnrɪ'strɪktɪd] *adj* illimité(e); **to have ~ access to** avoir librement accès *or* accès en tout temps à.

unrewarded [ˌʌnrɪ'wɔːdɪd] *adj* pas récompensé(e).

unripe [ʌn'raɪp] *adj* pas mûr(e).

unrivalled, (*US*) **unrivaled** [ʌn'raɪvəld] *adj* sans égal, incomparable.

unroll [ʌn'rəul] *vt* dérouler.

unruffled [ʌn'rʌfld] *adj* (*person*) imperturbable; (*hair*) qui n'est pas ébouriffé(e).

unruly [ʌn'ruːlɪ] *adj* indiscipliné(e).

unsafe [ʌn'seɪf] *adj* (*machine, wiring*) dangereux(euse); (*method*) hasardeux(euse); ~ **to drink/eat** non potable/comestible.

unsaid [ʌn'sed] *adj*: **to leave sth ~** passer qch sous silence.

unsaleable, (*US*) **unsalable** [ʌn'seɪləbl] *adj* invendable.

unsatisfactory [ˈʌnsætɪs'fæktərɪ] *adj* qui laisse à désirer.

unsavoury, (*US*) **unsavory** [ʌn'seɪvərɪ] *adj* (*fig*) peu recommandable, répugnant(e).

unscathed [ʌn'skeɪðd] *adj* indemne.

unscientific [ˈʌnsaɪən'tɪfɪk] *adj* non scientifique.

unscrew [ʌn'skruː] *vt* dévisser.

unscrupulous [ʌn'skruːpjuləs] *adj* sans scrupules.

unseat [ʌn'siːt] *vt* (*rider*) désarçonner; (*fig: official*) faire perdre son siège à.

unsecured [ˈʌnsɪ'kjuəd] *adj*: ~ **creditor** créancier/ière sans garantie.

unseeded [ʌn'siːdɪd] *adj* (*SPORT*) non classé(e).

unseemly [ʌn'siːmlɪ] *adj* inconvenant(e).

unseen [ʌn'siːn] *adj* (*person*) invisible; (*danger*) imprévu(e).

unselfish [ʌn'selfɪʃ] *adj* désintéressé(e).

unsettled [ʌn'setld] *adj* (*restless*) perturbé(e); (*unpredictable*) instable; incertain(e); (*not finalized*) non résolu(e).

unsettling [ʌn'setlɪŋ] *adj* qui a un effet perturbateur.

unshak(e)able [ʌn'ʃeɪkəbl] *adj* inébranlable.

unshaven [ʌn'ʃeɪvn] *adj* non *or* mal rasé(e).

unsightly [ʌn'saɪtlɪ] *adj* disgracieux(euse), laid(e).

unskilled [ʌn'skɪld] *adj*: ~ **worker** manœuvre *m*.

unsociable [ʌn'səuʃəbl] *adj* (*person*) peu sociable; (*behaviour*) qui manque de sociabilité.

unsocial [ʌn'səuʃl] *adj* (*hours*) en dehors de l'horaire normal.

unsold [ʌn'səuld] *adj* invendu(e), non vendu(e).

unsolicited [ˌʌnsə'lɪsɪtɪd] *adj* non sollicité(e).

unsophisticated [ˌʌnsə'fɪstɪkeɪtɪd] *adj* simple, naturel(le).

unsound [ʌn'saund] *adj* (*health*) chancelant(e); (*floor, foundations*) peu solide; (*policy, advice*) peu judicieux(euse).

unspeakable [ʌn'spiːkəbl] *adj* indicible; (*awful*) innommable.

unspoken [ʌn'spəukn] *adj* (*word*) qui n'est pas prononcé(e); (*agreement, approval*) tacite.

unsteady [ʌn'stedɪ] *adj* mal assuré(e), chancelant(e), instable.

unstinting [ʌn'stɪntɪŋ] *adj* (*support*) total(e), sans réserve; (*generosity*) sans limites.

unstuck [ʌn'stʌk] *adj*: **to come ~** se décoller; (*fig*) faire fiasco.

unsubstantiated [ˈʌnsəb'stænʃɪeɪtɪd] *adj* (*rumour*) qui n'est pas confirmé(e); (*accusation*) sans preuve.

unsuccessful [ˌʌnsək'sesful] *adj* (*attempt*) infructueux(euse); (*writer, proposal*) qui n'a pas de succès; (*marriage*) malheureux(euse), qui ne réussit pas; **to be ~** (*in attempting sth*) ne pas réussir; ne pas avoir de succès; (*application*) ne pas être retenu(e).

unsuccessfully [ˌʌnsək'sesfəlɪ] *adv* en vain.

unsuitable [ʌn'suːtəbl] *adj* qui ne convient pas, peu approprié(e); inopportun(e).

unsuited [ʌn'suːtɪd] *adj*: **to be ~ for** *or* **to** être inapte *or* impropre à.

unsung [ˈʌnsʌŋ] *adj*: **an ~ hero** un héros méconnu.

unsupported [ˌʌnsə'pɔːtɪd] *adj* (*claim*) non soutenu(e); (*theory*) qui n'est pas corroboré(e).

unsure [ʌn'ʃuə*] *adj* pas sûr(e); **to be ~ of o.s.** ne pas être sûr de soi, manquer de confiance en soi.

unsuspecting [ˌʌnsə'spektɪŋ] *adj* qui ne se méfie pas.

unsweetened [ʌn'swiːtnd] *adj* non sucré(e).

unswerving [ʌn'swɜːvɪŋ] *adj* inébranlable.

unsympathetic [ˈʌnsɪmpə'θetɪk] *adj* hostile; (*unpleasant*) antipathique; ~ **to** indifférent(e) à.

untangle [ʌn'tæŋgl] *vt* démêler, débrouiller.

untapped [ʌn'tæpt] *adj* (*resources*) inexploité(e).

untaxed [ʌn'tækst] *adj* (*goods*) non taxé(e); (*income*) non imposé(e).

unthinkable [ʌn'θɪŋkəbl] *adj* impensable, inconcevable.

unthinkingly [ʌn'θɪŋkɪŋlɪ] *adv* sans réfléchir.

untidy [ʌn'taɪdɪ] *adj* (*room*) en désordre; (*appearance*) désordonné(e), débraillé(e); (*person*) sans ordre, désordonné; débraillé; (*work*) peu soigné(e).

untie [ʌn'taɪ] *vt* (*knot, parcel*) défaire; (*prisoner, dog*) détacher.

until [ən'tɪl] *prep* jusqu'à; (*after negative*) avant ♦ *conj* jusqu'à ce que + *sub*, en attendant que + *sub*; (*in past, after negative*) avant que + *sub*; ~ **now** jusqu'à présent, jusqu'ici; ~ **then** jusque-là; **from morning** ~ **night** du matin au soir *or* jusqu'au soir.

untimely [ʌn'taɪmlɪ] *adj* inopportun(e); (*death*) prématuré(e).

untold [ʌn'təuld] *adj* incalculable; indescriptible.

untouched [ʌn'tʌtʃt] *adj* (*not used etc*) tel(le) quel(le), intact(e); (*safe: person*) indemne; (*unaffected*): ~ **by** indifférent(e) à.

untoward [ʌntə'wɔːd] *adj* fâcheux(euse), malencontreux(euse).

untrained [ʌn'treɪnd] *adj* (*worker*) sans formation; (*troops*) sans entraînement; **to the** ~ **eye** à l'œil non exercé.

untrammelled [ʌn'træmld] *adj* sans entraves.

untranslatable [ʌntrænz'leɪtəbl] *adj* intraduisible.

untrue [ʌn'truː] *adj* (*statement*) faux(fausse).

untrustworthy [ʌn'trʌstwəːðɪ] *adj* (*person*) pas digne de confiance, peu sûr(e).

unusable [ʌn'juːzəbl] *adj* inutilisable.

unused *adj* [ʌn'juːzd] (*new*) neuf(neuve); [ʌn'juːst]: **to be** ~ **to sth/to doing sth** ne pas avoir l'habitude de qch/de faire qch.

unusual [ʌn'juːʒuəl] *adj* insolite, exceptionnel(le), rare.

unusually [ʌn'juːʒuəlɪ] *adv* exceptionnellement, particulièrement.

unveil [ʌn'veɪl] *vt* dévoiler.

unwanted [ʌn'wɔntɪd] *adj* non désiré(e).

unwarranted [ʌn'wɔrəntɪd] *adj* injustifié(e).

unwary [ʌn'wɛərɪ] *adj* imprudent(e).

unwavering [ʌn'weɪvərɪŋ] *adj* inébranlable.

unwelcome [ʌn'wɛlkəm] *adj* importun(e); **to feel** ~ se sentir de trop.

unwell [ʌn'wɛl] *adj* indisposé(e), souffrant(e); **to feel** ~ ne pas se sentir bien.

unwieldy [ʌn'wiːldɪ] *adj* difficile à manier.

unwilling [ʌn'wɪlɪŋ] *adj*: **to be** ~ **to do** ne pas vouloir faire.

unwillingly [ʌn'wɪlɪŋlɪ] *adv* à contrecœur, contre son gré.

unwind [ʌn'waɪnd] *vb* (*irreg*) *vt* dérouler ♦ *vi* (*relax*) se détendre.

unwise [ʌn'waɪz] *adj* imprudent(e), peu judicieux(euse).

unwitting [ʌn'wɪtɪŋ] *adj* involontaire.

unworkable [ʌn'wəːkəbl] *adj* (*plan etc*) inexploitable.

unworthy [ʌn'wəːðɪ] *adj* indigne.

unwrap [ʌn'ræp] *vt* défaire; ouvrir.

unwritten [ʌn'rɪtn] *adj* (*agreement*) tacite.

unzip [ʌn'zɪp] *vt* ouvrir (la fermeture éclair de).

═══════════════════════════ KEYWORD

up [ʌp] *prep*: **he went** ~ **the stairs/the hill** il a monté l'escalier/la colline; **the cat was** ~ **a tree** le chat était dans un arbre; **they live further** ~ **the street** ils habitent plus haut dans la rue

♦ *vi* (*col*): **she** ~**ped and left** elle a fichu le camp sans plus attendre

♦ *adv* **1** en haut; en l'air; (*upwards, higher*): ~ **in the sky/the mountains** (là-haut) dans le ciel/les montagnes; **put it a bit higher** ~ mettez-le un peu plus haut; ~ **there** là-haut; ~ **above** au-dessus; **"this side** ~**"** "haut"

2: **to be** ~ (*out of bed*) être levé(e); (*prices*) avoir augmenté *or* monté; (*finished*): **when the year was** ~ à la fin de l'année; **time's** ~ c'est l'heure

3: ~ **to** (*as far as*) jusqu'à; ~ **to now** jusqu'à présent

4: **to be** ~ **to** (*depending on*): **it's** ~ **to you** c'est à vous de décider; (*equal to*): **he's not** ~ **to it** (*job, task etc*) il n'en est pas capable; (*inf: be doing*): **what is he** ~ **to?** qu'est-ce qu'il peut bien faire?

5 (*phrases*): **he's well** ~ **in** *or* **on ...** (*BRIT: knowledgeable*) il s'y connaît en ...; ~ **with Leeds United!** vive Leeds United!; **what's** ~**?** (*col*) qu'est-ce qui ne va pas?; **what's** ~ **with him?** (*col*) qu'est-ce qui lui arrive?

♦ *n*: ~**s and downs** hauts et bas *mpl*.

up-and-coming [ʌpənd'kʌmɪŋ] *adj* plein(e) d'avenir *or* de promesses.

upbeat ['ʌpbiːt] *n* (*MUS*) levé *m*; (*in economy, prosperity*) amélioration *f* ♦ *adj* (*optimistic*) optimiste.

upbraid [ʌp'breɪd] *vt* morigéner.

upbringing ['ʌpbrɪŋɪŋ] *n* éducation *f*.

upcoming ['ʌpkʌmɪŋ] *adj* tout(e) prochain(e).

update [ʌp'deɪt] *vt* mettre à jour.

upend [ʌp'ɛnd] *vt* mettre debout.

up-front [ʌp'frʌnt] *adj* franc(franche) ♦ *adv* (*pay*) d'avance.

upgrade [ʌp'greɪd] *vt* (*person*) promouvoir; (*job*) revaloriser; (*property, equipment*) moderniser.

upheaval [ʌp'hiːvl] *n* bouleversement *m*; branle-bas *m*; crise *f*.

uphill [ʌp'hɪl] *adj* qui monte; (*fig: task*) difficile, pénible ♦ *adv* (*face, move*) en amont, vers l'amont; (*go, move*) vers le haut, en haut; **to go** ~ monter.

uphold [ʌp'həuld] *vt irreg* maintenir; soutenir.

upholstery [ʌp'həulstərɪ] *n* rembourrage *m*; (*of car*) garniture *f*.

upkeep ['ʌpkiːp] *n* entretien *m*.

up-market [ˌʌpˈmɑːkɪt] *adj* (*product*) haut de gamme *inv*.

upon [əˈpɒn] *prep* sur.

upper [ˈʌpə*] *adj* supérieur(e); du dessus ♦ *n* (*of shoe*) empeigne *f*.

upper class *n*: **the** ~ ≈ la haute bourgeoisie ♦ *adj*: **upper-class** (*district*) élégant(e), huppé(e); (*accent, attitude*) caractéristique des classes supérieures.

uppercut [ˈʌpəkʌt] *n* uppercut *m*.

upper hand *n*: **to have the** ~ avoir le dessus.

Upper House *n*: **the** ~ (*in Britain*) la Chambre des Lords, la Chambre haute; (*in France, in the US etc*) le Sénat.

uppermost [ˈʌpəməʊst] *adj* le(la) plus haut(e); en dessus; **it was** ~ **in my mind** j'y pensais avant tout autre chose.

Upper Volta [-ˈvɒltə] *n* Haute Volta.

upright [ˈʌpraɪt] *adj* droit(e); vertical(e); (*fig*) droit, honnête ♦ *n* montant *m*.

uprising [ˈʌpraɪzɪŋ] *n* soulèvement *m*, insurrection *f*.

uproar [ˈʌprɔː*] *n* tumulte *m*, vacarme *m*.

uproarious [ʌpˈrɔːrɪəs] *adj* (*event etc*) désopilant(e); ~ **laughter** un brouhaha de rires.

uproot [ʌpˈruːt] *vt* déraciner.

upset *n* [ˈʌpset] dérangement *m* ♦ *vt* [ʌpˈset] (*irreg: like* **set**) (*glass etc*) renverser; (*plan*) déranger; (*person: offend*) contrarier; (: *grieve*) faire de la peine à; bouleverser ♦ *adj* [ʌpˈset] contrarié(e); peiné(e); (*stomach*) détraqué(e), dérangé(e); **to get** ~ (*sad*) devenir triste; (*offended*) se vexer; **to have a stomach** ~ (*BRIT*) avoir une indigestion.

upset price *n* (*US, Scottish*) mise *f* à prix, prix *m* de départ.

upsetting [ʌpˈsetɪŋ] *adj* (*offending*) vexant(e); (*annoying*) ennuyeux(euse).

upshot [ˈʌpʃɒt] *n* résultat *m*; **the** ~ **of it all was that ...** il a résulté de tout cela que ....

upside down [ˈʌpsaɪd-] *adv* à l'envers.

upstage [ˈʌpˈsteɪdʒ] *vt*: **to** ~ **sb** souffler la vedette à qn.

upstairs [ʌpˈstɛəz] *adv* en haut ♦ *adj* (*room*) du dessus, d'en haut ♦ *n*: **there's no** ~ il n'y a pas d'étage.

upstart [ˈʌpstɑːt] *n* parvenu/e.

upstream [ʌpˈstriːm] *adv* en amont.

upsurge [ˈʌpsɔːdʒ] *n* (*of enthusiasm etc*) vague *f*.

uptake [ˈʌpteɪk] *n*: **he is quick/slow on the** ~ il comprend vite/est lent à comprendre.

uptight [ʌpˈtaɪt] *adj* (*col*) très tendu(e), crispé(e).

up-to-date [ˈʌptəˈdeɪt] *adj* moderne; très récent(e).

upturn [ˈʌptɜːn] *n* (*in economy*) reprise *f*.

upturned [ˈʌptɜːnd] *adj* (*nose*) retroussé(e).

upward [ˈʌpwəd] *adj* ascendant(e); vers le haut ♦ *adv see* **upwards**.

upwardly-mobile [ˈʌpwədlɪˈməʊbaɪl] *adj* à mobilité sociale ascendante.

upwards [ˈʌpwədz] *adv* vers le haut; **and** ~ et plus, et au-dessus.

URA *n abbr* (*US*) = *Urban Renewal Administration.*

Ural Mountains [ˈjʊərəl-] *npl*: **the** ~ (*also*: **the Urals**) les monts *mpl* Oural, l'Oural *m*.

uranium [jʊəˈreɪnɪəm] *n* uranium *m*.

Uranus [jʊəˈreɪnəs] *n* Uranus *f*.

urban [ˈɜːbən] *adj* urbain(e).

urbane [əːˈbeɪn] *adj* urbain(e), courtois(e).

urbanization [əːbənaɪˈzeɪʃən] *n* urbanisation *f*.

urchin [ˈɜːtʃɪn] *n* gosse *m*, garnement *m*.

Urdu [ˈʊəduː] *n* ourdou *m*.

urge [ɜːdʒ] *n* besoin (impératif), envie (pressante) ♦ *vt* (*caution etc*) recommander avec insistance; (*person*): **to** ~ **sb to do** presser qn de faire, recommander avec insistance à qn de faire.

▶**urge on** *vt* pousser, presser.

urgency [ˈɜːdʒənsɪ] *n* urgence *f*; (*of tone*) insistance *f*.

urgent [ˈɜːdʒənt] *adj* urgent(e); (*plea, tone*) pressant(e).

urgently [ˈɜːdʒəntlɪ] *adv* d'urgence, de toute urgence; (*need*) sans délai.

urinal [ˈjʊərɪnl] *n* (*BRIT*) urinoir *m*.

urinate [ˈjʊərɪneɪt] *vi* uriner.

urine [ˈjʊərɪn] *n* urine *f*.

urn [ɜːn] *n* urne *f*; (*also*: **tea** ~) fontaine *f* à thé.

Uruguay [ˈjʊərəgwaɪ] *n* Uruguay *m*.

Uruguayan [jʊərəˈgwaɪən] *adj* uruguayen(ne) ♦ *n* Uruguayen/ne.

US *n abbr* = *United States.*

us [ʌs] *pron* nous.

USA *n abbr* = *United States of America*; (*MIL*) = *United States Army.*

usable [ˈjuːzəbl] *adj* utilisable.

USAF *n abbr* = *United States Air Force.*

usage [ˈjuːzɪdʒ] *n* usage *m*.

USCG *n abbr* = *United States Coast Guard.*

USDA *n abbr* = *United States Department of Agriculture.*

USDAW [ˈʌzdɔː] *n abbr* (*BRIT*: = *Union of Shop, Distributive and Allied Workers*) syndicat du commerce de détail et de la distribution.

USDI *n abbr* = *United States Department of the Interior.*

use *n* [juːs] emploi *m*, utilisation *f*; usage *m* ♦ *vt* [juːz] se servir de, utiliser, employer; **in** ~ en usage; **out of** ~ hors d'usage; **to be of** ~ servir, être utile; **to make** ~ **of sth** utiliser qch; **ready for** ~ prêt à l'emploi; **it's no** ~ ça ne sert à rien; **to have the** ~ **of** avoir l'usage de; **what's this** ~**d for?** à quoi est-ce que ça sert?; **she** ~**d to do it** elle le faisait (autrefois), elle avait coutume de le faire; **to be** ~**d to** avoir l'habitude de, être habitué(e) à; **to get** ~**d to** s'habituer à.

▶**use up** *vt* finir, épuiser; (*food*) consommer.

used [juːzd] *adj* (*car*) d'occasion.

useful ['ju:sful] *adj* utile; **to come in** ~ être utile.
usefulness ['ju:sfəlnɪs] *n* utilité *f*.
useless ['ju:slɪs] *adj* inutile.
user ['ju:zə*] *n* utilisateur/trice, usager *m*.
user-friendly ['ju:zə'frɛndlɪ] *adj* convivial(e), facile d'emploi.
USES *n abbr* = United States Employment Service.
usher ['ʌʃə*] *n* placeur *m* ♦ *vt*: **to** ~ **sb in** faire entrer qn.
usherette [ʌʃə'rɛt] *n* (*in cinema*) ouvreuse *f*.
USIA *n abbr* = United States Information Agency.
USM *n abbr* = United States Mail, United States Mint.
USN *n abbr* = United States Navy.
USPHS *n abbr* = United States Public Health Service.
USPO *n abbr* = United States Post Office.
USS *abbr* = United States Ship (or Steamer).
USSR *n abbr* = **Union of Soviet Socialist Republics.**
usu. *abbr* = **usually.**
usual ['ju:ʒuəl] *adj* habituel(le); **as** ~ comme d'habitude.
usually ['ju:ʒuəlɪ] *adv* d'habitude, d'ordinaire.
usurer ['ju:ʒərə*] *n* usurier/ière.
usurp [ju:'zə:p] *vt* usurper.
UT *abbr* (*US*) = Utah.
utensil [ju:'tɛnsl] *n* ustensile *m*; **kitchen** ~**s** batterie *f* de cuisine.
uterus ['ju:tərəs] *n* utérus *m*.
utilitarian [ju:tɪlɪ'tɛərɪən] *adj* utilitaire.
utility [ju:'tɪlɪtɪ] *n* utilité *f*; (*also*: **public** ~) service public.
utility room *n* buanderie *f*.
utilization [ju:tɪlaɪ'zeɪʃən] *n* utilisation *f*.
utilize ['ju:tɪlaɪz] *vt* utiliser; exploiter.
utmost ['ʌtməʊst] *adj* extrême, le(la) plus grand(e) ♦ *n*: **to do one's** ~ faire tout son possible; **of the** ~ **importance** d'une importance capitale, de la plus haute importance.
utter ['ʌtə*] *adj* total(e), complet(ète) ♦ *vt* prononcer, proférer; émettre.
utterance ['ʌtrns] *n* paroles *fpl*.
utterly ['ʌtəlɪ] *adv* complètement, totalement.
U-turn ['ju:'tə:n] *n* demi-tour *m*; (*fig*) volte-face *f inv*.
Uzbekistan [ʌzbɛkɪ'stɑ:n] *n* Ouzbékistan *m*.

V v

V, v [vi:] *n* (*letter*) V, v *m*; **V for Victor** V comme Victor.
v *abbr* (= *verse*, = *vide*: see) v.; (= *versus*) c.; (= *volt*) V.
VA, Va. *abbr* (*US*) = Virginia.
vac [væk] *n abbr* (*BRIT col*) = **vacation.**
vacancy ['veɪkənsɪ] *n* (*BRIT: job*) poste vacant; (*room*) chambre *f* disponible; **"no vacancies"** "complet".
vacant ['veɪkənt] *adj* (*post*) vacant(e); (*seat etc*) libre, disponible; (*expression*) distrait(e).
vacant lot *n* terrain inoccupé; (*for sale*) terrain à vendre.
vacate [və'keɪt] *vt* quitter.
vacation [və'keɪʃən] *n* (*esp US*) vacances *fpl*; **to take a** ~ prendre des vacances; **on** ~ en vacances.
vacation course *n* cours *mpl* de vacances.
vaccinate ['væksɪneɪt] *vt* vacciner.
vaccination [væksɪ'neɪʃən] *n* vaccination *f*.
vaccine ['væksi:n] *n* vaccin *m*.
vacuum ['vækjum] *n* vide *m*.
vacuum bottle *n* (*US*) = **vacuum flask.**
vacuum cleaner *n* aspirateur *m*.
vacuum flask *n* (*BRIT*) bouteille *f* thermos ®.
vacuum-packed ['vækjumpækt] *adj* emballé(e) sous vide.
vagabond ['vægəbɒnd] *n* vagabond/e; (*tramp*) chemineau *m*, clochard/e.
vagary ['veɪgərɪ] *n* caprice *m*.
vagina [və'dʒaɪnə] *n* vagin *m*.
vagrancy ['veɪgrənsɪ] *n* vagabondage *m*.
vagrant ['veɪgrənt] *n* vagabond/e, mendiant/e.
vague [veɪg] *adj* vague, imprécis(e); (*blurred: photo, memory*) flou(e); **I haven't the** ~**st idea** je n'en ai pas la moindre idée.
vaguely ['veɪglɪ] *adv* vaguement.
vain [veɪn] *adj* (*useless*) vain(e); (*conceited*) vaniteux(euse); **in** ~ en vain.
valance ['væləns] *n* (*of bed*) tour *m* de lit.
valedictory [vælɪ'dɪktərɪ] *adj* d'adieu.
valentine ['væləntaɪn] *n* (*also*: ~ **card**) carte *f* de la Saint-Valentin.
valet ['vælɪt] *n* valet *m* de chambre.
valet parking *n* parcage *m* par les soins du personnel (de l'hôtel *etc*).
valet service *n* (*for clothes*) pressing *m*; (*for car*) nettoyage complet.
valiant ['vælɪənt] *adj* vaillant(e), courageux(euse).
valid ['vælɪd] *adj* valide, valable; (*excuse*) valable.

validate ['vælɪdeɪt] *vt* (*contract, document*) valider; (*argument, claim*) prouver la justesse de, confirmer.

validity [və'lɪdɪtɪ] *n* validité *f*.

valise [və'liːz] *n* sac *m* de voyage.

valley ['vælɪ] *n* vallée *f*.

valour, (*US*) **valor** ['vælə*] *n* courage *m*.

valuable ['væljuəbl] *adj* (*jewel*) de grande valeur; (*time*) précieux(euse); ~s *npl* objets *mpl* de valeur.

valuation [vælju'eɪʃən] *n* évaluation *f*, expertise *f*.

value ['væljuː] *n* valeur *f* ♦ *vt* (*fix price*) évaluer, expertiser; (*cherish*) tenir à; **you get good ~ (for money) in that shop** vous en avez pour votre argent dans ce magasin; **to lose (in)** ~ (*currency*) baisser; (*property*) se déprécier; **to gain (in)** ~ (*currency*) monter; (*property*) prendre de la valeur; **to be of great ~ to sb** (*fig*) être très utile à qn.

value added tax (VAT) [-'ædɪd-] *n* (*BRIT*) taxe *f* à la valeur ajoutée (TVA).

valued ['væljuːd] *adj* (*appreciated*) estimé(e).

valuer ['væljuə*] *n* expert *m* (en estimations).

valve [vælv] *n* (*in machine*) soupape *f*, (*on tyre*) valve *f*; (*in radio*) lampe *f*.

vampire ['væmpaɪə*] *n* vampire *m*.

van [væn] *n* (*AUT*) camionnette *f*; (*BRIT RAIL*) fourgon *m*.

V and A *n abbr* (*BRIT*) = Victoria and Albert Museum.

vandal ['vændl] *n* vandale *m/f*.

vandalism ['vændəlɪzəm] *n* vandalisme *m*.

vandalize ['vændəlaɪz] *vt* saccager.

vanguard ['vængɑːd] *n* avant-garde *m*.

vanilla [və'nɪlə] *n* vanille *f* ♦ *cpd* (*ice cream*) à la vanille.

vanish ['vænɪʃ] *vi* disparaître.

vanity ['vænɪtɪ] *n* vanité *f*.

vanity case *n* sac *m* de toilette.

vantage ['vɑːntɪdʒ] *n*: ~ **point** bonne position.

vaporize ['veɪpəraɪz] *vt* vaporiser ♦ *vi* se vaporiser.

vapour, (*US*) **vapor** ['veɪpə*] *n* vapeur *f*; (*on window*) buée *f*.

vapo(u)r trail *n* (*AVIAT*) traînée *f* de condensation.

variable ['vɛərɪəbl] *adj* variable; (*mood*) changeant(e) ♦ *n* variable *f*.

variance ['vɛərɪəns] *n*: **to be at** ~ **(with)** être en désaccord (avec); (*facts*) être en contradiction (avec).

variant ['vɛərɪənt] *n* variante *f*.

variation [vɛərɪ'eɪʃən] *n* variation *f*; (*in opinion*) changement *m*.

varicose ['værɪkəus] *adj*: ~ **veins** varices *fpl*.

varied ['vɛərɪd] *adj* varié(e), divers(e).

variety [və'raɪətɪ] *n* variété *f*; (*quantity*): **a wide** ~ **of ...** une quantité *or* un grand nombre de ... (différent(e)s *or* divers(es)); **for a** ~ **of reasons** pour diverses raisons.

variety show *n* (spectacle *m* de) variétés *fpl*.

various ['vɛərɪəs] *adj* divers(e), différent(e); (*several*) divers, plusieurs; **at** ~ **times** (*different*) en diverses occasions; (*several*) à plusieurs reprises.

varnish ['vɑːnɪʃ] *n* vernis *m*; (*for nails*) vernis (à ongles) ♦ *vt* vernir; **to** ~ **one's nails** se vernir les ongles.

vary ['vɛərɪ] *vt, vi* varier, changer; **to** ~ **with** *or* **according to** varier selon.

varying ['vɛərɪɪŋ] *adj* variable.

vase [vɑːz] *n* vase *m*.

vasectomy [væ'sɛktəmɪ] *n* vasectomie *f*.

Vaseline ['væsɪliːn] *n* ® vaseline *f*.

vast [vɑːst] *adj* vaste, immense; (*amount, success*) énorme.

vastly ['vɑːstlɪ] *adv* infiniment, extrêmement.

vastness ['vɑːstnɪs] *n* immensité *f*.

VAT [væt] *n abbr* (*BRIT*) = **value added tax**.

vat [væt] *n* cuve *f*.

Vatican ['vætɪkən] *n*: **the** ~ le Vatican.

vatman ['vætmæn] *n* (*BRIT col*) contrôleur *m* de la T.V.A.

vault [vɔːlt] *n* (*of roof*) voûte *f*; (*tomb*) caveau *m*; (*in bank*) salle *f* des coffres; chambre forte; (*jump*) saut *m* ♦ *vt* (*also*: ~ **over**) sauter (d'un bond).

vaunted ['vɔːntɪd] *adj*: **much-**~ tant célébré(e).

VC *n abbr* = **vice-chairman**; (*BRIT*: = Victoria Cross*) distinction militaire.

VCR *n abbr* = **video cassette recorder**.

VD *n abbr* = **venereal disease**.

VDU *n abbr* = **visual display unit**.

veal [viːl] *n* veau *m*.

veer [vɪə*] *vi* tourner, virer.

veg. [vɛdʒ] *n abbr* (*BRIT col*) = **vegetable(s)**.

vegan ['viːgən] *n* végétalien/ne.

vegeburger ['vɛdʒɪbəːgə*] *n* burger végétarien.

vegetable ['vɛdʒtəbl] *n* légume *m* ♦ *adj* végétal(e).

vegetable garden *n* (jardin *m*) potager *m*.

vegetarian [vɛdʒɪ'tɛərɪən] *adj, n* végétarien(ne).

vegetate ['vɛdʒɪteɪt] *vi* végéter.

vegetation [vɛdʒɪ'teɪʃən] *n* végétation *f*.

vegetative ['vɛdʒɪtətɪv] *adj* (*lit*) végétal(e); (*fig*) végétatif(ive).

veggieburger ['vɛdʒɪbəːgə*] *n* = **vegeburger**.

vehemence ['viːɪməns] *n* véhémence *f*, violence *f*.

vehement ['viːɪmənt] *adj* violent(e), impétueux(euse); (*impassioned*) ardent(e).

vehicle ['viːɪkl] *n* véhicule *m*.

vehicular [vɪ'hɪkjulə*] *adj*: **"no** ~ **traffic"** "interdit à tout véhicule".

veil [veɪl] *n* voile *m* ♦ *vt* voiler; **under a** ~ **of secrecy** (*fig*) dans le plus grand secret.

veiled [veɪld] *adj* voilé(e).

vein [veɪn] *n* veine *f*; (*on leaf*) nervure *f*; (*fig: mood*) esprit *m*.

Velcro ['vɛlkrəu] *n* ® velcro *m* ®.

vellum ['vɛləm] n (*writing paper*) vélin m.
velocity [vɪ'lɔsɪtɪ] n vitesse f, vélocité f.
velour(s) [və'luə*] n velours m.
velvet ['vɛlvɪt] n velours m.
vending machine ['vɛndɪŋ-] n distributeur m automatique.
vendor ['vɛndə*] n vendeur/euse; **street** ~ marchand ambulant.
veneer [və'nɪə*] n placage m de bois; (*fig*) vernis m.
venerable ['vɛnərəbl] adj vénérable.
venereal [vɪ'nɪərɪəl] adj: ~ **disease (VD)** maladie vénérienne.
Venetian [vɪ'niːʃən] adj: ~ **blind** store vénitien.
Venezuela [vɛnɛ'zweɪlə] n Venezuela m.
Venezuelan [vɛnɛ'zweɪlən] adj vénézuélien(ne) ♦ n Vénézuélien/ne.
vengeance ['vɛndʒəns] n vengeance f; **with a** ~ (*fig*) vraiment, pour de bon.
vengeful ['vɛndʒful] adj vengeur(geresse).
Venice ['vɛnɪs] n Venise f.
venison ['vɛnɪsn] n venaison f.
venom ['vɛnəm] n venin m.
venomous ['vɛnəməs] adj venimeux(euse).
vent [vɛnt] n conduit m d'aération; (*in dress, jacket*) fente f ♦ vt (*fig: one's feelings*) donner libre cours à.
ventilate ['vɛntɪleɪt] vt (*room*) ventiler, aérer.
ventilation [vɛntɪ'leɪʃən] n ventilation f, aération f.
ventilation shaft n conduit m de ventilation or d'aération.
ventilator ['vɛntɪleɪtə*] n ventilateur m.
ventriloquist [vɛn'trɪləkwɪst] n ventriloque m/f.
venture ['vɛntʃə*] n entreprise f ♦ vt risquer, hasarder ♦ vi s'aventurer, se risquer; **a business** ~ une entreprise commerciale; **to** ~ **to do sth** se risquer à faire qch.
venture capital n capital-risques m.
venue ['vɛnjuː] n (*of conference etc*) lieu m de la réunion (*or manifestation etc*); (*of match*) lieu de la rencontre.
Venus ['viːnəs] n (*planet*) Vénus f.
veracity [və'ræsɪtɪ] n véracité f.
veranda(h) [və'rændə] n véranda f.
verb [vəːb] n verbe m.
verbal ['vəːbl] adj verbal(e); (*translation*) littéral(e).
verbally ['vəːbəlɪ] adv verbalement.
verbatim [vəː'beɪtɪm] adj, adv mot pour mot.
verbose [vəː'bəus] adj verbeux(euse).
verdict ['vəːdɪkt] n verdict m; ~ **of guilty/not guilty** verdict de culpabilité/de non-culpabilité.
verge [vəːdʒ] n bord m; "**soft ~s**" (*BRIT*) "accotements non stabilisés"; **on the** ~ **of doing** sur le point de faire.
▶**verge on** vt fus approcher de.
verger ['vəːdʒə*] n (*REL*) bedeau m.
verification [vɛrɪfɪ'keɪʃən] n vérification f.

verify ['vɛrɪfaɪ] vt vérifier.
veritable ['vɛrɪtəbl] adj véritable.
vermin ['vəːmɪn] npl animaux mpl nuisibles; (*insects*) vermine f.
vermouth ['vəːməθ] n vermouth m.
vernacular [və'nækjulə*] n langue f vernaculaire, dialecte m.
versatile ['vəːsətaɪl] adj polyvalent(e).
verse [vəːs] n vers mpl; (*stanza*) strophe f; (*in bible*) verset m; **in** ~ en vers.
versed [vəːst] adj: (**well-**)~ **in** versé(e) dans.
version ['vəːʃən] n version f.
versus ['vəːsəs] prep contre.
vertebra, pl ~**e** ['vəːtɪbrə, -briː] n vertèbre f.
vertebrate ['vəːtɪbrɪt] n vertébré m.
vertical ['vəːtɪkl] adj vertical(e) ♦ n verticale f.
vertically ['vəːtɪklɪ] adv verticalement.
vertigo ['vəːtɪgəu] n vertige m; **to suffer from** ~ avoir des vertiges.
verve [vəːv] n brio m; enthousiasme m.
very ['vɛrɪ] adv très ♦ adj: **the** ~ **book which** le livre même que; **the** ~ **thought (of it)** ... rien que d'y penser ...; **at the** ~ **end** tout à la fin; **the** ~ **last** le tout dernier; **at the** ~ **least** au moins; ~ **well** très bien; ~ **little** très peu; ~ **much** beaucoup.
vespers ['vɛspəz] npl vêpres fpl.
vessel ['vɛsl] n (*ANAT, NAUT*) vaisseau m; (*container*) récipient m.
vest [vɛst] n (*BRIT*) tricot m de corps; (*US*) gilet m ♦ vt: **to** ~ **sb with sth, to** ~ **sth in sb** investir qn de qch.
vested interest n: **to have a** ~ **in doing** avoir tout intérêt à faire; ~**s** npl (*COMM*) droits acquis.
vestibule ['vɛstɪbjuːl] n vestibule m.
vestige ['vɛstɪdʒ] n vestige m.
vestry ['vɛstrɪ] n sacristie f.
Vesuvius [vɪ'suːvɪəs] n Vésuve m.
vet [vɛt] n abbr (= *veterinary surgeon*) vétérinaire m/f ♦ vt examiner minutieusement; (*text*) revoir; (*candidate*) se renseigner soigneusement sur, soumettre à une enquête approfondie.
veteran ['vɛtərn] n vétéran m; (*also:* **war** ~) ancien combattant ♦ adj: **she's a** ~ **campaigner for** ... cela fait très longtemps qu'elle lutte pour ....
veteran car n voiture f d'époque.
veterinarian [vɛtrɪ'nɛərɪən] n (*US*) = **veterinary surgeon**.
veterinary ['vɛtrɪnərɪ] adj vétérinaire.
veterinary surgeon n (*BRIT*) vétérinaire m/f.
veto ['viːtəu] n (pl ~**es**) veto m ♦ vt opposer son veto à; **to put a** ~ **on** mettre (*or* opposer) son veto à.
vetting ['vɛtɪŋ] n: **positive** ~ enquête f de sécurité.
vex [vɛks] vt fâcher, contrarier.
vexed [vɛkst] adj (*question*) controversé(e).
VFD n abbr (*US*) = *voluntary fire department*.
VG n abbr (*BRIT: SCOL etc: = very good*) tb (= *très*

bien).

VHF *abbr* (= *very high frequency*) VHF.

VI *abbr* (*US*) = *Virgin Islands*.

via ['vaɪə] *prep* par, via.

viability [vaɪə'bɪlɪtɪ] *n* viabilité *f*.

viable ['vaɪəbl] *adj* viable.

viaduct ['vaɪədʌkt] *n* viaduc *m*.

vial ['vaɪəl] *m* fiole *f*.

vibes [vaɪbz] *npl* (*col*): **I get good/bad ~ about it** je le sens bien/ne le sens pas; **there are good/bad ~ between us** entre nous le courant passe bien/ne passe pas.

vibrant ['vaɪbrnt] *adj* (*sound, colour*) vibrant(e).

vibraphone ['vaɪbrəfəun] *n* vibraphone *m*.

vibrate [vaɪ'breɪt] *vi*: **to ~ (with)** vibrer (de); (*resound*) retentir (de).

vibration [vaɪ'breɪʃən] *n* vibration *f*.

vibrator [vaɪ'breɪtə*] *n* vibromasseur *m*.

vicar ['vɪkə*] *n* pasteur *m* (*de l'Église anglicane*).

vicarage ['vɪkərɪdʒ] *n* presbytère *m*.

vicarious [vɪ'kɛərɪəs] *adj* (*pleasure, experience*) indirect(e).

vice [vaɪs] *n* (*evil*) vice *m*; (*TECH*) étau *m*.

vice- [vaɪs] *prefix* vice-.

vice-chairman [vaɪs'tʃɛəmən] *n* vice-président/e.

vice-chancellor [vaɪs'tʃɑːnsələ*] *n* (*BRIT*) ≈ président/e d'université.

vice-president [vaɪs'prɛzɪdənt] *n* vice-président/e.

viceroy ['vaɪsrɔɪ] *n* vice-roi *m*.

vice squad *n* ≈ brigade mondaine.

vice versa ['vaɪsɪ'vɜːsə] *adv* vice versa.

vicinity [vɪ'sɪnɪtɪ] *n* environs *mpl*, alentours *mpl*.

vicious ['vɪʃəs] *adj* (*remark*) cruel(le), méchant(e); (*blow*) brutal(e); **a ~ circle** un cercle vicieux.

viciousness ['vɪʃəsnɪs] *n* méchanceté *f*, cruauté *f*; brutalité *f*.

vicissitudes [vɪ'sɪsɪtjuːdz] *npl* vicissitudes *fpl*.

victim ['vɪktɪm] *n* victime *f*; **to be the ~ of** être victime de.

victimization [vɪktɪmaɪ'zeɪʃən] *n* brimades *fpl*; représailles *fpl*.

victimize ['vɪktɪmaɪz] *vt* brimer; exercer des représailles sur.

victor ['vɪktə*] *n* vainqueur *m*.

Victorian [vɪk'tɔːrɪən] *adj* victorien(ne).

victorious [vɪk'tɔːrɪəs] *adj* victorieux(euse).

victory ['vɪktərɪ] *n* victoire *f*; **to win a ~ over sb** remporter une victoire sur qn.

video ['vɪdɪəu] *n* (~ *film*) vidéo *f*; (*also*: ~ **cassette**) vidéocassette *f*; (*also*: ~ **cassette recorder**) magnétoscope *m* ♦ *vt* (*with recorder*) enregistrer; (*with camera*) filmer ♦ *cpd* vidéo *inv*.

video camera *n* caméra *f* vidéo *inv*.

video cassette *n* vidéocassette *f*.

video (cassette) recorder *n* magnétoscope *m*.

videodisc ['vɪdɪəudɪsk] *n* vidéodisque *m*.

video game *n* jeu *m* vidéo *inv*.

video nasty *n* vidéo à caractère violent ou pornographique.

videophone ['vɪdɪəufəun] *n* visiophone *m*, vidéophone *m*.

video recording *n* enregistrement *m* (en) vidéo *inv*.

video tape *n* bande *f* vidéo *inv*; (*cassette*) vidéocassette *f*.

vie [vaɪ] *vi*: **to ~ with** lutter avec, rivaliser avec.

Vienna [vɪ'ɛnə] *n* Vienne.

Vietnam, Viet Nam ['vjɛt'næm] *n* Viêt-nam or Vietnam *m*.

Vietnamese [vjɛtnə'miːz] *adj* vietnamien(ne) ♦ *n* (*pl inv*) Vietnamien/ne; (*LING*) vietnamien *m*.

view [vjuː] *n* vue *f*; (*opinion*) avis *m*, vue ♦ *vt* (*situation*) considérer; (*house*) visiter; **on ~** (*in museum etc*) exposé(e); **in full ~ of sb** sous les yeux de qn; **to be within ~ (of sth)** être à portée de vue (de qch); **an overall ~ of the situation** une vue d'ensemble de la situation; **in my ~** à mon avis; **in ~ of the fact that** étant donné que; **with a ~ to doing sth** dans l'intention de faire qch.

viewdata ['vjuːdeɪtə] *n* (*BRIT*) télétexte *m* (*version téléphonique*).

viewer ['vjuːə*] *n* (*viewfinder*) viseur *m*; (*small projector*) visionneuse *f*; (*TV*) téléspectateur/trice.

viewfinder ['vjuːfaɪndə*] *n* viseur *m*.

viewpoint ['vjuːpɔɪnt] *n* point *m* de vue.

vigil ['vɪdʒɪl] *n* veille *f*; **to keep ~** veiller.

vigilance ['vɪdʒɪləns] *n* vigilance *f*.

vigilance committee *n* comité *m* d'autodéfense.

vigilant ['vɪdʒɪlənt] *adj* vigilant(e).

vigilante [vɪdʒɪ'læntɪ] *n* justicier ou membre *m* d'un groupe d'autodéfense.

vigorous ['vɪgərəs] *adj* vigoureux(euse).

vigour, (*US***) vigor** ['vɪgə*] *n* vigueur *f*.

vile [vaɪl] *adj* (*action*) vil(e); (*smell*) abominable; (*temper*) massacrant(e).

vilify ['vɪlɪfaɪ] *vt* calomnier, vilipender.

villa ['vɪlə] *n* villa *f*.

village ['vɪlɪdʒ] *n* village *m*.

villager ['vɪlɪdʒə*] *n* villageois/e.

villain ['vɪlən] *n* (*scoundrel*) scélérat *m*; (*criminal*) bandit *m*; (*in novel etc*) traître *m*.

VIN *n abbr* (*US*) = *vehicle identification number*.

vinaigrette [vɪneɪ'grɛt] *n* vinaigrette *f*.

vindicate ['vɪndɪkeɪt] *vt* défendre avec succès; justifier.

vindication [vɪndɪ'keɪʃən] *n*: **in ~ of** pour justifier.

vindictive [vɪn'dɪktɪv] *adj* vindicatif(ive), rancunier(ière).

vine [vaɪn] *n* vigne *f*; (*climbing plant*) plante grimpante.

vinegar ['vɪnɪgə*] *n* vinaigre *m*.

vine grower n viticulteur m.
vine-growing ['vaɪŋɡraʊɪŋ] adj viticole ♦ n viticulture f.
vineyard ['vɪnjɑːd] n vignoble m.
vintage ['vɪntɪdʒ] n (year) année f, millésime m; **the 1970 ~** le millésime 1970.
vintage car n voiture de grand cru.
vintage wine n vin m de grand cru.
vinyl ['vaɪnl] n vinyle m.
viola [vɪ'əʊlə] n alto m.
violate ['vaɪəleɪt] vt violer.
violation [vaɪə'leɪʃən] n violation f; **in ~ of** (rule, law) en infraction à, en violation de.
violence ['vaɪələns] n violence f; (POL etc) incidents violents.
violent ['vaɪələnt] adj violent(e); **a ~ dislike of sb/sth** une aversion profonde pour qn/qch.
violently ['vaɪələntlɪ] adv violemment; (ill, angry) terriblement.
violet ['vaɪələt] adj (colour) violet(te) ♦ n (plant) violette f.
violin [vaɪə'lɪn] n violon m.
violinist [vaɪə'lɪnɪst] n violoniste m/f.
VIP n abbr (= very important person) VIP m.
viper ['vaɪpə*] n vipère f.
viral ['vaɪərəl] adj viral(e).
virgin ['vɜːdʒɪn] n vierge f ♦ adj vierge; **she is a ~** elle est vierge; **the Blessed V~** la Sainte Vierge.
virginity [vɜː'dʒɪnɪtɪ] n virginité f.
Virgo ['vɜːɡəʊ] n la Vierge; **to be ~** être de la Vierge.
virile ['vɪraɪl] adj viril(e).
virility [vɪ'rɪlɪtɪ] n virilité f.
virtual ['vɜːtjʊəl] adj (COMPUT, PHYSICS) virtuel(le); (in effect): **it's a ~ impossibility** c'est quasiment impossible; **the ~ leader** le chef dans la pratique.
virtually ['vɜːtjʊəlɪ] adv (almost) pratiquement; **it is ~ impossible** c'est quasiment impossible.
virtual reality n réalité virtuelle.
virtue ['vɜːtjuː] n vertu f; (advantage) mérite m, avantage m; **by ~ of** par le fait de.
virtuosity [vɜːtjʊ'ɔsɪtɪ] n virtuosité f.
virtuoso [vɜːtjʊ'əʊzəʊ] n virtuose m/f.
virtuous ['vɜːtjʊəs] adj vertueux(euse).
virulent ['vɪrʊlənt] adj virulent(e).
virus ['vaɪərəs] n virus m.
visa ['viːzə] n visa m.
vis-à-vis [viːzə'viː] prep vis-à-vis de.
viscount ['vaɪkaʊnt] n vicomte m.
viscous ['vɪskəs] adj visqueux(euse), gluant(e).
vise [vaɪs] n (US TECH) = **vice**.
visibility [vɪzɪ'bɪlɪtɪ] n visibilité f.
visible ['vɪzəbl] adj visible; **~ exports/imports** exportations/importations fpl visibles.
visibly ['vɪzəblɪ] adv visiblement.
vision ['vɪʒən] n (sight) vue f, vision f; (foresight, in dream) vision.
visionary ['vɪʒənrɪ] n visionnaire m/f.

visit ['vɪzɪt] n visite f; (stay) séjour m ♦ vt (person) rendre visite à; (place) visiter; **on a private/official ~** en visite privée/officielle.
visiting ['vɪzɪtɪŋ] adj (speaker, team) invité(e), de l'extérieur.
visiting card n carte f de visite.
visiting hours npl heures fpl de visite.
visiting professor n ≈ professeur associé.
visitor ['vɪzɪtə*] n visiteur/euse; (in hotel) client/e.
visitors' book n livre m d'or; (in hotel) registre m.
visor ['vaɪzə*] n visière f.
VISTA ['vɪstə] n abbr (= Volunteers in Service to America) programme d'assistance bénévole aux régions pauvres.
vista ['vɪstə] n vue f, perspective f.
visual ['vɪzjʊəl] adj visuel(le).
visual aid n support visuel (pour l'enseignement).
visual arts npl arts mpl plastiques.
visual display unit (VDU) n console f de visualisation, visuel m.
visualize ['vɪzjʊəlaɪz] vt se représenter; (foresee) prévoir.
visually ['vɪzjʊəlɪ] adv visuellement; **~ handicapped** handicapé(e) visuel(le).
vital ['vaɪtl] adj vital(e); **of ~ importance (to sb/sth)** d'une importance capitale (pour qn/qch).
vitality [vaɪ'tælɪtɪ] n vitalité f.
vitally ['vaɪtəlɪ] adv extrêmement.
vital statistics npl (of population) statistiques fpl démographiques; (col: woman's) mensurations fpl.
vitamin ['vɪtəmɪn] n vitamine f.
vitiate ['vɪʃɪeɪt] vt vicier.
vitreous ['vɪtrɪəs] adj (china) vitreux(euse); (enamel) vitrifié(e).
vitriolic [vɪtrɪ'ɔlɪk] adj (fig) venimeux(euse).
viva ['vaɪvə] n (also: ~ **voce**) (examen) oral.
vivacious [vɪ'veɪʃəs] adj animé(e), qui a de la vivacité.
vivacity [vɪ'væsɪtɪ] n vivacité f.
vivid ['vɪvɪd] adj (account) frappant(e); (light, imagination) vif(vive).
vividly ['vɪvɪdlɪ] adv (describe) d'une manière vivante; (remember) de façon précise.
vivisection [vɪvɪ'sɛkʃən] n vivisection f.
vixen ['vɪksn] n renarde f; (pej: woman) mégère f.
viz [vɪz] abbr (= vide licet: namely) à savoir, c. à d.
VLF abbr = **very low frequency**.
V-neck ['viːnɛk] n décolleté m en V.
VOA n abbr (= Voice of America) voix f de l'Amérique (émissions de radio à destination de l'étranger).
vocabulary [vəʊ'kæbjʊlərɪ] n vocabulaire m.
vocal ['vəʊkl] adj vocal(e); (articulate) qui n'hésite pas à s'exprimer, qui sait faire entendre ses opinions; **~s** npl voix fpl.

vocal cords *npl* cordes vocales.
vocalist ['vəukəlɪst] *n* chanteur/euse.
vocation [vəu'keɪʃən] *n* vocation *f*.
vocational [vəu'keɪʃənl] *adj* professionnel(le); ~ **guidance/training** orientation/formation professionnelle.
vociferous [və'sɪfərəs] *adj* bruyant(e).
vodka ['vɔdkə] *n* vodka *f*.
vogue [vəug] *n* mode *f*; (*popularity*) vogue *f*; **to be in** ~ être en vogue *or* à la mode.
voice [vɔɪs] *n* voix *f*; (*opinion*) avis *m* ♦ *vt* (*opinion*) exprimer, formuler; **in a loud/soft** ~ à voix haute/basse; **to give** ~ **to** exprimer.
voice mail *n* (*system*) messagerie *f* vocale; (*device*) boîte *f* vocale.
voice-over ['vɔɪsəuvə*] *n* voix off *f*.
void [vɔɪd] *n* vide *m* ♦ *adj* (*invalid*) nul(le); (*empty*): ~ **of** vide de, dépourvu(e) de.
voile [vɔɪl] *n* voile *m* (*tissu*).
vol. *abbr* (= *volume*) vol.
volatile ['vɔlətaɪl] *adj* volatil(e); (*fig*) versatile.
volcanic [vɔl'kænɪk] *adj* volcanique.
volcano, ~es [vɔl'keɪnəu] *n* volcan *m*.
volition [və'lɪʃən] *n*: **of one's own** ~ de son propre gré.
volley ['vɔlɪ] *n* (*of gunfire*) salve *f*; (*of stones etc*) pluie *f*, volée *f*; (*TENNIS etc*) volée.
volleyball ['vɔlɪbɔːl] *n* volley(-ball) *m*.
volt [vəult] *n* volt *m*.
voltage ['vəultɪdʒ] *n* tension *f*, voltage *m*; **high/low** ~ haute/basse tension.
voluble ['vɔljubl] *adj* volubile.
volume ['vɔljuːm] *n* volume *m*; (*of tank*) capacité *f*; ~ **one/two** (*of book*) tome un/deux; **his expression spoke** ~**s** son expression en disait long.
volume control *n* (*RADIO, TV*) bouton *m* de réglage du volume.
voluminous [və'luːmɪnəs] *adj* volumineux(euse).
voluntarily ['vɔləntrɪlɪ] *adv* volontairement; bénévolement.
voluntary ['vɔləntərɪ] *adj* volontaire; (*unpaid*) bénévole.
voluntary liquidation *n* (*COMM*) dépôt *m* de bilan.
voluntary redundancy *n* (*BRIT*) départ *m* volontaire (*en cas de licenciements*).
volunteer [vɔlən'tɪə*] *n* volontaire *m/f* ♦ *vi* (*MIL*) s'engager comme volontaire; **to** ~ **to do** se proposer pour faire.
voluptuous [və'lʌptjuəs] *adj* voluptueux(euse).
vomit ['vɔmɪt] *n* vomissure *f* ♦ *vt, vi* vomir.
voracious [və'reɪʃəs] *adj* vorace; (*reader*) avide.
vote [vəut] *n* vote *m*, suffrage *m*; (*cast*) voix *f*, vote; (*franchise*) droit *m* de vote ♦ *vt* (*bill*) voter; (*chairman*) élire ♦ *vi* voter; **to put sth to the** ~, **to take a** ~ **on sth** mettre qch aux voix, procéder à un vote sur qch; ~ **for** *or* **in favour of/against** vote pour/contre; **to** ~ **to**

do sth voter en faveur de faire qch; ~ **of censure** motion *f* de censure; ~ **of thanks** discours *m* de remerciement.
voter ['vəutə*] *n* électeur/trice.
voting ['vəutɪŋ] *n* scrutin *m*.
voting paper *n* (*BRIT*) bulletin *m* de vote.
voting right *n* droit *m* de vote.
vouch [vautʃ]: **to** ~ **for** *vt fus* se porter garant de.
voucher ['vautʃə*] *n* (*for meal, petrol*) bon *m*; (*receipt*) reçu *m*; **travel** ~ bon *m* de transport.
vow [vau] *n* vœu *m*, serment *m* ♦ *vi* jurer; **to take** *or* **make a** ~ **to do sth** faire le vœu de faire qch.
vowel ['vauəl] *n* voyelle *f*.
voyage ['vɔɪɪdʒ] *n* voyage *m* par mer, traversée *f*.
voyeur [vwaː'jɔː*] *n* voyeur *m*.
VP *n abbr* = **vice-president**.
vs *abbr* (= *versus*) c.
VSO *n abbr* (*BRIT: = Voluntary Service Overseas*) ≈ coopération civile.
VT, Vt. *abbr* (*US*) = *Vermont*.
vulgar ['vʌlgə*] *adj* vulgaire.
vulgarity [vʌl'gærɪtɪ] *n* vulgarité *f*.
vulnerability [vʌlnərə'bɪlɪtɪ] *n* vulnérabilité *f*.
vulnerable ['vʌlnərəbl] *adj* vulnérable.
vulture ['vʌltʃə*] *n* vautour *m*.

W w

W, w ['dʌbljuː] *n* (*letter*) W, w *m*; **W for William** W comme William.
W *abbr* (= *west*) O; (*ELEC: = watt*) W.
WA *abbr* (*US*) = *Washington*.
wad [wɔd] *n* (*of cotton wool, paper*) tampon *m*; (*of banknotes etc*) liasse *f*.
wadding ['wɔdɪŋ] *n* rembourrage *m*.
waddle ['wɔdl] *vi* se dandiner.
wade [weɪd] *vi*: **to** ~ **through** marcher dans, patauger dans ♦ *vt* passer à gué.
wafer ['weɪfə*] *n* (*CULIN*) gaufrette *f*; (*REL*) pain *m* d'hostie; (*COMPUT*) tranche *f* (de silicium).
wafer-thin ['weɪfə'θɪn] *adj* ultra-mince, mince comme du papier à cigarette.
waffle ['wɔfl] *n* (*CULIN*) gaufre *f*; (*col*) rabâchage *m*; remplissage *m* ♦ *vi* parler pour ne rien dire; faire du remplissage.
waffle iron *n* gaufrier *m*.
waft [wɔft] *vt* porter ♦ *vi* flotter.
wag [wæg] *vt* agiter, remuer ♦ *vi* remuer; **the dog** ~**ged its tail** le chien a remué la queue.
wage [weɪdʒ] *n* (*also*: ~**s**) salaire *m*, paye *f* ♦ *vt*: **to** ~ **war** faire la guerre; **a day's** ~**s** un

jour de salaire.

wage claim n demande f d'augmentation de salaire.

wage differential n éventail m des salaires.

wage earner [-ə:nə*] n salarié/e; (bread-winner) soutien m de famille.

wage freeze n blocage m des salaires.

wage packet n (BRIT) (enveloppe f de) paye f.

wager ['weɪdʒə*] n pari m ♦ vt parier.

waggle ['wægl] vt, vi remuer.

wag(g)on ['wægən] n (horse-drawn) chariot m; (BRIT RAIL) wagon m (de marchandises).

wail [weɪl] n gémissement m; (of siren) hurlement m ♦ vi gémir; hurler.

waist [weɪst] n taille f, ceinture f.

waistcoat ['weɪskəut] n (BRIT) gilet m.

waistline ['weɪstlaɪn] n (tour m de) taille f.

wait [weɪt] n attente f ♦ vi attendre; **to ~ for sb/sth** attendre qn/qch; **to keep sb ~ing** faire attendre qn; **~ a minute!** un instant!; **"repairs while you ~"** "réparations minute"; **I can't ~ to ...** (fig) je meurs d'envie de ...; **to lie in ~ for** guetter.

►**wait behind** vi rester (à attendre).

►**wait on** vt fus servir.

►**wait up** vi attendre, ne pas se coucher; **don't ~ up for me** ne m'attendez pas pour aller vous coucher.

waiter ['weɪtə*] n garçon m (de café), serveur m.

waiting ['weɪtɪŋ] n: **"no ~"** (BRIT AUT) "stationnement interdit".

waiting list n liste f d'attente.

waiting room n salle f d'attente.

waitress ['weɪtrɪs] n serveuse f.

waive [weɪv] vt renoncer à, abandonner.

waiver ['weɪvə*] n dispense f.

wake [weɪk] vb (pt woke, ~d, pp woken, ~d [wəuk, 'wəukn]) vt (also: ~ up) réveiller ♦ vi (also: ~ up) se réveiller ♦ n (for dead person) veillée f mortuaire; (NAUT) sillage m; **to ~ up to sth** (fig) se rendre compte de qch; **in the ~ of** (fig) à la suite de; **to follow in sb's ~** (fig) marcher sur les traces de qn.

waken ['weɪkn] vt, vi = **wake**.

Wales [weɪlz] n pays m de Galles.

walk [wɔ:k] n promenade f; (short) petit tour; (gait) démarche f; (pace): **at a quick ~** d'un pas rapide; (path) chemin m; (in park etc) allée f ♦ vi marcher; (for pleasure, exercise) se promener ♦ vt (distance) faire à pied; (dog) promener; **10 minutes' ~ from** à 10 minutes de marche de; **to go for a ~** se promener; faire un tour; **I'll ~ you home** je vais vous raccompagner chez vous; **from all ~s of life** de toutes conditions sociales.

►**walk out** vi (go out) sortir; (as protest) partir (en signe de protestation); (strike) se mettre en grève; **to ~ out on sb** quitter qn.

walkabout ['wɔ:kəbaut] n: **to go (on a) ~** (VIP) prendre un bain de foule.

walker ['wɔ:kə*] n (person) marcheur/euse.

walkie-talkie ['wɔ:kɪ'tɔ:kɪ] n talkie-walkie m.

walking ['wɔ:kɪŋ] n marche f à pied; **it's within ~ distance** on peut y aller à pied.

walking holiday n vacances passées à faire de la randonnée.

walking shoes npl chaussures fpl de marche.

walking stick n canne f.

Walkman ['wɔ:kmən] n ® Walkman m ®.

walk-on ['wɔ:kɔn] adj (THEAT: part) de figurant/e.

walkout ['wɔ:kaut] n (of workers) grève-surprise f.

walkover ['wɔ:kəuvə*] n (col) victoire f or examen m etc facile.

walkway ['wɔ:kweɪ] n promenade f, cheminement piéton.

wall [wɔ:l] n mur m; (of tunnel, cave) paroi f; **to go to the ~** (fig: firm etc) faire faillite.

►**wall in** vt (garden etc) entourer d'un mur.

wall cupboard n placard mural.

walled [wɔ:ld] adj (city) fortifié(e).

wallet ['wɔlɪt] n portefeuille m.

wallflower ['wɔ:lflauə*] n giroflée f; **to be a ~** (fig) faire tapisserie.

wall hanging n tenture (murale), tapisserie f.

wallop ['wɔləp] vt (BRIT col) taper sur, cogner.

wallow ['wɔləu] vi se vautrer; **to ~ in one's grief** se complaire à sa douleur.

wallpaper ['wɔ:lpeɪpə*] n papier peint.

wall-to-wall ['wɔ:ltə'wɔ:l] adj: **~ carpeting** moquette f.

wally ['wɔlɪ] n (col) imbécile m/f.

walnut ['wɔ:lnʌt] n noix f; (tree) noyer m.

walrus, pl **~** or **~es** ['wɔ:lrəs] n morse m.

waltz [wɔ:lts] n valse f ♦ vi valser.

wan [wɔn] adj pâle; triste.

wand [wɔnd] n (also: **magic ~**) baguette f (magique).

wander ['wɔndə*] vi (person) errer, aller sans but; (thoughts) vagabonder; (river) serpenter ♦ vt errer dans.

wanderer ['wɔndərə*] n vagabond/e.

wandering ['wɔndrɪŋ] adj (tribe) nomade; (minstrel, actor) ambulant(e).

wane [weɪn] vi (moon) décroître; (reputation) décliner.

wangle ['wæŋgl] (BRIT col) vt se débrouiller pour avoir; carotter ♦ n combine f, magouille f.

wanker ['wæŋkə*] n (col!) branleur m (!).

want [wɔnt] vt vouloir; (need) avoir besoin de; (lack) manquer de ♦ n (poverty) pauvreté f, besoin m; **~s** npl (needs) besoins mpl; **for ~ of** par manque de, faute de; **to ~ to do** vouloir faire; **to ~ sb to do** vouloir que qn fasse; **you're ~ed on the phone** on vous demande au téléphone; **"cook ~ed"** "on demande un cuisinier".

want ads npl (US) petites annonces.

wanting ['wɔntɪŋ] adj: **to be ~ (in)** manquer (de); **to be found ~** ne pas être à la hauteur.

wanton ['wɔntn] *adj* capricieux(euse); dévergondé(e).

war [wɔ:*] *n* guerre *f*; **to go to** ~ se mettre en guerre.

warble ['wɔ:bl] *n* (*of bird*) gazouillis *m* ♦ *vi* gazouiller.

war cry *n* cri *m* de guerre.

ward [wɔ:d] *n* (*in hospital*) salle *f*; (*POL*) section électorale; (*LAW: child*) pupille *m/f*.

▶**ward off** *vt* parer, éviter.

warden ['wɔ:dn] *n* (*BRIT: of institution*) directeur/trice; (*of park, game reserve*) gardien/ne; (*BRIT: also: traffic* ~) contractuel/le.

warder ['wɔ:də*] *n* (*BRIT*) gardien *m* de prison.

wardrobe ['wɔ:drəub] *n* (*cupboard*) armoire *f*; (*clothes*) garde-robe *f*; (*THEAT*) costumes *mpl*.

warehouse ['wɛəhaus] *n* entrepôt *m*.

wares [wɛəz] *npl* marchandises *fpl*.

warfare ['wɔ:fɛə*] *n* guerre *f*.

war game *n* jeu *m* de stratégie militaire.

warhead ['wɔ:hɛd] *n* (*MIL*) ogive *f*.

warily ['wɛərɪlɪ] *adv* avec prudence, avec précaution.

warlike ['wɔ:laɪk] *adj* guerrier(ière).

warm [wɔ:m] *adj* chaud(e); (*person, greeting, welcome, applause*) chaleureux(euse); (*supporter*) ardent(e), enthousiaste; **it's** ~ il fait chaud; **I'm** ~ j'ai chaud; **to keep sth** ~ tenir qch au chaud; **with my** ~**est thanks/congratulations** avec mes remerciements/mes félicitations les plus sincères.

▶**warm up** *vi* (*person, room*) se réchauffer; (*water*) chauffer; (*athlete, discussion*) s'échauffer ♦ *vt* réchauffer; chauffer; (*engine*) faire chauffer.

warm-blooded ['wɔ:m'blʌdɪd] *adj* (*ZOOL*) à sang chaud.

war memorial *n* monument *m* aux morts.

warm-hearted [wɔ:m'hɑ:tɪd] *adj* affectueux(euse).

warmly ['wɔ:mlɪ] *adv* chaudement; chaleureusement.

warmonger ['wɔ:mʌŋgə*] *n* belliciste *m/f*.

warmongering ['wɔ:mʌŋgrɪŋ] *n* propagande *f* belliciste, bellicisme *m*.

warmth [wɔ:mθ] *n* chaleur *f*.

warm-up ['wɔ:mʌp] *n* (*SPORT*) période *f* d'échauffement.

warn [wɔ:n] *vt* avertir, prévenir; **to** ~ **sb not to do sth** *or* **against doing sth** prévenir qn de ne pas faire qch.

warning ['wɔ:nɪŋ] *n* avertissement *m*; (*notice*) avis *m*; **without (any)** ~ (*suddenly*) inopinément; (*without notifying*) sans prévenir; **gale** ~ (*METEOROLOGY*) avis de grand vent.

warning light *n* avertisseur lumineux.

warning triangle *n* (*AUT*) triangle *m* de présignalisation.

warp [wɔ:p] *n* (*TEXTILES*) chaîne *f* ♦ *vi* (*wood*) travailler, se voiler *or* gauchir ♦ *vt* voiler;

(*fig*) pervertir.

warpath ['wɔ:pɑ:θ] *n*: **to be on the** ~ (*fig*) être sur le sentier de la guerre.

warped [wɔ:pt] *adj* (*wood*) gauchi(e); (*fig*) perverti(e).

warrant ['wɔrnt] *n* (*guarantee*) garantie *f*; (*LAW: to arrest*) mandat *m* d'arrêt; (: *to search*) mandat de perquisition ♦ *vt* (*justify, merit*) justifier.

warrant officer *n* (*MIL*) adjudant *m*; (*NAUT*) premier-maître *m*.

warranty ['wɔrntɪ] *n* garantie *f*; **under** ~ (*COMM*) sous garantie.

warren ['wɔrən] *n* (*of rabbits*) terriers *mpl*, garenne *f*.

warring ['wɔ:rɪŋ] *adj* (*nations*) en guerre; (*interests etc*) contradictoire, opposé(e).

warrior ['wɔrɪə*] *n* guerrier/ière.

Warsaw ['wɔ:sɔ:] *n* Varsovie.

warship ['wɔ:ʃɪp] *n* navire *m* de guerre.

wart [wɔ:t] *n* verrue *f*.

wartime ['wɔ:taɪm] *n*: **in** ~ en temps de guerre.

wary ['wɛərɪ] *adj* prudent(e); **to be** ~ **about** *or* **of doing sth** hésiter beaucoup à faire qch.

was [wɔz] *pt of* **be**.

wash [wɔʃ] *vt* laver; (*sweep, carry: sea etc*) emporter, entraîner; (: *ashore*) rejeter ♦ *vi* se laver ♦ *n* (*paint*) badigeon *m*; (*washing programme*) lavage *m*; (*of ship*) sillage *m*; **to give sth a** ~ laver qch; **to have a** ~ se laver, faire sa toilette; **he was** ~**ed overboard** il a été emporté par une vague.

▶**wash away** *vt* (*stain*) enlever au lavage; (*subj: river etc*) emporter.

▶**wash down** *vt* laver; laver à grande eau.

▶**wash off** *vi* partir au lavage.

▶**wash up** *vi* faire la vaisselle; (*US: have a wash*) se débarbouiller.

Wash. *abbr* (*US*) = Washington.

washable ['wɔʃəbl] *adj* lavable.

washbasin ['wɔʃbeɪsn] *n* lavabo *m*.

washcloth ['wɔʃklɔθ] *n* (*US*) gant *m* de toilette.

washer ['wɔʃə*] *n* (*TECH*) rondelle *f*, joint *m*.

washing ['wɔʃɪŋ] *n* (*BRIT: linen etc*) lessive *f*.

washing line *n* (*BRIT*) corde *f* à linge.

washing machine *n* machine *f* à laver.

washing powder *n* (*BRIT*) lessive *f* (en poudre).

Washington ['wɔʃɪŋtən] *n* (*city, state*) Washington *m*.

washing-up [wɔʃɪŋ'ʌp] *n* (*BRIT*) vaisselle *f*.

washing-up liquid *n* (*BRIT*) produit *m* pour la vaisselle.

wash-out ['wɔʃaut] *n* (*col*) désastre *m*.

washroom ['wɔʃrum] *n* toilettes *fpl*.

wasn't ['wɔznt] = **was not**.

Wasp, WASP [wɔsp] *n abbr* (*US col*: = *White Anglo-Saxon Protestant*) surnom, *souvent péjoratif, donné à l'américain de souche anglo-saxonne, aisé et de tendance conser-*

vatrice.
wasp [wɔsp] n guêpe f.
waspish ['wɔspɪʃ] adj irritable.
wastage ['weɪstɪdʒ] n gaspillage m; (in manufacturing, transport etc) déchet m.
waste [weɪst] n gaspillage m; (of time) perte f; (rubbish) déchets mpl; (also: household ~) ordures fpl ♦ adj (material) de rebut; (energy, heat) perdu(e); (food) inutilisé(e); (land, ground: in city) à l'abandon; (: in country) inculte, en friche ♦ vt gaspiller; (time, opportunity) perdre; ~s npl étendue f désertique; it's a ~ of money c'est de l'argent jeté en l'air; to go to ~ être gaspillé(e); to lay ~ (destroy) dévaster.
▶**waste away** vi dépérir.
wastebasket ['weɪstbɑːskɪt] n = **wastepaper basket**.
waste disposal (unit) n (BRIT) broyeur m d'ordures.
wasteful ['weɪstful] adj gaspilleur(euse); (process) peu économique.
waste ground n (BRIT) terrain m vague.
wasteland ['weɪstlənd] n terres fpl à l'abandon; (in town) terrain(s) m(pl) vague(s).
wastepaper basket ['weɪstpeɪpə-] n corbeille f à papier.
waste pipe n (tuyau m de) vidange f.
waste products npl (INDUSTRY) déchets mpl (de fabrication).
waster ['weɪstə*] n (col) bon/ne à rien.
watch [wɔtʃ] n montre f; (act of watching) surveillance f; guet m; (guard: MIL) sentinelle f; (: NAUT) homme m de quart; (NAUT: spell of duty) quart m ♦ vt (look at) observer; (: match, programme) regarder; (spy on, guard) surveiller; (be careful of) faire attention à ♦ vi regarder; (keep guard) monter la garde; to keep a close ~ on sb/sth surveiller qn/qch de près; ~ what you're doing fais attention à ce que tu fais.
▶**watch out** vi faire attention.
watchband ['wɔtʃbænd] n (US) bracelet m de montre.
watchdog ['wɔtʃdɔg] n chien m de garde; (fig) gardien/ne.
watchful ['wɔtʃful] adj attentif(ive), vigilant(e).
watchmaker ['wɔtʃmeɪkə*] n horloger/ère.
watchman ['wɔtʃmən] n gardien m; (also: night ~) veilleur m de nuit.
watch stem n (US) remontoir m.
watch strap n bracelet m de montre.
watchword ['wɔtʃwəːd] n mot m de passe.
water ['wɔːtə*] n eau f ♦ vt (plant) arroser ♦ vi (eyes) larmoyer; **a drink of** ~ un verre d'eau; **in British** ~**s** dans les eaux territoriales Britanniques; **to pass** ~ uriner; **to make sb's mouth** ~ mettre l'eau à la bouche de qn.
▶**water down** vt (milk) couper d'eau; (fig: story) édulcorer.

water closet n (BRIT) w.-c. mpl, waters mpl.
watercolour, (US) **watercolor** ['wɔːtəkʌlə*] n aquarelle f; ~**s** npl couleurs fpl pour aquarelle.
water-cooled ['wɔːtəkuːld] adj à refroidissement par eau.
watercress ['wɔːtəkrɛs] n cresson m (de fontaine).
waterfall ['wɔːtəfɔːl] n chute f d'eau.
waterfront ['wɔːtəfrʌnt] n (seafront) front m de mer; (at docks) quais mpl.
water heater n chauffe-eau m.
water hole n mare f.
water ice n (BRIT) sorbet m.
watering can ['wɔːtərɪŋ-] n arrosoir m.
water level n niveau m de l'eau; (of flood) niveau des eaux.
water lily n nénuphar m.
waterline ['wɔːtəlaɪn] n (NAUT) ligne f de flottaison.
waterlogged ['wɔːtəlɔgd] adj détrempé(e); imbibé(e) d'eau.
water main n canalisation f d'eau.
watermark ['wɔːtəmɑːk] n (on paper) filigrane m.
watermelon ['wɔːtəmelən] n pastèque f.
water polo n water-polo m.
waterproof ['wɔːtəpruːf] adj imperméable.
water-repellent ['wɔːtərɪˈpɛlnt] adj hydrofuge.
watershed ['wɔːtəʃɛd] n (GEO) ligne f de partage des eaux; (fig) moment m critique, point décisif.
water-skiing ['wɔːtəskiːɪŋ] n ski m nautique.
water softener n adoucisseur m d'eau.
water tank n réservoir m d'eau.
watertight ['wɔːtətaɪt] adj étanche.
water vapour n vapeur f d'eau.
waterway ['wɔːtəweɪ] n cours m d'eau navigable.
waterworks ['wɔːtəwəːks] npl station f hydraulique.
watery ['wɔːtərɪ] adj (colour) délavé(e); (coffee) trop faible.
watt [wɔt] n watt m.
wattage ['wɔtɪdʒ] n puissance f or consommation f en watts.
wattle ['wɔtl] n clayonnage m.
wave [weɪv] n vague f; (of hand) geste m, signe m; (RADIO) onde f; (in hair) ondulation f; (fig: of enthusiasm, strikes etc) vague ♦ vi faire signe de la main; (flag) flotter au vent ♦ vt (handkerchief) agiter; (stick) brandir; (hair) onduler; **to** ~ **goodbye to sb** dire au revoir de la main à qn; **short/medium** ~ (RADIO) ondes courtes/moyennes; **long** ~ (RADIO) grandes ondes; **the new** ~ (CINE, MUS) la nouvelle vague.
▶**wave aside, wave away** vt (person): **to** ~ **sb aside** faire signe à qn de s'écarter; (fig: suggestion, objection) rejeter, repousser; (: doubts) chasser.

waveband ['weɪvbænd] *n* bande *f* de fréquences.
wavelength ['weɪvlɛŋθ] *n* longueur *f* d'ondes.
waver ['weɪvə*] *vi* vaciller; (*voice*) trembler; (*person*) hésiter.
wavy ['weɪvɪ] *adj* ondulé(e); onduleux(euse).
wax [wæks] *n* cire *f*; (*for skis*) fart *m* ♦ *vt* cirer; (*car*) lustrer ♦ *vi* (*moon*) croître.
waxen [wæksn] *adj* cireux(euse).
waxworks ['wækswɔːks] *npl* personnages *mpl* de cire; musée *m* de cire.
way [weɪ] *n* chemin *m*, voie *f*; (*path, access*) passage *m*; (*distance*) distance *f*; (*direction*) chemin, direction *f*; (*manner*) façon *f*, manière *f*; (*habit*) habitude *f*, façon; (*condition*) état *m*; **which** ~? — **this** ~ par où *or* de quel côté? — par ici; **to crawl one's** ~ **to ...** ramper jusqu'à ...; **to lie one's** ~ **out of it** s'en sortir par un mensonge; **to lose one's** ~ perdre son chemin; **on the** ~ **(to)** en route (pour); **to be on one's** ~ être en route; **to be in the** ~ bloquer le passage; (*fig*) gêner; **to keep out of sb's** ~ éviter qn; **it's a long** ~ **away** c'est loin d'ici; **the village is rather out of the** ~ le village est plutôt à l'écart *or* isolé; **to go out of one's** ~ **to do** (*fig*) se donner beaucoup de mal pour faire; **to be under** ~ (*work, project*) être en cours; **to make** ~ **(for sb/sth)** faire place (à qn/qch), s'écarter pour laisser passer (qn/qch); **to get one's own** ~ arriver à ses fins; **put it the right** ~ **up** (*BRIT*) mettez-le dans le bon sens; **to be the wrong** ~ **round** être à l'envers, ne pas être dans le bon sens; **he's in a bad** ~ il va mal; **in a** ~ d'un côté; **in some** ~**s** à certains égards; d'un côté; **in the** ~ **of** en fait de, comme; **by** ~ **of** (*through*) en passant par, via; (*as a sort of*) en guise de; **"~ in"** (*BRIT*) "entrée"; **"~ out"** (*BRIT*) "sortie"; **the** ~ **back** le chemin du retour; **this** ~ **and that** par-ci par-là; **"give** ~**"** (*BRIT AUT*) "cédez la priorité"; **no** ~! (*col*) pas question!
waybill ['weɪbɪl] *n* (*COMM*) récépissé *m*.
waylay ['weɪleɪ] *vt irreg* attaquer; (*fig*): **I got waylaid** quelqu'un m'a accroché.
wayside ['weɪsaɪd] *n* bord *m* de la route; **to fall by the** ~ (*fig*) abandonner; (*morally*) quitter le droit chemin.
way station *n* (*US RAIL*) petite gare.
wayward ['weɪwəd] *adj* capricieux(euse), entêté(e).
WC *n abbr* (*BRIT*: = *water closet*) w.-c. *mpl*, waters *mpl*.
WCC *n abbr* (= *World Council of Churches*) COE *m* (= *Conseil œcuménique des Églises*).
we [wiː] *pl pron* nous.
weak [wiːk] *adj* faible; (*health*) fragile; (*beam etc*) peu solide; (*tea, coffee*) léger(ère); **to grow** ~**(er)** s'affaiblir, faiblir.
weaken ['wiːkn] *vi* faiblir ♦ *vt* affaiblir.
weak-kneed ['wiːk'niːd] *adj* (*fig*) lâche, faible.
weakling ['wiːklɪŋ] *n* gringalet *m*; faible *m/f*.

weakly ['wiːklɪ] *adj* chétif(ive) ♦ *adv* faiblement.
weakness ['wiːknɪs] *n* faiblesse *f*; (*fault*) point *m* faible.
wealth [wɛlθ] *n* (*money, resources*) richesse(s) *f(pl)*; (*of details*) profusion *f*.
wealth tax *n* impôt *m* sur la fortune.
wealthy ['wɛlθɪ] *adj* riche.
wean [wiːn] *vt* sevrer.
weapon ['wɛpən] *n* arme *f*.
wear [wɛə*] *n* (*use*) usage *m*; (*deterioration through use*) usure *f*; (*clothing*): **sports/baby** ~ vêtements *mpl* de sport/pour bébés; **town/evening** ~ tenue *f* de ville/de soirée ♦ *vb* (*pt* **wore**, *pp* **worn** [wɔː*, wɔːn]) *vt* (*clothes*) porter; (*beard etc*) avoir; (*damage: through use*) user ♦ *vi* (*last*) faire de l'usage; (*rub etc through*) s'user; ~ **and tear** usure *f*; **to** ~ **a hole in sth** faire (à la longue) un trou dans qch.
▶**wear away** *vt* user, ronger ♦ *vi* s'user, être rongé(e).
▶**wear down** *vt* user; (*strength*) épuiser.
▶**wear off** *vi* disparaître.
▶**wear on** *vi* se poursuivre; passer.
▶**wear out** *vt* user; (*person, strength*) épuiser.
wearable ['wɛərəbl] *adj* mettable.
wearily ['wɪərɪlɪ] *adv* avec lassitude.
weariness ['wɪərɪnɪs] *n* épuisement *m*, lassitude *f*.
wearisome ['wɪərɪsəm] *adj* (*tiring*) fatigant(e); (*boring*) ennuyeux(euse).
weary ['wɪərɪ] *adj* (*tired*) épuisé(e); (*dispirited*) las(lasse); abattu(e) ♦ *vt* lasser ♦ *vi*: **to** ~ **of** il se lasser de.
weasel ['wiːzl] *n* (*ZOOL*) belette *f*.
weather ['wɛðə*] *n* temps *m* ♦ *vt* (*wood*) faire mûrir; (*tempest, crisis*) essuyer, être pris(e) dans; survivre à, tenir le coup durant; **what's the** ~ **like?** quel temps fait-il?; **under the** ~ (*fig: ill*) mal fichu(e).
weather-beaten ['wɛðəbiːtn] *adj* (*person*) hâlé(e); (*building*) dégradé(e) par les intempéries.
weather cock *n* girouette *f*.
weather forecast *n* prévisions *fpl* météorologiques, météo *f*.
weatherman ['wɛðəmæn] *n* météorologue *m*.
weatherproof ['wɛðəpruːf] *adj* (*garment*) imperméable; (*building*) étanche.
weather report *n* bulletin *m* météo, météo *f*.
weather vane [-veɪn] *n* = **weather cock**.
weave, *pt* **wove**, *pp* **woven** [wiːv, wəuv, 'wəuvn] *vt* (*cloth*) tisser; (*basket*) tresser ♦ *vi* (*fig: pt, pp* ~**d**: *move in and out*) se faufiler.
weaver ['wiːvə*] *n* tisserand/e.
weaving ['wiːvɪŋ] *n* tissage *m*.
web [wɛb] *n* (*of spider*) toile *f*; (*on foot*) palmure *f*; (*fabric, also fig*) tissu *m*; **the (World Wide) W**~ le Web.
webbed ['wɛbd] *adj* (*foot*) palmé(e).
webbing ['wɛbɪŋ] *n* (*on chair*) sangles *fpl*.

website ['wɛbsaɪt] n (COMPUT) site m Web.
wed [wɛd] vt (pt, pp **wedded**) épouser ♦ n: **the newly-~s** les jeunes mariés.
Wed. abbr (= Wednesday) me.
we'd [wiːd] = **we had, we would**.
wedded ['wɛdɪd] pt, pp of **wed**.
wedding ['wɛdɪŋ] n mariage m.
wedding anniversary n anniversaire m de mariage; **silver/golden ~** noces fpl d'argent/d'or.
wedding day n jour m du mariage.
wedding dress n robe f de mariée.
wedding present n cadeau m de mariage.
wedding ring n alliance f.
wedge [wɛdʒ] n (of wood etc) coin m; (under door etc) cale f; (of cake) part f ♦ vt (fix) caler; (push) enfoncer, coincer.
wedge-heeled shoes ['wɛdʒhiːld-] npl chaussures fpl à semelles compensées.
wedlock ['wɛdlɔk] n (union f du) mariage m.
Wednesday ['wɛdnzdɪ] n mercredi m; for phrases see also **Tuesday**.
wee [wiː] adj (Scottish) petit(e); tout(e) petit(e).
weed [wiːd] n mauvaise herbe ♦ vt désherber.
►**weed out** vt éliminer.
weed-killer ['wiːdkɪlə*] n désherbant m.
weedy ['wiːdɪ] adj (man) gringalet.
week [wiːk] n semaine f; **once/twice a ~** une fois/deux fois par semaine; **in two ~s' time** dans quinze jours; **Tuesday ~, a ~ on Tuesday** mardi en huit.
weekday ['wiːkdeɪ] n jour m de semaine; (COMM) jour ouvrable; **on ~s** en semaine.
weekend [wiːk'ɛnd] n week-end m.
weekend case n sac m de voyage.
weekly ['wiːklɪ] adv une fois par semaine, chaque semaine ♦ adj, n hebdomadaire (m).
weep, pt, pp wept [wiːp, wɛpt] vi (person) pleurer; (MED: wound etc) suinter.
weeping willow ['wiːpɪŋ-] n saule pleureur.
weepy ['wiːpɪ] n (col: film) mélo m.
weft [wɛft] n (TEXTILES) trame f.
weigh [weɪ] vt, vi peser; **to ~ anchor** lever l'ancre; **to ~ the pros and cons** peser le pour et le contre.
►**weigh down** vt (branch) faire plier; (fig: with worry) accabler.
►**weigh out** vt (goods) peser.
►**weigh up** vt examiner.
weighbridge ['weɪbrɪdʒ] n pont-bascule m.
weighing machine ['weɪŋ-] n balance f, bascule f.
weight [weɪt] n poids m ♦ vt alourdir; (fig: factor) pondérer; **sold by ~** vendu au poids; **to put on/lose ~** grossir/maigrir; **~s and measures** poids et mesures.
weighting ['weɪtɪŋ] n: **~ allowance** indemnité f de résidence.
weightlessness ['weɪtlɪsnɪs] n apesanteur f.
weightlifter ['weɪtlɪftə*] n haltérophile m.
weight training n musculation f.

weighty ['weɪtɪ] adj lourd(e).
weir [wɪə*] n barrage m.
weird [wɪəd] adj bizarre; (eerie) surnaturel(le).
weirdo ['wɪədəu] n (col) type m bizarre.
welcome ['wɛlkəm] adj bienvenu(e) ♦ n accueil m ♦ vt accueillir; (also: **bid ~**) souhaiter la bienvenue à; (be glad of) se réjouir de; **to be ~** être le(la) bienvenu(e); **to make sb ~** faire bon accueil à qn; **you're ~ to try** vous pouvez essayer si vous voulez; **you're ~!** (after thanks) de rien, il n'y a pas de quoi.
welcoming ['wɛlkəmɪŋ] adj accueillant(e); (speech) d'accueil.
weld [wɛld] n soudure f ♦ vt souder.
welder ['wɛldə*] n (person) soudeur m.
welding ['wɛldɪŋ] n soudure f (autogène).
welfare ['wɛlfɛə*] n bien-être m.
welfare state n État-providence m.
welfare work n travail social.
well [wɛl] n puits m ♦ adv bien ♦ adj: **to be ~** aller bien ♦ excl eh bien!; bon!; enfin!; ~ **done!** bravo!; **I don't feel ~** je ne me sens pas bien; **get ~ soon!** remets-toi vite!; **to do ~ in sth** bien réussir en or dans qch; **to think ~ of sb** penser du bien de qn; **as ~** (in addition) aussi, également; **you might as ~ tell me** tu ferais aussi bien de me le dire; **as ~ as** aussi bien que or de; en plus de; **~, as I was saying ...** donc, comme je disais ....
►**well up** vi (tears, emotions) monter.
we'll [wiːl] = **we will, we shall**.
well-behaved ['wɛlbɪ'heɪvd] adj sage, obéissant(e).
well-being ['wɛl'biːɪŋ] n bien-être m.
well-bred ['wɛl'brɛd] adj bien élevé(e).
well-built ['wɛl'bɪlt] adj (house) bien construit(e); (person) bien bâti(e).
well-chosen ['wɛl'tʃəuzn] adj bien choisi(e).
well-developed ['wɛldɪ'vɛləpt] adj (girl) bien fait(e).
well-disposed ['wɛldɪs'pəuzd] adj: **~ to(wards)** bien disposé(e) envers.
well-dressed ['wɛl'drɛst] adj bien habillé(e), bien vêtu(e).
well-earned ['wɛl'əːnd] adj (rest) bien mérité(e).
well-groomed ['wɛl'gruːmd] adj très soigné(e) de sa personne.
well-heeled ['wɛl'hiːld] adj (col: wealthy) fortuné(e), riche.
well-informed ['wɛlɪn'fɔːmd] adj (having knowledge of sth) bien renseigné(e); (having general knowledge) cultivé(e).
Wellington ['wɛlɪŋtən] n Wellington.
wellingtons ['wɛlɪŋtənz] npl (also: **wellington boots**) bottes fpl de caoutchouc.
well-kept ['wɛl'kɛpt] adj (house, grounds) bien tenu(e), bien entretenu(e); (secret) bien gardé(e); (hair, hands) soigné(e).
well-known ['wɛl'nəun] adj (person) bien connu(e).

well-mannered ['wɛl'mænəd] *adj* bien élevé(e).

well-meaning ['wɛl'miːnɪŋ] *adj* bien intentionné(e).

well-nigh ['wɛl'naɪ] *adv*: ~ **impossible** pratiquement impossible.

well-off ['wɛl'ɔf] *adj* aisé(e), assez riche.

well-read ['wɛl'rɛd] *adj* cultivé(e).

well-spoken ['wɛl'spəukn] *adj* (*person*) qui parle bien; (*words*) bien choisi(e).

well-stocked ['wɛl'stɔkt] *adj* bien approvisionné(e).

well-timed ['wɛl'taɪmd] *adj* opportun(e).

well-to-do ['wɛltə'duː] *adj* aisé(e), assez riche.

well-wisher ['wɛlwɪʃə*] *n* ami/e, admirateur/trice; **scores of ~s had gathered** de nombreux amis et admirateurs s'étaient rassemblés; **letters from ~s** des lettres d'encouragement.

well-woman clinic ['wɛlwumən-] *n* service de check-up pour les femmes dans un cabinet médical.

Welsh [wɛlʃ] *adj* gallois(e) ♦ *n* (*LING*) gallois *m*; **the ~** *npl* les Gallois.

Welshman, Welshwoman ['wɛlʃmən, -wumən] *n* Gallois/e.

Welsh rarebit *n* croûte *f* au fromage.

welter ['wɛltə*] *n* fatras *m*.

went [wɛnt] *pt of* **go**.

wept [wɛpt] *pt, pp of* **weep**.

were [wəː*] *pt of* **be**.

we're [wɪə*] = **we are**.

weren't [wəːnt] = **were not**.

werewolf, *pl* **-wolves** ['wɪəwulf, -wulvz] *n* loup-garou *m*.

west [wɛst] *n* ouest *m* ♦ *adj* ouest *inv*, de *or* à l'ouest ♦ *adv* à *or* vers l'ouest; **the W~** l'Occident *m*, l'Ouest.

westbound ['wɛstbaund] *adj* (*traffic*) en direction de l'ouest; (*carriageway*) ouest *inv*.

West Country *n*: **the ~** le sud-ouest de l'Angleterre.

westerly ['wɛstəlɪ] *adj* (*situation*) à l'ouest; (*wind*) d'ouest.

western ['wɛstən] *adj* occidental(e), de *or* à l'ouest ♦ *n* (*CINE*) western *m*.

westerner ['wɛstənə*] *n* occidental/e.

westernized ['wɛstənaɪzd] *adj* occidentalisé(e).

West German (*formerly*) *adj* ouest-allemand(e) ♦ *n* Allemand/e de l'Ouest.

West Germany *n* (*formerly*) Allemagne *f* de l'Ouest.

West Indian *adj* antillais(e) ♦ *n* Antillais/e.

West Indies [-'ɪndɪz] *npl*: **the ~** les Antilles *fpl*.

Westminster ['wɛstmɪnstə*] *n* (*BRIT PARLIAMENT*) Westminster *m*.

westward(s) ['wɛstwəd(z)] *adv* vers l'ouest.

wet [wɛt] *adj* mouillé(e); (*damp*) humide; (*soaked*) trempé(e); (*rainy*) pluvieux(euse) ♦ *vt*: **to ~ one's pants** *or* **o.s.** mouiller sa culotte, faire pipi dans sa culotte; **to get ~** se

mouiller; "*~* **paint**" "attention peinture fraîche".

wet blanket *n* (*fig*) rabat-joie *m inv*.

wetness ['wɛtnɪs] *n* humidité *f*.

wet suit *n* combinaison *f* de plongée.

we've [wiːv] = **we have**.

whack [wæk] *vt* donner un grand coup à.

whacked [wækt] *adj* (*BRIT col*: *tired*) crevé(e).

whale [weɪl] *n* (*ZOOL*) baleine *f*.

whaler ['weɪlə*] *n* (*ship*) baleinier *m*.

whaling ['weɪlɪŋ] *n* pêche *f* à la baleine.

wharf, *pl* **wharves** [wɔːf, wɔːvz] *n* quai *m*.

══════════════════════════ KEYWORD

what [wɔt] *adj* quel(le); ~ **size is he?** quelle taille fait-il?; ~ **colour is it?** de quelle couleur est-ce?; ~ **books do you need?** quels livres vous faut-il?; ~ **a mess!** quel désordre!

♦ *pron* **1** (*interrogative*) que, *prep* +quoi; ~ **are you doing?** que faites-vous?, qu'est-ce que vous faites?; ~ **is happening?** qu'est-ce qui se passe?, que se passe-t-il?; ~ **are you talking about?** de quoi parlez-vous?; ~ **is it called?** comment est-ce que ça s'appelle?; ~ **about me?** et moi?; ~ **about doing ...?** et si on faisait ...?

2 (*relative*: *subject*) ce qui; (: *direct object*) ce que; (: *indirect object*) ce +*prep* +quoi, ce dont; **I saw ~ you did/was on the table** j'ai vu ce que vous avez fait/ce qui était sur la table; **tell me ~ you remember** dites-moi ce dont vous vous souvenez; ~ **I want is a cup of tea** ce que je veux, c'est une tasse de thé

♦ *excl* (*disbelieving*) quoi!, comment!

──────────────────────────────

whatever [wɔt'ɛvə*] *adj*: ~ **book** quel que soit le livre que (*or* qui) + *sub*; n'importe quel livre ♦ *pron*: **do ~ is necessary** faites (tout) ce qui est nécessaire; ~ **happens** quoi qu'il arrive; **no reason ~** *or* **whatsoever** pas la moindre raison; **nothing ~** *or* **whatsoever** rien du tout.

whatsoever [wɔtsəu'ɛvə*] *adj see* **whatever**.

wheat [wiːt] *n* blé *m*, froment *m*.

wheatgerm ['wiːtdʒəːm] *n* germe *m* de blé.

wheatmeal ['wiːtmiːl] *n* farine bise.

wheedle ['wiːdl] *vt*: **to ~ sb into doing sth** cajoler *or* enjôler qn pour qu'il fasse qch; **to ~ sth out of sb** obtenir qch de qn par des cajoleries.

wheel [wiːl] *n* roue *f*; (*AUT: also*: **steering ~**) volant *m*; (*NAUT*) gouvernail *m* ♦ *vt* pousser, rouler ♦ *vi* (*also*: ~ **round**) tourner.

wheelbarrow ['wiːlbærəu] *n* brouette *f*.

wheelbase ['wiːlbeɪs] *n* empattement *m*.

wheelchair ['wiːltʃɛə*] *n* fauteuil roulant.

wheel clamp *n* (*AUT*) sabot *m* (de Denver).

wheeler-dealer ['wiːlə'diːlə*] *n* (*pej*) combinard/e, affairiste *m/f*.

wheelie-bin ['wiːlɪbɪn] *n* (*BRIT*) poubelle *f* à roulettes.

wheeling ['wiːlɪŋ] n: ~ **and dealing** (pej) manigances fpl, magouilles fpl.
wheeze [wiːz] n respiration bruyante (d'asthmatique) ♦ vi respirer bruyamment.
wheezy ['wiːzɪ] adj sifflant(e).

════════════════════════ KEYWORD

when [wen] adv quand; ~ **did he go?** quand est-ce qu'il est parti?
♦ conj **1** (at, during, after the time that) quand, lorsque; **she was reading ~ I came in** elle lisait quand or lorsque je suis entré
2 (on, at which): **on the day ~ I met him** le jour où je l'ai rencontré
3 (whereas) alors que; **I thought I was wrong ~ in fact I was right** j'ai cru que j'avais tort alors qu'en fait j'avais raison.

whenever [wen'evə*] adv quand donc ♦ conj quand; (every time that) chaque fois que; **I go ~ I can** j'y vais quand or chaque fois que je le peux.
where [wɛə*] adv, conj où; **this is ~** c'est là que; ~ **are you from?** d'où venez vous?
whereabouts ['wɛərəbauts] adv où donc ♦ n: **sb's ~** l'endroit où se trouve qn.
whereas [wɛər'æz] conj alors que.
whereby [wɛə'baɪ] adv (formal) par lequel (or laquelle etc).
whereupon [wɛərə'pɔn] adv sur quoi, et sur ce.
wherever [wɛər'evə*] adv où donc ♦ conj où que + sub; **sit ~ you like** asseyez-vous (là) où vous voulez.
wherewithal ['wɛəwɪðɔːl] n: **the ~ (to do sth)** les moyens mpl (de faire qch).
whet [wɛt] vt aiguiser.
whether ['wɛðə*] conj si; **I don't know ~ to accept or not** je ne sais pas si je dois accepter ou non; **it's doubtful ~** il est peu probable que; ~ **you go or not** que vous y alliez ou non.
whey [weɪ] n petit-lait m.

════════════════════════ KEYWORD

which [wɪtʃ] adj **1** (interrogative: direct, indirect) quel(le); ~ **picture do you want?** quel tableau voulez-vous?; ~ **one?** lequel(laquelle)?
2: in ~ case auquel cas
♦ pron **1** (interrogative) lequel(laquelle), lesquels(lesquelles) pl; **I don't mind ~** peu importe lequel; ~ **(of these) are yours?** lesquels sont à vous?; **tell me ~ you want** dites-moi lesquels or ceux que vous voulez
2 (relative: subject) qui; (: object) que, prep +lequel(laquelle); (NB: à + lequel = auquel; de + lequel = duquel); **the apple ~ you ate/~ is on the table** la pomme que vous avez mangée/qui est sur la table; **the chair on ~ you are sitting** la chaise sur laquelle vous êtes assis; **the book of ~ you spoke** le livre dont vous avez parlé; **he knew, ~ is true/I**

feared il le savait, ce qui est vrai/ce que je craignais; **after ~** après quoi.

whichever [wɪtʃ'evə*] adj: **take ~ book you prefer** prenez le livre que vous préférez, peu importe lequel; ~ **book you take** quel que soit le livre que vous preniez; ~ **way you** de quelque façon que vous + sub.
whiff [wɪf] n bouffée f; **to catch a ~ of sth** sentir l'odeur de qch.
while [waɪl] n moment m ♦ conj pendant que; (as long as) tant que; (as, whereas) alors que; (though) quoique + sub; **for a ~** pendant quelque temps; **in a ~** dans un moment; **all the ~** pendant tout ce temps-là; **we'll make it worth your ~** nous vous récompenserons de votre peine.
▶**while away** vt (time) (faire) passer.
whilst [waɪlst] conj = **while**.
whim [wɪm] n caprice m.
whimper ['wɪmpə*] n geignement m ♦ vi geindre.
whimsical ['wɪmzɪkl] adj (person) capricieux(euse); (look) étrange.
whine [waɪn] n gémissement m ♦ vi gémir, geindre; pleurnicher.
whip [wɪp] n fouet m; (for riding) cravache f; (POL: person) chef m de file (assurant la discipline dans son groupe parlementaire) ♦ vt fouetter; (snatch) enlever (or sortir) brusquement.
▶**whip up** vt (cream) fouetter; (col: meal) préparer en vitesse; (stir up: support) stimuler; (: feeling) attiser, aviver.

┌─────────────────────────────────────┐
│ Un **whip** est un député dont le rôle est, entre │
│ autres, de s'assurer que les membres de son │
│ parti sont régulièrement présents à la **House of** │
│ **Commons**, surtout lorsque les votes ont lieu. │
│ Les convocations que les whips envoient se │
│ distinguent, selon leur degré d'importance, par │
│ le fait qu'elles sont soulignées 1, 2 ou 3 fois (les │
│ "1-, 2-, ou 3-line whips"). │
└─────────────────────────────────────┘

whiplash ['wɪplæʃ] n (MED: also: ~ **injury**) coup m du lapin.
whipped cream [wɪpt-] n crème fouettée.
whipping boy ['wɪpɪŋ-] n (fig) bouc m émissaire.
whip-round ['wɪpraund] n (BRIT) collecte f.
whirl [wəːl] n tourbillon m ♦ vt faire tourbillonner; faire tournoyer ♦ vi tourbillonner.
whirlpool ['wəːlpuːl] n tourbillon m.
whirlwind ['wəːlwɪnd] n tornade f.
whirr [wə:*] vi bruire; ronronner; vrombir.
whisk [wɪsk] n (CULIN) fouet m ♦ vt fouetter, battre; **to ~ sb away** or **off** emmener qn rapidement.
whiskers ['wɪskəz] npl (of animal) moustaches fpl; (of man) favoris mpl.
whisky, (Irish, US) **whiskey** ['wɪskɪ] n whisky m.

whisper ['wɪspə*] n chuchotement m; (fig: of leaves) bruissement m; (rumour) rumeur f ♦ vt, vi chuchoter; **to ~ sth to sb** chuchoter qch à (l'oreille de) qn.

whispering ['wɪspərɪŋ] n chuchotement(s) m(pl).

whist [wɪst] n (BRIT) whist m.

whistle ['wɪsl] n (sound) sifflement m; (object) sifflet m ♦ vi siffler ♦ vt siffler, siffloter.

whistle-stop ['wɪslstɔp] adj: **to make a ~ tour of** (POL) faire la tournée électorale des petits patelins de.

Whit [wɪt] n la Pentecôte.

white [waɪt] adj blanc(blanche); (with fear) blême ♦ n blanc m; (person) blanc/blanche; **to turn** or **go ~** (person) pâlir, blêmir; (hair) blanchir; **the ~s** (washing) le linge blanc; **tennis ~s** tenue f de tennis.

whitebait ['waɪtbeɪt] n blanchaille f.

white coffee n (BRIT) café m au lait, (café) crème m.

white-collar worker ['waɪtkɔlə-] n employé/e de bureau.

white elephant n (fig) objet dispendieux et superflu.

white goods npl (appliances) (gros) électroménager m; (linen etc) linge m de maison.

white-hot [waɪt'hɔt] adj (metal) incandescent(e).

White House n (US): **the ~** la Maison-Blanche.

La **White House** est un grand bâtiment blanc situé à Washington D.C. où réside le président des États-Unis. Par extension, ce terme désigne l'exécutif américain.

---

white lie n pieux mensonge.

whiteness ['waɪtnɪs] n blancheur f.

white noise n son m blanc.

whiteout ['waɪtaut] n jour blanc.

white paper n (POL) livre blanc.

whitewash ['waɪtwɔʃ] n (paint) lait m de chaux ♦ vt blanchir à la chaux; (fig) blanchir.

whiting ['waɪtɪŋ] n (pl inv) (fish) merlan m.

Whit Monday n le lundi de Pentecôte.

Whitsun ['wɪtsn] n la Pentecôte.

whittle ['wɪtl] vt: **to ~ away, ~ down** (costs) réduire, rogner.

whizz [wɪz] vi aller (or passer) à toute vitesse.

whizz kid n (col) petit prodige.

WHO n abbr (= World Health Organization) OMS f (= Organisation mondiale de la Santé).

who [huː] pron qui.

whodunit [huː'dʌnɪt] n (col) roman policier.

whoever [huː'ɛvə*] pron: **~ finds it** celui(celle) qui le trouve (, qui que ce soit), quiconque le trouve; **ask ~ you like** demandez à qui vous voulez; **~ he marries** qui que ce soit or quelle que soit la personne qu'il épouse; **~**

told you that? qui a bien pu vous dire ça?, qui donc vous a dit ça?

whole [həul] adj (complete) entier(ière), tout(e); (not broken) intact(e), complet(ète) ♦ n (total) totalité f; (sth not broken) tout m; **the ~ lot (of it)** tout; **the ~ lot (of them)** tous (sans exception); **the ~ of the time** tout le temps; **the ~ of the town** la ville tout entière; **~ villages were destroyed** des villages entiers ont été détruits; **on the ~, as a ~** dans l'ensemble.

wholehearted [həul'hɑːtɪd] adj sans réserve(s), sincère.

wholemeal ['həulmiːl] adj (BRIT: flour, bread) complet(ète).

whole note n (US) ronde f.

wholesale ['həulseɪl] n (vente f en) gros m ♦ adj de gros; (destruction) systématique.

wholesaler ['həulseɪlə*] n grossiste m/f.

wholesome ['həulsəm] adj sain(e); (advice) salutaire.

wholewheat ['həulwiːt] adj = **wholemeal**.

wholly ['həulɪ] adv entièrement, tout à fait.

==================================== *KEYWORD*

whom [huːm] pron **1** (interrogative) qui; **~ did you see?** qui avez-vous vu?; **to ~ did you give it?** à qui l'avez-vous donné?
2 (relative) que, prep + qui; **the man ~ I saw/ to ~ I spoke** l'homme que j'ai vu/à qui j'ai parlé.

whooping cough ['huːpɪŋ-] n coqueluche f.

whoops [wuːps] excl (also: **~-a-daisy**) oups!, houp-là!

whoosh [wuʃ] n, vi: **the skiers ~ed past, the skiers came by with a ~** les skieurs passèrent dans un glissement rapide.

whopper ['wɔpə*] n (col: lie) gros bobard; (: large thing) monstre m, phénomène m.

whopping ['wɔpɪŋ] adj (col: big) énorme.

whore [hɔː*] n (col: pej) putain f.

==================================== *KEYWORD*

whose [huːz] adj **1** (possessive: interrogative): **~ book is this?** à qui est ce livre?; **~ pencil have you taken?** à qui est le crayon que vous avez pris?, c'est le crayon de qui que vous avez pris?; **~ daughter are you?** de qui êtes-vous la fille?
2 (possessive: relative): **the man ~ son we rescued** l'homme dont or de qui vous avez sauvé le fils; **the girl ~ sister you were speaking to** la fille à la sœur de qui or de laquelle vous parliez; **the woman ~ car was stolen** la femme dont la voiture a été volée ♦ pron à qui; **~ is this?** à qui est ceci?; **I know ~ it is** je sais à qui c'est.

Who's Who ['huːz'huː] n ≈ Bottin Mondain.

why [waɪ] adv pourquoi ♦ excl eh bien!, tiens!; **the reason ~** la raison pour laquelle; **~ is he**

late? pourquoi est-il en retard?

whyever [waɪ'ɛvə*] adv pourquoi donc, mais pourquoi.

WI n abbr (BRIT: = Women's Institute) amicale de femmes au foyer ♦ abbr (GEO) = West Indies; (US) = Wisconsin.

wick [wɪk] n mèche f (de bougie).

wicked ['wɪkɪd] adj foncièrement mauvais(e), inique; (mischievous: grin, look) espiègle, malicieux(euse); (terrible: prices, weather) épouvantable.

wicker ['wɪkə*] n osier m; (also: ~work) vannerie f.

wicket ['wɪkɪt] n (CRICKET) guichet m; espace compris entre les deux guichets.

wicket keeper n (CRICKET) gardien m de guichet.

wide [waɪd] adj large; (region, knowledge) vaste, très étendu(e); (choice) grand(e) ♦ adv: to open ~ ouvrir tout grand; to shoot ~ tirer à côté; it is 3 metres ~ cela fait 3 mètres de large.

wide-angle lens ['waɪdæŋgl-] n objectif m grand-angulaire.

wide-awake [waɪdə'weɪk] adj bien éveillé(e).

wide-eyed [waɪd'aɪd] adj aux yeux écarquillés; (fig) naïf(ïve), crédule.

widely ['waɪdlɪ] adv (different) radicalement; (spaced) sur une grande étendue; (believed) généralement; to be ~ read (author) être beaucoup lu(e); (reader) avoir beaucoup lu, être cultivé(e).

widen ['waɪdn] vt élargir.

wideness ['waɪdnɪs] n largeur f.

wide open adj grand(e) ouvert(e).

wide-ranging [waɪd'reɪndʒɪŋ] adj (survey, report) vaste; (interests) divers(e).

widespread ['waɪdsprɛd] adj (belief etc) très répandu(e).

widow ['wɪdəu] n veuve f.

widowed ['wɪdəud] adj (qui est devenu(e)) veuf(veuve).

widower ['wɪdəuə*] n veuf m.

width [wɪdθ] n largeur f; it's 7 metres in ~ cela fait 7 mètres de large.

widthways ['wɪdθweɪz] adv en largeur.

wield [wi:ld] vt (sword) manier; (power) exercer.

wife, pl **wives** [waɪf, waɪvz] n femme (mariée), épouse f.

wig [wɪg] n perruque f.

wigging ['wɪgɪŋ] n (BRIT col) savon m, engueulade f.

wiggle ['wɪgl] vt agiter, remuer ♦ vi (loose screw etc) branler; (worm) se tortiller.

wiggly ['wɪglɪ] adj (line) ondulé(e).

wild [waɪld] adj sauvage; (sea) déchaîné(e); (idea, life) fou(folle); extravagant(e); (col: angry) hors de soi, furieux(euse); (: enthusiastic): to be ~ about être fou(folle) or dingue de ♦ n: the ~ la nature; ~s npl régions fpl sauvages.

wild card n (COMPUT) caractère m de remplacement.

wildcat ['waɪldkæt] n chat m sauvage.

wildcat strike n grève f sauvage.

wilderness ['wɪldənɪs] n désert m, région f sauvage.

wildfire ['waɪldfaɪə*] n: to spread like ~ se répandre comme une traînée de poudre.

wild-goose chase [waɪld'gu:s-] n (fig) fausse piste.

wildlife ['waɪldlaɪf] n faune f (et flore f) sauvage(s).

wildly ['waɪldlɪ] adv (applaud) frénétiquement; (hit, guess) au hasard; (happy) follement.

wiles [waɪlz] npl ruses fpl, artifices mpl.

wilful, (US) **willful** ['wɪlful] adj (person) obstiné(e); (action) délibéré(e); (crime) prémédité(e).

═══════════════════════ *KEYWORD*

will [wɪl] (vt: pt, pp **willed**) aux vb **1** (forming future tense): I ~ **finish it tomorrow** je le finirai demain; I ~ **have finished it by tomorrow** je l'aurai fini d'ici demain; ~ **you do it? — yes I ~/no I won't** le ferez-vous? — oui/non; **you won't lose it,** ~ **you?** vous ne le perdrez pas, n'est-ce pas?

2 (in conjectures, predictions): **he ~** or **he'll be there by now** il doit être arrivé à l'heure qu'il est; **that ~ be the postman** ça doit être le facteur

3 (in commands, requests, offers): ~ **you be quiet!** voulez-vous bien vous taire!; ~ **you help me?** est-ce que vous pouvez m'aider?; ~ **you have a cup of tea?** voulez-vous une tasse de thé?; **I won't put up with it!** je ne le tolérerai pas!

♦ vt: **to ~ sb to do** souhaiter ardemment que qu fasse; **he ~ed himself to go on** par un suprême effort de volonté, il continua

♦ n volonté f; testament m; **to do sth of one's own free ~** faire qch de son propre gré; **against one's ~** à contre-cœur.

─────────────────────────────

willful ['wɪlful] adj (US) = **wilful.**

willing ['wɪlɪŋ] adj de bonne volonté, serviable ♦ n: **to show** ~ faire preuve de bonne volonté; **he's** ~ **to do it** il est disposé à le faire, il veut bien le faire.

willingly ['wɪlɪŋlɪ] adv volontiers.

willingness ['wɪlɪŋnɪs] n bonne volonté.

will-o'-the-wisp ['wɪləðə'wɪsp] n (also fig) feu follet m.

willow ['wɪləu] n saule m.

will power n volonté f.

willy-nilly ['wɪlɪ'nɪlɪ] adv bon gré mal gré.

wilt [wɪlt] vi dépérir.

Wilts [wɪlts] abbr (BRIT) = Wiltshire.

wily ['waɪlɪ] adj rusé(e).

wimp [wɪmp] n (col) mauviette f.

win [wɪn] n (in sports etc) victoire f ♦ vb (pt, pp **won** [wʌn]) vt (battle, money) gagner; (prize,

contract) remporter; (*popularity*) acquérir ♦ *vi* gagner.
►**win over**, (*BRIT*) **win round** *vt* gagner, se concilier.
wince [wɪns] *n* tressaillement *m* ♦ *vi* tressaillir.
winch [wɪntʃ] *n* treuil *m*.
Winchester disk ['wɪntʃɪstə-] *n* (*COMPUT*) disque *m* Winchester.
wind[1] [wɪnd] *n* (*also MED*) vent *m* ♦ *vt* (*take breath away*) couper le souffle à; **the ~(s)** (*MUS*) les instruments *mpl* à vent; **into** or **against the ~** contre le vent; **to get ~ of sth** (*fig*) avoir vent de qch; **to break ~** avoir des gaz.
wind[2], *pt*, *pp* **wound** [waɪnd, waʊnd] *vt* enrouler; (*wrap*) envelopper; (*clock, toy*) remonter ♦ *vi* (*road, river*) serpenter
►**wind down** *vt* (*car window*) baisser; (*fig: production, business*) réduire progressivement.
►**wind up** *vt* (*clock*) remonter; (*debate*) terminer, clôturer.
windbreak ['wɪndbreɪk] *n* brise-vent *m inv*.
windcheater ['wɪndtʃiːtə*], (*US*) **windbreaker** ['wɪndbreɪkə*] *n* anorak *m*.
winder ['waɪndə*] *n* (*BRIT*: *on watch*) remontoir *m*.
windfall ['wɪndfɔːl] *n* coup *m* de chance.
winding ['waɪndɪŋ] *adj* (*road*) sinueux(euse); (*staircase*) tournant(e).
wind instrument *n* (*MUS*) instrument *m* à vent.
windmill ['wɪndmɪl] *n* moulin *m* à vent.
window ['wɪndəʊ] *n* fenêtre *f*; (*in car, train, also*: ~**pane**) vitre *f*; (*in shop etc*) vitrine *f*.
window box *n* jardinière *f*.
window cleaner *n* (*person*) laveur/euse de vitres.
window dressing *n* arrangement *m* de la vitrine.
window envelope *n* enveloppe *f* à fenêtre.
window frame *n* châssis *m* de fenêtre.
window ledge *n* rebord *m* de la fenêtre.
window pane *n* vitre *f*, carreau *m*.
window-shopping ['wɪndəʊʃɔpɪŋ] *n*: **to go ~** faire du lèche-vitrines.
windowsill ['wɪndəʊsɪl] *n* (*inside*) appui *m* de la fenêtre; (*outside*) rebord *m* de la fenêtre.
windpipe ['wɪndpaɪp] *n* gosier *m*.
wind power *n* énergie éolienne.
windscreen ['wɪndskriːn], (*US*) **windshield** ['wɪndʃiːld] *n* pare-brise *m inv*.
windscreen washer *n* lave-glace *m inv*.
windscreen wiper [-waɪpə*] *n* essuie-glace *m inv*.
windsurfing ['wɪndsəːfɪŋ] *n* planche *f* à voile.
windswept ['wɪndswɛpt] *adj* balayé(e) par le vent.
wind tunnel *n* soufflerie *f*.
windy ['wɪndɪ] *adj* venté(e), venteux(euse); **it's ~** il y a du vent.

wine [waɪn] *n* vin *m* ♦ *vt*: **to ~ and dine sb** offrir un dîner bien arrosé à qn.
wind bar *n* bar *m* à vin.
wine cellar *n* cave *f* à vins.
wine glass *n* verre *m* à vin.
wine list *n* carte *f* des vins.
wine merchant *n* marchand/e de vins.
wine tasting [-teɪstɪŋ] *n* dégustation *f* (de vins).
wine waiter *n* sommelier *m*.
wing [wɪŋ] *n* aile *f*; (*in air force*) groupe *m* d'escadrilles; ~**s** *npl* (*THEAT*) coulisses *fpl*.
winger ['wɪŋə*] *n* (*SPORT*) ailier *m*.
wing mirror *n* (*BRIT*) rétroviseur latéral.
wing nut *n* papillon *m*, écrou *m* à ailettes.
wingspan ['wɪŋspæn] *n*, **wingspread** ['wɪŋsprɛd] *n* envergure *f*.
wink [wɪŋk] *n* clin *m* d'œil ♦ *vi* faire un clin d'œil; (*blink*) cligner des yeux.
winkle [wɪŋkl] *n* bigorneau *m*.
winner ['wɪnə*] *n* gagnant/e.
winning ['wɪnɪŋ] *adj* (*team*) gagnant(e); (*goal*) décisif(ive); (*charming*) charmeur(euse).
winning post *n* poteau *m* d'arrivée.
winnings ['wɪnɪŋz] *npl* gains *mpl*.
winsome ['wɪnsəm] *adj* avenant(e), engageant(e).
winter ['wɪntə*] *n* hiver *m* ♦ *vi* hiverner.
winter sports *npl* sports *mpl* d'hiver.
wintry ['wɪntrɪ] *adj* hivernal(e).
wipe [waɪp] *n* coup *m* de torchon (*or* de chiffon *or* d'éponge) ♦ *vt* essuyer; **to give sth a ~** donner un coup de torchon à qch; **to ~ one's nose** se moucher.
►**wipe off** *vt* essuyer.
►**wipe out** *vt* (*debt*) régler; (*memory*) oublier; (*destroy*) anéantir.
►**wipe up** *vt* essuyer.
wire ['waɪə*] *n* fil *m* (de fer); (*ELEC*) fil électrique; (*TEL*) télégramme *m* ♦ *vt* (*fence*) grillager; (*house*) faire l'installation électrique de; (*also*: ~ **up**) brancher.
wire brush *n* brosse *f* métallique.
wire cutters [-kʌtəz] *npl* cisaille *f*.
wireless ['waɪəlɪs] *n* (*BRIT*) télégraphie *f* sans fil; (*set*) T.S.F. *f*.
wire netting *n* treillis *m* métallique, grillage *m*.
wire service *n* (*US*) revue *f* de presse (*par téléscripteur*).
wire-tapping ['waɪə'tæpɪŋ] *n* écoute *f* téléphonique.
wiring ['waɪərɪŋ] *n* (*ELEC*) installation *f* électrique.
wiry ['waɪərɪ] *adj* noueux(euse), nerveux(euse).
Wis. *abbr* (*US*) = *Wisconsin*.
wisdom ['wɪzdəm] *n* sagesse *f*; (*of action*) prudence *f*.
wisdom tooth *n* dent *f* de sagesse.
wise [waɪz] *adj* sage, prudent(e), judicieux(euse); **I'm none the ~r** je ne suis pas

plus avancé(e) pour autant.
▶**wise up** *vi* (*col*): **to ~ up to** commencer à se rendre compte de.
...wise [waɪz] *suffix*: **time~** en ce qui concerne le temps, question temps.
wisecrack ['waɪzkræk] *n* sarcasme *m*.
wish [wɪʃ] *n* (*desire*) désir *m*; (*specific desire*) souhait *m*, vœu *m* ♦ *vt* souhaiter, désirer, vouloir; **best ~es** (*on birthday etc*) meilleurs vœux; **with best ~es** (*in letter*) bien amicalement; **give her my best ~es** faites-lui mes amitiés; **to ~ sb goodbye** dire au revoir à qn; **he ~ed.me well** il me souhaitait de réussir; **to ~ to do/sb to do** désirer *or* vouloir faire/que qn fasse; **to ~ for** souhaiter; **to ~ sth on sb** souhaiter qch à qn.
wishbone ['wɪʃbəun] *n* fourchette *f*.
wishful ['wɪʃful] *adj*: **it's ~ thinking** c'est prendre ses désirs pour des réalités.
wishy-washy ['wɪʃɪ'wɔʃɪ] *adj* (*col*: *person*) qui manque de caractère, falot(e); (: *ideas, thinking*) faiblard(e).
wisp [wɪsp] *n* fine mèche (*de cheveux*); (*of smoke*) mince volute *f*; **a ~ of straw** un fétu de paille.
wistful ['wɪstful] *adj* mélancolique.
wit [wɪt] *n* (*gen pl: intelligence*) intelligence *f*, esprit *m*; (*presence of mind*) présence *f* d'esprit; (*wittiness*) esprit; (*person*) homme/femme d'esprit; **to be at one's ~s' end** (*fig*) ne plus savoir que faire; **to have one's ~s about one** avoir toute sa présence d'esprit, ne pas perdre la tête; **to ~** *adv* à savoir.
witch [wɪtʃ] *n* sorcière *f*.
witchcraft ['wɪtʃkrɑːft] *n* sorcellerie *f*.
witch doctor *n* sorcier *m*.
witch-hunt ['wɪtʃhʌnt] *n* chasse *f* aux sorcières.

=== KEYWORD ===

with [wɪð, wɪθ] *prep* **1** (*in the company of*) avec; (*at the home of*) chez; **we stayed ~ friends** nous avons logé chez des amis; **I'll be ~ you in a minute** je suis à vous dans un instant
2 (*descriptive*): **a room ~ a view** une chambre avec vue; **the man ~ the grey hat/blue eyes** l'homme au chapeau gris/aux yeux bleus
3 (*indicating manner, means, cause*): **~ tears in her eyes** les larmes aux yeux; **to walk ~ a stick** marcher avec une canne; **red ~ anger** rouge de colère; **to shake ~ fear** trembler de peur; **to fill sth ~ water** remplir qch d'eau
4: **I'm ~ you** (*I understand*) je vous suis; **to be ~ it** (*col*: *up-to-date*) être dans le vent.

withdraw [wɪð'drɔː] *irreg vt* retirer ♦ *vi* se retirer; (*go back on promise*) se rétracter; **to ~ into o.s.** se replier sur soi-même.
withdrawal [wɪð'drɔːəl] *n* retrait *m*; (*MED*) état *m* de manque.

withdrawal symptoms *npl*: **to have ~** être en état de manque, présenter les symptômes *mpl* de sevrage.
withdrawn [wɪð'drɔːn] *pp of* **withdraw** ♦ *adj* (*person*) renfermé(e).
wither ['wɪðə*] *vi* se faner.
withered ['wɪðəd] *adj* fané(e), flétri(e); (*limb*) atrophié(e).
withhold [wɪθ'həuld] *vt irreg* (*money*) retenir; (*decision*) remettre; (*permission*): **to ~ (from)** refuser (à); (*information*): **to ~ (from)** cacher (à).
within [wɪð'ɪn] *prep* à l'intérieur de ♦ *adv* à l'intérieur; **~ sight of** en vue de; **~ a mile of** à moins d'un mille de; **~ the week** avant la fin de la semaine; **~ an hour from now** d'ici une heure; **to be ~ the law** être légal(e) *or* dans les limites de la légalité.
without [wɪð'aut] *prep* sans; **~ anybody knowing** sans que personne ne sache; **to go or do ~ sth** se passer de qch.
withstand [wɪθ'stænd] *vt irreg* résister à.
witness ['wɪtnɪs] *n* (*person*) témoin *m*; (*evidence*) témoignage *m* ♦ *vt* (*event*) être témoin de; (*document*) attester l'authenticité de; **to bear ~ to sth** témoigner de qch; **~ for the prosecution/defence** témoin à charge/à décharge; **to ~ to sth/having seen sth** témoigner de qch/d'avoir vu qch.
witness box, (*US*) **witness stand** *n* barre *f* des témoins.
witticism ['wɪtɪsɪzəm] *n* mot *m* d'esprit.
witty ['wɪtɪ] *adj* spirituel(le), plein(e) d'esprit.
wives [waɪvz] *npl of* **wife**.
wizard ['wɪzəd] *n* magicien *m*.
wizened ['wɪznd] *adj* ratatiné(e).
wk *abbr* = **week**.
Wm. *abbr* = **William**.
WO *n abbr* = **warrant officer**.
wobble ['wɔbl] *vi* trembler; (*chair*) branler.
wobbly ['wɔblɪ] *adj* tremblant(e); branlant(e).
woe [wəu] *n* malheur *m*.
woeful ['wəuful] *adj* (*sad*) malheureux(euse); (*terrible*) affligeant(e).
wok [wɔk] *n* wok *m*.
woke [wəuk] *pt of* **wake**.
woken ['wəukn] *pp of* **wake**.
wolf, *pl* **wolves** [wulf, wulvz] *n* loup *m*.
woman, *pl* **women** ['wumən, 'wɪmɪn] *n* femme *f* ♦ *cpd*: **~ doctor** femme *f* médecin; **~ friend** amie *f*; **~ teacher** professeur *m* femme; **young ~** jeune femme; **women's page** (*PRESS*) page *f* des lectrices.
womanize ['wumənaɪz] *vi* jouer les séducteurs.
womanly ['wumənlɪ] *adj* féminin(e).
womb [wuːm] *n* (*ANAT*) utérus *m*.
women ['wɪmɪn] *npl of* **woman**.
Women's (Liberation) Movement *n* (*also*: **women's lib**) mouvement *m* de libération de la femme, MLF *m*.
won [wʌn] *pt, pp of* **win**.

wonder ['wʌndə*] *n* merveille *f*, miracle *m*; (*feeling*) émerveillement *m* ♦ *vi*: **to ~ whether** se demander si; **to ~ at** s'étonner de; **s'émerveiller de; to ~ about** songer à; **it's no ~ that** il n'est pas étonnant que + *sub*.

wonderful ['wʌndəful] *adj* merveilleux(euse).

wonderfully ['wʌndəfəlɪ] *adv* (+ *adj*) merveilleusement; (+ *vb*) à merveille.

wonky ['wɒŋkɪ] *adj* (*BRIT col*) qui ne va *or* ne marche pas très bien.

wont [wəunt] *n*: **as is his/her ~** comme de coutume.

won't [wəunt] = **will not**.

woo [wu:] *vt* (*woman*) faire la cour à.

wood [wud] *n* (*timber, forest*) bois *m* ♦ *cpd* de bois, en bois.

wood carving *n* sculpture *f* en *or* sur bois.

wooded ['wudɪd] *adj* boisé(e).

wooden ['wudn] *adj* en bois; (*fig*) raide; inexpressif(ive).

woodland ['wudlənd] *n* forêt *f*, région boisée.

woodpecker ['wudpɛkə*] *n* pic *m* (*oiseau*).

wood pigeon *n* ramier *m*.

woodwind ['wudwɪnd] *n* (*MUS*) bois *m*; **the ~** (*MUS*) les bois.

woodwork ['wudwə:k] *n* menuiserie *f*.

woodworm ['wudwə:m] *n* ver *m* du bois; **the table has got ~** la table est piquée des vers.

woof [wuf] *n* (*of dog*) aboiement *m* ♦ *vi* aboyer; **~, ~!** oua, oua!

wool [wul] *n* laine *f*; **to pull the ~ over sb's eyes** (*fig*) en faire accroire à qn.

woollen, (*US*) **woolen** ['wulən] *adj* de laine; (*industry*) lainier(ière) ♦ *n*: **~s** lainages *mpl*.

woolly, (*US*) **wooly** ['wulɪ] *adj* laineux(euse); (*fig: ideas*) confus(e).

woozy ['wu:zɪ] *adj* (*col*) dans les vapes.

word [wə:d] *n* mot *m*; (*spoken*) mot, parole *f*; (*promise*) parole; (*news*) nouvelles *fpl* ♦ *vt* rédiger, formuler; **~ for ~** (*repeat*) mot pour mot; (*translate*) mot à mot; **what's the ~ for "pen" in French?** comment dit-on "pen" en français?; **to put sth into ~s** exprimer qch; **in other ~s** en d'autres termes; **to have a ~ with sb** toucher un mot à qn; **to have ~s with sb** (*quarrel with*) avoir des mots avec qn; **to break/keep one's ~** manquer à/tenir sa parole; **I'll take your ~ for it** je vous crois sur parole; **to send ~** of prévenir de; **to leave ~ {with sb/for sb} that** ... laisser un mot (à qn/pour qn) disant que ....

wording ['wə:dɪŋ] *n* termes *mpl*, langage *m*; libellé *m*.

word of mouth *n*: **by** *or* **through ~** de bouche à oreille.

word-perfect ['wə:d'pə:fɪkt] *adj*: **he was ~ (in his speech** *etc*), **his speech** *etc* **was ~** il savait son discours *etc* sur le bout du doigt.

word processing *n* traitement *m* de texte.

word processor [-prəusɛsə*] *n* machine *f* de traitement de texte.

wordwrap ['wə:dræp] *n* (*COMPUT*) retour *m*

(automatique) à la ligne.

wordy ['wə:dɪ] *adj* verbeux(euse).

wore [wɔ:*] *pt of* **wear**.

work [wə:k] *n* travail *m*; (*ART, LITERATURE*) œuvre *f* ♦ *vi* travailler; (*mechanism*) marcher, fonctionner; (*plan etc*) marcher; (*medicine*) agir ♦ *vt* (*clay, wood etc*) travailler; (*mine etc*) exploiter; (*machine*) faire marcher *or* fonctionner; **to go to ~** aller travailler; **to set to ~, to start ~** se mettre à l'œuvre; **to be at ~ (on sth)** travailler (sur qch); **to be out of ~** être au chômage; **to ~ hard** travailler dur; **to ~ loose** se défaire, se desserrer.

▶**work on** *vt fus* travailler à; (*principle*) se baser sur.

▶**work out** *vi* (*plans etc*) marcher; (*SPORT*) s'entraîner ♦ *vt* (*problem*) résoudre; (*plan*) élaborer; **it ~s out at £100** ça fait 100 livres.

workable ['wə:kəbl] *adj* (*solution*) réalisable.

workaholic [wə:kə'hɒlɪk] *n* bourreau *m* de travail.

workbench ['wə:kbɛntʃ] *n* établi *m*.

worked up [wə:kt-] *adj*: **to get ~** se mettre dans tous ses états.

worker ['wə:kə*] *n* travailleur/euse, ouvrier/ière; **office ~** employé/e de bureau.

work force *n* main-d'œuvre *f*.

work-in ['wə:kɪn] *n* (*BRIT*) occupation *f* d'usine *etc* (*sans arrêt de la production*).

working ['wə:kɪŋ] *adj* (*day, tools etc, conditions*) de travail; (*wife*) qui travaille; (*partner, population*) actif(ive); **in ~ order** en état de marche; **a ~ knowledge of English** une connaissance toute pratique de l'anglais.

working capital *n* (*COMM*) fonds *mpl* de roulement.

working class *n* classe ouvrière ♦ *adj*: **working-class** ouvrier(ière), de la classe ouvrière.

working man *n* travailleur *m*.

working party *n* (*BRIT*) groupe *m* de travail.

working week *n* semaine *f* de travail.

work-in-progress ['wə:kɪn'prəugrɛs] *n* (*COMM*) en-cours *m inv*; (: *value*) valeur *f* des en-cours.

workload ['wə:kləud] *n* charge *f* de travail.

workman ['wə:kmən] *n* ouvrier *m*.

workmanship ['wə:kmənʃɪp] *n* métier *m*, habileté *f*; facture *f*.

workmate ['wə:kmeɪt] *n* collègue *m/f*.

workout ['wə:kaut] *n* (*SPORT*) séance *f* d'entraînement.

work permit *n* permis *m* de travail.

works [wə:ks] *n* (*BRIT: factory*) usine *f* ♦ *npl* (*of clock, machine*) mécanisme *m*; **road ~** travaux *mpl* (d'entretien des routes).

works council *n* comité *m* d'entreprise.

work sheet *n* (*COMPUT*) feuille *f* de programmation.

workshop ['wə:kʃɒp] *n* atelier *m*.

work station *n* poste *m* de travail.

work study n étude f du travail.

worktop ['wɔːktɔp] n plan m de travail.

work-to-rule ['wɔːktə'ruːl] n (BRIT) grève f du zèle.

world [wɔːld] n monde m ♦ cpd (champion) du monde; (power, war) mondial(e); **all over the ~** dans le monde entier, partout dans le monde; **to think the ~ of sb** (fig) ne jurer que par qn; **what in the ~ is he doing?** qu'est-ce qu'il peut bien être en train de faire?; **to do sb a ~ of good** faire le plus grand bien à qn; **W~ War One/Two, the First/Second W~ War** la Première/Deuxième Guerre mondiale; **out of this ~** adj extraordinaire.

World Cup n: the ~ (FOOTBALL) la Coupe du monde.

world-famous [wɔːld'feɪməs] adj de renommée mondiale.

worldly ['wɔːldlɪ] adj de ce monde.

world music n world music f.

World Series n: the ~ (US: BASEBALL) le championnat national de baseball.

world-wide ['wɔːld'waɪd] adj universel(le) ♦ adv dans le monde entier.

worm [wɔːm] n ver m.

worn [wɔːn] pp of wear ♦ adj usé(e).

worn-out ['wɔːnaut] adj (object) complètement usé(e); (person) épuisé(e).

worried ['wʌrɪd] adj inquiet(ète); **to be ~ about sth** être inquiet au sujet de qch.

worrier ['wʌrɪə*] n inquiet/ète.

worrisome ['wʌrɪsəm] adj inquiétant(e).

worry ['wʌrɪ] n souci m ♦ vt inquiéter ♦ vi s'inquiéter, se faire du souci; **to ~ about** or **over sth/sb** se faire du souci pour or à propos de qch/qn.

worrying ['wʌrɪɪŋ] adj inquiétant(e).

worse [wɔːs] adj pire, plus mauvais(e) ♦ adv plus mal ♦ n pire m; **to get ~** (condition, situation) empirer, se dégrader; **a change for the ~** une détérioration; **he is none the ~ for it** il ne s'en porte pas plus mal; **so much the ~ for you!** tant pis pour vous!

worsen ['wɔːsn] vt, vi empirer.

worse off adj moins à l'aise financièrement; (fig): **you'll be ~ this way** ça ira moins bien de cette façon; **he is now ~ than before** il se retrouve dans une situation pire qu'auparavant.

worship ['wɔːʃɪp] n culte m ♦ vt (God) rendre un culte à; (person) adorer; **Your W~** (BRIT: to mayor) Monsieur le Maire; (: to judge) Monsieur le Juge.

worshipper ['wɔːʃɪpə*] n adorateur/trice; (in church) fidèle m/f.

worst [wɔːst] adj le(la) pire, le(la) plus mauvais(e) ♦ adv le plus mal ♦ n pire m; **at ~** au pis aller; **if the ~ comes to the ~** si le pire doit arriver.

worst-case ['wɔːstkeɪs] adj: the ~ scenario le pire scénario or cas de figure.

worsted ['wustɪd] n: **(wool)** ~ laine peignée.

worth [wɔːθ] n valeur f ♦ adj: **to be ~** valoir; **how much is it** ~? ça vaut combien?; **it's ~ it** cela en vaut la peine; **50 pence ~ of apples** (pour) 50 pence de pommes.

worthless ['wɔːθlɪs] adj qui ne vaut rien.

worthwhile ['wɔːθ'waɪl] adj (activity) qui en vaut la peine; (cause) louable; **a ~ book** un livre qui vaut la peine d'être lu.

worthy ['wɔːðɪ] adj (person) digne; (motive) louable; **~ of** digne de.

═══════════════════ KEYWORD

would [wud] aux vb **1** (conditional tense): **if you asked him he ~ do it** si vous le lui demandiez, il le ferait; **if you had asked him he ~ have done it** si vous le lui aviez demandé, il l'aurait fait

2 (in offers, invitations, requests): **~ you like a biscuit?** voulez-vous un biscuit?; **~ you close the door please?** voulez-vous fermer la porte, s'il vous plaît?

3 (in indirect speech): **I said I ~ do it** j'ai dit que je le ferais

4 (emphatic): **it WOULD have to snow today!** naturellement il neige aujourd'hui! or il fallait qu'il neige aujourd'hui!

5 (insistence): **she ~n't do it** elle n'a pas voulu or elle a refusé de le faire

6 (conjecture): **it ~ have been midnight** il devait être minuit

7 (indicating habit): **he ~ go there on Mondays** il y allait le lundi

would-be ['wudbiː] adj (pej) soi-disant.

wound vb [waund] pt, pp of wind ♦ n, vt [wuːnd] n blessure f ♦ vt blesser; **~ed in the leg** blessé à la jambe.

wove [wəuv] pt of weave.

woven ['wəuvn] pp of weave.

WP n abbr = **word processing, word processor** ♦ abbr (BRIT col) = **weather permitting.**

WPC n abbr (BRIT) = **woman police constable.**

wpm abbr (= words per minute) mots/minute.

WRAC n abbr (BRIT: = Women's Royal Army Corps) auxiliaires féminines de l'armée de terre.

WRAF n abbr (BRIT: = Women's Royal Air Force) auxiliaires féminines de l'armée de l'air.

wrangle ['ræŋgl] n dispute f ♦ vi se disputer.

wrap [ræp] n (stole) écharpe f; (cape) pèlerine f ♦ vt (also: ~ up) envelopper; **under ~s** (fig: plan, scheme) secret(ète).

wrapper ['ræpə*] n (BRIT: of book) couverture f; (on chocolate etc) papier m.

wrapping paper ['ræpɪŋ-] n papier m d'emballage; (for gift) papier cadeau.

wrath [rɔθ] n courroux m.

wreak [riːk] vt (destruction) entraîner; **to ~ havoc** faire des ravages; **to ~ vengeance on** se venger de, exercer sa vengeance sur.

wreath, ~s [riːθ, riːðz] n couronne f.

wreck [rɛk] n (*sea disaster*) naufrage m; (*ship*) épave f; (*pej: person*) loque (humaine) ♦ vt démolir; (*ship*) provoquer le naufrage de; (*fig*) briser, ruiner.

wreckage ['rɛkɪdʒ] n débris mpl; (*of building*) décombres mpl; (*of ship*) naufrage m.

wrecker ['rɛkə*] n (*US: breakdown van*) dépanneuse f.

WREN [rɛn] n abbr (*BRIT*) membre du WRNS.

wren [rɛn] n (*ZOOL*) troglodyte m.

wrench [rɛntʃ] n (*TECH*) clé f (à écrous); (*tug*) violent mouvement de torsion; (*fig*) arrachement m ♦ vt tirer violemment sur, tordre; **to ~ sth from** arracher qch (violemment) à or de.

wrest [rɛst] vt: **to ~ sth from sb** arracher or ravir qch à qn.

wrestle ['rɛsl] vi: **to ~ (with sb)** lutter (avec qn); **to ~ with** (*fig*) se débattre avec, lutter contre.

wrestler ['rɛslə*] n lutteur/euse.

wrestling ['rɛslɪŋ] n lutte f; (*also: all-in ~: BRIT*) catch m.

wrestling match n rencontre f de lutte (or de catch).

wretch [rɛtʃ] n pauvre malheureux/euse; **little ~!** (*often humorous*) petit(e) misérable!

wretched ['rɛtʃɪd] adj misérable; (*col*) maudit(e).

wriggle ['rɪgl] n tortillement m ♦ vi se tortiller.

wring, pt, pp wrung [rɪŋ, rʌŋ] vt tordre; (*wet clothes*) essorer; (*fig*): **to ~ sth out of** arracher qch à.

wringer ['rɪŋə*] n essoreuse f.

wringing ['rɪŋɪŋ] adj (*also: ~ wet*) tout mouillé(e), trempé(e).

wrinkle ['rɪŋkl] n (*on skin*) ride f; (*on paper etc*) pli m ♦ vt rider, plisser ♦ vi se plisser.

wrinkled ['rɪŋkld] adj, **wrinkly** ['rɪŋklɪ] adj (*fabric, paper*) froissé(e), plissé(e); (*surface*) plissé; (*skin*) ridé(e), plissé.

wrist [rɪst] n poignet m.

wristband ['rɪstbænd] n (*BRIT: of shirt*) poignet m; (: *of watch*) bracelet m.

wrist watch n montre-bracelet f.

writ [rɪt] n acte m judiciaire; **to issue a ~ against sb, serve a ~ on sb** assigner qn en justice.

write, pt wrote, pp written [raɪt, rəut, 'rɪtn] vt, vi écrire; **to ~ sb a letter** écrire une lettre à qn.

▶**write away** vi: **to ~ away for** (*information*) (écrire pour) demander; (*goods*) (écrire pour) commander.

▶**write down** vt noter; (*put in writing*) mettre par écrit.

▶**write off** vt (*debt*) passer aux profits et pertes; (*depreciate*) amortir; (*smash up: car etc*) démolir complètement.

▶**write out** vt écrire; (*copy*) recopier.

▶**write up** vt rédiger.

write-off ['raɪtɔf] n perte totale; **the car is a ~** la voiture est bonne pour la casse.

write-protect ['raɪtprə'tɛkt] vt (*COMPUT*) protéger contre l'écriture.

writer ['raɪtə*] n auteur m, écrivain m.

write-up ['raɪtʌp] n (*review*) critique f.

writhe [raɪð] vi se tordre.

writing ['raɪtɪŋ] n écriture f; (*of author*) œuvres fpl; **in ~** par écrit; **in my own ~** écrit(e) de ma main.

writing case n nécessaire m de correspondance.

writing desk n secrétaire m.

writing paper n papier m à lettres.

written ['rɪtn] pp of **write**.

WRNS n abbr (*BRIT*: = *Women's Royal Naval Service*) auxiliaires féminines de la marine.

wrong [rɔŋ] adj faux(fausse); (*incorrectly chosen: number, road etc*) mauvais(e); (*not suitable*) qui ne convient pas; (*wicked*) mal; (*unfair*) injuste ♦ adv faux ♦ n tort m ♦ vt faire du tort à, léser; **to be ~** (*answer*) être faux(fausse); (*in doing/saying*) avoir tort (de dire/faire); **you are ~ to do it** tu as tort de le faire; **it's ~ to steal, stealing is ~** c'est mal de voler; **you are ~ about that, you've got it ~** tu te trompes; **to be in the ~** avoir tort; **what's ~?** qu'est-ce qui ne va pas?; **there's nothing ~** tout va bien; **what's ~ with the car?** qu'est-ce qu'elle a, la voiture?; **to go ~** (*person*) se tromper; (*plan*) mal tourner; (*machine*) se détraquer.

wrongdoer ['rɔŋduːə*] n malfaiteur m.

wrong-foot [rɔŋ'fut] vt (*SPORT*) prendre à contre-pied; (*fig*) prendre au dépourvu.

wrongful ['rɔŋful] adj injustifié(e); **~ dismissal** (*INDUSTRY*) licenciement abusif.

wrongly ['rɔŋlɪ] adv à tort; (*answer, do, count*) mal, incorrectement; (*treat*) injustement.

wrong number n (*TEL*): **you have the ~** vous vous êtes trompé de numéro.

wrong side n (*of cloth*) envers m.

wrote [rəut] pt of **write**.

wrought [rɔːt] adj: **~ iron** fer forgé.

wrung [rʌŋ] pt, pp of **wring**.

WRVS n abbr (*BRIT*: = *Women's Royal Voluntary Service*) auxiliaires féminines bénévoles au service de la collectivité.

wry [raɪ] adj désabusé(e).

wt. abbr (= *weight*) pds.

WV, W. Va. abbr (*US*) = West Virginia.

WWW n abbr (= *World Wide Web*): **the ~** le Web.

WY, Wyo. abbr (*US*) = Wyoming.

WYSIWYG ['wɪzɪwɪg] abbr (*COMPUT*: = *what you see is what you get*) ce que vous voyez est ce que vous aurez.

X x

X, x [ɛks] n (letter) X, x m; (BRIT CINE: formerly) film interdit aux moins de 18 ans; **X for Xmas** X comme Xavier.
Xerox ['zɪərɔks] n ® (also: ~ **machine**) photocopieuse f; (photocopy) photocopie f ♦ vt photocopier.
XL abbr (= extra large) XL.
Xmas ['ɛksməs] n abbr = **Christmas**.
X-rated ['ɛks'reɪtɪd] adj (US: film) interdit(e) aux moins de 18 ans.
X-ray ['ɛksreɪ] n rayon m X; (photograph) radio(graphie) f ♦ vt radiographier.
xylophone ['zaɪləfəun] n xylophone m.

Y y

Y, y [waɪ] n (letter) Y, y m; **Y for Yellow,** (US) **Y for Yoke** Y comme Yvonne.
yacht [jɔt] n voilier m; (motor, luxury ~) yacht m.
yachting ['jɔtɪŋ] n yachting m, navigation f de plaisance.
yachtsman ['jɔtsmən] n yacht(s)man m.
yam [jæm] n igname f.
Yank [jæŋk], **Yankee** ['jæŋkɪ] n (pej) Amerloque m/f, Ricain/e.
yank [jæŋk] vt tirer d'un coup sec.
yap [jæp] vi (dog) japper.
yard [jɑːd] n (of house etc) cour f; (US: garden) jardin m; (measure) yard m (= 914 mm; 3 feet); **builder's** ~ chantier m.
yardstick ['jɑːdstɪk] n (fig) mesure f, critère m.
yarn [jɑːn] n fil m; (tale) longue histoire.
yawn [jɔːn] n bâillement m ♦ vi bâiller.
yawning ['jɔːnɪŋ] adj (gap) béant(e).
yd abbr = **yard**.
yeah [jɛə] adv (col) ouais.
year [jɪə*] n an m, année f; (SCOL etc) année; **every** ~ tous les ans, chaque année; **this** ~ cette année; **a** or **per** ~ par an; ~ **in,** ~ **out** année après année; **to be 8** ~**s old** avoir 8 ans; **an eight-**~**-old child** un enfant de huit ans.
yearbook ['jɪəbuk] n annuaire m.

yearly ['jɪəlɪ] adj annuel(le) ♦ adv annuellement; **twice** ~ deux fois par an.
yearn [jəːn] vi: **to** ~ **for sth/to do** aspirer à qch/à faire, languir après qch.
yearning ['jəːnɪŋ] n désir ardent, envie f.
yeast [jiːst] n levure f.
yell [jɛl] n hurlement m, cri m ♦ vi hurler.
yellow ['jɛləu] adj, n jaune (m).
yellow fever n fièvre f jaune.
yellowish ['jɛləuɪʃ] adj qui tire sur le jaune, jaunâtre (pej).
Yellow Pages npl ® pages fpl jaunes.
Yellow Sea n: **the** ~ la mer Jaune.
yelp [jɛlp] n jappement m; glapissement m ♦ vi japper; glapir.
Yemen ['jɛmən] n Yémen m.
yen [jɛn] n (currency) yen m; (craving): ~ **for/to do** grand(e) envie f or désir m de/de faire.
yeoman ['jəumən] n: **Y**~ **of the Guard** hallebardier m de la garde royale.
yes [jɛs] adv oui; (answering negative question) si ♦ n oui m; **to say** ~ **(to)** dire oui (à).
yesterday ['jɛstədɪ] adv, n hier (m); ~ **morning/evening** hier matin/soir; **the day before** ~ avant-hier; **all day** ~ toute la journée d'hier.
yet [jɛt] adv encore; déjà ♦ conj pourtant, néanmoins; **it is not finished** ~ ce n'est pas encore fini or toujours pas fini; **must you go just** ~? dois-tu déjà partir?; **the best** ~ le meilleur jusqu'ici or jusque-là; **as** ~ jusqu'ici, encore; **a few days** ~ encore quelques jours; ~ **again** une fois de plus.
yew [juː] n if m.
Y-fronts ['waɪfrʌnts] npl ® (BRIT) slip m kangourou.
YHA n abbr (BRIT) = Youth Hostels Association.
Yiddish ['jɪdɪʃ] n yiddish m.
yield [jiːld] n production f, rendement m; (FINANCE) rapport m ♦ vt produire, rendre, rapporter; (surrender) céder ♦ vi céder; (US AUT) céder la priorité; **a** ~ **of 5%** un rendement de 5%.
YMCA n abbr (= Young Men's Christian Association) ≈ union chrétienne de jeunes gens (UCJG).
yob(bo) ['jɔb(əu)] n (BRIT col) loubar(d) m.
yodel ['jəudl] vi faire des tyroliennes, jodler.
yoga ['jəugə] n yoga m.
yog(h)ourt, yog(h)urt ['jəugət] n yaourt m.
yoke [jəuk] n joug m ♦ vt (also: ~ **together**: oxen) accoupler.
yolk [jəuk] n jaune m (d'œuf).
yonder ['jɔndə*] adv là(-bas).
yonks [jɔŋks] npl (col): **for** ~ très longtemps; **we've been here for** ~ ça fait une éternité qu'on est ici; **we were there for** ~ on est resté là pendant des lustres.
Yorks [jɔːks] abbr (BRIT) = Yorkshire.

========================= KEYWORD

you [ju:] *pron* **1** (*subject*) tu; (*polite form*) vous; (*plural*) vous; ~ **French enjoy your food** vous autres Français, vous aimez bien manger; ~ **and I will go** toi et moi *or* vous et moi, nous irons
2 (*object: direct, indirect*) te, t' +*vowel*; vous; **I know** ~ je te *or* vous connais; **I gave it to** ~, je vous l'ai donné, je te l'ai donné
3 (*stressed*) toi; vous; **I told YOU to do it** c'est à toi *or* vous que j'ai dit de le faire
4 (*after prep, in comparisons*) toi; vous; **it's for** ~ c'est pour toi *or* vous; **she's younger than** ~ elle est plus jeune que toi *or* vous
5 (*impersonal: one*) on; **fresh air does** ~ **good** l'air frais fait du bien; ~ **never know** on ne sait jamais.

you'd [ju:d] = **you had, you would**.
you'll [ju:l] = **you will, you shall**.
young [jʌŋ] *adj* jeune ♦ *npl* (*of animal*) petits *mpl*; (*people*): **the** ~ les jeunes, la jeunesse; **a** ~ **man** un jeune homme; **a** ~ **lady** (*unmarried*) une jeune fille, une demoiselle; (*married*) une jeune femme *or* dame; **my** ~**er brother** mon frère cadet; **the** ~**er generation** la jeune génération.
youngish ['jʌŋɪʃ] *adj* assez jeune.
youngster ['jʌŋstə*] *n* jeune *m/f*; (*child*) enfant *m/f*.
your [jɔ:*] *adj* ton(ta), tes *pl*; (*polite form, pl*) votre, vos *pl*.
you're [juə*] = **you are**.
yours [jɔ:z] *pron* le(la) tien(ne), les tiens(tiennes); (*polite form, pl*) le(la) vôtre, les vôtres; **is it** ~? c'est à toi (*or* à vous)?; **a friend of** ~ un(e) de tes (*or* de vos) amis.
yourself [jɔ:'sɛlf] *pron* (*reflexive*) te; (: *polite form*) vous; (*after prep*) toi; vous; (*emphatic*) toi-même; vous-même; **you** ~ **told me** c'est vous qui me l'avez dit, vous me l'avez dit vous-même.
yourselves [jɔ:'sɛlvz] *pl pron* vous; (*emphatic*) vous-mêmes.
youth [ju:θ] *n* jeunesse *f*; (*young man: pl* ~**s** [ju:ðz]) jeune homme *m*; **in my** ~ dans ma jeunesse, quand j'étais jeune.
youth club *n* centre *m* de jeunes.
youthful ['ju:θful] *adj* jeune; (*enthusiasm etc*) juvénile; (*misdemeanour*) de jeunesse.
youthfulness ['ju:θfəlnɪs] *n* jeunesse *f*.
youth hostel *n* auberge *f* de jeunesse.
youth movement *n* mouvement *m* de jeunes.
you've [ju:v] = **you have**.
yowl [jaul] *n* hurlement *m*; miaulement *m* ♦ *vi* hurler; miauler.
YT *abbr* (*Canada*) = **Yukon Territory**.
Yugoslav ['ju:gəuslɑ:v] *adj* yougoslave ♦ *n* Yougoslave *m/f*.
Yugoslavia [ju:gəu'slɑ:vɪə] *n* Yougoslavie *f*.

Yugoslavian [ju:gəu'slɑ:vɪən] *adj* yougoslave.
Yule [ju:l]: ~ **log** *n* bûche *f* de Noël.
yuppie ['jʌpɪ] *n* yuppie *m/f*.
YWCA *n abbr* (= *Young Women's Christian Association*) union chrétienne féminine.

========================= **Z z**

Z, z [zɛd, (*US*) zi:] *n* (*letter*) Z, z *m*; **Z for Zebra** Z comme Zoé.
Zaïre [zɑ:'i:ə*] *n* Zaïre *m*.
Zambia ['zæmbɪə] *n* Zambie *f*.
Zambian ['zæmbɪən] *adj* zambien(ne) ♦ *n* Zambien/ne.
zany ['zeɪnɪ] *adj* farfelu(e), loufoque.
zap [zæp] *vt* (*COMPUT*) effacer.
zeal [zi:l] *n* (*revolutionary etc*) ferveur *f*; (*keenness*) ardeur *f*, zèle *m*.
zealot ['zɛlət] *n* fanatique *m/f*.
zealous ['zɛləs] *adj* fervent(e); ardent(e), zélé(e).
zebra ['zi:brə] *n* zèbre *m*.
zebra crossing *n* (*BRIT*) passage *m* pour piétons.
zenith ['zɛnɪθ] *n* (*ASTRONOMY*) zénith *m*; (*fig*) zénith, apogée *m*.
zero ['zɪərəu] *n* zéro *m* ♦ *vi*: **to** ~ **in on** (*target*) se diriger droit sur; **5° below** ~ 5 degrés au-dessous de zéro.
zero hour *n* l'heure *f* H.
zero option *n* (*POL*): **the** ~ l'option *f* zéro.
zero-rated ['zi:rəureɪtɪd] *adj* (*BRIT*) exonéré(e) de TVA.
zest [zɛst] *n* entrain *m*, élan *m*; (*of lemon etc*) zeste *m*.
zigzag ['zɪgzæg] *n* zigzag *m* ♦ *vi* zigzaguer, faire des zigzags.
Zimbabwe [zɪm'bɑ:bwɪ] *n* Zimbabwe *m*.
Zimbabwean [zɪm'bɑ:bwɪən] *adj* zimbabwéen(ne) ♦ *n* Zimbabwéen/ne.
Zimmer ['zɪmə*] *n* ® (*also*: ~ **frame**) déambulateur *m*.
zinc [zɪŋk] *n* zinc *m*.
Zionism ['zaɪənɪzəm] *n* sionisme *m*.
Zionist ['zaɪənɪst] *adj* sioniste ♦ *n* Sioniste *m/f*.
zip [zɪp] *n* (*also*: ~ **fastener,** (*US*) ~**per**) fermeture *f* éclair ® *or* à glissière; (*energy*) entrain *m* ♦ *vt* (*also*: ~ **up**) fermer (avec une fermeture éclair ®).
zip code *n* (*US*) code postal.
zither ['zɪðə*] *n* cithare *f*.
zodiac ['zəudɪæk] *n* zodiaque *m*.
zombie ['zɒmbɪ] *n* (*fig*): **like a** ~ avec l'air d'un zombie, comme un automate.
zone [zəun] *n* zone *f*.

zonked [zɔŋkt] *adj* (*col*) crevé(e), claqué(e).

zoo [zuː] *n* zoo *m*.

zoological [zuə'lɔdʒɪkl] *adj* zoologique.

zoologist [zu'ɔlədʒɪst] *n* zoologiste *m/f*.

zoology [zuː'ɔlədʒɪ] *n* zoologie *f*.

zoom [zuːm] *vi*: **to ~ past** passer en trombe; **to ~ in (on sb/sth)** (*PHOT, CINE*) zoomer (sur qn/qch).

zoom lens *n* zoom *m*, objectif *m* à focale variable.

zucchini [zuː'kiːnɪ] *n(pl)* (*US*) courgette(s) *f(pl)*.

Zulu ['zuːluː] *adj* zoulou ♦ *n* Zoulou *m/f*.

Zürich ['zjuərɪk] *n* Zurich.

L'ANGLAIS EN SITUATION

FRENCH IN ACTION

Collaborateurs/Contributors

Rose Rociola   Daphne Day

Coordination/Coordination

Isobel Gordon

INTRODUCTION

The aim of FRENCH IN ACTION is to help you express yourself simply but correctly in fluent, natural French.

The SENTENCE BUILDER section provides hundreds of phrases in which the key elements have been translated, providing an invaluable point of reference when you then construct your own sentences.

The section on correspondence provides practical models of personal and business letters, job applications and CVs, together with examples of standard opening and closing formulae and information on how to address an envelope. This section also offers guidance notes to help the user adapt these models to his/her needs.

A separate section covers fax and e-mail correspondence as well as all the expressions you might need to make different types of phone calls.

We hope you will find FRENCH IN ACTION both relevant and useful and that, used in conjunction with the dictionary, it will improve your understanding and enjoyment of French.

CONTENTS

INTRODUCTION

L'ANGLAIS EN SITUATION a pour objectif de vous aider à vous exprimer en anglais, dans un style simple et naturel.

Dans le MÉMO DES TOURNURES ESSENTIELLES, vous trouverez des centaines d'expressions anglaises de base, qui vous permettront de construire vos propres phrases dans toutes sortes de contextes.

La partie correspondance contient des modèles de lettres de tous genres, dont vous pourrez vous inspirer pour rédiger à votre tour vos lettres, que ce soit dans un contexte privé ou professionnel. Si vous êtes à la recherche d'un travail, vous y trouverez également des exemples de curriculum vitæ et de lettres de candidature. Pour vous permettre d'adapter ces modèles à vos besoins, nous vous donnons en outre une liste des formules de politesse employées en début et en fin de lettre.

La dernière partie est consacrée à la communication par télécopie, par courrier électronique et par téléphone, et comprend une liste des expressions de base les plus couramment utilisées au téléphone.

L'ANGLAIS EN SITUATION, complément indispensable de votre dictionnaire, vous permettra de vous exprimer avec aisance dans toutes les situations.

TABLE DES MATIÈRES

LIKES, DISLIKES AND PREFERENCES

Saying what you like

J'aime les gâteaux.	*I like ...*
J'aime que les choses soient à leur place.	*I like ...*
J'ai bien aimé le film.	*I liked ...*
J'adore sortir en boîte.	*I love ...*
Ce que je préfère chez Laurent, c'est son enthousiasme.	*What I like most ...*
Ce que j'aime par-dessus tout, c'est son sourire.	*What I like most of all is ...*
La visite des vignobles **m'a beaucoup plu.**	*I very much enjoyed ...*
J'ai un faible pour le chocolat.	*I've got a weakness for ...*
Rien ne vaut un bon café.	*You can't beat ...*
Rien de tel qu'un bon bain chaud !	*There's nothing better than ...*
Le couscous est **mon** plat **favori.**	*My favourite ...*
La lecture est **une de mes** activités **préférées.**	*... one of my favourite ...*
Cela ne me déplaît pas de sortir seule.	*I don't mind ...*

Saying what you dislike

Je n'aime pas le poisson.	*I don't like ...*
Je n'aime pas beaucoup parler en public.	*I'm not very keen on ...*
Je ne l'**aime pas du tout.**	*I don't like ... at all.*
Cette idée **ne m'emballe pas.**	*I'm not particularly keen on ...*
Je déteste la chimie.	*I hate ...*
J'ai horreur du sport.	*I loathe ...*
Je ne supporte pas qu'on me mente.	*I can't stand ...*
Sa façon d'agir **ne me plaît pas du tout.**	*I don't like ... at all.*
Ce que je déteste le plus, c'est le repassage.	*What I hate most is ...*

Saying what you prefer

Je préfère le rock **à** la musique classique.	*I prefer ... to ...*
Je préférerais vivre à Paris.	*I would rather ...*
J'aimerais mieux mourir de faim **que de** lui demander un service.	*I'd sooner ... than ...*

Expressing indifference

Ça m'est égal.	*It's all the same to me.*
Je n'ai pas de préférence.	*I have no preference either way.*
C'est comme vous voudrez.	*As you wish.*
Cela n'a aucune importance.	*It doesn't matter in the least.*
Peu importe.	*I don't mind.*

Asking what someone likes

Est-ce que vous aimez les frites ?	*Do you like ...*
Est-ce que vous aimez faire la cuisine ?	*Do you like ...*
Est-ce que cela vous plaît de vivre en ville ?	*Do you like ...*
Qu'est-ce que vous préférez : la mer ou la montagne ?	*Which do you like better ...*
Vous préférez lequel, le rouge ou le noir ?	*Which do you prefer ...*
Est-ce que vous préférez vivre à la campagne ou en ville ?	*Do you prefer ...*
Qu'est-ce que vous aimez le plus à la télévision ?	*What do you like best ...*

OPINIONS

Asking for opinions

Qu'en pensez-vous ?	*What do you think about it?*
Que pensez-vous de sa façon d'agir ?	*What do you think of ...*
Je voudrais savoir ce que vous pensez de son travail.	*I'd like to know what you think of ...*
J'aimerais connaître votre avis sur ce problème.	*I would like to know your views on ...*
Est-ce que vous pourriez me donner votre opinion sur cette émission ?	*What do you think of ...*
Quelle est votre opinion sur la peine de mort ?	*What is your opinion on ...*
À votre avis, hommes et femmes sont-ils égaux ?	*In your opinion ...*
Selon vous, faut-il donner plus de liberté aux jeunes ?	*In your opinion ...*

Expressing opinions

Vous avez raison.	*You are right.*
Il a tort.	*He is wrong.*
Il a eu tort de démissionner.	*He was wrong to ...*
Je pense que ce sera possible.	*I think ...*
Je crois que c'est un peu prématuré.	*I think ...*
Je trouve que c'est normal.	*I think ...*
Personnellement, je pense que c'est trop cher.	*Personally, I think that ...*
Il me semble que vous vous trompez.	*I think ...*
J'ai l'impression que ses parents ne la comprennent pas.	*I get the impression that ...*
Je suis certain qu'il est tout à fait sincère.	*I'm sure ...*
Je suis sûr que Marc va gagner.	*I'm sure ...*
Je suis persuadé qu'il y a d'autres solutions.	*I am convinced that ...*
À mon avis, il n'a pas changé.	*In my opinion ...*
D'après moi, il a fait une erreur.	*In my view ...*
Selon moi, c'est impossible.	*In my view ...*

Being noncommittal

Ça dépend.	*It depends.*
Tout dépend de ce que vous entendez par là.	*It all depends what you mean by ...*
Je ne peux pas me prononcer.	*I'd rather not express an opinion.*
Je n'ai pas d'opinion bien précise à ce sujet.	*I have no definite opinion on this.*
Je ne me suis jamais posé la question.	*I have never thought about it.*

APPROVAL AND AGREEMENT

Je trouve que c'est une excellente idée.	*I think it's an excellent idea.*
Quelle bonne idée !	*What a good idea!*
J'ai beaucoup apprécié son article.	*I was very impressed by ...*
C'est une très bonne chose.	*It's a very good thing.*
Je trouve que vous avez raison de vous méfier.	*I think you're right to ...*

Les journaux **ont raison de** publier ces informations.	*... are right to ...*
Vous avez bien fait de laisser vos bagages à la consigne.	*You were right to ...*
Vous n'avez pas tort de critiquer le gouvernement.	*You're quite justified in ...*
Je partage cette opinion.	*I share this view.*
Je partage votre inquiétude.	*I fully share your ...*
Nous sommes favorables à la création d'emplois.	*We are in favour of ...*
Nous sommes en faveur d'une Europe unie.	*We are in favour of ...*
Il est exact que c'est un risque à prendre.	*It is true that ...*
Il est vrai que cette erreur aurait pu être évitée.	*It is true that ...*
Je suis d'accord avec vous.	*I agree with you.*
Je suis entièrement d'accord avec toi.	*I entirely agree with you.*

DISAPPROVAL AND DISAGREEMENT

Je trouve qu'il a eu tort d'emprunter autant d'argent.	*I think he was wrong to ...*
Il est dommage qu'il ait réagi ainsi.	*It's a pity that ...*
Il est regrettable qu'ils ne nous aient pas prévenus.	*It is regrettable that ...*
Cette idée **me déplaît profondément.**	*I dislike ... intensely.*
Je ne supporte pas le mensonge.	*I can't stand ...*
Nous sommes contre la chasse.	*We are against ...*
Je refuse cette solution.	*I reject ...*
Je suis opposé à toute forme de censure.	*I am opposed to ...*
Je ne partage pas ce point de vue.	*I don't share this point of view.*
Je suis déçu par son attitude.	*I am disappointed by ...*
Je suis profondément déçu.	*I am deeply disappointed.*
Tu n'aurais pas dû lui parler sur ce ton.	*You shouldn't have ...*
Nous ne pouvons accepter de voir la situation se dégrader.	*We can't stand by and ...*
De quel droit agit–**il** de la sorte ?	*What gives him the right to ...*
Je ne suis pas d'accord.	*I disagree.*
Nous ne sommes pas d'accord avec eux.	*We don't agree with ...*
Je ne suis absolument pas d'accord avec ce qu'il a dit.	*I totally disagree with ...*
C'est faux de dire que cette erreur était inévitable.	*It is wrong to say that ...*
Vous vous trompez !	*You're wrong!*

APOLOGIES

How to say sorry

Excusez-moi.	*Sorry.*
Excusez-moi de vous déranger.	*Sorry to bother you.*
Oh, pardon ! J'ai dû faire un faux numéro.	*Oh, sorry!*
Je suis désolé de vous avoir réveillé.	*I am sorry I ...*
Je suis désolé pour tout ce qui s'est passé.	*I am sorry about ...*
Je vous prie de m'excuser.	*I do apologize.*
Nous prions nos lecteurs **de bien vouloir excuser** cette omission.	*We hope ... will excuse ...*

Admitting responsibility

C'est (de) ma faute : j'aurais dû partir plus tôt.	*It's my fault, I should have ...*
Je n'aurais pas dû me moquer d'elle.	*I shouldn't have ...*
Nous avons eu tort de ne pas vérifier cette information.	*We were wrong not to ...*
J'assume seul l'entière responsabilité de cette erreur.	*I take full responsibility for ...*
Si seulement j'avais préparé ma leçon !	*If only I had ...*

Disclaiming responsibility

Ce n'est pas (de) ma faute.	*It's not my fault.*
Ce n'est pas (de) ma faute si nous sommes en retard.	*It isn't my fault if ...*
Je ne l'ai pas fait exprès.	*I didn't do it on purpose.*
Je ne pouvais pas faire autrement.	*I had no other option.*
J'avais pourtant cru comprendre que je pouvais me garer là.	*But I thought that ...*
J'avais cru bien faire en le prévenant.	*I thought I was doing the right thing in ...*

Apologizing for being unable to do something

Je regrette, mais ce n'est pas possible.	*I'm sorry, but ...*
Je suis désolé, mais je ne peux pas vous aider.	*I'm sorry, but ...*
Il nous est malheureusement impossible d'accéder à votre demande.	*Unfortunately, it's impossible for us to ...*

EXPLANATIONS

Causes

Je n'ai rien acheté **parce que** je n'ai pas d'argent.	... because ...
Je suis arrivé en retard **à cause des** embouteillages.	... because of ...
Puisque tu insistes, je rentre dans une semaine.	Since ...
Comme j'habitais près de la bibliothèque, j'y allais souvent.	As ...
J'ai réussi à m'en sortir **grâce au** soutien de mes amis.	... thanks to ...
Je ne pourrai pas venir **car** je n'ai pas fini.	... as ...
Vu la situation actuelle, nous ne pouvons pas nous prononcer.	Given ...
Étant donné la crise, il est difficile de trouver du travail.	Given ...
C'est une rupture d'essieu **qui a provoqué** le déraillement.	It was ... that caused ...
Le théâtre va fermer **faute de** moyens.	... due to lack of ...
Il a donné sa démission **pour des raisons de** santé.	... for ... reasons.
Le projet a été abandonné **en raison de** problèmes juridiques.	... owing to ...
Le malaise des enseignants **est lié à** la difficulté de leur métier.	... is linked to ...
Le problème vient de ce que les gens ont peur des ordinateurs.	The problem is that ...
Le ralentissement des exportations **provient de** la chute de la demande européenne.	... is the result of ...
La haine **résulte de** l'incompréhension.	... results from ...

Consequences

Je dois partir ce soir. Je ne pourrai **donc** pas venir avec vous.	... so ...
La distribution a été améliorée, **de telle sorte que** les lecteurs trouveront leur journal plus tôt.	... so that ...
Le cidre nouveau est très peu fermenté et **par conséquent** très peu alcoolisé.	... consequently ...
Ce manque de concertation **a eu pour conséquence** une duplication inutile de nos efforts.	... has resulted in ...
Voilà pourquoi on s'en souvient.	That's why ...

COMPARISONS

On peut comparer la télévision **à** une drogue.	... can be compared to ...
C'est une très belle performance **que l'on peut comparer à** celle des meilleurs athlètes.	... which can be compared to ...
Le Centre Pompidou **est souvent comparé à** un paquebot.	... is often compared to ...
Le bruit **était comparable à** celui d'une moto dépourvue de silencieux.	... was comparable to ...
L'Afrique reste un continent sous-peuplé **comparé à** l'Asie.	... compared with ...
Par comparaison avec l'Islande, l'Irlande a un climat tropical.	Compared to ...
Les investissements publicitaires ont connu une légère progression **par rapport à** l'année dernière.	... compared to ...
Cette histoire **ressemble à** un conte de fées.	... is like ...
Il adorait cette campagne qui **lui rappelait** l'Irlande.	... reminded him of ...
Des taux de chômage effrayants, **rappelant ceux** des années 30.	... reminiscent of those ...
Il me fait penser à mon frère.	He reminds me of ...
Le surf des neiges **est l'équivalent** sur neige **de** la planche à roulettes.	... is the equivalent ... of ...
Cette somme **correspond à** six mois de salaire.	... corresponds to ...
C'est la même chose.	It's the same thing.
Cela revient au même.	It comes to the same thing.
Ce disque **n'est ni meilleur ni moins bon que** les autres.	... is no better and no worse than ...

Stressing differences

Aucune catastrophe **ne peut être comparée à** celle de Tchernobyl.	No ... can compare with ...
On ne peut pas comparer les usines modernes **à** celles où travaillaient nos grands-parents.	... cannot be compared with ...
Les actions de ce groupe **n'ont rien de comparable avec** les agissements des terroristes.	... are in no way comparable to ...
Sa démarche le **différencie de** son frère.	... distinguishes ... from ...
L'histoire des États-Unis **ne ressemble en rien à** la nôtre.	... in no way resembles ...
Il y a des événements bien plus tragiques que de perdre une finale de Coupe d'Europe.	There are worse things than ...
Le gruyère **est meilleur que** le comté.	... is better than ...

Son deuxième film **est moins** réussi **que** le premier.	... is less ... than ...
L'espérance de vie des femmes est de 81 ans, **tandis que** celle des hommes est de 72 ans.	... while ...
Alors que la consommation de vin et de bière diminue, l'eau minérale est un marché en expansion.	While ...

REQUESTS AND OFFERS

Requests

Je voudrais trois tartelettes.	I'd like ...
Je voudrais connaître les horaires des trains pour Lille.	I'd like to ...
Pourriez-vous nous donner un coup de main ?	Could you ...
Est-ce que vous pouvez annoncer la bonne nouvelle à Éliane ?	Can you ...
Est-ce que vous pourriez venir me chercher ?	Could you ...
Sois gentille, fais un saut chez le boulanger.	Be an angel ...
Auriez-vous l'amabilité de m'indiquer la sortie ?	Could you please ...
Auriez-vous la gentillesse de nous donner la recette ?	Would you be so kind as to ...
Auriez-vous l'obligeance de me garder ma place ?	Would you be very kind and ...
Puis-je vous demander de m'accorder un instant ?	Could you ...
Merci de bien vouloir patienter.	If you wouldn't mind ...
Est-ce que cela vous dérangerait d'ouvrir la fenêtre ?	Would you mind ...
Je vous serais reconnaissant de me prévenir dès que possible.	I would be grateful if you would ...
Je vous serais reconnaissant de bien vouloir me communiquer votre décision d'ici vendredi.	I would be grateful if you would ...

Offers

Je peux passer vous prendre, **si** vous voulez.	I can ... if ...
Je pourrais vous accompagner.	I could ...
Ça te dirait, une glace ?	Do you fancy ...
Ça vous dirait d'aller faire un tour ?	Would you like to ...
Que diriez-vous d'une balade en forêt ?	How do you fancy ...
Est-ce que vous voulez que j'aille chercher votre voiture ?	Do you want me to ...
Est-ce que vous voulez dîner avec nous un soir ?	Would you like to ...

ADVICE AND SUGGESTIONS

Asking for advice or suggestions

À ma place, que feriez-vous ?	*What would you do, if you were me?*
Quel est votre avis sur la question ?	*What's your opinion on the matter?*
Qu'est-ce que vous me conseillez, les Baléares ou les Canaries ?	*Which would you recommend ...*
Que me conseillez-vous de faire ?	*What would you advise me to do?*
Parmi les excursions à faire, **laquelle nous conseilleriez-vous ?**	*... which would you recommend?*
Quelle stratégie **proposez-vous ?**	*What ... do you suggest?*
Que proposez-vous pour réduire la pollution ?	*What, in your opinion, should be done to ...*
Qu'est-ce que vous proposez contre le chômage ?	*How would you deal with ...*

Offering advice or suggestions

À votre place, je me méfierais.	*If I were you ...*
Si j'étais toi, je ne dirais rien.	*If I were you ...*
Je peux vous donner un conseil : achetez votre billet à l'avance.	*If I may give you a bit of advice ...*
Un conseil : lisez le mode d'emploi.	*A word of advice ...*
Un bon conseil : n'attendez pas le dernier moment pour faire votre réservation.	*A useful tip ...*
Vous devriez voir un spécialiste.	*You should ...*
Vous feriez bien de consulter un avocat.	*You would do well to ...*
Vous feriez mieux d'acheter une nouvelle voiture.	*You would do better to ...*
Vous pourriez peut-être demander à quelqu'un de vous le traduire.	*You could perhaps ...*
Vous pourriez montrer un peu plus de compréhension.	*You could ...*
Pourquoi ne pas lui téléphoner ?	*Why don't you ...*

Il **faudrait peut-être** essayer autre chose.	*Perhaps we ought to ...*
Et si on allait au cinéma ?	*How about ...*
Je vous propose le 3 mars à 10 h 30.	*How about ...*
Il **vaudrait mieux** lui offrir de l'argent qu'un bijou.	*It might be better to ...*
Il **serait préférable d'**attendre le résultat.	*It would be better to ...*

Warnings

Je vous préviens, je ne me laisserai pas faire.	*I warn you ...*
Je te préviens que ça ne sera pas facile.	*I'd better warn you that ...*
N'oubliez pas de conserver le double de votre déclaration d'impôts.	*Don't forget to ...*
Méfiez-vous des apparences.	*Remember: appearances can be deceptive.*
Surtout, n'y allez **jamais** le samedi.	*Whatever you do, don't ...*
Si tu ne viens pas, **tu risques de** le regretter.	*... you risk ...*

INTENTIONS AND DESIRES

Asking what someone intends to do

Qu'est-ce que vous allez faire ?	*What are you going to do?*
Qu'est-ce que tu vas faire si tu rates ton examen ?	*What will you do if ...*
Qu'allez-vous faire en rentrant? **Avez-vous des projets ?**	*What are you going to do ... Do you have anything planned?*
Quels sont vos projets ?	*What are your plans?*
Est-ce que tu comptes passer tes vacances ici ?	*Are you planning to ...*
Vous comptez rester longtemps ?	*Are you planning on ...*
Que comptez-vous faire de votre collection ?	*What are you planning to do with ...*
Comment comptez-vous faire ?	*What are you thinking of doing?*
Tu as l'intention de passer des concours ?	*Do you intend to ...*
Songez-vous à refaire un film en Europe ?	*Are you thinking of ...*

Talking about intentions

Je comptais m'envoler pour Ajaccio le 8 juillet.	*I was planning to ...*
Elle prévoit de voyager pendant un an.	*She plans to ...*
Il est prévu de construire un nouveau stade.	*There are plans to ...*
Ils envisagent d'avoir plusieurs enfants.	*They are thinking of ...*
Cette banque **a l'intention de** fermer un grand nombre de succursales.	*... intends to ...*
Je songe à abandonner la politique.	*I am thinking of ...*
J'ai décidé de changer de carrière.	*I have decided to ...*
Je suis décidée à arrêter de fumer.	*I have made up my mind to ...*
Je me suis décidée à y aller.	*I have decided to ...*
C'est décidé, nous partons à la campagne.	*That's settled ...*
Il n'a jamais été dans nos intentions de lui cacher la vérité.	*We never had any intention of ...*
Il n'est pas question pour moi **de** renoncer à ce projet.	*There is no question of ...*

Wishes

Je veux faire du cinéma.	*I want to ...*
Je voudrais savoir jouer aussi bien que lui.	*I'd like to ...*
J'aimerais faire du deltaplane.	*I'd like to ...*
J'aimerais que mes photos soient publiées dans la presse.	*I would like ...*
J'aurais aimé avoir un frère.	*I would have liked to ...*
Lionel **voulait à tout prix** partir le soir-même.	*... wanted at all costs ...*
Nous souhaitons préserver notre indépendance.	*We wish to ...*
J'espère avoir des enfants.	*I hope to ...*
Nous espérons que les enfants regarderont cette émission avec leurs parents.	*We hope that ...*
Vous rêvez de faire le tour du monde ?	*Do you dream of ...*
Mon rêve serait d'avoir une grande maison.	*My dream would be to ...*

OBLIGATION

Il faut que je me trouve un logement. | *I must ...*

Il faut absolument qu'on se revoie avant le 23 ! | *We really must ...*

Si vous allez en Pologne, **vous devez** venir nous voir. | *... you must ...*

Les auteurs du détournement **ont exigé que** l'avion reparte vers New York. | *... demanded that ...*

Ça **me force à** faire de l'exercice. | *... makes me ...*

Une violente crise d'asthme **m'a obligé à** consulter un médecin. | *... forced me to ...*

Je suis obligé de partir. | *I have to ...*

Il est obligé de travailler, **il n'a pas le choix.** | *He has to ... he has no other option.*

On ne peut pas faire autrement que d'accepter. | *You have no choice but to ...*

L'école **est obligatoire** jusqu'à seize ans. | *... is compulsory ...*

Il est indispensable de voyager pour comprendre les autres. | *It is essential to ...*

PERMISSION

Asking for permission

Je peux téléphoner ? | *Can I ...*

Je peux vous demander quelque chose ? | *Can I ...*

Est-ce que je peux passer vous dire un petit bonjour tout à l'heure ? | *Can I ...*

Ça ne vous dérange pas si j'arrive en avance ? | *Is it alright if ...*

Ça ne vous dérange pas que je fume ? | *Do you mind if ...*

Est-ce que ça vous dérange si j'ouvre la fenêtre ? | *Do you mind if ...*

Vous permettez, Madame, **que** je regarde ce qu'il y a dans votre sac ? | *Would you mind if ...*

Giving permission

(Vous) faites comme vous voulez.	*Do as you please.*
Allez-y !	*Go ahead!*
Je n'y vois pas d'inconvénient.	*I have nothing against it.*
Vous avez le droit de porter plainte.	*You have the right to ...*

Saying something is not allowed

Je te défends de sortir !	*I forbid you to ...*
C'est défendu.	*It's forbidden.*
Il est interdit de fumer dans les toilettes.	*... is forbidden.*
Le travail des enfants **est formellement interdit par** une convention de l'ONU.	*... is strictly forbidden by ...*
Défense d'entrer.	*No entry.*
Stationnement interdit.	*No parking.*
Interdiction de stationner.	*No parking.*
C'est interdit.	*It's not allowed.*
Elle interdit à ses enfants **d'**ouvrir la porte.	*She forbids ... to ...*
Tu n'as pas le droit.	*You're not allowed.*
On n'avait pas le droit de manger ni de boire pendant le service.	*We weren't allowed to ...*
Il n'en est pas question.	*That's out of the question.*

CERTAINTY, PROBABILITY AND POSSIBILITY

Certainty

Il est certain qu'il y aura des problèmes.	*Undoubtedly ...*
Il ne fait aucun doute que ce produit connaîtra un réel succès.	*There is no doubt that ...*
Il est évident qu'il traverse une période difficile.	*Clearly ...*

C'est **de toute évidence** la seule chose à faire.	*Quite obviously ...*
Il est **indéniable qu'**il a eu tort d'agir ainsi.	*It is undeniable that ...*
Je suis sûre que mon frère te plaira.	*I am sure that ...*
Je suis sûr de gagner.	*I am sure that I ...*
Je suis certain que nous sommes sur la bonne voie.	*I am certain that ...*
J'ai la certitude qu'en travaillant avec lui, je ne m'ennuierai pas.	*I am sure that ...*
Je suis persuadé qu'il y a d'autres solutions.	*I am convinced that ...*

Probability

Il est probable que le prix du pétrole va continuer d'augmenter.	*... probably ...*
Le taux d'inflation dépassera **très probablement** les 10 %.	*... very probably ...*
80 % des problèmes de peau sont **sans doute** d'origine psychique.	*... undoubtedly ...*
Ils avaient **sans doute** raison.	*... no doubt ...*
Les travaux **devraient** débuter au mois d'avril.	*... should ...*
Il se pourrait bien qu'ils cherchent à tester nos réactions.	*It is quite possible that ...*
On dirait que tout lui est égal.	*It's as if ...*
Il a dû oublier d'ouvrir les fenêtres.	*He must have ...*

Possibility

C'est possible.	*It is possible.*
Il est possible que cela coûte plus cher.	*That might ...*
Il n'est pas impossible qu'il soit parti à Paris.	*It is not impossible that ...*
Il se pourrait que l'Amérique ait été découverte par des Chinois.	*It is possible that ...*
Il se peut que ce virus soit particulièrement virulent.	*... may ...*
En quelques mois tout **peut** changer.	*... could ...*
Il a **peut-être** mal compris.	*Maybe ...*
Peut-être que je me trompe.	*Perhaps ...*

DOUBT, IMPROBABILITY AND IMPOSSIBILITY

Doubt

Je ne suis pas sûr que ce soit utile.	*I'm not sure ...*
Je ne suis pas sûre d'y arriver.	*I'm not sure I'll ...*
Je ne suis pas certain d'avoir raison.	*I'm not sure I'm ...*
Il n'est pas certain que cela soit une bonne idée.	*I'm not sure that ...*
Il n'est pas certain qu'un vaccin puisse être mis au point.	*I'm not sure that ...*
Je me demande si nous avons fait beaucoup de progrès dans ce domaine.	*I wonder if ...*
Est-ce sage ? **J'en doute.**	*I doubt it.*
Il se mit à **douter de** la compétence de son médecin.	*... to have doubts about ...*
Je doute fort qu'il accepte de rester inactif.	*I very much doubt ...*
On ne sait pas exactement ce qui s'est passé.	*Nobody knows exactly ...*

Improbability

Il **ne** changera **probablement pas** d'avis.	*... probably won't ...*
Il est peu probable qu'il reste encore des places.	*It is unlikely that ...*
Ça m'étonnerait qu'ils aient ta pointure.	*I'd be surprised if ...*
Il serait étonnant que tout se passe conformément aux prévisions.	*It would be amazing if ...*
Nous ne risquons pas de nous ennuyer.	*There's no danger of ...*
Elles ne risquent pas d'avoir le prix Nobel d'économie.	*They are not likely to ...*
Il y a peu de chances que le taux de croissance dépasse 1,5 %.	*There is not much chance of ...*

Impossibility

C'est impossible.	*It's impossible.*
Il n'est pas possible qu'il n'y ait rien à faire.	*It is not possible that ...*
Il est impossible que ces renseignements soient faux.	*... cannot ...*
Il n'y a aucune chance qu'ils viennent à notre secours.	*There is no chance of ...*

GREETINGS

Bonjour !	*Hello!*
Bonsoir !	*Good evening!*
Salut !	*Hi!*
Comment allez-vous ?	*How are you?*
Comment ça va ?	*How's things?*

What to say in reply

Très bien, merci, et vous ?	*Fine thanks, and you?*
Ça va, et toi ?	*Fine thanks, and you?*
Super bien !	*Great!*
On fait aller.	*So-so.*
Couci-couça.	*So-so.*

Introductions

Je vous présente Charles.	*This is ...*
Je vous présente mon amie.	*May I introduce ...*
Marc ; Laurent	*Marc, this is Laurent; Laurent, Marc.*
Je ne crois pas que vous vous connaissiez.	*I don't believe you know one another.*

Replying to an introduction

Enchanté.	*Pleased to meet you.*
Enchanté or **Ravi de faire votre connaissance.**	*Pleased to meet you.*
Salut, moi c'est Dominique.	*Hi, I'm ...*

Leavetaking

Au revoir !	*Goodbye!*
Bonne nuit !	*Good night!*
Salut !	*Bye!*

Ciao !	See you!
À bientôt !	See you later!
À demain !	See you tomorrow!
À la semaine prochaine !	See you next week!
À jeudi !	See you Thursday!

Best wishes

Bon anniversaire !	Happy Birthday!
Joyeux Noël !	Merry Christmas!
Bonne année !	Happy New Year!
Félicitations !	Congratulations!
Bon voyage !	Safe journey!
Bonne chance !	Good luck!
Bienvenue !	Welcome!
Amusez-vous bien !	Have fun!
Bon appétit !	Enjoy your meal!
(À votre) santé !	Cheers!
Tchin-tchin !	Cheers!

CORRESPONDENCE

How to address an envelope

On the front

Stamp

There should always be a comma between the street number and street name.

Monsieur Léon Mougeot
45, avenue de la République
75010 Paris

On the back

Exp. Marcel Gautier
71, rue Montserrat
69000 Lyon

The postcode comes before the name of the town.

Common abbreviations used in addresses

av. = avenue   Exp. = expéditeur   pas. = passage
bd = boulevard   fg = faubourg   pl. = place

Standard opening and closing formulae

In personal correspondence

Cher Monsieur	Je vous envoie mes bien amicales pensées *(fairly formal)*
Chers Jean et Sylvie	Bien amicalement
Chère tante Laure	Je t'embrasse bien affectueusement
Mon cher Laurent	Grosses bises *(very informal)*

In formal correspondence

Monsieur le Directeur (or le Maire etc) Madame le Directeur	Je vous prie d'agréer, [. . .], l'assurance de ma considération distinguée
Messieurs Monsieur Madame	Je vous prie d'agréer, [. . .], l'assurance de mes sentiments distingués or Veuillez accepter, [. . .], l'expression de mes sentiments distingués
Cher Monsieur Chère Madame	Croyez, [. . .], à l'expression de mes sentiments les meilleurs

Starting a personal letter

Je te remercie de ta lettre ...
Thanks for your letter ...

J'ai été très content d'avoir de tes nouvelles.
It was lovely to hear from you.

Je suis désolé de ne pas vous avoir répondu plus vite.
I'm sorry I didn't reply sooner.

Starting a formal letter

Suite à ... je vous écris pour ...
Further to ... I am writing to ...

Je vous serais reconnaissant de ...
I would be grateful if you would ...

Je vous prie de ...
Please ...

Nous vous remercions de votre lettre ...
Thank you for your letter ...

Ending a personal letter

Transmettez mes amitiés à ...
Give my regards to ...

Dis bonjour à ... de ma part.
Say hello to ... for me.

... t'embrasse ...
... sends you his love ...

Embrasse ... pour moi.
Give my love to ...

Ending a formal letter

Dans l'attente de votre réponse ...
I look forward to hearing from you ...

Je demeure à votre entière disposition pour toute information complémentaire.
I will be happy to supply any further information you may require.

Je vous remercie dès à présent de ...
Thank you in advance for ...

THANK YOU LETTER

Name and address of sender.

The town or city from which the letter is being sent should be included along with the date. The article **le** should be included in the date.

Anne et Cyrille Legendre
25, rue des Grillons
69000 LYON

Lyon, le 24 octobre 1999

Chers oncle et tante,

Le grand jour, c'était il y a presqu'un mois déjà ...
Ce fut une merveilleuse fête et nous étions très
heureux de vous avoir parmi nous.

Nous tenons à vous remercier chaleureusement de
votre gentil cadeau et nous vous inviterons bientôt
pour inaugurer ce superbe service à raclette comme
il se doit.

Vous trouverez aussi ci-joint une photo-souvenir.

Nous vous embrassons tous les deux,

Anne et Cyrille

For alternatives see p21.

Name and address of letter's recipient.

Jeanne Judon
89, bd des Tertres
75008 PARIS

Hôtel Renoir
15, rue de Beaumanoir
59000 LILLE

Paris, le 3 novembre 1999

Madame ou Monsieur,

For alternatives see p22.

Me rendant à Lille le mois prochain à l'occasion du Salon de l'esthétique, j'aimerais réserver une chambre avec salle de bains pour deux nuits le mercredi 1er et le jeudi 2 décembre 1999.

Je vous saurais gré de me communiquer vos tarifs et de me confirmer que vous avez bien une chambre libre à cette époque.

Je vous prie de croire, Madame, Monsieur, à l'assurance de mes sentiments distingués.

Jeanne Judon

M et Mme DAUNAY
La Longue Haie
35135 CHANTEPIE

Hôtel "Au Bon Accueil"
17, rue Nationale
86000 POITIERS

Chantepie, le 29 décembre 1999

Madame, Monsieur,

Mon mari et moi avons passé la nuit du 23 décembre dans votre hôtel, où nous avions préalablement réservé une chambre. Nous tenons à vous faire savoir que nous avons été très déçus par vos services, en particulier par le bruit – nous avons pourtant demandé une chambre calme – et l'impossibilité de se faire servir un petit déjeuner avant notre départ à 6 h 30.

Cet arrêt dans votre hôtel qui devait nous permettre de nous reposer au cours d'un long voyage en voiture n'a fait que nous fatiguer davantage. Sachez que nous prendrons bien soin de déconseiller votre établissement à nos amis.

Je vous prie d'agréer, Madame, Monsieur, mes salutations distinguées.

For alternatives see p22.

In Canadian French **courriel** is used instead.

CURRICULUM VITÆ

LEGUEN Maxime
29, rue de Vannes
35000 RENNES
Tél : 56 02 71 28
Adresse électronique : mleguen@agriventes.com.fr

29 ans
célibataire
nationalité française

EXPÉRIENCE PROFESSIONNELLE

Du 10.3.95 à ce jour :   Adjointe du directeur à l'exportation,
Agriventes, Rennes

Du 8.10.93 au 30.1.95 : Secrétaire de direction,
France-Exportations, Cognac

DIPLÔMES

1993 : Diplôme de secrétaire bilingue, délivré par l'École de
commerce de Poitiers

1992 : Licence de langues étrangères appliquées (anglais et russe),
Université de Poitiers – plusieurs mentions

1988 : Baccalauréat (langues) – mention assez bien

AUTRES RENSEIGNEMENTS

Langues étrangères : anglais et russe (courant), allemand (bonnes
connaissances)

Stage d'information dans le cadre de la formation continue, 1995

Permis de conduire

Nombreux voyages en Europe et aux États-Unis

If you have British or American etc qualifications you should use wording such as **"équivalence baccalauréat (3 A-levels), équivalence licence de lettres (BA Hons)"** etc.

JOB APPLICATION

This is appropriate if you are writing to a company. However, if you are writing to the holder of a particular post use the following:

Monsieur (or Madame) le Directeur des ressources humaines
Société GERBAULT etc

and begin the letter:

Monsieur le Directeur des ressources humaines,

If you know the name of the person you should use the following:

Monsieur Alain Dupont
Directeur des ressources humaines
Société GERBAULT etc

and begin the letter:

Monsieur,

Maxime LEGUEN
29, rue de Vannes
35000 RENNES

Service du Personnel
Société GERBAULT
85, bd de la Liberté
35000 RENNES

Rennes, le 12 juillet 1999

Madame, Monsieur,

Votre annonce parue dans le Monde du 8 juillet concernant un poste d'assistante de direction dans votre service Import-Export m'a particulièrement intéressée.

Mon expérience de quatre ans en tant qu'assistante de direction dans le service d'exportation d'une petite entreprise m'a permis d'acquérir un sens des responsabilités ainsi qu'une grande capacité d'adaptation. Le poste que vous proposez m'intéresse tout particulièrement car j'aimerais beaucoup pouvoir utiliser ma connaissance de la langue et de la culture russe dans le cadre de mon travail.

Je me tiens à votre disposition pour vous apporter de plus amples renseignements sur ma formation et mon expérience.

Je vous prie, Madame, Monsieur, de bien vouloir agréer mes salutations distinguées.

Maxime Leguen

Maxime Leguen

P.J. : CV

= **pièces jointes.** You should add this if you are enclosing any other information with your letter eg a CV.

INVITATION TO INTERVIEW

SOCIÉTÉ GERBAULT

85, bd de la Liberté
35000 RENNES
TÉLÉPHONE : 02 99 45 32 88 • TÉLÉCOPIE : 02 99 45 32 90

Maxime LEGUEN
29, rue de Vannes
35000 RENNES

Rennes, le 19 juillet

Madame,

For alternatives see p22.

Votre candidature au poste d'assistante de direction au sein de notre Compagnie a retenu notre attention.

Nous vous proposons, dans le but de faire plus ample connaissance de part et d'autre, de rencontrer :

Monsieur LAURENT
notre Directeur Régional, le 26 juillet prochain, à 9 h, à l'adresse suivante :

2, bd de Lattre de Tassigny
35000 RENNES

Si cette date ne vous convenait pas, vous seriez aimable d'avertir notre secrétariat (Tél : 02 99 45 32 88) afin de convenir d'un autre rendez-vous.

Nous vous prions de croire, Madame, à l'expression de nos sentiments distingués.

Jean Minet

Jean Minet

FAX

France-Sanitaires S.A

55, rue de Strasbourg
75012 Paris
Téléphone : 01 63 13 84 20
Télécopie : 01 63 13 84 32

TELECOPIE

À : Mme Robin

Date : le 7 janvier 1999

De : M. Edmond
Service clientèle

Nombre de pages à suivre : 1

Réf. : Devis pour installation salle de bains.

Madame,

Suite à notre visite d'avant-hier, veuillez trouver ci-joint notre devis pour l'installation d'une salle de bains dans votre appartement. Les prix comprennent la fourniture du matériel ainsi que la main d'œuvre.

Dans l'attente de votre réponse, je vous prie, Madame, d'agréer l'expression de mes meilleurs sentiments,

Y. Edmond

Sending messages

Nouveau message		
Fichier Edition Affichage Outils **Composer** Aide Envoyer ✉		

A: fabienne@europost.fr	**Nouveau message**	
Cc:	**Répondre**	
Copie cachée:	**Répondre à tous**	
Objet: Réunion	**Faire suivre**	
	Fichier joint	

Est-ce qu'on pourrait se voir demain à 15 h pour faire un point sur les opérations en cours ? Si tu ne peux pas demain, je suis libre vendredi midi, on pourrait déjeuner ensemble.

À plus

Nadia

Fichier	File
Édition	Edit
Affichage	View
Outils	Tools
Composer	Compose
Aide	Help
Envoyer	Send
Nouveau message	New
Répondre	Reply to Sender

E-MAIL

Receiving messages

		Réunion			
Fichier	**Edition**	**Affichage**	**Outils**	**Composer**	**Aide**

De: Fabienne Mercier (fabienne@europost.fr)

Date: 30 novembre 1999 11 h 30

A: nadia.martin@europost.fr

Objet: Réunion

> In French, when telling someone your e-mail address you say : **"fabienne arrobas europost point fr"**.

C'est bon pour vendredi. Disons 13 h à la brasserie ?

Je ne serai pas joignable demain, je suis en formation toute la journée.

Bon courage et à vendredi.

Fabienne

Répondre à tous	Reply to All
Faire suivre	Forward
Fichier joint	Attachment
À	To
Cc	Cc (carbon copy)
Copie cachée	Bcc (blind carbon copy)
Objet	Subject
De	From
Date	Sent

TELEPHONE

Different types of call

Communication locale/interurbaine.	*Local/national call.*
Je voudrais appeler l'étranger.	*I want to make an international call.*
Je voudrais appeler Londres **en PCV.**	*I want to make a reverse charge call (Brit) to a ... number or I want to call a ... number collect (US).*
Comment est-ce que je peux téléphoner à l'extérieur ?	*How do I get an outside line?*

Asking for information

Quel est le numéro des renseignements ?	*What is the number for directory enquiries (Brit) or directory assistance (US)?*
Je voudrais le numéro de la société Europost, 20, rue de la Marelle, à Pierrefitte.	*Can you give me the number of ...*
Quel est l'indicatif de la Martinique ?	*What is the code for ...*
Quel est le numéro de l'horloge parlante ?	*What is the number for the speaking clock?*

Receiving information

Le numéro que vous avez demandé est le 01 40 32 37 12. *(zéro-un quarante trente-deux trente-sept douze)*	*The number you require is ...*
Je regrette, mais il n'y a pas d'abonné à ce nom.	*I'm sorry, there's no listing under that name.*
Le numéro que vous avez demandé est sur liste rouge.	*The number you require is ex-directory (Brit) or unlisted (US).*

When your number answers

Je voudrais parler à *or* **Pourrais-je parler à** M. Wolff, s'il vous plaît ?	*Could I speak to ...*
Pourriez-vous me passer le docteur Henderson, s'il vous plaît ?	*Could you put me through to ...*
Pourriez-vous me passer le poste 52 64, s'il vous plaît ?	*Can I have extension ...*
Je rappellerai dans une demi-heure.	*I'll call back in ...*
Pourriez-vous lui demander de me rappeler à son retour ?	*Would you ask him to ring me when he gets back?*

The switchboard operator speaks

C'est de la part de qui ?	*Who shall I say is calling?*
Je vous le passe.	*I'm putting you through.*
J'ai un appel de Tokyo **pour** Mme Thomson.	*I have a call from ... for ...*
J'ai Mlle Martin **en ligne.**	*I've got ... on the line.*
Le docteur Roberts **est en ligne, vous patientez ?**	*... is on another line. Do you want to wait?*
Ne quittez pas.	*Please hold.*
Ça ne répond pas.	*There's no reply.*
Voulez-vous laisser un message ?	*Would you like to leave a message?*

Recorded messages

Le numéro de votre correspondant n'est plus attribué. Veuillez consulter l'annuaire ou votre centre de renseignements.	*The number you have dialled has not been recognized. Please consult the directory or directory enquiries.*
Le numéro de votre correspondant a changé. Veuillez composer désormais le 33 42 21 70.	*The number you have dialled has been changed to ...*
Par suite de l'encombrement des lignes, votre appel ne peut aboutir. Veuillez rappeler ultérieurement.	*All the lines are busy right now. Please try again later.*
Bonjour, vous êtes en communication avec le service des ventes. **Veuillez patienter, nous allons donner suite à votre appel dans quelques instants.**	*Hello, you have reached ... Please wait, your call will be answered shortly.*
Bonjour, vous êtes bien chez M. et Mme Martin. **Laissez un message après le bip sonore et nous vous rappellerons dès notre retour.** Merci.	*Hello, you are through to ... Leave a message after the tone and we'll get back to you.*

Answering the telephone

Allô, c'est Anne **à l'appareil.**	*Hello, it's ... speaking.*
C'est moi or **lui-même** (or **elle-même**).	*Speaking.*
Qui est à l'appareil ?	*Who's speaking?*

When in trouble

Je n'arrive pas à avoir le numéro.	*I can't get through.*
Leur téléphone est en dérangement.	*Their phone is out of order.*
Nous avons été coupés.	*We have been cut off.*
J'ai dû faire un faux numéro.	*I must have dialled the wrong number.*
La ligne est très mauvaise.	*This is a very bad line.*

GOÛTS ET PRÉFÉRENCES

Pour dire ce que l'on aime

I like cakes.	J'aime ...
I like things to be in their proper place.	J'aime que ...
I really liked the film.	J'ai bien aimé ...
I love going to clubs.	J'adore ...
What I like best about Matthew are his eyes.	Ce que je préfère ...
What I enjoy most is an evening with friends.	Ce que j'aime par-dessus tout, c'est ...
I very much enjoyed the trip to the vineyards.	... m'a beaucoup plu.
I've never tasted **anything better than** this chicken.	... rien ... de meilleur que ...
I've got a weakness for chocolate cakes.	J'ai un faible pour ...
You can't beat a good cup of tea.	Rien ne vaut ...
There's nothing quite like a nice hot bath!	Rien de tel que ...
My favourite dish is lasagne.	... mon ... favori.
Reading is **one of my favourite** pastimes.	... une de mes ... préférées.
I don't mind being alone.	Cela ne me déplaît pas de ...

Pour dire ce que l'on n'aime pas

I don't like fish.	Je n'aime pas ...
I don't like him **at all.**	Je ne ... aime pas du tout.
I'm not very keen on speaking in public.	Je n'aime pas beaucoup ...
I'm not particularly keen on the idea.	... ne m'emballe pas.
I hate chemistry.	Je déteste ...
I loathe sport.	J'ai horreur du ...
I can't stand being lied to.	Je ne supporte pas que ...
If there's one thing I hate it's ironing.	Ce que je déteste le plus, c'est de ...

Préférences

I prefer pop **to** classical music.	Je préfère ... à ...

I **would rather** live in Paris.   *Je préférerais ...*
I'd rather starve **than** ask him a favour.   *J'aimerais mieux ... que de ...*

Indifférence

It's all the same to me.   *Ça m'est égal.*
I have no particular preference.   *Je n'ai pas de préférence.*
As you like.   *C'est comme vous voudrez.*
It doesn't matter in the least.   *Cela n'a aucune importance.*
I don't mind.   *Peu importe.*

Comment demander à quelqu'un ce qu'il aime

Do you like chocolate?   *Est-ce que vous aimez ...*
Do you like cooking?   *Est-ce que vous aimez ...*
Which do you like better: football or cricket?   *Qu'est-ce que vous préférez : ...*
Which would you rather have: the red one or the black one?   *Lequel préférez-vous : ...*
Do you prefer living in the town or in the country?   *Est-ce que vous préférez ...*
What do you like best on television?   *Qu'est-ce que vous aimez le plus ...*

OPINIONS

Comment demander l'avis de quelqu'un

What do you think about it?   *Qu'en pensez-vous ?*
What do you think about divorce?   *Que pensez-vous du ...*
What do you think of his behaviour?   *Que pensez-vous de ...*
I'd like to know what you think of his work.   *Je voudrais savoir ce que vous pensez de ...*
I would like to know your views on this.   *J'aimerais connaître votre avis sur ...*
What is your opinion on the team's chances of success?   *Quelle est votre opinion sur ...*
Could you give me your opinion on this proposal?   *Est-ce que vous pourriez me donner votre avis sur ...*
In your opinion, are men and women equal?   *À votre avis ...*
In your view, is this the best solution?   *Selon vous ...*

Comment donner son avis

You are right.	*Vous avez raison.*
He is wrong.	*Il a tort.*
He was wrong to resign.	*Il a eu tort de ...*
I think it ought to be possible.	*Je pense que ...*
I think it's a bit premature.	*Je crois que ...*
I think it's quite natural.	*Je trouve que ...*
Personally, I think that it's a waste of money.	*Personnellement, je pense que ...*
I have the impression that her parents don't understand her.	*J'ai l'impression que ...*
I'm sure he is completely sincere.	*Je suis certain que ...*
I'm convinced that there are other possibilities.	*Je suis persuadé que ...*
In my opinion, he hasn't changed.	*À mon avis ...*
In my view, he's their best player.	*Selon moi ...*

Comment éviter de donner son avis

It depends.	*Ça dépend.*
It all depends on what you mean by patriotism.	*Tout dépend de ce que vous entendez par ...*
I'd rather not express an opinion.	*Je préfère ne pas me prononcer.*
Actually, I've never thought about it.	*À vrai dire, je ne me suis jamais posé la question.*

APPROBATION ET ACCORD

I think it's an excellent idea.	*Je trouve que c'est une excellente idée.*
What a good idea!	*Quelle bonne idée !*
I was very impressed by his speech.	*J'ai beaucoup apprécié ...*
It's a very good thing.	*C'est une très bonne chose.*
I think you're right to be wary.	*Je trouve que vous avez raison de ...*
Newspapers **are right to** publish these stories.	*... ont raison de ...*

You were right to leave your bags in left-luggage.	*Vous avez bien fait de ...*
Third World countries **rightly believe that** most pollution comes from developed countries.	*... estiment à juste titre que ...*
You're quite justified in complaining.	*Vous avez bien raison de ...*
I share this view.	*Je partage cette opinion.*
I fully share your concern.	*Je partage ...*
We support the creation of jobs.	*Nous sommes favorables à ...*
We are in favour of a united Europe.	*Nous sommes en faveur de ...*
It is true that mistakes were made.	*Il est vrai que ...*
I agree with you.	*Je suis d'accord avec vous.*
I entirely agree with you.	*Je suis entièrement d'accord avec toi.*

DÉSAPPROBATION ET DÉSACCORD

I think he was wrong to borrow so much money.	*Je trouve qu'il a eu tort de ...*
It's a pity that you didn't tell me.	*Il est dommage que ...*
It is regrettable that they allowed this to happen.	*Il est regrettable que ...*
I dislike the idea **intensely.**	*... me déplaît profondément.*
I can't stand lies.	*Je ne supporte pas ...*
We are against hunting.	*Nous sommes contre ...*
We do not condone violence.	*Nous ne tolérons pas ...*
I am opposed to compulsory screening.	*Je suis opposé au ...*
I don't share this point of view.	*Je ne partage pas ce point de vue.*
I am disappointed by his attitude.	*Je suis déçu par ...*
I am deeply disappointed.	*Je suis profondément déçu.*
You shouldn't have said that.	*Tu n'aurais pas dû ...*
What gives him **the right to** act like this?	*De quel droit ...*
I disagree.	*Je ne suis pas d'accord.*
We don't agree with them.	*Nous ne sommes pas d'accord avec ...*
I totally disagree with what he said.	*Je ne suis absolument pas d'accord avec ...*

It is **not true to say that** the disaster was inevitable.	*C'est faux de dire que ...*
You are wrong!	*Vous vous trompez !*

EXCUSES

Pour s'excuser

Sorry.	*Excusez-moi.*
Oh, sorry! I've got the wrong number.	*Oh, pardon !*
Sorry to bother you.	*Excusez-moi de vous déranger.*
I'm sorry I woke you.	*Je suis désolé de ...*
I'm terribly sorry about the misunderstanding.	*Je suis navré de ...*
I do apologize.	*Je vous prie de m'excuser.*
We hope our readers **will excuse** this oversight.	*Nous prions ... de bien vouloir excuser ...*

En assumant la responsabilité de ce qui s'est passé

It's my fault; I should have left earlier.	*C'est (de) ma faute : j'aurais dû ...*
I shouldn't have laughed at her.	*Je n'aurais pas dû ...*
We were wrong not to check this information.	*Nous avons eu tort de ne pas ...*
I take full responsibility for what I did.	*J'assume seul l'entière responsabilité de ...*
If only I had done my homework!	*Si seulement j'avais ...*

En niant toute responsabilité

It's not my fault.	*Ce n'est pas (de) ma faute.*
It isn't my fault if we're late.	*Ce n'est pas (de) ma faute si ...*
I didn't do it on purpose.	*Je ne l'ai pas fait exprès.*
I had no option.	*Je ne pouvais pas faire autrement.*
But I thought that it was okay to park here.	*J'avais pourtant cru comprendre que ...*
I thought I was doing the right thing in warning him.	*J'avais cru bien faire en ...*

I'm sorry, but it's impossible.

Je regrette, mais ...

I'm afraid we're fully booked.

Je regrette, mais ...

Unfortunately we are unable to meet your request.

Il nous est malheureusement impossible de ...

EXPLICATIONS

Causes

I didn't buy anything **because** I had no money.

... parce que ...

I arrived late **because of** the traffic.

... à cause de ...

Since you insist, I'll come again tomorrow.

Puisque ...

As I lived near the library, I used it a lot.

Comme ...

I got through it **thanks to** the support of my friends.

... grâce à ...

Given the present situation, finding a job will be difficult.

Vu ...

Given that there is an economic crisis, it is difficult to find work.

Étant donné ...

Considering how many problems we had, we did well.

Étant donné ...

It was a broken axle **that caused** the derailment.

C'est ... qui a provoqué ...

He resigned **for** health **reasons.**

... pour des raisons de ...

The theatre is closing, **due to lack of** funds.

... faute de ...

The project was abandoned **owing to** legal problems.

... en raison de ...

Many cancers **are linked to** smoking.

... sont dus à ...

The problem is that people are afraid of computers.

Le problème vient de ce que ...

The drop in sales **is the result of** high interest rates.

... est due à ...

The quarrel **resulted from** a misunderstanding.

... a pour origine ...

Conséquences

I have to leave tonight; **so** I can't come with you.

... donc ...

Distribution has been improved **so that** readers now get their newspaper earlier.

... de telle sorte que ...

This cider is fermented for a very short time and is **consequently** low in alcohol.

... par conséquent ...

Our lack of consultation **has resulted in** a duplication of effort.	... a eu pour conséquence ...
That's why they are easy to remember.	Voilà pourquoi ...

COMPARAISONS

Gambling **can be compared to** a drug.	On peut comparer ... à ...
The gas has a smell **that can be compared to** rotten eggs.	... que l'on peut comparer à ...
The shape of Italy **is often compared to** a boot.	... est souvent comparé à ...
The noise **was comparable to** that of a large motorbike.	... était comparable à ...
Africa is still underpopulated **compared with** Asia.	... comparé à ...
In the UK, the rate of inflation increased slightly **compared to** the previous year.	... par rapport à ...
What is so special about a holiday in Florida **as compared to** one in Spain?	... par rapport à ...
This story **is like** a fairy tale.	... ressemble à ...
He loved this countryside, which **reminded him of** Ireland.	... lui rappelait ...
Frightening levels of unemployment, **reminiscent of those** of the 30s.	... rappelant ceux ...
The snowboard **is the equivalent** on snow **of** the skateboard.	... est l'équivalent ... de ...
This sum **corresponds to** six months' salary.	... correspond à ...
A 'bap'? **It's the same thing as** a bread roll.	C'est la même chose que ...
It comes to the same thing in terms of calories.	Ça revient au même ...
This record **is no better and no worse than** the others.	... n'est ni meilleur ni moins bon que ...

Pour souligner une différence

No catastrophe **can compare with** Chernobyl.	Aucune ... ne peut être comparée à ...
Modern factories **cannot be compared with** those our grandparents worked in.	On ne peut pas comparer ... à ...
The actions of this group **are in no way comparable to** those of terrorists.	... n'ont rien de comparable avec ...
The newspaper reports **differ** on this point.	... divergent ...

The history of the United States **in no way resembles** our own.	*... ne ressemble en rien à ...*
There are worse things than losing a European cup final.	*Il y a des événements bien plus tragiques que ...*
This film **is less** interesting **than** his first one.	*... est moins ... que ...*
Women's life expectancy is 81 years, **while** men's is 72.	*... tandis que ...*
While the consumption of wine and beer is decreasing, the consumption of bottled water is increasing.	*Alors que ...*

DEMANDES ET PROPOSITIONS

Demandes

I'd like another beer.	*Je voudrais ...*
I'd like to know the times of trains to Lille.	*Je voudrais ...*
Could you give us a hand?	*Pourriez-vous ...*
Can you tell Eleanor the good news?	*Est-ce que vous pouvez ...*
Could you please show me the way out?	*Auriez-vous l'obligeance de ...*
Could I ask you for a few minutes of your time?	*Puis-je vous demander de ...*
Be an angel, pop to the baker's for me.	*Sois gentille ...*
If you wouldn't mind waiting for a moment.	*Merci de bien vouloir ...*
Would you mind opening the window?	*Est-ce que cela vous dérangerait de ...*
Would you be very kind and save my seat for me?	*Auriez-vous l'obligeance de ...*
I would be grateful if you could reply as soon as possible.	*Je vous serais reconnaissant de ...*

Propositions

I can come and pick you up **if** you like.	*Je peux ... si ...*
I could go with you.	*Je pourrais ...*
Do you fancy a bit of Stilton?	*Ça te dit ...*
How about a pear tart?	*Que diriez-vous de ...*
Would you like to see my photos?	*Ça vous dirait de ...*

Would you like to have dinner with me one evening?

Est-ce que vous voulez ...

Do you want me to go and get your car?

Est-ce que vous voulez que ...

CONSEILS ET SUGGESTIONS

Comment demander conseil

What would you do, if you were me?

À ma place, que feriez-vous ?

Would you accept, **if you were me?**

À ma place ...

What's your opinion on this?

Quel est votre avis sur la question ?

What, in your opinion, should be done to reduce pollution?

Que proposez-vous pour ...

What would you advise?

Que me conseillez-vous ?

What would you advise me to do?

Que me conseillez-vous de faire ?

Which would you recommend, Majorca or Ibiza?

Qu'est-ce que vous me conseillez ...

If we were to sponsor a player, **who would you recommend?**

... lequel nous conseilleriez-vous ?

What strategy **do you suggest?**

Quelle ... proposez-vous ?

How would you deal with unemployment?

Qu'est-ce que vous proposez contre ...

Comment donner un conseil

If I were you, I'd be a bit wary.

À votre place ...

If I were you I wouldn't say anything.

À ta place ...

Take my advice, buy your tickets in advance.

Je vous conseille de ...

A word of advice: read the instructions.

Un conseil ...

A useful tip: always have some pasta in your cupboard.

Un bon conseil ...

As you like languages, **you ought to** study as a translator.

... vous devriez ...

You should see a specialist.

Vous devriez ...

You would do well to see a solicitor.

Vous feriez bien de ...

You would do better to spend the money on a new car.

Vous feriez mieux de ...

You could perhaps ask someone to go with you.	Vous pourriez peut-être ...
You could try being a little more understanding.	Vous pourriez ...
Perhaps you should speak to a plumber about it.	Il faudrait peut-être que ...
Perhaps we ought to try a different approach.	Il faudrait peut-être ...
Why don't you phone him?	Pourquoi ne pas ...
How about renting a video?	Et si on ...
How about 3 March at 10.30am?	... ça vous va ?
It might be better to give her money rather than jewellery.	Il vaudrait peut-être mieux ...
It would be better to wait a bit.	Il serait préférable de ...

Mises en garde

I warn you, I intend to get my own back.	Je vous préviens ...
I'd better warn you that he knows you did it.	Mieux vaut que je te prévienne ...
Don't forget to keep a copy of your income tax return.	N'oubliez pas de ...
Remember: appearances can be deceptive.	Méfiez-vous des apparences.
Beware of buying tickets from touts.	Attention ...
Whatever you do, don't leave your camera in the car.	Surtout, ne ... jamais ...
If you don't book early you risk being disappointed.	... tu risques de ...

INTENTIONS ET SOUHAITS

Pour demander à quelqu'un ce qu'il compte faire

What are you going to do?	Qu'est-ce que vous allez faire ?
What will you do if you fail your exams?	Qu'est-ce que tu vas faire si ...
What are you going to do when you get back? Do you have anything planned?	Qu'allez-vous faire ... Avez-vous des projets ?
Can we expect you next Sunday?	On compte sur vous ...
Are you planning to spend all of the holiday here?	Est-ce que tu comptes ...
Are you planning on staying long?	Vous comptez ...

What are you planning to do with your collection?	*Que comptez-vous faire de ...*
What are you thinking of doing?	*Que comptez-vous faire ?*
Do you intend to go into teaching?	*Est-ce que tu as l'intention de ...*
Are you thinking of making another film in Europe?	*Songez-vous à ...*

Pour dire ce qu'on a l'intention de faire

I was planning to go to Ajaccio on 8 July.	*Je comptais ...*
She plans to go to India for a year.	*Elle prévoit de ...*
There are plans to build a new stadium.	*Il est prévu de ...*
The bank **intends to** close a hundred branches.	*... a l'intention de ...*
I am thinking of giving up politics.	*Je songe à ...*
I have decided to get a divorce.	*J'ai décidé de ...*
I have made up my mind to stop smoking.	*Je suis décidé à ...*
We never had any intention of talking to the press.	*Il n'a jamais été dans nos intentions de ...*
That's settled, we'll go to Florida in May.	*C'est décidé ...*
For me, living abroad **is out of the question.**	*Il n'est pas question ... de ...*

Souhaits

I'd like to be able to play as well as him.	*Je voudrais ...*
I'd like to go hang-gliding.	*J'aimerais ...*
I would like my photos to be published.	*J'aimerais que ...*
I would like to have had a brother.	*J'aurais aimé ...*
I want to act in films.	*Je veux ...*
Ian **wanted at all costs** to prevent his boss finding out.	*... voulait à tout prix ...*
We wish to preserve our independence.	*Nous souhaitons ...*
I hope to have children.	*J'espère ...*
We hope that children will watch this programme with their parents.	*Nous espérons que ...*
Do you dream of winning the lottery?	*Vous rêvez de ...*
I dream of having a big house.	*Mon rêve serait de ...*

OBLIGATION

I must find somewhere to live.	*Il faut que je ...*
We really must see each other more often!	*Il faut absolument qu'on ...*
If you're going to Poland, **you must** learn Polish.	*... vous devez ...*
He **made** his secretary answer all his calls.	*... exigeait que ...*
My mother **makes me** eat spinach.	*... me force à ...*
The hijackers **demanded that** the plane fly to New York.	*... ont exigé que ...*
A serious illness **forced me to** cancel my holiday.	*... m'a obligé à ...*
He **was obliged to** borrow more and more money.	*... a été obligé de ...*
Mary **had no choice but to** invite him.	*... n'avait pas pu faire autrement que de ...*
The only thing you can do is say no.	*Tu ne peux pas faire autrement que de ...*
Many mothers **have to** work; **they have no other option.**	*... sont obligées de ... elles n'ont pas le choix.*
She had the baby adopted because **she had no other option.**	*... elle ne pouvait pas faire autrement.*
School **is compulsory** until the age of sixteen.	*... est obligatoire ...*
It is essential to know some history, if we are to understand the situation.	*Il est indispensable de ...*

PERMISSION

Comment demander la permission de faire quelque chose

Can I use the phone?	*Je peux ...*
Can I ask you something?	*Je peux ...*
Is it okay if I come now, or is it too early?	*Ça ne vous dérange pas si ...*
Do you mind if I smoke?	*Ça ne vous dérange pas que ...*
Do you mind if I open the window?	*Est-ce que ça vous dérange si ...*
Would you mind if I had a look in your briefcase, madam?	*Vous permettez ... que ...*
Could I have permission to leave early?	*Est-ce que je peux vous demander la permission de ...*

Do as you please.	*(Vous) faites comme vous voulez.*
Go ahead!	*Allez-y !*
No, of course I don't mind.	*Bien sûr que non.*
I have nothing against it.	*Je n'y vois pas d'inconvénient.*
Pupils **are allowed to** wear what they like.	*... ont le droit de ...*

Défense

I forbid you to go out!	*Je te défends de ...*
It's forbidden.	*C'est défendu.*
Smoking in the toilet **is forbidden.**	*Il est interdit de ...*
Child labour is **strictly forbidden by** a UN convention.	*... formellement interdit par ...*
No entry!	*Défense d'entrer !*
No parking.	*Stationnement interdit.*
It's not allowed.	*C'est interdit.*
You are not allowed to swim in the lake.	*Il est interdit de ...*
We weren't allowed to eat or drink while on duty.	*On n'avait pas le droit de ...*
That's out of the question.	*Il n'en est pas question.*

CERTITUDE, PROBABILITÉ ET POSSIBILITÉ

Certitude

Undoubtedly, there will be problems.	*Il est certain que ...*
There is no doubt that the country's image has suffered.	*Il ne fait aucun doute que ...*
It's bound to cause trouble.	*Cela va sûrement ...*
Clearly the company is in difficulties.	*Il est évident que ...*
A foreign tourist is **quite obviously** a rare sight here.	*... de toute évidence ...*
It is undeniable that she was partly to blame.	*Il est indéniable que ...*
I am sure you will like my brother.	*Je suis sûre que ...*
I am sure that I will win.	*Je suis sûr de ...*
I'm sure that I won't get bored working with him.	*J'ai la certitude que ...*

I am **certain that** we are on the right track.	*Je suis certain que ...*
I am **convinced that** there are other solutions.	*Je suis persuadé que ...*

Probabilité

The price of petrol will **probably** rise.	*Il est probable que ...*
Inflation will **very probably** exceed 10%.	*... très probablement ...*
It is highly probable that they will abandon the project.	*Il est fort probable que ...*
The trend **is likely** to continue.	*Il est probable que ...*
80% of skin problems **undoubtedly** have psychological origins.	*... sans doute ...*
They were **no doubt** right.	*... sans doute ...*
The construction work **should** start in April.	*... devrait ...*
He must have forgotten to open the windows.	*Il a dû ...*

Possibilité

It's possible.	*C'est possible.*
It is possible that they got your name from the electoral register.	*Il est possible que ...*
It is not impossible that he has gone to Paris.	*Il n'est pas impossible que ...*
That might be more expensive.	*Il se peut que ...*
He may have misunderstood.	*... peut-être ...*
This virus **may** be extremely infectious.	*Il se peut que ...*
It may be that it will take time to achieve peace.	*Il se peut que ...*
In a few months everything **could** change.	*... peut ...*
Perhaps I am mistaken.	*Peut-être que ...*

INCERTITUDE, IMPROBABILITÉ ET IMPOSSIBILITÉ

Incertitude

I'm not sure it's useful.	*Je ne suis pas sûr que ...*
I'm not sure I'll manage.	*Je ne suis pas certain de ...*
I'm not sure that it's a good idea.	*Je ne suis pas sûr que ...*

We **cannot be sure that** the problem will be solved.	*Il n'est pas sûr que ...*
I **very much doubt** he'll adapt to not working.	*Je doute fort que ...*
Is it wise? **I doubt it.**	*J'en doute.*
He began to **have doubts about** his doctor's competence.	*... douter de ...*
I **wonder if** we've made much progress in this area.	*Je me demande si ...*
There is no guarantee that a vaccine can be developed.	*Il n'est pas certain que ...*
Nobody knows exactly what happened.	*Personne ne sait exactement ...*

Improbabilité

He **probably won't** change his mind.	*... ne ... probablement pas ...*
It is unlikely that there'll be any tickets left.	*Il est peu probable que ...*
I'd be surprised if they had your size.	*Ça m'étonnerait que ...*
They are not likely to get the Nobel prize for Economics!	*Ils ne risquent pas de ...*
There is not much chance the growth rate will exceed 1.5%.	*Il y a peu de chances que ...*
There's no danger we'll get bored.	*Nous ne risquons pas de ...*
It would be amazing if everything went according to plan.	*Il serait étonnant que ...*

Impossibilité

It's impossible.	*C'est impossible.*
It is not possible for the government to introduce this Bill before the recess.	*Il n'est pas possible que ...*
This information **cannot be** wrong.	*Il est impossible que ...*
There is no chance of their helping us.	*Il n'y a aucune chance que ...*

SALUTATIONS

Hello!	*Bonjour !*
Hi!	*Salut !*
Good morning!	*Bonjour !*

Good afternoon!	Bonjour !
Good evening!	Bonsoir !
How's it going?	Comment ça va ?
How's things?	Comment (ça) va ?
How's life?	Comment (ça) va ?
How are you?	Comment allez-vous ?

Réponses

Very well, and you?	Très bien, merci, et vous ?
Fine, thanks.	Bien, merci.
Great!	Super bien !
So-so.	Comme ci comme ça.
Could be worse.	On fait aller.

Présentations

This is Charles.	Je te présente ...
Let me introduce you to my girlfriend.	Je vous présente ...
I'd like you to meet my husband.	Je vous présente ...
I don't believe you know one another.	Je ne crois pas que vous vous connaissiez.

Une fois qu'on a été présenté

Pleased to meet you.	Enchanté.
Hello, how do you do?	Enchanté de faire votre connaissance.
Hi, I'm Jane.	Salut, moi c'est ...

Pour prendre congé

Bye!	Au revoir !
Goodbye!	Au revoir !
Good night!	Bonne nuit !
See you!	Ciao !
See you later!	À tout à l'heure !

See you soon!	À bientôt !
See you tomorrow!	À demain !
See you next week!	À la semaine prochaine !
See you Thursday!	À jeudi !

Vœux et félicitations

Happy Birthday!	Bon anniversaire !
Many happy returns!	Bon anniversaire !
Merry Christmas!	Joyeux Noël !
Happy New Year!	Bonne année !
Happy Anniversary!	Bon anniversaire de mariage !
Congratulations!	Félicitations !
Welcome!	Soyez les bienvenus !
Good luck!	Bonne chance !
Safe journey!	Bon voyage !
Have fun!	Amusez-vous bien !
Get well soon!	Bon rétablissement !
Take care!	Fais bien attention à toi !
Cheers!	(À votre) santé !
Enjoy your meal!	Bon appétit !

CORRESPONDANCE

La rédaction de l'adresse en Grande-Bretagne

Timbre

Le code postal vient après le nom de la ville ou du département.

Mrs J.M. Mackintosh
129 Strathmore Ave
EDINBURGH
EH11 2AD
UK

La rédaction de l'adresse aux États-Unis

Timbre

MARK SMITH
968 MICHIGAN ST
SEATTLE WA   98060-1024
USA

Le code postal (zip code) vient après le nom de la ville et de l'État (en abrégé).

Abréviations couramment employées dans les adresses

Ave = avenue	Dr = drive	Pl = place	Sq = square
Cres = crescent	Gdns = gardens	Rd = road	St = street

Les formes d'adresse et les formules de politesse

Dans les lettres personnelles

Dear Mr and Mrs Roberts	Yours *(assez soutenu)*
Dear Kate and Jeremy	With best wishes
Dear Aunt Jane and Uncle Alan	Love from
Dear Granny	Lots of love from *(familier)*

Dans les lettres d'affaires

Dear Sirs Dear Sir Dear Madam Dear Sir or Madam Dear Professor Meldrum Dear Ms Gilmour	Yours faithfully Yours sincerely

Pour commencer une lettre personnelle

It was lovely to hear from you.	*Cela m'a fait plaisir d'avoir de vos nouvelles.*
Thanks for your letter ...	*Merci pour ta lettre ...*
Sorry I haven't written sooner.	*Je suis désolé de ne pas t'avoir écrit plus tôt.*

Pour commencer une lettre d'affaires

Thank you for your letter of ...	*Je vous remercie de votre lettre du ...*
In reply to your letter of ...	*En réponse à votre lettre du ...*
With reference to ...	*Suite à ...*
We are writing to you to ...	*Nous vous écrivons pour ...*
We are pleased to inform you ...	*Nous avons le plaisir de vous informer ...*
We regret to inform you ...	*Nous sommes au regret de vous informer ...*

Pour terminer une lettre personnelle

Write soon.	*Écris-moi vite.*
Give my regards to ...	*Transmettez mes amitiés à ...*
... sends his/her best wishes.	*... me charge de transmettre ses amitiés.*
Give my love to ...	*Embrasse ... de ma part.*

Pour terminer une lettre d'affaires

I look forward to hearing from you.	*Dans l'attente de votre réponse.*
Thanking you in advance for your help.	*En vous remerciant à l'avance pour votre aide.*
If you require any further information please do not hesitate to contact me.	*N'hésitez pas à me contacter pour toute information complémentaire.*

LETTRE DE REMERCIEMENT

Adresse de l'expéditeur.

18 Slateford Ave
Leeds
LS24 3PR

25th May 1999

Date

Dear Gran and Grandpa,

Thank you both very much for the CDs which you sent me for my birthday. They are two of my favourite groups and I'll really enjoy listening to them.

There's not much news here. I seem to be spending most of my time studying for my exams which start in two weeks. I'm hoping to pass all of them but I'm not looking forward to the Maths exam as that's my worst subject.

Mum says that you're off to Crete on holiday next week, so I hope that you have a great time and come back with a good tan.

Tony sends his love.

With love from

Voir également les formules p.51.

POUR RÉSERVER UNE CHAMBRE D'HÔTEL

109 Bellview Road
Cumbernauld
CA7 4TX

14th June 1999 ← **Date**

Mrs Elaine Crawford ← **Nom et adresse du destinataire.**
Manager
Poppywell Cottage
Westleigh
Devon
DV3 8SP

Dear Mrs Crawford,

My sister stayed with you last year and has highly recommended your guest house.

I would like to reserve a room for one week from 18th-24th August of this year. I would be obliged if you would let me know how much this would be for two adults and two children, and whether you have a room free on those dates.

On utilise cette formule lorsque l'on connaît le nom de la personne.

I hope to hear from you soon.

Yours sincerely,

Andrew Naismith

LETTRE DE RÉCLAMATION

Voir également les formules p.52.

85 Rush Lane
Triptown
Lancs
LC4 2DT

20th February 1999

Woodpecker Restaurant
145 Main Street
Triptown
Lancs
LC4 3EF

Dear Sir/Madam

I was to have dined in your restaurant last Thursday by way of celebrating my wedding anniversary with my wife and young son but am writing to let you know of our great dissatisfaction.

I had reserved a corner table for two with a view of the lake. However, when we arrived we had to wait for more than 20 minutes for a table and even then, not in the area which I had chosen. There was no highchair for my son as was promised and your staff made no effort whatsoever to accommodate our needs. In fact, they were downright discourteous. Naturally we went elsewhere, and not only have you lost any future custom from me, but I will be sure to advise my friends and colleagues against your establishment.

Yours faithfully

T. Greengage

On utilise cette formule lorsque l'on commence la lettre par **Dear Sir** etc.

CURRICULUM VITÆ

CURRICULUM VITAE

Pour les diplômes obtenus en France, mettre le nom du diplôme suivi d'une brève description en anglais entre parenthèses.

Name: Rosalind A. Williamson

Address: 11 North Street, Barnton NE6 2BT

Telephone: 01294 476230

E-mail: rosalind@metalcomp.co.uk

Date of Birth: 18/4/1973

Nationality: British

Marital Status: Single

CAREER

2/97 to date: Sales and Marketing Executive, Metal Company plc, Barnton

11/95-1/97: Marketing Assistant, Metal Company plc

QUALIFICATIONS

1991-1995: University of Newby
BA (Hons) Italian with French – 2:1

1984-1991: Barnton Comprehensive School
A-levels: English Literature (D), French (B), Italian (A)
GCSEs: Art, Chemistry, English Language, English Literature, French, German, Italian, Maths

OTHER SKILLS

Computer literate (Word for Windows, Excel, QuarkXPress), good keyboarding skills, full, clean driving licence.

INTERESTS

Travel (have travelled extensively throughout Europe and North Amercia), riding and sailing.

REFEREES

Ms Alice Bluegown
Sales and Marketing Manager
Metal Company plc
Barnton
NE4 3KL

Dr I.O. Sono
Department of Italian
University of Newby
Newby
S13 2RR

Il est d'usage d'indiquer sur son C.V. les noms de deux personnes prêtes à fournir une recommandation à l'employeur potentiel. L'une d'entre elles doit normalement être un ancien employeur, ou, pour les étudiants, un professeur.

LETTRE DE CANDIDATURE

11 North Street
Barnton
NE6 2BY

18 August 1999

The Personnel Director
Clifton Manufacturing Ltd
Firebrick House
Clifton
MK45 6RB

Dear Sir or Madam

> Lorsqu'on ignore si le destinataire est un homme ou une femme, il convient d'utiliser la formule ci-contre. Toutefois, si l'on connaît le nom de la personne, on utilise la présentation suivante :
> **Mrs Lynn Kerr**
> **Personnel Director**
> **Clifton Manufacturing Ltd** etc.
> Pour commencer votre lettre, la formule à employer est la suivante :
> **Dear Mrs Kerr**

With reference to your advertisement in the Guardian of 15 August, I wish to apply for the position of Marketing Manager in your company.

I am currently employed as a Sales and Marketing Executive for the Metal Company in Barnton where my main role is maintaining and developing links with our customers within the UK and producing material for marketing purposes.

I am interested in this position as it offers an opportunity to apply my sales and marketing skills in a new and challenging direction. I enclose my Curriculum Vitae for your consideration. Please do not hesitate to contact me if you require any further details.

Yours faithfully

> On utilise cette formule lorsque l'on commence la lettre par **Dear Sir or Madam** etc.

Rosalind Williamson

Enc.

> = **enclosures.** On ajoute ceci lorsque l'on joint d'autres pièces à la lettre, un C.V. par exemple.

POUR PROPOSER UN ENTRETIEN

Les coordonnées de l'expéditeur sont souvent mentionnées pour faciliter le classement de la correspondance.

CLIFTON MANUFACTURING LTD.

Firebrick House • Clifton MK45 6RB
Tel: (01367) 345 900 • Fax: (01367) 345 901
E-mail: personnel@cliftman.co.uk

Ref: RW/LK

27 August 1999

Ms Rosalind Williamson
11 North Street
Barnton
NE6 2BT

Dear Ms Williamson

Following your recent application for the position of Marketing Manager, I would like to invite you to attend an interview at the above office on Friday 3 September at 11am.

The interview will be conducted by the Sales and Marketing Director and myself and should last approximately one hour.

If this date does not suit please notify Jane Simpson on extension 3287 to arrange an alternative date.

We look forward to meeting you.

Yours sincerely

Lynn Kerr

Lynn Kerr (Mrs)
Personnel Director

On utilise cette formule lorsque l'on commence la lettre par **Dear Ms Williamson** etc.

Brown & Sons

Northport Enterprise Park
Birmingham B45 6JH
Tel: 0121 346 3287
Fax: 0121 346 3288
E-mail: orders@brownandsons.co.uk

FAX

To: Emma Scott, Westcott Hotel

Date: 6 November 1999

From: Malcolm Marshall

No. of pages to follow: 1

Re your order of 23 October for 100 tablecloths (Catalogue number 435789), I regret to inform you that these items are currently out of stock.

The next delivery will be in approximately four weeks' time. However, if this delay is unacceptable to you, please can you let me know so that I can cancel the order.

I am sorry for any inconvenience this may cause.

Regards

Malcolm Marshall

IF THERE ARE ANY PROBLEMS WITH THIS MESSAGE, PLEASE CONTACT
CLAIRE NEWPORT ON 0121 346 3287

COURRIER ÉLECTRONIQUE

Envoyer des messages

New Message						
File	Edit	View	Tools	**Compose**	Help	Send ✉

To: andrew@pmdesigns.co.uk	New	
Cc:	Reply to Sender	
Bcc:	Reply to All	
Subject: Meeting	Forward	
	Attachment	

Re our conversation this morning, would next Monday morning
10am be convenient for a meeting about the project's progress?
If this doesn't suit, I'm also free Wednesday morning.
Mark

New Message	Nouveau message
File	Fichier
Edit	Édition
View	Affichage
Tools	Outils
Compose	Composer
Help	Aide
Send	Envoyer
New	Nouveau message
Reply to Sender	Répondre

COURRIER ÉLECTRONIQUE

Recevoir des messages

Meeting	
File Edit View Tools Compose Help	

From: Andrew Collins (andrew@pmdesigns.co.uk)

Sent: 30 November 1999 08.30

To: mark.gordon@typo.co.uk

> En anglais, l'adresse électronique s'énonce de la manière suivante : **"andrew at pmdesigns dot co dot uk"**.

Subject: Meeting

Mark,

Unfortunately I'm away on business all next week. Would it be possible to arrange a working lunch, Thursday or Friday of this week?

Sorry about this!

Andrew

Reply to All	Répondre à tous
Forward	Faire suivre
Attachment	Fichier joint
To	À
Cc (carbon copy)	Cc
Bcc (blind carbon copy)	Copie cachée
Subject	Objet
From	De
Sent	Date

TÉLÉPHONE

Les différents types de communication

Local/national call.

Communication locale/ interurbaine.

I want to make an international call.

Je voudrais appeler l'étranger.

I want to make a reverse charge call *(Brit)* to a Paris **number** ou I want to call a Paris **number** collect *(US)*.

Je voudrais appeler ... en PCV.

How do I get an outside line?

Comment est-ce que je peux téléphoner à l'extérieur ?

Les renseignements

What is the number for directory enquiries *(Brit)* ou directory assistance *(US)*?

Quel est le numéro des renseignements ?

Can you give me the number of Europost, 20 Cumberland Street, Newquay?

Je voudrais le numéro de ...

What is the code for Martinique?

Quel est l'indicatif de ...

What is the number for the speaking clock?

Quel est le numéro de l'horloge parlante ?

Réponses

The number you require is 0181-613 3297. *(o-one-eight-one six-one-three three-two-nine-seven)*

Le numéro que vous avez demandé est le ...

I'm sorry, there's no listing under that name.

Je regrette, mais il n'y a pas d'abonné à ce nom.

The number you require is ex-directory *(Brit)* ou unlisted *(US)*.

Le numéro que vous avez demandé est sur liste rouge.

Lorsque l'abonné répond

Could I speak to Mr Sanderson, please?

Pourrais-je parler à ...

Could you put me through to Dr Evans, please?

Pourriez-vous me passer ...

Can I have extension 6578, please?

Pourriez-vous me passer le poste ...

I'll call back in half an hour.

Je rappellerai dans ...

Would you ask him to ring me when he gets back?

Pourriez-vous lui demander de me rappeler à son retour ?

Au standard

Who shall I say is calling?

C'est de la part de qui ?

I'm putting you through.

Je vous le passe.

I have a call from Tokyo for Mrs Thomson.

J'ai un appel de ... pour ...

I've got Miss Martin on the line.

J'ai ... en ligne.

Dr Roberts **is on another line. Do you want to wait?**	*... est en ligne, vous patientez ?*
Please hold.	*Ne quittez pas.*
There's no reply.	*Ça ne répond pas.*
Would you like to leave a message?	*Voulez-vous laisser un message ?*

Messages enregistrés

The number you have dialled has not been recognized. Please hang up.	*Le numéro de votre correspondant n'est plus attribué. Veuillez raccrocher.*
The number you have dialled has been changed to 0171-789 0044.	*Le numéro de votre correspondant a changé. Veuillez composer désormais le ...*
All the lines are busy right now. Please try again later.	*Par suite de l'encombrement des lignes, votre appel ne peut aboutir. Veuillez rappeler ultérieurement.*
Hello, you have reached Sunspot Insurance. **Please wait, your call will be answered shortly.**	*Bonjour, vous êtes en communication avec ... Veuillez patienter, nous allons donner suite à votre appel dans quelques instants.*
Hello, you are through to Emma and Matthew Hargreaves. **Please leave a message after the tone and we'll get back to you.** Thanks.	*Bonjour, vous êtes bien chez ... Laissez un message après le bip sonore et nous vous rappellerons dès notre retour.*

Pour répondre au téléphone

Hello, it's Anne **speaking.**	*Allô, c'est ... à l'appareil.*
Speaking.	*C'est moi.*
Who's speaking?	*Qui est à l'appareil ?*

En cas de difficulté

I can't get through.	*Je n'arrive pas à avoir le numéro.*
Their phone is out of order.	*Leur téléphone est en dérangement.*
We have been cut off.	*Nous avons été coupés.*
I must have dialled the wrong number.	*J'ai dû faire un faux numéro.*
We've got a crossed line.	*Il y a quelqu'un d'autre sur la ligne.*
This is a very bad line.	*La ligne est très mauvaise.*

